MICHIE'S
ANNOTATED CODE
OF THE PUBLIC GENERAL LAWS
OF MARYLAND

Maryland Rules

Prepared by the Editorial Staff of the Publisher

Volume 2

2012 Replacement Volume

*(Including amendments through November 7, 2011, and
annotations taken from posted decisions
as of October 24, 2011)*

LexisNexis®

44006-29

ISBN 978-1-4224-8851-5

Summary Table of Contents

Volume 1

SUMMARY TABLE OF CONTENTS

SUMMARY TABLE OF CONTENTS

SUMMARY TABLE OF CONTENTS

TABLE OF CONTENTS

Volume 1

COURT OF APPEALS AND APPELLATE JUDICIAL CIRCUITS

COURT OF APPEALS STANDING COMMITTEE ON RULES OF
PRACTICE AND PROCEDURE

IN THE COURT OF APPEALS OF MARYLAND

MARYLAND RULES

Title 1. General Provisions

TABLE OF CONTENTS

TABLE OF CONTENTS

TABLE OF CONTENTS

TABLE OF CONTENTS

TABLE OF CONTENTS

TABLE OF CONTENTS

TABLE OF CONTENTS

TABLE OF CONTENTS

TABLE OF CONTENTS

TABLE OF CONTENTS

TABLE OF CONTENTS

TABLE OF CONTENTS

TABLE OF CONTENTS

Volume 2

Title 9. Family Law Actions

Chapter 100. Adoption; Guardianship Terminating Parental Rights.

Chapter 200. Divorce, Annulment, Alimony, Child Support, and Child Custody.

Forms for Guardianships That Terminate Parental Rights and Adoptions.

TABLE OF CONTENTS

TABLE OF CONTENTS

TABLE OF CONTENTS

Title 11. Juvenile Causes

Title 12. Property Actions

Chapter 100. General Provisions.

Chapter 200. Condemnation.

TABLE OF CONTENTS

TABLE OF CONTENTS

TABLE OF CONTENTS

TABLE OF CONTENTS

TABLE OF CONTENTS

TABLE OF CONTENTS

TABLE OF CONTENTS

TABLE OF CONTENTS

TABLE OF CONTENTS

TABLE OF CONTENTS

Advocate.

Transactions With Persons Other Than Clients.

Law Firms and Associations.

Public Service.

Information About Legal Services.

Maintaining the Integrity of the Profession.

TABLE OF CONTENTS

TABLE OF CONTENTS

Index

INTERNAL OPERATING RULES OF THE COURT OF APPEALS OF MARYLAND

I. Preamble.

II. Conduct of Proceedings.

III. Extended Coverage.

Index

FEDERAL RULES OF PROCEDURE FOR UNITED STATES COURTS OF APPEALS; LOCAL RULES AND INTERNAL OPERATING PROCEDURES OF THE FOURTH CIRCUIT

Title I. Applicability of Rules.

Title II. Appeals From Judgments and Orders of District Courts.

TABLE OF CONTENTS

TABLE OF CONTENTS

TABLE OF CONTENTS

TABLE OF CONTENTS

TABLE OF CONTENTS

Fourth Circuit Forms.

RULES FOR JUDICIAL-CONDUCT AND JUDICIAL-DISABILITY PROCEEDINGS

Article I. General Provisions.

Article II. Initiation of a Complaint.

Article III. Review of a Complaint by the Chief Judge.

Article IV. Investigation and Report by Special Committee.

TABLE OF CONTENTS

RULES OF THE UNITED STATES DISTRICT COURT FOR THE DISTRICT OF MARYLAND

I. Civil.

II. Criminal.

TABLE OF CONTENTS

TABLE OF CONTENTS

TABLE OF CONTENTS

Part II.

Part III.

Part IV.

TABLE OF CONTENTS

TABLE OF CONTENTS

Appendix A. Local Bankruptcy Forms (LBF)

TABLE OF CONTENTS

MARYLAND RULES

TITLE 9. FAMILY LAW ACTIONS

Editor's note. — The Court of Appeals, by Order dated June 5, 1996, effective January 1, 1997, rescinded Subtitles A, D, E, J, P, Q, R, T, U, V, W, Y, Z, BB, BD, BE, BG, BH, BJ, BL, BP, BQ, BR, BS, BW, and BY of Chapter 1100 of the Maryland Rules of Procedure, rescinded Subtitles P, BB, BQ, and BW of the Maryland District Rules, and rescinded Forms 22a, 23, 24, 25, and 26. The Order substituted for certain of the rules and forms rescinded new Title 9, Chapter 100, Title 10, Title 12, Title 13, Title 14, and Title 15 of the Maryland Rules of Procedure. Furthermore, the Order transferred, without readoption, Chapter 900, Chapter 1200, and Subtitles S, BU, and BV of Chapter 1100 of the Maryland Rules of Procedure and Chapter 1200 of the Maryland District Rules to be Title 9, Chapter 200, Title 11, and Title 16 of the Maryland Rules of Procedure. The Order provides that the new rules shall "apply to all actions commenced on or after January 1, 1997, and insofar as practicable, to all actions then pending."

Many of the cases in the notes to the various rules were decided prior to the 1996 revision. These cases have been retained under pertinent rules of this title where it is thought that such cases will be of value in interpreting the present rules.

A table of comparable rules, relating those rules rescinded effective January 1, 1997, to the revised rules in Title 9 through Title 16 is to be found in Volume 2 following the end of the Maryland Rules.

CHAPTER 100. ADOPTION; GUARDIANSHIP TERMINATING PARENTAL RIGHTS.

Rule 9-101. Applicability; definitions.

(a) **Applicability.** The Rules in this Chapter apply to proceedings under Code, Family Law Article, Title 5, Subtitles 3 (Guardianship to and Adoption through Local Department), 3A (Private Agency Guardianship and Adoption), and 3B (Independent Adoption).

Committee note. — The Rules in this Chapter do not apply to the guardianship of persons and property of minors and disabled persons governed by Code, Estates and Trusts Article, § 13-101 *et seq.*

(b) **Definitions.** The terms used in this Chapter that are defined in Code, Family Law Article, Titles 1 and 5 shall have the meanings stated in those Titles. In addition, in this Chapter, the following definitions apply except as expressly otherwise provided or as necessary implication requires.

(1) Independent Adoption. "Independent Adoption" means an adoption under Code, Family Law Article, Title 5, Subtitle 3B.

(2) Private Agency Adoption. "Private Agency Adoption" means an adoption under Code, Family Law Article, Title 5, Subtitle 3A, Part III.

(3) Private Agency Guardianship. "Private Agency Guardianship" means a guardianship under Code, Family Law Article, Title 5, Subtitle 3A, Part II.

(4) Public Agency Adoption after TPR. "Public Agency Adoption after TPR" means an adoption under Code, Family Law Article, Title 5, Subtitle 3, Part IV, after termination of parental rights.

(5) Public Agency Adoption without Prior TPR. "Public Agency Adoption without Prior TRP" means an adoption under Code, Family Law Article, Title 5, Subtitle 3, Part III, without prior termination of parental rights.

(6) Public Agency Guardianship. "Public Agency Guardianship" means a guardianship under Code, Family Law Article, Title 5, Subtitle 3, Part II.

(7) TPR. "TPR" means termination of parental rights. (Amended June 4, 2007, effective July 1, 2007.)

Source. — This Rule is in part derived from former Rule D71 and is in part new.

Effect of amendments. — The 2007 amendment rewrote the rule.

Rule 9-102. Consents; revocation of consent.

(a) **Consents generally required.** Except when otherwise permitted, a judgment of adoption or guardianship may not be entered without the consents prescribed by Code, Family Law Article.

Cross references. — For provisions governing the authority to grant guardianships or adoptions and the validity of consents, see Code, Family Law Article, §§ 5-320 and 5-321 as to a Public Agency Guardianship; 5-338 and 5-339 as to a Public Agency Adoption without

Prior TPR; 5-350 and 5-351 as to a Public Agency Adoption after TPR; 5-3A-18 and 5-3A-19 as to a Private Agency Guardianship; 5-3A-35 as to a Private Agency Adoption; and 5-3B-20 and 5-3B-21 as to an Independent Adoption.

(b) **Form of consents, affidavits of attorneys, and disclosure vetoes.**
(1) Consent of parent. If signed on or after July 1, 2007, the consent of a parent to a guardianship or to an adoption shall be substantially in the applicable form set forth at the end of this Title as Form 9-102.1 (Consent of Parent to a Public Agency Guardianship), Form 9-102.2 (Consent of Parent to a Private Agency Guardianship), Form 9-102.3 (Consent of Parent to a Public Agency Adoption without Prior TPR), Form 9-102.4 (Consent of Parent to an Independent Adoption with Termination of Parental Rights), or Form 9-102.5 (Consent of Parent to an Independent Adoption without Termination of Parental Rights).

(2) Consent of child to adoption. If signed on or after July 1, 2007, the consent of a child to an adoption shall be substantially in the applicable form set forth at the end of this Title as Form 9-102.6 (Consent of Child to a Public Agency Adoption or Private Agency Adoption) or Form 9-102.7 (Consent of Child to an Independent Adoption).

(3) Attorney affidavit. When required and if signed on or after July 1, 2007, the affidavit by an attorney as to the validity of the consent of a parent to a guardianship or adoption or a child to an adoption shall be substantially in the applicable form set forth at the end of this Title as Form 9-102.8 (Attorney Affidavit as to Consent of a Parent to a Public Agency Guardianship or Private Agency Guardianship), Form 9-102.9 (Attorney Affidavit as to Consent of a Parent to Adoption), or Form 9-102.10 (Attorney Affidavit as to Consent of a Child to Adoption).

Cross references. — See Rule 9-106 (c).

(4) Disclosure vetoes. The disclosure vetoes that are required to be attached to the consent forms may be found on the website of the Maryland Department of Human Resources.

(c) **Revocation of consent.** (1) Time for revocation of consent. (A) By parent. The time for revocation of consent by a parent is as provided in Code, Family Law Article, § 5-321 (Public Agency Guardianship), § 5-339 (Public Agency Adoption without Prior TPR), § 5-3A-19 (Private Agency Guardianship), and § 5-3B-21 (Independent Adoption).

(B) By adoptee. The time for revocation of consent by an adoptee is as provided in Code, Family Law Article, § 5-339 (Public Agency Adoption without Prior TPR), § 5-351 (Public Agency Adoption after TPR), § 5-3A-35 (Private Agency Adoption), and § 5-3B-21 (Independent Adoption).

(C) By public or private agency or guardian. The time for revocation of consent by a public or private agency or guardian is as provided in Code, Family Law Article, § 5-339 (Public Agency Adoption without Prior TPR), § 5-351 (Public Agency Adoption after TPR), and § 5-3A-35 (Private Agency Adoption).

(2) Procedure for revocation of consent. (A) By parent — Delivery to clerk. A parent may revoke a consent to an adoption or guardianship only by a signed writing actually delivered by mail or in person to the clerk of the circuit court designated in the consent to receive the revocation. If the revocation is delivered to an agent of a public or private agency, the agent shall deliver the revocation promptly to the court.

(B) By agency, guardian, or adoptee. An agency, guardian, or adoptee may revoke consent to an adoption (i) in person or through counsel on the record at a hearing or (ii) in a writing signed by the executive head of the agency, the guardian, or the adoptee and filed with the court. If the revocation is delivered to an agent of a public or private agency, the agent shall deliver the revocation promptly to the court.

Cross references. — Rule 9-112.

(C) Notice. The court shall send to all parties, including the person who revoked the consent, a copy of the revocation and notice of a hearing scheduled pursuant to subsection (c)(2)(D) of this Rule.

(D) Court hearing upon revocation of consent. If a consent is revoked pursuant to this Rule, the court shall schedule an immediate hearing to determine the status of the petition and, if necessary, temporary custody of the child. (Amended Oct. 5, 1999; June 4, 2007, effective July 1, 2007.)

Source. — This Rule is derived in part from former Rule D73 and is in part new.

Effect of amendments. — The 1999 amendment inserted present (c) 7. and (c) 8. and redesignated the remaining subsections accordingly; substituted "Paragraph 10" for "Paragraph 8" in the third and fourth paragraphs of (c) 12.; inserted present (d) 4. and (d) 5. and redesignated the remaining subsections accordingly; and substituted "Paragraph 7" for "Paragraph 8" in the third and fourth paragraphs of (d) 9.

The 2007 amendment substituted "Revocation of consent" for "Requests for attorney or counseling" in the rule heading; in (a), added "Consents" and "Required", substituted a comma for "by Code, Family Law Article § 5-312, § 5-313, or § 5-313.1" near the bginning, deleted "§ 5-111 or § 5-317 (c) (2)" at the end, and rewrote the Cross reference note; added (b), and redesignated former (b) as present (c); in (c), substituted "Revocation of" for "Revoking" in (c)(1) and added (c)(1)(A) through (c)(1)(C), substituted "Revocation of Consent" for "Revoking" in (c)(2), designated previously undesignated language in (c)(2) as (c)(2)(A) and (c)(2)(B), added "By Parent - Delivery to Clerk", substituted "A parent" for "An individual" and added "If the ... to the court" in (c)(2)(A), rewrote (c)(2)(B), added (c)(2)(C), re-designated former (c)(3) as present (c)(2)(D), and rewrote (c)(2)(D); and deleted the form "CONSENT TO ADOPTIONUARDIANSHIP OR REQUEST FOR ATTORNEY OR COUNSELING".

Interests of child are paramount. — In both custody and adoption cases the interests of the child are paramount. Goodyear v. Cecil County Dep't of Social Servs., 11 Md. App. 280, 273 A.2d 644, rev'd on other grounds, 263 Md. 611, 284 A.2d 426 (1971); Nutwell v. Prince George's County Dep't of Social Servs., 21 Md. App. 100, 318 A.2d 563 (1974); Brendoff v. Titus, 22 Md. App. 412, 323 A.2d 612 (1974).

But adoption is not decreed over parental objection unless clearly justified. — But since the consequential loss to a natural parent in an adoption case is much more drastic than in a custody case, adoption will never be decreed over the objection of a natural parent or parents unless that course is clearly justified. Goodyear v. Cecil County Dep't of Social Servs., 11 Md. App. 280, 273 A.2d 644, rev'd on other grounds, 263 Md. 611, 284 A.2d 426 (1971); Nutwell v. Prince George's County Dep't of Social Servs., 21 Md. App. 100, 318 A.2d 563 (1974).

The Court of Appeals has indicated that it

will not permit trial courts to decree adoptions over the expressed objection of the natural parent or parents, save in very strong cases. Goodyear v. Cecil County Dep't of Social Servs., 11 Md. App. 280, 273 A.2d 644, rev'd on other grounds, 263 Md. 611, 284 A.2d 426 (1971); Nutwell v. Prince George's County Dep't of Social Servs., 21 Md. App. 100, 318 A.2d 563 (1974).

And welfare of child must be weighed against parental objection. — The welfare and best interests of the child must be weighed with great care against every just claim of an objecting parent. Goodyear v. Cecil County Dep't of Social Servs., 11 Md. App. 280, 273 A.2d 644, rev'd on other grounds, 263 Md. 611, 284 A.2d 426 (1971); Nutwell v. Prince George's County Dep't of Social Servs., 21 Md. App. 100, 318 A.2d 563 (1974).

The test as to what is to the best interests of the child necessarily depends on the facts and circumstances in each case. Schwartz v. Hudgins, 12 Md. App. 419, 278 A.2d 652 (1971).

No parental right to absolute, arbitrary veto. — Although the rights of the natural parent, or parents, must be closely considered, and although without a natural parent's consent the case for adoption must be strong, there is no right to an absolute, arbitrary veto on the part of the parent. Lloyd v. Schutes, 24 Md. App. 515, 332 A.2d 338, cert. denied, 275 Md. 752 (1975).

Determination whether parental consent is being withheld contrary to best interests of child necessarily depends on the facts of each particular case, but it is evident that willful abandonment, failure to contribute to support, neglect to see or visit, and unfitness of a natural parent are some of the more important factors to be considered by a court in reaching its conclusion. Goodyear v. Cecil County Dep't of Social Servs., 11 Md. App. 280, 273 A.2d 644, rev'd on other grounds, 263 Md. 611, 284 A.2d 426 (1971).

Factors to be considered in determining whether consent has been unjustifiably withheld are failure to contribute to support, neglect to see or visit the offspring and unfitness. Brendoff v. Titus, 22 Md. App. 412, 323 A.2d 612 (1974).

All of the facts and circumstances of the particular case must be considered in determining whether consent has been unjustifiably withheld and the natural rights of a natural parent, which have not been lost or forfeited, must be carefully weighed in deciding the question. Brendoff v. Titus, 22 Md. App. 412, 323 A.2d 612 (1974).

Where the evidence tends to show that mother's determination not to consent to the adoption of her baby daughter was born of a genuine concern that by consenting she would sever permanently the natural and legal rights and obligations binding parent and child, she did not lose or forfeit her parental rights, and did not unjustifiably withhold her consent contrary to the child's best interests. Brendoff v. Titus, 22 Md. App. 412, 323 A.2d 612 (1974).

Chancellor's finding that natural mother withheld her consent contrary to the best interest of her children was not supported where there was no evidence of wilful or intentional conduct on mother's part manifesting an intent to relinquish, renounce or forsake her parental right to her children. Nutwell v. Prince George's County Dep't of Social Servs., 21 Md. App. 100, 318 A.2d 563 (1974).

Agency's consent not withheld contrary to best interests of child. — In a case of a contested petition for adoption by an unmarried individual with whom contractual placement of a child had been made, which placement and adoption were contested by the placement agency, where the evidence revealed that the petitioner and her husband had jointly applied for placement, but they had been separated at time of placement, that neither the out-of-state nor the local agency was apprised of their marital difficulties which culminated in divorce, but rather this information appeared to be suppressed, that petitioner represented she had not previously been married, when in fact she had been twice married and twice divorced, and that sharp discrepancies existed with respect to her finances, the chancellor did not abuse his discretion in deciding that the agency's consent was not withheld contrary to the best interests of the child. Bernhardt v. Lutheran Social Servs. of Nat'l Capital Area, Inc., 39 Md. App. 334, 385 A.2d 1197 (1978).

Revocation of deemed consent arising due to untimely objection — When a mother failed to timely object to an agency's petitions for guardianship of the mother's children, after being served with orders to show cause which properly advised the mother of the consequences of such a failure, the mother's untimely objections to the petitions were properly stricken because the mother's failure to timely object gave rise to the mother's deemed consent to the petitions by operation of law, and that consent was not revocable within 30 days, as was a consent signed and filed with the court. In re Adoption/Guardianship of Audrey B., 186 Md. App. 454, 974 A.2d 965 (2009).

Applied in Att'y Griev. Comm'n v. Sabghir, 350 Md. 67, 710 A.2d 926 (1998).

Cited in In re Adoption No. 93321055, 344 Md. 458, 687 A.2d 681 (1997).

Rule 9-103. Petition.

(a) **Titling of case.** A proceeding shall be titled "In re Adoption/Guardianship of _____ (first name and first initial of last name of prospective adoptee or ward)."

(b) **Petition for adoption.** (1) Contents. A petition for adoption shall be signed and verified by each petitioner and shall contain the following information:

(A) The name, address, age, business or employment, and employer of each petitioner;

(B) The name, sex, and date and place of birth of the person to be adopted;

(C) The name, address, and age of each parent of the person to be adopted;

(D) Any relationship of the person to be adopted to each petitioner;

(E) The name, address, and age of each child of each petitioner;

(F) A statement of how the person to be adopted was located (including names and addresses of all intermediaries or surrogates), attaching a copy of all advertisements used to locate the person, and a copy of any surrogacy contract;

Committee note. — If the text of an advertisement was used verbatim more than once, the requirement that a copy of all advertisements be attached to the petition may be satisfied by attaching a single copy of the advertisement, together with a list of the publications in which the advertisement appeared and the dates on which it appeared.

(G) If the person to be adopted is a minor, the names and addresses of all persons who have had legal or physical care, custody, or control of the minor since the minor's birth and the period of time during which each of those persons has had care, custody, or control, but it is not necessary to identify the names and addresses of foster parents, other than a petitioner, who have taken care of the minor only while the minor has been committed to the custody of a child placement agency;

(H) If the person to be adopted is a minor who has been transported from another state to this State for purposes of placement for adoption, a statement of whether there has been compliance with the Interstate Compact on the Placement of Children (ICPC);

(I) If applicable, the reason why the spouse of the petitioner is not joining in the petition;

(J) If there is a guardian with the right to consent to adoption for the person to be adopted, the name and address of the guardian and a reference to the proceeding in which the guardian was appointed;

(K) Facts known to each petitioner that may indicate that a party has a disability that makes the party incapable of consenting or participating effectively in the proceedings, or, if no such facts are known to the petitioner, a statement to that effect;

(L) Facts known to each petitioner that may entitle the person to be adopted or a parent of that person to the appointment of an attorney by the court;

(M) If a petitioner desires to change the name of the person to be adopted, the name that is desired;

(N) As to each petitioner, a statement whether the petitioner has ever been convicted of a crime other than a minor traffic violation and, if so, the offense and the date and place of the conviction;

(O) That the petitioner is not aware that any required consent has been revoked; and

(P) If placement pending final action on the petition is sought in accordance with Code, Family Law Article, § 5-3B-12, a request that the court approve the proposed placement.

(2) Exhibits. (A) The following documents shall accompany the petition as exhibits:

(i) A certified copy of the birth certificate or "proof of live birth" of the person to be adopted;

(ii) A certified copy of the marriage certificate of each married petitioner;

(iii) A certified copy of all judgments of divorce of each petitioner;

(iv) A certified copy of any death certificate of a person whose consent would be required if that person were living;

(v) A certified copy of all orders concerning temporary custody or guardianship of the person to be adopted;

(vi) A copy of any existing adoption home study by a licensed child placement agency concerning a petitioner, criminal background reports, or child abuse clearances;

(vii) A document evidencing the annual income of each petitioner;

(viii) The original of all consents to the adoption, any required affidavits of translators or attorneys, and, if available, a copy of any written statement by the consenting person indicating a desire to revoke the consent, whether or not that statement constitutes a valid revocation;

Cross references. — *See* Code, Family Law Article, §§ 5-313, 5-320, and 5-321 as to a Public Agency Guardianship; 5-331, 5-338, and 5-339 as to a Public Agency Adoption without Prior TPR; 5-345, 5-350, and 5-351 as to a Public Agency Adoption after TPR; 5-3A-13, 5-3A-18, and 5-3A-19 as to a Private Agency Guardianship; 5-3A-35 as to a Private Agency Adoption; and 5-3B-20 and 5-3B-21 as to an Independent Adoption.

(ix) If applicable, proof of guardianship or relinquishment of parental rights granted by an administrative, executive, or judicial body of a state or other jurisdiction; a certification that the guardianship or relinquishment was granted in compliance with the jurisdiction's laws; and any appropriate translation of documents required to allow the child to enter the United States;

Cross references. — *See* Code, Family Law Article, §§ 5-305, 5-313, and 5-320 as to a Public Agency Guardianship; 5-305, 5-331, and 5-338 as to a Public Agency Adoption without Prior TPR; 5-305 and 5-345 as to a Public Agency Adoption after TPR; 5-3A-05, 5-3A-13, and 5-3A-18 as to a Private Agency Guardianship; 5-3A-05 as to a Private Agency Adoption; and 5-3B-04 and 5-3B-20 as to an Independent Adoption.

(x) If a parent of the person to be adopted cannot be identified or located, an affidavit of each petitioner and the other parent describing the attempts to identify and locate the unknown or missing parent;

Cross references. — *See* Code, Family Law Article, §§ 5-331 and 5-334 as to a Public Agency Adoption without Prior TPR and 5-3B-15 as to an Independent Adoption.

(xi) A copy of any agreement between a parent of the person to be adopted and a petitioner relating to the proposed adoption with any required redaction;

Cross references. — *See* Code, Family Law Article, §§ 5-308 and 5-331 as to a Public Agency Adoption without Prior TPR; 5-308 and 5-345 as to a Public Agency Adoption after TPR; 5-3A-08 as to a Private Agency Adoption; and 5-3B-07 as to an Independent Adoption.

(xii) If the adoption is subject to the Interstate Compact on the Placement of Children, the appropriate ICPC approval forms;

Cross references. — Code, Family Law Article, § 5-601.

(xiii) A brief statement of the health of each petitioner signed by a physician or other health care provider if applicable; and

(xiv) If required, a notice of filing as prescribed by Code, Family Law Article:

(1) § 5-313 in a Public Agency Guardianship;

(2) § 5-331 in a Public Agency Adoption without Prior TPR; or

(3) § 5-345 in a Public Agency Adoption after TPR.

(B) The following documents shall be filed before a judgment of adoption is entered:

(i) Any post-placement report relating to the adoption, if applicable;

Cross references. — *See* Code, Family Law Article, §§ 5-337 as to a Public Agency Adoption without Prior TPR; 5-349 as to a Public Agency Adoption after TPR; 5-3A-31 and 5-3A-34 as to a Private Agency Adoption; and 5-3B-16 as to an Independent Adoption.

(ii) A brief statement of the health of the child by a physician or other health care provider;

(iii) If required by law, an accounting of all payments and disbursements of any money or item of value made by or on behalf of each petitioner in connection with the adoption;

Cross references. — *See* Code, Family Law Article, § 5-3B-24 as to an Independent Adoption.

(iv) An affidavit of counsel for a parent, if required by Code, Family Law Article:

(1) §§ 5-307 and 5-321 in a Public Agency Guardianship;

(2) §§ 5-307 and 5-339 in a Public Agency Adoption without Prior TPR;

(3) §§ 5-3A-07 and 5-3A-19 in a Private Agency Guardianship; or

(4) §§ 5-3B-06 and 5-3B-21 in an Independent Adoption.

(v) An affidavit of counsel for a child, if the child is represented;

Cross references. — *See* Code, Family Law Article, §§ 5-307 and 5-338 as to a Public Agency Adoption without Prior TPR; 5-307 and 5-350 as to a Public Agency Adoption after

TPR; 5-3A-07 and 5-3A-35 as to a Private Agency Adoption; and 5-3B-06 and 5-3B-20 as to an Independent Adoption.

(vi) If the adoption is subject to the Interstate Compact on the Placement of Children, the required post-placement form;

(vii) A proposed judgment of adoption; and

(viii) A Department of Health and Mental Hygiene Certificate of Adoption Form.

Cross references. — Code, Health-General Article, § 4-211 (f).

(c) **Petition for guardianship.** A petition for guardianship shall state all facts required by subsection (b) (1) of this Rule, to the extent that the requirements are applicable and known to the petitioner. It shall be accompanied by all documents required to be filed as exhibits by subsection (b)(2) of this Rule, to the extent the documents are applicable. The petition shall also state the license number of the child placement agency.

Cross references. — *See* Code, Family Law Article, §§ 5-313 as to a Public Agency Guardianship and 5-3A-13 as to a Private Agency Guardianship.

(d) **If facts unknown or documents unavailable.** If a fact required by subsection (b) (1) or section (c) of this Rule is unknown to a petitioner or if a document required by subsection (b) (2) or section (c) is unavailable, the petitioner shall so state and give the reason in the petition or in a subsequent affidavit. If a document required to be submitted with the petition becomes available after the petition is filed, the petitioner shall file it as soon as it becomes available.

(e) **Disclosure of facts known to child placement agency.** If any fact required by subsection (b) (1) of this Rule to be stated is known to a child placement agency and the agency declines to disclose it to a petitioner, the agency shall disclose the fact to the court in writing at the time the petition is filed. (Amended Mar. 5, 2001, effective July 1, 2001; June 4, 2007, effective July 1, 2007.)

Source. — This Rule is derived in part from former Rule D72, in part from former Rule D80, and is in part new.

Effect of amendments. — The 2001 amendment inserted present (b) (1) (K) and redesignated former (b) (1) (K) through (O) as present (b) (1) (L) through (P).

The 2007 amendment rewrote (a); in (b), added "effectively" in (b)(1)(K), substituted "§ 5-3B-12" for "§ 5-507 (c)" in (b)(1)(P), in (b)(2)(A)(vi), substituted "existing ... agency" for "pre-placement report" and added "criminal ... clearances", added "any required affidavits of translators or attorneys" in (b)(2)(A)(viii), added "See" and substituted "§§ 5-313 ... Independent Adoption" for "§§ 5-311" in the Cross reference note of (b)(2)(A)(viii), added (b)(2)(A)(ix) and redesignated accordingly, added Cross reference in (b)(2)(A)(x), added "with any required redaction" and the Cross reference notes in (b)(2)(A)(xi), added "if applicable; and" in (b)(2)(A)(xiii), added (b)(2)(A)(xiv), and rewrote (b)(2)(B) and its

Cross reference notes; substituted "§§ 5-313
as to ... Guardianship" for "§ 5-317 (b)" in (c);
deleted former (e) and made related changes.

Rule 9-104. Notice of filing of petition; status conference.

(a) **Notice of filing of petition.** Notice of the filing of a petition for guardianship or adoption shall be given as required by Code, Family Law Article:

(1) § 5-315 in a Public Agency Guardianship;

(2) § 5-333 in a Public Agency Adoption without Prior TPR;

(3) § 5-346 in a Public Agency Adoption after TPR;

(4) § 5-3A-14 in a Private Agency Guardianship;

(5) § 5-3A-30 in a Private Agency Adoption; and

(6) § 5-3B-14 in an Independent Adoption.

(b) **Status conference.** In a public agency guardianship or adoption, at the time the notice of filing is sent, the court shall schedule a status conference no later than 60 days after the filing of the petition. (Amended June 4, 2007, effective July 1, 2007.)

Source. — This Rule is new.

Effect of amendments. — The 2007 amendment rewrote (a) and (b); and deleted (c).

Cited in In re Adoption/Guardianship Nos. 11387 & 11388, 354 Md. 574, 731 A.2d 972 (1999).

Rule 9-105. Show cause order; disability of a party; other notice.

(a) **Requirement for show cause order.** Promptly upon the filing of a petition for adoption or guardianship, the court shall issue a show cause order in substantially the form set forth in section (e) of this Rule when required by Code, Family Law Article:

(1) § 5-316 in a Public Agency Guardianship;

(2) § 5-334 in a Public Agency Adoption without Prior TPR;

(3) § 5-3A-15 in a Private Agency Guardianship; or

(4) § 5-3B-15 in an Independent Adoption.

If the petition seeks adoption of a minor, the show cause order shall not divulge the name of the petitioner. If the petition seeks appointment of a guardian, the show cause order shall state the name of the child placement agency seeking guardianship.

(b) **Appointment of attorney for disabled party.** (1) If the parties agree that a party who is not represented has a disability that makes the party incapable of consenting or participating effectively in the proceeding, the court shall appoint an attorney who shall represent the disabled party throughout the proceeding.

(2) If there is a dispute as to whether a party who is not represented has a disability that makes the party incapable of consenting or participating effectively in the proceeding, the court shall:

(A) hold a hearing promptly to resolve the dispute;

(B) appoint an attorney to represent the alleged disabled party at that hearing;

(C) provide notice of that hearing to all parties; and

(D) if the court finds at the hearing that the party has such a disability, appoint an attorney who shall represent the disabled party throughout the proceeding.

Cross references. — See Code, Family Law Article, §§ 5-307 as to a Public Agency Guardianship; 5-307 as to a Public Agency Adoption without Prior TPR; 5-3A-07 as to a Private Agency Guardianship; and 5-3B-06 as to an Independent Adoption. For eligibility of an individual for representation by the Office of the Public Defender, see Code, Family Law Article, § 5-307 and Code, Article 27A, § 4.

(c) **Service of show cause order.** (1) Method of service. The show cause order shall be served on those persons and in the manner required by Code, Family Law Article:

(A) § 5-316 in a Public Agency Guardianship;

(B) § 5-334 in a Public Agency Adoption without Prior TPR;

(C) § 5-3A-15 in a Private Agency Guardianship; or

(D) § 5-3B-15 in an Independent Adoption.

(2) Time for service. Unless the court orders otherwise, a show cause order shall be served within 90 days after the date it is issued. If service is not made within that period, a new show cause order shall be issued at the request of the petitioner.

(3) Notice of objection. A show cause order shall be served with two copies of a pre-captioned notice of objection form in substantially the form set forth in section (f) of this Rule. In a public agency guardianship or adoption, a copy of the petition shall be attached.

(d) **Notice of change of name.** If the person to be adopted is an adult and the petitioner desires to change the name of the person to be adopted to a surname other than that of the petitioner, notice of a proposed change of name shall also be given in the manner provided in Rule 15-901.

(e) **Form of show cause order.** Except as provided in section (g) of this Rule, the show cause order shall be substantially in the following form:

IMPORTANT

THIS IS A COURT ORDER. IF YOU DO NOT UNDERSTAND WHAT THE ORDER SAYS, HAVE SOMEONE EXPLAIN IT TO YOU. YOUR RIGHT TO AN ATTORNEY IS EXPLAINED IN PARAGRAPH 3 OF THIS ORDER. **IF YOU DO NOT MAKE SURE THAT THE COURT RECEIVES YOUR NOTICE OF OBJECTION ON OR BEFORE THE DEADLINE STATED IN PARAGRAPH 2 OF THIS ORDER, YOU HAVE AGREED TO A TERMINATION OF YOUR PARENTAL RIGHTS.**

(Note to Drafter of Show Cause Order: For the form of the caption of the Show Cause Order, see Rule 9-103 (a).)

SHOW CAUSE ORDER

TO:

_____

(name of person to be served)

_____

_____

(address, including county)

_____

(relationship of person served to individual who is the subject of the proceeding)

You are hereby notified that:

1. Filing of petition.

A petition has been filed for _____

(adoption/guardianship)

of _____ who

(name of individual who is the subject of the proceeding)

was born at _____ on _____.

(birthplace)   (date of birth)

(If the petition is for guardianship, include the following sentence: The petition was filed by _____).

(name of child placement agency seeking guardianship)

2. Right to object; time for objecting.

If you wish to object to the _____,

(adoption/guardianship)

you must file a notice of objection with the clerk of the court at

_____

(address of courthouse)

within _____ days after this Order is served on you. For your convenience, a form notice of objection is attached to this Order.

WHETHER THE PETITION REQUESTS ADOPTION OR GUARDIANSHIP, IF YOU DO NOT MAKE SURE THAT THE COURT RECEIVES YOUR NOTICE OF OBJECTION ON OR BEFORE THE DEADLINE STATED ABOVE, YOU HAVE AGREED TO A TERMINATION OF YOUR PARENTAL RIGHTS.

3. Right to an attorney. (a) You have the right to speak with an attorney and obtain independent legal advice.

(b) An attorney may already have been appointed for you. If you have been notified that an attorney has been appointed for you, you should speak immediately with that attorney.

(c) If an attorney has not already contacted you, you may be entitled to have the court appoint an attorney for you if:

(Note to Drafter of Show Cause Order: Include only those of the following paragraphs that are applicable to the type of guardianship or adoption proceeding that has been filed.)

[In a Public Agency Guardianship:]

You are a parent of the person for whom a guardian is sought and:

(A) you are under 18 years of age; or

(B) you have a disability that makes you unable to participate effectively in the case; or

(C) you object to the guardianship and cannot afford to hire an attorney because you are indigent.

[In a Public Agency Adoption without Prior TPR:]

(1) You are the person to be adopted;

OR

(2) You are a parent of the person to be adopted and:

(A) you are under 18 years of age; or

(B) you have a disability that makes you unable to participate effectively in the adoption case; or

(C) you object to the adoption and cannot afford to hire an attorney because you are indigent.

[In a Public Agency Adoption after TPR:]

You are the person to be adopted.

[In a Private Agency Guardianship:]

You are a parent of the person for whom a guardian is sought and:

(A) you are under 18 years of age; or

(B) you have a disability that makes you unable to participate effectively in the case.

[In a Private Agency Adoption:]

You are the person to be adopted and:

(A) you are at least 10 years old but are not yet 18; or

(B) you have a disability that makes you unable to participate effectively in the adoption case.

[In an Independent Adoption:]

(1) You are the person to be adopted and:

(A) you are at least 10 years old; and

(B) you have a disability that makes you unable to participate effectively in the adoption case;

OR

(2) You are a parent of the person to be adopted and:

(A) you are under 18 years of age; or

(B) you have a disability that makes you unable to participate effectively in the adoption case.

IF YOU BELIEVE YOU ARE ENTITLED TO HAVE THE COURT APPOINT AN ATTORNEY FOR YOU AND YOU WANT AN ATTORNEY, YOU MUST NOTIFY THE COURT BEFORE THE TIME YOUR NOTICE OF OBJECTION MUST BE FILED. HOWEVER, EVEN IF YOU HAVE OR WANT TO HAVE AN ATTORNEY, YOU MUST STILL FILE THE NOTICE OF OBJECTION ON

OR BEFORE THE DEADLINE STATED IN PARAGRAPH 2 OF THIS OR-DER. **IF YOU DO NOT MAKE SURE THAT THE COURT RECEIVES YOUR NOTICE OF OBJECTION ON OR BEFORE THE DEADLINE STATED, YOU HAVE AGREED TO THE TERMINATION OF YOUR PARENTAL RIGHTS.**

For your convenience, a request for appointment of an attorney is printed on the notice of objection form attached to this Order.

(d) You are entitled to consult an attorney chosen by you, even if you are not entitled to an attorney appointed by the court. If you employ an attorney, you may be responsible for any fees and costs charged by that attorney unless the court orders another party to pay all or part of those fees or expenses.

(e) If you wish further information concerning appointment of an attorney by the court or concerning adoption counseling and guidance, you may contact

_____

(name of court official)

_____

(address)

_____

(telephone number)

4. Option to receive adoption counseling. If this is an adoption proceeding, you also may have the option to receive adoption counseling and guidance. You may have to pay for that service unless another party agrees to pay or the court orders another party to pay all or part of those charges.

Date of issue: _____

_____

(Judge)

(f) **Form of notice of objection.** The notice of objection shall be substantially in the following form:

(Note to Drafter of the Notice of Objection/Request for Appointment of Attorney: For the caption of the form, see Rule 9-103 (a).)

NOTICE OF OBJECTION/REQUEST FOR APPOINTMENT OF
ATTORNEY

(Instructions to the person served with the show cause order:

IF YOU WISH TO OBJECT, YOU MUST MAKE SURE THAT THE COURT RECEIVES YOUR NOTICE OF OBJECTION ON OR BEFORE THE DEADLINE STATED IN THE SHOW CAUSE ORDER. You may use this form to do so. You need only sign this form, print or type your name, address, and telephone number underneath your signature, and mail or deliver it to the court at the address shown in paragraph 2 of the show cause order. **IF THE COURT HAS NOT RECEIVED YOUR NOTICE OF OB-JECTION ON OR BEFORE THE DEADLINE STATED IN PARAGRAPH 2 OF THE SHOW CAUSE ORDER, YOU HAVE AGREED TO THE TERMINATION OF YOUR PARENTAL RIGHTS.** If you wish to state your reasons, you may state them on this sheet.)

1. I object to the _____
                                        (adoption/guardianship)
of the above-named individual. My reasons for objecting are as follows:
_____
_____
_____
_____

2. I do/do not want the Court to appoint an attorney to represent me.
   (Circle one)

If I circled that I do want the court to appoint an attorney for me, I believe that
I am entitled to a court-appointed attorney because:
(Check appropriate box or boxes)

**(Note to Drafter of the Notice of Objection/Request for Appointment of
Attorney: Include only those of the following paragraphs which are
applicable to the type of guardianship or adoption proceeding that
has been filed.)**

[In a Public Agency Guardianship:]

[ ] I am the parent of the person for whom a guardian is sought and:
    [ ] I am under 18 years of age.
    [ ] I have a disability that makes me unable to participate effectively in
    the case.
    [ ] I object to the guardianship and cannot afford to hire an attorney
    because I am indigent.

[In a Public Agency Adoption without Prior TPR:]

[ ] I am the person to be adopted.
OR
[ ] I am the parent of the person to be adopted and:
    [ ] I am under 18 years of age.
    [ ] I have a disability that makes me unable to participate effectively in
    the adoption case.
    [ ] I object to the adoption and cannot afford to hire an attorney because
    I am indigent.

[In a Public Agency Adoption after TPR:]

[ ] I am the person to be adopted.

[In a Private Agency Guardianship:]

[ ] I am a parent of the person for whom a guardian is sought and:
    [ ] I am under 18 years of age.
    [ ] I have a disability that makes me unable to participate effectively in
    the case.

[In a Private Agency Adoption:]

[ ] I am the person to be adopted and:

[ ] I am at least 10 years old but am not yet 18.

[ ] I have a disability that makes me unable to participate effectively in the adoption case.

[In an Independent Adoption:]

[ ] I am the person to be adopted and:

[ ] I am at least 10 years old and I have a disability that makes me unable to participate effectively in the adoption case.

OR

[ ] I am the parent of the person to be adopted and:

[ ] I am under 18 years of age.

[ ] I have a disability that makes me unable to participate effectively in the adoption case.

_____
(Signature)

_____
(Name, printed or typed)

_____
(Address)

_____
(Telephone Number)

(g) **Form of notice for service by publication and posting.** The notice for service by publication and posting shall be in the form required by Code, Family Law Article:

(1) § 5-316 in a Public Agency Guardianship;

(2) § 5-334 in a Public Agency Adoption without Prior TPR;

(3) § 5-3A-15 in a Private Agency Guardianship; or

(4) § 5-3B-15 in an Independent Adoption. (Amended Mar. 5, 2001, effective July 1, 2001; Jan. 8, 2002, effective Feb. 1, 2002; Nov. 6, 2002, effective Jan. 1, 2003; June 4, 2007, effective July 1, 2007.)

Source. — This Rule is in part derived from former Rule D74 and is in part new.

Effect of amendments. — The 2001 amendment inserted "disability of a party" in the Rule heading; added (a) (2); in (e), substituted "A show cause order served" for "When the show cause order is served," deleted "it" preceding "shall," inserted "two copies of" following "accompanied by," and inserted "form" following "objection"; in (h), inserted heading "**IMPORTANT**" to form, added last 2 sentences to first paragraph following "**IMPORTANT**," rewrote paragraph preceding 3., and substituted present second sentence for former second sentence in the second paragraph of 3. (c) (3) (C); in (i), in the paragraph following "NOTICE OF OBJECTION," substituted "MUST MAKE SURE THAT THE COURT RECEIVES YOUR" for "MUST FILE YOUR" and inserted the present next to the last sentence, and deleted "(Signature)," "(Name, printed or typed)," "(Address)" and "(Telephone number)," respectively, from the last four blank lines; deleted the designation of "(j)," the introductory paragraph, and the heading of "REQUEST FOR APPOINTMENT OF AN ATTORNEY"; and substituted "I do/do not want the Court" for "I want the Court" and added a second sentence.

The first 2002 amendment rewrote this Rule.

The second 2002 amendment substituted "to

that parent by publication" for "by publication as to that parent" in (b)(1)(D); substituted "paragraph (2)(B), (2)(C), and (2)(D)" for "paragraphs (2)(B) and (2)(C)" in (b)(2)(A); in (b)(2)(C), substituted "If a person" for "The show cause order need not be served on: (i) a parent of a person for whom a guardian is to be appointed if the person," inserted "person's," and substituted "the court shall order notice to that parent by publication pursuant to section (c) of this Rule" for "or (ii) a person who has executed a written consent pursuant to Rule 9-102"; and added (b)(2)(D).

The 2007 amendment rewrote (a); rewrote (b) and its Cross reference notes; rewrote (c), deleted former (c) through (f) and redesignated accordingly; added "Except as ... Rule" and substituted "the" for "The" in the Show Cause Order form of present (e); in (f), deleted case name requirements in the introductory language, rewrote item 2 and item 3, substituted "another party agrees" for "the adoptive parents agree" and "another party" for "them" in item 4; deleted "in" and the case name language; added "REQUEST FOR APPOINTMENT OF ATTORNEY" to the "NOTICE OF OBJECTION" form title, rewrote item 2 of the form, and deleted the Committee note for the section of the rule.

Editor's note. — The Reporter's Note concerning this rule in the supplement to One Hundred Fifty-first Report of the Rules Committee, signed and filed by order of the Court of Appeals November 6, 2002, provides in part: "Chapter 496, Acts of 2001 (HB 705), modified notice to parents of persons to be adopted by providing that if the person to be adopted already has been adjudicated to be a child in need of assistance and the petitioner has made good faith efforts to serve a show cause order on the parent by certified mail and private process, the court shall order notice by publication, instead of waiving notice which the previous version of the statute allowed. Publication is to be in one or more newspapers of general circulation in the county in which the petition was filed. The same modifications also apply to notice to parents of persons for whom a guardian is to be appointed, and the appropriate parallel changes to subsection (b)(2) were inadvertently omitted when the Rule was initially revised."

Purpose of former Rule D74. — See Palmisano v. Baltimore County Welfare Bd., 249 Md. 94, 238 A.2d 251, cert. denied, 393 U.S. 853, 89 S. Ct. 93, 21 L. Ed. 2d 123 (1968).

Scope of Rule. — This Rule extends § 5-322 (a) of the Family Law Article and requires more detailed information. In re Adoption No. 93321055, 344 Md. 458, 687 A.2d 681 (1997).

Application of notice provisions. — The notice provisions of former Rule D74 applied to a proceeding for guardianship with the right to consent to long-term care short of adoption. 57 Op. Att'y Gen. 18 (1972).

The consent of the father of a child born out of wedlock and never legitimated is not necessary in a proceeding for guardianship preceding adoption nor is the father entitled to notice of the filing of a petition for such guardianship. 57 Op. Att'y Gen. 18 (1972).

Court-appointed counsel for child was entitled to a notice and hearing on a petition for guardianship. In re Adoption/Guardianship No. 3155, 103 Md. App. 300, 653 A.2d 521 (1995).

Mother could not be deemed to have consented to the termination of her parental rights when a municipal social services department mailed the notice of the guardianship proceeding and show cause order to an attorney in the same office with the mother's attorney who represented her in her daughter's children in need of assistance case. Accordingly, the mother did not consent to the termination of her parental rights, by operation of law, as her failure to file a timely notice of objection in the proceeding did not exist because the 30-day time period for the mother to file a notice of objection was tolled. In re Adoption/Guardianship of Genara A., 152 Md. App. 725, 834 A.2d 185 (2003).

When a mother failed to timely object to an agency's petitions for guardianship of the mother's children, after being served with orders to show cause which properly advised the mother of the consequences of such a failure, the mother's untimely objections to the petitions were properly stricken because the mother's failure to timely object gave rise to the mother's deemed consent to the petitions by operation of law, and that consent was not revocable within 30 days, as was a consent signed and filed with the court. In re Adoption/Guardianship of Audrey B., 186 Md. App. 454, 974 A.2d 965 (2009).

Child in need of assistance. — A child who has previously been adjudicated a child in need of assistance and who is subject to a guardianship petition is a party to the proceeding and entitled to notice and counsel. In re Adoption/Guardianship No. T97036005, 358 Md. 1, 746 A.2d 379 (2000).

Under subsection (h) of this Rule, the contents of a show cause order, when a petition for guardianship or adoption has been filed, must explain the nature of the proceeding, inform the natural parents of their right to object, and indicate the consequences to the parents of failing to object within the stated time limit. In re Adoption/Guardianship No. 6Z000045, 372 Md. 104, 812 A.2d 271 (2002).

Under this Rule, a guardianship or adoption petitioner must notify "each attorney who represented a parent" in a juvenile proceeding in which the child was adjudicated a child in need of assistance (CINA), and the Rule, in referring to "each attorney," acknowledges that a petitioner for guardianship may be required to notify more than one attorney if multiple attorneys represented a parent during the CINA proceedings, so such a requirement still commands notice to at least one attorney who represented the parent at the CINA proceed-ing. In re Adoption/Guardianship No. 6Z000045, 372 Md. 104, 812 A.2d 271 (2002).

Stated in In re Adoption/Guardianship No. TPR970011, 122 Md. App. 462, 712 A.2d 597 (1998).

Cited in In re Adoption Nos. T00130003 & T00130004, 370 Md. 250, 805 A.2d 254 (2002).

Rule 9-106. Appointment of attorney — Attorney affidavit — Investigation.

(a) **Appointment of attorney.** The court shall appoint an attorney for a party when required by Code, Family Law Article:

(1) § 5-307 in a Public Agency Guardianship;

(2) § 5-307 in a Public Agency Adoption without Prior TPR;

(3) § 5-307 in a Public Agency Adoption after TPR;

(4) § 5-3A-07 in a Private Agency Guardianship;

(5) § 5-3A-07 in a Private Agency Adoption; or

(6) § 5-3B-06 in an Independent Adoption.

(b) **Payment of attorney's fees.** Even if the prospective adoptee is not entitled to a court-appointed attorney, the person is entitled to consult an attorney chosen by that person. The adoptive parents or agency may agree to pay all or part of the attorney's fees on behalf of the person, or the court may order the adoptive parents or agency to do so.

Cross references. — See Code, Family Law Article, §§ 5-309 as to a Public Agency Guardianship; 5-309 as to a Public Agency Adoption without Prior TPR; 5-3A-09 as to a Private Agency Guardianship; and 5-3B-08 as to an Independent Adoption.

(c) **Affidavit of attorney.** (1) With a parental consent. The attorney shall file an affidavit in the applicable form set forth at the end of this Title with a consent signed by a parent when required by Code, Family Law Article:

(A) § 5-321 in a Public Agency Guardianship;

(B) § 5-339 in a Public Agency Adoption without Prior TPR;

(C) § 5-3A-19 in a Private Agency Guardianship; or

(D) § 5-3B-21 in an Independent Adoption.

(2) With a consent of a prospective adoptee. The attorney shall file an affidavit in the applicable form set forth at the end of this Title with a consent signed by a prospective adoptee if the adoptee is represented and

(A) is a minor; or

(B) has a disability that makes the prospective adoptee incapable of effectively participating in a case.

Cross references. — See Rule 9-102 (b)(3).

(d) **Investigation by court.** (1) Optional. The court may order an investigation as provided by Code, Family Law Article:

(A) § 5-317 in a Public Agency Guardianship;

(B) § 5-3A-16 in a Private Agency Guardianship; or

(C) § 5-3B-16 in an Independent Adoption.

(2) *Mandatory.* The court shall order an investigation in a nonconsensual Independent Adoption as provided in Code, Family Law Article, § 5-3B-16.

(3) *Recommendation of investigator.* If requested by the court, the report of any investigation may include the recommendation of the investigator.

(4) *In writing.* The report of any investigation shall be submitted to the court in writing and filed among the records of the proceeding. (Amended June 4, 2007, effective July 1, 2007.)

Source. — This Rule is new.

Effect of amendments. — The 2007 amendment rewrote the rule and the Cross reference.

Disclosure. — The court may order disclosure of information reported to it by its investigators to other government authorities; to the extent that disclosure is not connected with the State's administration of its foster care and adoption programs, however, the court should weigh its interest in disclosure against the privacy interests of the parties. In all cases, the court should limit disclosure to that information necessary to serve its interest. 79 Op. Att'y Gen. 179 (March 9, 1994).

Court may consider facts learned in proceedings to adopt another child of same father. — The chancellor did not err when she considered facts she had learned in an earlier case relating to the adoption of another of the objecting father's children, since the court may act without investigation in cases where it has personal knowledge of the facts. Walker v. Gardner, 221 Md. 280, 157 A.2d 273 (1960).

Investigation by court of county where former statute inapplicable. — There was nothing in repealed § 76 of Article 16 similar to this Rule, to prevent the court in any county in which the section did not apply from having proper investigation made as to the home, etc., of adoptive parents. Anderson v. Barkman, 195 Md. 94, 72 A.2d 709 (1950).

It was appropriate, and within the court's discretion to order an investigation, although this Rule mandates an investigation only in contested cases. In re Adoption No. 90072022/CAD, 87 Md. App. 630, 590 A.2d 1094 (1991).

Rule 9-107. Objection.

(a) **In general.** Any person having a right to participate in a proceeding for adoption or guardianship may file a notice of objection to the adoption or guardianship. The notice may include a statement of the reasons for the objection and a request for the appointment of an attorney.

Cross references. — *See* Rule 9-105 for Form of Notice of Objection.

(b) **Time for filing objection.** (1) *In general.* Except as provided by subsections (b) (2) and (b) (3) of this Rule, any notice of objection to an adoption or guardianship shall be filed within 30 days after the show cause order is served.

(2) *Service outside of the State.* If the show cause order is served outside the State but within the United States, the time for filing a notice of objection shall be within 60 days after service.

(3) *Service outside of the United States.* If the show cause order is served outside the United States, the time for filing a notice of objection shall be within 90 days after service.

(4) *Service by publication in a newspaper and on website.* If the court orders service by publication, the deadline for filing a notice of objection shall be not

less than 30 days from the later of (A) the date that the notice is published in a newspaper of general circulation or (B) the last day that the notice is published on the Maryland Department of Human Resources website.

(c) **Service.** The clerk shall serve a copy of any notice of objection on all parties in the manner provided by Rule 1-321.

(d) **Response.** Within 10 days after being served with a notice of objection, any party may file a response challenging the standing of the person to file the notice or the timeliness of the filing of the notice.

(e) **Hearing.** If any party files a response, the court shall hold a hearing promptly on the issues raised in the response.

(f) **Access to records.** If the court determines that the person filing the notice of objection has standing to do so and that the notice is timely filed, it shall enter an order permitting the person to inspect the papers filed in the proceeding subject to reasonable conditions imposed in the order. (Amended June 4, 2007, effective July 1, 2007; June 7, 2011, effective July 1, 2011.)

Source. — This Rule is derived in part from former Rule D76 and is in part new.

Effect of amendments. — The 2007 amendment rewrote (b)(4); substituted "all parties" for "the petitioner" in (c); substituted "any party" for "the petitioner" in (d) and (e); in (d), substituted "10" for "ten", added "the" before "notice", and deleted "of objection" at the end.

The 2011 amendment inserted "of general circulation" following "newspaper" in (b)(4).

Child in need of assistance. — A child who has previously been adjudicated a child in need of assistance and who is subject to a guardianship petition has a right to a hearing on the merits if he timely objects to the petition. In re Adoption/Guardianship No. T97036005, 358 Md. 1, 746 A.2d 379 (2000).

Revocation of deemed consent arising due to untimely objection — When a mother failed to timely object to an agency's petitions for guardianship of the mother's children, after being served with orders to show cause which properly advised the mother of the consequences of such a failure, the mother's untimely objections to the petitions were properly stricken because the mother's failure to timely object gave rise to the mother's deemed consent to the petitions by operation of law, and that consent was not revocable within 30 days, as was a consent signed and filed with the court. In re Adoption/Guardianship of Audrey B., 186 Md. App. 454, 974 A.2d 965 (2009).

Quoted in In re Adoption/Guardianship No. T00032005, 141 Md. App. 570, 786 A.2d 64 (2001).

Stated in In re Adoption No. 93321055, 344 Md. 458, 687 A.2d 681 (1997).

Cited in In re Adoption Nos. T00130003 & T00130004, 370 Md. 250, 805 A.2d 254 (2002).

Rule 9-108. Temporary custody.

The court may make an award of temporary custody of a minor prior to a hearing. (Amended June 4, 2007, effective July 1, 2007.)

Cross references. — See Code, Family Law Article, § 5-3B-12.

Source. — This Rule is derived from former Rule D78 (d).

Effect of amendments. — The 2007 amendment added the Cross reference.

The court may make a temporary award of custody prior to a hearing if it deems such actions in the child's best interests. Thumma v. Hartsook, 239 Md. 38, 210 A.2d 151 (1965).

Rule 9-109. Hearing on merits.

(a) **Requirement.** (1) Generally. The court shall hold a hearing and make findings on the record on the merits of a guardianship or adoption petition as provided by Code, Family Law Article:

(A) § 5-318 in a nonconsensual Public Agency Guardianship;

(B) § 5-335 in a Public Agency Adoption without Prior TPR;

(C) § 5-347 in a Public Agency Adoption after TPR;

(D) § 5-3A-32 in a Private Agency Adoption; or

(E) § 5-3B-17 in an Independent Adoption.

(2) Guardianship. The court may hold a hearing on the merits of a consensual Public or Private Agency Guardianship petition.

Cross references. — See Code, Family Law Article, § 5-318 as to Public Agency Guardianship.

(b) **Adoption.** (1) Persons present at hearing. Unless excused for good cause shown, each petitioner and the person to be adopted shall be present at the hearing on the merits in an adoption action. The hearing shall be conducted out of the presence of all persons other than the petitioners, the person to be adopted, and those persons whose presence the court deems necessary or desirable.

Committee note. — Social policy against public disclosure of adoption proceedings compels all hearings to be as private as possible. This Rule leaves to the discretion of the trial court the extent to which this consideration must be relaxed in the interest of fair trial.

(2) Considerations. In ruling on a petition for adoption, the court shall make the considerations required by Code, Family Law Article:

(A) § 5-337 in a Public Agency Adoption without Prior TPR;

(B) § 5-349 in a Public Agency Adoption after TPR;

(C) § 5-3A-34 in a Private Agency Adoption; or

(D) § 5-3B-19 in an Independent Adoption.

(3) Findings by the court. In an adoption action, the court shall determine on the record whether:

(A) Necessary consents have been filed;

(B) Any required consents have been revoked;

Cross references. — Rules 9-111 (b) and 9-112 (a).

(C) Appropriate notices have been served;

(D) Any investigative reports have been filed;

(E) All questioned or disputed issues have been resolved;

(F) In a nonconsensual independent adoption, whether the findings required by Code, Family Law Article, § 5-3B-21 have been met;

(G) The adoptive parents are fit and proper to be the parents of the person to be adopted;

(H) The best interests of the person to be adopted will be served by the adoption; and

(I) Other appropriate matters have been resolved. (Amended June 4, 2007, effective July 1, 2007.)

Cross references. — See Code, Family Law Article, §§ 5-337 as to a Public Agency Adoption without Prior TPR; 5-349 as to a Public Agency Adoption after TPR; 5-3A-34 as to a Private Agency Adoption; and 5-3B-19, 5-3B-22, and 5-3B-23 as to an Independent Adoption.

Source. — This Rule is in part derived from former Rule D77 and is in part new.

Effect of amendments. — The 2007 amendment rewrote (a); deleted former (b) and redesignated accordingly, added present (b)(2) and made related changes, in (b)(3)(D), added "Any" and substituted "have been filed" for "are in order" in (b)(3)(F), substituted "a nonconsensual independent adoption" for "a contested case" and "whether ... been met" for "where adoption will terminate a parent's rights, the parents are unfit or extraordinary circumstances exist"; and added the Cross reference.

Child entitled to hearing. — In termination of parental rights case in which only surviving parent was deemed to have consented to termination of parental rights, court erred in not affording a twelve year old child who had lived with the parent for five years and had developed an emotional relationship with the parent the opportunity to be heard on issue whether termination of child's filial relationship with parent was in child's best interest. In re Adoption No. 6Z970003, 127 Md. App. 33, 731 A.2d 467 (1999), rev'd on other grounds in part by In re Adoption/Guardianship No. T97036005, 358 Md. 1, 746 A.2d 379 (2000).

A child who has previously been adjudicated a child in need of assistance and who is subject to a guardianship petition has a right to a hearing on the merits if he timely objects to the petition. In re Adoption/Guardianship No. T97036005, 358 Md. 1, 746 A.2d 379 (2000).

Because the required factors in § 5-313 of the Family Law Article apply when a child objects to a guardianship petition and requests a hearing, the trial judge's refusal to grant a postponement to ascertain the child's views on the petition, based on the child's lack of standing, was an error of law. In re Adoption/Guardianship No. T97036005, 358 Md. 1, 746 A.2d 379 (2000).

No hearing was required on petition for visitation rights by natural mother. Weinschel v. Strople, 56 Md. App. 252, 466 A.2d 1301 (1983).

Rule 9-110. Accounting report.

(a) **Duty to file.** In an independent adoption other than an adoption by a stepparent or relative of the person to be adopted, each petitioner shall file an accounting report before the entry of a final judgment of adoption.

(b) **Contents.** The accounting report shall include:

(1) a statement of all payments and disbursements of money or anything of value, including benefits in kind, made by or on behalf of any petitioner in connection with the adoption;

(2) the approximate date the payment or disbursement was made or the benefit was provided;

(3) the name of the payee and the beneficiary; and

(4) the amount of the payment or disbursement or the reasonable value of the benefit provided.

The court may require the production of documentation to substantiate the accounting report. (Amended June 4, 2007, effective July 1, 2007.)

Cross references. — Code, Family Law Article, § 5-3B-24 as to an Independent Adoption.

Source. — This Rule is new.

Effect of amendments. — The 2007 amendment substituted "anything" for "any item" in (b)(1); and substituted "§ 5-3B-24 as to an Independent Adoption" for "§ 5-321 and 5-327 (c)" in the Cross reference note.

Rule 9-111. Judgment of adoption or guardianship.

(a) **Time.** The court may not enter a judgment of adoption or guardianship before the time set forth in Code, Family Law Article:

(1) § 5-319 in a Public Agency Guardianship;

(2) § 5-336 in a Public Agency Adoption without Prior TPR;

(3) § 5-348 in a Public Agency Adoption after TPR;

(4) § 5-3A-17 in a Private Agency Guardianship;

(5) § 5-3A-33 in a Private Agency Adoption; or

(6) § 5-3B-18 in an Independent Adoption.

(b) **Information from other court.** If a required consent indicates that any revocation of the consent must be filed in a court other than the trial court, the trial court may not enter a judgment of adoption or guardianship until it has obtained from the other court a copy of all papers filed in connection with the consent or an affidavit of the clerk of the other court that no papers were filed in connection with the consent.

(c) **Supplemental report.** Before entering a judgment of adoption or guardianship, the court may require a supplemental written report from the investigating officer or agency.

(d) **Change of name.** If the name of the person adopted is changed, the judgment of adoption shall state the new name of the person adopted and the names of the adopting parents.

(e) **Spouse of parent.** If the adopting parent is the spouse of a parent of the person to be adopted, the judgment shall specifically state whether and to what extent the parental rights of the parent are affected. (Amended June 4, 2007, effective July 1, 2007.)

Committee note. — Any attempt to set aside a judgment of adoption by reason of a procedural defect shall be filed with the court within one year following entry of the judgment. *See* Code, Family Law Article, §§ 5-342 as to a Public Agency Adoption without Prior TPR; 5-353 as to a Public Agency Adoption after TPR; 5-3A-37 as to a Private Agency Adoption; and 5-3B-26 as to an Independent Adoption.

An adoptive relationship created by a judgment of adoption in another jurisdiction shall be given full faith and credit by the courts of this State. *See* Code, Family Law Article, §§ 5-305 as to a Public Agency Adoption without Prior TPR; 5-305 as to a Public Agency Adoption after TPR; 5-3A-05 as to a Private Agency Adoption; and 5-3B-04 as to an Independent Adoption.

For the legal effect of adoption, see Code, Family Law Article, §§ 5-341 as to a Public Agency Adoption without Prior TPR; 5-352 as to a Public Agency Adoption after TPR; 5-3A-36 as to a Private Agency Adoption; and 5-3B-25 as to an Independent Adoption.

Source. — This Rule is derived in part from former Rule D79 and is in part new.

Effect of amendments. — The 2007 amendment rewrote (a); deleted "natural or biological" twice in (e); rewrote the Committee note; and added "in part" and "and is in part new" in the Source note.

Stated in In re Adoption No. 93321055, 344 Md. 458, 687 A.2d 681 (1997).

Rule 9-112. Court records.

(a) **Dockets.** The clerk shall keep separate dockets for (1) adoption and guardianship proceedings and (2) revocations of consent to adoption or guardianship for which there are no pending adoption or guardianship proceedings in that county. These dockets are not open to inspection by any person, including the parents, except upon order of court. If the index to a docket is kept apart from the docket itself, the index is open to inspection.

(b) **Sealing of records.** All pleadings and other papers in adoption and guardianship proceedings shall be sealed when they are filed and are not open to inspection by any person, including the parents, except upon an order of court. If a final decree of adoption was entered before June 1, 1947 and the record is not already sealed, the record may be sealed only on motion of a party. The clerk shall notify each person entitled to notice that the adoption has been finalized. (Amended June 4, 2007, effective July 1, 2007.)

Cross references. — *See* Code, Health-General Article, § 4-211, concerning the amendment and replacement of birth certificates following adoption and the requirement that the clerk transmit to the Department of Health and Mental Hygiene a report of adoption or revocation of adoption.

Source. — This Rule is derived from former Rule D80 a and c.

Effect of amendments. — The 2007 amendment added the third sentence in (b).

University of Baltimore Law Review. — For article, "The Adoption Trilemma: The Adult Adoptee's Emerging Search for his Ancestral Identity," see 8 U. Balt. L. Rev. 496 (1979).

Rule 9-113. Medical and mental health history.

Except in an adoption by a stepparent or relative, the person authorized to place a minor child for adoption shall affirm to the court that the person has made reasonable efforts to compile and make available to a prospective adoptive parent (1) all of the prospective adoptee's medical and mental health records that the person has or (2) a comprehensive medical and mental health history of the prospective adoptee and the prospective adoptee's parents, except that the records of the parents shall contain no identifying information unless identifying information was previously exchanged by agreement. (Amended June 4, 2007, effective July 1, 2007.)

Cross references. — *See* Code, Family Law Article, §§ 5-356 as to a Public Agency Adoption without Prior TPR; 5-356 as to a Public Agency Adoption after TPR; and 5-3A-39 as to a Private Agency Adoption.

Source. — This Rule is new.

Effect of amendments. — The 2007 amendment added "and mental health" to the rule heading; rewrote the introductory language; deleted (b) and made related changes;

added "See" and substituted "5-356 as ...
Agency Adoption" for "§ 5-320" in the Cross
reference note.

CHAPTER 200. DIVORCE, ANNULMENT, ALIMONY, CHILD SUPPORT, AND CHILD CUSTODY.

Rule 9-201. Scope.
The Rules in this Chapter are applicable to a circuit court action in which divorce, annulment, alimony, child support, custody, or visitation is sought. These Rules do not apply to actions in a juvenile court or actions brought solely under Code, Family Law Article, Title 4, Subtitle 5. (Added Mar. 5, 2001, effective July 1, 2001.)

Source. — This Rule is new.

Rule 9-202. Pleading.
(a) **Signing-telephone number.** A party shall personally sign each pleading filed by that party and, if the party is not represented by an attorney, shall state in the pleading a telephone number at which the party may be reached during ordinary business hours.

Cross references. — See Rule 1-202 (u).

(b) **Child custody.** When child custody is an issue, each party shall provide in the party's first pleading the information required by Code, Family Law Article, § 9.5-209 (a).

(c) **Amendment to complaint.** Except when a judgment of limited divorce has been entered, a complaint may be amended pursuant to Rule 2-341 to include a ground for divorce that by reason of the passage of sufficient time has become a ground for divorce after the filing of the complaint.

(d) **Supplemental complaint for absolute divorce after judgment of limited divorce.** A party who has obtained a judgment of limited divorce may file a supplemental complaint for an absolute divorce in the same action in which the limited divorce was granted if (1) the sole ground for the absolute divorce is that the basis of the limited divorce by reason of the lapse of sufficient time has become a ground for an absolute divorce and (2) the supplemental complaint is filed not later than two years after the entry of the judgment of limited divorce. Service of the supplemental complaint shall be in accordance with Rule 1-321 if the defendant has an attorney of record in the action at the time the supplemental complaint is filed. Otherwise, service of the supplemental complaint shall be in accordance with Rule 2-121 or in accordance with Rule 2-122.

Cross references. — For automatic termination of an attorney's appearance, see Rule 2-132.

(e) **Financial statement — Spousal support.** If spousal support is claimed by a party and either party alleges that no agreement regarding support exists, each party shall file a current financial statement in substantially the form set forth in Rule 9-203 (a). The statement shall be filed with the party's pleading making or responding to the claim. If the claim or the denial of an agreement is made in an answer, the other party shall file a financial statement within 15 days after service of the answer.

(f) **Financial statement — Child support.** If establishment or modification of child support is claimed by a party, each party shall file a current financial statement under affidavit. The statement shall be filed with the party's pleading making or responding to the claim. If the establishment or modification of child support in accordance with the guidelines set forth in Code, Family Law Article, §§ 12-201—12-204 is the only support issue in the action and no party claims an amount of support outside of the guidelines, the required financial statement shall be in substantially the form set forth in Rule 9-203 (b). Otherwise, the statement shall be in substantially the form set forth in Rule 9-203 (a). (Added Mar. 5, 2001, effective July 1, 2001; amended April 5, 2005, effective July 1, 2005; Feb. 10, 2009, effective May 1, 2009; June 7, 2011, effective July 1, 2011.)

Source. — This Rule is derived in part from former Rule S72 a, c, and f and is in part new.

Effect of amendments. — The 2005 amendment substituted "9.5-209 (a)" for "9-209" in (b).

The 2009 amendment substituted "Rule 1-202(t)" for "Rule 1-202(s) in the cross reference note to (a).

The 2011 amendment substituted "Rule 1-202 (u)" for "Rule 1-202 (t)" in the cross reference note.

Stated in Barnes v. Barnes, 181 Md. App. 390, 956 A.2d 770 (2008).

Cited in Potts v. Potts, 142 Md. App. 448, 790 A.2d 703 (2002), cert. denied, 369 Md. 181, 798 A.2d 553 (2002); Att'y Griev. Comm'n v. Kreamer, 404 Md. 282, 946 A.2d 500 (2008).

Rule 9-203. Financial statements.

(a) **Financial statement — General.** Unless section (b) of this Rule applies, a Financial Statement required by Rule 9-202 shall be in substantially the following form:

[caption of case]

FINANCIAL STATEMENT OF _____
(Name)

(General)

CHILDREN	**AGE**
_____	_____
_____	_____
_____	_____

_____ _____

MONTHLY EXPENSES

Item	SELF	CHILDREN	TOTAL
A. PRIMARY RESIDENCE			
Mortgage			
Insurance (homeowners)			
Rent/Ground Rent			
Taxes			
Gas & Electric			
Electric Only			
Heat (oil)			
Telephone			
Trash Removal			
Water Bill			
Cell Phone/Pager			
Repairs			
Lawn & Yard Care (snow removal)			
Replacement Furnishings/Appliances			
Condominium Fee (not included elsewhere)			
Painting/Wallpapering			
Carpet Cleaning			
Domestic Assistance/Housekeeper			
Pool			
Other:			
SUB TOTAL			
B. SECONDARY RESIDENCE (i.e. Summer Home/Rental)			
Mortgage			
Insurance (homeowners)			
Rent/Ground Rent			
Taxes			
Gas & Electric			
Electric Only			
Heat (oil)			
Telephone			
Trash Removal			
Water Bill			
Cell Phone/Pager			
Repairs			
Lawn & Yard Care (snow removal)			

Replacement
Furnishings/Appliances   _____   _____   _____
Condominium Fee
(not included elsewhere)   _____   _____   _____
Painting/Wallpapering   _____   _____   _____
Carpet Cleaning   _____   _____   _____
Domestic
Assistance/Housekeeper   _____   _____   _____
Pool   _____   _____   _____
Other: _____   _____   _____
SUB TOTAL   _____   _____   _____

C. OTHER HOUSEHOLD NECESSITIES
Food   _____   _____   _____
Drug Store Items   _____   _____   _____
Household Supplies   _____   _____   _____
Other: _____   _____   _____
SUB TOTAL   _____   _____   _____

D. MEDICAL/DENTAL
Health Insurance   _____   _____   _____
Therapist/Counselor   _____   _____   _____
Extraordinary Medical   _____   _____   _____
Dental/Orthodontia   _____   _____   _____
Ophthalmologist/Glasses   _____   _____   _____
Other: _____   _____   _____
SUB TOTAL   _____   _____   _____

E. SCHOOL EXPENSES
Tuition/Books   _____   _____   _____
School lunch   _____   _____   _____
Extracurricular activities   _____   _____   _____
Clothing/Uniforms   _____   _____   _____
Room & Board   _____   _____   _____
Daycare/Nursery School   _____   _____   _____
Other: _____   _____   _____
SUB TOTAL   _____   _____   _____

F. RECREATION & ENTERTAINMENT
Vacations   _____   _____   _____
Videos/Theater   _____   _____   _____
Dining Out   _____   _____   _____
Cable TV/Internet   _____   _____   _____
Allowance   _____   _____   _____
Camp   _____   _____   _____
Memberships   _____   _____   _____
Dance/Music Lessons etc.   _____   _____   _____
Horseback Riding   _____   _____   _____
Other: _____   _____   _____

SUB TOTAL _____ _____ _____

G. TRANSPORTATION EXPENSE
    Automobile Payment _____ _____ _____
    Automobile Repairs _____ _____ _____
    Maintenance/Tags/Tires/etc. _____ _____ _____
    Oil/Gas _____ _____ _____
    Automobile Insurance _____ _____ _____
    Parking Fees _____ _____ _____
    Bus/Taxi _____ _____ _____
    Other: _____ _____ _____
SUB TOTAL _____ _____ _____

H. GIFTS
    Holiday Gifts _____ _____ _____
    Birthdays _____ _____ _____
    Gifts to others _____ _____ _____
    Charities _____ _____ _____
SUB TOTAL _____ _____ _____

J. CLOTHING
    Purchasing _____ _____ _____
    Laundry _____ _____ _____
    Alterations/Dry Cleaning _____ _____ _____
    Other: _____ _____ _____
SUB TOTAL _____ _____ _____

K. INCIDENTALS
    Books & Magazines _____ _____ _____
    Newspapers _____ _____ _____
    Stamps/Stationery _____ _____ _____
    Banking Expense _____ _____ _____
    Other: _____ _____ _____
SUB TOTAL _____ _____ _____

L. MISCELLANEOUS/OTHER
    Alimony/Child Support
    (from a previous Order) _____ _____ _____
    Religious Contributions _____ _____ _____
    Hairdresser/Haircuts _____ _____ _____
    Manicure/Pedicure _____ _____ _____
    Pets/Boarding _____ _____ _____
    Life Insurance _____ _____ _____
    Other: _____ _____ _____
SUB TOTAL _____ _____ _____

TOTAL MONTHLY EXPENSES: _____ _____ _____

Number of Dependent Children, including children who have not attained the age of 19 years, are not married or self-supporting, and are enrolled in secondary school: _____

INCOME STATEMENT

GROSS MONTHLY WAGES: $_____
Deductions:
Federal $_____
State $_____
Medicare $_____
F.I.C.A. $_____
Retirement $_____

Total Deductions: $_____
NET INCOME FROM WAGES: $_____

**OTHER GROSS INCOME: (alimony,
part-time job, rentals etc.)** $_____
Deductions:
a. _____   _____
b. _____   _____
c. _____   _____
**Total deductions from Other
income:** $_____

NET OTHER INCOME: $_____

TOTAL MONTHLY INCOME $_____

ASSETS & LIABILITIES

ASSETS:

Real Estate $_____
Furniture (in the marital home) $_____
Bank Accounts/Savings $_____
U.S. Bonds $_____
Stocks/Investments $_____
Personal Property $_____
Jewelry $_____
Automobiles $_____
Boats $_____
Other: $_____

TOTAL ASSETS: $_____

LIABILITIES:

Mortgage $_____
Automobiles $_____
Notes payable to relatives $_____
Bank Loans $_____
Accrued Taxes $_____
Balance of Credit Card Accounts $_____
a. _____   _____

31

b. _____   _____

c. _____   _____

Other: _____

TOTAL LIABILITIES: $_____

TOTAL NET WORTH: $_____

SUMMARY:

TOTAL INCOME: $_____
TOTAL EXPENSES: $_____
EXCESS OR DEFICIT: $_____

I solemnly affirm under the penalties of perjury that the contents of the foregoing Financial Statement, Monthly Expense List, and Assets and Liabilities Statement are true to the best of my knowledge, information, and belief.

_____   _____

Date   Signature

(b) **Financial statement — Child support guidelines.** If the establishment or modification of child support in accordance with the guidelines set forth in Code, Family Law Article, §§ 12-201—12-204 is the only support issue in the action and no party claims an amount of support outside of the guidelines, the financial statement required by section (f) of Rule 9-202 shall be in substantially the following form:

[caption of case]

FINANCIAL STATEMENT
(Child Support Guidelines)

I, _____, state that:
          My name

I am the _____
          State Relationship (for example, mother, father, aunt, grandfather, guardian, etc.)

of the minor child(ren), including children who have not attained the age of 19 years, are not married or self-supporting, and are enrolled in secondary school:

Name	Date of Birth	Name	Date of Birth
Name	Date of Birth	Name	Date of Birth
Name	Date of Birth	Name	Date of Birth

The following is a list of my income and expenses (see below*):

See definitions on other side before filling out.
Total monthly income (before taxes) $_____
Child support I am paying for my other child(ren) each month   _____
Alimony I am paying each month to _____
                             (Name of Person(s))
Alimony I am receiving each month from _____
                             (Name of Person(s))

For the child or children listed above:
    The monthly health insurance premium   _____
    Work-related monthly child care expenses   _____
    Extraordinary monthly medical expenses   _____
    School and transportation expenses   _____

I solemnly affirm under the penalties of perjury that the contents of the foregoing paper are true to the best of my knowledge, information, and belief.

_____   _____
        Date   Signature

[side 2 of form]

Total Monthly Income: Include income from all sources including self-employment, rent, royalties, business income, salaries, wages, commissions, bonuses, dividends, pensions, interest, trusts, annuities, social security benefits, workers compensation, unemployment benefits, disability benefits, alimony or maintenance received, tips, income from side jobs, severance pay, capital gains, gifts, prizes, lottery winnings, etc. Do not report benefits from means-tested public assistance programs, such as food stamps or AFDC.

Extraordinary Medical Expenses: Uninsured expenses over $100 for a single illness or condition including orthodontia, dental treatment, asthma treatment, physical therapy, treatment for any chronic health problems, and professional counseling or psychiatric therapy for diagnosed mental disorders.

Child Care Expenses: Actual child care expenses incurred on behalf of a child due to employment or job search of either parent with amount to be determined by actual experience or the level required to provide quality care from a licensed source.

School and Transportation Expenses: Any expenses for attending a special or private elementary or secondary school to meet the particular needs of the child and expenses for transportation of the child between the homes of the parents.

  (c) **Amendment to financial statement.** If there has been a material change in the information furnished by a party in a financial statement filed

---

  * To figure the monthly amount of expenses, weekly expenses should be multiplied by 4.3 and yearly expenses should be divided by 12. If you do not pay the same amount each month for any of the categories listed, figure what your average monthly expense is.

pursuant to Rule 9-202, the party shall file an amended statement and serve a copy on the other party at least ten days before the scheduled trial date or by any earlier date fixed by the court.

(d) **Inspection of financial statements.** Except as provided in this section, inspection of a financial statement filed pursuant to the Rules in this Chapter is governed by Code, State Government Article, § 10-617 (a) and (f). A financial statement is open to inspection if it is an exhibit (1) attached to a motion that has been ruled upon by the court or (2) marked for identification at trial, whether or not offered in evidence, and if offered, whether or not admitted. A party who does not want the financial statement open to public inspection pursuant to this section may make a motion at any time to have it sealed. (Added Mar. 5, 2001, effective July 1, 2001; amended Oct. 31, 2002, effective Jan. 1, 2003; May 8, 2007, effective July 1, 2007.)

Cross references. — See Rule 16-1002 (c) and Rule 16-1009.

Source. — This Rule is new.

Effect of amendments. — The 2002 amendment added "including children who have not attained the age of 19 years, are not married or self-supporting, and are enrolled in secondary school" following "Number of Dependent Children" at the end of the "Monthly Expenses" form in (a) and beneath the "State Relationship" line near the beginning of the "Financial Statement" form in (b).

The 2007 amendment added the exception at the beginning, the second and third sentences, and the cross reference in (d).

Cited in Barnes v. Barnes, 181 Md. App. 390, 956 A.2d 770 (2008).

Rule 9-204. Educational seminar.

(a) **Applicability.** This Rule applies in an action in which child support, custody, or visitation is involved and the court determines to send the parties to an educational seminar designed to minimize disruptive effects of separation and divorce on the lives of children.

Cross references. — Code, Family Law Article, § 7-103.2.

(b) **Order to attend seminar.** (1) Subject to subsection (b) (2) of this Rule and as allowed or required by the county's case management plan required by Rule 16-202 b., the court may order the parties to attend an educational seminar within the time set forth in the plan. The content of the seminar shall be as prescribed in section (c) of this Rule. If a party who has been ordered to attend a seminar fails to do so, the court may not use its contempt powers to compel attendance or to punish the party for failure to attend, but may consider the failure as a factor in determining custody and visitation.

(2) A party who (A) is incarcerated, (B) lives outside the State in a jurisdiction where a comparable seminar or course is not available, or (C) establishes good cause for exemption may not be ordered to attend the seminar.

Committee note. — Code, Family Law Article, § 7-103.2 (c)(2)(v) prohibits exemption based on evidence of domestic violence, child abuse, or neglect.

(c) **Content.** The seminar shall consist of one or two sessions, totaling six hours. Topics shall include:

(1) the emotional impact of divorce on children and parents;

(2) developmental stages of children and the effects of divorce on children at different stages;

(3) changes in the parent-child relationship;

(4) discipline;

(5) transitions between households;

(6) skill-building in

(A) parental communication with children and with each other,

(B) explaining divorce to children,

(C) problem-solving and decision-making techniques,

(D) conflict resolution,

(E) coping strategies,

(F) helping children adjust to family changes,

(G) avoiding inappropriate interactions with the children, and

(H) developing constructive parenting arrangements; and

(7) resources available in cases of domestic violence, child abuse, and neglect.

(d) **Scheduling.** The provider of the seminar shall establish scheduling procedures so that parties in actions where domestic violence, child abuse, or neglect is alleged do not attend the seminar at the same time and so that any party who does not wish to attend a seminar at the same time as the opposing party does not have to do so.

(e) **Costs.** The fee for the seminar shall be set in accordance with Code, Courts Article, § 7-202. Payment may be compelled by order of court and assessed among the parties as the court may direct. For good cause, the court may waive payment of the fee. (Added Mar. 5, 2001, effective July 1, 2001.)

Source. — This Rule is new.

Rule 9-205. Mediation of child custody and visitation disputes.

(a) **Scope of Rule.** This Rule applies to any case under this Chapter in which the custody of or visitation with a minor child is an issue, including an initial action to determine custody or visitation, an action to modify an existing order or judgment as to custody or visitation, and a petition for contempt by reason of non-compliance with an order or judgment governing custody or visitation.

(b) **Duty of court.** (1) Promptly after an action subject to this Rule is at issue, the court shall determine whether:

(A) mediation of the dispute as to custody or visitation is appropriate and would likely be beneficial to the parties or the child; and

(B) a properly qualified mediator is available to mediate the dispute.

(2) If a party or a child represents to the court in good faith that there is a genuine issue of physical or sexual abuse of the party or child, and that, as a result, mediation would be inappropriate, the court shall not order mediation.

(3) If the court concludes that mediation is appropriate and feasible, it shall enter an order requiring the parties to mediate the custody or visitation

dispute. The order may stay some or all further proceedings in the action pending the mediation on terms and conditions set forth in the order.

Cross references. — With respect to subsection b (2) of this Rule, see Rule 1-341 and Rules 3.1 and 3.3 of the Maryland Lawyers' Rules of Professional Conduct.

(c) **Scope of mediation.** (1) The court's initial order may not require the parties to attend more than two mediation sessions. For good cause shown and upon the recommendation of the mediator, the court may order up to two additional mediation sessions. The parties may agree to further mediation.

(2) Mediation under this Rule shall be limited to the issues of custody and visitation unless the parties agree otherwise in writing.

(d) **If agreement.** If the parties agree on some or all of the disputed issues, the mediator may assist the parties in making a record of the points of agreement. The mediator shall provide copies of any memorandum of points of agreement to the parties and their attorneys for review and signature. If the memorandum is signed by the parties as submitted or as modified by the parties, a copy of the signed memorandum shall be sent to the mediator, who shall submit it to the court.

Committee note. — It is permissible for a mediator to make a brief record of points of agreement reached by the parties during the mediation and assist the parties in articulating those points in the form of a written memorandum, so that they are clear and accurately reflect the agreements reached. Mediators should act only as scribes recording the parties' points of agreement, and not as drafters creating legal memoranda.

(e) **If no agreement.** If no agreement is reached or the mediator determines that mediation is inappropriate, the mediator shall so advise the court but shall not state the reasons. If the court does not order mediation or the case is returned to the court after mediation without an agreement as to all issues in the case, the court promptly shall schedule the case for hearing on any pendente lite or other appropriate relief not covered by a mediation agreement.

(f) **Confidentiality.** Confidentiality of mediation communications under this Rule is governed by Rule 17-109.

Cross references. — For the definition of "mediation communication," see Rule 17-102 (e).

(g) **Costs.** Payment of the compensation, fees, and costs of a mediator may be compelled by order of court and assessed among the parties as the court may direct. In the order for mediation, the court may waive payment of the compensation, fees, and costs.

Cross references. — For the qualifications and selection of mediators, see Rule 17-104.

(Added Mar. 5, 2001, effective July 1, 2001; Nov. 1, 2001, effective Jan. 1, 2002; Feb. 8, 2005, effective July 1, 2005.)

Source. — This Rule is derived from former Rule S73A.

————

Effect of amendments. — The 2001 amendment rewrote (d) and added its committee note; and rewrote (f) and its cross reference note.

The 2005 amendment inserted "Lawyers'" before "Rules of Professional Conduct" in the cross references note in (b)(3).

Rule 9-205.0. Appointment of child's counsel .

(a) **Applicability.** This Rule applies to the appointment of child's counsel in actions involving child custody or child access.

Cross references. — See Code, Family Law Article, § 1-202 and the *Maryland Guidelines for Practice for Court-Appointed Lawyers Representing Children in Cases Involving Child Custody or Child Access.*

(b) **Factors.** In determining whether to appoint child's counsel, the court should consider the nature of the potential evidence to be presented, other available methods of obtaining information, including social service investigations and evaluations by mental health professionals, and available resources for payment. Appointment may be most appropriate in cases involving the following factors, allegations, or concerns:

(1) request of one or both parties;

(2) high level of conflict;

(3) inappropriate adult influence or manipulation;

(4) past or current child abuse or neglect;

(5) past or current mental health problems of the child or party;

(6) special physical, educational, or mental health needs of the child that require investigation or advocacy;

(7) actual or threatened family violence;

(8) alcohol or other substance abuse;

(9) consideration of terminating or suspending parenting time or awarding custody or visitation to a non-parent;

(10) relocation that substantially reduces the child's time with a parent, sibling, or both; or

(11) any other factor that the court considers relevant.

COMMENT

A court should provide for adequate and effective child's counsel in all cases in which an appointment is warranted, regardless of the economic status of the parties. The court should make the appointment as soon as practicable after it determines that the appointment is warranted. A court should appoint only lawyers who have agreed to serve in child custody and child access cases in the assigned role and have been trained in accordance with Guideline 4 of the Maryland Guidelines for Practice for Court-Appointed Lawyers Representing Children in Cases Involving Child Custody or Child Access. In making appointments, the court should fairly and equitably distribute cases among all qualified attorneys, taking into account the attorney's availability and caseload. Before asking an attorney to provide representation pro bono publico to a child, the court should consider the number of other similar cases the attorney has recently accepted on a pro bono basis from the court.

(c) **Appointment order.** (1) Content. An order appointing child's counsel shall:

(A) specify whether the attorney is to serve as a Child's Best Interest Attorney, Child's Advocate Attorney, or Child's Privilege Attorney;

(B) authorize the appointed attorney to have reasonable access to the child and to all otherwise privileged or confidential information about the child, without the necessity of any further order of court or the execution of a release;

(C) permit the attorney to participate in discovery under Title 2 of these Rules as though the child were a party;

(D) provide that the service and notice provisions in Title 1 of these Rules apply as though the child were a party;

(E) state any other duties or responsibilities required by the court;

(F) state when the appointment terminates; and

(G) unless the attorney has agreed to serve pro bono publico, include provisions concerning compensation for the attorney.

Cross references. — The court should write an appointment order in plain language, understandable to non-lawyers.

(2) Copies to parties and counsel. The court shall send a copy of the order appointing counsel to each attorney of record and to each party, whether or not represented by an attorney. (Added May 8, 2007, effective July 1, 2007.)

Cross references. — As to the attorney's compensation, see Guideline 6 of the Maryland Guidelines for Practice for Court-Appointed Lawyers Representing Children in Cases Involving Child Custody or Child Access.
Source. — This Rule is new.

Rule 9-205.2. Parenting Coordination.

(a) **Applicability.** This Rule applies to the appointment of parenting coordinators by a court and to consent orders approving the employment of parenting coordinators by the parties in actions under this Chapter.

Committee note. — Actions in which parenting coordination may be used include an initial action to determine custody or visitation and an action to modify an existing order or judgment as to custody or visitation.

(b) **Definitions.** In this Rule, the following definitions apply:

(1) Parenting Coordination. "Parenting coordination" means a process in which the parties work with a parenting coordinator to reduce the effects or potential effects of conflict on the parties' child. Although parenting coordination may draw upon alternative dispute resolution techniques, parenting coordination is not governed by the Rules in Title 17, except as otherwise provided in this Rule.

(2) Parenting Coordinator. "Parenting coordinator" means an impartial provider of parenting coordination services.

(c) **Qualifications of Parenting Coordinator.** (1) Age, Education, and Experience. To be designated or approved by the court as a parenting coordinator, an individual shall:

(A) be at least 21 years old and hold a bachelor's degree from an accredited college or university;

(B) hold a post-graduate degree in psychology, social work, counseling, negotiation, conflict management, or a related subject area, or from an accredited medical or law school;

(C) have at least three years of related professional experience undertaken after receiving the post-graduate degree; and

(D) hold a current license if required in the individual's area of practice.

(2) Parenting Coordination Training. A parenting coordinator also shall have completed:

(A) at least 20 hours of training in a family mediation training program meeting the requirements of Rule 17-106 (b); and

(B) at least 40 hours of accredited specialty training in topics related to parenting coordination, including conflict coaching, developmental stages of children, dynamics of high conflict families, family violence dynamics, parenting skills, problem-solving techniques, and the stages and effects of divorce.

Committee note. — The accredited specialty training requirement may be met by training offered by recognized national organizations such as the American Bar Association or the Association of Family and Conciliation Courts.

(3) Continuing Education. Within each calendar year, a parenting coordinator shall complete a minimum of four hours of continuing education approved by the Administrative Office of the Courts in one or more of the topics listed in subsection (c)(2) of this Rule and in recent developments in family law. The Administrative Office shall maintain a list of approved continuing education programs.

(d) **Parenting Coordinator Lists.** An individual who has the qualifications listed in section (c) of this Rule and seeks court appointment as a parenting coordinator shall submit an application to the family support services coordinator of the circuit court for each county in which the individual seeks appointment. The application shall document that the individual meets the qualifications required in section (c) of this Rule. If satisfied that the applicant meets the qualifications, the family support services coordinator shall place the applicant's name on a list of qualified individuals which, together with the information submitted by each individual on the list, shall be accessible to the public.

(e) **Approval of Parenting Coordinator Employed by Parties.** In any action in which the custody of or visitation with a child of the parties is or was at issue, the parties, by agreement, may employ a parenting coordinator to assist them in dealing with existing or future conflicts regarding their access to and responsibilities for the child. The parties may jointly request the court to enter a consent order approving the agreement. The court shall enter such an order if it finds that the parenting coordinator has the qualifications set forth in section (c) of this Rule and that the agreement:

(1) is in writing and signed by the parties and the parenting coordinator;

(2) states the services to be provided by the parenting coordinator;

(3) states the extent to which the parenting coordinator may receive confidential or privileged information pertaining to the child or the parties and any limitations on the use of that information by the parenting coordinator;

(4) states the amount or rate of compensation to be paid to the parenting coordinator, which may exceed the amount or rate provided for in section (k) of this Rule; and

(5) is otherwise consistent with the best interest of the child.

Committee note. — Parties who, by agreement, employ a parenting coordinator on their own initiative are not required to seek court approval. Section (e) of this Rule applies only if they request a court order approving the agreement.

(f) **Appointment of Parenting Coordinator by Court.** In an action in which the custody of or visitation with a child of the parties is in issue and the court determines that the level of conflict between the parties with respect to that issue so warrants, the court may appoint a parenting coordinator in accordance with this section.

(1) Appointment During Pendency of Action. On motion of a party, on joint request of the parties, or on the court's own initiative and after notice and hearing, the court may appoint a parenting coordinator during the pendency of the action. Unless sooner terminated in accordance with this Rule, the appointment shall terminate upon the entry of a judgment granting or modifying custody or visitation.

(2) Appointment Upon Entry of Judgment. Upon entry of a judgment granting or modifying custody or visitation, the court, with the consent of the parties and after a hearing, may appoint a parenting coordinator. The court may appoint the individual who served as a parenting coordinator during the pendency of the action. Unless sooner terminated in accordance with this Rule, the appointment of a post-judgment parenting coordinator shall not exceed two years unless the parties and the parenting coordinator agree in writing to an extension for a specified longer period.

Committee note. — Appointment of a parenting coordinator does not affect the applicability of Rules 9-204, 9-205, or 9-205.1, nor does the appointment preclude the use of an alternative dispute resolution process under Title 17 of these Rules.

(3) Selection. The court may not appoint an individual as a parenting coordinator unless the individual:

(A) has the qualifications listed in section (c) of this Rule,

(B) is willing to serve as the parenting coordinator in the action, and

(C) agrees not to charge or accept a fee in excess of that allowed in the applicable fee schedule adopted pursuant to subsection (k)(1) of this Rule.

(4) Contents of Order or Judgment. An order or judgment appointing a parenting coordinator shall include:

(A) the name, business address, e-mail address, and telephone number of the parenting coordinator;

(B) if there are allegations or findings of domestic violence committed by or against a party or child, any provisions the court deems necessary to address the safety and protection of the parties, all children of the parties, other children residing in the home of a party, and the parenting coordinator; and

Committee note. — The order must be consistent with the relevant provisions of any other existing order, such as a "no contact" requirement that is included in a civil protective order or is a condition of pre-trial release in a criminal case.

(C) if the appointment is of a post-judgment parenting coordinator, any decision-making authority of the parenting coordinator authorized pursuant to subsection (g)(9) of this Rule.

(g) **Services Permitted.** As appropriate, a parenting coordinator may:

(1) if there is no operative custody and visitation order, work with the parties to develop an agreed plan for custody and visitation;

(2) if there is an operative custody and visitation order, assist the parties in amicably resolving disputes about the interpretation of and compliance with the order and in making any joint recommendations to the court for any changes to the order;

(3) educate the parties about making and implementing decisions that are in the best interest of the child;

(4) assist the parties in developing guidelines for appropriate communication between them;

(5) suggest resources to assist the parties;

(6) assist the parties in modifying patterns of behavior and in developing parenting strategies to manage and reduce opportunities for conflict in order to reduce the impact of any conflict upon their child;

(7) in response to a subpoena issued at the request of a party or an attorney for a child of the parties, or upon action of the court pursuant to Rule 2-514 or 5-614, produce documents and testify in the action as a fact witness;

(8) if concerned that a party or child is in imminent physical or emotional danger, communicate with the court or court personnel to request an immediate hearing; and

(9) decide post-judgment disputes by making minor, temporary modifications to child access provisions ordered by the court if (A) the judgment or post-judgment order of the court authorizes such decision making, and (B) the parties have agreed in writing or on the record that the post-judgment parenting coordinator may do so.

Committee note. — Examples of such modifications include one-time or minor changes in the time or place for child transfer and one-time or minor deviations from access schedules to accommodate special events or circumstances.

(h) **Services Not Permitted.** A parenting coordinator may not:

(1) except as permitted by subsections (g)(7) and (8) of this Rule, communicate orally or in writing with the court or any court personnel regarding the substance of the action;

Committee note. — This subsection does not prohibit communications with respect to routine administrative matters; collection of fees, including submission of records of the number of contacts with each party and the duration of each contact; or resignation. Nothing in the subsection affects the duty to report child abuse or neglect under any provision of

federal or State law or the right of the parenting coordinator to defend against allegations of
misconduct or negligence.

(2) testify in the action as an expert witness; or Cross reference: See Rule
5-702 as to expert witnesses.

Cross references. — See Rule 5-702 as to
expert witnesses.

(3) except for decision making by a post-judgment parenting coordinator
authorized pursuant to subsection (g)(9) of this Rule, make parenting decisions
on behalf of the parties.

(i) **Confidential Information.** (a) Access to Case Records. Except as
otherwise provided in this subsection, the parenting coordinator shall have
access to all case records in the action. If a document or any information
contained in a case record is not open to public inspection under the Rules in
Title 16, Chapter 1000, the court shall determine whether the parenting
coordinator may have access to it and shall specify any conditions to that
access.

Cross references. — See Rule 16-1001 for
the definition of "case record."

(2) Other Confidential Information. (A) A parenting coordinator may not
require or coerce the parties or an attorney for the child to release any
confidential information that is not included in the case record

(B) Confidential or privileged information received by the parenting coordinator from a party or from a third person with the consent of a party may be
disclosed by the parenting coordinator to the other party, to an attorney for the
child, and in court pursuant to subsections (g)(7) and (8) of this Rule. Unless
otherwise required by law, the parenting coordinator may not disclose the
information to anyone else without the consent of the party who provided the
information or consented to a third person providing it.

(j) **Removal or Resignation of Parenting Coordinator.** (1) Removal.
The court shall remove a parenting coordinator:

(A) on motion of a party or an attorney for the child, if the court finds good
cause, or

(B) on a finding that continuation of the appointment is not in the best
interest of the child.

(2) Resignation. A parenting coordinator may resign at any time by written
notice sent by first-class mail to each party and any attorney for the child. The
notice shall state the effective date of the resignation and that the parties may
request the appointment of another parenting coordinator. The notice shall be
sent at least 15 days before the effective date of the resignation. Promptly after
mailing the notice, and at least seven days before the effective date of
resignation, the parenting coordinator shall file a copy of the notice with the
court.

(k) **Fees.** (1) Fee Schedules. Subject to the approval of the Chief Judge of the Court of Appeals, the county administrative judge of each circuit court may develop and adopt maximum fee schedules for parenting coordinators. In developing the fee schedules, the county administrative judge shall take into account the availability of qualified individuals willing to provide parenting coordination services and the ability of litigants to pay for those services. A parenting coordinator appointed by the court may not charge or accept a fee for parenting coordination services in that action in excess of the fee allowed by the applicable schedule. Violation of this subsection shall be cause for removal from all lists maintained pursuant to section (d) of this Rule, Rule 9-205, and the Rules in Title 17.

(2) Allocation of Fees and Expenses. Subject to any agreement entered into by the parties pursuant to section (e) of this Rule, the court shall designate how and by whom the parenting coordinator shall be paid. If the court finds that the parties have the financial means to pay the fees and expenses of the parenting coordinator, the court shall allocate the fees and expenses of the parenting coordinator between the parties and may enter an order against either or both parties for the reasonable fees and expenses. (Added June 7, 2011, effective July 1, 2011.)

Source. — This Rule is new.

Stated in Van Schaik v. Van Schaik, 200 Md. App. 126, 24 A.3d 241 (2011).

Rule 9-206. Child support guidelines.
(a) **Definitions.** The following definitions apply in this Rule:

(1) Shared physical custody. "Shared physical custody" has the meaning stated in Code, Family Law Article, § 12-201 (i).

(2) Worksheet. "Worksheet" means a document to compute child support under the guidelines set forth in Code, Family Law Article, Title 12, Subtitle 2.

(b) **Filing of worksheet.** In an action involving the establishment or modification of child support, each party shall file a worksheet in the form set forth in section (c) or (d) of this Rule. Unless the court directs otherwise, the worksheet shall be filed not later than the date of the hearing on the issue of child support.

Cross references. — See Code, Family Law Article, § 12-203 (a) and *Walsh v. Walsh*, 333 Md. 492 (1994).

(c) **Primary physical custody.** Except in cases of shared physical custody, the worksheet shall be in substantially the following form:

	In the
_____	Circuit Court for _____
v.	
_____	No. _____

WORKSHEET A — CHILD SUPPORT OBLIGATION:
PRIMARY PHYSICAL CUSTODY

Name of Child	Date of Birth	Name of Child	Date of Birth
Name of Child	Date of Birth	Name of Child	Date of Birth
Name of Child	Date of Birth	Name of Child	Date of Birth

	Mother	Father	Combined
1. MONTHLY ACTUAL INCOME (Before taxes) (Code, Family Law Article, § 12-201 (b))	$	$	/////////
a. Minus preexisting child support payment actually paid	-	-	/////////
b. Minus alimony actually paid	-	-	/////////
c. Plus/minus alimony awarded in this case	+/-	+/-	/////////
2. MONTHLY ADJUSTED ACTUAL INCOME	$	$	$
3. PERCENTAGE SHARE OF INCOME Divide each parent's income on line 2 by the combined income on line 2.	%	%	/////////
4. BASIC CHILD SUPPORT OBLIGATION (Apply line 2 Combined Income to Child Support Schedule.)	/////////	/////////	$
a. Work-Related Child Care Expenses (Code, Family Law Article § 12-204 (g))	$	$	+
b. Health Insurance Expenses (Code, Family Law Article § 12-204 (h) (1))	$	$	+

   c. Extraordinary Medical Expenses
     (Code, Family Law Article,
     § 12-204 (h) (2) $ $ +

   d. Cash Medical Support
     (Code, Family Law Article,
     §12-102 (c) — applies only to
     a child support order under
     Title IV, Part D of the Social
     Security Act) $ $ +

   e. Additional Expenses
     (Code, Family Law Article,
     § 12-204 (i)) $ $ +

5. TOTAL CHILD SUPPORT OBLIGATION   ////////   /////////
   (Add lines 4, 4a, 4b, 4c, 4d, and 4e).   ////////   //////// $

6. EACH PARENT'S CHILD SUPPORT   ////////
   OBLIGATION (Multiply line   ////////
   5 by line 3 for each parent.) $ $ ////////

7. TOTAL DIRECT PAY BY EACH PARENT   ////////
   (Add the expenses shows on lines   ////////
   4a, 4b, 4c, 4d, and 4e paid by   ////////
   each parent.) $ $ ////////

8. RECOMMENDED CHILD SUPPORT AMOUNT   ////////
   (Subtract line 7 from line 6 for each parent) $ $ ////////

9. RECOMMENDED CHILD SUPPORT ORDER   ////////
   (Bring down amount from line 8 for   ////////
   the non-custodial parent only.   ////////
   If this is a negative   ////////
   number, see Comment (2), below.) $ $ ////////

Comments or special adjustments, such as (1) any adjustment for certain third party benefits paid to or for the child of an obligor who is disabled, retired, or receiving benefits as a result of a compensable claim (see Code, Family Law Article, § 12-204 (j) or (2) that there is a negative dollar amount on line 9, which indicates a recommended child support order directing the custodial parent to reimburse the non-custodial parent this amount for "direct pay" expenses):

PREPARED BY: DATE:

(d) **Shared physical custody.** In cases of shared physical custody, the worksheet shall be in substantially the following form:

_____   In the
                                 Circuit Court for _____

          v.

_____   No. _____

WORKSHEET B — CHILD SUPPORT OBLIGATION: SHARED PHYSICAL CUSTODY

Name of Child	Date of Birth	Name of Child	Date of Birth
Name of Child	Date of Birth	Name of Child	Date of Birth
Name of Child	Date of Birth	Name of Child	Date of Birth

	Mother	Father	Combined
1. MONTHLY ACTUAL INCOME (Before taxes) (Code, Family Law Article, §12-201 (b))	$	$	///////// /////////
a. Minus preexisting child support payment actually paid	-	-	///////// /////////
b. Minus alimony actually paid	-	-	/////////
c. Plus/minus alimony awarded in this case	+/-	+/-	///////// /////////
2. MONTHLY ADJUSTED ACTUAL INCOME	$	$	$
3. PERCENTAGE SHARE OF INCOME Divide each parent's income on line 2 by the combined income on line 2.)	%	%	///////// ///////// ////////// //////////
4. BASIC CHILD SUPPORT OBLIGATION (Apply line 2 Combined Income to Child Support Schedule.)	//////// //////// ////////	//////// //////// ////////	$
5. ADJUSTED BASIC CHILD SUPPORT OBLIGATION (Multiply Line 4 by 1.5)	//////// ////////	//////// ////////	$
6. OVERNIGHTS with each parent (must total 365)			365

7. PERCENTAGE WITH EACH PARENT   ////////
    (Line 6 divided by 365)   A   % B   %   ////////

STOP HERE IF Line 7 is less than 35%   ////////   ////////   ////////
for either parent. Shared physical   ////////   ////////   ////////
custody does not apply. (Use   ////////   ////////   ////////
Worksheet A, instead.)   ////////   ////////   ////////

---

8. EACH PARENT'S THEORETICAL CHILD   ////////
    SUPPORT OBLIGATION (Multiply line   ////////
    5 by line 3 for each   ////////
    parent.)   A$ B$ ////////

---

9. BASIC CHILD SUPPORT OBLIGATION   ////////
    FOR TIME WITH OTHER PARENT   ////////
    (Multiply line 8A by line 7B   ////////
    and put answer on line 9A.)   ////////
    (Multiply line 8B by line 7A   ////////
    and put answer on line 9B.)   A$ B$ ////////

---

10. NET BASIC CHILD SUPPORT   ////////
    OBLIGATION (Subtract lesser   ////////
    amount from greater amount in   ////////
    line 9 and place answer here   ////////
    under column with greater amount   ////////
    in Line 9.) $ $ ////////

---

11. EXPENSES: ////////   ////////
    a. Work-Related Child Care   ////////   ////////
        Expenses   ////////   ////////
        (Code, Family Law Article,   ////////   ////////
        § 12-204 (g))   ////////   ////////   +

---

    b. Health Insurance Expenses   ////////   ////////
        (Code, Family Law Article   ////////   ////////
        (Code, Family Law Article   ////////   ////////
        § 12-204 (h) (1))   ////////   ////////   +

---

    c. Extraordinary Medical   ////////   ////////
        Expenses   ////////   ////////
        (Code, Family Law Article,   ////////   ////////
        § 12-204 (h) (2))   ////////   ////////   +

---

    d. Cash Medical Support   ////////   ////////
        (Code, Family Law Article,   ////////   ////////
        § 12-102 (c) — applies only to ////////   ////////
        a child support order under   ////////   ////////

47

Title IV, Part D of the Social	///////	///////	
Security Act)	///////	///////	+

e. Additional Expenses	///////	///////	
(Code, Family Law Article,	///////	///////	
§ 12-204 (i))	///////	///////	+

12. NET ADJUSTMENT FROM WORKSHEET   ///////////
C. Enter amount from line l,   ///////////
WORKSHEET C, if applicable. If   ///////////
not, continue to Line 13. $ $ ///////////

13. NET BASIC CHILD SUPPORT   ///////////
OBLIGATION (From Line 10,   ///////////
WORKSHEET B) $ $ ///////////

14. RECOMMENDED CHILD SUPPORT ORDER   ///////////
(If the same parent owes money   ///////////
under Lines 12 and 13, add   ///////////
these two figures to obtain   ///////////
the amount owed by that parent. If   ///////////
one parent owes money under   ///////////
Line 12 and the other owes   ///////////
money under Line 13, subtract   ///////////
the lesser amount from the   ///////////
greater amount to obtain the   ///////////
difference. The parent owing   ///////////
the greater of the two amounts   ///////////
on Lines 12 and 13 will owe   ///////////
that difference as the child   ///////////
support obligation. NOTE: The   ///////////
amount owed in a shared custody   ///////////
arrangement may not exceed the   ///////////
amount that would be owed if   ///////////
the obligor parent were a   ///////////
noncustodial parent. See   ///////////
WORKSHEET A). $ $ ///////////

PREPARED BY: DATE:

Comments, or special adjustments, such as any adjustment for certain third party benefits paid to or for the child of an obligor who is disabled, retired, or receiving benefits as a result of a compensable claim (see Code, Family Law Article, § 12-204 (j)):

INSTRUCTIONS FOR WORKSHEET C: Use Worksheet C ONLY if any of the Expenses listed in lines 11 a, 11 b, 11 c, 11 d, or 11 e is directly paid out or received by the parents in a different proportion than the percentage share of income entered on line 3 of Worksheet B. Example: If the mother pays all of the day care, or parents split education/medical costs 50/50 and line 3 is other than 50/50. If there is more than one 11 e expense, the calculations on lines i and j below must be made for each expense.

WORKSHEET C — FOR ADJUSTMENTS, LINE 12, WORKSHEET B

	Mother	Father
a. Total amount of direct payments made for Line 11a expenses multiplied by each parent's percentage of income (Line 3, WORKSHEET B) (Proportionate share)	$	$
b. The excess amount of direct payments made by the parent who pays more than the amount calculated in Line a, above. (The difference between amount paid and proportionate share)	$	$
c. Total amount of direct payments made for Line 11b expenses multiplied by each parent's percentage of income (Line 3, WORKSHEET B)	$	$
d. The excess amount of direct payments made by the parent who pays more than the amount calculated in Line c, above.	$	$
e. Total amount of direct payments made for Line 11 c expenses multiplied by each parent's percentage of income (Line 3, WORKSHEET B)	$	$
f. The excess amount of direct payments made by the parent who pays more than the amount calculated in Line e, above.	$	$
g. Total amount of direct payments made for Line 11 d expenses multiplied by each parent's percentage of income (Line 3, WORKSHEET B)	$	$
h. The excess amount of direct payments made by the parent who pays more than the amount calculated in Line g, above.	$	$

i. Total amount of direct payments made for Line 11 e expenses multiplied by

each parent's percentage of income
(Line 3, WORKSHEET B). $ $

---

j. The excess amount of direct payments
made by the parent who pays more than the
amount calculated in Line i, above. $ $

---

k. For each parent, add lines b, d, f, h, and j $ $

---

l. Subtract lesser amount from greater
amount in Line k, above. Place the answer
on this line under the lesser amount in
Line k. Also enter this answer on Line 12
of WORKSHEET B, in the same parent's
column. $ $

(Added Mar. 5, 2001, effective July 1, 2001; amended Dec. 4, 2007, effective
Jan. 1, 2008; amended Oct. 5, 2009, effective Oct. 5, 2009.)

Source. — This Rule is new.

Effect of amendments. — The December 4, 2007 Order, effective December 4, 2007, rewrote Worksheets A and B in (c) and (d), respectively.

The 2009 amendment in Worksheet A added 4 d ; in Worksheet B added 11 d; in Worksheet C added i and j; updated internal references accordingly; and made other related changes.

Cited in Att'y Griev. Comm'n v. Kreamer, 404 Md. 282, 946 A.2d 500 (2008).

Rule 9-207. Joint statement of marital and non-marital property.

(a) **When required.** When a monetary award or other relief pursuant to Code, Family Law Article, § 8-205 is an issue, the parties shall file a joint statement listing all property owned by one or both of them.

(b) **Form of property statement.** The joint statement shall be in substantially the following form:

JOINT STATEMENT OF PARTIES CONCERNING MARITAL AND NON-MARITAL PROPERTY

1. The parties agree that the following property is "marital property" as defined by Maryland Annotated Code, Family Law Article, § 8-201:

Description of Property		How Titled		Fair Market Value		Liens, Encumbrances, or Debt Directly Attributable	
Husband's Assertion	Wife's Assertion	Husband's Assertion	Wife's Assertion	Husband's Assertion	Wife's Assertion

2. The parties agree that the following property is not marital property because the property (a) was acquired by one party before marriage, (b) was acquired by one party by inheritance or gift from a third person, (c) has been excluded by valid agreement, or (d) is directly traceable to any of those sources:

Description of Property	How Titled	Fair Market Value	Liens, Encumbrances, or Debt Directly Attributable

Husband's Assertion	Wife's Assertion	Husband's Assertion	Wife's Assertion	Husband's Assertion	Wife's Assertion

3. The parties are not in agreement as to whether the following property is marital or non-marital:

Description of Property	How Titled	Fair Market Value	Liens, Encumbrances, or Debt Directly Attributable

Husband's Assertion	Wife's Assertion	Husband's Assertion	Wife's Assertion	Husband's Assertion	Wife's Assertion

Date _____

_____
Plaintiff or Attorney

Date _____

_____
Defendant or Attorney

INSTRUCTIONS:

1. If the parties do not agree about the title or value of any property, the parties shall set forth in the appropriate column a statement that the title or value is in dispute and each party's assertion as to how the property is titled or the fair market value.

2. In listing property that the parties agree is non-marital because the property is directly traceable to any of the listed sources of non-marital property, the parties shall specify the source to which the property is traceable.

(c) **Time for filing; procedure.** The joint statement shall be filed at least ten days before the scheduled trial date or by any earlier date fixed by the

51

court. At least 30 days before the joint statement is due to be filed, each party shall prepare and serve on the other party a proposed statement in the form set forth in section (b) of this Rule. At least 15 days before the joint statement is due, the plaintiff shall sign and serve on the defendant for approval and signature a proposed joint statement that fairly reflects the positions of the parties. The defendant shall timely file the joint statement, which shall be signed by the defendant or shall be accompanied by a written statement of the specific reasons why the defendant did not sign.

(d) **Sanctions.** If a party fails to comply with this Rule, the court, on motion or on its own initiative, may enter any orders in regard to the noncompliance that are just, including:

(1) an order that property shall be classified as marital or non-marital in accordance with the statement filed by the complying party;

(2) an order refusing to allow the noncomplying party to oppose designated assertions on the complying party's statement filed pursuant to this Rule, or prohibiting the noncomplying party from introducing designated matters in evidence.

Instead of or in addition to any order, the court, after opportunity for hearing, shall require the noncomplying party or the attorney advising the noncompliance or both of them to pay the reasonable expenses, including attorney's fees, caused by the noncompliance, unless the court finds that the noncompliance was substantially justified or that other circumstances make an award of expenses unjust.

Committee note. — The Joint Statement of Marital and Non-Marital Property is not intended as a substitute for discovery in domestic relations cases. (Added Mar. 5, 2001, effective July 1, 2001.)

Source. — This Rule is derived from former Rule S74.

Consideration of marital property. — Under § 8-205(a)(2)(iii) of the Family Law Article, a trial court lacked authority to order the transfer of title of a marital home, owned as tenants by the entirety, because § 8-205(a)(1) permitted a transfer only after a determination of what property was marital and the home was deemed non-marital property by the parties' Rule 9-207 statement. Brown v. Brown, 195 Md. App. 72, 5 A.3d 1144 (2010).

Property becoming non-marital distribution under this Rule should have been considered in making equitable distribu- tion. — Parties' agreement in a statement under this Rule as to certain property did not mean that the court could not consider such non-marital property in its equitable distribution of the remaining marital property. Flanagan v. Flanagan, 181 Md. App. 492, 956 A.2d 829 (2008).

Cited in Potts v. Potts, 142 Md. App. 448, 790 A.2d 703 (2002), cert. denied, 369 Md. 181, 798 A.2d 553 (2002); Gordon v. Gordon, 174 Md. App. 583, 923 A.2d 149 (2007); Murray v. Murray, 190 Md. App. 553, 989 A.2d 771 (2010); Murray v. Murray, 190 Md. App. 553, 989 A.2d 771 (2010).

Rule 9-208. Referral of matters to masters.

(a) **Referral.** (1) As of course. If a court has a full-time or part-time standing master for domestic relations matters and a hearing has been requested or is required by law, the following matters arising under this

Chapter shall be referred to the master as of course unless the court directs otherwise in a specific case:

(A) uncontested divorce, annulment, or alimony;

(B) alimony pendente lite;

(C) child support pendente lite;

(D) support of dependents;

(E) preliminary or pendente lite possession or use of the family home or family-use personal property;

(F) subject to Rule 9-205, pendente lite custody of or visitation with children or modification of an existing order or judgment as to custody or visitation;

(G) subject to Rule 9-205 as to child access disputes, constructive civil contempt by reason of noncompliance with an order or judgment relating to custody of or visitation with a minor child, the payment of alimony or support, or the possession or use of the family home or family-use personal property, following service of a show cause order upon the person alleged to be in contempt;

(H) modification of an existing order or judgment as to the payment of alimony or support or as to the possession or use of the family home or family-use personal property;

(I) counsel fees and assessment of court costs in any matter referred to a master under this Rule;

(J) stay of an earnings withholding order; and

(K) such other matters arising under this Chapter and set forth in the court's case management plan filed pursuant to Rule 16-202 b.

Committee note. — Examples of matters that a court may include in its case management plan for referral to a master under subsection (a) (1) (J) of this Rule include scheduling conferences, settlement conferences, uncontested matters in addition to the matters listed in subsection (a) (1) (A) of this Rule, and the application of methods of alternative dispute resolution.

(2) By order on agreement of the parties. By agreement of the parties, any other matter or issue arising under this Chapter may be referred to the master by order of the court.

(b) **Powers.** Subject to the provisions of an order referring a matter or issue to a master, the master has the power to regulate all proceedings in the hearing, including the power to:

(1) direct the issuance of a subpoena to compel the attendance of witnesses and the production of documents or other tangible things;

(2) administer oaths to witnesses;

(3) rule on the admissibility of evidence;

(4) examine witnesses;

(5) convene, continue, and adjourn the hearing, as required;

(6) recommend contempt proceedings or other sanctions to the court; and

(7) recommend findings of fact and conclusions of law.

(c) **Hearing.** (1) Notice. A written notice of the time and place of the hearing shall be sent to all parties.

(2) *Attendance of witnesses.* A party may procure by subpoena the attendance of witnesses and the production of documents or other tangible things at the hearing.

(3) *Record.* All proceedings before a master shall be recorded either stenographically or electronically, unless the making of the record is waived in writing by all parties. A waiver of the making of a record is also a waiver of the right to file exceptions that would require review of the record for their determination.

(d) **Contempt proceedings; referral for *de novo* hearing.** If, at any time during a hearing on a party's alleged constructive civil contempt, the master concludes that there are reasonable grounds to believe that the party is in contempt and that incarceration may be an appropriate sanction, the master shall (1) set a *de novo* hearing before a judge of the circuit court, (2) cause the alleged contemnor to be served with a summons to that hearing, and (3) terminate the master's hearing without making a recommendation. If the alleged contemnor is not represented by an attorney, the date of the hearing before the judge shall be at least 20 days after the date of the master's hearing and, before the master terminates the master's hearing, the master shall advise the alleged contemnor on the record of the contents of the notice set forth in Rule 15-206 (c) (2).

(e) **Findings and recommendations.** (1) *Generally.* Except as otherwise provided in section (d) of this Rule, the master shall prepare written recommendations, which shall include a brief statement of the master's findings and shall be accompanied by a proposed order. The master shall notify each party of the recommendations, either on the record at the conclusion of the hearing or by written notice served pursuant to Rule 1-321. In a matter referred pursuant to subsection (a) (1) of this Rule, the written notice shall be given within ten days after the conclusion of the hearing. In a matter referred pursuant to subsection (a) (2) of this Rule, the written notice shall be given within 30 days after the conclusion of the hearing. Promptly after notifying the parties, the master shall file the recommendations and proposed order with the court.

(2) *Supplementary report.* The master may issue a supplementary report and recommendations on the master's own initiative before the court enters an order or judgment. A party may file exceptions to new matters contained in the supplementary report and recommendations in accordance with section (f) of this Rule.

(f) **Exceptions.** Within ten days after recommendations are placed on the record or served pursuant to section (e) of this Rule, a party may file exceptions with the clerk. Within that period or within ten days after service of the first exceptions, whichever is later, any other party may file exceptions. Exceptions shall be in writing and shall set forth the asserted error with particularity. Any matter not specifically set forth in the exceptions is waived unless the court finds that justice requires otherwise.

(g) **Requirements for excepting party.** At the time the exceptions are filed, the excepting party shall do one of the following: (1) order a transcript of so much of the testimony as is necessary to rule on the exceptions, make an agreement for payment to ensure preparation of the transcript, and file a certificate of compliance stating that the transcript has been ordered and the agreement has been made; (2) file a certification that no transcript is necessary to rule on the exceptions; (3) file an agreed statement of facts in lieu of the transcript; or (4) file an affidavit of indigency and motion requesting that the court accept an electronic recording of the proceedings as the transcript. Within ten days after the entry of an order denying a motion under subsection (g) (4) of this section, the excepting party shall comply with subsection (g) (1). The transcript shall be filed within 30 days after compliance with subsection (g) (1) or within such longer time, not exceeding 60 days after the exceptions are filed, as the master may allow. For good cause shown, the court may shorten or extend the time for the filing of the transcript. The excepting party shall serve a copy of the transcript on the other party. The court may dismiss the exceptions of a party who has not complied with this section.

Cross references. — For the shortening or extension of time requirements, see Rule 1-204.

(h) **Entry of orders.** (1) In general. Except as provided in subsections (2) and (3) of this section,

(A) the court shall not direct the entry of an order or judgment based upon the master's recommendations until the expiration of the time for filing exceptions, and, if exceptions are timely filed, until the court rules on the exceptions; and

(B) if exceptions are not timely filed, the court may direct the entry of the order or judgment as recommended by the master.

(2) Immediate orders. This subsection does not apply to the entry of orders in contempt proceedings. If a master finds that extraordinary circumstances exist and recommends that an order be entered immediately, the court shall review the file and any exhibits and the master's findings and recommendations and shall afford the parties an opportunity for oral argument. The court may accept, reject, or modify the master's recommendations and issue an immediate order. An order entered under this subsection remains subject to a later determination by the court on exceptions.

(3) Contempt orders. (A) On recommendation by the master. On the recommendation by the master that an individual be found in contempt, the court may hold a hearing and direct the entry of an order at any time. The order may not include a sanction of incarceration.

(B) Following a *de novo* hearing. Upon a referral from the master pursuant to section (d) of this Rule, the court shall hold a *de novo* hearing and enter any appropriate order.

(i) **Hearing on exceptions.** (1) Generally. The court may decide exceptions without a hearing, unless a request for a hearing is filed with the exceptions or by an opposing party within ten days after service of the exceptions. The exceptions shall be decided on the evidence presented to the master unless: (A) the excepting party sets forth with particularity the additional evidence to be offered and the reasons why the evidence was not offered before the master, and (B) the court determines that the additional evidence should be considered. If additional evidence is to be considered, the court may remand the matter to the master to hear and consider the additional evidence or conduct a *de novo* hearing.

(2) *When hearing to be held.* A hearing on exceptions, if timely requested, shall be held within 60 days after the filing of the exceptions unless the parties otherwise agree in writing. If a transcript cannot be completed in time for the scheduled hearing and the parties cannot agree to an extension of time or to a statement of facts, the court may use the electronic recording in lieu of the transcript at the hearing or continue the hearing until the transcript is completed.

(j) **Costs.** The court, by order, may assess among the parties the compensation, fees, and costs of the master and of any transcript.

Committee note. — Compensation of a master paid by the State or a county is not assessed as costs.

(Added Mar. 5, 2001, effective July 1, 2001; amended Nov. 12, 2003, effective Jan. 1, 2004.)

Cross references. — See, Code, Family Law Article, § 10-131, prescribing certain time limits when a stay of an earnings withholding order is requested.

Source. — This Rule is derived in part from Rule 2-541 and former Rule S74A and is in part new.

Effect of amendments. — The 2003 amendment, in (a)(2), deleted "that is not triable of right before a jury" following "Chapter."

Referral to master proper. — Appellate court could not determine whether a paternity action was properly referred to a master under Md. R. 9-209(a)(1)(K) as the father failed to present the trial court's differentiated case management plan; in any event, Rule 9-208 is not a prohibition against referral to a master of proceedings that are not listed, and if a paternity action is not referable as of course to a master, it may be so referred by an exercise of the trial court's discretionary power under Md. R. 2-541(b)(2), which permits referrals to a master of any matter or issue, other than one specified in Md. R. 9-208, which is not triable of right before a jury. Stubbs v. Colandrea, 154 Md. App. 673, 841 A.2d 361 (2004).

Mother not denied notice. — As the record reflected that the master gave a lengthy discussion of his findings and recommendation at the conclusion of the hearing, and that he advised the parties of their rights to file exceptions, the mother was not deprived of notice. Green v. Green, 188 Md. App. 661, 982 A.2d 1150 (2009).

Adoption of master's recommendation prior to expiration of five-day period for filing exceptions in error. — In a juvenile proceedings involving a petition alleging that the parties' three children were in need of assistance, a trial court erred in adopting a master's recommendations changing custody of the parties' three children from the mother to the father prior to the expiration of the five days afforded by Rule 11-111(c) for the mother to file exceptions. Because California has assumed jurisdiction over the children's custody proceedings, however, the only remedy that the reviewing court was able to provide the mother was to reverse the lower courts' orders and dismiss the case, thereby relieving the mother of the collateral consequences she continued to suffer from the Maryland decision, which made no final disposition on the children in need of assistance allegations. In re Kaela C., 394 Md. 432, 906 A.2d 915 (2006).

Applied in Vogel v. Touhey, 151 Md. App. 682, 828 A.2d 268 (2003), cert. denied, 378 Md. 617, 837 A.2d 927 (2003).

Stated in Frase v. Barnhart, 379 Md. 100, 840 A.2d 114 (2003).

Cited in O'Brien v. O'Brien, 367 Md. 547, 790 A.2d 1 (2002); Fisher v. McCrary Crescent City, LLC, 186 Md. App. 86, 972 A.2d 954 (2009), cert. denied, 131 S. Ct. 637, 2010 U.S.

LEXIS 9156, 178 L. Ed. 2d 476 (U.S. 2010);
Bradford v. State, 199 Md. App. 175, 21 A.3d
123 (2011).

Rule 9-209. Testimony.

A judgment granting a divorce, an annulment, or alimony may be entered only upon testimony in person before an examiner or master or in open court. In an uncontested case, testimony shall be taken before an examiner or master unless the court directs otherwise. Testimony of a corroborating witness shall be oral unless otherwise ordered by the court for good cause. (Added Mar. 5, 2001, effective July 1, 2001.)

Cross references. — For the requirement of oral testimony by the plaintiff in a divorce action, see Code, Family Law Article, § 1-203 (c). For the requirement of corroboration, see Code, Family Law Article, § 7-101 (b). For default procedures, see Rule 2-613.

Source. — This Rule is derived from former Rules S73 and S75 a.

Rule 9-210. Attachment, seizure, and sequestration.

(a) **Alimony from a nonresident defendant.** A plaintiff who seeks alimony from a nonresident defendant under Code, Family Law Article § 11-104, may request an order for the attachment or sequestration of the defendant's property in accordance with the procedures of Rule 2-115. The court may enter any appropriate order regarding the property that is necessary to make the award effective.

(b) **Enforcement of an order awarding child support, alimony, attorney's fees, or a monetary award.** When the court has ordered child support, alimony, attorney's fees, or a monetary award, the property of a noncomplying obligor may be seized or sequestered in accordance with the procedures of Rules 2-648 and 2-651. (Added Mar. 5, 2001, effective July 1, 2001; amended Sept. 10, 2009, effective Oct. 1, 2009.)

Cross references. — For statewide Child Support Payment Incentive Program, see Code, Family Law Article, § 10-112.1.

Source. — This Rule is new.

Effect of amendments. — The 2009 amendment added the cross reference.

Applicability. — Because the husband in a divorce proceeding was not a noncomplying obligor pursuant to (b), and the law firm was not a transferee with knowledge pursuant to Rule 2-648(b), the circuit court, although purporting to grant the wife's emergency motion pursuant to Rule 2-535(b), erred in entering a money judgment for a monetary award granted to the wife against the husband's law firm, which had obtained a judgment against the proceeds from the sale of the marital home for its legal fees. De Arriz v. Klinger-De Arriz, 179 Md. App. 458, 947 A.2d 59 (2008).

FORMS FOR GUARDIANSHIPS THAT TERMINATE PARENTAL RIGHTS AND ADOPTIONS.

Form 9-102.1. Consent of parent to a public agency guardianship.

CONSENT OF PARENT TO GUARDIANSHIP WITH THE RIGHT TO
CONSENT TO ADOPTION OF _____ TO
THE _____ DEPARTMENT
OF SOCIAL SERVICES

INSTRUCTIONS

These instructions and attached consent form may be used only in cases where the child is a Child in Need of Assistance. Code, Family Law Article, Title 5, Subtitle 3, Part II.

The attached consent form is an important legal document. You must read all of these instructions BEFORE you sign the consent form. If you do not understand the instructions or the consent form, you should not sign it. If you are under 18 years old or if you have a disability that makes it difficult for you to understand, do not sign the consent form unless you have a lawyer.

A. Right to Have This Information in a Language You Understand

You have the right to have these instructions and the consent form translated into a language that you understand. If you cannot read or understand English, you should not sign the consent form. You should have this form translated for you into a language you do understand. The translated consent form is the one you should read and decide whether or not to sign. Any translation must have an affidavit attached in which the translator states that it is a true and accurate translation of this document.

B. Right to Speak with a Lawyer

You have the right to speak with a lawyer before you decide whether or not to consent.

If you are unable to afford a lawyer, you may be eligible for a lawyer through the Office of the Public Defender. You should contact the Office of the Public Defender, and ask for a lawyer to represent you in a D.S.S. (Department of Social Services) guardianship case.

You should not sign the consent form without a lawyer if you are under 18 years old or have a disability that makes it difficult for you to understand this document. If you are under 18 years old or have a disability that makes it difficult for you to understand this document, you are required to have a lawyer review the form with you before you can consent to the guardianship. You should contact the Office of the Public Defender, or let the Juvenile Court know that you need to have a lawyer appointed for you.

Even if you do not have the right to have the court appoint a lawyer for you or to be represented through the Office of the Public Defender, you have the right to speak with a lawyer you choose before you decide whether to consent.

C. Post-adoption Agreement

If you have made a written agreement with the adoptive parents for future contact (known as a post-adoption agreement), a copy of that agreement must be attached to the signed consent form. If you have a post-adoption agreement, and, after the adoption, the adoptive parents do not do what they agreed to do, it will not affect your consent to the guardianship or the adoption. However, if that happens, you have the right to ask a judge to make them do what they agreed to do. The judge can order you and the adoptive parents to go to mediation, order the adoptive parents to do what they agreed to do, or change the agreement if the judge decides that it is in the child's best interest.

D. Conditional Consent

If you decide to sign the consent form, you will have two choices:
(1) you can consent to the guardianship and the adoption of your child by a family approved by D.S.S.; or
(2) you can consent to the guardianship only if the child is adopted into a specific family. This is called a "conditional consent." If you sign a conditional consent, and the family whose name is on the consent cannot adopt the child, your consent will no longer be valid. The court will try to locate you to find out if you want to sign a new consent. If you do not sign a new consent, the court can have a trial to decide whether or not your parental rights should be ended (terminated) and whether or not guardianship with the right to consent to adoption should be granted to D.S.S., even without your consent.

E. Effect of Signing the Consent Form

IF YOU SIGN THE CONSENT FORM, AND THE GUARDIANSHIP IS GRANTED, YOU WILL BE GIVING UP ALL RIGHTS AND RESPONSI-BILITIES RELATING TO THE CHILD.

If you have a post-adoption agreement, you will keep only the rights the agreement gives you. Violation of the agreement will not affect your consent or the adoption.

After you sign the consent form, the person or agency to whom you give the form must file it in the Juvenile Court promptly. If a guardianship case has been filed, it will be filed in the guardianship case. If a guardianship case has not been filed, it will be filed in the child's CINA (Child in Need of Assistance) case. When it is filed, a copy of the filed consent form will be sent to you at the address you list at the end of the consent form. It is your responsibility to let the court know if your address changes.

F. Right to Revoke Consent

If you sign the consent form and then change your mind and no longer want to consent, you have the right to revoke (cancel) the consent **within 30 days after the date that it is filed in Juvenile Court**. The only way that you can revoke this consent is by giving a **signed written revocation statement** with the name, sex, and date of birth of the child (if you know it) to:

Juvenile Clerk, Circuit Court for _____, at
_____ (Address).

The written and signed revocation statement must be sent to the court, not to your social worker or lawyer. You may deliver your written revocation of consent in person or by mail. If it is not *received* by the Juvenile Clerk's office **within 30 days after the date the consent form was filed in court**, it will be too late, and you will not be able to withdraw the consent or stop the guardianship from being granted.

G. Further Notice of Guardianship and Adoption Proceedings

A petition for guardianship with the right to consent to adoption has been or will be filed in _____ Juvenile Court. If you sign the consent form, your written consent form will also be filed in the Juvenile Court. You have the right to be notified when the petition is filed, about any hearings before or after guardianship is granted, if and when guardianship is granted, and if and when the child is adopted. Any notices will be sent to the address given by you on the consent form, unless you write to the Juvenile Clerk at _____ (court's address) and give the clerk your new address. You may waive (give up) your right to notice if you wish to do so. Even if you give up your right to notice, someone from the court may contact you if further information is needed.

H. Compensation

Under Maryland law, you are not allowed to charge or receive money or compensation of any kind for the placement for adoption of your child or for your agreement to the adoptive parent having custody of your child, except that reasonable and customary charges or fees for adoption counseling, hospital, legal, or medical services may be paid.

I. Access to Birth and Adoption Records

When your child is at least 21 years old, your child, your child's other parent, or you may apply to the Maryland Secretary of the Department of Health and Mental Hygiene for access to certain birth and adoption records. If you do not want information about you to be disclosed (given) to that person, you have the right to prevent disclosure by filing a disclosure veto. Attached to this document is a copy of the form that you may use if you want to file a disclosure veto.

J. Adoption Search, Contact, and Reunion Services

When your child is at least 21 years old, your child, your child's other parent or siblings, or you may apply to the Director of the Social Services Administration of the Maryland Department of Human Resources for adoption search, contact, and reunion services.

K. Rights Under the Indian Child Welfare Act

If you or your child are members of or are eligible for membership in an Indian tribe, as defined by federal law, you have special legal rights under the Indian Child Welfare Act. You should not sign this consent form if you believe this may apply to you. You should tell the person requesting the consent or the court that you believe that your child's case should be handled under the Indian Child Welfare Act.

L. Authorization for Access to Medical and Mental Health Records

You may be asked to sign a separate form (authorization) to allow the adoptive parents and D.S.S. to get your child's medical and mental health records or your medical and mental health records. If you agree to allow access to this information, the records given to the adoptive parents will not include identifying information about you unless identifying information was previously exchanged by agreement.

M. Signature, Witness, and Copy

If you decide to complete and sign the consent form, you must have a witness present when you sign it. The witness must be someone 18 or older and should not be the child or the child's other parent. You must complete and sign the form with a pen and print or type in your name, address, and telephone number. The witness also must sign the form and print or type in the witness' name, address, and telephone number in the blanks on the last page.

If you have a post-adoption agreement, you must attach a copy to the signed consent form.

You have the right to receive a copy of the signed consent form.

STOP HERE IF YOU DID NOT UNDERSTAND SOMETHING YOU HAVE READ OR IF YOU WANT TO SPEAK WITH A LAWYER BEFORE YOU DECIDE IF YOU WANT TO SIGN THE CONSENT FORM.

If you wish to sign the consent form, you must also sign here to verify that you read these instructions and understand them:

_____   _____
(Signature)   (Date)

You must attach a copy of these signed instructions to the signed consent form.

CONSENT TO GUARDIANSHIP WITH THE RIGHT TO CONSENT TO
ADOPTION OF _____ TO
_____ DEPARTMENT
OF SOCIAL SERVICES

Use a pen to fill out this form. You must complete each section.

A. Identifying Information

1. Language.

I understand English, or this consent form has been translated into
_____ , a language that I under-
stand.
2. Name.
    My name is _____ .
3. Age.
    My date of birth is _____ .
4. Child.
    The child who is the subject of this consent was born on _____
                                                        (date)
    at _____ ,
        (name of hospital or address of birthplace)
    in _____ .
            (city, state, and county of birth)
5. Status as Parent. Check **all** that apply.
    (a) I am
        [ ] the mother of the child
        [ ] the father of the child
        [ ] alleged to be the father of the child
    (b) I was married to the mother of the child
        [ ] at the time of conception of the child
        [ ] at the time the child was born.

B. Right to Speak with a Lawyer

I WANT TO COMPLETE THIS CONSENT FORM BECAUSE:

Check **one** of the following
        [ ] I already have spoken with a lawyer whose name and telephone
            number are _____. I have read the instructions in front
            of this form, and I am ready to consent to the guardianship with the
            right to consent to adoption.
OR
        [ ] I am at least 18 years old and am able to understand this document.
            I have read the instructions at the front of this form, and I do not
            want to speak with a lawyer before I consent to the guardianship
            with the right to consent to adoption.

C. Consent

Check **one** of the following statements:
        [ ] I voluntarily and of my own free will consent to the ending
            (termination) of my parental rights and to the appointment of
            _____ Department of Social Services to be the
            guardian of my child, with the right of the guardian to consent to
            adoption.
OR
        [ ] I voluntarily and of my own free will consent to the ending
            (termination) of my parental rights and to the appointment of
            _____ Department of Social Services, to be the

guardian of my child as long as my child is adopted by
_____.

D. Notice

Check **one** of the following:

    [   ] I give up (waive) the right to any further notice of the guardianship case, any reviews after guardianship is granted, or when my child is adopted.

OR

    [   ] I give up (waive) the right to any further notice of the guardianship case or any reviews after guardianship is granted, but I want to be notified when my child is adopted.

OR

    [   ] I want to be notified about anything that happens in the guardianship case, any reviews after guardianship is granted, and when my child is adopted.

E. Revocation Rights

I understand that if I change my mind and no longer consent to the guardianship with the right to consent to adoption, I have the right to revoke this consent **within 30 days after it is filed in Juvenile Court**. I understand that the only way that I can revoke this consent is by giving a **signed written revocation** to the Juvenile Clerk, Circuit Court for _____ at _____.

F. Effect of this Consent

I UNDERSTAND THAT IF I SIGN THIS CONSENT FORM, AND GUARDIANSHIP IS GRANTED, I WILL BE GIVING UP ALL RIGHTS AND RESPONSIBILITIES RELATING TO THE CHILD, EXCEPT THOSE RIGHTS THAT I HAVE KEPT UNDER ANY WRITTEN POST-ADOPTION AGREEMENT.

G. Oath and Signature

I have read carefully and understand the instructions at the front of this consent form. I am signing this consent form voluntarily and of my own free will.

I solemnly affirm under the penalties of perjury that the contents of this consent form are true to the best of my knowledge, information, and belief.

_____
(Date)

_____
(Signature)

_____
(Printed Name)

_____
(Address)

_____
(City, State, Zip Code)

_____

(Telephone Number)

Witness:

_____   _____

(Signature)   (Date)

_____

(Printed Name)

_____

(Address)

_____

(City, State, Zip Code)

_____

(Telephone Number)

A COPY OF THE INSTRUCTIONS WITH YOUR SIGNATURE MUST BE ATTACHED TO THIS CONSENT FORM.

IF YOU HAVE A POST-ADOPTION AGREEMENT, ATTACH A COPY TO THIS CONSENT FORM. (Added June 4, 2007, effective July 1, 2007.)

Form 9-102.2. Consent of parent to a private agency guardianship.

CONSENT OF PARENT TO GUARDIANSHIP WITH THE RIGHT TO CONSENT TO ADOPTION OF _____ TO _____, A LICENSED PRIVATE ADOPTION AGENCY

INSTRUCTIONS

These instructions and attached consent form may be used only in cases where the child is being placed for adoption with the assistance of a licensed **private** adoption agency. Code, Family Law Article, Title 5, Subtitle 3A.

The attached consent form is an important legal document. You must read all of these instructions BEFORE you sign the consent form. If you do not understand the instructions or the consent form, you should not sign it. If you are under 18 years old or if you have a disability that makes it difficult for you to understand, do not sign the consent form unless you have a lawyer.

A. Right to Have This Information in a Language You Understand

You have the right to have these instructions and the consent form translated into a language that you understand. If you cannot read or understand English, you should not sign the consent form. You should have this form translated for you into a language you do understand. The translated consent form is the one you should read and decide whether or not to sign. Any translation must have an affidavit attached in which the translator states that it is a true and accurate translation of this document.

B. Right to Speak with a Lawyer

You have the right to speak with a lawyer before you decide whether or not to consent.

You should not sign the consent form without a lawyer if you are under 18 years old or have a disability that makes it difficult for you to understand this document. If you are under 18 years old or have a disability that makes it difficult for you to understand this document, you are required to have a lawyer review the form with you before you can consent to the guardianship.

Even if you are not required to have a lawyer, you have the right to speak with a lawyer you choose before you decide whether to consent.

You can ask the court to require the agency seeking guardianship of your child to pay the costs of the lawyer. The judge does not have to grant that request but may do so.

C. Post-adoption Agreement

If you have made a written agreement with the adoptive parents for future contact (known as a post-adoption agreement), a copy of that agreement must be attached to the signed consent form. If you have a post-adoption agreement, and, after adoption, the adoptive parents do not do what they agreed to do, it will not affect your consent to the guardianship or the adoption. However, if that happens, you have the right to ask a judge to make them do what they agreed to do. The judge can order you and the adoptive parents to go to mediation, order the adoptive parents to do what they agreed to do, or change the agreement if the judge decides that it is in the child's best interest.

D. Conditional Consent

If you decide to sign the consent form, you will have two choices:

(1) you can consent to the guardianship and the adoption of your child by a family approved by the adoption agency; or

(2) you can consent to the guardianship only if the child is adopted into a specific family. This is called a "conditional consent." If you sign a conditional consent, and the family whose name is on the consent cannot adopt the child, your consent will no longer be valid. The adoption agency will try to locate you to find out if you want to sign a new consent. If your parental rights have not been taken away (guardianship has not yet been granted), and you do not sign a new consent, the court will end the guardianship case. If your parental rights have been taken away (guardianship has been granted), and you do not sign a new consent, the court will decide whether it is in the child's best interests to continue the guardianship.

E. Effect of Signing the Consent Form

IF YOU SIGN THE CONSENT FORM, AND THE GUARDIANSHIP IS GRANTED, YOU WILL BE GIVING UP ALL RIGHTS AND RESPONSIBILITIES RELATING TO THE CHILD.

If you have a post-adoption agreement, you will keep only the rights the agreement gives you. Violation of the agreement will not affect your consent or the adoption.

65

F. Right to Revoke Consent

If you sign the consent form and then change your mind and no longer want to consent, you have the right to revoke (cancel) the consent **within 30 days after the date that you sign the consent form**. The only way that you can revoke this consent is by giving a **signed written revocation statement** with the name, sex, and date of birth of the child (if you know it) to:

Adoption Clerk, Circuit Court for _____, at _____ (Address).

The revocation must be sent to the court, not to the lawyers, or the agency, or the people adopting the child. You may deliver your written revocation of consent in person or by mail. If it is not **received** by the Adoption Clerk's office within 30 days after the date you signed the consent form, it will be too late, and you will not be able to withdraw the consent or stop the guardianship from being granted.

If you sign the consent form, and then revoke your consent, and then decide to consent to the guardianship again, you will not be able to revoke your second consent if you give your second consent in court within one year of your revocation of this consent.

G. Further Notice of Guardianship and Adoption Proceedings

A petition for guardianship with the right to consent to adoption has been or will be filed in _____ Circuit Court. If you sign the consent form, your written consent form will also be filed in the Circuit Court. You have the right to be notified when the petition is filed, about any hearings, if and when the guardianship is granted, and when the child is adopted. You also have the right to be notified if there is a delay in your child's adoption because:
1. The adoption agency does not place your child with an adoptive family within 270 days of being appointed the guardian of your child;
2. The adoption agency does not place your child with an adoptive family within 180 days of the disruption of a prior adoptive placement; or
3. The adoption is not completed within 2 years after your child's placement with the adoptive family.

Any notices will be sent to the address given by you on the consent form, unless you write to the Adoption Clerk at _____ (court's address) and give the clerk your new address. You may waive (give up) your right to notice if you wish to do so. Even if you give up your right to notice, someone from the court may contact you if further information is needed.

H. Compensation

Under Maryland law, you are not allowed to charge or receive money or compensation of any kind for the placement for adoption of your child or for your agreement to the adoptive parent having custody of your child, except that reasonable and customary charges or fees for adoption counseling, hospital, legal, or medical services may be paid.

I. Access to Birth and Adoption Records

When your child is at least 21 years old, your child, your child's other parent, or you may apply to the Maryland Secretary of the Department of Health and Mental Hygiene for access to certain birth and adoption records. If you do not want information about you to be disclosed (given) to that person, you have the right to prevent disclosure by filing a **disclosure veto.** Attached to this document is a copy of the form that you may use if you want to file a disclosure veto.

J. Adoption Search, Contact, and Reunion Services

When your child is at least 21 years old, your child, your child's other parent or siblings, or you may apply to the Director of the Social Services Administration of the Maryland Department of Human Resources for adoption search, contact, and reunion services.

K. Rights Under the Indian Child Welfare Act

If you or your child are members of or are eligible for membership in an Indian tribe, as defined by federal law, you have special legal rights under the Indian Child Welfare Act. You should not sign this consent form if you believe this may apply to you. You should tell the person requesting the consent or the court that you believe that your child's case should be handled under the Indian Child Welfare Act.

L. Authorization for Access to Medical and Mental Health Records

You may be asked to sign a separate form (authorization) to allow the adoptive parents and adoption agency to get your child's medical and mental health records or your medical and mental health records. If you agree to allow access to this information, the records given to the adoptive parents will not include identifying information about you unless identifying information was previously exchanged by agreement.

M. Signature, Witness, and Copy

If you decide to complete and sign the consent form, you must have a witness present when you sign it. The witness must be someone 18 or older and should not be the child or the child's other parent. You must complete and sign the form with a pen and print or type in your name, address, and telephone number. The witness also must sign the form and print or type in the witness' name, address, and telephone number in the blanks on the last page.

If you have a post-adoption agreement, you must attach a copy to the signed consent form.

You have the right to receive a copy of the signed consent form.

STOP HERE IF YOU DID NOT UNDERSTAND SOMETHING YOU HAVE READ OR IF YOU WANT TO SPEAK WITH A LAWYER BEFORE YOU DECIDE IF YOU WANT TO SIGN THE CONSENT FORM.

If you wish to sign the consent form, you must also sign here to verify that you read these instructions and understand them:

_____   _____
          (Signature)   (Date)

You must attach a copy of these signed instructions to the signed consent form.

CONSENT TO GUARDIANSHIP WITH THE RIGHT TO CONSENT TO ADOPTION OF _____ TO _____, A LICENSED PRIVATE ADOPTION AGENCY

Use a pen to fill out this form. You must complete each section.

A. Identifying Information

1. Language.
   I understand English, or this consent form has been translated into _____, a language that I under-stand.
2. Name.
   My name is _____.
3. Age.
   My date of birth is _____.
4. Child.
   The child who is the subject of this consent was born on _____
                                                          (date)
   at _____,
        (name of hospital or address of birthplace)
   in _____.
           (city, state, and county of birth)
5. Status as Parent. Check **all** that apply.
   (a) I am
   [   ] the mother of the child
   [   ] the father of the child
   [   ] alleged to be the father of the child
   (b) I was married to the mother of the child
   [   ] at the time of conception of the child
   [   ] at the time the child was born.

B. Right to Speak with a Lawyer

I WANT TO COMPLETE THIS CONSENT FORM BECAUSE:

Check **one** of the following
   [   ] I already have spoken with a lawyer whose name and telephone number are _____. I have read the instructions at the front of this form, and I am ready to consent to the guardianship with the right to consent to adoption.
OR
   [   ] I am at least 18 years old and am able to understand this document. I have read the instructions at the front of this form, and I do not

want to speak with a lawyer before I consent to the guardianship with the right to consent to adoption.

C. Consent

Check **one** of the following:

[ ] I voluntarily and of my own free will consent to the ending (termination) of my parental rights and to the appointment of _____, a licensed private adoption agency, to be the guardian of my child, with the right of the guardian to consent to adoption.

OR

[ ] I voluntarily and of my own free will consent to the ending (termination) of my parental rights and to the appointment of _____, a licensed private adoption agency, to be the guardian of my child as long as my child is adopted by _____.

D. Notice

Check **one** of the following:

[ ] I give up (waive) the right to any further notice of the guardianship case, any delays in the adoption of my child, or when my child is adopted.

OR

[ ] I give up (waive) the right to any further notice of the guardianship case or any delays in the adoption of my child, but I want to be notified when my child is adopted.

OR

[ ] I want to be notified about anything that happens in the guardianship case, any delays in the adoption of my child, and when my child is adopted.

E. Revocation Rights

I understand that if I change my mind and no longer consent to the guardianship with the right to consent to adoption, I have the right to revoke this consent **within 30 days after I sign this consent form**. I understand that the only way that I can revoke this consent is by giving a **signed written revocation** to the Adoption Clerk, Circuit Court for _____ at
_____ .

F. Effect of this Consent

I UNDERSTAND THAT IF I SIGN THIS CONSENT FORM, AND GUARDIANSHIP IS GRANTED, I WILL BE GIVING UP ALL RIGHTS AND RESPONSIBILITIES RELATING TO THE CHILD, EXCEPT THOSE RIGHTS THAT I HAVE KEPT UNDER ANY WRITTEN POST-ADOPTION AGREEMENT.

G. Oath and Signature

I have read carefully and understand the instructions at the front of this consent form. I am signing this consent form voluntarily and of my own free will.

I solemnly affirm under the penalties of perjury that the contents of this consent form are true to the best of my knowledge, information, and belief.

_____   _____
(Date)   (Signature)

                                        _____
                                        (Printed Name)

                                        _____
                                        (Address)

                                        _____
                                        (City, State, Zip Code)

                                        _____
                                        (Telephone Number)

Witness:

_____   _____
(Signature)   (Date)

_____
(Printed Name)

_____
(Address)

_____
(City, State, Zip Code)

_____
(Telephone Number)

A COPY OF THE INSTRUCTIONS WITH YOUR SIGNATURE MUST BE ATTACHED TO THIS CONSENT FORM.

IF YOU HAVE A POST-ADOPTION AGREEMENT, ATTACH A COPY TO THIS CONSENT FORM. (Added June 4, 2007, effective July 1, 2007.)

Form 9-102.3. Consent of parent to a public agency adoption without prior termination of parental rights.

CONSENT OF PARENT TO ADOPTION OF _____

Adoption of CINA without Prior Termination of Parental Rights

INSTRUCTIONS

These instructions and attached consent form may be used only in cases where the child is a Child in Need of Assistance **and** *the petitioner is seeking to adopt the child* **without** *prior termination of parental rights. Code, Family Law Article, Title 5, Subtitle 3, Part III.*

The attached consent form is an important legal document. You must read all of these instructions BEFORE you sign the consent form. If you do not understand the instructions or the consent form, you should not sign it. If you are under 18 years old or if you have a disability that makes it difficult for you to understand, do not sign the consent form unless you have a lawyer.

A. Right to Have This Information in a Language You Understand

You have the right to have these instructions and the consent form translated into a language that you understand. If you cannot read or understand English, you should not sign the consent form. You should have this form translated for you into a language you do understand. The translated consent form is the one you should read and decide whether or not to sign. Any translation must have an affidavit attached in which the translator states that it is a true and accurate translation of this document.

B. Right to Speak with a Lawyer

You have the right to speak with a lawyer before you decide whether or not to consent. If you are unable to afford a lawyer, you may be eligible for a lawyer through the Office of the Public Defender. You should contact the Office of the Public Defender, and ask for a lawyer to represent you in a D.S.S. (Department of Social Services) case.

You should not sign the consent form without a lawyer if you are under 18 years old or have a disability that makes it difficult for you to understand this document. If you are under 18 years old or have a disability that makes it difficult for you to understand this document, you are required to have a lawyer review the form with you before you can consent to the adoption. You should contact the Office of the Public Defender, or let the Juvenile Court know you need to have a lawyer appointed for you.

Even if you do not have the right to have the court appoint a lawyer for you or to be represented through the Office of the Public Defender, you have the right to speak with a lawyer you choose before you decide whether to consent.

C. Right to Adoption Counseling

You have the right to receive adoption counseling and guidance. The court may require D.S.S. or the adoptive parents to pay for the adoption counseling and guidance but does not have to do so. If you want adoption counseling or guidance, you should not complete this consent form until after you have gotten adoption counseling or guidance.

D. Post-adoption Agreement

If you have made a written agreement with the adoptive parents for future contact (known as a post-adoption agreement), a copy of that agreement must be attached to the signed consent form. If you have a post-adoption agreement, and, after the adoption, the adoptive parents do not do what they agreed to do, it will not affect the adoption or your consent to the adoption. However, if that happens, you have the right to ask a judge to make them do what they agreed to do. The judge can order you and the adoptive parents to go to mediation, order the adoptive parents to do what they agreed to do, or change the agreement if the judge decides that it is in the child's best interest.

E. Effect of Signing the Consent Form

IF YOU SIGN THE CONSENT FORM, AND ADOPTION IS GRANTED, YOU WILL BE GIVING UP ALL RIGHTS AND RESPONSIBILITIES RELATING TO THE CHILD. If you have a post-adoption agreement, you will keep only the rights the agreement gives you. Violation of the agreement will not affect your consent or the adoption.

F. Right to Revoke Consent

If you sign the consent form and then change your mind and no longer want to consent, you have the right to revoke (cancel) the consent. If the adoption case is already filed in court, you must revoke your consent **within 30 days after the date that you sign the consent form**. If the adoption case has not been filed in court, you must revoke your consent **within 30 days after the adoption petition is filed**. The only way that you can revoke this consent is by giving a **signed written revocation statement** with the name, sex, and date of birth of the child (if you know it) to:

Juvenile Clerk, Circuit Court for _____ at _____ (Address).

The revocation must be sent to the court, not to your social worker, lawyer, or the people adopting the child. You may deliver your written revocation of consent in person or by mail. If it is not **received** by the Juvenile Clerk's office within the later of 30 days after the date you sign the consent form or 30 days after the date the adoption petition is filed, it will be too late, and you will not be able to withdraw the consent or stop the adoption from being granted.

G. Further Notice of Adoption Proceedings

A petition for adoption has been or will be filed in the Circuit Court for _____. If you sign the consent form, your written consent will also be filed in the court. You have the right to be notified when the petition is filed, when any hearings are held before the adoption is granted, and if and when the adoption is granted. Any notices will be sent to the address given by you on the consent form, unless you write to the Juvenile Clerk at _____ (court's address) and give the clerk your new address. You may waive (give up) your right to notice if you wish to do so. Even if you give up your right to notice, someone from the court may contact you if further information is needed.

H. Compensation

Under Maryland law, you are not allowed to charge or receive money or compensation of any kind for the placement for adoption of your child or for your agreement to the adoptive parent having custody of your child, except that reasonable and customary charges or fees for adoption counseling, hospital, legal, or medical services may be paid.

I. Access to Birth and Adoption Records

When your child is at least 21 years old, your child, your child's other parent, or you may apply to the Maryland Secretary of the Department of Health and Mental Hygiene for access to certain birth and adoption records. If you do not want information about you to be disclosed (given) to that person, you have the right to prevent disclosure by filing a disclosure veto. Attached to this document is a copy of the form that you may use if you want to file a disclosure veto.

J. Adoption Search, Contact and Reunion Services

When your child is at least 21 years old, your child, your child's other parent or siblings, or you may apply to the Director of the Social Services Administration of the Maryland Department of Human Resources for adoption search, contact, and reunion services.

K. Rights under the Indian Child Welfare Act

If you or your child are members of or are eligible for membership in an Indian tribe, as defined by federal law, you have special legal rights under the Indian Child Welfare Act. You should not sign this consent form if you believe this may apply to you. You should tell the person requesting the consent or the court that you believe that your child's case should be handled under the Indian Child Welfare Act.

L. Authorization for Access to Medical and Mental Health Records

You may be asked to sign a separate form (authorization) to allow the adoptive parents to get your child's medical and mental health records or your medical and mental health records. If you agree to allow access to this information, the records given to the adoptive parents will not include identifying information about you unless identifying information was previously exchanged by agreement.

M. Signature, Witness, and Copy

If you decide to complete and sign the consent form, you must have a witness present when you sign it. The witness must be someone 18 or older and should not be the child or the child's other parent. You must complete and sign the form with a pen and print or type in your name, address, and telephone number. The witness also must sign the form and print or type in the witness' name, address, and telephone number in the blanks on the last page.

If you have a post-adoption agreement, you must attach a copy to the signed consent form.

You have the right to receive a copy of the signed consent form.

STOP HERE IF YOU DID NOT UNDERSTAND SOMETHING YOU HAVE READ OR IF YOU WANT TO SPEAK WITH A LAWYER OR GET ADOPTION COUNSELING BEFORE YOU DECIDE IF YOU WANT TO SIGN THE CONSENT FORM.

If you wish to sign the consent form, you must also sign here to verify that you read these instructions and understand them:

_____   _____
(Signature)   (Date)

You must attach a copy of these signed instructions to the signed consent form.

CONSENT OF PARENT TO ADOPTION OF _____

Adoption of CINA without Prior Termination of Parental Rights

Use a pen to fill out this form. You must complete each section.

A. Identifying Information

1. Language.
   I understand English, or this consent form has been translated into
   _____, a language that I under-
   stand.
2. Name.
   My name is _____.
3. Age.
   My date of birth is _____.
4. Child.
   The child who is the subject of this consent was born on _____
                                                                                    (date)
   at _____,
       (name of hospital or address of birthplace)
   in _____.
                    (city, state, and county of birth)
5. Status as Parent. Check **all** that apply.
   (a) I am
       [ ] the mother of the child
       [ ] the father of the child
       [ ] alleged to be the father of the child
   (b) I was married to the mother of the child
       [ ] at the time of conception of the child
       [ ] at the time the child was born.

B. Right to Speak with a Lawyer

I WANT TO COMPLETE THIS CONSENT FORM BECAUSE:

Check **one** of the following
       [ ] I already have spoken with a lawyer whose name and telephone
             number are _____
   _____.
   I have read the instructions at the front of this form, and I am ready to
   consent to the adoption.

OR

      [   ] I am at least 18 years old and am able to understand this document. I have read the instructions at the front of this form, and I do not want to speak with a lawyer before I consent to the adoption.

C. Right to Counseling and Guidance

I WANT TO COMPLETE THIS CONSENT FORM BECAUSE:

Check **one** of the following:

      [   ] I have already spoken with a counselor. I have read the instructions at the front of this form, and I am ready to consent to the adoption.

OR

      [   ] I do not want to speak with a counselor. I have read the instructions at the front of this form, and I am ready to consent to the adoption.

D. Consent

I voluntarily and of my own free will consent to the ending (termination) of my rights as parent to and to the adoption of my child, _____, by a person(s) known to me as _____.

E. Notice

Check **one** of the following:

      [   ] I give up (waive) the right to any further notice of the adoption case.

OR

      [   ] I want to be notified when the adoption case is filed, of any hearings, and if and when my child is adopted.

E. Revocation Rights

I understand that if I change my mind and no longer consent to the adoption, I have the right to revoke this consent **within the later of 30 days after I sign this form or 30 days after the adoption case is filed in court**. I understand that the only way that I can revoke this consent is by giving a **signed written revocation statement** to the Juvenile Clerk, Circuit Court for _____ at _____.

G. Effect of this Consent

I UNDERSTAND THAT IF I SIGN THIS CONSENT FORM, AND ADOPTION IS GRANTED, I WILL BE GIVING UP ALL RIGHTS AND RESPONSIBILITIES RELATING TO THE CHILD, EXCEPT THOSE RIGHTS THAT I HAVE KEPT UNDER ANY WRITTEN POST-ADOPTION AGREEMENT.

H. Oath and Signature

I have read carefully and understand the instructions in front of this consent form. I am signing this consent form voluntarily and of my own free will.

I solemnly affirm under the penalties of perjury that the contents of this consent form are true to the best of my knowledge, information, and belief.

_____   _____
(Date)   (Signature)

                            _____
                            (Printed Name)

                            _____
                            (Address)

                            _____
                            (City, State, Zip Code)

                            _____
                            (Telephone Number)

Witness:

_____   _____
(Signature)   (Date)

_____
(Printed Name)

_____
(Address)

_____
(City, State, Zip Code)

_____
(Telephone Number)

A COPY OF THE INSTRUCTIONS WITH YOUR SIGNATURE MUST BE ATTACHED TO THIS CONSENT FORM.

IF YOU HAVE A POST-ADOPTION AGREEMENT, ATTACH A COPY TO THIS CONSENT FORM. (Added June 4, 2007, effective July 1, 2007.)

Form 9-102.4. Consent of parent to an independent adoption with termination of parental rights.

CONSENT OF PARENT TO ADOPTION OF _____

Independent Adoption with Termination of Parental Rights

INSTRUCTIONS

These instructions and attached consent form may be used only in independent adoptions, not those that are arranged by an adoption agency. This form should only be used for a parent whose parental rights are being terminated. It should not be used for a parent who is retaining parental rights, for example, a custodial parent in a step-parent adoption. Code, Family Law Article, Title 5, Subtitle 3B.

The attached consent form is an important legal document. You must read all of these instructions BEFORE you sign the consent form. If you do not understand the instructions or the consent form, you should not sign it. If you are under 18 years old or if you have a

disability that makes it difficult for you to understand, do not sign the consent form unless you have a lawyer.

A. Right to Have This Information in a Language You Understand

You have the right to have these instructions and the consent form translated into a language that you understand. If you cannot read or understand English, you should not sign the consent form. You should have this form translated for you into a language you do understand. The translated consent form is the one you should read and decide whether or not to sign. Any translation must have an affidavit attached in which the translator states that it is a true and accurate translation of this document.

B. Right to Speak with a Lawyer

You have the right to speak with a lawyer before you decide whether or not to consent.

You should not sign the consent form without a lawyer if you are under 18 years old or have a disability that makes it difficult for you to understand this document. If you are under 18 years old or have a disability that makes it difficult for you to understand this document, you are required to have a lawyer review the form with you before you can consent to the adoption.

Even if you are not required to have a lawyer, you have the right to speak with a lawyer you choose before you decide whether to consent.

You can ask the court to require the people adopting your child to pay the costs of the lawyer. The judge does not have to grant that request but may do so.

C. Right to Adoption Counseling

You have the right to receive adoption counseling and guidance. The court may require the adoptive parents to pay for the adoption counseling and guidance but does not have to do so. If you want adoption counseling or guidance, you should not complete this consent form until after you have gotten adoption counseling or guidance.

D. Post-adoption Agreement

If you have made a written agreement with the adoptive parents for future contact (known as a post-adoption agreement), a copy of that agreement must be attached to the signed consent form. If you have a post-adoption agreement, and, after the adoption, the adoptive parents do not do what they agreed to do, it will not affect the adoption or your consent to the adoption. However, if that happens, you have the right to ask a judge to make them do what they agreed to do. The judge can order you and the adoptive parents to go to mediation, order the adoptive parents to do what they agreed to do, or change the agreement if the judge decides that it is in the child's best interest.

E. Effect of Signing the Consent Form

IF YOU SIGN THE CONSENT FORM, AND ADOPTION IS GRANTED, YOU WILL BE GIVING UP ALL RIGHTS AND RESPONSIBILITIES

RELATING TO THE CHILD. If you have a post-adoption agreement, you will keep only the rights the agreement gives you. Violation of the agreement will not affect your consent or the adoption.

F. Right to Revoke Consent

If you sign the consent form and then change your mind and no longer want to consent, you have the right to revoke (cancel) the consent **within 30 days after the date that you sign the consent form**. The only way that you can revoke this consent is by giving a **signed written revocation statement** with the name, sex, and date of birth of the child (if you know it) to:

Adoption Clerk, Circuit Court for _____, at _____ (Address).

The revocation must be sent to the court, not to the lawyers or the people adopting the child. You may deliver your written revocation of consent in person or by mail. If it is not **received** by the Adoption Clerk's office within 30 days after the date you signed the consent form, it will be too late, and you will not be able to withdraw the consent or stop the adoption from being granted.

If you sign this consent form, and then revoke your consent, and then decide to consent to the adoption again, you will not be able to revoke your second consent if you give your second consent in court within one year of your revocation of this consent.

G. Further Notice of Adoption Proceedings

A petition for adoption has been or will be filed in the Circuit Court for _____. If you sign the consent form, your written consent will also be filed in the court. You have the right to be notified when the petition is filed, when any hearings are held before the adoption is granted, and if and when the adoption is granted. Any notices will be sent to the address given by you on the consent form, unless you write to the Adoption Clerk at _____ (court's address) and give the clerk your new address. You may waive (give up) your right to notice if you wish to do so. Even if you give up your right to notice, someone from the court may contact you if further information is needed.

H. Compensation

Under Maryland law, you are not allowed to charge or receive money or compensation of any kind for the placement for adoption of your child or for your agreement to the adoptive parent having custody of your child, except that reasonable and customary charges or fees for adoption counseling, hospital, legal, or medical services may be paid.

I. Access to Birth and Adoption Records

When your child is at least 21 years old, your child, your child's other parent, or you may apply to the Maryland Secretary of the Department of Health and Mental Hygiene for access to certain birth and adoption records. If you do not want information about you to be disclosed (given) to that person, you have the right to prevent disclosure by filing a **disclosure veto**. Attached to this document is a copy of the form that you may use if you want to file a disclosure veto.

J. Adoption Search, Contact, and Reunion Services

When your child is at least 21 years old, your child, your child's other parent or siblings, or you may apply to the Director of the Social Services Administration of the Maryland Department of Human Resources for adoption search, contact, and reunion services.

K. Rights under the Indian Child Welfare Act

If you or your child are members of or are eligible for membership in an Indian tribe, as defined by federal law, you have special legal rights under the Indian Child Welfare Act. You should not sign this consent form if you believe this may apply to you. You should tell the person requesting the consent or the court that you believe that your child's case should be handled under the Indian Child Welfare Act.

L. Authorization for Access to Medical and Mental Health Records

You may be asked to sign a separate form (authorization) to allow the adoptive parents to get your child's medical and mental health records or your medical and mental health records. If you agree to allow access to this information, the records given to the adoptive parents will not include identifying information about you unless identifying information was previously exchanged by agreement.

M. Signature, Witness, and Copy

If you decide to complete and sign the consent form, you must have a witness present when you sign it. The witness must be someone 18 or older and should not be the child or the child's other parent. You must complete and sign the form with a pen and print or type in your name, address, and telephone number. The witness also must sign the form and print or type in the witness' name, address, and telephone number in the blanks on the last page.

If you have a post-adoption agreement, you must attach a copy to the signed consent form.

You have the right to receive a copy of the signed consent form.

STOP HERE IF YOU DID NOT UNDERSTAND SOMETHING YOU HAVE READ OR IF YOU WANT TO SPEAK WITH A LAWYER OR GET ADOPTION COUNSELING BEFORE YOU DECIDE IF YOU WANT TO SIGN THE CONSENT FORM.

If you wish to sign the consent form, you must also sign here to verify that you read these instructions and understand them:

_____   _____
(Signature)   (Date)

You must attach a copy of these signed instructions to the signed consent form.

CONSENT TO INDEPENDENT ADOPTION OF

_____

WITH TERMINATION OF PARENTAL RIGHTS

Use a pen to fill out this form. You must complete each section.

A. Identifying Information

1. Language.
   I understand English, or this consent form has been translated into
   _____, a language that I under-
   stand.
2. Name.
   My name is _____ .
3. Age.
   My date of birth is _____ .
4. Child.
   The child who is the subject of this consent was born on _____
                                              (date)
   at _____ ,
        (name of hospital or address of birthplace)
   in _____ .
           (city, state, and county of birth)
5. Status as Parent. Check **all** that apply.
   (a) I am
       [   ] the mother of the child
       [   ] the father of the child
       [   ] alleged to be the father of the child
   (b) I was married to the mother of the child
       [   ] at the time of conception of the child
       [   ] at the time the child was born.

B. Right to Speak with a Lawyer

I WANT TO COMPLETE THIS CONSENT FORM BECAUSE:

Check **one** of the following
    [   ] I already have spoken with a lawyer whose name and telephone
        number are _____

_____ .

  I have read the instructions at the front of this form, and I am ready to
consent to the adoption.
OR
    [   ] I am at least 18 years old and am able to understand this document.
        I have read the instructions at the front of this form, and I do not
        want to speak with a lawyer before I consent to the adoption.

C. Right to Counseling and Guidance

I WANT TO COMPLETE THIS CONSENT FORM BECAUSE:

Check **one** of the following:

[ ] I have already spoken with a counselor. I have read the instructions at the front of this form, and I am ready to consent to the adoption.

OR

[ ] I do not want to speak with a counselor. I have read the instructions at the front of this form, and I am ready to consent to the adoption.

D. Consent

I voluntarily and of my own free will consent to the ending (termination) of my rights as parent to and to the adoption of my child, _____, by person(s) known to me as _____. I also agree that such person(s) shall have temporary custody of the child until the completion of the adoption.

E. Notice

Check **one** of the following:

[ ] I give up (waive) the right to any further notice of the adoption case.

OR

[ ] I want to be notified when the adoption case is filed, of any hearings and if and when my child is adopted.

F. Revocation Rights

I understand that if I change my mind and no longer consent to the adoption, I have the right to revoke this consent **within 30 days after the date that I signed this consent form.** I understand that the only way that I can revoke this consent is by giving a **signed written revocation** to the Adoption Clerk, Circuit Court for _____at _____ .

G. Effect of this Consent

I UNDERSTAND THAT IF I SIGN THIS CONSENT FORM, AND ADOPTION IS GRANTED, I WILL BE GIVING UP ALL RIGHTS AND RESPONSIBILITIES RELATING TO THE CHILD, EXCEPT THOSE RIGHTS THAT I HAVE KEPT UNDER ANY WRITTEN POST-ADOPTION AGREEMENT.

H. Oath and Signature

I have read carefully and understand the instructions in front of this consent form. I am signing this consent form voluntarily and of my own free will.

I solemnly affirm under the penalties of perjury that the contents of this consent form are true to the best of my knowledge, information, and belief.

_____

(Date)

_____

(Signature)

_____

(Printed Name)

_____

(Address)

81

_____
(City, State, Zip Code)

_____
(Telephone Number)

Witness:

_____
(Signature)

_____
(Date)

_____
(Printed Name)

_____
(Address)

_____
(City, State, Zip Code)

_____
(Telephone Number)

A COPY OF THE INSTRUCTIONS WITH YOUR SIGNATURE MUST BE ATTACHED TO THIS CONSENT FORM.

IF YOU HAVE A POST-ADOPTION AGREEMENT, ATTACH A COPY TO THIS CONSENT FORM. (Added June 4, 2007, effective July 1, 2007.)

Form 9-102.5. Consent of parent to an independent adoption without termination of parental rights.

CONSENT OF PARENT TO ADOPTION OF _____

Independent Adoption without Termination of Parental Rights

INSTRUCTIONS

These instructions and attached consent form may be used only in independent adoptions, not those that are arranged by an adoption agency. This form should only be used for a parent whose parental rights are not being terminated. It should be used for a parent who is retaining parental rights, for example, a custodial parent in a step-parent adoption. Code, Family Law Article, Title 5, Subtitle 3B.

The attached consent form is an important legal document. You must read all of these instructions BEFORE you sign the consent form. If you do not understand the instructions or the consent form, you should not sign it. If you are under 18 years old or if you have a disability that makes it difficult for you to understand, do not sign the consent form unless you have a lawyer.

A. Right to Have This Information in a Language You Understand

You have the right to have these instructions and the consent form translated into a language that you understand. If you cannot read or understand English, you should not sign the consent form. You should have this form translated for you into a language you do understand. The translated consent form is the one you should read and decide whether or not to sign. Any translation must have an affidavit attached in which the translator states that it is a true and accurate translation of this document.

B. Right to Speak with a Lawyer

You have the right to speak with a lawyer before you decide whether or not to consent.

You should not sign the consent form without a lawyer if you are under 18 years old or have a disability that makes it difficult for you to understand this document. If you are under 18 years old or have a disability that makes it difficult for you to understand this document, you are required to have a lawyer review the form with you before you can consent to the adoption.

Even if you are not required to have a lawyer, you have the right to speak with a lawyer you choose before you decide whether to consent.

C. Right to Adoption Counseling

You have the right to receive adoption counseling and guidance. If you want adoption counseling or guidance, you should not complete this consent form until after you have gotten adoption counseling or guidance.

D. Effect of Signing the Consent Form

IF YOU SIGN THE CONSENT FORM, YOU WILL NOT BE GIVING UP ANY RIGHTS OR RESPONSIBILITIES RELATING TO THE CHILD.

E. Right to Revoke Consent

If you sign the consent form and then change your mind and no longer want to consent, you have the right to revoke (cancel) the consent **within 30 days after the date that you sign the consent form**. The only way that you can revoke this consent is by giving a **signed written revocation statement** with the name, sex, and date of birth of the child (if you know it) to:

Adoption Clerk, Circuit Court for _____, at
_____ (Address).

The revocation must be sent to the court, not to the lawyers or the people adopting the child. You may deliver your written revocation of consent in person or by mail. If it is not **received** by the Adoption Clerk's office within 30 days after the date you signed the consent form, it will be too late, and you will not be able to withdraw the consent or stop the adoption from being granted.

If you sign this consent form, and then revoke your consent, and then decide to consent to the adoption again, you will not be able to revoke your second consent if you give your second consent in court within one year of your revocation of this consent.

G. Further Notice of Adoption Proceedings

A petition for adoption has been or will be filed in the Circuit Court for _____. If you sign the consent form, your written consent will also be filed in the court. You have the right to be notified when the petition is filed, when any hearings are held before the adoption is granted, and if and when the adoption is granted. Any notices will be sent to the address given by you on the consent form, unless you write to the Adoption Clerk at _____ (court's address) and give the clerk your new address. You may waive (give up) your right to notice if you wish to do so. Even if you give up your right to notice, someone from the court may contact you if further information is needed.

H. Compensation

Under Maryland law, you are not allowed to charge or receive money or compensation of any kind for the placement for adoption of your child or for your agreement to the adoptive parent having custody of your child, except that reasonable and customary charges or fees for adoption counseling, hospital, legal, or medical services may be paid.

I. Access to Birth and Adoption Records

When your child is at least 21 years old, your child, your child's other parent, or you may apply to the Maryland Secretary of the Department of Health and Mental Hygiene for access to certain birth and adoption records. If you do not want information about you to be disclosed (given) to that person, you have the right to prevent disclosure by filing a **disclosure veto**. Attached to this document is a copy of the form that you may use if you want to file a disclosure veto.

J. Adoption Search, Contact, and Reunion Services

When your child is at least 21 years old, your child, your child's other parent or siblings, or you may apply to the Director of the Social Services Administration of the Maryland Department of Human Resources for adoption search, contact, and reunion services.

K. Rights under the Indian Child Welfare Act

If you or your child are members of or are eligible for membership in an Indian tribe, as defined by federal law, you have special legal rights under the Indian Child Welfare Act. You should not sign this consent form if you believe this may apply to you. You should tell the person requesting the consent or the court that you believe that your child's case should be handled under the Indian Child Welfare Act.

L. Signature, Witness, and Copy

If you decide to complete and sign the consent form, you must have a witness present when you sign it. The witness must be someone 18 or older and should not be the child or the child's other parent. You must complete and sign the form with a pen and print or type in your name, address, and telephone number. The witness also must sign the form and print or type in the witness' name, address, and telephone number in the blanks on the last page.

If you have a post-adoption agreement, you must attach a copy to the signed consent form.

You have the right to receive a copy of the signed consent form.

STOP HERE IF YOU DID NOT UNDERSTAND SOMETHING YOU HAVE READ OR IF YOU WANT TO SPEAK WITH A LAWYER OR GET ADOPTION COUNSELING BEFORE YOU DECIDE IF YOU WANT TO SIGN THE CONSENT FORM.

If you wish to sign the consent form, you must also sign here to verify that you read these instructions and understand them:

_____   _____
            (Signature)   (Date)

You must attach a copy of these signed instructions to the signed consent form.

CONSENT TO INDEPENDENT ADOPTION
WITHOUT TERMINATION OF PARENTAL RIGHTS

Use a pen to fill out this form. You must complete each section.

A. Identifying Information

    1. Language.
       I understand English, or this consent form has been translated into
       _____, a language that I under-
    stand.
    2. Name.
       My name is _____.
    3. Age.
       My date of birth is _____.
    4. Child.
       The child who is the subject of this consent was born on _____
                                                (date)
    at _____,
       (name of hospital or address of birthplace)
    in _____.
             (city, state, and county of birth)
    5. Status as Parent. Check **all** that apply.
       (a) I am
          [ ] the mother of the child
          [ ] the father of the child
          [ ] alleged to be the father of the child
       (b) I was married to the mother of the child
          [ ] at the time of conception of the child
          [ ] at the time the child was born.

B. Right to Speak with a Lawyer

I WANT TO COMPLETE THIS CONSENT FORM BECAUSE:

Check **one** of the following

[   ] I already have spoken with a lawyer whose name and telephone number are _____
_____ . I have read the instructions at the front of this form, and I am ready to consent to the adoption.

OR

[   ] I am at least 18 years old and am able to understand this document. I have read the instructions at the front of this form, and I do not want to speak with a lawyer before I consent to the adoption.

C. Right to Counseling and Guidance

I WANT TO COMPLETE THIS CONSENT FORM BECAUSE:

Check **one** of the following:

[   ] I have already spoken with a counselor. I have read the instructions at the front of this form, and I am ready to consent to the adoption.

OR

[   ] I do not want to speak with a counselor. I have read the instructions at the front of this form, and I am ready to consent to the adoption.

D. Consent

I voluntarily and of my own free will consent to the adoption of my child, _____, by _____ .

E. Notice

Check **one** of the following:

[   ] I give up (waive) the right to any further notice of the adoption case.

OR

[   ] I want to be notified when the adoption case is filed, of any hearings, and if and when my child is adopted.

F. Revocation Rights

I understand that if I change my mind and no longer consent to the adoption, I have the right to revoke this consent **within 30 days after the date that I signed this consent form.** I understand that the only way that I can revoke this consent is by giving a signed written revocation statement to the Adoption Clerk, Circuit Court for _____ at

_____ .

G. Effect of this Consent

I UNDERSTAND THAT IF I SIGN THIS CONSENT FORM, I WILL NOT BE GIVING UP ANY RIGHTS AND RESPONSIBILITIES RELATING TO THE CHILD.

H. Oath and Signature

I have read carefully and understand the instructions at the front of this consent form. I am signing this consent form voluntarily and of my own free will.

FAMILY LAW ACTIONS   **Form 9-102.6**

I solemnly affirm under the penalties of perjury that the contents of this consent form are true to the best of my knowledge, information, and belief.

_____   _____
(Date)   (Signature)

                             _____
                             (Printed Name)

                             _____
                             (Address)

                             _____
                             (City, State, Zip Code)

                             _____
                             (Telephone Number)

Witness:

_____   _____
(Signature)   (Date)

_____
(Printed Name)

_____
(Address)

_____
(City, State, Zip Code)

_____
(Telephone Number)

A COPY OF THE INSTRUCTIONS WITH YOUR SIGNATURE MUST BE ATTACHED TO THE CONSENT FORM. (Added June 4, 2007, effective July 1, 2007.)

Form 9-102.6. Consent of child to a public agency adoption or private agency adoption.

CONSENT OF _____ TO ADOPTION
                        (Name of Child)

INSTRUCTIONS

This consent form may be completed only after being reviewed with an attorney and should be completed only by a child who is in the custody of or under the guardianship of the Department of Social Services or under the guardianship of a private child placement agency. Code, Family Law Article, Title 5, Subtitle 3 or 3A.

1. I understand English, or this consent form has been translated into _____, a language that I understand.
2. My name is _____.
3 My date of birth is _____. I am _____ years old.

4. I understand that _____ have asked to adopt me.

5. I have a lawyer whose name and telephone number are _____. I have met with my lawyer who has gone over this consent form with me and explained to me what it means to be adopted.

6. I understand that if I agree to be adopted, and I am adopted, _____ will become my parents, and I will become their child.

7. I understand that I do not have to agree to be adopted. If I do not agree, the judge cannot approve the adoption. If the adoption is not approved, and I am not adopted by someone else, a judge will decide where I will live.

8. I voluntarily and of my own free will agree to being adopted by _____. I understand that if they are not able to complete the adoption, this consent form will no longer be valid and can no longer be used.

9. I understand that if I change my mind and do not want to be adopted, I must tell my lawyer, my social worker, or the judge immediately. I will have to sign a written statement or tell the judge in court that I do not want to be adopted **before** the adoption order is signed by a judge. This is called a revocation of consent.

10. I understand that when I am at least 21 years old, my birth parents or I may apply to the Secretary of the Maryland Department of Health and Mental Hygiene to get certain birth and adoption records. If I do not want information about me to be given to my birth parents, I have the right to file a form called a "disclosure veto." I have been given a form that I may use if I want to file a disclosure veto.

11. I understand that when I am at least 21 years old, my birth parents, my siblings, or I may apply to the Director of the Social Services Administration of the Maryland Department of Human Resources for adoption search, contact, and reunion services.

12. I have read this consent form or have had it read and explained to me in a language that I understand. I understand the meaning of this consent form.

13. I have not been promised anything in return for agreeing to be adopted.

14. I have signed this consent form of my own free will.

15. I understand that I will be given a copy of this signed consent form.

I solemnly affirm under the penalties of perjury that the contents of this consent to adoption form are true to the best of my knowledge, information, and belief.

_____
(Date)

_____
(Signature)

_____
(Printed Name)

_____
(Address)

_____
(City, State, Zip Code)

_____

(Telephone Number)

Witness:

_____

(Date)

_____

(Signature)

_____

(Printed Name)

_____

(Address)

_____

(City, State, Zip Code)

_____

(Telephone Number) (Added June 4, 2007, effective July 1, 2007.)

Form 9-102.7. Consent of child to independent adoption.

CONSENT OF _____ TO INDEPENDENT ADOPTION

(Name of child)

INSTRUCTIONS

This consent form should be completed only by a child who is being adopted in an independent adoption that is not being arranged by an adoption or child placement agency. Code, Family Law Article, Title 5, Subtitle 3B.

The attached consent form is an important legal document. You must read all of these instructions BEFORE you sign the form and agree to being adopted. If you do not understand the instructions or the consent form, you should not sign it. If you have a disability that makes it hard for you to understand this form, do not complete this consent form unless you have a lawyer.

A. Right to Have This Information in a Language You Understand

You have the right to have these instructions and the consent form translated into a language that you understand. If you cannot read or understand English, you should not sign the consent form.

B. Right to Speak with a Lawyer

If you have a disability that makes it hard for you to understand this consent form, **do not complete this form** because you must have a lawyer before you may complete this form and agree to be adopted.

Even if you do not have a problem understanding this consent form, you have the right to speak with a lawyer before you agree to be adopted. If you want to speak with a lawyer, do not complete this form until you have spoken with a lawyer.

C. What Happens if You Sign the Consent Form

If you sign the consent form, the people who want to adopt you will file an adoption case in the Circuit Court for _____. There probably will be a court hearing about your adoption. During that hearing, the judge probably will ask you if you want to be adopted. The judge will make the final decision about your adoption.

D. Right to Revoke Consent

If you sign this consent form and then change your mind and decide that you do not want to be adopted, you may take back or "revoke" your consent. However, **you must revoke your consent before the judge signs the adoption order,** and you must revoke it either in writing or in court in front of the judge. If you decide you do not want to be adopted, you should write the judge at _____ Circuit Court at _____ (address) immediately, or tell the judge before or at the beginning of your adoption hearing.

STOP HERE IF YOU DID NOT UNDERSTAND SOMETHING YOU HAVE READ OR IF YOU WANT TO SPEAK WITH A LAWYER BEFORE YOU DECIDE IF YOU WANT TO SIGN THE CONSENT FORM.

If you wish to sign the consent form, you must also sign here to verify that you read these instructions and understand them:

_____	_____
(Signature)	(Date)

You must attach a copy of these signed instructions to the signed consent form.

CONSENT OF _____ **TO INDEPENDENT ADOPTION**

(Name of Child)

Use a pen to fill out this form. If you decide to sign the consent form, you must have a witness present when you sign it. The witness must be someone 18 or older and should not be your parent or the person who is adopting you. You must fill in all the blanks, sign the form, and print your name, address, and telephone number, and the witness must sign and print the witness' name, address, and telephone number in the blanks on the last page.

1. I understand English, or this consent form has been translated into _____, a language that I understand.

2. My name is _____.

3. My date of birth is _____. I am _____ years old.

4. I understand that _____ have ask to adopt me.

5. Check **one**:

    [ ] I have a lawyer whose name and telephone number are _____. I have met with my lawyer who

has gone over this consent form with me and explained to me what it means to be adopted. I want to agree to be adopted.

OR

[ ] I do not have a lawyer. I have read the instructions in the front of this form, and I understand this consent form. I do not want to speak with a lawyer before I complete this form and agree to be adopted.

6. I understand that if I agree to be adopted, and I am adopted, _____ will become my parents, and I will become their child.

7. I understand that if I agree to be adopted, and I am adopted, _____ will no longer be my parents.

8. I understand that I do not have to agree to be adopted. If I do not agree, the court cannot approve the adoption.

9. I voluntarily and of my own free will agree to being adopted by _____. I understand that if they are not able to complete the adoption, this consent form will no longer be valid and can no longer be used.

10. I understand that if I change my mind and do not want to be adopted, I must tell the judge immediately. I will have to sign a written statement or tell the judge in court that I do not want to be adopted **before** the adoption order is signed.

11. I understand that when I am at least 21 years old, my birth parents or I may apply to the Secretary of the Maryland Department of Health and Mental Hygiene to get certain birth and adoption records. If I do not want information about me to be given to my birth parents, I have the right to file a form called a "disclosure veto." I have been given a form that I may use if I want to file a disclosure veto.

12. I understand that when I am at least 21 years old, my birth parents, my siblings, or I may apply to the Director of the Social Services Administration of the Maryland Department of Human Resources for adoption search, contact, and reunion services.

13. I have read this consent form or have had it read and explained to me in a language that I understand. I understand the meaning of this consent form.

14. I have not been promised anything in return for agreeing to be adopted.

15. I have signed this consent form of my own free will.

16. I understand that I will be given a copy of this signed consent form.

I solemnly affirm under the penalties of perjury that the contents of this consent to adoption form are true to the best of my knowledge, information, and belief.

_____   _____
(Date)   (Signature)

                                                           _____
                                                           (Printed Name)

                                                           _____
                                                           (Address)

_____
(City, State, Zip Code)

_____
(Telephone Number)

Witness:

_____   _____
(Date)   (Signature)

                             _____
                             (Printed Name)

                             _____
                             (Address)

                             _____
                             (City, State, Zip Code)

                             _____
                             (Telephone Number)

A COPY OF THE INSTRUCTIONS WITH YOUR SIGNATURE MUST BE ATTACHED TO THIS CONSENT FORM. (Added June 4, 2007, effective July 1, 2007.)

Form 9-102.8. Attorney affidavit as to consent of a parent to a public agency guardianship or private agency guardianship.

Affidavit by Attorney as to Consent of _____ (parent) to Guardianship with the Right to Consent to Adoption ("Guardianship") by _____ (agency) of _____ (child)

1. I am the attorney representing _____, a parent of _____, the child who is the subject of the consent.

2. The parent, at the time of the signing of the consent, was _____ years old. The parent's date of birth is _____.

3. (Check one of the following)

   [ ] The parent is not disabled or is disabled but the disability does not affect the parent's ability to understand the meaning of the consent to guardianship.

OR

   [ ] The parent is a minor or has a disability that could affect the parent's ability to understand the meaning of the consent to guardianship. The disability is _____
_____ .

   Despite the parent's age or disability, I believe that the parent understood the meaning of consenting to guardianship. The following additional steps were taken to ensure that the parent understood the meaning of the consent form prior to signing it: _____
_____ .

4. The parent understands English, or the consent form that the parent signed was translated into _____, a language that the parent understands.

5. I have explained to the parent that _____ (agency) has filed or plans to file a case to ask the court to grant it guardianship of the child with the right to consent to adoption by:

Check one of the following:

     [ ] a family approved by the agency.

OR

     [ ] _____ (name by which parent knows adoptive parent).

6. I reviewed the consent form thoroughly with the parent, and I believe that the parent desires to consent to the guardianship and has signed the consent form knowingly and voluntarily and not due to duress or coercion.

I solemnly affirm under the penalties of perjury that the contents of this affidavit are true to the best of my knowledge, information, and belief.

_____

(Date)

_____

(Signature)

_____

(Printed Name)

_____

(Address)

_____

(City, State, Zip Code)

_____

(Telephone Number) (Added June 4, 2007, effective July 1, 2007.)

Form 9-102.9. Attorney affidavit as to consent of a parent to adoption.

Affidavit by Attorney as to Consent of _____ (parent) to Adoption of _____

1. I am the attorney representing _____, a parent of _____, the child who is the subject of the consent.

2. The parent, at the time of the signing of the consent, was _____ years old. The parent's date of birth is _____.

3. (Check one of the following)

     [ ] The parent is not disabled or is disabled but the disability does not affect the parent's ability to understand the meaning of the consent to adoption.

OR

     [ ] The parent is a minor or has a disability that could affect the parent's ability to understand the meaning of the consent to adoption. The disability is _____.

Despite the parent's age or disability, I believe that the parent understood the meaning of consenting to adoption. The following additional steps were taken to ensure that the parent understood the meaning of the consent form prior to signing it: _____

_____.

4. The parent understands English, or the consent form that the parent signed was translated into _____, a language that the parent understands.

5. I have explained to the parent that _____ (name by which parent knows adoptive parent) has filed or plans to file a case to ask the court to permit that person to adopt the parent's child.

6. I reviewed the consent form thoroughly with the parent, and I believe that the parent desires to consent to the adoption and has signed the consent form knowingly and voluntarily and not due to duress or coercion.

I solemnly affirm under the penalties of perjury that the contents of this affidavit are true to the best of my knowledge, information, and belief.

_____

(Date)

(Signature)

_____

(Printed Name)

_____

(Address)

_____

(City, State, Zip Code)

_____

(Telephone Number) (Added June 4, 2007, effective July 1, 2007.)

Form 9-102.10. Attorney affidavit as to consent of a child to adoption.

Affidavit by Attorney as to Consent of _____ (Child) to Adoption

1. I am the attorney representing _____, the individual who is the subject of this adoption proceeding ("the child").

2. The child, at the time of the signing of the consent form, was _____ years old. The child's date of birth is _____. To the best of my knowledge, the child is not an Indian child subject to the provisions of the Indian Child Welfare Act.

3. (Check one of the following)

    [ ] The child is not disabled or is disabled but the disability would not affect the child's ability to understand the meaning of the consent to adoption.

OR

    [ ] The child has a disability that could affect the child's ability to understand the meaning of consenting to adoption. The disability is

_____.

Despite the child's disability, I believe that the child understands the meaning of the consenting adoption. The following additional steps

were taken to ensure that the child understood the meaning of the consent form prior to signing it: _____
_____.

4. The child understands English, or the consent form that the child signed has been translated into _____, a language that the child understands.

5. I have explained to the child that _____ have asked the court to be permitted to adopt the child, that the child has the right to decide whether or not the child wants to be adopted, and the possible options if the adoption is not approved.

6. I reviewed the consent form thoroughly with the child, and I believe that the child agrees to the adoption and has signed the consent form knowingly and voluntarily and not due to duress or coercion.

I solemnly affirm under the penalties of perjury that the contents of this affidavit are true to the best of my knowledge, information, and belief.

_____
(Date)

_____
(Signature)

_____
(Printed Name)

_____
(Address)

_____
(City, State, Zip Code)

_____
(Telephone Number) (Added June 4, 2007, effective July 1, 2007.)

TITLE 10. GUARDIANS AND OTHER FIDUCIARIES

Editor's note. — The Court of Appeals, by Order dated June 5, 1996, effective January 1, 1997, rescinded Subtitles A, D, E, J, P, Q, R, T, U, V, W, Y, Z, BB, BD, BE, BG, BH, BJ, BL, BP, BQ, BR, BS, BW, and BY of Chapter 1100 of the Maryland Rules of Procedure, rescinded Subtitles P, BB, BQ, and BW of the Maryland District Rules, and rescinded Forms 22a, 23, 24, 25, and 26. The Order substituted for certain of the rules and forms rescinded new Title 9, Chapter 100, Title 10, Title 12, Title 13, Title 14, and Title 15 of the Maryland Rules of Procedure. Furthermore, the Order transferred, without readoption, Chapter 900, Chapter 1200, and Subtitles S, BU, and BV of Chapter 1100 of the Maryland Rules of Procedure and Chapter 1200 of the Maryland District Rules to be Title 9, Chapter 200, Title 11, and Title 16 of the Maryland Rules of Procedure. The Order provides that the new rules shall "apply to all actions commenced on or after January 1, 1997, and insofar as practicable, to all actions then pending."

Many of the cases in the notes to the various rules were decided prior to the 1996 revision. These cases have been retained under pertinent rules of this title where it is thought that such cases will be of value in interpreting the present rules.

A table of comparable rules, relating those rules rescinded effective January 1, 1997, to the revised rules in Title 9 through Title 16 is to be found in Volume 2 following the end of the Maryland Rules.

CHAPTER 100. GENERAL PROVISIONS.

Rule 10-101. Applicability of title; jurisdiction.

(a) **Applicability.** Except as otherwise provided by law, the rules in this Title apply to proceedings concerning: (1) the guardianship of minors and disabled persons or their property; (2) a fiduciary estate; and (3) the distribution of property to an absent or unknown person.

(b) **Scope of jurisdiction.** In proceedings under this Title, the court may exercise its jurisdiction generally or for a limited purpose. An investment in a common trust fund by a fiduciary administering an estate subject to the jurisdiction of a court does not bring the administration of the common trust fund under the jurisdiction of the court.

Cross references. — For the definition of "common trust fund," *see* Code, Financial Institutions Article, § 3-501 (b).

Committee note. — The rules in this Title do not apply to a guardian with the right to consent to adoption (Code, Family Law Article, § 5-301 *et seq.* and Title 9, Chapter 100 of these rules); a trustee appointed to foreclose a mortgage or deed of trust or to make a judicial sale (Title 14, Chapters 200 and 300 of these rules); a trustee of a recovery by a minor in tort (Code, Estates and Trusts Article, § 13-401 *et seq.*); a custodian of property under the Maryland Uniform Transfers to Minors Act (Code, Estates and Trusts Article, § 13-301 *et seq.*); or a receiver or assignee for the benefit of creditors (Title 13 of these Rules).

Source. — This Rule is derived in part from former Rule V71 and is in part new.

Rule 10-102. Applicability of Titles 1 and 2.

(a) **Applicability of Title 1.** Except as otherwise provided in this Title, the rules in Title 1 apply to this Title.

(b) **Applicability of Title 2.** Any interested person may obtain discovery in a contested matter pursuant to Title 2, Chapter 400 of these Rules, unless otherwise ordered by the court. Except as otherwise provided in this Title, a court may apply any of the rules in Title 2 as appropriate.

Source. — This Rule is new.

Rule 10-103. Definitions.

In this Title the following definitions apply except as expressly otherwise provided or as necessary implication requires:

(a) **Court.** "Court" means the circuit court for any county and, where it has jurisdiction, the Orphans' Court.

Cross references. — *See* Code, Estates and Trusts Article, § 13-105 for the jurisdiction of the Orphans' Court over guardians of the person of a minor and protective proceedings for minors. *See also* 92 Op. Atty. Gen. 009 (March 20, 1992).

(b) **Disabled person.** (1) In connection with a guardianship of the person, "disabled person" means a person, other than a minor, who, because of mental disability, disease, habitual drunkenness, or addiction to drugs, has been adjudged by a court to lack sufficient understanding or capacity to make or communicate responsible decisions concerning himself or herself, such as provisions for health care, food, clothing, or shelter, and who, as a result of this inability, requires a guardian of the person.

(2) In connection with a guardianship of property, "disabled person" means a person, other than a minor, (A) who has been adjudged by a court to be unable to manage his or her property and affairs effectively because of physical or mental disability, disease, habitual drunkenness, addiction to drugs, imprisonment, compulsory hospitalization, confinement, detention by a foreign power, or disappearance, (B) who has or may be entitled to property or benefits that require proper management, and (C) who, as a result of this inability, requires a guardian of the property.

Cross references. — Code, Estates and Trusts Article, §§ 13-101, 13-705 (b) and 13-201 (c).

(c) **Fiduciary.** "Fiduciary" means (1) a guardian of the property of a minor or disabled person, (2) a guardian of the person of a minor or disabled person to the extent that the guardian exercises control over any property of the minor or disabled person, (3) a trustee acting under any inter vivos or testamentary trust over which the court has been asked to assume or has assumed jurisdiction, (4) a person administering an estate under appointment by a court as a "committee," "conservator," or the like, and (5) a personal representative of a decedent to the extent provided in Rules 10-703 and 10-711.

(d) **Fiduciary estate.** "Fiduciary estate" means real or personal property administered by a fiduciary.

(e) **Heir.** "Heir" means a person who would be entitled under the law of this State to inherit property if, at the applicable time, the owner of the property had died intestate.

(f) **Interested person.** (1) In connection with a guardianship of the person or the authorization of emergency protective services, "interested person" means the minor or the disabled person; the guardian and heirs of that person; a governmental agency paying benefits to that person or a person or agency eligible to serve as guardian of the person under Code, Estates and Trusts Article, § 13-707; the Department of Veterans Affairs as directed by Code,

Estates and Trusts Article, § 13-801; and any other person designated by the court.

(2) In connection with a guardianship of the property or other fiduciary proceedings, "interested person" means a person who would be an interested person under subsection (f) (1) of this Rule and a current income beneficiary of the fiduciary estate; a fiduciary and co-fiduciary of the fiduciary estate; and the creator of the fiduciary estate.

(3) If an interested person is a minor or disabled person, "interested person" includes a fiduciary appointed for that person, or, if none, the parent or other person who has assumed responsibility for the interested person.

Cross references. — Code, Estates and Trusts Article, § 13-101 (j) and § 13-801.

(g) **Minor.** "Minor" means a person who is under the age of eighteen.

(h) **Public guardian.** "Public guardian" means a guardian who is the director of a local department of social services, the State Department of Aging, or an area agency on aging.

(i) **Temporary guardian.** "Temporary guardian" means (1) a person appointed under Rule 10-210 in a proceeding for emergency protective services, (2) a person who has been authorized to preserve and apply the property of a minor or alleged disabled person pending a hearing on a petition for guardianship, and (3) a guardian of the person or property appointed by the court pending the appointment of a substituted or successor guardian. (Amended Oct. 5, 1999.)

Cross references. — Code, Estates and Trusts Article, §§ 13-203 and 13-709 (c) (4).
Source. — This Rule is derived as follows:
Section (a) is derived from former Rule R70 a.
Section (b) is derived from former Rule R70 b, and Code, Estates and Trusts Article, §§ 13-201 (c) (1) and 13-705 (b).
Section (c) is derived in part from former Rule V70 b and is in part new.
Section (d) is new.
Section (e) is derived from former Rule R70 c.

Section (f). Subsection (1) is derived in part from former Rule R70 d and in part from Code, Estates and Trusts Article, § 13-707.
Subsection (2) is derived from former Rule V70 c.
Section (g) is derived from former Rule R70 e.
Section (h) is derived from Code, Estates and Trusts Article, § 13-707 (a) (10).
Section (i) is derived in part from Code, Estates and Trusts Article, §§ 13-203 and 13-709 and is in part new.

Effect of amendments. — The 1999 amendment substituted "State Department of Aging" for "State Office on Aging" in (h).

Rule 10-104. Show cause orders.

Except as provided in Rules 10-209 (b), 10-213, and 10-705, upon the filing of a petition, the court shall issue a show cause order directing a person to show cause in writing on or before a specified date why the court should not take the action described in the order. Unless the court orders otherwise, the specified date shall be 20 days after the date prescribed for service in the order. The order shall also specify who is to be served and the method of service and, if a hearing is scheduled when the order is issued, the date, time, and place of the hearing. A copy of any related petition or document shall be served with a copy of the order. If required, the Advice of Rights form and the Notice to Interested Persons form shall also be served with the copy of the order. (Amended Feb. 10, 1998, effective July 1, 1998.)

Source. — This Rule is new.

Effect of amendments. — The 1998 amendment substituted "Notice" for "Advice" in the last sentence.

Quoted in Davis v. AG of Md., 187 Md. App. 110, 975 A.2d 362 (2009).

Rule 10-105. Waiver of notice.

(a) **Method of waiver.** An interested person other than a minor or disabled person may waive the right to any or all notices other than original notice by filing a signed waiver. A minor or disabled person may waive the right to any or all notices other than original notice by a waiver signed and filed by his or her attorney, which shall not be effective until approved by the court.

(b) **Revocation.** A waiver of notice may be revoked at any time by the filing of a revocation, which shall be effective from the date filed.

Source. — This Rule is derived from former Rule R70 f and Rule 6-126.

Rule 10-106. Appointment of attorney or investigator.

(a) **Appointment of attorney by the court.** Upon the filing of a petition for guardianship of the person or property of a disabled person or minor who is not represented by an attorney, the court shall promptly appoint an attorney for the disabled person and may appoint an attorney for the minor. The fee of an appointed attorney shall be fixed by the court and shall be paid out of the fiduciary estate or as the court shall direct. To the extent the estate is insufficient, the fee of an attorney appointed for a disabled person shall be paid by the State.

Cross references. — Code, Estates and Trusts Article, §§ 13-211 (b) and 13-705 (d). *See also* Rule 1.14 of the Maryland Lawyers' Rules of Professional Conduct with respect to the attorney's role and obligations.

(b) **Automatic termination of appointment; continuation of representation if public guardian appointed.** If no appeal is taken from a judgment dismissing the petition or appointing a guardian other than a public guardian, the attorney's appointment shall terminate automatically upon expiration of the time for filing an appeal unless the court orders otherwise. If a public guardian has been appointed for the disabled person, the court shall either continue the attorney's appointment or appoint another attorney to represent the disabled person before the Adult Public Guardianship Review Board.

Cross references. — Code, Family Law Article, § 14-404 (c) (2).

(c) **Investigator.** The court may appoint an independent investigator to investigate the facts of the case and report written findings to the court. The fee of an appointed investigator shall be fixed by the court and shall be paid out of the fiduciary estate or as the court shall direct. To the extent the estate is insufficient, the fee of an independent investigator appointed by the court shall be paid by the State.

Source. — This Rule is derived in part from former Rules R76 and V71 and is in part new.

Payment of costs and counsel fees in proceeding for construction of will. — The costs of the proceeding for construction of the will, including the fee of the trustee's counsel, may be paid from the assets of the trust estate, but not the fees of counsel for other parties, unless they were appointed by the court to represent infants or persons under some disability. Sollers v. Mercantile-Safe Deposit & Trust Co., 262 Md. 606, 278 A.2d 581 (1971).

Attorney fees. — Trusts out of which the fees of an alleged disabled person's attorney were ordered to be paid were not part of the person's fiduciary estate, under subsection (a) of this rule, because she only had a life interest in the income from those trusts. Owings v. Foote, 150 Md. App. 1, 818 A.2d 1149 (2002).

Rule 10-107. Assessment and waiver of fees and costs — Guardianships.

(a) **Assessment.** Upon a determination on the merits of a petition to appoint a guardian, the court may assess the filing fee and other court costs against the assets of the fiduciary estate or against the petitioner.

(b) **Waiver.** The court shall waive final costs and fees if the court finds that the person against whom the costs are assessed is unable to pay them by reason of poverty. The person may seek the waiver at the conclusion of the case in accordance with Rule 1-325 (a). If the person was granted a waiver pursuant to that Rule and remains unable to pay the costs, the affidavit required by Rule 1-325 (a) need only recite the existence of the prior waiver and the person's continued inability to pay.

Source. — This Rule is in part new and in part derived from Rule 2-603 (e).

Rule 10-108. Orders.

(a) **Order appointing guardian.** An order appointing a guardian shall state:

(1) Whether the guardianship is of the property or person or both;

(2) The name of the minor or disabled person;

(3) The name, address, and telephone number of the guardian;

(4) The reason for the guardianship;

(5) The amount of the guardian's bond, or that the bond is waived;

(6) The date upon which any annual report of the guardian shall be filed; and

(7) The specific powers and duties of the guardian and any limitations on those powers or duties. The order shall recite the powers and duties of the guardian either expressly or by referring to the specific paragraphs of an applicable statute containing those powers and duties.

Cross references. — Code, Estates and Trusts Article, §§ 13-201 (b) and (c), 13-213, 13-214, 15-102, 13-705 (b), and 13-708.

(b) **Letters of guardianship.** A court may issue letters of guardianship of the property which shall contain a list of any restrictions on the powers of the guardian.

Cross references. — Code, Estates and Trusts Article, §§ 13-215 and 13-217.

(c) **Orders assuming jurisdiction over a fiduciary estate other than a guardianship.** An order assuming jurisdiction over a fiduciary estate other than a guardianship shall state whether the court has assumed full jurisdiction over the estate. If it has not assumed full jurisdiction over the estate or if jurisdiction is contrary to the provisions in the instrument, the order shall state the extent of the jurisdiction assumed. The order shall state the amount of the fiduciary's bond or that the bond is waived.

(d) **Modifications.** The court may modify any order of a continuing nature in a guardianship or fiduciary estate upon the petition of an interested person or on its own initiative, and after notice and opportunity for hearing.

Source. — This Rule is derived as follows: *Section (a)* is derived in part from Code, Estates and Trusts Article, §§ 13-208 and 13-708 and is in part new.
Section (b) is derived from former Rule V77 c 3.
Section (c) is derived from former Rules V71 f 1 and f 2.
Section (d) is derived in part from former Rule R78 b and is in part new.

Court of equity assumes jurisdiction in guardianship matters to protect those who, because of illness or other disability, are unable to care for themselves. Kicherer v. Kicherer, 285 Md. 114, 400 A.2d 1097 (1979).

In reality court is guardian; an individual who is given that title is merely an agent or arm of that tribunal in carrying out its sacred responsibility. Kicherer v. Kicherer, 285 Md. 114, 400 A.2d 1097 (1979).

Stipulation not deemed decree. — A stipulation by the parties as to disability is not a specific finding by the court, so as to comply with this Rule. Kicherer v. Kicherer, 285 Md. 114, 400 A.2d 1097 (1979).

Rule 10-109. Transfer of action.

(a) **Proceedings initiated in the Orphans' Court.** Upon the petition of an interested person, the Orphans' Court may transfer a guardianship or protective proceeding for a minor to the circuit court.

Cross references. — Code, Estates and Trusts Article, § 13-105 (a); 92 Op. Atty. Gen. 009 (March 20, 1992).

(b) **Other proceedings.** During the course of an action, the court, on its own initiative or on the petition of an interested person, may transfer the action to any other circuit court if the transfer (1) is in the best interest of the minor or alleged disabled person; or (2) serves the convenience of the guardian, fiduciary, and other interested persons and witnesses, is not inconsistent with the best interest of the minor or alleged disabled person, and serves the interest of justice.

Source. — This Rule is derived from former Rule R72 d and Code, Estates and Trusts Article, § 13-105 (a).

Rule 10-110. Combination of guardianship petitions.

A petition for the appointment of a guardian of the person of a minor or alleged disabled person may also include a request for the appointment of a guardian of the person's property, and vice versa.

Source. — This Rule is derived from former Rule R71 a.

CHAPTER 200. GUARDIAN OF PERSON.

Rule 10-201. Petition for appointment of a guardian of person.

(a) **Who may file.** An interested person may file a petition requesting a court to appoint a guardian of a minor or alleged disabled person.

(b) **Venue.** (1) Resident. If the minor or alleged disabled person is a resident of Maryland, the petition shall be filed in the county where (A) the minor or alleged disabled person resides or (B) the person has been admitted for the purpose of medical care or treatment to either a general or a special hospital which is not a State facility as defined in Code, Health-General Article, § 10-406 or a licensed private facility as defined in Code, Health-General Article, §§ 10-501 to 10-511.

(2) Nonresident. If the minor or alleged disabled person does not reside in this State, a petition for guardianship of the person may be filed in any county in which the person is physically present.

(c) **Contents.** The petition shall be captioned, "In the Matter of ..." [stating the name of the minor or alleged disabled person]. It shall be signed and verified by the petitioner, may contain a request for the guardianship of property, and shall contain at least the following information:

(1) The petitioner's name, address, age, and telephone number.

(2) The petitioner's familial or other relationship to the minor or alleged disabled person.

(3) Whether the person who is the subject of the petition is a minor or alleged disabled person, and, if an alleged disabled person, a brief description of the alleged disability and how it affects the alleged disabled person's ability to function.

(4) The reasons why the court should appoint a guardian of the person and, if the subject of the petition is a disabled person, allegations demonstrating an inability of that person to make or communicate responsible decisions concern-

ing the person, including provisions for health care, food, clothing, or shelter, because of mental disability, disease, habitual drunkenness or addiction to drugs, and a description of less restrictive alternatives that have been attempted and have failed.

Cross references. — Code, Estates and Trusts Article, § 13-705 (b).

(5) An identification of any instrument nominating a guardian or constituting a durable power of attorney, with a copy attached to the petition, if possible, and, if not, an explanation of its absence.

Cross references. — Code, Estates and Trusts Article, § 13-701.

(6) If a guardian or conservator has been appointed for the alleged disabled person in another proceeding, the name and address of the guardian or conservator and the court that appointed the guardian or conservator. If a guardianship or conservatorship proceeding was previously filed in any other court, the name and address of the court, the case number, if known, and whether the proceeding is still pending in that court.

(7) A list of (A) the name, age, sex, and address of the minor or alleged disabled person, (B) the name and address of the persons with whom the minor or disabled person resides, and (C) if the minor or alleged disabled person resides with the petitioner, the name and address of another person on whom service can be made.

(8) The name, address, telephone number, and nature of interest of all other interested persons and all other persons exercising control of the minor or alleged disabled person, to the extent known or reasonably ascertainable.

(9) If the minor or alleged disabled person is represented by an attorney, the name and address of the attorney.

(10) A statement that the certificates required by Rule 10-202 are attached, or, if not, an explanation of their absence.

(11) If the petition also seeks a guardianship of the property, the additional information required by Rule 10-301.

(12) A statement of the relief sought.

Source. — This Rule is derived as follows:
Section (a) is derived from former Rule R71 a.
Section (b) is derived from former Rule R72 a and b.
Section (c) is derived in part from former Rule R73 a and in part from former Rule V71 c.

Rule 10-202. Certificates.

(a) **Generally required.** Except as provided in section (d), if guardianship of the person of a disabled person is sought, the petitioner shall file with the petition signed and verified certificates of (1) two physicians licensed to practice medicine in the United States who have examined the disabled person, or (2) one licensed physician or who has examined the disabled person and one licensed psychologist or certified clinical social worker who has seen and evaluated the disabled person. An examination or evaluation by at least one of the health care professionals under this subsection shall occur within 21 days before the filing of the petition.

(b) **Contents.** Each certificate shall state: (1) the name, address, and qualifications of the person who performed the examination or evaluation, (2) a brief history of the person's involvement with the disabled person, (3) the date of the last examination or evaluation of the disabled person, and (4) the person's opinion as to: (A) the cause, nature, extent, and probable duration of the disability, (B) whether institutional care is required, and (C) whether the disabled person has sufficient mental capacity to understand the nature of and consent to the appointment of a guardian.

(c) **Delayed filing of certificates.** (1) After refusal to permit examination. If the petition is not accompanied by the required certificate and the petition alleges that the disabled person is residing with or under the control of a person who has refused to permit examination by a physician or evaluation by a psychologist or certified clinical social worker, and that the disabled person may be at risk unless a guardian is appointed, the court shall defer issuance of a show cause order. The court shall instead issue an order requiring that the person who has refused to permit the disabled person to be examined or evaluated appear personally on a date specified in the order and show cause why the disabled person should not be examined or evaluated. The order shall be personally served on that person and on the disabled person.

(2) Appointment of health care professionals by court. If the court finds after a hearing that examinations are necessary, it shall appoint two physicians or one physician and one psychologist or certified clinical social worker to conduct the examinations or the examination and evaluation and file their reports with the court. If both health care professionals find the person to be disabled, the court shall issue a show cause order requiring the alleged disabled person to answer the petition for guardianship and shall require the petitioner to give notice pursuant to Rule 10-203. Otherwise, the petition shall be dismissed.

(d) **Beneficiary of the Department of Veterans Affairs.** If guardianship of the person of a disabled person who is a beneficiary of the United States Department of Veterans Affairs is being sought, the petitioner shall file with the petition, in lieu of the two certificates required by section (a) of this Rule, a certificate of the Secretary of that Department or an authorized representative of the Secretary stating that the person has been rated as disabled by the Department in accordance with the laws and regulations governing the Department of Veterans Affairs. The certificate shall be prima facie evidence of the necessity for the appointment. (Amended Feb. 10, 1998, effective July 1, 1998; Oct. 5, 1999; Nov. 12, 2003, effective Jan. 1, 2004; Dec. 4, 2007, effective Jan. 1, 2008.)

Cross references. — Code, Estates and Trusts Article, § 13-705. Rule 1-341.

Source. — This Rule is in part derived from former Rule R73 b 1 and b 2 and is in part new.

Effect of amendments. — The 1998 amendment added the (a) (1) designation and subsection heading; added (a) (2); and rewrote the source note.

The 1999 amendment deleted "Physicians'" from the section heading; rewrote (a) (1); substituted "the two certificates required" for "the certificates of two physicians required" in (a) (2); in (b) (1), inserted "or evaluation by a psychologist" in the first sentence, and inserted "or evaluated" following "examined" twice in the second sentence; and in (b) (2), substituted "health care professionals" for "physicians" in the heading and in the second sentence, and in the first sentence, inserted "or one physician and one psychologist" and "or the examination and evaluation."

The 2003 amendment in the first sentence of (a)(2), substituted "that Department" for "the Department of Veterans Affairs", substituted "an authorized representative of the Administrator stating" for "a duly authorized representative setting forth the fact."

The December 4, 2007 Order, effective January 1, 2008, in the heading, deleted "Requirement and Content"; added "or certified clinical social worker" throughout the section; in (a) rewrote the heading and redesignated the third sentence to be (b), and (a) (2) to be (d) and redesignated accordingly, added the exception at the beginning, in (a) (2) substituted "the petition" for "a petition for guardianship of a disabled person", and made related changes; and rewrote (b).

Compatibility with federal law. — Regulations of the Health Insurance Portability and Accountability Act of 1996 (HIPAA) and the requirements of the state guardianship law are not necessarily incompatible; thus, depending on the facts of the particular case, a physician or psychologist may well be able to disclose protected health information to a petitioner and a court in connection with a guardianship proceeding. 89 Op. Att'y Gen. 81 (Apr. 14, 2004).

Rule 10-203. Service; notice.

(a) **Service on minor or alleged disabled person.** The petitioner shall serve a show cause order issued pursuant to Rule 10-104 on the minor or alleged disabled person and on the parent, guardian, or other person having care or custody of the minor or alleged disabled person. Service shall be in accordance with Rule 2-121 (a). If the minor or alleged disabled person resides with the petitioner, service shall be made upon the minor or disabled person and on such other person as the court may direct. Service upon a minor under the age of ten years may be waived provided that the other service requirements of this section are met. The show cause order served on a disabled person shall be accompanied by an "Advice of Rights" in the form set forth in Rule 10-204.

(b) **Notice to other persons.** (1) To attorney. Unless the court orders otherwise, the petitioner shall mail a copy of the petition and show cause order by ordinary mail to the attorney for the minor or alleged disabled person.

(2) To interested persons. Unless the court orders otherwise, the petitioner shall mail by ordinary mail and by certified mail to all other interested persons a copy of the petition and show cause order and a "Notice to Interested Persons."

(c) **Notice to Interested Persons.** The Notice to Interested Persons shall be in the following form:

In the Matter of   In the Circuit Court for

_____   _____

(Name of minor or alleged   (County)
  disabled person)
                                    _____

                                          (docket reference)

NOTICE TO INTERESTED PERSONS

A petition has been filed seeking appointment of a guardian of the person of
_____, who is alleged to be a minor or disabled
person.

You are an "interested person," that is, someone who should receive notice of
this proceeding because you are related to or otherwise concerned with the
welfare of this person.

If the court appoints a guardian for the person, that person will lose certain
valuable rights to make individual decisions.

Please examine the attached papers carefully. If you object to the appointment of a guardian, please file a response in accordance with the attached
show cause order. (Be sure to include the case number). If you wish otherwise
to participate in this proceeding, notify the court and be prepared to attend any
hearing.

Each certificate filed pursuant to Rule 10-202 that is attached to the petition
will be admissible as substantive evidence without the presence or testimony
of the certifying health care professional unless you file a request that the
health care professional appear to testify. The request must be filed at least 10
days before the trial date, unless the trial date is less than 10 days from the
date your response is due. If the trial date is less than 10 days from the date
your response is due, the request may be filed at any time before trial.

If you believe you need further legal advice about this matter, you should
consult your attorney. (Amended Oct. 5, 1999; Dec. 4, 2007, effective Jan. 1,
2008.)

Source. — This Rule is in part derived from
former Rule R74 and Code, Estates and Trusts
Article, § 1-103 (b) and is in part new.

Effect of amendments. — The 1999
amendment, in the sixth paragraph of (c),
inserted "or psychologist's" following "physician's" near the beginning, and inserted "or
psychologist" following "physician" twice.

The December 4, 2007 Order, effective January 1, 2008, in (c) in the form, rewrote the
fifth paragraph.

Testimony of certifying physicians. —
The questionable adequacy of a physician's
certificates clearly illustrated the need for the
testimony of the doctors who prepared them,
and the trial court erred in not permitting the
doctors to testify. In re Lee, 132 Md. App. 696,
754 A.2d 426 (2000).

Rule 10-204. Advice of rights.

The Advice of Rights required to be served on an alleged disabled person
shall be in the following form:

TO _____ (Name).

A petition has been filed seeking appointment of a guardian of your person.

IF THE COURT APPOINTS A GUARDIAN OF YOUR PERSON, YOU WILL
LOSE CERTAIN VALUABLE RIGHTS, WHICH MAY INCLUDE THE RIGHT
TO MAKE DECISIONS FOR YOURSELF ABOUT WHERE YOU LIVE, HOW
YOU LIVE, AND WHAT MEDICAL CARE YOU RECEIVE.

YOU HAVE CERTAIN RIGHTS IN THIS CASE:

1. [ ] The petition alleges that _____

(Name of Attorney)

is your attorney. If that is not correct, notify the clerk immediately.

[ ] The court has appointed _____

(Name of Attorney)

as your attorney, but you may hire another attorney if you wish.

2. You will have a trial if you or your attorney object to the appointment of a guardian of your person. It will be a jury trial unless you give up the right to a jury trial.

3. You have the right to be present at the trial.

4. You have the right to present evidence on your own behalf and to cross-examine witnesses against you.

5. You have the right to suggest restrictions or limitations of the guardian's powers if a guardian is appointed.

6. The trial may be closed to the public if you so request.

The above statements cannot cover all possible situations. Please read the attached papers carefully. You should consult with your attorney to determine what is in your best interest. Your or your attorney should file a response on or before the deadline stated in the attached order.

Source. — This Rule is new.

Rule 10-205. Hearing.

(a) **Guardianship of the person of a minor.** (1) No response to show cause order. If no response to the show cause order is filed and the court is satisfied that the petitioner has complied with the provisions of Rule 10-203, the court may rule on the petition summarily.

(2) Response to show cause order. If a response to the show cause order objects to the relief requested, the court shall set the matter for trial, and shall give notice of the time and place of trial to all persons who have responded.

Cross references. — Code, Estates and Trusts Article, § 13-702.

(b) **Guardianship of alleged disabled person.** (1) Generally. When the petition is for guardianship of the person of an alleged disabled person, the court shall set the matter for jury trial. The alleged disabled person or the attorney representing the person may waive a jury trial at any time before trial. If a jury trial is held, the jury shall return a verdict pursuant to Rule 2-522 (c) as to any alleged disability. Each certificate filed pursuant to Rule 10-202 is admissible as substantive evidence without the presence or testimony of the certifying health care professional unless, not later than 10 days before trial, an interested person who is not an individual under a disability, or the attorney for the alleged disabled person, files a request that the health care professional appear to testify. If the trial date is less than 10 days from the date the response is due, a request that the health care professional appear may be filed at any time before trial. If the alleged disabled person asserts that, because of his or her disability, the alleged disabled person cannot attend a trial at the courthouse, the court may hold the trial at a place to which the alleged disabled person has reasonable access.

(2) Beneficiary of the Department of Veterans Affairs. If guardianship of the person of a disabled person who is a beneficiary of the United States Department of Veterans Affairs is being sought and no objection to the guardianship is made, a hearing shall not be held unless the Court finds that extraordinary circumstances require a hearing. (Amended Feb. 10, 1998, effective July 1, 1998; Jan. 20, 1999, effective July 1, 1999; Oct. 5, 1999; Nov. 1, 2001, effective Jan. 1, 2002; Dec. 4, 2007, effective Jan. 1, 2008.)

Source. — This Rule is in part derived from former Rule R77 and is in part new.

Effect of amendments. — The 1998 amendment added the (b) (1) designation and subsection heading; and added (b) (2).

The first 1999 amendment deleted the last sentence in (a) (2); and added the last sentence in (b) (1).

The second 1999 amendment, in (b) (1), in the fourth sentence, inserted "or psychologist's" following "physician's," and inserted "or psychologist" following "physician" twice; and inserted "or psychologist" following "physician" in the fifth sentence.

The 2001 amendment deleted "special" preceding "verdict" in the third sentence of (b)(1).

The December 4, 2007 Order, effective January 1, 2008, in (b) (1) rewrote the fourth sentence, and in the fifth sentence substituted "health care professional" for "physician or psychologist".

Editor's note. — The 1999 amendment of this Rule, set out in full in the 141st Report of the Standing Committee on Rules of Practice and Procedure, contained changes which did not coincide with the text of the Rule as it existed after its 1998 amendment. In addition, the version of this Rule as set out in the 1999 Edition inadvertently omitted a sentence at the end of (a) (2) and at the end of (b) (2). The Rule is set out above to correct all discrepancies as instructed by the Reporter of the Court of Appeals.

Hearing required. — This Rule clearly contemplates that a hearing will be held and evidence taken on the issue of competency, and a hearing on competency cannot be waived and must always be held for the petitioner to establish by "clear and convincing evidence" that the alleged disabled person is in need of a guardian. In re Lee, 132 Md. App. 696, 754 A.2d 426 (2000).

There is a rational basis for different treatment of the two classes of individuals who are subject to guardianship proceedings and individuals found not guilty by reason of insanity in that a guardianship proceeding, which strips the individual of voting and property rights, may be based on various disabling conditions, while the insanity acquittee has had the fact of his disablement at the time of the offense already determined by a jury when he comes before the court for a determination on the question of confinement. Dorsey v. Solomon, 435 F. Supp. 725 (D. Md. 1977), aff'd in part and rev'd in part, 604 F.2d 271 (4th Cir. 1979).

Rule 10-206. Annual report — Guardianship of a disabled person.

(a) **Report required.** A guardian, other than a temporary guardian, of a disabled person shall file an annual report in the action. The reporting year shall end on (1) the anniversary of the date the court assumed jurisdiction over the person or (2) any other date approved by the trust clerk or the court.

Cross references. — Code, Estates and Trusts Article, § 13-708 (b) (7).

(b) **Time for filing.** The report shall be filed not later than 60 days after the end of the reporting year, unless the court for good cause shown shall extend the time.

(c) **Copies to interested persons.** The guardian shall furnish a copy of the report to any interested person requesting it, unless the court orders otherwise.

(d) **Court approval.** The court shall review the report and either enter an order accepting the report and continuing the guardianship or take other appropriate action.

(e) **Form of annual report.** The guardian's report shall be in substantially the following form:

[CAPTION]

ANNUAL REPORT OF _____, GUARDIAN
OF _____

1. The name and permanent residence of the disabled person are: _____
_____ .

2. The disabled person currently resides or is physically present in:
_____ own home   _____ guardian's home
_____ nursing home   _____ hospital or medical facility
_____ foster or boarding   _____ relative's home: _____
     home   relationship
                     _____ other
(If other than disabled person's permanent home, state the name and address of the place where the disabled person lives _____
_____ .)

3. The disabled person has been in the current location since
_____. If the person has moved within the past year, the
     (date)
reasons for the change are: _____
_____ .

4. The physical and mental condition of the disabled person is as follows: ___
_____ .

5. During the past year, the disabled person's physical or mental condition has changed in the following respects: _____
_____
_____ .

6. The disabled person is presently receiving the following care: _____
_____ .

7. I have applied funds as follows from the estate of the disabled person for the purpose of support, care, or education: _____
_____
_____ .

8. The plan for the disabled person's future care and well being, including any plan to change the person's location, is: _____
_____ .

9. [   ] I have no serious health problems that affect my ability to serve as guardian.
   [   ] I have the following serious health problems that may affect my ability to serve as guardian: _____

10. This guardianship
    [ ] should be continued.
    [ ] should not be continued, for the following reasons: _____
_____.

11. My powers as guardian should be changed in the following respects and for the following reasons: _____
_____
_____.

12. The court should be aware of the following other matters relating to this guardianship: _____
_____
_____.

I solemnly affirm under the penalties of perjury that the contents of this report are true to the best of my knowledge, information, and belief.

_____   _____
Date   Guardian's Signature

                                            _____
                                            Guardian's Name (typed or printed)

                                            _____
                                            Street Address or Box Number

                                            _____
                                            City and State

                                            _____
                                            Telephone Number

ORDER

The foregoing Annual Report of a Guardian having been filed and reviewed, it is by the Court, this ____ day of _____, _____,
                                            (month)   (year)
ORDERED, that the report is accepted, and the guardianship is continued.

(or)

ORDERED, that a hearing shall be held in this matter on
_____.
    (date)

                                            _____
                                                          JUDGE

(Amended May 9, 2000, effective July 1, 2000.)

Source. — This Rule is new and is derived as follows:

Section (a) is derived from Code, Estates and Trusts Article, § 13-708 (b) (7) and former Rule V74 c 2 (b).

Section (b) is derived from former Rule V74 c 2 (b).

Section (c) is patterned after Rule 6-417 (d). *Sections (d) and (e)* are new.

Effect of amendments. — The 2000 amendment, in the paragraph following "ORDER" in (e), substituted "_____" for "19____" and added "(month)" and "(year)" notations.

Rule 10-207. Resignation of guardian of the person and appointment of substituted or successor guardian.

(a) **Commencement of action.** A petition to resign may be filed in accordance with this Rule by a guardian of the person who has exercised no control over any property of the minor or disabled person or by a public guardian. The petition shall state the reasons for the resignation and may request the appointment of a substitute or successor guardian. When a guardian of the person resigns, dies, is removed, or becomes otherwise incapable of filling the position, and there is no substituted or successor guardian of the person already named, the court may, on its own initiative or on the petition filed by any interested person, appoint a substituted or successor guardian of the person.

Committee note. — If the original guardian, other than a public guardian, has exercised control over any property of the minor or disabled person, resignation and appointment of a successor shall be in accordance with Rule 10-711.

(b) **Venue.** The petition to resign or to appoint a substituted or successor guardian shall be filed in the court that has assumed jurisdiction over the guardianship. If jurisdiction has not been assumed, the petition shall be filed pursuant to Rule 10-201 (b).

(c) **Notice.** The petitioner shall give notice to those interested persons designated by the court by mailing to them by ordinary mail a copy of the petition and a show cause order issued pursuant to Rule 10-104.

(d) **Termination of guardian's appointment.** Resignation of a guardian does not terminate the appointment of the guardian until the court enters an order accepting the resignation.

(e) **Proceedings.** The court may, and upon request shall, hold a hearing and shall grant or deny the relief sought in the petition. Pending the appointment of the successor guardian, the court may appoint a temporary guardian.

(f) **Other procedures.** This Rule is in addition to, and not in lieu of, any other procedure for the resignation or discharge of a guardian provided by law or by the instrument appointing the guardian.

Source. — This Rule is derived as follows:
Section (a) is derived from former Rule V81 a and former Rule V82 a.
Section (b) is derived from former Rule R72 a and b.
Section (c) is derived from former Rule V81 c 1.
Section (d) is new.
Section (e) is in part derived from former Rule V78 b 5 and is in part new.
Section (f) is derived from former Rule V81 e.

Rule 10-208. Removal for cause or other sanctions.

(a) **On court's initiative.** The court that has already assumed jurisdiction over the guardianship of the person may order a guardian to show cause why the guardian should not be removed or be subject to other sanctions for failure to perform the duties of that office.

(b) **On petition of interested persons.** An interested person may file a petition to remove a guardian of the person. The petition shall be filed in the court that has assumed jurisdiction or, if jurisdiction has not been assumed, pursuant to Rule 10-201 (b). The petition shall state the reasons why the guardian should be removed.

(c) **Notice and hearing.** The court shall issue a show cause order pursuant to Rule 10-104 which shall set a hearing date. If no petition for removal has been filed, the show cause order shall state the grounds asserted by the court for the removal. The order and a copy of any petition shall be served on the guardian, all interested persons, and any other persons as directed by the court. The court shall conduct a hearing for the purpose of determining whether the guardian should be removed.

(d) **Action by court.** If the court finds grounds for removal, it may remove the guardian and appoint a substituted or successor guardian as provided in Rule 10-207. Pending the appointment of the guardian, the court may appoint a temporary guardian.

Cross references. — As to the grounds for the removal of a fiduciary, *see* Code, Estates and Trusts Article, § 15-112.

(e) **Other sanctions.** In addition to or in lieu of removal, the Court may require the guardian to perform any neglected duties and may impose any other appropriate sanctions.

Source. — This Rule is derived as follows:

Section (a) is in part derived from former Rules V84 d and V74 e 1 (a) and is in part new.

Section (b) is in part derived from former Rule V84 d 1 and d 2 and in part from former Rule R72 a and b.

Section (c) is in part derived from former Rules V74 e 1 (a) and V84 e, and is in part new.

Section (d) is new.

Section (e) is in part derived from former Rule V74 e 2 and is in part new.

Conventional trustee has broad discretionary powers which may be exercised absent evidence of bad faith, misconduct or a want of ordinary skill or judgment. Shipley v. Crouse, 279 Md. 613, 370 A.2d 97 (1977).

First obligation of the trustees is to safeguard the trust estate, and in doing so they are called upon many times to exercise a judgment; hence the judgment exercised by the trustees that they would share the final contract and let the beneficiaries know when it was submitted to the court for ratification, but would not share the step-by-step negotiations with the beneficiaries, was not a breach of their duty, but, quite to the contrary, was in furtherance of their duty to try to do what, in their judgment, was in the best interests of the trust estate. Shipley v. Crouse, 279 Md. 613, 370 A.2d 97 (1977).

Receipt of information by beneficiaries not absolute. — While beneficiaries are entitled to receive complete and accurate information as to the administration of the trust and to know what the trust property is and how the trustee has dealt with it, this is not absolute, if the trustee renders periodic reports showing collection of income and disbursements, assuming the trustee is acting in good faith and is not abusing his discretionary powers. Shipley v. Crouse, 279 Md. 613, 370 A.2d 97 (1977).

Disclosure by trustees mandated. — When there is a confidential relationship between buyer and seller, or there is an element of self-dealing, the duty of loyalty mandates a full and frank disclosure by the trustees to the beneficiaries. Shipley v. Crouse, 279 Md. 613, 370 A.2d 97 (1977).

Where removal likely required. — Where because of a disagreement between coguardians a ward has not been permitted to leave the grounds of a nursing home in which she resides, receive new eyeglasses, have any change in the medication or medical care she requires or the like, it may well be that removal of one or both of the guardians will be required. Kicherer v. Kicherer, 285 Md. 114, 400 A.2d 1097 (1979).

Rule 10-209. Termination of a guardianship of the person.

(a) **Applicability.** When a guardian of the person has exercised no control over any property of the person or if the guardian of the person is a public guardian, the termination of the guardianship shall be according to this Rule.

Committee note. — If a guardian of the person, other than a public guardian, has exercised control over any property of the minor or disabled person, termination of the guardianship shall be in accordance with Rule 10-710.

(b) **Termination not requiring prior notice.** (1) Petition; grounds. Upon a petition filed in conformity with this section, the court shall terminate a guardianship of the person without prior notice upon a finding that either (A) a minor not otherwise disabled has attained the age of majority or (B) the minor or disabled person has died, and that (C) the guardian has exercised no control over any property of the disabled person. The petition may be filed by a minor not otherwise disabled or by the guardian of a minor or disabled person. It shall contain or be accompanied by the guardian's verified statement that the guardian has exercised no control over any property of the minor or disabled person, and shall also be accompanied by either a copy of the minor person's birth certificate or other satisfactory proof of age or a certified copy of the minor or disabled person's death certificate.

(2) Time for filing. A minor who is not disabled may file a petition at any time after attaining the age of majority. A guardian shall file a petition within 45 days after discovery that grounds for termination exists.

(3) Venue. The petition shall be filed in the court that appointed the guardian or that has assumed jurisdiction over the fiduciary estate.

(4) Copy of order. The court shall send a copy of the order terminating the guardianship to the guardian, the person whose minority has ended, and any other person whom the court designates.

(c) **Termination requiring notice.** (1) Cause for termination. A guardianship of the person may be terminated upon the filing of a petition in accordance with this section if the court, after notice and hearing, finds that any of the following grounds exist:

(A) the cessation of the disability;

(B) the emancipation of a minor who has not attained the age of majority; or

(C) any other good cause for termination.

(2) Time for filing — Who may file. Within 45 days after the guardian discovers that grounds for termination may exist, the guardian shall file a petition requesting the court to terminate the guardianship. At any time after discovery of the grounds for termination the minor or disabled person or any

other interested person may file a petition requesting the court to terminate the guardianship.

(3) Venue. The petition shall be filed in the court that appointed the guardian or that has assumed jurisdiction over the fiduciary estate.

(4) Contents. The petition shall be signed and verified by the petitioner and shall contain the following information:

(A) the petitioner's relationship to the minor or disabled person;

(B) the name and address of each interested person;

(C) a statement of facts establishing the grounds for termination; and

(D) a statement that the guardian has exercised no control over any property of the minor or disabled person.

(5) Documentation. (A) Medical certificate. If the cause for the termination of the guardianship is the cessation of the disability, the petitioner shall file with the petition a certificate, signed by a physician who has examined the person within 21 days of the filing of the petition, attesting to the cessation of the disability.

(B) Marriage certificate. If the cause for the termination of the guardianship is emancipation because of the marriage of the minor person, the petitioner shall file with the petition a copy of the marriage certificate.

(6) Notice. The petitioner shall give notice by mailing by ordinary mail to those persons designated by the court a copy of the petition and the show cause order issued pursuant to Rule 10-104.

(7) Proceedings and order. After the time for filing a response has expired, the court may, and upon request shall, hold a hearing and shall issue an order granting or denying the termination of the guardianship and the release of the guardian.

Source. — This Rule is in part derived from former Rule V78 and is in part new.

Rule 10-210. Petition for assumption of jurisdiction — Emergency protective services.

(a) **Who may file.** Any interested person may file a petition requesting a court to authorize emergency protective services.

Cross references. — For the statute providing for emergency protective services, *see* Code, Estates and Trusts Article, § 13-709.

(b) **Venue.** The petition shall be filed either in the county where the person alleged to need emergency services resides or where the person is physically present.

(c) **Contents.** The petition shall be captioned, "In the Matter of ..." [stating the name of the person alleged to need emergency protective services]. It shall be signed and verified by the petitioner and shall contain at least the following information:

(1) The name and address of the petitioner and the petitioner's relationship to the person alleged to be in need of emergency protective services.

(2) The name, address, and age of the person alleged to be in need of emergency protective services, and the name, address, and age of the proposed temporary guardian.

(3) A brief description of the disability.

(4) The proposed protective services.

(5) The reason for seeking the assumption of jurisdiction by the court and for the relief sought.

(6) A statement of reasons why the petitioner believes that:

(A) the person alleged to be in need of emergency protective services is living in conditions presenting a substantial risk of death or immediate and serious physical harm to that person or others;

(B) the person alleged to be in need of emergency protective services lacks the capacity to make or communicate responsible decisions; and

(C) no person authorized by law or court order to give consent is available to consent to emergency services.

(7) An explanation of steps taken by the petitioner to obtain the consent of the person alleged to be in need of emergency protective services to the proposed services and the response of the person.

(8) If the person alleged to be in need of emergency protective services is represented by an attorney, the name and address of the attorney. If the person is not represented by an attorney, a request that one be appointed.

Source. — This Rule is derived from Code, Estates and Trusts Article, § 13-709 and former Rule R72 a and b.

Rule 10-211. Notice of petition for emergency protective services.

(a) **To whom given.** Notice that a petition for emergency protective services has been filed or will be filed and the time and place of the court hearing shall be given by the petitioner to: (1) the person alleged to be in need of emergency protective services; (2) the person with whom the person is residing; (3) the attorney for the person; (4) the director of the local department of social services; and (5) those other interested persons as the court may direct.

(b) **Manner of notice.** The notice shall be in writing, unless the nature of the emergency makes written notice impracticable.

(c) **Timing of notice.** The notice shall be given at least 24 hours before the hearing unless the court shortens the time upon a finding that (1) immediate and reasonably foreseeable physical harm to the person or others will result from a 24-hour delay, and (2) reasonable attempts have been made to give notice.

Source. — This Rule is in part derived from Code, Estates and Trusts Article, § 13-709 (e) and in part new.

Rule 10-212. Hearing.

(a) **Hearing required.** The necessity for emergency protective services shall be determined by the court after a hearing.

(b) **Conduct of hearing.** The person alleged to be in need of emergency protective services is entitled to be present at the hearing unless the person has knowingly and voluntarily waived the right to be present. Waiver may not be presumed from nonappearance but shall be determined on the basis of factual information supplied by the person's attorney or a representative appointed by the court. Upon motion by or on behalf of the person alleged to be in need of emergency protective services that, because of his or her disability, the person cannot attend a hearing at the courthouse, the court may hold the hearing at a place to which the person has reasonable access. The person has a right to counsel and to present evidence and cross-examine witnesses.

Source. — This Rule is derived from Code, Estates and Trusts Article, § 13-709 (f).

Rule 10-213. Order.

(a) **Generally.** The court may issue an order authorizing the provision of protective services on an emergency basis after a finding on the record that the allegations required by Rule 10-210 (c) (6) are established by clear and convincing evidence. An order shall either be in writing or, if dictated into the record, transcribed by the court reporter immediately and placed into the record.

(b) **Appointment of temporary guardian.** In its order the court shall appoint a temporary guardian who can give consent on behalf of the disabled person for the approved protective services until the expiration of the order.

(c) **Duration of order.** The order shall expire 144 hours after it is issued, unless extended pursuant to section (d) of this Rule.

(d) **Extension of order.** The court may further extend the emergency order and the appointment of the temporary guardian until appointment of a guardian of the person upon (1) a petition of the temporary guardian filed before the expiration of the emergency order, accompanied by a petition for the appointment of a guardian of the person, and (2) a showing that the situation described in Rule 10-210 (c) (6) will probably continue or recur if the emergency order is not further extended. The petition for appointment of a guardian shall be heard on an expedited basis not later than 60 days after it is filed.

(e) **Report of temporary guardian.** When protective services are rendered on the basis of an emergency order, the temporary guardian shall submit a report to the court describing the services and outcome and any forcible entry used to obtain custody of the person. The report shall become a part of the court record. The temporary guardian shall also send a copy of the report to

(1) the disabled person and the attorney for the disabled person, and

(2) the director of the local department of social services if the disabled person is under 65, or

(3) the director of the local office on aging if the disabled person is 65 or older, and

(4) any other person or entity as required by the court or by law. (Amended Dec. 4, 2007, effective Jan. 1, 2008.)

Cross references. — Code, Human Services Article, Title 10.

Source. — This Rule is derived from Code, Estates and Trusts Article, § 13-709.

Effect of amendments. — The December 4, 2007 Order, effective January 1, 2008, in (e) in the Cross reference note substituted "Human Services Article, Title 10" for "Article 70B".

CHAPTER 300. GUARDIAN OF PROPERTY.

Rule 10-301. Petition for appointment of a guardian of property.

(a) **Who may file.** Any interested person may file a petition requesting a court to appoint a guardian of the property of a minor or an alleged disabled person.

(b) **Venue.** (1) Resident. If the minor or alleged disabled person is a resident of Maryland, the petition shall be filed in the county where the minor or alleged disabled person resides, even if the person is temporarily absent.

(2) Nonresident. If the minor or disabled person does not reside in this State, the petition shall be filed in the county in which a petition for guardianship of the person may be filed, or in the county where any part of the property is located. For purposes of determining the situs of property, the situs of tangible personal property is its location; the situs of intangible personal property is the location of the instrument, if any, evidencing a debt, obligation, stock or chose in action, or the residence of the debtor if there is no instrument evidencing a debt, obligation, stock, or chose in action; and the situs of an interest in property held in trust is located where the trustee may be sued.

(c) **Contents.** The petition shall be captioned "In the Matter of …" [stating the name of the minor or alleged disabled person]. It shall be signed and verified by the petitioner and shall contain at least the following information:

(1) The petitioner's name, address, age, and telephone number;

(2) The petitioner's familial or other relationship to the alleged disabled person;

(3) Whether the person who is the subject of the petition is a minor or an alleged disabled person and, if an alleged disabled person, a brief description of the alleged disability;

(4) The reasons why the court should appoint a guardian of the property and, if the subject of the petition is an alleged disabled person, allegations demonstrating an inability of the alleged disabled person to manage the person's property and affairs effectively because of physical or mental disability, disease, habitual drunkenness, addiction to drugs, imprisonment, compulsory hospitalization, confinement, detention by a foreign power, or disappearance;

Cross references. — Code, Estates and Trusts Article, § 13-201 (b) and (c).

(5) An identification of any instrument nominating a guardian for the minor or alleged disabled person or constituting a durable power of attorney;

Cross references. — Code, Estates and Trusts Article, § 13-207 (a) (2) and (5).

(6) If a guardian or conservator has been appointed for the alleged disabled person in another proceeding, the name and address of the guardian or conservator and the court that appointed the guardian or conservator. If a guardianship or conservatorship proceeding was previously filed in any other court, the name and address of the court, the case number, if known, and whether the proceeding is still pending in that court.

(7) The name, age, sex, and address of the minor or alleged disabled person, the name and address of the persons with whom the minor or alleged disabled person resides, and if the minor or alleged disabled person resides with the petitioner, the name and address of another person on whom service can be made;

(8) To the extent known or reasonably ascertainable, the name, address, telephone number, and nature of interest of all interested persons and all others exercising any control over the property of the estate;

(9) If the minor or alleged disabled person is represented by an attorney, the name, address, and telephone number of the attorney.

(10) The nature, value, and location of the property of the minor or alleged disabled person;

(11) A brief description of all other property in which the minor or alleged disabled person has a concurrent interest with one or more individuals;

(12) A statement that the exhibits required by section (d) of this Rule are attached or, if not attached, the reason that they are absent; and

(13) A statement of the relief sought.

(d) **Required exhibits.** The petitioner shall attach to the petition as exhibits (1) a copy of any instrument nominating a guardian; (2) (A) the certificates required by Rule 10-202, or (B) if guardianship of the property of a disabled person who is a beneficiary of the United States Department of Veterans Affairs is being sought, in lieu of the requirements of Rule 10-202, a certificate of the Secretary of that Department or an authorized representative of the Secretary stating that the person has been rated as disabled by the Department in accordance with the laws and regulations governing the Department of Veterans Affairs; and (3) if the petition is for the appointment of a guardian for a minor who is a beneficiary of the Department of Veterans Affairs, a certificate of the Secretary of that Department or any authorized representative of the Secretary, in accordance with Code, Estates and Trusts Article, § 13-802. (Amended Oct. 5, 1999; Nov. 12, 2003, effective Jan. 1, 2004; Dec. 4, 2007, effective Jan. 1, 2008.)

Source. — This Rule is derived as follows:
Section (a) is derived from former Rule R71 a.
Section (b) is derived from former Rule R72 a and b.
Section (c) is in part derived from former Rule R73 a and is in part new.
Section (d) is new.

Effect of amendments. — The 1999 amendment inserted "or psychologist's" following "physician's" in (d).

The 2003 amendment in (d), inserted the (1) (A) designation, inserted (B) and made a related minor change.

The December 4, 2007 Order, effective January 1, 2008, in (d) (2) (A) substituted "the certificates" for "any physician's or psychologist's certificates"; in (d) (2) (B) substituted "requirements of" for "certificates required by" and "Secretary" for "Administrator" in two places.

Compatibility with federal law. — Regulations of the Health Insurance Portability and Accountability Act of 1996 (HIPAA) and the requirements of the state guardianship law are not necessarily incompatible; thus, depending on the facts of the particular case, a physician or psychologist may well be able to disclose protected health information to a petitioner and a court in connection with a guardianship proceeding. 89 Op. Att'y Gen. 81 (Apr. 14, 2004).

Applied in Standard Fire Ins. Co. v. Berrett, 395 Md. 439, 910 A.2d 1072 (2006).

Stated in Att'y Griev. Comm'n v. Blum, 373 Md. 275, 818 A.2d 219 (2003).

Rule 10-302. Service; notice.

(a) **Service on minor or alleged disabled person.** The petitioner shall serve a show cause order issued pursuant to Rule 10-104 on the minor or alleged disabled person and on the parent, guardian, or other person having care or custody of the minor or alleged disabled person or of the estate belonging to the minor or alleged disabled person. Service shall be in accordance with Rule 2-121 (a). If the minor or alleged disabled person resides with the petitioner, service shall be made upon the minor or alleged disabled person and on such other person as the court may direct. Service upon a minor under the age of ten years may be waived provided that the other service requirements of this section are met. The show cause order served on an alleged disabled person shall be accompanied by an "Advice of Rights" in the form set forth in Rule 10-303.

(b) **Notice to other persons.** (1) To attorney. Unless the court orders otherwise, the petitioner shall mail a copy of the petition and show cause order by ordinary mail to the attorney for the minor or alleged disabled person.

(2) To interested persons. Unless the court orders otherwise, the petitioner shall mail by ordinary mail and by certified mail to all other interested persons a copy of the petition and show cause order and a "Notice to Interested Persons."

(c) **Notice to Interested Persons.** The Notice to Interested Persons shall be in the following form:

In the Matter of

_____

(Name of minor or alleged disabled person)

In the Circuit Court for

_____

(County)

_____

(docket reference)

NOTICE TO INTERESTED PERSONS

A petition has been filed seeking appointment of a guardian of the property of _____, who is alleged to be a minor or alleged disabled person.

You are an "interested person", that is, someone who should receive notice of this proceeding because you are related to or otherwise concerned with the welfare of this person.

If the court appoints a guardian of the property for _____, that person will lose the right to manage his or her property.

Please examine the attached papers carefully. If you object to the appointment of a guardian, please file a response in accordance with the attached show cause order. (Be sure to include the case number). If you wish otherwise to participate in this proceeding, notify the court and be prepared to attend any hearing.

Each certificate filed pursuant to Rule 10-202 that is attached to the petition will be admissible as substantive evidence without the presence or testimony of the certifying health care professional unless you file a request that the health care professional appear to testify. The request must be filed at least 10 days before the trial date, unless the trial date is less than 10 days from the date your response is due. If the trial date is less than 10 days from the date your response is due, the request may be filed at any time before trial.

If you believe you need further legal advice about this matter, you should consult your attorney. (Amended Oct. 5, 1999; Dec. 4, 2007, effective Jan. 1, 2008.)

Source. — This Rule is in part derived from former Rule R74 and Code, Estates and Trusts Article, § 1-103 (b) and is in part new.

Effect of amendments. — The 1999 amendment, in the sixth paragraph of (c), in the first sentence, inserted "or psychologist's" following "physician's," and inserted "or psychologist" following "physician" twice.

The December 4, 2007 Order, effective January 1, 2008, in (c) in the form rewrote the fifth paragraph.

Rule 10-303. Advice of rights.

The Advice of Rights required to be served on an alleged disabled person shall be in the following form:

TO _____ (Name):

A petition has been filed seeking appointment of a guardian of your property.

IF THE COURT APPOINTS A GUARDIAN OF YOUR PROPERTY, YOU WILL LOSE CERTAIN VALUABLE RIGHTS, INCLUDING YOUR RIGHT TO MANAGE YOUR PROPERTY AND TO DECIDE WHETHER AND HOW TO SPEND YOUR MONEY.

YOU HAVE CERTAIN RIGHTS IN THIS CASE:

1. [ ] The petition alleges that _____

(Name of Attorney)

is your attorney. If that is not correct, notify the clerk immediately.

   [ ] The court has appointed _____

(Name of Attorney)

as your attorney, but you may hire another attorney if you wish.

2. You will have a trial if you or your attorney object to the appointment of a guardian of your property.

3. You have the right to be present at the trial.

4. You have the right to present evidence on your own behalf and to cross-examine witnesses against you.

5. You have the right to suggest restrictions or limitations of the guardian's power if a guardian is appointed.

6. The trial may be closed to the public if you so request.

The above statements cannot cover all possible situations. Please read the attached papers carefully. You should consult with your attorney to determine what is in your best interest. You or your attorney should file a response on or before the deadline stated in the attached order.

Source. — This Rule is new.

Rule 10-304. Hearing.

(a) **No response to show cause order.** If no response to the show cause order is filed and the court is satisfied that the petitioner has complied with the provisions of Rule 10-302, the court may rule on the petition summarily.

(b) **Response to show cause order; place of trial.** If a response to the show cause order objects to the relief requested, the court shall set the matter for trial, and shall give notice of the time and place of trial to all persons who have responded. Upon motion by the alleged disabled person asserting that, because of his or her disability, the alleged disabled person cannot attend a trial at the courthouse, the court may hold the trial at a place to which the alleged disabled person has reasonable access.

Cross references. — Code, Estates and Trusts Article, § 13-211.

(c) **Request for attendance of health care professional.** When the petition is for guardianship of the property of a disabled person, each certificate filed pursuant to Rule 10-202 is admissible as substantive evidence without the presence or testimony of the health care professional unless, not later than 10 days before trial, an interested person who is not an individual under a disability, or the attorney for the disabled person, files a request that the health care professional appear to testify. If the trial date is less than 10 days from the date the response is due, a request that the health care professional appear may be filed at any time before trial. (Amended Oct. 5, 1999; Dec. 4, 2007, effective Jan. 1, 2008.)

Source. — This Rule is in part derived from former Rule R77 and is in part new.

Effect of amendments. — The 1999 amendment, in (c), inserted "or psychologist" following "physician" in the heading and throughout, and inserted "or psychologist's" following "physician's" in the first sentence.

The December 4, 2007 Order, effective January 1, 2008, in (c) substituted "health care professional" for "physician or psychologist" or variants throughout, and in the first sentence substituted "each certificate filed pursuant to" for "a physician's or psychologist's certificate that complies with" and added "to testify" at the end.

There is a rational basis for different treatment of the two classes of individuals who are subject to guardianship pro-

ceedings and individuals found not guilty by reason of insanity in that a guardianship proceeding, which strips the individual of voting and property rights, may be based on various disabling conditions, while the insanity acquittee has had the fact of his disable- ment at the time of the offense already determined by a jury when he comes before the court for a determination on the question of confinement. Dorsey v. Solomon, 435 F. Supp. 725 (D. Md. 1977), aff'd in part and rev'd in part, 604 F.2d 271 (4th Cir. 1979).

Rule 10-305. Administration of guardianship of the property.

A guardianship of the property shall be administered pursuant to Rules 10-702 through 10-712.

Source. — This Rule is new.

CHAPTER 400. STANDBY GUARDIAN.

Rule 10-401. Definitions.

(a) **Statutory definitions.** The definitions stated in Code, Estates and Trusts Article, § 13-901 are applicable to this Chapter.

(b) **Additional definition.** In this Chapter, "interested person" means the minor, the guardian of the minor, a person having parental rights over the minor pursuant to Code, Estates and Trusts Article, §§ 1-205 through 1-208, and includes any other person designated by the court. (Added Feb. 10, 1998, effective July 1, 1998.)

Source. — This Rule is new.

Rule 10-402. Petition by a parent for judicial appointment of a standby guardian.

(a) **Filing of petition.** Except for a petition filed by a standby guardian in accordance with Rule 10-403, a petition for the judicial appointment of a standby guardian of the person or property of a minor shall be filed by a parent of the minor. The petition shall contain the consent of each person having parental rights over the minor, unless a statement pursuant to subsection (c) (14) of this Rule is included in the petition.

(b) **Venue.** The petition shall be filed in the county where the minor resides or is physically present.

(c) **Contents.** The petition shall be captioned "In the Matter of ..." [stating the name of the minor]. It shall be signed and verified by the petitioner and shall include the following information:

(1) The petitioner's name, address, age, and telephone number;

(2) The petitioner's familial relationship to the minor;

(3) The name, address, and date of birth of the minor;

(4) Whether the minor has any siblings and, if so, their names and ages;

(5) The proposed standby guardian's name, address, age, and telephone number;

(6) The proposed standby guardian's relationship to the minor;

(7) A statement explaining why the appointment of the proposed standby guardian is in the best interests of the minor;

(8) Whether and under what circumstances the standby guardianship is to be of the minor's person, property, or both;

(9) If the standby guardian is to be a guardian of the property of the minor, the nature, value, and location of the property;

(10) A description of the duties and powers of the standby guardian, including whether the standby guardian is to have the authority to apply for, receive, and use public benefits and child support payable on behalf of the minor;

Cross references. — For a listing of the powers of a guardian of the person, see Code, Estates and Trusts Article, § 13-708 and for a guardian of the property, see Code, Estates and Trusts Article, § 15-102.

(11) Whether the authority of the standby guardian is to become effective on the petitioner's incapacity, death, or on the first of those circumstances to occur;

Cross references. — Code, Estates and Trust Article, § 13-906.

(12) A statement that there is a significant risk that the petitioner will become incapacitated or die within two years of the filing of the petition and the basis for the statement;

Cross references. — Code, Estates and Trusts Article, § 13-903 (a).

(13) If the petitioner is medically unable to appear in court for a hearing pursuant to Rule 10-404, a statement explaining why;

(14) If a person having parental rights does not join in the petition, (A) a statement that the identity or whereabouts of the person are unknown and a description of the reasonable efforts made in good faith to identify and locate the person or (B) a statement that the person is not willing to join in the petition or has not responded to a request to join in the petition and a description of the reasonable efforts made in good faith to inform the person about the petition; and

(15) If the petitioner believes that notice to the minor would be unnecessary or would not be in the best interests of the minor, a statement explaining why.

(d) **Notice.** Unless the court orders otherwise, the petitioner shall send by ordinary mail and by certified mail to all interested persons whose whereabouts are known a copy of the petition and a "Notice to Interested Persons" pursuant to section (e) of this Rule. Service upon a minor under the age of ten years may be waived provided that the other service requirements of this section are met. If the court is satisfied that the petitioner, after reasonable efforts made in good faith, has been unable to ascertain the whereabouts of a person having parental rights, the court may order, as to that individual, that the "Notice to Interested Persons Whose Whereabouts are Unknown," which is set out in section (f) of this Rule, be published one time in the county of that individual's last known residence or be posted at that county's courthouse door or on a bulletin board within its immediate vicinity.

(e) **Notice to Interested Persons.** The Notice to Interested Persons shall be in the following form:

In the Matter of In the Circuit Court for

_____ _____
(Name of minor) (County)

_____ _____
(Date of notice) (docket reference)

NOTICE TO INTERESTED PERSONS

A petition has been filed seeking the appointment of a standby guardian of the [person] [property] [person and property] of _____ , a minor.

You are receiving this because you are related to or otherwise concerned with the welfare of the minor.

Please examine the attached papers carefully. If you object to the appointment of a standby guardian, please file a response with the court at

_____
(address of courthouse)

no later than 30 days after the date of issue of this Notice. (Be sure to include the case number.) **If a response is not received by the court, the court may rule on the petition without a hearing. If you wish to participate in this proceeding in any way, notify the court and be prepared to attend any hearing.**

CERTIFICATE OF SERVICE

I certify that a copy of the petition and the "Notice to Interested Persons" was mailed, by ordinary mail, postage prepaid, and by certified mail, postage prepaid and return receipt requested, this _____ day of _____, to _____

_____
at _____ .

_____
Petitioner

_____
Name (printed)

_____
Address

_____
Telephone Number

(f) **Notice to Interested Persons Whose Whereabouts are Unknown.** The Notice to Interested Persons Whose Whereabouts are Unknown shall be in the following form:

In the Matter of

_____

(Name of minor)

_____

(Date of notice)

In the Circuit Court for

_____

(County)

_____

(docket reference)

NOTICE TO INTERESTED PERSONS WHOSE WHEREABOUTS ARE UNKNOWN

A petition has been filed seeking the appointment of a standby guardian of the [person] [property] [person and property] of _____, who is alleged to be a minor.

If you are related to or otherwise concerned with the welfare of the minor, you may obtain further information from the court at _____

_____.

(address of courthouse)

Any response must be received by the court no later than 30 days after the date of issue of this Notice. (Added Feb. 10, 1998, effective July 1, 1998.)

Source. — This Rule is new.

Rule 10-403. Petition by standby guardian for judicial appointment after parental designation.

(a) **Filing of petition.** If a parent designates a standby guardian by a written designation pursuant to Code, Estates and Trusts Article, § 13-904 and the standby guardian wishes to retain authority for a period of more than 180 days, the standby guardian shall file a petition for judicial appointment within 180 days after the effective date of the standby guardianship.

(b) **Venue.** The petition shall be filed in the county where the minor resides or is physically present.

(c) **Contents.** The petition shall be captioned "In the Matter of ..." [stating the name of the minor]. It shall be signed and verified by the petitioner and shall contain the following information:

(1) The petitioner's name, address, age, telephone number, and relationship to the minor;

(2) The name, address, and date of birth of the minor;

(3) Whether the minor has any siblings and, if so, their names and ages;

(4) A statement explaining why the appointment of the proposed standby guardian is in the best interests of the minor.

(5) Whether and under what circumstances the standby guardianship is to be of the minor's person, property, or of both;

(6) If the standby guardian is to be a guardian of the property of the minor, the nature, value, and location of the property;

(7) A description of the duties and powers of the standby guardian, including whether the standby guardian is to have the authority to apply for, receive, and use public benefits and child support payable on behalf of the minor; and

(8) If the petition is filed by a person designated by a parent as alternate standby guardian pursuant to Code, Estates and Trusts Article, § 13-904 (b) (2), a statement that the person designated as standby guardian is unwilling or unable to act as standby guardian and the basis for the statement.

(d) **Documentation.** The petitioner shall file with the petition:

(1) The written parental designation of the standby guardian signed, or consented to, by each person having parental rights over the child, if available, and, if not, the documentation required by Code, Estates and Trusts Article, § 13-904 (f) (4);

(2) A copy of a physician's determination of incapacity or debilitation of the parent pursuant to Code, Estates and Trusts Article, § 13-906; and

(3) If a determination of debilitation is filed pursuant to subsection (d) (2) of this Rule, a copy of the parental consent to the beginning of the standby guardianship pursuant to Code, Estates, and Trusts Article, § 13-904 (f).

(e) **Notice.** Unless the court orders otherwise, the petitioner shall send by ordinary mail and by certified mail to all interested persons a copy of the petition and a "Notice to Interested Persons" pursuant to section (f) of this Rule. Service upon a minor under the age of ten years may be waived provided that the other service requirements of this section are met. If the court is satisfied that the petitioner, after reasonable efforts made in good faith, has been unable to ascertain the whereabouts of a person having parental rights, the court may order, as to that individual, that the "Notice to Interested Persons Whose Whereabouts are Unknown," which is set out in section (g) of this Rule, be published one time in the county of that individual's last known residence or be posted at that county's courthouse door or on a bulletin board within its immediate vicinity.

(f) **Notice to Interested Persons.** The Notice to Interested Persons shall be in the following form:

In the Matter of   In the Circuit Court for

_____   _____
(Name of minor)   (County)

_____   _____
(Date of notice)   (docket reference)

NOTICE TO INTERESTED PERSONS

A petition has been filed seeking appointment of a standby guardian of the [person]   [property]   [person   and   property]   of
_____, a minor.

You are receiving this notice of this proceeding because you are related to or otherwise concerned with the welfare of the minor.

Please examine the attached papers carefully. If you object to the appointment of a standby guardian, please file a response with the court at

_____
(address of courthouse)

no later than 30 days after the date of issue of this Notice. (Be sure to include the case number.) **If a response is not received by the court, the court**

may rule on the petition without a hearing. If you wish to participate in this proceeding in any way, notify the court and be prepared to attend any hearing.

CERTIFICATE OF SERVICE

I certify that a copy of the petition and the "Notice to Interested Persons" was mailed, by ordinary mail, postage prepaid, and by certified mail, postage prepaid and return receipt requested, this _____ day of _____, to _____

at _____

_____.

_____
Petitioner

_____
Name (printed)

_____

_____
Address

_____
Telephone Number

(g) **Notice to Interested Persons Whose Whereabouts are Unknown.** The Notice to Interested Persons Whose Whereabouts are Unknown shall be in the following form:

In the Matter of   In the Circuit Court for

_____   _____
(Name of minor)   (County)

_____   _____
(Date of notice)   (docket reference)

NOTICE TO INTERESTED PERSONS WHOSE WHEREABOUTS ARE UNKNOWN

A petition has been filed seeking the appointment of a standby guardian of the   [person]   [property]   [person   and   property]   of _____, who is alleged to be a minor.

If you are related to or otherwise concerned with the welfare of the minor, you may obtain further information from the court at _____

_____

_____.

(address of courthouse)

Any response must be received by the court no later than 30 days after the date of issue of this Notice.

Cross references. — Code, Estates and Trusts Article, § 13-904(e) and (f).

(Added Feb. 10, 1998, effective July 1, 1998.)

Source. — This Rule is new.

Rule 10-404. Hearing.

(a) **No response to notice.** If no response to the notice is filed and the court is satisfied that the petitioner has complied with the provisions of Rules 10-402 or 10-403, the court may rule on the petition without a hearing.

(b) **Response to notice.** If a response is filed to the notice objecting to the appointment of the standby guardian, the court shall hold a hearing and shall give notice of the time and place of the hearing to all interested persons. Unless excused for good cause shown, the petitioner, the proposed standby guardian, and the minor named in the petition shall be present at the hearing. (Added Feb. 10, 1998, effective July 1, 1998.)

Source. — This Rule is new.

Rule 10-405. Order.

(a) **Judicial appointment of standby guardian.** After the filing of a petition for judicial appointment of a standby guardian pursuant to Code, Estates and Trusts Article, § 13-903 (a), the court shall enter an order appointing the person as a standby guardian if the court finds that the requirements of these Rules and Code, Estates and Trusts Article, § 13-903 (d) have been met.

(b) **Judicial appointment of standby guardian after parental designation.** After the filing of a petition for judicial appointment of a standby guardian who was previously designated as standby guardian or alternate standby guardian by a parent pursuant to Code, Estates and Trusts Article, § 13-904 (a), the court shall enter an order appointing the person as a standby guardian if the court finds that the requirements of these Rules and Code, Estates and Trusts Article, § 13-904 (g) have been met.

(c) **Order appointing a standby guardian.** (1) An order appointing a standby guardian shall state whether the standby guardianship is of the minor's person, property, or both, whether the guardian shall have the authority to apply for, receive, and use public benefits and child support payable on behalf of the minor, and any other duties and powers of the standby guardian; and

(2) When the order is entered pursuant to section (a) of this Rule, the order shall also

(A) Specify whether the authority of the standby guardian is effective on the receipt of a determination of the petitioner's incapacity pursuant to Code, Estates and Trusts Article, § 13-906, on the receipt of the certificate of the petitioner's death, or on whichever occurs first; and

(B) Provide that the authority of the standby guardian may become effective earlier on written consent of the petitioner in accordance with Code, Estates and Trusts Article, § 13-903 (e) (3).

(d) **Duty to file documentation.** A copy of the appropriate document referred to in subsection (c) (2) of this Rule shall be filed by the standby guardian with the court within 90 days after the standby guardian receives the document.

Cross references. — See Code, Estates and Trusts Article, § 13-906 concerning a written determination of incapacity.

(e) **Revocation of standby guardian's authority.** The court may revoke the standby guardian's authority for failure to file any of the required documentation. (Added Feb. 10, 1998, effective July 1, 1998.)

Source. — This Rule is new.

Rule 10-406. Accounting.

(a) **Records.** A court-appointed standby guardian of the property shall keep records of the fiduciary estate and, upon request of any interested person or of the court that has assumed jurisdiction over the standby guardianship of the property, shall make the records available for inspection.

(b) **Annual fiduciary accounts.** When the court has assumed jurisdiction over a standby guardianship of the property, the standby guardian shall file each year an account in substantially the form set forth in rule 10-708. The provisions of Rule 10-706 shall apply to the account, except that the end of the accounting year shall be the anniversary of the date upon which the court assumed jurisdiction over the standby guardianship. (Added Feb. 10, 1998, effective July 1, 1998.)

Source. — This Rule is new.

Rule 10-407. Removal for cause or other sanctions.

(a) **On court's initiative.** The court that has assumed jurisdiction over a standby guardianship may order the standby guardian to show cause why the guardian should not be removed or be subject to other sanctions for failure to perform the duties of that office.

(b) **On petition of interested persons.** An interested person may file a petition to remove a standby guardian. The petition shall be filed in the court that appointed the standby guardian or, if there is a written parental designation pursuant to Code, Estates and Trusts Article, § 13-904 (a) and the court has not yet assumed jurisdiction over the standby guardianship, in the county where the minor resides or is physically present. The petition shall state the reasons why the guardian should be removed.

(c) **Action by court.** The provisions of Rule 10-208 (c) and (e) shall apply to proceedings for removal of a standby guardian. If the court finds grounds for removal, it may remove the standby guardian and may appoint an alternate standby guardian pursuant to Code, Estates and Trusts Article, § 13-904 (b) (2). (Added Feb. 10, 1998, effective July 1, 1998.)

Source. — This Rule is new.

Rule 10-408. Revocation, renunciation, and resignation.

(a) **Revocation by parent.** A parent may file a petition to revoke a standby guardianship in the court that appointed the standby guardian. The petition shall state the reasons for the revocation and shall be served on the standby guardian and all interested persons. If an objection to the revocation is filed, the court shall hold a hearing prior to ruling on the petition.

(b) **Renunciation by standby guardian.** A person who is judicially appointed as a standby guardian may renounce the appointment at any time before the effective date of the person's authority by executing a written renunciation, filing the renunciation with the court that issued the order, and promptly notifying the parent in writing of the renunciation.

(c) **Resignation by standby guardian.** A person who has been judicially appointed as a standby guardian and whose authority has become effective may file a petition to resign in the court that appointed the standby guardian. The petition shall state the reasons for the resignation and shall be served on all interested persons. If an objection to the resignation is filed, the court shall hold a hearing prior to ruling on the petition. (Added Feb. 10, 1998, effective July 1, 1998.)

Source. — This Rule is new.

Rule 10-409. Bond.

The furnishing of a bond by a standby guardian shall be governed by the provisions of Code, Estates and Trusts Article, § 13-208. (Added Feb. 10, 1998, effective July 1, 1998.)

Source. — This Rule is new.

CHAPTER 500. FIDUCIARY ESTATES OTHER THAN GUARDIANSHIPS.

Rule 10-501. Petition for assumption of jurisdiction over a fiduciary estate other than a guardianship.

(a) **Who may file.** A fiduciary or other interested person may file a petition requesting a court to assume jurisdiction over a fiduciary estate other than a guardianship of the property of a minor or disabled person.

(b) **Venue.** The petition shall be filed in the county in which all or any part of the property of the estate is located or where the fiduciary, if any, resides, is regularly employed, or maintains a place of business.

(c) **Contents.** The petition shall be captioned "In the Matter of ..." [stating the name of the fiduciary estate]. It shall be signed and verified by the petitioner, and shall contain at least the following information:

(1) The petitioner's name, address, age, and telephone number.

(2) The reason for seeking the assumption of jurisdiction by the court and a statement of the relief sought, specifying the extent to which court jurisdiction over the fiduciary estate is desired.

(3) An identification of any instrument creating the estate, with a copy attached to the petition, if possible, and, if not, an explanation of its absence.

(4) The name, address, telephone number, and nature of interest of all interested persons and all others exercising control of any of the fiduciary estate, to the extent known or reasonably ascertainable.

(5) The nature of the interest of the petitioner.

(6) The nature, value, and location of the property comprising the fiduciary estate.

Source. — This Rule is derived from former Rule V71 a, b 1, and c.

Payment of costs and counsel fees in proceeding for construction of will. — The costs of the proceeding for construction of the will, including the fee of the trustee's counsel, may be paid from the assets of the trust estate, but not the fees of counsel for other parties, unless they were appointed by the court to represent infants or persons under some disability. Sollers v. Mercantile-Safe Deposit & Trust Co., 262 Md. 606, 278 A.2d 581 (1971); Davis v. AG of Md., 187 Md. App. 110, 975 A.2d 362 (2009).

Cited in Davis v. AG of Md., 187 Md. App. 110, 975 A.2d 362 (2009).

Rule 10-502. Notice.

The petitioner shall serve all interested persons and all others exercising control of any or all of the fiduciary estate by mailing to them by ordinary mail and by certified mail, unless the court directs otherwise, a copy of the petition and a show cause order issued pursuant to Rule 10-104.

Source. — This Rule is in part derived from former Rule V71 d and Code, Estates and Trusts Article, § 1-103 (b), and is in part new.

Rule 10-503. Hearing.

(a) **No response to show cause order.** If no response to the show cause order is filed, and the court is satisfied that the petitioner has complied with the provisions of Rule 10-502, the court may rule on the petition summarily.

(b) **Response to show cause order.** If a response to the show cause order objects to the relief requested, the court shall hold a hearing as in any contested matter, and shall give notice of the time and place of the hearing to all interested persons and to all others exercising control over any or all of the fiduciary estate.

Source. — This Rule is derived from former Rule R77 b 2.

There is a rational basis for different treatment of the two classes of individuals who are subject to guardianship proceedings and individuals found not guilty by reason of insanity in that a guardianship proceeding, which strips the individual of voting and property rights, may be based on various disabling conditions, while the insanity acquittee has had the fact of his disablement at the time of the offense already determined by a jury when he comes before the court for a determination on the question of confinement. Dorsey v. Solomon, 435 F. Supp. 725 (D. Md. 1977), aff'd in part and rev'd in part, 604 F.2d 271 (4th Cir. 1979).

Rule 10-504. Administration of fiduciary estates other than guardianships of the property.

A fiduciary estate other than a guardianship of property shall be administered pursuant to Rules 10-702 through 10-712.

Source. — This Rule is new.

Rule 10-505. Termination of jurisdiction.

(a) **Who may file.** Upon petition filed by any interested person, a court which has assumed jurisdiction over the administration of a fiduciary estate may relinquish jurisdiction.

(b) **Notice.** Unless the court orders otherwise, the petitioner shall serve all interested persons and all others exercising control over any of the fiduciary estate by mailing to them, by ordinary mail, a copy of the petition and a show cause order issued pursuant to Rule 10-104.

(c) **Proceedings.** (1) No response to show cause order. If no response to the show cause order is filed and the court is satisfied that the petitioner has complied with the provisions of section (b) of this Rule, the court may rule on the petition summarily.

(2) Response to show cause order. If a response to the show cause order objects to the relief requested, the court shall hold a hearing and shall give notice of the time and place of the hearing to all persons who have responded.

Source. — This Rule is derived from former Rule V72.

Vacating trust termination order for lack of proper notice. — Circuit court did not err or abuse its discretion in vacating a trust termination order and reassuming supervisory jurisdiction over a trust pursuant to § 6-408 of the Courts Article and Rule 2-535 when proper notice of termination was not given under (b) of this Rule. Davis v. AG of Md., 187 Md. App. 110, 975 A.2d 362 (2009).

CHAPTER 600. ABSENT OR UNKNOWN PERSONS.

Rule 10-601. Petition for assumption of jurisdiction — Person whose identity or whereabouts is unknown.

(a) **Who may file.** A fiduciary or interested person may file a petition requesting a court to assume jurisdiction over the fiduciary estate for the purpose of determining its distribution if the petitioner believes that there may be a person whose identity or present whereabouts is unknown who is entitled to share in the estate.

(b) **Venue.** The petition shall be filed in the court which has assumed jurisdiction over the fiduciary estate, or if jurisdiction has not been assumed, then in the county where any part of the property to be distributed is located or where the fiduciary, if any, resides, is regularly employed, or maintains a place of business.

(c) **Contents of petition.** In addition to any other material allegations, the petition shall contain at least the following information:

(1) The petitioner's name, address, and telephone number.

(2) The nature, value, and location of any property comprising the fiduciary estate.

(3) The reasons for seeking the assumption of jurisdiction by the court and the proposed distribution.

(4) An identification of any instrument creating the fiduciary estate, with a copy attached to the petition, if possible, and, if not, an explanation of its absence.

(5) The reason it is believed that there may be a person whose identity or whereabouts is unknown.

(6) Facts showing that the petitioner has searched diligently for the person whose identity or whereabouts is unknown.

Committee note. — For substantive law on absent persons, *see* Uniform Absent Persons Act, Code, Courts Article, §§ 3-101 to 3-110. For substantive law on abandoned property, *see* Uniform Disposition of Abandoned Property Act, Code, Commercial Law Article, §§ 17-301 to 17-324.

Source. — This Rule is in part derived from former Rules V71, V79, and R77 and is in part new.

Rule 10-602. Notice.

(a) **Known persons.** Unless the court orders otherwise, the petitioner shall give notice to those persons whose identity and interest in the property are known and to any others designated by the court by mailing to them by ordinary mail and by certified mail a copy of the petition and a show cause order issued pursuant to Rule 10-104.

(b) **Unknown persons.** If the court is satisfied that reasonable efforts have been made to ascertain the identity or whereabouts of a person, the court shall order that notice to those persons whose identity or whereabouts are unknown shall be made in the manner provided by Rule 2-122.

Source. — This Rule is derived from former Rule V79 b and c and from Code, Estates and Trusts Article, § 1-103 (b).

Rule 10-603. Hearing.

(a) **No response to show cause order.** If no response to the show cause order is filed, and if the court is satisfied that the petitioner has complied with the provisions of Rule 10-602, the court may rule on the petition summarily.

(b) **Response to show cause order.** If a response to the show cause order objects to the relief requested, the court shall set the matter for hearing and shall give notice of the time and place of the hearing to all persons who have responded.

Source. — This Rule is derived from former Rule R77 b 2.

There is a rational basis for different treatment of the two classes of individuals who are subject to guardianship proceedings and individuals found not guilty by reason of insanity in that a guardianship proceeding, which strips the individual of voting and property rights, may be based on various disabling conditions, while the insanity acquittee has had the fact of his disablement at the time of the offense already determined by a jury when he comes before the court for a determination on the question of confinement. Dorsey v. Solomon, 435 F. Supp. 725 (D. Md. 1977), aff'd in part and rev'd in part, 604 F.2d 271 (4th Cir. 1979).

Rule 10-604. Attorney for person whose identity or whereabouts is unknown.

The court may appoint an attorney to protect the interest of a person whose identity or whereabouts is unknown. The fee of the attorney shall be fixed by the court and paid out of the property or portion thereof to be distributed pursuant to court order.

Source. — This Rule is derived from former Rule V79 d.

Rule 10-605. Distribution.

(a) **Generally.** After the expiration of the time fixed in the order of publication for pleading by a person whose identity or whereabouts is unknown, the court may enter an appropriate order distributing the property.

(b) **To abandoned property fund.** If the court finds that all reasonable efforts have been made to locate a person whose identity or whereabouts is unknown and that person has not appeared, the court shall order the property distributable to that person, after allowing costs, to be distributed to the abandoned property fund pursuant to Code, Commercial Law Article, § 17-317.

(c) **Retention by fiduciary or distribution to trustee.** (1) Order. The court may order the fiduciary to retain or transfer to a trustee appointed by the court or to deposit with the clerk the share to which the person whose identity or whereabouts is unknown is entitled, and order any income to be accumulated for the time the court directs.

(2) Bond. The court may order a trustee to whom the property is transferred to furnish a bond to the State in an amount and for a time period prescribed by the court.

Source. — This Rule is derived from former Rule V79 e.

CHAPTER 700. FIDUCIARY ESTATES INCLUDING GUARDIANSHIPS OF THE PROPERTY.

Rule 10-701. Scope.

The rules in this Chapter apply to proceedings under the rules in Chapters 300, 500, and 600 of this Title. They do not apply to proceedings under the rules in Chapters 200 and 400 of this Title, except as otherwise provided in those rules. (Amended Feb. 10, 1998, effective July 1, 1998.)

Source. — This Rule is new.

Effect of amendments. — The 1998 amendment substituted "Chapters 200 and 400 of this Title, except as otherwise provided in those rules" for "Chapter 200 of this Title" in the second sentence.

Rule 10-702. Bond — Fiduciary estate.

(a) **When required or excused.** (1) Required by instrument. If the instrument nominating the fiduciary or creating the estate requires the fiduciary to give bond, the fiduciary, whether corporate or non-corporate, shall file a bond before commencing the performance of any fiduciary duties unless excused pursuant to subsection (5) of this section.

(2) Excused by instrument. If the instrument nominating the fiduciary or creating the estate excuses a noncorporate fiduciary from furnishing bond, the court shall not require a bond unless the court finds that, notwithstanding the provisions of the instrument, exceptional circumstances make a bond necessary for the protection of interested persons.

(3) Corporate fiduciary. Except as provided in subsection (1) of this section, a corporate fiduciary shall not be required to furnish a bond.

(4) Noncorporate fiduciary — Bond not mentioned in instrument — Court appointment. The court may require a non-corporate fiduciary, appointed by the court or nominated under an instrument that is silent as to bond, to file a bond if the court finds that exceptional circumstances make a bond necessary for the protection of interested persons.

(5) Fiduciary estate not exceeding $10,000. Unless the court finds that exceptional circumstances make a bond necessary for the protection of interested persons, the court shall not require a fiduciary to furnish or continue in effect a bond if the assets of the estate (A) do not exceed $10,000 in value, (B) cannot be transferred by the fiduciary without approval of the court, and (C) consist only of cash deposited in a restricted account pursuant to Rule 10-705, securities, or real property.

(b) **Petition to require or change amount of bond.** (1) Who may file. Subject to the provisions of section (a), any interested person may file a petition to require the fiduciary to file a bond if a bond has not previously been filed or to reduce any bond that has been filed.

(2) Where filed. If a court has assumed jurisdiction over the estate, the petition shall be filed in that court. Otherwise, it shall be filed in the county in which the fiduciary resides, is regularly employed, or maintains a place of business.

(3) Notice. Unless the court orders otherwise, the fiduciary shall mail by ordinary mail to all interested persons and all others exercising control of any of the fiduciary estate a copy of the petition and a show cause order issued pursuant to Rule 10-104.

(c) **Where bond to be filed.** (1) Required by court. If a court requires a bond, the bond shall be filed in that court, unless the court directs otherwise.

(2) Required by instrument. If a bond is required by the instrument that creates the fiduciary estate or nominates a fiduciary, the bond shall be filed in the following place:

(A) If the instrument specifies the county where the bond is to be filed, the bond shall be filed in the circuit court specified in the instrument;

(B) If the instrument does not specify a place or provide for a place to be selected, the bond shall be filed in the circuit court for the county where the instrument is recorded. If the instrument is not recorded, the bond shall be filed in the circuit court for the county where the estate will be administered.

(d) **Amount of bond — Other security.** (1) Generally. The amount of a fiduciary bond shall not be greater than the aggregate value of the property of the estate in the fiduciary's control, less the value of (A) securities, (B) money deposited in a financial institution as defined in Code, Estates and Trusts Article, § 13-301 (h) under arrangements requiring an order of court for their removal, and (C) real property which the fiduciary, by express limitation of power, lacks power to sell or convey without court authorization. In lieu of sureties on a bond, the court may accept other security for the performance of the bond, including a pledge of securities or a mortgage of real property. The court may at any time, subject to the maximum amount provided by this section, require the amount of the bond, or the type or value of security, to be changed. The approval of a new bond shall not discharge any liability that may have accrued under the existing bond before such approval.

(2) Specified by instrument. If the instrument creating the estate requires that the fiduciary file a bond in a specific amount, the bond shall be in the lesser of that amount or the maximum amount provided in subsection (1).

(e) **Terms of bond.** A fiduciary bond shall be to the State of Maryland and shall be conditioned upon the faithful discharge of the duties of the fiduciary as follows:

The condition of the above obligation is such, that if _____ shall well and truly perform the office of fiduciary as designated by the _____ and shall discharge the duties required by law as fiduciary without any injury or damage to any person interested in the faithful performance of the office, then the above obligation shall be void; it shall otherwise remain in full force and effect.

(f) **Payment of bond premium from income.** A fiduciary who is required to file a bond shall be entitled to pay and be allowed the cost of the premium out of the income of the estate, unless the court otherwise directs.

Cross references. — Code, Estates and Trusts Article, § 13-208.

Source. — This Rule is derived from former Rule V73, except for subsection (b) (3) which is in part derived from former Rule V71 d and is in part new.

Payment of costs and counsel fees in proceeding for construction of will. — The costs of the proceeding for construction of the will, including the fee of the trustee's counsel, may be paid from the assets of the trust estate, but not the fees of counsel for other parties, unless they were appointed by the court to represent infants or persons under some disability. Sollers v. Mercantile-Safe Deposit & Trust Co., 262 Md. 606, 278 A.2d 581 (1971).

Applied in Seaboard Sur. Co. v. Boney, 135 Md. App. 99, 761 A.2d 985 (2000), cert denied, 363 Md. 206, 768 A.2d 54 (2001).

Rule 10-703. Compromise of claim or dispute.

(a) **Petition.** A fiduciary may petition a court to authorize or ratify a compromise or settlement of any claim or matter relating to a fiduciary estate.

(b) **Venue.** The petition shall be filed in the court that has already assumed jurisdiction over the administration of the fiduciary estate or, if jurisdiction has not been assumed (A) if the petitioner is a personal representative, in the court of the county where letters of administration were issued or (B) if the petitioner is not a personal representative, by petition in the court in the county in which the fiduciary resides, is regularly employed, or maintains a place of business.

(c) **Notice.** The petitioner shall mail by ordinary mail to those interested persons designated by the court a copy of the petition and a show cause order issued pursuant to Rule 10-104.

(d) **Ratification.** The court may authorize or ratify the proposed compromise or settlement, imposing any appropriate terms and conditions, if satisfied that the action is in the best interest of the estate.

Cross references. — For the authority of the Orphans' court to authorize the compromise of any claim by a personal representative or guardian against or in favor of the estate, *see* Code, Estates and Trusts Article, § 2-102; *but see* Code, Estates and Trusts Article, § 7-401 (h), eliminating the necessity for court approval. *See* Code, Estates and Trusts Article, § 15-102 (o), which allows a fiduciary to employ an attorney, but requires court approval for attorney's fees exceeding $50 in a fiduciary estate administered under court jurisdiction. *See also* Rule 2-202 (c), authorizing the court to appoint an attorney to represent a person under disability.

Source. — This Rule is in part derived from former Rule V77 b 1, and is in part new.

Powers included in former Rule V77 applied applied to all trustees, whether or not such powers were included in the will or trust agreement. Mercantile-Safe Deposit & Trust Co. v. United States, 311 F. Supp. 670 (D. Md. 1970).

Trustee has no power to sell something he does not have. — The expansion of fiduciary powers which former Rule V77 accomplished did not confer upon a trustee a power to sell something he does not have. Jones v. Endslow, 23 Md. App. 578, 328 A.2d 339 (1974).

And therefore could not sell real property in which he held title to a life estate without prior approval. — A trustee could not sell real property placed in a trust by the testator without the approval of any beneficiary or of the court where, with respect to that property, the trustee held legal title to a life estate only. Jones v. Endslow, 23 Md. App. 578, 328 A.2d 339 (1974).

Rule 10-704. Titling of assets.

(a) **Form.** Unless otherwise ordered by the court, assets of a fiduciary estate shall be held in substantially the following form:

(1) Any account in any bank, savings and loan association, or other financial institution shall be held: A.B., (fiduciary) for _____ (or under the Will of _____).

(2) Any security held by a fiduciary shall be titled in accordance with subsection (a) (1) of this Rule or in the name of a nominee or in other form without disclosure of the interest of the fiduciary estate, but the fiduciary shall be liable for a wrongful act of the nominee in connection with the security so held.

Cross references. — Code, Estates and Trusts Article, § 15-102 (x).

(3) All other intangible assets and all tangible personal assets required to be titled shall be titled in a form similar to subsection (a) (1) of this Rule, unless it is impractical to do so.

(b) **Securities in name of disabled person.** Unless otherwise ordered by the court, nothing in section (a) of this Rule shall prohibit the fiduciary who has physical possession of securities from retaining them in the name of a disabled person.

(c) **Real estate.** Real estate need not be titled in the name of the fiduciary if (1) the real property lies in the county in which the court has assumed jurisdiction or (2) a copy of the court order or instrument naming the fiduciary has been filed in the land records in the Maryland county where the property is located (other than the county in which the court has assumed jurisdiction), or in the land records of another state where the property is located.

Cross references. — For authority of fiduciaries to deposit securities with a securities clearing corporation, *see* Code, Estates and Trusts Article, § 15-104.

Source. — This Rule is derived as follows: *Section (a)* is derived from former Rule V76 a.

Subsection (1) is derived from former Rule V76 a.

Subsection (2) is in part derived from former Rule V76 c, Code, Estates and Trusts Article, § 15-102 (x) and is in part new.

Section (b) is new.

Section (c) is new.

Rule 10-705. Restricted accounts.

(a) **Petition for restricted accounts.** When a fiduciary estate consists entirely of cash in an amount not exceeding $75,000, a fiduciary may petition the court for an order authorizing the deposit of cash in a federally insured financial institution in a single restricted account titled substantially in the following form: "A.B., (fiduciary), withdrawals subject to the order of the Circuit Court for _____ County."

(b) **Orders authorizing withdrawals.** The court may require a separate order prior to each withdrawal. The court may enter a continuing order authorizing withdrawals up to a specified amount. The continuing order may be for a definite period of time, not to exceed one year, and may on petition be renewed annually.

(c) **Proof of restricted account.** The fiduciary shall promptly provide proof of the opening of a restricted account to the trust clerk, who shall make note of it in the file.

(d) **When accounting not required.** If all of the assets of a fiduciary estate are deposited in a single restricted account in an amount not exceeding $10,000, no annual accounting is required unless the court orders otherwise.

Cross references. — For accounting requirements, *see* Rule 10-706.

Source. — This Rule is derived as follows: *Section (a)* is derived from former Rule V75 a and b.

Section (b) is derived from former Rule V75 c.

Section (c) is derived from former Rule V75 d.

Section (d) is derived from former Rule V74 c 2 (e).

Rule 10-706. Accounting.

(a) **Records.** A fiduciary shall keep records of the fiduciary estate and upon request of the court that has assumed jurisdiction over the fiduciary estate or any interested person, shall make the records available for inspection.

(b) **Annual fiduciary accounts.** (1) Generally. When the court has appointed a guardian of the property or has assumed jurisdiction over a fiduciary estate, the fiduciary shall file each year an account in substantially the form set forth in Rule 10-708. The end of the accounting year shall be (A) the anniversary of the date upon which the court assumed jurisdiction over the estate or appointed the fiduciary, or (B) any other anniversary date fixed with the consent of the trust clerk or the court. The account shall be filed not later than 60 days after the end of the accounting year, unless the court or trust clerk extends the time for good cause shown. The fiduciary shall furnish a copy of the account to any interested person who requests it.

(2) Beneficiary of the Department of Veterans Affairs. In the case of a beneficiary of the Department of Veterans Affairs, the fiduciary shall send a certified copy of the account to the Office of the Department of Veterans Affairs having jurisdiction over the area in which the court is located.

Cross references. — Code, Estates and Trusts Article, § 13-804 (c).

(3) When not required. Unless the court orders otherwise, the fiduciary of a fiduciary estate consisting entirely of cash in a restricted account under Rule 10-705 (d) need not file an annual account.

(4) Trust clerk — Report and recommendation. (A) Generally. The trust clerk shall examine each annual account, report to the court any irregularity in it, raise any other matters deemed appropriate, and make recommendations. The trust clerk may require the fiduciary to furnish proof of any transactions shown in the account.

(B) Beneficiary of the Department of Veterans Affairs. In the case of a beneficiary of the Department of Veterans Affairs, the trust clerk shall endorse on the account a certificate that any securities or investments shown on the account were exhibited to the trust clerk.

Cross references. — Code, Estates and Trusts Article, § 13-804 (b).

(5) Court approval. The court shall review every annual account and either enter an order approving the account or take other appropriate action.

(c) **Audit.** When the court has appointed a guardian of the property or has assumed jurisdiction over a fiduciary estate, the fiduciary account need not be audited by a private auditor unless specifically required by the court. Upon a petition filed by the fiduciary or upon the court's own initiative, the court may order an audit pursuant to Rule 2-543. A fiduciary may have a private audit conducted for any period but, unless the court orders otherwise, the cost of that audit shall be borne by the fiduciary and not the fiduciary estate.

Source. — This Rule is derived in part from former Rule V74 and is in part new.

———

Cited in Ashcraft & Gerel v. Shaw, 126 Md. App. 325, 728 A.2d 798 (1999).

Rule 10-707. Inventory and information report.

(a) **Duty to file.** Within 60 days after jurisdiction has been assumed or a fiduciary has been appointed, the fiduciary shall file an inventory and information report in substantially the following form:

Part I.

[CAPTION]

INVENTORY

The FIDUCIARY ESTATE now consists of the following assets:
    (attach additional sheets, if necessary; each item listed shall be valued by the fiduciary at its fair market value, as of the date of the appointment of the fiduciary or the assumption of jurisdiction by the court; unless the court otherwise directs, it shall not be necessary to employ an appraiser to make any valuation; state amount of any mortgages, liens, or other indebtedness, but do not deduct when determining estimated fair market value)

A. REAL ESTATE
(State location, liber/folio, balance of mortgage, and name of lender, if any)

ESTIMATED FAIR
MARKET VALUE

_____ $ _____

_____   _____

_____   _____

TOTAL $ _____

B. CASH AND CASH EQUIVALENTS
(State name of financial institution, account number, and type of account)

PRESENT FAIR
MARKET VALUE

_____ $ _____

_____   _____

TOTAL $ _____

C. PERSONAL PROPERTY
(Itemize motor vehicles, regardless of value; describe all other property generally if total value is under $1500; state amount of any lien; itemize, if total value is over $1500)

141

ESTIMATED FAIR
MARKET VALUE

_____ $ _____
_____   _____
_____   _____
                         TOTAL $ _____

D. STOCKS
(State number and class of shares, name of corporation)

PRESENT FAIR
MARKET VALUE

_____ $ _____
_____   _____
_____   _____
                         TOTAL $ _____

E. BONDS
(State face value, name of issuer, interest rate, maturity date)

PRESENT FAIR
MARKET VALUE

_____ $ _____
_____   _____
_____   _____
                         TOTAL $ _____

F. OTHER
(Describe generally, e.g., debts owed to estate, partnerships, cash value of life
   insurance policies, etc.)

ESTIMATED FAIR
MARKET VALUE

_____ $ _____
_____   _____
_____   _____
                         TOTAL $ _____

Part II.

INFORMATION REPORT

(1) Are there any assets in which the minor or disabled person holds a
present interest of any kind together with another person in any real or
personal property, including accounts in a credit union, bank, or other financial
institution?

[ ] No   [ ] Yes   If yes, give the following information as to all such
                     property:

Name, Address, and Relationship of Co-Owner	Nature of Property	Description of Interest	Total Value of Property
_____	_____	_____	_____
_____	_____	_____	_____
_____	_____	_____	_____
_____	_____	_____	_____
_____	_____	_____	_____

(2) Does the minor or disabled person hold an interest less than absolute in any other property which has not been disclosed in question (1) and has not been included in the inventory (e.g., interest in a trust, a term for years, a life estate)?

[ ] No [ ] Yes   If yes, give the following information as to each such interest:

Description of Interest
and Amount or Value

Date and Type of Instrument
Establishing Interest

_____   _____
_____   _____
_____   _____

VERIFICATION:

I solemnly affirm under the penalties of perjury that the contents of this inventory and information report are true and complete to the best of my knowledge, information, and belief.

_____   _____
Date   Date

_____   _____
Signature of Fiduciary   Signature of Fiduciary

_____   _____
Address   Address

_____   _____
Telephone Number   Telephone Number

_____
Name of Fiduciary's Attorney

_____
Address

_____
Telephone Number

(b) **Examination not required.** Unless the court otherwise directs, it shall not be necessary that the assets listed in the report be exhibited to or examined by the court, the trust clerk, or auditor.

(c) **Notice.** Unless the court orders otherwise, the trust clerk or fiduciary shall furnish a copy of the report to any interested person who has made a request for it.

Source. — This Rule is derived as follows: Section (a) is in part derived from former Rule V74 b 1 and 2 and is in part new.

Section (b) is derived from former Rule V74 b 3.
Section (c) is new.

Rule 10-708. Fiduciary's Account and report of trust clerk.

(a) **Form of account.** The Fiduciary's Account shall be filed in substantially the following form:

[CAPTION]

FIDUCIARY'S ACCOUNT

I, _____, make this [ ] periodic [ ] final Fiduciary's Account for the period from _____ to _____ .

Part I. The FIDUCIARY ESTATE now consists of the following assets: (attach additional sheets, if necessary; state amount of any mortgages, liens, or other indebtedness, but do not deduct when determining estimated fair market value)

A. REAL ESTATE
(State location, liber/folio, balance of mortgage, and name of lender, if any)

ESTIMATED FAIR
MARKET VALUE
_____ $ _____
_____   _____
_____   _____
TOTAL $ _____

B. CASH AND CASH EQUIVALENTS
(State name of financial institution, account number, and type of account)

PRESENT FAIR
MARKET VALUE
_____ $ _____
_____   _____
_____   _____
TOTAL $ _____

C. PERSONAL PROPERTY
(Itemize motor vehicles, regardless of value; describe all other property generally if total value is under $1500; state amount of any lien; itemize, if total value is over $1500)

ESTIMATED FAIR
MARKET VALUE
_____ $ _____
_____   _____
_____   _____
TOTAL $ _____

D. STOCKS
(State number and class of shares, name of corporation)

144

PRESENT FAIR
MARKET VALUE

_____ $ _____

_____   _____

_____   _____

TOTAL $ _____

E. BONDS

(State face value, name of issuer, interest rate, maturity date)

PRESENT FAIR
MARKET VALUE

_____ $ _____

_____   _____

TOTAL $ _____

F. OTHER

(Describe generally, e.g., debts owed to estate, partnerships, cash value of life
   insurance policies, etc.)

ESTIMATED FAIR
MARKET VALUE

_____ $ _____

_____   _____

_____   _____

TOTAL $ _____

Part II. The following income was collected and disbursements were made:
         (attach additional sheets, if necessary)

A. INCOME

(State type, e.g. pensions, social security, rent, annuities, dividends, interest,
   refunds)

AMOUNT

_____ $ _____

_____   _____

_____   _____

_____   _____

_____   _____

_____   _____

TOTAL $ _____

B. DISBURSEMENTS

(State to whom paid and purpose of payment)

AMOUNT

_____ $ _____

_____   _____

_____   _____

_____   _____

_____   _____

_____   _____

_____   _____

                                    TOTAL $ _____

C. SUMMARY

Total Income .... $ _____

Total Disbursements .... $ (_____)

Net Income/(Loss) .... $ _____

Part III. The following changes in the assets of the Fiduciary Estate have occurred since the last account: (attach additional sheets, if necessary)

A. ASSETS ADDED

Date	Description of Transaction	Gross Purchase Price	Value at date of acquisition if other than by purchase

B. ASSETS DELETED

Date	Description of Transaction	Gross Sale Proceeds	Selling Costs	Carrying Value	Gain (Loss)

A Summary of the Fiduciary Estate is as follows:

Type of Property	Value reported on last Fiduciary Account	Value reported on this Fiduciary Account
A. Real Estate	$ _____	$ _____
B. Cash and Cash Equivalents	$ _____	$ _____
C. Personal Property	$ _____	$ _____
D. Stocks	$ _____	$ _____
E. Bonds	$ _____	$ _____
F. Other	$ _____	$ _____
Total	$ _____	$ _____

The Fiduciary bond, if any, has been filed in this action in the amount of $ _____.

VERIFICATION:

I solemnly affirm under the penalties of perjury that the contents of this account are true and complete to the best of my knowledge, information, and belief.

Date

Signature of Fiduciary

Address

Telephone Number

Date

Signature of Fiduciary

Address

Telephone Number

Name of Fiduciary's Attorney

Address

Telephone Number

(b) **Report of the trust clerk and order of court.** The Report of the Trust Clerk and Order of Court shall be filed in substantially the following form:

REPORT OF TRUST CLERK AND ORDER OF COURT

I, the undersigned Trust Clerk, certify that I have examined the attached Fiduciary's Account in accordance with the Maryland Rules.

Matters to be called to the attention of the Court are as follows:

Date

Signature of Trust Clerk

Address of Trust Clerk

Telephone No. of Trust Clerk

ORDER

The foregoing Fiduciary's Account having been filed and reviewed, it is by the Court, this _____ day of _____, _____,

(month) (year)

ORDERED, that the attached Fiduciary's Account is accepted.

(or)

ORDERED, that a hearing shall be held in this matter on _____.

(date)

_____

JUDGE

(Amended May 9, 2000, effective July 1, 2000.)

Source. — This Rule is new.

_____

Effect of amendments. — The 2000 amendment, in the paragraph following "OR-DER" in (b), substituted "_____" for "19____" and added "(month)" and "(year)" notations.

Cited in Battley v. Banks, 177 Md. App. 638, 937 A.2d 846 (2007).

Rule 10-709. Transfer of fiduciary estate to a foreign fiduciary.

(a) **Who may file.** A fiduciary or any interested person may file a petition requesting a court to transfer a fiduciary estate to a foreign fiduciary.

(b) **Venue.** The petition shall be filed in the court that has assumed jurisdiction over the fiduciary estate, or if jurisdiction has not been assumed, in the county in which any part of the property is located, or where the transferor resides, is regularly employed, or maintains a place of business.

(c) **Contents.** The petition shall contain at least the following information:

(1) The name, address, telephone number, and interest of the petitioner.

(2) The name, address, telephone number, and interest of the foreign fiduciary.

(3) The place and date of the foreign fiduciary's appointment.

(4) The reasons why the transfer should be made.

(d) **Certificates.** A petition shall be accompanied by a certified copy of the instrument or court order appointing the foreign fiduciary, and proof that the appointment is still in effect.

(e) **Notice.** The petitioner shall give notice to all interested persons by mailing to them by ordinary mail a copy of the petition and a show cause order issued pursuant to Rule 10-104.

(f) **Final accounting.** No final accounting need be filed unless required by the court.

Source. — This Rule is in part derived from former Rule V80 and in part new.

Rule 10-710. Termination of a fiduciary estate — Final distribution.

(a) **Cause for termination.** Grounds for the termination of a fiduciary estate shall include:

(1) the occurrence of the event specified in the instrument creating the estate;

(2) the distribution by the fiduciary of all remaining assets of the estate in a manner authorized by the instrument creating the estate;

(3) the attainment by a minor of the age of majority;

(4) the emancipation of a minor who has not attained the age of majority;

(5) the cessation of a disability;

(6) the death of the minor or disabled person; or

(7) any other good cause for termination.

(b) **Time for filing — Who may file.** Within 45 days after the fiduciary discovers that the grounds for termination exist, the fiduciary shall file a petition requesting the court to terminate the estate. Thereafter, if the fiduciary has not timely filed the petition, an interested person may file a petition requesting the court to terminate the estate.

(c) **Venue.** The petition shall be filed in the court that has assumed jurisdiction over the fiduciary estate or if jurisdiction has not been assumed, in the county in which any part of the property is located, or where the fiduciary resides, is regularly employed, or maintains a place of business.

(d) **Contents.** The petition shall be signed and verified by the petitioner and shall contain the following information:

(1) the petitioner's interest in the estate;

(2) the name and address of each interested person entitled to notice of the petition;

(3) a statement of facts establishing the grounds for termination; and

(4) documentation as set forth in this Rule.

(e) **Documentation.** (1) Proof of age. If the cause for the termination of the guardianship of the property of a minor is the attainment of the age of majority, the petitioner shall file with the petition a copy of the minor person's birth certificate or other satisfactory proof of age.

(2) Marriage certificate. If the cause for the termination of the guardianship of the property of a minor is emancipation because of the marriage of the minor person, the petitioner shall file with the petition a copy of the marriage certificate.

(3) Medical certificate. If the cause for the termination of the guardianship of the property of a disabled person is the cessation of the disability, the petitioner shall file with the petition a certificate, signed by a physician who has examined the person within 21 days of the filing of the petition, attesting to the cessation of the disability.

(4) Death certificate. If the cause for the termination of the guardianship of the property is the death of the minor or disabled person, the petitioner shall file with the petition a copy of the death certificate.

(f) **Final accounting.** If the petitioner is the fiduciary, the petitioner shall file with the petition a final accounting containing the same information required in annual accountings by Rule 10-708, together with the proposed final distribution of any remaining assets of the estate. The accounting shall cover any period of the fiduciary's administration of the estate which has not been covered by annual accountings previously filed in the proceedings. If the petitioner is not the fiduciary, the fiduciary shall file an accounting as directed by the court.

Committee note. — For the right of a guardian to pay from the guardianship estate all commissions, fees, and expenses of the guardianship before the balance of the guardianship estate is paid out to the personal representative or other person entitled to it,

see Code, Estates and Trusts Article, § 13-214,
which abrogates the ruling in Battley v.
Banks, 177 Md. App. 638 (2007).

(g) **Notice.** The petitioner shall give notice of the filing of the petition to the persons named as distributees in the proposed final distribution, to the other persons entitled to notice of annual accounts, and to all other persons designated by the court. The notice shall consist of mailing by ordinary mail a copy of the petition and a show cause order issued pursuant to Rule 10-104. (Amended June 7, 2011, effective July 1, 201)

Source. — This Rule is in part derived from former Rule V78 and in part new.

———

Effect of amendments. — The 2011 amendment added the committee note following (f).

Cited in Battley v. Banks, 177 Md. App. 638, 937 A.2d 846 (2007); Davis v. AG of Md., 187 Md. App. 110, 975 A.2d 362 (2009).

Rule 10-711. Resignation of fiduciary and appointment of substituted or successor fiduciary.

(a) **Commencement of action.** A fiduciary may file a petition to resign. The petition shall state the reasons for the resignation and may request the appointment of a substituted or successor fiduciary. When a fiduciary resigns, dies, is removed, or becomes otherwise incapable of filling the position, and there is no substituted or successor fiduciary already named, the court may, on its own initiative or on petition filed by any interested person, appoint a substituted or successor fiduciary.

(b) **Venue.** (1) Guardianships of the property. The petition to resign or to appoint a substituted or successor fiduciary shall be filed in the court that has assumed jurisdiction over the guardianship. If jurisdiction has not been assumed, the petition shall be filed pursuant to Rule 10-301 (b).

(2) Other fiduciary proceedings. The petition shall be filed in the court that has assumed jurisdiction over the fiduciary estate, or if jurisdiction has not been assumed, in the county in which the property is situated, or where the fiduciary resides, is regularly employed, or maintains a place of business.

(c) **Account of resigning fiduciary.** The resigning fiduciary shall file with the petition an accounting pursuant to Rule 10-706 for any period not covered in any annual accountings previously filed, or, if none, from the date the fiduciary assumed the office.

In the case of an estate not previously subject to court jurisdiction, where all beneficiaries have filed a waiver or where the court does not require an accounting, an accounting need not be filed.

(d) **Notice.** The petitioner shall give notice to those interested persons designated by the court by mailing to them by ordinary mail a copy of the petition and a show cause order issued pursuant to Rule 10-104.

(e) **Termination of fiduciary's appointment.** Resignation of a fiduciary does not terminate the appointment of the fiduciary until the court enters an order accepting the resignation.

(f) **Proceedings.** The court may, and upon request shall, hold a hearing and shall grant or deny the relief sought in the petition. Pending the appointment of the successor fiduciary, the court may appoint a temporary fiduciary.

(g) **Resignation of co-fiduciary.** Unless otherwise ordered by the court, a co-fiduciary may resign the office pursuant to this Rule. The resigning co-fiduciary shall turn over all property belonging to the estate to the remaining co-fiduciary.

(h) **Duty of personal representative of the estate of deceased fiduciary or guardian of disabled fiduciary.** Upon the death or disability of a fiduciary, the personal representative or the guardian of the fiduciary, if any, shall, subject to order of court:

(1) Have the duty to protect all property belonging to the estate;

(2) Have the power to perform acts necessary for the protection of the estate;

(3) Immediately apply to the court for the appointment of a substituted or successor fiduciary;

(4) Upon appointment of a substituted or successor fiduciary have the duty to file an accounting pursuant to Rule 10-708 and deliver any property of the estate to the substituted or successor fiduciary.

Committee note. — Code, Estates and Trusts Article, § 13-220 (c) applies to deceased or disabled guardians of the property; section (i) of this Rule applies to all deceased or disabled fiduciaries.

(i) **Additional means of resignation.** This Rule is in addition to, and not in lieu of, any other procedure for the resignation or discharge of a fiduciary provided by law or by the instrument creating the estate or appointing the fiduciary.

Cross references. — See Code, Estates and Trusts Article, § 15-111.
Source. — This Rule is derived as follows:
Section (a) is derived from former Rule V81 a and former Rule V82 a.
Section (b)
Subsection (1) is derived from former Rule R72 a and b.
Subsection (2) is derived from former Rule V81 a.
Section (c) is in part derived from former Rule V81 b 1 and is in part new.
Section (d) is derived from former Rule V81 c 1.
Section (e) is new.
Section (f) is in part derived from former Rule V78 b 5 and is in part new.
Section (g) is new.
Section (h) is derived from former Rule V82 e.
Section (i) is derived from former Rule V81 e.

Rule 10-712. Removal for cause or other sanctions.

(a) **On court's initiative.** The court that has already assumed jurisdiction over the guardianship or estate may order a fiduciary to show cause why the fiduciary should not be removed or be subject to other sanctions for failure to perform the duties of that office.

(b) **On petition of interested persons.** An interested person may file a petition to remove a fiduciary. The petition shall state the reasons why the fiduciary should be removed.

(c) **Venue.** (1) Guardianships of the property. The petition shall be filed in the court that has already assumed jurisdiction or, if jurisdiction has not been assumed, pursuant to Rule 10-301 (b).

(2) *Other fiduciary proceedings.* The petition shall be filed in the court that has already assumed jurisdiction or, if jurisdiction has not been assumed, in the county in which the property is situated, or where the fiduciary resides, is regularly employed, or maintains a place of business.

(d) **Notice and hearing.** The court shall issue a show cause order pursuant to Rule 10-104 which shall set a hearing date. If no petition for removal has been filed, the show cause order shall state the grounds asserted by the court for the removal. The order and a copy of any petition shall be served on the fiduciary, the surety on any bond of the fiduciary, all interested persons, and any other persons as directed by the court. The court shall conduct a hearing for the purpose of determining whether the fiduciary should be removed.

(e) **Action by court.** If the court finds grounds for removal, it may remove the fiduciary and appoint a substituted or successor fiduciary as provided in Rule 10-711. Pending the appointment of the fiduciary, the court may appoint a temporary fiduciary.

Cross references. — As to the grounds for removal of a fiduciary, *see* Code, Estates and Trusts Article, § 15-112.

(f) **Final accounting and delivery of property.** Upon the appointment of a substituted or successor fiduciary, the removed fiduciary shall, within the time period specified by the Court,

(1) file an accounting, pursuant to section (f) of Rule 10-710; and

(2) deliver any property of the fiduciary estate to the substituted or successor fiduciary.

(g) **Other sanctions.** In addition to or in lieu of removal, the court may disallow any commissions from the time the court finds that the default began, require the fiduciary to perform the neglected duties, and impose any other appropriate sanctions.

Source. — This Rule is derived as follows:
Section (a) is in part derived from former Rules V84 d and V74 e 1 (a) and is in part new.
Section (b) is in part derived from former Rule V84 d 1 and d 2 and is in part new.
Section (c)
Subsection (1) is derived from former Rule R72 a and b.

Subsection (2) is derived from former Rule V84 c.
Section (d) is in part derived from former Rules V74 e 1 (a) and V84 e, and is in part new.
Section (e) is new.
Section (f) is derived from former Rule V84 f.
Section (g) is in part derived from former Rule V74 e 2 and is in part new.

Conventional trustee has broad discretionary powers which may be exercised absent evidence of bad faith, misconduct or a want of ordinary skill or judgment. Shipley v. Crouse, 279 Md. 613, 370 A.2d 97 (1977).

First obligation of the trustees is to safeguard the trust estate, and in doing so they are called upon many times to exercise a judgment; hence the judgment exercised by the trustees that they would share the final contract and let the beneficiaries know when it was submitted to the court for ratification, but would not share the step-by-step negotiations with the beneficiaries, was not a breach of their duty, but, quite to the contrary, was in furtherance of their duty to try to do what, in their judgment, was in the best interests of the trust estate. Shipley v. Crouse, 279 Md. 613, 370 A.2d 97 (1977).

Receipt of information by beneficiaries not absolute. — While beneficiaries are entitled to receive complete and accurate information as to the administration of the trust and to know what the trust property is and how the trustee has dealt with it, this is not absolute, if the trustee renders periodic reports showing collection of income and disbursements, assuming the trustee is acting in good faith and is not abusing his discretionary powers. Shipley v. Crouse, 279 Md. 613, 370 A.2d 97 (1977).

Disclosure by trustees mandated. — When there is a confidential relationship between buyer and seller, or there is an element of self-dealing, the duty of loyalty mandates a full and frank disclosure by the trustees to the beneficiaries. Shipley v. Crouse, 279 Md. 613, 370 A.2d 97 (1977).

Where removal likely required. — Where because of a disagreement between coguardians a ward has not been permitted to leave the grounds of a nursing home in which she resides, receive new eyeglasses, have any change in the medication or medical care she requires or the like, it may well be that removal of one or both of the guardians will be required. Kicherer v. Kicherer, 285 Md. 114, 400 A.2d 1097 (1979).

TITLE 11. JUVENILE CAUSES

Editor's note. — The Court of Appeals, by Order dated June 5, 1996, effective January 1, 1997, rescinded Subtitles A, D, E, J, P, Q, R, T, U, V, W, Y, Z, BB, BD, BE, BG, BH, BJ, BL, BP, BQ, BR, BS, BW, and BY of Chapter 1100 of the Maryland Rules of Procedure, rescinded Subtitles P, BB, BQ, and BW of the Maryland District Rules, and rescinded Forms 22a, 23, 24, 25, and 26. The Order substituted for certain of the rules and forms rescinded new Title 9, Chapter 100, Title 10, Title 12, Title 13, Title 14, and Title 15 of the Maryland Rules of Procedure. Furthermore, the Order transferred, without readoption, Chapter 900, Chapter 1200, and Subtitles S, BU, and BV of Chapter 1100 of the Maryland Rules of Procedure and Chapter 1200 of the Maryland District Rules to be Title 9, Chapter 200, Title 11, and Title 16 of the Maryland Rules of Procedure. The Order provides that the new rules shall "apply to all actions commenced on or after January 1, 1997, and insofar as practicable, to all actions then pending."

Many of the cases in the notes to the various rules were decided prior to the 1996 revision. These cases have been retained under pertinent rules of this title where it is thought that such cases will be of value in interpreting the present rules.

A table of comparable rules, relating those rules rescinded effective January 1, 1997, to the revised rules in Title 9 through Title 16 is to be found in Volume 2 following the end of the Maryland Rules.

Rule 11-101. Definitions.

a. **Statutory definitions.** The definitions stated in Section 3-801 of the Courts Article are applicable to this Title.

Cross references. — See § 3-801 of the Courts Article for definitions of "adjudicatory hearing," "adult," "child," "child in need of assistance," "child in need of supervision," "citation," "commit," "court," "custodian," "delinquent act," "delinquent child," "detention," "disposition hearing," "intake officer," "mentally handicapped child," "party," "shelter care," and "violation."

b. **Additional definitions.** The following words and phrases used in this Title are defined as follows:

1. Complaint. "Complaint" means a written statement made by any person or agency to an intake officer which, if true, would support the allegations of a juvenile petition.

2. Emergency detention or shelter care. "Emergency detention or shelter care" means detention or shelter care that is required at a time other than when a judge of the court having jurisdiction is available.

3. Juvenile petition. "Juvenile petition" means a petition filed pursuant to Section 3-810 of the Courts Article.

4. Parent. "Parent" includes a child's parent, guardian and custodian.

5. Probation. "Probation" means a status created by a court order under which a child adjudicated to be delinquent, or an adult convicted under Section 3-831 of the Courts Article, is to remain subject to supervision of the Court under conditions the Court or the agency designated by it deems proper, but is not removed from his home.

6. Respondent. "Respondent" means the person against whom a petition is filed.

7. Waiver petition. "Waiver petition" means a petition filed pursuant to Rule 11-113 (Waiver of Jurisdiction). (Amended Nov. 5, 1976, effective Jan. 1, 1977; June 5, 1996, effective Jan. 1, 1997.)

Source. — This Rule is former Rule 901.

Effect of amendments. — The 1996 amendment substituted "Title" for "Chapter" in a. and in the introductory language of b.; substituted "Rule 11-113" for "Rule 913" in b. 7.; and added the Source note.

Editor's note. — An Order dated June 5, 1996, effective Jan. 1, 1997, renumbered this Rule, which was formerly Rule 901.

University of Baltimore Law Forum. — For discussion of police investigative procedures and juveniles, see 16, No. 1 U. Balt. Law Forum 6 (1986).

Former Chapter 900 [see now this title] is exclusive rule relative to juvenile courts of this State; it does not provide for the right of intervention in a juvenile proceeding. In re Damien D., 50 Md. App. 411, 438 A.2d 932 (1982).

The Criminal Rules of Procedure under Title 4 of the Maryland Rules do not apply to an adjudicatory proceeding in a juvenile cause; juvenile delinquency proceedings are governed exclusively by this title. In re Victor B., 336 Md. 85, 646 A.2d 1012 (1994).

Preserving objection to admissibility of evidence. — In a juvenile proceeding, a pre-adjudicatory motion is not required to preserve an objection to the admissibility of evidence at an adjudicatory hearing. In re Victor B., 336 Md. 85, 646 A.2d 1012 (1994).

Rule 11-102. Complaint — Intake procedures.

a. **Complaint.** Any person or agency having knowledge of facts which may cause a person to be subject to the jurisdiction of the court may file a complaint with the Juvenile Services Agency intake officer assigned to the court having proper venue.

b. **Intake procedures.** The procedures for intake shall comply with provisions of Section 3-810 of the Courts Article. (Amended Nov. 5, 1976, effective Jan. 1, 1977; July 27, 1987, effective Aug. 17, 1987; June 5, 1996, effective Jan. 1, 1997.)

Source. — This Rule is former Rule 902.

Effect of amendments. — The 1996 amendment added the Source note.

Editor's note. — An Order dated June 5, 1996, effective Jan. 1, 1997, renumbered this Rule, which was formerly Rule 902.

Rule 11-102A. Transfer of jurisdiction from court exercising criminal jurisdiction.

a. **Applicability.** This Rule applies to actions for which a court exercising criminal jurisdiction has entered an order transferring jurisdiction pursuant to Rule 4-251 (c) (2) or 4-252 (h) (3).

Cross references. — Code, Criminal Procedure Article, § 4-202.

b. **Juvenile petition.** Within 10 days after a court exercising criminal jurisdiction enters an order transferring jurisdiction over a defendant to the juvenile court, the State's Attorney shall file a juvenile petition pursuant to Rule 11-103 and shall attach to the petition a copy of (1) the charging document that was filed in the court exercising criminal jurisdiction and (2) the order of the court transferring jurisdiction. If the petition is not so filed, the respondent shall be released from detention, shelter care, or all conditions of pretrial release, without prejudice to the right of the State's Attorney to file a petition thereafter.

c. **Effect of provisions in order transferring jurisdiction.** Except as provided in section b of this Rule and subject to Rules 11-112 and 11-114, any conditions of release of the respondent or any placement of the respondent in detention or shelter care set forth in the order transferring jurisdiction shall remain in effect and be enforceable by the juvenile court pending the adjudicatory hearing unless modified or abrogated by the juvenile court. (Added Sept. 11, 1995, effective Jan. 1, 1996; amended June 5, 1996, effective Jan. 1, 1997; Jan. 8, 2002, effective Feb. 1, 2002.)

Source. — This Rule is former Rule 902A.

Effect of amendments. — The 1996 amendment substituted "Rule 11-103" for "Rule 903" in b.; substituted "Rules 11-112 and 11-114" for "Rules 912 and 914" in c.; and added the Source note.

The 2002 amendment substituted "Criminal Procedure Article, § 4-202" for "Article 27, § 594A" in a.

Editor's note. — An Order dated June 5, 1996, effective Jan. 1, 1997, renumbered this Rule, which was formerly Rule 902A.

Rule 11-103. Juvenile petition.

a. **Form — Contents.** The juvenile petition shall be by the State of Maryland. It shall be in writing and shall comply with the requirements of this Rule.

1. Caption. The petition shall be captioned "Matter of ...."

2. Contents. The petition shall state:

(a) The respondent's name, address and date of birth. If the respondent is a child, it shall also state the name and address of his parent.

(b) Allegations providing a basis for the court's assuming jurisdiction over the respondent (e.g., that the respondent child is delinquent, in need of supervision, or in need of assistance; that the respondent adult violated Section 3-831 of the Courts Article; that the action arises under the Interstate Compact on Juveniles; or that the action arises under the compulsory public school attendance laws of this State).

(c) The facts, in clear and simple language, on which the allegations are based. If the commission of one or more delinquent acts or crimes is alleged, the petition shall specify the laws allegedly violated by the respondent.

(d) The name of each witness to be subpoenaed in support of the petition.

(e) Whether the respondent is in detention or shelter care; and if so, whether his parent has been notified and the date such detention or shelter care commenced. (Amended Mar. 3, 1987, effective July 1, 1987.)

3. Signature. Except in the case of a petition filed under the Interstate Compact on Juveniles, the petition shall be signed by the State's Attorney if delinquency or a violation of Section 3-831 of the Courts Article is alleged, or by the intake officer in other cases.

4. Interstate compact petitions. Juvenile petitions filed under Article IV of the Interstate Compact on Juveniles (Code, Article 83C, § 3-103) shall comply with the requirements of the Interstate Compact and must be verified by affidavit.

b. **Filing.** The petition shall be filed with the clerk of the court, in a sufficient number of copies to provide for service upon the parties. (Amended Nov. 5, 1976, effective Jan. 1, 1977; June 5, 1996, effective Jan. 1, 1997; May 9, 2000, effective July 1, 2000.)

Committee note. — Juvenile petitions filed under Article IV of the Interstate Compact on Juveniles Code, Article 83C, § 3-103, must be verified by affidavit.

Source. — This Rule is former Rule 903.

Effect of amendments. — The 1996 amendment added the Source note.

The 2000 amendment substituted "Article 83C, § 3-103" for "Health-General Article, § 6-303" in a 4 and in the Committee note following b.

Editor's note. — Former Health-General Article, § 6-303, referred to in this Rule, was transferred by ch. 290, Acts 1987, effective July 1, 1987, to be Article 41C, § 3-103. Section 8, ch. 6, Acts 1988, approved Feb. 18, 1988, and effective from date of passage, transferred former Article 41C to be present Article 83C.

An Order dated June 5, 1996, effective Jan. 1, 1997, renumbered this Rule, which was formerly Rule 903.

Juvenile court proceeding is initiated by filing of petition. — A proceeding before the juvenile court is not instituted at the time of arrest but thereafter by the filing of a petition by the State's Attorney or some other person having knowledge of the facts. Bean v. State, 234 Md. 432, 199 A.2d 773 (1964).

Although "any person or agency" may originate a delinquency proceeding, such proceedings are initiated by petition and such petitions must be prepared, signed and filed by the State's Attorney. United States v. Ramapuram, 432 F. Supp. 140 (D. Md. 1977), aff'd, 577 F.2d 738 (4th Cir.), cert. denied, 439 U.S. 926, 99 S. Ct. 309, 58 L. Ed. 2d 318 (1978).

And prior to filing of petition, State has right to conduct a normal investigation, including an interrogation of the defendant, in order to determine whether a petition would be appropriate, or whether the case was one for the grand jury. Bean v. State, 234 Md. 432, 199 A.2d 773 (1964).

This Rule indicates that reasons relied

on should be fully assigned, if only to prevent surprise. In re Cromwell, 232 Md. 409, 194 A.2d 88 (1963).

Delinquency petition satisfied form requirements. — Trial court erred in dismissing a juvenile delinquency petition, because the petition alleging that a juvenile made a false statement to a police officer in violation of § 9-501 of the Criminal Law Article satisfied the requirements of art. 21 of the Declaration of Rights, the specific dictates of § 3-8A-13(a) of the Courts Article and subsection (a)(2)(c) of this Rule, as the petition did more than merely state the elements of the charged offense, and

included specific facts concerning the alleged offense and the names and addresses of witnesses. In re Roneika S., 173 Md. App. 577, 920 A.2d 496 (2007).

Victim's petition for restitution. — The juvenile court does not have jurisdiction to hear a victim's petition for adjudication and restitution pursuant to CJ § 3-829. There is no jurisdiction in a juvenile delinquency case until a petition is filed by the State. Hart v. Bull, 69 Md. App. 229, 516 A.2d 1043 (1986).

Cited in In re Nahif A., 123 Md. App. 193, 717 A.2d 393 (1998); In re Kevin E., 402 Md. 624, 938 A.2d 826 (2008).

Rule 11-104. Duties of clerk.

a. **Separate Docket.** The clerk shall maintain a separate docket for Juvenile Causes. Upon the filing of a juvenile petition, or a petition for continued detention or shelter care the name of each respondent shall be entered on the docket and indexed.

b. **Scheduling of Hearing.** Upon the filing of a juvenile petition, or a petition for continued detention or shelter care the clerk shall promptly schedule a hearing.

c. **Process — Issuance — Service.** Unless the court otherwise directs, upon the filing of a juvenile petition, the clerk shall promptly issue a summons substantially in the form set forth in Form 904-S of the Appendix of Forms and returnable as provided by Rule 2-126 for each party except the petitioner and a respondent child alleged to be in need of assistance. Any summons addressed to a parent of a respondent child shall require the parent to produce the respondent child on the date and time named in the summons.

The summons, together with a copy of the juvenile petition, shall be served in the manner provided by Chapter 100 of Title 2 for service of process to obtain personal jurisdiction over a person within this State.

If the parent of the child is a nonresident, or for any reason cannot be served, notice of the pendency and nature of the proceeding shall be given as directed by the court, and proof of the steps taken to give notice that justice shall require.

d. **Subpoena.** The clerk shall issue a subpoena for each witness requested by any party, pursuant to Rule 2-510.

e. **The summons, together with a copy of the juvenile petition, shall be served in the manner provided by Chapter 100 of Title 2 for service of process to obtain personal jurisdiction over a person within this State.** The clerk shall accept for deposit security for the appearance of any person subject to the court's original jurisdiction, in the form and amount that the court determines.

f. **List of Open Hearings.** Prior to the convening of court on each day that the juvenile court is in session, the clerk shall prepare and make available to the public a list of the hearings scheduled for that day that are required by Code, Courts Article, § 3-8A-13(f) to be conducted in open court. The list shall include the full name of each respondent and the time and location of the hearing. (Amended Nov. 5, 1976, effective Jan. 1, 1977; Apr. 6, 1984, effective

July 1, 1984; June 5, 1996, effective Jan. 1, 1997; June 8, 1998, effective Oct. 1, 1998; Feb. 10, 2009, effective May 1, 2009.)

Source. — This Rules is former Rule 904, except that section f. is new.

Effect of amendments. — The 1996 amendment added the Source note.

The 1998 amendment substituted "the parent" for "him" in the second sentence in c.; added f.; and added "except that section f. is new" in the Source note.

The 2009 amendment substituted "§ 3-8A-13(f)" for "§ 3-812" in the first sentence in f.

Editor's note. — An Order dated June 5, 1996, effective Jan. 1, 1997, renumbered this Rule, which was formerly Rule 904.

A master himself is empowered to conduct an adjudicatory hearing. In re Brown, 13 Md. App. 625, 284 A.2d 441 (1971).

Rule 11-105. Physical and mental examination.

a. **Examination procedure.** 1. Order for examination. Any order for a physical or mental examination pursuant to Section 3-818 of the Courts Article shall specify the time, place, manner, conditions and scope of the examination and the person or persons by whom it is to be made. The court shall order that the examination be conducted on an outpatient basis if, considering the child's condition, that is feasible and appropriate. The order may regulate the filing of a report of findings and conclusions and the testimony at a hearing by the examining physician, psychiatrist, psychologist or other professionally qualified person, the payment of the expenses of the examination and any other relevant matters. (Amended Nov. 5, 1976, effective Jan. 1, 1977; Apr. 18, 1980, effective July 1, 1980.)

2. Service of copies of report. Copies of all studies and reports of examinations made to the court under this Rule shall be furnished by the court to counsel for the parties when received by the court, but not later than two days before any hearing at which the results of the examinations will be offered in evidence.

b. **Use of report.** The report of examination is admissible in evidence as set forth in Section 3-818 of the Courts Article.

c. **Admissibility of testimony.** 1. In delinquency and contributing cases. In delinquency cases and in cases in which an adult is charged with a violation of Section 3-831 of the Courts Article, testimony concerning a study or examination ordered under Section 3-818 of the Courts Article by persons who conducted the study or examination is admissible

(i) at waiver and disposition hearings, and

(ii) at an adjudicatory hearing on the issues of a respondent's competence to participate in the proceedings and his legal responsibility for his acts.

2. In all other cases. In all other cases, testimony concerning a study or examination ordered under Section 3-818 of the Courts Article by persons who conducted the study or examination is admissible at any hearing. (Amended Nov. 5, 1976, effective Jan. 1, 1977; June 5, 1996, effective Jan. 1, 1997.)

Source. — This Rule is former Rule 905.

Effect of amendments. — The 1996 amendment added the Source note.

Editor's note. — An Order dated June 5, 1996, effective Jan. 1, 1997, renumbered this Rule, which was formerly Rule 905.

University of Baltimore Law Forum. — For discussion of police investigative procedures and juveniles, see 16, No. 1 U. Balt. Law Forum 6 (1986).

Disposition hearing. — Section 3-818 (c) of the Courts and Judicial Proceedings Article and section c of this Rule create a hearsay exception for admission of evaluative reports at disposition hearings in Children in Need of Assistance cases. In re Wanda B., 69 Md. App. 105, 516 A.2d 615 (1986).

In a child in need of assistance proceeding, a parent as well as the State could move the court to order a psychiatric examination of the child, with the parent carrying the burden of showing good cause for an examiantion and that the child would not be harmed. In re Mark M., 365 Md. 687, 782 A.2d 332 (2001).

Consideration of agency study which accused's counsel has never received. — It is apparent that CJ § 3-818 and this Rule have been violated where, prior to any formal adjudication of delinquency, the court acknowledged that it had considered, and was still considering, the contents of an agency study, and where it was clear from the record that the accused's counsel had never received a copy of the report although the judge was considering disposition of the case. In re Jeffrey L., 50 Md. App. 268, 437 A.2d 255 (1981).

Denial of evaluation in child in need of assistance proceeding. — When a mother moved, at a permanency plan review hearing, for an independent evaluation of her bonding with her children, under § 3-816 of the Courts Article, the trial court's denial of that motion was not appealable because it was an interlocutory order, and it did not fit the exception in § 12-303(x) of the Courts Article allowing appeals of interlocutory orders depriving a parent of custody or modifying the terms of a prior custody order because, at the hearing at which the motion was made, the trial court merely maintained a previously approved permanency plan and granted the mother increased visitation, so the order from the hearing in question did not deprive the mother of custody or modify the terms of a prior custody order to her detriment. In re Samone H., 385 Md. 282, 869 A.2d 370 (2005).

Cited in In re Faith H., 409 Md. 625, 976 A.2d 336 (2009).

Rule 11-106. Right to counsel.

a. **In all proceedings — Appearance of out-of-state attorney.** The respondent is entitled to be represented in all proceedings under this Title by counsel retained by him, his parent, or appointed pursuant to the provisions of subsection b 2 and 3 of this Rule. An out-of-state attorney may enter his appearance and participate in a cause only after having been admitted in accordance with Rule 14 of the Rules Governing Admission to the Bar of Maryland (Special Admission of Out-of-State Attorneys). Once so admitted, his appearance and participation is limited by the restrictions of that Rule.

Cross references. — See Rule 14 of the Rules Governing Admission to the Bar of Maryland.

b. **Waiver of representation — Indigent cases — Non-indigent cases.** 1. Waiver procedure. If, after the filing of a juvenile petition, a respondent or his parent indicates a desire or inclination to waive representation for himself, before permitting the waiver the court shall determine, after appropriate questioning in open court and on the record, that the party fully comprehends:

(i) the nature of the allegations and the proceedings, and the range of allowable dispositions;

(ii) that counsel may be of assistance in determining and presenting any defenses to the allegations of the juvenile petition, or other mitigating circumstances;

(iii) that the right to counsel in a delinquency case, a child in need of supervision case, or a case in which an adult is charged with a violation of Section 3-831 of the Courts Article includes the right to the prompt assignment of an attorney, without charge to the party if he is financially unable to obtain private counsel;

(iv) that even if the party intends not to contest the charge or proceeding, counsel may be of substantial assistance in developing and presenting material which could affect the disposition; and

(v) that among the party's rights at any hearing are the right to call witnesses in his behalf, the right to confront and cross-examine witnesses, the right to obtain witnesses by compulsory process, and the right to require proof of any charges.

2. Representation of indigents in delinquency, child in need of supervision, and contributing cases. (a) Unless knowingly and intelligently waived, and unless counsel is otherwise provided, an indigent party, or an indigent child whose parents are either indigent or unwilling to employ counsel, shall be entitled to be represented by the Office of the Public Defender in a delinquency case, a child in need of supervision case, or a case in which an adult is charged with a violation of Section 3-831 of the Courts Article, at any stage in a waiver, adjudicatory or disposition hearing, or hearing under Rule 11-116 (Modification or Vacation of Order).

(b) Upon request or upon the court's own motion, the Office of the Public Defender shall appoint, in a delinquency case, a child in need of supervision case, or a case in which an adult is charged with a violation of Section 3-831 of the Courts Article, separate counsel to represent any indigent party other than the child if the interests of the child and those of the party appear to conflict, and if such counsel is necessary to meet the requirements of a fair hearing.

3. Child in need of assistance cases. A party in a child in need of assistance proceeding is entitled to the assistance of counsel as provided in Section 3-821 of the Courts Article.

Cross references. — See Appendix: The Maryland Lawyers' Rules of Professional Conduct, Rule 1.14 (Client with Diminished Capacity) and Appendix: Guidelines of Advocacy for Attorneys Representing Children in CINA and Related TPR and Adoption Cases.

4. Non-indigent cases. Upon motion of any party or upon the court's motion, the court may appoint an attorney to represent a child. Compensation for the services of the attorney may be assessed against any party. (Amended Nov. 5, 1976, effective Jan. 1, 1977; Nov. 4, 1977, effective Jan. 1, 1978; July 16, 1992; June 5, 1996, effective Jan. 1, 1997; Mar. 5, 2001, effective July 1, 2001; Feb. 8, 2005, effective July 1, 2005.)

Source. — This Rule is former Rule 906.

Effect of amendments. — The 1996 amendment substituted "Title" for "Chapter" in the first sentence of a.; substituted "Rule 11-116" for "Rule 916" in b. 2. (a); and added the Source note.

The 2001 amendment added the cross reference note for b. 3.

The 2005 amendment inserted "Lawyers'" before "Rules of Professional Conduct" and substituted "Client with Diminished Capacity" for "Client Under a Disability" in the cross references note in (b)(3).

Editor's note. — An Order dated June 5, 1996, effective Jan. 1, 1997, renumbered this Rule, which was formerly Rule 906.

Maryland Law Review. — For article, "Best Interests Equals Zealous Advocacy: A Not So Radical View of Holistic Representation of Children Accused of Crime," see 62 Md. L. Rev. 218 (2003).

University of Baltimore Law Forum. — For discussion of police investigative procedures and juveniles, see 16, No. 1 U. Balt. Law Forum 6 (1986).

Standard for waiver of counsel. — In order to safeguard a juvenile's right to counsel, it follows that the standard for waiver of counsel in a delinquency proceeding is necessarily as strict as the waiver standard that attaches in a criminal case. In re Christopher T., 129 Md. App. 28, 740 A.2d 69 (1999).

Section b must be satisfied for effective waiver. — Before the court may accept a juvenile's waiver of counsel, it must satisfy each mandate in section b of this Rule. Anything less will render the waiver void as unknowingly and unintelligently given. In re Appeal No. 101, 34 Md. App. 1, 366 A.2d 392 (1976).

Even if a juvenile had expressly waived his right to counsel, or done so by inaction, such a waiver would have been ineffective where the record plainly demonstrated that the court failed to provide the information mandated by this Rule. In re Christopher T., 129 Md. App. 28, 740 A.2d 69 (1999).

Judgment was vacated where the trial court failed to comply with this Rule by adequately advising a nine-year-old juvenile and his mother of the right to counsel, where the mother, once she realized that she had made a mistake by failing to secure counsel, made it clear to the court that she wanted legal representation for her son, and where the court never posed any questions directly to the juvenile nor sought to ensure that he actually understood his right to counsel. In re Christopher T., 129 Md. App. 28, 740 A.2d 69 (1999).

The use of the term "shall" in both Rule 4-215 and this Rule commands compliance. In re Christopher T., 129 Md. App. 28, 740 A.2d 69 (1999).

Before a trial court can accept a waiver of counsel by a juvenile, it must satisfy each aspect of (b)(1), and the record must reflect that a defendant is competent to waive the right to counsel and that the defendant did so

knowingly and intelligently after being made aware of the advantages and disadvantages of representing him or herself, and even if a defendant professes to waive counsel, where the defendant cannot or has ineffectively waived counsel, a court must take steps to ensure representation. In re Shawn P., 172 Md. App. 569, 916 A.2d 399 (2007).

Juvenile must comprehend rights and consequences. — The court must determine that the juvenile fully comprehends each of the rights and consequences delineated in this Rule. In re Appeal No. 101, 34 Md. App. 1, 366 A.2d 392 (1976).

Compliance with this Rule does not require that the court recite the full litany in the words of the Rule. Explanation, to assure full comprehension, is more important than recital. In re Appeal No. 101, 34 Md. App. 1, 366 A.2d 392 (1976).

A juvenile facing possible waiver of juvenile jurisdiction is entitled to advice of counsel. Kemplen v. Maryland, 428 F.2d 169 (4th Cir. 1970).

Waiver by inaction. — In contrast to Rule 4-215(d), which expressly permits the court to find waiver by inaction in the circuit court, section b of this Rule does not specifically provide for waiver by inaction. In re Christopher T., 129 Md. App. 28, 740 A.2d 69 (1999).

When a trial court found a juvenile waived counsel by failing to contact the public defender before coming to court, but did not make any of the inquiries about waiver of counsel required by (b)(1) of this Rule or § 3-8A-20(b)(3) of the Courts Article, and a public defender who happened to be present in court entered his apperance and unsuccessfully sought a continuance, the trial court abused its discretion because it did not grant counsel's motion for a continuance or, at the very least, allow counsel to confer with the juvenile before commencing an adjudicatory hearing. In re Shawn P., 172 Md. App. 569, 916 A.2d 399 (2007).

Review of commitment considered "proceedings" for counsel purposes. — Hearings before the juvenile court judge for "Review of Commitment for Placement" of a juvenile were "proceedings," and, therefore, there was a requirement that the juvenile be offered counsel. In re Glenn H., 43 Md. App. 510, 406 A.2d 444 (1979).

Order for psychiatric examination. — Since there is no requirement for a hearing prior to ordering a psychiatric examination of a child under § 3-818 of the Courts and Judicial Proceedings Article, the parent's entitlement to appointed counsel under section b 2 of this Rule is not implicated. In re Wanda B., 69 Md. App. 105, 516 A.2d 615 (1986).

Parents' responsibility for child's legal services deemed "necessaries." — Legal services provided to a minor may, in some circumstances, be deemed "necessaries" for which a parent may be required to pay, e.g., where they are reasonable and necessary for the protection or enforcement of the property rights of the minor or for his personal protection, liberty or relief. Serabian v. Alpern, 284 Md. 680, 399 A.2d 267 (1979).

Recoverable at law. — Recovery against the parent for "necessary" legal services provided to a minor must ordinarily be sought in an action at law. Serabian v. Alpern, 284 Md. 680, 399 A.2d 267 (1979).

Not applicable. — This rule did not apply in a Child in Need of Assistance action. In re Alijah Q., 195 Md. App. 491, 7 A.3d 106 (2010).

Cited in In re Elrich S., 416 Md. 15, 5 A.3d 27 (2010).

Rule 11-107. Responsive pleading or motion.

a. **Denial — Admission — Preliminary objection.** A respondent may file a pleading denying or admitting all or any facts alleged in the juvenile petition, or he may file a motion raising preliminary objection. Any allegation not admitted is deemed denied. If a respondent fails to file a pleading, his failure will be taken as a denial of the allegations in the petition.

b. **Uncontested responsive pleading.** If a respondent child has filed a pleading admitting the allegations of the juvenile petition or indicates to the court his intention not to deny those allegations, the court, before proceeding with an adjudicatory hearing, shall advise the child of the nature and possible consequence of his action or intended action. The court shall neither encourage or discourage the child with respect to his action or intended action, but shall ascertain to its satisfaction that the child understands the nature and possible consequences of failing to deny the allegations of the juvenile petition, and that he takes that action knowingly and voluntarily. These proceedings shall take place in open court and shall be on the record. If the respondent is an adult, the provisions of Title 4 shall apply. (Amended Nov. 5, 1976, effective Jan. 1, 1977; Apr. 6, 1984, effective July 1, 1984; June 5, 1996, effective Jan. 1, 1997.)

Source. — This Rule is former Rule 907.

Effect of amendments. — The 1996 amendment added the Source note.

Editor's note. — An Order dated June 5, 1996, effective Jan. 1, 1997, renumbered this Rule, which was formerly Rule 907.

Applicability. — This Rule is applicable whether or not the juvenile is represented by counsel. In re Montrail, 87 Md. App. 420, 589 A.2d 1318 (1991), aff'd, 325 Md. 527, 601 A.2d 1102 (1992).

This Rule makes no distinction between delinquency cases and other juvenile cases. In re Appeal No. 544, 25 Md. App. 26, 332 A.2d 680 (1975).

Failure to inform defendant of consequences of failing to deny allegation. — The court accepted defense counsel's word that defendant admitted that the allegation against him was true, without inquiring of defendant whether he understood the nature and possible consequences of failing to deny the allegation, and whether his admission was knowing and voluntary, in violation of this Rule. In re Montrail, 87 Md. App. 420, 589 A.2d 1318 (1991), aff'd, 325 Md. 527, 601 A.2d 1102 (1992).

Quoted in In re Nahif A., 123 Md. App. 193, 717 A.2d 393 (1998).

Rule 11-108. Amendment — Continuance.

a. **Juvenile petition.** A juvenile petition may be amended by or with the approval of the court at any time prior to the conclusion of the adjudicatory hearing.

b. **Other pleading.** A pleading other than a juvenile petition may be amended with the approval of the court at any time prior to the final disposition of that pleading.

c. **Continuance.** If a juvenile petition or other pleading is amended, the court shall grant the parties such continuance as justice may require in light of the amendment. (Amended Nov. 5, 1976, effective Jan. 1, 1977; June 5, 1996, effective Jan. 1, 1997.)

Source. — This Rule is former Rule 908.

Effect of amendments. — The 1996 amendment added the Source note.

Editor's note. — An Order dated June 5, 1996, effective Jan. 1, 1997, renumbered this Rule, which was formerly Rule 908.

Maryland Law Review. — For note, "Does a Juvenile Court Rehearing on the Record After a Master Has Made Proposed Findings Violate Double Jeopardy or Due Process?" see 39 Md. L. Rev. 395 (1979).

Amendment of State's petition deemed due process — When defendant, a juvenile, had been charged with engaging in prostitu-

tion under § 11-306(a) of the Criminal Law Article, it violated due process under the Fourteenth Amendment and art. 21 of the Declaration of Rights to allow the State, after it rested its case, to amend the petition under (a) of this Rule to allege solicitation. The amendment, after which defendant was immediately adjudicated delinquent based on the solicitation charge, deprived the defense of notice as to what she was called upon to defend and of the opportunity to properly prepare for the hearing. In re Areal B., 177 Md. App. 708, 938 A.2d 43 (2007).

Rule 11-109. Discovery and inspection.

a. **Delinquency and contributing cases.** 1. Definition of "State" and "Respondent." In this section, "State" means the State's Attorney, and "Respondent" includes his counsel where appropriate.

2. Scope of section. This section applies to proceedings in which by petition, a child is alleged to be delinquent, or an adult is alleged to have violated Section 3-831 of the Courts Article.

3. Discovery by the respondent. The State shall without the necessity of a request by the respondent, furnish to the Respondent:

(a) any material or information within the knowledge, possession or control of the State which tends to negate the involvement of the respondent as to the offense charged;

(b) any relevant material or information regarding

(1) specific searches and seizures;

(2) wiretaps and eavesdropping.

(3) the acquisition of statements made by the respondent; and

(4) prehearing identification of the respondent by a witness for the State;

(c) the name and address of each person whom the State intends to call as a witness at any hearing to prove its case in chief or to rebut alibi testimony to the extent then known;

(d) as to all statements made by the respondent to a State agent which the State intends to use at a hearing:

(1) a copy of each written or recorded statement; and

(2) the substance of each oral statement and a copy of all reports of each oral statement;

(e) as to all statements made by a co-respondent to a State agent which the State intends to use at a hearing, unless a severance has been ordered by the court:

(1) a copy of each written or recorded statement; and

(2) the substance of each oral statement and a copy of all reports of each oral statement;

(f) any written report or statement made in connection with the particular case by each expert consulted by the State, if the State intends to offer the testimony of the expert or the report at any hearing, including the written substance of any oral report and conclusion made in connection with the particular case by each expert consulted by the State and the results of any physical or mental examination, scientific test, experiment or comparison;

(g) any book, paper, document, recording, photograph and any tangible object which the State intends to use at any hearing, in order to permit the respondent to inspect, copy and photograph them; and

(h) any item obtained from or belonging to the respondent which the State intends to use at any hearing, in order to permit the respondent to inspect, copy and photograph it.

(i) The State's Attorney's obligations under this section extend to material and information in the possession or control of members of his staff and of any others who have participated in the investigation or evaluation of the case and who either regularly report or with reference to the particular case have reported to his office.

4. Compliance by the State. Subject to the provisions of subsections 8 and 9 of this section, the State may comply with subsection 3 of this section by advising the respondent in writing or on the record, that the respondent may inspect the entire file of the State and by allowing such inspection to occur at any time during normal business hours. However, if the State has any exculpatory information specified in subsection 3 (a) of this Rule, the State shall promptly furnish such information to the respondent, whether or not the respondent has made the inspection provided for by that subsection.

5. Matters not subject to discovery by respondent. This section does not require the State to disclose:

(a) any documents to the extent that they contain the opinions, theories, conclusions, or other work product of the State,

(b) the identity of a confidential informant, so long as the failure to disclose the informant's identity does not infringe on a constitutional right of the respondent, and the State does not intend to call the informant as a witness; and

(c) any matter which the court, under subsection 9 of this section, orders need not be disclosed.

6. Discovery by the State. Upon the request of the State, the respondent shall:

(a) appear in a lineup for identification;

(b) speak for identification;

(c) be fingerprinted;

(d) pose for photographs not involving reenactment of a scene;

(e) try on articles of clothing;

(f) permit the taking of specimens of material under his fingernails;

(g) permit the taking from his body of samples of blood, hair, and other material involving no unreasonable intrusion upon his person;

(h) provide specimens of his handwriting;

(i) submit to reasonable physical inspection of his body or mental examination;

(j) produce and permit the State to inspect and copy all written reports made in connection with the particular case by each expert who the respondent intends to call as a witness at the hearing, including the substance of any oral report and conclusion made in connection with the particular case by an expert which the respondent intends to use at the hearing and the results of any physical or mental examination, scientific test, experiment, or comparison;

(k) furnish, upon designation by the State of the time, place and date of the alleged occurrence, the name and address of each witness other than the respondent whom the respondent intends to call as a witness to show he was not present at the time, place and date designated by the State in its request.

7. Procedure for discovery — Time — Hearing on motion to compel. The State shall make the disclosure required under subsection 3 of this section, and shall request the discovery required under subsection 6 of this section, within five days after the earlier of the appearance of counsel, or the waiver of counsel under Rule 11-106. The respondent shall furnish the discovery required under this section within ten days after a request is made. The court, for good cause shown, may extend the time for discovery.

If discovery is not furnished as required, a motion to compel discovery may be filed which shall specify the items which have not been furnished. A hearing shall be held no later than three days after the motion is filed.

8. Continuing duty to disclose. If, subsequent to compliance with a request made under this Rule or with any order compelling discovery, a party learns of additional information previously requested and required to be furnished, he shall promptly furnish the information to the other party or his counsel. If the additional information is learned during a hearing, he shall, in addition to furnishing the information promptly to the other party or his counsel, notify the court that such matter is being furnished.

9. Protective orders. Upon motion and a showing of good cause, the court may order that specified disclosures be restricted. If, at any time during the proceedings, it is brought to the attention of the court that a party has failed to comply with this section or an order issued under this section, the court may:

(a) order such party to permit the discovery of the matters not previously disclosed;

(b) strike the testimony to which the undisclosed matter relates;

(c) grant a reasonable continuance;

(d) prohibit the party from introducing in evidence the matter not disclosed;

(e) grant a mistrial; or

(f) enter such other order as may be appropriate under the circumstances.

b. **All other cases.** In any proceeding in which a child is alleged to be in need of supervision or assistance, the court may, upon good cause shown, pass such orders in aid of discovery, and inspection of evidence as justice may require.

c. **Timely disclosure required.** All matters and information to which a party is entitled must be disclosed in time to permit its beneficial use. (Added Nov. 5, 1976, effective Jan. 1, 1977; amended June 5, 1996, effective Jan. 1, 1997.)

Source. — This Rule is former Rule 909.

Effect of amendments. — The 1996 amendment substituted "Rule 11-106" for "Rule 906" in the first sentence of a. 7.; and added the Source note.

Editor's note. — An Order dated June 5, 1996, effective Jan. 1, 1997, renumbered this Rule, which was formerly Rule 909.

University of Baltimore Law Forum. — For discussion of police investigative procedures and juveniles, see 16, No. 1 U. Balt. Law Forum 6 (1986).

Examination of victims. — The rules relating to juvenile proceedings contain no specific provisions for the mental or physical examination of victims. In re John M., 129 Md. App. 165, 741 A.2d 503 (1999).

Juvenile court erred in dismissing a child in need of assistance (CINA) petition based on its view that the local department of social services (DSS) had a unilateral right to withdraw its petition over a child's objection because the juvenile court should have declined DSS's dismissal request and conducted an adjudicatory hearing on the merits of the petition when the juvenile court was not precluded from considering a child's alleged infrequent and tardy school attendance at an adjudicatory hearing simply because the issue was not alleged in the CINA petition filed by the DSS. In re Najasha B., 409 Md. 20, 972 A.2d 845 (2009).

Harmless error. — If the State violated discovery requirements by calling a chemist to testify at an adjudicatory hearing on a petition alleging appellant, a juvenile, was a delinquent child, after appellant demanded the chemist's presence pursuant to § 10-1003 of the Courts Article, after the State indicated that an officer would be the State's only witness, when the State did not notify appellant, pursuant to (a)(3)(c), that the chemist would testify, it was not an abuse of the trial court's discretion to allow the witness to testify because appellant was not prejudiced, as (1) appellant's counsel reviewed the chemist's report prior to trial, and, (2) when the State raised the issue at trial, appellant did not ask

for a continuance to prepare for the chemist's testimony. In re Caitlin N., 192 Md. App. 251, 994 A.2d 454 (2010).

State's failure to give notice of chemist's trial testimony. — When a juvenile court allowed a chemist to testify at an adjudicatory hearing on a petition alleging appellant, a juvenile, was a delinquent child, after appellant demanded the chemist's presence pursuant to § 10-1003 of the Courts Article, after the State indicated that an officer would be the State's only witness, despite the State's failure to notify appellant, pursuant to (a)(3)(c), that the chemist would testify, any error was harmless because appellant's theory of the case primarily focused on (1) the credibility of an officer, (2) the fact that no drugs were found on appellant's person and no one witnessed an exchange of money, and (3) the fact that there might have been a chain of custody problem, as there was no indication that this theory was adversely impacted by the chemist's opinion that drugs involved in the case were marijuana. In re Caitlin N., 192 Md. App. 251, 994 A.2d 454 (2010).

It was not error for a juvenile court to allow a chemist to testify at an adjudicatory hearing on a petition alleging appellant, a juvenile, was a delinquent child, after appellant demanded the chemist's presence pursuant to § 10-1003 of the Courts Article, after the State indicated that an officer would be the State's only witness, despite the State's failure to notify appellant, pursuant to (a)(3)(c), that the chemist would testify, because (1) appellant was not prejudiced, as appellant's counsel reviewed the chemist's report prior to trial, and, (2) when the State raised the issue at trial, appellant did not ask for a continuance to prepare for the chemist's testimony, and (2) appellant's constitutional rights of confrontation and cross-examination were not violated, as there was no indication that appellant's ability or opportunity to question the witness at trial was restricted. In re Caitlin N., 192 Md. App. 251, 994 A.2d 454 (2010).

Rule 11-110. Hearings — Generally.

a. **Before master or judge — Proceedings recorded.** Hearings shall be conducted before a master or a judge without a jury. Proceedings shall be recorded by stenographic notes or by electronic, mechanical or other appropriate means.

b. **Place of hearing.** A hearing may be conducted in open court, in chambers, or elsewhere where appropriate facilities are available. The hearing may be adjourned from time to time and, except as otherwise required by Code, Courts Article, § 3-812, may be conducted out of the presence of all persons except those whose presence is necessary or desirable. If the court finds that it is in the best interest of a child who is the subject of the proceeding, the presence of the child may be temporarily excluded except when the child is alleged to have committed a delinquent act.

c. **Minimum five-day notice of hearing — Service — Exception.** Except in the case of a hearing on a petition for continued detention or shelter care pursuant to Rule 11-112 (Detention or Shelter Care), the clerk shall issue a notice of the time, place and purpose of any hearing scheduled pursuant to the provisions of this Title. This notice shall be served on all parties together with a copy of the petition or other pleading if any, in the manner provided by section c of Rule 11-104 (Duties of Clerk) at least five days prior to the hearing.

d. **Multiple petitions.** 1. Individual hearings. If two or more juvenile petitions are filed against a respondent, hearings on the juvenile petitions may be consolidated or severed as justice may require.

2. Consolidation. Hearings on juvenile petitions filed against more than one respondent arising out of the same incident or conditions, may be consolidated or severed as justice may require. However, (i) if prejudice may result to any respondent from a consolidation, the hearing on the juvenile petition against the respondent shall be severed and conducted separately; and (ii) if juvenile petitions are filed against a child and an adult, the hearing on the juvenile petition filed against the child shall be severed and conducted separately from the adult proceeding.

e. **Controlling conduct of person before the court.** 1. *Sua sponte* or on application. The court, upon its own motion or on application of any person, institution, or agency having supervision or custody of, or other interest in a respondent child, may direct, restrain or otherwise control the conduct of any person properly before the court in accordance with the provisions of Section 3-827 of the Courts Article.

2. Other remedies. Title 15, Chapter 200 of these Rules is applicable to juvenile causes, and the remedies provided therein are in addition to the procedures and remedies provided by subsection 1 of this section. (Amended Nov. 5, 1976, effective Jan. 1, 1977; June 5, 1996, effective Jan. 1, 1997; June 8, 1998, effective Oct. 1, 1998.)

Source. — This Rule is former Rule 910.

———————

Effect of amendments. — The 1996 amendment, in c., substituted "Rule 11-112" for "Rule 912" and substituted "Title" for "Chapter" in the first sentence and substituted "Rule 11-104" for "Rule 904" in the second sentence; substituted "Title 15, Chapter 200" for "Subtitle P (Contempt) of Chapter 1100" at the beginning of e. 2.; and added the Source note.

The 1998 amendment, in b., inserted "except as otherwise required by Code, Courts Article, § 3-812" in the second sentence and substituted "best interest of a child who is the subject of the proceeding, the presence of the child may be temporarily excluded except when the child" for "best interest and welfare of the child, his presence may be temporarily excluded except when he" in the third sentence; and substituted "the respondent" for "him" in the second sentence in d.2.

Editor's note. — An Order dated June 5, 1996, effective Jan. 1, 1997, renumbered this Rule, which was formerly Rule 910.

Maryland Law Review. — For note, "Does a Juvenile Court Rehearing on the Record After a Master Has Made Proposed Findings Violate Double Jeopardy or Due Process?" see 39 Md. L. Rev. 395 (1979).

"Hearings." — Private meetings between judge and children were hearings requiring compliance with the notice requirement of the rule where the Department of Social Services social worker was also present at the sessions and the foster mother was present at one, and they both made comments that were evidentiary in nature, although neither was under oath or subject to cross-examination and where the children's statements also were given considerable weight by the court. In re Barry E., 107 Md. App. 206, 667 A.2d 931 (1995).

Trial court erred in excluding the mother from child in need of assistance proceedings without making any specific factual findings as to the propriety of the exclusion; the mother's procedural due process rights under U.S. Const. amend. XIV, and Articles 19 and 24 of the Maryland Declaration of Rights were violated because the trial court assumed that the mother's presence would influence the child's testimony without determining that there existed a factual basis for that conclusion. In re Maria P., 393 Md. 661, 904 A.2d 432 (2006).

Juvenile is placed in jeopardy when the State begins to offer evidence in an adjudicatory hearing before a master. Aldridge v. Dean, 395 F. Supp. 1161 (D. Md. 1975).

A judge exercising jurisdiction under CJ § 3-829 may act only after a hearing under this Rule, wherein evidence, beyond a mere finding of delinquency of the juvenile, is produced which is legally sufficient to support a conclusion that damages authorized by it were wilfully or maliciously caused by or committed by a child under 18 years of age. In re Sorrell, 20 Md. App. 179, 315 A.2d 110, cert. denied, 271 Md. 740, 744 (1974).

Record of proceedings. — Where a juvenile court conducts proceedings under this section it must use a reliable recording system or conduct the session in such a manner to assure that the entire proceeding is properly and accurately recorded. In re Barry E., 107 Md. App. 206, 667 A.2d 931 (1995).

Access by press. — Although a juvenile court has the discretion to exclude the press from a juvenile proceeding, its discretion is not unlimited and must be exercised in accord with the purposes for which it was given and within applicable constitutional limitations. Baltimore Sun Co. v. State, 340 Md. 437, 667 A.2d 166 (1995).

While a court can place reasonable restrictions on the media's use of information obtained in a confidential juvenile proceeding, it cannot limit the media's publication of information which it legitimately collected from other sources, and cannot condition access to the juvenile proceeding upon the media's publication of material specified by the court. Baltimore Sun Co. v. State, 340 Md. 437, 667 A.2d 166 (1995).

Court records confidential. — Court records pertaining to juveniles are held in confidence, and can only be divulged by court order, or for limited educational purposes. Baltimore Sun Co. v. State, 340 Md. 437, 667 A.2d 166 (1995).

Closed proceedings. — Courts may close juvenile proceedings to the public in instances where closure would be impermissible in other court proceedings. Baltimore Sun Co. v. State, 340 Md. 437, 667 A.2d 166 (1995).

Ex parte proceedings. — In a children in need of assistance proceeding conducting a secret session with the children and social worker was error because of the lack of notice and proper recording equipment, not because it amounted to an improper ex parte proceeding. If a rule of court allows such a proceeding, as this section does, it is not per se improper. In re Barry E., 107 Md. App. 206, 667 A.2d 931 (1995).

Jury trial. — Where adults demanded and received a jury trial in Juvenile Court they acquiesced in and recognized the validity of that form of trial. Any error in granting a jury trial was waived by the appellants' being the movants in that seemingly procedural aberration. In re Jeannette L., 71 Md. App. 70, 523 A.2d 1048, cert. denied, 310 Md. 491, 530 A.2d 273 (1987).

Family counseling. — Even absent a "contributing" conviction, juvenile courts have the authority to require parents of children adjudicated "delinquent," "in need of supervision," or "in need of assistance," to participate in family counseling and to cite recalcitrant parents for contempt of court. 62 Op. Att'y Gen. 516 (1977).

Cited in In re Marcus J., 175 Md. App. 703, 931 A.2d 1146 (2007), aff'd, 2008 Md. LEXIS 322 (2008).

Rule 11-111. Masters.

a. **Authority.** 1. Detention or shelter care. A master is authorized to order detention or shelter care in accordance with Rule 11-112 (Detention or Shelter Care) subject to an immediate review by a judge if requested by any party.

2. Other matters. A master is authorized to hear any cases and matters assigned to him by the court, except a hearing on a waiver petition. The findings, conclusions and recommendations of a master do not constitute orders or final action of the court.

b. **Report to the court.** Within ten days following the conclusion of a disposition hearing by a master, he shall transmit to the judge the entire file in the case, together with a written report of his proposed findings of fact, conclusions of law, recommendations and proposed orders with respect to adjudication and disposition. A copy of his report and proposed order shall be served upon each party as provided by Rule 1-321.

c. **Review by court if exceptions filed.** Any party may file exceptions to the master's proposed findings, conclusions, recommendations or proposed orders. Exceptions shall be in writing, filed with the clerk within five days after the master's report is served upon the party, and shall specify those items to which the party excepts, and whether the hearing is to be de novo or on the record.

Upon the filing of exceptions, a prompt hearing shall be scheduled on the exceptions. An excepting party other than the State may elect a hearing de novo or a hearing on the record. If the State is the excepting party, the hearing shall be on the record, supplemented by such additional evidence as the judge considers relevant and to which the parties raise no objection. In either case the hearing shall be limited to those matters to which exceptions have been taken.

d. **Review by court in absence of exceptions.** In the absence of timely and proper exceptions, the master's proposed findings of fact, conclusions of law and recommendations may be adopted by the court and the proposed or other appropriate orders may be entered based on them. The court may remand the case to the master for further hearing, or may, on its own motion, schedule and conduct a further hearing supplemented by such additional evidence as the court considers relevant and to which the parties raise no objection. Action by the court under this section shall be taken within two days after the expiration of the time for filing exceptions. (Amended Nov. 5, 1976, effective Jan. 1, 1977; Apr. 6, 1984, effective July 1, 1984; June 5, 1996, effective Jan. 1, 1997.)

Source. — This Rule is former Rule 911.

Effect of amendments. — The 1996 amendment substituted "Rule 11-112" for "Rule 912" in a. 1.; and added the Source note.

Editor's note. — An Order dated June 5, 1996, effective Jan. 1, 1997, renumbered this Rule, which was formerly Rule 911.

Maryland Law Review. — For note, "Does a Juvenile Court Rehearing on the Record After a Master Has Made Proposed Findings Violate Double Jeopardy or Due Process?" see 39 Md. L. Rev. 395 (1979).

This Rule does not violate Fifth Amendment. — A proceeding under this Rule does not impinge on the purposes of the double jeopardy clause. Swisher v. Brady, 438 U.S. 204, 98 S. Ct. 2699, 57 L. Ed. 2d 705 (1978).

Purpose of Rule. — This Rule is a direct product of the desire of the State to continue using masters to meet the heavy burden of juvenile court caseloads while at the same time assuring that their use not violate the constitutional guarantee against double jeopardy. Swisher v. Brady, 438 U.S. 204, 98 S. Ct. 2699, 57 L. Ed. 2d 705 (1978).

Juvenile is placed in jeopardy when the State begins to offer evidence in an adjudicatory hearing before a master. Aldridge v. Dean, 395 F. Supp. 1161 (D. Md. 1975).

Court may hear testimony of victim. — This Rule permits the court to hear testimony of a victim if it chooses. Hazell v. State, 12 Md. App. 144, 277 A.2d 639, cert. denied, 263 Md. 715 (1971).

A juvenile master may be assigned by the court to hear cases involving waivers of juvenile jurisdiction. Hazell v. State, 12 Md. App. 144, 277 A.2d 639, cert. denied, 263 Md. 715 (1971).

Master may conduct adjudicatory hearing. — A master himself is empowered to conduct an adjudicatory hearing. In re Brown, 13 Md. App. 625, 284 A.2d 441 (1971).

Exceptions to master's proposed findings. — The double jeopardy clause of the federal Constitution does not prohibit State officials, acting in accordance with this Rule, from taking exceptions to a master's proposed findings. Swisher v. Brady, 438 U.S. 204, 98 S. Ct. 2699, 57 L. Ed. 2d 705 (1978).

State's highest court ruled that the public defender's petition for a writ of prohibition, writ of mandamus, or appropriate relief from the trial court's directive that parties meet certain procedural requirements in filing exceptions to the report of a master in juvenile cases or face dismissal of those exceptions had to be dismissed; the trial court, through court rules and statutory law, was delegated the authority to oversee the administration of juvenile cases and, more importantly, the issues with which the public defender was concerned were currently being considered in two cases before the state's intermediate appellate court,

which meant that the public defender had a chance to obtain the relief sough through those proceedings. Forster v. Hargadon, 398 Md. 298, 920 A.2d 1049 (2007).

It was error to dismiss defendant's exceptions to a master's report for failure to comply with a circuit court's exceptions policy that exceeded the requirements of this Rule and § 3-807(c) of the Courts Article; defendant's notice of exceptions complied with the plain language of the Rule and the statute since it pointed to the allegedly erroneous admission of opinion testimony, given by a police officer, who was not qualified as an expert, regarding the operability of the handgun defendant was alleged to have possessed. Although defendant's exception was stated broadly, it adequately communicated that defendant sought a de novo hearing on all issues. In re Marcus J., 175 Md. App. 703, 931 A.2d 1146 (2007), aff'd, 2008 Md. LEXIS 322 (2008).

There is no indication in (c) that the circuit court has discretion to decide whether to conduct a hearing on the exceptions to a master's report; this is consistent with the provision of § 3-807(c)(2) of the Courts Article that specifies that a juvenile who files exceptions may elect a hearing de novo. In re Marcus J., 175 Md. App. 703, 931 A.2d 1146 (2007), aff'd, 2008 Md. LEXIS 322 (2008).

When a master recommended the dismissal of charges against a juvenile based on the State's failure to present any evidence, after the State's motion to continue was denied, the State was entitled, under (c) and § 3-807 of the Courts Article to take exceptions to that recommendation. In re Kevin E., 402 Md. 624, 938 A.2d 826 (2008).

Time for filing exceptions. — In section c, phrase "within five days" of the service of the master's report means that the motion must be filed within a discrete five day period beginning with the date of that service. In re Danielle B., 78 Md. App. 41, 552 A.2d 570 (1989).

Adoption of master's recommendation prior to expiration of five-day period for filing exceptions in error. — In a juvenile proceedings involving a petition alleging that the parties' three children were in need of assistance, a trial court erred in adopting a master's recommendations changing custody of the parties' three children from the mother to the father prior to the expiration of the five days afforded by (c) for the mother to file exceptions. Because California has assumed jurisdiction over the children's custody proceedings, however, the only remedy that the reviewing court was able to provide the mother was to reverse the lower courts' orders and dismiss the case, thereby relieving the mother of the collateral consequences she continued to suffer from the Maryland decision, which made no final disposition on the children in need of assistance allegations. In re Kaela C., 394 Md. 432, 906 A.2d 915 (2006).

When a master recommended the dismissal of charges against a juvenile based on the State's failure to present any evidence, after the State's motion to continue was denied, it was error, under (c) and § 3-807(c)(3) of the Courts Article, for a trial court to adopt that recommendation without waiting the required five days, but, once the recommendation was adopted, that order, rightly or wrongly, became the final order of the court, from which an appeal could be taken, under Rule 8-602(a)(1), and the order was an acquittal, which barred further prosecution, because the order was based on the State's failure to produce sufficient evidence when trial was held as scheduled. In re Kevin E., 402 Md. 624, 938 A.2d 826 (2008).

Right to de novo hearing. — Juvenile was entitled to a de novo hearing, under § 3-807(c) of the Courts Article and this Rule, as to all the matters decided by a master because the juvenile took exception to all matters decided by the master and unequivocally stated that he requested that the matter be set for a hearing de novo. In re Marcus J., 405 Md. 221, 950 A.2d 787 (2008).

Double jeopardy clause precludes subsequent adjudicatory hearing where mistrial had been declared in a previous juvenile adjudicatory hearing, without manifest necessity and without the juvenile's consent. In re Mark R., 294 Md. 244, 449 A.2d 393 (1982).

Scope of review. — The report of a juvenile master is reviewed by the trial court on the same basis as that of any other master authorized by the court, except for the added burden placed on a juvenile judge by the special nature of his role. In re Danielle B., 78 Md. App. 41, 552 A.2d 570 (1989).

Where it was clear from the master's opinion that the conclusion that the state has failed to prove a prima facie case is premised upon not believing the testimony, the circuit court is bound to review the facts as they were presented before making it's own independent disposition of them. This review involves a two-step process: 1) the court must look to the fact and the conclusions reached by the master; 2) the court must make its own judgment of what those facts mean. In re Danielle B., 78 Md. App. 41, 552 A.2d 570 (1989).

Power of judge regarding master's proposals. — Regardless of which party is initially favored by the master's proposals, and regardless of the presence or absence of excep-

tions, the judge is empowered to accept, modify, or reject those proposals. Swisher v. Brady, 438 U.S. 204, 98 S. Ct. 2699, 57 L. Ed. 2d 705 (1978).

Findings of fact do not result in final judgment. — Findings of fact and rulings of law made by a master in juvenile proceedings do not result in a final judgment on the merits. Caldor, Inc. v. Bowden, 330 Md. 632, 625 A.2d 959 (1993).

Findings of fact and rulings of law do not result in final judgment. — In juvenile proceedings, although the master must make written findings of fact, conclusions of law, and recommendations with respect to adjudication and disposition, the master's findings and recommendations are not final orders of the court; it is the chancellor's role, and not the master's, to determine the ultimate rights of the parties. In re Michael G., 107 Md. App. 257, 667 A.2d 956 (1995).

Findings, conclusions and recommendations of a master do not constitute orders or final action of the court, under (a). In re Kevin E., 402 Md. 624, 938 A.2d 826 (2008).

Supplemental findings. — To the extent the juvenile court judge makes supplemental findings in a manner permitted by this Rule — either sua sponte, in response to the State's exceptions, or in response to the juvenile's exceptions, and either on the record or on a record supplemented by evidence to which the parties raise no objection — he does so without violating the constraints of the double jeopardy clause. Swisher v. Brady, 438 U.S. 204, 98 S. Ct. 2699, 57 L. Ed. 2d 705 (1978).

Additional evidence in de novo hearing. — It is not error to receive additional evidence as to a child in need of assistance (CINA) determination in a de novo hearing. In re Michael W., 89 Md. App. 612, 599 A.2d 458 (1991).

Authority to reject determination. — Juvenile court had authority to reject child in need of assistance (CINA) determination made by master, even though exception had been taken to proposed disposition and not to recommended adjudication, as the CINA determination was element of disposition hearing. In re Michael W., 89 Md. App. 612, 599 A.2d 458 (1991).

Rule governs over CJ § 3-813. — Although this Rule differs from CJ § 3-813, in significant aspects, under Maryland decisional law, the Rule governs. Swisher v. Brady, 438 U.S. 204, 98 S. Ct. 2699, 57 L. Ed. 2d 705 (1978).

Applied in In re Levon A., 124 Md. App. 103, 720 A.2d 1232 (1998).

Rule 11-112. Detention or shelter care.

a. **Emergency detention or shelter care.** 1. Authority. The court or an intake officer may authorize emergency detention or shelter care of a child taken into custody in accordance with Section 3-815 (b) of the Courts Article.

2. Report to court — Petition for continued detention or shelter care. If a child is placed in emergency detention or shelter care, the intake officer shall, on the next day the court is sitting:

(i) report that fact to the court, together with the circumstances that led to the child being placed in emergency detention or shelter care; and

(ii) if continued detention or shelter care is sought, file a petition for continued detention or shelter care showing cause why continued detention or shelter care is warranted.

3. Hearing. If a petition for continued detention or shelter care is filed pursuant to this Rule, a hearing shall be held on the day the petition is filed and the respondent shall be brought to court for the hearing. The hearing may be postponed or continued by the court for good cause shown, but it may not be postponed for more than eight days following the commencement of respondent's emergency detention or shelter care. Reasonable notice of the date and time of the hearing shall be given to the respondent, and if possible to his parent and his counsel, if known.

b. **Continued detention or shelter care pending adjudication or waiver.**

1. Finding. Detention or shelter care may not be continued beyond emergency detention or shelter care unless after a hearing the court finds that one or more of the circumstances stated in Section 3-815 (b) of the Courts Article exists.

2. Maximum period of detention or shelter care. Continued detention or shelter care pending the adjudicatory or waiver hearing may not be ordered for a period of more than thirty days.

c. **Continued detention or shelter care after waiver or adjudicatory hearing.** The court may, on petition or of its own motion, continue detention or shelter care for a period not longer than thirty days after a denial of a petition for waiver or an adjudicatory hearing.

d. **Title 5 not applicable.** Title 5 of these rules does not apply to detention or shelter care hearings. (Amended Nov. 5, 1976, effective Jan. 1, 1977; Dec. 15, 1993, effective July 1, 1994; June 5, 1996, effective Jan. 1, 1997.)

Cross references. — See Rule 11-113 (Waiver of Jurisdiction) for procedures following waiver.

Source. — This Rule is former Rule 912.

Effect of amendments. — The 1996 amendment substituted "Rule 11-113" for "Rule 913" in the Cross reference note; and added the Source note.

Editor's note. — An Order dated June 5, 1996, effective Jan. 1, 1997, renumbered this Rule, which was formerly Rule 912.

University of Baltimore Law Forum. — For discussion of police investigative procedures and juveniles, see 16, No. 1 U. Balt. Law Forum 6 (1986).

Right to present testimony. — In hearings under § 3-815(c)(2)(i) of the Courts Article and (a)(2) of this Rule, appellant mothers were entitled to present testimonial evidence to contest the allegations in appellee county agencies' petitions for orders for emergency shelter care. In re Damien F., 182 Md. App. 546, 958 A.2d 402 (2008).

Rule 11-113. Waiver of jurisdiction.

a. **Initiating waiver.** 1. On the court's own motion. Upon the filing of a juvenile petition alleging delinquency the court may on its own motion waive its exclusive original jurisdiction so that the respondent may be tried in the criminal court.

2. Petition by State's Attorney — Requirements. The State's Attorney may file a petition requesting the court to waive its exclusive jurisdiction over a juvenile respondent alleged to be delinquent. The petition shall:

(i) be filed with or after the filing of a juvenile petition, but before the commencement of an adjudicatory hearing;

(ii) comply with the provisions of Section 3-817 (a) of the Courts Article; and

(iii) state in clear, concise and specific language the reasons why the State's Attorney requests the waiver, taking into account the factors required to be considered by the court under Section 3-817 (c) and (d) of the Courts Article.

b. **Investigation.** Upon the filing of a waiver petition, the court shall order that a waiver investigation be made. The report of the waiver investigation shall include all social records that are to be made available to the court at the waiver hearing, and a copy of the report shall be served upon counsel for the parties at least two days before the hearing.

c. **Hearing.** 1. Hearing required — Exceptions. Except as provided by sections e and f of this Rule, the court may not waive its jurisdiction without first conducting a waiver hearing.

2. Time of hearing. The hearing shall take place

(i) after notice has been given pursuant to Rule 11-110 (Hearings — Generally).

(ii) prior to the commencement of an adjudicatory hearing.

3. Purpose of hearing. A waiver hearing is for the sole purpose of determining whether the court should waive its jurisdiction. The court shall assume, for purposes of that determination, that the respondent committed the delinquent act or crime alleged in the juvenile petition.

d. **Consideration in determining waiver.** In determining whether to waive its jurisdiction, the court shall comply with the provisions of Section 3-817 (c), (d), and (e) of the Courts Article. In the interest of justice, the court may decline to require strict application of the rules in Title 5, except those relating to the competency of witnesses.

e. **Summary review.** If the court has once waived its jurisdiction with respect to a respondent who again comes before the court on a juvenile petition alleging delinquency, the court, on its motion or on a waiver petition filed by the State's Attorney, may waive its jurisdiction in the subsequent proceeding after summary review and without a hearing.

f. **Adult respondent.** Jurisdiction over an adult respondent charged under Section 3-831 of the Courts Article shall be waived by the court upon the motion of the State's Attorney or the adult respondent. Jurisdiction may be waived by the court upon its own initiative or after a hearing upon the motion of any party, if charges against the adult respondent arising out of the same incident are pending in the criminal court.

g. **Order.** 1. Jurisdiction waived. If the court concludes that its jurisdiction should be waived, it shall:

(a) state the grounds for its decision on the record or in a written memorandum filed with the clerk.

(b) enter an order:

(i) waiving its jurisdiction and ordering the respondent held for trial under the appropriate criminal procedure;

(ii) placing the respondent in the custody of the sheriff or other appropriate officer in an adult detention facility pending a pretrial release hearing pursuant to Rule 4-222.

2. Juvenile petition a charging document pending bail hearing. The juvenile petition shall be considered a charging document for the purpose of detaining the respondent pending a bail hearing.

3. True copies to be furnished appropriate officer. A true copy of the juvenile petition and of the court's signed order shall be furnished forthwith by the clerk to the appropriate officer pending a bail hearing.

h. **Effect of appeal.** Deleted Mar. 3, 1987, effective July 1, 1987. (Amended Nov. 5, 1976, effective Jan. 1, 1977; Apr. 6, 1984, effective July 1, 1984; Mar. 3, 1987, effective July 1, 1987; Dec. 15, 1993, effective July 1, 1994; June 5, 1996, effective Jan. 1, 1997; Oct. 5, 1999.)

Source. — This Rule is former Rule 913.

Effect of amendments. — The 1996 amendment substituted "Rule 11-110" for "Rule 910" in c. 2. (i); and added the Source note.

The 1999 amendment substituted "Section 3-817 (c), (d), and (e)" for "Section 3-817 (c) and (d)" in d.

Editor's note. — An Order dated June 5, 1996, effective Jan. 1, 1997, renumbered this Rule, which was formerly Rule 913.

This Rule establishes procedural requirements for a waiver of jurisdiction. Thomas v. State, 10 Md. App. 458, 271 A.2d 197 (1970), cert. denied, 261 Md. 729 (1971).

Right to jury trial recognized. — Because the penalty prescribed for violation of CJ § 3-831 is substantial, a trial by jury is required, if demanded. CJ § 3-804 (c) and section f of this Rule are but recognition of that right. In re Jeannette L., 71 Md. App. 70, 523 A.2d 1048, cert. denied, 310 Md. 491, 530 A.2d 273 (1987).

Summary review to be conducted in proceeding meeting due process requirements. — Although a "full blown" hearing is not required to waive jurisdiction, the due process clause requires that summary review may only be conducted in a proceeding in

which the juvenile is provided at least with adequate notice, the right to counsel and the right to be present. In re Michael W., 53 Md. App. 271, 452 A.2d 1278 (1982).

Discretion of juvenile judge. — Waiver in a juvenile case is committed to the sound discretion of the juvenile judge, to be disturbed on appeal only upon a finding that such discretion has been abused. In re Appeal No. 646, 35 Md. App. 94, 369 A.2d 150 (1977).

Waiver hearing was improper. — A waiver hearing was patently improper at the stage where there had already been an adjudicatory hearing. In re Nawrocki, 15 Md. App. 252, 289 A.2d 846, cert. denied, 266 Md. 741 (1972).

Degree of proof. — Waiver is justified where a preponderance of the legally sufficient evidence shows that such a determination is proper in light of the factors to be considered under CJ § 3-817. Hazell v. State, 12 Md. App. 144, 277 A.2d 639 (1971).

Nothing in the Constitution, State or federal, requires the State to satisfy the court beyond a reasonable doubt that waiver is proper; the inquiry at the waiver hearing does not require a finding of guilt or innocence, or proof of the elements of any criminal offense.

Hazell v. State, 12 Md. App. 144, 277 A.2d 639, cert. denied, 263 Md. 715 (1971).

Statement of grounds for decision, separate from order of transfer, required when case is transferred to criminal court. — If a case is transferred to criminal court the statement by the court of the grounds for the decision, separate from the order of transfer, shall be made as required by this Rule. In re Toporzycki, 14 Md. App. 298, 287 A.2d 66 (1972).

Purpose of the statement required by section g 1 (a) of this Rule is to provide the parties and the reviewing court with the benefit of the trial court's reasons for its determination that the juvenile is an unfit subject for juvenile rehabilitative measures. In re Appeal No. 646, 35 Md. App. 94, 369 A.2d 150 (1977).

Contents of statement. — The statement required by section g 1 (a) of this Rule need not contain a point by point exposition of the trial court's consideration of each of the five enumerated criteria in CJ § 3-817. At a minimum, however, the statement should contain such factual findings as would permit the conclusion that the trial court has considered the criteria individually and in relation to each other and the basis on which it has reached its conclusion. In re Appeal No. 646, 35 Md. App. 94, 369 A.2d 150 (1977).

Suspension of lower court's jurisdiction pending appeal. — If an appeal is noted from an order of waiver in accordance with the Maryland Rules, the criminal court, pending the determination of the appeal has no jurisdiction over the case. The Court of Special Appeals is then vested with the exclusive power and jurisdiction over the subject matter of the proceedings, and the authority and control of the lower court with reference thereto are suspended. Aye v. State, 17 Md. App. 32, 299 A.2d 513 (1973).

When criminal court may proceed to try case. — Unless the authority over and control of a criminal case are suspended by an appeal to the Court of Special Appeals from an order of waiver, the criminal court may, upon termination of the period within which such appeal may be filed, then proceed to hear, try and determine the case against a child. Aye v. State, 17 Md. App. 32, 299 A.2d 513 (1973).

Bad faith not shown. — There was nothing in the record to show bad faith on the part of the State's Attorney in offering into evidence a waiver of jurisdiction by the juvenile court. Halstead v. State, 4 Md. App. 121, 241 A.2d 439 (1968).

No stenographic transcript. — See Jefferson v. State, 218 Md. 397, 147 A.2d 204 (1958).

Cited in Gaines v. State, — Md. App. —, — A.3d — (Sept. 7, 2011).

Rule 11-114. Adjudicatory hearing.

a. **Requirement.** After a juvenile petition has been filed, and unless jurisdiction has been waived, the court shall hold an adjudicatory hearing.

b. **Scheduling of hearing.** 1. Adjudicatory hearing. An adjudicatory hearing shall be held within sixty days after the juvenile petition is served on the respondent unless a waiver petition is filed, in which case an adjudicatory hearing shall be held within thirty days after the court's decision to retain jurisdiction at the conclusion of the waiver hearing. However, upon motion made on the record within these time limits by the petitioner or the respondent, the administrative judge of the county or a judge designated by him, for extraordinary cause shown, may extend the time within which the adjudicatory hearing may be held. The judge shall state on the record the cause which requires an extension and specify the number of days of the extension.

2. Prehearing detention or shelter care. If the respondent is in detention or shelter care, the adjudicatory hearing shall be held within thirty days from the date on which the court ordered continued detention or shelter care. If an adjudicatory hearing is not held within thirty days, the respondent shall be released on the conditions imposed by the court pending an adjudicatory hearing, which hearing shall be held within the time limits set forth in subsection 1 of this section.

c. **Presentation of evidence.** If the juvenile petition alleges delinquency, the State's Attorney shall present the evidence in support of it unless excused by the court. In all other cases the appropriate governmental or social agency or other persons authorized by the court shall present the evidence.

d. **Respondent's right to remain silent.** A respondent may remain silent as of right during an adjudicatory hearing on an allegation of delinquency and in all other cases where permitted on constitutional grounds; and the respondent shall be advised of this right by the court.

e. **Evidence — Proof of allegations of petition.** 1. Petition alleging delinquency. The allegations of a juvenile petition that the respondent has committed a delinquent act must be proved beyond a reasonable doubt. An uncorroborated extra judicial confession is not sufficient to establish that the respondent committed the delinquent act.

2. Petition alleging contributing. The allegations of a juvenile petition that an adult respondent violated Section 3-831 of the Courts Article must be proved beyond a reasonable doubt.

3. Other cases. All other allegations of a juvenile petition must be proved by a preponderance of the evidence.

f. **Adjudication — Finding — Adjudicatory order.** If the hearing is conducted by a judge, at its conclusion, he shall announce and dictate to the court stenographer or reporter, or prepare and file with the clerk, an adjudicatory order stating the grounds upon which he bases his adjudication. If the hearing is conducted by a master, the procedures set forth in Rule 11-111 (Masters) shall be followed. (Amended Nov. 5, 1976, effective Jan. 1, 1977; Nov. 13, 1981, effective Jan. 1, 1982; June 5, 1996, effective Jan. 1, 1997.)

Source. — This Rule is former Rule 914.

Effect of amendments. — The 1996 amendment substituted "Rule 11-111" for "Rule 911" in the second sentence of f.; and added the Source note.

Editor's note. — An Order dated June 5, 1996, effective Jan. 1, 1997, renumbered this Rule, which was formerly Rule 914.

University of Baltimore Law Forum. — For note, "Recent Development: In re Anthony W.: The Accomplice Corroboration Rule Applies to Juvenile Proceedings," see 36 U. Balt. L.F. 65 (2005).

Legislative intent. — The General Assembly intended to maintain the distinct functions of the adjudicatory hearing and the dispositional hearing by eliminating all inquiry into the child's need for guidance or treatment from the former, thereby preventing irrelevant and potentially prejudicial facts from being taken into consideration in the adjudication of pending charges. In re Ernest J., 52 Md. App. 56, 447 A.2d 97 (1982).

"Adjudicatory hearing." — The "adjudicatory hearing" is not that phase of the proceeding, frequently conducted ex parte and frequently conducted in camera, whereat the supervising judge ratifies, modifies or rejects

the findings and recommendations of the master. In re Brown, 13 Md. App. 625, 284 A.2d 441 (1971).

The clear contemplation of the Maryland law is that the "adjudicatory hearing" is that phase of the total proceeding whereto witnesses are summoned; whereat they are sworn, confronted with the alleged delinquent, examined and cross-examined; whereat their demeanor is observed, their credibility assessed and their testimony weighed; whereat the testimony is subject to the rules of evidence and is transcribed by a court reporter; whereat the alleged delinquent is represented by counsel and where he enjoys the right to remain silent; whereat the State's Attorney marshals and presents the evidence for the petitioner; and whereat the presiding judge or master makes and announces his finding including "a brief statement of the grounds upon which . . . [he] bases . . . [his] determination." In re Brown, 13 Md. App. 625, 284 A.2d 441 (1971).

"Held." — As used in this Rule, "held" does not mean completed, but means that the hearing should be initiated within thirty days and completed with a reasonable degree of continuity; by a reasonable degree of continuity, it is meant that a hearing once begun must continue, insofar as possible, on a day to day basis until completed. In re Vanessa C., 104 Md. App. 452, 656 A.2d 795 (1995).

Juvenile did not waive delay in holding adjudicatory hearing, and petition against juvenile had to be dismissed as "extraordinary circumstances" did not exist to justify the delay in completing the hearing, which the juvenile court stretched out over several months based solely on its crowded docket, as the law contemplated such a hearing would be completed within a reasonable time and, insofar as possible, would be conducted on a day-to-day basis. In re Ryan S., 369 Md. 26, 797 A.2d 39 (2002).

Primary purpose of adjudicatory hearing is to determine the merits of the allegation in the petition. In re Ernest J., 52 Md. App. 56, 447 A.2d 97 (1982).

A juvenile proceeding is not a criminal proceeding. Pennsylvania ex rel. Warren v. Warren, 204 Md. 467, 105 A.2d 488 (1954); Moquin v. State, 216 Md. 524, 140 A.2d 914 (1958).

The adjudicatory hearing is not a criminal proceeding. In re Appeal No. 544, 25 Md. App. 26, 332 A.2d 680 (1975).

Department of social services does not have unilateral right to withdraw CINA petition. — Juvenile court erred in dismissing a child in need of assistance (CINA) petition based on its view that the local department of social services (DSS) had a unilateral right to withdraw its petition over a child's objection because the juvenile court should have declined DSS's dismissal request and conducted an adjudicatory hearing on the merits of the petition when DSS did not have a unilateral right to withdraw a petition prior to an adjudication when the child objected, and the child was entitled to an adjudication to ensure that she was receiving proper care and attention; nothing in Title 11 of the Maryland Rules suggests that DSS, as the petitioner in a CINA proceeding, has a unilateral right to dismiss a CINA action after the petition has been filed. In re Najasha B., 409 Md. 20, 972 A.2d 845 (2009).

This Rule anticipates breach of its provisions in one part of its mandate, but imposes a sanction substantially less severe than dismissal of the petition. In re Howard L., 50 Md. App. 498, 438 A.2d 939 (1982).

Master is empowered to conduct an adjudicatory hearing. — A master himself is empowered to conduct an adjudicatory hearing. In re Brown, 13 Md. App. 625, 284 A.2d 441 (1971).

Time interval between waiver and adjudicatory hearings. — While setting forth no minimum time interval between a waiver

hearing and an adjudicatory hearing, section b 1 of this Rule sets forth a maximum period of 30 days from the conclusion of the waiver hearing. Parojinog v. State, 282 Md. 256, 384 A.2d 86 (1978).

Thirty-day requirement in this Rule must be read in conjunction with method for time computation set forth in Maryland Rules. In re Stephen J., 48 Md. App. 736, 429 A.2d 307 (1981).

Due process violated by delay. — Since neither the statutory provision nor the applicable court rule protected a juvenile against a delay in holding an adjudicatory proceeding where no petition had been served and the juvenile had not been detained, due process principles precluded holding of the delayed proceeding, where the juvenile and his mother had attempted to provide current address information to the authorities. In re Thomas J., 372 Md. 50, 811 A.2d 310 (2002).

Degree of proof. — Only in a determination that a child is delinquent and in cases in which an adult is charged under the subtitle "Juvenile Causes" in the Courts Article must the allegations be proved beyond a reasonable doubt. Woods v. Department of Social Servs., 11 Md. App. 10, 272 A.2d 92, cert. denied, 261 Md. 724, 730, 404 U.S. 965, 92 S. Ct. 340, 30 L. Ed. 2d 285 (1971).

Sufficient evidence demonstrated beyond a reasonable doubt that appellant, a juvenile, was involved in an attempt to possess marijuana, in violation of § 5-601(a) of the Criminal Law Article, because, although no marijuana was recovered from appellant's person, the facts support a rational inference that appellant engaged in multiple substantial steps towards the commission of illegal possession of marijuana. In re Caitlin N., 192 Md. App. 251, 994 A.2d 454 (2010).

Uncorroborated accomplice evidence insufficient basis for delinquency adjudication. — As a matter of policy, rather than constitutional or statutory interpretation, the rule applicable to adult criminal proceedings requiring corroboration of accomplice testimony was held applicable in the case of a young person who had been adjudicated delinquent for vandalizing a school bus based solely on the testimony of two companions; the fact that the companions were accused of theft rather than malicious destruction of property because they claimed to have entered the bus after the subject juvenile was of no significance to the holding. In re Anthony W., 159 Md. App. 514, 859 A.2d 679 (2004), rev'd on other grounds and remanded, 388 Md. 251, 879 A.2d 717, 2005 Md. LEXIS 458 (2005).

A disposition hearing separate and distinct from a delinquency adjudication hearing is required. — That a disposition hearing separate and distinct from the delinquency adjudication hearing is required subsequent to the finding of delinquency is plainly mandated by CJ §§ 3-819 and 3-820, and by the provisions of this Rule and Rule 915 (now Rule 11-115). In re Wooten, 13 Md. App. 521, 284 A.2d 32 (1971).

A disposition hearing separate and distinct from the delinquency adjudication hearing is required subsequent to the finding of delinquency and is plainly mandated by CJ §§ 3-819 and 3-820, and by the provisions of this Rule and Rule 915 (now Rule 11-115). The reason for such a bifurcated process is equally clear. The adjudicatory hearing is solely to determine the merits of the allegations of delinquency. In re Roberts, 13 Md. App. 644, 284 A.2d 621 (1971).

Interwoven adjudicatory and disposition hearing violated rules. — Where the adjudicatory hearing and disposition hearing were interwoven and the juveniles were actually ordered committed to the Maryland Training School before they were adjudged "delinquent," the hearing before the juvenile judge was violative of the rules. In re Arnold, 12 Md. App. 384, 278 A.2d 658 (1971).

Sanction for violation of Rule. — In determining whether dismissal is an appropriate sanction for violation of this Rule, such as a violation of the time limitations in this Rule, a judge presiding over a juvenile cause should examine the totality of the circumstances as required by Rule 1-201. In doing so, the judge must keep in mind the overriding purpose of the juvenile statute along with the fact that this purpose will ordinarily not be served by dismissal of the juvenile proceeding. Neither the juvenile nor society should be denied the benefits of the juvenile's rehabilitation because of a technical violation of scheduling requirements. In re Keith W., 310 Md. 99, 527 A.2d 35 (1987).

Rule not violated. — It was not error for a juvenile court to deny the motion of appellant, a juvenile, to hold an adjudicatory hearing within 60 days, which alleged that the 60-day time period within which an adjudicatory hearing had to be held, under (b), began running when appellant received formal notice of the allegations of a petition to find appellant was a delinquent child, because, under the plain language of the Rule, the 60-day period began when appellant was actually served with the petition, which occurred on the day of appellant's adjudicatory hearing. In re Caitlin N., 192 Md. App. 251, 994 A.2d 454 (2010).

Findings not res judicata in restitution proceeding. — Findings of adjudicatory proceeding against child were not res judicata as to parent in restitution proceeding. In re Appeal No. 769, 25 Md. App. 565, 335 A.2d 204 (1975), superseded on other grounds by statute as stated in In re Delric H., 150 Md. App. 234, 819 A.2d 1117 (2003).

Applied in In re Timothy C., 376 Md. 414, 829 A.2d 1024 (2003); In re Nathaniel A., 160 Md. App. 581, 864 A.2d 1066 (2005), cert. denied, — Md. —, 872 A.2d 47 (2005).

Quoted in In re Blessen H., 392 Md. 684, 898 A.2d 980 (2006).

Stated in In re Anthony W., 388 Md. 251, 879 A.2d 717 (2005).

Cited in In re Delric H., 150 Md. App. 234, 819 A.2d 1117 (2003); In re Lavar D., 189 Md. App. 526, 985 A.2d 102 (2009).

Rule 11-115. Disposition hearing.

a. **Hearing — Scheduling.** If after an adjudicatory hearing the court determines that the allegations of the petition at issue in the adjudicatory hearing have been sustained, it shall promptly schedule a separate disposition hearing. The disposition hearing shall be held no later than thirty days after the conclusion of the adjudicatory hearing.

b. **Disposition — Judge or master.** The disposition made by the court shall be in accordance with Section 3-820 (b) of the Courts Article. If the disposition hearing is conducted by a judge, and his order includes placement of the child outside the home, the judge shall announce in open court and shall prepare and file with the clerk, a statement of the reasons for the placement. If the hearing is conducted by a master, the procedures of Rule 11-111 shall be followed. In the interest of justice, the judge or master may decline to require strict application of the rules in Title 5, except those relating to the competency of witnesses. A commitment recommended by a master is subject to approval by the court in accordance with Rule 11-111, but may be implemented in advance of court approval.

c. **Placement in a State mental hospital.** 1. Standard for commitment. A court may not commit a child to the Department of Health and Mental Hygiene for inpatient care and treatment at a State mental hospital unless the court finds that

(a) the child has a mental disorder, and

(b) the child needs inpatient care and treatment for the protection of himself or others, and

(c) the child is unable or unwilling to be voluntarily admitted to such hospital, and

(d) there is no less restrictive form of intervention available which is consistent with the child's condition and welfare.

2. Order for evaluation. If the court has reason to believe that a child should be committed to the Department of Health and Mental Hygiene for inpatient care and treatment at a State mental hospital, it shall order that the child be evaluated, pursuant to Section 3-818 of the Courts Article and Rule 11-105. The order shall require the agency conducting the evaluation to submit a written report setting forth its findings regarding

(a) the extent to which the standard for commitment set forth in subsection c 1 of this Rule is met,

(b) the bases for these findings,

(c) its recommended disposition, and

(d) the reasons for its recommended disposition.

The evaluation shall be conducted on an outpatient basis if, considering the child's condition, that is feasible and appropriate. Where an inpatient evaluation is necessary, the court may authorize the admission of the child to a State mental hospital for a period not to exceed 30 days for the purpose of the evaluation.

3. Modification or vacation of commitment order. (a) Periodic review. A commitment order issued under section b of this Rule shall require the Department or the hospital to file progress reports with the court at six-month intervals throughout the commitment. The report shall comply with the requirements of an evaluation report under subsection c 2 of this Rule. A copy of each report shall be given to the child's attorney of record. The court shall review each report promptly and consider whether the commitment order should be modified or vacated. Upon the request of any party, the Department, or the hospital, or upon its own motion, the court shall grant a hearing for the purpose of hearing testimony pertinent to its review.

(b) Other review. In addition to the periodic review provided for in subsection c 3 (a) of this Rule, the court may at any time upon the petition of any party, the Department, or the hospital, or upon its own motion, modify or vacate its order, provided that the court may not modify or vacate its order without notice and opportunity for hearing.

d. **Commitment to Department of Social Services.** In cases in which a child is committed to a local department of social services for placement outside the child's home, the court, within 18 months after the original placement and periodically thereafter at intervals not greater than 18 months, shall conduct a review hearing to determine whether and under what circumstances the child's commitment to the local department of social services should continue. Considerations pertinent to the determination include whether the child should (1) be returned home, (2) be continued in foster care for a specified period, (3) be placed for adoption, or (4) because of the child's special needs or circumstances, be continued in foster care on a permanent or long-term basis. The hearing shall be conducted as prescribed in Rule 11-110 or, if conducted by a master, as prescribed in Rule 11-111, except that the child's presence shall not be required if presence at the hearing is likely to cause serious physical, mental, or emotional harm to the child. (Amended Nov. 5, 1976, effective Jan. 1, 1977; Apr. 18, 1980, effective July 1, 1980; June 23, 1983, effective July 1, 1983; Dec. 15, 1993, effective July 1, 1994; June 5, 1996, effective Jan. 1, 1997.)

Source. — This Rule is former Rule 915.

Effect of amendments. — The 1996 amendment substituted "Rule 11-111" for "Rule 911" twice in b.; substituted "Rule 11-105" for "Rule 905" in the introductory language of c. 2.; in d., substituted "Rule 11-110" for "Rule 910" and substituted "Rule 11-111" for "Rule 911"; and added the Source note.

Editor's note. — An Order dated June 5, 1996, effective Jan. 1, 1997, renumbered this Rule, which was formerly Rule 915.

Applicability of section b. — Section b applies to placement of a child outside of the home following a determination on allegations contained in a petition. In re Jessica M., 72 Md. App. 7, 527 A.2d 766 (1987), aff'd, 312 Md. 93, 538 A.2d 305 (1988).

Direction of dispositional process. — The dispositional process is directed toward the termination of a committal or other disposition when the juvenile court finds the child to be rehabilitated, and directed away from setting mandatory periods of commitment, which would be more in the nature of punishment. In re No. 1140, S.T. 1977, 39 Md. App. 609, 387 A.2d 315 (1978).

Finding that juvenile is not in need of services. — A judge is not authorized to retain jurisdiction after expressly finding at the disposition that a juvenile is not in need of services or treatment; therefore, the court erred in finding that the juvenile was a delinquent child and in failing to dismiss the delinquency petition. In re Charles K., 135 Md. App. 84, 761 A.2d 978 (2000).

A disposition hearing separate and distinct from a delinquency adjudication hearing is required. — That a disposition hearing separate and distinct from the delinquency adjudication hearing is required subsequent to the finding of delinquency is plainly mandated by CJ §§ 3-819 and 3-820, and by the provisions of former Rule 914 (now Rule 11-114) and this Rule. In re Wooten, 13 Md. App. 521, 284 A.2d 32 (1971).

A disposition hearing separate and distinct from the delinquency adjudication hearing is required subsequent to the finding of delinquency and is plainly mandated by CJ §§ 3-819 and 3-820, and by the provisions of former Rule 914 (now Rule 11-114) and this Rule. The reason for such a bifurcated process is equally clear. The adjudicatory hearing is solely to determine the merits of the allegations of delinquency. In re Roberts, 13 Md. App. 644, 284 A.2d 621 (1971).

Interwoven adjudicatory and disposition hearing violated rules. — Where the adjudicatory hearing and disposition hearing were interwoven and the juveniles were actually ordered committed to the Maryland Training School before they were adjudged "delinquent," the hearing before the juvenile judge was violative of the rules. In re Arnold, 12 Md. App. 384, 278 A.2d 658 (1971).

No requirement that disposition hearing be completed within 30 days. — No useful purpose is served by interpreting this Rule to require that the disposition hearing must be completed within 30 days of the adjudicatory hearing; all that this Rule necessitates is that the disposition hearing be commenced within that time frame, provided exigent circumstances do not foreclose that possibility. In re Phillip P., 50 Md. App. 235, 437 A.2d 892 (1981).

Unlike section b, section d does not require the court to announce its reasons in open court and to prepare a statement thereof. In re Jessica M., 72 Md. App. 7, 527 A.2d 766 (1987), aff'd, 312 Md. 93, 538 A.2d 305 (1988).

Dismissal of proceeding concerning ju-

venile is not proper sanction for violation of 30-day requirement of this Rule. In re Dewayne H., 290 Md. 401, 430 A.2d 76 (1981).

Adoption of master's recommendation prior to expiration of five-day period for filing exceptions in error. — In a juvenile proceedings involving a petition alleging that the parties' three children were in need of assistance, a trial court erred in adopting a master's recommendations changing custody of the parties' three children from the mother to the father prior to the expiration of the five days afforded by Md. R. 11-111(c) for the mother to file exceptions. Because California has assumed jurisdiction over the children's custody proceedings, however, the only remedy that the reviewing court was able to provide the mother was to reverse the lower courts' orders and dismiss the case, thereby relieving the mother of the collateral consequences she continued to suffer from the Maryland decision, which made no final disposition on the children in need of assistance allegations. In re Kaela C., 394 Md. 432, 906 A.2d 915 (2006).

Section b is mandatory. In re Virgil M., 46 Md. App. 654, 421 A.2d 105 (1980).

Reasons upon which disposition made. — Section b refers to CJ § 3-820 and indicates that among the reasons upon which the judge must base his determination as to the placement of a child are the best interests of the child and the feasibility of programs which allow the child to remain at home. In re Virgil M., 46 Md. App. 654, 421 A.2d 105 (1980).

Statement of reasons for placement outside home. — When the Court of Appeals adopted this Rule, it expected, desired and required by way of reasons under section b for placement of a child outside his home something more than perfunctory statements in the court's summary. In re Appeal No. 1327, 32 Md. App. 478, 361 A.2d 156 (1976).

When child is placed in custody of Department of Health and Mental Hygiene for inpatient care at a State mental hospital, section b of this Rule as well as CJ § 3-820 (h) (duplicated on April 18, 1980 as Md. Rule 915 c) spell out the prerequisites of such commitment, based upon clear and convincing evidence. In re Jeffrey L., 50 Md. App. 268, 437 A.2d 255 (1981).

Finding of fact sustained. — When a master or judge makes a finding of facts sustained, he or she determines that the allegations set forth in the State of Maryland's petition are supported by the evidence presented. In re Marcus J., 405 Md. 221, 950 A.2d 787 (2008).

Cited in In re Norberto C., 133 Md. App. 558, 758 A.2d 637 (2000); In re Damon M., 362 Md. 429, 765 A.2d 624 (2001); In re Delric H., 150 Md. App. 234, 819 A.2d 1117 (2003); In re Ashley E., 158 Md. App. 144, 854 A.2d 893 (2004), aff'd, 387 Md. 260, 874 A.2d 998 (2005).

Rule 11-116. Modification or vacation of order.

a. **Revisory power.** An order of the court may be modified or vacated if the court finds that action to be in the best interest of the child or the public, except in cases involving commitment of a child to the Department of Health and Mental Hygiene for placement in a State mental hospital. In cases involving such commitment the court shall proceed as provided in Rule 11-115. (Amended Nov. 7, 1976, effective Jan. 1, 1997; Apr. 18, 1980, effective July 1, 1980.)

b. **Sua sponte or on petition.** The court may proceed under section a of this Rule on its own motion, or on the petition of any party or other person, institution or agency having supervision or custody of the respondent, setting forth in concise terms the grounds upon which the relief is requested. If the court proceeds on its own motion, the order shall set forth the grounds on which it is based.

c. **Hearing — When required.** If the relief sought under section a of this Rule is for revocation of probation and for the commitment of a respondent, the court shall pass an order to show cause why the relief should not be granted and setting a date and time for a hearing. The clerk shall cause a copy of the petition and Show Cause Order to be served upon the parties. In all other cases, the court may grant or deny the relief, in whole or in part, without a hearing.

d. **Conduct of hearing.** In the interest of justice, at any hearing held pursuant to this Rule the court may decline to require strict application of the rules in Title 5, except those relating to the competency of witnesses. (Amended Nov. 5, 1976, effective Jan. 1, 1977; Dec. 15, 1993, effective July 1, 1994; June 5, 1996, effective Jan. 1, 1997.)

Source. — This Rule is former Rule 916.

Effect of amendments. — The 1996 amendment substituted "Rule 11-115" for "Rule 915" in the second sentence of a.; and added the Source note.

Editor's note. — An Order dated June 5, 1996, effective Jan. 1, 1997, renumbered this Rule, which was formerly Rule 916.

Maryland Law Review. — For article, "Maryland's Exchangeable Children: A Critique of Maryland's System of Providing Services to Mentally Handicapped Children," see 42 Md. L. Rev. 823 (1983).

Final, appealable order. — Court of appeals had jurisdiction to consider the appeal of petitioner, a juvenile, of a trial court's order denying petitioner's motion to vacate, under this Rule, a delinquency finding because the order was final, as (1) the trial court denied the motion in full, and (2) the record indicated that the trial court did not intend to take any further action on the motion. In re Elrich S., 416 Md. 15, 5 A.3d 27 (2010).

Constitutional considerations may preclude availability of relief. — Constitutional considerations other than the double jeopardy prohibition may preclude the availability of relief under this Rule; for example, due process principles would limit the time period within which reconsideration may be granted and would preclude the State from repeatedly seeking reconsiderations of the same petition. In re John P., 311 Md. 700, 537 A.2d 263 (1988).

Ineffective assistance of counsel. — When a trial court denied the motion of petitioner, a juvenile, to vacate a delinquency finding, the trial court did not fail to recognize that petitioner's claims of ineffective assistance of counsel could be a basis for relief, under this Rule, because, while the trial court expressed doubt about the use of this Rule as a post-conviction vehicle, the trial court so used

the Rule, acknowledging that the Rule gave the court revisory powers over delinquency orders. In re Elrich S., 416 Md. 15, 5 A.3d 27 (2010).

Operation of this Rule is unlimited with respect to the time running from the original order. In re No. 1140, S.T. 1977, 39 Md. App. 609, 387 A.2d 315 (1978).

But not guarantee of limited commitment. — Reliance on this Rule alone will not guarantee that children committed under CJ § 3-820 or the general involuntary admission provisions will remain committed only so long as is medically necessary. Johnson v. Solomon, 484 F. Supp. 278 (D. Md. 1979).

Granting motion for reconsideration did not violate Fifth Amendment or Maryland common law. — Granting motion for reconsideration of order dismissing "child in need of assistance" petitions on the merits did not violate the Double Jeopardy Clause of the Fifth Amendment or the Maryland common-law double jeopardy prohibition. In re John P., 311 Md. 700, 537 A.2d 263 (1988).

Reinstatement of restitution claim against juvenile. — The Juvenile Court has authority to vacate an order dismissing a restitution claim against a juvenile and to reinstate the claim. In re Darnell F., 71 Md. App. 584, 526 A.2d 971, aff'd, 311 Md. 144, 532 A.2d 1371 (1987).

Abuse of discretion. — Trial court's denial of the motion of petitioner, a juvenile, to vacate a delinquency finding was an abuse of discretion because the court did not address petitioner's arguments regarding whether (1) sufficient evidence supported the finding, or (2) petitioner received effective assistance of counsel. In re Elrich S., 416 Md. 15, 5 A.3d 27 (2010).

Quoted in In re Ashley E., 387 Md. 260, 874 A.2d 998 (2005).

Rule 11-117. Custody — Appointment of guardian — Pending support proceedings.

a. **Custody — Appointment of guardian of the person.** The court shall determine the custody or appoint a guardian of the person of a child only if the question arises in connection with a matter which is within its exclusive jurisdiction under Sections 3-804 and 3-805 (a) of the Courts Article, and the determination of the question is necessary to make an appropriate disposition.

b. **Pending support proceedings.** The court shall give due consideration to orders or proceedings pertaining to custody or support issued by or pending in other courts. However, this shall not affect the court's authority to detain, commit, or place in shelter care a child under its jurisdiction, or to exercise its authority in accordance with Sections 3-827 and 3-830 of the Courts Article. (Amended Nov. 5, 1976, effective Jan. 1, 1977; June 5, 1996, effective Jan. 1, 1997.)

Cross references. — For authority of a judge in juvenile proceedings to determine the custody or appoint a guardian "of a juvenile subject to the jurisdiction of equity courts," see § 3-820 (b) and (c) of the Courts Article. For procedure for exercise of appointment of a guardian, see Title 10, Chapter 100. For requirement of notice in the original summons with respect to custody and support payments, see subsection c of Rule 11-104 (Duties of Clerk). The notice, when given in accordance with that Rule, shall be sufficient to permit the consideration and determination of these questions at hearings held after service of the summons.

Source. — This Rule is former Rule 917.

Effect of amendments. — The 1996 amendment, in the Cross reference note, substituted "Title 10, Chapter 100" for "Subtitle R (Minors and Persons Under Disability)" in the second sentence and substituted "Rule 11-104" for "Rule 904" in the third sentence; and added the Source note.

Editor's note. — An Order dated June 5, 1996, effective Jan. 1, 1997, renumbered this Rule, which was formerly Rule 917.

Rule 11-118. Parents' liability — Hearing — Recording and effect.

a. **Hearing.** If, at any stage of a proceeding, the court believes a respondent has committed acts for which the respondent's parent or parents may be liable under Code, Criminal Law Article, §§ 4-503, 9-504, or 9-505 or Code, Criminal Procedure Article, § 11-607(b), the court shall summon the parent or parents in the manner provided by Chapter 100 of Title 2 for service of process to obtain personal jurisdiction over a person to appear at a hearing to determine liability. This hearing may be conducted contemporaneously with a disposition hearing, if appropriate.

b. **Recording.** Recordation of a judgment of restitution shall be governed by Code, Criminal Procedure Article, § 11-608. (Amended Nov. 5, 1976, effective Jan. 1, 1977; Apr. 6, 1984, effective July 1, 1984; June 5, 1996, effective Jan. 1, 1997; June 8, 1998, effective Oct. 1, 1998; Oct. 5, 1999; Jan. 8, 2002, effective Feb. 1, 2002; Oct. 31, 2002, effective Jan. 1, 2003.)

Source. — This Rule is derived in part from former Rule 918 and is in part new.

Effect of amendments. — The 1996 amendment added the Source note.

The 1998 amendment rewrote the Rule.

The 1999 amendment substituted "Article 27, §§ 807, 139D, 151A, or 151C" for "Article 27, § 807" in a.

The first 2002 amendment in a., deleted "807" preceding "139D" and inserted "or Code, Criminal Procedure Article, § 11-607(b)" after "151C" and substituted "Criminal Procedure Article, § 11-608" for "Article 27, § 807" in b.

The second 2002 amendment substituted

"Criminal Law Article, §§ 4-503, 9-504, or 9-505" for "Article 27, § 139D, 151A, or 151C" in a.

Editor's note. — An Order dated June 5, 1996, effective Jan. 1, 1997, renumbered this Rule, which was formerly Rule 918.

Matter of restitution should be considered and resolved no later than at a juvenile's disposition hearing. In re Yoldande L., 49 Md. App. 310, 431 A.2d 743 (1981).

Relief where parent not afforded proper notice of claim or fair opportunity to defend. — Where appellant's mother was not afforded proper notice of the claim for restitution to be asserted against her and a fair opportunity to defend the claim, judgment as to the mother must be vacated. On remand, she should be served with a copy of the delinquency petition, receive notice of the hearing, and be afforded a reasonable opportunity to be heard and to present evidence in her behalf. In re James B., 54 Md. App. 270, 458 A.2d 847 (1983).

Stated in In re Delric H., 150 Md. App. 234, 819 A.2d 1117 (2003).

Rule 11-119. Disposition of property brought into court.

Property brought into court shall be returned to the owner, or otherwise disposed of as the court may direct. (Amended Nov. 5, 1976, effective Jan. 1, 1977; June 5, 1996, effective Jan. 1, 1997.)

Source. — This Rule is former Rule 919.

Effect of amendments. — The 1996 amendment added the Source note.

Editor's note. — An Order dated June 5, 1996, effective Jan. 1, 1997, renumbered this Rule, which was formerly Rule 919.

Rule 11-120. Final order of termination.

A final order of termination of the proceedings may, in the court's discretion, be entered on the court's own motion at any time after the court's jurisdiction over the respondent is terminated, or upon the recommendation of the appropriate governmental or social agency exercising supervision over the respondent. (Amended Nov. 5, 1976, effective Jan. 1, 1977; June 5, 1996, effective Jan. 1, 1997.)

Source. — This Rule is former Rule 920.

Effect of amendments. — The 1996 amendment added the Source note.

Editor's note. — An Order dated June 5, 1996, effective Jan. 1, 1997, renumbered this Rule, which was formerly Rule 920.

Rule 11-121. Court records — Confidentiality.

a. **Sealing of records.** Files and records of the court in juvenile proceedings, including the docket entries and indices, are confidential and shall not be open to inspection except by order of the court or as otherwise expressly provided by law. On termination of the court's juvenile jurisdiction, the files and records shall be sealed pursuant to Section 3-828 (c) of the Courts Article, and all index references shall be marked "sealed." If a hearing is open to the public pursuant to Code, Courts Article, § 3-812, the name of the respondent and the date, time, and location of the hearing are not confidential.

b. **Unsealing of records.** Sealed files and records of the court in juvenile proceedings may be unsealed and inspected only by order of the court.

(Amended Nov. 5, 1976, effective Jan. 1, 1977; June 5, 1996, effective Jan. 1, 1997; June 8, 1998, effective October 1, 1998.)

Cross references. — For confidentiality in appellate proceedings, see Rule 8-121 (Appeals from Courts Exercising Juvenile Jurisdiction — Confidentiality).

Source. — This Rule is former Rule 921.

Effect of amendments. — The 1996 amendment added the Source note.

The 1998 amendment, in a., added "or as otherwise expressly provided by law" in the first sentence and added the last sentence.

Editor's note. — An Order dated June 5, 1996, effective Jan. 1, 1997, renumbered this Rule, which was formerly Rule 921.

Closed proceedings. — Courts may close juvenile proceedings to the public in instances where closure would be impermissible in other court proceedings. Baltimore Sun Co. v. State, 340 Md. 437, 667 A.2d 166 (1995).

Access to proceedings by press. — Although a juvenile court has the discretion to exclude the press from a juvenile proceeding, its discretion is not unlimited and must be exercised in accord with the purposes for which it was given and within applicable constitutional limitations. Baltimore Sun Co. v. State, 340 Md. 437, 667 A.2d 166 (1995).

While a court can place reasonable restrictions on the media's use of information obtained in a confidential juvenile proceeding, it cannot limit the media's publication of information which it legitimately collected from other sources, and cannot condition access to the juvenile proceeding upon the media's publication of material specified by the court. Baltimore Sun Co. v. State, 340 Md. 437, 667 A.2d 166 (1995).

Access by agents of Division of Parole and Probation. — Although court records pertaining to juveniles are to be maintained in a confidential manner as a general rule, agents of the Division of Parole and Probation may have access to such records when they are carrying out, at the direction of a court of competent jurisdiction, any of the Division's statutory duties. 63 Op. Att'y Gen. 502 (1978).

Opening or divulging court records. — Court records pertaining to juveniles are held in confidence, and can only be divulged by court order, or for limited educational purposes. Baltimore Sun Co. v. State, 340 Md. 437, 667 A.2d 166 (1995).

Trial court erred in finding that it lacked discretion to determine whether there was good cause under § 3-8A-27(c) of the Courts Article for defense counsel to review an agreed statement of facts used in a juvenile proceeding against a teenage child of the victims, which was confidential under § 3-8A-23(c) of the Courts Article; the trial court erred in interpreting this Rule as precluding even an in camera review of the statement to determine whether it contained cross-examination or impeachment material as the child was involved in the same altercation, was clearly a hostile witness. and was subject to impeachment under Md. R. 5-611(c)(2) and 5-607. Samie v. State, 181 Md. App. 59, 955 A.2d 794 (2008).

Rule 11-122. Intervention.

a. **Of right.** Upon timely application, any parent not served with original process shall be permitted to intervene for any purpose.

Cross references. — Rule 11-101 b 4.

b. **Permissive.** Upon timely application, any person, other than a parent, seeking custody or guardianship of the respondent child may be permitted to intervene for dispositional purposes only, including the filing of a petition to review, modify or vacate a disposition order. Any person permitted to intervene pursuant to this section shall not be deemed a "party" for the purposes of Rule 11-106, and for the purposes of Rule 11-105, counsel for the intervenor, upon request, shall only be entitled to be furnished copies of such studies and reports as directly relate to the intervenor's petition for custody or guardianship of the respondent child.

c. **Procedure.** 1. Motion. An application to intervene shall be made by motion. If the applicant claims a right of intervention under section a of this Rule, the motion shall be accompanied by an affidavit showing that the applicant is a parent of the respondent child.

2. Leave of court. Leave to intervene shall be granted only by court order. When intervention is pursuant to section b of this Rule the order shall designate the intervenor as a defendant for dispositional purposes only.

3. Service. A copy of the motion, the affidavit, any order thereon, and any pleading filed by the intervenor shall be served as provided by Rule 1-321. (Added Nov. 8, 1982, effective Jan. 1, 1983; amended Apr. 6, 1984, effective July 1, 1984; June 5, 1996, effective Jan. 1, 1997.)

Source. — This Rule is former Rule 922.

Effect of amendments. — The 1996 amendment substituted "Rule 11-101" for "Rule 901" in the Cross reference note in a.; in b., substituted "Rule 11-106" for "Rule 906" and substituted "Rule 11-105" for "Rule 905"; and added the Source note.

Editor's note. — An Order dated June 5, 1996, effective Jan. 1, 1997, renumbered this Rule, which was formerly Rule 922.

Intervention of non-parent. — This Rule does not require that a party, other than a parent, be permitted to intervene. In re Richard H., 128 Md. App. 71, 736 A.2d 1121 (1999).

Rule 11-501. Termination of parental rights and related adoption proceedings in the juvenile court.

(a) **Applicability of Rule.** This Rule applies to actions in which the juvenile court is exercising jurisdiction pursuant to Code, Courts Article, § 3-804 (a) (2).

(b) **Definition.** The word "guardianship" as used in this Rule has the meaning stated in Code, Family Law Article, § 5-301.

(c) **Applicability of Titles 1, 2, 5, and 9.** The Rules in Titles 1, 2, and 5 and Chapter 100 of Title 9 apply to actions under this Rule, except as otherwise provided by law or ordered by the court.

(d) **Petition.** A proceeding for adoption or guardianship shall be initiated by the filing of a petition in a new action, separate from any other proceedings involving the child who is the subject of the adoption or guardianship proceeding. In addition to complying with the requirements of Rule 9-103, the petition shall state the basis for the juvenile court's jurisdiction and the name of the court and case number of the proceeding in which the child was adjudicated a child in need of assistance.

(e) **Consolidation.** A proceeding for adoption or guardianship may be consolidated with, or severed from, any other case pending in the juvenile court involving the child who is the subject of the proceeding, as justice may require.

(f) **Hearing — Before whom held.** All hearings conducted pursuant to this Rule shall be held before a judge.

(g) **Judgments of adoption — Recording and indexing.** The clerk shall record and index each judgment of adoption entered by the juvenile court on or after October 1, 1996 in the adoption records of the circuit court for the county where the judgment was entered. (Amended June 10, 1997, effective July 1, 1997.)

Committee note. — Judgments of adoption under this section include judgments entered under former Rule 923.

Source. — This Rule is new.

Effect of amendments. — The 1997 amendment added (g) and the Committee note.

Editor's note. — The 1997 amendment takes effect July 1, 1997, and applies to all judgments entered by the juvenile court on or after October 1, 1996.

Former similar provisions embodied in Rule 923 were rescinded effective January 1, 1997.

Rule 11-601. Expungement of criminal charges transferred to the juvenile court.

(a) **Procedure.** A petition for expungement of records may be filed by a respondent who is eligible under Code, Criminal Procedure Article, § 10-106 to request expungement. Proceedings for expungement shall be in accordance with Title 4, Chapter 500 of these Rules, except that the petition shall be filed in the juvenile court and shall be substantially in the form set forth in section (b) of this Rule.

(b) **Form of petition.** A petition for expungement of records under this Rule shall be substantially in the following form:

(Caption)

PETITION FOR EXPUNGEMENT OF RECORDS

(Code*, Criminal Procedure Article, § 10-106)

1. On or about _____ , I was arrested by an officer of the _____

(Law Enforcement Agency)

at _____ , Maryland, as a result of the following incident ____ _____ .

2. I was charged with the offense of _____ _____ .

3. The charge was transferred to the juvenile court under former Code*, Article 27, § 594A or Code*, Criminal Procedure Article, § 4-202 and (check one of the following boxes):

☐ No petition under Code*, Courts Article, § 3-810 was filed;

☐ The decision on the juvenile petition was a finding of facts-not-sustained; or

☐ I was adjudicated delinquent and I am now at least 21 years of age.

WHEREFORE, I request the Court to enter an Order for Expungement of all police and court records pertaining to the above arrest, detention, confinement, and charges.

I solemnly affirm under the penalties of perjury that the contents of this Petition are true to the best of my knowledge, information and belief, and that the charge to which this Petition relates was not made for any nonincarcerable violation of the Vehicle Laws of the State of Maryland, or any traffic law, ordinance, or regulation, nor is it part of a unit the expungement of which is precluded under Code*, Criminal Procedure Article, § 10-107.

_____	_____
(Date)	Signature
	_____
	(Address)
	_____
	(Telephone No.)

* References to "Code" in this Petition are to the Annotated Code of Maryland.

(Added June 8, 1998, effective Oct. 1, 1998; amended Jan. 20, 1999, effective July 1, 1999; Jan. 8, 2002, effective Feb. 1, 2002.)

Source. — This Rule is new.

Effect of amendments. — The 1999 amendment inserted "nonincarcerable" in the last paragraph of the form in (b).

The 2002 amendment substituted "Criminal Procedure Article, § 10-106" for "Article 27, § 737(b)" in (a) and (b); in (b)3., inserted "former" preceding "Code" and added "or Code*, Criminal Procedure Article, § 4-402" near the end; and substituted "Criminal Procedure Article, § 10-107" for "Article 27, § 738" in the last paragraph.

TITLE 12. PROPERTY ACTIONS

Editor's note. — The Court of Appeals, by Order dated June 5, 1996, effective January 1, 1997, rescinded Subtitles A, D, E, J, P, Q, R, T, U, V, W, Y, Z, BB, BD, BE, BG, BH, BJ, BL, BP, BQ, BR, BS, BW, and BY of Chapter 1100 of the Maryland Rules of Procedure, rescinded Subtitles P, BB, BQ, and BW of the Maryland District Rules, and rescinded Forms 22a, 23, 24, 25, and 26. The Order substituted for certain of the rules and forms rescinded new Title 9, Chapter 100, Title 10, Title 12, Title 13, Title 14, and Title 15 of the Maryland Rules of Procedure. Furthermore, the Order transferred, without readoption, Chapter 900, Chapter 1200, and Subtitles S, BU, and BV of Chapter 1100 of the Maryland Rules of Procedure and Chapter 1200 of the Maryland District Rules to be Title 9, Chapter 200, Title 11, and Title 16 of the Maryland Rules of Procedure. The Order provides that the new rules shall "apply to all actions commenced on or after January 1, 1997, and insofar as practicable, to all actions then pending."

Many of the cases in the notes to the various rules were decided prior to the 1996 revision. These cases have been retained under pertinent rules of this title where it is thought that such cases will be of value in interpreting the present rules.

A table of comparable rules, relating those rules rescinded effective January 1, 1997, to the revised rules in Title 9 through Title 16 is to be found in Volume 2 following the end of the Maryland Rules.

CHAPTER 100. GENERAL PROVISIONS.

Rule 12-101. Writ of survey.

(a) **Availability.** On motion of a party in an action involving real property, the court may issue a writ of survey if it finds that a plat is necessary for illustration or that one of the following matters is in dispute: (1) the location of the property in dispute; (2) the location or extent of any property claimed to be damaged; or (3) the location of a dividing line if the parties are claiming under the same title. The motion shall contain a description sufficient to locate the property that is the subject of the claim. The court may condition issuance of the writ on the deposit by the moving party of the estimated cost of executing the writ.

(b) **Survey.** A writ of survey shall be issued to a surveyor designated by the court. The surveyor shall survey the property in accordance with the writ.

(c) **Plat.** The surveyor shall file the original and three copies of each plat with the clerk. Upon receiving payment of reasonable charges, the surveyor shall furnish a copy to any party.

Source. — This Rule is derived from former Rule T44.

The statutory source made radical changes in the practice. The court may, when it is satisfied that there is a dispute about boundaries, order a warrant of resurvey to be issued although defendant has not taken defense on warrant; when a warrant is so issued, the practice applicable to surveys made after defense on warrant is taken applies. The defendant may no longer take defense on warrant as a matter of right, and have a resurvey of the disputed land. Application must be made to court and warrant can only issue on its order or by agreement of parties. The warrant may be taken out at the instance of either party. The foregoing statements apply in an action of trespass q.c.f. Andrews v. Pitts, 126 Md. 328, 95 A. 203 (1915).

Application in action of trespass q.c.f. — An action of trespass q.c.f. is often resorted to in trying titles to land, and in actions involving locations it is much more satisfactory to have a warrant of resurvey. B & O R.R. v. Silbereisen, 121 Md. 407, 121 Md. 420, 88 A. 252, 89 A. 102 (1913).

Same — Lis pendens. — There was some indication in former §§ 34, 35 and 36 of Article 75 that the doctrine of lis pendens applied in a case of trespass quare clausum fregit, where a warrant of resurvey was issued. The point was not, however, decided in the case. Corey v. Carback, 201 Md. 389, 94 A.2d 629 (1953).

Bona fide dispute about location of property. — It is incumbent upon party applying for warrant of resurvey to furnish satisfactory evidence that there is a bona fide dispute about location of property or division line thereof. Where description of land sued for is identical with that claimed by defendant, and where both parties claim title from a common source, there is no necessity for issue of such warrant. Kelso v. Stigar, 75 Md. 376, 24 A. 18 (1892).

Mode of proof of land embraced within described boundaries not changed. — Former § 34 of Article 75 did not change laws and practice regulating surveys and locations, as to mode of proof of land actually embraced within boundaries described in patents, deeds, etc. Clary v. Kimmell, 18 Md. 246 (1862); Newman v. Young, 30 Md. 417 (1869).

Plats held to be authorized for illustration only. — See New York, P. & N.R.R. v. Jones, 94 Md. 24, 50 A. 423 (1901).

Plaintiff must locate every title paper in strict conformity with calls. — Since Acts 1852, ch. 177, gives defendant right to take defense on warrant, plaintiff must locate every title paper in strict conformity with the calls, etc., and if plats and explanations do not show them to be so located, they must be rejected at trial. Clary v. Kimmell, 18 Md. 246 (1862).

Rule 12-102. Lis pendens.

(a) **Scope.** This Rule applies to an action filed in a circuit court or in the United States District Court for the District of Maryland that affects title to or a leasehold interest in real property located in this State.

(b) **Creation — Constructive notice.** In an action to which the doctrine of lis pendens applies, the filing of the complaint is constructive notice of the lis pendens as to real property in the county in which the complaint is filed. In any other county, there is constructive notice only after the party seeking the lis pendens files either a certified copy of the complaint or a notice giving rise to the lis pendens, with the clerk in the other county.

(c) **Termination.** (1) While action is pending. On motion of a person in interest and for good cause, the court in the county in which the action is pending may enter an order terminating the lis pendens in that county or any other county in which the lis pendens has been created.

(2) Upon conclusion of action. If (A) the action is dismissed, or (B) judgment is entered in favor of the defendant and a timely appeal is not taken or the judgment is affirmed on appeal, or (C) judgment in favor of the plaintiff is reversed on appeal, vacated, or satisfied, the plaintiff shall file a certified copy of the appropriate docket entry with the clerk in each county in which a certified copy of the complaint or notice was filed pursuant to section (b) of this Rule. If the plaintiff fails to comply with this subsection, the court with jurisdiction over the action, on motion of any person in interest and upon such notice as the court deems appropriate in the circumstances, may enter an order terminating the lis pendens. In the order terminating the lis pendens, the court shall direct the plaintiff to pay the costs and expenses incurred by the person obtaining the order, including reasonable attorney's fees, unless the court finds that the plaintiff had a reason justifying the failure to comply.

(3) Duty of clerk. Upon entry of an order terminating a lis pendens, the clerk of the court of entry shall transmit a certified copy of the order to the clerk in any other county specified in the order.

Source. — This Rule is derived as follows: *Section (a)* is new.
Section (b) is derived from former Rule BD1 and BD2.

Section (c) is derived from former Rule BD3.

Maryland Law Review. — For comment, "Lis Pendens and Procedural Due Process: A Closer Look after Connecticut v. Doehr", see 51 Md. L. Rev. 1054 (1992).

University of Baltimore Law Review. — For discussion, "Property Disposition Upon Divorce in Maryland: An Analysis of the New Statute," see 8 U. Balt. L. Rev. 377 (1979).

Applicability. — In the State of Maryland, the lis pendens doctrine applies exclusively to real property and has no applicability except to proceedings directly relating to the title to the property transferred or in which the ultimate interest and object is to subject the property in question to the disposal of a decree of the court. Weston Builders & Developers, Inc. v. McBerry, LLC, 167 Md. App. 24, 891 A.2d 430 (2006), cert. denied, cert. denied, 898 A.2d 1005, 2006 Md. LEXIS 293 (2006).

Maryland doctrine of lis pendens is applicable to condemnation actions. Maryland-National Capital Park & Planning Comm'n v. Town of Wash. Grove, 408 Md. 37, 968 A.2d 552 (2009).

Debtors waived their constructive trust ob-jection to a bankruptcy court's order allowing a trustee to sell the property at issue because the debtors' filing of a State court suit seeking the imposition of a constructive trust did not operate as notice in accordance with (b), as the bankruptcy court, pursuant to 28 U.S.C.S. § 1334(e), retained exclusive jurisdiction, to the exclusion of other courts, over the property that was the subject of the constructive trust claim, and thus, the State court could not acquire or exercise jurisdiction over the property. As such, the doctrine of lis pendens, and by extension (b), did not apply to give constructive notice to the bankruptcy court of the debtors' constructive trust claim. Byrd v. Hoffman, 417 B.R. 320 (D. Md. 2008), aff'd, 2009 U.S. App. LEXIS 18063 (4th Cir. Md. 2009).

Complaint seeking to establish a constructive trust on specified real property is an action whose nature is such that it directly involves the property and is a proceeding directly relating to the title to the property transferred or in which the ultimate interest and object is to subject the property in question to the disposal of a decree of the court;

thus, such a complaint is within the ambit of Maryland's lis pendens doctrine. Stewart Title Guar. Co. v. Sanford Title Servs., LLC, — F. Supp. 2d — (D. Md. July 8, 2011).

In an action in which plaintiff, a title insurance company, alleged that certain real properties were illegitimately purchased with monies misappropriated from an escrow account and that plaintiff was required to make up a shortfall in the escrow account due to defendants' fraudulent conduct, plaintiff's complaint seeking to establish a constructive trust on the properties constituted a valid lis pendens on the properties because the complaint directly related to the title to the properties. Stewart Title Guar. Co. v. Sanford Title Servs., LLC, — F. Supp. 2d — (D. Md. July 8, 2011).

Filing includes indexing. — Compliance with filing requirement of this Rule was not enough to give receivers' lis pendens priority over interests of mortgage lenders, because that rule had to be read together with the filing/indexing requirements of §§ 3-301 and 3-302 of this subtitle; since the notices had not been properly indexed, there was no way a third party could receive notice, and the risk of loss of priority had to be placed on the receivers, the only parties who were in a position to monitor whether the filing and indexing had proceeded properly. Greenpoint Mortg. Fund-

ing, Inc. v. Schlossberg, 390 Md. 211, 888 A.2d 297 (2005).

Termination — Lis pendens is not automatically terminated with the entry of a trial court judgment as specific procedural steps must be undertaken to terminate the same as set forth in this section. Weston Builders & Developers, Inc. v. McBerry, LLC, 167 Md. App. 24, 891 A.2d 430 (2006), cert. denied, cert. denied, 898 A.2d 1005, 2006 Md. LEXIS 293 (2006).

Transfer of property during appeal. — In a specific performance action brought by a purchaser against a seller with regard to a real estate transaction involving 40 buildable lots, the judgment in favor of the seller was reversed on appeal since the appeal was not moot regardless of the fact that the seller had transferred the lots to a third party during the pendency of the appeal. Lis pendens had never been formally terminated in the action and did not automatically terminate upon entry of the judgment; therefore, the third-party purchaser was vulnerable to any adverse decision flowing from the appeal brought by the buyer. Weston Builders & Developers, Inc. v. McBerry, LLC, 167 Md. App. 24, 891 A.2d 430 (2006), cert. denied, cert. denied, 898 A.2d 1005, 2006 Md. LEXIS 293 (2006).

Cited in Wash. Mut. Bank v. Homan, 186 Md. App. 372, 974 A.2d 376 (2009).

Rule 12-103. Action for release of lien instrument.

When a mortgage or deed of trust remains unreleased of record, the mortgagor, grantor, or a successor in interest entitled by law to a release may file a complaint for release of the lien instrument in any county where the lien instrument is recorded. The person bringing the action shall include as defendants all other parties to the instrument unless their interest has been assigned or transferred of record, and in that case their successors in interest. If the court orders the lien instrument released of record, the clerk shall record the release in the manner prescribed by law. (Amended Nov. 12, 2003, effective Jan. 10, 2004.)

Cross references. — Code, Real Property Article, § 7-106 (e), § 3-105 (d), and 3-105.1 (e)(1).

Source. — This Rule is new.

Effect of amendments. — The 2003 amendment added "and 305.1 (e)(1)" and made related stylistic changes to the cross-reference note.

CHAPTER 200. CONDEMNATION.

Rule 12-201. Applicability.

The rules in this Chapter govern actions for acquisition of property by condemnation under the power of eminent domain.

Cross references. — Code, Real Property Article, §§ 12-101 and 12-102; Maryland Constitution, Article III, §§ 40 and 40A.

Committee note. — These rules are not intended to cover "condemnation" of property as hazardous to health, etc., or to repeal or supersede statutory or constitutional authority for "quick take" procedures.

Source. — This Rule is derived from former Rule U1.

Maryland Law Review. — For note, "The Maryland Survey: 2001-2002: Recent Decisions: The Court of Appeals of Maryland: VI. Eminent Domain," see 62 Md. L. Rev. 840 (2003).

University of Baltimore Law Review. — For article, "State Constitutional Law for Maryland Lawyers: Individual Civil Rights," see 7 U. Balt. L. Rev. 299 (1978).

Maryland statute controls in proceedings by federal government to condemn. — In proceedings by federal government to condemn land, the procedure is controlled by Maryland statute, except as modified by federal statute. United States v. Certain Parcels of Land, 40 F. Supp. 436 (D. Md. 1941).

Proceeding is one at law. — A condemnation proceeding for the acquisition of private property for public use has always been held to be a proceeding at law, and Article 33A (now RP, Title 12) of the Code does not change the proceeding into an equitable one. Ridgeley v. Mayor of Baltimore, 119 Md. 567, 87 A. 909 (1913).

Proceedings initiated by property owner. — Neither Title 12 of the Real Property Article, nor former Subtitle U of the Maryland Rules provides that proceedings may be initiated by a property owner who believes that his property has been taken, either by condemnation or by virtue of proceedings or governmental action short of condemnation. Millison v. Wilzack, 77 Md. App. 676, 551 A.2d 899, cert. denied, 315 Md. 307, 554 A.2d 393 (1989).

Order condemning property for railroad crossing. — When property is being condemned for a railroad crossing, the order of court should limit the condemnation to such purpose, and the condemnation should be subject to the rights of the public. Mayor of Hyattsville v. Washington, W. & G.R.R., 120 Md. 128, 87 A. 828 (1913).

When sanitary commission exercised power of eminent domain and paid jury's award to clerk of the court, all as authorized and directed by statute, it conducted the condemnation in conformity with former Subtitle U, and the award paid into court was for the use of the defendant. This being so, it was "paid or tendered" to the defendant, the person entitled thereto, before her private property was taken for public use, thus, gratifying Md. Const., article III, § 40. Payment to the clerk is payment to the court of which he is an agent, and payment to a court has been held to be payment to the litigant entitled thereto. Fitzgerald v. Somerset County San. Comm'n, 231 Md. 242, 189 A.2d 601 (1963).

Quoted in Maryland-National Capital Park & Planning Comm'n v. Town of Wash. Grove, 408 Md. 37, 968 A.2d 552 (2009).

Rule 12-202. Venue.

An action for condemnation shall be brought in the county where the property sought to be condemned is located. If the property lies in more than one county, the action for condemnation may be brought in any county where a part of the property lies. The court in which proceedings are first brought shall have jurisdiction over the entire property.

Cross references. — Code, Courts Article, § 6-203. For constructive notice of a proceeding in another county, see Rule 12-102. For limitations on the constitutional right of removal in condemnation cases, see Mayor and City Council of Baltimore v. Kane, 125 Md. 135 (1915) and Mayor and City Council of Baltimore v. Libowitz, 159 Md. 27 (1937).

Source. — This Rule is derived from former Rule U2.

Petition should be filed where land is situated. — A petition for condemnation should be filed in the county or the City of Baltimore, where property is situated. Park Land Corp. v. Mayor of Baltimore, 128 Md. 611, 98 A. 153 (1916).

Proceedings initiated by property owner. — Neither Title 12 of the Real Property Article, nor former Subtitle U of the Maryland Rules provides that proceedings may be initiated by a property owner who believes that his property has been taken, either by condemnation or by virtue of proceedings or governmental action short of condemnation. Millison v. Wilzack, 77 Md. App. 676, 551 A.2d 899, cert. denied, 315 Md. 307, 554 A.2d 393 (1989).

Removal. — The right of removal has no application to condemnation proceedings under Acts 1912, ch. 117. Mayor of Baltimore v. Kane, 125 Md. 135, 93 A. 393 (1915).

Rule 12-203. Required parties defendant.

An action for condemnation shall be brought against all persons, known or unknown, whose interest in the property is sought to be condemned.

Committee note. — *See Department of Natural Resources v. Welsh*, 308 Md. 54 (1986) relating to the consequences of failure to join required parties defendant.

Source. — This Rule is derived from former Rule U4 b.

Persons bound by proceeding. — A condemnation proceeding is a proceeding in rem and is binding upon all persons who are interested in the res even though they may not be, technically, parties to the suit. Bugg v. Maryland Transp. Auth., 31 Md. App. 622, 358 A.2d 562, cert. denied, 278 Md. 717 (1976), appeal dismissed, 429 U.S. 1082, 97 S. Ct. 1088, 51 L. Ed. 2d 529 (1977).

Right to proceed and to close in condemnation cases rests with condemnor. Harford Bldg. Corp. v. Mayor of Baltimore, 58 Md. App. 85, 472 A.2d 479, cert. denied, 300 Md. 153, 476 A.2d 722 (1984).

No statutory authority gives a property owner the status of a plaintiff with the corresponding right to open and close a case. Harford Bldg. Corp. v. Mayor of Baltimore, 58 Md. App. 85, 472 A.2d 479, cert. denied, 300 Md. 153, 476 A.2d 722 (1984).

Interest of owner not a party. — When the condemnation of land is effected by judicial decree, failure to designate in the petition (and to make a party respondent) the owner of any interest in the land taken whose title appears of record or is otherwise ascertainable on reasonable inquiry renders the proceedings ineffectual to transfer such interest to the condemnor. Department of Natural Resources v. Welsh, 308 Md. 54, 521 A.2d 313 (1986).

Suit to condemn common elements of condominium. — While a trial judge is correct in directing that condominium unit owners and any mortgagees be added as parties to a suit to condemn a portion of the general common elements of the condominium, he subsequently errs when he fails to include their names on the inquisition form submitted to the jury. Andrews v. City of Greenbelt, 293 Md. 69, 441 A.2d 1064 (1982).

It is not enough that the inquisition form submitted to the jury in a suit to condemn a portion of the general common elements of the condominium named the council of unit owners of the condominium as the defendant because, even though the council is a legal entity comprised of all unit owners, it does not have legal title to the collectively held property and nothing in § 11-109 of the Real Property Article allows the association, acting in a representative capacity for the unit owners, to transfer title to regime property. Andrews v. City of Greenbelt, 293 Md. 69, 441 A.2d 1064 (1982).

Quoted in Conrad v. Department of Natural Resources, 30 Md. App. 479, 352 A.2d 904, cert. denied, 278 Md. 719 (1976).

Cited in Department of Natural Resources v. Welsh, 308 Md. 54, 521 A.2d 313 (1986).

Rule 12-204. Acquisition of cemetery.

(a) **Notice by publication before filing complaint.** Before filing a complaint for condemnation of property used as a cemetery, the plaintiff shall give notice by publication in a newspaper of general circulation in each county where any part of the property is located.

(b) **Contents of notice.** The notice shall contain the following information:

(1) the name of the plaintiff,

(2) an identification of the cemetery and a description of the part that is sought to be condemned,

(3) the purpose for which the property is sought to be condemned, and

(4) the name of the court in which the complaint is to be filed.

(c) **Time of publication.** The notice shall be published at least once a week for three successive weeks, and the last publication shall be made at least seven days before the filing of a complaint.

(d) **Proof of publication.** The plaintiff shall file a certificate of publication as an exhibit to the original complaint.

(e) **Effect of failure to publish.** If it appears to the court at any time before entry of judgment that there has been a failure to comply with the provisions of this Rule, the court shall suspend further proceedings in the action until publication is made and may order any other means of notice that it deems appropriate in the circumstances. No objection based on failure to comply with this Rule shall be made after final judgment.

Committee note. — The notice required by this Rule is not a substitute for process pursuant to Chapter 100 of Title 2 of these Rules.

Source. — This Rule is in part derived from former Rule U5 and in part new.

Rule 12-205. Complaint.

An action for condemnation shall be commenced by filing a complaint complying with Rules 2-303 through 2-305 and containing:

(a) The names of all persons whose interest in the property is sought to be condemned. If any person is a nonresident or not known, that fact shall be stated. If any person is the unknown heir of a decedent, that person shall be described as the unknown heir of _____, deceased.

(b) A description of the property sought to be condemned. If the subject matter of the action is real property, the description shall be:

(1) by lot and block or square when an entire lot, block, or square shown on a subdivision map, plat, or record is sought to be condemned, or

(2) by metes and bounds when an entire tract is sought to be condemned, or

(3) by metes and bounds clearly and legibly set forth on a plat showing the area and stating the amount of land sought to be condemned. The plat shall set forth the beginning point for the description, referenced to an existing marker, call, monument, or point outside the area sought to be condemned, in a recorded deed or plat identified by liber and folio. The deed or plat shall be in the chain of title of the property sought to be condemned, but if no marker, call, monument, or point can be found in the chain of title, reference may be made to the chain of title of adjoining property.

(c) A statement of the nature of the interest that the plaintiff seeks to acquire by the proposed condemnation.

(d) A statement of the purpose for which the property is sought to be condemned.

(e) A statement that there is a public necessity for the proposed condemnation.

(f) A statement that the parties are unable to agree or that a defendant is unable to agree because that defendant is unknown or under legal disability.

(g) A statement of the amount of any money paid into court and the date of the payment.

(h) A statement of the date of taking if a taking has occurred.

(i) A request that the property be condemned.

Source. — This Rule is derived from former Rule U6.

Statement of purposes required. — The reason for the requirement that there be in the petition for condemnation a "statement of the purposes for which the property is sought to be condemned" is that without such a statement courts and litigants would not be able to determine whether a condemnation was proposed for a public purpose. Prince George's County v. Beard, 266 Md. 83, 291 A.2d 636 (1972).

A mere recital that a proposed property is needed for a particular public use is insufficient when dealing with the deprivation of private property rights. High Ridge Ass'n v. County Comm'rs, 105 Md. App. 423, 660 A.2d 951 (1995).

Corporation need not allege public necessity for construction for which land is petitioned to be condemned. Realty Imp. Co. v. Consolidated Gas Elec. Light & Power Co., 156 Md. 581, 144 A. 710 (1929).

Validity of ordinance relied on. — No rule of pleading requires that a city acting in reliance on an ordinance justify the validity of the ordinance in its petition for condemnation, nor need it allege the chain of legislative or constitutional authority of which the ordinance was the last link. Herzinger v. Mayor of Baltimore, 203 Md. 49, 98 A.2d 87 (1953).

Where authority to condemn is based on an ordinance, reliance thereon will make a prima facie case and shift the burden to the person attacking it to show that it is arbitrary and unreasonable. Herzinger v. Mayor of Baltimore, 203 Md. 49, 98 A.2d 87 (1953).

Amendment. — See Brack v. Mayor of Baltimore, 125 Md. 378, 93 A. 994 (1915).

Amendment to include parties necessary to obtain fee simple title. — There was no abuse of discretion on the part of the trial judge when he permitted the condemnor to file an amended petition for the purpose of including as parties defendant such parties as were claimed necessary to obtain a valid, fee simple title to the land sought to be condemned, which parties were not included in the original petition. D.C. Transit Sys. v. State Rds. Comm'n, 259 Md. 675, 270 A.2d 793 (1970).

Quoted in Maryland-National Capital Park & Planning Comm'n v. Town of Wash. Grove, 408 Md. 37, 968 A.2d 552 (2009).

Rule 12-206. Discovery.

(a) **Generally.** Except as otherwise provided in this Rule, discovery in actions for condemnation shall be conducted pursuant to Chapter 400 of Title 2 of these Rules.

(b) **Experts not expected to be called at trial; fees and expenses.** A party may obtain discovery of the identity, findings, and opinions of an expert, even though the expert is not expected to be called as a witness at trial, if the expert (1) was retained by another party in anticipation of litigation or preparation for trial and (2) has examined or appraised all or part of the property sought to be condemned for the purpose of determining its value or has prepared a report pertaining to its value. The court shall require the party seeking discovery to reimburse the other party for a fair portion of the fees and expenses reasonably incurred in obtaining findings and opinions from the expert.

Source. — This Rule is derived from former Rule U12 b and from Fed. R. Civ. P. 26 (b) (4).

Rule 12-207. Trial.

(a) **Trial by jury unless otherwise elected.** An action for condemnation shall be tried by a jury unless all parties file a written election submitting the case to the court for determination. All parties may file a written election submitting an issue of fact to the court for determination without submitting the whole action.

Committee note. — The issue of the plaintiff's right to condemn is a question of law for the court. *Bouton v. Potomac Edison Co.*, 288 Md. 305 (1980).

(b) **Opening statement.** Each party to the action may make an opening statement to the trier of fact. If the action for condemnation is not a "quick-take" pursuant to Maryland Constitution, Art. III, §§ 40A-40C, the opening statement may be made before the trier of fact views the property sought to be condemned. A plaintiff may reserve the opening statement until after a view. A defendant may reserve the opening statement until after a view or until the conclusion of the evidence offered by the plaintiff.

Cross references. — See Bern-Shaw Limited Partnership v. Mayor and City Council of Baltimore, 377 Md. 277 (2003), which held that section (c) of this Rule does not apply to a "quick-take" condemnation proceeding.

(c) **View.** Before the production of other evidence, the trier of fact shall view the property sought to be condemned unless the court accepts a written waiver filed by all parties or the condemnation is a "quick-take" proceeding. In a jury trial, each party shall inform the court, before the jury leaves for the view, of the name of the person to speak for that party at the view. Only one person shall represent all of the plaintiffs and only one person shall represent all of the defendants, unless the court orders otherwise for good cause. Only those persons shall be permitted to make any statement to the jury during the view, and the court shall so instruct the jury. These persons shall point out to the jury the property sought to be condemned, its boundaries, and any adjacent property of the owner claimed to be affected by the taking. They may also point out the physical features, before and after the taking, of the property taken and of any adjacent property of the owner claimed to be affected by the taking. The judge shall be present at and shall supervise the view unless the court accepts a written waiver filed by all parties.

The parties, their attorneys, and other representatives may be present during a view. A jury shall be transported to and attend a view as a body under the charge of an officer of the court, and the expense of transporting the jury shall be assessed as costs. (Amended April 5, 2005, effective July 1, 2005.)

Source. — This Rule is derived from former Rules U15, U17, and U18.

Effect of amendments. — The 2005 amendment rewrote (b) and added the cross references note after (b); and inserted "or the condemnation is a 'quick-take' proceeding" after "filed by all parties" in (c).

Editor's note. — See Mayor of Baltimore v. Kane, 125 Md. 135, 93 A. 393 (1915), regarding removal in condemnation proceedings.

Rule is valid regulation of court administration. — Former Rule U15 was a reasonable regulation in the matter of court administration, and is valid. Maryland Community Developers, Inc. v. State Rds. Comm'n, 261 Md. 205, 274 A.2d 641, appeal dismissed, 404 U.S. 803, 92 S. Ct. 62, 30 L. Ed. 2d 35 (1971).

Constitutional right to jury trial on damage issue. — Maryland Constitution, Article III, § 40, mandates that the issue of damages be tried by a jury, but the issue of the right to condemn remains for the court's determination. Bouton v. Potomac Edison Co., 288 Md. 305, 418 A.2d 1168 (1980).

Former Rule U15 was intended to implement Maryland Constitution, Article III, § 40, which provides for a jury on the issue of the quantum of compensation due. Bouton v. Potomac Edison Co., 288 Md. 305, 418 A.2d 1168 (1980).

Common law right to jury trial in civil proceedings does not include condemnation cases which are special proceedings. Bouton v. Potomac Edison Co., 288 Md. 305, 418 A.2d 1168 (1980).

The right to a jury trial may be subjected to reasonable regulation; indeed, it is generally acknowledged that it can, for all practical purposes, become meaningless to the individual and burdensome to the State unless the exercise of it is regulated to some extent. Maryland Community Developers, Inc. v. State Rds. Comm'n, 261 Md. 205, 274 A.2d 641, appeal dismissed, 404 U.S. 803, 92 S. Ct. 62, 30 L. Ed. 2d 35 (1971).

No guarantee of right to trial by court. — It is the right of trial by jury which is guaranteed by the Constitution, not the right of trial by court. Maryland Community Developers, Inc. v. State Rds. Comm'n, 261 Md. 205, 274 A.2d 641, appeal dismissed, 404 U.S. 803, 92 S. Ct. 62, 30 L. Ed. 2d 35 (1971).

But certain questions should not be submitted to jury. — The question of whether a modified line route for an overhead electric transmission line complies with a Public Service Commission order should not be submitted to a jury for it is a question for the court to decide. Bouton v. Potomac Edison Co., 288 Md. 305, 418 A.2d 1168 (1980).

Obligation of contract in charter not impaired. — The method of condemnation provided under former § 6 of Article 33A did not impair obligation of contract in Baltimore & O. R.R. charter, the section merely changing the remedy to enforce the right of condemnation. B & O R.R. v. Maughlin, 153 Md. 367, 138 A. 334 (1927).

View by jury not mandatory in quick-take proceedings. — In a quick-take proceeding, property owner had not received fair market value where trial court admitted evidence of the purchase price paid by the owner 18 years before the taking as a comparable sale; furthermore, the owner was prejudiced by the jury view of the property more than a year after the condemnor had taken possession of the property and left it empty and abandoned, prompting the court to hold that this Rule did not require a jury view in quick-take condemnations. Bern-Shaw Ltd. P'ship v. Mayor & City Council, 377 Md. 277, 833 A.2d 502 (2003).

Cited in Maryland-National Capital Park & Planning Comm'n v. Town of Wash. Grove, 408 Md. 37, 968 A.2d 552 (2009).

Rule 12-208. Inquisition — Form and contents.

(a) **Form and signature.** The trier of fact shall render a verdict in the form of an inquisition signed by each member of the jury or, if the action is tried without a jury, by the judge hearing the action.

(b) **Description of property.** The inquisition shall contain a description of the property condemned. If the property is real property, the description shall be in the form required by Rule 12-205 (b).

(c) **Nature of plaintiff's estate.** The inquisition shall state the nature of the interest in the property acquired by the plaintiff.

(d) **Award of damages.** The inquisition shall set forth the amount of any damages to which each defendant or class of defendants is entitled or, if the court so orders, the total amount of damages awarded, or both.

(e) **Other matters.** The inquisition shall contain findings on any other issues submitted by the court to the trier of fact for special findings. (Amended Nov. 1, 2001, effective Jan. 1, 2002.)

Cross references. — Code, Real Property Article, §§ 12-103, 12-108, 12-110, and 12-112.

Source. — This Rule is derived from former Rule U19.

Effect of amendments. — The 2001 amendment deleted "special" preceding "verdict" in (a).

Rule 12-209. Judgment.

(a) **Upon finding of right to condemn.** If the court decides that the plaintiff is entitled to condemn, the court, upon the return of the inquisition, shall enter judgment for the plaintiff for the property condemned and for each defendant or class of defendants against the plaintiff for the amount of damages and costs awarded to each defendant or class of defendants.

(b) **Upon finding of no right to condemn.** (1) After trial. If the court decides that the plaintiff is not entitled to condemn, the court shall enter judgment against the plaintiff and for each defendant or class of defendants for costs as provided in Code, Real Property Article, § 12-106.

(2) After appeal. If the final decision on appeal is that the plaintiff is not entitled to condemn, the trial court shall award a reasonable attorney's fee to the defendant and assess the fee against the plaintiff together with the other costs of the action.

Cross references. — Code, Real Property Article, § 12-107.

Source. — This Rule is derived from former Rules U21 and U25.

Procedure governing entry of judgment absolute under former Rule U21 appears identical with that governing other civil cases. State Rds. Comm'n v. Adams, 238 Md. 371, 209 A.2d 247 (1965).

Determination of damages. — While in conventional condemnation proceedings, an owner is entitled to interest from the date of the entry of judgment nisi until the time of payment, damages should not be determined by applying the State's rate of return on its investments during that period to the amount of the payment withheld, but rather by applying the legal rate of interest. Acting Dir., Dep't of Forests & Parks v. Walker, 39 Md. App. 298, 385 A.2d 806 (1978), aff'd, 284 Md. 357, 396 A.2d 262 (1979).

Cited in Maryland-National Capital Park & Planning Comm'n v. Town of Wash. Grove, 408 Md. 37, 968 A.2d 552 (2009).

Rule 12-210. Acquisition of title and possession.

At any time after entry of a judgment for the plaintiff for the property condemned and awarding compensation to the defendant, the plaintiff may obtain possession of the condemned property by (1) paying to the defendant or to the clerk of the court for the use of the defendant the amount awarded the defendant and the costs as determined by the judgment and (2) if the defendant files a timely appeal and the plaintiff is a person other than the State or any of its subdivisions or instrumentalities, filing a bond in an amount and with a surety approved by the court. The bond shall be conditioned on the plaintiff paying the defendant, if the judgment is reversed on appeal, all damages the plaintiff causes the defendant by taking possession of and using the property before final determination of the appeal.

Cross references. — *See* Maryland Constitution, Art. III, § 40 and Code, Real Property Article, §§ 12-102, 12-106, 12-108, 12-110, and 12-112.

Source. — This Rule is derived from former Rule U23.

Maryland Law Review. — For note, "The Maryland Survey: 2001-2002: Recent Decisions: The Court of Appeals of Maryland: VI. Eminent Domain," see 62 Md. L. Rev. 840 (2003).

Having recognized that an owner suffers additional damage when payment of a condemnation award is delayed, the General Assembly has authorized compensation for the loss of the use of money to the extent of the payment of interest from the date of the judgment nisi. Acting Dir., Dep't of Forests & Parks v. Walker, 39 Md. App. 298, 385 A.2d 806 (1978), aff'd, 284 Md. 357, 396 A.2d 262 (1979).

Liability to adverse claimant for compensation paid pursuant to award. — When a condemnor voluntarily pays to the wrong person, he does so at his peril, but when the compensation is paid pursuant to an award of court, the condemnor is not liable to an adverse claimant even though the court award may be erroneous. Bugg v. Maryland Transp. Auth., 31 Md. App. 622, 358 A.2d 562, cert. denied, 278 Md. 717 (1976), appeal dismissed, 429 U.S. 1082, 97 S. Ct. 1088, 51 L. Ed. 2d 529 (1977).

Rule 12-211. Abandonment.

(a) **Method.** A plaintiff may abandon an action for condemnation only by filing a written election to abandon it. A copy of the election shall be served as provided in Rule 1-321 upon each defendant over whom the court has obtained personal jurisdiction, and as the court may direct upon each other defendant.

(b) **When not allowed.** An action for condemnation may not be abandoned:

(1) after taking has occurred; or

(2) more than 120 days after the entry of judgment unless an appeal is taken; or

(3) if an appeal was taken, more than 120 days after the receipt by the clerk of the lower court of a mandate of the Court of Special Appeals or, if the Court of Appeals assumes jurisdiction, of the Court of Appeals evidencing (A) the dismissal of the appeal by the Court, (B) the affirmance of the judgment, (C) the entry of judgment pursuant to Rule 8-604 (e), or (D) the modification of the judgment without the award of a new trial. For purposes of this subsection, an appeal taken by the plaintiff that is stricken pursuant to Rule 8-203 or voluntarily dismissed shall be treated as if not taken, and the time allowed for abandonment shall be determined in accordance with subsections (1) and (2) of this section.

(c) **Effect.** The filing of the election shall reduce any money judgment entered in the civil action to a judgment for costs only, and the clerk shall make entries on the docket and judgment record necessary to reflect this effect. The filing of the election shall also annul any inquisition returned and any judgment entered in the action, to the extent that the inquisition or judgment affects the title of any defendant to the property that was sought to be condemned, and the clerk of any court where the inquisition has been recorded among the land records shall make a notation in the land records, in the same manner in which a release of a lien instrument is recorded, that the action has been abandoned.

(d) **Recovery of expenses.** Upon the abandonment of an action for condemnation, the defendant is entitled to recover from the plaintiff the reasonable legal, appraisal, and engineering fees actually incurred by the defendant because of the condemnation proceeding. If the parties agree on an amount, they shall file with the clerk statement of their agreement. If the parties cannot agree, the court shall determine the amount on motion of either party. The clerk shall enter the amount agreed upon or determined by the court as a part of the costs.

Cross references. — *See* Code, Real Property Article, § 12-109 relating to abandonment generally. *See also* Code, Real Property Article, § 12-102 as to when a "taking" occurs.

Source. — This Rule is derived from former Rule U26.

For circumstances under which amendment or abandonment in condemnation cases is permitted, see Concannon v. State Rds. Comm'n, 231 Md. 87, 188 A.2d 700 (1963).

Former Rule U26 d (see now section (d) of this Rule) is nearly identical to § 12-109 (e) of the Real Property Article. Southern Md. Elec. Coop. v. Albrittain, 256 Md. 39, 259 A.2d 311 (1969).

Any liability of condemning authority for extraordinary costs, such as are set forth in section (d) of this Rule and in § 12-109 (e) of the Real Property Article, is not automatic and must be supportable for reasons independent of the operation of former Rule 530 (now see Rule 2-507). 61 Op. Att'y Gen. 105 (1976).

Property taking — Trial court erred in granting the city's petitions to allow the city to take immediate possession of the property owner's properties using a procedure known as a "quick-take" possession where the city did not show any emergency that existed which required the city, in the public interest to take immediate possession of the properties; regular condemnation proceedings should have been used and if an acceptable price was reached, the condemnation proceedings could have been abandoned. Sapero v. Mayor of Baltimore, 398 Md. 317, 920 A.2d 1061 (2007).

A taking of property may occur without actual physical appropriation, entry or seizure. Hardesty v. State Rds. Comm'n of State Hwy. Admin., 276 Md. 25, 343 A.2d 884 (1975).

And without formally divesting owner of title. — There can be a taking of property giving rise to a vested right of compensation without formally divesting the owner of his title. Hardesty v. State Rds. Comm'n of State Hwy. Admin., 276 Md. 25, 343 A.2d 884 (1975).

Amending extent of taking to scenic easement. — See Hardesty v. State Rds. Comm'n of State Hwy. Admin., 276 Md. 25, 343 A.2d 884 (1975).

Cited in Utilities, Inc. v. Washington Sub. San. Comm'n, 362 Md. 37, 763 A.2d 129 (2000).

Rule 12-212. Recording.

(a) **Generally.** Upon the entry of judgment for the plaintiff for the property condemned and the filing of a certification by the plaintiff that the award has been paid to the defendant or into court, the clerk shall record the inquisition among the land records of the county in the same manner in which deeds are recorded. If the judgment is reversed on appeal or otherwise vacated or modified, the clerk shall make a notation to that effect in the land records in the same manner in which a release of a lien instrument is recorded, and if the judgment and inquisition have been recorded in any other county, the clerk shall give notice in the manner provided by Rule 2-622 (b).

(b) **Recording inquisition in other county.** Upon the entry of judgment in an action for condemnation of real or leasehold property located in more than one county, the plaintiff shall file with the clerk of the circuit court of each other county in which any part of the property is located a certified copy of the judgment, the docket entries, the complaint, and the inquisition. The clerk shall promptly record and index these documents in accordance with Rule 2-623.

Source. — This Rule is derived from former Rules U22 and U24b.

Condemning authority has no right to possession until condemnation judgment paid in full. — In conventional condemnation cases, no right to possession of the property is obtained by the condemning authority until it pays the full amount of the condemnation judgment, plus costs. King v. State Rds. Comm'n, 298 Md. 80, 467 A.2d 1032 (1983).

Rule 12-213. Board of property review procedure.

(a) **Scope.** This Rule applies to all actions under Code, Transportation Article, Title 8, Subtitle 3 that are certified to a board of property review.

Cross references. — The property review board procedure applies to acquisitions by condemnation by the State Roads Commission under Code, Transportation Article, Title 8, Subtitle 3.

(b) **Plats and maps.** In addition to any other requirements, plats and maps that are to be filed with the clerk of the court in proceedings subject to this Rule shall (1) state the amount of land sought to be taken, (2) refer to an existing permanent marker or monument outside the land sought to be taken from each owner, and (3) define and show the land sought to be taken from each owner so that its area may be computed with substantial accuracy from the plat or map.

Cross references. — *See* Code, Transportation Article, § 8-321.

(c) **Certificate to board.** (1) Filing. No later than six calendar months after the plats or maps referred to in section (b) of this Rule have been filed with the clerk of court as provided by law, a party may have the action referred to the board by filing a written notice to that effect with the clerk of the court.

(2) Duty of clerk. Upon the filing of the notice, the clerk shall certify the action promptly to the board by sending all pleadings and exhibits and a certified copy of the docket entries to the chairman of the board.

(d) **Hearing.** (1) Date. The board shall hear the action promptly but in no event later than three months after the filing of the notice of referral. Priority shall be given to an action involving a residence or commercial building.

(2) Notice. The board shall give each party at least ten days written notice of the date, time, and place of the hearing.

(3) Conduct — In general. The hearing may be conducted in an informal manner, and the board is not bound by the rules of evidence or procedure, except as provided in this Rule.

(4) Rights of parties. Each party has the right to be represented by counsel, to introduce evidence, to cross-examine, and to make oral argument upon the evidence.

(5) View. Unless waived in writing by all parties, the board shall view the property in question before taking testimony.

(6) *Witnesses to be sworn.* Witnesses shall be sworn by a member of the board or by some other person authorized to administer oaths.

(e) **Award.** As soon as practicable but in no event more than 30 days after the conclusion of the hearing, the board shall file with the clerk of the court a written award that explains the basis of its decision. The board shall serve the award pursuant to Rule 1-321 and file proof of service pursuant to Rule 1-323.

(f) **Case unheard or undetermined.** If the board has not heard the action within three months after the filing of the notice of referral or if the board has not filed a copy of its award with the clerk of the court within 30 days after the conclusion of the hearing, any party may serve upon the chairman of the board a written request that the board relinquish jurisdiction of the action. Upon service of the request, the board shall return to the clerk of the court the pleadings and exhibits in the action, and the case shall proceed as if notice of dissatisfaction with an award of the board was given.

(g) **Dissatisfaction with award.** (1) Notice — Time. Within 30 days after the filing of the award of the board with the clerk of the court, any dissatisfied party may file written notice of dissatisfaction with the clerk of the court.

(2) *Plaintiff's duty to file complaint.* Unless it has already done so, the condemning party shall file a complaint for condemnation within 30 days after the filing of notice of dissatisfaction. Except as provided in subsection (3) of this section, the action shall proceed thereafter as if the matter had never been certified to the board.

(3) *Extension of time to file description.* For good cause, the court may extend the time for filing the description required to be filed with the complaint for a period, not to exceed 90 days from the date of the filing of the complaint for condemnation, as may be just.

Cross references. — Code, Real Property Article, § 12-101 and Transportation Article, §§ 8-318 through 8-331.

Source. — This Rule is derived from former Rule U27.

Former Rule U27 was mandatory. State Rds. Comm'n v. Laurel Pines Country Club, 256 Md. 605, 261 A.2d 480 (1970).

Purpose of Rule. — The evident purpose of § 8-330 of the Transportation Article, and former Rule U27 was to give the Commission a defined and restricted limit within which to proceed to condemn. The owner cannot institute a condemnation suit so the law gave him the right to require the Commission, who can, to do so promptly, that is, within thirty days. First Nat'l Realty Corp. v. State Rds. Comm'n, 247 Md. 709, 234 A.2d 577 (1967).

The purpose of former Rule U27 could not be frustrated by filing a revised notice of the award, the avowed and single purpose of which was to extend the thirty-day period. State Rds. Comm'n v. Laurel Pines Country Club, 256 Md. 605, 261 A.2d 480 (1970).

The board of property review has only three months for a hearing. State Rds. Comm'n v. Orleans, 239 Md. 368, 211 A.2d 715 (1965).

And it has only an additional month to make an award. State Rds. Comm'n v. Orleans, 239 Md. 368, 211 A.2d 715 (1965).

The thirty-day provision under section (g) (2) is mandatory once the owner's notice of dissatisfaction is filed. First Nat'l Realty Corp. v. State Rds. Comm'n, 247 Md. 709, 234 A.2d 577 (1967).

Section (g) (2) requiring the condemning party to institute condemnation proceedings within thirty days after a notice of dissatisfaction is filed is mandatory, not directory. State Rds. Comm'n v. O'Boyle, 250 Md. 512, 243 A.2d 530 (1968).

Once the owner files a notice of dissatisfaction the Commission's duty to condemn within thirty days thereof is mandatory and ineluctable. State Rds. Comm'n v. O'Boyle, 250 Md. 512, 243 A.2d 530 (1968).

Discrepancy between section (g) and § 8-323 (a) (1) of the Transportation Article. — Under §§ 8-325 and 8-326 of the Transportation Article, referral to the board occurs after the petition for condemnation is filed but section (g) suggests that the petition is not filed until after the board has rendered its award or the case has been removed from its jurisdiction; it appears that the Commission has resolved this apparent inconsistency by referring to the first petition, that filed pursuant to § 8-323 of the Transportation Article, as an "informal" petition and regarding as the "formal" petition that actually commences the litigation that which is filed pursuant to the Rule. State Roads Comm'n v. G.L. Cornell Co., 85 Md. App. 765, 584 A.2d 1331 (1991), cert. denied, 325 Md. 248, 600 A.2d 418 (1992).

"Right of appeal." — The "right of appeal" given to a party dissatisfied with the award of a review board is the right of the owner to compel the filing of a condemnation case within thirty days of a demand therefor and the right of the condemnor to file a condemnation suit within thirty days of the review board's award. State Rds. Comm'n v. O'Boyle, 250 Md. 512, 243 A.2d 530 (1968).

Failure to file petition for condemnation. — Where the State files a notice of dissatisfaction and then fails to file its petition for condemnation within thirty days, under section (g) (2) it loses its right to have the Court of Appeals hear the petition. State Rds. Comm'n v. O'Boyle, 250 Md. 512, 243 A.2d 530 (1968).

Failure to hear case or make award within time provided by Rule. — If the case is not heard by the Board within three months or if an award is not made within thirty days after the hearing, either side may order the matter sent to court for the filing of a condemnation petition. State Rds. Comm'n v. Orleans, 239 Md. 368, 211 A.2d 715 (1965).

CHAPTER 300. MECHANICS' LIENS.

Rule 12-301. Applicability — Definitions.

(a) **Applicability.** The rules in this Chapter govern actions in which establishment and enforcement of a mechanics' lien are sought.

(b) **Definitions.** In this Chapter, the following definitions apply:

(1) Building. "Building" includes any unit of a nonresidential building that is leased or sold separately as a unit.

(2) Contract. "Contract" means an agreement of any kind or nature, express or implied, for doing work or furnishing material, for or about a building that may give rise to a mechanics' lien.

(3) Contractor. "Contractor" means a person who has a contract with an owner.

(4) Land. "Land" means the interest in land to which a mechanics' lien extends or the interest in land within the boundaries established by proceedings in accordance with Rule 12-308. "Land" includes the improvements to the land.

(5) Mechanics' lien or lien. "Mechanics' lien" or "lien" means a lien established pursuant to Code, Real Property Article, §§ 9-101 through 9-112.

(6) Owner. "Owner" means the owner of record of the land except that, when the contractor executes the contract with a tenant for life or for years, "owner" means the tenant.

(7) Subcontractor. "Subcontractor" means a person who has a contract with anyone except the owner or the owner's agent.

Cross references. — Code, Real Property Article, § 9-101.

Source. — This Rule is derived from former Rule BG70.

University of Baltimore Law Review. — For analysis of the new mechanics' lien law, see 6 U. Balt. L. Rev. 181 (1976).

For article, "The Maryland Rules — A Time for Overhaul," see 9 U. Balt. L. Rev. 1 (1979).

Notice to owner of property. — Notice is required under § 9-104 of the Real Property Article for the protection of the owner of the property; on receipt of notice, the owner is afforded an opportunity to withhold, from the sums due the contractor, the amount the owner ascertains to be due the subcontractor. National Glass, Inc. v. J.C. Penney Properties, Inc., 329 Md. 300, 619 A.2d 528 (1993).

Complaint defective for failure to name all condominium unit owners. — As a condominium regime lawfully existed at a building under § 11-102 of the Real Property Article, notice had to be given to all condominium unit owners under § 9-104 of the Real Property Article, and all such owners had to be parties to the case before a mechanic's lien could be established as against the entire building. Since only one of the two owners had been named a party, the trial court erred in entering an order establishing a mechanic's lien. S. Mgmt. Corp. v. Kevin Willes Constr. Co., 382 Md. 524, 856 A.2d 626 (2004).

Quoted in Wolf Org., Inc. v. Oles, 119 Md. App. 357, 705 A.2d 40 (1998).

Rule 12-302. Commencement of action.

(a) **How commenced.** An action to establish a mechanics' lien shall be commenced by filing a complaint in the county where all or any part of the land to be subject to the lien is located.

(b) **Complaint.** The complaint shall be under oath by the plaintiff or a person making oath on the plaintiff's behalf. It shall be accompanied by the original or sworn, certified, or photostatic copies of material papers that constitute the basis of the lien unless their absence is explained in the complaint. In addition to complying with Rules 2-303 through 2-305, the complaint shall set forth facts upon which the plaintiff claims entitlement to the lien in the amount specified and shall contain at least the following:

(1) the name and address of the plaintiff;

(2) the name and address of the owner;

(3) the kind of work done or the kind and amount of materials furnished, the time when the work was done or the materials furnished, the name of the person for whom the work was done or to whom the materials were furnished, and the amount claimed to be due, less any credit recognized by the plaintiff, and if the lien is sought to be established against two or more buildings on separate lots or parcels of land owned by the same person, a designation of the amount claimed to be due on each building;

Cross references. — *See* Code, Real Property Article, § 9-105 (a) (1) for the consequence of failing to make the designation required when multiple buildings on separate lots are involved.

(4) a description of the land, including, if part of the land is located in another county, a statement to that effect, and a description adequate to identify the building;

(5) if a building is not newly erected, a statement that it has been repaired, rebuilt, or improved to the extent of 15 percent of its value; and

(6) if the plaintiff is a subcontractor, facts showing that the notice required under Code, Real Property Article, § 9-104 was properly mailed or served upon the owner or, if so authorized, posted on the building.

(c) **Defendants.** The plaintiff shall bring an action to establish a mechanics' lien against the owner of the land against which the lien is sought to be established. The plaintiff may join, but is not required to join, any other person who has or may have an interest in the land and who may be entitled to share in the proceeds of a sale of the land.

Source. — This Rule is derived from former Rule BG71.

Maryland Law Review. — For article discussing mechanics' liens in Maryland after *Barry Properties*, see 36 Md. L. Rev. 733 (1977).

University of Baltimore Law Review. — For analysis of the new mechanics' lien law, see 6 U. Balt. L. Rev. 181 (1976).

For article, "The Maryland Rules — A Time for Overhaul," see 9 U. Balt. L. Rev. 1 (1979).

Proceeding in rem. — All proceedings for the enforcement of mechanics' liens are exclusively in rem. The subject matter adjudicated is the lien in favor of the claimant upon a specific piece of property. Gaybis v. Palm, 201 Md. 78, 93 A.2d 269 (1952).

Complaint defective for failing to name all condominium unit owners. — As a condominium regime lawfully existed at a building under § 11-102 of the Real Property Article, notice had to be given to all condominium unit owners under § 9-104 of the Real Property Article, and all such owners had to be parties to the case before a mechanic's lien could be established as against the entire building. Since only one of the two owners had been named a party, the trial court erred in entering an order establishing a mechanic's lien. S. Mgmt. Corp. v. Kevin Willes Constr. Co., 382 Md. 524, 856 A.2d 626 (2004).

Where a contractor's complaint to establish a mechanics' lien alleged that only one of two condominium owners and its managing agent were the owners of a building, but a second condominium owner had a separate property interest in the building, the complaint was deficient under § 9-105(a)(1)(ii) of the Real Property Article and subsection (b) of this Rule for not naming the second owner as an owner. S. Mgmt. Corp. v. Kevin Willes Constr. Co., 382 Md. 524, 856 A.2d 626 (2004).

Subcontractor entitled to presumption of indebtedness. — If a subcontractor who has supplied labor or material to a single family dwelling properly alleges that which is required under the law, it may be presumed that, at the time the contractor's notice was sent, the owner was indebted to the prime contractor in an amount at least equivalent to the subcontractor's claim, because of (i) the inference that the owner will not have settled in full with the prime contractor without an assurance that all subcontractors have been paid, (ii) the fact that between the owner and the subcontractor, any contrary information is

peculiarly within the knowledge of the owner, and (iii) the fact that the owner has an ample opportunity to raise the issue and present the relevant evidence. Winkler Constr. Co. v. Jerome, 355 Md. 231, 734 A.2d 212 (1999).

Complaint defective for failing to name all condominium unit owners. — As a condominium regime lawfully existed at a building under § 11-102 of the Real Property Article, notice had to be given to all condominium unit owners under § 9-104 of the Real Property Article, and all such owners had to be parties to the case before a mechanic's lien could be established as against the entire building. Since only one of the two owners had been named a party, the trial court erred in entering an order establishing a mechanic's lien. S. Mgmt. Corp. v. Kevin Willes Constr. Co., 382 Md. 524, 856 A.2d 626 (2004).

Action to establish mechanics' lien — Intermediate appellate court did not err in affirming the trial court's judgment that granted the contractor's petition to compel arbitration and found that under the totality of the circumstances, the contractor had not waived its right to arbitration merely by seeking and obtaining an interlocutory mechanics' lien; seeking and obtaining the lien was the contractor's way of protecting itself from a claim that it violated the time period for filing for a lien and as a means of insuring that it would be paid, and did not indicate any intent to waive the right to arbitrate. Brendsel v. Winchester Constr. Co., 392 Md. 601, 898 A.2d 472 (2006).

Assertion of adverse party's defense. — This Rule does not require that a party or an attorney assert an adverse party's defense, much less produce evidence in support of it, when the party disputes that defense. Winkler Constr. Co. v. Jerome, 355 Md. 231, 734 A.2d 212 (1999).

Setoff. — In a mechanics' lien action, the owner was allowed a setoff for failure to perform certain work properly, but not on account of an unusual water condition which made the specified construction inadequate, there being no warranty that the plans and specifications were sufficient. Gaybis v. Palm, 201 Md. 78, 93 A.2d 269 (1952).

No statement regarding owner's indebtedness required. — There is no requirement that a subcontractor's complaint include a statement regarding an owner's indebtedness to the prime contractor. Winkler Constr. Co. v. Jerome, 355 Md. 231, 734 A.2d 212 (1999).

Stated in Wolf Org., Inc. v. Oles, 119 Md. App. 357, 705 A.2d 40 (1998).

Rule 12-303. Amendment.

Pleadings in an action to establish a mechanics' lien may be amended pursuant to Rule 2-341, except that after the expiration of the period within which notice of the lien claim must be given, or the complaint to establish the lien must be filed if notice is not required, no amendment shall be permitted that will increase the amount of the claim or materially alter the description of the land.

Cross references. — Code, Real Property Article, § 9-112.

Source. — This Rule is derived from former Rule BG72.

Maryland Law Review. — For article discussing mechanics' liens in Maryland after *Barry Properties*, see 36 Md. L. Rev. 733 (1977).

University of Baltimore Law Review. — For analysis of the new mechanics' lien law, see 6 U. Balt. L. Rev. 181 (1976).

For article, "The Maryland Rules — A Time for Overhaul," see 9 U. Balt. L. Rev. 1 (1979).

Rights to amend are stated in § 9-112 of the Real Property Article and in this Rule. Mervin L. Blades & Son v. Lighthouse Sound Marina & Country Club, 37 Md. App. 265, 377 A.2d 523 (1977).

Rule prevails in conflict. — To the extent that there was a conflict between § 9-112 of the Real Property Article and former Rule BG72, the Rule prevailed until it was repealed

or modified by a subsequent statute or rule. Scott & Wimbrow, Inc. v. Wisterco Invs., Inc., 36 Md. App. 274, 373 A.2d 965 (1977).

It is difficult to imagine any more extensive power of amendment than that allowed in proceedings concerning mechanics' liens. Baltimore Contractors v. Valley Mall Assocs., 27 Md. App. 695, 341 A.2d 845 (1975).

Amendment held to materially alter description of property. — An amendment of the lien claim which would set forth the locality of the building, or buildings, and a description adequate to identify them, would materially alter the description of the property against which the lien claim was recorded. Mervin L. Blades & Son v. Lighthouse Sound Marina & Country Club, 37 Md. App. 265, 377 A.2d 523 (1977).

Rule 12-304. Proceedings.

(a) **Court review.** The court shall review the complaint and any exhibits and may require the plaintiff to supplement or explain any of the matters set forth in the complaint and exhibits.

(b) **Order.** (1) Entry; contents. If the court determines that there is a reasonable ground for the lien to attach, it shall enter an order directing the defendant to file an answer under oath on or before a date indicated in the order, showing cause why a lien for the amount claimed should not attach to the land described in the complaint, provided that a copy of the order together with copies of the pleadings and exhibits filed shall have been served on the defendant by the deadline for service specified in the order. The order also shall (A) set a date for hearing no later than 45 days from the date of the order, (B) advise the defendant of the defendant's right to appear and present evidence at the hearing, and (C) warn the defendant that if the defendant fails to file a timely answer, the facts set forth in the plaintiff's complaint shall be deemed admitted and the hearing waived, and the court may enter an order establishing the lien.

(2) Service. The order, together with copies of the pleadings and exhibits filed, shall be served on the defendant in the manner provided by Rule 2-121.

(c) **Answer; failure to file deemed admission.** A defendant may controvert any statement of fact in the plaintiff's complaint by filing an answer under oath. The failure to file an answer within the time allowed by the order shall constitute an admission for the purpose of the action of all statements of fact in the plaintiff's complaint, but shall not constitute an admission that the complaint is legally sufficient.

(d) **Hearing.** If the defendant fails to answer within the time allowed by the order, the court may at any time thereafter, without hearing and without further notice to the defendant, enter an order in conformity with section (e) of this Rule. If the defendant files an answer in compliance with the order, a hearing shall be held as scheduled.

(e) **Relief granted.** (1) Judgment if no genuine dispute. (A) If the pleadings and admissions on file and any evidence show that there is no genuine dispute as to any material fact and that the lien should attach as a matter of law, the court shall enter a judgment establishing the lien. If it appears that there is no genuine dispute as to a portion of the lien claim, the court shall enter an order establishing the validity of the lien as to that portion and the action shall proceed only on the disputed amount of the lien claim.

(B) If the pleadings and admissions on file and any evidence show that there is no genuine dispute as to any material fact and that the plaintiff, as a matter of law, has failed to establish a right to a lien, a judgment shall be entered denying the lien.

(2) Interlocutory order if probable cause. If the court determines from the pleadings and admissions on file and any evidence that a judgment under subsection (e)(1)(A) should not be entered, but that there is probable cause to believe the plaintiff is entitled to a lien, the court shall enter an interlocutory order that:

(A) establishes a lien;

(B) describes the land to which the lien attaches;

(C) states the amount of the claim for which probable cause is found;

(D) specifies the amount of a bond which may be filed by the defendant to have the land released from the lien; and

(E) assigns a date within six months for a trial of all matters that may be necessary to adjudicate the establishment of the lien.

The owner or any other person interested in the land may move at any time for modification or dissolution of the lien established by the interlocutory order.

(3) Probable cause not found. If no judgment or interlocutory order is entered under subsections (1) and (2), the court shall enter an order that the portion of the complaint seeking to establish the lien be dismissed unless the plaintiff, within 30 days thereafter, files a written request that the portion of the complaint seeking to establish the lien be assigned for trial.

(4) Bond by plaintiff. In an interlocutory order entered under subsection (2) of this section, the court may require the plaintiff to file a bond in an amount that the court determines to be sufficient for damages, including reasonable attorney's fees. The lien shall not attach until any required bond is filed.

(5) Trial. At the conclusion of the action a judgment shall be entered either continuing or terminating a lien established by an interlocutory order, or establishing or denying the lien.

Committee note. — This Rule renders impermissible an oral response to a show cause order previously permitted by Code, Real Property Article, § 9-106.

Source. — This Rule is derived from former Rule BG73.

Maryland Law Review. — For article discussing mechanics' liens in Maryland after *Barry Properties*, see 36 Md. L. Rev. 733 (1977).

University of Baltimore Law Review. — For analysis of the new mechanics' lien law, see 6 U. Balt. L. Rev. 181 (1976).

For article, "The Maryland Rules — A Time for Overhaul," see 9 U. Balt. L. Rev. 1 (1979).

Probable cause. — The probable cause determination is similar to a criminal case: whether, based on the pleadings and evidence before the trial judge, and weighing the facts, the trial judge believes that the petitioner is more or less likely to prevail at the trial on the merits. Reisterstown Lumber Co. v. Royer, 91 Md. App. 746, 605 A.2d 980, cert. denied, 327 Md. 626, 612 A.2d 257 (1992).

Trial court did not make a "no probable cause" finding under (a)(3) for the issuance of a mechanic's lien sought by the contractor against the building owner nor was it required to do so. The evidence showed that the contractor was an unlicensed home improvement contractor at the time it performed the relevant work and, thus, there was no question but that it could not enforce a home improvement contract by imposition of a mechanic's lien. Balt. St. Builders v. Stewart, 186 Md. App. 684, 975 A.2d 271 (2009).

Benefit of doubt. — In truly close cases, the benefit of the doubt at a show cause hearing should go to the materialman seeking the mechanics' lien, for two reasons. First, an owner burdened with a mechanics' lien may post a bond to have the lien removed, under former Rule BG76 a 1, while the materialman denied an interlocutory lien has no alternative means by which to protect himself. Second, to restrict a materialman's right to a mechanics' lien too severely would likely have a negative economic impact on the housing market, as materialmen would be less likely to extend credit to either general contractors or property owners. Reisterstown Lumber Co. v. Royer, 91 Md. App. 746, 605 A.2d 980, cert. denied, 327 Md. 626, 612 A.2d 257 (1992).

Admission. — Trial court did not err in entering a final order establishing a mechanics' lien in favor of the subcontractor and against the church in regard to a church building project; the church's failure to file an answer to the subcontractor's complaint for a mechanics' lien meant that the church was deemed to have admitted the facts in the complaint, which showed that the subcontractor was entitled to the lien on the church's property in the subcontractor's favor. Cottage City Mennonite Church, Inc. v. JAS Trucking, Inc., 167 Md. App. 694, 894 A.2d 609 (2006).

In determining whether there is genuine dispute of material fact and, if not, whether the claimant is, or is not, entitled to a lien as a matter of law, the court is in the same position as a judge passing upon a motion for summary judgment and it is not justified in weighing the evidence and adjudicating the case. E.L. Gardner, Inc. v. Bowie Joint Venture, 64 Md. App. 302, 494 A.2d 988, cert. denied, 304 Md. 296, 498 A.2d 1183 (1985).

Construction and weight of answer on motion to dismiss. — Answer to a mechanics' lien, which answer alleged the existence of other buildings on the property where the subject building was located, was not dispositive for purposes of a motion to dismiss because that allegation, unlike those in the petition, which were to be taken in the light most favorable to the subcontractor, need not have been viewed in the light most favorable to the owners. At best the answer created a dispute of fact, the resolution of which was a matter for the trier of fact pursuant to § 9-106(b) of the Real Property Article and (e) of this Rule. Arfaa v. Martino, 404 Md. 364, 946 A.2d 995 (2008).

Owner's pleadings valid and sufficient. — Order establishing a mechanic's lien was improper because both of the owner's verified answers were valid and sufficient under § 9-106(a)(2) of the Real Property Article, and an evidentiary hearing was required; pursuant to Rule 1-311, the owner's answers were valid because they were signed by counsel, and nothing in the North Carolina statutes prohibited the owner, acting through a manager, from authorizing the affiant to file an affidavit on its behalf. Even if N.C. Gen. Stat. § § 57C-3-24(a) required written authorization for the affidavit filed in this case, there was no requirement that the existence of the authorization be recited in the affidavit. T.W. Herring

Invs., LLC v. Atl. Builders Group, Inc., 186 Md. App. 673, 975 A.2d 264 (2009).

Entry of order — Trial court was authorized under (d) to enter a final order establishing a mechanics' lien in favor of the subcontractor and against the church in the church's building project; the church's failure to file an answer in regard to the subcontractor's complaint for entry of the lien pursuant to an arbitration award meant that the trial court had the power to enter an order granting that lien. Cottage City Mennonite Church, Inc. v. JAS Trucking, Inc., 167 Md. App. 694, 894 A.2d 609 (2006).

Applied in Jerome v. Winkler Constr. Co., 123 Md. App. 546, 720 A.2d 1 (1998); Winkler Constr. Co. v. Jerome, 355 Md. 231, 734 A.2d 212 (1999).

Rule 12-305. Enforcement of lien.

(a) **Time for filing motion to enforce.** A plaintiff may not enforce a lien or execute on a bond given to obtain a release of the lien until the lien has been established by a judgment. To enforce a lien or to execute on any bond given to obtain a release of the lien, the plaintiff shall file a motion in the original action within one year after the date on which the complaint to establish the lien was filed. The motion to enforce may be included in the original complaint to establish the lien.

(b) **Order.** An order granted pursuant to a motion to enforce shall direct that the land be sold unless the amount found to be due is paid on or before a date specified in the order, which shall be not more than 30 days after the date of the order.

(c) **Sale.** The sale shall be conducted pursuant to Title 14, Chapter 300 of these rules.

Source. — This Rule is derived from former Rule BG74.

Maryland Law Review. — For article discussing mechanics' liens in Maryland after *Barry Properties*, see 36 Md. L. Rev. 733 (1977).

University of Baltimore Law Review. — For analysis of the new mechanics' lien law, see 6 U. Balt. L. Rev. 181 (1976).

For article, "The Maryland Rules — A Time for Overhaul," see 9 U. Balt. L. Rev. 1 (1979).

A decree for enforcement of a mechanics' lien has the standing of any other decree in equity. Weinberg v. Fanning, 208 Md. 567, 119 A.2d 383 (1956).

Rule 12-306. Referral to auditor.

After a sale under Rule 12-305, the court shall refer the proceedings to an auditor pursuant to Rule 2-543 to state an account.

Source. — This Rule is derived from former Rule BG75.

Maryland Law Review. — For article discussing mechanics' liens in Maryland after *Barry Properties*, see 36 Md. L. Rev. 733 (1977).

University of Baltimore Law Review. —

For analysis of the new mechanics' lien law, see 6 U. Balt. L. Rev. 181 (1976).

For article, "The Maryland Rules — A Time for Overhaul," see 9 U. Balt. L. Rev. 1 (1979).

Rule 12-307. Release of lien.

(a) **Motion.** At any time after a complaint to establish a mechanics' lien is filed, the owner of the land or any other person interested in the land may move to have the land released from any lien that has been established by court order or that may thereafter be established.

(b) **Bond; order.** Unless a bond has previously been set pursuant to Rule 12-304, the court, after an opportunity for a hearing, shall determine the amount of bond sufficient to protect the plaintiff. Upon the filing of the bond in the amount set by the court, the court shall enter an order releasing the land from the lien.

(c) **Entry of satisfaction.** (1) By plaintiff. If the amount of a mechanics' lien is paid or otherwise satisfied, the plaintiff or plaintiff's successor in interest, upon payment of costs, shall file promptly an order of satisfaction of the lien in every court where the lien is a matter of record.

(2) Entry upon motion. If the plaintiff or plaintiff's successor in interest fails to file an order of satisfaction, the owner of the land or any other person interested therein may move for entry of an order of satisfaction pursuant to Rule 2-626.

Source. — This Rule is derived from former Rule BG76.

Maryland Law Review. — For article discussing mechanics' liens in Maryland after *Barry Properties*, see 36 Md. L. Rev. 733 (1977).

University of Baltimore Law Review. — For analysis of the new mechanics' lien law, see 6 U. Balt. L. Rev. 181 (1976).

For article, "The Maryland Rules — A Time for Overhaul," see 9 U. Balt. L. Rev. 1 (1979).

Order releasing lien is interlocutory and not expressly included as appealable. — An order granting a petition under section a of former Rule BG76, releasing a mechanics' lien upon the filing of a bond, is an interlocutory order not expressly included among the interlocutory orders of a court of equity which can be appealed before final judgment by virtue of former Article 5, § 7 (see now § 12-303 of the Courts Article). Maietta v. Greenfield, 267 Md. 287, 297 A.2d 244 (1972).

Rule 12-308. Designation of boundaries.

(a) **Before commencement of construction.** An owner of land who, before commencement of construction, desires to define the boundaries of the land in accordance with Code, Real Property Article, § 9-103 (b) shall file a notice to establish boundaries in an ex parte proceeding in the county in which the property is located. The notice shall be captioned, filed, and indexed as any other civil action under the name of the owner of the land and shall contain:

(1) a reference to the conveyance or other means by which the owner acquired title to the land;

(2) a description of the newly established boundaries sufficient to identify the land with reasonable certainty; and

(3) a brief description of the construction for which the boundaries are established.

(b) **After commencement of construction.** (1) Motion. After the commencement of construction of any improvement upon land that might be subject to a claim for a mechanics' lien, the owner of the land or any other person interested in the land, including anyone who has or might assert a mechanics' lien against the land by reason of the construction, may file a motion in the circuit court for the county where the land is located requesting the court to designate the boundaries pursuant to this Rule and to issue a writ of survey for that purpose. If the person filing the motion is a party to a proceeding to establish or enforce the lien, the motion shall be filed in the first proceeding to which the person became a party.

(2) Parties. A motion filed under this section shall be served on the owner of the land, each person who has moved for or established a mechanics' lien against the land, and any other person designated by the court in accordance with Rule 2-121, except that if the motion is filed in a pending proceeding, it shall be served in accordance with Rule 1-321.

(3) Surveyor. The court shall issue a writ to a surveyor directing the surveyor to make a report to the court in which the surveyor shall determine and describe the boundaries of the land, including within the boundaries as much of the land as is necessary for the use of the improvement thereon for the purpose for which it is designated or reasonably adaptable.

(4) Action on report. A copy of the surveyor's report shall be furnished to the moving party and to each person required to be served under section (b)(2) of this Rule. Within 15 days thereafter any person to whom the surveyor's report is required to be furnished may file a motion requesting the court to determine boundaries other than those that the surveyor has reported. After a hearing on the motion or upon expiration of the 15 day period for filing a motion if no motion is filed, the court shall determine the boundaries or approve the surveyor's report for filing in the proceedings.

Source. — This Rule is derived from former Rule BG77.

Maryland Law Review. — For article discussing mechanics' liens in Maryland after *Barry Properties*, see 36 Md. L. Rev. 733 (1977).

University of Baltimore Law Review. — For analysis of the new mechanics' lien law, see 6 U. Balt. L. Rev. 181 (1976).

Sufficiency of property description. — Trial court erred by dismissing a subcontractor's petition for a mechanic's lien as a matter of law for failing to adequately describe the property, because the subcontractor's petition included the street addresses with street numbers and the nine-digit zip code used by the postal service and by the owners themselves in describing the location of their home. The addresses, combined with the information in the state tax assessment print-out and the 141 photographs included with the petition, were sufficient to enable interested parties to identify the land and the building that were the subject of the lien claim; therefore, the subcontractor sufficiently pled a prima facie claim for a mechanic's lien. Martino v. Arfaa, 169 Md. App. 692, 906 A.2d 945 (2006), aff'd, 946 A.2d 995, 2008 Md. LEXIS 193 (2008).

Pursuant to Md. Code Ann., Real Prop. § 9-103 and its implementing rule, Md. R. 12-308, although a building that was subjected to a mechanics' lien arguably was situated on more land than was reasonably necessary for its use and enjoyment, the subcontractor did not have the burden of designating the boundaries of the land adjacent to the building that were necessary for the ordinary and useful purposes of the building. Arfaa v. Martino, 404 Md. 364, 946 A.2d 995 (2008).

CHAPTER 400. PARTITION.

Rule 12-401. Partition or sale in lieu of partition.

(a) **Scope.** This Rule applies in any action where the relief sought is the partition of real or personal property or the sale of real or personal property in lieu of partition.

Cross references. — *See* Code, Real Property Article, § 14-107.

(b) **Judgment for sale.** (1) When permitted. When the relief sought is a sale in lieu of partition, the court shall order a sale only if it determines that the property cannot be divided without loss or injury to the parties interested.

(2) Conduct of sale. The sale shall be conducted in the manner provided by Title 14, Chapter 300 of these rules.

(c) **Judgment for partition.** (1) Appointment of commissioners. When the court orders a partition, unless all the parties expressly waive the appointment of commissioners, the court shall appoint not less than three nor more than five disinterested persons to serve as commissioners for the purpose of valuing and dividing the property. On request of the court, each party shall suggest disinterested persons willing to serve as commissioners. The order appointing the commissioners shall set the date on or before which the commissioners' report shall be filed. The commissioners shall make oath before a person authorized to administer an oath that they will faithfully perform the duties of their commission. If the appointment of commissioners is waived by the parties, the court shall value and divide the property.

(2) Report of commissioners. Within the time prescribed by the order of appointment, the commissioners shall file a written report. At the time the report is filed the commissioners shall serve on each party pursuant to Rule 1-321 a copy of the report together with a notice of the times within which exceptions to the report may be filed.

(3) Exceptions to report. Within ten days after the filing of the report, a party may file exceptions with the clerk. Within that period or within three days after service of the first exceptions, whichever is later, any other party may file exceptions. Exceptions shall be in writing and shall set forth the asserted error with particularity. Any matter not specifically set forth in the exceptions is waived unless the court finds that justice requires otherwise. The court may decide the exceptions without a hearing, unless a request for a hearing is filed with the exceptions or by an opposing party within five days after service of the exceptions.

(d) **Costs.** Payment of the compensation, fees, and costs of the commissioners may be included in the costs of the action and allocated among the parties as the court may direct.

Source. — This Rule is derived as follows: *Section (a)* is new.

Section (b) is derived from former Rule BJ71.

Section (c) is derived from former Rule BJ72 and BJ73.

Section (d) is new.

Court determines whether property shall be partitioned in kind or be sold in lieu of partition. Boyd v. Boyd, 32 Md. App. 411, 361 A.2d 146 (1976).

And chancellor's determination is reversed only if clearly erroneous. — Because the determination of the propriety of partition is exclusively in the province of the chancellor, an appellate court can reverse his determination only if it were clearly erroneous. Boyd v. Boyd, 32 Md. App. 411, 361 A.2d 146 (1976).

Court must first conclude that partition in kind is proper. — The appointment of commissioners (unless waived by the parties) becomes a factor only after the court itself has concluded that partition in kind is proper. Boyd v. Boyd, 32 Md. App. 411, 361 A.2d 146 (1976).

The sole responsibility of the commissioners is to "value and divide" the property in question. Boyd v. Boyd, 32 Md. App. 411, 361 A.2d 146 (1976).

CHAPTER 500. REDEMPTION OF GROUND RENT.

Rule 12-501. Redemption of ground rent vested in trustee without power of sale.

(a) **Scope.** This Rule applies to the redemption of a ground rent, whether reserved by lease or sublease, that is vested in a trustee without a power of sale. As used in this Rule, "trustee" includes a trustee under a will, deed, or other instrument, a life tenant, and the holder of a defeasible estate.

(b) **When action may be brought — Venue — Parties.** When a ground rent that is or becomes redeemable is vested in a trustee without a power of sale, the owner of the leasehold or the trustee may file an action for redemption in the county where the land subject to the ground rent is located. The owner of the leasehold interest and the trustee are necessary parties. The plaintiff may join, but is not required to join, a remainderman or any other person who has or may have a beneficial interest in the land and who may be entitled to share in the redemption money.

(c) **Complaint — Content.** In addition to complying with Rules 2-303 through 2-305, the complaint shall be under oath and shall set forth:

(1) the location and description of the land;

(2) the date and place of record of the lease or sublease by which the reversion and rent were created;

(3) the amount of the annual rent and the redemption price of the leasehold interest;

(4) a statement that the owner of the leasehold desires to redeem the ground rent; and

(5) a statement that the notice required by law or by the lease has been given by the owner of the leasehold interest.

(d) **Bond.** Unless the trustee has previously given a bond that protects the redemption money or has been excused from filing a bond by the instrument creating the trust, the trustee shall file a bond as prescribed by Rule 10-702. Upon deposit of the redemption money by the trustee in the manner provided by Rule 10-705, the bond shall be released regardless of the amount of the entire estate or the amount of the redemption money.

(e) **Order of conveyance — Appointment of substitute trustee.** The court may order the trustee to convey the reversion in the land to the owner of the leasehold interest upon payment of the sum of money for which the ground rent is redeemable together with the amount of annual rent accrued to the date of payment. If the trustee is the owner of the leasehold interest, the court may appoint a substitute trustee to receive the redemption money and execute the deed.

(f) **Accounting and investment by trustee.** The trustee shall account promptly to the court for the redemption money received by the trustee. The court may order the redemption money invested for the purpose of holding it in place of the redeemed ground rent for the benefit of the persons entitled to the redeemed ground rent.

(g) **Costs.** If the relief sought in the complaint is granted, the court costs of the action, including the expenses of obtaining a bond, shall be paid out of the money received for the redemption. Otherwise, the court shall allocate costs pursuant to Rule 2-603.

Source. — This Rule is derived as follows:
Section (a) is derived from former Rules Y70 and Y71.
Section (b) is derived from former Rules Y71, Y72, and Y73.
Section (c) is derived from former Rule Y74.
Section (d) is derived from former Rule Y76.
Section (e) is derived from former Rule Y77.
Section (f) is derived from former Rule Y78.
Section (g) is derived from former Rule Y79.

Maryland Law Review. — For article, "The Law/Equity Dichotomy in Maryland," see 39 Md. L. Rev. 427 (1980).

CHAPTER 600. REPLEVIN AND DETINUE.

Rule 12-601. Possession of personal property before judgment — Replevin.

(a) **Action in District Court.** A person claiming the right to immediate possession of personal property may file an action under this Rule for possession before judgment. The action shall be filed in the District Court.

(b) **Defendant.** The action shall be brought against the person who has possession of the property at the time the complaint is filed. A person who obtains possession after the complaint is filed shall be joined as a defendant.

Cross references. — Rule 3-211.

(c) **Complaint.** In addition to complying with Rules 3-303 through 3-305, the complaint shall contain (1) a description of the property claimed and an allegation of its value, (2) an allegation that the defendant unjustly detains the property, (3) a claim for return of the property, and (4) any claim for damages to the property or for its detention.

(d) **Summons and notice.** (1) Upon the filing of the complaint, the clerk shall issue a summons as in other civil actions and a notice to the defendant.

(2) The notice shall:

(A) indicate the time within which the notice must be served;

(B) advise the defendant that before trial on the complaint a hearing will be held to determine the right to possession before judgment, if the notice, the complaint, and any exhibits are served within the time prescribed in the notice;

(C) indicate the date of the hearing on the right to possession before judgment, which may not be less than seven days after service of the notice on the defendant unless the court orders otherwise;

(D) advise the defendant of the right to appear and present evidence at the hearing; and

(E) warn the defendant that the court may grant the plaintiff's request for possession before judgment and direct the sheriff to place the plaintiff in possession of the property unless the defendant appears personally and shows cause why the property described in the complaint should not be immediately returned to the plaintiff.

(e) **Service.** The notice shall be served with the summons and complaint and any exhibits.

(f) **Hearing.** The hearing shall be held as scheduled and shall proceed ex parte if the defendant fails to appear in response to the notice.

Cross references. — *See* Code, Courts Article, § 4-402 (e) (2) regarding the jurisdiction of the District Court to conduct the show cause hearing, to enforce any ancillary injunction, and to issue, renew, and receive returns on the writ of possession even if a jury trial is demanded.

(g) **Decision.** If the court determines that the plaintiff is entitled to possession before judgment, the court shall order issuance of a writ directing the sheriff to place the plaintiff in possession of the property, provided that the plaintiff files a bond for the satisfaction of all costs and damages that may be awarded to the defendant or a claimant of the property by reason of the possession. The order shall prescribe the amount of and security for the bond. If the claimed property cannot be found and the writ is returned unexecuted, the plaintiff may request reissuance of the writ or may proceed pursuant to section (h) of this Rule.

(h) **Further proceedings pursuant to Rule 12-602.** After the issue of the right to possession before judgment is determined, the action shall proceed as an action for recovery of property after judgment under Rule 12-602. If the value of the property remains at issue and that value and any damages claimed exceed the monetary jurisdiction of the District Court or a timely demand for jury trial has been filed, the clerk shall transmit the record to the circuit court in accordance with the procedures set forth in Rule 3-325.

Committee note. — For a thorough history and explanation of the action of replevin and its relationship to actions of detinue and trover, *see Wallander v. Barnes*, 341 Md. 553 (1996).

Source. — This Rule is derived from former M.D.R. BQ41 through BQ45 and BQ49.

In a replevin suit damages are limited to the damage for detention of the property. Koch v. Mack Int'l Motor Truck Corp., 201 Md. 562, 95 A.2d 105 (1953).

Judgment against certain defendants for damages only. — In action against four defendants to recover shares of stock, or their value, or damages for detention, declaration was in form one of detinue, while only one of defendants (bank commissioner, as receiver) was in possession of stock, hence judgment against others could be for damages only; action for detinue cannot be joined with one for damages, but point was not raised in lower court. Mylander v. Page, 162 Md. 255, 159 A. 770 (1932).

When judgment final. — The requirements of former § 59 of Article 75 were not so fundamental in their nature as to prevent a judgment, if not entered strictly in accordance with its terms from being a valid final judgment subject to be appealed. Hartford Accident & Indem. Co. v. State ex rel. Ritter, 201 Md. 433, 94 A.2d 639 (1953).

Verdict held erroneous. — A verdict "in favor of the defendant for the return of the property replevied and one cent damages and costs" is erroneous. Standard Horseshoe Co. v. O'Brien, 88 Md. 335, 41 A. 898 (1898).

Correction of erroneous verdict. — Although the verdict as originally rendered is erroneous, if it is properly corrected by jury before its record, error is cured. Farmers' Packing Co. v. Alexander Brown & Sons, 87 Md. 1, 39 A. 625 (1898).

How irregularity in verdict should be raised. — See Standard Horseshoe Co. v. O'Brien, 88 Md, 335, 41 A. 898 (1898).

Case remanded in order that property might be valued, and judgment entered in accordance with former § 59 of Article 75. B & O R.R. v. Rueter, 114 Md. 687, 80 A. 220 (1911).

Cited in Furda v. State, 193 Md. App. 371, 997 A.2d 856 (2010).

Rule 12-602. Recovery of property or value after judgment — Detinue.

(a) **Action.** (1) A person claiming the right to possession of personal property may file an action under this Rule.

(2) The action:

(A) shall be brought in the District Court if the value of the property and any damages claimed are within the exclusive jurisdiction of that court;

(B) may be brought in either the District Court or a circuit court if the value of the property and any damages claimed are within the concurrent jurisdiction of those courts; and

(C) shall be brought in the circuit court if the value of the property and any damages claimed exceed the monetary jurisdiction of the District Court.

(3) If the plaintiff has brought an action under Rule 12-601, a separate action under this Rule shall not be brought. If required by Rule 2-326, a new complaint shall be filed in accordance with that Rule.

(b) **Defendant.** The action shall be brought against the person who has possession of the property at the time the complaint is filed. A person who obtains possession after the complaint is filed shall be joined as a defendant.

Cross references. — Rules 2-211 and 3-211.

(c) **Complaint.** In addition to complying with Rules 2-303 through 2-305 or 3-303 through 3-305, the complaint shall contain (1) a description of the property claimed and an allegation of its value, (2) an allegation that the defendant unjustly detains the property, (3) a claim for return of the property or payment of its value, and (4) any claim for damages to the property or for its detention.

(d) **Judgment.** (1) For plaintiff. A judgment for the plaintiff shall award possession of the property or, in the alternative, payment of its value. The judgment shall separately set forth the value of the property and any amount awarded for damage to or detention of the property. Unless the court orders otherwise for good cause or the plaintiff agrees on the record to accept the value of the property as fixed by the judgment instead of return of the property, the plaintiff may enforce return of the property pursuant to Rules 2-647 or 3-647. The plaintiff may also seek enforcement of any damages awarded pursuant to the rules contained in Chapter 600 of Title 2 or Title 3, as appropriate.

(2) For defendant. If a judgment is entered for the defendant after the plaintiff has obtained immediate possession of the property pursuant to Rule 12-601, the court shall order return of the property to the defendant. On motion filed within 15 days after entry of the judgment, the court shall enter judgment for any damages sustained by the defendant by reason of the plaintiff's possession.

Source. — This Rule is derived from former M.D.R. BQ51 and former Maryland Rule BQ 53.

Objection to defect in amount of bond. — A defect in the amount of a bond must be immediately objected to or such defect will be deemed waived. See Burrier v. Cunningham Piano Co., 135 Md. 135, 108 A. 492 (1919).

Bond forfeited on breach of conditions. — See Doogan v. Tyson, 6 G. & J. 453 (1834); Crabbs v. Koontz, 69 Md. 59, 13 A. 591 (1888). **Quoted** in Harris v. State, 420 Md. 300, 22 A.3d 886 (2011).

CHAPTER 700. SEVERED MINERAL INTERESTS.

Rule 12-701. Definitions.

In this Chapter, the terms "mineral," "mineral interest," "severed mineral interest," "surface estate," "surface owner," and "unknown or missing owner" have the meanings set forth in Code, Environment Article, § 15-1201. A "dormant mineral interest" is a mineral interest that satisfies the criteria set forth in Code, Environment Article, § 15-1203 (a)(2). (Added June 7, 2011, effective July 1, 2011.)

Source. — This Rule is new.

Rule 12-702. Scope.

This Chapter does not apply to a mineral interest:

(a) held by the United States or a Native American tribe, except to the extent permitted by federal law; or

(b) held by the State or an agency or political subdivision of the State, except to the extent permitted by State law. (Added June 7, 2011, effective July 1, 2011.)

Source. — This Rule is derived from Code, Environment Article, § 15-1202 (a)(2).

Rule 12-703. Trust for unknown or missing owner of severed mineral interest.

(a) **Petition to Create Trust.** (1) Generally. An owner in fee simple of a surface estate subject to a severed mineral interest that is vested, in whole or in part, in an unknown or missing owner may file a petition to place the mineral interest of the unknown or missing owner in trust. The petition shall be filed in the circuit court of any county in which the surface estate is located.

Cross references. — Code, Environment Article, §§ 15-1201 through 15-1206.

(2) Contents. The petition shall be captioned "In the Matter of ..." stating the location of the surface estate subject to the severed mineral interest. It shall be signed and verified by the petitioner and shall contain at least the following information:

(A) the petitioner's name, address, and telephone number;

(B) the name and address of all other surface owners;

(C) the reason for seeking the assumption of jurisdiction by the court and a statement of the relief sought;

(D) a legal description of the severed mineral interest;

(E) the name, address, telephone number, and nature of the interest of all persons with a legal interest in the severed mineral interest, including any unknown or missing owners, and their heirs, successors, or assignees;

(F) an affidavit of the petitioner stating that the identity or whereabouts of one or more owners are unknown and describing the reasonable efforts made in good faith to identify and locate each unknown or missing owner who is the subject of the petition;

(G) the nature of the interest of the petitioner;

(H) the nature and location of the surface estate subject to the severed mineral interest; and

(I) an affidavit of the petitioner, affirming fee simple ownership of the surface estate and including a reference to each recorded document establishing such ownership. If any person whose name is required information under this subsection is unknown, that fact shall be stated. If any person is the unknown heir of a decedent, that person shall be described as the unknown heir of _____, deceased.

(b) **Service.** The proceeding shall be deemed in rem or quasi in rem. A copy of the petition and attached documents shall be served on all persons with a legal interest in the severed mineral interest named in the petition and all surface owners who have not joined in the petition. Service on a person alleged to be unknown or missing shall be pursuant to Rule 2-122. Otherwise, service shall be pursuant to Rule 2-121.

(c) **Hearing.** The court shall hold a hearing on the petition.

(d) **Order Creating Trust.** If the court finds that the title to a severed mineral interest is vested, in whole or in part, in an unknown or missing owner, the court may enter an order:

(1) placing the severed mineral interest of the unknown or missing owner in trust;

(2) appointing a trustee for the unknown or missing owner;

(3) if it is likely that any revenue will accrue to the benefit of the unknown or missing owner, directing the trustee to create a separate trust bank account to manage all trust assets; and

(4) authorizing the trustee to lease the mineral interest to the owner of the surface estate, subject to any conditions the court deems appropriate.

Cross references. — See Rule 1-324 concerning notice of the order sent by the clerk to the parties.

(e) **Administration of Trust.** A trust created under this Rule shall be administered pursuant to Rules 10-702 to 10-712.

(f) **Termination of Trust.** (1) Petition by Unknown or Missing Owner. (A) Generally. An unknown or missing owner whose interest in a severed mineral interest has been placed in trust, at any time prior to the filing of a petition under subsection (f)(2) or (f)(3) of this Rule, may file a petition to terminate the trust and convey the interest to the petitioner. The petition shall be signed and verified by the petitioner, filed in the court that created the trust, and name as respondents the trustee, each surface owner, and each other person with a legal interest in the minerals.

(B) Contents. The petition shall be captioned "In the Matter of ..." and shall state:

(i) the petitioner's name, address, e-mail address, if any, and telephone number;

(ii) the name, address, e-mail address, if any, and telephone number of the trustee and each surface owner;

(iii) the nature and extent of the petitioner's legal interest in the severed mineral interest in trust and include a reference to each recorded document establishing that interest and be accompanied by any unrecorded document establishing that interest; and

(iv) whether, the petitioner has recorded or intends to record a notice of intent to preserve the mineral interest in accordance with Code, Environment Article, § 15-1204.

(C) Service. The petition shall be served on each respondent in accordance with the provisions of Rule 1-321 (a).

(D) Response. A respondent shall file a response to the petition within the time prescribed by Rule 2-321.

(E) Hearing. Unless waived in writing by all parties, the court shall hold a hearing on the petition.

(F) Order. If the court finds that the petitioner is the unknown or missing owner whose severed mineral interest was placed in the trust, that the petition is timely and in compliance with this Rule, and that the trust with respect to that mineral interest should be terminated, it shall enter an order (i) terminating the trust as to that mineral interest, (ii) directing the trustee to file a final accounting, convey the mineral interest to the petitioner, and distribute all proceeds in accordance with the accounting, as approved by the court, and (iii) assessing costs as it deems just under the circumstances.

(2) Petition by Trustee. (A) Generally. If the unknown or missing owner of a vested severed mineral interest to whom notice of the petition or order was given does not contest or move to terminate a trust created under this Rule on or before five years after the date that the court issued the order creating the trust, the trustee shall file a petition to terminate the trust and to convey to the surface owner title to the severed mineral interest. The petition shall name as respondents each surface owner and each person with a legal interest in the minerals, including any unknown or missing owners of the severed mineral interest.

(B) Contents. The petition shall be captioned "In the Matter of ..." stating the location of the surface estate subject to the severed mineral interest. It shall be signed and verified by the petitioner and shall contain at least the following information:

(i) a legal description of the severed mineral interest;

(ii) a description of the putative property interests of each party;

(iii) the last known address of each party;

(iv) an affidavit signed by each surface owner, affirming fee simple ownership of the surface estate and requesting the court to convey title to the severed mineral interest at issue; and

(v) an affidavit signed by the petitioner, affirming that after conducting a diligent inquiry, including a search in each county where the severed mineral interest is located, performed in accordance with generally accepted standards of title examination of the land records of the county, the records of the register of wills of the county, and the records of the circuit court for the county, the trustee cannot locate the unknown or missing owner.

(C) Service. The petition shall be served on each respondent in accordance with the provisions of Rule 1-321.

(D) Hearing. The court shall hold a hearing on the petition.

(E) Order Terminating Trust. The court shall enter an order requiring the trustee to convey the unknown or missing owner's mineral interest to the named surface owner if (i) the petition was filed more than five years after entry of the order creating the trust, (ii) the unknown or missing owner does not appear to contest the petition, and (iii) the court finds that the person named in the petition as surface owner is in fact the fee simple owner of the surface estate. After receiving the final report of the trustee as required by Code, Environment Article, § 15-1206, the court shall enter an order (a) terminating the trust as to that mineral interest, (b) directing the trustee to file a final accounting, convey the mineral interest to the surface owner, and distribute all proceeds in accordance with the accounting, as approved by the court, and (c) assessing costs as it deems just under the circumstances.

Committee note. — If the mineral interest is located in more than one county, conveyance by the trustee requires recordation in each county in which the surface estate is located.

Cross references. — See Rule 1-324 concerning notice of the order sent by the clerk to the parties.

(3) Petition by Surface Owner or Other Interested Person. If the trustee does not file the petition within the time prescribed in subsection (f)(2) of this

Rule, the surface owner or any person with a legal or beneficial interest in the severed mineral interest placed in trust may file a petition to direct the trustee to comply with subsection (f)(2) of this Rule or to appoint a substitute trustee to do so. The petition shall be served on the trustee in accordance with the provisions of Rule 2-121 and further proceedings shall be in accordance with subsection (f)(2) of this Rule. (Added June 7, 2011, effective July 1, 2011.)

Rule 12-704. Termination of dormant mineral interest.

(a) **Petition.** (1) Generally. At any time after October 1, 2011, a surface owner of real property that is subject to a severed mineral interest may initiate an action to terminate a dormant mineral interest by filing a petition in the circuit court of any county in which the surface estate is located, but if a trust created under Rule 12-703 is in existence, then in the county where the trust was created.

(2) Contents. The petition shall be captioned "In the Matter of ...," stating the location of each surface estate subject to the mineral interest. It shall be signed and verified by the petitioner and shall contain at least the following information:

(A) the petitioner's name, address, and telephone number;

(B) the name and address of all other surface owners;

(C) the reason for seeking the assumption of jurisdiction by the court and a statement of the relief sought;

(D) a legal description of the severed mineral interest;

(E) the name, address, telephone number, and nature of the interest of all interested persons, including each person who has previously recorded a notice of intent to preserve the mineral interest or a part of a mineral interest pursuant to Code, Environment Article, § 15-1204;

(F) the nature of the interest of the petitioner;

(G) the nature and location of the surface estate or estates subject to a severed mineral interest; and

(H) an affidavit signed by each surface owner affirming fee simple ownership of the surface estate, including a reference to each recorded document establishing such ownership. If any person whose name is required information under this subsection is unknown, that fact shall be stated. If any person is the unknown heir of a decedent, that person shall be described as the unknown heir of _____, deceased.

(b) **Service.** The proceeding shall be deemed in rem or quasi in rem. A copy of the petition and attached documents shall be served on all persons with a legal interest in the severed mineral interest named in the petition and all surface owners who have not joined in the petition. Service on a person alleged to be unknown or missing shall be pursuant to Rule 2-122. Otherwise, service shall be pursuant to Rule 2-121.

(c) **Late Notice of Intent to Preserve Interest.** Unless the mineral interest has been unused for a period of 40 years or more preceding the commencement of the action, the court shall permit the owner of the mineral interest to record a late notice of intent to preserve the mineral interest and dismiss the action, provided that the owner of the mineral interest pays the litigation expenses incurred by the surface owner of the real property that is subject to the mineral interest.

Cross references. — See Code, Environment Article, § 15-1203 (c) for actions constituting use of an entire mineral interest

(d) **Hearing.** The court, in its discretion, may hold a hearing on the petition.

(e) **Order.** The court shall enter an order granting or denying the petition. An order terminating a mineral interest shall describe each tract of the surface estate overlying the terminated mineral interest into which the mineral interest is merged, and shall describe the proportional shares, if any, of each surface owner in each tract. The clerk shall record a copy of the order of termination in the land records of each county in which the mineral interest is located. (Added June 7, 2011, effective July 1, 2011.)

Cross references. — See Code, Environment Article, § 15-1203 (d)(2) for the effects of an order terminating a mineral interest.

Source. — This Rule is new.

TITLE 13. RECEIVERS AND ASSIGNEES

Editor's note. — The Court of Appeals, by Order dated June 5, 1996, effective January 1, 1997, rescinded Subtitles A, D, E, J, P, Q, R, T, U, V, W, Y, Z, BB, BD, BE, BG, BH, BJ, BL, BP, BQ, BR, BS, BW, and BY of Chapter 1100 of the Maryland Rules of Procedure, rescinded Subtitles P, BB, BQ, and BW of the Maryland District Rules, and rescinded Forms 22a, 23, 24, 25 and 26. The Order substituted for certain of the rules and forms rescinded new Title 9, Chapter 100, Title 10, Title 12, Title 13, Title 14, and Title 15 of the Maryland Rules of Procedure. Furthermore, the Order transferred, without readoption, Chapter 900, Chapter 1200, and Subtitles S, BU, and BV of Chapter 1100 of the Maryland Rules of Procedure and Chapter 1200 of the Maryland District Rules to be Title 9, Chapter 200, Title 11, and Title 16 of the Maryland Rules of Procedure. The Order provides that the new rules shall "apply to all actions commenced on or after January 1, 1997, and insofar as practicable, to all actions then pending."

Many of the cases in the notes to the various rules were decided prior to the 1996 revision. These cases have been retained under pertinent rules of this title where it is thought that such cases will be of value in interpreting the present rules.

A table of comparable rules, relating those rules rescinded effective January 1, 1997, to the revised rules in Title 9 through Title 16 is to be found in Volume 2 following the end of the Maryland Rules.

CHAPTER 100. GENERAL PROVISIONS.

Rule 13-101. Definitions.

In this Title the following definitions apply except as expressly otherwise provided or as necessary implication requires:

(a) **Assignee.** "Assignee" means a person to whom a debtor has made a general assignment of property in trust for the benefit of creditors.

(b) **Court.** "Court" means the court that has appointed a receiver or that has assumed jurisdiction over the estate of an assignee.

(c) **Debtor.** "Debtor" means a person who has made a general assignment to an assignee or for whom a receiver has been appointed.

(d) **Estate.** "Estate" means property assigned to an assignee or administered by a receiver.

(e) **Receiver.** "Receiver" means a person, other than an assignee, appointed by a court to take charge of an estate that is within the scope of the rules in this Title.

> **Committee note.** — "General assignment" is a term of art used to describe an assignment of all or substantially all of a debtor's property for the benefit of creditors. The validity of a general assignment in a particular case is a matter of substantive law.
>
> **Source.** — This Rule is derived from former Rule BP1 a.

Cited in First Penn-Pacific Life Ins. Co. v. William R. Evans, Chtd., 304 F.3d 345 (4th Cir. 2002), cert. denied, 538 U.S. 944, 123 S. Ct. 1622, 155 L. Ed. 2d 484 (2003).

Rule 13-102. Scope.

(a) **Generally.** Except as provided in section (b), the rules in this Title apply in the circuit court to the estate of:

(1) an assignee;

(2) a receiver appointed under the general equitable power of a court to take charge of an estate;

(3) a receiver appointed under any statutory provision that specifically provides that these rules apply to the proceeding; and

(4) any other statutory receiver to the extent that (A) the rules in this Chapter are not inconsistent with the statutory provisions authorizing the appointment of the receiver, and (B) the court orders that the rules apply.

(b) **No application.** The rules in this Title do not apply to the estate of:

(1) a receiver appointed pursuant to the terms of a mortgage or deed of trust pending foreclosure who takes charge of only the property subject to that mortgage or deed of trust;

(2) a receiver appointed pursuant to the terms of a security agreement who takes charge of only the property subject to that agreement; or

(3) a person appointed for purposes of enforcement of health, housing, fire, building, electric, licenses and permits, plumbing, animal control, or zoning codes or for the purpose of abating a public nuisance. (Amended Dec. 16, 1999, effective Jan. 1, 2000; Dec. 4, 2007, effective Jan. 1, 2008.)

> **Cross references.** — For an example of a statute specifically providing that these rules apply, *see* Code, Financial Institutions Article, § 9-708. For examples of statutes authorizing the appointment of a receiver, *see* Code, Corporations and Associations Article, §§ 3-411, 3-414, 3-415, and 3-514; Financial Institutions Article, §§ 5-605 and 6-307; Commercial Law Article, §§ 6-106 and 15-210; Health-General Article, § 19-334; and Real Property Article, §§ 11-109.3 and 11B-111.5. This list is illustrative only.
>
> **Source.** — This Rule is derived in part from former Rule BP1 b.

> **Effect of amendments.** — The 1999 amendment inserted present (b) (2) and redesignated former (b) (2) as present (b) (3).
>
> The December 4, 2007 Order, effective Jan-

uary 1, 2008, in the Cross reference added
"and Real Property Article, §§ 11-109.3 and
11-111.5."

Rule 13-103. Applicability of other rules.

(a) **Discovery.** A receiver, an assignee, or any person in a contested matter
may obtain discovery pursuant to Title 2, Chapter 400 of these Rules. Any
other person having an interest in the estate may obtain discovery only upon
order of court.

(b) **Title 2 rules.** The Title 2 rules apply to proceedings under this Title
except to the extent that a rule in this Title is inconsistent with a particular
rule in Title 2 or the court determines that the application of a rule in Title 2
would be inappropriate.

(c) **Other rules.** Except as otherwise specifically provided in this Title, the
procedures for making a sale of property of the estate shall be governed by Title
14, Chapter 300 of these Rules.

Source. — This Rule is in part derived from
former Rule BP5 and is in part new.

Rule 13-104. Service.

Unless otherwise specifically provided by the rules in this Title or ordered by
the court, no paper required or permitted to be filed by a rule in this Title need
be served on any person.

Source. — This Rule is new.

Rule 13-105. Eligibility to serve as receiver, assignee, or professional.

(a) **Generally.** Except as otherwise provided by law or by section (b) of this
Rule, a person may not serve as a receiver or assignee, or as an attorney,
accountant, appraiser, auctioneer, or other professional representing or assisting the receiver or assignee, if the person:

(1) is a creditor or a holder of an equity security of the debtor;

(2) is or was an investment banker for any outstanding security of the
debtor;

(3) has been, within three years before the date of the appointment of a
receiver or the assumption of jurisdiction over the estate of an assignee, an
investment banker for a security of the debtor, or an attorney for such an
investment banker, in connection with the offer, sale, or issuance of a security
of the debtor;

(4) is or was, within two years before the date of the appointment of a
receiver or the assumption of jurisdiction over the estate of an assignee, a
director, an officer, or an employee of the debtor or of an investment banker
specified in subsection (2) or (3) of this section, except that an employee of the
debtor may serve as an assignee if the court finds that this is in the best
interest of the estate and that there is no actual conflict of interest by reason
of the employment;

(5) has an interest materially adverse to the interest of any class of creditors
or equity security holders by reason of any direct or indirect relationship to,

connection with, or interest in the debtor or an investment banker specified in subsection (2) or (3) of this section, or for any other reason;

(6) otherwise has or represents an interest adverse to the estate;

(7) has, at any time within five years before the date of the appointment of a receiver or the assumption of jurisdiction over the estate of an assignee, represented or been employed by the debtor or any secured creditor as an attorney, accountant, appraiser, or other professional, if the court finds an actual conflict of interest by reason of the representation or employment;

(8) is an "insider" as defined by 11 U.S.C. § 101; or

(9) represents or is employed by an unsecured creditor of the debtor and, on objection of a person in interest, the court finds an actual conflict of interest by reason of the representation or employment.

(b) **Special counsel or accountant.** An attorney or accountant who has represented or has been employed by the debtor is eligible to serve for a specified limited purpose if the employment is in the best interest of the estate and if the attorney or accountant does not represent or hold any interest materially adverse to the debtor or to the estate with respect to the purpose for which the attorney or accountant is to be employed.

(c) **Ineligibility no bar to assumption of jurisdiction.** The court shall not refuse to assume jurisdiction over the estate of a debtor solely because it finds that the assignee is ineligible to serve under this Rule. After assuming jurisdiction, the court shall remove the ineligible assignee pursuant to Rule 13-701 and may take any action permitted or required by Rule 13-703.

Source. — This Rule is derived in part from former Rule BP3 a and c and is in part derived from 11 U.S.C. § 101 and § 327.

Rule 13-106. Petition for assumption of jurisdiction over estate of an assignee.

(a) **Venue.** A petition requesting the court to assume jurisdiction over the estate of an assignee shall be filed in the county where the debtor resides, is employed, or maintains a place of business, or in any county where some part of the estate is located.

(b) **Contents of petition.** A petition for the assumption of jurisdiction over the estate of an assignee shall be signed by the petitioner and shall contain at least the following information:

(1) the name and address of the assignee;

(2) a statement that an assignment for the benefit of creditors has been executed;

(3) in the case of a corporation, a statement indicating that articles of transfer transferring assets to the assignee have been executed;

(4) in the case of a corporation, a statement indicating that required corporate resolutions have been executed; and

(5) the nature, approximate value, and location of the property comprising the estate, to the best of the petitioner's knowledge, information, and belief.

(c) **Exhibits to petition.** The petitioner shall attach to the petition a copy of the following documents or shall explain in the petition their absence:

(1) the executed assignment for the benefit of creditors;

(2) in the case of a corporation, the executed articles of transfer and the executed corporate resolutions of the corporation; and

(3) the affidavit of an assignee, as required by Rule 13-302.

Source. — This Rule is new.

Rule 13-107. Bond.

(a) **Duty to file.** Before taking charge of an estate, a receiver shall file a bond in the court in which the receiver has been appointed and an assignee shall file a bond in the court in which a petition to assume jurisdiction of the estate has been filed.

(b) **Amount of bond.** Notwithstanding any contrary provision in Rule 1-402, the amount of the bond shall be no greater than the net value of the property of the estate. In the event of a later sale of property by the receiver or assignee, the court shall evaluate the bond previously filed and may permit a decrease in the amount of the bond.

(c) **Motion to modify amount of bond; notice.** If a motion to modify the amount of a bond is filed pursuant to Rule 1-402, notice shall be given to such persons as the court may direct.

(d) **Terms of bond.** The bond shall be to the State of Maryland and shall be conditioned upon the faithful discharge of the duties of the receiver or assignee.

(e) **Payment of bond premium from estate.** Unless the court orders otherwise, a receiver or assignee is entitled to pay and be allowed the cost of the premium out of the estate.

Cross references. — Code, Commercial Law Article, § 15-103; Title 1, Chapter 400.

Source. — This Rule is derived in part from former Rule V73.

CHAPTER 200. NOTICE AND SCHEDULES.

Rule 13-201. Publication of notice to creditors.

(a) **Notice by receiver or assignee.** Promptly but in no event later than 5 days after the court appoints a receiver or assumes jurisdiction over the estate of an assignee, the receiver or assignee shall file a form of Notice to Creditors with the clerk, who shall issue the Notice. The receiver or assignee shall cause the Notice to be published.

(b) **Form of notice.** The Notice to Creditors shall be substantially in one of the following three forms, as applicable:

[CAPTION]

NOTICE TO CREDITORS
BY RECEIVER

TO ALL PERSONS INTERESTED IN THE ESTATE OF _____,
DEBTOR

Notice is given with respect to _____,
                                    (Name in bold type)
whose business address is _____
_____
and whose business is _____,
that this Court has appointed _____,
                                    (Name in bold type)
whose address is _____,
as Receiver.

All persons having claims against the Debtor should file them, under oath, with the Clerk of the Circuit Court at the address below not later than 120 days from the date this Notice was issued.

_____	_____
Date Notice Issued	Clerk of the Circuit Court for
	_____
	(County or Baltimore City)
	_____
	Address
_____	_____
Receiver	Attorney for Receiver
_____	_____
Address	Address
_____	_____
Telephone Number	Telephone Number

[CAPTION]

NOTICE TO CREDITORS
BY ASSIGNEE

TO ALL PERSONS INTERESTED IN THE ESTATE OF _____,
DEBTOR

Notice is given with respect to _____,
                                    (Name in bold type)
whose business address is _____
_____
and whose business is _____,
that the Debtor has executed an Assignment for the Benefit of Creditors and that _____,
                                    (Name in bold type)
whose address is _____
has been designated as Assignee.

The deed of assignment [ ] does [ ] does not contain a provision requiring creditors to release their claims against the debtor as a condition to (1) sharing in the distribution under the deed or (2) being accorded a preferred status over other creditors.

All persons having claims against the Debtor should file them, under oath, with the Clerk of the Circuit Court at the address below not later than 120 days from the date this Notice was issued.

_____	_____
Date Notice Issued	Clerk of the Circuit Court for
	_____
	(County or Baltimore City)
	_____
	Address
_____	_____
Assignee	Attorney for Assignee
_____	_____
Address	Address
_____	_____
Telephone Number	Telephone Number

[CAPTION]

NOTICE TO CREDITORS
OF BULK TRANSFER

TO ALL PERSONS INTERESTED IN THE ESTATE OF _____,
BULK TRANSFEROR

    Notice is given with respect to _____,
(Name in bold type)
whose business address is _____
_____
and whose business is _____,
that the Transferor has effected a bulk transfer of property to
_____, transferee, whose
(Name in bold type)
address is _____

and that _____ whose address is
(Name in bold type)
_____
has been appointed as Receiver pursuant to Code, Commercial Law Article,
§ 6-106.

    All persons having claims against the Transferor should file them, under
oath, with the Clerk of the Circuit Court at the address below not later than
120 days from the date this Notice was issued.

_____	_____
Date Notice Issued	Clerk of the Circuit Court for
	_____
	(County or Baltimore City)
	_____
	Address
_____	_____
Receiver	Attorney for Receiver
_____	_____
Address	Address

| Telephone Number | Telephone Number |

(c) **Where published; frequency.** A copy of the Notice to Creditors shall be published in a newspaper of general circulation in the county where the court is located. The Notice shall be published at least once a week in each of three successive weeks, and the last publication shall occur not less than ninety days before the date specified in the Notice as the last day for filing claims.

(d) **Certificate of publication.** On or before the last day for filing claims, the receiver or assignee shall file a certificate that publication has been made pursuant to this Rule. (Amended June 7, 2011, effective July 1, 2011.)

Source. — This Rule is derived from former Rule BP4 a 1.

Effect of amendments. — The 2011 amendment inserted "(County or Baltimore City)" and "Address" lines in the three forms in (b).

Late filing. — The present rules reflect the earlier case law that, absent laches amounting to prejudice to others, late filing is permitted as a matter of course as to undistributed funds in the hands of the court. Eastern Air Lines v. Phoenix Sav. & Loan Ass'n, 239 Md. 195, 210 A.2d 515 (1965).

A creditor who files late has an absolute right which does not, except to the extent that prejudice to others results from the late filing, depend on good cause shown to participate in funds in the hands of the court available for distribution. Eastern Air Lines v. Phoenix Sav. & Loan Ass'n, 239 Md. 195, 210 A.2d 515 (1965).

A creditor may come in and file his claim at any time before a distribution of the proceeds of sale has been actually made under a finally ratified auditor's account. Coppage v. Maryland Thrift Sav. & Loan Co., 253 Md. 238, 252 A.2d 869 (1969).

Where creditor's claim was timely filed, receiver could not object to claim on ground that he had been misled to believe claim had been paid. Coppage v. Maryland Thrift Sav. & Loan Co., 253 Md. 238, 252 A.2d 869 (1969).

Equitable principles will not bar creditor's claim where receiver's failure to follow procedures in the Maryland Rules allowed claim to be timely filed. Coppage v. Maryland Thrift Sav. & Loan Co., 253 Md. 238, 252 A.2d 869 (1969).

Rule 13-202. Mailing of notice to creditors.

(a) **After appointment of receiver or assumption of jurisdiction.** Within five days after the clerk issues the Notice to Creditors, the receiver or assignee shall send a copy of the Notice by first class mail, postage prepaid, to all known creditors of the debtor. The receiver or assignee shall file a certificate of mailing of the Notice within five days after the initial mailing.

(b) **After filing of schedule.** Within five days after the expiration of the time for the debtor to file the schedule required by Rule 13-203, the receiver or assignee shall send a copy of the Notice by first class mail, postage prepaid, to all creditors shown on the schedule to whom the Notice was not sent pursuant to section (a) of this Rule. Not later than the last day for filing claims, the receiver or assignee shall file a certificate of mailing.

(c) **Later-discovered creditors.** The receiver or assignee shall promptly send a copy of the Notice by first class mail, postage prepaid, to all creditors whose identity is discovered at any time after the schedule is filed or the expiration of the time for filing it. Not later than the last day for filing the final report and account, the receiver or assignee shall file a certificate of mailing.

Source. — This Rule is in part derived from former Rule BP4 a 2 and is in part new.

Late filing. — The present rules reflect the earlier case law that, absent laches amounting to prejudice to others, late filing is permitted as a matter of course as to undistributed funds in the hands of the court. Eastern Air Lines v. Phoenix Sav. & Loan Ass'n, 239 Md. 195, 210 A.2d 515 (1965).

A creditor who files late has an absolute right which does not, except to the extent that prejudice to others results from the late filing, depend on good cause shown to participate in funds in the hands of the court available for distribution. Eastern Air Lines v. Phoenix Sav. & Loan Ass'n, 239 Md. 195, 210 A.2d 515 (1965).

A creditor may come in and file his claim at any time before a distribution of the proceeds of sale has been actually made under a finally ratified auditor's account. Coppage v. Maryland Thrift Sav. & Loan Co., 253 Md. 238, 252 A.2d 869 (1969).

Where creditor's claim was timely filed, receiver could not object to claim on ground that he had been misled to believe claim had been paid. Coppage v. Maryland Thrift Sav. & Loan Co., 253 Md. 238, 252 A.2d 869 (1969).

Equitable principles will not bar creditor's claim where receiver's failure to follow procedures in the Maryland Rules allowed claim to be timely filed. Coppage v. Maryland Thrift Sav. & Loan Co., 253 Md. 238, 252 A.2d 869 (1969).

Cited in First Penn-Pacific Life Ins. Co. v. William R. Evans, Chtd., 304 F.3d 345 (4th Cir. 2002), cert. denied, 538 U.S. 944, 123 S. Ct. 1622, 155 L. Ed. 2d 484 (2003).

Rule 13-203. Schedule.

(a) **Preparation and filing by debtor.** Within fifteen days after the court appoints a receiver or assumes jurisdiction over the estate of an assignee, the debtor shall prepare and file with the clerk a schedule of property and debts under oath.

(b) **Form of schedule.** The debtor's schedule shall be in substantially the following form:

[CAPTION]

SCHEDULE OF PROPERTY AND DEBTS

Name of Debtor _____

Residence Address _____
_____

Occupation/Nature of Business _____

Business Address _____
_____

I solemnly affirm under the penalties of perjury that the contents of the attached schedule are true to the best of my knowledge, information, and belief.

_____   _____

Date   Signature of Debtor

A. Property of debtor.

Nature and description	Location	Estimated Market Value	Amount of Lien or Encumbrance

_____ _____ _____ _____
_____ _____ _____ _____
_____ _____ _____ _____
_____ _____ _____ _____

B. Debts and taxes owed by debtor.

	Name and address of creditor including taxing authority	Security held by creditor, if any	Whether claim is contingent, unliquidated, or disputed	Nature of and consideration for the debt	Amount due or claimed
1. Priority Claims					
A. Taxes	_____	_____	_____	_____	____
B. Wages	_____	_____	_____	_____	____
C. Other	_____	_____	_____	_____	____
2. Secured Creditors	_____	_____	_____	_____	____
3. General Unsecured Creditors	_____	_____	_____	_____	____

C. Recent transfers.

1. Did the Debtor transfer or dispose of any property, other than in the ordinary course of business, to a spouse during the three years immediately preceding the making of the assignment for the benefit of creditors or the appointment of the receiver?

_____ _____
Yes   No

2. Did the Debtor transfer or dispose of any property, other than in the ordinary course of business, to anyone other than a spouse during a period of one year immediately preceding the making of the assignment for the benefit of creditors or the appointment of the receiver?

_____ _____
Yes   No

3. If the answer to either of the above questions is "Yes," give the following information as to each transfer or disposition:

Date of transfer or disposition	Transferee and relation to debtor, if any	Description of property	Consideration and disposition thereof
_____	_____	_____	_____
_____	_____	_____	_____
_____	_____	_____	_____

D. Property claimed as exempt (applies only to individuals).

Nature and description	Location	Basis for exemption	Estimated market value
_____	_____	_____	_____
_____	_____	_____	_____
_____	_____	_____	_____
_____	_____	_____	_____

(c) **Preparation and filing by assignee or receiver.** If the debtor fails to file the schedule within the required time, the receiver or assignee to the extent able to supply the information shall prepare and file a schedule containing the information required by section (b) of this Rule. The schedule shall be filed within thirty days after the debtor's required filing date.

(d) **Failure of receiver or assignee to file schedule.** If a receiver or assignee who is required to file a schedule fails to do so within the required time, any person having an interest may file a report of the delinquency with the court. Upon the filing of a report or on its own initiative, the court may issue an order to the receiver or assignee to show cause in writing on or before a specified date why the receiver or assignee should not be compelled to file the schedule or be removed. Unless the court orders otherwise, the specified date shall be 20 days after the date prescribed for service in the order. The order shall also specify the persons to be served with the order, the method of service, and, if a hearing is scheduled when the order is issued, the date, time, and place of the hearing. Unless cause is shown or the schedule is filed, the court shall remove the receiver or assignee pursuant to Rule 13-701 and may take any action permitted or required by Rule 13-703.

(e) **Order compelling disclosure; sanction.** The court at any time may order the debtor, an officer or director of the debtor, or any other person who may have information that is necessary for the completion of the schedule to appear before the court or before an examiner pursuant to Rule 2-542 and to disclose the information. The debtor, an officer or director of a debtor, or other person who refuses to comply with an order compelling disclosure may be held in contempt pursuant to Title 15, Chapter 200 of these Rules.

Source. — This Rule is derived in part from former Rule BP2 a and b and is in part new.

Chancellor erred in issuing orders compelling president and sole shareholder of insolvent company to file schedules under former section a, by (1) ignoring the alternative provided by former section b in the event that the debtor fails to file a schedule; (2) issuing a contempt order for failure to comply with the Rule without any finding that such failure was wrongful as required by former subsection b 3; and (3) attempting to "pierce the corporate veil" of the debtor by ordering the director and shareholder to do that which was required of the corporate "debtor" under the provisions of former Rule BP 2. Rosenbloom v. Electric Motor Repair Co., 31 Md. App. 711, 358 A.2d 617 (1976).

Although officers of debtor corporation may be required to disclose information. — The officers of a corporation for which a receiver has been appointed may be compelled to disclose information to the receiver which is necessary for the preparation of the schedule under former section a, or to produce corporate records in their custody for that purpose. Rosenbloom v. Electric Motor Repair Co., 31 Md. App. 711, 358 A.2d 617 (1976).

And they are charged with knowledge of information required in schedules. — Both the president and the board chairman of a corporate insolvent are charged with the knowledge of all of the facts and information required in the schedule called for by former section a. Rosenbloom v. Electric Motor Repair Co., 31 Md. App. 711, 358 A.2d 617 (1976).

Former subsection b 2 contemplates a debtor who may fail to file for reasons that are not wrongful, i.e., delinquent but not wrongfully so. When read in conjunction with the next subsection, it brings into play the alternative provision for the receiver to assume the filing responsibility with the necessary information being compulsorily provided by the delinquent debtor. Rosenbloom v. Electric Motor Repair Co., 31 Md. App. 711, 358 A.2d 617 (1976).

Presumably, the penalty for contempt in former subsection b 3 is not available for mere delinquency in filing or simple refusal to disclose. Rather, to be punishable, the conduct must be wrongful. Before a judgment of wrongdoing may be rendered, the reasons for the failure to file (or the failure to disclose) must be ascertained by the court. Rosenbloom v. Electric Motor Repair Co., 31 Md. App. 711, 358 A.2d 617 (1976).

Court must be satisfied that failure was wrongful. — Before contempt is available as a punishment for failure to disclose under former subsection b 3, the court must first be satisfied by evidentiary offerings that the failure to disclose was wrongful. Rosenbloom v. Electric Motor Repair Co., 31 Md. App. 711, 358 A.2d 617 (1976).

CHAPTER 300. EMPLOYMENT OF PROFESSIONALS.

Rule 13-301. Employment of attorney, accountant, appraiser, auctioneer, or other professional.

(a) **Court approval required.** A receiver or assignee shall not employ an attorney, accountant, appraiser, auctioneer, or other professional without prior approval of the court. With the court's prior approval, a receiver or assignee may serve as attorney or accountant for the estate.

(b) **Application; contents.** An application requesting authority to employ an attorney, accountant, appraiser, auctioneer, or other professional shall be accompanied by the affidavit required by Rule 13-302 and shall set forth:

(1) the necessity for the employment; and

(2) in the event the schedule required by Rule 13-203 has not been filed, the nature and approximate amount of the debtor's property and debts.

(c) **Prior approval of compensation in certain instances.** If the application requesting authority to employ an attorney, accountant, appraiser, auctioneer, or other professional sets forth in reasonable detail the basis for the proposed compensation of the person to be employed, the court, by order, may authorize compensation to be paid without further order of court for work completed within stated limits. This section does not apply to a receiver or assignee who serves as attorney or accountant for the estate.

Source. — This Rule is derived in part from former Rule BP6 a and b and is in part new.

Cited in Ferguson v. Cramer, 349 Md. 760, 709 A.2d 1279 (1998).

Rule 13-302. Disclosures by receiver, assignee, and professionals.

(a) **Required disclosure by affidavit.** A receiver or assignee and each attorney, accountant, appraiser, auctioneer, or other professional to be employed by the assignee or receiver shall file an affidavit that states the following:

(1) whether the person has, within five years before the date of the appointment of a receiver or the assumption of jurisdiction over the estate of an assignee, represented or been employed by the debtor, an insider of the debtor as defined by 11 U.S.C. § 101, any secured or unsecured creditor of the debtor, or an investment banker of the debtor, and the nature of the representation or employment;

(2) if the debtor, insider, secured or unsecured creditor, or investment banker is a corporation, association, or partnership, whether the assignee,

receiver, accountant, appraiser, auctioneer, or other professional had, within five years before the date of the appointment of a receiver or the assumption of jurisdiction over the estate of an assignee, any financial interest in the corporation, association, or partnership and the extent of the financial interest; and

(3) that the person is not disqualified for any of the reasons set forth in Rule 13-105.

(b) **When filed.** The affidavit shall be filed:

(1) by an assignee, with the petition;

(2) by a receiver, prior to assuming the duties of office;

(3) by an attorney, accountant, appraiser, auctioneer, or other professional, with the application requesting authority to employ the person.

(c) **Supplemental disclosure.** A person who has filed an affidavit under this Rule and who learns that the information in the affidavit is inaccurate or incomplete shall promptly file a supplemental affidavit.

(d) **Penalty for failure to disclose required information.** In addition to any other remedies provided by law, the court, pursuant to Rule 13-701, may remove any person who fails to disclose any information required to be disclosed by this Rule and may take any action permitted or required by Rule 13-703.

Source. — This Rule is derived from former Rule BP3 a, b, and d.

Cited in Shapiro v. Greenfield, 136 Md. App. 1, 764 A.2d 270 (2000).

Rule 13-303. Compensation and expenses for receiver, assignee, or professional.

(a) **Application for allowance of compensation and expenses.** Before a receiver, assignee, or any person performing services for the estate pursuant to Rule 13-301 is paid compensation or reimbursed for expenses not previously approved by the court, the receiver or assignee shall file with the court an application for the allowance of compensation and expenses. The application shall include:

(1) the estimated gross amount of the estate;

(2) the estimated total of the sums to be paid for liens, preferences, and costs of administration;

(3) the estimated approximate sum for distribution among secured, priority, and unsecured creditors;

(4) a detailed description of the services rendered, time expended, and expenses incurred;

(5) the amount of compensation and expenses requested;

(6) the amount of any compensation or expenses previously allowed by the court;

(7) the amount of any compensation and expenses received from or to be paid by any source other than the estate; and

(8) a detailed description of any agreement or understanding for a division of the compensation between the person rendering services and any other person except those specifically permitted to share in compensation by section (c) of this Rule.

(b) **Allowance.** The court shall review the application and any evidence presented and shall determine the appropriate amount of compensation and expenses to be paid to the receiver, assignee, or person performing services for the receiver or assignee. In determining the amount, the court is not bound by any compensation or commission fixed in an assignment for the benefit of creditors or in any other agreement.

(c) **Sharing of compensation.** Without the express written approval of the court, a receiver, assignee, or person performing services for a receiver or assignee shall not, in any form or manner, share or agree to share compensation for services rendered with any person other than a partner, employer, or regular employee of the person rendering services.

Source. — This Rule is derived from former Rule BP7.

CHAPTER 400. CLAIMS.

Rule 13-401. Proof of claim.

(a) **Filing.** Any person who wishes to make a claim against the estate of a debtor shall file a verified proof of claim with the clerk. The proof of claim shall be filed within 120 days after the date the Notice to Creditors is issued by the clerk.

(b) **Form.** A proof of claim shall be in substantially the following form with supporting documentation attached as indicated:

[CAPTION]

CLAIM AGAINST DEBTOR

BY _____
Name of Claimant

The claimant certifies that the debtor owes the claimant the sum of $_____.

The consideration or basis for the debt is _____ .

The debt is:

[ ] an unsecured claim in the amount of $_____ (attach statement of account, invoices, promissory notes, or other evidence of claim); or

[ ] a secured claim in the amount of $_____ (attach evidence of perfection of security interest).

The undersigned certifies, in accordance with the verification below, that the debtor is indebted to the claimant in the amount shown, that there is no security for the debt other than that stated above or in an attachment to this claim form, that no unmatured interest is included, and that the undersigned is authorized to make this claim.

238

[ ] I solemnly affirm under the penalties of perjury and upon personal knowledge that the contents of the foregoing claim are true; or

[ ] I solemnly affirm under the penalties of perjury that I am employed by the claimant firm as _____ ;

(insert title)

that the claimant keeps regular books of account; that the keeping of these books is in my charge or under my supervision; that the entries in these books were made in the regular course of business; and that the entries show the facts set forth in this claim.

_____	_____
Name of Claimant	Signature of claimant or person authorized to make verifications on behalf of claimant
_____	_____
Name and Title of Person Signing Claim	Address
	_____
_____	_____
Date	Telephone Number

Instructions:

If the claim is based upon an obligation owed jointly to two or more persons, any one of the joint creditors may verify the claim. If the claimant is a corporation, association, or partnership, any officer, partner, or authorized agent may verify the claim. If the original and all copies of a written instrument securing a claim are lost or destroyed, the claimant must attach a statement explaining the circumstances of the loss or destruction.

(c) **Late filed claims.** (1) Before reference to auditor. A proof of claim that is filed late but before any reference to an auditor for the stating of an account is entitled to the same consideration for distribution as a timely filed proof of claim.

(2) After reference to auditor. A person who files a proof of claim after reference to an auditor is not entitled to participate in the next distribution unless the court on application of the claimant and for good cause shown orders otherwise. If the court permits participation, it may order the claimant to pay the cost of restating the account if the auditor must do so in whole or in part to include the claim. A proof of claim filed too late to be included in one or more auditor's accounts, if allowed, shall be included in any subsequent account, and the claimant is entitled to receive a distribution on the same basis as those already received by other creditors on prior accounts. The distribution shall be made before those creditors receive any further distribution. Thereafter, the claimant shall share with them in any future distributions.

Source. — This Rule is derived from former Rule BP4 b and c.

———

Late filing. — The present rules reflect the earlier case law that, absent laches amounting to prejudice to others, late filing is permitted as a matter of course as to undistributed funds in the hands of the court. Eastern Air Lines v. Phoenix Sav. & Loan Ass'n, 239 Md. 195, 210 A.2d 515 (1965).

A creditor who files late has an absolute right which does not, except to the extent that prejudice to others results from the late filing, depend on good cause shown to participate in funds in the hands of the court available for distribution. Eastern Air Lines v. Phoenix Sav. & Loan Ass'n, 239 Md. 195, 210 A.2d 515 (1965).

A creditor may come in and file his claim at any time before a distribution of the proceeds of sale has been actually made under a finally ratified auditor's account. Coppage v. Maryland Thrift Sav. & Loan Co., 253 Md. 238, 252 A.2d 869 (1969).

Where creditor's claim was timely filed, receiver could not object to claim on ground that he had been misled to believe claim had been paid. Coppage v. Maryland Thrift Sav. & Loan Co., 253 Md. 238, 252 A.2d 869 (1969).

Equitable principles will not bar creditor's claim where receiver's failure to follow procedures in the Maryland Rules allowed claim to be timely filed. Coppage v. Maryland Thrift Sav. & Loan Co., 253 Md. 238, 252 A.2d 869 (1969).

Cited in Allfirst Bank v. Department of Health & Mental Hygiene, 140 Md. App. 334, 780 A.2d 440 (2001).

Rule 13-402. Objections to claims.

An objection to a proof of claim may be filed at any time before final ratification of the auditor's account in which the claim is allowed. The grounds for the objection shall be stated with particularity. The objection shall be served pursuant to Rule 1-321 on the claimant and, unless the receiver or assignee is the objecting party, on the receiver or assignee. On request, the claimant or the objecting party is entitled to a hearing.

Source. — This Rule is derived from former Rule BP4 d.

Late filing. — The present rules reflect the earlier case law that, absent laches amounting to prejudice to others, late filing is permitted as a matter of course as to undistributed funds in the hands of the court. Eastern Air Lines v. Phoenix Sav. & Loan Ass'n, 239 Md. 195, 210 A.2d 515 (1965).

A creditor who files late has an absolute right which does not, except to the extent that prejudice to others results from the late filing, depend on good cause shown to participate in funds in the hands of the court available for distribution. Eastern Air Lines v. Phoenix Sav. & Loan Ass'n, 239 Md. 195, 210 A.2d 515 (1965).

A creditor may come in and file his claim at any time before a distribution of the proceeds of sale has been actually made under a finally ratified auditor's account. Coppage v. Maryland Thrift Sav. & Loan Co., 253 Md. 238, 252 A.2d 869 (1969).

Where creditor's claim was timely filed, receiver could not object to claim on ground that he had been misled to believe claim had been paid. Coppage v. Maryland Thrift Sav. & Loan Co., 253 Md. 238, 252 A.2d 869 (1969).

Equitable principles will not bar creditor's claim where receiver's failure to follow procedures in the Maryland Rules allowed claim to be timely filed. Coppage v. Maryland Thrift Sav. & Loan Co., 253 Md. 238, 252 A.2d 869 (1969).

Rule 13-403. Compromise of claim or dispute.

(a) **Application.** A receiver or assignee may file an application requesting the court to authorize or ratify a compromise or settlement of any claim or matter relating to an estate.

(b) **Ratification.** If satisfied that the action is in the best interest of the estate, the court may authorize or ratify the proposed compromise or settlement and may impose any appropriate terms and conditions.

Source. — This Rule is in part derived from former Rule V77 b 1 and is in part new.

Powers included in former Rule V77 applied to all trustees, whether or not such powers are included in the will or trust agreement. Mercantile-Safe Deposit & Trust Co. v. United States, 311 F. Supp. 670 (D. Md. 1970).

Trustee has no power to sell something he does not have. — The expansion of fiduciary powers which former Rule V77 accomplished did not confer upon a trustee a power to sell something he does not have. Jones v. Endslow, 23 Md. App. 578, 328 A.2d 339 (1974).

And therefore could not sell real prop- **erty in which he held title to a life estate without prior approval.** — A trustee could not sell real property placed in a trust by the testator without the approval of any beneficiary or of the court where, with respect to that property, the trustee held legal title to a life estate only. Jones v. Endslow, 23 Md. App. 578, 328 A.2d 339 (1974).

Cited in First Penn-Pacific Life Ins. Co. v. William R. Evans, Chtd., 304 F.3d 345 (4th Cir. 2002), cert. denied, 538 U.S. 944, 123 S. Ct. 1622, 155 L. Ed. 2d 484 (2003).

CHAPTER 500. REPORTS AND DISTRIBUTIONS.

Rule 13-501. Reports.

(a) **Annual and final report; filing.** A receiver or assignee shall file an annual report under oath within 60 days after the end of the reporting period. The reporting period shall be (1) the year ending on the anniversary of the date upon which the court appointed the receiver or assumed jurisdiction over the estate; (2) upon notice to the trust clerk, any other one-year period chosen by the receiver or assignee, provided that the interval between the last report (or appointment or assumption of jurisdiction) and the report submitted shall not exceed one year; or (3) any other period ordered by the court. Before any interim or final distribution of the estate may be made, the receiver or assignee shall file a report for the period from the closing date of the last annual report until the proposed date on which the estate will be partially or fully distributed.

(b) **Form of report.** A report shall be in substantially the following form:

[CAPTION]

REPORT OF RECEIVER OR ASSIGNEE

Name of Debtor   Name of Receiver or Assignee
Reporting Period _____, _____ to _____, _____.
         (month) (day) (year)   (month) (day) (year)

1. Summary of property held in fiduciary capacity at beginning of reporting period:

Nature and Description of Property	Estimated Market Value

2. Changes during the period covered by this report:

A. Collections and Receipts, including interest and dividends received:

Date	Description	Amount Received

Total Receipts $_____

B. Expenditures and distributions:

Date	Description	Amount Paid

Total Payments $_____

C. Property sold or otherwise transferred:

Date	Description	Court Order Reference	Transferee	Consideration Received

D. Property acquired:

Date	Description	Court Order Reference	Transferor	Consideration Paid

3. Summary of property held in fiduciary capacity at end of reporting period:

Nature and Description of Property	Estimated Market Value

4. Proposed distribution (distribution reports only):

Previous distributions were:

Date Autho- rized by Court	Amount of Distribution
_____	_____
_____	_____
_____	_____

Total distributions to date: _____

The amount available for [ ] partial [ ] final distribution is $_____ .

If the proposed distribution is partial, the amount proposed to be retained in estate is $_____.

(Include in final reports only) All property of the estate has been accounted for and the undersigned knows of no debts incurred during the administration of the estate other than those which have been paid or which are reflected in this Report.

(Include in all reports) I solemnly affirm under the penalties of perjury that the contents of this Report are true to the best of my knowledge, information, and belief.

Date: _____   _____

                                Receiver/Assignee

                                _____

                                Address

                                _____

(c) **Weekly report if conducting a business.** For each calendar week during which the receiver or assignee conducts the business of the debtor, the receiver or assignee shall also file a report listing the receipts and disbursements in reasonable detail. The report shall be filed not later than the third day after the end of the weekly reporting period.

(d) **Further accountability.** Nothing in this Rule shall be construed to abridge the power of the court to require a receiver or assignee to submit reports covering periods greater or lesser, or at times earlier or later, than those prescribed in this Rule or to require the submission of more detailed information than that which is prescribed in this Rule.

(e) **Failure to file reports; penalties.** (1) Order. If a receiver or assignee fails to file a timely annual report, the trust clerk shall inform the court in writing, and the court shall issue an order to the receiver or assignee to show cause within 15 days why the receiver or assignee should not be removed. The order shall be served on the receiver or assignee and a copy sent to the surety on the bond of the receiver or assignee in accordance with Rule 13-701 (b).

(2) Sanctions. If the receiver or assignee does not comply with the order by filing an answer and all overdue reports, the court may remove the receiver or assignee pursuant to Rule 13-701 and may take any action permitted or required by Rule 13-703.

(f) **Examination by trust clerk.** (1) Examination of reports. The trust clerk shall examine all reports submitted pursuant to this Rule, except those referred to an auditor pursuant to Rule 13-502. The trust clerk shall determine whether all of the required information has been submitted and whether the amount of and surety on the bond of the receiver or assignee are sufficient to protect the estate.

(2) Examination of property not required. Unless the court orders otherwise, the trust clerk need not examine the property of the estate.

(3) Report and recommendation. The trust clerk shall (A) report any irregularities in the report to the court, (B) bring to the court's attention any other matter that the trust clerk considers appropriate, and (C) make any appropriate recommendation. (Amended May 9, 2000, effective July 1, 2000.)

Source. — This Rule is derived from former Rule BP9 a, b, d, e, f, and g.

Effect of amendments. — The 2000 amendment, twice near the beginning of (b), substituted "_____" for "19____," added "(month) (day)" and "(year)" notations, and inserted a comma following the blank for the "(month) (day)."

When reference to auditor unnecessary. — If an account consists of very few items it may not be necessary to refer the case to the auditor for adjustment, but the court in its discretion may perform this duty and ascertain the proper amounts without the aid of an audit; and so, if there is but a single item to be determined, which the court may ascertain, a reference to an auditor is unnecessary. And where a sum for distribution was so small that it would be wholly consumed in the expense of stating an account, the court considered it proper to distribute it as interest among those entitled, without the expense of another audit. Coppage v. Maryland Thrift Sav. & Loan Co., 253 Md. 238, 252 A.2d 869 (1969).

Cited in First Penn-Pacific Life Ins. Co. v. William R. Evans, Chtd., 304 F.3d 345 (4th Cir. 2002), cert. denied, 538 U.S. 944, 123 S. Ct. 1622, 155 L. Ed. 2d 484 (2003).

Rule 13-502. Referral to auditor.

(a) **When required.** The court shall refer to an auditor pursuant to Rule 2-543 all papers filed for the purpose of making a partial or final distribution of the estate.

(b) **Action by auditor.** The auditor shall audit a final or interim distribution report filed pursuant to Rule 13-501 and shall state an account setting forth the distribution of the estate.

(c) **Notice by auditor.** (1) To whom given. The auditor shall give notice by first class mail, postage prepaid, to the debtor, the receiver or assignee, and each creditor who has filed a claim in the proceedings that an auditor's account has been stated.

(2) Contents. In addition to the requirements of Rule 2-543, the notice by the auditor shall contain the following information:

(A) the total amount of property stated in the account;

(B) the total amount of approved liens and priorities;

(C) the total costs of administration, including as separate items the court costs and the compensation of the receiver, assignee, or person employed as a professional;

(D) the amount available for distribution to general creditors;

(E) the percentage of the creditor's claim to be paid; and

(F) whether the distribution is final or partial.

(d) **Interim distribution.** On application of the receiver, assignee, or other person in interest, the court may direct such partial distribution as may be safely made from the money in the hands of the receiver or assignee to those creditors whose claims are not in dispute, reserving sufficient assets to secure, after final settlement of all claims, a proportionate distribution among all creditors whose claims are finally allowed.

Source. — This Rule is derived from former Rule BP9 b and c and BP10 b.

When reference to auditor unnecessary. — If an account consists of very few items it may not be necessary to refer the case to the auditor for adjustment, but the court in its discretion may perform this duty and ascertain the proper amounts without the aid of an audit; and so, if there is but a single item to be determined, which the court may ascertain, a reference to an auditor is unnecessary. And where a sum for distribution was so small that it would be wholly consumed in the expense of stating an account, the court considered it proper to distribute it as interest among those entitled, without the expense of another audit. Coppage v. Maryland Thrift Sav. & Loan Co., 253 Md. 238, 252 A.2d 869 (1969).

Rule 13-503. Distribution.

(a) **Final ratification required.** Until the final account has been audited pursuant to Rule 13-502 and finally ratified by the court, a final distribution shall not be made to creditors, the estate shall not be closed, and any bond of the receiver or assignee shall not be released.

(b) **Payment.** Promptly after final ratification of an auditor's account in which a distribution to creditors has been stated, the receiver or assignee shall make distribution as stated in the account.

(c) **Minimum Dividend.** Unless the court orders otherwise, the assignee or receiver shall not distribute to a creditor a dividend in an amount less than $5.00, but shall treat the dividend as unclaimed funds under section (d) of this Rule.

(d) **Disposition of unclaimed distributions.** The receiver or assignee shall pay into court any distributions that remain unclaimed for ninety days after final ratification of the auditor's final distribution account. The receiver or assignee shall file a list of the names and last known addresses of persons who have not claimed distributions, showing the amount of each person's distribution. The clerk shall issue a receipt for the payment, and the receipt shall release and discharge the receiver or assignee making the payment. Thereafter, the unclaimed distributions shall be subject to escheat as provided by law. (Amended April 5, 2005, effective July 1, 2005.)

Source. — This Rule is derived from former Rules BP9 b 2 and BP10.

Effect of amendments. — The 2005 amendment added present (c) and redesignated former (c) as (d).

When reference to auditor unnecessary. — If an account consists of very few items it may not be necessary to refer the case to the auditor for adjustment, but the court in its discretion may perform this duty and ascertain the proper amounts without the aid of an audit; and so, if there is but a single item to be determined, which the court may ascertain, a reference to an auditor is unnecessary. And where a sum for distribution was so small that it would be wholly consumed in the expense of stating an account, the court considered it proper to distribute it as interest among those entitled, without the expense of another audit. Coppage v. Maryland Thrift Sav. & Loan Co., 253 Md. 238, 252 A.2d 869 (1969).

Cited in First Penn-Pacific Life Ins. Co. v.

William R. Evans, Chtd., 304 F.3d 345 (4th Cir. 2002), cert. denied, 538 U.S. 944, 123 S. Ct. 1622, 155 L. Ed. 2d 484 (2003).

CHAPTER 600. ABANDONMENT OF PROPERTY AND RECORDS.

Rule 13-601. Abandonment of property and records.

(a) **Abandonment of property.** On application of a receiver, an assignee, or a creditor, the court may order the abandonment of any property of the debtor that is worthless, overburdened, or otherwise of inconsequential value and benefit to the estate.

(b) **Abandonment or destruction of books and records.** (1) Application. After the final ratification of an auditor's account that provides for the final distribution of the estate, the receiver or assignee may apply to the court for permission to destroy, return to the debtor, or otherwise dispose of all or part of the books and records of the debtor or of the estate.

(2) Notice to debtor and tax authorities. Notice of the application shall be given by first class mail, postage prepaid, to the Commissioner of Internal Revenue of the United States, the Comptroller of the Treasury of the State of Maryland, and the debtor at the debtor's last known address. If an objection is filed within 30 days after notice is given, the court shall hold a hearing.

Committee note. — This Rule does not address the consequences of destruction of books and records under state and federal revenue laws.

(3) Order. For good cause shown, the court may authorize the receiver or assignee to destroy, return to the debtor, or otherwise dispose of all or part of the books and records of the debtor or of the estate by or after a date fixed in the order.

Source. — This Rule is derived from former Rule BP8.

CHAPTER 700. REMOVAL AND RESIGNATION.

Rule 13-701. Removal of assignee, receiver, or professional.

(a) **On court's own initiative; by petition.** The court or any person having an interest in the estate may initiate proceedings to remove a receiver, assignee, or any person employed as a professional by the receiver or assignee. The court may initiate removal proceedings by filing an order pursuant to section (b) of this Rule and shall state in the order the reasons for the proposed removal. An interested person may initiate removal proceedings by filing a petition that shall state the reasons for the requested removal and may include a request for the appointment of a successor receiver, assignee, or professional.

(b) **Show cause order; service.** If removal proceedings are initiated, the court shall order the receiver, assignee, or professional to show cause why the receiver, assignee, or professional should not be removed or be subject to other sanctions. The order, together with a copy of any petition, shall be served pursuant to Rule 2-121 on the person sought to be removed or, if it is shown by affidavit that the whereabouts of the person sought to be removed are unknown and that reasonable efforts have been made in good faith to locate the person, the court may order service pursuant to Rule 2-122. Copies of the show cause order and any petition shall also be sent by first class mail, postage prepaid, to the surety on the bond of the receiver or assignee and to any other persons directed by the court.

(c) **Disposition.** After a hearing and for cause, including ineligibility, the court may remove a receiver, assignee, or professional.

Cross references. — As to the statutory grounds for the removal of a fiduciary, including a receiver or assignee, *see* Code, Estates and Trusts Article, § 15-112.

Source. — This Rule is in part derived from former Rule V84 and is in part new.

Conventional trustee has broad discretionary powers which may be exercised absent evidence of bad faith, misconduct or a want of ordinary skill or judgment. Shipley v. Crouse, 279 Md. 613, 370 A.2d 97 (1977).

First obligation of the trustees is to safeguard the trust estate, and in doing so they are called upon many times to exercise a judgment; hence the judgment exercised by the trustees that they would share the final contract and let the beneficiaries know when it was submitted to the court for ratification, but would not share the step-by-step negotiations with the beneficiaries, was not a breach of their duty, but, quite to the contrary, was in furtherance of their duty to try to do what, in their judgment, was in the best interests of the trust estate. Shipley v. Crouse, 279 Md. 613, 370 A.2d 97 (1977).

Receipt of information by beneficiaries not absolute. — While beneficiaries are entitled to receive complete and accurate information as to the administration of the trust and to know what the trust property is and how the trustee has dealt with it, this is not absolute, if the trustee renders periodic reports showing collection of income and disbursements, assuming the trustee is acting in good faith and is not abusing his discretionary powers. Shipley v. Crouse, 279 Md. 613, 370 A.2d 97 (1977).

Disclosure by trustees mandated. — When there is a confidential relationship between buyer and seller, or there is an element of self-dealing, the duty of loyalty mandates a full and frank disclosure by the trustees to the beneficiaries. Shipley v. Crouse, 279 Md. 613, 370 A.2d 97 (1977).

Where removal likely required. — Where because of a disagreement between coguardians a ward has not been permitted to leave the grounds of a nursing home in which she resides, receive new eyeglasses, have any change in the medication or medical care she requires or the like, it may well be that removal of one or both of the guardians will be required. Kicherer v. Kicherer, 285 Md. 114, 400 A.2d 1097 (1979).

Rule 13-702. Resignation of receiver or assignee.

(a) **Petition.** A receiver may file a petition for permission to resign in the court in which the receiver was appointed. An assignee may file a petition to resign in the court in which a petition to assume jurisdiction of the estate has been filed. The petition shall state the reasons for the proposed resignation and may include a request for the appointment of a successor receiver or assignee.

(b) **Report to be filed.** The receiver or assignee shall file with the petition a report pursuant to Rule 13-501 for any period not covered in an annual report previously filed or, if no annual report has been filed, from the date the receiver or assignee took charge of the estate.

(c) **Notice.** The receiver or assignee shall mail a copy of the petition by first class mail, postage prepaid, to those interested persons designated by the court.

(d) **Termination of appointment.** The resignation of a receiver or assignee does not terminate the appointment until the resignation has been approved by the court.

(e) **Proceedings.** The court may grant or deny the requested relief with or without a hearing. In an order granting the petition, the court may specify any conditions for the acceptance of the resignation that the nature of the case may require. (Amended March 9, 2010, effective July 1, 2010.)

Source. — This Rule is in part derived from former Rule V81 and is in part new.

Effect of amendments. — The 2010 amendment substituted "Rule 13-501" for "Rule 13-601" in (b).

Rule 13-703. Appointment of successors; forfeiture of compensation.

When a receiver, assignee, or professional dies, resigns, or is removed, the court may appoint a successor on its own initiative or on the petition of any person having an interest. The court shall order that all appropriate papers, records, and property be turned over to the successor and may order that a removed or resigning receiver or assignee file any report required by Rule 13-501. The court may order the person removed to forfeit any future compensation and return any compensation for services previously rendered.

Source. — This Rule is derived from former Rule V82 a.

TITLE 14. SALES OF PROPERTY

Editor's note. — The Court of Appeals, by Order dated June 5, 1996, effective January 1, 1997, rescinded Subtitles A, D, E, J, P, Q, R, T, U, V, W, Y, Z, BB, BD, BE, BG, BH, BJ, BL, BP, BQ, BR, BS, BW, and BY of Chapter 1100 of the Maryland Rules of Procedure, rescinded Subtitles P, BB, BQ, and BW of the Maryland District Rules, and rescinded Forms 22a, 23, 24, 25, and 26. The Order substituted for certain of the rules and forms rescinded new Title 9, Chapter 100, Title 10, Title 12, Title 13, Title 14, and Title 15 of the Maryland Rules of Procedure. Furthermore, the Order transferred, without readoption, Chapter 900, Chapter 1200, and Subtitles S, BU, and BV of Chapter 1100 of the Maryland Rules of Procedure and Chapter 1200 of the Maryland District Rules to be Title 9, Chapter 200, Title 11, and Title 16 of the Maryland Rules of Procedure. The Order provides that the new rules shall "apply to all actions commenced on or after January 1, 1997, and insofar as practicable, to all actions then pending."

Many of the cases in the notes to the various rules were decided prior to the 1996 revision. These cases have been retained under pertinent rules of this title where it is thought that such cases will be of value in interpreting the present rules.

A table of comparable rules, relating those rules rescinded effective January 1, 1997, to the revised rules in Title 9 through Title 16 is to be found in Volume 2 following the end of the Maryland Rules.

CHAPTER 100. GENERAL PROVISIONS.

Rule 14-101. Location of public sale of interest in real property.

Unless the court orders otherwise, a public sale of an interest in real property conducted pursuant to the Rules in this Title shall (a) take place in the county in which the property is located and (b) if the property is located in more than one county, take place in the county in which the action is pending.

The sale shall be conducted immediately outside the courthouse entrance, on the property being sold, or at any other place ordered by the court. (Added Feb. 10, 2009, effective May 1, 2009.)

Cross references. — See Rules 14-210 and 14-303(b) regarding notice of the place of sale.
Source. — This Rule is derived from the 2008 version of former Rules 14-101 and 14-207 (a).

Rule 14-102. Judgment awarding possession.

(a) **Motion.** (1) If the purchaser of an interest in real property at a sale conducted pursuant to the Rules in this Title is entitled to possession and the person in actual possession fails or refuses to deliver possession, the purchaser or a successor in interest who claims the right of immediate possession may file a motion for judgment awarding possession of the property.

(2) The motion shall state the legal and factual basis for the movant's claim of entitlement to possession.

(3) If the movant's right to possession arises from a foreclosure sale of a dwelling or residential property, the motion shall include averments, based on a reasonable inquiry into the occupancy status of the property and made to the best of the movant's knowledge, information, and belief, establishing either that the person in actual possession is not a bona fide tenant having rights under the Federal Protecting Tenants at Foreclosure Act of 2009 (P.L. 111-22) or Code, Real Property Article, §7-105.6 or, if the person in possession is such a bona fide tenant, that the notice required under these laws has been given and that the tenant has no further right to possession. If a notice pursuant to the Federal Act or Code, Real Property Article, §7-105.6 is required, the movant shall state the date the notice was given and attach a copy of the notice as an exhibit to the motion.

Committee note. — Unless the purchaser is a foreclosing lender or there is waste or other circumstance that requires prompt remediation, the purchaser ordinarily is not entitled to possession until the sale has been ratified and the purchaser has paid the full purchase price and received a deed to the property. See *Legacy Funding v. Cohn,* 396 Md. 511 (2007) and *Empire v. Hardy,* 386 Md. 628 (2005).

The Federal Protecting Tenants at Foreclosure Act of 2009 (P.L. 111-22) requires that a purchaser at a foreclosure sale of a dwelling or residential property give a 90-day notice to a "bona fide tenant" before any eviction and precludes the eviction if the tenant has a "bona fide lease or tenancy," unless the new owner of the property will occupy the property as a primary residence.

(b) **Affidavit and notice.** The motion shall be accompanied by:

(1) an affidavit that states:

(A) the name of the person in actual possession, if known;

(B) the actions taken to conduct a reasonable inquiry into the occupancy status of the property;

(C) whether the person in actual possession was a party to the action that resulted in the sale or to the instrument that authorized the sale;

(D) if the purchaser paid the full purchase price and received a deed to the property, the date the payment was made and the deed was received; and

(E) if the purchaser has not paid the full purchase price or has not received a deed to the property, the factual basis for the purchaser's claim of entitlement to possession; and

(2) if the person in actual possession was not a party to the action or instrument, a notice advising the person that any response to the motion must be filed within 30 days after being served or within any applicable longer time prescribed by Rule 2- 321 (b) for answering a complaint. A copy of Rule 2-321 (b) shall be attached to the notice.

(c) **No show cause order, summons, or other process.** The court shall not issue a show cause order, summons, or other process by reason of the filing of a motion pursuant to this Rule.

(d) **Service and response.** (1) On whom. The motion and all accompanying documents shall be served on the person in actual possession and on any other person affected by the motion.

(2) Party to action or instrument. (A) If the person to be served was a party to the action that resulted in the sale or to the instrument that authorized the sale, the motion shall be served in accordance with Rule 1-321.

(B) Any response shall be filed within the time set forth in Rule 2-311.

(3) Not a party to action or instrument. (A) If the person to be served was not a party to the action that resulted in the sale or a party to the instrument that authorized the sale, the motion shall be served:

(i) by personal delivery to the person or to a resident of suitable age and discretion at the dwelling house or usual place of abode of the person, or

(ii) if on at least two different days a good faith effort was made to serve the person under subsection (d)(3)(A)(i) of this Rule but the service was not successful, by (a) mailing a copy of the motion by certified and first-class mail to the person at the address of the property and (b) posting in a conspicuous place on the property a copy of the motion, with the date of posting conspicuously written on the copy.

(B) Any response shall be filed within the time prescribed by sections (a) and (b) of Rule 2-321 for answering a complaint. If the person asserts that the motion should be denied because the person is a bona fide tenant having a right of possession under the Federal Protecting Tenants at Foreclosure Act of 2009 (P.L. 111-22), or Code, Real Property Article, §7-105.6, the response shall (i) state the legal and factual basis for the assertion and (ii) be accompanied by a copy of any bona fide lease or documents establishing the existence of such a lease or state why the lease or documents are not attached.

(4) Judgment of possession. If a timely response to the motion is not filed and the court finds that the motion complies with the requirements of sections (a) and (b) of this Rule, the court may enter a judgment awarding possession.

(e) **Residential property; notice and affidavit.** After entry of a judgment awarding possession of residential property as defined in Rule 14-202 (i), but before executing on the judgment, the purchaser shall:

(1) send by first-class mail the notice required by Code, Real Property Article, § 7-105.9 (d) addressed to "All Occupants" at the address of the property; and

(2) file an affidavit that the notice was sent. (Added Feb. 10, 2009, effective May 1, 2009; amended June 16, 2009, effective June 17, 2009; amended June. 7, 2010, effective July 1, 2010.)

Cross references. — Rule 2-647 (Enforcement of Judgment Awarding Possession).
Source. — This Rule is derived in part from the 2008 version of former Rule 14-102 and is in part new.

Effect of amendments. — The 2009 amendment rewrote (a); added the second paragraph in the committee note in (a); added the second sentence in (d)(3)(B); in (d)(4) added "and the court finds that the motion complies with the requirements of sections (a) and (b) of this Rule"; and added (e).

The 2010 amendment added the (1) through (3) designations in (a) and rewrote (a)(3); added (b)(1)(B); redesignated accordingly; and added "or Code, Real Property Article, § 7-105.6" in (d)(3)(B).

Legislative history — Rule 14-102 provided the exclusive means for a purchaser at a foreclosure sale to seek the ouster of a mortgage debtor who refused to relinquish possession; it was clear from the legislative history of § 8-402.4 of the Real Property Article that the wrongful detainer action established in that provision applied solely where the person who remained in possession had formerly been the tenant of the party seeking to recover possession. Empire Properties, L.L.C. v. Hardy, 386 Md. 628, 873 A.2d 1187 (2005).

Motion for judgment of possession — Courts should inquire into the merits of a motion for judgment of possession and investigate the need for a hearing on the motion on a case-by-case basis; under the terms of the deed of trust, the lender was entitled to possession, and it was an abuse of discretion for the trial court to summarily deny the lender's motion for judgment of possession. G.E. Capital Mtg. Servs., Inc. v. Edwards, 144 Md. App. 449, 798 A.2d 1187 (2002).

Trial court properly denied a purchaser's action under § 8-402.4 of the Real Property Article, seeking possession of property purchased at a foreclosure sale; when a purchaser at a foreclosure sale sought to acquire actual possession of the purchased property though judicial means, the purchaser had to file a motion under Rule 14-102(a). Empire Properties, L.L.C. v. Hardy, 386 Md. 628, 873 A.2d 1187 (2005).

Although legal title to property purchased at a foreclosure sale did not vest in the purchaser until the buyer had fully performed by, for example, paying the purchase price, an entitlement to an award of immediate possession could arise as soon as equitable title vested in the buyer, upon ratification of the sale by a circuit court. Empire Properties, L.L.C. v. Hardy, 386 Md. 628, 873 A.2d 1187 (2005).

Purchaser who has not paid full purchase price. — Absent compelling circumstances, circuit courts should be wary of granting possession of foreclosed property pursuant to this Rule to a purchaser who has not yet paid the full purchase price. Legacy Funding LLC v. Cohn, 396 Md. 511, 914 A.2d 760 (2007).

Motion for surplus funds for denial of possession — Although a purchaser who, following conveyance of legal title, seeks only an order for possession may do so in a district court, if the purchaser intends to seek not just possession but a share of any surplus funds as compensation for wrongful detainer, the relief, for very practical reasons, should be sought in the foreclosure proceeding pursuant to Rule 14-208 and this Rule. Thus, it was entirely appropriate for a purchaser to seek relief in a foreclosure proceeding by asserting claims against surplus proceeds for the rental value of the mortgaged property between the date of the purchaser's demand for possession and the time the mortgagors vacated the property. Legacy Funding LLC v. Cohn, 396 Md. 511, 914 A.2d 760 (2007).

CHAPTER 200. FORECLOSURE OF LIEN INSTRUMENTS.

Rule 14-201. Applicability; Other Remedies.

(a) **Applicability.** The Rules in this Chapter apply to foreclosures under lien instruments and statutory liens.

(b) Not exclusive remedy; exception. The foreclosure procedure set forth in the Rules in this Chapter does not preclude other remedies available by law, except that the procedure is the sole remedy for the repossession of property sold under a land installment contract executed pursuant to Code, Real Property Article, Title 10, Subtitle 1 or its statutory predecessor. (Added Feb. 10, 2009, effective May 1, 2009.)

Source. — This Rule is derived from the 2008 version of former Rule 14-201(a).

Section (a) is derived from former Rules W70 b and W79 c.

Section (b) is in part derived from former Rule W70 a and in part new.

Former rules met due process requirements — Former Subtitle W Rules met due process requirements of the Fourteenth Amendment to the United States Constitution and Article 24 of the Maryland Declaration of Rights. Billingsley v. Lawson, 43 Md. App. 713, 406 A.2d 946 (1979), cert. denied, 446 U.S. 919, 100 S. Ct. 1853, 64 L. Ed. 2d 273 (1980).

Counterclaim by mortgagor. — Prior to 1984, when the distinctions between law and equity for purposes of pleadings, parties, court sittings, and dockets were eliminated, the foreclosure of a deed of trust pursuant to a power of sale contained therein was an exclusively equitable remedy; today, however, nothing in the Maryland Rules of Procedure prohibits a mortgagor who voluntarily appears in a mortgage foreclosure proceeding from filing a counterclaim. Fairfax Sav. v. Kris Jen Ltd. Partnership, 338 Md. 1, 655 A.2d 1265 (1995).

Notice may be given by attorney. — A notification given by an attorney, who is an agent with authority to act in the premises, is the act of the client. Bob Holding Corp. v. Normal Realty Corp., 223 Md. 260, 164 A.2d 457 (1960).

Where the plaintiff's attorney signed the notice required by former Article 21, § 113, instead of "the vendor," the notice was properly given. Bob Holding Corp. v. Normal Realty Corp., 223 Md. 260, 164 A.2d 457 (1960).

The fact that the letter of notification was signed by the attorney was not material. In so doing, he was acting as the attorney for and agent of the plaintiff. His act was the act of the plaintiff. The notice was by the "vendor" within the meaning of the statute. Bob Holding Corp. v. Normal Realty Corp., 223 Md. 260, 164 A.2d 457 (1960).

Form of notice is not prescribed. — The ingredients only, not the form of the notice, are prescribed by the statute. Bob Holding Corp. v. Normal Realty Corp., 223 Md. 260, 164 A.2d 457 (1960).

"Foreclosure" may be used instead of "terminate." — Where notice used the word "foreclosure" instead of the word "terminate," the notice was not defective, since there is no substantial difference between the meanings of the two words; foreclosure of mortgage meaning termination of all rights of mortgagor. Bob Holding Corp. v. Normal Realty Corp., 223 Md. 260, 164 A.2d 457 (1960).

Data from which time can be computed is sufficient — It is sufficient if data are furnished from which the time may be computed with certainty. Bob Holding Corp. v. Normal Realty Corp., 223 Md. 260, 164 A.2d 457 (1960).

Ejectment not permissible remedy — Ejectment is not a permissible remedy under the Land Installment Contracts Law. Hudson v. Maryland State Hous. Co., 207 Md. 320, 114 A.2d 421 (1955).

Ejectment proceedings do not invalidate contract. — The fact that vendor used ejectment proceedings against purchaser, which are not a permissible remedy under the statute, did not invalidate a land installment contract. Hudson v. Maryland State Hous. Co., 207 Md. 320, 114 A.2d 421 (1955).

Repossession only through foreclosure proceeding. — Although seller retained legal title to the subject property, which was indeed superior to any interest forfeited by the buyer under criminal statutes, that legal title only provided the seller with the right to enforce the buyer's obligation under the land installment contract, and if the seller wished to enforce the buyer's obligations and obtain an interest in the property greater than this lien or security interest, the seller would have had to foreclose the lien pursuant to the procedures established in the Maryland Rules. United States v. Schecter, 251 F.3d 490 (4th Cir. 2001).

Federal preemption — The Maryland insolvency law has been suspended by the federal bankruptcy law, except as to certain classes of persons not provided for by the federal law such as farmers, who may be proceeded against involuntarily under the State law. Old Town Bank v. McCormick, 96

Md. 341, 53 A. 934 (1903).

In a breach of contract suit brought by a mortgagor, the mortgagor was not permitted to advance a State law contract claim based on an asserted breach of the federal regulations alluded to in his Fair Housing Administration form deed of trust but was allowed to raise a violation as an affirmative defense in an injunction suit blocking foreclosure. Wells Fargo Home Mortg., Inc. v. Neal, — Md. —, — A.2d — (2007).

Rule 14-202. Definitions.

In the Rules in this Chapter, the following definitions apply except as expressly otherwise provided or as necessary implication requires:

(a) Assent to a decree. "Assent to a decree" means a provision in a lien instrument assenting, in the event of a specified default, to the entry of an order for the sale of the property subject to the lien.

(b) Borrower. "Borrower" means:

(1) a mortgagor;

(2) a grantor of a deed of trust;

(3) any person liable for the debt secured by the lien;

(4) a maker of a note secured by an indemnity deed of trust;

(5) a purchaser under a land installment contract;

(6) a person whose property is subject to a lien under Code, Real Property Article, Title 14, Subtitle 2 (Maryland Contract Lien Act); and

(7) a leasehold tenant under a ground lease, as defined in Code, Real Property Article, § 8-402.3 (a)(6).

(c) Debt. "Debt" means a monetary obligation secured by a lien.

(d) Final Loss Mitigation Affidavit. "Final loss mitigation affidavit" means an affidavit substantially in the form prescribed by regulation adopted by the Commissioner of Financial Regulation that:

(1) is made by a person authorized to act on behalf of a secured party to a mortgage or deed of trust on residential property that is the subject of a foreclosure action;

(2) certifies the completion of the final determination of loss mitigation analysis in connection with the mortgage or deed of trust or states why no loss mitigation analysis is required; and

(3) if a loan modification or other loss mitigation was denied, provides an explanation for the denial.

Committee note. — The Committee believes that a final loss mitigation affidavit should be filed in every action seeking foreclosure of a lien on residential property, whether or not the property is owner-occupied. If the affiant has determined that the property is not owner-occupied residential property and, therefore, no loss mitigation analysis is required, the affiant should so state. See Rule 14-207(b)(7). The definition set forth in Code, Real Property Article, §7-105.1 is supplemented to include this requirement, and it is clarified to include the requirement that the form of affidavit be substantially in the form prescribed by regulation adopted by the Commissioner of Financial Regulation. Other modifications to the definition are stylistic only.

If the property is owner-occupied residential property but the secured party, such as an individual purchase-money mortgagee, is not required to provide or participate in a loss mitigation program, the affiant should so state as an explanation for the denial of a loan modification or other loss mitigation.

Cross references. — See Chapter 485, Laws of 2010 (HB 472), Section 4 (3)(i) for the form of Final Loss Mitigation Affidavit required prior to the adoption of regulations by the Commissioner of Financial Regulation.

(e) Foreclosure Mediation. "Foreclosure mediation" means a conference at which the parties in a foreclosure action, their attorneys, additional representatives of the parties, or a combination of those persons appear before an impartial individual to discuss the positions of the parties in an attempt to reach agreement on a loss mitigation program for the mortgagor or grantor.

Committee note. — This is the definition stated in Code, Real Property Article, §7-105.1 (a)(3). Code, Real Property Article, §§7-105.1 (i), (j), (k), and (l) require that the foreclosure mediation be conducted by the Office of Administrative Hearings.

(f) Lien. "Lien" means a statutory lien or a lien upon property created or authorized to be created by a lien instrument.

(g) Lien instrument. "Lien instrument" means any instrument creating or authorizing the creation of a lien on property, including:

(1) a mortgage;

(2) a deed of trust;

(3) a land installment contract, as defined in Code, Real Property Article § 10-101(b);

(4) a contract creating a lien pursuant to Code, Real Property Article, Title 14, Subtitle 2;

(5) a deed or other instrument reserving a vendor's lien; or

(6) an instrument creating or authorizing the creation of a lien in favor of a homeowners' association, a condominium council of unit owners, a property owners' association, or a community association.

(h) Loss Mitigation Analysis. "Loss mitigation analysis" means an evaluation of the facts and circumstances of a loan secured by owner-occupied residential property to determine:

(1) whether a mortgagor or grantor qualifies for a loan modification; and

(2) if there will be no loan modification, whether any other loss mitigation program may be made available to the mortgagor or grantor.

(i) Loss Mitigation Program. "Loss mitigation program" means an option in connection with a loan secured by owner-occupied residential property that:

(1) avoids foreclosure through a loan modification or other changes to existing loan terms that are intended to allow the mortgagor or grantor to stay in the property;

(2) avoids foreclosure through a short sale, deed in lieu of foreclosure, or other alternative that is intended to simplify the relinquishment of ownership of the property by the mortgagor or grantor; or

(3) lessens the harmful impact of foreclosure on the mortgagor or grantor.

(j) Owner-Occupied Residential Property. "Owner-occupied residential property" means residential property in which at least one unit is occupied by an individual who has an ownership interest in the property and uses the property as the individual's primary residence.

(k) Power of sale. "Power of sale" means a provision in a lien instrument authorizing, in the event of a specified default, a sale of the property subject to the lien.

(l) Preliminary Loss Mitigation Affidavit. "Preliminary loss mitigation affidavit" means an affidavit substantially in the form prescribed by regulation adopted by the Commissioner of Financial Regulation that:

(1) is made by a person authorized to act on behalf of a secured party to a mortgage or deed of trust on owner-occupied residential property that is the subject of a foreclosure action;

(2) certifies the status of an incomplete loss mitigation analysis in connection with the mortgage or deed of trust; and

(3) includes reasons why the loss mitigation analysis is incomplete.

Cross references. — See Chapter 485, Laws of 2010 (HB 472), Section 4 (3)(ii) for the form of Preliminary Loss Mitigation Affidavit required prior to the adoption of regulations by the Commissioner of Financial Regulation.

(m) Property. "Property" means real and personal property of any kind located in this State, including a condominium unit and a time share unit.

(n) Record owner. "Record owner" of property means a person who as of 30 days before the date of providing a required notice holds record title to the property or is the record holder of the rights of a purchaser under a land installment contract.

(o) Residential property. "Residential property" means real property with four or fewer single family dwelling units that are designed principally and are intended for human habitation. It includes an individual residential condominium unit within a larger structure or complex, regardless of the total number of individual units in that structure or complex. "Residential property" does not include a time share unit.

Cross references. — See Code, Real Property Article, § 7-105.1(a).

(p) Sale. "Sale" means a foreclosure sale.

(q) Secured party. "Secured party" means any person who has an interest in property secured by a lien or any assignee or successor in interest to that person. The term includes:

(1) a mortgagee;

(2) the holder of a note secured by a deed of trust or indemnity deed of trust;

(3) a vendor under a land installment contract or holding a vendor's lien;

(4) a person holding a lien under Code, Real Property Article, Title 14, Subtitle 2;

(5) a condominium council of unit owners;

(6) a homeowners' association;

(7) a property owners' or community association; and

(8) a ground lease holder, as defined in Code, Real Property Article, § 8-402.3 (a)(3).

The term does not include a secured party under Code, Commercial Law Article, § 9-102 (a)(3).

(r) Statutory lien. "Statutory lien" means a lien on property created by a statute providing for foreclosure in the manner specified for the foreclosure of mortgages, including a lien created pursuant to Code, Real Property Article, § 8-402.3(d). (Added Feb. 10, 2009, effective May 1, 2009; amended June 16, 2009, effective June 17, 2009; amended June. 7, 2010, effective July 1, 2010.)

Committee note. — Liens created pursuant to Code, Real Property Article, Title 14, Subtitle 2 (Maryland Contract Lien Act) are to be foreclosed "in the same manner, and subject to the same requirements, as the foreclosure of mortgages or deeds of trust." See Code, Real Property Article, § 14-204(a). A lien for ground rent in arrears created pursuant to Code, Real Property Article, § 8-402.3(d) is to be foreclosed "in the same manner and subject to the same requirements, as the foreclosure of a mortgage or deed of trust containing neither a power of sale not an assent to decree." See Code, Real Property Article, § 8-402.3(n).

Source. — This Rule is derived in part from the 2008 version of former Rule 14-201 (b) and is in part new.

Effect of amendments. — The 2009 amendment added "that are designed principally and are intended for human habitation" in (i) and made stylistic changes.

The 2010 amendment added (d), (e), (h), (i), (j) and (l) and redesignated accordingly; following (d) added the committee note and the cross reference; following (e) added the committee note; and following (l) added the committee note.

"Mortgagor." — The word mortgagor, as customarily used, specifically refers to the maker or creator of a mortgage and not to one who is the grantee of or holds title under that person. Gaspin v. Browning, 265 Md. 552, 290 A.2d 507 (1972).

Rule 14-203. Venue and attachment of jurisdiction.

(a) **Venue.** An action to foreclose a lien shall be filed in the county in which all or any part of the property subject to the lien is located.

(b) **Attachment of jurisdiction.** The court's jurisdiction over the property subject to the lien attaches when an action to foreclose is filed. (Added Feb. 10, 2009, effective May 1, 2009.)

Source. — This Rule is derived from the 2008 version of former Rule 14-203(b) and (c).

When jurisdiction attaches — Former law. — Formerly in Maryland jurisdiction of the equity court in a case of foreclosure under a power of sale was not complete until the property was sold and the trustee under the mortgage had filed his report of the sale. In Warehime v. Carroll County Bldg. Ass'n, 44 Md. 512 (1876), it was said that, in the case of a sale under a power in a mortgage, the trust commenced with the filing of the trustee's bond; his report of sales was his first official intercourse with the court, and its supervisory power then commenced. In re Hurlock, 23 F.2d 500 (D. Md. 1928).

Former statute mandatory. — Former § 11 of Article 66, from which section b of former Rule W74 was derived, was mandatory, and if sale was not made in the county where the property lay, it would be set aside. Webb v. Haeffer, 53 Md. 187 (1880).

Former § 11 of Article 66 applied to technical mortgages. When an instrument was held not to be a technical mortgage, the application of the section was denied. Harrison v. Annapolis & E.R.R., 50 Md. 490 (1879).

Multiple mortgages on multiple parcels — Where multiple mortgages are secured by multiple parcels of property constituting one integrated business operation, the foreclosure sale of all of the property in one jurisdiction is proper. Federal Land Bank of Baltimore, Inc. v. Esham, 43 Md. App. 446, 406 A.2d 928 (1979).

Express waiver in regard to one sale applicable to other similar sales. — Since the two Worcester County properties were simultaneously sold at the Wicomico County sale, the express waiver of the objection to the place of sale of one of the properties operated to waive any similar objection to the sale of the other property. Federal Land Bank of Baltimore, Inc. v. Esham, 43 Md. App. 446, 406 A.2d 928 (1979).

Where location changed by annexation act. — Where a mortgage when executed covered property in Baltimore County, and subsequently annexation act changed geographical location of the property to Baltimore City, the sale thereafter should take place in the city. Chilton v. Brooks, 71 Md. 445, 18 A. 868 (1889).

Rule 14-204. Institution of action.

(a) **Who may file.** (1) Under power of sale. Subject to compliance with subsection (a)(3) of this Rule, any individual authorized to exercise a power of sale may institute an action to foreclose the lien.

(2) Under assent to decree. A secured party may file an action to foreclose the lien under an assent to a decree, except that an action to foreclose a deed of trust shall be instituted by the beneficiary of the deed of trust, any trustee appointed in the deed, or any successor trustee.

(3) Fractional owners of debt. Except when the lien instrument is a deed of trust, a power of sale may not be exercised, and the court may not enter an order for a sale under an assent to a decree, unless the power is exercised or application for an order is made or consented to by the holders of 25% or more of the entire debt due under the lien instrument.

(b) **Priority of actions.** If more than one party is authorized under these Rules to file an action to foreclose a lien, the first such party to file an action acquires the exclusive right to foreclose. (Added Feb. 10, 2009, effective May 1, 2009.)

Source. — This Rule is derived as follows:

Subsection (a)(1) is derived from the 2008 version of former Rule 14-202 (a)(1).

Subsection (a)(2) is derived from the 2008 version of former Rule 14-202 (a)(2).

Subsection (a)(3) is derived from the 2008 version of former Rule 14-202 (b)(1) and (c).

Section (b) is derived from the 2008 version of former Rule 14-202 (b)(2).

General creditor without lien not proper party — General creditor having no lien upon the property is not a proper party, initially or by intervention, to a foreclosure suit. Balance Ltd. v. Short, 35 Md. App. 10, 368 A.2d 1116 (1977).

Deed of trust is mortgage — For most purposes a deed of trust is a mortgage and is subject to some (but not all) statutory provisions relating to mortgages. Burroughs v. Garner, 43 Md. App. 302, 405 A.2d 301 (1979).

Obligor's interest after full payment. — Neither default nor institution of foreclosure in any way negates the fact that where full payment has been made, the obligor has, at the least, complete equitable ownership of the property, and the trustee has, at most, only bare legal title to it. Burroughs v. Garner, 43 Md. App. 302, 405 A.2d 301 (1979).

Exceptions to foreclosure sale. — When trustees initiated an action to foreclose on certain real property, a trial court was not required to overrule a mortgagor's exceptions to the foreclosure sale based on fraud when the mortgagor did not seek an injunction, prior to the 2009 revision which eliminated the injuction, prior to the sale, because the mortgagor could raise the issue in exceptions to the sale under Rule 14-305, and the trial court, as a court of equity, had full authority to hear and determine the issue. Bierman v. Hunter, 190 Md. App. 250, 988 A.2d 530 (2010), overruled in part on other grounds, Bates v. Cohn, 2010 Md. LEXIS 759 (Md. 2010).

Rule 14-205. Conditions precedent to the filing of an action.

(a) **Generally.** An action to foreclose may not be filed unless (1) the instrument creating or giving notice of the existence of the lien has been filed for record, and (2) there is a default that lawfully allows a sale.

Cross references. — Code, Real Property Article, Title 14, Subtitle 2 (Maryland Contract Lien Act).

(b) **Foreclosure of liens on residential property.** Unless otherwise ordered by the court pursuant to Rule 14-206, an action to foreclose a lien on residential property may not be filed until the later of (1) 90 days after a default for which the lien instrument lawfully allows a sale, or (2) 45 days after the notice of intent to foreclose required by Code, Real Property Article, § 7-105.1(c), together with all items required by that section to accompany the notice, has been sent in the manner required by that section.

Cross references. — For the form of the notice and any other information that the Commissioner of Financial Regulation requires, see COMAR 09.03.12.01 *et seq.*

(c) **Land installment contract.** (1) Notice. An action to foreclose a land installment contract on property other than residential property may not be filed until at least 30 days after the secured party has served written notice on the borrower, the record owner of the property, and, if different, the person in possession at the address of the property. The notice shall describe the default with particularity and state that foreclosure proceedings will be filed on or after a designated day, not less than 30 days after service of the notice, unless the default is cured prior to that day.

(2) Method of service. The secured party shall serve the notice required by subsection (1) of this section by (A) certified and first-class mail to the last known address of the person or (B) personal delivery to the person or to a resident of suitable age and discretion at the dwelling house or usual place of abode of the person. (Added Feb. 10, 2008, effective May 1, 2009; amended June. 7, 2010, effective July 1, 2010.)

Cross references. — For the definition of "land installment contract," see Code, Real Property Article, § 10-101(b).

Source. — This Rule is derived in part from the 2008 version of Rule 14-203(a) and is in part new.

Effect of amendments. — The 2010 amendment added "together with all items required by that section to accompany the notice" following "§ 7-105.1 (c)" in (b).

Purpose of foreclosure statutes. — One of the main objects of § 5 (now § 7-105 (a)) of the Real Property Article and repealed §§ 6 and 7 of Article 66, from which former Rules W72 and W74 were derived, was to bring sales made by their authority and the resulting equity proceedings under the cognizance and guidance of the court, and such proceedings are to be conducted and the validity of the sales tested as ordinary sales made by a trustee appointed by a decree of the court. Ex parte Aurora Fed. Sav. & Loan Ass'n, 223 Md. 135, 162 A.2d 739 (1960).

Order to docket is not pleading. — An order to docket is not a pleading. This is so in spite of the fact that it is the delivery of the order to the clerk which gives the equity court jurisdiction over the mortgaged property when a power of sale is being exercised. Saunders v.

Stradley, 25 Md. App. 85, 333 A.2d 604 (1975).

An order to docket need not make factual allegations sufficient to show a right to proceed. See Saunders v. Stradley, 25 Md. App. 85, 333 A.2d 604 (1975).

An order to docket is not designed to be answered, denied or traversed so as to arrive at issues. Saunders v. Stradley, 25 Md. App. 85, 333 A.2d 604 (1975).

No process is issued or served upon the filing of an order to docket. Saunders v. Stradley, 25 Md. App. 85, 333 A.2d 604 (1975).

Scope of court's function not affected by order to docket. — An order to docket neither broadens nor narrows the scope of the court's function in a case. Saunders v. Stradley, 25 Md. App. 85, 333 A.2d 604 (1975).

Default is condition precedent — A foreclosure-triggering default is a condition precedent to a Maryland mortgage foreclosure: ordinarily the existence of that essential will be demonstrated by the statement of mortgage debt that is required to accompany the order to docket the summary proceeding. Fairfax Sav. v. Kris Jen Ltd. Partnership, 338 Md. 1, 655 A.2d 1265 (1995).

No sale under decree until default. — Before the passage of former Rule W72, a decree might properly be entered at any time after the execution of a mortgage containing an assent to a decree, whether there was or not at the time a default on the part of the mortgagor in respect to the covenants of the mortgage, but there could be no sale under the decree until default. United States v. Eastern Woodworks, Inc., 151 F. Supp. 95 (D. Md. 1957); Better v. Williams, 203 Md. 613, 102 A.2d 750 (1954).

Time for sale. — Foreclosure pursuant to a power of sale is intended to be a summary, in rem proceeding. In that type of proceeding, a sale of the mortgaged property can be held in approximately twenty-one days after docketing. G.E. Capital Mtg. Servs., Inc. v. Levenson, 338 Md. 227, 657 A.2d 1170 (1995).

Tender of full amount due — Where a party interested in mortgaged property tenders mortgagee full amount due, for purpose of redeeming mortgage, as he has a right to do, mortgagee has no right to institute foreclosure proceedings thereafter, and may be enjoined from doing so. Kent Bldg. & Loan Co. v. Middleton, 112 Md. 10, 75 A. 967 (1910).

Sale not set aside because notes not filed — Sale will not be set aside because mortgage notes were not filed, no application having been made for that purpose and indebtedness and ownership of notes not being denied. Heider v. Bladen, 83 Md. 242, 34 A. 836 (1896).

Bankruptcy of mortgagor. — Where suit is entered in State court, to foreclose mortgage before petition in bankruptcy against mortgagor is filed foreclosure case may be prosecuted without interference of bankruptcy court; otherwise, however, where (as formerly the case where a mortgage was foreclosed under a power of sale) State court does not acquire jurisdiction until property sold and report of sale filed. In re Hurlock, 23 F.2d 500 (D. Md. 1928).

Notice may be given by attorney. — A notification given by an attorney, who is an agent with authority to act in the premises, is the act of the client. Bob Holding Corp. v. Normal Realty Corp., 223 Md. 260, 164 A.2d 457 (1960).

Where the plaintiff's attorney signed the notice required by former Article 21, § 113, instead of "the vendor," the notice was properly given. Bob Holding Corp. v. Normal Realty Corp., 223 Md. 260, 164 A.2d 457 (1960).

The fact that the letter of notification was signed by the attorney was not material. In so doing, he was acting as the attorney for and agent of the plaintiff. His act was the act of the plaintiff. The notice was by the "vendor" within the meaning of the statute. Bob Holding Corp. v. Normal Realty Corp., 223 Md. 260, 164 A.2d 457 (1960).

Form of notice is not prescribed. — The ingredients only, not the form of the notice, are prescribed by the statute. Bob Holding Corp. v. Normal Realty Corp., 223 Md. 260, 164 A.2d 457 (1960).

"Foreclosure" may be used instead of "terminate." — Where notice used the word "foreclosure" instead of the word "terminate," the notice was not defective, since there is no substantial difference between the meanings of the two words; foreclosure of mortgage meaning termination of all rights of mortgagor. Bob Holding Corp. v. Normal Realty Corp., 223 Md. 260, 164 A.2d 457 (1960).

Data from which time can be computed sufficient — It is sufficient if data are furnished from which the time may be computed with certainty. Bob Holding Corp. v. Normal Realty Corp., 223 Md. 260, 164 A.2d 457 (1960).

Ejectment not permissible remedy — Ejectment is not a permissible remedy under the Land Installment Contracts Law. Hudson v. Maryland State Hous. Co., 207 Md. 320, 114 A.2d 421 (1955).

Ejectment proceedings do not invalidate contract. — The fact that vendor used ejectment proceedings against purchaser, which are not a permissible remedy under the statute, did not invalidate a land installment contract. Hudson v. Maryland State Hous. Co., 207 Md. 320, 114 A.2d 421 (1955).

Rule 14-206. Petition for immediate foreclosure against residential property.

(a) **Right to file.** A secured party may file a petition to be excused from the time and notice requirements of Code, Real Property Article, § 7-105.1(b) and (c) and Rule 14-205(b) and for leave to file an action for immediate foreclosure of a lien against residential property if:

(1) the debt secured by the lien instrument was obtained by fraud or deception;

(2) no payments have ever been made on the debt;

(3) the property subject to the lien has been destroyed; or

(4) the default occurred after all stays have been lifted in a bankruptcy proceeding.

(b) **Contents of petition.** A petition filed under this Rule shall state with particularity the facts alleged in support of the petition and shall be under oath or supported by affidavit.

(c) **Notice to borrower and record owner.** The secured party shall send by certified and first-class mail a copy of the petition and all papers attached to it to each borrower and record owner of the property at the person's last known address, and, if the person's last known address is not the address of the property, to the person at the address of the property. The mailing shall include a notice that the addressee may file a response to the petition within 10 days after the date of the mailing. Promptly after the mailing, the secured party shall file an affidavit that states with particularity how compliance with this section was accomplished, including the date on which the petition was mailed and the names and addresses of the persons to whom it was mailed.

(d) **Response.** (1) Procedure. Within 10 days after the mailing pursuant to section (c) of this Rule, a borrower or record owner of the property may file a written response. The response shall state with particularity any defense to the petition and shall be under oath or supported by affidavit. A person who files a response shall serve a copy of the response and any supporting documents on the petitioner by first-class mail, and shall file proof of such service with the response.

Cross references. — See Rules 1-321(a) and 1-323.

(2) Non-waiver if no timely response filed. A person's failure to file a timely response to the petition does not waive the person's right to raise any defense in the action to foreclose, including a defense based upon noncompliance with the time or notice requirements of Code, Real Property Article, § 7-105.1(b) and (c).

(e) **Hearing.** The court may not grant the petition without a hearing if a response presents a genuine dispute of material fact as to whether the petitioner is entitled to the relief requested. Otherwise, the court may grant or deny the petition without a hearing.

(f) **Filing of order to docket or complaint.** An order to docket or complaint to foreclose shall be filed in the same action as the petition. (Added Feb. 10, 2009, effective May 1, 2009; amended June. 7, 2010, effective July 1, 2010.)

Committee note. — If this Rule applies in an action to foreclose a lien against owner-occupied residential property, the loss mitigation analysis and affidavit requirements of Code, Real Property Article, §7-105.1 are not applicable and foreclosure mediation under the statute is not available.

Source. — This Rule is new.

Effect of amendments. — The 2010 amendment added a committee note at the end of the section.

Nature of proceedings. — It is possible for a mortgage foreclosure proceeding in Maryland in which no deficiency decree is sought to be purely in rem: it is also possible, if the mortgagor voluntarily appears, for the proceeding to include judgments, in the form of rulings on exceptions to the sale and to the auditor's report, respectively, that have in personam collateral estoppel effect. Fairfax Sav. v. Kris Jen Ltd. Partnership, 338 Md. 1, 655 A.2d 1265 (1995).

Court order directing sale held not to change nature of proceedings. — The fact that the court entered an order directing the "trustees," not appointed by the court under a decree but so designated by, and acting pursuant to, the terms of the deed of trust, containing a power of sale, to sell the chattels described in the deed of trust did not change the proceedings from a foreclosure under power of sale pursuant to Article 66, former § 5 (see now § 7-105 of the Real Property Article), to a foreclosure under former § 6 of that article. United States v. Eastern Woodworks, Inc., 151 F. Supp. 95 (D. Md. 1957).

Cited in Wincopia Farm, LP v. Goozman, 188 Md. App. 519, 982 A.2d 868 (2009), cert. denied, 412 Md. 496, 988 A.2d 1010, 2010 Md. LEXIS 68 (2010).

Rule 14-207. Pleadings; service of certain affidavits, pleadings, and papers.

(a) **Pleadings allowed.** (1) Power of sale. An action to foreclose a lien pursuant to a power of sale shall be commenced by filing an order to docket. No process shall issue.

(2) Assent to a decree or lien instrument with no power of sale or assent to a decree. An action to foreclose a lien pursuant to an assent to a decree or pursuant to a lien instrument that contains neither a power of sale nor an assent to a decree shall be commenced by filing a complaint to foreclose. If the lien instrument contains an assent to a decree, no process shall issue.

(3) Lien instrument with both a power of sale and assent to a decree. If a lien instrument contains both a power of sale and an assent to a decree, the lien may be foreclosed pursuant to either.

(b) **Exhibits.** A complaint or order to docket shall include or be accompanied by:

(1) a copy of the lien instrument supported by an affidavit that it is a true and accurate copy, or, in an action to foreclose a statutory lien, a copy of a notice of the existence of the lien supported by an affidavit that it is a true and accurate copy;

Cross references. — See Code, Real Property Article, § 7-105.1 (d-1) concerning the contents of a lost note affidavit in an action to foreclose a lien on residential property.

(2) an affidavit by the secured party, the plaintiff, or the agent or attorney of either that the plaintiff has the right to foreclose and a statement of the debt remaining due and payable;

(3) a copy of any separate note or other debt instrument supported by an affidavit that it is a true and accurate copy and certifying ownership of the debt instrument;

(4) a copy of any assignment of the lien instrument for purposes of foreclosure or deed of appointment of a substitute trustee supported by an affidavit that it is a true and accurate copy of the assignment or deed of appointment;

(5) with respect to any defendant who is an individual, an affidavit in compliance with § 521 of the Servicemembers Civil Relief Act, 50 U.S.C. app. § 501 et seq.;

(6) a statement as to whether the property is residential property and, if so, statements in boldface type as to whether (A) the property is owner-occupied residential property, if known, and (B) a final loss mitigation affidavit is attached;

(7) if the property is residential property that is not owner-occupied residential property, a final loss mitigation affidavit to that effect;

(8) in an action to foreclose a lien instrument on residential property, to the extent not produced in response to subsections (b)(1) through (b)(7) of this Rule, the information and items required by Code, Real Property Article, § 7-105.1(d), except that (A) if the name and license number of the mortgage originator and mortgage lender is not required in the notice of intent to foreclose, the information is not required in the order to docket or complaint to foreclose; and (B) if the mortgage loan is owned, securitized, insured, or guaranteed by the Federal National Mortgage Association, Federal Home Loan Mortgage Corporation, or Federal Housing Administration, or if the servicing agent is participating in the federal Making Home Affordable Modification Program (also known as "HAMP"), providing documentation as required by those programs satisfies the requirement to provide a description of the eligibility requirement for the applicable loss mitigation program; and

Committee note. — Subsection (b)(8) of this Rule does not require the filing of any information or items that are substantially similar to information or items provided in accordance with subsections (b)(1) through (b)(7). For example, if a copy of a deed of appointment of substitute trustee, supported by an affidavit that it is a true and accurate copy, is filed, it is not necessary to file the original or a clerk-certified copy of the deed of appointment.

Cross references. — For the required form and sequence of documents, see Code, Real Property Article, § 7-105.1 (f)(1) and COMAR 09.03.12.01 et seq.

(9) in an action to foreclose a land installment contract on property other than residential property, an affidavit that the notice required by Rule 14-205 (c) has been given.

Cross references. — For statutory "notices" relating to liens, see, e.g., Code, Real Property Article, § 14-203 (b).

Committee note. — Pursuant to subsections (b)(7) and (8) of this Rule, a preliminary or final loss mitigation affidavit must be filed in all actions to foreclose a lien on residential property, even if a loss mitigation analysis is not required.

(c) **Service of certain affidavits, pleadings, and papers.** Any affidavit, pleading, or other paper that amends, supplements, or confirms a previously filed affidavit, pleading, or other paper shall be served on each party, attorney of record, borrower, and record owner in accordance with the methods provided by Rule 1-321, regardless of whether service of the original affidavit, pleading, or paper was required. (Added February 10, 2009, effective May 1, 2009; amended June 7, 2010, effective July 1, 2010; amended October 20, 2010, effective October 20, 2010; amended October 11, 2011, effective November 1, 2011.)

Committee note. — This Rule prevails over the provision in Rule 1- 321 (a) or any other Rule that purports, where a party is represented by an attorney, to permit service on only the attorney. This Rule requires service on both.

Source. — This Rule is derived in part from the 2008 version of former Rule 14-204(a) and (c) and is in part new.

Effect of amendments. — The 2010 amendment, effective July 1, 2010, in the introductory language of (b) added "include or"; rewrote (b)(6); added (b)(7) and redesignated accordingly; in (b)(8), substituted "(b)(7)" for "(b)(5)", "items" for "papers", added the (A) designation and added (B); in the committee note following (b)(8) substituted "(b)(8)" for "(b)(7)", "(b)(7)" for "(b)(5)" and "items" for "papers" throughout; and added a committee note at the end of the section.

The 2010 amendment, effective October 20, 2010, rewrote (c).

The 2011 amendment added cross reference notes after (b)(1) and (b)(8) and rewrote (b)(5).

Purpose of foreclosure statutes. — One of the main objects of § 5 (now § 7-105 (a)) of the Real Property Article and repealed §§ 6 and 7 of Article 66, from which former Rules W72 and W74 were derived, was to bring sales made by their authority and the resulting equity proceedings under the cognizance and guidance of the court, and such proceedings are to be conducted and the validity of the sales tested as ordinary sales made by a trustee appointed by a decree of the court. Ex parte Aurora Fed. Sav. & Loan Ass'n, 223 Md. 135, 162 A.2d 739 (1960).

Order to docket not a pleading. — An order to docket is not a pleading. This is so in spite of the fact that it is the delivery of the order to the clerk which gives the equity court jurisdiction over the mortgaged property when a power of sale is being exercised. Saunders v. Stradley, 25 Md. App. 85, 333 A.2d 604 (1975).

An order to docket need not make factual allegations sufficient to show a right to proceed. See Saunders v. Stradley, 25 Md. App. 85, 333 A.2d 604 (1975).

An order to docket is not designed to be answered, denied or traversed so as to arrive at issues. Saunders v. Stradley, 25 Md. App. 85, 333 A.2d 604 (1975).

No process is issued or served upon the filing of an order to docket. Saunders v. Stradley, 25 Md. App. 85, 333 A.2d 604 (1975).

Scope of court's function not affected by order to docket. — An order to docket neither broadens nor narrows the scope of the court's function in a case. Saunders v. Stradley, 25 Md. App. 85, 333 A.2d 604 (1975).

Default is condition precedent — A foreclosure-triggering default is a condition precedent to a Maryland mortgage foreclosure: ordinarily the existence of that essential will be demonstrated by the statement of mortgage debt that is required to accompany the order to docket the summary proceeding. Fairfax Sav. v. Kris Jen Ltd. Partnership, 338 Md. 1, 655 A.2d 1265 (1995).

No sale under decree until default. — Before the passage of former Rule W72, a decree might properly be entered at any time after the execution of a mortgage containing an assent to a decree, whether there was or not at the time a default on the part of the mortgagor in respect to the covenants of the mortgage, but there could be no sale under the decree until default. Better v. Williams, 203 Md. 613, 102 A.2d 750 (1954); United States v. Eastern Woodworks, Inc., 151 F. Supp. 95 (D. Md. 1957).

In a breach of contract suit brought by a mortgagor, the mortgagor was not permitted to advance a State law contract claim based on an asserted breach of the federal regulations alluded to in his Fair Housing Administration form deed of trust but was allowed to raise a violation as an affirmative defense in an injunction suit blocking foreclosure. Wells Fargo Home Mortg., Inc. v. Neal, — Md. —, —A.2d — (2007).

Exceptions to foreclosure sale. — When trustees initiated an action to foreclose on certain real property, a trial court was not required to overrule a mortgagor's exceptions to the foreclosure sale based on fraud when the mortgagor did not seek an injunction, prior to the 2009 revision which eliminated the injuction, prior to the sale, because the mortgagor could raise the issue in exceptions to the sale under Rule 14-305, and the trial court, as a court of equity, had full authority to hear and determine the issue. Bierman v. Hunter, 190 Md. App. 250, 988 A.2d 530 (2010), overruled in part on other grounds, Bates v. Cohn, 2010 Md. LEXIS 759 (Md. 2010).

Amendment of statement of mortgage debt after foreclosure. — Where a first mortgage lender amended the statement of mortgage debt after a foreclosure sale had been conducted and ratified, where the judgment of ratification had become final and unappealable, and where the amendment obliterated a surplus that would have been distributed to junior lienors, the first mortgage lender had the burden of proving that there was no prejudice in fact to junior lienors. Schaller v. Castle Dev. Corp., 347 Md. 90, 698 A.2d 1106 (1997).

Time for sale. — Foreclosure pursuant to a power of sale is intended to be a summary, in rem proceeding. In that type of proceeding, a sale of the mortgaged property can be held in approximately twenty-one days after docketing. G.E. Capital Mtg. Servs., Inc. v. Levenson, 338 Md. 227, 657 A.2d 1170 (1995).

Tender of full amount due — Where a party interested in mortgaged property tenders mortgagee full amount due, for purpose of redeeming mortgage, as he has a right to do, mortgagee has no right to institute foreclosure proceedings thereafter, and may be enjoined from doing so. Kent Bldg. & Loan Co. v. Middleton, 112 Md. 10, 75 A. 967 (1910).

No notice to loan guarantor required. — Debtors who executed an indemnity deed of trust to secure a creditor's loan to their daughter were not entitled to notice of a foreclosure or of an auditor's report under (b) of this Rule, Rule 14-305(b), and § 7-105 of the Real Property Article, because they were not record owners or holders of subordinate interests. In

re Cutaio, (Bankr. D. Md. 2007).

Sale not set aside because notes not filed — Sale will not be set aside because mortgage notes were not filed, no application having been made for that purpose and indebtedness and ownership of notes not being denied. Heider v. Bladen, 83 Md. 242, 34 A. 836 (1896).

Bankruptcy of mortgagor. — Where suit is entered in State court, to foreclose mortgage before petition in bankruptcy against mortgagor is filed foreclosure case may be prosecuted without interference of bankruptcy court; otherwise, however, where (as formerly the case where a mortgage was foreclosed under a power of sale) State court does not acquire jurisdiction until property sold and report of sale filed. In re Hurlock, 23 F.2d 500 (D. Md. 1928).

Res judicata. — Because the issue of the validity of the mortgagors' rescission claims had already been resolved in another action ending in a final judgment in a Maryland court in a foreclosure action, issue preclusion prevented a federal district court from considering the rescission claims once more. DeCosta v. U.S. Bancorp, — F. Supp. 2d — (D. Md. Sept. 27, 2010).

Rule 14-207.1. Court screening.

(a) **Generally.** The court may adopt procedures to screen pleadings and papers filed in an action to foreclose a lien. If the court determines that the pleadings or papers filed do not comply with all statutory and Rule requirements, it may give notice to the plaintiff and each borrower, record owner, party, and attorney of record that the action will be dismissed without prejudice or that some other appropriate order will be entered by reason of the non-compliance if the plaintiff does not demonstrate within 30 days that the papers are legally sufficient or that the deficiency has been cured.

Committee note. — This Rule prevails over the provision in Rule 1-321 (a) or any other Rule that purports, where a party is represented by an attorney, to permit service on only the attorney. This Rule requires service on both.

(b) **Review of affidavits.** (1) In this section, "affidavit" includes any attestation or certification by an attorney, borrower, record owner, party, or agent of the attorney, borrower, record owner, or party concerning the truth or accuracy of a pleading or paper.

Cross references. — See Rule 1-202 (b) for a general definition of "affidavit."

(2) If the court has reason to believe that an affidavit filed in the action may be invalid because the affiant has not read or personally signed the affidavit, because the affiant does not have a sufficient basis to attest to the accuracy of the facts stated in the affidavit, or, if applicable, because the affiant did not appear before the notary as stated, the court may order the party to show cause

why the affidavit should not be stricken, and, if it is stricken, why the action should not be dismissed or other relief granted.

(3) As part of the show cause order, the court may order that the affiant and any notary appear before the court at a time stated in the order for the affiant to attest under penalty of perjury that the affiant read and personally signed the affidavit and had a sufficient basis to attest to the accuracy of the facts stated in the affidavit, and, if applicable, for the affiant and the notary to attest that the affiant appeared before the notary and made the oath stated.

(4) A copy of the order shall be sent to the plaintiff and to each borrower, record owner, party, and attorney of record, together with a notice that they may appear and examine the affiant and notary. The court may further require that the plaintiff serve the order and any response thereto on each borrower, record owner, party, and attorney of record.

Cross references. — See Rule 1-341.

(c) **Special masters or examiners.** The court may designate one or more qualified Maryland lawyers to serve as a part-time special master or examiner to screen pleadings and papers under section (a) of this Rule, conduct proceedings under section (b) of this Rule, and make appropriate recommendations to the court. Subject to section (d) of this Rule, the costs and expenses of the special master or examiner may be assessed against one or more of the parties pursuant to Code, Courts Article, § 2-102 (c), Rule 2-541 (i), or Rule 2-542 (i). With his or her consent, the special master or examiner may serve on a pro bono basis.

(d) **Assessment of costs, expenses, and attorney's fees.** The costs, expenses, and attorney's fees of any proceeding under this Rule, including any costs or expense of a special master or examiner under section (c) of this Rule, shall not be assessed against the borrower or record owner either directly or as an expense of sale, unless the affidavit in question was filed by or on behalf of the borrower or record owner. (Added October 20, 2010, effective October 20, 2010.)

Committee note. — The exercise of the authority granted in this Rule is discretionary with the court. Nothing in this Rule precludes the court from using its own personnel for these purposes.

Source. — This Rule is new.

Rule 14-208. Subsequent proceedings if no power of sale or assent to a decree.

(a) **Process and service.** When a complaint is filed to foreclose a lien that has neither a power of sale nor an assent to a decree, process shall issue and be served in accordance with Title 2, Chapter 100 of these Rules, except that in an action to foreclose a lien on residential property, service shall be in accordance with Rule 14-209. Except as provided in section (b) of this Rule, the action shall proceed in the same manner as any other civil action.

(b) **Order directing immediate sale.** If after a hearing, the court finds that the interests of justice require an immediate sale of the property that is subject to the lien and that a sale would likely be ordered as a result of a judgment entered in the action, the court may order a sale of the property before judgment and shall appoint an individual to make the sale pursuant to Rule 14-214, provided any applicable requirements of Code, Real Property Article, §7-105.1 have been satisfied. The court shall order that the proceeds be deposited or invested pending distribution pursuant to judgment. (Amended June. 7, 2010, effective July 1, 2010.)

Source. — This Rule is derived from the 2008 version of former Rule 14-205 (a) and (b)(2).

Effect of amendments. — The 2010 amendment added "provided any applicable requirements of Code, Real Property Article, § 7-105.1 have been satisfied" and made related changes in (b).

Rule 14-209. Service in actions to foreclose on residential property; notice.

(a) **Service on borrower and record owner by personal delivery.** When an action to foreclose a lien on residential property is filed, the plaintiff shall serve on the borrower and the record owner a copy of all papers filed to commence the action, accompanied by the documents required by Code, Real Property Article, § 7-105.1 (f). Service shall be accomplished by personal delivery of the papers or by leaving the papers with a resident of suitable age and discretion at the borrower's or record owner's dwelling house or usual place of abode.

Cross references. — For the required form and sequence of documents, see Code, Real Property Article, § 7-105.1 (f)(1) and COMAR 09.03.12.01 et seq.

(b) **Service on borrower and record owner by mailing and posting.** If on at least two different days a good faith effort was made to serve a borrower or record owner under section (a) of this Rule and service was not successful, the plaintiff shall effect service by (1) mailing, by certified and first-class mail, a copy of all papers filed to commence the action, accompanied by the documents required by Code, Real Property Article, § 7-105.1 (f), to the last known address of each borrower and record owner and, if the person's last known address is not the address of the residential property, also to that person at the address of the property; and (2) posting a copy of the papers in a conspicuous place on the residential property. Service is complete when the property has been posted and the mailings have been made in accordance with this section.

Cross references. — For the required form and sequence of documents, see Code, Real Property Article, §7-105.1 (f)(1) and COMAR 09.03.12.01 et seq.

(c) **Notice to all occupants by first-class mail.** When an action to foreclose on residential property is filed, the plaintiff shall send by first-class mail addressed to "All Occupants" at the address of the property the notice required by Code, Real Property Article, §7-105.9 (b).

(d) **If notice required by local law.** When an action to foreclose on residential property is filed with respect to a property located within a county or a municipal corporation that, under the authority of Code, Real Property Article, §14-126 (c), has enacted a local law requiring notice of the commencement of a foreclosure action, the plaintiff shall give the notice in the form and manner required by the local law. If the local law does not provide for the manner of giving notice, the notice shall be sent by first-class mail.

(e) **Affidavit of service, mailing, and notice.** (1) Time for filing. An affidavit of service under section (a) or (b) of this Rule, mailing under section (c) of this Rule, and notice under section (d) of this Rule shall be filed promptly and in any event before the date of the sale.

(2) Service by an individual other than a sheriff. In addition to other requirements contained in this section, if service is made by an individual other than a sheriff, the affidavit shall include the name, address, and telephone number of the affiant and a statement that the affiant is 18 years of age or older.

(3) Contents of affidavit of service by personal delivery. An affidavit of service by personal delivery shall set forth the name of the person served and the date and particular place of service. If service was effected on a person other than the borrower or record owner, the affidavit also shall include a description of the individual served (including the individual's name and address, if known) and the facts upon which the individual making service concluded that the individual served is of suitable age and discretion.

(4) Contents of affidavit of service by mailing and posting. An affidavit of service by mailing and posting shall (A) describe with particularity the good faith efforts to serve the borrower or record owner by personal delivery; (B) state the date on which the required papers were mailed by certified and first-class mail and the name and address of the addressee; and (C) include the date of the posting and a description of the location of the posting on the property.

(5) Contents of affidavit of notice required by local law. An affidavit of the sending of a notice required by local law shall (A) state (i) the date the notice was given, (ii) the name and business address of the person to whom the notice was given, (iii) the manner of delivery of the notice, and (iv) a reference to the specific local law of the county or municipal corporation, or both, requiring the notice and (B) be accompanied by a copy of the notice that was given. (Added Feb. 10, 2009, effective May 1, 2009; amended June 16, 2009, effective June 17, 2009; amended October 11, 2011, effective November 1, 2011.)

Cross references. — See the Servicemembers Civil Relief Act, 50 U.S.C. app. §§ 501 *et seq.*

Source. — This Rule is derived in part from the 2008 version of former Rule 14-204 (b) and is in part new.

Effect of amendments. — The 2009 amendment rewrote (c); added (d); redesig- nated former (d) as (e); in the heading of (e) added "and notice; in the introductory language in (e) added "and notice under section (d) of this Rule"; added (e)(5); and made related changes.

The 2011 amendment added "accompanied by the documents required by Code, Real Property Article, § 7-105.1 (f)" in (a) and (b) and added cross reference notes after (a) and (b).

Debtor's rights. — Debtor may seek to enjoin a foreclosure sale from proceeding by filing a motion to enjoin prior to the sale, as provided for in Rule 14-209 but, if the debtor fails to do so and the sale occurs, the debtor's later filing of exceptions can only challenge any procedural irregularities regarding the sale, or the debtor can challenge the statement of indebtedness by filing exceptions to the auditor's statement of account. Ultimately, the foreclosure sale extinguishes a debtor's right of redemption, and substantial compliance by tendering a payment to satisfy the outstanding debt is insufficient once the decree of foreclosure has been declared. Greenbriar Condo. v. Brooks, 387 Md. 683, 878 A.2d 528 (2005).

Violations of the United States Department of Housing and Urban Development's regulations alleged of a mortgagee by the mortgagor could be asserted effectively as an affirmative defense within the injunctive apparatus provided in (b)(1). Wells Fargo Home Mortg., Inc. v. Neal, 398 Md. 705, 922 A.2d 538 (2007).

Denial of motion to stay not error. — Trial court did not err in denying the mortgagor's motion to stay a foreclosure sale where the mortgagor failed to comply with (b); strikingly absent from the motion to stay was any averment that the mortgagor did not owe any monies under the Indemnity Deed of Trust, a requirement for relief from the bond requirement of (b). Wincopia Farm, LP v. Goozman, 188 Md. App. 519, 982 A.2d 868 (2009), cert. denied, 412 Md. 496, 988 A.2d 1010, 2010 Md. LEXIS 68 (2010).

Setting aside foreclosure sale held in error. — When a petition to foreclose a mortgage pursuant to an assent to a decree is filed, stating simply that the mortgage is in default, such petition is sufficient to sustain the foreclosure proceeding so long as any one of the provisions of the mortgage, the violation of which can constitute a default under the terms of the mortgage, is in default. Pacific Mtg. & Inv. Group, Ltd. v. LaGuerre, 81 Md. App. 28, 566 A.2d 780 (1989).

The breach of a covenant to insure contained within a mortgage constitutes a default which allows acceleration under an acceleration clause. Pacific Mtg. & Inv. Group, Ltd. v. LaGuerre, 81 Md. App. 28, 566 A.2d 780 (1989).

Trial court erred by setting aside a second foreclosure sale with regard to a condominium unit, because the debtor failed to file an injunction prior to the sale and, upon completion of the sale, the debtor lost his right of redemption. The debtor should have sought to enjoin the sale from proceeding by filing a motion to enjoin under Md. R. 14-209.11-110, as substantial compliance by tendering a payment to satisfy the debt after the sale occurred was insufficient once the decree of foreclosure was entered. Greenbriar Condo. v. Brooks, 387 Md. 683, 878 A.2d 528 (2005).

Objections overruled. — Where a petition for an injunction alleged that the mortgage debt and interest were fully satisfied under the terms of an agreement, and appeal was from a final decree for a permanent injunction on that ground, the objection that the petition did not allege that the mortgage and all interest due thereon had been paid, and the contention that the bond filed as a prerequisite to issue of a preliminary injunction was not in the form prescribed by law, were properly overruled. Green v. Redmond, 132 Md. 166, 103 A. 431 (1918).

Bill held insufficient. Fowler v. Pendleton, 121 Md. 297, 88 A. 124 (1913).

Allegations in bill determine jurisdiction — Allegations in bill determine jurisdiction of court. Barrick v. Horner, 78 Md. 253, 27 A. 1111 (1893).

Amount due must be paid or brought into court. — Where the mortgagor admits in his bill that a balance is due mortgagee, that amount must be paid mortgagee or brought into court before mortgagor is entitled to an injunction. Talbott v. Laurel Bldg. Ass'n, 140 Md. 565, 118 A. 63 (1922).

Before court will grant an injunction to restrain a sale upon default in a mortgage, the mortgagor must pay into court amount admitted to be due. Buckner v. Cronhardt, 132 Md. 612, 104 A. 169 (1918).

Mortgagor seeking to raise a violation of the United States Department of Housing and Urban Development's (HUD's) loss mitigation regulations as a defense to foreclosure was not required to pay his or her debt in full in order to be granted an injunction under this Rule because under principles of equity, the mortgagee's commencement of a foreclosure proceeding on a Fair Housing Administration-insured mortgage, without first having adhered to the mandatory HUD loss mitigation regulations, may invalidate the mortgagee's declaration of default. Wells Fargo Home Mortg., Inc. v. Neal, 398 Md. 705, 922 A.2d 538 (2007).

Rule 14-209.1. Owner-Occupied Residential Property.

(a) **Applicability.** This rule applies to an action to foreclose a lien on residential property that is owner-occupied residential property, or where it is unknown whether the property is owner-occupied residential property at the time the action is filed.

(b) **Advertising of sale.** A sale may not be advertised until 30 days after a final loss mitigation affidavit is filed, but if a request for foreclosure mediation is filed within that time and not stricken, a sale may not be advertised until the report from the Office of Administrative Hearings is filed with the court.

(c) **Foreclosure mediation.** (1) Request; transmittal. (A) Filing of request. The borrower may file a request for foreclosure mediation within the time allowed by Code, Real Property Article, §7-105.1 (h)(1). The request shall contain the caption of the case and the names and addresses of the parties and be accompanied by the foreclosure mediation filing fee required by Code, Real Property Article, §7-105.1 (h)(1)(ii) or a written request in accordance with Rule 1-325 for an order waiving or reducing the fee. The borrower shall serve a copy of the request on the other parties. The clerk shall not accept for filing a request for foreclosure mediation that does not contain a certificate of service or is not accompanied by the required fee or request for an order waiving or reducing the fee.

Cross references. — See Rules 1-321 and 1-323. For the Request for Foreclosure Mediation form prescribed by regulation adopted by the Commissioner of Financial Regulation, see COMAR 09.03.12.05.

(B) Transmittal of request. Subject to section (e) of this Rule, the clerk shall transmit notice of the request to the Office of Administrative Hearings no later than five days after the request is filed.

Committee note. — The transmittal to the Office of Administrative Hearings shall be made within the time required by subsection (c)(1)(B) of this Rule, regardless of the status of a request for waiver or reduction of the foreclosure mediation filing fee.

(C) Ruling on request for fee waiver or reduction. The court promptly shall rule upon a request for an order waiving or reducing the foreclosure mediation filing fee. The court may make its ruling *ex parte* and without a hearing. If the court does not waive the fee in its entirety, the court shall specify in its order the dollar amount to be paid and the amount of time, not to exceed ten days, within which the sum shall be paid. The order shall direct the clerk to strike the request for foreclosure mediation if the sum is not paid within the time allowed and, if the request is stricken, to promptly notify the Office of Administrative Hearings that the request for foreclosure mediation has been stricken.

(2) Motion to strike request for foreclosure mediation. No later than 15 days after service of a request for foreclosure mediation, the secured party may file a motion to strike the request. The motion shall be accompanied by an affidavit that sets forth with particularity reasons sufficient to overcome the presumption that the borrower is entitled to foreclosure mediation and why foreclosure mediation is not appropriate.

(3) Response to motion to strike. No later than 15 days after service of the motion to strike, the borrower may file a response to the motion.

(4) Ruling on motion. After expiration of the time for filing a response, the court shall rule on the motion, with or without a hearing. If the court grants the motion, the clerk shall notify the Office of Administrative Hearings that the motion has been granted.

(d) **Notification from Office of Administrative Hearings.** (1) If extension granted. If the Office of Administrative Hearings extends the time for completing foreclosure mediation pursuant to Code, Real Property Article, §7-105.1 (i)(2)(ii), it shall notify the court no later than 67 days after the court transmitted the request for foreclosure mediation and specify the date by which mediation shall be completed. If the Office of Administrative Hearings extends the time for completing foreclosure mediation more than once, it shall notify the court of each extension and specify the new date by which mediation shall be completed.

(2) Outcome of foreclosure mediation. Within the time allowed by Code, Real Property Article, §7-105.1 (j)(3), the Office of Administrative Hearings shall file with the court a report that states (A) whether the foreclosure mediation was held and, if not, the reasons why it was not held, or (B) the outcome of the foreclosure mediation. The Office of Administrative Hearings promptly shall provide a copy of the report to each party to the foreclosure mediation.

(e) **Electronic transmittals.** By agreement between the Administrative Office of the Courts and the Office of Administrative Hearings, notifications required by this Rule may be transmitted by electronic means rather than by mail and by a department of the Administrative Office of the Courts rather than by the clerk, provided that an appropriate docket entry is made of the transmittal or the receipt of the notification.

(f) **Procedure following foreclosure mediation.** (1) If agreement results from foreclosure mediation. If the foreclosure mediation results in an agreement, the court shall take any reasonable action reasonably necessary to implement the agreement.

(2) If no agreement. If the foreclosure mediation does not result in an agreement, the secured party may advertise the sale, subject to the right of the borrower to file a motion pursuant to Rule 14- 211 to stay the sale and dismiss the action.

(3) If foreclosure mediation fails due to the fault of a party. (A) If the foreclosure mediation is not held or is terminated because the secured party failed to attend or failed to provide the documents required by regulation of the Commissioner of Financial Regulation, the court, after an opportunity for a hearing, may dismiss the action.

(B) If the foreclosure mediation is not held or is terminated because the borrower failed to attend or failed to provide the documents required by regulation of the Commissioner of Financial Regulation, the secured party may advertise the sale. (Added June. 7, 2010, effective July 1, 2010; amended October 11, 2011, effective November 1, 2011.)

Source. — This Rule is new.

Effect of amendments. — The 2011 amendment in (b) substituted "30 days" for "20 days"; in (c)(2) substituted "mediation and why" for "mediation why"; in (d)(1) substituted "67 days" for 65 days," added "and specify … shall be completed," and added the second sentence.

Rule 14-210. Notice prior to sale.

(a) **By publication.** Before selling property in an action to foreclose a lien, the individual authorized to make the sale shall publish notice of the time, place, and terms of the sale in a newspaper of general circulation in the county in which the action is pending. Notice of the sale of an interest in real property shall be published at least once a week for three successive weeks, the first publication to be not less than 15 days before the sale and the last publication to be not more than one week before the sale. Notice of the sale of personal property shall be published not less than five days nor more than 12 days before the sale.

(b) **By certified and first-class mail.** Before selling the property subject to the lien, the individual authorized to make the sale shall also send notice of the time, place, and terms of sale (1) by certified mail and by first-class mail to (A) the borrower, (B) the record owner of the property, and (C) the holder of any subordinate interest in the property subject to the lien and (2) by first-class mail to "All Occupants" at the address of the property. The notice to "All occupants" shall be in the form and contain the information required by Code, Real Property Article, §7-105.9 (c). Except for the notice to "All Occupants," the mailings shall be sent to the last known address of all such persons, including to the last address reasonably ascertainable from a document recorded, indexed, and available for public inspection 30 days before the date of the sale. The mailings shall be sent not more than 30 days and not less than ten days before the date of the sale.

(c) **To counties or municipal corporations.** In addition to any other required notice, not less than 15 days before the sale, the individual authorized to make the sale shall send written notice to the county or municipal corporation where the property subject to the lien is located. The notice shall include the name, address, and telephone number of the individual authorized to make the sale and the time, place, and terms of sale.

(d) **Holders of a subordinate interest.** If the individual authorized to make the sale receives actual notice at any time before the sale that there is a person holding a subordinate interest in the property and if the interest holder's identity and address are reasonably ascertainable, the individual authorized to make the sale shall give notice of the time, place, and terms of sale to the interest holder as promptly as reasonably practicable. The notice may be given in any manner reasonably calculated to apprise the interest holder of the sale, including by telephone or electronic transmission. This notice need not be given to anyone to whom notice was sent pursuant to section (b) of this Rule.

(e) **Affidavit of notice by mail.** An individual who is required by this Rule to give notice by mail shall file an affidavit stating that (1) the individual has complied with the mailing provisions of this Rule or (2) the identity or address of the borrower, record owner, or holder of a subordinate interest is not reasonably ascertainable. If the affidavit states that an identity or address is not reasonably ascertainable, the affidavit shall state in detail the reasonable, good faith efforts that were made to ascertain the identity or address. If notice was given to the holder of a subordinate interest in the property, the affidavit shall state the date, manner, and content of the notice. (Added Feb. 10, 2009, effective May 1, 2009; amended June 16, 2009, effective June 17, 2009; June 7, 2011, effective July 1, 2011.)

Source. — This Rule is derived in part from the 2008 version of former Rule 14-206 (b) and is in part new.

Effect of amendments. — The 2009 amendment in (b), in the first sentence, added the designations and substituted "by first-class mail to 'All Occupants'" for "Occupants" and made related changes; added the second sentence; and substituted "All Occupants" for "Occupants" in the third sentence.

The 2011 amendment deleted the committee note in (a).

Rule sets forth only notice required. — The only notice of a mortgage foreclosure proceeding which is required is that set forth in former Rule W74. Butler v. Daum, 245 Md. 447, 226 A.2d 261 (1967).

Constitutionality. — Section 7-105 of the Real Property Article and this Rule are not constitutionally infirm merely because they do not require the certified mail to be returned as undeliverable prior to requiring that notice be sent via first class mail. Griffin v. Bierman, 403 Md. 186, 941 A.2d 475 (2008).

Objective underlying notice requirement. — In recommending the adoption of section a 2 (b) of former Rule W74 to the Court of Appeals, the Rules Committee stated that it did not intend to create a burdensome requirement. Instead it indicated that its objective was to give notice to the original maker of the mortgage of both the sale and the fact that he can be called upon to pay any deficiency caused by the failure of the mortgaged property to produce sufficient funds necessary to extinguish the debt. Gaspin v. Browning, 265 Md. 552, 290 A.2d 507 (1972).

Strict compliance. — Former Rule W74, which replaced an earlier statute, makes more stringent and more precise the minimal requirements as to notice and must be strictly complied with. Fleisher Co. v. Grice, 245 Md. 248, 226 A.2d 153 (1967).

Hence, although the parties to a mortgage are free to contract in respect to the notice given, whatever else the terms agreed upon in the mortgage require the agent of the mortgagor to do in respect of the publication of the advertisement of sale, he must publish "at least once in each of three successive weeks" before the sale. The first of these three publications must be "not less than fifteen days" before the sale and the last of the same three publications must be "not more than one week" before the sale. Fleisher Co. v. Grice, 245 Md. 248, 226 A.2d 153 (1967).

Compliance with terms of decree. — Under former § 6 of Article 66 the terms of the decree were, by force of the statute, made a part of the statute and were to be as fully and strictly complied with as if they had been in terms embraced in the statute. United States v. Eastern Woodworks, Inc., 151 F. Supp. 95 (D. Md. 1957).

Rules controlling adequacy of advertisement. — In addition to the "time, place and terms" of sale, the cases state that the rules generally controlling the adequacy of an advertisement of a judicial sale are: (1) That the advertisement is sufficient if it describes the property so that it can be located by the exercise of ordinary intelligence and so that more detailed information concerning it can be obtained if desired; (2) the failure to mention or fully describe the nature and extent of the improvements will not vitiate a sale unless the exceptant meets the burden of overcoming the presumption of the validity of the sale by showing that the omission was prejudicial to the sale of the property at a fair and adequate sum and that a resale would be likely to produce a greater amount. Butler v. Daum, 245 Md. 447, 226 A.2d 261 (1967); Waring v. Guy, 248 Md. 544, 237 A.2d 763 (1968).

Notice in excess of requirements. — Notice of sale given by the trustees was sufficient and resulted in no injustice being done the defendant where notice in excess of that required by the statute and by the terms of the deed of trust was given. United States v. Eastern Woodworks, Inc., 151 F. Supp. 95 (D. Md. 1957).

Actual notice. — Where a mortgagor's property was sold at a foreclosure auction without her notice, her due process rights under the Fourteenth Amendment and art. 24 of the Declaration of Rights were not violated because the deed of trust trustees complied with the mailing requirement of § 7-105 of the Real Property Article, and due process did not require personal service. Griffin v. Bierman, 403 Md. 186, 941 A.2d 475 (2008).

Failure to describe improvements in advertisement. — In an advertisement of a foreclosure sale a failure to describe fully the nature and extent of improvements will not vitiate the sale, unless it is shown that the omission was prejudicial to the sale of the property at a fair and adequate sum, and that a resale would be likely to produce a greater amount. Hardy v. Gibson, 213 Md. 493, 133 A.2d 401 (1957); Waring v. Guy, 248 Md. 544, 237 A.2d 763 (1968).

Sufficiency of notice. — Trial court did not err by overruling the mortgagors' exceptions to a foreclosure sale and by ratifying the foreclosure sale because (1) the record contained an affidavit by the substitute trustees, stating that the substitute trustees gave notice of the foreclosure proceedings; and (2) attached to the affidavit were copies of the letter that was sent to the mortgagors and copies of the postal receipts for the mailings. Additionally, the mortgagors did not present any evidence to the contrary. Jones v. Rosenberg, 178 Md. App. 54, 940 A.2d 1109 (2008).

Personal notice not required prior to 1969. — No one (prior to 1969) was entitled to personal notice that foreclosure of a mortgage or deed of trust was pending. The only warning required to be given those affected by the proceedings, including the buying public, was through the published advertisements of sale mandated by section a 2 (b) of former Rule W74. Gaspin v. Browning, 265 Md. 552, 290 A.2d 507 (1972).

Personal notice of a mortgage foreclosure proceeding formerly was not necessary. Butler v. Daum, 245 Md. 447, 226 A.2d 261 (1967); Scott & Wimbrow, Inc. v. Calwell, 31 Md. App. 1, 354 A.2d 463, cert. denied, 278 Md. 733 (1976).

Attempt to give personal notice to mortgagor is now required. — The only requirement in section a 2 (c) of former Rule W74 is that an attempt be made to give personal notice to the original maker of the mortgage. Gaspin v. Browning, 265 Md. 552, 290 A.2d 507 (1972).

Although not to prior or subsequent lienholder. — Although the mortgagee, under paragraph (c) in subsection 2 of section a of former Rule W74, must endeavor to personally notify the mortgagor of the impending sale, no similar provision is contained in this Rule with respect to prior or subsequent lienholders. Scott & Wimbrow, Inc. v. Calwell, 31 Md. App. 1, 354 A.2d 463, cert. denied, 278 Md. 733 (1976).

Corporation that filed a petition for a mechanic's lien but had not obtained a lien was not entitled to notice that the property was going to be sold at a foreclosure sale, and the trial court ruled correctly that the lien which the corporation obtained after the property was sold at the foreclosure sale was extinguished when the sale was ratified. Redland Genstar, Inc. v. Mahase, 155 Md. App. 72, 841 A.2d 413 (2004).

Advertising deemed sufficient. — Advertising of sale held sufficient to meet the requirements of former subsection (c) of Article 66, § 5. deTamble v. Adkins, 210 Md. 414, 124 A.2d 276 (1956).

Time for sale. — Foreclosure pursuant to a power of sale is intended to be a summary, in rem proceeding. In that type of proceeding, a sale of the mortgaged property can be held in approximately twenty-one days after docketing. G.E. Capital Mtg. Servs., Inc. v. Levenson, 338 Md. 227, 657 A.2d 1170 (1995).

Procedure in Baltimore. — Compliance with the statutory provisions of former subsection (c) of Article 66, § 5, relative to notice, was held to be a compliance with the court's order that notice be given in the manner usually prescribed for advertising chattel foreclosure sales in Baltimore City. United States v. Eastern Woodworks, Inc., 151 F. Supp. 95 (D. Md. 1957).

Other cases under former statutes. — For other cases relating to notice and advertisement under former statutes, see White v. Malcolm, 15 Md. 529 (1860); Eichelberger v. Hardesty, 15 Md. 548 (1860); Warehime v. Carroll County Bldg. Ass'n, 44 Md. 512 (1876); Bank of Commerce v. Lanahan, 45 Md. 396 (1876); Roberts v. Loyola Perpetual Bldg. Ass'n, 74 Md. 1, 21 A. 684 (1891); Chilton v. Brooks, 71 Md. 445, 18 A. 868 (1889); Knapp v. Anderson, 89 Md. 189, 42 A. 933 (1899); Lewis v. Beale, 162 Md. 18, 158 A. 354 (1932); Preske v. Carroll, 178 Md. 543, 16 A.2d 291 (1940).

Quoted in Fagnani v. Fisher, 418 Md. 371, 15 A.3d 282 (2011).

Rule 14-211. Stay of the sale; dismissal of action.

(a) **Motion to stay and dismiss.** (1) Who may file. The borrower, a record owner, a party to the lien instrument, a person who claims under the borrower a right to or interest in the property that is subordinate to the lien being foreclosed, or a person who claims an equitable interest in the property may file in the action a motion to stay the sale of the property and dismiss the foreclosure action.

Cross references. — See Code, Real Property Article, §§7-101 (a) and 7-301 (f)(1).

(2) Time for filing. (A) Owner-occupied residential property. In an action to foreclose a lien on owner-occupied residential property, a motion by a borrower to stay the sale and dismiss the action shall be filed no later than 15 days after the last to occur of:

(i) the date the final loss mitigation affidavit is filed;

(ii) the date a motion to strike foreclosure mediation is granted; or

(iii) if foreclosure mediation was requested and the request was not stricken, the first to occur of:

(a) the date the foreclosure mediation was held;

(b) the date the Office of Administrative Hearings files with the court a report stating that no foreclosure mediation was held; or

(c) the expiration of 60 days after transmittal of the borrower's request for foreclosure mediation or, if the Office of Administrative Hearings extended the time to complete the foreclosure mediation, the expiration of the period of the extension.

(B) Other property. In an action to foreclose a lien on property, other than owner-occupied residential property, a motion by a borrower or record owner to stay the sale and dismiss the action shall be filed within 15 days after service pursuant to Rule 14-209 of an order to docket or complaint to foreclose. A motion to stay and dismiss by a person not entitled to service under Rule 14-209 shall be filed within 15 days after the moving party first became aware of the action.

(C) Non-compliance; extension of time. For good cause, the court may extend the time for filing the motion or excuse non-compliance.

Cross references. — See Rules 2-311 (b), 1-203, and 1-204, concerning the time allowed for filing a response to the motion.

(3) Contents. A motion to stay and dismiss shall:

(A) be under oath or supported by affidavit;

(B) state with particularity the factual and legal basis of each defense that the moving party has to the validity of the lien or the lien instrument or to the right of the plaintiff to foreclose in the pending action;

Committee note. — The failure to grant loss mitigation that should have been granted in an action to foreclose a lien on owner-occupied residential property may be a defense to the right of the plaintiff to foreclose in the pending action. If that defense is raised, the motion must state specific reasons why loss mitigation pursuant to a loss mitigation program should have been granted.

(C) be accompanied by any supporting documents or other material in the possession or control of the moving party and any request for the discovery of

275

any specific supporting documents in the possession or control of the plaintiff or the secured party;

(D) state whether there are any collateral actions involving the property and, to the extent known, the nature of each action, the name of the court in which it is pending, and the caption and docket number of the case;

(E) state the date the moving party was served or, if not served, when and how the moving party first became aware of the action; and

(F) if the motion was not filed within the time set forth in subsection (a)(2) of this Rule, state with particularity the reasons why the motion was not filed timely.

To the extent permitted in Rule 14-212, the motion may include a request for referral to alternative dispute resolution pursuant to Rule 14-212.

(b) **Initial determination by court.** (1) Denial of motion. The court shall deny the motion, with or without a hearing, if the court concludes from the record before it that the motion:

(A) was not timely filed and does not show good cause for excusing non-compliance with subsection (a)(2) of this Rule;

(B) does not substantially comply with the requirements of this Rule; or

(C) does not on its face state a valid defense to the validity of the lien or the lien instrument or to the right of the plaintiff to foreclose in the pending action.

Committee note. — A motion based on the failure to grant loss mitigation in an action to foreclose a lien on owner-occupied residential property must be denied unless the motion sets forth good cause why loss mitigation pursuant to a loss mitigation program should have been granted is stated in the motion.

(2) Hearing on the merits. If the court concludes from the record before it that the motion:

(A) was timely filed or there is good cause for excusing non-compliance with subsection (a)(2) of this Rule,

(B) substantially complies with the requirements of this Rule, and

(C) states on its face a defense to the validity of the lien or the lien instrument or to the right of the plaintiff to foreclose in the pending action, the court shall set the matter for a hearing on the merits of the alleged defense. The hearing shall be scheduled for a time prior to the date of sale, if practicable, otherwise within 60 days after the originally scheduled date of sale.

(c) **Temporary stay.** (1) Entry of stay; conditions. If the hearing on the merits cannot be held prior to the date of sale, the court shall enter an order that temporarily stays the sale on terms and conditions that the court finds reasonable and necessary to protect the property and the interest of the plaintiff. Conditions may include assurance that (1) the property will remain covered by adequate insurance, (2) the property will be adequately maintained, (3) property taxes, ground rent, and other charges relating to the property that become due prior to the hearing will be paid, and (4) periodic payments of principal and interest that the parties agree or that the court preliminarily finds will become due prior to the hearing are timely paid in a manner prescribed by the court. The court may require the moving party to provide reasonable security for compliance with the conditions it sets and may revoke the stay upon a finding of non-compliance.

(2) *Hearing on conditions.* The court may, on its own initiative, and shall, on request of a party, hold a hearing with respect to the setting of appropriate conditions. The hearing may be conducted by telephonic or electronic means.

(d) **Scheduling order.** In order to facilitate an expeditious hearing on the merits, the court may enter a scheduling order with respect to any of the matters specified in Rule 2-504 that are relevant to the action.

(e) **Final determination.** After the hearing on the merits, if the court finds that the moving party has established that the lien or the lien instrument is invalid or that the plaintiff has no right to foreclose in the pending action, it shall grant the motion and, unless it finds good cause to the contrary, dismiss the foreclosure action. If the court finds otherwise, it shall deny the motion. (Added Feb. 10, 2009, effective May 1, 2009; amended June. 7, 2010, effective July 1, 2010; amended October 11, 2011, effective November 1, 2011.)

Committee note. — If the court finds that the plaintiff has no right to foreclose in the pending action because loss mitigation should have been granted, the court may stay entry of its order of dismissal, pending further order of court, so that loss mitigation may be implemented.

Source. — This Rule is new.

Effect of amendments. — The 2010 amendment added (a)(2)(A) and redesignated formerly undesignated language of (a)(2) as (a)(2)(B) and (a)(2)(C); in (a)(2)(B) deleted "residential" and added "other than owner-occupied residential property"; following (a)(3)(B) added a committee note; to the undesignated paragraph following (a)(3)(F) added "To the extent permitted in Rule 14-212," and made related changes; following (b)(1)(C) added a committee note; and following (e) added a committee note.

The 2011 amendment in (a)(2)(A)(iii)(c) substituted "the expiration of the period of the extension" for "90 days after the date of the transmittal."

University of Baltimore Law Forum. — For a note, "Recent Development: Bates v. Cohn," see 41 U. Balt. L. F. 177 (2011).

Power to call off sale upon payment of past-due installments, etc. — An assignee, even though acting under the power of sale in a mortgage, has the right, when the past-due instalments and costs are paid, to call off a sale, thereby staying the sale of the property, and leave the equity proceedings open as a further security to enforce future payments. And, after a further default and he decides again to advertise the property for sale, he is not starting a new and independent proceeding, nor does he need an order of court to make the sale. Walsh v. Jefferson Fed. Sav. & Loan Ass'n, 216 Md. 131, 139 A.2d 847 (1958).

Setting aside foreclosure sale held in error. — Trial court erred by setting aside a second foreclosure sale with regard to a condominium unit, because the debtor failed to file an injunction prior to the sale and, upon completion of the sale, the debtor lost his right of redemption. The debtor should have sought to enjoin the sale from proceeding by filing a motion to enjoin under Md. R. 14-209, as substantial compliance by tendering a payment to satisfy the debt after the sale occurred was insufficient once the decree of foreclosure was entered. Greenbriar Condo. v. Brooks, 387 Md. 683, 878 A.2d 528 (2005).

Allegation of payment in cash not required. — An allegation of payment in cash is not required, and it is sufficient that a contract to cancel the mortgage debt in consideration of a transfer of the land to the mortgagee is alleged. Johnson v. Wheeler, 174 Md. 531, 199 A. 502 (1938).

When trustees initiated an action to foreclose on certain real property, a trial court was not required to overrule a mortgagor's exceptions to the foreclosure sale based on fraud when the mortgagor did not seek an injunction, prior to the 2009 revision which eliminated the injuction, prior to the sale, because the mortgagor could raise the issue in exceptions to the sale under Rule 14-305, and the trial court, as a court of equity, had full authority to hear and determine the issue. Bierman v. Hunter, 190 Md. App. 250, 988 A.2d 530 (2010), overruled in part on other grounds, Bates v. Cohn, 2010 Md. LEXIS 759 (Md. 2010).

Stranger instituting ejectment — A sale will not be stayed because a stranger has instituted ejectment, there being no allegation that his claim is valid. Gayle v. Fattle, 14 Md. 69 (1859).

Res judicata. — Because the issue of the validity of the mortgagors' rescission claims had already been resolved in another action ending in a final judgment in a Maryland court in a foreclosure action, issue preclusion prevented a federal district court from considering the rescission claims once more. DeCosta v. U.S. Bancorp, — F. Supp. 2d — (D. Md. Sept. 27, 2010).

Quoted in Bates v. Cohn, 417 Md. 309, 9 A.3d 846 (2010).

Rule 14-212. Alternative dispute resolution.

(a) **Applicability.** This Rule applies to actions that are ineligible for foreclosure mediation under Code, Real Property Article, §7- 105.1.

(b) **Referral to alternative dispute resolution.** In an action in which a motion to stay the sale and dismiss the action has been filed, and was not denied pursuant to Rule 14-211 (b)(1), the court at any time before a sale of the property subject to the lien may refer a matter to mediation or another appropriate form of alternative dispute resolution, subject to the provisions of Rule 17-103, and may require that individuals with authority to settle the matter be present or readily available for consultation. (Added Feb. 10, 2009, effective May 1, 2009; amended June. 7, 2010, effective July 1, 2010.)

Cross references. — For qualifications of a mediator other than one selected by agreement of the parties, see Rule 17-104(f).

Source. — This Rule is new.

Effect of amendments. — The 2010 amendment added (a) and redesignated formerly undesignated language as (b).

Rule 14-213. Bond by individual making sale.

Before selling property subject to a lien, the individual authorized to make the sale shall file a bond to the State of Maryland conditioned upon compliance with any court order that may be entered in relation to the sale of the property or distribution of the proceeds of the sale. Unless the court orders otherwise, the amount of the bond shall be $25,000. If the property is sold to a person other than the holder of the indebtedness or a person designated by the holder in a writing filed in the proceeding to take title on the holder's behalf, the individual authorized to make the sale shall increase the amount of the bond, before the sale is ratified, to the amount of the sale price as set forth in the report of sale. On application by a person having an interest in the property or by the individual authorized to make the sale, the court may increase or decrease the amount of the bond pursuant to Rule 1-402(d). (Added Feb. 10, 2009, effective May 1, 2009.)

Source. — This Rule is derived from the 2008 version of former Rule 14-206(a).

Party making sale to give bond — The bond must be given by the party making the sale and not by mortgagee. White v. Malcolm, 15 Md. 529 (1860).

Time of filing. — Where a bond is filed on the day of sale, the law presumes that it was filed before the sale. Hubbard v. Jarrell, 23 Md. 66 (1865); Hebb v. Mason, 143 Md. 345, 122 A. 318 (1923).

Second bond required where first inadequate. — Trustee appointed to sell at foreclosure proceedings may be required to give second bond on account of inadequacy of first bond. Employers' Liab. Assurance Corp. v. State ex rel. Hudgins, 163 Md. 119, 161 A. 249 (1932).

Defect raised by exception. — If a bond is defective, the defect must be raised by exceptions to ratification of sale, and cannot be inquired into collaterally. Cockey v. Cole, 28 Md. 276 (1868); Hebb v. Mason, 143 Md. 345, 122 A. 318 (1923).

Bond filed in wrong court — Bond filed in Circuit Court for Baltimore City conditioned to fulfill any order or decree of Baltimore County court is a nullity, and sale will be set aside. McCabe v. Ward, 18 Md. 505 (1862).

Who may bring suit. — Substituted trustee held to be among persons interested and entitled to institute suit on bond. Employers' Liab. Assurance Corp. v. State ex rel. Hudgins, 161 Md. 103, 155 A. 324 (1931).

Bond of trustee under former statute. — See Union Trust Co. v. Ward, 100 Md. 98, 59 A. 192 (1904); Real Estate Trust Co. v. Union Trust Co., 102 Md. 41, 61 A. 228 (1905); Cummings v. Wildman, 116 Md. 307, 81 A. 610 (1911); Richardson v. Malthan, 133 Md. 542, 105 A. 766 (1919); Briley v. Pinkston, 215 Md. 417, 136 A.2d 563 (1958).

Bond — See Thrift v. Bannon, 111 Md. 303, 73 A. 660 (1909); Wingert v. Brewer, 116 Md. 518, 82 A. 157 (1911); American Bonding Co. v. State ex rel. Com. & Farmers' Nat'l Bank, 120 Md. 305, 87 A. 922 (1913); Wolf v. Oldenburg, 154 Md. 353, 140 A. 494 (1928).

Rule 14-214. Sale.

(a) **Only by individual.** Only an individual may sell property pursuant to the Rules in this Chapter.

(b) **Under power of sale.** (1) Individual authorized to conduct a sale other than under a deed of trust. Except as provided in subsection (b)(2) of this Rule, a secured party authorized by the lien instrument to make the sale or any other individual designated by name in the lien instrument to exercise the power of sale shall conduct the sale.

(2) Individual authorized to conduct a sale under a deed of trust. An individual appointed as trustee in a deed of trust or as a substitute trustee shall conduct the sale of property subject to a deed of trust.

(3) Payment terms. A sale of property under a power of sale shall be made upon the payment terms specified in the lien instrument. If no payment terms are specified in the lien instrument, the sale shall be made upon payment terms that are reasonable under the circumstances.

(c) **Under assent to a decree.** (1) Individual authorized to sell. An individual appointed as a trustee in a lien instrument or as a substitute trustee shall conduct the sale of property pursuant to an assent to a decree.

(2) Payment terms. A sale of property under an order of court entered pursuant to an assent to a decree shall be made upon the payment terms provided in the order.

(d) **No power of sale or assent to decree.** (1) Individual authorized to sell. If there is no power or sale or assent to a decree in the lien instrument, or if the lien is a statutory lien, the sale shall be made by an individual trustee appointed by the court.

(2) Payment terms. The sale shall be made upon payment terms that are reasonable under the circumstances. (Added Feb. 10, 2009, effective May 1, 2009; amended June. 7, 2010, effective July 1, 2010.)

Cross references. — For requirements concerning the timing of the sale of residential property, see Code, Real Property Article, §7-105.1 (l).

Source. — This Rule is derived in part from the 2008 version of former Rule 14-207(b) and (c) and is in part new.

Effect of amendments. — The 2010 amendment added a cross reference to the timing of the sale of residential property.

Sales governed by same rules as other sales in equity. — Foreclosure sales under power of sale when brought within control of a court of equity are governed by same rules as other sales in equity. Warfield v. Dorsey, 39 Md. 299 (1874); Gaither v. Tolson, 84 Md. 637, 36 A. 449 (1897).

Foreclosure sales, when the proceedings are brought under the cognizance and guidance of the court, are to be conducted and determined in all respects as ordinary sales by a trustee appointed by decree of the court. Ivrey v. Karr, 182 Md. 463, 34 A.2d 847 (1943).

Proceedings are same for sale under power as for sale under decree. — The object of former § 7 of Article 66 was to confer upon courts the same jurisdiction, and to direct that the same proceedings should be had in sales made under a power in a mortgage, as if such sales had been made under a decree of the court. Patapsco Guano Co. v. Elder, 53 Md. 463 (1880); Beetem v. Garrison, 129 Md. 664, 99 A. 897 (1917); United States v. Eastern Woodworks, Inc., 151 F. Supp. 95 (D. Md. 1957); Walsh v. Jefferson Fed. Sav. & Loan Ass'n, 216 Md. 131, 139 A.2d 847 (1958).

Strict application of rules — Courts apply the rules more strictly to sales made under power of sale than to sales made under a decree in equity. Chilton v. Brooks, 69 Md. 584, 16 A. 273 (1888).

Court has power not to require strict compliance — The court has the power not to hold the trustee to strict compliance when it would be unjust and inequitable to do so. United States v. Eastern Woodworks, Inc., 151 F. Supp. 95 (D. Md. 1957).

Decree prior to sale not necessary — No decree prior to the sale is necessary to effectuate a valid sale under a power of sale. United States v. Eastern Woodworks, Inc., 151 F. Supp. 95 (D. Md. 1957).

Only the terms of the mortgage and the statute need be met in a foreclosure under a power of sale. Blanch v. Collison, 174 Md. 427, 199 A. 466 (1938); United States v. Eastern Woodworks, Inc., 151 F. Supp. 95 (D. Md. 1957).

Rights of mortgagors cease on day of sale. — All rights of mortgagors cease to exist on date of sale, unless satisfactory proof is shown before final ratification that sale should be set aside; hence, the right of redemption is divested by a valid foreclosure sale. Butler v. Daum, 245 Md. 447, 226 A.2d 261 (1967).

Although the jurisdiction of equity does not become complete until the filing of the report of sale, nevertheless the sale in effect forecloses the mortgage and divests the mortgagors of all right of redemption. Butler v. Daum, 245 Md. 447, 226 A.2d 261 (1967).

Sale under second mortgage A foreclosure sale under a second mortgage must be subject to the first mortgage, unless the first mortgagee is a party to the proceedings or intervenes therein, or unless he releases his mortgage or assents to a sale free and clear of it. Baltimore Fed. Sav. & Loan Ass'n v. Eareckson, 221 Md. 527, 158 A.2d 121 (1960).

Assignee of mortgage. — When an attorney is acting as the assignee of the mortgage and not as its agent, he need not be specially named in the power of sale in order to have the authority to act. Whitworth v. Algonquin Assocs., 75 Md. App. 479, 541 A.2d 1328 (1988).

There is no requirement that an assignee of a mortgage be specifically named in the mortgaged instrument to have the power to conduct a sale and that the assignee is an attorney is of no consequence under the applicable statute or rules and it is likewise of no consequence under the relevant case law. Whitworth v. Algonquin Assocs., 75 Md. App. 479, 541 A.2d 1328 (1988).

Statute of frauds. — A foreclosure sale under a power of sale in a mortgage is not within the fourth section of the statute of frauds. Warfield v. Dorsey, 39 Md. 299 (1874).

Writ of fieri facias not license to sell — Writ of fieri facias does not constitute license to sell property of debtors without regard to its value in relation to the bids offered. McCartney v. Frost, 282 Md. 631, 386 A.2d 784 (1978).

Terms of sale — Terms of sale held reasonable. White v. Malcolm, 15 Md. 529 (1860).

As to change in terms of sale, see Hubbard v. Jarrell, 23 Md. 66 (1865).

Invalidity of sale not presumed. — The invalidity of a mortgage sale, like other judicial sales, is not presumed, and the burden of proving the contrary is on the one attacking the sale. Butler v. Daum, 245 Md. 447, 226 A.2d 261 (1967).

Inadequacy of price must imply constructive fraud. — To justify a court of equity in setting aside an adequately advertised sale of property upon the ground of inadequacy of price, facts must be shown from which the conclusion arises that the price is so insignificant as to shock the conscience of the court. The facts must be such as to compel the conclusion that because of the inadequacy of the price, constructive fraud is implied. Butler v. Daum, 245 Md. 447, 226 A.2d 261 (1967).

Burden of proving inadequacy of price — The burden of proving inadequacy of price is on the exceptants. Butler v. Daum, 245 Md. 447, 226 A.2d 261 (1967).

Spread between fair market value and sale price indicates unfair sale. — While one does not expect a price produced at a forced sale to be commensurate with fair market value, the spread between a fair market value of $18,000 ($24,000 appraisal less mortgage of $6,000) and a $2,000 sale price is indicative of an unfair sheriff's sale, such as shocks the conscience of the court. McCartney v. Frost, 282 Md. 631, 386 A.2d 784 (1978).

Commissions. — See Johnson v. Glenn, 80 Md. 369, 30 A. 993 (1895); Goldberg v. Price, 218 Md. 602, 147 A.2d 745 (1959); Laney v. State, 379 Md. 522, 842 A.2d 773 (2004), cert. denied, — U.S. —, 125 S. Ct. 434, 160 L. Ed. 2d 335 (2004).

Rule 14-215. Post-sale procedures.

(a) **Procedure following sale.** The procedure following a sale made pursuant to this Chapter shall be as provided in Rules 14-305 and 14-306, except that an audit is mandatory.

(b) **Resale.** If the court sets a sale aside, the court may order that the property be resold by the individual who made the previous sale or by a special trustee appointed by the court.

(c) **Conveyance to purchaser.** (1) When made. After the court has finally ratified a sale and the purchase money has been paid, the individual making the sale shall convey the property to the purchaser or the purchaser's assignee. If the conveyance is to the purchaser's assignee, the purchaser shall join in the deed.

(2) Under power of sale — when vendor and purchaser are the same. If the individual making a sale and the purchaser at a sale made pursuant to a power of sale are the same person, the court shall appoint in the order of ratification a trustee to convey the property to the purchaser after payment of the purchase money. The trustee need not furnish a bond unless the court so provides in its order.

(3) To substituted purchaser. At any time after the sale and before a conveyance, the court, upon ex parte application and consent of the purchaser, substituted purchaser, and individual making the sale, may authorize the conveyance to be made to a substituted purchaser. (Added Feb. 10, 2009, effective May 1, 2009.)

Source. — This Rule is derived from the 2008 version of former Rule 14-207(d), (e), and (f).

Setting aside sale. — A sheriff's sale will not be set aside for mere inadequateness of price, but if the sale is so grossly inadequate as to shock the conscience of the court, or if there be but slight circumstances of unfairness in addition to great inadequateness of price, a sale will be set aside. McCartney v. Frost, 282 Md. 631, 386 A.2d 784 (1978).

Court not required to order resale — It is not absolutely necessary that court should order a resale, and a sale made without such order will not be set aside. Reeside v. Peter, 35 Md. 220 (1872).

Selling at private sale. — Where a trustee or attorney offers property at public sale in accordance with mortgage and withdraws it because he does not receive a satisfactory bid, he is authorized to sell property at private sale subject to ratification of court, and court has jurisdiction to set aside or ratify sale. Beetem

v. Garrison, 129 Md. 664, 99 A. 897 (1917).

Resale at risk of defaulting purchaser. — In case of resale ordered by court at defaulting purchaser's risk under former § 163 of Article 16, previous sale being under the foreclosure statutes and reported to court for rat-

ification, etc., court becomes vendor and assignee of mortgage is agent or trustee of court. Bilbrey v. Strahorn, 153 Md. 491, 138 A. 343 (1927).

Cited in Maddox v. Cohn, 199 Md. App. 63, 20 A.3d 153 (2011).

Rule 14-216. Proceeds of sale.

(a) **Distribution of surplus.** At any time after a sale of property and before final ratification of the auditor's account, any person claiming an interest in the property or in the proceeds of the sale of the property may file an application for the payment of that person's claim from the surplus proceeds of the sale. The court shall order distribution of the surplus equitably among the claimants.

(b) **Deficiency judgment.** At any time within three years after the final ratification of the auditor's report, a secured party or any appropriate party in interest may file a motion for a deficiency judgment if the proceeds of the sale, after deducting all costs and expenses allowed by the court, are insufficient to satisfy the debt and accrued interest. If the person against whom the judgment is sought is a party to the action, the motion shall be served in accordance with Rule 1-321. Otherwise, the motion shall be served in accordance with Rule 2-121 and shall be accompanied by a notice advising the person that any response to the motion must be filed within 30 days after being served or within any applicable longer time prescribed by Rule 2-321(b) for answering a complaint. A copy of Rule 2-321(b) shall be attached to the notice. (Added Feb. 10, 2009, effective May 1, 2009.)

Source. — This Rule is derived in part from the 2008 version of former Rule 14-208 and is in part new.

Mortgagee not paid on date of sale — A mortgagee is not actually paid his claim upon the date of the sale of the mortgaged premises. The sale must be reported to, and ratified by, the court; and the auditor must prepare his account, which must, likewise, be ratified before the proceeds of sale may be safely distributed. Ex parte Aurora Fed. Sav. & Loan Ass'n, 223 Md. 135, 162 A.2d 739 (1960).

Agreement of parties controls interest on mortgage debt. — The time during which interest on a mortgage runs is sometimes regulated by statute; but in the absence of statute the agreement of the parties controls. Ex parte Aurora Fed. Sav. & Loan Ass'n, 223 Md. 135, 162 A.2d 739 (1960).

Statute did not prohibit agreement to continue such interest after date of foreclosure sale. — The requirement in former § 6 of Article 66 that the proceeds of a sale should be distributed in the manner usual in cases of sales under decree did not prohibit the parties to a mortgage from agreeing that law-

ful interest on the mortgagor's indebtedness should continue after the date of foreclosure sale; and such requirement did not vary, by implication, such an agreement, so as to cut off interest on a mortgage after the date of the sale. Ex parte Aurora Fed. Sav. & Loan Ass'n, 223 Md. 135, 162 A.2d 739 (1960).

Thus, where mortgage stated that interest was payable from date of mortgage until principal and interest "shall be paid," the court held that, in the absence of statute, interest was payable beyond foreclosure sale until the auditor's report could be ratified. Ex parte Aurora Fed. Sav. & Loan Ass'n, 223 Md. 135, 162 A.2d 739 (1960).

Distribution of surplus generally. — Former § 10 of Article 66, from which section a of former Rule W75 is derived, was analogous to right existing on part of subsequent holders of liens in regard to sales under usual modes of proceeding in equity. Leonard v. Groome, 47 Md. 499 (1878).

Although a purchaser who, following conveyance of legal title, seeks only an order for possession may do so in a district court, if the purchaser intends to seek not just possession but a share of any surplus funds as compensation for wrongful detainer, the relief, for very practical reasons, should be sought in the foreclosure proceeding pursuant to Rule 14-102 and this Rule. Thus, it was entirely appropriate for a purchaser to seek relief in a foreclosure proceeding by asserting claims against surplus proceeds for the rental value of the mortgaged property between the date of the purchaser's demand for possession and the time the mortgagors vacated the property. Legacy Funding LLC v. Cohn, 396 Md. 511, 914 A.2d 760 (2007).

Purpose of former rule — The purpose of former Rule W75 was to require a sale of all ("all" in the sense used in this Rule being synonymous with or the equivalent of "whole") the mortgaged property that remains within reach of the mortgagee at the time of sale as a condition precedent to the right to move for a deficiency decree. Brown v. Fraley, 229 Md. 445, 184 A.2d 710 (1962).

Nature of proceedings. — It is possible for a mortgage foreclosure proceeding in Maryland in which no deficiency decree is sought to be purely in rem: it is also possible, if the mortgagor voluntarily appears, for the proceeding to include judgments, in the form of rulings on exceptions to the sale and to the auditor's report, respectively, that have in personam collateral estoppel effect. Fairfax Sav. v. Kris Jen Ltd. Partnership, 338 Md. 1, 655 A.2d 1265 (1995).

"Whole mortgaged property". — The term "whole mortgaged property" means only that property which has not been released from the lien of the mortgage. Brown v. Fraley, 229 Md. 445, 184 A.2d 710 (1962).

Decree in personam not barred by release of part of mortgaged property. — This Rule does state that "if, after a sale of the whole mortgaged property, the net proceeds of sale ... are insufficient to pay the mortgage debt and accrued interest, ... a motion for a deficiency decree may be made," but that does not mean that if some of the mortgaged property has been released, the mortgagee is barred from obtaining a decree in personam against the mortgagor. Brown v. Fraley, 229 Md. 445, 184 A.2d 710 (1962).

No distribution of surplus on claim that is not lien. — Claim which has not become an absolute lien upon the property cannot be considered in the disposition of any surplus, however equitable the claim may be. Balance Ltd. v. Short, 35 Md. App. 10, 368 A.2d 1116 (1977).

Liability of defaulting purchaser. — The liability of a defaulting purchaser under former Rule W75 was beyond the amount of the first lien on the real property sold. Funds in excess of the first lien accrue to secondary lienholders and then to owners of land. McCann v. McGinnis, 257 Md. 499, 263 A.2d 536 (1970).

Any money remaining after the satisfaction of the expenses of sale and the first lien would accrue to the underlying lienholders in order of priority and, if an excess still remained, to the owners of the land. Balance Ltd. v. Short, 35 Md. App. 10, 368 A.2d 1116 (1977).

Liability of guarantor not party to deed of trust. — Liability of guarantor not party to deed of trust can only be determined in an action at law on the note and guaranty agreement. Walde v. Capital Mtg. Invs., 286 Md. 343, 407 A.2d 1143 (1979).

First mortgagee not party to proceedings. — Where the first mortgagee was not a party to the proceedings and filed no claim therein, it was improper for the auditor to state an account distributing the net proceeds of a sale under the second mortgage, first to the payment of the first mortgage and the balance toward the second mortgage claim, leaving nothing for a judgment creditor who had filed a claim in the proceedings. Baltimore Fed. Sav. & Loan Ass'n v. Eareckson, 221 Md. 527, 158 A.2d 121 (1960).

Stipulation may transfer claims from chattels to proceeds of sale. — Where a stipulation of the parties was made before a sale was ratified, it transferred the claims of all of the parties to the chattels sold from the chattels to the proceeds of their sale. The stipulation effectively placed before the court the respective claims to the proceeds of the sale. Plaza Corp. v. Alban Tractor Co., 219 Md. 570, 151 A.2d 170 (1959).

Purpose of provisions for personal decree; does not affect right of action on covenants. — The portion of former § 156 of Article 16 relative to a personal decree was enacted to avoid the delay and expense of a separate suit, and such remedy is cumulative and does not affect the right of action on the covenants to pay the mortgage debt. Commercial Bldg. & Loan Ass'n v. Robinson, 90 Md. 615, 45 A. 449 (1900).

Provision for personal decree does not question whether covenants run with land. — Former § 156 of Article 16, authorizing a deficiency decree provided the mortgagee would be entitled to maintain an action on the covenants in the mortgage, did not affect the question whether covenants ran with the land. Commercial Bldg. & Loan Ass'n v. Robinson, 90 Md. 615, 45 A. 449 (1900).

Construction. — The provision for the entry of a deficiency decree should be strictly construed because it is in derogation of the common law, but as it is remedial it should be construed to accomplish the object for which it was designed whenever possible. Austraw v. Dietz, 185 Md. 245, 44 A.2d 437 (1945).

As former § 15 of Article 66 was remedial in nature, it should be interpreted so as to accomplish the object for which it was designed when possible. Boyd v. Goldstein, 223 Md. 255, 164 A.2d 336 (1960).

Mortgagee may proceed as common creditor unless estopped. — If sale of mortgaged property fails to satisfy mortgage debt, interest and costs, the mortgagee may proceed as common creditor against mortgagor for the balance unless he is estopped by his deed or acts in pais. Mizen v. Thomas, 156 Md. 313, 144 A. 479 (1929).

If a sale of mortgaged property does not produce enough to pay the mortgage debt, interest and costs, the mortgagee may proceed as any other creditor against the mortgagor for the balance of the indebtedness unless some element of estoppel is present. Brown v. Fraley, 229 Md. 445, 184 A.2d 710 (1962).

Former section b did not prevent separate action at law. — Section b of former Rule W75 provides that where there has been a sale at a mortgage foreclosure and the net proceeds of the sale are insufficient to pay the mortgage debt and the accrued interest, as found by the court upon the report of the auditor, a motion for a decree in personam for the deficiency may be made. This is really done as an accommodation to the mortgagee so that he may obtain a deficiency judgment in the same suit without having to institute a separate action. However, there is nothing in former Rule W75 to prevent the mortgagee from proceeding by a separate action at law. Katz v. Simcha Co., 251 Md. 227, 246 A.2d 555 (1968).

Lender's remedy against borrowers under a deed of trust for the borrowers' alleged default on a loan obligation evidenced by the deed of trust was not limited to a deficiency judgment in a foreclosure proceeding under (b). Since the deed of trust permitted the lender to pursue available legal remedies and the deed of trust's language showed that deed of trust was a separate, enforceable contract, the lender could file a contract action and was not limited merely to relief available under (b). Wellington Co. Profit Sharing Plan & Trust v. Shakiba, 180 Md. App. 576, 952 A.2d 328 (2008).

General creditor not entitled to attach distribution. — If a general creditor has no standing to intervene in the mortgage foreclosure, and if he has no standing to demand payment from any surplus, he is certainly not entitled to attack a distribution of funds from a sale after foreclosure. Balance Ltd. v. Short, 35 Md. App. 10, 368 A.2d 1116 (1977).

Junior lienholder of portion of property. — Where a foreclosure sale of property encumbered by a first mortgage produces a surplus, a junior lienholder of only a portion of that property should, in equity, receive only those proceeds derived from the sale of property encumbered to it. William H. Metcalfe & Sons v. Canyon Defined Benefit Trust, 318 Md. 565, 569 A.2d 669 (1990).

In personam judgment. — A deficiency judgment is an in personam judgment. Fairfax Sav. v. Kris Jen Ltd. Partnership, 338 Md. 1, 655 A.2d 1265 (1995).

Attorney named in mortgage to foreclose may obtain deficiency decree. — An attorney named in a mortgage to foreclose in default has the same functions as a person who is subsequently named as assignee of a mortgage for the purpose of foreclosure after default has occurred and consequently has the same rights as an assignee to obtain a deficiency decree in personam. Austraw v. Dietz, 185 Md. 245, 44 A.2d 437 (1945).

Decree entered only against party who might be sued Deficiency decree may be entered only against party who might be sued on covenants in mortgage, not against guarantor. Kushnick v. Lake Drive Bldg. & Loan Ass'n, 153 Md. 638, 139 A. 446 (1927).

When the General Assembly provided that the right to a deficiency decree should exist only where the mortgagee could have maintained an action at law upon the covenants contained in the mortgage, it meant that the right should exist only against the proper parties to the proceeding and such parties as were bound by the covenants and could have been sued at law thereon. Hence, as stated in Kushnick v. Lake Drive Bldg. & Loan Ass'n, 153 Md. 638, 139 A. 446 (1927), the right would not exist where the foreclosure suit was against an heir of the mortgagor, or was brought to foreclose a mortgage not under seal, because in such a case the person sought to be charged would not be liable on covenants in the mortgage and could not be sued thereon. Austraw v. Dietz, 185 Md. 245, 44 A.2d 437 (1945).

Deficiency decree against wife — Deficiency decree against wife was properly entered, though she might not have been fully aware of contents of note and mortgages. Bletzer v. Cooksey, 154 Md. 568, 141 A. 380 (1928).

Defenses — The mortgagor may raise any defense that could be made in an action at law on the covenants in the mortgage, when pressed for a deficiency decree; that is, any defense such as payment or release, or any other defense to the claim which has arisen since confirmation of the sale. McKenna v. Sachse, 225 Md. 595, 171 A.2d 732 (1961).

A deficiency decree is permitted where recovery could be had on the covenants of the mortgage in a suit at law and the same defenses that might be urged there may be set up. Kirsner v. Cohen, 171 Md. 687, 190 A. 520 (1937).

If mortgage is not under seal no decree in personam may be entered. — If the mortgage is not under the seal of the mortgagor, no decree in personam can be entered because no action of covenant could be maintained. McDonald v. Workingmen's Bldg. Ass'n, 60 Md. 589 (1883).

Assertion of fraud — Assertion of fraud does not extend right to intervene in the distribution of proceeds in an equity court. Balance Ltd. v. Short, 35 Md. App. 10, 368 A.2d 1116 (1977).

Cause of action is based upon covenants in mortgage. — When a deficiency decree is requested, the parties are in the same relative position as litigants at law, and for the party who requests the deficiency decree to prevail, he must show all of the requirements of a successful plaintiff at law, with his cause of action based upon the covenants in the mortgage. Boyd v. Goldstein, 223 Md. 255, 164 A.2d 336 (1960); Kirsner v. Cohen, 171 Md. 687, 190 A. 520 (1937).

A deficiency decree cannot be rendered against a debtor unless the party seeking the decree has a right to maintain an action at law on a covenant contained in the mortgage. Brown v. Fraley, 229 Md. 445, 184 A.2d 710 (1962).

Under the common law no implied covenant arises where deed of trust contains none. — Under the common law of Maryland, if a deed of trust is given as security for an indebtedness, but contains no covenant to pay the indebtedness, no implied covenant to do so arises. Boyd v. Goldstein, 223 Md. 255, 164 A.2d 336 (1960).

Obligation of mortgagor where mortgagee is purchaser at sale. — The Maryland Rule in regard to ameliorating the obligations of a mortgagor to pay a deficiency when the mortgagee buys in the property at foreclosure sale is clear and fixed: In the absence of fraud or breach of actual trust, it is well established that since the confirmation of a foreclosure sale is the final determination by the court that the mortgaged property was sold at a fair price, the defense of inadequacy of price cannot be raised in subsequent proceedings, and for the purpose of a deficiency decree the price obtained at the sale is conclusive on the question of the market value of the property. McKenna v. Sachse, 225 Md. 595, 171 A.2d 732 (1961).

Rights of mortgagee not lessened — Rights of mortgagee are not lessened because he is purchaser at foreclosure sale. McKenna v. Sachse, 225 Md. 595, 171 A.2d 732 (1961).

Mortgagee is not required to account for rents or profits. — Mortgagee who purchased at sale not required to account to mortgagor for rents or profits on property purchased by him after ratification of sale. Moss v. Annapolis Sav. Inst., 177 Md. 135, 8 A.2d 881 (1939).

The mortgagee is not required to account to the mortgagor for profit made upon resale. McKenna v. Sachse, 225 Md. 595, 171 A.2d 732 (1961).

Equitable chattel mortgage or implied covenant not excluded. — There is nothing in the provisions of former Rule W75 (as to who may make a motion for a deficiency decree) excluding an equitable chattel mortgage or an implied covenant. Brown v. Fraley, 229 Md. 445, 184 A.2d 710 (1962).

Even if there was no express covenant to pay the mortgage debt and interest, there was still a covenant sufficient to maintain an action of law under former Rule W75, since the bill of sale of a trucking business and its equipment was in substance a chattel mortgage and could be deemed to contain an implied covenant to pay the debt and interest specified therein pursuant to former Article 21, § 47, of the Code. Brown v. Fraley, 229 Md. 445, 184 A.2d 710 (1962).

Bill of sale and contract of sale, read as one instrument, contained sufficient covenant. — Where an express covenant to pay the mortgage debt and interest, though not included in the bill of sale of a trucking business and its equipment, was embodied in the contract of sale, which, as the Court of Appeals had already said, constituted one instrument, the Court of Appeals held that, when both instruments are read as one, the bill of sale — which was in substance a chattel mortgage — contained a covenant sufficient to maintain an action at law under former Rule W75. Brown v. Fraley, 229 Md. 445, 184 A.2d 710 (1962).

Rule 14-217. Release or assignment; insolvency.

(a) **Release or assignment of claim.** A person entitled to release or assign a claim under a lien may file a written release or assignment of the claim and of any order for the sale of the property entered in the action. The release or assignment shall be signed and acknowledged before an individual authorized to take acknowledgments of deeds. The release or assignment shall take effect at the time of entry on the docket.

(b) **Insolvency proceeding — Effect on foreclosure.** When property of an insolvent is subject to a lien, the institution of or pendency of insolvency proceedings by or against the insolvent under the laws of this State shall not stay a sale of property pursuant to a foreclosure action instituted prior to the insolvency proceeding. (Added Feb. 10, 2009, effective May 1, 2009.)

Source. — This Rule is derived from the 2008 version of former Rule 14-209 (a) and (c).

Rule 14-218. Removal of trustee under a deed of trust.

(a) **Inapplicable where procedure set forth in lien instrument.** The procedure for removal of a trustee under a deed of trust set forth in this Rule shall not supersede or nullify any procedure for the removal or substitution of a trustee that may be provided for in the deed of trust.

(b) **Motion to remove trustee.** When a trustee who has the right to institute a foreclosure action fails or refuses to do so, or if there is other good cause for the removal of the trustee under a deed of trust, secured parties holding not less than 25%, or any lesser percentage provided in the deed of trust, of the beneficial interest under the deed of trust may file a motion for the removal of the trustee and appointment of a new trustee. The motion shall be supported by affidavit and shall state the facts alleged to constitute grounds for removal. The motion may be filed in any court in which an action to foreclose may be instituted.

(c) **Notice to trustee.** Unless the court orders otherwise, notice of the filing of the motion shall be served on the trustee by mailing a copy of the motion by certified mail to the last known address of the trustee. (Added Feb. 10, 2009, effective May 1, 2009.)

Source. — This Rule is derived from the 2008 version of former Rule 14-210, with style changes.

Deed of trust is mortgage — For most purposes a deed of trust is a mortgage and is subject to some (but not all) statutory provisions relating to mortgages. Burroughs v. Garner, 43 Md. App. 302, 405 A.2d 301 (1979).

Obligor's interest after full payment. — Neither default nor institution of foreclosure in any way negates the fact that where full payment has been made, the obligor has, at the least, complete equitable ownership of the property, and the trustee has, at most, only bare legal title to it. Burroughs v. Garner, 43 Md. App. 302, 405 A.2d 301 (1979).

CHAPTER 300. JUDICIAL SALES.

Rule 14-301. Applicability.

Except as otherwise specifically provided in Rules 2-644 and 3-644 and Chapter 200 of this Title, the rules in this Chapter govern all sales of property that are subject to ratification by a court.

Source. — This Rule is derived from former Rule BR1.

University of Baltimore Law Review. — For article, "New Balance in the Rights of Creditors and Debtors: The Effect on Maryland Law," see 2 U. Balt. L. Rev. 236 (1973).

Property interest in seized property. — When property has been physically appropriated by a governmental entity from a property owner, the government must "justly" compensate the property owner. In addition, the full monetary equivalent to compensate a person deprived of his property interests by the government is based upon the fair market value of his property, which may be realized through a court ordered sale of the firearms, when firearms have been appropriated. Furda v. State, 193 Md. App. 371, 997 A.2d 856 (2010).

Quoted in Serio v. Baltimore County, 384 Md. 373, 863 A.2d 952 (2004).

Rule 14-302. Sales — Generally.

(a) **When court may order.** At any stage of an action, the court may order a sale if satisfied that the jurisdictional requisites have been met and that the sale is appropriate.

Cross references. — *See* Code, Family Law Article, § 11-104 and *Keen v. Keen*, 191 Md. 31 (1948) for sale of nonresidents' property to satisfy alimony decree; Code, Family Law Article, § 8-202 for sale of real or personal property incident to a divorce decree; Code, Business Regulation Article, § 5-505 for sale of burial grounds; Code, Real Property Article, § 14-107 for sale in lieu of partition; Code, Real Property Article, § 14-110 for sale of consecutive interests in land by agreement of parties; Code, Tax Property Article, §§ 14-808 through 14-854 for tax sales; and Code, Tax General Article, § 13-810 for sale to enforce income tax lien.

(b) **Appointment of trustee.** When the court orders a sale it may appoint a trustee to make the sale. The trustee shall be a natural person.

Cross references. — *See* Code, Courts Article, § 11-111 for the appointment of a trustee to execute a deed; Code, Real Property Article, § 4-202 (e) for a form of a trustee's deed under a decree; and Code, Estates and Trusts Article, § 14-101, for general jurisdiction of equity concerning trusts. Regarding fiduciaries generally, *see* Code, Estates and Trusts Article, § 15-101 *et seq.*

(Amended Jan. 20, 1999, effective July 1, 1999.)

Source. — This Rule is derived from former Rule BR2.

Effect of amendments. — The 1999 amendment in the cross reference note following (a), substituted "Business Regulation Article, § 5-505" for "Business Regulations Article, § 5-501" and deleted "Code, Article 16, § 159 for sale of personal property jointly owned" following "partition"; and in the first sentence of the cross reference note following (b), substituted "Courts Article, § 11-111" for "Article 16, § 107" and deleted "and Code, Article 16, § 114 for the appointment of a trustee to complete the collections of a sheriff or tax collector" from the end.

Object of statute providing for sale before final decree and effect of order of sale thereunder. — See Kelly v. Gilbert, 78 Md. 431, 28 A. 274 (1894).

Sale of decedent's real estate to pay debts. — It was the habit of the court to apply former § 161 of Article 16, authorizing a sale of property before final decree, in applications for sales of real estate to pay debts under former Article 16, § 157. Hammond v. Hammond, 2 Bland Ch. 306 (1830).

Sale of trust property where court has assumed jurisdiction of trust. — Where court has assumed jurisdiction of trust, it may order sale of trust property before final decree. Elkton Elec. Co. v. Perkins, 145 Md. 224, 125 A. 851 (1922), cert. denied, 266 U.S. 602, 45 S. Ct. 90, 69 L. Ed. 462, appeal dismissed, 266 U.S. 585, 45 S. Ct. 124, 69 L. Ed. 454 (1924).

Statute should be applied only in plain and unquestionable cases. — Former § 161 of Article 16 should never be applied except in very plain and unquestionable cases, and even then only after a full hearing. Kelly v. Gilbert, 78 Md. 431, 28 A. 274 (1894).

Where sale must inevitably be decreed at final hearing. — To justify a sale before final decree, it should appear beyond a reasonable doubt that a sale must be inevitably decreed at the final hearing. Donohue v. Daniel, 58 Md. 595 (1882).

Order of sale may be passed without waiting for defendant's appearance or answer. — Upon satisfactory proof as prescribed in the statute, the court may pass an order of sale at any time after bill filed, without waiting for the defendant's appearance or answer. Dorsey v. Dorsey, 30 Md. 522 (1869).

Bill of complaint may be amended after decree of sale. Kelly v. Gilbert, 78 Md. 431, 28 A. 274 (1894).

Order of sale is reviewable on appeal. — The discretion of the court in ordering a sale before final decree is reviewable on appeal. Dorsey v. Dorsey, 30 Md. 522 (1869).

But decree of sale cannot be inquired into collaterally. — A decree of sale under former § 161 of Article 16 could not be inquired into collaterally, provided the court had jurisdiction. Dorsey v. Garey, 30 Md. 489 (1869).

And no appeal lies from refusal or rescission of order of sale. — No appeal lay from the refusal to order a sale under former § 161 of Article 16, nor from the rescission of an order of sale. An appeal would lie, however, under former Article 5, § 7 (see now § 12-303 of the Courts Article), from an order directing a sale. Washington City & Point Lookout R.R. v. Southern Md. R.R., 55 Md. 153 (1880).

A sale held not to have been ordered under former § 161 of Article 16, and the proof did not justify a sale thereunder. Cornell v. McCann, 37 Md. 89 (1872).

Proof held insufficient to justify sale. — See Kelly v. Gilbert, 78 Md. 431, 28 A. 274 (1894).

The trustee is the mere attorney of the court acting under specially delegated authority. Andrews v. Scotton, 2 Bland Ch. 629 (1830).

A trustee may be appointed to execute an assignment of a patent, if the patentee fails to execute such assignment, as directed by a decree. Ager v. Murray, 105 U.S. 126, 26 L. Ed. 942 (1881).

Quoted in Serio v. Baltimore County, 384 Md. 373, 863 A.2d 952 (2004).

Rule 14-303. Procedure prior to sale.

(a) **Bond.** (1) Trustee appointed by court. Unless excused by the court, a trustee appointed by the court to make a sale shall file a bond with the clerk. The bond shall be to the State of Maryland in an amount determined by the court and conditioned on faithful performance and execution of the trust.

(2) Trustee appointed under certain instruments. Unless otherwise ordered by the court, the trustee need not file a bond if the sale is for the benefit of either the grantor of the trust instrument or a person who paid a valuable consideration for the deed of trust and who is entitled to the proceeds of sale.

Cross references. — For payment of the premium of the bond out of the estate being administered, *see* Rule 10-702 (f). *See also* Code, Commercial Law Article, § 15-103 (a) concerning bond requirements before passage of title to an assignee for the benefit of creditors.

(b) **Public sale — Advertisement.** Unless otherwise ordered by the court, a trustee proposing to make a public sale shall give notice by advertisement of the time, place, and terms of sale in a newspaper of general circulation in each county where any portion of the property is located. The notice shall describe the property to be sold sufficiently to identify it and shall be given as follows:

(1) for the sale of an interest in real property, at least once a week for three successive weeks, the first publication to be not less than 15 days before the sale and the last publication to be not more than one week before the sale; or

(2) for the sale of personal property, not less than five days nor more than 12 days before the sale.

(c) **Private sale; appraisal.** Before making a private sale, the person proposing to make it shall file in the proceedings an appraisal made by a competent appraiser within six months before the date of sale. An appraisal need not be filed if the filing is excused by order of the court or if the sale is made by a personal representative of an estate administered in the circuit court under a will that grants a power of sale without expressly requiring an appraisal.

Source. — This Rule is derived from former Rule BR3.

Complete accuracy in an advertisement is not required and a judicial sale will not be set aside without a clear showing that an omission misled anyone or had a prejudicial effect. Woelfel v. Tyng, 221 Md. 539, 158 A.2d 311 (1960).

Agreement to terms of notice. — Circuit court erred in ruling that a defaulting purchaser at a foreclosure sale was entitled to the surplus proceeds of the resale of the property because the parties by the terms expressly contracted out of the defaulting purchaser being entitled to the surplus proceeds from a resale due to a foreclosure by agreeing to shift the benefit of any surplus on a resale to the mortgage account. White v. Simard, 152 Md. App. 229, 831 A.2d 517 (2003), aff'd, 383 Md. 257, 859 A.2d 168 (2004).

Advertisement for the sale of property at auction run pursuant to (b) stated that, if settlement was delayed for any reason, there would be no abatement of the interest. As the advertisement was attached to the memorandum of sale signed by a foreclosure sale purchaser, the advertisement became part of the contract between the purchaser and the trustee. Thomas v. Dore, 183 Md. App. 388, 961 A.2d 655 (2008).

Sufficient description of real property.

— A description in an advertisement of a judicial sale of real property which describes the property so that it could be located by the exercise of ordinary intelligence and so that more detailed information concerning it could be obtained, if desired, is sufficient. Woelfel v. Tyng, 221 Md. 539, 158 A.2d 311 (1960).

Agreement to terms of notice. — Circuit court erred in ruling that a defaulting purchaser at a foreclosure sale was entitled to the surplus proceeds of the resale of the property because the parties by the terms expressly contracted out of the defaulting purchaser being entitled to the surplus proceeds from a resale due to a foreclosure by agreeing to shift the benefit of any surplus on a resale to the mortgage account. White v. Simard, 152 Md. App. 229, 831 A.2d 517 (2003), aff'd, 383 Md. 257, 859 A.2d 168 (2004).

Applied in Laney v. State, 379 Md. 522, 842 A.2d 773 (2004), cert. denied, — U.S. —, 125 S. Ct. 434, 160 L. Ed. 2d 335 (2004).

Quoted in Zorzit v. 915 W. 36th St., LLC, 197 Md. App. 91, 12 A.3d 698 (2011).

Cited in 91st St. Joint Venture v. Goldstein, 114 Md. App. 561, 691 A.2d 272 (1997); Goldberg v. Frick Elec. Co., 363 Md. 683, 770 A.2d 182 (2001); Griffin v. Shapiro, 158 Md. App. 337, 857 A.2d 519 (2004), cert. denied, 384 Md. 449, 863 A.2d 998 (2004).

Rule 14-304. Place of sale.

Unless otherwise ordered by the court, a sale shall be made in a county where all or a part of the property is located.

Source. — This Rule is derived from former Rule BR4.

Applied in Manigan v. Burson, 160 Md. App. 114, 862 A.2d 1037 (2004).

Rule 14-305. Procedure following sale.

(a) **Report of sale.** As soon as practicable, but not more than 30 days after a sale, the person authorized to make the sale shall file with the court a complete report of the sale and an affidavit of the fairness of the sale and the truth of the report.

(b) **Affidavit of purchaser.** Before a sale is ratified, unless otherwise ordered by the court for good cause, the purchaser shall file an affidavit setting forth:

(1) whether the purchaser is acting as an agent and, if so, the name of the principal;

(2) whether others are interested as principals and, if so, the names of the other principals; and

(3) that the purchaser has not directly or indirectly discouraged anyone from bidding for the property.

(c) **Sale of interest in real property; notice.** Upon the filing of a report of sale of real property or chattels real pursuant to section (a) of this Rule, the clerk shall issue a notice containing a brief description sufficient to identify the property and stating that the sale will be ratified unless cause to the contrary is shown within 30 days after the date of the notice. A copy of the notice shall be published at least once a week in each of three successive weeks before the expiration of the 30-day period in one or more newspapers of general circulation in the county in which the report of sale was filed.

(d) **Exceptions to sale.** (1) How taken. A party, and, in an action to foreclose a lien, the holder of a subordinate interest in the property subject to the lien, may file exceptions to the sale. Exceptions shall be in writing, shall set forth the alleged irregularity with particularity, and shall be filed within 30 days after the date of a notice issued pursuant to section (c) of this Rule or the filing of the report of sale if no notice is issued. Any matter not specifically set forth in the exceptions is waived unless the court finds that justice requires otherwise.

(2) Ruling on exceptions; hearing. The court shall determine whether to hold a hearing on the exceptions but it may not set aside a sale without a hearing. The court shall hold a hearing if a hearing is requested and the exceptions or any response clearly show a need to take evidence. The clerk shall send a notice of the hearing to all parties and, in an action to foreclose a lien, to all persons to whom notice of the sale was given pursuant to Rule 14-206 (b).

(e) **Ratification.** The court shall ratify the sale if (1) the time for filing exceptions pursuant to section (d) of this Rule has expired and exceptions to the report either were not filed or were filed but overruled, and (2) the court is satisfied that the sale was fairly and properly made. If the court is not satisfied that the sale was fairly and properly made, it may enter any order that it deems appropriate.

(f) **Referral to auditor.** Upon ratification of a sale, the court, pursuant to Rule 2-543, may refer the matter to an auditor to state an account.

(g) **Resale.** If the purchaser defaults, the court, on application and after notice to the purchaser, may order a resale at the risk and expense of the purchaser or may take any other appropriate action.

Source. — This Rule is derived from former Rule BR6.

———

University of Baltimore Law Forum. — For a note, "Recent Development: Bates v. Cohn," see 41 U. Balt. L. F. 177 (2011).

Former Rule BR6 was a restatement or recodification of preexisting practice in this State as was its statutory predecessor which came into being in 1841. McCann v. McGinnis, 257 Md. 499, 263 A.2d 536 (1970).

Scope of court's authority. — Section b 4 of former Rule BR6 gave the trial court the specific authority to ratify a foreclosure sale if the trial court finds that the sale was fairly and properly made and no exceptions are filed or exceptions are filed and overruled. If the trial judge finds that the sale was not fairly and properly held, then denial of ratification is appropriate. Former Rule BR6 provided no discretion or authority to do otherwise. Smith v. Lawler, 93 Md. App. 540, 613 A.2d 459 (1992), cert. denied, 329 Md. 110, 617 A.2d 1055 (1993).

Debtor may seek to enjoin a foreclosure sale from proceeding by filing a motion to enjoin prior to the sale, as provided for in Rule 14-209 but, if the debtor fails to do so and the sale occurs, the debtor's later filing of exceptions can only challenge any procedural irregularities regarding the sale, or the debtor can challenge the statement of indebtedness by filing exceptions to the auditor's statement of account. Ultimately, the foreclosure sale extinguishes a debtor's right of redemption, and substantial compliance by tendering a payment to satisfy the outstanding debt is insufficient once the decree of foreclosure has been declared. Greenbriar Condo. v. Brooks, 387 Md. 683, 878 A.2d 528 (2005).

Debtor may seek to enjoin a foreclosure sale from proceeding by filing a motion to enjoin prior to the sale, as provided for in Rule 14-209 but, if the debtor fails to do so and the sale occurs, the debtor's later filing of exceptions can only challenge any procedural irregularities regarding the sale, or the debtor can challenge the statement of indebtedness by filing exceptions to the auditor's statement of account. Ultimately, the foreclosure sale extinguishes a debtor's right of redemption, and substantial compliance by tendering a payment to satisfy the outstanding debt is insufficient once the decree of foreclosure has been declared. Greenbriar Condo. v. Brooks, 387 Md. 683, 878 A.2d 528 (2005).

Discovery. — Trial court properly granted substitute trustees' motion to quash the mortgagors' notices of deposition and subpoenas duces tecum because (1) the discovery of the lending documents was not necessary as the question of whether the loan was usurious or improper was not relevant to the hearing on exceptions to the sale; and (2) the mortgagors' counsel, upon entering an appearance, had sufficient time prior to the motions hearing to collect evidence on the issue of whether the mortgagors had received actual notice of the foreclosure sale. Jones v. Rosenberg, 178 Md. App. 54, 940 A.2d 1109 (2008).

Applicability. — Having failed to file a proper pre-sale injunction to a foreclosure sale under Rule 14-209(b), the mortgagors' next recourse was to file exceptions to the sale under (d) of this Rule. Jones v. Rosenberg, 178 Md. App. 54, 940 A.2d 1109 (2008).

Report of sale is merely an offer. — The sale is not a complete contract, and when reported is merely an offer not accepted until ratified by court. Hanover Fire Ins. Co. v. Brown, 77 Md. 64, 25 A. 989 (1893), reh'g overruled, 77 Md. 64, 27 A. 314 (1893).

Sale must be ratified to pass title. — Sale under a foreclosure decree did not pass the title to the property sold until the sale was ratified and confirmed. Before ratification, the transaction was merely an offer to purchase which had not been accepted. Plaza Corp. v. Alban Tractor Co., 219 Md. 570, 151 A.2d 170 (1958).

Since Maryland law provides that a mortgage foreclosure sale is subject to the approval of the court, such a sale does not pass title to the property until ratified by the court. Fisher v. Federal Nat'l Mtg. Ass'n, 360 F. Supp. 207 (D. Md. 1973).

Sale properly ratified. — Pursuant to § 7-105 of the Real Property Article and (d) of this Rule, a foreclosure sale was properly ratified and a property owner's exceptions thereto were properly overruled, as a concurrent interest holder had acquired the owner's promissory note, which was secured by a deed of trust on her one-half interest in the property, and when she defaulted on the note, her interest was freely devisable and properly foreclosed upon. Fagnani v. Fisher, 418 Md. 371, 15 A.3d 282 (2011).

When a mortgagor objected to the ratification of a foreclosure sale of the mortgagor's property on the grounds that an unauthorized fee was imposed on third-party purchasers, the sale was properly ratified because the mortgagor did not have standing to raise the issue, as (1) the mortgagor could only show injury if the mortgagor showed another bidder would pay more than the mortgagor owed but was deterred by an advertisement requiring the fee, which was not shown, and (2) the mortgagor did not show trustees committed fraud or acted deceptively by advertising the fee. Maddox v. Cohn, 199 Md. App. 63, 20 A.3d 153 (2011).

Report may be amended. — A case will not be reversed because report of sale does not state terms, nor compliance with them by purchasers — the report should be seasonably amended. White v. Malcolm, 15 Md. 529 (1860).

Report held correct. — Report held to be substantially correct. Hubbard v. Jarrell, 23 Md. 66 (1865).

Effect of filing report under former law. — Under the former statutes providing for foreclosure pursuant to a power of sale, the jurisdiction of the court became complete on the filing of the report of sale; until then the proceedings were ex parte. Warehime v. Carroll County Bldg. Ass'n, 44 Md. 512 (1876); Beetem v. Garrison, 129 Md. 664, 99 A. 897 (1917).

Motion to consolidate prior suit with foreclosure proceedings. — Appellees foreclosed a mortgage upon appellants' property, and appellants moved to consolidate with that proceeding a prior suit in which they had sought to have declared void the deed of trust upon which the foreclosure suit was based. The Court of Appeals affirmed the foreclosure sale, without prejudice to any proceedings remaining open in the prior suit to have the deed of trust declared void. Witt v. Zions, 194 Md. 186, 70 A.2d 594 (1949).

In absence of fraud or irregularity, court has no power to question sale sua sponte. — Where a mortgage foreclosure sale is ratified by the court without objection and the court authorizes the conveyance to be made to substituted purchasers, it is error for the court sua sponte to question the validity of such sale in the absence of fraud or illegality. Walker v. Ward, 65 Md. App. 443, 501 A.2d 83 (1985).

Res adjudicata Final ratification of mortgage foreclosure sale is res adjudicata as to validity of sale, except in case of fraud or illegality, and may not be attacked in collateral proceedings. Bachrach v. Washington United Coop., 181 Md. 315, 29 A.2d 822 (1943).

Order ratifying sale under deed of trust established the validity of the deed of trust and the title of the purchaser at the sale thereunder free of lien asserted by contract purchasers who had given down payment to mortgagor. Gerber v. Karr, 231 Md. 180, 189 A.2d 353 (1963).

Notice of foreclosure to guarantors of loan not required. — Debtors who executed an indemnity deed of trust to secure a creditor's loan to their daughter were not entitled to

notice of a foreclosure or of an auditor's report under (b) of this Rule, Rule 14-204(b), and § 7-105 of the Real Property Article, because they were not record owners or holders of subordinate interests. In re Cutaio, (Bankr. D. Md. 2007).

Interested persons may file objections. — Objections to the sale may be filed by any person interested in the property. Warfield v. Ross, 38 Md. 85 (1873); Albert v. Hamilton, 76 Md. 304, 25 A. 341 (1892).

The sale, when made, may be accepted to by the party authorized to redeem the mortgage and who made the tender. Kent Bldg. & Loan Co. v. Middleton, 112 Md. 10, 75 A. 967 (1910).

Exceptions cannot be filed by one who has no legal interest in, or record title to, property, but alleges a secret trust, person against whom the trust is sought to be enforced not being a party to proceedings. Bentley v. Beacham, 91 Md. 677, 47 A. 1024 (1900).

Holder of vendor's interest, under conditional sales contract, in hot water heating system, could not object to mortgage foreclosure sale of house, for if system was personalty, he had no interest in mortgaged property, and only persons interested in property can object to sale. Heating & Plumbing Fin. Corp. v. Glyndon Permanent Bldg. Ass'n, 167 Md. 222, 173 A. 198 (1934).

A person whose interest is not affected by the sale cannot intervene. Warfield v. Ross, 38 Md. 85 (1873).

Holder of prior mortgage has no standing to file exceptions — Ordinarily, the holder of a prior mortgage has no standing in court to file exceptions to the ratification of a sale made under a junior mortgage; because, generally, such a sale is made subject to the prior mortgage and does not affect the rights of the prior mortgagee. Plaza Corp. v. Alban Tractor Co., 219 Md. 570, 151 A.2d 170 (1958).

Defenses must be raised prior to foreclosure sale. — This rule and judicial opinions precluded the homeowner from challenging the lender's failure to satisfy loss mitigation requirements as an exception to the foreclosure sale; the homeowner had to assert known and ripe defenses to the conduct of the foreclosure sale prior to the sale. Bates v. Cohn, 417 Md. 309, 9 A.3d 846 (2010).

General creditor cannot object to sale — General creditor cannot object to sale of property under mortgage. Hannan v. Lyddane, 164 Md. 357, 165 A. 308 (1933).

Ordinarily, a general creditor has no standing to interpose objections to the ratification of a sale under a mortgage. Scott & Wimbrow, Inc. v. Calwell, 31 Md. App. 1, 354 A.2d 463, cert. denied, 278 Md. 733 (1976).

Consenting exceptant may not later challenge — An exceptant who consented and stipulated that the court ratify and confirm a sale and that the claims of all the parties to the chattels be transferred to the proceeds of the sale thereof, was in no position to challenge the power of the court below to make the sale. Plaza Corp. v. Alban Tractor Co., 219 Md. 570, 151 A.2d 170 (1958).

When exceptions may be filed. — Exceptions may be filed at any time before the ratification of the sale. Aukam v. Zantzinger, 94 Md. 421, 51 A. 93 (1902).

Objections not limited. — Objections are not limited to matters of irregularity in conduct of the sale, but extend to questions concerning validity of mortgage. Albert v. Hamilton, 76 Md. 304, 25 A. 341 (1892).

The mortgagors have a right in objecting to the ratification of the sale, to show that their title ought not to pass. Albert v. Hamilton, 76 Md. 304, 25 A. 341 (1892).

When trustees initiated an action to foreclose on certain real property, a trial court was not required to overrule a mortgagor's exceptions to the foreclosure sale based on fraud when the mortgagor did not seek an injunction, prior to the 2009 revision which eliminated the injuction, prior to the sale, because the mortgagor could raise the issue in exceptions to the sale under this Rule, and the trial court, as a court of equity, had full authority to hear and determine the issue. Bierman v. Hunter, 190 Md. App. 250, 988 A.2d 530 (2010), overruled in part on other grounds, Bates v. Cohn, 2010 Md. LEXIS 759 (Md. 2010).

Tender of full amount due — Where a party interested tenders mortgagee full amount due for purpose of redeeming mortgage as he has a right to do, the mortgagee has no right thereafter to foreclose mortgage, and party making tender may except to mortgage sale. Kent Bldg. & Loan Co. v. Middleton, 112 Md. 10, 75 A. 967 (1910).

Failure to file mortgage notes. — Where no exception is taken on ground that mortgage notes were not filed, and where there is no dispute about their ownership, or amount due on them, sale will not be set aside because notes were not filed. Heider v. Bladen, 83 Md. 242, 34 A. 836 (1896).

Objection that no decree authorizing sale — Objection that there was no decree authorizing sale is unavailing. Walker v. Cockey, 38 Md. 75 (1873).

Equity court has power to hear and determine objections — Equity court has full power to hear and determine all objections which may be filed against the sale. Fisher v. Federal Nat'l Mtg. Ass'n, 360 F. Supp. 207 (D. Md. 1973).

Bond on appeal from overruled exceptions. — Supersedeas bond on appeal from overruling of exceptions. See Scott & Wimbrow, Inc. v. Calwell, 31 Md. App. 1, 354 A.2d 463, cert. denied, 278 Md. 733 (1976).

Time for filing purchaser's affidavit. — There is no requirement that the purchaser's affidavit be filed 30 days after the sale although such an affidavit must obviously be filed before final ratification, unless otherwise ordered by the court for good cause shown. Southern Md. Oil, Inc. v. Kaminetz, 260 Md. 443, 272 A.2d 641 (1971).

The best obtainable offer accepted and reported by a trustee should be ratified in the absence of fraud, improper dealing or inadequacy of price as of the time the sale was made. Gilden v. Harris, 197 Md. 32, 78 A.2d 167 (1951); Standish Corp. v. Keane, 220 Md. 1, 150 A.2d 728 (1959).

Even though someone else is willing to give more. — The general rule is that if a trustee, acting diligently and without fraud, accepts an offer at private sale for the most that he is able to obtain for the property at the time, and reports that offer to the court, it will not be set aside merely because someone else is later willing to give more for the property. Standish Corp. v. Keane, 220 Md. 1, 150 A.2d 728 (1959).

Unless inadequate price is due to trustee's lack of diligence. — A sale should not be ratified if the inadequate price reported is attributable to a lack of diligence on the part of the person making the sale or to the failure of such person to make a thorough investigation of local conditions before fixing a price at which the property would be sold. Knight v. Nottingham Farms, Inc., 207 Md. 65, 113 A.2d 382 (1955); Webb & Knapp, Inc. v. Hanover Bank, 214 Md. 230, 133 A.2d 450 (1957); Standish Corp. v. Keane, 220 Md. 1, 150 A.2d 728 (1959).

Defaulting purchaser only liable for shortage between original price and first resale price. — Trial court erred in ratifying an auditor's report, finding a purchaser who defaulted on a sale of foreclosed property was liable for the shortage between the original price and an eventual resale price to a third purchaser, as pursuant to (g), the purchaser was only liable for a shortage between the original price and the first resale; a shortage that resulted from the second purchaser's default at resale, prompting a third sale/second resale, was the second purchaser's responsibility. Simard v. Burson, 197 Md. App. 396, 14 A.3d 6 (2011).

Sale reported by trustee named in deed or will. — The court is invested with the same powers with respect to a sale reported by a trustee named in a deed or will, as it would have had if the sale had been made by a trustee appointed by the court. Berry v. Foley, 92 Md. 311, 48 A. 146 (1901).

Sale does not pass title until ratified. — Since Maryland law provides that a mortgage foreclosure sale is subject to the approval of the court, such a sale does not pass title to the property until ratified by the court. Fisher v. Federal Nat'l Mtg. Ass'n, 360 F. Supp. 207 (D. Md. 1973).

A rescission of the order of ratification of the sale does not automatically relieve the purchaser of responsibility for any loss in the event of resale. McCann v. McGinnis, 257 Md. 499, 263 A.2d 536 (1970).

It is necessary for good cause to exist for relieving the original purchaser from further liability. McCann v. McGinnis, 257 Md. 499, 263 A.2d 536 (1970).

Res judicata. — The final ratification of the sale of property in foreclosure proceedings is res judicata as to the validity of such sale, except in case of fraud or illegality, and hence its regularity cannot be attacked in collateral proceedings. Ed Jacobsen, Jr., Inc. v. Barrick, 252 Md. 507, 250 A.2d 646 (1969).

Substantial compliance. — The purchaser's affidavit substantially complied with the provisions of former Rule BR6, where it stated that the purchaser bought the property as "principal and not as agent for anyone else," and that "neither he nor anyone connected with him directly or indirectly discouraged anyone from bidding on said property." Southern Md. Oil, Inc. v. Kaminetz, 260 Md. 443, 272 A.2d 641 (1971).

Sale procedurally proper. — Pursuant to this rule, a foreclosure sale was conducted properly procedurally, as the advertisement was sufficient because it adequately described the premises, and the price was not grossly inadequate in the circumstances. Fagnani v. Fisher, 418 Md. 371, 15 A.3d 282 (2011).

Former statute providing for resale was constitutional. Capron v. Devries, 83 Md. 220, 34 A. 251 (1896).

Object of statute; law prior to its adoption. — See Warfield v. Dorsey, 39 Md. 299 (1874).

It applied to sales under powers. — Former § 163 of Article 16, applied to sales under powers as well as to sales by trustees appointed by the court. The court is the vendor in a resale. Bilbrey v. Strahorn, 153 Md. 491, 138 A. 343 (1927).

Former § 163 of Article 16 applied to sales made under powers in mortgages. Middendorf v. Baltimore Refrigerating & Heating Co., 117 Md. 17, 82 A. 1047 (1911).

Sale to defaulting purchaser may be abandoned and rescinded. — Where a purchaser is insolvent a sale to him although finally ratified may be abandoned and rescinded, the property sold again and a clear title conveyed to the second purchaser. Sloan v. Safe Deposit & Trust Co., 73 Md. 239, 20 A. 922 (1890).

Bond given for balance of purchase money may be enforced. — Where a purchaser paid part of the purchase money in cash, and gave a bond for the balance, payment of the latter could be enforced by petition under former § 163 of Article 16. Stephens v. Magruder, 31 Md. 168 (1869).

Necessity for order nisi and service thereof on defaulting purchaser. — Judgment in personam entered before order *nisi* is passed and served on defaulting purchaser in case foreclosure sale is void, and may be collaterally attacked by creditor of defaulting purchaser. Mercantile Bank v. Maryland Title Guar. Co., 153 Md. 320, 138 A. 251 (1927).

Court may order resale at purchaser's risk. — Where purchaser has failed to comply with terms of sale, the court may, on application of trustee appointed to make the sale, order resale at purchaser's risk. Miller v. Mitnick, 163 Md. 113, 161 A. 157 (1932).

Purported common law rule entitling a defaulting purchaser at a foreclosure sale to any excess proceeds generated by resale of the subject property simply did not exist, and had resulted from a misapplication of decisions involving estate property, where there was no mortgagor whose interests required a court's protection; the defaulting purchaser was also not entitled to reimbursements for improvements made to the property. Simard v. White, 383 Md. 257, 859 A.2d 168 (2004).

Setting aside sheriff's sale. — A sheriff's sale will not be set aside for mere inadequateness of price, but if the sale is so grossly inadequate as to shock the conscience of the court, or if there be but slight circumstances of unfairness in addition to great inadequateness of price, a sale will be set aside. McCartney v. Frost, 282 Md. 631, 386 A.2d 784 (1978).

Trial court erred by setting aside a second foreclosure sale with regard to a condominium unit, because the debtor failed to file an injunction prior to the sale and, upon completion of the sale, the debtor lost his right of redemption. The debtor should have sought to enjoin the sale from proceeding by filing a motion to enjoin under Md. R. 14-209.11-110, as substantial compliance by tendering a payment to satisfy the debt after the sale occurred was insufficient once the decree of foreclosure was entered. Greenbriar Condo. v. Brooks, 387 Md. 683, 878 A.2d 528 (2005).

Trial court erred by setting aside a second foreclosure sale with regard to a condominium unit, because the debtor failed to file an injunction prior to the sale and, upon completion of the sale, the debtor lost his right of redemption. The debtor should have sought to enjoin the sale from proceeding by filing a motion to enjoin under Md. R. 14-209.11-110, as substantial compliance by tendering a payment to satisfy the debt after the sale occurred was insufficient once the decree of foreclosure was entered. Greenbriar Condo. v. Brooks, 387 Md. 683, 878 A.2d 528 (2005).

Delay in start time not prejudicial. — Even though the sale began 45 minutes late, the length of delay did not amount to the kind of irregularity that warranted an order setting aside the foreclosure sale where appellant failed to show any harm or prejudice from the delay, and where the vague contention that there were people present at the sale who left because the sale did not begin on time was not enough to establish harm or prejudice. J. Ashley Corp. v. Burson, 131 Md. App. 576, 750 A.2d 618 (2000).

Property is not regarded as belonging to defaulting purchaser. — Upon a resale the property is not to be regarded as belonging to the defaulting purchaser. Dalrymple v. Taneyhill, 4 Md. Ch. 171 (1853); Werner v. Clark, 108 Md. 627, 71 A. 305 (1908).

Order of resale not providing notice to purchaser. — The fact that an order for resale did not provide for notice to the purchaser and afford him an opportunity to show cause, although it might have been better practice for it to have done so, was held to be of no consequence where he received notice and had adequate opportunity to protest. Stofberg v. Levland, Inc., 213 Md. 477, 132 A.2d 122 (1957).

Mortgagor may except to ratification of resale. — Where a mortgage is being foreclosed, the mortgagor is entitled to except to the ratification of the resale. Dalrymple v. Taneyhill, 4 Md. Ch. 171 (1853); Werner v. Clark, 108 Md. 627, 71 A. 305 (1908).

There was no reversible error in order directing resale of property. Middendorf v. Baltimore Refrigerating & Heating Co., 117 Md. 17, 82 A. 1047 (1911).

Trustee's fees and commissions. — The trustee making the sale will be allowed his legal fee for filing the petition, and commissions on the proceeds of the resale, but no other compensation for the collection of the money. Farmers & Planters Bank v. Martin, 7 Md. 342 (1855).

Motion for equitable abatement of interest. — Foreclosure sale purchaser claimed the ratification of his purchase was delayed by the mortgagor's filing groundless exceptions to the sale under (d)(1). Although the contract between the purchaser and trustee stated that if settlement was delayed for any reason, there would be no abatement of the interest, the purchaser's motion for equitable abatement of interest should not have been denied without considering whether the delay in settlement was caused by the conduct of a person beyond the purchaser's power to control or ameliorate. Thomas v. Dore, 183 Md. App. 388, 961 A.2d 655 (2008).

Although a foreclosure sale purchaser was entitled to an equitable abatement of interest due to the filing of exceptions under (d)(1) by the former owners, a trial court abused its discretion in abating the interest from the date of the foreclosure sale to the date of settlement because only the time from the initial date set for final ratification to the actual date of final ratification constituted a delay caused by the former owners. Zorzit v. 915 W. 36th St., LLC, 197 Md. App. 91, 12 A.3d 698 (2011).

Acceptance of written bid from lender. — There is no blanket restriction in Maryland that bars a trustee from accepting a written bid on behalf of a lender, and the trustee did not act in place of the noteholder, but merely accepted its written offer to purchase the property. J. Ashley Corp. v. Burson, 131 Md. App. 576, 750 A.2d 618 (2000).

Dismissal of claims for allowances from proceeds of anticipated sale. — During a partition suit, dismissal of claims for allowances from the proceeds of an anticipated sale is without prejudice with regard to subsequent presentation to an auditor since a dismissal with prejudice would operate as an adjudication on the merits. Wooddy v. Wooddy, 270 Md. 23, 309 A.2d 754 (1973).

Waiver. — Where a debtor neither appeals the lifting of an automatic stay nor obtains a stay of a foreclosure sale, he can not later complain about the foreclosure of his property. Four Star Enters. Ltd. Partnership v. Council of Carousel Ctr. Condominium, Inc., 132 Md. App. 551, 752 A.2d 1272 (2000).

Applied in White v. Simard, 152 Md. App. 229, 831 A.2d 517 (2003), aff'd, 383 Md. 257, 859 A.2d 168 (2004); Laney v. State, 379 Md. 522, 842 A.2d 773 (2004), cert. denied, — U.S. —, 125 S. Ct. 434, 160 L. Ed. 2d 335 (2004); Manigan v. Burson, 160 Md. App. 114, 862 A.2d 1037 (2004); Seyed Mehran Mirjafari v. Cohn, 183 Md. App. 701, 963 A.2d 247 (2009), aff'd, 412 Md. 475, 988 A.2d 997, 2010 Md. LEXIS 17 (2010).

Quoted in Schaller v. Castle Dev. Corp., 111 Md. App. 40, 680 A.2d 528 (1996); G.E. Capital Mtg. Servs., Inc. v. Edwards, 144 Md. App. 449, 798 A.2d 1187 (2002).

Cited in 91st St. Joint Venture v. Goldstein, 114 Md. App. 561, 691 A.2d 272 (1997); Goldstein v. 91st St. Joint Venture, 153 Md. App. 171, 835 A.2d 239 (2003); Legacy Funding LLC v. Cohn, 396 Md. 511, 914 A.2d 760 (2007); Wells Fargo Home Mortg., Inc. v. Neal, 398 Md. 705, 922 A.2d 538 (2007).

Rule 14-306. Real property — Recording.

Upon the entry of a final order of ratification, the person making a sale of an interest in real property in a county other than one in which all of the property is located shall cause to be recorded among the land records of each county where any part of the property is located a certified copy of the docket entries, any complaint, the report of sale, the final order of ratification, and any other orders affecting the property. (Amended Nov. 12, 2003, effective Jan. 1, 2004.)

Committee note. — For special rules applying to properties in Baltimore City, see Code, Real Property Article, § 14-103 (f).

Source. — This Rule is derived from former Rule BR5.

Effect of amendments. — The 2003 amendment added the Committee note.

University of Baltimore Law Review. — For discussion, "Property Disposition Upon Divorce in Maryland: An Analysis of the New Statute," see 8 U. Balt. L. Rev. 377 (1979).

Cited in Simard v. White, 383 Md. 257, 859 A.2d 168 (2004); Piven v. Comcast Corp., 168 Md. App. 221, 895 A.2d 1118 (2006), aff'd, 397 Md. 278, 916 A.2d 984, 2007 Md. LEXIS 77 (2007).

CHAPTER 400. BURIAL GROUND.

Rule 14-401. Sale for other use.

(a) **Venue.** An action for sale of a burial ground for a use other than burial purposes shall be brought in the county in which the burial ground is located. When the burial ground is located in more than one county, the action may be brought in any county in which all or any part of the burial ground is located.

(b) **Complaint.** The action for sale of a burial ground shall be commenced by filing a complaint that, in addition to complying with Rules 2-303 through 2-305, shall contain:

(1) a description of the burial ground sufficient to enable it to be located,

(2) a statement that the ground has been dedicated and used for burial purposes,

(3) a statement that the burial ground has ceased to be used for burial purposes,

(4) a list of names and last known addresses of all known lot owners, or their assignees, if any, and

(5) a statement of the reasons why it is desirable to sell the burial ground for other uses.

Cross references. — *See* Code, Business Regulation Article, § 5-505, which authorizes a proceeding for the sale of a burial ground that has ceased to be used for such purposes.

For sale of cemeteries in Baltimore City where more than 75% of acreage has been abandoned or becomes a menace, *see* Code, Business Regulation Article, § 5-506.

As to certain cemeteries in Carroll County, *see* Code, Real Property Article, § 14-119.

As to exemption of lots held only for burial from attachment or execution and insolvency laws, *see* Code, Business Regulation Article, § 5-503.

As to condemnation of cemeteries, *see* Rule 12-204.

(c) **Notice — Publication and posting.** Upon the filing of the complaint, the clerk shall issue a notice instead of a summons. The notice shall be signed by the clerk and shall (1) include the caption of the action, (2) describe the substance of the complaint and the relief sought, and (3) inform all lot owners or other persons in interest of the latest date by which a response may be filed. The notice shall be published as provided in Rule 2-122, and a copy of the notice shall be posted in a conspicuous place on the property and at all principal gates or entrances to the burial ground. Additionally, a copy of the notice shall be sent by ordinary mail to each person whose name and last known address are listed in the complaint pursuant to subsection (b)(4) of this Rule.

(d) **Proceedings when no response filed.** If no party in interest appears in response to the notice, the action shall proceed ex parte. The court may order testimony to be taken and enter judgment as it deems proper. (Amended Jan. 20, 1999, effective July 1, 1999.)

Cross references. — For distribution of proceeds of sale among parties interested, *see* Code, Business Regulation Article, §§ 5-505 and 5-506.

For power of court before making distribution to order that part of proceeds may be set aside and applied to the removal and burial of any dead and the purchase of a lot in another cemetery, *see* Code, Business Regulation Article, §§ 5-505 and 5-506.

As to legal effect of judgment on title, *see* Code, Business Regulation Article, §§ 5-505 and 5-506.

Source. — This Rule is derived as follows:
Section (a) is derived from former Rule J71.
Section (b) is derived from former Rule J70.
Section (c) is derived from former Rule J72.
Section (d) is derived from former Rule J73.

Effect of amendments. — The 1999 amendment in the cross reference note following (b), substituted "Business Regulation Article, § 5-505" for "Business Regulations Article, § 5-501" in the first paragraph, substituted "Business Regulation Article, § 5-506" for "Business Regulations Article, § 5-502" in the second paragraph, and substituted "Business Regulation Article, § 5-503" for "Article 23, § 164" in the fourth paragraph; and in the cross reference note following (d), substituted "Business Regulation Article, §§ 5-505 and 5-506" for "Business Regulations Article, § 5-501" in all three paragraphs.

CHAPTER 500. TAX SALES.

Rule 14-501. Applicability.

The rules in this Chapter govern actions to foreclose the right of redemption in property sold at a tax sale.

Source. — This Rule is new.

Rule 14-502. Foreclosure of right of redemption — Complaint.

(a) **Contents.** In an action to foreclose the right of redemption in property sold at a tax sale, the complaint, in addition to complying with Rules 2-303 through 2-305, shall set forth:

(1) the fact of the issuance of the certificate of sale;

(2) a description of the property in substantially the same form as the description appearing on the certificate of tax sale;

(3) the fact that the property has not been redeemed by any party in interest; and

(4) a statement of the amount necessary for redemption.

(b) **Documents.** The complaint shall be accompanied by:

(1) the original certificate of sale, or a photocopy of the certificate;

(2) a copy of a title report supported by an affidavit by the person making the search that a complete search of the records has been performed in accordance with generally accepted standards of title examination for the period of at least 40 years immediately before the filing of the complaint; and

(3) a notice setting forth (A) the substance of the complaint and the relief sought, (B) a description of the property in substantially the same form as the description appearing on the collector's tax records, (C) the time within which a defendant must file an answer to the complaint or redeem the property, and (D) a statement that failure to answer or redeem the property within the time allowed may result in a judgment foreclosing the right of redemption.

Cross references. — *See* Code, Tax-Property Article, § 14-833 for provisions governing limitations on the time for bringing an action to foreclose the right of redemption and Code, Tax-Property Article, § 14-841 for the limitation on the number of certificates that may be joined in one action. *See also* Code, Tax-Property Article, §§ 14-836 and 14-837 governing parties to the action. For purchaser's obligations once a complaint has been filed, *see Scheve v. Shudder, Inc.*, 328 Md. 363 (1992).

Source. — This Rule is new but is consistent with Code, Tax-Property Article, §§ 14-835 and 14-838 and is derived in part from Code, Tax-Property Article, §§ 14-840 and 14-836.

Applied in Sallie v. Tax Sale Investors, Inc., 998 F. Supp. 612 (D. Md. 1998).

Quoted in Heartwood 88, Inc. v. Montgomery County, 156 Md. App. 333, 846 A.2d 1096 (2004).

Cited in Voltolina v. Property Homes, LLC, 198 Md. App. 590, 18 A.3d 944 (2011).

Rule 14-503. Process.

(a) **Notice to defendants whose whereabouts are known.** Upon the filing of the complaint, the clerk shall issue a summons as in any other civil action. The summons, complaint, and exhibits, including the notice prescribed by Rule 14-502 (b) (3), shall be served in accordance with Rule 2-121 on each defendant named in the complaint whose whereabouts are known.

(b) **Notice to defendants whose whereabouts are unknown, unknown owners, and unnamed interested persons.** When the complaint includes named defendants whose whereabouts are unknown, unknown owners, or unnamed persons having or claiming to have an interest in the property, the notice filed in accordance with Rule 14-502 (b) (3), after being issued and signed by the clerk, shall be served in accordance with Rule 2-122.

(c) **Posting of property.** Upon the filing of the complaint, the plaintiff shall cause a notice containing the information required by Rule 14-502 (b)(3) to be posted in a conspicuous place on the property. The posting may be made either by the sheriff or by a competent private person, appointed by the plaintiff, who is 18 years of age or older, including an attorney of record, but not a party to the action. A private person who posts the notice shall file with the court an affidavit setting forth the name and address of the affiant, the caption of the case, the date and time of the posting, and a description of the location of the posting and shall attach a photograph of the location showing the posted notice.

(d) **Notice to collector.** Upon the filing of the complaint, the plaintiff shall mail a copy of the complaint and exhibits to the collector of taxes in the county in which the property is located. (Amended Nov. 8, 2005, effective Jan. 1, 2006.)

Cross references. — For due process requirements, *see St. George Church v. Aggarwal*, 326 Md. 90 (1992).

Source. — This Rule is new. Section (a) is derived in part from Code, Tax-Property Article, § 14-839 (a). Section (b) is derived in part from Code, Tax-Property Article, § 14-840. Section (c) is new. Section (d) is derived from Code, Tax-Property Article, § 14-839 (c).

Effect of amendments. — The 2005 amendment, effective January 1, 2006, rewrote (c).

Homeowner given proper notice. — In a proceeding to foreclose a right of redemption as to property on which a tax lien was imposed, in which a homeowner moved to reopen a judgment of foreclosure, the purchaser's alleged non-compliance with affidavit and order provisions of Md. R. 2-122, when notice was published, did not require reopening the judgment because such non-compliance did not deprive the trial court of jurisdiction or work a constructive fraud on the homeowner, as the purchaser's affidavit showed reasonable and good faith efforts to serve the homeowner at the homeowner's last known address failed, and the purchaser posted, mailed, and published notice pursuant to default notice provisions of " 14-836, 14-839, 14-840 of the Tax — Property Article, and (c) of this Rule, so the homeowner was served in accordance with Md. R. 2-122. Voltolina v. Property Homes, LLC, 198 Md. App. 590, 18 A.3d 944 (2011).

Applied in Sallie v. Tax Sale Investors, Inc., 998 F. Supp. 612 (D. Md. 1998).

Rule 14-504. Notice to persons not named as defendants.

The plaintiff shall send the notice prescribed by Rule 14-502 (b) (3) to each person having a recorded interest, claim or judgment, or other lien who has not been made a defendant in the proceeding. If all or part of the property is a common area owned by or legally dedicated to a homeowners' association, the plaintiff shall also send the notice to the homeowners' association governing the property. The notice shall be sent to the person's last reasonably ascertainable address by certified mail, postage prepaid, return receipt requested, bearing a postmark from the United States Postal Service, and shall be accompanied by a copy of the complaint. The plaintiff shall file the return receipt from the notice or an affidavit that the provisions of this section have been complied with or that the address of the holder of the subordinate interest is not reasonably ascertainable. If the filing is made before final ratification of the sale, failure of a holder of a subordinate interest to receive the notice does not invalidate the sale. The plaintiff shall send notice to each tenant of the property, as required by Code, Tax-Property Article, § 14-836 (b) (4). (Amended Jan. 20, 1999, effective July 1, 1999.)

Source. — This Rule is new but is derived from Code, Tax-Property Article, § 14-836.

Effect of amendments. — The 1999 amendment added the last sentence.

Rule 14-505. Defense of invalidity.

Any issue as to the validity of the taxes, the proceedings to sell the property, or the sale, shall be raised by separate affirmative defense.

Cross references. — Rule 2-323.
Source. — This Rule is new but is consistent with Code, Tax-Property Article, § 14-842.

Quoted in Heartwood 88, Inc. v. Montgomery County, 156 Md. App. 333, 846 A.2d 1096 (2004).

Rule 14-506. Notice to tenant following judgment.

Notice to tenants after issuance of a judgment foreclosing the right of redemption is governed by Code, Tax Property Article, § 14-836 (b) (7). (Adopted Jan. 20, 1999, effective July 1, 1999.)

Source. — This Rule is new.

TITLE 15. OTHER SPECIAL PROCEEDINGS

Editor's note. — The Court of Appeals, by Order dated June 5, 1996, effective January 1, 1997, rescinded Subtitles A, D, E, J, P, Q, R, T, U, V, W, Y, Z, BB, BD, BE, BG, BH, BJ, BL, BP, BQ, BR, BS, BW, and BY of Chapter 1100 of the Maryland Rules of Procedure, rescinded Subtitles P, BB, BQ, and BW of the Maryland District Rules, and rescinded Forms 22a, 23, 24, 25, and 26. The Order substituted for certain of the rules and forms rescinded new Title 9, Chapter 100, Title 10, Title 12, Title 13, Title 14, and Title 15 of the Maryland Rules of

Procedure. Furthermore, the Order transferred, without readoption, Chapter 900, Chapter 1200, and Subtitles S, BU, and BV of Chapter 1100 of the Maryland Rules of Procedure and Chapter 1200 of the Maryland District Rules to be Title 9, Chapter 200, Title 11, and Title 16 of the Maryland Rules of Procedure. This Order provides that the new rules shall "apply to all actions commenced on or after January 1, 1997, and insofar as practicable, to all actions then pending."

Many of the cases in the notes to the various rules were decided prior to the 1996 revision. These cases have been retained under pertinent rules of this title where it is thought that such cases will be of value in interpreting the present rules.

A table of comparable rules, relating those rules rescinded effective January 1, 1997, to the revised rules in Title 9 through Title 16 is to be found in Volume 2 following the end of the Maryland Rules.

CHAPTER 100. ARBITRATION.

Rule 15-101. Application of Uniform Arbitration Act to certain proceedings.

(a) **Binding arbitration while court action pending.** (1) Not applicable to certain actions. This Rule does not apply to actions for judicial review of an order or action of an administrative agency.

(2) Consent; order of referral. If before trial all parties agree on the record or file a written stipulation agreeing to binding arbitration of the action or any issue, the court shall enter an order of referral to arbitration.

(3) Maryland Uniform Arbitration Act. Except to the extent provided otherwise in the order of referral, the Maryland Uniform Arbitration Act applies to the arbitration.

(b) **Court proceedings regarding binding arbitration not governed by Uniform Arbitration Act.** In connection with a binding arbitration conducted or sought to be conducted under common law or under a statute other than the Maryland Uniform Arbitration Act, unless otherwise required by applicable law, (1) court proceedings to confirm, vacate, modify, or enter judgment on a final written award are governed by the provisions of the Maryland Uniform Arbitration Act and (2) to the extent practicable, the procedure for obtaining other judicial relief shall be the same as the procedure in connection with an arbitration under the Maryland Uniform Arbitration Act.

Cross references. — Code, Courts Article, Title 3, Subtitles 2 and 2B.

Source. — This Rule is in part new and is derived in part from former Rules E2, E3, and E4.

University of Baltimore Law Review. — For article, "Confirmation of Out-of-State Arbitration Awards Under Maryland's Uniform Arbitration Act," see 9 U. Balt. L. Rev. 37 (1979).

Relationship between former Rule E2 and cases arising under § 301 of Labor Management Relations Act, 29 U.S.C. § 185. — See Brophy v. McLean Trucking Co., 552 F. Supp. 680 (D. Md. 1982).

Suit to recover the amount awarded, based on the award, was properly brought in the District Court. State of Md. Cent. Collection Unit v. Gettes, 321 Md. 671, 584 A.2d 689 (1991).

Authority of court. — Former Rule E3 gave the trial court authority to order litigants to submit to an arbitration that does not conform to the requirements of the Maryland Uniform Arbitration Act. Kovacs v. Kovacs, 98 Md. App. 289, 633 A.2d 425 (1993), cert. denied, 334 Md. 211, 638 A.2d 753 (1994).

Waiver. — Litigants may waive their rights under the Maryland Uniform Arbitration Act and submit to arbitration proceeding that do not meet all of the requirements of the Act. Kovacs v. Kovacs, 98 Md. App. 289, 633 A.2d 425 (1993), cert. denied, 334 Md. 211, 638 A.2d 753 (1994).

CHAPTER 200. CONTEMPT.

Rule 15-201. Applicability.

This Chapter applies to both civil and criminal contempts. It does not supersede or modify Code, Labor and Employment Article, § 4-322. (Amended Dec. 10, 1996, effective Jan. 1, 1997.)

Cross references. — As to the distinctions between civil and criminal contempt, see *State v. Roll and Scholl*, 267 Md. 714 (1973) and *Lynch v. Lynch*, 342 Md. 509 (1996).

Source. — This Rule is derived from former Rule P2 a and c.

Effect of amendments. — The 1996 amendment rewrote the cross reference.

University of Baltimore Law Review. — For comment, "A Pragmatic Look at Criminal Contempt and the Trial Attorney," see 12 U. Balt. L. Rev. 100 (1982).

The line of distinction between civil and criminal contempt is often indistinct. Often the same acts or omissions may constitute both or at least embrace aspects of each. State v. Roll, 267 Md. 714, 298 A.2d 867 (1973).

In this State, the distinction between the two types of contempt has been preserved and is important. State v. Roll, 267 Md. 714, 298 A.2d 867 (1973).

The form of punishment does not determine the nature of the contempt proceedings, but rather, from the nature of the proceedings flows the manner of punishment. Hare v. Hare, 21 Md. App. 71, 318 A.2d 234 (1974).

When contempt is civil or criminal. — If the punishment is coercive and the contemnors carry "the keys of their prison in their own pockets," it is civil, but if the sanction is to punish, it is criminal. State v. Roll, 267 Md. 714, 298 A.2d 867 (1973).

In this State, the nature of the contempt proceeding is determined before the time for imposing punishment is reached. State v. Roll, 267 Md. 714, 298 A.2d 867 (1973).

If any part of the contempt sentence is punishment, the contempt must be classified as a criminal one. Roll v. State, 15 Md. App. 31, 288 A.2d 605 (1972), modified and aff'd, 267 Md. 714, 298 A.2d 867 (1973).

Sentences in criminal and civil contempt distinguished. — The sentence in a criminal contempt is a determinate one while in a civil contempt the contemnor carries the keys to the prison in his pocket, that is, compliance with the courts' command effects his release. Roll v. State, 15 Md. App. 31, 288 A.2d 605 (1972), modified and aff'd, 267 Md. 714, 298 A.2d 867 (1973).

If it is a civil contempt the sanction is coercive and must allow for purging, but if it is criminal, it is punitive and must be determinate. State v. Roll, 267 Md. 714, 298 A.2d 867 (1973); Hare v. Hare, 21 Md. App. 71, 318 A.2d 234 (1974).

The penalty imposed in a criminal contempt is punishment for past misconduct which may not necessarily be capable of remedy. Therefore, such a penalty does not require a purging provision but may be purely punitive. State v. Roll, 267 Md. 714, 298 A.2d 867 (1973).

A penalty in a civil contempt must provide for purging. State v. Roll, 267 Md. 714, 298 A.2d 867 (1973).

When civil contempt indicated. — The five factors which generally point to a civil contempt are: (1) the complainant is usually a private person as opposed to the State; (2) the contempt proceeding is entitled in the original action and filed as a continuation thereof as opposed to a separate and independent action; (3) holding the defendant in contempt affords relief to a private party; (4) the relief requested is primarily for the benefit of the complainant; (5) the acts complained of do not of themselves constitute crimes or conduct by the defendant so willful or contumelious that the court is impelled to act on its own motion. State v. Roll, 267 Md. 714, 298 A.2d 867 (1973); Hare v. Hare, 21 Md. App. 71, 318 A.2d 234 (1974).

A civil contempt proceeding is intended to preserve and enforce the rights of private parties to a suit and to compel obedience to orders and decrees primarily made to benefit such parties. These proceedings are generally remedial in nature and are intended to coerce future compliance. State v. Roll, 267 Md. 714, 298 A.2d 867 (1973).

Procedure. — If unemployment is the

problem for a defendant's wilful failure to pay child support, a court, upon determining the cause, may, under Rule 15-207(e)(4), enter reasonable and specific directives to deal with it such as: ordering the defendant to pursue employment opportunities in a specific manner; ordering the defendant to pursue necessary education or a diploma, degree, certificate, or license that may be necessary or helpful in making the defendant eligible for meaningful employment; direct the defendant to seek a form of treatment for health or addiction problems that has a reasonable chance of dealing with the problem sufficiently to qualify the defendant for meaningful employment; require the defendant to report periodically and monitor compliance; or impose any directive that is specific and reasonable. If it appears that the defendant is wilfully not complying with the directives, the court may cause a criminal contempt proceeding to be filed, aimed at punishing defiance of the directives and, if as a result of that defiance, the underlying support order remains in arrears, the State's Attorney, if so inclined, may pursue a criminal action under § 10-203 of the Family Law Article. Arrington v. Dep't of Human Res., 402 Md. 79, 935 A.2d 432 (2007).

Proof required. — The degree of proof required to establish a civil contempt need be only by a preponderance of the evidence. State v. Roll, 267 Md. 714, 298 A.2d 867 (1973).

A criminal contempt must be shown beyond a reasonable doubt. State v. Roll, 267 Md. 714, 298 A.2d 867 (1973).

Maryland Rule 4-215 applies to civil contempt proceedings. Jones v. Johnson, 73 Md. App. 663, 536 A.2d 116 (1988).

If grand jury witnesses with immunity refused to testify and their refusals were contemptuous, their acts would be criminal contempts. State v. Roll, 267 Md. 714, 298 A.2d 867 (1973).

Criminal contemnor not entitled to grand jury indictment or jury trial. — A contemnor in a criminal contempt proceeding in Maryland is not entitled to indictment by a grand jury and may not have a right to a jury trial. State v. Roll, 267 Md. 714, 298 A.2d 867 (1973).

When civil contempt proceeding can terminate as criminal contempt. — Situations may arise where at a hearing held pursuant to an order to show cause in what properly began as a civil contempt, facts are presented which indicate that the alleged contemnor cannot comply with the order of the court that directed him to perform an act for the benefit and advantage of another party to the suit. If this inability to comply was caused by a deliberate effort or a wilful act of commission or omission by the alleged contemnor committed with the knowledge that it would frustrate the order of the court, the civil contempt proceeding should be terminated, and new proceedings may be instituted which can result in a finding of criminal contempt. State v. Roll, 267 Md. 714, 298 A.2d 867 (1973).

State's Attorney's discretion to dismiss or enter nolle prosequi without special court approval. — A State's Attorney designated to prosecute a contempt charge retains the usual prosecutorial discretion to dismiss, or enter a nolle prosequi of, a criminal charge without special court approval. However, in light of the intersection of branches of government on this matter, the State's Attorney should advise the initiating judge of the intention to nolle pros the charge so as to afford the judge an opportunity to appoint a substitute prosecutor. 84 Op. Att'y Gen. 73 (May 24, 1999).

Cited in Aronson v. Aronson, 115 Md. App. 78, 691 A.2d 785 (1997), cert. denied and appeal dismissed, 346 Md. 371, 697 A.2d 111 (1997); Archer v. State, 383 Md. 329, 859 A.2d 210 (2004); King v. State, 400 Md. 419, 929 A.2d 169 (2007).

Rule 15-202. Definitions.

(a) **Constructive contempt.** "Constructive contempt" means any contempt other than a direct contempt.

(b) **Direct contempt.** "Direct contempt" means a contempt committed in the presence of the judge presiding in court or so near to the judge as to interrupt the court's proceedings.

Source. — This Rule is derived from former Rule P1.

University of Baltimore Law Review. — For article "New Balance in the Rights of Creditors and Debtors: The Effect on Maryland Law," see 2 U. Balt. L. Rev. 236 (1973).

For discussion of child abduction by a relative and Maryland's misdemeanor offense to deter parental child stealing, see 8 U. Balt. L. Rev. 609 (1979).

For comment, "A Pragmatic Look at Criminal Contempt and the Trial Attorney," see 12 U. Balt. L. Rev. 100 (1982).

The purpose of the contempt power is to provide a means for a judge to uphold the dignity of the judicial process. This dignity is upheld in two related but distinct ways: first, by imposing punishment a judge makes a statement that what was done was improper and discourages others from engaging in similar acts; and second, the act of imposing punishment serves the purpose of maintaining control of the proceedings in the person of the judge. Johnson v. State, 100 Md. App. 553, 642 A.2d 259 (1994).

Classifications of contempts. — A contempt may be direct and civil, or direct and criminal, or constructive and civil, or constructive and criminal. Pearson v. State, 28 Md. App. 464, 347 A.2d 239 (1975).

Under what classification a contempt falls may be of the utmost importance, and the proper classification is often hard to come by. Pearson v. State, 28 Md. App. 464, 347 A.2d 239 (1975).

The two types of contempts, direct contempt and constructive contempt, may be further classified as civil or criminal; a civil contempt serves a remedial purpose, while a criminal contempt serves a punitive purpose. Johnson v. State, 100 Md. App. 553, 642 A.2d 259 (1994).

Contumacious intent. — In order to find someone guilty of a direct, criminal contempt, the behavior must be contemptuous on its face or it must be shown that the person possessed contumacious intent. Cameron v. State, 102 Md. App. 600, 650 A.2d 1376 (1994).

When an officer was found in direct criminal contempt, there was sufficient evidence of the officer's contumacious intent, based on the officer's false trial and pre-trial testimony and false affidavits, because the officer's admissions and sworn documents showed such intent, and the nature and extent of the officer's lying was pervasive enough to support a contempt finding. Espinosa v. State, 198 Md. App. 354, 17 A.3d 754 (2011).

Direct contempts may be summarily punished. State v. Roll, 267 Md. 714, 298 A.2d 867 (1973).

Conduct need not halt proceedings to constitute direct contempt. — In order to constitute direct contempt, it is not necessary that the conduct bring the proceedings in progress to a halt. Mitchell v. State, 320 Md. 756, 580 A.2d 196 (1990).

Occurrence of conduct in the course of judicial proceedings. — Where defendant directed gesture with middle finger at judge following sentencing and as he was being led out of the courtroom, conduct occurred in the course of judicial proceedings as judge was still on the bench and court remained in session. Mitchell v. State, 320 Md. 756, 580 A.2d 196 (1990).

Party cannot be held in criminal contempt, absent contemptuous behavior or a contumacious intent, merely for appearing in court in an intoxicated condition. Cameron v. State, 102 Md. App. 600, 650 A.2d 1376 (1994).

When an attorney (1) failed to appear at a hearing without telling the trial judge he would be late or explaining or apologizing for his absence, (2) repeatedly argued with a trial judge and opposing counsel in the course of a hearing, and (3) walked out of the courtroom while a trial judge was issuing his opinion, the attorney's conduct not only violated Md. R. Prof. Conduct 8.4(d), but it also constituted a direct contempt of court, under subsection (b) of this Rule. Att'y Griev. Comm'n v. Mahone, 398 Md. 257, 920 A.2d 458 (2007).

Before a party may be held in contempt of a court order, the order must be sufficiently definite, certain, and specific in its terms so that the party may understand precisely what conduct the order requires. Droney v. Droney, 102 Md. App. 672, 651 A.2d 415 (1995).

Failure of attorney to make appearance not direct criminal contempt. — Defendant's nonappearance in the circuit court when her case was called was not direct criminal contempt. Jones v. State, 61 Md. App. 94, 484 A.2d 1050 (1984).

Procedure explicit. — Once the initial decision is made as to whether to proceed as a direct or constructive contempt, the procedures to be followed are explicit. State v. Roll, 267 Md. 714, 298 A.2d 867 (1973).

Power not to be abused. — The power to immediately and summarily hold a person in contempt is awesome and abuses of it must be guarded against. State v. Roll, 267 Md. 714, 298 A.2d 867 (1973).

Constructive contempt was not an abuse of discretion. — Circuit court did not abuse its discretion in holding Carroll County in constructive contempt of an order, which enjoined the County from suspending its approval process for a developer's projects by means of a deferral ordinance, and ordering the County to resume the development review and approval process for the projects because the County, by retroactively applying a new adequate public facilities ordinance, sought to apply stricter public facilities conditions to the projects in an attempt to delay the subdivision approval and issuance of building permits. County Comm'rs v. Forty West Builders, Inc., 178 Md. App. 328, 941 A.2d 1181 (2008).

A summary contempt proceeding is only proper in cases where the action of

the alleged contemnor poses an open, serious threat to orderly procedure that instant, and summary punishment, as distinguished from due and deliberate procedures, is necessary. State v. Roll, 267 Md. 714, 298 A.2d 867 (1973).

If an attorney disrupts orderly proceedings by arriving late, summary punishment may be imposed immediately upon his arrival. But if the attorney fails to appear and the trial is simply postponed, there is no need for summary punishment. Hermina v. Baltimore Life Ins. Co., 128 Md. App. 568, 739 A.2d 893 (1999).

Summary punishment for direct contempt only. — Only a direct contempt may be punished summarily; if the contempt is constructive, the court must give the accused an opportunity to challenge the alleged basis for the contempt and show cause why a contempt order should not be entered. Betz v. State, 99 Md. App. 60, 635 A.2d 77 (1994).

Direct contempt procedures are designed to fill the need for immediate vindication of the dignity of the court. State v. Roll, 267 Md. 714, 298 A.2d 867 (1973).

Sufficient evidence of trial court's personal knowledge of officer's contemptuous behavior. — Trial court had sufficient personal knowledge of an officer's contemptuous behavior, when the officer lied in the officer's trial testimony and in the officer's pre-trial testimony and affidavits, because (1) the court heard the officer's trial testimony, and (2) the pre-trial testimony and affidavits were used extensively in cross-examining the officer and were considered when ruling on a summary judgment motion filed by the officer's opponent. Espinosa v. State, 198 Md. App. 354, 17 A.3d 754 (2011).

Combined single charging documents for criminal and civil contempt cases not authorized. — Although Rule 15-207(a) authorizes the consolidation for hearing of a constructive criminal contempt case and a constructive civil contempt case, nothing in the rules authorizes a combined single charging document. Dorsey v. State, 356 Md. 324, 739 A.2d 41 (1999).

Witness' refusal to answer in course of trial is direct contempt. — A witness commits a direct contempt when he refuses to answer a question when ordered to do so in the course of a trial. Roll v. State, 15 Md. App. 31, 288 A.2d 605 (1972), modified and aff'd, 267 Md. 714, 298 A.2d 867 (1973).

Reaction to sentence of incarceration. — When imposing a sentence, a sentencing judge must be sensitive to the fact that a sentence of incarceration is a ruling that may visit a most dramatic impact upon the emotions of a person who has just been deprived of his or her freedom; in certain situations, if a person believes the sentence to be unfair, it is quite possible that a flash of displeasure could be communicated in a manner that is contemptuous, and while such an outburst cannot be condoned, a judge needs to be sensitive to the reality that the language of the street is not the language of the courtroom. Johnson v. State, 100 Md. App. 553, 642 A.2d 259 (1994).

A refusal to testify before the grand jury is not in the "presence" of the lower court within the contemplation of the definition in former Rule P1, nor may it be deemed in any way as interrupting the lower court's proceedings. Roll v. State, 15 Md. App. 31, 288 A.2d 605 (1972), modified and aff'd, 267 Md. 714, 298 A.2d 867 (1973).

Procedure where witness refuses to testify before grand jury. — It is a customary procedure in Maryland that upon refusal of a witness to testify before the grand jury, the entire grand jury and the witness appear before the court. The court orders the witness to testify. The grand jury, to observe the requirements of secrecy, then retire with the witness. If he is adamant in his refusal to testify the entire grand jury and the witness again go before the court and the jury inform the court what occurred. The court may then cite the witness for contempt. Roll v. State, 15 Md. App. 31, 288 A.2d 605 (1972), modified and aff'd, 267 Md. 714, 298 A.2d 867 (1973).

Contemnor is entitled to trial by jury where sentence is six months or more. — In criminal contempts, both direct and constructive, where the sentence imposed is not petty, that is, the sentence imposed is six months or more, the alleged contemnor is entitled to a trial by jury, thus restricting, in the case of direct criminal contempts, the power of the court to inflict punishment summarily. Roll v. State, 15 Md. App. 31, 288 A.2d 605 (1972), modified and aff'd, 267 Md. 714, 298 A.2d 867 (1973).

Judicial review. — Decision of whether to hold a party in contempt is vested in the trial court; the reviewing court will only reverse such a decision upon a showing that a finding of fact upon which the contempt was imposed was clearly erroneous or that the court abused its discretion in finding particular behavior to be contemptuous. Droney v. Droney, 102 Md. App. 672, 651 A.2d 415 (1995).

Applied in Moguel v. State, 184 Md. App. 465, 966 A.2d 963 (2009).

Quoted in Ashford v. State, 358 Md. 552, 750 A.2d 35 (2000); Bahena v. Foster, 164 Md. App. 275, 883 A.2d 218 (2005); King v. State, 400 Md. 419, 929 A.2d 169 (2007); Usiak v. State, 413 Md. 384, 993 A.2d 39 (2010); Bradford v. State, 199 Md. App. 175, 21 A.3d 123 (2011).

Cited in Archer v. State, 383 Md. 329, 859 A.2d 210 (2004); Fisher v. McCrary Crescent

City, LLC, 186 Md. App. 86, 972 A.2d 954
(2009), cert. denied, 131 S. Ct. 637, 2010 U.S.
LEXIS 9156, 178 L. Ed. 2d 476 (U.S. 2010).

Rule 15-203. Direct civil and criminal contempt.

(a) **Summary imposition of sanctions.** The court against which a direct civil or criminal contempt has been committed may impose sanctions on the person who committed it summarily if (1) the presiding judge has personally seen, heard, or otherwise directly perceived the conduct constituting the contempt and has personal knowledge of the identity of the person committing it, and (2) the contempt has interrupted the order of the court and interfered with the dignified conduct of the court's business. The court shall afford the alleged contemnor an opportunity, consistent with the circumstances then existing, to present exculpatory or mitigating information. If the court summarily finds and announces on the record that direct contempt has been committed, the court may defer imposition of sanctions until the conclusion of the proceeding during which the contempt was committed.

Cross references. — As to possible constitutional limitations on summary imposition of sanctions, including the right to jury trial and the right to counsel, see *Codispoti v. Pennsylvania*, 418 U.S. 506 (1974); *Bloom v. Illinois*, 391 U.S. 194, 202 (1968); *Cheff v. Schnackenberg*, 384 U.S. 373 (1966); *Kawamura v. State*, 299 Md. 276, 292 (1984); *Wilkins v. State*, 293 Md. 335 (1982); *Dorsey v. State*, 56 Md. App. 54 (1983).

Committee note. — Sanctions may be imposed immediately upon the finding of the contempt, or, in the court's discretion, may be deferred to a later time in the proceeding. Deferral of a sanction does not affect its summary nature. The sanction remains summary in nature in that no hearing is required; the court simply announces and imposes the sanction.

(b) **Order of contempt.** Either before sanctions are imposed or promptly thereafter, the court shall issue a written order stating that a direct contempt has been committed and specifying:

(1) whether the contempt is civil or criminal,

(2) the evidentiary facts known to the court from the judge's own personal knowledge as to the conduct constituting the contempt, and as to any relevant evidentiary facts not so known, the basis of the court's findings,

(3) the sanction imposed for the contempt,

(4) in the case of civil contempt, how the contempt may be purged, and

(5) in the case of criminal contempt, (A) if the sanction is incarceration, a determinate term, and (B) any condition under which the sanction may be suspended, modified, revoked, or terminated.

(c) **Affidavits.** In a summary proceeding, affidavits may be offered for the record by the contemnor before or after sanctions have been imposed.

(d) **Record.** The record in cases of direct contempt in which sanctions have been summarily imposed shall consist of (1) the order of contempt; (2) if the proceeding during which the contempt occurred was recorded, a transcript of that part of the proceeding; and (3) any affidavits offered or evidence admitted in the proceeding. (Amended Dec. 10, 1996, effective Jan. 1, 1997.)

Source. — This Rule is derived from former Rule P3.

Effect of amendments. — The 1996 amendment, in (a), substituted "impose sanctions on" for "punish" near the beginning of the first sentence and substituted "sanctions" for "punishment" in the last sentence; substituted "sanction" for "penalty" and "punishment" throughout (b); substituted "contemnor before or after sanctions have" for "defendant before or after punishment has" in (c); substituted "in which sanctions have been summarily imposed" for "summarily punished" in (d); and made related changes in the cross reference and Committee note in (a).

University of Baltimore Law Review. — For comment, "A Pragmatic Look at Criminal Contempt and the Trial Attorney," see 12 U. Balt. L. Rev. 100 (1982).

The purpose of former Rule P3 was to enable the appellate court to determine, by an inspection of the record, whether a contempt has in fact been committed or whether the court had jurisdiction to punish it. Kandel v. State, 252 Md. 668, 250 A.2d 853 (1969); Jones v. State, 32 Md. App. 490, 362 A.2d 660 (1976).

Construction with statutes. — Although this Rule has the effect of creating an exception to Article 27, § 593A (see now § 6-101 of the Criminal Procedure Article) and § 12-401(g) of the Courts and Judicial Proceedings Article for direct criminal contempts summarily punished by the trial judge, there is no rule or statute creating an exception for other types of criminal contempt proceedings. Dorsey v. State, 356 Md. 324, 739 A.2d 41 (1999).

Classification of contempt determines punishment. — Whether the defendant is subject to summary punishment or is entitled to an adversary hearing hinges on whether the contempt is classified as direct or constructive. Murphy v. State, 46 Md. App. 138, 416 A.2d 748 (1980).

By holding a party in direct contempt the court vindicates its authority and punishes the offender. A.V. Laurins & Co. v. Prince George's County, 46 Md. App. 548, 420 A.2d 982 (1980).

Accused's intent. — A criminal contempt, and thus the accused's intent, must be shown beyond a reasonable doubt; this becomes an important factor in examining when it is permissible for a court to treat a criminal contempt as a direct contempt that may be punished summarily. Betz v. State, 99 Md. App. 60, 635 A.2d 77 (1994).

When an officer was found in direct criminal contempt, there was sufficient evidence of the officer's contumacious intent, based on the officer's false trial and pre-trial testimony and false affidavits, because the officer's admissions and sworn documents showed such intent, and the nature and extent of the officer's lying was pervasive enough to support a contempt finding. Espinosa v. State, 198 Md. App.

354, 17 A.3d 754 (2011).

One must look to the nature of the alleged contemptuous acts to determine whether they occurred in the presence of the court. Murphy v. State, 46 Md. App. 138, 416 A.2d 748 (1980).

A direct contempt occurs when the actions of the contemnor interrupt the order of the courtroom and interfere with the conduct of business. When such disruption occurs within the sensory perception of a presiding judge he will have a sufficient knowledge of the contemptuous act which tends to interrupt the proceedings and will not have to rely on other evidence to establish all the details, though some of them can be supplied by additional testimony. State v. Roll, 267 Md. 714, 298 A.2d 867 (1973); Murphy v. State, 46 Md. App. 138, 416 A.2d 748 (1980); Dorsey v. State, 295 Md. 217, 454 A.2d 353 (1983).

Individual retorts during single episode. — A trial judge could not order contempt convictions for each venomous retort hurled at him by the defendant during a single heated exchange. Johnson v. State, 100 Md. App. 553, 642 A.2d 259 (1994).

Determination whether refusal to testify is privileged required. — Because of the critical role which the right against compulsory self-incrimination plays in the legal system, a trial judge, before finding a witness in contempt, must ascertain, by inquiry when necessary, whether a refusal to testify is privileged. Kober v. State, 41 Md. App. 174, 395 A.2d 1228 (1979).

Where there had been no inquiry by the trial judge as to whether appellant's refusal to testify was privileged under his constitutional right against compulsory self-incrimination, there was no basis for a finding of contempt. Kober v. State, 41 Md. App. 174, 395 A.2d 1228 (1979).

Direct contempt not authorized where judge does not have personal knowledge of facts. — When the judge does not have personal knowledge of the facts and must learn of them totally from others, direct contempt proceedings are not authorized. State v. Roll, 267 Md. 714, 298 A.2d 867 (1973); Dorsey v. State, 295 Md. 217, 454 A.2d 353 (1983).

Error to hold officer in direct criminal contempt. — It was error for a trial court to summarily hold an officer in direct criminal contempt, under (a), because the evidence did not demonstrate that the officer's perjurious conduct, both in the officer's trial testimony and in the officer's pre-trial testimony and affidavits, interrupted the order of the court or interfered with the dignified conduct of the court's business, as required. Espinosa v. State, 198 Md. App. 354, 17 A.3d 754 (2011).

Sufficient evidence of trial court's personal knowledge of officer's contemptu-

ous behavior. — Trial court had sufficient personal knowledge of an officer's contemptuous behavior, when the officer lied in the officer's trial testimony and in the officer's pre-trial testimony and affidavits, because (1) the court heard the officer's trial testimony, and (2) the pre-trial testimony and affidavits were used extensively in cross-examining the officer and were considered when ruling on a summary judgment motion filed by the officer's opponent. Espinosa v. State, 198 Md. App. 354, 17 A.3d 754 (2011).

Proper to proceed under former Rule P4 where proof of contemptuous act not within knowledge of trial judge. — Although defendants were cited for direct contempt in violation of former Rule P3, where the proof was not within the knowledge of the trial judge, it was proper to proceed under the procedural requirements of former Rule P4. Dorsey v. State, 295 Md. 217, 454 A.2d 353 (1983).

An attorney's failure to attend court at the time appointed when he has a duty or obligation to be present may amount to, and be punishable as, contempt. Kandel v. State, 252 Md. 668, 250 A.2d 853 (1969).

Failure to appear in court in violation of an oral order is contemptuous on its face. Kandel v. State, 252 Md. 668, 250 A.2d 853 (1969).

Unjustified failure of an attorney to appear in court on time is at least misbehavior on the part of an officer of the court. Kandel v. State, 252 Md. 668, 250 A.2d 853 (1969); Murphy v. State, 46 Md. App. 138, 416 A.2d 748 (1980).

An attorney's unjustified failure to appear or to give reasonable notice thereof is a contempt committed in the presence of the court and, therefore, punishable summarily under this Rule. Murphy v. State, 46 Md. App. 138, 416 A.2d 748 (1980).

If an attorney disrupts orderly proceedings by arriving late, summary punishment may be imposed immediately upon arrival. But if the attorney fails to appear and the trial is simply postponed, there is no need for summary punishment. Hermina v. Baltimore Life Ins. Co., 128 Md. App. 568, 739 A.2d 893 (1999).

Lateness of attorney. — Since lateness of an attorney is misbehavior of an officer of the court, the guilty one may be punished summarily. Kandel v. State, 252 Md. 668, 250 A.2d 853 (1969).

Contempt procedures may be initiated because of a party's absence from court and must reveal sufficient evidence showing the party's requisite willful disobedience or deliberate disruption. A.V. Laurins & Co. v. Prince George's County, 46 Md. App. 548, 420 A.2d 982 (1980).

Direct contempt by juvenile. — Courts Article, § 3-804 (a), conferring exclusive original jurisdiction over a juvenile, is inapplicable to a case of direct contempt committed in another court and the court in which the contempt occurs possesses full power to deal with the contemptuous juvenile in the same manner as it would any adult person who had committed a similar offense. Thomas v. State, 21 Md. App. 572, 320 A.2d 538, cert. denied, 272 Md. 749 (1974).

Appeal from denial of motion to quash subpoena did not preclude issuance of contempt order against the custodian of certain dental records. In re Special Investigation No. 281, 299 Md. 181, 473 A.2d 1 (1984).

Written findings and court order are mandatory. — The requirements in former Rule P3, of written findings by the court, were mandatory. Thomas v. State, 99 Md. App. 47, 635 A.2d 71 (1994).

Where there were neither findings setting forth the basis for the contempt judgement nor a written order signed by the judge and entered in the record, judgment of contempt had to be reversed. Thomas v. State, 99 Md. App. 47, 635 A.2d 71 (1994).

Order court not be reissued. — Defective, but intended, order of direct and summary criminal contempt, with summary sanctions, that fails to comply with this Rule may not be re-issued as corrected on remand. Usiak v. State, 413 Md. 384, 993 A.2d 39 (2010).

Attorney was entitled to have a second contempt order, entered three months after original order, vacated because the defective, but intended, order of direct and summary criminal contempt, with summary sanctions, failed to comply with this Rule. Usiak v. State, 413 Md. 384, 993 A.2d 39 (2010).

Requirement of section b of former Rule P3 is more than mere formality. — The requirement that a summary order of contempt shall recite the facts is more than a formality. It is essential to disclosure of the basis of decision with sufficient particularity to permit an informed appellate review. Robinson v. State, 19 Md. App. 20, 308 A.2d 712 (1973).

The requirement of former section b is as much directed toward providing meaningful appellate review of a contempt conviction as it is aimed at assuring procedural protection for the defendant. Jones v. State, 32 Md. App. 490, 362 A.2d 660 (1976).

Summary contempt procedures where conduct directed at judge. — Trial judge was not precluded from using summary contempt procedures when the nature of the contempt was conduct directed toward him. Mitchell v. State, 320 Md. 756, 580 A.2d 196 (1990).

The purpose of the recitation of facts under section b of former Rule P3 is not to provide the reviewing court an opportunity to reevaluate and weigh the evidence, but to provide a basis for an assessment of its legal sufficiency. Jones v. State, 32 Md. App. 490, 362 A.2d 660 (1976).

The purpose of the rule's requirement of written findings is to enable the appellate court to determine whether a direct, criminal contempt has been committed and whether the court had jurisdiction to punish it. Thomas v. State, 99 Md. App. 47, 635 A.2d 71 (1994).

No man should be deprived of his liberty on the basis of judicial ipse dixits alone. To hold otherwise would be to ignore the language and clear purpose of former Rule P3 and flaunt due process. Robinson v. State, 19 Md. App. 20, 308 A.2d 712 (1973); Jones v. State, 32 Md. App. 490, 362 A.2d 660 (1976).

The specific facts constituting the contempt must be set out in the order; conclusionary language and general citations to the record will not suffice. Robinson v. State, 19 Md. App. 20, 308 A.2d 712 (1973).

Where an order finding an attorney in contempt did not specify the evidentiary facts known to the court from the judge's own personal knowledge as to the conduct constituting the contempt and as to the basis for the court's findings, the failure of compliance with the Rule rendered the order fatally defective in substance as well as form and required reversal. Hermina v. Baltimore Life Ins. Co., 128 Md. App. 568, 739 A.2d 893 (1999).

Failure to specify whether contempt was civil or criminal. — While the trial court had the authority to appoint the attorney, a public defender, to represent a criminal defendant, the trial court's contempt order had to be vacated because the order failed to specify whether the contempt was civil or criminal. Office of the Pub. Defender v. State, 413 Md. 411, 993 A.2d 55 (2010).

Otherwise appellate review will be pro tanto circumscribed. — The trial courts should remember that to the extent a contempt order does not specify those facts, appellate review of a conviction for summary contempt will be pro tanto circumscribed. Robinson v. State, 19 Md. App. 20, 308 A.2d 712 (1973); Jones v. State, 32 Md. App. 490, 362 A.2d 660 (1976).

It is contempt of court for a person to disregard an order, made by a court having authority to make it, of which he has knowledge. Weaver v. State, 244 Md. 640, 224 A.2d 684 (1966).

And the subtle defeat of an order of court is a contempt. Weaver v. State, 244 Md. 640, 224 A.2d 684 (1966).

That failure to comply with a judicial command was based on advice of counsel is generally held to be no justification. Weaver v. State, 244 Md. 640, 224 A.2d 684 (1966).

Contempt based on motion for disqualification of judge. — Where appellant made a good faith motion for disqualification, the

manner of delivery was not improper, and the language was not sufficient to constitute an "imminent threat to the administration of justice," contempt conviction could not withstand constitutional scrutiny. Cohen v. State, 19 Md. App. 85, 309 A.2d 294 (1973).

Person who voluntarily absents himself after his trial has commenced commits a constructive contempt. Pearson v. State, 28 Md. App. 464, 347 A.2d 239 (1975).

Proof in a direct contempt case must be shown beyond a reasonable doubt. Robinson v. State, 19 Md. App. 20, 308 A.2d 712 (1973); A.V. Laurins & Co. v. Prince George's County, 46 Md. App. 548, 420 A.2d 982 (1980).

Where a chancellor has stated conclusions as proof of a direct contempt but has not specified the facts which allegedly gave rise to contempt within the presence of the court, the reasonable doubt standard has not been met. A.V. Laurins & Co. v. Prince George's County, 46 Md. App. 548, 420 A.2d 982 (1980).

Opportunity for allocution before sentencing. — Where defendant was held in direct contempt for gesture directed at judge following sentencing and was immediately recalled to be sentenced for contempt, trial judge should have afforded defendant at least a brief opportunity for allocution before imposing sentence. Mitchell v. State, 320 Md. 756, 580 A.2d 196 (1990).

Due process does not require that an alleged contemnor must, in every instance, be given an opportunity to respond before an adjudication of direct criminal contempt is made in a summary proceeding. In some cases, affording a defendant an opportunity to speak in explanation of his conduct may only invite additional invective. Furthermore, where the conduct or speech is direct or unequivocal, there may be little or no room for helpful explanation. Mitchell v. State, 320 Md. 756, 580 A.2d 196 (1990).

Where the record clearly indicated that the case was one in which affording the defendant an opportunity to speak only invited additional invective, leaving little room for helpful explanation, this was not the sort of case in which the alleged contemnor had to be given an opportunity for allocution before imposition of sentence. Thomas v. State, 99 Md. App. 47, 635 A.2d 71 (1994).

Applied in Solomon v. Solomon, 118 Md. App. 96, 701 A.2d 1199 (1997).

Quoted in Ashford v. State, 358 Md. 552, 750 A.2d 35 (2000); King v. State, 400 Md. 419, 929 A.2d 169 (2007).

Cited in Fisher v. McCrary Crescent City, LLC, 186 Md. App. 86, 972 A.2d 954 (2009), cert. denied, 131 S. Ct. 637, 2010 U.S. LEXIS 9156, 178 L. Ed. 2d 476 (U.S. 2010); Att'y Griev. Comm'n v. Usiak, 418 Md. 667, 18 A.3d 1 (2011).

Rule 15-204. Direct contempt if no summary imposition of sanctions.

In any proceeding involving a direct contempt for which the court determines not to impose sanctions summarily, the judge, reasonably promptly after the conduct, shall issue a written order specifying the evidentiary facts within the personal knowledge of the judge as to the conduct constituting the contempt and the identity of the contemnor. Thereafter, the proceeding shall be conducted pursuant to Rule 15-205 or Rule 15-206, whichever is applicable, and Rule 15-207 in the same manner as a constructive contempt. (Amended Dec. 10, 1996, effective Jan. 1, 1997.)

Source. — This Rule is new.

Effect of amendments. — The 1996 amendment, in the first sentence, substituted "for which" for "which" and substituted "impose sanctions" for "punish."

Summary contempt proceedings. — Where the court did not attempt to punish an attorney's direct contempt summarily, initiating no contempt proceedings, and where the offending attorney had no warning that a subsequent motion hearing would evolve into an attempt by the court to conduct a summary contempt proceeding, the proceedings were flawed. Hermina v. Baltimore Life Ins. Co., 128 Md. App. 568, 739 A.2d 893 (1999).

When the trial court in the underlying criminal action decided not to find that the attorney committed a direct criminal contempt and impose sanctions summarily pursuant to Rule 15-203, the trial court forwent any opportunity to proceed summarily, and the later proceedings were subject to the compliance with Rule 15-205 and this Rule. King v. State, 400 Md. 419, 929 A.2d 169 (2007).

It was error for a trial court to summarily hold an officer in direct criminal contempt based on the officer's false trial and pre-trial testimony and false affidavits because it was not shown that such conduct interrupted the order of the court and interfered with the dignified conduct of the court's business, so the court was required to use the procedure provided in this Rule and Md. R. 15-205. Espinosa v. State, 198 Md. App. 354, 17 A.3d 754 (2011).

Procedural errors. — Petitioner received ineffective assistance of counsel when his attorney disclosed the nature of his advice to petitioner and his opinion regarding the application of the Fifth Amendment with regard to petitioner being summoned as a prosecution witness in a criminal case, therefore, petitioner's conviction for contempt pursuant to Rule 15-203 was reversed in a post-conviction proceeding. The trial judge committed multiple errors in characterizing the imposition of sanctions in the case as summary in nature and should have followed the procedures delineated in Rules 15-204, 15-205, 15-206, and 15-207. Smith v. State, 394 Md. 184, 905 A.2d 315 (2006). .

Quoted in Usiak v. State, 413 Md. 384, 993 A.2d 39 (2010).

Cited in Fisher v. McCrary Crescent City, LLC, 186 Md. App. 86, 972 A.2d 954 (2009), cert. denied, 131 S. Ct. 637, 2010 U.S. LEXIS 9156, 178 L. Ed. 2d 476 (U.S. 2010).

Rule 15-205. Constructive criminal contempt; commencement; prosecution.

(a) **Separate action.** A proceeding for constructive criminal contempt shall be docketed as a separate criminal action. It shall not be included in any action in which the alleged contempt occurred.

(b) **Who may institute.** (1) The court may initiate a proceeding for constructive criminal contempt by filing an order directing the issuance of a summons or warrant pursuant to Rule 4-212.

(2) The State's Attorney may initiate a proceeding for constructive criminal contempt committed against a trial court sitting within the county in which the State's Attorney holds office by filing a petition with that court.

(3) The Attorney General may initiate a proceeding for constructive criminal contempt committed (A) against the Court of Appeals or the Court of

Special Appeals, or (B) against a trial court when the Attorney General is exercising the authority vested in the Attorney General by Maryland Constitution, Art. V, § 3, by filing a petition with the court against which the contempt was allegedly committed.

(4) The State Prosecutor may initiate a proceeding for constructive criminal contempt committed against a court when the State Prosecutor is exercising the authority vested in the State Prosecutor by Code, State Government Article, § 9-1201 et seq., by filing a petition with the court against which the contempt was allegedly committed.

(5) The court or any person with actual knowledge of the facts constituting a constructive criminal contempt may request the State's Attorney, the Attorney General, or the State Prosecutor, as appropriate, to file a petition.

(c) **Appointment of prosecutor.** If the proceeding is commenced by a court on its own initiative, the court may appoint the State's Attorney of the county in which the court sits, the Attorney General, or the State Prosecutor to prosecute the charge.

(d) **Contents; service.** An order filed by the court pursuant to section (b)(1) of this Rule and a petition filed by the State's Attorney, the Attorney General, or the State Prosecutor shall contain the information required by Rule 4-202 (a). The order or petition shall be served, along with a summons or warrant, in the manner specified in Rule 4-212 or, if the proceeding is in the Court of Appeals or Court of Special Appeals, in the manner directed by that court.

(e) **Waiver of counsel.** The provisions of Rule 4-215 apply to constructive criminal contempt proceedings.

(f) **Jury trial.** The provisions of Rule 4-246 apply to constructive criminal contempt proceedings. (Amended May 9, 2000, effective July 1, 2000.)

Source. — This Rule is new.

Effect of amendments. — The 2000 amendment substituted "State Government Article, § 9-1201 et seq." for "Article 10, § 33B" in (b) (4).

Editor's note. — Article 10, § 33B, referred to in section (b) (4), has been revised as §§ 9-1202 through 9-1210 of the State Government Article.

Summary contempt proceedings. — Where the court did not attempt to punish an attorney's direct contempt summarily, initiating no contempt proceedings, and where the offending attorney had no warning that a subsequent motion hearing would evolve into an attempt by the court to conduct a summary contempt proceeding, the proceedings were flawed. Hermina v. Baltimore Life Ins. Co., 128 Md. App. 568, 739 A.2d 893 (1999).

When the trial court in the underlying criminal action decided not to find that the attorney committed a direct criminal contempt and impose sanctions summarily pursuant to Rule 15-203, the trial court forwent any opportunity to proceed summarily, and the later proceedings were subject to the compliance with Rule 15-204 and this Rule. King v. State, 400 Md. 419, 929 A.2d 169 (2007).

It was error for a trial court to summarily hold an officer in direct criminal contempt based on the officer's false trial and pre-trial testimony and false affidavits because it was not shown that such conduct interrupted the order of the court and interfered with the dignified conduct of the court's business, so the court was required to use the procedure provided in Md. R. 15-204 and this Rule. Espinosa v. State, 198 Md. App. 354, 17 A.3d 754 (2011).

Insufficiency of charging instrument. — Where neither the "criminal" paragraph nor the "civil" paragraph of a charging document were checked or otherwise marked, the document failed to notify the defendant that he was being charged with a crime, much less notify him of the nature of the particular offense. Dorsey v. State, 356 Md. 324, 739 A.2d 41 (1999).

Combined single charging documents for criminal and civil contempt cases not authorized. — Although Rule 15-207(a) authorizes the consolidation for hearing of a constructive criminal contempt case and a constructive civil contempt case, nothing in the rules authorizes a combined single charging document. Dorsey v. State, 356 Md. 324, 739 A.2d 41 (1999).

Procedural errors. — Petitioner received ineffective assistance of counsel when his attorney disclosed the nature of his advice to petitioner and his opinion regarding the application of the Fifth Amendment with regard to petitioner being summoned as a prosecution witness in a criminal case, therefore, petitioner's conviction for contempt pursuant to Rule 15-203 was reversed in a post-conviction proceeding. The trial judge committed multiple errors in characterizing the imposition of sanctions in the case as summary in nature and should have followed the procedures delineated in Rules 15-204, 15-205, 15-206, and 15-207. Smith v. State, 394 Md. 184, 905 A.2d 315 (2006).

Mid-trial conversion from civil to criminal contempt not permitted. — Compliance with Rules 15-205 and 4-202(a) requires some time lag between the termination of an exclusively civil contempt proceeding and the trial of a new constructive criminal contempt case, and thus a conversion from a civil to a criminal contempt proceeding mid-trial is not authorized. Dorsey v. State, 356 Md. 324, 739 A.2d 41 (1999).

Comparing Rules 15-205(b), 15-206(b), the Maryland Department of Social Services has no authority to file a petition for criminal contempt. Bryant v. Howard County Dep't of Soc. Servs., 387 Md. 30, 874 A.2d 457 (2005).

Jury trial. — This Rule does not provide an absolute right to a jury trial, but rather confers a right to a jury trial only when the defendant possesses a right to jury by the operation of other law. Barksdale v. State, 122 Md. App. 392, 712 A.2d 562 (1998).

Where the State converted the document charging defendant for failure to pay court-ordered child support from a civil contempt proceeding to a criminal contempt proceeding, the defendant was entitled to all common law, statutory, and constitutional safeguards for the criminally accused, and the trial court erred by denying the defendant a jury trial. Ashford v. State, 358 Md. 552, 750 A.2d 35 (2000).

Section (f) of this Rule does not grant a right to jury trial in constructive criminal contempt cases that does not otherwise exist by operation of other law. Barksdale v. State, 122 Md. App. 392, 712 A.2d 562 (1998).

An indefinite suspension was appropriate where, by his acts and omissions while representing his client, and specifically by his misrepresentations to the prosecutor and to the judge in seeking a continuance, an attorney engaged in misconduct as defined in Maryland Rule 16-701, was convicted in a case of criminal contempt, and violated Rules 1.3, 3.3 and 8.4 of the Maryland Rules of Professional Conduct. Att'y Griev. Comm'n v. Middleton, 360 Md. 34, 756 A.2d 565 (2000).

Evidence insufficient. — In limiting its proof to lack of compliance with a court order for payment of child support, the State failed to offer sufficient evidence to prove the crime of constructive criminal contempt beyond a reasonable doubt. Ashford v. State, 358 Md. 552, 750 A.2d 35 (2000).

Quoted in Usiak v. State, 413 Md. 384, 993 A.2d 39 (2010).

Cited in Archer v. State, 383 Md. 329, 859 A.2d 210 (2004); Fisher v. McCrary Crescent City, LLC, 186 Md. App. 86, 972 A.2d 954 (2009), cert. denied, 131 S. Ct. 637, 2010 U.S. LEXIS 9156, 178 L. Ed. 2d 476 (U.S. 2010); Bradford v. State, 199 Md. App. 175, 21 A.3d 123 (2011).

Rule 15-206. Constructive civil contempt.

(a) **Where filed.** A proceeding for constructive civil contempt shall be included in the action in which the alleged contempt occurred.

(b) **Who may initiate.** (1) The court may initiate a proceeding for constructive civil contempt by filing an order complying with the requirements of section (c) of this Rule.

(2) Any party to an action in which an alleged contempt occurred and, upon request by the court, the Attorney General, may initiate a proceeding for constructive civil contempt by filing a petition with the court against which the contempt was allegedly committed.

(3) In a support enforcement action where the alleged contempt is based on failure to pay spousal or child support, any agency authorized by law may bring the proceeding.

(c) **Content of order or petition.** (1) An order filed by the court pursuant to subsection (b) (1) of this Rule and a petition filed pursuant to subsection (b) (2) shall comply with Rule 2-303 and shall expressly state whether or not incarceration is sought.

(2) Unless the court finds that a petition for contempt is frivolous on its face, the court shall enter an order providing for (i) a prehearing conference, or (ii) a hearing, or (iii) both. The scheduled hearing date shall allow a reasonable time for the preparation of a defense and may not be less than 20 days after the prehearing conference. An order issued on a petition or on the court's own initiative shall state:

(A) the time within which any answer by the alleged contemnor shall be filed, which, absent good cause, may not be less than ten days after service of the order;

(B) the time and place at which the alleged contemnor shall appear in person for (i) a prehearing conference, or (ii) a hearing, or (iii) both and, if a hearing is scheduled, whether it is before a master pursuant to Rule 9-208 (a) (1) (G) or before a judge; and

(C) if incarceration to compel compliance with the court's order is sought, a notice to the alleged contemnor in the following form:

TO THE PERSON ALLEGED TO BE IN CONTEMPT OF COURT:

1. It is alleged that you have disobeyed a court order, are in contempt of court, and should go to jail until you obey the court's order.

2. You have the right to have a lawyer. If you already have a lawyer, you should consult the lawyer at once. If you do not now have a lawyer, please note:

(a) A lawyer can be helpful to you by:

(1) explaining the allegations against you;

(2) helping you determine and present any defense to those allegations;

(3) explaining to you the possible outcomes; and

(4) helping you at the hearing.

(b) Even if you do not plan to contest that you are in contempt of court, a lawyer can be helpful.

(c) If you want a lawyer but do not have the money to hire one, the Public Defender may provide a lawyer for you.

- To find out if the Public Defender will provide a lawyer for you, you must contact the Public Defender after any prehearing conference or master's hearing and **at least 10 business days before the date of a hearing before a judge.**

- If no prehearing conference or master's hearing is scheduled, you should contact the Public Defender as soon as possible, **at least 10 business days before the date of the hearing before the judge.**

- The court clerk will tell you how to contact the Public Defender.

(d) If you want a lawyer but you cannot get one and the Public Defender will not provide one for you, contact the court clerk as soon as possible.

(e) DO NOT WAIT UNTIL THE DATE OF YOUR COURT HEARING TO GET A LAWYER. If you do not have a lawyer before the court hearing date, the judge may find that you have waived your right to a lawyer, and the hearing may be held with you unrepresented by a lawyer.

314

3. IF YOU DO NOT APPEAR FOR A SCHEDULED PREHEARING CONFERENCE, MASTER'S HEARING, OR COURT HEARING BEFORE THE JUDGE, YOU WILL BE SUBJECT TO ARREST.

(d) **Service of order.** The order, together with a copy of any petition and other document filed in support of the allegation of contempt, shall be served on the alleged contemnor pursuant to Rule 2-121 or 3-121 or, if the alleged contemnor has appeared as a party in the action in which the contempt is charged, in the manner prescribed by the court.

(e) **Waiver of counsel if incarceration is sought.** (1) Applicability. This section applies if incarceration is sought and applies only to court hearings before a judge.

(2) Appearance in court without counsel. (A) If the alleged contemnor appears in court without counsel, the court shall make certain that the alleged contemnor has received a copy of the order containing notice of the right to counsel or was advised of the contents of the notice in accordance with Rule 9-208 (d);

(B) If the alleged contemnor indicates a desire to waive counsel, the court shall determine, after an examination of the alleged contemnor on the record, that the waiver is knowing and voluntary;

(C) If the alleged contemnor indicates a desire to have counsel and the court finds that the alleged contemnor received a copy of the order containing notice of the right to counsel or was advised of the contents of the notice pursuant to Rule 9-208 (d), the court shall permit the alleged contemnor to explain the appearance without counsel. If the court finds that there is a meritorious reason for the alleged contemnor's appearance without counsel, the court shall continue the action to a later time and advise the alleged contemnor that if counsel does not enter an appearance by that time, the action will proceed with the alleged contemnor unrepresented by counsel. If the court finds that there is no meritorious reason for the alleged contemnor's appearance without counsel, the court may determine that the alleged contemnor has waived counsel by failing or refusing to obtain counsel and may proceed with the hearing.

(3) Discharge of counsel. If an alleged contemnor requests permission to discharge an attorney whose appearance has been entered, the court shall permit the alleged contemnor to explain the reasons for the request. If the court finds that there is a meritorious reason for the alleged contemnor's request, the court shall permit the discharge of counsel, continue the action if necessary, and advise the alleged contemnor that if new counsel does not enter an appearance by the next scheduled hearing date, the action will be heard with the alleged contemnor unrepresented by counsel. If the court finds (A) that the alleged contemnor received a copy of the order containing notice of the right to counsel or was advised of the contents of the notice in accordance with Rule 9-208 (d) and (B) that there is no meritorious reason for the alleged contemnor's request, the court may permit the discharge of counsel but shall first inform the alleged contemnor that the hearing will proceed as scheduled with the alleged contemnor unrepresented by counsel. (Amended Dec. 10,

1996, effective Jan. 1, 1997; June 6, 2000, effective Oct. 1, 2000; Mar. 5, 2001, effective July 1, 2001.)

Source. — This Rule is new.

Effect of amendments. — The 1996 amendment substituted "alleged contemnor" for "defendant" and substituted "alleged contemnor's" for "defendant's" throughout the Rule; in (b) (3), substituted "may bring" for "to bring"; and substituted "an alleged contemnor" for "a defendant" in (e) (3).

The 2000 amendment rewrote (c); substituted "is sought and applies only to court hearings before a judge" for "to compel compliance is sought" in (e) (1); in (e) (2) (A), deleted "pursuant to the order" following "appears in court" and added "or was advised of the contents of the notice in accordance with Rule 9-207 d"; inserted "or was advised of the contents of the notice pursuant to Rule 9-207 d" in the first sentence of (e) (2) (C); and rewrote the third sentence of (e) (3).

The 2001 amendment substituted "9-208 (a) (1) (G)" for "9-207 a (1) (G)" in (c) (2) (B); and substituted "9-208 (d)" for "9-207 d" in (e) (2) (A), (C) and (e) (3).

Intent, standard of proof and defenses. — In non-support civil contempt cases, to find contempt, contumacious intent is not required, violation of an order must be established by only a preponderance of the evidence, and with respect to any penalties, inability to comply is a defense even if the inability to comply was willful. Howard County v. Pack Shack, Inc., 138 Md. App. 720, 773 A.2d 612 (2001), rev'd, remanded, on other grounds 371 Md. 243, 808 A.2d 795 (2002).

Right to Counsel — The trial court erred in finding that the contemnor waived his right to counsel; the trial court was duty bound to question the contemnor as to his economic circumstances before deciding whether his explanation had merit. Blackston v. Blackston, 145 Md. App. 348, 802 A.2d 1124 (2002).

Trial court erred in holding the mother in contempt for failure to pay child support and imposing a sentence of incarceration without first ascertaining that the mother had validly waived the mother's right to counsel pursuant to (e). Bradford v. State, 199 Md. App. 175, 21 A.3d 123 (2011).

Content of order. — The requirements of section (c) (2) (C) of this Rule were not met where the warnings to be given to an alleged contemnor were not communicated to him in his show cause order. Redmond v. Redmond, 123 Md. App. 405, 718 A.2d 668 (1998).

Procedure. — If unemployment is the problem for a defendant's wilful failure to pay child support, a court, upon determining the cause, may, under Rule 15-207(e)(4), enter reasonable and specific directives to deal with it such as: ordering the defendant to pursue employment opportunities in a specific manner; ordering the defendant to pursue necessary education or a diploma, degree, certificate, or license that may be necessary or helpful in making the defendant eligible for meaningful employment; direct the defendant to seek a form of treatment for health or addiction problems that has a reasonable chance of dealing with the problem sufficiently to qualify the defendant for meaningful employment; require the defendant to report periodically and monitor compliance; or impose any directive that is specific and reasonable. If it appears that the defendant is wilfully not complying with the directives, the court may cause a criminal contempt proceeding to be filed, aimed at punishing defiance of the directives and, if as a result of that defiance, the underlying support order remains in arrears, the State's Attorney, if so inclined, may pursue a criminal action under § 10-203 of the Family Law Article. Arrington v. Dep't of Human Res., 402 Md. 79, 935 A.2d 432 (2007).

Summary contempt proceedings. — Where the court did not attempt to punish an attorney's direct contempt summarily, initiating no contempt proceedings, and where the offending attorney had no warning that a subsequent motion hearing would evolve into an attempt by the court to conduct a summary contempt proceeding, the proceedings were flawed. Hermina v. Baltimore Life Ins. Co., 128 Md. App. 568, 739 A.2d 893 (1999).

Combined single charging documents for criminal and civil contempt cases not authorized. — Although Rule 15-207(a) authorizes the consolidation for hearing of a constructive criminal contempt case and a constructive civil contempt case, nothing in the rules authorizes a combined single charging document. Dorsey v. State, 356 Md. 324, 739 A.2d 41 (1999).

Because the constructive civil contempt order violated (e)(4) by including criminal sanctions and procedures and did not set a reasonable purge amount, highest court vacated the civil contempt order, but did not vacate the father's ongoing obligation to pay the child support and payments on arrearage that previously had been established and ordered. Bryant v. Howard County Dep't of Soc. Servs., 387

Md. 30, 874 A.2d 457 (2005).

Officer cannot file a petition for contempt. — Considering the language of Rule 15-206 and the penalty provision of § 4-509(b) of the Family Law Article, a police officer, in a case in which the officer is not a party, cannot initiate a constructive civil contempt proceeding by filing a petition for contempt. Zetty v. Piatt, 365 Md. 141, 776 A.2d 631 (2001).

Procedural errors. — Petitioner received ineffective assistance of counsel when his attorney disclosed the nature of his advice to petitioner and his opinion regarding the application of the Fifth Amendment with regard to petitioner being summoned as a prosecution witness in a criminal case, therefore, petitioner's conviction for contempt pursuant to Rule 15-203 was reversed in a post-conviction proceeding. The trial judge committed multiple errors in characterizing the imposition of sanctions in the case as summary in nature and should have followed the procedures delineated in Rules 15-204, 15-205, 15-206, and 15-207. Smith v. State, 394 Md. 184, 905 A.2d 315 (2006).

Comparing Rules 15-205(b), 15-206(b), the Maryland Department of Social Services has no authority to file a petition for criminal contempt. Bryant v. Howard County Dep't of Soc. Servs., 387 Md. 30, 874 A.2d 457 (2005).

Civil contempt order was reversed where the proceeding was initiated by a party who did not have the authority under Rule 15-206(b) to initiate the proceeding, and where the circuit court did not comply with Rule 15-206(e), which requires the court to confirm that the contemnor received a notice of the right to counsel and that he knowingly and voluntarily waived that right. Zetty v. Piatt, 365 Md. 141, 776 A.2d 631 (2001).

In non-support cases, absent a showing that the defendant can, in fact, meet a purge, no finding of contempt is permissible. Bryant v. Howard County Dep't of Soc. Servs., 387 Md. 30, 874 A.2d 457 (2005).

Applied in Solomon v. Solomon, 118 Md. App. 96, 701 A.2d 1199 (1997); Wright v. Phipps, 122 Md. App. 480, 712 A.2d 606 (1998), cert. dismissed, 351 Md. 661, 719 A.2d 1261 (1998).

Quoted in Usiak v. State, 413 Md. 384, 993 A.2d 39 (2010).

Cited in In re Blessen H., 392 Md. 684, 898 A.2d 980 (2006); Rodriguez v. Clarke, 400 Md. 39, 926 A.2d 736 (2007); King v. State, 400 Md. 419, 929 A.2d 169 (2007); R & D 2001, LLC v. Rice, 402 Md. 648, 938 A.2d 839 (2008); De Arriz v. Klinger-De Arriz, 179 Md. App. 458, 947 A.2d 59 (2008); Fisher v. McCrary Crescent City, LLC, 186 Md. App. 86, 972 A.2d 954 (2009), cert. denied, 131 S. Ct. 637, 2010 U.S. LEXIS 9156, 178 L. Ed. 2d 476 (U.S. 2010).

Rule 15-207. Constructive contempt; further proceedings.

(a) **Consolidation of criminal and civil contempts.** If a person has been charged with both constructive criminal contempt pursuant to Rule 15-205 and constructive civil contempt pursuant to Rule 15-206, the court may consolidate the proceedings for hearing and disposition.

(b) **When judge disqualified.** A judge who enters an order pursuant to Rule 15-204 or who institutes a constructive contempt proceeding on the court's own initiative pursuant to Rule 15-205 (b) (1) or Rule 15-206 (b) (1) and who reasonably expects to be called as a witness at any hearing on the matter is disqualified from sitting at the hearing unless (1) the alleged contemnor consents, or (2) the alleged contempt consists of a failure to obey a prior order or judgment in a civil action or a "judgment of restitution" as defined in Code, Criminal Procedure Article, § 11-601(g).

(c) **Hearing.** (1) Contempt of appellate court. Where the alleged contemnor is charged with contempt of an appellate court, that court, in lieu of conducting the hearing itself, may designate a trial judge as a special master to take evidence and make recommended findings of fact and conclusions of law, subject to exception by any party and approval of the appellate court.

(2) Failure of alleged contemnor to appear. If the alleged contemnor fails to appear personally at the time and place set by the court, the court may enter an order directing a sheriff or other peace officer to take custody of and bring the alleged contemnor before the court or judge designated in the order. If the

alleged contemnor in a civil contempt proceeding fails to appear in person or by counsel at the time and place set by the court, the court may proceed ex parte.

(d) **Disposition — Generally.** (1) Applicability. This section applies to all proceedings for contempt other than proceedings for constructive civil contempt based on an alleged failure to pay spousal or child support.

(2) Order. When a court or jury makes a finding of contempt, the court shall issue a written order that specifies the sanction imposed for the contempt. In the case of a civil contempt, the order shall specify how the contempt may be purged. In the case of a criminal contempt, if the sanction is incarceration, the order shall specify a determinate term and any condition under which the sanction may be suspended, modified, revoked, or terminated.

(e) **Constructive civil contempt — Support enforcement action.** (1) Applicability. This section applies to proceedings for constructive civil contempt based on an alleged failure to pay spousal or child support, including an award of emergency family maintenance under Code, Family Law Article, Title 4, Subtitle 5.

Committee note. — Sanctions for attorneys found to be in contempt for failure to pay child support may include referral to Bar Counsel pursuant to Rule 16-731. See Code, Family Law Article, § 10-119.3.

(2) Petitioner's burden of proof. Subject to subsection (3) of this section, the court may make a finding of contempt if the petitioner proves by clear and convincing evidence that the alleged contemnor has not paid the amount owed, accounting from the effective date of the support order through the date of the contempt hearing.

(3) When a finding of contempt may not be made. The court may not make a finding of contempt if the alleged contemnor proves by a preponderance of the evidence that (A) from the date of the support order through the date of the contempt hearing the alleged contemnor (i) never had the ability to pay more than the amount actually paid and (ii) made reasonable efforts to become or remain employed or otherwise lawfully obtain the funds necessary to make payment, or (B) enforcement by contempt is barred by limitations as to each unpaid spousal or child support payment for which the alleged contemnor does not make the proof set forth in subsection (3) (A) of this section.

Cross references. — Code, Family Law Article, § 10-102.

(4) Order. Upon a finding of constructive civil contempt for failure to pay spousal or child support, the court shall issue a written order that specifies (A) the amount of the arrearage for which enforcement by contempt is not barred by limitations, (B) any sanction imposed for the contempt, and (C) how the contempt may be purged. If the contemnor does not have the present ability to purge the contempt, the order may include directions that the contemnor make specified payments on the arrearage at future times and perform specified acts to enable the contemnor to comply with the direction to make payments.

(Amended Dec. 10, 1996, effective Jan. 1, 1997; Jan. 20, 1999, effective July 1, 1999; Jan. 8, 2002, effective Feb. 1, 2002; amended Sept. 10, 2009, effective Oct. 1, 2009.)

Committee note. — Section (e) modifies the holding in *Lynch v. Lynch*, 342 Md. 509 (1996), by allowing a court to make a finding of constructive civil contempt in a support enforcement action even if the alleged contemnor does not have the present ability to purge. In support enforcement cases, as in other civil contempt cases, after making a finding of contempt, the court may specify imprisonment as the sanction if the contemnor has the present ability to purge the contempt.

If the contemnor does not have the present ability to purge the contempt, an example of a direction to perform specified acts that a court may include in an order under subsection (e)(4) is a provision that an unemployed, able-bodied contemnor look for work and periodically provide evidence of the efforts made. If the contemnor fails, without just cause, to comply with any provision of the order, a criminal contempt proceeding may be brought based on a violation of that provision.

Cross references. — See *Arrington v. Department of Human Resources*, 402 Md. 79 (2007).

Source. — This Rule is derived in part from former Rule P4 c and d 2 and is in part new.

Effect of amendments. — The 1996 amendment rewrote the Rule.

The 1999 amendment substituted "a 'judgment of restitution' as defined in Code, Article 27, § 805A (i)" for "an 'order of restitution' as defined in Code, Article 27, § 640 (a) (9)" in (b).

The 2002 amendment substituted "Criminal Procedure Article, § 11-601(g)" for "Article 27, § 805A(i)" in (b).

The 2009 amendment added the cross reference at the end.

University of Baltimore Law Review. — For discussion of child abduction by a relative and Maryland's misdemeanor offense to deter parental child stealing, see 8 U. Balt. L. Rev. 609 (1979).

For comment, "A Pragmatic Look at Criminal Contempt and the Trial Attorney," see 12 U. Balt. L. Rev. 100 (1982).

University of Baltimore Law Forum. — Recent Development: Long v. State: Courts Cannot Modify a Consent Order Without Giving the Parties an Opportunity to Be Heard Because to Do Otherwise Would Violate the Parties Right to Due Process, see 33 U. Balt. Law Forum 33 (2002).

Section (e) may be applied retrospectively. — Section (e) of this Rule, regarding constructive civil contempt in support enforcement actions, may be applied retrospectively to its January 1, 1997, effective date to contempt proceedings initiated after the effective date, but relating to support orders entered before the effective date of the Rule. Rawlings v. Rawlings, 362 Md. 535, 766 A.2d 98 (2001).

Basic requirements of "due process" declared by former Rule P4. — Former Rule P4 is declaratory of the basic requirements of due process of law in the prosecution of constructive contempts. Reamer v. Reamer, 246 Md. 532, 229 A.2d 74 (1967).

The provisions of former Rule P4 are declaratory of the basic requirements of due process of law in the prosecution of constructive contempts. Savage v. State, 19 Md. App. 1, 308 A.2d 701 (1973).

Trial judge is not required to explain the nature of the contempt proceedings. — When an alleged civil contemnor in a support enforcement action is represented by counsel and has been informed that incarceration is a possibility, the trial judge is not required to explain the nature of the contempt proceedings, available defenses, or the consequences of a finding of contempt. Jones v. State, 351 Md. 264, 718 A.2d 222 (1998).

Classification of contempt determines punishment. — Whether the defendant is subject to summary punishment or is entitled to an adversary hearing hinges on whether the contempt is classified as direct or constructive. Murphy v. State, 46 Md. App. 138, 416 A.2d 748 (1980).

Combined single charging documents for criminal and civil contempt cases not authorized. — Although section (a) of this Rule authorizes the consolidation for hearing of a constructive criminal contempt case and a constructive civil contempt case, nothing in the rules authorizes a combined single charging document. Dorsey v. State, 356 Md. 324, 739 A.2d 41 (1999).

Procedure. — Subsection (a) permits a person to be charged separately with both a constructive civil and constructive criminal contempt and for the two proceedings to be consolidated for purposes of hearing and disposition. Arrington v. Dep't of Human Res., 402 Md. 79, 935 A.2d 432 (2007).

If unemployment is the problem for a defendant's wilful failure to pay child support, a court, upon determining the cause, may, under (e)(4), enter reasonable and specific directives to deal with it such as: ordering the defendant to pursue employment opportunities in a specific manner; ordering the defendant to pursue necessary education or a diploma, degree, certificate, or license that may be necessary or helpful in making the defendant eligible for meaningful employment; direct the defendant to seek a form of treatment for health or addiction problems that has a reasonable chance of dealing with the problem sufficiently to qualify the defendant for meaningful employment; require the defendant to report periodically and monitor compliance; or impose any directive that is specific and reasonable. If it appears that the defendant is wilfully not complying with the directives, the court may cause a criminal contempt proceeding to be filed, aimed at punishing defiance of the directives and, if as a result of that defiance, the underlying support order remains in arrears, the State's Attorney, if so inclined, may pursue a criminal action under § 10-203 of the Family Law Article. Arrington v. Dep't of Human Res., 402 Md. 79, 935 A.2d 432 (2007).

If a court desires to proceed with the civil contempt in a case involving the wilful refusal to pay child support but, due to the defendant's current inability to meet any meaningful purge, is precluded from imposing a sanction of incarceration, it should explore the reasons why the defendant is impecunious and attempt to deal with that situation. Arrington v. Dep't of Human Res., 402 Md. 79, 935 A.2d 432 (2007).

Procedural errors. — Petitioner received ineffective assistance of counsel when his attorney disclosed the nature of his advice to petitioner and his opinion regarding the application of the Fifth Amendment with regard to petitioner being summoned as a prosecution witness in a criminal case, therefore, petitioner's conviction for contempt pursuant to Rule 15-203 was reversed in a post-conviction proceeding. The trial judge committed multiple errors in characterizing the imposition of sanctions in the case as summary in nature and should have followed the procedures delineated in Rules 15-204, 15-205, 15-206, and 15-207. Smith v. State, 394 Md. 184, 905 A.2d 315 (2006).

Merging or conversion of civil and criminal contempt proceedings not allowed. — Civil contempt proceeding cannnot be merged into a criminal contempt proceeding or converted, mid-stream, into a criminal contempt proceeding. Bryant v. Howard County Dep't of Soc. Servs., 387 Md. 30, 874 A.2d 457 (2005).

It is the act itself which determines whether a contempt is constructive. Mur-

phy v. State, 46 Md. App. 138, 416 A.2d 748 (1980).

Summary contempt proceedings. — Where the court did not attempt to punish an attorney's direct contempt summarily, initiating no contempt proceedings, and where the offending attorney had no warning that a subsequent motion hearing would evolve into an attempt by the court to conduct a summary contempt proceeding, the proceedings were flawed. Hermina v. Baltimore Life Ins. Co., 128 Md. App. 568, 739 A.2d 893 (1999).

Summary punishment for direct contempt only. — Only a direct contempt may be punished summarily; if the contempt is constructive, the court must give the accused an opportunity to challenge the alleged basis for the contempt and show cause why a contempt order should not be entered. Betz v. State, 99 Md. App. 60, 635 A.2d 77 (1994).

Constructive contempts may not be summarily punished by the court. As they are contempts which are not committed in the presence of the court, or so near as to interrupt its proceedings, the court would not be a personal observer of the facts. Roll v. State, 15 Md. App. 31, 288 A.2d 605 (1972), modified and aff'd, 267 Md. 714, 298 A.2d 867 (1973).

There is no need for summarily disposing of an alleged contempt when the behavior of the accused is not personally known to the judge or does not occur so near to the court as to interrupt proceedings then being conducted by the judge. State v. Roll, 267 Md. 714, 298 A.2d 867 (1973).

Attachment of defendant. — Former Rule P4, setting forth the steps to be followed in constructive contempt proceedings, is silent on the question of whether the defendant may be subject to attachment to answer the alleged contempt. The Court of Appeals assumed without deciding that attachment was permissible where the court had reason to believe the defendant might conceal himself or flee the State to avoid personal service in the contempt proceeding. Reamer v. Reamer, 246 Md. 532, 229 A.2d 74 (1967).

Procedural safeguards violated by body attachment. — The lower court's incarceration of father, who was delinquent in his child support obligation, on a body attachment in June until his hearing in August violated the procedural safeguards afforded to alleged civil contemnors by the common law and Rule 15-207. Redden v. Department of Soc. Servs., 139 Md. App. 66, 773 A.2d 1094 (2001).

Subsection (c)(2) is clear, unambiguous, and requires no construction. The trial court may direct that a contemnor be arrested and brought before the court for a scheduled hearing, or the court may hold the hearing in his or her absence; it clearly does not speak to whether a court may order that the contemnor be arrested and detained while awaiting a subsequent hearing or set an unreasonable bond amount to secure via incarceration the contemnor's attendance. Young v. Fauth, 158 Md. App. 105, 854 A.2d 293 (2004).

Person who has allegedly violated an order of court is entitled to: (1) formal notice of the precise violation alleged, (2) an opportunity to be heard on the merits of that issue, and (3) the right to counsel if confinement is the sanction to be imposed for the violation. Reed v. Foley, 105 Md. App. 184, 659 A.2d 325 (1995).

Person who voluntarily absents himself after his trial has commenced commits a constructive contempt. Pearson v. State, 28 Md. App. 464, 347 A.2d 239 (1975).

Proper to proceed under former Rule P4 where proof of contemptuous act not within knowledge of trial judge. — Although defendants were cited for direct contempt in violation of former Rule P3, where the proof was not within the knowledge of the trial judge it was proper to proceed under the procedural requirements of former Rule P4. Dorsey v. State, 295 Md. 217, 454 A.2d 353 (1983).

Unexplained absence is not a contempt committed in the actual presence of the court. A.V. Laurins & Co. v. Prince George's County, 46 Md. App. 548, 420 A.2d 982 (1980).

Show cause order delivered in court complied with former Rule P4. — Delivery of unsigned copy of show cause order to defendant in open court as directed by judge complied with former Rule P4. Dorsey v. State, 56 Md. App. 54, 466 A.2d 546 (1983).

Incarceration where contemnor allegedly violated an order of court. — Incarceration cannot be imposed upon a civil contemnor for willfully failing to comply with a court order unless the contemnor has been given the opportunity to purge the contempt. Jones v. State, 351 Md. 264, 718 A.2d 222 (1998).

Where the trial court issued an arrest warrant in the contempt case against the father, the trial court acted within its jurisdiction to compel compliance with an order under § 1-202(a) of the Courts Article and (c)(2) of this Rule . Nnoli v. Nnoli, 389 Md. 315, 884 A.2d 1215 (2005).

Incarceration improper where no ability to pay purge was demonstrated. — The court's imposition of a prison term on father who was delinquent in child support payments was in error because the father demonstrated that he lacked the present ability to pay a purge, and a court may not incarcerate a civil contemnor unless he or she has the present ability to purge the contempt. Redden v. Department of Soc. Servs., 139 Md. App. 66, 773 A.2d 1094 (2001).

Where release from incarceration of a deadbeat father who could not possibly have purged the contempt was bargained for in a consent judgment, the intermediate court improperly interfered in the parties' settlement agreement by modifying it to add provisions that potentially exposed the father to a risk of further incarceration. Long v. State, 371 Md. 72, 807 A.2d 1 (2002).

Feasible purging provision required. — A civil contempt order must contain a purging provision with which the contemnor has the ability to comply. Furthermore, because the purpose of imprisoning the contemnor is remedial, i.e., to preserve and enforce the rights of private parties to a suit and to compel obedience to orders and decrees primarily to benefit such parties, a civil contemnor may be incarcerated only when he or she has been found to have the present ability to purge the contempt. Young v. Fauth, 158 Md. App. 105, 854 A.2d 293 (2004).

Ability to meet purge required. — In non-support cases, absent a showing that the defendant can, in fact, meet a purge, no finding of contempt is permissible. Bryant v. Howard County Dep't of Soc. Servs., 387 Md. 30, 874 A.2d 457 (2005).

Child support arrearage contempt order, which provided for release from detention if the father sold his memorabilia collection, was improper because he did not have the ability to comply with the purging provision when the order was issued. Young v. Fauth, 158 Md. App. 105, 854 A.2d 293 (2004).

Detention of a father under a writ of body attachment, pending the holding of a contempt hearing on child support arrearages, was improper; court can only direct that a contemnor be arrested and brought before the court for the scheduled hearing or hold a hearing in his or her absence. Young v. Fauth, 158 Md. App. 105, 854 A.2d 293 (2004).

Contemnor failed to establish her inability to purge her contempt for failure to pay child support, where she presented a bare affidavit which did not indicate her income from her present employment or how long she had been working, and where counter evidence was presented and the trial court found she voluntarily impoverished herself. Schwartz v. Wagner, 116 Md. App. 720, 698 A.2d 1222 (1997).

Where the contemnor's inability to comply with the support order is his/her lack of gainful employment or other access to available funds, a court may address that problem directly by ordering the contemnor to take reasonable steps to obtain such employment or access and, if warranted, enforcing those directives through criminal contempt proceedings; the court obviously has some flexibility in deciding what directives to issue (such as employment counseling and training). There are, of course, limits on how far a court may go in this regard; it cannot order things that are either inherently punitive in nature or that are so onerous, impractical, or unrelated to the objective of enabling the defendant to meet his/her obligation as to become punitive. Bryant v. Howard County Dep't of Soc. Servs., 387 Md. 30, 874 A.2d 457 (2005).

Refusal to borrow to pay obligation. — Contempt order was reversed where the chancellor's finding of contempt was incorrectly based upon the father's refusal to borrow $5,000 from a bank to pay his support obligations; the General Assembly did not intend that an obligor may be held in contempt when he has no income sufficient to pay a support obligation but, conceivably, could borrow the amount due from a relative, a friend, by the use of a credit card, or any other source that creates a debt. Rivera v. Zysk, 136 Md. App. 607, 766 A.2d 1049 (2001).

Requirements for purging contempt and bail amounts set too high. — Despite the trial court's understandable frustration with deadbeat father's longtime failure to appear, it erred in setting requirements for purging contempt and bail amounts that he could not possibly pay; the trial court's orders violated Rule 15-207(e)(4), which protects a parent against incarceration for contempt without giving the parent an opportunity to prove inability to pay, and Rule 15-207(c)(2), which provides remedies for a parent's failure to appear in a contempt proceeding that does not include immediate incarceration and the setting of an impossibly high bond. Wilson v. Holliday, 364 Md. 589, 774 A.2d 1123 (2001).

Vacation of civil order including criminal sanctions and procedures and lacking purge amount not changing obligations. — Because the constructive civil contempt order violated (e)(4) by including criminal sanctions and procedures and did not set a reasonable purge amount, highest court vacated the civil contempt order, but did not vacate the father's ongoing obligation to pay the child support and payments on arrearage that previously had been established and ordered. Bryant v. Howard County Dep't of Soc. Servs., 387 Md. 30, 874 A.2d 457 (2005).

Juveniles. — It was abuse of discretion to find juvenile guilty of criminal contempt for violation of court order to attend school without considering available alternatives which would have afforded the guidance, treatment or rehabilitation contemplated by CJ § 3-801 et seq. In re Ann M., 309 Md. 564, 525 A.2d 1054 (1987).

Finding of contempt proper — Trial court properly found a husband in contempt for refusing to consent to a wife's proposed order concerning the husband's military pension, because a master properly admitted expert testimony indicating that the terms of the proposed order were acceptable to the military under 10 U.S.C.S. § 1408, and the master complied with the requirements of (d)(2), as the master informed the husband that he would be required to pay the wife's counsel fees if he were found in contempt. Marquis v. Marquis, 175 Md. App. 734, 931 A.2d 1164 (2007).

When a landowner was found in civil contempt for non-compliance with an order to close a landfill, the landowner was not improperly found in civil contempt for a past failure to comply with a court order because a petition to hold the landowner in contempt required a trial court to find whether the landowner's past conduct violated a prior court order. Gertz v. Md. Dep't of the Env't, 199 Md. App. 413, 23 A.3d 236 (2011).

Landowner was properly fined, as a sanction for civil contempt, for failing to comply with a prior court order because the fine was designed to coerce compliance and provided for purging, as (1) a suspended part of the fine was a remedial sanction that could be purged, and, (2) a non-suspended part of the fine was a remedial incentive to comply with a prior order that could have been avoided, the landowner had consented to the fine, and the fine did not award compensatory damages. Gertz v. Md. Dep't of the Env't, 199 Md. App. 413, 23 A.3d 236 (2011).

It was not error to find that a landowner's delay in submitting a landfill closure plan was a willful violation of a prior court order, sufficient to support a finding that the landowner was in civil contempt, because ample evidence supported an inference that the delay was part of a deliberate strategy to avoid compliance with the order. Gertz v. Md. Dep't of the Env't, 199 Md. App. 413, 23 A.3d 236 (2011).

Fine imposed when a landowner was found in civil contempt was not an abuse of discretion because (1) relevant facts were considered, (2) the fine's range had previously induced the landowner to comply with an order requiring the landowner to close a landfill, so that range was reasonable, (3) the landowner did not actively pursue compliance with the order for four years, (4) the landowner had agreed to a trial court's discretion over the fine amount, and (5) the landowner could avoid a suspended part of the fine. Gertz v. Md. Dep't of the Env't, 199 Md. App. 413, 23 A.3d 236 (2011).

Contempt order was appealable, not moot. — Contempt order was appealable, and the father's appeal was not moot because the original adjudication of contempt was on the record and also provided for, although erroneously, various criminal penalties which were on the record and which could have a negative future impact on the father, for example, when applying for a job. Bryant v. Howard County Dep't of Soc. Servs., 387 Md. 30, 874 A.2d 457 (2005).

Ancillary orders. — When a landowner was found in civil contempt for non-compliance with an order related to the closure of a landfill on the landowner's land, a requirement that the landowner permit future inspection and monitoring of the landowner's land did not exceed a court's contempt powers because (1) the landowner agreed to such a requirement, and (2) the court could issue ancillary orders to facilitate compliance with the court's orders. Gertz v. Md. Dep't of the Env't, 199 Md. App. 413, 23 A.3d 236 (2011).

Applied in Wright v. Phipps, 122 Md. App. 480, 712 A.2d 606 (1998), cert. dismissed, 351 Md. 661, 719 A.2d 1261 (1998); State v. Stowe, 376 Md. 436, 829 A.2d 1036 (2003).

Quoted in Ott v. Frederick County Dep't of Social Servs., 345 Md. 682, 694 A.2d 101 (1997); In re Blessen H., 392 Md. 684, 898 A.2d 980 (2006); Usiak v. State, 413 Md. 384, 993 A.2d 39 (2010); Bradford v. State, 199 Md. App. 175, 21 A.3d 123 (2011).

Stated in Rosemann v. Salsbury, Clements, Bekman, Marder & Adkins, LLC, 412 Md. 308, 987 A.2d 48 (2010).

Cited in Dodson v. Dodson, 380 Md. 438, 845 A.2d 1194 (2004); Bahena v. Foster, 164 Md. App. 275, 883 A.2d 218 (2005); King v. State, 400 Md. 419, 929 A.2d 169 (2007); R & D 2001, LLC v. Rice, 402 Md. 648, 938 A.2d 839 (2008); De Arriz v. Klinger-De Arriz, 179 Md. App. 458, 947 A.2d 59 (2008); Hoile v. State, 404 Md. 591, 948 A.2d 30 (2008), cert. denied, 129 S. Ct. 257, 2008 U.S. LEXIS 5503, 172 L. Ed. 2d 146 (U.S. 2008); Fisher v. McCrary Crescent City, LLC, 186 Md. App. 86, 972 A.2d 954 (2009), cert. denied, 131 S. Ct. 637, 2010 U.S. LEXIS 9156, 178 L. Ed. 2d 476 (U.S. 2010).

Rule 15-208. Bail.

A contemnor committed for contempt is entitled to the same consideration with respect to bail pending appeal as a defendant convicted in a criminal proceeding. (Amended Dec. 10, 1996, effective Jan. 1, 1997.)

Cross references. — Rule 4-348.
Source. — This Rule is derived from former Rule P5.

Effect of amendments. — The 1996 amendment substituted "contemnor" for "defendant."

University of Baltimore Law Review. — For comment, "A Pragmatic Look at Criminal Contempt and the Trial Attorney," see 12 U. Balt. L. Rev. 100 (1982).

Procedure. — If unemployment is the problem for a defendant's wilful failure to pay child support, a court, upon determining the cause, may, under Rule 15-207(e)(4), enter reasonable and specific directives to deal with it such as: ordering the defendant to pursue employment opportunities in a specific manner; ordering the defendant to pursue necessary education or a diploma, degree, certificate, or license that may be necessary or helpful in making the defendant eligible for meaningful employment; direct the defendant to seek a form of treatment for health or addiction problems that has a reasonable chance of dealing with the problem sufficiently to qualify the defendant for meaningful employment; require the defendant to report periodically and monitor compliance; or impose any directive that is specific and reasonable. If it appears that the defendant is wilfully not complying with the directives, the court may cause a criminal contempt proceeding to be filed, aimed at punishing defiance of the directives and, if as a result of that defiance, the underlying support order remains in arrears, the State's Attorney, if so inclined, may pursue a criminal action under § 10-203 of the Family Law Article. Arrington v. Dep't of Human Res., 402 Md. 79, 935 A.2d 432 (2007).

Cited in King v. State, 400 Md. 419, 929 A.2d 169 (2007).

CHAPTER 300. HABEAS CORPUS.

Rule 15-301. Habeas corpus — Applicability.
The rules in this Chapter apply to all habeas corpus proceedings challenging the legality of the confinement or restraint of an individual.

Source. — This Rule is new.

___

Maryland Law Review. — For article, "Collateral Remedies in Criminal Cases in Maryland: An Assessment," see 64 Md. L. Rev. 968 (2005).

Rule 15-302. Petition.
(a) **Generally.** A petition for a writ of habeas corpus shall be supported by affidavit of the petitioner and shall include:

(1) a statement that the individual by or on behalf of whom the writ is sought is unlawfully confined or restrained;

(2) the place where the individual is confined or restrained, if known;

(3) the name and any official capacity of the person by whom the individual is confined or restrained or, if not known, a description sufficient to enable that person to be identified;

(4) the circumstances and the cause of the confinement; and

(5) if the confinement is pursuant to a judgment or order of a court, the name of the court, the date of the judgment or order, and the case number, if known.

(b) **Certain confinements.** If a petition is filed by or on behalf of an individual confined as a result of a sentence for a criminal offense, of an order in a juvenile proceeding, or of a judgment of contempt of court, the petition, in addition to complying with the provisions of section (a) of this Rule, shall state, to the best of the petitioner's knowledge, information, and belief:

(1) whether any previous petition for habeas corpus or other post conviction relief has been filed with respect to the confinement;

(2) with respect to each previous petition for habeas corpus or other post conviction relief: (A) the court or judge to whom the petition was directed, (B) all grounds of the petition, (C) the determination made on the petition, (D) whether any appeal or application for leave to appeal was filed from any order on the petition, and (E) any determination made on the appeal or application for leave to appeal; and

(3) all grounds for the issuance of the writ that were not asserted in any previous petition for habeas corpus or other post conviction relief.

Cross references. — Code, Courts Art., § 3-702 (a).

Source. — This Rule is derived from former Rule Z42.

___

Writ should issue where application conforms with former Rule Z42. — Where an application for the issuance of a writ was in conformance with former Rule Z42, the judge should have issued the writ, and, upon production of the applicant inquired into the legality and propriety of the confinement. Washburn v. Sheriff, Cecil County, 16 Md. App. 611, 298 A.2d 462 (1973).

Only custodian need be named in petition. — There is no provision in the Maryland Rules explicitly requiring the habeas corpus petitioner to name the person by whom he or she is confined as the respondent; the rules only require that the petitioner's custodian be named in the petition. Nnoli v. Nnoli, 101 Md. App. 243, 646 A.2d 1021 (1994).

Rule 15-303. Procedure on petition.

(a) **Generally.** Upon receiving a petition for a writ of habeas corpus, the judge immediately shall refer it as provided in section (c) of this Rule or act on the petition as provided in section (d) or (e) of this Rule, except that if the petition seeks a writ of habeas corpus for the purpose of determining admission to bail or the appropriateness of any bail set, the judge may proceed in accordance with section (b) of this Rule.

(b) **Bail.** (1) Pretrial. If a petition by or on behalf of an individual who is confined prior to or during trial seeks a writ of habeas corpus for the purpose of determining admission to bail or the appropriateness of any bail set, the judge to whom the petition is directed may deny the petition without a hearing if a judge has previously determined the individual's eligibility for pretrial release or the conditions for such release pursuant to Rule 4-216 and the petition raises no grounds sufficient to warrant issuance of the writ other than grounds that were raised when the earlier pretrial release determination was made.

Cross references. — Rule 4-213 (c).

(2) After conviction. (A) Except as otherwise provided in subsection (2)(B) of this section, if a petition by or on behalf of an individual confined as a result of a conviction pending sentencing or exhaustion of appellate review seeks a writ of habeas corpus for the purpose of determining admission to bail or the appropriateness of any bail set, the judge to whom the petition is directed may deny the writ and order that the petition be treated as a motion for release or for amendment of an order of release pursuant to Rule 4-349. Upon entry of the order, the judge shall transmit the petition, a certified copy of the order, and any other pertinent papers to the trial judge who presided at the proceeding as a result of which the individual was confined. Upon receiving of the transmittal, the trial judge shall proceed in accordance with Rule 4-349.

(B) If a petition directed to a circuit court judge is filed by or on behalf of an individual confined as a result of a conviction in the District Court that has been appealed to a circuit court, the circuit court judge shall act on the petition and may not transmit or refer the petition to a District Court judge.

(c) **Referral.** If the petition is made by or on behalf of an individual confined or restrained as the result of a prior judicial proceeding, a judge to whom the petition has been made may refer the petition, without taking other action, to the administrative judge of the court in which the prior proceeding was held. In exercising the discretion to refer the petition, the judge to whom the petition has been directed shall consider the interests and convenience of the parties and the State. Upon receiving the referral, the administrative judge shall assign the petition to a judge in accordance with the assignment procedures of that court, except that, without the written consent of the individual confined or restrained, the petition shall not be assigned to any judge who sat at the proceeding as a result of which the individual was confined or restrained. The judge to whom the petition has been assigned may not further refer the petition and shall act on it immediately pursuant to section (d) or (e) of this Rule.

(d) **Show cause order.** (1) Entry; contents. If the individual is confined as a result of a sentence in a criminal case, including a proceeding for criminal contempt other than a direct criminal contempt summarily punished, or as a result of a disposition or post-dispositional order following an adjudication of delinquency in a juvenile proceeding, the judge, prior to taking any further action, may enter an order directed to the person having custody of the individual to show cause why the writ should not issue. The show cause order may be entered regardless of whether the petition complies with Rule 15-302. The show cause order shall:

(A) state a date by which the order must be served upon the person having custody of the individual;

(B) state a date by which the person having custody may file a response and a date by which a copy of any response must be served on the petitioner in accordance with subsection (4) of this section;

(C) state that the petitioner may file a reply to the response within 30 days after service of the response; and

(D) require the petitioner to serve a copy of any reply on the person having custody by first class mail, postage prepaid.

(2) Service of show cause order. The show cause order, together with a copy of the petition, shall be served by certified mail on the person having custody of the individual confined. The show cause order shall be served by first class mail, postage prepaid, on the petitioner.

(3) Notice in response. A response to the show cause order shall include notice to the petitioner in substantially the following form:

NOTICE TO _____, PETITIONER
           (Name of Petitioner)
    This response alleges your petition for a writ of habeas corpus should be denied because (check all that apply):
    ☐ There is no good reason why new grounds now raised by the petition were not raised in previous proceedings.
    ☐ There has been unjustified delay in filing the petition and that delay has prejudiced the ability of _____
    (Name of person having custody of the individual confined) to respond to the petition.
    ☐ Other reasons for denial (specify):
    _____
    _____
    _____
    _____

You may file a reply to this response. Any reply must be filed with the court by _____ [Calendar Date] and you must mail a copy of your reply to _____.

(Name of person having custody)

If you do not file a reply by that date or if your reply does not show the court a good reason why the allegations in this response are wrong, the court may deny your petition.

Committee note. — The calendar date for a reply shall be 30 days after personal service is made or 33 days after service by mail is mailed.

(4) Service of response. The person having custody shall serve a copy of the response on the petitioner or the petitioner's attorney by first class mail, postage prepaid, or by hand-delivery. The response shall be accompanied by a certificate of service showing the date and manner of making service and, if service is by hand-delivery, the name of the individual making service.

(5) If show cause order or response not timely served. If (A) the show cause order was not timely served upon the person having custody and the person having custody has not filed a response or (B) the response was not timely served upon the petitioner and the petitioner has not filed a reply, the judge shall either reissue the show cause order or set the matter in for a hearing.

(e) **Action on petition.** (1) Preliminary determination. Unless the judge refers the petition pursuant to section (c) of this Rule, the judge shall first determine whether the petition complies with the provisions of Rule 15-302, except that if a show cause order was entered in accordance with section (d) of this Rule, the judge may defer making this determination until the time for a reply has expired. In determining whether the writ should be granted or denied, a judge shall consider any response or reply filed pursuant to a show cause order entered under section (d) of this Rule and may examine public records.

(2) Noncompliance with Rule 15-302. If the petition fails to comply with the provisions of Rule 15-302, the judge may (A) deny the petition; (B) permit the petition to be amended or supplemented; or (C) grant the writ if there is a sufficient showing of probable illegal confinement or restraint.

(3) Compliance with Rule 15-302. If the petition complies with the provisions of Rule 15-302, the judge shall grant the writ unless:

(A) the judge finds from the petition, any response, reply, document filed with the petition or with a response or reply, or public record that the individual confined or restrained is not entitled to any relief;

(B) the petition is made by or on behalf of an individual confined as a result of a sentence for a criminal offense, of an order in a juvenile proceeding, or of a judgment of contempt of court, the legality of the confinement was determined in a prior habeas corpus or other post conviction proceeding, and no new ground is shown sufficient to warrant issuance of the writ;

(C) there is no good reason why new grounds now raised by the petitioner were not raised in previous proceedings; or

(D) there has been an unjustified delay in filing the petition that has prejudiced the ability of the person having custody of the individual confined or restrained to respond to the petition.

(4) Exception; notice, reply. The judge may not deny the writ on a ground set forth in subsection (e) (3) (C) or (e) (3) (D) of this Rule unless the petitioner has been given notice of that ground and has had an opportunity to reply, either in accordance with section (d) of this Rule or as otherwise directed by the court. (Amended Sept. 10, 2009, effective Oct. 1, 2009.)

Cross references. — For victim notification procedures, see Code, Criminal Procedure Article, § § 11-104 and 11-503.

Source. — This Rule is derived in part from former Rules Z54, Z43, Z44, and Z52 and is in part new.

Effect of amendments. — The 2009 amendment deleted "or could have been" after "grounds that were" in (b)(1); rewrote (b)(2)(B); and added the cross reference.

Insufficient allegation of facts. — Order refusing petition for habeas corpus affirmed on appeal on ground that petitioner did not allege facts entitling him to relief. Nance v. Warden of Md. House of Cor., 189 Md. 112, 53 A.2d 554 (1947).

Prisoner's application for a writ of habeas corpus held not to make out a prima facie case for relief. Bernard v. Warden of Md. House of Cor., 187 Md. 273, 49 A.2d 737 (1946).

Dismissal of petition without hearing testimony. — In absence of evidence tending to show that trial was a sham, dismissal of petition without hearing testimony was within court's discretion. Reeder v. Warden of Md. Penitentiary, 196 Md. 683, 77 A.2d 1 (1950).

The fact that petitioner did not receive copy of indictment, as required by law, did not entitle him to release on habeas corpus. Ballam v. Warden of Md. House of Cor., 196 Md. 644, 75 A.2d 95 (1950).

Appeal from denial of relief from excessive bail. — From a denial of relief from excessive bail by the judge before whom the writ is returnable, petitioner has the right to file an application to the Court of Special Appeals under Code, § 3-707 of the Courts Article, for leave to appeal. Lewis v. Warden of Md. House of Cor., 16 Md. App. 339, 296 A.2d 428 (1972).

An examination of public records is authorized in habeas corpus petitions. White v. Warden of Md. Penitentiary, 211 Md. 623, 126 A.2d 294 (1956).

What are public records. — In passing upon a petition for a writ of habeas corpus, the trial judge properly had before him, and took into consideration, a certified copy of the docket entries in the court where petitioner was convicted, a transcript of the proceedings at the time of petitioner's arraignment and a copy of a medical report relating to him. These documents were public records. However, a letter from the judge before whom petitioner was tried was not a public record, and hence was not properly before the judge to whom application was made for the writ. Walker v. Warden of Md. House of Cor., 209 Md. 654, 121 A.2d 714 (1956).

Original commitment order. — Examination of the original commitment order in determining whether or not to grant the application is proper in habeas corpus. Roberts v. Warden of Md. House of Cor., 211 Md. 639, 126 A.2d 857 (1956), cert. denied, 355 U.S. 966, 78 S. Ct. 556, 2 L. Ed. 2d 540 (1958).

Hearing, etc., to determine complaints not refuted by docket entries. — Where petitioner made certain complaints on habeas corpus relating to his counsel and to the conduct of his criminal trial, which were not refuted by the docket entries in that trial, the only records of the trial before the judge who considered and denied the habeas corpus petition, there should have been a hearing or some further investigation of the records to determine whether or not petitioner had been deprived of any constitutional right, the denial of which would render his judgment of conviction a nullity. Bell v. Warden of Md. Penitentiary, 218 Md. 666, 146 A.2d 56 (1959).

Rule 15-304. Alternate remedy — Post Conviction Procedure Act.

When a petition for a writ of habeas corpus is filed by or on behalf of an individual confined as a result of a sentence for a criminal offense, including a criminal contempt, or a commitment order in a juvenile delinquency proceeding, the judge may order that the petition be treated as a petition under the Post Conviction Procedure Act if the individual confined consents in writing or on the record and the judge is satisfied that the post conviction proceeding is adequate to test the legality of the confinement. Upon entry of the order, the judge shall transmit the petition, a certified copy of the order, and any other pertinent papers to the court in which the sentence or judgment was entered. Subsequent procedure shall be as in a post conviction proceeding.

Cross references. — *See* Rules 4-401 through 4-408 and Code, Criminal Procedure Article, §§ 7-101 — 7-108 and §§ 7-201 — 7-204.

(Amended Jan. 8, 2002, effective Feb. 1, 2002.)

Source. — This Rule is derived from former Rule Z55.

Effect of amendments. — The 2002 amendment substituted "Criminal Procedure Article, §§ 7-101 — 7-108 and §§ 7-201 — 7-204" in the cross reference note.

Continued incarceration after expiration of sentence. — Applicant's continued incarceration after the expiration of his sentence was a proper subject for inquiry on a petition for a writ of habeas corpus; but since it was not attacked for any alleged infirmity in the judgment under which he was sentenced, or in the sentence itself, nor even in the order by which he was transferred to the Patuxent Institution for examination, it did not present any question cognizable under the Post Conviction Procedure Act. Roberts v. Director of Patuxent Inst., 226 Md. 643, 172 A.2d 880 (1961).

Rule 15-305. To whom writ directed — Before whom returnable.

A writ of habeas corpus shall be directed to the person having custody of the individual confined or restrained. The writ shall be returnable before the judge granting it or, in the discretion of that judge, before some other judge designated in the writ except that without the written consent of the individual confined or restrained, the judge designated in the writ shall not be a judge who sat at the proceeding as a result of which the individual was confined or restrained. In exercising the discretion granted by this Rule, the judge granting the writ shall consider the interests and convenience of the parties and the State.

Source. — This Rule is derived from former Rule Z45.

Conclusion that defendant lacked ability to comply held erroneous. — Habeas corpus judge erred in concluding upon the evidence heard by trial judge, but not heard by habeas corpus judge, that defendant charged with contempt lacked the present ability to comply with the court's order, a decision directly contrary to that reached by the trial judge who heard the evidence and had the opportunity to observe the demeanor of the witnesses. Nnoli v. Nnoli, 101 Md. App. 243, 646 A.2d 1021 (1994).

Quoted in Maryland House of Cor. v. Fields, 348 Md. 245, 703 A.2d 167 (1997).

Rule 15-306. Service of writ; appearance by individual; affidavit.

(a) **Service.** Except as provided in section (c) of this Rule, a writ of habeas corpus and a copy of the petition shall be served by delivering them to the person to whom the writ is directed or by mailing them by first class mail, postage prepaid, as ordered by the court.

Cross references. — *See* Rules 2-121 and 3-121.

(b) **Production of individual.** At the time stated in the writ, which, unless the court orders otherwise, shall not be later than three days after service of the writ, the person to whom the writ is directed shall cause the individual confined or restrained to be taken before the judge designated in the writ. If the petition is by or behalf of an individual confined or restrained pursuant to an isolation or quarantine directive or order issued under any federal, State, or local public health law or public emergency law, production of the individual may be by means of a telephonic conference call, live closed circuit television, live internet or satellite video conference transmission, or other available means of communication that reasonably permit the individual to participate in the proceedings.

Cross references. — For proceedings brought pursuant to Code, Health-General Article, § 18-906 and Code, Public Safety Article, § 14-3A-05, see the Rules in Title 15, Chapter 1100.

(c) **Immediate appearance.** Subject to section (b) of this Rule, if the judge finds probable cause to believe that the person having custody of the individual by or on whose behalf the petition was filed is about to remove the individual or would evade or disobey the writ, the judge shall include in the writ an order directing the person immediately to appear, together with the individual confined or restrained, before the judge designated in the writ. The sheriff to whom the writ is delivered shall serve the writ immediately, together with a copy of the petition, on the person having custody of the individual confined or restrained and shall bring that person, together with the individual confined or restrained, before the judge designated in the writ. (Amended May 9, 2000, effective July 1, 2000; June 7, 2011, effective July 1, 2011.)

Cross references. — *See* Code, Courts Article, § 2-305 for the penalty on a sheriff for failure to act as provided in section (b) of this Rule; *see* Code, Correctional Services Article, § 9-611 for the penalty on an officer or other person failing to furnish a copy of a warrant of commitment when demanded.

Source. — This Rule is derived in part from former Rules Z46 and Z47 and is in part new.

Effect of amendments. — The 2000 amendment substituted "Correctional Services Article, § 9-611" for "Article 27, § 617" in the cross reference note following (c).

The 2011 amendment, in (b), inserted the second sentence and added the cross reference note; inserted "Subject to section (b) of this Rule" at the beginning of (c); and in the source note, inserted "in part" following "derived" and added "and is in part new" at the end.

Rule 15-307. Absence of judge — Return to another court or judge.

If the judge designated in the writ is unavailable when the individual confined or restrained is produced, the individual shall be taken before another judge of the same judicial circuit. If the individual is confined or restrained as a result of a sentence for a criminal offense, including a criminal contempt, or as a result of an order in a juvenile proceeding, the individual shall not be taken before a judge who sat at any proceeding as a result of which the individual was confined or restrained unless the individual consents in writing.

Source. — This Rule is derived from former Rule Z49.

Lack of prejudice — When an inmate's habeas corpus petition was considered and dismissed by a judge who had previously sentenced him, contrary to the requirements of Md. R. 15-307, the inmate was not prejudiced because that dismissal was subsequently vacated, and the matter was assigned to a judge who had not previously sentenced the inmate, who also dismissed the petition. Jones v. Filbert, 155 Md. App. 568, 843 A.2d 908 (2004).

Rule 15-308. Notice to State's Attorney and Attorney General.

If a judge grants a writ with respect to an individual confined as a result of a sentence for a criminal offense, including a criminal contempt, or as a result of an order in a juvenile proceeding, the judge shall instruct the clerk to give notice of the time and place of the hearing to the State's Attorney for the county in which the sentence or order was entered. If the petition presents an issue of illegal confinement in the Division of Correction unrelated to the underlying conviction or order, notice shall also be directed to the Attorney General.

Cross references. — For the entry of judgment in a removed case, *see* Rule 4-254 (b) (3).

Source. — This Rule is derived from Rule Z50.

Stated in Maryland Correctional Institution-Women v. Lee, 362 Md. 502, 766 A.2d 80 (2001).

Rule 15-309. Hearing.

(a) **Generally.** Upon the production of the individual confined or restrained, the judge shall conduct a hearing immediately to inquire into the legality and propriety of the individual's confinement or restraint. The individual confined or restrained for whom the writ is issued may offer evidence to prove the lack of legal justification for the confinement or restraint, and evidence may be offered on behalf of the person having custody to refute the claim.

(b) **Conduct of Hearing If Isolation or Quarantine.** If, pursuant to an isolation or quarantine directive or order issued under any federal, State, or local public health law or public emergency law, one or more of the parties, their counsel, or witnesses are unable to appear personally at the hearing, and the fair and effective adjudication of the proceedings permits, the court may:

(1) admit documentary evidence submitted or proffered by courier, facsimile, or other electronic means;

(2) if feasible, conduct the proceedings by means of a telephonic conference call, live closed circuit television, live internet or satellite video conference transmission, or other available means of communication that reasonably permits the parties or their authorized representatives to participate in the proceedings; and

(3) decline to require strict application of the rules of evidence other than those relating to the competency of witnesses and lawful privileges. (Amended Sept. 10, 2009, effective Oct. 1, 2009; June 7, 2011, effective July 1, 2011.)

Cross references. — For right of a victim or victim's representative to address the court, see Code, Criminal Procedure Article, § 11-403.

Source. — This Rule is derived as follows: Section (a) is derived from former Rules Z46 b and Z48.
Section (b) is derived from Rule 15-1104 (d).

Effect of amendments. — The 2009 amendment added the cross reference.

The 2011 amendment designated the existing paragraph as (a), inserted "Generally" at the beginning of (a), added (b), and in the source note, inserted "is derived as follows: Section (a)" and added "Section (b) is derived from Rule 15-1104 (d)."

Generally. — The facts stated in the return may be controverted, and it may be shown that no judgment or execution in fact exists, or that the court had no jurisdiction. But if there is a judgment by a competent court, then there can be no inquiry as to whether judgment is erroneous. Habeas corpus is not a writ of error. Ex parte Maulsby, 13 Md. 625 (1859). See also In re Glenn, 54 Md. 572 (1880).

Rule 15-310. Disposition.

(a) **Appropriate remedy.** If the judge determines that the individual is confined or restrained without legal warrant or authority, the judge shall order that the individual be released or discharged immediately, or shall enter such other order as justice may require. If the judge determines that the confinement or restraint is lawful and proper, the individual shall be remanded to custody or admitted to bail pending trial or retrial.

(b) **Errors on face of commitment — Correction.** The judge to whom the writ is returned shall not discharge the individual confined or restrained merely because of errors, omissions, or irregularities on the face of the warrant or other written authority for commitment. The judge may direct that the warrant or other written authority be sent for correction to the court or judicial officer who issued it and that, after correction, it be redelivered to the person having custody of the individual.

Cross references. — See Rule 4-102 (f) for the definition of "judicial officer."

Source. — This Rule is derived from former Rules Z46 b and Z51.

Rule 15-311. Memorandum by judge.

The judge to whom the petition is made or referred shall prepare and file or dictate into the record a memorandum setting forth the grounds of the petition, the questions involved, and the reasons for the action taken. A copy of the memorandum or a transcription of the dictation shall be sent to the petitioner and the person having custody of the individual confined or restrained. (Amended Nov. 1, 2001, effective Jan. 1, 2002.)

Source. — This Rule is derived from former Rule Z53.

Effect of amendments. — The 2001 amendment inserted "prepare and file or" preceding "dictate" and deleted "or prepare and file" after "record" in the first sentence.

In habeas corpus proceedings concerning bail conducted prior to sentence, whether before or after conviction, it is equally essential that the hearing judge file a memorandum which shall include his reasons for the action taken by him. Hunter v. Warden, Baltimore City Jail, 17 Md. App. 86, 299 A.2d 846 (1973).

Where the record does not contain a statement by the judge, "setting forth the grounds of the application, the questions involved, and the reasons of the court for the action taken," ordinarily it might be necessary to remand the case so that such a statement might be supplied. However, where the record before the Court of Appeals shows that petitioner is lawfully imprisoned the reason for the court's action is apparent and it is unnecessary to remand the case. State ex rel. Kirby v. Warden of Md. House of Cor., 190 Md. 765, 59 A.2d 791 (1948); State ex rel. Sisk v. Warden of Md. House of Cor., 190 Md. 759, 59 A.2d 790 (1948).

Where petitioner in habeas corpus proceeding was discharged, and Superintendent of State Reformatory for Males appealed, but where papers were not transmitted until nearly 4 months thereafter, without any statement by judge of trial court and no brief, application for leave to appeal was denied.

Raymond v. Reed, 195 Md. 716, 73 A.2d 885 (1950).

Prior memorandum sufficient. — When the trial court denying a writ of habeas corpus failed to state any reason for doing so, but on a former application to a different judge on the same grounds an opinion had been filed and it appeared that the petitioner was lawfully imprisoned, it was not necessary to remand the case for that purpose. Agner v. Warden of Md. House of Cor., 203 Md. 665, 99 A.2d 735 (1953).

The dictation to a stenographer by a judge of a statement of his reasons for denying a writ, which statement the petitioners could have obtained from the stenographer, was sufficient. Mason v. Warden of Baltimore City Jail, 203 Md. 659, 99 A.2d 739 (1953).

Statement of judge held not to comply with statute. — Where the petition in a habeas corpus proceeding properly raised on its face constitutional questions that should have been resolved, but the judge to whom the petition was referred, in denying the writ, stated in an opinion filed only that the contention that the weight of the evidence was against the verdict was no ground for relief, this was not a compliance with former § 5 of Article 42. Webster v. Warden of Md. House of Cor., 211 Md. 632, 126 A.2d 613 (1956).

Applied in Lomax v. Warden, Md. Cor. Training Ctr., 120 Md. App. 314, 707 A.2d 395 (1998), aff'd, 356 Md. 569, 741 A.2d 476 (1999).

Cited in Smith v. State, 140 Md. App. 445, 780 A.2d 1199 (2001).

Rule 15-312. Discharge on ground of unconstitutionality — Review.

When an individual is released or discharged under a writ of habeas corpus on the ground that all or part of the statute or law under which the individual was convicted is unconstitutional, the memorandum or the transcription required by Rule 15-311 shall be filed by the judge within five days after the judge orders the release or discharge. The clerk shall promptly transmit the record to the Clerk of the Court of Special Appeals for further proceedings.

Cross references. — See Code, Courts Article, § 3-706 and Rule 8-413.

Committee note. — The provisions of Title 8 are applicable to proceedings under this Rule

except to the extent otherwise provided.

Source. — This Rule is derived from former Rule Z56.

Review. — Judge's order in a habeas corpus matter is not reviewable by the Court of Appeals, except in the event he declared a public law of the State to be unconstitutional. Simon v. Warden of Md. House of Cor., 238 Md. 27, 207 A.2d 484 (1965), overruled on other grounds, McMannis v. State, 311 Md. 534, 536 A.2d 652 (1988).

Order granting habeas corpus and releasing patient from Patuxent Institution was held not appealable in State v. Musgrove, 241 Md. 521, 217 A.2d 247 (1966)

Court of Special Appeals has no jurisdiction to review grant of writ of habeas corpus based on unconstitutionality of defective delinquent provisions as opposed to writ granted on basis of the unconstitutionality of statute under which petitioner was convicted. State v. Layman, 28 Md. App. 332, 345 A.2d 444 (1975).

CHAPTER 400. HEALTH CLAIMS ARBITRATION.

Rule 15-401. Judicial review — Health claims arbitration.

The rules in this Chapter apply to judicial review of an award determining a health care malpractice claim under Code, Courts Article, Title 3, Subtitle 2A and to an assessment of costs under an award.

Cross references. — *See* generally Code, Courts Article, §§ 3-2A-01 through 3-2A-09 (Health Care Malpractice Claims), relating to arbitration of certain claims against health care providers for medical injury.

Source. — This Rule is derived from former Rule BY1.

University of Baltimore Law Review. — For article, "The Health Care Malpractice Claims Statute: Maryland's Response to the Medical Malpractice Crisis," see 10 U. Balt. L. Rev. 74 (1980).

For article, "Health Claims Arbitration in Maryland: The Experiment Has Failed," see 14 U. Balt. L. Rev. 481 (1985).

For article, "Judicial Review of Health Claims Arbitration Awards: Practice and Pitfalls," see 17 U. Balt. L. Rev. 433 (1989).

Notice of action to nullify Health Claims Arbitration award is element of action itself and is governed by the Maryland Rules. Cherry v. Seymour Bros., 306 Md. 84, 507 A.2d 613 (1986).

Discretion of court. — The court abused its discretion when it dismissed the action because of an insubstantial noncompliance with this Subtitle — a noncompliance which in no way subverted the policy served by this Subtitle, and which amounted to little more than the filing of a complaint which would be subject to dismissal for failure to state a claim, but with leave to amend. Ott v. Kaiser-Georgetown Community Health Plan, Inc., 309 Md. 641, 526 A.2d 46 (1987).

Rule 15-402. Definitions.

In these Rules the following definitions apply except as expressly otherwise provided or as necessary implication requires:

(a) **Arbitration panel.** "Arbitration panel" means the arbitrators selected to determine a health care malpractice claim in accordance with Code, Courts Article, Title 3, Subtitle 2A.

(b) **Award.** "Award" means a final determination of a health care malpractice claim by an arbitration panel or by the panel chair.

Cross references. — For the authority of the panel chair to rule on issues of law, *see* Code, Courts Article, § 3-2A-05 (a).

(c) **Defendant.** "Defendant" means the health care provider.

(d) **Director.** "Director" means the Director of the Health Care Alternative Dispute Resolution Office.

(e) **Plaintiff.** "Plaintiff" means the party making a claim against a health care provider. (Amended Nov. 8, 2005, effective Jan. 1, 2006.)

Source. — This Rule is new.

Order constituted award. — Order by the panel chair of the Health Claims Alternative Dispute Resolution Office which dismissed plaintiffs' claims was a final determination which clearly disposed of the claims and thus, constituted an "award." Salvagno v. Frew, 388 Md. 605, 881 A.2d 660 (2005).

Rule 15-403. Action to reject health claims award or assessment of costs.

(a) **Rejection of award or costs.** A party may reject for any reason an award, the assessment of costs under an award, or both. An action to reject filed pursuant to this Rule constitutes the notice of rejection required by Code, Courts Article, § 3-2A-06 (a). An action to reject shall not impair the award or the assessment of costs as to any party before the arbitration panel who has not rejected the award or the assessment of costs and is not named as a defendant in the action.

(b) **Plaintiff's action to reject.** (1) How commenced. The plaintiff shall commence an action to reject by filing a complaint with a circuit court or with any other court of competent jurisdiction. The complaint shall (A) identify the award and state whether the award, the assessment of costs, or both are being rejected, (B) state that the plaintiff is the rejecting party, and (C) identify all defendants as to whom the plaintiff rejects the award, the assessment of the costs, or both. If the complaint is filed in a circuit court, it shall comply with Rules 2-303 through 2-305. The complaint may state that the amount of damages sought is more than the required jurisdictional amount, but the amount sought shall not be stated.

Committee note. — *See Ott v. Kaiser Georgetown Health Plan,* 309 Md. 641 (1987), recognizing that an action to reject an award may be filed in a United States District Court.

(2) Time for filing. The complaint shall be filed within the later of (A) 30 days after the Director serves the award or the assessment of costs or (B) ten days after service by the chair of the panel or the Director, whichever first occurs, of the disposition of a timely-filed application for modification or correction. A complaint filed before the disposition of an application does not deprive the panel of jurisdiction to dispose of the application. The action in the circuit court shall not proceed until the date a copy of the disposition is filed in that court. All time periods provided for in this Rule shall begin to run from that date.

(c) **Defendant's action to reject.** (1) How commenced. The defendant shall commence an action to reject an award, the assessment of costs, or both by filing a notice of action to reject with the Director. The notice shall (A) identify the award, state whether the award, the assessment of costs, or both are being rejected, (B) state that the defendant is the rejecting party, (C) identify all plaintiffs as to whom the defendant rejects the award, the assessment of costs, or both, and (D) allege that the monetary amount being rejected is more than the required jurisdictional amount.

(2) Time for filing. The notice shall be filed within the later of (A) 30 days after the Director serves the award or the assessment of costs or (B) ten days after service by the chair of the panel or the Director, whichever first occurs, of the disposition of a timely-filed application for modification or correction. A notice filed before the disposition of an application does not deprive the panel of jurisdiction to consider the application.

(3) Plaintiff to file complaint. When a defendant files a notice of action to reject, a plaintiff who desires to contest the action or reject the award or the assessment of costs shall file a complaint against any rejecting defendants and any defendants as to whom the plaintiff rejects the award or the assessment of costs. The complaint shall be filed within the later of (A) 30 days after service of the notice or (B) ten days after service by the chair of the panel or the Director, whichever first occurs, of the disposition of a timely-filed application for modification or correction. The complaint shall (A) identify the award and whether the award, the assessment of costs, or both are being rejected, (B) state who rejects the award, the assessment of costs, or both, and (C) identify all parties against whom the award, the assessment of costs, or both are rejected. If the complaint is filed in a circuit court, it shall comply with Rules 2-303 through 2-305. The complaint may state that the amount of damages sought is more than the required jurisdictional amount, but the amount sought shall not be stated.

(d) **Service.** (1) Of complaint. The plaintiff shall serve the complaint upon each defendant named in the complaint, the Director, and all other parties to the arbitration proceeding. Service upon the defendant shall be either in the manner prescribed by Rule 2-121 or, if the defendant was represented by counsel in the arbitration proceeding, on counsel by certified mail, return receipt requested. Service upon all other parties to the arbitration proceeding and upon the Director shall be in the manner prescribed by Rule 1-321.

(2) Of notice of action to reject. The defendant shall serve a copy of the notice to reject upon the plaintiff and all other parties to the arbitration proceeding. Service upon the plaintiff shall be either in the manner prescribed by Rule 2-121 or, if the plaintiff was represented by counsel in the arbitration proceeding, on counsel by certified mail, return receipt requested. Service upon all other parties to the arbitration proceeding shall be in the manner prescribed by Rule 1-321.

(e) **Modification, correction, or vacation of award or assessment of costs by court.** (1) Motion; when filed. In an action to reject, an allegation that an award or the assessment of costs is improper because of any ground stated in Code, Courts Article, § 3-223 (b), § 3-224 (b) (1), (2), (3), or (4), or § 3-2A-05 (h) shall be made by motion filed at least 30 days before trial, or the ground is waived. The court shall decide the motion before trial.

(2) Modification of award. If the court finds that a condition stated in Code, Courts Article, § 3-223 (b) exists, or that the award or assessment of costs was not appropriately modified in accordance with Code, Courts Article, § 3-2A-05 (h), it shall modify or correct the award or the assessment of costs. If the

rejecting party still desires to proceed with judicial review, the modified or corrected award or the assessment of costs shall be substituted for the original award.

(3) Vacation of award. If the court finds that a condition stated in Code, Courts Article, § 3-224 (b) (1), (2), (3), or (4) exists, it shall vacate the award or the assessment of costs, and trial of the case shall proceed as if there had been no award or assessment of costs.

Cross references. — *See* Code, Courts Article, § 3-2A-06 (c).

Source. — This Rule is in part derived from Rules BY2 through BY4 and in part new.

University of Baltimore Law Review. — For article, "The Health Care Malpractice Claims Statute: Maryland's Response to the Medical Malpractice Crisis," see 10 U. Balt. L. Rev. 74 (1980).

For article, "Health Claims Arbitration in Maryland: The Experiment Has Failed," see 14 U. Balt. L. Rev. 481 (1985).

For article, "Judicial Review of Health Claims Arbitration Awards: Practice and Pitfalls," see 17 U. Balt. L. Rev. 433 (1989).

Notice requirements mandatory. — Section 3-2A-06 of the Courts Article and former Rule BY2 require that the notice of rejection "must" be filed and the notice of action "shall" be filed within the prescribed time period. These sections imply that the notice requirements are mandatory, and that some sanction may be imposed for noncompliance therewith. Tranen v. Aziz, 59 Md. App. 528, 476 A.2d 1170 (1984), aff'd, 304 Md. 605, 500 A.2d 636 (1985).

Action to nullify arbitration award is two-step process: first, a notice of the action must be filed with the clerk of the court within 30 days after the award is served on the rejecting party; and second, a declaration must be filed setting forth the allegations to be proved entitling the aggrieved party to relief. Tranen v. Aziz, 304 Md. 605, 500 A.2d 636 (1985).

Action to nullify not notice. — Where an action to nullify is concerned only with the panel's allocation of costs, the action to nullify is not the notice of the action created by section (a) of former Rule BY2. State of Md. Cent. Collection Unit v. Gettes, 321 Md. 671, 584 A.2d 689 (1991).

When defendant files notice of action to nullify award in jurisdiction different from that in which plaintiff files declaration, the filing of the declaration with a certified copy of the defendant's notice of action amounts to an automatic consolidation of the two cases which, once the venue question is settled, divests the court in which defendants' notice of action was filed of venue; nothing in the statute or the rules required the defen-

dants to move to consolidate their filing with the plaintiff's case in another jurisdiction. Teimourian v. Spence, 59 Md. App. 74, 474 A.2d 919, cert. denied, 301 Md. 43 481 A.2d 802 (1984).

Action to nullify and complaint in a single document. — The requirement that judicial proceedings be commenced by filing an action to nullify, under § 3-2A-06 (b) of the Courts Article, may be met, by a single document which includes both the notice of action to nullify and the complaint required by this Subtitle, if it complies with the time, information, and service requirements of former Rule BY2 and former Rule BY4. Ott v. Kaiser-Georgetown Community Health Plan, Inc., 309 Md. 641, 526 A.2d 46 (1987).

Realignment of parties. — Former Maryland Rules of Procedure, BY2, BY3 and BY4, in conjunction with the Maryland Health Care Malpractice Claims Act (§ 3-2A-01 et seq. of the Courts Article), force a realignment of the parties to the adversarial positions in a traditional malpractice court action in those arbitrated cases in which the health care provider is aggrieved by the award on the merits, files a notice of rejection, and is required by § 3-2A-06 (b) (1) of the Courts Article to file an action in court to nullify the award. State of Md. Cent. Collection Unit v. Gettes, 321 Md. 671, 584 A.2d 689 (1991).

Miscaption on notice of action to nullify Health Claims Arbitration award held not misleading. — See Cherry v. Seymour Bros., 306 Md. 84, 507 A.2d 613 (1986).

Use of photocopy permissible. — In the absence of any provision in either Subtitle 2A of Title 3 of the Courts Article or the Maryland Rules prohibiting the use of a photocopy to institute a court action, the use of such a photocopy did not warrant dismissal. Cherry v. Seymour Bros., 306 Md. 84, 507 A.2d 613 (1986).

Failure to file declaration within 30-day period prescribed by subsection 1 of section a of former Rule BY4 does not require dismissal of the court action and automatic nullification of the arbitration award regardless of the circumstances. Golub v. Spivey, 70 Md. App. 147, 520 A.2d 394, cert. denied, 310 Md. 2, 526 A.2d 954 (1987).

Mere misappellation of a pleading should not ordinarily provide the predicate for a dismissal without leave to amend. Osheroff v. Chestnut Lodge, Inc., 62 Md. App. 519, 490 A.2d 720, cert. denied, 304 Md. 163, 497 A.2d 1163 (1985).

Failure to caption properly "Notice of Action to Nullify" so as to indicate that it was being filed in circuit court instead of with the Health Claims Arbitration Office was not fatal to the plaintiffs in a medical malpractice suit, where the notice to nullify, the notice of rejection, and the declaration were all filed at the same time and the declaration stated that the proceeding was in the circuit court. Brothers v. Sinai Hosp., 63 Md. App. 235, 492 A.2d 656 (1985), aff'd, 306 Md. 84, 507 A.2d 613 (1986).

Cited in Salvagno v. Frew, 388 Md. 605, 881 A.2d 660 (2005).

CHAPTER 500. INJUNCTIONS.

Rule 15-501. Injunctions — Definitions.

The following definitions apply in the rules in this Chapter:

(a) **Injunction.** "Injunction" means an order mandating or prohibiting a specified act.

(b) **Preliminary injunction.** "Preliminary injunction" means an injunction granted after opportunity for a full adversary hearing on the propriety of its issuance but before a final determination of the merits of the action.

(c) **Temporary restraining order.** "Temporary restraining order" means an injunction granted without opportunity for a full adversary hearing on the propriety of its issuance.

Source. — This Rule is derived from former Rule BB70.

Maryland Law Review. — For article, "Survey of Developments in Maryland Law, 1983-84," see 44 Md. L. Rev. 323 (1985).

Jurisdiction. — Court acquired jurisdiction to issue a prejudgment attachment-type interlocutory injunction based on the substantial evidence offered at the hearing which showed a substantial likelihood that: (1) the defendant had committed fraud, (2) he would dispose of assets before judgment and (3) the assets were fraudulently obtained; notwithstanding the defendant's opposition, as opposed to consent, to the injunction. Teferi v. Dupont Plaza Assocs., 77 Md. App. 566, 551 A.2d 477 (1989).

Considerations in entry of interlocutory injunction. — Trial court should consider four factors in determining whether entry of an interlocutory injunction is proper: 1) The likelihood that the plaintiff will succeed on the merits; 2) the "balance of convenience" determined by whether greater injury would be done to the defendant by granting the injunction than would result from its refusal; 3) whether plaintiff will suffer irreparable injury unless the injunction is granted; and 4) the public interest. Teferi v. Dupont Plaza Assocs., 77 Md. App. 566, 551 A.2d 477 (1989).

Prisoners' grievances not subject of Rules. — In the light of the passage of the Inmate Grievance Commission Act, the Court of Appeals finds it to have been the legislative intent that prisoners' grievances, even when involving constitutional rights, are not to be the subject of § 3-401 et seq. of the Courts Article, or former Rules BB70-BB80. State v. McCray, 267 Md. 111, 297 A.2d 265 (1972).

Order denying motion to stay Human Relations Commission decision. — Order of the circuit court denying motion to stay a decision of the Commission on Human Relations was not an "injunction" which could be appealed, and no party could be held in contempt for violating the order. LOOC, Inc. v. Kohli, 347 Md. 258, 701 A.2d 92 (1997).

Existence of some right which will be irreparably injured is prerequisite. — The mere existence of an injury, even if irreparable, is no guarantee that injunctive relief will issue. The existence of some right, which will be irreparably injured, is a prerequisite to the extraordinary relief of an injunction. Anne Arundel County v. Whitehall Venture, 39 Md. App. 197, 384 A.2d 780 (1978).

Mandatory or affirmative injunction should be issued with caution. — Although a mandatory or affirmative injunction should be issued with caution, and is ordinarily restricted to cases where adequate redress at law is not afforded, or where the injury is not compensable in damages, and in weighing the propriety of issuing it, a court should consider the relative convenience and inconvenience which will result to the parties from granting or refusing this form of injunctive relief, the issuance of a mandatory injunction may be peculiarly appropriate, as in this instance, for the erection of a fence. Maryland Trust Co. v. Tulip Realty Co., 220 Md. 399, 153 A.2d 275 (1959).

Under balance of convenience test, the benefits to plaintiff must be equal to or outweigh potential harm which defendant may incur if injunction is granted. Rowe v. C & P Tel. Co., 56 Md. App. 23, 466 A.2d 538 (1983).

Injunction restraining county from implementing charter section permitted. — Granting preliminary injunction to restrain county from implementing or enforcing charter section prohibiting county governments from purchasing and contracting for telephone services from certain company unless certain subscribers included was not clearly erroneous, arbitrary or capricious. Rowe v. C & P Tel. Co., 56 Md. App. 23, 466 A.2d 538 (1983).

Interlocutory injunction to prevent franchisor from terminating agreement expired, by operation of law, when judgment absolute was entered so that there was no valid restraining order in effect against franchisor, and franchisor could not be found in contempt. GMC v. Miller Buick, Inc., 56 Md. App. 374, 467 A.2d 1064 (1983), cert. denied, 299 Md. 136, 472 A.2d 999 (1984).

Preliminary injunction denial not error. — Voter was not entitled to the injunctive relief that the voter sought and which the trial court denied in a case where the voter received the voter's absentee ballot the evening of the day that administrative regulations dictated that the ballot had to be mailed and the voter waited until the next day, one day late, to mail the ballot; the voter did not have to be accommodated for not timely returning the voter's ballot, as it was necessary not to count noncompliant votes, as opposed to compliant votes, in order to safeguard the election process. Fritszche v. Md. State Bd. of Elections, 397 Md. 331, 916 A.2d 1015 (2007).

Appeal from interlocutory injunction not moot. — Although the appeal from an ex parte injunction is moot, the appeal from an interlocutory injunction is not. State Comm'n on Human Relations v. Suburban Hosp., 113 Md. App. 62, 686 A.2d 706 (1996).

Where property owners sought an injunction to enforce a restrictive covenant they had previously agreed to with a neighboring life care center, they only had to make the showing necessary to obtain specific performance, and did not have to prove irreparable injury. Chestnut Real Estate P'ship v. Huber, 148 Md. App. 190, 811 A.2d 389 (2002).

Quoted in Bond v. Slavin, 157 Md. App. 340, 851 A.2d 598 (2004); In re Kimmer, 392 Md. 251, 896 A.2d 1006 (2006); Motor Vehicle Admin. v. Baptist, 185 Md. App. 56, 968 A.2d 638 (2009).

Cited in Four Star Enters. Ltd. Partnership v. Council of Carousel Ctr. Condominium, Inc., 132 Md. App. 551, 752 A.2d 1272 (2000); Vu v. Allied Foot & Ankle, P.C., 180 Md. App. 663, 952 A.2d 379 (2008).

Rule 15-502. Injunctions — General provisions.

(a) **Exception to applicability — Labor disputes.** Rules 15-501 through 15-505 do not modify or supersede Code, Labor and Employment Article, Title 4, Subtitle 3 or affect the prerequisites for obtaining, or the jurisdiction to grant, injunctions under those Code sections.

(b) **Issuance at any stage.** Subject to the rules in this Chapter, the court, at any stage of an action and at the instance of any party or on its own initiative, may grant an injunction upon the terms and conditions justice may require.

(c) **Adequate remedy at law.** The court may not deny an injunction solely because the party seeking it has an adequate remedy in damages unless the adverse party has filed a bond with security that the court finds adequate to provide for the payment of all damages and costs that the adverse party might be adjudged to pay by reason of the alleged wrong.

(d) **Not binding without notice.** An injunction is not binding on a person until that person has been personally served with it or has received actual notice of it by any means.

(e) **Form and scope.** The reasons for issuance or denial of an injunction shall be stated in writing or on the record. An order granting an injunction shall (1) be in writing (2) be specific in terms, and (3) describe in reasonable detail, and not by reference to the complaint or other document, the act sought to be mandated or prohibited.

(f) **Modification or dissolution.** A party or any person affected by a preliminary or a final injunction may move for modification or dissolution of an injunction. (Amended Nov. 12, 2003, effective Jan. 1, 2004.)

Cross references. — For enforcement of an injunction, *see* Rule 2-648.

Source. — This Rule is derived from former Rules BB71, 76, 77, 78, and 79.

Effect of amendments. — The 2003 amendment, in (e), inserted the first sentence, substituted "(2)" for "or on the record (2) set forth the reasons for issuance (3)" and "(3)" for "(4)."

Rule does not interfere with court's power to issue injunctions. — While former Rule BB71 did not govern injunctions issued in divorce, alimony, support of wife or child, custody of child or annulment of marriage actions, it in no way purports to interfere with the right of a court to issue such injunctions if otherwise authorized. Winston v. Winston, 290 Md. 641, 431 A.2d 1330 (1981).

Legal remedy must be fully adequate. — To justify refusal of equitable relief on the ground that the appellant has a remedy at law, the legal remedy must be fully adequate and complete. The remedy at law which precludes relief in equity must be as practical and efficient to the ends of justice and its prompt administration as the remedy in equity. State v. Ficker, 266 Md. 500, 295 A.2d 231 (1972).

An "adequate remedy at law" must be adequate; for if at law it falls short of what the party is entitled to, that founds a jurisdiction in equity. And it must be complete, obtaining the full end and justice of the case. It must reach the whole mischief, and secure the whole right of the party in a perfect manner, at the present time and in the future; otherwise, equity will interfere and give such relief and aid as the exigency of the particular case may require. The jurisdiction of a court of equity is, therefore, sometimes concurrent with the jurisdiction of a court of law, it is sometimes exclusive of it; and it is sometimes auxiliary to it. State v. Ficker, 266 Md. 500, 295 A.2d 231 (1972).

Adequate remedy at law in the form of damages is not an absolute bar to injunctive relief. Anne Arundel County v. Whitehall Venture, 39 Md. App. 197, 384 A.2d 780 (1978).

Injunctive relief against commission of criminal acts. — Equity will enjoin criminal acts if such operate to the injury of complain-

ant's property rights or cause him pecuniary harm for which there is no adequate legal remedy. State v. Ficker, 266 Md. 500, 295 A.2d 231 (1972).

Where acts complained of are violations of the criminal law, courts of equity will not on that ground alone interfere by injunction to prevent their commission. Former Rule BB76, however, does not preclude injunctive relief against the commission of criminal acts which, unless enjoined, would operate to cause an irreparable injury to property or rights of a pecuniary nature. If criminal offenses are primarily and essentially an injury to property, preventive relief may be granted within the same limits as where the element of criminality is entirely absent. In such a case the court does not interfere to prevent the commission of crime, although that may incidentally result, but it exerts its force to protect individual property from destruction. State v. Ficker, 266 Md. 500, 295 A.2d 231 (1972).

Former § 98, Article 16, held not to justify the continuing of an injunction, since the evidence showed that the defendant had property in this State ample to meet any damages recovered. Bartlett v. Moyers, 88 Md. 715, 42 A. 204 (1898).

General contract creditor held not entitled to injunction. — Creditor, before judgment, who became such under a general contract, was not entitled to injunction or to have receiver appointed. Perlmutter v. Minskoff, 196 Md. 99, 75 A.2d 129 (1950).

Exclusive distribution contracts enforceable by injunction. — Exclusive distribution contracts are a recognized subject for enforcement by injunction. Plaintiff in the instant case was entitled to relief by injunction and to accounting for damages for sales made in violation of the contract. Foster-Porter Enters., Inc. v. De Mare, 198 Md. 20, 81 A.2d 325 (1951).

Jurisdiction to grant injunction on account of fraud. — Even if appellee could have sued appellant at law for fraud in view of former § 98, Article 16, the jurisdiction of equity to grant an injunction on account of such fraud was not affected. Michael v. Rigler, 142 Md. 125, 120 A. 382 (1923).

Injunctions against frivolous litigants. — Trial courts are authorized by (b) to issue a pre-filing order without the necessity of a complaint or motion. A pre-filing order is a sua sponte injunction and, if properly issued, is a remedy available to a Maryland court to control the actions of a vexatious or frivolous litigant. Riffin v. Circuit Court for Balt. County, 190 Md. App. 11, 985 A.2d 612 (2010).

Pre-filing order declaring appellant a frivolous litigant and requiring him to seek leave from the administrative judge before filing further pleadings was a sua sponte injunction authorized by (b) and thus was appealable under § 12-303(3)(i) of the Courts Article. Riffin v. Circuit Court for Balt. County, 190 Md. App. 11, 985 A.2d 612 (2010).

Intent. — See Conner v. Groh, 90 Md. 674, 45 A. 1024 (1900).

Former § 98, Article 16, was intended to reach the class of cases in which injunction or mandamus had been refused because the plaintiff could be compensated in damages in suits at law. Universal Realty Corp. v. Felser, 179 Md. 635, 22 A.2d 448 (1941); Frederick County Nat'l Bank v. Shafer, 87 Md. 54, 39 A. 320 (1898).

Applicable to cases where damages, not debt, are involved. — Former § 98, Article 16, related to cases where damages, as contradistinguished from debt, were involved. Frederick County Nat'l Bank v. Shafer, 87 Md. 54, 39 A. 320 (1898); Conner v. Groh, 90 Md. 674, 45 A. 1024 (1900).

Hearing and burden of proof. — Former § 98, Article 16, was not intended to be applicable on demurrer, but only after such hearing as might make it appear to the court that the defendants, in a given case, could respond to damages, or could give a bond, and that such relief would be adequate. The burden is on the defendants in this respect. Universal Realty Corp. v. Felser, 179 Md. 635, 22 A.2d 448 (1941).

Remedy at law held clearly inadequate. — Where illegal posting of political campaign signs in inordinate numbers in direct violation of a county ordinance caused irreparable injury to the county's rights of a pecuniary nature for which loss the criminal sanction was plainly inadequate, and where relief sought by the county — removal of the remaining illegal signs at the posting party's own expense, reimbursement for expenses previously incurred in removing the signs, and damages for injury to its property — would not have accrued to the county from successful criminal prosecution, the remedy at law was plainly inadequate. State v. Ficker, 266 Md. 500, 295 A.2d 231 (1972).

Injunction not embraced in prayer. — Former § 89 of Article 16, from which former Rule BB77 was derived, cured any defect arising out of an injunction not being embraced in the prayer for that writ. Board of County Sch. Comm'rs v. Board of County Sch. Comm'rs, 77 Md. 283, 26 A. 115 (1893); Supreme Lodge v. Simering, 88 Md. 276, 40 A. 723 (1898); B & O R.R. v. Silbereisen, 121 Md. 407, 88 A. 252, 89 A. 102 (1913).

Maryland Rule 15-502(b) allows the court, on its own initiative, at any stage in the proceedings, to grant an injunction upon the terms and conditions justice may require. Eller Media Co. v. Montgomery County, 143 Md. App. 562, 795 A.2d 728 (2002), cert. denied, 369 Md. 573, 801 A.2d 1033 (2002).

Issue and continuance of injunction upheld. — See Horner v. Nitsch, 103 Md. 498, 63 A. 1052 (1906).

Requiring injunction bond of county. — An appeal involving the right of the chancellor to require an injunction bond of a county was dismissed on other grounds, and the matter not decided in Montgomery County v. Maryland-Washington Metro. Dist., 200 Md. 525, 92 A.2d 350 (1952).

Role of court in granting injunctive relief. — It is not the role of the court in issuing an order granting injunctive relief to clarify hypothetical shades of meaning which the drafters of a regulation did not see fit to address. Chesapeake Outdoor Enters., Inc. v. Mayor of Baltimore, 89 Md. App. 54, 597 A.2d 503 (1991).

Trial court did not err in granting the cable television provider's motion to vacate a permanent injunction, the lifting of which allowed the cable television provider to collect future late fees in accordance with a law that the Maryland General Assembly recently enacted; the trial court was authorized to so act in order to comply with the new law, § 14-1315 of the Commercial Law Article, that provided for a rate other than that in art. III, § 57 of the Maryland Constitution, and the state's highest court of review, in coming to that conclusion, was authorized to pass on considering the cable customers' constitutional claim, as that claim was not raised in the trial court. Burch v. United Cable TV of Balt. Ltd. P'ship, 391 Md. 687, 895 A.2d 980 (2006).

Injunctive decree must not be broader than issue raised by pleadings. Rocks v. Brosius, 241 Md. 612, 217 A.2d 531 (1966).

Order which lacks specific terms and reasonable detail is too vague, too broad and failed to conform with the mandatory requirements of section a of former Rule BB78. Franzen v. Dubinok, 45 Md. App. 728, 415 A.2d 621 (1980), aff'd, 290 Md. 65, 427 A.2d 1002 (1981).

Order to restore land to original topography held too vague and overbroad. — An order requiring a party to restore land to its original topography, when there was no evidence in the record as to what that topography was and how the party is to comply, was too vague and overbroad to comply with former Rule BB78. Joy v. Anne Arundel County, 52 Md. App. 653, 451 A.2d 1237 (1982).

Scope of injunction in trade secret cases. — For a discussion of the two different American views as to the scope of an injunction in trade secret cases, see Space Aero Prods. Co. v. R.E. Darling Co., 238 Md. 93, 208 A.2d 74, cert. denied, 382 U.S. 843, 86 S. Ct. 77, 15 L. Ed. 2d 83 (1965).

Punishment for contempt where terms of injunction not specific and definite. — See Rocks v. Brosius, 241 Md. 612, 217 A.2d 531 (1966).

There may be remand for revision of a decree to comply with former Rule BB78 without upsetting effect of decree. — A matter may be remanded for revision of a decree to comply with the requirements of section a of former Rule BB78 without upsetting the effect of the decree. Arundel Supply Corp. v. Cason, 265 Md. 371, 289 A.2d 585 (1972).

Injunction held improper. — Trial court erred in enjoining automobile manufacturer from establishing a new dealership in proximity of existing dealer, where, although the existing dealer could lose a portion of its business without the injunction, the new dealership was certain to lose all of its business with the injunction in place, and the balance of hardships favored the new dealership. Antwerpen Dodge, Ltd. v. Herb Gordon Auto World, Inc., 117 Md. App. 290, 699 A.2d 1209 (1997).

Trial court erred in granting interlocutory injunction enjoining automobile manufacturer from establishing a new dealership in proximity of existing dealer, where existing dealer failed to demonstrate a strong likelihood it would be entitled to a permanent injunction based on § 15-207(d)(2) of the Transportation Code. Antwerpen Dodge, Ltd. v. Herb Gordon Auto World, Inc., 117 Md. App. 290, 699 A.2d 1209 (1997).

Trial court did not abuse its discretion by granting members of a homeowners association's board of directors a permanent injunction restraining a homeowner from verbally harassing them, communicating with them by mail, e-mail, or phone, or disrupting their meetings by using obscenities or loud and antagonistic tones, as the evidence showed a pattern of obscene and harassing communications from the homeowner to the members and his threatening and disruptive behavior against them. Davidson v. Seneca Crossing Section II Homeowner's Ass'n, 187 Md. App. 601, 979 A.2d 260 (2009).

Process improper. — Process employed by the trial court in staying a statutorily mandated suspension of the driver's license and allowing the driver to participate in the interlock program was improper, because the trial court issued a permanent injunction after an unrecorded, 20 minute telephonic hearing, without affording the Maryland Department of Transportation, Motor Vehicle Administration an opportunity for a trial on the merits, and without providing a basis for its ruling, as required by (e). Motor Vehicle Admin. v. Baptist, 185 Md. App. 56, 968 A.2d 638 (2009).

Temporary injunction properly dissolved. — Where, even accepting petitioner's allegations that the actions of the respondents in terminating his employment were arbitrary, capricious and without cause as true, his bill, nevertheless, failed to show that he would suffer irreparable injury, and the grievance procedure available under the Maryland Department of Personnel provided an adequate remedy, the temporary injunction was properly dissolved. Coster v. Department of Personnel, 36 Md. App. 523, 373 A.2d 1287, cert. denied, 281 Md. 735 (1977).

Cited in Sinclair v. State, 199 Md. App. 130, 20 A.3d 192 (2011).

Rule 15-503. Bond — Temporary restraining order and preliminary injunction.

(a) **Generally.** Except as otherwise provided in this Rule, a court may not issue a temporary restraining order or preliminary injunction unless a bond has been filed. The bond shall be in an amount approved by the court for the payment of any damages to which a party enjoined may be entitled as a result of the injunction.

(b) **State of Maryland.** If the injunction is sought by the State of Maryland, a political subdivision of the State of Maryland, or an officer or agency of the State or subdivision, the court may dispense with the requirement of a bond and shall do so when required by law.

(c) **Waiver.** On request, the court may dispense with the requirement of surety or other security for a bond if it is satisfied that (1) the person is unable to provide surety or other security for the bond, (2) substantial injustice would result if an injunction did not issue, and (3) the case is one of extraordinary hardship. The request shall be supported by an affidavit or testimony under oath stating the grounds for entitlement to the waiver.

Cross references. — Title 1, Chapter 400.
Source. — This Rule is derived from former Rule BB75.

Compliance with Rules required. — Equity courts should be especially alert to see that the parties comply with the applicable Rules before an ex parte injunction is ordered. Saunders v. Stradley, 25 Md. App. 85, 333 A.2d 604 (1975).

Motion to assess damages under bond properly denied. — Temporary restraining order (TRO) regarding a noncompete provision in an employment agreement was issued under the circuit court's general equity power and Rule 15-504, instead of under the Maryland Anti-Injunction Act, § 4-301 et seq. of the Labor and Employment Article. Therefore, any remedy by the employee was pursuant to this Rule, and the circuit court did not abuse its discretion by denying the employee's motion to assess damages under the bond posted by the employer in support of the TRO. Vu v. Allied Foot & Ankle, P.C., 180 Md. App. 663, 952 A.2d 379 (2008).

Cited in King v. State, 400 Md. 419, 929 A.2d 169 (2007); County Comm'rs v. Forty West Builders, Inc., 178 Md. App. 328, 941 A.2d 1181 (2008); Wincopia Farm, LP v. Goozman, 188 Md. App. 519, 982 A.2d 868 (2009), cert. denied, 412 Md. 496, 988 A.2d 1010, 2010 Md. LEXIS 68 (2010).

Rule 15-504. Temporary restraining order.

(a) **Standard for granting.** A temporary restraining order may be granted only if it clearly appears from specific facts shown by affidavit or other statement under oath that immediate, substantial, and irreparable harm will result to the person seeking the order before a full adversary hearing can be held on the propriety of a preliminary or final injunction.

(b) **Without notice.** A temporary restraining order may be granted without written or oral notice only if the applicant or the applicant's attorney certifies to the court in writing, and the court finds, that specified efforts commensurate with the circumstances have been made to give notice. Before ruling, the judge may communicate informally with other parties and any other person against whom the order is sought or their attorneys.

(c) **Contents and duration.** In addition to complying with Rule 15-502 (e), the order shall (1) contain the date and hour of issuance; (2) define the harm that the court finds will result if the temporary restraining order does not issue; (3) state the basis for the court's finding that the harm will be irreparable; (4) state that a party or any person affected by the order may apply for a modification or dissolution of the order on two days' notice, or such shorter notice as the court may prescribe, to the party who obtained the order; and (5) set forth an expiration date, which shall be not later than ten days after issuance for a resident and not later than 35 days after issuance for a nonresident. The order shall be promptly filed with the clerk. On motion filed pursuant to Rule 1-204, the court by order may extend the expiration date for no more than one additional like period, unless the person against whom the order is directed consents to an extension for a longer period. The order shall state the reasons for the extension.

(d) **Service; binding effect.** A temporary restraining order shall be served promptly on the person to whom it is directed, but it shall be binding on that person upon receipt of actual notice of it by any means.

(e) **Denial.** If the court denies a temporary restraining order, the clerk shall note the denial by docket entry in accordance with Rule 2-601 (b).

(f) **Modification or dissolution.** A party or person affected by the order may apply for modification or dissolution of the order on two days' notice to the party who obtained the temporary restraining order, or on such shorter notice as the court may prescribe. The court shall proceed to hear and determine the application at the earliest possible time. The party who obtained the temporary restraining order has the burden of showing that it should be continued. (Amended Nov. 12, 2003, effective Jan. 1, 2004.)

Source. — This Rule is derived from former Rules BB72, 73, and 79, and the 1987 version of Fed.R.Civ.P. 65 (b).

Effect of amendments. — The 2003 amendment changed the Source note to reflect the corresponding federal rule as of the date of adoption of the Maryland Rule. The amendment inserted "the 1987 version of" preceeding "Fed. R. Civ. P. 65 (b)".

University of Baltimore Law Review. — For article, "New Balance in the Rights of Creditors and Debtors: The Effect on Maryland Law," see 2 U. Balt. L. Rev. 236 (1973).

Compliance with Rules required. — Equity courts should be especially alert to see that the parties comply with the applicable Rules before an ex parte injunction is ordered. Saunders v. Stradley, 25 Md. App. 85, 333 A.2d 604 (1975).

Orders issued under former Rule BB72 are intended to suspend action until an opportunity is afforded the defendants to answer and defend. Harford County Educ. Ass'n v. Board of Educ., 281 Md. 574, 380 A.2d 1041 (1977).

Restrictions on injunctions in labor disputes. — Former Article 100, §§ 63 to 75 (now see § 4-301 et seq. of the Labor and Employment Article), places restrictions on the power of equity courts to grant injunctions in labor disputes. District 1199E, Nat'l Union of Hosp. & Health Care Employees v. Johns Hopkins Hosp., 293 Md. 343, 444 A.2d 448 (1982).

Since the Maryland Anti-Injunction Act only covers "labor disputes," ex parte injunctions still may be obtained in proceedings not covered by the Act; unlike an injunction obtained pursuant to the Act, ex parte injunctions can be obtained virtually immediately, and without extensive procedural prerequisites. Dis-

trict 1199E, Nat'l Union of Hosp. & Health Care Employees v. Johns Hopkins Hosp., 293 Md. 343, 444 A.2d 448 (1982).

Temporary restraining order filed under Rule, not Maryland Anti-Injunction Act Inapplicable. — Temporary restraining order regarding a noncompete provision in an employment agreement was issued under the circuit court's general equity power and this Rule, instead of under the Maryland Anti-Injunction Act, § 4-301 et seq. of the Labor and Employment Article. Vu v. Allied Foot & Ankle, P.C., 180 Md. App. 663, 952 A.2d 379 (2008).

Evidence. — In granting an injunction against a contemplated use of property which is not unlawful per se, the chancellor should require the plaintiff to present to the court strong prima facie evidence of the facts upon which his equity rests, and he must prove every material allegation by a preponderance of the evidence. Air Lift, Ltd. v. Board of County Comm'rs, 262 Md. 368, 278 A.2d 244 (1971).

In hearings under § 3-815(c)(2)(i) of the Courts Article and Rule 11-112(a)(2), appellant mothers were entitled to present testimonial evidence to contest the allegations in appellee county agencies' petitions for orders for emergency shelter care; other sections of the Maryland Code, such as §§ 4-504.1 and 4-505 of the Family Law Article and subsection (a) of this Rule, made clear the preference for evidentiary hearings. In re Damien F., 182 Md. App. 546, 958 A.2d 402 (2008).

Where terms of injunction are not specific and definite, a defendant will not be punished for contempt for noncompliance. Harford County Educ. Ass'n v. Board of Educ., 281 Md. 574, 380 A.2d 1041 (1977).

Collateral attack on violated injunction not permitted. — A party enjoined may not violate the terms of an injunction and then attack the injunction collaterally in a contempt proceeding, civil or criminal. Harford County Educ. Ass'n v. Board of Educ., 281 Md. 574, 380 A.2d 1041 (1977).

Temporary restraining order improperly issued. — Temporary restraining order of circuit court requiring compliance with administrative agency decision was not issued in accordance with the rules where the appellant was not given an opportunity for a hearing, and where the order did not contain an expiration date. LOOC, Inc. v. Kohli, 347 Md. 258, 701 A.2d 92 (1997).

Denial of temporary restraining order and preliminary injunction related to late absentee ballot filing — Voter was not entitled to the injunctive relief that the voter sought and which the trial court denied in a case where the voter received the voter's absentee ballot the evening of the day that administrative regulations dictated that the ballot had to be mailed and the voter waited until the next day, one day late, to mail the ballot; the voter did not have to be accommodated for not timely returning the voter's ballot, as it was necessary not to count noncompliant votes, as opposed to compliant votes, in order to safeguard the election process. Fritszche v. Md. State Bd. of Elections, 397 Md. 331, 916 A.2d 1015 (2007).

Temporary injunction properly dissolved. — Where, even accepting petitioner's allegations that the actions of the respondents in terminating his employment were arbitrary, capricious and without cause as true, his bill, nevertheless, failed to show that he would suffer irreparable injury, and the grievance procedure available under the Maryland Department of Personnel provided an adequate remedy, the temporary injunction was properly dissolved. Coster v. Department of Personnel, 36 Md. App. 523, 373 A.2d 1287, cert. denied, 281 Md. 735 (1977).

Trial court properly struck its temporary restraining order and directed an employer to pay the workers' compensation benefits awarded by the Maryland Workers' Compensation Commission, pending the resolution of the employer's appeal, as under § 9-741 of the Labor and Employment Article, an award of workers' compensation benefits could not be stayed; Rule 7-205 was inapplicable because a stay of an order of the Commission was prohibited by law, and Md. Regs. Code tit. 15, § 09.01.24A(4) was inapplicable as it referred specifically to the delayed payment of attorneys' fees. Gleneagles, Inc. v. Hanks, 156 Md. App. 543, 847 A.2d 520 (2004), aff'd, 385 Md. 492, 869 A.2d 852 (2005).

Quoted in Four Star Enters. Ltd. Partnership v. Council of Carousel Ctr. Condominium, Inc., 132 Md. App. 551, 752 A.2d 1272 (2000); Motor Vehicle Admin. v. Baptist, 185 Md. App. 56, 968 A.2d 638 (2009).

Cited in Phyllis J. Outlaw & Assocs. v. Graham, 172 Md. App. 16, 912 A.2d 64 (2006).

Rule 15-505. Preliminary injunction.

(a) **Notice.** A court may not issue a preliminary injunction without notice to all parties and an opportunity for a full adversary hearing on the propriety of its issuance.

(b) **Consolidation with trial on merits.** Before or after commencement of the hearing on the preliminary injunction, the court may order that a trial on the merits be advanced and consolidated with the preliminary injunction hearing, so long as any right to trial by jury is preserved. (Amended Nov. 12, 2003, effective Jan. 1, 2004.)

Cross references. — Rule 2-511 (a).
Source. — This Rule is derived from former Rule BB74 and the 1987 version of Fed.R.Civ.P. 65 (a).

Effect of amendments. — The 2003 amendment changed the Source note to reflect the corresponding federal rule as of the date of adoption of the Maryland Rule. The amendment inserted "the 1987 version of" preceeding "Fed. R. Civ. P. 65 (a)".

Permanent injunction is invalid without determination on merits. National Collegiate Athletic Ass'n v. John Hopkins Univ., 301 Md. 574, 483 A.2d 1272 (1984).

Temporary restraining order improperly issued. — Temporary restraining order of circuit court requiring compliance with administrative agency decision was not issued in accordance with the rules where the appellant was not given an opportunity for a hearing, and where the order did not contain an expiration date. LOOC, Inc. v. Kohli, 347 Md. 258, 701 A.2d 92 (1997).

Mootness. — Although the appeal from an ex parte injunction is moot, the appeal from an interlocutory injunction is not. State Comm'n on Human Relations v. Suburban Hosp., 113

Md. App. 62, 686 A.2d 706 (1996).

Quoted in Motor Vehicle Admin. v. Baptist, 185 Md. App. 56, 968 A.2d 638 (2009).

Cited in Four Star Enters. Ltd. Partnership v. Council of Carousel Ctr. Condominium, Inc., 132 Md. App. 551, 752 A.2d 1272 (2000); Riffin v. Circuit Court for Balt. County, 190 Md. App. 11, 985 A.2d 612 (2010).

CHAPTER 600. JUDICIAL RELEASE.

Rule 15-601. Judicial release of individuals confined for mental disorders.

(a) **Statutory definitions.** The definitions stated in Code, Health-General Article, § 10-101 are applicable to this Rule except that in this Rule, the term "facility" includes hospitals operated by the Department of Veterans Affairs.

(b) **Applicability.** This Rule applies to petitions filed pursuant to Code, Health-General Article, § 10-805 for release from a facility.

(c) **Contents of petition.** A petition for judicial release of a patient from a facility treating or caring for patients with mental disorders shall be titled "In the Matter of _____ for the Judicial Release From _____". The petition shall comply with Rules 2-303 through 2-305 and shall set forth:

(1) the name and address of the petitioner;

(2) the name of the patient and the facility at which the patient is confined;

(3) if the petition is filed by a person other than the patient, the petitioner's relationship to the patient and a description of the interest of the petitioner in the welfare of the patient;

(4) petitioner's best information as to the date of admission of the patient to the facility;

(5) whether the admission was voluntary or involuntary;

(6) the ground upon which the release is requested, which shall be that at the time the petition is filed one of the following is true: (A) the patient has no mental disorder; or (B) if the patient has a mental disorder, the disorder does not require inpatient medical care or treatment for the protection of the patient or others;

(7) a statement to the best of the petitioner's knowledge as to whether there were previous proceedings for the judicial release of the patient and, if so, a description of the proceedings, including a docket reference and any outcome; and

(8) if a jury trial is desired, a request for jury trial in the form prescribed in Rule 2-325.

Source. — This Rule is derived from former Rule R80 c 1.

CHAPTER 700. MANDAMUS.

Rule 15-701. Mandamus.

(a) **Applicability.** This Rule applies to actions for writs of mandamus other than administrative mandamus pursuant to Title 7, Chapter 400 of these Rules or mandamus in aid of appellate jurisdiction.

(b) **Commencement of action.** An action for a writ of mandamus shall be commenced by the filing of a complaint, the form and contents of which shall comply with Rules 2-303 through 2-305. The plaintiff shall have the right to claim and prove damages, but a demand for general relief shall not be permitted.

Committee note. — Because a mandamus action is similar to an ordinary civil proceeding, the discovery rules and the Rules in Title 5 apply. Code, Courts Article, § 3-8B-02 provides: "An action for a writ of mandamus shall be tried by a jury on request of either party." This has been judicially interpreted to apply to fact questions. See *Cicala v. Disability Review Board for Prince George's County,* 288 Md. 254 (1980).

(c) **Defendant's response.** The defendant may respond to the complaint as provided in Rule 2-322 or Rule 2-323. An answer shall fully and specifically set forth all defenses upon which the defendant intends to rely.

(d) **Amendment.** Amendment of pleadings shall be in accordance with Rule 2-341.

(e) **Writ of mandamus.** (1) Contents and compliance. The writ shall be peremptory in form and shall require the defendant to perform immediately the duty sought to be enforced, unless for good cause shown the court extends the time for compliance. The writ need not recite the reasons for its issuance.

(2) Certificate of compliance. Immediately after compliance, the defendant shall file a certificate stating that all the acts commanded by the writ have been fully performed.

(3) Enforcement. Upon application by the plaintiff, the court may proceed under Rule 2-648 against a party who disobeys the writ.

(f) **Adequate remedy at law.** The existence of an adequate remedy in damages does not preclude the issuance of the writ unless the defendant establishes that property exists from which damages can be recovered or files a sufficient bond to cover all damages and costs. (Amended Nov. 8, 2005, effective Jan. 1, 2006.)

Source. — This Rule is derived from former Rules BE40, BE41, BE43, BE44, BE45, and BE46.

Effect of amendments. — The 2005 amendment, effective January 1, 2006, added (a), deleted (d), and redesignated the remaining subsections accordingly; in (b) deleted "verified" before "complaint" and added the Committee note; in (c) deleted "shall be verified and" after "answer" and "but the defendant shall not assert any defense that the defendant might have relied upon in an answer to a previous complaint for mandamus by the same plaintiff for the same relief" after "rely"; and rewrote (e)(1) without substantive change.

I. In General.
II. When Mandamus Will Issue.
III. Procedure.

I. IN GENERAL.

Editor's note. — For definition of "affidavit," see Rule 1-202 (b). As to restrictions on writ of mandamus against State or officer thereof to prevent collection of tax, see TG § 13-505.

The following sections of the Code specifically authorize application for a writ of mandamus to be made for the purposes indicated:

Article 25, § 117 — To compel county drainage district or board of drainage commissioners to levy tax or special assessment in order to remedy default in payment of bond.

State Government, § 17-103 — To officeholder when there has been an inadvertent issuance of a commission.

University of Baltimore Law Review. — For article, "State Constitutional Law for Maryland Lawyers: Judicial Relief for Violations of Rights," see 10 U. Balt. L. Rev. 102 (1980).

Nature of writ. — Mandamus, while resembling in some respects a decree in equity for specific performance, is a common law process issued for the special purpose indicated in the writ, and the relief prayed cannot be modified according to circumstances, such as under a prayer for general relief in a bill in equity. The writ of mandamus depends upon the facts, circumstances, and conditions existing at the time the petition for mandamus is filed. Town of District Heights v. County Comm'rs, 210 Md. 142, 122 A.2d 489 (1956).

Mandamus is a remedy that is based upon reasons of justice and public policy to preserve peace, order and good government, and although the writ is issued by the law courts, it may be compared to a bill in equity for specific performance. Ipes v. Board of Fire Comm'rs, 224 Md. 180, 167 A.2d 337 (1961).

Mandamus is a writ in the nature of a prerogative writ, and is an extraordinary remedy. The writ is issued by the law courts. Ipes v. Board of Fire Comm'rs, 224 Md. 180, 167 A.2d 337 (1961).

The writ of mandamus, as generally used, is to compel inferior tribunals, public officials or administrative agencies to perform their function, or perform some particular duty imposed upon them which in its nature is imperative and to the performance of which duty the party applying for the writ has a clear legal right. Criminal Injuries Comp. Bd. v. Gould, 273 Md. 486, 331 A.2d 55 (1975); Rodgers v. Washington Sub. San. Comm'n, 32 Md. App. 664, 363 A.2d 633, cert. denied, 278 Md. 738 (1976).

Alternative writs and returns abol-ished. — The old alternative writs and returns are abolished, the respondent answers the petition, the petitioner is permitted to traverse the answer, and the case proceeds in much the same manner as do other actions. Ipes v. Board of Fire Comm'rs, 224 Md. 180, 167 A.2d 337 (1961).

Cited in O'Brien v. Bd. of License Comm'rs, 199 Md. App. 563, 23 A.3d 323 (2011).

II. WHEN MANDAMUS WILL ISSUE.

Generally. — Although mandamus is not a writ ex debito justitiae but rests in the sound discretion of the court, such discretion may not be exercised arbitrarily. The discretion must be exercised under the established rules of law and if under those rules a party is entitled to the writ, it must be issued. Weber v. Zimmerman, 23 Md. 45 (1865); Hardcastle v. Maryland & D.R.R., 32 Md. 32 (1870); Brooke v. Widdicombe, 39 Md. 386 (1874); Kinlein v. Mayor of Baltimore, 118 Md. 576, 85 A. 679 (1912).

Mandamus is not a writ of right, nor is it granted as of course, but only in the sound legal discretion of the judge who directs the issuance thereof, and, in approaching the question concerning the issuance, vel non, of the writ, the courts invoke equitable principles to reach the real merits of the controversy between the parties. Ipes v. Board of Fire Comm'rs, 224 Md. 180, 167 A.2d 337 (1961).

The writ will never be granted where it is unnecessary or would work injustice or be nugatory or introduce confusion into municipal administration. Kinlein v. Mayor of Baltimore, 118 Md. 576, 85 A. 679 (1912).

The writ will not be granted if it would be nugatory, or where it would demand an abstract right but not subserve any just or useful purpose. Town of District Heights v. County Comm'rs, 210 Md. 142, 122 A.2d 489 (1956).

Where the urgency of establishing a rule of future conduct in matters of important public concern is imperative and manifest, a departure from the general rule and practice of not deciding academic questions may be justified. Board of Educ. v. Montgomery County, 237 Md. 191, 205 A.2d 202 (1964).

Mandamus will lie to remedy arbitrary abuses of discretion. State Dep't of Health v. Walker, 238 Md. 512, 209 A.2d 555 (1965).

In absence of statutory provision for hearing or review. — Judicial review can properly be sought by a petition for writ of mandamus where there is no statutory provision for hearing or review. State Dep't of

Health v. Walker, 238 Md. 512, 209 A.2d 555 (1965).

But mandamus is not proper to review nonministerial acts of public officials or agencies. State Dep't of Health v. Walker, 238 Md. 512, 209 A.2d 555 (1965).

Nor to circumvent administrative remedies. — A person cannot circumvent possible administrative remedies by simply bringing an action for mandamus. Myers v. Chief of Baltimore County Fire Bureau, 237 Md. 583, 207 A.2d 467 (1965).

A ministerial duty may be enforced by mandamus. Sudler v. Lankford, 82 Md. 142, 33 A. 455 (1895).

But a discretionary duty may not be enforced by mandamus. Devin v. Belt, 70 Md. 352, 17 A. 375 (1889).

Where acts and duties necessarily call for the exercise of judgment and discretion on the part of officials, mandamus will not lie to direct the manner in which such discretion shall be exercised. Criminal Injuries Comp. Bd. v. Gould, 273 Md. 486, 331 A.2d 55 (1975).

Appropriate where law has established no specific remedy. — Mandamus is appropriate in all cases where the law has established no specific remedy, and where in justice there ought to be one. Harwood v. Marshall, 9 Md. 83 (1856); Legg v. Mayor of Annapolis, 42 Md. 203 (1875).

Mandamus will not lie when there is an adequate remedy at law. Brown v. Bragunier, 79 Md. 234, 29 A. 7 (1894).

Petitioner must show clear legal right and imperative duty on part of defendant. — Mandamus will not issue unless petitioner shows a clear legal right in himself and a corresponding imperative duty on part of defendant. Upshur v. Mayor of Baltimore, 94 Md. 743, 51 A. 953 (1902); County Comm'rs v. Fout, 110 Md. 165, 72 A. 765 (1909); Whittle v. Munshower, 221 Md. 258, 155 A.2d 670 (1959), cert. denied, 362 U.S. 981, 80 S. Ct. 1069, 4 L. Ed. 2d (1960); Myers v. Chief of Baltimore County Fire Bureau, 237 Md. 583, 207 A.2d 467 (1965).

To be entitled to the issuance of the writ of mandamus, the relator must have a real interest in the subject matter of the suit whether it be his alone or shared by a great number of people, and the respondent must owe him, or the group of which he is a member, an imperative duty. Rodgers v. Washington Sub. San. Comm'n, 32 Md. App. 664, 363 A.2d 633, cert. denied, 278 Md. 738 (1976).

Laches is a proper ground for refusing to issue a writ of mandamus. Ipes v. Board of Fire Comm'rs, 224 Md. 180, 167 A.2d 337 (1961).

Medical malpractice actions. — An order denying a motion for change in venue in a medical malpractice arbitration proceeding is not immediately reviewable in circuit court through an action for writ of mandamus or certiorari. Dorchester Gen. Hosp. v. Sober, 79 Md. App. 110, 555 A.2d 1074 (1989).

III. PROCEDURE.

Facts must be stated and proved or admitted. — In an application for mandamus all the facts necessary for the writ must be stated and proved or admitted on the record. McCurdy v. Jessup, 126 Md. 318, 95 A. 37 (1915); Potee v. County Comm'rs, 138 Md. 381, 113 A. 884 (1921); Brack v. Wells, 184 Md. 86, 40 A.2d 319 (1944).

Affidavit required. — Petition for writ of mandamus without affidavit of applicant was held to be insufficient. Brack v. Wells, 184 Md. 86, 40 A.2d 319 (1944).

The failure of petitioner to file exhibits is waived by answer not objecting on that score. Brooke v. Widdicombe, 39 Md. 386 (1874).

Former Rule BE41 replaces alternative writ of mandamus. — The answer required by former Rule BE41 stands in the place of the return to the alternative writ of mandamus under former practice, and seems to have been primarily directed to the degree of certainty and precision with which the defendant is required to set forth the facts relied upon by him in his answer. Ipes v. Board of Fire Comm'rs, 224 Md. 180, 167 A.2d 337 (1961).

Sufficiency of answer generally. — The exact degree of definiteness and certainty required in an answer in a mandamus case is difficult to determine. While undoubtedly the passage of former § 3 of Article 60 and similar statutes in other jurisdictions simplifying the procedure has caused a general relaxation of the old common-law rule, such action has not obviated the necessity for precision, nor has it entirely removed the strictness with which the courts have always dealt with the pleadings in such cases. Pennington v. Gilbert, 148 Md. 649, 129 A. 905 (1925).

If the answer sets up any good defense, it should not be quashed because it is in other respects evasive or irresponsive. Legg v. Mayor of Baltimore, 42 Md. 203 (1875).

Answer must state positive and definite facts. — If answer is indefinite and uncertain, relief will be granted. Pennington v. Gilbert, 148 Md. 649, 129 A. 905 (1925).

Answer held insufficient. — See Creager v. Hooper, 83 Md. 490, 35 A. 159 (1855).

The answer stands in the place of the return to the alternative writ under former practice, and seems to have been primarily directed to the degree of certainty and precision with which the defendant is required to set forth the facts relied upon by him in his answer. Ipes v. Board of Fire Comm'rs, 224 Md.

180, 167 A.2d 337 (1961).

Defense which could not have been relied on in previous case. — Former § 4 of Article 60, similar to section c of former Rule BE41, had no application where the defense could not have been relied upon in previous case. County Comm'rs v. Fout, 110 Md. 165, 72 A. 765 (1909).

Prerequisites to issuance of writ where defendant fails to answer. — When defendant fails to answer, the writ cannot issue without due proof of facts and judge's being satisfied on law. Legg v. Mayor of Annapolis, 42 Md. 203 (1875); Sudler v. Lankford, 82 Md. 142, 33 A. 455 (1895); Upshur v. Mayor of Baltimore, 94 Md. 743, 51 A. 953 (1902); Beasley v. Ridout, 94 Md. 641, 52 A. 61 (1902).

A statement in opinion of lower court that "at the hearing the questions at issue were waived or admitted" is equivalent to full proof. Beasley v. Ridout, 94 Md. 641, 52 A. 61 (1902).

Discretion of court to refuse writ. — Former § 9 of Article 60 did not take away the discretion of the court to refuse the writ of mandamus. Webber v. Zimmerman, 23 Md. 45 (1865).

A claim for costs and damages is inchoate, and cannot be considered as personal assets until judgment is entered. Booze v. Humbird, 27 Md. 1 (1867).

Attorney's fees incurred by successful party. — Provisions of former Rule BE44 do not authorize the assessment of attorney's fees incurred by a successful party in a mandamus action as damages or costs in such an action merely on the basis that the party against whom the attorney's fees are sought is the unsuccessful litigant. Hess Constr. Co. v.

Board of Educ., 102 Md. App. 736, 651 A.2d 446 (1995).

Mandamus will not issue where a plain, adequate remedy exists in an ordinary course of law. Walter v. Board of County Comm'rs, 179 Md. 665, 22 A.2d 472 (1941).

Mandamus will not lie to compel county commissioners to repair roads, as the legal remedy for damages in such cases is adequate. Walter v. Board of County Comm'rs, 179 Md. 665, 22 A.2d 472 (1941).

Intent. — See Conner v. Groh, 90 Md. 674, 45 A. 1024 (1900).

Former § 98, Article 16, was intended to reach the class of cases in which injunction or mandamus had been refused because the plaintiff could be compensated in damages in suits at law. Frederick County Nat'l Bank v. Shafer, 87 Md. 54, 39 A. 320 (1898); Universal Realty Corp. v. Felser, 179 Md. 635, 22 A.2d 448 (1941).

Applicable to cases where damages, not debt, are involved. — Former § 98, Article 16, related to cases where damages, as contradistinguished from debt, were involved. Frederick County Nat'l Bank v. Shafer, 87 Md. 54, 39 A. 320 (1898); Conner v. Groh, 90 Md. 674, 45 A. 1024 (1900).

Hearing and burden of proof. — Former § 98, Article 16, was not intended to be applicable on demurrer, but only after such hearing as might make it appear to the court that the defendants, in a given case, could respond to damages, or could give a bond, and that such relief would be adequate. The burden is on the defendants in this respect. Universal Realty Corp. v. Felser, 179 Md. 635, 22 A.2d 448 (1941).

CHAPTER 800. MARYLAND AUTOMOBILE INSURANCE FUND.

Rule 15-801. Actions involving the Maryland Automobile Insurance Fund.

The rules in this Chapter apply to actions involving the Maryland Automobile Insurance Fund that are authorized by Code, Insurance Article, § 20-601. (Amended May 9, 2000, effective July 1, 2000.)

Cross references. — For procedure governing claims against the Fund not rising to the level of a civil action, *see* C.O.M.A.R. 14.07.04.01 — .06, Uninsured Persons' Claims

for Compensation from the Maryland Automobile Insurance Fund.

Source. — This Rule is derived from former Rule BW1 b.

Effect of amendments. — The 2000 amendment substituted "Insurance Article,

§ 20-601" for "Article 48A, § 243H."

Editor's note. — Article 48A, § 243H,

which is referred to in this Rule, has been revised as §§ 20-601 and 20-603 through 20-608 of the Insurance Article.

Rule 15-802. Definitions.

In Rules 15-803 through 15-805 the following definitions apply:

(a) **Claimant.** "Claimant" means a person who claims damages resulting from an act or omission of a disappearing motorist, an unidentified motorist, or an uninsured motorist.

Cross references. — Code, Insurance Article, § 20-601.

(b) **Disappearing motorist.** "Disappearing motorist" means a motor vehicle owner or operator (1) whose identity is known but whose whereabouts cannot be ascertained for the purpose of serving process and (2) who was uninsured at the time of the act or omission or whose status as insured or uninsured cannot be ascertained, after all reasonable efforts have been made.

(c) **Executive Director.** "Executive Director" means the Executive Director of the Maryland Automobile Insurance Fund or a designee of the Executive Director.

(d) **Fund.** "Fund" means the Maryland Automobile Insurance Fund.

(e) **Unidentified motorist.** "Unidentified motorist" means a motor vehicle owner or operator whose identity and whereabouts are not known.

(f) **Uninsured motorist.** "Uninsured motorist" means a motor vehicle owner or operator whose whereabouts are ascertainable for the purpose of serving process, but who was uninsured at the time of the act or omission. (Amended May 9, 2000, effective July 1, 2000.)

Source. — This Rule is derived from former Rule BW1 a.

Effect of amendments. — The 2000 amendment substituted "Insurance Article, § 20-601" for "Article 48A, § 243H (a)" in the cross reference note following (a).

Editor's note. — Article 48A, § 243H (a), which is referred to in the Cross Reference note to section (a), has been revised as § 20-601 of the Insurance Article.

Rule 15-803. Uninsured motorist — Action against motorist.

(a) **Against whom brought.** An action on a claim against an uninsured motorist shall be brought against the uninsured motorist. The Fund shall not be named as a defendant.

(b) **Notice to Executive Director.** Within 15 days after the filing of the complaint, the claimant shall mail a copy of the complaint and summons to the Executive Director. Failure to give notice pursuant to this section shall not defeat the claim against the Fund if the Fund has reasonable notice of the pendency of the action and a reasonable opportunity to defend.

(c) **Order for payment.** (1) By consent. After entry of a money judgment against the uninsured motorist, the claimant may file with the court a stipulation, signed by the Executive Director, setting forth the deductions required by law and consenting to entry of an order directing payment of a specified amount by the Fund.

(2) On motion. After entry of a money judgment against the uninsured motorist, the claimant may file a motion for payment of a specified amount by the Fund. The motion shall be supported by affidavit, shall set forth the grounds for entitlement to payment by the Fund and all the deductions required by law, and shall be served on the Executive Director. (Amended May 9, 2000, effective July 1, 2000.)

Cross references. — *See* Code, Insurance Article, § 20-602, for required deductions from payment by the Fund.

Source. — This Rule is derived from former Rules BW4 and BW6.

Effect of amendments. — The 2000 amendment substituted "Insurance Article, § 20-602" for "Article 48A, § 243-I" in the cross reference note.

Editor's note. — Article 48A, § 243-I, which is referred to in the Cross Reference note to this Rule, has been been revised as § 20-602 of the Insurance Article.

Rule 15-804. Unidentified or disappearing motorist — Action against Fund.

(a) **Against whom brought.** An action on a claim against an unidentified or disappearing motorist shall be brought against the Fund.

(b) **Condition precedent to action against Fund.** Prior to bringing an action against the Fund for damages resulting from an act or omission of an unidentified motorist or a disappearing motorist, the claimant shall first present a request to the Executive Director, in the manner and form prescribed by the Executive Director, for a stipulation by the Fund that the claimant has met the procedural requirements for bringing an action against the Fund.

(c) **Venue.** The venue of an action against the Fund shall be either the county in which the claimant resides or the county in which the alleged act or omission by the unidentified motorist or disappearing motorist occurred.

(d) **Complaint.** In addition to complying with Rules 2-303 through 2-305, the complaint shall contain a statement as to whether the stipulation requested pursuant to section (b) of this Rule was granted or refused. If the stipulation was granted, a copy of the stipulation shall be filed with the complaint.

(e) **Motion to dismiss.** If the stipulation requested pursuant to section (b) of this Rule was refused, the Fund, within the time for filing an answer to the complaint, may file a motion to dismiss the complaint for failure of the claimant to meet the procedural requirements for bringing an action against the Fund. This defense may be joined with any other defense raised by motion pursuant to Rule 2-322 and is waived if not raised by motion before an answer is filed. When a motion is filed pursuant to this section, the time for filing an answer is extended without special order of the court to 15 days after entry of an order denying the motion.

(f) **Order for payment.** (1) By consent. After determination of the claimant's gross damages, the claimant may file a stipulation, signed by the

Executive Director, setting forth the deductions required by law and consenting to entry of an order directing payment of a specified amount by the Fund.

(2) On motion. After determination of the claimant's gross damages, either party may file a motion for an order directing payment by the Fund of a specified amount. The motion shall set forth the deductions required by law. (Amended May 9, 2000, effective July 1, 2000.)

Cross references. — Code, Insurance Article, § 20-602.

Source. — This Rule is derived from former Rules BW2, BW3, and BW5.

Effect of amendments. — The 2000 amendment substituted "Insurance Article, § 20-602" for "Article 48A, § 243-I" in the cross reference note.

Editor's note. — Article 48A, § 243-I, which is referred to in the Cross Reference note to this Rule, has been been revised as § 20-602 of the Insurance Article.

Rule 15-805. Consent judgment.

If the claimant and the Fund enter into a settlement agreement, in an action involving a claim for payment by the Fund, the court may enter a judgment by consent of the parties upon the filing of a motion setting forth the grounds for the claimant's entitlement to payment by the Fund, all the deductions required by law, and the amount of the agreed settlement. The motion shall be accompanied by a stipulation signed by the Executive Director consenting to entry of an order directing payment of a specified amount by the Fund.

Source. — This Rule is derived from former Rule BW7.

CHAPTER 900. NAME — CHANGE OF.

Rule 15-901. Action for change of name.

(a) **Applicability.** This Rule applies to actions for change of name other than in connection with an adoption or divorce.

(b) **Venue.** An action for change of name shall be brought in the county where the person whose name is sought to be changed resides.

(c) **Petition.** (1) Contents. The action for change of name shall be commenced by filing a petition captioned "In the Matter of ..." [stating the name of the person whose name is sought to be changed] "for change of name to ..." [stating the change of name desired]. The petition shall be under oath and shall contain at least the following information:

(A) the name, address, and date and place of birth of the person whose name is sought to be changed;

(B) whether the person whose name is sought to be changed has ever been known by any other name and, if so, the name or names and the circumstances under which they were used;

(C) the change of name desired;

(D) all reasons for the requested change;

(E) a certification that the petitioner is not requesting the name change for any illegal or fraudulent purpose;

(F) if the person whose name is sought to be changed is a minor, the names and addresses of that person's parents and any guardian or custodian; and

(G) whether the person whose name is sought to be changed has ever registered as a sexual offender and, if so, the full name(s) (including suffixes) under which the person was registered.

Cross references. — See Code, Criminal Procedure Article, § 11-705, which requires a registered sexual offender whose name has been changed by order of court to send written notice of the change to the Department of Public Safety and Correctional Services within seven days after the order is entered.

(2) *Documents to be attached to petition.* The petitioner shall attach to the petition a copy of a birth certificate or other documentary evidence from which the court can find that the current name of the person whose name is sought to be changed is as alleged.

(d) **Service of petition — When required.** If the person whose name is sought to be changed is a minor, a copy of the petition, any attachments, and the notice issued pursuant to section (e) of this Rule shall be served upon that person's parents and any guardian or custodian in the manner provided by Rule 2-121. When proof is made by affidavit that good faith efforts to serve a parent, guardian, or custodian pursuant to Rule 2-121 (a) have not succeeded and that Rule 2-121 (b) is inapplicable or that service pursuant to that Rule is impracticable, the court may order that service may be made by (1) the publication required by subsection (e)(2) of this Rule and (2) mailing a copy of the petition, any attachments, and notice by first class mail to the last known address of the parent, guardian, or custodian to be served.

(e) **Notice.** (1) *Issued by clerk.* Upon the filing of the petition, the clerk shall sign and issue a notice that (A) includes the caption of the action, (B) describes the substance of the petition and the relief sought, and (C) states the latest date by which an objection to the petition may be filed.

(2) *Publication.* Unless the court on motion of the petitioner orders otherwise, the notice shall be published one time in a newspaper of general circulation in the county in which the action was pending at least fifteen days before the date specified in the notice for filing an objection to the petition. The petitioner shall thereafter file a certificate of publication.

(f) **Objection to petition.** Any person may file an objection to the petition. The objection shall be filed within the time specified in the notice and shall be supported by an affidavit which sets forth the reasons for the objection. The affidavit shall be made on personal knowledge, shall set forth facts that would be admissible in evidence, and shall show affirmatively that the affiant is competent to testify to the matters stated in the affidavit. The objection and affidavit shall be served upon the petitioner in accordance with Rule 1-321. The petitioner may file a response within 15 days after being served with the objection and affidavit. A person desiring a hearing shall so request in the objection or response under the heading "Request for Hearing."

(g) **Action by court.** After the time for filing objections and responses has expired, the court may hold a hearing or may rule on the petition without a hearing and shall enter an appropriate order, except that the court shall not deny the petition without a hearing if one was requested by the petitioner. (Amended April 5, 2005, effective July 1, 2005; June 7, 2011, effective July 1, 2011.)

Source. — This Rule is derived in part from former Rules BH70 through BH75 and is in part new.

Effect of amendments. — The 2005 amendment added (c)(1)(G); and added the cross references note following (c)(1)(G).

The 2011 amendment inserted "in which the action was pending" in the first sentence in (e)(2).

Common law right to adopt name. — The common law recognizes the right of any person, absent a statute to the contrary, to adopt any name by which he may become known, and by which he may transact business and execute contracts and sue or be sued. Stuart v. Board of Supvrs. of Elections, 266 Md. 440, 295 A.2d 223 (1972).

In the absence of a statute to the contrary, a person may adopt any name by which he wishes to become known, as long as he does so consistently and nonfraudulently. Hardy v. Hardy, 269 Md. 412, 306 A.2d 244 (1973).

Right of married woman to retain birth-given name. — Maryland law permits a married woman to retain her birth-given name by the procedure of consistent, nonfraudulent use following her marriage. Stuart v. Board of Supvrs. of Elections, 266 Md. 440, 295 A.2d 223 (1972).

A married woman's surname does not become that of her husband where she evidences a clear intent to consistently and nonfraudulently use her birth-given name subsequent to her marriage. Stuart v. Board of Supvrs. of Elections, 266 Md. 440, 295 A.2d 223 (1972).

The mere fact of marriage does not, as a matter of law, operate to establish the custom and tradition of married women adopting their husbands' surname as their own. Stuart v. Board of Supvrs. of Elections, 266 Md. 440, 295 A.2d 223 (1972).

Woman not required to register to vote in surname of husband. — The provisions of Article 33, § 3-18 (a) (3) and (c) (see now § 3-505 of the Election Law Article), do not require that a married woman register to vote in the surname of her husband unless her name has been changed by legal proceedings under former Maryland Rules BH70-BH75, and Article 16, § 123, of the Annotated Code of Maryland. That section, even with the aid of a long-standing and uniform administrative practice, does not effect such a derogation of the common law. Stuart v. Board of Supvrs. of Elections, 266 Md. 440, 295 A.2d 223 (1972).

Child taking name of foster parents. — Where a court set aside a co-guardianship order, any advantage to the subject child in having the same last name as his foster parents no longer existed, and his name was not changed. In re Adoption/Guardianship No. 3155, 103 Md. App. 300, 653 A.2d 521 (1995).

The purpose of requiring publication is to apprise as many people as possible of the pendency of the petition so anyone who reasonably wishes to offer relevant information to aid the court in performing its functions can do so. Hardy v. Hardy, 269 Md. 412, 306 A.2d 244 (1973).

Waiver of publication in case involving infant. — It is difficult to imagine a case which has as its purpose the change of an infant's name under former Subtitle BH, as distinguished from other types of name change proceedings, where it would be proper to waive publication. Hardy v. Hardy, 269 Md. 412, 306 A.2d 244 (1973).

Where a motion seeking waiver of publication was based solely on the fact that a young child had no assets or liabilities, nor had he ever used his name for any instrument, while these grounds might form an appropriate basis for waiver of publication in a name change case involving an adult, they do not create a sufficient foundation for waiver on such a petition filed on behalf of an infant by another person under this subtitle. Hardy v. Hardy, 269 Md. 412, 306 A.2d 244 (1973).

Waiver or publication on motion of petitioner. — A court may waive publication under section (e) (2) of this Rule on motion of the petitioner, but not on its own initiative; in light of the disfavored status of waivers of publication, motions for waiver should be viewed by the court cautiously. 82 Op. Att'y Gen. 44 (August 21, 1997).

Cited in First Penn-Pacific Life Ins. Co. v. William R. Evans, Chtd., 304 F.3d 345 (4th Cir. 2002), cert. denied, 538 U.S. 944, 123 S. Ct. 1622, 155 L. Ed. 2d 484 (2003); In re Heilig, 372 Md. 692, 816 A.2d 68 (2003); Dorsey v. Tarpley, 381 Md. 109, 847 A.2d 445 (2004).

CHAPTER 1000. WRONGFUL DEATH.

Rule 15-1001. Wrongful death.

(a) **Applicability.** This Rule applies to an action involving a claim for damages for wrongful death.

Cross references. — *See* Code, Courts Article, §§ 3-901 through 3-904, relating to wrongful death claims generally. *See* Code, Courts Article, § 5-806, relating to wrongful death claims between parents and children arising out of the operation of a motor vehicle. *See also* Code, Labor and Employment Article, § 9-901 et seq. relating to wrongful death claims when workers' compensation may also be available, and Code, Insurance Article, § 20-601, relating to certain wrongful death claims against the Maryland Automobile Insurance Fund. *See also* Code, Estates and Trusts Article, § 8-103, relating to the limitation on presentation of claims against a decedent's estate.

(b) **Plaintiff.** If the wrongful act occurred in this State, all persons who are or may be entitled by law to damages by reason of the wrongful death shall be named as plaintiffs whether or not they join in the action. The words "to the use of" shall precede the name of any person named as a plaintiff who does not join in the action.

(c) **Notice to use plaintiff.** The party bringing the action shall mail a copy of the complaint by certified mail to any use plaintiff at the use plaintiff's last known address. Proof of mailing shall be filed as provided in Rule 2-126.

(d) **Complaint.** In addition to complying with Rules 2-303 through 2-305, the complaint shall state the relationship of each plaintiff to the decedent whose death is alleged to have been caused by the wrongful act. (Amended May 9, 2000, effective July 1, 2000; Jan. 8, 2002, effective Feb. 1, 2002.)

Source. — This Rule is derived as follows:
Section (a) is derived from former Rule Q40.
Section (b) is derived from former Rule Q41 a.

Section (c) is new.
Section (d) is derived from former Rule Q42.

Effect of amendments. — The 2000 amendment, in the cross reference note following (a), substituted "Code, Labor and Employment Article, § 9-901 et seq." for "Article 101, § 58," substituted "workers'" for "worker's," and substituted "Insurance Article, § 20-601" for "Article 48A, § 243H."

The 2002 amendment added the second sentence of the cross reference note following (a).

Editor's note. — Article 101, § 58, which is referred to in the Cross Reference note to section (a), has been been revised as § 9-901 et seq. of the Labor and Employment Article.

Article 48A, § 243H, which is referred to in the Cross Reference note to section (a), has been been revised as §§ 20-601 and 20-603 through 20-608 of the Insurance Article.

Maryland Law Review. — For note concerning person entitled to sue for wrongful death caused and occurring outside state of forum, see 2 Md. L. Rev. 168 (1938).

History and purpose of former Article 67, § 3. — See Kaufmann v. Service Trucking Co., 139 F. Supp. 1 (D. Md. 1956); Olewiler v. Fullerton Supply Co., 162 F. Supp. 563 (D. Md. 1958).

CJ § 3-903 must be read in conjunction with this Rule. Huber v. B & O R.R., 241 F. Supp. 646 (D. Md. 1965).

Rule not merely notice rule. — To interpret this Rule, concerning wrongful death actions, as simply a notice rule disregarded: (1) the representative nature of wrongful death actions; (2) the language of 3-904 (b) of the Courts Article, requiring that all persons who are or may be entitled by law to damages by reason of the wrongful death shall be named as plaintiffs whether or not the persons join in the action; and (3) the provisions of § 3-904(c) of the Courts Article relating to the award of damages to the statutory "beneficiaries" proportional to injury resulting from the wrongful death. Ace Am. Ins. Co. v. Williams, 418 Md. 400, 15 A.3d 761 (2011).

Suits must be filed in name of real parties in interest. — Since the adoption of former Rule Q41, suits under causes of action arising within this State must now be filed in the name of the real parties in interest, rather than in the name of the State. Robinson v. Lewis, 20 Md. App. 710, 317 A.2d 854 (1974).

When a decedent's second wife and the second wife's children settled a wrongful death suit, the judgment approving the settlement was reopened because (b), requiring that all statutory beneficiaries, under § 3-904 of the Courts Article, was not satisfied since the decedent's children by a prior marriage were not named as plaintiff's or "use" plaintiffs. Williams v. Work, 192 Md. App. 438, 995 A.2d 744 (2010), cert. granted, 415 Md. 607, 4 A.3d 512, 2010 Md. LEXIS 556 (2010); aff'd, 2011 Md. LEXIS 201 (Md. 2011) .

This Rule, concerning wrongful death actions, is in the nature of a joinder rule or a condition precedent that requires that all known statutory beneficiaries, i.e., the real parties in interest, be identified as parties to the litigation, and, although (b) does not require formal joinder, the failure to include a known statutory beneficiary as a plaintiff or a "use plaintiff" in a wrongful death action and to settle without providing for that beneficiary can be analogized to the failure to join a necessary party in an action where joinder is required, so, because of the one action rule, the failure to do so is a "defect" or "mistake" of jurisdictional proportions in the proceeding, which may be raised at any time, and that is true whether the failure to name the statutory beneficiary as a plaintiff or use plaintiff is attributed to a failure to file or to a clerk's error in docketing a filed pleading, as, in a situation where no financial provisions are made for known beneficiaries, the former is in the nature of a jurisdictional mistake and the latter is an irregularity of process or procedure, and either permit or require opening the judgment to protect the interests of those beneficiaries. Ace Am. Ins. Co. v. Williams, 418 Md. 400, 15 A.3d 761 (2011).

Division of damages. — Despite a wrongful death action being brought on behalf of three beneficiaries, only one action lies for a wrongful death, and the damages have to be divided among the beneficiaries, with all persons who are or may be entitled by law to damages being named as plaintiffs, whether or not they join in the action. Benjamin v. Union Carbide Corp., 162 Md. App. 173, 873 A.2d 463 (2005), aff'd, sub nom., 904 A.2d 511, 2006 Md. LEXIS 478 (2006).

Standing — There are today no Maryland statutory provisions with respect to standing to bring a wrongful death action, which con-firms the General Assembly's determination that standing to bring a wrongful death action is a procedural matter to be covered by rules and not an issue of substantive law. The Maryland Rules of Procedure adopted by the Court of Appeals, which are constitutionally limited to rules and regulations concerning the practice and procedure in and the administration of the appellate courts and the other courts of Maryland, and Article IV, § 18(a) of the Maryland Constitution, provide, in (b), that the statutory beneficiaries are the persons with standing to bring a wrongful death action if the wrongful act occurred in Maryland, but there is no longer a rule specifying standing to bring a wrongful death action when the wrongful act occurs outside of Maryland. Jones v. Prince George's County, 378 Md. 98, 835 A.2d 632 (2003).

Illinois administrator may sue in Maryland under Virginia statute. — A domiciliary administrator appointed in Illinois can maintain an action in a Maryland federal district court or any other court under the Virginia statute without qualifying in Virginia. Kaufmann v. Service Trucking Co., 139 F. Supp. 1 (D. Md. 1956).

Leave to amend should have been granted. — While the family did not comply with this Rule by sending notice of the action to the estranged, adopted son of the decedent, the trial court erred when it did not grant the family leave to amend their pleadings to name the estranged son as a "use plaintiff" without first considering whether the estranged son would be prejudiced thereby. Muti v. Univ. of Md. Med. Sys. Corp., 197 Md. App. 561, 14 A.3d 1179 (2011).

Determination of status of compensation insurer. — In a wrongful death case arising under the Maryland law where workmen's compensation benefits have been paid, the compensation insurer would be required to be a party plaintiff. Maryland, however, does not apply such a rule in a conflict of laws situation, but, rather, would look to the law of the jurisdiction in which the insurer's rights arose to determine its status as a party plaintiff. Maryland ex rel. Geils v. Baltimore Transit Co., 37 F.R.D. 34 (D. Md. 1965).

Consent to settlement. — The settlement by one wrongful death beneficiary requires the consent of the other joined beneficiaries or the approval of the court; the Wrongful Death Statute, § 3-901 et seq. of the Courts Article, and the rules relating to it implicitly require mutual consent or court approval. Walker v. Essex, 318 Md. 516, 569 A.2d 645 (1990).

It was error to approve a settlement of a wrongful death suit filed by a decedent's widow on behalf of two of the decedent's children because (1) the decedent's other children from a prior marriage were not identified as use plaintiffs, (2) a good faith effort to obtain the knowing and fully informed consent of the decedent's children from the prior marriage was not shown, so "court approval" without those children's consent was not appropriate, and (3) this Rule was not merely a notice requirement, but mandated a good faith attempt to obtain those children's consent. Ace Am. Ins. Co. v. Williams, 418 Md. 400, 15 A.3d 761 (2011).

Approval of settlement not required. — Settlement of a wrongful death suit was not required when two children of the decedent who had not been named as use plaintiffs or otherwise joined in the action stated the children did not wish to disturb the settlement because the children stated the children would have consented to the settlement had the children's own claims remained open to adjudication, which did not occur. Ace Am. Ins. Co. v. Williams, 418 Md. 400, 15 A.3d 761 (2011).

Cited in Jones v. Jones, 172 Md. App. 429, 915 A.2d 471 (2007), cert. denied, 925 A.2d 633, 2007 Md. LEXIS 454 (Md. 2007).

CHAPTER 1100. CATASTROPHIC HEALTH EMERGENCY.

Rule 15-1101. Construction.

The Rules in this Chapter shall be construed to facilitate the efficient adjudication of any proceedings brought pursuant to Code, Health-General Article, § 18-906 and Code, Public Safety Article, § 14-3A-05. These Rules do not prohibit an individual from seeking habeas corpus relief. (Added April 5, 2005, effective July 1, 2005.)

Source. — This Rule is new.

Rule 15-1102. Definitions.

The definitions set forth in Code, Health-General Article, §§ 1-101 and 18-901 and Code, Public Safety Article, §§ 1-101 and 14-3A-01, are incorporated in this Chapter by reference. (Added April 5, 2005, effective July 1, 2005.)

Source. — This Rule is new.

Rule 15-1103. Initiation of proceeding to contest isolation or quarantine.

(a) **Petition for Relief.** An individual or group of individuals required to go to or remain in a place of isolation or quarantine by a directive of the Secretary issued pursuant to Code, Health-General Article, § 18-906 or Code, Public Safety Article, § 14-3A-05, may contest the isolation or quarantine by filing a petition for relief in the circuit court for the county in which the isolation or quarantine is occurring or, if that court is not available, in any other circuit court.

Committee note. — Motions to seal or limit inspection of a case record are governed by Rule 16-1009. The right of a party to pro-ceed anonymously is discussed in Doe v. Shady Grove Hosp., 89 Md. App. 351, 360-66 (1991).

(b) **Order Assigning Judge and Setting Hearing.** The County Administrative Judge or that judge's designee shall enter an order (1) assigning the matter to a judge and (2) setting the date, time, and location of a hearing on the petition or directing the clerk to promptly set the hearing and notify the parties. The clerk shall provide a copy of the order to all parties, the State Court Administrator, and the Chief Judge of the Court of Appeals.

Cross references. — See Code, Health-General Article, § 18-906 (b), Code, Public Safety Article, § 14-3A-05 (c), and Rule 15- 1104 (c) concerning the time within which a hearing is to be conducted.

(c) **Notice.** No later than the day after the petition was filed, the clerk shall provide a copy of the petition and a notice of the date that it was filed to the Secretary or other official designated by the Secretary and to counsel to the Department of Health and Mental Hygiene.

(d) **Answer to Petition.** The Secretary or other official designated by the Secretary may file an answer to the petition. If an answer is not filed, the allegations of the petition shall be deemed denied. (Added April 5, 2005, effective July 1, 2005; June 7, 2011, effective July 1, 2011.)

Source. — This Rule is new.

Effect of amendments. — The 2011 amendment substituted "in the circuit court for the county in which the isolation or quarantine is occurring or, if that court is not available, in any other circuit court" for "with the Clerk of the Court of Appeals" in (a); in (b), in the first sentence, substituted "County Administrative Judge" for "Chief Judge of the Court of Appeals," deleted "of any circuit court to hear the action" following "matter to a judge," and substituted "the clerk to" for "that the clerk of the circuit court to which the action has been assigned," and in the second sentence, substituted "clerk" for "Clerk of the Court of Appeals" and added "the State Court Administrator, and the Chief Judge of the Court of Appeals" at the end; and substituted "clerk" for "Clerk of the Court of Appeals" in (c).

Rule 15-1104. Proceedings in circuit court.

(a) **Appointment of Counsel.** If a petition has been filed pursuant to Rule 15-1103 by an individual or group not represented by counsel and the petitioner does not decline court-appointed counsel, the circuit court shall appoint counsel in accordance with Code, Health-General Article, § 18-906 (c), or the Court of Appeals shall appoint counsel in accordance with Code, Public Safety Article, § 14-3A-05 (f)(2). The court making the appointment may order the Secretary to pay reasonable fees and costs of the court-appointed counsel.

(b) **Consolidation of Actions, Claims, and Issues.** Consolidation of actions, claims, and issues is governed by Rules 2-327 and 2-503 and by Code, Health General Article, § 18-906 (b)(7) or Code, Public Safety Article, § 14-3A-05 (f)(1).

(c) **Time for Hearing.** The circuit court shall conduct a hearing within three days after the date that the petition was filed, except that the court may extend the time for the hearing:

(1) upon a request by the Secretary or other designated official in accordance with Code, Health-General Article, § 18-906 (b)(4) or Code, Public Safety Article, § 14-3A-05 (c)(4);

(2) upon a request by a petitioner for good cause; or

(3) to effectuate the consolidation of proceedings.

(d) **Appearance at and Conduct of the Hearing.** If one or more of the parties, their counsel, or witnesses are unable to appear personally at the hearing, and the fair and effective adjudication of the proceedings permits, the court may:

(1) accept pleadings and admit documentary evidence submitted or proffered by courier, facsimile, or electronic mail;

(2) if feasible, conduct the proceedings by means of a telephonic conference call, live closed circuit television, live internet or satellite video conference transmission, or other available means of communication that reasonably permits the parties or their authorized representatives to participate fully in the proceedings; and

(3) decline to require strict application of the rules of evidence other than those relating to the competency of witnesses and lawful privileges. (Added April 5, 2005, effective July 1, 2005.)

Source. — This Rule is new.

Rule 15-1105. Decision and order.
(a) **Factors to be Considered.** In making its determination on the petition, the court shall consider the following factors:

(1) the means of transmission of the disease or outbreak that is believed to be caused by exposure to a deadly agent;

(2) the degree of contagion that is associated with exposure to a deadly agent;

(3) the degree of public exposure to the disease or outbreak;

(4) the risk and severity of the possible results from infection, injury, or death of an individual or group of individuals by a deadly agent;

(5) whether the petitioner or the group of individuals similarly situated to the petitioner may have been exposed to a deadly agent;

(6) the potential risk to the public health of an order enjoining the Secretary's directive or otherwise requiring the immediate release from isolation or quarantine of the petitioner or of an individual or group of individuals similarly situated; and

(7) any other material facts.

(b) **Decision.** The court shall order the release of the petitioner unless the court finds by a preponderance of the evidence that the Secretary's directive to isolate or quarantine is necessary and reasonable under the circumstances to prevent or reduce the spread of the disease or outbreak believed to have been caused by exposure to a deadly agent. Otherwise, the court shall deny the petition and issue an order authorizing the continued isolation or quarantine of the petitioners.

(c) **Statement of Reasons.** The court shall prepare and file or dictate into the record a brief statement of the reasons for its decision and enter an order in accordance with section (d) of this Rule. If dictated into the record, the statement shall be transcribed promptly.

(d) **Order.** (1) Generally. The order shall:

(A) be in writing;

360

(B) be filed no later than the next business day after the hearing concludes; and

(C) be given to the parties or their counsel of record, except as otherwise provided in subsection (d)(2)(A) of this Rule.

(2) Orders Authorizing Continued Isolation or Quarantine. An order authorizing continued isolation or quarantine of the individual or group of individuals shall:

(A) be served by the Secretary or the Secretary's designee on the individual or group of individuals specified in the order, unless service is impractical due to the number or geographical dispersion of the affected individuals, in which case the court shall provide for notice to the affected individuals by personal service or by any means available;

(B) be effective for a specific period of time not to exceed 30 days; and

(C) reasonably identify the isolated or quarantined individual or group of individuals by name or by shared characteristics; and

(D) specify all material findings of fact and conclusions of law and may incorporate by reference a transcript of the proceedings.

Committee note. — An order entered under section (d) of this Rule must either order the release of the petitioner (with or without a stay of that order) or authorize the continued isolation of quarantine imposed by the Secretary. Except as provided by Rule 15-1104 (a), the Rules is this Chapter do not authorize the court to grant any other relief.

(e) **Stay.** Upon request of the Secretary, the court may stay an order releasing the petitioner pending appellate review if the request is accompanied by an undertaking in writing or on the record that the Secretary will seek immediate appellate review of the order and the petitioner has been afforded an opportunity to be heard. (Added April 5, 2005, effective July 1, 2005.)

Source. — This Rule is new.

Rule 15-1106. Motion to continue order.

Before the expiration of a court order authorizing or continuing isolation or quarantine, the Secretary may move for a continuation of the order for another period not to exceed 30 days. The motion shall be filed in the court that entered the order. Unless the petitioner consents, the motion shall not be granted without a hearing. (Added April 5, 2005, effective July 1, 2005.)

Source. — This Rule is new.

Rule 15-1107. Appellate review.

A party adversely affected by the court's ruling on a petition for relief or on a subsequent motion to continue an order authorizing isolation or quarantine shall have the right of appellate review. The appellate court shall decide the appeal as soon as is reasonably practicable. In order to do so, the appellate court may modify the timing and filing requirements of any Rule in Title 8. (Added April 5, 2005, effective July 1, 2005.)

Source. — This Rule is new.

CHAPTER 1200. CORAM NOBIS.

Rule 15-1201. Applicability.

The Rules in this Chapter govern proceedings for a writ of coram nobis as to a prior judgment in a criminal action. (Added Nov. 8, 2005, effective Jan. 1, 2006.)

Committee note. — The Rules in this Chapter are not intended to apply to proceedings for a writ of coram nobis as to judgments in civil actions.

Source. — This Rule is new.

Applied in Moguel v. State, 184 Md. App. 465, 966 A.2d 963 (2009).

Rule 15-1202. Petition.

(a) **Filing; caption.** An action for a writ of error coram nobis is commenced by the filing of a petition in the court where the conviction took place. The caption of the petition shall state the case number of the criminal action to which the petition relates. If practicable, the petition shall be filed in the criminal action.

Committee note. — For the authority of the District Court to issue a writ of error *coram nobis*, see Code, Courts Article, § 1-609.

See Rule 1-301 (a) for captioning and titling requirements of court papers.

(b) **Content.** (1) The petition shall include:

(A) the identity of the petitioner as the person subject to the judgment and sentence;

(B) the place and date of trial, the offense for which the petitioner was convicted, and the sentence imposed;

(C) a statement of all previous proceedings, including appeals, motions for new trial, post conviction petitions, and previous petitions for writ of error coram nobis, and the results of those proceedings;

(D) the facts that would have resulted in the entry of a different judgment and the allegations of error upon which the petition is based;

(E) a statement that the allegations of error have not been waived;

Cross references. — See *Holmes v. State*, 401 Md. 429 (2007).

(F) the significant collateral consequences that resulted from the challenged conviction;

(G) the unavailability of appeal, post conviction relief, or other remedies; and

(H) a demand for relief.

(2) The petition may include a concise argument with citation to relevant authority.

(c) **Attachments.** The petitioner shall attach to the petition all relevant portions of the transcript or explain why the petitioner is unable to do so.

(d) **Service.** The petitioner shall serve a copy of the petition and any attachments on the State's Attorney pursuant to Rule 1-321 (a).

(e) **Amendment.** Amendment of the petition shall be freely allowed when justice so permits. (Added Nov. 8, 2005, effective Jan. 1, 2006; amended Sept. 10, 2009, effective Oct. 1, 2009.)

Source. — This Rule is new.

Effect of amendments. — The 2009 amendment added the cross reference following (b)(1)(E).

Rule 15-1203. Notice of petition.

Upon the filing of a petition for a writ of error coram nobis, the clerk promptly shall notify the State's Attorney that the petition has been filed and the case number of the criminal action to which the petition relates. (Added Nov. 8, 2005, effective Jan. 1, 2006.)

Source. — This Rule is new.

Rule 15-1204. Response.

The State's Attorney shall file a response to the petition within 30 days after the clerk gives notice of the filing, or within such other time as the court may order. (Added Nov. 8, 2005, effective Jan. 1, 2006.)

Source. — This Rule is new.

Rule 15-1205. Voluntary dismissal.

Voluntary dismissal of a petition is governed by Rules 2-506 and 3-506. (Added Nov. 8, 2005, effective Jan. 1, 2006.)

Source. — This Rule is new.

Rule 15-1206. Hearing.

(a) **Generally.** The court, in its discretion, may hold a hearing on the petition. The court may deny the petition without a hearing but may grant the petition only if a hearing is held. The court may permit evidence to be presented by affidavit, deposition, oral testimony, or any other manner that the court finds convenient and just. In the interest of justice, the court may decline to require strict application of the Rules in Title 5, except those relating to competency of witnesses.

(b) **Notice to victims.** The State's Attorney shall give notice to each victim and victim's representative who has filed a Crime Victim Notification Request form pursuant to Code, Criminal Procedure Article, § 11-104 or who has submitted a written request to the State's Attorney to be notified of subsequent proceedings as provided under Code, Criminal Procedure Article, § 11-503.

The notice shall state that (1) a petition for a writ of error coram nobis has been filed; (2) the petition has been denied without a hearing or the date, time, and location of the hearing; and (3) each victim or victim's representative may attend any hearing and request the opportunity to be heard. The court may allow the testimony of a victim or victim's representative if relevant to an issue before the court. (Added Nov. 8, 2005, effective Jan. 1, 2006.)

Source. — Added Nov. 8, 2005, effective Jan. 1, 2006.

———

Hearing not guaranteed. — Because defendant waited 23 years to file a coram nobis petition challenging the validity of his guilty plea and conviction, and because the State would be unfairly prejudiced by the delay, the doctrine of laches in Rule 2-323(g) barred the petition; defendant was not guaranteed a hearing on the merits under this Rule. Moguel v. State, 184 Md. App. 465, 966 A.2d 963 (2009).

Rule 15-1207. Statement and order of court.

(a) **Statement.** The judge shall prepare and file or dictate into the record a statement setting forth separately each ground on which the petition is based, the federal and state rights involved, the court's ruling with respect to each ground, and the reasons for the ruling.

(b) **Order of court.** The statement shall include or be accompanied by an order granting or denying relief. If the order is in favor of the petitioner, the court may provide for rearraignment, retrial, custody, bail, discharge, correction of sentence, or other matters that may be necessary and proper.

(c) **Copy to the parties.** A copy of the order shall be filed promptly with the clerk and sent to the petitioner, petitioner's counsel, and the State's Attorney.

(d) **Finality.** The order constitutes a final judgment when entered by the clerk. (Added Nov. 8, 2005, effective Jan. 1, 2006.)

Committee note. — An appeal from a District Court judgment under this Rule proceeds in accordance with the Rules in Title 7, Chapter 100 applicable in civil actions. An appeal from a circuit court judgment under this Rule proceeds in accordance with the Rules in Title 8.

Cross references. — See *Skok v. State,* 361 Md. 52 (2000).

Source. — This Rule is new.

TITLE 16. COURTS, JUDGES, AND ATTORNEYS

Editor's note. — The Court of Appeals, by Order dated June 5, 1996, effective January 1, 1997, rescinded Subtitles A, D, E, J, P, Q, R, T, U, V, W, Y, Z, BB, BD, BE, BG, BH, BJ, BL, BP, BQ, BR, BS, BW, and BY of Chapter 1100 of the Maryland Rules of Procedure, rescinded Subtitles P, BB, BQ, and BW of the Maryland District Rules, and rescinded Forms 22a, 23, 24, 25, and 26. The Order substituted for certain of the rules and forms rescinded new Title 9, Chapter 100, Title 10, Title 12, Title 13, Title 14, and Title 15 of the Maryland Rules of Procedure. Furthermore, the Order transferred, without readoption, Chapter 900, Chapter 1200, and Subtitles S, BU, and BV of Chapter 1100 of the Maryland Rules of Procedure and Chapter 1200 of the Maryland District Rules to be Title 9, Chapter 200, Title 11, and Title 16 of the Maryland Rules of Procedure. The Order provides that the new rules shall "apply to all actions commenced on or after January 1, 1997, and insofar as practicable, to all actions then pending."

Many of the cases in the notes to the various rules were decided prior to the 1996 revision. These cases have been retained under pertinent rules of this title where it is thought that such cases will be of value in interpreting the present rules.

A table of comparable rules, relating those

rules rescinded effective January 1, 1997, to the revised rules in Title 9 through Title 16 is to be found in Volume 2 following the end of the Maryland Rules.

CHAPTER 100. COURT ADMINISTRATIVE STRUCTURE, JUDICIAL DUTIES, ETC.

Rule 16-101. Administrative responsibility.

a. **Chief Judge of the Court of Appeals.** 1. Generally. The Chief Judge of the Court of Appeals has overall responsibility for the administration of the courts of this State. In the execution of that responsibility, the Chief Judge:

(A) may exercise the authority granted by the Rules in this Chapter or otherwise by law;

(B) shall appoint a State Court Administrator to serve at the pleasure of the Chief Judge;

(C) may delegate administrative duties to other persons within the judicial system, including retired judges recalled pursuant to Md. Constitution, Article IV, § 3A; and

(D) may assign a judge of any court other than an Orphans' Court to sit temporarily in any other court.

2. Pretrial proceeding in certain criminal cases. The Chief Judge of the Court of Appeals may, by Administrative Order, require in any county a pretrial proceeding in the District Court for an offense within the jurisdiction of the District Court punishable by imprisonment for a period in excess of 90 days. (Amended June 16, 1975, effective July 1, 1975.)

b. **Chief Judge of the Court of Special Appeals.** The Chief Judge of the Court of Special Appeals, subject to the direction of the Chief Judge of the Court of Appeals and pursuant to the provisions of this Title, shall be responsible for the administration of the Court of Special Appeals. In fulfilling that responsibility, the Chief Judge of the Court of Special Appeals shall possess, to the extent applicable, the authority granted to a County Administrative Judge in section d of this Rule. In the absence of the Chief Judge of the Court of Special Appeals, the provisions of this Rule shall be applicable to the senior judge present in the Court of Special Appeals.

c. **Circuit Administrative Judge.** 1. Designation. In each judicial circuit there shall be a Circuit Administrative Judge, who shall be appointed by order and serve at the pleasure of the Chief Judge of the Court of Appeals. In the absence of any such appointment, the Chief Judge of the judicial circuit shall be the Circuit Administrative Judge.

2. Duties. Each Circuit Administrative Judge shall be generally responsible for the administration of the several courts within the judicial circuit, pursuant to these Rules and subject to the direction of the Chief Judge of the Court of Appeals. Each Circuit Administrative Judge shall also be responsible for the supervision of the County Administrative Judges within the judicial circuit and may perform any of the duties of a County Administrative Judge. The Circuit Administrative Judge shall also call a meeting of all judges of the judicial circuit at least once every six months.

Cross references. — For more detailed provisions pertaining to the duties of Circuit Administrative Judges, see section (d) of Rule 4-344 (Sentencing — Review); Rule 16-103 (Assignment of Judges); and Rule 16-104 (Judicial Leave).

d. **County Administrative Judge.** 1. Designation. After considering the recommendation of the Circuit Administrative Judge, the Chief Judge of the Court of Appeals may appoint a judge of the Circuit Court for any county to be County Administrative Judge of the Circuit Court for that county. A County Administrative Judge shall serve in that capacity at the pleasure of the Chief Judge of the Court of Appeals.

2. Duties. Subject to the supervision of the Circuit Administrative Judge, a County Administrative Judge shall be responsible for the administration of justice and for the administration of the court for that county. The duties shall include:

(i) supervision of all judges, officers, and employees of the court, including the authority to assign judges within the court pursuant to Rule 16-103 (Assignment of Judges);

(ii) supervision and expeditious disposition of cases filed in the court and the control of the trial calendar and other calendars, including the authority to assign cases for trial and hearing pursuant to Rule 16-102 (Chambers Judge) and Rule 16-202 (Assignment of Actions for Trial);

(iii) preparation of the court's budget;

(iv) ordering the purchase of all equipment and supplies for the court and its ancillary services, such as master, auditor, examiner, court administrator, court reporter, jury commissioner, staff of the medical and probation offices, and all additional court personnel other than personnel comprising the Clerk of Court's office;

(v) supervision of and responsibility for the employment, discharge, and classification of court personnel and personnel of its ancillary services and the maintenance of personnel files, unless a majority of the judges of the court disapproves of a specific action. However, each judge (subject to budget limitations) shall have the exclusive right to employ and discharge the judge's personal secretary and law clerk; and

Committee note. — Article IV, § 9, of the Constitution gives the judges of any court the power to appoint officers and, thus, requires joint exercise of the personnel power. A similar provision was included in the July 17, 1967 Administrative and Procedure Regulation.

(vi) implementation and enforcement of all policies, rules and directives of the Court of Appeals, its Chief Judge, and the State Court Administrator, and performance of any other duties necessary for the effective administration of the judicial business of the court and the prompt disposition of litigation.

Cross references. — See also Rule 16-102 (Chambers Judge); Rule 16-103 (Assignment of Judges); Rule 16-201 (Motion Day — Calendar); Rule 16-202 (Assignment of Actions for Trial).

3. Power to delegate. (i) A County Administrative Judge may delegate to any judge, to any committee of judges, or to any officer or employee any of the

administrative responsibilities, duties and functions of the County Administrative Judge.

(ii) In the implementation of Code, Criminal Procedure Article, § 6-103 and Rule 4-271 (a), a County Administrative Judge may (A) with the approval of the Chief Judge of the Court of Appeals, authorize one or more judges to postpone criminal cases on appeal from the District Court or transferred from the District Court because of a demand for jury trial, and (B) except as provided in subsection d.3.(iii) of this Rule, authorize not more than one judge at a time to postpone all other criminal cases.

(iii) The administrative judge of the Circuit Court for Baltimore City may authorize one judge sitting in the Clarence M. Mitchell Courthouse to postpone criminal cases set for trial in that Courthouse and one judge sitting in Courthouse East to postpone criminal cases set for trial in that courthouse.

4. Single judge counties. In a county that has only one resident judge of the Circuit Court, that judge shall exercise the power and authority of a County Administrative Judge. (Amended Mar. 23, 1989, effective July 1, 1989; June 5, 1996, effective Jan. 1, 1997; Mar. 5, 2001, effective July 1, 2001; Jan. 8, 2002, effective Feb. 1, 2002; Nov. 12, 2003, effective Jan. 1, 2004; amended Sept. 10, 2009, effective Oct. 1, 2009; amended Sept. 8, 2011, effective Oct. 1, 2011.)

Source. — This Rule is derived from former Rule 1200.

Effect of amendments. — The 1996 amendment substituted "Title" for "Chapter" in b.; in c., rewrote the Cross reference note and substituted "Rule 16-103" for "Rule 1202" in the third sentence of the Committee note; substituted "Rule 16-103" for "Rule 1202" in d. 2. (i); in d. 2. (ii), substituted "Rule 16-202; for "Rule 1211"; and added the Source note.

The 2001 amendment rewrote the Rule.

The 2002 amendment substituted "Criminal Procedure Article, § 6-103" for "Article 27, § 591" in d. 3. (ii).

The 2003 amendment inserted "After considering the recommendation of the Circuit Administrative Judge" at the beginning of d. 1.; substituted "Circuit Administrative Judge" for "Chief Judge of the Court of Appeals" in d. 2.; and in d. 2. v., deleted "subject to the approval of a majority of the judges of the court" at the beginning and inserted "unless a majority of the judges of the court disapproves of a specific action" and made related stylistic changes.

The 2009 amendment substituted "reporter" for "stenographer" in d. 2. (iv).

The 2011 amendment in b. made a minor change in the first sentence, rewrote the second sentence, and added the third sentence; in d. 3. ii deleted "authorize" after "County Administrative Judge may", inserted "authorize" before "one or more judges" and added the exception; and added d. 3. (iii).

Editor's note. — An Order dated June 5, 1996, effective Jan. 1, 1997, renumbered this Rule, which was formerly Rule 1200.

Violation of subdivision d.3.(ii). — Compliance with subdivision d.3.(ii) of this Rule is mandatory and the appropriate sanction for its violation is dismissal of the charge; therefore, when a violation of Article 27, § 591 (see now § 6-103 of the Criminal Procedure Article) and Rule 4-271 is caused by a violation of this Rule, the proper sanction is dismissal of the charges. Goldring v. State, 358 Md. 490, 750 A.2d 1 (2000).

Courthouse security procedures. — A county administrative judge has authority to institute reasonable courthouse security procedures, and the State's Attorney and his staff may be required to adhere to those procedures. 78 Op. Att'y Gen. 103 (March 15, 1993).

Delegation of responsibility — State's highest court ruled that the public defender's petition for a writ of prohibition, writ of mandamus, or appropriate relief from the trial court's directive that parties meet certain procedural requirements in filing exceptions to the report of a master in juvenile cases or face dismissal of those exceptions had to be dismissed; the trial court, through court rules and statutory law, was delegated the authority to oversee the administration of juvenile cases and, more importantly, the issues with which the public defender was concerned were currently being considered in two cases before the State's intermediate appellate court, which meant that the public defender had a chance to obtain the relief sough through those proceedings. Forster v. Hargadon, 398 Md. 298, 920 A.2d 1049 (2007).

Improper to overrule assignment by administrative judge. — Circuit judge erred by ruling on defendant's motion for modification of sentence after an administrative judge assigned the matter to another judge because this Rule made it clear that the assignment of circuit judges for trials or hearings was entirely within the province of circuit and county administrative judges, subject only to the supervisory authority of the chief judge of the court of appeals and the administrative rules adopted by the court of appeals; Rules 16-101 through 16-103, 16-201, and 16-202 unambiguously vest in the chief judge of the court of appeals, circuit administrative judges, and county administrative judges, full authority to assign judges for trials or hearings in the circuit courts of the State, and there is no rule or opinion of the court of appeals that vests in a circuit judge of a particular county the authority to override or ignore an assignment by the administrative judge of that county or by the circuit administrative judge of the circuit that included that county. Strickland v. State, 407 Md. 344, 965 A.2d 887 (2009).

Cited in In re Marcus J., 175 Md. App. 703, 931 A.2d 1146 (2007), aff'd, 2008 Md. LEXIS 322 (2008).

Rule 16-102. Chambers judge.

a. **Generally.** 1. Designation. In a county with more than four resident judges, the County Administrative Judge shall, and in any other county may, designate one or more of the judges sitting in that county to sit as chambers judge.

2. Responsibility of County Administrative Judge. In any county where the designation of a chambers judge is mandatory pursuant to subsection 1 of this section, it shall be the responsibility of the County Administrative Judge to ensure that a chambers judge is on duty in the courthouse whenever the courthouse is open for the transaction of judicial business.

b. **Duties.** A chambers judge shall have primary responsibility for:

(i) Prompt disposition of motions and other preliminary matters which may be disposed of without hearing, except for motions made or filed during the course of a trial or on the day a case is set for trial, which motions shall be disposed of by the trial judge.

(ii) Consideration of and, when appropriate, signing show cause orders.

(iii) Conduct of pre-trial conferences and control of the pre-trial calendar, if one has been established.

(iv) Unless a different procedure is prescribed by the County Administrative Judge, consideration of and, when appropriate, signing orders and decrees in uncontested or ex parte cases, and the disposition of motions for continuances or postponements, except such motions made on the day of or during trial, which shall be disposed of by the trial judge. (Amended Apr. 6, 1984, effective July 1, 1984; June 5, 1996, effective Jan. 1, 1997; Dec. 16, 1999, effective Jan. 1, 2000.)

Committee note. — While a chambers judge, where one has been designated, will have primary responsibility for performing the duties set forth in this Rule, the Rule is not intended to affect the power of other judges to perform these duties should a chambers judge not be available. The Rule does contemplate that in those jurisdictions in which a chambers judge must be designated, some judge will be available to perform the duties of a chambers judge at all times during the normal 9:00 a.m. — 5:00 p.m. working day, Monday through Friday.

Source. — This Rule is former Rule 1201.

Effect of amendments. — The 1996 amendment substituted "Rule 16-101" for "Rule 1200" in the Cross reference note in a.; and added the Source note.

The 1999 amendment substituted "Generally" for "Designation" in the subheading for a; deleted former a 1 and redesignated former a 2 and a 3 as present a 1 and a 2; in a 1, substituted "Designation" for "Other judicial circuits" in the subheading, substituted "other county may, designate one or more of the judges sitting in that county to sit as chambers judge" for "other county, he may, from time to time designate one or more of the judges sitting in his court to sit therein as chambers judge"; and, in a 2, deleted "In the Eighth Judicial Circuit, and" from the beginning, inserted "the" preceding "designation," substituted "subsection 1" for "subsection 2," substituted "ensure" for "insure," deleted "therein" at the end, and deleted the cross reference note.

Editor's note. — An Order dated June 5, 1996, effective Jan. 1, 1997, renumbered this Rule, which was formerly Rule 1201.

Improper to overrule assignment by ad- ministrative judge. — Circuit judge erred by ruling on defendant's motion for modification of sentence after an administrative judge assigned the matter to another judge because Rule 16-101 made it clear that the assignment of circuit judges for trials or hearings was entirely within the province of circuit and county administrative judges, subject only to the supervisory authority of the chief judge of the court of appeals and the administrative rules adopted by the court of appeals; Rules 16-101 through 16-103, 16-201, and 16-202 unambiguously vest in the chief judge of the court of appeals, circuit administrative judges, and county administrative judges, full authority to assign judges for trials or hearings in the circuit courts of the State, and there is no rule or opinion of the court of appeals that vests in a circuit judge of a particular county the authority to override or ignore an assignment by the administrative judge of that county or by the circuit administrative judge of the circuit that included that county. Strickland v. State, 407 Md. 344, 965 A.2d 887 (2009).

Rule 16-103. Assignment of judges.

a. **Chief Judge of the Court of Appeals.** The Chief Judge of the Court of Appeals may by order assign any judge to sit temporarily in any court other than the one to which he was appointed or elected. The order of assignment shall specify the court in which the judge is to sit and the duration of the assignment. During the period of the assignment, the assigned judge shall possess all the power and authority of a judge of the court to which the judge is assigned.

COMMENT

This section, like the constitutional provision (article IV, § 18) on which it is based, gives the Chief Judge of the Court of Appeals full vertical and horizontal assignment power.

b. **Circuit Administrative Judge.** Except for assignments made pursuant to section a of this Rule, the Circuit Administrative Judge of each of the judicial circuits may assign any judge of that judicial circuit to sit as a judge of the Circuit Court of any county in the judicial circuit, in any specific case or cases or for any specified time. The assignments may be made orally or in writing.

c. **County Administrative Judge.** Except for assignments made pursuant to this Rule, assignment of judges within the Circuit Court for a county in which there is more than one resident judge shall be made by the County Administrative Judge. The assignments may be made orally or in writing.

d. **Use of assignment power.** The assignment power herein established shall be exercised to ensure full use of judicial personnel throughout the judicial system, to equalize, to the extent feasible, judicial workloads and to expedite the disposition of pending cases. (Amended June 5, 1996, effective Jan. 1, 1997; Dec. 16, 1999, effective Jan. 1, 2000.)

Source. — This Rule is former Rule 1202.

Effect of amendments. — The 1996 amendment added the Source note.

The 1999 amendment deleted former a 2 and b 2; in the last sentence of present a, substituted "the assignment" for "his assignment," and substituted "the judge" for "he"; in present b, deleted "first seven" preceding "judicial circuits," substituted "that judicial circuit" for "his judicial circuit," substituted "The" for "Such" in the last sentence, and deleted the cross reference note; in c, deleted "section a or subsection 1 of section b of" preceding "this Rule" in the first sentence, and substituted "The" for "Such" in the last sentence; and, in d, substituted "ensure" for "insure," substituted "personnel" for "manpower," and deleted the cross reference note.

Editor's note. — An Order dated June 5, 1996, effective Jan. 1, 1997, renumbered this Rule, which was formerly Rule 1202.

Article IV, § 32 of the Maryland Constitution, referred to in section b 2, was repealed by Acts 1980, ch. 523, ratified November 4, 1980.

Constitutionality. — Former Rule 1202, which grants a circuit administrative judge broad powers of assignment of judges, which power and authority encompass all facts of the internal management of the courts, does not violate Md. Const., art. IV, § 18. Whitaker v. Prince George's County, 307 Md. 368, 514 A.2d 4 (1986).

No new designation required. — No new designation under former Rule 1202 would be required for a District Court judge who sentenced the defendant to probation, while temporarily assigned to the circuit court, to preside over the hearing to revoke that probation; thus it would not be impractical to have the original sentencing judge preside at the revocation hearing. Peterson v. State, 73 Md. App. 459, 534 A.2d 1353 (1988), vacated on other grounds, 315 Md. 73, 553 A.2d 672 (1989).

Improper to overrule assignment by administrative judge. — Circuit judge erred by ruling on defendant's motion for modification of sentence after an administrative judge assigned the matter to another judge because Rule 16-101 made it clear that the assignment of circuit judges for trials or hearings was entirely within the province of circuit and county administrative judges, subject only to the supervisory authority of the chief judge of the court of appeals and the administrative rules adopted by the court of appeals; Rules 16-101 through 16-103, 16-201, and 16-202 unambiguously vest in the chief judge of the court of appeals, circuit administrative judges, and county administrative judges, full authority to assign judges for trials or hearings in the circuit courts of the State, and there is no rule or opinion of the court of appeals that vests in a circuit judge of a particular county the authority to override or ignore an assignment by the administrative judge of that county or by the circuit administrative judge of the circuit that included that county. Strickland v. State, 407 Md. 344, 965 A.2d 887 (2009).

Cited in Dep't of Human Res. v. Howard, 397 Md. 353, 918 A.2d 441 (2007).

Rule 16-104. Judicial leave.

a. **Definition of "judge."** In this Rule, "judge" means a judge of the Court of Appeals of Maryland, the Court of Special Appeals, a circuit court or the District Court of Maryland.

b. **Annual leave.** 1. In general. Subject to the provisions of subsection b 2 and section f of this Rule, a judge is entitled to annual leave of not more than 27 working days. The leave accrues as of the first day of the calendar year except that (1) during the first year of a judge's initial term of office, annual leave accrues at the rate of 2.25 days per month accounting from the date the judge qualifies for office, and (2) during the calendar year in which the judge retires, annual leave accrues at the rate of 2.25 days per month to the date the judge retires.

2. Calendar Year 2010. A. Subject to the provisions of subsection b 2 B and section f of this Rule, in calendar year 2010 a judge is entitled to annual leave of not more than 17 working days. The leave accrues as of the first day of the calendar year except that (1) during the first year of a judge's initial term of office, annual leave accrues at the rate of 1.42 days per month accounting from

the date the judge qualifies for office, and (2) during calendar year 2010, if the judge retires in that year, annual leave accrues at the rate of 1.42 days per month to the date the judge retires.

B. For each day, up to ten days, that a judge contributes to the State of Maryland an amount equal to the average daily compensation, after federal and state tax and FICA withholdings, of a judge serving on the court or level of court on which the judge serves, based on a 22-day work month, as calculated by the State Court Administrator, the judge shall be entitled to one additional day of annual leave. The judge shall make the contribution prior to taking the additional day of annual leave in the manner determined by the State Court Administrator.

3. Accumulation. If in any year a judge takes less than the full amount of annual leave the judge has accrued in that year, the judge may accumulate within any consecutive three year period, the difference between the leave accrued and the annual leave actually taken by the judge in any year during the period. However, no more than ten working days annual leave may be accumulated in any one year, and no judge may accumulate more than 20 working days annual leave in the aggregate.

4. Consecutive appointment — Leave status. A judge who is appointed or elected as a judge of another court, and whose term on the second court begins immediately following service on the first court has the same leave status as though the judge had remained on the first court.

c. **Personal leave.** 1. In general. In addition to annual leave as provided above and except as otherwise provided in subsection 2 of this section, a judge is entitled to six days of personal leave in each calendar year and personal leave accrues on the first day of each calendar year. Any personal leave unused at the end of the calendar year is forfeited.

2. First calendar year of initial term. During the first calendar year of a judge's initial term of office, the judge is entitled to:

A. six days of personal leave if the judge qualified for office in January or February,

B. five days of personal leave if the judge qualified for office in March or April,

C. four days of personal leave if the judge qualified for office in May or June, or

D. three days of personal leave if the judge qualified for office on or after July 1.

d. **Sick leave.** In addition to the annual leave and personal leave as provided for in this Rule, a judge: (1) is entitled to unlimited sick leave for any period of the judge's illness or disability that precludes the judge from performing judicial duties; and (2) may take a reasonable amount of sick leave (A) for the judge's medical appointments; (B) due to the illness or disability of family members; or (C) due to the birth, adoption, or foster care placement of a child with the judge, all subject to the definitions, conditions, limitations, and procedures in an Administrative Order issued by the Chief Judge of the Court of Appeals. Sick leave used for the purposes allowed by subsection (2) of this section, together with annual leave and personal leave taken for these purposes, may not exceed an aggregate total of 12 weeks for the calendar year. The Chief Judge of the Court of Appeals shall issue an Administrative Order implementing this section. The Order shall be posted on the Judiciary's website and otherwise made publicly available.

Committee note. — The authority of the Commission on Judicial Disabilities with respect to a disability as defined in Rule 16-803 is not affected by this Rule.

e. **Termination of judicial service.** A judge whose judicial service is terminated for any reason, and who is not elected or appointed to another court without break in service, loses any annual or personal leave unused as of the date of termination of service.

f. **Discretion of chief judge or administrative judge.** A judge's annual leave and personal leave shall be taken at the time or times prescribed or permitted by the chief judge of the judge's appellate court, if the judge is a judge of an appellate court; the Circuit Administrative Judge of the judge's judicial circuit, if the judge is a judge of a circuit court; or the Chief Judge of the District Court, if the judge is a judge of that court. In determining when a judge may take annual leave and for what period of time, the judge exercising supervisory authority under this Rule shall be mindful of the necessity of retention of sufficient judicial staffing in the court or courts under the judge's supervision to permit at all times the prompt and effective disposition of the business of that court or those courts. A request for leave at a certain time or for a certain period of time may be rejected by the judge exercising supervision under this Rule if the granting of the requested leave would prevent the prompt and effective disposition of business of that court or those courts, except that personal leave requested for observance of a religious holiday may not be denied.

g. **Supervision by Chief Judge of the Court of Appeals.** The operation of this Rule is at all times subject to the supervision and control of the Chief Judge of the Court of Appeals. (Amended Apr. 11, 1977, effective July 1, 1977; Nov. 13, 1981, effective Jan. 1, 1982; June 28, 1988, effective July 1, 1988; Dec. 31, 1991, effective Jan. 1, 1992; June 5, 1996, effective Jan. 1, 1997; Dec. 10, 1996, effective Jan. 1, 1997; Dec. 30, 2008, effective Jan. 1, 2009; Dec. 15, 2009, effective Jan. 1, 2010; Jan. 12, 2010, effective Jan. 12, 2010.)

Source. — This Rule is former Rule 1203.

Effect of amendments. — The first 1996 amendment added the Source note.

The second 1996 amendment rewrote the Rule.

The 2008 amendment added "subsection b 2 and" in the first sentence of b 1; and added b 2 and redesignated remaining paragraphs accordingly.

The 2009 amendment in b.(2) substituted "2010" for "2009" in the introductory language; in b.(2)A substituted "2010" for "2009" twice; substituted "17 working days" for "22 working days"; and substituted "1.42 days per month" for "1.83 days per month" twice; and in b.(2)B substituted "up to ten days" for "up to five days".

The 2010 amendment rewrote d and added the committee note.

Rule 16-105. Reports to be filed.

a. **Report by judge.** Every judge of the Circuit Court shall submit to the County Administrative Judge reports as the Chief Judge of the Court of Appeals may require, on forms prescribed and supplied by the State Court Administrator and approved by the Chief Judge of the Court of Appeals.

b. **Report by County Administrative Judge.** Each Circuit or County Administrative Judge shall furnish such other reports as may from time to time be required by the Chief Judge of the Court of Appeals. (Amended June 16, 1975, effective July 1, 1975; Nov. 8, 1982, effective Jan. 1, 1983; June 5, 1996, effective Jan. 1, 1997; Dec. 16, 1999, effective Jan. 1, 2000.)

Source. — This Rule is former Rule 1204.

Effect of amendments. — The 1996 amendment added the Source note.

The 1999 amendment, in a, substituted "County Administrative Judge" for "Circuit Administrative Judge," deleted "of his judicial circuit" following "Administrative Judge," deleted "may from time to time be required by" following "reports as," inserted "may require" following the first occurrence of "Appeals," deleted the comma following "Administrator," and deleted the former last sentence; and deleted the Committee note.

Editor's note. — An Order dated June 5, 1996, effective Jan. 1, 1997, renumbered this Rule, which was formerly Rule 1204.

Rule 16-106. Court sessions — Holidays — Time for convening.

a. **Court sessions — Holidays.** A court shall be in session each day from Monday through Friday except on holidays. On holidays, no trials or other court proceedings shall be conducted except in emergency matters or when ordered by the Chief Judge of the Court of Appeals or a judge of the particular court as the judicial business and public welfare may require. In an emergency and in the interest of the public welfare, the Chief Judge of the Court of Appeals may order a court to be closed on any day.

Cross references. — For the definition of "holiday," see Rule 1-202.

b. **Time for convening.** All scheduled proceedings will stand for hearing at 10:00 A.M. unless otherwise ordered by the court. (Amended Sept. 9, 1969; Oct. 13, 1970; Dec. 13, 1973; Nov. 5, 1976, effective Jan. 1, 1977; June 28, 1988, effective July 1, 1988; July 16, 1992; June 5, 1996, effective Jan. 1, 1997; Dec. 10, 1996, effective Jan. 1, 1997.)

Committee note. — This Rule is not intended to prevent the convening of court earlier than 10:00 o'clock A.M. when circumstances so require or when such a procedure is established under rules like Seventh Circuit Rules 507 and 707. However, if court is to convene at an earlier hour, reasonable notice should be furnished counsel. It is intended that conferences or other work in chambers shall not conflict with or postpone the regular time for convening court. It is contemplated that a court will remain in session for as long as is necessary for the effective disposition of the business before it.

Source. — This Rule is former Rule 1205.

Effect of amendments. — The first 1996 amendment added the Source note.

The second 1996 amendment rewrote the Rule.

Editor's note. — An Order dated June 5, 1996, effective Jan. 1, 1997, renumbered this Rule, which was formerly Rule 1205.

Pending before the Court of Appeals at press time is the One-Hundred Thirty-Third Report of the Court's Standing Committee on Rules of Practice and Procedure, which includes an amendment to this Rule to conform the holiday schedule of the Court to other divisions of State government in light of the General Assembly's passage of Chapter 347, Acts 1996, effective October 1, 1996.

Rule 16-107. Term of court and grand jury.

(a) **Term of court.** For accounting and statistical reporting purposes, each circuit court shall hold a single term each year beginning on July 1 and ending on the following June 30.

(b) **Term of grand jury; extension to complete investigation.** The jury plan of a county shall specify the term for a grand jury for the county. The term of service of any additional grand jury appointed pursuant to Code, Courts Article, § 8-413 shall be as determined by the county administrative judge. On motion of the State's Attorney, the county administrative judge or the jury judge may extend the term of a grand jury or additional grand jury so that it may complete an investigation specified by the judge in the order. The grand jury shall continue until it concludes its investigation or is sooner discharged by the judge, but is limited to the investigation specified in the order. In this Rule, "State's Attorney" includes the Attorney General, when using a grand jury pursuant to Article V, § 3 of the Maryland Constitution and the State Prosecutor, when using a grand jury pursuant to Code, Criminal Procedure Article, § 14-110. (Rescinded and new, Jan. 18, 1996, effective July 1, 1996; amended June 5, 1996, effective Jan. 1, 1997; Dec. 4, 2007, effective Jan. 1, 2008; Feb. 10, 2009, effective March 1, 2009.)

Cross references. — For the definition of "jury plan," see Code, Courts Article, § 8-101(c).

Source. — This Rule is derived in part from former Rule 1206 and is in part new.

Effect of amendments. — The 1996 amendment added the Source note.

The December 4, 2007 Order, effective January 1, 2008, rewrote the heading, deleted b, made related changes; and in the Source note added "derived from".

The 2009 amendment substituted "Term of court and grand jury" for "Single term of court" in the rule catchline; added the (a) designation and subsection heading; added (b) and the cross reference note; and inserted "in part " and "and is in part new" in the source note.

Editor's note. — An Order dated June 5, 1996, effective Jan. 1, 1997, renumbered this Rule, which was formerly Rule 1206.

Cited in State v. Griswold, 374 Md. 184, 821 A.2d 430 (2003).

Rule 16-108. Conference of Circuit Judges.

a. **Purpose.** There shall be a Conference of Circuit Judges that represents the interests of the circuit courts and is a policy advisory body to the Chief Judge of the Court of Appeals, the Court of Appeals, and other judicial branch agencies in all circuit court matters.

b. **Powers.** 1. Administration Policies. To fulfill its purpose, the Conference shall work collaboratively and in consultation with the Chief Judge of the Court of Appeals in developing policies affecting the administration of the circuit courts, including but not limited to:

(A) programs and practices that will enhance the administration of justice;

(B) the level of operational and judicial resources to be included in the Judiciary Budget;

(C) legislation that may affect the circuit courts; and

(D) the compensation and benefits of circuit court judges.

2. Consultants. With the approval of the Chief Judge, the Conference may retain consultants in matters relating to the circuit courts.

3. Consultation with Chief Judge of the Court of Appeals. The Conference shall consult with the Chief Judge of the Court of Appeals:

(A) on the appointment of circuit judges to committees of the Judicial Conference in accordance with Rule 16-802 f.2.; and

(B) to recommend circuit judges for membership on other committees and bodies of interest to the circuit courts.

4. Business and Technology Case Management Committee of Program Judges. The Conference shall appoint a committee of not less than three program judges to perform the duties required by Rule 17-107 (b) and generally to advise the Conference regarding the Business and Technology Case Management Program.

Cross references. — For the definition of "program judge," see Rule 16-205 (a)(3).

5. Majority Vote. The Conference and the Executive Committee of the Conference each shall exercise its powers and carry out its duties pursuant to a majority vote of its authorized membership.

c. **Membership and operation.** 1. Composition. The Conference shall comprise 16 members including the circuit administrative judge from each judicial circuit and one circuit judge from each judicial circuit who shall be elected every two years by majority vote of the circuit judges then authorized in the circuit.

2. Chair and Vice-Chair. The Conference shall elect from its members every two years a Chair and Vice-chair.

3. Quorum. A majority of the authorized membership of the Conference shall constitute a quorum.

4. Meetings. The Conference shall meet at least four times a year.

d. **Executive Committee.** 1. Power and Composition. There shall be an Executive Committee of the Conference. It shall consist of the Conference Chair and Vice-Chair and such other members as may be designated by the Conference and shall be empowered to act with the full authority of the Conference when the Conference is not in session. The actions of the Executive Committee will be reported fully to the Conference at its next meeting.

2. Quorum. A majority of the authorized membership of the Executive Committee shall constitute a quorum.

3. Convening the Executive Committee. The Executive Committee shall convene at the call of the Conference Chair. In the absence of the Chair, the Vice-Chair is authorized to convene the Executive Committee.

e. **Conference staff.** The Administrative Office of the Courts shall serve as staff to the Conference and its Executive Committee. (Added Mar. 14, 1972; amended Nov. 28, 1978; June 5, 1996, effective Jan. 1, 1997; June 8, 1998, effective Oct. 1, 1998; Nov. 12, 2003, effective Jan. 1, 2004.)

Source. — This Rule is new.

Effect of amendments. — The 1996 amendment added the Source note.

The 1998 amendment rewrote the Rule.

The 2003 amendment added new (b)(4); redesignated former (b)(4) as (b)(5); and added the cross reference following (b)(4).

Editor's note. — An Order dated June 5, 1996, effective Jan. 1, 1997, renumbered this Rule, which was formerly Rule 1207.

Rule 16-109. Photographing, recording, broadcasting or televising in courthouses.

a. **Definitions.** 1. "Extended coverage" means any recording or broadcasting of proceedings by the use of television, radio, photographic, or recording equipment by:

(i) the news media, or

(ii) persons engaged in the preparation of educational films or recordings with the written approval of the presiding judge.

2. "Local administrative judge" means the county administrative judge in the Circuit Court and the district administrative judge in the District Court.

3. "Party" means a named litigant of record who has appeared in the proceeding.

4. "Proceeding" means any trial, hearing, motion, argument on appeal or other matter held in open court which the public is entitled to attend.

5. "Presiding judge" means a trial judge designated to preside over a proceeding which is, or is intended to be the subject of extended coverage. Where action of a presiding judge is required by this rule, and no trial judge has been designated to preside over the proceeding, presiding judge means the local administrative judge. Presiding judge in an appellate court means the Chief Judge of that Court, or the senior judge of a panel of which the Chief Judge is not a member.

b. **General provisions.** 1. Unless prohibited by law or this Rule, extended coverage of proceedings in the trial and appellate courts of this State is permitted in accordance with this Rule.

Committee note. — Code, Criminal Procedure Article, § 1-201 prohibits extended coverage of criminal proceedings in a trial court or before a grand jury.

2. Outside a courtroom but within a courthouse or other facility extended coverage is prohibited of persons present for a judicial or grand jury proceeding, or where extended coverage is so close to a judicial or grand jury

proceeding that it is likely to interfere with the proceeding or its dignity and decorum.

3. Possession of an "electronic device" in a "court facility" as those terms are defined in Rule 16-110 is governed by that Rule.

4. Nothing in this rule is intended to restrict in any way the present rights of the media to report proceedings.

5. Extended coverage shall be conducted so as not to interfere with the right of any person to a fair and impartial trial, and so as not to interfere with the dignity and decorum which must attend the proceedings.

6. No proceeding shall be delayed or continued to allow for extended coverage, nor shall the requirements of extended coverage in any way affect legitimate motions for continuance or challenges to the judge.

7. This rule does not apply to:

(i) The use of electronic or photographic equipment approved by the court for the perpetuation of a court record;

(ii) Investiture or ceremonial proceedings, provided, however, that the local administrative judge of a trial court and the Chief Judge of an appellate court shall have complete discretion to regulate the presence and use of cameras, recorders, and broadcasting equipment at the proceedings.

(iii) The use of electronic or photographic equipment approved by the court to take the testimony of a child victim under Code, Criminal Procedure Article, § 11-303.

c. **Request for extended coverage.** 1. All requests for extended coverage shall be made in writing to the clerk of the court at which the proceeding is to be held at least five days before the proceeding is scheduled to begin and shall specifically identify the proceeding to be covered. For good cause a court may honor a request which does not comply with the requirements of this subsection. The clerk shall promptly give notice of a request to all parties to the proceeding.

Cross references. — For the computation of time before a day, act, or event, see Rule 1-203 (b).

2. Where proceedings are continued other than for normal or routine recesses, weekends, or holidays, it is the responsibility of the media to make a separate request for later extended coverage.

Cross references. — For the definition of "holiday," see Rule 1-202.

d. **Action on request.** The presiding judge shall grant or deny a request for extended coverage before the commencement of the proceeding. If the request is granted, the presiding judge shall promptly notify the local administrative judge who shall make whatever arrangements are necessary to accommodate the entry into and presence in the courthouse of the persons conducting the extended coverage and their equipment.

e. **Consent to extended coverage.** 1. Extended coverage shall not be permitted in any proceeding in a trial court unless all parties to the proceeding have filed their written consent in the record, except that consent need not be obtained from a party which is a federal, state, or local government, or an agency or subdivision thereof or an individual sued or suing in his official governmental capacity.

2. Consent once given may not be withdrawn, but any party may at any time move for termination or limitation of extended coverage in accordance with this rule.

3. Consent of the parties is not required for extended coverage in appellate courts, but any party may at any time move for termination or limitation of extended coverage in accordance with this rule.

f. **Restrictions on extended coverage.** 1. Extended coverage of all or any portion of a proceeding may be prohibited, terminated or limited, on the presiding judge's own initiative or on the request of a party, witness, or juror in the proceedings, where the judge finds that there is good cause for termination, prohibition, or limitation of extended coverage. There is a presumption that good cause exists in cases involving custody, divorce, minors, relocated witnesses, and trade secrets.

Committee note. — Examples of good cause include unfairness, danger to a person, undue embarrassment, or hindrance of proper law enforcement.

2. Extended coverage is not permitted of any proceeding which is by law closed to the public, or which may be closed to the public and has been closed by the judge.

3. Extended coverage in the judicial area of a courthouse or other facility is limited to proceedings in the courtroom in the presence of the presiding judge.

4. There shall be no audio coverage of private conferences, bench conferences, and conferences at counsel tables.

g. **Standards of conduct and technology.** 1. Television or movie camera equipment shall be positioned outside the rail of the courtroom, or if there is no rail, in the area reserved for spectators, at a location approved in advance by the presiding judge. Wherever possible, recording and broadcasting equipment which is not a component part of a television camera shall be located outside the courtroom in an area approved in advance by the presiding judge.

2. A still camera photographer shall be positioned outside the rail of the courtroom or if there is no rail, in the area reserved for spectators, at a location approved in advance by the presiding judge. The still camera photographer shall not photograph from any other place, and shall not engage in any movement or assume any body position that would be likely to attract attention or be distracting. Unless positioned in or beyond the last row of spectators' seats, or in an aisle to the outside of the spectators' seating area, the still photographer shall remain seated while photographing.

3. Broadcast media representatives shall not move about the courtroom while proceedings are in session, and microphones and recording equipment once positioned shall not be moved during the pendency of the proceeding.

4. Not more than one television camera, operated by not more than one person, shall be permitted in any trial court proceeding. Not more than two

stationary television cameras, operated by not more than one person each, shall be permitted in any appellate court proceeding.

5. Not more than one still photographer, utilizing not more than two still cameras with not more than two lenses for each camera and related equipment approved by the presiding judge shall be permitted in any proceeding in a trial or appellate court.

6. Not more than one audio system for broadcast purposes shall be permitted in any proceeding in a trial or appellate court. Audio pickup shall be accomplished from existing audio systems, except that if no technically suitable audio system exists, unobtrusive microphones and related wiring shall be located in places designated in advance by the presiding judge. Microphones located at the judge's bench and at counsel tables shall be equipped with temporary cutoff switches. A directional microphone may be mounted on the television or film camera, but no parabolic or similar microphones shall be used.

7. Any "pooling" arrangements among the media required by these limitations on equipment and personnel shall be the sole responsibility of the media without calling upon the presiding judge to mediate any dispute as to the appropriate media representative or equipment authorized to cover a particular proceeding. In the absence of advance media agreement on disputed equipment or personnel issues, the presiding judge shall exclude all contesting media personnel from extended coverage.

8. Only television, movie, and audio equipment that does not produce light or distracting sound shall be employed. No artificial lighting device of any kind shall be employed in connection with the television and movie cameras.

9. Only still camera equipment that does not produce distracting sound shall be employed to cover judicial proceedings. No artificial lighting device of any kind shall be employed in connection with a still camera.

10. It shall be the affirmative duty of media personnel to demonstrate to the presiding judge adequately in advance of any proceeding that the equipment sought to be utilized meets the sound and light criteria enunciated herein. A failure to obtain advance judicial approval for equipment shall preclude its use in any proceedings.

11. Photographic or audio equipment shall not be placed in or removed from the courtroom except prior to commencement or after adjournment of proceedings each day, or during a recess. Neither film magazines nor still camera film or lenses shall be changed within a courtroom except during a recess in the proceeding.

12. With the concurrence of the presiding judge, and before the commencement of a proceeding or during a recess, modifications and additions may be made in light sources existing in the courtroom provided such modifications or additions are installed and maintained without public expense. (Added November 10, 1980, effective January 1, 1981; amended June 5, 1996, effective January 1, 1997; December 10, 1996, effective January 1, 1997; December 16, 1999, effective January 1, 2000; May 8, 2007, effective July 1, 2007; amended October 20, 2010, effective January 1, 2011.)

Committee note. — Nothing in this Rule prohibits a judge from granting a reasonable request to use court-owned or court-controlled electronic or photographic equipment or materials.

Source. — This Rule is derived from former Rule 1209.

Effect of amendments. — The first 1996 amendment added the Source note.

The second 1996 amendment added the cross reference in c.

The 1999 amendment, in f 1, deleted "(film camera — 16 mm sound on film (self blimped) or video tape electronic camera)" following "television camera," substituted "one person" for "one camera person" twice, and inserted "stationary" preceding "television cameras"; inserted a comma following "audio system exists" in the second sentence of f 3; in f 5 and f 6, substituted "that does not" for "which does not," and deleted the former second sentences; substituted "that would be likely to attract attention" for "which would be likely to call attention to himself" in f 9; substituted "presiding judge" for "local administrative judge" in f 12; and deleted SCHEDULE A.

The 2007 amendment deleted "by" at the beginning of a.1(ii); in b.1 added "Unless prohibited by law or this Rule" and the Committee note, and deleted "unless prohibited or limited" after "permitted"; in b.3 added "including camera-equipped ... capturing images" and

"jury rooms"; added (b)(7)(iii), the Cross reference in c.1, and d, and redesignated accordingly; deleted previous f.1, redesignated accordingly, rewrote f.1 and added the Committee note; in g.4, deleted "portable" before "television"; and in g.12 added the Committee note and "derived from" in the Source note.

The 2010 amendment rewrote b.3.

Editor's note. — Extended coverage of criminal proceedings in the trial courts of Maryland is prohibited by Article 27, § 467B (see now § 1-201 of the Criminal Procedure Article) of the Maryland Code.

An Order dated June 5, 1996, effective Jan. 1, 1997, renumbered this Rule, which was formerly Rule 1209.

Rule stems from powers granted in article IV, § 18 (a) of Maryland Constitution. — This Rule — regulating the recording of court proceedings by the new media — is a rule of administration or procedure that falls within the concurrent rulemaking powers granted by article IV, § 18 (a) of the Maryland Constitution. 66 Op. Att'y Gen. 80 (1981).

Rule 16-110. Cell phones; other electronic devices; cameras.

(a) **Definitions.** In this Rule the following definitions apply:

(1) Court facility. "Court facility" means the building in which a circuit court or the District Court is located, but if the court is in a building that is also occupied by county or State executive agencies having no substantial connection with the court, then only that part of the building occupied by the court.

(2) Electronic device. "Electronic device" means (A) a cell phone, a computer, and any other device that is capable of transmitting, receiving, or recording messages, images, sounds, data, or other information by electronic means or that, in appearance, purports to be a cell phone, computer, or such other device; and (B) a camera, regardless of whether it operates electronically, mechanically, or otherwise and regardless of whether images are recorded by using digital technology, film, light-sensitive plates, or other means.

(3) Local administrative judge. "Local administrative judge" means the county administrative judge in a circuit court and the district administrative judge in the District Court.

(b) **Possession and use of electronic devices.** (1) Generally. Subject to inspection by court security personnel and the restrictions and prohibitions set forth in this section, a person may (A) bring an electronic device into a court facility and (B) use the electronic device for the purpose of sending and receiving phone calls and electronic messages and for any other lawful purpose not otherwise prohibited.

  (2) Restrictions and prohibitions. (A) Rule 5-615 Order. An electronic device may not be used to facilitate or achieve a violation of an order entered pursuant to Rule 5-615 (d).

  (B) Photographs and video. Except as permitted in accordance with this Rule, Rule 16-109, Rule 16-405, or Rule 16-504 or as expressly permitted by the local administrative judge, a person may not (i) take or record a photograph, video, or other visual image in a court facility, or (ii) transmit a photograph, video, or other visual image from or within a court facility.

Committee note. — The prohibition set forth in subsection (b)(2)(B) of this Rule includes still photography and moving visual images. It is anticipated that permission will be granted for the taking of photographs at ceremonial functions.

  (C) Interference with court proceedings or work. An electronic device shall not be used in a manner that interferes with court proceedings or the work of court personnel.

Committee note. — An example of a use prohibited by subsection (b)(2)(C) is a loud conversation on a cell phone near a court employee's work station or in a hallway near the door to a courtroom.

  (D) Jury deliberation room. An electronic device may not be brought into a jury deliberation room.

  (E) Courtroom. (i) Except with the express permission of the presiding judge or as otherwise permitted by this Rule, Rule 16-109, Rule 16-405, or Rule 16-504, all electronic devices inside a courtroom shall remain off and no electronic device may be used to receive, transmit, or record sound, visual images, data, or other information.

  (ii) Subject to subsection (b)(2)(F), the court shall liberally allow the attorneys in a proceeding currently being heard, their employees, and agents to make reasonable and lawful use of an electronic device in connection with the proceeding.

  (F) Security or privacy issues in a particular case. Upon a finding that the circumstances of a particular case raise special security or privacy issues that justify a restriction on the possession of electronic devices, the local administrative judge or the presiding judge may enter an order limiting or prohibiting the possession of electronic devices in a courtroom or other designated areas of the court facility. The order shall provide for notice of the designated areas and for the collection of the devices and their return when the individual who possessed the device leaves the courtroom or other area. No liability shall accrue to the security personnel or any other court official or employee for any loss or misplacement of or damage to the device.

  (c) **Violation of Rule.** (1) Security personnel or other court personnel may confiscate and retain an electronic device that is used in violation of this Rule, subject to further order of the court or until the owner leaves the building. No liability shall accrue to the security personnel or any other court official or employee for any loss or misplacement of or damage to the device.

(2) An individual who willfully violates this Rule or any reasonable limitation imposed by the local administrative judge or the presiding judge may be found in contempt of court and sanctioned in accordance with the Rules in Title 15, Chapter 200.

(d) **Notice.** Notice of the provisions of sections (b) and (c) of this Rule shall be:

(1) posted prominently at the court facility;

(2) included on the main judiciary website and the website of each court; and

(3) disseminated to the public by any other means approved in an administrative order of the Chief Judge of the Court of Appeals. (Added October 20, 2010, effective January 1, 20118; amended June 7, 2011, effective July 1, 2011; September 8, 2011, effective January 1, 2012.)

Source. — This Rule is new.

Effect of amendments. — The 2011 amendment, effective July 1, 2011, deleted (d)(2) and the (d)(1) designator.

The 2011 amendment, effective January 1, 2012, redesignated (d)(A) through (d)(C) as (d)(1) through (d)(3).

CHAPTER 200. THE CALENDAR — ASSIGNMENT AND DISPOSITION OF MOTIONS AND CASES.

Rule 16-201. Motion day — Calendar.

a. **Motion day.** Each County Administrative Judge may prescribe motion days on which all motions and other preliminary matters pending in that court and scheduled for hearing shall be heard.

b. **Motions calendar.** The clerk in each county shall maintain a motions calendar in such form as may be prescribed by the County Administrative Judge. Upon the filing of a response pursuant to Rule 2-311 (b), or upon the date on which such response should have been filed, the clerk will list the case on the motions calendar.

c. **Assignment when hearing required.** The County Administrative Judge in each county shall provide for review of the motions calendar at appropriate intervals and the determination of what matters thereon require hearings. The judge shall provide for assignment of hearing dates for such matters and notices thereof shall be given to all parties.

d. **Notice of lengthy hearing.** If it is anticipated that the hearing on a motion will exceed a total of 30 minutes, the parties shall inform the assignment clerk, in which event the motion may be calendared specially. (Amended June 30, 1973, effective July 1, 1973; Dec. 17, 1975, effective Jan. 1, 1976; Oct. 1, 1980, effective Jan. 1, 1981; Apr. 6, 1984, effective July 1, 1984; June 5, 1996, effective Jan. 1, 1997; Dec. 16, 1999, effective Jan. 1, 2000.)

Source. — This Rule is former Rule 1210.

Effect of amendments. — The 1996 amendment added the Source note.

The 1999 amendment substituted "Each County Administrative Judge may prescribe motion days" for "Each Circuit Administrative Judge shall prescribe for each court in his judicial circuit motion days" in a; in c, deleted "and the Circuit Administrative Judge of the Eighth Judicial Circuit" following "each county" in the first sentence, and substituted "The judge" for "He" in the last sentence; and deleted the Committee note.

Editor's note. — An Order dated June 5, 1996, effective Jan. 1, 1997, renumbered this Rule, which was formerly Rule 1210.

Improper to overrule assignment by administrative judge. — Circuit judge erred by ruling on defendant's motion for modification of sentence after an administrative judge assigned the matter to another judge because Rule 16-101 made it clear that the assignment of circuit judges for trials or hearings was entirely within the province of circuit and county administrative judges, subject only to the supervisory authority of the chief judge of the court of appeals and the administrative rules adopted by the court of appeals; Rules 16-101 through 16-103, 16-201, and 16-202 unambiguously vest in the chief judge of the court of appeals, circuit administrative judges, and county administrative judges, full authority to assign judges for trials or hearings in the circuit courts of the State, and there is no rule or opinion of the court of appeals that vests in a circuit judge of a particular county the authority to override or ignore an assignment by the administrative judge of that county or by the circuit administrative judge of the circuit that included that county. Strickland v. State, 407 Md. 344, 965 A.2d 887 (2009).

Rule 16-202. Assignment of actions for trial.

a. **Generally.** The County Administrative Judge in each county shall supervise the assignment of actions for trial to achieve the efficient use of available judicial personnel and to bring pending actions to trial and dispose of them as expeditiously as feasible. Procedures instituted in this regard shall be designed to:

(1) eliminate docket calls in open court;

(2) insure the prompt disposition of motions and other preliminary matters;

(3) provide for the use of scheduling and pretrial conferences, and the establishment of a calendar for that purpose, when appropriate;

(4) provide for the prompt disposition of uncontested and ex parte matters, including references to an examiner-master, when appropriate;

(5) provide for the disposition of actions under Rule 2-507;

(6) establish trial and motion calendars and other appropriate systems under which actions ready for trial will be assigned for trial and tried, after proper notice to parties, without necessity of a request for assignment from any party; and

Cross references. — *See* Rule 16-201 (Motion Day — Calendar).

(7) establish systems of regular reports which will indicate the status of all pending actions with respect to their readiness for trial, the disposition of actions, and the availability of judges for trial work.

b. **Case management plan; information report.** (1) The County Administrative Judge shall develop and, upon approval by the Chief Judge of the Court of Appeals, implement and monitor a case management plan for the prompt and efficient scheduling and disposition of actions in the circuit court. The plan shall include a system of differentiated case management in which actions are classified according to complexity and priority and are assigned to a scheduling category based on that classification. In courts that have a family division, the plan shall provide criteria for (A) requiring parties in an action assigned to the family division to attend a scheduling conference in accordance with Rule 2-504.1 (a) (1) and (B) identifying actions in the family division that are appropriate for assignment to a specific judge who shall be responsible for the entire case unless the County Administrative Judge subsequently decides to reassign it.

Cross references. — See Rule 9-204 for provisions that may be included in the case management plan concerning an educational seminar for parties in actions in which child support, custody, or visitation are involved.

(2) In developing and implementing the case management plan, the County Administrative Judge shall (i) consult with the Administrative Office of the Courts and with other county administrative judges who have developed or are in the process of developing such plans in an effort to achieve as much consistency and uniformity among the plans as is reasonably practicable, and (ii) seek the assistance of the county bar association and such other interested groups and persons as the judge deems advisable.

(3) As part of the plan, the clerk shall make available to the parties, without charge, a form approved by the County Administrative Judge that will provide the information necessary to implement the case management plan. The information contained in the information report shall not be used for any purpose other than case management.

(4) The clerk of each circuit court shall make available for public inspection a copy of the current administrative order of the Chief Judge of the Court of Appeals exempting categories of actions from the information report requirement of Rule 2-111 (a). (Amended Apr. 6, 1984, effective July 1, 1984; June 7, 1994, effective July 1, 1994; Jan. 10, 1995, effective Feb. 1, 1995; June 5, 1996, effective Jan. 1, 1997; Jan. 13, 1998, effective July 1, 1998; Mar. 5, 2001, effective July 1, 2001.)

Source. — This Rule is former Rule 1211.

Effect of amendments. — The 1996 amendment substituted "Rule 16-201" for "Rule 1210" in the Cross reference note to a. (6); and added the Source note.

The 1998 amendment, in b. (1), added the third sentence and the Cross reference.

The 2001 amendment substituted "9-204" for "9-204.1" in the cross reference of b. (1).

Editor's note. — An Order dated June 5, 1996, effective Jan. 1, 1997, renumbered this Rule, which was formerly Rule 1211.

Effect of assignment clerk's failure to set trial date and send notification thereof. — Even if an assignment clerk was responsible for setting a trial date and sending notification thereof under this Rule, and failed to do so, the plaintiff is not relieved of prosecuting his case and providing proof of proceedings therein on the record. Fact that the clerk has failed in his responsibility under one rule does not relieve appellants from their responsibility under another. Driver v. Parke-Davis & Co., 29 Md. App. 354, 348 A.2d 38, cert. denied, 277 Md. 736 (1975).

Improper to overrule assignment by administrative judge. — Circuit judge erred by ruling on defendant's motion for modification of sentence after an administrative judge assigned the matter to another judge because Rule 16-101 made it clear that the assignment of circuit judges for trials or hearings was entirely within the province of circuit and county administrative judges, subject only to the supervisory authority of the chief judge of the court of appeals and the administrative rules adopted by the court of appeals; Rules 16-101 through 16-103, 16-201, and 16-202 unambiguously vest in the chief judge of the court of appeals, circuit administrative judges, and county administrative judges, full authority to assign judges for trials or hearings in the circuit courts of the State, and there is no rule or opinion of the court of appeals that vests in a circuit judge of a particular county the authority to override or ignore an assignment by the administrative judge of that county or by the circuit administrative judge of the circuit that included that county. Strickland v. State, 407 Md. 344, 965 A.2d 887 (2009).

Supervision — State's highest court ruled that the public defender's petition for a writ of prohibition, writ of mandamus, or appropriate relief from the trial court's directive that parties meet certain procedural requirements in filing exceptions to the report of a master in juvenile cases or face dismissal of those excep-

tions had to be dismissed; the trial court, through court rules and statutory law, was delegated the authority to oversee the administration of juvenile cases and, more importantly, the issues with which the public defender was concerned were currently being considered in two cases before the State's intermediate appellate court, which meant that the public defender had a chance to obtain the relief sough through those proceedings. Forster v. Hargadon, 398 Md. 298, 920 A.2d 1049 (2007).

Cited in In re Marcus J., 175 Md. App. 703, 931 A.2d 1146 (2007), aff'd, 2008 Md. LEXIS 322 (2008); Davis v. State, 196 Md. App. 81, 7 A.3d 690 (2010).

Rule 16-203. Special docket for asbestos cases.

a. **Definition.** In this Rule, "asbestos case" means an action seeking money damages for personal injury or death allegedly caused by exposure to asbestos or products containing asbestos. It does not include an action seeking principally equitable relief or seeking principally damages for injury to property or for removal of asbestos or products containing asbestos from property.

b. **Special docket.** The Administrative Judge of the Circuit Court for Baltimore City may establish a special inactive docket for asbestos cases filed in or transferred to that court. The order:

(1) shall specify the criteria and procedures for placement of an asbestos case on the inactive docket and for removal of a case from the docket;

(2) may permit an asbestos case meeting the criteria for placement on the inactive docket to be placed on that docket at any time prior to trial; and

(3) with respect to any case placed on the inactive docket, may stay the time for filing responses to the complaint, discovery, and other proceedings until the case is removed from the docket.

c. **Transfer of cases from other counties.** (1) The circuit administrative judge for any other judicial circuit, by order, may

(A) adopt the criteria established in an order entered by the Administrative Judge of the Circuit Court for Baltimore City pursuant to section b of this Rule for placement of an asbestos case on the inactive docket for asbestos cases;

(B) provide for the transfer to the Circuit Court for Baltimore City, for placement on the inactive docket, of any asbestos case filed in a circuit court in that other circuit for which venue would lie in Baltimore City; and

(C) establish procedures for the prompt disposition in the circuit court where the action was filed of any dispute as to whether venue would lie in Baltimore City.

(2) If an action is transferred pursuant to this Rule, the clerk of the circuit court where the action was filed shall deliver the file or a copy of it to the clerk of the Circuit Court for Baltimore City, and, except as provided in subsection c (3) of this Rule, the action shall thereafter proceed as if initially filed in the Circuit Court for Baltimore City.

(3) Unless the parties agree otherwise, any action transferred pursuant to this section, upon removal from the inactive docket, shall be retransferred to

the circuit court in which it was originally filed and all further proceedings shall take place in that court.

d. **Exemption from Rule 2-507.** Any action placed on an inactive docket pursuant to this Rule shall not be subject to Rule 2-507 until the action is removed from that docket.

e. **Effect on Rule 2-327 (d).** To the extent of any inconsistency with Rule 2-327 (d), this Rule shall prevail.

Committee note. — This section e does not preclude a transfer under Rule 2-327 upon retransfer of an action under subsection c (3) of this Rule.

f. **Applicability of Rule.** This Rule shall apply only to actions filed on or after December 8, 1992. (Added Dec. 8, 1992; amended June 5, 1996, effective Jan. 1, 1997; Dec. 16, 1999, effective Jan. 1, 2000.)

Source. — This Rule is former Rule 1211A.

Effect of amendments. — The 1996 amendment added the Source note.

The 1999 amendment substituted "The Administrative Judge of the Circuit Court for Baltimore City" for "The Circuit Court for Baltimore City, by order entered by the Administrative Judge for the Eighth Judicial Circuit" in b; substituted "counties" for "circuits" in the subheading in c; and substituted "of the Circuit Court for Baltimore City" for "for the Eighth Judicial Circuit" in c (1) (A).

Editor's note. — An Order dated June 5, 1996, effective Jan. 1, 1997, renumbered this Rule, which was formerly Rule 1211A.

Rule 16-204. Family division and support services.

(a) **Family division.** (1) Established. In each county having more than seven resident judges of the circuit court authorized by law, there shall be a family division in the circuit court.

(2) Actions assigned. In a court that has a family division, the following categories of actions and matters shall be assigned to that division:

(A) dissolution of marriage, including divorce, annulment, and property distribution;

(B) child custody and visitation, including proceedings governed by the Maryland Uniform Child Custody Jurisdiction Act, Code, Family Law Article, Title 9, Subtitle 2, and the Parental Kidnapping Prevention Act, 28 U.S.C. § 1738A;

(C) alimony, spousal support, and child support, including proceedings under the Maryland Uniform Interstate Family Support Act;

(D) establishment and termination of the parent-child relationship, including paternity, adoption, guardianship that terminates parental rights, and emancipation;

(E) criminal nonsupport and desertion, including proceedings under Code, Family Law Article, Title 10, Subtitle 2 and Code, Family Law Article, Title 13;

(F) name changes;

(G) guardianship of minors and disabled persons under Code, Estates and Trusts Article, Title 13;

(H) involuntary admission to state facilities and emergency evaluations under Code, Health General Article, Title 10, Subtitle 6;

(I) family legal-medical issues, including decisions on the withholding or withdrawal of life-sustaining medical procedures;

(J) actions involving domestic violence under Code, Family Law Article, Title 4, Subtitle 5;

(K) juvenile causes under Code, Courts Article, Title 3, Subtitles 8 and 8A;

(L) matters assigned to the family division by the County Administrative Judge that are related to actions in the family division and appropriate for assignment to the family division; and

(M) civil and criminal contempt arising out of any of the categories of actions and matters set forth in subsection (a) (2) (A) through (a) (2) (L) of this Rule.

Committee note. — The jurisdiction of the circuit courts, the District Court, and the Orphan's Court is not affected by this section. For example, the District Court has concurrent jurisdiction with the circuit court over proceedings under Code, Family Law Article, Title 4, Subtitle 5.

(3) *Family support services.* Subject to the availability of funds, the following family support services shall be available through the family division for use when appropriate in a particular action:

(A) mediation in custody and visitation matters;

(B) custody investigations;

(C) trained personnel to respond to emergencies;

(D) mental health evaluations and evaluations for alcohol and drug abuse;

(E) information services, including procedural assistance to self-represented litigants;

Committee note. — This subsection is not intended to interfere with existing projects that provide assistance to self-represented litigants.

(F) information regarding lawyer referral services;

(G) parenting coordination services as permitted by Rule 9-205.2;

(H) parenting seminars; and

(I) any additional family support services for which funding is provided.

Committee note. — Examples of additional family support services that may be provided include general mediation programs, case managers, and family follow-up services.

(4) *Responsibilities of the County Administrative Judge.* The County Administrative Judge of the Circuit Court for each county having a family division shall:

(A) allocate sufficient available judicial resources to the family division so that actions are heard expeditiously in accordance with applicable law and the case management plan required by Rule 16-202 b;

Committee note. — This Rule neither requires nor prohibits the assignment of one or more judges to hear family division cases on a full-time basis. Rather, it allows each County Administrative Judge the flexibility to determine how that county's judicial assignments are to be made so that actions in the family division are heard expeditiously. Additional matters for county-by-county determination include whether and to what extent masters, special masters, and examiners are used to assist in the resolution of family division cases.

Nothing in this Rule affects the authority of a
circuit court judge to act on any matter within
the jurisdiction of the circuit court.

(B) provide in the case management plan required by Rule 16-202 b criteria
for:

(i) requiring parties in an action assigned to the family division to attend a
scheduling conference in accordance with Rule 2-504.1 (a) (1) and

(ii) identifying those actions in the family division that are appropriate for
assignment to a specific judge who shall be responsible for the entire case
unless the County Administrative Judge subsequently decides to reassign it;

Cross references. — For rules concerning
the referral of matters to masters as of course,
see Rules 2-541 and 9-208.

(C) appoint a family support services coordinator whose responsibilities
include:

(i) compiling, maintaining, and providing lists of available public and
private family support services,

(ii) coordinating and monitoring referrals in actions assigned to the family
division, and

(iii) reporting to the County Administrative Judge concerning the need for
additional family support services or the modification of existing services; and

(D) prepare and submit to the Chief Judge of the Court of Appeals, no later
than October 15 of each year, a written report that includes a description of
family support services needed by the court's family division, a fiscal note that
estimates the cost of those services for the following fiscal year, and, whenever
practicable, an estimate of the fiscal needs of the Clerk of the Circuit Court for
the county pertaining to the family division.

(b) **Circuit courts without a family division.** (1) Applicability. This
section applies to circuit courts for counties having less than eight resident
judges of the circuit court authorized by law.

(2) Family support services. Subject to availability of funds, the family
support services listed in subsection (a) (3) of this Rule shall be available
through the court for use when appropriate in cases in the categories listed in
subsection (a) (2) of this Rule.

(3) Family support services coordinator. The County Administrative Judge
shall appoint a full-time or part-time family support services coordinator
whose responsibilities shall be substantially as set forth in subsection (a) (4)
(C) of this Rule.

(4) Report to the Chief Judge of the Court of Appeals. The County Administrative Judge shall prepare and submit to the Chief Judge of the Court of
Appeals, no later than October 15 of each year, a written report that includes
a description of the family support services needed by the court, a fiscal note
that estimates the cost of those services for the following fiscal year, and,
whenever practicable, an estimate of the fiscal needs of the Clerk of the Circuit
Court for the county pertaining to family support services. (Added January 13,
1998, effective July 1, 1998; amended March 5, 2001, effective July 1, 2001;

January 8, 2002, effective Febuary 1, 2002; June 7, 2011, effective July 1, 2011; September 8, 2011, effective January 1, 2012.)

Source. — This Rule is new.

Effect of amendments. — The 2001 amendment substituted "9-208" for "9-207" in the cross reference of (a) (4) (B) (ii).

The 2002 amendment substituted "Subtitles 8 and 8A" for "Subtitle 8" in (a)(2)(K) and deleted ", and, in Montgomery ...Article, § 3-804" at the end of the committee note following (a)(2)(M).

The amendment effective July 1, 2011, inserted (a)(3)(G) and redesignated former (a)(3)(G) and (a)(3)(H) as (a)(3)(H) and (a)(3)(I) respectively.

The amendment effective January 1, 2012, substituted "self-represented" for "pro se" in (a)(3)(E) and in the cross reference note following (a)(3)(E) .

Rule 16-205. Business and technology case management program.

(a) **Definitions.** The following definitions apply in this Rule:

(1) ADR. "ADR" means "alternative dispute resolution" as defined in Rule 17-102.

(2) Program. "Program" means the business and technology case management program established pursuant to this Rule.

(3) Program judge. "Program judge" means a judge of a circuit court who is assigned to the program.

(b) **Program established.** Subject to the availability of fiscal and human resources, a program approved by the Chief Judge of the Court of Appeals shall be established to enable each circuit court to handle business and technology matters in a coordinated, efficient, and responsive manner and to afford convenient access to lawyers and litigants in business and technology matters. The program shall include:

(1) a program track within the differentiated case management system established under Rule 16-202;

(2) the procedure by which an action is assigned to the program;

(3) program judges who are specially trained in business and technology; and

(4) ADR proceedings conducted by persons qualified under Title 17 of these Rules and specially trained in business and technology.

Cross references. — See Rules 16-101 a and 16-103 a concerning the assignment of a judge of the circuit court for a county to sit as a program judge in the circuit court for another county.

(c) **Assignment of actions to the program.** On written request of a party or on the court's own initiative, the Circuit Administrative Judge of the circuit in which an action is filed or the Administrative Judge's designee may assign the action to the program if the judge determines that the action presents commercial or technological issues of such a complex or novel nature that specialized treatment is likely to improve the administration of justice. Factors that the judge may consider in making the determination include: (1) the nature of the relief sought, (2) the number and diverse interests of the parties, (3) the anticipated nature and extent of pretrial discovery and motions, (4) whether the parties agree to waive venue for the hearing of motions and other pretrial matters, (5) the degree of novelty and complexity of the factual and legal issues presented, (6) whether business or technology issues predominate over other issues presented in the action, and (7) the willingness of the parties to participate in ADR procedures.

(d) **Assignment to program judge.** Each action assigned to the program shall be assigned to a specific program judge. The program judge to whom the action is assigned shall hear all proceedings until the matter is concluded, except that, if necessary to prevent undue delay, prejudice, or injustice, the Circuit Administrative Judge or the Circuit Administrative Judge's designee may designate another judge to hear a particular pretrial matter. That judge shall be a program judge, if practicable.

(e) **Scheduling conference; Order.** Promptly after an action is assigned, the program judge shall (1) hold a scheduling conference under Rule 2-504.1 at which the program judge and the parties discuss the scheduling of discovery, ADR, and a trial date and (2) enter a scheduling order under Rule 2-504 that includes case management decisions made by the court at or as a result of the scheduling conference. (Added Oct. 31, 2002, effective Jan. 1, 2003.)

Source. — This Rule is new.

Cited in Boland v. Boland, 194 Md. App. 477, 5 A.3d 106 (2010).

Rule 16-206. Problem-solving court programs.

(a) **Applicability.** (1) Generally. This Rule applies to problem-solving court programs, which are specialized court dockets or programs that address matters under a court's jurisdiction through a multi-disciplinary and integrated approach incorporating collaboration by the court with other governmental entities, community organizations, and parties.

Committee note. — Problem-solving court programs include adult and juvenile drug treatment, DUI, mental health, truancy, and family recovery programs.

(2) Existing programs; programs submitted for approval on or after July 1, 2010. This Rule applies in its entirety to problem-solving court programs submitted for approval on or after July 1, 2010. Sections (d), (e), and (f) of this Rule apply also to problem-solving court programs in existence on July 1, 2010.

(b) **Submission of plan.** After consultation with the Office of Problem-Solving Courts and any officials whose participation in the program will be required, the County Administrative Judge of a circuit court or a District Administrative Judge of the District Court may prepare and submit to the State Court Administrator a detailed plan for a problem-solving program consistent with the protocols and requirements in an Administrative Order of the Chief Judge of the Court of Appeals.

Committee note. — Examples of officials to be consulted include individuals in the Office of the State's Attorney; Office of the Public Defender; Department of Juvenile Services; health, addiction, and education agencies; the Division of Parole and Probation; and the Department of Human Resources.

(c) **Approval of plan.** After review of the plan, the State Court Administrator shall submit the plan, together with any comments and a recommendation, to the Court of Appeals. The program shall not be implemented until it is approved by the Court of Appeals.

(d) **Acceptance of participant into program.** (1) Written agreement required; contents. As a condition of acceptance into a program and after the advice of counsel, if any, a prospective participant shall execute a written agreement that sets forth:

(A) the requirements of the program,

(B) the protocols of the program, including protocols concerning the authority of the judge to initiate, permit, and consider ex parte communications pursuant to Rule 2.9 of the Maryland Code of Judicial Conduct;

(C) the range of sanctions that may be imposed while the participant is in the program; and

(D) any rights waived by the participant, including any rights under Rule 4-215 or Code, Courts Article, § 3-8A-20.

Committee note. — The written agreement shall be in addition to any advisements that are required under Rule 4-215 or Code, Courts Article, § 3-8A-20, if applicable.

(2) Examination on the record. The court may not accept the prospective participant into the program until, after an examination of the prospective participant on the record, the court determines and announces on the record that the prospective participant knowingly and voluntarily enters into the agreement and understands it.

(3) Agreement to be made part of the record. A copy of the agreement shall be made a part of the record.

(e) **Immediate sanctions; loss of liberty or termination from program.** In accordance with the protocols of the program, the court may, for good cause, impose an immediate sanction on a participant, except that if the participant is considered for the imposition of a sanction involving the loss of liberty or termination from the program, the participant shall be afforded notice, an opportunity to be heard, and the right to be represented by counsel before the court makes its decision. If a hearing is required by this section and the participant is unrepresented by counsel, the court shall comply with Rule 4-215 in a criminal action or Code, Courts Article, § 3-8A-20 in a delinquency action before holding the hearing.

Committee note. — In considering whether a judge should be disqualified pursuant to Rule 2.11 of the Code of Judicial Conduct from post-termination proceedings involving a participant who has been terminated from a problem-solving court program, the judge should be sensitive to any exposure to ex parte communications or inadmissible information the judge may have received while the participant was in the program.

(f) **Credit for incarceration time served.** If a participant is terminated from a program, any period of time for which the participant was incarcerated as a sanction during participation in the program shall be credited against any sentence imposed or directed to be executed in the action. (Added March 9, 2010, effective July 1, 2010.)

Source. — This Rule is new.

CHAPTER 300. CIRCUIT COURT CLERKS' OFFICES.

Rule 16-301. Personnel in clerks' offices.
a. **Chief deputy clerk.** (1) The clerk may appoint a chief deputy clerk. The appointment is not subject to subsection (d) (3) of this Rule.

(2) Subject to paragraph (3) of this section, a chief deputy clerk serves at the pleasure of the clerk.

(3) The appointment, retention and removal of a chief deputy clerk shall be subject to the authority and approval of the Chief Judge of the Court of Appeals, after consultation with the County Administrative Judge.

b. **Other employees.** All other employees in the clerk's office shall be subject to a personnel system to be established by the State Court Administrator and approved by the Court of Appeals. The personnel system shall provide for equal opportunity, shall be based on merit principles, and shall include appropriate job classifications and compensation scales.

c. **Certain deputy clerks.** Persons serving as deputy clerks on July 1, 1991 who qualify for pension rights under Code, State Personnel and Pensions Article, § 23-404 shall hold over as deputy clerks but shall have no fixed term and shall in all respects be subject to the personnel system established pursuant to section (b) of this Rule.

d. **Personnel procedures.** (1) The State Court Administrator shall develop standards and procedures for the selection and appointment of new employees and the promotion, reclassification, transfer, demotion, suspension, discharge or other discipline of employees in the clerks' offices. These standards and procedures shall be subject to the approval of the Court of Appeals.

(2) If a vacancy occurs in a clerk's office, the clerk shall seek authorization from the State Court Administrator to fill the vacancy.

(3) The selection and appointment of new employees and the promotion, reclassification, transfer, demotion, suspension, discharge or other discipline of employees shall be in accordance with the standards and procedures established by the State Court Administrator.

(4) The State Court Administrator may review the selection or promotion of an employee to ensure compliance with the standards and procedures established pursuant to this Rule.

(5) An employee grievance shall be resolved in accordance with procedures established by the State Court Administrator. The clerk shall resolve a grievance within the clerk's office, but appeals of the grievance to the State Court Administrator or a designee of the State Court Administrator shall be allowed and shall constitute the final step in the grievance procedure.

(6) The Administrative Office of the Courts shall prepare the payroll and time and attendance reports for the clerks' offices. The clerks shall submit the information and other documentation that the Administrative Office requires for this purpose. (Added May 9, 1991, effective July 1, 1991; amended June 5, 1996, effective Jan. 1, 1997; Jan. 20, 1999, effective July 1, 1999.)

Source. — This Rule is former Rule 1212.

Effect of amendments. — The 1996 amendment rewrote the Source note.

The 1999 amendment substituted "State Personnel and Pensions Article, § 23-404" for "Article 73B, § 117" in c.

Editor's note. — An Order dated June 5, 1996, effective Jan. 1, 1997, renumbered this Rule, which was formerly Rule 1212.

Disclosure of personnel records. — Both the Clerk of the Circuit Court, as custodian of personnel records of employees of the Clerk's office, and Administrative Office of the Courts, as official custodian of personnel records relating to employees of the Clerk's offices, are prohibited from disclosing those records to a complainant or to a third person, such as a representative of the media. 78 Op. Att'y Gen. 291 (November 18, 1993).

Rule 16-302. Operations in clerks' offices.

a. **Procurement.** A clerk may not purchase, lease, or otherwise procure any service or property, including equipment, except in accordance with procedures established by the State Court Administrator. Unless otherwise provided by those procedures, the clerk shall submit all procurement requests to the State Court Administrator in the form and with the documentation that the Administrator requires.

b. **General operations.** The State Court Administrator shall develop policies, procedures, and standards for all judicial and non-judicial operations of the clerks' offices, including case processing, records management, forms control, accounting, budgeting, inventory, and data processing. The current data processing systems in Baltimore City, Prince George's County, and Montgomery County shall not be replaced except by order of the Chief Judge of the Court of Appeals.

c. **Audits.** The Administrative Office of the Courts may audit the operations and accounts of the clerks' offices.

d. **Submission of budget.** Each clerk shall submit an annual budget to the State Court Administrator for the review and approval of the Chief Judge of the Court of Appeals. The budget shall be submitted at the time specified by the State Court Administrator and shall be in the form prescribed by the Secretary of Budget and Fiscal Planning.

e. **County Administrative Judge to supervise certain functions.** The case assignment function and the jury selection process, whether or not located in the clerk's office, shall be subject to the overall supervision of the County Administrative Judge or a judge designated by the County Administrative Judge. (Added May 9, 1991, effective July 1, 1991; amended June 5, 1996, effective Jan. 1, 1997.)

Source. — This Rule is former Rule 1213.

Effect of amendments. — The 1996 amendment rewrote the Source note.

Editor's note. — An Order dated June 5, 1996, effective Jan. 1, 1997, renumbered this Rule, which was formerly Rule 1213.

Disclosure of personnel records. — Both the Clerk of the Circuit Court, as custodian of personnel records of employees of the Clerk's office, and Administrative Office of the Courts, as official custodian of personnel records relating to employees of the Clerks' offices, are prohibited from disclosing those records to a complainant or to a third person, such as a representative of the media. 78 Op. Att'y Gen. 291 (November 18, 1993).

Rule 16-303. Payment of money into court.

All money paid into court under an order or on account of a pending action shall be deposited by the clerk in a bank and noted in an appropriate record. The clerk shall disburse the money only upon order of the court and, unless the court otherwise directs, only by check payable to the order of the party entitled and the party's counsel of record. (Added Oct. 1, 1980, effective Jan. 1, 1981; amended June 5, 1996, effective Jan. 1, 1997.)

Source. — This Rule is former Rule 1214.

Effect of amendments. — The 1996 amendment added the Source note.

Editor's note. — An Order dated June 5, 1996, effective Jan. 1, 1997, renumbered this Rule, which was formerly Rule 1214.

Cited in Att'y Griev. Comm'n v. Tauber, — Md. —, 26 A.3d 967 (2011).

Rule 16-304. Clerks' offices — Hours.

The office of each clerk of court shall be open to the public for the transaction of all business of the court from at least 8:30 a.m. to 4:30 p.m. Monday through Friday of each week. Each clerk's office shall be open during the additional hours and on the additional days the judge or judges of the court shall prescribe. The office shall not be open on the holidays set forth in Rule 16-106 (Court Sessions — Holidays — Time for Convening) unless otherwise ordered by the County Administrative Judge. In the event of an emergency and in the interest of the public welfare, the Chief Judge of the Court of Appeals may order a clerk's office to be closed for the transaction of all business of the court on any day. (Amended Sept. 9, 1969; Dec. 13, 1973; July 1, 1974; May 19, 1978, effective July 1, 1978; June 5, 1996, effective Jan. 1, 1997; Dec. 10, 1996, effective Jan. 1, 1997.)

Source. — This Rule is former Rule 1215.

Effect of amendments. — The first 1996 amendment substituted "Rule 16-106" for "Rule 1205" in the third sentence; and added the Source note.

The second 1996 amendment substituted "each clerk" for "every clerk" in the first sentence; and deleted "legal" preceding "holidays" in the third sentence.

Editor's note. — An Order dated June 5, 1996, effective Jan. 1, 1997, renumbered this Rule, which was formerly Rule 1215.

Stated in Grayson v. State, 354 Md. 1, 728 A.2d 1280 (1999).

Rule 16-305. Dockets.

The clerks of the courts shall maintain such dockets in such form and containing such information as shall be prescribed by the Chief Judge of the Court of Appeals. (Amended June 5, 1996, effective Jan. 1. 1997.)

COMMENT

This will permit a uniform system of dockets in accordance with forms which are to be prescribed by the Chief Judge acting as administrative head of the judicial system. To permit maximum flexibility, the Rule does not specify what dockets shall be maintained. The general source of the Rule is proposed New Jersey Rule 1:32-2.

Source. — This Rule is former Rule 1216.

Effect of amendments. — The 1996 amendment added the Source note.

Editor's note. — An Order dated June 5, 1996, effective Jan. 1, 1997, renumbered this Rule, which was formerly Rule 1216.

Form for maintaining dockets in Seventh Judicial Circuit. — The following is an order of Chief Judge Murphy of the Court of Appeals.

"At the request and on the recommendation of the Judges of the Seventh Judicial Circuit of Maryland, it is, pursuant to Maryland Rule 1216, this 7th day of October, 1985.

"ORDERED, that the Clerks of the Circuit Courts in the Seventh Judicial Circuit may, at their option, discontinue the maintenance of docket books in equity, law and criminal cases, substituting therefor as the original docket, the entries made on the cover of the original Court file, or an equivalent electronic recordation. There will also be maintained a microfilm jacket known as a 'microfiche' which shall contain microphotographic images of every pleading, document and paper within each case."

Rule 16-306. Filing and removal of papers.

a. **Flat filing.** Any paper received by the clerk shall be filed flat in an appropriate folder. (Amended Apr. 6, 1984, effective July 1, 1984.)

b. **Docket entries.** Each case file shall include a copy of the docket entries pertaining to that case. (Amended Apr. 6, 1984, effective July 1, 1984.)

c. **Exhibits filed with pleadings.** The clerk shall, when practicable, file exhibits with the papers which they accompany. In other cases, the clerk shall file exhibits by such method as may be most convenient and practicable. (Amended Apr. 6, 1984, effective July 1, 1984.)

d. **Removal of papers and exhibits.** 1. Court papers and exhibits filed with pleadings. No paper or exhibit filed with a pleading in any case pending in or decided by the court shall be removed from the clerk's office, except by direction of a judge of the court, and except as authorized by rule or law; provided, however, that an attorney of record, upon signing a receipt, may withdraw any such paper or exhibit for presentation to the court, an auditor, or examiner-master, and an auditor or examiner-master, upon signing a receipt, may withdraw such paper or exhibit in connection with the performance of his official duties.

2. Exhibits filed during trial. All exhibits introduced in evidence or marked for identification during the trial of a case, and not filed as a part of or with the pleadings, shall be retained by the clerk of court or such other person as may be designated by the court. After either (i) the time for appeal has expired, or (ii) in the event of an appeal, the mandate has been received by the clerk, the clerk shall send written notice to all counsel of record advising them that if no

request to withdraw the exhibits is received within 30 days from the date of the notice, the exhibits will be disposed of. Unless a request is received by the clerk within 30 days from the date of notice, or unless the court within that period shall order otherwise, the clerk shall dispose of the exhibits in any manner, including destruction, as may be appropriate. (Amended Oct. 1, 1980, effective Jan. 1, 1981; Apr. 6, 1984, effective July 1, 1984.)

Committee note. — This subsection is intended to provide for the safeguarding of trial exhibits. In the absence of a request to withdraw such exhibits, the clerk is given discretion as to their disposition. It is assumed that exhibits such as hospital records, bank records, police records, etc., would normally be returned by the clerk to the proper custodian.

Other exhibits might be destroyed, although parties interested in preserving any exhibits could ask for appropriate action by the court. It should be noted that exhibits filed with the pleadings, even though admitted in evidence or marked for identification do not fall under the "disposition" provision of this subsection, but instead under subsection 1.

e. **Record of removed papers.** Whenever a court file or any paper contained therein is removed from the clerk's office pursuant to this Rule, the clerk shall maintain an appropriate record of its location while out of his hands, including a notation on the docket, if such file or papers are removed from the courthouse. (Amended Apr. 6, 1984, effective July 1, 1984; June 5, 1996, effective Jan. 1, 1997.)

COMMENT

The word "court" means the court of a circuit as defined in Rule 1-202 (e). The sources of this Rule are Supreme Bench Rule 331 and Montgomery County Rule 300. With respect to removal of exhibits introduced during trial, Baltimore County Rule 1.7 has been followed; see also Baltimore County Rule 1.12 and Seventh Circuit Rule 7.

In general, the Rule prohibits the withdrawal of exhibits filed with the pleadings without court order (compare Second Circuit Rule 9). However, exhibits introduced into evidence or marked for identification during a trial could be disposed of by the clerk of court or other person designated by the court after expiration of the time for appeal or after return of the mandate in the event of an appeal. The practice, now used in some areas, especially Baltimore City, of counsel removing exhibits after a trial would be prohibited.

Source. — This Rule is former Rule 1217.

Effect of amendments. — The 1996 amendment added the Source note.

Editor's note. — An Order dated June 5, 1996, effective Jan. 1, 1997, renumbered this Rule, which was formerly Rule 1217.

Parties permitted recovery of evidence. — This Rule does not permit a party to a case to recover the exhibit unless that party is the one who placed it in evidence, absent a showing of ownership. State v. Strickland, 42 Md. App. 357, 400 A.2d 451 (1979).

Nature of petition for return of money. — A petition for the return of money introduced into evidence, filed in the circuit court, is in the nature of trespass or trover for the determination of title and not replevin. State v. Strickland, 42 Md. App. 357, 400 A.2d 451 (1979).

And deemed civil proceeding. — A proceeding in the circuit court to recover money that was introduced into evidence in a bribery trial is civil in nature, and the State has the right to appeal an order of court directing that the money be paid over to the briber. State v. Strickland, 42 Md. App. 357, 400 A.2d 451 (1979).

Meaning of section d 2. — Section d 2 of this Rule means that the clerk of the court is required to notify all counsel in the case that the evidence will be disposed of in such manner as may be appropriate unless a motion for its return is filed within 30 days after the notice to counsel. State v. Strickland, 42 Md. App. 357, 400 A.2d 451 (1979).

Rule 16-307. Electronic filing of pleadings, papers and real property instruments.

a. **Applicability; conflicts with other rules.** This Rule applies to the electronic filing of pleadings and papers in a circuit court and to the electronic filing of instruments authorized or required by law to be recorded and indexed in the land records. A pleading, paper or instrument may not be filed by direct electronic transmission to the court except in accordance with this Rule. To the extent of any inconsistency with any other Rule, this Rule and any administrative order entered pursuant to it shall prevail.

Committee note. — Code, Real Property
Article, § 3-502.

b. **Submission of plan.** A County Administrative Judge may submit to the State Court Administrator a detailed plan for a pilot project for the electronic filing of pleadings and papers or of real property instruments. In developing the plan, the County Administrative Judge shall consult with the Clerk of the Circuit Court, appropriate vendors, the State Court Administrator, and any other judges, court clerks, members of the bar, vendors of electronic filing systems, and interested persons that the County Administrative Judge chooses to ensure that: (1) the proposed electronic filing system is compatible with the data processing systems, operational systems, and electronic filing systems used or expected to be used by the judiciary; (2) the installation and use of the proposed system does not create an undue financial or operational burden on the court; (3) the proposed system is reasonably available for use at a reasonable cost, or an efficient and compatible system of manual filing will be maintained; (4) the proposed system is effective, secure and not likely to break down; (5) the proposed system makes appropriate provision for the protection of privacy and for public access to public records; and (6) the court can discard or replace the system during or at the conclusion of a trial period without undue financial or operational burden. The State Court Administrator shall review the plan and make a recommendation to the Court of Appeals with respect to it.

Cross references. — For the definition of
"public record," see Code, State Government
Article, § 10-611.

c. **Approval; duration.** A plan may not be implemented unless approved by administrative order of the Court of Appeals. The plan shall terminate two years after the date of the administrative order unless the Court terminates it earlier or modifies or extends it by a subsequent administrative order.

d. **Evaluation.** The Chief Judge of the Court of Appeals may appoint a committee consisting of one or more judges, court clerks, lawyers, legal educators, bar association representatives, and other interested and knowledgeable persons to monitor and evaluate the plan. Before the expiration of the two-year period set forth in section c of this Rule, the Court of Appeals, after considering the recommendations of the committee, shall evaluate the operation of the plan.

e. **Public availability of plan.** The State Court Administrator and the Clerk of the Circuit Court shall make available for public inspection a copy of any current plan. (Added June 5, 1995, effective July 1, 1995; amended June 5, 1996, effective Jan. 1, 1997; Oct. 31, 2002, effective Jan. 1, 2003; Dec. 4, 2007, effective Jan. 1, 2008.)

Source. — This Rule is derived from former Rule 1217A.

Effect of amendments. — The 1996 amendment rewrote the Source note.

The 2002 amendment added "in a circuit court" at the end of the first sentence in a.; rewrote b.; inserted the cross-reference following b.; substituted "unless the Court terminates it earlier or modifies or extends it" for "approving it unless terminated earlier or extended" in the second sentence in c.; in d., substituted "may appoint" for "shall appoint" in the first sentence and substituted "Before" for "Prior to" at the beginning of the second sentence; deleted former e., which read, "By administrative order, the Court of Appeals may extend, modify, or terminate a plan at any time," and redesignated f. as present e.; and

inserted "derived from" in the Source note.

The December 4, 2007 Order, effective January 1, 2008, added "and real property instruments" to the heading and made related changes; in a added "and to the electronic filing of instruments authorized or required by law to be recorded and indexed in the land records" at the end of the first sentence, and "or instrument" in the second sentence, with related changes, and added the Cross reference note; and in b added "or of real property instruments".

Editor's note. — An Order dated June 5, 1996, effective Jan. 1, 1997, renumbered this Rule, which was formerly Rule 1217A.

Rule 16-308. Court information system.

a. **Report of docketing and disposition of cases.** The clerk shall promptly transmit to the Administrative Office of the Courts in a manner prescribed by the State Court Administrator the data elements concerning the docketing and disposition of criminal, juvenile and civil cases as may be designated by the State Court Administrator.

b. **Reporting and transmittal of criminal history record information.** 1. The Administrative Office of the Courts shall transmit to the Central Repository of Criminal History Record Information of the Department of Public Safety and Correctional Services the data elements of criminal history record information on offenses agreed to by the Secretary of the Department of Public Safety and Correctional Services and the Chief Judge of the Court of Appeals or his designee for purposes of completing a criminal history record maintained by the Central Repository of Criminal History Record Information.

2. Transmittal of reports of dispositions. (a) As directed by Administrative Order of the Chief Judge of the Court of Appeals, Judicial Information Systems shall report to the State Motor Vehicle Administration the conviction, forfeiture of bail, dismissal of an appeal or an acquittal in any case involving a violation of the Maryland Vehicle Law or other traffic law or ordinance, or any conviction for manslaughter or assault committed by means of an automobile, or of any felony involving the use of an automobile.

(b) When a defendant has been charged by citation and a conviction is entered by reason of his payment of a fine or forfeiture of collateral or bond before trial, the conviction is not a reportable event under Code, Criminal Procedure Article, § 10-215(a)(10).

c. **Inspection of criminal history record information contained in court records of public judicial proceedings.** Unless expunged, sealed, marked confidential or otherwise prohibited by statute, court rule or order, criminal history record information contained in court records of public judicial proceedings is subject to inspection by any person at the times and under conditions as the clerk of a court reasonably determines necessary for the protection of the records and the prevention of unnecessary interference with the regular discharge of the duties of his office.

Cross references. — See Code, Courts Article, §§ 2-203 and 13-101 (d) and (f), Criminal Procedure Article, §§ 10-201, 10-214, 10-217, and State Government Article, §§ 10-612 through 10-619.

(Added June 30, 1973, effective July 1, 1973; Nov. 4, 1977, effective Jan. 1, 1978; Dec. 21, 1977, effective Jan. 1, 1978; June 5, 1996, effective Jan. 1, 1997; Jan. 8, 2002, effective Feb. 1, 2002; Dec. 4, 2007, effective Jan. 1, 2008.)

Cross references. — For definition of court records see Rule 4-502 (d).

Committee note. — This Rule does not contemplate the reporting of parking violations.

Source. — This Rule is derived from former Rule 1218.

Effect of amendments. — The 1996 amendment added the Source note.

The 2002 amendment substituted "Code, Criminal Procedure Article, § 10-215(a)(10)" for "Article 27, Section 747(a)(10), Annotated Code of Maryland" in (b).

The December 4, 2007 Order, effective January 1, 2008, in b (2) (a) substituted "As directed by Administrative Order of the Chief Judge of the Court of Appeals, Judicial Information Systems shall report to the State Motor Vehicle Administration" for "Within 15 days after" and deleted "the clerk of the court shall forward to the State Motor Vehicle Administration a certified abstract of the record on a form furnished by the State Motor Vehicle Administration" at the end; and added "derived from" in the Source note.

Editor's note. — An Order dated June 5, 1996, effective Jan. 1, 1997, renumbered this Rule, which was formerly Rule 1218.

Rule 16-309. Notice to Court of Special Appeals.

By the third working day of each month, the clerk shall send or electronically transmit to the Clerk of the Court of Special Appeals a list of all cases in which, during the preceding calendar month, (1) a notice of appeal to the Court of Special Appeals has been filed, (2) a timely motion pursuant to Rule 2-532, 2-533, or 2-534 has been filed after the filing of a notice of appeal, or (3) an application for leave to appeal has been filed, or (4) a notice of appeal or an application for leave to appeal to the Court of Special Appeals has been stricken pursuant to Rule 8-203. The list shall include the title and docket number of the case, the name and address of counsel for appellant(s), and the date on which the notice of appeal, the motion, or the dismissal was filed. (Added May 5, 1976, effective July 1, 1976; amended May 7, 1982, effective July 1, 1982; Apr. 6, 1984, effective July 1, 1984; June 5, 1996, effective January 1, 1997; October 31, 2002, effective January 1, 2003; September 8, 2011, effective January 1, 2012.)

Source. — This Rule is derived from former Rule 1219.

Effect of amendments. — The 1996 amendment added the Source note.

The 2002 amendment substituted "a notice" for "an order" in (1); inserted present (2) and redesignated former (2) as (3); substituted "stricken pursuant to Rule 8-203" for "dismissed" in (3); and substituted "notice of appeal, the motion" for "order of appeal" in the last sentence.

The 2011 amendment in the first sentence

added "or electronically transmit"; added (3) and (4); made related changes; and added "derived from" in the Source note.

Editor's note. — An Order dated June 5, 1996, effective Jan. 1, 1997, renumbered this Rule, which was formerly Rule 1219.

University of Baltimore Law Review. — For article, "The Maryland Rules — A Time for Overhaul," see 9 U. Balt. L. Rev. 1 (1979).

CHAPTER 400. ATTORNEYS, OFFICERS OF COURT AND OTHER PERSONS.

Rule 16-401. Proscribed activities — Gratuities, etc.

a. **Giving prohibited.** No attorney shall give, either directly or indirectly, to an officer or employee of a court, or of an office serving a court, a gratuity, gift or any compensation related to his official duties and not expressly authorized by rule or law.

b. **Receiving prohibited.** No officer or employee of any court, or of any office serving a court, shall accept a gratuity or gift, either directly or indirectly, from a litigant, an attorney or any person regularly doing business with the court, or any compensation related to such officer's or employee's official duties and not expressly authorized by rule or law. (Amended, June 5, 1996, effective Jan. 1, 1997; Nov. 12, 2003, effective Jan. 1, 2004; Feb. 10, 2009, effective May 1, 2009; June 7, 2011, effective July 1, 2011.)

Cross references. — For definition of "person," see Rule 1-202(t).

Committee note. — This Rule is based in part on New Jersey Rule 1:34. It is intended as a broad prohibition against the exchange of gratuities, gifts or any compensation not expressly authorized by rule or law as between attorneys and court officials and employees, in connection with the official functions of such

persons. The Rule covers sheriffs and deputy sheriffs, as well as regular court officers, employees and other persons. This Rule is not intended to preclude contributions to or for elected public officials as authorized by and in conformance with the provisions of Code, Election Law Article, Title 13.

Source. — This Rule is derived from former Rule 1220.

Effect of amendments. — The 1996 amendment added the Source note.

The 2003 amendment substituted "(r)" for "(q)" in the cross reference; deleted "Among other things, it will prevent the practice, now existing in the courts of the Supreme Bench of Baltimore City, whereby certain portions of appearance fees are retained by the clerks by way of extra compensation or gratuities for the performance of their official duties" following "employees and other persons", and substituted "Code, Election Law Article, Title 13" for

"Article 33, §§26-1 through 26-20, Annotated Code of Maryland (1968 Cum. Supp)" in the Committee note; and inserted "derived from" in the Source note.

The 2009 amendment substituted "Rule 1-202(s)" for "Rule 1-202(r)" in the cross reference note.

The 2011 amendment substituted "Rule 1-202(t)" for "Rule 1-202(s)" in the cross reference note

Editor's note. — An Order dated June 5, 1996, effective Jan. 1, 1997, renumbered this

Rule, which was formerly Rule 1220.

The definition of "person" currently appears in Rule 1-202 (r).

University of Baltimore Law Review. — For article, "The Maryland Rules — A Time for Overhaul," see 9 U. Balt. L. Rev. 1 (1979).

Rule 16-402. Attorneys and other officers not to become sureties.

[Deleted Mar. 5, 2001, effective July 1, 2001.]

Rule 16-403. Trust clerk.

The circuit court for each county and the Supreme Bench of Baltimore City shall designate a trust clerk and shall determine the trust clerk's compensation. (Added Feb. 2, 1970; amended Oct. 1, 1980, effective Jan. 1, 1981; June 5, 1996, effective Jan. 1, 1997.)

Source. — This Rule is former Rule 1223.

Effect of amendments. — The 1996 amendment added the Source note.

Editor's note. — An Order dated June 5, 1996, effective Jan. 1, 1997, renumbered this Rule, which was formerly Rule 1223.

Practice of law. — An individual who is appointed a trust clerk pursuant to this rule is not, by that fact alone, prohibited from practicing law; only if the individual designated as trust clerk also is the Clerk of the Court or a member of one of the other classes expressly enumerated in BOP § 10-603 (b) (4) (e.g., an employee or appointee of the Clerk of the Court) is he or she prohibited from practicing law.

Rule 16-404. Administration of court reporters.

a. **Applicability.** Section b of this Rule applies to court reporters in the circuit courts and the District Court. Sections c, d, and e apply in the circuit courts only.

b. **Establishment of regulations and standards.** The Chief Judge of the Court of Appeals shall prescribe regulations and standards regarding court reporters and the system of reporting in the courts of the State. The regulations and standards may include:

(1) the selection, qualifications, and responsibilities of court reporters;

(2) procedures and regulations;

(3) preparation, typing, and format of transcripts;

(4) charges for transcripts and copies;

(5) preservation and maintenance of reporting notes and records, however recorded;

(6) equipment and supplies utilized in reporting; and

(7) procedures for filing and maintaining administrative records and reports.

Cross references. — Rule 16-504.

c. **Number of court reporters — Supervisory court reporter.** Each circuit court shall have the number of court reporters recommended by the County Administrative Judge and approved by the Chief Judge of the Court of Appeals. In a county with more than one court reporter, the County Administrative Judge shall designate one as supervisory court reporter, who shall serve at the pleasure of the County Administrative Judge. The Chief Judge of the Court of Appeals shall prescribe the duties of the supervisory court reporter.

d. **Supervision of court reporters.** Subject to the general supervision of the Chief Judge of the Court of Appeals, the County Administrative Judge shall have the supervisory responsibility for the court reporters in that county. The County Administrative Judge may delegate supervisory responsibility to the supervisory court reporter, including the assignment of court reporters.

e. **Methods of reporting — Proceedings to be recorded.** Each court reporter assigned to record a proceeding shall record verbatim by shorthand, stenotype, mechanical, or electronic audio recording methods, electronic word or text processing methods, or any combination of these methods, and shall maintain that record subject to regulations and standards prescribed by the Chief Judge of the Court of Appeals, except that a court reporter need not record an audio or audiovisual recording offered or used at a hearing or trial. All proceedings held in open court, including opening statements, closing arguments, and hearings on motions, shall be recorded in their entirety, unless the court and the parties agree otherwise. (Amended, June 5, 1996, effective Jan. 1, 1997; Dec. 16, 1999, effective Jan. 1, 2000; Mar. 5, 2001, effective July 1, 2001; April 5, 2005, effective July 1, 2005; amended Sept. 10, 2009, effective Oct. 1, 2009.)

Cross references. — See Rules 2-516 and 4-322. See also Rule 16-1006 (g), which provides that backup audio recordings made by any means, computer disks, and notes of a court reporter that have not been filed with the clerk or are not part of the official court record are not ordinarily subject to public inspection.

Source. — This Rule is derived from former Rule 1224.

Effect of amendments. — The 1996 amendment added the Source note.

The 1999 amendment made minor punctuation changes throughout; substituted "relating to" for "relative to" at the end of the introductory language of a; inserted "and records" in a (5); substituted "who shall serve at the pleasure of the County Administrative Judge" for "to serve at his pleasure" in b; in c, in the first sentence, deleted "and to the direct supervision of his Circuit Administrative Judge" following "Court of Appeals," and substituted "the county" for "his county" at the end, and deleted "to attend the record at each session of the court and every other proceeding as provided in this Rule or by order of the court" from the end of the second sentence; in the introductory language of d, inserted "electronic word or text processing methods," and inserted "and shall maintain that record"; and deleted "and the Circuit Administrative Judge" from the end of e.

The 2001 amendment deleted "circuit" preceding "court" from the Rule heading; added present a. and redesignated the remaining subsections accordingly; deleted former d. 1. through 2. and e.; in b., in the introductory paragraph, deleted "from time to time" following "shall," deleted "circuit" preceding "court reporters," and deleted "provisions relative to" from the end, inserted a comma following "qualifications" in (1), deleted "for court reporting" in (2), inserted a comma following "typing" in (3), added "and" at the end of (6), added (7) and added the cross reference following (7); in c., inserted "circuit" preceding "court shall" in the first sentence, and, in the second sentence, inserted a comma following the first occurrence of "reporter," and substituted "the pleasure of the County Administrative Judge" for "his pleasure"; in d., in the first sentence, deleted "the" following "shall have" and substituted "that county" for "his county" at the end; and added the second sentence to e.

The 2005 amendment substituted "audio" for "sound" in e.; and added the cross references note at the end of the rule.

The 2009 amendment in (e) added the exception in the first sentence and transferred "Unless the court and the parties agree otherwise" from the beginning of the second sentence to the end; in the cross reference added the first sentence and in the second sentence added "See also" and "which"; and made related changes.

Editor's note. — An Order dated June 5, 1996, effective Jan. 1, 1997, renumbered this Rule, which was formerly Rule 1224.

Purpose of section d of this Rule is to preserve a correct and precise account of the evidence and rulings at trial, and to assure the ability of courts and of counsel to perform their duties efficiently and completely. Smith v. State, 291 Md. 125, 433 A.2d 1143 (1981).

Responsibility of counsel under section d 1. — Since section d 1 of this Rule requires that opening statements and closing arguments be recorded, it is incumbent upon counsel, where all or part of the opening statements or closing arguments is challenged, to see that it is transcribed and made a part of the record for review. Blizzard v. State, 30 Md. App. 156, 351 A.2d 443, rev'd on other grounds, 278 Md. 556, 366 A.2d 1026 (1976).

Inability to prepare complete transcript not sufficient ground for reversal. — The inability to prepare a complete verbatim transcript of a criminal case, in and of itself, does not necessarily present a sufficient ground for reversal. Smith v. State, 291 Md. 125, 433 A.2d 1143 (1981).

Defective transcript imposes heavy burden on appeal. — Where there is some defect in the transcript of a trial not attributable to discrimination or inherent unfairness by the prosecution, an appellant carries a heavy burden on appeal. Smith v. State, 291 Md. 125, 433 A.2d 1143 (1981).

Effect of lack of adequate substitute for complete trial record. — Only when an adequate substitute for a complete record of a criminal trial cannot be made will a court consider an appellant's contention that he has been deprived of meaningful appellate review. Smith v. State, 291 Md. 125, 433 A.2d 1143 (1981).

Appellant's responsibility to perfect incomplete record. — Where the transcript of a criminal trial is incomplete an appellant has the responsibility to make a sincere effort to perfect the record. Smith v. State, 291 Md. 125, 433 A.2d 1143 (1981).

Cited in Gonzalez v. State, 388 Md. 63, 878 A.2d 604 (2005).

Rule 16-405. Electronic audio and audio-video recording of circuit court proceedings.

a. **Authorization.** The Circuit Administrative Judge for a judicial circuit, after consultation with the County Administrative Judge for a county, may authorize the electronic audio or audio-video recording in courtrooms or hearing rooms in that county of proceedings required or permitted to be recorded by Rule 16-404 e.

b. **Identification.** The or other designee of the court clerk shall affix to the electronic audio or audio-video recording a label containing the following information:

1. the name of the court;
2. the docket reference of each proceeding included on the recording;
3. the date on which the proceeding was recorded; and
4. any other identifying letters, marks, or numbers.

c. **Trial log; exhibit list.** The clerk or other designee of the court shall keep a written log identifying each proceeding recorded on an audio or audio-video recording and, for each proceeding recorded, a log listing the recording references for the beginning and end of each witness's testimony, an exhibit list, and any portion of the audio or audio-video recording that has been safeguarded pursuant to section d of this Rule. The original logs and exhibit list shall remain with the original papers in the circuit court. A copy of the logs and the exhibit list shall be kept with the audio or audio-video recording.

d. **Safeguarding Confidential or Non-Public Portions of Proceedings.** If a portion of a proceeding that is recorded by audio or audio-video recording involves placing on the record matters that would not be heard in open court or open to public inspection, the court shall direct that appropriate safeguards be placed on that portion of the recording.

e. **Presence of court reporter not necessary; conflicts with other rules.** 1. If circuit court proceedings are recorded by audio or audio-video recording, it is not necessary for a court reporter to be present in the courtroom.

2. In the event of a conflict between this Rule and another Rule, this Rule shall prevail. (Added Nov. 22, 1989, effective Jan. 1, 1990; amended July 16, 1992; June 5, 1996, effective Jan. 1, 1997; Oct. 31, 2002, effective Jan. 1, 2003; April 5, 2005, effective July 1, 2005.)

Source. — This Rule is derived from former Rule 1224A and is in part new.

Effect of amendments. — The 1996 amendment substituted "Rule 16-404 d" for "Rule 1224 d." in a.; and rewrote the Source note.

The 2002 amendment substituted "Rule 16-404 e" for "Rule 16-404 d" in a.

The 2005 amendment rewrote the rule to delete the word "videotape" from the title, to add references to audio and audio-video recording throughout the Rule and made other, related changes; and rewrote the Source note.

Editor's note. — An Order dated June 5, 1996, effective Jan. 1, 1997, renumbered this Rule, which was formerly Rule 1224A.

Cited in Walker v. State, 125 Md. App. 48, 723 A.2d 922 (1999); Gonzalez v. State, 388 Md. 63, 878 A.2d 604 (2005).

Rule 16-406. Access to electronic audio and audio-video recordings of proceedings in the circuit court.

a. **Control — In general.** Electronic audio and audio-video recordings made pursuant to Rules 16-404 and 16-405 are under the control of the court having custody of them. Access to and copying of those recordings are subject to the provisions of this Rule and Rule 16-405 d.

Cross references. — Code, State Government Article, § 10-615.

b. **Access - In General.** No person other than a duly authorized court official or employee shall have direct access to or possession of an official audio or audio-video recording. Subject to Rule 16-405 d and unless otherwise ordered by the court, any person may view an official audio-video recording at the times and places determined by the court having custody of the recording. Copies of audio recordings and, where practicable, the audio portion of audio-video recordings, may be purchased as provided in this Rule.

c. **Right to Obtain Copy of Audio Recording or Audio Portion of Audio-Video Recording.** Subject to Rule 16-405 d and unless otherwise ordered by the court, the authorized custodian of an official audio recording or the audio portion of an audio-video recording shall make a copy of the audio recording or, if practicable, the audio portion of the audio-video recording, or any portion thereof, available to any person upon written request and the payment of reasonable costs, unless payment is waived by the court.

d. **Right to copy of audio-video recording; restrictions.** 1. Upon written request and the payment of reasonable costs, the authorized custodian of an official videotape recording shall make a copy of the recording, or any part requested, available to:

(A) a party to the action or the party's attorney;

(B) a stenographer, court reporter, or transcription service designated by the court for the purpose of preparing an official transcript from the recording; and

(C) the Commission on Judicial Disabilities or its designee.

2. Unless authorized by an order of court, a person who receives a copy of an audio-video recording pursuant to this section shall not (A) make or cause to be made any additional copy of the recording or (B) except for a non-sequestered witness or an agent, employee, or consultant of the attorney, make the recording available to any person not entitled to it pursuant to this section.

e. **Other persons.** 1. This section does not apply to the audio-video recording of (A) a criminal proceeding, (B) a revocation of probation proceeding, or (C) any proceeding that is confidential by law. The right to obtain a copy of an audio-video recording in those proceedings is governed solely by section d of this Rule.

2. A person not entitled to a copy of an audio-video recording pursuant to section d of this Rule may file a request to obtain a copy pursuant to this section. The person shall file the request with the clerk of the circuit court in which the proceeding was conducted and shall serve a copy of the request pursuant to Rule 1-321 on each party to the action.

3. A party may file a written response to the request within five days after being served with the request. Any other interested person may file a response within 5 days after service of the request on the last party to be served.

4. The clerk shall refer the request and all responses to the judge who conducted the proceeding. If the action has been transferred to another circuit court, the clerk shall transfer the matter to that court.

5. If the action is still pending in the court, the court shall deny the request unless (A) all parties have affirmatively consented and no interested person has filed a timely objection or (B) the court finds good cause to grant the request. If judgment has been entered in the action, the court shall grant the request unless it finds good cause to the contrary, but the court may delay permission to obtain the copy until either all appellate proceedings are completed or the right to further appellate review has lapsed. (Added Nov. 22, 1989, effective Jan. 1, 1990; amended June 5, 1996, effective Jan. 1, 1997; Nov. 12, 2003, effective Jan. 1, 2004; April 5, 2005, effective July 1, 2005; amended Sept. 10, 2009, effective Oct. 1, 2009.)

Source. — This Rule is derived in part from former Rule 1224B and is in part new.

Effect of amendments. — The 1996 amendment substituted "Rule 16-405" for "Rule 1224A" in a.; and rewrote the Source note.

The 2003 amendment inserted (c) (1) (C) and made minor stylistic changes.

The 2005 amendment rewrote the rule to add references to audio recording throughout, to expand the access provision in b, to add section c, and make sections d and e applicable to audio-video recordings; and rewrote the Source note.

The 2009 amendment added "court reporter" in (d)(1)(B).

Editor's note. — An Order dated June 5, 1996, effective Jan. 1, 1997, renumbered this Rule, which was formerly Rule 1224B.

Cited in Walker v. State, 125 Md. App. 48, 723 A.2d 922 (1999); Gonzalez v. State, 388 Md. 63, 878 A.2d 604 (2005).

CHAPTER 500. COURT ADMINISTRATION — DISTRICT COURT.

Rule 16-501. Applicability.

The rules in this Chapter apply to the District Court.

Source. — This Rule is new.

Rule 16-502. Payment of money into court.

All money paid into court on account of a pending action shall be deposited by the clerk in a bank and noted in an appropriate record. The clerk shall disburse the money only upon order of the court and, unless the court otherwise directs, only by check payable to the order of the party entitled and the party's counsel of record. (Added May 14, 1992, effective July 1, 1992; amended June 5, 1996, effective Jan. 1, 1997.)

Source. — This Rule is former M.D.R. 1214.

Effect of amendments. — The 1996 amendment rewrote the Source note.

Editor's note. — An Order dated June 5, 1996, effective Jan. 1, 1997, renumbered this Rule, which was formerly Maryland District Rule 1214.

Rule 16-503. Court information system.

a. Reporting and transmittal of criminal history record information. 1. The District Court of Maryland shall transmit to the Central Repository of Criminal History Record Information of the Department of Public Safety and Correctional Services the data elements of criminal history record information on offenses agreed to by the Secretary of the Department of Public Safety and Correctional Services and the Chief Judge of the Court of Appeals or his designee for purposes of completing a criminal history record maintained by the Central Repository of Criminal History Record Information.

2. Transmittal of reports of dispositions. When a defendant has been charged by citation and a conviction is entered by reason of his payment of a fine or forfeiture of collateral before trial, the conviction is not a reportable event under Code, Criminal Procedure Article, § 10-215(a)(10).

b. Inspection of criminal history record information contained in court records of public judicial proceedings. Unless expunged, sealed, marked confidential or otherwise prohibited by statute, court rule or order, criminal history record information contained in court records of public judicial proceedings is subject to inspection by any person at the times and under conditions as the clerk of a court reasonably determines necessary for the protection of the records and the prevention of unnecessary interference with the regular discharge of the duties of his office.

Cross references. — See Code, Courts Article, §§ 2-203 and 13-101(d) and (f), Code, Criminal Procedure Article, §§ 10-201, 10-214, and 10-217, and Code, State Government Article, §§ 10-612 through 10-619. For definition of court records, see Rule 4-502(d).

(Added Dec. 21, 1977, effective Jan. 1, 1978; amended June 5, 1996, effective Jan. 1, 1997; Jan. 8, 2002, effective Feb. 1, 2002.)

Cross references. — For definition of court records see Rule 4-502 (d).

Source. — This Rule is former M.D.R. 1218.

Effect of amendments. — The 1996 amendment added the Source note.

The 2002 amendment substituted "Code, Criminal Procedure Article, § 10-215(a)(10)" for "Article 27, Section 747(a)(10), Annotated Code of Maryland" in a. 2. and in the cross reference note following b., substituted "Code, Criminal Procedure Article, §§ 10-201, 10-214, and 10-217" for "Article 27, §§ 743, 747, 748" and added "Code" preceding "State".

Editor's note. — An Order dated June 5, 1996, effective Jan. 1, 1997, renumbered this Rule, which was formerly Maryland District Rule 1218.

Rule 16-504. Recording of proceedings.

a. **Audio Recording Required.** All trials, hearings, and other proceedings before a judge in open court shall be recorded verbatim by an audio recording device provided by the Court. The Chief Judge of the District Court may authorize recording by additional means, including audio-video recording. The recording shall be filed among the court records. Audio-video recording of a proceeding and access to the audio-video recording shall be in accordance with Rules 16-405 and 16-406.

b. **Safeguarding Confidential or Non-Public Portions of Proceedings.** If a portion of a proceeding involves placing on the record matters that would not be heard in open court or open to public inspection, the Court shall direct that appropriate safeguards be placed on that portion of the audio recording. The clerk shall create a written log listing the recording references for the beginning and end of the safeguarded portions of the recording. The log shall be kept with the original papers in the Court and a copy of the log shall be kept with the audio recording.

c. **Access; Right to Obtain Copy of Audio Recording.** No person other than a duly authorized Court official or employee shall have direct access to or possession of an official audio recording. Subject to section b of this Rule and unless otherwise ordered by the Court, the authorized custodian of an official audio recording shall make a copy of the audio recording, or any portion thereof, available to any person upon written request and the payment of reasonable costs, unless payment is waived by the Court. (Added Apr. 6, 1984, effective July 1, 1984; amended June 5, 1996, effective Jan. 1, 1997; Mar. 5, 2001, effective July 1, 2001; April 5, 2005, effective July 1, 2005.)

Committee note. — In a proceeding from which, by law, an appeal is de novo, no transcript is provided by the Court. A copy of the audio recording of the proceeding may be obtained in accordance with section c of this Rule.

Cross references. — See Rule 16-404 b concerning regulations and standards applicable to court reporting in all courts of the State.

Source. — This Rule is derived in part from former M.D.R. 1224 and is in part new.

Effect of amendments. — The 1996 amendment added the Source note.

The 2001 amendment deleted b and rewrote the remaining paragraph.

The 2005 amendment rewrote the rule to provide that Rules 16-405 and 16-406 apply to any audio-visual recording; to add sections b and c; added the Committee note; and rewrote the Source note.

Editor's note. — An Order dated June 5, 1996, effective Jan. 1, 1997, renumbered this Rule, which was formerly Maryland District Rule 1224.

Cited in Gonzalez v. State, 388 Md. 63, 878 A.2d 604 (2005).

Rule 16-505. Disposition of records.

a. **Definitions.** In this Rule, unless the context or subject matter otherwise requires:

1. Dispose. "Dispose" means to either destroy or remove records.

2. Records. "Records" mean any original papers, official books, documents, and files, including but not limited to dockets, electronic recordings of testimony and exhibits within the custody of the clerk of the court.

Cross references. — See Code, §§ 9-1009 and 10-639 through 10-642 of the State Government Article.

3. Schedule. "Schedule" means the form known as the "Records Retention and Disposal Schedule" used by the Records Management Division of the Hall of Records Commission.

b. **Authority.** Subject to the provisions of this Rule, the clerk of the court, with the written approval of the Chief Judge of the District Court and in cooperation with the Hall of Records Commission, may dispose of records within his custody.

Cross references. — See § 2-206 of the Courts Article.

c. **Procedure.** 1. Schedule preparation — Hall of Records recommendation. The clerk of the court shall prepare a schedule for the disposition of court records and submit it to the Hall of Records Commission for its recommendation.

2. Chief Judge — Approval. The schedule, together with the recommendation of the Hall of Records Commission, shall be submitted for the written approval of the Chief Judge who may approve it in whole or in part, amend it or disapprove it.

3. Court order. Approval of the schedule by the Chief Judge shall be deemed an order of court providing for disposal of the records.

4. Contents of schedule. The schedule, as approved, shall set forth:

(i) The identification of the records.

(ii) The length of time the records are to be retained by the clerk of the court before disposition.

(iii) Whether the Hall of Records Commission declines to accept the records for preservation.

(iv) Whether the records are to be destroyed or removed.

(v) The place to which the records would be removed.

(vi) Whether the schedule shall be "standing" viz., operative until changed by further order of court.

5. Removal procedures — Hall of records. In those cases where the Hall of Records Commission accepts records, they shall be removed according to the Hall of Records Commission procedures.

6. Disposal if hall of records declines custody. In those cases where the Hall of Records Commission declines records, disposition shall be according to the terms set forth in the schedule as approved. If the records are to be destroyed the clerk shall obtain the approval of the Board of Public Works and upon destruction shall file a certificate of destruction with the Hall of Records Commission.

Cross references. — See Code, § 10-642 of the State Government Article.

Committee note. — This Rule is meant to allow periodic destruction of records without the necessity of obtaining Board of Public Works approval each time if such destruction of records or classes of records had been clearly approved by the Board of Public Works in a standing schedule.

d. **Limitations upon disposal of records.** 1. Indices, dockets, and books of account. The clerk shall retain permanently all indices, dockets, and books of account.

2. Emergency evaluation and domestic violence cases. The clerk shall retain for a period of 12 years after the case is closed all original papers and exhibits in any case containing a petition for emergency evaluation or a petition for protection from domestic violence.

3. Cases involving judgment for a sum certain. In any case in which a judgment for a sum certain is entered, the clerk shall retain all original papers, exhibits, and electronic recordings of testimony for a period of three years after entry of the judgment and shall continue to retain all original papers and exhibits in the file after that three year period until the judgment expires or is satisfied.

4. Criminal cases. (i) In any criminal case which is dismissed or in which a *nolle prosequi* or stet is entered, the clerk shall retain all original papers, exhibits, and electronic recordings of testimony for a period of three years after the case is so concluded.

(ii) In any criminal case in which judgment is entered or probation before judgment is granted, the clerk shall retain all original papers, exhibits, and electronic recordings of testimony for a period of three years after the case is so concluded, and if within that three year period the defendant fails to comply with the order of court, the clerk shall continue to retain the original papers and exhibits in the file until the failure is cured or an arrest warrant issued as a result of the failure is invalidated as permitted by law.

(iii) In any criminal case for a misdemeanor in which an arrest warrant issued on the charging document or as a result of the defendant's failure to appear for trial remains unserved three years after its issuance, the clerk shall retain all the original papers and exhibits in the file until the warrant is invalidated as permitted by law.

5. Other cases. Except as provided in subsection 1, 2, 3, or 4 of this section the clerk shall retain all original papers, exhibits, and electronic recordings of

testimony in a case for a period of three years after the case is concluded by dismissal, settlement, or entry of judgment.

6. Disposal if photographed, photocopied, or microphotographed — Traffic and criminal dockets. (i) Any of the records, except dockets, set forth in subsections 1 through 5 of this section may be disposed of at any time provided that the records have been photographed, photocopied or microphotographed in accordance with the Hall of Records Commission procedures and copies have been substituted therefor, including a master security negative which shall be retained permanently.

(ii) Traffic and criminal dockets may be disposed of after a period of five years if copies are retained in accordance with subsection 6 (i) above.

7. Retention by Hall of Records. Whenever this section requires the clerk to retain records, the requirement may be satisfied by retention of the records by the Hall of Records Commission. When records retained by the clerk are twenty-five years of age, if not previously transferred to the Hall of Records Commission, they shall be transferred to that Commission, or disposed of according to schedule. (Added June 16, 1975, effective July 1, 1975; amended Dec. 17, 1975, effective Jan. 1, 1976; May 6, 1977, effective July 1, 1977; June 23, 1983, effective Jan. 1, 1984; Nov. 19, 1987, effective July 1, 1988; Mar. 22, 1991, effective July 1, 1991; June 5, 1996, effective Jan. 1, 1997.)

Source. — This Rule is former M.D.R. 1299.

Effect of amendments. — The 1996 amendment added the Source note.

Editor's note. — An Order dated June 5, 1996, effective Jan. 1, 1997, renumbered this Rule, which was formerly Maryland District Rule 1299.

Section 2-206 of the Courts Article, which is referred to in the Cross Reference note to section b, has been transferred to be § 2-205 of the Courts Article.

Rule 16-506. Electronic filing of pleadings and papers.

(a) **Applicability; Conflicts with other Rules.** This Rule applies to the electronic filing of pleadings and papers in the District Court. A pleading or paper may not be filed by direct electronic transmission to the Court except in accordance with this Rule. This Rule and any administrative order entered pursuant to it prevail if inconsistent with any other Rule.

(b) **Submission of plan.** The Chief Judge of the District Court may submit to the Court of Appeals for approval a detailed plan for a pilot project for the electronic filing of pleadings and papers. In developing the plan, the Chief Judge shall consult with the District Administrative Judge and the District Administrative Clerk of each district included in the plan, the District Court Chief Clerk, appropriate vendors, the State Court Administrator, and any other judges, court clerks, members of the bar, vendors of electronic filing systems, and interested persons that the Chief Judge chooses to ensure that: (1) the proposed electronic filing system is compatible with the data processing systems, operational systems, and electronic filing systems used or expected to be used by the judiciary; (2) the installation and use of the proposed system does not create an undue financial or operational burden on the District Court;

(3) the proposed system is reasonably available for use at a reasonable cost or an efficient and compatible system of manual filing will be maintained; (4) the proposed system is effective, secure, and not likely to break down; (5) the proposed system makes appropriate provision for the protection of privacy and for public access to public records; and (6) the court can discard or replace the system during or at the conclusion of a trial period without undue financial or operational burden. The State Court Administrator shall review the plan and make a recommendation to the Court of Appeals with respect to it.

Cross references. — For the definition of "public record," see Code, State Government Article, § 10-611.

(c) **Approval; Duration.** A plan may not be implemented unless approved by administrative order of the Court of Appeals. The plan shall terminate two years after the date of the administrative order unless the Court terminates it earlier or modifies or extends it by a subsequent administrative order.

(d) **Evaluation.** The Chief Judge of the Court of Appeals may appoint a committee consisting of one or more judges, court clerks, lawyers, legal educators, bar association representatives, and other interested and knowledgeable persons to monitor and evaluate the plan. Before the expiration of the two-year period set forth in section (c) of this Rule, the Court of Appeals, after considering the recommendations of the committee, shall evaluate the operation of the plan.

(e) **Public availability of plan.** The Chief Clerk of the District Court shall make available for public inspection a copy of any current plan. (Added Oct. 31, 2002, effective Jan. 1, 2003.)

Source. — This Rule is new.

CHAPTER 600. ATTORNEY TRUST ACCOUNTS.

Rule 16-601. Applicability.
The Rules in this Chapter apply to all trust accounts required by law to be maintained by attorneys for the deposit of funds that belong to others, except that these Rules do not apply to a fiduciary account maintained by an attorney as personal representative, trustee, guardian, custodian, receiver, or committee, or as a fiduciary under a written instrument or order of court. (Amended June 5, 1996, effective Jan. 1, 1997; Feb. 8, 2005, effective July 1, 2005.)

Cross references. — Code, Business Occupations and Professions Article, § 10-301 et seq. and Rule 1.15 of the Maryland Lawyers' Rules of Professional Conduct.

Source. — This Rule is former Rule BU1.

Effect of amendments. — The 1996 amendment substituted "Chapter" for "Subtitle"; and added the Source note.
The 2005 amendment substituted "Code, Business Occupations and Professions Article," for "BOP" and inserted "Lawyers'" before "Rules of Professional Conduct" in the cross references note.

Editor's note. — An Order dated June 5, 1996, effective Jan. 1, 1997, renumbered this Rule, which was formerly Rule BU1.

Rule 16-602. Definitions.

In this Chapter, the following definitions apply, except as expressly otherwise provided or as necessary implication requires:

a. **Approved financial institution.** "Approved financial institution" means a financial institution approved by the Commission in accordance with these Rules.

b. **Attorney.** "Attorney" means any person admitted by the Court of Appeals to practice law.

c. **Attorney trust account.** "Attorney trust account" means an account, including an escrow account, maintained in a financial institution for the deposit of funds received or held by an attorney or law firm on behalf of a client or third person.

d. **Bar Counsel.** "Bar Counsel" means the person appointed by the Commission as the principal executive officer of the disciplinary system affecting attorneys. All duties of Bar Counsel prescribed by these Rules shall be subject to the supervision and procedural guidelines of the Commission.

e. **Client.** "Client" includes any individual, firm, or entity for which an attorney performs any legal service, including acting as an escrow agent or as a legal representative of a fiduciary. The term does not include a public or private entity of which an attorney is a full-time employee.

f. **Commission.** "Commission" means the Attorney Grievance Commission of Maryland, as authorized and created by Rule 16-711 (Attorney Grievance Commission).

g. **Financial institution.** "Financial institution" means a bank, trust company, savings bank, or savings and loan association authorized by law to do business in this State, in the District of Columbia, or in a state contiguous to this State, the accounts of which are insured by an agency or instrumentality of the United States.

h. **IOLTA.** "IOLTA" (Interest on Lawyer Trust Accounts) means interest on attorney trust accounts payable to the Maryland Legal Services Corporation Fund under Code, Business Occupations and Professions Article, § 10-303.

i. **Law firm.** "Law firm" includes a partnership of attorneys, a professional or nonprofit corporation of attorneys, and a combination thereof engaged in the practice of law. In the case of a law firm with offices in this State and in other jurisdictions, the Rules in this Chapter apply only to the offices in this State. (Amended June 28, 1989, effective July 1, 1989; June 5, 1996, effective Jan. 1, 1997; March 12, 2007, effective Jan. 1, 2008; Dec. 4, 2007, effective April 1, 2008.)

Source. — This Rule is derived from former Rule BU2.

Effect of amendments. — The 1996 amendment substituted "Rule 16-702" for "Rule BV2" in f.; and added the Source note.

The 2007 amendment, effective January 1, 2008, substituted "this Chapter" for "these rules" in the introductory language; in h. substituted "the Rules in this Chapter" for "these Rules"; and added "derived from" in the Source note.

The December 4, 2007, Order, effective April 1, 2008, added h and redesignated accordingly.

Editor's note. — An Order dated June 5, 1996, effective Jan. 1, 1997, renumbered this Rule, which was formerly Rule BU2.

The March 12, 2007, Order provided in part that "the rules changes hereby adopted by this Court shall take effect on January 1, 2008 and, from and after said date, shall govern the conduct of attorneys from and after that date".

Rule 16-603. Duty to maintain account.

An attorney or the attorney's law firm shall maintain one or more attorney trust accounts for the deposit of funds received from any source for the intended benefit of clients or third persons. The account or accounts shall be maintained in this State, in the District of Columbia, or in a state contiguous to this State, and shall be with an approved financial institution. Unless an attorney maintains such an account, or is a member of or employed by a law firm that maintains such an account, an attorney may not receive and accept funds as an attorney from any source intended in whole or in part for the benefit of a client or third person. (Amended, June 5, 1996, effective Jan. 1, 1997.)

Source. — This Rule is former Rule BU3.

Effect of amendments. — The 1996 amendment added the Source note.

Editor's note. — An Order dated June 5, 1996, effective Jan. 1, 1997, renumbered this Rule, which was formerly Rule BU3.

Approval of financial institutions handling trust accounts. Financial institution located in another state must be authorized to do business and establish a branch in either Maryland or a contiguous jurisdiction in order to handle attorney trust accounts. Unless the financial institution has such a branch or intends to open one before it accepts attorney trust accounts, the Commission may not approve that institution to handle those accounts. 92 OAG 171 (Nov. 14, 2007).

Failure to maintain accounts. — An attorney's failure to maintain separate accounts for the deposit of money advanced on behalf of his clients for future representation of those clients, his failure to maintain trust accounts, and his failure to cooperate with the grievance board constituted rules violations. Att'y Griev. Comm'n v. Briscoe, 357 Md. 554, 745 A.2d 1037 (2000).

Attorney violated Rules 16-603, 16-604, 16-606, 16-607, and 16-609 by failing to maintain an attorney trust account, failing to deposit client funds in such an account, failing to name or designate such an account in a manner that clearly identified it as such, and by using funds for an unauthorized purpose. Att'y Griev. Comm'n v. Daskalopoulos, 383 Md. 375, 859 A.2d 653 (2004).

Suspended attorney was disbarred because of his later (1) unjustified misappropriation of trust funds by not paying the clients' medical providers (as he had promised he would do) from clients' share settlement he retained in cash after he got clients' endorsements on settlement checks, received payable to him and to the clients, cashed the checks with the clients at a liquor store cashing service, retained cash to pay his one-third fee (that he reduced) and to pay listed medical providers according to a handwritten distribution summary given to the clients, and distributed the clients' share to them; (2) failure to have or to use an attorney trust account at a proper financial institution; and (3) failure to respond to the disciplinary committee's investigation or petition, or to the hearing judge's conclusions. The attorney's misappropriation of trust money was serious professional misconduct and was embezzlement, fraudulent misappropriation by a fiduciary, under 7-113 of the Criminal Law Article, representing professional misconduct that violated Md. R. Prof. Conduct 8.4(b)-(c); and his conducted also violated Md. R. Prof. Conduct 1.15, 8.1; Md. R. 16-812, 16-603, 16-604, §§ 10-302(a), 10-306 of the Business Occupations and Professions

Article. Att'y Griev. Comm'n v. Prichard, 386 Md. 238, 872 A.2d 81 (2005).

The failure to establish a proper trust account and the failure to use such an account as the depository for the recovery proceeds constituted a violation of Md. R. 16-603 and 604, and Md. R. Prof. Conduct 1.15, by failing to safeguard the property of others entrusted to the attorney. Att'y Griev. Comm'n v. Mitchell, 386 Md. 386, 872 A.2d 720 (2005).

Disciplinary proceedings. — Lawyer was indefinitely suspended from the practice of law where he failed to maintain a trust account, commingled client funds and his own, and failed to keep proper records regarding such funds; but, the violations were unintentional, resulting from lawyer's ignorance of his obligation to refrain from commingling, and he was not motivated to use client funds for his own benefit. Att'y Griev. Comm'n v. Awuah, 346 Md. 420, 697 A.2d 446 (1997).

Claimed ignorance of ethical duties and bookkeeping requirements is not a defense in disciplinary proceedings, but a finding with respect to the intent with which a violation was committed is relevant on the issue of the appropriate sanction. Att'y Griev. Comm'n v. Awuah, 346 Md. 420, 697 A.2d 446 (1997).

Disbarment was the appropriate sanction for an attorney who failed to maintain separate trust and escrow accounts, and placed funds he was holding for a client into an account he used for business and personal purposes, eventually draining it. Att'y Griev. Comm'n v. Gallagher, 371 Md. 673, 810 A.2d 996 (2002).

Quoted in Att'y Griev. Comm'n v. Jeter, 365 Md. 279, 778 A.2d 390 (2001).

Stated in Unnamed Att'y v. Att'y Griev. Comm'n, 349 Md. 391, 708 A.2d 667 (1998).

Cited in Att'y Griev. Comm'n v. Kreamer, 387 Md. 503, 876 A.2d 79 (2005). Att'y Griev. Comm'n v. Kreamer, 387 Md. 503, 876 A.2d 79 (2005).

Rule 16-604. Trust account — Required deposits.

Except as otherwise permitted by rule or other law, all funds, including cash, received and accepted by an attorney or law firm in this State from a client or third person to be delivered in whole or in part to a client or third person, unless received as payment of fees owed the attorney by the client or in reimbursement for expenses properly advanced on behalf of the client, shall be deposited in an attorney trust account in an approved financial institution. This Rule does not apply to an instrument received by an attorney or law firm that is made payable solely to a client or third person and is transmitted directly to the client or third person. (Amended, June 5, 1996, effective Jan. 1, 1997.)

Source. — This Rule is former Rule BU4.

Effect of amendments. — The 1996 amendment added the Source note.

Editor's note. — An Order dated June 5, 1996, effective Jan. 1, 1997, renumbered this Rule, which was formerly Rule BU4.

Failure to maintain accounts. — An attorney's failure to maintain separate accounts for the deposit of money advanced on behalf of his clients for future representation of those clients, his failure to maintain trust accounts, and his failure to cooperate with the grievance board constituted rules violations. Att'y Griev. Comm'n v. Briscoe, 357 Md. 554, 745 A.2d 1037 (2000).

Disbarment was the appropriate sanction for an attorney who failed to maintain separate trust and escrow accounts, and placed funds he was holding for a client into an account he used for business and personal purposes, eventually draining it. Att'y Griev. Comm'n v. Gallagher, 371 Md. 673, 810 A.2d 996 (2002).

Attorney violated Rules 16-603, 16-604, 16-606, 16-607, and 16-609 by failing to maintain an attorney trust account, failing to deposit client funds in such an account, failing to name or designate such an account in a manner that clearly identified it as such, and by using funds for an unauthorized purpose. Att'y Griev. Comm'n v. Daskalopoulos, 383 Md. 375, 859 A.2d 653 (2004).

Suspended attorney was disbarred because of his later (1) unjustified misappropriation of trust funds by not paying the clients' medical providers (as he had promised he would do) from clients' share settlement he retained in cash after he got clients' endorsements on settlement checks, received payable to him and to the clients, cashed the checks with the clients at a liquor store cashing service, retained cash to pay his one-third fee (that he reduced) and to pay listed medical providers according to a handwritten distribution summary given to the clients, and distributed the clients' share to them; (2) failure to have or to use an attorney trust account at a proper financial institution; and (3) failure to respond to the disciplinary committee's investigation or petition, or to the hearing judge's conclusions. The attorney's misappropriation of trust money was serious professional misconduct and was embezzlement, fraudulent misappropriation by a fiduciary, under 7-113 of the Criminal Law Article, representing professional misconduct that violated Md. R. Prof. Conduct 8.4(b)-(c); and his conducted also violated Md. R. Prof. Conduct 1.15, 8.1; Md. R. 16-812, 16-603, 16-604, §§ 10-302(a), 10-306 of the Business Occupations and Professions Article. Att'y Griev. Comm'n v. Prichard, 386 Md. 238, 872 A.2d 81 (2005).

The failure to establish a proper trust account and the failure to use such an account as the depository for the recovery proceeds constituted a violation of Md. R. 16-603 and 604, and Md. R. Prof. Conduct 1.15, by failing to safeguard the property of others entrusted to the attorney. Att'y Griev. Comm'n v. Mitchell, 386 Md. 386, 872 A.2d 720 (2005).

Attorney representing a client in a divorce action violated this Rule when he failed to deposit advanced fees into a trust account. Att'y Griev. Comm'n v. Rose, 391 Md. 101, 892 A.2d 469 (2006), cert. denied, 2006 U.S. LEXIS 5734, 166 L. Ed. 2d 22 (U.S. 2006).

Failure to deposit in attorney trust account — Attorney's misconduct in abusing the trust that the client placed in the attorney by placing the client's retainer check in the attorney's operating account rather than an attorney trust account, spending that money which belonged to the client on the attorney, in refusing to promptly refund to the client money that attorney admittedly owed to the client despite the client's refund request, and in failing to promptly answer bar counsel's request for information about the matter warranted the attorney's indefinite suspension. Att'y Griev. Comm'n v. McCulloch, 397 Md. 674, 919 A.2d 660 (2007).

Attorney was indefinitely suspended. — Hearing court's finding that an attorney did not use funds intended for certain clients for them supported a finding that the attorney violated § 10-306 of the Business Occupations and Professions Article and Rule 16-609, as well as the violations of Md. R. Prof. Conduct 1.15 and Rules 16-604 and 16-607 that were found by the hearing court; the attorney was indefinitely suspended, with a right to apply for readmission after 90 days. Att'y Griev. Comm'n v. Mba-Jonas, 397 Md. 690, 919 A.2d 669 (2007).

Attorney was indefinitely suspended from the practice of law with the right to reapply for admission after one year, as the attorney's act of threatening to withdraw from representation of a client if the client refused to pay additional legal fees constituted a violation of Md. R. Prof. Conduct 1.15 and 1.16, and constituted conduct involving dishonesty, fraud, deceit or misrepresentation in violation of Md. R. Prof. Conduct 8.4, and the flat fee charged violated Md. R. Prof. Conduct 1.5 as the attorney did not provide sufficient services to earn the fee, the attorney violated this Rule and Rule 16-609 by failing to place unearned attorney fees in his attorney trust account, and the attorney's failure to keep the client informed of the progress of the litigation violated Md. R. Prof. Conduct 1.4. Att'y Griev. Comm'n v. Lawson, 401 Md. 536, 933 A.2d 842 (2007).

Attorney disbarred. — Where the attorney, among other things, intentionally misappropriated client funds, forged a client's signature on a settlement check, lied under oath, and represented a client when the attorney was not licensed to do so, the attorney was disbarred for violating former, similar Md. R. Prof. Conduct 1.2(a), 1.3, 1.5(c), 1.15(a), (b), 3.3(a), 5.5, 8.1(a), (b), 8.4(a), (b), (c), (d), Md. R. 16-604, and §§ 10-304, -306 of the Business Occupations and Professions Article Att'y Griev. Comm'n v. Kapoor, 391 Md. 505, 894 A.2d 502 (2006).

Attorney violated this Rule and Md. Law. R. Prof. Conduct 1.2(a), 1.15(d), 8.4(c) and (d), Md. R. 16-609(c), and § 10-306 of the Business Occupations and Professions Article, and was disbarred, after misappropriating tens of thousands of dollars that should have been paid to a physical therapist and settling a client's claim without the client's knowledge or consent. Att'y Griev. Comm'n v. Stern, 419 Md. 525, 19 A.3d 904 (2011).

Applied in Att'y Griev. Comm'n v. Hollis, 347 Md. 547, 702 A.2d 223 (1997).

Quoted in Att'y Griev. Comm'n v. Adams, 349 Md. 86, 706 A.2d 1080 (1998); Att'y Griev. Comm'n v. Jeter, 365 Md. 279, 778 A.2d 390 (2001); Att'y Griev. Comm'n v. Snyder, 368 Md. 242, 793 A.2d 515 (2002); Att'y Griev. Comm'n v. Santos, 370 Md. 77, 803 A.2d 505 (2002); Att'y Griev. Comm'n v. Cafferty, 376 Md. 700, 831 A.2d 1042 (2003); Att'y Griev. Comm'n v. Seiden, 373 Md. 409, 818 A.2d 1108 (2003); Att'y Griev. Comm'n v. Braskey, 378 Md. 425, 836 A.2d 605 (2003); Att'y Griev. Comm'n v. Christopher, 383 Md. 624, 861 A.2d 692 (2004); Att'y Griev. Comm'n v. McCulloch, 404 Md. 388, 946 A.2d 1009 (2008); Att'y Griev. Comm'n v. Taylor, 405 Md. 697, 955 A.2d 755 (2008); Att'y Griev. Comm'n v. Thomas, 409 Md. 121, 973 A.2d 185 (2009); Att'y Griev. Comm'n v. Nwadike, 416 Md. 180, 6 A.3d 287 (2010).

Cited in Att'y Griev. Comm'n v. Stolarz, 379

Md. 387, 842 A.2d 42 (2004); Att'y Griev. Comm'n v. Sperling, 380 Md. 180, 844 A.2d 397 (2004); In re Powers, 838 A.2d 311 (2003); Att'y Griev. Comm'n v. Maignan, 390 Md. 287, 888 A.2d 344 (2005); Att'y Griev. Comm'n v. Obi, 393 Md. 643, 904 A.2d 422 (2006); Att'y Griev. Comm'n v. Mba-Jonas, 402 Md. 334, 936 A.2d 839 (2007); Att'y Griev. Comm'n v. Ugwuonye, 405 Md. 351, 952 A.2d 226 (2008); Att'y Griev. Comm'n v. Tauber, — Md. —, 26 A.3d 967 (2011).

Rule 16-605. Duty of attorney to notify institution.

An attorney may not exercise any authority to sign checks or disburse or withdraw funds from an attorney trust account until the attorney in writing:

a. Requests the financial institution to designate the account on its records as an attorney trust account, and

b. Authorizes the financial institution to report to Bar Counsel any dishonored instruments or overdrafts in the account as required by the agreement under Rule 16-610 between the institution and the Commission. (Amended, June 5, 1996, effective Jan. 1, 1997.)

Source. — This Rule is former Rule BU5.

Effect of amendments. — The 1996 amendment substituted "Rule 16-610" for "Rule BU10" in b; and added the Source note.

Editor's note. — An Order dated June 5, 1996, effective Jan. 1, 1997, renumbered this Rule, which was formerly Rule BU5.

Stated in Unnamed Att'y v. Att'y Griev. Comm'n, 349 Md. 391, 708 A.2d 667 (1998).

Rule 16-606. Name and designation of account.

An attorney or law firm shall maintain each attorney trust account with a title that includes the name of the attorney or law firm and that clearly designates the account as "Attorney Trust Account", "Attorney Escrow Account", or "Clients' Funds Account" on all checks and deposit slips. The title shall distinguish the account from any other fiduciary account that the attorney or law firm may maintain and from any personal or business account of the attorney or law firm. (Amended, June 5, 1996, effective Jan. 1, 1997.)

Source. — This Rule is former Rule BU6.

Effect of amendments. — The 1996 amendment added the Source note.

Editor's note. — An Order dated June 5, 1996, effective Jan. 1, 1997, renumbered this Rule, which was formerly Rule BU6.

Failure to properly designate attorney trust account — Attorney was disbarred as his failure to properly designate his attorney trust account as an attorney trust account, attorney escrow account, or client funds account violated this Rule. Att'y Griev. Comm'n v. Brown, 380 Md. 661, 846 A.2d 428 (2004).

Attorney violated Rules 16-603, 16-604, 16-606, 16-607, and 16-609 by failing to maintain an attorney trust account, failing to deposit client funds in such an account, failing to name or designate such an account in a manner that clearly identified it as such, and by using funds for an unauthorized purpose. Att'y Griev. Comm'n v. Daskalopoulos, 383 Md. 375, 859 A.2d 653 (2004).

Clear and convincing evidence was found that an attorney violated this Rule by titling her attorney trust account as an IOLTA account instead of designating the account as "Attorney Trust Account," "Attorney Escrow Account," or "Client's Funds Account." Att'y Griev. Comm'n v. Cherry-Mahoi, 388 Md. 124, 879 A.2d 58 (2005).

Attorney's failure to have checks and deposit tickets containing the necessary designation of Attorney Trust Account, Attorney Escrow Account, or Client's Fund Account amounted to a violation of this rule. Att'y Griev. Comm'n v.

Jarosinski, 411 Md. 432, 983 A.2d 477 (2009).

Disbarment required. — Attorney was disbarred, despite the mitigating factors of an absence of a prior disciplinary record and relative inexperience, for violating Md. R. Prof. Conduct 1.5(c), 1.15(b) and (c), 8.1(b), and 8.4(c) and (d), and Md. R. 16-606 and 16-609 in his intentionally dishonest conduct towards a third-party assignee/healthcare provider during the representation of a client in a personal injury claim and Maryland Bar Counsel and its investigator in the course of investigating the assignee's complaint. Att'y Griev. Comm'n v. Ellison, 384 Md. 688, 867 A.2d 259 (2005).

Attorney violated this Rule by designating his attorney trust account as "Jared K. Ellison, Esq. IOLTA" and Md. R. Prof. Conduct 1.15(a) for not complying with Title 16, ch. 600 of the Maryland Rules; the incorrectly designated account checks were sufficient to violate both this Rule and Md. R. Prof. Conduct 1.15(a). Att'y Griev. Comm'n v. Ellison, 384 Md. 688, 867 A.2d 259 (2005).

Applied in Att'y Griev. Comm'n v. Awuah, 346 Md. 420, 697 A.2d 446 (1997).

Quoted in Att'y Griev. Comm'n v. Blum, 373 Md. 275, 818 A.2d 219 (2003); Att'y Griev. Comm'n v. Braskey, 378 Md. 425, 836 A.2d 605 (2003); Att'y Griev. Comm'n v. Braskey, 378 Md. 425, 836 A.2d 605 (2003); Att'y Griev. Comm'n v. Calhoun, 391 Md. 532, 894 A.2d 518 (2006).

Stated in Unnamed Att'y v. Att'y Griev. Comm'n, 349 Md. 391, 708 A.2d 667 (1998).

Cited in Att'y Griev. Comm'n v. Gallagher, 371 Md. 673, 810 A.2d 996 (2002); In re Powers, 838 A.2d 311 (2003); Att'y Griev. Comm'n v. Maignan, 390 Md. 287, 888 A.2d 344 (2005); Att'y Griev. Comm'n v. Obi, 393 Md. 643, 904 A.2d 422 (2006).

Rule 16-606.1. Attorney trust account record-keeping.

(a) **Creation of records.** The following records shall be created and maintained for the receipt and disbursement of funds of clients or of third persons:

(1) Attorney trust account identification. An identification of all attorney trust accounts maintained, including the name of the financial institution, account number, account name, date the account was opened, date the account was closed, and an agreement with the financial institution establishing each account and its interest-bearing nature.

(2) Deposits and disbursements. A record for each account that chronologically shows all deposits and disbursements, as follows:

(A) for each deposit, a record made at or near the time of the deposit that shows (i) the date of the deposit, (ii) the amount, (iii) the identity of the client or third person for whom the funds were deposited, and (iv) the purpose of the deposit;

(B) for each disbursement, including a disbursement made by electronic transfer, a record made at or near the time of disbursement that shows (i) the date of the disbursement, (ii) the amount, (iii) the payee, (iv) the identity of the client or third person for whom the disbursement was made (if not the payee), and (v) the purpose of the disbursement;

(C) for each disbursement made by electronic transfer, a written memorandum authorizing the transaction and identifying the attorney responsible for the transaction.

Cross references. — See Rule 16-609 c, which provides that a disbursement that would create a negative balance with respect to any individual client matter or with respect to all client matters in the aggregate is prohibited.

(3) Client matter records. A record for each client matter in which the attorney receives funds in trust, as follows:

(A) for each attorney trust account transaction, a record that shows (i) the date of the deposit or disbursement; (ii) the amount of the deposit or disbursement; (iii) the purpose for which the funds are intended; (iv) for a disbursement, the payee and the check number or other payment identification; and (v) the balance of funds remaining in the account in connection with the matter; and

(B) an identification of the person to whom the unused portion of a fee or expense deposit is to be returned whenever it is to be returned to a person other than the client.

(4) Record of funds of the attorney. A record that identifies the funds of the attorney held in each attorney trust account as permitted by Rule 16-607 b.

(b) **Monthly reconciliation.** An attorney shall cause to be created a monthly reconciliation of all attorney trust account records, client matter records, records of funds of the attorney held in an attorney trust account as permitted by Rule 16-607 b, and the adjusted month-end financial institution statement balance. The adjusted month-end financial institution statement balance is computed by adding subsequent deposits to and subtracting subsequent disbursements from the financial institution's month-end statement balance.

(c) **Electronic records.** Whenever the records required by this Rule are created or maintained using electronic means, there must be an ability to print a paper copy of the records upon a reasonable request to do so.

Committee note. — Electronic records should be backed up regularly by an appropriate storage device.

(d) **Records to be maintained.** Financial institution month-end statements, any canceled checks or copies of canceled checks provided with a financial institution month-end statement, duplicate deposit slips or deposit receipts generated by the financial institution, and records created in accordance with section (a) of this Rule shall be maintained for a period of at least five years after the date the record was created. (Adopted March 12, 2007, effective January 1, 2008.)

Committee note. — An attorney or law firm may satisfy the requirements of section (d) of this Rule by maintaining any of the following items: original records, photocopies, microfilm, optical imaging, electronic records, or any other medium that preserves the required data for the required period of time and from which a paper copy can be printed.

Cross references. — Rule 1.15 (Safekeeping Property) of the Maryland Lawyers' Rules of Professional Conduct.

Source. — This Rule is new.

Editor's note. — The March 12, 2007, Order provided in part that "the rules changes hereby adopted by this Court shall take effect on January 1, 2008 and, from and after said date, shall govern the conduct of attorneys from and after that date".

Failure to create adequate records. — Attorney violated this Rule by failing to create a record for his trust account that chronologically showed all deposits and disbursements or describing the check number or other payment identification for disbursements. Att'y Griev. Comm'n v. Patterson, — Md. —, — A.3d — (Sept. 21, 2011).

Rule 16-607. Commingling of funds.

a. **General prohibition.** An attorney or law firm may deposit in an attorney trust account only those funds required to be deposited in that account by Rule 16-604 or permitted to be so deposited by section b. of this Rule.

b. **Exceptions.** 1. An attorney or law firm shall either (A) deposit into an attorney trust account funds to pay any fees, service charges, or minimum balance required by the financial institution to open or maintain the account, including those fees that cannot be charged against interest due to the Maryland Legal Services Corporation Fund pursuant to Rule 16-610 b 1 (D), or (B) enter into an agreement with the financial institution to have any fees or charges deducted from an operating account maintained by the attorney or law firm. The attorney or law firm may deposit into an attorney trust account any funds expected to be advanced on behalf of a client and expected to be reimbursed to the attorney by the client.

2. An attorney or law firm may deposit into an attorney trust account funds belonging in part to a client and in part presently or potentially to the attorney or law firm. The portion belonging to the attorney or law firm shall be withdrawn promptly when the attorney or law firm becomes entitled to the funds, but any portion disputed by the client shall remain in the account until the dispute is resolved.

3. Funds of a client or beneficial owner may be pooled and commingled in an attorney trust account with the funds held for other clients or beneficial owners. (Amended Sept. 11, 1995, effective Jan. 1, 1996; June 5, 1996, effective Jan. 1, 1997; June 10, 1997, effective July 1, 1997; Jan. 20, 1999, effective July 1, 1999.)

Cross references. — See Code, BOP §§ 10-301 et seq.

Source. — This Rule is former Rule BU7.

Effect of amendments. — The 1996 amendment substituted "Rule 16-604" for "Rule BU4" in a.; and added the Source note.

The 1997 amendment substituted "Rule 16-610" for "Rule BU10" in b.1.

The 1999 amendment inserted "Fund" following "Corporation" in b 1.

Editor's note. — An Order dated June 5, 1996, effective Jan. 1, 1997, renumbered this Rule, which was formerly Rule BU7.

Applicability. — Subdivision b 3, which permits commingling of the funds of several clients in a single attorney trust account, does not apply to a fiduciary account maintained by an attorney as personal representative, trustee, guardian, custodian, receiver, or committee, or as a fiduciary under a written instrument or order of court. Att'y Griev. Comm'n v. Owrutsky, 322 Md. 334, 587 A.2d 511 (1991).

Source of funds in designated account. — When an account is designated an attorney trust account, inquiry into the source of the funds within the account is irrelevant. Att'y Griev. Comm'n v. Webster, 348 Md. 662, 705 A.2d 1135 (1998).

Use of designated account. — Use of the attorney trust account for personal purposes while still designated a trust account, even if it was no longer intended that the account be used for trust purposes, is prohibited regardless of whether or not client funds are deposited in the account. Att'y Griev. Comm'n v. Webster, 348 Md. 662, 705 A.2d 1135 (1998).

Attorney was reprimanded for violating Rule 1.15 of the Rules of Professional Responsibility and this Rule because the attorney deposited personal funds into a trust account in excess of permissible amounts necessary to maintain the account, and the account was intended to be used to disburse personal and business related expense; the attorney's use of a trust account violated this Rule, even if no client funds were in the account, because the account was designated as an attorney trust account and constituted a holding out to the world that the monies contained in it were not subject to attachment and were beyond the reach of any creditors. Att'y Griev. Comm'n v. Taylor, 405 Md. 697, 955 A.2d 755 (2008).

Failure to remove fees from trust account — Attorney's failure to remove his earned fees promptly from his trust account violated Md. R. Prof. Conduct 1.15(a) and Md. R. 16-607(b)(2). Att'y Griev. Comm'n v. Zuckerman, 386 Md. 341, 872 A.2d 693 (2005).

Failure to use trust account — Attorney representing a client in a divorce action violated this Rule when he failed to deposit advanced fees into a trust account. Att'y Griev. Comm'n v. Rose, 391 Md. 101, 892 A.2d 469 (2006), cert. denied, 2006 U.S. LEXIS 5734, 166 L. Ed. 2d 22 (U.S. 2006).

Withdrawal of disputed funds. — When an attorney withdrew the entire amount of a settlement paid into his trust account as partial payment of his fee, billed on an hourly basis, he violated subdivision b 2 of this rule because his clients asserted that he had agreed to represent them on a contingency basis, so he was required to leave any disputed funds in the trust account until the dispute was resolved. Att'y Griev. Comm'n v. Culver, 371 Md. 265, 808 A.2d 1251 (2002).

Hiding personal funds in trust account. —Attorney's action in seeking to hide personal assets in an involuntary bankruptcy proceeding by depositing funds into his trust account was sufficient in itself to warrant disbarment, although in the case of the particularly attorney, disbarment could be justified on several other grounds as well. Att'y Griev. Comm'n v. Snyder, 368 Md. 242, 793 A.2d 515 (2002).

Failure to maintain separate accounts. — Where attorney deposited earned fees and money he received from his father into a bank account he titled as an attorney trust account, and used this account for personal and business purposes, such conduct constituted clear and convincing evidence of commingling in violation of both Md. R. Prof. Conduct 1.15(a) and Md. R. 16-607. Att'y Griev. Comm'n v. Powell, 369 Md. 462, 800 A.2d 782 (2002).

Attorney violated Rules 16-603, 16-604, 16-606, 16-607, and 16-609 by failing to maintain an attorney trust account, failing to deposit client funds in such an account, failing to name or designate such an account in a manner that clearly identified it as such, and by using funds for an unauthorized purpose. Att'y Griev. Comm'n v. Daskalopoulos, 383 Md. 375, 859 A.2d 653 (2004).

Attorney's conduct in taking funds from the attorney's escrow account holding client funds and using them to pay the attorney's law practice operating expenses violated this Rule, regarding the commingling of funds, and Rule 16-609, regarding prohibited transactions, as the escrow funds and the funds in the operating account were required to be kept separate. Att'y Griev. Comm'n v. Nussbaum, 401 Md. 612, 934 A.2d 1 (2007).

Unintentional violations are relevant to appropriate sanction. — Lawyer was indefinitely suspended from the practice of law where he failed to maintain a trust account, commingled client funds and his own, and failed to keep proper records regarding such funds; but, the violations were unintentional, resulting from lawyer's ignorance of his obligation to refrain from commingling, and he was not motivated to use client funds for his own benefit. Att'y Griev. Comm'n v. Awuah, 346 Md. 420, 697 A.2d 446 (1997).

Claimed ignorance of ethical duties and bookkeeping requirements is not a defense in disciplinary proceedings, but a finding with respect to the intent with which a violation was committed is relevant on the issue of the appropriate sanction. Att'y Griev. Comm'n v. Awuah, 346 Md. 420, 697 A.2d 446 (1997).

Attorney who operated his law practice using only a trust account was suspended, rather than disbarred, for commingling and misusing a client's funds, where the attorney had a 30-year spotless record, there was no intent to defraud, the one victim suffered no loss, and the attorney was candid and remorseful; the automatic disbarment rule for misappropriation did not apply, as this was not the kind of willful conduct to which the rule was directed or intended to reach. Att'y Griev. Comm'n v. Hayes, 367 Md. 504, 789 A.2d 119 (2002).

Court of Appeals of Maryland affirmed hearing judge's findings that an attorney mishandled funds in attorney trust account but held that because there was no finding of intentional misappropriation of funds and the attorney's clients did not suffer a financial loss, indefinite suspension was the appropriate sanction. Att'y Griev. Comm'n v. DiCicco, 369 Md. 662, 802 A.2d 1014 (2002).

Appropriate sanction. — Appropriate sanction for an attorney's violation of subdivision b 2 of this rule when he withdrew funds from his trust account to which his entitlement was disputed, was an indefinite suspension, with the right to apply for readmission in no less than 30 days, given his previous discipline and the fact that the disputed funds had neither been paid to his clients nor restored to his trust account. Att'y Griev. Comm'n v. Culver, 371 Md. 265, 808 A.2d 1251 (2002).

Attorney was indefinitely suspended. — Hearing court's finding that an attorney did not use funds intended for certain clients for them supported a finding that the attorney violated § 10-306 of the Business Occupations and Professions Article and Rule 16-609, as well as the violations of Md. R. Prof. Conduct

1.15 and Rules 16-604 and 16-607 that were found by the hearing court; the attorney was indefinitely suspended, with a right to apply for readmission after 90 days. Att'y Griev. Comm'n v. Mba-Jonas, 397 Md. 690, 919 A.2d 669 (2007).

Attorney was indefinitely suspended from practice of law for violating Md. R. Prof. Conduct 1.8, 1.15, 8.1, and 8.4, Rule 16-607 and this Rule, and § 10-306 of the Business Occupations and Professional Article, when the attorney advanced money to a client and the client's family members from the attorney's trust account, but did not hold any funds in escrow for those people, and commingled personal and trust funds in the same account. Att'y Griev. Comm'n v. McLaughlin, 409 Md. 304, 974 A.2d 315 (2009).

Disbarment ordered. — Disbarment was ordered where an attorney violated Md. R. Prof. Conduct 1.15(a), 8.1(a) and (b), and 8.4(c) and (d), and Md. R. 16-607, and had previously been sanctioned, receiving an indefinite suspension with the right to reapply in not less than six months for conduct amounting to negligent misappropriation of client funds. Att'y Griev. Comm'n v. Powell, 369 Md. 462, 800 A.2d 782 (2002).

Disbarment was the appropriate sanction for an attorney who failed to maintain separate trust and escrow accounts, and placed funds he was holding for a client into an account he used for business and personal purposes, eventually draining it. Att'y Griev. Comm'n v. Gallagher, 371 Md. 673, 810 A.2d 996 (2002).

Disbarment was the only appropriate sanction for an attorney who knowingly withdrew sums that should have been forwarded to a client from an attorney trust account for the attorney's personal use and failed to respond to the client's inquiries; the attorney's marital and drinking problems were not factors in mitigation. Att'y Griev. Comm'n v. Herman, 380 Md. 378, 844 A.2d 1181 (2004).

Where an attorney invaded trust funds being held for a client, and only scrambled to replace them when the client required reimbursement, the evidence was ample to show knowing misappropriation, and the only appropriate sanction was disbarment. Att'y Griev. Comm'n v. Zdravkovich, 381 Md. 680, 852 A.2d 82 (2004).

Intentional misappropriation of client funds by an attorney who failed to deposit client funds in an escrow account and used client funds for personal purposes warranted disbarment, especially where the attorney offered no evidence in mitigation. Att'y Griev. Comm'n v. James, 385 Md. 637, 870 A.2d 229 (2005).

Attorney violated this Rule by using trust account funds for peronal and business matters and was disbarred based on violation of

this Rule, Rule 16-609 and Md. R. Prof. Conduct 1.15(a), 8.1(b), 8.4 (a), (b), (c), (d), and §§ 10-306 and 10-606 of the Business Occupations and Professions Article. Att'y Griev. Comm'n v. Butler, 395 Md. 1, 909 A.2d 226 (2006).

Attorney, who, inter alia, failed to withdraw fees earned from the attorney's trust account and who withdrew funds from the trust account in excess of funds deposited on behalf of a client or for clients who did not contribute to the account at all, was disbarred for violating Md. Law. R. Prof. Conduct 1.15 and 8.4(a — d); §§ 10-306 and 307 of the Business Occupations and Professions Article; and Rule 16-609 and this Rule. Att'y Griev. Comm'n v. Thomas, 409 Md. 121, 973 A.2d 185 (2009).

Attorney was disbarred for violating Md. R. Prof. Conduct 1.15 and 8.4(a), (c), and (d), and this Rule because clear and convincing evidence established that he commingled personal and client funds and engaged in a pattern of dishonesty to hide his assets to avoid paying a judgment creditor. The evidence established that the attorney manipulated his corporate operations, his attorney escrow account, and his pension plan account to systematically avoid the judgment creditor's collection efforts and engaged in a pattern of behavior designed to conceal assets from attachment by the judgment creditor, which was conduct prejudicial to the administration of justice. Att'y Griev. Comm'n v. Foltz, 411 Md. 359, 983 A.2d 434 (2009).

Attorney was disbarred from the practice of law in Maryland for violating this section by failing to keep her earned feees and reimbursed expenses in her attorney trust account separate from her clients' and third parties' property, making a host of deposits and receiving electronic transfers into her trust account with any accounting, and commingling personal funds with her clients' monies in her trust account for more than four years. Att'y Griev. Comm'n v. Nwadike, 416 Md. 180, 6 A.3d 287 (2010).

Quoted in Att'y Griev. Comm'n v. Blum, 373 Md. 275, 818 A.2d 219 (2003); Att'y Griev. Comm'n v. Braskey, 378 Md. 425, 836 A.2d 605 (2003); Att'y Griev. Comm'n v. Christopher, 383 Md. 624, 861 A.2d 692 (2004); Att'y Griev. Comm'n v. Zakroff, 387 Md. 603, 876 A.2d 664 (2005), cert. denied, 2006 Md. LEXIS 561 (2006); cert. denied, 2006 Md. LEXIS 571 (Md. 2006); Att'y Griev. Comm'n v. Zakroff, 387 Md. 603, 876 A.2d 664 (2005), cert. denied, 2006 Md. LEXIS 561 (2006); cert. denied, 2006 Md. LEXIS 571 (Md. 2006); Att'y Griev. Comm'n v. Calhoun, 391 Md. 532, 894 A.2d 518 (2006); Att'y Griev. Comm'n v. Obi, 393 Md. 643, 904 A.2d 422 (2006); Att'y Griev. Comm'n v. Mba-Jonas, 402 Md. 334, 936 A.2d 839 (2007).

Cited in Att'y Griev. Comm'n v. McClain,

373 Md. 196, 817 A.2d 218 (2003); Att'y Griev. Comm'n v. McClain, 373 Md. 196, 817 A.2d 218 (2003); Att'y Griev. Comm'n v. Sperling, 380 Md. 180, 844 A.2d 397 (2004); In re Powers, 838 A.2d 311 (2003); Att'y Griev. Comm'n v.

Maignan, 390 Md. 287, 888 A.2d 344 (2005); Att'y Griev. Comm'n v. Adams, 404 Md. 1, 944 A.2d 1115 (2008); Att'y Griev. Comm'n v. Adams, 410 Md. 544, 979 A.2d 698 (2009).

Rule 16-608. Interest on funds in attorney trust accounts.

a. **Generally.** Any interest paid on funds deposited in an attorney trust account, after deducting service charges and fees of the financial institution, shall be credited and belong to the client or third person whose funds are on deposit during the period the interest is earned, except to the extent that interest is paid to the Maryland Legal Services Corporation Fund as authorized by law. The attorney or law firm shall have no right or claim to the interest.

Cross references. — See Rule 16-610 b 1 (D) providing that certain fees may not be deducted from interest that otherwise would be payable to the Maryland Legal Services Corporation Fund.

b. **Duty to report IOLTA participation.** (1) Required as a condition of practice. As a condition precedent to the practice of law, each lawyer admitted to practice in Maryland shall report annually in accordance with this Rule information concerning all IOLTA accounts, including name, address, location, and account number, on a form approved by the Court of Appeals.

(2) Oversight of the reporting process. The Court of Appeals shall designate an employee of the Administrative Office of the Courts to oversee the reporting process set forth in this Rule.

(3) Mailing by the Administrative Office of the Courts. On or before January 10 of each year, the Administrative Office of the Courts shall mail an IOLTA Compliance Report form to each lawyer on the list maintained by the Client Protection Fund of the Bar of Maryland. The addresses on that list shall be used for all notices and correspondence pertaining to the reports.

(4) Due date. IOLTA Compliance Reports for each year shall be filed with the Administrative Office of the Courts on or before February 15 of that year.

(5) Enforcement. (A) Notice of default. As soon as practicable after May 1 of each year, the Administrative Office of the Courts shall notify each defaulting lawyer of the lawyer's failure to file a report. The notice shall (i) state that the lawyer has not filed the IOLTA Compliance Report for that year, (ii) state that continued failure to file the Report may result in the entry of an order by the Court of Appeals prohibiting the lawyer from practicing law in the State, and (iii) be sent by first-class mail. The mailing of the notice of default shall constitute service.

(B) Additional discretionary notice of default. In addition to the mailed notice, the Administrative Office of the Courts may give additional notice to defaulting lawyers by any of the means enumerated in Rule 16-811 f 3.

(C) List of defaulting lawyers. As soon as practicable after July 1 of each year but no later than August 1, the Administrative Office of the Courts shall prepare, certify, and file with the Court of Appeals a list that includes the name and address of each lawyer engaged in the practice of law who has failed to file the IOLTA Compliance Report for that year.

(D) Certification of default; Order of Decertification. The Administrative Office of the Courts shall submit with the list a proposed Decertification Order stating the names and addresses of those lawyers who have failed to file their IOLTA Compliance Report. At the request of the Court of Appeals, the Administrative Office of the Courts also shall furnish additional information from its records or give further notice to the defaulting lawyers. If satisfied that the Administrative Office of the Courts has given the required notice to each lawyer named on the proposed Decertification Order, the Court of Appeals shall enter a Decertification Order prohibiting each of them from practicing law in the State.

(E) Mailing of Decertification Order. The Administrative Office of the Courts shall mail by first-class mail a copy of the Decertification Order to each lawyer named in the Order. The mailing of the copy of the Decertification Order shall constitute service.

(F) Recertification; restoration to good standing. If a lawyer thereafter files the outstanding IOLTA Compliance Report, the Administrative Office of the Courts shall request the Court of Appeals to enter an order that recertifies the lawyer and restores the lawyer to good standing. Upon entry of that order, the Administrative Office of the Courts promptly shall furnish confirmation to the lawyer. After a lawyer is recertified, the fact that the lawyer had been decertified need not be disclosed by the lawyer in response to a request for information as to whether the lawyer has been the subject of a disciplinary or remedial proceeding.

(G) Notices to clerks and Maryland Legal Services Corporation. The Clerk of the Court of Appeals shall send a copy of each Decertification Order and each order that recertifies a lawyer and restores the lawyer to good standing entered pursuant to this Rule to the Clerk of the Court of Special Appeals, the Clerk of each circuit court, the Chief Clerk of the District Court, and the Register of Wills for each county, and the Maryland Legal Services Corporation.

(H) Certain information furnished to the Maryland Legal Services Corporation. The Administrative Office of the Courts promptly shall submit to the Maryland Legal Services Corporation the data from electronically submitted IOLTA Compliance Reports and, upon request, shall forward the paper Compliance Reports.

(I) Confidentiality. Except as provided in subsection b 5 (H) of this Rule, IOLTA Compliance Reports, whether in paper or electronic form, are confidential and are not subject to inspection or disclosure under Code, State Government Article, § 10-615 (2) (iii). The Administrative Office of the Courts shall not release the Reports to any person or agency, except as provided in this Rule or upon order of the Court of Appeals. Nonidentifying information and data contained in a lawyer's IOLTA Compliance Report are not confidential.

(Amended Sept. 11, 1995, effective Jan. 1, 1996; June 5, 1996, effective Jan. 1, 1997; Jan. 20, 1999, effective July 1, 1999; Nov. 1, 2001, effective Jan. 1, 2002; Dec. 4, 2007, effective April 1, 2008; amended Sept. 10, 2009, effective Oct. 1, 2009.)

Cross references. — See Code, Business Occupations and Professions Article, § 10-303.

Source. — Section a of this Rule is former Rule BU8. Section b is new.

Effect of amendments. — The 1995 amendment added the cross reference.

The 1999 amendment inserted "Fund" following "Corporation" in the Rule and in the cross reference note; and substituted "Rule 16-610 b 1 (D)" for "Rule BU10 b 1 (D)" in the cross reference note.

The 2001 amendment added (b) and its cross reference note; and rewrote the source note.

The December 4, 2007, Order, effective April 1, 2008, in b deleted "(Interest on Lawyer Trust Accounts)" following "IOLTA".

The 2009 amendment rewrote (b).

Editor's note. — An Order dated June 5, 1996, effective Jan. 1, 1997, renumbered this Rule, which was formerly Rule BU8.

Applied in Att'y Griev. Comm'n v. Hollis, 347 Md. 547, 702 A.2d 223 (1997).

Quoted in Att'y Griev. Comm'n v. Zdravkovich, 381 Md. 680, 852 A.2d 82 (2004).

Rule 16-609. Prohibited transactions.

a. **Generally.** An attorney or law firm may not borrow or pledge any funds required by the Rules in this Chapter to be deposited in an attorney trust account, obtain any remuneration from the financial institution for depositing any funds in the account, or use any funds for any unauthorized purpose.

b. **No cash disbursements.** An instrument drawn on an attorney trust account may not be drawn payable to cash or to bearer, and no cash withdrawal may be made from an automated teller machine or by any other method. All disbursements from an attorney trust account shall be made by check or electronic transfer.

c. **Negative balance prohibited.** No funds from an attorney trust account shall be disbursed if the disbursement would create a negative balance with regard to an individual client matter or all client matters in the aggregate. (Amended, June 5, 1996, effective Jan. 1, 1997; March 12, 2007, effective January 1, 2008.)

Source. — This Rule is derived in part from former Rule BU9 and is in part new.

Effect of amendments. — The 1996 amendment added the Source note.

The 2007 amendment, effective January 1, 2008, added c. and the a. and b. designations and headings; in a. substituted "the Rules in this Chapter" for "these Rules"; and in b. added "and no cash withdrawal may be made from an automated teller machine or by any other method" at the end of the first sentence and added the second sentence; and in the Source note added "derived in part from" and "and is in part new".

Editor's note. — An Order dated June 5, 1996, effective Jan. 1, 1997, renumbered this Rule, which was formerly Rule BU9.

The March 12, 2007, Order provided in part that "the rules changes hereby adopted by this Court shall take effect on January 1, 2008 and, from and after said date, shall govern the conduct of attorneys from and after that date".

Intent not relevant to violation. — Attorney violated (c) when the attorney wrote checks for amounts that he knew exceeded the balance in his trust account, even though the second check was written after a bank teller told the attorney there was money in the account; there was no requirement that the attorney intentionally overdrew the account. Att'y Griev. Comm'n v. Patterson, — Md. —, — A.3d — (Sept. 21, 2011).

Unintentional violations are relevant to appropriate sanction. — Lawyer was indefinitely suspended from the practice of law where he failed to maintain a trust account, commingled client funds and his own, and failed to keep proper records regarding such funds; but, the violations were unintentional, resulting from lawyer's ignorance of his obligation to refrain from commingling, and he was not motivated to use client funds for his own benefit. Att'y Griev. Comm'n v. Awuah, 346 Md. 420, 697 A.2d 446 (1997).

Claimed ignorance of ethical duties and bookkeeping requirements is not a defense in disciplinary proceedings, but a finding with respect to the intent with which a violation was committed is relevant on the issue of the appropriate sanction. Att'y Griev. Comm'n v. Awuah, 346 Md. 420, 697 A.2d 446 (1997).

Attorney who operated his law practice using only a trust account was suspended, rather than disbarred, for commingling and misusing a client's funds, where the attorney had a 30-year spotless record, there was no intent to defraud, the one victim suffered no loss, and the attorney was candid and remorseful; the automatic disbarment rule for misappropriation did not apply, as this was not the kind of willful conduct to which the rule was directed or intended to reach. Att'y Griev. Comm'n v. Hayes, 367 Md. 504, 789 A.2d 119 (2002).

Court of Appeals of Maryland affirmed hearing judge's findings that an attorney mishandled funds in attorney trust account but held that because there was no finding of intentional misappropriation of funds and the attorney's clients did not suffer a financial loss, indefinite suspension was the appropriate sanction. Att'y Griev. Comm'n v. DiCicco, 369 Md. 662, 802 A.2d 1014 (2002).

Where violations of trust account rules were unintentional and relatively minor, but where the attorney had a history of such violations as well as of client neglect, which had also been found in the instant case, and a failure to initially cooperate with the grievance investigation had also been found, the appropriate sanction was an indefinite suspension with leave to reapply after six months. Att'y Griev. Comm'n v. Kreamer, 387 Md. 503, 876 A.2d 79 (2005).

Where violations of trust account rules were unintentional and relatively minor, but where the attorney had a history of such violations as well as of client neglect, which had also been found in the instant case, and a failure to initially cooperate with the grievance investigation had also been found, the appropriate sanction was an indefinite suspension with leave to reapply after six months. Att'y Griev. Comm'n v. Kreamer, 387 Md. 503, 876 A.2d 79 (2005).

Where the attorney violated this section and Md. R. Prof. Conduct 1.15(a), (b), 8.1(b) based on the attorney's failure to fully cooperate with the investigation and based on the attorney's inexperience and lack of knowledge in maintaining trust accounts, the attorney was suspended for 30 days. Att'y Griev. Comm'n v. Obi, 393 Md. 643, 904 A.2d 422 (2006).

Public reprimand. — Attorney was sanctioned by a public reprimand for technically violating this Rule regarding prohibited trans-

actions as a result of a negligent clerical error involving depositing some of his ex-girlfriend's funds into his operating account instead of his firm's escrow account, which error was corrected upon discovery and was not wilful. The Court of Appeals of Maryland further upheld the trial judge's finding of fact that no attorney client relationship existed between the attorney and his girlfriend to support the other violations asserted against him since he never charged his ex-girlfriend a fee for his services and was only helping her while she received treatment for her alcohol abuse. Att'y Griev. Comm'n v. Shoup, 410 Md. 462, 979 A.2d 120 (Aug. 28, 2009).

Attorney was indefinitely suspended. — Hearing court's finding that an attorney did not use funds intended for certain clients for them supported a finding that the attorney violated § 10-306 of the Business Occupations and Professions Article and this Rule, as well as the violations of Md. R. Prof. Conduct 1.15 and Rules 16-604 and 16-607 that were found by the hearing court; the attorney was indefinitely suspended, with a right to apply for readmission after 90 days. Att'y Griev. Comm'n v. Mba-Jonas, 397 Md. 690, 919 A.2d 669 (2007).

Attorney was indefinitely suspended from the practice of law for violating, inter alia, this Rule, when, on at least three occasions, the attorney disbursed funds to clients before settlement checks were deposited. Att'y Griev. Comm'n v. Goff, 399 Md. 1, 922 A.2d 554 (2007).

Attorney was indefinitely suspended from the practice of law with the right to reapply for admission after one year, as the attorney's act of threatening to withdraw from representation of a client if the client refused to pay additional legal fees constituted a violation of Md. R. Prof. Conduct 1.15 and 1.16, and constituted conduct involving dishonesty, fraud, deceit or misrepresentation in violation of Md. R. Prof. Conduct 8.4, and the flat fee charged violated Md. R. Prof. Conduct 1.5 as the attorney did not provide sufficient services to earn the fee, the attorney violated this Rule and Rule 16-604 by failing to place unearned attorney fees in his attorney trust account, and the attorney's failure to keep the client informed of the progress of the litigation violated Md. R. Prof. Conduct 1.4. Att'y Griev. Comm'n v. Lawson, 401 Md. 536, 933 A.2d 842 (2007).

Attorney was indefinitely suspended from practice of law for violating Md. R. Prof. Conduct 1.8, 1.15, 8.1, and 8.4, Rule 16-607 and this Rule, and § 10-306 of the Business Occupations and Professional Article, when the attorney advanced money to a client and the client's family members from the attorney's trust account, but did not hold any funds in escrow for those people, and commingled personal and trust funds in the same account. Att'y Griev. Comm'n v. McLaughlin, 409 Md. 304, 974 A.2d 315 (2009).

Attorney disbarred for violating rules. — Attorney was disbarred for violating Maryland Rules of Professional Conduct 1.1, 1.3, 1.4(a) and (b), 1.15(a), 3.3(a)(1), and 8.4(b) and (c), § 10-306 of the Business Occupations and Professions Article, and this Rule. Att'y Griev. Comm'n v. Williams, 335 Md. 458, 644 A.2d 490 (1994).

Attorney violated Rules 16-603, 16-604, 16-606, 16-607, and 16-609 by failing to maintain an attorney trust account, failing to deposit client funds in such an account, failing to name or designate such an account in a manner that clearly identified it as such, and by using funds for an unauthorized purpose. Att'y Griev. Comm'n v. Daskalopoulos, 383 Md. 375, 859 A.2d 653 (2004).

When an attorney acted as an escrow agent for a client which purportedly funded high-risk loans, and the attorney removed commitment fees deposited in the escrow account and disbursed them to parties unrelated to a contemplated loan, rather than either returning them to the depositors or disbursing them to parties providing loans, and failed to provide requested information to the grievance commission, he violated Md. R. Prof. Conduct 1.15(a) and (b), 8.1(b), and 8.4(a) and (c), §§ 10-306 and 10-606 of the Business Occupations and Professions Article, and this rule and, given the absence of mitigating circumstances, disbarment was the appropriate sanction. Att'y Griev. Comm'n v. Smith, 376 Md. 202, 829 A.2d 567 (2003).

Disbarment was the only appropriate sanction for an attorney who knowingly withdrew sums that should have been forwarded to a client from an attorney trust account for the attorney's personal use and failed to respond to the client's inquiries; the attorney's marital and drinking problems were not factors in mitigation. Att'y Griev. Comm'n v. Herman, 380 Md. 378, 844 A.2d 1181 (2004).

Attorney was disbarred, despite the mitigating factors of an absence of a prior disciplinary record and relative inexperience, for violating Md. R. Prof. Conduct 1.5(c), 1.15(b) and (c), 8.1(b), and 8.4(c) and (d), and Md. R. 16-606 and 16-609 in his intentionally dishonest conduct towards a third-party assignee/healthcare provider during the representation of a client in a personal injury claim and Maryland Bar Counsel and its investigator in the course of investigating the assignee's complaint. Att'y Griev. Comm'n v. Ellison, 384 Md. 688, 867 A.2d 259 (2005).

Attorney was disbarred under Rule 16-751 for misappropriation of client funds from his trust account, violating §§ 7-104 and 7-113 of the Criminal Law Article, § 10-306 of the

Business Occupations and Professions Article, this Rule, Rules 1.15 and 8.4 of the Maryland Lawyers Rules of Professional Conduct, and spousal abuse, violating § 3-203 of the Criminal Law Article. The attorney did not carry his burden to prove by a preponderance of the evidence any medical, psychiatric, or other condition to mitigate the findings of fact or conclusions of law. Att'y Griev. Comm'n v. Theriault, 390 Md. 202, 888 A.2d 292 (2005).

Attorney violated this Rule by withdrawing client funds from his trust account, to which he was in no way entitled, and was disbarred based on violation of Rule 16-607, this Rule, and Md. R. Prof. Conduct 1.15(a), 8.1(b), 8.4 (a), (b), (c), (d), and §§ 10-306 and 10-606 of the Business Occupations and Professions Article. Att'y Griev. Comm'n v. Butler, 395 Md. 1, 909 A.2d 226 (2006).

Attorney, who, inter alia, attempted to withdraw funds from an attorney trust account where the withdrawal was not against funds deposited for the subject client, was disbarred for violating Md. Law. R. Prof. Conduct 1.15 and 8.4(a — d); §§ 10-306 and 307 of the Business Occupations and Professions Article; and Rule 16-607 and this Rule. Att'y Griev. Comm'n v. Thomas, 409 Md. 121, 973 A.2d 185 (2009).

Attorney was disbarred for violating Md. R. Prof. Conduct 1.1, 1.3, 1.4, 1.15, and 8.4, this Rules, and §§ 10-306 and 10-606(b)of the Business and Professional Occupations Article as attorney misappropriated the clients' funds, performed no services whatsoever on the clients' behalf, lied to the clients about the status of their case, and provided them with a falsified administrative agency decision that was not issued by the agency. Att'y Griev. Comm'n v. Bahgat, 411 Md. 568, 984 A.2d 225 (2009).

Attorney's use of trust funds for unauthorized purposes, such as use of trust funds for other clients to pay himself fees and costs relating to settlements prior to the deposit of those settlement funds, supported a finding that he violated this Rule; attorney's violation of this and other rules, including Md. Law R. Prof. Conduct 1.15, 8.1, and 8.4; Rule 16-606; and § 10-306 of the Business Occupations and Professions supported disbarment. Att'y Griev. Comm'n v. Jarosinski, 411 Md. 432, 983 A.2d 477 (2009).

Attorney was disbarred for admittedly violating Md. Law. R. Prof. Conduct 1.1, 1.15(a) and (c), and 8.4(a) — (d), as well as this Rule and § 10-306 of the Business Occupations and Professions Article, by misappropriating client funds to make it appear as though the attorney's collected fees were higher than those fees actually were, when the attorney was being considered for partner in the attorney's firm, and by failing to file complaints in clients' cases, misrepresenting that the complaints were filed, and fabricating documents to hide the misrepresentations, because (1) disbarment was the presumed sanction for the misappropriation, and (2) the attorney did not show "compelling extenuating circumstances" justifying a lesser sanction, as the attorney showed no serious and debilitating mental condition, since the attorney was not diagnosed with a mental illness, the attorney did not show such a condition was the "root cause" of the attorney's misconduct by making the attorney unable to do day-to-day activities in a normal manner, and the attorney did not show such a condition caused an utter inability to conform the attorney's conduct to the law and the Maryland Rules of Professional Conduct, so any psychological issues the attorney had at the time of the attorney's misconduct did not mitigate the attorney's sanction. Att'y Griev. Comm'n v. Palmer, 417 Md. 185, 9 A.3d 37 (2010).

Attorney violated (c) and Md. Law. R. Prof. Conduct 1.2(a), 1.15(d), 8.4(c) and (d), Md. R. 16-604, and § 10-306 of the Business Occupations and Professions Article, and was disbarred, after misappropriating tens of thousands of dollars that should have been paid to a physical therapist and settling a client's claim without the client's knowledge or consent. Att'y Griev. Comm'n v. Stern, 419 Md. 525, 19 A.3d 904 (2011).

Use of funds. — Use of the attorney trust account for personal purposes while still designated a trust account, even if it was no longer intended that the account be used for trust purposes, is prohibited, regardless of whether or not client funds are deposited in the account. Att'y Griev. Comm'n v. Webster, 348 Md. 662, 705 A.2d 1135 (1998).

When an attorney acted as an escrow agent for a client which purportedly funded high-risk loans, and the attorney removed commitment fees deposited in the escrow account and disbursed them to parties unrelated to a contemplated loan, rather than either returning them to the depositors or disbursing them to parties providing loans, he violated this rule, prohibiting the unauthorized use of funds in an attorney trust account. Att'y Griev. Comm'n v. Smith, 376 Md. 202, 829 A.2d 567 (2003).

Attorney was disbarred as his misuse of a client's settlement monies violated Rules 8.4(a), (b), (c), and (d) of the Rules of Professional Conduct, Rule 16-609, and §§ 10-306 and 10-307 of the Business Occupations and Professions Article. Att'y Griev. Comm'n v. Brown, 380 Md. 661, 846 A.2d 428 (2004).

Clear and convincing evidence was found that an attorney violated this Rule by converting a client's personal injury protection fund monies to her personal use, having insufficient funds in her escrow account to pay the client's outstanding claims for reimbursement from such fund, and otherwise converting to her own use the fund, which should have been held in trust for the client. Disbarment was the sanction imposed, because the attorney did not protect her client's interests when she converted the funds and denied doing so, which constituted an intentional misrepresentation of a material fact in connection with a disciplinary matter. Att'y Griev. Comm'n v. Cherry-Mahoi, 388 Md. 124, 879 A.2d 58 (2005).

Where the attorney argued that the attorney did not violate this section, as the attorney did not issue any check or instrument on the client trust fund account to cash or bearer but only to the attorney and to an identifiable bank account, the attorney violated this section by using funds in the client trust fund account for personal expenses, an unauthorized purpose. Att'y Griev. Comm'n v. Obi, 393 Md. 643, 904 A.2d 422 (2006).

By delaying payment of settlement proceeds to a client and the client's medical providers, transferring the client's funds into his operating account, and using the money for his own personal needs, an attorney violated Md. R. Prof. Conduct 1.3, 1.15(a) and (b), and 8.4(c) and (d); Rule 16-609; and § 10-306 of the Business Occupations and Professions Article. The court acknowledged the mitigating factors of the attorney paying the client and the medical providers and reducing his fee, but concluded that disbarment for such deceit was warranted. Att'y Griev. Comm'n v. Roberts, 394 Md. 137, 904 A.2d 557 (2006).

Attorney's conduct in taking funds from the attorney's escrow account holding client funds and using them to pay the attorney's law practice operating expenses violated Rule 16-607, regarding the commingling of funds, and this Rule, regarding prohibited transactions, as the escrow funds and the funds in the operating account were required to be kept separate. Att'y Griev. Comm'n v. Nussbaum, 401 Md. 612, 934 A.2d 1 (2007).

Attorney was disbarred from the practice of law in Maryland for violating this section by continuously using trust money for purposes other than those for which her clients' monies were designated. Att'y Griev. Comm'n v. Nwadike, 416 Md. 180, 6 A.3d 287 (2010).

Failure to use trust account or return unearned fees — Attorney representing a client in a divorce action violated this Rule when he failed to deposit advanced fees into a trust account or return any unearned fees to the client after he was discharged. Att'y Griev. Comm'n v. Rose, 391 Md. 101, 892 A.2d 469 (2006), cert. denied, 2006 U.S. LEXIS 5734, 166 L. Ed. 2d 22 (U.S. 2006).

Disbursement to self and client prior to satisfying assignment to third party. — Attorney violated this Rule by disbursing unauthorized funds to himself and his client before satisfying an assignment of settlement funds to a third-party healthcare provider. Att'y Griev. Comm'n v. Ellison, 384 Md. 688, 867 A.2d 259 (2005).

Writing checks to "cash." — Violation of this Rule consisted of drawing checks on an escrow account made payable to "cash," since the purpose of the Rule's requirement is to enable one who is authorized to do so to trace the disposition of escrow funds. Att'y Griev. Comm'n v. Harper, 356 Md. 53, 737 A.2d 557 (1999).

Attorneys violated professional conduct rules by drawing a check payable to "cash" on an attorney trust account. Att'y Griev. Comm'n v. Franz, 355 Md. 752, 736 A.2d 339 (1999).

Clear and convincing evidence indicated that an attorney never set up a trust or escrow account at all, and that he drained the checking account into which he placed a client's check, in order to use the funds for his own purposes; therefore, disbarment was in order. Att'y Griev. Comm'n v. Gallagher, 371 Md. 673, 810 A.2d 996 (2002).

Applied in Att'y Griev. Comm'n v. Hollis, 347 Md. 547, 702 A.2d 223 (1997); Att'y Griev. Comm'n v. Ober, 350 Md. 616, 714 A.2d 856 (1998); Att'y Griev. Comm'n v. James, 385 Md. 637, 870 A.2d 229 (2005).

Quoted in Att'y Griev. Comm'n v. Snyder, 368 Md. 242, 793 A.2d 515 (2002); Att'y Griev. Comm'n v. Blum, 373 Md. 275, 818 A.2d 219 (2003); Att'y Griev. Comm'n v. Cafferty, 376 Md. 700, 831 A.2d 1042 (2003); Att'y Griev. Comm'n v. Braskey, 378 Md. 425, 836 A.2d 605 (2003); Att'y Griev. Comm'n v. Mininsohn, 380

Md. 536, 846 A.2d 353 (2004); Att'y Griev. Comm'n v. Zakroff, 387 Md. 603, 876 A.2d 664 (2005), cert. denied, 2006 Md. LEXIS 561 (2006); cert. denied, 2006 Md. LEXIS 571 (Md. 2006); Att'y Griev. Comm'n v. Zakroff, 387 Md. 603, 876 A.2d 664 (2005), cert. denied, 2006 Md. LEXIS 561 (2006); cert. denied, 2006 Md. LEXIS 571 (Md. 2006); Att'y Griev. Comm'n v. Calhoun, 391 Md. 532, 894 A.2d 518 (2006); Att'y Griev. Comm'n v. Mba-Jonas, 402 Md. 334, 936 A.2d 839 (2007); Att'y Griev. Comm'n v. Whitehead, 405 Md. 240, 950 A.2d 798 (2008).

Cited in Att'y Griev. Comm'n v. Gregory, 346 Md. 600, 697 A.2d 898 (1997); Att'y Griev. Comm'n v. Post, 379 Md. 60, 839 A.2d 718 (2003); In re Powers, 838 A.2d 311 (2003); Att'y Griev. Comm'n v. Whitehead, 390 Md. 663, 890 A.2d 751 (2006); Att'y Griev. Comm'n v. Kreamer, 404 Md. 282, 946 A.2d 500 (2008); Att'y Griev. Comm'n v. Tanko, 408 Md. 404, 969 A.2d 1010 (2009); Att'y Griev. Comm'n v. Khandpur, 421 Md. 1, 25 A.3d 165 (2011).

When an attorney deposited unearned funds received on a client's behalf in the attorney's operating account, rather than in a trust account, it was not error for a hearing judge not to find the attorney violated this Rule because (1) the attorney "drew against" the funds in the attorney's operating account, and (2) nothing showed those funds included the funds paid for the client, so no reasonable trier of fact could find by clear and convincing evidence that the attorney made an unauthorized use of the funds. Att'y Griev. Comm'n v. Tauber, — Md. —, 26 A.3d 967 (2011).

Rule 16-610. Approval of financial institutions.

a. **Written agreement to be filed with Commission.** The Commission shall approve a financial institution upon the filing with the Commission of a written agreement with the Maryland Legal Services Corporation (MLSC), complying with this Rule and in a form provided by the Commission, applicable to all branches of the institution that are subject to this Rule. The Commission may extend its approval of a previously approved financial institution for a reasonable period to allow the financial institution and the MLSC the opportunity to enter into a revised agreement that complies with this Rule.

b. **Contents of agreement.** 1. Duties to be performed. The agreement shall provide that the financial institution, as a condition of accepting the deposit of any funds into an attorney trust account, shall:

(A) Notify the attorney or law firm promptly of any overdraft in the account or the dishonor for insufficient funds of any instrument drawn on the account.

(B) Report the overdraft or dishonor to Bar Counsel as set forth in subsection b 1 (C) of this Rule.

(C) Use the following procedure for reports to Bar Counsel required under subsection b 1 (B) of this Rule:

(i) In the case of a dishonored instrument, the report shall be identical to the overdraft notice customarily forwarded to the institution's other regular account holders. The report shall be mailed to Bar Counsel within the time provided by law for notice of dishonor to the depositor and simultaneously with the sending of that notice.

(ii) If an instrument is honored but at the time of presentation the total funds in the account, both collected and uncollected, do not equal or exceed the amount of the instrument, the report shall identify the financial institution, the name and address of the attorney or law firm maintaining the account, the account name, the account number, the date of presentation for payment, and the payment date of the instrument, as well as the amount of the overdraft created. The report shall be mailed to Bar Counsel within five banking days after the date of presentation, notwithstanding any overdraft privileges that may attach to the account.

(D) Pay interest on its IOLTA accounts at a rate no less than the highest non-promotional interest rate generally available from the institution to its non-IOLTA customers at the same branch when the IOLTA account meets or exceeds the same minimum balance or other eligibility qualifications for its non-IOLTA accounts at that branch. In determining the highest interest rate generally available from the institution to its IOLTA customers at a particular branch, an approved institution may consider, in addition to the balance in the IOLTA account, factors customarily considered by the institution at that branch when setting interest rates for its non-IOLTA customers; provided, however, that these factors shall not discriminate between IOLTA accounts and non-IOLTA accounts, nor shall the factors include or consider the fact that the account is an IOLTA account.

(i) An approved institution may satisfy the requirement described in sub-section b 1 (D) of this Rule by establishing the IOLTA account in an account paying the highest rate for which the IOLTA account qualifies. The approved institution may deduct from interest earned on the IOLTA account Allowable Reasonable Fees as defined in subsection b 1 (d) (iii). This account may be any one of the following product option types, assuming the particular financial institution offers these account types to its non-IOLTA customers, and the particular IOLTA account qualifies to be established as this type of account at the particular branch:

(a) a business checking account with an automated investment feature, which is an overnight sweep and investment in repurchase agreements fully collateralized by U.S. Government securities, including securities of government-sponsored entities;

(b) checking accounts paying interest rates in excess of the lowest-paying interest-bearing checking account;

(c) any other suitable interest-bearing checking account offered by the approved institution to its non-IOLTA customers.

(ii) In lieu of the options provided in subsection b 1(D) (i), an approved financial institution may: (a) retain the existing IOLTA account and pay the equivalent applicable rate that would be paid at that branch on the highest-yield product for which the IOLTA account qualifies and deduct from interest earned on the IOLTA account Allowable Reasonable Fees; (b) offer a "safe harbor" rate that is equal to 55% of the Federal Funds Target Rate as reported in the Wall Street Journal on the first calendar day of the month on high-balance IOLTA accounts to satisfy the requirements described in subsection b 1 (D), but no fees may be deducted from the interest on a "safe harbor" rate account; or (c) pay a rate specified by the MLSC, if it chooses to specify a rate, which is agreed to by the financial institution and would be in effect for and remain unchanged during a period of twelve months from the agreement between the financial institution and MLSC to pay the specified rate. Allowable Reasonable Fees may be deducted from the interest on this "specified rate" account as agreed between MLSC and the financial institution.

(iii) "Allowable Reasonable Fees" means fees and service charges in amounts customarily charged to non-IOLTA customers with the same type of account and balance at the same branch, including per-check charges, per-deposit charges, a fee in lieu of a minimum balance, federal deposit insurance fees, and sweep fees, plus a reasonable IOLTA account administrative fee. Allowable Reasonable Fees may be deducted from interest earned on an IOLTA account only in amounts and in accordance with the customary practices of the approved institution for non-IOLTA customers at the particular branch. Fees or service charges are not Allowable Reasonable Fees if they are charged for the convenience of or arise due to errors or omissions by the attorney or law firm maintaining the IOLTA account or that attorney's or law firm's clients, including fees for wire transfers, certified checks, account reconciliation services, presentations against insufficient funds, overdrafts, or deposits of dishonored items.

(iv) Nothing in this Rule shall preclude an approved institution from paying a higher interest rate than described herein or electing to waive any fees and service charges on an IOLTA account.

(v) Fees that are not Allowable Reasonable Fees are the responsibility of, and may be charged to, the attorney or law firm maintaining the IOLTA account.

Cross references. — Rule 16-607 b 1.

(E) Allow reasonable access to all records of an attorney trust account if an audit of the account is ordered pursuant to Rule 16-722 (Audit of Attorney Accounts and Records).

2. Service charges for performing duties under agreement. Nothing in the agreement shall preclude an approved financial institution from charging the attorney or law firm maintaining an attorney trust account (1) a reasonable fee for providing any notice or record pursuant to the agreement or (2) fees and service charges other than the "Allowable Reasonable Fees" listed in subsection b 1 (D)(iii) of this Rule.

c. **Termination of agreement.** The agreement shall terminate only if:

1. The financial institution files a petition under any applicable insolvency law or makes an assignment for the benefit of creditors; or

2. the financial institution gives thirty days' notice in writing to the MLSC and to Bar Counsel that the institution intends to terminate the agreement

and its status as an approved financial institution on a stated date and that copies of the termination notice have been mailed to all attorneys and law firms that maintain trust accounts with any branch of that institution; or

3. after a complaint is filed by the MLSC or on its own initiative, the Commission finds, after prior written notice to the institution and adequate opportunity to be heard, that the institution has failed or refused without justification to perform a duty required by the agreement. The Commission shall notify the institution that the agreement and the Commission's approval of the institution are terminated.

d. **Exceptions.** Within 15 days after service of the notice of termination pursuant to subsection c 3 of this Rule, the institution may file with the Court of Appeals exceptions to the decision of the Commission. The institution shall file eight copies of the exceptions which shall conform to the requirements of Rule 8-112. The Court shall set a date for oral argument, unless oral argument is waived by the parties. Oral argument shall be conducted in accordance with Rule 8-522. The decision of the Court of Appeals is final and shall be evidenced by an order of the Court. (Amended Sept. 11, 1995, effective Jan. 1, 1996; June 5, 1996, effective Jan. 1, 1997; June 10, 1997, effective July 1, 1997; Jan. 20, 1999, effective July 1, 1999; Dec. 4, 2007, effective April 1, 2008.)

Source. — This Rule is derived from former Rule BU10.

Effect of amendments. — The 1996 amendment substituted "Rule 16-718" for "Rule BV18" in b 1(E); and added the Source note.

The 1997 amendment substituted "Rule 16-607" for "Rule BU7" in the Cross references.

The 1999 amendment inserted "Fund" following "Corporation" in b 1 (D).

The December 4, 2007, Order, effective April 1, 2008, in the first sentence of a added "with the Maryland Legal Services Corporation (MLSC)" and substituted "that are subject to this Rule" for "located in this State" and added the second sentence; in b 1 (C) (ii) in the first sentence added "name and address of the", rewrote b 1 (D), and in b 2 added "and service charges other than the 'Allowable Reasonable Fees'"; and added "(iii)" and made related changes; in c 2 added "the MLSC and to" and "and its status as an approved financial institution", in c 3 added "after a complaint is filed by the MLSC or on its own initiative" and added the second sentence; added d; and in the Source note added "derived from".

Editor's note. — An Order dated June 5, 1996, effective Jan. 1, 1997, renumbered this Rule, which was formerly Rule BU10.

Stated in Att'y Griev. Comm'n v. Zdravkovich, 381 Md. 680, 852 A.2d 82 (2004).

Cited in Att'y Griev. Comm'n v. Theriault, 390 Md. 202, 888 A.2d 292 (2005); Att'y Griev. Comm'n v. Obi, 393 Md. 643, 904 A.2d 422 (2006); Unnamed Atty. v. Att'y Griev. Comm'n, 409 Md. 509, 976 A.2d 267 (2009).

Rule 16-611. Notice of approved institutions.

The Commission shall cause to be published in the Maryland Register, at six-month intervals, a list that identifies:

1. All currently approved financial institutions; and

2. Any financial institution whose agreement has terminated since the previous list was published. (Amended June 5, 1996, effective Jan. 1, 1997; Dec. 10, 1996, effective Jan. 1, 1997.)

Source. — This Rule is former Rule BU11.

Effect of amendments. — The first 1996 amendment added the Source note.

The second 1996 amendment deleted former b. and the "a." designation.

Editor's note. — An Order dated June 5, 1996, effective Jan. 1, 1997, renumbered this Rule, which was formerly Rule BU11.

Rule 16-612. Enforcement.

Upon receipt of a report of overdraft on or dishonored instrument drawn on an attorney trust account, Bar Counsel shall contact the attorney or law firm maintaining the account and request an informal explanation for the overdraft or dishonored instrument. The attorney or law firm shall provide any records of the account necessary to support the explanation. If Bar Counsel has requested but has failed to receive a satisfactory explanation for any overdraft or dishonored check, or if good cause exists to believe that an attorney or law firm has failed to perform any duty under these Rules, Bar Counsel may secure compliance with these Rules by appropriate means approved by the Commission, including application for an audit pursuant to Rule 16-722 (Audit of Attorney Accounts and Records). (Amended June 5, 1996, effective Jan. 1, 1997.)

Source. — This Rule is former Rule BU12.

Effect of amendments. — The 1996 amendment substituted "Rule 16-718" for "Rule BV18" in the last sentence; and added the Source note.

Editor's note. — An Order dated June 5, 1996, effective Jan. 1, 1997, renumbered this Rule, which was formerly Rule BU12.

Cited in Unnamed Atty. v. Att'y Griev. Comm'n, 409 Md. 509, 976 A.2d 267 (2009).

CHAPTER 700. DISCIPLINE AND INACTIVE STATUS OF ATTORNEYS.

Rule 16-701. Definitions.

In this Chapter, the following definitions apply except as expressly otherwise provided or as necessary implication requires:

(a) **Attorney.** "Attorney" means a person admitted by the Court of Appeals to practice law in this State. For purposes of discipline or inactive status, the term also includes a person not admitted by the Court of Appeals who engages in the practice of law in this State, or who holds himself or herself out as practicing law in this State, or who has the obligation of supervision or control over another lawyer who engages in the practice of law in this State.

Cross references. — See Rule 8.5 of the Maryland Lawyers' Rules of Professional Conduct.

(b) **Circuit.** "Circuit" means Appellate Judicial Circuit.

(c) **Commission.** "Commission" means the Attorney Grievance Commission of Maryland.

(d) **Conditional diversion agreement.** "Conditional diversion agreement" means the agreement provided for in Rule 16-736.

(e) **Disbarment.** "Disbarment" means the unconditional termination of any privilege to practice law in this State and, when applied to an attorney not admitted by the Court of Appeals to practice law, means the unconditional exclusion from the admission to or the exercise of any privilege to practice law in this State.

(f) **Incapacity.** "Incapacity" means the inability to render adequate legal service by reason of mental or physical illness or infirmity, or addiction to or dependence upon an intoxicant or drug.

(g) **Office for the practice of law.** "Office for the practice of law" means an office in which an attorney usually devotes a substantial part of the attorney's time to the practice of law during ordinary business hours in the traditional work week.

(h) **Petition for disciplinary or remedial action.** "Petition for disciplinary or remedial action" means the initial pleading filed in the Court of Appeals against an attorney alleging that the attorney has engaged in professional misconduct or is incapacitated or both.

(i) **Professional misconduct.** "Professional misconduct" or "misconduct" has the meaning set forth in Rule 8.4 of the Maryland Lawyers' Rules of Professional Conduct, as adopted by Rule 16-812. The term includes the knowing failure to respond to a request for information authorized by this Chapter without asserting, in writing, a privilege or other basis for such failure.

(j) **Reinstatement.** "Reinstatement" means the termination of disbarment, suspension, or inactive status and the termination of any exclusion to practice law in this State.

(k) **Serious crime.** "Serious crime" means a crime that is in at least one of the following categories: (1) a felony under Maryland law, (2) a crime in another state or under federal law that would have been a felony under Maryland law had the crime been committed in Maryland, and (3) a crime under federal law or the law of any state that is punishable by imprisonment for three years or more.

(l) **State.** "State" means (1) a state, possession, territory, or commonwealth of the United States or (2) the District of Columbia.

(m) **Statement of charges.** "Statement of charges" means the document that alleges professional misconduct or incapacity and initiates disciplinary or remedial proceedings against an attorney pursuant to Rule 16-741.

(n) **Suspension.** "Suspension" means the temporary or indefinite termination of the privilege to practice law and, when applied to an attorney not admitted by the Court of Appeals to practice law, means the temporary or indefinite exclusion from the admission to or the exercise of any privilege to practice law in this State.

(o) **Warning.** "Warning" means a notice that warns an attorney about future misconduct. (Added Nov. 30, 2000, effective July 1, 2001; February 8, 2005, effective July 1, 2005.)

Source. — This Rule is derived in part from former Rule 16-701 (BV1) and is in part new.

Effect of amendments. — The 2005 amendment inserted "Lawyers'" before "Rules of Professional Conduct" in the cross references note in (a) and in (i).

Unauthorized practice by attorney licensed in other jurisdiction. — Disbarment was the appropriate remedy for an attorney, licensed in other jurisdictions, that opened an office, used letterhead, and represented clients in Maryland without being admitted or specially admitted, as this constituted misconduct. Att'y Griev. Comm'n v. Barneys, 370 Md. 566, 805 A.2d 1040 (2002).

Attorney was disbarred for his handling of a medical malpractice case for a wife, her common law husband, and her children, which had resulted in the attorney's disbarment in Georgia, for misconduct as defined in subsection (i) of this rule, and for violating the Maryland counterparts of the Georgia State Bar Standards he had been found to have violated, more specifically, the following rules of the Maryland Rules of Professional Conduct: 8.4 (misconduct), 1.5 (fees), 1.7 (conflict of interest: general rule), and 1.15 (safekeeping property). Att'y Griev. Comm'n v. Roberson, 373 Md. 328, 818 A.2d 1059 (2003).

Conspiracy to defraud federal government in immigration proceeding. — In an attorney disciplinary matter, the attorney was disbarred as a result of having violated Rule 8.4(a)-(d) of the Lawyer's Rules of Professional Conduct based on his guilty plea to the federal crimes involving conspiracy to defraud the government, in violation of 18 U.S.C.S. §§ 371 and 1546(a), based on his actions in knowingly filing a false letter with the United States Immigration and Naturalization Service on behalf of a client/immigrant in an immigration proceeding. The Court of Appeals of Maryland found no compelling extenuating circumstances, including the attorney's great remorse, to except him from disbarment based on his intention to commit fraud, to deceive, and to misrepresent. Att'y Griev. Comm'n v. Garcia, 410 Md. 507, 979 A.2d 146 (Aug. 28, 2009).

Applied in Att'y Griev. Comm'n v. Alsafty, 379 Md. 1, 838 A.2d 1213 (2003).

Quoted in Att'y Griev. Comm'n v. Barneys, 370 Md. 566, 805 A.2d 1040 (2002); Att'y Griev. Comm'n v. Roberson, 373 Md. 328, 818 A.2d 1059 (2003); Att'y Griev. Comm'n v. Velasquez, 380 Md. 651, 846 A.2d 422 (2004); Att'y Griev. Comm'n v. Daskalopoulos, 383 Md. 375, 859 A.2d 653 (2004); Att'y Griev. Comm'n v. Rose, 383 Md. 385, 859 A.2d 659 (2004); Att'y Griev. Comm'n v. Holt, 391 Md. 673, 894 A.2d 602 (2006); Att'y Griev. Comm'n v. Wingerter, 400 Md. 214, 929 A.2d 47 (2007); Att'y Griev. Comm'n v. Downey, 413 Md. 1, 990 A.2d 1070 (2010).

Stated in Att'y Griev. Comm'n v. Lee, 387 Md. 89, 874 A.2d 897 (2005); Att'y Griev. Comm'n v. Rose, 391 Md. 101, 892 A.2d 469 (2006), cert. denied, 2006 U.S. LEXIS 5734, 166 L. Ed. 2d 22 (U.S. 2006).

Cited in Att'y Griev. Comm'n v. Scroggs, 387 Md. 238, 874 A.2d 985 (2005); Att'y Griev. Comm'n v. Zuckerman, 403 Md. 695, 944 A.2d 525 (2008); Att'y Griev. Comm'n v. Kimmel, 405 Md. 647, 955 A.2d 269 (2008); Att'y Griev. Comm'n v. Johnson, 409 Md. 470, 976 A.2d 245 (2009).

Rule 16-709. Charges.

Editor's note. — This Rule was rescinded in the 2001 revision of Title 16, Chapter 700.

Rule 16-710. Hearings.

Editor's note. — This Rule was rescinded in the 2001 revision of Title 16, Chapter 700.

Stated in Att'y Griev. Comm'n v. Lee, 393 Md. 385, 903 A.2d 360 (2006).

Rule 16-711. Attorney Grievance Commission.

(a) **Creation and composition.** There is an Attorney Grievance Commission which shall consist of 12 members appointed by the Court of Appeals. Nine members shall be attorneys and three members shall not be attorneys.

(b) **Term.** Subject to section (f) of this Rule, the term of each member is three years. The terms of the members shall be staggered so that the terms of three attorney members and one non-attorney member expire each year.

(c) **Compensation.** A member of the Commission may not receive compensation for serving in that capacity but is entitled to reimbursement for expenses reasonably incurred in the performance of official duties in accordance with standard State travel regulations.

(d) **Chair and Vice Chair.** The Court of Appeals shall designate one attorney member as the Chair of the Commission and one attorney member as the Vice Chair. In the absence or disability of the Chair or upon an express delegation of authority by the Chair, the Vice Chair shall have the authority and perform the duties of the Chair.

(e) **Executive Secretary.** The Commission may select an attorney as Executive Secretary. The Executive Secretary shall serve at the pleasure of the Commission and receive the compensation set forth in the budget of the Commission. As directed by the Commission, the Executive Secretary shall (1) receive documents that are filed with the Commission and maintain the records of the Commission, (2) prepare the agenda of meetings of the Commission and before each meeting send to each Commission member a copy of the agenda and meeting materials, (3) serve as in-house counsel to the Commission, (4) serve as liaison to the Chair of the Peer Review Committee, and (5) have such other administrative powers and duties assigned by the Commission.

(f) **Removal.** The Court of Appeals may remove a member of the Commission at any time.

(g) **Quorum.** The presence of seven members of the Commission constitutes a quorum for the transaction of business. The concurrence of seven members is required for all actions taken by the Commission other than adjournment of a meeting for lack of a quorum.

(h) **Powers and duties.** The Commission has the powers and duties to:

(1) recommend to the Court of Appeals the adoption of procedural and administrative guidelines and policies consistent with these Rules;

(2) employ and prescribe the compensation of the Executive Secretary;

(3) with the approval of the Court of Appeals, appoint Bar Counsel;

(4) supervise the activities of Bar Counsel;

(5) authorize Bar Counsel to employ attorneys, investigators, and staff personnel and to prescribe their compensation;

(6) appoint special counsel as the need arises;

(7) appoint members of the Peer Review Committee, designate the Chair and one or more Vice Chairs, and remove any member for cause;

(8) employ and prescribe the compensation of personnel to assist the Chair of the Peer Review Committee;

(9) exercise the authority granted in the Rules in this Chapter with respect to the approval or disapproval of (A) the dismissal of a complaint or Statement of Charges, (B) the termination of a complaint with or without a warning, (C) a Conditional Diversion Agreement, (D) a reprimand, or (E) the filing of a Petition for Disciplinary or Remedial Action;

(10) grant or deny any requests for extensions of time permitted under the Rules of this Chapter or delegate to the Chair of the Commission the authority to grant or deny such requests;

(11) authorize the issuance of subpoenas in accordance with these Rules;

(12) perform the duties required by Title 16, Chapter 600 (Attorney Trust Accounts);

(13) administer the Disciplinary Fund;

(14) submit not later than September 1 of each year a report to the Court of Appeals accounting for the Disciplinary Fund, evaluating the effectiveness of the disciplinary system, and recommending any changes; and

(15) submit annually to the State Court Administrator for review and approval by the Court of Appeals a proposed budget for the disciplinary system.

(i) **Effect of Chair's decisions.** When a request for action under this Chapter is subject to the approval of the Chair of the Commission, the Chair's approval of the request is final and shall be reported to the Commission. If the Chair denies the request or refers it to the Commission for action, the Commission shall act upon the request at its next meeting. (Added Nov. 30, 2000, effective July 1, 2001.)

Source. — This Rule is derived from former Rules 16-702 a, b, and c (BV2 a, b, and c), and 16-703 (BV3).

University of Baltimore Law Forum. — For comment, "When Considering Whether Prior Criminal Convictions Are Admissible in Subsequent Civil Proceedings as a Hearsay Exception, Should Maryland Keep its Kuhl or Take a Walk on the Wald Side," see 36 U. Balt. L.F. 25 (2005).

Authority to bring action. — Subsection (h)(9) provides the authority for the Attorney Greivance Commission to bring an action against an attorney. Att'y Griev. Comm'n v. Pak, 400 Md. 567, 929 A.2d 546 (2007), cert. denied, 128 S. Ct. 905, 2008 U.S. LEXIS 126, 169 L. Ed. 2d 729 (U.S. 2008).

Attorney's failure to participate. — In an attorney disciplinary proceeding, an attorney's failure to respond to Bar Counsel's recommended disposition and/or to appear at oral argument will not be considered as any level of mitigation in the sound exercise of the Court of Appeals of Maryland's discretion as to what sanction is appropriate. Att'y Griev. Comm'n v. Duvall, 373 Md. 482, 819 A.2d 343 (2003).

Quoted in Att'y Griev. Comm'n v. Harris, 366 Md. 376, 784 A.2d 516 (2001); Att'y Griev. Comm'n v. Waters, — Md. —, — A.2d — (2001); Att'y Griev. Comm'n v. Garfield, 369 Md. 85, 797 A.2d 757 (2002); Att'y Griev. Comm'n v. McClain, 373 Md. 196, 817 A.2d 218 (2003); Att'y Griev. Comm'n v. Seiden, 373 Md. 409, 818 A.2d 1108 (2003); Att'y Griev. Comm'n v. Olver, 376 Md. 650, 831 A.2d 66 (2003).

Cited in Att'y Griev. Comm'n v. Sheinbein, 372 Md. 224, 812 A.2d 981 (2002); Att'y Griev. Comm'n v. Post, 379 Md. 60, 839 A.2d 718 (2003).

Rule 16-712. Bar Counsel.

(a) **Appointment.** Subject to approval by the Court of Appeals, the Commission shall appoint an attorney as Bar Counsel. Before appointing Bar Counsel, the Commission shall notify bar associations and the general public of the vacancy and consider any recommendations that are timely submitted. Bar Counsel shall serve at the pleasure of the Commission and shall receive the compensation set forth in the budget of the Commission.

(b) **Powers and duties.** Subject to the supervision and approval, if required, of the Commission, Bar Counsel has the powers and duties to:

(1) investigate professional misconduct or incapacity;

(2) issue subpoenas as provided by Rule 16-732;

(3) enter into and implement Conditional Diversion Agreements, issue notices, and administer warnings and reprimands;

(4) file statements of charges, participate in proceedings before Peer Review Panels, and prosecute all disciplinary and remedial proceedings;

(5) file and prosecute petitions for disciplinary and remedial actions in the name of the Commission;

(6) monitor and enforce compliance with all disciplinary and remedial orders of the Court of Appeals;

(7) investigate petitions for reinstatement and applications for resignation from the practice of law and represent the Commission in those proceedings;

(8) initiate, intervene in, and prosecute actions to enjoin the unauthorized practice of law;

(9) employ attorneys, investigators, and staff personnel as authorized by the Commission at the compensation set forth in the Commission's budget;

(10) discharge any employee;

(11) maintain dockets and records of all papers filed in disciplinary or remedial proceedings;

(12) make reports to the Commission; and

(13) perform other duties prescribed by the Commission, this Chapter, and the Rules in Title 16, Chapter 600 (Attorney Trust Accounts). (Added Nov. 30, 2000, effective July 1, 2001.)

Source. — This Rule is derived from former Rule 16-704 (BV4).

Consideration of mental health issues — Bar Counsel's recommendation of disbarment with regard to an attorney found to have violated Md. R. Prof. Conduct 1.15(a), (b), and (c), and Md. R.Prof. Conduct 8.4(b), (c), and (d), was not accepted by the Maryland Court of Appeals; the disciplinary matter was remanded for the Attorney Grievance Commission and Bar Counsel to reconsider entering into a conditional diversion agreement with the attorney because, even though the evidence supported the finding of wilful misconduct, the attorney's mental health and severe depression was a significant factor, and the Court of Appeal's interpretation of Rule 16-736 allowed diversion as a sanction in such cases where the professional misconduct was not solely the result of wilful or intentionally dishonest conduct. Att'y Griev. Comm'n v. Cappell, 389 Md. 402, 886 A.2d 112 (2005).

Bar Counsel's recommendation of disbarment with regard to an attorney found to have violated Md. R. Prof. Conduct 1.15(a), (b), and (c), and Md. R. Prof. Conduct 8.4(b), (c), and (d), was not accepted by the Maryland Court of Appeals; the disciplinary matter was remanded for the Attorney Grievance Commission and Bar Counsel to reconsider entering into a conditional diversion agreement with the attorney because, even though the evidence supported the finding of wilful miscon-

duct, the attorney's mental health and severe depression was a significant factor, and the Court of Appeal's interpretation of Rule 16-736 allowed diversion as a sanction in such cases where the professional misconduct was not solely the result of wilful or intentionally dishonest conduct. Att'y Griev. Comm'n v. Cappell, 389 Md. 402, 886 A.2d 112 (2005).

Motion to strike reinstatement order dismissed. — Because an attorney representing a litigant in proceedings involving a reinstated attorney did not have standing to move to vacate the order reinstating that attorney, rather, only Bar Counsel could do so, the plaintiff's attorney's motion to strike the court's order reinstating the suspended attorney had to be dismissed. Att'y Griev. Comm'n v. Adams, 404 Md. 1, 944 A.2d 1115 (2008).

Power to move to vacate reinstatement. — Attorney representing a litigant in proceedings involving a reinstated attorney does not have standing to move to vacate the order reinstating that attorney; only Bar Counsel may do so. Att'y Griev. Comm'n v. Adams, 404 Md. 1, 944 A.2d 1115 (2008).

Quoted in Att'y Griev. Comm'n v. Tinsky, 377 Md. 646, 835 A.2d 542 (2003); Att'y Griev. Comm'n v. Zdravkovich, 381 Md. 680, 852 A.2d 82 (2004).

Cited in Att'y Griev. Comm'n v. Pak, 400 Md. 567, 929 A.2d 546 (2007), cert. denied, 128

S. Ct. 905, 2008 U.S. LEXIS 126, 169 L. Ed. 2d
729 (U.S. 2008).

Rule 16-713. Peer Review Committee.

(a) **Creation.** There is a Peer Review Committee, the members of which are appointed to serve on Peer Review Panels pursuant to Rule 16-742.

(b) **Composition.** The Peer Review Committee consists of the number of persons in each circuit that the Commission determines is necessary to conduct the volume of peer review proceedings. Of the number of members determined for each circuit, one-third shall be residents of that circuit who are not attorneys and the remainder shall be attorneys who maintain offices for the practice of law within that circuit.

(c) **Persons ineligible for appointment as a lawyer member.** The Commission may not appoint as a lawyer member to the Peer Review Committee a person who:

(1) is not admitted by the Court of Appeals to practice law in Maryland;

(2) has not actively and lawfully engaged in the practice of law in Maryland for at least five years;

(3) is a judge of a court of record;

(4) is the subject of a pending statement of charges or petition for disciplinary or remedial action; or

(5) was ever disbarred or suspended by the Court of Appeals or by a disciplinary body or court of the United States or any State.

(d) **Persons ineligible for appointment as a non-lawyer member.** The Commission may not appoint as a non-lawyer member to the Peer Review Committee a person who:

(1) has been convicted of a serious crime and the conviction has not been reversed or vacated; or

(2) is the complainant in a pending matter against an attorney under the Rules in this Chapter.

(e) **Procedure for appointment.** Before appointing members of the Peer Review Committee, the Commission shall notify bar associations and the general public in the appropriate circuit and consider any applications and recommendations that are timely submitted. The Commission shall prepare a brief notice informing attorneys how they may apply to serve on the Peer Review Committee and deliver the notice to the Trustees of the Client Protection Fund of the Bar of Maryland, who at least once a year shall send a copy of the notice to each attorney who is required to pay an annual fee to the Fund.

(f) **Term.** The term of each member is two years. The Commission may extend the term of any member assigned to a Peer Review Panel until the completion of a pending matter. A member may be reappointed.

(g) **Chair and Vice Chair.** The Commission shall designate one attorney member of the Peer Review Committee as Chair and one or more attorney members as Vice Chairs. In the absence or disability of the Chair or upon express delegation of authority by the Chair, the Vice Chair shall have the authority and perform the duties of the Chair.

(h) **Compensation.** A member of the Peer Review Committee may not receive compensation for serving in that capacity but is entitled to reimbursement for expenses reasonably incurred in the performance of official duties in accordance with standard State travel regulations.

(i) **Removal.** The Commission may remove a member of the Peer Review Committee for cause. (Added Nov. 30, 2000, effective July 1, 2001; amended effective Nov. 6, 2002.)

Source. — This Rule is new.

Effect of amendments. — The 2002 amendment substituted "Client Protection Fund of the Bar of Maryland" for "Clients' Security Trust Fund" in (e).

Maryland suspension not greater than District of Columbia suspension. — In a disciplinary matter in Maryland that was not reciprocal in nature but that was based upon the attorney's 30-day suspension, with reinstatement conditioned upon a showing of fitness, in the District of Columbia, the attorney was suspended indefinitely for violating prior, similar Md. R. Prof. Conduct 8.1(b), 8.4(d), and the attorney's reinstatement to the Maryland bar was conditioned upon the attorney's reinstatement to the District of Columbia bar; the impact of the misconduct, which involved a refusal to respond to disciplinary charges in violation of D.C. R. Prof. Conduct 8.4(d), 8.1(b) and D.C. Bd. Prof. Resp. R. XI, § 2(b)(3), occurred in the District of Columbia, so the Maryland court decided to impose a suspension that, pursuant to Md. R. 16-713(a)(2), was not greater than the District of Columbia suspension. Att'y Griev. Comm'n v. Steinberg, 385 Md. 696, 870 A.2d 603 (2005).

Cited in Att'y Griev. Comm'n v. Bahgat, 411 Md. 568, 984 A.2d 225 (2009).

Rule 16-714. Disciplinary Fund.

(a) **Payment by attorneys.** There is a Disciplinary Fund to which, as a condition precedent to the practice of law, each attorney shall pay annually an amount prescribed by the Court of Appeals. The amount shall be in addition to and paid by the same date as other sums required to be paid pursuant to Rule 16-811. The Disciplinary Fund is created and administered pursuant to the Constitutional authority of the Court of Appeals to regulate the practice of law in the State of Maryland and to implement and enforce the Maryland Lawyers' Rules of Professional Conduct adopted by the Court. The Fund consists of contributions made by lawyers as a condition of their right to practice law in Maryland and income from those contributions. The principal and income of the Fund shall be dedicated exclusively to the purposes established by the Rules in this Title.

(b) **Collection and disbursement of Disciplinary Fund.** The treasurer of the Client Protection Fund of the Bar of Maryland shall collect and remit to the Commission the sums paid by attorneys to the Disciplinary Fund.

(c) **Audit.** There shall be an independent annual audit of the Disciplinary Fund. The expense of the audit shall be paid out of the Fund.

(d) **Enforcement.** Enforcement of payment of annual assessments of attorneys pursuant to this Rule is governed by the provisions of Rule 16-811 (g). (Added Nov. 30, 2000, effective July 1, 2001; amended effective Nov. 6, 2002; amended Sept. 8, 2011, effective Oct. 1, 2011.)

Source. — This Rule is derived from former Rule 16-702 d (BV2 d) and 16-703 b (vii) (BV3 b (vii)).

Effect of amendments. — The 2002 amendment substituted "Client Protection Fund" for "Clients' Security Trust Fund" in (b).

The 2011 amendment rewrote (a).

Cited in Att'y Griev. Comm'n v. Post, 379 Md. 60, 839 A.2d 718 (2003).

Rule 16-715. Costs.

Editor's note. — This rule was rescinded in the 2001 revision of Title 16, Chapter 700.

Applied in Att'y Griev. Comm'n v. Pak, 400 Md. 567, 929 A.2d 546 (2007), cert. denied, 128 S. Ct. 905, 2008 U.S. LEXIS 126, 169 L. Ed. 2d 729 (U.S. 2008); Att'y Griev. Comm'n v. Sapero, 400 Md. 461, 929 A.2d 483 (2007); Att'y Griev. Comm'n v. Floyd, 400 Md. 236, 929 A.2d 61 (2007).

Cited in Att'y Griev. Comm'n v. Zuckerman, 403 Md. 695, 944 A.2d 525 (2008); Att'y Griev. Comm'n v. Foltz, 411 Md. 359, 983 A.2d 434 (2009); Att'y Griev. Comm'n v. Usiak, 418 Md. 667, 18 A.3d 1 (2011); Att'y Griev. Comm'n v. Khandpur, 421 Md. 1, 25 A.3d 165 (2011); Att'y Griev. Comm'n v. Carithers, 421 Md. 28, 25 A.3d 181 (2011).

Rule 16-721. Sanctions and remedies for misconduct or incapacity.

(a) **Professional misconduct.** One or more of the following sanctions or remedies may be imposed upon an attorney for professional misconduct:

(1) disbarment by the Court of Appeals;

(2) suspension by the Court of Appeals;

(3) reprimand by the Court of Appeals or, with the attorney's consent, by the Commission;

(4) conditional diversion in accordance with a Conditional Diversion Agreement entered into pursuant to Rule 16-736; and

(5) termination of a disciplinary or remedial proceeding accompanied by a warning pursuant to Rule 16-735 (b).

(b) **Incapacity.** One of the following remedies may be imposed upon an attorney for incapacity:

(1) placement on inactive status, subject to further order of the Court, or

(2) conditional diversion in accordance with a Conditional Diversion Agreement entered pursuant to Rule 16-736.

(c) **Conditions.** An order, decision, or agreement that imposes a disciplinary sanction upon an attorney or places an attorney on inactive status may include one or more specified conditions, as authorized by Rules 16-736, 16-760, and 16-781. (Added Nov. 30, 2000, effective July 1, 2001.)

Source. — This Rule is new.

Certain factors may influence sanction to be imposed. — Factors such as the age and inexperience of an attorney and the lack of personal gain involved in an act of misconduct may in some circumstances influence the sanction to be imposed. Att'y Griev. Comm'n v. Kahn, 290 Md. 654, 431 A.2d 1336 (1981).

In determining whether an attorney has exhibited the requisite foundation for a sanction less than disbarment, the Court of Appeals considers whether the proffered circumstances diminish the degree of culpability inherent in his guilt. Att'y Griev. Comm'n v. Kahn, 290 Md. 654, 431 A.2d 1336 (1981).

Reprimand was proper sanction. — Proper sanction was a reprimand because the gravity of an attorney's violations was minimal and his intention, although misguided, was not to deceive. Att'y Griev. Comm'n v. Kalil, 402 Md. 358, 936 A.2d 854 (2007).

Indefinite suspension. — In a reciprocal discipline action, the attorney, who had been suspended in the District of Columbia for one year with six months stayed, followed by three years probationary period and participation in the District's Bar Practice Management Advisory Service, was indefinitely suspended in Maryland, with right to apply for readmission after reinstatement in the District, because the sanction imposed by the District of Columbia court was not within the Maryland spectrum of sanctions and the Court of Appeals of Maryland determined that indefinite suspension was the equivalent sanction and appropriate under the circumstances, where the attorney's conduct was negligence, rather that intentional acts. Att'y Griev. Comm'n v. Thaxton, 415 Md. 341, — A.2d —, 1 A.3d 470 (2010).

Attorney disbarred for abandoning clients — Attorney was disbarred for mishandling a client's bankruptcy, causing it to be dismissed, twice failing to appear for a client's criminal trial, abandoning his practice, and failing to return unearned fees. Att'y Griev. Comm'n v. Tinsky, 377 Md. 646, 835 A.2d 542 (2003).

Cited in Att'y Griev. Comm'n v. Saridakis, 402 Md. 413, 936 A.2d 886 (2007).

Rule 16-722. Audit of attorney accounts and records.

(a) **Action for audit.** Bar Counsel or the Trustees of the Client Protection Fund of the Bar of Maryland may file a petition requesting an audit of the accounts and records that an attorney is required by law or Rule to maintain. The petition may be filed in the circuit court in any county where the attorney resides or has an office for the practice of law. If the attorney has no established office and the attorney's residence is unknown, the petition may be filed in any circuit court.

(b) **Petition.** The petition shall state the facts showing that an audit is necessary and shall request the appointment of a Certified Public Accountant to conduct the audit. Proceedings under this Rule shall be sealed and stamped "confidential" at the time of filing, and the docket entries shall not divulge the name or otherwise identify the attorney against whom the petition is filed.

(c) **Caption.** The petition and all subsequent pleadings and papers filed in the action shall contain a caption, "In re: Application for Audit of an Attorney's Accounts and Records."

(d) **Show cause order; service.** The court shall enter an order giving the attorney notice of the action and directing the attorney to show cause on or before a stated date why an audit should not be conducted as requested. The order and the petition shall be served in the manner that the court directs so as to preserve the confidentiality of the action.

(e) **Response to petition.** The attorney may file a response to the petition and show cause order not later than the date stated in the order or, if no date is stated, within five days after being served.

(f) **Order directing audit.** After considering the petition and any response and upon a finding of good cause, the court may order any of the accounts and records required by law or Rule to be maintained by the attorney to be audited by a Certified Public Accountant designated in the order. The order directing the audit shall expressly require that the audit be conducted and a report be made in a manner that preserves the confidentiality of the proceedings and the attorney's confidential relation with the attorney's clients.

(g) **Finality of order.** An order granting or denying a petition for an audit is a final order for purposes of appeal.

(h) **Duty of clerk to preserve confidentiality.** The clerk shall maintain a separate docket with an index for proceedings under this Rule. Pleadings and other papers filed in the proceedings shall be sealed in accordance with Rule 16-723 (b) (9) at the time they are filed. The docket, index, and papers in the proceedings shall not be open to inspection by any person, including the parties, except upon order of court after reasonable notice and for good cause shown.

(i) **Cost of audit.** Upon completion of the audit, the court may order all or part of the costs of the audit and of the proceeding to be paid by any party to the proceeding, but costs shall not be assessed against the attorney if the audit fails to disclose any irregularity.

(j) **Remedy not exclusive.** Neither this Rule nor any proceeding under this Rule precludes any other remedy or cause of action while the audit is pending or thereafter. (Added Nov. 30, 2000, effective July 1, 2001; amended Oct. 31, 2002, effective Jan. 1, 2003; amended effective Nov. 6, 2002.)

Source. — This Rule is in part derived from former Rule 16-718 (BV18) and in part new.

Effect of amendments. — The first 2002 amendment substituted "Rule 16-723 (b) (9)" for "Rule 16-723 (b) (7)" in (h).

The second 2002 amendment substituted "Trustees of the Client Protection Fund of the Bar of Maryland" for "Clients' Security Trust Fund" in (a).

Quoted in Att'y Griev. Comm'n v. Zdravkovich, 381 Md. 680, 852 A.2d 82 (2004).

Rule 16-723. Confidentiality.

(a) **Confidentiality of peer review meetings.** All persons present at a peer review meeting shall maintain the confidentiality of all speech, writing, and conduct made as part of the meeting and may not disclose or be compelled to disclose the speech, writing, or conduct in any judicial, administrative, or other proceeding. Speech, writing, or conduct that is confidential under this Rule is privileged and not subject to discovery, but information otherwise admissible or subject to discovery does not become inadmissible or protected from disclosure solely by reason of its use at the peer review meeting.

(b) **Other confidential matters.** Except as otherwise provided in these Rules, the following records and proceedings are confidential and not open to public inspection and their contents may not be revealed by the Commission, the staff of the Commission, Bar Counsel, the staff and investigators of the Office of Bar Counsel, members of the Peer Review Committee, or any attorney involved in the proceeding:

(1) the records of an investigation by Bar Counsel, including the existence and content of any complaint;

(2) the records and proceedings of a Peer Review Panel;

(3) information that is the subject of a protective order;

(4) the contents of a warning issued by the Commission pursuant to Rule 16-735 (b), but the fact that a warning was issued shall be disclosed to the complainant;

(5) the contents of a prior private reprimand or Bar Counsel reprimand pursuant to the Attorney Disciplinary Rules in effect prior to July 1, 2001, but the fact that a private or Bar Counsel reprimand was issued and the facts underlying the reprimand may be disclosed to a peer review panel in a proceeding against the attorney alleging similar misconduct;

Committee note. — The peer review panel is not required to find that information disclosed under subsection (b)(5) is relevant under Rule 16-743 (c)(1).

(6) the contents of a Conditional Diversion Agreement entered into pursuant to Rule 16-736, but the fact that an attorney has signed such an agreement shall be public;

(7) the records and proceedings of the Commission on matters that are confidential under this Rule;

(8) a Petition for Disciplinary or Remedial Action based solely on the alleged incapacity of an attorney and records and proceedings other than proceedings in the Court of Appeals on that petition; and

(9) a petition for an audit of an attorney's accounts filed pursuant to Rule 16-722 and records and proceedings other than proceedings in the Court of Appeals on that petition.

(c) **Public proceedings and records.** The following records and proceedings are public and open to inspection:

(1) except as otherwise provided in subsection (b)(8) of this Rule, a Petition for Disciplinary or Remedial Action, all proceedings on that petition, and all documents or other items admitted into evidence at any hearing on the petition;

(2) an affidavit filed pursuant to Rule 16-772 that consents to discipline and an order that disbars, suspends, or reprimands the attorney by consent;

(3) a reprimand issued by the Commission pursuant to Rule 16-737; and

(4) except as otherwise provided by order of the Court of Appeals, all proceedings under this Chapter in the Court of Appeals.

(d) **Required disclosure by Bar Counsel.** (1) Reprimand by Commission. If an attorney is reprimanded by the Commission, Bar Counsel shall notify the Clerk of the Court of Appeals.

(2) Conviction of a serious crime. If Bar Counsel has received and verified information that an attorney has been convicted of a serious crime, Bar Counsel shall notify the Commission and the Clerk of the Court of Appeals.

(e) **Required disclosure by the Clerk of the Court of Appeals.** If an attorney resigns or is reprimanded, convicted of a serious crime, or, by order of the Court of Appeals, disbarred, suspended, reinstated, or transferred to inactive status, the Clerk of the Court of Appeals of Maryland shall notify the National Lawyer Regulatory Data Bank of the American Bar Association and the disciplinary authority of every other jurisdiction in which the attorney is admitted to practice.

(f) **Permitted disclosure.** (1) Written waiver of attorney. If the attorney has signed a written waiver of confidentiality, the Commission or Bar Counsel may disclose information to the extent permitted by the waiver.

(2) In preparation for a hearing. The parties to a disciplinary or remedial action may use confidential information other than the records and proceedings of a Peer Review Panel to the extent reasonably necessary to prepare for a public hearing in the action but shall preserve the confidentiality of the information in all other respects.

(3) Communications with complainant. Upon request of a complainant, Bar Counsel may disclose to the complainant the status of an investigation and of any disciplinary or remedial proceedings resulting from information from the complainant.

(4) Requests by authorities. Upon receiving a request that complies with this subsection, the Commission or Bar Counsel may disclose the pendency, subject matter, status, and disposition of disciplinary or remedial proceedings involving an attorney or former attorney that did not result in dismissal. The request must be made in writing by a judicial nominating commission, a bar admission authority, the President of the United States, the Governor of a state, territory, or district of the United States, or a committee of the General Assembly of Maryland or of the United States Congress. The requesting entity must represent that it is considering the nomination, appointment, confirmation, approval, or admission to practice of the attorney, or former attorney, and that the information will be treated as confidential and without the consent of the attorney may not be copied or disclosed to anyone other than the requesting entity.

(5) Explanatory statements. The Chair of the Commission may issue a brief explanatory statement necessary to correct any public misperception about actual or possible proceedings.

(6) Subpoena or court order. If satisfied that an attorney has received prior notice and an opportunity to object or move for a protective order, Bar Counsel may comply with a subpoena or order of a court of this State or the United States to produce records and disclose confidential information concerning the attorney.

(7) Information involving criminal activity. With the approval of the Chair of the Commission, Bar Counsel may provide to law enforcement and prosecuting officials information involving criminal activity, including information requested by a subpoena from a grand jury pursuant to Rule 4-643.

(8) Other disciplinary authorities. With the approval of the Chair of the Commission, Bar Counsel may provide to the disciplinary authority of any other jurisdiction in which an attorney is admitted to practice records and other confidential information concerning the attorney.

(9) Summarized information. In order to improve the administration of justice, the Commission and Bar Counsel may publish reports and summaries of confidential investigations, charges, and disciplinary or remedial proceedings, provided that the identity of attorneys, complainants, and witnesses is not revealed. (Added Nov. 30, 2000, effective July 1, 2001; amended by order effective Dec. 3, 2001; Oct. 31, 2002, effective Jan. 1, 2003; Nov. 12, 2003, effective July 1, 2004; April 5, 2005, effective July 1, 2005; June 16, 2009, effective June 17, 2009.)

Source. — This Rule is derived in part from former Rule 16-708 (BV8) and in part new.

Effect of amendments. — The 2002 amendment substituted "but the fact" for "except the fact" in (b)(4) and present (b)(6); inserted present (b)(5) and redesignated the remaining subsections accordingly; and inserted the Committee note following present (b)(5).

The 2005 rewrote the introductory language in (b) and (b)(1).

The 2009 amendment substituted "the Commission" for "Bar Counsel" in (b)(4).

Editor's note. — An Order dated Dec. 3, 2001, effective immediately, substituted "the Clerk of the Court of Appeals of Maryland" for "Bar Counsel" following "inactive status" in (d).

Constitutionality — Md. R. 16-723 is not unconstitutional. Att'y Griev. Comm'n v. Calhoun, 391 Md. 532, 894 A.2d 518 (2006).

Admissibility of Peer Review recommendations. — Hearing court did not err in refusing to admit into evidence the Peer Review Panel report; the Peer Review Panel were not meant to be admitted into evidence since its proceedings were confidential and the Peer Review Panel performed a limited function of reviewing disciplinary charges to make a preliminary determination of what disposition of them might be appropriate. Att'y Griev. Comm'n v. Kinnane, 390 Md. 324, 888 A.2d 1178 (2005).

Use to impeach complainant precluded. — Although the confidentiality provision of the peer review rules was drafted to protect against impeachment of respondent attorneys with their earlier statements during peer review, the purposes of peer review were best served by likewise applying the confidentiality rule, according to its plain language, where it was the complainant whose earlier statements were allegedly inconsistent; if a formal disciplinary ensued, a respondent attorney would still have an opportunity to depose and pursue other discovery as to witnesses whose evidence seemed questionable. Att'y Griev. Comm'n v. Lee, 387 Md. 89, 874 A.2d 897 (2005).

Bar Counsel's investigations not discoverable. — Attorney's Rule 2-432(b)(1)(G) motion was properly denied as Md. R. Prof. Conduct 1.15(b) placed an affirmative burden on the attorney to notify a third-party assignee upon the receipt of burdened funds and to deliver the proper amount due to the third party, a dispute over the amount due was not a defense to a disciplinary proceeding arising out of nonpayment to the assignee, and Maryland Bar Counsel's investigations of a complaint due to nonpayment were ordinarily not discoverable under (b). Att'y Griev. Comm'n v. Ellison, 384 Md. 688, 867 A.2d 259 (2005).

Applied in Att'y Griev. Comm'n v. Cappell, 389 Md. 402, 886 A.2d 112 (2005).

Quoted in Att'y Griev. Comm'n v. Pak, 400 Md. 567, 929 A.2d 546 (2007), cert. denied, 128 S. Ct. 905, 2008 U.S. LEXIS 126, 169 L. Ed. 2d 729 (U.S. 2008).

Cited in Att'y Griev. Comm'n v. Zdravkovich, 381 Md. 680, 852 A.2d 82 (2004); Att'y Griev. Comm'n v. Lee, 387 Md. 89, 874 A.2d 897 (2005); Att'y Griev. Comm'n v. Kreamer, 404 Md. 282, 946 A.2d 500 (2008); Att'y Griev. Comm'n v. Usiak, 418 Md. 667, 18 A.3d 1 (2011); Att'y Griev. Comm'n v. Keiner, — Md. —, — A.3d — (Aug. 19, 2011).

Rule 16-724. Service of papers on attorney.

(a) **Statement of Charges.** A copy of a Statement of Charges filed pursuant to Rule 16-741 shall be served on an attorney in the manner prescribed by Rule 2-121. If after reasonable efforts the attorney cannot be served personally, service may be made upon the employee designated by the Client Protection Fund of the Bar of Maryland pursuant to Rule 16-811 c 1 (x), who shall be deemed the attorney's agent for receipt of service. The Fund's employee shall send, by both certified mail and ordinary mail, a copy of the papers so served to the attorney at the address maintained in the Fund's records and to any other address provided by Bar Counsel.

(b) **Service of other papers.** Except as otherwise provided in this Chapter, other notices and papers may be served on an attorney in the manner provided by Rule 1-321 for service of papers after an original pleading.

Committee note. — The attorney's address contained in the records of the Client Protec- tion Fund of the Bar of Maryland may be the attorney's last known address.

(Added Nov. 30, 2000, effective July 1, 2001; amended effective November 6, 2002.)

Cross references. — See Rule 16-753 con- cerning service of a Petition for Disciplinary or Remedial Action.

Source. — This Rule is in part derived from former Rule 16-706 (BV6) and in part new.

Effect of amendments. — The 2002 amendment, in (a), in the first sentence sub- stituted "employee designated by the Client Protection Fund of the Bar of Maryland pur- suant to Rule 16-811 c 1 (x)" for "treasurer of the Clients' Security Trust" and in the second sentence substituted "Fund's employee" for "Treasurer" and deleted "Trust" preceding "Fund's records"; and substituted "Client Pro- tection Fund of the Bar of Maryland" for "Cli- ents' Security Trust Fund" in the Committee note.

Rule 16-731. Complaint; investigation by Bar Counsel.

(a) **Complaints.** A complaint alleging that an attorney has engaged in professional misconduct or is incapacitated shall be in writing and sent to Bar Counsel. Any written communication that includes the name and address of the person making the communication and states facts which, if true, would constitute professional misconduct by or demonstrate incapacity of an attorney constitutes a complaint. Bar Counsel also may initiate a complaint based on information from other sources.

(b) **Review of complaint.** (1) Bar Counsel shall make an appropriate investigation of every complaint that is not facially frivolous or unfounded.

(2) If Bar Counsel concludes that the complaint is either frivolous or unfounded or does not allege facts which, if true, would demonstrate either professional misconduct or incapacity, Bar Counsel shall dismiss the complaint and notify the complainant of the dismissal. Otherwise, Bar Counsel shall (A) open a file on the complaint, (B) acknowledge receipt of the complaint and explain in writing to the complainant the procedures for investigating and processing the complaint, (C) comply with the notice requirement of section (c) of this Rule, and (D) conduct an investigation to determine whether reasonable grounds exist to believe the allegations of the complaint.

Committee note. — Before determining whether a complaint is frivolous or unfounded, Bar Counsel may contact the attorney and obtain an informal response to the allegations.

(c) **Notice to attorney.** (1) Except as otherwise provided in this section, Bar Counsel shall notify the attorney who is the subject of the complaint that Bar Counsel is undertaking an investigation to determine whether the attorney has engaged in professional misconduct or is incapacitated. The notice shall be given before the conclusion of the investigation and shall include the name and address of the complainant and the general nature of the professional misconduct or incapacity under investigation. As part of the notice, Bar Counsel may demand that the attorney provide information and records that Bar Counsel deems appropriate and relevant to the investigation.

The notice shall state the time within which the attorney shall provide the information and any other information that the attorney may wish to present. The notice shall be served on the attorney in accordance with Rule 16-724 (b).

(2) Bar Counsel need not give notice of investigation to an attorney if, with the approval of the Commission, Bar Counsel proceeds under Rule 16-771, 16-773, or 16-774.

(d) **Time for completing investigation.** Unless the time is extended by the Commission for good cause, Bar Counsel shall complete an investigation within 90 days after opening the file on the complaint. Upon written request by Bar Counsel establishing good cause for an extension for a specified period, the Commission may grant one or more extensions. The Commission may not grant an extension, at any one time, of more than 60 days unless it finds specific good cause for a longer extension. If an extension exceeding 60 days is granted, Bar Counsel shall provide the Commission with a status report at least every 60 days. For failure to comply with the time requirements of this section, the Commission may take any action appropriate under the circumstances, including dismissal of the complaint and termination of the investigation. (Added Nov. 30, 2000, effective July 1, 2001.)

Source. — This Rule is new.

Time limits. — Time limits for conduct of ethical investigation were simply designed to move the investigation along; where more time was required to do a thorough job, dismissal, which was not mentioned in the rule as a response to delay, was not mandated. Att'y Griev. Comm'n v. Herman, 380 Md. 378, 844 A.2d 1181 (2004).

Relevant material had to be provided. — In the attorney disciplinary hearing, where the attorney asserted that there was no evidence that the materials requested by Bar Counsel were necessary to the investigation, this contention was immaterial, as the attorney's obligation under (c)(1) was to provide any relevant material requested in the course of the investigation. Att'y Griev. Comm'n v. Obi, 393 Md. 643, 904 A.2d 422 (2006).

Dismissal on request of complainant not proper. — Bar Counsel could not dismiss the complaint against the attorney merely because the complainant requested dismissal; Bar Counsel was obligated to investigate the

complaint once it was made, and could dismiss the complaint only if the evidence failed to show sanctionable professional misconduct or incapacity. Att'y Griev. Comm'n v. Lee, 393 Md. 546, 903 A.2d 895 (2006).

Bar Counsel investigation. — Trial court pursuant to Rule 2-510 could deny without granting a hearing the attorney's motion to quash the subpoena that the Commission sought to enforce in Bar Counsel's investigation under this Rule of an overdraft in the attorney's trust account. The attorney did not show that there was no reasonable possibility that relevant information would not be obtained from the material gathered pursuant to the subpoena. Unnamed Atty. v. Att'y Griev. Comm'n, 409 Md. 509, 976 A.2d 267 (2009).

Quoted in Att'y Griev. Comm'n v. Kreamer, 387 Md. 503, 876 A.2d 79 (2005); Att'y Griev. Comm'n v. Fox, 417 Md. 504, 11 A.3d 762 (2010). Att'y Griev. Comm'n v. Kreamer, 387 Md. 503, 876 A.2d 79 (2005).

Cited in Att'y Griev. Comm'n v. Lee, 387 Md. 89, 874 A.2d 897 (2005).

Rule 16-732. Investigative subpoena.

(a) **Approval and issuance.** (1) The Chair of the Commission may authorize Bar Counsel to issue a subpoena to compel the attendance of witnesses and the production of designated documents or other tangible things at a time and place specified in the subpoena if the Chair finds that (A) the subpoena is necessary to and in furtherance of an investigation being conducted by Bar

Counsel pursuant to Rule 16-731 or (B) the subpoena has been requested by a disciplinary authority of another jurisdiction pursuant to the law of that jurisdiction for use in a disciplinary or remedial proceeding in that jurisdiction to determine alleged professional misconduct or incapacity of a lawyer subject to the jurisdiction of that disciplinary authority.

(2) Upon approval, Bar Counsel may issue the subpoena.

(b) **Contents.** A subpoena shall comply with the requirements of Rule 2-510 (c), except that to the extent practicable, a subpoena shall not identify the attorney under investigation. A subpoena to compel attendance of a witness shall include or be accompanied by a notice that the witness (1) has the right to consult with an attorney with respect to the assertion of a privilege or any other matter pertaining to the subpoena and (2) may file a motion for judicial relief under Rule 2-510.

(c) **Service.** Except for service upon an attorney in accordance with Rule 16-724 (b), a subpoena shall be served in accordance with Rule 2-510. Promptly after service of a subpoena on a person other than the attorney under investigation and in addition to giving any other notice required by law, Bar Counsel shall serve a copy of the subpoena on the attorney under investigation.

Cross references. — For examples of other notice required by law, see Code, Financial Institutions Article, § 1-304, concerning notice to depositors of subpoenas for financial records; Code, Health General Article, § 4-306 concerning disclosure of medical records, and Code, Health General Article, § 4-307, concerning notice of a request for issuance of compulsory process seeking medical records related to mental health services.

(d) **Objection.** The person served with the subpoena or the attorney under investigation may file a motion in the circuit court for the county in which the subpoena was served for any order permitted by Rule 2-510 (e). The motion shall be filed promptly and, whenever practicable, at or before the time specified in the subpoena for compliance.

(e) **Enforcement.** On the motion of Bar Counsel, the court may enforce compliance with the subpoena.

(f) **Confidentiality.** Any paper filed in court with respect to a subpoena shall be sealed upon filing and shall be open to inspection only by order of the court. A hearing before the court on any motion shall be on the record and shall be conducted out of the presence of all persons other than Bar Counsel, the attorney, and those persons whose presence the court deems necessary.

(g) **Recording of statements.** Everything said by the witness at the time and place specified in the subpoena shall be contemporaneously recorded stenographically or electronically, and the witness shall be placed under oath. (Added Nov. 30, 2000, effective July 1, 2001.)

Source. — This Rule is new.

Relevant information. — Trial court pursuant to Rule 2-311(f) was not required to hold a hearing on the attorney's request to quash the Commission's subpoena in a case where the Commission was investigating an overdraft in the attorney's trust account. The trial court could deny the attorney's motion to quash without holding a hearing, as pursuant to (f) of this Rule, there was no reasonable possibility that the material the Commission sought would not produce relevant information. Unnamed Atty. v. Att'y Griev. Comm'n, 409 Md. 509, 976 A.2d 267 (2009).

Applied in Att'y Griev. Comm'n v. Alsafty, 379 Md. 1, 838 A.2d 1213 (2003).

Stated in Att'y Griev. Comm'n v.

Zdravkovich, 381 Md. 680, 852 A.2d 82 (2004); Att'y Griev. Comm'n v. Lee, 387 Md. 89, 874 A.2d 897 (2005).

Cited in Att'y Griev. Comm'n v. Adams, 404 Md. 1, 944 A.2d 1115 (2008); Att'y Griev. Comm'n v. Keiner, — Md. —, — A.3d — (Aug. 19, 2011).

Rule 16-733. Perpetuation of evidence before petition for disciplinary or remedial action.

Before a Petition for Disciplinary or Remedial Action is filed, Bar Counsel or an attorney who is or may be the subject of an investigation by Bar Counsel may perpetuate testimony or other evidence relevant to a claim or defense that may be asserted in the expected action. The perpetuation of evidence shall be governed by Rule 2-404 and the issuance of subpoenas and protective orders shall be governed by Rules 2-510 and 2-403. The Commission shall perform the functions that the court performs under those Rules. (Added Nov. 30, 2000, effective July 1, 2001.)

Source. — This Rule is new.

Rule 16-734. Procedure upon completion of investigation.

Upon completion of an investigation, Bar Counsel shall take one of the following actions:

(a) recommend to the Commission dismissal of the complaint or termination of the proceeding without discipline, with or without a warning, in accordance with Rule 16-735;

(b) recommend to the Commission approval of a Conditional Diversion Agreement signed by Bar Counsel and the attorney in accordance with Rule 16-736;

(c) recommend to the Commission a reprimand in accordance with Rule 16-737;

(d) file with the Commission a Statement of Charges with an election for peer review in accordance with Rule 16-741; or

(e) recommend to the Commission the immediate filing of a Petition for Disciplinary or Remedial Action, with or without collateral remedial proceedings, in accordance with Rules 16-771, 16-773, or 16-774. (Added Nov. 30, 2000, effective July 1, 2001.)

Consideration of mental health issues. — Bar Counsel's recommendation of disbarment with regard to an attorney found to have violated Md. R. Prof. Conduct 1.15(a), (b), and (c), and Md. R. Prof. Conduct 8.4(b), (c), and (d), was not accepted by the Maryland Court of Appeals; the disciplinary matter was remanded for the Attorney Grievance Commission and Bar Counsel to reconsider entering into a conditional diversion agreement with the attorney because, even though the evidence supported the finding of wilful misconduct, the attorney's mental health and severe depression was a significant factor, and the Court of Appeal's interpretation of Rule 16-736 allowed diversion as a sanction in such cases where the professional misconduct was not solely the result of wilful or intentionally dishonest conduct. Att'y Griev. Comm'n v. Cappell, 389 Md. 402, 886 A.2d 112 (2005).

Source. — This Rule is new.

Cited in Att'y Griev. Comm'n v. Lee, 387 Md.
89, 874 A.2d 897 (2005).

Rule 16-735. Dismissal or other termination of complaint.

(a) **Dismissal or termination.** (1) Upon completion of an investigation, Bar Counsel or, after a Peer Review Panel meeting, the Peer Review Panel, may recommend to the Commission that:

(A) the complaint be dismissed because Bar Counsel or the Panel has concluded that the evidence fails to show that the attorney has engaged in professional misconduct or is incapacitated; or

(B) the disciplinary or remedial proceeding be terminated, with or without a warning because Bar Counsel or the Panel has concluded that any professional misconduct on the part of the attorney (i) was not sufficiently serious to warrant discipline and (ii) is not likely to be repeated.

(2) If satisfied with the recommendation of Bar Counsel or the Panel, the Commission shall dismiss the complaint or otherwise terminate the disciplinary or remedial proceeding, as appropriate. If Bar Counsel or the Panel has recommended a warning, the matter shall proceed as provided in section (b) of this Rule.

(b) **Termination accompanied by warning.** (1) If Bar Counsel or the Panel concludes that the attorney may have engaged in some professional misconduct, that the conduct was not sufficiently serious to warrant discipline, but that a specific warning to the attorney would be helpful to ensure that the conduct is not repeated, Bar Counsel or the Panel may recommend that the termination be accompanied by a warning against repetition. If satisfied with the recommendation, the Commission shall proceed in accordance with subsection (b) (2) of this Rule and, if the warning is not rejected, accompany the termination of the disciplinary or remedial proceeding with a warning. A warning does not constitute discipline, but the complainant shall be notified that termination of the proceeding was accompanied by a warning against repetition of the conduct.

(2) At least 30 days before a warning is issued, the Commission shall mail to the attorney a notice that states the date on which it intends to issue the warning and the content of the warning. No later than five days before the intended date of issuance of the warning, the attorney may reject the warning by filing a written rejection with the Commission. If the warning is not rejected, the Commission shall issue it on or after the date stated in the initial notice to the attorney. If the warning is rejected, it shall not be issued, and Bar Counsel or the Commission may take any other action permitted under this Chapter. Neither the fact that a warning was proposed or rejected nor the contents of a warning that was not issued may be admitted into evidence.

(c) **Effect of dismissal or termination.** (1) Except as provided in subsection (c) (2) of this Rule, a dismissal or a termination under this Rule, with or without a warning, shall not be disclosed by the Commission or Bar Counsel in response to any request for information as to whether an attorney has been the subject of a disciplinary or remedial proceeding. The nature and existence of a proceeding terminated under this Rule, including any investigation by Bar

Counsel that led to the proceeding, need not be disclosed by an attorney in response to a request for information as to whether the attorney has been the subject of a disciplinary or remedial proceeding.

(2) The fact that a warning was issued in conjunction with the termination of a complaint shall be disclosed to the complainant, and the fact that a warning was issued and the facts underlying the warning may be disclosed in a subsequent proceeding against the attorney when relevant to a complaint alleging similar misconduct. (Added Nov. 30, 2000, effective July 1, 2001; amended Oct. 31, 2002, effective Jan. 1, 2003; Dec. 4, 2007, effective Jan. 1, 2008.)

Source. — This Rule is new.

Effect of amendments. — The 2002 amendment, in (c)(2), inserted "the fact that a warning was issued and the facts underlying the warning" and substituted "complaint alleging" for "subsequent complaint based on."

The December 4, 2007 Order, effective January 1, 2008, added "or the Panel" following "Bar Counsel" throughout the Rule; in (a) (1) added "or, after a Peer Review Panel meeting, the Peer Review Panel"; in (a) (2) substituted "the recommendation of Bar Counsel or the Panel" for "Bar Counsel's recommendation"; and added "or the Commission" or variant in (b) (2), fourth sentence, and (c) (1), first sentence.

Warning. — For a finding that an attorney violated Rule 1.15(b) of the Rules of Professional Conduct, the court of appeals remanded the case to the Attorney Grievance Commission for it to propose dismissal of the case with a warning to the attorney that his conduct in failing to notify a bank that settlement proceeds were paid to his client, and in failing to forward those proceeds to the bank, was a violation of Rule 1.15(b) that was not to be repeated. The warning was not discipline, but was simply an admonition against repetition of the conduct, and if the attorney rejected the warning, the court could consider an appropriate sanction. Att'y Griev. Comm'n v. Stolarz, 379 Md. 387, 842 A.2d 42 (2004).

Dismissal on request of complainant not proper. — Bar Counsel could not dismiss the complaint against the attorney merely because the complainant requested dismissal; Bar Counsel was obligated to investigate the complaint once it was made, and could dismiss the complaint only if the evidence failed to show sanctionable professional misconduct or incapacity. Att'y Griev. Comm'n v. Lee, 393 Md. 546, 903 A.2d 895 (2006).

Cited in Att'y Griev. Comm'n v. Saridakis, 402 Md. 413, 936 A.2d 886 (2007).

Rule 16-736. Conditional diversion agreement.

(a) **When appropriate.** Upon completing an investigation, Bar Counsel may agree to a Conditional Diversion Agreement if Bar Counsel concludes that:

(1) the attorney committed professional misconduct or is incapacitated;

(2) the professional misconduct or incapacity was not the result of any wilful or dishonest conduct and did not involve conduct that could be the basis for an immediate Petition for Disciplinary or Remedial Action pursuant to Rules 16-771, 16-773, or 16-774;

(3) the cause or basis of the professional misconduct or incapacity is subject to remediation or resolution through alternative programs or mechanisms, including (A) medical, psychological, or other professional treatment, counseling, or assistance, (B) appropriate educational courses or programs, (C) mentoring or monitoring services, or (D) dispute resolution programs; and

(4) the public interest and the welfare of the attorney's clients and prospective clients will not be harmed if, instead of the matter proceeding immediately

with a disciplinary or remedial proceeding, the attorney agrees to and complies with specific measures that, if pursued, will remedy the immediate problem and likely prevent any recurrence of it.

Committee note. — Examples of conduct that may be susceptible to conditional diversion include conduct arising from (A) unfamiliarity with proper methods of law office management, record-keeping, or accounting, (B) unfamiliarity with particular areas of law or legal procedure, (C) negligent management of attorney trust accounts or other financial matters, (D) negligent failure to maintain proper communication with clients, (E) negligent failure to provide proper supervision of employees, or (F) emotional stress or crisis or abuse of alcohol or other drugs.

(b) **Voluntary nature of Agreement; effect of rejection or disapproval.** Neither Bar Counsel nor an attorney is required to propose or enter into a Conditional Diversion Agreement. The Agreement shall state that the attorney voluntarily consents to its terms and promises to pay all expenses reasonably incurred in connection with its performance and enforcement. If a Conditional Diversion Agreement is proposed and rejected or if a signed Agreement is not approved by the Commission, Bar Counsel may take any other action permitted under this Chapter. Neither the fact that an Agreement was proposed, rejected, or not approved nor the contents of the Agreement may be admitted into evidence.

(c) **Terms of Conditional Diversion Agreement.** (1) A Conditional Diversion Agreement shall be in writing and signed by Bar Counsel, the attorney, and any monitor designated in the Agreement.

(2) The Agreement shall recite the basis for it, as set forth in section (a) of this Rule. By signing the Agreement, the attorney (A) acknowledges that the attorney has engaged in conduct that constitutes professional misconduct or is currently incapacitated, and (B) warrants that the attorney has not concealed from or misrepresented to Bar Counsel any material facts pertaining to the attorney's conduct or the Agreement.

(3) The Agreement shall state the particular course of remedial action that the attorney agrees to follow and a time for the performance or completion of that action. The Agreement is expressly conditioned on the attorney's not engaging in any further conduct that would constitute professional misconduct and may provide for any program or corrective action appropriate under the circumstances, including:

(A) mediation or binding arbitration of a fee dispute;

(B) restitution of unearned or excessive fees in a stipulated amount;

(C) public apology to designated individuals;

(D) law office management assistance, including temporary or continuing monitoring, mentoring, accounting, bookkeeping, financial, or other professional assistance, and completion of specific educational programs dealing with law office management;

(E) completion of specific legal education courses or curricula, including courses in legal ethics and professional responsibility;

(F) agreement not to practice in specific areas of the law (i) unless the attorney associates himself or herself with one or more other attorneys who are proficient in those areas, or (ii) until the attorney has successfully completed a designated course of study to improve the attorney's proficiency in those areas;

(G) specific course of treatment for emotional distress, mental disorder or disability, or dependence on alcohol or other drugs; and

(H) stipulated number of hours of pro bono legal services.

(4) The Agreement shall provide for a stay of any disciplinary or remedial proceeding pending satisfactory performance by the attorney. The Agreement may designate either a private monitor engaged at the attorney's expense or Bar Counsel to supervise performance and compliance. The Agreement shall authorize the monitor to request and receive all information and inspect any records necessary to verify compliance and, if a private monitor is selected, to report any violation or noncompliance to Bar Counsel. The Agreement shall specify the fees of any private monitor and the method and frequency of payment of those fees.

(d) **Approval by Commission.** A Conditional Diversion Agreement is not valid until approved by the Commission. Upon signing the Agreement, Bar Counsel and the attorney shall submit to the Commission the Agreement, any explanatory material that they believe relevant, and any further information that the Commission requests. The Commission may:

(1) approve the Agreement if satisfied that it is reasonable and in the public interest;

(2) disapprove the Agreement if not convinced that it is reasonable and in the public interest; or

(3) recommend amendments to the Agreement as a condition of approval, which the parties may accept or reject. If Bar Counsel and the attorney accept the amendments, they shall notify the Commission of the acceptance, and the Commission shall then approve the Agreement. If either party rejects a proposed amendment, the Agreement shall be deemed disapproved.

(e) **Amendment of Agreement.** A Conditional Diversion Agreement may be amended from time to time in a writing signed by Bar Counsel and the attorney and approved by the Commission.

(f) **Revocation of Agreement.** (1) Bar Counsel may declare a proposed default on a Conditional Diversion Agreement if Bar Counsel determines that the attorney (A) engaged in further professional misconduct while subject to the agreement, (B) wilfully misrepresented or concealed material facts during the negotiation of the Agreement that induced Bar Counsel to recommend approval of the Agreement, or (C) has failed in a material way to comply with the Agreement. Bar Counsel shall give written notice to the attorney of the proposed default and afford the attorney a reasonable opportunity to refute the determination.

(2) If the attorney fails to refute the charge or to offer an explanation or proposed remedy satisfactory to Bar Counsel, Bar Counsel shall file a petition with the Commission to revoke the Agreement and serve a copy of the petition on the attorney. The attorney may file a written response with the Commission within 15 days after service of the petition. The Commission may act upon the petition and response or may request the parties to supply additional information, in writing or in person.

(3) If the Commission concludes that the attorney is in material default of the Agreement, it shall revoke the Agreement, revoke the stay of the disciplin-

ary or remedial proceeding, and direct Bar Counsel to proceed in accordance with Rule 16-751, or as otherwise authorized by the Rules in this Chapter.

(g) **Satisfaction of Agreement.** If Bar Counsel determines that the attorney has complied in full with the requirements of the Agreement and that the disciplinary or remedial proceeding should be terminated, Bar Counsel shall inform the Commission and request that the disciplinary or remedial proceeding be terminated. If satisfied with Bar Counsel's recommendation, the Commission shall terminate the disciplinary or remedial proceeding.

(h) **Effect of Agreement.** (1) Approval by the Commission of a Conditional Diversion Agreement does not constitute discipline.

(2) Except as provided in subsections (h) (4) and (h) (5) of this Rule, the contents of the Agreement are confidential and may not be disclosed.

(3) Upon approval of an Agreement by the Commission, Bar Counsel shall inform the complainant that such an Agreement has been entered into and approved, that the disciplinary or remedial proceeding has been stayed in favor of the Agreement, and that, if the attorney complies with the Agreement, the proceeding will be terminated. The complainant shall also be notified of the potential for and consequences of noncompliance. Except to the extent that the Agreement requires the transfer of property to the complainant or other communication with the complainant, the terms of the Agreement shall not be disclosed.

(4) Upon revocation of an Agreement pursuant to section (f) of this Rule, the contents of the Agreement lose their confidentiality and may be disclosed in any ensuing disciplinary or remedial proceeding.

(5) The contents of an Agreement may be disclosed in a subsequent proceeding against the attorney when relevant to a subsequent complaint based on similar misconduct. (Added Nov. 30, 2000, effective July 1, 2001.)

Source. — This Rule is new.

Applicability — Even though an attorney's disciplinary proceeding was commenced and would normally have been governed by superseded procedures, the Court of Appeals directed that the case of an attorney with serious mental illness be dealt with, if appropriate, under new rules allowing for disposition by conditional diversion agreement, if one could be reached, or by placement on inactive status. Att'y Griev. Comm'n v. Olver, 376 Md. 650, 831 A.2d 66 (2003).

Construction — Even if disciplinary proceedings have already been commenced against an attorney, if competent evidence exists from which Bar Counsel and the Attorney Grievance Commission may conclude that the attorney's unprofessional conduct was not solely the result of wilful or intentionally dishonest conduct, conditional diversion may be an appropriate disposition. Att'y Griev. Comm'n v. Cappell, 389 Md. 402, 886 A.2d 112 (2005).

Even if disciplinary proceedings have already been commenced against an attorney, if competent evidence exists from which Bar Counsel and the Attorney Grievance Commission may conclude that the attorney's unprofessional conduct was not solely the result of wilful or intentionally dishonest conduct, conditional diversion may be an appropriate disposition. Att'y Griev. Comm'n v. Cappell, 389 Md. 402, 886 A.2d 112 (2005).

Consideration of mental health issues — Bar Counsel's recommendation of disbarment with regard to an attorney found to have violated Md. R. Prof. Conduct 1.15(a), (b), and (c), and Md. R.Prof. Conduct 8.4(b), (c), and (d), was not accepted by the Maryland Court of Appeals; the disciplinary matter was remanded for the Attorney Grievance Commission and Bar Counsel to reconsider entering into a conditional diversion agreement with the attorney because, even though the evidence supported the finding of wilful misconduct, the attorney's mental health and severe depression was a significant factor, and the Court of Appeal's interpretation of this Rule allowed diversion as a sanction in such cases where the professional misconduct was not solely the result of wilful or intentionally dishonest conduct. Att'y Griev. Comm'n v. Cappell, 389 Md. 402, 886 A.2d 112 (2005).

Bar Counsel's recommendation of disbarment with regard to an attorney found to have violated Md. R. Prof. Conduct 1.15(a), (b), and (c), and Md. R. Prof. Conduct 8.4(b), (c), and (d), was not accepted by the Maryland Court of Appeals; the disciplinary matter was remanded for the Attorney Grievance Commission and Bar Counsel to reconsider entering into a conditional diversion agreement with the attorney because, even though the evidence supported the finding of wilful misconduct, the attorney's mental health and severe depression was a significant factor, and the Court of Appeal's interpretation of this Rule allowed diversion as a sanction in such cases where the professional misconduct was not solely the result of wilful or intentionally dishonest conduct. Att'y Griev. Comm'n v. Cappell, 389 Md. 402, 886 A.2d 112 (2005).

Admissibility of evidence. — When an attorney was alleged to have violated Md. Law. R. Prof. Conduct 1.4(a) and (b) and 8.4(a), (b), (c), and (d), as well as § 7-302 of the Criminal Law Article by altering the attorney's employer law firm's electronic files to facilitate taking certain of the firm's clients with the attorney when the attorney left the firm, it was not error to rule that the report of a peer review panel and communications between the attorney's counsel and Bar Counsel about the possibility of a conditional diversion agreement were inadmissible because (1) the report and communications were irrelevant to the attorney's charged conduct and mitigation of the attorney's sanction, (2) the report was merely a recommendation to the Attorney Grievance Commission, and not the Court of Appeals, and (3) there was no authority to support remanding the case to reconsider the availability of a conditional diversion agreement. Att'y Griev. Comm'n v. Keiner, — Md. —, — A.3d — (Aug. 19, 2011).

Stated in Att'y Griev. Comm'n v. Lee, 387 Md. 89, 874 A.2d 897 (2005).

Cited in Att'y Griev. Comm'n v. James, 385 Md. 637, 870 A.2d 229 (2005); Att'y Griev. Comm'n v. Robertson, 400 Md. 618, 929 A.2d 576 (2007); Att'y Griev. Comm'n v. Khandpur, 421 Md. 1, 25 A.3d 165 (2011).

Rule 16-737. Reprimand by Commission.

(a) **Offer.** If Bar Counsel determines after completion of an investigation, or the Peer Review Panel determines after a Panel meeting, that an attorney has engaged in professional misconduct and that the appropriate sanction for the misconduct is a reprimand, Bar Counsel or the Panel shall serve on the attorney a written offer of a reprimand and a waiver of further disciplinary or remedial proceedings that is contingent upon acceptance of the reprimand by the attorney and approval of the reprimand by the Commission. The offer shall include the text of the proposed reprimand, the date when the offer will expire, a contingent waiver of further disciplinary or remedial proceedings, and advice that the offer, if accepted, is subject to approval by the Commission. The text of the proposed reprimand shall summarize the misconduct for which the reprimand is to be imposed and include a reference to any rule, statute, or other law allegedly violated by the attorney.

(b) **Response.** The attorney may accept the offer by signing the stipulation, endorsing the proposed reprimand, and delivering both documents to Bar Counsel or the Panel within the time stated in the notice or otherwise agreed to by Bar Counsel or the Panel. The attorney may (1) reject the offer expressly or by declining to return the documents timely, or (2) propose amendments to the proposed reprimand, which Bar Counsel or the Panel may accept, reject, or negotiate.

(c) **Action by Commission.** If the attorney agrees to a reprimand, Bar Counsel or the Panel shall submit the proposed reprimand to the Commission for approval. Bar Counsel or the attorney may submit also any explanatory material that either believes relevant and shall submit any further material that the Commission requests. Upon the submission, the Commission may take any of the following actions:

(1) the Commission may approve the reprimand, if satisfied that it is appropriate under the circumstances, in which event Bar Counsel shall promptly administer the reprimand to the attorney and terminate the disciplinary or remedial proceeding.

(2) the Commission may recommend amendments to the reprimand as a condition of approval, which the parties may accept or reject. If the parties accept the amendments, they shall notify the Commission of the acceptance, and the Commission shall then approve the reprimand. If either party rejects a proposed amendment, the reprimand shall be deemed disapproved.

(3) the Commission may disapprove the reprimand, if not satisfied that it is appropriate under the circumstances and direct Bar Counsel to proceed in another manner.

(d) **Effect of rejection or disapproval.** If a reprimand is proposed and rejected or if a reprimand to which the parties have stipulated is not approved by the Commission, the proceeding shall resume as if no reprimand had been proposed, and neither the fact that a reprimand was proposed, rejected, or not approved nor the contents of the reprimand and any stipulation may be admitted into evidence.

(e) **Effect of reprimand.** A reprimand constitutes discipline. (Added Nov. 30, 2000, effective July 1, 2001; Dec. 4, 2007, effective Jan. 1, 2008.)

Source. — This Rule is new.

Effect of amendments. — The December 4, 2007 Order, effective January 1, 2008, added "or the Panel" following "Bar Counsel" throughout the Rule; in (a), first and second sentences added "or the Peer Review Panel determines after a Panel meeting" and "that is contingent upon acceptance of the reprimand by the attorney and approval of the reprimand by the Commission" substituted "of a reprimand and a waiver" for "to administer a reprimand and enter into a joint waiver" and "a contingent waiver of" for "stipulation for waiving"; and in (c), first and second sentences substituted "attorney agrees" for "parties agree", "Bar Counsel or the Panel" for "they", "Bar Counsel or the attorney" for "The parties" and "either believes" for "they believe".

Recommendations inadmissible — Circuit court judge had not erred in refusing to admit evidence of Bar Counsel's proposed disposition and a peer review recommendation, as subsection (d) precluded their admission. Att'y Griev. Comm'n v. Brooke, 374 Md. 155, 821 A.2d 414 (2003).

Prior reprimand. — Attorney's conduct in violating State professional conduct rules in representing a client by not informing the client that the attorney would not be representing the client at a removal proceeding regarding the client's immigration status, plus the attorney's prior reprimand pursuant to this Rule, dictated that the attorney be disciplined. Att'y Griev. Comm'n v. Akpan, 405 Md. 277, 950 A.2d 820 (2008).

Rule 16-741. Statement of Charges.

(a) **Filing of Statement of Charges.** (1) Upon completion of an investigation, Bar Counsel shall file with the Commission a Statement of Charges if Bar Counsel determines that:

(A) the attorney either engaged in conduct constituting professional misconduct or is incapacitated;

(B) the professional misconduct or the incapacity does not warrant an immediate Petition for Disciplinary or Remedial Action;

(C) a Conditional Diversion Agreement is either not appropriate under the circumstances or the parties were unable to agree on one; and

(D) a reprimand is either not appropriate under the circumstances or (i) one was offered and rejected by the attorney, or (ii) a proposed reprimand was disapproved by the Commission and Bar Counsel was directed to file a Statement of Charges.

(2) Bar Counsel shall include with the Statement of Charges a fair summary of the evidence developed through the investigation, including any response that the attorney sent to Bar Counsel regarding the matter.

(b) **Service of Statement of Charges; Peer Review.** Bar Counsel shall serve on the attorney and send to the Chair of the Peer Review Committee a copy of the Statement of Charges, together with the supporting documentation filed pursuant to subsection (a) (2) of this Rule. The matter shall then proceed in accordance with Rules 16-742 and 16-743. (Added Nov. 30, 2000, effective July 1, 2001.)

Cross references. — See Rule 16-724 (a) concerning service of the Statement of Charges on the attorney.

Source. — This Rule is new.

Applicability — Even though an attorney's disciplinary proceeding was commenced and would normally have been governed by superseded procedures, the Court of Appeals directed that the case of an attorney with serious mental illness be dealt with, if appropriate, under new rules allowing for disposition by conditional diversion agreement, if one could be reached, or by placement on inactive status. Att'y Griev. Comm'n v. Olver, 376 Md. 650, 831 A.2d 66 (2003).

When formal charges exist. — Formal charges of misconduct do not exist against an attorney until a complaint is docketed in the Court of Appeals. Att'y Griev. Comm'n v. Bailey, 285 Md. 631, 403 A.2d 1261 (1979).

Purpose of written form. — The former rule concerning charges was designed to insure that the attorney is afforded notice and the opportunity to defend him or herself against the charges; the notice to which the attorney is entitled is of the factual allegations against which the attorney must defend. Att'y Griev. Comm'n v. Myers, 333 Md. 440, 635 A.2d 1315 (1994).

Charges must be sufficiently clear and specific. — While the former Rule governing charges did not require that the charges be set forth in any certain form or in extensive detail, it did establish a requirement that the charges be "sufficiently clear and specific" so as to make the attorney aware of what he is compelled to answer for and defend against. Bar Ass'n v. Cockrell, 270 Md. 686, 313 A.2d 816 (1974).

So long as the petition informs the attorney of the misconduct charged in language which is clear and sufficiently specific to enable the attorney to prepare a defense, the charges need not be set out in any particular form. Att'y Griev. Comm'n v. Fezell, 361 Md. 234, 760 A.2d 1108 (2000).

Any rule without such requirement would violate due process. — Any rule which did not require the degree of specificity of the charges prescribed in this Rule would violate the minimum requirements of constitutional due process mandated by the Maryland Declaration of Rights. Bar Ass'n v. Cockrell, 270 Md. 686, 313 A.2d 816 (1974).

Charges filed must embody disciplinary rule most probably violated. — See Att'y Griev. Comm'n v. Wright, 306 Md. 93, 507 A.2d 618 (1986).

Order disciplining lawyer in absence of charge. — Under the prior Rule governing "charges", any order disciplining a lawyer based on a finding by the hearing court of a particular form of professional misconduct would be a violation where the lawyer had not been charged in the Bar Association's petition with that particular misconduct, since it cannot be validly contended that the failure to allege that charge in any form is a charge in writing "sufficiently clear and specific reasonably to inform the attorney proceeded against" of the misconduct alleged. Bar Ass'n v. Cockrell, 270 Md. 686, 313 A.2d 816 (1974).

Indication that alleged conduct was vi-

olation of specific rule not required. — The command of the former Rule governing charges did not require Bar Counsel when he petitioned the Court of Appeals for disciplinary action against an attorney to say that the alleged conduct was a violation of a specific rule, but it was the factual allegation against which the individual had to defend himself. Att'y Griev. Comm'n v. McBurney, 282 Md. 116, 383 A.2d 58 (1978).

Authority of Bar Counsel. — The fact that the Review Board did not specify that Bar Counsel should file charges against defendant under Rules 8.4 (b) and (d) of the Rules of Professional Conduct, did not violate the former Rule; the charges were plainly related and within the authority vested in Bar Counsel. Att'y Griev. Comm'n v. Hamby, 322 Md. 606, 589 A.2d 53 (1991).

It was not improper for Bar Counsel to charge in a disciplinary petition a number of rule violations not specifically found by the former Review Board. Att'y Griev. Comm'n v. Goldsborough, 330 Md. 342, 624 A.2d 503 (1993).

The former Rule governing charges required the Bar Counsel, "acting at the direction of the Review Board," to file charges against an attorney. Att'y Griev. Comm'n v. Myers, 333 Md. 440, 635 A.2d 1315 (1994).

If Bar Counsel wished to specify a violation — Under prior Rule giverning "charges", if Bar Counsel wished to specify a violation of certain disciplinary rules in the petition to the Court of Appeals, then he should have selected all rules which conceivably might have had application to the facts of the particular case, because he was limited in the disciplinary action by such rules as he selected. Att'y Griev. Comm'n v. McBurney, 282 Md. 116, 383 A.2d 58 (1978).

Quoted in Att'y Griev. Comm'n v. McCoy, 369 Md. 226, 798 A.2d 1132 (2002); Att'y Griev. Comm'n v. Santos, 370 Md. 77, 803 A.2d 505 (2002); Att'y Griev. Comm'n v. McClain, 373 Md. 196, 817 A.2d 218 (2003); Att'y Griev. Comm'n v. McClain, 373 Md. 196, 817 A.2d 218 (2003); Att'y Griev. Comm'n v. DeMaio, 379 Md. 571, 842 A.2d 802 (2004); Att'y Griev. Comm'n v. Somerville, 379 Md. 586, 842 A.2d 811 (2004); Att'y Griev. Comm'n v. Sperling, 380 Md. 180, 844 A.2d 397 (2004); Att'y Griev. Comm'n v. Lee, 387 Md. 89, 874 A.2d 897 (2005); Att'y Griev. Comm'n v. Guberman, 392 Md. 131, 896 A.2d 337 (2006); Att'y Griev. Comm'n v. Lanocha, 392 Md. 234, 896 A.2d 996 (2006).

Cited in Att'y Griev. Comm'n v. Kinnane, 390 Md. 324, 888 A.2d 1178 (2005).

Rule 16-742. Peer Review Panel.

(a) **Appointment.** Within 30 days after receiving a copy of a Statement of Charges filed with the Commission, the Chair of the Peer Review Committee shall (1) appoint a Peer Review Panel, (2) notify the Commission, Bar Counsel, and the attorney of the appointment of the Panel and the names and addresses of its members, (3) send to the members of the Panel a copy of the Statement of Charges and the supporting material filed by Bar Counsel with the Commission, and (4) in accordance with Rule 16-743 (b), schedule a meeting of the Peer Review Panel.

(b) **Composition of Panel.** The Peer Review Panel shall consist of at least three members of the Peer Review Committee. A majority of the members of the Panel shall be attorneys, but at least one member shall not be an attorney. If practicable, the Chair shall appoint to the Panel members from the circuit in which the attorney who is the subject of the charges has an office for the practice of law or, if there is no such office, the circuit in which the last known address of the attorney, as reflected on the records of the Client Protection Fund of the Bar of Maryland, is located.

(c) **Panel Chair.** The Chair of the Peer Review Committee shall appoint an attorney member of the Panel as the Panel Chair.

(d) **Removal and recusal of members.** The Chair of the Peer Review Committee may remove a member of the Peer Review Panel for cause. A member of a Peer Review Panel shall not participate in any proceeding in which the member's impartiality might reasonably be questioned. A member who is required to recuse or who cannot attend the Peer Review meeting shall immediately notify the Chair of the Peer Review Committee, who shall promptly appoint another member.

(e) **Quorum.** The presence of any three members of the Peer Review Panel constitutes a quorum, whether or not a non-attorney member is present. With the consent of the Panel members who are present, Bar Counsel and the attorney may waive the quorum requirement. The concurrence of a majority of the members present is necessary to a recommendation to the Commission. (Added Nov. 30, 2000, effective July 1, 2001; amended effective Nov. 6, 2002.)

Source. — This Rule is new.

Effect of amendments. — The 2002 amendment substituted "Client Protection Fund of the Bar of Maryland" for "Clients' Security Trust Fund" in (b).

Stated in Att'y Griev. Comm'n v. Lee, 387 Md. 89, 874 A.2d 897 (2005).

Cited in Att'y Griev. Comm'n v. Guberman, 392 Md. 131, 896 A.2d 337 (2006); Att'y Griev. Comm'n v. Lanocha, 392 Md. 234, 896 A.2d 996 (2006); Att'y Griev. Comm'n v. Pak, 400 Md. 567, 929 A.2d 546 (2007), cert. denied, 128 S. Ct. 905, 2008 U.S. LEXIS 126, 169 L. Ed. 2d 729 (U.S. 2008).

Rule 16-743. Peer review process.

(a) **Purpose of peer review process.** The purpose of the peer review process is for the Peer Review Panel to consider the Statement of Charges and all relevant information offered by Bar Counsel and the attorney concerning it and to determine (1) whether the Statement of Charges has a substantial basis and there is reason to believe that the attorney has committed professional misconduct or is incapacitated, and, if so, (2) whether a Petition for Disciplinary or Remedial Action should be filed or some other disposition is appropriate. The peer review process is not intended to be an adversarial one and it is not the function of Peer Review Panels to hold evidentiary hearings, adjudicate facts, or write full opinions or reports.

Committee note. — If a Peer Review Panel concludes that the complaint has a substantial basis indicating the need for some remedy, some behavioral or operational changes on the part of the lawyer, or some discipline short of suspension or disbarment, part of the peer review process can be an attempt through both evaluative and facilitative dialogue, (A) to effectuate directly or suggest a mechanism for effecting an amicable resolution of the existing dispute between the lawyer and the complainant, and (B) to encourage the lawyer to recognize any deficiencies on his or her part that led to the problem and take appropriate remedial steps to address those deficiencies. The goal, in this setting, is not to punish or stigmatize the lawyer or to create a fear that any admission of deficiency will result in substantial harm, but rather to create an ambience for a constructive solution. The objective views of two fellow lawyers and a lay person, expressed in the form of advice and opinion rather than in the form of adjudication, may assist the lawyer (and the complainant) to retreat from confrontational positions and look at the problem more realistically.

(b) **Scheduling of meeting; notice to attorney.** (1) The Chair of the Peer Review Committee, after consultation with the members of the Peer Review Panel, Bar Counsel, and the attorney, shall schedule a meeting of the Panel.

(2) If, without substantial justification, the attorney does not agree to schedule a meeting within the time provided in subsection (b) (5) of this Rule, the Chair may recommend to the Commission that the peer review process be

terminated. If the Commission terminates the peer review process pursuant to this subsection, the Commission may take any action that could be recommended by the Peer Review Panel under section (e) of this Rule.

(3) The Chair shall notify Bar Counsel, the attorney, and each complainant of the time, place, and purpose of the meeting and invite their attendance.

(4) The notice to the attorney shall inform the attorney of the attorney's right to respond in writing to the Statement of Charges by filing a written response with the Commission and sending a copy of it to Bar Counsel and each member of the Peer Review Panel at least ten days before the scheduled meeting.

(5) Unless the time is extended by the Commission, the meeting shall occur within 60 days after appointment of the Panel.

(c) **Meeting.** (1) The Peer Review Panel shall conduct the meeting in an informal manner. It shall allow Bar Counsel, the attorney, and each complainant to explain their positions and offer such supporting information as the Panel finds relevant. Upon request of Bar Counsel or the attorney, the Panel may, but need not, hear from any other person. The Panel is not bound by any rules of evidence, but shall respect lawful privileges. The Panel may exclude a complainant after listening to the complainant's statement and, as a mediative technique, may consult separately with Bar Counsel or the attorney. The Panel may meet in private to deliberate.

(2) If the Panel determines that the Statement of Charges has a substantial basis and that there is reason to believe that the attorney has committed professional misconduct or is incapacitated, the Panel may (A) conclude the meeting and make an appropriate recommendation to the Commission or (B) inform the parties of its determination and allow the attorney an opportunity to consider a reprimand or a Conditional Diversion Agreement.

(3) The Panel may schedule one or more further meetings, but, unless the time is extended by the Commission, it shall make a recommendation to the Commission within 90 days after appointment of the Panel. If a recommendation is not made within that time or any extension granted by the Commission, the peer review process shall be terminated and the Commission may take any action that could be recommended by the Peer Review Panel under section (e) of this Rule.

(d) **Ex parte communications.** Except for administrative communications with the Chair of the Peer Review Committee and as allowed under subsection (c) (1) as part of the peer review meeting process, no member of the Panel shall participate in an ex parte communication concerning the substance of the Statement of Charges with Bar Counsel, the attorney, the complainant, or any other person.

(e) **Recommendation of Peer Review Panel.** (1) Agreed Upon Recommendation. If Bar Counsel and the attorney agree upon a recommended disposition, the Peer Review Panel shall transmit that recommendation to the Commission. If a Peer Review Panel determines that the attorney committed professional misconduct, or is incapacitated, and that the parties should enter into a Conditional Diversion Agreement, the Panel shall orally advise the parties of that determination and afford them an opportunity to enter into a

Conditional Diversion Agreement in accordance with Rule 16-736. If agreement is reached, the Conditional Diversion Agreement shall be the Panel's recommended disposition.

(2) If No Agreement. If there is no agreed-upon recommendation under subsection (e) (1) of this Rule, the Panel shall transmit to the Commission an independent recommendation, not subject to the approval of Bar Counsel, and shall accompany its recommendation with a brief explanatory statement. The Panel's recommendation shall be one of the following:

(A) the filing of a Petition for Disciplinary or Remedial Action;

(B) a reprimand in accordance with Rule 16-737;

(C) dismissal of the complaint or termination of the proceeding without discipline, but with a warning, in accordance with Rule 16-735; or

(D) dismissal of the complaint or termination of the proceeding without discipline and without a warning, in accordance with Rule 16-735.

(f) **Action by Commission.** The Commission may (1) direct Bar Counsel to file a Petition for Disciplinary or Remedial Action, (2) take any action on the Panel's recommendation that the Commission may take on a similar recommendation made by Bar Counsel under Rule 16-734, or (3) dismiss the Statement of Charges and terminate the proceeding. (Added Nov. 30, 2000, effective July 1, 2001; amended Oct. 31, 2002, effective Jan. 1, 2003; Dec. 4, 2007, effective Jan. 1, 2008.)

Source. — This Rule is new.

Effect of amendments. — The 2002 amendment, in (e), inserted "recommend to the Commission that a Petition for Disciplinary or Remedial Action be filed or" and substituted "or (c)" for "(c), or (e)"; and rewrote (f).

The December 4, 2007 Order, effective January 1, 2008, in (a) made an adjustment to the (2) designation, rewrote (e); and in (f) (1) substituted "direct Bar Counsel to file" for "approve the filing of".

Limited function — Hearing court did not err in refusing to admit into evidence the Peer Review Panel report; the Peer Review Panel were not meant to be admitted into evidence since its proceedings were confidential and the Peer Review Panel performed a limited function of reviewing disciplinary charges to make a preliminary determination of what disposition of them might be appropriate. Att'y Griev. Comm'n v. Kinnane, 390 Md. 324, 888 A.2d 1178 (2005).

Applied in Att'y Griev. Comm'n v. Duvall, 384 Md. 234, 863 A.2d 291 (2004).

Quoted in Att'y Griev. Comm'n v. MacDougall, 384 Md. 271, 863 A.2d 312 (2004); Att'y Griev. Comm'n v. Lee, 387 Md. 89, 874 A.2d 897 (2005); Att'y Griev. Comm'n v. Calhoun, 391 Md. 532, 894 A.2d 518 (2006); Att'y Griev. Comm'n v. Robertson, 400 Md. 618, 929 A.2d 576 (2007).

Cited in Att'y Griev. Comm'n v. Guberman, 392 Md. 131, 896 A.2d 337 (2006); Att'y Griev. Comm'n v. Lanocha, 392 Md. 234, 896 A.2d 996 (2006); Att'y Griev. Comm'n v. Hill, 398 Md. 95, 919 A.2d 1194 (2007); Att'y Griev. Comm'n v. Pak, 400 Md. 567, 929 A.2d 546 (2007), cert. denied, 128 S. Ct. 905, 2008 U.S. LEXIS 126, 169 L. Ed. 2d 729 (U.S. 2008); Att'y Griev. Comm'n v. Keiner, — Md. —, — A.3d — (Aug. 19, 2011).

Rule 16-751. Petition for disciplinary or remedial action.

(a) **Commencement of disciplinary or remedial action.** (1) Upon approval or direction of Commission. Upon approval or direction of the Commission, Bar Counsel shall file a Petition for Disciplinary or Remedial Action in the Court of Appeals.

(2) **Conviction of crime; reciprocal action.** If authorized by Rule 16-771 (b) or 16-773 (b), Bar Counsel may file a Petition for Disciplinary or Remedial Action in the Court of Appeals without prior approval of the Commission. Bar Counsel promptly shall notify the Commission of the filing. The Commission on review may direct the withdrawal of a petition that was filed pursuant to this subsection.

Cross references. — See Rule 16-723 (b) (8) concerning confidentiality of a petition to place an incapacitated attorney on inactive status.

(b) **Parties.** The petition shall be filed in the name of the Commission, which shall be called the petitioner. The attorney shall be called the respondent.

(c) **Form of petition.** The petition shall be sufficiently clear and specific to inform the respondent of any professional misconduct charged and the basis of any allegation that the respondent is incapacitated and should be placed on inactive status. (Added Nov. 30, 2000, effective July 1, 2001; amended Oct. 31, 2002, effective Jan. 1, 2003; Nov. 12, 2003, effective Jan. 1, 2004; amended Sept. 10, 2009, effective Oct. 1, 2009.)

Source. — This Rule is derived in part from former Rules 16-709 (BV9) and 16-711 b 2 (BV11 b 2) and is in part new.

Effect of amendments. — The 2002 amendment substituted "Rule 16-723 (b) (8)" for "Rule 16-723 (b) (7)" in the cross-reference following (a).

The 2003 amendment redesignated former (a) as (a)(1), added the heading, and inserted "or direction"; added (a)(2); and in the Source note, inserted "in part" and "and is in part new."

The 2009 amendment added "or direction" in subsection heading of (a)(1).

Petition. — Where an attorney disciplinary proceeding had been ongoing through many years of investigation, the court proceedings were properly initiated in accordance with former Rule 16-709, instead of pursuant to this rule et seq., since the old rules applied to pending matters. Att'y Griev. Comm'n v. Gallagher, 371 Md. 673, 810 A.2d 996 (2002).

Willful failure to file tax returns. — State supreme court found that an attorney who failed to file Maryland withholding tax forms for his professional corporation, and also failed to file individual federal and state income tax returns for 1998, 1999, and 2000, violated Md. R. Prof. Conduct 8.4(b) and (d), and it ordered that the attorney be suspended for 30 days. Att'y Griev. Comm'n v. O'Toole, 379 Md. 595, 843 A.2d 50 (2004).

Decertification. — There are no mandatory bar dues in Maryland, since Maryland does not have a mandatory bar. Decertification is the sanction for the failure to pay Client Protection Fund assessments under Rule 16-811(f)(4). Att'y Griev. Comm'n v. Theriault, 390 Md. 202, 888 A.2d 292 (2005).

Public reprimand. — Attorney was sanctioned by a public reprimand for technically violating Rule 16-609 regarding prohibited transactions as a result of a negligent clerical error involving depositing some of his ex-girlfriend's funds into his operating account instead of his firm's escrow account, which error was corrected upon discovery and was not wilful. The Court of Appeals of Maryland further upheld the trial judge's finding of fact that no attorney client relationship existed between the attorney and his girlfriend to support the other violations asserted against him since he never charged his ex-girlfriend a fee for his services and was only helping her while she received treatment for her alcohol abuse. Att'y Griev. Comm'n v. Shoup, 410 Md. 462, 979 A.2d 120 (Aug. 28, 2009).

Sixty-day suspension. — In an attorney disciplinary matter, it was held that the attorney violated Md. R. Prof. Conduct 3.3 by filing expungement petitions for a client knowing that the client's charges were ineligible for expungement and, as a result, he was suspended from the practice of law for 60 days. Additionally, the findings and conclusions of the hearing officer that the attorney did not fraudulently obtain a duplicate driver's license after having his original license taken away at a sobriety checkpoint were found not to be clearly erroneous, and no deficiencies were found with regard to the allegations in the petition providing sufficient notice to the attorney of the charges against him. Att'y Griev. Comm'n v. Tanko, 408 Md. 404, 969 A.2d 1010 (2009).

Indefinite suspension — In a disciplinary action filed by a grievance committee pursuant to this rule, an attorney was found to have violated multiple rules of professional conduct, and as a sanction the attorney was indefinitely suspended with permission to reapply no sooner than six months, as the attorney's conduct showed disregard and neglect for the client, and brought the client severe distress, loss, and inconvenience, as the client lost her home due to the attorney's failure to file a bankruptcy petition. Att'y Griev. Comm'n v. Granger, 374 Md. 438, 823 A.2d 611 (2003).

Disbarment. — Attorney was disbarred under this Rule for misappropriation of client funds from his trust account, violating §§ 7-104, 7-113 of the Criminal Law Article, § 10-306 of the Business Occupations and Professions Article, Rule 16-609, Rules 1.15, 8.4 of the Maryland Lawyers Rules of Professional Conduct, and spousal abuse, violating § 3-203 of the Criminal Law Article. The attorney did not carry his burden to prove by a preponderance of the evidence any medical, psychiatric, or other condition to mitigate the findings of fact or conclusions of law. Att'y Griev. Comm'n v. Theriault, 390 Md. 202, 888 A.2d 292 (2005).

In an action in which petitioner, the Attorney Grievance Commission of Maryland, acting pursuant to this Rule, filed a petition for disciplinary or remedial action against respondent attorney, the appropriate sanction was disbarment where the court found that, as a matter of law, that respondent violated Md. R. Prof. Conduct 1.3, 1.4, 1.16, and 8.1. Att'y Griev. Comm'n v. Baker, 396 Md. 15, 912 A.2d 651 (2006).

In an attorney disciplinary matter, the attorney was disbarred as a result of having violated Rule 8.4(a)-(d) of the Lawyer's Rules of Professional Conduct based on his guilty plea to the federal crimes involving conspiracy to defraud the government, in violation of 18 U.S.C.S. §§ 371 and 1546(a), based on his actions in knowingly filing a false letter with the United States Immigration and Naturalization Service on behalf of a client/immigrant in an immigration proceeding. The Court of Appeals of Maryland found no compelling extenuating circumstances, including the attorney's great remorse, to except him from disbarment based on his intention to commit fraud, to deceive, and to misrepresent. Att'y Griev.

Comm'n v. Garcia, 410 Md. 507, 979 A.2d 146 (Aug. 28, 2009).

Applied in Att'y Griev. Comm'n v. Alsafty, 379 Md. 1, 838 A.2d 1213 (2003); Att'y Griev. Comm'n v. Brown, 380 Md. 661, 846 A.2d 428 (2004); Att'y Griev. Comm'n v. Duvall, 384 Md. 234, 863 A.2d 291 (2004); Att'y Griev. Comm'n v. Cherry-Mahoi, 388 Md. 124, 879 A.2d 58 (2005); Att'y Griev. Comm'n v. Rose, 391 Md. 101, 892 A.2d 469 (2006), cert. denied, 2006 U.S. LEXIS 5734, 166 L. Ed. 2d 22 (U.S. 2006); Att'y Griev. Comm'n v. Sweitzer, 395 Md. 586, 911 A.2d 440 (2006); Att'y Griev. Comm'n v. Rees, 396 Md. 248, 913 A.2d 68 (2006); Att'y Griev. Comm'n v. Goff, 399 Md. 1, 922 A.2d 554 (2007); Att'y Griev. Comm'n v. Sapero, 400 Md. 461, 929 A.2d 483 (2007); Att'y Griev. Comm'n v. Pak, 400 Md. 567, 929 A.2d 546 (2007), cert. denied, 128 S. Ct. 905, 2008 U.S. LEXIS 126, 169 L. Ed. 2d 729 (U.S. 2008); Att'y Griev. Comm'n v. Robertson, 400 Md. 618, 929 A.2d 576 (2007); Att'y Griev. Comm'n v. Floyd, 400 Md. 236, 929 A.2d 61 (2007); Att'y Griev. Comm'n v. Wingerter, 400 Md. 214, 929 A.2d 47 (2007).

Quoted in Att'y Griev. Comm'n v. Sheinbein, 372 Md. 224, 812 A.2d 981 (2002); Att'y Griev. Comm'n v. Seiden, 373 Md. 409, 818 A.2d 1108 (2003); Att'y Griev. Comm'n v. Gansler, 377 Md. 656, 835 A.2d 548 (2003); Att'y Griev. Comm'n v. Ayres-Fountain, 379 Md. 44, 838 A.2d 1238 (2003); Att'y Griev. Comm'n v. DeMaio, 379 Md. 571, 842 A.2d 802 (2004); Att'y Griev. Comm'n v. Somerville, 379 Md. 586, 842 A.2d 811 (2004); Att'y Griev. Comm'n v. Sperling, 380 Md. 180, 844 A.2d 397 (2004); Att'y Griev. Comm'n v. Mininsohn, 380 Md. 536, 846 A.2d 353 (2004); Att'y Griev. Comm'n v. Link, 380 Md. 405, 844 A.2d 1197 (2004); Att'y Griev. Comm'n v. Velasquez, 380 Md. 651, 846 A.2d 422 (2004); Att'y Griev. Comm'n v. Daskalopoulos, 383 Md. 375, 859 A.2d 653 (2004); Att'y Griev. Comm'n v. Rose, 383 Md. 385, 859 A.2d 659 (2004); Att'y Griev. Comm'n v. MacDougall, 384 Md. 271, 863 A.2d 312 (2004); Att'y Griev. Comm'n v. Brisbon, 385 Md. 667, 870 A.2d 586 (2005); Att'y Griev. Comm'n v. Steinberg, 385 Md. 696, 870 A.2d 603 (2005); Att'y Griev. Comm'n v. Zuckerman, 386 Md. 341, 872 A.2d 693 (2005); Att'y Griev. Comm'n v. Mitchell, 386 Md. 386, 872 A.2d 720 (2005); Att'y Griev. Comm'n v. Jordan, 386 Md. 583, 873 A.2d 1161 (2005); Att'y Griev. Comm'n v. Scroggs, 387 Md. 238, 874 A.2d 985 (2005); Att'y Griev. Comm'n v. Zakroff, 387 Md. 603, 876 A.2d 664 (2005), cert. denied, 2006 Md. LEXIS 561 (2006); cert. denied, 2006 Md. LEXIS 571 (Md. 2006); Att'y Griev. Comm'n v. Kovacic, 389 Md. 233, 884 A.2d 673 (2005); Att'y Griev. Comm'n v. Muhammad, — Md. —, — A.2d — (2005); Att'y Griev. Comm'n v. Lee, 390 Md. 517, 890 A.2d 273 (2005); Att'y Griev. Comm'n v. Holt, 391 Md. 673, 894 A.2d 602

(2006); Att'y Griev. Comm'n v. Kapoor, 391 Md. 505, 894 A.2d 502 (2006); Att'y Griev. Comm'n v. Guberman, 392 Md. 131, 896 A.2d 337 (2006); Att'y Griev. Comm'n v. Lanocha, 392 Md. 234, 896 A.2d 996 (2006); Att'y Griev. Comm'n v. Obi, 393 Md. 643, 904 A.2d 422 (2006); Att'y Griev. Comm'n v. Ward, 394 Md. 1, 904 A.2d 477 (2006); Att'y Griev. Comm'n v. Butler, 395 Md. 1, 909 A.2d 226 (2006); Att'y Griev. Comm'n v. Hill, 398 Md. 95, 919 A.2d 1194 (2007); Att'y Griev. Comm'n v. Parsons, 404 Md. 175, 946 A.2d 437 (2008); Att'y Griev. Comm'n v. Kreamer, 404 Md. 282, 946 A.2d 500 (2008); Att'y Griev. Comm'n v. Whitehead, 405 Md. 240, 950 A.2d 798 (2008); Att'y Griev. Comm'n v. McClain, 406 Md. 1, 956 A.2d 135 (2008), cert. denied, 129 S. Ct. 1691, 2009 U.S. LEXIS 2433, 173 L. Ed. 2d 1036 (U.S. 2009); Att'y Griev. Comm'n v. Snyder, 406 Md. 21, 956 A.2d 147 (2008); Att'y Griev. Comm'n v. Byrd, 408 Md. 449, 970 A.2d 870 (2009); Att'y Griev. Comm'n v. Hall, 408 Md. 306, 969 A.2d 953 (2009); Att'y Griev. Comm'n v. McLaughlin, 409 Md. 304, 974 A.2d 315 (2009); Att'y Griev. Comm'n v. Gisriel, 409 Md. 331, 974 A.2d 331 (2009); Att'y Griev. Comm'n v. Jarosinski, 411 Md. 432, 983 A.2d 477 (2009); Att'y Griev. Comm'n v. Robaton, 411 Md. 415, 983 A.2d 467 (2009); Att'y Griev. Comm'n v. Kwarteng, 411 Md. 652, 984 A.2d 865 (2009); Att'y Griev. Comm'n v. Gordon, 413 Md. 46, 991 A.2d 51 (2010); Att'y Griev. Comm'n v. Bleecker, 414 Md. 147, 994 A.2d 928 (2010); Att'y Griev. Comm'n v. Thaxton, 415 Md. 341, — A.2d —, 1 A.3d 470 (2010); Att'y Griev. Comm'n v. Lara, 418 Md. 355, 14 A.3d 650 (2011); Att'y Griev. Comm'n v. Coppola, 419 Md. 370, 19 A.3d 431 (2011); Att'y Griev. Comm'n v. Stern, 419 Md. 525, 19 A.3d 904 (2011); Att'y Griev. Comm'n v. Khandpur, 421 Md. 1, 25 A.3d 165 (2011).

Stated in Att'y Griev. Comm'n v. Prichard, 386 Md. 238, 872 A.2d 81 (2005); Att'y Griev. Comm'n v. Zodrow, 419 Md. 286, 19 A.3d 381 (2011).

Cited in Att'y Griev. Comm'n v. Roberson, 373 Md. 328, 818 A.2d 1059 (2003); Att'y Griev. Comm'n v. Ayres-Fountain, 379 Md. 44, 838 A.2d 1238 (2003); Att'y Griev. Comm'n v. James, 385 Md. 637, 870 A.2d 229 (2005); Att'y Griev. Comm'n v. Parker, 389 Md. 142, 884 A.2d 104 (2005); Att'y Griev. Comm'n v. Weiss, 389 Md. 531, 886 A.2d 606 (2005); Att'y Griev. Comm'n v. Kinnane, 390 Md. 324, 888 A.2d 1178 (2005); Att'y Griev. Comm'n v. Calhoun, 391 Md. 532, 894 A.2d 518 (2006); Att'y Griev. Comm'n v. Manger, 396 Md. 134, 913 A.2d 1 (2006); Att'y Griev. Comm'n v. Ward, 396 Md. 203, 913 A.2d 41 (2006); Att'y Griev. Comm'n v. Muhammad, 395 Md. 676, 912 A.2d 588 (2006), cert. denied, 127 S. Ct. 2296, 2007 U.S. LEXIS 5292, 167 L. Ed. 2d 1103 (U.S. 2007); Att'y Griev. Comm'n v. Hodgson, 396 Md. 1, 912 A.2d 640 (2006); Att'y Griev. Comm'n v. McCulloch, 397 Md. 674, 919 A.2d 660 (2007); Att'y Griev. Comm'n v. Mba-Jonas, 397 Md. 690, 919 A.2d 669 (2007); Att'y Griev. Comm'n v. Mahone, 398 Md. 257, 920 A.2d 458 (2007); Att'y Griev. Comm'n v. Nussbaum, 401 Md. 612, 934 A.2d 1 (2007); Att'y Griev. Comm'n v. Webster, 402 Md. 448, 937 A.2d 161 (2007); Att'y Griev. Comm'n v. Harris, 403 Md. 142, 939 A.2d 732 (2008); Att'y Griev. Comm'n v. Zuckerman, 403 Md. 695, 944 A.2d 525 (2008); Att'y Griev. Comm'n v. Elmendorf, 404 Md. 353, 946 A.2d 542 (2008); Att'y Griev. Comm'n v. McCulloch, 404 Md. 388, 946 A.2d 1009 (2008); Att'y Griev. Comm'n v. Smith, 405 Md. 107, 950 A.2d 101 (2008); Att'y Griev. Comm'n v. Nichols, 405 Md. 207, 950 A.2d 778 (2008); Att'y Griev. Comm'n v. Foltz, 411 Md. 359, 983 A.2d 434 (2009); Att'y Griev. Comm'n v. Carithers, 421 Md. 28, 25 A.3d 181 (2011); Att'y Griev. Comm'n v. Keiner, — Md. —, — A.3d — (Aug. 19, 2011).

Rule 16-752. Order designating judge.

(a) **Order.** Upon the filing of a Petition for Disciplinary or Remedial Action, the Court of Appeals may enter an order designating a judge of any circuit court to hear the action and the clerk responsible for maintaining the record. The order of designation shall require the judge, after consultation with Bar Counsel and the attorney, to enter a scheduling order defining the extent of discovery and setting dates for the completion of discovery, filing of motions, and hearing.

(b) **Service of petition and order.** Upon entry of an order under section (a) of this Rule, the clerk of the Court of Appeals shall send two copies to Bar Counsel. Bar Counsel shall serve a copy of the order and a copy of the petition on the respondent. The copies shall be served in accordance with Rule 16-753 or as otherwise ordered by the Court of Appeals.

(c) **Motion to amend order.** Within 15 days after the respondent has been served, either party may file a motion in accordance with Rule 8-431 requesting that the Court of Appeals designate another judge. The motion shall not stay the time for filing an answer to the petition. (Added Nov. 30, 2000, effective July 1, 2001.)

Source. — This Rule is derived from former Rules 16-709 b (BV9 b), 16-709 e 1 (BV9 e 1) and 16-710 c (BV10 c).

Referral court's findings supported by evidence. — Where a disciplinary matter was referred to another court, pursuant to subsection (a) of this rule and findings of fact and conclusions of law were made without appearance or opposition by the attorney, the court found support in the record for such findings and noted that the attorney had failed to establish factual matters in defense of his position, which was required by a preponderance of the evidence pursuant to Rule 16-759; the attorney had asserted that the service upon him was lacking and violated due process, however, his failure to appear and present evidence in support of that exception was sufficient reason to overrule it, in addition to the finding that service pursuant to Rule 16-753(a) was properly made. Att'y Griev. Comm'n v. Faber, 373 Md. 173, 817 A.2d 205 (2003).

Applied in Att'y Griev. Comm'n v. Granger, 374 Md. 438, 823 A.2d 611 (2003); Att'y Griev. Comm'n v. Alsafty, 379 Md. 1, 838 A.2d 1213 (2003); Att'y Griev. Comm'n v. Hermina, 379 Md. 503, 842 A.2d 762 (2004); Att'y Griev. Comm'n v. O'Toole, 379 Md. 595, 843 A.2d 50 (2004); Att'y Griev. Comm'n v. Duvall, 384 Md. 234, 863 A.2d 291 (2004); Att'y Griev. Comm'n v. Cherry-Mahoi, 388 Md. 124, 879 A.2d 58 (2005); Att'y Griev. Comm'n v. Reinhardt, 391 Md. 209, 892 A.2d 533 (2006); Att'y Griev. Comm'n v. Lee, 393 Md. 546, 903 A.2d 895 (2006); Att'y Griev. Comm'n v. Rees, 396 Md. 248, 913 A.2d 68 (2006); Att'y Griev. Comm'n v. Sapero, 400 Md. 461, 929 A.2d 483 (2007); Att'y Griev. Comm'n v. Robertson, 400 Md. 618, 929 A.2d 576 (2007); Att'y Griev. Comm'n v. Floyd, 400 Md. 236, 929 A.2d 61 (2007); Att'y Griev. Comm'n v. Tanko, 408 Md. 404, 969 A.2d 1010 (2009); Att'y Griev. Comm'n v. Shoup, 410 Md. 462, 979 A.2d 120 (Aug. 28, 2009).

Quoted in Att'y Griev. Comm'n v. Wallace, 368 Md. 277, 793 A.2d 535 (2002); Att'y Griev. Comm'n v. Davis, 375 Md. 131, 825 A.2d 430 (2003); Att'y Griev. Comm'n v. Gansler, 377 Md. 656, 835 A.2d 548 (2003); Att'y Griev. Comm'n v. Stolarz, 379 Md. 387, 842 A.2d 42 (2004); Att'y Griev. Comm'n v. Mininsohn, 380 Md. 536, 846 A.2d 353 (2004); Att'y Griev. Comm'n v. Link, 380 Md. 405, 844 A.2d 1197 (2004); Att'y Griev. Comm'n v. Velasquez, 380 Md. 651, 846 A.2d 422 (2004); Att'y Griev. Comm'n v. Brown, 380 Md. 661, 846 A.2d 428 (2004); Att'y Griev. Comm'n v. Daskalopoulos, 383 Md. 375, 859 A.2d 653 (2004); Att'y Griev. Comm'n v. Rose, 383 Md. 385, 859 A.2d 659 (2004); Att'y Griev. Comm'n v. MacDougall, 384 Md. 271, 863 A.2d 312 (2004); Att'y Griev. Comm'n v. Brisbon, 385 Md. 667, 870 A.2d 586 (2005); Att'y Griev. Comm'n v. Steinberg, 385 Md. 696, 870 A.2d 603 (2005); Att'y Griev. Comm'n v. Mitchell, 386 Md. 386, 872 A.2d 720 (2005); Att'y Griev. Comm'n v. Jordan, 386 Md. 583, 873 A.2d 1161 (2005); Att'y Griev. Comm'n v. Zakroff, 387 Md. 603, 876 A.2d 664 (2005), cert. denied, 2006 Md. LEXIS 561 (2006); cert. denied, 2006 Md. LEXIS 571 (Md. 2006); Att'y Griev. Comm'n v. Zakroff, 387 Md. 603, 876 A.2d 664 (2005), cert. denied, 2006 Md. LEXIS 561 (2006); cert. denied, 2006 Md. LEXIS 571 (Md. 2006); Att'y Griev. Comm'n v. Kovacic, 389 Md. 233, 884 A.2d 673 (2005); Att'y Griev. Comm'n v. Weiss, 389 Md. 531, 886 A.2d 606 (2005); Att'y Griev. Comm'n v. Muhammad, — Md. —, — A.2d — (2005); Att'y Griev. Comm'n v. Lee, 390 Md. 517, 890 A.2d 273 (2005); Att'y Griev. Comm'n v. Holt, 391 Md. 673, 894 A.2d 602 (2006); Att'y Griev. Comm'n v. Rose, 391 Md. 101, 892 A.2d 469 (2006), cert. denied, 2006 U.S. LEXIS 5734, 166 L. Ed. 2d 22 (U.S. 2006); Att'y Griev. Comm'n v. Kapoor, 391 Md. 505, 894 A.2d 502 (2006); Att'y Griev. Comm'n v. Calhoun, 391 Md. 532, 894 A.2d 518 (2006); Att'y Griev. Comm'n v. Guberman, 392 Md. 131, 896 A.2d 337 (2006); Att'y Griev. Comm'n v. Lanocha, 392 Md. 234, 896 A.2d 996 (2006); Att'y Griev. Comm'n v. Butler, 395 Md. 1, 909 A.2d 226 (2006); Att'y Griev. Comm'n v. Sweitzer, 395 Md. 586, 911 A.2d 440 (2006); Att'y Griev. Comm'n v. Manger, 396 Md. 134, 913 A.2d 1 (2006); Att'y Griev. Comm'n v. Baker, 396 Md. 15, 912 A.2d 651 (2006); Att'y Griev. Comm'n v. Mba-Jonas, 397 Md. 690, 919 A.2d 669 (2007); Att'y Griev. Comm'n v. Hill, 398 Md. 95, 919 A.2d 1194 (2007); Att'y Griev. Comm'n v. Goff, 399 Md. 1, 922 A.2d 554 (2007); Att'y Griev. Comm'n v. Pak, 400 Md. 567, 929 A.2d 546 (2007), cert. denied, 128 S. Ct. 905, 2008 U.S. LEXIS 126, 169 L. Ed. 2d 729 (U.S. 2008); Att'y Griev. Comm'n v. Wingerter, 400 Md. 214, 929 A.2d 47 (2007); Att'y Griev. Comm'n v. Mba-Jonas, 402 Md.

334, 936 A.2d 839 (2007); Att'y Griev. Comm'n v. Kalil, 402 Md. 358, 936 A.2d 854 (2007); Att'y Griev. Comm'n v. Saridakis, 402 Md. 413, 936 A.2d 886 (2007); Att'y Griev. Comm'n v. Parsons, 404 Md. 175, 946 A.2d 437 (2008); Att'y Griev. Comm'n v. Kreamer, 404 Md. 282, 946 A.2d 500 (2008); Att'y Griev. Comm'n v. Whitehead, 405 Md. 240, 950 A.2d 798 (2008); Att'y Griev. Comm'n v. McClain, 406 Md. 1, 956 A.2d 135 (2008), cert. denied, 129 S. Ct. 1691, 2009 U.S. LEXIS 2433, 173 L. Ed. 2d 1036 (U.S. 2009); Att'y Griev. Comm'n v. Snyder, 406 Md. 21, 956 A.2d 147 (2008); Att'y Griev. Comm'n v. Harris, 403 Md. 142, 939 A.2d 732 (2008); Att'y Griev. Comm'n v. Byrd, 408 Md. 449, 970 A.2d 870 (2009); Att'y Griev. Comm'n v. Hall, 408 Md. 306, 969 A.2d 953 (2009); Att'y Griev. Comm'n v. Jarosinski, 411 Md. 432, 983 A.2d 477 (2009); Att'y Griev. Comm'n v. Robaton, 411 Md. 415, 983 A.2d 467 (2009); Att'y Griev. Comm'n v. Kwarteng, 411 Md. 652, 984 A.2d 865 (2009); Att'y Griev. Comm'n v. Khandpur, 421 Md. 1, 25 A.3d 165 (2011).

Stated in Att'y Griev. Comm'n v. Prichard, 386 Md. 238, 872 A.2d 81 (2005); Att'y Griev. Comm'n v. Theriault, 390 Md. 202, 888 A.2d 292 (2005).

Cited in Att'y Griev. Comm'n v. Walker-Turner, 372 Md. 85, 812 A.2d 260 (2002); Att'y Griev. Comm'n v. Braskey, 378 Md. 425, 836 A.2d 605 (2003); Att'y Griev. Comm'n v. Lichtenberg, 379 Md. 335, 842 A.2d 11 (2004); Att'y Griev. Comm'n v. Herman, 380 Md. 378, 844 A.2d 1181 (2004); Att'y Griev. Comm'n v. Christopher, 383 Md. 624, 861 A.2d 692 (2004); Att'y Griev. Comm'n v. James, 385 Md. 637, 870 A.2d 229 (2005); Att'y Griev. Comm'n v. Zuckerman, 386 Md. 341, 872 A.2d 693 (2005); Att'y Griev. Comm'n v. Kreamer, 387 Md. 503, 876 A.2d 79 (2005); Att'y Griev. Comm'n v. Kreamer, 387 Md. 503, 876 A.2d 79 (2005); Att'y Griev. Comm'n v. Parker, 389 Md. 142, 884 A.2d 104 (2005); Att'y Griev. Comm'n v. Maignan, 390 Md. 287, 888 A.2d 344 (2005); Att'y Griev. Comm'n v. Kinnane, 390 Md. 324, 888 A.2d 1178 (2005); Att'y Griev. Comm'n v. Obi, 393 Md. 643, 904 A.2d 422 (2006); Att'y Griev. Comm'n v. Roberts, 394 Md. 137, 904 A.2d 557 (2006); Att'y Griev. Comm'n v. Ward, 396 Md. 203, 913 A.2d 41 (2006); Att'y Griev. Comm'n v. Muhammad, 395 Md. 676, 912 A.2d 588 (2006), cert. denied, 127 S. Ct. 2296, 2007 U.S. LEXIS 5292, 167 L. Ed. 2d 1103 (U.S. 2007); Att'y Griev. Comm'n v. Hodgson, 396 Md. 1, 912 A.2d 640 (2006); Att'y Griev. Comm'n v. McCulloch, 397 Md. 674, 919 A.2d 660 (2007); Att'y Griev. Comm'n v. Mahone, 398 Md. 257, 920 A.2d 458 (2007); Att'y Griev. Comm'n v. Ficker, 399 Md. 445, 924 A.2d 1105 (2007); Att'y Griev. Comm'n v. Nussbaum, 401 Md. 612, 934 A.2d 1 (2007); Att'y Griev. Comm'n v. Maignan, 402 Md. 39, 935 A.2d 409 (2007); Att'y Griev. Comm'n v. Webster, 402 Md. 448, 937 A.2d 161 (2007); Att'y Griev. Comm'n v. Zuckerman, 403 Md. 695, 944 A.2d 525 (2008); Att'y Griev. Comm'n v. Adams, 404 Md. 1, 944 A.2d 1115 (2008); Att'y Griev. Comm'n v. Elmendorf, 404 Md. 353, 946 A.2d 542 (2008); Att'y Griev. Comm'n v. McCulloch, 404 Md. 388, 946 A.2d 1009 (2008); Att'y Griev. Comm'n v. Smith, 405 Md. 107, 950 A.2d 101 (2008); Att'y Griev. Comm'n v. Nichols, 405 Md. 207, 950 A.2d 778 (2008); Att'y Griev. Comm'n v. Akpan, 405 Md. 277, 950 A.2d 820 (2008); Att'y Griev. Comm'n v. Shryock, 408 Md. 105, 968 A.2d 593 (2009); Att'y Griev. Comm'n v. Palmer, 417 Md. 185, 9 A.3d 37 (2010); Att'y Griev. Comm'n v. Fox, 417 Md. 504, 11 A.3d 762 (2010); Att'y Griev. Comm'n v. Usiak, 418 Md. 667, 18 A.3d 1 (2011); Att'y Griev. Comm'n v. Zodrow, 419 Md. 286, 19 A.3d 381 (2011); Att'y Griev. Comm'n v. Carithers, 421 Md. 28, 25 A.3d 181 (2011); Att'y Griev. Comm'n v. Keiner, — Md. —, — A.3d — (Aug. 19, 2011); Att'y Griev. Comm'n v. Patterson, — Md. —, — A.3d — (Sept. 21, 2011).

Rule 16-753. Service of petition.

A copy of a Petition for Disciplinary or Remedial Action filed pursuant to Rule 16-751, and the order of the Court of Appeals designating a judge pursuant to Rule 16-752, shall be served on an attorney in the manner prescribed by Rule 2-121 or in any other manner directed by the Court of Appeals. If after reasonable efforts the attorney cannot be served personally, service may be made upon the employee designated by the Client Protection Fund of the Bar of Maryland pursuant to Rule 16-811 c 1 (x), who shall be deemed the attorney's agent for receipt of service. The Fund's employee shall send, by both certified mail and ordinary mail, a copy of the papers so served to the attorney at the address maintained in the Fund's records and to any other address provided by Bar Counsel. (Added Nov. 30, 2000, effective July 1, 2001; amended effective Nov. 6, 2002.)

Source. — This Rule is in part derived from former Rule 16-709 (BV9) and in part new.

Effect of amendments. — The 2002 amendment substituted "employee designated by the Client Protection Fund of the Bar of Maryland pursuant to Rule 16-811 c 1 (x)" for "treasurer of the Clients' Security Trust," substituted "Fund's employee" for "treasurer," and deleted "Trust" preceding "Fund's records."

Service proper where prior attempts failed. — Where a disciplinary matter was referred to another court, pursuant to Rule 16-752(a) and findings of fact and conclusions of law were made without appearance or opposition by the attorney, the court found support in the record for such findings and noted that the attorney had failed to establish factual matters in defense of his position, which was required by a preponderance of the evidence pursuant to Rule 16-759; the attorney had asserted that the service upon him was lacking and violated due process, however, his failure to appear and present evidence in support of that exception was sufficient reason to overrule it, in addition to the finding that service pursuant to (a) of this rule was properly made on the Treasurer of the Client Protection Fund. Att'y Griev. Comm'n v. Faber, 373 Md. 173, 817 A.2d 205 (2003).

Quoted in Att'y Griev. Comm'n v. Scroggs, 387 Md. 238, 874 A.2d 985 (2005).

Cited in Att'y Griev. Comm'n v. Weiss, 389 Md. 531, 886 A.2d 606 (2005); Att'y Griev. Comm'n v. Hodgson, 396 Md. 1, 912 A.2d 640 (2006).

Rule 16-754. Answer.

(a) **Timing; contents.** Within 15 days after being served with the petition, unless a different time is ordered, the respondent shall file with the designated clerk an answer to the petition and serve a copy on the petitioner. Sections (c) and (e) of Rule 2-323 apply to the answer. Defenses and objections to the petition, including insufficiency of service, shall be stated in the answer and not by preliminary motion.

(b) **Procedural defects.** It is not a defense or ground for objection to a petition that procedural defects may have occurred during disciplinary or remedial proceedings prior to the filing of the petition.

(c) **Failure to answer.** If the time for filing an answer has expired and the respondent has failed to file an answer in accordance with section (a) of this Rule, the court shall treat the failure as a default and the provisions of Rule 2-613 shall apply. (Added Nov. 30, 2000, effective July 1, 2001.)

Source. — This Rule is derived from former Rules 16-709 e (BV9 e) and 16-710 b (BV10 b) and is in part new.

Constitutionality — Md. R. 16-723 is not unconstitutional. Att'y Griev. Comm'n v. Calhoun, 391 Md. 532, 894 A.2d 518 (2006).

Default not set aside. — In an attorney disciplinary matter, a hearing judge properly concluded, from the totality of the circumstances, that the attorney did not proffer an adequate reason for his failure to file a responsive pleading where the attorney's assertion that he never received proper service was unsupported by any evidence in the record, other than his bare allegation that he was not served, and the petitioner, the Attorney Grievance Commission, on the other hand, provided an Affidavit of Service which specifically indicated that proper service was made. As a result, it was not an abuse of discretion for the hearing judge to deny the attorney's motion to vacate the default entered against him for failure to respond. Att'y Griev. Comm'n v. Steinberg, 395 Md. 337, 910 A.2d 429 (2006).

Factual averments deemed admitted due to failure to respond. — In an attorney disciplinary matter, factual averments in petitions filed by the Attorney Grievance Commission were deemed admitted, under Rules 2-323(e) and 2-613 and (c) of this Rule, because the attorney against whom the petitions were filed did not respond to the petitions or respond to requests for admissions of facts and genuineness of documents. Att'y Griev. Comm'n v. De La Paz, 418 Md. 534, 16 A.3d 181 (2011).

Waiver. — State's highest court found that the attorney should be disbarred, as clear and convincing evidence showed that the attorney falsely represented in a deposition that the business associate was a client of the attorney when that was not true, in violation of Md. R. Prof. Conduct 1.9, and that the attorney engaged in an impermissible conflict of interest in violation of Md. R. Prof. Conduct 8.4 when the attorney represented the corporation in a substantially similar matter in a lawsuit against the entity after the attorney had represented the entity for two years in matters that included the same matter that was the subject of the lawsuit; not only were the viola-

tions proven, but the attorney failed to prove the attorney's affirmative defense of waiver since the attorney presented a paucity of argument or evidence in that regard. Att'y Griev. Comm'n v. Siskind, 401 Md. 41, 930 A.2d 328 (2007).

Applied in Att'y Griev. Comm'n v. Lee, 390 Md. 517, 890 A.2d 273 (2005); Att'y Griev. Comm'n v. Sucklal, 418 Md. 1, 12 A.3d 650 (2011).

Quoted in Att'y Griev. Comm'n v. Wallace, 368 Md. 277, 793 A.2d 535 (2002); Att'y Griev. Comm'n v. Braskey, 378 Md. 425, 836 A.2d 605 (2003); Att'y Griev. Comm'n v. Herman, 380 Md. 378, 844 A.2d 1181 (2004); Att'y Griev. Comm'n v. Scroggs, 387 Md. 238, 874 A.2d 985 (2005).

Cited in Att'y Griev. Comm'n v. Nichols, 405 Md. 207, 950 A.2d 778 (2008).

Rule 16-755. Amendments to pleadings.

A party may amend a petition or an answer in accordance with the applicable provisions of Rule 2-341. (Added Nov. 30, 2000, effective July 1, 2001.)

Source. — This Rule is new.

Amendment of pleading to make additional charge. — Under the former Rule concerning charges, where the petition as filed did not contain the requisite allegations to support disciplinary sanctions based on a finding made by the hearing court that the respondent misappropriated his client's funds, the interest of justice required that the Bar Asso-

ciation be granted leave to amend its pleading so as to make the additional charge, without prejudice to the respondent's prerogative to raise an objection, first in the hearing court and then in the Court of Appeals, unless he elected to waive this right. Bar Ass'n v. Cockrell, 270 Md. 686, 313 A.2d 816 (1974).

Rule 16-756. Discovery.

After a Petition for Disciplinary or Remedial Action has been filed, discovery is governed by Title 2, Chapter 400, subject to any scheduling order entered pursuant to Rule 16-752 (a). (Added Nov. 30, 2000, effective July 1, 2001.)

Source. — This Rule is derived from former Rule 16-710 a (BV10 a).

Discovery in preference to introduction of inconsistent statements in peer review. — Although the confidentiality provision of the peer review rules was drafted to protect against impeachment of respondent attorneys with their earlier statements during peer review, the purposes of peer review were best served by likewise applying the confidentiality rule, according to its plain language, where it was the complainant whose earlier

statements were allegedly inconsistent; if a formal disciplinary ensued, a respondent attorney would still have an opportunity to depose and pursue other discovery as to witnesses whose evidence seemed questionable. Att'y Griev. Comm'n v. Lee, 387 Md. 89, 874 A.2d 897 (2005).

Unanswered request deemed admissions. — In an attorney disciplinary matter, when bar counsel gave the respondent attorney and his counsel a written request for admissions of fact and genuineness of documents, which went unanswered, and, at the hearing, the attorney's counsel conceded the truth of the matters contained in the request, the matters addressed in the request were deemed admitted, under Rules 16-756 and

2-424(b), for purposes of the disciplinary proceedings. Att'y Griev. Comm'n v. Guida, 391 Md. 33, 891 A.2d 1085 (2006).

Applied in Att'y Griev. Comm'n v. Steinberg, 395 Md. 337, 910 A.2d 429 (2006).

Cited in Att'y Griev. Comm'n v. Adams, 404 Md. 1, 944 A.2d 1115 (2008).

Rule 16-757. Judicial hearing.

(a) **Generally.** The hearing of a disciplinary or remedial action is governed by the rules of evidence and procedure applicable to a court trial in a civil action tried in a circuit court. Unless extended by the Court of Appeals, the hearing shall be completed within 120 days after service on the respondent of the order designating a judge. Before the conclusion of the hearing, the judge may permit any complainant to testify, subject to cross-examination, regarding the effect of the alleged misconduct. A respondent attorney may offer, or the judge may inquire regarding, evidence otherwise admissible of any remedial action undertaken relevant to the allegations. Bar Counsel may respond to any evidence of remedial action.

(b) **Burdens of proof.** The petitioner has the burden of proving the averments of the petition by clear and convincing evidence. A respondent who asserts an affirmative defense or a matter of mitigation or extenuation has the burden of proving the defense or matter by a preponderance of the evidence.

(c) **Findings and conclusions.** The judge shall prepare and file or dictate into the record a statement of the judge's findings of fact, including findings as to any evidence regarding remedial action, and conclusions of law. If dictated into the record, the statement shall be promptly transcribed. Unless the time is extended by the Court of Appeals, the written or transcribed statement shall be filed with the clerk responsible for the record no later than 45 days after the conclusion of the hearing. The clerk shall mail a copy of the statement to each party.

(d) **Transcript.** The petitioner shall cause a transcript of the hearing to be prepared and included in the record.

(e) **Transmittal of record.** Unless a different time is ordered by the Court of Appeals, the clerk shall transmit the record to the Court of Appeals within 15 days after the statement of findings and conclusions is filed. (Added Nov. 30, 2000, effective July 1, 2001; Nov. 1, 2001, effective Jan. 1, 2002.)

Source. — This Rule is derived from former Rules 16-710 d (BV10 d) and 16-711 a and b 1 (BV11 a and b 1).

Effect of amendments. — The 2001 amendment added "prepare and" preceding "file" in the first sentence of (c).

Action of court is judicial in character — Under prior Rule governing hearings, the action of a court in exercising its power to disbar is characterized as judicial in character and is essentially an inquiry in the nature of

an investigation by the court into the conduct of one of its own officers. The order which is entered is only an exercise of the disciplinary jurisdiction which a court has over its officers. It is recognized in this State and generally in America that in such an investigation mere forms not affecting the merits should not stand in the way of protecting the court and the public by appropriate action after a full hearing. Maryland State Bar Ass'n v. Boone, 255 Md. 420, 258 A.2d 438 (1969).

Power of local courts. — Statutes and rules have consistently confided to the local courts the power to act in both disciplinary proceedings and reinstatement proceedings. Maryland State Bar Ass'n v. Boone, 255 Md. 420, 258 A.2d 438 (1969).

The Court of Appeals has original and complete jurisdiction over disciplinary proceedings — The Court of Appeals has original and complete jurisdiction over disciplinary proceedings and renders the ultimate decision as to whether an attorney has engaged in misconduct. Att'y Griev. Comm'n v. Kent, 337 Md. 361, 653 A.2d 909 (1995).

Duty of Court of Appeals. — The Court of Appeals has the right and the duty ultimately to supervise the exercise of disciplinary and reinstatement powers of the local courts. Maryland State Bar Ass'n v. Boone, 255 Md. 420, 258 A.2d 438 (1969).

Purpose of disciplinary proceedings. — Purpose of disciplinary proceedings is not to punish the offending attorney but "is to protect the public from one who has demonstrated his unworthiness to continue the practice of law." Att'y Griev. Comm'n v. Howard, 282 Md. 515, 385 A.2d 1191 (1978).

The purpose of the proceeding under this Rule is to protect the public by determining a lawyer's fitness to practice law. Att'y Griev. Comm'n v. Green, 278 Md. 412, 365 A.2d 39 (1976).

The purpose of a disciplinary action is not to punish the offending attorney, but is to protect the public from one who has demonstrated his unworthiness to continue the practice of law. Att'y Griev. Comm'n v. Pollack, 279 Md. 225, 369 A.2d 61 (1977).

The purpose of a disciplinary proceeding is to protect the public, rather than to punish the erring attorney. Att'y Griev. Comm'n v. Kahn, 290 Md. 654, 431 A.2d 1336 (1981).

Disciplinary proceeding is neither action at law, nor criminal prosecution. — A disciplinary proceeding is neither an action at law, nor a criminal prosecution. Anne Arundel County Bar Ass'n v. Collins, 272 Md. 578, 325 A.2d 724 (1974), cert. denied, 364 Md. 536, 774 A.2d 409 (2001).

A disciplinary proceeding for professional misconduct is not the trial of an action at law. Maryland State Bar Ass'n v. Boone, 255 Md. 420, 258 A.2d 438 (1969); Kerpelman v. Bricker, 23 Md. App. 628, 329 A.2d 423 (1974).

A disciplinary proceeding for professional misconduct is not a proceeding of a criminal character. Kerpelman v. Bricker, 23 Md. App. 628, 329 A.2d 423 (1974).

Their purpose is to protect the public by determining a lawyer's fitness to practice law

and whether to institute disciplinary action against him. Att'y Griev. Comm'n v. Stewart, 285 Md. 251, 401 A.2d 1026, cert. denied, 444 U.S. 845, 100 S. Ct. 89, 62 L. Ed. 2d 58 (1979).

Constitutional guarantee of jury trial inapplicable. — Disciplinary proceedings against attorneys, in the absence of a rule or statute providing to the contrary, are not encompassed within the constitutional guarantees of trial by a jury, be that guarantee state or federal. Att'y Griev. Comm'n v. Kerpelman, 288 Md. 341, 420 A.2d 940 (1980), cert. denied, 450 U.S. 970, 101 S. Ct. 1492, 67 L. Ed. 2d 621 (1981).

Double jeopardy — Double jeopardy provisions of the Fifth Amendment of the Constitution of the United States are not applicable to disciplinary proceedings against lawyers since these proceedings are not criminal in nature. Att'y Griev. Comm'n v. Andresen, 281 Md. 152, 379 A.2d 159 (1977).

Notice and opportunity to defend. — As long as an attorney is given notice and opportunity to defend in a full and fair hearing following the institution of disciplinary proceedings, an irregularity in the proceedings before the Inquiry Panel and the Review Board ordinarily will not amount to a denial of due process. Att'y Griev. Comm'n v. Garland, 345 Md. 383, 692 A.2d 465 (1997).

Equity rules applicable. — Under prior rule governing hearings, the same rules of law, evidence and procedure as used in civil proceedings in equity were applicable in disciplinary hearings. Bar Ass'n v. Cockrell, 270 Md. 686, 313 A.2d 816 (1974).

The prior Rule governing hearings directed that post-charging discovery in an attorney grievance case proceed in accordance with Title 2, ch. 400 of the Maryland Rules, the rules for discovery in civil cases in the Maryland Circuit Courts; under subsection (d), the hearings are governed by the same rules of law, evidence and procedure as are applicable to the trial of civil proceedings in equity. Att'y Griev. Comm'n v. Ellison, 384 Md. 688, 867 A.2d 259 (2005).

Self-incrimination. — A disciplinary action against an attorney does not involve a potential criminal or quasi-criminal sanction for the purpose of the privilege against self-incrimination provided by the Fifth Amendment to the federal Constitution. Maryland State Bar Ass'n v. Sugarman, 273 Md. 306, 329 A.2d 1 (1974), cert. denied, 420 U.S. 974, 95 S. Ct. 1397, 43 L. Ed. 2d 654 (1975).

Attorney Grievance Commission's procedural guideline, warning attorney that Inquiry Panel may believe evidence which attorney does not contest, does not violate attorney's constitutional right against compelled self-incrimination. Att'y Griev. Comm'n v. Unnamed Att'y, 298 Md. 36, 467 A.2d 517 (1983).

Statute of limitations. — Disciplinary proceedings against attorneys are not barred by a general statute of limitations. Anne Arundel County Bar Ass'n v. Collins, 272 Md. 578, 325 A.2d 724 (1974), cert. denied, 364 Md. 536, 774 A.2d 409 (2001).

Delay in instituting disciplinary proceedings. — Where disciplinary proceedings against an attorney, which led to the three-judge panel's recommendation that the attorney in question be reprimanded, had not been instituted more closely on the heels of the events giving rise to them, it would not serve the underlying purpose of the proceedings to disbar or suspend the attorney. Att'y Griev. Comm'n v. Howard, 282 Md. 515, 385 A.2d 1191 (1978).

Dismissal of disciplinary petition for Commission's failure to proceed unwarranted. — Because the purpose of disciplinary action against an attorney is to protect the public, dismissal of the disciplinary petition for the sole reason that the Attorney Grievance Commission failed to proceed with the proper dispatch is manifestly unwarranted. Att'y Griev. Comm'n v. Kahn, 290 Md. 654, 431 A.2d 1336 (1981).

Lawyer charged with misconduct is entitled to basic elements of due process. — Notice and opportunity to defend in a full and fair hearing. Att'y Griev. Comm'n v. Stewart, 285 Md. 251, 401 A.2d 1026, cert. denied, 444 U.S. 845, 100 S. Ct. 89, 62 L. Ed. 2d 58 (1979).

Mitigation. — Attorney's mental condition was compelling extenuating circumstance where a disabling condition impeded the attorney from conducting his practice and which required treatment. Att'y Griev. Comm'n v. Burka, 292 Md. 221, 438 A.2d 514 (1981).

Maryland has a somewhat broader view of mitigation than Georgia, which may include an attorney's lack of prior record and his community involvement; subsection (b) of this rule permits an attorney in a disciplinary proceeding to provide proof of mitigating facts by a preponderance of evidence. Att'y Griev. Comm'n v. Roberson, 373 Md. 328, 818 A.2d 1059 (2003).

In an attorney disciplinary matter in which an attorney was charged with, inter alia, intentionally falsifying a court order and forging a judge's signature, the attorney's evidence that he suffered from severe depression at the time of his offense was not mitigating because the evidence showed that he knew that what he did was wrong, and he represented other clients at the same time, so his depression, and its related sequelae, were not so great that they satisfied the required standard of showing the condition affected his ability in normal day to day activities such that he was unable to accomplish the least of these activities in a normal fashion, so it was not shown that his condition was the "root cause" of his misconduct. Att'y Griev. Comm'n v. Guida, 391 Md. 33, 891 A.2d 1085 (2006).

Burden of proof — Under prior rule governing hearings, the burden of proof was on Commission as the petitioning party. Att'y Griev. Comm'n v. Bailey, 285 Md. 631, 403 A.2d 1261 (1979).

Under prior rule governing hearings, the "clear and convincing" standard applies to the measure of proof imposed upon the Attorney Grievance Commission in factual determinations essential to establishing its case against the attorney. It does not apply to factual matters sought to be established by the attorney in defense of the attorney's position, including whether mitigating circumstances have been shown; as to this, the preponderance of evidence standard is the applicable measure of proof. Att'y Griev. Comm'n v. Bakas, 322 Md. 603, 589 A.2d 52, modified, 323 Md. 395, 593 A.2d 1087 (1991).

Under prior rule governing hearings, where bar counsel introduced evidence solely to rebut mitigating circumstances, that evidence needed only to lessen or negate the weight of the attorney's mitigating evidence to the point that the fact finder was not persuaded by a preponderance of the evidence that the mitigating circumstances existed, and did not need to support the allegations of misconduct by clear and convincing evidence. Att'y Griev. Comm'n v. James, 355 Md. 465, 735 A.2d 1027 (1999).

State's highest court found that the attorney should be disbarred, as clear and convincing evidence showed that the attorney falsely represented in a deposition that the business associate was a client of the attorney when that was not true, in violation of Md. R. Prof. Conduct 1.9, and that the attorney engaged in an impermissible conflict of interest in violation of Md. R. Prof. Conduct 8.4 when the attorney represented the corporation in a substantially similar matter in a lawsuit against the entity after the attorney had represented the entity for two years in matters that included the same matter that was the subject of the lawsuit; not only were the violations proven, but the attorney failed to prove the attorney's affirmative defense of waiver since the attorney presented a paucity of argument or evidence in that regard. Att'y Griev. Comm'n v. Siskind, 401 Md. 41, 930 A.2d 328 (2007).

Attorney can be found to have erred by "clear and convincing evidence" — Under prior rule governing hearings, attorney can be found to have erred by "clear and convincing evidence" when the only evidence in the case is the testimonial evidence of the complaining witnesses. Att'y Griev. Comm'n v. Kerpelman, 288 Md. 341, 420 A.2d 940 (1980), cert. denied,

450 U.S. 970, 101 S. Ct. 1492, 67 L. Ed. 2d 621 (1981).

Under prior rule governing hearings, where there was clear and convincing evidence that an attorney had committed criminal acts, and where he pled guilty and was fined, there was a conviction within the meaning of this Rule. Att'y Griev. Comm'n v. Painter, 356 Md. 293, 739 A.2d 24 (1999).

Standard of proof in defense. — Under prior rule governing hearings, an attorney in a disciplinary proceeding need only establish factual matters in defense of the attorney's position by the preponderance of evidence, including whether mitigating circumstances existed at the time of the alleged misconduct. Att'y Griev. Comm'n v. Powell, 328 Md. 276, 614 A.2d 102 (1992).

Scope of review. — When exceptions to the hearing judge's findings are taken properly, the Court of Appeals of Maryland is required to determine whether the findings of fact have been proven by the requisite standards of proof set out in (b). Att'y Griev. Comm'n v. Stolarz, 379 Md. 387, 842 A.2d 42 (2004).

In deciding, in an attorney disciplinary matter, whether a hearing judge's findings of fact are clearly erroneous where exceptions are filed, the reviewing court looks first to Rule 16-759(b)(2)(B), which states that the Court of Appeals shall determine whether the findings of fact have been proven by the requisite standard of proof set out in subsection (b) of this Rule, and, under (b), where exceptions to findings of fact are filed by bar counsel, the reviewing court considers that bar counsel, before the hearing judge, had the burden of proving the averments of the petition by clear and convincing evidence, so, where the exceptions are filed to findings that were favorable to a respondent attorney, under (b), the court considers also that the attorney who asserts an affirmative defense or a matter of mitigation or extenuation has the burden of proving the defense or matter by a preponderance of the evidence. Att'y Griev. Comm'n v. Guida, 391 Md. 33, 891 A.2d 1085 (2006).

Factual findings of hearing judge are prima facie correct — Factual findings of hearing judge in attorney disciplinary proceeding are prima facie correct and will not be disturbed on review unless clearly erroneous. Att'y Griev. Comm'n v. Kahn, 290 Md. 654, 431 A.2d 1336 (1981); Att'y Griev. Comm'n v. Collins, 295 Md. 532, 457 A.2d 1134 (1983).

Findings of hearing judge not clearly erroneous; 60-day suspension was appropriate sanction. — In an attorney disciplinary matter, it was held that the attorney violated Md. R. Prof. Conduct 3.3 by filing expungement petitions for a client knowing that the client's charges were ineligible for expungement and, as a result, he was sus-

pended from the practice of law for 60 days. Additionally, the findings and conclusions of the hearing officer that the attorney did not fraudulently obtain a duplicate driver's license after having his original license taken away at a sobriety checkpoint were found not to be clearly erroneous, and no deficiencies were found with regard to the allegations in the petition providing sufficient notice to the attorney of the charges against him. Att'y Griev. Comm'n v. Tanko, 408 Md. 404, 969 A.2d 1010 (2009).

Discretion of judge not disturbed on appeal unless arbitrarily administered. — See Bar Ass'n v. Cockrell, 270 Md. 686, 313 A.2d 816 (1974).

Affirmance by divided panel is final judgment — Affirmance of attorney's conviction by equally divided panel of appellate court is final judgment for purposes of this Rule. Att'y Griev. Comm'n v. Mandel, 294 Md. 560, 451 A.2d 910 (1982).

Disbarment. — Pursuant to disciplinary proceedings against an attorney, arising from four separate incidents of misconduct which resulted in a finding that the attorney committed numerous violations of Maryland Rules of Professional Conduct, various statutory violations, including misappropriating of funds, the court adopted the hearing judge's determination pursuant to (c) to disbar the attorney; there were no compelling extenuating circumstances which required an exception to the rule of disbarment for misappropriation of funds, and the aggravating factors far outweighed the mitigating factors. Att'y Griev. Comm'n v. Mininsohn, 380 Md. 536, 846 A.2d 353 (2004).

State supreme court found that the attorney's misconduct, as charged in the grievance commission's petition and supported by the trial court's findings of fact and conclusions of law, warranted disbarment; the evidence established that the attorney failed to act with reasonable diligence and promptness in representing a client in a divorce case, that the attorney failed to keep the client reasonably informed about the status of the representation and did not respond to reasonable requests for information, that the attorney failed to respond to lawful demands for information from disciplinary counsel, and that the totality of the attorney's conduct was prejudicial to the administration of justice. Att'y Griev. Comm'n v. Hodgson, 396 Md. 1, 912 A.2d 640 (2006).

Attorney was disbarred for violating Md. R. Prof. Conduct 1.15 and 8.4(a), (c), and (d), and Rule 16-607, because clear and convincing evidence established that he commingled personal and client funds and engaged in a pattern of dishonesty to hide his assets to avoid paying a judgment creditor. The evidence established that the attorney manipulated his corporate operations, his attorney escrow account, and his pension plan account to systematically avoid the judgment creditor's collection efforts and engaged in a pattern of behavior designed to conceal assets from attachment by the judgment creditor, which was conduct prejudicial to the administration of justice. Att'y Griev. Comm'n v. Foltz, 411 Md. 359, 983 A.2d 434 (2009).

Applied in Att'y Griev. Comm'n v. Olver, 376 Md. 650, 831 A.2d 66 (2003); Att'y Griev. Comm'n v. Alsafty, 379 Md. 1, 838 A.2d 1213 (2003); Att'y Griev. Comm'n v. Christopher, 383 Md. 624, 861 A.2d 692 (2004); Att'y Griev. Comm'n v. Duvall, 384 Md. 234, 863 A.2d 291 (2004); Att'y Griev. Comm'n v. Cherry-Mahoi, 388 Md. 124, 879 A.2d 58 (2005); Att'y Griev. Comm'n v. Lee, 390 Md. 517, 890 A.2d 273 (2005); Att'y Griev. Comm'n v. Lanocha, 392 Md. 234, 896 A.2d 996 (2006); Att'y Griev. Comm'n v. Lee, 393 Md. 385, 903 A.2d 360 (2006); Att'y Griev. Comm'n v. Lee, 393 Md. 546, 903 A.2d 895 (2006); Att'y Griev. Comm'n v. Steinberg, 395 Md. 337, 910 A.2d 429 (2006); Att'y Griev. Comm'n v. Rees, 396 Md. 248, 913 A.2d 68 (2006); Att'y Griev. Comm'n v. Sapero, 400 Md. 461, 929 A.2d 483 (2007); Att'y Griev. Comm'n v. Pak, 400 Md. 567, 929 A.2d 546 (2007), cert. denied, 128 S. Ct. 905, 2008 U.S. LEXIS 126, 169 L. Ed. 2d 729 (U.S. 2008); Att'y Griev. Comm'n v. Robertson, 400 Md. 618, 929 A.2d 576 (2007); Att'y Griev. Comm'n v. Floyd, 400 Md. 236, 929 A.2d 61 (2007); Att'y Griev. Comm'n v. Harris, 403 Md. 142, 939 A.2d 732 (2008); Att'y Griev. Comm'n v. Kendrick, 403 Md. 489, 943 A.2d 1173 (2008); Att'y Griev. Comm'n v. Shoup, 410 Md. 462, 979 A.2d 120 (Aug. 28, 2009); Att'y Griev. Comm'n v. Fox, 417 Md. 504, 11 A.3d 762 (2010); Att'y Griev. Comm'n v. Sucklal, 418 Md. 1, 12 A.3d 650 (2011).

Quoted in Att'y Griev. Comm'n v. Davis, 375 Md. 131, 825 A.2d 430 (2003); Att'y Griev. Comm'n v. Gansler, 377 Md. 656, 835 A.2d 548 (2003); Att'y Griev. Comm'n v. DeMaio, 379 Md. 571, 842 A.2d 802 (2004); Att'y Griev. Comm'n v. Somerville, 379 Md. 586, 842 A.2d 811 (2004); Att'y Griev. Comm'n v. O'Toole, 379 Md. 595, 843 A.2d 50 (2004); Att'y Griev. Comm'n v. Sperling, 380 Md. 180, 844 A.2d 397 (2004); Att'y Griev. Comm'n v. Link, 380 Md. 405, 844 A.2d 1197 (2004); Att'y Griev. Comm'n v. Velasquez, 380 Md. 651, 846 A.2d 422 (2004); Att'y Griev. Comm'n v. Brown, 380 Md. 661, 846 A.2d 428 (2004); Att'y Griev. Comm'n v. Daskalopoulos, 383 Md. 375, 859 A.2d 653 (2004); Att'y Griev. Comm'n v. Rose, 383 Md. 385, 859 A.2d 659 (2004); Att'y Griev. Comm'n v. Zdravkovich, 381 Md. 680, 852 A.2d 82 (2004); Att'y Griev. Comm'n v. MacDougall, 384 Md. 271, 863 A.2d 312 (2004); Att'y Griev. Comm'n v. Brisbon, 385 Md. 667, 870 A.2d 586 (2005); Att'y Griev. Comm'n v. Steinberg, 385

Md. 696, 870 A.2d 603 (2005); Att'y Griev. Comm'n v. Mitchell, 386 Md. 386, 872 A.2d 720 (2005); Att'y Griev. Comm'n v. Jordan, 386 Md. 583, 873 A.2d 1161 (2005); Att'y Griev. Comm'n v. Lee, 387 Md. 89, 874 A.2d 897 (2005); Att'y Griev. Comm'n v. Kreamer, 387 Md. 503, 876 A.2d 79 (2005); Att'y Griev. Comm'n v. Zakroff, 387 Md. 603, 876 A.2d 664 (2005), cert. denied, 2006 Md. LEXIS 561 (2006); cert. denied, 2006 Md. LEXIS 571 (Md. 2006); Att'y Griev. Comm'n v. Kreamer, 387 Md. 503, 876 A.2d 79 (2005); Att'y Griev. Comm'n v. Zakroff, 387 Md. 603, 876 A.2d 664 (2005), cert. denied, 2006 Md. LEXIS 561 (2006); cert. denied, 2006 Md. LEXIS 571 (Md. 2006); Att'y Griev. Comm'n v. Kovacic, 389 Md. 233, 884 A.2d 673 (2005); Att'y Griev. Comm'n v. Weiss, 389 Md. 531, 886 A.2d 606 (2005); Att'y Griev. Comm'n v. Muhammad, — Md. —, — A.2d — (2005); Att'y Griev. Comm'n v. Holt, 391 Md. 673, 894 A.2d 602 (2006); Att'y Griev. Comm'n v. Rose, 391 Md. 101, 892 A.2d 469 (2006), cert. denied, 2006 U.S. LEXIS 5734, 166 L. Ed. 2d 22 (U.S. 2006); Att'y Griev. Comm'n v. Kapoor, 391 Md. 505, 894 A.2d 502 (2006); Att'y Griev. Comm'n v. Calhoun, 391 Md. 532, 894 A.2d 518 (2006); Att'y Griev. Comm'n v. Guberman, 392 Md. 131, 896 A.2d 337 (2006); Att'y Griev. Comm'n v. Butler, 395 Md. 1, 909 A.2d 226 (2006); Att'y Griev. Comm'n v. Sweitzer, 395 Md. 586, 911 A.2d 440 (2006); Att'y Griev. Comm'n v. Manger, 396 Md. 134, 913 A.2d 1 (2006); Att'y Griev. Comm'n v. Baker, 396 Md. 15, 912 A.2d 651 (2006); Att'y Griev. Comm'n v. Mba-Jonas, 397 Md. 690, 919 A.2d 669 (2007); Att'y Griev. Comm'n v. Hill, 398 Md. 95, 919 A.2d 1194 (2007); Att'y Griev. Comm'n v. Goff, 399 Md. 1, 922 A.2d 554 (2007); Att'y Griev. Comm'n v. Wingerter, 400 Md. 214, 929 A.2d 47 (2007); Att'y Griev. Comm'n v. Mba-Jonas, 402 Md. 334, 936 A.2d 839 (2007); Att'y Griev. Comm'n v. Kalil, 402 Md. 358, 936 A.2d 854 (2007); Att'y Griev. Comm'n v. Saridakis, 402 Md. 413, 936 A.2d 886 (2007); Att'y Griev. Comm'n v. Parsons, 404 Md. 175, 946 A.2d 437 (2008); Att'y Griev. Comm'n v. Kreamer, 404 Md. 282, 946 A.2d 500 (2008); Att'y Griev. Comm'n v. McCulloch, 404 Md. 388, 946 A.2d 1009 (2008); Att'y Griev. Comm'n v. Whitehead, 405 Md. 240, 950 A.2d 798 (2008); Att'y Griev. Comm'n v. McClain, 406 Md. 1, 956 A.2d 135 (2008), cert. denied, 129 S. Ct. 1691, 2009 U.S. LEXIS 2433, 173 L. Ed. 2d 1036 (U.S. 2009); Att'y Griev. Comm'n v. Snyder, 406 Md. 21, 956 A.2d 147 (2008); Att'y Griev. Comm'n v. Byrd, 408 Md. 449, 970 A.2d 870 (2009); Att'y Griev. Comm'n v. Hall, 408 Md. 306, 969 A.2d 953 (2009); Att'y Griev. Comm'n v. Pawlak, 408 Md. 288, 969 A.2d 311 (2009); Att'y Griev. Comm'n v. Thomas, 409 Md. 121, 973 A.2d 185 (2009); Att'y Griev. Comm'n v. Gisriel, 409 Md. 331, 974 A.2d 331 (2009); Att'y Griev. Comm'n v. Jarosinski, 411 Md. 432, 983 A.2d 477 (2009);

Att'y Griev. Comm'n v. Robaton, 411 Md. 415, 983 A.2d 467 (2009); Att'y Griev. Comm'n v. Kwarteng, 411 Md. 652, 984 A.2d 865 (2009); Att'y Griev. Comm'n v. Gordon, 413 Md. 46, 991 A.2d 51 (2010); Att'y Griev. Comm'n v. Bleecker, 414 Md. 147, 994 A.2d 928 (2010); Att'y Griev. Comm'n v. Lara, 418 Md. 355, 14 A.3d 650 (2011); Att'y Griev. Comm'n v. Coppola, 419 Md. 370, 19 A.3d 431 (2011); Att'y Griev. Comm'n v. Stern, 419 Md. 525, 19 A.3d 904 (2011); Att'y Griev. Comm'n v. Patterson, — Md. —, — A.3d — (Sept. 21, 2011).

Stated in Att'y Griev. Comm'n v. West, 378 Md. 395, 836 A.2d 588 (2003); Att'y Griev. Comm'n v. Braskey, 378 Md. 425, 836 A.2d 605 (2003); Att'y Griev. Comm'n v. Prichard, 386 Md. 238, 872 A.2d 81 (2005); Att'y Griev. Comm'n v. Theriault, 390 Md. 202, 888 A.2d 292 (2005).

Cited in Att'y Griev. Comm'n v. Post, 379 Md. 60, 839 A.2d 718 (2003); Att'y Griev. Comm'n v. Herman, 380 Md. 378, 844 A.2d 1181 (2004); Att'y Griev. Comm'n v. Gore, 380 Md. 455, 845 A.2d 1204 (2004); Att'y Griev. Comm'n v. James, 385 Md. 637, 870 A.2d 229 (2005); Att'y Griev. Comm'n v. Zuckerman, 386 Md. 341, 872 A.2d 693 (2005); Att'y Griev. Comm'n v. Kinnane, 390 Md. 324, 888 A.2d 1178 (2005); Att'y Griev. Comm'n v. Obi, 393 Md. 643, 904 A.2d 422 (2006); Att'y Griev. Comm'n v. Roberts, 394 Md. 137, 904 A.2d 557 (2006); Att'y Griev. Comm'n v. Ward, 396 Md. 203, 913 A.2d 41 (2006); Att'y Griev. Comm'n v.

Muhammad, 395 Md. 676, 912 A.2d 588 (2006), cert. denied, 127 S. Ct. 2296, 2007 U.S. LEXIS 5292, 167 L. Ed. 2d 1103 (U.S. 2007); Att'y Griev. Comm'n v. McCulloch, 397 Md. 674, 919 A.2d 660 (2007); Att'y Griev. Comm'n v. Mahone, 398 Md. 257, 920 A.2d 458 (2007); Att'y Griev. Comm'n v. Nussbaum, 401 Md. 612, 934 A.2d 1 (2007); Att'y Griev. Comm'n v. Webster, 402 Md. 448, 937 A.2d 161 (2007); Att'y Griev. Comm'n v. Zuckerman, 403 Md. 695, 944 A.2d 525 (2008); Att'y Griev. Comm'n v. Adams, 404 Md. 1, 944 A.2d 1115 (2008); Att'y Griev. Comm'n v. Elmendorf, 404 Md. 353, 946 A.2d 542 (2008); Att'y Griev. Comm'n v. Walker, 405 Md. 3, 948 A.2d 1263 (2008); Att'y Griev. Comm'n v. Nichols, 405 Md. 207, 950 A.2d 778 (2008); Att'y Griev. Comm'n v. Akpan, 405 Md. 277, 950 A.2d 820 (2008); Att'y Griev. Comm'n v. McLaughlin, 409 Md. 304, 974 A.2d 315 (2009); Att'y Griev. Comm'n v. Adams, 410 Md. 544, 979 A.2d 698 (2009); Att'y Griev. Comm'n v. Bahgat, 411 Md. 568, 984 A.2d 225 (2009); Att'y Griev. Comm'n v. Marcalus, 414 Md. 501, 996 A.2d 350 (2010); Att'y Griev. Comm'n v. Edib, 415 Md. 696, 4 A.3d 957 (2010); Att'y Griev. Comm'n v. Palmer, 417 Md. 185, 9 A.3d 37 (2010); Att'y Griev. Comm'n v. Elliott, 417 Md. 659, 12 A.3d 105 (2011); Att'y Griev. Comm'n v. Zodrow, 419 Md. 286, 19 A.3d 381 (2011); Att'y Griev. Comm'n v. Carithers, 421 Md. 28, 25 A.3d 181 (2011); Att'y Griev. Comm'n v. Tauber, — Md. —, 26 A.3d 967 (2011); Att'y Griev. Comm'n v. Keiner, — Md. —, — A.3d — (Aug. 19, 2011).

Rule 16-758. Post-hearing proceedings.

(a) **Notice of the filing of the record.** Upon receiving the record, the Clerk of the Court of Appeals shall notify the parties that the record has been filed.

(b) **Exceptions; recommendations.** Within 15 days after service of the notice required by section (a) of this Rule, each party may file (1) exceptions to the findings and conclusions of the hearing judge and (2) recommendations concerning the appropriate disposition under Rule 16-759 (c).

(c) **Response.** Within 15 days after service of exceptions or recommendations, the adverse party may file a response.

(d) **Form.** The parties shall file eight copies of any exceptions, recommendations, and responses. The copies shall conform to the requirements of Rule 8-112. (Added Nov. 30, 2000, effective July 1, 2001.)

Source. — This Rule is derived in part from former Rule 16-711 (BV11) and is in part new.

Applied in Att'y Griev. Comm'n v. Granger, 374 Md. 438, 823 A.2d 611 (2003); Att'y Griev. Comm'n v. Lee, 393 Md. 546, 903 A.2d 895 (2006); Att'y Griev. Comm'n v. Butler, 395 Md. 1, 909 A.2d 226 (2006); Att'y Griev. Comm'n v. Steinberg, 395 Md. 337, 910 A.2d 429 (2006); Att'y Griev. Comm'n v. Sapero, 400 Md. 461, 929 A.2d 483 (2007).

Quoted in Att'y Griev. Comm'n v. Tayback, 378 Md. 578, 837 A.2d 158 (2003); Att'y Griev. Comm'n v. Weiss, 389 Md. 531, 886 A.2d 606 (2005); Att'y Griev. Comm'n v. Calhoun, 391 Md. 532, 894 A.2d 518 (2006); Att'y Griev. Comm'n v. Lee, 393 Md. 385, 903 A.2d 360 (2006); Att'y Griev. Comm'n v. Goff, 399 Md. 1, 922 A.2d 554 (2007); Att'y Griev. Comm'n v. Pak, 400 Md. 567, 929 A.2d 546 (2007), cert. denied, 128 S. Ct. 905, 2008 U.S. LEXIS 126, 169 L. Ed. 2d 729 (U.S. 2008); Att'y Griev. Comm'n v. Hall, 408 Md. 306, 969 A.2d 953 (2009); Att'y Griev. Comm'n v. Khandpur, 421 Md. 1, 25 A.3d 165 (2011).

Stated in Att'y Griev. Comm'n v. Kreamer, 404 Md. 282, 946 A.2d 500 (2008).

Cited in Att'y Griev. Comm'n v. Seiden, 373 Md. 409, 818 A.2d 1108 (2003); Att'y Griev. Comm'n v. Mahone, 398 Md. 257, 920 A.2d 458 (2007); Att'y Griev. Comm'n v. Kendrick, 403 Md. 489, 943 A.2d 1173 (2008); Att'y Griev. Comm'n v. Smith, 405 Md. 107, 950 A.2d 101 (2008); Att'y Griev. Comm'n v. Marcalus, 414 Md. 501, 996 A.2d 350 (2010); Potomac Valley Orthopaedic Assocs. v. Md. State Bd. of Physicians, 417 Md. 622, 12 A.3d 84 (2011); Att'y Griev. Comm'n v. De La Paz, 418 Md. 534, 16 A.3d 181 (2011).

Rule 16-759. Disposition.

(a) **Oral argument.** The Court shall set a date for oral argument, unless oral argument is waived by the parties. Oral argument shall be conducted in accordance with Rule 8-522.

(b) **Review by Court of Appeals.** (1) Conclusions of law. The Court of Appeals shall review de novo the circuit court judge's conclusions of law.

(2) Findings of fact. (A) If no exceptions are filed. If no exceptions are filed, the Court may treat the findings of fact as established for the purpose of determining appropriate sanctions, if any.

(B) If exceptions are filed. If exceptions are filed, the Court of Appeals shall determine whether the findings of fact have been proven by the requisite standard of proof set out in Rule 16-757 (b). The Court may confine its review to the findings of fact challenged by the exceptions. The Court shall give due regard to the opportunity of the hearing judge to assess the credibility of witnesses.

(c) **Disposition.** The Court of Appeals may order (1) disbarment, (2) suspension, (3) reprimand, (4) inactive status, (5) dismissal of the disciplinary or remedial action, or (6) a remand for further proceedings.

(d) **Decision.** The decision of the Court of Appeals is final. The decision shall be evidenced by an order which the clerk shall certify under the seal of the Court. The order may be accompanied by an opinion. (Added Nov. 30, 2000, effective July 1, 2001.)

Source. — This Rule is derived in part from former Rule 16-711 (BV11) and is in part new.

Findings of fact supported by evidence. — Where a disciplinary matter was referred to another court, pursuant to Rule 16-752(a) of this rule and findings of fact and conclusions of law were made without appearance or opposition by the attorney, the court found support in the record for such findings and noted that the attorney had failed to establish factual matters in defense of his position, which was required by a preponderance of the evidence pursuant to this rule; the attorney had asserted that the service upon him was lacking and violated due process, however, his failure to appear and present evidence in support of that exception was sufficient reason to overrule it, in addition to the finding that service pursuant to Rule 16-753(a) was properly made on the Treasurer of the Client Protection Fund. Att'y Griev. Comm'n v. Faber, 373 Md. 173, 817 A.2d 205 (2003).

State supreme court found that the attorney's misconduct, as charged in the grievance commission's petition and supported by the trial court's findings of fact and conclusions of law, warranted disbarment; the evidence established that the attorney failed to act with reasonable diligence and promptness in representing a client in a divorce case, that the attorney failed to keep the client reasonably informed about the status of the representation and did not respond to reasonable requests for information, that the attorney failed to respond to lawful demands for information from disciplinary counsel, and that the totality of the attorney's conduct was prejudicial to the administration of justice. Att'y Griev. Comm'n v. Hodgson, 396 Md. 1, 912 A.2d 640 (2006).

In an attorney disciplinary matter, it was held that the attorney violated Md. R. Prof. Conduct 3.3 by filing expungement petitions for a client knowing that the client's charges were ineligible for expungement and, as a result, he was suspended from the practice of law for 60 days. Additionally, the findings and conclusions of the hearing officer that the attorney did not fraudulently obtain a duplicate driver's license after having his original license taken away at a sobriety checkpoint were found not to be clearly erroneous, and no deficiencies were found with regard to the allegations in the petition providing sufficient notice to the attorney of the charges against him. Att'y Griev. Comm'n v. Tanko, 408 Md. 404, 969 A.2d 1010 (2009).

Findings of fact and conclusions of law accepted due to parties' failures to file exceptions. — In an attorney disciplinary matter, a hearing judge's findings of fact and conclusions of law were accepted, under (b)(2)(A) of this Rule, for purposes of determining an appropriate sanction because neither the Attorney Grievance Commission nor the attorney against whom charges were brought filed exceptions to those findings and conclusions. Att'y Griev. Comm'n v. De La Paz, 418 Md. 534, 16 A.3d 181 (2011).

Scope of review. — When exceptions to the hearing judge's findings are taken properly, the Court of Appeals of Maryland is required to determine whether the findings of fact have been proven by the requisite standards of proof set out in (b). Att'y Griev. Comm'n v. Stolarz, 379 Md. 387, 842 A.2d 42 (2004).

In deciding, in an attorney disciplinary matter, whether a hearing judge's findings of fact are clearly erroneous where exceptions are filed, the reviewing court looks first to (b)(2)(B), which states that the Court of Appeals shall determine whether the findings of fact have been proven by the requisite standard of proof set out in Rule 16-757(b), and, under Rule 16-757(b), where exceptions to findings of fact are filed by bar counsel, the reviewing court considers that bar counsel, before the hearing judge, had the burden of proving the averments of the petition by clear and convincing evidence, so, where the excep-

tions are filed to findings that were favorable to a respondent attorney, under Rule 16-757(b), the court considers also that the attorney who asserts an affirmative defense or a matter of mitigation or extenuation has the burden of proving the defense or matter by a preponderance of the evidence. Att'y Griev. Comm'n v. Guida, 391 Md. 33, 891 A.2d 1085 (2006).

Although the trial court's conclusion that the record did not adequately support a finding that certain funds the attorney received were for legal fees or expenses was in error, the rest of the trial court's findings in a case where the attorney improperly commingled escrow account funds with operating expense account funds were supported by clear and convincing evidence, and, thus, would not be overturned by the state's highest court in the attorney's disciplinary proceeding. Att'y Griev. Comm'n v. Nussbaum, 401 Md. 612, 934 A.2d 1 (2007).

Hearing court's findings of fact based on the client's testimony about the attorney failing to inform the client that the attorney would not be representing the client at a removal hearing regarding the client's immigration status were not clearly erroneous. As a result, the State's highest court pursuant to (b) gave deference to the trial court's opportunity to assess the credibility of the witnesses in determining that the attorney's misconduct warranted a reprimand. Att'y Griev. Comm'n v. Akpan, 405 Md. 277, 950 A.2d 820 (2008).

Hearing judge's conclusion that an attorney violating Md. R. Prof. Conduct 1.1, 1.3, 8.1(a) and (b), and 8.4(a) and (d) was supported by clear and convincing evidence because the attorney's conduct in connection with an estate led to significant delay in closing the estate; the attorney owed the heirs to the estate competent and diligent representation but did not carry out either obligation, and after the attorney took over some responsibility for the property, his efforts on behalf of the estate were modest at best. Att'y Griev. Comm'n v. Pawlak, 408 Md. 288, 969 A.2d 311 (2009).

Indefinite suspension. — Following supplemental findings of fact and conclusions of law by the hearing court on remand, the Court of Appeals of Maryland considered earlier exceptions by an attorney which remained relevant, according to the standard of (b)(2)(B), as applied to the hearing judge's combined findings and conclusions. The court then indefinitely suspended the attorney because the court found that he (1) violated Md. R. Prof. Conduct 1.3 by largely neglecting his client's case; (2) violated Md. R. Prof. Conduct 1.4(a) by failing to keep his client reasonably informed; and (3) violated Md. R. Prof. Conduct 8.1(a) and 8.4(c) by misrepresenting to an investigator his reasons for inactivity. Att'y

Griev. Comm'n v. Lee, 393 Md. 385, 903 A.2d 360 (2006).

Disbarment — State's highest court found that the attorney should be disbarred, as clear and convincing evidence showed that the attorney falsely represented in a deposition that the business associate was a client of the attorney when that was not true, in violation of Md. R. Prof. Conduct 1.9, and that the attorney engaged in an impermissible conflict of interest in violation of Md. R. Prof. Conduct 8.4 when the attorney represented the corporation in a substantially similar matter in a lawsuit against the entity after the attorney had represented the entity for two years in matters that included the same matter that was the subject of the lawsuit; not only were the violations proven, but the attorney failed to prove the attorney's affirmative defense of waiver since the attorney presented a paucity of argument or evidence in that regard. Att'y Griev. Comm'n v. Siskind, 401 Md. 41, 930 A.2d 328 (2007).

Attorney was disbarred for violating Md. R. Prof. Conduct 1.15 and 8.4(a), (c), and (d), and Rule 16-607, because clear and convincing evidence established that he commingled personal and client funds and engaged in a pattern of dishonesty to hide his assets to avoid paying a judgment creditor. The evidence established that the attorney manipulated his corporate operations, his attorney escrow account, and his pension plan account to systematically avoid the judgment creditor's collection efforts and engaged in a pattern of behavior designed to conceal assets from attachment by the judgment creditor, which was conduct prejudicial to the administration of justice. Att'y Griev. Comm'n v. Foltz, 411 Md. 359, 983 A.2d 434 (2009).

Applied in Att'y Griev. Comm'n v. Maignan, 390 Md. 287, 888 A.2d 344 (2005); Att'y Griev. Comm'n v. Lee, 393 Md. 546, 903 A.2d 895 (2006); Att'y Griev. Comm'n v. Butler, 395 Md. 1, 909 A.2d 226 (2006); Att'y Griev. Comm'n v. Steinberg, 395 Md. 337, 910 A.2d 429 (2006); Att'y Griev. Comm'n v. Sweitzer, 395 Md. 586, 911 A.2d 440 (2006); Att'y Griev. Comm'n v. Sapero, 400 Md. 461, 929 A.2d 483 (2007); Att'y Griev. Comm'n v. Pak, 400 Md. 567, 929 A.2d 546 (2007), cert. denied, 128 S. Ct. 905, 2008 U.S. LEXIS 126, 169 L. Ed. 2d 729 (U.S. 2008); Att'y Griev. Comm'n v. Robertson, 400 Md. 618, 929 A.2d 576 (2007); Att'y Griev. Comm'n v. Floyd, 400 Md. 236, 929 A.2d 61 (2007); Att'y Griev. Comm'n v. Harris, 403 Md. 142, 939 A.2d 732 (2008); Att'y Griev. Comm'n v. Kendrick, 403 Md. 489, 943 A.2d 1173 (2008); Att'y Griev. Comm'n v. Kreamer, 404 Md. 282, 946 A.2d 500 (2008); Att'y Griev. Comm'n v. Snyder, 406 Md. 21, 956 A.2d 147 (2008); Att'y Griev. Comm'n v. Garcia, 410 Md. 507, 979 A.2d 146 (Aug. 28, 2009); Att'y Griev.

Comm'n v. Kwarteng, 411 Md. 652, 984 A.2d 865 (2009); Att'y Griev. Comm'n v. Lara, 418 Md. 355, 14 A.3d 650 (2011).

Quoted in Att'y Griev. Comm'n v. Davis, 375 Md. 131, 825 A.2d 430 (2003); Att'y Griev. Comm'n v. Gansler, 377 Md. 656, 835 A.2d 548 (2003); Att'y Griev. Comm'n v. Zdravkovich, 381 Md. 680, 852 A.2d 82 (2004); Att'y Griev. Comm'n v. Christopher, 383 Md. 624, 861 A.2d 692 (2004); Att'y Griev. Comm'n v. Brisbon, 385 Md. 667, 870 A.2d 586 (2005); Att'y Griev. Comm'n v. Jordan, 386 Md. 583, 873 A.2d 1161 (2005); Att'y Griev. Comm'n v. Zakroff, 387 Md. 603, 876 A.2d 664 (2005), cert. denied, 2006 Md. LEXIS 561 (2006); cert. denied, 2006 Md. LEXIS 571 (Md. 2006); Att'y Griev. Comm'n v. Zakroff, 387 Md. 603, 876 A.2d 664 (2005), cert. denied, 2006 Md. LEXIS 561 (2006); cert. denied, 2006 Md. LEXIS 571 (Md. 2006); Att'y Griev. Comm'n v. Mba-Jonas, 397 Md. 690, 919 A.2d 669 (2007); Att'y Griev. Comm'n v. Goff, 399 Md. 1, 922 A.2d 554 (2007); Att'y Griev. Comm'n v. Wingerter, 400 Md. 214, 929 A.2d 47 (2007); Att'y Griev. Comm'n v. Saridakis, 402 Md. 413, 936 A.2d 886 (2007); Att'y Griev. Comm'n v. Parsons, 404 Md. 175, 946 A.2d 437 (2008); Att'y Griev. Comm'n v. Whitehead, 405 Md. 240, 950 A.2d 798 (2008); Att'y Griev. Comm'n v. McClain, 406 Md. 1, 956 A.2d 135 (2008), cert. denied, 129 S. Ct. 1691, 2009 U.S. LEXIS 2433, 173 L. Ed. 2d 1036 (U.S. 2009); Att'y Griev. Comm'n v. Jarosinski, 411 Md. 432, 983 A.2d 477 (2009); Att'y Griev. Comm'n v. Robaton, 411 Md. 415, 983 A.2d 467 (2009); Att'y Griev. Comm'n v. Bleecker, 414 Md. 147, 994 A.2d 928 (2010); Att'y Griev. Comm'n v. Coppola, 419 Md. 370, 19 A.3d 431 (2011); Att'y Griev. Comm'n v. Stern, 419 Md. 525, 19 A.3d 904 (2011); Att'y Griev. Comm'n v. Khandpur, 421 Md. 1, 25 A.3d 165 (2011).

Cited in Att'y Griev. Comm'n v. McClain, 373 Md. 196, 817 A.2d 218 (2003); Att'y Griev. Comm'n v. Gore, 380 Md. 455, 845 A.2d 1204 (2004); Anne Arundel County v. Nes, 163 Md. App. 515, 881 A.2d 1161 (2005); Att'y Griev. Comm'n v. Weiss, 389 Md. 531, 886 A.2d 606 (2005); Att'y Griev. Comm'n v. Kinnane, 390 Md. 324, 888 A.2d 1178 (2005); Att'y Griev. Comm'n v. Lee, 390 Md. 517, 890 A.2d 273 (2005); Att'y Griev. Comm'n v. Ward, 396 Md. 203, 913 A.2d 41 (2006); Att'y Griev. Comm'n v. Mahone, 398 Md. 257, 920 A.2d 458 (2007); Att'y Griev. Comm'n v. Webster, 402 Md. 448, 937 A.2d 161 (2007); Att'y Griev. Comm'n v. Elmendorf, 404 Md. 353, 946 A.2d 542 (2008); Att'y Griev. Comm'n v. Nichols, 405 Md. 207, 950 A.2d 778 (2008); Att'y Griev. Comm'n v. Shryock, 408 Md. 105, 968 A.2d 593 (2009); Att'y Griev. Comm'n v. Hall, 408 Md. 306, 969 A.2d 953 (2009); Att'y Griev. Comm'n v. McLaughlin, 409 Md. 304, 974 A.2d 315 (2009); Att'y Griev. Comm'n v. Bahgat, 411 Md. 568, 984 A.2d 225 (2009); Att'y Griev. Comm'n

v. Marcalus, 414 Md. 501, 996 A.2d 350 (2010); Att'y Griev. Comm'n v. Edib, 415 Md. 696, 4 A.3d 957 (2010); Att'y Griev. Comm'n v. Usiak, 418 Md. 667, 18 A.3d 1 (2011); Att'y Griev. Comm'n v. Carithers, 421 Md. 28, 25 A.3d 181 (2011).

Rule 16-760. Order imposing discipline or inactive status.

(a) **Effective date of order.** Unless otherwise stated in the order, an order providing for the disbarment, suspension, or reprimand of a respondent or the placement of a respondent on inactive status shall take effect immediately. The order may provide that the disbarment, suspension, reprimand, or placement on inactive status be deferred for a specified period of time to allow the respondent a reasonable opportunity to comply with the requirements of section (c) of this Rule.

Cross references. — For the implementation of this Rule, see *Attorney Grievance Commission v. Maignan*, 402 Md. 39 (2007).

(b) **Reprimand.** Unless accompanied by a reported opinion, an order that reprimands the respondent shall summarize the misconduct for which the reprimand is imposed, include specific reference to any rule or statute violated by the respondent, and state any conditions imposed upon the respondent pursuant to section (h) of this Rule. Upon the entry of an order that reprimands a respondent, the Clerk of the Court of Appeals shall give the notice required by Rule 16-723 (e).

(c) **Duties of respondent.** Unless otherwise stated in the order, an order that disbars or suspends a respondent or places a respondent on inactive status shall operate as an immediate directive that the respondent perform each of the following duties in a timely manner:

(1) The respondent shall not accept any new clients or undertake any new or further representation of existing clients.

(2) The respondent shall take any action necessary to protect current clients.

(3) The respondent shall conclude any current client matters that can be concluded within 15 days after the date of the order.

(4) Within 15 days after the date of the order, the respondent shall supply to Bar Counsel or an attorney designated by Bar Counsel a list of the attorney's clients (by name, address, and telephone number) whose legal matters have not been concluded by the respondent and identify any client matters (by name, tribunal, and docket reference) currently pending in any court or agency.

(5) Within 15 days after the date of the order, the respondent shall mail a letter to each client whose legal matter has not been concluded, to counsel for any other party or to any unrepresented party in a pending action or proceeding, and to all attorneys with whom the respondent is associated in the practice of law, notifying each of them of the order and the fact that the respondent will be unable to practice law after the effective date of the order. The respondent shall supply copies of the letters to Bar Counsel or an attorney designated by Bar Counsel.

(6) Within 30 days after the date of the order, the respondent shall withdraw from all client matters.

(7) Unless suspended for a definite period of not more than one year, the respondent shall promptly request the publisher of any telephone directory or law listing to remove any listing or reference that suggests that the respondent is eligible to practice law.

(8) The respondent shall deliver promptly to clients with pending matters any papers or other property to which the clients are entitled or notify the clients and any co-counsel of a suitable time and place to obtain the papers and other property and call attention to any urgent need to obtain them.

(9) The respondent shall promptly notify the disciplinary authority in each jurisdiction in which the respondent is admitted to practice of the disciplinary sanction imposed by the Court of Appeals.

(10) Within 30 days of the effective date of the order, the respondent shall file with the Commission an affidavit that states (A) the manner and extent to which the respondent has complied with the order and the provisions of this section, (B) the names of all state and federal jurisdictions in which and administrative agencies before which the respondent has been admitted to practice, (C) the residence and any other address of the respondent to which future communications may be directed, (D) the policy number and the name and address of each insurer that provided malpractice insurance coverage to the respondent during the past five years and the inclusive dates of coverage, and (E) the date and manner that a copy of the affidavit required by this subsection was served upon Bar Counsel. The affidavit shall be accompanied by copies of the list required by subsection (c) (4) of this Rule and the letters mailed under subsection (c) (5) of this Rule.

(11) If the respondent is or becomes employed or retained by or associated with a lawyer, the respondent shall comply with Rule 5.3 (d) of the Maryland Lawyers' Rules of Professional Conduct and assist the supervising lawyer in complying with the supervising lawyer's obligations under the Rule.

(12) The respondent shall maintain records of the various steps taken to comply with this section and the order of the Court of Appeals and make those records available to Bar Counsel on request.

(d) **Effect of order; prohibited acts.** After the effective date of an order that disbars or suspends a respondent or places a respondent on inactive status, the respondent may not practice law, attempt to practice law, or offer to practice law in this State either directly or through an attorney, officer, director, partner, trustee, agent, or employee. Unless otherwise stated in an order of the Court of Appeals, the respondent shall not:

(1) occupy, share, or use office space in which an attorney practices law unless under circumstances clearly indicating to clients, prospective clients, and persons who may visit the office that the respondent is not a lawyer and is not permitted to practice law;

(2) use any business card, sign, or advertisement suggesting that the respondent is entitled to practice law or maintain, either alone or with another, an office for the practice of law;

(3) use any stationery, bank account, checks, or labels on which the respondent's name appears as an attorney or in connection with any office for the practice of law;

(4) solicit or procure any legal business or retainer for an attorney, whether or not for personal gain; and

(5) share in any fees for legal services performed by another attorney after the effective date of the order, but may be compensated for the reasonable value of services rendered prior to that date.

(e) **Duties of Clerk.** On the effective date of an order that disbars, suspends, or places the respondent on inactive status, the Clerk of the Court of Appeals shall strike the name of the respondent from the register of attorneys in that Court and shall certify that fact to the Trustees of the Client Protection Fund of the Bar of Maryland and the clerks of all courts in this State. The Clerk of the Court of Appeals also shall give the notice required by Rule 16-723 (e).

(f) **Duties of Bar Counsel.** Bar Counsel shall enforce the order of the Court of Appeals and the provisions of this Rule. In enforcing section (c) of this Rule, Bar Counsel may designate an attorney to monitor the respondent's compliance and to receive the list and copies of letters described in subsections (c) (4) and (c) (5) of this Rule. If Rule 16-777 is applicable, Bar Counsel may request the appointment of a conservator in accordance with that Rule.

(g) **Orders for suspension or inactive status.** (1) Definite period. An order of the Court of Appeals that suspends the respondent from the practice of law for a definite period of time may specify any conditions to be satisfied before or after the suspension expires.

(2) Indefinite suspension or inactive status. An order of the Court of Appeals that suspends the respondent from the practice of law indefinitely, or places the respondent on inactive status, may permit the respondent to apply for reinstatement in accordance with Rule 16-781 not earlier than a specified period of time after the effective date of the order.

(h) **Conditions.** An order entered under this Rule may impose one or more conditions to be satisfied by the respondent, whether as a condition precedent to reinstatement or a condition of probation after reinstatement, including a requirement that the respondent:

(1) demonstrate, by the report of a health care professional or other proper evidence, that the respondent is mentally and physically competent to resume the practice of law;

(2) upon reinstatement, engage an attorney satisfactory to Bar Counsel to monitor the respondent's legal practice pursuant to section (i) of this Rule;

(3) prove that every former client has been reimbursed for any part of fees paid in advance for legal services that were not completed;

(4) satisfy any judgment or reimburse the Client Protection Fund of the Bar of Maryland for any claim that arose out of the respondent's practice of law;

(5) make restitution to any client of any sum found to be due to the client;

(6) limit the nature or extent of the respondent's future practice of law;

(7) pay all costs assessed by the order and any mandate of the Court of Appeals;

(8) participate in a program tailored to individual circumstances that provides the respondent with law office management assistance, lawyer assistance or counseling, treatment for alcohol or substance abuse, psychological counseling, or specified courses in legal ethics, professional responsibility, or continuing legal education;

(9) issue an apology; and

(10) take any other corrective action that may be reasonable and appropriate.

(i) **Monitors.** An attorney engaged to monitor the respondent's legal practice pursuant to subsection (h) (2) of this Rule shall have access to client files, records of entrusted funds, and records of any attorney trust accounts maintained by the respondent. The respondent shall pay the reasonable fees and expenses of the monitor for the period of time stated in the order. The monitor shall make monthly or quarterly reports to Bar Counsel as Bar Counsel may direct.

(j) **Responsibility of affiliated attorneys.** After the effective date of an order that disbars or suspends a respondent or places a respondent on inactive status, no attorney may assist the respondent in any activity that constitutes the practice of law or in any activity prohibited under section (d) of this Rule. Upon notice of the order, an attorney affiliated with the respondent as a member of a law firm or shareholder of a professional corporation shall take reasonable action to ensure compliance with this Rule. The firm or corporation may give written notice to any client of the respondent's inability to practice law and of its willingness to represent the client with the client's consent.

Cross references. — Rule 5.5 of the Maryland Lawyers' Rules of Professional Conduct.

(k) **Non-admitted attorney.** (1) Duties of Clerk. On the effective date of an order by the Court of Appeals that disbars or suspends a non-admitted attorney, the Clerk of the Court of Appeals shall place the name of that attorney on a list maintained in that Court of non-admitted attorneys who are excluded from exercising in any manner the privilege of practicing law in the State. The Clerk also shall forward a copy of the order to the clerks of all courts in this State and to the State Court Administrator and the Board of Law Examiners to be maintained with the docket of out-of-state attorneys who are denied special admission to practice under the Rules Governing Admission to the Bar of Maryland. The Clerk shall give the notice required by Rule 16-723 (e).

(2) Effect of order. After the effective date of an order entered under this section, the attorney may not practice law in this State and is disqualified from admission to the practice of law in this State.

(l) **Modification of order.** Upon joint stipulation or verified motion filed by the respondent, the Court of Appeals may reduce a period of suspension, waive a requirement or condition imposed by this Rule or by order, or otherwise modify an order entered under this Rule. Relief shall be denied without a hearing unless it appears from the stipulation or from clear and convincing evidence submitted with the motion that the respondent is attempting in good faith to comply with the order but that full and exact compliance has become impossible or will result in unreasonable hardship. If necessary to resolve a genuine issue of material fact, the Court may enter an order designating a judge in accordance with Rule 16-752 to hold a hearing in accordance with Rule 16-757.

(m) **Sanctions for violations.** (1) Ineligibility for reinstatement. A petition for reinstatement filed pursuant to Rule 16-781 may be dismissed if the respondent fails to demonstrate (A) substantial compliance with sections (c) and (d) of this Rule and the order of the Court of Appeals, or (B) good cause for noncompliance.

(2) Disciplinary or remedial action. Upon receiving information from any source that a respondent has violated sections (c) or (d) of this Rule or the order of the Court of Appeals, and in addition to any other remedy, Bar Counsel may file a Petition for Disciplinary or Remedial Action pursuant to Rule 16-751 based upon the violation.

(3) Injunction against unauthorized practice. Upon receiving information from any source indicating that a respondent is violating section (d) of this Rule, Bar Counsel shall investigate the matter and may institute or intervene in an action in any court to enjoin the respondent from further violations.

(4) Contempt. If a respondent violates section (c) or (d) of this Rule or the order of the Court of Appeals, the Commission may request the initiation of a proceeding for constructive criminal contempt in accordance with the provisions of Rule 15-205 and may initiate a proceeding for constructive civil contempt in accordance with the provisions of Rule 15-206. (Added Nov. 30, 2000, effective July 1, 2001; amended effective Nov. 6, 2002; Nov. 12, 2003, effective Jan. 1, 2004; amended Sept. 10, 2009, effective Oct. 1, 2009.)

Source. — This Rule is derived in part from former Rules 16-713 (BV13) and 16-714 (BV14) and is in part new.

Effect of amendments. — The 2002 amendment substituted "Client Protection Fund of the Bar of Maryland" for "Clients' Security Trust Fund" in (e) and (h) (4).

The 2003 amendment added the last sentence in (b) and (e); deleted "Bar Counsel shall give the notice required by Rule 16-723 (d)" following the third sentence in (f); and in (k)(1), deleted "and Bar Counsel" in the subheading, substituted "Clerk shall also" for "Clerk also shall" in the second sentence, "The Clerk" for "Bar Counsel" and "(e)" for "(d)" in the last sentence.

The 2006 amendment added (c)(11) and redesignated former (c)(11) as present (c)(12); and deleted former (d)(2) and redesignated former (d)(3) as present (d)(2) and redesignated the remaining subsections accordingly.

The 2009 amendment added the cross reference following (a).

Editor's note. — The June, 2, 2005 court order lifted the stay on the application of (d)(2) effective August 31, 2005; however, by court order August 8, 2005, the stay was reinstated pending further action by the court which remanded the issue to the Committee for a revised recommendation.

Out-of-state attorneys sanctioned for failing to supervise in-State associate. — In a disciplinary proceeding against two supervising attorneys from out-of-state, who opened up a Maryland office and hired a Maryland associate, who ended up failing to respond to motions compelling discovery in 47 cases filed by her on behalf of the supervising attorneys' Maryland clients, the hearing judge was found to have properly determined that they violated Md. R. Prof. Conduct 5.1 and 1.4 and, therefore, they were suspended indefinitely, with the right to apply for reinstatement no sooner than 90 days after the effective date of the suspension. The findings and conclusions adequately found that the supervising attorneys failed to adequately supervise the relatively inexperienced associate they hired, failed to respond to her requests for paralegal help, failed to establish supervisory procedures designed deliberately to address the associate's inexperience and to counterbalance her physical distance from the ready availability of steadying interaction with peers and managers, failed to audit her case load, among other failings, as well as failed to directly communicate with a Maryland client regarding his case. Att'y Griev. Comm'n v. Kimmel, 405 Md. 647, 955 A.2d 269 (2008).

Further representation after suspension — Subsection (c)(1) is intended to make more specific the recommended prohibition against undertaking further legal matters, to make clear that, unless the order provided otherwise, the attorney could not undertake any further representation of existing clients. Unless the court affirmatively chose otherwise, a suspended or disbarred lawyer simply could not continue to practice law, even for existing clients. Att'y Griev. Comm'n v. Maignan, 402 Md. 39, 935 A.2d 409 (2007).

Further representation after suspension. — Subsection (c)(2) requires a lawyer to take any action necessary to protect current clients, which may require a very prompt notice to the client, to adverse or other interested parties, and to tribunals in which litigation is pending, expedited efforts to assist the client in obtaining new counsel, and, if necessary because of a true emergency, a request of the Court of Appeals of Maryland to consider a limited stay of the disbarment or suspension order; it cannot properly be read, however, as contravening the clear prohibition in (c)(1) against any further representation of a client. Att'y Griev. Comm'n v. Maignan, 402 Md. 39, 935 A.2d 409 (2007).

Applied in Att'y Griev. Comm'n v. Ficker, 399 Md. 445, 924 A.2d 1105 (2007); Att'y Griev. Comm'n v. Robertson, 400 Md. 618, 929 A.2d 576 (2007); Att'y Griev. Comm'n v. Sucklal, 418 Md. 1, 12 A.3d 650 (2011).

Cited in Att'y Griev. Comm'n v. Saridakis, 402 Md. 413, 936 A.2d 886 (2007); Att'y Griev. Comm'n v. Adams, 404 Md. 1, 944 A.2d 1115 (2008).

Rule 16-761. Costs.

(a) **Allowance and allocation.** Except as provided in Rule 16-781 (n), and unless the Court of Appeals orders otherwise, the prevailing party in proceedings under this Chapter is entitled to costs. The Court, by order, may allocate costs among the parties.

(b) **Judgment.** Costs of proceedings under this Chapter, including the costs of all transcripts, shall be taxed by the Clerk of the Court of Appeals and included in the order as a judgment. On motion, the Court may review the action of the Clerk.

(c) **Enforcement.** Rule 8-611 applies to proceedings under this Chapter. (Added Nov. 30, 2000, effective July 1, 2001; Nov. 12, 2003, effective Jan. 1, 2004.)

Source. — This Rule is in part derived from former Rule 16-715 (BV15) and in part new.

Effect of amendments. — The 2003 amendment substituted "(n)" for "(o)" in (a).

Bankruptcy. — Debts owed by an attorney as a result of disciplinary actions are nondischargeable under 11 U.S.C.S. § 523(a)(7); monetary judgment for costs entered by the state court in debtor's attorney disciplinary proceeding, initiated by the state attorney grievance commission and imposed under former Rule 16-715(c), was nondischargeable because the commission was a governmental unit and the purpose of imposing costs on the attorney was to protect the public by serving the deterrence and rehabilitative goals of the commission. Att'y Griev. Comm'n v. Smith (In re Smith), 317 B.R. 302 (Bankr. D. Md. 2004).

Applied in Att'y Griev. Comm'n v. Ficker, 399 Md. 445, 924 A.2d 1105 (2007); Att'y Griev. Comm'n v. Kalil, 402 Md. 358, 936 A.2d 854 (2007); Att'y Griev. Comm'n v. Parsons, 404 Md. 175, 946 A.2d 437 (2008).

Cited in Att'y Griev. Comm'n v. West, 378 Md. 395, 836 A.2d 588 (2003); Att'y Griev. Comm'n v. Braskey, 378 Md. 425, 836 A.2d 605 (2003); Att'y Griev. Comm'n v. Post, 379 Md. 60, 839 A.2d 718 (2003); Att'y Griev. Comm'n v. Stolarz, 379 Md. 387, 842 A.2d 42 (2004); Att'y Griev. Comm'n v. Hermina, 379 Md. 503, 842

A.2d 762 (2004); Att'y Griev. Comm'n v. Sperling, 380 Md. 180, 844 A.2d 397 (2004); Att'y Griev. Comm'n v. Velasquez, 380 Md. 651, 846 A.2d 422 (2004); Att'y Griev. Comm'n v. Brown, 380 Md. 661, 846 A.2d 428 (2004); Att'y Griev. Comm'n v. Rose, 383 Md. 385, 859 A.2d 659 (2004); Att'y Griev. Comm'n v. Muhammad, — Md. —, — A.2d — (2005); Att'y Griev. Comm'n v. Theriault, 390 Md. 202, 888 A.2d 292 (2005); Att'y Griev. Comm'n v. Maignan, 390 Md. 287, 888 A.2d 344 (2005); Att'y Griev. Comm'n v. Robertson, 400 Md. 618, 929 A.2d 576 (2007); Att'y Griev. Comm'n v. Wingerter, 400 Md. 214, 929 A.2d 47 (2007); Att'y Griev. Comm'n v. Mba-Jonas, 402 Md. 334, 936 A.2d 839 (2007); Att'y Griev. Comm'n v. Harris, 403 Md. 142, 939 A.2d 732 (2008); Att'y Griev. Comm'n v. Elmendorf, 404 Md. 353, 946 A.2d 542 (2008); Att'y Griev. Comm'n v. Kreamer, 404 Md. 282, 946 A.2d 500 (2008); Att'y Griev. Comm'n v. Walker, 405 Md. 3, 948 A.2d 1263 (2008); Att'y Griev. Comm'n v. Smith, 405 Md. 107, 950 A.2d 101 (2008); Att'y Griev. Comm'n v. Nichols, 405 Md. 207, 950 A.2d 778 (2008); Att'y Griev. Comm'n v. Akpan, 405 Md. 277, 950 A.2d 820 (2008); Att'y Griev. Comm'n v. Ugwuonye, 405 Md. 351, 952 A.2d 226 (2008); Att'y Griev. Comm'n v. Hall, 408 Md. 306, 969 A.2d 953 (2009); Att'y Griev. Comm'n v. Gisriel, 409 Md. 331, 974 A.2d 331 (2009); Att'y Griev. Comm'n v. Jarosinski, 411 Md. 432, 983 A.2d 477 (2009); Att'y Griev. Comm'n v. Robaton, 411 Md. 415, 983 A.2d 467 (2009); Att'y Griev. Comm'n v. Bahgat, 411 Md. 568, 984 A.2d 225 (2009); Att'y Griev. Comm'n v. Kwarteng, 411 Md. 652, 984 A.2d 865 (2009); Att'y Griev. Comm'n v. Gordon, 413 Md. 46, 991 A.2d 51 (2010); Att'y Griev. Comm'n v. Marcalus, 414 Md. 501, 996 A.2d 350 (2010); Armstead v. State, 195 Md. App. 599, 7 A.3d 169 (2010); Att'y Griev. Comm'n v. Elliott, 417 Md. 659, 12 A.3d 105 (2011); Att'y Griev. Comm'n v. Tauber, — Md. —, 26 A.3d 967 (2011); Att'y Griev. Comm'n v. Keiner, — Md. —, — A.3d — (Aug. 19, 2011).

Rule 16-771. Disciplinary or remedial action upon conviction of crime.

(a) **Duty of attorney charged.** An attorney charged with a serious crime in this State or any other jurisdiction shall promptly inform Bar Counsel in writing of the criminal charge. Thereafter, the attorney shall promptly notify Bar Counsel of the final disposition of the charge in each court that exercises jurisdiction over the charge.

Cross references. — Rule 16-701 (k).

(b) **Petition in Court of Appeals.** Upon receiving and verifying information from any source that an attorney has been convicted of a serious crime, Bar Counsel may file a Petition for Disciplinary or Remedial Action in the Court of Appeals pursuant to Rule 16-751 (a) (2). The petition may be filed whether the conviction resulted from a plea of guilty, nolo contendere, or a verdict after trial and whether an appeal or any other post-conviction proceeding is pending. The petition shall allege the fact of the conviction and include a request that the attorney be suspended immediately from the practice of law. A certified copy of the judgment of conviction shall be attached to the petition and shall be prima facie evidence of the fact that the attorney was convicted of the crime charged.

(c) **Temporary suspension of attorney.** Upon filing of the petition pursuant to section (b) of this Rule, the Court of Appeals shall issue an order requiring the attorney to show cause within 15 days from the date of the order why the attorney should not be suspended immediately from the practice of law until the further order of the Court of Appeals. If, after consideration of the petition and the answer to the order to show cause, the Court of Appeals determines that the attorney has been convicted of a serious crime, the Court may enter an order suspending the attorney from the practice of law until final disposition of the disciplinary or remedial action. The Court of Appeals shall vacate the order and terminate the suspension if the conviction is reversed or vacated at any stage of appellate or collateral review.

Cross references. — Rule 16-760.

(d) **Statement of Charges.** If the Court of Appeals denies a petition filed under section (b) of this Rule, Bar Counsel may file a Statement of Charges under Rule 16-741.

(e) **Further proceedings on petition.** When a petition filed pursuant to section (b) of this Rule alleges the conviction of a serious crime, the Court of Appeals may enter an order designating a judge pursuant to Rule 16-752 to hold a hearing in accordance with Rule 16-757.

(1) No appeal of conviction. If the attorney does not appeal the conviction, the hearing shall be held within a reasonable time after the time for appeal has expired.

(2) Appeal of conviction. If the attorney appeals the conviction, the hearing shall be delayed, except as provided in section (f), until the completion of appellate review.

(A) If, after completion of appellate review, the conviction is reversed or vacated, the judge to whom the action is assigned shall either dismiss the petition or hear the action on the basis of evidence other than the conviction.

(B) If, after the completion of appellate review, the conviction is not reversed or vacated, the hearing shall be held within a reasonable time after the mandate is issued.

(3) Effect of incarceration. If the attorney is incarcerated as a result of the conviction, the hearing shall be delayed until the termination of incarceration unless the attorney requests an earlier hearing and makes all arrangements (including financial arrangements) to attend the hearing or waives the right to attend.

(f) **Right to earlier hearing.** If the hearing on the petition has been delayed under subsection (e) (2) of this Rule and the attorney has been suspended from the practice of law under section (c) of this Rule, the attorney may request that the judge to whom the action is assigned hold an earlier hearing, at which the conviction shall be considered a final judgment.

(g) **Conclusive effect of final conviction of crime.** In any proceeding under this Chapter, a final judgment of any court of record convicting an attorney of a crime, whether the conviction resulted from a plea of guilty, nolo contendere, or a verdict after trial, is conclusive evidence of the guilt of the attorney of that crime. As used in this Rule, "final judgment" means a judgment as to which all rights to direct appellate review have been exhausted. The introduction of the judgment does not preclude the Commission or Bar Counsel from introducing additional evidence or the attorney from introducing evidence or otherwise showing cause why no discipline should be imposed. (Added Nov. 30, 2000, effective July 1, 2001; Nov. 12, 2003, effective Jan. 1, 2004.)

Source. — This Rule is in part derived from former Rules 16-710 e (BV10 e) and 16-716 (BV16) and in part new.

Effect of amendments. — The 2003 amendment, in (b), substituted "may" for "shall" in the first and second sentence and "(a)(2)" for "and serve the attorney in accordance with Rule 16-753."

Signing petition for expungement of arrest records of unmet person. — It was not dishonest, fraudulent or deceitful for an attorney to sign a petition for expungement of the arrest records of a person he had never met, when asked to do so as a favor for a deputy State's attorney. Att'y Griev. Comm'n v. Miles, 280 Md. 681, 374 A.2d 1159 (1977).

Final judgment — Final judgment of which this Rule speaks is one that exists when all avenues of direct appeal from the judgment of conviction and sentence are no longer open to the defendant. Maryland State Bar Ass'n v. Kerr, 272 Md. 687, 326 A.2d 180 (1974).

Conviction in a criminal case is final — Conviction in a criminal case, State or federal, is final for purposes of this Rule where a pending new trial motion was filed after the conviction had been affirmed on appeal and certiorari denied by the Supreme Court of the United States. Maryland State Bar Ass'n v. Rosenberg, 273 Md. 351, 329 A.2d 106 (1974).

The judgment entered by a California district court was conclusive evidence of the defendant's conviction for violating a federal statute. Att'y Griev. Comm'n v. Dechowitz, 358 Md. 184, 747 A.2d 657 (2000).

Conviction for misprison of felony. — Plea of guilty to misprison of a felony was conclusive evidence of guilt and supported a finding that the attorney violated Rule 8.4 of the Lawyers' Rules of Professional Conduct. Att'y Griev. Comm'n v. Wingerter, 400 Md. 214, 929 A.2d 47 (2007).

Integrity of criminal conviction cannot be attacked in disciplinary proceeding — Integrity of criminal conviction cannot be attacked in disciplinary proceeding by invoking the Court of Appeals to reweigh or to reevaluate the respondent's guilt or innocence. Att'y Griev. Comm'n v. Barnes, 286 Md. 474, 408 A.2d 719 (1979).

Nolo contendere plea is admissible in disciplinary proceedings affecting attorneys. — See Agnew v. State, 51 Md. App. 614, 446 A.2d 425 (1982).

Plea of nolo contendere tantamount to conviction. — Prior Rule provided that a plea of nolo contendere is tantamount to conviction for the purposes of disciplinary proceedings. Att'y Griev. Comm'n v. Brewster, 280 Md. 473, 374 A.2d 602 (1977).

When attorney is convicted of crime of moral turpitude, disbarment follows automatically — When attorney is convicted of crime of moral turpitude, disbarment follows automatically unless compelling extenuating circumstances are established. Att'y Griev. Comm'n v. Barnes, 286 Md. 474, 408 A.2d 719 (1979); Att'y Griev. Comm'n v. Kahn, 290 Md. 654, 431 A.2d 1336 (1981).

Attorney conduct which involves moral turpitude and is infected with fraud, deceit, or dishonesty shall require disbarment unless the attorney can demonstrate by clear and convincing evidence that there are compelling extenuating circumstances that merit a less onerous sanction. Att'y Griev. Comm'n v. Burka, 292 Md. 221, 438 A.2d 514 (1981).

"Moral turpitude" — "Moral turpitude" is an act of baseness, vileness, or depravity in the private and social duties which a man owes to his fellow men, or to society in general, contrary to the accepted and customary rule of right and duty between man and man. Att'y Griev. Comm'n v. Barnes, 286 Md. 474, 408 A.2d 719 (1979).

Bribery may be deemed conduct involving moral turpitude. — Where circumstances clearly permit an inference of corrupt intent, bribery may be deemed to be conduct involving moral turpitude so as to justify disbarment of an attorney in the absence of compelling circumstances justifying a lesser sanction. Att'y Griev. Comm'n v. Spector, 293 Md. 324, 443 A.2d 965 (1982).

Convictions involving moral turpitude. — An attorney's convictions of obtaining money under false pretenses with intent to defraud and of fraudulent and willful appropriation of trust assets necessarily meant establishment of a fraudulent intent, and hence involves moral turpitude. Att'y Griev. Comm'n v. Andresen, 281 Md. 152, 379 A.2d 159 (1977).

Final adjudication of attorney's misconduct by foreign court — Final adjudication of attorney's misconduct by foreign court is conclusive proof of the misconduct in the hearing of charges pursuant to this Rule. Att'y Griev. Comm'n v. Hines, 304 Md. 625, 500 A.2d 646 (1985).

Though New York applies a lower standard of proof in attorney discipline cases, there is no reason to believe that New York courts treat such matters less seriously or wholly inconsistently with the manner exercised by the Maryland Court of Appeals; accordingly, there is no problem in accepting a New York court's findings in attorney discipline cases based on the different standard of proof. Att'y Griev. Comm'n v. Moore, 301 Md. 169, 482 A.2d 497 (1984).

Final judgment in D.C. Court of Appeals conclusive in this State. — Under prior Rule 1, the final adjudication of an attorney's misconduct by the District of Columbia Court of Appeals is conclusive proof of that misconduct in a Maryland hearing. Att'y Griev. Comm'n v. Moore, 301 Md. 169, 482 A.2d 497 (1984); Att'y Griev. Comm'n v. Gittens, 346 Md. 316, 697 A.2d 83 (1997).

Affirmation of agency finding not same as judicial finding. — Affirmation of an administrative agency finding by the U.S. Court of Appeals is not tantamount to a finding by a judicial tribunal. See Att'y Griev. Comm'n v. Miller, 310 Md. 163, 528 A.2d 481 (1987).

Suspension denied. — Attorney Grievance Commission of Maryland's request that attorney be suspended from practice of law was denied, because the offense that the attorney stood convicted of in the District of Columbia, engaging in the transmission of money without a license, did not reveal anything about the attorney's character, and the evidence showed that the attorney did not intend to violate the law but actually tried to comply with it by hiring an attorney for that purpose. Att'y Griev. Comm'n v. Downey, 413 Md. 1, 990 A.2d 1070 (2010).

Disbarment. — In an attorney disciplinary matter, the attorney was disbarred as a result of having violated Rule 8.4(a)-(d) of the Lawyer's Rules of Professional Conduct based on his guilty plea to the federal crimes involving conspiracy to defraud the government, in violation of 18 U.S.C.S. §§ 371 and 1546(a), based on his actions in knowingly filing a false letter with the United States Immigration and Naturalization Service on behalf of a client/immigrant in an immigration proceeding. The Court of Appeals of Maryland found no compelling extenuating circumstances, including the attorney's great remorse, to except him from disbarment based on his intention to commit fraud, to deceive, and to misrepresent. Att'y Griev. Comm'n v. Garcia, 410 Md. 507, 979 A.2d 146 (Aug. 28, 2009).

Quoted in Att'y Griev. Comm'n v. Tayback, 378 Md. 578, 837 A.2d 158 (2003); Att'y Griev. Comm'n v. Ayres-Fountain, 379 Md. 44, 838 A.2d 1238 (2003).

Stated in Att'y Griev. Comm'n v. Olver, 376 Md. 650, 831 A.2d 66 (2003).

Cited in Rourke v. Amchem Prods., Inc., 153 Md. App. 91, 835 A.2d 193 (2003), aff'd, 384 Md. 329, 863 A.2d 926 (2004).

Rule 16-772. Consent to discipline or inactive status.

(a) **General requirement.** An attorney may consent to discipline or placement on inactive status in accordance with this Rule.

(b) **Consent to discipline for misconduct.** (1) Joint petition. An attorney may consent to disbarment or other discipline by joining with Bar Counsel in a petition for an order disbarring the attorney, suspending the attorney from the practice of law, or reprimanding the attorney. The petition shall be signed by the attorney and Bar Counsel and filed in the Court of Appeals. If a suspension is requested, the petition shall state whether the suspension should be indefinite or for a stated period and shall set forth any conditions that the parties agree should be imposed. If a reprimand is requested, the petition shall state the proposed text of the reprimand and any conditions.

(2) Affidavit required. A joint petition filed under subsection (b) (1) of this Rule shall be accompanied by an affidavit by the attorney that certifies that the attorney:

(A) is aware that an investigation or proceeding is currently pending involving allegations of professional misconduct, the nature of which shall be specifically set forth;

(B) knows that if a hearing were to be held, sufficient evidence could be produced to sustain the allegations of misconduct;

(C) consents to the disbarment or other discipline stated in the petition;

(D) gives the consent freely and voluntarily without coercion or duress;

(E) is aware of the effects of the disbarment or other discipline to which the attorney is consenting; and

(F) agrees to comply with Rule 16-760 and any conditions stated in the petition that the Court of Appeals may impose.

(3) Order of the Court of Appeals. Upon the filing of the joint petition and the affidavit, the Court of Appeals may enter an order, signed by the Chief Judge or a judge designated by the Chief Judge, disbarring the attorney by consent from the practice of law in the State, suspending the attorney by consent from the practice of law, or reprimanding the attorney by consent and imposing any conditions stated in the petition. The provisions of Rule 16-760 apply to an order entered under this subsection.

(c) **Consent to placement on inactive status.** (1) Joint petition. An attorney may consent to placement on inactive status by joining with Bar Counsel in a petition for an order placing the attorney on inactive status. The petition shall be signed by the attorney and Bar Counsel and filed in the Court of Appeals. The petition shall state whether the inactive status should be indefinite or until the occurrence of a specified event and shall set forth any conditions that the parties agree should be imposed.

(2) Affidavit required. A joint petition filed under subsection (c) (1) of this Rule shall be accompanied by an affidavit by the attorney that certifies that the attorney:

(A) consents to the placement on inactive status;

(B) gives the consent freely and voluntarily without coercion or duress;

(C) is currently incapacitated and unable to render adequate legal service;

(D) knows that if a hearing were to be held, Bar Counsel would have the burden of proving by clear and convincing evidence that the attorney is so incapacitated as to require the attorney to be placed on inactive status;

(E) understands that being placed on inactive status, if ordered by the Court of Appeals, terminates the attorney's privilege to practice law in this State until otherwise ordered by the Court;

(F) agrees to comply with Rule 16-760 and any conditions stated in the petition that the Court of Appeals may impose;

(G) understands that the attorney may not be reinstated to practice law unless the attorney is able to prove by a preponderance of the evidence that the attorney has regained the ability to render adequate legal services, that inactive status should be terminated, and that the attorney should be reinstated to active practice;

(H) has disclosed to Bar Counsel the name of every physician, other health care provider, and health care facility by whom or at which the attorney has been examined, evaluated, or treated; and

(I) has furnished Bar Counsel with written consent to the release of such health care information and records as Bar Counsel has requested and waived any privilege as to such information and records.

(3) Order of the Court of Appeals. Upon the filing of the joint petition and affidavit, the Court of Appeals may enter an order, signed by the Chief Judge or a judge designated by the Chief Judge, placing the attorney on inactive status by consent pending further order of the Court and imposing any conditions stated in the petition. The provisions of Rule 16-760 apply to an order entered under this section.

(d) **Duty of Clerk.** When an attorney has been disbarred, suspended, or placed on inactive status under this Rule, the Clerk of the Court of Appeals shall strike the name of the attorney from the register of attorneys in that Court and shall certify to the Trustees of the Client Protection Fund of the Bar of Maryland and the clerks of all courts in this State that the attorney's name has been so stricken.

(e) **Effect of denial.** If the Court of Appeals denies a joint petition for discipline or inactive status, the investigation or disciplinary or remedial proceeding shall resume as if no consent had been given. Neither the joint petition nor the affidavit may be admitted in evidence. (Added Nov. 30, 2000, effective July 1, 2001; amended effective Nov. 6, 2002.)

Source. — This Rule is in part derived from former Rules 16-712 d (BV12 d) and 16-713 a (BV13 a) and in part new.

Effect of amendments. — The 2002 amendment substituted "Client Protection Fund of the Bar of Maryland" for "Clients' Security Trust Fund" in (d).

Applied in Att'y Griev. Comm'n v. Scroggs, 387 Md. 238, 874 A.2d 985 (2005).

Rule 16-773. Reciprocal discipline or inactive status.

(a) **Duty of attorney.** An attorney who in another jurisdiction (1) is disbarred, suspended, or otherwise disciplined, (2) resigns from the bar while disciplinary or remedial action is threatened or pending in that jurisdiction, or (3) is placed on inactive status based on incapacity shall inform Bar Counsel promptly of the discipline, resignation, or inactive status.

(b) **Petition in Court of Appeals.** Upon receiving and verifying information from any source that in another jurisdiction an attorney has been disciplined or placed on inactive status based on incapacity, Bar Counsel may file a Petition for Disciplinary or Remedial Action in the Court of Appeals pursuant to Rule 16-751(a)(2). A certified copy of the disciplinary or remedial order shall be attached to the Petition, and a copy of the Petition and order shall be served on the attorney in accordance with Rule 16-753.

(c) **Show cause order.** When a petition and certified copy of a disciplinary or remedial order have been filed, the Court of Appeals shall order that Bar Counsel and the attorney, within 15 days from the date of the order, show cause in writing based upon any of the grounds set forth in section (e) of this Rule why corresponding discipline or inactive status should not be imposed.

(d) **Temporary suspension of attorney.** When the petition and disciplinary or remedial order demonstrate that an attorney has been disbarred or is currently suspended from practice by final order of a court in another jurisdiction, the Court of Appeals may enter an order, effective immediately, suspending the attorney from the practice of law, pending further order of Court. The provisions of Rule 16-760 apply to an order suspending an attorney under this section.

(e) **Exceptional circumstances.** Reciprocal discipline shall not be ordered if Bar Counsel or the attorney demonstrates by clear and convincing evidence that:

(1) the procedure was so lacking in notice or opportunity to be heard as to constitute a deprivation of due process;

(2) there was such infirmity of proof establishing the misconduct as to give rise to a clear conviction that the Court, consistent with its duty, cannot accept as final the determination of misconduct;

(3) the imposition of corresponding discipline would result in grave injustice;

(4) the conduct established does not constitute misconduct in this State or it warrants substantially different discipline in this State; or

(5) the reason for inactive status no longer exists.

(f) **Action by Court of Appeals.** Upon consideration of the petition and any answer to the order to show cause, the Court of Appeals may immediately impose corresponding discipline or inactive status, may enter an order designating a judge pursuant to Rule 16-752 to hold a hearing in accordance with Rule 16-757, or may enter any other appropriate order. The provisions of Rule 16-760 apply to an order under this section that disbars or suspends an attorney or that places the attorney on inactive status.

(g) **Conclusive effect of adjudication.** Except as provided in subsections (e) (1) and (e) (2) of this Rule, a final adjudication in a disciplinary or remedial proceeding by another court, agency, or tribunal that an attorney has been guilty of professional misconduct or is incapacitated is conclusive evidence of that misconduct or incapacity in any proceeding under this Chapter. The introduction of such evidence does not preclude the Commission or Bar Counsel from introducing additional evidence or preclude the attorney from introducing evidence or otherwise showing cause why no discipline or lesser discipline should be imposed.

(h) **Effect of stay in other jurisdiction.** If the other jurisdiction has stayed the discipline or inactive status, any proceedings under this Rule shall be deferred until the stay is no longer operative and the discipline or inactive status becomes effective. (Added Nov. 30, 2000, effective July 1, 2001; amended Nov. 12, 2003, effective Jan. 1, 2004.)

Source. — This Rule is in part derived from former Rule 16-710 e (BV10 e) and in part new.

Effect of amendments. — The 2003 amendment rewrote (b).

University of Baltimore Law Forum. — For note, "Recent Development: Att'y Grievance Comm'n of Md. v. Midlen: Maryland Attorneys Run the Risk of Having to Serve a Consecutive, Rather Than Concurrent Suspension, When They Fail to Promptly Notify Bar Counsel That They Have Been Suspended in Another Jurisdiction," see 37 U. Balt. L.F. 131 (2007).

Appeals; reciprocal discipline cases. — Subsection (g) of this rule, by its terms, limits challenges to the original adjudication in reciprocal discipline cases to notice and opportu-

nity to be heard or infirmity of proof, and the Maryland Court of Appeals, even prior to the adoption of this rule, has recognized that a respondent is not allowed to collaterally attack either the findings of fact or the judgment rendered by the original jurisdiction; further, a respondent's remorse, although a factor that may be considered in fashioning a sanction, also does not come within an exception to the mandate of reciprocal discipline when properly proven. Att'y Griev. Comm'n v. Roberson, 373 Md. 328, 818 A.2d 1059 (2003).

Court of Appeals of Maryland concludes that, where a respondent's most serious misconduct involves misrepresentations, and those misrepresentations are to the supreme court of the state in which he or she principally practices and that sanctioned him or her, it ordinarily is appropriate to defer to that court, notwithstanding that the sanction it imposed is not identical to the one that may have been imposed by the Court of Appeals of Maryland were the same conduct to have occurred in Maryland. Att'y Griev. Comm'n v. Ayres-Fountain, 379 Md. 44, 838 A.2d 1238 (2003).

In a reciprocal disciplinary proceeding, the Court of Appeals of Maryland suspended an attorney who stipulated in the Delaware proceeding to longstanding and protracted violations of federal and state tax laws where the attorney was primarily a Delaware lawyer, the misrepresentations upon which the Attorney Grievance Commission principally relied were made to the Supreme Court of Delaware, and that court was fully informed of the facts and consequences of the attorney's conduct when it imposed a three-year suspension. Att'y Griev. Comm'n v. Ayres-Fountain, 379 Md. 44, 838 A.2d 1238 (2003).

Due process not denied in original disciplinary proceeding. — Attorney was suspended from the practice of law for 18 months in a reciprocal disciplinary proceeding, under (b), as the attorney was not denied the right to due process in the original disciplinary proceeding. While a hearing committee in the attorney's original disciplinary proceeding made findings of fact and then determined that the facts did not establish that there was a fee dispute, a review board and the reviewing court then concluded that those same facts did establish that there was a fee dispute; thus, the attorney was not denied due process in the original disciplinary proceeding. Att'y Griev. Comm'n v. Midlen, 395 Md. 628, 911 A.2d 852 (2006).

Failure to inform Bar Counsel of suspension and resignation in other state pending proceedings in that state. — Attorney violated (a) and was disbarred, after he failed to promptly inform Bar Counsel of his suspension and resignation pending disciplinary proceedings that occurred in Oklahoma. Att'y Griev. Comm'n v. Scroggs, 387 Md. 238, 874 A.2d 985 (2005).

Concurrent reciprocal suspension preferred. — If an attorney who is suspended in another state promptly notifies the Maryland Bar Counsel of that suspension, as required by (a), and promptly ceases the practice of law in Maryland during the period of that suspension, any corresponding, reciprocal period of suspension ordered by the Court of Appeals of Maryland, ordinarily, should be concurrent with that imposed in the other state, whether through the device of retroactive commencement of the reciprocal discipline or by terminating our suspension upon termination of the

suspension to which it is reciprocal. Concurrence in the reciprocal suspension of an attorney is not a matter of right but of the Court of Appeals of Maryland's discretion and practice, to be used when the circumstances warrant. Att'y Griev. Comm'n v. Midlen, 395 Md. 628, 911 A.2d 852 (2006).

Attorney's reciprocal suspension not to run concurrently. — Court of Appeals of Maryland found no basis under (e) for not imposing an 18-month suspension based on the findings and conclusions of the District of Columbia Court of Appeals in imposing the same sanction on the attorney because it was not clear from the record when the attorney notified the Maryland Bar Counsel of his suspension in the District of Columbia or whether he continued to practice law in Maryland after commencement of that suspension. Therefore, the court had no evidentiary basis at that point for making its suspension concurrent with that imposed in the District of Columbia, and the court commenced the suspension upon the issuance of its opinion to run for its full term of 18 months. Att'y Griev. Comm'n v. Midlen, 395 Md. 628, 911 A.2d 852 (2006).

Disciplinary matter not reciprocal in nature. — Where a disciplinary matter was instituted in Maryland based upon the disciplinary rules violation committed by the attorney in the District of Columbia, because the Maryland matter was not initiated as a reciprocal discipline matter, the case was not a reciprocal discipline matter under Md. R. 16-773. Att'y Griev. Comm'n v. Steinberg, 385 Md. 696, 870 A.2d 603 (2005).

Conclusive effect of findings — Maryland's Court of Appeals accepted as binding for reciprocal disciplinary purposes a determination by the District of Columbia Court of Appeals that an attorney misappropriated client funds, even though the evidence indicated that the attorney's senior partner took the lead in the illicit activity; since the misconduct was intentional, disbarment was mandated. Att'y Griev. Comm'n v. Cafferty, 376 Md. 700, 831 A.2d 1042 (2003).

Where an attorney paid himself funds as and for legal fees out of medical malpractice settlement proceeds that he was the conservator for in a District of Columbia matter without first obtaining court approval, wherein he was removed from that position and he consented to disbarment, the court in Maryland chose not to impose the same discipline due to the Maryland disciplinary precedents and the need for consistency; rather, the factual findings of the attorney's actions were given great deference, but under Maryland precedent, the proper sanction was a suspension. Att'y Griev. Comm'n v. Whitehead, 390 Md. 663, 890 A.2d 751 (2006).

Same sanction not required — This Rule

was interpreted by the Maryland Court of Appeals in a reciprocal discipline case to provide that where an attorney was sanctioned in a foreign state, the attorney can be sanctioned in Maryland for the same misconduct, but the same sanction is not mandatorily imposed; rather, based on the reasonable interpretation of the rule, the court gives deference to the foreign state's factual findings, it examines the other state's sanctions and determines whether they are consistent with Maryland precedent, and it imposes a different sanction than that imposed by the foreign state if Maryland precedent requires it for purposes of consistency.

Out-of-state attorneys sanctioned for failing to supervise in-state associate. — In a disciplinary proceeding against two supervising attorneys from out-of-state, who opened up a Maryland office and hired a Maryland associate, who ended up failing to respond to motions compelling discovery in 47 cases filed by her on behalf of the supervising attorneys' Maryland clients, the hearing judge was found to have properly determined that they violated Md. R. Prof. Conduct 5.1 and 1.4 and, therefore, they were suspended indefinitely, with the right to apply for reinstatement no sooner than 90 days after the effective date of the suspension. The findings and conclusions adequately found that the supervising attorneys failed to adequately supervise the relatively inexperienced associate they hired, failed to respond to her requests for paralegal help, failed to establish supervisory procedures designed deliberately to address the associate's inexperience and to counterbalance her physical distance from the ready availability of steadying interaction with peers and managers, failed to audit her case load, among other failings, as well as failed to directly communicate with a Maryland client regarding his case. Att'y Griev. Comm'n v. Kimmel, 405 Md. 647, 955 A.2d 269 (2008).

Indefinite suspension imposed after attorney suspended followed by probation in District of Columbia — In a reciprocal discipline action, the attorney, who had been suspended in the District of Columbia for one year with six months stayed, followed by three years probationary period and participation in the District's Bar Practice Management Advisory Service, was indefinitely suspended in Maryland, with right to apply for readmission after reinstatement in the District, because the sanction imposed by the District of Colum-

bia court was not within the Maryland spectrum of sanctions and the Court of Appeals of Maryland determined that indefinite suspension was the equivalent sanction and appropriate under the circumstances, where the attorney's conduct was negligence, rather that intentional acts. Att'y Griev. Comm'n v. Thaxton, 415 Md. 341, — A.2d —, 1 A.3d 470 (2010).

Suspension imposed. — In a reciprocal discipline action, the attorney, who had been publicly reprimanded in Texas, was suspended from the practice of law in Maryland for 45 days for misrepresenting that a document was an original signature page, but later admitting that the document was signed five years after the original contract, on the eve of summary judgment, because such conduct warranted substantially different discipline in Maryland. Att'y Griev. Comm'n v. Gordon, 413 Md. 46, 991 A.2d 51 (2010).

Disbarment required. — Even though a lawyer had only been suspended from practice for a few years in the District of Columbia after having admitted to misappropriating title insurance agency fees that should have been turned over the the law firm as part of the attorney's handling of real estate transactions, the imposition of precisely reciprocal discipline in Maryland was inappropriate in light of the severe penalties imposed on Maryland attorneys who misappropriated funds from anyone; disbarment was the only possible sanctions, since the attorney presented no evidence that compelling circumstances were the root cause of the misconduct. Att'y Griev. Comm'n v. Weiss, 389 Md. 531, 886 A.2d 606 (2005).

In a reciprocal disciplinary action, the attorney, who had been suspended from the practice of law for one year and one day in Colorado, was disbarred for violating Md. Law. R. Prof. Conduct 3.3(a)(1), 3.4(c), and 8.4(a), (b), (c), and (d), based on the attorney's own admission that he failed to make pertinent disclosures during a personal bankruptcy case and gave false testimony that case. Att'y Griev. Comm'n v. Zodrow, 419 Md. 286, 19 A.3d 381 (2011).

Quoted in Att'y Griev. Comm'n v. Roberson, 373 Md. 328, 818 A.2d 1059 (2003); Att'y Griev. Comm'n v. Baker, 396 Md. 15, 912 A.2d 651 (2006).

Stated in Att'y Griev. Comm'n v. Olver, 376 Md. 650, 831 A.2d 66 (2003).

Cited in Att'y Griev. Comm'n v. Garcia, 410 Md. 507, 979 A.2d 146 (Aug. 28, 2009); Att'y Griev. Comm'n v. Keiner, — Md. —, — A.3d — (Aug. 19, 2011).

Rule 16-774. Summary placement on inactive status.

(a) **Grounds.** An attorney may be summarily placed on inactive status for an indefinite period if the attorney has been judicially determined to be mentally incompetent or to require a guardian of the person for any of the reasons stated in Code, Estates and Trusts Article, § 13-705 (b), or, in accordance with law, has been involuntarily admitted to a facility for inpatient care treatment of a mental disorder.

(b) **Procedure.** (1) Petition for summary placement; confidentiality. Bar Counsel, with the approval of the Commission, may file in accordance with Rule 16-751 a petition to summarily place an attorney on inactive status. The petition shall be supported by a certified copy of the judicial determination or involuntary admission. The petition and all other papers filed in the Court of Appeals shall be sealed and stamped "confidential" in accordance with Rule 16-723 (b) (8).

(2) Service. The petition and all papers filed with the petition shall be served upon the attorney in accordance with Rule 16-753 and, in addition, upon any guardian of the person of the attorney and the director of any facility to which the attorney has been admitted. Proof of service shall be made in accordance with Rule 2-126.

(c) **Order of the Court of Appeals.** Upon consideration of the petition and any answer, the Court of Appeals may immediately place the attorney on inactive status for an indefinite period pending further order of the Court, may enter an order designating a judge in accordance with Rule 16-752 to hold a hearing in accordance with Rule 16-757, or may enter any other appropriate order. The provisions of Rule 16-760 apply to an order that places an attorney on inactive status. Copies of the order shall be served upon Bar Counsel and each person named in the proof of service of the petition.

(d) **Effect on disciplinary or remedial proceeding.** If a disciplinary or remedial proceeding for alleged misconduct is pending against the attorney, the entry of an order under this section shall stay the proceeding until the further order of the Court.

(e) **Termination of inactive status.** When an attorney who has been placed on inactive status under section (c) of this Rule is judicially determined to be competent or is judicially released after involuntary admission, the Court of Appeals shall terminate the inactive status and either dismiss the petition or enter an order designating a judge in accordance with Rule 16-752 to hold a hearing in accordance with Rule 16-757. (Added Nov. 30, 2000, effective July 1, 2001; amended Oct. 31, 2002, effective Jan. 1, 2003.)

Source. — This Rule is new.

Effect of amendments. — The 2002 amendment substituted "Rule 16-723 (b) (8)" for "Rule 16-723 (b) (7)" in (b)(1).

Quoted in Att'y Griev. Comm'n v. Olver, 376 Md. 650, 831 A.2d 66 (2003).

Rule 16-775. Resignation of attorney.

(a) **Application.** An application to resign from the practice of law in this State shall be submitted in writing under oath to the Court of Appeals, with a copy to Bar Counsel. The application shall state that the resignation is not being offered to avoid disciplinary action and that the attorney has no knowledge of any pending investigation, action, or proceedings in any jurisdiction involving allegations of professional misconduct by the attorney.

(b) **When attorney may not resign.** An attorney may not resign while the attorney is the subject of a disciplinary investigation, action, or proceeding involving allegations of professional misconduct. An application to resign does not prevent or stay any disciplinary action or proceeding against the attorney.

(c) **Procedure.** Upon receiving a copy of the application submitted in accordance with section (a) of this Rule, Bar Counsel shall investigate the application and file a response with the Clerk of the Court.

(d) **Order of the Court of Appeals.** The Court of Appeals shall enter an order accepting or denying the resignation. A resignation is effective only upon entry of an order accepting it.

(e) **Duty of clerk.** When the Court enters an order accepting an attorney's resignation, the Clerk of the Court of Appeals shall strike the name of the attorney from the register of attorneys in that Court and shall certify that fact to the Trustees of the Client Protection Fund of the Bar of Maryland and the clerks of all courts in this State. The Clerk shall give any notice required by Rule 16-723 (e).

(f) **Effect of resignation.** An attorney may not practice law in this State after entry of an order accepting the attorney's resignation.

(g) **Motion to vacate.** On motion of Bar Counsel, the Court may vacate or modify the order in case of intrinsic or extrinsic fraud. (Added Nov. 30, 2000, effective July 1, 2001; amended effective Nov. 6, 2002; Nov. 12, 2003, effective Jan. 1, 2004.)

Source. — This Rule is in part derived from former Rules 16-712 (BV12) and 16-713 a (BV13 a) and in part new.

Effect of amendments. — The 2002 amendment substituted "Client Protection Fund of the Bar of Maryland" for "Clients' Security Trust" in (e).

The 2003 amendment added the last sentence to (e) and deleted "Bar Counsel shall give any notice required by Rule 16-723 (d)" at the end of (f).

Rule 16-776. Injunction; expedited disciplinary or remedial action.

(a) **Injunction to prevent serious harm.** (1) Authority of Commission. Upon receiving information that an attorney is engaging in professional misconduct and poses an immediate threat of causing (A) death or substantial bodily harm to another, (B) substantial injury to the financial interest or property of another, or (C) substantial harm to the administration of justice, Bar Counsel, with approval of the Chair of the Commission, may apply in accordance with the provisions of Title 15, Chapter 500 for appropriate injunctive relief against the attorney. The relief sought may include restricting the attorney's practice of law, limiting or prohibiting withdrawals from any account in any financial institution, and limiting or prohibiting transfers of funds or property.

Committee note. — Except as otherwise provided in this Rule, Rules 15-501 through 15-505, the rules relating to temporary restraining orders and injunctions, apply. The appealability of injunctions under this Rule is governed by Code, Courts Article, § 12-303.

Cross references. — See Rule 16-777 for the right of Bar Counsel to request the appointment of a conservator when an attorney no longer can practice.

(2) Parties. The action for injunction shall be brought in the name of the Commission against the attorney whose conduct is alleged to be causing or threatening the harm and against any other person alleged to be assisting or acting in concert with the attorney.

(3) Effect of investigation or disciplinary or remedial proceeding. A court may not delay or deny an injunction solely because the misconduct is or may become the subject of an investigation under Rule 16-731 or the basis for a Statement of Charges under Rule 16-741.

(4) Order granting injunction. In addition to meeting the requirements of Rule 15-502 (e), an order granting a preliminary or permanent injunction pursuant to this section shall include specific findings by a preponderance of the evidence that the attorney has engaged in the professional misconduct alleged and poses the threat alleged in the complaint. A bond shall not be required except in exceptional circumstances.

(5) Service of injunction on financial institution. An order granting an injunction under this section that limits or prohibits withdrawals from any account or that limits or prohibits transfers of funds or property is effective against any financial institution upon which it is served from the time of service.

(b) **Expedited disciplinary or remedial action.** When an injunction has issued in accordance with this Rule, and regardless of any pending appeal or motion to modify or dissolve the injunction, Bar Counsel shall immediately commence an action against the attorney by filing in the Court of Appeals a Petition for Disciplinary or Remedial Action pursuant to Rule 16-751. A certified copy of the order granting the injunction shall be attached to the petition. The action shall proceed in accordance with Rules 16-751 through 16-761. The Court of Appeals may assign the petition for hearing to the judge who granted the injunction. (Added Nov. 30, 2000, effective July 1, 2001.)

Source. — This Rule is new.

Rule 16-777. Conservator of client matters.

(a) **Appointment; when authorized.** If an attorney dies, disappears, or has been disbarred, suspended, or placed on inactive status, or has abandoned the practice of law, and no personal representative, partner, or other responsible party capable of conducting the former attorney's affairs is known to exist, Bar Counsel may file a petition requesting the appointment of a conservator to inventory the attorney's files and to take other appropriate action to protect the attorney's clients.

(b) **Petition and order.** The petition to appoint a conservator may be filed in the circuit court in any county in which the attorney maintained an office for the practice of law. Upon such proof of the facts as the court may require, the court may enter an order appointing an attorney approved by Bar Counsel to serve as conservator subject to further order of the court.

(c) **Inventory.** Promptly upon accepting the appointment, the conservator shall take possession and prepare an inventory of the former attorney's files, take control of the attorney's trust and business accounts, review the files and accounts, identify open matters, and note the matters requiring action.

(d) **Disposition of files.** With the consent of the client or the approval of the court, the conservator may assist the client in finding new counsel, assume responsibility for specific matters, or refer the client's open matters to attorneys willing to handle them.

(e) **Sale of law practice.** With the approval of the court, the conservator may sell the attorney's law practice in accordance with Rule 1.17 of the Maryland Lawyers' Rules of Professional Conduct.

(f) **Compensation.** The conservator shall be entitled to periodic payment from the attorney's assets or estate for reasonable hourly attorney's fees and reimbursement for expenditures reasonably incurred in carrying out the order of appointment. Upon verified motion served upon the attorney at the attorney's last known address or, if the attorney is deceased, upon the personal representative of the attorney, the court may order payment to the conservator and enter judgment against the attorney or personal representative for the reasonable fees and expenses of the conservator. If the conservator is unable to obtain full payment within one year after entry of judgment, the Commission in its sole discretion may authorize payment from the Disciplinary Fund in an amount not exceeding the amount of the judgment that remains unsatisfied. If payment is made from the Disciplinary Fund, the conservator shall assign the judgment to the Commission for the benefit of the Disciplinary Fund.

(g) **Confidentiality.** A conservator shall not disclose any information contained in a client's file without the consent of the client, except as necessary to carry out the order of appointment. (Added Nov. 30, 2000, effective July 1, 2001; Feb. 8, 2005, effective July 1, 2005.)

Source. — This Rule is in part derived from former Rule 16-717 (BV17) and in part new.

Effect of amendments. — The 2005 amendment inserted "Lawyers'" before "Rules of Professional Conduct" in (e).

Rule 16-778. Referral from Child Support Enforcement Administration.

(a) **Referral.** The Commission promptly shall transmit to Bar Counsel a referral from the Child Support Enforcement Administration pursuant to Code, Family Law Article, § 10-119.3 (e)(3) and direct Bar Counsel to file a Petition for Disciplinary or Remedial Action in the Court of Appeals pursuant to Rule 16-751 (a)(1). A copy of the Administration's referral shall be attached to the Petition, and a copy of the Petition and notice shall be served on the attorney in accordance with Rule 16-753.

Committee note. — The procedures set out in Code, Family Law Article, § 10-119.3 (f)(1), (2), and (3) are completed before the referral to the Attorney Grievance Commission.

(b) **Show cause order.** When a petition and notice of referral have been filed, the Court of Appeals shall order that Bar Counsel and the attorney, within 15 days from the date of the order, show cause in writing why the attorney should not be suspended from the practice of law.

(c) **Action by the court of appeals.** Upon consideration of the petition and any answer to the order to show cause, the Court of Appeals may enter an order: (1) immediately and indefinitely suspending the attorney from the practice of law, (2) designating a judge pursuant to Rule 16-752 to hold a hearing in accordance with Rule 16-757, or (3) containing any other appropriate provisions. The provisions of Rule 16-760 apply to an order under this section that suspends an attorney.

(d) **Presumptive effect of referral.** A referral from the Child Support Enforcement Administration to the Attorney Grievance Commission is presumptive evidence that the attorney falls within the criteria specified in Code, Family Law Article, § 10-119.3 (e)(1), but the introduction of such evidence does not preclude Bar Counsel or the attorney from introducing additional evidence or otherwise showing cause why no suspension should be imposed.

(e) **Termination of suspension.** (1) On notification by the Child Support Enforcement Administration. Upon notification by the Child Support Enforcement Administration that the attorney has complied with the provisions of Code, Family Law Article, § 10-119.3 (j), the Court of Appeals shall order the attorney reinstated to the practice of law, unless other grounds exist for the suspension to remain in effect.

(2) On verified petition by attorney. In the absence of a notification by the Child Support Enforcement Administration pursuant to subsection (e)(1) of this Rule, the attorney may file with the Court of Appeals a verified petition for reinstatement. The petition shall allege under oath that (A) the attorney is in compliance with the provisions of Code, Family Law Article, § 10-119.3 (j) and is not currently in arrears in the payment of child support, (B) at least 15 days prior to filing the verified petition, the attorney gave written notice of those facts to the Child Support Enforcement Administration and requested that the Child Support Enforcement Administration notify the Court, (C) the Child Support Enforcement Administration has failed or refused to file such a notification, and (D) the attorney is entitled to be reinstated. All relevant documents shall be attached to the petition as exhibits. A copy of the petition

and exhibits shall be served on Bar Counsel, who shall file an answer within 15 days after service. Upon consideration of the petition and answer, the Court of Appeals may enter an order reinstating the attorney, an order denying the petition, or any other appropriate order.

(f) **Other disciplinary proceedings.** Proceedings under this Rule shall not preclude (1) the use of the facts underlying the referral from the Child Support Enforcement Administration when relevant to a pending or subsequent disciplinary proceeding against the attorney or (2) prosecution of a disciplinary action based upon a pattern of conduct adverse to the administration of justice. (Added Sept. 10, 2009, effective Oct. 1, 2009.)

Source. — This Rule is new.

Rule 16-781. Reinstatement.

(a) **Petition.** A petition for reinstatement to the practice of law shall be filed in the Court of Appeals. It shall be verified and include docket references to all prior disciplinary or remedial actions to which the petitioner was a party. A copy of the order that disbarred or suspended the petitioner from the practice of law, placed the petitioner on inactive status, or accepted the petitioner's resignation shall be attached, together with any opinion of the Court that accompanied the order. The petition shall certify that the petitioner has complied in all respects with the provisions of Rule 16-760 and with the terms and conditions of the disciplinary or remedial order. Except as provided in section (e) of this Rule, the petition shall allege facts describing the petitioner's original misconduct, subsequent conduct and reformation, present character, present qualifications and competence to practice law, and ability to satisfy the criteria specified in section (g) of this Rule.

(b) **Processing fee.** Upon filing the petition, the petitioner shall pay any filing fee or costs prescribed by law. Except as provided in section (e) of this Rule, the petitioner also shall deposit with the Clerk of the Court of Appeals a non-refundable processing fee set by the Commission and approved by the Court of Appeals payable to the Disciplinary Fund.

(c) **Service.** The petition shall be served upon Bar Counsel pursuant to Rule 2-121 and upon any other person designated by order of the Court of Appeals on request of Bar Counsel.

(d) **Requirement to provide information to Bar Counsel.** (1) Petitioner disbarred or suspended indefinitely or for more than six months. A petitioner who has been disbarred or suspended indefinitely or for more than six months shall provide the following information to Bar Counsel at the time of filing the petition:

(A) the petitioner's current address and telephone number;

(B) the address of each residence during the period of discipline, with inclusive dates of each residence;

(C) documentary evidence supporting the petitioner's claim that the criteria specified in section (g) have been satisfied;

(D) the name, address, and telephone number of each employer, associate, and partner of the petitioner during the period of discipline, with the inclusive dates of each employment, association, and partnership, the positions held, the names of all supervisors, and, if applicable, reasons for terminating the employment, association, or partnership;

(E) the case caption, general nature, and disposition of each civil and criminal action pending during the period of discipline to which the petitioner was a party or in which the petitioner claimed an interest;

(F) a statement of monthly earnings and all other income during the period of discipline, including the source;

(G) a statement of the petitioner's assets and financial obligations;

(H) the names and addresses of all creditors;

(I) a statement that any required restitution has been made and the amounts paid;

(J) a statement indicating whether the petitioner has applied for reinstatement in any other jurisdiction and the present status of each application;

(K) a statement identifying all other business or occupational licenses or certificates applied for during the period of discipline and the current status of each application;

(L) the name and address of each financial institution at which the petitioner maintained or was signatory on any account, safe deposit box, deposit, or loan during the period of discipline;

(M) written authorization for Bar Counsel to secure financial records pertaining to any account, safe deposit box, deposit, or loan at any financial institution identified in subsection (d) (1) (L) of this Rule;

(N) copies of the petitioner's state and federal income tax returns for the three years preceding the effective date of discipline and each year thereafter; and

(O) any other information that the petitioner believes is relevant to determining whether the petitioner possesses the character and fitness necessary for reinstatement.

(2) Petitioner on inactive status for incapacity. A petitioner who has been placed on inactive status for incapacity shall provide the following information to Bar Counsel at the time of filing the petition:

(A) information that complies with the requirements of subsections (d) (1) (A), (d) (1) (C), (d) (1) (J), and (d) (1) (O) of this Rule;

(B) a statement of the name, address, and telephone number of each health care provider and institution that examined or treated the petitioner for incapacity during the period of inactive status; and

(C) a written waiver of any physician-patient privilege with respect to each health care provider named in subsection (d) (2) (A) of this Rule.

(e) **Expedited reinstatement.** If the petitioner is an attorney who has been suspended for a definite period and the period has elapsed, Bar Counsel may consent to reinstatement by filing with the Clerk of the Court of Appeals a written notice that Bar Counsel is satisfied that the attorney has complied in all respects with the provisions of Rule 16-760 and with the terms and conditions of the order imposing the suspension. Upon receiving Bar Counsel's consent, the Clerk shall proceed in accordance with the applicable provisions of section (l) of this Rule. If Bar Counsel does not consent, Bar Counsel shall respond to the petition in accordance with section (f) of this Rule and shall state the particular grounds for withholding consent. The processing fee required by section (b) of this Rule does not apply to a petition filed under this section.

(f) **Response to petition.** Bar Counsel shall file a response to the petition within 30 days after being served unless a different time is ordered. The response shall admit or deny the averments of the petition in accordance with Rule 2-323 (c) and may include a statement of Bar Counsel's recommendations and reasons for supporting or opposing the petition.

(g) **Criteria for reinstatement.** The Court of Appeals shall consider the nature and circumstances of the petitioner's original conduct, the petitioner's subsequent conduct and reformation, the petitioner's current character, and the petitioner's current qualifications and competence to practice law. The Court may order reinstatement if the petitioner meets each of the following criteria or presents sufficient reasons why the petitioner should nonetheless be reinstated:

(1) The petitioner has complied in all respects with the provisions of Rule 16-760 and with the terms and conditions of prior disciplinary or remedial orders;

(2) The petitioner has not engaged or attempted or offered to engage in the unauthorized practice of law and has not engaged in any other professional misconduct during the period of suspension, disbarment, or inactive status;

(3) If the petitioner was placed on inactive status, the incapacity or infirmity (including alcohol or drug abuse) does not now exist and is not reasonably likely to recur in the future;

(4) If the petitioner was disbarred or suspended, the petitioner recognizes the wrongfulness and seriousness of the professional misconduct for which discipline was imposed;

(5) The petitioner has not engaged in any other professional misconduct since the imposition of discipline;

(6) The petitioner currently has the requisite honesty and integrity to practice law;

(7) The petitioner has kept informed about recent developments in the law and is competent to practice law; and

(8) The petitioner has paid all sums previously assessed by the order of the Court of Appeals.

(h) **Disposition.** Upon review of the petition and Bar Counsel's response, the Court of Appeals may order (1) dismissal without a hearing, (2) reinstatement, or (3) further proceedings in accordance with section (i) of this Rule.

(i) **Further proceedings.** If the Court of Appeals orders further proceedings, the Court shall enter an order designating a judge in accordance with Rule 16-752 to hold a hearing. The judge shall allow reasonable time for Bar Counsel to investigate the petition and, subject to Rule 16-756, take depositions and complete discovery. The applicable provisions of Rule 16-757 shall govern the hearing, including the requirement that the petitioner shall have the burden of proving the averments of the petition by clear and convincing evidence. The applicable provisions of Rules 16-758 and 16-759, except section (c) of Rule 16-759, shall govern any subsequent proceedings in the Court of

Appeals. The Court may order (1) reinstatement, (2) dismissal of the petition, or (3) a remand for further proceedings.

(j) **Conditions of reinstatement.** An order that reinstates a petitioner may require that the petitioner fulfill, either as a condition precedent to reinstatement or a condition of probation after reinstatement, one or more of the provisions set forth in Rule 16-760 (h) and one or more of the following requirements:

(1) take the oath of attorneys required by Code, Business Occupations and Professions Article, § 10-212;

(2) attend a bar review course approved by Bar Counsel and submit to Bar Counsel satisfactory evidence of attendance;

(3) successfully complete a professional ethics course at an accredited law school;

(4) attend the professionalism course required for newly-admitted attorneys;

(5) pass either the regular comprehensive Maryland bar examination or an attorney examination administered by the Board of Law Examiners; and

(6) pay all costs assessed in accordance with section (n) of this Rule.

(k) **Effective date of reinstatement order.** An order that reinstates the petitioner may provide that it shall become effective immediately or on a date stated in the order. If no effective date is stated, the order shall take effect on the date that Bar Counsel gives written notice to the Clerk of the Court of Appeals that the petitioner has complied with all conditions precedent to reinstatement set forth in the order.

(l) **Duties of Clerk.** (1) Generally. Promptly after the effective date of an order that reinstates a petitioner, the Clerk of the Court of Appeals shall give any notice required by Rule 16-723 (e).

(2) Attorney admitted to practice. Upon receiving a reinstatement notice authorized by section (e) of this Rule, or on the effective date of an order or notice that reinstates a petitioner admitted by the Court of Appeals to the practice of law, the Clerk of the Court of Appeals shall place the name of the petitioner on the register of attorneys in that Court and shall certify that fact to the Trustees of the Client Protection Fund of the Bar of Maryland and to the clerks of all courts in the State.

(3) Attorney not admitted to practice. Upon receiving a reinstatement notice authorized by section (e) of this Rule, or on the effective date of an order or notice that reinstates a petitioner not admitted by the Court of Appeals to practice law, the Clerk of the Court of Appeals shall remove the petitioner's name from the list maintained in that Court of non-admitted attorneys who are ineligible to practice law in this State, and shall certify that fact to the Board of Law Examiners and the clerks of all courts in the State.

(m) **Motion to vacate reinstatement.** Bar Counsel may file a motion to vacate an order that reinstates the petitioner if (1) the petitioner has failed to demonstrate substantial compliance with the order, including any condition of reinstatement imposed under Rule 16-760 (h) or section (j) of this Rule or (2) the petition filed under section (a) of this Rule contains a false statement or omits a material fact, the petitioner knew the statement was false or the fact was omitted, and the true facts were not disclosed to Bar Counsel prior to entry of the order. The petitioner may file a verified response within 15 days after service of the motion, unless a different time is ordered. If there is a factual dispute to be resolved, the court may enter an order designating a judge in accordance with Rule 16-752 to hold a hearing. The judge shall allow reasonable time for the parties to prepare for the hearing and may authorize discovery pursuant to Rule 16-756. The applicable provisions of Rule 16-757 shall govern the hearing. The applicable provisions of Rules 16-758 and 16-759, except section (c) of Rule 16-759, shall govern any subsequent proceedings in the Court of Appeals. The Court may reimpose the discipline that was in effect when the order was entered or may impose additional or different discipline.

(n) **Costs.** In proceedings for reinstatement, unless the Court of Appeals orders otherwise, the petitioner shall pay all court costs and costs of investigation and other proceedings on the petition, including the costs of physical and mental examinations, transcripts, and other expenditures incurred by Bar Counsel that were reasonably necessary to evaluate the petition. (Added Nov. 30, 2000, effective July 1, 2001; amended effective Nov. 6, 2002; Nov. 12, 2003, effective Jan. 1, 2004.)

Source. — This Rule is in part derived from former Rules 16-713 a 2 (BV13 a 2), 16-714 (BV14), 16-715 b (BV15 b), and in part new.

Effect of amendments. — The 2002 amendment substituted "Client Protection Fund of the Bar of Maryland" for "Clients' Security Trust Fund" in (l) (1).

The 2003 amendment, in (l), inserted (l)(1) and redesignated the following subparagraphs accordingly; deleted (m) and redesignated following subsections accordingly.

Power to move to vacate reinstatement. — Attorney representing a litigant in proceedings involving a reinstated attorney does not have standing to move to vacate the order reinstating that attorney; only Bar Counsel may do so. Att'y Griev. Comm'n v. Adams, 404 Md. 1, 944 A.2d 1115 (2008).

Motion to strike reinstatement order dismissed. — Because an attorney representing a litigant in proceedings involving a reinstated attorney did not have standing to move to vacate the order reinstating that attorney, rather, only Bar Counsel could do so, the plaintiff's attorney's motion to strike the court's order reinstating the suspended attorney had to be dismissed. Att'y Griev. Comm'n v. Adams, 404 Md. 1, 944 A.2d 1115 (2008).

Motion to revoke reinstatement denied. — Bar Counsel's motion to revoke the attorney's reinstatement under this Rule was denied, because Bar Counsel was fully aware, or should have been, of the nature and gravity of the allegations being made against the attorney in federal litigation involving the attorney's alleged forging of another person's name on an offer to purchase and contract of sale. Att'y Griev. Comm'n v. Adams, 410 Md. 544, 979 A.2d 698 (2009).

Indefinite suspension with opportunity to apply for reinstatement. — Indefinite suspension with opportunity to apply for reinstatement after 60 days, rather than suspension for an indefinite period, was the appropriate sanction in the case of attorney who never acknowledged anything unethical about nonresponsive behavior toward two co-personal representatives with whom the attorney was serving both as the third personal representative and as attorney for the estate; although the attorney had an otherwise clean record and there was evidently a private basis for the attorney's sudden change in behavior toward the other two, it was nonetheless important that the attorney reflect on the importance of responsiveness to any client, during the period of preparing to apply for reinstatement. Att'y Griev. Comm'n v. MacDougall, 384 Md. 271, 863 A.2d 312 (2004).

Applied in In re R.M.W., 428 F. Supp. 2d 389 (D. Md. 2006).

Cited in Att'y Griev. Comm'n v. Robertson, 400 Md. 618, 929 A.2d 576 (2007); Att'y Griev.

Comm'n v. Kimmel, 405 Md. 647, 955 A.2d 269
(2008).

CHAPTER 800. MISCELLANEOUS.

Rule 16-801. Promulgation of rules.

a. **Promulgation by Rules Order.** Rules of the Court of Appeals shall be promulgated by a Rules Order approved by a majority of the members of the Court of Appeals.

b. **Rules committee.** To assist the Court of Appeals in developing rules in the exercise of its rule-making power, the Court has appointed a standing committee on rules of practice and procedure, usually and herein referred to as the "Rules Committee," composed of judges, lawyers and persons familiar with judicial administration appointed for a three year term or at the Court's pleasure. The Court has also appointed a member of the bar to serve as Reporter to the Rules Committee, and from time to time, such assistant or special reporters as may be required to assist the Rules Committee in discharging its assigned responsibilities. Unless otherwise determined by the Court of Appeals, every suggestion for the adoption, amendment, or rescission of a rule shall be referred to the Rules Committee for consideration. The Rules Committee may also consider rules changes on its own initiative, and shall make its recommendations with respect to rules changes to the Court of Appeals by two or more written reports each year, submitted on or before March 31 and September 30. A copy of each report shall be transmitted to the Maryland Register for publication under a thirty day notice of proposed rules changes soliciting public comment.

Cross references. — See §§ 13-301 to 13-303 of the Courts Article of the Annotated Code of Maryland.

Committee note. — The Rules Committee was originally appointed by order of the Court of Appeals dated January 22, 1946, to succeed an *ad hoc* predecessor Committee on Rules of Practice and Procedure appointed by order of the Court dated March 5, 1940.

c. **Publication of rules changes.** Unless the Court of Appeals determines that some emergency requires the promulgation of a rules change to take effect prior to either of the dates specified in section d of this Rule, a copy of every Rules Order adopting, amending, or rescinding a rule shall be published in the Maryland Register at least thirty days before its effective date under a notice of rules changes, and may also be published in such other publication as the Court of Appeals may direct. A Rules Order adopting or amending a rule in the form previously published in the Maryland Register as a proposed rule change shall cite the number and page of the Maryland Register on which the proposed rules change appears, and in that case the text of the rule adopted or amended need not be re-published with the order of adoption or amendment. If, however, the Court of Appeals should further amend a rule proposed for adoption or amendment during the course of the rule-making process, either in response to comment received, or of its own motion, the full text of the rule or amendment as adopted and showing such further amendment shall be republished with the Rules Order.

If the Court of Appeals determines that an emergency exists and that a rules change is required to take effect prior to either of the dates specified in section d of this Rule, it shall direct such special publication as it considers appropriate to notify the judiciary, the clerks and members of the bar.

d. **Effective date of rules changes.** Unless the Court of Appeals determines that an emergency exists, and otherwise directs, rules changes shall become effective not earlier than the first day of January or the first day of July, whichever first occurs after the entry and appropriate publication of the order promulgating the rules changes.

e. **Record of rules.** The Clerk of the Court of Appeals shall maintain a separate record designated as the "Maryland Rules of Procedure," which shall contain all rules and amendments adopted by the Court. (Added May 5, 1976, effective July 1, 1976; amended Nov. 5, 1976, effective Jan. 1, 1977; Apr. 6, 1984, effective July 1, 1984; Nov. 19, 1987, effective July 1, 1988; June 5, 1996, effective Jan. 1, 1997.)

Source. — This Rule is former Rule 1225.

Effect of amendments. — The 1996 amendment added the Source note.

Editor's note. — An Order dated June 5, 1996, effective Jan. 1, 1997, renumbered this Rule, which was formerly Rule 1225.

University of Baltimore Law Forum. — For an article, "The Idealist Discourse of Legal Professionalism in Maryland: Delineating the Omissions and Eloquent Silences as a Progres-

sive Critique," see 41 U. Balt. L. F. 120 (2011).

Section c of this Rule does not apply to local or circuit rules; this Rule, like its predecessor, former Rule 4, by its very terms applies only to the Court of Appeals. Walker v. Haywood, 65 Md. App. 1, 498 A.2d 1198 (1985).

Cited in Hudson v. Hous. Auth., 402 Md. 18, 935 A.2d 395 (2007); In re Alijah Q., 195 Md. App. 491, 7 A.3d 106 (2010).

Rule 16-802. Maryland Judicial Conference and Council.

(a) **Conference and Council Established.** There is a Judicial Conference, known as "The Maryland Judicial Conference," to consider the status of judicial business in the various courts, appropriate legislation, and changes in rules and to exchange ideas with respect to the improvement of the administration of justice in Maryland and the judicial system in Maryland. There is a Judicial Council, which is part of the Maryland Judicial Conference. The Judicial Council guides the Maryland Judicial Conference in maintaining the cohesiveness, leadership, and efficacy of the judiciary.

(b) **Membership of Conference.** The members of the Judicial Conference are the judges of the Court of Appeals of Maryland, Court of Special Appeals, circuit courts of the counties, and District Court of Maryland.

(c) **Chair.** The Chief Judge of the Court of Appeals of Maryland is the Chair of the Judicial Conference and the Judicial Council.

(d) **Duties and Members of the Judicial Council.** (1) Duties. Between plenary sessions of the Maryland Judicial Conference, the Judicial Council shall perform the functions of the Conference and:

(A) shall submit recommendations for the improvement of the administration of justice in Maryland to the Chief Judge, the Court of Appeals, and the full Conference, as appropriate;

(B) may submit recommendations to the Governor, the General Assembly, or both, but only through the Chief Judge and the Court of Appeals, who shall forward them with any comments or additional recommendations that the Chief Judge or the Court deems appropriate;

(C) shall establish committees of the Judicial Conference pursuant to section (f) of this Rule, and approve and coordinate the work of those committees;

(D) plan educational programs to improve the administration of justice in Maryland; and

(E) plan sessions of the Conference in conjunction with the Conference Chair.

(2) Members. (A) The Judicial Council consists of 16 members, namely, the Chief Judge, the Chief Judge of the Court of Special Appeals, the Chair of the Conference of Circuit Judges, the Chief Judge of the District Court, the State Court Administrator, the Chair of the Conference of Circuit Court Clerks, the Chief Clerk of the District Court, and nine members appointed by the Chief Judge pursuant to subsection (d) (2) (B) of this Rule.

(B) The members of the Judicial Council appointed by the Chief Judge are four circuit court judges, consisting of two circuit administrative judges and two elected members from the Conference of Circuit Court Judges; four District Court judges, consisting of two District Administrative judges and two elected members of the Administrative Judges Committee; and one court administrator of a circuit court.

(3) Terms. The term of each appointed member is two years. The terms of the members shall be staggered.

(4) Vacancies. If a vacancy occurs on the Judicial Council because an appointed member resigns from the Council, leaves judicial office, or is appointed or elected to a judicial office other than the office the member held when appointed to the Council, the Chair shall appoint a replacement member to serve for the unexpired balance of the predecessor's term.

(e) **Secretariat.** The Administrative Office of the Courts is the secretariat for the Conference.

(f) **Committees.** (1) Establishment. In consultation with the Chair of the Judicial Conference, the Judicial Council shall establish the committees of the Conference it considers necessary or desirable from time to time and appoint the chair and members of each committee.

(2) Duties. At the time or times each committee's chair designates, the committee shall meet to receive, discuss, and consider suggestions pertaining to its area of responsibility. Each committee shall make reports to the Judicial Council as required by the Council and submit an annual report to the Judicial Conference through the Judicial Council.

(g) **Sessions of the conference.** Unless otherwise ordered by the Court of Appeals, the Conference shall meet in general session at least once a year at the time and place designated by the Judicial Council. Each session of the Conference shall be for the number of days the work of the Conference may require. (Amended June 28, 1971, effective Sept. 1, 1971; June 1, 1981; Nov. 7, 1990; June 5, 1996, effective Jan. 1, 1997; Dec. 16, 1999, effective July 1, 2000; Mar. 5, 2001, effective July 1, 2001.)

Source. — This Rule is derived in part from former Rule 1226 and is in part new.

Effect of amendments. — The 1996 amendment substituted "Rule 16-801" for "Rule 1225" in the last sentence of the Comment in c.; and added the Source note.

The 1999 amendment deleted "and the Supreme Bench of Baltimore City" from the end of b 3; in c, substituted "Chair" and "Vice Chair" for "chairman" and "vice-chairman" respectively, throughout, substituted "in the absence of the Chair" for "in his absence" at the end, and deleted the comment note; substituted "19 members" for "18 members" in d 1 (a); substituted "Chair" for "Chairman" at the end of d 1 (b) (4); rewrote d 2; substituted "a successor" for "his successor" in the first sentence of d 3; in d 4 (a), substituted "county administrative" for "circuit administrative," and inserted "appellate" preceding "judicial circuit"; in d 4 (c), inserted "appellate" preceding "judicial circuit" four times, deleted "(and of the Supreme Bench of Baltimore City in the Eighth Judicial Circuit)" following the first occurrence of "judicial circuit," and deleted "/Supreme Bench" following "circuit court" in the second sentence; in d 4 (d), inserted "Chief Judge of the" preceding "Court of Special," substituted "circuit court judge who has been elected from each appellate judicial circuit" for "circuit administrative judge of each judicial circuit," and substituted "from that court" for "from his court" at the end; in d 5 (a), substituted "the member held" for "he held," substi-

tuted "the county administrative judges of the appropriate appellate judicial circuit" for "the circuit administrative judge of the appropriate judicial circuit," and deleted "or of the Supreme Bench of Baltimore City" following "of a circuit court"; in d 5 (b), deleted "or of the Supreme Bench" following "circuit court," inserted "appellate" preceding "judicial circuit," inserted "appellate judicial" following the second occurrence of "appropriate," substituted "the judge's predecessor" for "his predecessor," and substituted "the predecessor's term, and until a successor" for "his predecessor's term, and until his successor" near the end; substituted "Chair" and "Vice Chair" for "chairman" and "vice-chairman" respectively, throughout d 6 and f; in d 6 (b), substituted "If the position of Chair and Vice Chair become vacant, it shall be" for "A vacancy in the chairmanship or vice-chairmanship shall be," substituted "the predecessor's term" for "his predecessor's term," and substituted "a successor" for "his successor" near the end, and deleted the comment note; and, deleted the comment note in f.

The 2001 amendment rewrote this Rule and in the Source note, inserted "derived in part from" and "and is in part new," respectively.

Editor's note. — An Order dated June 5, 1996, effective Jan. 1, 1997, renumbered this Rule, which was formerly Rule 1226.

Maryland Law Review. — For note, "Discipline of Judges in Maryland," see 34 Md. L. Rev. 612 (1974).

Rule 16-803. Commission on judicial disabilities — Definitions.

The following definitions apply in Rules 16-804 through 16-810 except as expressly otherwise provided or as necessary implication requires:

(a) **Address of Record.** "Address of record" means a judge's current home address or another address designated by the judge.

Cross references. — See Rule 16-810 (a)(1) concerning confidentiality of a judge's home address.

(b) **Board.** "Board" means the Judicial Inquiry Board appointed pursuant to Rule 16-804.1.

(c) **Charges.** "Charges" means the charges filed with the Commission by Investigative Counsel pursuant to Rule 16-808.

(d) **Commission.** "Commission" means the Commission on Judicial Disabilities.

(e) **Commission Record.** "Commission record" means all documents pertaining to the judge who is the subject of charges that are filed with the Commission or made available to any member of the Commission.

(f) **Complainant.** "Complainant" means a person who has filed a complaint.

(g) **Complaint.** "Complaint" means a communication alleging that a judge has a disability or has committed sanctionable conduct.

(h) **Disability.** "Disability" means a mental or physical disability that seriously interferes with the performance of a judge's duties and is, or is likely to become, permanent.

(i) **Formal Complaint.** "Formal Complaint" means a written communication under affidavit signed by the complainant, alleging facts indicating that a judge has a disability or has committed sanctionable conduct.

Committee note. — The complainant may comply with the affidavit requirement of this section by signing a statement in the following form: "I solemnly affirm under the penalties of perjury that the contents of the foregoing paper are true to the best of my knowledge, information, and belief." It is not required that the complainant appear before a notary public.

(j) **Judge.** "Judge" means a judge of the Court of Appeals, the Court of Special Appeals, a circuit court, the District Court, or an orphans' court, and a retired judge during any period that the retired judge has been approved to sit.

Cross references. — See Md. Const., Art. 4, § 3A and Code, Courts Article, § 1-302.

(k) **Sanctionable conduct.** (1) "Sanctionable conduct" means misconduct while in office, the persistent failure by a judge to perform the duties of the judge's office, or conduct prejudicial to the proper administration of justice. A judge's violation of any of the provisions of the Maryland Code of Judicial Conduct promulgated by Rule 16-813 may constitute sanctionable conduct.

(2) Unless the conduct is occasioned by fraud or corrupt motive or raises a substantial question as to the judge's fitness for office, "sanctionable conduct" does not include:

(A) making an erroneous finding of fact, reaching an incorrect legal conclusion, or misapplying the law; or

(B) failure to decide matters in a timely fashion unless such failure is habitual. (Added May 9, 1995, effective July 1, 1995; amended June 5, 1996, effective Jan. 1, 1997; June 6, 2000, effective Jan. 1, 2001; May 8, 2007, effective July 1, 2007.)

Committee note. — Sanctionable conduct does not include a judge's making wrong decisions — even very wrong decisions — in particular cases.

Cross references. — Md. Const., Art. IV, § 4B (b)(1).

For powers of the Commission in regard to any investigation or proceeding under § 4B of Article IV of the Constitution, see Code, Courts Article §§ 13-401 to 13-403.

Source. — This Rule is in part derived from former Rule 1227 (adopted 1995) and is in part new.

Effect of amendments. — The 1996 amendment rewrote the Rule heading; substituted "Rules 16-804 through 16-810" for "Rules 1227A through 1227G" in the introductory language; substituted "Rule 16-808" for "Rule 1227E" in (a); substituted "Rule 16-813" for "Rule 1231" in the second sentence of (g); substituted "Rule 16-803 g" for "Rule 1227 g" in the Cross reference note; and rewrote the Source note.

The 2000 amendment rewrote this Rule.

The 2007 amendment added (b) and redesignated accordingly.

Editor's note. — An Order dated June 5, 1996, effective Jan. 1, 1997, renumbered this Rule, which was formerly Rule 1227.

Maryland Law Review. — For note, "Discipline of Judges in Maryland," see 34 Md. L. Rev. 612 (1974).

For a recent decision, "The Court of Appeals of Maryland Diggs v. State: A Not-So-Plain Error?," see 69 U. Md. L. Rev. 680 (2010).

Rule was adopted pursuant to direction contained in former § 45 of Article 40. In re Diener, 268 Md. 659, 304 A.2d 587 (1973), cert. denied, 415 U.S. 989, 94 S. Ct. 1586, 39 L. Ed. 2d 885 (1974).

Power to conduct preliminary investigation on own motion. — Commission on Judicial Disabilities has the power, on its own motion, to conduct a preliminary investigation concerning a complaint against a judge which has been brought to its attention. In re Diener, 268 Md. 659, 304 A.2d 587 (1973), cert. denied, 415 U.S. 989, 94 S. Ct. 1586, 39 L. Ed. 2d 885 (1974).

Power to recommend censure. — The grant to the Commission on Judicial Disabilities of the greater power to recommend retirement or removal impliedly includes the lesser power to recommend censure. In re Diener, 268 Md. 659, 304 A.2d 587 (1973), cert. denied, 415 U.S. 989, 94 S. Ct. 1586, 39 L. Ed. 2d 885 (1974).

Notice held sufficient. — See In re Diener, 268 Md. 659, 304 A.2d 587 (1973), cert. denied, 415 U.S. 989, 94 S. Ct. 1586, 39 L. Ed. 2d 885 (1974).

Judge's failure to disclose loan from bail bondsman. — Where a judge borrowed money from a bail bondsman and failed to include information relative to this loan in his financial disclosure statements for the two years during which the loan was outstanding, Rule 8 of the former Rules of Judicial Ethics was violated and the judge was subject to censure. In re Hormes, 291 Md. 673, 436 A.2d 457 (1981).

Rules of evidence inapplicable in Commission proceedings. — The ordinary rules of evidence do not apply in a proceeding before the Judicial Disabilities Commission. In re Bennett, 301 Md. 517, 483 A.2d 1242 (1984).

Indictment by grand jury not required for Commission to bring charges against judge. — Failure of the grand jury to indict a judge does not prevent the bringing of charges by the Judicial Disabilities Commission. In re Bennett, 301 Md. 517, 483 A.2d 1242 (1984).

Rule 16-804. Commission.

(a) **Chair and Vice Chair.** The Commission shall select one of its members to serve as Chair and another to serve as Vice Chair for such terms as the Commission shall determine. The Vice Chair shall perform the duties of the Chair whenever the Chair is disqualified or otherwise unable to act.

(b) **Interested member.** A member of the Commission shall not participate as a member in any proceeding in which (1) the member is a complainant, (2) the member's disability or sanctionable conduct is in issue, (3) the member's impartiality might reasonably be questioned, (4) the member has personal knowledge of disputed evidentiary facts involved in the proceeding, or (5) the recusal of a judicial member would otherwise be required by the Maryland Code of Judicial Conduct.

Cross references. — See Md. Const., Article IV, § 4B (a), providing that the Governor shall appoint a substitute member of the Commission for the purpose of a proceeding against a member of the Commission.

(c) **Executive Secretary.** The Commission may select an attorney as Executive Secretary. The Executive Secretary shall serve at the pleasure of the Commission, advise and assist the Commission, have other administrative powers and duties assigned by the Commission, and receive the compensation set forth in the budget of the Commission.

(d) **Investigative Counsel; assistants.** The Commission shall appoint an attorney as Investigative Counsel. Before appointing Investigative Counsel, the Commission shall notify bar associations and the general public of the vacancy and shall consider any recommendations that are timely submitted. Investigative Counsel shall serve at the pleasure of the Commission and shall receive the compensation set forth in the budget of the Commission. Investigative Counsel shall have the powers and duties set forth in these rules and shall report and make recommendations to the Commission as directed by the Commission. As the need arises and to the extent funds are available in the Commission's budget, the Commission may appoint additional attorneys or other persons to assist Investigative Counsel. Investigative Counsel shall keep an accurate record of the time and expenses of additional persons employed and ensure that the cost does not exceed the amount allocated by the Commission.

(e) **Quorum.** The presence of a majority of the members of the Commission constitutes a quorum for the transaction of business, provided that at least one judge, one lawyer, and one public member are present. At a hearing on charges held pursuant to Rule 16-808 (i), a Commission member is present only if the member is physically present in person. Under all other circumstances, a member may be present in person or by telephone or video conferencing. Other than adjournment of a meeting for lack of a quorum, no action may be taken by the Commission without the concurrence of a majority of members of the Commission.

(f) **Record.** The Commission shall keep a record of all proceedings concerning a judge.

(g) **Annual report.** The Commission shall submit an annual report to the Court of Appeals, not later than September 1, regarding its operations and including statistical data with respect to complaints received and processed, subject to the provisions of Rule 16-810.

(h) **Request for home address.** Upon request by the Commission or the Chair of the Commission, the Administrative Office of the Courts shall supply to the Commission the current home address of each judge. (Added May 9, 1995, effective July 1, 1995; amended June 5, 1996, effective Jan. 1, 1997; Dec. 10, 1996, effective Jan. 1, 1997; June 6, 2000, effective Jan. 1, 2001; amended May 8, 2007, effective July 1, 2007.)

Cross references. — See Rules 16-803 (a) and 16-810 (a)(1).

Source. — This Rule is derived from former Rule 1227A.

Effect of amendments. — The first 1996 amendment substituted "Rule 16-810" for "Rule 1227G" in (g); and rewrote the Source note.

The second 1996 amendment substituted "a majority of the" for "four" twice in (e).

The 2000 amendment rewrote this Rule.

The 2007 amendment added the second and third sentences in (e).

Editor's note. — An Order dated June 5, 1996, effective Jan. 1, 1997, renumbered this Rule, which was formerly Rule 1227A.

Section (e) of this Rule provides that four members of the Commission on Judicial Disabilities constitute a quorum for the transaction of business. Pending before the Court of Appeals at press-time is the One-Hundred Thirty-Fifth Report of the Court's Standing Committee on Rules of Practice and Procedure which recommends an amendment to this Rule in light of Art. IV, §§ 4A and 4B of the Maryland Constitution as amended by Chapter 113, Acts 1995, which was approved by the voters on November 5, 1996.

Rule 16-804.1. Judicial inquiry board.

(a) **Creation and composition.** The Commission shall appoint a Judicial Inquiry Board consisting of two judges, two attorneys, and three public members who are not attorneys or judges. No member of the Commission may serve on the Board.

(b) **Compensation.** A member of the Board may not receive compensation for serving in that capacity but is entitled to reimbursement for expenses reasonably incurred in the performance of official duties in accordance with standard State travel regulations.

(c) **Chair.** The Chair of the Commission shall designate a member of the Board who is a lawyer or judge to serve as Chair of the Board.

(d) **Removal.** The Commission by majority vote may remove or replace members of the Board at any time.

(e) **Quorum.** The presence of a majority of the members of the Board constitutes a quorum for the transaction of business, so long as at least one judge, one lawyer, and one public member are present. A member of the Board may be present in person or by telephone or video conferencing. Other than adjournment of a meeting for lack of a quorum, no action may be taken by the Board without the concurrence of a majority of members of the Board.

(f) **Powers and duties.** The powers and duties of the Board are set forth in Rules 16-805 and 16-806.

(g) **Record.** The Executive Secretary of the Commission shall attend the Board meetings and keep a record in the form that the Commission requires. (Added May 8, 2007, effective July 1, 2007.)

Source. — This Rule is new.

Rule 16-805. Complaints; preliminary investigations.

(a) **Complaints.** All complaints against a judge shall be sent to Investigative Counsel. Upon receiving a complaint that does not qualify as a formal complaint but indicates that a judge may have a disability or have committed sanctionable conduct, Investigative Counsel shall, if possible: (1) inform the complainant of the right to file a formal complaint; (2) inform the complainant that a formal complaint must be supported by affidavit and provide the complainant with the appropriate form of affidavit; and (3) inform the complainant that unless a formal complaint is filed within 30 days after the date of the notice, Investigative Counsel is not required to take action, and the complaint may be dismissed.

(b) **Formal Complaints.** Investigative Counsel shall number and open a file on each formal complaint received and promptly in writing (1) acknowledge receipt of the complaint and (2) explain to the complainant the procedure for investigating and processing the complaint.

(c) **Dismissal by Investigative Counsel.** If Investigative Counsel concludes that the complaint does not allege facts that, if true, would constitute a disability or sanctionable conduct and that there are no reasonable grounds for a preliminary investigation, Investigative Counsel shall dismiss the complaint. If a complainant does not file a formal complaint within the time stated in section (a) of this Rule, Investigative Counsel may dismiss the complaint.

Upon dismissing a complaint, Investigative Counsel shall notify the complainant and the Commission that the complaint has been dismissed. If the judge has learned of the complaint and has requested notification, Investigative Counsel shall also notify the judge that the complaint has been dismissed.

(d) **Inquiry.** Upon receiving information from any source indicating that a judge may have a disability or may have committed sanctionable conduct, Investigative Counsel may open a file and make an inquiry. An inquiry may include obtaining additional information from the complainant and any potential witnesses, reviewing public records, obtaining transcripts of court proceedings, and communicating informally with the judge. Following the inquiry, Investigative Counsel shall (1) close the file and dismiss any complaint in conformity with section (c) of this Rule or (2) proceed as if a formal complaint had been filed and undertake a preliminary investigation in accordance with section (e) of this Rule.

(e) **Preliminary investigation.** (1) If a complaint is not dismissed in accordance with section (c) or (d) of this Rule, Investigative Counsel shall conduct a preliminary investigation to determine whether there are reasonable grounds to believe that the judge may have a disability or may have committed sanctionable conduct. Investigative Counsel shall promptly inform the Board or Commission that the preliminary investigation is being undertaken.

(2) Upon application by Investigative Counsel and for good cause, the Chair of the Commission may authorize Investigative Counsel to issue a subpoena to obtain evidence during a preliminary investigation.

(3) During a preliminary investigation, Investigative Counsel may recommend to the Board or Commission that the complaint be dismissed without notifying the judge that a preliminary investigation has been undertaken.

(4) Unless directed otherwise by the Board or Commission for good cause, Investigative Counsel shall notify the judge before the conclusion of the preliminary investigation (A) that Investigative Counsel has undertaken a preliminary investigation into whether the judge has a disability or has committed sanctionable conduct; (B) whether the preliminary investigation was undertaken on Investigative Counsel's initiative or on a complaint; (C) if the investigation was undertaken on a complaint, of the name of the person who filed the complaint and the contents of the complaint; (D) of the nature of the disability or sanctionable conduct under investigation; and (E) of the judge's rights under subsection (e)(5) of this Rule. The notice shall be given by first class mail or by certified mail requesting "Restricted Delivery — show to whom, date, address of delivery" addressed to the judge at the judge's address of record.

(5) Except when Investigative Counsel has recommended that the complaint be dismissed without notifying the judge and the Board or Commission has accepted the recommendation, before the conclusion of the preliminary investigation, Investigative Counsel shall afford the judge a reasonable opportunity to present, in person or in writing, such information as the judge chooses.

(6) Investigative Counsel shall complete a preliminary investigation within 90 days after the investigation is commenced. Upon application by Investiga-

513

tive Counsel within the 90-day period and for good cause, the Board shall extend the time for completing the preliminary investigation for an additional 30-day period. For failure to comply with the time requirements of this section, the Commission may dismiss any complaint and terminate the investigation.

(f) **Recommendation by Investigative Counsel.** Upon completion of a preliminary investigation, Investigative Counsel shall report to the Board the results of the investigation in the form that the Commission requires. The report shall include one of the following recommendations: (1) dismissal of any complaint and termination of the investigation, with or without a warning, (2) entering into a private reprimand or a deferred discipline agreement, (3) authorization of a further investigation, or (4) the filing of charges.

(g) **Monitoring and review by board.** The Board shall monitor investigations by, and review the reports and recommendations of, Investigative Counsel.

(h) **Authorization of further investigation.** The Board may authorize a further investigation to be conducted pursuant to Rule 16-806.

(i) **Informal meeting with judge.** The Board may meet informally with the judge for the purpose of discussing an appropriate disposition.

(j) **Board's report to commission.** (1) Contents. Upon receiving Investigative Counsel's final report and recommendation concerning a further investigation or a preliminary investigation if no further investigation was conducted and subject to subsection (j)(2) of this Rule, the Board shall submit to the Commission a report that includes one of the following recommendations: (A) dismissal of any complaint and termination of the investigation with or without a warning; (B) entering into a private reprimand or deferred discipline agreement; or (C) upon a determination of probable cause, the filing of charges, unless the Board determines that there is a basis for private disposition under the standards of Rule 16-807. The Board may not recommend a dismissal with a warning, a private reprimand, or a deferred discipline agreement unless the respondent judge has consented to this remedy.

(2) Limitation on contents of report. The information transmitted by the Board to the Commission shall be limited to a proffer of evidence that the Board has determined would be likely to be admitted at a plenary hearing. The Chair of the Board may consult with the Chair of the Commission in making the determination as to what information is transmitted to the Commission.

(3) Time for submission of report. Unless the time is extended by the Chair of the Commission, the Board shall transmit the report to the Commission within 45 days after the date the Board receives Investigative Counsel's report and recommendation. Upon written request by the Chair of the Board, the Chair of the Commission may grant one 30-day extension of time for transmission of the report. If the Board does not issue its report within the time allowed, the Chair of the Commission and Investigative Counsel shall conform the report and recommendation of Investigative Counsel to the requirements of subsection (j)(2) of this Rule and refer the matter to the Commission, which may proceed, using the report and recommendation of Investigative Counsel.

(4) Copy to investigative counsel and judge. Upon receiving the report and recommendation, the Commission promptly shall transmit a copy of it to Investigative Counsel and to the judge.

(k) **Filing of objections.** Investigative Counsel and the judge shall file with the Commission any objections to the report and recommendation within 15 days of the date the Commission transmitted the report and recommendation unless Investigative Counsel, the judge, and the Chair of the Commission agree to an extension of the time for filing an objection.

(l) **Action by commission.** The Commission shall review the report and recommendation and any timely filed objections. Upon written request by the judge, with a copy provided to Investigative Counsel, the Commission may permit the judge to appear before the Commission on terms and conditions established by the Commission. Unless the Commission authorizes further investigation in accordance with Rule 16-806, disposition by the Commission shall be in accordance with Rule 16-807 or 16-808 (a), as appropriate. (Added May 9, 1995, effective July 1, 1995; amended June 5, 1996, effective Jan. 1, 1997; June 6, 2000, effective Jan. 1, 2001; May 8, 2007, effective July 1, 2007.)

Source. — This Rule is derived from former Rule 1227B.

Effect of amendments. — The 1996 amendment substituted "Rule 16-803(d)" for "Rule 1227(d)" in (a); and rewrote the Source note.

The 2000 amendment rewrote this Rule.

The 2007 amendment in (d) redesignated the Committee note as the second sentence, and in the third sentence substituted (c) for (b) and (e) for (d); in (e)(1) added "Board or"; in (e)(2) added "Chair of the"; added (e)(3) and (e)(5) and redesignated accordingly including an internal cross reference; in (e)(6) substituted "Board" for "Commission" in the second

sentence; in (f) substituted "Upon completion of" for "Within the time for completing", added "to the Board" and "with or without a warning" and substituted "entering into" for "the offer of"; and added (g) through (l).

Editor's note. — An Order dated June 5, 1996, effective Jan. 1, 1997, renumbered this Rule, which was formerly Rule 1227B.

Maryland Law Review. — For a recent decision, "The Court of Appeals of Maryland Diggs v. State: A Not-So-Plain Error?," see 69 U. Md. L. Rev. 680 (2010).

Rule 16-806. Further investigation.

(a) **Notice to judge.** Upon approval of a further investigation by the Board or Commission, Investigative Counsel promptly shall notify the judge (1) that the Board or Commission has authorized the further investigation, (2) of the specific nature of the disability or sanctionable conduct under investigation, and (3) that the judge may file a written response within 30 days of the date on the notice. The notice shall be given (1) by first class mail to the judge's address of record, or (2) if previously authorized by the judge, by first class mail to an attorney designated by the judge. The Board or Commission, for good cause, may defer the giving of notice, but notice must be given not less than 30 days before Investigative Counsel makes a recommendation as to disposition.

(b) **Subpoenas.** (1) Upon application by Investigative Counsel and for good cause, the Chair of the Commission may authorize Investigative Counsel to issue a subpoena to compel the attendance of witnesses and the production of documents or other tangible things at a time and place specified in the subpoena. Promptly after service of the subpoena and in addition to any other notice required by law, Investigative Counsel shall provide to the judge under investigation notice of the service of the subpoena. The notice to the judge shall be sent by first class mail to the judge's address of record or, if previously authorized by the judge, by first class mail to an attorney designated by the judge.

(2) The judge or the person served with the subpoena may file a motion for a protective order pursuant to Rule 2-510 (e). The motion shall be filed in the circuit court for the county in which the subpoena was served or, if the judge under investigation is a judge serving on that circuit court, another circuit court designated by the Commission. The court may enter any order permitted by Rule 2-510 (e). Upon a failure to comply with a subpoena issued pursuant to this Rule, the court, on motion of Investigative Counsel, may compel compliance with the subpoena.

(3) To the extent practicable, a subpoena shall not divulge the name of the judge under investigation. Files and records of the court pertaining to any motion filed with respect to a subpoena shall be sealed and shall be open to inspection only upon order of the Court of Appeals. Hearings before the circuit court on any motion shall be on the record and shall be conducted out of the presence of all persons except those whose presence is necessary.

Cross references. — See Code, Courts Article, §§ 13-401 - 403.

(c) **Completion.** Investigative Counsel shall complete a further investigation within 60 days after it is authorized by the Board or Commission. Upon application by Investigative Counsel made within the 60-day period and served by first class mail upon the judge or counsel of record, the Commission, for good cause, may extend the time for completing the further investigation for a specified reasonable time. The Commission may dismiss the complaint and terminate the investigation for failure to comply with the time requirements of this section.

(d) **Recommendation by Investigative Counsel.** Within the time for completing a further investigation, Investigative Counsel shall report the results of the investigation to the Board or the Commission in the form that the Commission requires. The report shall include one of the following recommendations: (1) dismissal of any complaint and termination of the investigation, with or without a warning, (2) entering into a private reprimand or a deferred discipline agreement, or (3) the filing of charges. (Added May 9, 1995, effective July 1, 1995; amended June 5, 1996, effective Jan. 1, 1997; June 6, 2000, effective Jan. 1, 2001; May 8, 2007, effective July 1, 2007.)

Source. — This Rule is derived from former Rule 1227C.

Effect of amendments. — The 1996 amendment rewrote the Source note.

The 2000 amendment rewrote this Rule.

The 2007 amendment added "Board or" throughout (a); in (b)(1) added "Chair of the"; in (d) added "Board or the" and "with or without a warning" in (1) and substituted "entering into" for "the offer of" in (2).

Editor's note. — An Order dated June 5, 1996, effective Jan. 1, 1997, renumbered this Rule, which was formerly Rule 1227C.

Rule 16-807. Disposition without proceedings on charges.

(a) **Dismissal.** (1) Evidence Fails to Show Disability or Sanctionable Conduct. The Commission shall dismiss a complaint if, after an investigation, it concludes that the evidence fails to show that the judge has a disability or has committed sanctionable conduct. The Commission shall notify the judge and each complainant of the dismissal.

(2) Sanctionable Conduct Not Likely to be Repeated. If the Commission determines that any sanctionable conduct that may have been committed by the judge will be sufficiently addressed by the issuance of a warning, the Commission may accompany a dismissal with a warning against future sanctionable conduct. The contents of the warning are private and confidential, but the Commission has the option of notifying the complainant of the fact that a warning was given to the judge. At least 30 days before a warning is issued, the Commission shall mail to the judge a notice that states (A) the date on which it intends to issue the warning, (B) the content of the warning, and (C) whether the complainant is to be notified of the warning. Before the intended date of issuance of the warning, the judge may reject the warning by filing a written rejection with the Commission. If the warning is not rejected, the Commission shall issue it on or after the date stated in the initial notice to the judge. If the warning is rejected, it shall not be issued, the proceeding shall resume as if no warning had been proposed, and the fact that a warning was proposed or rejected may not be admitted into evidence.

Committee note. — A warning by the Commission under this section is not a reprimand and does not constitute discipline.

(b) **Private reprimand.** (1) The Commission may issue a private reprimand to the judge if, after an investigation:

(A) the Commission concludes that the judge has committed sanctionable conduct that warrants some form of discipline;

(B) the Commission further concludes that the sanctionable conduct was not so serious, offensive, or repeated as to warrant formal proceedings and that a private reprimand is the appropriate disposition under the circumstances; and

(C) the judge, in writing on a copy of the reprimand retained by the Commission, (i) waives the right to a hearing before the Commission and subsequent proceedings before the Court of Appeals and the right to challenge the findings that serve as the basis for the private reprimand, and (ii) agrees that the reprimand may be admitted in any subsequent disciplinary proceeding against the judge to the extent that it is relevant to the charges at issue or the sanction to be imposed.

(2) Upon the issuance of a private reprimand, the Commission shall notify the complainant of that disposition.

(c) **Deferred discipline agreement.** (1) The Commission and the judge may enter into a deferred discipline agreement if, after an investigation:

(A) The Commission concludes that the alleged sanctionable conduct was not so serious, offensive, or repeated as to warrant formal proceedings and that the appropriate disposition is for the judge to undergo specific treatment, participate in one or more specified educational programs, issue an apology to the complainant, or take other specific corrective or remedial action; and

(B) The judge, in the agreement, (i) agrees to the specified conditions, (ii) waives the right to a hearing before the Commission and subsequent proceedings before the Court of Appeals, and (iii) agrees that the deferred discipline agreement may be revoked for noncompliance in accordance with the provisions of subsection (c)(2) of this Rule.

(2) The Commission shall direct Investigative Counsel to monitor compliance with the conditions of the agreement and may direct the judge to document compliance. Investigative Counsel shall give written notice to the judge of the nature of any alleged failure to comply with a condition of the agreement. If after affording the judge at least 15 days to respond to the notice, the Commission finds that the judge has failed to satisfy a material condition of the agreement, the Commission may revoke the agreement and proceed with any other disposition authorized by these rules.

(3) The Commission shall notify the complainant that the complaint has resulted in an agreement with the judge for corrective or remedial action. Unless the judge consents in writing, the terms of the agreement shall remain confidential and not be disclosed to the complainant or any other person. An agreement under this section does not constitute discipline or a finding that sanctionable conduct was committed.

(4) Upon notification by Investigative Counsel that the judge has satisfied all conditions of the agreement, the Commission shall terminate the proceedings. (Added May 5, 1995, effective July 1, 1995; amended June 5, 1996, effective Jan. 1, 1997; June 6, 2000, effective Jan. 1, 2001.)

Source. — This Rule is in part derived from former Rule 1227D and in part new.

Effect of amendments. — The 1996 amendment rewrote the Source note.

The 2000 amendment rewrote this Rule.

Editor's note. — An Order dated June 5, 1996, effective Jan. 1, 1997, renumbered this Rule, which was formerly Rule 1227D.

Maryland Law Review. — For a recent decision, "The Court of Appeals of Maryland Diggs v. State: A Not-So-Plain Error?," see 69 U. Md. L. Rev. 680 (2010).

Rule 16-808. Proceedings before Commission.

(a) **Charges.** After considering the report and recommendation of the Board or Investigative Counsel submitted pursuant to Rule 16-805 (j), and upon a finding by the Commission of probable cause to believe that a judge has a disability or has committed sanctionable conduct, the Commission may direct Investigative Counsel to initiate proceedings against the judge by filing with the Commission charges that the judge has a disability or has committed sanctionable conduct. The charges shall (1) state the nature of the alleged disability or sanctionable conduct, including each Rule of the Maryland Code of Judicial Conduct allegedly violated by the judge, (2) allege the specific facts upon which the charges are based, and (3) state that the judge has the right to file a written response to the charges within 30 days after service of the charges.

(b) **Service; notice.** The charges may be served upon the judge by any means reasonably calculated to give actual notice. A return of service of the charges shall be filed with the Commission pursuant to Rule 2-126. Upon service, the Commission shall notify any complainant that charges have been filed against the judge.

Cross references. — See Md. Const., Article IV, § 4B (a).

(c) **Response.** Within 30 days after service of the charges, the judge may file with the Commission an original and 11 copies of a response.

(d) **Notice of hearing.** Upon the filing of a response or upon expiration of the time for filing it, the Commission shall notify the judge of the date, time, and place of a hearing. Unless the judge has agreed to an earlier hearing date, the notice shall be mailed at least 60 days before the date set for the hearing. If the hearing is on a charge of sanctionable conduct, the Commission shall also notify the complainant and publish a notice in the Maryland Register that is limited to (1) the name of the judge, (2) the date, time, and place of the hearing, and (3) a statement that the charges and any response by the judge are available for inspection at the office of the Commission.

Cross references. — See Rule 16-810 (a)(3).

(e) **Extension of time.** The Commission may extend the time for filing a response and for the commencement of a hearing.

(f) **Procedural rights of judge.** The judge has the right to inspect and copy the Commission Record, to a prompt hearing on the charges, to be represented by an attorney, to the issuance of subpoenas for the attendance of witnesses and for the production of designated documents and other tangible things, to present evidence and argument, and to examine and cross-examine witnesses.

(g) **Exchange of information.** (1) Upon request of the judge at any time after service of charges upon the judge, Investigative Counsel shall promptly (A) allow the judge to inspect the Commission Record and to copy all evidence accumulated during the investigation and all statements as defined in Rule 2-402 (f) and (B) provide to the judge summaries or reports of all oral statements for which contemporaneously recorded substantially verbatim recitals do not exist, and

(2) Not later than 30 days before the date set for the hearing, Investigative Counsel and the judge shall each provide to the other a list of the names, addresses, and telephone numbers of the witnesses that each intends to call and copies of the documents that each intends to introduce in evidence at the hearing.

(3) Discovery is governed by Title 2, Chapter 400 of these Rules, except that the Chair of the Commission, rather than the court, may limit the scope of discovery, enter protective orders permitted by Rule 2-403, and resolve other discovery issues.

(4) When disability of the judge is an issue, on its own initiative or on motion for good cause, the Chair of the Commission may order the judge to submit to a mental or physical examination pursuant to Rule 2-423.

(h) **Amendments.** At any time before the hearing, the Commission on motion may allow amendments to the charges or the response. If an amendment to the charges is made less than 30 days before the hearing, the judge, upon request, shall be given a reasonable time to respond to the amendment and to prepare and present any defense.

(i) **Hearing.** (1) At a hearing on charges, the applicable provisions of Rule 16-806 (b) shall govern subpoenas.

(2) At the hearing, Investigative Counsel shall present evidence in support of the charges.

(3) The Commission may proceed with the hearing whether or not the judge has filed a response or appears at the hearing.

(4) Except for good cause shown, a motion for recusal of a member of the Commission shall be filed not less than 30 days before the hearing.

(5) The hearing shall be conducted in accordance with the rules of evidence in Title 5 of these rules.

(6) The proceedings at the hearing shall be stenographically recorded. Except as provided in section (k) of this Rule, the Commission is not required to have a transcript prepared. The judge may, at the judge's expense, have the record of the proceedings transcribed.

(7) With the approval of the Chair of the Commission, the judge and Investigative Counsel may each submit proposed findings of fact and conclusions of law within the time period set by the Chair.

(j) **Commission findings and action.** If the Commission finds by clear and convincing evidence that the judge has a disability or has committed sanctionable conduct, it shall either issue a public reprimand for the sanctionable conduct or refer the matter to the Court of Appeals pursuant to section (k) of this Rule. Otherwise, the Commission shall dismiss the charges filed by the Investigative Counsel and terminate the proceeding.

(k) **Record.** If the Commission refers the case to the Court of Appeals, the Commission shall:

(1) make written findings of fact and conclusions of law with respect to the issues of fact and law in the proceeding, state its recommendations, and enter those findings and recommendations in the record in the name of the Commission;

(2) cause a transcript of all proceedings at the hearing to be prepared and included in the record;

(3) make the transcript available for review by the judge and the judge's attorney in connection with the proceedings or, at the judge's request, provide a copy to the judge at the judge's expense;

(4) file with the Court of Appeals the entire hearing record which shall be certified by the Chair of the Commission and shall include the transcript of the

proceedings, all exhibits and other papers filed or marked for identification in the proceeding, and all dissenting or concurring statements by Commission members; and

(5) promptly mail to the judge at the judge's address of record notice of the filing of the record and a copy of the findings, conclusions, and recommendations and all dissenting or concurring statements by Commission members.

(l) **Discipline by consent.** After the filing of charges alleging sanctionable conduct and before a decision by the Commission, the judge and Investigative Counsel may enter into an agreement in which the judge (1) admits to all or part of the charges; (2) as to the charges admitted, admits the truth of all facts constituting sanctionable conduct as set forth in the agreement, (3) agrees to take any corrective or remedial action provided for in the agreement; (4) consents to the stated sanction; (5) states that the consent is freely and voluntarily given; and (6) waives the right to further proceedings before the Commission and subsequent proceedings before the Court of Appeals. The agreement shall be submitted to the Court of Appeals, which shall either approve or reject the agreement. Until approved by the Court of Appeals, the agreement is confidential and privileged. If the Court approves the agreement and imposes the stated sanction, the agreement shall be made public. If the Court rejects the stated sanction, the proceeding shall resume as if no consent had been given, and all admissions and waivers contained in the agreement are withdrawn and may not be admitted into evidence. (Added May 9, 1995, effective July 1, 1995; amended June 5, 1996, effective Jan. 1, 1997; June 6, 2000, effective Jan. 1, 2001; Nov. 12, 2003, effective Jan. 1, 2004; May 8, 2007, effective July 1, 2007; Dec. 4, 2007, effective Jan. 1, 2008; June 7, 2011, effective July 1, 2011.)

Source. — This Rule is in part derived from former Rule 1227E and in part new.

Effect of amendments. — The 1996 amendment rewrote the Source note.

The 2000 amendment rewrote this Rule.

The 2003 amendment substituted "(e)" for "(d)" in (g)(1).

The 2007 amendment in (a), added "report and", "the Board or" and "submitted pursuant to Rule 16-805 (j)" near the beginning of the first sentence.

The December 4, 2007 Order, effective January 1, 2008, in (g) (1) substituted "Rule 2-402 (f)" for "Rule 2-402 (e)".

The 2011 amendment substituted "Rule of the Maryland Code of Judicial Conduct" for "Canon of Judicial Conduct" in the second sentence in (a).

Editor's note. — An Order dated June 5, 1996, effective Jan. 1, 1997, renumbered this Rule, which was formerly Rule 1227E.

Maryland Law Review. — For a recent decision, "The Court of Appeals of Maryland Diggs v. State: A Not-So-Plain Error?," see 69 U. Md. L. Rev. 680 (2010).

Rule 16-809. Proceedings in Court of Appeals.

(a) **Expedited consideration.** Upon receiving the hearing record file pursuant to Rule 16-808 (k), the Clerk of the Court of Appeals shall docket the case for expedited consideration.

(b) **Exceptions.** The judge may except to the findings, conclusions, or recommendation of the Commission by filing with the Court of Appeals eight copies of exceptions within 30 days after service of the notice of filing of the record. The exceptions shall set forth with particularity all errors allegedly committed by the Commission and the disposition sought. A copy of the exceptions shall be served on the Commission in accordance with Rules 1-321 and 1-323.

(c) **Response.** The Commission shall file eight copies of a response within 15 days after service of the exceptions. The Commission shall be represented in the Court of Appeals by its Executive Secretary or such other counsel as the Commission may appoint. A copy of the response shall be served on the judge in accordance with Rules 1-321 and 1-323.

(d) **Hearing.** If exceptions are filed, upon the filing of a response or the expiration of the time for filing it, the Court shall set a schedule for filing memoranda in support of the exceptions and response and a date for a hearing. The hearing on exceptions shall be conducted in accordance with Rule 8-522. If no exceptions are filed or if the judge files with the Court a written waiver of the judge's right to a hearing, the Court may decide the matter without a hearing.

(e) **Disposition.** The Court of Appeals may (1) impose the sanction recommended by the Commission or any other sanction permitted by law; (2) dismiss the proceeding; or (3) remand for further proceedings as specified in the order of remand.

Cross references. — For rights and privileges of the judge after disposition, see Md. Const., Article IV, § 4B (b).

(f) **Decision.** The decision shall be evidenced by the order of the Court of Appeals, which shall be certified under the seal of the Court by the Clerk and shall be accompanied by an opinion. Unless the case is remanded to the Commission, the record shall be retained by the Clerk of the Court of Appeals. (Added May 9, 1995, effective July 1, 1995; amended June 5, 1996, effective Jan. 1, 1997; June 6, 2000, effective Jan. 1, 2001.)

Source. — This Rule is in part derived from former Rule 1227F and in part new.

Effect of amendments. — The 1996 amendment rewrote the Source note.

The 2000 amendment rewrote this Rule.

Editor's note. — An Order dated June 5, 1996, effective Jan. 1, 1997, renumbered this Rule, which was formerly Rule 1227F.

Grievance Commission's recommended sanction modified — Severe alcoholism for which respondent attorney had received extensive treatment was a mitigator in determining whether disbarment was an appropriate sanc-tion for failure to keep track of client funds and other professional misconduct; although the commission had recommended disbarment, the court of appeals extended the respondent's suspension indefinitely, and set high standards for a showing of fitness to practice before reinstatement would be allowed. Att'y Griev. Comm'n v. Christopher, 383 Md. 624, 861 A.2d 692 (2004).

Cited in Anne Arundel County v. Nes, 163 Md. App. 515, 881 A.2d 1161 (2005).

Rule 16-810. Public access.

(a) **Generally.** Except as otherwise expressly provided by these rules, proceedings and information relating to a complaint or charges shall be open to the public or confidential, as follows:

(1) Address of Record. The judge's current home address shall remain confidential at all stages of proceedings under these rules. Any other address of record shall be open to the public if the charges and proceedings are open to the public.

(2) Complaints and Investigations. All proceedings under Rules 16-805 and 16-806 shall be confidential.

(3) Upon Filing of a Response or Expiration of the Time for Filing a Response. After the filing of a response to charges alleging sanctionable conduct, whether or not joined with charges of disability, or expiration of the time for filing a response, the charges and all subsequent proceedings before the Commission on them shall be open to the public. If the charges allege only that the judge has a disability, the charges and all proceedings before the Commission on them shall be confidential.

(4) Work product and deliberations. Investigative counsel's work product and records not admitted into evidence before the Commission, the Commission's deliberations, and records of the Commission's deliberations shall be confidential.

(5) Proceedings in the Court of Appeals. Unless otherwise ordered by the Court of Appeals, the record of Commission proceedings filed with that Court and any proceedings before that Court shall be open to the public.

(b) **Permitted release of information by Commission.** (1) Written waiver. The Commission may release confidential information upon a written waiver by the judge.

(2) Explanatory statement. The Commission may issue a brief explanatory statement necessary to correct any public misperception about actual or possible proceedings before the Commission.

(3) Nominations; appointments; approvals. (A) Permitted disclosures. Upon a written application made by a judicial nominating commission, a Bar Admission authority, the President of the United States, the Governor of a state, territory, district, or possession of the United States, or a committee of the General Assembly of Maryland or of the United States Senate which asserts that the applicant is considering the nomination, appointment, confirmation, or approval of a judge or former judge, the Commission shall disclose to the applicant:

(i) Information about any completed proceedings that did not result in dismissal, including reprimands and deferred discipline agreements; and

(ii) The mere fact that a formal complaint is pending.

(B) Restrictions. When the Commission furnishes information to an applicant under this section, the Commission shall furnish only one copy of the material and it shall be furnished under seal. As a condition to receiving the material, the applicant shall agree (i) not to copy the material or permit it to be copied; (ii) that when inspection of the material has been completed, the applicant shall seal and return the material to the Commission; and (iii) not to disclose the contents of the material or any information contained in it to anyone other than another member of the applicant.

(C) Copy to judge. The Commission shall send the judge a copy of all documents disclosed under this subsection. (Added May 9, 1995, effective July 1, 1995; amended June 5, 1996, effective Jan. 1, 1997; June 6, 2000, effective Jan. 1, 2001.)

Cross references. — For the powers of the Commission in an investigation or proceeding under Md. Const., Article IV, § 4B, see Code, Courts Article, §§ 13-401, 402, and 403.

Source. — This Rule is derived from former Rule 1227G.

Effect of amendments. — The 1996 amendment rewrote the Source note.

The 2000 amendment rewrote this Rule.

Editor's note. — An Order dated June 5, 1996, effective Jan. 1, 1997, renumbered this Rule, which was formerly Rule 1227G.

Rule 16-811. Client Protection Fund of the Bar of Maryland.

a. **Name, operation, and purpose.** 1. Name. Effective July 1, 2002, the name of the Clients' Security Trust Fund of the Bar of Maryland, promulgated pursuant to Chapter 779, Laws of Maryland (1965), shall be changed to the "Client Protection Fund of the Bar of Maryland" (the "Fund").

2. **Cross references.** — See Code, Business Occupations and Professions Article, §§ 10-310 et seq.

2. Operation. The Fund shall be operated and administered in accordance with this Rule by nine trustees, appointed as hereinafter provided. The trustees shall be known as the "Trustees of the Client Protection Fund of the Bar of Maryland."

3. Purpose. The purpose of the Fund shall be to maintain the integrity and protect the good name of the legal profession by reimbursing, to the extent authorized by this Rule and deemed proper and reasonable by the trustees, losses caused by defalcations of members of the Bar of the State of Maryland or out-of-state attorneys authorized to practice in this State under Rule 15 of the Rules Governing Admission to the Bar, acting either as attorneys or as fiduciaries (except to the extent to which they are bonded). (Amended July 3, 1980; June 22, 1990.)

b. **Appointment and compensation of trustees and officers.** 1. Number. There shall be nine trustees appointed by the Court of Appeals, eight to be members of the Bar of this State, and one who shall not be a member of the Bar.

2. Appointment. One trustee who is a member of the Bar of this State shall be appointed from each of the seven appellate judicial circuits. The eighth trustee who is a member of the Bar and the trustee who is not a member of the Bar shall be appointed at large. Each appointment shall be for a term of seven years. (Amended June 4, 1979, effective July 1, 1979; June 5, 1995, effective July 1, 1995.)

3. Officers. The trustees shall from time to time elect from their membership a chair, a treasurer, and such other officers as they deem necessary or appropriate.

4. Removal. A trustee may be removed by the Court at any time in its discretion.

5. Vacancies. Vacancies shall be filled by appointment by the Court for the unexpired term.

6. Compensation. The trustees shall serve without compensation, but shall be entitled to reimbursement from the Fund, if no other source of funds is available, for their expenses reasonably incurred in performance of their duties as trustees, including transportation costs.

c. **Powers and duties of trustees.** 1. Additional powers and duties. In addition to the powers granted elsewhere in this Rule, the trustees shall have the following powers and duties:

(i) To receive, hold, manage, and distribute, pursuant to this Rule, the funds raised hereunder, and any other monies that may be received by the Fund through voluntary contributions or otherwise.

(ii) To authorize payment of claims in accordance with this Rule.

(iii) To adopt regulations for the administration of the Fund and the procedures for the presentation, consideration, recognition, rejection and payment of claims, and to adopt bylaws for conducting business. A copy of the regulations shall be filed with the Clerk of the Court of Appeals, who shall mail a copy of them to the clerk of the circuit court for each county and to all Registers of Wills.

(iv) To enforce claims for restitution, arising by subrogation or assignment or otherwise.

(v) To invest the Fund, or any portion thereof, in such investments as they may deem appropriate, and to cause funds to be deposited in any bank, banking institution or federally insured savings and loan association in this State, provided however, that the trustees shall have no obligation to cause the Fund or any portion thereof to be invested.

(vi) To employ and compensate consultants, agents, legal counsel and employees.

(vii) To delegate the power to perform routine acts which may be necessary or desirable for the operation of the Fund, including the power to authorize disbursements for routine operating expenses of the Fund, but authorization for payments of claims shall be made only as provided in section h (Claims) of this Rule.

(viii) To sue or be sued in the name of the Fund without joining any or all individual trustees.

(ix) To comply with the requirements of Rules 16-713 (e), 16-714 (b), 16-724 (a), and 16-753.

(x) To designate an employee to perform the duties set forth in Rules 16-724 (a) and 16-753 and notify Bar Counsel of that designation.

(xi) To perform all other acts necessary or proper for fulfillment of the purposes of the Fund and its efficient administration.

2. Report and audit — Filing. At least once each year, and at such additional times as the Court of Appeals may order, the trustees shall file with the Court

of Appeals a written report, which shall include the audit made pursuant to subsection 3 of section i (Powers of Court of Appeals — Arrange Audit) of this Rule of the management and operation of the Fund. (Amended June 5, 1995, effective July 1, 1995.)

    d. **Meetings and quorum.** 1. Time. Meetings of the trustees shall be held at the call of the chair or a majority of the trustees, and shall be held at least once each year, upon reasonable notice.

    2. Number. Five trustees shall constitute a quorum. A majority of the trustees present at a duly constituted meeting may exercise any powers held by the trustees, except to the extent that this Rule provides otherwise. (Amended June 4, 1979, effective July 1, 1979.)

    e. **Payments to fund.** 1. Definition. In this section, "local bar association" means (A) in Baltimore City, the Bar Association of Baltimore City; or (B) in each county, the bar association with the greatest number of members who are residents of the county and who maintain their principal office for the practice of law in that county.

    2. Payment required as condition of practice; exception. Except as otherwise provided in this section, each lawyer admitted to practice before the Court of Appeals or issued a certificate of special authorization under Rule 15 of the Rules Governing Admission to the Bar of Maryland, shall, as a condition precedent to the practice of law (as from time to time defined in Code, Business Occupations and Professions Article) in this State, pay annually to the treasurer of the Fund the sum, including all applicable late charges, the Court may fix. The trustees may provide in their regulations reasonable and uniform deadline dates for receipt of payments of assessments or applications for change to inactive/retired status. A lawyer on inactive/retired status may engage in the practice of law without payment to the Fund if (A) the lawyer is on inactive/retired status solely as a result of having been approved for that status by the trustees and not as a result of any action against the attorney pursuant to Title 16, Chapter 700 of these Rules and (B) the lawyer's practice is limited to representing clients without compensation, other than reimbursement of reasonable and necessary expenses, as part of the lawyer's participation in a legal services or pro bono publico program sponsored or supported by a local bar association, the Maryland State Bar Association, Inc., an affiliated bar foundation, or the Maryland Legal Services Corporation. (Amended Dec. 8, 1992; Sept. 11, 1995, effective Jan. 1, 1996.)

    3. Change of address. It is the obligation of each lawyer to give written notice to the trustees of every change in the lawyer's resident address, business address, or telephone numbers within 30 days of the change. The trustees shall have the right to rely on the latest information received by them for all billing and other correspondence. (Added Sept. 11, 1995, effective Jan. 1, 1996.)

    4. Due date. Payments for any fiscal year shall be due on July 1st of each such year. (Amended June 22, 1990; Dec. 8, 1992; Sept 11, 1995, effective Jan. 1, 1996.)

    5. Dishonor. If any check to the Fund in payment of an annual assessment is dishonored, the treasurer of the Fund shall promptly notify the attorney of

the dishonor. The attorney shall be responsible for all additional charges assessed by the trustees. (Amended Aug. 30, 1989; Dec. 8, 1992; Sept. 11, 1995, effective Jan. 1, 1996.)

f. **Enforcement.** 1. List by trustees of unpaid assessments. As soon as practical after January 1, but no later than February 15 of each calendar year, the trustees shall prepare, certify, and file with the Court of Appeals a list showing:

(i) the name and account number, as it appears on their records, of each lawyer who, to the best of their information, is engaged in the practice of law and without valid reason or justification has failed or refused to pay (a) one or more annual assessments, (b) penalties for late payment, (c) any charge for a dishonored check, or (d) reimbursement of publication charges; and

(ii) the amount due from that lawyer to the Fund.

2. Notice of default by trustees. (i) The trustees shall give notice of delinquency promptly to each lawyer on the list by first class mail addressed to the lawyer at the lawyer's last address appearing on the records of the trustees. The notice shall state the amount of the obligation to the Fund, that payment is overdue, and that failure to pay the amount to the Fund within 30 days following the date of the notice will result in the entry of an order by the Court of Appeals prohibiting the lawyer from practicing law in the State.

(ii) The mailing by the trustees of the notice of default shall constitute service.

3. Additional discretionary notice. In addition to the mailed notice, the trustees may give any additional notice to the lawyers on the delinquency list as the trustees in their discretion deem desirable. Additional notice may include publication in one or more newspapers selected by the trustees; telephone, facsimile, or other transmission to the named lawyers; dissemination to local bar associations or other professional associations; posting in State court houses; or any other means deemed appropriate by the trustees. Additional notice may be statewide, regional, local, or personal to a named lawyer as the trustees may direct.

4. Certification of default by trustees; order of Temporary Suspension by the Court of Appeals. (i) Promptly after expiration of the deadline date stated in the mailed notice, the trustees shall submit to the Court of Appeals a proposed Temporary Suspension Order stating the names and account numbers of those lawyers whose accounts remain unpaid. The trustees also shall furnish additional information from their records or give further notice as the Court of Appeals may direct. The Court of Appeals, on being satisfied that the trustees have given the required notice to the lawyers remaining in default, shall enter a Temporary Suspension Order prohibiting each of them from practicing law in the State. The trustees shall mail by first class mail a copy of the Temporary Suspension Order to each lawyer named in the order at the lawyer's last address as it appears on the records of the trustees. The mailing of the copy shall constitute service of the order.

(ii) A lawyer who has been served with a copy of a Temporary Suspension Order and has not been restored to good standing may not practice law and shall comply with the requirements of Rule 16-760 (c). In accordance with the provisions of Title 15, Chapter 200 (Contempt) and any other applicable provision of law or as the Court of Appeals shall direct, an action for contempt of court may be brought against a lawyer who practices law in violation of a Temporary Suspension Order.

(iii) Upon written request from any Maryland lawyer, judge, or litigant to confirm whether a Maryland lawyer named in the request has been temporarily suspended and has not been restored to good standing, the trustees shall furnish confirmation promptly by informal means and, if requested, by written confirmation. On receiving confirmation by the trustees that a Maryland lawyer attempting to practice law has been and remains temporarily suspended, a Maryland judge shall not permit the lawyer to practice law in the State until the Court of Appeals enters an order that terminates the Temporary Suspension Order and restores the lawyer to good standing.

5. Payment. Upon payment in cash or by certified or bank official's check to the Fund by a lawyer of all amounts due by the lawyer, including all related costs that the Court of Appeals or the trustees may prescribe from time to time, the trustees shall remove the lawyer's name from their list of delinquent lawyers and, if a Temporary Suspension Order has been entered, request the Court of Appeals to enter an order that terminates the temporary suspension and restores the lawyer to good standing. If requested by a lawyer affected by the action, the trustees shall furnish confirmation promptly.

6. Bad check; interim Temporary Suspension Order. (i) If a check payable to the Fund is dishonored, the treasurer of the Fund shall notify the lawyer immediately by the quickest available means. Within 7 business days following the date of the notice, the lawyer shall pay to the treasurer of the Fund, in cash or by certified or bank official's check, the full amount of the dishonored check plus any additional charge that the trustees in their discretion shall prescribe from time to time.

(ii) The treasurer of the Fund promptly (but not more often than once each calendar quarter) shall prepare and submit to the Court of Appeals a proposed interim Temporary Suspension Order stating the name and account number of each lawyer who remains in default of payment for a dishonored check and related charges. The Court of Appeals shall enter an interim Temporary Suspension Order prohibiting the practice of law in the State by each lawyer as to whom it is satisfied that the treasurer has made reasonable and good faith efforts to give notice concerning the dishonored check. The treasurer shall mail by first class mail a copy of the interim Temporary Suspension Order to each lawyer named in the order at the lawyer's last address as it appears on the records of the trustees, and the mailing of the copy shall constitute service of the order. (Amended June 5, 1995, effective July 1, 1995.)

7. Notices to clerks. The Clerk of the Court of Appeals shall send a copy of each Temporary Suspension Order and order that terminates a temporary suspension and restores the lawyer to good standing entered pursuant to this Rule to the Clerk of the Court of Special Appeals, the clerk of each circuit court, the Chief Clerk of the District Court, and the Register of Wills for each county. (Amended Oct. 12, 1970; June 30, 1973, effective July 1, 1973; Nov. 8, 1982, effective Jan. 1, 1983; Dec. 8, 1992; June 7, 1994, effective Oct. 1, 1994.)

g. **Treasurer's duties.** 1. Separate account. The Fund shall be maintained by the treasurer in a separate account.

2. Disbursements. The treasurer shall disburse monies from the Fund only upon the action of the trustees pursuant to this Rule.

3. Bond. The treasurer shall file annually with the trustees a bond for the proper execution of the duties of the office of treasurer of the Fund in an amount established from time to time by the trustees and with such surety as may be approved by the trustees. (Amended Nov. 20, 1984, effective Jan. 1, 1985; Dec. 8, 1992.)

4. Other duties. The treasurer shall comply with the requirements of Rule 16-714 (b).

h. **Claims.** 1. Power of trustees. The trustees are invested with the power to determine whether a claim merits reimbursement from the Fund, and if so, the amount of such reimbursement, the time, place, and manner of its payment, the conditions upon which payment shall be made, and the order in which payments shall be made. The trustees' powers under this section may be exercised only by the affirmative vote of at least five trustees.

2. No rights in Fund. No claimant or other person or organization has any right in the Fund as beneficiary or otherwise.

3. Exercise of discretion — Factors. In exercising their discretion the trustees may consider, together with such other factors as they deem appropriate, the following:

(i) The amounts available and likely to become available to the Fund for payment of claims.

(ii) The size and number of claims which are likely to be presented in the future.

(iii) The total amount of losses caused by defalcations of any one attorney or associated group of attorneys.

(iv) The unreimbursed amounts of claims recognized by the trustees in the past as meriting reimbursement, but for which reimbursement has not been made in the total amount of the loss sustained.

(v) The amount of the claimant's loss as compared with the amount of the losses sustained by others who may merit reimbursement from the Fund.

(vi) The degree of hardship the claimant has suffered by the loss.

(vii) Any negligence of the claimant which may have contributed to the loss.

4. Additional powers of trustees. In addition to other conditions and requirements the trustees may require each claimant, as a condition of payment, to execute such instruments, to take such action, and to enter such agreements as the trustees may desire, including assignments, subrogation agreements, trust agreements and promises to cooperate with the trustees in making and prosecuting claims or charges against any person.

5. Investigation of claims — Assistance. The trustees may request individual lawyers, bar associations, and other organizations of lawyers to assist the trustees in the investigation of claims. (Amended Sept. 15, 1976; July 3, 1980; Dec. 8, 1992.)

i. **Powers of Court of Appeals.** 1. To change rule. The Court of Appeals may amend, modify, or repeal this Rule at any time without prior notice, and may provide for the dissolution and winding up of the affairs of the Fund.

2. Judicial review. A person aggrieved by a final determination of the trustees may seek judicial review of the determination pursuant to Title 7, Chapter 200 of these Rules. On any judicial review, the decision of the trustees shall be deemed prima facie correct and shall be affirmed unless the decision was arbitrary, capricious, unsupported by substantial evidence on the record considered as a whole, beyond the authority vested in the trustees, made upon unlawful procedure, or unconstitutional or otherwise illegal. Any party, including the Fund, aggrieved by the judgment of the circuit court may appeal the judgment to the Court of Special Appeals.

3. Arrange audit. The trustees shall arrange for auditing of the accounts of the Fund by state or private auditors, and the Court of Appeals may at any time arrange for such an audit to be made. The cost of any such audit shall be paid by the Fund if no other source of funds is available.

4. Administrative Advice. The trustees may apply to the Court of Appeals, in its nonadjudicatory, supervisory capacity, for interpretation of this Rule and for advice as to their powers and as to the proper administration of the Fund. Any final order issued by the Court in response to any such application shall finally bind and determine all rights with respect to the matters covered therein. (Amended Sept. 15, 1976; June 5, 1996, effective Jan. 1, 1997; Dec. 10, 1996, effective Jan. 1, 1997; Nov. 30, 2000, effective Jan. 1, 2001; Nov. 30, 2000, effective July 1, 2001; effective Nov. 6, 2002; May 8, 2007, effective July 1, 2007.)

Source. — This Rule is in part derived from former Rule 1228 and is in part new.

Effect of amendments. — The first 1996 amendment, in f.1., substituted "Title 16, Chapter 700" for "Subtitle BV" and substituted "Rule 16-701 b" for "Rule BV1 b"; substituted "Title 15, Chapter 200" for "Subtitle P" in g.4.(ii); and added the Source note.

The second 1996 amendment substituted "nine" for "eight" in the first sentence of b 2.

The first 2000 amendment redesignated former d.1.(ix) as present d.1.(x) and inserted present d.1.(ix); and added h.4.

The second 2000 amendment substituted "16-713 (e), 16-714 (b), 16-724 (a), and 16-753" for "16-702 j and 16-709 d" at the end of d.1.(ix); inserted present f.1. and redesignated the remaining subsections accordingly; deleted "as defined by Rule 16-701 b." following "local Bar Association" near the end of f.2.; and substituted "16-713 (e), 16-714 (b), 16-724 (a), and 16-753" for "16-702 j and 16-709 d" at the end of h.4.

The 2002 amendment substituted "the Fund" for "the trust fund" throughout the rule; deleted former a. and redesignated the remaining subsections and changed internal references accordingly; rewrote a. 1. and inserted the cross-reference thereafter; substituted "Client Protection Fund" for "Clients' Security Trust Fund" in a. 2.; inserted present c. 1. (x) and redesignated former c. 1. (x) as c. 1. (xi); substituted "all applicable late charges" for "any late charges" in present e. 2.; substituted "Rule 16-714 (b)" for "Rules 16-713 (e), 16-714 (b), 16-724 (a), and 16-753" in present g. 4.; rewrote present i. 2; and made stylistic changes.

The 2007 amendment substituted "Temporary Suspension" for "Decertification" and variants throughout f, rewrote f.4.(ii); in f.4.(iii) substituted "restored to good standing" for "reinstated" and "Court of Appeals ... good standing" for "lawyer's default has been cured"; in f.5. substituted "enter an order ... good standing" for "rescind its Decertification Order as to that lawyer"; and in f.7. deleted "rescission" before "order" and added "that terminates ... good standing".

Editor's note. — An Order dated June 5, 1996, effective Jan. 1, 1997, renumbered this Rule, which was formerly Rule 1228.

The November 30, 2000 order made amendments to this Rule effective on both January 1, 2001, and July 1, 2001.

Maryland Law Review. — For note on

rules governing the administration of Clients' Security Trust Fund in Maryland, see 26 Md. L. Rev. 369 (1966).

University of Baltimore Law Review. — For article, "The Maryland Rules — A Time for Overhaul," see 9 U. Balt. L. Rev. 1 (1979).

Narrow interpretation. — The history of the Clients' Security Trust Fund suggests a carefully tailored and rather narrow expansion of the desire to provide some protection to clients from defalcations by their attorneys, rather than a broad-brush attempt to compensate for any type of loss caused by an attorney. Monumental Life Ins. Co. v. Trustees of Clients' Sec. Trust Fund, 322 Md. 442, 588 A.2d 340 (1991).

Eligibility for reimbursement. — To be eligible for reimbursement by the Clients' Security Trust Fund a claimant must be the client of, or in a fiduciary relationship with, the defaulting attorney. Monumental Life Ins. Co. v. Trustees of Clients' Sec. Trust Fund, 322 Md. 442, 588 A.2d 340 (1991).

Inactive status — Inactive status in the sense contemplated by Md. R. 16-811, allowing an attorney to voluntarily become inactive, does not insulate an attorney from reciprocal discipline resulting from his or her misconduct in another state. Att'y Griev. Comm'n v. Ruffin, 369 Md. 238, 798 A.2d 1139 (2002).

Fiduciary for non-client. — An attorney acts as a fiduciary for a non-client within the meaning of § 10-312 (b) (1) of the Business Occupations and Professions Article and section (b) (3) of this Rule when the attorney disburses client funds from the attorney's trust account to a non-client, at the instructions of the client and pursuant to the obligations recognized in Rule 1.15 of the Rules of Professional Conduct. Advance Fin. Co. v. Trustees of Clients' Sec. Trust Fund, 337 Md. 195, 652 A.2d 660 (1995).

Claim that former Rule BV2 (now Rule 16-702) and this Rule are impermissible taxes may or may not be correct, but even if the point is well taken, it would not be an excuse for unethical conduct on the part of a member of the bar, nor would it be a defense to charges relative to such conduct. Att'y Griev. Comm'n v. Kerpelman, 288 Md. 341, 420 A.2d 940 (1980), cert. denied, 450 U.S. 970, 101 S. Ct. 1492, 67 L. Ed. 2d 621 (1981).

Trustees are granted wide discretion. Folly Farms I, Inc. v. Trustees of Clients' Sec. Trust Fund, 282 Md. 659, 387 A.2d 248 (1978).

In exercising their discretion, the trustees are to consider a number of factors, including the amounts available and likely to become available to the trust fund for payment of claims, the size and number of claims likely to be presented, the total amount of losses caused by defalcations of any one attorney, the unreimbursed amounts of claims recognized by the trustees in the past as meriting reimbursement but for which reimbursement has not been made in the total amount of the loss sustained, the amount of the claimant's loss as compared with the amount of the losses sustained by others who may merit reimbursement from the trust fund, the degree of hardship the claimant has suffered by the loss, and any negligence of the claimant which may have contributed to the loss. Folly Farms I, Inc. v. Trustees of Clients' Sec. Trust Fund, 282 Md. 659, 387 A.2d 248 (1978).

It is not negligence under subsection i 3 of this Rule to trust one's attorney in the absence of facts which put one on notice or ought to put the client on notice that inquiry should be made. Folly Farms I, Inc. v. Trustees of Clients' Sec. Trust Fund, 282 Md. 659, 387 A.2d 248 (1978).

Deprivation of right to counsel. — Defendant was not deprived of his constitutional right to counsel because the lawyer who conducted his defense was then under suspension from the practice of law in Maryland for failure to pay an annual assessment required by law. Jones v. State, 328 Md. 654, 616 A.2d 422 (1992).

"Defalcation." — Converting the funds of a client, or the funds held for another in a fiduciary capacity, clearly comes within the meaning of "defalcation"; however, obtaining money from a third party by means of a fraud does not. Monumental Life Ins. Co. v. Trustees of Clients' Sec. Trust Fund, 322 Md. 442, 588 A.2d 340 (1991).

Standard of judicial review. — The standard of judicial review of decisions of the trustees of the Clients' Security Trust Fund set forth in section (j) (2) of this Rule is analogous to the standard of review applicable to administrative agencies: whether a reasonable mind could have reached the factual conclusion the agency reached. Advance Fin. Co. v. Trustees of Clients' Sec. Trust Fund, 337 Md. 195, 652 A.2d 660 (1995).

Rule 16-812. Maryland Lawyers' Rules of Professional Conduct.

The Maryland Lawyers' Rules of Professional Conduct, as set forth in Appendix: Maryland Lawyers' Rules of Professional Conduct, are hereby adopted. (Added Oct. 13, 1970; amended Dec. 9, 1976, effective Jan. 1, 1977; Mar. 8, 1978, effective May 1, 1978; Apr. 15, 1986, effective Jan. 1, 1987; June 5, 1996, effective Jan. 1, 1997; Feb. 8, 2005, effective July 1, 2005.)

Source. — This Rule is derived from former Rule 1230.

Effect of amendments. — The 1996 amendment added the Source note.

The 2005 amendment inserted "Lawyers'" before "Rules of Professional Conduct" in the Rule heading; inserted "Lawyers'" before "Rules of Professional Conduct", substituted "Maryland Lawyers Rules of Professional Conduct" for "Rules of Professional Conduct of the Maryland Rules" in the undesignated paragraph; and added "derived from" after "This Rule is" in the Source note.

Editor's note. — An Order dated June 5, 1996, effective Jan. 1, 1997, renumbered this Rule, which was formerly Rule 1230.

Maryland Law Review. — For article, "Group Legal Services and Canon II," see 34 Md. L. Rev. 541 (1974).

For note, "Applying the Sherman Act to Restrictive Practices of the Legal Profession," see 34 Md. L. Rev. 571 (1974).

For comment, "Discipline of Attorneys in Maryland," see 35 Md. L. Rev. 236 (1975).

For article, "The Law of Disbarment and Reinstatement in Maryland," see 36 Md. L. Rev. 703 (1977).

For article, "Survey of Developments in Maryland Law, 1987-88," see 48 Md. L. Rev. 551 (1989).

University of Baltimore Law Review. — For article on fee schedules and prepaid legal services, see 4 U. Balt. L. Rev. 80 (1974).

For article, "The Maryland Rules — A Time for Overhaul," see 9 U. Balt. L. Rev. 1 (1979).

Application. — This Rule simply adopts the Maryland Rules of Professional Conduct, as set forth in the appendix of the Maryland Rules of Procedure, and does not constitute a discrete provision establishing a standard of conduct itself which one may be said to have violated. Att'y Griev. Comm'n v. Guida, 391 Md. 33, 891 A.2d 1085 (2006).

Purpose of sanctions imposed in disciplinary proceedings. — Sanctions imposed in disciplinary proceedings against an attorney are not for the purpose of punishing the individual, but are intended as protection to the public. Att'y Griev. Comm'n v. Pattison, 292 Md. 599, 441 A.2d 328 (1982).

Professional service corporations. — When the conduct of a lawyer in a professional service corporation is called into question with reference to the attorney-client relationship, the Rules of Professional Conduct will apply and not those of an ordinary business corporation. Where, however, the situation involves a dispute between shareholders of the professional service corporation, the corporate law

should not be disregarded in favor of partnership law. Langhoff v. Marr, 81 Md. App. 438, 568 A.2d 844 (1990), vacated on other grounds and remanded, 322 Md. 657, 589 A.2d 470 (1991).

Attorney accepts clients' moneys and properties in trust. — The relationship existing between an attorney and his client is one that of necessity requires mutual trust and confidence. An attorney accepts moneys and properties belonging to his clients in trust and is strictly accountable for his conduct in administering that trust, so he dares not appropriate those funds and properties for his personal use. The misappropriation by an attorney of funds of others entrusted to his care, be the amount small or large, is of great concern and represents the gravest form of professional misconduct. Att'y Griev. Comm'n v. Pattison, 292 Md. 599, 441 A.2d 328 (1982).

Fiduciary may not make loan to himself. — It is fundamental that a fiduciary, including an attorney administering a decedent's estate, may not make a loan secured or unsecured, unto himself. Att'y Griev. Comm'n v. Pattison, 292 Md. 599, 441 A.2d 328 (1982).

Disbarment sanction for converting funds. — Absent extenuating circumstances, disbarment is the sanction which should be imposed upon an attorney for converting the funds of his client to his own use, even if he intended to repay the funds. Att'y Griev. Comm'n v. Pattison, 292 Md. 599, 441 A.2d 328 (1982).

Suspended attorney was disbarred because of his later (1) unjustified misappropriation of trust funds by not paying the clients' medical providers (as he had promised he would do) from clients' share settlement he retained in cash after he got clients' endorsements on settlement checks, received payable to him and to the clients, cashed the checks with the clients at a liquor store cashing service, retained cash to pay his one-third fee (that he reduced) and to pay listed medical providers according to a handwritten distribution summary given to the clients, and distributed the clients' share to them; (2) failure to have or to use an attorney trust account at a proper financial institution; and (3) failure to respond to the disciplinary committee's investigation or petition, or to the hearing judge's conclusions. The attorney's misappropriation of trust money was serious professional misconduct and was embezzlement, fraudulent misappropriation by a fiduciary, under 7-113 of the Criminal Law Article, representing professional misconduct that violated Md. R. Prof. Conduct 8.4(b)-(c); and his conducted also violated Md. R. Prof. Conduct 1.15, 8.1; Md. R. 16-812, 16-603, 16-604, §§ 10-302(a), 10-306 of the Business Occupations and Professions Article. Att'y Griev. Comm'n v. Prichard, 386 Md. 238, 872 A.2d 81 (2005).

Disbarment was an appropriate sanction for an attorney who had violated various of the Maryland Rules of Professional Conduct, as adopted by this Rule. No mitigating evidence had been presented and there was a disciplinary history that evidenced recent similar misconduct of placing an unearned fee in her operating account, spending it for personal purposes before it was earned, failing to communicate with her client, retaining the fee even after the case in which she was retained had been dismissed for lack of prosecution, and failing to respond to Bar Counsel's inquiries as to her client's complaint. Att'y Griev. Comm'n v. McCulloch, 404 Md. 388, 946 A.2d 1009 (2008).

When defendant tells his attorney before trial that he committed crime charged and the attorney is convinced that his client is telling the truth, the attorney is precluded under this Rule from calling or presenting alibi witnesses who would offer perjured testimony. State v. Lloyd, 48 Md. App. 535, 429 A.2d 244 (1981).

Applied in Cole v. State, 378 Md. 42, 835 A.2d 600 (2003); Att'y Griev. Comm'n v. Alsafty, 379 Md. 1, 838 A.2d 1213 (2003); Att'y Griev. Comm'n v. Rees, 396 Md. 248, 913 A.2d 68 (2006); Att'y Griev. Comm'n v. Parsons, 404 Md. 175, 946 A.2d 437 (2008); In re Gulczynski, (Bankr. D. Md. 2008).

Quoted in Att'y Griev. Comm'n v. Baker, 396 Md. 15, 912 A.2d 651 (2006).

Stated in United States v. Gray, 189 F. Supp. 2d 279 (D. Md. 2002).

Cited in Att'y Griev. Comm'n of Maryland v. Mooney, 359 Md. 56, 753 A.2d 17 (2000); Att'y Griev. Comm'n v. Post, 379 Md. 60, 839 A.2d 718 (2003); Att'y Griev. Comm'n v. Link, 380 Md. 405, 844 A.2d 1197 (2004); Att'y Griev. Comm'n v. Daskalopoulos, 383 Md. 375, 859 A.2d 653 (2004); Att'y Griev. Comm'n v. Christopher, 383 Md. 624, 861 A.2d 692 (2004); Att'y Griev. Comm'n v. MacDougall, 384 Md. 271,

863 A.2d 312 (2004); Att'y Griev. Comm'n v. Brisbon, 385 Md. 667, 870 A.2d 586 (2005); Att'y Griev. Comm'n v. Steinberg, 385 Md. 696, 870 A.2d 603 (2005); Att'y Griev. Comm'n v. Mitchell, 386 Md. 386, 872 A.2d 720 (2005); Att'y Griev. Comm'n v. Jordan, 386 Md. 583, 873 A.2d 1161 (2005); Att'y Griev. Comm'n v. Kovacic, 389 Md. 233, 884 A.2d 673 (2005); Att'y Griev. Comm'n v. Muhammad, — Md. —, — A.2d — (2005); Att'y Griev. Comm'n v. Lee, 390 Md. 517, 890 A.2d 273 (2005); Att'y Griev. Comm'n v. Holt, 391 Md. 673, 894 A.2d 602 (2006); Att'y Griev. Comm'n v. Rose, 391 Md. 101, 892 A.2d 469 (2006), cert. denied, 2006 U.S. LEXIS 5734, 166 L. Ed. 2d 22 (U.S. 2006); Att'y Griev. Comm'n v. Calhoun, 391 Md. 532, 894 A.2d 518 (2006); Att'y Griev. Comm'n v. Guberman, 392 Md. 131, 896 A.2d 337 (2006); Att'y Griev. Comm'n v. Manger, 396 Md. 134, 913 A.2d 1 (2006); Att'y Griev. Comm'n v. Ward, 396 Md. 203, 913 A.2d 41 (2006); Att'y Griev. Comm'n v. Muhammad, 395 Md. 676, 912 A.2d 588 (2006), cert. denied, 127 S. Ct. 2296, 2007 U.S. LEXIS 5292, 167 L. Ed. 2d 1103 (U.S. 2007); Att'y Griev. Comm'n v. Hodgson, 396 Md. 1, 912 A.2d 640 (2006); Att'y Griev. Comm'n v. Mba-Jonas, 397 Md. 690, 919 A.2d 669 (2007); Att'y Griev. Comm'n v. Hill, 398 Md. 95, 919 A.2d 1194 (2007); Att'y Griev. Comm'n v. Goff, 399 Md. 1, 922 A.2d 554 (2007); Att'y Griev. Comm'n v. Robertson, 400 Md. 618, 929 A.2d 576 (2007); Att'y Griev. Comm'n v. Wingerter, 400 Md. 214, 929 A.2d 47 (2007); Att'y Griev. Comm'n v. Adams, 404 Md. 1, 944 A.2d 1115 (2008); Att'y Griev. Comm'n v. Elmendorf, 404 Md. 353, 946 A.2d 542 (2008); Att'y Griev. Comm'n v. Hall, 408 Md. 306, 969 A.2d 953 (2009); Att'y Griev. Comm'n v. Tanko, 408 Md. 404, 969 A.2d 1010 (2009); Att'y Griev. Comm'n v. McLaughlin, 409 Md. 304, 974 A.2d 315 (2009); Att'y Griev. Comm'n v. Johnson, 409 Md. 470, 976 A.2d 245 (2009); Att'y Griev. Comm'n v. Adams, 410 Md. 544, 979 A.2d 698 (2009); Att'y Griev. Comm'n v. Kwarteng, 411 Md. 652, 984 A.2d 865 (2009); Att'y Griev. Comm'n v. Downey, 413 Md. 1, 990 A.2d 1070 (2010); Louis Fireison & Assocs., P.A. v. Alkire, 195 Md. App. 461, 6 A.3d 945 (2010); Monmouth Meadows Homeowners Ass'n v. Hamilton, 416 Md. 325, 7 A.3d 1 (Oct. 25, 2010).

Rule 16-812.1. Judicial Ethics Committee.

(a) **Definitions.** In this Rule the following definitions apply except as expressly otherwise provided or as necessary implication requires:

(1) Committee. "Committee" means the Judicial Ethics Committee.

(2) Ethics provision. "Ethics provision" means:

(A) a provision of Code, State Government Article, Title 15, Subtitle 5 or 6;

(B) as to a judge, also a provision of the Maryland Code of Judicial Conduct; and

(C) as to a judicial appointee as defined in Rule 16-814, also a provision of the Maryland Code of Conduct for Judicial Appointees.

(3) State Official in Judicial Branch. "State official in the Judicial Branch" means an individual who is in the Judicial Branch and is a State official, as defined in Code, State Government Article, § 15-102.

(b) **Creation.** There is a Judicial Ethics Committee.

(c) **Composition.** The Committee consists of 11 members appointed by the Chief Judge of the Court of Appeals. Of the 11 members:

(1) one shall be a judge of the Court of Special Appeals;

(2) two shall be circuit court judges;

(3) two shall be judges of the District Court;

(4) one shall be a judge of an orphans' court;

(5) one shall be a former judge who is approved for recall for temporary service under Maryland Constitution, Article IV, § 3A;

(6) one shall be a clerk of a circuit court;

(7) one shall be a judicial appointee as defined in Rule 16-814; and

(8) two shall not be a judge or other officer or employee of the Judicial Branch of the State government or a lawyer.

(d) **Term.** (1) The term of a member is three years and begins on July 1, except that the former judge appointed pursuant to subsection (c)(5) of this Rule shall not have a term and shall serve at the pleasure of the Chief Judge of the Court of Appeals.

(2) The terms of the members shall be staggered so that the terms of not more than four members expire each year.

(3) At the end of a term, a member continues to serve until a successor is appointed.

(4) A member who is appointed after a term has begun serves only for the rest of the term and until a successor is appointed.

(5) A member appointed on or after July 1, 2005, may not serve more than two consecutive three-year terms.

(e) **Chair and Vice Chair.** The Chief Judge of the Court of Appeals shall designate one judicial member as the Chair of the Committee and one judicial member as the Vice Chair. In the absence or disability of the Chair or upon an express delegation of authority by the Chair, the Vice Chair shall have the authority and perform the duties of the Chair.

(f) **Meetings.** The Committee shall meet at the times and places that the Chair directs.

(g) **Quorum.** The presence of a majority of the members then serving constitutes a quorum for the transaction of all business other than adjournment of a meeting for lack of a quorum.

(h) **Committee Staff.** The Committee shall have staff as the State Court Administrator directs.

(i) **Duties.** In addition to its other duties imposed by law, the Committee:

(1) shall give advice, as provided in this Rule, with respect to the application or interpretation of the Maryland Code of Judicial Conduct and the Maryland Code of Conduct for Judicial Appointees;

(2) is designated as the body to give advice with respect to the application or interpretation of any provision of Code, State Government Article, Title 15, Subtitles 5 and 6, to a State official in the Judicial Branch;

(3) shall review timely appeals from the State Court Administrator's decision not to extend, under Rule 16-815 or 16-816, the period for filing a financial disclosure statement;

(4) shall determine, under Rule 16-815 f or Rule 16-816 g, whether to allow a judge or judicial appointee to correct a deficiency as to a financial disclosure statement or to refer the matter, as to a judge, to the Commission on Judicial Disabilities or, as to a judicial appointee, to the State Ethics Commission; and

(5) shall submit to the Court of Appeals recommendations for necessary or desirable changes in any ethics provision.

(j) (1) Requester. A request for the opinion of the Committee may be made only by:

(A) a State official in the Judicial Branch, as to the proper interpretation of an ethics provision as applied to that State official; or

(B) the Chief Judge of the Court of Appeals, as to the proper interpretation of an ethics provision.

(2) Form of Request. Each request for an opinion of the Committee shall:

(A) be in writing;

(B) describe the act or activity about which the opinion is requested;

(C) include all documentation or other information necessary for the Committee to perform its function, which may include citation to rules, statutes, and published opinions of the Committee that the requester believes to be relevant to the request; and

(D) include an address to which the Committee shall direct correspondence.

(3) Opinion. The Committee may render an opinion, in writing, with regard to any request made under this Rule and shall decide whether an opinion is to be published or unpublished. The Chair shall cause to be prepared an edited version of each opinion designated to be published, in which the identity and specific court or geographical location of the requester and the identity of other persons mentioned in the opinion shall not be disclosed and shall have the opinion published in the manner that the State Court Administrator deems proper.

(4) Letter of Advice. If the Chair decides that the full Committee cannot provide a timely written opinion or that prior opinions of the Committee render full Committee review unnecessary, a panel of not less than three members appointed by the Chair may issue a written letter of advice, which shall not be published and shall have no precedential effect.

(5) Protection from a Charge of Violation. A State official in the Judicial Branch who requests an opinion as to application of an ethics provision and is in compliance with an opinion of, or letter of advice issued for, the Committee is protected from a charge of violation of that ethics provision.

Committee note. — The Judicial Ethics Committee noted that, given the binding effect of opinions, they generally should be issued only to a State official in the Judicial Branch requesting advice as to the official's own conduct. This practice would avoid comment either on hypothetical conduct or conduct incompletely or inaccurately described. However, there may be instances, such as those in which an opinion would affect numerous State officials in the Judicial Branch or the implementation of administrative duties, that make it appropriate to have a mechanism for requesting an interpretation of an ethics provision but not an opinion as to its application. Therefore, language in former Maryland Code of Judicial

Conduct (1987), Canon 7 suggesting that persons other than a State official in the Judicial Branch could request an opinion has been omitted, but a provision for the Chief Judge of the Court of Appeals to request guidance on interpretation has been added. The addition is patterned on the practice for requesting an opinion from the Attorney General.

(6) Filing; Confidentiality. The Chair shall file with the State Court Administrator every opinion of, and letter of advice issued for, the Committee. A request and the letter of advice or the opinion, other than the edited version designated to be published, filed in response are confidential and, unless otherwise directed by the Court of Appeals or required by law, are not public information. (Added December 2, 2004, effective July 1, 2005; February 10, 2009, effective July 1, 2009.)

Cross references. — See Rule 16-813 (Maryland Code of Judicial Conduct) and Rule 16-814 (Maryland Code of Conduct for Judicial Appointees).
Source. — This Rule is derived from former

Maryland Code of Judicial Conduct (1987), Canon 7, as it was set forth in former Rule 1231 (renumbered Rule 16-813 by Rules Order dated January 18, 1996, effective July 1, 1996).

Effect of amendments. — The 2009 amendment in (c) substituted "11 members" for "nine members" in two places in the introductory paragraph; added (c)(5) and redesig-

nated accordingly; in (c)(8) substituted "two shall" for "one shall"; in (d)(1) added the exception at the end; and in (d)(2) substituted "not more than four members" for "three members".

Rule 16-813. Maryland Code of Judicial Conduct.
TABLE OF CONTENTS

GENERAL PROVISIONS, DEFINITIONS, AND PREAMBLE

A. GENERAL PROVISIONS

A-101 — The Maryland Code of Judicial Conduct is divided into five Parts. This introductory Part contains General Provisions, Definitions, and a Preamble. The remaining Parts, titled as Sections 1 through 4, contain both substantive Rules of Judicial Conduct that articulate specific ethical standards and Comments that provide guidance in interpreting those Rules. Those Sections are organized as follows:

Section 1. Rules Governing Judicial Integrity and the Avoidance of Impropriety (Rules 1.1 through 1.3)

Section 2. Rules Governing the Performance of Judicial Duties (Rules 2.1 through 2.16)

Section 3. Rules Governing Non-Judicial Activities (Rules 3.1 through 3.15)

Section 4. Rules Governing Political Activity (Rules 4.1 through 4.6)

A-102 — This Code is based in large part on the 2007 Model Code of Judicial Conduct proposed by the American Bar Association (hereafter referred to as "2007 ABA Code"), although this Code differs from the 2007 ABA Code in a number of respects. Some differences are substantive; others are matters of style or organization. Three differences are worthy of general note:

Consolidation of Prefatory Provisions

This Code consolidates and reorganizes the Preamble, Scope, Application, and Terminology provisions of the 2007 ABA Code into this introductory Part on General Provisions, Definitions, and Preamble. Although these provisions are not in the form of Rules, they are part of this Code.

Elimination of Canons

The 2007 ABA Code proposed a new and much different structure and format. The enforceable ethical commands in previous Codes were stated in the form of specific Canons, to which were appended interpretative Comments. The enforceable ethical commands in the 2007 ABA Code are stated in the form of Rules that are supplemented by interpretative Comments and headed by very brief and general statements denominated as Canons.

The 2007 ABA Code acknowledges that a judge may be disciplined only for violating a Rule, but it regards the Canons as providing guidance in interpreting the Rules. That, however, is more precisely the function of the Comments under each Rule. The Canons themselves appear to be merely descriptive of the subject matter of the Rules. To avoid any ambiguity over the significance of the Canons and to make clear that attention must be focused on the Rules and the Comments, this Code eliminates the Canons and uses instead a descriptive statement of the Rules in each Section.

Political Activity

The 2007 ABA Code contains provisions regarding political activity and financial disclosure by judges. This Code reorganizes those provisions and conforms them to the different manners in which judges are selected and retained in Maryland and to requirements enacted by the Maryland General Assembly or adopted by the Court of Appeals. The intent is to make more clear to each judge and candidate for judicial office what is allowed and what is not allowed.

A-103 — A judge may be disciplined only for violating a Rule. If a Rule contains a permissive term, such as "may" or "should" the conduct being addressed is committed to the personal and professional discretion of the judge or candidate in question, and no disciplinary action should be taken for action or inaction within the bounds of that discretion.

Source. — This provision is derived from the Scope section of the 2007 ABA Code.

A-104 — The Comments that accompany the Rules contain explanatory material and, in some instances, provide examples of permitted or prohibited conduct.

Comments neither add to nor subtract from the binding obligations set forth in the Rules. Therefore, when a Comment contains the term "must," it does not mean that the Comment itself is binding or enforceable but merely signifies that the Rule in question, properly understood, is obligatory as to the conduct at issue.

The Comments also may identify aspirational goals for judges. To implement fully the principles of this Code, judges should hold themselves to the highest ethical standards and seek to achieve those aspirational goals, thereby enhancing the dignity of the judicial office.

Source. — These provisions are derived from the Scope section of the 2007 ABA Code.

A-105 — The Rules in this Code are rules of reason that should be applied in a manner consistent with Constitutional requirements, statutes, other Court Rules, and decisional law and with due regard for all relevant circumstances. The Rules should not be interpreted to impinge upon the essential **independence** of judges in making judicial decisions.

Source. — This provision is derived from the Scope section of the 2007 ABA Code.

A-106 — Although the text of the Rules is binding and enforceable, it is not contemplated that every transgression will result in the imposition of discipline. Whether discipline should be imposed should be determined through a reasonable and reasoned application of the Rules and should depend upon factors such as the seriousness of the transgression, the facts and circumstances that existed at the time of the transgression, the extent of any pattern of improper activity, whether there have been previous violations, and the effect of the improper activity upon the judicial system or others.

Source. — This provision is derived from the Scope section of the 2007 ABA Code.

A-107 — This Code is not designed or intended as a basis for civil or criminal liability. It is also not intended to be the basis for litigants to seek collateral remedies against each other or to obtain tactical advantages in proceedings before a court.

Source. — This provision is derived from the Scope section of the 2007 ABA Code.

A-108 — In interpreting this Code, attention should be given to the opinions of the Judicial Ethics Committee and, if appropriate, that Committee should be asked for a written letter of advice or a binding opinion. *See* Rule 16-812.1 (j)(5), protecting a judge from a charge of violating an ethics provision in this Code if the judge has requested and received an opinion or advice letter from the Committee and is in compliance with that opinion or advice letter.

Source. — This provision is derived from the Preamble to the former Maryland Code of Judicial Conduct.

A-109 — This Code applies to:

(1) Incumbent judges of the Court of Appeals, the Court of Special Appeals, the Circuit Courts, and the District Court;

(2) Except as otherwise expressly provided in specific Rules, incumbent judges of the Orphans' Courts;

(3) Except as otherwise expressly provided in specific Rules, retired judges who are approved for recall for temporary service pursuant to Maryland Constitution, Art. IV, § 3A.; and

(4) Candidates and applicants for judicial office as defined in Rule 4.1, to the extent that a Rule expressly applies to such candidates or applicants. *See* Section 4 and Rule 2.11.

Source. — This provision is new.

B. DEFINITIONS

B-101 — Domestic Partner

"Domestic partner" means a person with whom another person maintains a household and an intimate relationship, other than a person to whom he or she is legally married. *See* Rules 2.11, 2.13, 3.13, and 3.14.

Source. — This definition is derived from the Terminology section of the 2007 ABA Code.

B-102 — Fiduciary

"Fiduciary" includes relationships such as administrator, attorney-in-fact by power of attorney, personal representative, and trustee. *See* Rules 2.11, 3.2, and 3.8.

Source. — This definition is derived from the Terminology section of the 2007 ABA Code.

B-103 — Gift

(a) Except as provided in paragraph (b), **"gift"** means the transfer of anything of economic value, regardless of form, without adequate and lawful consideration.

(b) **"Gift"** does not include the solicitation, acceptance, receipt, or regulation of a political contribution that is regulated in accordance with:

(1) the Election Law Article of the Maryland Code; or

(2) any other Maryland law regulating the conduct of elections or the receipt of political contributions. *See* Rule 3.13.

Source. — This definition is derived from Code, State Government Article, § 15-102 (p).

B-104 — Impartial

"Impartial," "impartiality," and **"impartially"** mean absence of bias or prejudice in favor of, or against, particular parties or classes of parties, as well as maintenance of an open mind in considering issues that may come before a judge. *See* Rules 1.2, 2.2, 2.10, 2.11, 2.13, 3.1, 3.12, 3.13, 4.4, and 4.5.

Source. — This definition is derived from the Terminology section of the 2007 ABA Code.

B-105 — Impending Matter

"Impending matter" means a matter that is imminent or expected to occur in the near future. *See* Rules 2.9, 2.10, 3.13, 4.4, and 4.5

Source. — This definition is derived from the Terminology section of the 2007 ABA Code.

B-106 — Independence

"Independence" means a judge's freedom from influence or controls other than those established by law. *See* Rules 1.2, 3.1, 3.12, 3.13, 4.4, and 4.5.

Source. — This definition is derived from the Terminology section of the 2007 ABA Code.

B-107 — Knowingly

"Knowingly," "knowledge," "known," and **"knows"** mean actual **knowledge** of the fact in question. A person's **knowledge** may be inferred from circumstances. *See* Rules 2.11, 2.13. 2.15, 2.16, 3.6, and 4.4, and 4.5.

Source. — This definition is derived from the Terminology section of the 2007 ABA Code.

B-108 — Member of judge's or candidate's family

"Member of a [judge's] [candidate's] family" means a spouse, **domestic partner,** child, grandchild, parent, grandparent, or other relative or person with whom the judge or candidate maintains a close familial relationship. *See* Rules 3.7, 3.8, 3.10, and 3.11.

Source. — This definition is derived from the Terminology section of the 2007 ABA Code.

B-109 — Member of judge's or candidate's household

"Member of [judge's] [candidate's] household" means:

(a) if sharing the judge's or candidate's legal residence, the judge's or candidate's spouse, **domestic partner,** child, ward, financially dependent parent, or other financially dependent relative; or

(b) the judge's or candidate's spouse, child, ward, parent, or other relative, over whose financial affairs the judge or candidate has legal or actual control. *See* Rule 3.13.

Source. — This definition is derived from Maryland Code, State Government Article, § 15-102 (z).

B-110 — Pending matter
"Pending matter" means a matter that has commenced. A matter continues to be pending through any appellate process until final disposition. *See* Rules 2.9, 2.10, 3.13, and 4.4, and 4.5.

Source. — This definition is derived from the Terminology section of the 2007 ABA Code.

B-111 — Significant financial interest
(a) **"Significant financial interest"** means ownership of:

(1) an interest as the result of which the owner has received within the past three years, is currently receiving, or in the future is entitled to receive, more than $1,000 per year;

(2) more than 3% of a business entity; or

(3) a security of any kind that represents, or is convertible into, more than 3% of a business entity.

(b) In applying this definition:

(1) ownership of an interest in a mutual or common investment fund that holds a security is not ownership of the security unless:

(i) the judge participates in the management of the fund; or

(ii) there is before the judge a **pending matter** or an **impending matter** that could substantially affect the value of the interest;

(2) ownership of a government security is not a **significant financial interest** in the issuer unless there is before the judge a **pending matter** or an **impending matter** that could substantially affect the value of the security;

(3) neither a deposit in a financial institution nor a proprietary interest such as or similar to that of a depositor in a mutual savings association, member of a credit union, or policy holder in a mutual insurance company is a **significant financial interest** in the entity unless there is before the judge a **pending matter** or an **impending matter** that could substantially affect the value of the deposit or interest; and

(4) an ownership interest in a security held by a charitable, civic, educational, fraternal, sororal, or religious organization will not be imputed to a judge merely because the judge or the judge's child, parent, or spouse is an adviser to or director or officer of, or otherwise actively participates in, the organization.

Source. — This definition is derived from the former Maryland Code of Judicial Conduct.

B-112 — Third Degree of Relationship

"Third degree of relationship" includes the following persons: great-grandparent, grandparent, parent, uncle, aunt, brother, sister, child, grandchild, great-grandchild, nephew, and niece. *See* Rules 2.11 and 2.13.

Source. — This definition is derived from the Terminology section of the 2007 ABA Code.

C. PREAMBLE

C-101 — An independent, fair, competent, and **impartial** judiciary composed of men and women of integrity who will interpret and apply the law that governs our society is indispensable to our system of justice. Thus, the judiciary plays a central role in preserving the principles of justice and the rule of law. Inherent in all the Rules contained in this Code are the precepts that judges, individually and collectively, must respect and honor the judicial office as a public trust and strive to maintain and enhance confidence in the legal system.

C-102 — Judges should maintain the dignity of judicial office at all times, and avoid both impropriety and the appearance of impropriety in their professional and personal lives. They should aspire at all times to conduct that ensures the greatest possible public confidence in their **independence, impartiality,** integrity, and competence.

C-103 — This Code of Judicial Conduct establishes standards for the ethical conduct of judges and judicial candidates. It is not intended as an exhaustive guide for the conduct of judges and judicial candidates, who are governed in their judicial and personal conduct by general ethical standards as well as by this Code. This Code is intended, however, to provide guidance and assist judges in maintaining the highest standards of judicial and personal conduct, and to provide a basis for regulating their conduct through disciplinary agencies.

Source. — This Preamble is derived from the Preamble section of the 2007 ABA Code.

SECTION 1.

RULES GOVERNING JUDICIAL INTEGRITY AND THE AVOIDANCE OF IMPROPRIETY

Rule 1.1. COMPLIANCE WITH THE LAW

A judge shall comply with the law, including this Code of Judicial Conduct.

Source. — This Rule is derived from Rule 1.1 of the 2007 ABA Code.

Rule 1.2. PROMOTING CONFIDENCE IN THE JUDICIARY

(a) A judge shall act at all times in a manner that promotes public confidence in the **independence,** integrity, and **impartiality** of the judiciary.

(b) A judge shall avoid conduct that would create in reasonable minds a perception of impropriety.

COMMENT

[1] Public confidence in the judiciary is eroded by improper conduct and conduct that creates the appearance of impropriety. This principle applies to both the professional and personal conduct of a judge.

[2] A judge should expect to be the subject of public scrutiny that might be viewed as burdensome if applied to other persons, and must accept the restrictions imposed by this Code.

[3] Conduct that compromises or appears to compromise the **independence,** integrity, and **impartiality** of a judge undermines public confidence in the judiciary. Because it is not practicable to list all such conduct, the Rule is necessarily cast in general terms.

[4] Judges should participate in activities that promote ethical conduct among judges and lawyers, support professionalism within the judiciary and the legal profession, and promote access to justice for all.

[5] Actual improprieties include violations of law, court rules, and this Code. The test for appearance of impropriety is whether the conduct would create in reasonable minds a perception that the judge's ability to carry out judicial responsibilities with competence, **impartiality,** and integrity is impaired.

[6] A judge should initiate and participate in community outreach activities for the purpose of promoting public understanding of and confidence in the administration of justice. In conducting such activities, the judge must act in a manner consistent with this Code.

Source. — This Rule is derived from Rule 1.2 of the 2007 ABA Code. Comments [1], [2], [3], [4], and [6] are derived from the ABA Comments to that Rule. Comment [5] is derived in part from ABA Comment [5] to that Rule and is in part new.

Rule 1.3. AVOIDING LENDING THE PRESTIGE OF JUDICIAL OFFICE

A judge shall not lend the prestige of judicial office to advance the personal or economic interests of the judge or others, or allow others to do so.

COMMENT

[1] It is improper for a judge to use or attempt to use his or her position to gain personal advantage or deferential treatment of any kind. For example, it would be improper for a judge to allude to his or her judicial status to gain favorable treatment in encounters with traffic officials. Similarly, a judge must not use a judicial letterhead to gain an advantage in conducting his or her personal business.

[2] A judge may provide a reference or recommendation for an individual based upon the judge's personal **knowledge.** The judge may use an official letterhead if the judge indicates that the reference is personal and if there is no likelihood that the use of the letterhead would reasonably be perceived as an attempt to exert pressure by reason of the judicial office.

[3] Judges may participate in the process of judicial selection by cooperating with appointing authorities and screening committees and by responding to inquiries from such entities concerning the professional qualifications of a person being considered for judicial office.

Cross references. — *See* Rule 4.3.

[4] Special considerations arise when judges write or contribute to publications of for-profit entities, whether related or unrelated to the law. A judge should not permit anyone associated with the publication of such materials to exploit the judge's office in a manner that violates this Rule or other applicable law. In contracts for publication of a judge's writing, the judge should retain sufficient control over the advertising to avoid such exploitation.

Source. — This Rule is derived from Rule 1.3 of the 2007 ABA Code. The Comments are derived from the ABA Comments to that Rule.

SECTION 2.

RULES GOVERNING THE PERFORMANCE OF JUDICIAL DUTIES

Rule 2.1. GIVING PRECEDENCE TO THE DUTIES OF JUDICIAL OFFICE

The duties of judicial office, as prescribed by law, shall take precedence over a judge's personal and extrajudicial activities.

COMMENT

[1] To ensure that judges are available to fulfill their judicial duties, judges must conduct their personal and extrajudicial activities to minimize the risk of conflicts that would result in frequent disqualification.

[2] Although it is not a duty of judicial office unless prescribed by law, judges are encouraged to participate in activities that promote public understanding of and confidence in the justice system.

[3] With respect to time devoted to personal and extrajudicial activities, this Rule must be construed in a reasonable manner. Family obligations, illnesses, emergencies, and per-

missible extrajudicial activities may require a judge's immediate attention. Attending to those obligations and situations, temporary in nature, is not prohibited by this Rule and should be dealt with in accordance with applicable vacation, sick leave, and administrative leave policies.

Source. — This Rule is derived from Rule 2.1 of the 2007 ABA Code, except that the words "all of" in that Code have been deleted. Comments [1] and [2] are derived from the ABA Comments to that Rule. Comment [3] is new.

Rule 2.2. IMPARTIALITY AND FAIRNESS

A judge shall uphold and apply the law and shall perform all duties of judicial office **impartially** and fairly.

COMMENT

[1] To ensure **impartiality** and fairness to all parties, a judge must be objective and open-minded.

[2] Although each judge comes to the bench with a unique background and personal philosophy, a judge must interpret and apply the law without regard to whether the judge approves or disapproves of the law in question.

[3] When applying and interpreting the law, a judge sometimes may make good-faith errors of fact or law. Errors of this kind do not violate this Rule.

[4] It is not a violation of this Rule for a judge to make reasonable accommodations to ensure self-represented litigants the opportunity to have their matters fairly heard.

Cross references. — *See* Rule 2.6 Comment [2].

Source. — This Rule is derived from Rule 2.2 of the 2007 ABA Code. The Comments are derived from the ABA Comments to that Rule.

Rule 2.3. BIAS, PREJUDICE, AND HARASSMENT

(a) A judge shall perform the duties of judicial office, including administrative duties, without bias or prejudice.

(b) A judge shall not, in the performance of judicial duties, by words or conduct, manifest bias, prejudice, or harassment based upon race, sex, gender, religion, national origin, ethnicity, disability, age, sexual orientation, marital status, socioeconomic status, or political affiliation. A judge shall require lawyers in proceedings before the court, court staff, court officials, and others subject to the judge's direction and control to refrain from similar conduct.

(c) The restrictions of paragraph (b) do not preclude judges or lawyers from making legitimate references to the listed factors, or similar factors, when they are relevant to an issue in a proceeding.

COMMENT

[1] A judge who manifests bias or prejudice in a proceeding impairs the fairness of the

proceeding and brings the judiciary into disrepute.

[2] A judge must avoid conduct that may reasonably be perceived as prejudiced or biased. Examples of manifestations of bias or prejudice include epithets; slurs; demeaning nicknames; negative stereotyping; attempted humor based upon stereotypes; threatening, intimidating, or hostile acts; suggestions of connections between race, ethnicity, or nationality and crime; and irrelevant references to personal characteristics. Even facial expressions and body language can convey to parties and lawyers in the proceeding, jurors, the media, and others an appearance of bias or prejudice.

[3] Harassment, as referred to in paragraph (b), is verbal or physical conduct that denigrates or shows hostility or aversion toward a person on bases such as race, sex, gender, religion, national origin, ethnicity, disability, age, sexual orientation, marital status, socioeconomic status, or political affiliation.

[4] Sexual harassment includes sexual advances, requests for sexual favors, and other verbal or physical conduct of a sexual nature that is unwelcome.

Source. — This Rule is derived from Rule 2.3 of the 2007 ABA Code with certain style changes. The Comments are derived from the ABA Comments to that Rule with certain style changes.

Rule 2.4. EXTERNAL INFLUENCES ON JUDICIAL CONDUCT

(a) A judge shall not be swayed by public clamor or fear of criticism.

(b) A judge shall not permit family, social, political, financial, or other interests or relationships to influence the judge's judicial conduct or judgment.

(c) A judge shall not convey or permit others to convey the impression that any person or organization is in a position to influence the judge.

COMMENT

[1] An independent judiciary requires that judges decide cases according to the law and facts, without regard to whether particular laws or litigants are popular or unpopular with the public, the media, government officials, or the judge's friends or family. Confidence in the judiciary is eroded if judicial decision-making is perceived to be subject to inappropriate outside influences.

Source. — This Rule is derived from Rule 2.4 of the 2007 ABA Code. The Comments are derived from the ABA Comments to that Rule.

Rule 2.5. COMPETENCE, DILIGENCE, AND COOPERATION

(a) A judge shall perform judicial and administrative duties competently, diligently, promptly, and without favoritism or nepotism.

(b) A judge shall cooperate with other judges and court officials in the administration of court business.

(c) A judge shall not wilfully fail to comply with administrative rules or reasonable directives of a judge with supervisory authority.

COMMENT

[1] Competence in the performance of judicial duties requires the legal **knowledge,** skill, thoroughness, and preparation reasonably necessary to perform a judge's responsibilities of judicial office.

[2] A judge should seek the necessary docket time, court staff, expertise, and resources to discharge all adjudicative and administrative responsibilities.

[3] Prompt disposition of the court's business requires a judge to devote adequate time to judicial duties, to be punctual in attending court and expeditious in determining matters under submission, and to take reasonable measures to ensure that court officials, litigants, and their lawyers cooperate with the judge to that end.

[4] In disposing of matters promptly and efficiently, a judge must demonstrate due regard for the rights of parties to be heard and to have issues resolved without unnecessary cost or delay. A judge should monitor and supervise cases in ways that reduce or eliminate dilatory practices, avoidable delays, and unnecessary costs.

Source. — Paragraphs (a) and (b) of this Rule are derived from Rule 2.5 of the 2007 ABA

Code. Paragraph (c) is new. The Comments are derived from the ABA Comments to that Rule.

Rule 2.6. ENSURING THE RIGHT TO BE HEARD

(a) A judge shall accord to every person who has a legal interest in a proceeding, or that person's lawyer, the right to be heard according to law.

(b) A judge may encourage parties to a proceeding and their lawyers to settle matters in dispute but shall not act in a manner that coerces any party into settlement.

COMMENT

[1] The right to be heard is an essential component of a fair and **impartial** system of justice. Substantive rights of litigants can be protected only if procedures protecting the right to be heard are observed.

[2] Increasingly, judges have before them self-represented litigants whose lack of **knowledge** about the law and about judicial procedures and requirements may inhibit their ability to be heard effectively. A judge's obligation under Rule 2.2 to remain fair and **impartial** does not preclude the judge from making reasonable accommodations to protect a self-represented litigant's right to be heard, so long as those accommodations do not give the self-represented litigant an unfair advantage. This Rule does not require a judge to make any particular accommodation.

[3] Settlement conferences and referrals to alternative dispute resolution may play an important role in the administration of justice. The judge plays an important role in overseeing the settlement of disputes, but should be careful that efforts to further settlement do not undermine any party's right to be heard according to law. Among the factors that a judge should consider when deciding upon an appropriate settlement practice for a case are (a) whether the parties have requested or voluntarily consented to a certain level of participation by the judge in settlement discussions, (b) whether the parties and their counsel are relatively sophisticated in legal matters, (c) whether the case will be tried by the judge or a jury, (d) whether the parties participate with their counsel in settlement discussions, (e) whether any parties are self-represented, and (f) the nature of the proceeding.

[4] Judges must be mindful of the effect settlement discussions can have, not only on their objectivity and **impartiality,** but also on the appearance of their objectivity and **impartiality.** A judge should keep in mind the effect that the judge's participation in settlement discussions may have on both the judge's own views of the case and the perceptions of the lawyers and the parties if the case remains with the judge after settlement efforts are unsuccessful. Despite a judge's best efforts, there may be instances when information obtained during settlement discussions could influence a judge's decision making during trial, and, in such instances, the judge should consider whether disqualification may be appropriate. *See* Rule 2.11 (a) (1).

Source. — This Rule is derived from Rule 2.6 of the 2007 ABA Code. Comments [1], [3], and [4] are derived from the ABA Comments to that Rule, with some modifications. Comment [2] is new.

Rule 2.7. RESPONSIBILITY TO DECIDE

A judge shall hear and decide matters assigned to the judge unless recusal is appropriate.

COMMENT

[1] Although there are times when disqualification is necessary or appropriate to protect the rights of litigants and preserve public confidence in the **independence,** integrity, and **impartiality** of the judiciary, judges must be available to decide matters that come before the courts. The dignity of the court, the judge's respect for fulfillment of judicial duties, and a proper concern for the burdens that may be imposed upon the judge's colleagues require that a judge not use disqualification to avoid cases that present difficult, controversial, or unpopular issues.

Source. — This Rule is derived from Rule 2.7 of the 2007 ABA Code, but substitutes the test of whether "recusal is appropriate" for whether disqualification "is required by Rule 2.11 or other law." The Comment is derived from the ABA Comment to Rule 2.7 but adds "or appropriate" in the first sentence.

Rule 2.8. DECORUM, DEMEANOR, AND COMMUNICATION WITH JURORS

(a) A judge shall require order and decorum in proceedings before the court.

(b) A judge shall be patient, dignified, and courteous to litigants, jurors, witnesses, lawyers, court staff, court officials, and others with whom the judge deals in an official capacity, and shall require similar conduct of lawyers, court staff, court officials, and others subject to the judge's direction and control.

(c) A judge shall not commend or criticize jurors for their verdict other than in a court order or opinion in a proceeding.

COMMENT

[1] The duty to hear all proceedings with patience and courtesy is not inconsistent with the duty imposed in Rule 2.5 to dispose promptly of the business of the court. Judges can be efficient and businesslike while being patient and deliberate.

[2] Commending or criticizing jurors for their verdict may imply a judicial expectation in future cases and may impair a juror's ability to be fair and **impartial** in a subsequent case.

[3] A judge who is not otherwise prohibited by law from doing so may meet with jurors who choose to remain after trial but should be careful not to discuss the merits of the case.

Source. — This Rule is derived from Rule 2.8 of the 2007 ABA Code. The Comments are derived from the ABA Comments to that Rule.

Rule 2.9. EX PARTE COMMUNICATIONS

(a) A judge shall not initiate, permit, or consider ex parte communications, or consider other communications made to the judge out of the presence of the parties or their lawyers, concerning a pending or **impending matter,** except as follows:

(1) A judge may initiate, permit, or consider any ex parte communication when expressly authorized by law to do so.

(2) When circumstances require it, ex parte communication for scheduling, administrative, or emergency purposes, which does not address substantive matters, is permitted, provided:

(A) the judge reasonably believes that no party will gain a procedural, substantive, or tactical advantage as a result of the ex parte communication; and

(B) the judge makes provision promptly to notify all other parties of the substance of the ex parte communication, and gives the parties an opportunity to respond.

(3) A judge may obtain the advice of a disinterested expert on the law applicable to a proceeding if the judge (A) makes provision promptly to notify all of the parties as to the expert consulted and the substance of the advice, and (B) affords the parties a reasonable opportunity to respond.

(4) A judge may consult with court staff and court officials whose functions are to aid the judge in carrying out the judge's adjudicative responsibilities, or with other judges, provided the judge does not decide a case based on adjudicative facts that are not made part of the record, and does not abrogate the responsibility personally to decide the matter.

Cross references. — *See* Comment [1] to Rule 3.9, permitting a judge to engage in settlement conferences.

(5) A judge may, with the consent of the parties, confer separately with the parties and their lawyers as part of a settlement conference conducted pursuant to Rules 17-102 (h) and 17-105 (b).

(6) When serving in a problem-solving court program of a Circuit Court or the District Court pursuant to Rule 16-206, a judge may initiate, permit, and consider ex parte communications in conformance with the established protocols for the operation of the program if the parties have expressly consented to those protocols.

(b) If a judge inadvertently receives an unauthorized ex parte communication bearing upon the substance of a matter, the judge shall make provision promptly to notify the parties of the substance of the communication and provide the parties with an opportunity to respond.

(c) A judge shall not investigate adjudicative facts in a matter independently, and shall consider only the evidence in the record and any facts that may properly be judicially noticed.

(d) A judge shall make reasonable efforts, including providing appropriate supervision, to ensure that this Rule is not violated by court staff, court officials, and others subject to the judge's direction and control.

COMMENT

[1] To the extent reasonably possible, all parties or their lawyers shall be included in communications with a judge.

[2] Whenever the presence of a party or notice to a party is required by this Rule, it is the party's lawyer, or if the party is self-represented, the party, who is to be present or to whom notice is to be given.

[3] The proscription against communications concerning a proceeding includes communications with lawyers, law teachers, and other persons who are not participants in the proceeding, except to the limited extent permitted by this Rule.

[4] A judge may consult with other judges on **pending matters,** including a retired judge approved for recall, but must avoid ex parte discussions of a case with judges who have previously been disqualified from hearing the matter, and with judges who have appellate jurisdiction over the matter.

[5] The prohibition against a judge investigating adjudicative facts in a matter extends to information available in all mediums, including electronic.

[6] A judge may consult ethics advisory committees, outside counsel, or legal experts concerning the judge's compliance with this Code. Such consultations are not subject to the restrictions of paragraph (a) (2).

Source. — This Rule is derived in part from Rule 2.9 of the 2007 ABA Code and in part from Canon 3B (6) (e) of the former Maryland Code of Judicial Conduct, except paragraph (a) (6) is new. Comments [1], [2], [3], [4], [5], and [6] are derived from the ABA Comments to that Rule.

Rule 2.10. JUDICIAL STATEMENTS ON PENDING AND IMPENDING CASES

(a) A judge shall abstain from public comment that relates to a proceeding pending or impending in any court and that might reasonably be expected to affect the outcome or impair the fairness of that proceeding and shall require similar abstention on the part of court personnel subject to the judge's direction and control. This Rule does not prohibit a judge from making public statements in the course of official duties or from explaining for public information the procedures of the court.

(b) With respect to a case, controversy, or issue that is likely to come before the court, a judge shall not make a commitment, pledge, or promise that is inconsistent with the **impartial** performance of the adjudicative duties of the office.

(c) Notwithstanding the restrictions in paragraphs (a) and (b), a judge may make public statements in the course of official duties, may explain court procedures, and may comment on any proceeding in which the judge is a litigant in a non-judicial capacity.

COMMENT

[1] This Rule's restrictions on judicial speech are essential to the maintenance of the **independence,** integrity, and **impartiality** of the judiciary.

[2] This Rule does not prohibit a judge from commenting on proceedings in which the judge is a litigant in a personal capacity. In cases in which the judge is a litigant in an official capacity, such as a writ of mandamus, the judge must not comment publicly.

[3] "Court personnel," as used in paragraph (a) of this Rule does not include the lawyers in a proceeding before the judge. The comment of lawyers in this regard is governed by Rule 3.6 of the Maryland Lawyers' Rules of Professional Conduct.

Source. — This Rule is derived principally from Canon 3B (8) and (9) of the former Maryland Code of Judicial Conduct, which is largely consistent with Rule 2.10 of the 2007 ABA Code. Comments [1] and [2] are derived from the ABA Comments to Rule 2.10 of the 2007 ABA Code. Comment [3] is new.

Rule 2.11. DISQUALIFICATION

(a) A judge shall disqualify himself or herself in any proceeding in which the judge's **impartiality** might reasonably be questioned, including the following circumstances:

(1) The judge has a personal bias or prejudice concerning a party or a party's lawyer, or personal **knowledge** of facts that are in dispute in the proceeding.

(2) The judge **knows** that the judge, the judge's spouse or **domestic partner,** or a person within the **third degree of relationship** to either of them, or the spouse or **domestic partner** of such a person:

(A) is a party to the proceeding, or an officer, director, general partner, managing member, or trustee of a party;

(B) is acting as a lawyer in the proceeding;

(C) is a person who has more than a de minimis interest that could be substantially affected by the proceeding; or

(D) is likely to be a material witness in the proceeding.

(3) The judge **knows** that he or she, individually or as a **fiduciary,** or any of the following persons has a **significant financial interest** in the subject matter in controversy or in a party to the proceeding:

(A) the judge's spouse **or domestic partner;**

(B) a person within the **third degree of relationship** to the judge; or

(C) any other **member of the judge's family** residing in the judge's household.

(4) The judge, while a judge or a judicial candidate, has made a public statement, other than in a court proceeding, judicial decision, or opinion, that commits or appears to commit the judge to reach a particular result or rule in a particular way in the proceeding or controversy.

(5) The judge:

(A) served as a lawyer in the matter in controversy, or was associated with a lawyer who participated substantially as a lawyer in the matter during such association;

(B) served in governmental employment, and in such capacity participated personally and substantially as a lawyer or public official concerning the proceeding, or has publicly expressed in such capacity an opinion concerning the merits of the particular matter in controversy;

(C) previously presided as a judge over the matter in another court; or

(D) is a retired judge who is subject to recusal under Rule 3.9.

(b) A judge shall keep informed about the judge's personal and **fiduciary** economic interests and make a reasonable effort to keep informed about the personal economic interests of the judge's spouse and minor children residing in the judge's household.

(c) A judge subject to disqualification under this Rule, other than for bias or prejudice under paragraph (a) (1), may disclose on the record the basis of the judge's disqualification and may ask the parties and their lawyers to consider, outside the presence of the judge and court personnel, whether to waive disqualification. If, following the disclosure, the parties and lawyers agree, without participation by the judge or court personnel, that the judge should not be disqualified, the judge may participate in the proceeding. The agreement shall be incorporated into the record of the proceeding.

COMMENT

[1] Under this Rule, a judge is disqualified whenever the judge's **impartiality** might reasonably be questioned, regardless of whether any of the specific provisions of paragraphs (a) (1) through (5) apply. In this Rule, "disqualification" has the same meaning as "recusal."

[2] A judge's obligation not to hear or decide matters in which disqualification is required applies regardless of whether a motion to disqualify is filed.

[3] By decisional law, the rule of necessity may override the rule of recusal. For example, a judge might be required to participate in judicial review of a judicial salary statute or might be the only judge available in a matter requiring immediate judicial action, such as a hearing on probable cause or a temporary restraining order. When the rule of necessity does override the rule of recusal, the judge must disclose on the record the basis for possible disqualification and, if practicable, use reasonable efforts to transfer the matter to another judge.

[4] A judge should disclose on the record information that the judge believes the parties or their lawyers might reasonably consider relevant to a possible motion for disqualification, even if the judge believes there is no basis for disqualification.

[5] This procedure gives the parties an opportunity to waive the recusal if the judge agrees. The judge may comment on possible waiver but must ensure that consideration of the question of waiver is made independently of the judge. A party may act through counsel if counsel represents on the record that the party has been consulted and consents. As a practical matter, a judge may request that all parties and their lawyers sign a waiver agreement.

Source. — This Rule is derived in part from Rule 2.11 of the 2007 ABA Code and in part from Canon 3D of the former Maryland Code of Judicial Conduct. Comments [1], [2], and [3] are derived from the ABA Comments to Rule 2.11 of the 2007 ABA Code, with some modifications. Comments [4] and [5] are new. ABA Rule 2.11 (a) (4) and ABA Comment [6] are not included.

Rule 2.12. SUPERVISORY DUTIES

(a) A judge shall require court staff, court officials, and others subject to the judge's direction and control to act in a manner consistent with the judge's obligations under this Code.

(b) A judge with supervisory authority for the performance of other judges shall take reasonable measures to ensure that those judges properly discharge their judicial responsibilities, including the prompt disposition of matters before them.

COMMENT

[1] A judge is responsible for his or her own conduct and for the conduct of others, such as staff, when those persons are acting at the judge's direction or control. A judge may not direct court personnel to engage in conduct on the judge's behalf or as the judge's representative when such conduct would violate this Code if undertaken by the judge.

[2] Public confidence in the judicial system depends upon timely justice. To promote the efficient administration of justice, a judge with supervisory authority must take the steps needed to ensure that judges under his or her supervision administer their workloads promptly.

Source. — This Rule is derived from Rule 2.12 of the 2007 ABA Code. The Comments are derived from the ABA Comments to that Rule.

Rule 2.13. ADMINISTRATIVE APPOINTMENTS

(a) In making administrative appointments, a judge:

(1) shall exercise the power of appointment **impartially** and on the basis of merit; and

(2) shall avoid nepotism, favoritism, and unnecessary appointments.

(b) A judge shall not approve compensation of appointees beyond the fair value of services rendered.

COMMENT

[1] Appointees of a judge include assigned counsel, officials such as commissioners, special masters, receivers, and guardians, and personnel such as clerks, secretaries, and bailiffs. Consent by the parties to an appointment or an award of compensation does not relieve the judge of the obligation prescribed by paragraph (a).

[2] Unless otherwise defined by law, nepotism is the appointment or hiring of any relative within **the third degree of relationship** to either the judge or the judge's spouse or **domestic partner,** or the spouse or **domestic partner** of such relative.

Source. — This Rule is derived generally from Rule 2.13 of the 2007 ABA Code, although paragraph (b) of that Rule is not included. Comments [1] and [2] are derived from the ABA Comments to that Rule, although ABA Comment [3] is not included.

Rule 2.14. DISABILITY AND IMPAIRMENT OF OTHERS

A judge having a reasonable belief that the performance of a lawyer or another judge is impaired by drugs or alcohol or by a mental, emotional, or physical condition, shall take appropriate action, which may include a confidential referral to a lawyer or judicial assistance program.

COMMENT

[1] "Appropriate action" means action intended and reasonably likely to help the judge or lawyer in question to address the problem and prevent harm to the justice system. Depending upon the circumstances, appropriate action may include speaking directly to the impaired person, notifying an individual with supervisory responsibility over the impaired person, or making a referral to an assistance program.

[2] Taking or initiating corrective action by way of referral to an assistance program may satisfy a judge's responsibility under this Rule. Assistance programs have many approaches for offering help to impaired judges and lawyers, such as intervention, counseling, or re-

ferral to appropriate health care professionals. Depending upon the gravity of the conduct that has come to the judge's attention, however, the judge may be required to take other action, such as reporting the impaired judge or lawyer to the appropriate authority, agency, or body. *See* Rule 2.15.

Source. — This Rule is derived from Rule 2.14 of the 2007 ABA Code. The Comments are derived from the ABA Comments to that Rule.

Rule 2.15. RESPONDING TO JUDICIAL AND LAWYER MISCONDUCT

(a) A judge shall take or initiate appropriate corrective measures with respect to the unprofessional conduct of another judge or a lawyer.

(b) If other corrective measures are not appropriate or, if attempted, were not successful, a judge shall inform the Commission on Judicial Disabilities of facts **known** to that judge that raise a substantial question as to another judge's fitness for office.

(c) If other corrective measures are not appropriate or, if attempted, were not successful, a judge shall inform the Attorney Grievance Commission of facts **known** to the judge that raise a substantial question as to a lawyer's honesty, trustworthiness, or fitness as a lawyer in other respects.

(d) Acts of a judge required or permitted by paragraphs (a), (b), and (c) of this Rule shall be absolutely privileged.

COMMENT

[1] Permitting a judge to take "corrective" measures gives the judge a wide range of options to deal with unprofessional conduct. Appropriate corrective measures may include direct communication with the judge or lawyer who is believed to have committed the violation or other direct action if available. There may be instances of professional misconduct that would warrant a private admonition or referral to a bar association counseling service.

Source. — This Rule is derived from Canon 3F of the former Maryland Code of Judicial Conduct.

Rule 2.16. COOPERATION WITH DISCIPLINARY AUTHORITIES

(a) A judge shall cooperate and be candid and honest with judicial and lawyer disciplinary agencies.

(b) A judge shall not retaliate, directly or indirectly, against a person **known** or suspected to have assisted or cooperated with an investigation of a judge or a lawyer.

COMMENT

[1] Cooperation with investigations and proceedings of judicial and lawyer discipline agencies, as required in paragraph (a) of this Rule, instills confidence in judges' commitment to the integrity of the judicial system and the protection of the public.

Source. — This Rule is derived from Rule 2.16 of the 2007 ABA Code. The Comment is derived from the ABA Comment to that Rule.

SECTION 3.

RULES GOVERNING EXTRAJUDICIAL ACTIVITY

Rule 3.1. EXTRAJUDICIAL ACTIVITIES IN GENERAL

A judge may engage in extrajudicial activities, except as prohibited by law or this Code. When engaging in extrajudicial activities, a judge shall not:

(a) participate in activities that will interfere with the proper performance of the judge's judicial duties;

(b) participate in activities that will lead to frequent disqualification of the judge;

(c) participate in activities that would appear to a reasonable person to undermine the judge's **independence,** integrity, or **impartiality;**

(d) engage in conduct that would appear to a reasonable person to be coercive; or

(e) make inappropriate use of court premises, staff, stationery, equipment, or other resources.

COMMENT

[1] To the extent that time permits, and judicial **independence** and **impartiality** are not compromised, judges are encouraged to engage in appropriate extrajudicial activities. Judges are uniquely qualified to engage in extrajudicial activities that concern the law, the legal system, and the administration of justice, such as by speaking, writing, teaching, or participating in scholarly research projects. In addition, judges are permitted and encouraged to engage in educational, religious, charitable, fraternal, or civic extrajudicial activities not conducted for profit, even when the activities do not involve the law. *See* Rule 3.7.

[2] Participation in both law-related and other extrajudicial activities helps integrate judges into their communities and furthers public understanding of and respect for courts and the judicial system.

[3] Discriminatory actions and expressions of bias or prejudice by a judge, even outside the judge's official or judicial actions, are likely to appear to a reasonable person to call into question the judge's integrity and **impartiality.** Examples include jokes or other remarks that demean individuals based upon their race, sex, gender, religion, national origin, ethnicity, disability, age, sexual orientation, or socioeconomic status. For the same reason, a judge's extrajudicial activities must not be conducted in connection or affiliation with an organization that practices invidious discrimination. *See* Rule 3.6.

[4] While engaged in permitted extrajudicial activities, judges must not coerce others or take action that would reasonably be perceived as coercive. For example, depending upon the circumstances, a judge's solicitation of contributions or memberships for an organization, even as permitted by Rule 3.7 (a), might create the risk that the person solicited would feel obligated to respond favorably, or would do so to curry favor with the judge.

Source. — This Rule is derived from Rule 3.1 of the 2007 ABA Code. The Comments are derived from the ABA Comments to that Rule.

Rule 3.2. APPEARANCES BEFORE GOVERNMENTAL BODIES AND CONSULTATION WITH GOVERNMENT OFFICIALS

A judge shall not appear voluntarily at a public hearing before, or otherwise consult with, an executive or a legislative body or official, except:

(a) in connection with matters concerning the law, the legal system, or the administration of justice;

(b) in connection with matters about which the judge acquired **knowledge** or expertise in the course of the judge's judicial duties; or

(c) when the judge is acting self-represented in a matter involving the judge's legal or economic interests, or when the judge is acting in a **fiduciary** capacity.

COMMENT

[1] Judges possess special expertise in matters of law, the legal system, and the administration of justice, and may properly share that expertise with governmental bodies and executive or legislative branch officials.

[2] In appearing before governmental bodies or consulting with government officials, judges must be mindful that they remain subject to other provisions of this Code, such as Rule 1.3, prohibiting judges from using the prestige of office to advance their own or others' interests, Rule 2.10, governing public comment on pending and **impending matters,** and Rule 3.1 (c), prohibiting judges from engaging in extrajudicial activities that would appear to a reasonable person to undermine the judge's **independence,** integrity, or **impartiality.**

[3] In general, it would be an unnecessary and unfair burden to prohibit judges from appearing before governmental bodies or consulting with government officials on matters that are likely to affect them as private persons, such as zoning proposals affecting their real property. In engaging in such activities, however, judges must not refer to their judicial positions, and must otherwise exercise caution to avoid using the prestige of judicial office.

Source. — This Rule is derived from Rule 3.2 of the 2007 ABA Code. The Comments are derived from the ABA Comments to that Rule.

Rule 3.3. TESTIFYING AS A CHARACTER WITNESS

A judge shall not testify as a character witness in a judicial, administrative, or other adjudicatory proceeding or otherwise vouch for the character of a person in a legal proceeding, except when duly summoned.

COMMENT

[1] A judge who, without being subpoenaed, testifies as a character witness abuses the prestige of judicial office to advance the interests of another. *See* Rule 1.3. Except in unusual circumstances where the demands of justice require, a judge should discourage a party from requiring the judge to testify as a character witness.

Source. — This Rule is derived from Rule 3.3 of the 2007 ABA Code. The Comment is derived from the ABA Comment to that Rule.

Rule 3.4. APPOINTMENT TO GOVERNMENTAL POSITIONS

A judge shall not accept appointment to a governmental committee, board, commission, or other governmental position, unless it is one that concerns the law, the legal system, or the administration of justice.

COMMENT

[1] Rule 3.4 implicitly acknowledges the value of judges accepting appointments to entities that concern the law, the legal system, or the administration of justice. Even in such instances, however, a judge should assess the appropriateness of accepting an appointment, paying particular attention to the subject matter of the appointment and the availability and allocation of judicial resources, including the judge's time commitments, and giving due regard to the requirements of the **independence** and **impartiality** of the judiciary.

[2] A judge may not accept a governmental appointment that could interfere with the effectiveness and **independence** of the judiciary, assume or discharge an executive or legislative power, or hold another "office" under the Constitution or laws of the United States or the State of Maryland. *See* Maryland Declaration of Rights, Articles 8, 33, and 35.

[3] A judge may represent his or her country, State, or locality on ceremonial occasions or in connection with historical, educational, or cultural activities. Such representation does not constitute acceptance of a government position.

Committee note. — Although the Judicial Ethics Committee has concluded that the Supremacy Clause of the U.S. Constitution may

555

allow service in reserve components of the armed forces that otherwise might be precluded under this Code, such as service as a judge advocate or military judge, the Attorney General, rather than the Judicial Ethics Committee, traditionally has rendered opinions with regard to issues of dual or incompatible offices.

Source. — This Rule is derived from Rule 3.4 of the 2007 ABA Code. Comments [1] and [3] are derived from the ABA Comments to that Rule. Comment [2] and the Committee note are derived from the Comment and Committee note to Canon 4C of the former Maryland Code of Judicial Conduct.

Rule 3.5. USE OF NONPUBLIC INFORMATION

A judge shall not intentionally disclose or use nonpublic information acquired in a judicial capacity for any purpose unrelated to the judge's judicial duties. Nonpublic information means information that is not available to the public. It may include information that is (a) sealed or shielded pursuant to law or court order, (b) impounded, (c) communicated in camera, or (d) offered in grand jury proceedings, pre-sentencing reports, dependency cases, or psychiatric reports.

COMMENT

[1] In the course of performing judicial duties, a judge may acquire information of commercial or other value that is unavailable to the public. The judge must not reveal or use such information for personal gain or for any purpose unrelated to his or her judicial duties.

[2] This Rule is not intended, however, to affect a judge's ability to act on information as necessary to protect the health or safety of the judge or a **member of a judge's family,** court personnel, or other judicial officers.

Source. — The first sentence of this Rule is derived from Rule 3.5 of the 2007 ABA Code. The second sentence is derived from the Terminology section of the 2007 ABA Code. The Comments are derived from the ABA Comments to Rule 3.5 of the 2007 ABA Code, except that Comment [2] is modified to eliminate the words "if consistent with other provisions of this Code."

Rule 3.6. AFFILIATION WITH DISCRIMINATORY ORGANIZATIONS

(a) A judge shall not hold membership in any organization that practices invidious discrimination on the basis of race, sex, gender, religion, national origin, ethnicity, or sexual orientation.

(b) A judge shall not use the benefits or facilities of an organization if the judge **knows** or should **know** that the organization practices invidious discrimination on one or more of the bases identified in paragraph (a). A judge's attendance at an event in a facility of an organization that the judge is not permitted to join is not a violation of this Rule when the judge's attendance is an isolated event that could not reasonably be perceived as an endorsement of the organization's practices.

COMMENT

[1] A judge's public manifestation of approval of invidious discrimination on any basis gives rise to the appearance of impropriety and diminishes public confidence in the integrity and **impartiality** of the judiciary. A judge's membership in an organization that practices invidious discrimination creates the perception that the judge's **impartiality** is impaired.

[2] An organization is generally said to discriminate invidiously if it arbitrarily excludes

from membership on the basis of race, sex, gender, religion, national origin, ethnicity, or sexual orientation persons who would otherwise be eligible for admission. Whether an organization practices invidious discrimination is a complex question to which judges should be attentive. The answer cannot be determined from a mere examination of an organization's current membership rolls, but rather, depends upon how the organization

556

selects members, as well as other relevant factors, such as whether the organization is dedicated to the preservation of religious, ethnic, or cultural values of legitimate common interest to its members, or whether it is an intimate, purely private organization whose membership limitations could not constitutionally be prohibited.

[3] When a judge learns that an organization to which the judge belongs engages in invidious discrimination, the judge must re-sign immediately from the organization.

[4] A judge's membership in a religious organization as a lawful exercise of the freedom of religion is not a violation of this Rule.

[5] This Rule does not apply to national or state military service.

Source. — This Rule is derived from Rule 3.6 of the 2007 ABA Code. The Comments are derived from the ABA Comments to that Rule.

Rule 3.7. PARTICIPATION IN EDUCATIONAL, RELIGIOUS, CHARITABLE, FRATERNAL, OR CIVIC ORGANIZATIONS AND ACTIVITIES

(a) Subject to the requirements of Rules 3.1 and 3.6, a judge may participate in activities sponsored by organizations or governmental entities concerned with the law, the legal system, or the administration of justice, and those sponsored by or on behalf of educational, religious, charitable, fraternal, or civic organizations not conducted for profit, including the following activities:

(1) assisting such an organization or entity in planning related to fund-raising, and participating in the management and investment of the organization's or entity's funds;

(2) soliciting contributions for such an organization or entity, but only from **members of the judge's family,** or from judges over whom the judge does not exercise supervisory or appellate authority;

(3) soliciting membership for such an organization or entity, even though the membership dues or fees generated may be used to support the objectives of the organization or entity, but only if the organization or entity is concerned with the law, the legal system, or the administration of justice;

(4) appearing or speaking at, receiving an award or other recognition at, being featured on the program of, and permitting his or her title to be used in connection with an event of such an organization or entity, but if the event serves a fund-raising purpose, the judge may participate only if the event concerns the law, the legal system, or the administration of justice;

(5) making recommendations to such a public or private fund-granting organization or entity in connection with its programs and activities, but only if the organization or entity is concerned with the law, the legal system, or the administration of justice; and

(6) serving as an officer, director, trustee, or nonlegal advisor of such an organization or entity, unless it is likely that the organization or entity:

(A) will be engaged in proceedings that would ordinarily come before the judge; or

(B) will frequently be engaged in adversary proceedings in the court of which the judge is a member, or in any court subject to the appellate jurisdiction of the court of which the judge is a member.

(b) A judge may encourage but not coerce lawyers to provide pro bono publico legal services.

[1] The activities permitted by paragraph (a) generally include those sponsored by or undertaken on behalf of public or private not-for-profit educational institutions, and other not-for-profit organizations, including law-related, charitable, and other organizations.

[2] Even for law-related organizations, a judge should consider whether the membership and purposes of the organization or the nature of the judge's participation in or association with the organization would conflict with the judge's obligation to refrain from activities that reflect adversely upon a judge's **independence,** integrity, and **impartiality.**

[3] Mere attendance at an event, whether or not the event serves a fund-raising purpose, does not constitute a violation of paragraph (a) (4). It is also generally permissible for a judge to serve as an usher or a food server or preparer, or to perform similar functions, at fund-raising events sponsored by educational, religious, charitable, fraternal, or civic organizations. Such activities are not solicitation and do not present an element of coercion

or abuse the prestige of judicial office.

[4] Identification of a judge's position in educational, religious, charitable, fraternal, or civic organizations on letterhead used for fund-raising or membership solicitation does not violate this Rule. The letterhead may list the judge's title or judicial office if comparable designations are used for other persons.

[5] In addition to appointing lawyers to serve as counsel for indigent parties in individual cases, a judge may promote broader access to justice by encouraging lawyers to participate in pro bono publico legal services, if in doing so the judge does not employ coercion, or abuse the prestige of judicial office. Such encouragement may take many forms, including providing lists of available programs, training lawyers to do pro bono publico legal work, and participating in events recognizing lawyers who have done pro bono publico work.

Source. — This Rule is derived from Rule 3.7 of the 2007 ABA Code with some modifications. The Comments are derived from the ABA Comments to that Rule.

Rule 3.8. APPOINTMENTS TO FIDUCIARY POSITIONS

(a) A judge shall not accept appointment to serve in a **fiduciary** position, such as executor, administrator, trustee, guardian, attorney in fact, or other personal representative, except for the estate, trust, or person of a **member of the judge's family,** and then only if such service will not interfere with the proper performance of judicial duties.

(b) A judge shall not serve in a **fiduciary** position if the judge as **fiduciary** will likely be engaged in proceedings that would ordinarily come before the judge, or if the estate, trust, or ward becomes involved in adversary proceedings in the court on which the judge serves, or one under its appellate jurisdiction.

(c) A judge acting in a **fiduciary** capacity shall be subject to the same restrictions on engaging in financial activities that apply to a judge personally.

(d) If a person who is serving in a **fiduciary** position becomes a judge, he or she must comply with this Rule as soon as reasonably practicable, but in no event later than one year after becoming a judge.

(e) Paragraph (a) of this Rule does not apply to retired judges approved for recall under Maryland Constitution, Article IV, § 3A.

[1] A judge should recognize that other restrictions imposed by this Code may conflict with a judge's obligations as a **fiduciary;** in such circumstances, a judge should resign as **fiduciary.** For example, serving as a **fiduciary** might require frequent disqualification of a judge under Rule 2.11 because a judge is deemed to have an economic interest in shares

of stock held by a trust if the amount of stock held is more than de minimis.

Source. — Paragraphs (a) through (d) of this Rule are derived from Rule 3.8 of the 2007 ABA Code. Paragraph (e) is derived from Canon 6C of the former Maryland Code of Judicial Conduct. The Comment is derived from the ABA Comment to Rule 3.8 of the 2007 ABA Code.

Rule 3.9. SERVICE AS ARBITRATOR OR MEDIATOR

(a) A judge shall not act as an arbitrator or a mediator or perform other judicial functions apart from the judge's official duties unless expressly authorized by law.

(b) A retired judge who is approved for recall for temporary service under Maryland Constitution, Article IV, §3A may conduct alternative dispute resolution (ADR) proceedings in a private capacity only if the judge:

(1) conducts no ADR proceedings in a private capacity relating to a case in which the judge currently is presiding;

(2) is not affiliated with a law firm, regardless of whether the law firm also offers ADR services;

(3) discloses to the parties in each judicial proceeding over which the judge presides:

(A) the judge's professional association with any entity that is engaged in offering ADR services;

(B) whether the judge is conducting, or has conducted within the previous 12 months, an ADR proceeding involving any party, attorney, or law firm involved in the judicial proceeding pending before the judge; and

(C) any negotiations or agreements for future ADR services involving the judge and any of the parties or counsel to the case; and

(4) except if there is no disqualification by agreement as permitted by Rule 2.11 (c), does not preside over a judicial proceeding in which the judge's **impartiality** might reasonably be questioned because of ADR services engaged in or offered by the judge.

Committee note. — A retired judge approved for recall may affiliate with an entity that exclusively is engaged in offering ADR services but may not affiliate with any entity that also is engaged in the practice of law.

COMMENT

[1] Except as provided in paragraph (b), this Rule does not prohibit a judge from participating in arbitration, mediation, or settlement conferences performed as part of assigned judicial duties. Rendering dispute resolution services apart from those duties, whether or not for economic gain, is prohibited unless it is expressly authorized by law.

Source. — Paragraph (a) of this Rule is derived from Rule 3.9 of the 2007 ABA Code. Paragraph (b) and the Committee note are derived from Canon 4F (2) of the former Maryland Code of Judicial Conduct and the Committee note thereto. The Comment is derived from the ABA Comment to Rule 3.9 of the 2007 ABA Code.

Rule 3.10. PRACTICE OF LAW

(a) **In General.** Except as expressly allowed by this Rule, a judge shall not practice law.

(b) **Exceptions.** (1) A judge may act self-represented in a matter involving the judge or the judge's interest and, if without compensation, may give legal advice to and draft or review documents for a **member of the judge's family.**

(2) To the extent expressly allowed by law and subject to other applicable provisions of this Code, a part-time judge of an orphans' court who is a lawyer may practice law, provided that:

(A) the judge shall not use the judge's judicial office to further the judge's success in the practice of law; and

(B) the judge shall not practice or appear as an individual in a matter involving the judge or the judge's interest in the court on which the judge serves, even if another judge is presiding.

Cross references. — *See* Code, Estates and Trusts Article, § 2-109 for restrictions on the practice of law by a part-time judge of an orphans' court.

COMMENT

[1] A judge may act self-represented in all legal matters, including matters involving litigation and matters involving appearances before or other dealings with governmental bodies. A judge must not use the prestige of office to advance the judge's personal or family interests. *See* Rule 1.3.

[2] Paragraphs (a) and (b) (1) of this Rule limit the practice of law in a representative capacity but not in a self- represented capacity. A judge may act for himself or herself in all legal matters, including matters involving litigation and matters involving appearances before or other dealings with legislative and other governmental bodies. In so doing, however, a judge must not abuse the prestige of office for any reason, including advancement of an interest of the judge or the judge's family.

See Rules 2.4 (b) and 3.2 (c).

[3] This Rule allows a judge to give legal advice to, and draft legal documents for, a **member of the judge's family.** Except for a part-time orphans' court judge allowed to practice law, however, a judge must not receive any compensation from, or act as an advocate or negotiator for, a **member of the judge's family** in a legal matter.

Source. — This Rule is derived from Canon 4G of the former Maryland Code of Judicial Conduct. Comment [1] is derived from the ABA Comment to Rule 3.10 of the 2007 ABA Code. Comments [2] and [3] are derived from the Comment to Canon 4G of the former Maryland Code of Judicial Conduct.

Rule 3.11. FINANCIAL, BUSINESS, OR REMUNERATIVE ACTIVITIES

(a) A judge may hold and manage investments of the judge and **members of the judge's family.**

(b) Except as permitted by Rule 3.7, a judge shall not serve as an officer, director, manager, general partner, advisor, or employee of any business entity except that a judge may manage or participate in:

(1) a business closely held by the judge or **members of the judge's family;** or

(2) a business entity primarily engaged in investment of the financial resources of the judge or **members of the judge's family.**

(c) A judge shall not engage in financial activities permitted under paragraphs (a) or (b) if they will:

(1) interfere with the proper performance of judicial duties;

(2) lead to frequent disqualification of the judge;

(3) involve the judge in frequent transactions or continuing business relationships with lawyers or other persons likely to come before the court on which the judge serves; or

(4) result in violation of other provisions of this Code.

(d) This Rule does not apply to retired judges approved for recall under Maryland Constitution, Article IV, § 3A.

COMMENT

[1] Judges are generally permitted to engage in financial activities, including managing real estate and other investments for themselves or for members of their families. Participation in these activities, like participation in other extrajudicial activities, is subject to the requirements of this Code. For example, it would be improper for a judge to spend so much time on business activities that it interferes with the performance of judicial duties. *See* Rule 2.1. Similarly, it would be improper for a judge to use his or her official title or appear in judicial robes in business advertising, or to conduct his or her business or financial affairs in such a way that disqualification is frequently required. *See* Rules 1.3 and 2.11.

[2] As soon as practicable without serious financial detriment, the judge must divest himself or herself of investments and other financial interests that might require frequent disqualification or otherwise violate this Rule.

Source. — Paragraphs (a), (b), and (c) of this Rule are derived from Rule 3.11 of the 2007 ABA Code and the Comments are derived from the ABA Comments to that Rule. Paragraph (d) is derived from Canon 6C of the former Maryland Code of Judicial Conduct.

Rule 3.12. COMPENSATION FOR EXTRAJUDICIAL ACTIVITIES

A judge may accept reasonable compensation for extrajudicial activities permitted by this Code or other law unless such acceptance would appear to a reasonable person to undermine the judge's **independence,** integrity, or **impartiality.**

Cross references. — *See* Rule 3.9 requiring certain disclosures and action by retired judges approved for recall who provide alternative dispute resolution services.

COMMENT

[1] A judge is permitted to accept honoraria, stipends, fees, wages, salaries, royalties, or other compensation for speaking, teaching, writing, and other extrajudicial activities, provided the compensation is reasonable and commensurate with the task performed. The judge should be mindful, however, that judicial duties must take precedence over other activities. *See* Rule 2.1, Code, Family Law Article, §§ 2-406 and 2-410, and Md. Rules 16-821 through 16-824.

[2] Compensation derived from extrajudicial activities may be subject to public reporting. *See* Rule 3.15.

Source. — This Rule is derived from Rule 3.12 of the 2007 ABA Code. The Comments are derived from the ABA Comments to that Rule.

Rule 3.13. ACCEPTANCE OF GIFTS, LOANS, BEQUESTS, BENEFITS, OR OTHER THINGS OF VALUE

(a) A judge shall not accept any **gifts,** loans, bequests, benefits, or other things of value, if acceptance is prohibited by law or would appear to a reasonable person to undermine the judge's **independence,** integrity, or **impartiality.**

(b) Unless otherwise prohibited by law, or by paragraph (a), a judge may accept the following:

(1) items with little intrinsic value, such as plaques, certificates, trophies, and greeting cards;

(2) **gifts,** loans, bequests, benefits, or other things of value from friends, relatives, or other persons, including lawyers, whose appearance or interest in a proceeding pending or impending before the judge would in any event require disqualification of the judge under Rule 2.11;

(3) ordinary social hospitality;

(4) commercial or financial opportunities and benefits, including special pricing and discounts, and loans from lending institutions in their regular course of business, if the same opportunities and benefits or loans are made available on the same terms to similarly situated persons who are not judges;

(5) rewards and prizes given to competitors or participants in random drawings, contests, or other events that are open to persons who are not judges;

(6) scholarships, fellowships, and similar benefits or awards, if they are available to similarly situated persons who are not judges, based upon the same terms and criteria;

(7) books, magazines, journals, audiovisual materials, and other resource materials supplied by publishers on a complimentary basis for official use;

(8) **gifts,** awards, or benefits associated with the business, profession, or other separate activity of a spouse, a **domestic partner,** or other family member of a judge residing in the judge's household, but that incidentally benefit the judge;

(9) **gifts** incident to a public testimonial; or

(10) invitations to the judge and the judge's spouse, **domestic partner,** or guest to attend without charge:

(A) an event associated with a bar-related function or other activity relating to the law, the legal system, or the administration of justice; or

(B) an event associated with any of the judge's educational, religious, charitable, fraternal or civic activities permitted by this Code, if the same invitation is offered to nonjudges who are engaged in similar ways in the activity as is the judge.

COMMENT

[1] Whenever a judge accepts a **gift** or other thing of value without paying fair market value, there is a risk that the benefit might be viewed as intended to influence the judge's decision in a case. Rule 3.13 imposes restrictions upon the acceptance of such benefits, according to the magnitude of the risk. Paragraph (b) identifies circumstances in which the risk that the acceptance would appear to undermine the judge's **independence,** integrity, or **impartiality** is low. As the value of the benefit or the likelihood that the source of the benefit will appear before the judge increases, the judge is prohibited under paragraph (a) from accepting the **gift.**

[2] Gift-giving between friends and relatives is a common occurrence, and ordinarily does not create an appearance of impropriety or cause reasonable persons to believe that the judge's **independence,** integrity, or **impartiality** has been compromised. In addition, when the appearance of friends or relatives in a case would require the judge's disqualification under Rule 2.11, there would be no opportunity for a gift to influence the judge's decision-making. Paragraph (b)(2) places no restrictions upon the ability of a judge to accept **gifts** or other things of value from friends or relatives under these circumstances.

[3] Businesses and financial institutions frequently make available special pricing, discounts, and other benefits, either in connection with a temporary promotion or for preferred customers, based upon longevity of the relationship, volume of business transacted, and other factors. A judge may freely accept such benefits if they are available to the general public, or if the judge qualifies for the special price or discount according to the same criteria as are applied to persons who are not judges. As an example, loans provided at generally prevailing interest rates are not **gifts,** but a judge could not accept a loan from a financial institution at below-market interest rates unless the same rate was being made available to the general public for a certain period of time or only to borrowers with specified qualifications that the judge also possesses.

[4] Rule 3.13 applies only to acceptance of **gifts** or other things of value by a judge. Nonetheless, if a **gift** or other benefit is given to the judge's spouse, **domestic partner,** or **member of the judge's family** residing in the judge's household, it may be viewed as an

attempt to evade Rule 3.13 and influence the judge indirectly. Where the **gift** or benefit is being made primarily to such other persons, and the judge is merely an incidental beneficiary, this concern is reduced. A judge should, however, remind family and household members of the restrictions imposed upon judges and urge them to take these restrictions into account when making decisions about accepting such **gifts** or benefits.

[5] Rule 3.13 does not apply to contributions to a judge's campaign for judicial office.

Source. — This Rule is derived from Rule 3.13 of the 2007 ABA Code, except that paragraph (c) (3) is eliminated, paragraphs (c) (1) and (2) are added to paragraph (b) and provisions relating to the reporting of **gifts** are covered in Rule 3.15. The Comments are derived from the ABA Comments to Rule 3.13 of the 2007 ABA Code.

Rule 3.14. REIMBURSEMENT OF EXPENSES AND WAIVERS OF FEES OR CHARGES

(a) Unless otherwise prohibited by Rule 3.1, Rule 3.13 (a), or other law, a judge may accept reimbursement of necessary and reasonable expenses for travel, food, lodging, or other incidental expenses, or a waiver or partial waiver of fees or charges for registration, tuition, and similar items, from sources other than the judge's employing entity, if the expenses or charges are associated with the judge's participation in extrajudicial activities permitted by this Code.

(b) Reimbursement of expenses for necessary travel, food, lodging, or other incidental expenses shall be limited to the actual costs reasonably incurred by the judge and, when appropriate to the occasion, by the judge's spouse, **domestic partner,** or guest.

COMMENT

[1] Educational, civic, religious, fraternal, and charitable organizations often sponsor meetings, seminars, symposia, dinners, awards ceremonies, and similar events. Judges are encouraged to attend educational programs, as both teachers and participants, in law-related and academic disciplines, in furtherance of their duty to remain competent in the law. Participation in a variety of other extrajudicial activities is also permitted and encouraged by this Code.

[2] Not infrequently, sponsoring organizations invite certain judges to attend seminars or other events on a fee-waived or partial-fee-waived basis, and sometimes include reimbursement for necessary travel, food, lodging, or other incidental expenses. A judge's decision whether to accept reimbursement of expenses or a waiver or partial waiver of fees or charges in connection with these or other extrajudicial activities must be based upon an assessment of all the circumstances. The judge must undertake a reasonable inquiry to obtain the information necessary to make an informed judgment about whether acceptance would be consistent with the requirements of this Code.

[3] A judge must assure himself or herself that acceptance of reimbursement or fee waivers would not appear to a reasonable person to undermine the judge's **independence,** integrity, or **impartiality.** The factors that a judge should consider when deciding whether to accept reimbursement or a fee waiver for attendance at a particular activity include:

(a) whether the sponsor is an accredited educational institution or bar association rather than a trade association or a for-profit entity;

(b) whether the funding comes largely from numerous contributors rather than from a single entity and is earmarked for programs with specific content;

(c) whether the content is related or unrelated to the subject matter of litigation pending or impending before the judge, or to matters that are likely to come before the judge;

(d) whether the activity is primarily educational rather than recreational, and whether the costs of the event are reasonable and comparable to those associated with similar events sponsored by the judiciary, bar associations, or similar groups;

(e) whether information concerning the activity and its funding sources is available upon inquiry;

(f) whether the sponsor or source of funding is generally associated with particular parties or interests currently appearing or likely to appear in the judge's court, thus possibly requiring disqualification of the judge under Rule 2.11;

(g) whether differing viewpoints are presented; and

(h) whether a broad range of judicial and nonjudicial participants are invited, whether a large number of participants are invited, and whether the program is designed specifically for judges.

Source. — This Rule is derived from Rule 3.14 of the 2007 ABA Code. The Comments are derived from the ABA Comments to that Rule.

Rule 3.15. REPORTING REQUIREMENTS

A judge must accurately complete and timely file an annual Statement of Financial Interests on the form and as otherwise prescribed by the Court of Appeals pursuant to Md. Rule 16-815.

Source. — This Rule is derived from Md. Rule 16-815.

SECTION 4.

RULES GOVERNING POLITICAL ACTIVITY

Rule 4.1. DEFINITIONS

(a) **Applicant**

(1) **"Applicant"** means a person who has applied for appointment by the Governor to a judicial office.

(2) The person becomes an **applicant** when the person files an application with a judicial nominating commission and remains an **applicant** until the Governor makes an appointment to that judicial office unless, prior to that time, the person formally withdraws the application.

(3) If the person is not appointed but, pursuant to an Executive Order of the Governor or other law, remains eligible for appointment to another judicial office without a further application to or recommendation from the judicial nominating commission, the person remains an **applicant** until the Governor makes an appointment to that other judicial office, unless, prior to that time, the person formally withdraws the application.

Cross references. — Executive Order 01.01.2008.04

(b) **Candidate**

"Candidate" means a **candidate for election** or a **District Court candidate for retention**.

(c) **Candidate for election**

(1) **"Candidate for election"** means a person who:

(A) seeks initial election to a Circuit Court or an Orphans' Court;

(B) is an incumbent judge of a Circuit Court or Orphans' Court and seeks to retain that office through an election conducted pursuant to Art. IV, § 3, 5, or 40 of the Maryland Constitution; or

(C) is an incumbent judge of the Court of Appeals or Court of Special Appeals and seeks to retain that office through a retention election conducted pursuant to Art. IV, § 5A of the Maryland Constitution.

(2) A person becomes a **candidate for election**:

(A) as to a newly appointed judge, from the date the judge takes the oath of office;

(B) as to any other incumbent judge, from the earlier of:

(i) the date two years prior to the general election pertaining to that judge's re-election or subsequent retention; or

(ii) the date on which a newly appointed judge to that court becomes a **candidate** in the same general election.

(C) as to a judge who seeks election to another judicial office, the earlier of:

(i) the date on which the judge files a certificate of candidacy in accordance with Maryland election laws, but no earlier than two years prior to the general election for that office; or

(ii) the date on which a newly appointed judge to that court becomes a **candidate** in the same general election; and

(D) as to a lawyer who seeks a judicial office, the date on which the lawyer files a certificate of candidacy in accordance with Maryland election laws, but no earlier than two years prior to the general election for the office.

(3) A person who becomes a **candidate** under paragraph (c) remains a **candidate** until the general election for the office unless, prior to that time, the person files a formal withdrawal of candidacy in accordance with Maryland election laws.

(d) District Court Candidate for Retention

"District Court candidate for retention" means an incumbent judge of the District Court who seeks retention for an additional term pursuant to Art. IV, § 41D of the Maryland Constitution. A District Court judge becomes a **candidate** for retention from the date one year prior to the expiration of the judge's current term.

(e) Political organization

"Political organization" includes a political party, a political committee, and a partisan organization, as those terms are defined in Maryland Code, Election Article, § 1-101.

Source. — These definitions are new.

COMMENT

[1] This Rule is new. It is intended to reflect and focus on the different ways in which judges in Maryland are selected and retained. *See* Maryland Constitution, Art. IV, § 5A (appellate judges), §§ 3 and 5 (Circuit Court judges), § 41D (District Court judges), and § 40 (Orphans' Court judges).

(a) In all cases, a vacancy is filled by appointment by the Governor. The appointment of appellate, District Court, and Orphans' Court judges requires the advice and consent of the Senate; the appointment of Circuit Court judges does not.

(b) Appellate judges then face an uncontested plebiscite election (yes or no for continuance in office) for an additional 10-year term, following which they face another such election for a succeeding term.

(c) Circuit Court judges face a potentially contested primary and general election for a 15-year term, at the end of which, in order to remain in office, they must be appointed by the Governor for a "bridge" term until the next election and then prevail in that election.

(d) District Court judges do not face election but receive a 10-year term, at the end of which, they must be reappointed by the Governor subject to confirmation by the Senate.

(e) Orphans' Court judges face a potentially contested primary and general election every four years.

[2] The first context, applicable to all appellate, Circuit Court, and District Court judges and many Orphans' Court judges, is initial

appointment by the Governor to fill a vacancy. Except for Orphans' Court judges, that requires an application to and consideration by a judicial nominating commission, which normally interviews the **applicants,** receives information and recommendations from Bar Associations, other interested groups, and members of the public, and sends to the Governor a list of recommended **applicants.** The Governors have agreed, expressly or tacitly, to appoint from the list of applicants recommended by the applicable nominating commission. The applicants may be lawyers seeking initial appointment to the Bench, incumbent Circuit Court judges seeking reappointment, upon the expiration of their 15-year term, for a "bridge" period until the next election, or other judges seeking appointment to a different court. Rule 4.1 (a) defines those persons as **"applicants."**

[3] A person seeking election, either through a potentially contested election (Circuit Court and Orphans' Court) or through a plebiscite-type retention election (appellate judges), is defined in Rule 4.1 (c) as a **"candidate for election."** A District Court judge, at the end of the 10-year term, faces confirmation by the Senate for an additional term. That judge is not a **candidate for election** but is defined in Rule 4.1 (d) as a **"District Court candidate for retention."**

[4] The remaining Rules in Section 4 specify the political activity allowed or not allowed to persons falling within those categories, as well as to incumbent judges who are not within any of them.

[5] Even when subject to election, a judge plays a role different from that of a legislator or executive branch official. Rather than making decisions based on the expressed views or preferences of the electorate, a judge makes decisions based on the law and the facts of each case. In furtherance of that interest, judges and **candidates** for judicial office must, to the greatest extent possible, be free and appear to be free from political influence and political pressure. The Rules in Section 4 impose narrowly tailored restrictions on the political and campaign activities of all judges and **candidates** for judicial office.

Source. — This Rule and Comments [1] through [4] are new. Comment [5] is derived from ABA Comment [1] to Rule 4.1 of the 2007 ABA Code.

Rule 4.2. POLITICAL CONDUCT OF JUDGE WHO IS NOT A CANDIDATE

(a) A judge who is not a **candidate** shall not engage in any partisan political activity.

(b) A judge shall resign when the judge becomes a **candidate** for a non-judicial office, except that a judge may continue to hold judicial office while a **candidate for election** as a delegate to a Maryland Constitutional Convention.

Source. — Rule 4.2 is derived from former Md. Code of Judicial Conduct Canon 5A.

Rule 4.3. POLITICAL CONDUCT OF APPLICANT

An **applicant** for judicial office may initiate communications or contact with a judicial nominating commission or its members and may seek endorsements for the appointment from any other person or organization, other than a **political organization.**

COMMENT

[1] Rule 4.3 is derived in part from Rule 4.3 of the 2007 ABA Code but departs from it in one important respect. Under Rule 4.3, an **applicant** may initiate communications or contact with a judicial nominating commission or its members, but neither the Commission nor its members are obliged to respond to such communications or contact. **Applicants** may appear for interviews before the commission and may respond to questions or inquiries from commission members, and they may solicit endorsements from other persons or organizations (other than a **political organization**). If they have a question regarding the procedure or their application, they may contact the Administrative Office of the Courts.

Source. — This Rule is derived from Rule 4.3 of the 2007 ABA Code. The Comment is new.

Rule 4.4. POLITICAL CONDUCT OF CANDIDATE FOR ELECTION

A **candidate for election:**

(a) shall comply with all applicable election laws and regulations;

(b) shall act at all times in a manner consistent with the **independence, integrity,** and **impartiality** of the judiciary and maintain the dignity appropriate to judicial office;

(c) subject to the other provisions of this Rule, may engage in partisan political activity allowed by law with respect to such candidacy, and, in that regard:

(1) may publicly endorse or oppose **candidates** for the same judicial office;

(2) may attend or purchase tickets for dinners or other events sponsored by a **political organization** or a **candidate** for public office; and

(3) may seek, accept, and use endorsements from any person or organization; but

(4) shall not act as a leader in or hold office in a **political organization,** make a speech for a **candidate** or **political organization,** or publicly endorse a **candidate** for non- judicial office.

(d) As to statements and materials made or produced during a campaign:

(1) shall review, approve, and be responsible for the content of all campaign statements and materials produced by the **candidate** or by the **candidate's** campaign committee or other authorized agents;

(2) shall take reasonable measures to ensure that other persons do not undertake on behalf of the **candidate** activities that the **candidate** is prohibited from doing by this Rule;

(3) with respect to a case, controversy, or issue that is likely to come before the court, shall not make a commitment, pledge, or promise that is inconsistent with the **impartial** performance of the adjudicative duties of the office;

(4) shall not make any statement that would reasonably be expected to affect the outcome or impair the fairness of a matter pending or impending in any court;

(5) shall not **knowingly,** or with reckless disregard for the truth, misrepresent the **candidate's** identity or qualifications, the identity or qualifications of an opponent, or any other fact, or make any false or misleading statement;

(6) may speak or write on behalf of the candidate's candidacy through any medium, including advertisements, websites, or other campaign literature; and

(7) subject to paragraph (b) of this Rule, may respond to a personal attack or an attack on the **candidate's** record.

COMMENT

[1] This Rule is derived in part from former Md. Code of Judicial Conduct Canon 5B and from the 2007 ABA Code, but it has been substantially reorganized into three basic segments: general requirements (paragraphs (a) and (b)); the extent to which **candidates for election** may engage in partisan political conduct (paragraph (c)); and the rules governing campaign statements (paragraph (d)).

[2] Rule 4.4 (a) requires **candidates for election** to comply with all election laws and regulations. The Election Law Article of the

Maryland Code contains laws governing **candidates,** campaign contributions, finance, expenditures, and reporting. Those requirements are supplemented by regulations adopted by the State Board of Elections. **Candidates for election** must become familiar with applicable laws and regulations and comply with them.

[3] Public confidence in the **independence** and **impartiality** of the judiciary is eroded if judges or **candidates** for judicial office are perceived to be subject to political influence. Although they may register to vote as members of a political party, they are prohibited by Rule 4.4 (c) (4) from assuming leadership roles in **political organizations.**

[4] Rule 4.4 (c) (4) also prohibits **candidates for election** from making speeches on behalf of **political organizations** or publicly endorsing or opposing **candidates** for public office, to prevent them from abusing the prestige of judicial office to advance the interests of others. *See* Rule 1.3. Rule 4.4 does not prohibit **candidates for election** from (a) campaigning on their own behalf, (b) endorsing or opposing **candidates for election** to the same judicial office for which they are running, or (c) from having their name on the same sample ballot as a **candidate** for another public office.

[5] Although members of the families of **candidates for election** are free to engage in their own political activity, including running for public office, there is no "family exception" to the prohibition in Rule 4.4 (c) (4) against publicly endorsing **candidates** for public office. A **candidate for election** must not become involved in, or be publicly associated with, a family member's political activity or campaign for public office. To avoid public misunderstanding, **candidates for election** should take, and should urge members of their families to take, reasonable steps to avoid any implication that they endorse any family member's candidacy or other political activity.

[6] Judicial **candidates** must be scrupulously fair and accurate in all statements made by them and by their campaign committees. Rule 4.4 (d) (5) obligates them to refrain from making statements that are false or mis-

leading, or that omit facts necessary to make the communication considered as a whole not materially misleading. Rule 4.4 (d) (1) requires the **candidate** to review and approve the content of statements made by the **candidate's** campaign committee or other authorized agents and makes the **candidate** responsible for those statements.

[7] **Candidates for election** are sometimes the subject of false, misleading, or unfair allegations made by opposing **candidates,** third parties, or the media. As long as the **candidate for election** does not violate Rule 4.4 (d), he or she may make a factually accurate public response, although it is preferable for someone else to respond if the allegations relate to a pending case. If an independent third party has made unwarranted attacks on a **candidate for election's** opponent, the **candidate for election** may disavow the attacks and request the third party to cease and desist.

[8] Rule 4.4 (d) (3) prohibits **candidates for election,** with regard to cases or issues likely to come before the court, from making a commitment, promise, or pledge that is inconsistent with the **impartial** performance of the adjudicative duties of the office. The making of a commitment, promise, or pledge is not dependent on, or limited to, the use of any specific words or phrases. The totality of the statement must be examined to determine if a reasonable person would believe that the **candidate** has specifically undertaken to reach a particular result. Commitments, promises, and pledges must be contrasted with statements or announcements of personal views on legal, political, or other issues, which are not prohibited. When making such statements, a judge should acknowledge the overarching judicial obligation to apply and uphold the law, without regard to his or her personal views.

Source. — This Rule is derived in part from Rule 4.1 of the 2007 ABA Code and in part from Canon 5 of the former Maryland Code of Judicial Conduct. The Comments are derived from the ABA Comments to Rule 4.1 of the 2007 ABA Code.

Rule 4.5. POLITICAL CONDUCT OF DISTRICT COURT CANDIDATE FOR RETENTION

A **District Court candidate for retention:**

(a) may contact and communicate with the Governor and members of the State Senate regarding the **candidate's** reconfirmation;

(b) may seek, accept, and use endorsements from any person or organization;

(c) shall act at all times in a manner consistent with the **independence,** integrity, and **impartiality** of the judiciary and maintain the dignity appropriate to judicial office;

(d) subject to paragraph (c) of this Rule, may respond to a personal attack or an attack on the **candidate's** record;

(e) with respect to a case, controversy, or issue that is likely to come before the court, shall not make a commitment, pledge, or promise that is inconsistent with the **impartial** performance of the adjudicative duties of the office; and

(f) shall not **knowingly** or with reckless disregard for the truth misrepresent the **candidate's** identity or qualifications or any other fact.

COMMENT

[1] Because a **District Court candidate for retention** does not face an election, the political activity allowed is much more limited. It is reasonable to permit the judge to contact the Governor, who must transmit the judge's name to the Senate, and members of the Senate, regarding the judge's reconfirmation, and to seek endorsements that may be helpful to the judge in that regard. The constraints in paragraphs (c) through (f), which are taken from Rule 4.4, are applicable as well to even this political activity.

Source. — This Rule and the Comment are new.

Rule 4.6. APPLICABILITY AND DISCIPLINE

(a) A **candidate** who is a judge shall comply with the Rules in this Section 4. A **candidate** who is a lawyer shall comply with Rule 8.2 of the Maryland Lawyers' Rules of Professional Conduct (Maryland Rule 16-812).

(b) A successful **candidate** and a judge who unsuccessfully sought a different judicial office are subject to judicial discipline for campaign conduct. An unsuccessful **candidate** who is a lawyer is subject to attorney discipline for campaign conduct (Added March 9, 2010, effective July 1, 2010; June 7, 2011, effective July 1, 2011.)

Source. — This Rule is derived from Canon 5D of the former Maryland Code of Judicial Conduct.

Effect of amendments. — The 2011 amendment inserted "former" preceding "Maryland Code of Judicial Conduct" in the second sentence of the source note under Rule 3.8.

University of Baltimore Law Forum. — For an article, "The Selection and Election of Circuit Judges in Maryland: A Time for Change," see 40 U. Balt. L. F. 39 (2010).

Maryland Law Review. — For a recent decision, "The Court of Appeals of Maryland Diggs v. State: A Not-So-Plain Error?," see 69 U. Md. L. Rev. 680 (2010).

Recusal. — Trial court's discussions with the State Public Defender regarding an internal review by the Office of the Public Defender (OPD) of the OPD's employees' performance did not require the trial court's recusal when the trial court questioned a self-condemning affidavit submitted by trial counsel employed by the OPD in support of the motion of petitioner, a juvenile, to vacate a delinquency finding, alleging counsel's ineffective assistance, because (1) the discussions were unrelated to petitioner's case, so nothing in the record suggested the judge had any specific knowledge as to whether counsel had been the subject of such an evaluation or whether the rumored consequences of such assessments affected counsel's decision to submit a self-condemning affidavit, and (2) the judge's knowledge of the evaluations did not relate to the issue of whether counsel actually provided effective assistance at petitioner's delinquency hearing, but rather led the judge to inquire on the record regarding a potential conflict and

the voluntariness of the affidavit. In re Elrich
S., 416 Md. 15, 5 A.3d 27 (2010).

Rule 16-814. Maryland Code Of Conduct For Judicial Appointees.
TABLE OF CONTENTS

Rule 3.12. COMPENSATION FOR EXTRA-OFFICIAL ACTIVITIES

Rule 3.13. ACCEPTANCE OF GIFTS, LOANS, BEQUESTS, BENEFITS, OR OTHER THINGS OF VALUE

Rule 3.14. REIMBURSEMENT OF EXPENSES AND WAIVERS OF FEES OR CHARGES

Rule 3.15. REPORTING REQUIREMENTS

SECTION 4. RULES GOVERNING POLITICAL ACTIVITY

Rule 4.1. DEFINITIONS

Rule 4.2. POLITICAL CONDUCT OF JUDICIAL APPOINTEE WHO IS NOT A CANDIDATE

Rule 4.3. POLITICAL CONDUCT OF APPLICANT

Rule 4.4. POLITICAL CONDUCT OF CANDIDATE FOR ELECTION

Rule 4.5. APPLICABILITY AND DISCIPLINE

PREAMBLE

This Code of Conduct for **Judicial Appointees** governs the conduct of judicial appointees. It is patterned after the Maryland Code of Judicial Conduct (MCJC) set forth in Rule 16-813, and the provisions of this Code should be read in a consistent manner with parallel provisions in the MCJC.

This Code sets forth minimum standards and is not intended as a limitation on an appointing authority's power to impose additional requirements.

DEFINITIONS

(a) **Judicial Appointee. "Judicial appointee"** means:

(1) an auditor, examiner, or master appointed by a court of this State; and

Cross references. — *See* Rules 2-541, 2-542, and 2-543.

(2) a District Court commissioner appointed pursuant to Article IV, § 41G of the Maryland Constitution.

Source. — With style changes this definition is derived from the former Code of Conduct for Judicial Appointees.

Cross references. — For the definition of "judicial appointee" for purposes of filing a financial disclosure statement, *see* Rule 16-816.

(b) **Member of Judicial Appointee's Family. "Member of judicial appointee's family"** means a spouse, **domestic partner,** child, grandchild, parent, grandparent, or other relative or person with whom the **judicial appointee** maintains a close familial relationship.

Source. — This definition is derived from Section B-108 of the MCJC.

(c) **Member of Judicial Appointee's Household. "Member of judicial appointee's household"** means:

(1) if sharing the **judicial appointee's** legal residence, the **judicial appointee's** spouse, **domestic partner,** child, ward, financially dependent parent, or other financially dependent relative; or

(2) the **judicial appointee's** spouse, **domestic partner,** child, ward, parent, or other relative over whose financial affairs the **judicial appointee** has legal or actual control.

Source. — This definition is derived from Section B-109 of the MCJC.

(d) **Other Definitions.** As to a **judicial appointee, "domestic partner," "fiduciary," "gift," "impartial, impartiality, and impartially," "impending matter," "independence," "knowingly, knowledge, known, and knows," "pending matter," "significant financial interest,"** and **"third degree of relationship"** have the meanings set forth, respectively, in Sections B-101, B-102, B-103, B-104, B-105, B-106, B-107, B-110, and B-111, and B-112 of the MCJC.

APPLICATION

(a) **District Court Commissioners and Full-time Standing Masters, Examiners, and Auditors.** This Code applies in its entirety to District Court Commissioners and full-time standing masters, examiners, and auditors.

(b) **Part-time Standing Masters, Examiners, and Auditors.** Except as otherwise provided in a specific Rule, this Code applies in its entirety to part-time standing masters, examiners, and auditors.

(c) **Special Masters, Examiners, and Auditors.** During the period of their serving in that capacity, special masters, examiners, and auditors are subject only to the Rules in Sections 1 and 2, to Rule 3.5, and to such of the Comments to those Rules as are relevant, given the limited duration of the service. Special masters, examiners, and auditors shall, however, on request of a party or the appointing authority, disclose any extra-official activity or interests covered by the other Rules in this Code that may be grounds for a motion to recuse under Rule 2.11.

Source. — This provision is new.

Committee note. — District Court Commissioners, despite the number of hours they may actually be on duty, are regarded as full-time judicial appointees. Auditors, examiners, and masters may fall into several categories.

Under Code, Courts Article, § 2-102, all courts may appoint a master, examiner, or auditor in "a specific proceeding." Under Code, Courts Article, § 2-501, the judges of the circuit courts have more general authority to employ masters, examiners, and auditors. That authority is extended and made more specific in Rules 2-541 (masters), 2-542 (examiners), and 2-543 (auditors).

Rules 2-541, 2-542, and 2-543 create two categories of masters, examiners, and auditors — standing and special. Standing masters, examiners, and auditors are employed to deal with whatever cases are referred to them on an on-going basis, but their employment by the court may be full-time or part-time. Special masters, examiners, and auditors are appointed "for a particular action," and thus, like appointments made under Courts Article, § 2-102, their service is limited to the particular action or proceeding. During that period of service, however, it is possible that they may work full-time or part-time, as necessary or as directed by the court. A master, examiner, or auditor may therefore be standing full-time, standing part-time, special full-time, or special part-time.

This Code, in its entirety, applies to District Court Commissioners and full-time standing masters, examiners, and auditors. Because their employment by the court is full-time and more-or-less permanent, it is appropriate to limit some of their extra-official activities in the same manner as judges. Standing masters, examiners, and auditors who work only part-time but whose employment is also more-or-less permanent and who handle whatever cases are referred to them also need to be subject to most or the requirements and limitations in the Code, but it is impractical to preclude them from engaging in other lawful remunerative activities, such as practicing law or accounting or providing ADR services. They are subject to the entire Code, except as pro-vided in specific Rules. Special masters, examiners, and auditors, appointed for only one proceeding, are subject to those Rules governing such things as fairness, impartiality, integrity, and diligence during the period of their service, but it is impractical and unnecessary to subject them across-the-board to the Rules in Section 4 or most of the Rules in Section 3 (political and extra-official activities), provided that, upon request of a party or the appointing authority, they disclose any activity or interest that may be cause for recusal.

SECTION 1.

RULES GOVERNING INTEGRITY AND THE AVOIDANCE OF IM-PROPRIETY

Rule 1.1. COMPLIANCE WITH THE LAW

A **judicial appointee** shall comply with the law, including the Rules in this Code of Conduct for Judicial Appointees that are applicable.

Source. — This Rule is derived from Rule 1.1 of the MCJC.

Rule 1.2. PROMOTING CONFIDENCE IN THE JUDICIARY

(a) A **judicial appointee** shall act at all times in a manner that promotes public confidence in the **independence,** integrity, and **impartiality** of the judiciary.

(b) A **judicial appointee** shall avoid conduct that would create in reasonable minds a perception of impropriety.

COMMENT

[1] Public confidence in the judiciary is eroded by improper conduct and conduct that creates the appearance of impropriety. This principle applies to both the professional and personal conduct of a **judicial appointee.**

[2] A **judicial appointee** should expect to be the subject of public scrutiny that might be viewed as burdensome if applied to other citizens, and must accept the restrictions imposed by this Code.

[3] Conduct that compromises or appears to compromise the **independence,** integrity, and **impartiality** of a **judicial appointee** undermines public confidence in the judiciary. Because it is not practicable to list all such conduct, the Rule is necessarily cast in general terms.

[4] **Judicial appointees** should participate in activities that promote ethical conduct among **judicial appointees** and lawyers, support professionalism within the judiciary and the legal profession, and promote access to justice for all.

[5] Actual improprieties include violations of law, court rules, and this Code. The test for appearance of impropriety is whether the conduct would create in reasonable minds a perception that the **judicial appointee's** ability to carry out the responsibilities of the **judicial appointee's** position with competence, **impartiality,** and integrity is impaired.

[6] A **judicial appointee** should, where appropriate, initiate and participate in community outreach activities for the purpose of promoting public understanding of and confidence in the administration of justice. In conducting such activities, the **judicial appointee** must act in a manner consistent with this Code.

Source. — This Rule is derived from Rule 1.2 of the MCJC.

Rule 1.3. AVOIDING LENDING THE PRESTIGE OF THE POSITION

A **judicial appointee** shall not lend the prestige of the **judicial appointee's** position to advance the personal or economic interests of the **judicial appointee** or others, or allow others to do so.

COMMENT

[1] It is improper for a **judicial appointee** to use or attempt to use his or her position to gain personal advantage or deferential treatment of any kind. For example, it would be improper for a **judicial appointee** to allude to his or her official status to gain favorable treatment in encounters with traffic officials. Similarly, a **judicial appointee** must not use an official letterhead to gain an advantage in conducting his or her personal business.

[2] A **judicial appointee** may provide a reference or recommendation for an individual based upon the **judicial appointee's** personal **knowledge.** The **judicial appointee** may use an official letterhead if the **judicial appointee** indicates that the reference is personal and if there is no likelihood that the use of the letterhead would reasonably be perceived as an attempt to exert pressure by reason of the **judicial appointee's** position.

[3] **Judicial appointees** may participate in the process of judicial selection by cooperating with appointing authorities and screening committees and by responding to inquiries from such entities concerning the professional qualifications of a person being considered for judicial office.

[4] Special considerations arise when **judicial appointees** write or contribute to publications of for-profit entities, whether related or unrelated to the law. A **judicial appointee** should not permit anyone associated with the publication of such materials to exploit the **judicial appointee's** position in a manner that violates this Rule or other applicable law. In contracts for publication of a **judicial appointee's** writing, the **judicial appointee** should retain sufficient control over the advertising to avoid such exploitation.

Source. — This Rule is derived from Rule 1.3 of MCJC.

SECTION 2.

RULES GOVERNING THE PERFORMANCE OF A JUDICIAL APPOINTEE'S DUTIES

Rule 2.1. GIVING PRECEDENCE TO THE DUTIES OF POSITION

The duties of **the judicial appointee's** position, as prescribed by law and by the conditions and requirements imposed by the appointing authority, shall take precedence over a **judicial appointee's** personal and extra-official activities.

COMMENT

[1] To ensure that **judicial appointees** are available to fulfill their official duties, **judicial appointees** must conduct their personal and extra-official activities to minimize the risk of conflicts that would result in frequent disqualification.

[2] Although it is not a duty of a **judicial appointee's** position unless prescribed by law, **judicial appointees** are encouraged to participate in activities that promote public understanding of and confidence in the justice system.

[3] With respect to time devoted to personal and extra-official activities, this Rule must be construed in a reasonable manner. Family obligations, illnesses, emergencies, and other permissible extra-official activities may require a **judicial appointee's** immediate attention. Attending to those obligations and situations, temporary in nature, is not prohibited by this Rule and should be dealt with in accordance with applicable vacation, sick leave, and administrative leave policies. Judicial appointees must not permit their other activities to interfere with their ability to perform the duties of their public position.

Source. — This Rule is derived from Rule 2.1 of MCJC. The last sentence of Comment [3] is new.

Rule 2.2. IMPARTIALITY AND FAIRNESS

A **judicial appointee** shall uphold and apply the law and shall perform all duties of the position impartially and fairly.

COMMENT

[1] To ensure **impartiality** and fairness to all parties, a **judicial appointee** must be objective and open-minded.

[2] Although each **judicial appointee** comes to the position with a unique background and personal philosophy, a **judicial appointee** must interpret and apply the law without regard to whether the **judicial appointee** approves or disapproves of the law in question.

[3] When applying and interpreting the law, a **judicial appointee** sometimes may make good-faith errors of fact or law. Errors of this kind do not violate this Rule.

[4] It is not a violation of this Rule for a **judicial appointee** to make reasonable accommodations to ensure self-represented litigants the opportunity to have their matters fairly heard.

Cross references. — *See* Rule 2.6 Comment [2].

Source. — This Rule is derived from Rule 2.2 of MCJC.

Rule 2.3. BIAS, PREJUDICE, AND HARASSMENT

(a) A **judicial appointee** shall perform the duties of the position, including administrative duties, without bias or prejudice.

(b) A **judicial appointee** shall not, in the performance of the **judicial appointee's** duties, by words or conduct, manifest bias, prejudice, or harassment based upon race, sex, gender, religion, national origin, ethnicity, disability, age, sexual orientation, marital status, socioeconomic status, or political affiliation. A **judicial appointee** shall require lawyers in proceedings before the **judicial appointee,** court staff, court officials, and others subject to the **judicial appointee's** direction and control to refrain from similar conduct.

(c) The restrictions of paragraph (b) do not preclude **judicial appointees** or lawyers from making legitimate references to the listed factors, or similar factors, when they are relevant to an issue in a proceeding.

COMMENT

[1] A **judicial appointee** who manifests bias or prejudice in a proceeding impairs the fairness of the proceeding and brings the judiciary into disrepute.

[2] A **judicial appointee** must avoid conduct that may reasonably be perceived as prejudiced or biased. Examples of manifestations of bias or prejudice include epithets, slurs, demeaning nicknames, negative stereotyping, attempted humor based upon stereotypes, threatening, intimidating, or hostile acts, suggestions of connections between race, ethnicity, or nationality and crime, and irrelevant references to personal characteristics. Even facial expressions and body language can convey to parties and lawyers in the proceed-ing, the media, and others an appearance of bias or prejudice.

[3] Harassment, as referred to in paragraph (b), is verbal or physical conduct that denigrates or shows hostility or aversion toward a person on bases such as race, sex, gender, religion, national origin, ethnicity, disability, age, sexual orientation, marital status, socioeconomic status, or political affiliation.

[4] Sexual harassment includes sexual advances, requests for sexual favors, and other verbal or physical conduct of a sexual nature that is unwelcome.

Source. — This Rule is derived from Rule 2.3 of the MCJC.

Rule 2.4. EXTERNAL INFLUENCES ON PROFESSIONAL CONDUCT

(a) A **judicial appointee** shall not be swayed by public clamor or fear of criticism.

(b) A **judicial appointee** shall not permit family, social, political, financial, or other interests or relationships to influence the **judicial appointee's** official conduct or judgment.

(c) A **judicial appointee** shall not convey or permit others to convey the impression that any person or organization is in a position to influence the **judicial appointee.**

COMMENT

[1] An independent judiciary requires that **judicial appointees** decide matters according to the law and facts, without regard to whether particular laws or litigants are popular or unpopular with the public, the media, government officials, or the **judicial appointee's** friends or family. Confidence in the judiciary is eroded if a **judicial appointee's** decision-making is perceived to be subject to inappropriate outside influences.

Source. — This Rule is derived from Rule 2.4 of the MCJC.

Rule 2.5. COMPETENCE, DILIGENCE, AND COOPERATION

(a) A **judicial appointee** shall perform the duties of the position competently, diligently, promptly, and without favoritism or nepotism.

(b) A **judicial appointee** shall cooperate with judges, other **judicial appointees** of the court, and court officials in the administration of court business.

(c) A **judicial appointee** shall not wilfully fail to comply with administrative rules or reasonable directives of a judge or other **judicial appointee** with supervisory authority.

COMMENT

[1] Competence in the performance of a **judicial appointee's** duties requires the legal **knowledge,** skill, thoroughness, and preparation reasonably necessary to perform the responsibilities of the position.

[2] A **judicial appointee** should seek the necessary docket time, court staff, expertise, and resources to discharge the **judicial appointee's** responsibilities.

[3] Prompt disposition of the court's business requires a **judicial appointee** to devote adequate time to the position in accordance with the requirements imposed by the appointing authority, to be punctual in attendance and expeditious in determining matters

under submission, and to take reasonable measures to ensure that court officials, litigants, and their lawyers cooperate with the **judicial appointee** to that end.

[4] In disposing of matters promptly and efficiently, a **judicial appointee** must demonstrate due regard for the rights of parties to be heard and to have issues resolved without unnecessary cost or delay. A **judicial appointee** should monitor and supervise cases in ways that reduce or eliminate dilatory practices, avoidable delays, and unnecessary costs.

Source. — This Rule is derived from Rule 2.5 of the MCJC.

Rule 2.6. ENSURING THE RIGHT TO BE HEARD

(a) A **judicial appointee** shall accord to every person who has a legal interest in a proceeding, or that person's lawyer, the right to be heard according to law.

(b) A **judicial appointee** may encourage parties to a proceeding and their lawyers to settle matters in dispute but shall not act in a manner that coerces any party into settlement.

[1] The right to be heard is an essential component of a fair and **impartial** system of justice. Substantive rights of litigants can be protected only if procedures protecting the right to be heard are observed.

[2] Increasingly, **judicial appointees** have before them self-represented litigants whose lack of **knowledge** about the law and about judicial procedures and requirements may inhibit their ability to be heard effectively. A **judicial appointee's** obligation under Rule 2.2 to remain fair and **impartial** does not preclude the **judicial appointee** from making reasonable accommodations to protect a self-represented litigant's right to be heard, so long as those accommodations do not give the self-represented litigant an unfair advantage. This Rule does not require a **judicial appointee** to make any particular accommodation.

[3] Settlement conferences and referrals to alternative dispute resolution may play an important role in the administration of justice. A **judicial appointee** may play an important role in overseeing the settlement of disputes, but should be careful that efforts to further settlement do not undermine any party's right to be heard according to law. Among the factors that a **judicial appointee** should consider when deciding upon an appropriate settlement practice for a case are (a) whether the parties have requested or voluntarily consented to a certain level of participation by the **judicial appointee** in settlement discussions, (b) whether the parties and their counsel are relatively sophisticated in legal matters, (c) whether the case will be tried by a judge or a jury, (d) whether the parties participate with their counsel in settlement discussions, (e) whether any parties are self-represented, and (f) the nature of the proceeding.

[4] **Judicial appointees** must be mindful of the effect settlement discussions can have, not only on their objectivity and **impartiality,** but also on the appearance of their objectivity and **impartiality.** A **judicial appointee** should keep in mind the effect that the **judicial appointee's** participation in settlement discussions may have on both the **judicial appointee's** own views of the case and the perceptions of the lawyers and the parties if the case remains with the **judicial appointee** after settlement efforts are unsuccessful. Despite a **judicial appointee's** best efforts, there may be instances when information obtained during settlement discussions could influence a **judicial appointee's** decision making during proceedings, and, in such instances, the **judicial appointee** should consider whether disqualification may be appropriate. *See* Rule 2.11 (a) (1).

Source. — This Rule is derived from Rule 2.6 of the MCJC.

Rule 2.7. RESPONSIBILITY TO DECIDE

A **judicial appointee** shall hear and decide matters assigned to the **judicial appointee** unless recusal is appropriate.

[1] Although there are times when disqualification is necessary or appropriate to protect the rights of litigants and preserve public confidence in the **independence,** integrity, and **impartiality** of the judiciary, **judicial appointees** must be available to decide matters that come before them. The dignity of the court, the **judicial appointee's** respect for fulfillment of the duties of the position, and a proper concern for the burdens that may be imposed upon the judges and the **judicial appointee's** colleagues require that a **judicial appointee** not use disqualification to avoid cases that present difficult, controversial, or unpopular issues.

Source. — This Rule is derived from Rule 2.7 of the MCJC.

Rule 2.8. DECORUM AND DEMEANOR

(a) A **judicial appointee** shall require order and decorum in proceedings before the **judicial appointee.**

(b) A **judicial appointee** shall be patient, dignified, and courteous to litigants, witnesses, lawyers, court staff, court officials, and others with whom the **judicial appointee** deals in an official capacity, and shall require similar conduct of lawyers, court staff, court officials, and others subject to the **judicial appointee's** direction and control.

COMMENT

[1] The duty to hear all proceedings with patience and courtesy is not inconsistent with the duty imposed in Rule 2.5 to dispose promptly of the business of the court. **Judicial appointees** can be efficient and businesslike while being patient and deliberate.

Source. — This Rule is derived from Rule 2.8 of the MCJC, except that Comments [2] and [3] were deleted.

Rule 2.9. EX PARTE COMMUNICATIONS

(a) A **judicial appointee** shall not initiate, permit, or consider ex parte communications, or consider other communications made to the **judicial appointee** out of the presence of the parties or their lawyers, concerning a pending or **impending matter,** except as follows:

(1) A **judicial appointee** may initiate, permit, or consider any ex parte communication when expressly authorized by law to do so.

(2) When circumstances require it, ex parte communication for scheduling, administrative, or emergency purposes, which does not address substantive matters, is permitted, provided:

(A) the **judicial appointee** reasonably believes that no party will gain a procedural, substantive, or tactical advantage as a result of the ex parte communication; and

(B) the **judicial appointee** makes provision promptly to notify all other parties of the substance of the ex parte communication, and gives the parties an opportunity to respond.

(3) A **judicial appointee** may obtain the advice of a disinterested expert on the law applicable to a proceeding if the **judicial appointee** (A) makes provision promptly to notify all of the parties as to the expert consulted and the substance of the advice, and (B) affords the parties a reasonable opportunity to respond.

(4) A **judicial appointee** may consult with court staff and court officials whose functions are to aid the **judicial appointee** in carrying out the **judicial appointee's** adjudicative responsibilities, or with a judge, provided the **judicial appointee** does not make a decision based on adjudicative facts that are not made part of the record, and does not abrogate the responsibility personally to decide the matter.

(5) A **judicial appointee** may, with the consent of the parties, confer separately with the parties and their lawyers as part of a settlement conference conducted pursuant to Rules 17-102 (h) and 17-105 (b).

(6) When serving in a problem-solving court program of a Circuit Court or the District Court pursuant to Rule 16-206, a **judicial appointee** may initiate, permit, and consider ex parte communications in conformance with the established protocols for the operation of the program if the parties have expressly consented to those protocols.

(b) If a **judicial appointee** inadvertently receives an unauthorized ex parte communication bearing upon the substance of a matter, the **judicial appointee** shall make provision promptly to notify the parties of the substance of the communication and provide the parties with an opportunity to respond.

(c) Unless expressly authorized by law, a **judicial appointee** shall not investigate adjudicative facts in a matter independently, and shall consider only the evidence presented and any facts that may properly be judicially noticed.

Cross references. — *See* Code, Courts Article, § 2-607 (c) (2) authorizing District Court Commissioners to conduct investigations and inquiries into the circumstances of matters presented to determine if probable cause exists for the issuance of a charging document, warrant, or criminal summons.

(d) A **judicial appointee** shall make reasonable efforts, including providing appropriate supervision, to ensure that this Rule is not violated by court staff, court officials, and others subject to the **judicial appointee's** direction and control.

COMMENT

[1] To the extent reasonably possible, all parties or their lawyers shall be included in communications with a **judicial appointee.**

[2] Whenever the presence of a party or notice to a party is required by this Rule, it is the party's lawyer, or if the party is self-represented, the party, who is to be present or to whom notice is to be given.

[3] The proscription against communications concerning a proceeding includes communications with lawyers, law teachers, and other persons who are not participants in the proceeding, except to the limited extent permitted by this Rule.

[4] A **judicial appointee** may consult with judges or other **judicial appointees** on **pending matters,** including a retired judge approved for recall, but must avoid ex parte discussions of a case with judges or **judicial appointees** who have previously been disqualified from hearing the matter or with a judge whom the **judicial appointee knows** has been assigned to hear exceptions to the **judicial appointee's** recommendation in the matter.

[5] The prohibition against a **judicial appointee** investigating adjudicative facts in a matter extends to information available in all mediums, including electronic.

[6] A **judicial appointee** may consult ethics advisory committees, outside counsel, or legal experts concerning the **judicial appointee's** compliance with this Code. Such consultations are not subject to the restrictions of paragraph (a) (2).

Source. — This Rule is derived in part from Rule 2.9 of the MCJC.

Rule 2.10. STATEMENTS ON PENDING AND IMPENDING CASES

(a) A **judicial appointee** shall abstain from public comment that relates to a proceeding **pending or impending** in any court and that might reasonably be expected to affect the outcome or impair the fairness of that proceeding and shall require similar abstention on the part of court personnel subject to the **judicial appointee's** direction and control. This Rule does not prohibit a **judicial appointee** from making public statements in the course of official duties or from explaining for public information the procedures of the court.

(b) With respect to a case, controversy, or issue that is likely to come before the court, a **judicial appointee** shall not make a commitment, pledge, or promise that is inconsistent with the **impartial** performance of the adjudicative duties of the office.

(c) Notwithstanding the restrictions in paragraphs (a) and (b), a **judicial appointee** may make public statements in the course of official duties, may explain court procedures, and may comment on any proceeding in which the **judicial appointee** is a litigant in a non-official capacity.

[1] This Rule's restrictions are essential to the maintenance of the **independence**, integrity, and **impartiality** of the judiciary.

[2] This Rule does not prohibit a **judicial appointee** from commenting on proceedings in which the **judicial appointee** is a litigant in a personal capacity. In cases in which the **judicial appointee** is a litigant in an official capacity, such as a writ of mandamus, the **judicial appointee** must not comment publicly.

[3] "Court personnel," as used in paragraph (a) of this Rule does not include the lawyers in a proceeding before the **judicial appointee.** The comment of lawyers in this regard is governed by Rule 3.6 of the Maryland Lawyers' Rules of Professional Conduct.

Source. — This Rule is derived from Rule 2.10 of the MCJC.

Rule 2.11. DISQUALIFICATION

(a) A **judicial appointee** shall disqualify himself or herself in any proceeding in which the **judicial appointee's impartiality** might reasonably be questioned, including the following circumstances:

(1) The **judicial appointee** has a personal bias or prejudice concerning a party or a party's lawyer, or personal **knowledge** of facts that are in dispute in the proceeding.

(2) The **judicial appointee knows** that the **judicial appointee,** the **judicial appointee's** spouse or **domestic partner,** or a person within the third degree of relationship to either of them, or the spouse or **domestic partner** of such a person:

(A) is a party to the proceeding, or an officer, director, general partner, managing member, or trustee of a party;

(B) is acting as a lawyer in the proceeding;

(C) is a person who has more than a de minimis interest that could be substantially affected by the proceeding; or

(D) is likely to be a material witness in the proceeding.

(3) The **judicial appointee knows** that he or she, individually or as a **fiduciary,** or any of the following persons has a **significant financial interest** in the subject matter in controversy or in a party to the proceeding:

(A) the **judicial appointee's** spouse **or domestic partner;**

(B) a person within the third degree of relationship to the **judicial appointee;** or

(C) any other **member of the judicial appointee's family** residing in the **judicial appointee's** household.

(4) The **judicial appointee,** while a **judicial appointee** or as an applicant for the position, has made a public statement, other than in a court proceeding, decision, or opinion, that commits or appears to commit the **judicial appointee** to reach a particular result or rule in a particular way in the proceeding or controversy.

(5) The **judicial appointee:**

(A) served as a lawyer in the matter in controversy, or was associated with a lawyer who participated substantially as a lawyer in the matter during such association; or

(B) served in governmental employment, and in such capacity participated personally and substantially as a lawyer or public official concerning the proceeding, or has publicly expressed in such capacity an opinion concerning the merits of the particular matter in controversy.

(6) If the **judicial appointee** is part-time, the **judicial appointee** or any attorney with whom the **judicial appointee** is associated represents a party or otherwise has an interest in the proceeding.

(b) A **judicial appointee** shall keep informed about the **judicial appointee's** personal and **fiduciary** economic interests and make a reasonable effort to keep informed about the personal economic interests of the **judicial appointee's** spouse and minor children residing in the **judicial appointee's** household.

(c) A **judicial appointee** subject to disqualification under this Rule, other than for bias or prejudice under paragraph (a) (1), may disclose on the record the basis of the **judicial appointee's** disqualification and may ask the parties and their lawyers to consider, outside the presence of the **judicial appointee** and court personnel, whether to waive disqualification. If, following the disclosure, the parties and lawyers agree, without participation by the **judicial appointee** or court personnel, that the **judicial appointee** should not be disqualified, the **judicial appointee** may participate in the proceeding. The agreement shall be incorporated into the record of the proceeding.

COMMENT

[1] Under this Rule, a **judicial appointee** is disqualified whenever the **judicial appointee's impartiality** might reasonably be questioned, regardless of whether any of the specific provisions of paragraphs (a) (1) through (5) apply. In this Rule, "disqualification" has the same meaning as "recusal."

[2] A **judicial appointee's** obligation not to hear or decide matters in which disqualification is required applies regardless of whether a motion to disqualify is filed.

[3] A **judicial appointee** should disclose on the record information that the **judicial appointee** believes the parties or their lawyers might reasonably consider relevant to a possible motion for disqualification, even if the **judicial appointee** believes there is no basis for disqualification.

[4] This procedure gives the parties an opportunity to waive the recusal if the **judicial appointee** agrees. The **judicial appointee** may comment on possible waiver but must ensure that consideration of the question of waiver is made independently of the **judicial appointee.** A party may act through counsel if counsel represents on the record that the party has been consulted and consents. As a practical matter, a **judicial appointee** may request that all parties and their lawyers sign a waiver agreement.

Source. — This Rule is derived from Rule 2.11 of the MCJC, except that Comment [3] was deleted. Paragraph (a) (6) is derived from Canon 3D (1) (b) (ii) of the former Code of Conduct for Judicial Appointees.

Rule 2.12. SUPERVISORY DUTIES

(a) A **judicial appointee** shall require court staff, court officials, and others subject to the **judicial appointee's** direction and control to act in a manner consistent with the **judicial appointee's** obligations under this Code.

(b) A **judicial appointee** with supervisory authority for the performance of other **judicial appointees** shall take reasonable measures to ensure that those **judicial appointees** properly discharge their **official** responsibilities, including the prompt disposition of matters before them.

COMMENT

[1] A **judicial appointee** is responsible for his or her own conduct and for the conduct of others, such as staff, when those persons are acting at the **judicial appointee's** direction

or control. A **judicial appointee** may not direct court personnel to engage in conduct on the **judicial appointee's** behalf or as the **judicial appointee's** representative when such conduct would violate this Code if undertaken by the **judicial appointee.**

[2] Public confidence in the judicial system depends upon timely justice. To promote the efficient administration of justice, a **judicial appointee** with supervisory authority must take the steps needed to ensure that **judicial appointees** under his or her supervision administer their workloads promptly.

Source. — This Rule is derived from Rule 2.12 (a) of the MCJC.

Rule 2.13. ADMINISTRATIVE APPOINTMENTS

(a) In making **official** administrative appointments, a **judicial appointee:**

(1) shall exercise the power of appointment impartially and on the basis of merit; and

(2) shall avoid nepotism, favoritism, **personal benefit,** and unnecessary appointments.

(b) A **judicial appointee** shall not approve compensation of appointees beyond the fair value of services rendered.

COMMENT

[1] Consent by the parties to an appointment or an award of compensation does not relieve the **judicial appointee** of the obligation prescribed by paragraph (a).

[2] Unless otherwise defined by law, nepotism is the appointment or hiring of any relative within the third degree of relationship to either the **judicial appointee** or the **judicial appointee's** spouse or **domestic partner,** or the spouse or **domestic partner** of such relative.

[3] Rule 2.13 does not apply to the appointment or compensation of an employee in the private office of a part-time **judicial appointee.**

Source. — This Rule is derived from Rule 2.13 of the MCJC, except that the first sentence of Comment [1] was deleted.

Rule 2.14. DISABILITY AND IMPAIRMENT OF OTHERS

A **judicial appointee** having a reasonable belief that the performance of a lawyer, a judge, or another **judicial appointee** is impaired by drugs or alcohol or by a mental, emotional, or physical condition, shall take appropriate action, which may include a confidential referral to a lawyer or judicial assistance program.

COMMENT

[1] "Appropriate action" means action intended and reasonably likely to help the judge, **judicial appointee,** or lawyer in question to address the problem and prevent harm to the justice system. Depending upon the circumstances, appropriate action may include speaking directly to the impaired person, notifying an individual with supervisory responsibility over the impaired person, or making a referral to an assistance program.

[2] Taking or initiating corrective action by way of referral to an assistance program may satisfy a **judicial appointee's** responsibility under this Rule. Assistance programs have many approaches for offering help to impaired judges and lawyers, such as intervention, counseling, or referral to appropriate health care professionals. Depending upon the gravity of the conduct that has come to the **judicial appointee's** attention, however, the **judicial appointee** may be required to take other action, such as reporting the impaired judge, **judicial appointee,** or lawyer to the appropriate authority, agency, or body. *See* Rule 2.15.

Source. — This Rule is derived from Rule 2.14 of the MCJC.

582

Rule 2.15. RESPONDING TO JUDICIAL AND LAWYER MISCONDUCT

(a) A **judicial appointee** shall take or initiate appropriate corrective measures with respect to the unprofessional conduct of a judge, another **judicial appointee,** or a lawyer.

(b) If other corrective measures are not appropriate or, if attempted, were not successful, a **judicial appointee:**

(1) shall inform the Commission on Judicial Disabilities of facts known to the **judicial appointee** that raise a substantial question as to a judge's fitness for office;

(2) shall inform the Attorney Grievance Commission of facts **known** to the **judicial appointee** that raise a substantial question as to a lawyer's honesty, trustworthiness, or fitness as a lawyer in other respects; and

(3) shall inform the appointing authority of facts **known** to the **judicial appointee** that raise a substantial question as to another **judicial appointee's** fitness for the position.

(c) Acts of a **judicial appointee** required or permitted by paragraphs (a) or (b) of this Rule shall be absolutely privileged.

COMMENT

[1] Permitting a **judicial appointee** to take "corrective" measures gives the **judicial appointee** a wide range of options to deal with unprofessional conduct. Appropriate corrective measures may include direct communication with the judge, lawyer, or other **judicial appointee** who is believed to have committed the violation or other direct action if available. There may be instances of professional misconduct that would warrant a private admonition or referral to a bar association counseling service.

Source. — This Rule is derived from Rule 2.15 of the MCJC, except that paragraph (b) (3) is new.

Rule 2.16. COOPERATION WITH DISCIPLINARY AUTHORITIES

(a) A **judicial appointee** shall cooperate and be candid and honest with judicial and lawyer disciplinary agencies.

(b) A **judicial appointee** shall not retaliate, directly or indirectly, against a person **known** or suspected to have assisted or cooperated with an investigation of a judge, another **judicial appointee,** or a lawyer.

COMMENT

[1] Cooperation with investigations and proceedings of judicial and lawyer discipline agencies, as required in paragraph (a) of this Rule, instills confidence in **judicial appointees'** commitment to the integrity of the judicial system and the protection of the public.

Source. — This Rule is derived from Rule 2.16 of the MCJC.

SECTION 3.

RULES GOVERNING EXTRA-OFFICIAL ACTIVITY

Rule 3.1. EXTRA-OFFICIAL ACTIVITIES IN GENERAL

A **judicial appointee** may engage in extra-official activities, except as prohibited by law or this Code. When engaging in extra-official activities, a **judicial appointee** shall not:

(a) participate in activities that will interfere with the proper performance of the **judicial appointee's** official duties;

(b) participate in activities that will lead to frequent disqualification of the **judicial appointee;**

(c) participate in activities that would appear to a reasonable person to undermine the **judicial appointee's independence,** integrity, or **impartiality;**

(d) engage in conduct that would appear to a reasonable person to be coercive; or

(e) make inappropriate use of court premises, staff, stationery, equipment, or other resources.

COMMENT

[1] To the extent that time permits, and **independence** and **impartiality** are not compromised, **judicial appointees** are encouraged to engage in appropriate extra-official activities. **Judicial appointees** are uniquely qualified to engage in extra-official activities that concern the law, the legal system, and the administration of justice, such as by speaking, writing, teaching, or participating in scholarly research projects. In addition, **judicial appointees** are permitted and encouraged to engage in educational, religious, charitable, fraternal, or civic extra-official activities not conducted for profit, even when the activities do not involve the law. *See* Rule 3.7.

[2] Participation in both law-related and other extra-official activities helps integrate **judicial appointees** into their communities and furthers public understanding of and respect for courts and the judicial system.

[3] Discriminatory actions and expressions of bias or prejudice by a **judicial appointee,** even outside the **judicial appointee's** official actions, are likely to appear to a reasonable person to call into question the **judicial appointee's** integrity and **impartiality.** Examples include jokes or other remarks that demean individuals based upon their race, sex, gender, religion, national origin, ethnicity, disability, age, sexual orientation, or socioeconomic status. For the same reason, a **judicial appointee's** extra-official activities must not be conducted in connection or affiliation with an organization that practices invidious discrimination. *See* Rule 3.6.

[4] While engaged in permitted extra-official activities, **judicial appointees** must not coerce others or take action that would reasonably be perceived as coercive. For example, depending upon the circumstances, a **judicial appointee's** solicitation of contributions or memberships for an organization, even as permitted by Rule 3.7 (a), might create the risk that the person solicited would feel obligated to respond favorably, or would do so to curry favor with the **judicial appointee.**

Source. — This Rule is derived from Rule 3.1 of the MCJC.

Rule 3.2. APPEARANCES BEFORE GOVERNMENTAL BODIES AND CONSULTATION WITH GOVERNMENT OFFICIALS

A **judicial appointee** shall not appear voluntarily at a public hearing before, or otherwise consult with, an executive or a legislative body or official, except:

(a) in connection with matters concerning the law, the legal system, or the administration of justice;

(b) in connection with matters about which the **judicial appointee** acquired **knowledge** or expertise in the course of the **judicial appointee's** official duties;

(c) when the **judicial appointee** is acting self-represented in a matter involving the **judicial appointee's** legal or economic interests, or when the **judicial appointee** is acting in a **fiduciary** capacity; or

(d) as permitted by Rule 3.10.

[1] **Judicial appointees** possess special expertise in matters of law, the legal system, and the administration of justice, and may properly share that expertise with governmental bodies and executive or legislative branch officials.

[2] In appearing before governmental bodies or consulting with government officials, **judicial appointees** must be mindful that they remain subject to other provisions of this Code, such as Rule 1.3, prohibiting them from using the prestige of office to advance their own or others' interests, Rule 2.10, governing public comment on **pending and impending matters,** and Rule 3.1 (c), prohibiting **judicial appointees** from engaging in extra-official activities that would appear to a reason-

able person to undermine the **judicial appointee's** independence, integrity, or **impartiality.**

[3] In general, it would be an unnecessary and unfair burden to prohibit **judicial appointees** from appearing before governmental bodies or consulting with government officials on matters that are likely to affect them as private citizens, such as zoning proposals affecting their real property. In engaging in such activities, however, **judicial appointees** must not refer to their official positions, and must otherwise exercise caution to avoid using the prestige of their position.

Source. — This Rule is derived from Rule 3.2 of the MCJC.

Rule 3.3. TESTIFYING AS A CHARACTER WITNESS

A **judicial appointee** shall not testify as a character witness in a judicial, administrative, or other adjudicatory proceeding or otherwise vouch for the character of a person in a legal proceeding, except when duly summoned.

[1] A **judicial appointee** who, without being subpoenaed, testifies as a character witness abuses the prestige of the position to advance the interests of another. *See* Rule 1.3. Except in unusual circumstances where the demands of justice require, a **judicial ap-**

pointee should discourage a party from requiring the **judicial appointee** to testify as a character witness.

Source. — This Rule is derived from Rule 3.3 of the MCJC.

Rule 3.4. APPOINTMENT TO GOVERNMENTAL POSITIONS

A **judicial appointee** shall not accept appointment to: (a) a Judicial Nominating Commission or (b) any other governmental committee, board, commission, or position, unless it is one that concerns the law, the legal system, or the administration of justice.

[1] Rule 3.4 implicitly acknowledges the value of **judicial appointees** accepting appointments to entities that concern the law, the legal system, or the administration of justice. Even in such instances, however, a **judicial appointee** should assess the appropriateness of accepting an appointment, paying particular attention to the subject matter of the appointment and the availability and allocation of judicial resources, including the **judicial appointee's** time commitments, and giving due regard to the requirements of the **independence** and **impartiality** of the judiciary.

[2] A **judicial appointee** may not accept a governmental appointment that could interfere with the effectiveness and **independence**

of the judiciary, assume or discharge an executive or legislative power, or hold another "office" under the Constitution or laws of the United States or the State of Maryland. *See* Maryland Declaration of Rights, Articles 8, 33, and 35.

[3] A **judicial appointee** may represent his or her country, State, or locality on ceremonial occasions or in connection with historical, educational, or cultural activities. Such representation does not constitute acceptance of a government position.

Committee note. — Although the Judicial Ethics Committee has concluded that the Supremacy Clause of the U.S. Constitution may allow service in reserve components of the armed forces that otherwise might be precluded under this Code, such as service as a judge advocate or military judge, the Attorney General, rather than the Judicial Ethics Committee, traditionally has rendered opinions

with regard to issues of dual or incompatible offices.

Source. — This Rule is derived from Rule 3.4 of the MCJC.

Rule 3.5. USE OF NONPUBLIC INFORMATION

A **judicial appointee** shall not intentionally disclose or use nonpublic information acquired in an official capacity for any purpose unrelated to the **judicial appointee's** official duties. Nonpublic information means information that is not available to the public. It may include information that is (a) sealed or shielded pursuant to law or court order, (b) impounded, (c) communicated in camera, or (d) offered in grand jury proceedings, pre-sentencing reports, dependency cases, or psychiatric reports.

COMMENT

[1] In the course of performing official duties, a **judicial appointee** may acquire information of commercial or other value that is unavailable to the public. The **judicial appointee** must not reveal or use such information for personal gain or for any purpose unrelated to his or her official duties.

[2] This Rule is not intended, however, to affect a **judicial appointee's** ability to act on information as necessary to protect the health or safety of the **judicial appointee** or a member of a **judicial appointee's family,** court personnel, or other judicial officers.

Source. — This Rule is derived from Rule 3.5 of the MCJC.

Rule 3.6. AFFILIATION WITH DISCRIMINATORY ORGANIZATIONS

(a) A **judicial appointee** shall not hold membership in any organization that practices invidious discrimination on the basis of race, sex, gender, religion, national origin, ethnicity, or sexual orientation.

(b) A **judicial appointee** shall not use the benefits or facilities of an organization if the **judicial appointee knows** or should **know** that the organization practices invidious discrimination on one or more of the bases identified in paragraph (a). A **judicial appointee's** attendance at an event in a facility of an organization that the **judicial appointee** is not permitted to join is not a violation of this Rule when the **judicial appointee's** attendance is an isolated event that could not reasonably be perceived as an endorsement of the organization's practices.

COMMENT

[1] A **judicial appointee's** public manifestation of approval of invidious discrimination on any basis gives rise to the appearance of impropriety and diminishes public confidence in the integrity and **impartiality** of the judiciary. A **judicial appointee's** membership in an organization that practices invidious discrimination creates the perception that the **judicial appointee's impartiality** is impaired.

[2] An organization is generally said to discriminate invidiously if it arbitrarily excludes from membership on the basis of race, sex, gender, religion, national origin, ethnicity, or sexual orientation persons who would other-

wise be eligible for admission. Whether an organization practices invidious discrimination is a complex question to which **judicial appointees** should be attentive. The answer cannot be determined from a mere examination of an organization's current membership rolls, but rather, depends upon how the organization selects members, as well as other relevant factors, such as whether the organization is dedicated to the preservation of religious, ethnic, or cultural values of legitimate common interest to its members, or whether it is an intimate, purely private organization whose membership limitations could not constitutionally be prohibited.

[3] When a **judicial appointee** learns that an organization to which the **judicial appointee** belongs engages in invidious discrimination, the **judicial appointee** must resign immediately from the organization.

[4] A **judicial appointee's** membership in a religious organization as a lawful exercise of the freedom of religion is not a violation of this Rule.

[5] This Rule does not apply to national or state military service.

Source. — This Rule is derived from Rule 3.6 of the MCJC.

Rule 3.7. PARTICIPATION IN EDUCATIONAL, RELIGIOUS, CHARITABLE, FRATERNAL, OR CIVIC ORGANIZATIONS AND ACTIVITIES

(a) Subject to the requirements of Rules 3.1 and 3.6, a **judicial appointee** may participate in activities sponsored by organizations or governmental entities concerned with the law, the legal system, or the administration of justice, and those sponsored by or on behalf of educational, religious, charitable, fraternal, or civic organizations not conducted for profit, including the following activities:

(1) assisting such an organization or entity in planning related to fundraising, and participating in the management and investment of the organization's or entity's funds;

(2) soliciting contributions for such an organization or entity, but only from **members of the judicial appointee's family,** judges, or other **judicial appointees** over whom the **judicial appointee** does not exercise supervisory authority;

(3) soliciting membership for such an organization or entity, even though the membership dues or fees generated may be used to support the objectives of the organization or entity, but only if the organization or entity is concerned with the law, the legal system, or the administration of justice;

(4) appearing or speaking at, receiving an award or other recognition at, being featured on the program of, and permitting his or her title to be used in connection with an event of such an organization or entity, but if the event serves a fund-raising purpose, the **judicial appointee** may participate only if the event concerns the law, the legal system, or the administration of justice;

(5) making recommendations to such a public or private fund-granting organization or entity in connection with its programs and activities, but only if the organization or entity is concerned with the law, the legal system, or the administration of justice; and

(6) serving as an officer, director, trustee, or nonlegal advisor of such an organization or entity, unless it is likely that the organization or entity:

(A) will be engaged in proceedings that would ordinarily come before the **judicial appointee;** or

(B) will frequently be engaged in adversary proceedings in the appointing court.

(b) A **judicial appointee** may encourage but not coerce lawyers to provide pro bono publico legal services.

COMMENT

[1] The activities permitted by paragraph (a) generally include those sponsored by or undertaken on behalf of public or private not-for-profit educational institutions, and other not-for-profit organizations, including law-related, charitable, and other organizations.

[2] Even for law-related organizations, a **judicial appointee** should consider whether the membership and purposes of the organization or the nature of the **judicial appointee's** participation in or association with the organization would conflict with the **judicial appointee's** obligation to refrain from activities that reflect adversely upon a **judicial appointee's independence,** integrity, and **impartiality.**

[3] Mere attendance at an event, whether or not the event serves a fund-raising purpose, does not constitute a violation of paragraph (a)(4). It is also generally permissible for a **judicial appointee** to serve as an usher or a food server or preparer, or to perform similar functions, at fund-raising events sponsored by educational, religious, charitable, fraternal, or civic organizations. Such activities are not solicitation and do not present an element of coercion or abuse the prestige of the **judicial appointee's** position.

[4] Identification of a **judicial appointee's** position in educational, religious, charitable, fraternal, or civic organizations on letterhead used for fund-raising or membership solicitation does not violate this Rule. The letterhead may list the **judicial appointee's** title or position if comparable designations are used for other persons.

[5] A **judicial appointee** may promote access to justice by encouraging lawyers to participate in pro bono publico legal services, if in doing so the **judicial appointee** does not employ coercion, or abuse the prestige of the **judicial appointee's** position. Such encouragement may take many forms, including providing lists of available programs, training lawyers to do pro bono publico legal work, and participating in events recognizing lawyers who have done pro bono publico work.

Source. — This Rule is derived from Rule 3.7 of the MCJC.

Rule 3.8. APPOINTMENTS TO FIDUCIARY POSITIONS

(a) Except as provided in paragraph (b), a **judicial appointee** may hold a **fiduciary** position, such as executor, administrator, trustee, guardian, attorney in fact, or other personal representative.

(b) A **judicial appointee** shall not hold a **fiduciary** position if:

(1) doing so would interfere with the proper performance of the **judicial appointee's** official duties; or

(2) the **fiduciary** will likely be engaged in proceedings that would ordinarily come before the **judicial appointee,** or if the estate, trust, or ward becomes involved in adversary proceedings in the appointing court.

(c) A **judicial appointee** acting in a **fiduciary** capacity shall be subject to the same restrictions on engaging in financial activities that apply to a **judicial appointee** personally.

(d) If a person who is serving in a **fiduciary** position becomes a **judicial appointee,** he or she must comply with this Rule as soon as reasonably practicable, but in no event later than one year after becoming a **judicial appointee.**

COMMENT

[1] A **judicial appointee** should recognize that other restrictions imposed by this Code may conflict with the **judicial appointee's** obligations as a **fiduciary;** in such circumstances, a **judicial appointee** should resign as **fiduciary.** For example, serving as a **fiduciary** might require frequent disqualification of a **judicial appointee** under Rule 2.11 because a **judicial appointee** is deemed to have an economic interest in shares of stock held by a trust if the amount of stock held is more than de minimis.

Source. — This Rule is derived in part from Rule 3.8 of the MCJC but permits **judicial appointees** to serve as a **fiduciary** in situations in which a judge is not permitted to serve.

Rule 3.9. SERVICE AS ARBITRATOR OR MEDIATOR

(a) A full-time **judicial appointee** shall not act as an arbitrator or a mediator or perform other alternative dispute resolution functions apart from the **judicial appointee's** official duties unless expressly authorized by law.

(b) A part-time **judicial appointee** may conduct alternative dispute resolution (ADR) proceedings in a private capacity only if the **judicial appointee:**

(1) conducts no ADR proceedings in a private capacity relating to a matter currently assigned to the **judicial appointee;**

(2) discloses to the parties in each matter assigned to the **judicial appointee:**

(A) the **judicial appointee's** professional association with any entity that is engaged in offering ADR services;

(B) whether the **judicial appointee** is conducting, or has conducted within the previous 12 months, an ADR proceeding involving any party, attorney, or law firm involved in the matter assigned to the **judicial appointee;** and

(C) any negotiations or agreements for future ADR services involving the **judicial appointee** and any of the parties or counsel to the case; and

(3) except if there is no disqualification by agreement as permitted by Rule 2.11 (c), does not participate in a matter in which the **judicial appointee's impartiality** might reasonably be questioned because of ADR services engaged in or offered by the **judicial appointee.**

COMMENT

[1] This Rule does not prohibit a part-time **judicial appointee** from participating in arbitration, mediation, or other alternative dispute resolution services in a private capacity. *See,* however, Rule 3.1.

[2] Masters may conduct settlement conferences pursuant to Rules 17-102 (h) and 17-105 (b) as part of assigned official duties. Full-time **judicial appointees** shall not otherwise render dispute resolution services, whether or not for economic gain, unless expressly authorized by law.

Source. — This Rule is derived in part from Canon 4F of the former Code of Conduct for Judicial Appointees.

Rule 3.10. PRACTICE OF LAW

(a) **In General.** Except as expressly allowed by this Rule, a **judicial appointee** shall not practice law.

(b) **Exceptions.** (1) A **judicial appointee** may act self-represented in a matter involving the **judicial appointee** or the **judicial appointee's** interest and, if without compensation, may give legal advice to and draft or review documents for a **member of the judicial appointee's family.**

(2) To the extent **not** expressly prohibited by law or by the appointing authority and subject to other applicable provisions of this Code, a part-time **judicial appointee** who is a lawyer may practice law, provided that:

(A) the **judicial appointee** shall not use his or her position to further the **judicial appointee's** success in the practice of law; and

(B) the **judicial appointee** shall not practice or appear as an individual in a matter involving the **judicial appointee** or the **judicial appointee's** interest in the appointing court.

(c) Prior to assuming official duties, a full-time **judicial appointee** shall enter into an agreement for payments relating to the **judicial appointee's** former law practice. A payment period limited to a maximum of five years is presumptively reasonable.

COMMENT

[1] A **judicial appointee** may act self-represented in all legal matters, including matters involving litigation and matters involving appearances before or other dealings with governmental bodies. A **judicial appointee** must not use the prestige of office to advance the **judicial appointee's** personal or family interests. *See* Rule 1.3.

Source. — This Rule is derived from Canon 4G of the former Maryland Code of Conduct for Judicial Appointees.

Rule 3.11. FINANCIAL, BUSINESS, OR REMUNERATIVE ACTIVITIES

(a) A **judicial appointee** may hold and manage investments of the **judicial appointee** and **members of the judicial appointee's family.**

(b)(1) Except as permitted by Rule 3.7, a **judicial appointee** shall not serve as an officer, director, manager, general partner, advisor, or employee of any business entity except that a **judicial appointee** may manage or participate in:

(A) a business closely held by the **judicial appointee** or **members of the judicial appointee's family;** or

(B) a business entity primarily engaged in investment of the financial resources of the **judicial appointee** or **members of the judicial appointee's family.**

(2) This section does not apply to a part-time **judicial appointee.**

(c) A **judicial appointee** shall not engage in financial activities permitted under paragraphs (a) or (b) if they will:

(1) interfere with the proper performance of the **judicial appointee's** official duties;

(2) lead to frequent disqualification of the **judicial appointee;**

(3) involve the **judicial appointee** in frequent transactions or continuing business relationships with lawyers or other persons likely to come before the appointing court; or

(4) result in violation of other provisions of this Code.

COMMENT

[1] **Judicial appointees** are generally permitted to engage in financial activities, including managing real estate and other investments for themselves or for members of their families. Participation in these activities, like participation in other extra-official activities, is subject to the requirements of this Code. For example, it would be improper for a **judicial appointee** to spend so much time on business activities that it interferes with the performance of the **judicial appointee's** official duties. *See* Rule 2.1. Similarly, it would be improper for a **judicial appointee** to use his or her official title or conduct his or her business or financial affairs in such a way that disqualification is frequently required. *See* Rules 1.3 and 2.11.

[2] As soon as practicable without serious financial detriment, the **judicial appointee** must divest himself or herself of investments and other financial interests that might require frequent disqualification or otherwise violate this Rule.

Source. — This Rule is derived from Rule 3.11 of the MCJC.

Rule 3.12. COMPENSATION FOR EXTRA-OFFICIAL ACTIVITIES

A **judicial appointee** may accept reasonable compensation for extra-official activities permitted by this Code or other law unless such acceptance would appear to a reasonable person to undermine the **judicial appointee's independence,** integrity, or **impartiality.**

COMMENT

[1] A **judicial appointee** is permitted to accept honoraria, stipends, fees, wages, salaries, royalties, or other compensation for speaking, teaching, writing, and other extrajudicial activities, provided the compensation is reasonable and commensurate with the task performed. The **judicial appointee** should be mindful, however, that official duties must take precedence over other activities.

[2] Compensation derived from extra-official activities may be subject to public reporting. *See* Rule 3.15.

Source. — This Rule is derived from Rule 3.12 of the MCJC.

Rule 3.13. ACCEPTANCE OF GIFTS, LOANS, BEQUESTS, BENEFITS, OR OTHER THINGS OF VALUE

(a) A **judicial appointee** shall not accept any **gifts,** loans, bequests, benefits, or other things of value, if acceptance is prohibited by law or would appear to a reasonable person to undermine the **judicial appointee's independence,** integrity, or **impartiality.**

(b) Unless otherwise prohibited by law, or by paragraph (a), a **judicial appointee** may accept the following:

(1) items with little intrinsic value, such as plaques, certificates, trophies, and greeting cards;

(2) **gifts,** loans, bequests, benefits, or other things of value from friends, relatives, or other persons, including lawyers, whose appearance or interest in a proceeding **pending or impending** before the **judicial appointee** would in any event require disqualification of the **judicial appointee** under Rule 2.11;

(3) ordinary social hospitality;

(4) commercial or financial opportunities and benefits, including special pricing and discounts, and loans from lending institutions in their regular course of business, if the same opportunities and benefits or loans are made available on the same terms to similarly situated persons who are not **judicial appointees;**

(5) rewards and prizes given to competitors or participants in random drawings, contests, or other events that are open to persons who are not **judicial appointees;**

(6) scholarships, fellowships, and similar benefits or awards, if they are available to similarly situated persons who are not **judicial appointees,** based upon the same terms and criteria;

(7) books, magazines, journals, audiovisual materials, and other resource materials supplied by publishers on a complimentary basis for official use; or

(8) **gifts,** awards, or benefits associated with the business, profession, or other separate activity of a spouse, a **domestic partner,** or other family member of a **judicial appointee** residing in the **judicial appointee's** household, but that incidentally benefit the **judicial appointee.**

(9) **gifts** incident to a public testimonial;

591

(10) invitations to the **judicial appointee** and the **judicial appointee's** spouse, **domestic partner,** or guest to attend without charge:

(A) an event associated with a bar-related function or other activity relating to the law, the legal system, or the administration of justice; or

(B) an event associated with any of the **judicial appointee's** educational, religious, charitable, fraternal or civic activities permitted by this Code, if the same invitation is offered to persons who are not **judicial appointees** who are engaged in similar ways in the activity as is the **judicial appointee.**

COMMENT

[1] Whenever a **judicial appointee** accepts a **gift** or other thing of value without paying fair market value, there is a risk that the benefit might be viewed as intended to influence the **judicial appointee's** decision in a case. Rule 3.13 imposes restrictions upon the acceptance of such benefits, according to the magnitude of the risk. Paragraph (b) identifies circumstances in which the risk that the acceptance would appear to undermine the **judicial appointee's independence,** integrity, or **impartiality** is low. As the value of the benefit or the likelihood that the source of the benefit will appear before the **judicial appointee** increases, the **judicial appointee** is prohibited under paragraph (a) from accepting the **gift.**

[2] **Gift** - giving between friends and relatives is a common occurrence, and ordinarily does not create an appearance of impropriety or cause reasonable persons to believe that the **judicial appointee's independence,** integrity, or **impartiality** has been compromised. In addition, when the appearance of friends or relatives in a case would require the **judicial appointee's** disqualification under Rule 2.11, there would be no opportunity for a **gift** to influence the **judicial appointee's** decision-making. Paragraph (b) (2) places no restrictions upon the ability of a **judicial appointee** to accept **gifts** or other things of value from friends or relatives under these circumstances.

[3] Businesses and financial institutions frequently make available special pricing, discounts, and other benefits, either in connection with a temporary promotion or for preferred customers, based upon longevity of the relationship, volume of business transacted, and other factors. A **judicial appointee** may freely accept such benefits if they are available to the general public, or if the **judicial appointee** qualifies for the special price or discount according to the same criteria as are applied to persons who are not **judicial appointees.** As an example, loans provided at generally prevailing interest rates are not **gifts,** but a **judicial appointee** could not accept a loan from a financial institution at below-market interest rates unless the same rate was being made available to the general public for a certain period of time or only to borrowers with specified qualifications that the **judicial appointee** also possesses.

[4] Rule 3.13 applies only to acceptance of **gifts** or other things of value by a **judicial appointee.** Nonetheless, if a **gift** or other benefit is given to the **judicial appointee's** spouse, **domestic partner,** or **member of the judicial appointee's family** residing in the **judicial appointee's** household, it may be viewed as an attempt to evade Rule 3.13 and influence the **judicial appointee** indirectly. Where the **gift** or benefit is being made primarily to such other persons, and the **judicial appointee** is merely an incidental beneficiary, this concern is reduced. A **judicial appointee** should, however, remind **family and household members** of the restrictions imposed upon **judicial appointees** and urge them to take these restrictions into account when making decisions about accepting such **gifts** or benefits.

[5] Rule 3.13 does not apply to contributions to a **judicial appointee's** campaign for judicial office.

Source. — This Rule is derived from Rule 3.13 of the MCJC.

Rule 3.14. REIMBURSEMENT OF EXPENSES AND WAIVERS OF FEES OR CHARGES

(a) Unless otherwise prohibited by Rule 3.1, Rule 3.13 (a), or other law, a **judicial appointee** may accept reimbursement of necessary and reasonable expenses for travel, food, lodging, or other incidental expenses, or a waiver or partial waiver of fees or charges for registration, tuition, and similar items, from sources other than the **judicial appointee's** employing entity, if the expenses or charges are associated with the **judicial appointee's** participation in extra-official activities permitted by this Code.

(b) Reimbursement of expenses for necessary travel, food, lodging, or other incidental expenses shall be limited to the actual costs reasonably incurred by the **judicial appointee** and, when appropriate to the occasion, by the **judicial appointee's** spouse, **domestic partner,** or guest.

COMMENT

[1] Educational, civic, religious, fraternal, and charitable organizations often sponsor meetings, seminars, symposia, dinners, awards ceremonies, and similar events. **Judicial appointees** are encouraged to attend educational programs, as both teachers and participants, in law-related and academic disciplines, in furtherance of their duty to remain competent in the law. Participation in a variety of other extra-official activities is also permitted and encouraged by this Code.

[2] Not infrequently, sponsoring organizations invite certain **judicial appointees** to attend seminars or other events on a fee-waived or partial-fee-waived basis, and sometimes include reimbursement for necessary travel, food, lodging, or other incidental expenses. A **judicial appointee's** decision whether to accept reimbursement of expenses or a waiver or partial waiver of fees or charges in connection with these or other extra-official activities must be based upon an assessment of all the circumstances. The **judicial appointee** must undertake a reasonable inquiry to obtain the information necessary to make an informed judgment about whether acceptance would be consistent with the requirements of this Code.

[3] A **judicial appointee** must assure himself or herself that acceptance of reimbursement or fee waivers would not appear to a reasonable person to undermine the **judicial appointee's independence,** integrity, or **impartiality.** The factors that a **judicial appointee** should consider when deciding whether to accept reimbursement or a fee waiver for attendance at a particular activity include:

(a) whether the sponsor is an accredited educational institution or bar association rather than a trade association or a for-profit entity;

(b) whether the funding comes largely from numerous contributors rather than from a single entity and is earmarked for programs with specific content;

(c) whether the content is related or unrelated to the subject matter of litigation **pending or impending** before the **judicial appointee,** or to matters that are likely to come before the **judicial appointee;**

(d) whether the activity is primarily educational rather than recreational, and whether the costs of the event are reasonable and comparable to those associated with similar events sponsored by the judiciary, bar associations, or similar groups;

(e) whether information concerning the activity and its funding sources is available upon inquiry;

(f) whether the sponsor or source of funding is generally associated with particular parties or interests currently appearing or likely to appear in the **judicial appointee's** court, thus possibly requiring disqualification of the **judicial appointee** under Rule 2.11;

(g) whether differing viewpoints are presented; and

(h) whether a broad range of judicial and nonjudicial participants are invited, whether a large number of participants are invited, and whether the program is designed specifically for judges or **judicial appointees.**

Source. — This Rule is derived from Rule 3.14 of the MCJC.

Rule 3.15. REPORTING REQUIREMENTS

A **judicial appointee** must accurately complete and timely file an annual Statement of Financial Interests on the form and as otherwise prescribed by the Court of Appeals pursuant to Md. Rule 16-816.

Source. — This Rule is derived from Rule 3.14 of the MCJC.

SECTION 4.

RULES GOVERNING POLITICAL ACTIVITY

Rule 4.1. DEFINITIONS

(a) **Applicant**

(1) **"Applicant"** means a **judicial appointee** who has applied for appointment by the Governor to a judicial office.

(2) **A judicial appointee** becomes an **applicant** when the **judicial appointee** files an application with a judicial nominating commission and remains an **applicant** until the Governor makes an appointment to that judicial office unless, prior to that time, the **judicial appointee** formally withdraws the application.

(3) If the **judicial appointee** is not appointed but, pursuant to an Executive Order of the Governor or other law, remains eligible for appointment to another judicial office without a further application to or recommendation from the judicial nominating commission, the **judicial appointee** remains an **applicant** until the Governor makes an appointment to that other judicial office, unless, prior to that time, the **judicial appointee** formally withdraws the application.

Cross references. — Executive Order 01.01.2008.04

(b) **Candidate for election**

(1) **"Candidate for election"** means a **judicial appointee** who seeks initial election to a Circuit Court or an Orphans' Court.

(2) A **judicial appointee** becomes a **candidate for election** on the date on which the **judicial appointee** files a certificate of candidacy in accordance with Maryland election laws, but no earlier than two years prior to the general election for that office.

(3) A **judicial appointee** who becomes a **candidate for election** under paragraph (c) remains a **candidate for election** until the general election for the office unless, prior to that time, the **judicial appointee** files a formal withdrawal of candidacy in accordance with Maryland election laws.

(c) **Political organization**

"Political organization" includes a political party, a political committee, and a partisan organization, as those terms are defined in Maryland Code, Election Article, § 1-101.

Source. — These definitions are derived from Rule 4.1 of the MCJC.

Rule 4.2. POLITICAL CONDUCT OF JUDICIAL APPOINTEE WHO IS NOT A CANDIDATE

(a) A **judicial appointee** who is not a **candidate for election** shall not engage in any partisan political activity.

(b) A **judicial appointee** shall resign when the **judicial appointee** becomes a candidate for a non-judicial office, except that a **judicial appointee** may continue to hold the appointed position while a **candidate for election** as a delegate to a Maryland Constitutional Convention.

Source. — Rule 4.2 is derived from Rule 4.2 of the MCJC.

Rule 4.3. POLITICAL CONDUCT OF APPLICANT

An **applicant** for judicial office may initiate communications or contact with a judicial nominating commission or its members and may seek endorsements for the appointment from any other person or organization, other than a **political organization.**

COMMENT

[1] An **applicant** may initiate communications or contact with a judicial nominating commission or its members, but neither the commission nor its members are obliged to respond to such communications or contact. **Applicants** may appear for interviews before the commission and may respond to questions or inquiries from commission members, and they may solicit endorsements from other per-sons or organizations (other than a **political organization**). If they have a question regarding the procedure or their application, they may contact the Administrative Office of the Courts.

Source. — This Rule is derived from Rule 4.3 of the MCJC.

Rule 4.4. POLITICAL CONDUCT OF CANDIDATE FOR ELECTION

A **candidate for election:**

(a) shall comply with all applicable election laws and regulations;

(b) shall act at all times in a manner consistent with the **independence,** integrity, and **impartiality** of the judiciary and maintain the dignity appropriate to judicial office;

(c) subject to the other provisions of this Rule, may engage in partisan political activity allowed by law with respect to such candidacy, and, in that regard:

(1) may publicly endorse or oppose candidates for the same judicial office;

(2) may attend or purchase tickets for dinners or other events sponsored by a **political organization** or a candidate for public office; and

(3) may seek, accept, and use endorsements from any person or organization; but

(4) shall not act as a leader in or hold office in a **political organization,** make a speech for a candidate or **political organization,** or publicly endorse a candidate for non-judicial office.

(d) As to statements and materials made or produced during a campaign:

(1) shall review, approve, and be responsible for the content of all campaign statements and materials produced by the **candidate** or by the **candidate's** campaign committee or other authorized agents;

(2) shall take reasonable measures to ensure that other persons do not undertake on behalf of the **candidate** activities that the **candidate** is prohibited from doing by this Rule;

(3) with respect to a case, controversy, or issue that is likely to come before the **judicial appointee,** shall not make a commitment, pledge, or promise

that is inconsistent with the **impartial** performance of the adjudicative duties of the office;

(4) shall not make any statement that would reasonably be expected to affect the outcome or impair the fairness of a matter **pending or impending** in any court;

(5) shall not **knowingly,** or with reckless disregard for the truth, misrepresent the **candidate's** identity or qualifications, the identity or qualifications of an opponent, or any other fact, or make any false or misleading statement;

(6) may speak or write on behalf of the **candidate's** candidacy through any medium, including advertisements, websites, or other campaign literature; and

(7) subject to paragraph (b) of this Rule, may respond to a personal attack or an attack on the **candidate's** record.

COMMENT

[1] This Rule is derived from Rule 4.4 of the MCJC.

[2] Rule 4.4 (a) requires **candidates for election** to comply with all election laws and regulations. The Election Law Article of the Maryland Code contains laws governing candidates, campaign contributions, finance, expenditures, and reporting. Those requirements are supplemented by regulations adopted by the State Board of Elections. **Candidates for election** must become familiar with applicable laws and regulations and comply with them.

[3] Public confidence in the **independence** and **impartiality** of the judiciary is eroded if **judicial appointees,** as **candidates** for judicial office, are perceived to be subject to political influence. Although they may register to vote as members of a political party, they are prohibited by Rule 4.4 (c) (4) from assuming leadership roles in **political organizations.**

[4] Rule 4.4 (c) (4) also prohibits **candidates for election** from making speeches on behalf of **political organizations** or publicly endorsing or opposing candidates for public office, to prevent them from abusing the prestige of judicial office to advance the interests of others. *See* Rule 1.3. Rule 4.4 does not prohibit **candidates for election** from (a) campaigning on their own behalf, (b) endorsing or opposing **candidates for election** to the same judicial office for which they are running, or (c) from having their name on the same sample ballot as a candidate for another public office.

[5] Although members of the families of **candidates for election** are free to engage in their own political activity, including running for public office, there is no "family exception" to the prohibition in Rule 4.4 (c) (4) against publicly endorsing candidates for public office. A **candidate for election** must not become involved in, or be publicly associated with, a family member's political activity or campaign for public office. To avoid public misunderstanding, **candidates for election** should take, and should urge members of their families to take, reasonable steps to avoid any implication that they endorse any family member's candidacy or other political activity.

[6] Judicial **candidates** must be scrupulously fair and accurate in all statements made by them and by their campaign committees. Rule 4.4 (d) (5) obligates them to refrain from making statements that are false or misleading, or that omit facts necessary to make the communication considered as a whole not materially misleading. Rule 4.4 (d) (1) requires the **candidate** to review and approve the content of statements made by the **candidate's** campaign committee or other authorized agents and makes the **candidate** responsible for those statements.

[7] **Candidates for election** are sometimes the subject of false, misleading, or unfair allegations made by opposing candidates, third parties, or the media. As long as the **candidate for election** does not violate Rule 4.4 (d), he or she may make a factually accurate public response, although it is preferable for someone else to respond if the allegations relate to a pending case. If an independent third party has made unwarranted attacks on a **candidate for election's** opponent, the **candidate for election** may disavow the attacks and request the third party to cease and desist.

[8] Rule 4.4 (d) (3) prohibits **candidates for election,** with regard to cases or issues likely to come before the court, from making a commitment, promise, or pledge that is inconsistent with the **impartial** performance of the duties of the office. The making of a commitment, promise, or pledge is not dependent on, or limited to, the use of any specific words or

phrases. The totality of the statement must be examined to determine if a reasonable person would believe that the candidate has specifically undertaken to reach a particular result. Commitments, promises, and pledges must be contrasted with statements or announcements of personal views on legal, political, or other issues, which are not prohibited. When mak-

ing such statements, a **candidate for election** should acknowledge the overarching judicial obligation to apply and uphold the law, without regard to his or her personal views.

Source. — This Rule is derived from Rule 4.4 of the MCJC.

Rule 4.5. APPLICABILITY AND DISCIPLINE

(a) A **judicial appointee** shall comply with the Rules in this Section 4 and with Rule 8.2 of the Maryland Lawyers' Rules of Professional Conduct (Maryland Rule 16-812). If successful as a **candidate for election,** the **judicial appointee** is subject to judicial discipline for campaign conduct. If unsuccessful, the **judicial appointee** is subject to attorney discipline for campaign conduct. (Added March 9, 2010, effective July 1, 2010.)

Source. — This Rule is derived from Rule 4.6 of the MCJC.

Rule 16-815. Financial disclosure statement.

a. For purposes of this Rule, former judge means a former judge approved for recall for temporary service under Maryland Constitution, Article IV, § 3A.

b. Each judge and each former judge shall file with the State Court Administrator an annual financial disclosure statement on the form prescribed by the Court of Appeals. When filed, a financial disclosure statement is a public record.

c. Except as provided in paragraph d of this Rule:

1. The initial financial disclosure statement shall be filed on or before April 15, 1987 and shall cover the period beginning on January 1, 1986 and ending on December 31, 1986.

2. A subsequent statement shall be filed annually on or before April 15 of each year and shall cover the preceding calendar year or that portion of the preceding calendar year during which the judge held office.

3. A financial disclosure statement is presumed to have been filed unless the State Court Administrator, on April 16, notifies a judge that the judge's statement for the preceding calendar year or portion thereof has not been received.

d. If a judge or other person who files a certificate of candidacy for nomination for an election to an elected judgeship has filed a statement pursuant to § 15-610 (b) of the State Government Article, Annotated Code of Maryland, the person need not file for the same period of time the statement required by paragraph c of this Rule.

e. The State Court Administrator is designated as the person to receive statements from the State Administrative Board of Election Laws pursuant to § 15-610 (b) of the State Government Article.

f. **Extension of time for filing.** 1. Except when the judge or former judge is required to file a statement pursuant to § 15-610 (b) of the State Government Article, Annotated Code of Maryland, a judge or former judge may apply to the State Court Administrator for an extension of time for filing the statement. The application shall be submitted prior to the deadline for filing the statement, and shall set forth in detail the reasons an extension is requested and the date upon which a completed statement will be filed.

2. For good cause shown, the State Court Administrator may grant a reasonable extension of time for filing the statement. Whether the State Court Administrator grants or denies the request, the State Court Administrator shall furnish the judge or former judge and the Judicial Ethics Committee with a written statement of the State Court Administrator's reasons for the decision and the facts upon which the decision is based.

3. A judge or former judge who is dissatisfied with the State Court Administrator's decision may seek review of the decision by the Judicial Ethics Committee by filing with the Committee a statement of reasons for the judge's or former judge's dissatisfaction within ten days from the date of the State Court Administrator's decision. The Committee may take the action it deems appropriate with or without a hearing or the consideration of additional documents.

g. **Failure to file statement — Incomplete statement.** 1. A judge or former judge who fails to file a timely statement, or who files an incomplete statement, shall be notified in writing by the State Court Administrator, and given a reasonable time, not to exceed ten days, within which to correct the deficiency. If the deficiency has not been corrected within the time allowed, the State Court Administrator shall report the matter to the on Judicial Ethics Committee.

2. If the Committee finds, after inquiry, that the failure to file or the omission of information was either inadvertent or in a good faith belief that the omitted information was not required to be disclosed, the Committee shall give the judge or former judge a reasonable period, not to exceed 15 days, within which to correct the deficiency. Otherwise, the Committee shall refer the matter to the Commission on Judicial Disabilities. If a judge or former judge who has been allowed additional time within which to correct a deficiency fails to do so within that time, the matter shall also be referred to the Commission on Judicial Disabilities.

h. This rule applies to each judge of a court named in Rule 16-813, Maryland Code of Judicial Conduct, A-109 (General Provisions) who has resigned or retired in any calendar year, with respect to the portion of that calendar year prior to the judge's resignation or retirement and to each former judge with respect to the previous calendar year. (Added Nov. 21, 1986, effective July 1, 1987; amended Nov. 21, 1995, effective Dec. 1, 1995; June 5, 1996, effective Jan. 1, 1997; Dec. 2, 2004, effective July 1, 2005; Dec. 4, 2007, effective Jan. 1, 2008; June 7, 2011, effective July 1, 2011.)

Source. — This Rule is derived from former Rule 1233.

Effect of amendments. — The 1996 amendment rewrote the Source note.

The 2004 amendment substituted "Judicial Ethics Committee" for "Committee on Judicial Ethics" in f.1.

The December 4, 2007 Order, effective January 1, 2008, added a and redesignated accordingly including internal cross references in c and d; added "or former judge" or variants throughout the Rule; in b added "and each former judge" and made related and other minor changes; in f 2 added "the State Court Administrator" or variants in two places and in f 2 and f 3 added "for the decision" and made other minor changes; in h added "and to each former judge with respect to the previous calendar year" and made minor changes; and in

the Source note added "derived from".

The 2011 amendment substituted "Rule 16-813, Maryland Code of Judicial Conduct, A-109 (General Provisions)" for "Canon 6A" in h.

Editor's note. — An Order dated June 5, 1996, effective Jan. 1, 1997, renumbered this Rule, which was formerly Rule 1233.

Canon 6 A, which is referred to in section g, is incorporated as part of Rule 16-813.

Rule 16-816. Financial disclosure statement — Judicial appointees.

a. For purposes of this Rule, judicial appointee means (1) a full- or part-time master, (2) a commissioner appointed by a District Administrative Judge with the approval of the Chief Judge of the District Court of Maryland, and (3) an auditor or examiner who is full-time or who earns in any calendar year, by reason of the judicial appointee's official position, compensation at least equal to the pay provided for the base step of State Pay Grade 16, as in effect on July 1 of that calendar year. If an auditor or examiner has served as such for only a portion of a calendar year, a pro rata determination of compensation shall be applied.

Cross references. — For the definition of judicial appointee for purposes of applying the Maryland Code of Conduct for Judicial Appoin- tees, see the Terminology section of Rule 16-814.

b. Every judicial appointee shall file with the State Court Administrator an annual financial statement on the form prescribed by the Court of Appeals. When filed, a financial disclosure statement is a public record.

c. Except as provided in paragraph d of this Rule:

(i) The initial financial disclosure statement shall be filed on or before April 15, 1989, and shall cover the period beginning on January 1, 1988, and ending on December 31, 1988.

(ii) A subsequent statement shall be filed annually on or before April 15 of each year, and shall cover the preceding calendar year or that portion of the preceding calendar year during which the judicial appointee held office.

(iii) A financial disclosure statement is presumed to have been filed unless the State Court Administrator, on April 16, notifies a judicial appointee that the judicial appointee's statement for the preceding calendar year or portion thereof has not been received.

d. If a judicial appointee who files a certificate of candidacy for nomination for an elected office has filed a statement pursuant to § 15-605 or § 15-610 (b) of the State Government Article, Annotated Code of Maryland, the judicial appointee need not file for the same period of time the statement required by paragraph c of this Rule.

e. The State Court Administrator is designated as the person to receive statements from the State Administrative Board of Election Laws pursuant to § 15-610 (b) of the State Government Article.

f.(i) Except when the judicial appointee is required to file a statement pursuant to § 15-605 or § 15-610 (b) of the State Government Article,

Annotated Code of Maryland, a judicial appointee may apply to the State Court Administrator for an extension of time for filing the judicial appointee's statement. The application shall be submitted prior to the deadline for filing the statement, and shall set forth in detail the reasons an extension is requested and the date upon which a completed statement will be filed.

(ii) For good cause shown, the State Court Administrator may grant a reasonable extension of time for filing the statement. Whether the request is denied or approved, the State Court Administrator shall furnish the judicial appointee and the Judicial Ethics Committee with a written statement of the State Court Administrator's reasons, and the facts upon which this decision is based.

(iii) A judicial appointee who is dissatisfied with the State Court Administrator's decision may seek review by the Judicial Ethics Committee by filing with the Committee a statement of reasons for the judicial appointee's dissatisfaction within ten days from the date of the State Court Administrator's decision. The Committee may take the action it deems appropriate with or without a hearing or the consideration of additional documents.

g.(i) A judicial appointee who fails to file a timely statement, or who files an incomplete statement, shall be notified in writing by the State Court Administrator, and given a reasonable time, not to exceed ten days, within which to correct the deficiency. If the deficiency has not been corrected within the time allowed, the State Court Administrator shall report the matter to the Judicial Ethics Committee.

(ii) If the Committee finds, after inquiry, that failing to file or the omission of information was either inadvertent or in good faith belief that the omitted information was not required to be disclosed, the Committee shall give the judicial appointee a reasonable period, not to exceed 15 days, within which to correct the deficiency. Otherwise, the Committee shall refer the matter to the State Ethics Commission. If a judicial appointee who has been allowed additional time within which to correct a deficiency fails to do so within that time, the matter shall also be referred to the State Ethics Commission.

h. Violation of this Rule is grounds for disciplinary action, including removal, by the appointing authority. (Added Oct. 14, 1988, effective Jan. 1, 1989; amended Nov. 21, 1995, effective Dec. 1, 1995; June 5, 1996, effective Jan. 1, 1997; Dec. 2, 2004, effective July 1, 2005; amended March 9, 2010, effective July 1, 2010.)

Source. — This Rule is derived from former Rule 1234 and is part new.

Effect of amendments. — The 1996 amendment substituted "Rule 16-814" for "Rule 1233" in the first sentence of a.; and added the Source note.

The 2004 amendment rewrote a.; added the cross references note after a.; added "judicial" before "appointee" in b.; substituted "a judi-cial" for "an" in d.; substituted "Judicial Ethics Committee" for "Committee on Judicial Ethics" in g.(i), added "judicial" before "appointee" and substituted "a judicial" for "an" in g.(ii); and rewrote the Source note.

The 2010 amendment in a in the first sentence deleted "full- or part-time" preceding "commissioner" and deleted "or referee" following "examiner" twice; and made stylistic changes.

Editor's note. — An Order dated June 5, 1996, effective Jan. 1, 1997, renumbered this Rule, which was formerly Rule 1234.

Rule 16-817. Appointment of bail bond commissioner — Licensing and regulation of bail bondsmen.

A majority of the judges of the circuit courts in any appellate judicial circuit may appoint a bail bond commissioner and license and regulate bail bondsmen and acceptance of bail bonds. Each bail bond commissioner appointed pursuant to this Rule shall prepare, maintain, and periodically distribute to all District Court commissioners and clerks within the jurisdiction of the appellate judicial circuit for posting in their respective offices, to the State Court Administrator, and to the Chief Clerk of the District Court, an alphabetical list of bail bondsmen licensed to write bail bonds within the appellate judicial circuit, showing the bail bondsman's name, business address and telephone number, and any limit on the amount of any one bond, and the aggregate limit on all bonds, each bail bondsman is authorized to write. (Added Jan. 1, 1977, effective July 1, 1977; amended June 5, 1996, effective Jan. 1, 1997; Mar. 5, 2001, effective July 1, 2001.)

Source. — This Rule is former Rule 1285.

Effect of amendments. — The 1996 amendment added the Source note.

The 2001 amendment, in the first sentence, inserted "the circuit courts" and "appellate," respectively; in the second sentence, inserted a comma following "maintain," substituted "the" for "his," inserted "of the appellate judicial circuit" following "jurisdiction," deleted "and" following "respective offices," inserted "and to the Chief Clerk of the District Court" following "Administrator," and inserted "appellate" preceding the second occurrence of "judicial circuit."

Editor's note. — An Order dated June 5, 1996, effective Jan. 1, 1997, renumbered this Rule, which was formerly Rule 1285.

Rule 16-818. Disposition of records.

a. **Definitions.** In this Rule, unless the context or subject matter otherwise requires:

1. Dispose. "Dispose" means to either destroy or remove records.

2. Records. "Records" mean any original papers, official books, documents, files, including but not limited to dockets, electronic recordings of testimony and exhibits within the custody of the clerk of the court.

Cross references. — See Code, §§ 9-1009 and 10-639 through 10-642 of the State Government Article.

3. Schedule. "Schedule" means the form known as the "Records Retention and Disposal Schedule" used by the Records Management Division of the Hall of Records Commission.

b. **Authority.** Subject to the provisions of this Rule, the clerk of the court, with the written approval of the County Administrative Judge and in cooperation with the Hall of Records Commission, may dispose of records within his custody.

Cross references. — See § 2-205 of the
Courts Article.

c. **Procedure.** 1. Schedule preparation — Hall of Records recommendation. The clerk of the court shall prepare a schedule for the disposition of court records and submit it to the Hall of Records Commission for its recommendation.

2. Administrative judge — Approval. The schedule, together with the recommendation of the Hall of Records Commission, shall be submitted for the written approval of the County Administrative Judge who may approve it in whole or in part, amend it or disapprove it.

3. Court order. Approval of the schedule by the County Administrative Judge shall be deemed an order of court providing for disposal of the records.

4. Contents of schedule. The schedule, as approved, shall set forth:

(i) The identification of the records.

(ii) The length of time the records are to be retained by the clerk of the court before disposition.

(iii) Whether the Hall of Records Commission declines to accept the records for preservation.

(iv) Whether the records are to be destroyed or removed.

(v) The place to which the records would be removed.

(vi) Whether the schedule shall be "standing" viz., operative until changed by further order of court.

5. Removal procedures — Hall of Records. In those cases where the Hall of Records Commission accepts records, they shall be removed according to the Hall of Records Commission procedures.

6. Disposal if Hall of Records declines custody. In those cases where the Hall of Records Commission declines records, disposition shall be according to the terms set forth in the schedule as approved. If the records are to be destroyed the clerk shall obtain the approval of the Board of Public Works and upon destruction shall file a certificate of destruction with the Hall of Records Commission.

Cross references. — See Code, § 10-642 of the State Government Article.

Committee note. — This Rule is meant to allow periodic destruction of records without the necessity of obtaining Board of Public Works approval each time if such destruction of records or classes of records had been clearly approved by the Board of Public Works in a standing schedule.

d. **Limitations upon disposal of records.** 1. Permanent retention — Clerks or Hall of Records. Records which shall be retained permanently either by the clerks or the Hall of Records Commission:

(i) Permanent books of account.

(ii) Indices and dockets maintained by the clerks.

(iii) Other records as designated on a schedule as approved.

2. Permanent retention — Clerks. Records which shall be retained permanently by the clerk:

(i) Records affecting title to real estate.

3. Records destruction after certain periods. Records which may be destroyed by the clerk after the following minimum periods of time:

(i) Motor vehicle and natural resources cases — three years after case is closed and audit performed, if required; except for convictions of offenses which carry subsequent offender penalties which cases shall be retained as permanent records.

(ii) Landlord/Tenant cases — three years in cases involving restitution of premises where there is no money judgment.

(iii) Other records — according to times designated on a schedule as approved — twelve years.

4. Disposal if photographed, photocopied, or microphotographed. Any of the records set forth in subsections 1, 2, and 3 of this section may be disposed of at any time provided that the records have been photographed, photocopied or microphotographed in accordance with the Hall of Records Commission procedures and copies have been substituted therefor. (Added June 16, 1975, effective July 1, 1975; amended Dec. 17, 1975, effective Jan. 1, 1976; May 6, 1977, effective July 1, 1977; June 5, 1996, effective Jan. 1, 1997.)

Source. — This Rule is former Rule 1299.

Effect of amendments. — The 1996 amendment added the Source note.

Editor's note. — An Order dated June 5, 1996, effective Jan. 1, 1997, renumbered this Rule, which was formerly Rule 1299.

Rule 16-819. Court interpreters.

(a) **Definitions.** The following definitions apply in this Rule:

(1) Certified interpreter. "Certified Interpreter" means an interpreter who is certified by:

(A) the Maryland Administrative Office of the Courts;

(B) a member of the Consortium for State Court Interpreter Certification; or

(C) the Federal Administrative Office of the Courts.

(2) Interpreter. "Interpreter" means an adult who has the ability to render a complete and accurate interpretation or sight translation, without altering, omitting, or adding anything to what is stated or written and without explanation.

(3) Interpreter eligible for certification. "Interpreter eligible for certification" means an interpreter who is not a certified interpreter but who:

(A) has submitted to the Administrative Office of the Courts a completed Maryland State Judiciary Information Form for Spoken and Sign Language Court Interpreters and a statement swearing or affirming compliance with the Maryland Code of Conduct for Court Interpreters;

(B) has attended the Maryland Judiciary's orientation workshop on court interpreting; and

(C) does not have, in a state or federal court of record, a pending criminal charge or conviction on a charge punishable by a fine of more than $500 or imprisonment for more than six months unless pardoned or expunged in accordance with law.

(4) Non-certified interpreters. "Non-certified interpreter" means an interpreter other than a certified interpreter or an interpreter eligible for certification.

(5) Person who needs an interpreter. "Person who needs an interpreter" means a party or a witness who is deaf or unable adequately to understand or express himself or herself in spoken or written English.

(b) **Application for the appointment of an interpreter.** A person who needs an interpreter may apply to the court for the appointment of an interpreter. As far as practicable, an application for the appointment of an interpreter shall be (1) presented on a form approved by administrative order of the Court of Appeals and available from the clerk of the court and (2) submitted not less than 30 days before the proceeding for which the interpreter is requested.

(c) **Procedures to determine the need for interpreters.** (1) Sign language interpreter. The court shall determine whether a sign language interpreter is needed in accordance with the requirements of the Americans with Disabilities Act, 42 U.S.C. § 12101, et seq.; Code, Courts Article, § 9-114; and Code, Criminal Procedure Article, §§ 1-202 and 3-103.

(2) Spoken language interpreter. (A) Examination of party or witness. To determine whether a spoken language interpreter is needed, the court, on request or on its own initiative, shall examine a party or witness on the record. The court shall appoint a spoken language interpreter if the court determines that:

(i) the party does not understand English well enough to participate fully in the proceedings and to assist counsel, or

(ii) the party or a witness does not speak English well enough to be understood by counsel, the court, and the jury.

(B) Scope of examination. The court's examination of the party or witness should include questions relating to:

(i) identification;

(ii) active vocabulary in vernacular English; and

(iii) the court proceedings.

Committee note. — Examples of matters relating to identification are: name, address, birth date, age, and place of birth. Examples of questions that elicit active vocabulary in vernacular English are: How did you come to court today? What kind of work do you do? Where did you go to school? What was the highest grade you completed? What do you see in the courtroom? Examples of questions relating to the proceedings are: What do you understand this case to be about? What is the purpose of what we are doing here in court? What can you tell me about the rights of the parties to a court case? What are the responsibilities of a court witness? Questions should be phrased to avoid "yes or no" replies.

(d) **Selection and appointment of interpreters.** (1) Certified interpreter required; exceptions. When the court determines that an interpreter is needed, the court shall make a diligent effort to obtain the services of a certified interpreter. If a certified interpreter is not available, the court shall make a diligent effort to obtain the services of an interpreter eligible for certification. The court may appoint a non-certified interpreter only if neither a certified interpreter nor an interpreter eligible for certification is available.

A person related by blood or marriage to a party or to the person who needs an interpreter may not act as an interpreter.

Committee note. — The court should be cautious about appointing a non-certified interpreter and should consider carefully the seriousness of the case and the availability of resources before doing so.

(2) Inquiry of prospective interpreter. Before appointing an interpreter under this Rule, the court shall conduct an appropriate inquiry of the prospective interpreter on the record.

Committee note. — The court should use the interpreter inquiry questions promulgated by the Maryland Judicial Conference Advisory Committee on Interpreters and published, together with suggested responses, in the October 20, 1998 Report of the Advisory Committee. The questions and suggested responses are reprinted as an Appendix to these Rules.

(3) Oath. Upon appointment by the court and before acting as an interpreter in the proceeding, the interpreter shall solemnly swear or affirm under the penalties of perjury to interpret accurately, completely, and impartially and to refrain from knowingly disclosing confidential or privileged information obtained while serving in the proceeding. If the interpreter is to serve in a grand jury proceeding, the interpreter also shall take and subscribe an oath that the interpreter will keep secret all matters and things occurring before the grand jury.

(4) Multiple interpreters in the same language. At the request of a party or on its own initiative, the court may appoint more than one interpreter in the same language to ensure the accuracy of the interpretation or to preserve confidentiality if:

(A) the proceedings are expected to exceed three hours;

(B) the proceedings include complex issues and terminology or other such challenges; or

(C) an opposing party requires an interpreter in the same language.

Committee note. — To ensure accurate interpretation, after interpreting for a period of forty-five minutes, an interpreter ordinarily should be granted a reasonable rest period.

(e) **Removal from proceeding.** A court interpreter may be removed from a proceeding by a judge or judicial appointee within the meaning of Rule 16-814 (e)(1), who shall then notify the Administrative Office of the Courts that the action was taken.

(f) **Compensation of court interpreters.** Compensation for interpreters shall be in accordance with Code, Criminal Procedure Article, §§ 1-202 and 3-103 and Code, Courts Article, § 9-114. (Added Oct. 31, 2002, effective Jan. 1, 2003; Amended April 5, 2005, effective July 1, 2005; May 8, 2007, effective July 1, 2007; amended Sept. 10, 2009, effective Oct. 1, 2009.)

Committee note. — Code, Courts Article, § 9-114 provides for the appointment of interpreters for certain parties and witnesses, generally. Code, Criminal Procedure Article, §§ 1-202 and 3-103 provide for the appointment of interpreters for certain defendants in criminal proceedings and proceedings under Title 3 of that Article.

Source. — This Rule is new.

Effect of amendments. — The 2005 amendment substituted "As far as...is requested" for "The application shall be made by providing the information required by Form 1-332 in the Appendix to these Rules" in (b).

The 2007 amendment added the second sentence in (d)(3); and rewrote (e).

The 2009 amendment substituted "30 days" for "five days" in the second sentence of (b)(2).

Quoted in Kang v. State, 393 Md. 97, 899 A.2d 843 (2006).

Rule 16-821. Performance of marriage ceremonies by judges — Applicability of rules.

Rules 16-821 through 16-824 apply to all Maryland judges of the District Court, a circuit court, the Court of Special Appeals, and the Court of Appeals, including retired judges approved for recall pursuant to Maryland Constitution, Article IV, § 3A and Code, Courts Article, § 1-302, who wish to perform marriage ceremonies. (Added Nov. 12, 2003, effective Jan. 1, 2004; amended April 5, 2005, effective July 1, 2005.)

Cross references. — Code, Family Law Article, § 2-406.

Source. — This Rule is new.

Effect of amendments. — The 2005 amendment added "approved for recall...§ 1-302" after "retired judges" in the undesignated paragraph.

Rule 16-822. Scheduling.

(a) **Clerk's responsibilities.** A judge who has agreed to perform a marriage ceremony shall notify the clerk of the circuit court for the county in which the ceremony is to take place. The clerk is responsible for recording and reporting the marriage. The parties are responsible for making all other arrangements.

Committee note. — Except for communications necessary to determine a judge's willingness and availability to perform the ceremony, a judge's staff should not be used to make arrangements for a marriage ceremony.

(b) **Non-interference with court functions.** Ceremonies shall be scheduled so as not to interfere with the prompt disposition of cases and other judicial and administrative duties of the judge, and the use of public resources shall be reasonable and consistent with the security of the courthouse.

(c) **Place of ceremony.** A judge may perform a marriage ceremony at a location other than in a Courthouse.

(d) **Time of ceremony.** A judge may perform a marriage ceremony at any time, including on a court holiday or after regular court hours. (Added Nov. 12, 2003, effective Jan. 1, 2004.)

Source. — This Rule is new.

Rule 16-823. Judicial action.

(a) **Ceremony.** A judge who performs a marriage ceremony shall include substantially the form of ceremony used by the clerk of the circuit court for the county where the marriage is to be performed. If the parties request, and the judge agrees, the ceremony may include reference to matters not typically found in the clerk's ceremony. A judge may participate in performing a marriage ceremony with another person authorized under Maryland law to perform marriage ceremonies.

(b) **License.** A judge may not perform a marriage ceremony unless a license has been issued by the clerk of the circuit court in the county where the ceremony is to be performed. A judge who performs a marriage ceremony shall (1) complete the certificate of marriage, (2) provide a copy of the certificate to the parties, and (3) return the completed certificate to the issuing clerk of court for recordation and reporting of the marriage as required by law. A judge who grants a request for the issuance of a marriage license under Code, Family Law Article, §2-405 (d) also may perform the marriage.

(c) **Refusal to perform ceremony.** A judge may decline to perform a marriage ceremony. (Added Nov. 12, 2003, effective Jan. 1, 2004.)

Source. — This Rule is new.

Rule 16-824. Restrictions.

(a) **Judge's own ceremony.** A judge may not perform his or her own marriage ceremony.

(b) **Compensation.** A judge may receive no compensation, remuneration, or gift for performing a marriage ceremony.

Committee note. — See Code, Family Law Article, § 2-410, as to the fees a clerk or deputy clerk shall collect for performing a marriage ceremony.

(c) **Advertising or other solicitations.** A judge may not give or offer to give any reward to any person as an inducement to have the judge perform a marriage ceremony. A judge may not advertise or otherwise solicit individuals contemplating marriage to choose the judge to perform the ceremony. (Added Nov. 12, 2003, effective Jan. 1, 2004; amended March 9, 2010, effective July 1, 2010.)

Source. — This Rule is new.

Effect of amendments. — The 2010 amendment substituted "shall collect" for "may collect" in the committee note in (b).

CHAPTER 900. PRO BONO LEGAL SERVICE.

Rule 16-901. State Pro Bono Committee and Plan.

(a) **Standing Committee on Pro Bono Legal Service.** (1) Creation. There is a Standing Committee of the Court of Appeals on Pro Bono Legal Service.

(2) Members. The Standing Committee consists of the following members appointed by the Court of Appeals:

(A) eight members of the Maryland Bar, including one from each appellate judicial circuit and one selected from the State at large;

(B) a maximum of three Circuit Court judges selected from nominees submitted by the Conference of Circuit Judges;

(C) a maximum of three District Court judges selected from nominees submitted by the Chief Judge of the District Court;

(D) the Public Defender or a designee of the Public Defender;

(E) a representative from the Legal Aid Bureau, Maryland Volunteer Lawyers Service, Pro Bono Resource Center of Maryland, and one other pro bono referral organization; and

(F) a member of the general public.

(3) Terms; chair. The term of each member is three years. A member may be reappointed to serve one or more additional terms. The Court of Appeals shall designate one of the members as chair.

(4) Consultants. The Standing Committee may designate a reasonable number of consultants from among court personnel or representatives of other organizations or agencies concerned with the provision of legal services to persons of limited means.

(b) **Functions of the Standing Committee.** (1) Required. The Standing Committee shall:

(A) develop standard forms for use by the Local Pro Bono Committees in developing and articulating the Local Pro Bono Action Plans and making their annual reports;

(B) recommend uniform standards for use by the Local Pro Bono Committees to assess the need for pro bono legal services in their communities;

(C) review and evaluate the Local Pro Bono Action Plans and the annual reports of the Local Pro Bono Committees;

(D) collect and make available to Local Pro Bono Committees information about pro bono projects;

(E) at the request of a Local Pro Bono Committee, provide guidance about the Rules in this Chapter and Rule 6.1 of the Maryland Lawyers' Rules of Professional Conduct;

(F) file with the Court of Appeals an annual report and recommendations about the implementation and effectiveness of the Local Pro Bono Action Plans, the Rules in this Chapter, and Rule 6.1 of the Maryland Lawyers' Rules of Professional Conduct; and

(G) prepare a State Pro Bono Action Plan as provided in section (c) of this Rule.

(2) Permitted. The Standing Committee may make recommendations to the Court of Appeals concerning the appointment and reappointment of its members.

(c) **State Pro Bono Action Plan.** (1) Generally. Within three years after the effective date of this Rule, the Standing Committee shall submit to the Court of Appeals a State Pro Bono Action Plan to promote increased efforts on the part of lawyers to provide legal assistance to persons of limited means. In developing the Plan, the Standing Committee shall:

(A) review and assess the results of the Local Pro Bono Action Plans;

(B) assess the data generated by the reports required by Rule 16-903;

(C) gather and consider information pertinent to the existence, nature, and extent of the need for pro bono legal services in Maryland; and

(D) provide the opportunity for one or more public hearings.

(2) Contents. The State Pro Bono Action Plan may include a recommendation for increasing or decreasing the aspirational goals for pro bono publico legal service set forth in Rule 6.1 of the Maryland Lawyers' Rules of Professional Conduct. The Plan should include suggestions for the kinds of pro bono activities that will be most helpful in meeting the need for pro bono legal service throughout the State and should address long-range pro bono service issues.

Committee note. — Examples of long-range issues that may be addressed include opportunities for transactional lawyers, government lawyers, business lawyers, and in-house counsel to render pro bono legal service; opportunities for pro bono legal service by lawyers who are unable to provide direct client representation; "collective responsibility" for pro bono legal service when a law firm designates certain lawyers to handle only pro bono matters; and encouraging pro bono legal service among law students and in the legal academic setting.

(d) **Publication.** The Clerk of the Court of Appeals shall cause the State Action Plan submitted by the Standing Committee to be published in the Maryland Register and such other publications as the Court directs and shall establish a reasonable period for public comment.

(e) **Consideration by the Court of Appeals.** After the comment period, the Court of Appeals shall hold a public hearing and take appropriate action on the Plan. (Added April 9, 2002, effective July 1, 2002; amended October 20, 2010, effective October 20, 2010.)

Source. — This Rule is new.

Effect of amendments. — The 2010 amendment rewrote (a)(2) and (a)(3); in (b) substituted "Functions" for "Duties" in the subheading; adding the subheading in (b)(1); added (b)(2); and made related, stylistic changes.

Cited in Henriquez v. Henriquez, 185 Md. App. 465, 971 A.2d 345 (2009), aff'd, 992 A.2d 446, 2010 Md. LEXIS 138 (Md. 2010).

Rule 16-902. Local Pro Bono Committees and Plans.

(a) **Local Pro Bono Committees.** (1) Creation. There is a Local Pro Bono Committee for each county.

(2) Members. The Local Pro Bono Committee consists of at least two representatives nominated by legal services organizations and pro bono referral organizations that provide services in the county and selected by the County Administrative Judge and the District Administrative Judge, and no more than nine additional members, as follows:

(A) the District Public Defender for the county or an assistant public defender selected by the District Public Defender;

(B) at least three but no more than five lawyers, appointed by the president of the county bar association, who practice in the county and at least one of whom is an officer of the county bar association;

(C) at least one but no more than two persons from the general public, appointed jointly by the County Administrative Judge and the District Administrative Judge; and

(D) at least one but no more than two trial court judges, with the selection of any circuit court judge made by the County Administrative Judge and the selection of any District Court judge made by the County Administrative Judge with the concurrence of the Chief Judge of the District Court.

(3) Term. Each Committee shall establish a procedure for new membership, including articulating length of terms, to ensure member rotation and involvement.

(4) Chair. The County Administrative Judge shall appoint a member of the Committee to serve as temporary chair. The temporary chair shall convene a meeting at which the Committee shall elect a member to serve as chair. Each Committee shall establish a procedure by which its chair will be replaced.

(5) Full Membership. On at least an annual basis, the County Administrative Judge shall assess the composition of the Committee and take steps to ensure full membership of the Committee.

(6) Consultants. The Committee may designate a reasonable number of consultants from among court personnel or representatives of other organizations or agencies concerned with the provision of legal services to persons of limited means. Each consultant should be encouraged to attend meetings and participate as a member, providing input and assisting in the development and implementation of the plan, where appropriate, without being a voting member of the Committee.

(b) **Duties of the Committee.** (1) The local pro bono committee shall:. assess the needs in the county for pro bono legal service, including the needs of non-English speaking, minority, and isolated populations;

(2) determine the nature and extent of existing and proposed free or low-cost legal services, both staff and volunteer, for persons of limited means in the county;

(3) establish goals and priorities for pro bono legal service in the county;

(4) prepare a Local Pro Bono Action Plan as provided in section (c) of this Rule;

(5) in accordance with the policies and directives established by the Standing Committee or the Court of Appeals, implement or monitor the implementation of the Plan; and

(6) submit an annual report about the Plan to the Standing Committee by May 1.

(c) **Local Pro Bono Action Plans.** (1) Generally. The Local Pro Bono Committee shall develop, in coordination with existing legal services organizations and pro bono referral organizations that provide services in the county, a detailed Local Pro Bono Action Plan to promote pro bono legal service to meet the needs of persons of limited means in the county. The Plan shall be submitted to the Standing Committee within one year after creation of the Local Committee. The Local Pro Bono Committees of two or more adjoining counties may collaborate and form a Regional Pro Bono Committee with approval of the Administrative Judges of the counties that wish to collaborate. With the approval of the Standing Committee, a single joint Pro Bono Action Plan may be developed for two or more adjoining counties, by collaboration of the Local Pro Bono Committees.

(2) Contents. The Local Pro Bono Action Plan shall address the following matters:

(A) screening applicants for pro bono representation and referring them to appropriate referral sources or panels of participating attorneys;

(B) establishing or expanding attorney referral panels;

(C) continuing and supporting current services provided by existing pro bono and legal services organizations;

(D) a procedure for matching cases with individual attorney expertise, including specialized panels;

(E) support for participating attorneys, including

(i) providing litigation resources and out-of-pocket expenses for pro bono cases;

(ii) providing or supplementing legal malpractice insurance for participating attorneys;

(iii) providing legal education and training for participating attorneys in specialized areas of the law relevant to pro bono legal service, including consultation services with attorneys who have expertise in areas of law in which participating attorneys seek to provide pro bono service; and

(iv) recommending court scheduling and docketing preferences for pro bono cases;

(F) methods of informing lawyers about the ways in which they may provide pro bono legal service;

Committee note. — Ways in which lawyers may provide pro bono legal service include assisting in the screening and intake process; interviewing prospective clients and providing basic consultation; participating in self-represented clinics or other programs in which lawyers provide advice and counsel, assist persons in drafting letters or documents, or assist persons in planning transactions or resolving disputes without the need for litigation; representing clients through case referral; acting as co-counsel with legal service providers or other participating attorneys; providing consultation to legal service providers for case reviews and evaluations; training or consulting with other participating attorneys or staff attorneys affiliated with a legal service provider; engaging in legal research and writing; and, if qualified through training and experience, serving as a mediator, arbitrator, or neutral evaluator.

(G) coordinating implementation of the Plan with the courts, county bar associations, and other agencies and organizations;

(H) the number of hours of pro bono legal services needed annually to meet the needs of persons of limited means in the county; and

(I) programs to recognize lawyers who provide pro bono legal services. (Added April 9, 2002, effective July 1, 2002; April 10, 2007, effective July 1, 2007; September 8, 2011, effective January 1, 2012.)

Source. — This Rule is new.

Effect of amendments. — The 2007 amendment in (a)(2) rewrote (A) as introductory language, redesignated (i) — (iv) as (B) — (C), deleted former (iii) and added (D); added (a)(3) and (a)(5), rewrote (a)(4), and in (a)(6) added the second sentence; in (b)(6) added "by May 1"; and in (c)(1) added the third sentence.

The 2011 amendment substituted "self-represented" for "pro se" in the Committee note

Rule 16-903. Reporting Pro Bono Legal Service.

(a) **Required as a condition of practice.** As a condition precedent to the practice of law, each lawyer admitted to practice in Maryland shall file annually with the Administrative Office of the Courts, in accordance with this Rule, a Pro Bono Legal Service Report on a form approved by the Court of Appeals. The form shall not require the identification of pro bono clients.

Committee note. — The purpose of pro bono legal service reporting is to document the pro bono legal service performed by lawyers in Maryland and determine the effectiveness of the Local Pro Bono Action Plans, the State Pro Bono Action Plan, the Rules in this Chapter, and Rule 6.1 of the Maryland Lawyers' Rules of Professional Conduct.

(b) **Oversight of the reporting process.** The Court of Appeals shall designate an employee of the Administrative Office of the Courts to oversee the reporting process set forth in this Rule.

(c) **Mailing by the Administrative Office of the Courts.** On or before January 10 of each year, the Administrative Office of the Courts shall mail a Pro Bono Legal Service Report form to each lawyer on the list maintained by the Client Protection Fund of the Bar of Maryland. The addresses on that list shall be used for all notices and correspondence pertaining to the reports.

(d) **Due date.** Pro Bono Legal Service Reports for a given calendar year shall be filed with the Administrative Office of the Courts on or before February 15 of the following calendar year.

(e) **Enforcement.** (1) Notice of default. As soon as practicable after May 1 of each year, the Administrative Office of the Courts shall notify each defaulting lawyer of the lawyer's failure to file a report. The notice shall (A) state that the lawyer has not filed the Pro Bono Legal Service Report for the previous calendar year, (B) state that continued failure to file the Report may result in the entry of an order by the Court of Appeals prohibiting the lawyer from practicing law in the State, and (C) be sent by first class mail. The mailing of the notice of default shall constitute service.

(2) Additional discretionary notice of default. In addition to the mailed notice, the Administrative Office of the Courts may give additional notice to defaulting lawyers by any of the means enumerated in Rule 16-811 f 3.

(3) List of defaulting lawyers. As soon as practicable after July 1 of each year but no later than August 1, the Administrative Office of the Courts shall prepare, certify, and file with the Court of Appeals a list that includes the name and address of each lawyer engaged in the practice of law who has failed to file the Pro Bono Legal Service Report for the previous year.

(4) Certification of default; Order of Decertification. The Administrative Office of the Courts shall submit with the list a proposed Decertification Order stating the names and addresses of those lawyers who have failed to file their Pro Bono Legal Service Reports for the specified calendar year. At the request of the Court of Appeals, the Administrative Office ofthe Courts also shall furnish additional information from its records or give further notice to the defaulting lawyers. If satisfied that the Administrative Office of the Courts has given the required notice to each lawyer named on the proposed Decertification Order, the Court of Appeals shall enter a Decertification Order prohibiting each of them from practicinglaw in the State.

(5) Mailing of Decertification Order. The Administrative Office of the Courts shall mail by first class mail a copy of the Decertification Order to each lawyer named in the Order. The mailing of the copy of the Decertification Order shall constitute service.

(6) Recertification; restoration to good standing. If a lawyer thereafter files the outstanding Pro Bono Legal Service Report, the Administrative Office of the Courts shall request the Court of Appeals to enter an order that recertifies the lawyer and restores the lawyer to good standing. Upon entry of that order, the Administrative Office of the Courts promptly shall furnish confirmation to the lawyer. After a lawyer is recertified, the fact that the lawyer had been decertified need not be disclosed by the lawyer in response to a request for information as to whether the lawyer has been the subject of a disciplinary or remedial proceeding.

(7) Notices to Clerks. The Clerk of the Court of Appeals shall send a copy of each Decertification Order and each order that recertifies a lawyer and restores the lawyer to good standing entered pursuant to this Rule to the Clerk of the Court of Special Appeals, the Clerk of each circuit court, the Chief Clerk of the District Court, and the Register of Wills for each county.

(f) **Certain Information Furnished to the Standing Committee on Pro Bono Legal Service.** The Administrative Office of the Courts shall submit promptly to the Standing Committee on Pro Bono Legal Service a compilation of non-identifying information and data from the Pro Bono Legal Service Reports.

(g) **Confidentiality.** Pro Bono Legal Service Reports are confidential and are not subject to inspection or disclosure under Code, State Government Article, § 10-615 (2) (iii). The Administrative Office of the Courts shall not release the Reports to any person or agency, except upon order of the Court of

Appeals. Nonidentifying information and data contained in a lawyer's Pro Bono Legal Service Report are not confidential. (Added Apr. 9, 2002, effective July 1, 2002; May 8, 2007, effective July 1, 2007; amended Sept. 10, 2009, effective Oct. 1, 2009.)

Source. — This Rule is new.

Effect of amendments. — The 2007 amendment rewrote (e)(6); and in (e)(7) substituted "order that ... good standing" for "Rescission Order".

The 2009 amendment in the first sentence of (a) substituted "admitted to practice" for "authorized to practice law" and added "in accordance with this Rule"; substituted "Oversight of the Reporting Process" for "Designated Employee of the Administrative Office of the Courts" in the subsection heading for (b); in the first sentence of (c) substituted "Client Protection Fund of the Bar of Maryland" for "Clients' Security Trust Fund"; in the first sentence of (e)(1) substituted "notify" for "give

notice of the failure to file a report to" and added "of the lawyer's failure to file a report"; in (e)(2) substituted "Rule 16-811 f 3" for "Rule 16-811 g 3"; in (e)(6) added "thereafter" in the first sentence, deleted "that recertifies the lawyer and restores the lawyer to good standing" before "the Administrative Office" in the second sentence, and added the last sentence; and made stylistic changes.

Applied in Henriquez v. Henriquez, 413 Md. 287, 992 A.2d 446 (2010).

Cited in Att'y Griev. Comm'n v. Brisbon, 385 Md. 667, 870 A.2d 586 (2005); Touzeau v. Deffinbaugh, 394 Md. 654, 907 A.2d 807 (2006).

CHAPTER 1000. ACCESS TO COURT RECORDS.

Rule 16-1001. Definitions.

In this Chapter, the following definitions apply except as expressly otherwise provided or as necessary implication requires.

(a) **Administrative record.** (1) Except as provided in subsection (a)(3) of this Rule, "administrative record" means a record that:

(A) pertains to the administration of a court, another judicial agency, or the judicial system of the State; and

(B) is not otherwise a case record.

(2) "Administrative record" includes:

(A) a rule adopted by a court pursuant to Rule 1-102;

(B) an administrative order, policy, or directive that governs the operation of a court, including an order, policy, or directive that determines the assignment of one or more judges to particular divisions of the court or particular kinds of cases;

(C) an analysis or report, even if derived from court records, that is:

(i) prepared by or for a court or other judicial agency;

(ii) used by the court or other judicial agency for purposes of judicial administration; and

(iii) not filed, and not required to be filed, with the clerk of a court.

(D) a jury plan adopted by a court;

(E) a case management plan adopted by a court;

(F) an electronic filing plan adopted by a court; and

(G) an administrative order issued by the Chief Judge of the Court of Appeals pursuant to Rule 16-1002.

(3) "Administrative record" does not include a document or information gathered, maintained, or stored by a person or entity other than a court or other judicial agency, to which a court or other judicial agency has access but which is not a case record.

(b) **Business license record.** (1) "Business license record" means a court record pertaining to an application for a business license issued by the clerk of a court, and includes the application for the license and a copy of the license.

(2) "Business license record" does not include a court record pertaining to a marriage license.

(c) **Case record.** (1) Except as otherwise provided in this Rule, "case record" means:

(A) a document, information, or other thing that is collected, received, or maintained by a court in connection with one or more specific judicial actions or proceedings;

(B) a copy of a marriage license issued and maintained by the court, including, after the license is issued, the application for the license;

(C) a miscellaneous record filed with the clerk of the court pursuant to law that is not a notice record.

(2) "Case record" does not include a document or information described in subsection (a)(3) of this Rule.

(d) **Court.** "Court" means the Court of Appeals of Maryland, the Court of Special Appeals, a circuit court, the District Court of Maryland, and an orphans' court of Maryland.

(e) **Court record.** "Court record" means a record that is:

(1) an administrative record;

(2) a business license record;

(3) a case record; or

(4) a notice record.

(f) **Custodian.** "Custodian" means:

(1) the clerk of a court; and

(2) any other authorized individual who has physical custody and control of a court record.

(g) **Individual.** "Individual" means a human being.

(h) **Judicial agency.** "Judicial agency" means a unit within the Judicial Branch of the Maryland Government.

(i) **Notice record.** "Notice record" means a record that is filed with a court pursuant to statute for the principal purpose of giving public notice of the record. It includes deeds, mortgages, and other documents filed among the land records; financing statements filed pursuant to Code, Commercial Law Article, Title 9; and tax and other liens filed pursuant to statute.

(j) **Person.** "Person" means an individual, sole proprietorship, partnership, firm, association, corporation, or other entity.

(k) **Remote access.** "Remote access" means the ability to inspect, search, or copy a court record by electronic means from a location other than the location where the record is stored. (Added Mar. 4, 2004, effective Oct. 1, 2004.)

Committee note. — The Rules in this Chapter recognize that court records can be of four types: (1) those, like land records, that are filed with the court, not in connection with any litigation, but for the sole purpose of providing public notice of them; (2) those that are essentially administrative in nature — that are created by the court or judicial agency itself and relate to the internal operation of a court or other judicial agency as an agency of Government; (3) those that are filed or created in connection with business licenses (excluding marriage licenses) issued by the clerk; and (4) those that are filed with the court in connection with a judicial action or the issuance of a marriage license. The premise of the Rules in this Chapter is that, although the presumption of openness applies to all four kinds of records, they need to be treated differently in some respects.

Land records and other similar kinds of records that are filed with the clerk for the sole purpose of giving public notice of them are court records, but, because the court's only function with respect to those records is to preserve them and make and keep them available for public inspection, there is no justification for shielding them, or any part of them, from public inspection. Those kinds of records are defined as "notice records," and it is the intent of the Rules in this Chapter that there be no substantive (content) restrictions on public access to them.

The Rules in this Chapter assume that the kinds of internal administrative records maintained by a court or other Judicial Branch agency, mostly involving personnel, budgetary, and operational management, are similar in nature and purpose to the kinds of administrative records maintained by Executive Branch agencies and that records pertaining to business licenses issued by a court clerk are similar in nature to records kept by Executive Branch agencies that issue licenses of one kind or another. The Rules in this Chapter thus treat those kinds of records more or less the same as comparable Executive Branch records. The Public Information Act ("PIA") provides the most relevant statement of public policy regarding those kinds of records, and, as a general matter, the Rules in this Chapter apply the PIA to those kinds of records.

A different approach is taken with respect to case records — those that come into the court's possession as the result of their having been filed by litigants in judicial actions. As to them, the Rules in this Chapter carve out only those exceptions to public access that are felt particularly applicable. The exceptions, for the most part, are much narrower than those provided by the PIA. Categorical exceptions are limited to those that (1) have an existing basis, either by statute other than the PIA, or by specific Rule, or (2) present some compelling need for non-access. In an attempt to remove discretion from clerical personnel to deny public access and require that closure be examined by a judge on a case-by-case basis, the Rules in this Chapter require that all other exclusions be by court order.

To achieve the differentiation between these various kinds of court records, four categories are specifically defined in this Rule — "administrative records," "business license records," "case records," and "notice records." Some principles enunciated in the Rules in this Chapter apply to all four categories, and, for that purpose, the term "court records," which includes all four categories, is used.

Source. — This Rule is new.

University of Baltimore Law Review. — For comment, "Access to Court Records: Shifting the Privacy Burden Away from Witnesses and Victims," see 36 U. Balt. L. Rev. 419 (2007).

Access to DVD and audiotape of confession. — Trial court had jurisdiction in a criminal case to determine a motion for access filed by a television station to obtain a copy of a DVD and audiotape of the defendant's confession as by intervening in the criminal matter was deemed the appropriate method, and the trial court did not abuse its discretion by authorizing the release of the same since the media already had full transcripts of the tapes and it balanced the public's right to access court records with the defendant's fair trial concerns, and the concerns of the victim's family by permitting redacted copies of the DVD and audiotape. State v. WBAL-TV, 187 Md. App. 135, 975 A.2d 909 (2009), cert. denied, 410 Md. 701, 980 A.2d 482, 2009 Md. LEXIS 752 (2009).

Cited in Marks v. Crim. Injuries Comp. Bd., 196 Md. App. 37, 7 A.3d 665 (2010).

Rule 16-1002. General policy.

(a) **Presumption of openness.** Court records maintained by a court or by another judicial agency are presumed to be open to the public for inspection. Except as otherwise provided by or pursuant to the Rules in this Chapter, the custodian of a court record shall permit a person, upon personal appearance in the office of the custodian during normal business hours, to inspect the record.

(b) **Protection of records.** To protect court records and prevent unnecessary interference with the official business and duties of the custodian and other court personnel,

(1) a clerk is not required to permit inspection of a case record filed with the clerk for docketing in a judicial action or a notice record filed for recording and indexing until the document has been docketed or recorded and indexed; and

(2) the Chief Judge of the Court of Appeals, by administrative order, a copy of which shall be filed with and maintained by the clerk of each court, may adopt procedures and conditions, not inconsistent with the Rules in this Chapter, governing the timely production, inspection, and copying of court records.

Committee note. — It is anticipated that, by Administrative Order, entered pursuant to section (b) of this Rule, the Chief Judge of the Court of Appeals will direct that, if the clerk does not permit inspection of a notice record prior to recording and indexing of the record, (1) persons filing a notice record for recording and indexing include a separate legible copy of those pages of the document necessary to identify the parties to the transaction and the property that is the subject of the transaction and (2) the clerk date stamp that copy and maintain it in a separate book that is subject to inspection by the public.

(c) **Exhibit attached to motion or marked for identification.** Unless a judicial action is not open to the public or the court expressly orders otherwise, a court record that consists of an exhibit (1) attached to a motion that has been ruled upon by the court or (2) marked for identification at trial, whether or not offered in evidence, and if offered, whether or not admitted, is subject to inspection, notwithstanding that the record otherwise would not have been subject to inspection under the Rules in this Chapter.

Cross references. — Rule 2-516.

(d) **Fees.** (1) In this Rule, "reasonable fee" means a fee that bears a reasonable relationship to the actual or estimated costs incurred or likely to be incurred in providing the requested access.

(2) Unless otherwise expressly permitted by the Rules in this Chapter, a custodian may not charge a fee for providing access to a court record that can be made available for inspection, in paper form or by electronic access, with the expenditure of less than two hours of effort by the custodian or other judicial employee.

(3) A custodian may charge a reasonable fee if two hours or more of effort is required to provide the requested access.

(4) The custodian may charge a reasonable fee for making or supervising the making of a copy or printout of a court record.

(5) The custodian may waive a fee if, after consideration of the ability of the person requesting access to pay the fee and other relevant factors, the custodian determines that the waiver is in the public interest.

(e) **New court records.** (1) Except as expressly required by other law and subject to Rule 16-1008, neither a custodian nor a court or other judicial agency is required by the Rules in this Chapter to index, compile, re-format, program, or reorganize existing court records or other documents or information to create a new court record not necessary to be maintained in the ordinary course of business. The removal, deletion, or redaction from a court record of information not subject to inspection under the Rules in this Chapter in order to make the court record subject to inspection does not create a new record within the meaning of this Rule.

(2) If a custodian, court, or other judicial agency (A) indexes, compiles, re-formats, programs, or reorganizes existing court records or other documents or information to create a new court record, or (B) comes into possession of a new court record created by another from the indexing, compilation, re-formatting, programming, or reorganization of other court records, documents, or information, and there is no basis under the Rules in this Chapter to deny inspection of that new court record or some part of that court record, the new court record or a part for which there is no basis to deny inspection shall be subject to inspection.

(f) **Access by judicial employees, parties, and counsel of record.** The Rules in this Chapter address access to court records by the public at large. The Rules do not limit access to court records by judicial officials or employees in the performance of their official duties, or to a case record by a party or counsel of record in the action. (Added Mar. 4, 2004, effective Oct. 1, 2004; amended March 7, 2006, effective July 1, 2006; May 8, 2007, effective July 1, 2007.)

Source. — This Rule is new.

Effect of amendments. — The 2006 amendment added "parties, and counsel of record" in the heading of (f), and in (f), changed the text to be two sentences, added "The Rules" at the beginning of the second sentence; and added "or to a case record by a party or counsel of record in the action" and made related changes.

The 2007 amendment rewrote (c) and added the Cross reference.

Quoted in Marks v. Crim. Injuries Comp. Bd., 196 Md. App. 37, 7 A.3d 665 (2010).

Rule 16-1003. Copies.

(a) Except as otherwise expressly provided by law, a person who is entitled to inspect a court record is entitled to have a copy or printout of the court record. The copy or printout may be in paper form or, subject to Rule 16-1008 (a)(3), in electronic form.

(b) To the extent practicable, a copy or printout in paper form shall be made where the court record is kept and while the court record is in the custody of the custodian. (Added Mar. 4, 2004, effective Oct. 1, 2004.)

Source. — This Rule is new.

Rule 16-1004. Access to notice, administrative, and business license records.

(a) **Notice records.** A custodian may not deny inspection of a notice record that has been recorded and indexed by the clerk.

(b) **Administrative and business license records.** (1) Except as otherwise provided by the Rules in this Chapter, the right to inspect administrative and business license records is governed by Code, State Government Article, §§ 10-611 through 10-626.

(2)(A) A custodian shall deny inspection of an administrative record used by the jury commissioner in the jury selection process, except (i) as a trial judge orders in connection with a challenge under Code, Courts Article, §§ 8-408 and 8-409; and (ii) as provided in (B) and (C) of this subsection.

(B) A custodian shall, upon request, disclose the names and zip codes of the sworn jurors contained on a jury list after the jury has been impaneled and sworn, unless otherwise ordered by the trial judge.

(C) After a source pool of qualified jurors has been emptied and re-created in accordance with Code, Courts Article, § 8-207, and after every person selected to serve as a juror from that pool has completed the person's service, a trial judge shall, upon request, disclose the name, zip code, age, sex, education, occupation, and spouse's occupation of each person whose name was selected from that pool and placed on a jury list, unless, in the interest of justice, the trial judge determines that this information remain confidential in whole or in part.

(D) A jury commissioner may provide jury lists to the Health Care Alternative Dispute Resolution Office as required by that Office in carrying out its duties, subject to that Office adopting regulations to ensure against improper dissemination of juror data.

(E) At intervals acceptable to the jury commissioner, a jury commissioner shall provide the State Board of Elections and State Motor Vehicle Administration with data about prospective, qualified, or sworn jurors needed to correct erroneous or obsolete information, such as that related to a death or change of address, subject to the Board's and Administration's adoption of regulations to ensure against improper dissemination of juror data.

(c) **Personnel records — Generally.** Except as otherwise permitted by the Maryland Public Information Act or by this Rule, a custodian shall deny to a person other than the person who is the subject of the record inspection of the personnel records of an employee of the court or other judicial agency or of an individual who has applied for employment with the court or other judicial agency. The following records or information are not subject to this exclusion and shall be open to inspection:

(1) The full name of the individual;

(2) The date of the application for employment and the position for which application was made;

(3) The date employment commenced;

(4) The name, location, and telephone number of the court or judicial agency to which the individual has been assigned;

(5) The current and previous job titles and salaries of the individual during employment by the court or judicial agency;

(6) The name of the individual's current supervisor;

(7) The amount of monetary compensation paid to the individual by the court or judicial agency and a description of any health, insurance, or other fringe benefit that the individual is entitled to receive from the court or judicial agency;

(8) Unless disclosure is prohibited by law, other information authorized by the individual to be released; and

(9) A record that has become a case record.

(d) **Personnel records — Retirement.** Unless inspection is permitted under the Maryland Public Information Act or the record has become a case record, a custodian shall deny inspection of a retirement record of an employee of the court or other judicial agency.

(e) **Certain administrative records.** A custodian shall deny inspection of the following administrative records:

(1) Judicial work product, including drafts of documents, notes, and memoranda prepared by a judge or other court personnel at the direction of a judge and intended for use in the preparation of a decision, order, or opinion;

(2) An administrative record that is:

(A) prepared by or for a judge or other judicial personnel;

(B) either (i) purely administrative in nature but not a local rule, policy, or directive that governs the operation of the court or (ii) a draft of a document intended for consideration by the author or others and not intended to be final in its existing form; and

(C) not filed with the clerk and not required to be filed with the clerk. (Added Mar. 4, 2004, effective Oct. 1, 2004; Dec. 4, 2007, effective Jan. 1, 2008.)

Source. — This Rule is new.

Effect of amendments. — The December 4, 2007 Order, effective January 1, 2008, rewrote (b) (2).

Rule 16-1005. Case records — Required denial of inspection — In general.

(a) A custodian shall deny inspection of a case record or any part of a case record if inspection would be contrary to:

(1) The Constitution of the United States, a Federal statute, or a Federal regulation adopted under a Federal statute and having the force of law;

(2) The Maryland Constitution;

(3) A provision of the Maryland Public Information Act that is expressly adopted in the Rules in this Chapter;

(4) A rule adopted by the Court of Appeals; or

(5) An order entered by the court having custody of the case record or by any higher court having jurisdiction over

(A) the case record, or

(B) the person seeking inspection of the case record.

(b) Unless inspection is otherwise permitted by the Rules in this Chapter, a custodian shall deny inspection of a case record or any part of a case record if inspection would be contrary to a statute enacted by the Maryland General Assembly, other than the Maryland Public Information Act (Code, State Government Article, §§10-611 through 10-626), that expressly or by necessary implication applies to a court record. (Added Mar. 4, 2004, effective Oct. 1, 2004.)

Committee note. — Subsection (a)(5) allows a court to seal a record or otherwise preclude its disclosure. So long as a court record is under seal or subject to an order precluding or limiting disclosure, it may not be disclosed except in conformance with the order. The authority to seal a court record must be exercised in conformance with the general policy of these Rules and with supervening standards enunciated in decisions of the United States Supreme Court and the Maryland Court of Appeals.

Source. — This Rule is new.

Applied in Clark v. O'Malley, 186 Md. App. 194, 973 A.2d 821 (2009).

Rule 16-1006. Required denial of inspection — Certain categories of case records.

Except as otherwise provided by law, court order, or the Rules in this Chapter, the custodian shall deny inspection of:

(a) All case records filed in the following actions involving children:

(1) Actions filed under Title 9, Chapter 100 of the Maryland Rules for:

(A) Adoption;

(B) Guardianship; or

(C) To revoke a consent to adoption or guardianship for which there is no pending adoption or guardianship proceeding in that county.

(2) Delinquency, child in need of assistance, and child in need of supervision actions in Juvenile Court, except that, if a hearing is open to the public pursuant to Code, Courts Article, § 3-8A-13 (f), the name of the respondent and the date, time, and location of the hearing are open to inspection.

(b) The following case records pertaining to a marriage license:

(1) A certificate of a physician or certified nurse practitioner filed pursuant to Code, Family Law Article, § 2-301, attesting to the pregnancy of a child under 18 years of age who has applied for a marriage license.

(2) Until a license becomes effective, the fact that an application for a license has been made, except to the parent or guardian of a party to be married.

Cross references. — See Code, Family Law Article, § 2-402 (f).

(c) Case records pertaining to petitions for relief from abuse filed pursuant to Code, Family Law Article, § 4-504, which shall be sealed until the earlier of 48 hours after the petition is filed or the court acts on the petition.

(d) In any action or proceeding, a record created or maintained by an agency concerning child abuse or neglect that is required by statute to be kept confidential.

Committee note. — Statutes that require child abuse or neglect records to be kept confidential include Code, Human Services Article, §§ 1-202 and 1-203 and Code, Family Law Article, § 5-707.

(e) The following case records in actions or proceedings involving attorneys or judges:

(1) Records and proceedings in attorney grievance matters declared confidential by Rule 16-723 (b).

(2) Case records with respect to an investigative subpoena issued by Bar Counsel pursuant to Rule 16-732;

(3) Subject to the provisions of Rule 19 (b), (c), and (d) of the Rules Governing Admission to the Bar, case records relating to bar admission proceedings before the Accommodations Review Committee and its panels, a Character Committee, the State Board of Law Examiners, and the Court of Appeals.

(4) Case records consisting of IOLTA Compliance Reports filed by an attorney pursuant to Rule 16-608 and Pro Bono Legal Service Reports filed by an attorney pursuant to Rule 16-903.

(5) Case records relating to a motion filed with respect to a subpoena issued by Investigative Counsel for the Commission on Judicial Disabilities pursuant to Rule 16-806.

(f) The following case records in criminal actions or proceedings:

(1) A case record that has been ordered expunged pursuant to Rule 4-508.

(2) The following case records pertaining to search warrants:

(A) The warrant, application, and supporting affidavit, prior to execution of the warrant and the filing of the records with the clerk.

(B) Executed search warrants and all papers attached thereto filed pursuant to Rule 4-601.

(3) The following case records pertaining to an arrest warrant:

(A) A case record pertaining to an arrest warrant issued under Rule 4-212 (d) and the charging document upon which the warrant was issued until the conditions set forth in Rule 4-212 (d)(3) are satisfied.

(B) Except as otherwise provided in Code, State Government Article, §10-616 (q), a case record pertaining to an arrest warrant issued pursuant to a grand jury indictment or conspiracy investigation and the charging document upon which the arrest warrant was issued.

(4) A case record maintained under Code, Courts Article, § 9-106, of the refusal of a person to testify in a criminal action against the person's spouse.

(5) A presentence investigation report prepared pursuant to Code, Correctional Services Article, § 6-112.

(6) A case record pertaining to a criminal investigation by (A) a grand jury, (B) a State's Attorney pursuant to Code, Criminal Procedure Article, § 15-108, or (C) the State Prosecutor pursuant to Code, Criminal Procedure Article, § 14-110.

Committee note. — Although this Rule shields only case records pertaining to a criminal investigation, there may be other laws that shield other kinds of court records pertaining to such investigations. This Rule is not intended to affect the operation or effectiveness of any such other law.

(g) A transcript, tape recording, audio, video, or digital recording of any court proceeding that was closed to the public pursuant to rule or order of court.

(h) Backup audio recordings made by any means, computer disks, and notes of a court reporter that are in the possession of the court reporter and have not been filed with the clerk.

(i) The following case records containing medical information:

(1) A case record, other than an autopsy report of a medical examiner, that (A) consists of a medical or psychological report or record from a hospital, physician, psychologist, or other professional health care provider, and (B) contains medical or psychological information about an individual.

(2) A case record pertaining to the testing of an individual for HIV that is declared confidential under Code, Health-General Article, § 18-338.1 or § 18-338.2.

(3) A case record that consists of information, documents, or records of a child fatality review team, to the extent they are declared confidential by Code, Health-General Article, § 5-709.

(4) A case record that contains a report by a physician or institution concerning whether an individual has an infectious disease, declared confidential under Code, Health-General Article, § 18-201 or § 18-202.

(5) A case record that contains information concerning the consultation, examination, or treatment of a developmentally disabled person, declared confidential by Code, Health-General Article, § 7-1003.

(6) A case record relating to a petition for an emergency evaluation made under Code, Health-General Article, § 10-622 and declared confidential under Code, Health-General Article, § 10-630.

(j) A case record that consists of the federal or Maryland income tax return of an individual.

(k) A case record that:

(1) a court has ordered sealed or not subject to inspection, except in conformance with the order; or

(2) in accordance with Rule 16-1009 (b), is the subject of a motion to preclude or limit inspection.

(l) As provided in Rule 9-203 (d), a case record that consists of a financial statement filed pursuant to Rule 9-202. (Added Mar. 4, 2004, effective Oct. 1, 2004; amended April 5, 2005, effective July 1, 2005; amended Jan. 10, 2006, effective Jan. 10, 2006; May 8, 2007, effective July 1, 2007; Dec. 4, 2007, effective Jan. 1, 2008; June 16, 2009, effective June 17, 2009; amended Sept. 10, 2009, effective Oct. 1, 2009; amended March 9, 2010, effective July 1, 2010.)

Source. — This Rule is new.

Effect of amendments. — The 2005 amendment rewrote the first undesignated paragraph; and substituted "Backup audio recordings made by any means, computer disks, and notes" for "Notes or a computer disk" in (g).

The 2006 amendment, effective January 10, 2006, rewrote (c) and added the committee note following (c).

The 2007 amendment added (k).

The December 4, 2007 Order, effective January 1, 2008, in the Committee note following (c) substituted "Human Services Article, §§ 1-202 and 1-203" for "Article 88A, §§ 6 (b) and 6A"; and added (h) (6).

The June 17, 2009, amendment added the designations in (e)(6); updated the statutory reference in (e)(6)(B); added (e)(6)(C); and made related changes.

The October 1, 2009, amendment rewrote (d)(3); and in (d)(4) added "IOLTA Compliance Reports filed by an attorney pursuant to Rule 16-608 and".

The 2010 amendment in (b)(1) substituted "certificate of a physician or certified nurse practitioner" for "physician's certificate"; in (b)(2) substituted "becomes effective" for "is issued"; added the cross reference following (b); and added (c) and redesignated accordingly.

Rule 16-1007. Required denial of inspection — Specific information in case records.

Except as otherwise provided by law, the Rules in this Chapter, or court order, a custodian shall deny inspection of a case record or a part of a case record that would reveal:

(a) The name, address, telephone number, e-mail address, or place of employment of a person who reports the abuse of a vulnerable adult pursuant to Code, Family Law Article, § 14-302.

(b) Except as provided in Code, State Government Article, § 10-617 (e), the home address or telephone number of an employee of the State or a political subdivision of the State.

(c) Any part of the social security or Federal Identification Number of an individual, other than the last four digits.

(d) Information about a person who has received a copy of a sex offender's or sexual predator's registration statement. (Added Mar. 4, 2004, effective Oct. 1, 2004; amended July 25, 2006, effective July 25, 2006.)

Cross references. — See Rule 16-1009 (b)(2) concerning information shielded upon a request authorized by Code, Courts Article, Title 3, Subtitle 15 (peace orders) or Code, Family Law Article, Title 4, Subtitle 5 (domestic violence) and in criminal actions.

Source. — This Rule is new.

Effect of amendments. — The 2006 amendment added the cross references note.

Rule 16-1008. Electronic records and retrieval.

(a) **In general.** (1) Subject to the conditions stated in this Rule, a court record that is kept in electronic form is open to inspection to the same extent that the record would be open to inspection in paper form.

(2) Subject to the other provisions of this Rule and any other law or any administrative order of the Chief Judge of the Court of Appeals, a custodian, court, or other judicial agency, for the purpose of providing public access to court records in electronic form, is authorized but not required:

(A) to convert paper court records into electronic court records;

(B) to create new electronic records, databases, programs, or computer systems;

(C) to provide computer terminals or other equipment for use by the public;

(D) to create the ability to inspect or copy court records through remote access; or

(E) to convert, supplement, modify, or replace an existing electronic storage or retrieval system.

(3)(A) Subject to the other provisions of this Rule, a custodian may limit access to court records in electronic form to the manner, form, and program that the electronic system used by the custodian, without modification, is capable of providing. If a custodian, court, or other judicial agency converts paper court records into electronic court records or otherwise creates new electronic records, databases, or computer systems, it shall, to the extent practicable, design those records, databases, or systems to facilitate access to court records that are open to inspection under the Rules in this Chapter.

(B)(i) Subject to subsection (a)(3)(B)(ii) of this Rule and except for identifying information relating to law enforcement officers, other public officials or employees acting in their official capacity, and expert witnesses, a custodian shall prevent remote access to the name, address, telephone number, date of birth, e-mail address, and place of employment of a victim or nonparty witness in (1) a criminal action, (2) a juvenile delinquency action under Title 3, Subtitle 8A of the Courts Article, (3) an action under Title 4, Subtitle 5 of the Family Law Article (domestic violence), or (4) an action under Title 3, Subtitle 15 of the Courts Article (peace order).

(ii) A person who files or otherwise causes to be placed in a court record identifying information relating to a witness shall give the custodian written notice whether the identifying information is not subject to remote access under subsection (a)(3)(B)(i) of this Rule. In the absence of written notice, a custodian is not liable for allowing remote access to the information.

(4) Subject to subsection (a)(3)(B) of this Rule and procedures and conditions established by administrative order of the Chief Judge of the Court of Appeals, a person may view and copy electronic court records that are open to inspection under the Rules in this Chapter:

(A) at computer terminals that a court or other judicial agency makes available for public use at the court or other judicial agency; or

(B) by remote access that the court or other judicial agency makes available through dial-up modem, web site access, or other technology.

(b) **Current programs providing electronic access to databases.** Any electronic access to a database of court records that is provided by a court or other judicial agency and is in effect on October 1, 2004 may continue in effect, subject to review by the Technology Oversight Board for consistency with the Rules in this Chapter. After review, the Board may make or direct any changes that it concludes are necessary to make the electronic access consistent with the Rules in this Chapter.

(c) **New requests for electronic access to or information from databases.** (1) A person who desires to obtain electronic access to or information from a database of court records to which electronic access is not then immediately and automatically available shall submit to the Office of Communications and Public Affairs a written application that describes the court records to which access is desired and the proposed method of achieving that access.

(2) The Office of Communications and Public Affairs shall review the application and may consult the Judicial Information Systems. Without undue delay and, unless impracticable, within 30 days after receipt of the application, the Office of Communications and Public Affairs shall take one of the following actions:

(A) The Office of Communications and Public Affairs shall approve the application if it determines that the application does not request access to court records not subject to inspection under the Rules in this Chapter and will not impose a significant fiscal, personnel, or operational burden on any court or judicial agency. The approval may be conditioned on the applicant's paying or reimbursing the court or agency for any additional expense that may be incurred in implementing the application.

(B) If the Office of Communications and Public Affairs is unable to make the findings provided for in subsection (c)(2)(A), it shall inform the applicant and:

(i) deny the application;

(ii) offer to confer with the applicant about amendments to the application that would meet the concerns of the Office of Communications and Public Affairs; or

(iii) if the applicant requests, refer the application to the Technology Oversight Board for its review.

(C) If the application is referred to the Technology Oversight Board, the Board shall determine whether approval of the application would be likely to permit access to court records or information not subject to inspection under the Rules in this Chapter, create any undue burden on a court, other judicial agency, or the judicial system as a whole, or create undue disparity in the ability of other courts or judicial agencies to provide equivalent access to court records. In making those determinations, the Board shall consider, to the extent relevant:

(i) whether the data processing system, operational system, electronic filing system, or manual or electronic storage and retrieval system used by or planned for the court or judicial agency that maintains the records can currently provide the access requested in the manner requested and in conformance with Rules 16-1001 through 16-1007, and, if not, what changes or effort would be required to make those systems capable of providing that access;

(ii) any changes to the data processing, operational electronic filing, or storage or retrieval systems used by or planned for other courts or judicial agencies in the State that would be required in order to avoid undue disparity in the ability of those courts or agencies to provide equivalent access to court records maintained by them;

(iii) any other fiscal, personnel, or operational impact of the proposed program on the court or judicial agency or on the State judicial system as a whole;

(iv) whether there is a substantial possibility that information retrieved through the program may be used for any fraudulent or other unlawful purpose or may result in the dissemination of inaccurate or misleading information concerning court records or individuals who are the subject of court records and, if so, whether there are any safeguards to prevent misuse of disseminated information and the dissemination of inaccurate or misleading information; and

(v) any other consideration that the Technology Oversight Board finds relevant.

(D) If, upon consideration of the factors set forth in subsection (c)(2)(C) of this Rule, the Technology Oversight Board concludes that the proposal would create (i) an undue fiscal, personnel, or operational burden on a court, other judicial agency, or the judicial system as a whole, or (ii) an undue disparity in the ability of other courts or judicial agencies to provide equivalent access to judicial records, the Board shall inform the Office of Communications and Public Affairs and the applicant in writing of its conclusions. The Office of Communications and Public Affairs and the applicant may then discuss amendments to the application to meet the concerns of the Board, including changes in the scope or method of the requested access and arrangements to bear directly or reimburse the appropriate agency for any expense that may be incurred in providing the requested access and meeting other conditions that may be attached to approval of the application. The applicant may amend the application to reflect any agreed changes. The application, as amended, shall be submitted to the Technology Oversight Board for further consideration. (Added Mar. 4, 2004, effective Oct. 1, 2004; amended March 7, 2006, effective July 1, 2006; June 16, 2009, effective June 17, 2009.)

Source. — This Rule is new.

Effect of amendments. — The 2005 amendment in the first sentence of (c)(2)(A), substituted "application does not request" for "proposal will not permit" before "access", deleted "that are" following "records", substituted "impose" for "involve", and deleted "it shall approve the application" after "agency", and substituted "application" for "proposal" at the end of the second sentence; and in the first sentence of (c)(2)(C), substituted "approval of the application would be" for "the proposal is" after "whether" and deleted "that are" after "information."

The 2006 amendment, effective March 7, 2006, added the (a)(3)(A) designation; added (a)(3)(B); and inserted "subsection (a)(3)(B) of this Rule and" before "procedures" in (a)(4).

The 2006 amendment, effective April 10, 2006, added the (a)(3)(B)(i) designation; in (a)(3)(B)(i), added "Subject to subsection (a)(3)(B)(ii) of this Rule and" at the beginning, substituted "except" for "Except" before "for identifying", inserted "or employees" before "acting", inserted "name" before "address", and made a related change; and added (a)(3)(B)(ii).

The 2009 amendment substituted "Office of Communications and Public Affairs" for "Court Information Office" throughout (c).

University of Baltimore Law Review. — For comment, "Access to Court Records: Shifting the Privacy Burden Away from Witnesses and Victims," see 36 U. Balt. L. Rev. 419 (2007).

Quoted in Marks v. Crim. Injuries Comp. Bd., 196 Md. App. 37, 7 A.3d 665 (2010).

Rule 16-1009. Court order denying or permitting inspection of case record.

(a) **Motion.** (1) A party to an action in which a case record is filed, including a person who has been permitted to intervene as a party, and a person who is the subject of or is specifically identified in a case record may file a motion:

(A) to seal or otherwise limit inspection of a case record filed in that action that is not otherwise shielded from inspection under the Rules in this Chapter; or

(B) to permit inspection of a case record filed in that action that is not otherwise subject to inspection under the Rules in this Chapter.

(2) The motion shall be filed with the court in which the case record is filed and shall be served on:

(A) all parties to the action in which the case record is filed; and

(B) each identifiable person who is the subject of the case record.

(b) **Shielding upon motion or request.** (1) Preliminary shielding upon motion. Upon the filing of a motion to seal or otherwise limit inspection of a case record pursuant to section (a) of this Rule, the custodian shall deny inspection of the case record for a period not to exceed five business days, including the day the motion is filed, in order to allow the court an opportunity to determine whether a temporary order should issue.

(2) Shielding upon request. If a request to shield information in a case record is filed by or on behalf of a person entitled to request the shielding under Code, Courts Article, Title 3, Subtitle 15 (peace orders) or Code, Family Law Article, Title 4, Subtitle 5 (domestic violence), and the request is granted, or if a request to shield the address or telephone number of a victim, victim's representative, or witness is filed in a criminal action, and the request is granted, a custodian shall deny inspection of the shielded information. The shield remains in effect until terminated or modified by order of court. If the request is denied, the person seeking to shield information may file a motion under section (a) of this Rule.

Committee note. — If a court or District Court Commissioner grants a request to shield information under subsection (b)(2) of this Rule, no adversary hearing is held unless a person seeking inspection of the shielded information files a motion under section (a) of this Rule.

(c) **Temporary order precluding or limiting inspection.** (1) The court shall consider a motion filed under this Rule on an expedited basis.

(2) In conformance with the provisions of Rule 15-504 (Temporary Restraining Order), the court may enter a temporary order precluding or limiting inspection of a case record if it clearly appears from specific facts shown by affidavit or other statement under oath that (A) there is a substantial basis for believing that the case record is properly subject to an order precluding or limiting inspection, and (B) immediate, substantial, and irreparable harm will result to the person seeking the relief if temporary relief is not granted before a full adversary hearing can be held on the propriety of a final order precluding or limiting inspection.

(3) A court may not enter a temporary order permitting inspection of a case record that is not otherwise subject to inspection under the Rules in this Chapter in the absence of an opportunity for a full adversary hearing.

(d) **Final order.** (1) After an opportunity for a full adversary hearing, the court shall enter a final order:

(A) precluding or limiting inspection of a case record that is not otherwise shielded from inspection under the Rules in this Chapter;

(B) permitting inspection, under such conditions and limitations as the court finds necessary, of a case record that is not otherwise subject to inspection under the Rules in this Chapter; or

(C) denying the motion.

(2) A final order shall include findings regarding the interest sought to be protected by the order.

(3) A final order that precludes or limits inspection of a case record shall be as narrow as practicable in scope and duration to effectuate the interest sought to be protected by the order.

(4) In determining whether to permit or deny inspection, the court shall consider:

(A) if the motion seeks to preclude or limit inspection of a case record that is otherwise subject to inspection under the Rules in this Chapter, whether a special and compelling reason exists to preclude or limit inspection of the particular case record; and

(B) if the motion seeks to permit inspection of a case record that is otherwise not subject to inspection under the Rules in this Chapter, whether a special and compelling reason exists to permit inspection.

(C) if the motion seeks to permit inspection of a case record that has been previously sealed by court order under subsection (d)(1)(A) of this Rule and the movant was not a party to the case when the order was entered, whether the order satisfies the standards set forth in subsections (d)(2), (3), and (4)(A) of this Rule.

(5) Unless the time is extended by the court on motion of a party and for good cause, the court shall enter a final order within 30 days after a hearing was held or waived.

(e) **Filing of order.** A copy of any preliminary or final order shall be filed in the action in which the case record in question was filed and shall be subject to public inspection.

(f) **Non-exclusive remedy.** This Rule does not preclude a court from exercising its authority at any time to enter an order that seals or limits inspection of a case record or that makes a case record subject to inspection. (Added Mar. 4, 2004, effective Oct. 1, 2004; amended July 25, 2006, effective July 25, 2006.)

Source. — This Rule is new.

Effect of amendments. — The 2006 amendment added (b)(2) and the committee note following (b)(2) and made related changes.

University of Baltimore Law Review. — For comment, "Access to Court Records: Shifting the Privacy Burden Away from Witnesses and Victims," see 36 U. Balt. L. Rev. 419 (2007).

Access to DVD and audiotape of confession. — Trial court had jurisdiction in a criminal case to determine a motion for access filed by a television station to obtain a copy of a DVD and audiotape of the defendant's confession as by intervening in the criminal matter was deemed the appropriate method, and the trial court did not abuse its discretion by authorizing the release of the same since the media already had full transcripts of the tapes and it balanced the public's right to access court records with the defendant's fair trial concerns, and the concerns of the victim's family by permitting redacted copies of the DVD and audiotape. State v. WBAL-TV, 187 Md. App. 135, 975 A.2d 909 (2009), cert. denied, 410 Md. 701, 980 A.2d 482, 2009 Md. LEXIS 752 (2009).

Rule 16-1010. Procedures for compliance.

(a) **Duty of person filing record.** (1) A person who files or authorizes the filing of a case record shall inform the custodian, in writing, whether, in the person's judgment, the case record, any part of the case record, or any information contained in the case record is confidential and not subject to inspection under the Rules in this Chapter.

(2) The custodian is not bound by the person's determination that a case record, any part of a case record, or information contained in a case record is not subject to inspection and shall permit inspection of a case record unless, in the custodian's independent judgment, subject to review as provided in Rule 16-1011, the case record is not subject to inspection.

(3) Notwithstanding subsection (b)(2) of this Rule, a custodian may rely on a person's failure to advise that a case record, part of a case record, or information contained in a case record is not subject to inspection, and, in default of such advice, the custodian is not liable for permitting inspection of the case record, part of the case record, or information, even if the case record, part of the case record, or information in the case record is not subject to inspection under the Rules in this Chapter.

(b) **Duty of clerk.** (1) In conformance with procedures established by administrative order of the Chief Judge of the Court of Appeals, the clerk shall make a reasonable effort, promptly upon the filing or creation of a case record, to shield any information that is not subject to inspection under the Rules in this Chapter and that has been called to the attention of the custodian by the person filing or authorizing the filing of the case record, in order that the case record, as shielded, may be subject to inspection.

(2) Persons who filed or authorized the filing of a case record filed prior to October 1, 2004 may advise the custodian in writing whether any part of the case record is not subject to inspection. The custodian is not bound by that determination. The custodian shall make a reasonable effort, as time and circumstances allow, to shield from those case records any information that is not subject to inspection under the Rules in this Chapter and that has been called to the attention of the custodian, in order that those case records, as shielded, may be subject to inspection. The duty under this subsection is subordinate to all other official duties of the custodian. (Added Mar. 4, 2004, effective Oct. 1, 2004.)

Source. — This Rule is new.

Rule 16-1011. Resolution of disputes by administrative or chief judge.

(a) If, upon a request for inspection of a court record, a custodian is in doubt whether the record is subject to inspection under the Rules in this Chapter, the custodian, after making a reasonable effort to notify the person seeking inspection and each person to whom the court record pertains, shall apply in writing for a preliminary judicial determination whether the court record is subject to inspection.

(1) If the record is in an appellate court or an orphans' court, the application shall be to the chief judge of the court.

(2) If the record is in a circuit court, the application shall be to the county administrative judge.

(3) If the record is in the District Court, the application shall be to the district administrative judge.

(4) If the record is in a judicial agency other than a court, the application shall be to the Chief Judge of the Court of Appeals, who may refer it to the county administrative judge of a circuit court.

(b) After hearing from or making a reasonable effort to communicate with the person seeking inspection and each person to whom the court record pertains, the court shall make a preliminary determination of whether the record is subject to inspection. Unless the court extends the time for good cause, the preliminary determination shall be made within 10 days after the court receives the written request.

(c) If the court determines that the record is subject to inspection, the court shall file an order to that effect. If a person to whom the court record pertains objects, the judge may stay the order to permit inspection for not more than five working days in order to allow the person an opportunity to file an appropriate action to enjoin the inspection. An action under this section shall be filed within 30 days after the order is filed, and the person who requested inspection of the record shall be made a party. If such an action is timely filed, it shall proceed in accordance with Rules 15-501 through 15-505.

(d) If the court determines that the court record is not subject to inspection, the court shall file an order to that effect and the person seeking inspection may file an action under the Public Information Act or on the basis of the Rules in this Chapter to compel the inspection. An action under this section shall be filed within thirty days after the order is filed.

(e) If a timely action is filed under section (c) or (d) of this Rule, the preliminary determination by the court shall not have a preclusive effect under any theory of direct or collateral estoppel or law of the case. If a timely action is not filed, the order shall be final and conclusive. (Added Mar. 4, 2004, effective Oct. 1, 2004.)

Source. — This Rule is new.

Copying of criminal case exhibits. — Trial court had jurisdiction in a criminal case to determine a motion for access filed by a television station to obtain a copy of a DVD and audiotape of the defendant's confession as by intervening in the criminal matter was deemed the appropriate method, and the trial court did not abuse its discretion by authorizing the release of the same since the media already had full transcripts of the tapes and it balanced the public's right to access court records with the defendant's fair trial concerns, and the concerns of the victim's family by permitting redacted copies of the DVD and audiotape. State v. WBAL-TV, 187 Md. App. 135, 975 A.2d 909 (2009), cert. denied, 410 Md. 701, 980 A.2d 482, 2009 Md. LEXIS 752 (2009).

TITLE 17. ALTERNATIVE DISPUTE RESOLUTION

CHAPTER 100. PROCEEDINGS IN CIRCUIT COURT.

Editor's note. — This Chapter was added Oct. 9, 1998, effective January 1, 1999.

Rule 17-101. Applicability.

(a) **Generally.** The rules in this Chapter apply to all civil actions in circuit court except (1) they do not apply to actions or orders to enforce a contractual agreement to submit a dispute to alternative dispute resolution and (2) other than Rule 17-104, they do not apply to health care malpractice claims.

Committee note. — Alternative dispute resolution proceedings in a health care malpractice claim are governed by Code, Courts Article, § 3-2A-06C.

(b) **Rules governing qualifications and selection.** The rules governing the qualifications and selection of a person designated to conduct court-ordered alternative dispute resolution proceedings apply only to a person designated by the court in the absence of an agreement by the parties. They do not apply to a master, examiner, auditor, or parenting coordinator appointed under Rules 2-541, 2-542, 2-543, or 9-205.2. (Amended Nov. 8, 2005, effective Jan. 1, 2006; June 7, 2011, effective July 1, 2011.)

Source. — This Rule is new.

Effect of amendments. — The 2005 amendment, effective January 1, 2006, in (a) combined the two sentences into one, added the (1) designation, substituted "apply to all civil actions" for "apply only to civil actions" and "court except (1) they" for the second instance of "The rules in this Chapter", added (2) and the Committee note, and made related changes.

The 2011 amendment, in the second sentence in (b), substituted "auditor, or parenting coordinator" for "or auditor" and substituted "2-543, or 9-205.2" for "or 2-543."

Rule 17-102. Definitions.

In this Chapter, the following definitions apply except as expressly otherwise provided or as necessary implication requires:

(a) **Alternative dispute resolution.** "Alternative dispute resolution" means the process of resolving matters in pending litigation through a

632

settlement conference, neutral case evaluation, neutral fact-finding, arbitration, mediation, other non-judicial dispute resolution process, or combination of those processes.

Committee note. — Nothing in these Rules is intended to restrict the use of consensus-building to assist in the resolution of disputes. Consensus-building means a process generally used to prevent or resolve disputes or to facilitate decision making, often within a multi-party dispute, group process, or public policy-making process. In consensus-building processes, one or more neutral facilitators may identify and convene all stakeholders or their representatives and use techniques to open communication, build trust, and enable all parties to develop options and determine mutually acceptable solutions.

(b) **Arbitration.** "Arbitration" means a process in which (1) the parties appear before one or more impartial arbitrators and present evidence and argument supporting their respective positions, and (2) the arbitrators render a decision in the form of an award that is not binding, unless the parties agree otherwise in writing.

Committee note. — Under the Federal Arbitration Act, the Maryland Uniform Arbitration Act, at common law, and in common usage outside the context of court-referred cases, arbitration awards are binding unless the parties agree otherwise.

(c) **Fee-for-service.** "Fee-for-service" means that a party will be charged a fee by the person or persons conducting the alternative dispute resolution proceeding.

(d) **Mediation.** "Mediation" means a process in which the parties work with one or more impartial mediators who, without providing legal advice, assist the parties in reaching their own voluntary agreement for the resolution of the dispute or issues in the dispute. A mediator may identify issues and options, assist the parties or their attorneys in exploring the needs underlying their respective positions, and, upon request, record points of agreement reached by the parties. While acting as a mediator, the mediator does not engage in arbitration, neutral case evaluation, neutral fact-finding, or other alternative dispute resolution processes and does not recommend the terms of an agreement.

(e) **Mediation communication.** "Mediation communication" means speech, writing, or conduct made as part of a mediation, including communications made for the purpose of considering, initiating, continuing, or reconvening a mediation or retaining a mediator.

(f) **Neutral case evaluation.** "Neutral case evaluation" means a process in which (1) the parties, their attorneys, or both appear before an impartial person and present in summary fashion the evidence and arguments supporting their respective positions, and (2) the impartial person renders an evaluation of their positions and an opinion as to the likely outcome of the dispute or issues in the dispute if the action is tried.

(g) **Neutral fact-finding.** "Neutral fact-finding" means a process in which (1) the parties, their attorneys, or both appear before an impartial person and present evidence and arguments supporting their respective positions as to particular disputed factual issues, and (2) the impartial person makes findings of fact as to those issues. Unless the parties otherwise agree in writing, those findings are not binding.

(h) **Settlement conference.** "Settlement conference" means a conference at which the parties, their attorneys, or both appear before an impartial person to discuss the issues and positions of the parties in the action in an attempt to resolve the dispute or issues in the dispute by agreement or by means other than trial. A settlement conference may include neutral case evaluation and neutral fact-finding, and the impartial person may recommend the terms of an agreement. (Amended Nov. 1, 2001, effective Jan. 1, 2002.)

Source. — This Rule is new.

Effect of amendments. — The 2001 amendment added the committee note after (a); rewrote (b) and added its committee note; rewrote (d); added (e) and redesignated the remaining sections accordingly; and added "of the dispute or issues in the dispute" after "outcome" in present (f).

University of Baltimore Law Forum. — For article, "The New Maryland Rules of Professional Conduct and Mediation: Perplexing Questions Answered and Perplexing Questions That Remain," see 36 U. Balt. L.F. 1 (2005).

Rule 17-103. General procedures and requirements.

(a) **In general.** A court may not require a party or the party's attorney to participate in an alternative dispute resolution proceeding except in accordance with this Rule.

(b) **Minimum qualifications required for court designees.** A court may not require a party or the party's attorney to participate in an alternative dispute resolution proceeding conducted by a person designated by the court unless (1) that person possesses the minimum qualifications prescribed in the applicable rules in this Chapter, or (2) the parties agree to participate in the process conducted by that person.

(c) **Procedure.** (1) Inapplicable to Child Access Disputes. This section does not apply to proceedings under Rule 9-205.

(2) Objection. If the court enters an order or determines to enter an order referring a matter to an alternative dispute resolution process, the court shall give the parties a reasonable opportunity (A) to object to the referral, (B) to offer an alternative proposal, and (C) to agree on a person to conduct the proceeding. The court may provide that opportunity before the order is entered or upon request of a party filed within 30 days after the order is entered.

(3) Ruling on Objection. The court shall give fair consideration to an objection to a referral and to any alternative proposed by a party. The court may not require an objecting party or the attorney of an objecting party to participate in an alternative dispute resolution proceeding other than a non-fee-for-service settlement conference.

(4) Designation of Person to Conduct Procedure. In an order referring an action to an alternative dispute resolution proceeding, the court may tentatively designate any person qualified under these rules to conduct the proceeding. The order shall set a reasonable time within which the parties may inform the court that (A) they have agreed on another person to conduct the

proceeding, and (B) that person is willing and able to conduct the proceeding. If, within the time allowed by the court, the parties inform the court of their agreement on another person willing and able to conduct the proceeding, the court shall designate that person. Otherwise, the referral shall be to the person designated in the order. In making a designation when there is no agreement by the parties, the court is not required to choose at random or in any particular order from among the qualified persons. Although the court should endeavor to use the services of as many qualified persons as possible, the court may consider whether, in light of the issues and circumstances presented by the action or the parties, special training, background, experience, expertise, or temperament may be helpful and may designate a person possessing those special qualifications.

Source. — This Rule is new.

Immunity of settlement officer. — An attorney appointed by the court as a settlement officer has the benefit of official immunity. 93 Op. Att'y Gen. 68 (May 1, 2008).

Rule 17-104. Qualifications and selection of mediators.

(a) **Qualifications in general.** To be designated by the court as a mediator, other than by agreement of the parties, a person must:

(1) unless waived by the court, be at least 21 years old and have at least a bachelor's degree from an accredited college or university;

Committee note. — This subsection permits a waiver because the quality of a mediator's skill is not necessarily measured by age or formal education.

(2) have completed at least 40 hours of mediation training in a program meeting the requirements of Rule 17-106;

(3) complete in every two-year period eight hours of continuing mediation-related education in one or more of the topics set forth in Rule 17-106;

(4) abide by any standards adopted by the Court of Appeals;

(5) submit to periodic monitoring of court-ordered mediations by a qualified mediator designated by the county administrative judge; and

(6) comply with procedures and requirements prescribed in the court's case management plan filed under Rule 16-202 b. relating to diligence, quality assurance, and a willingness to accept a reasonable number of referrals on a reduced-fee or pro bono basis upon request by the court.

(b) **Additional qualifications — Child access disputes.** To be designated by the court as a mediator with respect to issues concerning child access, the person must:

(1) have the qualifications prescribed in section (a) of this Rule;

(2) have completed at least 20 hours of training in a family mediation training program meeting the requirements of Rule 17-106; and

(3) have observed or co-mediated at least eight hours of child access mediation sessions conducted by persons approved by the county administrative judge, in addition to any observations during the training program.

(c) **Additional qualifications — Business and Technology Case Management Program cases.** To be designated by the court as a mediator of Business and Technology Program cases, other than by agreement of the parties, the person must:

(1) have the qualifications prescribed in section (a) of this Rule;

(2) within the two-year period preceding application for approval pursuant to Rule 17-107, have completed as a mediator at least five non-domestic circuit court mediations or five non-domestic non-circuit court mediations of comparable complexity (A) at least two of which are among the types of cases that are assigned to the Business and Technology Case Management Program or (B) have co-mediated an additional two cases from the Business and Technology Case Management Program with a mediator already approved to mediate these cases;

(3) agree to serve as co-mediator with at least two mediators each year who seek to meet the requirements of subsection (c)(2)(B) of this Rule; and

(4) agree to complete any continuing education training required by the Circuit Administrative Judge or that judge's designee.

(d) **Additional qualifications — Marital property issues.** To be designated by the court as a mediator in divorce cases with marital property issues, the person must:

(1) have the qualifications prescribed in section (a) of this Rule;

(2) have completed at least 20 hours of skill-based training in mediation of marital property issues; and

(3) have observed or co-mediated at least eight hours of divorce mediation sessions involving marital property issues conducted by persons approved by the county administrative judge, in addition to any observations during the training program.

(e) **Additional qualifications — Health care malpractice claims.** To be designated by the court as a mediator of health care malpractice claims, other than by agreement of the parties, the person must:

(1) have the qualifications prescribed in section (a) of this Rule;

(2) have completed as a mediator at least five non domestic circuit court mediations or five non domestic non circuit court mediations of comparable complexity;

(3) be knowledgeable about health care malpractice claims because of experience, training, or education; and

(4) agree to complete any continuing education training required by the court.

(f) **Additional qualifications — Proceedings to foreclose lien instruments.** To be designated by the court as a mediator in a proceeding to foreclose a lien instrument, other than by agreement of the parties, the person must:

(1) have the qualifications prescribed in section (a) of this Rule;

(2) have completed as a mediator at least five non-domestic circuit court mediations or five non-domestic non-circuit court mediations of comparable complexity;

(3) be knowledgeable about lien instruments and foreclosure proceedings because of experience, training, or education; and

(4) agree to complete any continuing education training required by the court. (Amended Nov. 1, 2001, effective Jan. 1, 2002; Nov. 12, 2003, effective Jan. 1, 2004; amended Nov. 8, 2005, effective Jan. 1, 2006; Feb. 10, 2009, effective May 1, 2009.)

Cross references. — Code, Courts Article, § 3-2A-06C (c).

Source. — This Rule is new.

Effect of amendments. — The 2001 amendment rewrote this Rule.

The 2003 amendment substituted "one or more of the topics set forth in" for "a program meeting the requirements of" in (a)(3); added a new (c) and redesignated former (c) as present (d).

The 2005 amendment, effective January 1, 2006, in (c)(2)(B) deleted "on a non-paid basis" after "co-mediated"; and added (e) and the cross reference note.

The 2009 amendment added (f).

Rule 17-105. Qualifications and selection of persons other than mediators and neutral experts.

(a) **Generally.** Except as provided in section (b) of this Rule, to be designated by the Court to conduct an alternative dispute resolution proceeding other than mediation, a person, unless the parties agree otherwise, must:

(1) abide by any standards adopted by the Court of Appeals;

(2) submit to periodic monitoring of court-ordered alternative dispute resolution proceedings by a qualified person designated by the county administrative judge;

(3) comply with procedures and requirements prescribed in the court's case management plan filed under Rule 16-202 b. relating to diligence, quality assurance, and a willingness to accept a reasonable number of referrals on a reduced-fee or pro bono basis upon request by the court;

(4) either (A) be a member in good standing of the Maryland bar and have at least five years experience in the active practice of law as (i) a judge, (ii) a practitioner, (iii) a full-time teacher of law at a law school accredited by the American Bar Association, or (iv) a Federal or Maryland administrative law judge, or (B) have equivalent or specialized knowledge and experience in dealing with the issues in dispute; and

(5) unless waived by the court, have completed a training program that consists of at least eight hours and has been approved by the county administrative judge.

(b) **Judges and masters.** A judge or master of the court may conduct a non-fee-for-service settlement conference. (Amended Nov. 1, 2001, effective Jan. 1, 2002; Nov. 12, 2003, effective Jan. 1, 2004; December 2, 2004, effective July 1, 2005; June 7, 2011, effective July 1, 2011.)

Cross references. — Rule 16-813, Maryland Code of Judicial Conduct, Rule 3.9 and Rule 16-814, Maryland Code of Conduct for Judicial Appointees, Rule 3.9.

Source. — This Rule is new.

Effect of amendments. — The 2001 amendment deleted "agree to" from the beginning of (a)(1) through (a)(3); substituted "any standards adopted" for "a code of ethics approved" in (a)(1); deleted "reasonable" preceding "procedures" in (a)(3); in (a)(5), inserted "unless waived by the court," at the beginning, deleted "either" preceding "completed", and substituted "that consists of ... county administrative judge" for "specified by the circuit administrative judge or conducted at least two alternative dispute resolution proceedings with respect to actions pending in a circuit court".

The 2003 amendment rewrote the heading of the Rule.

The 2004 amendment rewrote the cross references note.

The 2011 amendment substituted "Rule 3.9" for "Canon 4F" in two places in the cross reference note.

Cited in Dickerson v. Longoria, 414 Md. 419, 995 A.2d 721 (2010).

Rule 17-105.1. Neutral experts.

(a) **Definition.** A "neutral expert" means a person who has special expertise to provide impartial technical background information, an impartial opinion, or both in a specific area.

(b) **Selection.** When a court-appointed alternative dispute resolution practitioner or one or both of the parties believe that it would be helpful to have the assistance of a neutral expert, the practitioner may select a neutral expert, with the consent of the parties and at their expense, to be present at or participate in the mediation at the request of the practitioner.

(c) **Confidentiality.** (1) Mediation proceedings. In a mediation, the provisions of sections (a), (b), and (e) of Rule 17-109 apply to the neutral expert.

(2) Other alternative dispute resolution proceedings. In all other alternative dispute resolution proceedings, the parties and the alternative dispute resolution practitioner may require the neutral expert to enter into a written agreement binding the neutral expert to confidentiality. The written agreement may include provisions stating that the expert may not disclose or be compelled to disclose any communications related to the alternative dispute resolution proceeding in any judicial, administrative, or other proceedings. Communications related to the alternative dispute resolution proceeding that are confidential under an agreement allowed by this subsection are privileged and not subject to discovery, but information otherwise admissible or subject to discovery does not become inadmissible or protected from disclosure solely by reason of its use related to the alternative dispute resolution proceeding. (Added Nov. 12, 2003, effective Jan. 1, 2004.)

Source. — This Rule is new.

Rule 17-106. Mediation training programs.

(a) **In general.** To qualify under Rule 17-104 (a)(2), a mediation training program must include the following:

(1) conflict resolution and mediation theory, including causes of conflict, interest-based versus positional bargaining, and models of conflict resolution;

(2) mediation skills and techniques, including information gathering skills, communication skills, problem solving skills, interaction skills, conflict management skills, negotiation techniques, caucusing, cultural and gender issues, and power balancing;

(3) mediator conduct, including conflicts of interest, confidentiality, neutrality, ethics, and standards of practice;

(4) rules, statutes, and practice governing mediation in the circuit courts; and

(5) simulations and role-playing, monitored and critiqued by experienced mediator trainers.

(b) **Child access mediation training.** To qualify under Rule 17-104 (b)(2), a mediation training program must include the following:

(1) Maryland law relating to separation, divorce, annulment, child custody and visitation, child and spousal support;

(2) emotional aspects of separation and divorce on adults and children;

(3) screening for and addressing domestic violence;

(4) introduction to family systems and child development theory; and

(5) inter-relationship of custody and child support.

Source. — This Rule is new.

Editor's note. — This rule is set out above to correct the content of (a)(5), which inadvertently duplicated (a)(4) in the bound volume.

Rule 17-107. Procedure for approval.

(a) **Generally.** (1) Filing application. A person seeking designation to conduct alternative dispute resolution proceedings pursuant to Rule 2-504 in actions other than those assigned to the Business and Technology Case Management Program shall file an application with the clerk of the circuit court from which the person is willing to accept referrals. The application shall be substantially in the form approved by the State Court Administrator and shall be available from the clerk of each circuit court. If the person is applying for designation as a mediator, the application shall be accompanied by documentation demonstrating that the applicant has the qualifications required by Rule 17-104. If the person is applying for designation to conduct alternative dispute resolution proceedings other than mediation, the application shall be accompanied by documentation demonstrating that the applicant has the qualifications required by Rule 17-105 (a). The State Court Administrator may require the application and documentation to be provided in a word processing file or other electronic format.

(2) Action on application. After any investigation that the county administrative judge deems appropriate, the county administrative judge shall notify each applicant of the approval or disapproval of the application and the reasons for a disapproval.

(3) Approved lists. The clerk shall prepare a list of mediators found by the county administrative judge to meet the qualifications required by Rule 17-104 and a list of persons found by the county administrative judge to meet the qualifications required by Rule 17-105 (a). The lists, together with the applications of the persons on the lists, shall be kept current by the clerk and be available in the clerk's office to the public.

(4) Removal from list. After notice and a reasonable opportunity to respond, the county administrative judge shall remove a person from a list for failure to

maintain the applicable qualifications of Rule 17-104 or Rule 17-105 (a) or for other good cause.

(b) **Business and Technology Case Management Program.** (1) Filing application. A person seeking designation to conduct alternative dispute resolution proceedings pursuant to Rule 2-504 in actions assigned to the Business and Technology Case Management Program shall file an application with the Administrative Office of the Courts, which shall transmit the application to the Committee of Program Judges appointed pursuant to Rule 16-108 b. 4. The application shall be substantially in the form approved by the State Court Administrator and shall be available from the clerk of each circuit court. If the person is applying for designation as a mediator, the application shall be accompanied by documentation demonstrating that the applicant has the qualifications required by Rule 17-104. If the person is applying for designation to conduct alternative dispute resolution proceedings other than mediation, the application shall be accompanied by documentation demonstrating that the applicant has the qualifications required by Rule 17-105 (a). The State Court Administrator may require the application and documentation to be provided in a word processing file or other electronic format.

(2) Action on application. After any investigation that the Committee of Program Judges deems appropriate, the Committee shall notify the Administrative Office of the Courts that the application has been approved or disapproved, and if disapproved, shall state the reasons for the disapproval. The Administrative Office of the Courts shall notify each applicant of the action of the Committee and the reasons for a disapproval.

(3) Approved lists. The Administrative Office of the Courts shall prepare a list of mediators found by the Committee to meet the qualifications required by Rule 17-104 and a list of persons found by the Committee to meet the qualifications required by Rule 17-105 (a). The Administrative Office of the Courts shall (A) attach to the lists such additional information as the State Court Administrator specifies; (B) keep the lists current; and (C) transmit a copy of each current list to the clerk of each circuit court, who shall make them available to the public.

Committee note. — Examples of information that the State Court Administrator may specify as attachments to the lists made pursuant to this subsection include information about the person's qualifications, experience, and background and any other information that would be helpful to litigants selecting a person best qualified to conduct alternative dispute resolution proceedings in a specific case.

(4) Removal from list. After notice and a reasonable opportunity to respond, the Committee of Program Judges shall remove a person from a list for failure to maintain the applicable qualifications of Rule 17-104 or Rule 17-105 (a) or for other good cause. (Amended Nov. 12, 2003, effective Jan. 1, 2004.)

Source. — This Rule is new.

Effect of amendments. — The 2003 amendment rewrote the Rule.

Rule 17-108. Fee schedules.

Subject to the approval of the Chief Judge of the Court of Appeals, the circuit administrative judge of each circuit court may develop and adopt maximum fee schedules for persons conducting each type of alternative dispute resolution proceeding other than on a volunteer basis. In developing the fee schedules, the circuit administrative judge shall take into account the availability of qualified persons willing to provide those services and the ability of litigants to pay for those services. A person designated by the court, other than with the agreement of the parties, to conduct an alternative dispute resolution proceeding under Rule 2-504 may not charge or accept a fee for that proceeding in excess of that allowed by the applicable schedule. Violation of this Rule shall be cause for removal from all lists. (Amended Nov. 12, 2003, effective Jan. 1, 2004.)

Committee note. — The rates in a fee schedule may vary based on the type the alternative dispute resolution proceeding, the complexity of the action, and the qualifications of the alternative dispute resolution practitioner.

Source. — This Rule is new.

Effect of amendments. — The 2003 amendment, in the first and second sentences, substituted "circuit" for "county"; and in the third sentence, substituted "with" for "on," inserted "applicable"; and added the Committee note.

Rule 17-109. Mediation confidentiality.

(a) **Mediator.** Except as provided in sections (c) and (d) of this Rule, a mediator and any person present or otherwise participating in the mediation at the request of the mediator shall maintain the confidentiality of all mediation communications and may not disclose or be compelled to disclose mediation communications in any judicial, administrative, or other proceeding.

(b) **Parties.** Subject to the provisions of sections (c) and (d) of this Rule, (1) the parties may enter into a written agreement to maintain the confidentiality of all mediation communications and to require any person present or otherwise participating in the mediation at the request of a party to maintain the confidentiality of mediation communications and (2) the parties and any person present or otherwise participating in the mediation at the request of a party may not disclose or be compelled to disclose mediation communications in any judicial, administrative, or other proceeding.

(c) **Signed document.** A document signed by the parties that reduces to writing an agreement reached by the parties as a result of mediation is not confidential, unless the parties agree in writing otherwise.

Cross references. — See Rule 9-205 (d) concerning the submission of a memorandum of the points of agreement to the court in a child access case.

(d) **Permitted disclosures.** In addition to any disclosures required by law, a mediator and a party may disclose or report mediation communications to a potential victim or to the appropriate authorities to the extent that they believe it necessary to help:

(1) prevent serious bodily harm or death,

(2) assert or defend against allegations of mediator misconduct or negligence, or

(3) assert or defend against a claim or defense that because of fraud, duress, or misrepresentation a contract arising out of a mediation should be rescinded.

Cross references. — For the legal requirement to report suspected acts of child abuse, see Code, Family Law Article, § 5-705.

(e) **Discovery; admissibility of information.** Mediation communications that are confidential under this Rule are privileged and not subject to discovery, but information otherwise admissible or subject to discovery does not become inadmissible or protected from disclosure solely by reason of its use in mediation. (Amended Nov. 12, 2003, effective Jan. 1, 2004; amended Nov. 8, 2005, effective Jan. 1, 2006.)

Committee note. — A neutral expert appointed pursuant to Rule 17-105.1 is subject to the provisions of sections (a), (b), and (e) of this Rule.

Source. — This Rule is new.

Effect of amendments. — The 2003 amendment inserted "or otherwise participating in the mediation" once in (a) and twice in (b) and added the Committee note.

The 2005 amendment, effective January 1, 2006, added (d)(3).

University of Baltimore Law Forum. —

For article, "The New Maryland Rules of Professional Conduct and Mediation: Perplexing Questions Answered and Perplexing Questions That Remain," see 36 U. Balt. L.F. 1 (2005).

Stated in Att'y Griev. Comm'n v. Lee, 387 Md. 89, 874 A.2d 897 (2005).

APPENDIX: FORMS

Introductory statement.

Introductory statement.

The forms contained in this Appendix are limited in number and intended to illustrate some of the more commonly used forms in modern practice. Rule 1-302 provides that the forms in this Appendix are not mandatory except as otherwise expressly provided by rule or statute.

Forms 1 to 21.

Rescinded April 6, 1984, effective July 1, 1984.

Form 22. Notice of appeal.
  (Rule 8-201)

(Caption)

NOTICE OF APPEAL

_____ notes an appeal to the Court of
Special Appeals in the above-captioned action.

(Signature and Certificate of Service)

Editor's note. — This form was amended
Feb. 10, 1998, effective July 1, 1998.

Forms 22a to 26.
  Rescinded June 5, 1996, effective January 1, 1997.

Forms 27 to 36. Juvenile causes.
  New forms substituted.

Editor's note. — Forms 903-P/C to 920-   Order of the Court of Appeals dated June 18,
FOT were substituted for Forms 27 to 36 by   1975.

Form 611. Notice of judgment by default or decree pro confesso.
  Rescinded April 6, 1984, effective July 1, 1984.

Form 1-332. Notification of need for accommodation or interpreter.
  Rescinded April 5, 2005, effective July 1, 2005.

FORMS FOR JUVENILE CAUSES.

Form 903-P/C. Juvenile petition — Child.
MATTER OF
....
        (Respondent)

IN THE .... COURT
FOR .... CITY/COUNTY
SITTING AS A JUVENILE
COURT
        Case Number ....

JUVENILE PETITION — CHILD

TO THE HONORABLE JUDGE OF THE COURT:

The Petition of the State of Maryland respectfully shows:
1. That:
(a) The Respondent's home address is ....
....

644

(b) He resides with ....
    at that address.

(c) The name and address of his parent, guardian, or custodian is ....
....

(d) The Respondent's date of birth is ....

2. That the State alleges the Respondent is
    ☐ Delinquent   ☐ In need of supervision
    ☐ In need of assistance

3. That the facts on which the allegation is based are as follows: ....
....
in violation of ....
                        (specify law violated, if applicable)

4. That pending these proceedings, the Respondent:
    ☐ was released in the custody of ....
....
                            (name and address)
    ☐ has been in detention/shelter care since ....
                                                (date)
and that his parent, guardian, or custodian has/has not been notified of the
detention or shelter care.

WHEREFORE, the State asks that the Court make appropriate findings and
dispositions under the Juvenile Causes Law (Title 3, Subtitle 8, Courts Article,
Annotated Code of Maryland).

                            STATE OF MARYLAND
                            by ....
                            State's Attorney/Intake Officer
                            for .... City/County
                            Petitioner

The names of each witness to be summoned in support of this petition are:

Rev. 9/76

Editor's note. — By Order dated Nov. 5, 1976, effective Jan. 1, 1977, the Court of Appeals adopted the Fifty-sixth Report of the Standing Committee on Rules of Practice and Procedure, including the present Forms for juvenile causes.

Form 903-P/A. Juvenile petition — Adult.

(Caption)

JUVENILE PETITION — ADULT

TO THE HONORABLE JUDGE OF THE COURT:

The Petition of the State of Maryland respectfully shows:

1. That the Respondent was born on .... and is an adult residing at

....

2. That your petitioner alleges that the Respondent has willfully committed an act, omission, or condition which contributed to, encouraged, caused or tended to cause .... to be brought within the jurisdiction of the Courts as a

     ☐ delinquent child.
     ☐ child in need of supervision.
     ☐ child in need of assistance.

3. That the facts on which the allegation is based are as follows:

....

in violation of section 3-831 of the Courts Article of the Annotated Code of Maryland.

4. That pending these proceedings, the Respondent was
     ☐ not arrested on this charge
     ☐ released on recognizance
     ☐ detained in default of $...... bail.

WHEREFORE, the State asks that the Court make appropriate findings and dispositions under the Juvenile Causes Law (Title 3, Subtitle 8, Courts Article, Annotated Code of Maryland).

                      STATE OF MARYLAND
                      By ....
                      State's Attorney for
                      .... City/County
                      Petitioner

The names of each witness to be summoned in support of this petition are:
Rev. 9/76

Editor's note. — Section 3-831 of the Courts Article, referred to in paragraph 3, was redesignated by § 6, ch. 415, Acts 2001, to be § 3-8A-30 of the Courts Article.

Form 904-R. Recognizance of parent, guardian, or custodian.

RECOGNIZANCE OF PARENT, GUARDIAN, OR CUSTODIAN

I hereby acknowledge:

1. That I am the parent, guardian, or custodian of ....;
2. That the child was released into my custody at .... o'clock on ...., 19 ..., pending possible proceedings in the .... Court for .... City/County, sitting as a Juvenile Court;
3. That, as a condition of the child's release, I hereby assume the responsibility for retaining custody and control of the child and for bringing him before the court when ordered to do so;
4. That I have posted $...... as security for the child's appearance in court, and that all or part of it may be forfeited if I fail to produce the child when ordered to do so;

5. That the child may be taken into custody and I may be proceeded against for contempt of court if I fail to produce the child before the court when ordered to do so.

6. That I will immediately notify the Clerk of the Juvenile Court at ...., ..., of any new address for me or the child.

Address   Telephone

....
Witness

....
Parent/Guardian/Custodian

....
Address

....
Date

....
Telephone Number

Rev. 9/76

Form 904-S. Summons.

(Caption)

SUMMONS

STATE OF MARYLAND ....   City/County
TO: ....

....
     (Address)

....

....

You are hereby summoned to attend a ....
                      (specify type)
hearing in this case at ...., 19 ..., at ....., Maryland.

IF YOU FAIL TO ATTEND, YOU MAY BE ARRESTED.
ISSUED the .... day of .... , 19 ....
WITNESS the Honorable .... Judge of the ....
                                       (place)

Court for .... City/County, Maryland.

....
     (SEAL)   Clerk

TO THE PERSON SUMMONED: TAKE NOTICE that the Court may, at this or any later hearings, consider and pass orders concerning but not limited to the detention, shelter care, commitment, custody, treatment, and supervision of the respondent child; responsibility for his support; restitution by the respondent and/or his parents in an amount not to exceed $10,000; controlling the conduct of persons before the court; and assessment of court costs.

You may, if you wish, retain a lawyer to represent you or the child; if you do, be sure to show this Summons to him. If you cannot afford a lawyer, contact the Office of the Public Defender on any weekday between 8:30 and 4:30 at: .... Telephone Number: .... A postponement will NOT be granted because you fail to contact a lawyer.

Form 904-R/WS   MARYLAND RULES

If you do not want a lawyer, but you wish to subpoena witnesses on your behalf or on behalf of the respondent child, you must list their names and addresses neatly on the enclosed Request for Witness Subpoena Form, and mail it promptly to the Clerk at the address shown on the form.

RETURN OF SERVICE

SUMMONED ....   Non Est: ....
by personal service and delivering   Other ....
a copy of this Summons and the   ....
attached ....   ATTEMPTS AT SERVICE

....
to the said   Date   Time   Date   Time
.... at   ....

....
this .... day of ....   By: ....
19 ...   Sheriff

Rev. 9/76, 7/87, 12/95

Editor's note. — This form was amended April 6, 1984, effective July 1, 1984; March 3, 1987, effective July 1, 1987; and Nov. 21, 1995, effective Dec. 1, 1995.

Form 904-R/WS. Request for witness subpoena.

(Caption)

REQUEST FOR WITNESS SUBPOENA

Clerk, Juvenile Court for .... City/County

....
   (address)

....

Please subpoena the following:

Name: ....   Address: ....
     ....
     ....
     ....
     ....
to testify for the respondent at the hearing in this case.

         Signed ....
         Respondent, Parent, Guardian,
         Custodian or Attorney
         (Circle appropriate status)

Rev. 9/76

Editor's note. — This form was amended April 6, 1984, effective July 1, 1984.

Form 904-WS. Witness subpoena.

(Caption)

WITNESS SUBPOENA

STATE OF MARYLAND .... City/County:

TO: ....

....

(Address)

....

You are hereby subpoenaed to attend a hearing in this case at .... M. on

(time)

.... at ...., Maryland, to testify on behalf of the

    date   place

State/Respondent.

IF YOU FAIL TO ATTEND, YOU MAY BE ARRESTED.

ISSUED the ...... day of ...., 19 ....

WITNESS the Honorable ...., Judge of the .... Court for
.... City/County, Maryland.

....

    (SEAL)   Clerk

RETURN OF SERVICE

SUBPOENAED	Non Est: ....
by personal service of a copy	Other: ....
of this Subpoena	
Subpoenaed on the said	Date Time Date Time
.... at	....
....	....
this ...... day of	By: ....
19 ...	Sheriff

Rev. 9/76

Editor's note. — This form was amended April 6, 1984, effective July 1, 1984.

Form 904-WA. Writ of attachment.

(Caption)

WRIT OF ATTACHMENT

TO THE SHERIFF OF .... CITY/COUNTY

WHEREAS, the Respondent ...., was released in the custody of his parent, guardian or custodian on recognizance pending further proceedings, and his parent, guardian or custodian has failed to produce the Respondent at a hearing before the Court, you are commanded to take the said Respondent into custody and deliver him before the Court.

ISSUED this ...... day of ...., 19 ... by the .... Court for .... City/County, Maryland.

....
Clerk

CIPI this ...... day of ...., 19 ..., at ... M. and copy of writ delivered. NON EST ....

....
Sheriff

Rev. 9/76

Form 905-OE. Order for physical or mental examination of respondent.

(Caption)

ORDER FOR PHYSICAL OR MENTAL EXAMINATION OF RESPONDENT

WHEREAS, the Respondent is before this Court on a Juvenile Petition alleging that he is:

☐ delinquent
☐ in need of supervision
☐ in need of assistance; and

The Court believing that the Respondent should be examined in order to assist the Court in making a proper adjudication and disposition, it is thereupon

ORDERED, this ...... day of ...., 19 ..., by the .... Court for .... City/County, Maryland, sitting as a Juvenile Court, that the Respondent .... be examined by a qualified .... at .... on or before ...., 19 ..., for the purpose of advising the Court as to

☐ his competence to participate in these proceedings

☐ his responsibility for the alleged acts
☐ his general mental and physical condition
☐ the propriety of the Court waiving its jurisdiction
☐ any physical or mental condition that may require treatment

and it is further

ORDERED, that the Report of the examination be delivered to Court; and it is further

ORDERED, that the cost of the examination be paid by ....; and it is further

ORDERED, that a copy of this Order be served on the Respondent and on ....

Recommended:

....
Master for Juvenile Causes

                                    ....
                                    Judge

Rev. 9/76

Form 912-A. Authorization for emergency detention or shelter care pending hearing.

(Caption)

AUTHORIZATION FOR EMERGENCY DETENTION OR
SHELTER CARE PENDING HEARING

TO: ....
....
(Address)
....

WHEREAS, it has been determined that .... requires emergency

☐ detention, having been alleged delinquent;
☐ shelter care, having been alleged to be delinquent, in need of supervision, or in need of assistance

you are hereby authorized to receive and keep the child in your care and custody pending a hearing in this case on ....
                                    (Date)

Dated ...., 19 ....

                        STATE OF MARYLAND
                        By ....
                        Juvenile Services Intake Officer

Form 912-N MARYLAND RULES

Rev. 9/76

Form 912-N. Notice of emergency detention/shelter care and notice of hearing.

(Caption)

NOTICE OF EMERGENCY DETENTION/SHELTER CARE
AND NOTICE OF HEARING

TO: ....

....
(Address)

....
Parent, Guardian or Custodian
of ....

TAKE NOTICE that .... has been taken into custody for the reason that he is alleged to be

☐ delinquent
☐ in need of supervision
☐ in need of assistance

and that he was at ... M. on .... placed in emergency detention/shelter care at ...., Maryland, for the reasons indicated below:

☐ to protect the child, or the person and property of others;
☐ the child is believed likely to leave the jurisdiction of the Court;
☐ there appears to be no parent, guardian or custodian able to provide supervision and care for the child when required.

A hearing has been scheduled for ... M. on ...., 19 ..., before the .... Court for .... City/County, Maryland, to determine whether the said child should remain in detention or shelter care.

AS THE PARENT, GUARDIAN, OR CUSTODIAN OF THE CHILD, YOU ARE DIRECTED TO BE PRESENT AT THE HEARING.

If you wish, you may contact the Juvenile Services Agency Intake Officer at .... Maryland, Telephone No. ....

STATE OF MARYLAND
By ....
Juvenile Services Intake Officer
for .... City/County

Rev. 9/76, 8/87

Editor's note. — This form was amended July 27, 1987, effective August 17, 1987.

Form 912-P/CDSC. Petition for continued detention or shelter care.

(Caption)

PETITION FOR CONTINUED DETENTION OR SHELTER CARE
TO THE HONORABLE JUDGE OF THE COURT:

The Petition of the State of Maryland respectfully shows:

1. That the Respondent was taken into custody as the result of certain facts and conditions that indicate that he may be a

    ☐ delinquent child
    ☐ child in need of supervision
    ☐ child in need of assistance

2. That the Respondent was placed in emergency detention or shelter care at ... M. on ...., 19 ..., at ....
                                (place)

3. That an investigation is now being made to determine whether a Juvenile Petition should be filed with respect to the Respondent.

4. That pending the possible filing of Juvenile Petition, the Respondent should remain in detention or shelter care

    ☐ to protect the child, or the person and property of others;
    ☐ the child is believed likely to leave the jurisdiction of the Court;
    ☐ there appears to be no parent, guardian, or custodian able to provide supervision and care for the child and to return him to Court when required.

WHEREFORE, the State asks that the Court pass an Order continuing the detention or shelter care of the Respondent for a period not to exceed ...... days.

                  STATE OF MARYLAND
                  By ....
                  Juvenile Services Intake Officer
                  for ....City/County

Rev. 9/76

Form 912-O/CDSC. Order for continued detention or shelter care.

(Caption)

ORDER FOR CONTINUED DETENTION OR SHELTER CARE

WHEREAS, the Respondent having been alleged/adjudicated to be delinquent/in need of supervision/in need of assistance, and the Court, after a hearing, having found that the respondent's continued detention or shelter care is necessary pending further proceedings in this case; it is

ORDERED, this .... day of ...., 19 ..., by the .... Court for .... City/County, Maryland, sitting as a Juvenile Court, that the detention/shelter care of the Respondent at .... Maryland be continued pending the further order of this Court or the expiration of 30 days from the date of this Order, whichever first occurs; and it is further

ORDERED, that .... be, and hereby is, authorized and directed to retain the Respondent in its care and custody, with the right to consent to such medical, surgical and hospital care and treatment as may from time to time be determined to be in Respondent's best interests, subject to the further order of this Court; and it is further

ORDERED, that .... deliver the Respondent to the appropriate detention/shelter care facility and it is further

ORDERED, that a copy of this Order be served on the Respondent .... and ....

Recommended:

....
Master for Juvenile Causes

....
                                                                Judge

Form 913-P/W. Petition for waiver of juvenile jurisdiction.

(Caption)

PETITION FOR WAIVER OF JUVENILE JURISDICTION

TO THE HONORABLE JUDGE OF THE COURT:

The Petition of the State of Maryland respectfully shows:

1. That the Respondent was born on ....

2. That the petition filed in these proceedings alleges that the respondent is a delinquent child.

3. That the Respondent is an unfit subject for juvenile rehabilitative measures because:

☐   he is .... years of age and

☐   by reason of his physical and mental condition or past experience, he is not amenable to treatment in any institution, facility, or program available to delinquents;

☐   of the seriousness of the alleged offense;

☐   of the degree of his alleged participation in the offense;

☐   of the requirements of public safety;

☐   the Court has previously waived its jurisdiction with respect to the Respondent on another petition alleging delinquency.

WHEREFORE, the State asks that the Court waive its exclusive original jurisdiction so that the Respondent may be tried in the criminal court.

STATE OF MARYLAND

Form 914-O/A

By ....
State's Attorney
for ....City/County

Rev. 9/76

Form 913-O/W. Order waiving juvenile jurisdiction.

(Caption)

ORDER WAIVING JUVENILE JURISDICTION

WHEREAS,

☐ a waiver hearing having been held, upon petition by the State of Maryland/Motion of the Court,

☐ after summary review pursuant to § 3-817 of the Courts Article, it is ORDERED, this .... day of ...., 19 ..., by the .... Court for .... City/County, Maryland, sitting as a Juvenile Court, that this Court's exclusive original jurisdiction over the Respondent .... be, and it hereby is, waived; and it is further

ORDERED, that the Respondent be held for action under the appropriate criminal procedure; and it is further

ORDERED, that the Respondent be placed in the custody of the sheriff or other appropriate officer in an adult detention facility pending a bail hearing pursuant to Rule 4-222; and it is further

ORDERED, that a copy of this Order be served upon the Respondent, the State's Attorney for .... City/County, Maryland, and the sheriff or other custodian of the adult detention facility.

....
Judge

Rev. 9/76

Form 914-O/A. Order of adjudication.

(Caption)

ORDER OF ADJUDICATION

THIS cause having come on for an adjudicatory hearing on notice to all parties, the Court finds that the allegations of the petition have been proved

☐ beyond a reasonable doubt, that the respondent is a delinquent child;

☐ by a preponderance of the evidence, that the respondent is a child in need of supervision;

☐ by a preponderance of the evidence, that the respondent is a child in need of assistance;

and it is thereupon

ADJUDGED, ORDERED and DECREED, this .... day of ...., 19 ..., by the .... Court for .... City/County, Maryland, sitting as

655

a Juvenile Court, that the Respondent .... be and hereby is made and declared to be a ward of this Court; and it is further

ORDERED, that a copy of   this Order   be served upon the Respondent and ....

Recommended:

....
Master for Juvenile Causes

....
Judge

Rev. 9/76

Form 915-O/PDC. Order for probation of delinquent child.

(Caption)

ORDER FOR PROBATION OF DELINQUENT CHILD

WHEREAS, the Respondent has been adjudicated as a delinquent child, and the Court believes that the Respondent should be placed on probation, it is

ORDERED, this .... day of ...., 19 ..., by the .... Court for .... City/County, Maryland, sitting as a Juvenile Court, that the Respondent .... be, and hereby is placed on probation in the custody of .... but under the supervision of .... and subject to the following special conditions:

....
....

and to the further order of this Court; and it is further

ORDERED, that a copy of this Order be served on the Respondent and

Recommended:

....
Master for Juvenile Causes

....
Judge

Rev. 9/76

Form 915-O/CJ. Order for commitment of juvenile.

(Caption)

ORDER FOR COMMITMENT OF JUVENILE

WHEREAS, the Respondent was made a ward of this Court on ...., 19 ..., and the Court finds that the best interests of both the Respondent and the public would be served by removing the Respondent from his present environment, it is thereupon

ORDERED, this .... day of ...., 19 ..., by the .... Court for .... City/County, Maryland, sitting as a Juvenile Court, that the Respondent .... be, and hereby is committed to the care and custody of .... with the right of the custodian to consent to such medical, surgical, and hospital care and treatment as may from time to time be determined to be in the Respondent's best interest, subject to the further Order of this Court; and it is further

ORDERED, that .... shall deliver the Respondent to the appropriate detention/shelter care facility; and it is further

ORDERED, that a copy of this Order be served upon the Respondent and ....

Recommended:

....

Master for Juvenile Causes

....
                                   Judge

Rev. 9/76

Form 915-O/PS. Order for protective supervision.

(Caption)

ORDER FOR PROTECTIVE SUPERVISION

WHEREAS, the Respondent has been adjudicated as a child in need of supervision/assistance, and the Court believes that the Respondent should be placed in protective supervision, it is thereupon,

ORDERED, this .... day of ...., 19 ..., by the .... Court for .... City/County, Maryland, sitting as a Juvenile Court, that the Respondent .... be, and hereby is, placed in protective supervision in the custody of .... but under the supervision of .... subject to the following special conditions: ....

....

and to the further order of this Court; and it is further

ORDERED, that a copy of this Order be served upon the Respondent and ....

Recommended:

....

Master for Juvenile Causes

....
                                   Judge

Rev. 9/76

Form 915-O/PA. Order for probation — Adult.

(Caption)

ORDER FOR PROBATION — ADULT

WHEREAS, the Respondent has been convicted of violating Section 3-831 of the Courts Article, and the Court believes that the Respondent should be placed on probation under the conditions set forth in this Order, it is thereupon

ORDERED, this .... day of ...., 19 ..., by the .... Court for .... City/County, Maryland, sitting as a Juvenile Court, that the Respondent .... be, and hereby is, placed on probation for a period of .... under the supervision of .... subject to the following special conditions:

....
....

and to the further order of this Court; and it is further

ORDERED, that a copy of this Order be served upon the Respondent and

....

Recommended:

....

Master for Juvenile Causes

....
                                              Judge

Rev. 9/76

Form 916-P/RPC. Petition for revocation of probation and for commitment of delinquent child.

(Caption)

PETITION FOR REVOCATION OF PROBATION
AND FOR COMMITMENT OF DELINQUENT CHILD

TO THE HONORABLE JUDGE OF THE COURT:

The Petition of the State of Maryland respectfully shows:

1. That the Respondent was placed on probation in the custody of and under supervision of .... by Order of this Honorable Court dated ...., 19 ..., subject to the following special conditions .... and to the further Order of the Court.

2. That the Respondent has violated the following conditions of probation

....
....

WHEREFORE, the State asks that an Order be passed directing the Respondent to appear and show cause why his probation should not be revoked and why he should not be committed.

STATE OF MARYLAND

Form 916-SCO

By ....
....
(Agency)
Petitioner

Rev. 9/76

Form 916-P/RPSC. Petition for revocation of protective supervision and for commitment.

(Caption)

PETITION FOR REVOCATION OF PROTECTIVE SUPERVISION
AND FOR COMMITMENT

TO THE HONORABLE JUDGE OF THE COURT:

The Petition of the State of Maryland respectfully shows:

1. That the Respondent was placed in protective supervision in the custody of .... and under supervision of .... by Order of this Honorable Court on ...., 19 ..., subject to the following special conditions .... and subject to the further Order of the Court.

2. That the following conditions of protective supervision have been violated
....

WHEREFORE, the State asks that an Order be passed directing the Respondent to appear and show cause why the protective supervision should not be revoked and why he should not be committed.

STATE OF MARYLAND
By ....
....
(Agency)
Petitioner

Rev. 9/76

Form 916-SCO. Show cause order.

(Caption)

SHOW CAUSE ORDER

UPON consideration of the petition of the State of Maryland/the Motion of the Court, it is

ORDERED, this .... day of ...., 19 ..., by the .... Court for .... City/County, sitting as a Juvenile Court, that the Respondent ....

be, and hereby is, directed to appear in this Court at .... .M. on .... 19 ...,
and show cause why the Order for Probation or Protective Supervision passed
on ...., 19 ..., should not be rescinded and why the Respondent should not
be committed; provided that a copy of this Order and the petition of the State,
if any, be served upon the Respondent and on .... on or before ....,
19 ...

Recommended:

....
Master for Juvenile Causes

....
Judge

Rev. 9/76

**Form 916-O/RCAS. Order rescinding commitment and for aftercare
supervision.**

(Caption)

ORDER RESCINDING COMMITMENT AND FOR
AFTERCARE SUPERVISION

WHEREAS, the Respondent was committed by this Court to .... on
............, 19 ..., and the Court having found, upon the petition of ....,
that the interests of the Respondent and the public would best be served by the
Respondent's release from commitment and placement in protective supervision, it is thereupon

ORDERED, this ...... day of ...., 19 ..., by the .... Court for
.... City/County, Maryland, sitting as a Juvenile Court, that the commitment of the Respondent .... be, and it hereby is, rescinded, and that the
Respondent be released into the custody of .... effective ...., 19 ...;
and it is further

ORDERED, that the Respondent be, and hereby is, placed under the
supervision of .... subject to the following special conditions
....
and subject to the further Order of this Court; and it is further

ORDERED, that a copy of this Order be served on the Respondent, and on
....

Recommended:

....
Master for Juvenile Causes

....
Judge

Rev. 9/76

Form 918-O/S

Form 916-O/TPPS. Order   terminating   probation/protective supervision.

(Caption)

ORDER TERMINATING PROBATION/PROTECTIVE SUPERVISION

WHEREAS, the Respondent was placed on probation/in protective supervision by Order of this Court on ...., 19 ..., and the Court having found that the interests of the Respondent and the public would best be served by releasing the Respondent from that status, it is thereupon

ORDERED, this .... day of ...., 19 ..., by the .... Court for .... City/County, Maryland, sitting as a Juvenile Court, that the aforementioned Order for Probation/Protective Supervision be, and hereby is, rescinded, and the Respondent be, and hereby is, released from Probation/Protective Supervision; and it is further

ORDERED, that a copy of this Order be served on the Respondent and on

....

Recommended:

....

Master for Juvenile Causes

....

Judge

Rev. 9/76

Form 918-O/S. Order for support.

(Caption)

ORDER FOR SUPPORT

ORDERED, this .... day of ...., 19 ..., by the .... Court for .... City/County, Maryland, sitting as a Juvenile Court, that .... be, and hereby is, directed to pay the sum of $.......... per .... toward the support and maintenance of ...., a child subject to the jurisdiction of this Court, subject to the further Order of the Court; and it is further

ORDERED, that this sum be paid to ....; and it is further

ORDERED, that a copy of this Order be served on .... and ....

Recommended:

....

Master for Juvenile Causes

....

Judge

Rev. 9/76

Form 918-O/JR. Order for judgment of restitution.

(Caption)

ORDER FOR JUDGMENT OF RESTITUTION

WHEREAS, the Court having found that the Respondent child
☐ stole, damaged, destroyed, converted, unlawfully obtained, or substantially decreased the value of the property of .in the amount of $ ....;
☐ inflicted personal injury on ....
requiring that person to incur medical, dental, hospital, funeral or burial expenses in the amount of $ ....;
and that .... is the Respondent child or the parent of the Respondent child, it is thereupon
ORDERED, this .... day of ...., 19 ..., by the Court for .... City/County, Maryland, sitting as a Juvenile Court, that Judgment of Restitution in the amount of $ .... be, and it hereby is, entered against .... jointly and severally in favor of ...., pursuant to Section 3-829 of the Courts Article, and that the judgment debtor pay the costs of this proceeding; and it is further
ORDERED, that a copy of this Order be served on the Respondent, on .... and on ....
Recommended:

....
Master for Juvenile Causes

....
Judge

Rev. 9/76, 7/87, 8/87

Editor's note. — This form was amended March 3, 1987, effective July 1, 1987, and July 27, 1987, effective August 17, 1987.

Form 920-FOT. Final order of termination.

(Caption)

FINAL ORDER OF TERMINATION

ORDERED, this .... day of ...., 19 ..., by the .... Court for .... City/County, Maryland, sitting as a Juvenile Court, that this proceeding be, and it hereby is, terminated; and it is further
ORDERED, that a copy of this Order be served on the Respondent and on

....
Recommended:

....
Master for Juvenile Causes

....
Judge

Rev. 9/76

FORMS FOR EXPUNGEMENT OF RECORDS.

Rescinded April 6, 1984, effective July 1, 1984.

Editor's note. — Forms 4-503.1 through 4-503.4, 4-504.1 through 4-504.3, and 4-508.1 through 4-508.3, the present forms for ex- pungement of records, appear in Volume 1 of the Maryland Rules, following revised Title 4 and the Bail Bond forms.

BAIL BOND FORMS.

Rescinded April 6, 1984, effective July 1, 1984.

Editor's note. — Forms 4-217.1 and 4-217.2, the present bail bond forms, appear in Volume 1 of the Maryland Rules, following revised Title 4.

FORMS FOR SPECIAL ADMISSION OF OUT-OF-STATE ATTORNEY.

Form RGAB-14/M. Motion for special admission of out-of-state attorney under Rule 14 of the Rules Governing Admission to the Bar of Maryland.

(Caption)

MOTION FOR SPECIAL ADMISSION OF OUT-OF-STATE ATTORNEY UNDER RULE 14 OF THE RULES GOVERNING ADMISSION TO THE BAR OF MARYLAND

I, ..., attorney of record in this case, move that the court admit, ... of ...., an out-of-state attorney who is a member
  (name)   (address)
in good standing of the Bar of ....,
for the limited purpose of appearing and participating in this case as co-counsel with me.

Unless the court has granted a motion for reduction or waiver, the $100.00 fee required by Code, Courts and Judicial Proceedings Article, § 7-202 (e) is attached to this motion.

I ☐ do ☐ do not request that my presence be waived under Rule 14 (d) of the Rules Governing Admission to the Bar of Maryland.

....
Signature of Moving Attorney
....
Name
....
Address

663

....
Telephone

Attorney for ....

CERTIFICATE AS TO SPECIAL ADMISSIONS

I, ..., certify on this .... day of ...., ..., that during the preceding twelve months, I have been specially admitted in the State of Maryland .... times.

....
Signature of
Out-of-State Attorney

....
Name

....
Address

....
Telephone

(Certificate of Service)

(Amended September 8, 2011, effective January 1, 2012.)

Editor's note. — This form was renumbered (formerly appeared as Form RGAB-20/M) and amended Feb. 10, 1998, effective July 1, 1998.

Form RGAB-14/O. Order.

(Caption)

ORDER

ORDERED, this ...... day of ...., ..., by the .... Court for ...., Maryland, that

☐ .... is admitted specially for the limited purpose of appearing and participating in this case as co-counsel for .... The presence of the Maryland lawyer ☐ is ☐ is not waived.

☐ That the Special Admission of .... is denied for the following reasons: ....
.... and the Clerk shall return any fee paid for the Special Admission and it is further

ORDERED, that the Clerk forward a true copy of the Motion and of this Order to the State Court Administrator.

....
Judge

(Amended September 8, 2011, effective January 1, 2012.)

Editor's note. — This form was renumbered (formerly appeared as Form RGAB-20/O) and amended Feb. 10, 1998, effective July 1, 1998.

FORM INTERROGATORIES.

Committee note. — The following forms have been prepared to facilitate the exchange of meaningful information with a minimum of controversy. They are designed to be appropriate in a large percentage of cases, and the Committee encourages their use. In the context of some cases, however, they may be overly burdensome or otherwise inappropriate. The forms are not designed to limit the parties' right to frame their own interrogatories.

Rule 2-421 (a) provides that each form interrogatory contained in the appendix to these rules shall count as a single interrogatory even though some of the interrogatories, were it not for the rule, might constitute more than a single interrogatory for counting purposes. While use of the form interrogatories contained in this appendix may provide a safe harbor from the counting rules, that protection may be lost if any change is made to the interrogatory or in any of the instructions or definitions contained in this appendix.

It is suggested that when a form contained in this appendix is being used, that fact should be indicated in a parenthetical reference at the end of the form so that opposing counsel and the court may be aware that a form interrogatory is being used.

Editor's note. — Interrogatories, Forms 1 through 8 were adopted by Order of the Court of Appeals, dated January 18, 1996 and effective July 1, 1996.

Form 1. Instructions.

TO: [Name of party to answer interrogatories]

FROM: [Name of party propounding interrogatories]

Instructions

Pursuant to Rule 2-421, you are required to answer the following interrogatories within 30 days or within the time otherwise required by court order or by the Maryland Rules:

(a) In accordance with Rule 2-421 (b), your response shall set forth the interrogatory, and shall set forth the answer to the interrogatory "separately and fully in writing under oath" or "shall state fully the grounds for refusal to answer any interrogatory." The response shall be signed by you. (Standard Instruction (a).)

(b) Also in accordance with Rule 2-421 (b), your answers "shall include all information available" to you "directly or through agents, representatives, or attorneys." (Standard Instruction (b).)

(c) Pursuant to Rule 2-401 (e), these interrogatories are continuing. If you obtain further material information before trial you are required to supplement your answers promptly. (Standard Instruction (c).)

(d) If pursuant to Rule 2-421 (c), you elect to specify and produce business records of yours in answer to any interrogatory, your specification shall be in sufficient detail to enable the interrogating party to locate and identify the records from which the answer may be ascertained. (Standard Instruction (d).)

(e) If you perceive any ambiguities in a question, instruction, or definition, set forth the matter deemed ambiguous and the construction used in answering. (Standard Instruction (e).)

Committee note. — These instructions are designed to be used in virtually all cases.

Form 2. General definitions.

Definitions

In these interrogatories, the following definitions apply:

(a) **Document** includes electronically stored information and any writing, drawing, graph, chart, photograph, sound recording, image, and other data or data compilation stored in any medium from which information can be obtained, translated, if necessary, through detection devices into reasonably usable form. (Standard General Definition (a).)

(b) **Identify, identity,** or **identification**, (1) when used in reference to a natural **person**, means that **person's** full name, last known address, home and business telephone numbers, and present occupation or business affiliation; (2) when used in reference to a **person** other than a natural **person**, means that **person's** full name, a description of the nature of the **person** (that is, whether it is a corporation, partnership, etc. under the definition of **person** below), and the **person's** last known address, telephone number, and principal place of business; (3) when used in reference to any **person** after the **person** has been properly **identified** previously means the **person's** name; and (4) when used in reference to a **document**, requires you to state the date, the author (or, if different, the signer or signers), the addressee, the **identity** of the present custodian of the **document**, and the type of **document** (e.g., letter, memorandum, telegram, or chart) or to attach an accurate copy of the **document** to your answer, appropriately labeled to correspond to the interrogatory. (Standard General Definition (b).)

(c) **Person** includes an individual, general or limited partnership, joint stock company, unincorporated association or society, municipal or other corporation, incorporated association, limited liability partnership, limited liability company, the State, an agency or political subdivision of the State, a court, and any other governmental entity. (Standard General Definition (c).) (Amended June 10, 1997, effective July 1, 1997; Mar. 5, 2001, effective July 1, 2001; amended Sept. 10, 2009, effective Oct. 1, 2009.)

Committee note. — These definitions are designed to be used in virtually all cases. In order to flag the use of a defined term in the actual interrogatories and alert the responding party to the need to consult the definition, defined terms have been printed in bold type.

Effect of amendments. — The 1997 amendment substituted "means that **person's** full name, a description of the nature of the **person**" for "includes a description of the nature of the **person**" in (b) (2).

The 2001 amendment, in (b) (4), inserted "the **identity** of the present custodian of the **document**" following "addressee," inserted a comma following "e.g." and substituted "telegram or chart" for "telegram, chart, etc."

The 2009 amendment in (a) added "electronically stored information and any," "sound," "or data," and "stored in any medium."

Form 3. General interrogatories.

Interrogatories

1. **Identify** each **person**, other than a person intended to be called as an expert witness at trial, having discoverable information that tends to support a position that you have taken or intend to take in this action, including any claim for damages, and state the subject matter of the information possessed by that **person**. (Standard General Interrogatory No. 1.)

2. **Identify** each **person** whom you expect to call as an expert witness at trial, state the subject matter on which the expert is expected to testify, state the substance of the findings and opinions to which the expert is expected to testify and a summary of the grounds for each opinion, and, with respect to an expert whose findings and opinions were acquired in anticipation of litigation or for trial, summarize the qualifications of the expert, state the terms of the expert's compensation, and attach to your answers any available list of publications written by the expert and any written report made by the expert concerning the expert's findings and opinions. (Standard General Interrogatory No. 2.)

3. If you intend to rely upon any **documents,** electronically stored information, or tangible things to support a position that you have taken or intend to take in the action, including any claim for damages, provide a brief description, by category and location, of all such **documents,** electronically stored information, and tangible things, and **identify** all **persons** having possession, custody, or control of them. (Standard General Interrogatory No. 3.)

4. Itemize and show how you calculate any economic damages claimed by you in this action, and describe any non-economic damages claimed. (Standard General Interrogatory No. 4.)

5. If any **person** carrying on an insurance business might be liable to satisfy part or all of a judgment that might be entered in this action or to indemnify or reimburse for payments made to satisfy the judgment, **identify** that **person**, state the applicable policy limits of any insurance agreement under which the **person** might be liable, and describe any question or challenge raised by the **person** relating to coverage for this action. (Standard General Interrogatory No. 5.) (Amended Nov. 12, 2003, effective Jan. 1, 2004; Dec. 4, 2007, effective Jan. 1, 2008.)

Committee note. — These interrogatories are general in nature and are designed to be used in a broad range of cases.

Effect of amendments. — The 2003 amendment, in 2, inserted "and with respect to an expert whose findings and opinions were acquired in anticipation of litigation or for trial, summarize the qualifications of the ex-pert, state the terms of the expert's compensation" and "any available list of publications written by the expert and" and substituted "the expert's" for "those."

The December 4, 2007 Order, effective Jan-

uary 1, 2008, in 3, substituted "electronically
stored information, or tangible things" for "or
other tangible things" in two places.

Form 4. Domestic relations definitions.

Definitions

(a) **Employer** means any **person** that has compensated, or is obligated to
compensate, you for services. (Standard Domestic Relations Definition (a).)

(b) **Fringe benefits** include: (1) contributions made by your **employer** to
health insurance, life insurance, disability insurance, pension, profit sharing,
or retirement plans; and (2) **employer** reimbursements or payments that
reduce your personal living expenses such as use of a company car, expense
accounts, and housing. (Standard Domestic Relations Definition (b).)

(c) **Property** includes:

(1) accounts in any financial institution or brokerage, including certificates
of deposit;

(2) cash;

(3) debts owed to you, secured or unsecured, actual or contingent;

(4) home furnishings, jewelry, furs, stamp or coin collections, antiques, and
works of art;

(5) intellectual property, including patents, royalties, and copyrights;

(6) interests in any entity, including partnerships, joint ventures, and
corporations;

(7) interest in improved or unimproved real property, including leaseholds,
condominiums, and time share interests;

(8) life insurance and annuities;

(9) military or federal retirement benefits;

(10) pension plans, profit sharing plans, individual retirement accounts,
and retirement plans;

(11) securities, including stocks, bonds, mutual funds, United States Government obligations, options, and debentures;

(12) vehicles, boats, aircraft, equipment, machinery, crops, livestock, and
poultry;

(13) workers' compensation claims and tort or contract claims against
another; and

(14) any other interest or asset. (Standard Domestic Relations Definition
(c).)

(d) **Wages** include hourly **wages**, salary, bonuses, tips, incentive awards,
fees, commissions, self-employment income, and overtime pay. (Standard
Domestic Relations Definition (d).)

Committee note. — These definitions, in
addition to the General Definitions, are designed to be used in domestic relations cases.

Form 5. Domestic relations interrogatories.

Interrogatories

1. **Identify** yourself and all individuals with whom you reside. For each individual other than yourself, state that individual's age, relationship to you, and marital status. State your own birth date and social security number. (Standard Domestic Relations Interrogatory No. 1.)

2. Describe your educational background. Include in your answer the highest grade you completed; the name and date of any degree, diploma, or certificate you received, and the name of the institution conferring the degree, diploma, or certificate; and any specialized training you have received. (Standard Domestic Relations Interrogatory No. 2.)

3. If you are currently employed in any capacity, **identify** each current **employer** and, for each employment, state: (a) your job title, (b) your duties, (c) the number of hours in your average work week, (d) your regular pay period, (e) your gross **wages** per pay period, and (f) the deductions per pay period made by your **employer** from your **wages**. If overtime work was available to you during the past 12 months, state: (a) the number of overtime hours you worked during the 12 months and your rate of pay for those hours and (b) the number of overtime hours that were available to you during the 12 months but that you did not work and the rate of pay you would have received if you had worked those hours. (Standard Domestic Relations Interrogatory No. 3.)

4. Describe the nature and amount of any **fringe benefits** that you receive as a result of your employment. (Standard Domestic Relations Interrogatory No. 4.)

5. If you are unemployed, describe your efforts to obtain employment since you became unemployed, **identify** each prospective **employer** and employment agency you have contacted while seeking employment and state the date of each contact. (Standard Domestic Relations Interrogatory No. 5.)

6. If you claim you are physically or mentally unable to work or your capacity to work is limited, state the facts upon which your claim is based and **identify** all **persons** with personal knowledge of those facts. (Standard Domestic Relations Interrogatory No. 6.)

7. For each employment that you have had during the past five years other than any current employment, **identify** each **employer** and for each employment state: (a) the dates of employment, (b) your duties, (c) your **wages**, and (d) your reason for leaving the job. If you were unemployed for any period of time, specify the amount and source of any income that you received while unemployed. (Standard Domestic Relations Interrogatory No. 7.)

8. **Identify** the sources and amounts of all taxable and non-taxable income you received during the past five years. (Standard Domestic Relations Interrogatory No. 8.)

9. **Identify** the sources and amounts of any other moneys and credit(s) you received during the past five years with an aggregate value in excess of $250 in any one year, including gifts, loans from others, loans repaid to you by others, sales of assets, and untaxed distributions. (Standard Domestic Relations Interrogatory No. 9.)

10. List each item of **property** in which you have any interest. For each item listed, state how it is titled, its value, the amount of any present lien or mortgage on the **property**, the date of acquisition of the **property**, and the **identity** of any other **person** with an interest in the **property**. If you claim that any **property** listed is not marital **property**, state the facts upon which you base your claim, including all sources of funds used for the acquisition of the **property** and **identify** all **persons** with personal knowledge of those facts. (Standard Domestic Relations Interrogatory No. 10.)

11. If you, either alone or with anyone other than your spouse, transferred **property** during the last five years of your marriage with a value in excess of $250 to any **person** other than your spouse without receiving full consideration in money or money's worth for the **property** transferred, **identify** each **person** to whom a transfer was made and the **property** transferred, giving the date and method of transfer and the value of the **property** at the time of transfer. (Standard Domestic Relations Interrogatory No. 11.)

12. If the information contained on your financial statement submitted pursuant to Rule 9-202 (e) or (f) has changed, describe each change. (Standard Domestic Relations Interrogatory No. 12.)

13. State by type and amount all support provided by you for your spouse and children since the date of your separation. (Standard Domestic Relations Interrogatory No. 13.)

14. State the date on which you separated from your spouse and describe the circumstances of the separation. (Standard Domestic Relations Interrogatory No. 14.)

15. If you contend that you are entitled to a divorce because your spouse's conduct toward you or your minor child was cruel or vicious or that your spouse constructively deserted you, describe your spouse's conduct and state the date and nature of any injuries sustained by you or your minor child and the date, nature, and provider of health care services rendered regarding the injuries. **Identify** all **persons** with personal knowledge of your spouse's conduct and all **persons** with knowledge of any injuries you or your minor child sustained as a result of that conduct. (Standard Domestic Relations Interrogatory No. 15.)

16. State the date on which you and your spouse last had sexual relations with each other. (Standard Domestic Relations Interrogatory No. 16.)

17. If you have had sexual relations with a **person** other than your spouse during your marriage, **identify** the **person(s)** with whom you have had sexual relations, state the date of each act of sexual relations, and state the location where each act took place. If you refuse to answer this interrogatory as framed because the answer would tend to incriminate you, so state and answer for the period ending one year prior to the date of your answers. (Standard Domestic Relations Interrogatory No. 17.)

18. If you have had sexual relations with a **person** other than your spouse during the marriage and you contend that your spouse has forgiven or condoned your actions, state the facts upon which your contention is based. (Standard Domestic Relations Interrogatory No. 18.)

19. If you contend that your spouse is unfit to have custody of the children, state the facts upon which your contention is based and **identify** all **persons**

having personal knowledge of these facts. If your contention is based on the use of controlled dangerous substances or the abuse of alcohol on specific occasions, **identify** the substance used, the other **persons** present at the time of the use, and the date, time, and place of the use. If your contention is based on the repeated use of controlled dangerous substances or the repeated abuse of alcohol, **identify** the substance and all **persons** with personal knowledge of the repeated use or abuse. (Standard Domestic Relations Interrogatory No. 19.)

20. If you have sought or received treatment or therapy at any time during the past 10 years for any physical, mental, or emotional condition, including drug addiction or alcoholism, describe the condition and the treatment or therapy provided, state the date or dates of treatment or therapy, and **identify** all **persons** providing treatment or therapy. (Standard Domestic Relations Interrogatory No. 20.)

21. If you contend that placing the children in your sole, shared, or joint custody will be in their best interest, specify the facts and circumstances upon which you rely. (Standard Domestic Relations Interrogatory No. 21.)

22. Describe the child care plan you intend to follow when the children are with you. Include in your answer a description of the place where the children will reside, specifying the number of bedrooms, bathrooms, and other rooms, the distance to the school which the children will attend, and the **identity** of all other **persons** who will be residing in that household. **Identify** all **persons** who will care for the children in your absence, state the hours during which they will care for the children, and the location where the care will be provided. (Standard Domestic Relations Interrogatory No. 22.) (Amended Dec. 16, 1999, effective Jan. 1, 2000; Nov. 12, 2003, effective Jan. 1, 2004.)

Effect of amendments. — The 1999 amendment substituted "Rule 9-203 f" for "Rule S72 f" in 12.

The 2003 amendment substituted "9-202 (e) or (f)" for "9-203 f" in 12 and rewrote 15.

Form 6. Motor vehicle tort definitions.

Definitions

(a) The term **occurrence**, unless otherwise indicated, means the collision or other event complained of in the pleadings. (Standard Motor Vehicle Tort Definition (a).)

(b) The phrase **in [a, the, or that] vehicle** includes entering, exiting, and being in or on a vehicle. (Standard Motor Vehicle Tort Definition (b).)

(c) The term **possession** includes possession, custody, or control. (Standard Motor Vehicle Tort Definition (c).)

Committee note. — These definitions, in addition to the General Definitions, are designed to be used in motor vehicle tort cases.

Form 7. Motor vehicle tort interrogatories.

Interrogatories

1. **Identify** yourself and state all names by which you have been known, your date of birth, your marital status, and the **identity** of your spouse. (Standard Motor Vehicle Tort Interrogatory No. 1.)

2. State all addresses at which you have resided for the past five years and the date that you resided at each. (Standard Motor Tort Interrogatory No. 2.)

3. Describe in detail how the **occurrence** took place. (Standard Motor Vehicle Tort Interrogatory No. 3.)

4. **Identify** all **persons** who were witnesses to the **occurrence** and state their location at the time of the **occurrence**.

5. **Identify** all **persons** who were at or near the scene at the time of the **occurrence**. (Standard Motor Vehicle Tort Interrogatory No. 5.)

6. If you were **in a vehicle** at the time of the **occurrence**, **identify** all other **persons** who were **in that vehicle**. (Standard Motor Vehicle Tort Interrogatory No. 6.)

7. **Identify** all **persons** who arrived at the scene within two hours after the **occurrence**. (Standard Motor Vehicle Tort Interrogatory No. 7.)

8. If you were **in a vehicle** at the time of the **occurrence**, state the itinerary of the vehicle, including the time and place of the beginning of the trip, the time and duration of each stop, the destination, and the expected time of arrival. (Standard Motor Vehicle Tort Interrogatory No. 8.)

9. If you were engaged in any activity for an employer or other **person** at the time of the **occurrence**, state the nature of the activity and **identify** the employer or other **person**. (Standard Motor Vehicle Tort Interrogatory No. 9.)

10. If a report with respect to the **occurrence** was made in the ordinary course of business, state the date on which the report was made, the **identity** of the **person** who made the report, and whether the report was written, oral, or in some other form. **Identify** each **document** containing information concerning the report and the custodian of the **document**. (Standard Motor Vehicle Tort Interrogatory No. 10.)

11. **Identify** all photographs, videotapes, plats, diagrams, or other depictions of the scene or of things connected with the **occurrence** that are in your **possession**. (Standard Motor Vehicle Tort Interrogatory No. 11.)

12. Identify all persons who have given you "statements," as that term is defined in Rule 2-402 (f), concerning the action or its subject matter. For each statement, state the date on which it was given and **identify** the custodian. (Standard Motor Vehicle Tort Interrogatory No. 12.)

13. If you were charged with any offenses arising out of the **occurrence**, state the nature of the charges, the court and case number, and the disposition of the charges. (Standard Motor Vehicle Tort Interrogatory No. 13.)

14. If you contend that any party to this action caused or contributed to the **occurrence**, state concisely the facts on which you rely. (Standard Motor Vehicle Tort Interrogatory No. 14.)

15. If you contend that a **person** not a party to this action caused or contributed to the **occurrence**, **identify** each such **person** and state con-

cisely the facts upon which you rely. (Standard Motor Vehicle Tort Interrogatory No. 15.)

16. If you owned or were **in a vehicle** damaged as a result of the **occurrence**, describe any damage to the vehicle. If the vehicle was repaired, **identify** the **person** who performed the repairs, the dates of the repairs, and the cost. If the vehicle is unrepaired, state the address where and the hours when it may be seen. (Standard Motor Vehicle Tort Interrogatory No. 16.)

17. If you owned or were **in a vehicle** involved in the **occurrence**, state: when the vehicle was last repaired before the **occurrence**; the nature, dates, and costs of the repairs; the **identity** of the **persons** making the repairs; and the extent of any unrepaired damage to the vehicle immediately prior to the **occurrence**. (Standard Motor Vehicle Tort Interrogatory No. 17.)

18. If you contend that mechanical failure caused or contributed to the **occurrence**, state concisely the facts upon which you rely. (Standard Motor Vehicle Tort Interrogatory No. 18.)

19. If you were **in a vehicle** at the time of the **occurrence**, **identify** the owner and the driver of the vehicle. If you were not the owner, state whether you had the permission of the owner to be **in the vehicle** and the purpose for which permission was given. (Standard Motor Vehicle Tort Interrogatory No. 19.)

20. If you were the driver of a vehicle involved in the **occurrence**, state whether you have or have ever had any disability, illness, disease, or injury that could affect your ability to operate a motor vehicle, and describe its nature and extent. If treated or evaluated, **identify** all treating or examining health care providers and the approximate date of each examination or treatment. (Standard Motor Vehicle Tort Interrogatory No. 20.)

21. State whether you used any alcoholic beverages or drugs, whether controlled or otherwise, within 24 hours before the **occurrence**, the places where they were obtained, the places where they were used, and the nature and amount used. (Standard Motor Vehicle Tort Interrogatory No. 21.)

22. State the substance of all discussions concerning the **occurrence** that you or others in your presence had with any party to this case. State when and where each discussion took place and **identify** all **persons** who were present. (Standard Motor Vehicle Tort Interrogatory No. 22.)

23. State whether you have **possession** or knowledge of any recordings or transcripts of testimony in any proceeding arising out of the **occurrence**. If so, state the date and subject matter, and **identify** each **person** who recorded the testimony and the custodian of each recording or transcript. (Standard Motor Vehicle Tort Interrogatory No. 23.)

24. If you were **in a vehicle** involved in the **occurrence**, state whether the driver of the vehicle has a current driver's license. If so, state when and where the license was issued, the nature of any restrictions on the license, and whether the license was ever suspended or revoked. (Standard Motor Vehicle Tort Interrogatory No. 24.)

25. State whether, at any time during the fifteen year period preceding the date of your answers to these interrogatories, you have been convicted of any crime other than a minor traffic offense. If so, for each conviction **identify** the

court in which you were convicted and state the amount of any fine and the date and length of any incarceration imposed. For purposes of this interrogatory, a conviction includes a plea of *nolo contendere* followed by a sentence, whether or not the sentence is suspended. (Standard Motor Vehicle Tort Interrogatory No. 25.)

26. If you were **in a vehicle** at the time of the **occurrence**, state whether there were any electronic devices capable of two-way voice, text, data, or image transmission **in the vehicle** and for each device:

(a) state the type of device (e.g., cellular telephone, personal digital assistant, citizens' band radio, mobile data terminal);

(b) **identify** the owner of the device;

(c) **identify** the **person** who had **possession** of the device at the time of the **occurrence**;

(d) state whether the device was in use at the time of the **occurrence**;

(e) **identify** the service provider for the device;

(f) state the account number with the service provider; and

(g) if the device has a telephone number, state the number, including the area code. (Standard Motor Vehicle Tort Interrogatory No. 26) (Amended Mar. 5, 2001, effective July 1, 2001; Nov. 12, 2003, effective Jan. 1, 2004; Dec. 4, 2007, effective Jan. 1, 2008; amended Sept. 10, 2009, effective Oct. 1, 2009.)

Effect of amendments. — The 2001 amendment rewrote 10.

The 2003 amendment substituted "(e)" for "(d)" in 12.

The December 4, 2007 Order, effective January 1, 2008, in 12, substituted "Rule 2-402 (f)" for "Rule 2-402 (e)".

The 2009 amendment added 26.

Form 8. Personal injury interrogatories.

Interrogatories

1. Describe each injury sustained by you as a result of the **occurrence**, and state whether the injury was temporary or is permanent. (Standard Personal Injury Interrogatory No. 1.)

2. Describe all current symptoms, disabilities, and other physical or mental conditions that you claim are a result of the **occurrence**. (Standard Personal Injury Interrogatory No. 2.)

3. **Identify** each health care provider who has examined or treated you as a result of the **occurrence**, and for each provider state the date and purpose of each examination or treatment. (Standard Personal Injury Interrogatory No. 3.)

4. **Identify** all hospitals or other facilities at which you have been examined or treated as a result of the **occurrence**, and for each state the dates of your examinations or treatments and, if you were admitted, the dates of your admissions and discharges. (Standard Personal Injury Interrogatory No. 4.)

5. **Identify** all health care providers, other than those otherwise **identified** in your answers, who have examined or treated you during the period commencing five years before the **occurrence** and extending to the present, **identify** all hospitals and other facilities at which you were examined or

treated, and describe the condition for which you were examined or treated. (Standard Personal Injury Interrogatory No. 5.)

6. State whether you claim past or future loss of earnings or earning capacity as a result of the **occurrence** and, if so, state for each category the amount claimed, the method by which you computed that amount, the figures used in that computation, and the facts and assumptions upon which your claim is based. (Standard Personal Injury Interrogatory No. 6.)

7. State the amount you reported as earned income on your federal income tax returns for each of the past three years and whether you have a copy of the returns. (Standard Personal Injury Interrogatory No. 7.)

8. Itemize all expenses and other economic damages, past and future, that you claim are a result of the **occurrence** and as to each item claimed **identify** the item, the amount claimed for that item, the method, if any, by which you computed the amount, the figures used in that computation, and the facts and assumptions upon which your claim is based. (Standard Personal Injury Interrogatory No. 8.)

9. State whether prior or subsequent to the **occurrence** you have sustained any accidental injury for which you received medical care or treatment. If so, describe the date and circumstances of the accidental injury and **identify** all health care providers, including hospitals and other institutions, that furnished care to you. (Standard Personal Injury Interrogatory No. 9.)

10. State whether you have applied for any Medicare, Medicaid, or other federally funded benefits with respect to the injuries or **occurrence** complained of in this action, and if so, for each such application:

(a) state the type of benefits involved;

(b) **identify** the funding source to which you applied;

(c) state the case number, policy number, or other identifier assigned to your application;

(d) state the amount of benefits paid, if any; and

(e) **identify** all **documents** that contain any of the information requested in this interrogatory. (Standard Personal Injury Interrogatory No. 10.) (Amended Jan. 8, 2002, effective Feb. 1, 2002; amended Sept. 10, 2009, effective Oct. 1, 2009.)

Effect of amendments. — The 2002 amendment substituted "disabilities" for "handicaps" in 2. The 2009 amendment added 10.

Form 9. Product liability definitions.

Definitions

(a) **Component** means a part or ingredient. (Standard Product Liability Definition (a).)

(b) **Component(s) at issue** means the [insert description of the alleged defective **component(s)** of **The Product**, e.g., "the steering mechanism"] alleged to be defective in this action. If **The Product** has only one **component**, the **component at issue** is **The Product**. (Standard Product Liability Definition (b).)

(c) **Component substantially similar to the component(s) at issue** means ... [insert fact-specific description of "component substantially similar to the component(s) at issue"].

(d) **Occurrence**, unless otherwise indicated, means the accident or other event complained of in the pleadings. (Standard Product Liability Definition (d).)

(e) **Product information** means an instruction or warning as to use or risks of a product. (Standard Product Liability Definition (e).)

(f) **Substantially similar product** means ... [insert fact-specific definition of "substantially similar product"].

(g) **The Product** means the particular [insert description of product, e.g., "XYZ Motors 1999 Dreammobile bearing Vehicle Identification Number ABCD1234EFG56"] alleged in the pleadings to have been involved in the **occurrence**. (Standard Product Liability Definition (g).) (Added Mar. 5, 2001, effective July 1, 2001.)

Committee note. — Definitions (a), (b), (d), (e), and (g), in addition to the General Definitions, are designed to be used in product liability cases. Optional Definition (c) is designed to be used in conjunction with Standard Product Liability Interrogatories Nos. 39, 40, 44, and 45, and optional Definition (f) is designed to be used in conjunction with Nos. 5, 9, 32, 33, 34, 36, and 40. The Committee has concluded that it is not possible to formulate generic definitions for the terms **"component substantially similar to the component(s) at issue"** and **"substantially similar product."** If an interrogating party elects to include the optional references to "substantially similar" products or components in the standard interrogatories, the interrogator should define those terms with sufficient particularity in the context of the facts at issue. If Definition (c) is not used, Interrogatory No. 39 and the bracketed language in Interrogatories Nos. 40, 44, and 45 should be omitted. If Definition (f) is not used, the bracketed language in Interrogatories Nos. 5, 9, 32, 33, 34, 36, and 40 should be omitted.

Form 10. Product liability interrogatories.

Interrogatories For Use by Either Party

1. **Identify** the specific provision(s) of each governmental or industry regulation, standard, guideline, recommendation, accepted practice, or custom that you contend was applicable to the design, manufacture, performance, testing, certification, or safety of the **component(s) at issue** at the time **The Product** left the manufacturer's control. (Standard Product Liability Interrogatory No. 1.)

2. State whether **The Product** underwent any change in its condition between the time it left the manufacturer's control and the time of the **occurrence** and, if so, describe each change in condition. (Standard Product Liability Interrogatory No. 2.)

3. State whether **The Product** underwent any change in its condition between the time of the **occurrence** and the present and, if so, describe each change in condition. (Standard Product Liability Interrogatory No. 3.)

4. State whether, at any time after the **occurrence**, you or any **person** on your behalf examined **The Product** or any of its **components** and, if so, describe the nature and results of each examination, **identify** the person who performed it, and **identify** each **document** that refers to it. (Standard Product Liability Interrogatory No. 4.)

5. State whether, at any time, you or any **person** on your behalf conducted any test, study, or other analysis concerning possible safety or health hazards of **The Product** [or of any **substantially similar product**] and, if so, describe the nature and results of each test, study, or analysis, state when it was performed, **identify** each **person** who performed it, and **identify** each **document** that refers to it. (Standard Product Liability Interrogatory No. 5.)

6. If you intend to use at trial a simulation (computer or actual), experiment, test, or analysis, describe each simulation, experiment, test, or analysis, **identify** the **person** who created or performed it or who intends to perform it, and **identify** each **document** that refers to it. (Standard Product Liability Interrogatory No. 6.)

7. **Identify** each **document** that depicts or purports to depict the **occurrence** or scene of the **occurrence**. (Standard Product Liability Interrogatory No. 7.)

8. **Identify** each document that depicts or purports to depict the condition of **The Product** or any of its **components** at the time of or after the **occurrence**. (Standard Product Liability Interrogatory No. 8.)

9. State the date, place, and circumstances under which you first became aware that exposure to or use of **The Product** [or any **substantially similar product**] may be harmful or hazardous, **identify** each source of information leading to your awareness, and identify the harm or hazards of which you became aware. (Standard Product Liability Interrogatory No. 9.)

(10) **Identify** each **person** (other than your attorney or an expert retained in anticipation of litigation or preparation for trial who is not expected to be called as a witness at trial) who has made any written or oral report, memorandum, or statement to you or anyone acting on your behalf regarding the cause of the **occurrence**, and **identify** each **document** that constitutes or refers to each such report, memorandum, or statement. (Standard Product Liability Interrogatory No. 10.)

Interrogatories To Defendant From Plaintiff

31. If you contend that any **product information** was or should have been provided with **The Product** at the time of its sale or distribution to the end user, state the subject matter of the **product information**, **identify** the **person** responsible for providing the **product information**, and **identify** each **document** that constitutes or refers to the **product information**. (Standard Product Liability Interrogatory No. 31.)

32. **Identify** and describe each study, experiment, test, or analysis, performed by you or on your behalf, that mentions any adverse effects of the use of **The Product** [or any **substantially similar product**]. (Standard Product Liability Interrogatory No. 32.)

33. State whether any **product information** concerning [insert a description of the particular use or risk at issue in the case] was changed in any way with respect to **The Product** [or any **substantially similar product**] during the period [date] through [date]. (Standard Product Liability Interrogatory No. 33.)

34. **Identify** each safety-related **product information**, sign, display, or other **document** furnished by you to sellers for display in their sales facilities from [date] through [date] that concerned **The Product** [or any **substantially similar product**]. (Standard Product Liability Interrogatory No. 34.)

35. Describe each change that was made to each item identified in your answer to the preceding Interrogatory, state whether the change was furnished by you to sellers of **The Product** or their customers, and state when the change was furnished to the sellers or their customers. (Standard Product Liability Interrogatory No. 35.)

36. If at any time before the **occurrence** you or anyone on your behalf made any statement regarding the safety of **The Product** [or any **substantially similar product**]:

(a) state the date, time, place, and substance of each statement, the circumstances or occasion when the statement was made, and whether the statement was written or oral;

(b) **identify** each **person** making the statement;

(c) **identify** reach **person** to whom the statement was made; and,

(d) **identify** each **document** that constitutes or refers to the statement. (Standard Product Liability Interrogatory No. 36.)

37. If you contend that the plaintiff was given any written or oral **product information** concerning **The Product** at any time before the **occurrence**, as to each **product information**:

(a) state the substance of the **product information**;

(b) state the date on which the plaintiff was given the **product information**;

(c) **identify** the **person** who gave the plaintiff the **product information**;

(d) describe the manner in which the **product information** was given to the plaintiff; and

(e) **identify** each **document** that constitutes or refers to the **product information**. (Standard Product Liability Interrogatory No. 37.)

38. If you or anyone on your behalf provided to the plaintiff any technical literature, product brochure, or promotional literature concerning **The Product** at any time before the **occurrence**:

(a) **identify** the literature or brochure;

(b) **identify** the **person** who provided the literature or brochure to the plaintiff; and

(c) state the date the literature or brochure was given to the plaintiff. (Standard Product Liability Interrogatory No. 38.)

39. If you are aware of any lawsuit or other claim based upon an allegation that a defect in a **component substantially similar to the component(s) at issue** was a cause of any personal injury, death, or property damage, as to each:

(a) state the date you became aware of the lawsuit or claim;

(b) state the date and location of the incident involved in the lawsuit or claim and describe the [product(s)] and [component(s)] involved and the nature of the defect alleged;

(c) **identify** the **person** bringing the lawsuit or claim; and

(d) if a lawsuit, **identify** the court, case caption, and docket number. (Standard Product Liability Interrogatory No. 39.)

40. If there has been any federal or state governmental or industry investigation of the safety of **The Product** or [any **substantially similar product** or] the **component(s) at issue** [or any **component substantially similar to the component(s) at issue**]:

(a) state the date of the investigation;

(b) **identify** the governmental or industry entity that conducted the investigation;

(c) **describe** the nature and subject matter of the investigation;

(d) **identify** each **person** who responded on your behalf to the investigation; and,

(e) **identify** each **document** that refers to the investigation. (Standard Product Liability Interrogatory No. 40.)

41. If you or any agent or employee of yours expressly warranted or guaranteed **The Product**, state the exact words of each warranty or guarantee, and when, where, and by what means the warranty or guarantee was given. (Standard Product Liability Interrogatory No. 41.)

42. If you contend that you or any agent or employee of yours disclaimed any warranty or guarantee of **The Product**, state the exact words of each disclaimer, whether you contend that the person harmed by **The Product** was or should have been aware of the disclaimer, and when, where, and by what means the disclaimer was made. (Standard Product Liability Interrogatory No. 42.)

43. Explain the meaning of each code word, code number, or other symbol appearing on **The Product**, including any that identifies the place of manufacture, the date of manufacture, the lot or batch of which **The Product** was a part, or any test or examination of **The Product**. (Standard Product Liability Interrogatory No. 43.)

44. If there was a change after the date of manufacture of **The Product** in the design of the **component(s) at issue** [or **component substantially similar to the component(s) at issue**]:

(a) state the nature of the change;

(b) state the reason for the change;

(c) state the date of the change;

(d) **identify** each **person** who directed the change; and

(e) **identify** each **document** that implements the change. (Standard Product Liability Interrogatory No. 44.)

45. If there was a change after the date of manufacture of **The Product** in the manufacturing process of the **component(s) at issue** [or **component substantially similar to the component(s) at issue**]:

(a) state the nature of the change;

(b) state the reason for the change;

(c) state the date of the change;

(d) **identify** each **person** who directed the change; and

(e) **identify** each **document** that implements the change. (Standard Product Liability Interrogatory No. 45.)

46. **Identify** all **persons** who (a) were directly responsible for the design, testing, certification, or safety of the **component(s) at issue**, (b) are most knowledgeable about the design, testing, certification, or safety of the **component(s) at issue**, (c) manufactured the **component(s) at issue**, or (d) assembled the component(s) at issue into **The Product**. As to each **person**, state the area of that **person's** responsibility or knowledge (e.g., design, testing, certification, or safety). (Standard Product Liability Interrogatory No. 46.)

Interrogatories to Plaintiff from Defendant

61. Name each **component at issue** and:

(a) state whether you contend that its alleged defect is one of design, manufacture, or a failure to provide adequate **product information**;

(b) describe the specific nature of each alleged design, manufacturing, or **product information** defect;

(c) state the facts that support your contention; and

(d) **identify** each **person** and **document** having or containing information that supports your contention. (Standard Product Liability Interrogatory No. 61.)

62. With respect to each **component at issue** for which you contend there was a defect in design, state the particulars of each alternative design that you contend could and should have been employed and state the cost of the alternative design. (Standard Product Liability Interrogatory No. 62.)

63. With respect to each **component at issue** for which you contend there was a defect in manufacture, **identify** the applicable manufacturing specifications for the **component at issue** and state how you contend it failed to meet the prescribed manufacturing specifications. (Standard Product Liability Interrogatory No. 63.)

64. If you contend that this defendant failed to provide adequate **product information** for **The Product**, state how the **product information** was inadequate and how you contend the defendant could and should have made it adequate. (Standard Product Liability Interrogatory No. 64.)

65. State the facts that support your contention that **The Product** was defective and unreasonably dangerous, state how long the alleged defective or unreasonably dangerous condition existed before the **occurrence**, and **identify** each **person** and **document** having or containing information that supports your contentions. (Standard Product Liability Interrogatory No. 65.)

66. **Identify** each **person** who you contend is responsible for causing the alleged defective or unreasonably dangerous condition of **The Product**, and **identify** each **person** and **document** having or containing information that supports your contention. (Standard Product Liability Interrogatory No. 66.)

67. State the facts that support your contention that **The Product** reached you without substantial change in the condition in which it was manufactured, and **identify** each **person** and **document** having or containing information that supports your contention. (Standard Product Liability Interrogatory No. 67.)

68. State the facts that support your contention that the alleged defect in **The Product** was a proximate cause of the harm alleged in this action. (Standard Product Liability Interrogatory No. 68.)

69. If you contend that **The Product** was not properly installed before the **occurrence**, state the facts that support your contention and **identify** each **person** and **document** having or containing information that supports your contention. (Standard Product Liability Interrogatory No. 69.)

70. If you contend that this defendant before the **occurrence** had notice of any defect or unreasonably dangerous condition of **The Product**, state the facts that support your contention and **identify** each **person** and **document** having or containing information that supports your contention. (Standard Product Liability Interrogatory No. 70.)

71. Describe each complaint about **The Product**, if any, made at any time by you or any other **person** to this defendant, and **identify** each **person** and **document** having or containing information about the complaint. (Standard Product Liability Interrogatory No. 71.)

72. Describe the negligent acts or omissions for which you contend that this defendant is responsible with respect to **The Product**, state the facts that support your contention, state how each negligent act or omission could and should have been avoided, and **identify** each **person** and **document** having or containing information that supports your contention. (Standard Product Liability Interrogatory No. 72.)

73. If you contend that this defendant violated any statute, regulation, ordinance, standard, or guideline with respect to the manufacture or design of **The Product** or with respect its **product information**, for each statute, regulation, ordinance, standard, or guideline provide:

(a) the name of the publication in which it appears;

(b) the volume and page number of the publication in which it appears;

(c) the specific provision that you contend was violated; and

(d) its promulgation date and effective date. (Standard Product Liability Interrogatory No. 73.)

74. If you contend that the violation of any statute, regulation, ordinance, standard, or guideline set forth in your answer to the preceding Interrogatory proximately caused any harm alleged in this action, state the facts that support your contention. (Standard Product Liability Interrogatory No. 74.)

75. If you contend that this defendant had a duty to test but failed to test **The Product**, state the facts that support your contention and **identify** each **person** and **document** having or containing information that supports your contention. (Standard Product Liability Interrogatory No. 75.)

76. **Identify** the **person** who sold **The Product** to the **person** who owned **The Product** at the time of the **occurrence**, and state the sales price, the date of sale, and whether **The Product** was sold in a "new" or "used" condition. If **The Product** was sold in a "used" condition, **identify** each **person** who owned **The Product** at any time from the date of its manufacture to the present and state when the **person** owned it. (Standard Product Liability Interrogatory No. 76.)

77. **Identify** each **person** who has or had custody of **The Product** or any **component at issue** from the date of the **occurrence** to the present. For

each **person** identified, state the time during which that **person** had custody and the exact location, including any street address, at which **The Product** or **component at issue** was kept. (Standard Product Liability Interrogatory No. 77.)

78. If you have knowledge of any maintenance or repair that was contemplated, recommended, or conducted, or should have been conducted, on **The Product** before the **occurrence**, state the knowledge you have concerning any such maintenance or repair and **identify** each **person** and **document** having or containing any information concerning the maintenance or repair. (Standard Product Liability Interrogatory No. 78.)

79. If you have knowledge of any photograph, video, motion picture, drawing, model, or other image made of **The Product** or any **component at issue** at any time, describe the medium on which the image is recorded, **identify** each **person** who participated in that process, state the date when the image was made, and **identify** the **person** who has present custody of the image. (Standard Product Liability Interrogatory No. 79.) (Added Mar. 5, 2001, effective July 1, 2001.)

Form 11. Medical Malpractice Definitions.

Definitions

(a) **Defendant** includes the agents, servants, and employees of the defendant. (Standard Medical Malpractice Definition (a).)

(b) **Patient** means the individual, whether alive or dead, whose medical care is the subject of this action. (Standard Medical Malpractice Definition (b).) (Added Sept. 10, 2009, effective Oct. 1, 2009.)

Form 12. Medical Malpractice Interrogatories.

Interrogatories for Use by Either Party

1. If you intend to rely upon or use in direct examination any medical article, treatise, or other publication, **identify** the **document** and state:

(a) the title of the publication, journal, magazine, or treatise in which each **document** was published,

(b) the name and address of the publisher,

(c) the date of publication, and

(d) the volume and page or section referenced. (Standard Medical Malpractice Interrogatory No. 1.)

Interrogatories to Defendant from Plaintiff

31. Describe the nature and duration of the professional or business relationship between you and any other Defendant. (Standard Medical Malpractice Interrogatory No. 31.)

32. State your professional medical training, qualifications and experience, including:

(a) each university or college you attended, each degree awarded to you, and the date of each award;

(b) each hospital with which you have been affiliated at any time up to the present, and the nature and inclusive dates of each affiliation.

(c) each medical society or association of which you have ever been a member, and the inclusive dates of your membership;

(d) each specialty or subspecialty for which you have been certified by an American speciality or subspecialty board, and the date of each certification; and

(e) a bibliography of all your publications, including titles, dates and publishers. (Standard Medical Malpractice Interrogatory No. 32.)

33. List, by date and time of day, each occasion on which you saw the **Patient,** and as to each occasion, describe in detail:

(a) nature and scope of your examination of the **Patient**;

(b) the nature and scope of any conversation you had with the **Patient** or with anyone who accompanied the **Patient**;

(c) what you observed or were told about the **Patient's** condition; and

(d) the treatment you provided or ordered to be provided for the **Patient**. (Standard Medical Malpractice Interrogatory No. 33.)

34. Describe in detail and chronological order each test, procedure, or other treatment performed or ordered as part of your care of the **Patient**, and for each:

(a) **identify** all **persons** present during the test, procedure, or treatment and state the **person's** professional relationship to you, if any; and

(b) state the reasons for, and result of, the test, procedure, or treatment. (Standard Medical Malpractice Interrogatory No. 34.)

35. For each conversation you had with any other physician or medical professional relating in any way to the care and treatment of the **Patient**, state the substance, date, time, and place of the conversation, and **identify** all **persons** involved. (Standard Medical Malpractice Interrogatory No. 35.)

36. **Identify**, in chronological order, each writing or dictation known to you and prepared by anyone concerning the treatment of the **Patient** and made since you first undertook care of the **Patient**, and set forth as to each:

(a) the date on which the writing or dictation was made;

(b) the **identity** of the person who made it;

(c) the meanings, in both lay and medical terms, of all abbreviations and symbols used in it; and

(d) attach a copy or transcription of it to your answers to these interrogatories. (Standard Medical Malpractice Interrogatory No. 36.)

37. Summarize in detail each conversation that you had with the **Patient** or with any Plaintiff about any aspect of the **Patient's** diagnosis, treatment, care or medical condition, and state the date and place of each such conversation. (Standard Medical Malpractice Interrogatory No. 37.)

38. If you gave any advice, instruction, or warning that the **Patient** did not follow, state:

(a) the advice, instruction, or warning that was given;

(b) the **identity** of all **persons** to whom you gave the advice, instruction, or warning;

(c) when and where the advice, instruction, or warning was given; and

(d) all reasons given, if any, for not following the advice, instruction or warning. (Standard Medical Malpractice Interrogatory No. 38.)

39. If you contend that, by any act or omission occurring at any time during or following the **Patient's** care and treatment, the **Patient** caused or contributed to the **Patient's** injury or death, state the facts that support your contention. (Standard Medical Malpractice Interrogatory No. 39.)

40. State your contention as to each cause of the **Patient's** death or injury that is alleged in the complaint and, as to each cause:

(a) state the facts upon which you rely;

(b) **identify** each **document** containing information that supports your contention;

(c) **Identify** each **person** who you contend is responsible, in whole or in part, for the **Patient's** death or injury that is alleged in the complaint and your reasons for contending that the **person** is responsible; and

(d) state the professional relationship to you, if any, of each **person** named in your response to this Interrogatory. (Standard Medical Malpractice Interrogatory No. 40.)

41. List by author, title, publisher or publication, any texts, treaties, articles or other works which, at the time the **Patient** was under your care, you regarded as reliable authority with respect to the care that you rendered to the **Patient**. (Standard Medical Malpractice Interrogatory No. 41.)

42. **Identify** each instance in which you have been named a defendant, or have testified as an expert witness, in any other claim or suit for personal injury, negligence, or medical malpractice, including in your answer to this Interrogatory:

(a) the **identity** of the **person** or organization who brought each claim or suit;

(b) the date of the filing of each claim or suit;

(c) the identifying number of each claim or suit;

(d) the date, place, and nature of the occurrence from which the claim or suit arose; and

(e) the final disposition of each claim or suit. (Standard Medical Malpractice Interrogatory No. 42.)

43. **Identify** each **person** that undertook an investigation of the events surrounding the **Patient's** death, and for each also state:

(a) the **person's** title or position;

(b) the date(s) upon which the **person** conducted the investigation;

(c) the **identity** of each **person** contacted or to whom the investigator spoke regarding the events giving rise to this action;

(d) any remedial or corrective action taken as a result of the investigation; and

(e) whether there is a written report or other **document** containing the results of the investigation. (Standard Medical Malpractice Interrogatory No. 43.)

Interrogatories to Plaintiff from Defendant

61. State chronologically and in detail:

(a) the cause and origin of the injuries alleged in the complaint;

(b) if you contend the injuries changed or worsened over time, state how and when;

(c) the course of the treatment provided by each **defendant**;

(d) each procedure that was performed by each **defendant**;

(e) the substance of your conversations with each **defendant** prior to and after each procedure or other treatment, including how the proposed procedure or treatment was described to you; and

(f) the extent of your knowledge of, and consent to, each procedure or other treatment. **Identify** all sources of information about the procedure or other treatment that you consulted before it was performed or rendered, including any sources on the Internet. (Standard Medical Malpractice Interrogatory No. 61.)

62. With respect to **defendant** [insert name], describe in detail each act or omission that you contend constitutes a breach of the applicable standard of professional care for the **Patient** or that otherwise forms a basis for your claim against the **defendant**, and for each such act or omission:

(a) explain how you contend it caused or contributed to the **Patient's** injuries or death alleged in the Complaint; and

(b) **identify** each **person** and **document** having or containing information that supports your contention. (Standard Medical Malpractice Interrogatory No. 62.)

63. If you contend that any portion of any medical record, chart, or report is inaccurate, false, or altered:

(a) **identify** each **document** and each part of it that you contend is inaccurate, false, or altered, and

(b) as to each contention, state the factual basis for it. (Standard Medical Malpractice Interrogatory No. 63.)

64. State the substance of all written and oral advice, instructions, and warnings you received from **defendant** [insert name] before and after each procedure or other treatment, and attach a copy of each written advice, instruction, or warning. If you no longer have the document, summarize your recollection of its substance. (Standard Medical Malpractice Interrogatory No. 64.) (Added Sept. 10, 2009, effective Oct. 1, 2009.)

APPENDIX: THE MARYLAND LAWYERS' RULES OF PROFESSIONAL CONDUCT:

Preamble: A lawyer's responsibilities.

Scope.

Editor's note. — The Court of Appeals, by Order dated April 15, 1986, adopted the Maryland Rules of Professional Conduct, effective January 1, 1987. The Order provides that "the Maryland Rules of Professional Conduct shall govern the conduct of attorneys from and after said date; provided, however, that the Code of Professional Responsibility as set forth in Appendix F of the Maryland Rules shall continue in full force and effect and shall govern the conduct of attorneys until January 1, 1987."

Annotations from cases appearing under the

new Rules were decided under the former Code of Professional Responsibility, and have been retained where it is thought they will be of value in construing the new Rules.

An Order filed February 8, 2005, provided in part that the rules changes hereby adopted by this Court shall take effect on July 1, 2005, and that "the Maryland Lawyers' Rules of Professional Conduct shall govern the conduct of attorneys from and after said date; pro-vided, however, that the current Maryland Rules of Professional Conduct as set forth in Appendix: Rules of Professional Conduct of the Maryland Rules shall continue in full force and effect and shall govern the conduct of attorneys until July 1, 2005; and attorneys shall continue on and after July 1, 2005 to be subject to discipline for violations of the current Maryland Rules of Professional Conduct occurring prior to July 1, 2005."

Preamble: A lawyer's responsibilities.

[1] A lawyer, as a member of the legal profession, is a representative of clients, an officer of the legal system and a public citizen having special responsibility for the quality of justice.

[2] As a representative of clients, a lawyer performs various functions. As advisor, a lawyer provides a client with an informed understanding of the client's legal rights and obligations and explains their practical implications. As advocate, a lawyer zealously asserts the client's position under the rules of the adversary system. As negotiator, a lawyer seeks a result advantageous to the client but consistent with requirements of honest dealing with others. As evaluator, a lawyer acts by examining a client's legal affairs and reporting about them to the client or to others.

[3] In addition to these representational functions, a lawyer may serve as a third-party neutral, a nonrepresentational role helping the parties to resolve a dispute or other matter. Some of these Rules apply directly to lawyers who are or have served as third-party neutrals. See, e.g., Rules 1.12 and 2.4. In addition, there are Rules that apply to lawyers who are not active in the practice of law or to practicing lawyers even when they are acting in a nonprofessional capacity. For example, a lawyer who commits fraud in the conduct of a business is subject to discipline for engaging in conduct involving dishonesty, fraud, deceit or misrepresentation. See Rule 8.4.

[4] In all professional functions a lawyer should be competent, prompt and diligent. A lawyer should maintain communication with a client concerning the representation. A lawyer should keep in confidence information relating to representation of a client except so far as disclosure is required or permitted by the Maryland Lawyers' Rules of Professional Conduct or other law.

[5] A lawyer's conduct should conform to the requirements of the law, both in professional service to clients and in the lawyer's business and personal affairs. A lawyer should use the law's procedures only for legitimate purposes and not to harass or intimidate others. A lawyer should demonstrate respect for the legal system and for those who serve it, including judges, other lawyers and public officials. While it is a lawyer's duty, when necessary, to challenge the rectitude of official action, it is also a lawyer's duty to uphold legal process.

[6] As a public citizen, a lawyer should seek improvement of the law, access to the legal system, the administration of justice and the quality of service rendered by the legal profession. As a member of a learned profession, a lawyer should cultivate knowledge of the law beyond its use for clients, employ that

knowledge in reform of the law and work to strengthen legal education. In addition, a lawyer should further the public's understanding of and confidence in the rule of law and the justice system because legal institutions in a constitutional democracy depend on popular participation and support to maintain their authority. A lawyer should be mindful of deficiencies in the administration of justice and of the fact that the poor, and sometimes persons who are not poor, cannot afford adequate legal assistance. Therefore, all lawyers should devote professional time and resources and use civic influence to ensure equal access to our system of justice for all those who because of economic or social barriers cannot afford or secure adequate legal counsel. A lawyer should aid the legal profession in pursuing these objectives and should help the bar regulate itself in the public interest.

[7] Many of a lawyer's professional responsibilities are prescribed in the Maryland Lawyers' Rules of Professional Conduct, as well as substantive and procedural law. However, a lawyer is also guided by personal conscience and the approbation of professional peers. A lawyer should strive to attain the highest level of skill, to improve the law and the legal profession and to exemplify the legal profession's ideals of public service.

[8] A lawyer's responsibilities as a representative of clients, an officer of the legal system and a public citizen are usually harmonious. Thus, when an opposing party is well represented, a lawyer can be a zealous advocate on behalf of a client and at the same time assume that justice is being done. So also, a lawyer can be sure that preserving client confidences ordinarily serves the public interest because people are more likely to seek legal advice, and thereby heed their legal obligations, when they know their communications will be private.

[9] In the nature of law practice, however, conflicting responsibilities are encountered. Virtually all difficult ethical problems arise from conflict between a lawyer's responsibilities to clients, to the legal system and to the lawyer's own interest in remaining an ethical person while earning a satisfactory living. The Maryland Lawyers' Rules of Professional Conduct often prescribe terms for resolving such conflicts. Within the framework of these Rules, however, many difficult issues of professional discretion can arise. Such issues must be resolved through the exercise of sensitive professional and moral judgment guided by the basic principles underlying the Rules. These principles include the lawyer's obligation zealously to protect and pursue a client's legitimate interests, within the bounds of the law, while maintaining a professional, courteous and civil attitude toward all persons involved in the legal system.

[10] The legal profession is largely self-governing. Although other professions also have been granted powers of self-government, the legal profession is unique in this respect because of the close relationship between the profession and the processes of government and law enforcement. This connection is manifested in the fact that ultimate authority over the legal profession is vested largely in the courts.

[11] To the extent that lawyers meet the obligations of their professional calling, the occasion for government regulation is obviated. Self-regulation also

helps maintain the legal profession's independence from government domination. An independent legal profession is an important force in preserving government under law, for abuse of legal authority is more readily challenged by a profession whose members are not dependent on government for the right to practice.

[12] The legal profession's relative autonomy carries with it special responsibilities of self-government. The profession has a responsibility to assure that its regulations are conceived in the public interest and not in furtherance of parochial or self-interested concerns of the bar. Every lawyer is responsible for observance of the Maryland Lawyers' Rules of Professional Conduct. A lawyer should also aid in securing their observance by other lawyers. Neglect of these responsibilities compromises the independence of the profession and the public interest which it serves.

[13] Lawyers play a vital role in the preservation of society. The fulfillment of this role requires an understanding by lawyers of their relationship to our legal system. The Maryland Lawyers' Rules of Professional Conduct, when properly applied, serve to define that relationship.

Scope.

[14] The Maryland Lawyers' Rules of Professional Conduct are rules of reason. They should be interpreted with reference to the purposes of legal representation and of the law itself. Some of the Rules are imperatives, cast in the terms "shall" or "shall not." These define proper conduct for purposes of professional discipline. Others, generally cast in the term "may," are permissive and define areas under the Rules in which the lawyer has discretion to exercise professional judgment. No disciplinary action should be taken when the lawyer chooses not to act or acts within the bounds of such discretion. Other Rules define the nature of relationships between the lawyer and others. The Rules are thus partly obligatory and disciplinary and partly constitutive and descriptive in that they define a lawyer's professional role. Many of the Comments use the term "should." Comments do not add obligations to the Rules but provide guidance for practicing in compliance with the Rules.

[15] The Rules presuppose a larger legal context shaping the lawyer's role. That context includes court rules and statutes relating to matters of licensure, laws defining specific obligations of lawyers and substantive and procedural law in general. The Comments are sometimes used to alert lawyers to their responsibilities under such other law.

[16] Compliance with the Rules, as with all law in an open society, depends primarily upon understanding and voluntary compliance, secondarily upon reinforcement by peer and public opinion and finally, when necessary, upon enforcement through disciplinary proceedings. The Rules do not, however, exhaust the moral and ethical considerations that should inform a lawyer, for no worthwhile human activity can be completely defined by legal rules. The Rules simply provide a framework for the ethical practice of law.

[17] Furthermore, for purposes of determining the lawyer's authority and responsibility, principles of substantive law external to these Rules determine

689

whether a client-lawyer relationship exists. Most of the duties flowing from the client-lawyer relationship attach only after the client has requested the lawyer to render legal services and the lawyer has agreed to do so. But there are some duties, such as that of confidentiality under Rule 1.6, that attach when the lawyer agrees to consider whether a client-lawyer relationship shall be established. See Rule 1.18. Whether a client-lawyer relationship exists for any specific purpose can depend on the circumstances and may be a question of fact.

[18] Under various legal provisions, including constitutional, statutory and common law, the responsibilities of government lawyers may include authority concerning legal matters that ordinarily reposes in the client in private client-lawyer relationships. For example, a lawyer for a government agency may have authority on behalf of the government to decide upon settlement or whether to appeal from an adverse judgment. Such authority in various respects is generally vested in the attorney general and the state's attorney in state government, and their federal counterparts, and the same may be true of other government law officers. Also, lawyers under the supervision of these officers may be authorized to represent several government agencies in intra-governmental legal controversies in circumstances where a private lawyer could not represent multiple private clients. These Rules do not abrogate any such authority.

[19] Failure to comply with an obligation or prohibition imposed by a Rule is a basis for invoking the disciplinary process. The Rules presuppose that disciplinary assessment of a lawyer's conduct will be made on the basis of the facts and circumstances as they existed at the time of the conduct in question and in recognition of the fact that a lawyer often has to act upon uncertain or incomplete evidence of the situation. Moreover, the Rules presuppose that whether or not discipline should be imposed for a violation, and the severity of a sanction, depend on all the circumstances, such as the willfulness and seriousness of the violation, extenuating factors and whether there have been previous violations.

[20] Violation of a Rule does not itself give rise to a cause of action against a lawyer nor does it create any presumption that a legal duty has been breached. In addition, violation of a Rule does not necessarily warrant any other non-disciplinary remedy, such as disqualification of a lawyer in pending litigation. The Rules are designed to provide guidance to lawyers and to provide a structure for regulating conduct through disciplinary agencies. They are not designed to be a basis for civil liability. Furthermore, the purpose of the Rules can be subverted when they are invoked by opposing parties as procedural weapons. The fact that a Rule is a just basis for a lawyer's self-assessment, or for sanctioning a lawyer under the administration of a disciplinary authority, does not imply that an antagonist in a collateral proceeding or transaction has standing to seek enforcement of the Rule. Nevertheless, in some circumstances, a lawyer's violation of a Rule may be evidence of breach of the applicable standard of conduct. Nothing in this Preamble and Scope is intended to detract from the holdings of the Court of Appeals in Post v. Bregman, 349 Md. 142 (1998) and Son v. Margolius, Mallios, Davis, Rider & Tomar, 349 Md. 441 (1998).

[21] The Comment accompanying each Rule explains and illustrates the meaning and purpose of the Rule. The Preamble and this note on Scope provide general orientation. The Comments are intended as guides to interpretation, but the text of each Rule is authoritative.

(Amended May 8, 2007, effective July 1, 2007.)

Effect of amendments. — The 2007 amendment in [20], substituted "should" for "does" twice, and deleted "in such a case" following "any presumption" in the first sentence.

Model Rules Comparison — With the exception of wording changes to paragraph [20], the Preamble and Scope are substantially similar to the language of the Ethics 2000 Amendments to the ABA Model Rules of Professional Conduct.

Rule 1.0. Terminology.

(a) "Belief" or "believes" denotes that the person involved actually supposed the fact in question to be true. A person's belief may be inferred from circumstances.

(b) "Confirmed in writing," when used in reference to the informed consent of a person, denotes informed consent that is given in writing by the person or a writing that a lawyer promptly transmits to the person confirming an oral informed consent. See paragraph (f) for the definition of "informed consent." If it is not feasible to obtain or transmit the writing at the time the person gives informed consent, then the lawyer must obtain or transmit it within a reasonable time thereafter.

(c) "Consult" or "consultation" denotes communication of information reasonably sufficient to permit the client to appreciate the significance of the matter in question.

(d) "Firm" or "law firm" denotes:

(1) an association of a lawyer or lawyers in a law partnership, professional corporation, sole proprietorship or other association formed for the practice of law; or

(2) a legal services organization or the legal department of a corporation, government or other organization.

(e) "Fraud" or "fraudulent" denotes conduct that is fraudulent under the substantive or procedural law of the applicable jurisdiction and has a purpose to deceive.

(f) "Informed consent" denotes the agreement by a person to a proposed course of conduct after the lawyer has communicated adequate information and explanation about the material risks of and reasonably available alternatives to the proposed course of conduct.

(g) "Knowingly," "known," or "knows" denotes actual knowledge of the fact in question. A person's knowledge may be inferred from circumstances.

(h) "Law firm." See Rule 1.0(d).

(i) "Partner" denotes a member of a partnership, a shareholder in a law firm organized as a professional corporation, or a member of an association authorized to practice law.

(j) "Reasonable" or "reasonably" when used in relation to conduct by a lawyer denotes the conduct of a reasonably prudent and competent lawyer.

(k) "Reasonable belief" or "reasonably believes" when used in reference to a lawyer denotes that the lawyer believes the matter in question and that the circumstances are such that the belief is reasonable.

(l) "Reasonably should know" when used in reference to a lawyer denotes that a lawyer of reasonable prudence and competence would ascertain the matter in question.

(m) "Screened" denotes the isolation of a lawyer from any participation in a matter through the timely imposition of procedures within a firm that are reasonably adequate under the circumstances to protect information that the isolated lawyer is obligated to protect under these Rules or other law.

(n) "Substantial" when used in reference to degree or extent denotes a material matter of clear and weighty importance.

(o) "Tribunal" denotes a court, an arbitrator in a binding arbitration proceeding or a legislative body, administrative agency or other body acting in an adjudicative capacity. A legislative body, administrative agency or other body acts in an adjudicative capacity when a neutral official, after the presentation of evidence or legal argument by a party or parties, will render a binding legal decision directly affecting a party's interests in a particular matter.

(p) "Writing" or "written" denotes a tangible or electronic record of a communication or representation, including handwriting, typewriting, printing, photostating, photography, audio or video-recording and e-mail. A "signed" writing includes an electronic sound, symbol or process attached to or logically associated with a writing and executed or adopted by a person with the intent to sign the writing.

COMMENT

Confirmed in Writing. — [1] If it is not feasible to obtain or transmit a written confirmation at the time the client gives informed consent, then the lawyer must obtain or transmit it within a reasonable time thereafter. If a lawyer has obtained a client's informed consent, the lawyer may act in reliance on that consent so long as it is confirmed in writing within a reasonable time thereafter.

Firm. — [2] Whether two or more lawyers constitute a firm within paragraph (c) can depend on the specific facts. For example, two practitioners who share office space and occasionally consult or assist each other ordinarily would not be regarded as constituting a firm. However, if they present themselves to the public in a way that suggests that they are a firm or conduct themselves as a firm, they should be regarded as a firm for purposes of the Rules. The terms of any formal agreement between associated lawyers are relevant in determining whether they are a firm, as is the fact that they have mutual access to information concerning the clients they serve. Furthermore, it is relevant in doubtful cases to consider the underlying purpose of the Rule that is involved. A group of lawyers could be regarded as a firm for purposes of the Rule providing that the same lawyer should not represent opposing parties in litigation, while it might not be so regarded for purposes of the Rule that information acquired by one lawyer is attributed to another.

[3] With respect to the law department of an organization, including the government, there is ordinarily no question that the members of the department constitute a firm within the meaning of the Maryland Lawyers' Rules of Professional Conduct. There can be uncertainty, however, as to the identity of the client. For example, it may not be clear whether the law department of a corporation represents a subsidiary or an affiliated corporation, as well as the corporation by which the members of the department are directly employed. A similar question can arise concerning an unincorporated association and its local affiliates.

[4] Similar questions can also arise with respect to lawyers in legal aid and legal services organizations. Depending upon the structure of the organization, the entire organization or different components of it may constitute a firm or firms for purposes of these Rules.

Fraud. — [5] When used in these Rules, the terms "fraud" or "fraudulent" refer to conduct that is characterized as such under the substantive or procedural law of the applicable jurisdiction and has a purpose to deceive. This does not include merely negligent misrepresentation or negligent failure to apprise another of relevant information. For purposes of these Rules, it is not necessary that anyone has suffered damages or relied on the misrepresentation or failure to inform.

Informed Consent. — [6] Many of the Maryland Lawyers' Rules of Professional Conduct require the lawyer to obtain the informed consent of a client or other person (e.g., a former client or, under certain circumstances, a prospective client) before accepting or continuing representation or pursuing a course of conduct. See, e.g., Rules 1.2(c), 1.6(a) and 1.7(b). The communication necessary to obtain such consent will vary according to the Rule involved and the circumstances giving rise to the need to obtain informed consent. The lawyer must make reasonable efforts to ensure that the client or other person possesses information reasonably adequate to make an informed decision. Ordinarily, this will require communication that includes a disclosure of the facts and circumstances giving rise to the situation, any explanation reasonably necessary to inform the client or other person of the material advantages and disadvantages of the proposed course of conduct and a discussion of the client's or other person's options and alternatives. In some circumstances it may be appropriate for a lawyer to advise a client or other person of facts or implications already known to the client or other person to seek the advice of other counsel. A lawyer need not inform a client or other person of facts or implications already known to the client or other person; nevertheless, a lawyer who does not personally inform the client or other person assumes the risk that the client or other person is inadequately informed and the consent is invalid. In determining whether the information and explanation provided are reasonably adequate, relevant factors include whether the client or other person is experienced in legal matters generally and in making decisions of the type involved, and whether the client or other person is independently represented by other counsel in giving the consent. Normally, such persons need less information and explanation than others, and generally a client or other person who is independently represented by other counsel in giving the consent should be assumed to have given informed consent.

[7] Obtaining informed consent will usually require an affirmative response by the client or other person. In general, a lawyer may not assume consent from a client's or other person's silence. Consent may be inferred, however, from the conduct of the client or other person who has reasonably adequate information about the matter. A number of Rules require that a person's consent be confirmed in writing. See Rules 1.7(b) and 1.9(a). For a definition of "writing" and "confirmed in writing," see paragraphs (p) and (b). Other Rules require that a client's consent be obtained in a writing signed by the client. See, e.g., Rules 1.5(c) and 1.8(a). For a definition of "signed," see paragraph (p).

Screened. — [8] This definition applies to situations where screening of a personally disqualified lawyer is permitted to remove imputation of a conflict of interest under Rules 1.10, 1.11, 1.12 or 1.18.

[9] The purpose of screening is to assure the affected parties that confidential information known by the personally disqualified lawyer remains protected. The personally disqualified lawyer should acknowledge the obligation not to communicate with any of the other lawyers in the firm with respect to the matter. Similarly, other lawyers in the firm who are working on the matter should be informed that the screening is in place and that they may not communicate with the personally disqualified lawyer with respect to the matter. Additional screening measures that are appropriate for the particular matter will depend on the circumstances. To implement, reinforce and remind all affected lawyers of the presence of the screening, it may be appropriate for the firm to undertake such procedures as a written undertaking by the screened lawyer to avoid any communication with other firm personnel and any contact with any firm files or other materials relating to the matter, written notice and instructions to all other firm personnel forbidding any communication with the screened lawyer relating to the matter, denial of access by the screened lawyer to firm files or other materials relating to the matter and periodic reminders of the screen to the screened lawyer and all other firm personnel.

[10] In order to be effective, screening measures must be implemented as soon as practical after a lawyer or law firm knows or reasonably should know that there is a need for screening.

Model Rules Comparison. — Rule 1.0 is substantially similar to the language of the Ethics 2000 Amendments to the ABA Model Rules of Professional Conduct except for the retention of the definition of "consult" and "consultation," the addition of a cross reference to "law firm," and the appropriate redesignation of subsections.

Editor's note. — An Order filed February 8, 2005, provided in part that "the rules changes hereby adopted by this Court shall take effect on July 1, 2005, and that the Maryland Lawyers' Rules of Professional Conduct shall govern the conduct of attorneys from and after said date; provided, however, that the current Maryland Rules of Professional Conduct as set forth in Appendix: Rules of Professional Conduct of the Maryland Rules shall continue in full force and effect and shall govern the conduct of attorneys until July 1, 2005; and attorneys shall continue on and after July 1, 2005 to be subject to discipline for violations of the current Maryland Rules of Professional Conduct occurring prior to July 1, 2005."

Screen was sufficient. — Corporation's motion to disqualify a law firm from representing an individual because an attorney and a secretary who worked for the firm were previously part of the legal team that represented the corporation was denied because (1) Md. R. Prof. Conduct 1.10(c) addressed the situation because the corporation became a former client of the attorney when his former law firm withdrew from the case, and, at that point, the attorney was prohibited from representing an adverse client such as the individual without the corporation's consent by Md. R. Prof. Conduct 1.9; (2) the fact that the attorney could have no longer represented the individual did not mean that his new law firm could not have represented the individual; (3) such representation could have taken place so long as the tainted lawyer had been timely screened and he would not have been apportioned a fee from that client; (4) the corporation failed to show any concrete flaws in the screening process, other than what it called "the appearance of impropriety," and the court was not persuaded that an appearance of impropriety was enough to disqualify the firm; (5) the firm tailored its screen to fit the guidelines set forth by subsection (m) of this Rule; (6) the firm set up a sufficient screen so that the attorney and the secretary would not have tainted the firm's defense of the individual in the suit initiated by the corporation; and (7) as long as the screen was in place, the firm could have represented the individual. Compass Mktg. v. Schering-Plough Corp., — F. Supp. 2d — (D. Md. 2006).

Cited in Att'y Griev. Comm'n v. Edib, 415 Md. 696, 4 A.3d 957 (2010); Att'y Griev. Comm'n v. De La Paz, 418 Md. 534, 16 A.3d 181 (2011); Att'y Griev. Comm'n v. Keiner, — Md. —, — A.3d — (Aug. 19, 2011).

CLIENT-LAWYER RELATIONSHIP.

Rule 1.1. Competence.

A lawyer shall provide competent representation to a client. Competent representation requires the legal knowledge, skill, thoroughness and preparation reasonably necessary for the representation.

COMMENT

Legal knowledge and skill. — [1] In determining whether a lawyer employs the requisite knowledge and skill in a particular matter, relevant factors include the relative complexity and specialized nature of the matter, the lawyer's general experience, the lawyer's training and experience in the field in question, the preparation and study the lawyer is able to give the matter and whether it is feasible to refer the matter to, or associate or consult with, a lawyer of established competence in the field in question. In many instances, the required proficiency is that of a general practitioner. Expertise in a particular field of law may be required in some circumstances.

[2] A lawyer need not necessarily have special training or prior experience to handle legal problems of a type with which the lawyer is unfamiliar. A newly admitted lawyer can be as competent as a practitioner with long experience. Some important legal skills, such as the analysis of precedent, the evaluation of evidence and legal drafting, are required in all legal problems. Perhaps the most fundamental legal skill consists of determining what kind of legal problems a situation may involve, a skill that necessarily transcends any particular specialized knowledge. A lawyer can provide adequate representation in a wholly novel field through necessary study. Competent representation can also be provided through the association of a lawyer of established competence in the field in question.

[3] In an emergency a lawyer may give advice or assistance in a matter in which the lawyer does not have the skill ordinarily required where referral to or consultation or association with another lawyer would be impractical. Even in an emergency, however, assistance should be limited to that reasonably necessary in the circumstances, for ill-consid-

ered action under emergency conditions can jeopardize the client's interest.

[4] A lawyer may accept representation where the requisite level of competence can be achieved by reasonable preparation. This applies as well to a lawyer who is appointed as counsel for an unrepresented person. See also Rule 6.2.

Thoroughness and preparation. — [5] Competent handling of a particular matter includes inquiry into and analysis of the factual and legal elements of the problem, and use of methods and procedures meeting the standards of competent practitioners. It also includes adequate preparation. The required attention and preparation are determined in part by what is at stake; major litigation and complex transactions ordinarily require more extensive treatment than matters of lesser complexity. An agreement between the lawyer and the client regarding the scope of the representation may limit the matters for which the lawyer is responsible. See Rule 1.2(c).

Maintaining competence. — [6] To maintain the requisite knowledge and skill, a lawyer should keep abreast of changes in the law and its practice, engage in continuing study and education and comply with all continuing legal education requirements to which the lawyer is subject.

Model Rules Comparison. — Rule 1.1 is substantially similar to the language of the Ethics 2000 Amendments to the ABA Model Rules of Professional Conduct.

Editor's note. — An Order filed February 8, 2005, provided in part that "the rules changes hereby adopted by this Court shall take effect on July 1, 2005, and that the Maryland Lawyers' Rules of Professional Conduct shall govern the conduct of attorneys from and after said date; provided, however, that the current Maryland Rules of Professional Conduct as set forth in Appendix: Rules of Professional Conduct of the Maryland Rules shall continue in full force and effect and shall govern the conduct of attorneys until July 1, 2005; and attorneys shall continue on and after July 1, 2005 to be subject to discipline for violations of the current Maryland Rules of Professional Conduct occurring prior to July 1, 2005."

Maryland Law Review. — For symposium, expanding pro bono legal assistance in civil cases to Maryland's poor, see 49 Md. L. Rev. 1 (1990).

University of Baltimore Law Forum. — For discussion of the code of ethics, see 17, No. 1 U. Balt. Law Forum 31 (1986).

For Recent Development, "Attorney Grievance Commission of Maryland v. Mooney: Indefinite Suspension is Warranted Where an Attorney Fails to Provide Competent Representation," see 31 U. Balt. Law Forum 44 (2000).

In general. — Where clients consulted him with the knowledge that he was a practicing attorney and he made no attempt to inform them that he was dealing with them in any restricted capacity, the attorney will be held accountable to the ethical and performance standards of his profession. Att'y Griev. Comm'n v. Martin, 308 Md. 272, 518 A.2d 1050 (1987).

A person's use of the term "Esq." in correspondence with a client's guardian provides an insufficient basis, standing alone, for the finding that the respondent held herself out as a lawyer in violation of the Rule. Att'y Griev. Comm'n v. Shaw, 354 Md. 636, 732 A.2d 876 (1999).

Lawyers are disciplined for conduct occurring when they are not practicing law only if that conduct is dishonest or is conduct that reflects adversely on the profession, not each time they may undertake tasks for which they are under qualified or may be inexperienced. Att'y Griev. Comm'n v. Shaw, 354 Md. 636, 732 A.2d 876 (1999).

Lawyer's failure to file an accounting, despite being ordered to do so, and taking no substantial action to administer a client's estate, for which he was appointed as personal representative, was a violation of Md. R. Prof. Conduct 1.1. Att'y Griev. Comm'n v. Sullivan, 369 Md. 650, 801 A.2d 1077 (2002).

Bar counsel failed to show that an attorney had violated Md. R. Prof. Conduct 1.1, 1.3, 1.5(a), 1.16(d), 3.1, 5.1, 5.3(a) and (c), and 8.4(a) and (d) where the attorney had informed the client that he no longer wished to represent him after the client changed his mind with respect to a settlement agreement and the attorney had discharged the associate after discovering that she had subsequently file additional motions. Att'y Griev. Comm'n v. Maignan, 402 Md. 39, 935 A.2d 409 (2007).

Thoroughness and preparation. — Absent some compelling extenuating circumstance, it is ordinarily unacceptable for a lawyer to appear in court for a trial or other proceeding unprepared, and doing so may constitute a violation of this rule. Att'y Griev. Comm'n v. Ficker, 349 Md. 13, 706 A.2d 1045 (1998).

An indefinite suspension was appropriate where, among other violations, attorney violated this Rule in that he lacked the "thoroughness and preparation necessary" in order to faithfully represent his client, and through his failure to apply and grasp basic and fundamental areas of bankruptcy law that were essential to faithfully represent other clients. Att'y Griev. Comm'n v. Cohen, 361 Md. 161, 760 A.2d 706 (2000).

Disbarment was the proper sanction for an attorney who dragged out representation of two different clients for many years, dooming their causes by failure to comply with applicable laws, and pretended to be continuing representation efforts, in one case, even falsifying a letter after the fact to give the impression that the client had received proper communications; the attorney had also failed to notify clients of a suspension and make other arrangements with them, and to supply information needed by a grievance commission investigator. Att'y Griev. Comm'n v. Davis, 375 Md. 131, 825 A.2d 430 (2003).

Attorney's multiple violations of the Maryland Rules of Professional Conduct, including violation of this Rule for failing to timely request for an emergency hearing, warranted disbarment. The client retained the attorney to file for such a hearing and even though the attorney told the client the attorney did so, the attorney did not comply with that request. Att'y Griev. Comm'n v. Webster, 402 Md. 448, 937 A.2d 161 (2007).

Professional service corporations. — When the conduct of a lawyer in a professional service corporation is called into question with reference to the attorney-client relationship, the Rules of Professional Conduct will apply and not those of an ordinary business corporation. Where, however, the situation involves a dispute between shareholders of the professional service corporation, the corporate law should not be disregarded in favor of partnership law. Langhoff v. Marr, 81 Md. App. 438, 568 A.2d 844 (1990), vacated on other grounds and remanded, 322 Md. 657, 589 A.2d 470 (1991).

Competence in specialty areas. — Each member of the Bar should be on notice to consider his or her own competence prior to undertaking employment involving a particularly complex area of the law and should, if deemed appropriate, either decline the employment, or with the consent of the client, accept the employment and associate a lawyer who is competent in the matter. Att'y Griev. Comm'n v. Brown, 308 Md. 219, 517 A.2d 1111 (1986).

Single mistake does not necessarily result in a violation of Md. Law. R. Prof. Conduct 1.1, and may constitute negligence but not misconduct under the rule. Att'y Griev. Comm'n v. Pennington, 387 Md. 565, 876 A.2d 642 (2005).

Single mistake does not necessarily result in a violation of Md. Law. R. Prof. Conduct 1.1, and may constitute negligence but not miscon-

duct under the rule. Att'y Griev. Comm'n v. Pennington, 387 Md. 565, 876 A.2d 642 (2005).

Attorney violated this Rule by the attorney's abject failure to understand and comprehend how to calculate child support. Although the attorney claimed that the majority of the attorney's practice was family law, the attorney had no idea how or when to deduct child health care insurance costs when calculating child support. Att'y Griev. Comm'n v. Kreamer, 404 Md. 282, 946 A.2d 500 (2008).

Public reprimand was imposed upon an attorney for violating Rules 1.1 and 1.16 because the attorney failed to make adequate investigate into a client's eligibility for cancellation of removal from the United States and to pursue that relief, and he failed to promptly return the fees a client paid him even though the client requested a refund; the attorney did recognize the error of his ways and returned the entire fee plus interest, he had no prior disciplinary history in his over 37 years as a member of the Maryland Bar, and he was genuinely remorseful. Att'y Griev. Comm'n v. Snyder, 406 Md. 21, 956 A.2d 147 (2008).

Numerous trivial and inconsequential errors. — Seven errors, each taken separately trivial and inconsequential, taken together amounted to collective incompetence and violations of former disciplinary rules. Att'y Griev. Comm'n v. Brown, 308 Md. 219, 517 A.2d 1111 (1986).

Loss of file. — The loss of a client's file and the failure to reconstruct it in a timely fashion amounted to a violation of this Rule. Att'y Griev. Comm'n v. Ober, 350 Md. 616, 714 A.2d 856 (1998).

Mishandling escrow account. — Indefinite suspension was appropriate sanction for attorneys mishandling of escrow account, including the failure to pay claims due from the account and the failure to refund moneys to clients. Att'y Griev. Comm'n v. Singleton, 311 Md. 1, 532 A.2d 157 (1987); Att'y Griev. Comm'n v. Bakas, 323 Md. 395, 593 A.2d 1087 (1991).

Attorney was suspended indefinitely with the right to reapply after 30 days where the court found that the attorney routinely failed to pay clients after settlement for period of years due to lack of established procedures to property maintain his trust account. Att'y Griev. Comm'n v. Zuckerman, 386 Md. 341, 872 A.2d 693 (2005).

Failure to maintain client's settlement monies. — Attorney was disbarred as his failure to properly maintain a client's settlement monies in his escrow account demonstrated incompetence. Att'y Griev. Comm'n v. Brown, 380 Md. 661, 846 A.2d 428 (2004).

Failure to file affidavit. — A lawyer engaged in default judgment proceedings who fails to file a military affidavit or to adequately comply with the content requirements of Maryland Rule 2-613(a) is not incompetent; such failure is, at best, indicative of the lawyer's carelessness or negligence. Att'y Griev. Comm'n v. Kemp, 335 Md. 1, 641 A.2d 510 (1994).

Failure to file bankruptcy petition constituted violation of Rule. — Attorney violated this Rule, as the attorney did not provide competent representation to a client; the attorney agreed to represent a client in a bankruptcy proceeding, and since the attorney testified he specialized in debtor law, the attorney possessed the legal knowledge and skill to handle the case, the attorney was familiar with the procedure he would use to file the petition, to time lines, to meeting at the trustee's office, to the information and documents he would require, but the attorney failed to file a bankruptcy petition, and took no further action to protect the client's home from foreclosure. Att'y Griev. Comm'n v. Granger, 374 Md. 438, 823 A.2d 611 (2003).

Incompetent handling of bankruptcy case — Attorney acted incompetently in violation of this Rule by failing to submit the required schedules and statement of financial affairs along with his client's bankruptcy petition, by failing to provide these materials when requested by the court, and by failing to file a timely and appropriate opposition to the dismissal of the client's petition. Att'y Griev. Comm'n v. Tinsky, 377 Md. 646, 835 A.2d 542 (2003).

Failure to appear in court. — Attorney twice failed to appear in court for scheduled proceedings for which he was retained, and he provided no acceptable explanation for these absences; this constituted incompetent representation. Att'y Griev. Comm'n v. Harris, 366 Md. 376, 784 A.2d 516 (2001).

Failure to appear for trial — Attorney's failure to appear at his client's criminal trial on two occasions was incompetent representation and showed lack of diligence, in violation of the prior, similar Rule and prior, similar Rule 1.3. Att'y Griev. Comm'n v. Tinsky, 377 Md. 646, 835 A.2d 542 (2003).

Failure to withdraw and inform client of suspension did not support violation of this Rule. — Failure to withdraw from a client matter after being suspended from the practice of law for 90 days and failure to inform the client did not address, and was not dispositive of, a lawyer's competence to handle a particular matter and thus could not support a finding that the attorney violated this Rule. Att'y Griev. Comm'n v. Robertson, 400 Md. 618, 929 A.2d 576 (2007).

Alcoholism, drug addiction or mental disorder. — When a lawyer's misconduct is caused by alcoholism, drug addiction, or a mental disorder, the usual sanction is indefi-

nite suspension. This provides the requisite protection for the public, for it prevents the lawyer from practicing law until such time (if ever) that he or she can demonstrate that he or she is free from the effects of the ailment and able to practice competently. At the same time, the lawyer is spared the ultimate sanction of disbarment, a sanction which would be unfair to apply where the lawyer's conduct is caused by factors beyond his or her control. Att'y Griev. Comm'n v. Powers, 314 Md. 484, 551 A.2d 465 (1989).

An indefinite suspension was the proper sanction in the case of a misappropriation of client funds caused by alcoholism; however, in the future, absent truly compelling circumstances, alcoholism will usually not be permitted to mitigate where an attorney commits a violation of ethical or legal rules which would ordinarily warrant disbarment. Att'y Griev. Comm'n v. Kenney, 339 Md. 578, 664 A.2d 854 (1995).

Incompetence found. — Attorney's professed inability to render an accounting of what happened in his law practice and his escrow account, coupled with his loss of memory on everything from money entrusted to him to the names of his secretaries, cast doubt on his ability to adequately carry out the functions of an attorney. Att'y Griev. Comm'n v. Kramer, 325 Md. 39, 599 A.2d 100 (1991).

State supreme court found that an attorney who failed to maintain adequate records, commingled funds, and accepted commissions without prior court approval when he served as an estate's representative, violated the prior, similar Rule, and it ordered that the attorney be suspended from the practice of law in Maryland, with the right to reapply for permission to practice law at the end of one year. Att'y Griev. Comm'n v. Thompson, 376 Md. 500, 830 A.2d 474 (2003).

Attorney violated the prior, similar Rule by his failure file a timely motion and/or appeal on a client's behalf in an immigration matter. Further, the attorney's suggestion that the client consent to deportation was not competent advice or in his client's best interest. Att'y Griev. Comm'n v. Awuah, 374 Md. 505, 823 A.2d 651 (2003).

When it was not shown that an attorney, who had agreed to represent his clients in an adoption case, did not have the skill to handle such a case, he nonetheless violated this Rule by doing virtually nothing to pursue the case. Att'y Griev. Comm'n v. Guida, 391 Md. 33, 891 A.2d 1085 (2006).

Attorney's representation of a divorce client was incompetent where the attorney did not abide by his client's objectives, failed to act diligently, did not keep the client informed, did not deposit advanced fees in an attorney trust account, and failed to return unearned fees.

Att'y Griev. Comm'n v. Rose, 391 Md. 101, 892 A.2d 469 (2006), cert. denied, 2006 U.S. LEXIS 5734, 166 L. Ed. 2d 22 (U.S. 2006).

Attorney violated Md. R. Prof. Conduct 1.1 and 1.3 by failing to exhibit competence and diligence in pursuing a client's sexual harassment action efficiently and within a reasonable time period; the attorney did not file a complaint for nine to 12 months after agreeing to represent the client. Att'y Griev. Comm'n v. Calhoun, 391 Md. 532, 894 A.2d 518 (2006).

In an attorney disciplinary matter wherein the attorney was ordered disbarred, the attorney was found to have violated Rule 1.4 when he failed to file a Chapter 13 bankruptcy petition, and took no further action to protect the client's home in an impending foreclosure sale, therefore, breaching his duty to provide competent representation. Att'y Griev. Comm'n v. Steinberg, 395 Md. 337, 910 A.2d 429 (2006).

Clear and convincing evidence showed that the attorney acted incompetently when the attorney accepted a case that required filing in a jurisdiction where the attorney was not admitted to practice, and when the attorney failed to service notice to defendant, that the attorney failed to act with reasonable diligence and promptness in representing the client when the attorney failed to file the estate in the proper jurisdiction, that the attorney failed to communicate the truth when the attorney told the client that the attorney was admitted to practice in a certain jurisdiction when the attorney was not admitted there and when the attorney failed to communicate to the client that the attorney intended to seek other counsel in the District of Columbia to assist the attorney, that the attorney's fees were unreasonable because the attorney charged and accepted fees when no work was performed in furtherance of the case, and that the attorney's actions were prejudicial to the administration of justice; even though the attorney was absolved of the charge that the attorney did not properly terminate the representation because the evidence showed that the attorney returned all unearned advance fees to the client after the client retained new counsel, the attorney's violations, which included intentionally dishonest conduct, warranted disbarment, especially since the attorney had a prior disciplinary history. Att'y Griev. Comm'n v. Ward, 396 Md. 203, 913 A.2d 41 (2006).

Where a client, facing incarceration for driving under the influence, was virtually abandoned until the eve of trial and then was represented by an associate who had not read the entire file, who was unaware that his client had two prior convictions, and who first presented the available options to her in the lobby of the courthouse on the day of trial, the supervising attorney violated Md. R. Prof.

Conduct 1.1, 1.3, and 5.1. Att'y Griev. Comm'n v. Ficker, 399 Md. 445, 924 A.2d 1105 (2007).

Where a disciplinary hearing judge found that an attorney's stubbornness over the past eight years to find the guidance necessary to close an estate amounted to incompetence, the record clearly supported the hearing judge's conclusion that the attorney had violated this Rule. Despite the eight years of problems that she had experienced with several courts in administering the estate, she refused to admit her ignorance of the probate procedures involved or to seek and accept help from qualified legal professionals in getting her problems solved. Att'y Griev. Comm'n v. Kendrick, 403 Md. 489, 943 A.2d 1173 (2008).

Attorney's failure to turn over the fee that the attorney retained from a personal injury settlement, when that fee amount belonged to the bankruptcy estate and the attorney had not obtained approval regarding it, amounted to incompetence in violation of this Rule. As a result of that misconduct and other related misconduct, the proper sanction was the attorney's indefinite suspension from the practice of law. Att'y Griev. Comm'n v. Nichols, 405 Md. 207, 950 A.2d 778 (2008).

Attorney provided incompetent representation in two separate cases in violation of this Rule where, in the first case, the attorney did not remove himself from the case even though the attorney did not respond to requests from the trial court to file a response in a discrimination case in order to avoid dismissal and did not communicate to the client of the need to respond, and, in the second case, took and pursued a case that was patently without merit. Since the attorney's conduct was merely negligent rather than deceitful, a 90-day suspension from the practice of law was warranted. Att'y Griev. Comm'n v. Ugwuonye, 405 Md. 351, 952 A.2d 226 (2008).

Attorney's failure to adequately represent the client in all of the client's matters, and the attorney's concealment of the error from the client and the trial court, reflected a lack of competent representation in violation of this rule. Att'y Griev. Comm'n v. Bleecker, 414 Md. 147, 994 A.2d 928 (2010).

While the attorney's drafting of a complaint that did not specifically comply with all the technical requirements did not violate this section, the attorney did violate this section when the attorney failed to enter an appearance in an action until the trial date, did not learn of the looming trial date until the client informed the attorney of it several days before trial, and did not give the client accurate information about the status of the case. Att'y Griev. Comm'n v. Patterson, — Md. —, — A.3d — (Sept. 21, 2011).

Violation found. — Attorney violated this Rule failing to appear for a scheduled court proceeding, by failing to serve interrogatory answers under oath, and by filing an untimely appeal. Att'y Griev. Comm'n v. Byrd, 408 Md. 449, 970 A.2d 870 (2009).

Attorney violated this Rule in two cases because, (1) in a civil case in which the attorney was retained to defend a client, the attorney never entered the attorney's appearance or contact the plaintiff, and did not appear for a hearing, leaving the client to enter into a consent judgment without the aid of counsel, and, (2) in a personal injury case, after discovering that a defendant was deceased, the attorney did not open an estate or otherwise act to protect a client's claim, which was eventually dismissed for a failure to prosecute. Att'y Griev. Comm'n v. De La Paz, 418 Md. 534, 16 A.3d 181 (2011).

No violation found. — In an attorney discipline proceeding, there was no violation of the prior, similar Rule where the only basis was a bare finding that the attorney's failure to file a request for interrogatories adversely affected the attorney's ability to prepare for trial. Att'y Griev. Comm'n v. Hermina, 379 Md. 503, 842 A.2d 762 (2004).

Though an attorney was found to have violated numerous Maryland Rules of Professional Conduct as a result of converting a client's personal injury protection funds to her personal use, the attorney was found not to have violated this Rule with regard to competence, because there was no suggestion or evidence that the attorney did not handle the subject matter of the action, an automobile tort, without lawyerly skill and ability. Att'y Griev. Comm'n v. Cherry-Mahoi, 388 Md. 124, 879 A.2d 58 (2005).

Despite the fact that the attorney did not follow the client's exact instructions with regard to arranging bail for the client, the attorney did not violate this Rule, because the attorneys's actions were reasonable. Att'y Griev. Comm'n v. Ward, 394 Md. 1, 904 A.2d 477 (2006).

Bar counsel failed to show that an attorney had violated Md. R. Prof. Conduct 1.1, 1.3, 1.4(a) and (b), 1.5, 1.16(d), 3.1, 5.1, 5.3, and 8.4(a), (c), and (d) where it was possible to find, based on the testimony, that the attorney had relied on the clients' representations that they intended to handle the appeal pro se, and as a result, Bar counsel had failed to prove that the attorney had represented the two clients in an appeal. Att'y Griev. Comm'n v. Maignan, 402 Md. 39, 935 A.2d 409 (2007).

Attorney was sanctioned by a public reprimand for technically violating Rule 16-609 regarding prohibited transactions as a result of a negligent clerical error involving depositing some of his ex-girlfriend's funds into his operating account instead of his firm's escrow account, which error was corrected upon dis-

covery and was not wilful. The Court of Appeals of Maryland further upheld the trial judge's finding of fact that no attorney client relationship existed between the attorney and his girlfriend to support the other violations asserted against him since he never charged his ex-girlfriend a fee for his services and was only helping her while she received treatment for her alcohol abuse. Att'y Griev. Comm'n v. Shoup, 410 Md. 462, 979 A.2d 120 (Aug. 28, 2009).

Breach of rule of professional liability not basis of cause of action — Maryland law refuses to impose liability for a breach of a rule of professional conduct; violation of a rule does not give rise to a cause of action and does not create a presumption that a legal duty has been breached. Maryland Nat'l Bank v. Resolution Trust Corp., 895 F. Supp. 762 (D. Md. 1995).

Disbarment was proper sanction. — Attorney was properly disbarred for violating prior, similar Maryland Rules of Professional Conduct 1.1, 1.3, 1.4(a) and (b), 1.15(a), 3.3(a)(1), and 8.4(b) and (c), § 10-306 of the Business Occupations and Professions Article, and Rule BU9 (now Rule 16-609) of the Maryland Rules of Procedure. Att'y Griev. Comm'n v. Williams, 335 Md. 458, 644 A.2d 490 (1994).

Attorney was disbarred for violating, inter alia, this Rule by failing to prepare and answer interrogatories in a client's case for damages arising from a fire, and by failing to preserve the client's right of appeal in an employment discrimination matter. Att'y Griev. Comm'n v. Kwarteng, 411 Md. 652, 984 A.2d 865 (2009).

Disbarment of attorney was appropriate where there were serious and repeated violations of the prior, similar Rule and other provisions of the Maryland Rules of Professional Conduct. Att'y Griev. Comm'n v. Milliken, 348 Md. 486, 704 A.2d 1225 (1998).

Disbarment was the proper sanction for an attorney who dragged out representation of two different clients for many years, dooming their causes by failure to comply with applicable laws, and pretended to be continuing representation efforts, in one case, even falsifying a letter after the fact to give the impression that the client had received proper communications; the attorney had also failed to notify clients of a suspension and make other arrangements with them, and to supply information needed by a grievance commission investigator. Att'y Griev. Comm'n v. Davis, 375 Md. 131, 825 A.2d 430 (2003).

In an attorney disciplinary matter wherein the attorney was ordered disbarred, the attorney was found to have violated this Rule when he failed to appear at one client meeting, arrived an hour late each to two mediation sessions, and participated unprepared in the second mediation session. Such actions did not reflect the thoroughness or preparation that the legal profession demanded and such neglect also constituted a violation of Rule 8.4(d), which prohibited conduct that was prejudicial to the administration of justice as failure to be punctual in a scheduled court appearance was not only detrimental to the administration of justice but also constituted discourteous conduct degrading to the tribunal. Att'y Griev. Comm'n v. Steinberg, 395 Md. 337, 910 A.2d 429 (2006).

Disbarment was an appropriate sanction for an attorney whose client's divorce case had been dismissed following the attorney's failure to take any action in response to a notice of contemplated dismissal, pursuant to Rule 2-507. The attorney (1) showed a lack of legal knowledge to obtain a hearing on an emergency basis; (2) failed to consult Rule 1-351, which provided that she certify that all parties had been given notice of the time and place of her presentation of her application for the hearing; (3) was unaware of the requirement of Rule 2-311(d) that a motion based on facts not in the record had to be supported by an affidavit setting forth the necessary facts under oath and had to advise the opposing party that the request would be heard at a particular time; and (4) subjected her client to a motion for counsel fees. Att'y Griev. Comm'n v. McCulloch, 404 Md. 388, 946 A.2d 1009 (2008).

Where the attorney, while decertified, entered appearances on behalf of defendants, and either showed up late or did not show up at all for court proceedings, the attorney violated Md. R. Prof. Conduct 1.1, 1.3, and 8.4(d) by failing to appear for court proceedings. As a result of (1) those violations, (2) the fact that the attorney was decertified at the time the violations were committed, and (3) the fact that the attorney violated other professional conduct rules, also while decertified, the state's highest court had little choice but to disbar the attorney. Att'y Griev. Comm'n v. Walker, 405 Md. 3, 948 A.2d 1263 (2008).

Attorney was disbarred for violating Md. R. Prof. Conduct 1.1, 3.1, 3.2, 3.3(a), 4.4, 8.2(a), and 8.4(c) and (d) because his representation of a client in the court of special appeals was incompetent; the attorney wasintentionally dishonest with both the trial court and the court of special appeals, which showed a systematic effort to mislead the courts, and his history of sanctions for violating the Maryland Rules of Professional Conduct (MRPC) showed an ongoing disregard for the MRPC. Att'y Griev. Comm'n v. McClain, 406 Md. 1, 956 A.2d 135 (2008), cert. denied, 129 S. Ct. 1691, 2009 U.S. LEXIS 2433, 173 L. Ed. 2d 1036 (U.S. 2009).

Attorney was disbarred for violating Md. R. Prof. Conduct 1.1, 1.3, 1.4, 1.15, 3.1, 8.1, and 8.4, when the attorney, inter alia, failing to file an opposition to a motion to dismiss filed in an underlying action and failed to appear for the hearing on that motion. Att'y Griev. Comm'n v. Gisriel, 409 Md. 331, 974 A.2d 331 (2009).

Attorney was disbarred for violating Md. R. Prof. Conduct 1.1, 1.3, 1.4, 1.15, and 8.4, Rule 16-609, and §§ 10-306 and 10-606(b)of the Business and Professional Occupations Article as attorney misappropriated the clients' funds, performed no services whatsoever on the clients' behalf, lied to the clients about the status of their case, and provided them with a falsified administrative agency decision that was not issued by the agency. Att'y Griev. Comm'n v. Bahgat, 411 Md. 568, 984 A.2d 225 (2009).

Attorney violated this rule by completely neglecting a case after filing a complaint, such that the case was dismissed, and by effectively abandoning a second case for six years; the attorney was disbarred for violating this rule along with Md. Law. R. Prof. Conduct 1.2(a), 1.3, 1.4(a), 1.16(d), 8.1(b), and 8.4(a), (c), and (d). Att'y Griev. Comm'n v. Fox, 417 Md. 504, 11 A.3d 762 (2010).

Attorney was disbarred for admittedly violating Md. Law. R. Prof. Conduct 1.1, 1.15(a) and (c), and 8.4(a) — (d), as well as Rule 16-609 and § 10-306 of the Business Occupations and Professions Article, by misappropriating client funds to make it appear as though the attorney's collected fees were higher than those fees actually were, when the attorney was being considered for partner in the attorney's firm, and by failing to file complaints in clients' cases, misrepresenting that the complaints were filed, and fabricating documents to hide the misrepresentations, because (1) disbarment was the presumed sanction for the misappropriation, and (2) the attorney did not show "compelling extenuating circumstances" justifying a lesser sanction, as the attorney showed no serious and debilitating mental condition, since the attorney was not diagnosed with a mental illness, the attorney did not show such a condition was the "root cause" of the attorney's misconduct by making the attorney unable to do day-to-day activities in a normal manner, and the attorney did not show such a condition caused an utter inability to conform the attorney's conduct to the law and the Maryland Rules of Professional Conduct, so any psychological issues the attorney had at the time of the attorney's misconduct did not mitigate the attorney's sanction. Att'y Griev. Comm'n v. Palmer, 417 Md. 185, 9 A.3d 37 (2010).

One year suspension was proper sanction. — Attorney was suspended from the practice of law for a period of one year because of failure to cooperate with bar counsel in violation of prior, similar Rule 8.1, performing services in an incompetent manner in violation of the prior, similar Rule, charging an excessive fee in violation of prior, similar Rule 1.5, and engaging in conduct prejudicial to the administration of justice in violation of prior, similar Rule 8.4. Att'y Griev. Comm'n v. Shaw, 363 Md. 1, 766 A.2d 1028 (2001).

Indefinite suspension was proper sanction. — Where respondent attorney's representation of four clients was marked by serious neglect and inattention; where he failed to return a fee which was unearned for a period of nine months; where he failed to timely remit funds he received on behalf of a client; where he failed to communicate with his clients; and in connection with the investigation of three of the complaints, where respondent failed to answer Bar Counsel's requests for information, the proper sanction was that the attorney be indefinitely suspended from the practice of law, with the right to apply for reinstatement after the suspension had been in effect for six months, conditioned upon his payment of all costs and upon the monitoring of respondent's practice. Att'y Griev. Comm'n v. David, 331 Md. 317, 628 A.2d 178 (1993).

An attorney's practice of assigning and handling cases in such a manner that the lawyer ultimately charged with actually representing the client went into court unprepared, or missed scheduled trial dates entirely, resulted in clients not being afforded competent representation, and justified an indefinite suspension from the practice of law. Att'y Griev. Comm'n v. Ficker, 349 Md. 13, 706 A.2d 1045 (1998).

An attorney who on several separate occasions failed to file legal documents which he had drafted, failed to communicate with clients in these matters, and failed to return attorney's fees he collected in connection with these matters, was rightly found to have violated prior, similar Rules of Professional Conduct 1.1, 1.3, 1.4, 1.16, and 8.4. The appropriate sanction was an indefinite suspension with the right to apply for reinstatement after 60 days, conditioned upon his payment of all costs associated with the matter, reimbursement of the unearned legal fees, and his hiring of an attorney to oversee his practice for a period of one year. Att'y Griev. Comm'n v. Brugh, 353 Md. 475, 727 A.2d 913 (1999).

Attorney was suspended indefinitely for failing to appear on behalf of a client, failing to file a petition on behalf of a client, providing a client with incorrect information that the client did not have to appear for a scheduled trial, and failing to subpoena witness and to obtain medical records that may have exculpated his client. Att'y Griev. Comm'n of Maryland v. Mooney, 359 Md. 56, 753 A.2d 17 (2000).

Attorney's license to practice law was indefinitely suspended for his failure to provide competent, diligent, and communicative representation to his client, for charging unreasonable fees, for pursuing a frivolous proceeding, and for engaging in conduct prejudicial to the administration of justice. Att'y Griev. Comm'n v. Zdravkovich, 362 Md. 1, 762 A.2d 950 (2000).

Hearing court's finding that an attorney who, in connection with a foreclosure action, failed to conduct a title search and discover IRS liens on the subject property, had not been incompetent, was affirmed; there was no rule requiring such a title search, and the court had not been obliged to accept the opinion of a foreclosure expert that the attorney had acted incompetently. Att'y Griev. Comm'n v. McClain, 373 Md. 196, 817 A.2d 218 (2003).

Disciplinary proceedings which charged that an attorney who represented a very difficult client in an estate matter, and who deducted his fee from settlement proceeds without having filed a fee petition and obtaining the court's approval prior to taking his portion, culminated in a determination by clear and convincing evidence that the attorney had violated prior, similar Rules 1.1, 1.15, and 8.4 and the imposition of an indefinite suspension against him upon a finding that his actions were not intentional; however, where the attorney was not charged with violating prior, similar Rule 8.4, it was a violation of due process for the hearing judge to determine that he had violated all of prior, similar Rule 8.4 because he had never received notice of those alleged charges and accordingly, was not held to have violated those rules. Att'y Griev. Comm'n v. Seiden, 373 Md. 409, 818 A.2d 1108 (2003).

Attorney violated the Maryland Rules of Professional Conduct by failing to advise a client of court dates at which the client was to appear, by failing to expeditiously obtain service on the two parties that his client was suing, and by showing a significant lack of preparation and thoroughness. Att'y Griev. Comm'n v. Harris, 371 Md. 510, 810 A.2d 457 (2002).

Where an attorney was retained in two separate bankruptcy matters, was paid the retainer fee, and thereafter neglected the matters, misinformed the clients as to the status of their actions, and failed to properly communicate with them, it was found that he violated prior, similar Rules 1.1, 1.2, 1.3, 1.4, 1.16, and where the attorney had a prior history of disciplinary violations, the court imposed the sanction of disbarment. Att'y Griev. Comm'n v. Faber, 373 Md. 173, 817 A.2d 205 (2003).

Substantial evidence did not support a hearing judge's determinations that an attorney had not violated prior, similar Rules 1.1, 1.15(b), and 8.4 by commingling a client's settlement proceeds with other funds in the attorney's operating account and delaying disbursement of the proceeds for several months, where the hearing judge had ignored the evidence on the back of the check itself and in bank records; although the conduct was egregious, it had not been shown to be intentional, so an indefinite suspension was the appropriate sanction. Att'y Griev. Comm'n v. Maignan, 390 Md. 287, 888 A.2d 344 (2005).

Indefinite suspension, rather than disbarment, was the proper sanction for the attorney's violation of Md. R. Prof. Conduct 1.1, 1.2, 1.3, 1.4, 3.2, and 8.4, where there was no evidence he acted out of fraudulent or selfish motive, he cooperated with Bar Counsel, he engaged in negotiations with the client's attorney regarding restitution, and he expressed great remorse. Att'y Griev. Comm'n v. Reinhardt, 391 Md. 209, 892 A.2d 533 (2006).

Attorney was indefinitely suspended after he conceded violating, inter alia, this Rule by his conduct of the representation of the complainant, acknowledging, "on reflection, the relevant rules of court, rules of evidence, case law, and the Maryland Rules of Professional Conduct demonstrate that his theory of the case, strategy, tactics and time expended on the matter were erroneous, misplaced, and did not rise to the level of competent representation. Att'y Griev. Comm'n v. Manger, 396 Md. 134, 913 A.2d 1 (2006).

Combination of the attorney's lackadaisical handling of trust funds, unreliable recordkeeping system, failure to routinely back up a computer, and lack of urgency in correcting the errors once discovered rose the level of incompetent representation supported a finding that the attorney violated this Rule and justified, in combination with other violations, an indefinite suspension from the practice of law. Att'y Griev. Comm'n v. Goff, 399 Md. 1, 922 A.2d 554 (2007).

Attorney's failure to promptly pay individuals who had funds on deposit in the attorney's trust account was a violation of Md. R. Prof. Conduct 1.1, 1.3, 1.15(d), and 8.4(d). That misconduct, along with the attorney's misconduct in paying clients before funds belonging to them were deposited in the attorney's trust account and failing to supervise an employee, warranted an indefinite suspension from the practice of law with the right to apply for reinstatement after 90 days. Att'y Griev. Comm'n v. Zuckerman, 403 Md. 695, 944 A.2d 525 (2008).

Attorney was suspended indefinitely because his conduct in connection with an estate led to significant delay in closing the estate and violated Md. R. Prof. Conduct 1.1, 1.3, 8.1(a) and (b), and 8.4(a) and (d); the attorney owed the heirs to the estate competent and diligent representation but did not carry out either obligation, and indefinite suspension was the appropriate sanction due to the number and sort of violations, the mitigating factors, and the attorney's seeming failure to follow through on his promise to the hearing judge that he would attempt to "make things right" in the matter. Att'y Griev. Comm'n v. Pawlak, 408 Md. 288, 969 A.2d 311 (2009).

Indefinite suspension with leave to apply for readmission. — Attorney was indefinitely suspended, with leave to apply for readmission after six months, where the attorney violated this Rule and Md. R. Prof. Conduct 1.3, 3.3(a)(1), 5.5(a), and 8.4(c) and (d), by, inter alia, appearing at a meeting of creditors when not authorized to practice before the district court, failing to appear at a confirmation hearing, and failing to disclose fees the client paid to a bankruptcy preparer and attorney. Att'y Griev. Comm'n v. Robaton, 411 Md. 415, 983 A.2d 467 (2009).

Reprimand for negligent handling of personal injury case. — Lawyer was reprimanded for violations of Md. R. Prof. Conduct 1.1, 1.3, 8.1(b) for his negligent handing of a client's case, and his four month delay in acknowledging Bar Counsel's request for information; the commission's request for an indefinite suspension was rejected because there was no reason to believe that the lawyer's misconduct would have been repeated, and the lawyer was honest with his client about his mistakes, advised the client to seek representation for a claim against him, and entered into a settlement in which he paid $ 30,000 to the client from his own funds without resort to his malpractice carrier. The case did not involve either an obstinate refusal to cooperate or a denial of access to relevant documents, and the court was able to protect the public and deter other lawyers from misconduct without disrupting the lawyer's practice. Att'y Griev. Comm'n v. Queen, 407 Md. 556, 967 A.2d 198 (2009).

Applied in Att'y Griev. Comm'n v. James, 385 Md. 637, 870 A.2d 229 (2005); Att'y Griev. Comm'n v. Kapoor, 391 Md. 505, 894 A.2d 502 (2006); Att'y Griev. Comm'n v. Roberts, 394 Md. 137, 904 A.2d 557 (2006).

Quoted in Att'y Griev. Comm'n v. Christopher, 383 Md. 624, 861 A.2d 692 (2004); Att'y Griev. Comm'n v. Mitchell, 386 Md. 386, 872 A.2d 720 (2005); Att'y Griev. Comm'n v. Scroggs, 387 Md. 238, 874 A.2d 985 (2005); Att'y Griev. Comm'n v. Kreamer, 387 Md. 503, 876 A.2d 79 (2005); Att'y Griev. Comm'n v. Kreamer, 387 Md. 503, 876 A.2d 79 (2005); Att'y Griev. Comm'n v. Muhammad, — Md. —, — A.2d — (2005); Att'y Griev. Comm'n v. Mba-Jonas, 402 Md. 334, 936 A.2d 839 (2007).

Cited in Att'y Griev. Comm'n v. Lee, 387 Md. 89, 874 A.2d 897 (2005); Att'y Griev. Comm'n v. Lee, 393 Md. 385, 903 A.2d 360 (2006); Att'y Griev. Comm'n v. Muhammad, 395 Md. 676, 912 A.2d 588 (2006), cert. denied, 127 S. Ct. 2296, 2007 U.S. LEXIS 5292, 167 L. Ed. 2d 1103 (U.S. 2007); Att'y Griev. Comm'n v. McCulloch, 397 Md. 674, 919 A.2d 660 (2007);

Bland v. Hammond, 177 Md. App. 340, 935 A.2d 457 (2007); Att'y Griev. Comm'n v. Akpan, 405 Md. 277, 950 A.2d 820 (2008); Abramson v. Wildman, 184 Md. App. 189, 964 A.2d 703 (2009); Att'y Griev. Comm'n v. Tanko, 408 Md. 404, 969 A.2d 1010 (2009); Att'y Griev. Comm'n v. Edib, 415 Md. 696, 4 A.3d 957 (2010).

Rule 1.2. Scope of Representation and Allocation of Authority Between Client and Lawyer.

(a) Subject to paragraphs (c) and (d), a lawyer shall abide by a client's decisions concerning the objectives of the representation and, when appropriate, shall consult with the client as to the means by which they are to be pursued. A lawyer may take such action on behalf of the client as is impliedly authorized to carry out the representation. A lawyer shall abide by a client's decision whether to settle a matter. In a criminal case, the lawyer shall abide by the client's decision, after consultation with the lawyer, as to a plea to be entered, whether to waive jury trial and whether the client will testify.

(b) A lawyer's representation of a client, including representation by appointment, does not constitute an endorsement of the client's political, economic, social or moral views or activities.

(c) A lawyer may limit the scope of the representation if the limitation is reasonable under the circumstances and the client gives informed consent.

(d) A lawyer shall not counsel a client to engage, or assist a client, in conduct that the lawyer knows is criminal or fraudulent, but a lawyer may discuss the legal consequences of any proposed course of conduct with a client and may counsel or assist a client to make a good faith effort to determine the validity, scope, meaning or application of the law.

COMMENT

Scope of Representation. — [1] Both lawyer and client have authority and responsibility in the objectives and means of representation. The client has ultimate authority to determine the purposes to be served by legal representation, within the limits imposed by law and the lawyer's professional obligations. Within those limits, a client also has a right to consult with the lawyer about the means to be used in pursuing those objectives. At the same time, a lawyer is not required to pursue objectives or employ means simply because a client may wish that the lawyer do so. A clear distinction between objectives and means sometimes cannot be drawn, and in many cases the client-lawyer relationship partakes of a joint undertaking. In questions of means, the lawyer should assume responsibility for technical and legal tactical issues, but should defer to the client regarding such questions as the expense to be incurred and concern for third persons who might be adversely affected.

[2] On occasion, however, a lawyer and a client may disagree about the means to be used to accomplish the client's objectives. Because of the varied nature of the matters about which a lawyer and client might disagree and because the actions in question may implicate the interests of a tribunal or other persons, this Rule does not prescribe how such disagreements are to be resolved. Other law, however, may be applicable and should be consulted by the lawyer. The lawyer should also consult with the client and seek a mutually acceptable resolution of the disagreement. If such efforts are unavailing and the lawyer has a fundamental disagreement with the client, the lawyer may withdraw from the representation. See Rule 1.16(b)(4). Conversely, the client may resolve the disagreement by discharging the lawyer. See Rule 1.16(a)(3).

[3] At the outset of a representation, the client may authorize the lawyer to take specific action on the client's behalf without further consultation. Absent a material change in circumstances and subject to Rule 1.4, a lawyer may rely on such an advance authorization. The client may, however, revoke such authority at any time.

[4] In a case in which the client appears to be suffering diminished capacity, the lawyer's duty to abide by the client's decisions is to be guided by reference to Rule 1.14.

Independence from Client's Views or Activities. — [5] Legal representation should not be denied to people who are unable to afford legal services, or whose cause is controversial or the subject of popular disapproval. By the same token, representing a client does not constitute approval of the client's views or activities.

Agreements Limiting Scope of Representation. — [6] The scope of services to be provided by a lawyer may be limited by agreement with the client or by the terms under which the lawyer's services are made available to the client. When a lawyer has been retained by an insurer to represent an insured, for example, the representation may be limited to matters related to the insurance coverage. A limited representation may be appropriate because the client has limited objectives for the representation. In addition, the terms upon which representation is undertaken may exclude specific means that might otherwise be used to accomplish the client's objectives. Such limitations may exclude actions that the client thinks are too costly or that the lawyer regards as repugnant or imprudent.

[7] Although this Rule affords the lawyer and client substantial latitude to limit the representation, the limitation must be reasonable under the circumstances. If, for example, a client's objective is limited to securing general information about the law the client needs in order to handle a common and typically uncomplicated legal problem, the lawyer and client may agree that the lawyer's services will be limited to a brief telephone consultation. Such a limitation, however, would not be reasonable if the time allotted was not sufficient to yield advice upon which the client could rely. Although an agreement for a limited representation does not exempt a lawyer from the duty to provide competent representation, the limitation is a factor to be considered when determining the legal knowledge, skill, thoroughness and preparation reasonably necessary for the representation. See Rule 1.1.

[8] All agreements concerning a lawyer's representation of a client must accord with the Maryland Lawyers' Rules of Professional Conduct and other law. See, e.g., Rule 1.1, 1.8 and 5.6.

Criminal, Fraudulent and Prohibited Transactions. — [9] Paragraph (d) prohibits a lawyer from knowingly counseling or assisting a client to commit a crime or fraud. This prohibition, however, does not preclude the lawyer from giving an honest opinion about the actual consequences that appear likely to result from a client's conduct. The fact that a client uses advice in a course of action that is criminal or fraudulent does not, of itself, make a lawyer a party to the course of action. There is a critical distinction between presenting an analysis of legal aspects of questionable conduct and recommending the means by which a crime or fraud might be committed with impunity.

[10] When the client's course of action has already begun and is continuing, the lawyer's responsibility is especially delicate. The lawyer is required to avoid assisting the client, for example, by drafting or delivering documents that the lawyer knows are fraudulent or by suggesting how the wrongdoing might be concealed. A lawyer may not continue assisting a client in conduct that the lawyer originally supposed was legally proper but then discovers is criminal or fraudulent. The lawyer must, therefore, withdraw from the representation of the client in the matter. See Rule 1.16(a). In some cases withdrawal alone might be insufficient. It may be necessary for the lawyer to give notice of the fact of withdrawal and to disaffirm any opinion, document, affirmation or the like. See Rules 1.6, 4.1.

[11] Where the client is a fiduciary, the lawyer may be charged with special obligations in dealings with a beneficiary.

[12] Paragraph (d) applies whether or not the defrauded party is a party to the transaction. Hence, a lawyer must not participate in a transaction to effectuate criminal or fraudulent avoidance of tax liability. Paragraph (d) does not preclude undertaking a criminal defense incident to a general retainer for legal services to a lawful enterprise. The last clause of paragraph (d) recognizes that determining the validity or interpretation of a statute or regulation may require a course of action involving disobedience of the statute or regulation or of the interpretation placed upon it by governmental authorities.

[13] If a lawyer comes to know or reasonably should know that a client expects assistance not permitted by the Maryland Lawyers' Rules of Professional Conduct or other law or if the lawyer intends to act contrary to the client's instructions, the lawyer must consult with the client regarding the limitations on the lawyer's conduct. See Rule 1.4(a)(4).

Model Rules Comparison. — Rule 1.2 is substantially similar to the language of the Ethics 2000 Amendments to the ABA Model Rules of Professional Conduct except for wording changes in Rule 1.2(a) and the retention of existing Maryland language in Comment [1].

Maryland Law Review. — For symposium, expanding pro bono legal assistance in civil cases to Maryland's poor, see 49 Md. L. Rev. 1 (1990).

Client's dissatisfaction. — A client's dissatisfaction with an attorney's representation alone did not establish a violation of this Rule. Att'y Griev. Comm'n v. Briscoe, 357 Md. 554,

745 A.2d 1037 (2000).

Assisting client in criminal conduct. — Although attorney's conduct in assisting a former client in breaking into the home of his wife was an aberration, the egregious nature of that conduct warranted the imposition of a significant sanction such that the attorney was suspended indefinitely from the practice of law with the right to apply for reinstatement not less than one year from the date of filing the opinion. Att'y Griev. Comm'n v. Protokowicz, 329 Md. 252, 619 A.2d 100 (1993).

Failure to abide by represenation objectives. — Attorney's representation of a divorce client violated former version of this Rule, where the attorney did not abide by the client's representation objectives. Att'y Griev. Comm'n v. Rose, 391 Md. 101, 892 A.2d 469 (2006), cert. denied, 2006 U.S. LEXIS 5734, 166 L. Ed. 2d 22 (U.S. 2006).

Attorney violated this Rule by failing to do anything on behalf of the attorney's client for over one year, the attorney's failure to abide by the client's request that a dissolution be filed on behalf of the client's corporation, and by failing to act in a reasonable time to conclude the representation. Att'y Griev. Comm'n v. Kreamer, 404 Md. 282, 946 A.2d 500 (2008).

Attorney violated this Rule because, (1) after a client signed a contract to be represented by the attorney's employer, the attorney did not respect that decision when the attorney asserted that the client hired the attorney personally, and (2) the attorney took action on the client's behalf that the client did not authorize when the attorney substituted the attorney's name as payee on the client's check made payable to the attorney's employer. Att'y Griev. Comm'n v. Elliott, 417 Md. 659, 12 A.3d 105 (2011).

Requirement to abide by criminal defendant's decision concerning services to be performed. — Trial court did not violate Md. R. 4-215(a)(3) when defendant said defendant did not want counsel to represent defendant because the trial court could rely on counsel's statement "I'm still in the case," and did not have to inquire further, as this Rule required counsel to abide by defendant's decision concerning the services to be performed on defendant's behalf, and Md. R. Prof. Conduct 3.3 prohibited counsel from making a false statement to the trial court. Garner v. State, 414 Md. 372, 995 A.2d 694 (2010).

Failure to file bankruptcy petition as requested by client — Attorney violated the prior, similar Rule, as the attorney did not abide by his client's decision to immediately file the petition for bankruptcy after the client made it clear that her purpose in hiring the attorney was to save her home from foreclosure, and after the attorney assured her on numerous occasions he would protect her home, but failed to take the necessary steps to abide by the client's decision to file for bankruptcy. Att'y Griev. Comm'n v. Granger, 374 Md. 438, 823 A.2d 611 (2003).

In an attorney disciplinary matter wherein the attorney was ordered disbarred, the attorney was found to have violated Rule 1.4 when he failed to file a Chapter 13 bankruptcy petition, and took no further action to protect the client's home in an impending foreclosure sale, therefore, breaching his duty to provide competent representation. Further, the attorney violated Rule 1.2 by reassuring his client on several occasions that the petition had been filed, he failed to do so, which was in direct contravention of the client's wishes to file for bankruptcy. Att'y Griev. Comm'n v. Steinberg, 395 Md. 337, 910 A.2d 429 (2006).

Disbarment was an appropriate sanction for an attorney who did not abide by her client's decision regarding the objective to obtain a divorce. Instead of pursuing this objective, the attorney allowed the case to be dismissed and stopped pursuing the matter altogether, thus, failing to abide by the client's decisions regarding the objective of the representation and violating Md. R. Prof. Conduct 1.2. Att'y Griev. Comm'n v. McCulloch, 404 Md. 388, 946 A.2d 1009 (2008).

Defense of criminal responsibility. — A defendant who is competent is entitled to decide whether the defense of criminal responsibility is to be interposed at that trial, and absent the most unusual circumstances, this decision binds both counsel and the trial judge. Treece v. State, 313 Md. 665, 547 A.2d 1054 (1988).

Disbarment was proper sanction. — Where an attorney was retained in two separate bankruptcy matters, was paid the retainer fee, and thereafter neglected the matters, misinformed the clients as to the status of their actions, and failed to properly communicate with them, it was found that he violated prior, similar Rules 1.1, 1.2, 1.3, 1.4, 1.16, and where the attorney had a prior history of disciplinary violations, the court imposed the sanction of disbarment. Att'y Griev. Comm'n v. Faber, 373 Md. 173, 817 A.2d 205 (2003).

Where the attorney, among other things, intentionally misappropriated client funds, forged a client's signature on a settlement check, lied under oath, and represented a client when the attorney was not licensed to do so, the attorney was disbarred for violating former, similar Md. R. Prof. Conduct1.2(a), 1.3, 1.5(c), 1.15(a), (b), 3.3(a), 5.5, 8.1(a), (b), 8.4(a), (b), (c),(d), Md. R. 16-604, and §§ 10-304, -306 of the Business Occupations and Professions Article. Att'y Griev. Comm'n v. Kapoor, 391 Md. 505, 894 A.2d 502 (2006).

Attorney violated this rule by failing to abide by the decisions of his clients in one action and failing to pursue their matter after the complaint was filed, and by failing to consult with a client in a second action about the settlement agreement reached with an insurer; the attorney was disbarred for violating this rule along with Md. Law. R. Prof. Conduct 1.1, 1.3, 1.4(a), 1.16(d), 8.1(b), and 8.4(a), (c), and (d). Att'y Griev. Comm'n v. Fox, 417 Md. 504, 11 A.3d 762 (2010).

Attorney was disbarred for violating (d) and Md. Law. R. Prof. Conduct 8.4(a), (b), (c), and (d), when the attorney empowered a client's child to forge the client's signature on estate documents, notarized falsely executed and initialed estate documents, and directed the attorney's employees to falsely attest to the signature; the attorney suffered no cognitive deficits and new what he was doing was wrong. Att'y Griev. Comm'n v. Coppola, 419 Md. 370, 19 A.3d 431 (2011).

Attorney violated (a) and Md. Law. R. Prof. Conduct 1.15(d), 8.4(c) and (d), Md. R. 16-604 and 16-609(c), and § 10-306 of the Business Occupations and Professions Article, and was disbarred, after misappropriating tens of thousands of dollars that should have been paid to a physical therapist and settling a client's claim without the client's knowledge or consent. Att'y Griev. Comm'n v. Stern, 419 Md. 525, 19 A.3d 904 (2011).

Indefinite suspension was proper sanction. — Indefinite suspension, rather than disbarment, was the proper sanction for the attorney's violation of Md. R. Prof. Conduct 1.1, 1.2, 1.3, 1.4, 3.2, and 8.4, where there was no evidence he acted out of fraudulent or selfish motive, he cooperated with Bar Counsel, he engaged in negotiations with the client's attorney regarding restitution, and he expressed great remorse. Att'y Griev. Comm'n v. Reinhardt, 391 Md. 209, 892 A.2d 533 (2006).

In a reciprocal discipline action, the attorney, who admitted to the wrongdoing which led to a finding that D.C. R. Prof. Conduct 1.2(a), 1.4(a), 1.4(b), 1.4(c), 1.5(c), 1.15(a), 1.15(b), 1.15(c), and 8.4(d) had been violated based on the attorney's negligence misrepresentation of settlement funds in one case and interference with the administration of justice in another case, amounting to violations of Md. Law. R. Prof. Conduct Rules 1.2(a), 1.4(a)(2) and (3), 1.4(b), 1.5(c), 1.15(a), 1.15(d), 1.15(e), and 8.4(d), was indefinitely suspended in Maryland, with right to apply for readmission after reinstatement in the District in Columbia. Att'y Griev. Comm'n v. Thaxton, 415 Md. 341, — A.2d —, 1 A.3d 470 (2010).

Applied in Att'y Griev. Comm'n v. Roberts, 394 Md. 137, 904 A.2d 557 (2006).

Quoted in Att'y Griev. Comm'n v. Scroggs, 387 Md. 238, 874 A.2d 985 (2005); Att'y Griev. Comm'n v. Muhammad, — Md. —, — A.2d — (2005); Att'y Griev. Comm'n v. Ward, 394 Md. 1, 904 A.2d 477 (2006); Att'y Griev. Comm'n v. Kwarteng, 411 Md. 652, 984 A.2d 865 (2009).

Cited in Att'y Griev. Comm'n v. Muhammad, 395 Md. 676, 912 A.2d 588 (2006), cert. denied, 127 S. Ct. 2296, 2007 U.S. LEXIS 5292, 167 L. Ed. 2d 1103 (U.S. 2007); Att'y Griev. Comm'n v. McCulloch, 397 Md. 674, 919 A.2d 660 (2007); Att'y Griev. Comm'n v. Elmendorf, 404 Md. 353, 946 A.2d 542 (2008); Att'y Griev. Comm'n v. Ugwuonye, 405 Md. 351, 952 A.2d 226 (2008); State v. Northam, — Md. —, 26 A.3d 344 (2011).

Rule 1.3. Diligence.

A lawyer shall act with reasonable diligence and promptness in representing a client.

COMMENT

[1] A lawyer should pursue a matter on behalf of a client despite opposition, obstruction or personal inconvenience to the lawyer, and may take whatever lawful and ethical measures are required to vindicate a client's cause or endeavor. A lawyer must also act with commitment and dedication to the interests of the client and with zeal in advocacy upon the client's behalf. A lawyer is not bound, however, to press for every advantage that might be realized for a client. For example, a lawyer may have authority to exercise professional discretion in determining the means by which a matter should be pursued. See Rule 1.2. The lawyer's duty to act with reasonable diligence does not require the use of offensive tactics or permit treating any person involved in the legal process without courtesy and respect.

[2] A lawyer's workload must be controlled so that each matter can be handled competently.

[3] Perhaps no professional shortcoming is more widely resented than procrastination. A client's interests often can be adversely affected by the passage of time or the change of conditions; in extreme instances, as when a lawyer overlooks a statute of limitations, the client's legal position may be destroyed. Even when the client's interests are not affected in substance, however, unreasonable delay can cause a client needless anxiety and undermine confidence in the lawyer's trustworthiness. A lawyer's duty to act with reasonable promptness, however, does not preclude the lawyer

from agreeing to a reasonable request for a postponement that will not prejudice the lawyer's client.

[4] Unless the relationship is terminated as provided in Rule 1.16, a lawyer should carry through to conclusion all matters undertaken for a client. If a lawyer's employment is limited to a specific matter, the relationship terminates when the matter has been resolved. If a lawyer has served a client over a substantial period in a variety of matters, the client sometimes may assume that the lawyer will continue to serve on a continuing basis unless the lawyer gives notice of withdrawal. Doubt about whether a client-lawyer relationship still exists should be clarified by the lawyer, preferably in writing, so that the client will not mistakenly suppose the lawyer is looking after the client's affairs when the lawyer has ceased to do so. For example, if a lawyer has handled a judicial or administrative proceeding that produced a result adverse to the client and the lawyer and client have not agreed that the lawyer will handle the matter on appeal, the lawyer must consult with the client about the possibility of appeal before relinquishing responsibility for the matter. See Rule 1.4. Similarly, the lawyer must inform the client if, following a result favorable to the client, another party files an appeal. Whether the lawyer is obligated to prosecute the appeal for the client depends on the scope of the representation the lawyer has agreed to provide to the client. See Rule 1.2.

[5] To prevent neglect of client matters in the event of a sole practitioner's death or disability, the duty of diligence may require that each sole practitioner prepare a plan, in conformity with applicable rules, that designates another competent lawyer to review client files, notify each client of the lawyer's death or disability, and determine whether there is a need for immediate protective action. Cf. Md. Rule 16-777 (providing for appointment of a conservator to inventory the files of an attorney who is deceased or has abandoned the practice of law, and to take other appropriate action to protect the attorney's clients in the absence of a plan to protect clients' interests).

Model Rules Comparison. — Rule 1.3 is substantially similar to the language of the Ethics 2000 Amendments to the ABA Model Rules of Professional Conduct except for Comment [5], which incorporates Maryland law.

Maryland Law Review. — For note discussing whether, under third-party beneficiary theory, a nonclient can sue attorney for negligent misrepresentation without proof of privity of contract, see 16 U. Balt. L. Rev. 354 (1987).

For symposium, expanding pro bono legal assistance in civil cases to Maryland's poor, see 49 Md. L. Rev. 1 (1990).

University of Baltimore Law Forum. — For article, "Code of Ethics Revisited," see 19.2 U. Balt. Law Forum 14 (1989).

For Recent Development, "Attorney Grievance Commission of Maryland v. Mooney: Indefinite Suspension is Warranted Where an Attorney Fails to Provide Competent Representation," see 31 U. Balt. Law Forum 44 (2000).

Alcoholism, drug addiction or mental disorder. — When alcoholism is, to a substantial extent, the cause of the misconduct by an attorney, we view the misconduct in a somewhat different light; under this circumstance the appropriate sanction is indefinite suspension and the focus shifts to questions of rehabilitation and the imposition of conditions sufficient to protect the public if the lawyer is allowed to resume practice. Att'y Griev. Comm'n v. Reid, 308 Md. 646, 521 A.2d 743 (1987).

When a lawyer's misconduct is caused by alcoholism, drug addiction, or a mental disorder, the usual sanction is indefinite suspension. This provides the requisite protection for the public, for it prevents the lawyer from practicing law until such time (if ever) that he or she can demonstrate that he or she is free from the effects of the ailment and able to practice competently. At the same time, the lawyer is spared the ultimate sanction of disbarment, a sanction which would be unfair to apply where the lawyer's conduct is caused by factors beyond his or her control. Att'y Griev. Comm'n v. Powers, 314 Md. 484, 551 A.2d 465 (1989).

An indefinite suspension was the proper sanction in the case of a misappropriation of client funds caused by alcoholism; however, in the future, absent truly compelling circumstances, alcoholism will usually not be permitted to mitigate where an attorney commits a violation of ethical or legal rules which would ordinarily warrant disbarment. Att'y Griev. Comm'n v. Kenney, 339 Md. 578, 664 A.2d 854 (1995).

Workaholism. — Acceptance of "workaholism" as an excuse for lack of diligence would effectively gut this Rule. Att'y Griev. Comm'n v. Drew, 341 Md. 139, 669 A.2d 1344 (1996).

Failure to carry out contract of employment. — Ninety-day suspension was appropriate sanction for attorney's failure to timely file or adequately investigate action on behalf of her client, and for misrepresenting to her client that the suit had been filed on her behalf and was proceeding to trial where the client paid the attorney only part of the costs involved in the work the attorney did do and the attorney did not consider the gratuitous client to be a client; an attorney-client relationship did exist and, thus, the attorney failed to carry out her contract of employment. Att'y Griev. Comm'n v. Pinkney, 311 Md. 137, 532 A.2d 1367 (1987).

Attorney's multiple violations of the Maryland Rules of Professional Conduct, including violation of this Rule for failing to timely request for an emergency hearing, warranted disbarment. The client retained the attorney to file for such a hearing and even though the attorney told the client the attorney did so, the attorney did not comply with that request. Att'y Griev. Comm'n v. Webster, 402 Md. 448, 937 A.2d 161 (2007).

Failure to handle clients' matters in a reasonably diligent manner. — Attorney violated this rule by not handling matters for which he had been retained in a reasonably diligent fashion, in that the attorney did little work on a client's immigration case, not being diligent in responding to her requests for information about the status of her case, and failing to deliver the client's file to her despite the repeated requests of the client and her new counsel. Additionally, the attorney violated the rule by failing to file a timely motion and/or appeal on behalf of another immigration client. Attorney violated the prior, similar Rule by not handling matters for which he had been retained in a reasonably diligent fashion, in that the attorney did little work on a client's immigration case, not being diligent in responding to her requests for information about the status of her case, and failing to deliver the client's file to her despite the repeated requests of the client and her new counsel. Additionally, the attorney violated the rule by failing to file a timely motion and/or appeal on behalf of another immigration client. Att'y Griev. Comm'n v. Awuah, 374 Md. 505, 823 A.2d 651 (2003).

Attorney was disbarred as he violated the prior, similar Rule when, having been engaged to provide legal services to a client, the attorney failed to act with reasonable diligence and promptness in carrying out that representation. Att'y Griev. Comm'n v. Velasquez, 380 Md. 651, 846 A.2d 422 (2004).

Attorney violated Md. R. Prof. Conduct 1.3, 1.4(a), (b), 8.1 and 8.4(d) when she failed to administratively close a client's asylum application and refile it in proper form as directed by the immigration judge and the client, and failed to respond to requests for information in connection with the related disciplinary investigation. Indefinite suspension was proper

given the egregious nature of the attorney's misconduct and her failure to present anything by way of mitigation to the appellate court. Att'y Griev. Comm'n v. Brisbon, 385 Md. 667, 870 A.2d 586 (2005).

Attorney violated this Rule because he agreed to represent his clients in an adoption matter but did virtually no work in the case, such as filing a petition. Att'y Griev. Comm'n v. Guida, 391 Md. 33, 891 A.2d 1085 (2006).

Attorney violated Md. R. Prof. Conduct 1.1 and 1.3 by failing to exhibit competence and diligence in pursuing a client's sexual harassment action efficiently and within a reasonable time period; the attorney did not file a complaint for nine to 12 months after agreeing to represent the client. Att'y Griev. Comm'n v. Calhoun, 391 Md. 532, 894 A.2d 518 (2006).

Attorney violated this Rule because he neglected his client's matter as evidenced by his failure to review case documents until nearly two years after he was retained, failure to manage his case workload in a manner which would have allowed for the timely research, review, evaluation, and pursuit of the matters for which he was retained, and failure to prepare any written pleadings or papers in the pursuit of the matter as promised to the client in correspondence. Att'y Griev. Comm'n v. Lee, 393 Md. 385, 903 A.2d 360 (2006).

Where a client, facing incarceration for driving under the influence, was virtually abandoned until the eve of trial and then was represented by an associate who had not read the entire file, who was unaware that his client had two prior convictions, and who first presented the available options to her in the lobby of the courthouse on the day of trial, the supervising attorney violated Md. R. Prof. Conduct 1.1, 1.3, 1.4, and 5.1. Att'y Griev. Comm'n v. Ficker, 399 Md. 445, 924 A.2d 1105 (2007).

Where a client, facing criminal charges that could have resulted in incarceration, was abandoned by her attorney on what she assumed would be a trial date, the attorney violated Md. R. Prof. Conduct 1.3 and 8.4(d). Att'y Griev. Comm'n v. Ficker, 399 Md. 445, 924 A.2d 1105 (2007).

Bar counsel failed to show that an attorney had violated Md. R. Prof. Conduct 1.1, 1.3, 1.5(a), 1.16(d), 3.1, 5.1, 5.3(a) and (c), and 8.4(a) and (d) where the attorney had informed the client that he no longer wished to represent him after the client changed his mind with respect to a settlement agreement and the attorney had discharged the associate after discovering that she had subsequently file additional motions. Att'y Griev. Comm'n v. Maignan, 402 Md. 39, 935 A.2d 409 (2007).

Where there was evidence in a disciplinary hearing judge's record an attorney repeatedly failed to properly file a required Third and

Final Administration Account, the record supported a finding that the attorney had violated this Rule. The attorney was not diligent in responding to the guidance given concerning the correct procedure or form for submission of an account and was not diligent in timely filing documents with the Register of Wills. Att'y Griev. Comm'n v. Kendrick, 403 Md. 489, 943 A.2d 1173 (2008).

Attorney violated this Rule by failing to advise the attorney's client for over three months of a judge's order fixing child support and a wage lien against the client. Att'y Griev. Comm'n v. Kreamer, 404 Md. 282, 946 A.2d 500 (2008).

Attorney failed to act with diligence and promptness as required by Md. R. Prof. Conduct 1.3. She abandoned efforts to serve a defendant in her client's divorce case and took no action after receiving the notice of contemplated dismissal; this was an extreme lack of diligence and a violation of Rule 1.3 . Att'y Griev. Comm'n v. McCulloch, 404 Md. 388, 946 A.2d 1009 (2008).

Attorney's inattentiveness to the clients' interests, including the attorney's failure to respond to a motion to dismiss filed against the clients in an undelrying case, supported a finding that the attorney violated this Rule. Att'y Griev. Comm'n v. Gisriel, 409 Md. 331, 974 A.2d 331 (2009).

Attorney was disbarred for violating, inter alia, this Rule by failing to communicate with the client in the two matters the attorney represented the client on and abandoning the client, demonstrating a lack of diligence. Att'y Griev. Comm'n v. Kwarteng, 411 Md. 652, 984 A.2d 865 (2009).

Attorney violated this section when the attorney failed to enter an appearance in an action until the trial date, did not learn of the looming trial date until the client informed the attorney of it several days before trial, and did not give the client accurate information about the status of the case. Att'y Griev. Comm'n v. Patterson, — Md. —, — A.3d — (Sept. 21, 2011).

Failure to represent adequately. — Counsel failed to represent debtors adequately with respect to their objections to the prepetition arrearage claim filed by the deed of trust holder where counsel committed debtors to pay the full disputed claim in an amended plan without taking any action either to evaluate the objection or question the amount of the disputed claim. By doing nothing in response to debtors' express desire to object to the claim, it appeared that counsel violated this Rule. In re Bramble, (Bankr. D. Md. 2006).

Attorney violated this Rule in two cases because, (1) in a civil case in which the attorney was retained to defend a client, the attorney never entered the attorney's appearance or contact the plaintiff, and did not appear for a hearing, leaving the client to enter into a consent judgment without the aid of counsel, and, (2) in a personal injury case, after discovering that a defendant was deceased, the attorney did not open an estate or otherwise act to protect a client's claim, which was eventually dismissed for a failure to prosecute. Att'y Griev. Comm'n v. De La Paz, 418 Md. 534, 16 A.3d 181 (2011).

Failure to pursue legal authority — Failure to pursue applicable legal authority in timely fashion may well constitute a violation of this Rule. Massey v. Prince George's County, 907 F. Supp. 138 (D. Md. 1995).

The prior, similar Rule's requirement of diligence includes pursuing applicable legal authority in timely fashion. Massey v. Prince George's County, 918 F. Supp. 905 (D. Md. 1996).

Handling of bankruptcy case. — Attorney did not act with reasonable diligence in his representation of a client, in violation of this Rule, by delaying over two years after he was retained before filing the bankruptcy petition, then not filing additional materials requested by the court in a timely manner, and by failing to file a motion to strike the dismissal order within the time permitted. Att'y Griev. Comm'n v. Tinsky, 377 Md. 646, 835 A.2d 542 (2003).

Failure to file bankruptcy petition in a timely fashion — Attorney violated prior, similar Rule, as the attorney did not act with reasonable diligence or promptness; in agreeing to represent a client in a bankruptcy matter, the attorney fully understood that acting promptly was of the utmost importance, and due diligence required the attorney, when faced with questions about seeing the client's home listed for sale in the paper, having a potential buyer come to the home, and being advised that someone had purchased the home, to immediately check on the case by confirming receipt by the bankruptcy court of the bankruptcy petition, but the attorney never made any inquiries to ensure that the petition had been properly filed. Att'y Griev. Comm'n v. Granger, 374 Md. 438, 823 A.2d 611 (2003).

Failure to file divorce complaint in timely manner. — Attorney violated this Rule when he failed to act diligently in providing the requested representation. It took the attorney about six weeks to file a complaint in the client's divorce action. Att'y Griev. Comm'n v. Rose, 391 Md. 101, 892 A.2d 469 (2006), cert. denied, 2006 U.S. LEXIS 5734, 166 L. Ed. 2d 22 (U.S. 2006).

Failure to timely file asylum application. — Attorney violated this Rule by failing to file a client's asylum application on time; while the attorney argued that the late filing was due to the client's failure to timely provide essential information, the Court of Appeals concluded that a reasonably diligent attorney would have submitted as complete an application as possible before the deadline. Att'y Griev. Comm'n v. Khandpur, 421 Md. 1, 25 A.3d 165 (2011).

Failure to reschedule hearing. — An attorney's failure to reschedule in a timely fashion a hearing that had been postponed previously was sufficient grounds to find that the attorney had violated this Rule. Att'y Griev. Comm'n v. Ober, 350 Md. 616, 714 A.2d 856 (1998).

Tardiness or absence from trial. — Since being late for a scheduled court appearance interferes with the administration of justice, it is obvious that being altogether absent from a scheduled trial does so as well; however, the circumstances surrounding the failure to appear and the actual consequences of that failure are matters that go to the question of sanction. Att'y Griev. Comm'n v. Ficker, 319 Md. 305, 572 A.2d 501 (1990).

Attorney's failure to appear at his client's criminal trial on two occasions was incompetent representation and showed lack of diligence, in violation of prior, similar Rule 1.1 and this Rule. Att'y Griev. Comm'n v. Tinsky, 377 Md. 646, 835 A.2d 542 (2003).

Given the duty of zealous representation that a lawyer owes the client, a failure to appear caused by poor office practices or simple forgetfulness may constitute neglect. Att'y Griev. Comm'n v. Ficker, 319 Md. 305, 572 A.2d 501 (1990).

A single inadvertent failure to appear may constitute neglect of a legal matter. Att'y Griev. Comm'n v. Ficker, 319 Md. 305, 572 A.2d 501 (1990).

Attorney violated the Maryland Rules of Professional Conduct by failing to appear for scheduled trials on three dates and by failing to notify his client about those dates and if his client was or was not to appear in court on those dates. Att'y Griev. Comm'n v. Harris, 371 Md. 510, 810 A.2d 457 (2002).

Attorney violated this Rule by failing to appear for a scheduled court proceeding. Att'y Griev. Comm'n v. Byrd, 408 Md. 449, 970 A.2d 870 (2009).

Repeated failure to attend hearings or produce documents. — Attorney who repeatedly failed to appear in court and to produce documents as directed by court order violated prior, similar Rule 3.4, as his claim that he did not appear on one occasion due to an ice storm but that he called the court clerk was not substantiated by the court record; he was also found to have violated the prior, similar Rule by failing to have prepared an order in a family court matter, as directed by the court, as his claim that he thought his

opposing counsel was preparing the order conflicted with documents indicating that the attorney knew it was his obligation to prepare it. Att'y Griev. Comm'n v. Mininsohn, 380 Md. 536, 846 A.2d 353 (2004).

Mishandling escrow account. — Indefinite suspension was appropriate sanction for attorney's mishandling of escrow account, including the failure to pay claims due from the account and the failure to refund moneys to clients. Att'y Griev. Comm'n v. Singleton, 311 Md. 1, 532 A.2d 157 (1987); Att'y Griev. Comm'n v. Bakas, 323 Md. 395, 593 A.2d 1087 (1991).

Attorney's failure to pay medical bills in a timely manner and to disburse client funds demonstrated a lack of reasonable diligence. Att'y Griev. Comm'n v. Zuckerman, 386 Md. 341, 872 A.2d 693 (2005).

Attorney was less than diligent when he failed to inform his client that he received settlement proceeds, moved his office without notifying clients, and stole a client's money. Att'y Griev. Comm'n v. Mitchell, 386 Md. 386, 872 A.2d 720 (2005).

Clear and convincing evidence was found that an attorney violated this Rule by converting a client's personal injury protection fund monies to her personal use, having insufficient funds in her escrow account to pay the client's outstanding claims for reimbursement from such fund, and otherwise converting to her own use the fund, which should have been held in trust for the client. Att'y Griev. Comm'n v. Cherry-Mahoi, 388 Md. 124, 879 A.2d 58 (2005).

Failure to file affidavit. — A lawyer engaged in default judgment proceedings who fails to file a military affidavit or to adequately comply with the content requirements of former Maryland Rule 2-613 (a) (now Rule 2-613 (b)) is not incompetent; such failure is, at best, indicative of the lawyer's carelessness or negligence. Att'y Griev. Comm'n v. Kemp, 335 Md. 1, 641 A.2d 510 (1994).

Failure to file testimony and serve defendant. — Attorney violated the prior, similar Rule when it took him four years to obtain a divorce for his client, and where his repeated failure to file testimony timely and to serve the defendant demonstrated a lack of reasonable diligence. Att'y Griev. Comm'n v. Fezell, 361 Md. 234, 760 A.2d 1108 (2000).

Failure to file in proper jurisdiction and failure to perfect service on defendant — Clear and convincing evidence showed that the attorney acted incompetently when the attorney accepted a case that required filing in a jurisdiction where the attorney was not admitted to practice, and when the attorney failed to service notice to defendant, that the attorney failed to act with reasonable diligence and promptness in representing the client when the attorney failed to file the estate in the proper jurisdiction, that the attorney failed to communicate the truth when the attorney told the client that the attorney was admitted to practice in a certain jurisdiction when the attorney was not admitted there and when the attorney failed to communicate to the client that the attorney intended to seek other counsel in the District of Columbia to assist the attorney, that the attorney's fees were unreasonable because the attorney charged and accepted fees when no work was performed in furtherance of the case, and that the attorney's actions were prejudicial to the administration of justice; even though the attorney was absolved of the charge that the attorney did not properly terminate the representation because the evidence showed that the attorney returned all unearned advance fees to the client after the client retained new counsel, the attorney's violations, which included intentionally dishonest conduct, warranted disbarment, especially since the attorney had a prior disciplinary history. Att'y Griev. Comm'n v. Ward, 396 Md. 203, 913 A.2d 41 (2006).

Failure to secure client's financial interests. — An attorney was reprimanded where she failed to take action to secure her client's interest in a retirement plan until several months following the client's complaint to the Grievance Commission and where she failed to communicate with her client and explain adequately that she would not be taking any further action on the client's behalf. Att'y Griev. Comm'n v. Tolar, 357 Md. 569, 745 A.2d 1045 (2000).

Failure to include attestation clause and witness signature on will. — Failure to include attestation clause and witness signature lines on will and neglecting to inform the client of these necessities constitute neglect of a legal matter. Att'y Griev. Comm'n v. Myers, 302 Md. 571, 490 A.2d 231 (1985).

Violation not found. — When an attorney filed for a labor certification on behalf of a client, but did not advise the client of a more expeditious procedure the attorney had used in another case, the hearing court did not find the attorney guilty of a violation of this Rule because the court was not convinced the attorney failed to act with reasonable diligence and promptness, noting testimony that but for the attorney's timely filing, the client would not have received a labor certification. Att'y Griev. Comm'n v. Alsafty, 379 Md. 1, 838 A.2d 1213 (2003).

Attorney's failure to inform a client that attorney had to withdraw from representation because of a suspension did not support a violation of this Rule, because the attorney could not, by virtue of the suspension, have represented the complainant. Att'y Griev.

Comm'n v. Robertson, 400 Md. 618, 929 A.2d 576 (2007).

Bar counsel failed to show that an attorney had violated Md. R. Prof. Conduct 1.1, 1.3, 1.4(a) and (b), 1.5, 1.16(d), 3.1, 5.1, 5.3, and 8.4(a), (c), and (d) where it was possible to find, based on the testimony, that the attorney had relied on the clients' representations that they intended to handle the appeal pro se, and as a result, Bar counsel had failed to prove that the attorney had represented the two clients in an appeal. Att'y Griev. Comm'n v. Maignan, 402 Md. 39, 935 A.2d 409 (2007).

No violation found. — In an attorney discipline proceeding, there was no violation of the rule where the only basis was a bare finding that the attorney's failure to file a request for interrogatories adversely affected the attorney's ability to prepare for trial. Att'y Griev. Comm'n v. Hermina, 379 Md. 503, 842 A.2d 762 (2004).

Public reprimand. — Attorney was found to have violated Md. R. Prof. Conduct 1.3 and was sanctioned with a public reprimand where he accepted a retainer from an inmate to handle post-conviction proceedings on his behalf and failed to meet with the inmate until almost a year after he had been retained. Att'y Griev. Comm'n v. Lee, 390 Md. 517, 890 A.2d 273 (2005).

Reprimand for negligent handling of personal injury case. — Lawyer was reprimanded for violations of Md. R. Prof. Conduct 1.1, 1.3, 8.1(b) for his negligent handing of a client's case, and his four month delay in acknowledging Bar Counsel's request for information; the commission's request for an indefinite suspension was rejected because there was no reason to believe that the lawyer's misconduct would have been repeated, and the lawyer was honest with his client about his mistakes, advised the client to seek representation for a claim against him, and entered into a settlement in which he paid $ 30,000 to the client from his own funds without resort to his malpractice carrier. The case did not involve either an obstinate refusal to cooperate or a denial of access to relevant documents, and the court was able to protect the public and deter other lawyers from misconduct without disrupting the lawyer's practice. Att'y Griev. Comm'n v. Queen, 407 Md. 556, 967 A.2d 198 (2009).

Thirty-day suspension. — Attorney was suspended for 30 days for violating Md. R. Prof. Conduct 1.3, 1.4, 8.1(b), and 8.4(d) after the attorney failed to prepare an eligible domestic relations order for client one, and failed to timely prepare a consent order for client two, and then submitted it to opposing counsel and the trial court without allowing client two to review it, since there were mitigating factors, the attorney had expressed remorse, and there was testimony that the conduct was out of the attorney's character. Att'y Griev. Comm'n v. Hill, 398 Md. 95, 919 A.2d 1194 (2007).

Ninety-day suspension. — Ninety-day suspension was appropriate sanction for attorney's neglect of client's cases, falsifying client's signature on a complaint, and causing the complaint with the false signature to be notarized and filed. Att'y Griev. Comm'n v. Parsons, 310 Md. 132, 527 A.2d 325 (1987).

Attorney's failure to respond to subsequent notices from the trial court that a response was necessary or the client's case would. be dismissed, failure to communicate the trial court's intention to the client, and failure in a separate case to keep the client informed about developments meant that the attorney violated this Rule regarding diligence. Since the attorney's conduct was merely negligent rather than deceitful, a 90-day suspension from the practice of law was warrented. Att'y Griev. Comm'n v. Ugwuonye, 405 Md. 351, 952 A.2d 226 (2008).

One-year suspension. — One-year suspension was warranted where attorney's neglect of case was continuous over three-year period and his misconduct ultimately prejudiced his client's right to seek damages for her injuries. Att'y Griev. Comm'n v. Sinclair, 302 Md. 581, 490 A.2d 236 (1985).

Three-year suspension. — Three-year suspension was warranted where attorney prepared defective will for his client and later excoriated her and attempted to mislead an investigator and inquiry panel for the Attorney Grievance Commission. Att'y Griev. Comm'n v. Myers, 302 Md. 571, 490 A.2d 231 (1985).

Disbarment was proper sanction. — Attorney was properly disbarred for violating prior, similar Maryland Rules of Professional Conduct 1.1, 1.3, 1.4, 1.15, 3.3, and 8.4, § 10-306 of the Business Occupations and Professions Article, and Rule BU9 (now Rule 16-609) of the Maryland Rules of Procedure. Att'y Griev. Comm'n v. Williams, 335 Md. 458, 644 A.2d 490 (1994).

Evidence justified findings of misconduct, and disbarment was warranted. Att'y Griev. Comm'n v. Mazelis, 309 Md. 50, 522 A.2d 913 (1987); Att'y Griev. Comm'n v. Manning, 318 Md. 697, 569 A.2d 1250 (1990).

Disbarment of attorney was appropriate where there were serious and repeated violations of the prior, similar Rule and other provisions of the Maryland Rules of Professional Conduct. Att'y Griev. Comm'n v. Milliken, 348 Md. 486, 704 A.2d 1225 (1998).

Because the attorney engaged in several acts of professional misconduct following an earlier suspension by accepting fees from clients but by failing to diligently to pursue their cases, the sanction of disbarment was held to be appropriate. Att'y Griev. Comm'n v. Fallin, 371 Md. 237, 808 A.2d 791 (2002).

Where an attorney was retained in two separate bankruptcy matters, was paid the retainer fee, and thereafter neglected the matters, misinformed the clients as to the status of their actions, and failed to properly communicate with them, it was found that he violated prior, similar Rules 1.1, 1.2, 1.3, 1.4, 1.16, and where the attorney had a prior history of disciplinary violations, the court imposed the sanction of disbarment. Att'y Griev. Comm'n v. Faber, 373 Md. 173, 817 A.2d 205 (2003).

Disbarment was the proper sanction for an attorney who dragged out representation of two different clients for many years, dooming their causes by failure to comply with applicable laws, and pretended to be continuing representation efforts, in one case, even falsifying a letter after the fact to give the impression that the client had received proper communications; the attorney had also failed to notify clients of a suspension and make other arrangements with them, and to supply information needed by a grievance commission investigator. Att'y Griev. Comm'n v. Davis, 375 Md. 131, 825 A.2d 430 (2003).

Disbarment was the only appropriate sanction for an attorney who withdrew sums that should have been forwarded to a client from an attorney trust account for the attorney's personal use and failed to respond to the client's inquiries; the attorney's marital and drinking problems were not factors in mitigation. Att'y Griev. Comm'n v. Herman, 380 Md. 378, 844 A.2d 1181 (2004).

An attorney's pursuit of a claim for the torts of either criminal conversation or adultery was pursuit of a baseless claim and his failure to communicate with the client after accepting representation despite repeated attempts by the client to contact the attorney constituted misconduct that warranted disbarment. Att'y Griev. Comm'n v. James, 385 Md. 637, 870 A.2d 229 (2005).

Where the attorney abandoned his representation of the client and refused to engage in further communications with the client after terminating his representation via electronic mail, and the attorney engaged in other misconduct which included not being admitted to practice in forums where the attorney was representing the client and not responding to the disciplinary commission's lawful demands for information regarding the investigation of the attorney, disbarment was warranted. Att'y Griev. Comm'n v. Logan, 390 Md. 313, 888 A.2d 359 (2005).

Where the attorney, among other things, intentionally misappropriated client funds, forged a client's signature on a settlement check, lied under oath, and represented a client when the attorney was not licensed to do so, the attorney was disbarred for violating former, similar Md. R. Prof. Conduct 1.2(a), 1.3, 1.5(c), 1.15(a), (b), 3.3(a), 5.5, 8.1(a), (b), 8.4(a), (b), (c), (d), Md. R. 16-604, and §§ 10-304, -306 of the Business Occupations and Professions Article Att'y Griev. Comm'n v. Kapoor, 391 Md. 505, 894 A.2d 502 (2006).

By delaying payment of settlement proceeds to a client and the client's medical providers, transferring the client's funds into his operating account, and using the money for his own personal needs, an attorney violated Md. R. Prof. Conduct 1.3, 1.15(a) and (b), and 8.4(c) and (d); Rule 16-609; and § 10-306 of the Business Occupations and Professions Article. The court acknowledged the mitigating factors of the attorney paying the client and the medical providers and reducing his fee, but concluded that disbarment for such deceit was warranted. Att'y Griev. Comm'n v. Roberts, 394 Md. 137, 904 A.2d 557 (2006).

In an attorney disciplinary matter wherein the attorney was ordered disbarred, the attorney was found to have violated this Rule where he failed to deliver his client's file after termination of the representation, despite repeated requests from the client and did not return her papers until much later, which during such time the client was forced to represent herself during ongoing litigation and suffered significant set-backs in her efforts to overturn the sanctions imposed upon her due to the omissions of attorney. Additionally, the attorney's inexcusable six-month delay in withdrawing formally from the court case, after his representation was terminated, demonstrated a lack of requisite diligence and promptness. Att'y Griev. Comm'n v. Steinberg, 395 Md. 337, 910 A.2d 429 (2006).

In an action in which petitioner, the Attorney Grievance Commission of Maryland, acting pursuant to Rule 16-751, filed a petition for disciplinary or remedial action against respondent attorney, the appropriate sanction was disbarment where the court found that, as a matter of law, respondent violated Md. R. Prof. Conduct 1.3, 1.4, 1.16, and 8.1; respondent violated Rule 1.3 by not by not acting with diligence and promptness in either filing a claim for a client or informing her that he was not going to file a claim because he did not believe there was a substantial basis for doing so. Att'y Griev. Comm'n v. Baker, 396 Md. 15, 912 A.2d 651 (2006).

State supreme court found that the attorney's misconduct, as charged in the grievance commission's petition and supported by the trial court's findings of fact and conclusions of law, warranted disbarment; the evidence established that the attorney failed to act with reasonable diligence and promptness in representing a client in a divorce case, that the attorney failed to keep the client reasonably informed about the status of the representation and did not respond to reasonable requests for information, that the attorney failed to respond to lawful demands for information from disciplinary counsel, and that the totality of the attorney's conduct was prejudicial to the administration of justice. Att'y Griev. Comm'n v. Hodgson, 396 Md. 1, 912 A.2d 640 (2006).

Where the attorney, while decertified, entered appearances on behalf of defendants, and either showed up late or did not show up at all for court proceedings, the attorney violated Md. R. Prof. Conduct 1.1, 1.3, and 8.4(d) by failing to appear for court proceedings. As a result of (1) those violations, (2) the fact that the attorney was decertified at the time the violations were committed, and (3) the fact that the attorney violated other professional conduct rules, also while decertified, the state's highest court had little choice but to disbar the attorney. Att'y Griev. Comm'n v. Walker, 405 Md. 3, 948 A.2d 1263 (2008).

Attorney was disbarred for violating Md. R. Prof. Conduct 1.1, 1.3, 1.4, 1.15, and 8.4, Rule 16-609, and §§ 10-306 and 10-606(b) of the Business Professions and Occupations Article as an attorney misappropriated the clients' funds, performed no services whatsoever on the clients' behalf, lied to the clients about the status of their case, and provided them with a falsified administrative agency decision that was not issued by the agency. Att'y Griev. Comm'n v. Bahgat, 411 Md. 568, 984 A.2d 225 (2009).

Attorney was disbarred for violating this section and Md. Law. R. Prof. Conduct 1.1, 1.4(a) and (b), 1.16(a), 8.1(b), and 8.4(a) and (d), where the attorney, inter alia, failed to timely file a complaint in a client's personal injury action and concealed the error from the client and the court. Att'y Griev. Comm'n v. Bleecker, 414 Md. 147, 994 A.2d 928 (2010).

Attorney violated this rule by failing to diligently pursue an action for two clients after the complaint was filed and failing to monitor the action, and by allowing a second action to languish for over six years while an insurer sent over 50 checks to the attorneys' office; the attorney was disbarred for violating this rule along with Md. Law. R. Prof. Conduct 1.1, 1.2(a), 1.4(a), 1.16(d), 8.1(b), and 8.4(a), (c), and (d). Att'y Griev. Comm'n v. Fox, 417 Md. 504, 11 A.3d 762 (2010).

Attorney was disbarred for violating this section and Md. Law. R. Prof. Conduct 1.4(a) and (b), 1.15(a), (c), and (d), 1.16(d), 8.1(b), and 8.4(a) and (d), after the attorney received advance fee payments from two clients, deposited the money in a personal account, rather than a trust account, having not earned the fees, and abandoned the clients without performing work for the clients. Att'y Griev. Comm'n v. Lara, 418 Md. 355, 14 A.3d 650 (2011).

Indefinite suspension was proper sanction. — Where respondent attorney's representation of four clients was marked by serious neglect and inattention; where he failed to return a fee which was unearned for a period of nine months; where he failed to timely remit funds he received on behalf of a client; where he failed to communicate with his clients; and in connection with the investigation of three of the complaints, where respondent failed to answer Bar Counsel's requests for information, the proper sanction was that the attorney be indefinitely suspended from the practice of law, with the right to apply for reinstatement after the suspension had been in effect for six months, conditioned upon his payment of all costs and upon the monitoring of respondent's practice. Att'y Griev. Comm'n v. David, 331 Md. 317, 628 A.2d 178 (1993).

An attorney who on several separate occasions failed to file legal documents which he had drafted, failed to communicate with clients in these matters, and failed to return attorney's fees he collected in connection with these matters, was rightly found to have violated prior, similar Rules of Professional Conduct 1.1, 1.3, 1.4, 1.16, and 8.4. The appropriate sanction was an indefinite suspension with the right to apply for reinstatement after 60 days, conditioned upon his payment of all costs associated with the matter, reimbursement of the unearned legal fees, and his hiring of an attorney to oversee his practice for a period of one year. Att'y Griev. Comm'n v. Brugh, 353 Md. 475, 727 A.2d 913 (1999).

An indefinite suspension was appropriate where, by his acts and omissions while representing his client, and specifically by his misrepresentations to the prosecutor and to the judge in seeking a continuance, an attorney engaged in misconduct as defined in Maryland Rule 16-701, was convicted in a case of criminal contempt, and violated prior, similar Rules 1.3, 3.3 and 8.4 of the Maryland Rules of Professional Conduct. Att'y Griev. Comm'n v. Middleton, 360 Md. 34, 756 A.2d 565 (2000).

Attorney's license to practice law was indefinitely suspended for his failure to provide competent, diligent, and communicative representation to his client, for charging unreasonable fees, for pursuing a frivolous proceeding, and for engaging in conduct prejudicial to the administration of justice. Att'y Griev. Comm'n v. Zdravkovich, 362 Md. 1, 762 A.2d 950 (2000).

When attorney represented that he would complete the simple legal task of preparing a deed by changing an existing owner's name and adding another name as co-owner in three weeks, but never completed the task, he violated the prior, similar Rule. Taking into consideration the attorney's past disciplinary proceedings, an indefinite suspension was proper for attorney's violation of the prior, similar Rule and Rule 1.4. Att'y Griev. Comm'n v. Cassidy, 362 Md. 689, 766 A.2d 632 (2001).

An indefinite suspension was appropriate where, among other violations, attorney violated the prior, similar Rule by failing to return telephone calls to his client, by failing to file another client's tax returns, by failing to pay a court fee that initially prevented the processing of another client's motion, and by claiming to have sent various letters to his clients and to taxing authorities which were not received by any of the parties. Att'y Griev. Comm'n v. Cohen, 361 Md. 161, 760 A.2d 706 (2000).

Indefinite suspension was appropriate where attorney was retained to represent a client in filing for alien labor certifications for three of its employees, but where the attorney never prepared or filed an application for one employee and prepared but did not file applications for the other two, where he provided his client with altered documents making it appear he had done the work, and where the attorney never refunded the money paid to him and refused to cooperate with the investigation of his actions. Att'y Griev. Comm'n v. Koven, 361 Md. 337, 761 A.2d 881 (2000).

Indefinite suspension was proper sanction where attorney violated prior, similar Md. R. Prof. Conduct 1.3 by his failure to diligently pursue the legal matter which he undertook on behalf of his client, and prior, similar Md. R. Prof. Conduct 1.4 for failing to promptly comply with reasonable requests for information about a legal matter by a client and failing to fully and truthfully explain his actions, or inaction, to permit the client to make informed decisions regarding the representation; further, the attorney violated prior, similar Md. R. Prof. Conduct 1.16 by effectively terminating the representation of the client, but failing to take such steps to reasonably protect his client's interest. Att'y Griev. Comm'n v. Harrington, 367 Md. 36, 785 A.2d 1260 (2001).

Even though the hearing judge was mistaken in finding that respondent attorney had failed to file a proper petition for an absolute divorce for the client, the record still supported the judge's findings that while the attorney had not been altogether incompetent, the attorney had been negligent and unresponsive; in light of the fact that the attorney had some previous disciplinary history involving client neglect, a indefinite suspension with leave to apply for reinstatement after six months was imposed. Att'y Griev. Comm'n v. Kreamer, 387 Md. 503, 876 A.2d 79 (2005).

Even though the hearing judge was mistaken in finding that respondent attorney had failed to file a proper petition for an absolute divorce for the client, the record still supported the judge's findings that while the attorney had not been altogether incompetent, the attorney had been negligent and unresponsive; in light of the fact that the attorney had some previous disciplinary history involving client neglect, a indefinite suspension with leave to apply for reinstatement after six months was imposed. Att'y Griev. Comm'n v. Kreamer, 387 Md. 503, 876 A.2d 79 (2005).

Although an attorney in a similar case had only been reprimanded after having similarly abandoned a client in a divorce case, the more severe sanction of indefinite suspension was the best way to protect the public where the mitigators present in the earlier case had not been shown to be present, where there had been no expressions of remorse from the attorney, and where, moreover, the attorney had not even respondent to inquiries in early stages of the investigation. Att'y Griev. Comm'n v. Kovacic, 389 Md. 233, 884 A.2d 673 (2005).

Indefinite suspension, rather than disbarment, was the proper sanction for the attorney's violation of Md. R. Prof. Conduct 1.1, 1.2, 1.3, 1.4, 3.2, and 8.4, where there was no evidence he acted out of fraudulent or selfish motive, he cooperated with Bar Counsel, he engaged in negotiations with the client's attorney regarding restitution, and he expressed great remorse. Att'y Griev. Comm'n v. Reinhardt, 391 Md. 209, 892 A.2d 533 (2006).

Attorney was indefinitely suspended from the practice of law for violating Md. R. Prof. Conduct 1.3, 1.4, 1.16(d), 3.2, 8.1(b), and 8.4(d) in connection with the attorney's representation of a client in a bankruptcy matter. The complaint could not be dismissed based on the complainant's request because the evidence did not fail to show sanctionable professional misconduct. Att'y Griev. Comm'n v. Lee, 393 Md. 546, 903 A.2d 895 (2006).

Attorney was indefinitely suspended from the practice of law in Maryland for violating this Rule, by failing to act with reasonable diligence and promptness in recording a deed conveying land to a client, and Md. R. Prof. Conduct 8.4(b) and (c), when the attorney presented a Gift Certification Form containing the forged signature of the attorney's former wife to the Motor Vehicle Administration. The court needed to consider both violations and impose a single sanction. Att'y Griev. Comm'n v. Sweitzer, 395 Md. 586, 911 A.2d 440 (2006).

Attorney was indefinitely suspended for violating Md. R. Prof. Conduct 1.1, 1.3, 1.15(a) and (b), 8.1(b), and 8.4(d), Md. R. 16-609, and § 10-306 of the Business Occupations and Professions Article, in connection with handling of client funds in connection with an estate matter. Att'y Griev. Comm'n v. Goff, 399 Md. 1, 922 A.2d 554 (2007).

Attorney's failure to promptly pay individuals who had funds on deposit in the attorney's trust account was a violation of Md. R. Prof.

Conduct 1.1, 1.3, 1.15(d), and 8.4(d). That misconduct, along with the attorney's misconduct in paying clients before funds belonging to them were deposited in the attorney's trust account and failing to supervise an employee, warranted an indefinite suspension from the practice of law with the right to apply for reinstatement after 90 days. Att'y Griev. Comm'n v. Zuckerman, 403 Md. 695, 944 A.2d 525 (2008).

Attorney's misconduct in taking six months to turn over the client's file to a new attorney after the client had terminated the attorney's services amounted to a failure on the attorney's part to act with reasonable diligence and promptness in violation of this Rule. As a result of that misconduct and related misconduct, the sanction of indefinite suspension was warranted. Att'y Griev. Comm'n v. Nichols, 405 Md. 207, 950 A.2d 778 (2008).

Attorney was suspended indefinitely because his conduct in connection with an estate led to significant delay in closing the estate and violated Md. R. Prof. Conduct 1.1, 1.3, 8.1(a) and (b), and 8.4(a) and (d); the attorney owed the heirs to the estate competent and diligent representation but did not carry out either obligation, and indefinite suspension was the appropriate sanction due to the number and sort of violations, the mitigating factors, and the attorney's seeming failure to follow through on his promise to the hearing judge that he would attempt to "make things right" in the matter. Att'y Griev. Comm'n v. Pawlak, 408 Md. 288, 969 A.2d 311 (2009).

Indefinite suspension with leave to apply for readmission. — Attorney was indefinitely suspended, with leave to apply for readmission after six months, where the attorney violated this Rule and Md. R. Prof. Conduct 1.1, 3.3(a)(1), 5.5(a), and 8.4(c) and (d), by, inter alia, failing to appear at a confirmation hearing, despite the attorney's knowledge of the hearing. Att'y Griev. Comm'n v. Robaton, 411 Md. 415, 983 A.2d 467 (2009).

Quoted in Att'y Griev. Comm'n v. MacDougall, 384 Md. 271, 863 A.2d 312 (2004); Att'y Griev. Comm'n v. Christopher, 383 Md. 624, 861 A.2d 692 (2004); Att'y Griev. Comm'n v. Lee, 387 Md. 89, 874 A.2d 897 (2005); Att'y Griev. Comm'n v. Scroggs, 387 Md. 238, 874 A.2d 985 (2005); Att'y Griev. Comm'n v. Zakroff, 387 Md. 603, 876 A.2d 664 (2005), cert. denied, 2006 Md. LEXIS 561 (2006); cert. denied, 2006 Md. LEXIS 571 (Md. 2006); Att'y Griev. Comm'n v. Zakroff, 387 Md. 603, 876 A.2d 664 (2005), cert. denied, 2006 Md. LEXIS 561 (2006); cert. denied, 2006 Md. LEXIS 571 (Md. 2006); Att'y Griev. Comm'n v. Muhammad, — Md. —, — A.2d — (2005); Att'y Griev. Comm'n v. Ward, 394 Md. 1, 904 A.2d 477 (2006); Att'y Griev. Comm'n v. Manger, 396 Md. 134, 913 A.2d 1 (2006); Att'y Griev.

Comm'n v. Taylor, 405 Md. 697, 955 A.2d 755 (2008); Att'y Griev. Comm'n v. Hall, 408 Md. 306, 969 A.2d 953 (2009).

Cited in Att'y Griev. Comm'n v. Maignan, 390 Md. 287, 888 A.2d 344 (2005); Att'y Griev. Comm'n v. Muhammad, 395 Md. 676, 912 A.2d 588 (2006), cert. denied, 127 S. Ct. 2296, 2007 U.S. LEXIS 5292, 167 L. Ed. 2d 1103 (U.S. 2007); Att'y Griev. Comm'n v. McCulloch, 397 Md. 674, 919 A.2d 660 (2007); Att'y Griev. Comm'n v. Akpan, 405 Md. 277, 950 A.2d 820 (2008).

Rule 1.4. Communication.

(a) A lawyer shall:

(1) promptly inform the client of any decision or circumstance with respect to which the client's informed consent, as defined in Rule 1.0(f), is required by these Rules;

(2) keep the client reasonably informed about the status of the matter;

(3) promptly comply with reasonable requests for information; and

(4) consult with the client about any relevant limitation on the lawyer's conduct when the lawyer knows that the client expects assistance not permitted by the Maryland Lawyers' Rules of Professional Conduct or other law.

(b) A lawyer shall explain a matter to the extent reasonably necessary to permit the client to make informed decisions regarding the representation.

COMMENT

[1] Reasonable communication between the lawyer and the client is necessary for the client effectively to participate in the representation.

Communicating with Client. — [2] If these Rules require that a particular decision about the representation be made by the client, paragraph (a)(1) requires that the lawyer promptly consult with and secure the client's consent prior to taking action unless prior discussions with the client have resolved what action the client wants the lawyer to take. For example, a lawyer who receives from opposing counsel an offer of settlement in a civil controversy or a proffered plea bargain in a criminal case must promptly inform the client of its substance unless the client has previously indicated that the proposal will be acceptable or unacceptable or has authorized the lawyer to accept or to reject the offer. See Rule 1.2(a).

[3] Under Rule 1.2(a), a lawyer is required, when appropriate, to consult with the client about the means to be used to accomplish the client's objectives. In some situations - depending on both the importance of the action under consideration and the feasibility of consulting with the client - this duty will require consultation prior to taking action. In other circumstances, such as during a trial when an immediate decision must be made, the exigency of the situation may require the lawyer to act without prior consultation. In such cases the lawyer must nonetheless act reasonably to inform the client of actions the lawyer has taken on the client's behalf. Additionally, paragraph (a)(2) requires that the lawyer keep the client reasonably informed about the status of the matter, such as significant developments affecting the timing or the substance of the representation.

[4] A lawyer's regular communication with clients will minimize the occasions on which a client will need to request information concerning the representation. When a client makes a reasonable request for information, however, paragraph (a)(3) requires prompt compliance with the request, or if a prompt response is not feasible, that the lawyer, or a member of the lawyer's staff, acknowledge receipt of the request and advise the client when a response may be expected. Client telephone calls should be promptly returned or acknowledged.

Explaining Matters. — [5] The client should have sufficient information to participate intelligently in decisions concerning the objectives of the representation and the means by which they are to be pursued, to the extent the client is willing and able to do so. Adequacy of communication depends in part on the kind of advice or assistance that is involved. For example, where there is time to explain a proposal made in a negotiation, the lawyer should review all important provisions with the client before proceeding to an agreement. In litigation a lawyer should explain the general strategy and prospects of success and ordinarily should consult the client on tactics that are likely to result in significant expense or to injure or coerce others. On the other hand, a lawyer ordinarily will not be expected to describe trial or negotiation strategy in detail. The guiding principle is that the lawyer should fulfill reasonable client expectations for information consistent with the duty to act in the client's best interests, and the client's overall requirements as to the character of representation. In certain circumstances, such as when a lawyer asks a client to consent to a representation affected by a conflict of interest, the client must give informed consent, as defined in Rule 1.0(f).

[6] Ordinarily, the information to be provided is that appropriate for a client who is a comprehending and responsible adult. However, fully informing the client according to this standard may be impracticable, for example, where the client is a child or suffers from diminished capacity. See Rule 1.14. When the client is an organization or group, it is often impossible or inappropriate to inform every one of its members about its legal affairs; ordinarily, the lawyer should address communications to the appropriate officials of the organization. See Rule 1.13. Where many routine matters are involved, a system of limited or occasional reporting may be arranged with the client.

Withholding Information. — [7] In some circumstances, a lawyer may be justified in delaying transmission of information when the client would be likely to react imprudently to an immediate communication. Thus, a lawyer might withhold a psychiatric diagnosis of a client when the examining psychiatrist indicates that disclosure would harm the client. A lawyer may not withhold information to serve the lawyer's own interest or convenience or the interests or convenience of another person. Rules or court orders governing litigation may provide that information supplied to a lawyer may not be disclosed to the client. Rule 3.4(c) directs compliance with such rules or orders.

Model Rules Comparison. — Rule 1.4 is substantially similar to the language of the Ethics 2000 Amendments to the ABA Model Rules of Professional Conduct except for the deletion of Model Rule 1.4(a)(2) and the redesignation of subsections as appropriate, and wording changes to Comment [3].

University of Baltimore Law Forum. — For Recent Development, "Attorney Grievance Commission of Maryland v. Mooney: Indefinite Suspension is Warranted Where an Attorney Fails to Provide Competent Representation," see 31 U. Balt. Law Forum 44 (2000).

Misrepresentation of status of case to client. — Ninety-day suspension was appropriate sanction for attorney's failure to timely file or adequately investigate action on behalf of her client, and for misrepresenting to her client that the suit had been filed on her behalf and was proceeding to trial where the client paid the attorney only part of the costs involved in the work the attorney did do and the attorney did not consider the gratuitous client to be a client; an attorney-client relationship did exist and, thus, the attorney failed to carry out her contract of employment. Att'y Griev. Comm'n v. Pinkney, 311 Md. 137, 532 A.2d 1367 (1987).

Attorney violated the prior, similar Rule by not keeping a client reasonably informed of the status of her case and not responding honestly or, at a minimum, without negligence to the client's request for information about the security of her ownership in her home, as the attorney repeatedly told the client that her home was safe and not to worry, and that a bankruptcy petition had been filed when, in fact, none of that was true. Att'y Griev. Comm'n v. Granger, 374 Md. 438, 823 A.2d 611 (2003).

Disbarment was the proper sanction for an attorney who dragged out representation of two different clients for many years, dooming their causes by failure to comply with applicable laws, and pretended to be continuing representation efforts, in one case, even falsifying a letter after the fact to give the impression that the client had received proper communications; the attorney had also failed to notify clients of a suspension and make other arrangements with them, and to supply information needed by a grievance commission investigator. Att'y Griev. Comm'n v. Davis, 375 Md. 131, 825 A.2d 430 (2003).

After an attorney agreed to represent clients in an adoption case, he violated (a) and (b) because he misrepresented to them that the case had been filed, failed, on occasion, to communicate with them at all by staying away from his office, and prepared a false court order, on which he forged a judge's signature, representing to his clients that it was valid. Att'y Griev. Comm'n v. Guida, 391 Md. 33, 891 A.2d 1085 (2006).

Attorney's multiple violations of the Maryland Rules of Professional Conduct, including violation of this Rule for failing to timely request for an emergency hearing, warranted disbarment. The client retained the attorney to file for such a hearing and even though the attorney told the client the attorney did so, the attorney did not comply with that request. Att'y Griev. Comm'n v. Webster, 402 Md. 448, 937 A.2d 161 (2007).

Failure to communicate with client. — An attorney was reprimanded where she failed to take action to secure her client's interest in a retirement plan until several months following the client's complaint to the Grievance

Commission and where she failed to communicate with her client and explain adequately that she would not be taking any further action on the client's behalf. Att'y Griev. Comm'n v. Tolar, 357 Md. 569, 745 A.2d 1045 (2000).

Attorney's lack of candor with respect to his payment of his client's obligation, after representing that he would do so, resulting in his failure to inform the client as to the status of settlement payment or explain to him what actually transpired with respect to it and his failure to keep a second client informed concerning settlement proceeds, misleading him by falsely advising him that the funds were placed in the attorney's trust account, constituted communications violations under the prior, similar Rule. Att'y Griev. Comm'n v. Daskalopoulos, 383 Md. 375, 859 A.2d 653 (2004).

Attorney violated the prior, similar Rule through his pervasive failure to inform his client of the status of her case where, throughout the four years of representation, the client never received anything in writing from the attorney, and she had to obtain information regarding her divorce from the clerk's office. Att'y Griev. Comm'n v. Fezell, 361 Md. 234, 760 A.2d 1108 (2000).

Attorney violated the Maryland Rules of Professional Conduct by failing to keep his client reasonably informed of the status of her case to the extent reasonably necessary for her to make informed decisions regarding his representation and by not informing his client that her case was dismissed directly because of his lack of prosecution, nor did he tell her of two motions to vacate that were denied, in one instance because he simply failed to sign the motion. Att'y Griev. Comm'n v. Harris, 371 Md. 510, 810 A.2d 457 (2002).

When an attorney filed for a labor certification on behalf of a client, but did not keep the client advised of the status of the matter or comply with the client's reasonable requests for information, the attorney violated the prior, similar Rule. Att'y Griev. Comm'n v. Alsafty, 379 Md. 1, 838 A.2d 1213 (2003).

Violation of (a) should have been found in addition to violation of (b), where an attorney admitted having failed to initiate communication with, or respond to inquiries from, co-personal representatives of an estate that the attorney was administering. Att'y Griev. Comm'n v. MacDougall, 384 Md. 271, 863 A.2d 312 (2004).

Attorney violated prior, similar Md. R. Prof. Conduct 1.3, 1.4(a), (b), 8.1 and 8.4(d) when she failed to administratively close a client's asylum application and refile it in proper form as directed by the immigration judge and the client, and failed to respond to requests for information in connection with the related disciplinary investigation. Indefinite suspension was proper given the egregious nature of the attorney's misconduct and her failure to present anything by way of mitigation to the appellate court. Att'y Griev. Comm'n v. Brisbon, 385 Md. 667, 870 A.2d 586 (2005).

Where the attorney abandoned his representation of the client and refused to engage in further communications with the client after terminating his representation via electronic mail, and the attorney engaged in other misconduct which included not being admitted to practice in forums where the attorney was representing the client and not responding to the disciplinary commission's lawful demands for information regarding the investigation of the attorney, disbarment was warranted. Att'y Griev. Comm'n v. Logan, 390 Md. 313, 888 A.2d 359 (2005).

Due to an attorney's default in disciplinary proceedings, averments in the Attorney Grievance Commission's petition were deemed admitted pursuant to Md. R. 2-613(f) and 2-323(e); therefore, the circuit court improperly failed to find that a violation of Md. R. Prof. Conduct 1.4 was not proven by clear and convincing evidence based on the admitted facts that the attorney failed to communicate with an inmate who had retained him to handle post-conviction proceedings for almost a year. The attorney was sanctioned with a public reprimand. Att'y Griev. Comm'n v. Lee, 390 Md. 517, 890 A.2d 273 (2005).

Attorney violated this Rule when he failed keep his divorce client informed of the status of his case or reply to inquiries made by the client; among other things, the attorney moved his office and failed to inform the client. Att'y Griev. Comm'n v. Rose, 391 Md. 101, 892 A.2d 469 (2006), cert. denied, 2006 U.S. LEXIS 5734, 166 L. Ed. 2d 22 (U.S. 2006).

Attorney violated this Rule by the attorney's failure to communicate effectively with the client concerning the settlement as well as by the attorney's inadequate monthly billing statements. Att'y Griev. Comm'n v. Calhoun, 391 Md. 532, 894 A.2d 518 (2006).

Clear and convincing evidence showed that the attorney acted incompetently when the attorney accepted a case that required filing in a jurisdiction where the attorney was not admitted to practice, and when the attorney failed to service notice to defendant, that the attorney failed to act with reasonable diligence and promptness in representing the client when the attorney failed to file the estate in the proper jurisdiction, that the attorney failed to communicate the truth when the attorney told the client that the attorney was admitted to practice in a certain jurisdiction when the attorney was not admitted there and when the attorney failed to communicate to the client that the attorney intended to seek other counsel in the District of Columbia to assist the attorney, that the attorney's fees were unreasonable because the attorney charged and accepted fees when no work was performed in furtherance of the case, and that the attorney's actions were prejudicial to the administration of justice; even though the attorney was absolved of the charge that the attorney did not properly terminate the representation because the evidence showed that the attorney returned all unearned advance fees to the client after the client retained new counsel, the attorney's violations, which included intentionally dishonest conduct, warranted disbarment, especially since the attorney had a prior disciplinary history. Att'y Griev. Comm'n v. Ward, 396 Md. 203, 913 A.2d 41 (2006).

State supreme court found that the attorney's misconduct, as charged in the grievance commission's petition and supported by the trial court's findings of fact and conclusions of law, warranted disbarment; the evidence established that the attorney failed to act with reasonable diligence and promptness in representing a client in a divorce case, that the attorney failed to keep the client reasonably informed about the status of the representation and did not respond to reasonable requests for information, that the attorney failed to respond to lawful demands for information from disciplinary counsel, and that the totality of the attorney's conduct was prejudicial to the administration of justice. Att'y Griev. Comm'n v. Hodgson, 396 Md. 1, 912 A.2d 640 (2006).

Attorney's misconduct in abusing the trust that the client placed in the attorney by placing the client's retainer check in the attorney's operating account rather than an attorney trust account, spending that money which belonged to the client on the attorney, in refusing to promptly refund to the client money that attorney admittedly owed to the client despite the client's refund request, and in failing to promptly answer bar counsel's request for information about the matter warranted the attorney's indefinite suspension. Att'y Griev. Comm'n v. McCulloch, 397 Md. 674, 919 A.2d 660 (2007).

Where a client, facing incarceration for driving under the influence, was virtually abandoned until the eve of trial and then was represented by an associate who had not read the entire file, who was unaware that his client had two prior convictions, and who first presented the available options to her in the lobby of the courthouse on the day of trial, the supervising attorney violated Md. R. Prof. Conduct 1.1, 1.3, 1.4, and 5.1. Att'y Griev. Comm'n v. Ficker, 399 Md. 445, 924 A.2d 1105 (2007).

Attorney violated this Rule by failing to maintain communications with a client and failing to return the client's telephone calls during a five-month lapse between the time the attorney was retained by the client and the first letter the attorney sent to the client's husband in a divorce matter. Att'y Griev. Comm'n v. Kreamer, 404 Md. 282, 946 A.2d 500 (2008).

Attorney violated this Rule when she failed to communicate with her client about the client's divorce case, advise her of the status of service on her husband or of the contemplated dismissal of her case or the dismissal itself. The attorney had changed her e-mail address without telling her client, thus inhibiting communication. Att'y Griev. Comm'n v. McCulloch, 404 Md. 388, 946 A.2d 1009 (2008).

In a disciplinary proceeding against two supervising attorneys from out of State, who opened up a Maryland office and hired a Maryland associate, who ended up failing to respond to motions compelling discovery in 47 cases filed by her on behalf of the supervising attorneys' Maryland clients, the hearing judge was found to have properly determined that they violated Md. R. Prof. Conduct 5.1 and 1.4 and, therefore, they were suspended indefinitely, with the right to apply for reinstatement no sooner than 90 days after the effective date of the suspension. The findings and conclusions adequately found that the supervising attorneys failed to adequately supervise the relatively inexperienced associate they hired, failed to respond to her requests for paralegal help, failed to establish supervisory procedures designed deliberately to address the associate's inexperience and to counterbalance her physical distance from the ready availability of steadying interaction with peers and managers, failed to audit her case load, among other failings, as well as failed to directly communicate with a Maryland client regarding his case. Att'y Griev. Comm'n v. Kimmel, 405 Md. 647, 955 A.2d 269 (2008).

Attorney's ignorance did not absolve him of his responsibility for violating (b) for failing to appreciate the negative impact that his personal relationship with a client could have had on his representation of her, nor would his ignorance be viewed as a mitigating factor, because the attorney's previous violation of this rule in a disciplinary action should have made the attorney even more cautious about his actions with the client. Att'y Griev. Comm'n v. Hall, 408 Md. 306, 969 A.2d 953 (2009).

Attorney violated (a)(2) by failing, without good reason, to notify the attorney's client of a trial date. Att'y Griev. Comm'n v. Byrd, 408 Md. 449, 970 A.2d 870 (2009).

Attorney's failure to communicate with the clients regarding the attorney's receipt of a check, made payable solely to the clients, for two months supported a finding that the attorney violated this Rule. Att'y Griev. Comm'n v.

Rule 1.4   MARYLAND RULES

Gisriel, 409 Md. 331, 974 A.2d 331 (2009).

Lawyer violated this Rule because (1) this Rule applied to former clients, and (2) the lawyer failed to promptly comply with reasonable requests for information, under (a)(3) when the lawyer failed to surrender documents to which the client was entitled, when the lawyer did not give the client's file to the client's new lawyer. Att'y Griev. Comm'n v. Edib, 415 Md. 696, 4 A.3d 957 (2010).

Attorney violated this Rule, in two cases, because (1) the attorney did not respond to clients' telephone messages or letters, (2) the attorney did not tell a client that the client's case had been dismissed, and (3) the attorney did not tell clients the attorney had moved the attorney's practice or provide the clients with new contact information. Att'y Griev. Comm'n v. De La Paz, 418 Md. 534, 16 A.3d 181 (2011).

Attorney violated (b) when the attorney failed to give the client accurate information about the status of the case, in particular, when failing to tell the client that witnesses the client wished to have testify at trial wanted to be compensated as "experts." Att'y Griev. Comm'n v. Patterson, — Md. —, — A.3d — (Sept. 21, 2011).

Inadequate communication. — Even though, as the hearing judge found, the respondent attorney had adequately communicated with the clients during the period of ostensible representation, the judge should have found a failure to communicate regarding the representation where the attorney later gave the clients a mortgage for property purchased from them and attempted to pay it off with commissions that the attorney had not established entitlement to as a result of the earlier representation. Att'y Griev. Comm'n v. Parker, 389 Md. 142, 884 A.2d 104 (2005).

Attorney violated (a) because he failed to keep his client reasonably informed of the status of his case and failed to respond promptly or meaningfully to his client's reasonable requests for information. Att'y Griev. Comm'n v. Lee, 393 Md. 385, 903 A.2d 360 (2006).

Attorney's failure to make the client aware that the attorney would not be representing the client at a removal proceeding regarding the client's immigration status because such representation was not covered by their retainer agreement violated this Rule about keeping a client reasonably informed. Such misconduct warranted a reprimand of the attorney. Att'y Griev. Comm'n v. Akpan, 405 Md. 277, 950 A.2d 820 (2008).

Failure to disclose fee. — Respondent, who was not licensed to practice law in Maryland, violated Md. Law. R. Prof. Conduct 1.4(b) and 1.5(a) and (b) by suing a client for fees at an excessive hourly rate that she had not disclosed and he had not agreed to pay. Att'y

Griev. Comm'n v. Sucklal, 418 Md. 1, 12 A.3d 650 (2011).

Attorney's unilateral decision to make firm's client attorney's personal client. — Attorney violated (a)(1) because (1) the attorney made a unilateral decision to make a client the attorney's personal client although the client had entered into a written agreement to retain the law firm which employed the attorney, and (2) the attorney decided to change the payee on the client's check from the firm to the attorney without discussing the change and obtaining the client's consent. Att'y Griev. Comm'n v. Elliott, 417 Md. 659, 12 A.3d 105 (2011).

When an attorney altered the attorney's law firm employer's electronic files to facilitate the attorney taking certain of the firm's clients with the attorney when the attorney left the firm, the attorney admittedly violated (a) and (b) because the attorney failed to communicate with the attorney's clients regarding a material change in the clients' representation. Att'y Griev. Comm'n v. Keiner, — Md. —, — A.3d — (Aug. 19, 2011).

Professional obligation in advising about merits of claim. — A client may certainly consent to an action that has only a modest chance of success in court; nonetheless, an attorney has both professional and contractual obligations to exercise reasonable care in advising his or her client about the merits of a claim. Taylor v. Feissner, 103 Md. App. 356, 653 A.2d 947 (1995).

Mishandling escrow account. — Indefinite suspension was appropriate sanction for attorney's mishandling of escrow account, including the failure to pay claims due from the account and the failure to refund moneys to clients. Att'y Griev. Comm'n v. Singleton, 311 Md. 1, 532 A.2d 157 (1987).

Disbarment was the appropriate sanction for an attorney who commingled the client's funds with his own, and continued to handle them that way even after establishing a purported escrow account; further, as the attorney drained the account of funds, he failed to communicate with the client about the disbursements he was making. Att'y Griev. Comm'n v. Gallagher, 371 Md. 673, 810 A.2d 996 (2002).

Attorney's failure to pay medical bills in a timely manner and to disburse client funds demonstrated a failure to keep his client informed about the status of their cases. Att'y Griev. Comm'n v. Zuckerman, 386 Md. 341, 872 A.2d 693 (2005).

Attorney was less than diligent when he failed to inform his client that he received settlement proceeds, moved his office without notifying clients, and stole a client's money. Att'y Griev. Comm'n v. Mitchell, 386 Md. 386, 872 A.2d 720 (2005).

Mishandling of bankruptcy case. — Where an attorney filed deficient bankruptcy papers, causing the bankruptcy case to be dismissed, his failure to keep his client informed of the status of the case and to respond to his inquires regarding the case violated the prior, similar Rule. Att'y Griev. Comm'n v. Tinsky, 377 Md. 646, 835 A.2d 542 (2003).

Use of expert testimony in establishing likely conclusions of reasonable attorney. — Expert testimony was indispensable in establishing what conclusions a reasonably competent workers' compensation attorney would have reached under all the facts and circumstances, including the state of Maryland law at the time of the representation, to determine whether the attorney was negligent in advising his client not to appeal. Ankney v. Franch, 103 Md. App. 83, 652 A.2d 1138 (1995), rev'd on other grounds, 341 Md. 350, 670 A.2d 951 (1996).

Ruling of violation could not be sustained. — Hearing court's conclusion that the attorney violated this Rule could not be sustained because it was based on the allowance of testimony by a witness for the Attorney Grievance Commision of Maryland that was inconsistent with a request for admission that was not timely denied, in which the attorney alleged that he told the cleint he would be away from his practice and introduce the client to new counsel, and therefore, should have been deemed admitted. Att'y Griev. Comm'n v. Robertson, 400 Md. 618, 929 A.2d 576 (2007).

No violation found. — Bar counsel failed to show that an attorney had violated Md. R. Prof. Conduct 1.1, 1.3, 1.4(a) and (b), 1.5, 1.16(d), 3.1, 5.1, 5.3, and 8.4(a), (c), and (d) where it was possible to find, based on the testimony, that the attorney had relied on the clients' representations that they intended to handle the appeal pro se, and as a result, Bar counsel had failed to prove that the attorney had represented the two clients in an appeal. Att'y Griev. Comm'n v. Maignan, 402 Md. 39, 935 A.2d 409 (2007).

Attorney was sanctioned by a public reprimand for technically violating Rule 16-609 regarding prohibited transactions as a result of a negligent clerical error involving depositing some of his ex-girlfriend's funds into his operating account instead of his firm's escrow account, which error was corrected upon discovery and was not wilful. The Court of Appeals of Maryland further upheld the trial judge's finding of fact that no attorney client relationship existed between the attorney and his girlfriend to support the other violations asserted against him since he never charged his ex-girlfriend a fee for his services and was only helping her while she received treatment for her alcohol abuse. Att'y Griev. Comm'n v.

Shoup, 410 Md. 462, 979 A.2d 120 (Aug. 28, 2009).

Finding of no violation not clearly erroneous. — Hearing judge's finding that a lawyer did not violate this Rule was not clearly erroneous under circumstances in which the hearing officer rejected permissible inferences which might have been drawn from the evidence by another trier of the facts; the hearing judge's findings and conclusions included a footnote stating that the client was unclear as to how often she had spoken with the lawyer, and forgot that she had filed the instant grievance and that she had settled her claim against the lawyer. Att'y Griev. Comm'n v. Queen, 407 Md. 556, 967 A.2d 198 (2009).

Thirty-day suspension. — Attorney was suspended for 30 days for violating Md. R. Prof. Conduct 1.3, 1.4, 8.1(b), and 8.4(d) after the attorney failed to prepare an eligible domestic relations order for client one, and failed to timely prepare a consent order for client two, and then submitted it to opposing counsel and the trial court without allowing client two to review it, since there were mitigating factors, the attorney had expressed remorse, and there was testimony that the conduct was out of the attorney's character. Att'y Griev. Comm'n v. Hill, 398 Md. 95, 919 A.2d 1194 (2007).

Ninety-day suspension. — Ninety-day suspension was appropriate sanction for attorney's neglect of client's cases, falsifying client's signature on a complaint, and causing the complaint with the false signature to be notarized and filed. Att'y Griev. Comm'n v. Parsons, 310 Md. 132, 527 A.2d 325 (1987).

Attorney's failure to comply with reasonable client requests for information and display of an overall lack of communication with the attorney's client in one case, and empty promises made to a second client in a separarte case that the attorney would provide prompt communications when the attorney did not do so meant that the attorney violated this Rule regarding communications to clients. Since the attorney's conduct was negligent rather than deceitful, a 90-day suspension was warranted. Att'y Griev. Comm'n v. Ugwuonye, 405 Md. 351, 952 A.2d 226 (2008).

Disbarment was proper sanction. — Attorney was properly disbarred for violating prior, similar Maryland Rules of Professional Conduct 1.1, 1.3, 1.4, 1.15, 3.3, and 8.4, § 10-306 of the Business Occupations and Professions Article, and former Rule BU9 (now Rule 16-609) of the Maryland Rules of Procedure. Att'y Griev. Comm'n v. Williams, 335 Md. 458, 644 A.2d 490 (1994).

Disbarment of attorney was appropriate where there were serious and repeated violations of the prior, similar Rule and other provisions of the Maryland Rules of Professional

Conduct. Att'y Griev. Comm'n v. Milliken, 348 Md. 486, 704 A.2d 1225 (1998).

Attorney was disbarred for failing to keep clients apprised of their matters and failing to respond to their calls, for failing to return their retainer to them although he did little or no work on their matters, for failing to keep their funds separate and in a trust fund, for failing to avoid a conflict of interest with respect to their matters, all in violation of prior, similar Md. R. Prof. Conduct 1.4, 1.5, 1.7, 1.8, 1.15, and 1.16; his conduct was especially egregious where his clients were the elderly and their families and where he was so blatant in his continued actions. Att'y Griev. Comm'n v. McLaughlin, 372 Md. 467, 813 A.2d 1145 (2002).

Because the attorney engaged in several acts of professional misconduct following an earlier suspension by accepting fees from clients but by failing to diligently to pursue their cases, the sanction of disbarment was held to be appropriate. Att'y Griev. Comm'n v. Fallin, 371 Md. 237, 808 A.2d 791 (2002).

Where an attorney was retained in two separate bankruptcy matters, was paid the retainer fee, and thereafter neglected the matters, misinformed the clients as to the status of their actions, and failed to properly communicate with them, it was found that he violated prior, similar Rules 1.1, 1.2, 1.3, 1.4, 1.16, and where the attorney had a prior history of disciplinary violations, the court imposed the sanction of disbarment. Att'y Griev. Comm'n v. Faber, 373 Md. 173, 817 A.2d 205 (2003).

Disbarment was the only appropriate sanction for an attorney who withdrew sums that should have been forwarded to a client from an attorney trust account for the attorney's personal use and failed to respond to the client's inquiries; the attorney's marital and drinking problems were not factors in mitigation. Att'y Griev. Comm'n v. Herman, 380 Md. 378, 844 A.2d 1181 (2004).

Attorney was disbarred as he violated (a) and (b) where he did not keep his client informed as to the status of the representation or inform him that the attorney was not licensed to practice law in Virginia. Att'y Griev. Comm'n v. Velasquez, 380 Md. 651, 846 A.2d 422 (2004).

An attorney's pursuit of a claim for the torts of either criminal conversation or adultery was pursuit of a baseless claim, and his failure to communicate with the client after accepting representation despite repeated attempts by the client to contact the attorney constituted misconduct that warranted disbarment. Att'y Griev. Comm'n v. James, 385 Md. 637, 870 A.2d 229 (2005).

In an attorney disciplinary matter wherein the attorney was ordered disbarred, the attorney was found to have violated this Rule by presenting the contents of an offer made by opposing counsel to his client's brother but failing to communicate the contents of the offer to the client directly. The attorney also violated this Rule by failing to communicate on at least two occasions the status of depositions to the client. Att'y Griev. Comm'n v. Steinberg, 395 Md. 337, 910 A.2d 429 (2006).

In an action in which petitioner, the Attorney Grievance Commission of Maryland, acting pursuant to Rule 16-751, filed a petition for disciplinary or remedial action against respondent attorney, the appropriate sanction was disbarment where the court found that, as a matter of law, respondent violated Md. R. Prof. Conduct 1.3, 1.4, 1.16, and 8.1; respondent violated Rule 1.4 by not keeping the client informed about the status, or lack thereof, of her case. Att'y Griev. Comm'n v. Baker, 396 Md. 15, 912 A.2d 651 (2006).

In an action in which petitioner, the Attorney Grievance Commission of Maryland, acting pursuant to Rule 16-751, filed a petition for disciplinary or remedial action against respondent attorney, the appropriate sanction was disbarment where the court found that, as a matter of law, respondent violated Md. R. Prof. Conduct 1.4 in failing to address a client's request for information as well as Md. R. Prof. Conduct 8.1 in failing to answer the repeated queries of Bar Counsel. Att'y Griev. Comm'n v. Baker, 396 Md. 15, 912 A.2d 651 (2006).

Attorney was disbarred for violating Md. R. Prof. Conduct 1.1, 1.3, 1.4, 1.15, and 8.4, Rule 16-609, and §§ 10-306 and 10-606(b) of the Business Professions and Occupations Article as attorney misappropriated the clients' funds, performed no services whatsoever on the clients' behalf, lied to the clients about the status of their case, and provided them with a falsified administrative agency decision that was not issued by the agency. Att'y Griev. Comm'n v. Bahgat, 411 Md. 568, 984 A.2d 225 (2009).

Attorney was disbarred for violating, inter alia, this Rule by failing to communicate with the client and keep him informed of the status of his cases despite the client's repeated efforts to speak with him. Att'y Griev. Comm'n v. Kwarteng, 411 Md. 652, 984 A.2d 865 (2009).

Attorney was disbarred for violating this section and Md. Law. R. Prof. Conduct 1.1, 1.4(a) and (b), 1.16(a), 8.1(b), and 8.4(a) and (d), where the attorney, inter alia, failed to timely file a complaint in a client's personal injury action and concealed the error from the client and the court. Att'y Griev. Comm'n v. Bleecker, 414 Md. 147, 994 A.2d 928 (2010).

Attorney violated this rule by failing to keep his clients informed about the status of their cases, including the dismissal of one case, which the attorney himself was not aware of, and by failing to respond promptly to requests for information about the subject actions; the attorney was disbarred for violating this rule along with Md. Law. R. Prof. Conduct 1.1, 1.2(a), 1.3, 1.16(d), 8.1(b), and 8.4(a), (c), and (d). Att'y Griev. Comm'n v. Fox, 417 Md. 504, 11 A.3d 762 (2010).

Attorney was disbarred for violating (a) and (b) and Md. Law. R. Prof. Conduct 1.3, 1.15(a), (c), and (d), 1.16(d), 8.1(b), and 8.4(a) and (d), after the attorney received advance fee payments from two clients, deposited the money in a personal account, rather than a trust account, having not earned the fees, and abandoned the clients without performing work for the clients. Att'y Griev. Comm'n v. Lara, 418 Md. 355, 14 A.3d 650 (2011).

When an attorney altered the attorney's law firm employer's electronic files to facilitate the attorney taking certain of the firm's clients with the attorney when the attorney left the firm, the proper sanction for the attorney's admitted violations of Md. Law. R. Prof. Conduct 8.4(a), (b), (c), and (d), and (a) and (b) of this Rule, as well as Md. Code Ann., Crim. Law § 7-302, was disbarment because (1) the attorney's conduct was dishonest, intentional, and solely motivated by a desire for personal gain, so disbarment was presumed, and (2) the attorney's mental disabilities of depression and alcohol dependency were not "compelling extenuating circumstances" warranting a lesser sanction as the disabilities did not result in an utter inability to conform the attorney's conduct to the law and the Rules of Professional Conduct. Att'y Griev. Comm'n v. Keiner, — Md. —, — A.3d — (Aug. 19, 2011).

Indefinite suspension was proper sanction. — Where respondent attorney's representation of four clients was marked by serious neglect and inattention; where he failed to return a fee which was unearned for a period of nine months; where he failed to timely remit funds he received on behalf of a client; where he failed to communicate with his clients; and in connection with the investigation of three of the complaints, where respondent failed to answer Bar Counsel's requests for information, the proper sanction was that the attorney be indefinitely suspended from the practice of law, with the right to apply for reinstatement after the suspension had been in effect for six months, conditioned upon his payment of all costs and upon the monitoring of respondent's practice. Att'y Griev. Comm'n v. David, 331 Md. 317, 628 A.2d 178 (1993).

An attorney who on several separate occasions failed to file legal documents which he had drafted, failed to communicate with clients in these matters, and failed to return attorney's fees he collected in connection with these matters, was rightly found to have violated prior, similar Rules of Professional Conduct 1.1, 1.3, 1.4, 1.16, and 8.4. The appropriate sanction was an indefinite suspension with the right to apply for reinstatement after 60 days, conditioned upon his payment of all costs associated with the matter, reimbursement of the unearned legal fees, and his hiring of an attorney to oversee his practice for a period of one year. Att'y Griev. Comm'n v. Brugh, 353 Md. 475, 727 A.2d 913 (1999).

Attorney was suspended indefinitely for failing to appear on behalf of a client, failing to file a petition on behalf of a client, providing a client with incorrect information that the client did not have to appear for a scheduled trial, and failing to subpoena witness and to obtain medical records that may have exculpated his client. Att'y Griev. Comm'n of Maryland v. Mooney, 359 Md. 56, 753 A.2d 17 (2000).

Taking into consideration prior disciplinary history, an indefinite suspension was proper where attorney violated the prior, similar Rule by demonstrating a complete disregard for his client's inquiries when he failed to return numerous phone calls over a 6-month period of time, and failed to inform his clients, when they finally visited him at his office, that he had been suspended from the practice of law for 18 months. If attorney had disclosed his suspension, his clients could have made the informed choice to seek another attorney. Att'y Griev. Comm'n v. Cassidy, 362 Md. 689, 766 A.2d 632 (2001).

Attorney's license to practice law was indefinitely suspended for his failure to provide competent, diligent, and communicative representation to his client, for charging unreasonable fees, for pursuing a frivolous proceeding, and for engaging in conduct prejudicial to the administration of justice. Att'y Griev. Comm'n v. Zdravkovich, 362 Md. 1, 762 A.2d 950 (2000).

An indefinite suspension was appropriate where, among other violations, attorney violated the prior, similar Rule through his pervasive failure to inform his clients of the status of their cases. Att'y Griev. Comm'n v. Cohen, 361 Md. 161, 760 A.2d 706 (2000).

Indefinite suspension was appropriate where attorney was retained to represent a client in filing for alien labor certifications for three of its employees, but where the attorney never prepared or filed an application for one employee and prepared but did not file applications for the other two, where he provided his client with altered documents making it appear he had done the work, and where the attorney never refunded the money paid to him and refused to cooperate with the investigation of his actions. Att'y Griev. Comm'n v. Koven, 361 Md. 337, 761 A.2d 881 (2000).

Indefinite suspension was proper sanction where attorney violated prior, similar Md. R. Prof. Conduct 1.3 by his failure to diligently pursue the legal matter which he undertook on behalf of his client, and prior, similar Md. R. Prof. Conduct 1.4 for failing to promptly comply with reasonable requests for information about a legal matter by a client and failing to fully and truthfully explain his actions, or inaction, to permit the client to make informed decisions regarding the representation; further, the attorney violated prior, similar Md. R. Prof. Conduct 1.16 by effectively terminating the representation of the client, but failing to take such steps to reasonably protect his client's interest. Att'y Griev. Comm'n v. Harrington, 367 Md. 36, 785 A.2d 1260 (2001).

Even though the hearing judge was mistaken in finding that respondent attorney had failed to file a proper petition for an absolute divorce for the client, the record still supported the judge's findings that while the attorney had not been altogether incompetent, the attorney had been negligent and unresponsive; in light of the fact that the attorney had some previous disciplinary history involving client neglect, a indefinite suspension with leave to apply for reinstatement after six months was imposed. Att'y Griev. Comm'n v. Kreamer, 387 Md. 503, 876 A.2d 79 (2005).

Even though the hearing judge was mistaken in finding that respondent attorney had failed to file a proper petition for an absolute divorce for the client, the record still supported the judge's findings that while the attorney had not been altogether incompetent, the attorney had been negligent and unresponsive; in light of the fact that the attorney had some previous disciplinary history involving client neglect, a indefinite suspension with leave to apply for reinstatement after six months was imposed. Att'y Griev. Comm'n v. Kreamer, 387 Md. 503, 876 A.2d 79 (2005).

Although an attorney in a similar case had only been reprimanded after having similarly abandoned a client in a divorce case, the more severe sanction of indefinite suspension was the best way to protect the public where the mitigators present in the earlier case had not been shown to be present, where there had been no expressions of remorse from the attorney, and where, moreover, the attorney had not even respondent to inquiries in early stages of the investigation. Att'y Griev. Comm'n v. Kovacic, 389 Md. 233, 884 A.2d 673 (2005).

Indefinite suspension, rather than disbarment, was the proper sanction for the attorney's violation of Md. R. Prof. Conduct 1.1, 1.2, 1.3, 1.4, 3.2, and 8.4, where there was no evidence he acted out of fraudulent or selfish motive, he cooperated with Bar Counsel, he engaged in negotiations with the client's attorney regarding restitution, and he expressed great remorse. Att'y Griev. Comm'n v. Reinhardt, 391 Md. 209, 892 A.2d 533 (2006).

Attorney was indefinitely suspended from the practice of law for violating Md. R. Prof. Conduct 1.3, 1.4, 1.16(d), 3.2, 8.1(b), and 8.4(d)

in connection with the attorney's representation of a client in a bankruptcy matter. The complaint could not be dismissed based on the complainant's request because the evidence did not fail to show sanctionable professional misconduct. Att'y Griev. Comm'n v. Lee, 393 Md. 546, 903 A.2d 895 (2006).

Attorney was indefinitely suspended from the practice of law with the right to reapply for admission after one year, as the attorney's act of threatening to withdraw from representation of a client if the client refused to pay additional legal fees constituted a violation of Md. R. Prof. Conduct 1.15 and 1.16, and constituted conduct involving dishonesty, fraud, deceit or misrepresentation in violation of Md. R. Prof. Conduct 8.4, and the flat fee charged violated Md. R. Prof. Conduct 1.5 as the attorney did not provide sufficient services to earn the fee, the attorney violated Rules 16-604 and 16-609 by failing to place unearned attorney fees in his attorney trust account, and the attorney's failure to keep the client informed of the progress of the litigation violated this Rule. Att'y Griev. Comm'n v. Lawson, 401 Md. 536, 933 A.2d 842 (2007).

In a reciprocal discipline action, the attorney, who admitted to the wrongdoing which led to a finding that D.C. R. Prof. Conduct 1.2(a), 1.4(a), 1.4(b), 1.4(c), 1.5(c), 1.15(a), 1.15(b), 1.15(c), and 8.4(d) had been violated based on the attorney's negligence misrepresentation of settlement funds in one case and interference with the administration of justice in another case, amounting to violations of Md. Law. R. Prof. Conduct Rules 1.2(a), 1.4(a)(2) and (3), 1.4(b), 1.5(c), 1.15(a), 1.15(d), 1.15(e), and 8.4(d), was indefinitely suspended in Maryland, with right to apply for readmission after reinstatement in the District in Columbia. Att'y Griev. Comm'n v. Thaxton, 415 Md. 341, — A.2d —, 1 A.3d 470 (2010).

Alcoholism, drug addiction or mental disorder. — When a lawyer's misconduct is caused by alcoholism, drug addiction, or a mental disorder, the usual sanction is indefinite suspension. This provides the requisite protection for the public, for it prevents the lawyer from practicing law until such time (if ever) that he or she can demonstrate that he or she is free from the effects of the ailment and able to practice competently. At the same time, the lawyer is spared the ultimate sanction of disbarment, a sanction which would be unfair to apply where the lawyer's conduct is caused by factors beyond his or her control. Att'y Griev. Comm'n v. Powers, 314 Md. 484, 551 A.2d 465 (1989).

An indefinite suspension was the proper sanction in the case of a misappropriation of client funds caused by alcoholism; however, in the future, absent truly compelling circumstances, alcoholism will usually not be permitted to mitigate where an attorney commits a violation of ethical or legal rules which would ordinarily warrant disbarment. Att'y Griev. Comm'n v. Kenney, 339 Md. 578, 664 A.2d 854 (1995).

Applied in Att'y Griev. Comm'n v. Duvall, 384 Md. 234, 863 A.2d 291 (2004); Att'y Griev. Comm'n v. Kapoor, 391 Md. 505, 894 A.2d 502 (2006); Merzbacher v. Shearin, 732 F. Supp. 2d 527 (D. Md. 2010).

Quoted in Att'y Griev. Comm'n v. Lee, 387 Md. 89, 874 A.2d 897 (2005); Att'y Griev. Comm'n v. Scroggs, 387 Md. 238, 874 A.2d 985 (2005); Att'y Griev. Comm'n v. Muhammad, — Md. —, — A.2d — (2005); Att'y Griev. Comm'n v. Ward, 394 Md. 1, 904 A.2d 477 (2006); Att'y

Griev. Comm'n v. Manger, 396 Md. 134, 913 A.2d 1 (2006); Att'y Griev. Comm'n v. Taylor, 405 Md. 697, 955 A.2d 755 (2008); Att'y Griev. Comm'n v. Khandpur, 421 Md. 1, 25 A.3d 165 (2011).

Cited in Att'y Griev. Comm'n v. Maignan, 390 Md. 287, 888 A.2d 344 (2005); Att'y Griev. Comm'n v. Roberts, 394 Md. 137, 904 A.2d 557 (2006); Att'y Griev. Comm'n v. Muhammad, 395 Md. 676, 912 A.2d 588 (2006), cert. denied, 127 S. Ct. 2296, 2007 U.S. LEXIS 5292, 167 L. Ed. 2d 1103 (U.S. 2007); Att'y Griev. Comm'n v. Rees, 396 Md. 248, 913 A.2d 68 (2006); Att'y Griev. Comm'n v. Sapero, 400 Md. 461, 929 A.2d 483 (2007); Bland v. Hammond, 177 Md. App. 340, 935 A.2d 457 (2007).

Rule 1.5. Fees.

(a) A lawyer shall not make an agreement for, charge, or collect an unreasonable fee or an unreasonable amount for expenses. The factors to be considered in determining the reasonableness of a fee include the following:

(1) the time and labor required, the novelty and difficulty of the questions involved, and the skill requisite to perform the legal service properly;

(2) the likelihood, if apparent to the client, that the acceptance of the particular employment will preclude other employment of the lawyer;

(3) the fee customarily charged in the locality for similar legal services;

(4) the amount involved and the results obtained;

(5) the time limitations imposed by the client or by the circumstances;

(6) the nature and length of the professional relationship with the client;

(7) the experience, reputation, and ability of the lawyer or lawyers performing the services; and

(8) whether the fee is fixed or contingent.

(b) The scope of the representation and the basis or rate of the fee and expenses for which the client will be responsible shall be communicated to the client, preferably in writing, before or within a reasonable time after commencing the representation, except when the lawyer will charge a regularly represented client on the same basis or rate. Any changes in the basis or rate of the fee or expenses shall also be communicated to the client.

(c) A fee may be contingent on the outcome of the matter for which the service is rendered, except in a matter in which a contingent fee is prohibited by paragraph (d) or other law. A contingent fee agreement shall be in a writing signed by the client and shall state the method by which the fee is to be determined, including the percentage or percentages that shall accrue to the lawyer in the event of settlement, trial or appeal; litigation and other expenses to be deducted from the recovery; and whether such expenses are to be deducted before or after the contingent fee is calculated. The agreement must clearly notify the client of any expenses for which the client will be responsible whether or not the client is the prevailing party. Upon conclusion of a contingent fee matter, the lawyer shall provide the client with a written statement stating the outcome of the matter, and, if there is a recovery, showing the remittance to the client and the method of its determination.

(d) A lawyer shall not enter into an arrangement for, charge, or collect:

(1) any fee in a domestic relations matter, the payment or amount of which is contingent upon the securing of a divorce or custody of a child or upon the amount of alimony or support or property settlement, or upon the amount of an award pursuant to Md. Code, Family Law Article, §§ 8-201 through 213; or

(2) a contingent fee for representing a defendant in a criminal case.

(e) A division of a fee between lawyers who are not in the same firm may be made only if:

(1) the division is in proportion to the services performed by each lawyer or each lawyer assumes joint responsibility for the representation;

(2) the client agrees to the joint representation and the agreement is confirmed in writing; and

(3) the total fee is reasonable.

COMMENT

Reasonableness of Fee and Expenses. — [1] Paragraph (a) requires that lawyers charge fees that are reasonable under the circumstances. The factors specified in (1) through (8) are not exclusive. Nor will each factor be relevant in each instance. Paragraph (a) also requires that expenses for which the client will be charged must be reasonable. A lawyer may seek reimbursement for the cost of services performed in-house, such as copying, or for other expenses incurred in-house, such as telephone charges, either by charging a reasonable amount to which the client has agreed in advance or by charging an amount that reasonably reflects the cost incurred by the lawyer.

Basis or Rate of Fee. — [2] When the lawyer has regularly represented a client, they ordinarily will have evolved an understanding concerning the basis or rate of the fee and the expenses for which the client will be responsible. In a new client-lawyer relationship, however, an understanding as to fees and expenses must be promptly established. Generally, it is desirable to furnish the client with at least a simple memorandum or copy of the lawyer's customary fee arrangements that states the general nature of the legal services to be provided, the basis, rate, or total amount of the fee and whether and to what extent the client will be responsible for any costs, expenses or disbursements in the course of representation. A written statement concerning the terms of the engagement reduces the possibility of misunderstanding.

[3] Contingent fees, like any other fees, are subject to the reasonableness standard of paragraph (a) of this Rule. In determining whether a particular contingent fee is reasonable, or whether it is reasonable to charge any form of contingent fee, a lawyer must consider the factors that are relevant under the circumstances. Applicable law may impose limitations on contingent fees, such as a ceiling on the percentage allowable, or may require a lawyer to offer clients an alternative basis for the fee. Applicable law may also apply to situations other than a contingent fee, for example, government regulations regarding fees in certain tax matters.

Terms of Payment. — [4] A lawyer may require advance payment of a fee, but is obliged to return any unearned portion. See Rule 1.15(c); Comment [3] to Rule 1.15; Rule 1.16(d). A lawyer may accept property in payment for services, such as an ownership interest in an enterprise, providing this does not involve acquisition of a proprietary interest in the cause of action or subject matter of the litigation contrary to Rule 1.8(i). However, a fee paid in property instead of money may be subject to the requirements of Rule 1.8(a) because such fees often have the essential qualities of a business transaction with the client.

[5] An agreement may not be made whose terms might induce the lawyer improperly to curtail services for the client or perform them in a way contrary to the client's interest. For example, a lawyer should not enter into an agreement whereby services are to be provided only up to a stated amount when it is foreseeable that more extensive services probably will be required, unless the situation is adequately explained to the client. Otherwise, the client might have to bargain for further assistance in the midst of a proceeding or transaction. However, it is proper to define the extent of services in light of the client's ability to pay. A lawyer should not exploit a fee arrangement based primarily on hourly charges by using wasteful procedures.

Prohibited Contingent Fees. — [6] Paragraph (d) prohibits a lawyer from charging a contingent fee in a domestic relations matter when payment is contingent upon the securing of a divorce or upon the amount of alimony or support or property settlement to be obtained. This provision does not preclude a contract for a contingent fee for legal representation in connection with the recovery of post-judgment balances due under support, alimony or other financial orders because such contracts do not implicate the same policy concerns.

Division of Fee. — [7] A division of fee is a single billing to a client covering the fee of two or more lawyers who are not in the same firm. A division of fee facilitates association of more than one lawyer in a matter in which neither alone could serve the client as well, and most often is used when the fee is contingent and the division is between a referring lawyer and a trial specialist. Paragraph (e) permits the lawyers to divide a fee on either the basis of the proportion of services they render or by agreement between the participating lawyers if all assume responsibility for the representation as a whole and the client agrees to the joint representation, which is confirmed in writing. Contingent fee agreements must be in a writing signed by the client and must otherwise comply with paragraph (c) of this Rule. Joint responsibility for the representation entails financial and ethical responsibility for the representation as if the lawyers were associated in a partnership. A lawyer should only refer a matter to a lawyer whom the referring lawyer reasonably believes is competent to handle the matter. See Rule 1.1.

[8] Paragraph (e) does not prohibit or regulate division of fees to be received in the future for work done when lawyers were previously associated in a law firm.

Disputes over Fees. — [9] If a procedure has been established for resolution of fee disputes, such as an arbitration or mediation procedure established by the bar, the lawyer must comply with the procedure when it is mandatory, and even when it is voluntary, the lawyer should conscientiously consider submitting to it. Law may prescribe a procedure for determining a lawyer's fee, for example, in representation of an executor or administrator, a class or a person entitled to a reasonable fee as part of the measure of damages. The lawyer entitled to such a fee and a lawyer representing another party concerned with the fee should comply with the prescribed procedure.

Cross references. — See *Post v. Bregman,* 349 Md. 142 (1998) and *Son v. Margolius,* 349 Md. 441 (1998).

Model Rules Comparison. — Rule 1.5 is substantially similar to the language of the Ethics 2000 Amendments to the ABA Model Rules of Professional Conduct except that it retains existing Maryland language in Rule 1.5(d)(1) and adds wording changes to Rule 1.5(e)(2) and Comment [7].

Maryland Law Review. — For article, "Survey of Developments in Maryland Law, 1987-88," see 48 Md. L. Rev. 551 (1989).

For note, "Recent Decisions, The Maryland Court of Appeals," see 54 Md. L. Rev. 670 (1995).

University of Baltimore Law Forum. — For article, "Code of Ethics Revisited," see 19.2 U. Balt. Law Forum 14 (1989).

Recent Developments: Post v. Bregman: Rule of Professional Conduct Regarding the Splitting of Attorney's Fees May Extend Beyond Disciplinary Proceedings, 28.2 U. Balt. Law Forum 33 (1998).

For note, "Recent Development: Attorney Grievance Comm'n of Md. v. Kinnane: Disbarment of Attorney Based on Rules 1.5(E) and 8.4(B) & (C) of the Maryland Rules of Professional Conduct Held Proper Where Violations Are Established and No Mitigating or Compelling Extenuating Circumstances Exist," see 36 U. Balt. L.F. 165 (2006).

Focus of Rule. — The focus of the prior, similar Rule is clearly upon excessive fees. Att'y Griev. Comm'n v. Eisenstein, 333 Md. 464, 635 A.2d 1327 (1994).

Limits on fees. — The prior, similar Rule puts a limit on what a lawyer may charge his or her own client; it is generally a violation of the rule for the attorney's stake in the result to exceed the client's stake. Friolo v. Frankel, 373 Md. 501, 819 A.2d 354 (2003).

Delineation of basis for fee. — Where the fee request is based primarily on time spent, a form of lodestar, the best evidence ordinarily would be a clear delineation in the attorney's billings of the time spent and expenses incurred with respect to the particular claims upon which the fee request is based. Because such a precise delineation may not always be practicable, however, it is not regarded as a sine qua non of the right to recover, for to conclude otherwise would, in many cases, deny all recovery where some recovery is clearly warranted. Diamond Point Plaza L.P. v. Wells Fargo Bank, N.A., 400 Md. 718, 929 A.2d 932 (2007).

Bank's claim of attorneys' fees should not have been denied in its entirety based on the trial court's finding insufficient evidence due to a lack of delineation, especially where a retailer, which was found to be liable to the bank, had shown an attorney fee liability of $280,000. Diamond Point Plaza L.P. v. Wells Fargo Bank, N.A., 400 Md. 718, 929 A.2d 932 (2007).

Where prevailing parties merely presented a compilation of hours multiplied by fixed hourly rates in support of their request for attorney fees, the parties did not meet their burden of production as to the services performed, by whom they were performed, the time expended thereon, and the hourly rates charged under Maxima; further, the trial court did not apply the reasonableness factors articulated in Md. R. Prof. Conduct 1.5 espoused in Maxima. Long v. Burson, 182 Md. App. 1, 957 A.2d 173 (2008).

Trial court erred in awarding attorney's fees where, in analyzing the evidence before it, the trial court did not apply the reasonableness factors articulated in this Rule; the trial court focused only on the amount of work that was put into this case as detailed in the testimony, as well as the sellers' billing records and the appellate court's opinion in the first appeal. The trial court failed to consider the time and labor required, the novelty and difficulty of the questions involved, and the skill requisite to perform the legal services properly; and the amount involved and the results obtained. Long v. Burson, 182 Md. App. 1, 957 A.2d 173 (2008).

Percentage fees not allowed. — As a bank presented no evidence that it agreed to pay attorneys' fees other than on an hourly rate basis or concerning the fees it would incur in future collection efforts, the court did not err in awarding the bank only the reasonable fees it incurred as of the date of judgment instead of fees equal to 15 percent of principal amount owed, as the parties' loan agreement provided. SunTrust Bank v. Goldman, — Md. App. —, — A.3d — (Sept. 30, 2011).

Fee approved by court. — Attorney could not be found to have violated the prior, similar Rule by taking a fee for representing an estate where the fee had been approved by the Orphans' Court, the fee was actually smaller than the amount authorized under probate laws, and there had never been any allegation that the court had abused its discretion in awarding the fee. Att'y Griev. Comm'n v. MacDougall, 384 Md. 271, 863 A.2d 312 (2004).

Interest and penalty not allowed where not provided for in representation agreement — Attorney violated Md. R. Prof. Conduct 1.5 by attempting to charge interest and penalty fees which were not in his representation agreement as well as building up excessive fees through her delaying of the litigation. Att'y Griev. Comm'n v. Calhoun, 391 Md. 532, 894 A.2d 518 (2006).

Factors considered. — In Maryland, the lodestar approach includes consideration of the factors set forth in the prior, similar Rule, among which are the novelty and difficulty of the questions involved and the skill requisite to perform the legal service adequately; those factors are more judgmental than fact-based and therefore more apt to be within the expertise of a judge than of lay jurors. Friolo v. Frankel, 373 Md. 501, 819 A.2d 354 (2003).

The prior, similar Rule requires that a lawyer's fee be reasonable and sets out factors to be considered in determining the reasonableness of a fee; most of them are identical or similar to the factors enumerated in Johnson, which the Hensley Court indicated are relevant even in a lodestar analysis. Friolo v. Frankel, 373 Md. 501, 819 A.2d 354 (2003).

The key inquiry in determining a reasonable amount of attorneys' fees is the degree of success achieved by the plaintiff; thus, if a plaintiff has obtained excellent results, the attorney should recover a fully compensatory fee, but if the plaintiff has achieved only partial or limited success, the product of hours reasonably spent on the litigation times the hourly rate may be an excessive amount, even where the claims were interrelated, nonfrivolous, and raised in good faith. Garcia v. Foulger Pratt Dev., Inc., 155 Md. App. 634, 845 A.2d 16 (2003).

Appellees were not entitled to attorney's fees in their declaratory judgment action where the only portion of the action that reached a substantive conclusion was decided in favor of appellant and the two prior appeals were decided unfavorably to appellees. The trial court should have taken into consideration that a significant portion of appellees' attorney's fees were accumulated in connection with the unsuccessful litigation. Long v. Burson, 182 Md. App. 1, 957 A.2d 173 (2008).

Calculation of fees in homeowners' association assessment dispute. — While lodestar method did not apply when calculating attorneys' fees in homeowners' associations' assessment dispute because no fee-shifting statute finding that such litigation promoted a public policy was involved, the trial court properly used the rubric of this rule to determining a reasonable fee. Monmouth Meadows Homeowners Ass'n v. Hamilton, 416 Md. 325, 7 A.3d 1 (Oct. 25, 2010).

Effect of violation of Rule. — A violation of the prior, similar Rule does not necessarily invalidate an otherwise valid court order. Goldman, Skeen & Wadler v. Cooper, Beckman & Tuerk, 122 Md. App. 29, 712 A.2d 1 (1998).

"Excessive fee." — Receipt of one-third of $5,000 paid under an insured client's medical payment coverage as a contingency fee was clearly an "excessive fee." Att'y Griev. Comm'n v. Kemp, 303 Md. 664, 496 A.2d 672 (1985).

A fee based on results in a domestic relations case which is one and one-half times the lodestar fee was excessive. Head v. Head, 66 Md. App. 655, 505 A.2d 868 (1986).

If attorney's contingent fee was clearly excessive in violation of former DR 2-106, then he also failed to stay within the exception to the prohibition of former DR 5-103(A) against acquiring a proprietary interest in the clients' causes of action. Att'y Griev. Comm'n v. Korotki, 318 Md. 646, 569 A.2d 1224 (1990).

A $20,000, nonrefundable engagement retainer that was not intended to pay for future services was excessive and therefore unreasonable under the prior, similar Rule. In re Printing Dimensions, Inc., 153 Bankr. 715 (Bankr. D. Md. 1993).

Attorney violated the Maryland Rules of Professional Conduct by accepting and retaining the entire settlement payment procured on behalf of his client in representing the client in a suit against the client's former employer, while claiming that the money was also applied to the payment of back rent that the client owed the attorney. Att'y Griev. Comm'n v. Harris, 371 Md. 510, 810 A.2d 457 (2002).

Maryland Court of Appeals has stated that it is generally a violation of the rules of professional conduct for the attorney's stake in the result to exceed the client's stake. Att'y Griev. Comm'n v. Roberson, 373 Md. 328, 818 A.2d 1059 (2003).

Attorney violated the prior, similar Rule and Ga. St. Bar Stand. 31.a by including future medical services' valuation, which were not yet provided, in the contingency fee, boosting the attorneys' fee share of actual cash to 72 percent. Att'y Griev. Comm'n v. Roberson, 373 Md. 328, 818 A.2d 1059 (2003).

Attorney violated this Rule when the amount of attorney's fees she collected for representing a decedent's estate as co-personal representative far exceeded the fee customarily charged for estates of similar size, under §§ 7-601 and 7-602 of the Estates and Trusts Article. That a portion of the fees collected was for reducing the amount due on a credit card balance was not reasonable in light of the time and labor she must have spent in reducing the balance, which could not have been more than a couple of hours on the phone with a credit card company representative. Att'y Griev. Comm'n v. Kendrick, 403 Md. 489, 943 A.2d 1173 (2008).

Attorney violated this Rule by taking a client's case that had no merit, obtaining a retainer check, and charging a grossly excessive fee that used up all of the retainer check amount when the attorney should have declined representation. Since the attorney's conduct was merely negligent rather than deceitful, a 90-day suspension from the practice of law was warranted. Att'y Griev. Comm'n v. Ugwuonye, 405 Md. 351, 952 A.2d 226 (2008).

Attorney violated (a) when the attorney charged a client for the execution of a judgment, when there was no judgment. Att'y Griev. Comm'n v. Patterson, — Md. —, — A.3d — (Sept. 21, 2011).

Unreasonable fee. — Attorney's fee for representing client in parole proceeding was unreasonable as a matter of law in that evidence showed he performed almost no services in return for the money paid by the client's mother; restitution of the fee was one of the conditions for the attorney's reinstatement after suspension. Att'y Griev. Comm'n v. Monfried, 368 Md. 373, 794 A.2d 92 (2002).

When an attorney agreed to represent clients in an adoption case, and they paid him an agreed fee, while that fee was not, on its face, unreasonable for handling such a case, it became unreasonable, under (a), because the attorney did virtually no work after he received the fee. Att'y Griev. Comm'n v. Guida, 391 Md. 33, 891 A.2d 1085 (2006).

Clear and convincing evidence showed that the attorney acted incompetently when the attorney accepted a case that required filing in a jurisdiction where the attorney was not admitted to practice, and when the attorney failed to service notice to defendant, that the attorney failed to act with reasonable diligence and promptness in representing the client when the attorney failed to file the estate in the proper jurisdiction, that the attorney failed to communicate the truth when the attorney told the client that the attorney was admitted to practice in a certain jurisdiction when the attorney was not admitted there and when the attorney failed to communicate to the client that the attorney intended to seek other counsel in the District of Columbia to assist the attorney, that the attorney's fees were unreasonable because the attorney charged and accepted fees when no work was performed in furtherance of the case, and that the attorney's actions were prejudicial to the administration of justice; even though the attorney was absolved of the charge that the attorney did not properly terminate the representation because the evidence showed that the attorney returned all unearned advance fees to the client after the client retained new counsel, the attorney's violations, which included intentionally dishonest conduct, warranted disbarment, especially since the attorney had a prior disciplinary history. Att'y Griev. Comm'n v. Ward, 396 Md. 203, 913 A.2d 41 (2006).

Attorney violated this Rule by unreasonably charging the client for such things as file organization, time sheet maintenance, reimbursement of fees and review and revise accounting. These were matters of overhead in any law office. Att'y Griev. Comm'n v. Kreamer, 404 Md. 282, 946 A.2d 500 (2008).

Attorney violated this Rule by charging clients for "accounting services" — billing clients for time spent completing time sheets and calculating bills therefrom. Att'y Griev. Comm'n v. Kreamer, 404 Md. 282, 946 A.2d 500 (2008).

Attorney's failure to turn over the fee that the attorney retained from a personal injury settlement, when that fee amount belonged to the bankruptcy estate and the attorney had not obtained approval regarding it, meant that the attorney collected an unreasonable fee in violation of (a). As a result of that misconduct and other related misconduct, the proper sanction was the attorney's indefinite suspension from the practice of law. Att'y Griev. Comm'n v. Nichols, 405 Md. 207, 950 A.2d 778 (2008).

Respondent, who was not licensed to practice law in Maryland, violated Md. Law. R. Prof. Conduct 1.4(b) and 1.5(a) and (b) by suing a client for fees at an $ 375 per hour, a rate that she had not disclosed and he had not agreed to pay. Att'y Griev. Comm'n v. Sucklal, 418 Md. 1, 12 A.3d 650 (2011).

Attorney violated this Rule because the attorney's fee, collected in advance, that was otherwise reasonable, became unreasonable when the attorney did no work to earn the fee. Att'y Griev. Comm'n v. De La Paz, 418 Md. 534, 16 A.3d 181 (2011).

Reasonable fee award. — Trial court did not abuse its discretion in calculating the amount and reasonableness of a fee award to a partner who recovered a development fee from co-partners on behalf of the partnership where: (1) the trial court had before it an extensive line-by-line accounting of all the fees generated pursuant to each claim, and had the opportunity to review that document before making its determination; (2) the trial court found that the partner had partially succeeded, and granted fees for the prevailing claim and those fees reasonably related to that claim but denied the partner's request for 1/3 of the time and services "related predominantly" to the ownership interest because the partner did not prevail on that claim; and (3) the trial court denied all fees on a misrepresentation count as it was neither successful nor reasonably related; furthermore, the court's use of the lodestar approach instead of the percentage method was clearly justified, and the court relied on the factors set forth in (a) to ensure a reasonable fee award. Garcia v. Foulger Pratt Dev., Inc., 155 Md. App. 634, 845 A.2d 16 (2003).

It is a circuit court's obligation to ensure that an attorneys' fee award is reasonable under this Rule and §§ 3-427 and 3-507.1 of the Labor and Employment Article, as appropriate adjustments to a lodestar approach can produce a fee that would be reasonable under both the rule and the statutes. Frankel v. Friolo, 170 Md. App. 441, 907 A.2d 363 (2006), aff'd, remanded, 403 Md. 443, 942 A.2d 1242, 2008 Md. LEXIS 107 (2008).

Bar counsel failed to show that an attorney had violated Md. R. Prof. Conduct 1.1, 1.3, 1.5(a), 1.16(d), 3.1, 5.1, 5.3(a) and (c), and

8.4(a) and (d) where the attorney had informed the client that he no longer wished to represent him after the client changed his mind with respect to a settlement agreement and the attorney had discharged the associate after discovering that she had subsequently file additional motions. Att'y Griev. Comm'n v. Maignan, 402 Md. 39, 935 A.2d 409 (2007).

Since only an employer's claim for breach of contract gave rise to attorney's fees and that claim shared a factual element with extracontractual claims, and the "common core of facts" doctrine comported with Maryland law, the fees were reasonable and properly awarded. Weichert Co. of Md. v. Faust, 191 Md. App. 1, 989 A.2d 1227 (2010), aff'd, 2011 Md. LEXIS 225 (Md. 2011).

When a tenant successfully sued a landlord, but the trial court's judgment was reversed and the case was remanded for a second trial, at which the tenant again prevailed, the tenant was entitled to an award of fees and costs incurred at the second trial because (1) the tenant did not engage in unreasonable conduct at the first trial which necessitated the second trial, and (2) the second trial was, instead, necessitated by the trial court's erroneous rulings at the first trial. Cong. Hotel Corp. v. Mervis Diamond Corp., — Md. App. —, — A.3d — (Sept. 2, 2011).

Failure to provide settlement statement in timely manner. — Attorney violated (c) by failing to provide clients with a settlement sheet at the time of the settlement of the clients' tort claims; to provide a settlement sheet to the clients more than three years after the conclusion of the contingent fee matter was not sufficient to comply with (c). Att'y Griev. Comm'n v. Sapero, 400 Md. 461, 929 A.2d 483 (2007).

Partial success. — Where a partner sought fees for unsucccssful claims of conversion and breach of fiduciary duty that were reasonably related to a successful claim of obtaining the development fee for his partnership against commercial development entities, the court adopted the "reasonably related" argument but deducted fees for two claims, misrepresentation and punitive damages, because they were neither successful nor reasonably related. Garcia v. Foulger Pratt Dev., Inc., 155 Md. App. 634, 845 A.2d 16 (2003).

Attorney was disbarred for failing to keep clients apprised of their matters and failing to respond to their calls, for failing to return their retainer to them although he did little or no work on their matters, for failing to keep their funds separate and in a trust fund, for failing to avoid a conflict of interest with respect to their matters, all in violation of prior, similar Rules 1.4, 1.5, 1.7, 1.8, 1.15, and 1.16; his conduct was especially egregious where his clients were the elderly and their families and where he was so blatant in his continued actions. Att'y Griev. Comm'n v. McLaughlin, 372 Md. 467, 813 A.2d 1145 (2002).

Agreements for division of fees. — Compliance with the prior, similar Rule is not implied in every fee-sharing agreement between attorneys. Post v. Bregman, 112 Md. App. 738, 686 A.2d 665 (1996).

Fee-sharing violations. — A violation of the prior, similar Rule, whether regarded as an external defense or as incorporated into the contract itself, is an equitable defense and the principles of equity ought to be applied. Post v. Bregman, 349 Md. 142, 707 A.2d 806 (1998).

Appellate court ordered that the attorney be disbarred, as the evidence showed that he violated, inter alia, (e), by sharing a fee with an alleged lawyer from a corporation without performing any services for the corporation; the fee was part of a scheme to steal money from the corporation in the guise of providing a retainer to the attorney, with a plan to have the attorney kick back some of the "retainer" as payment for future consulting services, which constituted felony theft in the corporation's place of business. Att'y Griev. Comm'n v. Kinnane, 390 Md. 324, 888 A.2d 1178 (2005).

Other than proportionally splitting a fee with petitioner per the fee-splitting agreement, respondent did not owe petitioner any other duties under contractual and tort principles; respondent was not required to consult or communicate with petitioner under the agreement, which provided that respondent had primary responsibility for the case and petitioner would act as co-counsel and perform tasks as requested by respondent. Blondell v. Littlepage, 413 Md. 96, 991 A.2d 80 (2010).

Applicability to agreements between attorneys. — This Rule does not apply to a case involving one lawyer's attempt to enforce an agreement he made with another. Vogelhut v. Kandel, 66 Md. App. 170, 502 A.2d 1120, aff'd, 308 Md. 183, 517 A.2d 1092 (1986).

The prior, similar Rule constitutes a supervening statement of public policy to which fee-sharing agreements by lawyers are subject; its enforcement is not limited to disciplinary proceedings, and may render fee-sharing arrangements in clear and flagrant violation of the prior, similar Rule unenforceable. Post v. Bregman, 349 Md. 142, 707 A.2d 806 (1998).

A trial court erred in not allowing a law firm to present an equitable defense based on a violation of the prior, similar Rule during litigation regarding a fee-sharing agreement. Goldman, Skeen & Wadler v. Cooper, Beckman & Tuerk, 122 Md. App. 29, 712 A.2d 1 (1998).

Court may not set attorneys' fees. — It is inappropriate for attorney to ask court to set attorney's fees as the attorney is in the best position to assess the skill, time, labor and effort the case requires and set the value of his or her own services. Head v. Head, 66 Md. App. 655, 505 A.2d 868 (1986).

Unilateral increase of fees improper. — Unilateral increase of attorney's fees by the attorney after a fee arrangement is agreed upon by client is inappropriate. Head v. Head, 66 Md. App. 655, 505 A.2d 868 (1986).

Inflation of attorney's claimed normal fee. — A three-year suspension was warranted where an attorney promised a client a fifteen percent discount on billing time and then systematically inflated his normal rate by the same fifteen percent. Att'y Griev. Comm'n v. Hess, 352 Md. 438, 722 A.2d 905 (1999).

Modification of fee arrangement permissible. — Where an attorney and client have a special fee arrangement they may, after disclosures appropriate to the existing confidential relationship, agree on a modification of that arrangement. Att'y Griev. Comm'n v. Wright, 306 Md. 93, 507 A.2d 618 (1986).

There was not necessarily any impropriety, in the context of a long-term representation, for the attorney representing clients in a real estate matter to switch from billing by the hour to a commission arrangement; the impropriety occurred later on, when the attorney attempted to recover another commission, to which there was no entitlement. Att'y Griev. Comm'n v. Parker, 389 Md. 142, 884 A.2d 104 (2005).

Even where contingency fee agreement was void, firm was awarded reasonable fees. — Where the law firm's failure to deal candidly with its client weighed heavily in the court's determination to void the contingency fee agreement, considering the ultimate favorable outcome of the litigation, the court believed the law firm's reasonable hourly fees to be a fair award pursuant to prior, similar Md. R. Prof. Conduct 1.5. United States Postal Serv. v. Haselrig Constr. Co., 349 F. Supp. 2d 955 (D. Md. 2004).

Fees based on preclusion of other employment. — In the relation of attorney and client, if a fee for work requiring only modest legal ability is to be based on the higher value of more complex legal work which the attorney is capable of performing, but which he is unable to perform because of the employment, then some kind of effective disclosure to the client is required as part of the terms of the engagement. Att'y Griev. Comm'n v. Wright, 306 Md. 93, 507 A.2d 618 (1986).

Attorney's violations resulting in default judgment. — Where a default judgment directly resulted from attorney's violations, at a minimum, the loss suffered by a client included the expense incurred by her in engaging counsel to appeal the default judgment and to appear in circuit court where successor counsel was able to have that default judgment vacated. Att'y Griev. Comm'n v. Dietz,

331 Md. 637, 629 A.2d 678 (1993).

Unreasonableness argument not considered absent findings of fact. — Appellate court refused to consider insurance company's argument that insured's legal fees were unreasonable where, even assuming the insurer had standing to question the fee's reasonableness, such a determination would require a factual hearing and findings of fact, neither of which had occurred. Medical Mut. Liab. Ins. Soc'y v. Evans, 330 Md. 1, 622 A.2d 103 (1993).

Cumulative violations. — Although a fee that is not permitted by law is by definition an unreasonable fee, where other rules more specifically and completely address the specifically and completely address the improper conduct, adding a cumulative violation for the same conduct will serve no useful purpose. Att'y Griev. Comm'n v. Eisenstein, 333 Md. 464, 635 A.2d 1327 (1994).

Quantum meruit fees. — Where a client has a good faith basis to terminate the attorney-client relationship but there is no serious misconduct warranting forfeiture of any fee, the attorney is entitled to compensation based on the reasonable value of services rendered prior to discharge, considering as factors the reasonable value of the benefits the client obtained as a result of the services rendered prior to discharge and the nature and gravity of the cause that led to the attorney's discharge. Somuah v. Flachs, 352 Md. 241, 721 A.2d 680 (1998).

Class action contingent fee agreement. — Because the percentage of a contingent fee in a contract between counsel for the class of plaintiffs and the named plaintiffs was not binding on a circuit court, since the vast majority of class members did not consent to the agreement, the proper procedure was for the court to determine the approximate percentage of a multi-million dollar recovery a business person would have been able to negotiate with counsel of the caliber of the plaintiffs' counsel in a case of comparable complexity. United Cable Television of Baltimore Ltd. Partnership v. Burch, 354 Md. 658, 732 A.2d 887 (1999).

Post judgment attorney fees. — If a contract calls for the shifting of attorneys' fees incurred in post judgment collection efforts, and assuming that it does not avoid the doctrine of merger, a trial court should permit the requesting party to put on evidence of fees that will, with certainty, be incurred in addition to those actually incurred at that time. SunTrust Bank v. Goldman, — Md. App. —, — A.3d — (Sept. 30, 2011).

Evidence sufficient. — Evidence justified findings of misconduct, and disbarment was warranted. Att'y Griev. Comm'n v. Mazelis, 309 Md. 50, 522 A.2d 913 (1987); Att'y Griev.

Comm'n v. Manning, 318 Md. 697, 569 A.2d 1250 (1990).

Clear and convincing evidence was found that an attorney violated this Rule by knowingly taking a greater fee than that which she had agreed upon. The attorney was entitled to the amount of $ 3,663 as her fee but she withdrew $ 2,962 beyond the $ 3,663, even though she knew those monies were to have been maintained for payment of various medical bills on behalf of her client, and the bank statements for the account reflected that the attorney wrote a multitude of checks to herself and a check for cash on the escrow account, totaling $ 6,625. Att'y Griev. Comm'n v. Cherry-Mahoi, 388 Md. 124, 879 A.2d 58 (2005).

Attorney's attempt to collect a fee in excess of the agreed upon flat fee amounted to a violation of this Rule. Att'y Griev. Comm'n v. Ward, 394 Md. 1, 904 A.2d 477 (2006).

Evidence was insufficient to support a finding of a violation — Evidence was insufficient to find a violation of the prior, similar Rule regarding an attorney's representation of a client because no testimony or evidence was presented regarding fees customarily charged in the locality for similar legal services or as to the novelty or difficulty of the questions involved. Furthermore, no credible testimony or evidence was presented regarding the actual amount billed to and paid by the client. Att'y Griev. Comm'n v. Awuah, 374 Md. 505, 823 A.2d 651 (2003).

Insufficient findings for award of statutory attorney's fees. — Award of attorney's fees to buyer under §§ 14-1502 and 13-408(b) of the Commercial Law Article was improper because, in considering the reasonableness of the fee request, the trial court did not make sufficient findings of fact with regard to the lodestar factors under this Rule. Hyundai Motor America v. Alley, 183 Md. App. 261, 960 A.2d 1257 (2008).

Contingency fee agreement not in writing. — As a matter of law an attorney violated conduct rules where he did not describe his contingency fee in writing, failed to deposit settlement funds into any account, failed to pay bills as he had promised, and failed to cooperate with the Grievance Commission. Att'y Griev. Comm'n v. Briscoe, 357 Md. 554, 745 A.2d 1037 (2000).

Attorney undertook representation of a client in a personal injury action without a written fee agreement, which was a violation of prior, similar Rule, which permitted a contingent fee, but required that its terms be communicated to the client in writing, stating the method by which the fee was to be determined, including the percent or percentages that would accrue to the lawyer in the event of settlement, trial or appeal, litigation and other expenses to be deducted from the recovery, and whether such expenses were to be deducted before or after the contingent fee was calculated. Att'y Griev. Comm'n v. Jeter, 365 Md. 279, 778 A.2d 390 (2001).

When an attorney agreed to modify his fee arrangement with clients to provide solely for a contingency fee, the attorney violated the prior, similar Rule by not reducing the agreement to writing. Att'y Griev. Comm'n v. Culver, 371 Md. 265, 808 A.2d 1251 (2002).

Attorney violated the prior, similar Rule where a client retained a firm with regard to his personal injury claim and then terminated that representation, and the terminated contingency fee arrangement with the firm did not meet the requirements for a written fee arrangement between the attorney, acting outside the firm, and the client, even though the attorney had an oral arrangement with the client for a contingency fee; further, the attorney did not create a written settlement statement. Att'y Griev. Comm'n v. Ellison, 384 Md. 688, 867 A.2d 259 (2005).

In an attorney disciplinary matter wherein the attorney was ordered disbarred, the attorney was found to have violated (c), among other rules of professional conduct, when he failed to memorialize a contingency fee agreement in writing, signed by the client. Implicit in that failure was the absence of memorialization of the method by which the fee was determined, the percentage(s) that would have accrued to the attorney in the event of settlement, and an allocation of responsibility for the litigation expenses. Att'y Griev. Comm'n v. Steinberg, 395 Md. 337, 910 A.2d 429 (2006).

Contingent fee not availaible for recovery on implied in law contracts. — Calculation of recovery may not be computed on the basis of a contingent fee in a case where the theory of recovery is that of a contract implied in law. Slick v. Reinecker, 154 Md. App. 312, 839 A.2d 784 (2003).

Contingent fee agreement not unreasonable. — A retainer agreement with contingent elements unknown at the time the agreement was made did not violate the prior, similar Rule, where the primary objective of the client was to obtain a managerial position, and thus the value of the case was greater than the monetary recovery made. Att'y Griev. Comm'n v. Pennington, 355 Md. 61, 733 A.2d 1029 (1999).

Contingency fee of 40% reasonable. — Attorney's 40% contingency fee agreement was reasonable where it was negotiated by sophisticated, experienced parties on both sides, was approved in advance by the court, and was not a contingency fee agreement where the attorney possessed undue leverage because of superior knowledge and sophistication. In re Mer-ry-Go-Round Enters., 244 Bankr. 327 (Bankr. D. Md. 2000).

No violation found — Bar counsel failed to show that an attorney had violated Md. R. Prof. Conduct 1.1, 1.3, 1.4(a) and (b), 1.5, 1.16(d), 3.1, 5.1, 5.3, and 8.4(a), (c), and (d) where it was possible to find, based on the testimony, that the attorney had relied on the clients' representations that they intended to handle the appeal pro se, and as a result, Bar counsel had failed to prove that the attorney had represented the two clients in an appeal. Att'y Griev. Comm'n v. Maignan, 402 Md. 39, 935 A.2d 409 (2007).

When a lawyer agreed with a client that the lawyer would be entitled to 15 percent of the value of any lost property the lawyer recovered for the client, and then a real estate broker charged the client a real estate commission after allegedly promising that no commission would be charged, the lawyer's 15 percent commission did not become an unreasonable fee, in violation of (a), nor did the lawyer, as a result, violate Md. Law. R. Prof. Conduct 8.4(c), because the lawyer never attempted to increase the lawyer's fees beyond the 15 percent contingent fee. Att'y Griev. Comm'n v. Edib, 415 Md. 696, 4 A.3d 957 (2010).

When a lawyer agreed with a client that the lawyer would be entitled to 15 percent of the value of any lost property the lawyer recovered for the client, and then a real estate broker charged the client a real estate commission after allegedly promising that no commission would be charged, the lawyer's 15 percent commission did not become an unreasonable fee, in violation of (a), nor did the lawyer, as a result, violate Md. Law. R. Prof. Conduct 8.4(c), because (1) the commission paid to the broker was not part of an analysis of whether the lawyer had a larger stake in the outcome of the undertaken services than the client, and (2) the client obtained substantially the result that the client desired. Att'y Griev. Comm'n v. Edib, 415 Md. 696, 4 A.3d 957 (2010).

When a lawyer agreed with a client that (1) the lawyer would serve as administrator of the client's deceased brother's estate, and (2) the lawyer would be entitled to 15 percent of the value of any lost property the lawyer recovered for the client, after which a real estate broker charged the client a real estate commission after allegedly promising that no commission would be charged, the lawyer's 15 percent commission did not become an unreasonable fee, in violation of (a), nor did the lawyer, as a result, violate Md. Law. R. Prof. Conduct 8.4(c), when the lawyer's fee allegedly exceeded a fee schedule for administrators in the jurisdiction in which the lawyer administered the estate because the lawyer was not administering an estate when the lawyer sold real property for the client since the property passed directly to the client upon the client's brother's death, outside of probate, so the fee schedule was not violated. Att'y Griev. Comm'n v. Edib, 415 Md. 696, 4 A.3d 957 (2010).

When a lawyer agreed with a client that (1) the lawyer would serve as administrator of the client's deceased brother's estate, and (2) the lawyer would be entitled to 15 percent of the value of any lost property the lawyer recovered for the client, after which a real estate broker charged the client a real estate commission after allegedly promising that no commission would be charged, the lawyer did not violate (a) or Md. Law. R. Prof. Conduct 8.4(c), when the lawyer's fee allegedly exceeded a Maryland fee schedule for estate administrators because the lawyer was not acting as an estate administrator when the sold the brother's properties for the client, since those properties passed to the client outside of probate, so the Maryland fee schedule for an estate administrator did not bear heavily on an analysis under (a)(3) as the sale of property and the administration of an estate, where conducted separately, were not sufficiently analogous legal services. Att'y Griev. Comm'n v. Edib, 415 Md. 696, 4 A.3d 957 (2010).

When a lawyer agreed with a client that (1) the lawyer would serve as administrator of the client's deceased brother's estate, and (2) the lawyer would be entitled to 15 percent of the value of any lost property the lawyer recovered for the client, after which a real estate broker charged the client a real estate commission after allegedly promising that no commission would be charged, the lawyer did not violate (a) or Md. Law. R. Prof. Conduct 8.4(c) on the theory that any fees charged by the lawyer for the liquidation of real estate in the brother's estate were unreasonable, since the lawyer performed no actual "legal services" in doing so, because this Rule made no mention of "legal services," and this Rule only implicated attorneys who made an agreement for, charged, or collected an unreasonable fee, so an attorney was entitled to a reasonable fee whether or not the attorney was performing "legal services" per se. Att'y Griev. Comm'n v. Edib, 415 Md. 696, 4 A.3d 957 (2010).

When a lawyer agreed with a client that (1) the lawyer would serve as administrator of the client's deceased brother's estate, and (2) the lawyer would be entitled to 15 percent of the value of any lost property the lawyer recovered for the client, after which a real estate broker charged the client a real estate commission after allegedly promising that no commission would be charged, the lawyer did not violate (a) or Md. Law. R. Prof. Conduct 8.4(c), based on a weighing of the applicable factors in (a), because the fact that the time and labor involved in dealing with the client's various requests, ranging from asset liquidation to

finding lost property, was unknown at the inception; that the lawyer achieved the client's desired result (the liquidation of real property); and, that the lawyer was particularly capable of performing the services required by the client, all bore on (a)(1), (4), and (7), respectively, and suggested that the lawyer's fee was reasonable. Att'y Griev. Comm'n v. Edib, 415 Md. 696, 4 A.3d 957 (2010).

One-year suspension was proper sanction. — Under the prior, similar Rules, attorney was suspended from the practice of law for a period of one year because of failure to cooperate with bar counsel in violation of Rule 8.1, performing services in an incompetent manner in violation of Rule 1.1, charging an excessive fee in violation of the prior, similar Rule, and engaging in conduct prejudicial to the administration of justice in violation of Rule 8.4. Att'y Griev. Comm'n v. Shaw, 363 Md. 1, 766 A.2d 1028 (2001).

Indefinite suspension was proper sanction. — Where respondent attorney's representation of four clients was marked by serious neglect and inattention; where he failed to return a fee which was unearned for a period of nine months; where he failed to timely remit funds he received on behalf of a client; where he failed to communicate with his clients; and in connection with the investigation of three of the complaints, where respondent failed to answer Bar Counsel's requests for information, the proper sanction was that the attorney be indefinitely suspended from the practice of law, with the right to apply for reinstatement after the suspension had been in effect for six months, conditioned upon his payment of all costs and upon the monitoring of respondent's practice. Att'y Griev. Comm'n v. David, 331 Md. 317, 628 A.2d 178 (1993).

Attorney's license to practice law was indefinitely suspended for his failure to provide competent, diligent, and communicative representation to his client, for charging unreasonable fees, for pursuing a frivolous proceeding, and for engaging in conduct prejudicial to the administration of justice. Att'y Griev. Comm'n v. Zdravkovich, 362 Md. 1, 762 A.2d 950 (2000).

Attorney was indefinitely suspended for violating, inter alia, (a), based on his bills to the complainant being excessive and unreasonable, consisting of billings that included extensive activity that would not further the goals of the client, constituting general background readings not billable to a client, and clerical and administrative tasks that should be a part of the attorney's general overhead. Att'y Griev. Comm'n v. Manger, 396 Md. 134, 913 A.2d 1 (2006).

Attorney was indefinitely suspended from the practice of law with the right to reapply for admission after one year, as the attorney's act of threatening to withdraw from representation of a client if the client refused to pay additional legal fees constituted a violation of Md. R. Prof. Conduct 1.15 and 1.16, and constituted conduct involving dishonesty, fraud, deceit or misrepresentation in violation of Md. R. Prof. Conduct 8.4, and the flat fee charged violated this Rule as the attorney did not provide sufficient services to earn the fee, the attorney violated Rules 16-604 and 16-609 by failing to place unearned attorney fees in his attorney trust account, and the attorney's failure to keep the client informed of the progress of the litigation violated Md. R. Prof. Conduct 1.4. Att'y Griev. Comm'n v. Lawson, 401 Md. 536, 933 A.2d 842 (2007).

In a reciprocal discipline action, the attorney, who admitted to the wrongdoing which led to a finding that D.C. R. Prof. Conduct 1.2(a), 1.4(a), 1.4(b), 1.4(c), 1.5(c), 1.15(a), 1.15(b), 1.15(c), and 8.4(d) had been violated based on the attorney's negligence misrepresentation of settlement funds in one case and interference with the administration of justice in another case, amounting to violations of Md. Law. R. Prof. Conduct Rules 1.2(a), 1.4(a)(2) and (3), 1.4(b), 1.5(c), 1.15(a), 1.15(d), 1.15(e), and 8.4(d), was indefinitely suspended in Maryland, with right to apply for readmission after reinstatement in the District in Columbia. Att'y Griev. Comm'n v. Thaxton, 415 Md. 341, — A.2d —, 1 A.3d 470 (2010).

Disbarment was proper sanction. — Because the attorney engaged in several acts of professional misconduct following an earlier suspension by accepting fees from clients but by failing to diligently to pursue their cases, the sanction of disbarment was held to be appropriate. Att'y Griev. Comm'n v. Fallin, 371 Md. 237, 808 A.2d 791 (2002).

Attorney was disbarred where he lacked a license to practice law in Virginia, failed to render any meaningful services in connection with the representation he had undertaken, and collected and retained a fee for the representation. Att'y Griev. Comm'n v. Velasquez, 380 Md. 651, 846 A.2d 422 (2004).

Attorney was disbarred, despite the mitigating factors of an absence of a prior disciplinary record and relative inexperience, for violating prior, similar Md. R. Prof. Conduct 1.5(c), 1.15(b) and (c), 8.1(b), and 8.4(c) and (d), and Md. R. 16-606 and 16-609 in his intentionally dishonest conduct towards a third-party assignee/healthcare provider during the representation of a client in a personal injury claim and Maryland Bar Counsel and its investigator in the course of investigating the assignee's complaint. Att'y Griev. Comm'n v. Ellison, 384 Md. 688, 867 A.2d 259 (2005).

Where the attorney, among other things, intentionally misappropriated client funds, forged a client's signature on a settlement check, lied under oath, and represented a client when the attorney was not licensed to do so, the attorney was disbarred for violating former, similar Md. R. Prof. Conduct 1.2(a), 1.3, 1.5(c), 1.15(a), (b), 3.3(a), 5.5, 8.1(a), (b), 8.4(a), (b), (c), (d), Md. R. 16-604, and §§ 10-304, -306 of the Business Occupations and Professions Article Att'y Griev. Comm'n v. Kapoor, 391 Md. 505, 894 A.2d 502 (2006).

Reciprocal discipline. — Attorney was disbarred for his handling of a medical malpractice case for a wife, her common-law husband, and her children, which had resulted in the attorney's disbarment in Georgia, for misconduct as defined in Maryland Rule 16-701(i), and for violating the Maryland counterparts of the Georgia State Bar Standards he had been found to have violated, more specifically, prior, similar Rules 8.4 (misconduct), 1.5 (fees), 1.7 (conflict of interest: general rule), and 1.15 (safekeeping property). Att'y Griev. Comm'n v. Roberson, 373 Md. 328, 818 A.2d 1059 (2003).

Applied in Att'y Griev. Comm'n v. Duvall, 384 Md. 234, 863 A.2d 291 (2004); Blondell v. Littlepage, 185 Md. App. 123, 968 A.2d 678 (2009), aff'd, 991 A.2d 80, 2010 Md. LEXIS 80 (Md. 2010); Friolo v. Frankel, — Md. App. —, — A.3d — (Sept. 7, 2011).

Stated in Wells Fargo Bank, N.A. v. Diamond Point Plaza L.P., 185 Md. App. 489, 971 A.2d 360 (2009), cert. denied, 410 Md. 559, 979 A.2d 707, 2009 Md. LEXIS 833 (2009).

Quoted in Att'y Griev. Comm'n v. Zuckerman, 386 Md. 341, 872 A.2d 693 (2005); Stevenson v. Branch Banking & Trust Corp., 159 Md. App. 620, 861 A.2d 735 (2004); Att'y Griev. Comm'n v. Christopher, 383 Md. 624, 861 A.2d 692 (2004); Att'y Griev. Comm'n v. Lee, 387 Md. 89, 874 A.2d 897 (2005); Att'y Griev. Comm'n v. Scroggs, 387 Md. 238, 874 A.2d 985 (2005); Att'y Griev. Comm'n v. Muhammad, — Md. —, — A.2d — (2005); Friolo v. Frankel, 403 Md. 443, 942 A.2d 1242 (2008); Att'y Griev. Comm'n v. Taylor, 405 Md. 697, 955 A.2d 755 (2008).

Cited in Att'y Griev. Comm'n v. Zuckerman, 386 Md. 341, 872 A.2d 693 (2005); Broccoli v. Echostar Communs. Corp., 229 F.R.D. 506 (D. Md. 2005); Att'y Griev. Comm'n v. Maignan, 390 Md. 287, 888 A.2d 344 (2005); Att'y Griev. Comm'n v. Lee, 393 Md. 385, 903 A.2d 360 (2006); Att'y Griev. Comm'n v. Muhammad, 395 Md. 676, 912 A.2d 588 (2006), cert. denied, 127 S. Ct. 2296, 2007 U.S. LEXIS 5292, 167 L. Ed. 2d 1103 (U.S. 2007); Att'y Griev. Comm'n v. Rees, 396 Md. 248, 913 A.2d 68 (2006); Att'y Griev. Comm'n v. McCulloch, 397 Md. 674, 919 A.2d 660 (2007); Att'y Griev. Comm'n v. Akpan, 405 Md. 277, 950 A.2d 820 (2008); Att'y Griev. Comm'n v. Snyder, 406 Md. 21, 956 A.2d 147 (2008); Att'y Griev. Comm'n v. Tanko, 408 Md. 404, 969 A.2d 1010 (2009); Louis Fireison & Assocs., P.A. v. Alkire, 195 Md. App. 461, 6 A.3d 945 (2010).

Rule 1.6. Confidentiality of Information.

(a) A lawyer shall not reveal information relating to representation of a client unless the client gives informed consent, the disclosure is impliedly authorized in order to carry out the representation, or the disclosure is permitted by paragraph (b).

(b) A lawyer may reveal information relating to the representation of a client to the extent the lawyer reasonably believes necessary:

(1) to prevent reasonably certain death or substantial bodily harm;

(2) to prevent the client from committing a crime or fraud that is reasonably certain to result in substantial injury to the financial interests or property of another and in furtherance of which the client has used or is using the lawyer's services;

(3) to prevent, mitigate, or rectify substantial injury to the financial interests or property of another that is reasonably certain to result or has resulted from the client's commission of a crime or fraud in furtherance of which the client has used the lawyer's services;

(4) to secure legal advice about the lawyer's compliance with these Rules, a court order or other law;

(5) to establish a claim or defense on behalf of the lawyer in a controversy between the lawyer and the client, to establish a defense to a criminal charge, civil claim, or disciplinary complaint against the lawyer based upon conduct in which the client was involved or to respond to allegations in any proceeding concerning the lawyer's representation of the client; or

(6) to comply with these Rules, a court order or other law.

COMMENT

[1] This Rule governs the disclosure by a lawyer of information relating to the representation of a client during the lawyer's representation of the client. See Rule 1.18 for the lawyer's duties with respect to information provided to the lawyer by a prospective client, Rule 1.9(c)(2) for the lawyer's duty not to reveal information relating to the lawyer's prior representation of a former client and Rules 1.8(b) and 1.9(c)(1) for the lawyer's duties with respect to the use of such information to the disadvantage of clients and former clients.

[2] A fundamental principle in the client-lawyer relationship is that, in the absence of the client's informed consent, the lawyer must not reveal information relating to the representation. See Rule 1.0(f) for the definition of informed consent. This contributes to the trust that is the hallmark of the client-lawyer relationship. The client is thereby encouraged to seek legal assistance and to communicate fully and frankly with the lawyer even as to embarrassing or legally damaging subject matter. The lawyer needs this information to represent the client effectively and, if necessary, to advise the client to refrain from wrongful conduct. Almost without exception, clients come to lawyers in order to determine their rights and what is, in the complex of laws and regulations, deemed to be legal and correct. Based upon experience, lawyers know that almost all clients follow the advice given, and the law is upheld.

[3] The principle of client-lawyer confidentiality is given effect by related bodies of law: the attorney-client privilege, the work product doctrine and the rule of confidentiality established in professional ethics. The attorney-client privilege and work-product doctrine apply in judicial and other proceedings in which a lawyer may be called as a witness or otherwise required to produce evidence concerning a client. The rule of client-lawyer confidentiality applies in situations other than those where evidence is sought from the lawyer through compulsion of law. The confidentiality rule, for example, applies not only to matters communicated in confidence by the client but also to all information relating to the representation, whatever its source. A lawyer may not disclose such information except as authorized or required by the Maryland Lawyers' Rules of Professional Conduct or other law. See also Scope.

[4] Paragraph (a) prohibits a lawyer from

revealing information relating to the representation of a client. This prohibition also applies to disclosures by a lawyer that do not in themselves reveal protected information but could reasonably lead to the discovery of such information by a third person. A lawyer's use of a hypothetical to discuss issues relating to the representation is permissible so long as there is no reasonable likelihood that the listener will be able to ascertain the identity of the client or the situation involved.

Implied Authority to Disclose. — [5] Except to the extent that the client's instructions or special circumstances limit that authority, a lawyer is impliedly authorized to make disclosures about a client when appropriate in carrying out the representation. In some situations, for example, a lawyer may be impliedly authorized to admit a fact that cannot properly be disputed, or to make a disclosure that facilitates a satisfactory conclusion to a matter. Lawyers in a firm may, in the course of the firm's practice, disclose to each other information relating to a client of the firm, unless the client has instructed that particular information be confined to specified lawyers.

Disclosure Adverse to Client. — [6] Although the public interest is usually best served by a strict rule requiring lawyers to preserve the confidentiality of information relating to the representation of their clients, the confidentiality rule is subject to limited exceptions. Paragraph (b), however, permits disclosure only to the extent the lawyer reasonably believes the disclosure is necessary to accomplish one of the purposes specified. Where practicable, the lawyer should first seek to persuade the client to take suitable action to obviate the need for disclosure. In any case, a disclosure adverse to the client's interest should be no greater than the lawyer reasonably believes necessary to accomplish the purpose. If the disclosure will be made in connection with a judicial proceeding, the disclosure should be made in a manner that limits access to the information to the tribunal or other persons having a need to know it and appropriate protective orders or other arrangements should be sought by the lawyer to the fullest extent practicable.

[7] Paragraph (b) permits, but does not require the disclosure of information relating to a client's representation to accomplish the purposes specified in paragraphs (b)(1) through (b)(6). In exercising the discretion conferred by this Rule, the lawyer may consider such factors as the nature of the lawyer's relationship with the client and with those who might be injured by the client, the lawyer's own involvement in the transaction and factors that may extenuate the conduct in question. A lawyer's decision not to disclose as permitted by paragraph (b) does not violate this Rule. Disclosure may be required, however, by other Rules regardless of whether the disclosure is permitted by Rule 1.6. See Rules 1.2(d), 3.3(a)(4), 4.1(b), 8.1 and 8.3. A lawyer representing an organization may in some circumstances be permitted to disclose information regardless of whether the disclosure is permitted by Rule 1.6(b). See Rule 1.13(c).

[8] Paragraph (b)(1) recognizes the overriding value of life and physical integrity and permits disclosure reasonably believed necessary to prevent reasonably certain death or substantial bodily harm. Such harm is reasonably certain to occur if it will be suffered imminently or if there is a present and substantial threat that a person will suffer such harm at a later date if the lawyer fails to take action necessary to eliminate the threat. Thus, a lawyer who knows that a client has accidentally discharged toxic waste into a town's water supply may reveal this information to the authorities if there is a present and substantial risk that a person who drinks the water will contract a life-threatening or debilitating disease, and the lawyer reasonably believes disclosure is necessary to eliminate the threat or reduce the number of victims.

[9] Paragraph (b)(2) is a limited exception to the rule of confidentiality that permits the lawyer to reveal information to the extent necessary to enable affected persons or appropriate authorities to prevent the client from committing a crime or a fraud, as defined in Rule 1.0(e), that is reasonably certain to result in substantial injury to the financial or property interests of another and in furtherance of which the client has used or is using the lawyer's services. Such a serious abuse of the client lawyer relationship by the client forfeits the protection of this Rule. The client can, of course, prevent such disclosure by refraining from the wrongful conduct. Although paragraph (b)(2) does not require the lawyer to reveal the client's misconduct, the lawyer may not counsel or assist the client in conduct the lawyer knows is criminal or fraudulent. See Rule 1.2(d). See also Rule 1.16 with respect to the lawyer's obligation or right to withdraw from the representation of the client in such circumstances. Where the client is an organization, the lawyer should consult Rule 1.13(b).

[10] Paragraph (b)(3) addresses the situation in which the lawyer does not learn of a client's criminal or fraudulent act in furtherance of which the lawyer's services were used until after the act has occurred. Although the client no longer has the option of preventing disclosure by refraining from the wrongful conduct, there will be situations in which the loss suffered by the affected person can be prevented, rectified or mitigated. In such situations, the lawyer may disclose information relating to the representation to the extent

necessary to enable the affected persons to prevent or mitigate reasonably certain losses or to attempt to recoup their losses. Paragraph (b)(3) does not apply when a person who has committed a crime or fraud thereafter employs a lawyer for representation concerning that offense.

[11] A lawyer's confidentiality obligations do not preclude a lawyer from securing confidential legal advice about the lawyer's personal responsibility to comply with these Rules, a court order or other law. In most situations, disclosing information to secure such advice will be impliedly authorized for the lawyer to carry out the representation. Even when the disclosure is not impliedly authorized, paragraph (b)(4) permits such disclosure because of the importance of a lawyer's compliance with the law.

Withdrawal. — [12] If the lawyer knows that the lawyer's services will be used by the client in materially furthering a course of criminal or fraudulent conduct, the lawyer must withdraw, as stated in Rule 1.16 (a)(1). After withdrawal the lawyer is required to refrain from making disclosure of the client's confidences, except as otherwise provided in Rule 1.6 or in other Rules.

[13] If the lawyer knows that despite the withdrawal the client is continuing in conduct that is criminal or fraudulent, and is making use of the fact that the lawyer was involved in the matter, the lawyer may have to take positive steps to avoid being held to have assisted the conduct. See Rules 1.2(d) and 4.1(b). In other situations not involving such assistance, the lawyer has discretion to make disclosure of otherwise confidential information only in accordance with Rules 1.6 and 1.13(c). Neither this Rule nor Rule 1.8(b) nor Rule 1.16(d) prevents the lawyer from giving notice of the fact of withdrawal, and the lawyer may also withdraw or disaffirm any opinion, document, affirmation, or the like.

Dispute Concerning Lawyer's Conduct. — [14] Where a legal claim or disciplinary charge alleges complicity of the lawyer in a client's conduct or other misconduct of the lawyer involving representation of the client, the lawyer may respond to the extent the lawyer reasonably believes necessary to establish a defense. The same is true with respect to a claim involving the conduct or representation of a former client. Such a charge can arise in a civil, criminal, disciplinary or other proceeding and can be based on a wrong allegedly committed by the lawyer against the client or on a wrong alleged by a third person, for example, a person claiming to have been defrauded by the lawyer and client acting together. The lawyer's right to respond arises when an assertion of such complicity has been made. Paragraph (b)(5) does not require the lawyer to await the commencement of an action or proceeding that charges such complicity, so that the defense may be established by responding directly to a third party who has made such an assertion. The right to defend also applies, of course, where a proceeding has been commenced.

[15] A lawyer entitled to a fee is permitted by paragraph (b)(5) to prove the services rendered in an action to collect it. This aspect of the rule expresses the principle that the beneficiary of a fiduciary relationship may not exploit it to the detriment of the fiduciary.

Disclosures Otherwise Required or Authorized. — [16] As noted in Comment 7, Rules 3.3(b) and 4.1(b) require disclosure in some circumstances regardless of whether the disclosure is permitted by Rule 1.6. Circumstances may be such that disclosure is required under other Rules, for example, Rule 1.2(d), in order to avoid assisting a client to perpetrate a crime or fraud.

[17] Other law may require that a lawyer disclose information about a client. Whether such a law supersedes Rule 1.6 is a question of law beyond the scope of these Rules. When disclosure of information relating to the representation appears to be required by other law, the lawyer must discuss the matter with the client to the extent required by Rule 1.4. If, however, the other law supersedes this Rule and requires disclosure, paragraph (b)(6) permits the lawyer to make such disclosures as are necessary to comply with the law.

[18] A lawyer may be ordered to reveal information relating to the representation of a client by a court or by another tribunal or governmental entity claiming authority pursuant to other law to compel the disclosure. Absent informed consent of the client to do otherwise, the lawyer should assert on behalf of the client all nonfrivolous claims that the order is not authorized by other law or that the information sought is protected against disclosure by the attorney-client privilege or other applicable law. In the event of an adverse ruling, the lawyer must consult with the client about the possibility of appeal to the extent required by Rule 1.4. Unless review is sought, however, paragraph (b)(6) permits the lawyer to comply with the court's order.

Acting Competently to Preserve Confidentiality. — [19] A lawyer must act competently to safeguard information relating to the representation of a client against inadvertent or unauthorized disclosure by the lawyer or other persons who are participating in the representation of the client or who are subject to the lawyer's supervision. See Rules 1.1, 5.1 and 5.3.

[20] When transmitting a communication that includes information relating to the representation of a client, the lawyer must take reasonable precautions to prevent the infor-

mation from coming into the hands of unintended recipients. This duty, however, does not require that the lawyer use special security measures if the method of communication affords a reasonable expectation of privacy. Special circumstances, however, may warrant special precautions. Factors to be considered in determining the reasonableness of the lawyer's expectation of confidentiality include the sensitivity of the information and the extent to which the privacy of the communication is protected by law or by a confidentiality agreement. A client may require the lawyer to implement special security measures not required by this Rule or may give informed consent to the use of a means of communication that would otherwise be prohibited by this Rule.

Former Client. — [21] The duty of confidentiality continues after the client-lawyer relationship has terminated. See Rule 1.9(c)(2). See Rule 1.9(c)(1) for the prohibition against using such information to the disadvantage of the former client.

Model Rules Comparison. — Rule 1.6 retains elements of former Rule 1.6 language, incorporates some changes from the Ethics 2000 Amendments to the ABA Model Rules, and incorporates further revisions.

Maryland Law Review. — For comment discussing the need for a consensus on the proper scope of the attorney-client privilege where a client attempts to use an attorney's services for fraudulent or illegal purposes, see 46 Md. L. Rev. 436 (1987).

For article, "Conducting Informal Discovery of a Party's Former Employees: Legal and Ethical Concerns and Constraints," see 51 Md. L. Rev. 239 (1992).

For survey, "Developments in Maryland Law, 1991-92," see 52 Md. L. Rev. 530 (1993).

For survey, "Developments in Maryland Law, 1992-93," see 53 Md. L. Rev. 616 (1994).

For a recent decision, "Blackwell v. Wyeth: It's Our Courtroom and We'll Frye (Only) if We Want to — The Maryland Court of Appeals's Unstated Adoption of Daubert," see 69 U. Md. L. Rev. 195 (2010).

University of Baltimore Law Forum. — For article, "Code of Ethics Revisited," see 19.2 U. Balt. Law Forum 14 (1989).

For note, "Recent Development: Newman v. State: An Attorney's Disclosure Under Rule 1.6 of the Maryland Rules of Professional Conduct Does Not Defeat a Client's Assertion of the Attorney-Client Privilege," see 35 U. Balt. L.F. 171 (2005).

For article, "The New Maryland Rules of Professional Conduct and Mediation: Perplexing Questions Answered and Perplexing Questions That Remain," see 36 U. Balt. L.F. 1 (2005).

The prior, similar Rule is permissive. — The prior, similar Rule is permissive; failure to reveal that which may be revealed, as opposed to that which must be revealed, is not a basis for disciplinary action. Att'y Griev. Comm'n v. Rohrback, 323 Md. 79, 591 A.2d 488 (1991).

Application. — This Rule prohibits disclosure of any information pertaining to the representation of a client, but does not operate to render information inadmissible at a judicial proceeding, as only communications subject to the attorney-client privilege cannot be disclosed under judicial compulsion. Newman v. State, 384 Md. 285, 863 A.2d 321 (2004).

Crime-fraud exception. — Crime-fraud exception to Md. R. Prof. Conduct 1.6 applies in the State of Maryland to exempt communications by a client to an attorney seeking advice or aid in furtherance of a crime or fraud. Newman v. State, 384 Md. 285, 863 A.2d 321 (2004).

Crime-fraud exception. — To trigger the crime-fraud exception to the attorney-client privilege, more than a mere statement of intent to commit a crime or fraud is required. The test is whether there is reasonable cause to believe that the attorney's services are sought to be utilized in furtherance of the activity in question. Newman v. State, 384 Md. 285, 863 A.2d 321 (2004).

Procedure. — Once the attorney-client privilege is invoked, a trial court should make a preliminary inquiry and hear testimony relative thereto out of the presence of the jury, looking at the surrounding facts and circumstances pursuant to Md. R. 5-104(c). At that preliminary hearing, which should be in camera, a trial court must decide, as a matter of law, whether the elements of the privilege are present and if so, whether the communication, absent an exception, is privileged without the disclosure of the communication at issue. Newman v. State, 384 Md. 285, 863 A.2d 321 (2004).

Burden of proof. — Party seeking the protection of the attorney-client privilege bears the burden of establishing its existence. Newman v. State, 384 Md. 285, 863 A.2d 321 (2004).

Public defenders. — Public defenders owe their clients the same duty to maintain confidentiality of information that all lawyers owe to their clients under this Rule. Harris v. Baltimore Sun Co., 330 Md. 595, 625 A.2d 941 (1993).

Only client has power to waive. — Where a third party is acting at the attorney's behest, the client's consent to the third party's continued presence does not constitute waiver of the privilege because the decision to include the third party was not made by the client, but rather by the attorney, as only the client has the power to waive the attorney-client privilege. Newman v. State, 384 Md. 285, 863 A.2d 321 (2004).

Allegations of breach insufficient. — With respect to allegations that an attorney communicated information to various government organizations, the plaintiff's amended complaint failed to allege facts which would explain how that attorney breached his duty by speaking to these government organizations; the bald allegation that the attorney's revelations to government agencies constituted a breach of duty was clearly insufficient. Alleco Inc. v. Harry & Jeanette Weinberg Found., Inc., 340 Md. 176, 665 A.2d 1038 (1995).

Prohibition against disclosure. — Under the structure of the prior, similar Rule, the lawyer who reveals confidential information, reasonably believing the revelation to be necessary in order to comply with other law, is not in violation of the general prohibition against disclosure and is not subject to professional discipline. Harris v. Baltimore Sun Co., 330 Md. 595, 625 A.2d 941 (1993).

A lawyer can never violate one part of the prior, similar Rule's prohibition against disclosure by refusing to produce requested public records, even if production would not violate a separate provision in the Rule allowing permissive disclosure. Harris v. Baltimore Sun Co., 330 Md. 595, 625 A.2d 941 (1993).

Attorney who failed to make any showing regarding how disclosure of bank records would have prejudiced the client whose funds the attorney was suspected of having misappropriated could not convincingly claim that confidentiality considerations precluded cooperation with a disciplinary investigation. Att'y Griev. Comm'n v. Zdravkovich, 381 Md. 680, 852 A.2d 82 (2004).

Failure to inform authorities of completed crimes. — When client revealed to attorney that he had operated a motor vehicle when his license was expired, and that, unbeknownst to the arresting officer, he had given a fictitious name when arrested on DWI charge, attorney had no duty to inform authorities, as

these were completed crimes; the attorney had a duty not to disclose them. Att'y Griev. Comm'n v. Rohrback, 323 Md. 79, 591 A.2d 488 (1991).

Previous work with corporation. — Attorney's previous work with corporation as labor attorney and labor relations lawyer which made him familiar with the corporation's personnel policies and procedures held sufficiently related to his representation of employee in an age discrimination case to work to the corporation's disadvantage; therefore attorney held disqualified from further participation in the age discrimination case. Stitz v. Bethlehem Steel Corp., 650 F. Supp. 914 (D. Md. 1987).

In-house counsel claims against former employers. — Motion of an in-house counsel's former employer, the Baltimore Police Department (BPD), to seal the record in a discrimination and retaliation action filed by counsel, the employee, was denied because attorney conduct was governed by Md. R. Prof. Conduct 1.6, a rule that allowed disclosure of client secrets to establish a claim or defense against the former client, and because the BPD waived the attorney-client privilege by producing the same documents to the Equal Employment Opportunity Commission. Hoffman v. Balt. Police Dep't, 379 F. Supp. 2d 778 (D. Md. 2005).

Disclosure of fee arrangement. — Whether a fee arrangement is protected from disclosure in judicial proceedings is governed by the attorney-client privilege, and not by the Rules of Professional Conduct. In re Criminal Investigation No. 1/242Q, 326 Md. 1, 602 A.2d 1220 (1992).

The attorney-client privilege is generally not violated by requiring disclosure of the payment of attorney's fees and expenses. In re Criminal Investigation No. 1/242Q, 326 Md. 1, 602 A.2d 1220 (1992).

Quoted in Att'y Griev. Comm'n v. Hall, 408 Md. 306, 969 A.2d 953 (2009).

Cited in Att'y Griev. Comm'n v. Muhammad, 395 Md. 676, 912 A.2d 588 (2006), cert. denied, 127 S. Ct. 2296, 2007 U.S. LEXIS 5292, 167 L. Ed. 2d 1103 (U.S. 2007); Att'y Griev. Comm'n v. Mba-Jonas, 402 Md. 334, 936 A.2d 839 (2007); Att'y Griev. Comm'n v. Tanko, 408 Md. 404, 969 A.2d 1010 (2009); Att'y Griev. Comm'n v. De La Paz, 418 Md. 534, 16 A.3d 181 (2011).

Rule 1.7. Conflict of Interest: General Rule.

(a) Except as provided in paragraph (b), a lawyer shall not represent a client if the representation involves a conflict of interest. A conflict of interest exists if:

(1) the representation of one client will be directly adverse to another client; or

(2) there is a significant risk that the representation of one or more clients will be materially limited by the lawyer's responsibilities to another client, a former client or a third person or by a personal interest of the lawyer.

(b) Notwithstanding the existence of a conflict of interest under paragraph (a), a lawyer may represent a client if:

(1) the lawyer reasonably believes that the lawyer will be able to provide competent and diligent representation to each affected client;

(2) the representation is not prohibited by law;

(3) the representation does not involve the assertion of a claim by one client against another client represented by the lawyer in the same litigation or other proceeding before a tribunal; and

(4) each affected client gives informed consent, confirmed in writing.

COMMENT

General Principles. — [1] Loyalty and independent judgment are essential elements in the lawyer's relationship to a client. Conflicts of interest can arise from the lawyer's responsibilities to another client, a former client or a third person or from the lawyer's own interests. For specific Rules regarding certain conflicts of interest, see Rule 1.8. For former client conflicts of interest, see Rule 1.9. For conflicts of interest involving prospective clients, see Rule 1.18. For definitions of "informed consent" and "confirmed in writing," see Rule 1.0(f) and (b).

[2] Resolution of a conflict of interest problem under this Rule requires the lawyer to: 1) clearly identify the client or clients; 2) determine whether a conflict of interest exists; 3) decide whether the representation may be undertaken despite the existence of a conflict, i.e., whether the conflict is consentable; and 4) if so, consult with the clients affected under paragraph (a) and obtain their informed consent, confirmed in writing. The clients affected under paragraph (a) include both of the clients referred to in paragraph (a)(1) and the one or more clients whose representation might be materially limited under paragraph (a)(2).

[3] A conflict of interest may exist before representation is undertaken, in which event the representation must be declined, unless the lawyer obtains the informed consent of each client under the conditions of paragraph (b). To determine whether a conflict of interest exists, a lawyer should adopt reasonable procedures, appropriate for the size and type of firm and practice, to determine in both litigation and non-litigation matters the persons and issues involved. See also Comment to Rule 5.1. Ignorance caused by a failure to institute such procedures will not excuse a lawyer's violation of this Rule. As to whether a client-lawyer relationship exists or, having once been established, is continuing, see Comment to Rule 1.3 and Scope.

[4] If a conflict arises after representation has been undertaken, the lawyer ordinarily must withdraw from the representation, unless the lawyer has obtained the informed consent of the client under the conditions of paragraph (b). See Rule 1.16. Where more than one client is involved, whether the lawyer may continue to represent any of the clients is determined both by the lawyer's ability to comply with duties owed to the former client and by the lawyer's ability to represent adequately the remaining client or clients, given the lawyer's duties to the former client. See Rule 1.9. See also Comments [5] and [29].

[5] Unforeseeable developments, such as changes in corporate and other organizational affiliations or the addition or realignment of parties in litigation, might create conflicts in the midst of a representation, as when a company sued by the lawyer on behalf of one client is bought by another client represented by the lawyer in an unrelated matter. Depending on the circumstances, the lawyer may have the option to withdraw from one of the representations in order to avoid the conflict. The lawyer must seek court approval where necessary and take steps to minimize harm to the clients. See Rule 1.16. The lawyer must continue to protect the confidences of the client from whose representation the lawyer has withdrawn. See Rule 1.9(c).

Identifying Conflicts of Interest: Directly Adverse. — [6] Loyalty to a current client prohibits undertaking representation directly adverse to that client without that client's informed consent. Thus, absent consent, a lawyer may not act as an advocate in one matter against a person the lawyer represents in some other matter, even when the matters are wholly unrelated. The client as to whom the representation is directly adverse is likely to feel betrayed, and the resulting damage to the client-lawyer relationship is likely to impair the lawyer's ability to represent the client effectively. In addition, the client on whose behalf the adverse representation is undertaken reasonably may fear that the lawyer will pursue that client's case less effectively out of deference to the other client, i.e., that the representation may be materially limited by the lawyer's interest in retaining the current client. Similarly, a directly adverse conflict may arise when a lawyer is required to cross-examine a client who appears as a witness in a lawsuit involving another client, as when the testimony will be damaging to the client who is represented in the lawsuit. On the other hand, simultaneous representation in unrelated matters of clients whose interests are only economically adverse, such as representation of competing economic enterprises in unrelated litigation, does not ordinarily constitute a conflict of interest and thus may not require consent of the respective clients.

[7] Directly adverse conflicts can also arise in transactional matters. For example, if a lawyer is asked to represent the seller of a business in negotiations with a buyer represented by the lawyer, not in the same transaction but in another, unrelated matter, the lawyer could not undertake the representation without the informed consent of each client.

Identifying Conflicts of Interest: Material Limitation. — [8] Even where there is no direct adverseness, a conflict of interest exists if there is a significant risk that a lawyer's ability to consider, recommend or carry out an appropriate course of action for the client will be materially limited as a result of the lawyer's other responsibilities or interests. For example, a lawyer asked to represent several individuals seeking to form a joint venture is likely to be materially limited in the lawyer's ability to recommend or advocate all possible positions that each might take because of the lawyer's duty of loyalty to the others. The conflict in effect forecloses alternatives that would otherwise be available to the client. The mere possibility of subsequent harm does not itself require disclosure and consent. The critical questions are the likelihood that a difference in interests will eventuate and, if it does, whether it will materially interfere with the lawyer's independent professional judgment in considering alternatives or foreclose courses of action that reasonably should be pursued on behalf of the client.

Lawyer's Responsibilities to Former Clients and Other Third Persons. — [9] In addition to conflicts with other current clients, a lawyer's duties of loyalty and independence may be materially limited by responsibilities to former clients under Rule 1.9 or by the lawyer's responsibilities to other persons, such as fiduciary duties arising from a lawyer's service as a trustee, executor or corporate director.

Personal Interest Conflicts. — [10] The lawyer's own interests should not be permitted to have an adverse effect on representation of a client. For example, if the probity of a lawyer's own conduct in a transaction is in serious question, it may be difficult or impossible for the lawyer to give a client detached advice. Similarly, when a lawyer has discussions concerning possible employment with an opponent of the lawyer's client, or with a law firm representing the opponent, such discussions could materially limit the lawyer's representation of the client. In addition, a lawyer may not allow related business interests to affect representation, for example, by referring clients to an enterprise in which the lawyer has an undisclosed financial interest. See Rule 1.8 for specific Rules pertaining to a number of personal interest conflicts, including business transactions with clients. See also Rule 1.10 (personal interest conflicts under Rule 1.7 ordinarily are not imputed to other lawyers in a law firm).

[11] When lawyers representing different clients in the same matter or in substantially related matters are closely related by blood or marriage, there may be a significant risk that client confidences will be revealed and that the lawyer's family relationship will interfere with both loyalty and independent professional judgment. As a result, each client is entitled to know of the existence and implications of the relationship between the lawyers before the lawyer agrees to undertake the representation. Thus, a lawyer related to another lawyer, e.g., as parent, child, sibling or spouse, ordinarily may not represent a client in a matter where that lawyer is representing another party, unless each client gives informed consent. The disqualification arising from a close family relationship is personal and ordinarily is not imputed to members of firms with whom the lawyers are associated. See Rule 1.10.

[12] A sexual relationship with a client, whether or not in violation of criminal law, will create an impermissible conflict between the interests of the client and those of the lawyer if (1) the representation of the client would be materially limited by the sexual relationship and (2) it is unreasonable for the lawyer to believe the lawyer can provide competent and diligent representation. Under those circumstances, informed consent by the client is ineffective. See also Rule 8.4.

Interest of Person Paying for a Lawyer's Service. — [13] A lawyer may be paid from a source other than the client, including a co-client, if the client is informed of that fact and consents and the arrangement does not compromise the lawyer's duty of loyalty or independent judgment to the client. See Rule 1.8(f). If acceptance of the payment from any other source presents a significant risk that the lawyer's representation of the client will be materially limited by the lawyer's own interest in accommodating the person paying the lawyer's fee or by the lawyer's responsibilities to a payer who is also a co-client, then the lawyer must comply with the requirements of paragraph (b) before accepting the representation, including determining whether the conflict is consentable and, if so, that the client has adequate information about the material risks of the representation.

Prohibited Representations. [14] Ordinarily, clients may consent to representation notwithstanding a conflict. However, as indicated in paragraph (b), some conflicts are nonconsentable, meaning that the lawyer involved cannot properly ask for such agreement or provide representation on the basis of the client's consent. When the lawyer is representing more than one client, the question of consentability must be resolved as to each client.

[15] Consentability is typically determined by considering whether the interests of the clients will be adequately protected if the clients are permitted to give their informed consent to representation burdened by a conflict of interest. Thus, under paragraph (b)(1), representation is prohibited if in the circumstances the lawyer cannot reasonably conclude that the lawyer will be able to provide competent and diligent representation. See Rule 1.1 (competence) and Rule 1.3 (diligence).

[16] Paragraph (b)(2) describes conflicts that are nonconsentable because the representation is prohibited by applicable law. For example, in some states substantive law provides that the same lawyer may not represent more than one defendant in a capital case, even with the consent of the clients, and under federal criminal statutes certain representations by a former government lawyer are prohibited, despite the informed consent of the former client. In addition, decisional law in some states limits the ability of a governmental client, such as a municipality, to consent to a conflict of interest.

[17] Paragraph (b)(3) describes conflicts that are nonconsentable because of the institutional interest in vigorous development of each client's position when the clients are aligned directly against each other in the same litigation or other proceeding before a tribunal. Whether clients are aligned directly against each other within the meaning of this paragraph requires examination of the context of the proceeding. Although this paragraph does not preclude a lawyer's multiple representation of adverse parties to a mediation (because mediation is not a proceeding before a "tribunal" under Rule 1.0(o)), such representation may be precluded by paragraph (b)(1).

Informed Consent. — [18] Informed consent requires that each affected client be aware of the relevant circumstances and of the material and reasonably foreseeable ways that the conflict could have adverse effects on the interests of that client. See Rule 1.0(f) (informed consent). The information required depends on the nature of the conflict and the nature of the risks involved. When representation of multiple clients in a single matter is undertaken, the information must include the implications of the common representation, including possible effects on loyalty, confidentiality and the attorney-client privilege and the advantages and risks involved. See Comments [30] and [31] (effect of common representation on confidentiality).

[19] Under some circumstances it may be impossible to make the disclosure necessary to obtain consent. For example, when the lawyer represents different clients in related matters and one of the clients refuses to consent to the disclosure necessary to permit the other client to make an informed decision, the lawyer cannot properly ask the latter to consent. In some cases the alternative to common representation can be that each party may have to obtain separate representation with the possibility of incurring additional costs. These costs, along with the benefits of securing separate representation, are factors that may be considered by the affected client in determining whether common representation is in the client's interests.

Consent Confirmed in Writing. — [20] Paragraph (b) requires the lawyer to obtain the informed consent of the client, confirmed in writing. Such a writing may consist of a document executed by the client or one that the lawyer promptly records and transmits to the client following an oral consent. See Rule 1.0(b). See also Rule 1.0(p) (writing includes electronic transmission). If it is not feasible to obtain or transmit the writing at the time the client gives informed consent, then the lawyer must obtain or transmit it within a reasonable time thereafter. See Rule 1.0(b). The requirement of a writing does not supplant the need in most cases for the lawyer to talk with the client, to explain the risks and advantages, if any, of representation burdened with a conflict of interest, as well as reasonably available alternatives, and to afford the client a reasonable opportunity to consider the risks and alternatives and to raise questions and concerns. Rather, the writing is required in order to impress upon clients the seriousness of the decision the client is being asked to make and to avoid disputes or ambiguities that might later occur in the absence of a writing.

Revoking Consent. — [21] A client who has given consent to a conflict may revoke the consent and, like any other client, may terminate the lawyer's representation at any time. Whether revoking consent to the client's own representation precludes the lawyer from continuing to represent other clients depends on the circumstances, including the nature of the conflict, whether the client revoked consent because of a material change in circumstances, the reasonable expectations of the other client and whether material detriment to the other clients or the lawyer would result.

Consent to Future Conflict. — [22] Whether a lawyer may properly request a client to waive conflicts that might arise in the future is subject to the test of paragraph (b). The effectiveness of such waivers is generally determined by the extent to which the client reasonably understands the material risks that the waiver entails. The more comprehensive the explanation of the types of future representations that might arise and the actual and reasonably foreseeable adverse consequences of those representations, the greater the likelihood that the client will have the requisite understanding. Thus, if the client agrees to consent to a particular type of conflict with which the client is already familiar, then the consent ordinarily will be effective with regard to that type of conflict. If the consent is general and open-ended, then the consent ordinarily will be ineffective, because it is not reasonably likely that the client will have understood the material risks involved. On the other hand, if the client is an experienced user of the legal services involved and is reasonably informed regarding the risk that a conflict may arise, such consent is more likely to be effective, particularly if, e.g., the client is independently represented by other counsel in giving consent and the consent is limited to future conflicts unrelated to the subject of the representation. In any case, advance consent cannot be effective if the circumstances that materialize in the future are such as would make the conflict nonconsentable under paragraph (b).

Conflicts in Litigation. — [23] Paragraph (b)(3) prohibits representation of opposing parties in the same litigation, regardless of the clients' consent. On the other hand, simultaneous representation of parties whose interests in litigation may conflict, such as coplaintiffs or codefendants, is governed by paragraph (a)(2). A conflict may exist by reason of substantial discrepancy in the parties' testimony, incompatibility in positions in relation to an opposing party or the fact that there are substantially different possibilities of settlement of the claims or liabilities in question. Such conflicts can arise in criminal cases as well as civil. The potential for conflict of interest in representing multiple defendants in a criminal case is so grave that ordinarily a lawyer should decline to represent more than one codefendant. On the other hand, common representation of persons having similar interests in civil litigation is proper if the requirements of paragraph (b) are met.

[24] Ordinarily a lawyer may take inconsistent legal positions in different tribunals at different times on behalf of different clients. The mere fact that advocating a legal position on behalf of one client might create precedent adverse to the interests of a client represented by the lawyer in an unrelated matter does not create a conflict of interest. A conflict of interest exists, however, if there is a significant risk that a lawyer's action on behalf of one client will materially limit the lawyer's effectiveness in representing another client in a different case; for example, when a decision favoring one client will create a precedent likely to seriously weaken the position taken on behalf of the other client. Factors relevant in determining whether the clients need to be advised of the risk include: where the cases are pending, whether the issue is substantive or procedural, the temporal relationship between the matters, the significance of the issue to the immediate and long-term interests of the clients involved and the clients' reasonable expectations in retaining the lawyer. If there is significant risk of material limitation, then absent informed consent of the affected clients, the lawyer must refuse one of the representations or withdraw from one or both matters.

[25] When a lawyer represents or seeks to represent a class of plaintiffs or defendants in a class-action lawsuit, unnamed members of the class are ordinarily not considered to be clients of the lawyer for purposes of applying paragraph (a)(1) of this Rule. Thus, the lawyer does not typically need to get the consent of such a person before representing a client suing the person in an unrelated matter. Similarly, a lawyer seeking to represent an opponent in a class action does not typically need the consent of an unnamed member of the class whom the lawyer represents in an unrelated matter.

Nonlitigation Conflicts. — [26] Conflicts of interest under paragraphs (a)(1) and (a)(2) arise in contexts other than litigation. For a discussion of directly adverse conflicts in transactional matters, see Comment [7]. Relevant factors in determining whether there is significant potential for material limitation include the duration and intimacy of the lawyer's relationship with the client or clients involved, the functions being performed by the lawyer, the likelihood that disagreements will arise and the likely prejudice to the client from the conflict. The question is often one of proximity and degree. See Comment [8].

[27] For example, conflict questions may arise in estate planning and estate administration. A lawyer may be called upon to prepare wills for several family members, such as husband and wife, and, depending upon the circumstances, a conflict of interest may be

present. In estate administration the identity of the client may be unclear under the law of a particular jurisdiction. Under one view, the client is the fiduciary; under another view the client is the estate or trust, including its beneficiaries. In order to comply with conflict of interest rules, the lawyer should make clear the lawyer's relationship to the parties involved.

[28] Whether a conflict is consentable depends on the circumstances. For example, a lawyer may not represent multiple parties to a negotiation whose interests are fundamentally antagonistic to each other, but common representation is permissible where the clients are generally aligned in interest even though there is some difference in interest among them. Thus, a lawyer may seek to establish or adjust a relationship between clients on an amicable and mutually advantageous basis; for example, in helping to organize a business in which two or more clients are entrepreneurs, working out the financial reorganization of an enterprise in which two or more clients have an interest or arranging a property distribution in settlement of an estate. The lawyer seeks to resolve potentially adverse interests by developing the parties' mutual interests. Otherwise, each party might have to obtain separate representation, with the possibility of incurring additional cost, complication or even litigation. Given these and other relevant factors, the clients may prefer that the lawyer act for all of them.

Special Considerations in Common Representation. — [29] In considering whether to represent multiple clients in the same matter, a lawyer should be mindful that if the common representation fails because the potentially adverse interests cannot be reconciled, the result can be additional cost, embarrassment and recrimination. Ordinarily, the lawyer will be forced to withdraw from representing all of the clients if the common representation fails. In some situations, the risk of failure is so great that multiple representation is plainly impossible. For example, a lawyer cannot undertake common representation of clients where contentious litigation or negotiations between them are imminent or contemplated. Moreover, because the lawyer is required to be impartial between commonly represented clients, representation of multiple clients is improper when it is unlikely that impartiality can be maintained. Generally, if the relationship between the parties has already assumed antagonism, the possibility that the clients' interests can be adequately served by common representation is not very good. Other relevant factors are whether the lawyer subsequently will represent both parties on a continuing basis and whether the situation involves creating or terminating a relationship between the parties.

[29.1] Rule 1.7 may not apply to an attorney appointed by a court to serve as a Child's Best Interest Attorney in the same way that it applies to other attorneys. For example, because the Child's Best Interest Attorney is not bound to advocate a client's objective, siblings with conflicting views may not pose a conflict of interest for a Child's Best Interest Attorney, provided that the attorney determines the siblings' best interests to be consistent. A Child's Best Interest Attorney should advocate for the children's best interests and ensure that each child's position is made a part of the record, even if that position is different from the position that the attorney advocates. See Md. Rule 9-205.1 and Appendix to the Maryland Rules: *Maryland Guidelines for Practice for Court-appointed Lawyers Representing Children in Cases Involving Child Custody or Child Access.*

[30] A particularly important factor in determining the appropriateness of common representation is the effect on client-lawyer confidentiality and the attorney-client privilege. With regard to the attorney-client privilege, the prevailing rule is that, as between commonly represented clients, the privilege does not attach. Hence, it must be assumed that if litigation eventuates between the clients, the privilege will not protect any such communications, and the clients should be so advised.

[31] As to the duty of confidentiality, continued common representation will almost certainly be inadequate if one client asks the lawyer not to disclose to the other client information relevant to the common representation. This is so because the lawyer has an equal duty of loyalty to each client, and each client has the right to be informed of anything bearing on the representation that might affect that client's interests and the right to expect that the lawyer will use that information to that client's benefit. See Rule 1.4. The lawyer should, at the outset of the common representation and as part of the process of obtaining each client's informed consent, advise each client that information will be shared and that the lawyer will have to withdraw if one client decides that some matter material to the representation should be kept from the other. In limited circumstances, it may be appropriate for the lawyer to proceed with the representation when the clients have agreed, after being properly informed, that the lawyer will keep certain information confidential. For example, the lawyer may reasonably conclude that failure to disclose one client's trade secrets to another client will not adversely affect representation involving a joint venture between the clients and agree to keep that infor-

mation confidential with the informed consent of both clients.

[32] When seeking to establish or adjust a relationship between clients, the lawyer should make clear that the lawyer's role is not that of partisanship normally expected in other circumstances and, thus, that the clients may be required to assume greater responsibility for decisions than when each client is separately represented. Any limitations on the scope of the representation made necessary as a result of the common representation should be fully explained to the clients at the outset of the representation. See Rule 1.2(c).

[33] Subject to the above limitations, each client in the common representation has the right to loyal and diligent representation and the protection of Rule 1.9 concerning the obligations to a former client. The client also has the right to discharge the lawyer as stated in Rule 1.16.

Organizational Clients. — [34] A lawyer who represents a corporation or other organization does not, by virtue of that representation, necessarily represent any constituent or affiliated organization, such as a parent or subsidiary. See Rule 1.13(a). Thus, the lawyer for an organization is not barred from accepting representation adverse to an affiliate in an unrelated matter, unless the circumstances are such that the affiliate should also be considered a client of the lawyer, there is an understanding between the lawyer and the organizational client that the lawyer will avoid representation adverse to the client's affiliates, or the lawyer's obligations to either the organizational client or the new client are likely to limit materially the lawyer's representation of the other client.

[35] A lawyer for a corporation or other organization who is also a member of its board of directors should determine whether the responsibilities of the two roles may conflict. The lawyer may be called on to advise the corporation in matters involving actions of the directors. Consideration should be given to the frequency with which such situations may arise, the potential intensity of the conflict, the effect of the lawyer's resignation from the board and the possibility of the corporation's obtaining legal advice from another lawyer in such situations. If there is material risk that the dual role will compromise the lawyer's independence of professional judgment, the lawyer should not serve as a director or should cease to act as the corporation's lawyer when conflicts of interest arise. The lawyer should advise the other members of the board that in some circumstances matters discussed at board meetings while the lawyer is present in the capacity of director might not be protected by the attorney-client privilege and that conflict of interest considerations might require the lawyer's recusal as a director or might require the lawyer and the lawyer's firm to decline representation of the corporation in a matter.

Model Rules Comparison. — Rule 1.7 is substantially similar to the language of the Ethics 2000 Amendments to the ABA Model Rules of Professional Conduct except for omitting the word "concurrent" in Rule 1.7(a) and (b) and Comment [1], and retaining most of existing Maryland language in Comment [12].

Effect of amendments. — The 2007 amendment added Comment [29.1].

Maryland Law Review. — For note discussing whether, under third-party beneficiary theory, a nonclient can sue attorney for negligent misrepresentation without proof of privity of contract, see 16 U. Balt. L. Rev. 354 (1987).

University of Baltimore Law Forum. — For note, "Recent Development: Attorney Grievance Commission of Maryland v. Culver: Attorney's Sexual Relationship with his Client Violated the Maryland Rules of Professional Conduct," see 35 U. Balt. L.F. 52 (2004).

For article, "The New Maryland Rules of Professional Conduct and Mediation: Perplexing Questions Answered and Perplexing Questions That Remain," see 36 U. Balt. L.F. 1 (2005).

Office of public defender. — Attorneys employed by a public defender who are required to practice their profession side by side are, literally and figuratively, members of a "firm"; where the practice of each attorney is so separated from the other's that the interchange of confidential information can be avoided or where it is possible to create such a separation, there need be no relationship between them analogous to that of a law firm and there would be no inherent ethical bar to their representation of antagonistic interests. Graves v. State, 94 Md. App. 649, 619 A.2d 123 (1993), rev'd on other grounds, 334 Md. 30, 637 A.2d 1197 (1994).

Public defender (or assistant public defender representing a particular defendant) is required to do no more than merely ascertain that there is hostility or adversity between defendants represented by his office before filing a motion to withdraw; it is also his duty to ascertain, as a condition precedent to the filing of that motion, that counseling of such defendants by different members of the staff cannot be done without conflict of interest.

Graves v. State, 94 Md. App. 649, 619 A.2d 123 (1993), rev'd on other grounds, 334 Md. 30, 637 A.2d 1197 (1994).

Where a public defender concludes that a potential conflict of interest is such that it is required that other counsel be assigned, the case may be assigned to a panel attorney, or the court may be requested to assign counsel; in addition, the case may be transferred to another district public defender's office. Graves v. State, 94 Md. App. 649, 619 A.2d 123 (1993), rev'd on other grounds, 334 Md. 30, 637 A.2d 1197 (1994).

The public defender may make changes within a specific office that could sufficiently insulate, from each other, assistant public defenders who operate from the same office and who are simultaneously representing co-defendants. These institutional changes could include early screening of the cases, structural and procedural separation of the units, assignments to completely separate units in the same office, and other innovations in the handling of cases involving co-defendants that would be conducive to the avoidance of any conflict of interest. Graves v. State, 94 Md. App. 649, 619 A.2d 123 (1993), rev'd on other grounds, 334 Md. 30, 637 A.2d 1197 (1994).

Administrative judge erred in failing to grant a postponement to allow defense counsel a reasonable time to resolve an issue because there existed a conflict of interest when a public defender represented defendant while another attorney from the public defender's district office was representing a person in an unrelated proceeding whom defendant contended was the actual guilty party, and defense counsel requested a continuance prior to trial. Defendant's right to the effective assistance of counsel under U.S. Const. amend. VI and Md. Const. Decl. Rights art. 21 was thus violated by the conflict of interest; furthermore, because an actual conflict existed, the administrative judge had a duty to determine whether defendant waived the conflict before the judge allowed defense counsel to continue her representation of defendant. Duvall v. State, 399 Md. 210, 923 A.2d 81 (2007).

County Attorney. — An attorney in the office of the County Attorney may represent a county official or agency before the County Board of Appeals while another attorney in the same office serves as counsel to the Board; however, procedures should be employed to separate the two roles and to ensure the fairness of proceedings before the Board. 87 Op. Att'y Gen. 126 (Aug. 27, 2002).

Representation not simultaneous. — When representation is not simultaneous, this Rule's prohibition is not absolute; a lawyer is not necessarily prohibited from representing a client whose interests are adverse to a former client. Gaumer v. McDaniel, 811 F. Supp. 1113 (D. Md. 1991), aff'd, 23 F.3d 400 (4th Cir. 1994).

Representation of multiple defendants. — Representation of multiple defendants in a criminal case by the same attorney or law partners is not per se an actual conflict of interest; the potential, however, for conflict of interest is present. Graves v. State, 94 Md. App. 649, 619 A.2d 123 (1993), rev'd on other grounds, 334 Md. 30, 637 A.2d 1197 (1994).

The trial court had no affirmative duty to inquire or determine whether there was a conflict of interest in joint representation where there was no objection by defense counsel to the multiple representation and where the conflict, if any, was merely a potential one. Pugh v. State, 103 Md. App. 624, 654 A.2d 888 (1995).

An attorney's contact with his client's represented criminal codefendant was deemed a violation of the prior, similar Rule and resulted in disbarment. Att'y Griev. Comm'n v. Kent, 337 Md. 361, 653 A.2d 909 (1995).

As a general rule, whenever one co-defendant makes a statement which is exculpatory or inculpatory of a co-defendant, conflict of interest prevents them being represented by the same attorney. Lettley v. State, 358 Md. 26, 746 A.2d 392 (2000).

Representation by members of single firm. — Representation of co-defendants by members of a single law firm is treated the same, for purposes of conflict of interest analysis, as representation of co-defendants by one attorney. Graves v. State, 94 Md. App. 649, 619 A.2d 123 (1993), rev'd on other grounds, 334 Md. 30, 637 A.2d 1197 (1994).

Consent to multiple representation. — Where the record revealed an affidavit from both represented parties, stating that they were apprised of the alleged conflict that could arise concerning the planned scope of employment defense, and where they consented to the continued joint representation by counsel, any conflict of interest that may have occurred was consented to by the parties. Fearnow v. C & P Tel. Co., 104 Md. App. 1, 655 A.2d 1 (1995), rev'd on other grounds, 342 Md. 363, 676 A.2d 65 (1996).

Appointment of substitute counsel. — Although it was proper for court to prohibit attorney from representing the corporation, the directors and the majority stockholders because of a conflict of interest, it was error for the court to appoint counsel for the corporation and prohibit the corporation from selecting its own counsel. Tydings v. Berk Enters., 80 Md. App. 634, 565 A.2d 390 (1989).

Requirement that borrower use and pay for specific lawyer at settlement. — Pertinent rules of legal ethics do not bar a lender from requiring that a specific settlement lawyer be used and that the borrower pay for the lawyer's settlement services. 72 Op. Att'y Gen. 72 (1987).

Separation agreement, or divorce. — Where husband and wife are contemplating a separation agreement or divorce, it should be obvious to an attorney that he cannot adequately represent the interests of both parties; attorney should not attempt to represent both parties in these matters. Hale v. Hale, 74 Md. App. 555, 539 A.2d 247, cert. denied, 313 Md. 30, 542 A.2d 857 (1988).

Sexual relationship with client. — Attorney's representation of a client in her employment discrimination action created a conflict of interests because the attorney's sexual relationship with the client had the potential to prejudice her employment discrimination claim; if the attorney's the sexual relationship with the client became known to the client's former employer, it was likely that the attorney would have been requested to provide potentially damaging testimony that could have harmed any chance that the client could have had in succeeding on her employment discrimination claim. Att'y Griev. Comm'n v. Hall, 408 Md. 306, 969 A.2d 953 (2009).

Lawyer as potential witness in the action. — A lawyer's acceptance of a representation in a matter where it was likely that he would be required to testify, and that his testimony would likely be harmful to his client, constituted violations of prior, similar Rules 1.7 and 3.7. Klupt v. Krongard, 126 Md. App. 179, 728 A.2d 727 (1999), cert. denied, 355 Md. 612, 735 A.2d 1107 (1999).

Representation of indigent defendants. — If the public defender's office is unable to represent an indigent defendant because of a conflict, and if funds for the provision of panel attorneys are unavailable, the defendant would be represented by an attorney appointed by the court. To the extent of available funds, the county in which the prosecution is brought would be responsible for paying the fees set by the court for the appointed attorney's services. 76 Op. Att'y Gen. 341 (October 4, 1991).

Attorney's reliance on advice of counsel from a lawyer not admitted to practice in the State of Maryland was not a defense to her violations of Md. Law. R. Prof. Conduct 8.4(c) and (d), or to Md. Law. R. Prof. Conduct 1.7(d), or, for that matter, any of her conduct in the case. Att'y Griev. Comm'n v. Pennington, 387 Md. 565, 876 A.2d 642 (2005).

Attorney's reliance on advice of counsel from a lawyer not admitted to practice in the State of Maryland was not a defense to her violations of Md. Law. R. Prof. Conduct 8.4(c) and (d), or to Md. Law. R. Prof. Conduct 1.7(d), or, for that matter, any of her conduct in the case. Att'y Griev. Comm'n v. Pennington, 387 Md. 565, 876 A.2d 642 (2005).

Conflict of interest not found — An actual conflict of interest was not shown where appellants' defenses were not necessarily incompatible or inconsistent. Pugh v. State, 103 Md. App. 624, 654 A.2d 888 (1995).

Motion for disqualification was denied because defendants failed to raise the conflict of interest in a timely manner and the attorneys did not represent a new client, but rather, represented their longstanding clients against the buyer of the clients' business. Gross v. SES Americom, Inc., 307 F. Supp. 2d 719 (D. Md. 2004).

Fact that the State's Attorney prosecuting defendant had, several years before, represented defendant in two matters as a public defender did not automatically create a conflict of interest per se that required disqualification; the trial court appropriately exercised its discretion in conducting a thorough inquiry into whether the matters were substantially similar, finding that they were not, even though two controlled substance cases were involved, ascertained that the prosecutor had little recollection of the earlier cases, and assured that no confidential information gleaned in prior matters was used for impeachment purposes, before properly determining that disqualification was not required. Gatewood v. State, 388 Md. 526, 880 A.2d 322 (2005).

Plaintiff's attorney would not be disqualified because the attorney, while he worked for the city, was not substantially and personally involved in the termination of plaintiff, the attorney only spent a hour on a draft of a memorandum regarding the ability of the city to discipline and fire command level officers, and the police commissioners had waived any attorney-client privilege regarding the memorandum because they produced it during discovery. Furthermore, the memorandum would not be sufficient to overcome the former commissioner's defense of qualified immunity, so there would be no need for the attorney to testify regarding the former commissioner's knowledge of the memorandum at the time he terminated plaintiff. Franklin v. Clark, 454 F. Supp. 2d 356 (D. Md. 2006).

Hearing judge's conclusions that an attorney violated Md. R. Prof. Conduct 1.1, 3.1, 3.2, 3.3(a), 4.4, 8.2(a), and 8.4(c) and (d) but not Rule 1.7(b) were supported by clear and convincing evidence because the attorney reasonably believed that he could provide competent and diligent representation while serving as his client's counsel and real estate broker; there was no showing that the attorney's role as broker posed a significant risk of materially limiting his ability to consider, recommend, or carry out an appropriate course of action for his client or that it prohibited his ability to give detached legal advice. Att'y Griev. Comm'n v. McClain, 406 Md. 1, 956 A.2d 135

(2008), cert. denied, 129 S. Ct. 1691, 2009 U.S. LEXIS 2433, 173 L. Ed. 2d 1036 (U.S. 2009).

Attorney was sanctioned by a public reprimand for technically violating Rule 16-609 regarding prohibited transactions as a result of a negligent clerical error involving depositing some of his ex-girlfriend's funds into his operating account instead of his firm's escrow account, which error was corrected upon discovery and was not wilful. The Court of Appeals of Maryland further upheld the trial judge's finding of fact that no attorney client relationship existed between the attorney and his girlfriend to support the other violations asserted against him since he never charged his ex-girlfriend a fee for his services and was only helping her while she received treatment for her alcohol abuse. Att'y Griev. Comm'n v. Shoup, 410 Md. 462, 979 A.2d 120 (Aug. 28, 2009).

Conflict of interest found. — Attorney active in a corporation had a conflict of interest where he confessed judgment against the corporation and its other principals, in favor of his wife, and advised one of the principals that he need do nothing about the action. Att'y Griev. Comm'n v. Hines, 366 Md. 277, 783 A.2d 656 (2001).

Attorney had a conflict of interest where his firm prepared a confessed judgment note in favor of his wife, obligating a corporation in which he was active and the other corporate principals, which contained a signature line for him, but did not obligate him on the note. Att'y Griev. Comm'n v. Hines, 366 Md. 277, 783 A.2d 656 (2001).

Attorney had a conflict of interest where he confessed a judgment in favor of his wife against a corporation in which he was active, but delayed service even though the corporation had offices in his building. Att'y Griev. Comm'n v. Hines, 366 Md. 277, 783 A.2d 656 (2001).

Attorney violated the Maryland Rules of Professional Conduct by purchasing at a foreclosure sale the home of the client the attorney was representing in a bankruptcy, permitting the client to continue to reside in the home, representing the client in a suit that was brought against the client by an insurer, representing the client in a suit brought by the client against the client's former employer, and suing the client for back rent and garnishing the client's wages as the attorney's conduct created a conflict of interest with the client. Att'y Griev. Comm'n v. Harris, 371 Md. 510, 810 A.2d 457 (2002).

Attorney was disbarred for failing to keep clients apprised of their matters and failing to respond to their calls, for failing to return their retainer to them although he did little or no work on their matters, for failing to keep their funds separate and in a trust fund, for failing to avoid a conflict of interest with respect to their matters, all in violation of prior, similar Rules 1.4, 1.5, 1.7, 1.8, 1.15, and 1.16; his conduct was especially egregious where his clients were the elderly and their families and where he was so blatant in his continued actions. Att'y Griev. Comm'n v. McLaughlin, 372 Md. 467, 813 A.2d 1145 (2002).

Attorney violated a prior, similar Rule 1.7 and Ga. St. Bar Stand. 30 by failing to disclose a conflict of interest when he did not tell his client that the inflation of future medical expenses might result in an increase in counsel fees in the attorney's interest and to the detriment of the client. Att'y Griev. Comm'n v. Roberson, 373 Md. 328, 818 A.2d 1059 (2003).

Attorney violated the prior, similar Rule and Ga. St. Bar Stand. 36 by providing multiple representation to a wife, her husband, both individually and as the wife's guardian, as well as the wife's children, although there was no written agreement as to representation or attorney's fees as to the children; the attorney's professional judgment was clearly impaired in the multiple representation in that he: (1) paid the husband and his sister a portion of the settlement funds without prior court authorization; and (2) failed to complete arrangements agreed upon to deposit a portion of settlement funds into trust for benefit of the children. Att'y Griev. Comm'n v. Roberson, 373 Md. 328, 818 A.2d 1059 (2003).

Lawyer's conduct in purchasing real property from two elderly clients and then taking back a mortgage that the lawyer apparently intended from the first to pay off out of commissions to which the lawyer was not entitled, without advising the clients even to consult a lawyer but simply referring them to a banker of the lawyer's acquaintance who was not familiar with the details of the transaction presented a clear conflict of interest and was grossly unfair to the clients. Att'y Griev. Comm'n v. Parker, 389 Md. 142, 884 A.2d 104 (2005).

Attorney's conduct, while the attorney was decertified, of undertaking to represent a defendant with whom the attorney had been arrested for possession of cocaine and marijuana on charges arising out of the arrest violated Md. R. Prof. Conduct 1.7 that partly provided that a lawyer could not undertake representation involving a conflict of interest. That the attorney committed the misconduct (1) while the attorney was decertified and (2) at a time when the attorney violated other professional misconduct rules meant that the state's highest court had little choice but to disbar the attorney. Att'y Griev. Comm'n v. Walker, 405 Md. 3, 948 A.2d 1263 (2008).

Sanction held proper. — The appropriate sanction for an attorney's improper administration of a trust in violation of the prior, similar Rule and § 10-306 of the Business Occupations and Professions Article would be indefinite suspension from the practice of law for not less than one year with the right to reapply, conditioned upon restitution and appropriate monitoring. Att'y Griev. Comm'n v. Sachse, 345 Md. 578, 693 A.2d 806 (1997).

Disbarment was the appropriate sanction where an out-of-state attorney practiced law in the State of Maryland without a license, failed to acknowledge his jurisdictional limitations on his firm letterhead, acted against the interests of his purported clients during and after the sale of their home to him, filed a bankruptcy petition on those clients' behalf, but without their consent or knowledge, and forged the signatures of the clients and another attorney in his office on court papers and filings, in violation of prior, similar Rules of

Professional Conduct 1.7, 3.3, 5.5, 7.1, 7.5, and 8.4. Att'y Griev. Comm'n v. Johnson, 363 Md. 598, 770 A.2d 130 (2001).

Attorney was disbarred for his handling of a medical malpractice case for a wife, her common-law husband, and her children, which had resulted in the attorney's disbarment in Georgia, for misconduct as defined in Maryland Rule 16-701(i), and for violating the Maryland counterparts of the Georgia State Bar Standards he had been found to have violated, more specifically, prior, similar Rules 8.4 (misconduct), 1.5 (fees), 1.7 (conflict of interest: general rule), and 1.15 (safekeeping property). Att'y Griev. Comm'n v. Roberson, 373 Md. 328, 818 A.2d 1059 (2003).

Stated in De Arriz v. Klinger-De Arriz, 179 Md. App. 458, 947 A.2d 59 (2008).

Rule 1.8. Conflict of Interest: Current Clients: Specific Rules.

(a) A lawyer shall not enter into a business transaction with a client unless:

(1) the transaction and terms on which the lawyer acquires the interest are fair and reasonable to the client and are fully disclosed and transmitted in writing in a manner that can be reasonably understood by the client;

(2) the client is advised in writing of the desirability of seeking and is given a reasonable opportunity to seek the advice of independent legal counsel on the transaction; and

(3) the client gives informed consent, in a writing signed by the client, to the essential terms of the transaction and the lawyer's role in the transaction, including whether the lawyer is representing the client in the transaction.

(b) A lawyer shall not use information relating to representation of a client to the disadvantage of the client unless the client gives informed consent, except as permitted or required by these Rules.

(c) A lawyer shall not solicit any substantial gift from a client, including a testamentary gift, or prepare on behalf of a client an instrument giving the lawyer or a person related to the lawyer any substantial gift unless the lawyer or other recipient of the gift is related to the client. For purposes of this paragraph, related persons include a spouse, child, grandchild, parent, grandparent or other relative or individual with whom the lawyer or the client maintains a close, familial relationship.

(d) Prior to the conclusion of representation of a client, a lawyer shall not make or negotiate an agreement giving the lawyer literary or media rights to a portrayal or account based in substantial part on information relating to the representation.

(e) A lawyer shall not provide financial assistance to a client in connection with pending or contemplated litigation, except that:

(1) a lawyer may advance court costs and expenses of litigation, the repayment of which may be contingent on the outcome of the matter; and

(2) a lawyer representing an indigent client may pay court costs and expenses of litigation on behalf of the client.

(f) A lawyer shall not accept compensation for representing a client from one other than the client unless:

(1) the client gives informed consent;

(2) there is no interference with the lawyer's independence of professional judgment or with the client-lawyer relationship; and

(3) information relating to representation of a client is protected as required by Rule 1.6.

(g) A lawyer who represents two or more clients shall not participate in making an aggregate settlement of the claims of or against the clients, or in a criminal case an aggregated agreement as to guilty or nolo contendere pleas, unless each client gives informed consent, in a writing signed by the client or confirmed on the record before a tribunal. The lawyer's disclosure shall include the existence and nature of all the claims or pleas involved and of the participation of each person in the settlement.

(h) A lawyer shall not:

(1) make an agreement prospectively limiting the lawyer's liability to a client for malpractice unless the client is independently represented in making the agreement; or

(2) settle a claim or potential claim for such liability with an unrepresented client or former client unless that person is advised in writing of the desirability of seeking and is given a reasonable opportunity to seek the advice of independent legal counsel in connection therewith.

(i) A lawyer shall not acquire a proprietary interest in the cause of action or subject matter of litigation the lawyer is conducting for a client, except that the lawyer may:

(1) acquire a lien authorized by law to secure the lawyer's fee or expenses; and

(2) subject to Rule 1.5, contract with a client for a reasonable contingent fee in a civil case.

(j) While lawyers are associated in a firm, a prohibition in the foregoing paragraphs (a) through (i) that applies to any one of them shall apply to all of them.

COMMENT

Business Transactions Between Client and Lawyer. — [1] A lawyer's legal skill and training, together with the relationship of trust and confidence between lawyer and client, create the possibility of overreaching when the lawyer participates in a business, property or financial transaction with a client, for example, a loan or sales transaction or a lawyer investment on behalf of a client. The requirements of paragraph (a) must be met even when the transaction is not closely related to the subject matter of the representation, as when a lawyer drafting a will for a client learns that the client needs money for unrelated expenses and offers to make a loan to the client. Paragraph (a) also applies to lawyers purchasing property from estates they represent. It does not apply to ordinary fee arrangements between client and lawyer, which are governed by Rule 1.5, although its requirements must be met when the lawyer accepts an interest in the client's business or other nonmonetary property as payment of all or part of a fee. In addition, the Rule does not apply to standard commercial transactions between the lawyer and the client for products or services that the client generally markets to others, for example, banking or brokerage services, medical services, products manufactured or distributed by the client, and utilities' services. In such transactions, the lawyer has no advantage in dealing with the client, and the restrictions in paragraph (a) are unnecessary and impracticable. For restrictions regarding lawyers engaged in the sale of goods or services related to the practice of law, see Rule 5.7.

[2] Paragraph (a)(1) requires that the transaction itself be fair to the client and that its essential terms be communicated to the client, in writing, in a manner that can be reasonably

understood. Paragraph (a)(2) requires that the client also be advised, in writing, of the desirability of seeking the advice of independent legal counsel. It also requires that the client be given a reasonable opportunity to obtain such advice. Paragraph (a)(3) requires that the lawyer obtain the client's informed consent, in a writing signed by the client, both to the essential terms of the transaction and to the lawyer's role. When necessary, the lawyer should discuss both the material risks of the proposed transaction, including any risk presented by the lawyer's involvement, and the existence of reasonably available alternatives and should explain why the advice of independent legal counsel is desirable. See Rule 1.0(f) (definition of informed consent).

[3] The risk to a client is greatest when the client expects the lawyer to represent the client in the transaction itself or when the lawyer's financial interest otherwise poses a significant risk that the lawyer's representation of the client will be materially limited by the lawyer's financial interest in the transaction. Here the lawyer's role requires that the lawyer must comply, not only with the requirements of paragraph (a), but also with the requirements of Rule 1.7. Under that Rule, the lawyer must disclose the risks associated with the lawyer's dual role as both legal adviser and participant in the transaction, such as the risk that the lawyer will structure the transaction or give legal advice in a way that favors the lawyer's interests at the expense of the client. Moreover, the lawyer must obtain the client's informed consent. In some cases, the lawyer's interest may be such that Rule 1.7 will preclude the lawyer from seeking the client's consent to the transaction.

[4] If the client is independently represented in the transaction, paragraph (a)(2) of this Rule is inapplicable, and the paragraph (a)(1) requirement for full disclosure is satisfied either by a written disclosure by the lawyer involved in the transaction or by the client's independent counsel. The fact that the client was independently represented in the transaction is relevant in determining whether the agreement was fair and reasonable to the client as paragraph (a)(1) further requires.

Use of Information Related to Representation. — [5] Use of information relating to the representation to the disadvantage of the client violates the lawyer's duty of loyalty. Paragraph (b) applies when the information is used to benefit either the lawyer or a third person, such as another client or business associate of the lawyer. For example, if a lawyer learns that a client intends to purchase and develop several parcels of land, the lawyer may not use that information to purchase one of the parcels in competition with the client or to recommend that another client make such a purchase. The

Rule does not prohibit uses that do not disadvantage the client. For example, a lawyer who learns a government agency's interpretation of trade legislation during the representation of one client may properly use that information to benefit other clients. Paragraph (b) prohibits disadvantageous use of client information unless the client gives informed consent, except as permitted or required by these Rules. See Rules 1.2(d), 1.6, 1.9(c), 3.3, 4.1(b), 8.1 and 8.3.

Gifts to Lawyers. — [6] A lawyer may accept a gift from a client, if the transaction meets general standards of fairness. For example, a simple gift such as a present given at a holiday or as a token of appreciation is permitted. If a client offers the lawyer a more substantial gift, paragraph (c) does not prohibit the lawyer from accepting it, although such a gift may be voidable by the client under the doctrine of undue influence, which treats client gifts as presumptively fraudulent. In any event, due to concerns about overreaching and imposition on clients, a lawyer may not suggest that a substantial gift be made to the lawyer or for the lawyer's benefit, except where the lawyer is related to the client as set forth in paragraph (c).

[7] If effectuation of a substantial gift requires preparing a legal instrument such as a will or conveyance, the client should have the detached advice that another lawyer can provide. The sole exception to this Rule is where the client is a relative of the donee.

[8] This Rule does not prohibit a lawyer from seeking to have the lawyer or a partner or associate of the lawyer named as executor of the client's estate or to another potentially lucrative fiduciary position. Nevertheless, such appointments will be subject to the general conflict of interest provision in Rule 1.7 when there is a significant risk that the lawyer's interest in obtaining the appointment will materially limit the lawyer's independent professional judgment in advising the client concerning the choice of an executor or other fiduciary. In obtaining the client's informed consent to the conflict, the lawyer should advise the client concerning the nature and extent of the lawyer's financial interest in the appointment, as well as the availability of alternative candidates for the position.

Literary Rights. — [9] An agreement by which a lawyer acquires literary or media rights concerning the conduct of the representation creates a conflict between the interests of the client and the personal interests of the lawyer. Measures suitable in the representation of the client may detract from the publication value of an account of the representation. Paragraph (d) does not prohibit a lawyer representing a client in a transaction concerning literary property from agreeing that the lawyer's fee shall consist of a share in ownership in the property, if the arrangement conforms to Rule 1.5 and paragraphs (a) and (i).

Financial Assistance. — [10] Lawyers may not subsidize lawsuits or administrative proceedings brought on behalf of their clients, including making or guaranteeing loans to their clients for living expenses, because to do so would encourage clients to pursue lawsuits that might not otherwise be brought and because such assistance gives lawyers too great a financial stake in the litigation. These dangers do not warrant a prohibition on a lawyer lending a client court costs and litigation expenses, including the expenses of medical examination and the costs of obtaining and presenting evidence, because these advances are virtually indistinguishable from contingent fees and help ensure access to the courts. Similarly, an exception allowing lawyers representing indigent clients to pay court costs and litigation expenses regardless of whether these funds will be repaid is warranted.

Person Paying for a Lawyer's Services. — [11] Lawyers are frequently asked to represent a client under circumstances in which a third person will compensate the lawyer, in whole or in part. The third person might be a relative or friend, an indemnitor (such as a liability insurance company) or a co-client (such as a corporation sued along with one or more of its employees). Because third-party payers frequently have interests that differ from those of the client, including interests in minimizing the amount spent on the representation and in learning how the representation is progressing, lawyers are prohibited from accepting or continuing such representations unless the lawyer determines that there will be no interference with the lawyer's independent professional judgment and there is informed consent from the client. See also Rule 5.4(c) (prohibiting interference with a lawyer's professional judgment by one who recommends, employs or pays the lawyer to render legal services for another).

[12] Sometimes, it will be sufficient for the lawyer to obtain the client's informed consent regarding the fact of the payment and the identity of the third-party payer. If, however, the fee arrangement creates a conflict of interest for the lawyer, then the lawyer must comply with Rule. 1.7. The lawyer must also conform to the requirements of Rule 1.6 concerning confidentiality. Under Rule 1.7(a), a conflict of interest exists if there is significant risk that the lawyer's representation of the client will be materially limited by the lawyer's own interest in the fee arrangement or by the lawyer's responsibilities to the third-party payer (for example, when the third-party payer is a co-client). Under Rule 1.7(b), the lawyer may accept or continue the representation with the informed consent of each affected client, unless the conflict is nonconsentable under that paragraph. Under Rule 1.7(b), the informed consent must be confirmed in writing.

Aggregate Settlements. — [13] Differences in willingness to make or accept an offer of settlement are among the risks of common representation of multiple clients by a single lawyer. Under Rule 1.7, this is one of the risks that should be discussed before undertaking the representation, as part of the process of obtaining the clients' informed consent. In addition, Rule 1.2(a) protects each client's right to have the final say in deciding whether to accept or reject an offer of settlement and in deciding whether to enter a guilty or nolo contendere plea in a criminal case. The rule stated in this paragraph is a corollary of both these Rules and provides that, before any settlement offer or plea bargain is made or accepted on behalf of multiple clients, the lawyer must inform each of them about all the material terms of the settlement, including what the other clients will receive or pay if the settlement or plea offer is accepted. See also Rule 1.0(f) (definition of informed consent). Lawyers representing a class of plaintiffs or defendants, or those proceeding derivatively, may not have a full client-lawyer relationship with each member of the class; nevertheless, such lawyers must comply with applicable rules regulating notification of class members and other procedural requirements designed to ensure adequate protection of the entire class.

Limiting Liability and Settling Malpractice Claims. — [14] Agreements prospectively limiting a lawyer's liability for malpractice are prohibited unless the client is independently represented in making the agreement because they are likely to undermine competent and diligent representation. Also, many clients are unable to evaluate the desirability of making such an agreement before a dispute has arisen, particularly if they are then represented by the lawyer seeking the agreement. This paragraph does not, however, prohibit a lawyer from entering into an agreement with the client to arbitrate existing legal malpractice claims, provided the client is fully informed of the scope and effect of the agreement. Nor does this paragraph limit the ability of lawyers to practice in the form of a limited-liability entity, where permitted by law, provided that each lawyer remains personally liable to the client for his or her own conduct and the firm complies with any conditions required by law, such as provisions requiring client notification or maintenance of adequate liability insurance. Nor does it prohibit an agreement in accordance with Rule 1.2 that defines the scope of the representation, although a definition of scope that makes the obligations of representation illusory will amount to an attempt to limit liability.

[15] Agreements settling a claim or a potential claim for malpractice are not prohibited by this Rule. Nevertheless, in view of the danger that a lawyer will take unfair advantage of an unrepresented client or former client, the lawyer must first advise such a person in writing of the appropriateness of independent representation in connection with such a settlement. In addition, the lawyer must give the client or former client a reasonable opportunity to find and consult independent counsel.

Acquiring Proprietary Interest in Litigation. — [16] Paragraph (i) states the traditional general rule that lawyers are prohibited from acquiring a proprietary interest in litigation. Like paragraph (e), the general rule has its basis in common law champerty and maintenance and is designed to avoid giving the lawyer too great an interest in the representation. In addition, when the lawyer acquires an ownership interest in the subject of the representation, it will be more difficult for a client to discharge the lawyer if the client so desires. The Rule is subject to specific exceptions developed in decisional law and continued in these Rules. The exception for certain advances of the costs of litigation is set forth in paragraph (e). In addition, paragraph (i) sets forth exceptions for liens authorized by law to

secure the lawyer's fees or expenses and contracts for reasonable contingent fees. The law of each jurisdiction determines which liens are authorized by law. These may include liens granted by statute, liens originating in common law and liens acquired by contract with the client. When a lawyer acquires by contract a security interest in property other than that recovered through the lawyer's efforts in the litigation, such an acquisition is a business or financial transaction with a client and is governed by the requirements of paragraph (a). Contracts for contingent fees in civil cases are governed by Rule 1.5.

Imputation of Prohibitions. — [17] Under paragraph (i), a prohibition on conduct by an individual lawyer in paragraphs (a) through (i) also applies to all lawyers associated in a firm with the personally prohibited lawyer. For example, one lawyer in a firm may not enter into a business transaction with a client of another member of the firm without complying with paragraph (a), even if the first lawyer is not personally involved in the representation of the client.

Model Rules Comparison. — Rule 1.8 is substantially similar to the language of the Ethics 2000 Amendments to the ABA Model Rules of Professional Conduct, except for wording changes to Rule 1.8(a), (g), (i)(2) and Comments [1], [14] and [17], and the omission of Model Rule 1.8(j) with appropriate redesignation of subsections.

Closely tailored to Model Rules. — The prior, similar Rule is closely tailored to the model rule adopted by the American Bar Association, under which the only exception to the rule's prohibition of drafting self-benefitting instruments is where the attorney is related to the client; in contrast, the Kutak Commission version of this Rule, adopted by the Maryland Court of Appeals, contains an additional exception for situations where the client is represented by independent counsel in connection with the gift. Att'y Griev. Comm'n v. Stein, 373 Md. 531, 819 A.2d 372 (2003).

Rule is absolute prohibition. — Even under the less stringent form of the prior, similar Rule, the Rule remains an absolute prohibition against substantial transactions not covered by the two limited exceptions. Att'y Griev. Comm'n v. Stein, 373 Md. 531, 819 A.2d 372 (2003).

Attorney's exception to hearing court's finding that the attorney violated (c) was overruled where the attorney drafted a will that bequeathed the residue of his client's estate to the attorney's daughter; the attorney did not meet any of the qualifiers to that rule that would have allowed the attorney to draft the

will since: (1) the bequest was a substantial gift; (2) the client was not related to the attorney; and (3) the client did not consult with independent counsel regarding the will. Compliance with the rule was mandatory and absolute, and was not excused by the attorney's ignorance if the rule; reprimand was ordered as the appropriate sanction rather than suspension, which was the more common sanction for such a violation, because the attorney did not orchestrate the bequest with any undue influence or duress and the client rejected the attorney's advice to consult with independent counsel. Att'y Griev. Comm'n v. Lanocha, 392 Md. 234, 896 A.2d 996 (2006).

Prohibition same as in prior rule. — Although the wording of this Rule is different from that of its predecessor, the prohibition intended is essentially the same as the reach of the prior rule. Att'y Griev. Comm'n v. Pennington, 355 Md. 61, 733 A.2d 1029 (1999).

Independent counsel requirement. — The prior, similar Rule is qualified in only three ways: (1) if the gift is not substantial, (2) if the client is related to the attorney, or (3) if the client has consulted with independent counsel. Unlike the provision under the ethical considerations of Maryland's prior rule, this provision and prohibition is express and mandatory, and the independent counsel required by the rule must be truly independent, which may not be satisfied by consultation with an attorney who is a partner of, shares space with, or is a close associate of the attorney-drafter. Att'y Griev. Comm'n v. Stein, 373 Md. 531, 819 A.2d 372 (2003).

Compliance with the requirements of (c) is mandatory and contains no provision for waiver of the provision to consult with independent counsel. This Rule is qualified in only three ways: (1) if the gift is not substantial, (2) if the client is related to the attorney, or (3) if the client has consulted with independent counsel. Att'y Griev. Comm'n v. Lanocha, 392 Md. 234, 896 A.2d 996 (2006).

No provision of waiver of independent counsel requirement. — The prior, similar Rule provides that a lawyer shall not prepare an instrument, including a testamentary gift, giving the lawyer any substantial gift from a client except where the lawyer is related to the client or where the client is represented by independent counsel; the rule is mandatory and contains no provision for waiver of the requirement to consult with independent counsel. Att'y Griev. Comm'n v. Stein, 373 Md. 531, 819 A.2d 372 (2003).

Courts of equity look upon transactions between attorney and client with great solicitude, and exercise the most exact scrutiny to be certain that the attorney has not taken any unfair advantage of his client. When a transaction between attorney and client is attacked, the presumption of fraud or unfairness can be overcome only by the clearest and most satisfactory evidence, and where the attorney is in a position to exercise strong influence, and the client is not skilled in business and is easily influenced, the burden on the attorney to sustain the transaction with his client is extremely stringent. Att'y Griev. Comm'n v. Stein, 373 Md. 531, 819 A.2d 372 (2003).

Any challenged transaction between an attorney and client is prima facie fraudulent and void, and the burden is cast upon the attorney to show that he used no undue influence or deception, that the transaction was fully understood, and that it was fair in all respects; this rule is founded upon public policy, because the confidential and fiduciary relationship enables an attorney to exercise a very strong influence over his client and often affords him opportunities to obtain undue advantage by availing himself of the client's necessities, credulity and liberality. Att'y Griev. Comm'n v. Stein, 373 Md. 531, 819 A.2d 372 (2003).

Limitations on the purposes of advances. — Although there are differences between the former DR 5-1038 and the prior, similar Rule, the limitations on the purposes

for which advances may be made remain essentially the same. Att'y Griev. Comm'n v. Eisenstein, 333 Md. 464, 635 A.2d 1327 (1994).

Excessive fee. — If attorney's contingent fee was clearly excessive in violation of former DR 2-106, then he also failed to stay within the exception to the prohibition of former DR 5-103(A) against acquiring a proprietary interest in the clients' causes of action. Att'y Griev. Comm'n v. Korotki, 318 Md. 646, 569 A.2d 1224 (1990).

Attorney violated the Maryland Rules of Professional Conduct by purchasing at a foreclosure sale the home of the client the attorney was representing in a bankruptcy, permitting the client to continue to reside in the home, representing the client in a suit that was brought against the client by an insurer, representing the client in a suit brought by the client against the client's former employer and retaining the entire amount of the settlement payment, and suing the client for back rent and garnishing the client's wages as the attorney's conduct created a conflict of interest with the client. Att'y Griev. Comm'n v. Harris, 371 Md. 510, 810 A.2d 457 (2002).

Requirement that borrower use and pay for specific lawyer at settlement. — Pertinent rules of legal ethics do not bar a lender from requiring that a specific settlement lawyer be used and that the borrower pay for the lawyer's settlement services. 72 Op. Att'y Gen. 72 (1987).

Client loan to attorney not violative of this Rule. — Trial court's finding that client's loan to her attorney was a fair and equitable personal loan to a close friend which did not violate this rule was not clearly erroneous. Att'y Griev. Comm'n v. Powell, 328 Md. 276, 614 A.2d 102 (1992).

But an interest-free loan made by a client to an attorney was violation. — An interest-free loan from a client to an attorney who did not advise the client to see independent counsel constituted a violation; the fact that the client was a close personal friend did not save the attorney from the violation. Att'y Griev. Comm'n v. Ober, 350 Md. 616, 714 A.2d 856 (1998).

Advancing funds to client. — Attorney's advancement of funds to client for medical treatment, or for transportation to a medical office for treatment, violated former DR 5-103 (B). Att'y Griev. Comm'n v. Kandel, 317 Md. 274, 563 A.2d 387 (1989).

Advancement of living expenses violation of Rule. — Attorney suspended for 2 years for violating the prior, similar Rule, inter alia, by advancing certain living expenses to the claimant during the pendency of the litigation. Att'y Griev. Comm'n v. Eisenstein, 333 Md. 464, 635 A.2d 1327 (1994).

Representation of several parties to a

settlement. — The Rule does not require that a settlement be set aside because certain parties were not aware of the precise eventual shares of an aggregate settlement that they were to receive, where the total settlement amount was well known, a method for formulating the eventual shares had been agreed to, the resulting settlement would be known to the parties, and there was no obvious injustice in upholding the settlement. Scamardella v. Illiano, 126 Md. App. 76, 727 A.2d 421 (1999).

Merger. — Where an attorney prepared a will for a client in which he was sole legatee, the circuit court judge erred by concluding that the attorney's violations of prior, similar 1.8 and 8.4 Appendix: Maryland Lawyers' Rules of Professional Conduct merged; since the attorney's conduct constituted separate rule violations, "merger" was improper. Att'y Griev. Comm'n v. Brooke, 374 Md. 155, 821 A.2d 414 (2003).

Preparation of will in which attorney is legatee — Though respondent attorney was indefinitely suspended for violating the prior, similar Rule by drafting a will for a client in which he was the sole legatee, it was not appropriate to condition his reinstatement upon his renunciation of the bequest, since, inter alia, disciplinary proceedings were not the appropriate forum to determine the proper distribution of an estate. Att'y Griev. Comm'n v. Brooke, 374 Md. 155, 821 A.2d 414 (2003).

Conflict of interest found. — Attorney was disbarred for failing to keep clients apprised of their matters and failing to respond to their calls, for failing to return their retainer to them although he did little or no work on their matters, for failing to keep their funds separate and in a trust fund, for failing to avoid a conflict of interest with respect to their matters, all in violation of prior, similar Rules 1.4, 1.5, 1.7, 1.8, 1.15, and 1.16; his conduct was especially egregious where his clients were the elderly and their families and where he was so blatant in his continued actions. Att'y Griev. Comm'n v. McLaughlin, 372 Md. 467, 813 A.2d 1145 (2002).

Lawyer's conduct in purchasing real property from two elderly clients and then taking back a mortgage that the lawyer apparently intended from the first to pay off out of commissions to which the lawyer was not entitled, without advising the clients even to consult a lawyer but simply referring them to a banker of the lawyer's acquaintance who was not familiar with the details of the transaction presented a clear conflict of interest and was grossly unfair to the clients. Att'y Griev. Comm'n v. Parker, 389 Md. 142, 884 A.2d 104 (2005).

Attorney was sanctioned by a public reprimand for technically violating Rule 16-609 regarding prohibited transactions as a result of a negligent clerical error involving depositing some of his ex-girlfriend's funds into his operating account instead of his firm's escrow account, which error was corrected upon discovery and was not wilful. The Court of Appeals of Maryland further upheld the trial judge's finding of fact that no attorney client relationship existed between the attorney and his girlfriend to support the other violations asserted against him since he never charged his ex-girlfriend a fee for his services and was only helping her while she received treatment for her alcohol abuse. Att'y Griev. Comm'n v. Shoup, 410 Md. 462, 979 A.2d 120 (Aug. 28, 2009).

Suspension appropriate. — Courts in other jurisdictions have found suspension proper for attorneys who draft instruments in which they are named beneficiaries; although some courts have imposed a reprimand for attorneys who draft such instruments, such decisions typically are under the Canons of Professional Ethics as opposed to the more stringent subsection (c) of this Rule. Att'y Griev. Comm'n v. Stein, 373 Md. 531, 819 A.2d 372 (2003).

Indefinite suspension appropriate — Attorney was indefinitely suspended from practice of law for violating this Rule and Md. R. Prof. Conduct 1.15, 8.1, and 8.4, Rules 16-607 and 16-609, and § 10-306 of the Business Occupations and Professional Article, when the attorney lent money to a client and the client's family members but failed to advise them to seek the advice of independent counsel, and the attorney required the client to repay the loan the attorney made to the client's mother as a condition of the attorney loaning the client money. Att'y Griev. Comm'n v. McLaughlin, 409 Md. 304, 974 A.2d 315 (2009).

Disbarment appropriate. — In an attorney disciplinary matter wherein the attorney was ordered disbarred, the attorney was found to have violated this Rule, after the hearing judge found that the attorney sought to have a client, without the assistance of independent counsel, execute a release of any malpractice claims. Att'y Griev. Comm'n v. Steinberg, 395 Md. 337, 910 A.2d 429 (2006).

Attorney was indefinitely suspended for drafting self-benefitting will. — Attorney was indefinitely suspended for drafting a self-benefitting will under which he was to receive a substantial sum, but was not required to disclaim the gift as a condition to reinstatement, where: (1) the attorney was not aware of subsection (c) of this Rule; (2) there was no evidence of undue influence; (3) he was 69 years old and was admitted to the bar in 1961; (4) he was semi-retired; and (5) he had no prior disciplinary sanction imposed against him. Att'y Griev. Comm'n v. Stein, 373 Md.

531, 819 A.2d 372 (2003).

Attorney violated (c) by preparing a will for a client in which the attorney was named the beneficiary of a substantial bequest and having counsel that the attorney shared office space with review the will with the client and gauge the client's competency, because it created the potential for the appearance of impropriety and thus, also amounted to a violation of Md. R. Prof. Conduct 8.4(d). Because the attorney was unlikely to repeat the actions in a similar situation, had no prior disciplinary history, and had made a good faith effort to comply with subsection (c) of this Rule, a warning was issued. Att'y Griev. Comm'n v. Saridakis, 402 Md. 413, 936 A.2d 886 (2007).

Preparation of will — Circuit court judge properly found that respondent attorney violated the prior, similar Rule and Md. R. Prof.

Conduct 8.4, as clear and convincing evidence established the existence of an attorney-client relationship between the attorney and a testator with respect to a will prepared by the attorney, in which he was sole legatee; the attorney was indefinitely suspended. Att'y Griev. Comm'n v. Brooke, 374 Md. 155, 821 A.2d 414 (2003).

Quoted in Att'y Griev. Comm'n v. Zuckerman, 386 Md. 341, 872 A.2d 693 (2005); De Arriz v. Klinger-De Arriz, 179 Md. App. 458, 947 A.2d 59 (2008).

Cited in Att'y Griev. Comm'n v. Muhammad, 395 Md. 676, 912 A.2d 588 (2006), cert. denied, 127 S. Ct. 2296, 2007 U.S. LEXIS 5292, 167 L. Ed. 2d 1103 (U.S. 2007); Att'y Griev. Comm'n v. Bleecker, 414 Md. 147, 994 A.2d 928 (2010).

Rule 1.9. Duties to Former Clients.

(a) A lawyer who has formerly represented a client in a matter shall not thereafter represent another person in the same or a substantially related matter in which that person's interests are materially adverse to the interests of the former client unless the former client gives informed consent, confirmed in writing.

(b) A lawyer shall not knowingly represent a person in the same or a substantially related matter in which a firm with which the lawyer formerly was associated had previously represented a client

(1) whose interests are materially adverse to that person; and

(2) about whom the lawyer had acquired information protected by Rules 1.6 and 1.9(c) that is material to the matter; unless the former client gives informed consent, confirmed in writing.

(c) A lawyer who has formerly represented a client in a matter or whose present or former firm has formerly represented a client in a matter shall not thereafter:

(1) use information relating to the representation to the disadvantage of the former client except as these Rules would permit or require with respect to a client, or when the information has become generally known; or

(2) reveal information relating to the representation except as these Rules would permit or require with respect to a client.

COMMENT

[1] After termination of a client-lawyer relationship, a lawyer has certain continuing duties with respect to confidentiality and conflicts of interest and thus may not represent another client except in conformity with this Rule. Under this Rule, for example, a lawyer could not properly seek to rescind on behalf of a new client a contract drafted on behalf of the former client. So also a lawyer who has prosecuted an accused person could not properly represent the accused in a subsequent civil action against the government concerning the same transaction. Nor could a lawyer who has represented multiple clients in a matter represent one of the clients against the others in the same or a substantially related matter after a dispute arose among the clients in that matter, unless all affected clients give informed consent. See Comment [9]. Current and former government lawyers must comply with this Rule to the extent required by Rule 1.11.

[2] The scope of a "matter" for purposes of this Rule depends on the facts of a particular

situation or transaction. The lawyer's involvement in a matter can also be a question of degree. When a lawyer has been directly involved in a specific transaction, subsequent representation of other clients with materially adverse interests in that transaction clearly is prohibited. On the other hand, a lawyer who recurrently handled a type of problem for a former client is not precluded for that reason alone from later representing another client in a factually distinct problem of that type even though the subsequent representation involves a position adverse to the prior client. Similar considerations can apply to the reassignment of military lawyers between defense and prosecution functions within the same military jurisdictions. The underlying question is whether the lawyer was so involved in the matter that the subsequent representation can be justly regarded as a changing of sides in the matter in question.

[3] Matters are "substantially related" for purposes of this Rule if they involve the same transaction or legal dispute or if there otherwise is a substantial risk that confidential factual information as would normally have been obtained in the prior representation would materially advance the client's position in the subsequent matter. For example, a lawyer who has represented a businessperson and learned extensive private financial information about that person may not then represent that person's spouse in seeking a divorce. Similarly, a lawyer who has previously represented a client in securing environmental permits to build a shopping center would be precluded from representing neighbors seeking to oppose rezoning of the property on the basis of environmental considerations; however, the lawyer would not be precluded, on the grounds of substantial relationship, from defending a tenant of the completed shopping center in resisting eviction for nonpayment of rent. Information that has been disclosed to the public or to other parties adverse to the former client ordinarily will not be disqualifying. Information acquired in a prior representation may have been rendered obsolete by the passage of time, a circumstance that may be relevant in determining whether two representations are substantially related. In the case of an organizational client, general knowledge of the client's policies and practices ordinarily will not preclude a subsequent representation; on the other hand, knowledge of specific facts gained in a prior representation that are relevant to the matter in question ordinarily will preclude such a representation. A former client is not required to reveal the confidential information learned by the lawyer in order to establish a substantial risk that the lawyer has confidential information to use in the subsequent matter. A conclusion about the possession of such information may be based on the nature of the services the lawyer provided the former client and information that would in ordinary practice be learned by a lawyer providing such services.

Lawyers Moving Between Firms. — [4] When lawyers have been associated within a firm but then end their association, the question of whether a lawyer should undertake representation is more complicated. There are several competing considerations. First, the client previously represented by the former firm must be reasonably assured that the principle of loyalty to the client is not compromised. Second, the rule should not be so broadly cast as to preclude other persons from having reasonable choice of legal counsel. Third, the rule should not unreasonably hamper lawyers from forming new associations and taking on new clients after having left a previous association. In this connection, it should be recognized that today many lawyers practice in firms, that many lawyers to some degree limit their practice to one field or another, and that many move from one association to another several times in their careers. If the concept of imputation were applied with unqualified rigor, the result would be radical curtailment of the opportunity of lawyers to move from one practice setting to another and of the opportunity of clients to change counsel.

[5] Paragraph (b) operates to disqualify the lawyer only when the lawyer involved has actual knowledge of information protected by Rules 1.6 and 1.9(c). Thus, if a lawyer while with one firm acquired no knowledge or information relating to a particular client of the firm, and that lawyer later joined another firm, neither the lawyer individually nor the second firm is disqualified from representing another client in the same or a related matter even though the interests of the two clients conflict. See Rule 1.10(b) for the restrictions on a firm once a lawyer has terminated association with the firm.

[6] Application of paragraph (b) depends on a situation's particular facts, aided by inferences, deductions or working presumptions that reasonably may be made about the way in which lawyers work together. A lawyer may have general access to files of all clients of a law firm and may regularly participate in discussions of their affairs; it should be inferred that such a lawyer in fact is privy to all information about all the firm's clients. In contrast, another lawyer may have access to the files of only a limited number of clients and participate in discussions of the affairs of no other clients; in the absence of information to the contrary, it should be inferred that such a lawyer in fact is privy to information about the clients actually served but not those of other clients. In such an inquiry, the burden of proof

ordinarily rests upon the firm whose disqualification is sought.

[7] Independent of the question of disqualification of a firm, a lawyer changing professional association has a continuing duty to preserve confidentiality of information about a client formerly represented. See Rules 1.6 and 1.9(c).

[8] Paragraph (c) provides that information acquired by the lawyer in the course of representing a client may not subsequently be used or revealed by the lawyer to the disadvantage of the client. However, the fact that a lawyer has once served a client does not preclude the lawyer from using generally known information about that client when later representing another client.

[9] The provisions of this Rule are for the protection of former clients and can be waived if the client gives informed consent, which consent must be confirmed in writing under paragraphs (a) and (b). See Rule 1.0(f). With regard to the effectiveness of an advance waiver, see Comment [22] to Rule 1.7. With regard to disqualification of a firm with which a lawyer is or was formerly associated, see Rule 1.10.

Model Rules Comparison. — Rule 1.9 is substantially similar to the language of the Ethics 2000 Amendments to the ABA Model Rules of Professional Conduct except for wording changes to Comments [2] and [6].

Maryland Law Review. — For note, "The Maryland Survey: 2004-2005: Recent Decisions: The Court of Appeals of Maryland: VII. Legal Ethics, see 65 Md. L. Rev. 1222 (2006).

Duty of court. — A court must examine the nature and scope of the prior and present representation and determine whether confidences might have been disclosed in the course of the prior representation which could be relevant to the present action. Buckley v. Airshield Corp., 908 F. Supp. 299 (D. Md. 1995), appeal dismissed, 86 F.3d 1175 (Fed. Cir. 1996).

Fact that the State's Attorney prosecuting defendant had, several years before, represented defendant in two matters as a public defender did not automatically create a conflict of interest per se that required disqualification; the trial court appropriately exercised its discretion in conducting a thorough inquiry into whether the matters were substantially similar, finding that they were not, even though two controlled substance cases were involved, ascertained that the prosecutor had little recollection of the earlier cases, and assured that no confidential information gleaned in prior matters was used for impeachment purposes, before properly determining that disqualification was not required. Gatewood v. State, 388 Md. 526, 880 A.2d 322 (2005).

Same or substantially related matter. — In order to show a substantial relationship for the purposes of this rule it is not necessary that two lawsuits involve the same operative facts, so long as there is a sufficient similarity of issues. Buckley v. Airshield Corp., 908 F. Supp. 299 (D. Md. 1995), appeal dismissed, 86 F.3d 1175 (Fed. Cir. 1996).

As defendant corporation's attorney previously performed tasks on behalf of the patent holder in furtherance of a patent application that was a "substantially related" matter to the patent at issue in the patent infringement suit, the patent holder's motion to disqualify was granted. Stratagene v. Invitrogen Corp., 225 F. Supp. 2d 608 (D. Md. 2002).

Attorney-client relationship existed between defendant corporation's attorney and the attorney during her time at another law office even if her work was limited to what the corporation characterized as "administrative tasks;" the attorney performed tasks on behalf of the patent in furtherance of its patent application sufficient to establish an attorney-client relationship. Stratagene v. Invitrogen Corp., 225 F. Supp. 2d 608 (D. Md. 2002).

Defendant corporation's attorney had unrestricted access to all of the attorney's former law office's files containing attorney-client confidences regarding the patent holder's '767 application and because the '767 continuation application derived from the original parent patent application, which also ultimately resulted in patent number '772 that was the patent at issue, the '772 patent and the '767 continuation application were "substantially related" matters for the purposes of this Rule. Stratagene v. Invitrogen Corp., 225 F. Supp. 2d 608 (D. Md. 2002).

Where plaintiff two, a deceased singer's parents, had decided to cooperate with an individual in licensing the musical works of the deceased singer to a producer planning a film about the singer, but plaintiff one, a record company, disagreed, contending that it had the exclusive rights to all works by the deceased singer, including her appearance in a musical group, the court determined that the attorney, who stated that the attorney could continue representing the record company after the parents had terminated its relationship with the attorney, could no longer represent the record company; the dispute was material and centered on the core issues of the case, and it had not been waived. Cassidy v. Lourim, 311 F. Supp. 2d 456 (D. Md. 2004).

Prosecutor's prior representation of defendant while serving as an assistant public defender did not require disqualifiction where the matter was not "substantially related" to the case sub judice. Gatewood v. State, 158 Md. App. 458, 857 A.2d 590 (2004), aff'd, — Md. —, 880 A.2d 322 (2005).

State's highest court found that the attorney should be disbarred, as clear and convincing evidence showed that the attorney falsely represented in a deposition that the business associate was a client of the attorney when that was not true, in violation of Md. R. Prof. Conduct 1.9, and that the attorney engaged in an impermissible conflict of interest in violation of Md. R. Prof. Conduct 8.4 when the attorney represented the corporation in a substantially similar matter in a lawsuit against the entity after the attorney had represented the entity for two years in matters that included the same matter that was the subject of the lawsuit; not only were the violations proven, but the attorney failed to prove the attorney's affirmative defense of waiver since the attorney presented a paucity of argument or evidence in that regard. Att'y Griev. Comm'n v. Siskind, 401 Md. 41, 930 A.2d 328 (2007).

No conflict of interest found — Disqualification was not required for an attorney who had previously represented an advertising and marketing agency in drafting contracts and whose law firm represented the agency's former client in a suit alleging breach of contract and copyright infringement, because there was no conflict of interest under thbis Rule since the attorney only performed limited work in drafting a form contract for the agency, the agency's owner made substantial revisions to the document, and the attorney did not have access to the agency's files while performing this limited work. Nichols Agency, Inc. v. Enchanted Child Care, Inc., 537 F. Supp. 2d 774 (D. Md. Feb. 26, 2008).

Disqualification of an insured's attorney and her law firm was not warranted under Rules 1.9(a) and 1.10(a) where the insurer only showed that the attorney had previously represented other insureds; it failed to show that it also stood in an attorney-client relationship with the attorney. Pa. Nat'l Mut. Cas. Ins. Co. v. Perlberg, — F. Supp. 2d — (D. Md. May 20, 2011).

Disqualification of an insured's attorney was not warranted under (a) where the attorney's prior representation of other insureds was in matters that were not at all related to a coverage issue, which was the subject matter of the present dispute that the insurer was involved in against other insureds. Pa. Nat'l Mut. Cas. Ins. Co. v. Perlberg, — F. Supp. 2d —

(D. Md. May 20, 2011).

Previous work with corporation. — Attorney's previous work with corporation as labor attorney and labor relations lawyer which made him familiar with the corporation's personnel policies and procedures held sufficiently related to his representation of employee in an age discrimination case to work to the corporation's disadvantage; therefore attorney held disqualified from further participation in the age discrimination case. Stitz v. Bethlehem Steel Corp., 650 F. Supp. 914 (D. Md. 1987).

Longstanding clients. — Motion for disqualification was denied because defendants failed to raise the conflict of interest in a timely manner and the attorneys did not represent a new client, but rather, represented their longstanding clients against the buyer of the clients' business. Gross v. SES Americom, Inc., 307 F. Supp. 2d 719 (D. Md. 2004).

Attorney's new law firm not disqualified. — Corporation's motion to disqualify a law firm from representing an individual because an attorney and a secretary who worked for the firm were previously part of the legal team that represented the corporation was denied because (1) Md. R. Prof. Conduct 1.10(c) addressed the situation because the corporation became a former client of the attorney when his former law firm withdrew from the case, and, at that point, the attorney was prohibited from representing an adverse client such as the individual without the corporation's consent by this Rule; (2) the fact that the attorney could have no longer represented the individual did not mean that his new law firm could not have represented the individual; (3) such representation could have taken place so long as the tainted lawyer had been timely screened and he would not have been apportioned a fee from that client; (4) the corporation failed to show any concrete flaws in the screening process, other than what it called "the appearance of impropriety," and the court was not persuaded that an appearance of impropriety was enough to disqualify the firm; (5) the firm tailored its screen to fit the guidelines set forth by Md. R. Prof. Conduct 1.0(m); (6) the firm set up a sufficient screen so that the attorney and the secretary would not have tainted the firm's defense of the individual in the suit initiated by the corporation; and (7) as long as the screen was in place, the firm could have represented the individual. Compass Mktg. v. Schering-Plough Corp., — F. Supp. 2d — (D. Md. 2006).

Cited in Duvall v. State, 399 Md. 210, 923 A.2d 81 (2007); State v. Goldsberry, 419 Md. 100, 18 A.3d 836 (2011).

Rule 1.10. Imputation of Conflicts of Interest: General Rule.

(a) While lawyers are associated in a firm, none of them shall knowingly represent a client when any one of them practicing alone would be prohibited from doing so by Rules 1.7 or 1.9, unless the prohibition is based on a personal interest of the prohibited lawyer and does not present a significant risk of materially limiting the representation of the client by the remaining lawyers in the firm.

(b) When a lawyer has terminated an association with a firm, the firm is not prohibited from thereafter representing a person with interests materially adverse to those of a client represented by the formerly associated lawyer and not currently represented by the firm, unless:

(1) the matter is the same or substantially related to that in which the formerly associated lawyer represented the client; and

(2) any lawyer remaining in the firm has information protected by Rules 1.6 and 1.9(c) that is material to the matter.

(c) When a lawyer becomes associated with a firm, no lawyer associated in the firm shall knowingly represent a person in a matter in which the newly associated lawyer is disqualified under Rule 1.9 unless the personally disqualified lawyer is timely screened from any participation in the matter and is apportioned no part of the fee therefrom.

(d) A disqualification prescribed by this rule may be waived by the affected client under the conditions stated in Rule 1.7.

(e) The disqualification of lawyers associated in a firm with former or current government lawyers is governed by Rule 1.11.

COMMENT

Definition of "Firm" — [1] A "firm" is defined in Rule 1.0(d). Whether two or more lawyers constitute a firm within this definition can depend on the specific facts. See Rule 1.0, Comments [2] - [4]. A lawyer is deemed associated with a firm if held out to be a partner, principal, associate, of counsel, or similar designation. A lawyer ordinarily is not deemed associated with a firm if the lawyer no longer practices law and is held out as retired or emeritus. A lawyer employed for short periods as a contract attorney ordinarily is deemed associated with the firm only regarding matters to which the lawyer gives substantive attention.

Principles of Imputed Disqualification. — [2] The rule of imputed disqualification stated in paragraph (a) gives effect to the principle of loyalty to the client as it applies to lawyers who practice in a law firm. Such situations can be considered from the premise that a firm of lawyers is essentially one lawyer for purposes of the rules governing loyalty to the client, or from the premise that each lawyer is vicariously bound by the obligation of loyalty owed by each lawyer with whom the lawyer is associated. Paragraph (a) operates only among the lawyers currently associated in a firm. When a lawyer moves from one firm to another, the situation is governed by Rules 1.9(b), 1.10(b) and 1.10(c).

[3] The rule in paragraph (a) does not prohibit representation where neither questions of client loyalty nor protection of confidential information are presented. Where one lawyer in a firm could not effectively represent a given client because of strong political beliefs, for example, but that lawyer will do no work on the case and the personal beliefs of the lawyer will not materially limit the representation by others in the firm, the firm should not be disqualified. On the other hand, if an opposing party in a case were owned by a lawyer in the law firm, and others in the firm would be materially limited in pursuing the matter because of loyalty to that lawyer, the personal disqualification of the lawyer would be imputed to all others in the firm.

[4] The rule in paragraph (a) also does not prohibit representation by others in the law firm where the person prohibited from involvement in a matter is a nonlawyer, such as a paralegal or legal secretary. Nor does paragraph (a) prohibit representation if the lawyer is prohibited from acting because of events before the person became a lawyer, for exam-

761

ple, work that the person did while a law student. Such persons, however, ordinarily must be screened from any personal participation in the matter to avoid communication to others in the firm of confidential information that both the nonlawyers and the firm have a legal duty to protect. See Rules 1.0(m) and 5.3.

[5] Rule 1.10(b) operates to permit a law firm, under certain circumstances, to represent a person with interests directly adverse to those of a client represented by a lawyer who formerly was associated with the firm. The Rule applies regardless of when the formerly associated lawyer represented the client. However, the law firm may not represent a person with interests adverse to those of a present client of the firm, which would violate Rule 1.7. Moreover, the firm may not represent the person where the matter is the same or substantially related to that in which the formerly associated lawyer represented the client and any other lawyer currently in the firm has material information protected by Rules 1.6 and 1.9(c).

[6] Where the conditions of paragraph (c) are met, imputation is removed, and consent to the new representation is not required. Lawyers should be aware, however, that courts may impose more stringent obligations in ruling upon motions to disqualify a lawyer from pending litigation.

[7] Requirements for screening procedures are stated in Rule 1.0(m). Paragraph (c) does not prohibit the screened lawyer from receiving a salary or partnership share established by prior independent agreement, but that lawyer may not receive compensation directly related to the matter in which the lawyer is disqualified.

[8] Rule 1.10(d) removes imputation with the informed consent of the affected client or former client under the conditions stated in Rule 1.7. The conditions stated in Rule 1.7 require the lawyer to determine that the representation is not prohibited by Rule 1.7(b) and that each affected client or former client has given informed consent to the representation, confirmed in writing. In some cases, the risk may be so severe that the conflict may not be cured by client consent. For a discussion of the effectiveness of client waivers of conflicts that might arise in the future, see Rule 1.7, Comment [22]. For a definition of informed consent, see Rule 1.0(f).

[9] Where a lawyer has joined a private firm after having represented the government, imputation is governed by Rule 1.11(b) and (c), not this Rule. Under Rule 1.11(d), where a lawyer represents the government after having served clients in private practice, nongovernmental employment or in another government agency, former-client conflicts are not imputed to government lawyers associated with the individually disqualified lawyer.

[10] Where a lawyer is prohibited from engaging in certain transactions under Rule 1.8, paragraph (j) of that Rule, and not this Rule, determines whether that prohibition also applies to other lawyers associated in a firm with the personally prohibited lawyer.

Model Rules Comparison. — Rule 1.10 is substantially similar to the language of the Ethics 2000 Amendments to the ABA Model Rules of Professional Conduct except for changes to Comment [1] and to provide for screening in Rule 1.10(c) and Comments [6] and [7], with the appropriate redesignation of paragraphs. These screening provisions, along with Rule 1.0(m) and Comments [8]-[10] under Rule 1.0 are substantially the same as former Rule 1.10(b) (adopted January 1, 2000) with additional guidance on how to make screening effective.

An "unrelated" law firm must be disqualified when there is some evidence of the possibility that the tainted lawyer, either consciously or unconsciously, transmitted some confidence to a previously untainted firm; however, where law firm had met only briefly with the disqualified attorney and it was unlikely that tainted information was discussed at that meeting, the law firm was not disqualified. Stitz v. Bethlehem Steel Corp., 650 F. Supp. 914 (D. Md. 1987).

Firm not sheltered from imputed disqualification. — Defendant corporation did not show that its attorney received no confidential information from plaintiff patent holder while working at another law office and the imputation of disqualification rule did not apply because the attorney's present law office clearly did not screen the attorney from participation in the case, the attorney's present law firm was disqualified from representing the corporation regarding the patent infringement at issue in this case as it had not sheltered itself from imputed disqualification in the manners described in the prior, similar Rule. Stratagene v. Invitrogen Corp., 225 F. Supp. 2d 608 (D. Md. 2002).

Representation of multiple defendants. — Representation of multiple defendants in a criminal case, by the same attorney or law partners, is not per se an actual conflict of interest; however, an actual conflict of interest exists where an attorney, or law partners, represent, in the same criminal case, both the defendant and a codefendant (or other individual) who testifies adversely to the defendant.

Austin v. State, 327 Md. 375, 609 A.2d 728 (1992).

Office of public defender. — Administrative judge erred in failing to grant a postponement to allow defense counsel a reasonable time to resolve an issue because there existed a conflict of interest when a public defender represented defendant while another attorney from the public defender's district office was representing a person in an unrelated proceeding whom defendant contended was the actual guilty party, and defense counsel requested a continuance prior to trial. Defendant's right to the effective assistance of counsel under U.S. Const. amend. VI and Md. Const. Decl. Rights art. 21 was thus violated by the conflict of interest. Duvall v. State, 399 Md. 210, 923 A.2d 81 (2007).

Firm could have represented individual. — Corporation's motion to disqualify a law firm from representing an individual because an attorney and a secretary who worked for the firm were previously part of the legal team that represented the corporation was denied because (1) subsection (c) of this Rule addressed the situation because the corporation became a former client of the attorney when his former law firm withdrew from the case, and, at that point, the attorney was prohibited from representing an adverse client such as the individual without the corporation's consent by Md. R. Prof. Conduct 1.9; (2)

the fact that the attorney could have no longer represented the individual did not mean that his new law firm could not have represented the individual; (3) such representation could have taken place so long as the tainted lawyer had been timely screened and he would not have been apportioned a fee from that client; (4) the corporation failed to show any concrete flaws in the screening process, other than what it called "the appearance of impropriety," and the court was not persuaded that an appearance of impropriety was enough to disqualify the firm; (5) the firm tailored its screen to fit the guidelines set forth by Md. R. Prof. Conduct 1.0(m); (6) the firm set up a sufficient screen so that the attorney and the secretary would not have tainted the firm's defense of the individual in the suit initiated by the corporation; and (7) as long as the screen was in place, the firm could have represented the individual. Compass Mktg. v. Schering-Plough Corp., — F. Supp. 2d — (D. Md. 2006).

No conflict of interest found. — Disqualification of an insured's attorney and her law firm was not warranted under Rules 1.9(a) and 1.10(a) where the insurer only showed that the attorney had previously represented other insureds; it failed to show that it also stood in an attorney-client relationship with the attorney. Pa. Nat'l Mut. Cas. Ins. Co. v. Perlberg, — F. Supp. 2d — (D. Md. May 20, 2011).

Cited in Att'y Griev. Comm'n v. Carithers, 421 Md. 28, 25 A.3d 181 (2011).

Rule 1.11. Special Conflicts of Interest for Former and Current Government Officers and Employees.

(a) Except as law may otherwise expressly permit, a lawyer who has formerly served as a public officer or employee of the government:

(1) is subject to Rule 1.9(c); and

(2) shall not otherwise represent a client in connection with a matter in which the lawyer participated personally and substantially as a public officer or employee, unless the appropriate government agency gives its informed consent, confirmed in writing, to the representation.

(b) When a lawyer is disqualified from representation under paragraph (a), no lawyer in a firm with which that lawyer is associated may knowingly undertake or continue representation in such a matter unless:

(1) the disqualified lawyer is timely screened from any participation in the matter and is apportioned no part of the fee therefrom; and

(2) written notice is promptly given to the appropriate government agency to enable it to ascertain compliance with the provisions of this Rule.

(c) Except as law may otherwise expressly permit, a lawyer having information that the lawyer knows is confidential government information about a person acquired when the lawyer was a public officer or employee, may not represent a private client whose interests are adverse to that person in a matter in which the information could be used to the material disadvantage of that person. As used in this Rule, the term "confidential government information" means information that has been obtained under governmental authority and which, at the time this Rule is applied, the government is prohibited by law from disclosing to the public or has a legal privilege not to disclose and which is not otherwise available to the public. A firm with which that lawyer is associated may undertake or continue representation in the matter only if the disqualified lawyer is timely screened from any participation in the matter and is apportioned no part of the fee therefrom.

(d) Except as law may otherwise expressly permit, a lawyer currently serving as a public officer or employee:

(1) is subject to Rules 1.7 and 1.9; and

(2) shall not:

(i) participate in a matter in which the lawyer participated personally and substantially while in private practice or non-governmental employment, unless the appropriate government agency gives its informed consent, confirmed in writing; or

(ii) negotiate for private employment with any person who is involved as a party or as lawyer for a party in a matter in which the lawyer is participating personally and substantially, except that a lawyer serving as a law clerk to a judge, other adjudicative officer or arbitrator may negotiate for private employment as permitted by Rule 1.12(b) and subject to the conditions stated in Rule 1.12(b).

(e) As used in this Rule, the term "matter" includes:

(1) any judicial or other proceeding, application, request for a ruling or other determination, contract, claim, controversy, investigation, charge, accusation, arrest or other particular matter involving a specific party or parties, and

(2) any other matter covered by the conflict of interest rules of the appropriate government agency.

COMMENT

[1] A lawyer who has served or is currently serving as a public officer or employee is personally subject to the Maryland Lawyers' Rules of Professional Conduct, including the prohibition against concurrent conflicts of interest stated in Rule 1.7. In addition, such a lawyer may be subject to statutes and government regulations regarding conflict of interest. Such statutes and regulations may circumscribe the extent to which the government agency may give consent under this Rule. See Rule 1.0(f) for the definition of informed consent.

[2] Paragraphs (a)(1), (a)(2) and (d)(1) restate the obligations of an individual lawyer who has served or is currently serving as an officer or employee of the government toward a former government or private client. Rule 1.10 is not applicable to the conflicts of interest addressed by this Rule. Rather, paragraph (b) sets forth a special imputation rule for former government lawyers that provides for screening and notice. Because of the special problems raised by imputation within a government agency, paragraph (d) does not impute the conflicts of a lawyer currently serving as an officer or employee of the government to other associated government officers or employees, although ordinarily it will be prudent to screen such lawyers.

[3] Paragraphs (a)(2) and (d)(2) apply regardless of whether a lawyer is adverse to a former client and are thus designed not only to protect the former client, but also to prevent a lawyer from exploiting public office for the advantage of another client. For example, a lawyer who has pursued a claim on behalf of the government may not pursue the same claim on behalf of a later private client after the lawyer has left government service, except when authorized to do so by the government agency under paragraph (a). Similarly, a lawyer who has pursued a claim on behalf of a private client may not pursue the claim on behalf of the government, except when authorized to do so by paragraph (d). As with para-

graphs (a)(1) and (d)(1), Rule 1.10 is not applicable to the conflicts of interest addressed by these paragraphs.

[4] This Rule represents a balancing of interests. On the one hand, where the successive clients are a government agency and another client, public or private, the risk exists that power or discretion vested in that agency might be used for the special benefit of the other client. A lawyer should not be in a position where benefit to the other client might affect performance of the lawyer's professional functions on behalf of the government. Also, unfair advantage could accrue to the other client by reason of access to confidential government information about the client's adversary obtainable only through the lawyer's government service. On the other hand, the rules governing lawyers presently or formerly employed by a government agency should not be so restrictive as to inhibit transfer of employment to and from the government. The government has a legitimate need to attract qualified lawyers as well as to maintain high ethical standards. Thus a former government lawyer is disqualified only from particular matters in which the lawyer participated personally and substantially. The provisions for screening and waiver in paragraph (b) are necessary to prevent the disqualification rule from imposing too severe a deterrent against entering public service. The limitation of disqualification in paragraphs (a)(2) and (d)(2) to matters involving a specific party or parties, rather than extending disqualification to all substantive issues on which the lawyer worked, serves a similar function.

[5] When a lawyer has been employed by one government agency and then moves to a second government agency, it may be appropriate to treat that second agency as another client for purposes of this Rule, as when a lawyer is employed by a city and subsequently is employed by a federal agency. However, because the conflict of interest is governed by paragraph (d), the latter agency is not required to screen the lawyer as paragraph (b) requires a law firm to do. The question of whether two government agencies should be regarded as the same or different clients for conflict of interest purposes is beyond the scope of these Rules. See Rule 1.13 Comment [8].

[6] Paragraphs (b) and (c) contemplate a screening arrangement. See Rule 1.0(m) (requirements for screening procedures). These paragraphs do not prohibit a lawyer from receiving a salary or partnership share established by prior independent agreement, but that lawyer may not receive compensation directly relating the lawyer's compensation to the fee in the matter in which the lawyer is disqualified.

[7] Notice, including a description of the screened lawyer's prior representation and of the screening procedures employed, generally should be given as soon as practicable after the need for screening becomes apparent.

[8] Paragraph (c) operates only when the lawyer in question has knowledge of the information, which means actual knowledge; it does not operate with respect to information that merely could be imputed to the lawyer.

[9] Paragraphs (a) and (d) do not prohibit a lawyer from jointly representing a private party and a government agency when doing so is permitted by Rule 1.7 and is not otherwise prohibited by law.

[10] For purposes of paragraph (e) of this Rule, a "matter" may continue in another form. In determining whether two particular matters are the same, the lawyer should consider the extent to which the matters involve the same basic facts, the same or related parties, and the time elapsed.

Model Rules Comparison. — Rule 1.11 is substantially similar to the language of the Ethics 2000 Amendments to the ABA Model Rules of Professional Conduct.

Conflict of interest not shown. — Plaintiff's attorney would not be disqualified because the attorney, while he worked for the city, was not substantially and personally involved in the termination of plaintiff, the attorney only spent a hour on a draft of a memorandum regarding the ability of the city to discipline and fire command level officers, and the police commissioners had waived any attorney-client privilege regarding the memo-randum because they produced it during discovery. Furthermore, the memorandum would not be sufficient to overcome the former commissioner's defense of qualified immunity, so there would be no need for the attorney to testify regarding the former commissioner's knowledge of the memorandum at the time he terminated plaintiff. Franklin v. Clark, 454 F. Supp. 2d 356 (D. Md. 2006).

Rule 1.12. Former Judge, Arbitrator, Mediator or Other Third-Party Neutral.

(a) Except as stated in paragraph (d), a lawyer shall not represent anyone in connection with a matter in which the lawyer participated personally and substantially as a judge or other adjudicative officer or law clerk to such a person or as an arbitrator, mediator or other third-party neutral, unless all parties to the proceeding give informed consent, confirmed in writing.

(b) A lawyer shall not negotiate for employment with any person who is involved as a party or as lawyer for a party in a matter in which the lawyer is participating personally and substantially as a judge or other adjudicative officer or as an arbitrator, mediator or other third-party neutral. A lawyer serving as a law clerk to a judge or other adjudicative officer may negotiate for employment with a party or lawyer involved in a matter in which the clerk is participating personally and substantially, but only after the lawyer has notified the judge or other adjudicative officer.

(c) If a lawyer is disqualified by paragraph (a), no lawyer in a firm with which that lawyer is associated may knowingly undertake or continue representation in the matter unless:

(1) the disqualified lawyer is timely screened from any participation in the matter and is apportioned no part of the fee therefrom; and

(2) written notice is promptly given to the parties and any appropriate tribunal to enable them to ascertain compliance with the provisions of this Rule.

(d) An arbitrator selected as a partisan of a party in a multimember arbitration panel is not prohibited from subsequently representing that party.

COMMENT

[1] This Rule generally parallels Rule 1.11. The term "personally and substantially" signifies that a judge who was a member of a multimember court, and thereafter left judicial office to practice law, is not prohibited from representing a client in a matter pending in the court, but in which the former judge did not participate. So also the fact that a former judge exercised administrative responsibility in a court does not prevent the former judge from acting as a lawyer in a matter where the judge had previously exercised remote or incidental administrative responsibility that did not affect the merits. Compare the Comment to Rule 1.11.

[2] The term "adjudicative officer" includes such officials as judges pro tempore, referees, special masters, hearing officers and other parajudicial officers, and also lawyers who serve as part-time judges. See Md. Rule 16-814, Maryland Code of Conduct for Judicial Appointees.

[3] Like former judges, lawyers who have served as arbitrators, mediators or other third-party neutrals may be asked to represent a client in a matter in which the lawyer participated personally and substantially. This Rule forbids such representation unless all of the parties to the proceedings give their informed consent, confirmed in writing. See Rule 1.0(f) and (b). Other law or codes of ethics governing third-party neutrals may impose more stringent standards of personal or imputed disqualification. See Rule 2.4.

[4] Although lawyers who serve as third-party neutrals do not have information concerning the parties that is protected under Rule 1.6, they typically owe the parties an obligation of confidentiality under law or codes of ethics governing third-party neutrals. Thus, paragraph (c) provides that conflicts of the personally disqualified lawyer will be imputed to other lawyers in a law firm unless the conditions of this paragraph are met.

[5] Requirements for screening procedures are stated in Rule 1.0(m). Paragraph (c)(1) does not prohibit the screened lawyer from receiving a salary or partnership share established by prior independent agreement, but that lawyer may not receive compensation directly related to the matter in which the lawyer is disqualified.

[6] Notice, including a description of the screened lawyer's prior representation and of

the screening procedures employed, generally should be given as soon as practicable after the need for screening becomes apparent.

Model Rules Comparison. — Apart from redesignating the paragraphs of the Com-

ments to this Rule, Rule 1.12 is substantially similar to the language of the Ethics 2000 Amendments to the ABA Model Rules of Professional Conduct.

University of Baltimore Law Forum. — "The New Maryland Rules of Professional Conduct and Mediation: Perplexing Questions

Answered and Perplexing Questions That Remain," see 36 U. Balt. L.F. 1 (2005).

Rule 1.13. Organization as Client.

(a) A lawyer employed or retained by an organization represents the organization acting through its duly authorized constituents.

(b) If a lawyer for an organization knows that an officer, employee or other person associated with the organization is engaged in action, intends to act or refuses to act in a matter related to the representation that is a violation of a legal obligation to the organization, or a violation of law that reasonably might be imputed to the organization, and is likely to result in substantial injury to the organization, the lawyer shall proceed as is reasonably necessary in the best interest of the organization. Unless the lawyer reasonably believes that it is not necessary in the best interest of the organization to do so, the lawyer shall refer the matter to higher authority in the organization, including, if warranted by the circumstances, to the highest authority that can act on behalf of the organization as determined by applicable law.

(c) When the organization's highest authority insists upon action, or refuses to take action, that is clearly a violation of a legal obligation to the organization, or a violation of law which reasonably might be imputed to the organization, and is reasonably certain to result in substantial injury to the organization, the lawyer may take further remedial action that the lawyer reasonably believes to be in the best interest of the organization. Such action may include revealing information otherwise protected by Rule 1.6 only if the lawyer reasonably believes that:

(1) the highest authority in the organization has acted to further the personal or financial interests of members of the authority which are in conflict with the interests of the organization; and

(2) revealing the information is necessary in the best interest of the organization.

(d) In dealing with an organization's directors, officers, employees, members, shareholders or other constituents, a lawyer shall explain the identity of the client when the lawyer knows or reasonably should know that the organization's interests are adverse to those of the constituents with whom the lawyer is dealing.

(e) A lawyer representing an organization may also represent any of its directors, officers, employees, members, shareholders or other constituents, subject to the provisions of Rule 1.7. If the organization's consent to the dual representation is required by Rule 1.7, the consent shall be given by an appropriate official of the organization other than the individual who is to be represented, or by the shareholders.

COMMENT

The Entity as the Client. — [1] An organizational client is a legal entity, but it cannot act except through its officers, directors, employees, shareholders and other constituents.

[2] Officers, directors, employees and shareholders are the constituents of the corporate organizational client. The duties created by this Rule apply equally to unincorporated associations. "Other constituents" as used in this Comment means the positions equivalent to officers, directors, employees and shareholders held by persons acting for organizational clients that are not corporations.

[3] When one of the constituents of an organizational client communicates with the organization's lawyer in that person's organizational capacity, the communication is protected by Rule 1.6. Thus, for example, if an organizational client requests its lawyer to investigate allegations of wrongdoing, interviews made in the course of that investigation between the lawyer and the client's employees or other constituents are covered by Rule 1.6. This does not mean, however, that constituents of an organizational client are the clients of the lawyer. The lawyer may not disclose to such constituents information relating to the representation except for disclosures explicitly or impliedly authorized by the organizational client in order to carry out the representation or as otherwise permitted by Rule 1.6.

[4] When constituents of the organization make decisions for it, the decisions ordinarily must be accepted by the lawyer even if their utility or prudence is doubtful. Decisions concerning policy and operations, including ones entailing serious risk, are not as such in the lawyer's province. However, different considerations arise when the lawyer knows that the organization is likely to be substantially injured by action of a constituent that is in violation of law. In such a circumstance, it may be reasonably necessary for the lawyer to ask the constituent to reconsider the matter. If that fails, or if the matter is of sufficient seriousness and importance to the organization, it may be reasonably necessary for the lawyer to take steps to have the matter reviewed by a higher authority in the organization, depending on the seriousness of the matter and whether the constituent in question has apparent motives to act at variance with the organization's interest. Review by the chief executive officer or by the board of directors may be required when the matter is of importance commensurate with their authority. At some point it may be useful or essential to obtain an independent legal opinion.

[5] The organization's highest authority to whom a matter may be referred ordinarily will be the board of directors or similar governing body. However, applicable law may prescribe that under certain conditions the highest authority reposes elsewhere; for example, in the independent directors of a corporation.

[6] If a lawyer can take remedial action without a disclosure of information that might adversely affect the organization, the lawyer as a matter of professional discretion may take such action as the lawyer reasonably believes to be in the best interest of the organization. For example, a lawyer for a close corporation may find it reasonably necessary to disclose misconduct by the Board to the shareholders. However, taking such action could entail disclosure of information relating to the representation with consequent risk of injury to the client; when such is the case, the organization is threatened by alternative injuries; the injury that may result from the governing Board's action or refusal to act, and the injury that may result if the lawyer's remedial efforts entail disclosure of confidential information. The lawyer may pursue remedial efforts even at the risk of disclosure in the circumstances stated in paragraphs (c)(1) and (c)(2).

Relation to Other Rules. — [7] The authority and responsibility provided in this Rule are concurrent with the authority and responsibility provided in other Rules. Paragraph (c) of this Rule supplements Rule 1.6(b) by providing an additional basis upon which the lawyer may reveal information relating to the representation, but does not modify, restrict, or limit the provisions of Rule 1.6(b)(1)-(6). Under paragraph (c) the lawyer may reveal such information only when the organization's highest authority insists upon or fails to address threatened or ongoing action that is clearly a violation of law, and then only to the extent the lawyer reasonably believes necessary to prevent reasonably certain substantial injury to the organization. It is not necessary that the lawyer's services be used in furtherance of the violation as it is under Rules 1.6(b)(2) and 1.6(b)(3), but it is required that the matter be related to the lawyer's representation of the organization. In particular, this Rule does not limit or expand the lawyer's responsibility under Rules 1.8, 1.16, 3.3 or 4.1. If the lawyer's services are being used by an organization to further a crime or fraud by the organization, Rules 1.6(b)(2) and 1.6(b)(3) may permit the lawyer to disclose information otherwise protected by Rule 1.6(a). In such circumstances, Rule 1.2(d) may also be applicable.

Government Agency. — [8] The duty defined in this Rule applies to governmental organizations. Defining precisely the identity of the client and prescribing the resulting obligations of such lawyers may be more difficult in the government context and is a matter beyond the scope of these Rules. See Scope [18]. Although in some circumstances the client may be a specific agency, it may also be a branch of government, such as the executive branch, or the government as a whole. For example, if the action or failure to act involves the head of a bureau, either the department of which the bureau is a part or the relevant branch of government may be the client for purposes of this Rule. Moreover, in a matter involving the conduct of government officials, a government lawyer may have authority under applicable law to question such conduct more extensively than that of a lawyer for a private organization in similar circumstances. Thus, when the client is a governmental organization, a different balance may be appropriate between maintaining confidentiality and assuring that the wrongful act is prevented or rectified, for public business is involved. In addition, duties of lawyers employed by the government or lawyers in military service may be defined by statutes and regulation. This Rule does not limit that authority. See Scope.

Clarifying the Lawyer's Role. — [9] There are times when the organization's interest may be or become adverse to those of one or more of its constituents. In such circumstances the lawyer should advise any constituent, whose interest the lawyer finds adverse to that of the organization of the conflict or potential conflict of interest, that the lawyer cannot represent such constituent, and that such person may wish to obtain independent representation. Care must be taken to assure that the individual understands that, when there is such adversity of interest, the lawyer for the organization cannot provide legal representation for that constituent individual, and that

discussions between the lawyer for the organization and the individual may not be privileged.

[10] Whether such a warning should be given by the lawyer for the organization to any constituent individual may turn on the facts of each case.

Dual Representation. — [11] Paragraph (e) recognizes that a lawyer for an organization may also represent a principal officer or major shareholder.

Derivative Actions. — [12] Under generally prevailing law, the shareholders or members of a corporation may bring suit to compel the directors to perform their legal obligations in the supervision of the organization. Members of unincorporated associations have essentially the same right. Such an action may be brought nominally by the organization, but usually is, in fact, a legal controversy over management of the organization.

[13] The question can arise whether counsel for the organization may defend such an action. The proposition that the organization is the lawyer's client does not alone resolve the issue. Most derivative actions are a normal incident of an organization's affairs, to be defended by the organization's lawyer like any other suit. However, if the claim involves serious charges of wrongdoing by those in control of the organization, a conflict may arise between the lawyer's duty to the organization and the lawyer's relationship with the board. In those circumstances, Rule 1.7 governs who may represent the directors and the organization.

Model Rules Comparison. — Rule 1.13 retains elements of existing Maryland language, incorporates further revisions, and incorporates language in Rule 1.13(d) and Comments [5] and [8] from the Ethics 2000 Amendments to the ABA Model Rules.

Relationship of county attorney with citizens of county served. — St. Mary's County, as a corporate entity, is the client of the St. Mary's County Attorney, and the County Attorney may, under appropriate circumstances, invoke the attorney-client and other privileges to maintain the confidentiality of documents encompassed by those privileges; although the County Attorney should act with due regard for the public interest, an attorney-client relationship as such does not ordinarily exist between the County Attorney and the citizens of the County. 82 Op. Att'y Gen. — (December 16, 1997).

Rule 1.14. Client with Diminished Capacity.

(a) When a client's capacity to make adequately considered decisions in connection with a representation is diminished whether because of minority, mental impairment or for some other reason, the lawyer shall, as far as reasonably possible, maintain a normal client-lawyer relationship with the client.

(b) When the lawyer reasonably believes that the client has diminished capacity, is at risk of substantial physical, financial, or other harm unless action is taken and cannot adequately act in the client's own interest, the lawyer may take reasonably necessary protective action, including consulting with individuals or entities that have the ability to take action to protect the client and, in appropriate cases, seeking the appointment of a guardian ad litem, conservator, or guardian.

(c) Information relating to the representation of a client with diminished capacity is protected by Rule 1.6. When taking protective action pursuant to paragraph (b), the lawyer is impliedly authorized under Rule 1.6(a) to reveal information about the client, but only to the extent reasonably necessary to protect the client's interests.

COMMENT

[1] The normal client-lawyer relationship is based on the assumption that the client, when properly advised and assisted, is capable of making decisions about important matters. When the client is a minor or suffers from a diminished mental capacity, however, maintaining the ordinary client-lawyer relationship may not be possible in all respects. In particular, a severely incapacitated person may have no power to make legally binding decisions. Nevertheless, to an increasing extent the law recognizes intermediate degrees of competence. Indeed, a client with diminished capacity often has the ability to understand, deliberate upon, and reach conclusions about matters affecting the client's own well-being. For example, it is recognized that some persons of advanced age can be quite capable of handling routine financial matters while needing special legal protection concerning major transactions. In addition, children as young as five or six years of age, and certainly those of ten or twelve, are regarded as having opinions that are entitled to weight in legal proceedings concerning their custody. Consideration of and, when appropriate, deference to these opinions are especially important in cases involving children in Child In Need of Assistance (CINA) and related Termination of Parental Rights (TPR) and adoption proceedings. With respect to these categories of cases, the Maryland Foster Care Court Improvement Project has prepared Guidelines of Advocacy for Attorneys Representing Children in CINA and Related TPR and Adoption Proceedings. The Guidelines are included in an appendix to the Maryland Rules. Also included in an Appendix to the Maryland Rules are *Maryland Guidelines for Practice for Court-Appointed Lawyers Representing Children in Cases Involving Child Custody or Child Access*, developed by the Maryland Judicial Conference Committee on Family Law.

[2] The fact that a client suffers a disability does not diminish the lawyer's obligation to treat the client with attention and respect. Even if the person has a legal representative, the lawyer should as far as possible accord the represented person the status of client, particularly in maintaining communication.

[3] The client may wish to have family members or other persons participate in discussions with the lawyer. When necessary to assist in the representation, the presence of such persons generally does not affect the applicability of the attorney-client evidentiary privilege. Nevertheless, the lawyer must keep the client's interests foremost and, except for protective action authorized under paragraph (b), must look to the client, and not family members, to make decisions on the client's behalf.

[4] If a legal representative has already been appointed for the client, the lawyer should ordinarily look to the representative for decisions on behalf of the client. In matters involving a minor, whether the lawyer should look to the parents as natural guardians may depend on the type of proceeding or matter in which the lawyer is representing the minor. If the lawyer represents the guardian as distinct from the ward, and is aware that the guardian is acting adversely to the ward's interest, the lawyer may have an obligation to prevent or rectify the guardian's misconduct. See Rule 1.2(d).

Taking Protective Action. — [5] If a lawyer reasonably believes that a client is at risk of substantial physical, financial or other harm unless action is taken, and that a normal client-lawyer relationship cannot be maintained as provided in paragraph (a) because the client lacks sufficient capacity to communicate or to make adequately considered decisions in connection with the representation, then paragraph (b) permits the lawyer to take protective measures deemed necessary. Such measures could include: consulting with family members, delaying action if feasible to permit clarification or improvement of circumstances, using voluntary surrogate decision-making tools such as durable powers of attorney or consulting with support groups, professional services, adult-protective agencies or other individuals or entities that have the ability to protect the client. In taking any protective action, the lawyer should be guided by such factors as the wishes and values of the client to the extent known, the client's best interests and the goals of intruding into the client's decision-making autonomy to the least extent feasible, maximizing client capacities and respecting the client's family and social connections.

[6] In determining the extent of the client's diminished capacity, the lawyer should consider and balance such factors as: the client's ability to articulate reasoning leading to a decision; variability of state of mind and ability to appreciate consequences of a decision; the substantive fairness of a decision; and the consistency of a decision with the known long-term commitments and values of the client. In appropriate circumstances, the lawyer may seek guidance from an appropriate diagnostician.

[7] If a legal representative has not been appointed, the lawyer should consider whether appointment of a guardian ad litem, conservator or guardian is necessary to protect the client's interests. Thus, if a client with diminished capacity has substantial property that should be sold for the client's benefit, effective completion of the transaction may require appointment of a legal representative. In addition, rules of procedure in litigation sometimes provide that minors or persons with diminished capacity must be represented by a guardian or next friend if they do not have a general guardian. In many circumstances, however, appointment of a legal representative may be more expensive or traumatic for the client than circumstances in fact require. Evaluation of such circumstances is a matter entrusted to the professional judgment of the lawyer. In considering alternatives, however, the lawyer should be aware of any law that requires the lawyer to advocate the least restrictive action on behalf of the client.

Disclosure of the Client's Condition. — [8] Disclosure of the client's diminished capacity could adversely affect the client's interests. For example, raising the question of diminished capacity could, in some circumstances, lead to proceedings for involuntary commitment. Information relating to the representa-

tion is protected by Rule 1.6. Therefore, unless authorized to do so, the lawyer may not disclose such information. When taking protective action pursuant to paragraph (b), the lawyer is impliedly authorized to make the necessary disclosures, even when the client directs the lawyer to the contrary. Nevertheless, given the risks of disclosure, paragraph (c) limits what the lawyer may disclose in consulting with other individuals or entities or seeking the appointment of a legal representative. At the very least, the lawyer should determine whether it is likely that the person or entity consulted with will act adversely to the client's interests before discussing matters related to the client. The lawyer's position in such cases is an unavoidably difficult one.

Emergency Legal Assistance. — [9] In an emergency where the health, safety or a financial interest of a person with seriously diminished capacity is threatened with imminent and irreparable harm, a lawyer may take legal action on behalf of such a person even though the person is unable to establish a client-lawyer relationship or to make or express considered judgments about the matter, when the person or another acting in good faith on that person's behalf has consulted with the lawyer. Even in such an emergency, however, the lawyer should not act unless the lawyer reasonably believes that the person has no other lawyer, agent or other representative available. The lawyer should take legal action on behalf of the person only to the extent reasonably necessary to maintain the status quo or otherwise avoid imminent and irreparable harm. A lawyer who undertakes to represent a person in such an exigent situation has the same duties under these Rules as the lawyer would with respect to a client.

[10] A lawyer who acts on behalf of a person with seriously diminished capacity in an emergency should keep the confidences of the person as if dealing with a client, disclosing them only to the extent necessary to accomplish the intended protective action. The lawyer should disclose to any tribunal involved and to any other counsel involved the nature of his or her relationship with the person. The lawyer should take steps to regularize the relationship or implement other protective solutions as soon as possible.

Model Rules Comparison. — Rule 1.14 is substantially similar to the language of the Ethics 2000 Amendments to the ABA Model Rules of Professional Conduct, with the exception of retaining elements of existing Maryland language in Comment [1] and further revising Comments [5] and [10].

Effect of amendments. — The 2007 amendment added the last sentence in Comment [1].

Rule 1.15. Safekeeping Property.

(a) A lawyer shall hold property of clients or third persons that is in a lawyer's possession in connection with a representation separate from the lawyer's own property. Funds shall be kept in a separate account maintained pursuant to Title 16, Chapter 600 of the Maryland Rules, and records shall be created and maintained in accordance with the Rules in that Chapter. Other property shall be identified specifically as such and appropriately safeguarded, and records of its receipt and distribution shall be created and maintained. Complete records of the account funds and of other property shall be kept by the lawyer and shall be preserved for a period of at least five years after the date the record was created.

(b) A lawyer may deposit the lawyer's own funds in a client trust account only as permitted by Rule 16-607 b.

(c) Unless the client gives informed consent, confirmed in writing, to a different arrangement, a lawyer shall deposit legal fees and expenses that have been paid in advance into a client trust account and may withdraw those funds for the lawyer's own benefit only as fees are earned or expenses incurred.

(d) Upon receiving funds or other property in which a client or third person has an interest, a lawyer shall promptly notify the client or third person. Except as stated in this Rule or otherwise permitted by law or by agreement with the client, a lawyer shall deliver promptly to the client or third person any funds or other property that the client or third person is entitled to receive and, upon request by the client or third person, shall render promptly a full accounting regarding such property.

(e) When a lawyer in the course of representing a client is in possession of property in which two or more persons (one of whom may be the lawyer) claim interests, the property shall be kept separate by the lawyer until the dispute is resolved. The lawyer shall distribute promptly all portions of the property as to which the interests are not in dispute. (Amended March 12, 2007, effective January 1, 2008.)

COMMENT

[1] A lawyer should hold property of others with the care required of a professional fiduciary. Securities should be kept in a safe deposit box, except when some other form of safekeeping is warranted by special circumstances. All property of clients or third persons, including prospective clients, must be kept separate from the lawyer's business and personal property and, if money, in one or more trust accounts. Separate trust accounts may be warranted when administering estate money or acting in similar fiduciary capacities. A lawyer should maintain on a current basis books and records in accordance with generally accepted accounting practice and the Rules in Title 16, Chapter 600 and comply with any other record-keeping rules established by law or court order.

Normally it is impermissible to commingle the lawyer's own funds with client funds, and paragraph (b) provides that it is permissible only as permitted by Rule 16-607 b. Accurate records must be kept regarding which part of the funds are the lawyer's.

[3] Paragraph (c) of Rule 1.15 permits advances against unearned fees and unincurred costs to be treated as either the property of the client or the property of the lawyer. Unless the client gives informed consent, confirmed in writing, to a different arrangement, the Rule's default position is that such advances be treated as the property of the client, subject to

the restrictions provided in paragraph (a). In any case, at the termination of an engagement, advances against fees that have not been incurred must be returned to the client as provided in Rule 1.16(d).

[4] Lawyers often receive funds from which the lawyer's fee will be paid. The lawyer is not required to remit the client funds that the lawyer reasonably believes represent fees owed. However, a lawyer may not hold funds to coerce a client into accepting the lawyer's contention. The disputed portion of the funds must be kept in a trust account and the lawyer should suggest means for prompt resolution of the dispute, such as arbitration. The undisputed portion of the funds shall be distributed promptly.

[5] Paragraph (e) also recognizes that third parties may have lawful claims against specific funds or other property in a lawyer's custody, such as a client's creditor who has a lien on funds recovered in a personal injury action. A lawyer may have a duty under applicable law to protect such third-party claims against wrongful interference by the client. In such cases, when the third-party claim is not frivolous under applicable law, the lawyer must refuse to surrender the funds or property to the client until the claims are resolved. A lawyer should not unilaterally assume to arbitrate a dispute between the client and the third party, but, when there are substantial grounds for dispute as to the person entitled to the funds, the lawyer may file an action to have a court resolve the dispute.

[6] The obligations of a lawyer under this Rule are independent of those arising from activity other than rendering legal services. For example, a lawyer who serves only as an escrow agent is governed by the applicable law relating to fiduciaries even though the lawyer does not render legal services in the transaction and is not governed by this Rule.

Model Rules Comparison. — Rule 1.15 is substantially similar to the language of the Ethics 2000 Amendments to the ABA Model Rules of Professional Conduct, with the exception of changes to Rule 1.15(c), the addition of Comment [3], and the omission of ABA Comment [6].

I. GENERAL CONSIDERATION.

A. In General.

Effect of amendments. — The 2007 amendment, effective January 1, 2008, in (a) added "and records shall be created and maintained in accordance with the Rules in that Chapter" at the end of the second sentence, added "specifically" and "and records of its receipt and distribution shall be created and maintained" in the third sentence, and added "at least" and substituted "the date the record was created" for "termination of the representation" in the third sentence and made stylistic changes; in (b) substituted "only as permitted by Rule 16-607 b" for "for the sole purpose of paying bank service charges on that account but only in an amount necessary for the purpose"; in (c) added "legal fees and expenses that have been paid in advance" and substituted "and may withdraw those funds for the lawyer's own benefit" for "to be withdrawn by the lawyer" and made stylistic changes; made nonsubstantive, stylistic changes in (d) and (e); and in the Comment, in [1] substituted "money" for "monies" throughout, deleted "that is the property" after "property" at the beginning of the third sentence, and added "and the Rules in Title 16, Chapter 600" and "other" in the fifth sentence; in the first sentence of [2] substituted "only as permitted by Rule 16-607 b" for "when necessary to pay bank service charges on that account" and made stylistic changes; made stylistic changes in [4]; and added "funds or" in the third sentence of [5].

Editor's note. — The March 12, 2007, Order provided in part that "the rules changes hereby adopted by this Court shall take effect on January 1, 2008 and, from and after said date, shall govern the conduct of attorneys from and after that date".

University of Baltimore Law Forum. — For article "The Regulation of Attorney Escrow Accounts ... Boon or Overkill?", see 17, No. 3 U. Balt. Law Forum 9 (1987).

In general. — Lawyer's failure to respond to inquiries from the legatees of an estate for which he was personal representative, or their counsel, or provide necessary information to the estate's accountant, or comply with a subpoena to produce estate records, only producing those records when he was specifically ordered to, violated prior, similar Md. R. Prof. Conduct 1.15. Att'y Griev. Comm'n v. Sullivan, 369 Md. 650, 801 A.2d 1077 (2002).

Abandonment of matter. — Attorney violated this Rule and Ga. St. Bar Stand. 44 by failing to fund a special needs trust for his client and a trust for the benefit of her children, although he had a settlement check replaced with checks to fund the trusts. Att'y Griev. Comm'n v. Roberson, 373 Md. 328, 818 A.2d 1059 (2003).

Attorney acting as title insurance broker — Attorney, who was acting outside the practice of law when he placed funds received as a title insurance broker into his title insurance company account, could not be disciplined for violations of the Maryland rules of professional conduct related to an attorney's handling of client funds where it was not clear that the attorney had violated any of the statutes regarding a title insurance broker's handling of client funds. Since the attorney had received the client's consent to place interest on funds he was holding into this title insurance company's account, he may not have violated any of the rules regulating brokers, but was nevertheless not acting as an attorney and could not be subjected to attorney disciplinary proceedings. Att'y Griev. Comm'n v. Lichtenberg, 379 Md. 335, 842 A.2d 11 (2004).

Fiduciary for non-client. — An attorney acts as a fiduciary for a non-client within the meaning of § 10-312 (b) (1) of the Business Occupations and Professions Article and of former Md. Rule 1228 b 3 (now Rule 16-811 b 3), relating to the Clients' Security Trust Fund, when the attorney disburses client funds from the attorney's trust account to a non-client, at the instructions of the client and pursuant to the obligations recognized in the prior, similar Rule. Advance Fin. Co. v. Trustees of Clients' Sec. Trust Fund, 337 Md. 195, 652 A.2d 660 (1995).

A lawyer should hold settlement funds with the care of a professional fiduciary. Where a bank had an interest in settlement proceeds owed to an attorney's client, the prior, similar Rule imposed on the attorney the ethical duties of notification, payment, and accounting to that creditor; the attorney must recognize the creditor's interest in the settlement funds in his possession. Att'y Griev. Comm'n v. Stolarz, 379 Md. 387, 842 A.2d 42 (2004).

When an attorney acted as a settlement agent at a real estate closing, and another attorney supervised the first attorney, the agent was properly found to have violated (b) because the agent assumed fiduciary obligations when the agent signed a certification stating how sale proceeds were to be distributed, and a violation of those obligations by not distributing the proceeds in the manner stated in the certification violated the Rule. Att'y Griev. Comm'n v. Johnson, 409 Md. 470, 976 A.2d 245 (2009).

When an attorney acted as a settlement agent at a real estate closing, and another attorney supervised the first attorney, both attorneys were properly found to have violated (b) when sale proceeds were not distributed in the manner stated in a settlement statement because the fact that the attorneys were not practicing law was not a defense, as the Rule applied generally to the attorneys' fiduciary obligations related to holding "any property." Att'y Griev. Comm'n v. Johnson, 409 Md. 470, 976 A.2d 245 (2009).

When an attorney acted as a settlement agent at a real estate closing, and another attorney supervised the first attorney, the supervisor was properly found to have violated (b) when sale proceeds were not distributed in the manner stated in a settlement statement because the supervisor was ultimately responsible for the distribution of the proceeds. Att'y Griev. Comm'n v. Johnson, 409 Md. 470, 976 A.2d 245 (2009).

Unapproved accounts. — Respondent violated § 10-302 of the Business Occupations & Professions Article, the prior, similar Rule and Rule 8.4 by placing trust account money in an unapproved account. Att'y Griev. Comm'n v. Boyd, 333 Md. 298, 635 A.2d 382 (1994).

Attorney violated Rule 16-606 by designating his attorney trust account as "Jared K. Ellison, Esq. IOLTA" and the prior, similar Rule for not complying with Title 16, ch. 600 of the Maryland Rules; the incorrectly designated account checks were sufficient to violate both Md. R. 16-606 and the prior, similar Rule. Att'y Griev. Comm'n v. Ellison, 384 Md. 688, 867 A.2d 259 (2005).

Prima facie showing of violation. — The mere fact that the balance in an attorney trust account falls below the total amounts held in trust supports a prima facie finding of violation of the Rule. Att'y Griev. Comm'n v. Glenn, 341 Md. 448, 671 A.2d 463 (1996).

Unintentional violations. — An unintentional violation of the prior, similar Rule, with certain limited exceptions is still a violation of the attorney's affirmative duties imposed by the Rule. Att'y Griev. Comm'n v. Glenn, 341 Md. 448, 671 A.2d 463 (1996).

Bar Counsel failed to prove by clear and convincing evidence violations of the prior, similar Rule or prior, similar Rule 8.4, or § 10-306 of the Business Occupations and Professions Article, where judge found lawyer's use of funds from trust account for operating expenses was motivated by ignorance of his obligations and not by fraud, dishonesty or deceit. Att'y Griev. Comm'n v. Awuah, 346 Md. 420, 697 A.2d 446 (1997).

Disputed fee. — Attorney's arguably good faith belief that funds withdrawn from a trust account were due as fees could be offered in mitigation of charges of having violated prior, similar Md. R. Prof. Conduct 1.15, but it did not make the attorney's actions not a violation. Att'y Griev. Comm'n v. Braskey, 378 Md. 425, 836 A.2d 605 (2003).

An unintentional violation of the rule is still a violation of the attorney's affirmative duties imposed by the rule. An attorney's oversight in either notifying or paying a bank the proceeds of a settlement his client received, though without intent to deceive, was still a violation and still subjected the attorney to possible sanctions. Att'y Griev. Comm'n v. Stolarz, 379 Md. 387, 842 A.2d 42 (2004).

Applied in Att'y Griev. Comm'n v. Ficker, 399 Md. 445, 924 A.2d 1105 (2007).

Quoted in Att'y Griev. Comm'n v. Christopher, 383 Md. 624, 861 A.2d 692 (2004); Att'y Griev. Comm'n v. Scroggs, 387 Md. 238, 874 A.2d 985 (2005); Att'y Griev. Comm'n v. Whitehead, 390 Md. 663, 890 A.2d 751 (2006); Att'y Griev. Comm'n v. Lanocha, 392 Md. 234, 896 A.2d 996 (2006); Att'y Griev. Comm'n v. Mba-Jonas, 402 Md. 334, 936 A.2d 839 (2007); Att'y Griev. Comm'n v. Kreamer, 404 Md. 282, 946 A.2d 500 (2008).

Stated in Att'y Griev. Comm'n v. Midlen, 395 Md. 628, 911 A.2d 852 (2006).

Cited in Att'y Griev. Comm'n v. Sweitzer, 395 Md. 586, 911 A.2d 440 (2006); Phyllis J. Outlaw & Assocs. v. Graham, 172 Md. App. 16, 912 A.2d 64 (2006); Att'y Griev. Comm'n v. Adams, 404 Md. 1, 944 A.2d 1115 (2008); Att'y Griev. Comm'n v. Snyder, 406 Md. 21, 956 A.2d 147 (2008); Att'y Griev. Comm'n v. Tanko, 408 Md. 404, 969 A.2d 1010 (2009); Unnamed Atty. v. Att'y Griev. Comm'n, 409 Md. 509, 976 A.2d 267 (2009); Att'y Griev. Comm'n v. Adams, 410 Md. 544, 979 A.2d 698 (2009); Att'y Griev. Comm'n v. Tauber, — Md. —, 26 A.3d 967 (2011).

B. Failure to Act.

Failure to deliver funds to client. — Attorney violated the prior, similar Rule and Ga. St. Bar Stand. 61 by: (1) (1) failing to deposit $ 600,000 in funds left in the hands of the defendant doctor's attorney; (2) improperly paying the client's settlement funds to her husband and his sister; and (3) taking excessive counsel fees for himself and his co-counsel. Att'y Griev. Comm'n v. Roberson, 373 Md. 328, 818 A.2d 1059 (2003).

Misleading client by falsely advising him that funds were being placed in the attorney's trust account when they, in fact, were not, and failing to keep client apprised of status of settlement funds constituted a violation of the prior, similar Rule. Att'y Griev. Comm'n v. Daskalopoulos, 383 Md. 375, 859 A.2d 653 (2004).

Attorney violated the prior, similar Rule when he failed to deliver client funds to her for more than a year; his claim that he failed to finalize disbursements because he was negotiating a reduction of one of the liens did not excuse him from the obligation of "prompt delivery." Att'y Griev. Comm'n v. Mininsohn, 380 Md. 536, 846 A.2d 353 (2004).

Attorney was disbarred as his failure to hold a client's money in his escrow account and his failure to promptly deliver the money to his client violated the prior, similar Rule. Att'y Griev. Comm'n v. Brown, 380 Md. 661, 846 A.2d 428 (2004).

Failure to use trust account or return unearned fees — Attorney representing a client in a divorce action violated this Rule when he failed to deposit advanced fees into a trust account and failed to promptly return unearned fees to the client after the client discharged the attorney. Att'y Griev. Comm'n v. Rose, 391 Md. 101, 892 A.2d 469 (2006), cert. denied, 2006 U.S. LEXIS 5734, 166 L. Ed. 2d 22 (U.S. 2006).

Attorney's conduct violated this Rule and § 10-304 of the Business Occupations and Professions Article where she had placed a client's entire payment in an operating account at the time it was paid. The fee was for the entire representation and, because the attorney's only substantive action was to file the divorce complaint, most of it was unearned at the time it was deposited in her operating account; therefore, some portion of the unearned fee belonged to the client and met the definition of "trust money" as defined in § 10-301(d) of the Business Occupations and Professions Article. Att'y Griev. Comm'n v. McCulloch, 404 Md. 388, 946 A.2d 1009 (2008).

Failure to contact assignee of client's settlement proceeds. — Attorney violated the prior, similar Rule where he made no effort to contact a third-party healthcare provider, who was an assignee of a client's settlement proceeds, after he received the settlement funds and in fact, made substantial efforts to avoid such contact. Att'y Griev. Comm'n v. Ellison, 384 Md. 688, 867 A.2d 259 (2005).

Failure to keep adequate records. — Attorney violated the prior, similar Rule and Ga. St. Bar Stand. 63 by keeping no records of the receipt and disbursement of a client's funds other than bank statements and cancelled checks such that it was impossible to determine how much money the attorney received on the client's behalf and where it all went; the settlement statement falsely reflected the receipt of $600,000 on behalf of the client's children, as the attorney returned the funds, and that the attorney paid an attorney to set up the children's trust, as the payment was never actually made. Att'y Griev. Comm'n v. Roberson, 373 Md. 328, 818 A.2d 1059 (2003).

Where the attorney argued that the failure to maintain a client ledger sheet with regard to the client trust fund account did not necessarily constitute a violation of (a) if the attorney maintained equivalent information, the attorney's argument failed; the attorney violated (a) and (b) by commingling personal funds with the account and by failing to maintain a complete record of the account, as the attorney's cash receipt journal, check register, statement of account, and cancelled checks failed to provide an adequate accounting of the origin of the funds in the attorney's escrow account, and the documents the attorney produced failed to provide a complete record of the receipt and disbursement of client funds in the attorney's possession. Att'y Griev. Comm'n v. Obi, 393 Md. 643, 904 A.2d 422 (2006).

Failure to provide accounting. — Attorney violated the prior, similar Rule and Ga. St. Bar Stand. 65.a by failing to provide an accounting for all settlement funds to his client or her guardian, which the attorney, as her attorney, held in trust. Att'y Griev. Comm'n v. Roberson, 373 Md. 328, 818 A.2d 1059 (2003).

Failure to deliver funds and records to client. — Attorney's failure to safekeep estate assets and financial records of an estate and to turn them over to a successor personal representative was a clear violation of this Rule. Att'y Griev. Comm'n v. Kendrick, 403 Md. 489, 943 A.2d 1173 (2008).

Failure to maintain separate accounts. — An attorney's failure to maintain separate accounts for the deposit of money advanced on behalf of his clients for future representation of those clients, his failure to maintain trust accounts, and his failure to cooperate with the Grievance Board constituted rules violations. Att'y Griev. Comm'n v. Briscoe, 357 Md. 554, 745 A.2d 1037 (2000).

Attorney violated the prior, similar Rule when he undertook representatation of a client in a personal injury action, and deposited monies received into his operating account because he did not have a trust or escrow account. Att'y Griev. Comm'n v. Jeter, 365 Md. 279, 778 A.2d 390 (2001).

Where attorney deposited earned fees and money he received from his father into a bank account he titled as an attorney trust account, and used this account for personal and business purposes, such conduct constituted clear and convincing evidence of commingling in violation of both the prior, similar Rule and Md. R. 16-607. Att'y Griev. Comm'n v. Powell, 369 Md. 462, 800 A.2d 782 (2002).

State supreme court found that an attorney who failed to maintain adequate records, commingled funds, and accepted commissions without prior court approval when he served as an estate's representative, violated prior, similar Maryland Rules of Professional Conduct 1.1, and it ordered that the attorney be suspended from the practice of law in Maryland, with the right to reapply for permission to practice law at the end of one year. Att'y Griev. Comm'n v. Thompson, 376 Md. 500, 830 A.2d 474 (2003).

Suspended attorney was disbarred because of his later (1) unjustified misappropriation of trust funds by not paying the clients' medical providers (as he had promised he would do) from clients' share settlement he retained in cash after he got clients' endorsements on settlement checks, received payable to him and to the clients, cashed the checks with the clients at a liquor store cashing service, retained cash to pay his one-third fee (that he reduced) and to pay listed medical providers according to a handwritten distribution summary given to the clients, and distributed the clients' share to them; (2) failure to have or to use an attorney trust account at a proper financial institution; and (3) failure to respond to the disciplinary committee's investigation or petition, or to the hearing judge's conclusions. The attorney's misappropriation of trust money was serious professional misconduct and was embezzlement, fraudulent misappropriation by a fiduciary, under 7-113 of the Criminal Law Article, representing professional misconduct that violated prior, similar Rule 8.4(b)-(c); and his conducted also violated prior, similar Rules 1.15, 8.1; Maryland Rules 16-812, 16-603, 16-604, and §§ 10-302(a), 10-306 of the Business Occupations and Professions Article. Att'y Griev. Comm'n v. Prichard, 386 Md. 238, 872 A.2d 81 (2005).

The failure to establish a proper trust account and the failure to use such an account as the depository for the recovery proceeds constituted a violation Maryland Rules 16-603 and 604, and prior, similar Rule 1.15, by failing to safeguard the property of others entrusted to the attorney. Att'y Griev. Comm'n v. Mitchell, 386 Md. 386, 872 A.2d 720 (2005).

Substantial evidence did not support a hearing judge's determinations that an attorney had not violated prior, similar Rules 1.1, 1.15(b), and 8.4 by commingling a client's settlement proceeds with other funds in the attorney's operating account and delaying disbursement of the proceeds for several months, where the hearing judge had ignored the evidence on the back of the check itself and in bank records; although the conduct was egregious, it had not been shown to be intentional, so an indefinite suspension was the appropriate sanction. Att'y Griev. Comm'n v. Maignan, 390 Md. 287, 888 A.2d 344 (2005).

Attorney violated this Rule by failing to properly label her trust account and depositing two payments into that account and, especially, by her deposit of a settlement check into her personal checking account. Att'y Griev. Comm'n v. Calhoun, 391 Md. 532, 894 A.2d 518 (2006).

Failure to hold withholding tax funds in trust for State. — Where an attorney was found to have willfully and regularly failed to comply with his obligation as an employer for several years because he failed to withhold state income tax from the wages of his employees and to hold such funds in trust for the State, he was found to have violated prior, similar Rule 8.4 and this Rule, as well as §§ 13-1007(b) and (c) and 10-906(a) and (b) of the Tax - General Article; however, the hearing judge erred in finding that although the attorney technically violated prior, similar Rule 8.4, he did not exhibit conduct that violated those rules, as there were tax liens filed against the attorney and he failed to file required periodic reports, which conduct exhibited a willful failure to comply with his tax obligations. Att'y Griev. Comm'n v. Mininsohn, 380 Md. 536, 846 A.2d 353 (2004).

Disbarment was the only appropriate sanction for an attorney who withdrew sums that should have been forwarded to a client from an attorney trust account for the attorney's personal use and failed to respond to the client's inquiries; the attorney's marital and drinking problems were not factors in mitigation. Att'y Griev. Comm'n v. Herman, 380 Md. 378, 844 A.2d 1181 (2004).

Duty to notify assignee. — Attorney's Rule 2-432(b)(1)(G) motion was properly denied as (b) placed an affirmative burden on the attorney to notify a third-party assignee upon the receipt of burdened funds and to deliver the proper amount due to the third party, a dispute over the amount due was not a defense to a disciplinary proceeding arising out of nonpayment to the assignee, and Maryland Bar Counsel's investigations of a complaint due to nonpayment were ordinarily not discoverable under Rule 16-723(b). Att'y Griev. Comm'n v. Ellison, 384 Md. 688, 867 A.2d 259 (2005).

Failure to advise. — It was a violation of professional conduct rules for an attorney to fail to advise a client of the receipt of a refunded deposit from the bankruptcy trustee. Att'y Griev. Comm'n v. Harris-Smith, 356 Md. 72, 737 A.2d 567 (1999).

C. Misappropriation or Mishandling of Funds.

Misappropriation of funds. — Misappropriation of client's funds involves conduct constituting moral turpitude. Att'y Griev. Comm'n v. Moore, 301 Md. 169, 482 A.2d 497 (1984).

Clear and convincing evidence was found that an attorney violated this Rule by converting a client's personal injury protection fund monies to her personal use, having insufficient funds in her escrow account to pay the client's outstanding claims for reimbursement from such fund, and otherwise converting to her own use the fund, which should have been held in trust for the client. Att'y Griev. Comm'n v. Cherry-Mahoi, 388 Md. 124, 879 A.2d 58 (2005).

Attorney's misconduct in abusing the trust that the client placed in the attorney by placing the client's retainer check in the attorney's operating account rather than an attorney trust account, spending that money which belonged to the client on the attorney, in refusing to promptly refund to the client money that attorney admittedly owed to the client despite the client's refund request, and in failing to promptly answer bar counsel's request for information about the matter warranted the attorney's indefinite suspension. Att'y Griev. Comm'n v. McCulloch, 397 Md. 674, 919 A.2d 660 (2007).

Attorney's conduct in taking client funds placed in the attorney's escrow account out of that account and using them to cover the attorney's law practice operating expenses was a violation of this Rule and merited disbarment, as the escrow funds and the account used to pay the law practice's operating expenses had to be maintained separately. Att'y Griev. Comm'n v. Nussbaum, 401 Md. 612, 934 A.2d 1 (2007).

Attorney's exceptions to a judge's finding that he had violated Md. R. Prof. Conduct 1.1, 1.15(a), and 8.4(a) and (d) were overruled where the findings were based on the credibility of the client's testimony with respect to the attorney's handling of a retainer. Att'y Griev. Comm'n v. Maignan, 402 Md. 39, 935 A.2d 409 (2007).

Attorney's conduct in violating multiple Maryland Rules of Professional Conduct, including violation of (a) of this Rule by not properly depositing funds the client gave to the attorney for the client's representation, warranted disbarment. The attorney committed the violation by depositing the funds in the attorney's general operating account rather than in the attorney's escrow account. Att'y Griev. Comm'n v. Webster, 402 Md. 448, 937 A.2d 161 (2007).

Attorney violated this Rule because (1) the attorney did not enter a client's name into the database of the firm by which the attorney was employed, (2) the attorney did not record the client's retainer payment, (3) the attorney did not forward that payment to the firm's main office, (4) the attorney substituted the attorney's name as payee on a check that the client issued to the firm, and deposited that check in the attorney's personal account, and (5) the attorney did not relinquish the funds deposited in the attorney's personal account to the firm until after the attorney was confronted by a supervisor. Att'y Griev. Comm'n v. Elliott, 417 Md. 659, 12 A.3d 105 (2011).

Attorney violated (a) of this Rule and 10-304(a) of the Business Occupations and Professions Article because, when the attorney maintained an unauthorized side practice while being employed "of counsel" for a law firm, the attorney (1) did not keep a trust account for clients represented in that practice, and (2) deposited unearned retainers from that practice in the attorney's personal account. Att'y Griev. Comm'n v. Carithers, 421 Md. 28, 25 A.3d 181 (2011).

What constitutes commingling. — Deposit of a check from a client's insurer, payable to the client and attorney, into the attorney's personal account constituted a prohibited commingling of funds, even though the attorney disbursed funds to the client less than three weeks later. Att'y Griev. Comm'n v. Kemp, 303 Md. 664, 496 A.2d 672 (1985).

Attorney violated (a) by failing to remove earned fees from the attorney's trust account and thereby commingling the attorney's own funds with those of the attorney's clients. The attorney was only reprimanded because the act was unintentional. Att'y Griev. Comm'n v. Sapero, 400 Md. 461, 929 A.2d 483 (2007).

Mishandling escrow account. — Indefinite suspension was appropriate sanction for attorneys mishandling of escrow account, including the failure to pay claims due from the account and the failure to refund moneys to clients. Att'y Griev. Comm'n v. Singleton, 311 Md. 1, 532 A.2d 157 (1987).

Attorney who, in connection with a foreclosure action he filed on behalf of his clients, failed to safeguard the bidder's deposit and used of part of the funds for his own purposes, was suspended for 30 days; his violation of this Rule was not wilful, and he had no prior record. Att'y Griev. Comm'n v. McClain, 373 Md. 196, 817 A.2d 218 (2003).

Disciplinary proceedings which charged that an attorney who represented a very difficult client in an estate matter, and who deducted his fee from settlement proceeds without having filed a fee petition and obtaining the court's approval prior to taking his portion, culminated in a determination by clear and convincing evidence that the attorney had violated prior, similar Rules 1.1, 1.15, and 8.4, and the imposition of an indefinite suspension against him upon a finding that his actions were not intentional; however, where the attorney was not charged with violating a part of prior, similar Rule 8.4, it was a violation of due process for the hearing judge to determine that he had violated all of prior, similar Rule 8.4 because he had never received notice of those alleged charges and accordingly, was not held to have violated those rules. Att'y Griev. Comm'n v. Seiden, 373 Md. 409, 818 A.2d 1108 (2003).

When an attorney acted as an escrow agent for a client which purportedly funded high-risk loans, the attorney violated subsections (a) and (b) when he removed commitment fees deposited in the escrow account and disbursed them to parties unrelated to a contemplated loan, rather than either returning them to the depositors or disbursing them to parties providing loans. Att'y Griev. Comm'n v. Smith, 376 Md. 202, 829 A.2d 567 (2003).

Where an attorney invaded trust funds being held for a client, and only scrambled to replace them when the client required reimbursement, the evidence was ample to show knowing misappropriation, and the only appropriate sanction was disbarment. Att'y Griev. Comm'n v. Zdravkovich, 381 Md. 680, 852 A.2d 82 (2004).

Attorney was suspended for thirty days for withdrawing part of a retainer fee from her escrow account before earning the fee in violation of (a) and § 10-306 of the Business Occupations and Professions Article and for making a billing error that resulted in a refund being owed to the clients under (b) and Md. R. Prof. Conduct 1.16(d). Additionally, the attorney's inexcusable and untimely delay in responding to a bar counsel's request for information in answer to allegations made by two disgruntled clients in an adoption matter violated Md. R. Prof. Conduct 8.1(b). Att'y Griev. Comm'n v. Rees, 396 Md. 248, 913 A.2d 68 (2006).

Attorney was indefinitely suspended from the practice of law for violating, inter alia, (a) and (b) of this Rule when, on at least three occasions, the attorney disbursed funds to clients before settlement checks were deposited. Att'y Griev. Comm'n v. Goff, 399 Md. 1, 922 A.2d 554 (2007).

Mishandling attorney trust account. — Court of Appeals of Maryland affirmed hearing judge's findings that an attorney mishandled funds in attorney trust account but held that because there was no finding of intentional misappropriation of funds and the attorney's clients did not suffer a financial loss, indefinite suspension was the appropriate sanction. Att'y Griev. Comm'n v. DiCicco, 369 Md. 662, 802 A.2d 1014 (2002).

Even though an attorney's clients lost no funds because of a trust account shortfall resulting from failure to properly monitor the account, or even to balance the checkbook, and even though the attorney never touched any of the funds in question for personal or business use, because the shortfall was large and was not made up for a considerable length of time, and because of certain prior disciplinary problems, an indefinite suspension with permission to reapply after three months was imposed. Att'y Griev. Comm'n v. Sperling, 380 Md. 180, 844 A.2d 397 (2004).

Indefinite suspension with right to apply for reinstatement after six months was the sanction imposed on an attorney who knowingly allowed trust account to be overdrawn and failed to respond to bar counsel inquiries; the court cautioned the attorney that allegations of suffering from depression would have to be addressed if and when the attorney sought reinstatement, as this could affect the capacity to practice law. Att'y Griev. Comm'n v. Rose, 383 Md. 385, 859 A.2d 659 (2004).

Attorney's failure to remove his earned fees promptly from his trust account and his disbursement of fund to clients before their settlement checks had been deposited into the trust account violated the prior, similar Rule. Att'y Griev. Comm'n v. Zuckerman, 386 Md. 341, 872 A.2d 693 (2005).

Attorney violated prior, similar Rule 1.15(a) and § 10-306 of the Business Occupations and Professions Article when he disbursed funds to his clients from his trust account before their settlement checks had been deposited into the trust account. Att'y Griev. Comm'n v. Zuckerman, 386 Md. 341, 872 A.2d 693 (2005).

Despite evidence that respondent attorney suffered from depression and a mood disorder, disbarment was the only appropriate sanction for misconduct that included misleading both clients and their health care providers about the status of settlement negotiations and concealing a possible asset of a bankrupt client from the bankruptcy trustee; the mental problems were not the root cause of the misconduct, and the attorney, whose practice had been quite successful, had known quite well that mishandling of client trust funds to cover practice expenses and misleading the bankruptcy court were wrong. Att'y Griev. Comm'n v. Zakroff, 387 Md. 603, 876 A.2d 664 (2005), cert. denied, 2006 Md. LEXIS 561 (2006); cert. denied, 2006 Md. LEXIS 571 (Md. 2006).

Where violations of trust account rules were unintentional and relatively minor, but where the attorney had a history of such violations as well as of client neglect, which had also been found in the instant case, and a failure to initially cooperate with the grievance investigation had also been found, the appropriate sanction was an indefinite suspension with leave to reapply after six months. Att'y Griev. Comm'n v. Kreamer, 387 Md. 503, 876 A.2d 79 (2005).

Despite evidence that respondent attorney suffered from depression and a mood disorder, disbarment was the only appropriate sanction for misconduct that included misleading both clients and their health care providers about the status of settlement negotiations and concealing a possible asset of a bankrupt client from the bankruptcy trustee; the mental problems were not the root cause of the misconduct, and the attorney, whose practice had been quite successful, had known quite well that mishandling of client trust funds to cover

practice expenses and misleading the bankruptcy court were wrong. Att'y Griev. Comm'n v. Zakroff, 387 Md. 603, 876 A.2d 664 (2005), cert. denied, 2006 Md. LEXIS 561 (2006); cert. denied, 2006 Md. LEXIS 571 (Md. 2006).

Where violations of trust account rules were unintentional and relatively minor, but where the attorney had a history of such violations as well as of client neglect, which had also been found in the instant case, and a failure to initially cooperate with the grievance investigation had also been found, the appropriate sanction was an indefinite suspension with leave to reapply after six months. Att'y Griev. Comm'n v. Kreamer, 387 Md. 503, 876 A.2d 79 (2005).

Attorney was disbarred under Rule 16-751 for misappropriation of client funds from his trust account, violating §§ 7-104 and 7-113 of the Criminal Law Article, § 10-306 of the Business Occupations and Professions Article, Rule 16-609, Rules 1.15 and 8.4 of the Maryland Lawyers Rules of Professional Conduct, and spousal abuse, violating § 3-203 of the Criminal Law Article. The attorney did not carry his burden to prove by a preponderance of the evidence any medical, psychiatric, or other condition to mitigate the findings of fact or conclusions of law. Att'y Griev. Comm'n v. Theriault, 390 Md. 202, 888 A.2d 292 (2005).

By delaying payment of settlement proceeds to a client and the client's medical providers, transferring the client's funds into his operating account, and using the money for his own personal needs, an attorney violated Md. R. Prof. Conduct 1.3, 1.15(a) and (b), and 8.4(c) and (d); Rule 16-609; and § 10-306 of the Business Occupations and Professions Article. The court acknowledged the mitigating factors of the attorney paying the client and the medical providers and reducing his fee, but concluded that disbarment for such deceit was warranted. Att'y Griev. Comm'n v. Roberts, 394 Md. 137, 904 A.2d 557 (2006).

Attorney was reprimanded for violating this Rule and Rule 16-607 because the attorney's use of a trust account to pay an office phone bill and his subsequent deposit to cover the overdraft violated Rule 1.15, notwithstanding the circuit court's finding that there was no commingling with or misuse of client funds; the attorney recognized that he violated Rule 1.15 by depositing personal funds into the trust account in excess of the amount needed to cover bank charges. Att'y Griev. Comm'n v. Taylor, 405 Md. 697, 955 A.2d 755 (2008).

Attorney, who, inter alia, failed to withdraw fees earned from the attorney's trust account and who withdrew funds from the trust account in excess of funds deposited on behalf of a client or for clients who did not contribute to the account at all, was disbarred for violating Rule 8.4(a - d) and this Rule; §§ 10-306 and

307 of the Business Occupations and Professions Article; and Rules 16-607 and 16-609. Att'y Griev. Comm'n v. Thomas, 409 Md. 121, 973 A.2d 185 (2009).

Failure to deposit unearned funds into trust account. — Attorney violated (a) by failing to keep adequate records and failing to deposit a client's unearned deposit into his trust account; the trial judge did not believe that the attorney could have performed substantial work on the matter, entitling him to half of the total fee at the time the deposit was made. Att'y Griev. Comm'n v. Khandpur, 421 Md. 1, 25 A.3d 165 (2011).

Disbursement of fee prior to receipt of settlement funds. — Attorney's use of client trust funds to cover the shortfalls in the attorney's trust account and the disbursement of funds to the attorney before depositing settlement funds amounted to violations of (a) and, along with the attorney's other misconduct, supported disbarment. Att'y Griev. Comm'n v. Jarosinski, 411 Md. 432, 983 A.2d 477 (2009).

Failure to provide accounting. — Attorney violate (d) when the attorney failed to provide a full accounting to a client who had demanded a refund of the fee paid. Att'y Griev. Comm'n v. Patterson, — Md. —, — A.3d — (Sept. 21, 2011).

II. SANCTIONS.

Alcoholism, drug addiction or mental disorder. — When alcoholism is, to a substantial extent, the cause of the misconduct by an attorney, the court views the misconduct in a somewhat different light; under this circumstance the appropriate sanction is indefinite suspension and the focus shifts to questions of rehabilitation and the imposition of conditions sufficient to protect the public if the lawyer is allowed to resume practice. Att'y Griev. Comm'n v. Reid, 308 Md. 646, 521 A.2d 743 (1987).

When a lawyer's misconduct is caused by alcoholism, drug addiction, or a mental disorder, the usual sanction is indefinite suspension. This provides the requisite protection for the public, for it prevents the lawyer from practicing law until such time (if ever) that he or she can demonstrate that he or she is free from the effects of the ailment and able to practice competently. At the same time, the lawyer is spared the ultimate sanction of disbarment, a sanction which would be unfair to apply where the lawyer's conduct is caused by factors beyond his or her control. Att'y Griev. Comm'n v. Powers, 314 Md. 484, 551 A.2d 465 (1989).

Where alcoholism is allegedly implicated in cases involving misappropriation of trust or client funds, a sanction less severe than disbarment may be imposed if the evidence discloses that the alcoholism, to a substantial extent, was the responsible, precipitating, and root cause of the misappropriation. Att'y Griev. Comm'n v. White, 328 Md. 412, 614 A.2d 955 (1992).

Simply to show that an attorney was in the throes of alcoholism at the time he misappropriated client funds and that his thinking was "alcoholically impaired" to the point where he rationalized his behavior as acceptable, even though he knew it was not, is insufficient mitigation in and of itself to justify a sanction less than disbarment. Att'y Griev. Comm'n v. White, 328 Md. 412, 614 A.2d 955 (1992).

An indefinite suspension was the proper sanction in the case of a misappropriation of client funds caused by alcoholism; however, in the future, absent truly compelling circumstances, alcoholism will usually not be permitted to mitigate where an attorney commits a violation of ethical or legal rules which would ordinarily warrant disbarment. Att'y Griev. Comm'n v. Kenney, 339 Md. 578, 664 A.2d 854 (1995).

Bar Counsel's recommendation of disbarment with regard to an attorney found to have violated (a), (b), and (c) of this Rule and Md. R. Prof. Conduct 8.4(b), (c), and (d), was not accepted by the Maryland Court of Appeals; the disciplinary matter was remanded for the Attorney Grievance Commission and Bar Counsel to reconsider entering into a conditional diversion agreement with the attorney because, even though the evidence supported the finding of wilful misconduct, the attorney's mental health and severe depression was a significant factor, and the Court of Appeal's interpretation of Rule 16-736 allowed diversion as a sanction in such cases where the professional misconduct was not solely the result of wilful or intentionally dishonest conduct. Att'y Griev. Comm'n v. Cappell, 389 Md. 402, 886 A.2d 112 (2005).

Warning. — For a finding that an attorney violated the rule, the court of appeals remanded the case to the Attorney Grievance Commission for it to propose dismissal of the case with a warning to the attorney that his conduct in failing to notify a bank that settlement proceeds were paid to his client, and in failing to forward those proceeds to the bank, was a violation of the prior, similar Rule that was not to be repeated. The warning was not discipline, but was simply an admonition against repetition of the conduct, and if the attorney rejected the warning, the court could consider an appropriate sanction. Att'y Griev. Comm'n v. Stolarz, 379 Md. 387, 842 A.2d 42 (2004).

No violation found. — Attorney was sanctioned by a public reprimand for technically violating Rule 16-609 regarding prohibited transactions as a result of a negligent clerical error involving depositing some of his ex-girlfriend's funds into his operating account instead of his firm's escrow account, which error was corrected upon discovery and was not wilful. The Court of Appeals of Maryland further upheld the trial judge's finding of fact that no attorney client relationship existed between the attorney and his girlfriend to support the other violations asserted against him since he never charged his ex-girlfriend a fee for his services and was only helping her while she received treatment for her alcohol abuse. Att'y Griev. Comm'n v. Shoup, 410 Md. 462, 979 A.2d 120 (Aug. 28, 2009).

Disbarment was proper sanction. — Attorney was properly disbarred for violating prior, similar Maryland Rules of Professional Conduct 1.1, 1.3, 1.4, 1.15, 3.3, and 8.4, § 10-306 of the Business Occupations and Professions Article, and former Rule BU9 (now Rule 16-609) of the Maryland Rules of Procedure. Att'y Griev. Comm'n v. Williams, 335 Md. 458, 644 A.2d 490 (1994).

Disbarment of attorney was appropriate where there were serious and repeated violations of the prior, similar Rule and other provisions of the Maryland Rules of Professional Conduct. Att'y Griev. Comm'n v. Milliken, 348 Md. 486, 704 A.2d 1225 (1998).

Attorney was disbarred where he had demonstrated an alarming propensity for deceit and dishonesty that infested a large part of his dealings spanning a short period of time, and where he engaged in deceitful conduct, was less than candid in testimony, and violated a medley of rules and statutes concerned with protecting trust funds. Att'y Griev. Comm'n v. Tomaino, 362 Md. 483, 765 A.2d 653 (2001).

Disbarment was ordered where an attorney violated prior, similar Md. R. Prof. Conduct 1.15, 8.1, and 8.4, and Md. R. 16-607, and had previously been sanctioned, receiving an indefinite suspension with the right to reapply in not less than six months for conduct amounting to negligent misappropriation of client funds. Att'y Griev. Comm'n v. Powell, 369 Md. 462, 800 A.2d 782 (2002).

Disbarment was the appropriate sanction for an attorney who failed to maintain separate trust and escrow accounts, and placed funds he was holding for a client into an account he used for business and personal purposes, eventually draining it. Att'y Griev. Comm'n v. Gallagher, 371 Md. 673, 810 A.2d 996 (2002).

Attorney was disbarred for failing to keep clients apprised of their matters and failing to respond to their calls, for failing to return their retainer to them although he did little or no work on their matters, for failing to keep their funds separate and in a trust fund, for failing to avoid a conflict of interest with respect to their matters, all in violation of prior, similar Rules 1.4, 1.5, 1.7, 1.8, 1.15, and 1.16; his conduct was especially egregious where his clients were the elderly and their families and where he was so blatant in his continued actions. Att'y Griev. Comm'n v. McLaughlin, 372 Md. 467, 813 A.2d 1145 (2002).

Attorney was disbarred for his handling of a medical malpractice case for a wife, her common-law husband, and her children, which had resulted in the attorney's disbarment in Georgia, for misconduct as defined in Maryland Rule 16-701(i), and for violating the Maryland counterparts of the Georgia State Bar Standards he had been found to have violated, more specifically, prior, similar Rules 8.4 (misconduct), 1.5 (fees), 1.7 (conflict of interest: general rule), and 1.15 (safekeeping property). Att'y Griev. Comm'n v. Roberson, 373 Md. 328, 818 A.2d 1059 (2003).

When an attorney acted as an escrow agent for a client which purportedly funded high-risk loans, and the attorney removed commitment fees deposited in the escrow account and disbursed them to parties unrelated to a contemplated loan, rather than either returning them to the depositors or disbursing them to parties providing loans, and failed to provide requested information to the grievance commission, he violated prior, similar Maryland Rules of Professional Conduct 1.15, 8.1, and 8.4, §§ 10-306 and 10-606 of the Business Occupations and Professions Article, and Rule 16-609 of the Maryland Rules of Procedure, and, given the absence of mitigating circumstances, disbarment was the appropriate sanction. Att'y Griev. Comm'n v. Smith, 376 Md. 202, 829 A.2d 567 (2003).

Attorney was disbarred as he violated the prior, similar Rule where he failed to hold a client's fee in an escrow account separate from the attorney's personal funds, until earned. Att'y Griev. Comm'n v. Velasquez, 380 Md. 651, 846 A.2d 422 (2004).

Attorney was disbarred, despite the mitigating factors of an absence of a prior disciplinary record and relative inexperience, for violating prior, similar Md. R. Prof. Conduct 1.5(c), 1.15(b) and (c), 8.1(b), and 8.4(c) and (d), and Md. R. 16-606 and 16-609 in his intentionally dishonest conduct towards a third-party assignee/healthcare provider during the representation of a client in a personal injury claim and Maryland Bar Counsel and its investigator in the course of investigating the assignee's complaint. Att'y Griev. Comm'n v. Ellison, 384 Md. 688, 867 A.2d 259 (2005).

Intentional misappropriation of client funds by an attorney who failed to deposit client funds in an escrow account and used client funds for personal purposes warranted disbarment, especially where the attorney offered no evidence in mitigation. Att'y Griev. Comm'n v. James, 385 Md. 637, 870 A.2d 229 (2005).

Where the attorney, among other things, intentionally misappropriated client funds, forged a client's signature on a settlement check, lied under oath, and represented a client when the attorney was not licensed to do so, the attorney was disbarred for violating former, similar Md. R. Prof. Conduct 1.2(a), 1.3, 1.5(c), 1.15(a), (b), 3.3(a), 5.5, 8.1(a), (b), 8.4(a), (b), (c), (d), Md. R. 16-604, and §§ 10-304, -306 of the Business Occupations and Professions Article Att'y Griev. Comm'n v. Kapoor, 391 Md. 505, 894 A.2d 502 (2006).

Attorney who failed to properly hold runds in escrow to cover a child support check written to a client's ex-wife violated (a) and was disbarred based on violation of this Rule and Md. R. Prof. Conduct 8.1(b), 8.4 (a), (b), (c), (d), Rules 16-607 and 16-609, and §§ 10-306 and 10-606 of the Business Occupations and Professions Article. Att'y Griev. Comm'n v. Butler, 395 Md. 1, 909 A.2d 226 (2006).

Attorney was disbarred from the practice of law because he violated this Rule and Rule 8.4(a), (c), and (d) and §§ 10-306 and 10-307 of the Business Occupations and Professions Article when he withdrew $ 600,000 of conservatorship assets to purchase property that was titled in his name and that of his business partner. Att'y Griev. Comm'n v. Whitehead, 405 Md. 240, 950 A.2d 798 (2008).

Attorney was disbarred for violating Md. R. Prof. Conduct 1.1, 1.3, 1.4, 1.15, 3.1, 8.1, and 8.4, when the attorney, inter alia, deposit a check made out solely to the cleints into the attorney's operating account, not a trust account. Att'y Griev. Comm'n v. Gisriel, 409 Md. 331, 974 A.2d 331 (2009).

Attorney was disbarred for violating Md. R. Prof. Conduct 1.1, 1.3, 1.4, 1.15, and 8.4, Rule 16-609, and §§ 10-306 and 10-606(b) of the Business Professions and Occupations Article as attorney misappropriated the clients' funds, performed no services whatsoever on the clients' behalf, lied to the clients about the status of their case, and provided them with a falsified administrative agency decision that was not issued by the agency. Att'y Griev. Comm'n v. Bahgat, 411 Md. 568, 984 A.2d 225 (2009).

Attorney was disbarred for violating this Rule, Rule 16-607, and Md. R. Prof. Conduct 8.4(a), (c), and (d) because clear and convincing evidence established that he commingled personal and client funds and engaged in a pattern of dishonesty to hide his assets to avoid paying a judgment creditor. The evidence established that the attorney manipulated his corporate operations, his attorney escrow account, and his pension plan account to systematically avoid the judgment creditor's collection efforts and engaged in a pattern of behavior designed to conceal assets from attachment by the judgment creditor, which was conduct prejudicial to the administration of justice. Att'y Griev. Comm'n v. Foltz, 411 Md. 359, 983 A.2d 434 (2009).

Attorney was disbarred from the practice of law in Maryland for violating, inter alia, (a) by failing to keep her earned feees and reimbursed expenses in her attorney trust account separate from her clients' and third parties' property, making a host of deposits and receiving electronic transfers into her trust account with any accounting, and commingling personal funds with her clients' monies in her trust account for more than four years. Att'y Griev. Comm'n v. Nwadike, 416 Md. 180, 6 A.3d 287 (2010).

Attorney was disbarred for admittedly violating Md. Law. R. Prof. Conduct 1.1, 1.15(a) and (c), and 8.4(a) — (d), as well as Rule 16-609 and § 10-306 of the Business Occupations and Professions Article, by misappropriating client funds to make it appear as though the attorney's collected fees were higher than those fees actually were, when the attorney was being considered for partner in the attorney's firm, and by failing to file complaints in clients' cases, misrepresenting that the complaints were filed, and fabricating documents to hide the misrepresentations, because (1) disbarment was the presumed sanction for the misappropriation, and (2) the attorney did not show "compelling extenuating circumstances" justifying a lesser sanction, as the attorney showed no serious and debilitating mental condition, since the attorney was not diagnosed with a mental illness, the attorney did not show such a condition was the "root cause" of the attorney's misconduct by making the attorney unable to do day-to-day activities in a normal manner, and the attorney did not show such a condition caused an utter inability to conform the attorney's conduct to the law and the Maryland Rules of Professional Conduct, so any psychological issues the attorney had at the time of the attorney's misconduct did not mitigate the attorney's sanction. Att'y Griev. Comm'n v. Palmer, 417 Md. 185, 9 A.3d 37 (2010).

Attorney was disbarred for violating (a), (c) and (d), and Md. Law. R. Prof. Conduct 1.3, 1.4(a) and (b)1.16(d), 8.1(b), and 8.4(a) and (d), after the attorney received advance fee payments from two clients, deposited the money in a personal account, rather than a trust account, having not earned the fees, and abandoned the clients without performing work for the clients. Att'y Griev. Comm'n v. Lara, 418 Md. 355, 14 A.3d 650 (2011).

Attorney violated (d) and Md. Law. R. Prof. Conduct 1.2(a), 8.4(c) and (d), Md. R. 16-604 and 16-609(c), and § 10-306 of the Business Occupations and Professions Article, and was disbarred, after misappropriating tens of thousands of dollars that should have been paid to a physical therapist and settling a client's claim without the client's knowledge or consent. Att'y Griev. Comm'n v. Stern, 419 Md. 525, 19 A.3d 904 (2011).

Indefinite suspension was proper sanction. — Where respondent attorney's representation of four clients was marked by serious neglect and inattention; where he failed to return a fee which was unearned for a period of nine months; where he failed to timely remit funds he received on behalf of a client; where he failed to communicate with his clients; and in connection with the investigation of three of the complaints, where respondent failed to answer Bar Counsel's requests for information, the proper sanction was that the attorney be indefinitely suspended from the practice of law, with the right to apply for reinstatement after the suspension had been in effect for six months, conditioned upon his payment of all costs and upon the monitoring of respondent's practice. Att'y Griev. Comm'n v. David, 331 Md. 317, 628 A.2d 178 (1993).

Attorney who operated his law practice using only a trust account was suspended, rather than disbarred, for commingling and misusing a client's funds, where the attorney had a 30-year spotless record, there was no intent to defraud, the one victim suffered no loss, and the attorney was candid and remorseful; the automatic disbarment rule for misappropriation did not apply, as this was not the kind of willful conduct to which the rule was directed or intended to reach. Att'y Griev. Comm'n v. Hayes, 367 Md. 504, 789 A.2d 119 (2002).

Hearing court's finding that an attorney did not use funds intended for certain clients for them supported a finding that the attorney violated § 10-306 of the Business Occupations and Professions Article and Rule 16-609, as well as the violations of Md. R. Prof. Conduct 1.15 and Rules 16-604 and 16-607 that were found by the hearing court; the attorney was indefinitely suspended, with a right to apply for readmission after 90 days. Att'y Griev. Comm'n v. Mba-Jonas, 397 Md. 690, 919 A.2d 669 (2007).

Attorney was indefinitely suspended from the practice of law with the right to reapply for admission after one year, as the attorney's act of threatening to withdraw from representation of a client if the client refused to pay additional legal fees constituted a violation of this Rule and Md. R. Prof. Conduct 1.16, and constituted conduct involving dishonesty, fraud, deceit or misrepresentation in violation of Md. R. Prof. Conduct 8.4, and the flat fee charged violated Md. R. Prof. Conduct 1.5 as the attorney did not provide sufficient services to earn the fee, the attorney violated Rules 16-604 and 16-609 by failing to place unearned attorney fees in his attorney trust account, and the attorney's failure to keep the client informed of the progress of the litigation violated

Md. R. Prof. Conduct 1.4. Att'y Griev. Comm'n v. Lawson, 401 Md. 536, 933 A.2d 842 (2007).

Attorney's failure to promptly pay individuals who had funds on deposit in the attorney's trust account was a violation of Md. R. Prof. Conduct 1.1, 1.3, 1.15(d), and 8.4(d). That misconduct, along with the attorney's misconduct in paying clients before funds belonging to them were deposited in the attorney's trust account and failing to supervise an employee, warranted an indefinite suspension from the practice of law with the right to apply for reinstatement after 90 days. Att'y Griev. Comm'n v. Zuckerman, 403 Md. 695, 944 A.2d 525 (2008).

Attorney's failure to turn over the fee that the attorney retained from a personal injury settlement, when that fee amount belonged to the bankruptcy estate and the attorney had not obtained approval regarding it, meant that the attorney violated (d) and (e) by placing the fee amount in the attorney's escrow account rather than keeping that property separate from the attorney's own property. As a result of that misconduct and other related misconduct, the proper sanction was the attorney's indefinite suspension from the practice of law. Att'y Griev. Comm'n v. Nichols, 405 Md. 207, 950 A.2d 778 (2008).

Attorney was indefinitely suspended from practice of law for violating this section and Md. R. Prof. Conduct 1.8, 8.1, and 8.4, Rules 16-607 and 16-609, and § 10-306 of the Business Occupations and Professional Article, when the attorney advanced money to a client and the client's family members from the attorney's trust account, but did not hold any funds in escrow for those people, and commingled personal and trust funds in the same account. Att'y Griev. Comm'n v. McLaughlin, 409 Md. 304, 974 A.2d 315 (2009).

In a reciprocal discipline action, the attorney, who admitted to the wrongdoing which led to a finding that D.C. R. Prof. Conduct 1.2(a), 1.4(a), 1.4(b), 1.4(c), 1.5(c), 1.15(a), 1.15(b), 1.15(c), and 8.4(d) had been violated based on the attorney's negligence misrepresentation of settlement funds in one case and interference with the administration of justice in another case, amounting to violations of Md. Law. R. Prof. Conduct Rules 1.2(a), 1.4(a)(2) and (3), 1.4(b), 1.5(c), 1.15(a), 1.15(d), 1.15(e), and 8.4(d), was indefinitely suspended in Maryland, with right to apply for readmission after reinstatement in the District in Columbia. Att'y Griev. Comm'n v. Thaxton, 415 Md. 341, — A.2d —, 1 A.3d 470 (2010).

Two-year suspension justified. — Attorney suspended for 2 years for violating the prior, similar Rule, inter alia, and by the manner in which he collected fees and handled the funds of a client. Att'y Griev. Comm'n v. Eisenstein, 333 Md. 464, 635 A.2d 1327 (1994).

Thirty-day suspension. — Where the attorney violated Rule 16-609 and (a) and (b) of this Rule and Md. R. Prof. Conduct 8.1(b) based on the attorney's failure to fully cooperate with the investigation and based on the attorney's inexperience and lack of knowledge in maintaining trust accounts, the attorney was suspended for 30 days. Att'y Griev. Comm'n v. Obi, 393 Md. 643, 904 A.2d 422 (2006).

Ninety-day suspension was warranted. — Attorney's conduct violated this Rule, regarding the safekeeping of client property, where the attorney took a client's case that patently had no merit, obtained a retainer check, and the attorney then deposited that retainer check in the attorney's operating account rather than placing it where the attorney should have placed, in the attorney's trust account. Since the attorney's conduct was merely negligent rather than deceitful, a 90-day suspension from the practice of law was warranted. Att'y Griev. Comm'n v. Ugwuonye, 405 Md. 351, 952 A.2d 226 (2008).

Sufficiency of evidence. — Evidence justified findings of misconduct, and disbarment was warranted. Att'y Griev. Comm'n v. Mazelis, 309 Md. 50, 522 A.2d 913 (1987); Att'y Griev. Comm'n v. Kolodner, 321 Md. 545, 583 A.2d 724 (1991).

Attorney's professed inability to render an accounting of what happened in his law practice and his escrow account, coupled with his loss of memory on everything from money entrusted to him to the names of his secretaries, cast doubt on his ability to adequately carry out the functions of an attorney. Att'y Griev. Comm'n v. Kramer, 325 Md. 39, 599 A.2d 100 (1991).

An attorney who failed to preserve complete trust account records of a client's money for a period of five years was guilty of violating this Rule. Att'y Griev. Comm'n v. Ober, 350 Md. 616, 714 A.2d 856 (1998).

The prior, similar Rule was violated by an attorney who failed to keep separate collected funds, applied settlement funds for his own professional or personal use, and demanded payments in arrears from one of his client's debtors and then used them for business and professional purposes. Att'y Griev. Comm'n of Md. v. Sheridan, 357 Md. 1, 741 A.2d 1143 (1999).

As a matter of law an attorney violated conduct rules where he did not describe his contingency fee in writing, failed to deposit settlement funds into any account, failed to pay bills as he had promised, and failed to cooperate with the Grievance Commission. Att'y Griev. Comm'n v. Briscoe, 357 Md. 554, 745 A.2d 1037 (2000).

When an attorney agreed to represent clients in an adoption case, and they paid him an agreed fee, he violated Md. Code Prof. Resp. 1.15(a) when he did not deposit the fee into a trust account because the fee had not been earned. Att'y Griev. Comm'n v. Guida, 391 Md. 33, 891 A.2d 1085 (2006).

Rule 1.16. Declining or Terminating Representation.

(a) Except as stated in paragraph (c), a lawyer shall not represent a client or, where representation has commenced, shall withdraw from the representation of a client if:

(1) the representation will result in violation of the Maryland Lawyers' Rules of Professional Conduct or other law;

(2) the lawyer's physical or mental condition materially impairs the lawyer's ability to represent the client; or

(3) the lawyer is discharged.

(b) Except as stated in paragraph (c), a lawyer may withdraw from representing a client if:

(1) withdrawal can be accomplished without material adverse effect on the interests of the client;

(2) the client persists in a course of action involving the lawyer's services that the lawyer reasonably believes is criminal or fraudulent;

(3) the client has used the lawyer's services to perpetrate a crime or fraud;

(4) the client insists upon action or inaction that the lawyer considers repugnant or with which the lawyer has a fundamental disagreement;

(5) the client fails substantially to fulfill an obligation to the lawyer regarding the lawyer's services and has been given reasonable warning that the lawyer will withdraw unless the obligation is fulfilled;

(6) the representation will result in an unreasonable financial burden on the lawyer or has been rendered unreasonably difficult by the client; or

(7) other good cause for withdrawal exists.

(c) A lawyer must comply with applicable law requiring notice to or permission of a tribunal when terminating representation. When ordered to do so by a tribunal, a lawyer shall continue representation notwithstanding good cause for terminating the representation.

(d) Upon termination of representation, a lawyer shall take steps to the extent reasonably practicable to protect a client's interests, such as giving reasonable notice to the client, allowing time for employment of other counsel, surrendering papers and property to which the client is entitled and refunding any advance payment of fee or expense that has not been earned or incurred. The lawyer may retain papers relating to the client to the extent permitted by other law.

COMMENT

[1] A lawyer should not accept representation in a matter unless it can be performed competently, promptly, without improper conflict of interest and to completion. Ordinarily, a representation in a matter is completed when the agreed-upon assistance has been concluded. See Rules 1.2(c) and 6.5. See also Rule 1.3, Comment [4].

Mandatory Withdrawal. — [2] A lawyer ordinarily must decline or withdraw from representation if the client demands that the lawyer engage in conduct that is illegal or violates the Maryland Lawyers' Rules of Professional Conduct or other law. The lawyer is not obliged to decline or withdraw simply because the client suggests such a course of conduct; a client may make such a suggestion in the hope that a lawyer will not be constrained by a professional obligation.

[3] When a lawyer has been appointed to represent a client, withdrawal ordinarily requires approval of the appointing authority. See also Rule 6.2. Similarly, court approval or notice to the court is often required by applicable law before a lawyer withdraws from pending litigation. Difficulty may be encountered if withdrawal is based on the client's demand that the lawyer engage in unprofessional conduct. The court may request an explanation for the withdrawal, while the lawyer may be bound to keep confidential the facts that would constitute such an explanation. The lawyer's statement that professional considerations require termination of the representation ordinarily should be accepted as sufficient. Lawyers should be mindful of their obligation to both clients and the court under Rules 1.6 and 3.3.

Discharge. — [4] A client has a right to discharge a lawyer at any time, with or without cause, subject to liability for payment for the lawyer's services. Where future dispute about the withdrawal may be anticipated, it may be advisable to prepare a written statement reciting the circumstances.

[5] Whether a client can discharge appointed counsel may depend on applicable law. A client seeking to do so should be given a full explanation of the consequences. These consequences may include a decision by the appointing authority that appointment of successor counsel is unjustified, thus requiring self-representation by the client.

[6] If the client has severely diminished capacity, the client may lack the legal capacity to discharge the lawyer, and in any event the discharge may be seriously adverse to the client's interests. The lawyer should make special effort to help the client consider the consequences and may take reasonably necessary protective action as provided in Rule 1.14.

Optional Withdrawal. — [7] A lawyer may withdraw from representation in some circumstances. The lawyer has the option to withdraw if it can be accomplished without material adverse effect on the client's interests. Withdrawal is also justified if the client persists in a course of action that the lawyer reasonably believes is criminal or fraudulent, for a lawyer is not required to be associated with such conduct even if the lawyer does not further it. Withdrawal is also permitted if the lawyer's services were misused in the past even if that would materially prejudice the client. The lawyer may also withdraw where the client insists on taking action or inaction that the lawyer considers repugnant or with which the lawyer has a fundamental disagreement.

[8] A lawyer may withdraw if the client refuses to abide by the terms of an agreement relating to the representation, such as an

agreement concerning fees or court costs or an agreement limiting the objectives of the representation.

Assisting the Client Upon Withdrawal. — [9] Even if the lawyer has been unfairly discharged by the client, a lawyer must take all reasonable steps to mitigate the consequences to the client. The lawyer may retain papers as security for a fee only to the extent permitted by law, subject to the limitations in paragraph (d) of this Rule. See Rule 1.15.

Model Rules Comparison. — Rule 1.16 is substantially similar to the language of the Ethics 2000 Amendments to the ABA Model Rules of Professional Conduct with the exception of the addition of "or inaction" to Rule 1.16(b)(4) and Comment [7], and the addition of "subject to the limitations in paragraph (d) of this Rule" to Comment [9].

Maryland Law Review. — For comment discussing the need for a consensus on the proper scope of the attorney-client privilege where a client attempts to use an attorney's services for fraudulent or illegal purposes, see 46 Md. L. Rev. 436 (1987).

Advance payment fees. — Most courts that have considered the issue have determined that advance payment fees must be placed in a trust account as opposed to an operating account; it is beyond question that the prior, similar Rule requires that any portion of an advance payment fee that is unearned must be returned to the client. Att'y Griev. Comm'n v. Milliken, 348 Md. 486, 704 A.2d 1225 (1998).

Failure to refund fee. — Where the bankruptcy papers an attorney filed for a client were deficient, causing the bankruptcy case to be dismissed, and he never refunded the client's fee, he violated the prior, similar Rule by not refunding his unearned fee and by abandoning his practice. Att'y Griev. Comm'n v. Tinsky, 377 Md. 646, 835 A.2d 542 (2003).

Attorney representing a client in a divorce action violated this Rule when he failed to promptly return unearned fees to the client after the client discharged the attorney. Att'y Griev. Comm'n v. Rose, 391 Md. 101, 892 A.2d 469 (2006), cert. denied, 2006 U.S. LEXIS 5734, 166 L. Ed. 2d 22 (U.S. 2006).

Attorney was suspended for thirty days for withdrawing part of a retainer fee from her escrow account before earning the fee in violation of Md. R. Prof. Conduct 1.15(a) and § 10-306 of the Business Occupations and Professions Article and for making a billing error that resulted in a refund being owed to the clients under Md. R. Prof. Conduct 1.15(b) and 1.16(d). Additionally, the attorney's inexcusable and untimely delay in responding to a bar counsel's request for information in answer to allegations made by two disgruntled clients in an adoption matter violated Md. R. Prof. Conduct 8.1(b). Att'y Griev. Comm'n v. Rees, 396 Md. 248, 913 A.2d 68 (2006).

Attorney's misconduct in abusing the trust that the client placed in the attorney by placing the client's retainer check in the attorney's operating account rather than an attorney trust account, spending that money which belonged to the client on the attorney, in refusing to promptly refund to the client money that attorney admittedly owed to the client despite the client's refund request, and in failing to promptly answer bar counsel's request for information about the matter warranted the attorney's indefinite suspension. Att'y Griev. Comm'n v. McCulloch, 397 Md. 674, 919 A.2d 660 (2007).

Attorney's conduct in violating multiple Maryland Rules of Professional Conduct, including violation of (d) of this Rule for the attorney's failure to return unearned fees given to the attorney, warranted disbarment. Two clients were involved, and the attorney was unable to perform the requested work for one while the attorney did not return the fees to the other until a disciplinary complaint was filed against the attorney. Att'y Griev. Comm'n v. Webster, 402 Md. 448, 937 A.2d 161 (2007).

Attorney violated this Rule when she did only a portion of the work required by a divorce client, did not achieve the client's objective of obtaining a divorce, and kept the entire fee without earning it. Her failure to refund a portion of the fee violated (d). Att'y Griev. Comm'n v. McCulloch, 404 Md. 388, 946 A.2d 1009 (2008).

Attorney violated (d), regarding the termination of representation, by taking a client's case that patently had no merit, obtaining a retainer check and depositing it in the attorney's operating account rather than trust account, and failing to refund the retainer check amount when representation ended and the attorney had not performed work of any value. Since the attorney's conduct was merely negligent rather than deceitful, a 90-day suspension from the practice of law was warranted. Att'y Griev. Comm'n v. Ugwuonye, 405 Md. 351, 952 A.2d 226 (2008).

Public reprimand was imposed upon an attorney for violating Rules 1.1 and 1.16 because the attorney failed to make adequate investigate into a client's eligibility for cancellation of removal from the United States and to pursue that relief, and he failed to promptly return the fees a client paid him even though the client requested a refund; the attorney did recognize the error of his ways and returned the entire fee plus interest, he had no prior disciplinary history in his over 37 years as a member of the Maryland Bar, and he was genuinely remorseful. Att'y Griev. Comm'n v. Snyder, 406 Md. 21, 956 A.2d 147 (2008).

No record of work completed. — It was not clearly erroneous for a judge to find a violation of professional conduct rules where an attorney presented no record of time spent on a client's case, nor of any legal work she had completed to justify retention of a retainer. Att'y Griev. Comm'n v. Harris-Smith, 356 Md. 72, 737 A.2d 567 (1999).

Failure to provide case file to former client. — An attorney violated the prior, similar Rule by failing to provide a case file to a client or to the client's new attorney after the client had terminated her relationship with the attorney. Att'y Griev. Comm'n v. Ober, 350 Md. 616, 714 A.2d 856 (1998).

Lawyer violated (d) by not turning over a client's file to the client's new attorney, despite the lawyer's claim that the client was given all documents the client needed or was entitled to, because the client was entitled to the documents since the client was a former client and the sole heir of the estate that the lawyer administered, so the refusal to surrender the requested papers constituted a failure to take reasonable and practicable steps to protect the client's interest. Att'y Griev. Comm'n v. Edib, 415 Md. 696, 4 A.3d 957 (2010).

Abandonment of client. — Attorney's failure to notify his client of his closing of his office, his taking a fee without appearing at trial, and his disappearance while his client's criminal cases were pending violated this Rule pertaining to termination of representation. Att'y Griev. Comm'n v. Tinsky, 377 Md. 646, 835 A.2d 542 (2003).

Where the attorney abandoned his representation of the client and refused to engage in further communications with the client after terminating his representation via electronic mail, and the attorney engaged in other misconduct which included not being admitted to practice in forums where the attorney was representing the client and not responding to the disciplinary commission's lawful demands for information regarding the investigation of the attorney, disbarment was warranted. Att'y Griev. Comm'n v. Logan, 390 Md. 313, 888 A.2d 359 (2005).

Attorney violated this Rule in two cases because (1) the attorney moved the attorney's practice without notifying a client, and, upon termination of the client's case, did not return an unearned fee, and, (2) in a personal injury case in which it was learned that the defendant was deceased, the attorney did not open

an estate or otherwise prevent the dismissal of a client's case for failure to prosecute. Att'y Griev. Comm'n v. De La Paz, 418 Md. 534, 16 A.3d 181 (2011).

Failure to assist not found. — Attorney could not be found to have failed to assist a client upon being discharged where the attorney was serving as counsel to the estate but was also one of three co-personal representatives of the estate; since all three had to agree on decisions regarding retention or discharge of any attorney, and since the attorney did not agree with the discharge decision and no court order mandated removal, there was no withdrawal and no related duty to assist the client. Att'y Griev. Comm'n v. MacDougall, 384 Md. 271, 863 A.2d 312 (2004).

No violation found — Clear and convincing evidence showed that the attorney acted incompetently when the attorney accepted a case that required filing in a jurisdiction where the attorney was not admitted to practice, and when the attorney failed to service notice to defendant, that the attorney failed to act with reasonable diligence and promptness in representing the client when the attorney failed to file the estate in the proper jurisdiction, that the attorney failed to communicate the truth when the attorney told the client that the attorney was admitted to practice in a certain jurisdiction when the attorney was not admitted there and when the attorney failed to communicate to the client that the attorney intended to seek other counsel in the District of Columbia to assist the attorney, that the attorney's fees were unreasonable because the attorney charged and accepted fees when no work was performed in furtherance of the case, and that the attorney's actions were prejudicial to the administration of justice; even though the attorney was absolved of the charge that the attorney did not properly terminate the representation because the evidence showed that the attorney returned all unearned advance fees to the client after the client retained new counsel, the attorney's violations, which included intentionally dishonest conduct, warranted disbarment, especially since the attorney had a prior disciplinary history. Att'y Griev. Comm'n v. Ward, 396 Md. 203, 913 A.2d 41 (2006).

Bar counsel failed to show that an attorney had violated Md. R. Prof. Conduct 1.1, 1.3, 1.5(a), 1.16(d), 3.1, 5.1, 5.3(a) and (c), and 8.4(a) and (d) where the attorney had informed the client that he no longer wished to represent him after the client changed his mind with respect to a settlement agreement and the attorney had discharged the associate after discovering that she had subsequently file additional motions. Att'y Griev. Comm'n v. Maignan, 402 Md. 39, 935 A.2d 409 (2007).

Bar counsel failed to show that an attorney

had violated Md. R. Prof. Conduct 1.1, 1.3, 1.4(a) and (b), 1.5, 1.16(d), 3.1, 5.1, 5.3, and 8.4(a), (c), and (d) where it was possible to find, based on the testimony, that the attorney had relied on the clients' representations that they intended to handle the appeal pro se, and as a result, Bar counsel had failed to prove that the attorney had represented the two clients in an appeal. Att'y Griev. Comm'n v. Maignan, 402 Md. 39, 935 A.2d 409 (2007).

Although the attorney was found to have committed violations of the State professional misconduct rules about keeping a client reasonably informed and not engaging in conduct prejudicial to the administration of justice, the attorney did not violate (d) regarding the termination of representation of a client. No violation was shown because the evidence did not show that the client terminated the attorney's representation of the client. Att'y Griev. Comm'n v. Akpan, 405 Md. 277, 950 A.2d 820 (2008).

Attorney did not violate (d) as there was no evidence before the State's highest court concerning declining or terminating representation. Att'y Griev. Comm'n v. Bahgat, 411 Md. 568, 984 A.2d 225 (2009).

Failure to find violation deemed error. — An attorney who admitted to failing to deposit a retainer in her escrow account, to spending it on her rent, and to failing return the unearned portion to her client, and who was found guilty of violating the prior, similar Rule 1.15, should have also been found guilty of violating § 10-306 of the Business Occupations and Professions Article and subsection (d) of this Rule. Att'y Griev. Comm'n v. Duvall, 373 Md. 482, 819 A.2d 343 (2003).

Disbarment was proper sanction. — Disbarment of attorney was appropriate where there were serious and repeated violations of this Rule and other provisions of the Maryland Rules of Professional Conduct. Att'y Griev. Comm'n v. Milliken, 348 Md. 486, 704 A.2d 1225 (1998).

Because the attorney engaged in several acts of professional misconduct following an earlier suspension by accepting fees from clients but by failing to diligently to pursue their cases, the sanction of disbarment was held to be appropriate. Att'y Griev. Comm'n v. Fallin, 371 Md. 237, 808 A.2d 791 (2002).

Attorney was disbarred for failing to keep clients apprised of their matters and failing to respond to their calls, for failing to return their retainer to them although he did little or no work on their matters, for failing to keep their funds separate and in a trust fund, for failing to avoid a conflict of interest with respect to their matters, all in violation of prior, similar Rules 1.4, 1.5, 1.7, 1.8, 1.15, and 1.16; his conduct was especially egregious where his clients were the elderly and their families and

where he was so blatant in his continued actions. Att'y Griev. Comm'n v. McLaughlin, 372 Md. 467, 813 A.2d 1145 (2002).

Where an attorney was retained in two separate bankruptcy matters, was paid the retainer fee, and thereafter neglected the matters, misinformed the clients as to the status of their actions, and failed to properly communicate with them, it was found that he violated prior, similar Rules 1.1, 1.2, 1.3, 1.4, 1.16, and where the attorney had a prior history of disciplinary violations, the court imposed the sanction of disbarment. Att'y Griev. Comm'n v. Faber, 373 Md. 173, 817 A.2d 205 (2003).

Disbarment was the proper sanction for an attorney who dragged out representation of two different clients for many years, dooming their causes by failure to comply with applicable laws, and pretended to be continuing representation efforts, in one case, even falsifying a letter after the fact to give the impression that the client had received proper communications; the attorney had also failed to notify clients of a suspension and make other arrangements with them, and to supply information needed by a grievance commission investigator. Att'y Griev. Comm'n v. Davis, 375 Md. 131, 825 A.2d 430 (2003).

Attorney was disbarred where he abandoned his representation of a client, without giving reasonable notice or returning the unearned fee. Att'y Griev. Comm'n v. Velasquez, 380 Md. 651, 846 A.2d 422 (2004).

Clear and convincing evidence was found that an attorney violated this Rule by converting a client's personal injury protection fund monies to her personal use, having insufficient funds in her escrow account to pay the client's outstanding claims for reimbursement from such fund, and otherwise converting to her own use the fund, which should have been held in trust for the client. Disbarment was the sanction imposed, because the attorney did not protect her client's interests when she converted the funds. Att'y Griev. Comm'n v. Cherry-Mahoi, 388 Md. 124, 879 A.2d 58 (2005).

In an attorney disciplinary matter wherein the attorney was ordered disbarred, the attorney was found to have violated this Rule where the testimony of the attorney's former counsel and opposing counsel in a case indicated that the attorney's representation was terminated in February 2004, both the client and opposing counsel repeatedly requested that the attorney formally withdraw from the caveat proceeding, but the motion to withdraw was not filed until August 13, 2004. Therefore, the attorney violated this Rule when he failed to withdraw in a timely fashion despite the client having terminated his representation of her. Att'y Griev. Comm'n v. Steinberg, 395 Md. 337, 910 A.2d 429 (2006).

In an action in which petitioner, the Attorney Grievance Commission of Maryland, acting pursuant to Rule 16-751, filed a petition for disciplinary or remedial action against respondent attorney, the appropriate sanction was disbarment where the court found that, as a matter of law, respondent violated Md. R. Prof. Conduct 1.3, 1.4, 1.16, and 8.1; respondent violated Rule 1.16 in failing to inform the client that he was shutting the doors to his law practice and failing to return to the client her documents and photographs. Att'y Griev. Comm'n v. Baker, 396 Md. 15, 912 A.2d 651 (2006).

Attorney was disbarred for violating, inter alia, this Rule by failing to pursue a client's cases, thereby abandoning the attorney's representation of the client. Att'y Griev. Comm'n v. Kwarteng, 411 Md. 652, 984 A.2d 865 (2009).

Attorney was disbarred for violating this section and Md. Law. R. Prof. Conduct 1.1, 1.3, 1.4(a) and (b), 8.1(b), and 8.4(a) and (d), where the attorney, inter alia, failed to withdraw from representation after the attorney failed to timely file a complaint in a personal injury action and failed to inform the client to seek independent counsel concerning a potential malpractice claim. Att'y Griev. Comm'n v. Bleecker, 414 Md. 147, 994 A.2d 928 (2010).

Attorney violated this rule by effectively terminating his representation of clients in two action by abandoning the cases; the attorney was disbarred for violating this rule along with Md. Law. R. Prof. Conduct 1.1, 1.2(a), 1.3, 1.4(a), 8.1(b), and 8.4(a), (c), and (d). Att'y Griev. Comm'n v. Fox, 417 Md. 504, 11 A.3d 762 (2010).

Attorney was disbarred for violating (d) and Md. Law. R. Prof. Conduct 1.3, 1.4(a) and (b), 1.15(a), (c), and (d), 8.1(b), and 8.4(a) and (d), after the attorney received advance fee payments from two clients, deposited the money in a personal account, rather than a trust account, having not earned the fees, and abandoned the clients without performing work for the clients. Att'y Griev. Comm'n v. Lara, 418 Md. 355, 14 A.3d 650 (2011).

Indefinite suspension was proper sanction. — Where respondent attorney's representation of four clients was marked by serious neglect and inattention; where he failed to return a fee which was unearned for a period of nine months; where he failed to timely remit funds he received on behalf of a client; where he failed to communicate with his clients; and in connection with the investigation of three of the complaints, where respondent failed to answer Bar Counsel's requests for information, the proper sanction was that the attorney be indefinitely suspended from the practice of law, with the right to apply for reinstatement after the suspension had been in effect for six months, conditioned upon his payment of all costs and upon the monitoring of respondent's

practice. Att'y Griev. Comm'n v. David, 331 Md. 317, 628 A.2d 178 (1993).

An attorney who on several separate occasions failed to file legal documents which he had drafted, failed to communicate with clients in these matters, and failed to return attorney's fees he collected in connection with these matters, was rightly found to have violated prior, similar Rules of Professional Conduct 1.1, 1.3, 1.4, 1.16, and 8.4. The appropriate sanction was an indefinite suspension with the right to apply for reinstatement after 60 days, conditioned upon his payment of all costs associated with the matter, reimbursement of the unearned legal fees, and his hiring of an attorney to oversee his practice for a period of one year. Att'y Griev. Comm'n v. Brugh, 353 Md. 475, 727 A.2d 913 (1999).

Indefinite suspension was appropriate where attorney was retained to represent a client in filing for alien labor certifications for three of its employees, but where the attorney never prepared or filed an application for one employee and prepared but did not file applications for the other two, where he provided his client with altered documents making it appear he had done the work, and where the attorney never refunded the money paid to him and refused to cooperate with the investigation of his actions. Att'y Griev. Comm'n v. Koven, 361 Md. 337, 761 A.2d 881 (2000).

Indefinite suspension was proper sanction where attorney violated prior, similar Md. R. Prof. Conduct 1.3 by his failure to diligently pursue the legal matter which he undertook on behalf of his client, and prior, similar Md. R. Prof. Conduct 1.4, for failing to promptly comply with reasonable requests for information about a legal matter by a client and failing to fully and truthfully explain his actions, or inaction, to permit the client to make informed decisions regarding the representation; further, the attorney violated prior, similar Md. R. Prof. Conduct 1.16 by effectively terminating the representation of the client, but failing to take such steps to reasonably protect his client's interest. Att'y Griev. Comm'n v. Harrington, 367 Md. 36, 785 A.2d 1260 (2001).

Where violations of trust account rules were unintentional and relatively minor, but where the attorney had a history of such violations as well as of client neglect, which had also been found in the instant case, and a failure to initially cooperate with the grievance investigation had also been found, the appropriate sanction was an indefinite suspension with leave to reapply after six months. Att'y Griev. Comm'n v. Kreamer, 387 Md. 503, 876 A.2d 79 (2005).

Where violations of trust account rules were unintentional and relatively minor, but where the attorney had a history of such violations as well as of client neglect, which had also been found in the instant case, and a failure to initially cooperate with the grievance investigation had also been found, the appropriate sanction was an indefinite suspension with leave to reapply after six months. Att'y Griev. Comm'n v. Kreamer, 387 Md. 503, 876 A.2d 79 (2005).

Attorney was indefinitely suspended from the practice of law for violating Md. R. Prof. Conduct 1.3, 1.4, 1.16(d), 3.2, 8.1(b), and 8.4(d) in connection with the attorney's representation of a client in a bankruptcy matter. The complaint could not be dismissed based on the complainant's request because the evidence did not fail to show sanctionable professional misconduct. Att'y Griev. Comm'n v. Lee, 393 Md. 546, 903 A.2d 895 (2006).

Attorney was indefinitely suspended from the practice of law with the right to reapply for admission after one year, as the attorney's act of threatening to withdraw from representation of a client if the client refused to pay additional legal fees constituted a violation of this Rule and Md. R. Prof. Conduct 1.15, and constituted conduct involving dishonesty, fraud, deceit or misrepresentation in violation of Md. R. Prof. Conduct 8.4, and the flat fee charged violated Md. R. Prof. Conduct 1.5 as the attorney did not provide sufficient services to earn the fee, the attorney violated Rules 16-604 and 16-609 by failing to place unearned attorney fees in his attorney trust account, and the attorney's failure to keep the client in-

formed of the progress of the litigation violated Md. R. Prof. Conduct 1.4. Att'y Griev. Comm'n v. Lawson, 401 Md. 536, 933 A.2d 842 (2007).

Attorney's failure to turn over the attorney's file to the client's new attorney for six months after the client terminated the attorney's services regarding personal injury and bankruptcy matters violated (d). As a result of that misconduct and other related misconduct, the proper sanction was the attorney's indefinite suspension from the practice of law. Att'y Griev. Comm'n v. Nichols, 405 Md. 207, 950 A.2d 778 (2008).

Applied in Att'y Griev. Comm'n v. Duvall, 384 Md. 234, 863 A.2d 291 (2004); Att'y Griev. Comm'n v. Kreamer, 404 Md. 282, 946 A.2d 500 (2008).

Quoted in Att'y Griev. Comm'n v. Lee, 387 Md. 89, 874 A.2d 897 (2005); Att'y Griev. Comm'n v. Scroggs, 387 Md. 238, 874 A.2d 985 (2005); Att'y Griev. Comm'n v. Muhammad, — Md. —, — A.2d — (2005); Att'y Griev. Comm'n v. Lee, 390 Md. 517, 890 A.2d 273 (2005); Att'y Griev. Comm'n v. Stern, 419 Md. 525, 19 A.3d 904 (2011).

Stated in Att'y Griev. Comm'n v. Midlen, 395 Md. 628, 911 A.2d 852 (2006).

Cited in Att'y Griev. Comm'n v. Lee, 393 Md. 385, 903 A.2d 360 (2006); Att'y Griev. Comm'n v. Muhammad, 395 Md. 676, 912 A.2d 588 (2006), cert. denied, 127 S. Ct. 2296, 2007 U.S. LEXIS 5292, 167 L. Ed. 2d 1103 (U.S. 2007); Att'y Griev. Comm'n v. Patterson, — Md. —, — A.3d — (Sept. 21, 2011).

Rule 1.17. Sale of Law Practice.

(a) Subject to paragraph (b), a law practice, including goodwill, may be sold if the following conditions are satisfied:

(1) Except in the case of death, disability, or appointment of the seller to judicial office, the entire practice that is the subject of the sale has been in existence at least five years prior to the date of sale;

(2) The practice is sold as an entirety to another lawyer or law firm; and

(3) Written notice has been mailed to the last known address of the seller's current clients regarding:

(A) the proposed sale;

(B) the terms of any proposed change in the fee arrangement;

(C) the client's right to retain other counsel, to take possession of the file, and to obtain any funds or other property to which the client is entitled; and

(D) the fact that the client's consent to the new representation will be presumed if the client does not take any action or does not otherwise object within sixty (60) days of mailing of the notice.

(b) If a notice required by paragraph (a)(3) is returned and the client cannot be located, the representation of that client may be transferred to the purchaser only by an order of a court of competent jurisdiction authorizing the transfer. The seller may disclose to the court in camera information relating to the representation only to the extent necessary to obtain an order authorizing the transfer.

COMMENT

[1] The practice of law is a profession, not merely a business. Clients are not commodities that can be purchased and sold at will. Pursuant to this Rule, when a lawyer or an entire firm ceases to practice and another lawyer or firm takes over the representation, the selling lawyer or firm may obtain compensation for the reasonable value of the practice as may withdrawing partners of law firms. See Rules 5.4 and 5.6

Termination of Practice by the Seller. — [2] The requirement that all of the private practice be sold is satisfied if the seller in good faith makes the entire practice available for sale to the purchaser. The fact that a number of the seller's clients decide not to be represented by the purchaser but take their matters elsewhere does not therefore result in a violation. The purchase agreement for the sale of a law practice may allow for restrictions on the scope and time of the seller's reentry into practice.

Single Purchaser. — [3] The Rule requires a single purchaser. The prohibition against piecemeal sale of a practice protects those clients whose matters are less lucrative and who might find it difficult to secure other counsel if a sale could be limited to substantial fee-generating matters. The purchaser is required to undertake all client matters in the practice, subject to client consent. If, however, the purchaser is unable to undertake all client matters because of a conflict of interest in a specific matter respecting which the purchaser is not permitted by Rule 1.7 or another rule to represent the client, the requirement that there be a single purchaser is nevertheless satisfied.

Client Confidences, Consent and Notice. — [4] Negotiations between seller and prospective purchaser prior to disclosure of information relating to a specific representation of an identifiable client no more violate the confidentiality provisions of Rule 1.6 than do preliminary discussions concerning the possible association of another lawyer or mergers between firms, with respect to which client consent is not required. Providing the purchaser access to client-specific information relating to the representation and to the file, however, requires client consent. The Rule provides that before such information can be disclosed by the seller to the purchaser, written notice of the contemplated sale must be mailed to the client. The notice must include the identity of the purchaser and any proposed change in the terms of future representation, and must tell the client that the decision to consent or make

other arrangements must be made within 60 days. If nothing is heard from the client within that time, consent to the new representation is presumed.

[5] A lawyer or law firm ceasing to practice cannot be required to remain in practice because some clients cannot be given actual notice of the proposed purchase. Since these clients cannot themselves consent to the new representation or direct any other disposition of their files, the Rule requires an order from a court having jurisdiction authorizing their transfer or other disposition. The Court can be expected to determine whether reasonable efforts to locate the client have been exhausted, and whether the absent client's legitimate interests will be served by authorizing the transfer of the file so that the purchaser may continue the representation. Preservation of client confidences requires that the petition for a court order be considered in camera.

[6] All the elements of client autonomy, including the client's absolute right to discharge a lawyer and transfer the representation to another, survive the sale of the practice. Additionally, the transfer of the practice does not operate to change the attorney-client privilege.

Other Applicable Ethical Standards. — [7] Lawyers participating in the sale of a law practice are subject to the ethical standards applicable to the involvement of another lawyer in the representation of a client. These include, for example, the seller's obligation to exercise competence in identifying a purchaser qualified to assume the practice and the purchaser's obligation to undertake the representation competently (see Rule 1.1); the obligation to avoid disqualifying conflicts, and to secure the client's informed consent for those conflicts which can be agreed to (see Rule 1.7 regarding conflicts and Rule 1.0(f) for the definition of informed consent); and the obligation to protect information relating to the representation (see Rules 1.6 and 1.9).

[8] If approval of the substitution of the purchasing attorney for the selling attorney is required by the rules of any tribunal in which a matter is pending, that approval must be obtained before the matter can be included in the sale (see Rule 1.16).

Applicability of the Rule. — [9] This Rule applies to the sale of a law practice by representatives of a deceased or disabled lawyer, or one who has disappeared. Thus, the seller may be represented by a non-lawyer representative not subject to these Rules. Since, however, no lawyer may participate in a sale of a law practice which does not conform to the requirements of this Rule, the representatives of the seller as well as the purchasing lawyer can be expected to see to it that they are met.

[10] Admission to or retirement from law partnership or professional association, retirement plans and similar arrangements, and a sale of tangible assets of a law practice, do not constitute a sale or purchase governed by this Rule.

[11] This Rule does not apply to the transfers of legal representation between lawyers when such transfers are unrelated to the sale of a practice. This Rule does not prohibit an attorney from selling his or her interest in a law practice.

Committee note. — The sale of a practice does not mean that the appearance of a lawyer who is in a case will be stricken.

Model Rules Comparison. — This Rule substantially retains Maryland language as it existed prior to the Ethics 2000 Amendments to the ABA Model Rules of Professional Conduct except for incorporating ABA changes to Comments [2] and [3].

Rule 1.18. Duties to Prospective Client.

(a) A person who discusses with a lawyer the possibility of forming a client-lawyer relationship with respect to a matter is a prospective client.

(b) Even when no client-lawyer relationship ensues, a lawyer who has had discussions with a prospective client shall not use or reveal information learned in the consultation, except as Rule 1.9 would permit with respect to information of a former client.

(c) A lawyer subject to paragraph (b) shall not represent a client with interests materially adverse to those of a prospective client in the same or a substantially related matter if the lawyer received information from the prospective client that could be significantly harmful to that person in the matter, except as provided in paragraph (d). If a lawyer is disqualified from representation under this paragraph, no lawyer in a firm with which that lawyer is associated may knowingly undertake or continue representation in such a matter, except as provided in paragraph (d).

(d) Representation is permissible if both the affected client and the prospective client have given informed consent, confirmed in writing, or the disqualified lawyer is timely screened from any participation in the matter and is apportioned no part of the fee therefrom.

COMMENT

[1] Prospective clients, like clients, may disclose information to a lawyer, place documents or other property in the lawyer's custody, or rely on the lawyer's advice. A lawyer's discussions with a prospective client usually are limited in time and depth and leave both the prospective client and the lawyer free (and sometimes required) to proceed no further. Hence, prospective clients should receive some but not all of the protection afforded clients.

[2] Not all persons who communicate information to a lawyer are entitled to protection under this Rule. For example, a person who communicates information unilaterally to a lawyer, without any reasonable expectation that the lawyer is willing to discuss the possibility of forming a client-lawyer relationship, is not a "prospective client" within the meaning of paragraph (a).

[3] It is often necessary for a prospective client to reveal information to the lawyer during an initial consultation prior to the decision about formation of a client-lawyer relationship. The lawyer often must learn such information to determine whether there is a conflict of interest with an existing client and whether the matter is one that the lawyer is willing to undertake. Paragraph (b) prohibits the lawyer from using or revealing that information, except as permitted by Rule 1.9, even if the client or lawyer decides not to proceed with the representation. The duty exists regardless of how brief the initial conference may be.

[4] In order to avoid acquiring disqualifying information from a prospective client, a lawyer considering whether or not to undertake a new matter should limit the initial interview to only such information as reasonably appears necessary for that purpose. Where the information indicates that a conflict of interest or other reason for non-representation exists, the lawyer should so inform the prospective client

or decline the representation. If the prospective client wishes to retain the lawyer, and if consent is possible under Rule 1.7, then consent from all affected present or former clients must be obtained before accepting the representation.

[5] A lawyer may condition conversations with a prospective client on the person's informed consent that no information disclosed during the consultation will prohibit the lawyer from representing a different client in the matter. See Rule 1.0(f) for the definition of informed consent. If the agreement expressly so provides, the prospective client may also consent to the lawyer's subsequent use of information received from the prospective client.

[6] Even in the absence of an agreement, under paragraph (c), the lawyer is not prohibited from representing a client with interests adverse to those of the prospective client in the same or a substantially related matter unless the lawyer has received from the prospective client information that could be significantly harmful if used in the matter.

[7] Under paragraph (c), the prohibition in this Rule is imputed to other lawyers as provided in Rule 1.10, but, under paragraph (d),

imputation may be avoided if the lawyer obtains the informed consent, confirmed in writing, of both the prospective and affected clients. In the alternative, imputation may be avoided if, under paragraph (d), all disqualified lawyers are timely screened. See Rule 1.0(m) (requirements for screening procedures). Paragraph (d) does not prohibit the screened lawyer from receiving a salary or partnership share established by prior independent agreement, but that lawyer may not receive compensation directly related to the matter in which the lawyer is disqualified.

[8] For the duty of competence of a lawyer who gives assistance on the merits of a matter to a prospective client, see Rule 1.1. For a lawyer's duties when a prospective client entrusts valuables or papers to the lawyer's care, see Rule 1.15.

Model Rules Comparison. — This Rule, newly added to the Model Rules by the Ethics 2000 Amendments to the ABA Model Rules of Professional Conduct, is substantially similar to the ABA Rule, with the exception of omitting portions of ABA Model Rule 1.18(d) and Comment [7], and omitting ABA Comment [8] with appropriate redesignation of the Comment paragraph thereafter.

Motion to disqualify denied. — Debtor's motion to disqualify a first attorney and a law firm from representing a creditor pursuant to Md. R. Prof. Conduct 1.18 was denied where (1) while the debtor argued that he was a prospective client because a consultant for a company was acting as his agent when she spoke with a second attorney at the firm, and her purpose was to discuss the possibility of the firm representing him, the debtor had not clearly established that the consultant qualified as an intermediary acting on his personal behalf, as opposed to continuing her role on behalf of the company, (2) even if the debtor succeeded on this point, however, the debtor's motion would have failed because, if the consultant was the debtor's agent, then her actions as his agent would have been imputed to the debtor, (3) the debtor waived the issue because the debtor did not file the motion to disqualify for more than five months after the first attorney filed his notice of appearance in the bankruptcy case, a delay in the debtor's bankruptcy case would have been to the tactical advantage of the debtor, and the creditor would have been prejudiced by the disqualifi-

cation of the first attorney and the firm, particularly because of the long and complex history of litigation relating to two companies, and the first attorney's prior involvement, and (4) the debtor had not shown that any information shared with the firm qualified as significantly harmful. Modanlo v. Ahan (In re Modanlo), 342 B.R. 230 (D. Md. 2006).

Improper disqualification of defendant's chosen counsel. — Trial court committed structural error by violating defendant's right to counsel of defendant's choice by disqualifying one of defendant's retained attorneys because, after it was represented that the attorney had spoken to a co-defendant before trial and that the attorney was a potential witness, due to a grand jury witness's testimony that the attorney attempted to "coach" the witness, the trial court did not conduct an evidentiary hearing to determine whether there was an actual or serious potential for conflict, at which the court could balance defendant's right to counsel of defendant's choice against interests of fairness and maintenance of ethical standards. State v. Goldsberry, 419 Md. 100, 18 A.3d 836 (2011).

COUNSELOR.

Rule 2.1. Advisor.

In representing a client, a lawyer shall exercise independent professional judgment and render candid advice. In rendering advice, a lawyer may refer not only to law but to other considerations such as moral, economic, social and political factors, that may be relevant to the client's situation.

COMMENT

Scope of Advice. — [1] A client is entitled to straightforward advice expressing the lawyer's honest assessment. Legal advice often involves unpleasant facts and alternatives that a client may be disinclined to confront. In presenting advice, a lawyer endeavors to sustain the client's morale and may put advice in as acceptable a form as honesty permits. However, a lawyer should not be deterred from giving candid advice by the prospect that the advice will be unpalatable to the client.

[2] Advice couched in narrow legal terms may be of little value to a client, especially where practical considerations, such as cost or effects on other people, are predominant. Purely technical legal advice, therefore, can sometimes be inadequate. It is proper for a lawyer to refer to relevant moral and ethical considerations in giving advice. Although a lawyer is not a moral advisor as such, moral and ethical considerations impinge upon most legal questions and may decisively influence how the law will be applied.

[3] A client may expressly or impliedly ask the lawyer for purely technical advice. When such a request is made by a client experienced in legal matters, the lawyer may accept it at face value. When such a request is made by a client inexperienced in legal matters, however, the lawyer's responsibility as advisor may include indicating that more may be involved than strictly legal considerations.

[4] Matters that go beyond strictly legal questions may also be in the domain of another profession. Family matters can involve problems within the professional competence of psychiatry, clinical psychology or social work; business matters can involve problems within the competence of the accounting profession or of financial specialists. Where consultation with a professional in another field is itself something a competent lawyer would recommend, the lawyer should make such a recommendation. At the same time, a lawyer's advice at its best often consists of recommending a course of action in the face of conflicting recommendations of experts.

Offering Advice. — [5] In general, a lawyer is not expected to give advice until asked by the client. However, when a lawyer knows that a client proposes a course of action that is likely to result in substantial adverse legal consequences to the client, the lawyer's duty to the client under Rule 1.4 may require that the lawyer offer advice if the client's course of action is related to the representation. Similarly, when a matter is likely to involve litigation and, in the opinion of the lawyer, one or more forms of alternative dispute resolution are reasonable alternatives to litigation, the lawyer should advise the client about those reasonable alternatives. A lawyer ordinarily has no duty to initiate investigation of a client's affairs or to give advice that the client has indicated is unwanted, but a lawyer may initiate advice to a client when doing so appears to be in the client's interest.

Model Rules Comparison. — Rule 2.1 is substantially similar to the language of the Ethics 2000 Amendments to the ABA Model Rules of Professional Conduct.

Effect of amendments. — The 2007 amendment substituted "and in the opinion of the lawyer ... reasonable alternatives" for "it may be necessary under Rule 1.4 to inform the client of forms of dispute resolution that might constitute reasonable alternatives to litigation" in the Comment, Offering Advice - [5].

Editor's note. — See note to Rule 1.1.

University of Baltimore Law Forum. — For discussion of the code of ethics, see 17, No. 1 U. Balt. Law Forum 31 (1986).

For article, "The New Maryland Rules of Professional Conduct and Mediation: Perplexing Questions Answered and Perplexing Questions That Remain," see 36 U. Balt. L.F. 1 (2005).

Rule 2.2. Intermediary.
Deleted effective July 1, 2005.

Model Rules Comparison. — This Rule has been deleted in conformity with the Ethics 2000 Amendments to the ABA Model Rules of Professional Conduct.

Rule 2.3. Evaluation for Use by Third Parties.

(a) A lawyer may provide an evaluation of a matter affecting a client for the use of someone other than the client if the lawyer reasonably believes that making the evaluation is compatible with other aspects of the lawyer's relationship with the client.

(b) When the lawyer knows or reasonably should know that the evaluation is likely to affect the client's interests materially and adversely, the lawyer shall not provide the evaluation unless the client gives informed consent.

(c) Except as disclosure is authorized in connection with a report of an evaluation, information relating to the evaluation is otherwise protected by Rule 1.6.

COMMENT

Definition. — [1] An evaluation may be performed at the client's direction or when impliedly authorized in order to carry out the representation. See Rule 1.2. Such an evaluation may be for the primary purpose of establishing information for the benefit of third parties; for example, an opinion concerning the title of property rendered at the behest of a vendor for the information of a prospective purchaser, or at the behest of a borrower for the information of a prospective lender. In some situations, the evaluation may be required by a government agency; for example, an opinion concerning the legality of the securities registered for sale under the securities laws. In other instances, the evaluation may be required by a third person, such as a purchaser of a business.

[2] A legal evaluation should be distinguished from an investigation of a person with whom the lawyer does not have a client-lawyer relationship. For example, a lawyer retained by a purchaser to analyze a vendor's title to property does not have a client-lawyer relationship with the vendor. So also, an investigation into a person's affairs by a government lawyer, or by special counsel employed by the government, is not an evaluation as that term is used in this Rule. The question is whether the lawyer is retained by the person whose affairs are being examined. When the lawyer is retained by that person, the general rules concerning loyalty to client and preservation of confidences apply, which is not the case if the lawyer is retained by someone else. For this reason, it is essential to identify the person by whom the lawyer is retained. This should be made clear not only to the person under examination, but also to others to whom the results are to be made available.

Duties Owed to Third Person and Client. — [3] When the evaluation is intended for the information or use of a third person, a legal duty to that person may or may not arise. That legal question is beyond the scope of this Rule. However, since such an evaluation involves a departure from the normal client-lawyer relationship, careful analysis of the situation is required. The lawyer must be satisfied as a matter of professional judgment that making the evaluation is compatible with other functions undertaken in behalf of the client. For example, if the lawyer is acting as advocate in defending the client against charges of fraud, it would normally be incompatible with that responsibility for the lawyer to perform an evaluation for others concerning the same or a related transaction. Assuming no such impediment is apparent, however, the lawyer should advise the client of the implications of the evaluation, particularly the lawyer's responsibilities to third persons and the duty to disseminate the findings.

Access to and Disclosure of Information. — [4] The quality of an evaluation depends on the freedom and extent of the investigation upon which it is based. Ordinarily a lawyer should have whatever latitude of investigation seems necessary as a matter of professional judgment. Under some circumstances, however, the terms of the evaluation may be limited. For example, certain issues or sources may be categorically excluded, or the scope of search may be limited by time constraints or the noncooperation of persons having relevant information. Any such limitations which are material to the evaluation should be described in the report. If after a lawyer has commenced an evaluation, the client refuses to comply with the terms upon which it was understood the evaluation was to have been made, the lawyer's obligations are determined by law, having reference to the terms of the client's agreement and the surrounding circumstances. In no circumstances is the lawyer permitted to knowingly make a false statement of material fact or law in providing an evaluation under this Rule. See Rule 4.1.

Obtaining Client's Informed Consent. — [5] Information relating to an evaluation is protected by Rule 1.6. In many situations, providing an evaluation to a third party poses no significant risk to the client; thus the lawyer may be impliedly authorized to disclose information to carry out the representation. See Rule 1.6(a). Where, however, it is reasonably likely that providing the evaluation will affect the client's interests materially and adversely,

the lawyer must first obtain the client's consent after the client has been adequately informed concerning the important possible effects on the client's interests. See Rules 1.6(a) and 1.0(f).

Financial Auditors' Requests for Information. — [6] When a question concerning the legal situation of a client arises at the instance of the client's financial auditor and the question is referred to the lawyer, the lawyer's response may be made in accordance with procedures recognized in the legal profession. Such a procedure is set forth in the American Bar Association Statement of Policy Regarding Lawyers' Responses to Auditors' Requests for Information.

Model Rules Comparison. — Rule 2.3 is substantially similar to the language of the Ethics 2000 Amendments to the ABA Model Rules of Professional Conduct.

Rule 2.4. Lawyer Serving as Third-Party Neutral.

(a) A lawyer serves as a third-party neutral when the lawyer assists two or more persons who are not clients of the lawyer to reach a resolution of a dispute or other matter that has arisen between them. Service as a third-party neutral may include service as an arbitrator, a mediator or in such other capacity as will enable the lawyer to assist the parties to resolve the matter.

(b) A lawyer serving as a third-party neutral shall inform unrepresented parties that the lawyer is not representing them. When the lawyer knows or reasonably should know that a party does not understand the lawyer's role in the matter, the lawyer shall explain the difference between the lawyer's role as a third-party neutral and a lawyer's role as one who represents a client.

COMMENT

[1] Alternative dispute resolution has become a substantial part of the civil justice system. Aside from representing clients in dispute-resolution processes, lawyers often serve as third-party neutrals. A third-party neutral is a person, such as a mediator, arbitrator, conciliator or evaluator, who assists the parties, represented or unrepresented, in the resolution of a dispute or in the arrangement of a transaction. Whether a third-party neutral serves primarily as a facilitator, evaluator or decision maker depends on the particular process that is either selected by the parties or mandated by a court.

[2] The role of a third-party neutral is not unique to lawyers, although, in some court-connected contexts, only lawyers are allowed to serve in this role or to handle certain types of cases. In performing this role, the lawyer may be subject to court rules or other law that apply either to third-party neutrals generally or to lawyers serving as third-party neutrals. See Md. Rules 17-101-17-109. Lawyer-neu-

trals may also be subject to various codes of ethics, such as the Maryland Standards of Conduct for Mediators, Arbitrators and Other ADR Practitioners adopted by the Maryland Court of Appeals or the Code of Ethics for Arbitration in Commercial Disputes prepared by a joint committee of the American Bar Association and the American Arbitration Association.

[3] Unlike nonlawyers who serve as third-party neutrals, lawyers serving in this role may experience unique problems as a result of differences between the role of a third-party neutral and a lawyer's service as a client representative. The potential for confusion is significant when the parties are unrepresented in the process. Thus, paragraph (b) requires a lawyer-neutral to inform unrepresented parties that the lawyer is not representing them. For some parties, particularly parties who frequently use dispute-resolution processes, this information will be sufficient. For others, particularly those who are using

the process for the first time, more information may be required. Where appropriate, the lawyer should inform unrepresented parties of the important differences between the lawyer's role as third-party neutral and a lawyer's role as a client representative, including the inapplicability of the attorney-client evidentiary privilege. The extent of disclosure required under this paragraph will depend on the particular parties involved and the subject matter of the proceeding, as well as the particular features of the dispute-resolution process selected.

[4] A lawyer who serves as a third-party neutral subsequently may be asked to serve as a lawyer representing a client in the same matter. The conflicts of interest that arise for both the individual lawyer and the lawyer's law firm are addressed in Rule 1.12.

[5] Lawyers who represent clients in alternative dispute-resolution processes are governed by the Maryland Lawyers' Rules of Professional Conduct. When the dispute-resolution process takes place before a tribunal, as in binding arbitration (see Rule 1.0(o)), the lawyer's duty of candor is governed by Rule 3.3. Otherwise, the lawyer's duty of candor toward both the third-party neutral and other parties is governed by Rule 4.1.

Model Rules Comparison. — This Rule, newly added to the Model Rules by the Ethics 2000 Amendments to the ABA Model Rules of Professional Conduct, is substantially similar to the ABA Rule, with the exception of changing "will" to "may" in the fifth sentence of Comment [3].

University of Baltimore Law Forum. — For article, "The New Maryland Rules of Professional Conduct and Mediation: Perplexing Questions Answered and Perplexing Questions That Remain," see 36 U. Balt. L.F. 1 (2005).

ADVOCATE.

Rule 3.1. Meritorious Claims and Contentions.

A lawyer shall not bring or defend a proceeding, or assert or controvert an issue therein, unless there is a basis for doing so that is not frivolous, which includes, for example, a good faith argument for an extension, modification or reversal of existing law. A lawyer may nevertheless so defend the proceeding as to require that every element of the moving party's case be established.

COMMENT

[1] The advocate has a duty to use legal procedure for the fullest benefit of the client's cause, but also a duty not to abuse legal procedure. The law, both procedural and substantive, establishes the limits within which an advocate may proceed. However, the law is not always clear and never is static. Accordingly, in determining the proper scope of advocacy, account must be taken of the law's ambiguities and potential for change.

[2] The filing of an action or defense or similar action taken for a client is not frivolous merely because the facts have not first been fully substantiated or because the lawyer expects to develop vital evidence only by discovery. What is required of lawyers, however, is that they inform themselves about the facts of their clients' cases and the applicable law and determine that they can make good faith arguments in support of their clients' positions.

Such action is not frivolous even though the lawyer believes that the client's position ultimately will not prevail. The action is frivolous, however, if the lawyer is unable either to make a good faith argument on the merits of the action taken or to support the action taken by a good faith argument for an extension, modification or reversal of existing law.

[3] The lawyer's obligations under this Rule are subordinate to federal or state constitutional law that entitles a defendant in a criminal matter to the assistance of counsel in presenting a claim that otherwise would be prohibited by this Rule.

Model Rules Comparison. — This Rule substantially retains Maryland language as it existed prior to the Ethics 2000 Amendments to the ABA Model Rules of Professional Conduct except for: 1) adding "for example" to the text of the Rule; and 2) incorporating ABA changes to Comments [2] and [3].

Editor's note. — See note to Rule 1.1.

Maryland Law Review. — For symposium, expanding pro bono legal assistance in civil cases to Maryland's poor, see 49 Md. L. Rev. 1 (1990).

For article, "The Devolution of the Legal Profession: A Demand Side Perspective," see 49 Md. L. Rev. 869 (1990).

University of Baltimore Law Forum. — For discussion of the code of ethics, see 17, No. 1 U. Balt. Law Forum 31 (1986).

For article, "Code of Ethics Revisited," see 19.2 U. Balt. Law Forum 14 (1989).

Frivolous or unjustified motions. — The frivolous and unjustified filing of any motion, including one under Md. Rule 1-341, may not only be grounds for sanctions under that rule, but may also constitute a violation of the prior, similar Rule. Gunther v. Smith, 78 Md. App. 508, 553 A.2d 1314 (1989).

Attorney's license to practice law was indefinitely suspended for his failure to provide competent, diligent, and communicative representation to his client, for charging unreasonable fees, for pursuing a frivolous proceeding, and for engaging in conduct prejudicial to the administration of justice. Att'y Griev. Comm'n v. Zdravkovich, 362 Md. 1, 762 A.2d 950 (2000).

Prosecutor's promise to prosecute bomb threat cases against juveniles. — Prosecutor did not commit a violation of the prior, similar Rule by commenting on future prosecutions of juveniles who phoned bomb threats, despite clear evidence in the juvenile prosecutions, because by making the comments about prosecuting bomb threats, the prosecutor intended to communicate that his office must try hard cases. Att'y Griev. Comm'n v. Gansler, 377 Md. 656, 835 A.2d 548 (2003).

Rule does not preclude department of social services from maintaining CINA petition through adjudicatory hearing stage. — This Rule does not preclude the maintenance of a child in need of assistance petition by a local department of social services (DSS) through the adjudicatory hearing stage of a case, despite changed circumstances that throw doubt on the facts that supported the original petition because in the face of such change, DSS is still well within the bounds of professional responsibility in maintaining its petition when the child seeks an adjudication under § 3-817 of the Courts Article; at the hearing, DSS may argue that court intervention is no longer in the child's best interests, thereby complying with its responsibility under this Rule to only maintain an action with substantial justification. In re Najasha B., 409 Md. 20, 972 A.2d 845 (2009).

Trial court sanction as evidence of violation. — A sanction by a trial court for the filing of a frivolous complaint is insufficient, in and of itself, to find a violation of the prior, similar Rule. Att'y Griev. Comm'n v. Brown, 353 Md. 271, 725 A.2d 1069 (1999).

Violations. — Sanctions warranted where the actions of an attorney, including pressing claims that were completely without foundation, keeping a party in a suit for no other reason except to unnecessarily burden them, and knowingly failing to respond to a lawful demand for information from a disciplinary authority. Att'y Griev. Comm'n v. Alison, 349 Md. 623, 709 A.2d 1212 (1998).

Disbarment was the proper sanction for an attorney who dragged out representation of two different clients for many years, dooming their causes by failure to comply with applicable laws, and pretended to be continuing representation efforts, in one case, even falsifying a letter after the fact to give the impression that the client had received proper communications; the attorney had also failed to notify clients of a suspension and make other arrangements with them, and to supply information needed by a grievance commission investigator. Att'y Griev. Comm'n v. Davis, 375 Md. 131, 825 A.2d 430 (2003).

In an attorney disciplinary matter wherein the attorney was ordered disbarred, the attorney was found to have violated Rules 3.1 and 3.3 when he filed a motion to reconsider ratification and confirmation of a trustee's sale and to set aside a sale in a foreclosure case, supporting the motion with an assertion that his client had not received timely notice of the sale, which was not true and the attorney knew that his client had notice of the sale. Further, the statements in the affidavit violated Rule 3.3, which prohibited a lawyer from knowingly making a false statement of material fact or law to a tribunal. Att'y Griev. Comm'n v. Steinberg, 395 Md. 337, 910 A.2d 429 (2006).

Bringing an action for defamation against a former client, without having conducted legal research into its viability and without appreciating that Maryland law provides for a broad privilege for allegedly defamatory statements in judicial proceedings, or that doing so likely would erode the public confidence in the legal profession, sufficiently supported the finding that the attorney violated this Rule and Rule 8.4(d). Att'y Griev. Comm'n v. Manger, 396 Md. 134, 913 A.2d 1 (2006).

Attorney was disbarred for violating Md. R. Prof. Conduct 1.1, 3.1, 3.2, 3.3(a), 4.4, 8.2(a), and 8.4(c) and (d) because he had no basis for filing certain motions, and he continued to file motions relying on the same facts, same argument, and same legal theory after being advised that they had no merit; the attorney was intentionally dishonest with both the trial court and the court of special appeals, which showed a systematic effort to mislead the courts, and his history of sanctions for violating the Maryland Rules of Professional Conduct (MRPC) showed an ongoing disregard for the MRPC. Att'y Griev. Comm'n v. McClain, 406 Md. 1, 956 A.2d 135 (2008), cert. denied, 129 S. Ct. 1691, 2009 U.S. LEXIS 2433, 173 L. Ed. 2d 1036 (U.S. 2009).

Attorney was disbarred for violating Md. R. Prof. Conduct 1.1, 1.3, 1.4, 1.15, 3.1, 8.1, and 8.4, when the attorney, inter alia, filed an action for the clients knowing that the clients were bound by the real estate contract to mediate any dispute. Att'y Griev. Comm'n v. Gisriel, 409 Md. 331, 974 A.2d 331 (2009).

Violation not found. — Bar counsel failed to show that an attorney had violated Md. R. Prof. Conduct 1.1, 1.3, 1.4(a) and (b), 1.5, 1.16(d), 3.1, 5.1, 5.3, and 8.4(a), (c), and (d) where it was possible to find, based on the testimony, that the attorney had relied on the clients' representations that they intended to handle the appeal pro se, and as a result, Bar counsel had failed to prove that the attorney

had represented the two clients in an appeal. Att'y Griev. Comm'n v. Maignan, 402 Md. 39, 935 A.2d 409 (2007).

Bar counsel failed to show that an attorney had violated Md. R. Prof. Conduct 1.1, 1.3, 1.5(a), 1.16(d), 3.1, 5.1,. 5.3(a) and (c), and 8.4(a) and (d) where the attorney had informed the client that he no longer wished to represent him after the client changed his mind with respect to a settlement agreement and the attorney had discharged the associate after discovering that she had subsequently file additional motions. Att'y Griev. Comm'n v. Maignan, 402 Md. 39, 935 A.2d 409 (2007).

Quoted in Dove v. Montgomery County Bd. of Educ., 178 Md. App. 702, 943 A.2d 662 (2008).

Cited in Att'y Griev. Comm'n v. Bleecker, 414 Md. 147, 994 A.2d 928 (2010); Ross v. Chakrabarti, 194 Md. App. 526, 5 A.3d 135 (2010).

Rule 3.2. Expediting litigation.

A lawyer shall make reasonable efforts to expedite litigation consistent with the interests of the client.

COMMENT

[1] Dilatory practices bring the administration of justice into disrepute. Although there will be occasions when a lawyer may properly seek a postponement for personal reasons, it is not proper for a lawyer to routinely fail to expedite litigation solely for the convenience of the advocates. Nor will a failure to expedite be reasonable if done for the purpose of frustrating an opposing party's attempt to obtain rightful redress or repose. It is not a justification that similar conduct is often tolerated by

the bench and bar. The question is whether a competent lawyer acting in good faith would regard the course of action as having some substantial purpose other than delay. Financial or other benefit from otherwise improper delay in litigation is not a legitimate interest of the client.

Model Rules Comparison. — Rule 3.3 is substantially similar to the language of the Ethics 2000 Amendments to the ABA Model Rules of Professional Conduct.

Failure to timely file or adequately investigate action. — Ninety day suspension was appropriate sanction for attorney's failure to timely file or adequately investigate action on behalf of her client, and for misrepresenting to her client that the suit had been filed on her behalf and was proceeding to trial where the client paid the attorney only part of the costs involved in the work the attorney did do and the attorney did not consider the gratuitous client to be a client; an attorney-client relationship did exist and, thus, the attorney failed to carry out her contract of employment. Att'y Griev. Comm'n v. Pinkney, 311 Md. 137, 532 A.2d 1367 (1987).

Failure to serve defendant and inappropriate pleadings. — Attorney violated this Rule by failing to obtain an uncontested divorce within four years where he repeatedly

failed to serve the defendant throughout the four years of representation, unreasonably delaying his client's divorce, and where testimony had to be taken on three separate occasions due to attorney error; as a result, court time was spent unnecessarily in filing and reviewing inappropriate pleadings and testimony. Att'y Griev. Comm'n v. Fezell, 361 Md. 234, 760 A.2d 1108 (2000).

Attorney was found to be guilty of violating the prior, similar Maryland Rules of Professional Conduct by failing to obtain service against a taxicab company that his client was suing and by failing to obtain service against the driver of the taxicab until nearly three years after the suit was served. Att'y Griev. Comm'n v. Harris, 371 Md. 510, 810 A.2d 457 (2002).

Violation of Rule shown. — Bar Counsel's

exception to judge's failure to find a violation of the prior, similar Rule, requiring a lawyer to make reasonable efforts to expedite litigation consistent with the interests of the client, was granted. Att'y Griev. Comm'n v. Dietz, 331 Md. 637, 629 A.2d 678 (1993).

Attorney violated this Rule when he failed to act diligently in providing the requested representation. It took the attorney about six weeks to file a complaint in the client's divorce action. Att'y Griev. Comm'n v. Rose, 391 Md. 101, 892 A.2d 469 (2006), cert. denied, 2006 U.S. LEXIS 5734, 166 L. Ed. 2d 22 (U.S. 2006).

In an attorney disciplinary matter wherein the attorney was found to have violated Rules 3.2 and 3.4 by engaging in a pattern of delay with opposing counsel in a will competency case which included unreturned phone calls, unanswered letters, cryptic excuses for lack of communication, and failure to comply with reasonable requests to depose his client. The attorney's behavior also displayed an unwillingness to comply with discovery, in violation of Rules 3.2 and 3.4, wherein the attorney twice contacted opposing counsel on the eve of two scheduled deposition dates giving a cryptic excuse that a sick relative required medical attention in the first instance, and in the second instance, misrepresenting that his client refused to attend. Att'y Griev. Comm'n v. Steinberg, 395 Md. 337, 910 A.2d 429 (2006).

Attorney violated this section by failing to expedite a tort action, taking no effort to serve process upon either defendant and undertaking no discovery. Att'y Griev. Comm'n v. Patterson, — Md. —, — A.3d — (Sept. 21, 2011).

Violation of rule not shown. — In an attorney discipline proceeding, an attorney did not violate the rule by failing to cooperate in a pretrial conference to produce a joint statement because the failure to produce the statement had no effect on the trial; however, the attorney's conduct did constitute a violation of prior, similar Rule 3.4. Att'y Griev. Comm'n v. Hermina, 379 Md. 503, 842 A.2d 762 (2004).

Disbarment was proper sanction. — Disbarment of attorney was appropriate where there were serious and repeated violations of the prior, similar Rule and other provisions of the Maryland Rules of Professional Conduct. Att'y Griev. Comm'n v. Milliken, 348 Md. 486, 704 A.2d 1225 (1998).

Because the attorney engaged in several acts of professional misconduct following an earlier suspension by accepting fees from clients but by failing to diligently to pursue their cases, the sanction of disbarment was held to be appropriate. Att'y Griev. Comm'n v. Fallin,

371 Md. 237, 808 A.2d 791 (2002).

Disbarment was the proper sanction for an attorney who dragged out representation of two different clients for many years, dooming their causes by failure to comply with applicable laws, and pretended to be continuing representation efforts, in one case, even falsifying a letter after the fact to give the impression that the client had received proper communications; the attorney had also failed to notify clients of a suspension and make other arrangements with them, and to supply information needed by a grievance commission investigator. Att'y Griev. Comm'n v. Davis, 375 Md. 131, 825 A.2d 430 (2003).

Attorney was disbarred for violating Md. R. Prof. Conduct 1.1, 3.1, 3.2, 3.3(a), 4.4, 8.2(a), and 8.4(c) and (d) because he employed dilatory tactics, including unwarranted motions and false representations that settlement had occurred, to prevent the sale of property, thereby frustrating the opposing party's attempt to obtain rightful redress; the attorney was intentionally dishonest with both the trial court and the court of special appeals, which showed a systematic effort to mislead the courts, and his history of sanctions for violating the Maryland Rules of Professional Conduct (MRPC) showed an ongoing disregard for the MRPC. Att'y Griev. Comm'n v. McClain, 406 Md. 1, 956 A.2d 135 (2008), cert. denied, 129 S. Ct. 1691, 2009 U.S. LEXIS 2433, 173 L. Ed. 2d 1036 (U.S. 2009).

Indefinite suspension was proper sanction. — Indefinite suspension, rather than disbarment, was the proper sanction for the attorney's violation of Md. R. Prof. Conduct 1.1, 1.2, 1.3, 1.4, 3.2, and 8.4, where there was no evidence he acted out of fraudulent or selfish motive, he cooperated with Bar Counsel, he engaged in negotiations with the client's attorney regarding restitution, and he expressed great remorse. Att'y Griev. Comm'n v. Reinhardt, 391 Md. 209, 892 A.2d 533 (2006).

Attorney was indefinitely suspended from the practice of law for violating Md. R. Prof. Conduct 1.3, 1.4, 1.16(d), 3.2, 8.1(b), and 8.4(d) in connection with the attorney's representation of a client in a bankruptcy matter. The complaint could not be dismissed based on the complainant's request because the evidence did not fail to show sanctionable professional misconduct. Att'y Griev. Comm'n v. Lee, 393 Md. 546, 903 A.2d 895 (2006).

Quoted in Att'y Griev. Comm'n v. Scroggs, 387 Md. 238, 874 A.2d 985 (2005); Att'y Griev. Comm'n v. Taylor, 405 Md. 697, 955 A.2d 755 (2008).

Rule 3.3. Candor Toward the Tribunal.

(a) A lawyer shall not knowingly:

(1) make a false statement of fact or law to a tribunal or fail to correct a false statement of material fact or law previously made to the tribunal by the lawyer;

(2) fail to disclose a material fact to a tribunal when disclosure is necessary to avoid assisting a criminal or fraudulent act by the client;

(3) fail to disclose to the tribunal legal authority in the controlling jurisdiction known to the lawyer to be directly adverse to the position of the client and not disclosed by opposing counsel; or

(4) offer evidence that the lawyer knows to be false. If a lawyer has offered material evidence and comes to know of its falsity, the lawyer shall take reasonable remedial measures.

(b) The duties stated in paragraph (a) continue to the conclusion of the proceeding, and apply even if compliance requires disclosure of information otherwise protected by Rule 1.6.

(c) A lawyer may refuse to offer evidence that the lawyer reasonably believes is false.

(d) In an ex parte proceeding, a lawyer shall inform the tribunal of all material facts known to the lawyer which will enable the tribunal to make an informed decision, whether or not the facts are adverse.

(e) Notwithstanding paragraphs (a) through (d), a lawyer for an accused in a criminal case need not disclose that the accused intends to testify falsely or has testified falsely if the lawyer reasonably believes that the disclosure would jeopardize any constitutional right of the accused.

COMMENT

[1] This Rule governs the conduct of a lawyer who is representing a client in the proceedings of a tribunal. See Rule 1.0(o) for the definition of "tribunal." It also applies when the lawyer is representing a client in an ancillary proceeding conducted pursuant to the tribunal's adjudicative authority, such as a deposition. Thus, for example, paragraph (a)(4) requires a lawyer to take reasonable remedial measures if the lawyer comes to know that a client who is testifying in a deposition has offered evidence that is false.

[2] This Rule sets forth special duties of lawyers as officers of the court to avoid conduct that undermines the integrity of the adjudicative process. A lawyer acting as an advocate in an adjudicative proceeding has an obligation to present the client's case with persuasive force. Performance of that duty while maintaining confidences of the client, however, is qualified by the advocate's duty of candor to the tribunal. Consequently, although a lawyer in an adversary proceeding is not required to present an impartial exposition of the law or to vouch for the evidence submitted in a cause, the lawyer must not allow the tribunal to be misled by false statements of law or fact or evidence that the lawyer knows to be false.

Representations by a Lawyer. — [3] An advocate is responsible for pleadings and other documents prepared for litigation, but is usually not required to have personal knowledge of matters asserted therein, for litigation documents ordinarily present assertions by the client, or by someone on the client's behalf, and not assertions by the lawyer. Compare Rule 3.1. However, an assertion purporting to be on the lawyer's own knowledge, as in an affidavit by the lawyer or in a statement in open court, may properly be made only when the lawyer knows the assertion is true or believes it to be true on the basis of a reasonably diligent inquiry. There are circumstances where failure to make a disclosure is the equivalent of an affirmative misrepresentation. The obligation prescribed in Rule 1.2(d) not to counsel a client to commit or assist the client in committing a fraud applies in litigation. Regarding compliance with Rule 1.2(d), see the Comment to that Rule. See also the Comment to Rule 8.4(b).

Misleading Legal Argument. — [4] Legal argument based on a knowingly false representation of law constitutes dishonesty toward the tribunal. A lawyer is not required to make a disinterested exposition of the law, but must recognize the existence of pertinent legal authorities. Furthermore, as stated in paragraph (a)(3), an advocate has a duty to disclose directly adverse authority in the controlling jurisdiction which has not been disclosed by the opposing party. The underlying concept is that legal argument is a discussion seeking to determine the legal premises properly applicable to the case.

False Evidence. — [5] When evidence that a lawyer knows to be false is provided by a person who is not the client, the lawyer must refuse to offer it regardless of the client's wishes.

[6] When false evidence is offered by the client, however, a conflict may arise between the lawyer's duty to keep the client's revelations confidential and the duty of candor to the court. Upon ascertaining that material evidence is false, the lawyer should seek to persuade the client that the evidence should not be offered or, if it has been offered, that its false character should immediately be disclosed. If the persuasion is ineffective, the lawyer must take reasonable remedial measures.

[7] Except in the defense of a criminal accused, the rule generally recognized is that, if necessary to rectify the situation, an advocate must disclose the existence of the client's deception to the court or to the other party. Such a disclosure can result in grave consequences to the client, including not only a sense of betrayal but also loss of the case and perhaps a prosecution for perjury. But the alternative is that the lawyer cooperate in deceiving the court, thereby subverting the truth-finding process which the adversary system is designed to implement. See Rule 1.2(d). Furthermore, unless it is clearly understood that the lawyer will act upon the duty to disclose the existence of false evidence, the client can simply reject the lawyer's advice to reveal the false evidence and insist that the lawyer keep silent. Thus the client could in effect coerce the lawyer into being a party to fraud on the court.

Perjury by a Criminal Defendant. — [8] Whether an advocate for a criminally accused has the same duty of disclosure has been intensely debated. While it is agreed that the lawyer should seek to persuade the client to refrain from perjurious testimony, there has been dispute concerning the lawyer's duty when that persuasion fails. If the confrontation with the client occurs before trial, the lawyer ordinarily can withdraw. Withdrawal before trial may not be possible, however, either because trial is imminent, or because the confrontation with the client does not take place until the trial itself, or because no other counsel is available.

[9] The most difficult situation, therefore, arises in a criminal case where the accused insists on testifying when the lawyer knows that the testimony is perjurious. The lawyer's effort to rectify the situation can increase the likelihood of the client's being convicted as well as opening the possibility of a prosecution for perjury. On the other hand, if the lawyer does not exercise control over the proof, the lawyer participates, although in a merely passive way, in deception of the court.

[10] Three resolutions of this dilemma have been proposed. One is to permit the accused to testify by a narrative without guidance through the lawyer's questioning. This compromises both contending principles; it exempts the lawyer from the duty to disclose false evidence but subjects the client to an implicit disclosure of information imparted to counsel. Another suggested resolution, of relatively recent origin, is that the advocate be entirely excused from the duty to reveal perjury if the perjury is that of the client. This is a coherent solution but makes the advocate a knowing instrument of perjury.

[11] The other resolution of the dilemma is that the lawyer must reveal the client's perjury if necessary to rectify the situation. A criminal accused has a right to the assistance of an advocate, a right to testify and a right of confidential communication with counsel. However, an accused should not have a right to assistance of counsel in committing perjury. Furthermore, an advocate has an obligation, not only in professional ethics but under the law as well, to avoid implication in the commission of perjury or other falsification of evidence. See Rule 1.2(d).

Remedial Measures. — [12] If perjured testimony or false evidence has been offered, the advocate's proper course ordinarily is to remonstrate with the client confidentially. If that fails, the advocate should seek to withdraw if that will remedy the situation. If withdrawal will not remedy the situation or is impossible, the advocate should make disclosure to the court. It is for the court then to determine what should be done — making a statement about the matter to the trier of fact, ordering a mistrial or perhaps nothing. If the false testimony was that of the client, the client may controvert the lawyer's version of their communication when the lawyer discloses the situation to the court. If there is an issue whether the client has committed perjury, the lawyer cannot represent the client in resolution of the issue, and a mistrial may be unavoidable. An unscrupulous client might in this way attempt to produce a series of mistrials and thus escape prosecution. However, a second such encounter could be construed as a deliberate abuse of the right to counsel and as such a waiver of the right to further representation.

Constitutional Requirements. — [13] The general rule — that an advocate must disclose the existence of perjury with respect to a material fact, even that of a client — applies to defense counsel in criminal cases, as well as in other instances. However, the definition of the lawyer's ethical duty in such a situation may be qualified by constitutional provisions for due process and the right to counsel in criminal cases. Paragraph (e) is intended to protect from discipline the lawyer who does not make disclosures mandated by paragraphs (a) through (d) only when the lawyer acts in the "reasonable belief" that disclosure would jeopardize a constitutional right of the client. For a definition of "reasonable belief," see Rule 1.0(k).

Duration of Obligation. — [14] A practical time limit on the obligation to rectify the presentation of false evidence has to be established. The conclusion of the proceeding is a reasonably definite point for the termination of the obligation. After that point, however, the lawyer may be permitted to take certain actions pursuant to Rule 1.6(b)(3).

Refusing to Offer Proof Believed to Be False. — [15] Generally speaking, a lawyer has authority to refuse to offer testimony or other proof that the lawyer reasonably believes is false. Offering such proof may reflect adversely on the lawyer's ability to discriminate in the quality of evidence and thus impair the lawyer's effectiveness as an advocate. In criminal cases, however, a lawyer may, in some jurisdictions, be denied this authority by constitutional requirements governing the right to counsel.

Ex Parte Proceedings. — [16] Ordinarily, an advocate has the limited responsibility of presenting one side of the matters that a tribunal should consider in reaching a decision; the conflicting position is expected to be presented by the opposing party. However, in an ex parte proceeding, such as an application for a temporary restraining order, there is no balance of presentation by opposing advocates. The object of an ex parte proceeding is nevertheless to yield a substantially just result. The judge has an affirmative responsibility to accord the absent party just consideration. The lawyer for the represented party has the correlative duty to make disclosures of material facts known to the lawyer and that the lawyer reasonably believes are necessary to an informed decision.

Model Rules Comparison. — Rule 3.3 has been rewritten to retain elements of existing Maryland language and to incorporate some changes from the Ethics 2000 Amendments to the ABA Model Rules.

Maryland Law Review. — For article, "The Devolution of the Legal Profession: A Demand Side Perspective," see 49 Md. L. Rev. 869 (1990).

University of Baltimore Law Forum. — For note, "Recent Development: Attorney Grievance Commission of Maryland v. Goodman: Disbarment Imposed in Cases Involving Intentionally Dishonest Conduct Unless Compelling Extenuating Circumstances Mitigate Against Such Sanction," see 35 U. Balt. L.F. 56 (2004).

For article, "The New Maryland Rules of Professional Conduct and Mediation: Perplexing Questions Answered and Perplexing Questions That Remain," see 36 U. Balt. L.F. 1 (2005).

Nature of practice. — Fact that attorney had nonlawyers working for him did not transform his business from that of a law practice to a title business. Prahinski v. Prahinski, 75 Md. App. 113, 540 A.2d 833 (1988), aff'd, 321 Md. 227, 582 A.2d 784 (1990).

Important character traits. — Candor and truthfulness are two of the most important moral character traits of a lawyer. Att'y Griev. Comm'n v. Myers, 333 Md. 440, 635 A.2d 1315 (1994).

Comments from bench. — Comments from bench may be reversible error, even if counsel violates his ethical duty toward the court. Spencer v. State, 76 Md. App. 71, 543 A.2d 851 (1988).

Misrepresentation in complaint. — Attorney's failure to correct the misstatement in the complaint as to the date of the accident amounted to a violation of (a)(1). Att'y Griev. Comm'n v. Bleecker, 414 Md. 147, 994 A.2d 928 (2010).

Citation of relevant Fourth Circuit cases. — In this district, whenever a case from the Fourth Circuit comes anywhere close to being relevant to a disputed issue, the better part of wisdom is to cite it and attempt to distinguish it, and the matter will then be left for the judge to decide. While attorneys may still in time be judged unsuccessful in their attempt to distinguish the case, they will never be judged ethically omissive for failing to cite it. Massey v. Prince George's County, 918 F. Supp. 905 (D. Md. 1996).

Failure to inform authorities of completed crimes. — When client revealed to attorney that he had operated a motor vehicle when his license was expired, and that, unbeknownst to the arresting officer, he had given a fictitious name when arrested on DWI charge, attorney had no duty to inform authorities, as these were completed crimes; the attorney had a duty not to disclose them. Att'y Griev.

Comm'n v. Rohrback, 323 Md. 79, 591 A.2d 488 (1991).

Failure to disclose client's use of fictitious name at presentence investigation interview. — A client awaiting sentencing has no constitutional right to counsel at presentence investigation interview; therefore, attorney's failure to disclose client's use of a fictitious name to the agent conducting the presentence investigation did not fall within the exception under the prior, similar Rule, to the requirement of candor toward a tribunal. Att'y Griev. Comm'n v. Rohrback, 323 Md. 79, 591 A.2d 488 (1991).

Representation of multiple defendants in a criminal case. — An attorney's contact with his client's represented criminal codefendant was deemed a violation of this Rule and resulted in disbarment. Att'y Griev. Comm'n v. Kent, 337 Md. 361, 653 A.2d 909 (1995).

Assertion of adverse party's defense. — The prior, similar Rule does not require that a party or an attorney assert an adverse party's defense, much less produce evidence in support of it, when the party disputes that defense. Winkler Constr. Co. v. Jerome, 355 Md. 231, 734 A.2d 212 (1999).

Respondent was deemed to have displayed a lack of candor to the tribunal. — Respondent was deemed to have displayed a lack of candor to the tribunal where subsequent testimony to an inquiry board contradicted his testimony to the hearing court. Att'y Griev. Comm'n v. Kent, 337 Md. 361, 653 A.2d 909 (1995).

Failure to disclose bankruptcy debtors' dissipation of sale proceeds. — Order to show cause why the Chapter 13 debtors' counsel should not have been sanctioned for violating his duty of candor to the tribunal in violation of (a)(1) was sustained because counsel waited until the 11th hour, the hearing on the motion to sell, to apprise the court and trustee that the debtors had already spent a substantial portion of the proceeds from the sale of timber on their land and could not consummate the sale and retire the plan base, even though counsel was aware of that material fact for two months. In re Gulczynski, (Bankr. D. Md. 2008).

Failing to mail on dates represented on certificates of service. — Attorney violated (a)(1) by failing to mail documents on the dates represented in the certificates of service. Att'y Griev. Comm'n v. Byrd, 408 Md. 449, 970 A.2d 870 (2009).

False evidence. — When perjured testimony or false evidence has been offered, and that fact has been disclosed to the court (by the client or by the client's lawyer), it is for the court then to determine what should be done — making a statement about the matter to the trier of fact, ordering a mistrial or perhaps

nothing. Holden v. Blevins, 154 Md. App. 1, 837 A.2d 1053 (2003).

The prior, similar Rule, regarding a lawyer's obligation to disclose his or her client's false testimony, in pertinent part, provides that the duties continue to the conclusion of a proceeding, and, for purposes of the Rule, a "proceeding" has not concluded until the appeal rights of every party to that proceeding have been exhausted, including the right to petition for certiorari. Holden v. Blevins, 154 Md. App. 1, 837 A.2d 1053 (2003).

Issue of whether false evidence is "material" must be decided by a trial judge rather than by a lawyer who thinks the evidence is material, i.e. important to the client's case, at the point when the lawyer offered it. Holden v. Blevins, 154 Md. App. 1, 837 A.2d 1053 (2003).

In a will contest, when a residuary beneficiary defending the submitted will testified falsely that he had received various awards during his military career, and revealed this to the appellate court, under former Md. Code Prof. Resp. DR 7-102(B)(1) of the Maryland Code of Professional Responsibility, now this Rule, after the trial court had denied the new trial motion filed by his opposing siblings, this revelation was newly discovered evidence which required the appellate court, under Rule 8-604(d) of the Maryland Rules of Procedure, to remand the matter to the trial court to reconsider the new trial motion upon a factually accurate record. Holden v. Blevins, 154 Md. App. 1, 837 A.2d 1053 (2003).

Prohibition against making false statement to tribunal. — Trial court did not violate Md. R. 4-215(a)(3) when defendant said defendant did not want counsel to represent defendant because the trial court could rely on counsel's statement "I'm still in the case," and did not have to inquire further, as Md. R. Prof. Conduct 1.2 required counsel to abide by defendant's decision concerning the services to be performed on defendant's behalf, and this Rule prohibited counsel from making a false statement to the trial court. Garner v. State, 414 Md. 372, 995 A.2d 694 (2010).

Fraud action. — One may not use the Maryland Rules of Professional Conduct as the basis of a fraud action. Maryland Nat'l Bank v. Resolution Trust Corp., 895 F. Supp. 762 (D. Md. 1995).

Maryland law refuses to impose liability for a breach of a rule of professional conduct. — Maryland law refuses to impose liability for a breach of a rule of professional conduct; violation of a rule does not give rise to a cause of action and does not create a presumption that a legal duty has been breached. Maryland Nat'l Bank v. Resolution Trust Corp., 895 F. Supp. 762 (D. Md. 1995).

Rule not violated. — In an attorney discipline proceeding, a finding that an attorney violated the rule by misleading a judge in asserting that certain discovery had been timely sent could not stand because there was some independent evidence to support the attorney's belief. Att'y Griev. Comm'n v. Hermina, 379 Md. 503, 842 A.2d 762 (2004).

Attorney's exception to the violation of Md. R. Prof. Conduct 3.3(a)(1) was sustained because such a finding was inconsistent with the hearing judge's conclusion that the Commission failed to prove that the attorney made any false statement of material fact. Att'y Griev. Comm'n v. Ward, 394 Md. 1, 904 A.2d 477 (2006).

Forty-five day suspension. — In a reciprocal discipline action, the attorney, who had been publicly reprimanded in Texas, was suspended from the practice of law in Maryland for 45 days for misrepresenting that a document was an original signature page, but later admitting that the document was signed five years after the original contract, on the eve of summary judgment, conduct that amounted to violations of Md. Law. R. Prof. Conduct 3.3(a)(1) and (4) and 8.4(c), because such conduct warranted substantially different discipline in Maryland. Att'y Griev. Comm'n v. Gordon, 413 Md. 46, 991 A.2d 51 (2010).

Forty-five day suspension. — In a reciprocal discipline action, the attorney, who had been publicly reprimanded in Texas, was suspended from the practice of law in Maryland for 45 days for misrepresenting that a document was an original signature page, but later admitting that the document was signed five years after the original contract, on the eve of summary judgment, conduct that amounted to violations of Md. Law. R. Prof. Conduct 3.3(a)(1) and (4) and 8.4(c), because such conduct warranted substantially different discipline in Maryland. Att'y Griev. Comm'n v. Gordon, 413 Md. 46, 991 A.2d 51 (2010).

Indefinite suspension was proper sanction — Attorney's indefinite suspension for violating Md. R. Prof. Conduct 3.3(a)(1), 5.5(a), and 8.4(a), (c), and (d) was appropriate where, pursuant to Rule 16-760(c)(2), he should have advised the court that he was not permitted to continue his representation of a client as soon as he learned of his suspension. Att'y Griev. Comm'n v. Maignan, 402 Md. 39, 935 A.2d 409 (2007).

Indefinite suspension with leave to apply for readmission. — Attorney was indefinitely suspended, with leave to apply for readmission after six months, where the attorney violated (a)(1) and Md. R. Prof. Conduct 1.1, 1.3, 5.5(a), and 8.4(c) and (d), by, inter alia, appearing at a meeting of creditors when not authorized to practice before district court and failing to disclose fees the client paid to a bankruptcy preparer and attorney. Att'y Griev.

Comm'n v. Robaton, 411 Md. 415, 983 A.2d 467 (2009).

Disbarment appropriate. — Where an attorney violated the prior, similar Rule and prior, similar Rule 8.4 when he gave a false response to a question posed by a District Court judge concerning his traffic record due to his previous history of misconduct, he was disbarred. Att'y Griev. Comm'n v. Myers, 333 Md. 440, 635 A.2d 1315 (1994).

Despite evidence that respondent attorney suffered from depression and a mood disorder, disbarment was the only appropriate sanction for misconduct that included misleading both clients and their health care providers about the status of settlement negotiations and concealing a possible asset of a bankrupt client from the bankruptcy trustee; the mental problems were not the root cause of the misconduct, and the attorney, whose practice had been quite successful, had known quite well that mishandling of client trust funds to cover practice expenses and misleading the bankruptcy court were wrong. Att'y Griev. Comm'n v. Zakroff, 387 Md. 603, 876 A.2d 664 (2005), cert. denied, 2006 Md. LEXIS 561 (2006); cert. denied, 2006 Md. LEXIS 571 (Md. 2006).

Despite evidence that respondent attorney suffered from depression and a mood disorder, disbarment was the only appropriate sanction for misconduct that included misleading both clients and their health care providers about the status of settlement negotiations and concealing a possible asset of a bankrupt client from the bankruptcy trustee; the mental problems were not the root cause of the misconduct, and the attorney, whose practice had been quite successful, had known quite well that mishandling of client trust funds to cover practice expenses and misleading the bankruptcy court were wrong. Att'y Griev. Comm'n v. Zakroff, 387 Md. 603, 876 A.2d 664 (2005), cert. denied, 2006 Md. LEXIS 561 (2006); cert. denied, 2006 Md. LEXIS 571 (Md. 2006).

Where the attorney, among other things, intentionally misappropriated client funds, forged a client's signature on a settlement check, lied under oath, and represented a client when the attorney was not licensed to do so, the attorney was disbarred for violating former, similar Md. R. Prof. Conduct 1.2(a), 1.3, 1.5(c), 1.15(a), (b), 3.3(a), 5.5, 8.1(a), (b), 8.4(a), (b), (c), (d), Md. R. 16-604, and §§ 10-304, -306 of the Business Occupations and Professions Article Att'y Griev. Comm'n v. Kapoor, 391 Md. 505, 894 A.2d 502 (2006).

In an attorney disciplinary matter wherein the attorney was ordered disbarred, the attorney was found to have violated Rules 3.1 and 3.3 when he filed a motion to reconsider ratification and confirmation of a trustee's sale and to set aside a sale in a foreclosure case, supporting the motion with an assertion that his client had not received timely notice of the sale, which was not true and the attorney knew that his client had notice of the sale. Further, the statements in the affidavit violated Rule 3.3, which prohibited a lawyer from knowingly making a false statement of material fact or law to a tribunal. Att'y Griev. Comm'n v. Steinberg, 395 Md. 337, 910 A.2d 429 (2006).

Attorney was disbarred for violating Md. R. Prof. Conduct 1.1, 3.1, 3.2, 3.3(a), 4.4, 8.2(a), and 8.4(c) and (d) because he knowingly made false statements when representing that settlement had occurred, and he relied on misleading statements of fact regarding a trial judge when appealing sanctions that were imposed upon him; the attorney was intentionally dishonest with both the trial court and the court of special appeals, which showed a systematic effort to mislead the courts, and his history of sanctions for violating the Maryland Rules of Professional Conduct (MRPC) showed an ongoing disregard for the MRPC. Att'y Griev. Comm'n v. McClain, 406 Md. 1, 956 A.2d 135 (2008), cert. denied, 129 S. Ct. 1691, 2009 U.S. LEXIS 2433, 173 L. Ed. 2d 1036 (U.S. 2009).

In a reciprocal disciplinary action, the attorney, who had been suspended from the practice of law for one year and one day in Colorado, was disbarred for violating Md. Law. R. Prof. Conduct 3.3(a)(1), 3.4(c), and 8.4(a), (b), (c), and (d), based on the attorney's own admission that he failed to make pertinent disclosures during a personal bankruptcy case and gave false testimony that case. Att'y Griev. Comm'n v. Zodrow, 419 Md. 286, 19 A.3d 381 (2011).

Sixty-day suspension was proper sanction. — In an attorney disciplinary matter, it was held that the attorney violated this Rule by filing expungement petitions for a client knowing that the client's charges were ineligible for expungement and, as a result, he was suspended from the practice of law for 60 days. Additionally, the findings and conclusions of the hearing officer that the attorney did not fraudulently obtain a duplicate driver's license after having his original license taken away at a sobriety checkpoint were found not to be clearly erroneous, and no deficiencies were found with regard to the allegations in the petition providing sufficient notice to the attorney of the charges against him. Att'y Griev. Comm'n v. Tanko, 408 Md. 404, 969 A.3d 1010 (2009).

Ninety-day suspension. — Ninety-day suspension was appropriate sanction for attorney's neglect of client's cases, falsifying client's signature on a complaint, and causing the complaint with the false signature to be notarized and filed. Att'y Griev. Comm'n v. Parsons, 310 Md. 132, 527 A.2d 325 (1987).

Disbarment was proper sanction. — Attorney was properly disbarred for violating prior, similar Maryland Rules of Professional Conduct 1.1, 1.3, 1.4, 1.15, 3.3, and 8.4, § 10-306 of the Business Occupations and Professions Article, and former Rule BU9 (now Rule 16-609) of the Maryland Rules of Procedure. Att'y Griev. Comm'n v. Williams, 335 Md. 458, 644 A.2d 490 (1994).

An attorney's giving false testimony during a deposition taken in a federal District Court proceeding and as a witness in a Maryland post conviction proceeding about her improper representation of private clients while an Assistant Public Defender violated prior, similar Rule 3.3 and Rule 8.4. The Court of Appeals held disbarment was the appropriate sanction. Att'y Griev. Comm'n v. White, 354 Md. 346, 731 A.2d 447 (1999).

Disbarment was the appropriate sanction where an out-of-state attorney practiced law in the State of Maryland without a license, failed to acknowledge his jurisdictional limitations on his firm letterhead, acted against the interests of his purported clients during and after the sale of their home to him, filed a bankruptcy petition on those clients' behalf, but without their consent or knowledge, and forged the signatures of the clients and another attorney in his office on court papers and filings, in violation of prior, similar Rules of Professional Conduct 1.7, 3.3, 5.5, 7.1, 7.5, and 8.4. Att'y Griev. Comm'n v. Johnson, 363 Md. 598, 770 A.2d 130 (2001).

Attorney was disbarred after it was found that the attorney violated, inter alia, former, similar version of this Rule, by lying about when funds used to purchase property were wired and failing to disclose the source of the funds used to purchase the subject property. Att'y Griev. Comm'n v. Pak, 400 Md. 567, 929 A.2d 546 (2007), cert. denied, 128 S. Ct. 905, 2008 U.S. LEXIS 126, 169 L. Ed. 2d 729 (U.S. 2008).

Quoted in Att'y Griev. Comm'n v. Christopher, 383 Md. 624, 861 A.2d 692 (2004); Att'y Griev. Comm'n v. Kalil, 402 Md. 358, 936 A.2d 854 (2007); Att'y Griev. Comm'n v. Kreamer, 404 Md. 282, 946 A.2d 500 (2008).

Stated in Blake v. State, 418 Md. 445, 15 A.3d 787 (2011).

Cited in Barufaldi v. Ocean City, 196 Md. App. 1, 7 A.3d 643 (2010); Att'y Griev. Comm'n v. Coppola, 419 Md. 370, 19 A.3d 431 (2011); State v. Northam, — Md. —, 26 A.3d 344 (2011).

Rule 3.4. Fairness to Opposing Party and Counsel.

A lawyer shall not:

(a) unlawfully obstruct another party's access to evidence or unlawfully alter, destroy or conceal a document or other material having potential evidentiary value. A lawyer shall not counsel or assist another person to do any such act;

(b) falsify evidence, counsel or assist a witness to testify falsely, or offer an inducement to a witness that is prohibited by law;

(c) knowingly disobey an obligation under the rules of a tribunal except for an open refusal based on an assertion that no valid obligation exists;

(d) in pretrial procedure, make a frivolous discovery request or fail to make reasonably diligent effort to comply with a legally proper discovery request by an opposing party;

(e) in trial, allude to any matter that the lawyer does not reasonably believe is relevant or that will not be supported by admissible evidence, assert personal knowledge of facts in issue except when testifying as a witness, or state a personal opinion as to the justness of a cause, the credibility of a witness, the culpability of a civil litigant or the guilt or innocence of an accused; or

(f) request a person other than a client to refrain from voluntarily giving relevant information to another party unless:

(1) the person is a relative or an employee or other agent of a client; and

(2) the lawyer reasonably believes that the person's interests will not be adversely affected by refraining from giving such information.

COMMENT

[1] The procedure of the adversary system contemplates that the evidence in a case is to be marshalled competitively by the contending parties. Fair competition in the adversary system is secured by prohibitions against destruction or concealment of evidence, improperly influencing witnesses, obstructive tactics in discovery procedure, and the like.

[2] Documents and other items of evidence are often essential to establish a claim or defense. Subject to evidentiary privileges, the right of an opposing party, including the government, to obtain evidence through discovery or subpoena is an important procedural right. The exercise of that right can be frustrated if relevant material is altered, concealed or destroyed. Applicable law in many jurisdictions makes it an offense to destroy material for purpose of impairing its availability in a pending proceeding or one whose commencement can be foreseen. Falsifying evidence is also generally a criminal offense. Paragraph (a)

applies to evidentiary material generally, including computerized information.

[3] With regard to paragraph (b), it is not improper to pay a witness's expenses, including lost earnings, or to compensate an expert witness on terms permitted by law. The common law rule in most jurisdictions is that it is improper to pay an occurrence witness any fee for testifying and that it is improper to pay an expert witness a contingent fee.

[4] Paragraph (f) permits a lawyer to advise employees of a client to refrain from giving information to another party, for the employees may identify their interests with those of the client. See also Rule 4.2.

Model Rules Comparison. — Rule 3.4 is substantially similar to the language of the Ethics 2000 Amendments to the ABA Model Rules of Professional Conduct except that "including lost earnings" has been added to Comment [3] and the last two sentences of Comment [2] have been deleted.

University of Baltimore Law Forum. — For note, "Recent Development: Attorney

Grievance Commission of Maryland v. Goodman: Disbarment Imposed in Cases Involving

Intentionally Dishonest Conduct Unless Compelling Extenuating Circumstances Mitigate Against Such Sanction," see 35 U. Balt. L.F. 56 (2004).

Failure to report to facility. — Failure to report to a D.W.I. facility following a D.W.I. conviction was conduct prejudicial to the administration of justice and in violation of the Rules of Professional Conduct. Att'y Griev. Comm'n v. Garland, 345 Md. 383, 692 A.2d 465 (1997).

Representation of multiple defendants in a criminal case. — An attorney's contact with his client's represented criminal codefendant was deemed a violation of this Rule and resulted in disbarment. Att'y Griev. Comm'n v. Kent, 337 Md. 361, 653 A.2d 909 (1995).

Professional obligation to meet agreed upon extended deadline. — A lawyer who has requested and received an extension of time in which to answer interrogatories has a concomitant professional obligation to meet the agreed upon extended deadline, and failure to do so absent extenuating circumstances may well violate this Rule. Jayne H. Lee, Inc. v. Flagstaff Indus. Corp., 173 F.R.D. 651 (D. Md. 1997).

Failure to appear in court or produce documents. — Attorney who repeatedly failed to appear in court and to produce documents as directed by court order violated the prior, similar Rule, as his claim that he did not appear on one occasion due to an ice storm but that he called the court clerk was not substantiated by the court record; he was also found to have violated prior, similar Rule 1.3 by failing to have prepared an order in a family court matter, as directed by the court, as his claim that he thought his opposing counsel was preparing the order conflicted with documents indicating that the attorney knew it was his obligation to prepare it. Att'y Griev. Comm'n v. Mininsohn, 380 Md. 536, 846 A.2d 353 (2004).

Destruction of evidence and giving false testimony constituted violation. — Attorney sanctioned in the United States District Court for her destruction of evidence and giving false testimony in a case before that court was held to have violated prior, similar Maryland Rules of Professional Conduct 3.4 and 8.4. The Court of Appeals held disbarment was the appropriate sanction. Att'y Griev. Comm'n v. White, 354 Md. 346, 731 A.2d 447 (1999).

Rule violated. — In an attorney discipline proceeding, an attorney violated the rule by failing to cooperate in a pretrial conference to produce a joint statement. Att'y Griev. Comm'n v. Hermina, 379 Md. 503, 842 A.2d 762 (2004).

In an attorney disciplinary matter wherein the attorney was ordered disbarred, the attorney was found to have violated Rules 3.2 and 3.4 by engaging in a pattern of delay with opposing counsel in a will competency case which included unreturned phone calls, unanswered letters, cryptic excuses for lack of communication, and failure to comply with reasonable requests to depose his client. The attorney's behavior also displayed an unwillingness to comply with discovery, in violation of Rules 3.2 and 3.4, wherein the attorney twice contacted opposing counsel on the eve of two scheduled deposition dates giving a cryptic excuse that a sick relative required medical attention in the first instance, and in the second instance, misrepresenting that his client refused to attend. Att'y Griev. Comm'n v. Steinberg, 395 Md. 337, 910 A.2d 429 (2006).

Attorney violated (c) when the attorney knowingly and intentionally contravened a bankruptcy court's orders to allow access by the trustee to the attorney's property and to vacate the premises in the attorney's own bankruptcy proceeding. Att'y Griev. Comm'n v. Byrd, 408 Md. 449, 970 A.2d 870 (2009).

In the course of the employee's deposition, the employee's counsel instructed the employee not to answer on grounds other than privilege or court-ordered limitation, in violation of Fed. R. Civ. P. 30(d)(3) and this Rule. Mezu v. Morgan State Univ., 269 F.R.D. 565 (D. Md. 2010).

Over the course of the employee's deposition, her counsel objected more than 50 times, and counsel interjected frequently to answer questions for the employee; the frequency of counsel's objections and interjections and the length of the ensuing discussions impeded the deposition and frustrated the examination of the employee in violation of this Rule. Mezu v. Morgan State Univ., 269 F.R.D. 565 (D. Md. 2010).

Rule not violated — The prior, similar Rule was not violated where an attorney stated that "one learns to expect to get jerked around" when dealing with an insurance company, and called a driver in the case an "idiot." Att'y Griev. Comm'n v. Alison, 349 Md. 623, 709 A.2d 1212 (1998).

Although an attorney intentionally misrepresented his identity on a witness' voice mail as being a police officer, he did not intentionally misrepresent that a warrant had issued for a witness' arrest; the attorney had acted on a mistaken belief that a warrant had been issued and he would not have made the call had he not honestly believed the warrant had been issued. That conduct, standing alone, was not a violation of this Rule or Rule 8.4(a)-(d), as it did not cause the witness to be unavailable for trial (although the attorney did intend that the witness would be unavailable to the State by invoking his Fifth Amendment privilege), actually interfere with the administration of justice, or obstruct the State's access to evidence. Att'y Griev. Comm'n v. Smith, 405

Md. 107, 950 A.2d 101 (2008).

Acts not resulting in criminal conviction. — An attorney may be disciplined for acts which are criminal but do not result in a criminal conviction if Bar Counsel proves the underlying conduct at the disciplinary hearing. Att'y Griev. Comm'n v. Garland, 345 Md. 383, 692 A.2d 465 (1997).

Suspension warranted. — Although attorney's conduct was an aberration, the egregious nature of assisting a former client in breaking into the home of his wife in an attempt to recover evidence warranted the imposition of a significant sanction such that the attorney was suspended indefinitely from the practice of law with the right to apply for reinstatement not less than one year from the date of filing the opinion. Att'y Griev. Comm'n v. Protokowicz, 329 Md. 252, 619 A.2d 100 (1993).

Disbarment appropriate. — In a reciprocal disciplinary action, the attorney, who had been suspended from the practice of law for one year and one day in Colorado, was disbarred for violating Md. Law. R. Prof. Conduct 3.3(a)(1), 3.4(c), and 8.4(a), (b), (c), and (d), based on the attorney's own admission that he failed to make pertinent disclosures during a personal bankruptcy case and gave false testimony that case. Att'y Griev. Comm'n v. Zodrow, 419 Md. 286, 19 A.3d 381 (2011).

Applied in Md. Transp. Auth. Police Lodge # 34 of FOP, Inc. v. Md. Transp. Auth., 195 Md. App. 124, 5 A.3d 1174 (2010).

Quoted in Att'y Griev. Comm'n v. MacDougall, 384 Md. 271, 863 A.2d 312 (2004); Evans v. State, 174 Md. App. 549, 922 A.2d 620 (2007), cert. denied, 929 A.2d 890, 2007 Md. LEXIS 563 (Md. 2007); Att'y Griev. Comm'n v. McCulloch, 404 Md. 388, 946 A.2d 1009 (2008); Att'y Griev. Comm'n v. Taylor, 405 Md. 697, 955 A.2d 755 (2008); Falik v. Hornage, 413 Md. 163, 991 A.2d 1234 (2010); Att'y Griev. Comm'n v. Khandpur, 421 Md. 1, 25 A.3d 165 (2011).

Cited in Att'y Griev. Comm'n v. Baker, 396 Md. 15, 912 A.2d 651 (2006); Att'y Griev. Comm'n v. Ficker, 399 Md. 445, 924 A.2d 1105 (2007).

Rule 3.5. Impartiality and Decorum of the Tribunal.

(a) A lawyer shall not:

(1) seek to influence a judge, prospective, qualified, or sworn juror, or other official by means prohibited by law;

(2) before the trial of a case with which the lawyer is connected, communicate outside the course of official proceedings with anyone known to the lawyer to be on the jury list for trial of the case;

(3) during the trial of a case with which the lawyer is connected, communicate outside the course of official proceedings with any member of the jury;

(4) during the trial of a case with which the lawyer is not connected, communicate outside the course of official proceedings with any member of the jury about the case;

(5) after discharge of a jury from further consideration of a case with which the lawyer is connected, ask questions of or make comments to a jury member that are calculated to harass or embarrass the jury member or to influence the jury member's actions in future jury service;

(6) conduct a vexatious or harassing investigation of any prospective, qualified, or sworn juror;

(7) communicate ex parte about an adversary proceeding with the judge or other official before whom the proceeding is pending, except as permitted by law;

(8) discuss with a judge potential employment of the judge if the lawyer or a firm with which the lawyer is associated has a matter that is pending before the judge; or

(9) engage in conduct intended to disrupt a tribunal.

(b) A lawyer who has knowledge of any violation of paragraph (a) of this Rule, any improper conduct by a prospective, qualified, or sworn juror or any improper conduct by another towards a prospective, qualified, or sworn juror, shall report it promptly to the court or other appropriate authority. (Amended Dec. 4, 2007, effective Jan. 1, 2008.)

COMMENT

[1] Many forms of improper influence upon a tribunal are proscribed by criminal law. Others are specified in Rule 16-813, Maryland Code of Judicial Conduct, with which an advocate should be familiar. A lawyer is required to avoid contributing to a violation of such provisions.

[2] The advocate's function is to present evidence and argument so that the cause may be decided according to law. Refraining from abusive or obstreperous conduct is a corollary of the advocate's right to speak on behalf of litigants. A lawyer may stand firm against abuse by a judge but should avoid reciprocation; the judge's default is no justification for similar dereliction by an advocate. An advocate can present the cause, protect the record for subsequent review and preserve professional integrity by patient firmness no less effectively than by belligerence or theatrics.

[3] With regard to the prohibition in paragraph (a)(2) of this Rule against communications with anyone on "the jury list," see Md. Rules 2-512(c) and 4-312(c).

Model Rules Comparison. — Rule 3.5 retains the former Maryland Rule text and comments, except that paragraph (a)(8) is new and the reference in Comment [1] is to the Code of Judicial Conduct. Changes in ABA Model Rule 3.5 were not adopted.

Effect of amendments. — The December 4, 2007 Order, effective January 1, 2008, in (a)(1), (a)(6), and (b) substituted "prospective, qualified, or sworn juror" for "juror, prospective juror"; in (a)(2) substituted "jury list for trial" for "list from which the jurors will be selected for the trial"; in (a)(5) substituted "jury member" for "member of that jury" or "juror" and variants in three places; in (b) substituted "paragraph (a)" for "section (a)" and "qualified or sworn juror" for "juror or prospective juror"; and in the Comment, [3] substituted "paragraph (a)(2)" for "section (a)(2)" and "jury list" for "list from which the jurors will be selected".

Ex parte communications. — Counsel's discussion with dentist member of arbitration panel, which occurred within the 30-day period during which a party may ask the arbitration panel to modify or correct an award, did not constitute an ex parte communication in violation of both the regulations of the Health Claims Arbitration Office and the Maryland Rules of Professional Conduct. Counsel's contact with dentist came subsequent to the pendency of the arbitration, at least as it concerned dentist. Carrion v. Linzey, 342 Md. 266, 675 A.2d 527 (1996).

In an attorney discipline proceeding, a finding that an attorney had violated the prior, similar Rule by objecting to the introduction of documents on the basis that they had not been disclosed when in fact they had, by moving for a mistrial on an assertion that the opposing party had not answered interrogatories that were allegedly not sent, and by moving to disqualify a judge for unsupportable reasons, could not stand because there were no deliberate misstatements and there was no evidence demonstrating that the attorney's actions were made to disrupt the trial or tribunal. Att'y Griev. Comm'n v. Hermina, 379 Md. 503, 842 A.2d 762 (2004).

Rule 3.6. Trial Publicity.

(a) A lawyer who is participating or has participated in the investigation or litigation of a matter shall not make an extrajudicial statement that the lawyer knows or reasonably should know will be disseminated by means of public communication and will have a substantial likelihood of materially prejudicing an adjudicative proceeding in the matter.

(b) Notwithstanding paragraph (a), a lawyer may state:

(1) the claim, offense or defense involved and, except when prohibited by law, the identity of the persons involved;

(2) information contained in a public record;

(3) that an investigation of a matter is in progress;

(4) the scheduling or result of any step in litigation;

(5) a request for assistance in obtaining evidence and information necessary thereto;

(6) a warning of danger concerning the behavior of a person involved, when there is reason to believe that there exists the likelihood of substantial harm to an individual or to the public interest; and

(7) in a criminal case, in addition to subparagraphs (1) through (6):

(i) the identity, residence, occupation and family status of the accused;

(ii) if the accused has not been apprehended, information necessary to aid in apprehension of that person;

(iii) the fact, time and place of arrest; and

(iv) the identity of investigating and arresting officers or agencies and the length of the investigation.

(c) Notwithstanding paragraph (a), a lawyer may make a statement that a reasonable lawyer would believe is required to protect a client from the substantial undue prejudicial effect of recent publicity not initiated by the lawyer or the lawyer's client. A statement made pursuant to this paragraph shall be limited to such information as is necessary to mitigate the recent adverse publicity.

(d) No lawyer associated in a firm or government agency with a lawyer subject to paragraph (a) shall make a statement prohibited by paragraph (a).

COMMENT

[1] It is difficult to strike a balance between protecting the right to a fair trial and safeguarding the right of free expression. Preserving the right to a fair trial necessarily entails some curtailment of the information that may be disseminated about a party prior to trial, particularly where trial by jury is involved. If there were no such limits, the result would be the practical nullification of the protective effect of the rules of forensic decorum and the exclusionary rules of evidence. On the other hand, there are vital social interests served by the free dissemination of information about events having legal consequences and about legal proceedings themselves. The public has a right to know about threats to its safety and measures aimed at assuring its security. It also has a legitimate interest in the conduct of judicial proceedings, particularly in matters of general public concern. Furthermore, the subject matter of legal proceedings is often of direct significance in debate and deliberation over questions of public policy.

[2] Special rules of confidentiality may validly govern proceedings in juvenile, domestic relations and mental disability proceedings, and perhaps other types of litigation. Rule 3.4(c) requires compliance with such rules.

[3] The Rule sets forth a basic general prohibition against a lawyer's making statements that the lawyer knows or should know will have a substantial likelihood of materially prejudicing an adjudicative proceeding. Recog-

nizing that the public value of informed commentary is great and the likelihood of prejudice to a proceeding by the commentary of a lawyer who is not involved in the proceeding is small, the rule applies only to lawyers who are, or who have been involved in the investigation or litigation of a case, and their associates.

[4] Paragraph (b) identifies specific matters about which a lawyer's statements would not ordinarily be considered to present a substantial likelihood of material prejudice, and should not in any event be considered prohibited by the general prohibition of paragraph (a). Paragraph (b) is not intended to be an exhaustive listing of the subjects upon which a lawyer may make a statement, but statements on other matters may be subject to paragraph (a).

[5] There are, on the other hand, certain subjects that are more likely than not to have a material prejudicial effect on a proceeding, particularly when they refer to a civil matter triable to a jury, a criminal matter, or any other proceeding that could result in incarceration. These subjects relate to:

(1) the character, credibility, reputation or criminal record of a party, suspect in a criminal investigation or witness, or the identity of a witness, or the expected testimony of a party or witness;

(2) in a criminal case or proceeding that could result in incarceration, the possibility of a plea of guilty to the offense or the existence

or contents of any confession, admission, or statement given by a defendant or suspect or that person's refusal or failure to make a statement;

(3) the performance or results of any examination or test or the refusal or failure of a person to submit to an examination or test, or the identity or nature of physical evidence expected to be presented;

(4) any opinion as to the guilt or innocence of a defendant or suspect in a criminal case or proceeding that could result in incarceration;

(5) information that the lawyer knows or reasonably should know is likely to be inadmissible as evidence in a trial and that would, if disclosed, create a substantial risk of prejudicing an impartial trial; or

(6) the fact that a defendant has been charged with a crime, unless there is included therein a statement explaining that the charge is merely an accusation and that the defendant is presumed innocent until and unless proven guilty.

[6] Another relevant factor in determining prejudice is the nature of the proceeding involved. Criminal jury trials will be most sensitive to extrajudicial speech. Civil trials may be less sensitive. Non-jury hearings and arbitration proceedings may be even less affected. The Rule will still place limitations on prejudicial comments in these cases, but the likelihood of prejudice may be different depending on the type of proceeding.

[7] Finally, extrajudicial statements that might otherwise raise a question under this Rule may be permissible when they are made in response to statements made publicly by another party, another party's lawyer, or third persons, where a reasonable lawyer would believe a public response is required in order to avoid prejudice to the lawyer's client. When prejudicial statements have been publicly made by others, responsive statements may have the salutary effect of lessening any resulting adverse impact on the adjudicative proceeding. Such responsive statements should be limited to contain only such information as is necessary to mitigate undue prejudice created by the statements made by others.

[8] See Rule 3.8(e) for additional duties of prosecutors in connection with extrajudicial statements about criminal proceedings.

Model Rules Comparison. — Rule 3.6 is substantially similar to the language of the Ethics 2000 Amendments to the ABA Model Rules of Professional Conduct.

Attorneys' statements about litigation. — When the owner of a title company sued attorneys for defamation related to statements made in a class action lawsuit against the owner's company, the suit was properly dismissed, under Rule 2-322(b)(2), because, even if the owner had standing to bring the suit, the allegedly defamatory statements were protected by absolute privilege, as (1) the statements were made in the context of litigation, and (2) the republication on the Internet of complaints filed against the company did not void the privilege, as the statements that were republished were not extra-judicial statements, the complaints were public documents to which the public was allowed to have access, under §§ 10-612 and 10-613 of the State Government Article, (b) of this Rule applied this legislative direction to court proceedings by allowing attorneys to state a claim offense, defense, and persons involved in a complaint as well as information contained in the public record, and the judge presiding over the class action expressly allowed the attorneys to use the Internet to communicate with class members. Norman v. Borison, 192 Md. App. 405, 994 A.2d 1019 (2010), aff'd, 2011 Md. LEXIS 210 (Md. 2011) .

Disclosure of criminal record information. — Because of the strong prejudicial impact of the public disclosure of criminal record information, future respondents will have the burden of establishing that such information was contained in a bona fide public court record accessible to the general public. Att'y Griev. Comm'n v. Gansler, 377 Md. 656, 835 A.2d 548 (2003).

Defendant's prior conviction a public record. — Prosecutor's extrajudicial reference to the defendant's prior convictions qualified for the protection of the public record safe harbor; thus, the prosecutor did not violate the prior, similar Rule. Att'y Griev. Comm'n v. Gansler, 377 Md. 656, 835 A.2d 548 (2003).

Prosecutor's extrajudicial comments. — Prosecutor violated the prior, similar Rule in various cases by making extrajudicial comments to the press concerning one defendant's confession, by discussing a plea offer concerning one defendant, and by providing his opinion as to the guilt of two defendants. Att'y Griev. Comm'n v. Gansler, 377 Md. 656, 835 A.2d 548 (2003).

Rule 3.7. Lawyer as Witness.

(a) A lawyer shall not act as advocate at a trial in which the lawyer is likely to be a necessary witness unless:

(1) the testimony relates to an uncontested issue;

(2) the testimony relates to the nature and value of legal services rendered in the case; or

(3) disqualification of the lawyer would work substantial hardship on the client.

(b) A lawyer may act as advocate in a trial in which another lawyer in the lawyer's firm is likely to be called as a witness unless precluded from doing so by Rule 1.7 or Rule 1.9.

COMMENT

[1] Combining the roles of advocate and witness can prejudice the tribunal and the opposing party and can also involve a conflict of interest between the lawyer and client.

Advocate Witness Rule. — [2] The tribunal has proper objection when the trier of fact may be confused or misled by a lawyer serving as both advocate and witness. The opposing party has proper objection where the combination of roles may prejudice that party's rights in the litigation. A witness is required to testify on the basis of personal knowledge, while an advocate is expected to explain and comment on evidence given by others. It may not be clear whether a statement by an advocate-witness should be taken as proof or as an analysis of the proof.

[3] To protect the tribunal, paragraph (a) prohibits a lawyer from simultaneously serving as advocate and necessary witness except in those circumstances specified in paragraphs (a)(1) through (a)(3). Paragraph (a)(1) recognizes that if the testimony will be uncontested, the ambiguities in the dual role are purely theoretical. Paragraph (a)(2) recognizes that where the testimony concerns the extent and value of legal services rendered in the action in which the testimony is offered, permitting the lawyers to testify avoids the need for a second trial with new counsel to resolve that issue. Moreover, in such a situation the judge has firsthand knowledge of the matter in issue; hence, there is less dependence on the adversary process to test the credibility of the testimony.

[4] Apart from these two exceptions, paragraph (a)(3) recognizes that a balancing is required between the interests of the client and those of the tribunal and the opposing party. Whether the tribunal is likely to be misled or the opposing party is likely to suffer prejudice depends on the nature of the case, the importance and probable tenor of the lawyer's testimony, and the probability that the lawyer's testimony will conflict with that of other witnesses. Even if there is risk of such prejudice, in determining whether the lawyer should be disqualified due regard must be given to the effect of disqualification on the lawyer's client. It is relevant that one or both parties could reasonably foresee that the lawyer would probably be a witness. The conflict of interest principles stated in prior, similar Rules 1.7, 1.9 and 1.10 have no application to this aspect of the problem.

[5] Because the tribunal is not likely to be misled when a lawyer acts as advocate in a trial in which another lawyer in the lawyer's firm will testify as a necessary witness, paragraph (b) permits the lawyer to do so except in situations involving a conflict of interest.

Conflict of Interest. — [6] In determining if it is permissible to act as advocate in a trial in which the lawyer will be a necessary witness, the lawyer must also consider that the dual role may give rise to a conflict of interest that will require compliance with Rules 1.7 or 1.9. For example, if there is likely to be substantial conflict between the testimony of the client and that of the lawyer, the representation involves a conflict of interest that requires compliance with Rule 1.7. This would be true even though the lawyer might not be prohibited by paragraph (a) from simultaneously serving as advocate and witness because the lawyer's disqualification would work a substantial hardship on the client. Similarly, a lawyer who might be permitted to simultaneously serve as an advocate and a witness by paragraph (a)(3) might be precluded from doing so by Rule 1.9. The problem can arise whether the lawyer is called as a witness on behalf of the client or is called by the opposing party. Determining whether or not such a conflict exists is primarily the responsibility of the lawyer involved. If there is a conflict of interest, the lawyer must secure the client's informed consent, confirmed in writing. In some cases, the lawyer will be precluded from seeking the client's consent. See Rule 1.7. See

Rule 1.0(b) for the definition of "confirmed in writing" and Rule 1.0(f) for the definition of "informed consent."

[7] Paragraph (b) provides that a lawyer is not disqualified from serving as an advocate because a lawyer with whom the lawyer is associated in a firm is precluded from doing so by paragraph (a). If, however, the testifying lawyer would also be disqualified by Rule 1.7 or Rule 1.9 from representing the client in the matter, other lawyers in the firm will be precluded from representing the client by Rule 1.10 unless the client gives informed consent under the conditions stated in Rule 1.7.

Model Rules Comparison. — Rule 3.7 is substantially similar to the language of the Ethics 2000 Amendments to the ABA Model Rules of Professional Conduct.

Defense counsel as State's witness. — Allowing defense counsel to be called as State's witness does not constitute a per se violation of either this section or the Constitution. Venable v. State, 108 Md. App. 395, 672 A.2d 123 (1996).

Although the issue of whether a party can call opposing counsel to testify is ordinarily within the discretion of the trial judge, in exercising that discretion during a criminal trial the judge must weigh the materiality of defense counsel's testimony versus the defendant's constitutional rights, and must also consider the extent to which defense counsel's credibility as an advocate will be adversely affected. Venable v. State, 108 Md. App. 395, 672 A.2d 123 (1996).

Whenever the prosecutor calls defense counsel to the stand, the trial judge must (1) require that the prosecutor make a detailed and complete proffer of what he or she expects defense counsel's testimony will be; (2) afford defense counsel an opportunity to respond; and (3) consider alternate methods of presenting any evidence that the prosecutor is entitled to introduce through defense counsel's testimony. If the court determines that the State is entitled to defense counsel's testimony, the court must next determine whether the defendant — not defense counsel — wants the assistance of another lawyer while defense counsel is on the stand. Venable v. State, 108 Md. App. 395, 672 A.2d 123 (1996).

Putting a defense counsel in the position of a prosecution witness is something that should be avoided whenever possible because defense counsel is called to testify as a State's witness, (1) it is impossible for the defendant to consult with the attorney; (2) the defendant cannot call attention to any inaccuracy in the attorney's testimony or suggest proper questions for cross-examination; (3) it is difficult, to say the least, for the lawyer, as a witness, to determine what objections should be made to questions asked him; (4) it is difficult for the lawyer to determine what questions to ask himself on cross-examination, and if he attempts to cross-examine himself the proceedings may take on a ludicrous appearance, and (5) it is difficult for the lawyer to answer questions so as to not antagonize the jury and still maintain a favorable impression. Venable v. State, 108 Md. App. 395, 672 A.2d 123 (1996).

Testimony of attorney that would likely be harmful to his client. — A lawyer's acceptance of a representation in a matter where it was likely that he would be required to testify, and that his testimony would likely be harmful to his client, constituted violations of prior, similar Rules 1.7 and 3.7. Klupt v. Krongard, 126 Md. App. 179, 728 A.2d 727 (1999), cert. denied, 355 Md. 612, 735 A.2d 1107 (1999).

Attorney was not allowed to disregard the general provisions of (a) prohibiting serving as both an advocate and a witness because he had been named on his own client's witness list, had weeks if not months to prepare new counsel, and had both outside and associate counsel available to assist if necessary. Schlossberg v. Fischer (In re Fischer), (Bankr. D. Md. 2006).

Testimony not required. — Plaintiff's attorney would not be disqualified because the attorney, while he worked for the city, was not substantially and personally involved in the termination of plaintiff, the attorney only spent a hour on a draft of a memorandum regarding the ability of the city to discipline and fire command level officers, and the police commissioners had waived any attorney-client privilege regarding the memorandum because they produced it during discovery. Furthermore, the memorandum would not be sufficient to overcome the former commissioner's defense of qualified immunity, so there would be no need for the attorney to testify regarding the former commissioner's knowledge of the memorandum at the time he terminated plaintiff. Franklin v. Clark, 454 F. Supp. 2d 356 (D. Md. 2006).

Testimony before an administrative agency. — Attorney was allowed to give evidence before an administrative agency, but needed to have been under oath as a sworn witness; where an attorney was not sworn, his statements were argument, not evidence, and should not have been considered by a county board of appeals in determining whether to grant a special use exception. Heard v. Foxshire Assocs., 145 Md. App. 695, 806 A.2d 348 (2002).

Prosecutorial vouching and advocate-witness. — Mistrial should have been declared when the prosecutor impeached a witness with questions about a prior conversation between the witness and the prosecutor; the prosecutor was in effect testifying, but could not be cross-examined by defendant. Walker v. State, 373 Md. 360, 818 A.2d 1078 (2003).

Where prosecutor testifies as to exercise of peremptory juror challenges. — Although this rule may suggest the advisability of having a second prosecutor available, whenever practicable, to argue the matter of alleged racial discrimination in exercising peremptory juror challenges when another prosecutor has been required to formally testify, this rule would in no way impair the ability of the testifying prosecutor to proceed with the trial on the merits. Gray v. State, 317 Md. 250, 562 A.2d 1278 (1989).

Improper disqualification of defendant's chosen counsel. — Trial court committed structural error by violating defendant's right to counsel of defendant's choice by disqualifying one of defendant's retained attorneys because, after it was represented that the attorney had spoken to a co-defendant before trial and that the attorney was a potential witness, due to a grand jury witness's testimony that the attorney attempted to "coach" the witness, the trial court did not conduct an evidentiary hearing to determine whether there was an actual or serious potential for conflict, at which the court could balance defendant's right to counsel of defendant's choice against interests of fairness and maintenance of ethical standards. State v. Goldsberry, 419 Md. 100, 18 A.3d 836 (2011).

Rule 3.8. Special Responsibilities of a Prosecutor.

The prosecutor in a criminal case shall:

(a) refrain from prosecuting a charge that the prosecutor knows is not supported by probable cause;

(b) make reasonable efforts to assure that the accused has been advised of the right to, and the procedure for obtaining, counsel and has been given reasonable opportunity to obtain counsel;

(c) not seek to obtain from an unrepresented accused a waiver of important pretrial rights, such as the right to a preliminary hearing;

(d) make timely disclosure to the defense of all evidence or information known to the prosecutor that tends to negate the guilt of the accused or mitigates the offense, and, in connection with sentencing, disclose to the defense and to the tribunal all unprivileged mitigating information known to the prosecutor, except when the prosecutor is relieved of this responsibility by a protective order of the tribunal; and

(e) except for statements that are necessary to inform the public of the nature and extent of the prosecutor's action and that serve a legitimate law enforcement purpose, refrain from making extrajudicial comments that have a substantial likelihood of heightening public condemnation of the accused and exercise reasonable care to prevent an employee or other person under the control of the prosecutor in a criminal case from making an extrajudicial statement that the prosecutor would be prohibited from making under Rule 3.6 or this Rule. (Amended September 8, 2011, effective January 1, 2012.)

COMMENT

[1] A prosecutor has the responsibility of a minister of justice and not simply that of an advocate. This responsibility carries with it specific obligations to see that the defendant is accorded procedural justice and that guilt is decided upon the basis of sufficient evidence. Precisely how far the prosecutor is required to go in this direction is a matter of debate and varies in different jurisdictions. Many jurisdictions have adopted the ABA Standards of Criminal Justice Relating to Prosecution Function, which in turn are the product of prolonged and careful deliberation by lawyers experienced in both criminal prosecution and defense. See also Rule 3.3(d), governing ex parte proceedings, among which grand jury

proceedings are included. Applicable law may require other measures by the prosecutor and knowing disregard of those obligations or a systematic abuse of prosecutorial discretion could constitute a violation of Rule 8.4.

[2] Paragraph (c) does not apply to an accused appearing self-represented with the approval of the tribunal. Nor does it forbid the lawful questioning of a suspect who has knowingly waived the rights to counsel and silence.

[3] The exception in paragraph (d) recognizes that a prosecutor may seek an appropriate protective order from the tribunal if disclosure of information to the defense could result in substantial harm to an individual or to the public interest.

[4] Paragraph (e) supplements Rule 3.6, which prohibits extrajudicial statements that have a substantial likelihood of prejudicing an adjudicatory proceeding. In the context of a criminal prosecution, a prosecutor's extrajudicial statement can create the additional problem of increasing public condemnation of the accused. Although the announcement of an indictment, for example, will necessarily have severe consequences for the accused, a prosecutor can, and should, avoid comments which have no legitimate law enforcement purpose and have a substantial likelihood of increasing public opprobrium of the accused. Nothing in this Comment is intended to restrict the statements which a prosecutor may make which comply with Rule 3.6(b) or 3.6(c).

[5] Like other lawyers, prosecutors are subject to Rules 5.1 and 5.3, which relate to responsibilities regarding lawyers and nonlawyers who work for or are associated with the lawyer's office. Paragraph (e) reminds the prosecutor of the importance of these obligations in connection with the unique dangers of improper extrajudicial statements in a criminal case. In addition, paragraph (e) requires a prosecutor to exercise reasonable care to prevent persons assisting or associated with the prosecutor from making improper extrajudicial statements, even when such persons are not under the direct supervision of the prosecutor. Ordinarily, the reasonable care standard will be satisfied if the prosecutor issues the appropriate cautions to law-enforcement personnel and other relevant individuals.

Model Rules Comparison. — Rule 3.8 has been rewritten to retain elements of existing Maryland language and to incorporate some changes from the Ethics 2000 Amendments to the ABA Model Rules. ABA Model Rule 3.8(e) has not been adopted.

Effect of amendments. — The 2011 amendment substituted "self-represented" for "pro se" in paragraph [2] of the Comment.

Prosecutorial vouching and advocate-witness. — Mistrial should have been declared when the prosecutor impeached a witness with questions about a prior conversation between the witness and the prosecutor; the prosecutor was in effect testifying, but could not be cross-examined by defendant. Walker v. State, 373 Md. 360, 818 A.2d 1078 (2003).

Prosecutor's promise to prosecute bomb threat cases against juveniles. — Prosecutor did not commit a violation of prior, similar Rule 3.1 by commenting on future prosecutions of juveniles who phoned bomb threats, despite the lack of clear evidence against the juveniles, because by making the comments about prosecuting bomb threats, the prosecutor intended to communicate that his office must try hard cases. Att'y Griev. Comm'n v. Gansler, 377 Md. 656, 835 A.2d 548 (2003).

Cited in Adams v. State, 192 Md. App. 469, 995 A.2d 763 (2010).

Rule 3.9. Advocate in Nonadjudicative Proceedings.

A lawyer representing a client before a legislative body or administrative agency in a nonadjudicative proceeding shall disclose that the appearance is in a representative capacity and shall conform to the provisions of Rules 3.3(a) through (c), 3.4(a) through (c), and 3.5.

COMMENT

[1] In representation before bodies such as legislatures, municipal councils, and executive and administrative agencies acting in a rule-making or policy-making capacity, lawyers engage in activities that are comparable to those of an advocate appearing before a tribunal. For example, lawyers present facts, formulate issues and advance argument in the matters under consideration. The decision-making body, like a court, should be able to rely on the integrity of the submissions made to it. A lawyer appearing before such a body should deal with it honestly and in conformity with applicable rules of procedure.

[2] Given these policies, this Rule requires that a lawyer who appears before legislative bodies or administrative agencies in such non-adjudicative proceedings must adhere to Rules 3.3(a) through (c), 3.4(a) through (c), and 3.5. Lawyers appearing under these circumstances must also adhere to all other applicable Rules, including Rules 4.1 through 4.4.

[3] Lawyers have no exclusive right to appear before nonadjudicative bodies, as they do before a court. The requirements of this Rule therefore may subject lawyers to regulations inapplicable to advocates who are not lawyers.

[4] Not all appearances before a legislative body or administrative agency are nonadjudicative within the meaning of this Rule. This Rule only applies when a lawyer represents a client in connection with an official or formal hearing or meeting to which the lawyer or the lawyer's client is presenting evidence or argument. Thus, this Rule does not apply to representation of a client in a negotiation or other bilateral transaction with a governmental agency; or in connection with an application for a license or other privilege or the client's compliance with generally applicable reporting requirements, such as the filing of income-tax returns. Nor does it apply to the representation of a client in connection with an investigation or examination of the client's affairs conducted by government investigators or examiners. Representation in such matters is governed by Rules 4.1 through 4.4.

[5] When a lawyer appears before a legislative body or administrative agency acting in an adjudicative capacity, the legislative body or administrative agency is considered a "Tribunal" for purposes of these Rules, and all Rules relating to representation by a lawyer before a Tribunal apply. See Rule 1.0(o) for the definition of "Tribunal."

Model Rules Comparison. — Rule 3.9 has been rewritten to retain elements of existing Maryland language, to incorporate some changes from the Ethics 2000 Amendments to the ABA Model Rules, and to incorporate further revisions.

TRANSACTIONS WITH PERSONS OTHER THAN CLIENTS.

Rule 4.1. Truthfulness in Statements to Others.

(a) In the course of representing a client a lawyer shall not knowingly:

(1) make a false statement of material fact or law to a third person; or

(2) fail to disclose a material fact when disclosure is necessary to avoid assisting a criminal or fraudulent act by a client.

(b) The duties stated in this Rule apply even if compliance requires disclosure of information otherwise protected by Rule 1.6.

COMMENT

Misrepresentation. — [1] A lawyer is required to be truthful when dealing with others on a client's behalf, but generally has no affirmative duty to inform an opposing party of relevant facts. A misrepresentation can occur if the lawyer incorporates or affirms a statement of another person that the lawyer knows is false. Misrepresentations can also occur by partially true but misleading statements or omissions that are the equivalent of affirmative false statements. For dishonest conduct that does not amount to a false statement or for misrepresentations by a lawyer other than in the course of representing a client, see Rule 8.4.

Statements of Fact. — [2] This Rule refers to statements of fact. Whether a particular statement should be regarded as one of fact can depend on the circumstances. Under generally accepted conventions in negotiation, certain types of statements ordinarily are not taken as statements of material fact. Estimates of price or value placed on the subject of a transaction and a party's intentions as to an acceptable settlement of a claim are ordinarily in this category, and so is the existence of an undisclosed principal except where nondisclosure of the principal would constitute fraud. Lawyers should be mindful of their obligations under applicable law to avoid criminal or tortious misrepresentation.

Fraud by Client. — [3] Under Rule 1.2(d), a lawyer is prohibited from counseling or assisting a client in conduct that the lawyer knows is criminal or fraudulent. Paragraph (a)(2) states a specific application of the principle set forth in Rule 1.2(d) and addresses the situation where a client's crime or fraud takes the form of a lie or misrepresentation. Sometimes a lawyer can avoid assisting a client's crime or fraud by withdrawing from the representation. It also may be necessary for the lawyer to give notice of the fact of withdrawal and to disaffirm an opinion, document, affirmation or the like. In extreme cases, however, substantive law may require a lawyer to disclose information relating to the representation to avoid being deemed to have assisted the client's crime or fraud. If the lawyer can avoid assisting a client's crime or fraud only by disclosing this information, then under paragraph (b) the lawyer is required to do so, even though the disclosure otherwise would be prohibited by Rule 1.6.

Disclosure. — [4] As noted in the comment to Rule 1.6, the duty imposed by Rule 4.1 may require a lawyer to disclose information that otherwise is confidential and to correct or withdraw a statement. However, the constitutional rights of defendants in criminal cases may limit the extent to which counsel for a defendant may correct a misrepresentation that is based on information provided by the client. See Comment to Rule 3.3.

Model Rules Comparison. — Rule 4.1 has been rewritten to retain elements of existing Maryland language, to incorporate some changes from the Ethics 2000 Amendments to the ABA Model Rules, and to incorporate further revisions.

Editor's note. — See note to Rule 1.1.

University of Baltimore Law Forum. — For discussion of the code of ethics, see 17, No. 1 U. Balt. Law Forum 31 (1986).

For article, "The New Maryland Rules of Professional Conduct and Mediation: Perplexing Questions Answered and Perplexing Questions That Remain," see 36 U. Balt. L.F. 1 (2005).

Failure to inform authorities of completed crimes. — When client revealed to attorney that he had operated a motor vehicle when his license was expired, and that, unbeknownst to the arresting officer, he had given a fictitious name when arrested on DWI charge, attorney had no duty to inform authorities, as these were completed crimes; the attorney had a duty not to disclose them. Att'y Griev. Comm'n v. Rohrback, 323 Md. 79, 591 A.2d 488 (1991).

Failure to disclose client's use of fictitious name at presentence investigation interview. — A client awaiting sentencing has no constitutional right to counsel at presentence investigation interview; therefore, attorney's failure to disclose client's use of a fictitious name to the agent conducting the presentence investigation did not fall within the exception under prior, similar Rule 3.3 to the requirement of candor toward a tribunal. Att'y Griev. Comm'n v. Rohrback, 323 Md. 79, 591 A.2d 488 (1991).

Ninety-day suspension. — Ninety-day suspension was appropriate sanction for attorney's neglect of client's cases, falsifying client's signature on a complaint, and causing the complaint with the false signature to be notarized and filed. Att'y Griev. Comm'n v. Parsons, 310 Md. 132, 527 A.2d 325 (1987).

Disbarment for misrepresentation — Disbarment was the appropriate remedy for an attorney, licensed in other jurisdictions, who opened an office, used letterhead, and represented clients in Maryland without being admitted or specially admitted, as this constituted misconduct; in addition, the attorney misled a third party into believing he had represented a client in a worker's compensation action, when he had not. Att'y Griev. Comm'n v. Barneys, 370 Md. 566, 805 A.2d 1040 (2002).

In an attorney disciplinary matter wherein the attorney was ordered disbarred, the attorney was found to have violated this Rule by falsely representing to opposing counsel that his client refused to attend a deposition and also when, after his discharge, he falsely represented to his former client and opposing counsel that he had filed a motion to withdraw, when in fact he did not file the same until months later. Att'y Griev. Comm'n v. Steinberg, 395 Md. 337, 910 A.2d 429 (2006).

Attorney was disbarred for violating, inter alia, former, similar version of this Rule by lying about when funds were sent in a real property transaction and knowingly allowing opposing counsel to rely upon an incorrect record. Att'y Griev. Comm'n v. Pak, 400 Md. 567, 929 A.2d 546 (2007), cert. denied, 128 S. Ct. 905, 2008 U.S. LEXIS 126, 169 L. Ed. 2d 729 (U.S. 2008).

Quoted in Att'y Griev. Comm'n v. Gordon, 413 Md. 46, 991 A.2d 51 (2010).

Cited in In re Gulczynski, (Bankr. D. Md. 2008); Att'y Griev. Comm'n v. Elmendorf, 404 Md. 353, 946 A.2d 542 (2008).

Rule 4.2. Communication with Person Represented by Counsel.

(a) Except as provided in paragraph (c), in representing a client, a lawyer shall not communicate about the subject of the representation with a person who the lawyer knows is represented in the matter by another lawyer unless the lawyer has the consent of the other lawyer or is authorized by law or court order to do so.

(b) If the person represented by another lawyer is an organization, the prohibition extends to each of the organization's (1) current officers, directors, and managing agents and (2) current agents or employees who supervise, direct, or regularly communicate with the organization's lawyers concerning the matter or whose acts or omissions in the matter may bind the organization for civil or criminal liability. The lawyer may not communicate with a current agent or employee of the organization unless the lawyer first has made inquiry to ensure that the agent or employee is not an individual with whom communication is prohibited by this paragraph and has disclosed to the individual the lawyer's identity and the fact that the lawyer represents a client who has an interest adverse to the organization.

(c) A lawyer may communicate with a government official about matters that are the subject of the representation if the government official has the authority to redress the grievances of the lawyer's client and the lawyer first makes the disclosures specified in paragraph (b).

Committee note. — The use of the word "person" for "party" in paragraph (a) is not intended to enlarge or restrict the extent of permissible law enforcement activities of government lawyers under applicable judicial precedent.

COMMENT

[1] This Rule contributes to the proper functioning of the legal system by protecting a person who has chosen to be represented by a lawyer in a matter against possible overreaching by other lawyers who are participating in the matter, interference by those lawyers with the lawyer-client relationship, and the uncounseled disclosure of information relating to the representation.

[2] This Rule does not prohibit communication with a person, or an employee or agent of the person, concerning matters outside the representation. For example, the existence of a controversy between two organizations does not prohibit a lawyer for either from communicating with nonlawyer representatives of the other regarding a separate matter. Also, parties to a matter may communicate directly with each other and a lawyer having independent justification or legal authorization for communicating with a represented person is permitted to do so.

[3] Communications authorized by law include communications in the course of investigative activities of lawyers representing governmental entities, directly or through investigative agents, before the commencement of criminal or civil enforcement proceedings if there is applicable judicial precedent holding either that the activity is permissible or that the Rule does not apply to the activity. The term "civil enforcement proceedings" includes administrative enforcement proceedings. Except to the extent applicable judicial precedent holds otherwise, a government lawyer who communicates with a represented criminal defendant must comply with this Rule.

[4] A lawyer who is uncertain whether a communication with a represented person is permissible may seek a court order in exceptional circumstances. For example, when a represented criminal defendant expresses a desire to speak to the prosecutor without the knowledge of the defendant's lawyer, the prosecutor may seek a court order appointing substitute counsel to represent the defendant with respect to the communication.

[5] This Rule applies to communications with any person, whether or not a party to a formal adjudicative proceeding, contract, or negotiation, who is represented by counsel concerning the matter to which the communication relates. The Rule applies even though the represented person initiates or consents to the communication. A lawyer must immediately terminate communication with a person if, after commencing communication, the lawyer learns that the person is one with whom communication is not permitted by this Rule.

[6] If an agent or employee of a represented person that is an organization is represented in the matter by his or her own counsel, the consent by that counsel to a communication

will be sufficient for purposes of this Rule. Compare Rule 3.4 (f). In communicating with a current agent or employee of an organization, a lawyer must not seek to obtain information that the lawyer knows or reasonably should know is subject to an evidentiary or other privilege of the organization. Regarding communications with former employees, see Rule 4.4(b).

[7] The prohibition on communications with a represented person applies only if the lawyer has actual knowledge that the person in fact is represented in the matter to be discussed. Actual knowledge may be inferred from the circumstances. The lawyer cannot evade the requirement of obtaining the consent of counsel by ignoring the obvious.

[8] Rule 4.3 applies to a communication by a lawyer with a person not known to be represented by counsel.

[9] Paragraph (c) recognizes that special considerations come into play when a lawyer is seeking to redress grievances involving the government. Subject to certain conditions, it permits communications with those in govern-ment having the authority to redress the grievances (but not with any other government personnel) without the prior consent of the lawyer representing the government in the matter. Paragraph (c) does not, however, permit a lawyer to bypass counsel representing the government on every issue that may arise in the course of disputes with the government. Rather, the paragraph provides lawyers with access to decision makers in government with respect to genuine grievances, such as to present the view that the government's basic policy position with respect to a dispute is faulty or that government personnel are conducting themselves improperly with respect to aspects of the dispute. It does not provide direct access on routine disputes, such as ordinary discovery disputes or extensions of time.

Model Rules Comparison. — This Rule substantially retains Maryland language as it existed prior to the Ethics 2000 Amendments to the ABA Model Rules of Professional Conduct except for dividing Rule 4.2(b) into Rule 4.2(b) and (c) with no change in wording.

Maryland Law Review. — For article, "Conducting Informal Discovery of a Party's Former Employees: Legal and Ethical Concerns and Constraints," see 51 Md. L. Rev. 239 (1992).

Purpose of Rule. — Protection of information covered by the attorney-client privilege (as well as the work product privilege) has been traditionally cited as one of the prime objectives of the no-contact rule. Camden v. Maryland, 910 F. Supp. 1115 (D. Md. 1996).

Representation of multiple defendants in a criminal case. — An attorney's contact with his client's represented criminal codefendant was deemed a violation of the prior, similar Rule and resulted in disbarment. Att'y Griev. Comm'n v. Kent, 337 Md. 361, 653 A.2d 909 (1995).

Other interested parties. — Other interested parties, for purposes of determining whether a lawyer may have ex parte contact with a former employee of an interested party, include corporations and other organizations. Camden v. Maryland, 910 F. Supp. 1115 (D. Md. 1996).

Plaintiff's counsel violated rule by engaging in ex parte contact with a former employee of the defendants whom plaintiff's counsel well knew had been extensively exposed to confidential information; accordingly, appropriate remedy for violation of rule was disqualification of counsel from any further representation in the matters covered by lawsuit. Zachair, Ltd. v. Driggs, 965 F. Supp. 741 (D. Md. 1997), aff'd, 141 F.3d 1162 (4th Cir. 1998).

Inapplicable to certain investigations and persons. — This Rule did not apply to criminal investigation of corporation and certain of its employees where corporation sought ex parte injunction to prevent interviews of any of its employees by Attorney General's office without consent and presence of corporation counsel. In re Criminal Investigation No. 13, 82 Md. App. 609, 573 A.2d 51 (1990).

Rule does not apply to communication from attorney to children otherwise represented by a guardian. — Although the prior, similar Rule applies to communications with minors for whom guardians have been appointed, an attorney who communicated with children he was hired to represent was not improper even though the children were already "represented" in the matter by a guardian. This is because of the ages, intelligence, and maturity of the children in question and the real or perceived inability of the guardian ad litem to be the investigative arm of the court and reporter of the children's preferences to the court, while simultaneously acting as advocate for appellants. Auclair v. Auclair, 127 Md. App. 1, 730 A.2d 1260 (1999).

Rule did not apply to purchaser of bankruptcy claims. — Representative of a company that was in the business of buying and selling bankruptcy claims did not violate this Rule when he approached union members about obtaining an assignment of their claims against their employer because he was not acting as an attorney and, even had he been, he had no reason to know that the union members were represented by counsel. Moreover, even if there had been a violation of the Rule, a civil remedy was not appropriate. Preston Trucking Co. v. Liquidity Solutions, Inc.(In re Preston Trucking Co.), 333 B.R. 315 (Bankr. D. Md. 2005), criticized in, 390 Bankr. 667, 2008 Bankr. LEXIS 1855 (Bankr. D. Ariz. 2008); aff'd, 392 Bankr. 623, 2008 U.S. Dist. LEXIS 63951 (2008).

Attorney acting as executive, not as attorney. — Whether the individual violated a cannon of ethics was irrelevant to the enforceability of the assignment contracts; further, although a licensed attorney, he was acting as an executive of the purchaser, not an attorney, when negotiating the assignment contracts. If a lawyer pursues his own business interests, he is not acting in a representative capacity, and the anti-contact rule, therefore, did not apply. Preston Trucking Co. v. Liquidity Solutions, Inc. (In re Preston Trucking Co.), 392 B.R. 623 (D. Md. 2008).

Use of hired informant. — A prosecutor's use of a wired informant for the purpose of recording conversations with the represented target of a criminal investigation, even to the point of suggesting topics to be discussed, does not violate professional disciplinary rules. United States v. Marcus, 849 F. Supp. 417 (D. Md. 1994), aff'd, 82 F.3d 606 (4th Cir. 1996).

Detective's communication with represented defendant. — When defendant sought the suppression of defendant's incriminating statement to a detective, while the Maryland Lawyers' Rules of Professional Conduct did not control the interpretation of applicable constitutional provisions, this Rule underscored the importance of communicating with represented parties through counsel because the Rule provided that lawyers should not communicate with a person known to be represented about the subject of the representation. Adams v. State, 192 Md. App. 469, 995 A.2d 763 (2010).

Improper disqualification of defendant's chosen counsel. — Trial court committed structural error by violating defendant's right to counsel of defendant's choice by disqualifying one of defendant's retained attorneys because, after it was represented that the attorney had spoken to a co-defendant before trial and that the attorney was a potential witness, due to a grand jury witness's testimony that the attorney attempted to "coach" the witness, the trial court did not conduct an evidentiary hearing to determine whether there was an actual or serious potential for conflict, at which the court could balance defendant's right to counsel of defendant's choice against interests of fairness and maintenance of ethical standards. State v. Goldsberry, 419 Md. 100, 18 A.3d 836 (2011).

Rule 4.3. Dealing with Unrepresented Person.

In dealing on behalf of a client with a person who is not represented by counsel, a lawyer shall not state or imply that the lawyer is disinterested. When the lawyer knows or reasonably should know that the unrepresented person misunderstands the lawyer's role in the matter, the lawyer shall make reasonable efforts to correct the misunderstanding.

COMMENT

[1] An unrepresented person, particularly one not experienced in dealing with legal matters, might assume that a lawyer is disinterested in loyalties or is a disinterested authority on the law even when the lawyer represents a client. In order to avoid a misunderstanding, a lawyer will typically need to identify the lawyer's client and, where necessary, explain that the client has interests opposed to those of the unrepresented person. For misunderstandings that sometimes arise when a lawyer for an organization deals with an unrepresented constituent, see Rule 1.13(d).

[2] A lawyer should not give legal advice to an unrepresented person, other than the advice to secure counsel, if the lawyer knows or reasonably should know that the interests of such a person are or have a reasonable possibility of being in conflict with the interests of the client. This distinguishes between situations involving unrepresented persons whose interests may be adverse to those of the lawyer's client and those in which the person's interests are not in conflict with the client's. In the former situation, the possibility that the lawyer will compromise the unrepresented person's interests is so great that the lawyer should not give any advice, apart from the advice to obtain counsel. Whether a lawyer is giving impermissible advice may depend on the experience and sophistication of the unrepresented person, as well as the setting in which the behavior and comments occur. This Rule does not prohibit a lawyer from negotiating the terms of a transaction or settling a dispute with an unrepresented person. So long as the lawyer has explained that the lawyer represents an adverse party and is not representing the person, the lawyer may inform the

person of the terms on which the lawyer's client will enter into an agreement or settle a matter, prepare documents that require the person's signature and explain the lawyer's own view of the meaning of the document or the lawyer's view of the underlying legal obligations.

Model Rules Comparison. — Rule 4.3 has been rewritten to retain elements of existing Maryland language, to incorporate some changes from the Ethics 2000 Amendments to the ABA Model Rules, and to incorporate further revisions.

Rule 4.4. Respect for Rights of Third Persons.

(a) In representing a client, a lawyer shall not use means that have no substantial purpose other than to embarrass, delay, or burden a third person, or use methods of obtaining evidence that the lawyer knows violate the legal rights of such a person.

(b) In communicating with third persons, a lawyer representing a client in a matter shall not seek information relating to the matter that the lawyer knows or reasonably should know is protected from disclosure by statute or by an established evidentiary privilege, unless the protection has been waived. The lawyer who receives information that is protected from disclosure shall (1) terminate the communication immediately and (2) give notice of the disclosure to any tribunal in which the matter is pending and to the person entitled to enforce the protection against disclosure.

Committee note. — If the person entitled to enforce the protection against disclosure is represented by counsel, the notice required by this Rule shall be given to the person's counsel. See Md. Rule 1-331 and Maryland Lawyers' Rules of Professional Conduct, Rule 4.2.

COMMENT

[1] Responsibility to a client requires a lawyer to subordinate the interests of others to those of the client, but that responsibility does not imply that a lawyer may disregard the rights of third persons. It is impractical to catalogue all such rights, but they include legal restrictions on methods of obtaining evidence from third persons.

[2] Third persons may possess information that is confidential to another person under an evidentiary privilege or under a law providing specific confidentiality protection, such as trademark, copyright, or patent law. For example, present or former organizational employees or agents may have information that is protected as a privileged attorney-client communication or as work product. A lawyer may not knowingly seek to obtain confidential information from a person who has no authority to waive the privilege. Regarding current employees of a represented organization, see also Rule 4.2.

Model Rules Comparison. — This Rule substantially retains Maryland language as amended November 1, 2001 and does not adopt Ethics 2000 Amendments to the ABA Model Rules of Professional Conduct.

Maryland Law Review. — For a recent decision, "Blackwell v. Wyeth: It's Our Courtroom and We'll Frye (Only) if We Want to — The Maryland Court of Appeals's Unstated Adoption of Daubert," see 69 U. Md. L. Rev. 195 (2010).

Use of abusive language outside litigation setting. — Attorney's abusive outburst at a motor vehicle administration office expressing rage at delays in accessing insurance information on behalf of a personal injury client was outrageous and rude, but it did not rise to the level of conduct prejudicial to the administration of justice; therefore, a petition for imposition of appropriate discipline was dismissed. Att'y Griev. Comm'n v. Link, 380 Md. 405, 844 A.2d 1197 (2004).

Disbarment appropriate. — Attorney was disbarred for violating Md. R. Prof. Conduct 1.1, 3.1, 3.2, 3.3(a), 4.4, 8.2(a), and 8.4(c) and (d) because his actions were pursued in total disregard for their substantial cost to the opposing party, were intentionally dilatory, and were without legal basis; the attorney was intentionally dishonest with both the trial court and the court of special appeals, which showed a systematic effort to mislead the courts, and his history of sanctions for violating the Maryland Rules of Professional Conduct (MRPC) showed an ongoing disregard for the MRPC. Att'y Griev. Comm'n v. McClain, 406 Md. 1, 956 A.2d 135 (2008), cert. denied, 129 S. Ct. 1691, 2009 U.S. LEXIS 2433, 173 L. Ed. 2d 1036 (U.S. 2009).

Applied in Md. Transp. Auth. Police Lodge # 34 of FOP, Inc. v. Md. Transp. Auth., 195 Md. App. 124, 5 A.3d 1174 (2010).

Cited in Att'y Griev. Comm'n v. Hall, 408 Md. 306, 969 A.2d 953 (2009).

LAW FIRMS AND ASSOCIATIONS.

Rule 5.1. Responsibilities of Partners, Managers, and Supervisory Lawyers.

(a) A partner in a law firm, and a lawyer who individually or together with other lawyers possesses comparable managerial authority in a law firm, shall make reasonable efforts to ensure that the firm has in effect measures giving reasonable assurance that all lawyers in the firm conform to the Maryland Lawyers' Rules of Professional Conduct.

(b) A lawyer having direct supervisory authority over another lawyer shall make reasonable efforts to ensure that the other lawyer conforms to the Maryland Lawyers' Rules of Professional Conduct.

(c) A lawyer shall be responsible for another lawyer's violation of the Maryland Lawyers' Rules of Professional Conduct if:

(1) the lawyer orders or, with knowledge of the specific conduct, ratifies the conduct involved; or

(2) the lawyer is a partner or has comparable managerial authority in the law firm in which the other lawyer practices, or has direct supervisory authority over the other lawyer, and knows of the conduct at a time when its consequences can be avoided or mitigated but fails to take reasonable remedial action.

COMMENT

[1] Paragraphs (a) applies to lawyers who have managerial authority over the professional work of a firm. See Rule 1.0(d). This includes members of a partnership, the shareholders in a law firm organized as a professional corporation, and members of other associations authorized to practice law; lawyers having comparable managerial authority in a legal services organization or a law department of an enterprise or government agency; and lawyers who have intermediate managerial responsibilities in a firm. Paragraph (b) applies to lawyers who have supervisory authority over the work of other lawyers in a firm.

[2] Paragraph (a) requires lawyers with managerial authority within a firm to make reasonable efforts to establish internal policies and procedures designed to provide reasonable assurance that all lawyers in the firm will conform to the Maryland Lawyers' Rules of Professional Conduct. Such policies and procedures include those designed to detect and resolve conflicts of interest, identify dates by which actions must be taken in pending matters, account for client funds and property and ensure that inexperienced lawyers are properly supervised.

[3] Other measures that may be required to fulfill the responsibility prescribed in paragraph (a) can depend on the firm's structure and the nature of its practice. In a small firm of experienced lawyers, informal supervision and periodic review of compliance with the required systems ordinarily will suffice. In a large firm, or in practice situations in which difficult ethical problems frequently arise, more elaborate measures may be necessary. Some firms, for example, have a procedure whereby junior lawyers can make confidential referral of ethical problems directly to a designated senior partner or special committee. See Rule 5.2. Firms, whether large or small, may also rely on continuing legal education in pro-

fessional ethics. In any event, the ethical atmosphere of a firm can influence the conduct of all its members and the partners may not assume that all lawyers associated with the firm will inevitably conform to the Rules.

[4] Paragraph (c) expresses a general principle of personal responsibility for acts of another. See also Rule 8.4(a).

[5] Paragraph (c)(2) defines the duty of a partner or other lawyer having comparable managerial authority in a law firm, as well as a lawyer who has direct supervisory authority over performance of specific legal work by another lawyer. Whether a lawyer has supervisory authority in particular circumstances is a question of fact. Partners and lawyers with comparable authority have at least indirect responsibility for all work being done by the firm, while a partner or manager in charge of a particular matter ordinarily also has supervisory responsibility for the work of other firm lawyers engaged in the matter. Appropriate remedial action by a partner or managing lawyer would depend on the immediacy of that lawyer's involvement and the seriousness of the misconduct. A supervisor is required to intervene to prevent avoidable consequences of misconduct if the supervisor knows that the misconduct occurred. Thus, if a supervising lawyer knows that a subordinate misrepresented a matter to an opposing party in negotiation, the supervisor as well as the subordinate has a duty to correct the resulting misapprehension.

[6] Professional misconduct by a lawyer under supervision could reveal a violation of paragraph (b) on the part of the supervisory lawyer even though it does not entail a violation of paragraph (c) because there was no direction, ratification or knowledge of the violation.

[7] Apart from this Rule and Rule 8.4(a), a lawyer does not have disciplinary liability for the conduct of a partner, associate or subordinate. Whether a lawyer may be liable civilly or criminally for another lawyer's conduct is a question of law beyond the scope of these Rules.

[8] The duties imposed by this Rule on managing and supervising lawyers do not alter the personal duty of each lawyer in a firm to abide by the Maryland Lawyers' Rules of Professional Conduct. See Rule 5.2(a).

Model Rules Comparison. — Rule 5.1 is substantially similar to the language of the Ethics 2000 Amendments to the ABA Model Rules of Professional Conduct.

Editor's note. — See note to Rule 1.1.

University of Baltimore Law Forum. — For discussion of the code of ethics, see 17, No. 1 U. Balt. Law Forum 31 (1986).

For article, "Recent Developments," see 18.3 U. Balt. Law Forum 32 (1988).

For Recent Development, "Attorney Grievance Commission of Maryland v. Mooney: Indefinite Suspension is Warranted Where an Attorney Fails to Provide Competent Representation," see 31 U. Balt. Law Forum 44 (2000).

Delegation of workload. — An attorney's practice of assigning and handling cases in such a manner that the lawyer ultimately charged with actually representing the client went into court unprepared, or missed scheduled trial dates entirely, resulted in clients not being afforded competent representation, and justified an indefinite suspension from the practice of law. Att'y Griev. Comm'n v. Ficker, 349 Md. 13, 706 A.2d 1045 (1998).

Bar counsel failed to show that an attorney had violated Md. R. Prof. Conduct 1.1, 1.3, 1.5(a), 1.16(d), 3.1, 5.1, 5.3(a) and (c), and 8.4(a) and (d) where the attorney had informed the client that he no longer wished to represent him after the client changed his mind with respect to a settlement agreement and the attorney had discharged the associate after discovering that she had subsequently file additional motions. Att'y Griev. Comm'n v. Maignan, 402 Md. 39, 935 A.2d 409 (2007).

Failure to supervise associate. — Where a client, facing incarceration for driving under the influence, was virtually abandoned until the eve of trial and then was represented by an associate who had not read the entire file, who was unaware that his client had two prior convictions, and who first presented the available options to her in the lobby of the courthouse on the day of trial, the supervising attorney violated Md. R. Prof. Conduct 1.1, 1.3, 1.4, and 5.1. Att'y Griev. Comm'n v. Ficker, 399 Md. 445, 924 A.2d 1105 (2007).

In a disciplinary proceeding against two supervising attorneys from out-of-state, who opened up a Maryland office and hired a Maryland associate, who ended up failing to respond to motions compelling discovery in 47 cases filed by her on behalf of the supervising attorneys' Maryland clients, the hearing judge was found to have properly determined that they violated Md. R. Prof. Conduct 5.1 and 1.4 and, therefore, they were suspended indefinitely, with the right to apply for reinstatement no sooner than 90 days after the effective date of the suspension. The findings and conclusions adequately found that the supervising attorneys failed to adequately supervise the relatively inexperienced associate they hired, failed to respond to her requests for paralegal help, failed to establish supervisory procedures designed deliberately to address the associate's inexperience and to counterbalance her physical distance from the ready availability of steadying interaction with peers and managers, failed to audit her case load, among other failings, as well as failed to directly communicate with a Maryland client regarding his case. Att'y Griev. Comm'n v. Kimmel, 405 Md. 647, 955 A.2d 269 (2008).

Violation found. — When an attorney acted as a settlement agent at a real estate closing, and another attorney supervised the first attorney, the supervisor was properly found to have violated this Rule, when the agent did not distribute sale proceeds in the manner stated in a settlement statement, because (1) an employer-employee relationship did not have to exist between the supervisor and the attorney supervised, so the fact that the supervised attorney was an independent contractor was not a defense, and (2) the supervisor did not have to be engaged in the practice of law at the time of the supervised attorney's misconduct. Att'y Griev. Comm'n v. Johnson, 409 Md. 470, 976 A.2d 245 (2009).

Violation not found. — Bar counsel failed to show that an attorney had violated Md. R. Prof. Conduct 1.1, 1.3, 1.4(a) and (b), 1.5, 1.16(d), 3.1, 5.1, 5.3, and 8.4(a), (c), and (d) where it was possible to find, based on the testimony, that the attorney had relied on the clients' representations that they intended to handle the appeal pro se, and as a result, Bar counsel had failed to prove that the attorney had represented the two clients in an appeal. Att'y Griev. Comm'n v. Maignan, 402 Md. 39, 935 A.2d 409 (2007).

Rule 5.2. Responsibilities of a Subordinate Lawyer.

(a) A lawyer is bound by the Maryland Lawyers' Rules of Professional Conduct notwithstanding that the lawyer acted at the direction of another person.

(b) A subordinate lawyer does not violate the Maryland Lawyers' Rules of Professional Conduct if that lawyer acts in accordance with a supervisory lawyer's reasonable resolution of an arguable question of professional duty.

COMMENT

[1] Although a lawyer is not relieved of responsibility for a violation by the fact that the lawyer acted at the direction of a supervisor, that fact may be relevant in determining whether a lawyer had the knowledge required to render conduct a violation of the Rules. For example, if a subordinate filed a frivolous pleading at the direction of a supervisor, the subordinate would not be guilty of a professional violation unless the subordinate knew of the document's frivolous character.

[2] When lawyers in a supervisor-subordinate relationship encounter a matter involving professional judgment as to ethical duty, the supervisor may assume responsibility for making the judgment. Otherwise a consistent course of action or position could not be taken. If the question can reasonably be answered only one way, the duty of both lawyers is clear and they are equally responsible for fulfilling it. However, if the question is reasonably arguable, someone has to decide upon the course of action. That authority ordinarily reposes in the supervisor, and a subordinate may be guided accordingly. For example, if a question arises whether the interests of two clients conflict under Rule 1.7, the supervisor's reasonable resolution of the question should protect the subordinate professionally if the resolution is subsequently challenged.

Model Rules Comparison. — Given that the Ethics 2000 Amendments to the ABA Model Rules of Professional Conduct made no changes to this Rule, Rule 5.2 has not been amended and remains substantially similar to Model Rule 5.2.

Rule 5.3. Responsibilities Regarding Nonlawyer Assistants.

With respect to a nonlawyer employed or retained by or associated with a lawyer:

(a) a partner, and a lawyer who individually or together with other lawyers possesses comparable managerial authority in a law firm shall make reasonable efforts to ensure that the firm has in effect measures giving reasonable assurance that the person's conduct is compatible with the professional obligations of the lawyer;

(b) a lawyer having direct supervisory authority over the nonlawyer shall make reasonable efforts to ensure that the person's conduct is compatible with the professional obligations of the lawyer;

(c) a lawyer shall be responsible for conduct of such a person that would be a violation of the Maryland Lawyers' Rules of Professional Conduct if engaged in by a lawyer if:

(1) the lawyer orders or, with the knowledge of the specific conduct, ratifies the conduct involved; or

(2) the lawyer is a partner or has comparable managerial authority in the law firm in which the person is employed, or has direct supervisory authority over the person, and knows of the conduct at a time when its consequences can be avoided or mitigated but fails to take reasonable remedial action; and

(d) a lawyer who employs or retains the services of a nonlawyer who (i) was formerly admitted to the practice of law in any jurisdiction and (ii) has been and remains disbarred, suspended, or placed on inactive status because of incapacity shall comply with the following requirements:

(1) all law-related activities of the formerly admitted lawyer shall be (A) performed from an office that is staffed on a full-time basis by a supervising lawyer and (B) conducted under the direct supervision of the supervising lawyer, who shall be responsible for ensuring that the formerly admitted lawyer complies with the requirements of this Rule.

(2) the lawyer shall take reasonable steps to ensure that the formerly admitted lawyer does not:

(A) represent himself or herself to be a lawyer;

(B) render legal consultation or advice to a client or prospective client;

(C) appear on behalf of or represent a client in any judicial, administrative, legislative, or alternative dispute resolution proceeding;

(D) appear on behalf of or represent a client at a deposition or in any other discovery matter;

(E) negotiate or transact any matter on behalf of a client with third parties;

(F) receive funds from or on behalf of a client or disburse funds to or on behalf of a client; or

(G) perform any law-related activity for (i) a law firm or lawyer with whom the formerly admitted lawyer was associated when the acts that resulted in the disbarment or suspension occurred or (ii) any client who was previously represented by the formerly admitted lawyer.

(3) the lawyer, the supervising lawyer, and the formerly admitted lawyer shall file jointly with Bar Counsel (A) a notice of employment identifying the supervising lawyer and the formerly admitted lawyer and listing each jurisdiction in which the formerly admitted lawyer has been disbarred, suspended, or placed on inactive status because of incapacity; and (B) a copy of an executed written agreement between the lawyer, the supervising lawyer, and the formerly admitted lawyer that sets forth the duties of the formerly admitted lawyer and includes an undertaking to comply with requests by Bar Counsel for proof of compliance with the terms of the agreement and this Rule. As to a formerly admitted lawyer employed as of July 1, 2006, the notice and agreement shall be filed no later than September 1, 2006. As to a formerly

admitted lawyer hired after July 1, 2006, the notice and agreement shall be filed within 30 days after commencement of the employment. Immediately upon the termination of the employment of the formerly admitted lawyer, the lawyer and the supervising lawyer shall file with Bar Counsel a notice of the termination.

COMMENT

[1] Lawyers generally employ assistants in their practice, including secretaries, investigators, law student interns, and paraprofessionals. Such assistants, whether employees or independent contractors, act for the lawyer in rendition of the lawyer's professional services. A lawyer must give such assistants appropriate instruction and supervision concerning the ethical aspects of their employment, particularly regarding the obligation not to disclose information relating to representation of the client, and should be responsible for their work product. The measures employed in supervising nonlawyers should take account of the fact that they do not have legal training and are not subject to professional discipline.

[2] Paragraph (a) requires lawyers with managerial authority within a law firm to make reasonable efforts to establish internal policies and procedures designed to provide reasonable assurance that nonlawyers in the firm will act in a way compatible with the Maryland Lawyers' Rules of Professional Conduct. See Comment [1] to Rule 5.1. Paragraph (b) applies to lawyers who have supervisory authority over the work of a nonlawyer. Paragraph (c) specifies the circumstances in which a lawyer is responsible for conduct of a nonlawyer that would be a violation of the Maryland Lawyers' Rules of Professional Conduct if engaged in by a lawyer.

[3] Paragraph (d) addresses formerly admitted lawyers engaging in law-related activities and does not establish a standard for what constitutes the unauthorized practice of law.

Model Rules Comparison. — The language of Rule 5.3 (a) through (c) is substantially similar to the language of the Ethics 2000 Amendments to the ABA Model Rules of Professional Conduct. Paragraph (d) and Comment [3] are in part derived from Rule 217 (j) of the Pennsylvania Rules of Disciplinary Enforcement and in part new.

Effect of amendments. — The 2006 amendment added (d) and made related changes; added Comment [3]; and in the Model Rules Comparison note, added "The language of" and "(a) through (c)"; and added the last sentence.

Disclosure of client list. — It was not clearly erroneous for a judge to conclude that proper training of lay staff in keeping client matters confidential would have avoided the unauthorized disclosure of an attorney's client list to a mortgage lender. Att'y Griev. Comm'n v. Harris-Smith, 356 Md. 72, 737 A.2d 567 (1999).

Failure to supervise law clerk. — An inexperienced attorney did not act intentionally when she assured a court, and other attorneys, that her client's bankruptcy had been filed, and a reprimand was an appropriate sanction for her failure to supervise the law clerk who was supposed to have filed the bankruptcy petition. Att'y Griev. Comm'n v. Jaseb, 364 Md. 464, 773 A.2d 516 (2001).

Failure to supervise associate. — In a disciplinary proceeding against two supervising attorneys from out-of-state, who opened up a Maryland office and hired a Maryland associate, who ended up failing to respond to motions compelling discovery in 47 cases filed by her on behalf of the supervising attorneys' Maryland clients, the hearing judge was found to have properly determined that they violated Md. R. Prof. Conduct 5.1 and 1.4 and, therefore, they were suspended indefinitely, with the right to apply for reinstatement no sooner than 90 days after the effective date of the suspension. The findings and conclusions adequately found that the supervising attorneys failed to adequately supervise the relatively inexperienced associate they hired, failed to respond to her requests for paralegal help, failed to establish supervisory procedures designed deliberately to address the associate's inexperience and to counterbalance her physical distance from the ready availability of steadying interaction with peers and managers, failed to audit her case load, among other failings, as well as failed to directly communicate with a Maryland client regarding his case. Att'y Griev. Comm'n v. Kimmel, 405 Md. 647, 955 A.2d 269 (2008).

Indefinite suspension was proper sanction. — Where respondent attorney's representation of four clients was marked by serious neglect and inattention; where he failed to return a fee which was unearned for a period of nine months; where he failed to timely remit funds he received on behalf of a client; where he failed to communicate with his clients; and where, in connection with the investigation of three of the complaints, respondent failed to answer Bar Counsel's requests for information, the proper sanction was that the attorney be indefinitely suspended from the practice of law, with the right to apply for reinstatement after the suspension had been in effect for six months, conditioned upon his payment of all costs and upon the monitoring of respondent's practice. Att'y Griev. Comm'n v. David, 331 Md. 317, 628 A.2d 178 (1993).

Disbarment was proper sanction. — Disbarment of attorney was appropriate where there were serious and repeated violations of the prior, similar Rule and other provisions of the prior, similar Maryland Rules of Professional Conduct. Att'y Griev. Comm'n v. Milliken, 348 Md. 486, 704 A.2d 1225 (1998).

Duty to determine that employees perform competently. — An attorney may not escape responsibility to his clients by blithely saying that any shortcomings are solely the fault of his employee; an attorney must ascertain that his or her employees perform their responsibilities in a competent manner. Att'y Griev. Comm'n v. Glenn, 341 Md. 448, 671 A.2d 463 (1996).

Violation found. — Attorney violated (c) when the attorney asked the attorney's legal assistant, who was under the attorney's supervision, to notarize a power of attorney when the signatory was not actually present at the moment of notarization. Att'y Griev. Comm'n v. Ward, 394 Md. 1, 904 A.2d 477 (2006).

Attorney's failure to instruct his employees of the proper management of the trust account and to inform himself of the status of his employees' efforts to monitor the funds in the account constituted a violation of prior, similar 5.3(a) and (b) because the attorney did not make reasonable efforts to ensure that his employees' conduct complied with his own professional obligations. Att'y Griev. Comm'n v. Zuckerman, 386 Md. 341, 872 A.2d 693 (2005).

When an attorney acted as a settlement agent at a real estate closing, and another attorney supervised the first attorney, the supervisor was properly found to have violated this Rule, based on the conduct of a nonlawyer employee of the supervisor's title company, because (1) the supervisor was in a management position, and (2) the employee's conduct would have constituted violations of Md. R. Prof. Conduct 1.15(b) and 8.4(c) had the supervisor engaged in such acts. Att'y Griev. Comm'n v. Johnson, 409 Md. 470, 976 A.2d 245 (2009).

Violation not found. — Bar counsel failed to show that an attorney had violated Md. R. Prof. Conduct 1.1, 1.3, 1.5(a), 1.16(d), 3.1, 5.1, 5.3(a) and (c), and 8.4(a) and (d) where the attorney had informed the client that he no longer wished to represent him after the client changed his mind with respect to a settlement agreement and the attorney had discharged the associate after discovering that she had subsequently file additional motions. Att'y Griev. Comm'n v. Maignan, 402 Md. 39, 935 A.2d 409 (2007).

Bar counsel failed to show that an attorney had violated Md. R. Prof. Conduct 1.1, 1.3, 1.4(a) and (b), 1.5, 1.16(d), 3.1, 5.1, 5.3, and 8.4(a), (c), and (d) where it was possible to find, based on the testimony, that the attorney had relied on the clients' representations that they intended to handle the appeal pro se, and as a result, Bar counsel had failed to prove that the attorney had represented the two clients in an appeal. Att'y Griev. Comm'n v. Maignan, 402 Md. 39, 935 A.2d 409 (2007).

Quoted in Att'y Griev. Comm'n v. Goff, 399 Md. 1, 922 A.2d 554 (2007).

Cited in Att'y Griev. Comm'n v. Lee, 387 Md. 89, 874 A.2d 897 (2005); Att'y Griev. Comm'n v. Maignan, 390 Md. 287, 888 A.2d 344 (2005); Att'y Griev. Comm'n v. Lee, 393 Md. 385, 903 A.2d 360 (2006); Att'y Griev. Comm'n v. Zuckerman, 403 Md. 695, 944 A.2d 525 (2008); Adams v. State, 192 Md. App. 469, 995 A.2d 763 (2010); Att'y Griev. Comm'n v. Khandpur, 421 Md. 1, 25 A.3d 165 (2011).

Rule 5.4. Professional Independence of a Lawyer.

(a) A lawyer or law firm shall not share legal fees with a nonlawyer, except that:

(1) an agreement by a lawyer with the lawyer's firm, partner, or associate may provide for the payment of money, over a reasonable period of time after the lawyer's death, to the lawyer's estate or to one or more specified persons;

(2) a lawyer who purchases the practice of a lawyer who is deceased or disabled or who has disappeared may, pursuant to the provisions of Rule 1.17, pay the purchase price to the estate or representative of the lawyer.

(3) a lawyer who undertakes to complete unfinished legal business of a deceased, retired, disabled, or suspended lawyer may pay to that lawyer or

that lawyer's estate the proportion of the total compensation which fairly represents the services rendered by the former lawyer;

(4) a lawyer or law firm may include nonlawyer employees in a compensation or retirement plan, even though the plan is based in whole or in part on a profit-sharing arrangement; and

(5) a lawyer may share court-awarded legal fees with a nonprofit organization that employed, retained or recommended employment of the lawyer in the matter.

(b) A lawyer shall not form a partnership with a nonlawyer if any of the activities of the partnership consist of the practice of law.

(c) A lawyer shall not permit a person who recommends, employs, or pays the lawyer to render legal services for another to direct or regulate the lawyer's professional judgment in rendering such legal services.

(d) A lawyer shall not practice with or in the form of a professional corporation or association authorized to practice law for a profit, if:

(1) a nonlawyer owns any interest therein, except that a fiduciary representative of the estate of a lawyer may hold the stock or interest of the lawyer for a reasonable time during administration;

(2) a nonlawyer is a corporate director or officer thereof or occupies the position of similar responsibility in any form of association other than a corporation; or

(3) a nonlawyer has the right to direct or control the professional judgment of a lawyer.

Cross references. — Md. Rule 16-760(d)(6).

COMMENT

[1] The provisions of this Rule express traditional limitations on sharing fees. These limitations are to protect the lawyer's professional independence of judgment. Where someone other than the client pays the lawyer's fee or salary, or recommends employment of the lawyer, that arrangement does not modify the lawyer's obligation to the client. As stated in paragraph (c), such arrangements should not interfere with the lawyer's professional judgment.

[2] This Rule also expresses traditional limitations on permitting a third party to direct or regulate the lawyer's professional judgment in rendering legal services to another. See also

Rule 1.8(f) (lawyer may accept compensation from a third party as long as there is no interference with the lawyer's independent professional judgment and the client gives informed consent).

Model Rules Comparison. — Rule 5.4 is substantially similar to the language of the Ethics 2000 Amendments to the ABA Model Rules of Professional Conduct with the exception of: 1) retaining existing Maryland language in Rule 5.4(a)(2); 2) retaining existing Maryland language in Rule 5.4(a)(3) with appropriate redesignation of the subparagraphs of Rule 5.4(a).

University of Baltimore Law Forum. — For article, "The New Maryland Rules of Professional Conduct and Mediation: Perplexing Questions Answered and Perplexing Questions That Remain," see 36 U. Balt. L.F. 1 (2005).

Professional service corporations. —

When the conduct of a lawyer in a professional service corporation is called into question with reference to the attorney-client relationship, the prior, similar Rules of Professional Conduct will apply and not those of an ordinary business corporation. Where, however, the situation involves a dispute between shareholders of the professional service corporation, the corporate law should not be disregarded in favor of partnership law. Langhoff v. Marr, 81 Md. App. 438, 568 A.2d 844 (1990), vacated and remanded, 322 Md. 657, 589 A.2d 470 (1991).

Agent of nonlawyer. — Defendant was an agent for Burrus trading as Life Investors. Although he improperly participated in a referral arrangement, this does not amount to a partnership with a nonlawyer. Att'y Griev. Comm'n v. Martin, 308 Md. 272, 518 A.2d 1050 (1987).

Nonlawyer spouse as partner. — Because nonlawyer spouse could not be a partner in the attorney's spouse's practice, she could not claim a partner's interest in the practice upon her divorce from her lawyer husband, and therefore the goodwill of the practice could not be included as marital property. Prahinski v. Prahinski, 321 Md. 227, 582 A.2d 784 (1990).

Attorney violated prior, similar (a) and (d) when he agreed with his non-lawyer spouse, a law graduate who was not admitted to the bar, to form a law firm and to share fees with the non-lawyer. Att'y Griev. Comm'n v. Mitchell,

386 Md. 386, 872 A.2d 720 (2005).

Suspended attorney as colleague. — This Rule was violated by an attorney who worked with a suspended attorney who represented himself as the attorney for a client, acted as though he was an attorney, and led the client to believe he was an attorney; this was true even though the role that the suspended lawyer eventually took with regard to the case was quite limited in scope. Att'y Griev. Comm'n v. Brennan, 350 Md. 489, 714 A.2d 157 (1998).

Illegal contract claims. — The Rules of Professional Conduct are not statements of public policy on which an illegal contract claim may be founded. Son v. Margolius, Mallios, Davis, Rider & Tomar, 114 Md. App. 190, 689 A.2d 645 (1997).

Disbarment was proper sanction. — Disbarment of attorney was appropriate where there were serious and repeated violations of the prior, similar Rule and other provisions of the Maryland Rules of Professional Conduct. Att'y Griev. Comm'n v. Milliken, 348 Md. 486, 704 A.2d 1225 (1998).

Rule 5.5. Unauthorized Practice of Law; Multijurisdictional Practice of Law.

(a) A lawyer shall not practice law in a jurisdiction in violation of the regulation of the legal profession in that jurisdiction, or assist another in doing so.

(b) A lawyer who is not admitted to practice in this jurisdiction shall not:

(1) except as authorized by these Rules or other law, establish an office or other systematic and continuous presence in this jurisdiction for the practice of law; or

(2) hold out to the public or otherwise represent that the lawyer is admitted to practice law in this jurisdiction.

(c) A lawyer admitted in another United States jurisdiction, and not disbarred or suspended from practice in any jurisdiction, may provide legal services on a temporary basis in this jurisdiction that:

(1) are undertaken in association with a lawyer who is admitted to practice in this jurisdiction and who actively participates in the matter;

(2) are in or reasonably related to a pending or potential proceeding before a tribunal in this or another jurisdiction, if the lawyer, or a person the lawyer is assisting, is authorized by law or order to appear in such proceeding or reasonably expects to be so authorized;

(3) are in or reasonably related to a pending or potential arbitration, mediation, or other alternative dispute resolution proceeding in this or another jurisdiction, if the services arise out of or are reasonably related to the lawyer's practice in a jurisdiction in which the lawyer is admitted to practice and are not services for which the forum requires pro hac vice admission; or

(4) are not within paragraphs (c)(2) or (c)(3) and arise out of or are reasonably related to the lawyer's practice in a jurisdiction in which the lawyer is admitted to practice.

(d) A lawyer admitted in another United States jurisdiction, and not disbarred or suspended from practice in any jurisdiction, may provide legal services in this jurisdiction that:

(1) are provided to the lawyer's employer or its organizational affiliates and are not services for which the forum requires pro hac vice admission; or

(2) are services that the lawyer is authorized to provide by federal law or other law of this jurisdiction. (Amended September 8, 2011, effective January 1, 2012.)

COMMENT

[1] A lawyer may practice law only in a jurisdiction in which the lawyer is authorized to practice. A lawyer may be admitted to practice law in a jurisdiction on a regular basis or may be authorized by court rule or order or by law to practice for a limited purpose or on a restricted basis. Paragraph (a) applies to unauthorized practice of law by a lawyer, whether through the lawyer's direct action or by the lawyer's assisting another person.

[2] The definition of the practice of law is established by law and varies from one jurisdiction to another. Whatever the definition, limiting the practice of law to members of the bar protects the public against rendition of legal services by unqualified persons. This Rule does not prohibit a lawyer from employing the services of paraprofessionals and delegating functions to them, so long as the lawyer supervises the delegated work and retains responsibility for their work. See Rule 5.3.

[3] A lawyer may provide professional advice and instruction to nonlawyers whose employment requires knowledge of law; for example, claims adjusters, employees of financial or commercial institutions, social workers, accountants and persons employed in government agencies. Lawyers also may assist independent nonlawyers, such as paraprofessionals, who are authorized by the law of a jurisdiction to provide particular law-related services. In addition, a lawyer may counsel nonlawyers who wish to proceed self-represented .

[4] Other than as authorized by law or this Rule, a lawyer who is not admitted to practice generally in this jurisdiction violates paragraph (b) if the lawyer establishes an office or other systematic and continuous presence in this jurisdiction for the practice of law. Presence may be systematic and continuous even if the lawyer is not physically present here. Such a lawyer must not hold out to the public or otherwise represent that the lawyer is admitted to practice law in this jurisdiction. See also Rules 7.1(a) and 7.5(b).

[5] There are occasions in which a lawyer admitted to practice in another United States jurisdiction, and not disbarred or suspended from practice in any jurisdiction, may provide legal services on a temporary basis in this jurisdiction under circumstances that do not create an unreasonable risk to the interests of their clients, the public or the courts. Paragraph (c) identifies four such circumstances. The fact that conduct is not so identified does not imply that the conduct is or is not authorized.

[6] There is no single test to determine whether a lawyer's services are provided on a "temporary basis" in this jurisdiction, and may therefore be permissible under paragraph (c). Services may be "temporary" even though the lawyer provides services in this jurisdiction on a recurring basis, or for an extended period of time, as when the lawyer is representing a client in a single lengthy negotiation or litigation.

[7] Paragraphs (c) and (d) apply to lawyers who are admitted to practice law in any United States jurisdiction, which includes the District of Columbia and any state, territory or commonwealth of the United States. The word "admitted" in paragraph (c) contemplates that the lawyer is authorized to practice in the jurisdiction in which the lawyer is admitted and excludes a lawyer who while technically admitted is not authorized to practice, because, for example, the lawyer is on inactive status.

[8] Paragraph (c)(1) recognizes that the interests of clients and the public are protected if a lawyer admitted only in another jurisdiction associates with a lawyer licensed to practice in this jurisdiction. For this paragraph to apply, however, the lawyer admitted to practice in this jurisdiction must actively participate in and share responsibility for the representation of the client.

[9] Lawyers not admitted to practice gener-

ally in a jurisdiction may be authorized by law or order of a tribunal or an administrative agency to appear before the tribunal or agency. This authority may be granted pursuant to formal rules governing admission pro hac vice or pursuant to informal practice of the tribunal or agency. Under paragraph (c)(2), a lawyer does not violate this Rule when the lawyer appears before a tribunal or agency pursuant to such authority. A lawyer who is not admitted to practice in this jurisdiction must obtain admission pro hac vice before appearing before a tribunal or administrative agency, as provided by Rule 14 of the Rules Governing Admission to the Bar of Maryland. See also Md. Code, Business Occupations and Professions Article, § 10-215.

[10] Paragraph (c)(2) also provides that a lawyer rendering services in this jurisdiction on a temporary basis does not violate this Rule when the lawyer engages in conduct in anticipation of a proceeding or hearing in a jurisdiction in which the lawyer is authorized to practice law or in which the lawyer reasonably expects to be admitted *pro hac vice*. Examples of such conduct include meetings with the client, interviews of potential witnesses, and the review of documents. Similarly, a lawyer admitted only in another jurisdiction may engage in conduct temporarily in this jurisdiction in connection with pending litigation in another jurisdiction in which the lawyer is or reasonably expects to be authorized to appear, including taking depositions in this jurisdiction.

[11] When a lawyer has been or reasonably expects to be admitted to appear before a court or administrative agency, paragraph (c)(2) also permits conduct by lawyers who are associated with that lawyer in the matter, but who do not expect to appear before the court or administrative agency. For example, subordinate lawyers may conduct research, review documents, and attend meetings with witnesses in support of the lawyer responsible for the litigation.

[12] Paragraph (c)(3) permits a lawyer admitted to practice law in another jurisdiction to perform services on a temporary basis in this jurisdiction if those services are in or reasonably related to a pending or potential arbitration, mediation, or other alternative dispute resolution proceeding in this or another jurisdiction, if the services arise out of or are reasonably related to the lawyer's practice in a jurisdiction in which the lawyer is admitted to practice. The lawyer, however, must obtain permission *pro hac vice* in the case of a court-annexed arbitration or mediation or otherwise if court rules or law so require. See Rule 14 of the Rules Governing Admission to the Bar of Maryland regarding admission to appear in arbitrations.

[13] Paragraph (c)(4) permits a lawyer ad-

mitted in another jurisdiction to provide certain legal services on a temporary basis in this jurisdiction that arise out of or are reasonably related to the lawyer's practice in a jurisdiction in which the lawyer is admitted but are not within paragraphs (c)(2) or (c)(3). These services include both legal services and services that non-lawyers may perform but that are considered the practice of law when performed by lawyers.

[14] Paragraphs (c)(3) and (c)(4) require that the services arise out of or be reasonably related to the lawyer's practice in a jurisdiction in which the lawyer is admitted. A variety of factors evidence such a relationship. The lawyer's client may have been previously represented by the lawyer, or may be resident in or have substantial contacts with the jurisdiction in which the lawyer is admitted. The matter, although involving other jurisdictions, may have a significant connection with that jurisdiction. In other cases, significant aspects of the lawyer's work might be conducted in that jurisdiction or a significant aspect of the matter may involve the law of that jurisdiction. The necessary relationship might arise when the client's activities or the legal issues involve multiple jurisdictions, such as when the officers of a multinational corporation survey potential business sites and seek the services of their lawyer in assessing the relative merits of each. In addition, the services may draw on the lawyer's recognized expertise developed through the regular practice of law on behalf of clients in matters involving a particular body of federal, nationally-uniform, foreign, or international law.

[15] Paragraph (d) identifies two circumstances in which a lawyer who is admitted to practice in another United States jurisdiction, and is not disbarred or suspended from practice in any jurisdiction, may establish an office or other systematic and continuous presence in this jurisdiction for the practice of law as well as provide legal services on a temporary basis.

[16] Paragraph (d)(1) applies to a lawyer who is employed by a client to provide legal services to the client or its organizational affiliates, i.e., entities that control, are controlled by, or are under common control with the employer. This paragraph does not authorize the provision of personal legal services to the employer's officers or employees. The paragraph applies to in-house corporate lawyers, government lawyers and others who are employed to render legal services to the employer. The lawyer's ability to represent the employer outside the jurisdiction in which the lawyer is licensed generally serves the interests of the employer and does not create an unreasonable risk to the client and others because the employer is well situated to assess the lawyer's

qualifications and the quality of the lawyer's work.

[17] If an employed lawyer establishes an office or other systematic presence in this jurisdiction for the purpose of rendering legal services to the employer, the lawyer is governed by Md. Code, Business Occupations and Professions Article, § 1-206(d). In general, the employed lawyer is subject to disciplinary proceedings under the Maryland Rules and must comply with Md. Code, Business Occupations and Professions Article, § 10-215 (and Rule 14 of the Rules Governing Admission to the Bar of Maryland) for authorization to appear before a tribunal. See also Rule 15 of the Rules Governing Admission to the Bar of Maryland (as to legal services attorneys).

[18] Paragraph (d)(2) recognizes that a lawyer may provide legal services in a jurisdiction in which the lawyer is not licensed when authorized to do so by federal or other law, which includes statute, court rule, executive regulation or judicial precedent.

[19] A lawyer who practices law in this jurisdiction pursuant to paragraph (c) or (d) or otherwise is subject to the disciplinary authority of this jurisdiction. See Rule 8.5(a) and Md. Rules 16-701 and 16-731.

[20] In some circumstances, a lawyer who practices law in this jurisdiction pursuant to paragraph (c) or (d) may have to inform the client that the lawyer is not licensed to practice law in this jurisdiction. For example, that may be required when the representation occurs primarily in this jurisdiction and requires knowledge of the law of this jurisdiction. See Rule 1.4(b).

[21] Paragraphs (c) and (d) do not authorize communications advertising legal services to prospective clients in this jurisdiction by lawyers who are admitted to practice in other jurisdictions. Rules 7.1 to 7.5 govern whether and how lawyers may communicate the availability of their services to prospective clients in this jurisdiction.

Model Rules Comparison. — Rule 5.5 is substantially similar to the language of the Ethics 2000 Amendments to the ABA Model Rules of Professional Conduct.

Effect of amendments. — The 2011 amendment substituted "self-represented" for "pro se" paragraph [3] of the Comment.

University of Baltimore Law Forum. — For article, "The New Maryland Rules of Professional Conduct and Mediation: Perplexing Questions Answered and Perplexing Questions That Remain," see 36 U. Balt. L.F. 1 (2005).

Purpose. — The purpose of the prior, similar Rule is to protect the public from being preyed upon by those not competent to practice law – from incompetent, unethical, or irresponsible representation; that goal is achieved by emphasizing the insulation of the unlicensed person from the public and from tribunals such as courts and certain administrative agencies. Att'y Griev. Comm'n v. Hallmon, 343 Md. 390, 681 A.2d 510 (1996).

Engaging in practice of law. — To determine whether an individual has engaged in the practice of law, the focus of the inquiry should be on whether the activity in question required legal knowledge and skill in order to apply legal principles and precedent; where trial work is not involved but the preparation of legal documents, their interpretation, the giving of legal advice, or the application of legal principles to problems of any complexity is involved, these activities are still the practice of law. Att'y Griev. Comm'n v. Hallmon, 343 Md. 390, 681 A.2d 510 (1996).

Attorney's conduct in, inter alia, representing another person in a real estate matter while the attorney's license to practice law was suspended constituted the unauthorized practice of law. That conduct violated (a), and that as well as the attorney's overall misconduct warranted the attorney's disbarment from the practice of law in Maryland. Att'y Griev. Comm'n v. Shryock, 408 Md. 105, 968 A.2d 593 (2009).

Respondent violated Md. Law. R. Prof. Conduct 5.5, 7.1, and 7.5 by establishing a law firm in Maryland and holding herself out as an attorney without being licensed to practice there. Att'y Griev. Comm'n v. Sucklal, 418 Md. 1, 12 A.3d 650 (2011).

Out-of-state attorneys. — A Maryland attorney was subject to sanction under the prior, similar Rule where he associated with an out-of-state attorney, included his signature on pleadings, and introduced him to a hearing examiner as his "co-counsel." Att'y Griev. Comm'n v. Brown, 353 Md. 271, 725 A.2d 1069 (1999).

Reciprocal discipline was imposed on an attorney for his unauthorized practice as an out-of-state attorney in the District of Columbia, where he was not licensed; clear and convincing evidence indicated that he violated the District's unauthorized practice rules by attempting to practice indefinitely under the putative supervision of a District attorney and assured clients that he could be admitted pro hac vice if need arose, even though his maintenance of an office in the District made him ineligible for such admission. Att'y Griev. Comm'n v. Walker-Turner, 372 Md. 85, 812 A.2d 260 (2002).

Unauthorized practice by attorney licensed in other jurisdictions. — Disbarment was the appropriate remedy for an attorney, licensed in other jurisdictions, that opened an office, used letterhead, and represented clients in Maryland without being admitted or specially admitted. Att'y Griev. Comm'n v. Barneys, 370 Md. 566, 805 A.2d 1040 (2002).

When an attorney admitted to practice in New York started practicing in the State and federal courts of Maryland before being admitted to practice in either court, he violated this Rule as, even after he was admitted to practice in federal court, his business cards, which were available at various locations, signs and stationery did not indicate his practice was limited to federal court, nor did he advise clients that his practice was so limited. Att'y Griev. Comm'n v. Alsafty, 379 Md. 1, 838 A.2d 1213 (2003).

Where the attorney abandoned his representation of the client and refused to engage in further communications with the client after terminating his representation via electronic mail, and the attorney engaged in other misconduct which included not being admitted to practice in forums where the attorney was representing the client and not responding to the disciplinary commission's lawful demands for information regarding the investigation of the attorney, disbarment was warranted. Att'y Griev. Comm'n v. Logan, 390 Md. 313, 888 A.2d 359 (2005).

Unauthorized practice of law in another jurisdiction. — Attorney was disbarred as he violated (a) where he engaged in activity constituting the practice of law in Virginia, where he was not authorized to practice law; the unauthorized practice of law in Virginia was prohibited under Va. Sup. Ct. R. pt. 6, § I, and was a crime under Va. Code Ann. § 54.1-3904, and therefore, coupled with the attorney's failure to disclose the fact that he was not licensed in Virginia to the client and his acceptance of a fee for representation that he could not perform, was conduct involving dishonesty, fraud, deceit, or misrepresentation for the purposes of prior, similar Rule 8.4. Att'y Griev. Comm'n v. Velasquez, 380 Md. 651, 846 A.2d 422 (2004).

Lay advocates. — A lay advocate who provides certain services to victims of domestic violence may provide basic information about the existence of legal rights and remedies; may provide basic information about the manner in which judicial proceedings are conducted; may assist victims in preparing legal pleadings or other legal documents on her own behalf by defining unfamiliar terms on a form, explaining where on a form the victim is to provide certain information, and if necessary transcribing or otherwise recording the victim's

own words verbatim; may sit with a victim at trial table, if permitted by the court; and may engage in the general advocacy of the rights of battered women as a group. 80 Op. Att'y Gen. — (Dec. 19, 1995).

Except under the supervision of an attorney, a lay advocate may not provide any advice relating to a victim's rights or remedies, including whether a victim's particular circumstances suggest that she should pursue a particular remedy; may not provide information about the legal aspects of judicial proceedings, such as how to present a case, call witnesses, introduce evidence, and the like; may not use the advocate's own language in preparing or filling out form pleadings or other legal documents; or may not engage in advocacy before any governmental representative on behalf of an individual victim. 80 Op. Att'y Gen. — (Dec. 19, 1995).

Law clerks and paralegals. — Law clerks and paralegals perform a variety of services for attorneys but they may not give legal advice, accept cases, set fees, appear in court, plan strategy, make legal decisions, or chart the direction of a case. Att'y Griev. Comm'n v. Hallmon, 343 Md. 390, 681 A.2d 510 (1996).

Adequate supervision of legal assistants is an ethical requirement. Att'y Griev. Comm'n v. Hallmon, 343 Md. 390, 681 A.2d 510 (1996).

Hearing record demonstrated by clear and convincing evidence an abdication of supervision by subject attorney and that a lay legal assistant was unauthorizedly practicing law. Att'y Griev. Comm'n v. Hallmon, 343 Md. 390, 681 A.2d 510 (1996).

Lack of supervision. — An attorney who was admitted in another jurisdiction, but not in Maryland, violated the professional conduct rules by practicing law in partnership with a Maryland attorney out of an office maintained by the partnership in the State, without the supervision of the admitted attorney. Att'y Griev. Comm'n v. Harper, 356 Md. 53, 737 A.2d 557 (1999).

Limitation of practice to bankruptcy proceedings. — Where, although an attorney not admitted to practice in the State claimed that she "pinpointed" bankruptcy cases, the evidence was that she analyzed matters that came to her to determine whether action in the district bankruptcy court was the proper course of action, and where she did not advise clients that she was limiting her legal representation to bankruptcy proceedings, she was found in violation of professional conduct rules. Att'y Griev. Comm'n v. Harris-Smith, 356 Md. 72, 737 A.2d 567 (1999).

Admission of evidence. — Where evidence was not introduced to prove additional violations of the professional conduct rules by an attorney suspended from the practice of law in order to impose discipline on him for those uncharged violations, but was introduced to rebut the attorney's evidence of mitigation, the Rule's purpose as a filter for charges was not violated. Att'y Griev. Comm'n v. James, 355 Md. 465, 735 A.2d 1027 (1999).

Suspended license. — The prior, similar Rule was violated where a suspended attorney represented himself as an attorney to a client, acted as though he was an attorney, and led the client to believe he was an attorney, even though the role he eventually took on the case was quite limited in scope. Att'y Griev. Comm'n v. Brennan, 350 Md. 489, 714 A.2d 157 (1998).

An attorney was suspended for 30 days where he could not reasonably have believed that lending his name to an unadmitted attorney's partnership scheme would convert an unauthorized practice into an authorized one. Att'y Griev. Comm'n v. Harper, 356 Md. 53, 737 A.2d 557 (1999).

Attorney violated this rule by continuing to practice law after the attorney was suspended in Maryland as the attorney continued to represent clients for months in immigration matters after his suspension in Maryland and his later suspension in the District of Columbia; furthermore, the attorney used his legal letterhead and business cards, which stated that his practice encompassed more than immigration law, and did not inform clients that he had been disbarred. Att'y Griev. Comm'n v. Awuah, 374 Md. 505, 823 A.2d 651 (2003).

Attorney was indefinitely suspended from practice of law for violating Rule 8.4 and this Rule, by preparing a response to a summary judgment motion in a separate action while suspended from the practice of law for 90 days, and by failing to inform the client in that other action that the attorney had been suspended, thereby engaging in conduct prejudicial to administration of justice. Att'y Griev. Comm'n v. Robertson, 400 Md. 618, 929 A.2d 576 (2007).

Indefinite suspension with leave to apply for readmission. — Attorney was indefinitely suspended, with leave to apply for readmission after six months, where the attorney violated (a) and Md. R. Prof. Conduct 1.1, 1.3, 3.3(a)(1), and 8.4(c) and (d), by, inter alia, appearing at a meeting of creditors when not authorized to practice before the district court. Att'y Griev. Comm'n v. Robaton, 411 Md. 415, 983 A.2d 467 (2009).

Disbarment. — Disbarment was the appropriate sanction for an attorney who, motivated by greed, set up an office for the general practice of law even though he was not admitted to practice in Maryland. Att'y Griev. Comm'n v. Harper, 356 Md. 53, 737 A.2d 557 (1999).

Disbarment was the appropriate sanction where an out-of-state attorney practiced law in

the State of Maryland without a license, failed to acknowledge his jurisdictional limitations on his firm letterhead, acted against the interests of his purported clients during and after the sale of their home to him, filed a bankruptcy petition on those clients' behalf, but without their consent or knowledge, and forged the signatures of the clients and another attorney in his office on court papers and filings, in violation of prior, similar Rules of Professional Conduct 1.7, 3.3, 5.5, 7.1, 7.5, and 8.4. Att'y Griev. Comm'n v. Johnson, 363 Md. 598, 770 A.2d 130 (2001).

Because the attorney engaged in several acts of professional misconduct following an earlier suspension by accepting fees from clients but by failing to diligently to pursue their cases, the sanction of disbarment was held to be appropriate. Att'y Griev. Comm'n v. Fallin, 371 Md. 237, 808 A.2d 791 (2002).

Where the attorney, among other things, intentionally misappropriated client funds, forged a client's signature on a settlement check, lied under oath, and represented a client when the attorney was not licensed to do so, the attorney was disbarred for violating former, similar Md. R. Prof. Conduct 1.2(a), 1.3, 1.5(c), 1.15(a), (b), 3.3(a), 5.5, 8.1(a), (b), 8.4(a), (b), (c), (d), Md. R. 16-604, and §§ 10-304, -306 of the Business Occupations and Professions Article Att'y Griev. Comm'n v. Kapoor, 391 Md. 505, 894 A.2d 502 (2006).

Attorney was disbarred for violating, inter alia, former similar version of this Rule by signing the attorney's name to a motion to dismiss filed in a federal district court where the attorney had not been admitted to practice. Att'y Griev. Comm'n v. Pak, 400 Md. 567, 929 A.2d 546 (2007), cert. denied, 128 S. Ct. 905, 2008 U.S. LEXIS 126, 169 L. Ed. 2d 729 (U.S. 2008).

Attorney was disbarred because the attorney made knowingly false statements concerning the attorney's bar admission status, proceeded to act as general counsel for clients, and acted to mislead and defraud investors in violation of Md. R. Prof. Conduct 5.5 and 8.4. Att'y Griev. Comm'n v. Parsons, 404 Md. 175, 946 A.2d 437 (2008).

Attorney's conduct, while the attorney was decertified, of representing at least two defendants after making them believe that the attorney was authorized to practice law in Maryland, violated Md. R. Prof. Conduct 5.5(a). As a result of the attorney (1) being decertified, (2) practicing law while the attorney was decertified, and (3) other violation of the rules of professional conduct, the state's highest court had little choice but to disbar the attorney. Att'y Griev. Comm'n v. Walker, 405 Md. 3, 948 A.2d 1263 (2008).

Attorney violated (b)(2) through the unauthorized maintenance of an attorney trust account while the attorney was suspended from the practice of law, as well as the attorney's conduct in holding out that the attorney was admitted to practice of law in Maryland. That conduct, and other professional misconduct, warranted the attorney's disbarment from the practice of law in Maryland. Att'y Griev. Comm'n v. Shryock, 408 Md. 105, 968 A.2d 593 (2009).

Quoted in Att'y Griev. Comm'n v. Mitchell, 386 Md. 386, 872 A.2d 720 (2005).

Cited in Att'y Griev. Comm'n v. MacDougall, 384 Md. 271, 863 A.2d 312 (2004); Att'y Griev. Comm'n v. Lee, 387 Md. 89, 874 A.2d 897 (2005); Att'y Griev. Comm'n v. Lee, 393 Md. 385, 903 A.2d 360 (2006); Abrams v. Lamone, 398 Md. 146, 919 A.2d 1223 (2007).

Rule 5.6. Restrictions on Right to Practice.

A lawyer shall not participate in offering or making:

(a) a partnership, shareholders, operating, employment, or other similar type of agreement that restricts the right of a lawyer to practice after termination of the relationship, except an agreement concerning benefits upon retirement; or

(b) an agreement in which a restriction on the lawyer's right to practice is part of the settlement of a client controversy.

COMMENT

[1] An agreement restricting the right of lawyers to practice after leaving a firm not only limits their professional autonomy but also limits the freedom of clients to choose a lawyer. Paragraph (a) prohibits such agreement except for restrictions incident to provisions concerning retirement benefits for service with the firm.

[2] Paragraph (b) prohibits a lawyer from agreeing not to represent other persons in connection with settling a claim on behalf of a client.

[3] This Rule does not apply to prohibit restrictions that may be included in the terms of the sale of a law practice pursuant to Rule 1.17.

Model Rules Comparison. — Rule 5.6 is substantially similar to the language of the Ethics 2000 Amendments to the ABA Model Rules of Professional Conduct.

Maryland Law Review. — For survey, "Developments in Maryland Law, 1990-91," see 51 Md. L. Rev. 507 (1992).

Rule 5.7. Responsibilities Regarding Law-Related Services.

(a) A lawyer shall be subject to the Maryland Lawyers' Rules of Professional Conduct with respect to the provision of law-related services, as defined in paragraph (b), if the law-related services are provided:

(1) by the lawyer in circumstances that are not distinct from the lawyer's provision of legal services to clients; or

(2) in other circumstances by an entity controlled by the lawyer individually or with others if the lawyer fails to take reasonable measures to assure that a person obtaining the law-related services knows that the services are not legal services and that the protections of the client-lawyer relationship do not exist.

(b) The term "law-related services" denotes services that might reasonably be performed in conjunction with and in substance are related to the provision of legal services, and that are not prohibited as unauthorized practice of law when provided by a nonlawyer.

COMMENT

[1] When a lawyer performs law-related services or controls an organization that does so, there exists the potential for ethical problems. Principal among these is the possibility that the person for whom the law-related services are performed fails to understand that the services may not carry with them the protections normally afforded as part of the client-lawyer relationship. The recipient of the law-related services may expect, for example, that the protection of client confidences, prohibitions against representation of persons with conflicting interests, and obligations of a lawyer to maintain professional independence apply to the provision of law-related services when that may not be the case.

[2] Rule 5.7 applies to the provision of law-related services by a lawyer even when the lawyer does not provide any legal services to the person for whom the law-related services are performed and whether the law-related services are performed through a law firm or a separate entity. The Rule identifies the circumstances in which all of the Maryland Lawyers' Rules of Professional Conduct apply to the provision of law-related services. Even when those circumstances do not exist, however, the conduct of a lawyer involved in the provision of law-related services is subject to those Rules that apply generally to lawyer conduct, regardless of whether the conduct involves the provision of legal services. See, e.g., Rule 8.4.

[3] When law-related services are provided by a lawyer under circumstances that are not distinct from the lawyer's provision of legal services to clients, the lawyer in providing the law-related services must adhere to the requirements of the Maryland Lawyers' Rules of Professional Conduct as provided in paragraph (a)(1). Even when the law-related and legal services are provided in circumstances that are distinct from each other, for example through separate entities or different support staff within the law firm, the Maryland Lawyers' Rules of Professional Conduct apply to the lawyer as provided in paragraph (a)(2) unless the lawyer takes reasonable measures to assure that the recipient of the law-related services knows that the services are not legal services and that the protections of the client-lawyer relationship do not apply.

[4] Law-related services also may be provided through an entity that is distinct from that through which the lawyer provides legal services. If the lawyer individually or with others has control of such an entity's operations, the Rule requires the lawyer to take reasonable measures to assure that each person using the services of the entity knows that the services provided by the entity are not legal services and that the Maryland Lawyer's Rules of Professional Conduct that relate to the client-lawyer relationship do not apply. A lawyer's control of an entity extends to the ability to direct its operation. Whether a lawyer has such control will depend upon the circumstances of the particular case.

[5] A lawyer is not required to comply with Rule 1.8(a) when referring a person to a separate law-related entity owned or controlled by the lawyer for the purpose of providing services to the person. If the lawyer also is providing legal services to the person, the lawyer must exercise independent professional judgment in making the referral. See Rule 2.1. Moreover, the lawyer must explain the matter to the person to the extent necessary for the person to make an informed decision to accept the lawyer's recommendation. See Rule 1.4(b).

[6] In taking the reasonable measures referred to in paragraph (a)(2) to assure that a person using law-related services understands the practical effect or significance of the inapplicability of the Maryland Lawyers' Rules of Professional Conduct, the lawyer should communicate to the person receiving the law-related services, in a manner sufficient to assure that the person understands the significance of the fact, that the relationship of the person to the business entity will not be a client-lawyer relationship. The communication should be made before entering into an agreement for provision of or providing law-related services, and preferably should be in writing.

[7] The burden is upon the lawyer to show that the lawyer has taken reasonable measures under the circumstances to communicate the desired understanding. For instance, a sophisticated user of law-related services, such as a publicly held corporation, may require a lesser explanation than someone unaccustomed to making distinctions between legal services and law-related services, such as an individual seeking tax advice from a lawyer-accountant or investigative services in connection with a lawsuit.

[8] Regardless of the sophistication of potential recipients of law-related services, a lawyer should take special care to keep separate the provision of law-related and legal services in order to minimize the risk that the recipient will assume that the law-related services are legal services. The risk of such confusion is especially acute when the lawyer renders both types of services with respect to the same matter. Under some circumstances the legal and law-related services may be so closely entwined that they cannot be distinguished

from each other, and the requirement of disclosure and consultation imposed by paragraph (a)(2) of the Rule cannot be met. In such a case a lawyer will be responsible for assuring that both the lawyer's conduct and, to the extent required by Rule 5.3, that of nonlawyer employees in the distinct entity that the lawyer complies in all respects with the Maryland Lawyers' Rules of Professional Conduct.

[9] A broad range of economic and other interests of clients may be served by lawyers' engaging in the delivery of law-related services. Examples of law-related services include providing title insurance, financial planning, accounting, trust services, real estate counseling, legislative lobbying, economic analysis, social work, psychological counseling, tax preparation, and patent, medical or environmental consulting.

[10] When a lawyer is obliged to accord the recipients of such services the protections of those Rules that apply to the client-lawyer relationship, the lawyer must take special care to heed the proscriptions of the Rules addressing conflict of interest (Rules 1.7 through 1.11, especially Rules 1.7(a)(2) and 1.8(b) and (f)), and to scrupulously adhere to the requirements of Rule 1.6 relating to disclosure of confidential information. The promotion of the law-related services must also in all respects comply with Rules 7.1 through 7.3, dealing with advertising and solicitation. In that regard, lawyers should take special care to identify the obligations that may be imposed as a result of a jurisdiction's decisional law.

[11] When the full protections of all of the Maryland Lawyers' Rules of Professional Conduct do not apply to the provision of law-related services, principles of law external to the Rules, for example, the law of principal and agent, govern the legal duties owed to those receiving the services. Those other legal principles may establish a different degree of protection for the recipient with respect to confidentiality of information, conflicts of interest and permissible business relationships with clients. See also Rule 8.4 (Misconduct).

[12] Regarding a lawyer's referrals of clients to non-lawyer professionals, see Rule 7.2(c) and related Comment.

Model Rules Comparison. — This Rule, newly added to the Model Rules by the Ethics 2000 Amendments to the ABA Model Rules of Professional Conduct, is substantially similar to the ABA Rule, with the exception of changes to Comment [5] and the addition of Comment [12].

University of Baltimore Law Forum. — For article, "The New Maryland Rules of Professional Conduct and Mediation: Perplexing Questions Answered and Perplexing Questions That Remain," see 36 U. Balt. L.F. 1 (2005).

PUBLIC SERVICE.

Rule 6.1. Pro Bono Publico Service.

(a) **Professional Responsibility.** A lawyer has a professional responsibility to render pro bono publico legal service.

(b) **Discharge of Professional Responsibility.** A lawyer in the full-time practice of law should aspire to render at least 50 hours per year of pro bono publico legal service, and a lawyer in part-time practice should aspire to render at least a pro rata number of hours.

(1) Unless a lawyer is prohibited by law from rendering the legal services described below, a substantial portion of the applicable hours should be devoted to rendering legal service, without fee or expectation of fee, or at a substantially reduced fee, to:

(A) people of limited means;

(B) charitable, religious, civic, community, governmental, or educational organizations in matters designed primarily to address the needs of people of limited means;

(C) individuals, groups, or organizations seeking to secure or protect civil rights, civil liberties, or public rights; or

(D) charitable, religious, civic, community, governmental, or educational organizations in matters in furtherance of their organizational purposes when the payment of the standard legal fees would significantly deplete the organization's economic resources or would otherwise be inappropriate.

(2) The remainder of the applicable hours may be devoted to activities for improving the law, the legal system, or the legal profession.

(3) A lawyer also may discharge the professional responsibility set forth in this Rule by contributing financial support to organizations that provide legal services to persons of limited means.

(c) **Effect of Noncompliance.** This Rule is aspirational, not mandatory. Noncompliance with this Rule shall not be grounds for disciplinary action or other sanctions.

Cross references. — For requirements regarding reporting pro bono legal service, see Md. Rule 16-903.

COMMENT

[1] The ABA House of Delegates has formally acknowledged "the basic responsibility of each lawyer engaged in the practice of law to provide public interest legal services" without fee, or at a substantially reduced fee, in one or more of the following areas: poverty law, civil rights law, public rights law, charitable organization representation, and the administration of justice. This Rule expresses that policy but is not intended to be enforced through the disciplinary process.

[2] The rights and responsibilities of individuals and organizations in the United States are increasingly defined in legal terms. As a consequence, legal assistance in coping with the web of statutes, rules, and regulations is imperative for persons of modest and limited means, as well as for the relatively well-to-do.

[3] The basic responsibility for providing legal services for those unable to pay ultimately rests upon the individual lawyer, and personal involvement in the problems of the disadvantaged can be one of the most rewarding experiences in the life of a lawyer. Every lawyer, regardless of professional prominence or professional workload, should find time to participate in or otherwise support the provision of legal services to the disadvantaged. The provision of free legal services to those unable to pay reasonable fees continues to be an obligation of each lawyer as well as the profession generally, but the efforts of individual lawyers are often not enough to meet the need. Thus, it has been necessary for the profession, the government, and the courts to institute additional programs to provide legal services. Accordingly, legal aid offices, lawyer referral services, and other related programs have been developed, and more will be developed by the profession, the government, and the courts. Every lawyer should support all proper efforts to meet this need for legal services.

[4] The goal of 50 hours per year for pro bono legal service established in paragraph (b) of this Rule is aspirational; it is a goal, not a requirement. The number used is intended as an average yearly amount over the course of the lawyer's career.

[5] A lawyer in government service who is prohibited by constitutional, statutory, or regulatory restrictions from performing the pro bono legal services described in paragraph (b)(1) of the Rule may discharge the lawyer's responsibility by participating in activities described in paragraph (b)(2).

Model Rules Comparison. — This Rule substantially retains Maryland language as amended April 9, 2002, effective July 1, 2002, and does not adopt Ethics 2000 Amendments to the ABA Model Rules of Professional Conduct.

Editor's note. — See note to Rule 1.1.

Maryland Law Review. — For symposium, expanding pro bono legal assistance in civil cases to Maryland's poor, see 49 Md. L. Rev. 1 (1990).

University of Baltimore Law Forum. — For discussion of the code of ethics, see 17, No. 1 U. Balt. Law Forum 31 (1986).

For article, "Code of Ethics Revisited," see 19.2 U. Balt. Law Forum 14 (1989).

For article, "Pro Bono for the Non-Litigator," see 20.2 U. Balt. Law Forum 13 (1990).

Applied in Henriquez v. Henriquez, 413

Md. 287, 992 A.2d 446 (2010).

Cited in Touzeau v. Deffinbaugh, 394 Md. 654, 907 A.2d 807 (2006).

Rule 6.2. Accepting Appointments.

A lawyer shall not seek to avoid appointment by a tribunal to represent a person except for good cause, such as:

(a) representing the client is likely to result in violation of the Maryland Lawyers' Rules of Professional Conduct or other law;

(b) representing the client is likely to result in an unreasonable financial burden on the lawyer; or

(c) the client or the cause is so repugnant to the lawyer as to be likely to impair the client-lawyer relationship or the lawyer's ability to represent the client.

COMMENT

[1] A lawyer ordinarily is not obliged to accept a client whose character or cause the lawyer regards as repugnant. The lawyer's freedom to select clients is, however, qualified. All lawyers have a responsibility to assist in providing pro bono publico service. See Rule 6.1. An individual lawyer fulfills this responsibility by accepting a fair share of unpopular matters or indigent or unpopular clients. A lawyer may also be subject to appointment by a court to serve unpopular clients or persons unable to afford legal services.

Appointed Counsel. — [2] For good cause a lawyer may seek to decline an appointment to represent a person who cannot afford to retain counsel or whose cause is unpopular. Good cause exists if the lawyer could not handle the matter competently, see Rule 1.1, or if undertaking the representation would result in an improper conflict of interest, for example, when the client or the cause is so repugnant to

the lawyer as to be likely to impair the client-lawyer relationship or the lawyer's ability to represent the client. A lawyer may also seek to decline an appointment if acceptance would be unreasonably burdensome, for example, when it would impose a financial sacrifice so great as to be unjust.

[3] An appointed lawyer has the same obligations to the client as retained counsel, including the obligations of loyalty and confidentiality, and is subject to the same limitations on the client-lawyer relationship, such as the obligation to refrain from assisting the client in violation of the Rules.

Model Rules Comparison. — Given that the Ethics 2000 Amendments to the ABA Model Rules of Professional Conduct made no changes to this Rule, Rule 6.2 has not been amended and remains substantially similar to Model Rule 6.2.

Maryland Law Review. — For symposium, expanding pro bono legal assistance in civil cases to Maryland's poor, see 49 Md. L. Rev. 1 (1990).

Rule 6.3. Membership in Legal Services Organization.

A lawyer may serve as a director, officer or member of a legal services organization, apart from the law firm in which the lawyer practices, notwithstanding that the organization serves persons having interests adverse to a client of the lawyer. The lawyer shall not knowingly participate in a decision or action of the organization:

(a) if participating in the decision would be incompatible with the lawyer's obligations to a client under Rule 1.7; or

(b) where the decision could have a material adverse effect on the representation of a client of the organization whose interests are adverse to a client of the lawyer.

COMMENT

[1] Lawyers should be encouraged to support and participate in legal service organizations. A lawyer who is an officer or a member of such an organization does not thereby have a client-lawyer relationship with persons served by the organization. However, there is potential conflict between the interests of such persons and the interests of the lawyer's clients. If the possibility of such conflict disqualified a lawyer from serving on the board of a legal services organization, the profession's involvement in such organizations would be severely curtailed.

[2] It may be necessary in appropriate cases to reassure a client of the organization that the representation will not be affected by conflicting loyalties of a member of the board. Established, written policies in this respect can enhance the credibility of such assurances.

Model Rules Comparison. — Given that the Ethics 2000 Amendments to the ABA Model Rules of Professional Conduct made no changes to this Rule, Rule 6.3 has not been amended and remains substantially similar to Model Rule 6.3.

Rule 6.4. Law Reform Activities Affecting Client Interests.

A lawyer may serve as a director, officer or member of an organization involved in reform of the law or its administration notwithstanding that the reform may affect the interests of a client of the lawyer. When the lawyer knows that the interests of a client may be materially benefited by a decision in which the lawyer participates, the lawyer shall disclose that fact but need not identify the client.

COMMENT

[1] Lawyers involved in organizations seeking law reform generally do not have a client-lawyer relationship with the organization. Otherwise, it might follow that a lawyer could not be involved in a bar association law reform program that might indirectly affect a client. See also Rule 1.2(b). For example, a lawyer specializing in antitrust litigation might be regarded as disqualified from participating in drafting revisions of rules governing that subject. In determining the nature and scope of participation in such activities, a lawyer should be mindful of obligations to clients

under other Rules, particularly Rule 1.7. A lawyer is professionally obligated to protect the integrity of the program by making an appropriate disclosure within the organization when the lawyer knows a private client might be materially benefited.

Model Rules Comparison. — Given that the Ethics 2000 Amendments to the ABA Model Rules of Professional Conduct made no changes to this Rule, Rule 6.4 has not been amended and remains substantially similar to Model Rule 6.4.

Rule 6.5. Nonprofit and Court-Annexed Limited Legal Services Programs.

(a) A lawyer who, under the auspices of a program sponsored by a nonprofit organization or court, provides short-term limited legal services to a client without expectation by either the lawyer or the client that the lawyer will provide continuing representation in the matter:

(1) is subject to Rules 1.7 and 1.9(a) only if the lawyer knows that the representation of the client involves a conflict of interest; and

(2) is subject to Rule 1.10 only if the lawyer knows that another lawyer associated with the lawyer in a law firm is disqualified by Rule 1.7 or 1.9(a) with respect to the matter.

(b) Except as provided in paragraph (a)(2), Rule 1.10 is inapplicable to a representation governed by this Rule. (Amended September 8, 2011, effective January 1, 2012.)

COMMENT

[1] Legal services organizations, courts and various nonprofit organizations have established programs through which lawyers provide short-term limited legal services — such as advice or the completion of legal forms — that will assist persons to address their legal problems without further representation by a lawyer. In these programs, such as legal-advice hotlines, advice-only clinics, self-represented counseling programs, or programs in which lawyers represent clients on a pro bono basis for the purposes of mediation only, a client-lawyer relationship is established, but there is no expectation that the lawyer's representation of the client will continue beyond the limited consultation.

[2] A lawyer who provides short-term limited legal services pursuant to this Rule must secure the client's informed consent to the limited scope of the representation. See Rule 1.2(c). If a short-term limited representation would not be reasonable under the circumstances, the lawyer may offer advice to the client but must also advise the client of the need for further assistance of counsel. Except as provided in this Rule, the Maryland Lawyers' Rules of Professional Conduct, including Rules 1.6 and 1.9(c), are applicable to the limited representation.

[3] Because the limited nature of the ser-

vices significantly reduces the risk of conflicts of interest with other matters being handled by the lawyer's firm, paragraph (b) provides that Rule 1.10 is inapplicable to a representation governed by this Rule except as provided by paragraph (a)(2). Paragraph (a)(2) requires the participating lawyer to comply with Rule 1.10 when the lawyer knows that the lawyer's firm is disqualified by Rules 1.7 or 1.9(a). By virtue of paragraph (b), however, a lawyer's participation in a short-term limited legal services program will not preclude the lawyer's firm from undertaking or continuing the representation of a client with interests adverse to a client being represented under the program's auspices. Nor will the personal disqualification of a lawyer participating in the program be imputed to other lawyers participating in the program.

[4] If, after commencing a short-term limited representation in accordance with this Rule, a lawyer undertakes to represent the client in the matter on an ongoing basis, Rules 1.7, 1.9(a) and 1.10 become applicable.

Model Rules Comparison. — This Rule, newly added to the Model Rules by the Ethics 2000 Amendments to the ABA Model Rules of Professional Conduct, is substantially similar to the ABA Rule, with the exception of changes to Comment [1] and the omission of ABA Comment [3].

Effect of amendments. — The 2011 amendment substituted "self-represented" for "pro se" in paragraph [1] of the Comment.

University of Baltimore Law Forum. — For article, "The New Maryland Rules of Pro-

fessional Conduct and Mediation: Perplexing Questions Answered and Perplexing Questions That Remain," see 36 U. Balt. L.F. 1 (2005).

INFORMATION ABOUT LEGAL SERVICES.

Rule 7.1. Communications Concerning a Lawyer's Services.

A lawyer shall not make a false or misleading communication about the lawyer or the lawyer's services. A communication is false or misleading if it:

(a) contains a material misrepresentation of fact or law, or omits a fact necessary to make the statement considered as a whole not materially misleading;

(b) is likely to create an unjustified expectation about results the lawyer can achieve, or states or implies that the lawyer can achieve results by means that violate the Maryland Lawyers' Rules of Professional Conduct or other law; or

(c) compares the lawyer's services with other lawyers' services, unless the comparison can be factually substantiated.

COMMENT

[1] This Rule governs all communications about a lawyer's services, including advertising and direct personal contact with potential clients permitted by Rules 7.2 and 7.3. Whatever means are used to make known a lawyer's services, statements about them should be truthful. The prohibition in paragraph (b) of statements that may create "unjustified expectations" would ordinarily preclude advertisements about results obtained on behalf of a client, such as the amount of a damage award or the lawyer's record in obtaining favorable verdicts, and advertisements containing client endorsements. Such information may create the unjustified expectation that similar results can be obtained for others without reference to the specific factual and legal circumstances.

[2] A communication will be regarded as false or misleading if it (1) asserts the lawyer's record in obtaining favorable awards, verdicts, judgments, or settlements in prior cases, un-less it also expressly and conspicuously states that each case is different and that the past record is no assurance that the lawyer will be successful in reaching a favorable result in any future case, or (2) contains an endorsement or testimonial as to the lawyer's legal services or abilities by a person who is not a bona fide pre-existing client of the lawyer and has not in fact benefited as such from those services or abilities.

[3] See also Rule 8.4(f) for the prohibition against stating or implying an ability to influence a government agency or official or to achieve results by means that violate the Maryland Lawyers' Rules of Professional Conduct or other law.

Model Rules Comparison. — This Rule substantially retains existing Maryland language and does not adopt Ethics 2000 Amendments to the ABA Model Rules of Professional Conduct.

Editor's note. — See note to Rule 1.1.

University of Baltimore Law Forum. — For discussion of the code of ethics, see 17, No. 1 U. Balt. Law Forum 31 (1986).

For article, "Code of Ethics Revisited," see 19.2 U. Balt. Law Forum 14 (1989).

Trade names. — The Court of Appeals lacks the jurisdiction to render advisory ethics opinions, and has no authority either to approve of or disapprove a contemplated trade name. In re Attorney's Use of Trade Name, 333 Md. 488, 635 A.2d 1338 (1994).

Letterhead information. — Failure of a Maryland attorney to include on his letterhead that an attorney who was associated with him was not licensed to practice law in the state of Maryland constituted a violation of the prior, similar Rule and Rule 7.5. Att'y Griev. Comm'n v. Brown, 353 Md. 271, 725 A.2d 1069 (1999).

Professional conduct rules were violated where an unadmitted attorney's letterhead created the false impression that the attorney was lawfully engaged in the practice of law in Maryland from a principal office in the State, and where a letter implied that the attorney could settle a Maryland resident's claim. Att'y Griev. Comm'n v. Harper, 356 Md. 53, 737 A.2d 557 (1999).

Attorney grievance commission's exceptions to a hearing court's finding that an attorney violated prior, similar Rule 7.5, prohibiting the use of firm names and letterhead in violation of the prior, similar Rule, and § 10-602 of the Business Occupations and Professions Article, prohibiting the use of titles indicating authorization to practice, by failing to indicate on his letterhead that his practice was limited to the federal courts of Maryland, were sustained; such violations were not alleged in the petition seeking the attorney's discipline. Att'y Griev. Comm'n v. Alsafty, 379 Md. 1, 838 A.2d 1213 (2003).

Use of business cards and execution of retainer agreement by nonlawyer. — The use of a business card which indicated that a law graduate who had not passed the bar was a J.D., the execution of a retainer agreement by that person, and the setting of fees were violations of prior, similar 7.1 and 8.4 because the attorney knew, and in fact, sponsored the arrangement undertaken by the nonlawyer. Att'y Griev. Comm'n v. Mitchell, 386 Md. 386, 872 A.2d 720 (2005).

Failure to advise of lack of admission. — An attorney violated professional conduct rules where she did not advise prospective clients that she was not admitted to practice in Maryland, and where her professional card gave an in-state address for her office, thereby indicating that she was a Maryland lawyer. Att'y Griev. Comm'n v. Harris-Smith, 356 Md. 72, 737 A.2d 567 (1999).

When an attorney's business cards, which were available at various locations, signs and stationery did not indicate his practice was limited to federal court, nor did he advise clients that his practice was so limited, he violated the prior, similar Rule by making misleading communications about his services. Att'y Griev. Comm'n v. Alsafty, 379 Md. 1, 838 A.2d 1213 (2003).

Tasteless advertisement did not violate

Rule. — Attorney's advertisements regarding palimony suits, although deemed to be tasteless, were not in violation of this Rule. Att'y Griev. Comm'n v. Ficker, 319 Md. 305, 572 A.2d 501 (1990).

Unauthorized practice of law. — Respondent violated Md. Law. R. Prof. Conduct 5.5, 7.1, and 7.5 by establishing a law firm in Maryland and holding herself out as an attorney without being licensed to practice there. Potomac Valley Orthopaedic Assocs. v. Md. State Bd. of Physicians, 417 Md. 622, 12 A.3d 84 (2011).

Cited in Att'y Griev. Comm'n v. Carithers, 421 Md. 28, 25 A.3d 181 (2011).

Rule 7.2. Advertising.

(a) Subject to the requirements of Rules 7.1 and 7.3(b), a lawyer may advertise services through public media, such as a telephone directory, legal directory, newspaper or other periodical, outdoor, radio or television advertising, or through communications not involving in person contact.

(b) A copy or recording of an advertisement or such other communication shall be kept for at least three years after its last dissemination along with a record of when and where it was used.

(c) A lawyer shall not give anything of value to a person for recommending the lawyer's services, except that a lawyer may

(1) pay the reasonable cost of advertising or written communication permitted by this Rule;

(2) pay the usual charges of a legal service plan or a not-for-profit lawyer referral service;

(3) pay for a law practice purchased in accordance with Rule 1.17; and

(4) refer clients to a non-lawyer professional pursuant to an agreement not otherwise prohibited under these Rules that provides for the other person to refer clients or customers to the lawyer, if

(i) the reciprocal agreement is not exclusive, and

(ii) the client is informed of the existence and nature of the agreement.

(d) Any communication made pursuant to this Rule shall include the name of at least one lawyer responsible for its content.

(e) An advertisement or communication indicating that no fee will be charged in the absence of a recovery shall also disclose whether the client will be liable for any expenses.

Cross references. — Maryland Lawyers'
Rules of Professional Conduct, Rule 1.8(e).

(f) A lawyer, including a participant in an advertising group or lawyer referral service or other program involving communications concerning the lawyer's services, shall be personally responsible for compliance with the provisions of Rules 7.1, 7.2, 7.3, 7.4, and 7.5 and shall be prepared to substantiate such compliance.

COMMENT

[1] To assist the public in obtaining legal services, lawyers should be allowed to make known their services not only through reputation but also through organized information campaigns in the form of advertising. Advertising involves an active quest for clients, contrary to the tradition that a lawyer should not seek clientele. However, the public's need to know about legal services can be fulfilled in part through advertising. This need is particularly acute in the case of persons of moderate means who have not made extensive use of

legal services. The interest in expanding public information about legal services ought to prevail over considerations of tradition. Nevertheless, advertising by lawyers entails the risk of practices that are misleading or overreaching.

[2] This Rule permits public dissemination of information concerning a lawyer's name or firm name, address and telephone number; the kinds of services the lawyer will undertake; the basis on which the lawyer's fees are determined, including prices for specific services and payment and credit arrangements; a lawyer's foreign language ability; names of references and, with their consent, names of clients regularly represented; and other information that might invite the attention of those seeking legal assistance.

[3] Questions of effectiveness and taste in advertising are matters of speculation and subjective judgment. Some jurisdictions have had extensive prohibitions against television advertising, against advertising going beyond specified facts about a lawyer, or against "undignified" advertising. Television is now one of the most powerful media for getting information to the public, particularly persons of low and moderate income; prohibiting television advertising, therefore, would impede the flow of information about legal services to many sectors of the public. Limiting the information that may be advertised has a similar effect and assumes that the bar can accurately forecast the kind of information that the public would regard as relevant.

[4] Neither this Rule nor Rule 7.3 prohibits communications authorized by law, such as notice to members of a class in class action litigation.

[5] Paragraph (a) permits communication by mail to a specific individual as well as general mailings, but does not permit contact by telephone or in person delivery of written material except through the postal service or other delivery service.

Record of Advertising. — [6] Paragraph (b) requires that a record of the content and use of advertising be kept in order to facilitate enforcement of this Rule. It does not require that advertising be subject to review prior to dissemination. Such a requirement would be burdensome and expensive relative to its possible benefits, and may be of doubtful constitutionality.

Paying Others to Recommend a Lawyer. — [7] A lawyer is allowed to pay for advertising permitted by this Rule and for the purchase of a law practice in accordance with the provisions of Rule 1.17, but otherwise is not permitted to pay another person for channeling professional work. This restriction does not prevent an organization or person other than the lawyer from advertising or recommending

the lawyer's services. Thus, a legal aid agency or prepaid legal services plan may pay to advertise legal services provided under its auspices. Likewise, a lawyer may participate in not-for-profit lawyer referral programs and pay the usual fees charged by such programs. Paragraph (c) does not prohibit paying regular compensation to an assistant, such as a secretary, to prepare communications permitted by this Rule.

Assignments or Referrals from a Legal Services Plan or Lawyer Referral Service. — [8] A lawyer who accepts assignments or referrals from a legal services plan or referrals from a lawyer referral service must act reasonably to assure that the activities of the plan or service are compatible with the lawyer's professional obligations. See Rule 5.3. Legal service plans and lawyer referral services may communicate with prospective clients, but such communications must be in conformity with these Rules. Thus, advertising must not be false or misleading, as would be the case if the communications of a group advertising program or a group legal services plan would mislead prospective clients to think that it was lawyer referral service sponsored by a state agency or bar association. Nor could the lawyer allow in-person, telephonic, or real-time contacts that would violate Rule 7.3.

Reciprocal Referral Agreements with Non-lawyer Professionals. — [9] A lawyer may agree to refer clients to a non-lawyer professional, in return for the undertaking of that person to refer clients or customers to the lawyer to provide them with legal services. Such reciprocal referral arrangements must not be exclusive or otherwise interfere with the lawyer's professional judgment as to making referrals or as to providing substantive legal services. See Rules 2.1 and 5.4(c). The client must also be informed of the existence and nature of the referral agreement. Reciprocal referral agreements should not be of indefinite duration and should be reviewed periodically to determine whether they comply with these Rules. Conflicts of interest created by such arrangements are governed by Rule 1.7. Referral agreements between lawyers who are not in the same firm are governed by Rule 1.5(e).

Responsibility for Compliance. — [10] Every lawyer who participates in communications concerning the lawyer's services is responsible for assuring that the specified Rules are complied with and must be prepared to substantiate compliance with those Rules. That may require retaining records for more than the three years specified in paragraph (b) of this Rule.

Model Rules Comparison. — This Rule substantially retains existing Maryland language and does not adopt Ethics 2000 Amendments to the ABA Model Rules of Professional Conduct, with the exception of: 1) adding in substantial part ABA Rule 7.2(c)(4) as adopted by the ABA House of Delegates on August 13, 2002; 2) adding ABA Comment [7] (Comment [8] above); 3) adding ABA Comment [8] (Comment [9] above).

University of Baltimore Law Forum. — For article, "Code of Ethics Revisited," see 19.2 U. Balt. Law Forum 14 (1989).

For comment, "Lawyer Television Advertising—What's the Big Deal?," see 19.3 U. Balt. Law Forum 31 (1989).

Illegal contract claims. — The Rules of Professional Conduct are not statements of public policy on which an illegal contract claim may be founded. Son v. Margolius, Mallios, Davis, Rider & Tomar, 114 Md. App. 190, 689 A.2d 645 (1997).

Application of prohibition against solicitation must not offend constitutional guarantees. — A general prohibition against solicitation must be tested against the individual facts of each case to determine whether the application of that prohibition would offend constitutional guarantees of free speech and the right of association. Att'y Griev. Comm'n v. Gregory, 311 Md. 522, 536 A.2d 646 (1988).

Prohibition of in-person solicitation for pecuniary gain does not offend constitutional guarantees of free speech and the right of association. Att'y Griev. Comm'n v. Gregory, 311 Md. 522, 536 A.2d 646 (1988).

Referrals by nonlawyers. — Referrals by nonlawyers are permitted under certain conditions, but not where an attorney accepts a referral from a profit-making organization where the attorney is employed or selected by the organization, except where the organization has ultimate legal responsibility for the person referred. Att'y Griev. Comm'n v. Martin, 308 Md. 272, 518 A.2d 1050 (1987).

Law firm employees. — There is no violation of the prohibition against a lawyer's giving "anything of value to a person for recommending the lawyer's services" if the lawyer's employee engages in conduct in which the lawyer permissibly may directly engage. Att'y Griev. Comm'n v. Willis, 348 Md. 633, 705 A.2d 1121 (1998).

Improper solicitation of defendants in criminal cases. — Ninety-day suspension was warranted where attorney engaged in improper solicitation of defendants in criminal cases by in-person solicitation where attorney had earlier received a reprimand for similar conduct. Att'y Griev. Comm'n v. Gregory, 311 Md. 522, 536 A.2d 646 (1988).

Attorney's practice of initiating personal contacts with criminal defendants outside courtrooms where those defendants had just been advised of their right to counsel, and then introducing himself as an attorney, handing the defendants a letter soliciting their business, suggesting that they call him, and accepting employment from these defendants was improper. Att'y Griev. Comm'n v. Gregory, 311 Md. 522, 536 A.2d 646 (1988).

Rule 7.3. Direct Contact with Prospective Clients.

(a) A lawyer shall not by in-person, live telephone or real-time electronic contact solicit professional employment from a prospective client when a significant motive for the lawyer's doing so is the lawyer's pecuniary gain, unless the person contacted:

(1) is a lawyer; or

(2) has a family, close personal, or prior professional relationship with the lawyer.

(b) A lawyer shall not solicit professional employment from a prospective client by written, recorded or electronic communication or by in-person, telephone, or real-time electronic contract even when not otherwise prohibited by paragraph (a), if:

(1) the lawyer knows or reasonably should know that the physical, emotional or mental state of the prospective client is such that the prospective client could not exercise reasonable judgment in employing a lawyer;

(2) the prospective client has made known to the lawyer a desire not to be solicited by the lawyer; or

(3) the solicitation involves coercion, duress, or harassment.

(c) Every written, recorded, or electronic communication from a lawyer soliciting professional employment from a prospective client known to be in need of legal services in a particular matter shall include the words "Advertising Material" on the outside envelope, if any, and at the beginning and ending of any recorded or electronic communication, unless the recipient of the communication is a person specified in paragraphs (a)(1) or (a)(2).

(d) Notwithstanding the prohibitions in paragraph (a), a lawyer may participate with a prepaid or group legal service plan operated by an organization not owned or directed by the lawyer that uses in-person or telephone contact to solicit memberships or subscriptions for the plan from persons who are not known to need legal services in a particular matter covered by the plan.

Cross references. — For additional restrictions and requirements for certain communications, see Md. Code, Business Occupations and Professions Article, §§ 10-605.1 and 10-605.2.

COMMENT

[1] There is a potential for abuse inherent in direct in-person, live telephone or real-time electronic contact by a lawyer with a prospective client known to need legal services. These forms of contact between a lawyer and a prospective client subject the layperson to the private importuning of the trained advocate in a direct interpersonal encounter. The prospective client, who may already feel overwhelmed by the circumstances giving rise to the need for legal services, may find it difficult fully to evaluate all available alternatives with reasoned judgment and appropriate self-interest in the face of the lawyer's presence and insistence upon being retained immediately. The situation is fraught with the possibility of undue influence, intimidation, and over-reaching.

[2] This potential for abuse inherent in direct in-person, live telephone or real-time electronic solicitation of prospective clients justifies its prohibition, particularly since lawyer advertising and written and recorded communication permitted under Rule 7.2 offer alternative means of conveying necessary information to those who may be in need of legal services. Advertising and written and recorded communications which may be mailed or autodialed make it possible for a prospective client to be informed about the need for legal services, and about the qualifications of available lawyers and law firms, without subjecting the prospective client to direct in-person, telephone or real-time electronic persuasion that may overwhelm the client's judgment.

[3] The use of general advertising and written, recorded or electronic communications to transmit information from lawyer to prospective client, rather than direct in-person, live telephone or real-time electronic contact, will help to assure that the information flows cleanly as well as freely. The contents of advertisements and communications permitted under Rule 7.2 can be permanently recorded so that they cannot be disputed and may be shared with others who know the lawyer. This potential for informal review is itself likely to help guard against statements and claims that might constitute false and misleading communications, in violation of Rule 7.1. The contents of direct in-person, live telephone or real-time electronic conversations between a lawyer and a prospective client can be disputed and may not be subject to third-party scrutiny. Consequently, they are much more likely to approach (and occasionally cross) the dividing line between accurate representations and those that are false and misleading.

[4] There is far less likelihood that a lawyer would engage in abusive practices against an individual who is a former client, or with whom the lawyer has a close personal or family relationship, or in situations in which the lawyer is motivated by considerations other than the lawyer's pecuniary gain. Nor is there a serious potential for abuse when the person contacted is a lawyer. Consequently, the general prohibition in Rule 7.3(a) and the requirements of Rule 7.3(c) are not applicable in those situations. Also, paragraph (a) is not intended to prohibit a lawyer from participating in constitutionally protected activities of public or charitable legal-service organizations or bona fide political, social, civic, fraternal, employee or trade organizations whose purposes include providing or recommending legal services to its members or beneficiaries.

[5] But even permitted forms of solicitation can be abused. Thus, any solicitation which contains information which is false or mislead-

ing within the meaning of Rule 7.1, which involves coercion, duress or harassment within the meaning of Rule 7.3(b)(2), or which involves contact with a prospective client who has made known to the lawyer a desire not to be solicited by the lawyer within the meaning of Rule 7.3(b)(2) is prohibited. Moreover, if after sending a letter or other communication to a client as permitted by Rule 7.2 the lawyer receives no response, any further effort to communicate with the prospective client may violate the provisions of Rule 7.3(b).

[6] This Rule is not intended to prohibit a lawyer from contacting representatives of organizations or groups that may be interested in establishing a group or prepaid legal plan for their members, insureds, beneficiaries or other third parties for the purpose of informing such entities of the availability of and details concerning the plan or arrangement which the lawyer or lawyer's firm is willing to offer. This form of communication is not directed to a prospective client. Rather, it is usually addressed to an individual acting in a fiduciary capacity seeking a supplier of legal services for others who may, if they choose, become prospective clients of the lawyer. Under these circumstances, the activity which the lawyer undertakes in communicating with such representatives and the type of information transmitted to the individual are functionally similar to and serve the same purpose as advertising permitted under Rule 7.2.

[7] The requirement in Rule 7.3(c) that certain communications be marked "Advertising Material" does not apply to communications sent in response to requests of potential clients or their spokespersons or sponsors. General announcements by lawyers, including changes in personnel or office location, do not constitute communications soliciting professional employment from a client known to be in need of legal services within the meaning of this Rule.

[8] Paragraph (d) of this Rule permits a lawyer to participate with an organization which uses personal contact to solicit members for its group or prepaid legal service plan, provided that the personal contact is not undertaken by any lawyer who would be a provider of legal services through the plan. The organization must not be owned by or directed (whether as manager or otherwise) by any lawyer or law firm that participates in the plan. For example, paragraph (d) would not permit a lawyer to create an organization controlled directly or indirectly by the lawyer and use the organization for the in-person or telephone solicitation of legal employment of the lawyer through memberships in the plan or otherwise. The communication permitted by these organizations also must not be directed to a person known to need legal services in a particular matter, but is to be designed to inform potential plan members generally of another means of affordable legal services. Lawyers who participate in a legal service plan must reasonably assure that the plan sponsors are in compliance with Rules 7.1, 7.2 and 7.3(b). See 8.4(a).

Model Rules Comparison. — Rule 7.3 is substantially similar to the language of the Ethics 2000 Amendments to the ABA Model Rules of Professional Conduct, with the exception of retaining existing Maryland language in 7.3(b)(1) and accordingly redesignating the subsections of Rule 7.3(b).

University of Baltimore Law Forum. — For article, "Recent Developments," see 19.1 U. Balt. Law Forum 29 (1988).

For article, "Code of Ethics Revisited," see 19.2 U. Balt. Law Forum 14 (1989).

Application of prohibition must not offend constitutional guarantees. — A general prohibition against solicitation must be tested against the individual facts of each case to determine whether the application of that prohibition would offend constitutional guarantees of free speech and the right of association. Att'y Griev. Comm'n v. Gregory, 311 Md. 522, 536 A.2d 646 (1988).

Validity. — The prior, similar Rule, which improperly focuses solely on the condition of the recipient of the solicitation, has questionable validity. Unnamed Att'y v. Att'y Griev. Comm'n, 313 Md. 357, 545 A.2d 685 (1988).

Written modes of solicitation (as opposed to in-person solicitation) are protected by the First Amendment, regardless of the recipient's condition, so long as such communication is neither false, misleading, nor overreaching. Unnamed Att'y v. Att'y Griev. Comm'n, 313 Md. 357, 545 A.2d 685 (1988).

Insofar as former Code of Professional Responsibility DR 2-103 (B) constituted a blanket prohibition against targeted direct mail solicitation, it was unconstitutional. Unnamed Att'y v. Att'y Griev. Comm'n, 313 Md. 357, 545 A.2d 685 (1988).

Initiation of in-person contacts. — Attorneys violated professional conduct rules by initiating in-person contacts with prospective clients for the purpose of obtaining professional employment. Att'y Griev. Comm'n v. Franz, 355 Md. 752, 736 A.2d 339 (1999).

Improper solicitation of criminal defendants. — Ninety-day suspension was warranted where attorney engaged in improper solicitation of defendants in criminal cases by in-person solicitation where attorney had earlier received a reprimand for similar conduct.

Att'y Griev. Comm'n v. Gregory, 311 Md. 522, 536 A.2d 646 (1988).

Reprimand. — Where attorneys, within a short time of its occurrence, recognized the impropriety of their having made direct contact with the victims of a train accident and immediately withdrew as counsel for those clients, where they cooperated with those former clients and new counsel, where they neither charged, nor accepted, a fee for their work, and where they self reported their misconduct to the grievance commission, a reprimand was the appropriate sanction. Att'y Griev. Comm'n v. Franz, 355 Md. 752, 736 A.2d 339 (1999).

Rule 7.4. Communication of Fields of Practice.

(a) A lawyer may communicate the fact that the lawyer does or does not practice in particular fields of law, subject to the requirements of Rule 7.1. A lawyer shall not hold himself or herself out publicly as a specialist.

(b) A lawyer admitted to engage in patent practice before the United States Patent and Trademark Office may use the designation "Patent Attorney" or a substantially similar designation.

COMMENT

[1] This Rule permits a lawyer to indicate areas of practice in communications about the lawyer's services; for example, in a telephone directory or other advertising. If a lawyer practices only in such fields, or will not accept matters except in such fields, the lawyer is permitted so to indicate.

[2] Paragraph (b) recognizes the long-established policy of the Patent and Trademark Office for the designation of lawyers practicing before the Office.

Model Rules Comparison. — This Rule substantially retains existing Maryland language and does not adopt Ethics 2000 Amendments to the ABA Model Rules of Professional Conduct, with the exception of: 1) adding ABA Rule 7.4(c) (incorporated as Rule 7.4(b) above); 2) the first sentence of ABA Comment [2] (included as Comment [2] above).

Rule 7.5. Firm Names and Letterheads.

(a) A lawyer shall not use a firm name, letterhead or other professional designation that violates Rule 7.1. A trade name may be used by a lawyer in private practice if it does not imply a connection with a government agency or with a public or charitable legal services organization and is not otherwise in violation of Rule 7.1.

(b) A law firm with offices in more than one jurisdiction may use the same name in each jurisdiction, but identification of the lawyers in an office of the firm shall indicate the jurisdictional limitations on those not licensed to practice in the jurisdiction where the office is located.

(c) The name of a lawyer holding a public office shall not be used in the name of a law firm, or in communications on its behalf, during any substantial period in which the lawyer is not actively and regularly practicing with the firm.

(d) Lawyers may state or imply that they practice in a partnership or other organization only when that is the fact.

COMMENT

[1] A firm may be designated by the names of all or some of its members, by the names of deceased or retired members where there has been a continuing succession in the firm's identity or by a trade name such as the "ABC Legal Clinic." A firm may not be designated by the names of non-lawyers. See Rule 5.4. Although the United States Supreme Court has held that legislation may prohibit the use of trade names in professional practice, use of such names in law practice is acceptable so long as it is not misleading. It may be observed

that any firm name including the name of a deceased partner is, strictly speaking, a trade name. The use of such names to designate law firms has proven a useful means of identification. However, it is misleading to use the name of a lawyer not associated with the firm or a predecessor of the firm, or the name of a nonlawyer.

[2] A lawyer in private practice may not practice under a name which implies any connection with the government or any agency of the federal government, any state or any political subdivision, or with a public or charitable legal services organization. This is to prevent a situation where nonlawyers might conclude that they are dealing with an agency established or sanctioned by the government, or one funded by either the government or public contributions and thus charging lower fees. The use of any of the following ordinarily would violate this Rule:

(1) The proper name of a government unit, whether or not identified with the type of unit. Thus, a name could be the basis of a disciplinary proceeding if it included the designation "Annapolis" or "City of Annapolis," "Baltimore," or "Baltimore County," "Maryland," or "Maryland State" (which could be a violation as a confusing although mistaken reference to the state or under the third application of this instruction below).

(2) The generic name of any form of government unit found in the same area where the firm practices, e.g. national, state, county, or municipal.

(3) The name of or a reference to a college, university, or other institution of higher learning, regardless of whether it has a law school, unless the provider of legal higher learning.

For example, the names "Georgetown Legal Clinic (or "Law Office," etc.)" and "U.B. Legal Clinic (or "Law Office," etc.)" could both violate this Rule if used by unaffiliated organizations.

(4) The words "public," "government," "civic," "legal aid," "community," "neighborhood," or other words of similar import suggesting that the legal services offered are at least in part publicly funded. Although names such as "Neighborhood Legal Clinic of John Doe" might otherwise appear unobjectionable, the terms "legal aid," "community" and "neighborhood" have become so associated with public or charitable legal services organizations as to form the basis of disciplinary proceedings.

[3] Firm names which include geographical names which are not also government units, or adjectives merely suggesting the context of the practice (e.g., "urban," "rural") ordinarily would not violate Rule 7.5. The acceptability of the use of a proper or generic name of a government unit when coupled with an adjective or further description (beyond mere reference to the provision of legal services) should be judged by the general policy underlying Rule 7.5, and any doubt regarding the misleading connotations of a name may be resolved against use of the name.

[4] With regard to paragraph (d), lawyers sharing office facilities, but who are not in fact partners, may not denominate themselves as, for example, "Smith and Jones," for that title suggests partnership in the practice of law.

Model Rules Comparison. — This Rule substantially retains existing Maryland language and does not adopt Ethics 2000 Amendments to the ABA Model Rules of Professional Conduct, with the exception of changes to Comment [1].

Trade names. — The Court of Appeals lacks the jurisdiction to render advisory ethics opinions, and has no authority either to approve of or disapprove a contemplated trade name. In re Attorney's Use of Trade Name, 333 Md. 488, 635 A.2d 1338 (1994).

Misleading information. — An attorney violated professional conduct rules where she did not advise prospective clients that she was not admitted to practice in Maryland, and where her professional card gave an in-state address for her office, thereby indicating that she was a Maryland lawyer. Att'y Griev. Comm'n v. Harris-Smith, 356 Md. 72, 737 A.2d 567 (1999).

Disbarment was the appropriate sanction where an out-of-state attorney practiced law in the State of Maryland without a license, failed to acknowledge his jurisdictional limitations on his firm letterhead, acted against the interests of his purported clients during and after

the sale of their home to him, filed a bankruptcy petition on those clients' behalf, but without their consent or knowledge, and forged the signatures of the clients and another attorney in his office on court papers and filings, in violation of prior, similar Rules of Professional Conduct 1.7, 3.3, 5.5, 7.1, 7.5, and 8.4. Att'y Griev. Comm'n v. Johnson, 363 Md. 598, 770 A.2d 130 (2001).

Letterhead information. — Failure of a Maryland attorney to include on his letterhead that an attorney who was associated with him was not licensed to practice law in the state of Maryland constituted a violation of prior, similar Rule 7.1 and this Rule. Att'y Griev. Comm'n v. Brown, 353 Md. 271, 725 A.2d 1069 (1999).

Professional conduct rules were violated where an unadmitted attorney's letterhead created the false impression that the attorney was lawfully engaged in the practice of law in

Maryland from a principal office in the state, and where a letter implied that the attorney could settle a Maryland resident's claim. Att'y Griev. Comm'n v. Harper, 356 Md. 53, 737 A.2d 557 (1999).

Attorney grievance commission's exceptions to a hearing court's finding that an attorney violated subsection (a), prohibiting the use of firm names and letterhead in violation of prior, similar Rule 7.1, and § 10-602 of the Business Occupations and Professions Article, prohibiting the use of titles indicating authorization to practice, by failing to indicate on his letterhead that his practice was limited to the federal courts of Maryland, were sustained;

such violations were not alleged in the petition seeking the attorney's discipline. Att'y Griev. Comm'n v. Alsafty, 379 Md. 1, 838 A.2d 1213 (2003).

Unauthorized practice of law. — Respondent violated Md. Law. R. Prof. Conduct 5.5, 7.1, and 7.5 by establishing a law firm in Maryland and holding herself out as an attorney without being licensed to practice there. Att'y Griev. Comm'n v. Sucklal, 418 Md. 1, 12 A.3d 650 (2011).

Applied in Att'y Griev. Comm'n v. Mitchell, 386 Md. 386, 872 A.2d 720 (2005).

Cited in Att'y Griev. Comm'n v. Carithers, 421 Md. 28, 25 A.3d 181 (2011).

MAINTAINING THE INTEGRITY OF THE PROFESSION.

Rule 8.1. Bar Admission and Disciplinary Matters.

An applicant for admission or reinstatement to the bar, or a lawyer in connection with a bar admission application or in connection with a disciplinary matter, shall not:

(a) knowingly make a false statement of material fact; or

(b) fail to disclose a fact necessary to correct a misapprehension known by the person to have arisen in the matter, or knowingly fail to respond to a lawful demand for information from an admissions or disciplinary authority, except that this Rule does not require disclosure of information otherwise protected by Rule 1.6.

COMMENT

[1] The duty imposed by this Rule extends to persons seeking admission or reinstatement to the bar as well as to lawyers. Hence, if a person makes a material false statement in connection with an application for admission or for reinstatement, it may be the basis for subsequent disciplinary action if the person is admitted or reinstated, and in any event may be relevant in a subsequent admission application. The duty imposed by this Rule applies to a lawyer's own admission or discipline as well as that of others. Thus, it is a separate professional offense for a lawyer to knowingly make a misrepresentation or omission in connection with a disciplinary investigation of the lawyer's own conduct. This Rule also requires affirmative clarification of any misunderstanding on the part of the admissions or disciplinary authority of which the person involved becomes aware.

[2] The Court of Appeals has considered this Rule applicable when information is sought by the Attorney Grievance Commission from any

lawyer on any matter, whether or not the lawyer is personally involved. See *Attorney Grievance Commission v. Oswinkle,* 364 Md. 182 (2001).

[3] This Rule is subject to the provisions of the Fifth Amendment of the United States Constitution and corresponding provisions of state constitutions. A person relying on such a provision in response to a question, however, should do so openly and not use the right of nondisclosure as a justification for failure to comply with this Rule.

[4] A lawyer representing an applicant for admission to the bar, or representing a lawyer who is the subject of a disciplinary inquiry or proceeding, is governed by the rules applicable to the client-lawyer relationship.

Cross references. — Md. Rule 16-701(j) (defining "Reinstatement").

Model Rules Comparison. — This Rule substantially retains existing Maryland language with some further revisions and does not adopt Ethics 2000 Amendments to the ABA Model Rules of Professional Conduct.

Editor's note. — See note to Rule 1.1.

University of Baltimore Law Forum. — For discussion of the code of ethics, see 17, No. 1 U. Balt. Law Forum 31 (1986).

For note, *"Attorney Grievance Commission v. Gilbert:* Attorney Disbarred for Failure to Disclose Material Information on His Bar Application", see 17, No. 3 U. Balt. Law Forum 27 (1987).

For article, "The New Maryland Rules of Professional Conduct and Mediation: Perplexing Questions Answered and Perplexing Questions That Remain," see 36 U. Balt. L.F. 1 (2005).

Comparison with prior, similar Rule 8.4. — Dishonesty before disciplinary authorities could fall under both the narrow proscription of this Rule as well as under the broader proscription of prior, similar Rule 8.4. Att'y Griev. Comm'n v. Goldsborough, 330 Md. 342, 624 A.2d 503 (1993).

Bar admission applications. — For determining the materiality under former DR 1-101 (A) of an omission or false statement on a bar admission application, the standard was whether the omission had the effect of inhibiting the efforts of the bar to determine an applicant's fitness to practice law. Att'y Griev. Comm'n v. Gilbert, 307 Md. 481, 515 A.2d 454 (1986).

Material, deliberate omission. — Attorney's failure to disclose in his application for admission to the Maryland Bar that, although he had a Pennsylvania license and a Pennsylvania office, he worked full-time for a Baltimore corporation and only worked at his legal practice 10-15 hours per week was material, deliberate omission for which disbarment was the appropriate sanction. Att'y Griev. Comm'n v. Keehan, 311 Md. 161, 533 A.2d 278 (1987).

Written responses. — Where an attorney allegedly did not respond in writing to a request for a response to a complaint filed against him by the Grievance Commission of Maryland, it was held that he had submitted at least a partial response, in writing, and that the Rule, by its terms, did not indicate that a written response was mandated or even that there was a preference for such a response. Att'y Griev. Comm'n v. Jeter, 365 Md. 279, 778 A.2d 390 (2001).

Attorney's failure to respond in writing to bar counsel's request for information violated this Rule. Att'y Griev. Comm'n v. Daskalopoulos, 383 Md. 375, 859 A.2d 653 (2004).

In a disciplinary matter in Maryland that was not reciprocal in nature but that was based upon the attorney's 30-day suspension, with reinstatement conditioned upon a showing of fitness, in the District of Columbia, the attorney was suspended indefinitely for violating prior, similar Md. R. Prof. Conduct 8.1(b), 8.4(d), and the attorney's reinstatement to the Maryland bar was conditioned upon the attorney's reinstatement to the District of Columbia bar; the impact of the misconduct, which involved a refusal to respond to disciplinary charges in violation of D.C. R. Prof. Conduct 8.4(d), 8.1(b) and D.C. Bd. Prof. Resp. R. XI, § 2(b)(3), occurred in the District of Columbia, so the Maryland court decided to impose a suspension that, pursuant to Md. R. 16-713(a)(2), was not greater than the District of Columbia suspension. Att'y Griev. Comm'n v. Steinberg, 385 Md. 696, 870 A.2d 603 (2005).

No matter how busy a respondent attorney was, a tardy oral response to inquiries in a grievance matter did not excuse failure to respond as originally requested, particularly given the time constraints applicable to such investigations. Att'y Griev. Comm'n v. Kreamer, 387 Md. 503, 876 A.2d 79 (2005).

"Lawful demand" does not require subpoena. — Although the prior, similar Rule does not define a "lawful demand" from a disciplinary authority, it is identical to Rule 8.1 of the ABA Model Rules of Professional Conduct, and universally, the ABA Model Rule has been interpreted to require an attorney to respond to letters or telephone calls from the disciplinary authority without the use of a subpoena. Att'y Griev. Comm'n v. Fezell, 361 Md. 234, 760 A.2d 1108 (2000).

Failure to respond as grounds for sanction. — An attorney's knowing failure to respond to a lawful demand for information from a disciplinary authority constituted grounds for sanction. Att'y Griev. Comm'n v. Shaw, 354 Md. 636, 732 A.2d 876 (1999).

Suspended attorney was disbarred because of his later (1) unjustified misappropriation of trust funds by not paying the clients' medical providers (as he had promised he would do) from clients' share settlement he retained in cash after he got clients' endorsements on settlement checks, received payable to him and to the clients, cashed the checks with the clients at a liquor store cashing service, retained cash to pay his one-third fee (that he reduced) and to pay listed medical providers according to a handwritten distribution summary given to the clients, and distributed the clients' share to them; (2) failure to have or to use an attorney trust account at a proper financial institution; and (3) failure to respond to the disciplinary committee's investigation or petition, or to the hearing judge's conclusions. The attorney's misappropriation of trust money was serious professional misconduct and was embezzlement, fraudulent misappropriation by a fiduciary, under 7-113 of the Criminal Law Article, representing professional misconduct that violated prior, similar Rule 8.4(b)-(c); and his conducted also violated Rules 1.15, 8.1; Maryland Rules R. 16-812,

16-603, 16-604, and §§ 10-302(a), 10-306 of the Business Occupations and Professions Article. Att'y Griev. Comm'n v. Prichard, 386 Md. 238, 872 A.2d 81 (2005).

Attorney was disbarred as he violated the prior, similar Rule where he knowingly failed to respond to the Attorney Grievance Commission of Maryland's lawful demand for information. Att'y Griev. Comm'n v. Velasquez, 380 Md. 651, 846 A.2d 422 (2004).

When an attorney did not respond to a complaint alleging violations of the Rules of Professional Conduct against him, to letters from bar counsel, or to the attempts of the grievance commission's investigator to interview him, he violated prior, similar Md. R. Prof. Conduct 8.1. Att'y Griev. Comm'n v. Sullivan, 369 Md. 650, 801 A.2d 1077 (2002).

Attorney was disbarred as his failure to respond to the Attorney Grievance Commission of Maryland's letters and to attend a scheduled interview violated the prior, similar Rule. Att'y Griev. Comm'n v. Brown, 380 Md. 661, 846 A.2d 428 (2004).

Where the attorney abandoned his representation of the client and refused to engage in further communications with the client after terminating his representation via electronic mail, and the attorney engaged in other misconduct which included not being admitted to practice in forums where the attorney was representing the client and not responding to the disciplinary commission's lawful demands for information regarding the investigation of the attorney, disbarment was warranted. Att'y Griev. Comm'n v. Logan, 390 Md. 313, 888 A.2d 359 (2005).

Attorney violated (b) because he admitted that he did not respond in a timely manner to the request of bar counsel for information about the attorney's representation of clients who filed a grievance against the attorney. Att'y Griev. Comm'n v. Guida, 391 Md. 33, 891 A.2d 1085 (2006).

Where the attorney violated Rule 16-609 and Md. R. Prof. Conduct 1.15(a) and (b) and subsection (b) of this Rule based on the attorney's failure to fully cooperate with the investigation and based on the attorney's inexperience and lack of knowledge in maintaining trust accounts, the attorney was suspended for 30 days. Att'y Griev. Comm'n v. Obi, 393 Md. 643, 904 A.2d 422 (2006).

In an attorney disciplinary matter, regardless of what the attorney believed about the necessity of documents requested, because the attorney knowingly failed to respond to a lawful demand from a disciplinary authority in connection with a disciplinary matter, the attorney violated (b). Att'y Griev. Comm'n v. Obi, 393 Md. 643, 904 A.2d 422 (2006).

Attorney violated (b) when he knowingly and repeatedly failed to respond to lawful demand for information from the officer of Bar Counsel. Att'y Griev. Comm'n v. Butler, 395 Md. 1, 909 A.2d 226 (2006).

Attorney violated this Rule by failing to respond timely to the Attorney Grievance Commission's requests for information relating to the three complaints. The Commission sent out five letters asking for the attorney to respond as well as attempted telephone contact, to which the attorney did not respond. Att'y Griev. Comm'n v. Steinberg, 395 Md. 337, 910 A.2d 429 (2006).

Attorney was suspended for thirty days for withdrawing part of a retainer fee from her escrow account before earning the fee in violation of Md. R. Prof. Conduct 1.15(a) and § 10-306 of the Business Occupations and Professions Article and for making a billing error that resulted in a refund being owed to the clients under Md. R. Prof. Conduct 1.15(b) and 1.16(d). Additionally, the attorney's inexcusable and untimely delay in responding to a bar counsel's request for information in answer to allegations made by two disgruntled clients in an adoption matter violated Md. R. Prof. Conduct 8.1(b). Att'y Griev. Comm'n v. Rees, 396 Md. 248, 913 A.2d 68 (2006).

Attorney's misconduct in abusing the trust that the client placed in the attorney by placing the client's retainer check in the attorney's operating account rather than an attorney trust account, spending that money which belonged to the client on the attorney, in refusing to promptly refund to the client money that attorney admittedly owed to the client despite the client's refund request, and in failing to promptly answer bar counsel's request for information about the matter warranted the attorney's indefinite suspension. Att'y Griev. Comm'n v. McCulloch, 397 Md. 674, 919 A.2d 660 (2007).

Attorney's conduct violated (b) and subjected her to sanction when she ignored letters from the Maryland Attorney Grievance Commission, there was evidence that she had received the letters, and she filed no answer even though she told the Commission's investigator that she believed that she had mailed in an answer to both of the complaints that were the subject of an action for disciplinary or remedial action. Att'y Griev. Comm'n v. McCulloch, 404 Md. 388, 946 A.2d 1009 (2008).

Because Bar Counsel sent four letters to an attorney before he replied in an incomplete fashion nearly three months after Bar Counsel's initial letter, the untimely response did not excuse the attorney's failure to timely respond even though the attorney could have ultimately responded thoroughly and openly to the letters; Bar Counsel's persistence will not absolve an attorney of the responsibility to make a reasonably prompt reply. Att'y Griev.

Comm'n v. Taylor, 405 Md. 697, 955 A.2d 755 (2008).

Attorney violated this rule when the attorney failed to response to Bar Counsel's three letters requesting information related to the disciplinary investigation. Att'y Griev. Comm'n v. Bleecker, 414 Md. 147, 994 A.2d 928 (2010).

Hearing judge erred in failing to find a violation of this Rule, as the evidence showed the attorney did not produce financial records despite two clear and specific demands by Bar Counsel. Att'y Griev. Comm'n v. Khandpur, 421 Md. 1, 25 A.3d 165 (2011).

Failure to correct "misapprehensions." — Attorney violated the prior, similar Rule where an attorney knew that there was a question regarding his representation, fee arrangement, and disbursement of settlement proceeds to the client, was on notice of misrepresentations of Bar Counsel and its investigator, and did not make the appropriate disclosures to correct Bar Counsel's "misapprehensions" throughout the investigation. Att'y Griev. Comm'n v. Ellison, 384 Md. 688, 867 A.2d 259 (2005).

Cooperation with bar counsel — Attorney's conduct in violating multiple Maryland Rules of Professional Conduct in representing two separate clients warranted the attorney's disbarment. Although the attorney cited the attorney's cooperation with bar counsel regarding the investigation in the attorney's misconduct, the cooperation was not a mitigating factor since of this Rule required that cooperation. Att'y Griev. Comm'n v. Webster, 402 Md. 448, 937 A.2d 161 (2007).

Attorney violated this Rule because the attorney did not respond to requests for information from the Attorney Grievance Commission about a client's disciplinary complaint. Att'y Griev. Comm'n v. De La Paz, 418 Md. 534, 16 A.3d 181 (2011).

Deliberate misrepresentations to disciplinary counsel. — Attorney's conduct in showing disciplinary counsel ledgers that misrepresented the fact that the attorney was using the attorney's escrow account holding client funds to pay the attorney's law practice operating expenses violated this Rule, as an attorney was not permitted to make false statements in connection with a disciplinary matter, and that violation along with other violations warranted the attorney's disbarment. Att'y Griev. Comm'n v. Nussbaum, 401 Md. 612, 934 A.2d 1 (2007).

Attorney violated (a) because (1) the attorney represented to Bar Counsel that a client had retained the attorney personally (as opposed to the firm by which the attorney was employed) when the attorney knew that the client had executed a written contract with the firm and the attorney had signed the same

contract on behalf of the firm, and (2) the attorney misrepresented to Bar Counsel that the client had authorized the attorney to change the payee on a check the client issued to the firm. Att'y Griev. Comm'n v. Elliott, 417 Md. 659, 12 A.3d 105 (2011).

Failure to respond as grounds for reprimand. — An attorney's knowing failure to respond to a lawful demand for information from a disciplinary authority constituted grounds for reprimand. Prior, similar Rule 8.1 places an obligation on an attorney to respond to a lawful demand from the bar counsel, and the Rule does not distinguish between attorneys who fail to respond due to dilatoriness, on the one hand, and those on the other hand, who intentionally fail to respond. An attorney's obligation to respond to these lawful demands applies when the attorney upon whom the demand is made is the focus of the investigation or when the investigation relates to the conduct of another attorney. Att'y Griev. Comm'n v. Oswinkle, 364 Md. 182, 772 A.2d 267 (2001).

Attorney violated the prior, similar Rule where he resisted efforts to investigate complaints against him, and then attempted to justify his recalcitrance by a formalistic interpretation of procedural rules. Att'y Griev. Comm'n v. Fezell, 361 Md. 234, 760 A.2d 1108 (2000).

Four month delay in acknowledging request for information. — Lawyer was reprimanded for violations of Md. R. Prof. Conduct 1.1, 1.3, 8.1(b) for his negligent handing of a client's case, and his four month delay in acknowledging Bar Counsel's request for information; the commission's request for an indefinite suspension was rejected because there was no reason to believe that the lawyer's misconduct would have been repeated, and the lawyer was honest with his client about his mistakes, advised the client to seek representation for a claim against him, and entered into a settlement in which he paid $ 30,000 to the client from his own funds without resort to his malpractice carrier. The case did not involve either an obstinate refusal to cooperate or a denial of access to relevant documents, and the court was able to protect the public and deter other lawyers from misconduct without disrupting the lawyer's practice. Att'y Griev. Comm'n v. Queen, 407 Md. 556, 967 A.2d 198 (2009).

Failure to communicate with client. — An attorney was reprimanded where she failed to take action to secure her client's interest in a retirement plan until several months following the client's complaint to the Grievance Commission and where she failed to communicate with her client and explain adequately that she would not be taking any further action on the client's behalf. Att'y Griev.

Comm'n v. Tolar, 357 Md. 569, 745 A.2d 1045 (2000).

An attorney's pursuit of a claim for the torts of either criminal conversation or adultery was pursuit of a baseless claim that constituted misconduct. Moreover, the attorney's failure to communicate with the client after accepting representation and his failure to respond to letters from the bar counsel was also misconduct; the combination of those instances of misconduct along with misappropriation of client funds warranted disbarment. Att'y Griev. Comm'n v. James, 385 Md. 637, 870 A.2d 229 (2005).

Attorney's conduct violated (b) where (1) her fee agreement called for a flat fee to handle a divorce case; (2) she filed the case but was unable to serve the defendant and eventually abandoned the representation without advising the client that the case was dismissed for lack of prosecution; and (3) she did only a portion of the work required, did not achieve the client's objective, and kept the entire fee. The attorney did not earn the entire fee, was not entitled to retain all of it, and her failure to refund a portion of it violated Md. R. Prof. Conduct 1.16 (d). Att'y Griev. Comm'n v. McCulloch, 404 Md. 388, 946 A.2d 1009 (2008).

Mishandling escrow account. — Indefinite suspension was appropriate sanction for attorney's mishandling of escrow account, including the failure to pay claims due from the account and the failure to refund moneys to clients. Att'y Griev. Comm'n v. Singleton, 311 Md. 1, 532 A.2d 157 (1987).

When an attorney acted as an escrow agent for a client which purportedly funded high-risk loans, and the attorney removed commitment fees deposited in the escrow account and disbursed them to parties unrelated to a contemplated loan, rather than either returning them to the depositors or disbursing them to parties providing loans, he violated the prior, similar Rule when, after the grievance commission requested documents relating to allegations that he had failed to return commitment fees, he did not provide those documents. Att'y Griev. Comm'n v. Smith, 376 Md. 202, 829 A.2d 567 (2003).

Attorney who failed to make any showing regarding how disclosure of bank records would have prejudiced the client whose funds the attorney was suspected of having misappropriated could not convincingly claim that confidentiality considerations precluded cooperation with a disciplinary investigation. Att'y Griev. Comm'n v. Zdravkovich, 381 Md. 680, 852 A.2d 82 (2004).

Clear and convincing evidence was found that an attorney violated this Rule by converting a client's personal injury protection fund monies to her personal use, having insufficient funds in her escrow account to pay the client's outstanding claims for reimbursement from such fund, and otherwise converting to her own use the fund, which should have been held in trust for the client. Disbarment was the sanction imposed, because the attorney did not protect her client's interests when she converted the funds and denied doing so, which constituted an intentional misrepresentation of a material fact in connection with a disciplinary matter. Att'y Griev. Comm'n v. Cherry-Mahoi, 388 Md. 124, 879 A.2d 58 (2005).

Alcoholism, drug addiction and mental disorders. — An indefinite suspension was the proper sanction in the case of a misappropriation of client funds caused by alcoholism; however, in the future, absent truly compelling circumstances, alcoholism will usually not be permitted to mitigate where an attorney commits a violation of ethical or legal rules which would ordinarily warrant disbarment. Att'y Griev. Comm'n v. Kenney, 339 Md. 578, 664 A.2d 854 (1995).

Violation and mitigating factor shown. — Attorney violated/Aa(b) by failing to respond to Bar Counsel's demand for information, and the attorney established his multiple sclerosis as a mitigating factor for his violation of (b). Att'y Griev. Comm'n v. Patterson, — Md. —, — A.3d — (Sept. 21, 2011).

Testimony found credible. — Attorney's exception to a hearing judge's finding that he had violated this Rule was overruled where the hearing judge had had the opportunity to weigh the credibility of the witnesses and had found an investigator's testimony regarding the attorney's statements to be credible. Att'y Griev. Comm'n v. Mba-Jonas, 402 Md. 334, 936 A.2d 839 (2007).

Finding that attorney did not fraudulently obtain duplicate driver's license not clearly erroneous. — In an attorney disciplinary matter, it was held that the attorney violated Md. R. Prof. Conduct 3.3 by filing expungement petitions for a client knowing that the client's charges were ineligible for expungement and, as a result, he was suspended from the practice of law for 60 days. Additionally, the findings and conclusions of the hearing officer that the attorney did not fraudulently obtain a duplicate driver's license after having his original license taken away at a sobriety checkpoint were found not to be clearly erroneous, and no deficiencies were found with regard to the allegations in the petition providing sufficient notice to the attorney of the charges against him. Att'y Griev. Comm'n v. Tanko, 408 Md. 404, 969 A.2d 1010 (2009).

Thirty-day suspension. — Attorney was suspended for 30 days for violating Md. R. Prof. Conduct 1.3, 1.4, 8.1(b), and 8.4(d) after the attorney failed to prepare an eligible domestic relations order for client one, and failed to timely prepare a consent order for client two, and then submitted it to opposing counsel and the trial court without allowing client two to review it, since there were mitigating factors, the attorney had expressed remorse, and there was testimony that the conduct was out of the attorney's character. Att'y Griev. Comm'n v. Hill, 398 Md. 95, 919 A.2d 1194 (2007).

One-year suspension was proper sanction. — Attorney was suspended from the practice of law for a period of one year because of failure to cooperate with bar counsel in violation of the prior, similar Rule, performing services in an incompetent manner in violation of prior, similar Rule 1.1, charging an excessive fee in violation of prior, similar Rule 1.5, and engaging in conduct prejudicial to the administration of justice in violation of prior, similar Rule 8.4. Att'y Griev. Comm'n v. Shaw, 363 Md. 1, 766 A.2d 1028 (2001).

Indefinite suspension was proper sanction. — Where respondent attorney's representation of four clients was marked by serious neglect and inattention; where he failed to return a fee which was unearned for a period of nine months; where he failed to timely remit funds he received on behalf of a client; where he failed to communicate with his clients; and where, in connection with the investigation of three of the complaints, respondent failed to answer Bar Counsel's requests for information, the proper sanction was that the attorney be indefinitely suspended from the practice of law, with the right to apply for reinstatement after the suspension had been in effect for six months, conditioned upon his payment of all costs and upon the monitoring of respondent's practice. Att'y Griev. Comm'n v. David, 331 Md. 317, 628 A.2d 178 (1993).

Indefinite suspension was appropriate where attorney was retained to represent a client in filing for alien labor certifications for three of its employees, but where the attorney never prepared or filed an application for one employee and prepared but did not file applications for the other two, where he provided his client with altered documents making it appear he had done the work, and where the attorney never refunded the money paid to him and refused to cooperate with the investigation of his actions. Att'y Griev. Comm'n v. Koven, 361 Md. 337, 761 A.2d 881 (2000).

Indefinite suspension was appropriate sanction where attorney violated prior, similar Md. R. Prof. Conduct 8.1 by failing to respond to bar counsel's repeated requests for information in connection with investigation of complaints, which further violated prior, similar Md. R. Prof. Conduct 8.4 as conduct prejudicial to the administration of justice; failure to respond exacerbated other violations of the Maryland Rules of Professional Conduct. Att'y

Griev. Comm'n v. Harrington, 367 Md. 36, 785 A.2d 1260 (2001).

Indefinite suspension with right to apply for reinstatement after six months was the sanction imposed on an attorney who knowingly allowed trust account to be overdrawn and failed to respond to bar counsel inquiries; the court cautioned the attorney that allegations of suffering from depression would have to be addressed if and when the attorney sought reinstatement, as this could affect the capacity to practice law. Att'y Griev. Comm'n v. Rose, 383 Md. 385, 859 A.2d 659 (2004).

Although an attorney in a similar case had only been reprimanded after having similarly abandoned a client in a divorce case, the more severe sanction of indefinite suspension was the best way to protect the public where the mitigators present in the earlier case had not been shown to be present, where there had been no expressions of remorse from the attorney, and where, moreover, the attorney had not even respondent to inquiries in early stages of the investigation. Att'y Griev. Comm'n v. Kovacic, 389 Md. 233, 884 A.2d 673 (2005).

Attorney was indefinitely suspended from the practice of law for violating Md. R. Prof. Conduct 1.3, 1.4, 1.16(d), 3.2, 8.1(b), and 8.4(d) in connection with the attorney's representation of a client in a bankruptcy matter. The complaint could not be dismissed based on the complainant's request because the evidence did not fail to show sanctionable professional misconduct. Att'y Griev. Comm'n v. Lee, 393 Md. 546, 903 A.2d 895 (2006).

Attorney was indefinitely suspended for violating Md. R. Prof. Conduct 1.1, 1.3, 1.15(a) and (b), 8.1(b), and 8.4(d), Md. R. 16-609, and § 10-306 of the Business Occupations and Professions Article, in connection with handling of client funds in connection with an estate matter. Att'y Griev. Comm'n v. Goff, 399 Md. 1, 922 A.2d 554 (2007).

Attorney's failure to respond to a disciplinary investigation filed after the client alleged that the attorney violated professional conduct rules in representing the client in personal injury and bankruptcy matters violated (b). As a result of that misconduct and other related misconduct, the proper sanction was the attorney's indefinite suspension from the practice of law. Att'y Griev. Comm'n v. Nichols, 405 Md. 207, 950 A.2d 778 (2008).

Attorney was suspended indefinitely because his conduct in connection with an estate led to significant delay in closing the estate and violated Md. R. Prof. Conduct 1.1, 1.3, 8.1(a) and (b), and 8.4(a) and (d); the attorney owed the heirs to the estate competent and diligent representation but did not carry out either obligation, and indefinite suspension was the appropriate sanction due to the number and sort of violations, the mitigating factors, and the attorney's seeming failure to follow through on his promise to the hearing judge that he would attempt to "make things right" in the matter. Att'y Griev. Comm'n v. Pawlak, 408 Md. 288, 969 A.2d 311 (2009).

Attorney was indefinitely suspended from practice of law for violating Md. R. Prof. Conduct 1.8, 1.15, 8.4, and this Rule, Rules 16-607 and 16-609, and § 10-306 of the Business Occupations and Professional Article, when the attorney, inter alai, misrepresented to Bar Counsel that certain expenses were paid from personal funds rather than escrow funds. Att'y Griev. Comm'n v. McLaughlin, 409 Md. 304, 974 A.2d 315 (2009).

Disbarment required. — Willful misconduct of attorney where there was no causal relation between the misconduct and alcoholism and no evidence of any extenuating circumstances for misconduct warranted disbarment. Att'y Griev. Comm'n v. Kolodner, 321 Md. 545, 583 A.2d 724 (1991).

Representations and omissions made by an attorney in connection with his application for admission to the Bar of this State violated prior, similar Rules 8.1 and 8.4 of the Maryland Rules of Professional Conduct and warranted disbarment. Att'y Griev. Comm'n v. Joehl, 335 Md. 83, 642 A.2d 194 (1994).

Disbarment of attorney was appropriate where there were serious and repeated violations of the prior, similar Rule and other provisions of the prior, similar Maryland Rules of Professional Conduct. Att'y Griev. Comm'n v. Milliken, 348 Md. 486, 704 A.2d 1225 (1998).

Disbarment was ordered where an attorney violated prior, similar Md. R. Prof. Conduct 1.15, 8.1, and 8.4, and Md. R. 16-607, and had previously been sanctioned, receiving an indefinite suspension with the right to reapply in not less than six months for conduct amounting to negligent misappropriation of client funds. Att'y Griev. Comm'n v. Powell, 369 Md. 462, 800 A.2d 782 (2002).

Disbarment was the proper sanction for an attorney who dragged out representation of two different clients for many years, dooming their causes by failure to comply with applicable laws, and pretended to be continuing representation efforts, in one case, even falsifying a letter after the fact to give the impression that the client had received proper communications; the attorney had also failed to notify clients of a suspension and make other arrangements with them, and to supply information needed by a grievance commission investigator. Att'y Griev. Comm'n v. Davis, 375 Md. 131, 825 A.2d 430 (2003).

When an attorney acted as an escrow agent for a client which purportedly funded high-risk loans, and the attorney removed commitment fees deposited in the escrow account and disbursed them to parties unrelated to a contemplated loan, rather than either returning them to the depositors or disbursing them to parties providing loans, and failed to provide requested information to the grievance commission, he violated prior, similar Md. R. Prof. Conduct 1.15, 8.1, and 8.4, §§ 10-306 and 10-606 of the Business Occupations and Professions Article, and Rule 16-609 of the Maryland Rules of Procedure, and, given the absence of mitigating circumstances, disbarment was the appropriate sanction. Att'y Griev. Comm'n v. Smith, 376 Md. 202, 829 A.2d 567 (2003).

Attorney was disbarred, despite the mitigating factors of an absence of a prior disciplinary record and relative inexperience, for violating prior, similar Md. R. Prof. Conduct 1.5(c), 1.15(b) and (c), 8.1(b), and 8.4(c) and (d), and Md. R. 16-606 and 16-609 in his intentionally dishonest conduct towards a third-party assignee/healthcare provider during the representation of a client in a personal injury claim and Maryland Bar Counsel and its investigator in the course of investigating the assignee's complaint. Att'y Griev. Comm'n v. Ellison, 384 Md. 688, 867 A.2d 259 (2005).

Where the attorney, among other things, intentionally misappropriated client funds, forged a client's signature on a settlement check, lied under oath, and represented a client when the attorney was not licensed to do so, the attorney was disbarred for violating former, similar Md. R. Prof. Conduct 1.2(a), 1.3, 1.5(c), 1.15(a), (b), 3.3(a), 5.5, 8.1(a), (b), 8.4(a), (b), (c), (d), Md. R. 16-604, and §§ 10-304, -306 of the Business Occupations and Professions Article Att'y Griev. Comm'n v. Kapoor, 391 Md. 505, 894 A.2d 502 (2006).

In an action in which petitioner, the Attorney Grievance Commission of Maryland, acting pursuant to Rule 16-751, filed a petition for disciplinary or remedial action against respondent attorney, the appropriate sanction was disbarment where the court found that, as a matter of law, respondent violated Md. R. Prof. Conduct 1.3, 1.4, 1.16, and 8.1; respondent violated Rule 1.16 in failing to inform the client that he was shutting the doors to his law practice and failing to return to the client her documents and photographs. Att'y Griev. Comm'n v. Baker, 396 Md. 15, 912 A.2d 651 (2006).

In an action in which petitioner, the Attorney Grievance Commission of Maryland, acting pursuant to Rule 16-751, filed a petition for disciplinary or remedial action against respondent attorney, the appropriate sanction was disbarment where the court found that, as a matter of law, respondent violated Md. R. Prof. Conduct 1.4 in failing to address a client's request for information as well as Md. R. Prof. Conduct 8.1 in failing to answer the repeated queries of Bar Counsel. Att'y Griev. Comm'n v. Baker, 396 Md. 15, 912 A.2d 651 (2006).

State supreme court found that the attorney's misconduct, as charged in the grievance commission's petition and supported by the trial court's findings of fact and conclusions of law, warranted disbarment; the evidence established that the attorney failed to act with reasonable diligence and promptness in representing a client in a divorce case, that the attorney failed to keep the client reasonably informed about the status of the representation and did not respond to reasonable requests for information, that the attorney failed to respond to lawful demands for information from disciplinary counsel, and that the totality of the attorney's conduct was prejudicial to the administration of justice. Att'y Griev. Comm'n v. Hodgson, 396 Md. 1, 912 A.2d 640 (2006).

Attorney was disbarred after the court found that the attorney violated Md. R. Prof. Conduct 8.1(a) and 8.4(c) when the attorney executed a transfer authorization that changed the title of an account the attorney had with the attorney's ex-wife from ownership as tenants in common to sole ownership in the attorney's name following the death of the ex-wife. Att'y Griev. Comm'n v. Harris, 403 Md. 142, 939 A.2d 732 (2008).

Attorney's conduct, while the attorney was decertified, of failing to respond to lawful demands for information from the state attorney disciplinary commission violated Md. R. Prof. Conduct 8.1. As a result of (1) that misconduct, (2) the violations of other professional conduct rules, and (3) all occurring at a time when the attorney was decertified, the state's highest court had little choice but to disbar the attorney. Att'y Griev. Comm'n v. Walker, 405 Md. 3, 948 A.2d 1263 (2008).

Attorney's misconduct warranted disbarment, as the attorney engaged in the unauthorized practice of law in violation of (b) by representing another person in a real estate matter while the attorney's license to practice law was suspended. Disbarment was reasonable since the attorney's conduct was punishable by time in jail, a fine, or both pursuant to § 10-606(a)(3) of the Business Occupations and Professions Article and the attorney had also failed to respond to bar counsel's lawful demand for information, which was another violation of (b). Att'y Griev. Comm'n v. Shryock, 408 Md. 105, 968 A.2d 593 (2009).

Attorney was disbarred for violating, inter alia, this Rule, after the attorney failed to return Bar Counsel's telephone messages during an investigation in the client's complaints. Att'y Griev. Comm'n v. Kwarteng, 411 Md. 652, 984 A.2d 865 (2009).

Attorney violated this rule by failing to timely respond to Bar Counsel's requests for information despite being granted two extensions and failing to produce a file duirng an interview, as requested ahead of time; the attorney was disbarred for violating this rule along with Md. Law. R. Prof. Conduct 1.1, 1.2(a), 1.3, 1.4(a), 1.16(d). and 8.4(a), (c), and (d). Att'y Griev. Comm'n v. Fox, 417 Md. 504, 11 A.3d 762 (2010).

Attorney was disbarred for violating (b) and Md. Law. R. Prof. Conduct 1.3, 1.4(a) and (b), 1.15(a), (c), and (d), 1.16(d), and 8.4(a) and (d), after the attorney received advance fee payments from two clients, deposited the money in a personal account, rather than a trust account, having not earned the fees, and abandoned the clients without performing work for the clients. Att'y Griev. Comm'n v. Lara, 418 Md. 355, 14 A.3d 650 (2011).

Four criteria in evaluating petition for readmission to Bar. — Four principal criteria have to be evaluated in a petition for readmission to the Maryland Bar: (1) the nature and circumstances of petitioner's original misconduct; (2) petitioner's subsequent conduct and reformation; (3) petitioner's present character; and (4) petitioner's present qualifications and competence to practice law. In re Keehan, 342 Md. 121, 674 A.2d 510 (1996).

Disbarred attorney, in light of evidence exhibiting compliance with readmission criteria except as to his present qualifications and competence to practice law, demonstrated his fitness to become a member of the Maryland Bar, but only after taking and passing the regular comprehensive Maryland Bar examination. In re Keehan, 342 Md. 121, 674 A.2d 510 (1996).

Rule violations shown. — An attorney's failure to maintain separate accounts for the deposit of money advanced on behalf of his clients for future representation of those clients, his failure to maintain trust accounts, and his failure to cooperate with the Grievance Board constituted rules violations. Att'y Griev. Comm'n v. Briscoe, 357 Md. 554, 745 A.2d 1037 (2000).

As a matter of law an attorney violated conduct rules where he did not describe his contingency fee in writing, failed to deposit settlement funds into any account, failed to pay bills as he had promised, and failed to cooperate with the Grievance Commission. Att'y Griev. Comm'n v. Briscoe, 357 Md. 554, 745 A.2d 1037 (2000).

There was clear and convincing evidence that respondent violated the prior, similar Rule by knowingly making false representations of material facts and failing to timely respond to demands for information from bar counsel where an attorney, when asked to explain the cause of the overdraft on his attorney trust account, first delayed in providing the requested records and then, in a letter, made false statements of material fact to bar counsel concerning the transactions. Att'y Griev. Comm'n v. Powell, 369 Md. 462, 800 A.2d 782 (2002).

Attorney who admitted to failing to respond to investigators and to lying to the inquiry panel about placing a retainer in her escrow account was properly found by the hearing judge to have violated the prior, similar Rule, but he erred in not also finding violation of other provisions of this Rule. Att'y Griev. Comm'n v. Duvall, 373 Md. 482, 819 A.2d 343 (2003).

Attorney violated the prior, similar Rule, as the attorney misrepresented to bar counsel that a client was to come back to the attorney's office and sign paperwork, and that the client was to come back to the attorney's office prior to the filing of a bankruptcy petition to pay the attorney a fee. Att'y Griev. Comm'n v. Granger, 374 Md. 438, 823 A.2d 611 (2003).

Attorney violated Md. R. Prof. Conduct 1.3, 1.4(a), (b), 8.1 and 8.4(d) when she failed to administratively close a client's asylum application and refile it in proper form as directed by the immigration judge and the client, and failed to respond to requests for information in connection with the related disciplinary investigation. Indefinite suspension was proper given the egregious nature of the attorney's misconduct and her failure to present anything by way of mitigation to the appellate court. Att'y Griev. Comm'n v. Brisbon, 385 Md. 667, 870 A.2d 586 (2005).

Attorney violated this Rule when he failed to respond to Bar Counsel's reasonable demands for information relating to a complaint made by a former divorce client. Att'y Griev. Comm'n v. Rose, 391 Md. 101, 892 A.2d 469 (2006), cert. denied, 2006 U.S. LEXIS 5734, 166 L. Ed. 2d 22 (U.S. 2006).

Where the attorney forged the client's signature on a check, where the attorney was dishonest in communicating with bar counsel during the course of the disciplinary investigation, and where the attorney lied on several occasions during disciplinary proceedings, the attorney violated former, similar Md. R. Prof. Conduct 8.1, 8.4(a). Att'y Griev. Comm'n v. Kapoor, 391 Md. 505, 894 A.2d 502 (2006).

Attorney violated (a) of this Rule and Rule 8.4(c) because he misrepresented his reasons for inactivity in his client's case. The attorney intentionally misled an investigator by implying, through emphatic statements of fact, that the reasons for the case's delay was due to unavailable transcripts and the complainant's

late delivery of transcripts. Att'y Griev. Comm'n v. Lee, 393 Md. 385, 903 A.2d 360 (2006).

Attorney's disorganization in the attorney's record keeping practices did not excuse the attorney from complying with a subpoena in a timely manner, and the attorney's failure to timely produce the requested documents in a format that permitted their use by Bar Counsel constituted a violation of (b). Att'y Griev. Comm'n v. Sapero, 400 Md. 461, 929 A.2d 483 (2007).

Attorney violated this rule when the attorney failed to respond in a timely manner to Deputy Bar Counsel's letters. Att'y Griev. Comm'n v. Jarosinski, 411 Md. 432, 983 A.2d 477 (2009).

Rule violation not shown. — While less than cooperative and reasonable in his responses to Bar Counsel's investigation of the charges against him, an attorney's conduct fell short of a violation of the provisions of the prior, similar Rule. Att'y Griev. Comm'n v. Powell, 328 Md. 276, 614 A.2d 102 (1992).

Attorney did not violate (a) where it was the attorney's inexperience that led to the complaints; none of the errors or misrepresentations appeared to be knowing or intentional. Att'y Griev. Comm'n v. Ward, 394 Md. 1, 904 A.2d 477 (2006).

Applied in Att'y Griev. Comm'n v. Duvall, 384 Md. 234, 863 A.2d 291 (2004).

Quoted in Att'y Griev. Comm'n v. MacDougall, 384 Md. 271, 863 A.2d 312 (2004); Att'y Griev. Comm'n v. Mitchell, 386 Md. 386, 872 A.2d 720 (2005); Att'y Griev. Comm'n v. Lee, 387 Md. 89, 874 A.2d 897 (2005); Att'y Griev. Comm'n v. Scroggs, 387 Md. 238, 874 A.2d 985 (2005); Att'y Griev. Comm'n v. Muhammad, — Md. —, — A.2d — (2005); Att'y Griev. Comm'n v. Calhoun, 391 Md. 532, 894 A.2d 518 (2006); Att'y Griev. Comm'n v. Lanocha, 392 Md. 234, 896 A.2d 996 (2006); Att'y Griev. Comm'n v. Mba-Jonas, 397 Md. 690, 919 A.2d 669 (2007); Att'y Griev. Comm'n v. Kreamer, 404 Md. 282, 946 A.2d 500 (2008); Att'y Griev. Comm'n v. Gisriel, 409 Md. 331, 974 A.2d 331 (2009); Att'y Griev. Comm'n v. Stern, 419 Md. 525, 19 A.3d 904 (2011).

Cited in Att'y Griev. Comm'n v. Maignan, 390 Md. 287, 888 A.2d 344 (2005); Att'y Griev. Comm'n v. Muhammad, 395 Md. 676, 912 A.2d 588 (2006), cert. denied, 127 S. Ct. 2296, 2007 U.S. LEXIS 5292, 167 L. Ed. 2d 1103 (U.S. 2007); Att'y Griev. Comm'n v. Parsons, 404 Md. 175, 946 A.2d 437 (2008); Att'y Griev. Comm'n v. Snyder, 406 Md. 21, 956 A.2d 147 (2008).

Rule 8.2. Judicial and Legal Officials.

(a) A lawyer shall not make a statement that the lawyer knows to be false or with reckless disregard as to its truth or falsity concerning the qualifications or integrity of a judge, adjudicatory officer or public legal officer, or of a candidate for election or appointment to judicial or legal office.

(b) Rule 4.1 (c)(2)(D) of the Maryland Code of Judicial Conduct, set forth in Rule 16-813, provides that a lawyer becomes a candidate for a judicial office when the lawyer files a certificate of candidacy in accordance with Maryland election laws, but no earlier than two years prior to the general election for that office. A candidate for a judicial office:

(1) shall maintain the dignity appropriate to the office and act in a manner consistent with the impartiality, independence and integrity of the judiciary;

(2) with respect to a case, controversy, or issue that is likely to come before the court, shall not make a commitment, pledge, or promise that is inconsistent with the impartial performance of the adjudicative duties of the office;

Committee note. — Rule 8.2(b)(2) does not prohibit a candidate from making a commitment, pledge, or promise respecting improvements in court administration or the faithful and impartial performance of the duties of the office.

(3) shall not knowingly misrepresent his or her identity or qualifications, the identity or qualifications of an opponent, or any other fact;

(4) shall not allow any other person to do for the candidate what the candidate is prohibited from doing; and

(5) may respond to a personal attack or an attack on the candidate's record as long as the response does not otherwise violate this Rule. (Amended June 7, 2011, effective July 1, 2011.)

COMMENT

[1] Assessments by lawyers are relied on in evaluating the professional or personal fitness of persons being considered for election or appointment to judicial office and to public legal offices, such as attorney general, prosecuting attorney and public defender. Expressing honest and candid opinions on such matters contributes to improving the administration of justice. Conversely, false statements by a lawyer can unfairly undermine public confidence in the administration of justice.

[2] To maintain the fair and independent administration of justice, lawyers are encouraged to continue traditional efforts to defend judges and courts unjustly criticized.

Model Rules Comparison. — Rule 8.2 revises prior Maryland language without adopting Ethics 2000 Amendments to the ABA Model Rules of Professional Conduct.

Effect of amendments. — The 2011 amendment substituted "Rule 4.1 (c)(2)(D)" for "Canon 5C (4)" at the beginning of (b).

Accusation of ex parte communication violated rule. — In an attorney discipline proceeding, an attorney violated the rule by falsely accusing a judge of having an improper ex parte conference. Att'y Griev. Comm'n v. Hermina, 379 Md. 503, 842 A.2d 762 (2004).

Disbarment appropriate. — Attorney was disbarred for violating Md. R. Prof. Conduct 1.1, 3.1, 3.2, 3.3(a), 4.4, 8.2(a), and 8.4(c) and

(d) because his use of misleading statements to support the assertion that a trial judge was motivated by personal bias improperly called the judge's integrity into question; the attorney was intentionally dishonest with both the trial court and the court of special appeals, which showed a systematic effort to mislead the courts, and his history of sanctions for violating the Maryland Rules of Professional Conduct (MRPC) showed an ongoing disregard for the MRPC. Att'y Griev. Comm'n v. McClain, 406 Md. 1, 956 A.2d 135 (2008), cert. denied,

129 S. Ct. 1691, 2009 U.S. LEXIS 2433, 173 L. Ed. 2d 1036 (U.S. 2009).

Rule 8.3. Reporting Professional Misconduct.

(a) A lawyer who knows that another lawyer has committed a violation of the Maryland Lawyers' Rules of Professional Conduct that raises a substantial question as to that lawyer's honesty, trustworthiness or fitness as a lawyer in other respects, shall inform the appropriate professional authority.

(b) A lawyer who knows that a judge has committed a violation of applicable rules of judicial conduct that raises a substantial question as to the judge's fitness for office shall inform the appropriate authority.

(c) This Rule does not require disclosure of information otherwise protected by Rule 1.6 or information gained by a lawyer or judge while participating in a lawyer or judge assistance or professional guidance program.

COMMENT

[1] Self-regulation of the legal profession requires that members of the profession initiate disciplinary investigation when they know of a violation of the Maryland Lawyers' Rules of Professional Conduct. Lawyers have a similar obligation with respect to judicial misconduct. An apparently isolated violation may indicate a pattern of misconduct that only a disciplinary investigation can uncover. Reporting a violation is especially important where the victim is unlikely to discover the offense. For the definition of "knows" under these Rules, see Rule 1.0(g).

[2] A report about misconduct is not required where it would involve violation of Rule 1.6. However, a lawyer should encourage a client to consent to disclosure where prosecution would not substantially prejudice the client's interests.

[3] If a lawyer were obliged to report every violation of the Rules, the failure to report any violation would itself be a professional offense. Such a requirement existed in many jurisdictions but proved to be unenforceable. This Rule limits the reporting obligation to those offenses that a self-regulating profession must vigorously endeavor to prevent. A measure of judgment is, therefore, required in complying with the provisions of this Rule. The term "substantial" refers to the seriousness of the possible offense and not the quantum of evidence of which the lawyer is aware. A report should be made to the bar disciplinary agency unless some other agency, such as a peer review agency, is more appropriate in the circumstances. Similar considerations apply to the reporting of judicial misconduct.

[4] The duty to report professional misconduct does not apply to a lawyer retained to represent a lawyer whose professional conduct is in question. Such a situation is governed by the rules applicable to the client-lawyer relationship.

[5] Information about a lawyer's or judge's misconduct or fitness may be received by a lawyer in the course of that lawyer's participation in an approved lawyer or judge assistance or professional guidance program. In that circumstance, providing for an exception to the reporting requirements of paragraphs (a) and (b) of this Rule encourages lawyers and judges to seek assistance through such a program. Conversely, without such an exception, lawyers and judges may hesitate to seek assistance from these programs, which may then result in harm to their professional careers and injury to the welfare of client and the public. These Rules do not otherwise address the confidentiality of information received by a lawyer or judge participating in such programs; such an obligation, however, may be imposed by the rules of the program or other law.

Model Rules Comparison. — Rule 8.3 is substantially similar to the Ethics 2000 Amendments to the ABA Model Rules of Professional Conduct, with the exception of wording changes to Rule 8.3(c) and Comment [5].

Practice without a license. — Failure to report the continued practice of law by a suspended lawyer constituted a violation of the prior, similar Rule. Att'y Griev. Comm'n v. Brennan, 350 Md. 489, 714 A.2d 157 (1998).

Charges filed must embody rule most

probably violated. — See Att'y Griev.
Comm'n v. Wright, 306 Md. 93, 507 A.2d 618
(1986).

Rule 8.4. Misconduct.

It is professional misconduct for a lawyer to:

(a) violate or attempt to violate the Maryland Lawyers' Rules of Professional Conduct, knowingly assist or induce another to do so, or do so through the acts of another;

(b) commit a criminal act that reflects adversely on the lawyer's honesty, trustworthiness or fitness as a lawyer in other respects;

(c) engage in conduct involving dishonesty, fraud, deceit or misrepresentation;

(d) engage in conduct that is prejudicial to the administration of justice;

(e) knowingly manifest by words or conduct when acting in a professional capacity bias or prejudice based upon race, sex, religion, national origin, disability, age, sexual orientation or socioeconomic status when such action is prejudicial to the administration of justice, provided, however, that legitimate advocacy is not a violation of this paragraph;

(f) state or imply an ability to influence improperly a government agency or official or to achieve results by means that violate the Maryland Lawyers' Rules of Professional Conduct or other law; or

(g) knowingly assist a judge or judicial officer in conduct that is a violation of applicable rules of judicial conduct or other law. (Amended June 7, 2011, effective July 1, 2011.)

COMMENT

[1] Lawyers are subject to discipline when they violate or attempt to violate the Maryland Lawyers' Rules of Professional Conduct, knowingly assist or induce another to do so or do so through the acts of another, as when they request or instruct an agent to do so on the lawyer's behalf. Paragraph (a), however, does not prohibit a lawyer from advising a client concerning action the client is legally entitled to take.

[2] Many kinds of illegal conduct reflect adversely on fitness to practice law, such as offenses involving fraud and the offense of willful failure to file an income tax return. However, some kinds of offense carry no such implication. Traditionally, the distinction was drawn in terms of offenses involving "moral turpitude." That concept can be construed to include offenses concerning some matters of personal morality, such as adultery and comparable offenses, that have no specific connection to fitness for the practice of law. Although a lawyer is personally answerable to the entire criminal law, a lawyer should be professionally answerable only for offenses that indicate lack of those characteristics relevant to law practice. Offenses involving violence, dishonesty, or breach of trust, or serious interference with the administration of justice are in that category. A pattern of repeated offenses, even ones of minor significance when considered separately, can indicate indifference to legal obligation.

[3] Sexual misconduct or sexual harassment involving colleagues, clients, or co-workers may violate paragraph (d) or (e). This could occur, for example, where coercion or undue influence is used to obtain sexual favor in exploitation of these relationships. See *Attorney Grievance Commission v. Goldsborough*, 330 Md. 342 (1993). See also Rule 1.7.

[4] Paragraph (e) reflects the premise that a commitment to equal justice under the law lies at the very heart of the legal system. As a result, even when not otherwise unlawful, a lawyer who, while acting in a professional capacity, engages in the conduct described in paragraph (e) and by so doing prejudices the administration of justice commits a particularly egregious type of discrimination. Such conduct manifests a lack of character required of members of the legal profession. A trial judge's finding that peremptory challenges were exercised on a discriminatory basis does

not alone establish a violation of this rule. A judge, however, must require lawyers to refrain from the conduct described in paragraph (e). See Md. Rule 16-813, Maryland Code of Judicial Conduct, Rule 2.3.

[5] A lawyer may refuse to comply with an obligation imposed by law upon a good faith belief that no valid obligation exists. The provisions of Rule 1.2(d) concerning a good faith challenge to the validity, scope, meaning or application of the law apply to challenges of legal regulation of the practice of law.

[6] Lawyers holding public office assume legal responsibilities going beyond those of other citizens. A lawyer's abuse of public office

can suggest an inability to fulfill the professional role of attorney. The same is true of abuse of positions of private trust such as trustee, executor, administrator, guardian, agent and officer, director or manager of a corporation or other organization.

Model Rules Comparison. — Rule 8.4 is substantially similar to the language of the Ethics 2000 Amendments to the ABA Model Rules of Professional Conduct, with the exception of adding Rule 8.4(e) and redesignating the subsections of Rule 8.4 as appropriate, adding Comment [4] above, and retaining Comment [3] above from existing Maryland language.

Effect of amendments. — The 2011 amendment substituted "Rule 2.3" for "Canon 3 B (11)" at the end of comment [4].

I. General Consideration.
II. What constitutes violation.
   A. In general.
   B. Criminal Acts.
   C. Tax-related issues.
   D. Handling clients' funds.
   E. Forgery, fraud, and false pretenses.
   F. Misfeasance.
III. Evidence and sanctions.

I. GENERAL CONSIDERATION.

University of Baltimore Law Forum. — Attorney Grievance Comm'n of Maryland v. Painter: An Attorney Who Commits Repeated Domestic Violence and Has Been Convicted for Similar Conduct Is Subject to Disbarment, see 30 U. Balt. Law Forum 71 (1999).

For Recent Development, "Attorney Grievance Comm'n of Maryland v. Painter: An Attorney Who Commits Repeated Domestic Violence and Has Been Convicted for Similar Conduct Is Subject to Disbarment," see 30 U. Balt. Law Forum 71 (1999).

For Recent Development, "Attorney Grievance Commission of Maryland v. Mooney: Indefinite Suspension is Warranted Where an Attorney Fails to Provide Competent Representation," see 31 U. Balt. Law Forum 44 (2000).

Recent Development: Attorney Grievance Commission v. Santos: An Attorney May Not Be Disbarred for Failing to Return Unearned Fees, Absent Fraud, Deceit or Misrepresentation, see 33 U. Balt. Law Forum 17 (2002).

For note, "Recent Development: Attorney Grievance Commission of Maryland v. Goodman: Disbarment Imposed in Cases Involving Intentionally Dishonest Conduct Unless Compelling Extenuating Circumstances Mitigate

Against Such Sanction," see 35 U. Balt. L.F. 56 (2004).

For note, "Recent Development: Attorney Grievance Comm'n of Md. v. Kinnane: Disbarment of Attorney Based on Rules 1.5(E) and 8.4(B) & (C) of the Maryland Rules of Professional Conduct Held Proper Where Violations Are Established and No Mitigating or Compelling Extenuating Circumstances Exist," see 36 U. Balt. L.F. 165 (2006).

Comparison with prior, similar Rule 8.1. — Dishonesty before disciplinary authorities could fall under both the narrow proscription of prior, similar Rule 8.1 as well as under the broader proscription of this Rule. Att'y Griev. Comm'n v. Goldsborough, 330 Md. 342, 624 A.2d 503 (1993).

Merger. — Where an attorney prepared a will for a client in which he was sole legatee, the circuit court judge erred by concluding that the attorney's violations of prior, similar Md. R. 1.8 and 8.4 merged; since the attorney's conduct constituted separate rule violations, "merger" was improper. Att'y Griev. Comm'n v. Brooke, 374 Md. 155, 821 A.2d 414 (2003).

Imposition of sanctions protects the public interest. — The imposition of a sanction for misconduct protects the public interest because it demonstrates to members of the legal profession the type of conduct which will not be tolerated. Att'y Griev. Comm'n v. Hamby, 322 Md. 606, 589 A.2d 53 (1991).

Purpose of disciplinary proceedings. — The purpose of disciplinary proceedings is to protect the public rather then to punish the erring attorney, although concepts of general and specific deterrence are consistent with that primary goal. Att'y Griev. Comm'n v. Owrutsky, 322 Md. 334, 587 A.2d 511 (1991).

Purpose of disciplinary proceedings is not to punish the offending attorney but "is to protect the public from one who has demonstrated his unworthiness to continue the practice of law." Att'y Griev. Comm'n v. Howard, 282 Md. 515, 385 A.2d 1191 (1978).

Conduct during civil litigation. — In an attorney discipline proceeding, where an attorney violated prior, similar Rule 3.3 by misrepresenting the content and effect of a judge's pre-trial protective order and falsely claiming that he had been precluded from conducting discovery, prior, similar Rule 3.4, by failing to respond to discovery requests and by failing to participate in a pre-trial conference and cooperate in preparing a joint pre-trial statement, and prior, similar Rule 8.2 by recklessly accusing a judge of participating in an inappropriate ex parte conference, those conclusions sufficed to establish a violation of the prior, similar Rule. Att'y Griev. Comm'n v. Hermina, 379 Md. 503, 842 A.2d 762 (2004).

Actions reflecting adversely on fitness to practice law. — Lawyer's neglect of divorce matter prior to his suspension from the practice of law, and his subsequent failure to advise client to obtain other counsel after suspension, constituted conduct prejudicial to the administration of justice reflecting adversely on his fitness to practice in violation of former DR 1-102 (A) (5) (6). Att'y Griev. Comm'n v. Singleton, 315 Md. 1, 553 A.2d 222 (1989).

Because misappropriation of client's funds was criminal conduct which adversely reflected on the attorney's honesty, trustworthiness or fitness to practice law, it constituted a violation of the prior, similar Rule. Such conduct was prejudicial to the administration of justice in violation of the prior, similar Rule and constituted a violation of the prior, similar Rules of Professional Conduct. Att'y Griev. Comm'n v. Daskalopoulos, 383 Md. 375, 859 A.2d 653 (2004).

Because the attorney was found to have violated prior, similar Rules 1.1, 1.3, 1.4, and 3.2, the Court of Appeals of Maryland could find that the attorney violated this Rule because of the same conduct that was a violation of the other rules. Additionally, because the attorney lined the attorney's own pockets in representations and relationships with another client that resulted in conflicts of interest with the client, the Court of Appeals could

also find for that reason that the attorney had committed misconduct. Att'y Griev. Comm'n v. Harris, 371 Md. 510, 810 A.2d 457 (2002).

When an attorney employed by another lawyer deleted the firm's computer records of two clients the attorney had brought to the firm, before ending his employment with the firm, because he feared his employer would try to use this information to require the attorney to pay the employer certain compensation, the attorney violated § 7-302 of the Criminal Law Article by exceeding his authorized access to a computer for the purpose of destroying data stored on the computer, and this reflected adversely on his honesty and trustworthiness, was dishonest and deceitful, and was prejudicial to the administration of justice, contrary to the prior, similar Rule; thus, the attorney was suspended from the practice of law for 90 days. Att'y Griev. Comm'n v. Potter, 380 Md. 128, 844 A.2d 367 (2004).

When an attorney employed by another lawyer deleted the firm's computer records of two clients the attorney had brought to the firm, before ending his employment with the firm, because he feared his employer would try to use this information to require the attorney to pay the employer certain compensation, the attorney violated § 7-302 of the Criminal Law Article by exceeding his authorized access to a computer for the purpose of destroying data stored on the computer, and this reflected adversely on his honesty and trustworthiness, was dishonest and deceitful, and was prejudicial to the administration of justice, contrary to the prior, similar Rule; the attorney's motivation in committing this offense was irrelevant. Att'y Griev. Comm'n v. Potter, 380 Md. 128, 844 A.2d 367 (2004).

When an attorney employed by another lawyer deleted the firm's computer records of two clients the attorney had brought to the firm, before ending his employment with the firm, because he feared his employer would try to use this information to require the attorney to pay the employer certain compensation, the attorney violated § 7-302 of the Criminal Law Article by exceeding his authorized access to a computer for the purpose of destroying data stored on the computer, and this reflected adversely on his honesty and trustworthiness, was dishonest and deceitful, and was prejudicial to the administration of justice, contrary to the prior, similar Rule; thus, the attorney was suspended from the practice of law for 90 days because even though the clients were not harmed, the attorney's employer was potentially harmed by having no records of his firm's representation of these clients which he could use to defend himself in a potential malpractice suit or against which he could exert a retaining lien, under Md. R. 2-652(a) to secure payment of any sums to which he was entitled.

Att'y Griev. Comm'n v. Potter, 380 Md. 128, 844 A.2d 367 (2004).

When an attorney altered the attorney's law firm employer's electronic files to facilitate the attorney taking certain of the firm's clients with the attorney when the attorney left the firm, the attorney admittedly violated (a), (b), (c), and (d) because (1) the attorney's acts of altering and deleting documents within the firm's client files constituted criminal acts in violation of § 7-302 of the Criminal Law Article and, therefore, violated these Rules, (2) the attorney's criminal conduct reflected adversely on the attorney's honesty, trustworthiness and fitness as a lawyer, (3) the attorney's conduct was deceitful and prejudicial to the administration of justice as the attorney carried out the deception after hours, when others would not observe the attorney's actions, as the attorney understood the attorney's actions to be inappropriate and unauthorized. Att'y Griev. Comm'n v. Keiner, — Md. —, — A.3d — (Aug. 19, 2011).

Disciplinary proceedings for professional misconduct are not criminal proceedings. — Their purpose is to protect the public by determining a lawyer's fitness to practice law and whether to institute disciplinary action against him. Att'y Griev. Comm'n v. Stewart, 285 Md. 251, 401 A.2d 1026, cert. denied, 444 U.S. 845, 100 S. Ct. 89, 62 L. Ed. 2d 58 (1979).

Criminal prosecution not required to find violation. — Although criminal prosecution is certainly a factor weighing heavily in favor of finding a violation of the prior, similar Rule, its absence does not necessarily mean the Rule has not been violated. Att'y Griev. Comm'n v. Breschi, 340 Md. 590, 667 A.2d 659 (1995).

What is required is clear and convincing evidence of conduct that constitutes a commission of the offense. Att'y Griev. Comm'n v. Proctor, 309 Md. 412, 524 A.2d 773 (1987).

An attorney may be disciplined for acts which are criminal but do not result in a criminal conviction if Bar Counsel proves the underlying conduct at the disciplinary hearing. Att'y Griev. Comm'n v. Garland, 345 Md. 383, 692 A.2d 465 (1997).

The burden on Bar Counsel in a disciplinary proceeding is to prove the violation of a Rule of Professional Conduct by clear and convincing evidence, and this standard of proof is not heightened to proof beyond a reasonable doubt where Bar Counsel's theory of the case is that a Rule of Professional Conduct has been violated by conduct which constitutes a crime, although there has been no criminal conviction. Att'y Griev. Comm'n v. Childress, 364 Md. 48, 770 A.2d 685 (2001).

Although an attorney who also owned a title insurance company could have been disciplined even in the absence of a finding of violation of law with regard to the company's drawing of interest on certain amounts that moved through the settlement trust account, in the absence of any interpretation of statutory and regulatory requirements by insurance regulators, it was impossible to determine whether anything had been amiss at all; in that circumstance, the petition for discipline was dismissed. Att'y Griev. Comm'n v. Davis, 379 Md. 361, 842 A.2d 26 (2004).

Conduct constituting crime in another jurisdiction. — Attorney was disbarred as he violated prior, similar Rule 5.5 where he engaged in activity constituting the practice of law in Virginia, where he was not authorized to practice law; the unauthorized practice of law in Virginia was prohibited under Va. Sup. Ct. R. pt. 6, § I, and was a crime under Va. Code Ann. § 54.1-3904, and therefore, coupled with the attorney's failure to disclose the fact that he was not licensed in Virginia to the client and his acceptance of a fee for representation that he could not perform, was conduct involving dishonesty, fraud, deceit, or misrepresentation for the purposes of prior, similar Rule 8.4. Att'y Griev. Comm'n v. Velasquez, 380 Md. 651, 846 A.2d 422 (2004).

Moral turpitude irrelevant under current Rule. — The only difference under this Rule and the rule that existed before 1987 is that a crime's moral turpitude now irrelevant to whether a lawyer is guilty of misconduct; under the current rule, a lawyer's commission of a crime or conduct enumerated therein will subject that lawyer to discipline irrespective of whether the crime is also one of moral turpitude. Att'y Griev. Comm'n v. Casalino, 335 Md. 446, 644 A.2d 43 (1994).

A lawyer's commission of a crime or conduct enumerated in the prior, similar Rule will subject him to discipline irrespective of whether the crime is also one of moral turpitude. Att'y Griev. Comm'n v. Bereano, 357 Md. 321, 744 A.2d 35 (2000).

Honest mistake not a violation. — It was not clearly erroneous for a judge to find that the prior, similar Rule was not violated where the record demonstrated that an attorney was attempting to conduct a bankruptcy practice in a lawful manner by limiting her court appearances to the federal district, even though the attorney was mistaken in her conclusion that this was permissible. Att'y Griev. Comm'n v. Harris-Smith, 356 Md. 72, 737 A.2d 567 (1999).

Reliance on advice of out-of-state attorney not defense. — Attorney's reliance on advice of counsel from a lawyer not admitted to practice in the State of Maryland was not a defense to her violations of Md. Law. R. Prof. Conduct 8.4(c) and (d), or to Md. Law. R. Prof. Conduct 1.7(d), or, for that matter, any of her conduct in the case. Att'y Griev. Comm'n v. Pennington, 387 Md. 565, 876 A.2d 642 (2005).

Violation Found — Attorney was found to have violated Md. R. Prof. Conduct 8.4 based on evidence that the attorney failed to serve defendants in a personal injury action filed for a client, lost the client's file, and failed to respond to the client's inquiries; suspension rather than disbarment was proper where there was no evidence he acted out of fraudulent or selfish motive. Att'y Griev. Comm'n v. Reinhardt, 391 Md. 209, 892 A.2d 533 (2006).

Quoted in Att'y Griev. Comm'n v. Christopher, 383 Md. 624, 861 A.2d 692 (2004); Att'y Griev. Comm'n v. MacDougall, 384 Md. 271, 863 A.2d 312 (2004); Att'y Griev. Comm'n v. Lee, 387 Md. 89, 874 A.2d 897 (2005); Att'y Griev. Comm'n v. Scroggs, 387 Md. 238, 874 A.2d 985 (2005); Att'y Griev. Comm'n v. Kreamer, 387 Md. 503, 876 A.2d 79 (2005); Att'y Griev. Comm'n v. Muhammad, — Md. —, — A.2d — (2005); Att'y Griev. Comm'n v. Whitehead, 390 Md. 663, 890 A.2d 751 (2006); Att'y Griev. Comm'n v. Obi, 393 Md. 643, 904 A.2d 422 (2006); Att'y Griev. Comm'n v. Sapero, 400 Md. 461, 929 A.2d 483 (2007); Att'y Griev. Comm'n v. Mba-Jonas, 402 Md. 334, 936 A.2d 839 (2007); Att'y Griev. Comm'n v. Taylor, 405 Md. 697, 955 A.2d 755 (2008); Att'y Griev. Comm'n v. Kwarteng, 411 Md. 652, 984 A.2d 865 (2009).

Stated in Att'y Griev. Comm'n v. Prichard, 386 Md. 238, 872 A.2d 81 (2005); Att'y Griev. Comm'n v. Midlen, 395 Md. 628, 911 A.2d 852 (2006).

Cited in Att'y Griev. Comm'n v. Muhammad, 395 Md. 676, 912 A.2d 588 (2006), cert. denied, 127 S. Ct. 2296, 2007 U.S. LEXIS 5292, 167 L. Ed. 2d 1103 (U.S. 2007); Att'y Griev. Comm'n v. Baker, 396 Md. 15, 912 A.2d 651 (2006); Att'y Griev. Comm'n v. Rees, 396 Md. 248, 913 A.2d 68 (2006); Att'y Griev. Comm'n v. Nussbaum, 401 Md. 612, 934 A.2d 1 (2007).

II. WHAT CONSTITUTES VIOLATION.

A. In general.

Violation of several Maryland Rules of Professional Conduct. — When an attorney has violated several Maryland Rules of Professional Conduct, he necessarily violates (a) of this Rule as well, which finds professional misconduct where a lawyer violates or attempts to violate the Maryland Rules of Professional Conduct. Att'y Griev. Comm'n v. Foltz, 411 Md. 359, 983 A.2d 434 (2009).

Attorney violated (a) because, when the attorney maintained an unauthorized side practice while being employed "of counsel" for a law firm, and deposited unearned retainers from clients in that side practice in the attorney's personal account, the attorney violated Md. R. Prof. Conduct 1.15(a) and (b) — (d) of this Rule. Att'y Griev. Comm'n v. Carithers, 421 Md. 28, 25 A.3d 181 (2011).

Failure to disclose nonattorney status. — Failure of a lawyer to inform a client that his "associate" was suspended from the practice of law was sufficient to find a violation of the prior, similar Rule. Att'y Griev. Comm'n v. Brennan, 350 Md. 489, 714 A.2d 157 (1998).

The use of a business card which indicated that a law graduate who had not passed the bar was a J.D., the execution of a retainer agreement by that person, and the setting of fees were violations of prior, similar 7.1 and 8.4 because the attorney knew, and in fact, sponsored the arrangement undertaken by the nonlawyer. Att'y Griev. Comm'n v. Mitchell, 386 Md. 386, 872 A.2d 720 (2005).

Conduct prejudicial to administration of justice. — Violation of this Rule was supported by the attorney's failure to promptly, completely and truthfully respond to Bar Counsel's requests for information, to keep his client advised of the status of the representation and to diligently represent the complainant constitutes; such conduct tends to bring the legal profession into disrepute and is therefore prejudicial to the administration of justice. Att'y Griev. Comm'n v. Rose, 391 Md. 101, 892 A.2d 469 (2006), cert. denied, 2006 U.S. LEXIS 5734, 166 L. Ed. 2d 22 (U.S. 2006).

Attorney violated (d) when he was repeatedly disruptive and disrespectful to a trial judge in the course of a hearing, even though his client was not prejudiced, because the court had to address that offensive and disruptive conduct during the court proceedings, and his conduct undermined the judicial system and the public's faith in the system and constituted a lack of respect for the judicial process. Att'y Griev. Comm'n v. Mahone, 398 Md. 257, 920 A.2d 458 (2007).

Attorney violated (d) when he left the courtroom while a trial judge was announcing his opinion, even though his client was not prejudiced and was represented by someone else for the remainder of the hearing, because he abandoned his client, in violation of his duty to represent her interests, as there was no evidence to suggest that he knew another attorney would be available to represent his client, and because this was an overt and public display of disdain for the court and a disrespect for the administration of justice. Att'y Griev. Comm'n v. Mahone, 398 Md. 257, 920 A.2d 458 (2007).

When an attorney left a courtroom after a trial court disagreed with the attorney's position that the court had no authority to deny the State's uncontested motion to stet a criminal charge against the attorney's client, under Md. R. 4-248, despite the trial court's instruction that the case was not concluded, the attorney was properly found to have violated (d) because the attorney's conduct wasted judicial resources and was prejudicial to the administration of justice. Att'y Griev. Comm'n v. Usiak, 418 Md. 667, 18 A.3d 1 (2011).

When an attorney left a courtroom after a trial court disagreed with the attorney's position that the court had no authority to deny the State's uncontested motion to stet a criminal charge against the attorney's client, under Md. R. 4-248, despite the trial court's instruction that the case was not concluded, the attorney was properly found to have violated (d) because (1) the attorney's interpretation of Md. R. 4-248 was plainly wrong, and, (2) even if the attorney's interpretation were correct, the attorney's conduct was prejudicial to the administration of justice. Att'y Griev. Comm'n v. Usiak, 418 Md. 667, 18 A.3d 1 (2011).

Attorney violated (d) because, when the attorney maintained an unauthorized side practice while being employed "of counsel" for a law firm, the attorney (1) stole fees that were owed to the firm, when the attorney represented and received fees from clients who owed the firm fees. Att'y Griev. Comm'n v. Carithers, 421 Md. 28, 25 A.3d 181 (2011).

Conduct not prejudicial to the administration of justice — Attorney Grievance Commission's exception to a judge's findings and conclusion that an attorney did not violate (d) and argument that the attorney's representation, that he was acting on behalf of the District of Columbia Bar Counsel, was conduct prejudicial to the administration of justice were overruled because the judge's findings that the attorney's telephone calls were minimally intrusive and that they did not disrupt the work of the Merit Systems Protection Board were not clearly erroneous, and these findings supported the conclusion that the calls did not result in conduct that was prejudicial to the administration of justice as was required for a violation of (d). Att'y Griev. Comm'n v. Kalil, 402 Md. 358, 936 A.2d 854 (2007).

Nonconsensual kissing and/or spanking clients or employees. — Attorney who was soliciting sex over the Internet from young girls, after imploring them to keep the meeting a secret from their parents, violated the prior, similar Rule because his behavior was prejudicial to the administration of justice; the exhibition of such behavior is likely to impair public confidence in the profession, impact on the image of the legal profession, and engender disrespect for the court. Att'y Griev. Comm'n v. Childress, 360 Md. 373, 758 A.2d 117 (2000).

Sexual relationship with client. — Attorney's conduct was prejudicial to the administration of justice and brought disrepute to the legal profession because the attorney inappropriately continued his sexual relationship with a client while continuing to represent her, despite his knowledge of her fragile emotional state; if attorneys take advantage of a client's emotional fragility by having a sexual relationship with that client, the court of appeals will not hesitate to impose disciplinary sanctions. Att'y Griev. Comm'n v. Hall, 408 Md. 306, 969 A.2d 953 (2009).

Soliciting underage sex over Internet. — Attorney who was soliciting sex over the Internet from young girls, after imploring them to keep the meeting a secret from their parents, violated the prior, similar Rule because his behavior was prejudicial to the administration of justice; the exhibition of such behavior is likely to impair public confidence in the profession, impact on the image of the legal profession, and engender disrespect for the court. Att'y Griev. Comm'n v. Childress, 360 Md. 373, 758 A.2d 117 (2000).

Engaging in sexual chat room conversations. — Attorney who was involved in sexual chat room conversations with minors followed by in-person meetings was indefinitely suspended from the practice of law, without the right to apply for the termination of the suspension for a period of one year from the effective date of the suspension. Att'y Griev. Comm'n v. Childress, 364 Md. 48, 770 A.2d 685 (2001).

Sexual attraction to minors. — Attorney, who admitted sexual attraction to pubescent boys, was suspended indefinitely for stalking a 13-year-old boy, as actions reflected adversely on attorney's fitness to practice law, under the prior, similar Rule; trust was an inseparable element of any attorney's practice, and the attorney's actions were not those of a trustworthy adult. Att'y Griev. Comm'n v. Thompson, 367 Md. 315, 786 A.2d 763 (2001).

Claimed ignorance of ethical duties and bookkeeping requirements. — Claimed ignorance of ethical duties and bookkeeping requirements is not a defense in disciplinary proceedings, but a finding with respect to the intent with which a violation was committed is relevant on the issue of the appropriate sanction. Att'y Griev. Comm'n v. Awuah, 346 Md. 420, 697 A.2d 446 (1997).

Use of colorful language. — The prior, similar Rule was not violated where an attorney stated that "one learns to expect to get jerked around" when dealing with an insurance company, and called a driver in the case an idiot. Att'y Griev. Comm'n v. Alison, 349 Md. 623, 709 A.2d 1212 (1998).

Prosecutor's promise to prosecute bomb threat cases against juveniles. — Prosecutor did not commit a violation of prior, similar Rule 3.1 by commenting on future prosecutions of juveniles who phoned bomb threats, despite the lack of clear evidence as to the juveniles' actions, because by making the comments about prosecuting bomb threats, the prosecutor intended to communicate that his office must try hard cases. Att'y Griev. Comm'n v. Gansler, 377 Md. 656, 835 A.2d 548 (2003).

Use of abusive language outside litigation setting. — Attorney's abusive outburst at a motor vehicle administration office expressing rage at delays in accessing insurance information on behalf of a personal injury client was outrageous and rude, but it did not rise to the level of conduct prejudicial to the administration of justice; therefore, a petition for imposition of appropriate discipline was dismissed. Att'y Griev. Comm'n v. Link, 380 Md. 405, 844 A.2d 1197 (2004).

Violations may show intent with regard to good faith or honest belief defense. — Where the defendant in a criminal proceeding introduces evidence of possible Disciplinary Code violations as evidence of a good faith or honest belief defense, whether a violation in fact occurred is relevant to the jury's determination of the defendant's intent or lack thereof; thus, instructions to that effect were correct. Cardin v. State, 73 Md. App. 200, 533 A.2d 928 (1987), cert. denied, 488 U.S. 827, 109 S. Ct. 78, 102 L. Ed. 2d 55 (1988).

Finding that attorney did not fraudulently obtain duplicate driver's license not clearly erroneous. — In an attorney disciplinary matter, it was held that the attorney violated Md. R. Prof. Conduct 3.3 by filing expungement petitions for a client knowing that the client's charges were ineligible for expungement and, as a result, he was suspended from the practice of law for 60 days. Additionally, the findings and conclusions of the hearing officer that the attorney did not fraudulently obtain a duplicate driver's license after having his original license taken away at a sobriety checkpoint were found not to be clearly erroneous, and no deficiencies were found with regard to the allegations in the petition providing sufficient notice to the attorney of the charges against him. Att'y Griev. Comm'n v. Tanko, 408 Md. 404, 969 A.2d 1010 (2009).

Failure to report. — Failure to report to a D.W.I. facility following a D.W.I. conviction was conduct prejudicial to the administration of justice and in violation of the Rules of Professional Conduct. Att'y Griev. Comm'n v. Garland, 345 Md. 383, 692 A.2d 465 (1997).

Failure to cooperate with disciplinary investigation. — Attorney violated prior, similar Md. R. Prof. Conduct 1.3, 1.4(a), (b), 8.1 and 8.4(d) when she failed to administratively close a client's asylum application and refile it in proper form as directed by the immigration judge and the client, and failed to respond to requests for information in connection with the related disciplinary investigation. Indefinite suspension was proper given the egregious nature of the attorney's misconduct and her failure to present anything by way of mitigation to the appellate court. Att'y Griev. Comm'n v. Brisbon, 385 Md. 667, 870 A.2d 586 (2005).

Where the attorney abandoned his representation of the client and refused to engage in further communications with the client after terminating his representation via electronic mail, and the attorney engaged in other misconduct which included not being admitted to practice in forums where the attorney was representing the client and not responding to the disciplinary commission's lawful demands for information regarding the investigation of the attorney, disbarment was warranted. Att'y Griev. Comm'n v. Logan, 390 Md. 313, 888 A.2d 359 (2005).

Conviction for accepting illegal gratuity under federal statute was not crime involving moral turpitude. — Where an individual who was both a member of the State bar and a former United States Senator from Maryland stood convicted of accepting an illegal gratuity under 18 U.S.C. § 201(g) (now § 201(c)(1)(B)), this was not a crime involving moral turpitude, and a petition for disciplinary action charging him only with conviction of a crime involving moral turpitude must be dismissed. Att'y Griev. Comm'n v. Brewster, 280 Md. 473, 374 A.2d 602 (1977).

B. Criminal Acts.

Violation of § 5-602 of the Criminal Law Article. — Although conduct in violation of Article 27, § 286 (see now § 5-602 of the Criminal Law Article) will ordinarily involve moral turpitude, each case must be decided on its own facts. Att'y Griev. Comm'n v. Proctor, 309 Md. 412, 524 A.2d 773 (1987).

It was not error for a hearing judge to conclude that an attorney violated (b) because (1) the attorney committed a crime, in violation of § 5-602(l) of the Criminal Law Article, when the attorney gave another person Vicodin in exchange for oral sex, as Vicodin contained compounds listed on the schedules of controlled dangerous substances, under § 5-404 of the Criminal Law Article, and (2) such conduct adversely reflected on the attorney's fitness to practice law. Att'y Griev. Comm'n v. Marcalus, 414 Md. 501, 996 A.2d 350 (2010).

It was not error for a hearing judge to conclude that an attorney violated (d) because (1) the attorney committed a crime, in violation of § 5-602(l) of the Criminal Law Article, when the attorney gave another person Vicodin in exchange for oral sex, as Vicodin contained compounds listed on the schedules of controlled dangerous substances, under § 5-

404 of the Criminal Law Article, and (2) the fact that the attorney's statements to police revealing this conduct assisted in the administration of justice did not require a different conclusion since the disciplinary complaint filed against the attorney was not based on the attorney's statements to police but on the attorney's crime. Att'y Griev. Comm'n v. Marcalus, 414 Md. 501, 996 A.2d 350 (2010).

Acts constituting felony theft. — Appellate court ordered that the attorney be disbarred, as the evidence showed that he violated, inter alia, Rule 1.5(e), by sharing a fee with an alleged lawyer from a corporation without performing any services for the corporation; the fee was part of a scheme to steal money from the corporation in the guise of providing a retainer to the attorney, with a plan to have the attorney kick back some of the "retainer" as payment for future consulting services, which constituted felony theft in the corporation's place of business. Att'y Griev. Comm'n v. Kinnane, 390 Md. 324, 888 A.2d 1178 (2005).

Attorney violated (b) because, when the attorney maintained an unauthorized side practice while being employed "of counsel" for a law firm, the attorney engaged in criminal conduct, under § 7-104(a) of the Criminal Law Article, by stealing the firm's fees, when the attorney represented and received fees from clients who owed the firm fees. Att'y Griev. Comm'n v. Carithers, 421 Md. 28, 25 A.3d 181 (2011).

Federal theft charges. — Attorney who pleaded guilty to federal theft charges violated the prior, similar Rule, and engaged in misconduct as defined in former Rule BV1k (see now Maryland Rule 16-701). Att'y Griev. Comm'n v. Gittens, 346 Md. 316, 697 A.2d 83 (1997).

Conspiracy to defraud the federal government in immigration proceeding. — In an attorney disciplinary matter, the attorney was disbarred as a result of having violated Rule 8.4(a)-(d) of the Lawyer's Rules of Professional Conduct based on his guilty plea to the federal crimes involving conspiracy to defraud the government, in violation of 18 U.S.C.S. §§ 371 and 1546(a), based on his actions in knowingly filing a false letter with the United States Immigration and Naturalization Service on behalf of a client/immigrant in an immigration proceeding. The Court of Appeals of Maryland found no compelling extenuating circumstances, including the attorney's great remorse, to except him from disbarment based on his intention to commit fraud, to deceive, and to misrepresent. Att'y Griev. Comm'n v. Garcia, 410 Md. 507, 979 A.2d 146 (Aug. 28, 2009).

Misprison of felony. — Attorney was disbarred from the practice of law for a violation of this Rule, after pleading guilty of misprison

of a felony; the attorney admitted being aware that the named co-defendants were engaging in immigration fraud, making false statements, and encouraging aliens to enter the country illegally and not reporting the crimes to the proper authorities. Att'y Griev. Comm'n v. Wingerter, 400 Md. 214, 929 A.2d 47 (2007).

Intentional failure to maintain funds in trust account — When the attorney deposited client funds in his trust account and intentionally failed to maintain those funds in his account, he committed a criminal act in violation of (b). Att'y Griev. Comm'n v. Butler, 395 Md. 1, 909 A.2d 226 (2006).

Acceptance of unapproved fees was criminal conduct. — Attorney's act in taking unapproved worker's compensation fees in violation of 33 U.S.C. § 928(e) amounted to "criminal conduct" within the meaning of the prior, similar Rule. Att'y Griev. Comm'n v. Eisenstein, 333 Md. 464, 635 A.2d 1327 (1994).

Drug use — Attorney was indefinitely suspended from the practice of law in Maryland after the hearing court found that he violated Md. R. Prof. Conduct 8.4(b) and (d), by possessing and using cocaine on more than once occasion, and took into account the fact that the attorney suffered a set back after his first attempt to recover for using drugs. Att'y Griev. Comm'n v. Holt, 391 Md. 673, 894 A.2d 602 (2006).

Intentional misrepresentation that warrant had been issued. — Although an attorney intentionally misrepresented his identity on a witness' voice mail as being a police officer, he did not intentionally misrepresent that a warrant had issued for a witness' arrest; the attorney had acted on a mistaken belief that a warrant had been issued and he would not have made the call had he not honestly believed the warrant had been issued. That conduct, standing alone, was not a violation of Md. R. Prof. Conduct 3.4 or 8.4(a)-(d), as it did not cause the witness to be unavailable for trial (although the attorney did intend that the witness would be unavailable to the State by invoking his Fifth Amendment privilege), actually interfere with the administration of justice, or obstruct the State's access to evidence. Att'y Griev. Comm'n v. Smith, 405 Md. 107, 950 A.2d 101 (2008).

Misrepresentation that attorney was police officer. — Attorney committed a criminal act that reflected adversely on his fitness as a lawyer, thereby violating (b). He falsely represented himself to a State's trial witness in a criminal prosecution that he was a police officer, a violation of § 3-502 of the Public Safety Article, in an attempt to influence a witness, a violation of § 9-305 of the Criminal Law Article. Att'y Griev. Comm'n v. Smith, 405 Md. 107, 950 A.2d 101 (2008).

Reversal of violation of criminal con-

victions not precluding finding violation under (b). — Reversal of an attorney's convictions for impersonating a police officer and influencing a witness, violations of § 3-502 of the Public Safety Article and § 9-305 of the Criminal Law Article, did not preclude finding a violation of (b), or any other applicable provisions of the rules of professional conduct. Att'y Griev. Comm'n v. Smith, 405 Md. 107, 950 A.2d 101 (2008).

C. Tax-related issues.

Willful tax evasion. — Willful tax evasion is a crime involving moral turpitude and dishonesty; accordingly, the court held that disbarment was the appropriate sanction. Att'y Griev. Comm'n v. Clinton, 308 Md. 701, 521 A.2d 1202 (1987).

Willful tax evasion is a crime infested with fraud, deceit and dishonesty, and will result in automatic disbarment absent clear and convincing evidence of a compelling reason to the contrary; the exemplary character or activities of an attorney is not sufficient to avoid disbarment. Att'y Griev. Comm'n v. Casalino, 335 Md. 446, 644 A.2d 43 (1994).

Since a conviction for tax evasion is not a necessary predicate to support a finding of dishonesty, a hearing court correctly determined that an attorney's failure to fulfill her income tax duties constituted a violation of this Rule. Att'y Griev. Comm'n v. Atkinson, 357 Md. 646, 745 A.2d 1086 (2000).

An attorney's misconduct exhibited a dishonest character where she purposefully avoided almost all contact with both State and federal income taxing authorities and at no point exhibited, over a period of 11 years, any real intention to fulfill her duties of filing the required returns and paying the taxes due. Att'y Griev. Comm'n v. Atkinson, 357 Md. 646, 745 A.2d 1086 (2000).

Failure to file State income tax returns not considered in determining sanction for failure to file federal returns. — Attorney's failure to file Maryland income tax returns since 1965, not mentioned in the disciplinary charge brought against respondent and disclosed for the first time at a remand hearing, was properly not considered in determining the sanction to be imposed for failure to file federal returns since the requirement of procedural due process, which is applicable in disciplinary proceedings, mandates sufficiently clear and specific notice of the charges being brought before disciplinary sanctions can be imposed against an attorney. Att'y Griev. Comm'n v. Walman, 280 Md. 453, 374 A.2d 354 (1977).

Willful failure to file withholding tax returns — Willful failure to file withholding tax returns may seriously impair public confi-

dence in the entire profession; therefore, where there were no extenuating circumstances, and the defendant had previously been reprimanded and suspended, the defendant's conduct was prejudicial to the administration of justice. Att'y Griev. Comm'n v. Baldwin, 308 Md. 397, 519 A.2d 1291 (1987).

Failure to report and remit income taxes withheld from employees' wages did not show dishonesty or conduct involving moral turpitude, due to the effect the defendant's financial and family problems and alcoholism had on his intent, together with the absence of any evidence that defendant falsified or did not maintain records. Att'y Griev. Comm'n v. Baldwin, 308 Md. 397, 519 A.2d 1291 (1987).

While an attorney's failure to file timely withholding tax returns was a "criminal act" within the meaning of the prior, similar Rule, it did not "adversely reflect on his fitness" as an attorney within the meaning of the Rule. Att'y Griev. Comm'n v. Post, 350 Md. 85, 710 A.2d 935 (1998).

The proper sanction for an attorney found to have willfully failed to make required withholding tax payments was indefinite suspension with the right to apply for re-admission after 30 days. Att'y Griev. Comm'n v. Post, 350 Md. 85, 710 A.2d 935 (1998).

Although the attorney's disbarment was primarily due to his neglect of client matters and nonresponsiveness to bar counsel's investigation, his continuing failure to remit employee withholding taxes or to file returns was an aggravating factor in determining the appropriate sanction. Att'y Griev. Comm'n v. Angst, 369 Md. 404, 800 A.2d 747 (2002).

State supreme court found that an attorney who did not withhold income taxes from his employees or pay those taxes to the state and federal governments, and who also provided incompetent representation and accepted commissions without prior court approval when he served as an estate's representative, violated this rule, and it ordered that the attorney be suspended from the practice of law in Maryland, with the right to reapply for permission to practice law at the end of one year. Att'y Griev. Comm'n v. Thompson, 376 Md. 500, 830 A.2d 474 (2003).

Attorney's actions over many years of willfully failing to file tax returns and pay taxes was prejudicial to the administration of justice and constituted violations of (d). Att'y Griev. Comm'n v. Tayback, 378 Md. 578, 837 A.2d 158 (2003).

State supreme court found that an attorney who failed to file Maryland withholding tax forms for his professional corporation, and also failed to file individual federal and state income tax returns for 1998, 1999, and 2000, violated the prior, similar Rule, and it ordered that the attorney be suspended for 30 days.

Att'y Griev. Comm'n v. O'Toole, 379 Md. 595, 843 A.2d 50 (2004).

Where an attorney was found to have willfully and regularly failed to comply with his obligation as an employer for several years because he failed to withhold state income tax from the wages of his employees and to hold such funds in trust for the State, he was found to have violated the prior, similar Rules 8.4 and 1.15, and §§ 13-1007(b) and (c) and 10-906(a) and (b) of the Tax - General Article; however, the hearing judge erred in finding that although the attorney technically violated the prior, similar Rule, he did not exhibit conduct that violated those rules, as there were tax liens filed against the attorney and he failed to file required periodic reports, which conduct exhibited a willful failure to comply with his tax obligations. Att'y Griev. Comm'n v. Mininsohn, 380 Md. 536, 846 A.2d 353 (2004).

Falsifying tax returns. — Knowingly falsifying income tax returns is illegal conduct involving moral turpitude. Att'y Griev. Comm'n v. Jacob, 303 Md. 172, 492 A.2d 905, cert. denied, 474 U.S. 905, 106 S. Ct. 272, 88 L. Ed. 2d 234 (1985).

A conviction of making a fraudulent return with the intent to defeat the payment of taxes is a crime of moral turpitude and warrants disbarment. Att'y Griev. Comm'n v. Tayback, 378 Md. 578, 837 A.2d 158 (2003).

Willful delay in correcting tax delinquencies amounted to Rule violation. — An attorney's willful delay in correcting tax delinquencies spanning from two to six years from the date he first became aware of them constituted "conduct prejudicial to the administration of justice." Att'y Griev. Comm'n v. Gavin, 350 Md. 176, 711 A.2d 193 (1998).

Failure to pay sales taxes in another jurisdiction. — Attorney was disbarred in Maryland, as his actions in failing to file sales tax returns or remit collected sales tax from a restaurant in the District of Columbia violated the prior, similar Rule, as the attorney's failure to pay the taxes was intentional, and his act of tendering a check for the payment of the taxes which was dishonored for insufficient funds involved fraud and deceit. Att'y Griev. Comm'n v. Gore, 380 Md. 455, 845 A.2d 1204 (2004).

Eventual payment of moneys due. — Eventual late payment of all monies due to a taxing authority does not preclude disciplinary action under the prior, similar Rule consequences of the illegal action, but does not mitigate the act itself and therefore does not erase a potential disciplinary violation.

D. Handling clients' funds.

Handling funds of clients. — Misappropriation of client's funds involves conduct con-

stituting "moral turpitude." Att'y Griev. Comm'n v. Moore, 301 Md. 169, 482 A.2d 497 (1984).

An attorney's violations of the prior, similar Md. R. Prof. Conduct 1.15 by misappropriating client funds necessarily resulted in a violation of prior, similar Md. R. Prof. Conduct 8.4(a) as well and resulted in his disbarment. Att'y Griev. Comm'n v. James, 385 Md. 637, 870 A.2d 229 (2005).

Suspended attorney was disbarred because of his later (1) unjustified misappropriation of trust funds by not paying the clients' medical providers (as he had promised he would do) from clients' share settlement he retained in cash after he got clients' endorsements on settlement checks, received payable to him and to the clients, cashed the checks with the clients at a liquor store cashing service, retained cash to pay his one-third fee (that he reduced) and to pay listed medical providers according to a handwritten distribution summary given to the clients, and distributed the clients' share to them; (2) failure to have or to use an attorney trust account at a proper financial institution; and (3) failure to respond to the disciplinary committee's investigation or petition, or to the hearing judge's conclusions. The attorney's misappropriation of trust money was serious professional misconduct and was embezzlement, fraudulent misappropriation by a fiduciary, under 7-113 of the Criminal Law Article, representing professional misconduct that violated prior, similar Rule 8.4(b)-(c); and his conducted also violated prior, similar Rules 1.15, 8.1; Maryland Rules 16-812, 16-603, 16-604, and §§ 10-302(a), 10-306 of the Business Occupations and Professions Article. Att'y Griev. Comm'n v. Prichard, 386 Md. 238, 872 A.2d 81 (2005).

Attorney's misconduct in abusing the trust that the client placed in the attorney by placing the client's retainer check in the attorney's operating account rather than an attorney trust account, spending that money which belonged to the client on the attorney, in refusing to promptly refund to the client money that attorney admittedly owed to the client despite the client's refund request, and in failing to promptly answer bar counsel's request for information about the matter warranted the attorney's indefinite suspension. Att'y Griev. Comm'n v. McCulloch, 397 Md. 674, 919 A.2d 660 (2007).

By spending fiduciary funds on herself, an attorney engaged in dishonest conduct in violation of (c). Att'y Griev. Comm'n v. McCulloch, 404 Md. 388, 946 A.2d 1009 (2008).

Attorney violated this Rule when he took a client's settlement proceeds, purchased a car and tried to avoid any responsibility in the matter. Att'y Griev. Comm'n v. Mitchell, 386 Md. 386, 872 A.2d 720 (2005).

Subsequent approval of unauthorized advance. — Arguing that an unauthorized "advance" from estate funds was later approved as a fee is little better than arguing that a fiduciary may dip into the client's funds for a "loan " as long as the money is later repaid. Att'y Griev. Comm'n v. Owrutsky, 322 Md. 334, 587 A.2d 511 (1991).

Lending funds to self as breach of trust. — It is a breach of trust for a trustee to lend trust funds to himself. Att'y Griev. Comm'n v. Owrutsky, 322 Md. 334, 587 A.2d 511 (1991).

Placing trust account money in unapproved account. — Respondent violated § 10-302 of the Business Occupations & Professions Article of the Annotated Code, prior, similar Rule 1.15 and this Rule, by placing trust account money in an unapproved account. Att'y Griev. Comm'n v. Boyd, 333 Md. 298, 635 A.2d 382 (1994).

Communications about settlement funds. — Attorney violated (a) because of the attorney's deceit and misrepresentation in communications with the client concerning the settlement funds. Att'y Griev. Comm'n v. Calhoun, 391 Md. 532, 894 A.2d 518 (2006).

Actions in attempt to avoid payment to judgment creditor. — Attorney was disbarred for violating Md. R. Prof. Conduct 1.15, Rule 16-607, and (a), (c), and (d) of this Rule because clear and convincing evidence established that he commingled personal and client funds and engaged in a pattern of dishonesty to hide his assets to avoid paying a judgment creditor. The evidence established that the attorney manipulated his corporate operations, his attorney escrow account, and his pension plan account to systematically avoid the judgment creditor's collection efforts and engaged in a pattern of behavior designed to conceal assets from attachment by the judgment creditor, which was conduct prejudicial to the administration of justice. Att'y Griev. Comm'n v. Foltz, 411 Md. 359, 983 A.2d 434 (2009).

Unintentional commingling of funds. — Lawyer was indefinitely suspended from the practice of law where he failed to maintain a trust account, commingled client funds and his own, and failed to keep proper records regarding such funds; but, the violations were unintentional, resulting from lawyer's ignorance of his obligation to refrain from commingling, and he was not motivated to use client funds for his own benefit. Att'y Griev. Comm'n v. Awuah, 346 Md. 420, 697 A.2d 446 (1997).

Bar Counsel failed to prove by clear and convincing evidence violations of prior, similar Rule 1.15 and this Rule, or § 10-306 of the Business Occupations and Professions Article, where lawyer's use of funds from trust account for operating expenses was motivated by ignorance of his obligations and not by fraud, dishonesty or deceit. Att'y Griev. Comm'n v. Awuah, 346 Md. 420, 697 A.2d 446 (1997).

Substantial evidence did not support a hearing judge's determinations that an attorney had not violated prior, similar Rules 1.1, 1.15(b), and 8.4 1.1, 1.15(b), and 8.4 by commingling a client's settlement proceeds with other funds in the attorney's operating account and delaying disbursement of the proceeds for several months, where the hearing judge had ignored the evidence on the back of the check itself and in bank records; although the conduct was egregious, it had not been shown to be intentional, so an indefinite suspension was the appropriate sanction. Att'y Griev. Comm'n v. Maignan, 390 Md. 287, 888 A.2d 344 (2005).

Misappropriation of client's funds. — When a lawyer drew several checks on the account of an estate for which he was personal representative, payable to himself, he violated prior, similar Md. R. Prof. Conduct 8.4. Att'y Griev. Comm'n v. Sullivan, 369 Md. 650, 801 A.2d 1077 (2002).

Misappropriation of entrusted funds is an act infected with deceit and dishonesty, and, in the absence of compelling extenuating circumstances justifying a lesser sanction, will result in disbarment. Att'y Griev. Comm'n v. Somerville, 379 Md. 586, 842 A.2d 811 (2004).

Attorney was disbarred as his misuse of a client's settlement monies violated prior, similar Rule 8.4 of the Rules of Professional Conduct, Rule 16-609, and §§ 10-306 and 10-307 of the Business Occupations and Professions Article. Att'y Griev. Comm'n v. Brown, 380 Md. 661, 846 A.2d 428 (2004).

Attorney was disbarred as his misappropriation of his client's funds was an act of theft and dishonesty, which violated the prior, similar Rule. Att'y Griev. Comm'n v. Brown, 380 Md. 661, 846 A.2d 428 (2004).

Attorney was disbarred under Rule 16-751 for misappropriation of client funds from his trust account, violating §§ 7-104 and 7-113 of the Criminal Law Article, § 10-306 of the Business Occupations and Professions Article, Rule 16-609, Rules 1.15 and 8.4 of the Maryland Lawyers Rules of Professional Conduct, and spousal abuse, violating § 3-203 of the Criminal Law Article. The attorney did not carry his burden to prove by a preponderance of the evidence any medical, psychiatric, or other condition to mitigate the findings of fact or conclusions of law. Att'y Griev. Comm'n v. Theriault, 390 Md. 202, 888 A.2d 292 (2005).

Where the attorney misappropriated client funds in two cases by signing a settlement check and depositing the proceeds into a personal account and by cashing a personal injury protection check sent by the client's insurer and spending it, the attorney's conduct was dishonest, deceitful, and criminal in violation of former, similar Md. R. Prof. Conduct 8.4(a)-

(d). Att'y Griev. Comm'n v. Kapoor, 391 Md. 505, 894 A.2d 502 (2006).

Where the attorney forged the client's signature on a check, where the attorney was dishonest in communicating with bar counsel during the course of the disciplinary investigation, and where the attorney lied on several occasions during disciplinary proceedings, the attorney violated former, similar Md. R. Prof. Conduct 8.1, 8.4(a). Att'y Griev. Comm'n v. Kapoor, 391 Md. 505, 894 A.2d 502 (2006).

By delaying payment of settlement proceeds to a client and the client's medical providers, transferring the client's funds into his operating account, and using the money for his own personal needs, an attorney violated Md. R. Prof. Conduct 1.3, 1.15(a) and (b), and 8.4(c) and (d); Rule 16-609; and § 10-306 of the Business Occupations and Professions Article. The court acknowledged the mitigating factors of the attorney paying the client and the medical providers and reducing his fee, but concluded that disbarment for such deceit was warranted. Att'y Griev. Comm'n v. Roberts, 394 Md. 137, 904 A.2d 557 (2006).

Attorney engaged in criminal acts that reflected adversely on the attorney's honesty, trustworthiness, or fitness as a lawyer in other respects when the attorney knowingly used trust funds for unauthorized purposes, such as teh payment of fees to himself before receiving settlement funds and use of client trust funds to pay other clients' fees. Att'y Griev. Comm'n v. Jarosinski, 411 Md. 432, 983 A.2d 477 (2009).

Mishandling attorney trust account. — Court of Appeals of Maryland affirmed hearing judge's findings that an attorney mishandled funds in attorney trust account but held that because there was no finding of intentional misappropriation of funds and the attorney's clients did not suffer a financial loss, indefinite suspension was the appropriate sanction. Att'y Griev. Comm'n v. DiCicco, 369 Md. 662, 802 A.2d 1014 (2002).

Even though an attorney's clients lost no funds because of a trust account shortfall resulting from failure to properly monitor the account, or even to balance the checkbook, and even though the attorney never touched any of the funds in question for personal or business use, because the shortfall was large and was not made up for a considerable length of time, and because of certain prior disciplinary problems, an indefinite suspension with permission to reapply after three months was imposed. Att'y Griev. Comm'n v. Sperling, 380 Md. 180, 844 A.2d 397 (2004).

Disbarment was the only appropriate sanction for an attorney who withdrew sums that should have been forwarded to a client from an attorney trust account for the attorney's personal use and failed to respond to the client's inquiries; the attorney's marital and drinking problems were not factors in mitigation. Att'y Griev. Comm'n v. Herman, 380 Md. 378, 844 A.2d 1181 (2004).

Where an attorney invaded trust funds being held for a client, and only scrambled to replace them when the client required reimbursement, the evidence was ample to show knowing misappropriation, and the only appropriate sanction was disbarment. Att'y Griev. Comm'n v. Zdravkovich, 381 Md. 680, 852 A.2d 82 (2004).

Attorney's repeated failure to pay either clients or medical providers as he was required to do was conduct prejudicial to the administration of justice. Att'y Griev. Comm'n v. Zuckerman, 386 Md. 341, 872 A.2d 693 (2005).

Attorney was disbarred from the practice of law because he violated Md. R. Prof. Conduct 1.15 and (a), (c), and (d) of this Rule and §§ 10-306 and 10-307 of the Business Occupations and Professions Article when he withdrew $600,000 of conservatorship assets to purchase property that was titled in his name and that of his business partner; the attorney's removal of the funds without court approval, was clearly a misappropriation in violation of (c), and the utilization of the funds, or lack thereof, did not alter the character of the misappropriation. Att'y Griev. Comm'n v. Whitehead, 405 Md. 240, 950 A.2d 798 (2008).

Attorney was disbarred from the practice of law because he violated Md. R. Prof. Conduct 1.15 and (a), (c), and (d) of this Rule and §§ 10-306 and 10-307 of the Business Occupations and Professions Article when he withdrew $600,000 of conservatorship assets to purchase property that was titled in his name and that of his business partner; the attorney violated (d) by engaging in self-dealing, which was prejudicial to the administration of justice, because his behavior undermined public confidence that an attorney would maintain entrusted funds as a fiduciary and as required by law. Att'y Griev. Comm'n v. Whitehead, 405 Md. 240, 950 A.2d 798 (2008).

Attorney was disbarred from the practice of law because he violated Md. R. Prof. Conduct 1.15 and (a), (c), and (d) of this Rule and §§ 10-306 and 10-307 of the Business Occupations and Professions Article when he withdrew $600,000 of conservatorship assets to purchase property that was titled in his name and that of his business partner; the attorney's violation of Md. R. Prof. Conduct 1.15, to which he failed to file an exception, as well as (c) and (d) of this Rule also constituted a violation of (a). Att'y Griev. Comm'n v. Whitehead, 405 Md. 240, 950 A.2d 798 (2008).

Attorney was disbarred from the practice of law because he violated Md. R. Prof. Conduct 1.15 and (a), (c), and (d) of this Rule and §§ 10-306 and 10-307 of the Business Occupations and Professions Article when he withdrew $600,000 of conservatorship assets to purchase property that was titled in his name and that of his business partner; the attorney's removal of the funds without court approval, was clearly a misappropriation in violation of (c), and his motivation did not affect the violation of (c) because he intentionally took the money out of the conservatorship. Att'y Griev. Comm'n v. Whitehead, 405 Md. 240, 950 A.2d 798 (2008).

Attorney violated (d) by falsely stating to the investigator that he had deposited prepaid funds into his trust account and by failing to produce complete records, in a timely manner, after a legitimate demand by Bar Counsel, to show the receipt and distribution of trust funds. Att'y Griev. Comm'n v. Khandpur, 421 Md. 1, 25 A.3d 165 (2011).

Attorney disbarred. — Attorney who, inter alia, intentionally misrepresented that much of the funds the attorney withdrew from the attorney's trust account were for fees earned from clients who contributed significantly less, or not at all, to the trust account, was disbarred for violating Md. Law. R. Prof. Conduct 1.15 and (a — d) of this Rule; §§ 10-306 and 307 of the Business Occupations and Professions Article; and Rules 16-607 and 16-609. Att'y Griev. Comm'n v. Thomas, 409 Md. 121, 973 A.2d 185 (2009).

Mishandling of escrow account. — Indefinite suspension was appropriate sanction for attorney's mishandling of escrow account, including the failure to pay claims due from the account and the failure to refund moneys to clients. Att'y Griev. Comm'n v. Singleton, 311 Md. 1, 532 A.2d 157 (1987).

When an attorney acted as an escrow agent for a client which purportedly funded high-risk loans, and the attorney removed commitment fees deposited in the escrow account and disbursed them to parties unrelated to a contemplated loan, rather than either returning them to the depositors or disbursing them to parties providing loans, he violated the prior, similar Rule because his conduct violated the Maryland Rules of Professional Conduct and it involved dishonesty, fraud, deceit and misrepresentation. Att'y Griev. Comm'n v. Smith, 376 Md. 202, 829 A.2d 567 (2003).

Escrow account violations. — An attorney who failed to observe the requirements with regard to an escrow account violated the prior, similar Rule and Rule 1.15 of the Rules of Professional Conduct, former Rule BV9 (now Rule 16-709) and § 10-306 of the Business Occupations and Professions Article, and was suspended for a minimum of one year. Att'y Griev. Comm'n v. Drew, 341 Md. 139, 669 A.2d 1344 (1996).

Attorney's repeated conduct in taking client funds from the attorney's escrow account and using them to pay the operating expenses of the attorney's law practice was intentional conduct that was criminalized pursuant to § 10-606 of the Business Occupations and Professions Article, regarding penalties for misuse of trust money, because such intentional conduct was willful and, thus, supported a finding that the attorney had committed misconduct pursuant to this Rule. Att'y Griev. Comm'n v. Nussbaum, 401 Md. 612, 934 A.2d 1 (2007).

E. Forgery, fraud, and false pretenses.

Providing false information. — Where attorney was aware that clients were declining disbursement for the purpose of secreting the settlement funds, and where he willfully complied with their plan to provide false information by withholding their funds, attorney engaged in dishonest and deceitful conduct prohibited by this Rule. Att'y Griev. Comm'n v. Glenn, 341 Md. 448, 671 A.2d 463 (1996).

Bar Counsel's failure to present evidence that attorney's clients actually filed a false financial aid application, that the false information was relied upon, or that their son actually received a benefit from such a representation was immaterial to finding that attorney was in violation of this Rule as it was sufficient if attorney aided the clients in their efforts to defraud or mislead college authorities in assessing their financial picture. Att'y Griev. Comm'n v. Glenn, 341 Md. 448, 671 A.2d 463 (1996).

Where the case was a disciplinary proceeding and not a criminal case, Bar Counsel did not need to prove fraud or false pretenses, nor prove that attorney specifically intended to defraud the college authorities in order to establish that attorney's conduct was dishonest or deceitful. Att'y Griev. Comm'n v. Glenn, 341 Md. 448, 671 A.2d 463 (1996).

The prior, similar Rule is broad enough to include intentionally deceptive or misleading testimony, even if it does not relate to a material matter. Att'y Griev. Comm'n v. Willis, 348 Md. 633, 705 A.2d 1121 (1998).

An attorney who gave false testimony during a deposition taken in the federal District Court proceeding and as a witness in a Maryland post conviction proceeding about her improper representation of private clients while an Assistant Public Defender violated prior, similar Rule 3.3 and Rule 8.4. The Court of Appeals held disbarment was the appropriate sanction. Att'y Griev. Comm'n v. White, 354 Md. 346, 731 A.2d 447 (1999).

Attorney violated the prior, similar Rule and Ga. St. Bar Stand. 4 for misrepresenting the estimate of a wife's future medical expenses to the husband, the court, and an expert economist (for use in an affidavit), and for paying the husband and his sister money belonging to the wife, while not properly disclosing the basis for the payments for the court's approval. Att'y Griev. Comm'n v. Roberson, 373 Md. 328, 818 A.2d 1059 (2003).

Attorney was disbarred for violating this Rule when she submitted fraudulent documents to her homeowner's insurance company, which resulted in compensation for rent she was purportedly paying, on property she actually owned, while water damage to her home was being fixed. Att'y Griev. Comm'n v. Jordan, 386 Md. 583, 873 A.2d 1161 (2005).

In attorney disciplinary proceedings, there is intentionally a high bar for a respondent attorney in a case where the flagship violation is of (c) (conduct involving dishonesty, fraud, deceit or misrepresentation) before the sanction of such a violation will be excused or mitigated based on the attorney's mental or physical condition at the time of commission of the conduct constituting the violation. Att'y Griev. Comm'n v. Guida, 391 Md. 33, 891 A.2d 1085 (2006).

Attorney violated Rule 8.1(a) and (c) of this Rule because he misrepresented his reasons for inactivity in his client's case. The attorney intentionally misled an investigator by implying, through emphatic statements of fact, that the reasons for the case's delay was due to unavailable transcripts and the complainant's late delivery of transcripts. Att'y Griev. Comm'n v. Lee, 393 Md. 385, 903 A.2d 360 (2006).

Attorney's exception to a judge's factual finding that the attorney represented to others that he was an agent of the District of Columbia (D.C.) Bar Counsel when he made telephone calls was without merit because (1) whether the attorney intended to deceive the recipients of his calls or misrepresent himself did not alter the judge's finding and conclusion that, regardless of the attorney's intentions, his actions of representing that he was calling on behalf of the D.C. Bar Counsel were deceitful and untrue; and (2) the judge's factual finding regarding the manner in which the attorney represented himself to the Merit Systems Protection Board was not clearly erroneous, and the conclusion of law that the attorney violated (c) was supported by the record. Att'y Griev. Comm'n v. Kalil, 402 Md. 358, 936 A.2d 854 (2007).

Attorney violated this Rule by committing perjury when the attorney filed false business reports under oath in the attorney's bankruptcy proceeding. Att'y Griev. Comm'n v. Byrd, 408 Md. 449, 970 A.2d 870 (2009).

When an attorney acted as a settlement agent at a real estate closing, and another attorney supervised the first attorney, both attorneys were properly found to have violated (c), when sale proceeds were not distributed as stated in a settlement statement, because the fact that the attorneys were not engaged in the practice of law was not a defense, as the Rule applied whether or not the attorney were engaged in the practice of law. Att'y Griev. Comm'n v. Johnson, 409 Md. 470, 976 A.2d 245 (2009).

Failure to inform prospective employer of nature of relationship with source of employment offer. — Attorney violated (c), and was suspended from the practice of law for 90 days, when the attorney concealed the nature of the attorney's relationship with the attorney's husband, also an attorney, from a prospective employer, the Federal Trade Commission, in order to establish a higher starting salary. Att'y Griev. Comm'n v. Floyd, 400 Md. 236, 929 A.2d 61 (2007).

Stealing employer's fees. — Attorney violated (c) because, when the attorney maintained an unauthorized side practice while being employed "of counsel" for a law firm, the attorney (1) stole fees that were owed to the firm, when the attorney represented and received fees from clients who owed the firm fees, (2) used the firm's resources for the attorney's side practice, and (2) put unearned fees from the side practice in the attorney's personal account. Att'y Griev. Comm'n v. Carithers, 421 Md. 28, 25 A.3d 181 (2011).

Destruction of evidence and giving false testimony. — Attorney sanctioned in the United States District Court for her destruction of evidence and giving false testimony in a case before that court was held to have violated prior, similar Maryland Rules of Professional Conduct 3.4 and 8.4. The Court of Appeals held disbarment was the appropriate sanction. Att'y Griev. Comm'n v. White, 354 Md. 346, 731 A.2d 447 (1999).

Misrepresentation under Md. Law R. Prof. Conduct 8.4(c) does not require specific intent. Att'y Griev. Comm'n v. Pennington, 387 Md. 565, 876 A.2d 642 (2005).

Misrepresentation of endorsement. — An attorney's misrepresentation of an endorsement constituted forgery which warranted suspension. Att'y Griev. Comm'n v. James, 333 Md. 174, 634 A.2d 48 (1993).

Attestation of false signature. — Ninety-day suspension was proper sanction for deliberate falsification of the notary certificate and knowing attestation of a false signature on a deed as genuine. Att'y Griev. Comm'n v. Maxwell, 307 Md. 600, 516 A.2d 570 (1986).

Forging another judge's name. — Forging another judge's name to change of disposition in a traffic case in return for political support warranted disbarment. Att'y Griev. Comm'n v. Bennett, 304 Md. 120, 497 A.2d 1140 (1985).

Attorney violated (c) and (d) when he forged a judge's signature on a false order purportedly from an adoption case he had agreed to handle for his clients and represented to his clients that it was a genuine order because this was dishonest, fraudulent, deceitful and a gross misrepresentation, in violation of Md. R. Prof. Conduct 8.4(c), and it was clearly prejudicial to the administration of justice, in violation of Md. R. Prof. Conduct 8.4(d), as he intended for his clients to rely on the order, and he violated both sections by his continuing misrepresentations amounting to outright lies to the clients concerning the status of their case and his representation that the order was genuine. Att'y Griev. Comm'n v. Guida, 391 Md. 33, 891 A.2d 1085 (2006).

Use of pseudonyms — Attorney Grievance Commission's exception to a judge's conclusion that an attorney's use of pseudonyms did not violate (c) was overruled because the judge found that the attorney's use of pseudonyms were not material and did nothing to mislead the call recipients to their detriment, the record did not show that the judge's findings of fact pertaining to the use of pseudonyms were clearly erroneous, and these facts supported the conclusion that the attorney's use of alternate names did not rise to the level necessary for a violation of (c). Att'y Griev. Comm'n v. Kalil, 402 Md. 358, 936 A.2d 854 (2007).

Misconduct not found. — Attorney was not shown to have violated (c) because the attorney's conduct in retaining an attorney fee from the client's personal injury case, despite the fee belonging to the bankruptcy estate, was a result of incompetence rather than intentional misconduct. However, given the attorney's other violations of professional conduct rules, the proper sanction was the attorney's indefinite suspension from the practice of law. Att'y Griev. Comm'n v. Nichols, 405 Md. 207, 950 A.2d 778 (2008).

F. Misfeasance.

Neglect of administration of estate. — Neglect of administration of estate which was continuous over several years and which ultimately prejudiced the right of at least one legatee under the will from receiving a monetary bequest was sufficient to warrant a 45-day suspension. Att'y Griev. Comm'n v. Gallagher, 306 Md. 107, 507 A.2d 625 (1986).

Failure to carry out contract of employment. — Ninety-day suspension was appropriate sanction for attorney's failure to timely file or adequately investigate action on behalf of her client, and for misrepresenting to her client that the suit had been filed on her behalf and was proceeding to trial where the client paid the attorney only part of the costs involved in the work the attorney did do and the attorney did not consider the gratuitous client to be a client; an attorney-client relationship did exist and, thus, the attorney failed to carry out her contract of employment. Att'y Griev. Comm'n v. Pinkney, 311 Md. 137, 532 A.2d 1367 (1987).

An attorney violated prior, similar Md. R. Prof. Conduct 8.4 by committing professional misconduct when he engaged in dishonesty, deceit and misrepresentation by leading his client to believe he had filed a law suit on her behalf, when in fact he had not, and accounted for the delay because he was waiting for a court date; indefinite suspension was appropriate sanction for this violation, coupled with other violations, especially failure to respond to repeated requests from bar counsel. Att'y Griev. Comm'n v. Harrington, 367 Md. 36, 785 A.2d 1260 (2001).

Abandonment of client. — Attorney's failure to appear in court and abandonment of his client, who was facing criminal charges in two cases, was conduct prejudicial to the administration of justice, in violation of the prior, similar Rule. Att'y Griev. Comm'n v. Tinsky, 377 Md. 646, 835 A.2d 542 (2003).

Where a client, facing criminal charges that could have resulted in incarceration, was abandoned by her attorney on what she assumed would be a trial date, the attorney violated Md. R. Prof. Conduct 1.3 and 8.4(d). Att'y Griev. Comm'n v. Ficker, 399 Md. 445, 924 A.2d 1105 (2007).

Where a client had an arrest warrant issued against him because his attorney failed to notify him that the trial had not been continued, and neither the attorney nor client appeared, the attorney violated (d). Att'y Griev. Comm'n v. Ficker, 399 Md. 445, 924 A.2d 1105 (2007).

Attorney's failure to make the client aware that the attorney would not be representing the client at a removal proceeding regarding the client's immigration status because such representation was not covered by their retainer agreement violated not only Md. R. Prof. Conduct 1.4 about keeping a client reasonably informed, but also (d) of this Rule regarding conduct prejudicial to the administration of justice. Such misconduct warranted a reprimand of the attorney. Att'y Griev. Comm'n v. Akpan, 405 Md. 277, 950 A.2d 820 (2008).

Concealment of information from client. — Attorney's concealment of material information regarding the dismissal of a client's case from the client amounted to a violation of (c). Att'y Griev. Comm'n v. Bleecker, 414 Md. 147, 994 A.2d 928 (2010).

Unwarranted claims. — Evidence that a lawyer had filed a RICO action that had "absolutely no foundation of facts" in the hope of obtaining treble damages was sufficient to justify sanction. Att'y Griev. Comm'n v. Alison, 349 Md. 623, 709 A.2d 1212 (1998).

Delegation of responsibility. — An attorney's practice of assigning and handling cases in such a manner that the lawyer ultimately charged with actually representing the client went into court unprepared or missed scheduled trial dates entirely, resulted in clients not being afforded competent representation, and justified an indefinite suspension from the practice of law. Att'y Griev. Comm'n v. Ficker, 349 Md. 13, 706 A.2d 1045 (1998).

Tardiness or absence from trial. — Since being late for a scheduled court appearance interferes with the administration of justice, it is obvious that being altogether absent from a scheduled trial does so as well; however, the circumstances surrounding the failure to appear and the actual consequences of that failure are matters that go to the question of sanction. Att'y Griev. Comm'n v. Ficker, 319 Md. 305, 572 A.2d 501 (1990).

Attorney twice failed to appear for scheduled court proceedings for which he was retained; this constituted a violation of prior, similar Md. R. Prof. Conduct 8.4. Att'y Griev. Comm'n v. Harris, 366 Md. 376, 784 A.2d 516 (2001).

Attorney violated (d) when he failed to appear for a hearing, even though his absence appeared to be unintentional, and his client was not prejudiced, because (1) he did not notify the trial court that he would be tardy, (2) he did not explain or apologize for his tardiness to the trial court, and (3) he failed to be present to protect his client's interests. Att'y Griev. Comm'n v. Mahone, 398 Md. 257, 920 A.2d 458 (2007).

Misrepresentations with respect to failure to file bankruptcy petition. — Attorney violated the prior, similar Rule by misrepresenting material facts to both bar counsel and to a client regarding the attorney's failure to file the client's bankruptcy petition, and moreover, this failure to truthfully report the facts regarding the client's representation of the client to bar counsel was conduct prejudicial to the administration of justice, which comprised a violation of the prior, similar Rule. Att'y Griev. Comm'n v. Granger, 374 Md. 438, 823 A.2d 611 (2003).

Improper handling of bankruptcy case. — Attorney's lack of any effective action on behalf of his client in connection with a bankruptcy case, particularly in failing to supply information requested by the court and his untimely filing of a motion to strike, was conduct prejudicial to the administration of justice in violation of the prior, similar Rule. Att'y Griev. Comm'n v. Tinsky, 377 Md. 646, 835 A.2d 542 (2003).

Negligent handling of personal injury case not violation. — Under circumstances in which a lawyer was honest with his client about his mistakes in handling the client's personal injury case, advised his client to hire counsel to assert a claim against him for his negligence in handling the client's case, and entered into a settlement in which he paid $ 30,000 to the client from his own funds without resort to his malpractice carrier, the hearing judge was not clearly erroneous in finding that the client was fairly and fully compensated, and the lawyer's negligent handling of the case did not constitute a violation of (d). Att'y Griev. Comm'n v. Queen, 407 Md. 556, 967 A.2d 198 (2009).

Practicing law while license was suspended. — Attorney violated prior, similar Md. R. Prof. Conduct 5.5 by continuing to practice law after the attorney was suspended in Maryland as the client continued to represent clients for months in immigration matters after his suspension in Maryland and his later suspension in the District of Columbia; furthermore, the attorney used his legal letterhead and business cards, which stated that his practice encompassed more than immigration law, and did not inform clients that he had been disbarred. Att'y Griev. Comm'n v. Awuah, 374 Md. 505, 823 A.2d 651 (2003).

Clients of other attorneys. — It was not a violation of former DR 1-102 (A) (4) for attorney not to have advised the clients of other attorneys that the recording undertaken by those attorneys was possibly ineffective. Att'y Griev. Comm'n v. Clements, 319 Md. 289, 572 A.2d 174 (1990).

Misrepresenting ownership of funds and failure to open probate estate. — Attorney's use of an account titled in the name of his father for personal and business purposes after his father's death, thereby misrepresenting the ownership of the funds in both these accounts, and his failure to open an estate to probate the father's assets in an effort to hide assets from creditors' collection efforts was clear and convincing evidence of conduct involving dishonesty, fraud, deceit and or misrepresentation. Att'y Griev. Comm'n v. Powell, 369 Md. 462, 800 A.2d 782 (2002).

Taking more than double payment of fees. — Hearing judge should not have been able to determine, from the evidence presented, that an attorney's actions in trying to set off earned commissions against a mortgage debt for property purchased from elderly clients could possibly be characterized as a "mistake"; the attorney had already been paid for handling another transaction for the client, and the evidence clearly indicated the attorney would never have refunded the overpayment if the clients' grown child had not launched an investigation, so disbarment was absolutely mandated. Att'y Griev. Comm'n v. Parker, 389 Md. 142, 884 A.2d 104 (2005).

Representation of multiple defendants in a criminal case. — An attorney's contact with his client's represented criminal codefendant was deemed a violation of the prior, similar Rule and resulted in disbarment. Att'y Griev. Comm'n v. Kent, 337 Md. 361, 653 A.2d 909 (1995).

III. EVIDENCE AND SANCTIONS.

Violation not found by Review Board. — It was not improper for Bar Counsel to charge in a disciplinary petition a number of rule violations not specifically found by the Review Board. Att'y Griev. Comm'n v. Goldsborough, 330 Md. 342, 624 A.2d 503 (1993).

Violation found. — Attorney violated the prior, similar Rule in informing a third-party assignee that his firm no longer represented a client and to direct all future inquiries to the client and misrepresented the attorney's ongoing representation of the client with an intent to nullify the assignment and allow the attorney to avoid paying the assignee; further, the attorney's misrepresentation of the facts to Maryland Bar Counsel's investigator supported a finding of a violation. Att'y Griev. Comm'n v. Ellison, 384 Md. 688, 867 A.2d 259 (2005).

Attorney violated the prior, similar Rule by failing to disclose to Maryland Bar Counsel and its investigator his continued representation of a client (and his fee), until faced with producing the ultimate documentation of his violation; his dishonest and deceitful conduct regarding a third-party assignee and an assignment of settlement proceeds not only violated his obligations under the Maryland Rules of Professional Conduct, but also engendered a public disrespect for attorneys and the courts that was connected inherently with his practice. Att'y Griev. Comm'n v. Ellison, 384 Md. 688, 867 A.2d 259 (2005).

Bar counsel's exception to hearing court's findings of fact and conclusions of law was sustained where the hearing court found that an attorney violated Md. R. Prof. Conduct 1.8(c), but did not find a violation of this Rule. The attorney's violation of Md. R. Prof. Conduct 1.8(c) was considered a serious violation, and the attorney's violation of this Rule could properly be based on the attorney's violation of another rule of professional conduct. Att'y Griev. Comm'n v. Lanocha, 392 Md. 234, 896 A.2d 996 (2006).

Attorney violated Md. R. Prof. Conduct 5.3(c), when the attorney asked the attorney's legal assistant, who was under the attorney's supervision, to notarize a power of attorney when the signatory was not actually present at the moment of notarization. Att'y Griev. Comm'n v. Ward, 394 Md. 1, 904 A.2d 477 (2006).

Bringing an action for defamation against a former client, without having conducting legal research into its viability and without appreciating that Maryland law provides for a broad privilege for allegedly defamatory statements in judicial proceedings, or that doing so likely would erode the public confidence in the legal profession, sufficiently supported the finding that the attorney violated (d) of this Rule and Rule 3.1. Att'y Griev. Comm'n v. Manger, 396 Md. 134, 913 A.2d 1 (2006).

Clear and convincing evidence showed that the attorney acted incompetently when the attorney accepted a case that required filing in a jurisdiction where the attorney was not admitted to practice, and when the attorney failed to service notice to defendant, that the attorney failed to act with reasonable diligence and promptness in representing the client when the attorney failed to file the estate in the proper jurisdiction, that the attorney failed to communicate the truth when the attorney told the client that the attorney was admitted to practice in a certain jurisdiction when the attorney was not admitted there and when the attorney failed to communicate to the client that the attorney intended to seek other counsel in the District of Columbia to assist the attorney, that the attorney's fees were unreasonable because the attorney charged and accepted fees when no work was performed in furtherance of the case, and that the attorney's actions were prejudicial to the administration of justice; even though the attorney was absolved of the charge that the attorney did not properly terminate the representation because the evidence showed that the attorney returned all unearned advance fees to the client after the client retained new counsel, the attorney's violations, which included intentionally dishonest conduct, warranted disbarment, especially since the attorney had a prior disciplinary history. Att'y Griev. Comm'n v. Ward, 396 Md. 203, 913 A.2d 41 (2006).

State's highest court found that the attorney should be disbarred, as clear and convincing evidence showed that the attorney falsely represented in a deposition that the business associate was a client of the attorney when that was not true, in violation of Md. R. Prof. Conduct 1.9, and that the attorney engaged in an impermissible conflict of interest in violation of Md. R. Prof. Conduct 8.4 when the attorney represented the corporation in a substantially similar matter in a lawsuit against the entity after the attorney had represented the entity for two years in matters that included the same matter that was the subject of the lawsuit; not only were the violations proven, but the attorney failed to prove the attorney's affirmative defense of waiver since the attorney presented a paucity of argument or evidence in that regard. Att'y Griev.

Comm'n v. Siskind, 401 Md. 41, 930 A.2d 328 (2007).

Attorney's conduct in violating multiple Maryland Rules of Professional Conduct, including violation of (a),(b), and (d) of this Rule for knowing misappropriation of client funds and lying to clients, warranted the attorney's disbarment. The attorney did (1) not place fees advanced into the attorney's trust account, (2) not file a complaint for an emergency hearing when the attorney told the client the attorney had done so, and (3) not return fees paid that the attorney had not earned. Att'y Griev. Comm'n v. Webster, 402 Md. 448, 937 A.2d 161 (2007).

Attorney violated (c) by misrepresenting to the client that the attorney had never been in trouble with the bar. When asked that question by the client the attorney clearly replied no, knowing full well that there were at least two prior formal disciplinary actions by the Court of Appeals against the attorney. Att'y Griev. Comm'n v. Kreamer, 404 Md. 282, 946 A.2d 500 (2008).

Attorney violated (c) by taking a $ 100 non-refundable "engagement fee" upon representation and a $ 200 retainer and then never contacting the client at all or keeping the client up to date on the attorney's progress. The attorney took the money with obviously no intent to pursue the matter. Att'y Griev. Comm'n v. Kreamer, 404 Md. 282, 946 A.2d 500 (2008).

Respondent violated (a) — (d) in her dealings with a client and a person from whom she borrowed money by, inter alia, falsely claiming to be licensed to practice law in Maryland. Att'y Griev. Comm'n v. Sucklal, 418 Md. 1, 12 A.3d 650 (2011).

Attorney violated this Rule in two cases because, (1) in a personal injury case in which it was learned that the defendant was deceased, the attorney's failure to petition to open an estate for the deceased defendant resulted in the dismissal of a client's complaint, and the attorney delayed the client's pursuit of the complaint by promising to petition to open the estate by a certain date, neglecting to do so, and then failing to inform the client of the complaint's dismissal, and, (2) in another case, despite soliciting a client, the attorney never entered the attorney's appearance on the client's behalf, and then failed to appear at a hearing for which the attorney was retained. Att'y Griev. Comm'n v. De La Paz, 418 Md. 534, 16 A.3d 181 (2011).

Attorney violated (a) — (d) because the attorney (1) intentionally took funds belonging to the firm by which the attorney was employed, consisting of a client's check issued to the firm, and placed the funds in the attorney's personal bank account, (2) commingled the funds with the attorney's own personal funds and later transferred a portion of the funds to another personal bank account without the knowledge or consent of the client or the law firm to whom the funds belonged, (3) failed to advise the law firm of payments made by the client, and (4) did not relinquish the funds to the firm until after the attorney was confronted by a supervisor. Att'y Griev. Comm'n v. Elliott, 417 Md. 659, 12 A.3d 105 (2011).

Violation not found. — Attorney's indefinite suspension for violating Md. R. Prof. Conduct 3.3(a)(1), 5.5(a), and 8.4(a), (c), and (d) was appropriate where, pursuant to Rule 16-760(c)(2), he should have advised the court that he was not permitted to continue his representation of a client as soon as he learned of his suspension. Att'y Griev. Comm'n v. Maignan, 402 Md. 39, 935 A.2d 409 (2007).

Bar counsel failed to show that an attorney had violated Md. R. Prof. Conduct 1.1, 1.3, 1.5(a), 1.16(d), 3.1, 5.1, 5.3(a) and (c), and 8.4(a) and (d) where the attorney had informed the client that he no longer wished to represent him after the client changed his mind with respect to a settlement agreement and the attorney had discharged the associate after discovering that she had subsequently file additional motions. Att'y Griev. Comm'n v. Maignan, 402 Md. 39, 935 A.2d 409 (2007).

Bar counsel failed to show that an attorney had violated Md. R. Prof. Conduct 1.1, 1.3, 1.4(a) and (b), 1.5, 1.16(d), 3.1, 5.1, 5.3, and 8.4(a), (c), and (d) where it was possible to find, based on the testimony, that the attorney had relied on the clients' representations that they intended to handle the appeal pro se, and as a result, Bar counsel had failed to prove that the attorney had represented the two clients in an appeal. Att'y Griev. Comm'n v. Maignan, 402 Md. 39, 935 A.2d 409 (2007).

Attorney was not in violation of (b) as the allegation that the attorney committed a criminal act was not proven by the State Attorney Grievance Commission; the court was not satisfied that the attorney engaged in conduct involving dishonesty, fraud, deceit or misrepresentation, and the court believed that the attorney's conduct was motivated by stubbornness, not greed, and therefore found that the attorney was not in violation of (c). Att'y Griev. Comm'n v. Kendrick, 403 Md. 489, 943 A.2d 1173 (2008).

Petition alleging that the attorney violated Md. R. Prof. Conduct 8.4, based on claims that the attorney sought reimbursement for expenditures not made or for amounts in excess of expenditures, lacked merit, because no client was asked to pay more than reasonable costs for travel, lodging, and incidental expenses, and the attorney never asked for education expenses in excess of amounts the attorney believed the attorney was entitled. Att'y Griev.

Comm'n v. Walter, 407 Md. 670, 967 A.2d 783 (2009).

Attorney's lies to a client about being faithful to her were wholly unrelated to the actual practice of law and did not warrant a finding of a Rule 8.4(c) violation; an attorney's lies to his client concerning his romantic relationships with others is a completely different creature than an attorney's lies to his client about matters related directly to his legal representation of that client, and Comment 2 to this rule makes clear that offenses involving "moral turpitude" that are unrelated to an attorney's fitness to practice law are outside the bounds of sanctionable conduct under this rule. Att'y Griev. Comm'n v. Hall, 408 Md. 306, 969 A.2d 953 (2009).

Attorney was sanctioned by a public reprimand for technically violating Rule 16-609 regarding prohibited transactions as a result of a negligent clerical error involving depositing some of his ex-girlfriend's funds into his operating account instead of his firm's escrow account, which error was corrected upon discovery and was not wilful. The Court of Appeals of Maryland further upheld the trial judge's finding of fact that no attorney client relationship existed between the attorney and his girlfriend to support the other violations asserted against him since he never charged his ex-girlfriend a fee for his services and was only helping her while she received treatment for her alcohol abuse. Att'y Griev. Comm'n v. Shoup, 410 Md. 462, 979 A.2d 120 (Aug. 28, 2009).

When a lawyer agreed with a client that the lawyer would be entitled to 15 percent of the value of any lost property the lawyer recovered for the client, and then a real estate broker charged the client a real estate commission after allegedly promising that no commission would be charged, the lawyer's 15 percent commission did not become an unreasonable fee, in violation of Md. Law. R. Prof. Conduct 1.5(a), nor did the lawyer, as a result, violate (c) of this Rule, because the lawyer never

When a lawyer agreed with a client that the lawyer would be entitled to 15 percent of the value of any lost property the lawyer recovered for the client, and then a real estate broker charged the client a real estate commission after allegedly promising that no commission would be charged, the lawyer's 15 percent commission did not become an unreasonable fee, in violation of Md. Law. R. Prof. Conduct 1.5(a), nor did the lawyer, as a result, violate (c) of this Rule, because the lawyer never

attempted to increase the lawyer's fees beyond the 15 percent contingent fee. Att'y Griev. Comm'n v. Edib, 415 Md. 696, 4 A.3d 957 (2010).

When a lawyer agreed with a client that (1) the lawyer would serve as administrator of the client's deceased brother's estate, and (2) the lawyer would be entitled to 15 percent of the value of any lost property the lawyer recovered for the client, after which a real estate broker charged the client a real estate commission after allegedly promising that no commission would be charged, the lawyer's 15 percent commission did not become an unreasonable fee, in violation of Md. Law. R. Prof. Conduct 1.5(a), nor did the lawyer, as a result, violate (c) of this Rule, when the lawyer's fee allegedly exceeded a fee schedule for administrators in the jurisdiction in which the lawyer administered the estate because the lawyer was not administering an estate when the lawyer sold real property for the client since the property passed directly to the client upon the client's brother's death, outside of probate, so the fee schedule was not violated. Att'y Griev. Comm'n v. Edib, 415 Md. 696, 4 A.3d 957 (2010).

When a lawyer agreed with a client that (1) the lawyer would serve as administrator of the client's deceased brother's estate, and (2) the lawyer would be entitled to 15 percent of the value of any lost property the lawyer recovered for the client, after which a real estate broker charged the client a real estate commission after allegedly promising that no commission would be charged, the lawyer did not violate Md. Law. R. Prof. Conduct 1.5(a) or (c) of this Rule, when the lawyer's fee allegedly exceeded a Maryland fee schedule for estate administrators because the lawyer was not acting as an estate administrator when the sold the brother's properties for the client, since those properties passed to the client outside of probate, so the Maryland fee schedule for an estate administrator did not bear heavily on an analysis under Md. Law. R. Prof. Conduct 1.5(a)(3) as the sale of property and the administration of an estate, where conducted separately, were not sufficiently analogous legal services. Att'y Griev. Comm'n v. Edib, 415 Md. 696, 4 A.3d 957 (2010).

When a lawyer agreed with a client that (1) the lawyer would serve as administrator of the client's deceased brother's estate, and (2) the lawyer would be entitled to 15 percent of the value of any lost property the lawyer recovered for the client, after which a real estate broker charged the client a real estate commission after allegedly promising that no commission would be charged, the lawyer did not violate Md. Law. R. Prof. Conduct 1.5(a) or (c) of this Rule on the theory that any fees charged by the lawyer for the liquidation of real estate in the brother's estate were unreasonable, since the lawyer performed no actual "legal services" in doing so, because Md. Law. R. Prof. Conduct 1.5 made no mention of "legal services," and Rule 1.5 only implicated attorneys who made an agreement for, charged, or collected an unreasonable fee, so an attorney was entitled to a reasonable fee whether or not the attorney was performing "legal services" per se. Att'y Griev. Comm'n v. Edib, 415 Md. 696, 4 A.3d 957 (2010).

When a lawyer agreed with a client that (1) the lawyer would serve as administrator of the client's deceased brother's estate, and (2) the lawyer would be entitled to 15 percent of the value of any lost property the lawyer recovered for the client, after which a real estate broker charged the client a real estate commission after allegedly promising that no commission would be charged, the lawyer did not violate Md. Law. R. Prof. Conduct 1.5(a) or (c) of this Rule, based on a weighing of the applicable factors in Md. Law. R. Prof. Conduct 1.5(a), because the fact that the time and labor involved in dealing with the client's various requests, ranging from asset liquidation to finding lost property, was unknown at the inception; that the lawyer achieved the client's desired result (the liquidation of real property); and, that the lawyer was particularly capable of performing the services required by the client, all bore on Md. Law. R. Prof. Conduct 1.5(a)(1), (4), and (7), respectively, and suggested that the lawyer's fee was reasonable. Att'y Griev. Comm'n v. Edib, 415 Md. 696, 4 A.3d 957 (2010).

When a lawyer was properly found to have violated Md. Law. R. Prof. Conduct 1.4 and 1.16(d) by not turning over a former client's file to the client's new attorney, when requested, the lawyer also violated (a) of this Rule because it was a violation of (a) to violate another rule of professional conduct. Att'y Griev. Comm'n v. Edib, 415 Md. 696, 4 A.3d 957 (2010).

When an attorney deposited unearned funds received on a client's behalf in the attorney's operating account, rather than in a trust account, it was not error for a hearing judge not to find the attorney violated (c) because the hearing judge (1) could accept the attorney's explanation that the attorney believed the attorney was allowed to deposit the funds in the operating account and that the attorney opened a trust account as soon as the attorney learned the attorney was required to have a trust account, (2) found no indication of the attorney's dishonest intent, and (3) based the finding on a credibility assessment of the attorney, so the finding was deferred to. Att'y Griev. Comm'n v. Tauber, — Md. —, 26 A.3d 967 (2011).

Mitigating circumstances. — While disbarment usually follows a conviction of a crime of moral turpitude which involves fraud or dishonesty, a lesser sanction may be justified when compelling mitigating circumstances exist. Att'y Griev. Comm'n v. Mandel, 316 Md. 197, 557 A.2d 1329 (1989).

Where an attorney's neglect of clients, including misrepresenting the status of their litigation to them, was almost certainly causally related to the attorney's serious illness, and the attorney's record was otherwise distinguished, the court imposed an indefinite suspension instead of disbarment. Att'y Griev. Comm'n v. West, 378 Md. 395, 836 A.2d 588 (2003).

The traumatic events in attorney's life during the period for which he failed to file tax returns, together with the fact he acknowledged and regretted his errors and felt tremendous remorse, warranted the unusually lenient sanction of a six-month suspension. Att'y Griev. Comm'n v. Breschi, 340 Md. 590, 667 A.2d 659 (1995).

Alcoholism, drug addiction or mental disorder. — When alcoholism is, to a substantial extent, the cause of the misconduct by an attorney, we view the misconduct in a somewhat different light; under this circumstance the appropriate sanction is indefinite suspension and the focus shifts to questions of rehabilitation and the imposition of conditions sufficient to protect the public if the lawyer is allowed to resume practice. Att'y Griev. Comm'n v. Reid, 308 Md. 646, 521 A.2d 743 (1987).

When a lawyer's misconduct is caused by alcoholism, drug addiction, or a mental disorder, the usual sanction is indefinite suspension. This provides the requisite protection for the public, for it prevents the lawyer from practicing law until such time (if ever) that he or she can demonstrate that he or she is free from the effects of the ailment and able to practice competently. At the same time, the lawyer is spared the ultimate sanction of disbarment, a sanction which would be unfair to apply where the lawyer's conduct is caused by factors beyond his or her control. Att'y Griev. Comm'n v. Powers, 314 Md. 484, 551 A.2d 465 (1989).

Where alcoholism is allegedly implicated in cases involving misappropriation of trust or client funds, a sanction less severe than disbarment may be imposed if the evidence discloses that the alcoholism, to a substantial extent, was the responsible, precipitating, and root cause of the misappropriation. Att'y Griev. Comm'n v. White, 328 Md. 412, 614 A.2d 955 (1992).

Simply to show that an attorney was in the throes of alcoholism at the time he misappropriated client funds and that his thinking was "alcoholically impaired" to the point where he rationalized his behavior as acceptable, even though he knew it was not, is insufficient mitigation in and of itself to justify a sanction less than disbarment. Att'y Griev. Comm'n v. White, 328 Md. 412, 614 A.2d 955 (1992).

An indefinite suspension was the proper sanction in the case of a misappropriation of client funds caused by alcoholism; however, in the future, absent truly compelling circumstances, alcoholism will usually not be permitted to mitigate where an attorney commits a violation of ethical or legal rules which would ordinarily warrant disbarment. Att'y Griev. Comm'n v. Kenney, 339 Md. 578, 664 A.2d 854 (1995).

An attorney who had been convicted of possession of cocaine, but whose offenses were not directly related to the practice of law, whose first disciplinary proceeding this was, and who had made efforts to overcome his addiction, was suspended for thirty days. Att'y Griev. Comm'n v. Gilbert, 356 Md. 249, 739 A.2d 1 (1999).

Bar Counsel's recommendation of disbarment with regard to an attorney found to have violated Md. R. Prof. Conduct 1.15(a), (b), and (c), and (b), (c), and (d) of this Rule, was not accepted by the Maryland Court of Appeals; the disciplinary matter was remanded for the Attorney Grievance Commission and Bar Counsel to reconsider entering into a conditional diversion agreement with the attorney because, even though the evidence supported the finding of wilful misconduct, the attorney's mental health and severe depression was a significant factor, and the Court of Appeal's interpretation of Rule 16-736 allowed diversion as a sanction in such cases where the professional misconduct was not solely the result of wilful or intentionally dishonest conduct. Att'y Griev. Comm'n v. Cappell, 389 Md. 402, 886 A.2d 112 (2005).

Lawyer's criminal behavior. — Lawyer's criminal behavior, which was causally related to psychiatric disorder, warranted imposition of indefinite suspension. Att'y Griev. Comm'n v. Mitchell, 308 Md. 653, 521 A.2d 746 (1987).

Cocaine conviction. — Attorney convicted of possession of cocaine was sanctioned with an indefinite suspension for his violation of the prior, similar Rule because it was his first disciplinary proceeding and his conviction did not reflect on his honesty or the quality of legal services he rendered to clients. Att'y Griev. Comm'n v. Black, 362 Md. 574, 766 A.2d 119 (2001).

Misconduct during disciplinary hearing. — The hearing court's determination that an attorney violated the prior, similar Rule by misleading the hearing court during the disciplinary hearing was inappropriate because conduct before the court at a disciplinary hearing cannot be the basis for a separate finding of a violation of the Rule in the same proceeding.

Att'y Griev. Comm'n of Maryland v. Mooney, 359 Md. 56, 753 A.2d 17 (2000).

Sanctions for misrepresentation. — A misrepresentation need not involve fraud or deceit; and in such a circumstance a sanction other than disbarment is justified and has been imposed; when, in addition to the misrepresentation, a finding of fraud is made and is supported by the evidence, disbarment would follow as a matter of course absent compelling extenuating circumstances. Att'y Griev. Comm'n v. Myers, 333 Md. 440, 635 A.2d 1315 (1994).

Disbarment was the only appropriate sanction against an attorney where the hearing court had articulated the basis for its conclusion that the attorney had violated (b) and (c), had considered the character testimony presented by the attorney, the absence of other evidence indicating that the attorney had taken client monies for his own use, and the attorney's medical conditions in reaching those findings, had properly refused to credit the attorney's mitigation evidence with respect to intent and the seriousness of the attorney's medical conditions, and there were no other compelling extenuating circumstances sufficient to avoid the automatic disbarment rule for misappropriation. Att'y Griev. Comm'n v. Post, 379 Md. 60, 839 A.2d 718 (2003).

Practicing law while license was suspended. — Attorney violated prior, similar Md. R. Prof. Conduct 5.5 by continuing to practice law after the attorney was suspended in Maryland as the client continued to represent clients for months in immigration matters after his suspension in Maryland and his later suspension in the District of Columbia; furthermore, the attorney used his legal letterhead and business cards, which stated that his practice encompassed more than immigration law, and did not inform clients that he had been disbarred. Att'y Griev. Comm'n v. Awuah, 374 Md. 505, 823 A.2d 651 (2003).

Attorney's conduct in providing advice to another person on a real estate matter and then falsely stating that the attorney was representing the attorney's own interests in the matter, done while the attorney's license to practice law was already suspended, violated (a),(b), and (c) making it wrong for an attorney to engage in misconduct. Since the attorney's provision of legal services to another constituted the practice of law pursuant to pursuant to §§ 10-101 and 10-602 of the Business Occupations and Professions Article and was done while the attorney's license was suspended, disbarment was a proper sanction. Att'y Griev. Comm'n v. Shryock, 408 Md. 105, 968 A.2d 593 (2009).

Reciprocal discipline. — Attorney was disbarred for his handling of a medical malpractice case for a wife, her common-law husband, and her children, which had resulted in the attorney's disbarment in Georgia, for misconduct as defined in Maryland Rule 16-701(i), and for violating the Maryland counterparts of the Georgia State Bar Standards he had been found to have violated, more specifically, prior, similar Rules 8.4 (misconduct), 1.5 (fees), 1.7 (conflict of interest: general rule), and 1.15 (safekeeping property). Att'y Griev. Comm'n v. Roberson, 373 Md. 328, 818 A.2d 1059 (2003).

Even though a lawyer had only been suspended from practice for a few years in the District of Columbia after having admitted to misappropriating title insurance agency fees that should have been turned over the the law firm as part of the attorney's handling of real estate transactions, the imposition of precisely reciprocal discipline in Maryland was inappropriate in light of the severe penalties imposed on Maryland attorneys who misappropriated funds from anyone; disbarment was the only possible sanction, since the attorney presented no evidence that compelling circumstances were the root cause of the misconduct. Att'y Griev. Comm'n v. Weiss, 389 Md. 531, 886 A.2d 606 (2005).

Attorney violated Md. R. Prof. Conduct 1.8(c) by preparing a will for a client in which the attorney was named the beneficiary of a substantial bequest and having counsel that the attorney shared office space with review the will with the client and gauge the client's competency, because it created the potential for the appearance of impropriety and thus, also amounted to a violation of subsection (d) of this Rule. Because the attorney was unlikely to repeat the actions in a similar situation, had no prior disciplinary history, and had made a good faith effort to comply with Md. R. Prof. Conduct 1.8(c), a warning was issued. Att'y Griev. Comm'n v. Saridakis, 402 Md. 413, 936 A.2d 886 (2007).

In a reciprocal discipline action, the attorney, who admitted to the wrongdoing which led to a finding that D.C. R. Prof. Conduct 1.2(a), 1.4(a), 1.4(b), 1.4(c), 1.5(c), 1.15(a), 1.15(b), 1.15(c), and 8.4(d) had been violated based on the attorney's negligence misrepresentation of settlement funds in one case and interference with the administration of justice in another case, amounting to violations of Md. Law. R. Prof. Conduct Rules 1.2(a), 1.4(a)(2) and (3), 1.4(b), 1.5(c), 1.15(a), 1.15(e), and 8.4(d), was indefinitely suspended in Maryland, with right to apply for readmission after reinstatement in the District in Columbia. Att'y Griev. Comm'n v. Thaxton, 415 Md. 341, — A.2d —, 1 A.3d 470 (2010).

In a reciprocal disciplinary action, the attorney, who had been suspended from the practice of law for one year and one day in Colorado, was disbarred for violating Md. Law. R. Prof. Conduct 3.3(a)(1), 3.4(c), and 8.4(a), (b), (c), and (d), based on the attorney's own admission that he failed to make pertinent disclosures during a personal bankruptcy case and gave false testimony that case. Att'y Griev. Comm'n v. Zodrow, 419 Md. 286, 19 A.3d 381 (2011).

Reprimand was proper sanction. — An inexperienced attorney did not act intentionally when she assured a court, and other attorneys, that her client's bankruptcy had been filed, and a reprimand was an appropriate sanction for her failure to supervise the law clerk who was supposed to have filed the bankruptcy petition. Att'y Griev. Comm'n v. Jaseb, 364 Md. 464, 773 A.2d 516 (2001).

A reprimand was issued to an attorney who violated prior, similar Rules 5.5, 7.1, 7.5, 8.1, 8.4, and § 10-602 of the Business Occupations and Professions Article. Att'y Griev. Comm'n v. Bridges, 360 Md. 489, 759 A.2d 233 (2000).

When an attorney (1) failed to appear at a hearing without telling the trial judge he would be late or explaining or apologizing for his absence, (2) repeatedly argued with a trial judge and opposing counsel in the course of a hearing, and (3) walked out of the courtroom while a trial judge was issuing his opinion, the attorney's conduct violated (d), and a reprimand was the appropriate sanction. Att'y Griev. Comm'n v. Mahone, 398 Md. 257, 920 A.2d 458 (2007).

Only the attorney's e-mail response to a social acquaintance that the social acquaintance and spouse could represent to the trial court that they had in fact been separated the required one year to obtain a no-fault divorce merited discipline in a case involving two separate disciplinary investigations. The attorney's representation violated (d) because it left the social acquaintance with the impression that she could mislead the trial court and warranted a reprimand, especially since the advice was not given with the intent that it be followed and the social acquaintance had not seen the response. Att'y Griev. Comm'n v. Elmendorf, 404 Md. 353, 946 A.2d 542 (2008).

Suspension denied. — Attorney Grievance Commission of Maryland's request that attorney be suspended from practice of law was denied, because the offense that the attorney stood convicted of in the District of Columbia, engaging in the transmission of money without a license, did not reveal anything about the attorney's character, and the evidence showed that the attorney did not intend to violate the law but actually tried to comply with it by hiring an attorney for that purpose. Att'y Griev. Comm'n v. Downey, 413 Md. 1, 990 A.2d 1070 (2010).

Thirty-day suspension. — Attorney was suspended for 30 days for violating Md. R. Prof. Conduct 1.3, 1.4, 8.1(b), and 8.4(d) after the attorney failed to prepare an eligible domestic relations order for client one, and failed to timely prepare a consent order for client two, and then submitted it to opposing counsel and the trial court without allowing client two to review it, since there were mitigating factors, the attorney had expressed remorse, and there was testimony that the conduct was out of the attorney's character. Att'y Griev. Comm'n v. Hill, 398 Md. 95, 919 A.2d 1194 (2007).

Attorney was suspended from the practice of law for 30 days for depositing unearned funds received on a client's behalf in an operating account, rather than a trust account, because (1) the attorney violated (d) by not having a trust account, (2) it was found the attorney mistakenly thought the attorney properly handled the funds and that the attorney's failure to put the funds in a trust account was not done with an intent to be dishonest, (3) there was a potential for injury, (4) an indefinite suspension was too harsh, as there was no misappropriation, and (5) a reprimand was inadequate. Att'y Griev. Comm'n v. Tauber, — Md. —, 26 A.3d 967 (2011).

Forty-five day suspension. — In a reciprocal discipline action, the attorney, who had been publicly reprimanded in Texas, was suspended from the practice of law in Maryland for 45 days for misrepresenting that a document was an original signature page, but later admitting that the document was signed five years after the original contract, on the eve of summary judgment, conduct that amounted to violations of Md. Law. R. Prof. Conduct 3.3(a)(1) and (4) and 8.4(c), because such conduct warranted substantially different discipline in Maryland. Att'y Griev. Comm'n v. Gordon, 413 Md. 46, 991 A.2d 51 (2010).

Ninety-day suspension was appropriate sanction. — Ninety-day suspension was appropriate sanction for attorney's neglect of client's cases, falsifying client's signature on a complaint, and causing the complaint with the false signature to be notarized and filed. Att'y Griev. Comm'n v. Parsons, 310 Md. 132, 527 A.2d 325 (1987).

Attorney's failure in one case to take any action in response to a notice from the trial court that the attorney had to respond or face dismissal of the client's case showed a lack of both competence and diligence, and the attorney's conduct in a second, separate case where the attorney took a meritless case, charged a fee that grossly outweighed the work accomplished, and failed to communicate with the client meant that the attorney violated (d) regarding actions prejudicial to the administration of justice. Since the attorney's conduct was merely negligent rather than deceitful, a 90-day suspension from the practice of law was warranted. Att'y Griev. Comm'n v. Ugwuonye, 405 Md. 351, 952 A.2d 226 (2008).

Indefinite suspension with leave to apply for reinstatement. — Indefinite suspension with leave to apply for reinstatement in one year was warranted where the attorney had served sentence for federal offenses in California, had been suspended and reinstated by the California Bar, and had, both prior to and after the federal charges, no other misconduct or disciplinary problems. Att'y Griev. Comm'n v. Sparrow, 314 Md. 421, 550 A.2d 1150 (1988).

Indefinite suspension with leave to apply for reinstatement after 90 days was warranted, where defendant pleaded guilty to possessing cocaine and drug paraphernalia, resisting arrest, and assault and battery upon an officer, and had a long history of abuse of controlled substances. Att'y Griev. Comm'n v. Hamby, 322 Md. 606, 589 A.2d 53 (1991).

In a disciplinary matter in Maryland that was not reciprocal in nature but that was based upon the attorney's 30-day suspension, with reinstatement conditioned upon a showing of fitness, in the District of Columbia, the attorney was suspended indefinitely for violating prior, similar Md. R. Prof. Conduct 8.1(b), 8.4(d), and the attorney's reinstatement to the Maryland bar was conditioned upon the attorney's reinstatement to the District of Columbia bar; the impact of the misconduct, which involved a refusal to respond to disciplinary charges in violation of D.C. R. Prof. Conduct 8.4(d), 8.1(b) and D.C. Bd. Prof. Resp. R. XI, § 2(b)(3), occurred in the District of Columbia, so the Maryland court decided to impose a suspension that, pursuant to Md. R. 16-713(a)(2), was not greater than the District of Columbia suspension. Att'y Griev. Comm'n v. Steinberg, 385 Md. 696, 870 A.2d 603 (2005).

Attorney was indefinitely suspended from the practice of law with the right to reapply for admission after one year, as the attorney's act of threatening to withdraw from representation of a client if the client refused to pay additional legal fees constituted a violation of Md. R. Prof. Conduct 1.15 and 1.16, and constituted conduct involving dishonesty, fraud, deceit or misrepresentation in violation of this Rule, and the flat fee charged violated Md. R. Prof. Conduct 1.5 as the attorney did not provide sufficient services to earn the fee, the attorney violated Rules 16-604 and 16-609 by failing to place unearned attorney fees in his attorney trust account, and the attorney's failure to keep the client informed of the progress of the litigation violated Md. R. Prof. Conduct 1.4. Att'y Griev. Comm'n v. Lawson, 401 Md. 536, 933 A.2d 842 (2007).

Clear and convincing evidence showed that the attorney failed to promptly pay individuals who had funds on deposit in the attorney's trust account, which was a violation of Md. R. Prof. Conduct 1.1, 1.3, 1.15(d), and 8.4(d). That misconduct, along with the attorney's misconduct in paying clients before funds belonging to them were deposited in the attorney's trust account and failing to supervise an employee, warranted an indefinite suspension from the practice of law with the right to apply for reinstatement after 90 days. Att'y Griev. Comm'n v. Zuckerman, 403 Md. 695, 944 A.2d 525 (2008).

Clear and convincing evidence showed that the attorney's failure to adequately supervise the attorney's employee, by delegating to her the task of dealing with the consequences of an original theft in addition to management of the trust accounts day-to-day operations, allowed the employee to steal from the attorney's trust account in the same manner as the previous employee. That misconduct in violation of (d), along with the attorney's payment to clients before the attorney deposited the corresponding settlement payments owed to clients in the attorney's trust account and the attorney's failure to promptly disburse to individuals funds held in the attorney's trust account for those individuals, warranted an indefinite suspension with the right to apply for reinstatement after 90 days. Att'y Griev. Comm'n v. Zuckerman, 403 Md. 695, 944 A.2d 525 (2008).

Indefinite suspension from the practice of law in Maryland was the appropriate sanction for an attorney who had been convicted in New Jersey of fourth degree stalking and suspended from the practice of law in that State because the attorney would not be readmitted to the Bar of New Jersey until the Supreme Court of New Jersey was persuaded that he was once again fit to practice law, and the New Jersey Disciplinary Review Board provided additional protection to the public by requesting that the New Jersey Office of Attorney Ethics compel the attorney to undergo a medical examination pursuant to N.J. Ct. R. 1:20-12; because the attorney conceded that he suffered from mental illness and represented that he was continuing to receive treatment, the court of appeals did not reject the possibility that he could at some point in the future persuade it that he was once again fit to practice law in Maryland. Att'y Griev. Comm'n v. Beatty, 409 Md. 11, 972 A.2d 840 (2009).

Attorney was indefinitely suspended, with leave to apply for readmission after six months, where the attorney violated (c) and (d) and Md. R. Prof. Conduct 1.1, 1.3, 3.3(a)(1), and 5.5(a), by, inter alia, appearing at a meeting of creditors when not authorized to practice before the district court and failing to disclose fees the client paid to a bankruptcy preparer and attorney. Att'y Griev. Comm'n v. Robaton, 411 Md. 415, 983 A.2d 467 (2009).

Indefinite suspension was proper sanction. — Where respondent attorney's representation of four clients was marked by serious neglect and inattention; where he failed to return a fee which was unearned for a period of nine months; where he failed to timely remit funds he received on behalf of a client; where he failed to communicate with his clients; and where in connection with the investigation of three of the complaints, respondent failed to answer Bar Counsel's requests for information, the proper sanction was that the attorney be indefinitely suspended from the practice of law, with the right to apply for reinstatement after the suspension had been in effect for six months, conditioned upon his payment of all costs and upon the monitoring of respondent's practice. Att'y Griev. Comm'n v. Hamby, 322 Md. 606, 589 A.2d 53 (1991).

An attorney who on several separate occasions failed to file legal documents which he had drafted, failed to communicate with clients in these matters, and failed to return attorney's fees he collected in connection with these matters, was rightly found to have violated prior, similar Rules of Professional Conduct 1.1, 1.3, 1.4, 1.16, and 8.4. The appropriate sanction was an indefinite suspension with the right to apply for reinstatement after 60 days, conditioned upon his payment of all costs associated with the matter, reimbursement of the unearned legal fees, and his hiring of an attorney to oversee his practice for a period of one year. Att'y Griev. Comm'n v. Brugh, 353 Md. 475, 727 A.2d 913 (1999).

Attorney was suspended indefinitely for failing to appear on behalf of a client, failing to file a petition on behalf of a client, providing a client with incorrect information that the client did not have to appear for a scheduled trial, and failing to subpoena witness and to obtain medical records that may have exculpated his client. Att'y Griev. Comm'n of Maryland v. Mooney, 359 Md. 56, 753 A.2d 17 (2000).

An indefinite suspension was appropriate where, by his acts and omissions while representing his client, and specifically by his misrepresentations to the prosecutor and to the judge in seeking a continuance, an attorney engaged in misconduct as defined in Maryland Rule 16-701, was convicted in a case of criminal contempt, and violated prior, similar Rules 1.3, 3.3 and 8.4 of the Maryland Rules of Professional Conduct. Att'y Griev. Comm'n v. Middleton, 360 Md. 34, 756 A.2d 565 (2000).

Indefinite suspension was appropriate where attorney was retained to represent a client in filing for alien labor certifications for three of its employees, but where the attorney never prepared or filed an application for one employee and prepared but did not file applications for the other two, where he provided his client with altered documents making it appear he had done the work, and where the attorney never refunded the money paid to him and refused to cooperate with the investigation of his actions. Att'y Griev. Comm'n v.

Koven, 361 Md. 337, 761 A.2d 881 (2000).

An indefinite suspension was appropriate where, among other violations, attorney violated the prior, similar Rule by not filing his client's tax returns despite indicating to the court, and on the debtors' certificate, that the clients had filed their tax returns, and by careless business practices in failing to keep a contemporaneous activity log. Att'y Griev. Comm'n v. Cohen, 361 Md. 161, 760 A.2d 706 (2000).

Attorney's license to practice law was indefinitely suspended for his failure to provide competent, diligent, and communicative representation to his client, for charging unreasonable fees, for pursuing a frivolous proceeding, and for engaging in conduct prejudicial to the administration of justice. Att'y Griev. Comm'n v. Zdravkovich, 362 Md. 1, 762 A.2d 950 (2000).

Indefinite suspension was appropriate sanction where attorney prior, similar violated Md. R. Prof. Conduct 8.1 by failing to respond to bar counsel's repeated requests for information in connection with investigation of complaints, which further violated prior, similar Md. R. Prof. Conduct 8.4 as conduct prejudicial to the administration of justice; failure to respond exacerbated other violations of the Maryland Rules of Professional Conduct. Att'y Griev. Comm'n v. Harrington, 367 Md. 36, 785 A.2d 1260 (2001).

Attorney was indefinitely suspended from the practice of law for violating Md. R. Prof. Conduct 1.3, 1.4, 1.16(d), 3.2, 8.1(b), and 8.4(d) in connection with the attorney's representation of a client in a bankruptcy matter. The complaint could not be dismissed based on the complainant's request because the evidence did not fail to show sanctionable professional misconduct. Att'y Griev. Comm'n v. Lee, 393 Md. 546, 903 A.2d 895 (2006).

Attorney was indefinitely suspended from the practice of law in Maryland for violating Md. R. Prof. Conduct 1.3, by failing to act with reasonable diligence and promptness in recording a deed conveying land to a client, and (b) and (c) of this Rule, when the attorney presented a Gift Certification From containing the forged signature of the attorney's former wife to the Motor Vehicle Administration. The court need to consider both violations and impose a single sanction. Att'y Griev. Comm'n v. Sweitzer, 395 Md. 586, 911 A.2d 440 (2006).

Attorney's conduct in overdrawing the attorney's trust account on several occasions, in managing the attorney's escrow account carelessly, failing to reconcile it monthly, maintaining inaccurate settlement sheets, and keeping very few records was conduct prejudicial to the administration of justice for purposes of (d); the attorney was indefinitely suspended, with a right to apply for readmission after 90 days. Att'y Griev. Comm'n v. Mba-Jonas, 397 Md.

690, 919 A.2d 669 (2007).

Attorney was indefinitely suspended from the practice of law for violating, inter alia, (d) of this Rule when the attorney ignored requests for an accounting of trust funds relating to the estate. Att'y Griev. Comm'n v. Goff, 399 Md. 1, 922 A.2d 554 (2007).

Attorney was indefinitely suspended from practice of law for violating Rule 5.5 and this Rule by preparing a response to a summary judgment motion in a separate action while suspended from the practice of law for 90 days, and by failing to inform the client in that other action that the attorney had been suspended, thereby engaging in conduct prejudicial to administration of justice. Att'y Griev. Comm'n v. Robertson, 400 Md. 618, 929 A.2d 576 (2007).

Attorney was suspended indefinitely because his conduct in connection with an estate led to significant delay in closing the estate and violated Md. R. Prof. Conduct 1.1, 1.3, 8.1(a) and (b), and 8.4(a) and (d); the attorney owed the heirs to the estate competent and diligent representation but did not carry out either obligation, and indefinite suspension was the appropriate sanction due to the number and sort of violations, the mitigating factors, and the attorney's seeming failure to follow through on his promise to the hearing judge that he would attempt to "make things right" in the matter. Att'y Griev. Comm'n v. Pawlak, 408 Md. 288, 969 A.2d 311 (2009).

Attorney was indefinitely suspended from practice of law for violating Md. R. Prof. Conduct 1.8, 1.15, 8.1, and this Rule, Rules 16-607 and 16-609, and § 10-306 of the Business Occupations and Professional Article, when the attorney commingled funds for over four years, negligently misappropriated funds, failed to pay third party providers timely on behalf of his clients, and misrepresented that certain expenses were paid from personal funds rather than escrow funds. Att'y Griev. Comm'n v. McLaughlin, 409 Md. 304, 974 A.2d 315 (2009).

Suspension of one year required; disbarment was not appropriate sanction. — Suspension of one year required; disbarment was not appropriate sanction, considering the nature of the controlled dangerous substances involved, the absence of a finding of actual distribution, and all other surrounding circumstances. Att'y Griev. Comm'n v. Proctor, 309 Md. 412, 524 A.2d 773 (1987).

One-year suspension appropriate. — Although attorney's conduct in assisting a former client in breaking into the home of his wife was an aberration, the egregious nature of that conduct warranted the imposition of a significant sanction such that the attorney was suspended indefinitely from the practice of law with the right to apply for reinstatement not less than one year from the date of filing the opinion. Att'y Griev. Comm'n v. Protokowicz, 329 Md. 252, 619 A.2d 100 (1993).

Attorney was suspended from the practice of law for a period of one year because of failure to cooperate with bar counsel in violation of prior, similar Rule 8.1, performing services in an incompetent manner in violation of prior, similar Rule 1.1, charging an excessive fee in violation of prior, similar Rule 1.5, and engaging in conduct prejudicial to the administration of justice in violation of the prior, similar Rule. Att'y Griev. Comm'n v. Shaw, 363 Md. 1, 766 A.2d 1028 (2001).

Two-year suspension appropriate. — Attorney suspended for 2 years for violating the prior, similar Rule, inter alia, by the manner in which he collected fees and handled the funds of a client. Att'y Griev. Comm'n v. Eisenstein, 333 Md. 464, 635 A.2d 1327 (1994).

Three-year suspension appropriate. — Where an attorney, who had been practicing for nearly 30 years and had no record of previous misconduct, had been negligent and careless in handling estates and trusts, had taken fees from the estates before, and in some cases without, approval of the Orphans' Court and had made a loan to himself from the trust funds, a three-year suspension from the practice of law was the appropriate sanction. Att'y Griev. Comm'n v. Owrutsky, 322 Md. 334, 587 A.2d 511 (1991).

Three-year suspension was warranted where attorney prepared defective will or his client and later excoriated her and attempted to mislead an investigator and inquiry panel for the Attorney Grievance Commission. Att'y Griev. Comm'n v. Myers, 302 Md. 571, 490 A.2d 231 (1985).

Evidence justified findings of misconduct, and disbarment was warranted. — See Att'y Griev. Comm'n v. Mazelis, 309 Md. 50, 522 A.2d 913 (1987).

Because the four terms "dishonesty, fraud, deceit or misrepresentation" constitute separate categories, denoting differences in meaning or degree, an attorney violated the prior, similar Rule where his violations of other rules exhibited a lack of probity, integrity and straightforwardness, even though a judge's finding of fraud was not affirmed by the reviewing court. Att'y Griev. Comm'n of Md. v. Sheridan, 357 Md. 1, 741 A.2d 1143 (1999).

Clear and convincing evidence justified the hearing judge's findings that an attorney obstructed police investigation into a murder committed by his son while he arranged for the son to flee to Israel; this conduct which served to undermine confidence in the profession and obstructed justice could only be punishable by disbarment. Att'y Griev. Comm'n v. Sheinbein, 372 Md. 224, 812 A.2d 981 (2002).

Disbarment was the proper sanction for an attorney who dragged out representation of two different clients for many years, dooming their causes by failure to comply with applicable laws, and pretended to be continuing representation efforts, in one case, even falsifying a letter after the fact to give the impression that the client had received proper communications; the attorney had also failed to notify clients of a suspension and make other arrangements with them, and to supply information needed by a grievance commission investigator. Att'y Griev. Comm'n v. Davis, 375 Md. 131, 825 A.2d 430 (2003).

Disbarment required. — Illegal conduct involving moral turpitude, dishonesty, fraud, deceit, or misrepresentation; and conduct prejudicial to the administration of justice, adversely reflected on attorney's fitness to practice law and warranted disbarment. Att'y Griev. Comm'n v. Ezrin, 312 Md. 603, 541 A.2d 966 (1988).

Attorney Grievance Commission of Maryland's recommendation was adopted and an attorney was disbarred for violating Md. R. Prof. Conduct 8.4(c) and (d) where: (1) he falsely represented to his supervisor and other members of his firm that he had filed an appeal in a case, (2) he filed appellate pleadings in the firm's files containing what appeared to be, but were not, court file receipts, and (3) he gave monthly status reports on the appellate case. Att'y Griev. Comm'n v. Guberman, 392 Md. 131, 896 A.2d 337 (2006).

Misappropriation of funds by an attorney involves moral turpitude; it is an act infected with deceit and dishonesty and will result in disbarment in the absence of compelling extenuating circumstances justifying a lesser sanction. Att'y Griev. Comm'n v. Ezrin, 312 Md. 603, 541 A.2d 966 (1988).

Absent compelling extenuating circumstances justifying a lesser sanction, misappropriation by an attorney of funds entrusted to the attorney's care warrants disbarment, and this is true even where the misappropriation is committed in a nonprofessional capacity, since it involves a breach of trust or a fiduciary relationship and bears upon the fitness of a lawyer to practice his profession. Att'y Griev. Comm'n v. Lazerow, 320 Md. 507, 578 A.2d 779 (1990).

Disbarment was appropriate sanction where attorney executed documents without ex-spouse's authority in order to obtain for himself the proceeds of the sale of property. Att'y Griev. Comm'n v. Pearson, 322 Md. 154, 586 A.2d 25 (1991).

Representations and omissions made by an attorney in connection with his application for admission to the Bar of this State violated prior, similar Rules 8.1 and 8.4 of the Maryland Rules of Professional Conduct and warranted disbarment. Att'y Griev. Comm'n v.

Joehl, 335 Md. 83, 642 A.2d 194 (1994).

Attorney was properly disbarred for violating prior, similar Maryland Rules of Professional Conduct 1.1, 1.3, 1.4, 1.15, 3.3, and 8.4, § 10-306 of the Business Occupations and Professions Article, and former Rule BU9 (now Rule 16-609) of the Maryland Rules of Procedure. Att'y Griev. Comm'n v. Williams, 335 Md. 458, 644 A.2d 490 (1994).

Where an attorney violated prior, similar Rule 3.3 and the prior, similar Rule when he gave a false response to a question posed by a District Court judge concerning his traffic record, due to his previous history of misconduct, he was disbarred. Att'y Griev. Comm'n v. Myers, 333 Md. 440, 635 A.2d 1315 (1994).

Disbarment of attorney was appropriate where there were serious and repeated violations of the prior, similar Rule and other provisions of the Maryland Rules of Professional Conduct. Att'y Griev. Comm'n v. Milliken, 348 Md. 486, 704 A.2d 1225 (1998).

Where an attorney committed acts of violence, to some of which he pled guilty, on both his wife and children, where he violated court ordered probation, and where his conduct was a repetition of past conduct, disbarment was the appropriate sanction. Att'y Griev. Comm'n v. Painter, 356 Md. 293, 739 A.2d 24 (1999).

Attorney was disbarred where he had demonstrated an alarming propensity for deceit and dishonesty that infested a large part of his dealings spanning a short period of time, and where he engaged in deceitful conduct, was less than candid in testimony, and violated a medley of rules and statutes concerned with protecting trust funds. Att'y Griev. Comm'n v. Tomaino, 362 Md. 483, 765 A.2d 653 (2001).

Disbarment was the appropriate sanction where an out-of-state attorney practiced law in the State of Maryland without a license, failed to acknowledge his jurisdictional limitations on his firm letterhead, acted against the interests of his purported clients during and after the sale of their home to him, filed a bankruptcy petition on those clients' behalf, but without their consent or knowledge, and forged the signatures of the clients and another attorney in his office on court papers and filings, in violation of prior, similar Rules of Professional Conduct 1.7, 3.3, 5.5, 7.1, 7.5, and 8.4. Att'y Griev. Comm'n v. Johnson, 363 Md. 598, 770 A.2d 130 (2001).

Attorney was disbarred for taking money from her employer while working outside the profession of law where there was little evidence that attorney was not able to handle every day economic affairs of life and where her mental problems did not affect her ability to be a competent thief. Att'y Griev. Comm'n v. Vanderlinde, 364 Md. 376, 773 A.2d 463 (2001).

Disbarment was ordered where an attorney violated prior, similar Md. R. Prof. Conduct 1.15, 8.1, and 8.4, and Md. R. 16-607, and had previously been sanctioned, receiving an indefinite suspension with the right to reapply in not less than six months for conduct amounting to negligent misappropriation of client funds. Att'y Griev. Comm'n v. Powell, 369 Md. 462, 800 A.2d 782 (2002).

When an attorney acted as an escrow agent for a client which purportedly funded high-risk loans, and the attorney removed commitment fees deposited in the escrow account and disbursed them to parties unrelated to a contemplated loan, rather than either returning them to the depositors or disbursing them to parties providing loans, and failed to provide requested information to the grievance commission, he violated prior, similar Md. R. Prof. Conduct 1.15, 8.1, and this Rule, §§ 10-306 and 10-606 of the Business Occupations and Professions Article, and Rule 16-609 of the Maryland Rules of Procedure and, given the absence of mitigating circumstances, disbarment was the appropriate sanction. Att'y Griev. Comm'n v. Smith, 376 Md. 202, 829 A.2d 567 (2003).

Taken in its entirety, an attorney's representation of a Virginia client, on a Virginia matter, his failure to provide effective representation, his abandonment of the client without notice or returning the unearned fee, his failure to deposit his fee in an attorney escrow account, and his failure to respond to the Attorney Grievance Commission of Maryland's request for information, constituted conduct prejudicial to the administration of justice and violated the prior, similar Rule; the appropriate sanction was disbarment, especially since the attorney had previously been disbarred and reinstated. Att'y Griev. Comm'n v. Velasquez, 380 Md. 651, 846 A.2d 422 (2004).

Appropriate sanction against attorney was disbarment. Making accusations in petitions to the court seeking their removal, impugning the integrity of the chief judge of the court of special appeals and the clerk of that court, without justification or even an attempt at justification beyond conjecture and speculation, and repeating those accusations during the disciplinary hearing, again without an attempt at justification, were themselves cause for disbarment and constituted conduct that prejudiced the administration of justice seriously and most directly. Att'y Griev. Comm'n v. DeMaio, 379 Md. 571, 842 A.2d 802 (2004).

Attorney was disbarred, despite the mitigating factors of an absence of a prior disciplinary record and relative inexperience, for violating prior, similar Md. R. Prof. Conduct 1.5(c), 1.15(b) and (c), 8.1(b), and 8.4(c) and (d), and Md. R. 16-606 and 16-609 in his intentionally dishonest conduct towards a third-party assignee/healthcare provider during the representation of a client in a personal injury claim and Maryland Bar Counsel and its investigator in the course of investigating the assignee's complaint. Att'y Griev. Comm'n v. Ellison, 384 Md. 688, 867 A.2d 259 (2005).

Despite evidence that respondent attorney suffered from depression and a mood disorder, disbarment was the only appropriate sanction for misconduct that included misleading both clients and their health care providers about the status of settlement negotiations and concealing a possible asset of a bankrupt client from the bankruptcy trustee; the mental problems were not the root cause of the misconduct, and the attorney, whose practice had been quite successful, had known quite well that mishandling of client trust funds to cover practice expenses and misleading the bankruptcy court were wrong. Att'y Griev. Comm'n v. Zakroff, 387 Md. 603, 876 A.2d 664 (2005), cert. denied, 2006 Md. LEXIS 561 (2006); cert. denied, 2006 Md. LEXIS 571 (Md. 2006).

Despite evidence that respondent attorney suffered from depression and a mood disorder, disbarment was the only appropriate sanction for misconduct that included misleading both clients and their health care providers about the status of settlement negotiations and concealing a possible asset of a bankrupt client from the bankruptcy trustee; the mental problems were not the root cause of the misconduct, and the attorney, whose practice had been quite successful, had known quite well that mishandling of client trust funds to cover practice expenses and misleading the bankruptcy court were wrong. Att'y Griev. Comm'n v. Zakroff, 387 Md. 603, 876 A.2d 664 (2005), cert. denied, 2006 Md. LEXIS 561 (2006); cert. denied, 2006 Md. LEXIS 571 (Md. 2006).

Clear and convincing evidence was found that an attorney violated this Rule by converting a client's personal injury protection fund monies to her personal use, having insufficient funds in her escrow account to pay the client's outstanding claims for reimbursement from such fund, and otherwise converting to her own use the fund, which should have been held in trust for the client. Disbarment was the sanction imposed, because the attorney did not protect her client's interests when she converted the funds and denied doing so, which constituted an intentional misrepresentation of a material fact in connection with a disciplinary matter. Att'y Griev. Comm'n v. Cherry-Mahoi, 388 Md. 124, 879 A.2d 58 (2005).

In an attorney disciplinary matter wherein the attorney was ordered disbarred, the attorney was found to have violated Md. R. Prof. Conduct 1.1 when he failed to appear at one client meeting, arrived an hour late each to two mediation sessions, and participated unprepared in the second mediation session.

Such actions did not reflect the thoroughness or preparation that the legal profession demanded, and such neglect also constituted a violation of subsection (d) of this Rule, which prohibited conduct that was prejudicial to the administration of justice as failure to be punctual in a scheduled court appearance was not only detrimental to the administration of justice but also constituted discourteous conduct degrading to the tribunal. Att'y Griev. Comm'n v. Steinberg, 395 Md. 337, 910 A.2d 429 (2006).

State supreme court found that the attorney's misconduct, as charged in the grievance commission's petition and supported by the trial court's findings of fact and conclusions of law, warranted disbarment; the evidence established that the attorney failed to act with reasonable diligence and promptness in representing a client in a divorce case, that the attorney failed to keep the client reasonably informed about the status of the representation and did not respond to reasonable requests for information, that the attorney failed to respond to lawful demands for information from disciplinary counsel, and that the totality of the attorney's conduct was prejudicial to the administration of justice. Att'y Griev. Comm'n v. Hodgson, 396 Md. 1, 912 A.2d 640 (2006).

Attorney was disbarred for violating, inter alia, former, similar (c) and (d) by creating shell corporations to transfer property to in an effort to delay, hinder, or defraud the attorney's parents' creditors. Att'y Griev. Comm'n v. Pak, 400 Md. 567, 929 A.2d 546 (2007), cert. denied, 128 S. Ct. 905, 2008 U.S. LEXIS 126, 169 L. Ed. 2d 729 (U.S. 2008).

Attorney was disbarred after the court found that the attorney violated Md. R. Prof. Conduct 8.1(a) and 8.4(c) when the attorney executed a transfer authorization that changed the title of an account the attorney had with the attorney's ex-wife from ownership as tenants in common to sole ownership in the attorney's name following the death of the ex-wife. Att'y Griev. Comm'n v. Harris, 403 Md. 142, 939 A.2d 732 (2008).

Attorney was disbarred because the attorney made knowingly false statements concerning the attorney's bar admission status, proceeded to act as general counsel for clients, and acted to mislead and defraud investors in violation of Md. R. Prof. Conduct 5.5 and 8.4. Att'y Griev. Comm'n v. Parsons, 404 Md. 175, 946 A.2d 437 (2008).

Where the attorney, while decertified, entered appearances on behalf of defendants, and either showed up late or did not show up at all for court proceedings, the attorney violated Md. R. Prof. Conduct 1.1, 1.3, and 8.4(d) by failing to appear for court proceedings. As a result of (1) those violations, (2) the fact that the attorney was decertified at the time the violations were committed, and (3) the fact that the attorney violated other professional conduct rules, also while decertified, the state's highest court had little choice but to disbar the attorney. Att'y Griev. Comm'n v. Walker, 405 Md. 3, 948 A.2d 1263 (2008).

Attorney was disbarred for violating Md. R. Prof. Conduct 1.1, 3.1, 3.2, 3.3(a), 4.4, 8.2(a), and 8.4(c) and (d) because the attorney advised a trial court that his client had entered into a settlement agreement when he had not, and his frivolous motions, intentionally dilatory tactics, and misrepresentations were prejudicial to the administration of justice; the attorney was intentionally dishonest with both the trial court and the court of special appeals, which showed a systematic effort to mislead the courts, and his history of sanctions for violating the Maryland Rules of Professional Conduct (MRPC) showed an ongoing disregard for the MRPC. Att'y Griev. Comm'n v. McClain, 406 Md. 1, 956 A.2d 135 (2008), cert. denied, 129 S. Ct. 1691, 2009 U.S. LEXIS 2433, 173 L. Ed. 2d 1036 (U.S. 2009).

Attorney violated this Rule by committing perjury when the attorney filed false business reports under oath in the attorney's bankruptcy proceeding. Accordingly, when considered with the attorney's other violations, the disbarment of the attorney was the appropriate sanction. Att'y Griev. Comm'n v. Byrd, 408 Md. 449, 970 A.2d 870 (2009).

Attorney was disbarred for violating Md. R. Prof. Conduct 1.1, 1.3, 1.4, 1.15, 3.1, 8.1, and 8.4, when the attorney, inter alia, failed to oppose a motion to dismiss filed against clients in an underlying action and did not attend a hearing on that motion, and forged the clients' names on a check made out only to them and deposited it in the attorney's operating account, not trust account. Att'y Griev. Comm'n v. Gisriel, 409 Md. 331, 974 A.2d 331 (2009).

Attorney was disbarred for violating Md. R. Prof. Conduct 1.1, 1.3, 1.4, 1.15, and 8.4, Rule 16-609, and §§ 10-306 and 10-606(b) of the Business Professions and Occupations Article as attorney misappropriated the clients' funds, performed no services whatsoever on the clients' behalf, lied to the clients about the status of their case, and provided them with a falsified administrative agency decision that was not issued by the agency. Att'y Griev. Comm'n v. Bahgat, 411 Md. 568, 984 A.2d 225 (2009).

Attorney was disbarred from the practice of law in Maryland for violating this section by consciously acting dishonestly with regard to a contract for the sale and purchase of real property and failing to depict the true agreement between the parties and intentionally concealing the identity of her brother, for whom she had held funds in her trust account. Att'y Griev. Comm'n v. Nwadike, 416 Md. 180, 6 A.3d 287 (2010).

Attorney violated this rule by failign to diligently and competently oversee an action failing to communicate the clients in two actions, and failing to obtain a client's consent for settlement; the attorney was disbarred for violating this rule along with Md. Law. R. Prof. Conduct 1.1, 1.2(a), 1.3, 1.4(a), 1.16(d). and 8.1(b) Att'y Griev. Comm'n v. Fox, 417 Md. 504, 11 A.3d 762 (2010).

Attorney was disbarred for admittedly violating Md. Law. R. Prof. Conduct 1.1, 1.15(a) and (c), and 8.4(a) — (d), as well as Rule 16-609 and § 10-306 of the Business Occupations and Professions Article, by misappropriating client funds to make it appear as though the attorney's collected fees were higher than those fees actually were, when the attorney was being considered for partner in the attorney's firm, and by failing to file complaints in clients' cases, misrepresenting that the complaints were filed, and fabricating documents to hide the misrepresentations, because (1) disbarment was the presumed sanction for the misappropriation, and (2) the attorney did not show "compelling extenuating circumstances" justifying a lesser sanction, as the attorney showed no serious and debilitating mental condition, since the attorney was not diagnosed with a mental illness, the attorney did not show such a condition was the "root cause" of the attorney's misconduct by making the attorney unable to do day-to-day activities in a normal manner, and the attorney did not show such a condition caused an utter inability to conform the attorney's conduct to the law and the Maryland Rules of Professional Conduct, so any psychological issues the attorney had at the time of the attorney's misconduct did not mitigate the attorney's sanction. Att'y Griev. Comm'n v. Palmer, 417 Md. 185, 9 A.3d 37 (2010).

Attorney was disbarred for violating (a) and (d) and Md. Law. R. Prof. Conduct 1.3, 1.4(a) and (b), 1.15(a), (c), and (d), 1.16(d), and 8.1(b), after the attorney received advance fee payments from two clients, deposited the money in a personal account, rather than a trust account, having not earned the fees, and abandoned the clients without performing work for the clients. Att'y Griev. Comm'n v. Lara, 418 Md. 355, 14 A.3d 650 (2011).

Attorney was disbarred for violating (a), (b), (c), and (d) and Md. Law. R. Prof. Conduct 1.2, when the attorney empowered a client's child to forge the client's signature on estate documents, notarized falsely executed and initialed estate documents, and directed the attorney's employees to falsely attest to the signature; the attorney suffered no cognitive deficits and new what he was doing was wrong. Att'y Griev. Comm'n v. Coppola, 419 Md. 370, 19 A.3d 431 (2011).

Attorney violated (c) and (d), and Md. Law. R. Prof. Conduct 1.2(a), 1.15(d), Md. R. 16-604 and 16-609(c), and § 10-306 of the Business Occupations and Professions Article, and was disbarred, after misappropriating tens of thousands of dollars that should have been paid to a physical therapist and settling a client's claim without the client's knowledge or consent. Att'y Griev. Comm'n v. Stern, 419 Md. 525, 19 A.3d 904 (2011).

When an attorney altered the attorney's law firm employer's electronic files to facilitate the attorney taking certain of the firm's clients with the attorney when the attorney left the firm, the proper sanction for the attorney's admitted violations of Md. Law. R. Prof. Conduct 1.4(a) and (b) and (a), (b), (c), and (d) of this Rule, as well as Md. Code Ann., Crim. Law § 7-302, was disbarment because (1) the attorney's conduct was dishonest, intentional, and solely motivated by a desire for personal gain, so disbarment was presumed, and (2) the attorney's mental disabilities of depression and alcohol dependency were not "compelling extenuating circumstances" warranting a lesser sanction as the disabilities did not result in an utter inability to conform the attorney's conduct to the law and the Rules of Professional Conduct. Att'y Griev. Comm'n v. Keiner, — Md. —, — A.3d — (Aug. 19, 2011).

Reinstatement proceedings. — The essential factors to be considered in any reinstatement proceeding are: (1) the nature and circumstances of the petitioner's original misconduct; (2) the petitioner's subsequent conduct and reformation; (3) the petitioner's present character; and (4) the petitioner's present qualifications and competence to practice.

Although the attorney was not prosecuted for failure to maintain a trust account, and his failure to do so was a misdemeanor in Maryland, his violation of numerous ethical rules was sufficient basis to find that he had violated this Rule. Att'y Griev. Comm'n v. Gallagher, 371 Md. 673, 810 A.2d 996 (2002).

Although the attorney was not prosecuted for failure to maintain a trust account, and his failure to do so was a misdemeanor in Maryland, his violation of numerous ethical rules was sufficient basis to find that he had violated this Rule. Att'y Griev. Comm'n v. Gallagher, 371 Md. 673, 810 A.2d 996 (2002).

Disciplinary proceedings which charged that an attorney who represented a very difficult client in an estate matter, and who deducted his fee from settlement proceeds without having filed a fee petition and obtaining the court's approval prior to taking his portion, culminated in a determination by clear and convincing evidence that the attorney had violated prior, similar Rules 1.1, 1.15, and 8.4 and the imposition of an indefinite suspension against him upon a finding that his actions were not intentional; however, where the attorney was not charged with violating this Rule, it was a violation of due process for the hearing judge to determine that he had violated all of the prior, similar Rule because he had never received notice of those alleged charges and accordingly, was not held to have violated those rules. Att'y Griev. Comm'n v. Seiden, 373 Md. 409, 818 A.2d 1108 (2003).

Rule 8.5. Disciplinary Authority; Choice of Law.

(a) **Disciplinary Authority.** (1) A lawyer admitted by the Court of Appeals to practice in this State is subject to the disciplinary authority of this State, regardless of where the lawyer's conduct occurs.

(2) A lawyer not admitted to practice in this State is also subject to the disciplinary authority of this State if the lawyer

(i) provides or offers to provide any legal services in this State,

(ii) holds himself or herself out as practicing law in this State, or

(iii) has an obligation to supervise or control another lawyer practicing law in this State whose conduct constitutes a violation of these Rules.

Cross references. — Md. Rule 16-701(a).

(3) A lawyer may be subject to the disciplinary authority of both this State and another jurisdiction for the same conduct.

(b) **Choice of Law.** In any exercise of the disciplinary authority of this State, the rule of professional conduct to be applied shall be as follows:

(1) for conduct in connection with a matter pending before a tribunal, the rules of the jurisdiction in which the tribunal sits, unless the rules of the tribunal provide otherwise; and

(2) for any other conduct, the rules of the jurisdiction in which the lawyer's conduct occurred, or, if the predominant effect of the conduct is in a different jurisdiction, the rules of that jurisdiction shall be applied to the conduct. A lawyer shall not be subject to discipline if the lawyer's conduct conforms to the rules of a jurisdiction in which the lawyer reasonably believes the predominant effect of the lawyer's conduct will occur.

COMMENT

Disciplinary Authority. — [1] It is longstanding law that the conduct of a lawyer admitted to practice in this State is subject to the disciplinary authority of this State. Extension of the disciplinary authority of this State to other lawyers who provide or offer to provide legal services in this State is for the protection of the citizens of this State. Reciprocal enforcement of a jurisdiction's disciplinary findings and sanctions will further advance the purposes of this Rule. A lawyer who is subject to the disciplinary authority of this State under Rule 8.5(a) appoints an official to be designated by this Court to receive service of process in this State.

Choice of Law. — [2] A lawyer may be potentially subject to more than one set of rules of professional conduct which impose different obligations. The lawyer may be licensed to practice in more than one jurisdiction with differing rules, or may be admitted to practice before a particular court with rules that differ from those of the jurisdiction or jurisdictions in which the lawyer is licensed to practice. Additionally, the lawyer's conduct may involve significant contacts with more than one jurisdiction.

[3] Paragraph (b) seeks to resolve such potential conflicts. Its premise is that minimizing conflicts between rules, as well as uncertainty about which rules are applicable, is in the best interest of both clients and the profession (as well as the bodies having authority to regulate the profession). Accordingly, it takes the approach of (i) providing that any particular conduct of a lawyer shall be subject to only one set of rules of professional conduct, (ii) making the determination of which set of rules applies to particular conduct as straightforward as possible, consistent with recognition of appropriate regulatory interests of relevant jurisdictions, and (iii) providing protection from discipline for lawyers who act reasonably in the face of uncertainty.

[4] Paragraph (b)(1) provides that as to a lawyer's conduct relating to a proceeding pending before a tribunal, the lawyer shall be subject only to the rules of professional conduct of that tribunal. As to all other conduct, including conduct in anticipation of a proceeding not yet pending before a tribunal, paragraph (b)(2) provides that a lawyer shall be subject to the rules of the jurisdiction in which the lawyer's conduct occurred, or, if the predominant effect of the conduct is in another jurisdiction, the rules of that jurisdiction shall be applied to the conduct. In the case of conduct in anticipation of a proceeding that is likely to be before a tribunal, the predominant effect of such conduct could be where the conduct occurred, where the tribunal sits or in another jurisdiction.

[5] When a lawyer's conduct involves significant contacts with more than one jurisdiction, it may not be clear whether the predominant effect of the lawyer's conduct will occur in a jurisdiction other than the one in which the conduct occurred. So long as the lawyer's conduct conforms to the rules of a jurisdiction in which the lawyer reasonably believes the predominant effect will occur, the lawyer shall not be subject to discipline under this Rule.

[6] If two admitting jurisdictions were to proceed against a lawyer for the same conduct, they should, applying this Rule, identify the same governing ethics rules. They should take all appropriate steps to see that they do apply the same rule to the same conduct, and in all events should avoid proceeding against a lawyer on the basis of two inconsistent rules.

[7] The choice of law provision applies to lawyers engaged in transnational practice, unless international law, treaties or other agreements between competent regulatory authorities in the affected jurisdiction provide otherwise.

Model Rules Comparison. — Rule 8.5(a) combines the substance of former Rules 8.5(a) and 8.5(b). Rule 8.5(b) is substantially similar to ABA Model Rule 8.5(b). The Comments are substantially similar to the ABA Comments with the exception of omitting the final sentence of ABA Comment [1].

Failure to supervise associate by unlicensed supervising attorneys from out-of-state. — In a disciplinary proceeding against two supervising attorneys from out-of-state, who opened up a Maryland office and hired a Maryland associate, who ended up failing to respond to motions compelling discovery in 47 cases filed by her on behalf of the supervising attorneys' Maryland clients, the hearing judge was found to have properly determined that they violated Md. R. Prof. Conduct 5.1 and 1.4 and, therefore, they were suspended indefinitely, with the right to apply for reinstatement no sooner than 90 days after the effective date of the suspension. The findings and conclusions adequately found that the supervising attorneys failed to adequately supervise the relatively inexperienced associate they hired, failed to respond to her requests for paralegal help, failed to establish supervisory procedures designed deliberately to address the associate's inexperience and to counterbalance her physical distance from the ready availability of steadying interaction with peers and managers, failed to audit her case load, among other failings, as well as failed to directly communicate with a Maryland client regarding his case. Att'y Griev. Comm'n v. Kimmel, 405 Md. 647, 955 A.2d 269 (2008).

APPENDIX: IDEALS OF PROFESSIONALISM

Professionalism is the combination of the core values of personal integrity, competency, civility, independence, and public service that distinguish lawyers as the caretakers of the rule of law.

These Ideals of Professionalism emanate from and complement the Maryland Lawyers' Rules of Professional Conduct ("MLRPC"), the overall thrust of which is well-summarized in this passage from the Preamble to those Rules:

> "A lawyer should use the law's procedures only for legitimate purposes and not to harass or intimidate others. A lawyer should demonstrate respect for the legal system and for those who serve it, including judges, other lawyers, and public officials."

A failure to observe these Ideals is not of itself a basis for disciplinary sanctions, but the conduct that constitutes the failure may be a basis for disciplinary sanctions if it violates a provision of the MLRPC or other relevant law.

Preamble

Lawyers are entrusted with the privilege of practicing law. They take a firm vow or oath to uphold the Constitution and laws of the United States and the State of Maryland. Lawyers enjoy a distinct position of trust and confidence that carries the significant responsibility and obligation to be caretakers for the system of justice that is essential to the continuing existence of a civilized society. Each lawyer, therefore, as a custodian of the system of justice, must be conscious of this responsibility and exhibit traits that reflect a personal responsibility to recognize, honor, and enhance the rule of law in this society. The Ideals and some characteristics set forth below are representative of a value system that lawyers must demand of themselves as professionals in order to maintain and enhance the role of legal professionals as the protectors of the rule of law.

Ideals of Professionalism

A lawyer should aspire:

(1) to put fidelity to clients before self-interest;

(2) to be a model for others, and particularly for his or her clients, by showing respect due to those called upon to resolve disputes and the regard due to all participants in the dispute resolution processes;

(3) to avoid all forms of wrongful discrimination in all of his or her activities, including discrimination on the basis of race, sex, gender, religion, national origin, ethnicity, disability, age, sexual orientation, marital status, socioeconomic status, or political affiliation, with equality and fairness as the goals;

(4) to preserve and improve the law, the legal system, and other dispute resolution processes as instruments for the common good;

(5) to make the law, the legal system, and other dispute resolution processes available to all;

(6) to practice law with a personal commitment to the rules governing the profession and to encourage others to do the same;

(7) to preserve the dignity and the integrity of the profession by his or her conduct, because the dignity and the integrity of the profession are an inheritance that must be maintained by each successive generation of lawyers;

(8) to strive for excellence in the practice of law to promote the interests of his or her clients, the rule of law, and the welfare of society; and

(9) to recognize that the practice of law is a calling in the spirit of public service, not merely a business pursuit.

Accountability and Trustworthiness

A lawyer should understand the principles set forth in this section.

(1) Punctuality promotes the credibility of a lawyer. Tardiness and neglect denigrate the individual, as well as the legal profession.

(2) Personal integrity is essential to the honorable practice of law. Lawyers earn the respect of clients, opposing counsel, and the courts when they keep their commitments and perform the tasks promised.

(3) Honesty and, subject to legitimate requirements of confidentiality, candid communications promote credibility with clients, opposing counsel, and the courts.

(4) Monetary pressures that cloud professional judgment and should be resisted.

Education, Mentoring, and Excellence

A lawyer should:

(1) make constant efforts to expand his or her legal knowledge and to ensure familiarity with changes in the law that affect a client's interests;

(2) willingly take on the responsibility of promoting the image of the legal profession by educating each client and the public regarding the principles underlying the justice system, and, as a practitioner of a learned art, by conveying to everyone the importance of professionalism;

(3) attend continuing legal education programs to demonstrate a commitment to keeping abreast of changes in the law;

(4) as a senior lawyer, accept the role of mentor and teacher, whether through formal education programs or individual mentoring of less experienced lawyers; and

(5) understand that mentoring includes the responsibility for setting a good example for another lawyer, as well as an obligation to ensure that each mentee learns the principles enunciated in these Ideals and adheres to them in practice.

A Calling to Service

A lawyer should:

(1) serve the public interest by communicating clearly with clients, opposing counsel, judges, and the general public;

(2) consider the impact on others when scheduling events. Reasonable requests for schedule changes should be accommodated if, in the view of the lawyer, such requests do not impact adversely the merits of the client's position;

(3) maintain an open and respectful dialogue with clients and opposing counsel;

(4) respond to all communications promptly, even if more time is needed to formulate a complete answer, and understand that delays in returning telephone calls or answering mail may leave the impression that the communication was unimportant or that the message was lost, and such delays increase tension and frustration;

(5) keep a client apprised of the status of important matters affecting the client and inform the client of the frequency with which information will be provided, understanding that some matters will require regular contact, while others will require only occasional communication;

(6) always explain a client's options or choices with sufficient detail to help the client make an informed decision;

(7) reflect a spirit of respect in all interactions with opposing counsel, parties, staff, and the court; and

(8) accept responsibility for ensuring that justice is available to every person and not just those with financial means.

Fairness, Civility, and Courtesy

A lawyer should:

(1) act fairly in all dealings as a way of promoting the system of justice;

(2) understand that an excess of zeal may undermine a client's cause and hamper the administration of justice and that a lawyer can advocate zealously a client's cause in a manner that remains fair and civil;

(3) know that zeal requires only that the client's interests are paramount and therefore warrant use of negotiation and compromise, when appropriate, to achieve a beneficial outcome, understanding that yelling, intimidating, issuing ultimatums, and using an "all or nothing" approach may constitute bullying, not zealous advocacy;

(4) seek to remain objective when advising a client about the strengths and weaknesses of the client's case or work;

(5) not allow a client's improper motives, unethical directions, or ill-advised wishes to influence a lawyer's actions or advice, such as when deciding whether to consent to an extension of time requested by an opponent, and make that choice based on the effect, if any, on the outcome of the client's case and not on the acrimony that may exist between the parties;

(6) when appropriate and consistent with duties to the client, negotiate in good faith in an effort to avoid litigation and, where indicated, suggest alternative dispute resolution;

(7) use litigation tools to strengthen the client's case, but avoid using litigation tactics in a manner solely to harass, intimidate, or overburden an opposing party; and

(8) note explicitly any changes made to documents submitted for review by opposing counsel, understanding that fairness is undermined by attempts to insert or delete language without notifying the other party or the party's lawyer.

A lawyer should understand that:

(1) professionalism requires civility in all dealings, showing respect for differing points of view, and demonstrating empathy for others;

(2) courtesy does not reflect weakness; rather, it promotes effective advocacy by ensuring that parties have the opportunity to participate in the process without personal attacks or intimidation;

(3) maintaining decorum in every venue, especially in the courtroom, is neither a relic of the past nor a sign of weakness; it is an essential component of the legal process;

(4) professionalism is enhanced by preparing scrupulously for meetings and court appearances and by showing respect for the court, opposing counsel, and the parties through courteous behavior and respectful attire;

(5) courtesy and respect should be demonstrated in all contexts, not just with clients and colleagues, or in the courtroom, but also with support staff and court personnel;

(6) hostility between clients should not become grounds for a lawyer to show hostility or disrespect to a party, opposing counsel, or the court;

(7) patience enables a lawyer to exercise restraint in volatile situations and to defuse anger, rather than elevate the tension and animosity between parties or lawyers; and

(8) the Ideals of Professionalism are to be observed in all manner of communication, and a lawyer should resist the impulse to respond uncivilly to electronic communications in the same manner as he or she would resist such impulses in other forms of communication. (Added March 9, 2010, effective July 1, 2010.)

APPENDIX: GUIDELINES OF ADVOCACY FOR ATTORNEYS REPRESENTING CHILDREN IN CINA AND RELATED TPR AND ADOPTION PROCEEDINGS

STATEMENT OF THE ISSUE

The Maryland Foster Care Court Improvement Project has developed these Guidelines of Advocacy for Attorneys Representing Children in Child in Need of Assistance (CINA) and Related Termination of Parental Rights (TPR) and Adoption Proceedings. The court's ability to protect the interests of children rests in large part upon the skill and expertise of the advocate. An attorney should represent a child who is the subject of a CINA or a related TPR or adoption proceeding in accordance with these Guidelines. Nothing contained in the Guidelines is intended to modify, amend, or alter the fiduciary duties that an attorney owes to a client pursuant to the Maryland Lawyers' Rules of Professional Conduct. For purposes of these Guidelines, the word "child" refers to the client of the attorney.

A. ADVOCATE FOR THE CHILD

GUIDELINE A. ROLE OF THE CHILD'S COUNSEL

The attorney should determine whether the child has considered judgment as defined in Guideline B1. If the child has considered judgment, the attorney should so state in open court and should advocate a position consistent with the child's wishes in the matter. If the attorney determines that the child lacks considered judgment, the attorney should so inform the court. The attorney should then advocate a position consistent with the best interests of the child as defined in Guideline B2.

B. CONSIDERED JUDGMENT

GUIDELINE B1. ASSESSING CONSIDERED JUDGMENT

The attorney should advocate the position of a child unless the attorney reasonably concludes that the child is unable to express a reasoned choice about issues that are relevant to the particular purpose for which the attorney is representing the child. If the child has the ability to express a reasoned choice, the child is regarded as having considered judgment.

a. To determine whether the child has considered judgment, the attorney should focus on the child's decision-making process, rather than the child's decision. The attorney should determine whether the child can understand the risks and benefits of the child's legal position and whether the child can reasonably communicate the child's wishes. The attorney should consider the following factors when determining whether the child has considered judgment:

(1) the child's developmental stage:

(a) cognitive ability,

(b) socialization, and

(c) emotional and mental development;

(2) the child's expression of a relevant position:

(a) ability to communicate with the attorney, and

(b) ability to articulate reasons for the legal position; and

(3) relevant and available reports such as reports from social workers, psychiatrists, psychologists, and schools.

b. A child may be capable of considered judgment even though the child has a significant cognitive or emotional disability.

c. At every interview with the child, the attorney should assess whether the child has considered judgment regarding each relevant issue. In making a determination regarding considered judgment, the attorney may seek guidance from professionals, family members, school officials, and other concerned persons. The attorney should also determine if any evaluations are needed and advocate them when appropriate. At no time shall the attorney compromise the attorney-client privilege.

d. An attorney should be sensitive to cultural, racial, ethnic, or economic differences between the attorney and the child because such differences may inappropriately influence the attorney's assessment of whether the child has considered judgment.

GUIDELINE B2. BEST INTEREST STANDARD

When an attorney representing a child determines that the child does not have considered judgment, the attorney should advocate for services and safety measures that the attorney believes to be in the child's best interests, taking into consideration the placement that is the least restrictive alternative. The attorney may advocate a position different from the child's wishes if the attorney finds that the child does not have considered judgment at that time. The attorney should make clear to the court that the attorney is adopting the best interest standard for that particular proceeding and state the reasons for adopting the best interest standard as well as the reasons for any change from a previously adopted standard of representation. Even if the attorney advocates a position different from the child's wishes, the attorney should ensure that the child's position is made a part of the record.

C. CLIENT CONTACT

GUIDELINE C1. GENERAL

The attorney should meet in the community with the child at each key stage of the representation to conduct a meaningful interview. The attorney should meet the child in preparation for a hearing, regardless of the child's age or disability, in an environment that will facilitate reasonable attorney-client communications. The attorney is encouraged to meet with the child in multiple environments, including the child's school, placement, each subsequent placement, or home.

When face-to-face contact with a child is not reasonably possible or not necessary, the attorney still should have meaningful contact with the child. These situations may include: (a) a child placed out-of-state; (b) a teenager with whom the attorney has established a sufficient attorney-client relationship; or (c) a child under the age of three at the shelter care proceeding. The attorney, however, should have face-to-face contact with the child prior to the adjudication hearing.

When a communication with the child requires a sign or spoken language interpreter, the attorney should try to use the services of a court-related interpreter or other qualified interpreter other than the child's family, friends, or social workers.

GUIDELINE C2. DETERMINATIONS

After conducting one or more interviews with a child and giving reasonable consideration to the child's age and cognitive and emotional development, the attorney should determine, at a minimum:

a. whether the child has considered judgment;

b. whether the presence of the child at the proceedings will be waived, i.e., whether the child wants or needs to be present at the hearing or whether the child will be harmed by appearing in court;

c. the child's position on the agency's petition, court report(s), and other relevant issues, including the permanency plan and placement;

d. the child's position on evidence that may be offered at the hearing, including evidence that may be offered on behalf of the child;

e. the child's legal position at the hearing;

f. whether there is a conflict of interest that requires the attorney to move to withdraw from representing one or all of the clients as, for example, when the attorney represents siblings;

g. whether the child should be called as a witness, after considering such factors as (1) the child's age, (2) the child's cognitive and emotional development, (3) the child's need or desire to testify, (4) the likelihood of emotional trauma or repercussions to the child, (5) the necessity of the child's direct testimony, and (6) the availability of other evidence, hearsay exceptions, proffers, or stipulations that can substitute for direct testimony; and

h. if the child will be called as a witness, the setting of the child's testimony; for example, whether the child should testify in open court, open chambers, closed chambers, or another location.

GUIDELINE C3. ANCILLARY CONTACT WITH THE CHILD

The attorney should have meaningful contact with the child at least every six months, even if a court hearing is not scheduled. The attorney should seek to obtain notice of emergencies and significant events involving the child between court hearings. Upon receiving notice of such an event (for example, a change of placement), the attorney should interview or observe the child within a reasonable time. As necessary or appropriate to the representation, the attorney should attend treatment, placement, and administrative hearings, and other proceedings, as well as school case conferences or staffing conferences concerning the child.

GUIDELINE C4. CONTINUITY OF REPRESENTATION

The attorney should continue to represent the child after the initial court proceeding, including at disposition review hearings, permanency planning hearings, and related TPR and adoption proceedings.

D. ATTORNEY INVESTIGATION

GUIDELINE D1. INDEPENDENT INVESTIGATION

The child's attorney should conduct a thorough and independent investigation as necessary or appropriate to the representation. This investigation may include the following:

a. obtaining and reviewing the child's social services, psychiatric, psychological, drug and alcohol, medical, law enforcement, school, and other records relevant to the case;

b. interviewing or observing the child before all court hearings and when apprised of emergencies or significant events affecting the child;

c. interviewing school personnel and other professionals and potential witnesses;

d. interviewing the child's caretaker(s), with the permission of their attorney when necessary, concerning the type of services the child currently receives and the type of services the child needs; and

e. reviewing all relevant evidence.

At each stage of the investigation, the attorney should be familiar with the child's position.

GUIDELINE D2. NON-VERBAL CHILD WITHOUT CONSIDERED JUDGMENT

For a non-verbal child who does not have considered judgment, the attorney should observe that child in the child's environment and conduct a thorough investigation. The investigation should include, at a minimum, contact with the child's caretaker, teacher, physician, and caseworker to obtain information about the status of the child.

E. INVOLVEMENT IN THE COURT PROCESS

GUIDELINE E1. PRE-TRIAL STAGES

a. If the child has considered judgment, the attorney should develop a position and strategy concerning every relevant aspect of the proceedings. When developing the child's legal position, the attorney should ensure that the child is given advice and guidance and all information necessary to make an informed decision.

b. The attorney should explain to the child in a manner appropriate to the child's level of development what is expected to happen before, during, and after each hearing.

c. Consistent with the child's wishes, or the best interests of a child without considered judgment, the attorney should seek to obtain appropriate services, including services for children with physical, mental, or developmental disabilities.

GUIDELINE E2. TRIAL STAGES

a. The attorney should attend all hearings involving the child and participate in all telephone or other conferences with the court unless a particular hearing involves issues completely unrelated to the child.

b. The attorney should present a case and make appropriate motions, including, when appropriate, introducing independent evidence and witnesses and cross-examining witnesses.

c. During all hearings, the attorney should preserve legal issues for appeal, as appropriate.

d. Consistent with the wishes of a child with considered judgment, the attorney should try to ensure timely hearings and oppose unwarranted continuances or postponements.

GUIDELINE E3. POST-TRIAL STAGES

a. Following the hearing, if consistent with the attorney's representation of the child's position, the attorney should seek a written court order to be given to the parties, containing at a minimum:

(1) required findings of fact and conclusions of law;

(2) the date and time of the next hearing;

(3) required notices;

(4) actions to be taken by each party, including the agency(ies), and custodians;

(5) appropriate statutory timelines; and

(6) the names of the parties who were present at the hearing.

b. The attorney should consider and discuss with the child the possibility and ramifications of an appeal and, when appropriate, take all steps necessary to note an appeal or participate in an appeal filed by another party.

F. LAWYER TRAINING

GUIDELINE F1. INITIAL TRAINING OR EXPERIENCE

Before accepting a case, a lawyer who does not have sufficient experience in providing legal representation to children in CINA and related TPR and adoption cases should participate in formal training and education related to this area of practice. The lawyer should satisfy the court and, if applicable, the entity responsible for payment of the lawyer that the lawyer has sufficient skill and experience in child advocacy. The lawyer should participate in available training and education, including in-house training.

GUIDELINE F2. SUBSTANCE OF TRAINING

Lawyers who seek to represent children in these proceedings are encouraged to seek training and education in such subjects as:

a. the role of child's counsel;

b. assessing considered judgment;

c. basic interviewing techniques;

d. child development: cognitive, emotional, and mental stages;

e. federal and state statutes, regulations, rules, and case law;

f. overview of the court process and key personnel in child-related litigation;

g. applicable guidelines and standards of representation;

h. family dynamics and dysfunction, including substance abuse and mental illness;

i. related issues, such as domestic violence, special education, mental health, developmental disability systems, and adult guardianships;

j. social service agencies, child welfare programs, and medical, educational, and mental health resources for the child and family; and

k. written materials, including related motions, court orders, pleadings, and training manuals.

G. ROLE OF THE COURT

If the court becomes aware that an attorney is not following these Guidelines, the court may encourage compliance by taking one or more of the following steps, as appropriate:

(1) alert the individual attorney that the attorney is not in compliance with the Guidelines;

(2) alert relevant government agencies or firms that the attorney is not complying with the Guidelines;

(3) alert the entity(ies) responsible for administering the contracts for children's representation that the attorney appointed to represent children is not complying with the Guidelines; and

(4) appoint another attorney for the child. (Added Mar. 5, 2001, effective July 1, 2001.)

APPENDIX: MARYLAND GUIDELINES FOR PRACTICE FOR COURT-APPOINTED LAWYERS REPRESENTING CHILDREN IN CASES INVOLVING CHILD CUSTODY OR CHILD ACCESS

Introduction and Scope

These Guidelines are intended to promote good practice and consistency in the appointment and performance of lawyers for children in cases involving child custody and child access decisions. However, the failure to follow a Guideline does not itself give rise to a cause of action against a lawyer nor does it create any presumption that a legal duty has been breached. These Guidelines apply to divorce, custody, visitation, domestic violence, and other civil cases where the court may be called upon to decide issues relating to child custody or access. Nothing contained in the Guidelines is intended to modify, amend, or alter the fiduciary duty that an attorney owes to a client pursuant to the Maryland Lawyers' Rules of Professional Conduct.

These Guidelines do not apply to Child In Need of Assistance ("CINA"), Termination of Parental Rights ("TPR"), or adoption cases. The appointment and performance of attorneys appointed to represent children in those cases is addressed by the Guidelines of Advocacy for Attorneys Representing Children in CINA and Related TPR and Adoption Proceedings.

1. **Definitions**. A court that appoints counsel for a minor child in a case involving child custody or child access issues should clearly indicate in the appointment order, and in all communications with the attorney, the parties, and other counsel, the role expected of child's counsel. The terminology and roles used should be in accordance with the definitions in Guidelines 1.1 — 1.3.

1.1. Child's Best Interest Attorney. "Child's Best Interest Attorney" means a lawyer appointed by a court for the purpose of protecting a child's best interests, without being bound by the child's directives or objectives. This term replaces the term "guardian ad litem." The Child's Best Interest Attorney makes an independent assessment of what is in the child's best interest and advocates for that before the court, even if it requires the disclosure of confidential information. The best interest attorney should ensure that the child's position is made a part of the record whether or not different from the position that the attorney advocates.

1.2. Child's Advocate Attorney. "Child's Advocate Attorney" means a lawyer appointed by a court to provide independent legal counsel for a child. This term replaces the less specific phrase, "child's attorney." A Child's Advocate Attorney owes the child the same duties of undivided loyalty, confidentiality, and competent representation as are due an adult client. A Child's Advocate Attorney should be appointed when the child is need of a voice in court, such as in relocation cases, when there are allegations of child abuse, or where the child is sufficiently mature and sees his or her interests as distinct from the interests of the child's parents.

1.3. Child's Privilege Attorney. "Child's Privilege Attorney" means a lawyer appointed by a court in a case involving child custody or child access to decide whether to assert or waive, on behalf of a minor child, any privilege that the child if an adult would be entitled to assert or waive. This term replaces the term "*Nagle v. Hooks* Attorney." (*Nagle v. Hooks*, 296 Md. 123 (1983)). The court may combine the roles of Child's Privilege Attorney with either of the other two roles.

2. **Responsibilities**. 2.1. Determining considered judgment. The attorney should determine whether the child has considered judgment. To determine whether the child has considered judgment, the attorney should focus on the child's decision-making process, rather than the child's decision. The attorney should determine whether the child can understand therisks and benefits of the child's legal position and whether the child can reasonably communicate the child's wishes. The attorney should consider the following factors when determining whether the child has considered judgment:

(1) the child's developmental stage:

(a) cognitive ability,

(b) socialization, and

(c) emotional and mental development;

(2) the child's expression of a relevant position:

(a) ability to communicate with the attorney, and

(b) ability to articulate reasons for the legal position; and

(3) relevant and available reports, such as reports from social workers, psychiatrists, psychologists, and schools.

A child may be capable of considered judgment even though the child has a significant cognitive or emotional disability.

In determining considered judgment, the attorney may seek guidance from professionals, family members, school officials, and other concerned persons. The attorney also should determine whether any evaluations are needed and request them when appropriate.

An attorney should be sensitive to cultural, racial, ethnic, or economic differences between the attorney and the child.

2.2. Child's Best Interest Attorney. A Child's Best Interest Attorney advances a position that the attorney believes is in the child's best interest. Even if the attorney advocates a position different from the child's wishes, the attorney should ensure that the child's position is made a part of the record. A Child's Best Interest Attorney may perform the following duties in exercising the attorney's obligation to the client and the court, as appropriate:

(a) Meet with and interview the child, and advise the child of the scope of the representation.

(b) Investigate the relative abilities of the parties in their roles as parents or custodians.

(c) Visit the child in each home.

(d) Conduct individual interviews with parents, other parties, and collateral witnesses.

(e) Observe the child's interactions with each parent and each other party, individually.

(f) Review educational, medical, dental, psychiatric, psychological, or other records.

(g) Interview school personnel, childcare providers, healthcare providers, and mental health professionals involved with the child or family.

(h) File and respond to pleadings and motions.

(i) Participate in discovery.

(j) Participate in settlement negotiations.

(k) Participate in the trial, including calling witnesses and presenting evidence and argument, as appropriate.

(l) If the child is to meet with the judge or testify, prepare the child, familiarizing the child with the places, people, procedures, and questioning that the child will be exposed to, and seek to minimize any harm to the child from the process.

(m) Inform the child in a developmentally appropriate manner when the representation is ending.

A Child's Best Interest Attorney shall not testify at trial or file a report with the court.

2.3. Child's Advocate Attorney. If a Child's Advocate Attorney determines that the child has considered judgment, the attorney advances the child's wishes and desires in the pending matter. If a Child's Advocate Attorney determines that the child does not have considered judgment, the Child's Advocate Attorney should petition the court to (1) alter the attorney's role to permit the attorney to serve as a Child's Best Interest Attorney or (2) appoint a separate Child's Best Interest Attorney. A Child's Advocate Attorney may perform the following duties in exercising the attorney's obligation to the child and the court, as appropriate:

(a) Meet with and interview the child, and advise the child of the scope of the representation.

(b) Investigate the relative abilities of the parties in their role as parents or custodians.

(c) Visit the child in each home.

(d) Conduct individual interviews with parents, other parties, and collateral witnesses.

(e) Observe the child's interactions with each parent and each other party, individually.

(f) Review educational, medical, dental, psychiatric, psychological, or other records.

(g) Interview school personnel, childcare providers, healthcare providers, and mental health professionals involved with the child or family.

(h) File and respond to pleadings and motions.

(i) Participate in discovery.

(j) Participate in settlement negotiations.

(k) Participate in the trial, including calling witnesses and presenting evidence and argument, as appropriate.

(l) If the child is to meet with the judge or testify, prepare the child, familiarizing the child with the places, people, procedures, and questioning that the child will be exposed to, and seek to minimize any harm to the child from the process.

(m) Inform the child in a developmentally appropriate manner when the representation ends.

A Child's Advocate Attorney shall not testify at trial or file a report with the court.

2.4. Child's Privilege Attorney. A Child's Privilege Attorney notifies the court and the parties of the attorney's decision to waive or assert the child's privilege by (1) filing a document with the court prior to the hearing or trial at which the privilege is to be asserted or waived or (2) placing the waiver or assertion of privilege on the record at a pretrial proceeding or the trial.

A Child's Privilege Attorney may perform the following duties in exercising the attorney's obligation to the child and the court, as appropriate:

(a) Meet with and interview the child, and advise the child of the scope of the representation.

(b) Interview any witnesses necessary to assist the attorney in determining whether to assert or waive the privilege.

(c) Review educational, medical, dental, psychiatric, psychological, or other records.

3. **Conflicts of interest**. An attorney who has been appointed to represent two or more children should remain alert to the possibility of a conflict that could require the attorney to decline representation or withdraw from representing all of the children.

If a conflict of interest develops, the attorney should bring the conflict to the attention of the court as soon as possible, in a manner that does not compromise either client's interests.

4. **Training and continuing education**. Unless waived by the court, an attorney appointed as a Child's Best Interest Attorney, Child's Advocate Attorney, or Child's Privilege Attorney should have completed at least six hours of training that includes the following topics:

(a) applicable representation guidelines and standards;

(b) children's development, needs, and abilities at different stages;

(c) effectively communicating with children;

(d) preparing and presenting a child's viewpoint, including child testimony and alternatives to direct testimony;

(e) recognizing, evaluating, and understanding evidence of child abuse and neglect;

(f) family dynamics and dysfunction, domestic violence, and substance abuse;

(g) recognizing the limitations of attorney expertise and the need for other professional expertise, which may include professionals who can provide information on evaluation, consultation, and testimony on mental health, substance abuse, education, special needs, or other issues; and

(h) available resources for children and families in child custody and child access disputes.

Each court should require attorneys seeking appointments as child counsel to maintain their knowledge of current law and complete a specific amount of additional training over a defined interval.

5. **Qualifications**. An attorney appointed to serve as a Child's Best Interest Attorney, Child's Advocate Attorney, or Child's Privilege Attorney should, as a minimum:

(a) be a member of the Maryland Bar in good standing, with experience in family law, or have been approved to represent children through a pro bono program approved by the bench; and

(b) unless waived by the court, have successfully completed the six hours of training specified in Guideline 4.

In addition, courts should seek to appoint attorneys who:

(a) are willing to take at least one pro bono appointment as child counsel per year, and

(b) have at least three years of family law experience or other relevant experience. In evaluating relevant experience, the court may consider the attorney's experience in social work, education, child development, mental health, healthcare, or other related fields.

6. **Compensation**. 6.1. Compensation structure. Each court should develop a compensation structure for the three roles of child counsel: Child's Best Interest Attorneys, Child's Advocate Attorneys, and Child's Privilege Attorneys.

6.2. Compensation mechanism. Each court should take steps to ensure that child counsel are compensated adequately and in a timely fashion, unless the attorney has been asked to serve pro bono publico. Courts may use the following mechanisms to ensure attorney compensation:

(a) Require one or more of the parties to deposit a significant retainer amount or a fixed fee determined by the court into an attorney escrow account or the court's registry.

(b) If a party qualifies for a fee waiver, compensate child counsel out of available funds. See Guideline 6.3.

(c) Enter a judgment for any unpaid fees.

6.3. Fee waivers. Each court should prepare its budget to ensure that it has sufficient funds to cover the expense of counsel fees for children when the parties are not able to pay the full fees, or the court should develop a pro bono publico component to its program to provide counsel for children.

Each court should apply the same fee waiver procedure, forms, and standard for the appointment of child counsel that are set forth in the Guidelines for Grant Recipients for all family services funded by the Family Division amily Services Program Grants. If a fee waiver is granted, the court should apply a cap on compensation that is appropriate to the role for which child counsel is appointed. (Added May 8, 2007, effective July 1, 2007.)

APPENDIX: MARYLAND CODE OF CONDUCT FOR COURT INTERPRETERS:

Preamble

In the absence of a court interpreter, many persons who come before the courts are partially or completely excluded from full participation in the proceedings because they have limited proficiency in the English language, have a speech impairment, or are deaf or hard of hearing. It is essential that the resulting communication barrier be removed, as far as possible, so that these persons are placed in the same position and enjoy equal access to justice as similarly situated persons for whom there is no such barrier. As officers of the court, interpreters help to ensure that these persons enjoy equal access to justice and that court proceedings and court support services function efficiently and effectively.

Applicability

This Code shall guide and be binding upon all certified interpreters and interpreters eligible for certification, as those terms are defined in Rule 16-819, and all agencies and organizations that administer, supervise the use of, or deliver interpreting services in the courts of this State.

Canon 1
Accuracy and Completeness

Interpreters shall render a complete and accurate interpretation or sight translation, without altering, omitting, or adding anything to what is stated or written and without explanation.

Commentary

The interpreter has a twofold duty: 1) to ensure that the proceedings reflect precisely what was said, and 2) to place the person with limited English proficiency on an equal footing with those who understand English. This creates an obligation to conserve every element of information contained in a source language communication when it is rendered in the target language.

Therefore, interpreters are obligated to apply their best skills and judgment to preserve faithfully the meaning of what is said in court, including the style or register of speech. Verbatim, "word for word," or literal oral interpretations are not appropriate if they distort the meaning of the source language, but every spoken statement, even if it appears non-responsive, obscene, rambling, or incoherent, should be interpreted. This includes apparent misstatements.

Interpreters should never interject their own words, phrases, or expressions. If the need arises to explain an interpreting problem (*e.g.*, a term or phrase with no direct equivalent in the target language or a misunderstanding that

909

only the interpreter can clarify), the interpreter should ask the court's permission to provide an explanation. Interpreters should convey the emotional emphasis of the speaker without reenacting or mimicking the speaker's emotions or dramatic gestures.

Sign language interpreters, however, *must* employ all of the visual cues that the language that they are interpreting requires — including facial and spatial grammar.

The obligation to preserve accuracy includes the interpreter's duty to correct any error of interpretation discovered by the interpreter during the proceeding.

Interpreters should demonstrate their professionalism by objectively analyzing any challenge to their performance.

Canon 2
Representation of Qualifications

Interpreters shall accurately and completely represent their certifications, training, and pertinent experience.

Commentary

Acceptance of a case by an interpreter conveys linguistic and interpreting competency in legal settings. Withdrawing or being asked to withdraw from a case after it begins causes a disruption of court proceedings and is wasteful of scarce public resources. It is therefore essential that, prior to appointment, interpreters present a complete and truthful account of their training, certification, and experience, so the officers of the court can fairly evaluate their qualifications for delivering interpreting services.

Canon 3
Impartiality and Avoidance of Conflict of Interest

Interpreters shall be impartial and unbiased and shall refrain from conduct that may give an appearance of bias. Interpreters shall disclose any real or perceived conflict of interest.

Commentary

The interpreter serves as an officer of the court, and the interpreter's duty in a court proceeding is to serve the court and the public to which the court is a servant. This is true regardless of whether the interpreter is retained publicly at government expense or privately at the expense of one of the parties.

Interpreters should avoid any conduct or behavior that presents the appearance of favoritism toward any of the parties. Interpreters should maintain professional relationships with the participants and should not take an active part in any of the proceedings.

During the course of the proceedings, interpreters should not converse with parties, witnesses, prospective, qualified, or sworn jurors, attorneys, or law enforcement officers or with friends or relatives of any party, except in the discharge of official functions. It is especially important that interpreters who are familiar with courtroom personnel refrain from casual and personal conversations that may convey an appearance of a special relationship with or partiality to any of the court participants.

Interpreters should strive for professional detachment. Verbal and non-verbal displays of personal attitudes, prejudices, emotions, or opinions should be avoided at all times.

Whenever an interpreter becomes aware that a proceeding participant views the interpreter as having a bias or being biased, the interpreter should disclose that knowledge to the appropriate judicial authority and counsel.

Any condition that interferes with the objectivity of an interpreter constitutes a conflict of interest. Before providing services in a matter, court interpreters must disclose to all parties and presiding officials any prior involvement, whether personal or professional, that could be reasonably construed as a conflict of interest. This disclosure should not include privileged or confidential information.

The following are circumstances that are presumed to create actual or apparent conflicts of interest for interpreters so that they should not serve:

1. The interpreter is a friend, associate, or relative of a party or counsel involved in the proceedings;
2. The interpreter has served in an investigative capacity for any party to the case;
3. The interpreter was retained by a law enforcement agency to assist in the preparation of the civil or criminal case at issue;
4. The interpreter or the interpreter's spouse or child has a financial interest in the subject matter in controversy or in a party to the proceeding or has any other interest that would be affected by the outcome of the case;
5. The interpreter has been involved in the choice of counsel or law firm for that case.

Interpreters should disclose to the court and other parties whenever they have been retained previously for private employment by one of the parties in the case.

Interpreters should not serve in any matter in which payment for their services is contingent upon the outcome of the case.

An interpreter who is also an attorney should not serve in both capacities in the same matter.

Canon 4
Professional Demeanor

Interpreters shall conduct themselves in a manner consistent with the dignity of the court and shall be as unobtrusive as possible.

Commentary

Interpreters should know and observe the established protocol, rules, and procedures for delivering interpreting services. Interpreters should work without drawing undue or inappropriate attention to themselves.

911

Interpreters should avoid obstructing the view of any of the individuals involved in the proceedings. However, the positioning of interpreters should be conducive to receiving effective communications.

Canon 5
Confidentiality

Interpreters shall protect the confidentiality of all privileged and other confidential information.

Commentary

The interpreter must protect and uphold the confidentiality of all privileged information obtained during the course of her or his duties. It is especially important that the interpreter understand and uphold the attorney-client privilege, which requires confidentiality with respect to any communication between attorney and client. This rule also applies to other types of privileged communications.

Interpreters must also refrain from repeating or disclosing information that is obtained by them in the course of their employment and that may be relevant to the legal proceeding.

In the event that an interpreter becomes aware of information that suggests imminent harm to someone or relates to a crime being committed during the course of the proceedings, the interpreter should immediately disclose the information to an appropriate authority within the judiciary who is not involved in the proceeding and seek advice in regard to the potential conflict in professional responsibility.

Canon 6
Restriction of Public Comment

Interpreters shall not publicly discuss, report, or offer an opinion concerning a matter in which they are or have been engaged, even when that information is not privileged or required by law to be confidential.

Canon 7
Scope of Practice

While serving as interpreters, interpreters shall limit themselves to interpreting or translating and shall not give legal advice, express personal opinions to individuals for whom they are interpreting, or engage in any other activities which may be construed to constitute a service other than interpreting or translating.

Commentary

Since interpreters are responsible only for enabling others to communicate, they should limit themselves to the activity of interpreting or translating.

Interpreters should refrain from initiating communications while interpreting, except as necessary for ensuring an accurate and faithful interpretation.

Interpreters may be required to initiate communications during a proceeding when they find it necessary to seek assistance in performing their duties. Examples of such circumstances include seeking direction when unable to understand or express a word or thought, requesting speakers to moderate their rate of communication or to repeat or rephrase something, correcting their own interpreting errors, or notifying the court of reservations about their ability to satisfy an assignment competently. In such instances, interpreters should make it clear that they are speaking for themselves.

An interpreter may convey legal advice from an attorney to a person only while that attorney is giving it. An interpreter should not explain the purpose of forms or services or otherwise act as counselors or advisors but, rather, merely interpret for someone who is acting in that official capacity. The interpreter may translate language on a form for a person who is filling out the form but may not explain the form or its purpose for such a person.

The interpreter should not perform acts that are the official responsibility of other court officials including, but not limited to, court clerks, pretrial release investigators or interviewers, or probation counselors.

Canon 8
Assessing and Reporting Impediments to Performance

Interpreters shall assess at all times their ability to deliver their services. When interpreters have any reservation about their ability to satisfy an assignment competently, they shall immediately convey that reservation to the appropriate judicial authority.

Commentary

Interpreters should notify the appropriate judicial authority whenever the communication mode or language of the persons with limited English proficiency cannot be interpreted readily.

Interpreters should notify the appropriate judicial authority about any environmental or physical limitation that impedes or hinders their ability to deliver interpreting services adequately (*e.g.*, the courtroom is not quiet enough for the interpreter to hear or be heard, more than one person at a time is speaking, or principals or witnesses are speaking too rapidly for the interpreter to interpret adequately). Sign language interpreters must ensure that, prior to commencement of the proceeding, they are positioned visually in the most appropriate position for the deaf or hard of hearing person to convey and receive the communication. The proceeding should not begin, even by permitting the attorneys to identify themselves for the record, until the sign language interpreter is positioned properly. Immediately after the attorneys have identified themselves, the interpreter oath should be administered, regardless of the type of proceeding.

Interpreters should notify the presiding officer of the need to take periodic breaks to maintain mental and physical alertness and to prevent interpreter fatigue. Interpreters should recommend and encourage the use of a relay interpreter and/or interpreter teams as necessary.

Interpreters are required to inquire as to the nature of a case before accepting an assignment. This enables interpreters to match their professional qualifications, skills, and experience more closely to potential assignments, to assess more accurately their ability to satisfy those assignments competently, and to identify any personal bias arising from the nature of the case.

Even competent and experienced interpreters may encounter situations in which routine proceedings involve unanticipated technical or specialized terminology unfamiliar to the interpreter (*e.g.*, the unscheduled testimony of an expert witness). When such instances occur, interpreters should request a recess for a sufficient amount of time to familiarize themselves with the terminology. If familiarity with the terminology requires extensive time or more intensive research, interpreters should inform the presiding officer.

Interpreters should refrain from accepting a case whenever they feel the language or subject matter of that case is likely to exceed their skills or capacities. Interpreters should feel no compunction about notifying the presiding officer if they feel unable to perform competently, due to lack of familiarity with terminology, lack of preparation, or difficulty in understanding a witness or defendant.

Canon 9
Duty to Report Ethical Violations

Interpreters shall report to the proper judicial authority any effort to impede their compliance with any law, any provision of this Code, or any other official policy governing court interpreting and legal translating.

Commentary

Since users of interpreting services frequently misunderstand the proper role of the interpreter, they may ask or expect the interpreter to perform duties or engage in activities that run counter to the provisions of this Code or of laws, regulations, or policies governing court interpreters. It is incumbent upon the interpreter to inform such persons of his or her professional obligations. If, having been apprised of these obligations, the person persists in demanding that the interpreter violate them, the interpreter should ask a supervisory interpreter, a judge, or another official with jurisdiction over interpreter matters to resolve the situation.

Canon 10
Professional Development

Interpreters shall continually improve their skills and knowledge and advance the profession through activities such as professional training and education and interaction with colleagues and specialists in related fields.

Commentary

Interpreters must continually strive to increase their knowledge of the languages in which they work professionally, including past and current trends in technical, vernacular, and regional terminology as well as their application within court proceedings.

Interpreters should keep informed of all statutes, rules of courts and policies of the judiciary that relate to the performance of their professional duties.

Interpreters should seek to elevate the standards of the profession through participation in workshops, professional meetings, interaction with colleagues, and reading of current literature in the field.

Canon 11
Compliance

After notice and a reasonable opportunity to respond, the Administrative Office of the Courts may remove an interpreter from the list of court interpreters. (Amended May 8, 2007, effective July 1, 2007; Dec. 4, 2007, effective Jan. 1, 2008.)

Effect of amendments. — The 2007 amendment rewrote the Canon 11 Compliance and deleted the Commentary.

The December 4, 2007 Order, effective January 1, 2008, in the third paragraph of the Commentary to Canon 3 added "prospective, qualified, or sworn".

APPENDIX: COURT INTERPRETER INQUIRY QUESTIONS

Following is an excerpt from the October 20, 1998 Report of the Maryland Judicial Conference Advisory Committee on Interpreters.

Interpreter Voir Dire Questions*:

These questions are intended to elicit from a prospective interpreter, whether sign or spoken, the information that the Court needs to determine whether an individual is a competent court interpreter and whether the individual is the appropriate interpreter for the particular case. A few questions are appropriate only to a sign or a spoken language interpreter. In the event that the interpreter is considered "certified" in Maryland, the *voir dire* need not be as extensive.

(1) State your full name and address.

(2) Where are you employed currently?

(3) How long have you known [sign/spoken language]?

(4) Where did you learn [sign/spoken language]?

(5) Can you communicate fluently in [sign/spoken language]?

(6) What is your educational background?

(7) What formal interpreter training have you undertaken?

(8) What formal legal interpreter training have you undertaken?

(9) What knowledge and skill areas did you study?

(10) Have you attended the Maryland Judiciary's Orientation Workshop for Court Interpreters?

(11) Are you certified? By whom? What is your certification called?

(12) Please explain the certification process?

Questions 13 through 19 need not be asked if the interpreter is "certified" for purposes of Maryland courts.

(13) Have you spent time in a country where your spoken language is used?

(14) Are you active in any professional organization?

(15) What do "RID" and "NAJIT" mean?

(16) How many times have you interpreted in court and in what kinds of situations have you interpreted?

(17) Have you met _____ (the person for whom interpreter services are to be provided)?

(18) Were you able to establish communication?

(19) How could you determine that you were being understood and that communication was established?

(20) What language does the person use?

---

* Adapted from William Mitchell School of Law, Legal Interpreting Workshop, 1981, conducted by Anna Witter-Merithew and Jill Hartman. Revised in 1986 by the authors. Revised in 1994 by the Maryland Judicial Conference's Task Force on Interpreters. Revised in May, 1997 by the Advisory Committee on Interpreters' Subcommittee on Court Interpreter Fees, Qualification Standards and usage.

(21) How did you determine the language used?

(22) How long did it take you to determine the language used?

(23) In your opinion, is the deaf person American Sign Language-English bilingual?

Questions 24 through 30 need not be asked if the interpreter is "certified" for purposes of Maryland courts.

(24) Please explain the difference between interpreting and transliterating. Between interpreting and translation.

(25) Can you define "minimal language skills"?

(26) Is it possible to sign in American Sign Language at the same time you are speaking in English?

(27) Will the interpretation you provide today be verbatim?

(28) What process would you use to inform the Court of an error in your interpretation?

(29) Can you explain the difference between simultaneous and consecutive interpretation?

(30) What issues significantly affect your interpreting in court?

(31) Have you submitted to the Administrative Office of the Courts a completed information form, a statement swearing or affirming compliance with the Maryland Code of Conduct for Court Interpreters and a statement subscribing to the Interpreter's Oath?

(32) Have you, in a state or federal court of record, a pending criminal charge or criminal conviction on a charge punishable by a fine of more than $500 or imprisonment for more than 6 months and not pardoned or expunged?

(33) Are you a potential witness in this case?

(34) Do you have any other potential conflicts of interests that you have not yet mentioned to the Court?

(35) Are you ready to take the oath for interpreters?

Explanation of Responses to *Voir Dire* Questions for Interpreters*:

The following is an explanation or suggested responses to the *voir dire* questions used to determine the qualifications of interpreters working in Maryland courts. In some instances, the appropriateness of the response will depend on whether a sign or spoken language interpreter is being questioned.

(1) *State your full name and address.*

No explanation needed.

(2) *Where are you employed currently?*

The Court needs to determine whether there is any potential conflict due to full- or part-time employment of an interpreter or assignments as an indepen-

---

* Adapted from William Mitchell School of Law, Legal Interpreting Workshop, 1981, conducted by Anna Witter-Merithew and Jill Hartman. Revised in 1986 by the authors. Revised in 1994 by the Maryland Judicial Conference's Task Force on Interpreters. Revised in May, 1997 by the Advisory Committee on Interpreters' Subcommittee on Court Interpreter Fees, Qualification Standards and usage.

dent contractor. For example, some police forces employ bilingual officers who freelance as interpreters. The Court may need to evaluate whether a conflict arises from that employment in, *e.g.*, a vehicle tort case.

Interpreters may be self employed, "freelance" interpreters, may work through interpreter service agencies, or do both. In certain localities, such as Frederick or Columbia, a number of certified interpreters work full-time at the schools for the deaf and freelance on a part-time basis.

(3) *How long have you known [sign / spoken] language?*

Research indicates that it takes between 6 to 10 years of language study before an individual has the language skills necessary to learn the interpreting process in his or her second language.

An interpreter may indicate that the signed or spoken language is his or her first language.

(4) *Where did you learn [sign / spoken language]?*

The answer to this question reinforces the answer to question 3, indicating whether the language was learned in the home in which the interpreter was raised, in school, or in some combination of these or other settings. A mix of formal and informal language training is an asset. For a second language, 6 to 10 years' use should be expected.

(5) *Can you communicate fluently in [sign / spoken language]?*

The answer to this question should be "yes".

On occasion, a deaf person will use a language other than American Sign Language (ASL) such as French Sign Language, and an interpreter may be available in that language. Thus, if the Court inquires about ASL specifically, the answer may be "No, I do not use American Sign Language; however, the individual for whom I am to interpret uses French Sign Language, which I do use."

(6) *What is your educational background?*

Formal education may vary dramatically among interpreters, depending on their cultural heritage, but the Court should realize the complexity of interpreting. For this reason, the Court is urged not to accept an interpreter on the basis of a *voir dire* examination unless the interpreter has at least a high school education or its cultural equivalent.

(7) *What formal interpreter training have you undertaken?*

The advent of formal postsecondary programs for interpreters is relatively recent, but the number of programs are growing in recognition that interpreter training differs from general, non-interpreting language training.

Such programs for sign language interpreting degree programs have been offered since the 1970's, usually at a 2-year associate of arts level. About 10, 4-year interpreting programs exist throughout the country and, within the vicinity of Maryland, 2 master's degree interpreting programs are available. Additionally or in the alternative, the interpreter may have less formal training such as completion of workshops through professional organizations.

An individual with no formal interpreter training should be questioned to

document non-formal training.

(8) *What formal legal interpreter training have you undertaken?*

Resources for formal training in legal interpreting have not stabilized. Over the past 10 years, intensive programs have been offered through California State University/Northridge (6 weeks), Advancement Seminars Inc. (3 weeks), Haury Institute for Court Interpreting (3 weeks), and Montclair State University (3 weeks). Less intensive courses include those of the Galluadet University School of Professional and Sign Language Studies Department (4 days), Potomac Chapter of the Registry of Interpreters for the Deaf (4 days), and the Bicultural Center formerly of Riverdale, Maryland (2 days).

(9) *What knowledge and skill areas did you study?*

Interpreters who have had legal training have studied the vocabulary of the law and the manner in which language is used in the courtroom. In addition, these interpreters have spent considerable time interpreting legal texts. The interpreter training programs for legal interpreting include course work on courtroom protocol and legal interpreting ethics. Interpreters also should have successfully participated in supervised fieldwork prior to completing the program. Each of these subject areas is extensive and a competent interpreter should be able to explain each thoroughly.

Sign language interpreters also study how deaf people use American Sign Language to discuss legal topics.

(10) *Have you attended the Maryland Judiciary's Orientation Workshop for Court Interpreters?*

The answer should be "yes", as this is required under the Administrative Order issued on December 7, 1995. This workshop includes components on legal terminology, ethics, and skills but is merely a 2-day overview and not an intensive course.

(11) *Are you certified? By whom? What is your certification called?*

The answer to the first of these questions preferably is "yes", but the Court should be aware that "certified" often is used loosely. Refer to the next answer for an explanation of the various types of certification credentials.

For a sign language interpreter, certification is offered throughout the United States by the Registry of Interpreters for the Deaf, Inc. (RID), which has several types of certificates. Additionally, the National Association of the Deaf (NAD), the Mid-Atlantic Quality Assurance Test developed by the Kansas Commission for the Hearing Impaired in cooperation with the Johnson County Community College, and some states also establish levels that some courts use in determining competency in sign language interpretation and that may denote an interpreter as "certified". As these categories are not in general use in this area at this time, however, the following discussion describes RID certification. As the RID certification process is in transition, you may wish to contact its FAX on Demand number (800-711-3691) for a document entitled "Explanation of Certificates".

After a lapse of almost 10 years, RID has renewed testing for skills and specialized knowledge of legal settings and terminology, as evidenced by a Specialist Certificate: Legal (SC:L). RID previously issued Specialist Certificate: Legal (SC:L) but discontinued doing so when the reliability of the testing procedures were questioned. Various training programs were instituted, leading to the Provisional Specialist Certificate: Legal (Prov. SC:L) for intensive training and testing, the Conditional Legal Interpreting Permit (CLIP) and Conditional Legal Interpreting Permit-Relay (CLIP-R) certificates for training followed by a supervision component.

A revamped SC:L examination has been developed. SC:L Prov. and CLIP holders must take and pass the new examination to retain specialized certification in legal settings. CLIP-R certificates will remain valid until RID develops an appropriate examination.

Other current RID certificates are: the Certificate of Interpretation (CI), which is indicative of a demonstrated ability to interpret between American Sign Language and spoken English, both in sign-to-voice and voice-to-sign; the Certificate of Transliteration (CT), which denotes a demonstrated ability to transliterate between an English-based sign language (traditionally, but inaccurately, termed Signed English, Pidgin Sign Language, Ameslan or otherwise) and spoken English, both in sign-to-voice and voice-to-sign; the combined Certificate of Interpretation and Certificate of Translation (CI and CT); the Oral Transliteration Certificate (OTC), which denotes a demonstrated ability to transliterate a spoken message from a hearing person to, and to understand and repeat the message and intent of the speech and mouth movements of, a deaf or hard of hearing person; the Certified Deaf Interpreter (CDI), which denotes testing of a deaf or hard of hearing person with at least 1 year's work experience and 16 hours of training in interpreting; and the Certified Deaf Interpreter-Provisional (CDI-P), which is awarded for partial completion of CDI testing.

RID certificates that no longer are issued, but may remain valid so long as RID continuing education requirements are met, include: the Master Comprehensive Skills Certificate (MCSC), which denotes testing both of American Sign Language (ASL) and other varieties of sign language that do not conform to ASL grammar; the Comprehensive Skills Certificate (CSC), which denotes the same testing as the MCSC, at a lower level but comparable to the current, combined CI and CT; the Interpretation Certificate/Transliteration Certificate (IC/TC); the Interpretation Certificate (IC) and the Transliteration Certificate (TC), which were awarded to persons not scoring sufficiently high marks for the full CSC and, for holders who are deaf interpreters, is being replaced by the CDI and the CDI-P certificates; the Reverse Skills Certificate (RSC), which also was awarded to persons not scoring sufficiently high marks; the Oral Interpreting Certificate: Comprehensive (OIC:C), the Oral Interpreting Certificate: Spoken to Visible (OIC:S/V) and the Oral Interpreting Certificate: Visible to Spoken (OIC:V/S), being phased out by the OIC; and the Specialist Certificate: Performing Arts (SC:PA).

Due to the limitations on the availability of these tests for deaf interpreters and the unique need for these interpreters for some assignments, some deaf interpreters may have extensive experience without certification. However, this situation should change with renewed RID testing.

Similarly, for spoken language interpreters, a number of forms of recognition exist, which are informally or formally denoted as certification. For purposes of court interpretation, however, an interpreter should be listed in the Maryland Administrative Office of the Courts' Registry of Court Interpreters as certified, because Maryland certification standards require, in addition to passing an examination of the United States Administrative Office of the Courts or State Court Interpreter Certification Consortium, attendance at a Maryland orientation workshop and, if practicable, a background check.

(12) *Please explain the certification process?*

RID certification involves written testing of knowledge as to the ethics of interpreting, the history of interpreting, the culture of deaf people, the protocol of the interpreting process and the business of interpreting, followed by an interpretation skills evaluation, and/r transliteration evaluation. This process is not directed at interpretation in a legal setting, which is evaluated by written and practical test for the specialist certificate.

(13) *Have you spent time in a country where the spoken language is used?*

This question is intended to elicit information about time that afforded intensive exposure to, and use of, the spoken language.

(14) *Are you active in any professional organization?*

The answer to this question should be "yes". See question 15.

(15) *What do "RID" and "NAJIT" mean?*

"RID" is the acronym for The Registry of Interpreters for the Deaf, Inc., a professional membership organization formed in 1964, and certifying sign language interpreters.

"NAJIT" is the National Association of Judiciary Interpreters and Translators.

(16) *How many times have you interpreted in court and in what kinds of situations have you interpreted?*

While usage of interpreters in court seems to be growing for every language, it still will be a rarity to encounter an interpreter with hundred hours of court interpreting experience even in the most frequently used languages. Furthermore, experience may run the gamut of court proceedings and is not a guarantee of quality skills. Consequently, the Court needs to elicit whether an interpreter has professional experience and evaluate that experience in light of the interpreter's education and testing and the particular court assignment.

(17) *Have you met* _____
                        (the person for whom interpreter services are to be provided)?
The answer should be "yes", for two reasons.

First, an interpreter needs to establish his or her ability to communicate with the person and to identify any potential communication barriers deriving from the person's unique language patterns.

Second, the Code of Conduct for Court Interpreters requires an interpreter to disclose prior contact with the person, in order to have the Court determine whether there is or may appear to be a conflict of interest. The deaf community and various linguistic groups, and their respective pools of interpreters, can be very limited in number, and meeting with the person may remind the interpreter of an earlier contact.

(18) *Were you able to establish communication?*

The answer should be "yes", or the interpreter cannot fulfill the function of the job.

For example, a deaf person who uses an idiosyncratic variation of sign language may require that a deaf and hearing interpreter be used as a team. Deaf people with limited English or American Sign Language skills often benefit from this type of arrangement.

Communication must not only be established but maintained, and the interpreter should bring to the attention of the Court any difficulty in communicating that subsequently arises, as soon as the difficulty becomes apparent to the interpreter. Furthermore, the interpreter should suggest that the Court check on a continuous basis with the individual for whom interpreter services are being provided, to monitor whether communication is maintained.

(19) *How could you determine that you were being understood and that*

communication was established?

During the initial meeting between an interpreter and an individual with limited English proficiency, the interpreter should ask open-ended questions about neutral topics unrelated to the case, such as the individual's life, current events, or the community, to determine whether the interpreter and individual understand one another. "Yes" or "no" questions do not suffice. A perceived problem should be explored by asking the individual to rephrase his or her questions. If the individual answers appropriately, the interpreter is assured that communication has been established.

(20) *What language does the person use?*

The Court needs to establish on the record which language or combination of the 5,000 plus extant languages is being used. For example, a deaf person may be monolingual-American Sign Language, monolingual-English, monolingual-other signed language, or bilingual American Sign Language and English. Most deaf persons are somewhat bilingual by virtue of the fact that they live in an English speaking environment; however, most are not equally fluent in both languages. The majority of deaf Americans are described accurately as "American Sign Language dominant bilingual."

(21) *How did you determine the language used?*

The answer of a sign language interpreter should discuss the linguistic features that would indicate whether the person uses American Sign Language (ASL). For example, an ASL user would use a subject-object-verb or object-subject-verb sentence structure; time and tense markers would be at or near the beginning of the utterances; adverbs and other grammar would take place on the face and not in separate signs; complex features, such as sentence structure that incorporates topic-comment eyebrow markers, would be used; rhetorical question eyebrow markers would be employed; relative clause eyebrow and head-tilt markers would be used; verbs would incorporate pronouns; and pronouns would be performed by eye-gaze and not by signs.

(22) *How long did it take you to determine the language used?*

The answer will vary. If no communication difficulties arise, a reasonable time allows the interpreter and individual for whom interpreter services are to be provided to become comfortable communicating. It can, however, take a considerable amount of time, so that the interpreter and individual should be allowed to decide, within limits, the amount of time they need.

The crucial point is to allow enough time for the interpreter and individual, as well as the Court and attorneys, to feel comfortable that communication is effective.

(23) *In your opinion, is the deaf person American Sign Language-English bilingual?*

The answer will vary, depending on the deaf person. The question is intended to determine the interpreter's grasp of bilingualism.

(24) *Please explain the difference between interpreting and transliterating. Between interpreting and translation.*

Interpretation involves working between two formal languagestransmitting a message from a source language into an appropriate equivalent message in a target language. Interpreting requires rearrangement of the syntax of both languages in order to convey the message faithfully.

Transliterating involves changing the form of a single language. Thus, an interpreter might listen to spoken English or watch a variation of sign language that approximates English and convey the message in either a signed or spoken form. Transliterating does not necessarily involve fluency in American Sign Language. Approximately 30% of deaf Americans can be accommodated satisfactorily with a transliteration.

Translation involves transmitting a message from written form to written form between languages.

Sight translation is a hybrid of interpretation and translation, whereby an interpreter translates a written document into a spoken or signed rendition.

(25) *Can you define "minimal language skills"?*

"Minimal language skills" refers to an absence of, or limitation on, language skills due to limited education and/or minimal exposure to a community of language users. By virtue of isolation, an individual may lack fluency in a formal language system such as American Sign Language. If the Court encounters such an individual, a linguistic evaluation should be performed to determine the best method of interpretation for that individual.

(26) *Is it possible to sign in American Sign Language at the same time you are speaking in English?*

No. American Sign Language and English differ significantly in syntax, making it no more possible to use American Sign Language and speak English at the same time than to use two spoken languages simultaneously.

The question derives from the common experience of people who do in fact sign and speak at the same time in what is called "simultaneous communication", a practice of speaking English while attempting to sign in a language that approximates English. As 70% of deaf Americans use American Sign Language and simultaneous communication supposedly is a form of English, most deaf persons cannot rely on simultaneous communication as an effective means of courtroom interpretation.

(27) *Will the interpretation you provide today be verbatim?*

The answer should be "no". Some interpreters will answer "yes" and assume that the Court's intention is to determine whether, as required by the Code of Conduct for Court Interpreters, they will interpret the message accurately while retaining the nuances of the language. However, the assumption may not be clear to counsel or other persons interested in the role of the interpreter.

Verbatim means "word-for-word", which is impossible in interpreting since it would necessitate a disregard for grammar and other features unique to a language. The interpreter's task is to convey the source message in the target language appropriately. A proper interpretation will retain the mood, tone, nuances, and meaning of the speaker to the extent that the target language has an appropriate equivalent.

(28) *What process would you use to inform the Court of an error in your interpretation?*

An interpreter has an ethical duty to inform the Court of an error of substance made in interpretation, and the interpreter should construe "substance" broadly. On the other hand, an interpreter should not continually interrupt the proceedings to refine the interpretation. Furthermore, the Court should be notified as soon as possible with the least disruption of the proceedings.

If the interpreter realizes an error while still interpreting, the proper manner to inform the Court is to speak in the third person and state something like, "The interpreter erred in conveying the last question, may Counsel please repeat?" or "The interpreter has erred in interpreting the last response, the correct interpretation is ...." Otherwise, the interpreter should apprise the Court by note, during the next break or in some other, unobtrusive manner.

A second interpreter who realizes an error may apprise the first interpreter. Should the first interpreter refuse to correct a substantive error, the second interpreter has an ethical obligation to do so.

(29) *Can you explain the difference between simultaneous and consecutive interpretation?*

Simultaneous interpretation occurs when continuous spoken text is interpreted while the speaker or signer convey their message. Notwithstanding the word "simultaneous", the interpreter may allow a lag time of up to two or three sentences, in order to comprehend the message to be interpreted. The Nuremberg trials were the first notable example of the use of simultaneous interpretation in court and involved the entire proceedings, but now simultaneous interpretation is used most often during opening and closing statements, jury instructions or other relatively uninterrupted segments of spoken text. As explained below, it should not be used during questioning of a witness.

In consecutive interpreting, an interpreter listens or watches an entire message before beginning to convey the interpretation. Accordingly, consecutive interpreting can be more accurate, by obviating the need to guess at the entire message and allowing time to refine the interpretation after the pressure of continued spoken or signed text is removed. Accordingly, it should always be used during examination of a witness.

(30) *What issues significantly affect your interpreting in court?*

Interpreters may view these issues as too numerous to list, but among the obstacles are: the interpreter's lack of familiarity with legal terminology, process, protocol, and ethics specifically relating to court interpretation; the Court's, counsels' or parties' lack of understanding of the role of the interpreter; positioning in the room; and the speed of the spoken text.

(31) *Have you submitted to the Administrative Office of the Courts a completed information form, a statement swearing or affirming compliance with the Maryland Code of Conduct for Court Interpreters and a statement subscribing to the Interpreter's Oath?*

The answer to this question should be "yes" as to the information form, as this is required under the Administrative Order dated December 7, 1995. The remaining documents will be required should the Subcommittee report be adopted.

(32) *Have you, in a state or federal court of record, a pending criminal charge or criminal conviction on a charge punishable by a fine of more than $500 or imprisonment for more than 6 months and not pardoned or expunged?*

The answer should be "no". This is the standard for juror qualification, although Courts Article § 8-204 as to disclosures by prospective jurors contains an exclusion for traffic offenses.

(33) *Are you a potential witness in this case?*

The answer should be "no".

(34) *Do you have any other potential conflicts of interests that you have not yet mentioned to the Court?*

In addition to conflicts that may stem from the interpreter's employment or a prior relationship with the individual for whom he or she would be interpreting, the interpreter may raise issues of financial interest in the proceedings or other actual or potential conflicts.

(35) *Are you ready to take the oath for interpreters?*

This question presents the prospective interpreter with a final opportunity to raise with the Court any points of concern about undertaking the role of court interpreter in this particular case, and the Court should note any hesitancy that may indicate unresolved issues that could disrupt the proceedings if the interpreter later must be replaced.

APPENDIX: TABLES OF COMPARABLE RULES

TABLE I — 1984 Revision

(Table II — 1997 Revision follows)

THIS TABLE SHOWS THOSE FORMER MARYLAND
RULES OF PROCEDURE AND MARYLAND DIS-
TRICT RULES RESCINDED EFFECTIVE
JULY 1, 1984, FROM WHICH COR-
RESPONDING MARYLAND RULES
IN TITLE 1 THROUGH
TITLE 4 HAVE BEEN
DERIVED

RESCINDED RULE	REVISED RULE	RESCINDED RULE	REVISED RULE
CJ § 7-201	1-325	104 b 1 (i), (ii)	2-124 (a)
1 f	1-102	104 b 2	2-121 (a), 2-126 (a)
1 g	1-201 (c)	104 c	2-125
1 h, i	1-201 (b)	104 h 1	2-121 (b)
2 b	1-201 (e)	104 h 2	2-123 (a)
2 c	1-201 (d)	104 h 3 (c)	2-126 (g)
3	1-312 (a)	104 i	2-121 (d)
3 a	1-331	105 a	2-121 (a)
3 d	1-103	105 b	2-122 (a)
5 a	1-202 (a)	105 b 1 (a)	2-126 (b), 3-126 (b)
5 c	1-202 (b), 1-303, 1-304	105 b 2	2-122 (b), 2-126 (b), 3-126 (b)
5 e	1-202 (e)	106 b, c	2-124 (c)
5 f	1-202 (f)	106 e 1, 2	2-124 (c)
5 g	1-202 (g)	106 e 3	2-321 (b) (3)
5 h	1-202 (h)	107 a 1	2-121 (a)
5 m	1-202 (j)	107 a 2	2-121 (a), 2-126 (a)
5 n	1-202 (l)	107 a 3	2-121 (b)
5 o	1-202 (m)	107 a 4	2-121 (a)
5 q	1-202 (p)	107 b	2-321 (b) (1), (5)
5 r	1-202 (k)	107 c	2-121 (d)
5 v	1-202 (o)	108 a	2-124 (f), 3-124 (f)
5 w	1-202 (r)	108 b	2-124 (g), 3-124 (g)
5 y	1-202 (s)	108 d	2-321 (b) (4)
5 z	1-202 (t)	111 a	2-122 (a)
5 aa	1-202 (d)	114 a, b	2-510 (c)
5 cc	1-202 (v)	114 d	2-510 (h)
5 ee	1-202 (w)	115 a	2-510 (c)
5 ff	1-202 (y)	115 b	2-510 (e)
8 a	1-203 (a)	116 a	2-123 (a), (b)
8 b	1-203 (b)	116 b	2-510 (d)
18 (b)	2-522 (a)	116 c 1, 2	2-126 (a)
21	1-303	116 c 3	2-126 (g)
103 b	2-111 (b)	117 a, b	2-123 (c)
103 c	2-112 (a)	119	2-124 (b)
103 e	2-112 (a)	124	2-131, 3-131
103 f	2-114	125 a	2-132 (b)
103 g	2-111 (a)	125 c 2	2-132 (b)
103 j	2-112 (b), 3-112 (b)	125 d	2-132 (c)
104 a	2-510 (d)	125 e	2-132 (d)
104 a (2)	2-126 (f)	140 a	2-101
104 a (4)	2-645 (d)	170 a	2-101
104 b	2-510 (d)	203 a-c	2-201
104 b 1	2-121 (a), 2-123 (a)	205 c, d	2-202 (b)

Appendix

RESCINDED RULE	REVISED RULE	RESCINDED RULE	REVISED RULE
205 e 1, 2	2-202 (c)	323 a 1-4	2-322 (a)
208 b 1	2-214 (b) (1)	323 a 5	2-323 (f)
208 b 2	2-214 (b) (2)	323 b	2-322 (a), 2-324 (a)
208 c	2-214 (c)	340 a	2-305
209 a	2-231 (a)	342 b 1, 2	2-323 (d)
209 d	2-231 (h)	342 c 1, 2	2-323 (f), (g)
220	2-241 (a)	343 a	2-325 (a)
220 c-e	2-241 (b)	343 d	2-325 (d)
220 f	2-241 (d)	343 e	2-325 (f)
222	2-241 (a), 3-241 (a)	370 a 3	2-305
240	2-241 (a)	372 a 2	2-323 (c)
301 b	2-303 (b), (d), 3-303 (d)	372 b	2-323 (e)
301 c	2-304 (c), 2-305	372 b 1	2-323 (e)
301 d	2-303 (c), 3-303 (c)	379	2-341 (c), 3-341 (c)
301 e	1-301 (a)	400 c	2-402 (a)
301 f	1-311 (a)	400 d	2-402 (c)
301 g	1-313	400 e	2-402 (d), 2-432 (c)
301 h	1-301 (a)	400 f	2-402 (c) (1)
301 j	2-322 (e)	401	2-411
301 k	1-301 (f)	402	2-404 (a) (1)
301 l	1-302	403 a	2-414 (a)
302 a	1-311 (a)	403 b	2-414 (b)
302 b	1-311 (b)	403 c	2-414 (c)
302 c 1	1-312 (b)	403 d	2-414 (d)
302 c 2, 3	1-312 (a)	404	2-401 (e)
303 a	1-301 (f)	405 a 1	2-412 (a)
306 a 1	1-321 (a)	405 a 2 (a)	2-412 (a)
306 a 2	1-323	405 a 2 (b)	2-412 (d), 2-510 (c)
306 b	1-321 (b)	405 b 1, 2	2-417 (a)
306 c	1-321 (a)	406 a	2-403 (a)
306 d	1-323	407 a	3-510 (a)
307 a 2	2-321 (b) (2)	408	2-413
307 c (4)	2-321 (b) (1)	409 a	2-415 (b)
309	1-204 (a)	409 b	2-417 (b)
311 a	2-323 (f)	409 c	2-415 (a)
312 b	2-323 (e)	409 c 2	2-415 (g), 2-416 (g)
313 a	2-212 (a), 2-303 (c), 3-212 (a), 3-303 (c)	410	2-416 (a)-(f), (h), (i)
313 c-e	2-212 (a), 3-212 (a)	410 c	2-412 (b)
314 a 1, 2	2-331 (a)	411 a	2-415 (d)
314 b	2-331 (b)	411 b 1, 2	2-415 (c)
314 c	2-331 (c), 3-331 (c)	411 b 3	2-415 (c)
314 d 2	2-331 (d)	411 b 4	2-415 (f)
314 d 3	2-331 (c), 3-331 (c)	411 b 5	2-415 (e)
315 a	2-332 (a)	412 a	2-412 (e)
315 b	2-332 (e)	412 b	2-414 (e)
315 c 1, 2	2-332 (b)	412 c 1, 2	2-415 (g)
315 d	2-332 (c), 3-332 (c)	412 c 3	2-417 (c)
315 d 1	2-332 (b)	412 d	2-415 (i)
315 f 1, 2	2-332 (d), 3-332 (d)	412 e	2-415 (d), (i)
317	2-327 (b)	413	2-419
319	2-311 (c)	413 a 5	2-401 (d)
320	2-341 (a), 3-341 (a)	413 c	2-416 (g)
320 a 2-4	2-341 (c), 3-341 (c)	414	2-434
320 b 1	2-341 (c), 3-341 (c)	417 a 1, 2	2-421 (a)
320 d 5	2-341 (c), 3-341 (c)	417 a 3	2-401 (c)
321 a	2-311 (a)	417 b 1, 2	2-421 (b)
321 b	2-311 (d)	417 c 1	2-432 (d)
321 d	2-311 (e)	417 d	2-421 (d)
322	2-322 (e)	417 f	2-421 (c)
		419	2-422

RESCINDED RULE	REVISED RULE	RESCINDED RULE	REVISED RULE
420	2-423	563 a	2-532 (a)
421 a	2-424 (a)	563 a 2	2-532 (b)
421 b 1, 2	2-424 (b)	563 a 3	2-532 (c)
421 c	2-424 (d)	563 a 4	2-532 (d)
421 d	2-424 (c)	563 b	2-532 (e)
421 e	2-424 (e)	563 b 3	2-533 (c)
421 f	2-424 (d)	563 c	2-532 (f)
422 a 1	2-432 (e)	567 b	2-533 (b)
422 a 2	2-415 (h), 2-432 (b)	567 c	2-533 (c)
422 a 3, 4	2-432 (b)	567 e	2-533 (d)
422 a 5-7	2-433 (c)	580 a, b	2-542 (a)
422 b	2-433 (b)	580 c	2-542 (c)
422 c 1	2-432 (a), 2-433 (a)	580 d	2-542 (d) (1)
422 c 2	2-433 (a)	580 g 1	2-542 (d) (5)
422 c 3	2-432 (a)	580 l 1, 2	2-542 (d) (3)
422 d	2-431	580 m 1	2-542 (f)
501 a	2-503 (b)	580 n	2-542 (f)
501 b	2-212 (b)	580 q	2-542 (i)
502	2-502	582 b	2-506 (d), 3-506 (e)
503	2-503 (a)	595 a	2-543 (c)
504 a-c	2-504	595 d	2-543 (d) (1)
515 a	2-327 (a)	595 e	2-543 (c)
517	2-511 (d)	595 h	2-543 (h)
521	2-514, 3-514	596 b	2-541 (a), 2-542 (a), 2-543 (a)
522 a	2-517 (d), 3-517 (d)	596 c	2-541 (b)
522 b, c	2-517 (c), 3-517 (c)	596 d	2-541 (d), 2-542 (c), 2-543 (c)
522 d	2-517 (a), 3-517 (a)	596 e	2-541 (e)
526	2-508 (b)	596 e 1	2-542 (d) (2), 2-543 (d) (2)
527 a 1	2-508 (a)	596 e 2	2-543 (d) (3)
527 b	2-508 (d), 3-508 (c)	596 f	2-541 (f)
527 c 1-4	2-508 (c)	596 g	2-541 (g)
527 e	2-508 (e), 3-508 (d)	596 h 1, 2	2-541 (h), 2-543 (f)
528	2-536, 3-536	596 h 3	2-541 (h)
530	2-507	596 h 3 (c), (d)	2-543 (f)
536	2-513 (a), 3-513 (a)	596 h 4	2-541 (h), 2-543 (f)
541 b	2-506 (b), 3-506 (b), (d)	596 h 5, 6	2-541 (i), 2-543 (g)
541 c	2-506 (c)	596 h 7	2-541 (h)
541 d	2-506 (d), 3-506 (e)	596 h 8	2-541 (j), 2-542 (i), 2-543 (h)
542 a 1, 2	2-505 (a)	596 i	2-541 (j)
542 c 1	2-505 (b)	604 a	2-603 (a), (b)
542 c 4	2-505 (b)	604 b	1-341
542 d 1	2-505 (c)	604 c	2-603 (d), 3-603 (c)
542 g	2-505 (d)	605 a	2-602
542 i	2-505 (e)	605 b	2-615, 3-615
543 a 3, 4	2-512 (h)	605 d	2-614
543 a 8	2-511 (c)	606	2-503 (a)
543 d	2-512 (d)	607	2-632 (c)
544	2-511 (b)	610 a 1	2-501 (a)
545	2-325 (e)	610 a 3	2-501 (a)
548	2-509	610 b	2-501 (c)
550 a	2-515 (b)	610 d 1	2-501 (e)
550 d	2-515 (c)	610 d 2	2-501 (d)
554 a	2-520 (a)	610 d 4	2-501 (f)
554 b 1	2-520 (c)	619 a	2-623
554 b 2	2-520 (d)	620 a	2-621 (a)
554 d	2-520 (e)	622 e	2-641 (a)
558 a, b	2-521 (a)	622 h 1	2-641 (b)
558 d	2-521 (a)	622 h 2	2-126 (f), 2-642 (e)
560	2-522 (c)	622 h 3	2-641 (b)
561	2-503 (a)	625 a	2-535 (a), (b)

Appendix

RESCINDED RULE	REVISED RULE	RESCINDED RULE	REVISED RULE
625 b	2-535 (c)	733	4-243
627	2-633 (a)	734	4-245
628 b	2-633 (b)	735	4-246
635 b	2-516, 3-516	736	4-252
645	2-115 (d)	737 b	4-266 (b)
645 a	2-611 (a)	740 a	4-261 (b)
645 c	2-611 (c)	740 b	4-267 (e)
645 d	2-611 (d)	740 c	4-261 (c)
659	2-115 (k)	740 d	4-261 (d)
681	2-535 (d), 3-535 (d)	740 e	4-261 (e)
685 a	2-648, 3-648	740 f	4-261 (f)
701	1-201 (a), (c), 4-101	740 g	4-261 (g)
702 a	4-102 (a)	740 h	4-261 (h)
702 b	4-102 (c)	740 i	4-261 (i)
702 c	4-102 (d)	740 j	4-261 (b)
702 d	4-102 (e)	741 a 1, 2	4-263 (a)
702 e	4-102 (g)	741 a 3	4-263 (g)
702 f	4-102 (j)	741 b	4-263 (b)
702 g	4-102 (k)	741 c	4-263 (c)
702 h	4-102 (l)	741 d	4-263 (d)
710 a	4-201 (a)	741 e 1	4-263 (e)
710 e	4-201 (d)	741 e 2	4-263 (f)
711 a	4-202 (a)	741 f	4-263 (h)
711 b	4-202 (c)	741 g	4-263 (i)
711 c	4-202 (b)	742 a	4-264
711 d, e	4-202 (d)	742 b	4-265
712 a	4-203 (a)	742 c	4-266 (a)
712 b	4-203 (b)	742 d	4-266 (c)
713 a	4-204	742 e	2-510 (h), 4-266 (d)
713 c	4-204	743	4-267 (a)-(d)
720 a	4-212 (a), (b)	744	4-254 (b)
720 b	4-212 (c)	745 b	4-253 (b)
720 c	4-212 (d)	745 c	4-253 (c)
720 d, e	4-212 (e)	746 a, b	4-271 (a)
720 f	4-212 (f)	750 a	4-361 (b)
721 a	4-216 (a)	750 b	4-361 (a)
721 b	4-216 (d)	751 a	4-311 (b)
721 c	4-216 (e)	751 b	2-512 (b), 4-312 (b)
721 d	4-216 (f)	751 c	4-312 (h)
721 e	4-216 (h)	751 d	2-512 (i), 4-312 (h)
721 f	4-216 (i)	751 e	4-311 (c)
721 g	4-216 (j)	752	2-512 (d), 4-312 (d)
722	4-217	753	4-313
723	4-215 (b)	753 b 1	2-512 (g), 4-312 (g)
723 a	4-213 (c)	753 b 3	2-512 (i)
723 b 1-3	4-215 (a)	754 a	2-512 (a), 4-312 (a)
723 b 7	4-215 (a)	754 b	2-512 (e), 4-312 (b), (e)
723 c 1	4-215 (a)	755 a	4-321 (a)
724	4-231	755 b	2-513 (b), 3-513 (b), 4-321 (b)
725	4-214	755 c	4-321 (a)
730	4-241	755 d	2-513 (c), 3-513 (c), 4-321 (c)
731 a	4-242 (a)	756	4-324
731 b 1	4-242 (b) (1)	757 a	4-325 (b)
731 b 2	4-242 (b) (3)	757 b	4-325 (c)
731 b 3	4-242 (b) (4)	757 c	2-520 (d), 4-325 (d)
731 c	4-242 (c)	757 d	4-325 (a)
731 d	4-242 (d)	757 e	4-326 (a)
731 e	4-242 (e)	757 f	4-325 (e)
731 f	4-242 (f)	757 g	4-325 (f)
732	4-244	757 h	4-325 (e)

RESCINDED RULE	REVISED RULE	RESCINDED RULE	REVISED RULE
758 a	4-326 (a)	H3 b	1-402 (e)
758 b	2-521 (a), 4-326 (a)	H4 a, b	1-402 (d)
758 c	2-521 (b), 4-326 (b)	H5	1-406
758 d	2-521 (c), 4-326 (c)	H6 a	1-403 (a)
759	4-327	H6 b	1-403 (b)
759 a	2-522 (b)	H6 c 1, 2	1-403 (a), (b)
759 e	2-522 (b)	H7 a, b	1-402 (c)
760	4-328	H8	1-405
764	4-353	U12 b	2-402 (e) (2)
770	4-331	U18 a	2-515 (a)
771	4-341	U18 b	2-515 (c)
772 a	4-342 (a)	U18 c-e	2-515 (a)
772 b	4-342 (b)	BK40	4-401
772 c	4-342 (c)	BK41 a	4-402 (a)
772 d	4-342 (d), 4-343 (d)	BK41 c	4-402 (b)
772 e	4-342 (e)	BK41 d	4-402 (c)
772 f	4-342 (f)	BK41 e	4-403
772 h	4-342 (g)	BK43 a	4-404
772 A	4-343 (a)-(c), (e)-(g)	BK43 b	4-404, 4-405
773	4-344	BK44 c	4-406 (b)
774	4-345	BK44 d	4-406 (c)
775	4-346	BK44 e	4-406 (d)
776 a	4-348 (a)	BK45 a	4-407 (b)
776 b	4-348 (c)	BK45 b	4-407 (a)
776 c	4-348 (b)	BK45 c	4-407 (d)
777	4-351	BK45 d	4-407 (c)
778 a	4-347	BK46	4-408
778 b	4-348 (c)	BU70	2-221 (a)
780	4-601	BU72	2-221 (b)
781	4-611	BU73	2-221 (c)
782 a, b	4-247	BU74	2-221 (d)
782 c, d	4-248	EX1	4-502
784	4-621	EX2	4-501
785	4-631	EX3 a	4-503
F6 a	2-646 (a)	EX3 b	4-504
F6 b	2-646 (c)	EX3 c	4-504
F6 c	2-645 (d), 2-646 (d)	EX3 c 1, 2	4-503
F6 d	2-646 (e)	EX4	4-505
F6 e	2-646 (g)	EX5	4-506
F6 f	2-646 (f)	EX6	4-507
F6 g	2-646 (h)	EX7	4-508
F6 h	2-646 (i)	EX8	4-509
F6 i	2-646 (k)	EX9	4-510
F6 j	2-646 (j)	EX10	4-511
F6 k	2-646 (e)	EX11	4-512
G40 a, b	2-115 (a)	1219	1-324
G40 b 4	2-641 (a)	M.D.R. 1 b	3-711
G43	2-115 (b)	M.D.R. 100	3-101
G44	2-115 (c)	M.D.R. 101 a	3-102 (a)
G45	2-115 (d)	M.D.R. 102	1-325
G49 a	2-641 (a), 2-642 (a), (b)	M.D.R. 103 b	3-111 (b)
G51	2-115 (g), 2-643 (b), (c)	M.D.R. 103 c	3-112 (a)
G52 a, b	2-645 (e)	M.D.R. 103 d 2	3-126 (d)
G56	2-645 (h)	M.D.R. 103 e	3-102 (b), 3-112 (a)
G59	2-115 (k)	M.D.R. 103 f	3-114
G60	2-115 (i)	M.D.R. 103 g	3-102 (c)
H1	1-401	M.D.R. 103 h	3-111 (a)
H2 a	1-402 (a), (f)	M.D.R. 104 a	3-510 (d)
H2 b 1, 2	1-402 (b)	M.D.R. 104 a (ii)	3-126 (f)
H3 a 2	1-402 (e)	M.D.R. 104 a (iii)	3-645 (d)

Appendix

RESCINDED RULE	REVISED RULE	RESCINDED RULE	REVISED RULE
M.D.R. 104 b	3-510 (d)	M.D.R. 401 b	3-401
M.D.R. 104 b 1	3-121 (a), 3-123 (a)	M.D.R. 402	3-431
M.D.R. 104 b 1 (i), (ii)	3-124 (a)	M.D.R. 405	3-401
M.D.R. 104 b 2	3-121 (a), 3-126 (a)	M.D.R. 417 a	3-421 (b)
M.D.R. 104 c	3-125	M.D.R. 417 b	3-421 (d)
M.D.R. 104 h 1	3-121 (b)	M.D.R. 417 c	3-421 (g)
M.D.R. 104 h 2	3-123 (a)	M.D.R. 417 d	3-421 (h)
M.D.R. 104 h 3 (a)	3-126 (a)	M.D.R. 417 e	3-421 (a)
M.D.R. 104 h 3 (c)	3-126 (g)	M.D.R. 417 e 4	3-421 (e)
M.D.R. 104 i	3-121 (d)	M.D.R. 417 f	3-421 (c)
M.D.R. 106 b, c	3-124 (c)	M.D.R. 417 g	3-421 (i)
M.D.R. 106 e 1, 2	3-124 (c)	M.D.R. 501	3-503
M.D.R. 106 f	3-124 (h)	M.D.R. 504	3-504
M.D.R. 107 a 1	3-121 (a)	M.D.R. 526	3-508 (b)
M.D.R. 107 a 2	3-121 (a), 3-126 (a)	M.D.R. 527	3-508 (a)
M.D.R. 107 a 3	3-121 (b)	M.D.R. 530	3-507
M.D.R. 107 b	3-121 (d)	M.D.R. 541 b	3-506 (c)
M.D.R. 114 a, b	3-510 (c)	M.D.R. 542	3-505
M.D.R. 114 d	3-510 (h)	M.D.R. 564 c	3-522
M.D.R. 115 a	3-510 (c)	M.D.R. 567 b	3-533 (b)
M.D.R. 115 b	3-510 (e)	M.D.R. 567 c	3-533 (c)
M.D.R. 116 a	3-123 (a), (b)	M.D.R. 567 d	3-533 (d)
M.D.R. 116 b	3-510 (d)	M.D.R. 568	3-701
M.D.R. 116 c 1, 2	3-126 (a)	M.D.R. 604	3-603 (a)
M.D.R. 116 c 3	3-126 (g)	M.D.R. 605 a	3-602
M.D.R. 117 a, b	3-123 (c)	M.D.R. 605 b	3-632 (c)
M.D.R. 119	3-124 (b)	M.D.R. 605 d	3-614
M.D.R. 125 a	3-132 (a), (b)	M.D.R. 610 a	3-306 (a)
M.D.R. 125 b	3-132 (c)	M.D.R. 610 b, c	3-306 (b)
M.D.R. 203	3-201	M.D.R. 610 d	3-306 (b), (d)
M.D.R. 205 c, d	3-202 (b)	M.D.R. 610 e	3-306 (c)
M.D.R. 205 e	3-202 (c)	M.D.R. 619 b	3-601 (c)
M.D.R. 208 b 1	3-214 (b) (1)	M.D.R. 620 a	4-354
M.D.R. 208 b 2	3-214 (b) (2)	M.D.R. 620 b	3-621 (a)
M.D.R. 208 c	3-214 (c)	M.D.R. 620 c	3-621 (b)
M.D.R. 220	3-241 (a)	M.D.R. 621 b, c	3-621 (c)
M.D.R. 220 b-d	3-241 (b)	M.D.R. 622 e	3-641 (a)
M.D.R. 220 e	3-241 (d)	M.D.R. 622 h 1	3-641 (b)
M.D.R. 240	3-241 (a)	M.D.R. 622 h 2	3-126 (f), 3-642 (e)
M.D.R. 300 b	3-303 (a)	M.D.R. 622 h 3	3-641 (b)
M.D.R. 301 a	3-303 (b)	M.D.R. 622 i	3-641 (a)
M.D.R. 301 a (i)	3-304	M.D.R. 625 a	3-535 (a), (b)
M.D.R. 301 a (ii)	3-305	M.D.R. 625 b	3-535 (c)
M.D.R. 302	3-307	M.D.R. 627	3-633 (a)
M.D.R. 302 a	3-308, 3-332 (b)	M.D.R. 628 b	3-633 (b)
M.D.R. 314 a	3-331 (a)	M.D.R. 645 a	3-611 (a)
M.D.R. 314 b	3-331 (b)	M.D.R. 645 c	3-611 (c)
M.D.R. 314 c	3-331 (d)	M.D.R. 645 d	3-611 (d)
M.D.R. 314 g	3-331 (e)	M.D.R. 645 j	3-611 (f)
M.D.R. 314 h	3-331 (f)	M.D.R. 648	3-509
M.D.R. 315 a	3-332 (a), (e)	M.D.R. 701	4-101
M.D.R. 315 b	3-332 (a)	M.D.R. 702 a	4-102 (a)
M.D.R. 317	3-326	M.D.R. 702 c	4-102 (b)
M.D.R. 321 a	3-311 (a), (b)	M.D.R. 702 d	4-102 (c)
M.D.R. 321 b	3-311 (d)	M.D.R. 702 e	4-102 (e)
M.D.R. 321 d	3-311 (c)	M.D.R. 702 f	4-102 (f)
M.D.R. 343 a	3-325 (b)	M.D.R. 702 g	4-102 (g)
M.D.R. 343 b, c	3-325 (a)	M.D.R. 702 h	4-102 (h)
M.D.R. 343 d	3-325 (c)	M.D.R. 702 i	4-102 (i)
M.D.R. 401 a	3-701, 3-711	M.D.R. 702 j	4-102 (j)

RESCINDED RULE	REVISED RULE	RESCINDED RULE	REVISED RULE
M.D.R. 702 l	4-102 (k)	M.D.R. 746	4-271 (b)
M.D.R. 702 m	4-102 (l)	M.D.R. 750	4-361 (a)
M.D.R. 710 a	4-201 (a)	M.D.R. 751	4-301 (a)
M.D.R. 710 b-d	4-201 (b), (c)	M.D.R. 755 a	4-321 (a)
M.D.R. 710 e	4-201 (d)	M.D.R. 755 b	4-321 (b)
M.D.R. 711 a	4-202 (a)	M.D.R. 755 c	4-321 (a)
M.D.R. 711 b 1	4-202 (c)	M.D.R. 755 d	4-321 (c)
M.D.R. 711 b 2	4-202 (b)	M.D.R. 756	4-324
M.D.R. 711 c, d	4-202 (d)	M.D.R. 760	4-328
M.D.R. 712	4-203 (a)	M.D.R. 764	4-353
M.D.R. 713 a, b	4-204	M.D.R. 770	4-331
M.D.R. 720 a, b	4-211 (b)	M.D.R. 771	4-341
M.D.R. 720 c	4-212 (a), (b)	M.D.R. 772 a	4-342 (b)
M.D.R. 720 d	4-212 (c)	M.D.R. 772 b	4-342 (c)
M.D.R. 720 e	4-212 (d)	M.D.R. 772 c	4-342 (d), 4-343 (d)
M.D.R. 720 f	4-212 (e)	M.D.R. 772 d	4-342 (e)
M.D.R. 720 g	4-212 (g)	M.D.R. 772 e	4-342 (f)
M.D.R. 720 h	4-212 (f)	M.D.R. 772 g	4-342 (g)
M.D.R. 720 i	4-211 (a), 4-212 (h)	M.D.R. 774	4-345
M.D.R. 721 a	4-216 (a)	M.D.R. 775	4-346
M.D.R. 721 b	4-216 (b)	M.D.R. 776 a	4-348 (a)
M.D.R. 721 c	4-216 (d)	M.D.R. 776 b	4-348 (c)
M.D.R. 721 d	4-216 (e)	M.D.R. 776 c	4-348 (b)
M.D.R. 721 e	4-216 (f)	M.D.R. 777	4-351
M.D.R. 721 f	4-216 (g)	M.D.R. 778 a	4-347
M.D.R. 721 g	4-216 (i)	M.D.R. 778 b	4-348 (c)
M.D.R. 721 h	4-216 (j)	M.D.R. 780	4-601
M.D.R. 722	4-217	M.D.R. 782 a, b	4-247
M.D.R. 723	4-213 (a)	M.D.R. 782 c, d	4-248
M.D.R. 723 a	4-212 (e)	M.D.R. 784	4-621
M.D.R. 723 b 4	4-216 (c)	M.D.R. 785	4-631
M.D.R. 724	4-231	M.D.R. F6 a	3-646 (a)
M.D.R. 725	4-214	M.D.R. F6 b	3-646 (c)
M.D.R. 726 d	4-215 (c)	M.D.R. F6 c	3-645 (d), 3-646 (d)
M.D.R. 727	4-221	M.D.R. F6 d	3-646 (e)
M.D.R. 728	4-222	M.D.R. F6 e	3-646 (g)
M.D.R. 731 a	4-242 (a)	M.D.R. F6 f	3-646 (f)
M.D.R. 731 b 1	4-242 (b) (1)	M.D.R. F6 g	3-646 (h)
M.D.R. 731 b 2	4-242 (b) (4)	M.D.R. F6 h	3-646 (i)
M.D.R. 731 c	4-242 (c)	M.D.R. F6 i	3-646 (k)
M.D.R. 731 d	4-242 (d)	M.D.R. F6 j	3-646 (j)
M.D.R. 731 e	4-242 (f)	M.D.R. F6 k	3-646 (e)
M.D.R. 732	4-244	M.D.R. G40 a, b	3-115 (a)
M.D.R. 733	4-243	M.D.R. G40 b 4	3-641 (a)
M.D.R. 734	4-245	M.D.R. G43	3-115 (b)
M.D.R. 736	4-251	M.D.R. G44	3-115 (c)
M.D.R. 737 b	4-266 (b)	M.D.R. G45	3-115 (d)
M.D.R. 742 a	4-265	M.D.R. G47 c	3-115 (e)
M.D.R. 742 b	4-266 (a)	M.D.R. G49 a	3-641 (a), 3-642 (a), (b)
M.D.R. 742 c	4-266 (c)	M.D.R. G51	3-115 (h), 3-643 (b), (c)
M.D.R. 742 d	3-510 (h), 4-266 (d)	M.D.R. G52 a, b	3-645 (e)
M.D.R. 743	4-267 (a)-(d)	M.D.R. G56	3-645 (h)
M.D.R. 744	4-254 (a)	M.D.R. G59	3-115 (l)
M.D.R. 745 a	4-253 (a)	M.D.R. G60	3-115 (j)
M.D.R. 745 b	4-253 (b)		
M.D.R. 745 c	4-253 (c)		

Table II — 1997 Revision

(Table I — 1984 Revision precedes this table)

THIS TABLE SHOWS THOSE FORMER MARYLAND
RULES OF PROCEDURE AND MARYLAND DIS-
TRICT RULES RESCINDED EFFECTIVE
JANUARY 1, 1997, FROM WHICH
CORRESPONDING MARYLAND
RULES IN TITLE 9
THROUGH TITLE 16
HAVE BEEN
DERIVED.

RESCINDED RULE	REVISED RULE	RESCINDED RULE	REVISED RULE
901	11-101	Q40	15-1001 (a)
902	11-102	Q41 a	15-1001 (b)
902A	11-102A	Q42	15-1001 (d)
903	11-103	R70 a	10-103 (a)
904	11-104	R70 b	10-103 (b)
905	11-105	R70 c	10-103 (e)
906	11-106	R70 d	10-103 (f) (1)
907	11-107	R70 e	10-103 (g)
908	11-108	R70 f	10-105
909	11-109	R71 a	10-110, 10-201 (a), 10-301 (a)
910	11-110	R72 a & b	10-201 (b), 10-207 (b),
911	11-111		10-208 (b), 10-210, 10-301 (b),
912	11-112		10-711 (b) (1), 10-712 (c) (1)
913	11-113	R72 d	10-109
914	11-114	R73 a	10-201 (c), 10-301 (c)
915	11-115	R73 b 1	10-202
916	11-116	R74	10-203, 10-302
917	11-117	R76	10-106
918	11-118	R77	10-205, 10-304, 10-601
919	11-119	R77 b 2	10-503, 10-603
920	11-120	R78 b	10-108 (d)
921	11-121	R80 c 1	15-601
922	11-122	S70	9-201
D71	9-101	S71	9-202
D72	9-103	S72	9-203
D73	9-102	S73	9-204
D74	9-105	S73A	9-205
D75	9-106	S74	9-206
D76	9-107	S74A	9-207
D77	9-109	S75	9-208
D78(d)	9-108	S76	9-209
D79	9-111	S77	9-210
D80	9-103; 9-112	T44	12-101
E2	15-101	U1	12-201
E3	15-101	U2	12-202
E4	15-101	U4 b	12-203
J70	14-401 (b)	U5	12-204
J71	14-401 (a)	U6	12-205
J72	14-401 (c)	U12 b	12-206
J73	14-401 (d)	U15	12-207
P1	15-202	U17	12-207
P2 a & c	15-201	U18	12-207
P3	15-203	U19	12-208
P4 c & d 2	15-207	U21	12-209
P5	15-208	U22	12-212

RESCINDED RULE	REVISED RULE	RESCINDED RULE	REVISED RULE
U23	12-210	W77 d	14-210
U24 b	12-212	W79	14-203
U25	12-209	W79 c	14-201(a)
U26	12-211	Y70	12-501 (a)
U27	12-213	Y71	12-501 (a), (b)
V70 b	10-103 (c)	Y72	12-501 (b)
V70 c	10-103 (f) (2)	Y73	12-501 (b)
V71	10-101, 10-106, 10-601	Y74	12-501 (c)
V71 a & b 1	10-501	Y76	12-501 (d)
V71 c	10-201 (c), 10-501	Y77	12-501 (e)
V71 d	10-502, 10-702 (b) (3)	Y78	12-501 (f)
V71 f 1 & f 2	10-108 (c)	Y79	12-501 (g)
V72	10-505	Z42	15-302
V73	10-702, 13-107	Z43	15-303
V74	10-706	Z44	15-303
V74 b 1 & 2	10-707 (a)	Z45	15-305
V74 b 3	10-707 (b)	Z46	15-306
V74 c 2 (b)	10-206 (a) & (b)	Z46 b	15-309, 15-310
V74 c 2 (e)	10-705 (d)	Z47	15-306
V74 e 1 (a)	10-208 (a) & (c), 10-712 (a) & (d)	Z48	15-309
V74 e 2	10-208 (e), 10-712 (g)	Z49	15-307
V75 a & b	10-705 (a)	Z50	15-308
V75 c	10-705 (b)	Z51	15-310
V75 d	10-705 (c)	Z52	15-303
V76 a	10-704, 10-704 (a) (1)	Z53	15-311
V76 c	10-704 (a) (2)	Z54	15-303
V77 b 1	10-703, 13-403	Z55	15-304
V77 c 3	10-108 (b)	Z56	15-312
V78	10-209, 10-710	Z47	14-203
V78 b 5	10-207 (e), 10-711 (f)	Z48 c-e	14-204
V79	10-601	Z51	14-205
V79 b & c	10-602	Z52	14-206
V79 d	10-604	Z53 b-g	14-207
V79 e	10-605	Z54 a	14-208
V80	10-709	Z55	14-209
V81	13-702	BB70	15-501
V81 a	10-207 (a), 10-711 (a) & (b) (2)	BB71	15-502
V81 b 1	10-711 (c)	BB72	15-504
V81 c 1	10-207 (c), 10-711 (d)	BB73	15-504
V81 e	10-207 (f), 10-711 (i)	BB74	15-505
V82 a	10-207 (a), 10-711 (a), 13-703	BB75	15-503
V82 e	10-711 (h)	BB76	15-502
V84	13-701	BB77	15-502
V84 c	10-712 (c) (2)	BB78	15-502
V84 d	10-208 (a), 10-712 (a)	BB79	15-502, 15-504
V84 d 1 & 2	10-208 (b), 10-712 (b)	BD1	12-102(b)
V84 e	10-208 (c), 10-712 (d)	BD2	12-102(b)
V84 f	10-712 (f)	BD3	12-102(c)
W70 a	14-201(b)	BE40	15-701
W70 b	14-201(a)	BE41	15-701
W71	14-202	BE43	15-701
W72	14-203	BE44	15-701
W72 c-e	14-204	BE45	15-701
W73	14-205	BE46	15-701
W74	14-206	BG70	12-301
W74 b-g	14-207	BG71	12-302
W75 a	14-208	BG72	12-303
W76	14-209	BG73	12-304
W77 b	14-202(c)	BG74	12-305
		BG75	12-306

Appendix

RESCINDED RULE	REVISED RULE	RESCINDED RULE	REVISED RULE
BG76	12-307	BV10	16-710
BG77	12-308	BV11	16-711
BH70	15-901	BV12	16-712
BH71	15-901	BV13	16-713
BH72	15-901	BV14	16-714
BH73	15-901	BV15	16-715
BH74	15-901	BV16	16-716
BH75	15-901	BV17	16-717
BJ71	12-401 (b)	BV18	16-718
BJ72	12-401 (c)	BW1 a	15-802
BJ73	12-401 (c)	BW1 b	15-801
BP1 a	13-101	BW2	15-804
BP1 b	13-102	BW3	15-804
BP2 a & b	13-203	BW4	15-803
BP3 a, b & d	13-302	BW5	15-804
BP3 a & c	13-105	BW6	15-803
BP4 a 1	13-201	BW7	15-805
BP4 a 2	13-202	BY2	15-403
BP4 b & c	13-401	BY3	15-403
BP4 d	13-402	BY4	15-403
BP5	13-103	1200	16-101
BP6 a & b	13-301	1201	16-102
BP7	13-303	1202	16-103
BP8	13-601	1203	16-104
BP9 a, b, d-g	13-501	1204	16-105
BP9 b & c	13-401	1205	16-106
BP9 b 2	13-503	1206	16-107
BP10	13-502	1207	16-108
BP10 b	13-503	1209	16-109
BR1	14-301	1210	16-201
BR2	14-302	1211	16-202
BR3	14-303	1211A	16-203
BR4	14-304	1212	16-301
BR5	14-306	1213	16-302
BR6	14-305	1214	16-303
BQ41-45	12-601	1215	16-304
BQ49	12-601	1216	16-305
BQ51	12-602	1217	16-306
BQ53	12-602	1217A	16-307
BU1	16-601	1218	16-308
BU2	16-602	1219	16-309
BU3	16-603	1220	16-401
BU4	16-604	1221	16-402
BU5	16-605	1223	16-403
BU6	16-606	1224	16-404
BU7	16-607	1224A	16-405
BU8	16-608	1224B	16-406
BU9	16-609	1225	16-801
BU10	16-610	1226	16-802
BU11	16-611	1227	16-803
BU12	16-612	1227A	16-804
BV1	16-701	1227B	16-805
BV2	16-702	1227C	16-806
BV3	16-703	1227D	16-807
BV4	16-704	1227E	16-808
BV5	16-705	1227F	16-809
BV6	16-706	1227G	16-810
BV7	16-707	1228	16-811
BV8	16-708	1230	16-812
BV9	16-709	1231	16-813

RESCINDED RULE	REVISED RULE	RESCINDED RULE	REVISED RULE
1232	16-814	M.D.R. 1214	16-502
1233	16-815	M.D.R. 1218	16-503
1234	16-816	M.D.R. 1224	16-504
1285	16-817	M.D.R. 1299	16-505
1299	16-818		

Index to Maryland Rules

INDEX

INDEX

943

INDEX

INDEX

INDEX

INDEX

INDEX

INDEX

APPEARANCE —Cont'd
Defendants.
Initial appearance of defendant, Crim Rule
4-213.
Effect.
Circuit courts, CivProCir Rule 2-131.
District Court, CivProDist Rule 3-131.
Entry of appearance.
How entered.
Circuit courts, CivProCir Rule 2-131.
Executors and administrators.
Settlement of decedents' estates.
Presence of personal representative,
Estates Rule 6-131.
Habeas corpus.
Production of person, SpecPro Rule 15-306.
How appearance entered.
District Court, CivProDist Rule 3-131.
Initial appearance of defendant, Crim
Rule 4-213.
Juvenile causes.
Right to counsel.
Out-of-state attorney, Juv Rule 11-106.
Motions.
Striking attorney's appearance.
Circuit courts, CivProCir Rule 2-132.
District Court, CivProDist Rule 3-132.
Notice.
Striking attorney's appearance.
Circuit courts, CivProCir Rule 2-132.
District Court, CivProDist Rule 3-132.
Preliminary hearings.
Initial appearance of defendant.
Advice of preliminary hearing, Crim Rule
4-213.
Pretrial release.
Initial appearance of defendant.
Determination of pretrial release, Crim
Rule 4-213.
Proper person.
Circuit courts, CivProCir Rule 2-131.
District Court, CivProDist Rule 3-131.
Striking of attorney's appearance.
Circuit courts, CivProCir Rule 2-132.
District Court, CivProDist Rule 3-132.
Summons and process.
Initial appearance of defendant.
Circuit court following arrest or
summons, Crim Rule 4-213.
District Court following summons, Crim
Rule 4-213.
Termination of appearance.
Automatic termination.
District Court, CivProDist Rule 3-132.
Video conferencing.
Initial appearance, Crim Rule 4-231.

APPRAISALS.
Appraisers.
Receivers.
Compensation and fees, Receivers Rule
13-303.
Employment, Receivers Rule 13-301.

APPRAISALS —Cont'd
Executors and administrators.
Settlement of decedents' estates.
Application to fix inheritance tax on
non-probate assets.
Form, Estates Rule 6-405.
Basis, Estates Rule 6-403.
Content.
Required content, Estates Rule 6-403.
Forms, Estates Rule 6-403.
Application to fix inheritance tax on
non-probate assets, Estates Rule
6-405.
Forms.
Executors and administrators.
Settlement of decedents' estates.
Application to fix inheritance tax on
non-probate assets, Estates Rule
6-405.
Inventory, Estates Rule 6-403.

ARBITRATION AND AWARD.
Alternative dispute resolution generally,
ADR Rules 17-101 to 17-109.
See ALTERNATIVE DISPUTE
RESOLUTION.
Health care malpractice claims, SpecPro
Rules 15-401 to 15-403.
See MALPRACTICE.
Uniform arbitration act.
Applicability to certain proceedings,
SpecPro Rule 15-101.

ARRAY.
Jury trial.
Challenge to the array.
Circuit courts, CivProCir Rule 2-512.

ARREST.
Circuit courts.
Initial appearance of defendant, Crim Rule
4-213.
Procedure when defendant in custody.
Other offenses, Crim Rule 4-212.
Same offense, Crim Rule 4-212.
Statement of charges.
Filing, Crim Rule 4-211.
District Court.
Initial appearance after arrest, Crim Rule
4-213.
Pretrial release.
Bench warrant for violation of conditions of
release, Crim Rule 4-216.
Warrantless arrest.
Pretrial release, Crim Rule 4-216.

ASBESTOS DOCKET, CJA Rule 16-203.

ASSAULT.
Peace orders.
Petition for peace order.
Form, CivProDist Rule 3-731.
Spousal privilege.
Record of assertion, Crim Rule 4-632.

INDEX

INDEX

960

INDEX

INDEX

INDEX

C

CHARGING DOCUMENTS.
Appearances.
Initial appearance of defendant.
District Court following arrest.
Advice of charges, Crim Rule 4-213.
Circuit courts.
Motions in circuit courts in criminal cases,
Crim Rule 4-252.
Use, Crim Rule 4-201.
Citations.
Content, Crim Rule 4-202.
Defined, Crim Rule 4-102.
Docket in place of citation, Crim Rule
4-201.
Content.
Citations, Crim Rule 4-202.
Indictments, Crim Rule 4-202.
Matters not required, Crim Rule 4-202.
Requirements.
General requirements, Crim Rule 4-202.
Signatures, Crim Rule 4-202.
Specific requirements, Crim Rule 4-202.
Criminal rules.
Defined, Crim Rule 4-102.
Definitions, Crim Rule 4-102.
District Court.
Use, Crim Rule 4-201.
Dockets.
Citations.
Docket in place of citation, Crim Rule
4-201.
Indictments.
Content, Crim Rule 4-202.
Defined, Crim Rule 4-102.
Informations.
Defined, Crim Rule 4-102.
**Inspection by public of files and records
pertaining to,** Crim Rule 4-212.
Joinder.
Multiple offenses, Crim Rule 4-203.
Offenses.
Multiple offenses, Crim Rule 4-203.
Juvenile causes.
Waiver of jurisdiction.
Filing of charging document, Crim Rule
4-222.
Motions.
Mandatory motions in circuit courts.
Criminal rules, Crim Rule 4-252.
Offenses.
Joinder.
Multiple offenses, Crim Rule 4-203.
**Public inspection of files and records
pertaining to,** Crim Rule 4-212.
Requirements.
Content.
General requirements, Crim Rule 4-202.
Use, Crim Rule 4-201.
Sealing charging document, Crim Rule
4-201.
Signatures, Crim Rule 4-202.
Statement of charges.
Defined, Crim Rule 4-102.

CHARGING DOCUMENTS —Cont'd
Use.
Circuit courts, Crim Rule 4-201.
District Court, Crim Rule 4-201.
Requirements, Crim Rule 4-201.

CHILD CUSTODY.
Attorneys at law.
Appointment of child's counsel, FamLaw
Rule 9-205.1.
Guidelines for practice.
See COURT-APPOINTED LAWYERS
REPRESENTING CHILDREN.
Divorce, FamLaw Rule 9-203.
Educational seminars, FamLaw Rule 9-204.
Guidelines for support, FamLaw Rule
9-206.
Mediation of child custody and visitation
disputes, FamLaw Rule 9-205.
Pleadings, FamLaw Rule 9-202.
Family division and support services,
CJA Rule 16-204.
Parenting coordination, FamLaw Rule
9-205.2.

CHILD IN NEED OF ASSISTANCE.
Attorneys at law.
Representing children, guidelines, ChildAdv
Appx.

CHILDREN.
Access to court records.
Denial of inspection, cases involving, CJA
Rule 16-1006.
Juvenile causes, Juv Rules 11-101 to
11-122.
See JUVENILE CAUSES.
Minors.
General provisions.
See MINORS.
Support and maintenance generally.
See SUPPORT AND MAINTENANCE.

CHILD SUPPORT.
Divorce.
Guidelines for support, FamLaw Rule
9-206.
Enforcement of orders.
Seizure or sequestration of property,
FamLaw Rule 9-210.
Parenting coordination, FamLaw Rule
9-205.2.

CIRCUIT COURTS.
Administration of courts, CJA Rules
16-101 to 16-824.
See ADMINISTRATION OF COURTS.
Appeals.
Applicability of rules, Rule 1-101.
Form of court papers, Rule 1-301.
From District Court to circuit court,
AppRevCir Rules 7-101 to 7-116.
See APPEALS FROM DISTRICT COURT
TO CIRCUIT COURT.

INDEX

INDEX

INDEX

INDEX

INDEX

CRIMINAL RULES —Cont'd
Verdicts —Cont'd
Jury trial, Crim Rule 4-327.
Video conferencing.
Initial appearance, Crim Rule 4-231.
Waiver.
Attorneys at law.
Waiver of counsel, Crim Rule 4-215.
Jury trial.
Circuit courts, Crim Rule 4-246.
Warrants.
Defined, Crim Rule 4-102.
Execution.
Defendant not in custody, Crim Rule
4-212.
Issuance, Crim Rule 4-212.
Circuit courts, Crim Rule 4-212.
District Court, Crim Rule 4-212.
Procedure when defendant in custody.
Other offenses, Crim Rule 4-212.
Search warrants, Crim Rule 4-601.
Service.
Return of service, Crim Rule 4-212.
Witnesses.
Body attachment of material witness, Crim
Rule 4-267.

CROSS-CLAIMS.
Allowed pleadings, CivProCir Rule 2-302.
District Court, CivProDist Rule 3-302.
Answers.
Statement indicating filing or expectation to
file cross-claim, CivProCir Rule 2-323.
Filing.
Time for filing.
Circuit courts, CivProCir Rule 2-331.
District Court, CivProDist Rule 3-331.
Joinder.
Circuit courts, CivProCir Rule 2-331.
District Court, CivProDist Rule 3-331.
Judgments.
Multiple claims.
Circuit courts, CivProCir Rule 2-602.
Jurisdiction.
Exceeding jurisdictional amount.
District Court, CivProDist Rule 3-331.
Parties.
Circuit courts, CivProCir Rule 2-331.
District Court, CivProDist Rule 3-331.
Joinder of additional parties.
Circuit courts, CivProCir Rule 2-331.
District Court, CivProDist Rule 3-331.
Pleadings.
Against co-parties.
Circuit courts, CivProCir Rule 2-331.
District Court, CivProDist Rule 3-331.
Allowed pleadings, CivProDist Rule 3-302.
Answers.
Statement indicating filing or expectation
of filing cross-claim, CivProCir Rule
2-323.
Filing.
Time for filing.
Circuit courts, CivProCir Rule 2-331.

CROSS-CLAIMS —Cont'd
Pleadings —Cont'd
Filing —Cont'd
Time for filing —Cont'd
District Court, CivProDist Rule 3-331.
Joinder of additional parties.
Circuit courts, CivProCir Rule 2-331.
District Court, CivProDist Rule 3-331.
Jurisdiction.
Exceeding jurisdictional amount.
District Court, CivProDist Rule 3-331.
Parties.
Joinder of additional parties.
Circuit courts, CivProCir Rule 2-331.
Time for filing.
Circuit courts, CivProCir Rule 2-331.
District Court, CivProDist Rule 3-331.
Time of trial.
District Court, CivProDist Rule 3-331.
Trial.
Time of trial.
District Court, CivProDist Rule 3-331.
Small claim actions.
District Court, CivProDist Rule 3-701.
Time for filing.
Circuit courts, CivProCir Rule 2-331.
District Court, CivProDist Rule 3-331.
Trial.
District Court, CivProDist Rule 3-331.
Trial.
Time.
District Court, CivProDist Rule 3-331.
Voluntary dismissal.
Circuit courts, CivProCir Rule 2-506.
District Court, CivProDist Rule 3-506.

CROSS-EXAMINATION.
Depositions.
Circuit courts, CivProCir Rule 2-415.

CUSTODY.
Attorneys at law.
Appointment of child's counsel, FamLaw
Rule 9-205.1.
Guidelines for practice.
See COURT-APPOINTED LAWYERS
REPRESENTING CHILDREN.
Child custody.
Attorneys at law.
Appointment of child's counsel, FamLaw
Rule 9-205.1.
Guidelines for practice.
See COURT-APPOINTED LAWYERS
REPRESENTING CHILDREN.
Divorce.
Child custody, FamLaw Rule 9-203.
Attorneys at law.
Appointment of child's counsel,
FamLaw Rule 9-205.1.
Guidelines for practice.
See COURT-APPOINTED LAWYERS
REPRESENTING CHILDREN.
Educational seminars, FamLaw Rule
9-204.

INDEX

INDEX

INDEX

INDEX

INDEX

INDEX

INDEX

INDEX

INDEX

EVIDENCE —Cont'd

Impeachment, Evid Rule 5-616.
Bias, Evid Rule 5-616.
Capacity, Evid Rule 5-616.
Character evidence, Evid Rule 5-608.
Computer-generated evidence used to impeach, CivProCir Rule 2-504.3.
Conduct of witness, Evid Rules 5-608, 5-616.
Nonwaiver of privilege against self-incrimination, Evid Rule 5-608.
Conviction of crime, Evid Rule 5-609.
Extrinsic evidence, Evid Rule 5-616.
Personal knowledge, Evid Rule 5-616.
Prejudice, Evid Rule 5-616.
Prior statements of witnesses, Evid Rules 5-613, 5-616.
Rehabilitation, Evid Rule 5-616.
Religious beliefs or opinions, Evid Rule 5-610.
Who may impeach, Evid Rule 5-607.
Inconsistent statements.
Witnesses, Evid Rule 5-613.
Injuries.
Payment of medical, hospital or similar expenses.
Admissibility to prove liability for injury, Evid Rule 5-409.
Instructions to the jury.
Reference to evidence.
Circuit courts, CivProCir Rule 2-520.
Criminal rules, Crim Rule 4-325.
Insurance.
Liability insurance.
Admissibility, Evid Rule 5-411.
Interrogation of witnesses.
By court, Evid Rule 5-614.
Mode and order, Evid Rule 5-611.
Prior statements, Evid Rule 5-613.
Irrelevant evidence.
Inadmissible, Evid Rule 5-402.
Judges.
Competency as witness, Evid Rule 5-605.
Explanation of ruling on evidence, Evid Rule 5-103.
Functions of court and jury.
Writings, recordings or photographs, Evid Rule 5-1008.
Judgments.
Boundaries.
Hearsay exceptions, Evid Rule 5-803.
General history.
Hearsay exceptions, Evid Rule 5-803.
Personal or family history.
Hearsay exceptions, Evid Rule 5-803.
Revisory power of court.
Newly-discovered evidence.
District Court, CivProDist Rule 3-535.
Judicial notice, Evid Rule 5-201.
Jury.
Competency of juror as witness, Evid Rule 5-606,

EVIDENCE —Cont'd

Jury —Cont'd
Functions of court and jury.
Writings, recordings or photographs, Evid Rule 5-1008.
Hearing of jury.
Inadmissible evidence suggested to the jury, Evid Rule 5-103.
Preliminary questions, Evid Rule 5-104.
Judicial notice.
Instructing jury, Evid Rule 5-201.
Limited admissibility.
Instructing jury, Evid Rule 5-105.
Misleading the jury.
Relevance.
Exclusion of relevant evidence on grounds of misleading the jury, Evid Rule 5-403.
Writings, recordings or photographs.
Functions of court and jury, Evid Rule 5-1008.
Jury trial.
Exhibits.
Circuit courts, CivProCir Rule 2-516.
Instructions to jury.
Reference to evidence.
Circuit courts, CivProCir Rule 2-520.
Criminal rules, Crim Rule 4-325.
Items taken to jury room.
Review of evidence.
Circuit courts, CivProCir Rule 2-521.
Criminal rules, Crim Rule 4-326.
Jury request to review.
Criminal rules, Crim Rule 4-326.
Objections to evidence.
Continuing objections to evidence.
Criminal rules, Crim Rule 4-323.
Method of making.
Criminal rules, Crim Rule 4-323.
Production of evidence.
When court may require production of evidence.
Circuit courts, CivProCir Rule 2-514.
Recordings.
Circuit courts, CivProCir Rule 2-516.
Review of evidence.
Circuit courts, CivProCir Rule 2-521.
Items taken to jury room.
Criminal rules, Crim Rule 4-326.
Jury request to review evidence.
Criminal rules, Crim Rule 4-326.
Juvenile causes.
Adjudicatory hearing.
Presentation of evidence, Juv Rule 11-114.
Proof of allegations of petition, Juv Rule 11-114.
Detention or shelter care hearings, Juv Rule 11-112.
Disposition hearings, Juv Rule 11-115.
Modification or vacation of order, Juv Rule 11-116.
Waiver of jurisdiction, Juv Rule 11-113.

1008

INDEX

INDEX

INDEX

EVIDENCE —Cont'd
Writings —Cont'd
Self-authentication, Evid Rule 5-902.
Summaries, Evid Rule 5-1006.
Writ of actual innocence.
Newly discovered evidence, Crim Rule
4-332.

EXAMINATIONS.
Depositions.
Circuit courts, CivProCir Rule 2-415.
Written questions.
Circuit courts, CivProCir Rule 2-417.
Discovery.
Mental or physical examination of persons.
Circuit courts, CivProCir Rule 2-423.
Examiners.
Order to complete.
Circuit courts, CivProCir Rule 2-542.
Judgments.
Discovery in aid of enforcement.
Circuit courts, CivProCir Rule 2-633.
District Court, CivProDist Rule 3-633.
Jury trial.
Jurors.
Circuit courts, CivProCir Rule 2-512.
Criminal rules, Crim Rule 4-312.
Juvenile causes.
Order for physical and mental examination
of respondent.
Forms, Form 905-OE.
Physical and mental examination, Juv Rule
11-105.
Mental or physical examinations of
persons.
Discovery provisions.
Circuit courts, CivProCir Rule 2-423.
Juvenile causes, Juv Rule 11-105.

EXAMINERS.
Administration of courts.
Financial disclosure statements, CJA Rule
16-816.
Appointment, CivProCir Rule 2-542.
Hearings, CivProCir Rule 2-542.
Judgments.
Discovery in aid of enforcement.
Examination before judge or examiner.
Circuit courts, CivProCir Rule 2-633.
District Court, CivProDist Rule 3-633.
Special examiners, CivProCir Rule 2-542.
Standing examiners, CivProCir Rule 2-542.

EXCITED UTTERANCES.
Hearsay exceptions, Evid Rule 5-803.

EXCLUSION OF WITNESSES, Evid Rule
5-615.

EXECUTIONS.
Bonds, surety.
Levy.
Release of property from levy.
Posting of bond.
Circuit courts, CivProCir Rule 2-643.

EXECUTIONS —Cont'd
Bonds, surety —Cont'd
Levy —Cont'd
Release of property from levy —Cont'd
Posting of bond —Cont'd
District Court, CivProDist Rule
3-643.
Sheriff's bond.
Circuit courts, CivProCir Rule 2-641.
District Court, CivProDist Rule 3-641.
Content of writ.
Generally.
Circuit courts, CivProCir Rule 2-641.
District Court, CivProDist Rule 3-641.
Ejectment.
Warrant of resurvey, PropAct Rule 12-101.
Election of rights and remedies.
Levy.
Release of property from levy.
Election of exemption by judgment
debtor.
Circuit courts, CivProCir Rule 2-643.
District Court, CivProDist Rule
3-643.
Exemptions.
Levy.
Release of property from levy.
Election of exemption by judgment
debtor.
Circuit courts, CivProCir Rule 2-643.
District Court, CivProDist Rule
3-643.
Hearings.
Levy.
Release of property from levy.
Circuit courts, CivProCir Rule 2-643.
District Court, CivProDist Rule 3-643.
Issuance of writ.
Generally.
Circuit courts, CivProCir Rule 2-641.
District Court, CivProDist Rule 3-641.
Judgments.
Levy, CivProCir Rule 2-642.
District Court, CivProDist Rule 3-642.
Release of property from levy, CivProCir
Rule 2-643.
Writ of execution.
Circuit courts, CivProCir Rules 2-641,
2-642.
District Court, CivProDist Rules 3-641,
3-642.
Levy.
Circuit courts, CivProCir Rule 2-642.
District Court, CivProDist Rule 3-642.
Release of levy.
Circuit courts, CivProCir Rule 2-643.
District Court, CivProDist Rule 3-643.
Sale of property under levy.
Circuit courts, CivProCir Rule 2-644.
District Court, CivProDist Rule 3-644.

INDEX

INDEX

GUILTY PLEAS —Cont'd
Withdrawn or unaccepted pleas.
Evidentiary effect, Evid Rule 5-410.

H

HABEAS CORPUS.
Absence of judge.
Return to another court or judge, SpecPro
Rule 15-307.
Alternative remedies.
Post conviction procedure.
Consent required, SpecPro Rule 15-304.
Determination by judge, SpecPro Rule
15-304.
No consent, SpecPro Rule 15-304.
Applicability of rules, SpecPro Rule 15-301.
Bail and recognizance, SpecPro Rule
15-303.
Before whom returnable, SpecPro Rule
15-305.
Commitment.
Errors on face.
Correction, SpecPro Rule 15-310.
Constitutional law.
Discharge for unconstitutionality of law.
Review by court of special appeals review,
SpecPro Rule 15-312.
Disposition, SpecPro Rule 15-310.
Errors on face of commitment.
Correction, SpecPro Rule 15-310.
Evasion of writ.
Immediate appearance may be ordered,
SpecPro Rule 15-306.
Hearings, SpecPro Rule 15-309.
Issuance of writ.
Production of person, SpecPro Rule 15-306.
Service of process.
Procedure following issuance of writ,
SpecPro Rule 15-306.
Judges.
Absence of judge.
Return to another court or judge, SpecPro
Rule 15-307.
Memorandum by judge, SpecPro Rule
15-311.
Notice.
State's attorney to be notified, SpecPro Rule
15-308.
Petitions.
Generally, SpecPro Rule 15-302.
Procedure upon receipt, SpecPro Rule
15-303.
Post conviction procedure.
Alternative remedy to writ, SpecPro Rule
15-304.
Referral of petition, SpecPro Rule 15-303.
Service of process, SpecPro Rule 15-303.
Issuance of writ.
Procedure following issuance of writ,
SpecPro Rule 15-306.
Show cause orders, SpecPro Rule 15-303.

HABEAS CORPUS —Cont'd
State's attorney.
Notice to state's attorney, SpecPro Rule
15-308.
To whom rent directed, SpecPro Rule
15-305.

HABIT.
Evidentiary effect, Evid Rule 5-406.

HABITUAL OFFENDERS.
Generally, Crim Rule 4-245.

HALL OF RECORDS.
Administration of courts.
Disposition of records, CJA Rule 16-818.

HANDWRITING.
Authentication or identification.
Nonexpert, Evid Rule 5-901.

HEADINGS.
Construction and interpretation, Rule
1-201.

HEALTH CARE MALPRACTICE CLAIMS,
SpecPro Rules 15-401 to 15-403.
See MALPRACTICE.

HEALTH CARE PROVIDERS.
Records.
Subpoenas.
Circuit courts, CivProCir Rule 2-510.

HEARINGS.
Administration of courts.
Motion day.
Assignment when hearing required, CJA
Rule 16-201.
**Administrative agency decisions, judicial
review,** AppRevCir Rule 7-208.
Adoption.
Procedure, FamLaw Rule 9-109.
Appeals.
Dismissal of appeals.
Motion to dismiss, AppRev Rule 8-603.
Motions, AppRev Rule 8-431.
Auditors.
Exception to account or report.
Circuit courts, CivProCir Rule 2-543.
Notice.
Circuit courts, CivProCir Rule 2-543.
Record of hearing.
Circuit courts, CivProCir Rule 2-543.
Witnesses.
Attendance.
Circuit courts, CivProCir Rule 2-543.
Certiorari in circuit court, AppRevCir
Rule 7-301.
Computer-generated evidence, CivProCir
Rule 2-504.3.
Coram nobis proceedings, SpecPro Rule
15-1206.
Criminal rules.
Preliminary hearings.
See CRIMINAL RULES.

INDEX

INDEX

INDEX

INDEX

INDEX

1048

INDEX

INDEX

INDEX

INDEX

INDEX

INDEX

1065

MAIL —Cont'd
Service of process.
Return.
Circuit courts, CivProCir Rule 2-126.
Service by delivery or mail.
Return.
District Court, CivProDist Rule 3-126.
Time.
Additional time after service by mail,
Rule 1-203.

MALPRACTICE.
Health care malpractice claims.
Alternative dispute resolution.
Mediators, special qualifications, ADR
Rule 17-104.
Construction and interpretation.
Scope of provisions, SpecPro Rule 15-401.
Definitions, SpecPro Rule 15-402.
Modification of award, SpecPro Rule 15-403.
Offers of judgment, CivProCir Rule 2-605.
Rejection of award or costs, SpecPro Rule
15-403.
Scope of provisions, SpecPro Rule 15-401.
Service of process, SpecPro Rule 15-403.
Vacation of award, SpecPro Rule 15-403.

MANDAMUS, SpecPro Rule 15-701.
Administrative mandamus, AppRevCir
Rules 7-401 to 7-403.
Administrative agency defined, AppRevCir
Rule 7-401.
Applicability, AppRevCir Rule 7-401.
Discovery, AppRevCir Rule 7-402.
Disposition of cases, AppRevCir Rule 7-403.
Procedure, AppRevCir Rule 7-402.
Record, AppRevCir Rule 7-402.
Stay, AppRevCir Rule 7-402.

MANDATE.
Appeals.
General provisions.
See APPEALS.
Mandamus.
See MANDAMUS.

MARRIAGE.
Divorce.
See DIVORCE.
**Performance of marriage ceremonies by
judge.**
Advertising, CJA Rule 16-824.
Applicability of rules, CJA Rule 16-821.
Ceremony, CJA Rule 16-823.
Clerk's responsibilities, CJA Rule 16-822.
Compensation, CJA Rule 16-824.
License required, CJA Rule 16-823.
Place and time of ceremony, CJA Rule
16-822.
Refusal to perform, CJA Rule 16-823.
Restrictions, CJA Rule 16-824.
Scheduling, CJA Rule 16-822.

MARRIAGE CERTIFICATES.
Access to court records.
Denial of inspection, CJA Rule 16-1006.

MARRIAGE CERTIFICATES —Cont'd
Hearsay exceptions, Evid Rule 5-803.

**MARYLAND AUTOMOBILE INSURANCE
FUND.**
General provisions, SpecPro Rules 15-801
to 15-805.
See AUTOMOBILE INSURANCE FUND.

MASTERS.
Administration of courts.
Financial disclosure statements, CJA Rule
16-816.
Alimony.
Referral of matters to masters, FamLaw
Rules 9-207, 9-208.
Alternative dispute resolution.
Authority to conduct settlement
conferences, ADR Rule 17-105.
Appointment.
Special masters.
Circuit courts, CivProCir Rule 2-541.
Standing masters.
Circuit courts, CivProCir Rule 2-541.
Child support.
Referral of matters to masters, FamLaw
Rules 9-207, 9-208.
Clerks of court.
Referral as of course.
Circuit courts, CivProCir Rule 2-541.
Compensation.
Special masters.
Circuit courts, CivProCir Rule 2-541.
Standing masters.
Circuit courts, CivProCir Rule 2-541.
Contempt.
Time of entry of order.
Circuit courts, CivProCir Rule 2-541.
Costs.
Circuit courts, CivProCir Rule 2-541.
Divorce.
Referral of matters to masters, FamLaw
Rules 9-207, 9-208.
Domestic relations.
Referral of cases, CivProCir Rule 2-541.
Exceptions.
Circuit courts, CivProCir Rule 2-541.
Hearings.
Attendance of witnesses.
Circuit courts, CivProCir Rule 2-541.
Notice, CivProCir Rule 2-541.
Records.
Circuit courts, CivProCir Rule 2-541.
Juvenile causes.
Authority.
Generally, Juv Rule 11-111.
Disposition hearing, Juv Rule 11-115.
Emergency detention.
Authority of masters, Juv Rule 11-111.
Hearings, Juv Rule 11-110.
Report to the court, Juv Rule 11-111.
Shelter care.
Authority of masters, Juv Rule 11-111.

INDEX

MOTIONS —Cont'd

Satisfaction of money judgments.

Entry upon motion.

Circuit courts, CivProCir Rule 2-626.

District Court, CivProDist Rule 3-626.

Searches and seizures.

Mandatory motions in circuit courts.

Criminal rules, Crim Rule 4-252.

Service of process.

Preliminary motions.

Mandatory motions.

Circuit courts, CivProCir Rule 2-322.

Sovereign immunity.

Preliminary motions.

Permissive motions.

Circuit courts, CivProCir Rule 2-322.

Statement of grounds.

Circuit courts, CivProCir Rule 2-311.

District Court, CivProDist Rule 3-311.

Striking.

Motion to strike.

Circuit courts, CivProCir Rule 2-322.

Summary judgment.

Circuit courts, CivProCir Rule 2-501.

Summons and process.

Preliminary motions.

Mandatory motions.

Circuit courts, CivProCir Rule 2-322.

Telephone.

Testimony taken by telephone, CivProCir
Rule 2-513, CivProDist Rule 3-513.

Time.

Shortening or extending time requirements.

Ex parte order, Rule 1-204.

Service, Rule 1-204.

Generally, Rule 1-204.

Trial.

Acquittal.

Motion for judgment of acquittal, Crim
Rule 4-324.

Disqualification of judge.

Circuit courts, CivProCir Rule 2-505.

District Court, CivProDist Rule 3-505.

Judgments.

Altering or amending judgments.

Court trials, CivProCir Rule 2-534.

Mandatory motions in circuit courts.

Joint or separate trial of defendants or
offenses.

Criminal rules, Crim Rule 4-252.

Motion for judgment.

District Court, CivProDist Rule 3-519.

Venue.

Preliminary motions.

Mandatory motions.

Circuit courts, CivProCir Rule 2-322.

Waiver.

Certain defenses not waived.

Circuit courts, CivProCir Rule 2-324.

MOTOR VEHICLES.

Insurance.

Automobile insurance fund.

General provisions, SpecPro Rules 15-801
to 15-805.

See AUTOMOBILE INSURANCE
FUND.

Interrogatories in tort actions,
Interrogatories Forms 6, 7.

Pleadings.

Demand for proof.

District Court, CivProDist Rule 3-308.

MUTE.

**Appeals from District Court to circuit
court.**

Dismissal of appeal, AppRevCir Rule 7-114.

N

NAME.

Change of name, SpecPro Rule 15-901.

Adoption.

Notice, FamLaw Rule 9-105.

Family division and support services, CJA
Rule 16-204.

Jury.

Jurors addressed by juror number, not
name, in open court, Crim Rule 4-312.

NE EXEAT.

Divorce, annulment and alimony.

Affidavit required, FamLaw Rule 9-203.

NEGLIGENCE.

Interrogatories.

Motor vehicle tort actions, Interrogatories
Forms 6, 7.

Personal injury actions, Interrogatories
Form 8.

NEWLY DISCOVERED EVIDENCE, Crim
Rule 4-331.

Death penalty cases, Crim Rule 4-331.

New trial, Crim Rule 4-331.

Writ of actual innocence, Crim Rule 4-332.

**NEWSPAPER OF GENERAL
CIRCULATION.**

Defined, Rule 1-202.

NEW TRIAL.

**Appeals from District Court to circuit
court.**

Time for filing.

Notice of appeal, AppRevCir Rule 7-104.

Costs.

Circuit courts, CivProCir Rule 2-533.

District Court, CivProDist Rule 3-533.

Criminal rules, Crim Rule 4-331.

Death penalty cases.

Newly discovered evidence, Crim Rule
4-331.

INDEX

INDEX

O

OATHS.
Depositions.
Officer before whom deposition taken.
In state, CivProCir Rule 2-414.
Procedure.
Circuit courts, CivProCir Rule 2-415.
Forms, Rule 1-303.
Interpreters, CJA Rule 16-819.
Witnesses, Evid Rule 5-603.

OIL AND GAS.
Severed mineral interests, PropAct Rules 12-701 to 12-704.

OPENING ESTATES, Estates Rules 6-301 to 6-351.
See EXECUTORS AND ADMINISTRATORS.

OPINIONS.
Appeals.
General provisions.
See APPEALS.
Unreported opinions.
Citation, Rule 1-104.
No authority, Rule 1-104.
Appeals from District Court to circuit court.
Appeals heard on the record, AppRevCir Rule 7-113.
Court of special appeals.
Reporting, AppRev Rule 8-605.1.
Unreported opinions.
Appeals.
Citation, Rule 1-104.

OPINION TESTIMONY.
Experts.
Bases of opinion, Evid Rule 5-703.
Mental state of criminal defendant, Evid Rule 5-704.
Right to challenge, Evid Rule 5-703.
Underlying facts or data, Evid Rule 5-705.
Handwriting, Evid Rule 5-901.
Impeachment, Evid Rule 5-616.
Lay witnesses, Evid Rule 5-701.
Ultimate issue, Evid Rule 5-704.

ORAL ARGUMENTS.
Appeals from District Court to circuit court.
Appeals heard on the record, AppRevCir Rule 7-113.
Death penalty cases, AppRev Rule 8-306.

ORDERS OF COURT.
Administration of courts.
Clients' security fund.
Show cause order, CJA Rule 16-811.
Disposition of records.
Court order, CJA Rule 16-818.
Promulgation of rules.
Promulgation by rules order, CJA Rule 16-801.

ORDERS OF COURT —Cont'd
Adoption.
Show cause order, FamLaw Rule 9-105.
Appeals.
Court of appeals.
Certification procedure.
Federal courts and other state courts as certifying courts, AppRev Rule 8-305.
Emergency orders.
Authority of court to rule on party's motion before expiration of time for response, AppRev Rule 8-431.
Entry of order.
Clerk entering, AppRev Rule 8-432.
Court entering, AppRev Rule 8-432.
Time extensions in court of special appeals, AppRev Rule 8-432.
Forms, Form 22.
Mandate.
Evidence of order of court, AppRev Rule 8-606.
Auditors.
Referral by order.
Circuit courts, CivProCir Rule 2-543.
Automobile insurance fund.
Judgments.
Actions against fund.
Payment of judgments.
Show cause order, SpecPro Rule 15-804.
Bail and recognizance.
Pretrial release.
Amendment of pretrial release order, Crim Rule 4-216.
Review of order, Crim Rule 4-216.
Bar admissions.
Out-of-state attorneys.
Special admission.
Form, Form RGAB-14/O.
Catastrophic health emergency.
Contest of isolation or quarantine.
Decision and order, SpecPro Rule 15-1105.
Certiorari in circuit court.
Show cause orders, AppRevCir Rule 7-301.
Class actions.
Conduct of class actions.
Circuit courts, CivProCir Rule 2-231.
Computer-generated evidence, CivProCir Rule 2-504.3.
Contempt, SpecPro Rules 15-203, 15-204.
Child or spousal support nonpayment, SpecPro Rule 15-207.
Coram nobis proceedings, SpecPro Rule 15-1207.
Default judgments.
Orders of default.
Circuit courts, CivProCir Rule 2-613.
Depositions.
Contents.
Criminal rules, Crim Rule 4-261.

INDEX

INDEX

INDEX

INDEX

INDEX

INDEX

INDEX

INDEX

INDEX

INDEX

INDEX

1109

SUNDAYS AND HOLIDAYS.
Definition of "holiday," Rule 1-202.
Service of process.
Circuit courts, CivProCir Rule 2-125.
District Court, CivProDist Rule 3-125.

SUPERSEDEAS BONDS.
Appeals.
Amount, AppRev Rule 8-423.
Conditions, AppRev Rule 8-423.
Disposition of property.
Amount of bond, AppRev Rule 8-423.
Money judgment not otherwise secured.
Amount of bond, AppRev Rule 8-423.
Appeals from District Court to circuit court, AppRevCir Rule 7-111.

SUPPORT AND MAINTENANCE.
Contempt for failure to pay spousal or child support.
Constructive civil contempt, SpecPro Rule 15-207.
Family division and support services, CJA Rule 16-204.
Juvenile causes.
Order for support.
Forms, Form 918-O/S.
Pending support proceedings, Juv Rule 11-117.
Masters.
Referral of matters to masters, FamLaw Rules 9-207, 9-208.
Sentence and punishment.
Revisory power of court.
Desertion and non-support cases, Crim Rule 4-345.

SURVEYS AND SURVEYORS.
Ejectment.
Warrant of resurvey, PropAct Rule 12-101.
Mechanics' liens.
Boundaries.
Designation after commencement of construction, PropAct Rule 12-308.

T

TAPE RECORDINGS.
Administration of courts.
Photographing, recording, broadcasting or televising in courthouses, CJA Rule 16-109.
Depositions.
Videotape and audiotape depositions.
Certification.
Circuit courts, CivProCir Rule 2-416.
Custody.
Circuit courts, CivProCir Rule 2-416.
Deferral.
Circuit courts, CivProCir Rule 2-416.
Expert witnesses.
Use of depositions.
Circuit courts, CivProCir Rule 2-419.

TAPE RECORDINGS —Cont'd
Depositions —Cont'd
Videotape and audiotape depositions —Cont'd
Notice.
Circuit courts, CivProCir Rule 2-412.
Objections.
Circuit courts, CivProCir Rule 2-416.
Operation of equipment.
Circuit courts, CivProCir Rule 2-416.
Operator.
Circuit courts, CivProCir Rule 2-416.
Permitted, CivProCir Rule 2-416.
Physical arrangements.
Circuit courts, CivProCir Rule 2-416.
Procedure generally.
Circuit courts, CivProCir Rule 2-416.
Electronic audio and audio-video recording.
Circuit court proceedings, CJA Rule 16-405.
Access to videotape recording, CJA Rule 16-406.
Executors and administrators.
Settlement of decedents' estates.
Electronic recording of proceedings.
Orphans' court, Estates Rule 6-114.
Videotape recording.
Appeals.
Record on appeal, AppRev Rule 8-415.
Depositions. See within this heading, "Depositions."

TAXATION.
Access to court records.
Denial of inspection, CJA Rule 16-1006.
Executors and administrators.
Settlement of decedents' estate.
Inheritance tax.
Application to fix inheritance tax on non-probate assets.
Form, Estates Rule 6-405.
Application to set inheritance tax.
Certification of publication, Estates Rule 6-501.
Form, Estates Rule 6-501.
Notice of appointment of foreign personal representative, Estates Rule 6-501.
Publication of notice, Estates Rule 6-501.
Forms.
Executors and administrators.
Settlement of decedents' estate.
Application to fix inheritance tax on non-probate assets, Estates Rule 6-405.
Inheritance tax.
Application by foreign personal representative to set inheritance tax, Estates Rule 6-501.
Notice to creditors of appointment of foreign personal representative, Estates Rule 6-501.

TAX SALES.
Applicability of rules, PropSales Rule
14-501.
Defenses.
Invalidity, PropSales Rule 14-505.
Foreclosure of right of redemption,
PropSales Rule 14-502.
Notice.
Persons not names and defendants,
PropSales Rule 14-504.
Process, PropSales Rule 14-503.
Service of process, PropSales Rule 14-503.

TELEGRAPH AND TELEPHONE
COMPANIES.
Depositions.
Deposition by telephone.
Circuit courts, CivProCir Rule 2-418.

TELEPHONE CONVERSATIONS.
Authentication or identification, Evid
Rule 5-901.
Evidence.
Testimony taken by telephone, CivProCir
Rule 2-513, CivProDist Rule 3-513.

TELEVISION.
Administration of courts.
Photographing, recording, broadcasting or
televising in courthouses, CJA Rule
16-109.
Extended coverage.
Circuit courts.
See CIRCUIT COURTS.

TEMPORARY RESTRAINING ORDERS.
Generally, SpecPro Rule 15-504.
Injunctions, SpecPro Rule 15-503.
General provisions, SpecPro Rules 15-501 to
15-505.
See INJUNCTIONS.

TERMINATION OF PARENTAL RIGHTS,
FamLaw Rules 9-101 to 9-113, Juv Rule
11-501.
Attorneys at law.
Representing children in termination
proceedings, guidelines, ChildAdv
Appx.
Family division and support services,
CJA Rule 16-204.

THIRD PARTIES.
Answers.
Statement indicating filing or expectation of
filing third party claim, CivProCir Rule
2-323.
Attachment.
Prejudgment attachment.
Claim of property by third person.
Circuit courts, CivProCir Rule 2-115.
District Court, CivProDist Rule 3-115.
Circuit court civil rules, CivProCir Rule
2-332.
Complaints.
Allowed pleadings.
Circuit courts, CivProCir Rule 2-302.

THIRD PARTIES —Cont'd
Complaints —Cont'd
Allowed pleadings —Cont'd
District Court, CivProDist Rule 3-302.
District Court civil rules, CivProDist Rule
3-332.
Executions.
Levy.
Possession of personal property by third
person.
Circuit courts, CivProCir Rule 2-642.
District Court, CivProDist Rule 3-642.
Release of property from levy.
Claim of third person.
Circuit courts, CivProCir Rule 2-643.
District Court, CivProDist Rule
3-643.
Filing.
Time for filing third-party claim.
Circuit courts, CivProCir Rule 2-332.
District Court, CivProDist Rule 3-341.
Garnishment.
Property.
Claim by third person.
Circuit courts, CivProCir Rule 2-645.
District Court, CivProDist Rule 3-645.
Judgments.
Multiple claims.
Circuit courts, CivProCir Rule 2-602.
Levy.
Personal property in possession of third
person.
Circuit courts, CivProCir Rule 2-642.
District Court, CivProDist Rule 3-642.
Release of property from levy.
Claim of third person.
Circuit courts, CivProCir Rule 2-643.
District Court, CivProDist Rule 3-643.
Pleadings.
Additional parties.
Circuit courts, CivProCir Rule 2-332.
District Court, CivProDist Rule 3-332.
Allowed pleadings, CivProCir Rule 2-302.
District Court, CivProDist Rule 3-302.
Amendment of pleadings, CivProCir Rule
2-341, CivProDist Rule 3-341.
Answers.
Statement indicating filing or expectation
of filing third party claim, CivProCir
Rule 2-323.
Defendant's claim against third party.
Circuit courts, CivProCir Rule 2-332.
District Court, CivProDist Rule 3-332.
Response by third party.
Circuit courts, CivProCir Rule 2-332.
District Court, CivProDist Rule 3-332.
Plaintiff's claim against third party.
Circuit courts, CivProCir Rule 2-332.
District Court, CivProDist Rule 3-332.
Time for filing.
Circuit courts, CivProCir Rule 2-332.
District Court, CivProDist Rule 3-332.

INDEX

VICTIMS —Cont'd

Character of victim.

Admissibility to prove conduct, Evid Rule 5-404.

Coram nobis proceedings.

Notice to victims, hearings, SpecPro Rule 15-1206.

Plea agreements.

Notice to victim, Crim Rule 4-243.

Reduction or revision of sentence.

Notice to and participation of victims, Crim Rule 4-345.

Restitution by parents, Crim Rule 4-342.

Sentencing.

Notice and right to address court, Crim Rule 4-342.

Service of process.

Victims and victim representatives, Rule 1-326.

Sexual offense cases.

Rape shield, Evid Rule 5-412.

VIDEO CONFERENCING.

Administrative agency decisions, judicial review.

Hearing conducted by video conferencing or other electronic means, AppRevCir Rule 7-208.

Initial appearance, Crim Rule 4-231.

VIDEOTAPE.

Depositions.

Expert witnesses.

Use of depositions.

Circuit courts, CivProCir Rule 2-419.

Generally.

Circuit courts, CivProCir Rule 2-416.

Notice.

Circuit courts, CivProCir Rule 2-412.

VIDEOTAPE RECORDING.

Administration of courts.

Circuit court proceedings, CJA Rule 16-405.

Appeals.

Record on appeal, AppRev Rule 8-415.

Circuit court proceedings, CJA Rule 16-405.

Access to videotape recordings, CJA Rule 16-406.

Evidence, trial.

Civil rules, CivProCir Rule 2-516.

Criminal rules, Crim Rule 4-322.

VIEW BY JURY.

Circuit courts, CivProCir Rule 2-515.

VIEWS.

Eminent domain.

Board of property review, PropAct Rule 12-213.

VISITATION.

Attorneys at law.

Appointment of child's counsel, FamLaw Rule 9-205.1.

Guidelines for practice.

See COURT-APPOINTED LAWYERS REPRESENTING CHILDREN.

VISITATION —Cont'd

Educational seminars, FamLaw Rule 9-204.

Family division and support services, CJA Rule 16-204.

Mediation of child custody and visitation disputes, FamLaw Rule 9-205.

VITAL STATISTICS.

Hearsay exceptions, Evid Rule 5-803.

VOICE IDENTIFICATION, Evid Rule 5-901.

VOLUNTARY DISMISSAL.

Circuit courts, CivProCir Rule 2-506.

Coram nobis proceedings, SpecPro Rule 15-1205.

District Court, CivProDist Rule 3-506.

W

WAIVER.

Attorneys at law.

Criminal rules, Crim Rule 4-215.

Executors and administrators.

Opening estates.

Personal representative.

Bond of personal representative, Estates Rule 6-312.

Settlement of decedents' estates.

Waiver of notice.

Generally, Estates Rule 6-126.

Expungement of records.

General waiver and release, Form 4-503.2.

Disposition of expunged records, Crim Rule 4-512.

Fees.

Filing.

Prepayment of filing fees, Rule 1-325.

Filing.

Fees.

Prepayment of filing fees, Rule 1-325.

Forms.

Executors and administrators.

Settlement of decedents' estates.

Waiver of notice, Estates Rule 6-126.

Jurisdiction.

Juvenile courts.

Procedure upon waiver, Crim Rule 4-222.

Jury trial.

Circuit courts, CivProCir Rule 2-325.

Criminal rules, Crim Rule 4-246.

Demand for jury trial.

Circuit courts, CivProCir Rule 2-325.

Criminal rules, Crim Rule 4-301.

District Court, CivProDist Rule 3-325.

District Court, CivProDist Rule 3-325.

Juvenile causes.

Emergency detention or shelter care.

Continued detention or shelter care, Juv Rule 11-112.

Jurisdiction, Juv Rule 11-113.

Order for waiver of jurisdiction.

Forms, Form 913-O/W.

INDEX

MARYLAND DISTRICT RULES

Rescinded or transferred.

Editor's note. — The Court of Appeals, by Order dated April 6, 1984, rescinded Chapters 1 through 700 and Subtitles F, G, H, BT, and EX of Chapter 1100 of the Maryland Rules of Procedure and the Maryland District Rules, Rules U12 and U18, Subtitles BF and BK, Rule BQ50, and Subtitle BU of Chapter 1100 of the Maryland Rules of Procedure, and Forms 1 through 21, 611, the Bail Bond Forms, and the Forms for Expungement of Records in the Appendix of Forms, and substituted for the rescinded rules and forms Titles 1 through 4 of the Maryland Rules and related forms, effective July 1, 1984. The Order also approved and adopted, effective July 1, 1984, amendments to certain rules in Chapters 800 through 1300 of the Maryland Rules of Procedure and the Appendix of Forms and in Chapters 1100 and 1200 of the Maryland District Rules, submitted by the Court's Standing Committee on Rules of Practice and Procedure in its Eighty-second, Eighty-seventh and Eighty-eighth Reports and the Supplement to the Eighty-second Report, together with amendments made thereto by the Court. The Order provides that the new rules and forms shall "apply to all actions commenced on and after July 1, 1984, and insofar as practicable, to all actions then pending."

A table of comparable rules, relating those rules rescinded effective July 1, 1984, to the revised rules in Title 1 through Title 4, may be found in this volume as an appendix following the Maryland Rules.

The Court of Appeals, by Order dated June 5, 1996, effective January 1, 1997, rescinded Subtitles A, D, E, J, P, Q, R, T, U, V, W, Y, Z, BB, BD, BE, BG, BH, BJ, BL, BP, BQ, BR, BS, BW, and BY of Chapter 1100 of the Maryland Rules of Procedure, rescinded Subtitles P, BB, BQ, and BW of the Maryland District Rules, and rescinded Forms 22a, 23, 24, 25, and 26. The Order substituted for certain of the rules and forms rescinded new Title 9, Chapter 100, Title 10, Title 12, Title 13, Title 14, and Title 15 of the Maryland Rules of Procedure. Furthermore, the Order transferred, without readoption, Chapter 900, Chapter 1200, and Subtitles S, BU, and BV of Chapter 1100 of the Maryland Rules of Procedure and Chapter 1200 of the Maryland District Rules to be Title 9, Chapter 200, Title 11, and Title 16 of the Maryland Rules of Procedure. The Order provides that the new rules shall "apply to all actions commenced on or after January 1, 1997, and insofar as practicable, to all actions then pending."

A table of comparable rules, relating those rules rescinded effective January 1, 1997, to the revised rules in Title 9 through Title 16 may be found in this volume as an appendix following the Maryland Rules.

RULES GOVERNING ADMISSION TO THE BAR OF MARYLAND

This Court's Standing Committee on Rules of Practice and Procedure having submitted its Ninety-ninth Report to the Court recommending rescission of the current Rules Governing Admission to the Bar of the Maryland Rules of Procedure, the adoption of certain Proposed Rules in substitution therefor, and the adoption of conforming amendments to Rules BV2 and 1228, all as set forth in that Report published in the *Maryland Register,* Vol. 15, Issue 6, Pages 722-734 (March 11, 1988); and

The Rules Committee having submitted a Supplement to the Ninety-ninth Report, recommending adoption of proposed new Bar Admission Rules 11, 17, and 22 and certain amendments to proposed revised Bar Admission Rule 13, Rule BV2, and Rule 1228, all as set forth in that Supplement published in the *Maryland Register,* Vol. 17, Issue 10, Pages 1210-1216 (May 18, 1990); and

This Court having considered at open meetings, notice of which was posted as prescribed by law, all those proposed rules changes, together with the comments received and certain further amendments subsequently submitted by the Rules Committee, and having on its own motion amended certain of the proposed rules, it is this 28th day of June, 1990, ORDERED, by the Court of Appeals of Maryland, that the Rules Governing Admission to the Bar of Maryland adopted March 30, 1970, and all subsequent amendments thereto be, and they are hereby, rescinded effective August 1, 1990; and it is further

ORDERED, that proposed new Bar Admission Rule 17, Legal Assistance by Law Graduates, as set forth in the Supplement to the Ninety-ninth Report, be, and it is hereby, rejected; and it is further

ORDERED, that in substitution for the rules hereby rescinded, the Maryland Rules annexed to this Order be, and they are hereby, adopted in the form annexed hereto; and it is further

ORDERED, that the Rules amendments hereby adopted by this Court shall take effect August 1, 1990, and it is further

ORDERED, that a copy of this Order be published in the next issue of the *Maryland Register.*

ROBERT C. MURPHY
JOHN C. ELDRIDGE
HARRY A. COLE
LAWRENCE F. RODOWSKY
JOHN F. MCAULIFFE
WILLIAM H. ADKINS II
HOWARD S. CHASANOW

This Court having considered a proposed amendment to Bar Admission Rule 11 (Required Course on Professionalism) of the Maryland Rules of Procedure at an open meeting, notice of which was posted as prescribed by law, and finding that an emergency does in fact exist with reference to the proposed rules change, it is this 18th day of August, 1994

ORDERED, by the Court of Appeals of Maryland, that Bar Admission Rule 11 (Required Course on Professionalism) be, and it is hereby, amended and adopted in the form attached hereto, and it is further

ORDERED, that the rules change hereby adopted by this Court shall govern all courts of this State and all parties and their attorneys in all actions and proceedings; and shall take effect and apply to all actions commenced on and after August 18, 1994 and insofar as practicable to all actions then pending; and it is further

ORDERED, that a copy of this Order be published in the next issue of the *Maryland Register.*

ROBERT C. MURPHY
JOHN C. ELDRIDGE
LAWRENCE F. RODOWSKY
*
ROBERT L. KARWACKI
ROBERT M. BELL
IRMA S. RAKER
*Judge Chasanow declined to sign the Order.

The Court, by a Rules Order dated July 14, 1995, having extended the operation of Rule 11 of the Rules Governing Admission to the Bar of Maryland until December 31, 1995 pending a decision by the Court to extend, make permanent or rescind Rule 11, and

The Professionalism Course Evaluation Committee having been appointed by the Court to study the Professionalism Course as mandated by Rule 11 and to make recommendations to the Court concerning the continuation of the requirements of Rule 11 and the Committee having filed its report recommending that the requirements of Rule 11 be extended for a period of five years with provision for an additional evaluation by the Court at the end of that time, and

This Court having considered, at an open meeting, notice of which was posted as prescribed by law, the report and recommendation of the Professionalism Course Evaluation Committee, it is this 21st day of November 1995

ORDERED, by the Court of Appeals of Maryland, that Rule 11 (Required Course on Professionalism) be, and it is hereby, amended

and adopted in the form attached hereto and it is further

ORDERED, that the rule change hereby adopted by this Court shall govern all courts of this State and all parties and their attorneys in all actions and proceedings; and shall take effect and apply to all actions commenced on and after January 1, 1996 and insofar as practicable to all actions then pending; and it is further

ORDERED, that a copy of this Order be published in the next issue of the *Maryland Register.*

ROBERT C. MURPHY
*
LAWRENCE F. RODOWSKY
*
ROBERT L. KARWACKI
ROBERT M. BELL
IRMA S. RAKER
*For reasons set forth in the attached dissenting opinion Judge Eldridge and Judge Chasanow declined to approve the adoption of the amendment to Rule 11(c).

Chasanow, J., dissents:

Although I believe that the professionalism course is an excellent and meaningful program, I dissent from Rule 11 because I believe that the course should be mandatory for all members of the bar, rather than just new admittees. The course was instituted because there is a perceived lack of professionalism among some members of the bar. To correct the problem, the course should be given to all lawyers, including those who are responsible for this perceived problem. Moreover, new graduates fresh from their professional responsibility courses in law school probably have less need for a professionalism course than older attorneys, many of whom were not required to take an ethics course in law school. New graduates are also likely to have acquired some sensitivity to minority and gender concerns, which constitute a significant part of the course. Senior members of the bar who began practicing law in a different era may need more guidance in these areas. Any experienced trial judge knows that as a general rule the new, eager, young lawyers, in their first year of practice tend to be respectful, diligent and conscientious practitioners. It is at least a year or so before any potential lack of professionalism begins to emerge.

The course is mandated at a time when the new graduates may be less than receptive; it is taken during the hectic, numbing period following successful completion of the bar examination, but before admission to the bar. It might be more meaningful after the new admittees have had some exposure to the practice of law. The lack of professionalism among some lawyers that the course is designed to address most likely developed during the practice of law, rather than before admission to the bar. Requiring the course for new graduates creates a false sense of security if the Court assumes it has solved the problem of lack of professionalism.

When Rule 11 was first adopted, many people anticipated that the course requirement would eventually be expanded to include all members of the bar. To date, this has not occurred. A proposed amendment to make the course a requirement for all lawyers has been rejected by the Court of Appeals by a five-to-two vote. The professionalism course is an admirable undertaking by the Maryland State Bar Association, but it is expensive. Costs of the course, over and above the fees paid by attendees, continue to grow every year and are currently in excess of thirty-thousand dollars per year. If the course were mandatory for all lawyers, these excess costs might be reduced since senior attorneys could afford to pay a higher fee. Further, any expenditures by the Bar Association would have a far greater impact on the profession. We senior members of the bar ought not impose a requirement on new admittees that we are unwilling to impose on ourselves. I respectfully dissent from the adoption of Rule 11, although the professionalism course is an excellent idea, it targets the least needy audience.

Judge Eldridge authorizes me to state that he joins in the views expressed in this dissenting opinion.

ADOPTED BY
THE COURT OF APPEALS
OF
MARYLAND

June 28, 1990, effective August 1, 1990, with amendments through November 15, 1997

State Board of Law Examiners

State of Maryland

Jonathan A. Azrael

Chairman

John F. Mudd
Robert H. Reinhart
Christopher B. Kehoe
Robert L. Bloom
Maurene Epps Webb
Katherine D. Savage

Forms for admission to the Bar are supplied by the State Board of Law Examiners, upon request.

FOR FURTHER INFORMATION ADDRESS

Bedford T. Bentley, Jr., Secretary

State Board of Law Examiners

People's Resource Center

Room 1210

100 Community Place

Crownsville, Maryland 21032-2026

Telephone: (410) 514-7044

The Court, by a Rules Order dated July 14, 1995, having extended the operation of Rule 11 of the Rules Governing Admission to the Bar of Maryland until December 31, 2000 pending a decision by the Court to extend, make permanent or rescind Rule 11, and

The Maryland State Bar Association Committee on Professionalism, having recommended that the expiration provision of Rule 11 be repealed and that Rule 11 be made permanent, and

The Court, after consideration, having concluded that Rule 11 should be extended for a period of ten years, it is the 2nd day of November, 2000,

ORDERED, by the Court of Appeals of Maryland, that Rule 11 (Required Course on Professionalism) be, and it is hereby, amended to extend the operation of Rule 11 for a period of ten years, until December 31, 2010 and it is further

ORDERED, that the Rule change adopted by this Court in the form attached hereto shall govern all courts of this State and all parties and their attorneys in all actions and proceedings and shall take effect and apply to all actions commenced on and after January 1, 2001 and insofar as practicable to all actions then pending, and it is further

ORDERED, that a copy of this Order be published in the next issue of the *Maryland Register*.

ROBERT M. BELL
JOHN C. ELDRIDGE
LAWRENCE F. RODOWSKY
IRMA S. RAKER
ALAN M. WILNER
DALE R. CATHELL
GLENN T. HARRELL, JR.

The State Board of Law Examiners having submitted to this Court proposed amendments to Rules 1, 7, and 8 of the Rules Governing Admission to the Bar of Maryland, as published in the Maryland Register, Vol. 32, Issue

15, Pages 1311-1312 (July 22, 2005), and

This Court having considered at an open meeting, notice of which was posted as prescribed by law, all those proposed rules changes, together with the comments received, it is this 13th day of September, 2005

ORDERED, by the Court of Appeals of Maryland, that amendments to Rules 1, 7, and 8 of the Rules Governing Admission to the Bar of Maryland be, and they are hereby, adopted in the form previously published; and it is further

ORDERED that the rules changes hereby adopted by this Court shall take effect on January 1, 2007 and apply to Maryland Bar Examinations administered thereafter; and it is further

ORDERED that a copy of this Order be published in the next issue of the *Maryland Register.*

ROBERT M. BELL

IRMA S. RAKER

ALAN M. WILNER

DALE R. CATHELL

*GLENN T. HARRELL, JR.

LYNNE A. BATTAGLIA

CLAYTON GREENE, JR.

* Judge Harrell declined to sign the Order. See attached dissent.

Harrell, J., dissenting:

Although I have no quarrel with the substance of the subject changes to the Rules Governing Admission to the Bar of Maryland (either as to the substitution of the Multistate Performance Test ("MPT") for some essay questions in the Bar examination or the elimination of the authority of the State Board of Law Examiners (the "Board") to provide for carry over from prior examinations of a passing score on either the essay or Multistate Bar Examination ("MBE") portion), I dissent from the Order approving those changes because the Majority of the Court refuses concurrently to raise by an appropriate amount the Bar application fee, provided for in § 10-208(b)(2) of the Business Occupations and Professions Article of the Maryland Code,[1] to offset the costs associated with adding the MPT component to the examination. The effect of this refusal will exacerbate an already intolerable and substantial budgetary deficit incurred each year, over the last twelve years, in administering the Bar examination and admission process.

The total expenses of the Board substantially have outpaced the Board's total revenues since at least 1993.[2] In 2002, the last time it was calculated, the Board's deficit was pro-jected to be $311,900 for fiscal year ("FY") 2003.[3] Although a number of Board activities not directly involved in administering the Bar examination contribute to the creation of the annual deficit,[4] the cost of administering the Bar examination is by far the largest single contributor.[5] The substitution of the MPT component affected by the Rule change approved by the Court today will increase further annual deficits because there will be additional expenditures incurred (some only at the inception of the MPT and others on a recurring basis) in the implementation and administration of the MPT, according to my understanding of what the Board informs us. Although the Board's projected additional expenditures related to the MPT appear reasonable, the Court Majority's apparent comfort with further expansion of the deficit is unreasonable.

The annual deficit is not the fault of the Board, which lacks unilateral power to regulate its revenue stream. Rather, the Legislature and the Maryland Judicial Conference shied away twice in relatively recent history from increasing the fees associated with admission to the Bar. The first instance was in 1999 when the Legislature considered a proposal to increase the Bar examination fee, which it exclusively regulates under § 10-208(b)(1), from $100 to $200 and require that the Board be financially self-supporting,[6] as recommended by the Department of Legislative Service.[7] The Judicial Conference, however, expressed its concern over both the $100 increase and the self-supporting requirement, citing a generalized desire that Bar admission be affordable to all applicants and that the public should bear some of the cost of ADA compliance.[8] In response, the Legislature enacted an amended bill to increase the Bar examination fee only to $150 and remove entirely from the bill the self-supporting language. Obviously, the $50 increase to the legislatively-controlled fee in 1999 fell far short of addressing the fiscal situation.

In 2003, the Legislature considered a proposal submitted by the Judicial Conference, the latter reversing its position from 1999 (probably in the face of the escalating deficit calculated to reach an all-time high in FY 2003 of $311,900), to increase the § 10-208(b)(1) examination fee from $150 to $325 in an effort to eliminate future Board deficits. Both House Bill (H.B.) 56-2003 and Senate Bill (S.B.) 142-2003 died, for no apparent reason, in their respective committees. Had not the Board spoken in support of the bills at the respective committee meetings, one would think from an examination of the public record that this "initiative" was a parentless child.

I do not propose at this time that the Court increase the § 10-208(b)(2) Bar application fee, entrusted to its discretion, to such a level as to eradicate virtually assured future deficits. That would be overreaching until a better understanding is put on the record for why the two branches of government have been unable to agree on a fiscally responsible approach to this situation. Nonetheless, we should authorize a modest fee increase sufficient to cover the estimated cost of introducing and administering the new MPT component.

As it stands today, only five other states have a Bar admission fee schedule lower than Maryland's fee structure.[9] The Court is authorized to increase the § 10-208(b)(2) Bar application fee, for which no other approval is required nor "cap" imposed by the Legislature. The Court has not increased this fee since 1999. With the authority to regulate the fee comes the responsibility to administer the Bar admission process in a responsible fiscal manner. If a concern lingers that admission to the Bar may become unaffordable to some applicants, we have the means to address individual cases of merit through deferred payment or other creative measures. The Court's unwillingness to engage in meaningful discussion of solutions is puzzling.

[1] Unless otherwise provided, all statutory references are to sections within Maryland Code (1989, 2004 Repl. Vol.), Business Occupations and Professions, § 10-208.

[2] 2 DEPARTMENT OF LEGISLATIVE SERVICES, EVALUATION OF THE STATE BOARD OF LAW EXAMINERS, Exhibit 3.2, 28 (1998). The annual deficits identified by the Department in this document were: FY 1993 ($6,721), FY 1994 ($717), FY 1995 ($100,141), FY 1996 ($120,780), FY 1997 ($161,095), FY 1998 ($206,955), and FY 1999 ($262,935). *Id.*

[3] Letter from Bedford T. Bentley, Esq., Executive Secretary, State Board of Bar Examiners to Laura McCarty, Principal Analyst, Office of Policy Analysis of the Department of Legislative Services (Oct. 7, 2002).

[4] The annual deficit is 'covered' by the General Fund of the State.

[5] DEPARTMENT OF LEGISLATIVE SERVICES, EVALUATION OF THE STATE BOARD OF LAW EXAMINERS, Exhibit 3.3, at 29-30. Some of the other factors contributing to the Board's operating deficit include "[salary and fringe benefit] inflation, increased character committee reimbursement, the use of multiple test sites, increased board compensation,increased cost of the MBE, and ADA compliance." *Id.*at 27.

[6] Senate Bill (S.B.) 82-1999, as reported favorably, with amendments, by the Senate Judicial Proceedings Committee.

[7] The Department of Legislative Service recommended that the Court "increase the fees collected by the [B]oard to a level that places the [B]oard's revenues in balance with its expenditures," increase the § 10-208(b)(1) ex-

amination fee from $90 to $180, and increase by $50 the § 10-208(b)(2) application fee from $125 for timely filed applications to $175 and from $175 for late applications to $225. DEPARTMENT OF LEGISLATIVE SERVICES, EVALUATION OF THE STATE BOARD OF LAW EXAMINERS, at 33.

[8] Letter from the Honorable Robert M. Bell, Chief Judge, Court of Appeals, to the Honorable Leo E. Green, Vice Chairman, Senate Judicial Proceedings Committee, Maryland General Assembly (Apr. 7, 1999).

[9] *See* NATIONAL CONFERENCE OF BAR EXAMINERS AND AMERICAN BAR ASSOCIATION SECTION OF LEGAL EDUCATION AND ADMISSIONS TO THE BAR, COMPREHENSIVE GUIDE TO BAR ADMISSION REQUIREMENTS, Chart XI: Bar Admission Fee, 5 (2005), at http://www.abanet.org/legaled/publications/compguide2005/chart11.pdf (listing the Bar registration and examination fees for each state and jurisdiction).

This Court having been requested by the Maryland State Bar Association and the American Bar Association to accommodate the needs of attorneys licensed in Louisiana, Mississippi, and Alabama who have been displaced by Hurricane Katrina and have relocated to Maryland, and

This Court having considered that request at an open meeting, notice of which was posted as prescribed by law, and finding that an emergency exists with reference to the displaced lawyers and that it is in the interests of justice to permit them to continue to practice while temporarily residing in Maryland, it is this 29th day of September, 2005,

ORDERED, by the Court of Appeals of Maryland, that new Rule 15.1 of the Rules Governing Admission to the Bar of Maryland be, and it is hereby, adopted in the form attached to this Order; and it is further

ORDERED that the rule change hereby adopted by this Court shall take effect September 29, 2005 and that a copy of this Order be published in the next issue of the *Maryland Register.*

ROBERT M. BELL

IRMA S. RAKER

ALAN M. WILNER

DALE R. CATHELL

GLENN T. HARRELL, JR.

LYNNE A. BATTAGLIA

CLAYTON GREENE, JR.

Rule 1. Definitions.

In these Rules, the following definitions apply, except as expressly otherwise provided or as necessary implication requires:

(a) **ADA.** "ADA" means the Americans with Disabilities Act, 42 U.S.C. § 12101, *et seq.*

(b) **Board.** "Board" means the Board of Law Examiners of the State of Maryland.

(c) **Court.** "Court" means the Court of Appeals of Maryland.

(d) **Code, Reference to.** Reference to an article and section of the Code means the article and section of the Annotated Code of Public General Laws of Maryland as from time to time amended.

(e) **Filed.** "Filed" means received in the office of the Secretary of the Board during normal business hours.

(f) **MBE.** "MBE" means the Multi-state Bar Examination published by the National Conference of Bar Examiners.

(g) **MPT.** "MPT" means the Multistate Performance Test published by the National Conference of Bar Examiners.

(h) **Oath.** "Oath" means a declaration or affirmation made under the penalties of perjury that a certain statement or fact is true.

(i) **State.** "State" means (1) a state, possession, territory, or commonwealth of the United States or (2) the District of Columbia. (Amended Sept. 13, 2005, effective Jan. 1, 2006.)

Source. — This Rule is derived from former Rule 1.

Effect of amendments. — The 2005 amendment, effective January 1, 2006, added (f) and redesignated the remaining paragraphs accordingly.

The December 4, 2007 Order, effective April 1, 2008, added (a) and redesignated accordingly.

Rule 2. Application for admission and preliminary determination of eligibility.

(a) **By application.** A person who meets the requirements of Rules 3 and 4 may apply for admission to the Bar of this State by filing an application for admission, accompanied by the prescribed fee, with the Board.

Committee note. — The application is the first step in the admission process. These steps include application for admission, proof of character, proof of graduation from an approved law school, application to take a particular bar examination, and passing of that examination.

(b) **Form of application.** The application shall be on a form prescribed by the Board and shall be under oath. The form shall elicit the information the Board considers appropriate concerning the applicant's character, education, and eligibility to become a candidate for admission. The application shall include an authorization for release of confidential information pertaining to character and fitness for the practice of law to a Character Committee, the Board, and the Court.

(c) **Time for filing.** (1) Without intent to take particular examination. At any time after the completion of pre-legal studies, a person may file an application for the purpose of determining whether there are any existing impediments to the applicant's qualifications for admission.

Committee note. — Subsection (c)(1) of this Rule is particularly intended to encourage persons whose eligibility may be in question for reasons pertaining to character and sufficiency of pre-legal education to seek early review by the Character Committee and Board.

(2) With intent to take particular examination. An applicant who intends to take the examination in July shall file the application no later than the preceding January 16 or, upon payment of the required late fee, no later than the preceding May 20. An applicant who intends to take the examination in February shall file the application no later than the preceding September 15 or, upon payment of the required late fee, no later than the preceding December 20.

(3) Acceptance of late application. Upon written request of the applicant and for good cause shown, the Board may accept an application filed after the applicable deadline for a late filing prescribed in subsection (c)(2) of this Rule. If the Board rejects the application, the applicant may file an exception with the Court within five days after notice of the rejection.

(d) **Preliminary determination of eligibility.** On receipt of an application, the Board shall determine whether the applicant has met the pre-legal education requirements set forth in Rule 3 and in Code, Business Occupations and Professions Article, § 10-207. If the Board concludes that the requirements have been met, it shall forward the character questionnaire portion of the application to a Character Committee. If the Board concludes that the requirements have not been met, it shall promptly notify the applicant in writing.

(e) **Withdrawal of application.** At any time, an applicant may withdraw as a candidate for admission by filing written notice of withdrawal with the Board. No fees will be refunded.

(f) **Subsequent application.** A person who reapplies for admission after an earlier application has been withdrawn or rejected pursuant to Rule 5 must retake and pass the bar examination even if the person passed the examination when the earlier application was pending. If the person failed the examination when the earlier application was pending, the failure will be counted under Rule 9.

Source. — This Rule is derived as follows:
Section (a) is in part derived from the first sentence of former Rule 2 b and in part new.
Section (b) is new.
Section (c) is derived from former Rule 2 a, 2 b, and f.
Section (d) is in part derived from former Rule 2 g and in part new.
Section (e) is derived from former Rule 2 h.
Section (f) is new.

Application denied. — Application for admission denied. In re Charles M., 313 Md. 168, 545 A.2d 7 (1988).

Despite the recommendation of the State Board of Law Examiners to accept an applicant to the Maryland Bar in a four-to-three decision, the Court of Appeals of Maryland denied the application for admission upon concluding that the applicant failed to meet his burden of proving that he possessed the good moral character and fitness required for admission to the Bar. The denial was based on the Court's findings that the applicant failed to disclose a bank fraud conviction and job termination on his law school application, had failed to satisfy the restitution he was ordered to pay for the bank fraud, failed to pay a tax debt, and represented himself as an attorney to a bank employee in his attempt to resolve the outstanding restitution matter. In re Brown, 392 Md. 44, 895 A.2d 1050 (2006).

Applicant for admission to practice law did not show that he had been rehabilitated from his prior financial misconduct because he satisfied his creditors only from the resources of others, specifically, a loan from his mother and gifts received after his graduation. Absent the exigency of the Bar admission process, the applicant likely would have continued to ignore his financial obligations to repay his debt;

he had allowed his debts to increase, and made very few efforts, if any, to resolve his financial obligations, even when it appeared he had the means to do so. In re Stern, 403 Md. 615, 943 A.2d 1247 (2008).

Applicant for admission to the bar did not currently possesses the requisite moral character and fitness for the practice of law, because he had shown a pattern of financial irresponsibility, had not been candid in disclosures on his law school and Bar applications, and had an in appropriate sexual relationship with a 15-year-old female. In re Stern, 403 Md. 615, 943 A.2d 1247 (2008).

Applicant for admission to practice law did not show that he had been rehabilitated from his prior moral misconduct with an underage female who was not emotionally mature enough to enter into, much less maintain, her relationship with the applicant; his claims that he was attracted to her and engaged in a sexual relationship with her belied his claims that he stayed with her for seven or eight years because he was a father figure to her and wanted to help her. In re Stern, 403 Md. 615, 943 A.2d 1247 (2008).

Stated in In re Hyland, 339 Md. 521, 663 A.2d 1309 (1995).

Cited in Abrams v. Lamone, 398 Md. 146, 919 A.2d 1223 (2007).

Rule 3. Pre-legal education.

An applicant for admission must have completed the pre-legal education necessary to meet the minimum requirements for admission to an American Bar Association approved law school.

Source. — This Rule is new.

Rule 4. Eligibility to take bar examination.

(a) **Legal education.** (1) In order to take the bar examination of this State a person either shall have graduated or shall be unqualifiedly eligible for graduation from a law school.

(2) The law school shall be located in a state and shall be approved by the American Bar Association.

(b) **Waiver.** The Board shall have discretion to waive the requirements of subsection (a)(2) of this Rule and of Rule 3 for any person who (1) has passed the bar examination of another state and is a member in good standing of the Bar of that state and (2) in the Board's opinion is qualified by reason of education, experience, or both to take the bar examination.

(c) **Minors.** If otherwise qualified a person who is under 18 years of age is eligible to take the bar examination but shall not be admitted to the Bar until 18 years of age.

Source. — This Rule is derived as follows: *Section (a)* is derived from former Rule 5 b.

Section (b) is derived from former Rule 5 c. *Section (c)* is derived from former Rule 5 d.

Rule 5. Character review.

(a) **Burden of proof.** The applicant bears the burden of proving to the Character Committee, the Board, and the Court the applicant's good moral character and fitness for the practice of law. Failure or refusal to answer fully and candidly any question set forth in the application or any relevant question asked by a member of the Character Committee, the Board, or the Court is sufficient cause for a finding that the applicant has not met this burden.

(b) **Investigation and report of character committee.** (1) On receipt of a character questionnaire forwarded by the Board pursuant to Rule 2 (d), the Character Committee shall (A) through one of its members, personally interview the applicant, (B) verify the facts stated in the questionnaire, contact the applicant's references, and make any further investigation it finds necessary or desirable, (C) evaluate the applicant's character and fitness for the practice of law, and (D) transmit to the Board a report of its investigation and a recommendation as to the approval or denial of the application for admission.

(2) If the Committee concludes that there may be grounds for recommending denial of the application, it shall notify the applicant and schedule a hearing. The hearing shall be conducted on the record and the applicant shall have the right to testify, to present witnesses, and to be represented by counsel. A transcript of the hearing shall be transmitted by the Committee to the Board along with the Committee's report. The Committee's report shall set forth findings of fact on which the recommendation is based and a statement supporting the conclusion. The Committee shall mail a copy of its report to the applicant, and a copy of the hearing transcript shall be furnished to the applicant upon payment of reasonable charges.

(c) **Hearing by board.** If the Board concludes after review of the Committee's report and the transcript that there may be grounds for recommending denial of the application, it shall promptly afford the applicant the opportunity for a hearing on the record made before the Committee. The Board shall mail a copy of its report and recommendation to the applicant and the Committee. If the Board decides to recommend denial of the application in its report to the Court, the Board shall first give the applicant an opportunity to withdraw the application. If the applicant withdraws the application, the Board shall retain the records. Otherwise, it shall transmit to the Court a report of its proceedings and a recommendation as to the approval or denial of the application together with all papers relating to the matter.

(d) **Review by court.** (1) If the applicant elects not to withdraw the application, after the Board submits its report and adverse recommendation the Court shall require the applicant to show cause why the application should not be denied.

(2) If the Board recommends approval of the application contrary to an adverse recommendation by the Committee, within 30 days after the filing of the Board's report the Committee may file with the Court exceptions to the Board's recommendation. The Committee shall mail copies of its exceptions to the applicant and the Board.

(3) Proceedings in the Court under this section shall be on the records made before the Character Committee and the Board. If the Court denies the application, the Board shall retain the records.

(e) **Continuing review.** All applicants remain subject to further Committee review and report until admitted to the Bar.

Source. — This Rule is derived as follows:
Section (a) is in part derived from the first sentence of former Rule 2 d and in part new.
Section (b) is in part derived from former Rule 4 b and in part new.
Section (c) is in part derived from former Rule 4 c and in part new.
Section (d) is in part derived from former Rule 4 c and in part new.
Section (e) is in part derived from former Rule 4 d.

Role of Court of Appeals. — The conclusion of the State Board of Law Examiners that an applicant does not possess the requisite moral character is entitled to great weight; to properly exercise its responsibility in regulating the conduct of attorneys, however, the Court of Appeals must independently evaluate the applicant's present moral character based upon the records made by the Character Committee and the Board. In re Hyland, 339 Md. 521, 663 A.2d 1309 (1995).

Evidence sufficient to find applicant failed to satisfy requirements. — Applicant was deemed to have failed to satisfy his burden that he possessed those qualities that comprise good moral character necessary for the practice of law where the applicant did not appreciate the fiduciary responsibility incumbent upon an attorney when entrusted with the monies of another person, where he did not appreciate the analogy between tax obligations and client trust account responsibilities, and where, in addition to his lack of candor and contradictory testimony on critical issues, the applicant displayed an inability to recognize his dereliction of a moral duty inherent in his past behaviors. In re Hyland, 339 Md. 521, 663 A.2d 1309 (1995).

Despite the recommendation of the State Board of Law Examiners to accept an applicant to the Maryland Bar in a four-to-three decision, the Court of Appeals of Maryland denied the application for admission upon concluding that the applicant failed to meet his burden of proving that he possessed the good moral character and fitness required for admission to the Bar. The denial was based on the Court's findings that the applicant failed to disclose a bank fraud conviction and job termination on his law school application, had failed to satisfy the restitution he was ordered to pay for the bank fraud, failed to pay a tax debt, and represented himself as an attorney to a bank employee in his attempt to resolve the outstanding restitution matter. In re Brown, 392 Md. 44, 895 A.2d 1050 (2006).

Attorney seeking admission to the Maryland Bar did not meet the attorney's burden to show, under (a), that the attorney had the present moral character and fitness for the practice of law, required for admission to the Maryland Bar, because the attorney did not observe the attorney's mandatory duty to supplement the attorney's application for admission with the attorney's serious traffic offense arrest, convictions, or sentence, which occurred after the attorney originally completed the application. In re Strzempek, 407 Md. 102, 962 A.2d 988 (2008).

Supplementation of application — Disclosure of information on an application for admission to the Maryland Bar and immediate and full supplementation after an incident warranting exposition is mandatory, not voluntary, and it is not the choice of a candidate for admission whether to disclose and under what conditions. In re Strzempek, 407 Md. 102, 962 A.2d 988 (2008).

Quoted in In re Kimmer, 392 Md. 251, 896 A.2d 1006 (2006).

Cited in In re Worthington, 336 Md. 555, 649 A.2d 599 (1994); In re Stern, 403 Md. 615, 943 A.2d 1247 (2008).

Rule 6. Petition to take a scheduled examination.

(a) **Filing.** An applicant may file a petition to take a scheduled bar examination if the applicant (1) is eligible under Rule 4 to take the bar examination and (2) has applied for admission pursuant to Rule 2 and the application has not been withdrawn or rejected pursuant to Rule 5. The petition shall be under oath and shall be filed on the form prescribed by the Board.

(b) **Request for Test Accommodation.** An applicant who seeks a test accommodation under the ADA for the bar examination shall file with the

Board an "Accommodation Request" on a form prescribed by the Board, together with any supporting documentation that the Board requires. The form and documentation shall be filed no later than the deadline stated in section (c) of this Rule for filing a petition to take a scheduled bar examination.

Committee note. — An applicant who may need a test accommodation is encouraged to file an Accommodation Request as early as possible.

Cross references. — See Rule 6.1 for the procedure to appeal a denial of a request for a test accommodation.

(c) **Time for filing.** A petitioner who intends to take the examination in July shall file the petition no later than the preceding May 20. A petitioner who intends to take the examination in February shall file the petition no later than the preceding December 20. Upon written request of a petitioner and for good cause shown, the Board may accept a petition filed after that deadline. If the Board rejects the petition, the petitioner may file an exception with the Court within five days after notice of the rejection.

(d) **Affirmation and verification of eligibility.** The petition to take an examination shall contain a signed, notarized statement affirming that the petitioner is eligible to take the examination. No later than the first day of September following an examination in July or the fifteenth day of March following an examination in February, the petitioner shall cause to be sent to the Office of the State Board of Law Examiners a transcript that reflects the date of the award of a Juris Doctor degree to the petitioner.

(e) **Voiding of examination results for ineligibility.** If an applicant who is not eligible under Rule 4 takes an examination, the applicant's petition will be deemed invalid and the applicant's examination results will be voided. No fees will be refunded.

(f) **Certification by law school.** Promptly following each bar examination, the Board shall submit a list of petitioners who identified themselves as graduates of a particular law school and who sat for the most recent bar examination to the law school for certification of graduation and good moral character. Not later than 45 days after each examination, the law school dean or other authorized official shall certify to the Board in writing (1) the date of graduation of each of its graduates on the list or shall state that the petitioner is unqualifiedly eligible for graduation at the next commencement exercise, naming the date; and (2) that each of the petitioners on the list, so far as is known to that official, has not been guilty of any criminal or dishonest conduct other than minor traffic offenses and is of good moral character, except as otherwise noted.

(g) **Refunds.** If a petitioner withdraws the petition or fails to attend and take the examination, the examination fee will not be refunded except for good cause shown. The examination fee may not be applied to a subsequent examination unless the petitioner is permitted by the Board to defer taking the examination. (Amended Nov. 12, 2003, effective March 1, 2004.)

Source. — This Rule is new, except that section (a) is derived from former Rule 5 (a).

Effect of amendments. — The 2003 amendment deleted former (b); redesignated former (c) as present (b), and substituted the present first and second sentences for the former first sentence; added present (c) through (e); and redesignated former (d) as (f); and in the Source note deleted "derived from

former Rule 5 a with the exception of section (d), which is" preceding "new" and added ", except that section (a) is derived from former Rule 5 (a)".

The December 4, 2007 Order, effective June 1, 2008, added (b) with a Committee note and Cross reference and redesignated accordingly.

Rule 6.1. Appeal of Denial of ADA Test Accommodation Request.

(a) **Definition.** In this Rule, "applicant" includes a petitioner under Rule 13 who seeks a test accommodation under the ADA for the attorney examination.

(b) **Accommodations Review Committee.** (1) Creation and Composition. There is an Accommodations Review Committee that shall consist of nine members appointed by the Court of Appeals. Six members shall be lawyers who are not members of the Board. Three members shall not be lawyers. Each non-lawyer member shall be a licensed psychologist or physician who during the member's term does not serve the Board as a consultant or in any capacity other than as a member of the Committee. The Court shall designate one lawyer member as Chair of the Committee and one lawyer member as the Vice Chair. In the absence or disability of the Chair or upon express delegation of authority by the Chair, the Vice Chair shall have the authority and perform the duties of the Chair.

(2) Term. Subject to subsection (b)(4) of this Rule, the term of each member is five years. A member may serve more than one term.

(3) Reimbursement; Compensation. A member is entitled to reimbursement for expenses reasonably incurred in the performance of official duties in accordance with standard State travel regulations. In addition, the Court may provide compensation for the members.

(4) Removal. The Court of Appeals may remove a member of the Accommodations Review Committee at any time.

(c) **Procedure for Appeal.** (1) Notice of Appeal. An applicant whose request for a test accommodation pursuant to the ADA is denied in whole or in part by the Board may note an appeal to the Accommodations Review Committee by filing a Notice of Appeal with the Board.

Committee note. — It is likely that an appeal may not be resolved before the date of the scheduled bar examination that the applicant has petitioned to take. No applicant "has the right to take a particular bar examination at a particular time, nor to be admitted to the bar at any particular time." Application of Kimmer, 392 Md. 251, 272 (2006). After an appeal has been resolved, the applicant may file a timely petition to take a later scheduled bar examination with the accommodation, if any, granted as a result of the appeal process.

(2) Transmittal of Record. Upon receiving a notice of appeal, the Board promptly shall (A) transmit to the Chair of the Accommodations Review Committee a copy of the applicant's request for a test accommodation, all documentation submitted in support of the request, the report of each expert retained by the Board to analyze the applicant's request, and the Board's letter denying the request and (B) mail to the applicant notice of the transmittal and a copy of each report of an expert retained by the Board.

(3) Hearing. The Chair of the Accommodations Review Committee shall appoint a panel of the Committee, consisting of two lawyers an done non-lawyer, to hold a hearing at which the applicant and the Board have the right to present witnesses and documentary evidence and be represented by counsel. In the interest of justice, the panel may decline to require strict application of the Rules in Title 5, other than those relating to the competency of witnesses. Lawful privileges shall be respected. The hearing shall be recorded verbatim by shorthand, stenotype, mechanical, or electronic audio recording methods, electronic word or text processing methods, or any combination of those methods.

(4) Report. The panel shall (A) file with the Board a report containing its recommendation, the reasons for the recommendation, and findings of fact upon which the recommendation is based, (B) mail a copy of its report to the applicant, and (C) provide a copy of the report to the Chair of the Committee.

(d) **Exceptions.** Within 30 days after the report of the panel is filed with the Board, the applicant or the Board may file with the Chair of the Committee exceptions to the recommendation and shall mail a copy of the exceptions to the other party. Upon receiving the exceptions, the Chair shall cause to be prepared a transcript of the proceedings and transmit to the Court of Appeals the record of the proceedings, which shall include the transcript and the exceptions. The Chair shall notify the applicant and the Board of the transmittal to the Court and provide to each party a copy of the transcript.

(e) **Proceedings in the Court of Appeals.** Proceedings in the Court of Appeals shall be on the record made before the panel. The Court shall require the party who filed exceptions to show cause why the exceptions should not be denied.

(f) **If No Exceptions Filed.** If no exceptions pursuant to section (d) of this Rule are timely filed, no transcript of the proceedings before the panel shall be prepared, the panel shall transmit its record to the Board, and the Board shall provide the test accommodation, if any, recommended by the panel. (Added December 4, 2007, effective June 1, 2008.)

Source. — This Rule is new.

Editor's note. — The December 4, 2007 Order provides that the section shall take effect June 1, 2008.

Rule 7. Bar examination.

(a) **Scheduling.** The Board shall administer a written examination twice annually, once in February and once in July. The examination shall be held on two successive days. The total duration of the examination shall be not more than 12 hours nor less than nine hours. The Board shall publish notice of the dates, times, and place or places of the examination no later than the preceding December 1 for the February examination and no later than the preceding May 1 for the July examination.

(b) **Purpose of examination.** It is the policy of the Court that no quota of successful examiners be set, but that each examinee be judged for fitness to be a member of the Bar as demonstrated by the examination answers. To this end, the examination shall be designed to test the examinee's knowledge of legal principles in the subjects on which examined and the examinee's ability to recognize, analyze, and intelligibly discuss legal problems and to apply that knowledge in reasoning their solution. The examination will not be designed primarily to test information, memory, or experience.

(c) **Format and scope of examination.** The Board shall prepare the examination and may adopt the MBE and the MPT as part of it. The examination shall include an essay test. The Board shall define by rule the subject matter of the essay test, but the essay test shall include at least one question dealing in whole or part with professional conduct.

(d) **Grading.** (1) The Board shall grade the examination and shall by rule establish passing grades for the examination. The Board may provide by rule that an examinee may satisfy the MBE part of the Maryland examination requirement by applying a grade on an MBE taken in another jurisdiction at the same examination.

(2) At any time before it notifies examinees of the results, the Board, in its discretion and in the interest of fairness, may lower, but not raise, the passing grades it has established for any particular examination. (Amended Nov. 12, 2003, effective March 1, 2004; amended Sept. 13, 2005, effective Jan. 1, 2006.)

Source. — This Rule is derived as follows: *Section (a)* is derived from former Rule 7 a, and b.
Section (b) is derived from former Rule 7 c.

Section (c) is derived from former Rule 7 d and e.
Section (d) is derived from former Rule 7 e.

Effect of amendments. — The 2003 amendment, in the last sentence of (a), deleted "at least 30 days before an examination" following "The Board shall publish" and added "no later than the preceding December 1 for the February examination and no later than the preceding May 1 for the July examination" at the end.

The 2005 amendment, effective January 1, 2006, in (c) combined the former first and second sentences and fourth and fifth sentences; in the first sentence deleted "and grade" after "prepare" and added "and the MPT" and made related changes; substituted "The examination shall include an essay test" for "Essay answers shall be required on all parts of examination except the MBE part" as the second sentence; in the third sentence substituted "test, but the essay test" for "examination. An examination" and made minor, stylistic changes; and in (d) deleted the former second sentence "If the examination includes the MBE, the Board may provide by rule that an examinee who fails one part (the MBE or the essay test) but passes the other may carry over the passing score to the next examination only" and deleted "also" before "provide" and "or the immediately preceding" after "same".

Cited in Abrams v. Lamone, 398 Md. 146, 919 A.2d 1223 (2007).

Rule 8. Notice of grades and review procedure.

(a) **Notice of grades; alteration.** Notice of examination results shall be sent to each examinee by regular mail, postage prepaid. Successful examinees shall be notified only that they have passed. Unsuccessful examinees shall be given their grades in the detail the Board considers appropriate. Thereafter, the Board may not alter any examinee's grades except when necessary to correct a clerical error.

(b) **Review procedure.** On written request filed with the Board within 60 days after the mailing date of examination results, unsuccessful examinees, in accordance with the procedures prescribed by the Board, may (1) review their essay test answer books and the Board's analysis for the essay test, (2) review their MPT answer books, (3) order the National Conference of Bar Examiners' MPT Point Sheet and Grading Guidelines, and (4) upon payment of the required costs, obtain confirmation of their MBE scores. No further review of the MBE will be permitted. (Amended Sept. 13, 2005, effective Jan. 1, 2006.)

Source. — This Rule is derived as follows: *Section (a)* is derived in part from former Rule 7 f and in part new.

Section (b) is derived from former Rule 8 b.

Effect of amendments. — The 2005 amendment, effective January 1, 2006, in (b) moved "may (1)" from following "examinees," substituted "essay test answer books" for "examination books," added (2) and (3) and redesignated former (2) as (4) and made related changes.

Rule 9. Re-examination after failure.

(a) **Petition for re-examination.** An unsuccessful examinee may file a petition to take another scheduled examination. The petition shall be on the form prescribed by the Board and shall be accompanied by the required examination fee.

(b) **Request for Test Accommodation.** An applicant who seeks a test accommodation under the ADA for the bar examination shall file with the Board an "Accommodation Request" on a form prescribed by the Board, together with any supporting documentation that the Board requires. The form and documentation shall be filed no later than the deadline stated in section (c) of this Rule for filing a petition to take a scheduled bar examination.

Committee note. — An applicant who may need a test accommodation is encouraged to file an Accommodation Request as early as possible.

Cross references. — See Rule 6.1 for the procedure to appeal a denial of a request for a test accommodation.

(c) **Time for filing.** A petitioner who intends to take the July examination shall file the petition, together with the prescribed fee, no later than the preceding May 20. A petitioner who intends to take the examination in February shall file the petition, together with the prescribed fee, no later than the preceding December 20. Upon written request of a petitioner and for good cause shown, the Board may accept a petition filed after that deadline. If the Board rejects the petition, the petitioner may file an exception with the Court within five days after notice of the rejection.

(d) **Deferment of re-examination.** To meet scheduling needs at either the July or the February examination, the Board may require a petitioner to defer re-examination for one setting.

(e) **Three or more failures — Re-examination conditional.** If a person fails three or more examinations, the Board may condition retaking of the examination on the successful completion of specified additional study.

(f) **No refunds.** If a petitioner withdraws the petition or fails to attend and take the examination, the examination fee will not be refunded and may not be applied to a subsequent examination unless the petitioner is required by the Board to defer retaking the examination or establishes good cause for the withdrawal or failure to attend. (Amended Nov. 12, 2003, effective March 1, 2004.)

Source. — This Rule is derived as follows: Section (a) is derived from former Rule 8 a. Section (b) is new.

Sections (c) and (d) are derived from former Rule 8 c.

Effect of amendments. — The 2003 amendment, in (b), deleted "The petition shall be filed at least 20 days before the scheduled examination" and inserted the first two sentences; and in the Source note rewrote the section (a) note and inserted the section (b) note.

The December 4, 2007 Order, effective June 1, 2008, added (b) with a Committee note and Cross reference and redesignated accordingly.

Rule 10. Report to court — Order.

(a) **Report and recommendations as to candidates.** As soon as practicable after each examination, the Board shall file with the Court a report of the names of the successful candidates and the Board's recommendation for admission. If proceedings as to the character of a candidate are pending, the Board's recommendation of that candidate shall be conditioned on the outcome of the proceedings.

(b) **Order of ratification.** On receipt of the Board's report, the Court shall enter an order fixing a date at least 30 days after the filing of the report for ratification of the Board's recommendations. The order shall include the names and addresses of all persons who are recommended for admission, including those who are conditionally recommended. The order shall state generally that all recommendations are conditioned on character approval, but shall not identify those persons as to whom proceedings are still pending. The order shall be published in the Maryland Register at least once before ratification of the Board's recommendations.

(c) **Exceptions.** Before ratification of the Board's report, any person may file with the Court exceptions relating to any relevant matter. For good cause shown the Court may permit the filing of exceptions after ratification of the Board's report and before the candidate's admission to the Bar. The Court shall give notice of the filing of exceptions to the candidate, the Board, and the Character Committee that passed on the candidate's application. A hearing on the exceptions shall be held to allow the exceptant and candidate to present evidence in support of or in opposition to the exceptions and the Board and Character Committee to be heard. The Court may hold the hearing or may refer the exceptions to the Board, the Character Committee, or an examiner for hearing. The Board, Character Committee, or examiner hearing the exceptions shall file with the Court, as soon as practicable after the hearing, a report of the proceedings. The Court may decide the exceptions without further hearing.

(d) **Ratification of board's report.** On expiration of the time fixed in the order entered pursuant to section (b) of this Rule, the Board's report and recommendations shall be ratified subject to the conditions stated in the recommendations and to any exceptions noted under section (c) of this Rule.

Source. — This Rule is derived as follows: Section (a) is derived from former Rule 11. Section (b) is derived from former Rule 12 a.

Section (c) is derived from former Rule 12 b. Section (d) is derived from former Rule 12 c.

Quoted in In re Thompson, 363 Md. 469, 769 A.2d 905 (2001); In re Kimmer, 392 Md. 251, 896 A.2d 1006 (2006).

Rule 11. Required course on professionalism [Expires January 1, 2016].

(a) **Course on legal professionalism — Development and approval.** The Chief Judge of the Court of Appeals may designate a unit within the Judicial Branch, or any other qualified person or entity willing to undertake the responsibility, to develop for consideration and approval by the Court the structure and features of a course on legal professionalism, including (1) the course content, (2) recommended faculty and support staff, (3) the times and places at which the course will be given, (4) estimated expenses for conducting the course, (5) a proposed fee, which shall be adequate to meet the estimated expenses, and (6) any other desirable and appropriate feature. The proposal shall require that the course be given at least twice each year, during the period between the announcement of the Bar examination results and the scheduled Bar admission ceremonies next following that announcement, in the number of locations determined from time to time by the Court. In its discretion, the Court may develop the structure and features of the course on its own.

(b) **Course presentation.** The approved plan shall be implemented as directed by the Court of Appeals.

(c) **Duty to complete course.** Before admission to the Bar, an individual recommended for admission pursuant to Rule 10 shall successfully complete a course on legal professionalism approved by the Court of Appeals. For good cause shown, the Court may admit an individual who has not completed the course, on condition that the individual complete the next regularly scheduled course. If the attorney does not successfully complete the next post-admission course, the Court shall enter a Decertification Order prohibiting the individual from practicing law in the State and shall mail, by first-class mail, a copy of the order to the individual. Mailing of the copy shall constitute service. The decertification shall remain in effect until the Court, after having received satisfactory proof that the individual has successfully completed the course, enters a Recertification Order that restores the individual to good standing. The Clerk of the Court of Appeals shall send a copy of each Decertification Order and each Recertification Order to the Clerk of the Court of Special Appeals, the Clerk of each circuit court, the Chief Clerk of the District Court, and the Register of Wills of each county.

(d) **Duration of requirement; evaluation.** This Rule shall remain in effect until January 1, 2016. Prior to that date, the Court of Appeals shall evaluate the results of the course requirement to determine whether to extend this Rule. The Court of Appeals may appoint a committee consisting of one or more judges, lawyers, legal educators, bar association representatives, and other interested and knowledgeable individuals to assist the Court in the evaluation and make appropriate recommendations to the Court. (Amended effective August 18, 1994; July 14, 1995; November 21, 1995, effective January 1, 1996; November 2, 2000, effective January 1, 2001; March 7, 2011, effective March 7, 2011.)

Source. — This Rule is new.

Effect of amendments. — The 1994 amendment substituted "five" for "three" in the first sentence of (c).

The first 1995 amendment substituted "until December 31, 1995" for "for a period of five years from the effective date of this Rule" in the first sentence of (c).

The second 1995 amendment substituted "for a period of five years beginning January 1, 1996 and ending December 31, 2000" for "until December 31, 1995" in the first sentence of (c).

The 2000 amendment substituted "ten years beginning January 1, 2001 and ending December 31, 2010" for "five years beginning January 1, 1996 and ending December 31, 2000" in the first sentence of (c).

The 2011 amendment rewrote the Rule.

Applied in Att'y Griev. Comm'n v. Reamer, 328 Md. 32, 612 A.2d 895 (1992); In re Wyatt, 342 Md. 117, 673 A.2d 1356 (1996).

Cited in In re Kahn, 328 Md. 698, 616 A.2d 882 (1992); In re McManus, 335 Md. 19, 641 A.2d 870 (1994); In re Reinstatement of Clinton, 338 Md. 481, 659 A.2d 875 (1995).

Rule 12. Order of admission; time limitation.

When the Court has determined that a candidate is qualified to practice law and is of good moral character, it shall enter an order directing that the candidate be admitted to the Bar on taking the oath required by law. A candidate who has passed the Maryland bar examination may not take the oath of admission to the Bar later than 24 months after the date that the Court of Appeals ratified the Board's report for that examination. For good cause, the Board may extend the time for taking the oath, but the candidate's failure to take action to satisfy admission requirements does not constitute good cause. A candidate who fails to take the oath within the required time period shall reapply for admission and retake the bar examination, unless excused by the Court. (Amended June 5, 1996, effective Jan. 1, 1997; Nov. 1, 2001, effective Jan. 1, 2002; effective Nov. 6, 2002.)

Cross references. — See Code, Business Occupations and Professions Article, § 10-212, for form of oath. See also Maryland Rule 16-811 e (Client Protection Fund of the Bar of Maryland — Payments to Fund) and Maryland Rule 16-714 (Disciplinary Fund), which require persons admitted to the Maryland Bar, as a condition precedent to the practice of law in this State, to pay an annual assessment to the Client Protection Fund of the Bar of Maryland and the Attorney Grievance Commission Disciplinary Fund.

Source. — This Rule is in part derived from former Rule 13 and is in part new.

Effect of amendments. — The 1996 amendment, in the Cross reference note, substituted "Rule 16-811 f" for "Rule 1228 f" and substituted "Rule 16-702" for "Rule BV2."

The 2001 amendment rewrote this Rule.

The 2002 amendment, in the cross-reference, substituted "16-811 e" for "16-811 f" and substituted "Client Protection Fund of the Bar of Maryland" for "Clients' Security Fund" twice.

Rule 13. Out-of-state attorneys.

(a) **Eligibility for admission by attorney examination — Generally.** A person is eligible for admission to the Bar of this State under this Rule if the person

(1) is a member of the Bar of a state;

(2) has passed a written bar examination in a state;

(3) has the professional experience required by this Rule;

(4) successfully completes the attorney examination prescribed by this Rule; and

(5) possesses the good moral character and fitness necessary for the practice of law.

(b) **Required professional experience.** The professional experience required for admission under this Rule shall be on a full time basis as (1) a practitioner of law as provided in section (c) of this Rule; (2) a teacher of law at a law school approved by the American Bar Association; (3) a judge of a court of record in a state; or (4) a combination thereof.

(c) **Practitioner of law.** (1) Subject to paragraphs (2) and (3) of this section, a practitioner of law is a person who has regularly engaged in the authorized practice of law

(A) in a state;

(B) as the principal means of earning a livelihood; and

(C) whose professional experience and responsibilities have been sufficient to satisfy the Board that the petitioner should be admitted under this Rule.

(2) As evidence of the requisite professional experience, for purposes of subsection (c) (1) (C) of this Rule, the Board may consider, among other things:

(A) the extent of the petitioner's experience in general practice;

(B) the petitioner's professional duties and responsibilities, the extent of contacts with and responsibility to clients or other beneficiaries of the petitioner's professional skills, the extent of professional contacts with practicing lawyers and judges, and the petitioner's professional reputation among those lawyers and judges; and

(C) if the petitioner is or has been a specialist, the extent of the petitioner's experience and reputation for competence in such specialty, and any professional articles or treatises that the petitioner has written.

(3) The Board may consider as the equivalent of practice of law in a state practice outside the United States if the Board concludes that the nature of the practice makes it the functional equivalent of practice within a state.

(d) **Duration of professional experience.** (1) A person shall have the professional experience required by section (b) of this Rule for (A) a total of ten years, or (B) at least five of the ten years immediately preceding the filing of a petition pursuant to this Rule.

(e) **Exceptional cases.** In exceptional cases, the Board may treat a petitioner's actual experience, although not meeting the literal requirements of subsections (c) (1) or (d) of this Rule, as the equivalent of the professional experience otherwise required by this Rule.

(f) **Petition.** (1) The petitioner shall file with the Board a petition under oath on a form prescribed by the Board, accompanied by the fees required by

1143

the Board and the costs assessed for the character and fitness investigation and report by the National Conference of Bar Examiners.

(2) The petitioner shall state (A) each jurisdiction in which the petitioner has been admitted to the Bar and whether each admission was by examination, by diploma privilege or on motion; and (B) the additional facts showing that the petitioner meets the requirements of section (a) of this Rule or should be qualified under section (e) of this Rule.

(3) The petitioner shall file with the petition the supporting data required by the Board as to the petitioner's professional experience, character, and fitness to practice law.

(4) The petitioner shall be under a continuing obligation to report to the Board any material change in information previously furnished.

(g) **Request for Test Accommodation.** A petitioner who seeks a test accommodation under the ADA for the attorney examination shall file with the Board an "Accommodation Request" on a form prescribed by the Board, together with any supporting documentation that the Board requires. The form and documentation shall be filed no later than the deadline stated in section (i) of this Rule for filing a petition to take a scheduled attorney examination.

Committee note. — A petitioner who may need a test accommodation is encouraged to file an Accommodation Request as early as possible.

Cross references. — See Rule 6.1 for the procedure to appeal a denial of a request for a test accommodation.

(h) **Refunds.** If the Board determines on the face of the petition that the applicant is not qualified to sit for the attorney's examination and the petitioner elects to withdraw the petition without further proceedings, all fees shall be refunded. If in other circumstances a petitioner withdraws the petition or fails to attend and take the examination without permission from the Board, no fees will be refunded and the examination fee may not be applied to a subsequent examination unless the petitioner establishes good cause for the withdrawal or failure to attend.

(i) **Time for filing.** The petition shall be filed at least 60 days before the scheduled attorney examination that the petitioner wishes to take. On written request of the petitioner and for good cause shown, the Board may accept a petition filed after the deadline. If the Board rejects the petition, the petitioner may file an exception with the Court within five days after notice of the rejection.

(j) **Standard for admission and burden of proof.** (1) The petitioner bears the burden of proving to the Board and the Court that the petitioner is qualified on the basis of professional experience and possesses the good moral character and fitness necessary to practice law in this State.

(2) The Board shall recommend rejection of a petition if it is not satisfied that the petitioner possesses good moral character and fitness and that the contents of the petition are true and correct. Failure or refusal to answer fully and candidly any relevant questions asked by the Board, either orally or in writing, is sufficient cause for rejection of the petition.

(k) **Action by board on petition.** The Board shall investigate the matters set forth in the petition. (1) If the Board decides that the petition should be accepted, it shall mail notice of its decision to recommend acceptance of the petition to the petitioner. (2) If the Board concludes that there may be grounds for rejecting the petition, the Board shall notify the petitioner and shall afford the petitioner an opportunity for a hearing. The hearing will not be held until after the National Conference of Bar Examiners completes its investigation of the petitioner's character and fitness to practice law and reports to the Board. The petitioner may be represented by an attorney at the hearing. Promptly after the Board makes its final decision to recommend acceptance or rejection of the petition, the Board shall mail notice of its decision to the petitioner. (3) If the Board decides to recommend rejection of the petition, it shall file with the Court a report of its decision and all papers relating to the matter.

(l) **Exceptions.** Within 30 days after the Board mails notice of its adverse decision to the petitioner, the petitioner may file with the Court exceptions to the Board's decision. The petitioner shall mail or deliver to the Board a copy of the exceptions. The Court may hear the exceptions or may appoint an examiner to hear the evidence and shall afford the Board an opportunity to be heard on the exceptions.

(m) **Attorney examination.** The petitioner must pass an attorney examination prescribed by the Board. The Board shall define, by rule, the subject matter of the examination, prepare the examination, and establish the passing grade. The Board shall administer the attorney examination on a date and at a time during the administration of the regular examination pursuant to Rule 7 and shall publish at least 30 days in advance notice of the date and time of the examination. The Board shall grade the examination and shall send notice of examination results to each examinee by regular mail, postage prepaid. Successful examinees shall be notified only that they have passed. Unsuccessful examinees shall be given their grades in the detail the Board considers appropriate. Review by unsuccessful examinees shall be in accordance with the provisions of Rule 8 (b).

(n) **Re-examination.** In the event of failure on the first examination, a petitioner may file a petition to retake the examination, but a petitioner may not be admitted under this Rule after failing four examinations. A petition for re-examination shall be accompanied by the required fees. Failure to pass the attorney examination shall not preclude any person from taking the regular examination.

(o) **Report to court — Order.** The Board shall file a report and recommendations pursuant to Rule 10. Proceedings on the report, including the disposition of any exceptions filed, shall be as prescribed in that Rule. If the Court determines that the petitioner has met all the requirements of this Rule, it shall enter an order directing that the petitioner be admitted to the Bar of Maryland on taking the oath required by law.

(p) **Required course on professionalism.** A petitioner recommended for admission pursuant to section (n) of this Rule shall comply with Rule 11.

(q) **Time limitation for admission to the Bar.** A petitioner under this Rule is subject to the time limitation of Rule 12. (Amended June 5, 1996, effective January 1, 1997; November 1, 2001, effective January 1, 2002; effective November 6, 2002; amended October 20, 2010, effective January 1, 2011.)

Cross references. — See Code, Business Occupations and Professions Article, § 10-212, for the form of oath. See also Maryland Rule 16-811 e (Client Protection Fund of the Bar of Maryland — Payments to Fund) and Maryland Rule 16-714 (Disciplinary Fund) which require persons admitted to the Maryland Bar, as a condition precedent to the practice of law in this State, to pay an annual assessment to the Client Protection Fund of the Bar of Maryland and the Attorney Grievance Commission Disciplinary Fund.

Source. — This Rule is derived in part from former Rule 14 and is in part new.

Effect of amendments. — The 1996 amendment, in the Cross reference note, substituted "Rule 16-811 f" for "Rule 1228 f" and substituted "Rule 16-702" for "Rule BV2."

The 2001 amendment added (p).

The 2002 amendment, in the cross-reference, substituted "for the form" for "for form," substituted "16-811 e" for "16-811 f," and substituted "Client Protection Fund of the Bar of Maryland" for "Clients' Security Fund" twice.

The December 4, 2007 Order, effective June 1, 2008, added (g) with a Committee note and Cross reference and redesignated accordingly.

The 2010 amendment substituted "paragraphs (2) and (3)" for "paragraphs (2), (3), and (4)" in (c)(1).

Maryland Law Review. — For article, "Survey of Developments in Maryland Law, 1984-85," see 45 Md. L. Rev. 473 (1986).

"Practice of law". — "Practice of law" is a term of art connoting much more than merely working with legally related matters. In re Mark W., 303 Md. 1, 491 A.2d 576 (1985).

Employment as a hearing examiner for the Maryland Department of Employment and Training does not constitute practice of law so as to permit an individual to become a member of the Maryland Bar without taking the usual bar examination. In re Mark W., 303 Md. 1, 491 A.2d 576 (1985).

Purpose of the Rule is to require only enough "practice" (practical experience) to demonstrate no need to take a "full" bar examination. In re R.G.S., 312 Md. 626, 541 A.2d 977 (1988).

Applicant for admission was practicing law, within the meaning of Rule, and period of practice, added to his full-time professorship, added up to the requisite number of years within the required time span prior to the date applicant submitted petition for admission. In re R.G.S., 312 Md. 626, 541 A.2d 977 (1988).

"Practice of law" as used in the unauthorized practice statutes need not be read as synonymous with "practice of law" as used in this Rule. In re R.G.S., 312 Md. 626, 541 A.2d 977 (1988).

Work of attorney was actual practice within the meaning of this Rule, but was not unauthorized practice within the meaning of former Art. 10, § 1. In re R.G.S., 312 Md. 626, 541 A.2d 977 (1988).

Disclosure of material facts required. — This Rule is designed to afford a benefit to lawyers who have practiced lawfully for at least a minimum period of time. The reason for this privilege rests on the assumption that a lawyer who has regularly engaged in the practice of law has sufficient legal knowledge to demonstrate at least minimum competence; it is, therefore, of basic importance that the Board of Law Examiners have before it information from which it can determine whether an applicant has engaged in practice to the extent required by the Rule and it is important that an applicant disclose to the Board all facts bearing on this subject. Att'y Griev. Comm'n v. Keehan, 311 Md. 161, 533 A.2d 278 (1987).

Material, deliberate omission. — Attorney's failure to disclose in his application for admission to the Maryland Bar that, although he had a Pennsylvania license and a Pennsylvania office, he worked full-time for a Baltimore corporation and only worked at his legal practice 10-15 hours per week was material, deliberate omission for which disbarment was the appropriate sanction. Att'y Griev. Comm'n v. Keehan, 311 Md. 161, 533 A.2d 278 (1987).

Quoted in In re Kimmer, 392 Md. 251, 896 A.2d 1006 (2006).

Cited in Abrams v. Lamone, 398 Md. 146, 919 A.2d 1223 (2007).

Rule 14. Special admission of out-of-state attorneys.

(a) **Motion for special admission.** A member of the Bar of this State who is an attorney of record in an action pending in any court of this State, or before an administrative agency of this State or any of its political subdivisions, or representing a client in an arbitration taking place in this State involving the application of Maryland law, may move, in writing, that an attorney who is a member in good standing of the Bar of another state be admitted to practice in this State for the limited purpose of appearing and participating in the action as co-counsel with the movant. If the action is pending in a court, the motion shall be filed in that court. If the action is pending before an administrative agency or arbitration panel, the motion shall be filed in the circuit court for the county in which the principal office of the agency is located or in which the arbitration hearing is located or in any other circuit to which the action may be appealed and shall include the movant's signed certification that copies of the motion have been furnished to the agency or the arbitration panel, and to all parties of record.

Cross references. — For the definition of "arbitration," see Rule 17-102 (b). See Forms RGAB-14/M and RGAB/14-O for the form of a motion and order for the Special Admission of an out-of-state attorney.

(b) **Certification by out-of-state attorney.** The attorney whose special admission is moved shall certify in writing the number of times the attorney has been specially admitted during the twelve months immediately preceding the filing of the motion. The certification may be filed as a separate paper or may be included in the motion under an appropriate heading.

(c) **Order.** The court by order may admit specially or deny the special admission of an attorney. In either case, the clerk shall forward a copy of the order to the State Court Administrator, who shall maintain a docket of all attorneys granted or denied special admission. When the order grants or denies the special admission of an attorney in an action pending before an administrative agency, the clerk also shall forward a copy of the order to the agency.

(d) **Limitations on out-of-state attorney's practice.** An attorney specially admitted may act only as co-counsel for a party represented by an attorney of record in the action who is admitted to practice in this State. The specially admitted attorney may participate in the court or administrative proceedings only when accompanied by the Maryland attorney, unless the latter's presence is waived by the judge or administrative hearing officer presiding over the action. Any out-of-state attorney so admitted is subject to the Maryland Lawyers' Rules of Professional Conduct. (Amended March 5, 2001, effective July 1, 2001; effective November 6, 2002; Febuary 8, 2005, effective July 1, 2005; September 8, 2011, effective January 1, 2012..)

Cross references. — See Code, Business Occupations and Professions Article, § 10-215.
Committee note. — The Committee has not recommended a numerical limitation on the number of appearances pro hac vice to be allowed any attorney. Specialized expertise of out-of-state attorneys or other special circumstances may be important factors to be considered by judges in assessing whether Maryland litigants have access to effective representa-

tion. This Rule is not intended, however, to permit extensive or systematic practice by attorneys not licensed in Maryland. The Committee is concerned primarily with ensuring professional responsibility of attorneys in Maryland by avoiding circumvention of Rule 13 (Out-of-State Attorneys) or *Kemp Pontiac Cadillac, Inc. et al v. S & M Construction Co.,* *Inc.,* 33 Md. App. 516 (1976). The Committee also noted that payment to the Client Protection Fund of the Bar of Maryland by an attorney admitted specially for the purposes of an action is not required by existing statute or rule of court.

Source. — This Rule is derived from former Rule 20.

Effect of amendments. — The 2001 amendment, in (a), in the first sentence, substituted a comma for "or" following the second occurrence of "this State" and inserted "or representing a client in an arbitration taking place in this State involving the application of Maryland law" following "subdivisions," in the last sentence, inserted "or arbitration panel" following the first occurrence of "agency" and inserted "or in which the arbitration hearing is located" following "agency is located" and added the cross reference note.

The 2002 amendment, in the Committee note, substituted "concerned primarily with ensuring" for "primarily concerned with assuring" and substituted "Client Protection Fund" for "Clients' Security Trust Fund."

The 2005 amendment substituted "subject" for "subjected" and inserted "Lawyers'" before "Rules of Professional Conduct" in the last sentence in (d).

The 2011 amendment add the second sentence in the Cross reference note after (a).

Editor's note. — For forms for motion and order for special admission of out-of-state attorneys, see Forms RGAB 14/M and RGAB 14/O in Appendix: Forms following the Maryland Rules in this volume.

Petition for readmission. — Four principal criteria have to be evaluated in a petition for readmission to the Maryland bar: (1) the nature and circumstances of petitioner's original misconduct; (2) petitioner's subsequent conduct and reformation; (3) petitioner's present character; and (4) petitioner's present qualifications and competence to practice law. In re Keehan, 342 Md. 121, 674 A.2d 510 (1996).

Applied in Att'y Griev. Comm'n v. Ray, 343 Md. 254, 680 A.2d 1101 (1996).

Cited in Att'y Griev. Comm'n v. James, 340 Md. 318, 666 A.2d 1246 (1995); Turkey Point Property Owners' Ass'n v. Anderson, 106 Md. App. 710, 666 A.2d 904 (1995); Abrams v. Lamone, 398 Md. 146, 919 A.2d 1223 (2007).

Rule 15. Special authorization for out-of-state attorneys to practice in this state.

(a) **Eligibility.** Subject to the provisions of this Rule, a member of the Bar of another state who is employed by or associated with an organized legal services program that is sponsored or approved by Legal Aid Bureau, Inc. may practice in this State pursuant to that organized legal services program, if (1) the individual is a graduate of a law school meeting the requirements of Rule 4 (a) (2), (2) the legal services program provides legal assistance to indigents in this State, and (3) the individual will practice under the supervision of a member of the Bar of this State.

(b) **Proof of eligibility.** To obtain authorization to practice under this Rule the out-of-state attorney shall file with the Clerk of the Court of Appeals a written request accompanied by (1) evidence of graduation from a law school as defined in Rule 4 (a) (2), (2) a certificate of the highest court of another state certifying that the attorney is a member in good standing of the Bar of that state, and (3) a statement signed by the Executive Director of Legal Aid Bureau, Inc., that the attorney is currently employed by or associated with an approved organized legal services program.

(c) **Certificate of authorization to practice.** Upon the filing of the proof of eligibility required by this Rule, the Clerk of the Court of Appeals shall issue a certificate under the seal of the Court certifying that the attorney is authorized to practice under this Rule. The certificate shall contain the effective date and expiration date of the special authorization to practice. The expiration date shall be no later than two years after the effective date.

(d) **Automatic termination before expiration.** Authorization to practice under this Rule is automatically terminated before its expiration date if the attorney ceases to be employed by or associated with an approved organized legal services program in this State. Within five days after cessation of the attorney's employment or association, the Executive Director of Legal Aid Bureau, Inc. shall file with the Clerk of the Court of Appeals notice of the termination of authorization.

(e) **Revocation or suspension.** At any time, the Court, in its discretion, may revoke or suspend authorization to practice under this Rule either by written notice to the attorney or by amendment or deletion of this Rule.

(f) **Special authorization not admission.** Out-of-state attorneys authorized to practice under this Rule are not, and shall not represent themselves to be, members of the Bar of this State, except in connection with practice that is authorized under this Rule. They shall be required to make payments to the Client Protection Fund of the Bar of Maryland and the Disciplinary Fund. (Amended effective Nov. 6, 2002.)

Source. — This Rule is derived from former Rule 19.

Effect of amendments. — The 2002 amendment substituted "Client Protection Fund of the Bar of Maryland" for "Clients' Security Trust Fund" in (f).

Cited in Abrams v. Lamone, 398 Md. 146, 919 A.2d 1223 (2007).

Rule 15.1. Authorization for attorneys displaced by Hurricane Katrina to practice from Maryland.
Expired.

Rule 16. Legal assistance by law students.
(a) **Definitions.** As used in this Rule, the following terms have the following meanings:

(1) Law school. "Law school" means a law school meeting the requirements of Rule 4 (a) (2).

(2) Clinical program. "Clinical program" means a law school program for credit, in which a student obtains experience in the operation of the legal system by engaging in the practice of law, that is (A) under the direction of a faculty member of the school and (B) has been approved by the Section Council of the Section of Legal Education and Admissions to the Bar of the Maryland State Bar Association, Inc.

(3) Supervising attorney. "Supervising attorney" means an attorney who is a member in good standing of the Bar of this State and whose service as a supervising attorney for the clinical program is approved by the dean of the law school in which the law student is enrolled or by the dean's designee.

(b) **Eligibility.** A law student enrolled in a clinical program is eligible to engage in the practice of law as provided in this Rule if the student:

(1) is enrolled in a law school;

(2) has read and is familiar with the Maryland Lawyers' Rules of Professional Conduct and the relevant Maryland Rules of Procedure; and

(3) has been certified in accordance with section (c) of this Rule.

(c) **Certification.** (1) Contents and filing. The dean of the law school shall file the certification of a student with the Clerk of the Court of Appeals. It shall state that the student is in good academic standing and has successfully completed legal studies in the law school amounting to the equivalent of at least one-third of the total credit hours required to complete the law school program. It shall also state its effective date and expiration date, which shall be no later than one year after the effective date.

(2) Withdrawal or suspension. The dean may withdraw the certificate at any time by mailing a notice to that effect to the Clerk of the Court of Appeals. It shall automatically be suspended upon the issuance of an unfavorable report of the Character Committee made in connection with the student's application for registration as a candidate for admission to the Bar. Upon reversal of the Character Committee, the certification shall be reinstated.

(d) **Practice.** In connection with a clinical program, a law student for whom a certificate is in effect may appear in any trial court or the Court of Special Appeals or otherwise engage in the practice of law in Maryland provided that the supervising attorney (1) is satisfied that the student is competent to perform the duties assigned, (2) assumes responsibility for the quality of the student's work, (3) directs and assists the student to the extent necessary, in the supervising attorney's professional judgment, to ensure that the student's participation is effective on behalf of the client the student represents, and (4) accompanies the student when the student appears in court or before an administrative agency. The law student shall neither ask for nor receive personal compensation of any kind for service rendered under this Rule. (Amended Feb. 8, 2005, effective July 1, 2005.)

Source. — This Rule is derived from former Rule 18.

Effect of amendments. — The 2005 amendment inserted "Lawyers'" before "Rules of Professional Conduct" in (b)(2).

Maryland Law Review. — For article,

"Missed Manners in Courtroom Decorum," see 50 Md. L. Rev. 945 (1991).

Cited in Abrams v. Lamone, 398 Md. 146, 919 A.2d 1223 (2007).

Rule 17. Character committees.

The Court shall appoint a Character Committee for each of the seven Appellate Judicial Circuits of the State. Each Character Committee shall consist of not less than five members whose terms shall be five years each, except that in the Sixth Appellate Judicial Circuit the term of each member shall be two years. The terms shall be staggered. The Court shall designate the chair of each Committee, and may provide compensation to the members. (Amended June 6, 2000, effective July 1, 2000.)

Source. — This Rule is derived from former Rule 4 a and e.

Effect of amendments. — The 2000 amendment rewrote this Rule.

Cited in In re Hyland, 339 Md. 521, 663 A.2d 1309 (1995).

Rule 18. Fees.

The Board shall prescribe the fees, subject to approval by the Court, to be paid by applicants under Rules 2 and 7 and by petitioners under Rule 13.

Cross references. — See Code, Business Occupations and Professions Article, § 10-208 (b) for maximum examination fee allowed by law.

Source. — This Rule is new and replaces former Rules 2 e, 6, 8 a, and 14 c.

Rule 19. Confidentiality.

(a) **Proceedings before committee or board; general policy.** Except as provided in sections (b), (c), and (d) of this Rule, the proceedings before the Accommodations Review Committee and its panels, a Character Committee, and the Board and the related papers, evidence, and information are confidential and shall not be open to public inspection or subject to court process or compulsory disclosure.

(b) **Right of applicant.** (1) Except as provided in paragraph (2) of this section, an applicant has the right to attend all hearings before a panel of the Accommodations Review Committee, a Character Committee, and the Board pertaining to his or her application and to be informed of and inspect all papers, evidence, and information received or considered by the panel, Committee or the Board pertaining to the applicant.

(2) This section does not apply to (A) papers or evidence received or considered by a Character Committee of the Board if the Committee or Board, without a hearing, recommends the applicant's admission; (B) personal memoranda, notes, and work papers of members or staff of a Character Committee or the Board; (C) correspondence between or among members or staff of a Character Committee or the Board; or (D) an applicant's bar examination grades and answers, except as authorized in Rule 8 and Rule 13.

(c) **When disclosure authorized.** The Board may disclose:

(1) statistical information that does not reveal the identity of an individual applicant;

(2) the fact that an applicant has passed the bar examination and the date of the examination;

(3) any material pertaining to an applicant that the applicant would be entitled to inspect under section (b) of this Rule if the applicant has consented in writing to the disclosure;

(4) any material pertaining to an applicant requested by

(A) a court of this State, another state, or the United States;

(B) Bar Counsel, the Attorney Grievance Commission, or the attorney disciplinary authority in another state;

(C) the authority in another jurisdiction responsible for investigating the character and fitness of an applicant for admission to the bar of that jurisdiction, or

(D) Investigative Counsel, the Commission on Judicial Disabilities, or the judicial disciplinary authority in another jurisdiction for use in:

(i) a pending disciplinary proceeding against the applicant as an attorney or judge;

(ii) a pending proceeding for reinstatement of the applicant as an attorney after disbarment; or

(iii) a pending proceeding for original admission of the applicant to the Bar;

(5) any material pertaining to an applicant requested by a judicial nominating commission or the Governor of this State, a committee of the Senate of Maryland, or a committee of the United States Senate in connection with an application by or nomination of the applicant for judicial office;

(6) to a law school, the names of persons who graduated from that law school who took a bar examination and whether they passed or failed the examination;

(7) to the Maryland State Bar Association and to each entity selected to give the course on legal professionalism required by Rule 11, the name and address of a person recommended for bar admission pursuant to Rule 10;

(8) to the National Conference of Bar Examiners, the following information regarding persons who have filed applications for admission pursuant to Rule 2 or petitions to take the attorney's examination pursuant to Rule 13: the applicant's name and aliases, applicant number, birthdate, Law School Admission Council number, law school, date that a juris doctor degree was conferred, bar examination results and pass/fail status, and the number of bar examination attempts;

(9) to any member of a Character Committee, the report of any Character Committee or the Board following a hearing on an application; and

(10) to the Child Support Enforcement Administration, upon its request, the name, Social Security number, and address of a person who has filed an application pursuant to Rule 2 or a petition to take the attorney's examination pursuant to Rule 13.

Unless information disclosed pursuant to paragraphs (4) and (5) of this section is disclosed with the written consent of the applicant, an applicant shall receive a copy of the information and may rebut, in writing, any matter contained in it. Upon receipt of a written rebuttal, the Board shall forward a copy to the person or entity to whom the information was disclosed.

(d) **Proceedings and access to records in the court of appeals.**
(1) Subject to reasonable regulation by the Court of Appeals, Bar Admission ceremonies shall be open.

(2) Unless the Court otherwise orders in a particular case:

(A) hearings in the Court of Appeals shall be open, and

(B) if the Court conducts a hearing regarding a bar applicant, any report by the Accommodations Review Committee, a Character Committee, or the Board filed with the Court, but no other part of the applicant's record, shall be subject to public inspection.

(3) The Court of Appeals may make any of the disclosures that the Board may make pursuant to section (c) of this Rule.

(4) Except as provided in paragraphs (1), (2), and (3) of this section or as otherwise required by law, proceedings before the Court of Appeals and the related papers, evidence, and information are confidential and shall not be open to public inspection or subject to court process or compulsory disclosure. (Amended September 10, 2009, effective October 1, 2009; March 7, 2011, effective March 7, 2011.)

Source. — This Rule is new.

Effect of amendments. — The 2009 amendment rewrote the rule.

The 2011 amendment added (c)(7) and made minor, stylistic changes throughout (c).

Rule 20. The Board.

(a) **Authority to adopt rules.** The Board may adopt rules to carry out the requirements of these Rules and to facilitate the conduct of examinations. The Rules of the Board shall be published in the Code, Maryland Rules, following these Rules.

(b) **Amendment of Board rules — Publication.** Any amendment of the Board's rules shall be published at least once in a daily newspaper of general circulation in this State. The amendment shall be published at least 45 days before the examination at which it is to become effective, except that an amendment that substantially increases the area of subject-matter knowledge required for any examination shall be published at least one year before the examination.

(c) **Assistants.** The Board may appoint the assistants necessary for the proper conduct of its business. Each assistant shall be an attorney admitted by the Court of Appeals and shall serve at the pleasure of the Board.

(d) **Compensation of Board members and assistants.** The members of the Board and assistants shall receive the compensation fixed from time to time by the Court.

(e) **Secretary to the Board.** The Court may appoint a secretary to the Board, to hold office during the pleasure of the Court. The secretary shall have the administrative powers and duties that the Board may prescribe.

Source. — This Rule is derived as follows:
Section (a) is derived from former Rule 7 h and 9 a.
Section (b) is derived from former Rule 7 h and i.

Section (c) is derived from former Rule 9 c.
Section (d) is derived from former Rule 16.
Section (e) is derived from former Rule 17.

Rule 21. Suspension or revocation of license of attorney ineligible for admission.

If an attorney admitted to the Bar of this State is discovered to have been ineligible for admission under circumstances that do not warrant disbarment or other disciplinary proceedings, the Court of Appeals may, upon a recommendation by the Board and after notice and opportunity to be heard, suspend or revoke the attorney's license. In the case of a suspension the Court shall specify in its order the duration of the suspension and the conditions upon which the suspension may be lifted.

Source. — This Rule is new.

License revoked for failing to disclose material fact of disbarment. — Attorney's Maryland license was revoked where he applied to take the examination and passed it while disciplinary proceedings against him were on appeal in another state, but was disbarred in the other state before being admitted in Maryland. There was a failure at the time of admission of one of the essential requirements for admission, membership in the bar of a state, and there was a failure to disclose the material fact of the disbarment. In re Thompson, 363 Md. 469, 769 A.2d 905 (2001).

Rule 22. Subpoena power of board and character committees.

(a) **Subpoena.** In any proceeding before the Board or a Character Committee pursuant to Bar Admission Rule 5 or Bar Admission Rule 13, the Board or Committee, on its own motion or the motion of an applicant, may cause a subpoena to be issued by a clerk pursuant to Rule 2-510. The subpoena shall issue from the Circuit Court for Anne Arundel County if incident to Board proceedings or from the circuit court in the county in which Character Committee proceedings are pending, and the proceedings may not be docketed in court. The subpoena shall not divulge the name of the applicant, except to the extent this requirement is impracticable. The sheriff's return shall be made as directed in the subpoena. The Character Committee or the Board, as applicable, shall maintain dockets and files of all papers filed in the proceedings.

(b) **Sanctions.** If a person is subpoenaed to appear and give testimony or to produce books, documents, or other tangible things and fails to do so, the party who requested the subpoena, by motion that does not divulge the name of the applicant (except to the extent that this requirement is impracticable), may request the court to issue an attachment pursuant to Rule 2-510(j), or to cite the person for contempt pursuant to Title 15, Chapter 200 of the Maryland Rules, or both.

(c) **Court rules.** All court costs in proceedings under this Rule shall be assessable to and paid by the State. (Added June 7, 1994, effective Oct. 1, 1994; amended June 5, 1996, effective Jan. 1, 1997.)

Source. — This Rule is new.

Effect of amendments. — The 1996 amendment substituted "Title 15, Chapter 200" for "Subtitle P, Chapter 1100" in (b).

The December 4, 2007 Order, effective June 1, 2008, in (b) substituted "Rule 2-510(j)" for "Rule 2-510(h)".

RULES OF THE BOARD.

The State Board of Law Examiners of Maryland adopted revised **Board Rules 1 and 3** *on December 9, 2008.*

The "Notice of Amendments to Rules of the Board, Rules Governing Admission to the Bar of Maryland" related to Rule changes adopted November 11, 2005, provides that "On November 11, 2005, the State Board of Law Examiners adopted a new **Board Rule 3. Test Accommodations Pursuant to the Americans with Disabilities Act** and amended **Board Rule 4. Examination Format, Scoring, and Passing Standard.** Former **Board Rules 3, 4, and 5** were renumbered as **Board Rules 4, 5, and 6.** These amendments to the Board Rules are adopted pursuant to Rule 20 of the Rules Governing Admission to the Bar of Maryland adopted by the Court of Appeals of Maryland on June 28, 1990."

Pursuant to Rule 20 of the Court of Appeals' Rules Governing Admission to the Bar of Maryland, the State Board of Law Examiners adopted the following Rules of the Board on October 8, 1990 to be effective immediately and superseding all previous Rules of the Board:

Board Rule 1. Application fees.

a. **General Bar examination.** 1. An Application filed pursuant to the Court's Bar Admission Rule 2 shall be accompanied by a check or money order payable to the State Board of Law Examiners in the amount of:

(i) $225 if timely filed, or

(ii) $275 if filed late.

2. A petition to take a scheduled bar examination pursuant to the Court's Bar Admission Rule 6 shall be accompanied by a check or money order in the amount of $250.

b. **Out-of-state attorney examination.** 1. A petition filed pursuant to the Court's Bar Admission Rule 13 shall be accompanied by a check or money order payable to the State Board of Law Examiners in the amount of $700 and a separate check, money order, or credit card authorization for the National Conference of Bar Examiners in such amount as required to cover the cost of the character and fitness investigation and report.

2. A petition for re-examination filed pursuant to the Court's Bar Admission Rule 13 shall be accompanied by a check or money order payable to the State Board of Law Examiners in the amount of $250.

c. **Effective date.** The fees prescribed in sections a. and b. of this rule apply to all applications and petitions filed on or after January 1, 2009. "Filed" means received in the office of the Secretary of the Board during normal business hours. (Amended December 8, 2008, effective December 8, 2008.)

Effect of amendments. — The 2008 amendment increased fees throughout the Rule and changed the applicability date.

Board Rule 2. Filing late for good cause.

An applicant's written request for acceptance of an application or petition filed late for good cause pursuant to the Court's Bar Admission Rule 2 c (3), Rule 6 or Rule 13 h shall include a statement indicating:

(a) whether the applicant's failure to timely file was due to facts and circumstances beyond the applicant's control and stating those facts and circumstances,

(b) whether the applicant presently has a bar application pending with any other jurisdiction,

(c) whether the applicant presently is a member of the Bar of any other jurisdiction, and

(d) the specific nature of the hardship which would result if the applicant's request is denied.

Board Rule 3. Test accommodations pursuant to the Americans with Disabilities Act.

a. **Definition.** In this Rule, "applicant" includes a petitioner under Bar Admission Rule 13 who seeks test accommodations under the ADA for the attorney examination.

b. **Policy.** In accordance with the ADA, the Board shall provide test accommodations to an applicant taking the Maryland bar examination, to the extent that such accommodations are reasonable, consistent with the nature and purpose of the examination and necessitated by the applicant's disability.

c. **Requesting test accommodations.** An individual must be an applicant for admission to the Bar of Maryland prior to requesting test accommodations. In order to request test accommodations an applicant must file a completed Applicant's Accommodations Request Form along with the specified supporting documentation. The Applicant's Accommodations Request Form must be filed not later than the deadline for filing the petition to sit for the bar examination pursuant to Bar Admission 6, 9, or 13.

d. **Review by board.** 1. Initial review for sufficiency. The Board's staff shall conduct an initial review of a request for test accommodations. The Board's staff shall reject a request if the request fails to adequately specify the test accommodations required or if the supporting documentation is substantially incomplete or is otherwise deficient. If the request is rejected, the Board's staff shall advise the applicant in writing of the deficiencies in the request and supporting documents.

2. Board determination. If there is uncertainty about whether the requested test accommodation is warranted pursuant to the ADA, the applicant's request and all supporting documentation may be referred to a qualified expert retained by the Board to review and analyze whether the applicant has documented a disability and requested a reasonable accommodation. Thereafter, a designated member of the Board shall determine whether test accommodations should be granted after examining the applicant's request and the report of the Board's expert. The Board's staff shall advise the applicant in writing whether the request for test accommodations is granted or denied in whole or in part.

e. **Appeal to the Accommodations Review Committee.** If the board denies a request for test accommodations in whole or in part, the applicant may file an appeal with the Accommodations Review Committee pursuant to Bar Admission Rule 6.1 (Adopted November 11, 2005, effective November 11, 2005; amended December 8, 2008, effective December 8, 2008.)

Effect of amendments. — The 2008 amendment rewrote the Rule.

Board Rule 4. Examination — Subject matter.

Pursuant to section c of Rule 7 (Bar Examination), Rules Governing Admission to the Bar of Maryland, the subject matter of the Maryland Bar Examination is defined as follows:

AGENCY

The law of agency will be included on the examination only to the extent provided in the definitions of Business Associations, Contracts and Torts.

BUSINESS ASSOCIATIONS

The legal principles pertaining to forming, organizing, operating and dissolving business entities in Maryland and related principles of agency. The business entities include: (a) corporations, (b) close corporations, (c) limited liability companies, (d) professional service corporations, (e) general, limited, and limited liability partnerships, (f) joint ventures, (g) unincorporated associations, and (h) sole proprietorships. The subject also includes: (a) the rights, powers, duties and liabilities of owners, partners, member, shareholders, managers, directors, officers, (b) the issuance of shares or other ownership interests in business entities, (c) the distribution of dividends and assets, and (d) the allocation of profits and losses from business entities. (Amended February 25, 1998)

COMMERCIAL TRANSACTIONS

The law governing commercial transactions including negotiable instruments, sales and sales financing, secured transactions, rights and remedies of buyers and sellers with emphasis on the Uniform Commercial Code as the prevailing commercial legislation.

CONSTITUTIONAL LAW

The interpretation of the Constitution of the United States and its amendments, division of powers between the states and national government, powers of the President, the Congress, and the Supreme Court, limitations on the powers of the state and national government.

CONTRACTS

The consideration of agreements enforceable at law. The subject includes: (a) formation of contracts — offer and acceptance, mistake, fraud, misrepresentation or duress, contractual capacity, effect of illegality, consideration; informal contracts; (b) third-party beneficiary contracts; (c) assignment of contracts; (d) statute of frauds; (e) parol evidence rule, interpretation of contracts; (f) performance-conditions, failure of consideration, aleatory promises, rights of defaulting plaintiff, substantial performance, specific performance, (g) breach of contract and remedies therefor, including measure of damages; (h) impossibility of performance, frustration of purpose; and (i) discharge of contracts. This subject may also include law dealing with an agent's ability to bind a principal to a contract, and the agent's personal liability on a contract made for a principal.

CRIMINAL LAW AND PROCEDURE

The law of crimes against the person; crimes against public peace and morals; property crimes; crimes involving the breach of public trust or civic duty, obstruction of justice; criminal responsibility, causation, justification and other defenses; constitutional limitations and protections.

EVIDENCE

The law governing the proof of issues of fact in civil and criminal trials including functions of the court and jury; competence of witnesses; examination, cross-examination and impeachment of witnesses; presumptions, burden of producing evidence and burden of persuasion; privileges against disclosure of information; relevancy; demonstrative, experimental and scientific evidence; opinion evidence; admissibility of writings; parol evidence rule; hearsay rule; judicial notice. The Board's Test will cover only the Maryland substantive Law of Evidence, including the *Maryland Rules of Evidence,* common law and statute. (Amended November 11, 2004.)

FAMILY LAW

The principles of Maryland law regarding creation of (or the existence of) the marriage relationship; termination of the marriage; alimony and support of the marriage partner; support and custody of children; marital property issues; and prenuptial agreements. Includes both statutory and common law principles of Maryland law and procedure except for matters of adoption, paternity, and juvenile law. (Adopted April 8, 1992, effective beginning with the July 1993 bar examination.)

MARYLAND CIVIL PROCEDURE

The various procedural steps and matters involved in an action at law or in equity, from commencement of the action to final disposition on appeal. The subject includes: (a) jurisdiction of courts; (b) venue; (c) parties and process; (d) forms of pleadings; (e) motions and other means of raising procedural objections and defenses, including affirmative defenses and counter-claims; (f) discovery and other pre-trial procedures; (g) trial practice; (h) entry, effect and enforcement of judgments; (i) methods of taking appeal or otherwise securing appellate review; and (j) appellate practice and procedure. The subject embraces civil procedure and practice in the State courts. Federal Rules of practice and procedure are not covered on the examination. (Amended Nov. 11, 2004, effective Nov. 11, 2004.)

PROFESSIONAL CONDUCT

The Maryland Lawyers' Rules of Professional Conduct as adopted by Maryland Rule 16-812. These are contained in the *Maryland Rules,* Appendix. (Amended Nov. 11, 2004, effective Nov. 11, 2004; and April 15, 2005; effective April 15, 2005.)

PROPERTY

The fundamentals of real property law including concepts of possession; concurrent and consecutive future estates in land (and their counterparts in testamentary and *inter vivos* trusts); leaseholds and landlord-tenant relationships; fixtures and the distinction between real and personal property; covenants enforceable in equity; easements, profits and licenses; rights of user and exploitation in land (including rights to lateral and subjacent support); contracts of sale of real estate; the statute of limitations on real actions (adverse possession) and prescription; conveyancing priorities and recording (including marketable title); remedies. Problems of rules against perpetuities will appear only on the MBE test (Board Rule 4).

TORTS

The law of civil wrongs. The subject includes, but is not limited to: (a) negligent torts including causation, standard of care, primary negligence, comparative and contributory negligence, assumption of risk, limitations on liability, contribution and indemnity; impact of insurance; (b) intentional torts; (c) strict liability, products liability; (d) nuisance; (e) invasion of privacy; (f) defamation; (g) vicarious liability; and (h) defenses, immunity and privilege, and damages in connection with any of these areas. (Amended Nov. 11, 2005, effective Nov. 11, 2005.)

Effect of amendments. — The 1992 amendment, effective beginning with the July 1993 bar examination, adds Family Law to the list of essay examination subjects.

The 1998 amendment rewrote the paragraph conncering business associations.

The 2004 amendment, in the paragraph concerning Maryland civil procedure, substituted "of pleadings" for "of pleading" in (d) and "and defenses" for "or defenses" in (e); and in the paragraph concerning professional conduct, substituted "the *Maryland Rules*" for "*Maryland Rules* Volume 2."

The 2005 amendment, adopted November 11, 2005 and effective immediately, added new Rule 3 and redesignated the following rules accordingly.

Editor's note. — Concerning the Nov. 11, 2004 amendment, the board notes: "The amendment to Board Rule 3 recognizes explicitly that certain Maryland Rules of Evidence are codified as Title 5. Evidence in the *Maryland Rules,* Annotated Code of Maryland. This revision does not change the scope of the Maryland Bar examination; it states explicitly the location of certain statutory evidence rules. This change is effective immediately."

Not preempted. — Fact that 28 U.S.C.S. § 1331 permits state courts to hear Americans with Disabilities Act (ADA), 42 U.S.C.S. § 12101 et seq., claims does not preempt the state high court's exclusive jurisdiction over bar admission andits procedures under Md. Bd. R. 3 (now 4) for applicants seeking ADA accommodations; the ADA does not mandate specific state court procedures. In re Kimmer, 392 Md. 251, 896 A.2d 1006 (2006).

Board Rule 5. Examination format, scoring and passing standard.

a. **Authority.** Pursuant to section (c) of Rule 7, Bar Examination, of the *Rules Governing Admission to the Bar of Maryland adopted by the Court of Appeals of Maryland,* the State Board of Law Examiners adopts the Multistate Bar Examination and the Multistate Performance Test as part of the Maryland Bar Examination. Pursuant to section (d) of the Court's Bar Admission Rule 7, the Board establishes the policies and standards set forth in the following sections of this Board Rule to govern the format, scoring, and passing standard for the Maryland Bar Examination.

b. **Multistate Bar Examination (MBE).** (i) One part of the Maryland Bar Examination is the Multistate Bar Examination (MBE). The MBE is published and scored by the National Conference of Bar Examiners (NCBE) and its agents.

(ii) The MBE is a multiple choice test. An applicant's MBE raw score is the number of questions answered correctly. MBE raw scores are scaled to adjust for possible differences in average question difficulty across administrations of the exam. As a result of scaling, a given MBE scale score indicates about the same level of performance regardless of the particular administration of the examination on which it is earned.

c. **Written Test: Board's essay test and the Multistate Performance Test (MPT).** (i) The other part of the Maryland Bar Examination is the Written Test, which comprises the Board's Essay Test and one MPT question. The Board will prepare and grade the Board's Essay test. The MPT is published by the NCBE and graded by the Board.

(ii) The Board's Essay test will consist entirely of questions requiring essay answers. Questions will not be labeled by subject matter. Single questions may involve two or more subject matters from the list in Board Rule 4.

(iii) The format and specifications for the MPT are determined by the NCBE.

(iv) The raw score for the Written Test will be calculated as follows:
Written Test raw score = Sum of Board's Essay test raw scores + (MPT raw score x 2)

(v) The Written Test raw score will be converted to the same scale of measurement as that used on the MBE to adjust for possible differences in average question difficulty across administrations of the examination.

d. **Combining MBE and Written Test scores to calculate total examination score.** (i) For purposes of calculating an applicant's total scale score, both the MBE and Written scale scores will be rounded to the nearest whole number.

(ii) The Written Test shall be weighted twice as much as the MBE in the computation of the total scale score. The following formula will be used to compute an applicant's total scale score on the Maryland Bar Examination:
Total Test Scale Score = (Written Scale Score x 2) + MBE Scale Score

e. **Passing standard.** In order to pass the Maryland Bar Examination, an applicant must achieve a total scale score, as defined in section d(ii), of 406 or higher.

f. **No carryover of MBE score or written score from prior examinations.** An applicant must achieve both the MBE and Written Test scale scores on the same administration of the Bar Examination for purposes of the Board's calculation of the total scale score and determination of the applicant's pass/fail status.

g. **Recognition of MBE score achieved concurrently in another jurisdiction.** The Board will accept an MBE score which an applicant achieves in another jurisdiction in an administration of the MBE which is concurrent with Maryland's administration of the Written Test to the applicant. The concurrent MBE score will be treated exactly as though it were achieved in Maryland for purposes of the Board's calculation of the total scale score and determination of the applicant's pass/fail status.

h. **Adjustment of passing standard.** For any particular examination, the Board may, in the interest of justice, lower (but not raise) the passing score standard at any time before notices of the examination results are mailed. (Amended January 22, 2000; Nov. 11, 2005, effective Nov. 11, 2005, and Jan. 1, 2007.)

Effect of amendments. — The 2000 amendment deleted the former last sentences of b (ii) and c (ii), which read: "The maximum possible MBE scale score is 200." and "The maximum possible Essay scale score is 200." respectively.

The 2005 amendment, adopted November 11, 2005 and effective immediately, added new Rule 3 and redesignated the following rules accordingly.

The 2005 amendment, adopted November 11, 2005 and applicable to bar examinations beginning with examinations administered after January 1, 2007, in a. added "and the Multistate Performance Test"; in c. added "Written Test" and "and the Multistate Performance Test (MPT)" to the heading; in c(i) substituted "Written Test, which comprises the Board's Essay Test and one MPT question" for "Board's Essay Test", rewrote the second sentence and added the third sentence; in c(ii) substituted "Rule 4" for "Rule 3" and deleted the former second sentence concerning conversion and balancing of raw scores; added c(iii) — (v); and in d, f, and g substituted "Written Test" for "Essay Test"; and updated the historical citation at the end.

Editor's note. — The "Notice of Amendments to Rules of the Board, Rules Governing Admission to the Bar of Maryland" related to Rules changes adopted November 11, 2005, provides that "Former Board Rule 4, renumbered Board Rule 5, revises the format and scoring provisions for the bar examination to provide for the incorporation of the Multistate Performance Test as a component of the bar examination beginning with examinations administered after January 1, 2007."

Board Rule 6. Out-of-state attorney examination.

a. **Subject matter.** The out-of-state attorney examination will be prepared and graded by the Board and will consist entirely of questions requiring essay answers. It will relate to:

(i) Maryland Rules of Procedure governing practice and procedure in civil cases and criminal causes in all the Courts of the State of Maryland, including the Appendix of forms (*Maryland Rules*),

(ii) the Maryland Lawyers' Rules of Professional Conduct, as adopted by Maryland Rule 16-812 (*Maryland Rules*),

(iii) the provisions of the *Courts and Judicial Proceedings Article* of the Annotated Code of Maryland, and

(iv) the provisions of the *Criminal Procedure Article* of the Annotated Code of Maryland.

b. **Time — Duration.** The attorney examination shall be conducted during a part of the essay day of each regularly scheduled bar examination and will have a total of three hours writing time for the entire test. The point score allotted for each question will be noted on the examination sheet.

c. **Requirement for passing.** In order to pass the examination, a petitioner shall attain a score of at least 70% of the total point score allotted to the entire test. (Amended effective Dec. 14, 1994; Nov. 11, 2004, effective Nov. 11, 2004; Nov. 11, 2005, effective Nov. 11, 2005.)

Effect of amendments. — The 1994 amendment rewrote a.

The 2004 amendment, in a.(1), substituted "civil cases and criminal causes" for "civil and criminal cases" and deleted "Volumes 1 and 2" in the parentheses; in a.(ii), deleted "Volume 2" in the parentheses.

The 2005 amendment, adopted November 11, 2005 and effective immediately, added new Rule 3 and redesignated the following rules accordingly.

Editor's note. — The 2004 amendment adds a.(iv), which says, "the provisions of the Criminal Procedure Article of the Annotated Code of Maryland," which is effective for examinations administered after Jan. 1, 2006.

The "Notice of Amendments to Rules of the Board, Rules Governing Admission to the Bar of Maryland" related to Rules changes adopted November 11, 2005, provides that "Subsection a. (iv) is effective for examinations administered after January 1, 2006."

Index to Rules Governing Admission to the Bar of Maryland

INDEX

INTERNAL OPERATING RULES OF THE COURT OF APPEALS OF MARYLAND

I. PREAMBLE.

A recent amendment to the Open Meetings Act, State Government Article, Section 10-507 (b), provides: "[a] public body shall adopt and enforce reasonable rules regarding the conduct of persons attending its meetings and the videotaping, televising, photographing, broadcasting, or recording of its meetings." In accordance with this provision, the following rules have been adopted by the Court of Appeals of Maryland effective January 1, 1992.

II. CONDUCT OF PROCEEDINGS.

Rule 1. Open meeting.

The Court shall conduct all proceedings involving the exercise of its authority under Md. Constitution, Art. IV, Section 18 (a) to adopt or modify Rules of Practice and Procedure at a meeting open to the public. The meeting may be in the Courtroom, in the Court's conference room, or at any other suitable place designated by the Court. Advance notice of the meeting shall be given in the manner designated by the Court.

Rule 2. Opportunity for comment.

(a) **Written comment.** If the proposed changes have been included in a Report from the Court's Standing Committee on Rules of Practice and Procedure that has been published in the Md. Register, written comments may be filed within the time and in the manner specified in the Notice published in the Md. Register. If the proposed changes have not been published in the Md. Register, written comments may be filed within the time and in the manner specified by the Court. Comments not filed in accordance with this section will ordinarily not be considered by the Court.

(b) **Oral comment.** (1) The Court may conduct a public hearing with respect to proposed changes in the Md. Rules. Persons desiring to be heard must notify the Clerk of Court at least two days before the hearing of their desire to be heard and of the amount of time needed to address the Court. The Court may prescribe a shorter period for oral presentation and may pose questions to the person addressing the Court.

(2) If the Court does not conduct a public hearing, persons attending the open meeting may not address the Court unless requested by the Court.

Rule 3. Record of proceedings.

The Clerk of the Court of Appeals shall serve as recording secretary at all public hearings and open meetings. The Clerk shall monitor an audio recording of the proceedings which the Clerk shall retain as a permanent record and make available upon request. Tape recording or videotaping by persons in attendance is prohibited.

Rule 4. Doors.

In order to furnish the public easy access to rules proceedings, doors to the court or conference room shall remain open at all times during all public hearings and open meetings.

Rule 5. Personal conduct.

Persons attending rules proceedings are prohibited from smoking, eating, or drinking during the proceedings. Anyone who violates this rule may be removed from the vicinity.

Rule 6. Disruptive behavior.

If the Chief Judge determines that the behavior of a person is disrupting a rules proceeding, the Chief Judge may have the person removed.

III. EXTENDED COVERAGE.

Rule 7. Nature and extent.

Extended coverage, as defined in Maryland Rule 16-109a1, shall be permitted during rules proceedings unless prohibited or limited in accordance with these rules.

Rule 8. Coverage at public hearing.

Ordinarily, extended coverage will be permitted at a public hearing provided a request for coverage is made to the Clerk of Court at least five days before the proceeding to be covered. For good cause shown the Court may honor a request which does not comply with the requirements of this subsection.

Rule 9. Coverage at open meeting.

Absent exceptional circumstances, extended coverage shall not be permitted during open meetings. If coverage is sought, a request must be made in writing at least five days before the meeting and shall set forth the exceptional circumstances warranting extended coverage. A decision by the Court denying coverage is not intended to restrict the right of the media to report the proceedings.

Rule 10. Standards of conduct and technology.

Anyone who is permitted to conduct extended coverage of a rules proceeding must adhere to the standards of conduct and technology set forth in Maryland Rule 16-109 f.

Index to Internal Operating Rules of the Court of Appeals of Maryland

---

FEDERAL RULES OF APPELLATE PROCEDURE FOR UNITED STATES COURTS OF APPEALS; LOCAL RULES AND INTERNAL OPERATING PROCEDURES OF THE FOURTH CIRCUIT

TITLE I. APPLICABILITY OF RULES.

Rule 1. Scope of rules; Title.

(a) **Scope of rules.** (1) These rules govern procedure in the United States courts of appeals.

(2) When these rules provide for filing a motion or other document in the district court, the procedure must comply with the practice of the district court.

(b) [Abrogated].

(c) **Title.** These rules are to be known as the Federal Rules of Appellate Procedure. (Amended by order adopted April 30, 1979, effective August 1, 1979; by order adopted April 25, 1989, corrected May 1, 1989, effective December 1, 1989; by order adopted April 29, 1994, effective December 1, 1994; by order adopted April 24, 1998, effective December 1, 1998; and by order adopted April 29, 2002, effective December 1, 2002.)

Editor's note. — Subdivision (c) of this rule was formerly codified as FRAP 48.

This rule is set out herein with proposed amendments submitted to Congress by the Supreme Court on April 29, 2002. In the absence of Congressional action to the contrary, the rule, as amended, becomes effective on December 1, 2002.

Rule 2. Suspension of rules.

On its own or a party's motion, a court of appeals may — to expedite its decision or for other good cause — suspend any provision of these rules in a particular case and order proceedings as it directs, except as otherwise provided in Rule 26(b). (Amended by order adopted April 24, 1998, effective December 1, 1998.)

TITLE II. APPEALS FROM JUDGMENTS AND ORDERS OF DISTRICT COURTS.

Rule 3. Appeal as of right — How taken.

(a) **Filing the notice of appeal.** (1) An appeal permitted by law as of right from a district court to a court of appeals may be taken only by filing a notice of appeal with the district clerk within the time allowed by Rule 4. At the time of filing, the appellant must furnish the clerk with enough copies of the notice to enable the clerk to comply with Rule 3(d).

(2) An appellant's failure to take any step other than the timely filing of a notice of appeal does not affect the validity of the appeal, but is ground only for the court of appeals to act as it considers appropriate, including dismissing the appeal.

(3) An appeal from a judgment by a magistrate judge in a civil case is taken in the same way as an appeal from any other district court judgment.

(4) An appeal by permission under 28 U.S.C. § 1292(b) or an appeal in a bankruptcy case may be taken only in the manner prescribed by Rules 5 and 6, respectively.

(b) **Joint or consolidated appeals.** (1) When two or more parties are entitled to appeal from a district-court judgment or order, and their interests make joinder practicable, they may file a joint notice of appeal. They may then proceed on appeal as a single appellant.

(2) When the parties have filed separate timely notices of appeal, the appeals may be joined or consolidated by the court of appeals.

(c) **Content of the notice of appeal.** (1) The notice of appeal must:

(A) specify the party or parties taking the appeal by naming each one in the caption or body of the notice, but an attorney representing more than one party may describe those parties with such terms as "all plaintiffs," "the defendants," "the plaintiffs A, B, et al.," or "all defendants except X";

(B) designate the judgment, order, or part thereof being appealed; and

(C) name the court to which the appeal is taken.

(2) A pro se notice of appeal is considered filed on behalf of the signer and the signer's spouse and minor children (if they are parties), unless the notice clearly indicates otherwise.

(3) In a class action, whether or not the class has been certified, the notice of appeal is sufficient if it names one person qualified to bring the appeal as representative of the class.

(4) An appeal must not be dismissed for informality of form or title of the notice of appeal, or for failure to name a party whose intent to appeal is otherwise clear from the notice.

(5) Form 1 in the Appendix of Forms is a suggested form of a notice of appeal.

(d) **Serving the notice of appeal.** (1) The district clerk must serve notice of the filing of a notice of appeal by mailing a copy to each party's counsel of record — excluding the appellant's — or, if a party is proceeding pro se, to the party's last known address. When a defendant in a criminal case appeals, the clerk must also serve a copy of the notice of appeal on the defendant, either by personal service or by mail addressed to the defendant. The clerk must promptly send a copy of the notice of appeal and of the docket entries — and any later docket entries — to the clerk of the court of appeals named in the notice. The district clerk must note, on each copy, the date when the notice of appeal was filed.

(2) If an inmate confined in an institution files a notice of appeal in the manner provided by Rule 4(c), the district clerk must also note the date when the clerk docketed the notice.

(3) The district clerk's failure to serve notice does not affect the validity of the appeal. The clerk must note on the docket the names of the parties to whom the clerk mails copies, with the date of mailing. Service is sufficient despite the death of a party or the party's counsel.

(e) **Payment of fees.** Upon filing a notice of appeal, the appellant must pay the district clerk all required fees. The district clerk receives the appellate docket fee on behalf of the court of appeals. (Amended by order adopted April 30, 1979, effective August 1, 1979; by order adopted March 10, 1986, effective July 1, 1986; by order adopted April 25, 1989, effective December 1,1989; by order adopted April 22, 1993, effective December 1, 1993; by order adopted April 29, 1994, effective December 1, 1994; and by order adopted April 24, 1998, effective December 1, 1998.)

Local Rule 3(a). Filing and docket fees.

Upon filing a notice of appeal appellant shall pay the clerk of the district court a fee of $455, which includes a $5 filing fee for the notice of appeal, and a $450 fee for docketing the appeal in this Court. (Amended October 9, 2003, effective November 1, 2003 and April 27, 2006, effective April 9, 2006.)

Effect of amendments. — The 2003 amendment subsituted "$255" for "105.00," "$5" for "$5.00" and "$250" for "100." The 2006 amendment substituted "$455" for "$255" and substituted "$450" for "$250."

Local Rule 3(b). Docketing statement.

To assist counsel in giving prompt attention to the substance of an appeal, to help reduce the ordering of unnecessary transcripts, to provide the Clerk of the Court of Appeals at the commencement of an appeal with the information needed for effective case management, and to provide necessary information for any mediation conference conducted under Local Rule 33, counsel filing a notice of appeal, petition for review, or application for enforcement for any direct or cross-appeal must complete a docketing statement (form available at www.ca4.uscourts.gov) and file it with the Clerk of the Court of Appeals within 14 days of docketing of the appeal. A copy of the docketing statement must be served on the opposing party or parties.

The docketing statement shall have attached to it any transcript order.

Although a party will not be precluded from raising additional issues, counsel will should every effort to include in the docketing statement all of the issues that will be presented to the Court. Failure to file the docketing statement within the time set forth above will cause the Court to initiate the process for dismissing a case under Local Rule 45.

If an opposing party concludes that the docketing statement is in any way inaccurate, incomplete, or misleading, the Clerk's Office should be informed in writing of any errors and any proposed additions or corrections within 10 days of service of the docketing statement, with copies to all other parties. (Amended by order effective September 28, 1994; by order effective December 1, 1995; by order effective March 12, 1998; by order effective April 1, 2008; and amended effective December 1, 2009.)

COMMENT

Proposed Local Rule 3(b) changes the "each party" requirement of existing I.O.P. 3.2 to "counsel" to reflect this Court's practice of not requiring docketing statements from parties proceedings pro se.

Effect of amendments. — The 2008 amendment substituted "The orginial docketing statement" for "Two copies of the docketing statment", added "petition for review, or application for enforcement, with copies", and deleted "party or" before "parties", and made minor, stylistic changes in the first sentence of the second paragraph, rewrote the third paragraph, and substituted "should" for "will" in the first sentence of the fourth paragraph.

The 2009 amendment in the first paragraph added "petition for review, or application for enforcement", deleted "must complete and file a docketing statement, using the form provided by the clerk of the district court" following "cross-appeal", and deleted the former second sentence; incorporated the second paragraph into the first paragraph and rewrote that portion of the text; and in the last paragraph substituted "10 days" for "7 days".

Rule 3.1. Appeal from a judgment of a magistrate judge in a civil case.
[Abrogated by order adopted April 24, 1998, effective December 1, 1998.]

Editor's note. — Rule 3.1, which was adopted effective July 1, 1986; and amended by order adopted April 22, 1993, effective December 1, 1993, was abrogated by order adopted April 24, 1998, effective December 1, 1998.

I.O.P. 3.1. Transmission of district court order.
The clerk of the district court shall transmit to the Clerk of the Court of Appeals a copy of the order appealed from, along with copies of the materials required by FRAP 3(d)(1). (Amended effective December 1, 1998.)

Rule 4. Appeal as of right — When taken.
(a) **Appeal in a civil case.** (1) Time for filing a notice of appeal. (A) In a civil case, except as provided in Rules 4(a)(1)(B), 4(a)(4), and 4(c), the notice of appeal required by Rule 3 must be filed with the district clerk within 30 days after the judgment or order appealed from is entered.

(B) When the United States or its officer or agency is a party, the notice of appeal may be filed by any party within 60 days after the judgment or order appealed from is entered.

(C) (C) An appeal from an order granting or denying an application for a writ of error *coram nobis* is an appeal in a civil case for purposes of Rule 4(a).

(2) Filing before entry of judgment. A notice of appeal filed after the court announces a decision or order — but before the entry of the judgment or order — is treated as filed on the date of and after the entry.

(3) Multiple appeals. If one party timely files a notice of appeal, any other party may file a notice of appeal within 14 days after the date when the first notice was filed, or within the time otherwise prescribed by this Rule 4(a), whichever period ends later.

(4) Effect of a motion on a notice of appeal. (A) If a party timely files in the district court any of the following motions under the Federal Rules of Civil Procedure, the time to file an appeal runs for all parties from the entry of the order disposing of the last such remaining motion:

(i) for judgment under Rule 50(b);

(ii) to amend or make additional factual findings under Rule 52(b), whether or not granting the motion would alter the judgment;

(iii) for attorney's fees under Rule 54 if the district court extends the time to appeal under Rule 58;

(iv) to alter or amend the judgment under Rule 59;

(v) for a new trial under Rule 59; or

(vi) for relief under Rule 60 if the motion is filed no later than 10 days after the judgment is entered.

(B)(i) If a party files a notice of appeal after the court announces or enters a judgment — but before it disposes of any motion listed in Rule 4(a)(4)(A) — the notice becomes effective to appeal a judgment or order, in whole or in part, when the order disposing of the last such remaining motion is entered.

(ii) A party intending to challenge an order disposing of any motion listed in Rule 4(a)(4)(A), or a judgment altered or amended upon such a motion, must file a notice of appeal, or an amended notice of appeal — in compliance with Rule 3(c) — within the time prescribed by this Rule measured from the entry of the order disposing of the last such remaining motion.

(iii) No additional fee is required to file an amended notice.

(5) Motion for extension of time. (A) The district court may extend the time to file a notice of appeal if:

(i) a party so moves no later than 30 days after the time prescribed by this Rule 4(a) expires; and

(ii) regardless of whether its motion is filed before or during the 30 days after the time prescribed by this Rule 4(a) expires, that party shows excusable neglect or good cause.

(B) A motion filed before the expiration of the time prescribed in Rule 4(a)(1) or (3) may be *ex parte* unless the court requires otherwise. If the motion is filed after the expiration of the prescribed time, notice must be given to the other parties in accordance with local rules.

(C) No extension under this Rule 4(a)(5) may exceed 30 days after the prescribed time or 10 days after the date when the order granting the motion is entered, whichever is later.

(6) Reopening the time to file an appeal. The district court may reopen the time to file an appeal for a period of 14 days after the date when its order to reopen is entered, but only if all the following conditions are satisfied:

(A) the motion is filed within 180 days after the judgment or order is entered or within 7 days after the moving party receives notice of the entry, whichever is earlier;

(B) the court finds that the moving party was entitled to notice of the entry of the judgment or order sought to be appealed but did not receive the notice from the district court or any party within 21 days after entry; and

(C) the court finds that no party would be prejudiced.

(7) Entry defined. (A) A judgment or order is entered for purposes of this Rule 4(a):

(i) if Federal Rule of Civil Procedure 58(a)(1) does not require a separate document, when the judgment or order is entered in the civil docket under Federal Rules of Civil Procedure 79(a); or

(ii) if Federal Rule of Civil Procedure 58(a)(1) requires a separate document, when the judgment or order is entered in the civil docket under Federal Rule of Civil Procedure 79(a) and when the earlier of these events occurs:

1. the judgment or order is set forth on a separate document, or

2. 150 days have run from entry of the judgment or order in the civil docket under Federal Rule of Civil Procedure 79(a).

(B) A failure to set forth a judgment or order on a separate document when required by Federal Rule of Civil Procedure 58(a)(1) does not affect the validity of an appeal from that judgment or order.

(b) **Appeal in a criminal case.** (1) Time for filing a notice of appeal. (A) In a criminal case, a defendant's notice of appeal must be filed in the district court within 10 days after the later of:

(i) the entry of either the judgment or the order being appealed; or

(ii) the filing of the government's notice of appeal.

(B) When the government is entitled to appeal, its notice of appeal must be filed in the district court within 30 days after the later of:

(i) the entry of the judgment or order being appealed; or

(ii) the filing of a notice of appeal by any defendant.

(2) Filing before entry of judgment. A notice of appeal filed after the court announces a decision, sentence, or order — but before the entry of the judgment or order — is treated as filed on the date of and after the entry.

(3) Effect of a motion on a notice of appeal. (A) If a defendant timely makes any of the following motions under the Federal Rules of Criminal Procedure, the notice of appeal from a judgment of conviction must be filed within 10 days after the entry of the order disposing of the last such remaining motion, or within 10 days after the entry of the judgment of conviction, whichever period ends later. This provision applies to a timely motion:

(i) for judgment of acquittal under Rule 29;

(ii) for a new trial under Rule 33, but if based on newly discovered evidence, only if the motion is made no later than 10 days after the entry of the judgment; or

(iii) for arrest of judgment under Rule 34.

(B) A notice of appeal filed after the court announces a decision, sentence, or order — but before it disposes of any of the motions referred to in Rule 4(b)(3)(A) — becomes effective upon the later of the following:

(i) the entry of the order disposing of the last such remaining motion; or

(ii) the entry of the judgment of conviction.

(C) A valid notice of appeal is effective — without amendment — to appeal from an order disposing of any of the motions referred to in Rule 4(b)(3)(A).

(4) *Motion for extension of time.* Upon a finding of excusable neglect or good cause, the district court may — before or after the time has expired, with or without motion and notice — extend the time to file a notice of appeal for a period not to exceed 30 days from the expiration of the time otherwise prescribed by this Rule 4(b).

(5) *Jurisdiction.* The filing of a notice of appeal under this Rule 4(b) does not divest a district court of jurisdiction to correct a sentence under Federal Rule of Criminal Procedure 35(c), nor does the filing of a motion under 35(c) affect the validity of a notice of appeal filed before the entry of the order disposing of the motion. The filing of a motion under Federal Rule of Criminal Procedure 35(a) does not suspend the time for filing a notice of appeal from a judgment of conviction.

(6) *Entry defined.* A judgment or order is entered for purposes of this Rule 4(b) when it is entered on the criminal docket.

(c) **Appeal by an inmate confined in an institution.** (1) If an inmate confined in an institution files a notice of appeal in either a civil or a criminal case, the notice is timely if it is deposited in the institution's internal mail system on or before the last day for filing. If an institution has a system designed for legal mail, the inmate must use that system to receive the benefit of this rule. Timely filing may be shown by a declaration in compliance with 28 U.S.C. § 1746 or by a notarized statement, either of which must set forth the date of deposit and state that first-class postage has been prepaid.

(2) If an inmate files the first notice of appeal in a civil case under this Rule 4(c), the 14-day period provided in Rule 4(a)(3) for another party to file a notice of appeal runs from the date when the district court dockets the first notice.

(3) When a defendant in a criminal case files a notice of appeal under this Rule 4(c), the 30-day period for the government to file its notice of appeal runs from the entry of the judgment or order appealed from or from the district court's docketing of the defendant's notice of appeal, whichever is later.

(d) **Mistaken filing in the court of appeals.** If a notice of appeal in either a civil or a criminal case is mistakenly filed in the court of appeals, the clerk of that court must note on the notice the date when it was received and send it to the district clerk. The notice is then considered filed in the district court on the date so noted. (Amended by order adopted April 30, 1979, effective August 1, 1979; by P.L. 100-690, § 7111, signed November 18, 1988; by order adopted April 30, 1991, effective December 1, 1991; by order adopted April 22, 1993, effective December 1, 1993; by order adopted April 27, 1995, effective December 1, 1995; by order adopted April 24, 1998, effective December 1, 1998; and by order adopted April 29, 2002, effective December 1, 2002.)

Broad construction favored. — In general, courts have construed Rule 4(a)(1) broadly. Buonocore v. Harris, 65 F.3d 347 (4th Cir. 1995).

Subdivision (b) considered mandatory and jurisdictional. — In the absence of extraordinary circumstances, subdivision (b) of this rule is considered mandatory and jurisdictional. Morin v. United States, 522 F.2d 8 (4th Cir. 1975).

Compliance with subdivision (b) is mandatory and jurisdictional. United States v. Schuchardt, 685 F.2d 901 (4th Cir. 1982).

Notice of appeal in a civil suit must be filed within thirty days of the entry of judgment. This limitation is mandatory and jurisdictional. Thompson v. E.I. DuPont de Nemours & Co., 76 F.3d 530 (4th Cir. 1996).

60-day period applies to all parties, not just United States. — Where the United

States is a "party," the 60-day period in which to appeal applies to all parties to the case, not just the United States. Buonocore v. Harris, 65 F.3d 347 (4th Cir. 1995).

Order granting motion to quash subpoenas was criminal proceeding. — In an appeal where the district court granted movant's motion to quash subpoenas issued by two grand juries with respect to certain papers in its possession, and where the effect of the district court's order was that movant's subsidiary had to turn over all of the papers in its possession to the grand jury, proceeding was criminal rather than civil so that subdivision (b) applied to the proceeding rather than subdivision (a). United States v. Under Seal, 902 F.2d 244 (4th Cir. 1990).

Entry of judgment for purposes of notice of appeal. — A notice of appeal must be filed within thirty days of entry of judgment. Entry of judgment consists of two steps: Creation of a document setting out the judgment and a notation of the document on the docket sheet. The thirty-day period does not begin to run until after the document is entered on the docket sheet. Wilson v. Murray, 806 F.2d 1232 (4th Cir. 1986), cert. denied, 484 U.S. 870, 108 S. Ct. 197, 98 L. Ed. 2d 149 (1987).

Pro se prisoners' notices of appeal deemed filed on delivery to prison authorities. — Pro se prisoners' notices of appeal are deemed filed with the district court when delivered to prison authorities for forwarding and filing. Wilder v. Chairman of Cent. Classification Bd., 926 F.2d 367 (4th Cir.), cert. denied, 926 U.S. 367, 112 S. Ct. 109, 116 L. Ed. 2d 78 (1991).

Bare notice of appeal not construed as motion for extension. — A bare notice of appeal cannot be construed as a motion for extension of time under subdivision (a)(5). Wilder v. Chairman of Cent. Classification Bd., 926 F.2d 367 (4th Cir.), cert. denied, 926 U.S. 367, 112 S. Ct. 109, 116 L. Ed. 2d 78 (1991).

Extension of filing period under subdivisions (a) and (b) compared. — Unlike subdivision (a), the language of subdivision (b) empowers the district court to extend the filing period with or without motion. United States v. Reyes, 759 F.2d 351 (4th Cir.), cert. denied, 474 U.S. 857, 106 S. Ct. 164, 88 L. Ed. 2d 136 (1985).

Opportunity to show excusable neglect for late filing. — A criminal defendant who has filed his notice of appeal beyond the time specified in subdivision (b), but within the thirty-day permissible extension period, should have the opportunity to seek relief by showing excusable neglect. United States v. Reyes, 759 F.2d 351 (4th Cir.), cert. denied, 474 U.S. 857, 106 S. Ct. 164, 88 L. Ed. 2d 136 (1985).

Move to vacate temporary restraining order qualifies as motion "to alter or amend judgment." — The plaintiff's contention that the notice of appeal, filed February 14, 1975, was filed more than thirty days after entry of the temporary restraining order (TRO) on December 31, 1974, overlooked the fact that defendants moved to vacate the TRO on January 6, 1975, which qualifies as a motion "to alter or amend judgment" within the meaning of Rule 59, Federal Rules of Civil Procedure. By the terms of Rule 4(a), Federal Rules of Appellate Procedure, the "full time for appeal (thirty days) ... commences to run and is to be computed from the entry of (the) ... (order) granting or denying a motion under Rule 59 to alter or amend the judgment ...." January 20, 1975, was thus the date that the appeal period of thirty days began to run, and February 14, 1975, was within the period. Virginia v. Tenneco, Inc., 538 F.2d 1026 (4th Cir. 1976).

Court of appeals lacks jurisdiction where notice not given in time. — By virtue of subdivision (b) a court of appeals does not have jurisdiction to treat the issues sought to be raised on appeal where notice of appeal was not given within ten days after entry of the judgment, the time was not otherwise extended by order of the district court, and the subsequent motion for a new trial based on newly discovered evidence was not made before or within ten days after entry of the judgment. United States v. Williams, 415 F.2d 232 (4th Cir. 1969).

Belated appeal may be allowed where defendant is prevented from complying. — The original ten-day appeal period prescribed by the federal rules of court as to filing the notice of appeal in criminal cases is jurisdictional. But if a defendant attempted to exercise his right to appeal within the ten-day period specified by the rules and, without fault on his part, was prevented from effective communication with the clerk or the district judge, the defendant may be allowed a belated appeal. United States v. Meyers, 406 F.2d 1015 (4th Cir. 1969) (construing former Fed. R. Crim. P. 37(a)).

Court may extend ten-day period on showing of "excusable neglect." — Subdivision (b) permits a district court upon a showing of "excusable neglect" before or after the expiration of the ten-day appeal time to extend the time for filing a notice of appeal for an additional thirty days. United States v. Meyers, 406 F.2d 1015 (4th Cir. 1969).

Non-prisoner litigant who entrusts filing with postal service. — A non-prisoner litigant who entrusts his filing with the postal processes, without taking further steps to ensure that the notice of appeal is timely filed with the district court, cannot establish excusable neglect. Thompson v. E.I. DuPont de

Nemours & Co., 76 F.3d 530 (4th Cir. 1996).

Applicability of good cause standard. — The good cause standard is only applicable to motions for enlargement of time filed within thirty days of entry of judgment. Thompson v. E.I. DuPont de Nemours & Co., 76 F.3d 530 (4th Cir. 1996).

Notice to pro se litigant of right to extension. — When a pro se litigant files a notice of appeal that is untimely but within the period during which an extension of time might be granted pursuant to this rule, the litigant must be informed of the rule and provided an opportunity to establish excusable neglect. Shah v. Hutto, 704 F.2d 717 (4th Cir. 1983), cert. denied, 466 U.S. 975, 104 S. Ct. 2354, 80 L. Ed. 2d 827 (1984).

No jurisdiction to reconsider and va- **cate own final order.** — District court has no jurisdiction to reconsider and vacate an order of that court which has become final in a criminal case because of the expiration of the time to appeal. United States v. Breit, 754 F.2d 526 (4th Cir. 1985).

Correction of error as to matter not dealt with below. — Without filing a cross-appeal, an appellee may not attack the decree with a view either to enlarging his own rights thereunder or of lessening the rights of his adversary, where what he seeks is to correct an error or to supplement the decree with respect to a matter not dealt with below. Thurston v. United States, 810 F.2d 438 (4th Cir. 1987).

Applied in United States v. Bodden, 736 F.2d 142 (4th Cir. 1984).

Rule 5. Appeal by permission.

(a) **Petition for permission to appeal.** (1) To request permission to appeal when an appeal is within the court of appeals' discretion, a party must file a petition for permission to appeal. The petition must be filed with the circuit clerk with proof of service on all other parties to the district-court action.

(2) The petition must be filed within the time specified by the statute or rule authorizing the appeal or, if no such time is specified, within the time provided by Rule 4(a) for filing a notice of appeal.

(3) If a party cannot petition for appeal unless the district court first enters an order granting permission to do so or stating that the necessary conditions are met, the district court may amend its order, either on its own or in response to a party's motion, to include the required permission or statement. In that event, the time to petition runs from entry of the amended order.

(b) **Contents of the petition; answer or cross-petition; oral argument.** (1) The petition must include the following:

(A) the facts necessary to understand the question presented;

(B) the question itself;

(C) the relief sought;

(D) the reasons why the appeal should be allowed and is authorized by a statute or rule; and

(E) an attached copy of:

(i) the order, decree, or judgment complained of and any related opinion or memorandum, and

(ii) any order stating the district court's permission to appeal or finding that the necessary conditions are met.

(2) A party may file an answer in opposition or a cross-petition within 7 days after the petition is served.

(3) The petition and answer will be submitted without oral argument unless the court of appeals orders otherwise.

(c) **Form of papers; number of copies.** All papers must conform to Rule 32(c)(2). Except by the court's permission, a paper must not exceed 20 pages, exclusive of the disclosure statement, the proof of service, and the accompanying documents required by Rule 5(b)(1)(E). An original and 3 copies must be filed unless the court requires a different number by local rule or by order in a particular case.

(d) **Grant of permission; fees; cost bond; filing the record.** (1) Within 10 days after the entry of an order granting permission to appeal, the appellant must:

(A) pay the district clerk all required fees; and

(B) file a cost bond if required under Rule 7.

(2) A notice of appeal need not be filed. The date when the order granting permission to appeal is entered serves as the date of the notice of appeal for calculating time under these rules.

(3) The district clerk must notify the circuit clerk once the petitioner has paid the fees. Upon receiving this notice, the circuit clerk must enter the appeal on the docket. The record must be forwarded and filed in accordance with Rules 11 and 12(c). (Amended by order adopted April 30, 1979, effective August 1, 1979; by order adopted April 29, 1994, effective December 1, 1994; by order adopted April 24, 1998, effective December 1, 1998; and by order adopted April 29, 2002, effective December 1, 2002.)

Applied in Peanut Corp. of Am. v. Hollywood Brands, Inc., 696 F.2d 311 (4th Cir. 1982); City of Va. Beach v. Roanoke River Basin Ass'n, 776 F.2d 484 (4th Cir. 1985).

Local Rule 5. Interlocutory orders.

The Court of Appeals will initially enter a petition for permission to appeal upon the miscellaneous docket; a docket fee shall not be required unless the petition is granted. A Disclosure of Corporate Affiliations statement must be filed with the petition and answer. See FRAP 26.1 and Local Rule 26.1. Upon granting the petition, the Court of Appeals will notify the district court by copy of the order and transfer the case to the regular docket. (Amended effective December 1, 2009.)

Effect of amendments. — The 2009 amendment substituted "Disclosure of Corporate Affiliations statement" for "Disclosure of Corporate Affiliations and Other Entities with a Direct Financial Interest in Litigation statement" in the second sentence; at the end of the third sentence, deleted "and Form A"; and made related changes.

Rule 5.1. Appeal by leave under 28 U.S.C. § 636(c)(5).

[Abrogated.]

Editor's note. — Rule 5.1 which was adopted March 10, 1986, effective July 1, 1986; amended by order adopted April 22, 1993, effective December 1, 1993; and by order adopted April 29, 1994, effective December 1, 1994 was abrogated by order adopted April 24, 1998, effective December 1, 1998.

Rule 6. Appeal in a bankruptcy case from a final judgment, order, or decree of a district court or of a bankruptcy appellate panel.

(a) **Appeal from a judgment, order or decree of a district court exercising original jurisdiction in a bankruptcy case.** An appeal to a court of appeals from a final judgment, order or decree of a district court exercising jurisdiction under 28 U.S.C. § 1334 is taken as any other civil appeal under these rules.

(b) **Appeal from a judgment, order or decree of a district court or bankruptcy appellate panel exercising appellate jurisdiction in a bankruptcy case.** (1) Applicability of other rules. These rules apply to an appeal to a court of appeals under 28 U.S.C. § 158(d) from a final judgment, order or decree of a district court or bankruptcy appellate panel exercising appellate jurisdiction under 28 U.S.C. § 158(a) or (b). But there are 3 exceptions:

(A) Rules 4(a)(4), 4(b), 9, 10, 11, 12(b), 13-20, 22-23, and 24(b) do not apply;

(B) the reference in Rule 3(c) to "Form 1 in the Appendix of Forms" must be read as a reference to Form 5; and

(C) when the appeal is from a bankruptcy appellate panel, the term "district court" as used in any applicable rule means "appellate panel".

(2) Additional rules. In addition to the rules made applicable by Rule 6(b)(1), the following rules apply:

(A) Motion for rehearing. (i) If a timely motion for rehearing under Bankruptcy Rule 8015 is filed, the time to appeal for all parties runs from the entry of the order disposing of the motion. A notice of appeal filed after the district court or bankruptcy appellate panel announces or enters a judgment, order, or decree — but before disposition of the motion for rehearing — becomes effective when the order disposing of the motion for rehearing is entered.

(ii) Appellate review of the order disposing of the motion requires the party, in compliance with Rules 3(c) and 6(b)(1)(B), to amend a previously filed notice of appeal. A party intending to challenge an altered or amended judgment, order, or decree must file a notice of appeal or amended notice of appeal within the time prescribed by Rule 4 — excluding Rules 4(a)(4) and 4(b) — measured from the entry of the order disposing of the motion.

(iii) No additional fee is required to file an amended notice.

(B) The record on appeal. (i) Within 10 days after filing the notice of appeal, the appellant must file with the clerk possessing the record assembled in accordance with Bankruptcy Rule 8006 — and serve on the appellee — a statement of the issues to be presented on appeal and a designation of the record to be certified and sent to the circuit clerk.

(ii) An appellee who believes that other parts of the record are necessary must, within 10 days after being served with the appellant's designation, file with the clerk and serve on the appellant a designation of additional parts to be included.

(iii) The record on appeal consists of:

• the redesignated record as provided above;

• the proceedings in the district court or bankruptcy appellate panel; and

• a certified copy of the docket entries prepared by the clerk under Rule 3(d).

(C) Forwarding the record. (i) When the record is complete, the district clerk or bankruptcy appellate panel clerk must number the documents constituting the record and send them promptly to the circuit clerk together with a list of the documents correspondingly numbered and reasonably identified. Unless directed to do so by a party or the circuit clerk, the clerk will not send to the court of appeals documents of unusual bulk or weight, physical exhibits other than documents, or other parts of the record designated for omission by local rule of the court of appeals. If the exhibits are unusually bulky or heavy, a party must arrange with the clerks in advance for their transportation and receipt.

(ii) All parties must do whatever else is necessary to enable the clerk to assemble and forward the record. The court of appeals may provided by rule or order that a certified copy of the docket entries be sent in place of the redesignated record, but any party may request at any time during the pendency of the appeal that the redesignated record be sent.

(D) Filing the record. Upon receiving the record — or a certified copy of the docket entries sent in place of the redesignated record — the circuit clerk must file it and immediately notify all parties of the filing date. (Amended by order adopted April 30, 1979, effective August 1, 1979; by order adopted April 25, 1989, effective December 1, 1989; by order adopted April 30, 1991, effective December 1,1991; by order adopted April 22, 1993, effective December 1, 1993; and by order adopted April 24, 1998, effective December 1 1998.)

I.O.P. 6.1. Bankruptcy appeals.

The Fourth Circuit has not established panels of three bankruptcy judges to hear appeals from bankruptcy courts pursuant to 28 U.S.C. § 158.

Rule 7. Bond for costs on appeal in a civil case.

In a civil case, the district court may require an appellant to file a bond or provide other security in any form and amount necessary to ensure payment of costs on appeal. Rule 8(b) applies to a surety on a bond given under this rule. (Amended by order adopted April 30, 1979, effective August 1, 1979; and by order adopted April 24, 1998, effective December 1, 1998.)

Rule 8. Stay or injunction pending appeal.

(a) **Motion for stay.** (1) Initial motion in the district court. A party must ordinarily move first in the district court for the following relief:

(A) a stay of the judgment or order of a district court pending appeal;

(B) approval of a supersedeas bond; or

(C) an order suspending, modifying, restoring, or granting an injunction while an appeal is pending.

(2) Motion in the Court of Appeals; conditions on relief. A motion for the relief mentioned in Rule 8(a)(1) may be made to the court of appeals or to one of its judges.

(A) The motion must:

(i) show that moving first in the district court would be impracticable; or

(ii) state that, a motion having been made, the district court denied the motion or failed to afford the relief requested and state any reasons given by the district court for its action.

(B) The motion must also include:

(i) the reasons for granting the relief requested and the facts relied on;

(ii) originals or copies of affidavits or other sworn statements supporting facts subject to dispute; and

(iii) relevant parts of the record.

(C) The moving party must give reasonable notice of the motion to all parties.

(D) A motion under this Rule 8(a)(2) must be filed with the circuit clerk and normally will be considered by a panel of the court. But in an exceptional case in which time requirements make that procedure impracticable, the motion may be made to and considered by a single judge.

(E) The court may condition relief on a party's filing a bond or other appropriate security in the district court.

(b) **Proceeding against a surety.** If a party gives security in the form of a bond or stipulation or other undertaking with one or more sureties, each surety submits to the jurisdiction of the district court and irrevocably appoints the district clerk as the surety's agent on whom any papers affecting the surety's liability on the bond or undertaking may be served. On motion, a surety's liability may be enforced in the district court without the necessity of an independent action. The motion and any notice that the district court prescribes may be served on the district clerk, who must promptly mail a copy to each surety whose address is known.

(c) **Stay in a criminal case.** Rule 38 of the Federal Rules of Criminal Procedure governs a stay in a criminal case. (Amended by order adopted March 10, 1986, effective July 1, 1986; by order adopted April 27, 1995, effective December 1, 1995; and by order adopted April 24, 1998, effective December 1, 1998.)

Applied in City of Alexandria v. Helms, 719 F.2d 699 (4th Cir. 1983); Morris v. City of Danville, 744 F.2d 1041 (4th Cir. 1984); Kennedy v. Block, 784 F.2d 1220 (4th Cir. 1986).

Local Rule 8. Stay or injunction pending appeal.

Filing a notice of appeal does not automatically stay the operation of the judgment, order or decision for which review is sought. If an application to the district court for temporary relief pending appeal is not practicable, counsel must make a specific showing of the reasons the application was not made to the district court in the first instance. Any motion to the Court of Appeals should include copies of all previous applications for relief and their outcome and any relevant parts of the record. A Disclosure of Corporate Affiliations statement must accompany the motion and any response unless the parties have previously filed disclosure statements with the Court in the case. See FRAP 26.1 and Local Rule 26.1. Filing and assignment of emergency motions for stay or injunction pending appeal are governed by Local Rule 27(e). An order granting a stay or injunction pending appeal remains in effect until issuance of the mandate or further order of the Court and may be conditioned upon the filing of a supersedeas bond in the district court. (Redesignated by order effective December 1, 1995; amended by order effective February 1, 2001; amended effective December 1, 2009.)

Effect of amendments. — The 2009 amendment added "and any relevant parts of the record" in the third sentence; in the fourth sentence substituted "Disclosure of Corporate Affiliations statement" for "Disclosure of Corporate Affiliations and Other Entities with a Direct Financial Interest in Litigation statement"; at the end of the fifth sentence deleted "and Form A"; deleted the former sixth sentence; and made related changes.

Rule 9. Release in a criminal case.

(a) **Release before judgment of conviction.** (1) The district court must state in writing, or orally on the record, the reasons for an order regarding release or detention of a defendant in a criminal case. A party appealing from the order must file with the court of appeals a copy of the district court's order and the court's statement of reasons as soon as practicable after filing the notice of appeal. An appellant who questions the factual basis for the district court's order must file a transcript of the release proceedings or an explanation of why a transcript was not obtained.

(2) After reasonable notice to the appellee, the court of appeals must promptly determine the appeal on the basis of the papers, affidavits, and parts of the record that the parties present or the court requires. Unless the court so orders, briefs need not be filed.

(3) The court of appeals or one of its judges may order the defendant's release pending the disposition of the appeal.

(b) **Release after judgment of conviction.** A party entitled to do so may obtain review of a district-court order regarding release after a judgment of conviction by filing a notice of appeal from that order in the district court, or by filing a motion in the court of appeals if the party has already filed a notice of appeal from the judgment of conviction. Both the order and the review are subject to Rule 9(a). The papers filed by the party seeking review must include a copy of the judgment of conviction.

(c) **Criteria for release.** The court release must make its decision regarding release in accordance with the applicable provisions of 18 U.S.C. §§ 3142, 3143, and 3145(c). (Amended by order adopted April 24, 1972, effective October 1, 1972; by order effective October 12, 1984; by order adopted April 29, 1994, effective December 1, 1994; and by order adopted April 24, 1998, effective December 1, 1998.)

Local Rule 9(a). Release prior to judgment of conviction.

A criminal defendant may be released in accordance with the conditions set by the district court prior to judgment of conviction. If the district court refuses to release the prisoner, or sets conditions for release that cannot be met, the order is appealable as a matter of right and will be given prompt consideration by the Court of Appeals. Counsel should submit memoranda in support of their position on appeal and, in cases involving corporate defendants, Disclosure of Corporate Affiliations statements required by FRAP 26.1 and Local Rule 26.1. The appeal is usually decided without oral argument upon the materials presented by the parties. A motion for release pending determination of the appeal may be filed and will be assigned as provided in Local Rule 27(e). (Redesignated by order effective December 1, 1995; amended by order effective February 1, 2001; amended effective December 1, 2009.)

Effect of amendments. — The 2009 amendment in the third sentence substituted "Disclosure of Corporate Affiliations statements" for "Disclosure of Corporate Affiliations and Other Entities with a Direct Financial Interest in Litigation statements" and deleted "and Form A" at the end; and made related changes.

Local Rule 9(b). Release after conviction and notice of appeal.

After the district court has ruled on a motion for bail or reduction of bail pending appeal, the appellant may renew the motion for release, or for a modification of the conditions of release, before the Court of Appeals without noting an additional appeal. A copy of the district court statement of reasons should accompany the motion. The motion will be submitted to a three-judge panel for decision.

Local Rule 9(c). Recalcitrant witnesses.

When an appeal arises from the incarceration of a witness who refuses to testify or produce evidence in any court or grand jury proceeding, the Court of Appeals is required by statute, 28 U.S.C. § 1826, to decide the appeal within 30 days of the filing of the notice of appeal. Therefore, counsel should immediately contact the Clerk's Office regarding all such witness contempt matters so that the appeal may be expedited for resolution within the statutory guidelines.

Rule 10. The record on appeal.

(a) **Composition of the record on appeal.** The following items constitute the record on appeal:

(1) the original papers and exhibits filed in the district court;

(2) the transcript of proceedings, if any; and

(3) a certified copy of the docket entries prepared by the district clerk.

(b) **The transcript of proceedings.** (1) Appellant's duty to order. Within 10 days after filing the notice of appeal or entry of an order disposing of the last timely remaining motion of a type specified in Rule 4(a)(4)(A), whichever is later, the appellant must do either of the following:

(A) order from the reporter a transcript of such parts of the proceedings not already on file as the appellant considers necessary, subject to a local rule of the court of appeals and with the following qualifications:

(i) the order must be in writing;

(ii) if the cost of the transcript is to be paid by the United States under the Criminal Justice Act, the order must so state; and

(iii) the appellant must, within the same period, file a copy of the order with the district clerk; or

(B) file a certificate stating that no transcript will be ordered.

(2) Unsupported finding or conclusion. If the appellant intends to urge on appeal that a finding or conclusion is unsupported by the evidence or is contrary to the evidence, the appellant must include in the record a transcript of all evidence relevant to that finding or conclusion.

(3) Partial transcript. Unless the entire transcript is ordered:

(A) the appellant must — within the 10 days provided in Rule 10(b)(1) — file a statement of the issues that the appellant intends to present on the appeal and must serve on the appellee a copy of both the order or certificate and the statement;

1187

(B) if the appellee considers it necessary to have a transcript of other parts of the proceedings, the appellee must, within 10 days after the service of the order or certificate and the statement of the issues, file and serve on the appellant a designation of additional parts to be ordered; and

(C) unless within 10 days after service of that designation the appellant has ordered all such parts, and has so notified the appellee, the appellee may within the following 10 days either order the parts or move in the district court for an order requiring the appellant to do so.

(4) Payment. At the time of ordering, a party must make satisfactory arrangements with the reporter for paying the cost of the transcript.

(c) **Statement of the evidence when the proceedings were not recorded or when a transcript is unavailable.** If the transcript of a hearing or trial is unavailable, the appellant may prepare a statement of the evidence or proceedings from the best available means, including the appellant's recollection. The statement must be served on the appellee, who may serve objections or proposed amendments within 10 days after being served. The statement and any objections or proposed amendments must then be submitted to the district court for settlement and approval. As settled and approved, the statement must be included by the district clerk in the record on appeal.

(d) **Agreed statement as the record on appeal.** In place of the record on appeal as defined in Rule 10(a), the parties may prepare, sign, and submit to the district court a statement of the case showing how the issues presented by the appeal arose and were decided in the district court. The statement must set forth only those facts averred and proved or sought to be proved that are essential to the court's resolution of the issues. If the statement is truthful, it —together with any additions that the district court may consider necessary to a full presentation of the issues on appeal — must be approved by the district court and must then be certified to the court of appeals as the record on appeal. The district clerk must then send it to the circuit clerk within the time provided by Rule 11. A copy of the agreed statement may be filed in place of the appendix required by Rule 30.

(e) **Correction or modification of the record.** (1) If any difference arises about whether the record truly discloses what occurred in the district court, the difference shall be submitted to and settled by that court and the record conformed accordingly.

(2) If anything material to either party is omitted from or misstated in the record by error or accident, the omission or misstatement may be corrected and a supplemental record may be certified and forwarded:

(A) on stipulation of the parties;

(B) by the district court before or after the record has been forwarded; or

(C) by the court of appeals.

(3) All other questions as to the form and content of the record must be presented to the court of appeals. (Amended by order adopted April 30, 1979, effective August 1, 1979; by order adopted March 10, 1986, effective July 1, 1986; by order adopted April 30, 1991, effective December 1, 1991; by order adopted April 22, 1993, effective December 1, 1993; by order adopted April 27, 1995, effective December 1, 1995; and by order adopted April 24, 1998, effective December 1, 1998.)

Authority to conform record. — Subdivision (e) of this rule vests authority in the district court to conform the record to what occurred in the district court either by supplying what has been omitted or correcting what has been erroneously transcribed. This power exists before or after the record is transmitted to the court of appeals, and the court of appeals on its own initiative may direct, inter alia, that any omission from the record be supplied. United States v. Greenwell, 418 F.2d 845 (4th Cir. 1969).

Direction to certify security measures in criminal trial. — District judge directed to certify statement regarding security measures used at criminal trial. See United States v. Greenwell, 418 F.2d 845 (4th Cir. 1969).

Applied in Mullins Coal Co. v. Clark, 759 F.2d 1142 (4th Cir. 1985).

Local Rule 10(a). Retention of the record on appeal in the district court.

In cases in which all parties are represented by counsel on appeal, the district court clerk will transmit with the notice of appeal sent to the Court of Appeals a certificate that the record of docket entries is available upon request. The district court clerk will notify the Court of Appeals of the subsequent filing of any transcript in the case. The district court will then retain the record on appeal until and unless a judge of this Court asks the Clerk of this Court to obtain it. Upon receipt of a request from the Clerk of the Court of Appeals, the clerk of the district court will assemble and transmit the record on appeal within 48 hours. (Amended by order effective April 1, 2008.)

Effect of amendments. — The 2008 amendment rewrote the Rule.

Local Rule 10(b). Records on appeal.

The preparation and transmittal of the record on appeal is the obligation of the clerk of the lower court, board or agency, and any questions concerning form or content should be addressed to the trial forum in the first instance. Parties should check with the clerk of the lower court, board or agency to determine whether everything relevant to the issues on appeal will be included initially in the record on appeal in order to obviate motions to supplement the record. The record is transmitted to the appellate court as soon as it is complete, except as provided in Local Rule 10(a). Local Rule 10(a) does not apply to records in cases in which one or more parties are proceeding without counsel on appeal. (Amended effective December 1, 2009.)

Effect of amendments. — The 2009 amendment deleted the former second sentence.

Local Rule 10(c). Transcripts.

(1) **Responsibilities and designation.** The appellant has the duty of ordering transcript of all parts of the proceedings material to the issues to be raised on appeal whether favorable or unfavorable to appellant's position. Appellant should complete the transcript order (form available at www.ca4.uscourts.gov) and distribute the form to the Clerk of the Court of Appeals, the court reporter, the clerk of the district court, and the appellee.

Before the transcript order is distributed, appellant must make appropriate financial arrangements with the court reporter for either immediate payment in full or in other form acceptable to the court reporter, payment pursuant to the Criminal Justice Act, or at government expense pursuant to 28 U.S.C. § 753(f).

In cross-appeals each party must order those parts of the transcript pertinent to the issues of such appeals. The parties are encouraged to agree upon those parts of the transcript jointly needed and to apportion the cost, with additional portions being ordered and paid for by the party considering them essential to that party's appeal.

If the entire transcript of proceedings is not to be prepared, the appellant's docketing statement filed pursuant to Local Rule 3(b) may constitute the statement of issues required by FRAP 10(b)(3)(A).

(2) **Monitoring and receipt by clerk.** Failure to order timely a transcript, failure to make satisfactory financial arrangements with the court reporter, or failure to specify in adequate detail those proceedings to be transcribed will subject the appeal to dismissal by the clerk for want of prosecution pursuant to Local Rule 45. The Clerk's Office is charged with monitoring the status of transcripts pending with court reporters.

(3) **Statement in lieu of transcript.** The parties may prepare and sign a statement of the case in lieu of the transcript or the entire record on appeal. The use of a statement in lieu of a transcript of a hearing substantially accelerates the appellate process. The statement should contain a description of the essential facts averred and proved or sought to be proved and a summary of pertinent testimony.

(4) **Guidelines for preparation of appellate transcripts in the Fourth Circuit.** The Fourth Circuit Judicial Council has adopted guidelines to define the obligations of appellants, appellees, clerks of the district court, court reporters and the Clerk of the Court of Appeals in the ordering, preparation, and filing of transcripts completed pursuant to these rules. (Amended effective December 1, 2009.)

Effect of amendments. — The 2009 amendment in the first paragraph of (1), deleted the former second sentence and substituted "transcript order (form available at www.ca4.uscourts.gov) and distribute the form" for "form and distribute the appropriate parts of the form" in the second sentence; in the second paragraph of (1) substituted "distributed" for "mailed"; and in (4) substituted "The Fourth Circuit Judicial Council has adopted guidelines" for "An appendix to these rules contains the guidelines adopted by the Fourth Circuit Judicial Council".

Local Rule 10(d). Supplemental records, modification or correction.

Disputes concerning the accuracy or composition of the record on appeal should be resolved in the trial court in the first instance, although the Court of Appeals has the power, either on motion or of its own accord, to require that the record be corrected or supplemented. It is unnecessary to seek permission of the Court of Appeals to supplement the record and the record may be supplemented by the parties by stipulation or by order of the district court at any time during the appellate process. (Redesignated by order effective April 16, 2007)

Effect of amendments. — The 2007
amendment redesignated 10(e) as 10(d).

Rule 11. Forwarding the record.

(a) **Appellant's duty.** An appellant filing a notice of appeal must comply with Rule 10(b) and must do whatever else is necessary to enable the clerk to assemble and forward the record. If there are multiple appeals from a judgment or order, the clerk must forward a single record.

(b) **Duties of reporter and district clerk.** (1) Reporter's duty to prepare and file a transcript. The reporter must prepare and file a transcript as follows:

(A) Upon receiving an order for a transcript, the reporter must enter at the foot of the order the date of its receipt and the expected completion date and send a copy, so endorsed, to the circuit clerk.

(B) If the transcript cannot be completed within 30 days of the reporter's receipt of the order, the reporter may request the circuit clerk to grant additional time to complete it. The clerk must note on the docket the action taken and notify the parties.

(C) When a transcript is complete, the reporter must file it with the district clerk and notify the circuit clerk of the filing.

(D) If the reporter fails to file the transcript on time, the circuit clerk must notify the district judge and do whatever else the court of appeals directs.

(2) District clerk's duty to forward. When the record is complete, the district clerk must number the documents constituting the record and send them promptly to the circuit clerk together with a list of the documents correspondingly numbered and reasonably identified. Unless directed to do so by a party or the circuit clerk, the district clerk will not send to the court of appeals documents of unusual bulk or weight, physical exhibits other than documents, or other parts of the record designated for omission by local rule of the court of appeals. If the exhibits are unusually bulky or heavy, a party must arrange with the clerks in advance for their transportation and receipt.

(c) **Retaining the record temporarily in the district court for use in preparing the appeal.** The parties may stipulate, or the district court on motion may order, that the district clerk retain the record temporarily for the parties to use in preparing the papers on appeal. In that event the district clerk must certify to the circuit clerk that the record on appeal is complete. Upon receipt of the appellee's brief, or earlier if the court orders or the parties agree, the appellant must request the district clerk to forward the record.

(d) [Abrogated by order adopted April 24, 1998, effective December 1, 1998.]

(e) **Retaining the record by court order.** (1) The court of appeals may, by order or local rule, provide that a certified copy of the docket entries be forwarded instead of the entire record. But a party may at any time during the appeal request that designated parts of the record be forwarded.

(2) The district court may order the record or some part of it retained if the court needs it while the appeal is pending, subject, however, to call by the court of appeals.

(3) If part or all of the record is ordered retained, the district clerk must send to the court of appeals a copy of the order and the docket entries together

with the parts of the original record allowed by the district court and copies of any parts of the record designated by the parties.

(f) **Retaining parts of the record in the district court by stipulation of the parties.** The parties may agree by written stipulation filed in the district court that designated parts of the record be retained in the district court subject to call by the court of appeals or request by a party. The parts of the record so designated remain a part of the record on appeal.

(g) **Record for a preliminary motion in the court of appeals.** If, before the record is forwarded, a party makes any of the following motions in the court of appeals:

- for dismissal;
- for release;
- for a stay pending appeal;
- for additional security on the bond on appeal or on a supersedeas bond; or
- for any other intermediate order —

the district clerk must send the court of appeals any parts of the record designated by any party. (Amended by order adopted April 30, 1979, effective August 1, 1979; by order adopted March 10, 1986, effective July 1, 1986; and by order adopted April 24, 1998, effective December 1, 1998.)

Local Rule 11(a). Transcript acknowledgments.

Upon receipt of an order for a transcript, the Clerk of the Court of Appeals will prepare for the reporter a transcript order acknowledgment which will set forth the date the transcript order was received in the Clerk's Office and the transcript due date, computed from the order receipt date in accordance with the time limits set forth in the applicable district court reporter management plan. If the transcript order is correct in all respects, except for an order date error in the reporter's favor, no response will be required from the reporter. If the reporter believes that there is a problem with the transcript order, he or she must complete a copy of the acknowledgment form noting the problem and return it to the Court of Appeals within 7 days of receipt of the form by the reporter, or within such further time as the Court of Appeals allows. The time for completion of the transcript will automatically cease to run until the problem has been remedied. The Clerk of the Court of Appeals will send a new transcript order acknowledgment setting forth new transcript order and filing dates taking into account the delay caused by resolving the problem with the original transcript order.

Local Rule 11(b). Time limits for filing transcripts.

Although FRAP 11(b)(1)(B) requires that transcripts be completed within 30 days from the purchase order date, this Court routinely uses instead the time limits set forth in the district court reporter management plans. All of the plans establish a 60-day period for preparation of transcripts, with the following exceptions:

(1) Special provisions adopted by the Fourth Circuit Judicial Council for appeals by incarcerated criminal defendants.

(a) transcripts of 1000 pages or less shall be filed within 30 days of transcript order and completion of satisfactory financial arrangements.

(b) transcripts of more than 1000 pages shall be filed within the time ordered by the Clerk of the Court of Appeals.

(2) Special circumstances, such as

(a) bail appeals,

(b) death penalty cases, or

(c) other expedited procedures in which the transcript shall be filed within the time ordered by the Clerk of the Court of Appeals.

Local Rule 11(c). Exhibits.

Counsel should be aware that certain portions of the record will not be transmitted to the Court of Appeals as part of the record. If bulky documents and physical exhibits are required by a party for oral argument, the party must make advance arrangements with the clerks of both courts for their transportation and receipt. Such arrangements are best made after the completion of the briefing schedule on appeal and receipt of notice of oral argument.

Local Rule 11(d). Access of counsel to original record.

Counsel desiring to use the record on appeal in preparing their case should make arrangements with the clerk of the district court for access to the record. Under Local Rule 10(a), records in cases in which all parties are represented by counsel are retained by the district court clerk during appeal unless a judge of the Court of Appeals requests that they be obtained. If the record is transmitted to the Court of Appeals, the record may be withdrawn upon proper application and returned to the trial court or the nearest district court clerk's office for counsel's review. Law professors representing indigents by Court appointment may request that the record be sent to the law school for their review.

I.O.P. 11.1. Sanctions for court reporter's failure to file a timely transcript.

The Fourth Circuit Judicial Council has implemented a resolution of the Judicial Conference of the United States which mandates sanctions for the late delivery of transcripts. For transcripts not delivered within the time limits set forth in Local Rule 11(b), the reporter may charge only 90 percent of the prescribed fee; for a transcript not delivered within 30 days after that time the reporter may charge only 80 percent of the prescribed fee. The time period in criminal proceedings for the preparation of transcripts that are ordered before sentencing shall not begin to run until after entry of the judgment and commitment order. (Amended by order effective December 1, 1995, and by order effective December 1, 2002.)

COMMENT

New I.O.P. 11.1 incorporates proposed language which would, in combination with proposed changes to the Fourth Circuit Guidelines for Preparation of Appellate Transcripts, permit preparation of transcript to begin after conviction but before sentencing upon certification by counsel that the defendant intends to appeal. If transcript is ordered prior to sentencing, the court reporter's time limits for filing the transcript would not begin to run until after entry of the judgment and commitment order.

Rule 12. Docketing the appeal; filing a representation statement; filing the record.

(a) **Docketing the appeal.** Upon receiving the copy of the notice of appeal and the docket entries from the district clerk under Rule 3(d), the circuit clerk must docket the appeal under the title of the district-court action and must identify the appellant, adding the appellant's name if necessary.

(b) **Filing a representation statement.** Unless the court of appeals designates another time, the attorney who filed the notice of appeal must, within 10 days after filing the notice, file a statement with the circuit clerk naming the parties that the attorney represents on appeal.

(c) **Filing the record, partial record, or certificate.** Upon receiving the record, partial record, or district clerk's certificate as provided in Rule 11, the circuit clerk must file it and immediately notify all parties of the filing date. (Amended by order adopted April 30, 1979, effective August 1, 1979; by order adopted March 10, 1986, effective July 1, 1986; by order adopted April 22, 1993, effective December 1, 1993; and by order adopted April 24, 1998, effective December 1, 1998.)

Local Rule 12(a). Appeals by aggrieved non-parties in the lower court.

If the appellant was not a party to the lower court proceeding, the appeal shall be styled "In re _____, Appellant," and the title of the action in the district court shall also be given.

Local Rule 12(b). Joint appeals/cross-appeals and consolidations.

For the purpose of identifying consolidated appeals and cross-appeals, the earliest docketed appeal will be designated the lead case and identified by an "L" following its docket number. The parties should designate lead counsel for each side and communicate lead counsel's identity in writing to the clerk within 14 days of the consolidation order. Although most consolidations will be on the Court's own motion, a party is not precluded from filing a request. (Amended effective December 1, 2009.)

Effect of amendments. — The 2009 amendment substituted "14 days" for "10 days" in the second sentence.

Local Rule 12(c). Expedition of appeals.

The Court on its own motion or on motion of the parties may expedite an appeal for briefing and oral argument. Any motion to expedite should state clearly the reasons supporting expedition, the ability of the parties to present the appeal on the existing record, and the need for oral argument. (Amended by order effective December 1, 1998.)

COMMENT

The last sentence of Local Rule 12(c) has been deleted because Local Rule 10(a) does not require that the record be transmitted to the court of appeals.

Local Rule 12(d). Abeyance.

In the interest of docket control the Court may, either on its own motion or upon request, place a case in abeyance pending disposition of matters before this Court or other courts which may affect the ultimate resolution of an appeal. During the period of time a case is held in abeyance the appeal remains on the docket but nothing is done to advance the case to maturity and resolution. If a case is held in abeyance for cases other than a Fourth Circuit case, the parties will be required to make periodic status reports.

Local Rule 12(e). Intervention.

A party who appeared as an intervenor in a lower court proceeding shall be considered a party to the appeal upon filing a notice of appearance. Otherwise, a motion for leave to intervene must be filed with the Court of Appeals. Any notice of appearance or motion to intervene should indicate the side upon which the movant proposes to intervene. The provisions of FRAP 15(d) govern intervention in appeals from administrative agencies. Intervenors are required to join in the brief for the side which they support unless leave to file a separate brief is granted by the Court.

I.O.P. 12.1. Organization of the Court's docket.

[Deleted effective December 1, 1998.]

COMMENT

I.O.P. 12.1 has been deleted. The court has, in the past, made several adjustments to docket assignments to reflect changes in the court's caseload. Since the docket assignment information in the I.O.P. is not of significant import to persons practicing before the court, the proposed draft would delete the I.O.P. rather than continue the practice of modifying it.

TITLE III. REVIEW OF DECISIONS OF THE UNITED STATES TAX COURT.

Rule 13. Review of a decision of the Tax Court.

(a) **How obtained; time for filing notice of appeal.** (1) Review of a decision of the United States Tax Court is commenced by filing a notice of appeal with the Tax Court clerk within 90 days after the entry of the Tax Court's decision. At the time of filing, the appellant must furnish the clerk with enough copies of the notice to enable the clerk to comply with Rule 3(d). If one party files a timely notice of appeal, any other party may file a notice of appeal within 120 days after the Tax Court's decision is entered.

(2) If, under Tax Court rules, a party makes a timely motion to vacate or revise the Tax Court's decision, the time to file a notice of appeal runs from the entry of the order disposing of the motion or from the entry of a new decision, whichever is later.

(b) **Notice of appeal; how filed.** The notice of appeal may be filed either at the Tax Court clerk's office in the District of Columbia or by mail addressed to the clerk. If sent by mail the notice is considered filed on the postmark date, subject to § 7502 of the Internal Revenue Code, as amended, and the applicable regulations.

(c) **Contents of the notice of appeal; service; effect of filing and service.** Rule 3 prescribes the contents of a notice of appeal, the manner of service, and the effect of its filing and service. Form 2 in the Appendix of Forms is a suggested form of a notice of appeal.

(d) **The record on appeal; forwarding; filing.** (1) An appeal from the Tax Court is governed by the parts of Rules 10, 11, and 12 regarding the record on appeal from a district court, the time and manner of forwarding and filing, and the docketing in the court of appeals. References in those rules and in Rule 3 to the district court and district clerk are to be read as referring to the Tax Court and its clerk.

(2) If an appeal from a Tax Court decision is taken to more than one court of appeals, the original record must be sent to the court named in the first notice of appeal filed. In an appeal to any other court of appeals, the appellant must apply to that other court to make provision for the record. (Amended by order adopted April 30, 1979, effective August 1, 1979; by order adopted April 29, 1994, effective December 1, 1994; and by order adopted April 24, 1998, effective December 1, 1998.)

Rule 14. Applicability of other rules to the review of a Tax Court decision.

All provisions of these rules, except Rules 4-9, 15-20, and 22-23, apply to the review of a Tax Court decision. (Amended by order adopted April 24, 1998, effective December 1, 1998.)

TITLE IV. REVIEW AND ENFORCEMENT OF ORDERS OF ADMINISTRATIVE AGENCIES, BOARDS, COMMISSIONS AND OFFICERS.

Rule 15. Review or enforcement of an agency order — How obtained; intervention.

(a) **Petition for review; joint petition.** (1) Review of an agency order is commenced by filing, within the time prescribed by law, a petition for review with the clerk of a court of appeals authorized to review the agency order. If their interests make joinder practicable, two or more persons may join in a petition to the same court to review the same order.

(2) The petition must:

(A) name each party seeking review either in the caption or the body of the petition — using such terms as "et al.," "petitioners," or "respondents" does not effectively name the parties;

(B) name the agency as a respondent (even though not named in the petition, the United States is a respondent if required by statute); and

(C) specify the order or part thereof to be reviewed.

(3) Form 3 in the Appendix of Forms is a suggested form of a petition for review.

(4) In this rule "agency" includes an agency, board, commission, or officer; "petition for review" includes a petition to enjoin, suspend, modify, or otherwise review, or a notice of appeal, whichever form is indicated by the applicable statute.

(b) **Application or cross-application to enforce an order; answer; default.** (1) An application to enforce an agency order must be filed with the clerk of a court of appeals authorized to enforce the order. If a petition is filed to review an agency order that the court may enforce, a party opposing the petition may file a cross-application for enforcement.

(2) Within 20 days after the application for enforcement is filed, the respondent must serve on the applicant an answer to the application and file it with the clerk. If the respondent fails to answer in time, the court will enter judgment for the relief requested.

(3) The application must contain a concise statement of the proceedings in which the order was entered, the facts upon which venue is based, and the relief requested.

(c) **Service of the petition or application.** The circuit clerk must serve a copy of the petition for review, or an application or cross-application to enforce an agency order, on each respondent as prescribed by Rule 3(d), unless a different manner of service is prescribed by statute. At the time of filing, the petitioner must:

(1) serve, or have served, a copy on each party admitted to participate in the agency proceedings, except for the respondents;

(2) file with the clerk a list of those so served; and

(3) give the clerk enough copies of the petition or application to serve each respondent.

(d) **Intervention.** Unless a statute provides another method, a person who wants to intervene in a proceeding under this rule must file a motion for leave to intervene with the circuit clerk and serve a copy on all parties. The motion — or other notice of intervention authorized by statute — must be filed within 30 days after the petition for review is filed and must contain a concise statement of the interest of the moving party and the grounds for intervention.

(e) **Payment of fees.** When filing any separate or joint petition for review in a court of appeals, the petitioner must pay the circuit clerk all required fees. (Amended by order adopted April 22, 1993, effective December 1, 1993; and by order adopted April 24, 1998, effective December 1, 1998.)

Local Rule 15(a). Docketing fee.

Upon filing a petition for review of an agency order, petitioner shall pay the prescribed docketing fee of $450, payable to the Clerk, U.S. Court of Appeals, or submit a properly executed application for leave to proceed in forma pauperis. (Added by order effective September 28, 1994; added by order effective December 4, 1996; amended October 9, 2003, effective November 1, 2003 and amended April 27, 2006, effective April 9, 2006.)

Effect of amendments. — The 2003 amendment substituted "$250" for "$100." The 2006 amendment substituted "$450" for "$250."

Local Rule 15(b). Petitions for review.

Whenever filing a petition for review or an application or cross-application for enforcement, the party shall attach to the petition, application or cross-application a copy of the agency order for which review or enforcement is sought. The petition, application or cross-application shall also be accompanied by a list of respondents specifically identifying the respondents' names and the addresses where respondents may be served with copies of the petition, application or cross-application. (Adopted by order effective December 4, 1996.)

Rule 15.1. Briefs and oral argument in National Labor Relations Board proceedings.

In either an enforcement or a review proceeding, a party adverse to the National Labor Relations Board proceeds first on briefing and at oral argument, unless the court orders otherwise. (Adopted by order adopted March 10, 1986, effective July 1, 1986; and amended by order adopted April 24, 1998, effective December 1, 1998.)

Rule 16. The record on review or enforcement.

(a) **Composition of the record.** The record on review or enforcement of an agency order consists of:

(1) the order involved;

(2) any findings or report on which it is based; and

(3) the pleadings, evidence, and other parts of the proceedings before the agency.

(b) **Omissions from or misstatements in the record.** The parties may at any time, by stipulation, supply any omission from the record or correct a misstatement, or the court may so direct. If necessary, the court may direct that a supplemental record be prepared and filed. (Amended by order adopted April 24, 1998, effective December 1, 1998.)

Rule 17. Filing of the record.

(a) **Agency to file; time for filing; notice of filing.** The agency must file the record with the circuit clerk within 40 days after being served with a petition for review, unless the statute authorizing review provides otherwise, or within 40 days after it files an application for enforcement unless the respondent fails to answer or the court orders otherwise. The court may shorten or extend the time to file the record. The clerk must notify all parties of the date when the record is filed.

(b) **Filing; what constitutes.** (1) The agency must file:

(A) the original or a certified copy of the entire record or parts designated by the parties; or

(B) a certified list adequately describing all documents, transcripts of testimony, exhibits, and other material constituting the record, or describing those parts designated by the parties.

(2) The parties may stipulate in writing that no record or certified list be filed. The date when the stipulation is filed with the circuit clerk is treated as the date when the record is filed.

(3) The agency must retain any portion of the record not filed with the clerk. All parts of the record retained by the agency are a part of the record on review for all purposes and, if the court or a party so requests, must be sent to the court regardless of any prior stipulation. (Amended by order adopted April 24, 1998, effective December 1, 1998.)

Rule 18. Stay pending review.

(a) **Motion for a stay.** (1) Initial motion before the agency. A petitioner must ordinarily move first before the agency for a stay pending review of its decision or order.

(2) Motion in the court of appeals. A motion for a stay may be made to the court of appeals or one of its judges.

(A) The motion must:

(i) show that moving first before the agency would be impracticable; or

(ii) state that, a motion having been made, the agency denied the motion or failed to afford the relief requested and state any reasons given by the agency for its action.

(B) The motion must also include:

(i) the reasons for granting the relief requested and the facts relied on;

(ii) originals or copies of affidavits or other sworn statements supporting facts subject to dispute; and

(iii) relevant parts of the record.

(C) The moving party must give reasonable notice of the motion to all parties.

(D) The motion must be filed with the circuit clerk and normally will be considered by a panel of the court. But in an exceptional case in which time requirements make that procedure impracticable, the motion may be made to and considered by a single judge.

(b) **Bond.** The court may condition relief on the filing of a bond or other appropriate security. (Amended by order adopted April 24, 1998, effective December 1, 1998.)

Local Rule 18. Procedures.

This Court's local rules accompanying FRAP 8 and 27 apply also to applications for stays under FRAP 18.

COMMENT

The proposed Local Rule simply revises the language of existing I.O.P. 18 which cross-references the procedures found in FRAP 8 and 27.

Rule 19. Settlement of a judgment enforcing an agency order in part.

When the court files an opinion directing entry of judgment enforcing the agency's order in part, the agency must within 14 days file with the clerk and serve on each other party a proposed judgment conforming to the opinion. A party who disagrees with the agency's proposed judgment must within 7 days file with the clerk and serve the agency with a proposed judgment that the party believes conforms to the opinion. The court will settle the judgment and direct entry without further hearing or argument. (Amended by order adopted March 10, 1986, effective July 1, 1986; and by order adopted April 24, 1998, effective December 1, 1998.)

Rule 20. Applicability of rules to the review or enforcement of an agency order.

All provisions of these rules, except Rules 3-14 and 22-23, apply to the review or enforcement of an agency order. In these rules, "appellant" includes a petitioner or applicant, and "appellee" includes a respondent. (Amended by order adopted April 24, 1998, effective December 1, 1998.)

TITLE V. EXTRAORDINARY WRITS.

Rule 21. Writs of mandamus and prohibition, and other extraordinary writs.

(a) **Mandamus or prohibition to a court: petition, filing, service, and docketing.** (1) A party petitioning for a writ of mandamus or prohibition directed to a court must file a petition with the circuit clerk with proof of service on all parties to the proceeding in the trial court. The party must also provide a copy to the trial-court judge. All parties to the proceeding in the trial court other than the petitioner are respondents for all purposes.

(2) (A) The petition must be titled "In re [name of petitioner]."

(B) The petition must state:

(i) the relief sought;

(ii) the issues presented;

(iii) the facts necessary to understand the issue presented by the petition; and

(iv) the reasons why the writ should issue.

(C) The petition must include a copy of any order or opinion or parts of the record that may be essential to understand the matters set forth in the petition.

(3) Upon receiving the prescribed docket fee, the clerk must docket the petition and submit it to the court.

(b) **Denial; order directing answer; briefs; precedence.** (1) The court may deny the petition without an answer. Otherwise, it must order the respondent, if any, to answer within a fixed time.

(2) The clerk must serve the order to respond on all persons directed to respond.

(3) Two or more respondents may answer jointly.

(4) The court of appeals may invite or order the trial-court judge to address the petition or may invite an amicus curiae to do so. The trial-court judge may request permission to address the petition but may not do so unless invited or ordered to do so by the court of appeals.

(5) If briefing or oral argument is required, the clerk must advise the parties, and when appropriate, the trial-court judge or amicus curiae.

(6) The proceeding must be given preference over ordinary civil cases.

(7) The circuit clerk must send a copy of the final disposition to the trial-court judge.

(c) **Other extraordinary writs.** An application for an extraordinary writ other than one provided for in Rule 21(a) must be made by filing a petition with the circuit clerk with proof of service on the respondents. Proceedings on the application must conform, so far as is practicable, to the procedures prescribed in Rule 21(a) and (b).

(d) **Form of papers; number of copies.** All papers must conform to Rule 32(c)(2). Except by the court's permission, a paper must not exceed 30 pages, exclusive of the disclosure statement, the proof of service, and the accompanying documents required by Rule 21(a)(2)(C). An original and 3 copies must be filed unless the court requires the filing of a different number by local rule or by order in a particular case. (Amended by order adopted April 29, 1994, effective December 1, 1994; by order adopted April 23, 1996, effective December 1, 1996; by order adopted April 24, 1998, effective December 1, 1998; and by order adopted April 29, 2002, effective December 1, 2002.)

Mandamus preferred method of review of orders restricting press activity. — Mandamus is preferred method of review for orders restricting press activity related to criminal proceedings, but an appeal would be treated as a petition for mandamus if the party seeking review has standing and has substantially complied with the requirements of subdivision (a) of this rule concerning mandamus. Washington Post Co. v. United States, 807 F.2d 383 (4th Cir. 1986).

Local Rule 21(a). Case captions for extraordinary writs.

A petition for a writ of mandamus or writ of prohibition shall not bear the name of the district judge, but shall be entitled simply "In re _____, Petitioner." To the extent that relief is requested of a particular judge, unless otherwise ordered, the judge shall be represented pro forma by counsel for the party opposing the relief, who shall appear in the name of the party and not that of the judge.

Local Rule 21(b). Petitions for mandamus or prohibition.

Strict compliance with the requirements of FRAP 21 is required of all petitioners, even pro se litigants. Petitioner must pay the prescribed docket fee of $450, payable to the Clerk, U.S. Court of Appeals; submit the forms required by Local Rule 21(c)(1) for cases subject to that Local Rule; or submit a properly executed application for leave to proceed in forma pauperis. The parties are required to submit Disclosure of Corporate Affiliations statements with the petition and answer. See FRAP 26.1 and Local Rule 26.1.

After docketing, the clerk shall submit the application to a three-judge panel. A motion for emergency relief pending determination of the petition may be filed and will be assigned in accordance with Local Rule 27(e).

If the Court believes the writ should not be granted, it will deny the petition without requesting an answer. Otherwise the Court will direct the clerk to obtain an answer. After an answer has been filed, the Court ordinarily will decide the merits of the petition on the materials submitted without oral argument. Occasionally, however, briefs may be requested and the matter set for oral argument. (Amended by order effective September 25, 1996; amended by order effective February 1, 2001; amended October 9, 2003, effective

November 1, 2003; amended April 27, 2006, effective April 9, 2006; and amended effective December 1, 2009.)

<table>
<tr><td>

Effect of amendments. — The 2003 amendment substituted "$250" for "100" in the second sentence of the first paragraph.

The 2006 amendment substituted "$450" for "$250" in the first paragraph.

The 2009 amendment in the first paragraph substituted "Disclosure of Corporate Affilia-

</td><td>

tions statements" for "Disclosure of Corporate Affiliations and Other Entities with a Direct Financial Interest in Litigation statements" in the third sentence and deleted "and Form A" at the end of the last sentence; and made related changes.

</td></tr>
</table>

Local Rule 21(c). Fees and costs for prisoner petitions for mandamus, prohibition, or other extraordinary relief.

(1) **Proceedings arising out of civil matters.** A prisoner filing a petition for writ of mandamus, prohibition, or other extraordinary relief in a matter arising out of a civil case must pay the full $450 docket fee. A prisoner who is unable to prepay this fee may apply to pay the fee in installments by filing with the Court of Appeals (1) an application to proceed without prepayment of fees; (2) a certified copy of the prisoner's trust fund account statement for the six-month period immediately preceding the filing of the notice of appeal, obtained from the appropriate official of each prison at which the prisoner is or was confined; and (3) a form consenting to the collection of fees from the prisoner's trust account.

The Court of Appeals will assess an initial partial filing fee of 20% of the greater of:

(a) the average monthly deposits to the prisoner's account for the six-month period immediately preceding the filing of the petition; or

(b) the average monthly balance in the prisoner's account for the six-month period immediately preceding the filing of the petition.

The Court will direct the agency having custody of the prisoner to collect this initial partial fee from the prisoner's trust account, and to collect the remainder of the $450 fee, as well as any other fees, costs, or sanctions imposed by the Court, in monthly installments of 20% of the preceding month's deposits credited to the prisoner's account. The agency having custody of the prisoner shall forward payments from the prisoner's account to the Clerk, U.S. Court of Appeals, each time the amount in the account exceeds $10 until all fees, costs, and sanctions are paid for the petition.

If a prisoner proceeding under this rule fails to file the forms or make the payments required by the Court, the appeal will be dismissed pursuant to Local Rule 45.

(2) **Effect of prior actions and appeals on proceedings arising out of civil matters.** A prisoner who has, on three or more prior occasions, while incarcerated or detained in any facility, brought an action or appeal in a court of the United States that was dismissed on the grounds that it was frivolous, malicious, or failed to state a claim upon which relief could be granted, may not proceed in a matter arising out of a civil case without prepayment of fees unless the prisoner is under imminent danger of serious physical injury.

(3) **Proceedings arising out of criminal matters.** A prisoner who is unable to prepay the full $450 docket fee for a petition for writ of mandamus,

prohibition, or other extraordinary relief arising out of a criminal case may apply to proceed without the prepayment of fees by filing an application for leave to proceed in forma pauperis. (Adopted by order effective September 25, 1996; amended October 9, 2003, effective November 1, 2003; and amended April 27, 2006, effective April 9, 2006.)

Effect of amendments. — The 2003 amendment substituted "$250" for "$100" three times.

The 2006 amendment substituted "$450" for "$250" in (1), the second paragraph of (b) and (3).

Local Rule 21(d). Petitions for writ of mandamus pursuant to 18 U.S.C. § 3771, Crime Victims' Rights.

A petition for writ of mandamus asserting the rights of a crime victim pursuant to 18 U.S.C.§ 3771(d)(3) shall bear the caption "PETITION FOR WRIT OF MANDAMUS PURSUANT TO 18 U.S.C. § 3771, CRIME VICTIMS' RIGHTS." Before filing such a petition, the petitioner must notify the Court of Appeals that such a petition will be filed and must arrange for immediate service of the petition on the relevant parties. Such notification must be by telephone call to the Office of the Clerk during normal office hours (804-916-2700).

A failure to comply with these requirements will adversely affect the Court's ability to decide the petition within 72 hours as required by 18 U.S.C. § 3771(d)(3). (Added June 1, 2006, effective August 1, 2006.)

TITLE VI. HABEAS CORPUS; PROCEEDINGS IN FORMA PAUPERIS.

Rule 22. Habeas corpus and section 2255 proceedings.

(a) **Application for the original writ.** An application for a writ of habeas corpus must be made to the appropriate district court. If made to a circuit judge, the application must be transferred to the appropriate district court. If a district court denies an application made or transferred to it, renewal of the application before a circuit judge is not permitted. The applicant may, under 28 U.S.C. § 2253, appeal to the court of appeals from the district court's order denying the application.

(b) **Certificate of appealability.** (1) In a habeas corpus proceeding in which the detention complained of arises from process issued by a state court, or in a 28 U.S.C. § 2255 proceeding, the applicant cannot take an appeal unless a circuit justice or a circuit or district judge issues a certificate of appealability under 28 U.S.C. § 2253(c). If an applicant files a notice of appeal, the district judge who rendered the judgment must either issue a certificate of appealability or state why a certificate should not issue. The district clerk must send the certificate or statement to the court of appeals with the notice of appeal and the file of the district-court proceedings. If the district judge has denied the certificate, the applicant may request a circuit judge to issue the certificate.

(2) A request addressed to the court of appeals may be considered by a circuit judge or judges, as the court prescribes. If no express request for a

certificate is filed, the notice of appeal constitutes a request addressed to the judges of the court of appeals.

(3) A certificate of appealability is not required when a state or its representative or the United States or its representative appeals. (Amended by order adopted April 24, 1998, effective December 1, 1998.)

Local Rule 22(a). Certificates of appealability.

All applications for certificates of appealability shall either be in the form of a motion under FRAP 27(a) or be accompanied by informal briefs pursuant to Local Rule 34(b), regardless of whether the petitioner is represented by counsel. An application for a certificate of appealability may be referred to a panel of three judges. If all the judges on the panel conclude that the certificate should not issue, the certificate will be denied; but if any judge of such panel is of the opinion that the applicant has made a substantial showing of the denial of a constitutional right, the certificate will issue. The certificate shall indicate which specific issue or issues satisfy the required showing. If the Court grants a certificate of appealability, it may thereafter affirm, reverse or remand without further briefing or direct full briefing and oral argument. (Amended by order effective December 1, 1995; amended by order effective June 5, 1996; and amended by order effective December 1, 1998.)

COMMENT

Local Rule 22(a) has been amended to delete reference to an accompanying memorandum of law because FRAP 27(a)(2)(c)(i) bars memoranda in support of motions.

Local Rule 22(b). Death penalty cases and motions for stay of execution.

(1) **Statement certifying existence of sentence of death.** Whenever a petition for writ of habeas corpus or motion to vacate a federal sentence in which a sentence of death is involved is filed in the district court or the Court of Appeals, the petitioner shall file with the petition a statement certifying the existence of a sentence of death and the emergency nature of the proceedings and listing any proposed date of execution, any previous cases filed by petitioner in federal court and any cases filed by petitioner pending in any other court. The clerk of the district court shall immediately forward to the Court of Appeals a copy of any such statement filed, and shall immediately notify by telephone the Court of Appeals upon issuance of a final order in that case. If a notice of appeal is filed, the clerk of the district court shall transmit the available record forthwith. The clerk of the Court of Appeals will maintain a special docket for such cases and these cases shall be presented to the Court of Appeals on an expedited basis.

(2) **Lodging of documents.** In cases in which an execution date has been set, counsel shall lodge with the clerk of the Court of Appeals all district court documents as they are filed and any pertinent state court materials. If an execution date is imminent, counsel may also lodge proposed appellate papers in anticipation of having to seek emergency appellate relief.

(3) **Motion for stay of execution.** Any motion for stay of execution shall be considered initially in conjunction with any pending application for a certifi-

cate of appealability. Should a party file a motion to stay execution or a motion to vacate an order granting a stay of execution, the following documents shall accompany such motion:

(a) The habeas petition or motion to vacate filed in the district court;

(b) Each brief or memorandum of authorities filed by either party in the district court;

(c) Any available transcript of proceedings before the district court;

(d) The memorandum opinion giving the reasons advanced by the district court for denying relief;

(e) The district court judgment denying relief;

(f) The application to the district court for stay;

(g) Any certificate of appealability or order denying a certificate of appealability;

(h) The district court order granting or denying a stay and a statement of reasons for its action; and

(i) A copy of the docket entries of the district court. (Amended by order effective December 1, 1995; and effective June 5, 1996.)

COMMENT

Local Rule 22(b) has been modified to include within its procedures federal death penalty cases filed pursuant to 28 U.S.C. § 2255.

Local Rule 22(c). Petitions for rehearing in death penalty cases.

(1) **All death penalty cases.** Once the Court's mandate has issued in a death penalty case, any petition for panel or en banc rehearing should be accompanied by a motion to recall the mandate and motion to stay the execution.

Generally, the Court will not enter a stay of execution solely to allow for additional time for counsel to prepare, or for the Court to consider, a petition for rehearing. Consequently, counsel should take all possible steps to assure that any such petition is filed sufficiently in advance of the scheduled execution date to allow it to be considered by the Court. Counsel should notify the Clerk's Office promptly of their intention to file a petition for rehearing so that arrangements can be made in advance for the most expeditious consideration of the matter by the Court.

(2) **Emergency petitions.** In extraordinary circumstances, when the petition cannot be filed earlier than three days before a scheduled execution date, the Clerk's Office will endeavor to inform the members of the panel that issued the Court's decision of the filing of a petition for panel or en banc rehearing within a shorter period of time. At the direction of a panel member, similar efforts will be made to inform the full Court of the matter. The Clerk's Office will give notice to counsel by telephone of the Court's decision on such petitions. (Amended by order effective December 1, 1995; by order effective December 1, 1998; by order effective July 29, 1999; and by order effective December 1, 2002.)

Local Rule 22(d). Motions for authorization.

Any individual seeking to file in the district court a second or successive application for relief pursuant to 28 U.S.C. § 2254 or § 2255 shall first file a motion with the Court of Appeals for authorization as required by 28 U.S.C. § 2244, on the form provided by the clerk for such motions. The motion shall be entitled "In re _____, Movant." The motion must be accompanied by copies of the § 2254 or § 2255 application which movant seeks authorization to file in the district court, as well as all prior § 2254 or § 2255 applications challenging the same conviction and sentence, all court opinions and orders disposing of those applications, and all magistrate judge's reports and recommendations issued on those applications. The movant shall serve a copy of the motion with attachments on the respondent named in the proposed application and shall file an original and three copies of the motion with attachments in the Court of Appeals. Failure to provide the requisite information and attachments may result in denial of the motion for authorization.

If the Court requires a response to the motion, it will direct that the response be received by the clerk for filing within no more than seven days. The Court will enter an order granting or denying authorization within 30 days of receipt of the motion by the clerk for filing, and the clerk will certify a copy of the order to the district court. If authorization is granted, a copy of the application will be attached to the certified order for filing in the district court. No motion or request for reconsideration, petition for rehearing, or any other paper seeking review of the granting or denial of authorization will be allowed. (Adopted by order effective June 5, 1996; amended by order effective December 1, 2002; and amended effective December 1, 2009.)

Effect of amendments. — The 2009 amendment substituted "seven days" for "seven calendar days" in the first sentence of the last paragraph.

I.O.P. 22.1. Death penalty cases.

Once a notice of appeal has been filed in a case involving a sentence of death where an execution date has been set, a panel of three judges will be promptly identified for consideration of all matters related to the case. The position of coordinator of case information in death penalty cases has been established in the Clerk's Office of the Court of Appeals for the purpose of establishing personal liaison with district court personnel and counsel to aid in the expeditious treatment of appeals involving a sentence of death. An expedited briefing schedule will be established when necessary to allow the Court the opportunity to review all issues presented. (Amended by order effective June 1, 1999.)

Rule 23. Custody or release of a prisoner in a habeas corpus proceeding.

(a) **Transfer of custody pending review.** Pending review of a decision in a habeas corpus proceeding commenced before a court, justice, or judge of the United States for the release of a prisoner, the person having custody of the prisoner must not transfer custody to another unless a transfer is directed in accordance with this rule. When, upon application, a custodian shows the need for a transfer, the court, justice, or judge rendering the decision under review may authorize the transfer and substitute the successor custodian as a party.

(b) **Detention or release pending review of decision not to release.** While a decision not to release a prisoner is under review, the court or judge rendering the decision, or the court of appeals, or the Supreme Court, or a judge or justice of either court, may order that the prisoner be:

(1) detained in the custody from which release is sought;

(2) detained in other appropriate custody; or

(3) released on personal recognizance, with or without surety.

(c) **Release pending review of decision ordering release.** While a decision ordering the release of a prisoner is under review, the prisoner must — unless the court or judge rendering the decision, or the court of appeals, or the Supreme Court, or a judge or justice of either court orders otherwise — be released on personal recognizance, with or without surety.

(d) **Modification of the initial order on custody.** An initial order governing the prisoner's custody or release, including any recognizance or surety, continues in effect pending review unless for special reasons shown to the court of appeals or the Supreme Court, or to a judge or justice of either court, the order is modified or an independent order regarding custody, release, or surety is issued. (Amended by order adopted March 10, 1986, effective July 1, 1986, and by order adopted April 29, 1994, effective December 1, 1994, and by order adopted April 23, 1996, effective December 1, 1996 and by order adopted April 24, 1998, effective December 1, 1998.)

Rule 24. Proceeding in forma pauperis.

(a) **Leave to proceed in forma pauperis.** (1) Motion in the district court. Except as stated in Rule 24(a)(3), a party to a district-court action who desires to appeal in forma pauperis must file a motion in the district court. The party must attach an affidavit that:

(A) shows in the detail prescribed by Form 4 of the Appendix of Forms, the party's inability to pay or to give security for fees and costs;

(B) claims an entitlement to redress; and

(C) states the issues that the party intends to present on appeal.

(2) Action on the motion. If the district court grants the motion, the party may proceed on appeal without prepaying or giving security for fees and costs, unless a statute provides otherwise. If the district court denies the motion, it must state its reasons in writing.

(3) Prior approval. A party who was permitted to proceed in forma pauperis in the district-court action, or who was determined to be financially unable to obtain an adequate defense in a criminal case, may proceed on appeal in forma pauperis without further authorization, unless:

(A) the district court — before or after the notice of appeal is filed — certifies that the appeal is not taken in good faith or finds that the party is not otherwise entitled to proceed in forma pauperis and states in writing its reasons for the certification or finding; or

(B) a statute provides otherwise.

(4) Notice of district court's denial. The district clerk must immediately notify the parties and the court of appeals when the district court does any of the following:

(A) denies a motion to proceed on appeal in forma pauperis;

(B) certifies that the appeal is not taken in good faith; or

(C) finds that the party is not otherwise entitled to proceed in forma pauperis.

(5) Motion in the court of appeals. A party may file a motion to proceed on appeal in forma pauperis in the court of appeals within 30 days after service of the notice prescribed in Rule 24(a)(4). The motion must include a copy of the affidavit filed in the district court and the district court's statement of reasons for its action. If no affidavit was filed in the district court, the party must include the affidavit prescribed by Rule 24(a)(1).

(b) **Leave to proceed in forma pauperis on appeal or review of an administrative-agency proceeding.** When an appeal or review of a proceeding before an administrative agency, board, commission, or officer (including for the purpose of this rule the United States Tax Court) proceeds directly in a court of appeals, a party may file in the court of appeals a motion for leave to proceed on appeal in forma pauperis with an affidavit prescribed by Rule 24(a)(1).

(c) **Leave to use original record.** A party allowed to proceed on appeal in forma pauperis may request that the appeal be heard on the original record without reproducing any part. (Amended by order adopted April 30, 1979, effective August 1, 1979; by order adopted March 10, 1986, effective July 1, 1986; by order adopted April 24, 1998, effective December 1, 1998; and by order adopted April 29, 2002, effective December 1, 2002.)

Local Rule 24. Prisoner appeals.

(a) **Payment of fees and costs required.** A prisoner appealing a judgment in a civil action must pay in full the $455 fee required for commencement of the appeal. A prisoner who is unable to prepay this fee may apply to pay the fee in installments by filing with the Court of Appeals (1) an application to proceed without prepayment of fees; (2) a certified copy of the prisoner's trust fund account statement or institutional equivalent for the six-month period immediately preceding the filing of the notice of appeal, obtained from the appropriate official of each prison at which the prisoner is or was confined; and (3) a form consenting to the collection of fees from the prisoner's trust account.

The Court of Appeals will assess an initial partial filing fee of 20% of the greater of:

(1) the average monthly deposits to the prisoner's account for the six-month period immediately preceding the filing of the notice of appeal; or

(2) the average monthly balance in the prisoner's account for the six-month period immediately preceding the filing of the notice of appeal.

Based upon the prisoner's consent, the Court will direct the agency having custody of the prisoner to collect this initial partial fee from the prisoner's trust account, and to collect the remainder of the $455 filing fee, as well as any other fees, costs, or sanctions imposed by the Court of Appeals, in monthly installments of 20% of the preceding month's deposits credited to the prisoner's account. The agency having custody of the prisoner shall forward payments from the prisoner's account to the clerk of the district court each time the amount in the account exceeds $10 until all fees, costs, and sanctions are paid for the appeal.

If a prisoner proceeding under this rule fails to file the forms or make the payments required by the Court, the appeal will be dismissed pursuant to Local Rule 45.

(b) **Effect of prior actions and appeals.** A prisoner who has, on three or more prior occasions, while incarcerated or detained in any facility, brought an action or appeal in a court of the United States that was dismissed on the grounds that it was frivolous, malicious, or failed to state a claim upon which relief could be granted, may not proceed on appeal without prepayment of fees unless the prisoner is under imminent danger of serious physical injury. (Adopted by order effective June 5, 1996; amended October 9, 2003, effective November 1, 2003; amended April 27, 2006, effective April 9, 2006.)

Effect of amendments. — The 2003 amendment substituted "$255" for "$105" in the introductory sentence in (a) and in (a)(2).

The 2006 amendment substituted "$455" for "$255" in (a) and the second paragraph of (a)(2).

TITLE VII. GENERAL PROVISIONS.

Rule 25. Filing and service.

(a) **Filing.** (1) Filing with the clerk. A paper required or permitted to be filed in a court of appeals must be filed with the clerk.

(2) Filing: Method and timeliness. (A) In general. Filing may be accomplished by mail addressed to the clerk, but filing is not timely unless the clerk receives the papers within the time fixed for filing.

(B) A brief or appendix. A brief or appendix is timely filed, however, if on or before the last day for filing, it is:

(i) mailed to the clerk by First-Class Mail, or other class of mail that is at least as expeditious, postage prepaid; or

(ii) dispatched to a third-party commercial carrier for delivery to the clerk within 3 calendar days.

(C) Inmate filing. A paper filed by an inmate confined in an institution is timely if deposited in the institution's internal mailing system on or before the last day for filing. If an institution has a system designed for legal mail, the inmate must use that system to receive the benefit of this rule. Timely filing may be shown by a declaration in compliance with 28 U.S.C. § 1746 or by a notarized statement, either of which must set forth the date of deposit and state that first-class postage has been prepaid.

(D) Electronic filing. A court of appeals may by local rule permit or require papers to be filed, signed, or verified by electronic means that are consistent with technical standards, if any, that the Judicial Conference of the United States establishes. A local rule may require filing by electronic means only if reasonable exceptions are allowed. A paper filed by electronic means in compliance with a local rule constitutes a written paper for the purpose of applying these rules.

(3) Filing a motion with a judge. If a motion requests relief that may be granted by a single judge, the judge may permit the motion to be filed with the judge; the judge must note the filing date on the motion and give it to the clerk.

(4) Clerk's refusal of documents. The clerk must not refuse to accept for filing any paper presented for that purpose solely because it is not presented in proper form as required by these rules or by any local rule or practice.

(b) **Service of all papers required.** Unless a rule requires service by the clerk, a party must, at or before the time of filing a paper, serve a copy on the other parties to the appeal or review. Service on a party represented by counsel must be made on the party's counsel.

(c) **Manner of service.** (1) Service may be any of the following:

(A) personal, including delivery to a responsible person at the office of counsel;

(B) by mail,

(C) by third-party commercial carrier for delivery within 3 calendar days; or

(D) by electronic means, if the party being served consents in writing.

(2) If authorized by local rule, a party may use the court's transmission equipment to make electronic service under Rule 25(c)(1)(D).

(3) When reasonably considering such factors as the immediacy of the relief sought, distance, and cost, service on a party must be by a manner at least as expeditious as the manner used to file the paper with the court.

(4) Service by mail or by commercial carrier is complete on mailing or delivery to the carrier. Service by electronic means is complete on transmission, unless the party making service is notified that the paper was not received by the party served.

(d) **Proof of service.** (1) A paper presented for filing must contain either of the following:

(A) an acknowledgment of service by the person served; or

(B) proof of service consisting of a statement by the person who made service certifying:

(i) the date and manner of service;

(ii) the names of the persons served; and

(iii) their mail or electronic addresses, facsimile numbers, or the addresses of the places of delivery, as appropriate for the manner of service.

(2) When a brief or appendix is filed by mailing or dispatch in accordance with Rule 25(a)(2)(B), the proof of service must also state the date and manner by which the document was mailed or dispatched to the clerk.

(3) Proof of service may appear on or be affixed to the papers filed.

(e) **Number of copies.** When these rules require the filing or furnishing of a number of copies, a court may require a different number by local rule or by order in a particular case. (Amended by order effective July 1, 1986; by order adopted April 30, 1991, effective December 1, 1991; by order adopted April 22, 1993, effective December 1, 1993; by order adopted April 29, 1994, effective December 1, 1994; by order adopted April 23, 1996, effective December 1, 1996; by order adopted April 24, 1998, effective December 1, 1998; by order adopted

April 29, 2002, effective December 1, 2002; amended effective December 1, 2006.)

Effect of amendments. — The 2006 amendment, in (a)(2)(D), added "or require" in the first sentence and added "A local rule may require filing by electronic means only if reasonable exceptions are allowed."

Editor's note. — As to electronic filing of documents with federal courts in the Fourth Circuit, see CM/ECF Docket at www.ca4.uscourts.gov.

Local Rule 25(a). Electronic case filing system.

As authorized by FRAP 25(a)(2)(D) & (c)(2), the Court has established procedures requiring electronic filing of documents, with certain exceptions, and authorizing electronic service of documents using the Court's transmission equipment, as set forth in Administrative Order 08-01. (Amended by order effective December 1, 1995; by order effective December 1, 1998; and by order effective April 1, 2008.)

COMMENT

Local Rule 25(a) has been amended to delete the reference to typeset briefs because FRAP 32(a) no longer provides for typeset briefs.

Effect of amendments. — The 2008 amendment rewrote the Rule.

Editor's note. — As to electronic filing of documents with federal courts in the Fourth Circuit, see CM/ECF docket at www.ca4.uscourts.gov.

Local Rule 25(b). Filing documents, use of facsimile equipment, service, certificate of service.

(1) **Filing documents.** Documents, except briefs, appendices, and inmate filings, are not timely filed unless actually received by the Clerk's Office within the time fixed for filing. Documents are deemed filed upon receipt by the Clerk's Office.

(2) **Use of Facsimile Equipment.** Documents may be transmitted for filing by use of facsimile transmission equipment only when an emergency situation exists and advance permission has been obtained to use the Clerk's Office facsimile equipment. Several printing services in Richmond will accept documents by facsimile for filing with the Court. Their telephone numbers may be obtained from the Clerk's Office. When a facsimile copy is filed, the original, signed document need not be filed.

(3) **Service.** Service on a party represented by counsel must be on all counsel of record.

(4) **Certificate of service.** All documents must be accompanied by a valid certificate of service. The certificate of service of a brief should be bound with the brief as the last, unnumbered page. A certificate of service can be prepared in advance of actual service. If service is not actually accomplished in the manner and on the date stated in the certificate, an amended certificate of service is required. (Amended by order effective December 1, 1995; order effective December 1, 1998; order effective April 1, 2008.)

COMMENT

The first sentence of the last paragraph of Rule 25(b)(1) has been moved to Local Rule 27(d) because it refers to the filing of responses to motions. The final sentence of Local Rule 25(b)(1) has been deleted because it duplicates the information in the first sentence of Local Rule 27(d)(1).

Effect of amendments. — The 2008 amendment substituted "documents, use of facsimile equipment" for "papers" in the title; rewrote (1); added (2) and redesignated accordingly; and in (4) substituted "documents" for "papers" in the first sentence and in the third sentence substituted the second instance of "service" for "mailing or hand delivery of the paper served".

Local Rule 25(c). Confidential and sealed materials.

(1) **Certificates of confidentiality.** At the time of filing any appendix, brief, motion, or other document containing or otherwise disclosing materials held under seal by another court or agency, counsel or a *pro se* party shall file a certificate of confidentiality.

(A) Record material held under seal by another court or agency remains subject to that seal on appeal unless modified or amended by the Court of Appeals.

(B) A certificate of confidentiality must accompany any filing which contains or would otherwise disclose sealed materials. The certificate of confidentiality shall:

(i) identify the sealed material;

(ii) list the dates of the orders sealing the material or, if there is no order, the lower court or agency's general authority to treat the material as sealed;

(iii) specify the terms of the protective order governing the information; and

(iv) identify the appellate document that contains the sealed information.

(2) **Motions to seal.** Motions to seal all or any part of the record are presented to and resolved by the lower court or agency in accordance with applicable law during the course of trial, hearing, or other proceedings below.

(A) A motion to seal may be filed with the Court of Appeals when:

(i) a change in circumstances occurs during the pendency of an appeal that warrants reconsideration of a sealing issue decided below;

(ii) the need to seal all or part of the record on appeal arises in the first instance during the pendency of an appeal; or

(iii) additional material filed for the first time on appeal warrants sealing.

(B) Any motion to seal filed with the Court of Appeals shall:

(i) identify with specificity the documents or portions thereof for which sealing is requested;

(ii) state the reasons why sealing is necessary;

(iii) explain why a less drastic alternative to sealing will not afford adequate protection; and

(iv) state the period of time the party seeks to have the material maintained under seal and how the material is to be handled upon unsealing.

(C) A motion to seal filed with the Court of Appeals will be placed on the public docket for at least 5 days before the Court rules on the motion, but the materials subject to a motion to seal will be held under seal pending the Court's disposition of the motion.

(3) **Filing of Confidential and Sealed Material.** (A) Appendices: When sealed material is included in the appendix, it must be segregated from other portions of the appendix and filed in a separate, sealed volume of the appendix.

(B) Briefs, Motions, and Other Documents: When sealed material is included in a brief, motion, or any document other than an appendix, two versions of the document must be filed:

(i) a complete version under seal in which the sealed material has been distinctively marked and

(ii) a redacted version of the same document for the public file.

(C) Personal Data Identifying Information: Personal data identifying information, such as an individual's social security number, an individual's tax identification number, a minor's name, a person's birth date, a financial account number, and (in a criminal case) a person's home address, shall be filed in accordance with section 205(c)(3) of the E-Government Act of 2002 and FRAP 25(a)(5).

(D) Marking of Sealed and Ex Parte Material: The first page of any appendix, brief, motion, or other document tendered or filed under seal shall be conspicuously marked SEALED and all copies shall be placed in an envelope marked SEALED. If filed ex parte, the first page and the envelope shall also be marked EX PARTE.

(E) Method of Filing. (i) Appendices: Appendices are filed in paper form only, with sealed material placed in a separate, sealed volume, accompanied by a certificate of confidentiality or motion to seal. A Notice of paper filing and either a certificate of confidentiality or a motion to seal are filed in electronic form.

(ii) Formal Briefs: The sealed and public versions of formal briefs are filed in both paper and electronic form. The sealed version is accompanied by a certificate of confidentiality or motion to seal, that is also filed in both paper and electronic form. The electronic sealed version of the brief is filed using the entry SEALED BRIEF FILED, which automatically restricts electronic access to the Court. The electronic public version of the brief is filed using the entry BRIEF FILED.

(iii) Other Documents: Any other sealed document is filed electronically using the entry SEALED DOCUMENT FILED, which automatically restricts electronic access to the Court. A certificate of confidentiality or motion to seal is also filed electronically. If filed electronically, paper copies of the sealed document are not required unless requested by the Court.

(F) Number of Paper Copies Filed and Served: Sealed documents must be served in paper form because electronic access to sealed documents is restricted to the Court.

(i) Appendices: Sealed volumes - File four and serve one on each party separately represented. Unsealed volumes - File six (five if counsel was appointed, four if party is proceeding in forma pauperis without appointed counsel) and serve one on each party separately represented.

(ii) Formal Briefs: Sealed version – File four and serve one on each party separately represented. Public version – File eight (six if counsel was appointed, four if party is proceeding in forma pauperis without appointed counsel).

(iii) Other Documents: Sealed version – File one (none if filed electronically) and serve one paper copy on each party separately represented. Public version – File one (none if filed electronically).

(G) Responsibility for Compliance: The responsibility for following the required procedures in filing confidential and sealed material rests solely with counsel and the parties. The clerk will not review each filing for compliance with this rule.

(H) Public Access: Parties must remember that any personal information not otherwise protected by sealing or redaction may be made available over the internet. Counsel should notify clients of this fact so that an informed decision may be made on what information is to be included in a document filed with the Court. (Redesignated and amended by order effective April 16, 2007; by order effective April 1, 2008; and amended effective December 1, 2009.)

Effect of amendments. — The 2007 amendment redesignated former 10(d) as present 25(c); added "and sealed" to the heading; in (1) substituted "At the time of filing ... or otherwise disclosing materials" for "At the time of filing any motion, brief, appendix or other document containing or otherwise disclosing materials" and added "or a pro se party"; rewrote (2)(A)(i); and rewrote (3).

The 2008 amendment in (3)(C) substituted "FRAP 25(a)(5)" for "rules adopted thereunder"; added (3)(E), and redesignated accordingly; and rewrote (3)(F).

The 2009 amendment substituted "5 days" for "5 calendar days" in (2)(C).

Rule 26. Computing and extending time.

(a) **Computation of time.** The following rules apply in computing any period of time specified in these rules or in any local rule, court order, or applicable statute:

(1) Exclude the day of the act, event, or default that begins the period.

(2) Exclude intermediate Saturdays, Sundays, and legal holidays when the period is less than 11 days, unless stated in calendar days.

(3) Include the last day of the period unless it is a Saturday, Sunday, legal holiday, or — if the act to be done is filing a paper in court — a day on which the weather or other conditions make the clerk's office inaccessible.

(4) As used in this rule, "legal holiday" means New Year's Day, Martin Luther King, Jr.'s Birthday, Presidents' Day, Memorial Day, Independence Day, Labor Day, Columbus Day, Veterans' Day, Thanksgiving Day, Christmas Day, and any other day declared a holiday by the President, Congress, or the state in which is located either the district court that rendered the challenged judgment or order, or the circuit clerk's principal office.

(b) **Extending time.** For good cause, the court may extend the time prescribed by these rules or by its order to perform any act, or may permit an act to be done after that time expires. But the court may not extend the time to file:

(1) a notice of appeal (except as authorized in Rule 4) or a petition for permission to appeal; or

(2) a notice of appeal from or a petition to enjoin, set aside, suspend, modify, enforce, or otherwise review an order of an administrative agency, board,

commission, or officer of the United States, unless specifically authorized by law.

(c) **Additional time after service.** When a party is required or permitted to act within a prescribed period after a paper is served on that party, 3 calendar days are added to the prescribed period unless the paper is delivered on the date of service stated in the proof of service. For purposes of this Rule 26(c), a paper that is served electronically is not treated as delivered on the date of service stated in the proof of service. (Amended by order adopted March 1, 1971, effective July 1, 1971; by order effective July 1, 1986; by order adopted April 25, 1989, effective December 1, 1989; by order adopted April 30, 1991, effective December 1, 1991; by order adopted April 23, 1996, effective December 1, 1996; by order adopted April 24, 1998, effective December 1, 1998; and by order adopted April 24, 2002, effective December 1, 2002.)

Extension granted merely to prevent unduly harsh result for failure to comply with Rule 41 FRAP. — See Caperton v. Beatrice Pocahontas Coal Co., 585 F.2d 683 (4th Cir. 1978).

Applied in United States v. Breit, 754 F.2d 526 (4th Cir. 1985).

Local Rule 26. State holidays and inclement weather.

Whenever a party in computing a filing or service date relies upon an extension of time due to the inaccessibility of the Clerk's Office because of inclement weather or other conditions, or due to a state holiday, counsel must certify such reliance in the certificate of service or by separate written declaration.

Rule 26.1. Corporate disclosure statement.

(a) **Who must file.** Any nongovernmental corporate party to a proceeding in a court of appeals must file a statement that identifies any parent corporation and any publicly held corporation that owns 10% or more of its stock or states that there is no such corporation.

(b) **Time for filing; Supplemental filing.** A party must file the Rule 26.1(a) statement with the principal brief or upon filing a motion, response, petition, or answer in the court of appeals, whichever occurs first, unless a local rule requires earlier filing. Even if the statement has already been filed, the party's principal brief must include the statement before the table of contents. A party must supplement its statement whenever the information that must be disclosed under Rule 26.1(a) changes.

(c) **Number of copies.** If the Rule 26.1(a) statement is filed before the principal brief, or if a supplemental statement is filed, the party must file an original and 3 copies unless the court requires a different number by local rule or by order in a particular case. (Adopted by order April 25, 1989, effective December 1, 1989; amended by order adopted April 30, 1991, effective December 1, 1991; by order adopted April 29, 1994, effective December 1, 1994; by order adopted April 24, 1998, effective December 1, 1998; and by order adopted April 29, 2002, effective December 1, 2002.)

Local Rule 26.1. Disclosure of corporate affiliations and other entities with a direct financial interest in litigation.

(a) **Disclosure requirements applicable to parties, including intervenors.** (1) Who must file. (A) Civil, agency, bankruptcy, and mandamus cases. A party in a civil, agency, bankruptcy, or mandamus case, other than the United States or a party proceeding in *forma pauperis,* must file a disclosure statement, except that a state or local government is not required to file a disclosure statement in a case in which the opposing party isproceeding without counsel.

(B) Criminal and post-conviction cases. A corporate party in a criminal or post-conviction case must file a disclosure statement.

(2) Information to be disclosed by parties, including intervenors. (A) Information Required by FRAP 26.1. A party must identify any parent corporation and any publicly held corporation that owns 10% or more of the party's stock, or state that there is no such corporation.

(B) Information about other finanacial interests. A party must identify any publicly held corporation, whether or not a party to the present litigation, that has a direct financial interest in the outcome of the litigation by reason of a franchise, lease, other profit sharing agreement, insurance, or indemnity agreement, or state that there is no such corporation.

(C) Information about other publicly held legal entities. Whenever required by FRAP 26.1 or this rule to disclose information about a corporation that has issued shares to the public, a party shall also disclose information about similarly situated master limited partnerships, real estate investment trusts, or other legal entities whose shares are publicly held or traded, or state that there are no such entities.

(D) Information about trade association members. A party trade association must identify any publicly held member whose stock or equity value could be affected substantially by the outcome of the proceeding or whose claims the trade association is pursuing in a representative capacity, or state that there is no such member.

(b) **Disclosure requirements applicable to corporate *amicus curiae*.** (1) Who must file. If an *amicus curiae* is a corporation, the *amicus curiae* brief must include a disclosure statement.

(2) Information to be disclosed by corporate *amicus curiae*. A corporate *amicus curiae* must disclose the same information that sections (a)(2)(A), (B) and (C) require parties to disclose.

(c) **Form.** The disclosure statement shall be on a form provided by the clerk. A negative statement is required if a filer has no disclosures to make.

(d) **Time of filing.** A party's disclosure statement must be filed within 14 days of docketing of the appeal, unless earlier pleadings are submitted for the Court's consideration, in which case the disclosure statement shall be filed at that time.

(e) **Amendment.** Filers are required to amend their disclosure statements whennecessary to maintain their current accuracy. (Amended by order adopted June 9, 2008, effective August 11, 2008.)

Effect of amendments. — The 2008 amendment rewrote the Rule.

Rule 27. Motions.

(a) **In general.** (1) Application for relief. An application for an order or other relief is made by motion unless these rules prescribe another form. A motion must be in writing unless the court permits otherwise.

(2) Contents of a motion. (A) Grounds and relief sought. A motion must state with particularity the grounds for the motion, the relief sought, and the legal argument necessary to support it.

(B) Accompanying documents. (i) Any affidavit or other paper necessary to support a motion must be served and filed with the motion.

(ii) An affidavit must contain only factual information, not legal argument.

(iii) A motion seeking substantive relief must include a copy of the trial court's opinion or agency's decision as a separate exhibit.

(C) Documents barred or not required. (i) A separate brief supporting or responding to a motion must not be filed.

(ii) A notice of motion is not required.

(iii) A proposed order is not required.

(3) Response. (A) Time to file. Any party may file a response to a motion; Rule 27(a)(2) governs its contents. The response must be filed within 8 days after service of the motion unless the court shortens or extends the time. A motion authorized by Rules 8, 9, 18, or 41 may be granted before the 8-day period runs only if the court gives reasonable notice to the parties that it intends to act sooner.

(B) Request for affirmative relief. A response may include a motion for affirmative relief. The time to respond to the new motion, and to reply to that response, are governed by Rule 27(a)(3)(A) and (a)(4). The title of the response must alert the court to the request for relief.

(4) Reply to response. Any reply to a response must be filed within 5 days after service of the response. A reply must not present matters that do not relate to the response.

(b) **Disposition of a motion for a procedural order.** The court may act on a motion for a procedural order — including a motion under Rule 26(b) — at any time without awaiting a response, and may, by rule or by order in a particular case, authorize its clerk to act on specified types of procedural motions. A party adversely affected by the court's, or the clerk's, action may file a motion to reconsider, vacate, or modify that action. Timely opposition filed after the motion is granted in whole or in part does not constitute a request to reconsider, vacate, or modify the disposition; a motion requesting that relief must be filed.

(c) **Power of a single judge to entertain a motion.** A circuit judge may act alone on any motion, but may not dismiss or otherwise determine an appeal or other proceeding. A court of appeals may provide by rule or by order in a particular case that only the court may act on any motion or class of motions. The court may review the action of a single judge.

(d) **Form of papers; page limits; and number of copies.** (1) Format. (A) Reproduction. A motion, response, or reply may be reproduced by any process that yields a clear black image on light paper. The paper must be opaque and unglazed. Only one side of the paper may be used.

(B) Cover. A cover is not required but there must be a caption that includes the case number, the name of the court, the title of the case, and a brief descriptive title indicating the purpose of the motion and identifying the party or parties for whom it is filed. If a cover is used, it must be white.

(C) Binding. The document must be bound in any manner that is secure, does not obscure the text, and permits the document to lie reasonably flat when open.

(D) Paper size, line spacing, and margins. The document must be on 8½ by 11 inch paper. The text must be double-spaced, but quotations more than two lines long may be indented and single-spaced. Headings and footnotes may be single-spaced. Margins must be at least one inch on all four sides. Page numbers may be placed in the margins, but no text may appear there.

(2) Page limits. A motion or a response to a motion must not exceed 20 pages, exclusive of the corporate disclosure statement and accompanying documents authorized by Rule 27(a)(2)(B), unless the court permits or directs otherwise. A reply to a response must not exceed 10 pages.

(3) Number of copies. An original and 3 copies must be filed unless the court requires a different number by local rule or by order in a particular case.

(e) **Oral argument.** A motion will be decided without oral argument unless the court orders otherwise. (Amended by order adopted April 30, 1979, effective August 1, 1979; by order adopted April 25, 1989, effective December 1, 1989; by order adopted April 29, 1994, effective December 1, 1994; by order adopted April 24, 1998, effective December 1, 1998; and by order adopted April 29, 2002, effective December 1, 2002.)

Local Rule 27(a). Content of motions, notification and consent.

In cases where all parties are represented by counsel, all motions shall contain a statement by counsel that counsel for the other parties to the appeal have been informed of the intended filing of the motion. The statement shall indicate whether the other parties consent to the granting of the motion, or intend to file responses in opposition. (Redesignated and amended by order effective December 1, 1998.)

COMMENT

Former Local Rule 27(a) has been deleted as unnecessary because the provision has been incorporated into FRAP 27(e).

Local Rule 27(b). Procedural orders acted on by clerk; reconsideration thereof.

Motions and applications for orders if consented to, or if unopposed after due notice to all interested parties has been given or waived, or if the orders sought are procedural or relate to the preparation or printing of the appendix and briefs on appeal, or are such as are ordinarily granted as of course and without notice or hearing, need not be submitted to the Court, or to a judge thereof.

Such orders may be entered for the Court by the clerk, who shall forthwith send copies thereof to the parties.

Any party adversely affected by an order entered by the clerk pursuant to this rule shall be entitled to request reconsideration of the clerk's action by the Court, if within 14 days after entry of the order, such party shall file with the clerk and serve upon the parties to the proceedings a request, in writing, for reconsideration, vacation or modification of the order, stating the grounds for such request. The clerk shall thereupon submit to the Court the request for reconsideration, vacation or modification, the motion or application upon which the order was entered, and any responses by other parties which may have been filed in support or opposition to the request. The Court may thereafter take such action as may be proper.

COMMENT

Local Rule 27(c) has been designated as 27(b), and the title has been changed from "Non-Controversial orders granted by the clerk" to "Procedural orders acted on by the clerk." The change better characterizes the clerk's delegation of authority.

Local Rule 27(c). Form of motions.

A Disclosure of Corporate Affiliations statement must accompany the motion unless previously filed with the Court. See FRAP 26.1 and Local Rule 26.1. Counsel should always review carefully the specific rule which authorizes relief to ascertain the requirements and any motion should contain or be accompanied by any supporting documents required by a specific rule. If a motion is supported by attachments, these materials should also be served and filed with the motion. The parties should not make requests for procedural and substantive relief in a single motion, but should make each request in a separate motion. (Redesignated and amended by order effective December 1, 1998; by order effective April 1, 2008; and amended effective December 1, 2009.)

Effect of amendments. — The 2008 amendment substituted "motions" for "papers; number of copies" in the title; deleted the former second sentence which required three copies to be filed; and deleted "with each copy of" before "the motion" in the fifth sentence.

The 2009 amendment deleted the former first sentence; in the first sentence substituted "Disclosure of Corporate Affiliations statement" for "Disclosure of Corporate Affiliations and Other Entities with a Direct Financial Interest in Litigation statement"; at the end of the second sentence deleted "and Form A"; and made related changes.

Local Rule 27(d). Responses; replies.

(1) **Responses.** Although any party may file a response to a motion, a party need not respond to a motion until requested to do so by the Court. The three-day mailing period permitted by FRAP 26(c) does not apply to responses requested by the Court or clerk by letter wherein a response date is set forth in the request. A Disclosure of Corporate Affiliations statement must accompany any response to a motion unless previously filed with the Court. See FRAP 26.1 and Local Rule 26.1. If the Court acts upon a motion without a response, any party adversely affected by such action may by application to the Court request reconsideration, vacation or modification of the Court's action.

(2) **Replies.** The Court will not ordinarily await the filing of a reply before reviewing a motion and response. If movant intends to file a reply and does not want the Court to actively consider the motion and response until a reply is filed, movant shall notify the clerk in writing of the intended filing of the reply and request that this Court not act on the motion until the reply is received. (Amended by order effective December 1, 1995; and redesignated and amended by order effective December 1, 1998; and amended effective December 1, 2009.)

COMMENT

Local Rule 27(e) has been redesignated Local Rule 27(d) and the seven-day period for filing a response has been deleted from the local rule because FRAP 27(a)(3)(A) now affords ten days for a response. Reference in the local rule to the absence of a standard time period for filing a reply is deleted because FRAP 27(a)(4) now provides a seven-day reply period. The local rule retains, however, the statement that the court will ordinarily not await the filing of a reply before reviewing the motion or response. Replies are not routinely filed and waiting an additional seven days before actively considering a matter simply delays the disposition of motions by the court. The local rule is amended to provide that when a movant intends to file a reply, the movant shall inform the clerk that a reply is forthcoming and specifically request that the motion not be considered until a reply is received. Subsection 3 of the local rule has been deleted because the statement is now contained in FRAP 27(a)(2)(C)(iii).

Effect of amendments. — The 2009 amendment in (1), substituted "Disclosure of Corporate Affiliations statement" for "Disclosure of Corporate Affiliations and Other Financial Entities with a Direct Financial Interest in Litigation statement" in the third sentence and deleted "and Form A" at the end of the fourth sentence; and made related changes.

Local Rule 27(e). Panel assignments and emergency motions.

There is a strong presumption that the Court will act, in all but routine procedural matters, through panels or en banc, as prescribed by 28 U.S.C. § 46(c). Ordinarily, counsel shall present all motions to the clerk for presentation to the Court. Application to a single judge should be made only in exceptional circumstances where action by a panel would be impractical due to the requirements of time. In such exceptional circumstances, counsel shall attempt to notify the clerk's office that application is being made directly to a single judge, and copies of all papers presented to the judge shall be presented to the clerk as soon as practical for filing.

When a single judge determines to act, the matter will be referred to a panel as early in the process as is practical. As soon as a matter has been assigned to a panel, any action in the matter will be decided by the panel.

The selection of motion panels is similar to the process set forth in I.O.P. 34.1 for hearing panels. In a case where a request for single judge action is made to the clerk and action by a panel is not feasible, the clerk will assign the matter to a judge selected at random. In cases where a single judge, selected at random, has found it necessary to act, the clerk will fill out the panel with the at-random selection of two additional judges. In cases in which a single judge, selected by counsel, has found it necessary to act, the clerk will assign the matter to a three-judge panel selected at random, which may or may not include the single judge who acted in the case. (Redesignated by order effective December 1, 1998; amended by order effective February 1, 2001.)

Local Rule 27(f). Motions for summary disposition.

Motions for summary affirmance, reversal or dismissal are reserved for extraordinary cases only and should not be filed routinely. Counsel contemplating filing a motion to dispose summarily of an appeal should carefully consider whether the issues raised on appeal are in fact manifestly unsubstantial and appropriate for disposition by motion. Motions for summary affirmance or reversal are seldom granted.

Motions for summary disposition should be made only after briefs are filed. If such motions are submitted before the completion of the briefing schedule, the Court will defer action on the motion until the case is mature for full consideration.

Motions to dismiss based upon the ground that the appeal is not within the jurisdiction of the Court or for other procedural grounds may be filed at anytime. The Court may also sua sponte summarily dispose of any appeal at any time. (Redesignated by order effective December 1, 1998.)

Rule 28. Briefs.

(a) **Appellant's brief.** The appellant's brief must contain, under appropriate headings and in the order indicated:

(1) a corporate disclosure statement if required by Rule 26.1;

(2) a table of contents, with page references;

(3) a table of authorities — cases (alphabetically arranged), statutes, and other authorities — with references to the pages of the brief where they are cited;

(4) a jurisdictional statement, including:

(A) the basis for the district court's or agency's subject-matter jurisdiction, with citations to applicable statutory provisions and stating relevant facts establishing jurisdiction;

(B) the basis for the court of appeals' jurisdiction, with citations to applicable statutory provisions and stating relevant facts establishing jurisdiction;

(C) the filing dates establishing the timeliness of the appeal or petition for review; and

(D) an assertion that the appeal is from a final order or judgment that disposes of all parties' claims, or information establishing the court of appeals' jurisdiction on some other basis;

(5) a statement of the issues presented for review;

(6) a statement of the case briefly indicating the nature of the case, the course of proceedings, and the disposition below;

(7) a statement of facts relevant to the issues submitted for review with appropriate references to the record (see Rule 28(e));

(8) a summary of the argument, which must contain a succinct, clear, and accurate statement of the arguments made in the body of the brief, and which must not merely repeat the argument headings;

(9) the argument, which must contain:

(A) appellant's contentions and the reasons for them, with citations to the authorities and parts of the record on which the appellant relies; and

(B) for each issue, a concise statement of the applicable standard of review (which may appear in the discussion of the issue or under a separate heading placed before the discussion of issues);

(10) a short conclusion stating the precise relief sought; and

(11) the certificate of compliance, if required by Rule 32(a)(7).

(b) **Appellee's brief.** The appellee's brief must conform to the requirements of Rule 28(a)(1)-(9) and (11), except that none of the following need appear unless the appellee is dissatisfied with the appellant's statement:

(1) the jurisdictional statement;

(2) the statement of the issues;

(3) the statement of the case;

(4) the statement of the facts; and

(5) the statement of the standard of review.

(c) **Reply brief.** The appellant may file a brief in reply to the appellee's brief. An appellee who has cross-appealed may file a brief in reply to the appellant's response to the issues presented by the cross-appeal. Unless the court permits, no further briefs may be filed. A reply brief must contain a table of contents, with page references, and a table of authorities — cases (alphabetically arranged), statutes, and other authorities — with references to the pages of the reply brief where they are cited.

(d) **References to parties.** In briefs and at oral argument, counsel should minimize use of the terms "appellant " and "appellee." To make briefs clear, counsel should use the parties' actual names or the designations used in the lower court or agency proceeding, or such descriptive terms as "the employee," "the injured person," "the taxpayer," "the ship," "the stevedore."

(e) **References to the record.** References to the parts of the record contained in the appendix filed with the appellant's brief must be to the pages of the appendix. If the appendix is prepared after the briefs are filed, a party referring to the record must follow one of the methods detailed in Rule 30(c). If the original record is used under Rule 30(f) and is not consecutively paginated, or if the brief refers to an unreproduced part of the record, any reference must be to the page of the original document. For example:

- Answer p. 7;
- Motion for Judgment p. 2;
- Transcript p. 231.

Only clear abbreviations may be used. A party referring to evidence whose admissibility is in controversy must cite the pages of the appendix or of the transcript at which the evidence was identified, offered, and received or rejected.

(f) **Reproduction of statutes, rules, regulations, etc.** If the court's determination of the issues presented requires the study of statutes, rules, regulations, etc., the relevant parts must be set out in the brief or in an addendum at the end, or may be supplied to the court in pamphlet form.

(g) [Reserved]

(h) **Briefs in a case involving a cross-appeal.** If a cross-appeal is filed, the party who files a notice of appeal first is the appellant for the purposes of this rule and Rules 30, 31, and 34. If notices are filed on the same day, the plaintiff in the proceeding below is the appellant. These designations may be modified by agreement of the parties or by court order. With respect to appellee's cross-appeal and response to appellant's brief, appellee's brief must conform to the requirements of Rule 28(a)(1)-(11). But an appellee who is satisfied with appellant's statement need not include a statement of the case or of the facts.

(i) **Briefs in a case involving multiple appellants or appellees.** In a case involving more than one appellant or appellee, including consolidated cases, any number of appellants or appellees may join in a brief, and any party may adopt by reference a part of another's brief. Parties may also join in reply briefs.

(j) **Citation of supplemental authorities.** If pertinent and significant authorities come to a party's attention after the party's brief has been filed — or after oral argument but before decision — a party may promptly advise the circuit clerk by letter, with a copy to all other parties, setting forth the citations. The letter must state the reasons for the supplemental citations, referring either to the page of the brief or to a point argued orally. The body of the letter must not exceed 350 words. Any response must be made promptly and must be similarly limited. (Amended by order adopted April 30, 1979, effective August 1, 1979; by order adopted June 30, 1979, effective August 1, 1979; by order adopted March 10, 1986, effective July 1, 1986; by order adopted April 25, 1989, corrected May 1, 1989, effective December 1, 1989; by order adopted April 30, 1991, effective December 1, 1991; by order adopted April 22, 1993, effective December 1, 1993; by order adopted April 29, 1994, effective December 1, 1994; by order adopted April 24, 1998, effective December 1, 1998; and by order adopted April 29, 2002, effective December 1, 2002.)

Court will not search through record to find material which parties failed to provide. — United States Court of Appeals will not sift through the record to piece together support for computer corporation's contentions that a computer program developed by one of its competitors, infringed upon the copyrights it held in its "Claims Express" and "EDI Link" computer programs where it had not identified any evidence demonstrating that district court clearly erred in finding that the program developed by competitor was not substantially similar to either Claims Express or EDI Link. Comprehensive Technologies Int'l, Inc. v. Software Artisans, Inc., 3 F.3d 730 (4th Cir. 1993).

Failure to include contentions constitute abandonment of claims. — Where none of the briefs filed by either party contains "contentions" about the application of the Virginia Constitution's Declaration of Rights or the Virginia Act for Religious Freedom to the instant case, or citations to authorities that might illuminate the special rights that state charter and religious-freedom statute are said to guarantee, the parties failed to appeal the district court's grant of summary judgment with respect to these state-law theories of recovery; failure of this nature constitutes abandonment of the claims, and precludes appellate court from considering them further herein. Rosenberger v. Rector & Visitors of Univ. of Va., 18 F.3d 269 (4th Cir. 1994).

Applied in Columbus-America Discovery Group v. Atlantic Mut. Ins. Co., 56 F.3d 556 (4th Cir. 1995); Winfield v. Bass, 67 F.3d 529 (4th Cir. 1995).

Local Rule 28(a). Consolidated cases and briefs.

Related appeals or petitions for review will be consolidated in the Office of the Clerk, with notice to all parties, at the time a briefing schedule is established. One brief shall be permitted per side, including parties permitted to intervene, in all cases consolidated by Court order, unless leave to the contrary is granted upon good cause shown. In consolidated cases lead counsel shall be selected by the attorneys on each side and that person's identity made known in writing to the clerk within 14 days of the date of the order of consolidation. In the absence of an agreement by counsel, the clerk shall designate lead counsel. The individual so designated shall be responsible for the coordination, preparation and filing of the briefs and appendix. (Amended effective December 1, 2009.)

Effect of amendments. — The 2009 amendment substituted "14 days" for "10 days" in the third sentence.

Local Rule 28(b). Addenda and attachments to briefs.

A party may comply with the requirements of FRAP 28(f) and FRAP 32.1(b) by including material or items designated therein in an addendum at the end of the brief or by supplying them to the Court under separate cover. Should a party wish to supplement the brief with matters other than those designated in FRAP 28(f) or FRAP 32.1(b), the additional material must be presented to the Court under separate cover, accompanied by a motion for leave to file such supplemental material as an attachment to the brief. (Amended by order effective December 1, 1998; December 1, 2006; and August 20, 2007.)

Effect of amendments. — The 2006 amendment substituted "amended June 1, 2006, effective December 1, 2006" for "Local Rule 36(c)" in the second sentence.

The 2007 Order, effective September 24, 2007, added "Addenda and" to the heading, rewrote the first and third sentences, deleted the second sentence, and deleted the Comment note at the end.

Local Rule 28(c). Responsibilities of counsel listed on a brief.

The Court will interpret the listing of an attorney on a brief as a representation that he or she is capable of arguing the appeal if lead counsel is unavailable.

Local Rule 28(d). Joint appeals and consolidations.

Where multiple parties are directed to file a consolidated brief, counsel on the same side of the case should confer and agree upon a means for assuring that the positions of all parties are addressed within the length limits allowed and that each counsel will have an opportunity to review and approve the consolidated brief before it is filed.

Motions to file separate briefs are not favored by the Court and are granted only upon a particularized showing of good cause, such as, but not limited to, cases in which the interests of the parties are adverse. Generally unacceptable grounds for requests to file separate briefs include representations that the issues presented require a brief in excess of the length limitations established by FRAP 32(a)(7) (appropriately addressed by a motion to exceed length limit), that counsel cannot coordinate their efforts due to different geographical locations, or that the participation of separate counsel in the proceedings below entitles each party to separate briefs on appeal.

If a motion to file separate briefs is granted, the length of such briefs may be limited by the Court. The parties shall continue to share the time allowed for oral argument. (Amended by order effective December 1, 1995; redesignated and amended by order effective December 1, 1998.)

COMMENT

Proposed Local Rule 28(e) adds language to existing I.O.P. 28.2 to cross-reference the 40-page proportional type requirement contained in proposed Local Rule 28(d) (existing I.O.P. 28.1).

[Former] Local Rule 28(d) has been moved to Local Rule 32(b) and amended to conform to FRAP 32(a)(7).

Local Rule 28(e). Citation of additional authorities.

Counsel may, without leave of Court, present a letter drawing the Court's attention to supplemental authorities under Rule 28(j) and serve a copy on all counsel of record. The Court may grant leave for or direct the filing of additional memoranda, which may include additional argument before, during or after oral argument. (Redesignated by order effective December 1, 1998; amended by order effective December 1, 2002; and by order effective April 1, 2008.)

Effect of amendments. — The 2008 amendment added "and serve a copy on all counsel of record" in the first sentence and deleted the second sentence with read "An original and three copies of the letter should be filed with the clerk and a copy of the letter should be mailed to all counsel of record".

Local Rule 28(f). Statement of facts.

Every opening brief filed by appellants in this court shall include a separate section, the title which is STATEMENT OF FACTS. In this section the attorneys will prepare a narrative statement of all of the facts necessary for the Court to reach the conclusion which the brief desires. The said STATEMENT OF FACTS will include exhibit, record, transcript, or appendix references showing the source of the facts stated. An appellee's brief shall also include a STATEMENT OF FACTS so prepared unless appellee is satisfied with appellant's statement of facts. (Adopted by order effective June 5, 1996; amended by order effective December 4, 1996; and redesignated and amended by order effective December 1, 1998.)

COMMENT

Local Rule 28(g), which has been redesignated as 28(f), has been amended to conform to FRAP 28(a)(7) (listing the statement of facts as a separate section) and FRAP 28(b) (providing that appellee is not required to include a statement of facts unless appellee is dissatisfied with appellant's statement).

Rule 29. Brief of an amicus curiae.

(a) **When permitted.** The United States or its officer or agency, or a State, Territory, Commonwealth, or the District of Columbia may file an amicus-curiae brief without the consent of the parties or leave of court. Any other amicus curiae may file a brief only by leave of court or if the brief states that all parties have consented to its filing.

(b) **Motion for leave to file.** The motion must be accompanied by the proposed brief and state:

(1) the movant's interest; and

(2) the reason why an amicus brief is desirable and why the matters asserted are relevant to the disposition of the case.

(c) **Contents and form.** An amicus brief must comply with Rule 32. In addition to the requirements of Rule 32, the cover must identify the party or parties supported and indicate whether the brief supports affirmance or reversal. If an amicus curiae is a corporation, the brief must include a disclosure statement like that required of parties by Rule 26.1. An amicus brief need not comply with Rule 28, but must include the following:

(1) a table of contents, with page references;

(2) a table of authorities — cases (alphabetically arranged), statutes and other authorities — with references to the pages of the brief where they are cited;

(3) a concise statement of the identity of the amicus curiae, its interest in the case, and the source of its authority to file;

(4) an argument, which may be preceded by a summary and which need not include a statement of the applicable standard of review; and

(5) a certificate of compliance, if required by Rule 32(a)(7).

(d) **Length.** Except by the court's permission, an amicus brief may be no more than one-half the maximum length authorized by these rules for a party's principal brief. If the court grants a party permission to file a longer brief, that extension does not affect the length of an amicus brief.

(e) **Time for filing.** An amicus curiae must file its brief, accompanied by a motion for filing when necessary, no later than 7 days after the principal brief of the party being supported is filed. An amicus curiae that does not support either party must file its brief no later than 7 days after the appellant's or petitioner's principal brief is filed. A court may grant leave for later filing, specifying the time within which an opposing party may answer.

(f) **Reply brief.** Except by the court's permission, an amicus curiae may not file a reply brief.

(g) **Oral argument.** An amicus curiae may participate in oral argument only with the court's permission. (Amended by order adopted April 24, 1998, effective December 1, 1998.)

Local Rule 29. Motion for leave to file brief as amicus curiae.

[Deleted.]

COMMENT

Local Rule 29 has been deleted because the federal rule now details the filing requirements for amicus curiae briefs.

Rule 30. Appendix to the briefs.

(a) **Appellant's responsibility.** (1) Contents of the appendix. The appellant must prepare and file an appendix to the briefs containing:

(A) the relevant docket entries in the proceeding below;

(B) the relevant portions of the pleadings, charge, findings, or opinion;

(C) the judgment, order, or decision in quesstion; and

(D) other parts of the record to which the parties wish to direct the court's attention.

(2) Excluded material. Memoranda of law in the district court should not be included in the appendix unless they have independent relevance. Parts of the record may be relied on by the court or the parties even though not included in the appendix.

(3) Time to file; Number of copies. Unless filing is deferred under Rule 30(c), the appellant must file 10 copies of the appendix with the brief and must serve one copy on counsel for each party separately represented. An unrepresented party proceeding in forma pauperis must file 4 legible copies with the clerk, and one copy must be served on counsel for each separately represented party. The court may by local rule or by order in a particular case require the filing or service of a different number.

(b) **All parties' responsibilities.** (1) Determining the contents of the appendix. The parties are encouraged to agree on the contents of the appendix. In the absence of an agreement, the appellant must, within 10 days after the record is filed, serve on the appellee a designation of the parts of the record the appellant intends to include in the appendix and a statement of the issues the appellant intends to present for review. The appellee may, within 10 days after receiving the designation, serve on the appellant a designation of additional parts to which it wishes to direct the court's attention. The appellant must include the designated parts in the appendix. The parties must not engage in unnecessary designation of parts of the record, because the entire record is available to the court. This paragraph applies also to a cross-appellant and a cross-appellee.

(2) Costs of appendix. Unless the parties agree otherwise, the appellant must pay the cost of the appendix. If the appellant considers parts of the record designated by the appellee to be unnecessary, the appellant may advise the appellee, who must then advance the cost of including those parts. The cost of the appendix is a taxable cost. But if any party causes unnecessary parts of the record to be included in the appendix, the court may impose the cost of those parts on that party. Each circuit must, by local rule, provide for sanctions against attorneys who unreasonably and vexatiously increase litigation costs by including unnecessary material in the appendix.

(c) **Deferred appendix.** (1) Deferral until after briefs are filed. The court may provide by rule for classes of cases or by order in a particular case that preparation of the appendix may be deferred until after the briefs have been filed and that the appendix may be filed 21 days after the appellee's brief is served. Even though the filing of the appendix may be deferred, Rule 30(b) applies; except that a party must designate the parts of the record it wants included in the appendix when it serves its brief, and need not include a statement of the issues presented.

(2) References to the record. (A) If the deferred appendix is used, the parties may cite in their briefs the pertinent pages of the record. When the appendix is prepared, the record pages cited in the briefs must be indicated by inserting record page numbers, in brackets, at places in the appendix where those pages of the record appear.

(B) A party who wants to refer directly to pages of the appendix may serve and file copies of the brief within the time required by Rule 31(a), containing appropriate references to pertinent pages of the record. In that event, within 14 days after the appendix is filed, the party must serve and file copies of the brief, containing references to the pages of the appendix in place of or in addition to the references to the pertinent pages of the record. Except for the correction of typographical errors, no other changes may be made to the brief.

(d) **Format of the appendix.** The appendix must begin with a table of contents identifying the page at which each part begins. The relevant docket entries must follow the table of contents. Other parts of the record must follow chronologically. When pages from the transcript of proceedings are placed in the appendix, the transcript page numbers must be shown in brackets immediately before the included pages. Omissions in the text of papers or of the transcript must be indicated by asterisks. Immaterial formal matters (captions, subscriptions, acknowledgments, etc.) should be omitted.

(e) **Reproduction of exhibits.** Exhibits designated for inclusion in the appendix may be reproduced in a separate volume, or volumes, suitably indexed. Four copies must be filed with the appendix and one copy shall be served on counsel for each separately represented party. If a transcript of a proceeding before an administrative agency, board, commission, or officer used in an action in the district court action and has been designated for inclusion in the appendix, the transcript must be places in the appendix as an exhibit.

(f) **Appeal on the original record without an appendix.** The court may, either by rule for all cases or classes of cases or by order in a particular case, dispense with the appendix and permit an appeal to proceed on the original record with any copies of the record, or relevant parts, that the court may order the parties to file. (Amended by order adopted March 30, 1970, effective July 1, 1970; by order adopted March 10, 1986, effective July 1, 1986; by order adopted April 30, 1991, effective December 1,1991; by order adopted April 29, 1994, effective December 1, 1994; and by order adopted April 24, 1998, effective December 1, 1998.)

Appellant has obligation to file appendix. — The obligation to file an appendix is clearly that of the appellant. United States v. Seaboard Coast Line R.R., 517 F.2d 881 (4th Cir. 1975).

Appeal dismissed where appendix failed to meet minimum requirements. — The government's appeal from an order dismissing a complaint in an action under the Carmack amendment was dismissed, where the brief filed by the government purported to include an appendix, but the appendix failed to meet the minimum requirements of subdivi-

sion (a), where the appendix to the government's brief consisted of two pages reproducing only two bills of lading and where the government neither sought nor obtained an order under subdivision (c) which authorizes the filing of a deferred appendix, nor did it seek or obtain an order under subdivision (f) authorizing an appeal to be heard on the original record. United States v. Seaboard Coast Line R.R., 517 F.2d 881 (4th Cir. 1975).

Applied in Sivertsen v. Guardian Life Ins. Co., 423 F.2d 443 (4th Cir. 1970); Webb v. Hutto, 720 F.2d 375 (4th Cir. 1983).

Local Rule 30(a). Attorney sanctions for unnecessary appendix designations.

The Court, on its own motion or on motion of any party, may impose sanctions against attorneys who unreasonably and vexatiously increase the costs of litigation through the inclusion of unnecessary material in the appendix. Attorneys shall receive reasonable notice and opportunity to respond before the imposition of any sanction. A party's motion for the imposition of sanctions will be entertained only if filed within 14 days after entry of judgment and only if counsel for the moving party previously objected to the designation of the allegedly unnecessary material in writing to opposing counsel within 14 days of the material's designation. (Amended effective December 1, 2009.)

Effect of amendments. — The 2009 amendment substituted "14 days of" for "10 days of" in the last sentence.

Local Rule 30(b). Appendix contents; number of copies.

(1) **Required Contents:.** In designating or agreeing upon the contents of the appendix, and in assembling the appendix, the parties should avoid unnecessary duplication of materials. The appellee's designation should only include those additional parts of the record to which it wishes to direct the Court's attention that have not already been designated by the appellant.

The use of a selectively abridged record allows the judges to refer easily to relevant parts of the record and saves the parties the considerable expense of reproducing the entire record. Although there is no limit on the length of the appendix except as provided in Local Rule 32(a), it is unnecessary to include everything in the appendix. The appendix should, however, contain the final order or order appealed from, the complaint or petition, as finally amended (civil appeals) or indictment (criminal appeals), as well as all other parts of the record which are vital to the understanding of the basic issues on appeal. Although the entire record is available to the Court should it believe that additional portions are important to a full understanding of the issues, citations to portions of the record not included in the appendix is not favored.

(2) **Table of Contents; Witness Names and Type of Examination:.** The table of contents to the appendix should be sufficiently detailed to be helpful to the Court. Referring to the transcript of a trial under a single reference to "proceeding" or "trial transcript" is not sufficient. When the testimony of a witness is included in the appendix, the testimony should be clearly identified in the table of contents, beneath the proceeding in which it occurred. The name of the testifying witness and the type of examination (e.g., direct, cross, redirect, or recross) should also be clearly indicated at the top of each page of the appendix where the witness's testimony appears. Exhibits should be listed in the table of contents by number or letter and by name or brief description.

(3) **Sentencing Guideline Appeals:.** In all criminal appeals seeking review of the application of the sentencing guidelines, appellant shall include the sentencing hearing transcript and presentence report in the appendix. The presentence report must be included in a separate sealed volume, stamped

"SEALED" on the volume itself and on the envelope containing it, and be accompanied by a certificate stating that the volume contains sealed material.

(4) **Number of Copies.** (a) Filing: Six paper copies of the appendix and any supplemental appendix must be filed. Appointed counsel may file five copies of an appendix or supplemental appendix, and any party proceeding in forma pauperis who is not represented by Court-appointed counsel may file four copies.

(b) Service: One paper copy of the appendix must be served on lead counsel for each party separately represented and on any party not represented by counsel.

(c) Sealed Appendix Volumes: For sealed volumes of the appendix, four paper copies must be filed and one paper copy must be served on lead counsel for each party separately represented who is authorized to have access to the sealed volume and on any party not represented by counsel who is authorized to have access to the sealed volume. (Amended by order effective December 1, 1995; by order effective December 1, 1998; by order effective April 16, 2007; by order effective April 1, 2008; and by order effective September 1, 2011.)

COMMENT

Proposed Local Rule 30(b) adds language to existing I.O.P. 30.1 by cross-referencing the 250-page limitation on appendices in court-appointed criminal cases as provided in proposed Local Rule 32(b) (existing I.O.P. 32.1).

Effect of amendments. — The 2007 amendment added the first and third paragraphs; rewrote the second paragraph; and added the second sentence in the fourth paragraph.

The 2008 amendment in the last paragraph in the third sentence substituted "their final briefs in electronic form only" for "four page-proof copies of the brief in lieu of the requisite number of copies"; in the fourth sentence substituted "file their final briefs in electronic form in addition to filing the requisite number of paper copies" for "must replace their page-proof copies with the requisite number of copies of their final brief" and changed the last clause regarding references to the appendix into a free-standing sentence.

The 2011 amendment added the (1), (2), and (3) designations and headings; and rewrote the former last paragraph as (4).

Editor's note. — Local Rule 30(b) cross-references the 250-page limitation on appendices in court-appointed criminal cases as provided in Local Rule 32(a).

Local Rule 30(c). Responsibility of parties.

Notwithstanding that FRAP 30 provides that the appellant shall prepare and file the appendix, the Court considers the coordination of preparing the appendix to be the responsibility of both sides. The failure of a side to designate does not absolve the other side from the responsibility.

Except under the most extraordinary circumstances, supplementary appendices will not be accepted. If the appellant omits from the appendix the portions designated by the appellee, the appellant will be required to file a corrected appendix incorporating such material, and to bear the cost regardless of the outcome of the appeal.

If a party files a motion for leave to file a supplemental appendix, the motion must specifically identify the contents of the supplemental appendix, state that the items are matters of record, and set forth good cause why the original appendix should not be returned for insertion of the additional materials.

Local Rule 30(d). Dispensing with appendix.

Motions to proceed on the original record pursuant to FRAP 30(f) are carefully reviewed in the Fourth Circuit and are not usually granted unless the appellant is proceeding in forma pauperis, the record is short, or the appeal is expedited. Even if the motion is granted, counsel must include an abbreviated appendix consisting of:

i. pertinent district court docket entries,

ii. indictment or complaint,

iii. judgment or order being appealed,

iv. notice of appeal,

v. any crucial portions of the transcript of proceedings referred to in appellant's brief,

vi. a copy of the order granting leave to proceed on the original record.

The requisite number of copies of the abbreviated appendix as set forth in Local Rule 30(b) must be filed with the brief. (Amended by order effective December 1, 1995; and by order effective April 1, 2008.)

Effect of amendments. — The 2008 amendment deleted "but it may be included as part of the brief rather than being reproduced separately" at the end.

Rule 31. Serving and filing briefs.

(a) **Time to serve and file a brief.** (1) The appellant must serve and file a brief within 40 days after the record is filed. The appellee must serve and file a brief within 30 days after the appellant's brief is served. The appellant may serve and file a reply brief within 14 days after service of the appellee's brief but a reply must be filed at least 3 days before argument, unless the court, for good cause, allows a later filing.

(2) A court of appeals that routinely considers cases on the merits promptly after the briefs are filed may shorten the time to serve and file briefs, either by local rule or by order in a particular case.

(b) **Number of copies.** Twenty-five copies of each brief must be filed with the clerk and 2 copies must be served on each unrepresented party and on counsel for each separately represented party. An unrepresented party proceeding in forma pauperis must file 4 legible copies with the clerk, and one copy must be served on each unrepresented party and on counsel for each separately represented party. The court may by local rule or by order in a particular case require the filing or service of a different number.

(c) **Consequence of failure to file.** If an appellant fails to file a brief within the time provided by this rule, or within an extended time, an appellee may move to dismiss the appeal. An appellee who fails to file a brief will not be heard at oral argument unless the court grants permission. (Amended by order adopted March 30, 1970, effective July 1, 1970; by order adopted March 10, 1986, effective July 1, 1986; by order adopted April 29, 1994, effective December 1, 1994; by order adopted April 24, 1998, effective December 1, 1998; and by order adopted April 29, 2002, effective December 1, 2002.)

Local Rule 31(a). Shortened time for service and filing of briefs in criminal cases.

Pursuant to the authority conferred by FRAP 31(a)(2), the time for serving and filing briefs in criminal appeals is shortened as follows: the appellant shall serve and file appellant's brief and appendix within thirty-five days after the date on which the briefing order is filed; the appellee shall serve and file appellee's brief within twenty-one days after service of the brief of the appellant; the appellant may serve and file a reply brief within ten days after service of the brief of the appellee. (Amended by order effective December 1, 1995; by order effective December 1, 1998; by order effective December 1, 2002; and amended effective December 1, 2009.)

Effect of amendments. — The 2009 amendment substituted "ten days" for "ten calendar days".

Local Rule 31(b). Briefing orders.

A formal briefing schedule shall be sent to the parties upon receipt of the record or determination by the Clerk that the record is complete — whichever occurs first. Thus, the time for designating the contents of the joint appendix and the filing of briefs is controlled by the briefing order and not the receipt of the record as provided in FRAP 31(a)(1). (Amended by order effective December 4, 1991; by order effective December 1, 1995; by order effective December 1, 1998; and amended effective December 1, 2009.)

Effect of amendments. — The 2009 amendment substituted "or determination by the Clerk that the record is complete" for "notification that the record is complete pursuant to Local Rule 10(a), or when the Clerk determines that no hearing was held for which a transcript is necessary" in the first sentence.

Editor's note. — Rule 31(b) reflects that the establishment of a briefing schedule triggers the time for designation of the joint appendix.

Local Rule 31(c). Filing and service.

Briefs and appendices are deemed filed on the date of mailing if first class mail or other classes of mail at least as expeditious are used. If a courier service is used, the briefs and appendices are deemed timely filed if the briefs and appendices are given to the courier service on or before the due date to be dispatched to the Clerk's Office for delivery within three days. Filing must be within the time allowed by the briefing order. A brief must be accompanied by a valid certificate of service, which should be bound with the brief as the last, unnumbered page. A certificate of service can be prepared in advance of actual service. If service is not actually accomplished in the manner and on the date stated in the certificate, an amended certificate of service is required.

Extensions will be granted only when extraordinary circumstances exist. A motion for an extension of time to file a brief must be filed well in advance of the date the brief is due and must set forth the additional time requested and the reasons for the request. The Court discourages these motions and may deny the motion entirely or grant a lesser period of time than the time requested. (Amended effective December 4, 1996; by order effective April 1, 2008; and amended effective December 1, 2009.)

Effect of amendments. — The 2008 amendment substituted "service" for "mailing or hand delivery of the paper served" in the fifth sentence of the first paragraph.

The 2009 amendment substituted "three days" for "three calendar days" in the second sentence of the first paragraph.

Local Rule 31(d). Number of copies.

(1) **Filing:.** In addition to the electronic brief, each party must file eight paper copies of the brief with the clerk, except that appointed counsel may file six copies, and any party proceeding in forma pauperis who is not represented by Court-appointed counsel may file four copies. Service of paper copies of briefs on opposing counsel is not required unless counsel was not served electronically.

(2) **Service:.** Service of paper copies of briefs is not required if the brief was served electronically on counsel and on any party not represented by counsel. If the brief was not served electronically, one paper copy must be served on lead counsel for each party separately represented and on any party not represented by counsel.

(3) **Sealed Briefs:.** For sealed briefs, four paper copies of the sealed version must be filed and one paper copy must be served on lead counsel for each party separately represented who is authorized to have access to the sealed version and on any party not represented by counsel who is authorized to have access to the sealed version. Filing and service of the public version of the brief are governed by (1) and (2) above.

(4) **Page-Proof Briefs:.** If the Court allows a deferred appendix, the parties are required to file their page-proof briefs in electronic form only. After the deferred appendix is filed, filing and service of final briefs are governed by (1) and (2) above. (Amended effective December 4, 1991; December 1, 1998; July 1, 2010; and September 1, 2011.)

Effect of amendments. — The 2010 amendment rewrote the Rule.
The 2011 amendment added the (1) and (2) designations and headings; rewrote (2); deleted the former second paragraph; and added (3) and (4).

Rule 32. Form of briefs, appendices and other papers.

(a) **Form of a brief.** (1) Reproduction. (A) A brief may be reproduced by any process that yields a clear black image on light paper. The paper must be opaque and unglazed. Only one side of the paper may be used.

(B) Text must be reproduced with a clarity that equals or exceeds the output of a laser printer.

(C) Photographs, illustrations, and tables may be reproduced by any method that results in a good copy of the original; a glossy finish is acceptable if the original is glossy.

(2) Cover. Except for filings by unrepresented parties, the cover of the appellant's brief must be blue; the appellee's, red; an intervenor's or amicus curiae's, green; any reply brief, gray; and any supplemental brief, tan. The front cover of a brief must contain:

(A) the number of the case centered at the top;

(B) the name of the court;

(C) the title of the case (see Rule 12(a));

(D) the nature of the proceeding (e.g., Appeal, Petition for Review) and the name of the court, agency, or board below;

(E) the title of the brief, identifying the party or parties for whom the brief is filed; and

(F) the name, office address, and telephone number of counsel representing the party for whom the brief is filed.

(3) Binding. The brief must be bound in any manner that is secure, does not obscure the text, and permits the brief to lie reasonably flat when open.

(4) Paper size, line spacing, and margins. The brief must be on 8 ½ by 11 inch paper. The text must be double-spaced, but quotations more than two lines long may be indented and single-spaced. Headings and footnotes may be single-spaced. Margins must be at least one inch on all four sides. Page numbers may be placed in the margins, but no text may appear there.

(5) Typeface. Either a proportionally spaced or a monospaced face may be used.

(A) A proportionally spaced face must include serifs, but sans-serif type may be used in headings and captions. A proportionally spaced face must be 14-point or larger.

(B) A monospaced face may not contain more than 10 ½ characters per inch.

(6) Type styles. A brief must be set in a plain, roman style, although italics or boldface may be used for emphasis. Case names must be italicized or underlined.

(7) Length. (A) Page limitation. A principal brief may not exceed 30 pages, or a reply brief 15 pages, unless it complies with Rule 32(a)(7)(B) and (C).

(B) Type-volume limitation. (i) A principal brief is acceptable if:

• it contains no more than 14,000 words; or

• it uses a monospaced face and contains no more than 1,300 lines of text.

(ii) A reply brief is acceptable if it contains no more than half of the type volume specified in Rule 32(a)(7)(B)(i).

(iii) Headings, footnotes, and quotations count toward the word and line limitations. The corporate disclosure statement, table of contents, table of citations, statement with respect to oral argument, any addendum containing statutes, rules or regulations, and any certificates of counsel do not count toward the limitation.

(C) Certificate of compliance. (i) A brief submitted under Rule 32(a)(7)(B) must include a certificate by the attorney, or an unrepresented party, that the brief complies with the type-volume limitation. The person preparing the certificate may rely on the word or line count of the word-processing system used to prepare the brief. The certificate must state either:

• the number of words in the brief; or

• the number of lines of monospaced type in the brief.

(ii) Form 6 in the Appendix of Forms is a suggested form of a certificate of compliance. Use of Form 6 must be regarded as sufficient to meet the requirements of Rule 32(a)(7)(C)(i).

(b) **Form of an appendix.** An appendix must comply with Rule 32(a)(1), (2), (3), and (4), with the following exceptions:

(1) The cover of a separately bound appendix must be white.

(2) An appendix may include a legible photocopy of any document found in the record or of a printed judicial or agency decision.

(3) When necessary to facilitate inclusion of odd-sized documents such as technical drawings, an appendix may be a size other than 8 ½ by 11 inches, and need not lie reasonably flat when opened.

(c) **Form of other papers.** (1) Motion. The form of a motion is governed by Rule 27(d).

(2) Other papers. Any other paper, including a petition for panel rehearing and a petition for hearing or rehearing en banc, and any response to such a petition, must be reproduced in the manner prescribed by Rule 32(a), with the following exceptions:

(A) A cover is not necessary if the caption and signature page of the paper together contain the information required by Rule 32(a)(2). If a cover is used, it must be white.

(B) Rule 32(a)(7) does not apply.

(d) **Signature.** Every brief, motion, or other paper filed with the court must be signed by the party filing the paper or, if the party is represented, by one of the party's attorneys.

(e) **Local variation.** Every court of appeals must accept documents that comply with the form requirements of this rule. By local rule or order in a particular case a court of appeals may accept documents that do not meet all of the form requirements of this rule. (Amended by order adopted April 24, 1998, effective December 1, 1998; and by order adopted April 29, 2002, effective December 1, 2002.)

Local Rule 32(a). Reproduction of briefs and appendices.

Double-sided copying of appendices is preferred in all cases. If an appendix is prepared by a commercial printer in a court-appointed case, the materials contained in the appendix should be reproduced on both sides of a sheet because reimbursement for copying expenses will be limited to 35 cents per double-sided sheet of the joint appendix. No joint appendix in a court-appointed case should exceed 250 sheets without advance permission from the Court; unless such permission is granted, reimbursement of copy expenses will limited to 250 sheets. (Amended by order effective December 1, 1992; by order effective December 1, 1995; by order effective December 1, 1998; and by order effective December 1, 2002.)

Local Rule 32(b). Length of briefs.

The Fourth Circuit encourages short, concise briefs. Under no circumstances may a brief exceed the limits set forth in FRAP 32 (a)(7) without the Court's advance permission.

A motion for permission to submit a longer brief must be made to the Court of Appeals at least 10 days prior to the due date of the brief and must be supported by a statement of reasons. These motions are not favored and will be granted only for exceptional reasons. (Amended by order effective January 1, 1994; by order effective December 1, 1995; by order effective December 1, 1998; by order effective December 1, 2002; and amended effective December 1, 2009.)

Effect of amendments. — The 2009 amendment substituted "10 days" for "10 calendar days" in the first sentence of the second paragraph.

Local Rule 32(c). Correction of briefs and appendices.

If briefs, appendices, or other papers are illegible or are not in the form required by the federal rules or by this Court's local rules or standards when filed, counsel will be required to file corrected copies of the document. If the corrected copies are not submitted within the time allowed by the clerk, they must be accompanied by a motion to file out of time. (Amended by order effective December 1, 1998.)

COMMENT

Proposed Local Rule 32(d) changes the procedure set forth in existing I.O.P. 32.4 to reflect that the clerk no longer returns briefs for correction, but instead requires the submission of a corrected brief. Counsel may contact the clerk to make arrangements for the return of the original briefs at counsel's expense rather than filing an entirely new set.

Former Local Rule 32(a) has been deleted in its entirety as superseded by FRAP 32(a)(7).

Former Local Rule 32(b) has been redesignated Local Rule 32(a). Consistent with the FRAP amendments, it deletes reference to typeset briefs. It recasts as a preference the court's former requirement that materials in the joint appendix be reproduced on both sides of a sheet in court-appointed cases. FRAP 32(d) requires the court to accept any document in conformity with the requirements of FRAP but permits the court by local rule or order in a particular case to accept documents that do not meet all the FRAP form requirements. FRAP 32(a)(1) and 32(b) provide that briefs and appendices should be copied on only one side of the paper. Several years ago, the Court adopted a double-sided copying requirement and limited the size of the appendix to control excessive reproduction costs in Criminal Justice Act cases. The provision has proved an effective cost reduction mechanism which should be retained if possible. The amended local rule does this by stating that reimbursement will be limited to $.35 per double-sided sheet if the appendix is reproduced by a commercial printer, and that reimbursement will be limited to 250 sheets (500 pages) unless counsel obtained leave to file a longer appendix.

Local Rule 32(b) contains some of the information previously found in old Local Rule 28(d), but deletes the second sentence of old Local Rule 28(d), which was superseded by limits set forth in FRAP 32(a)(7). The last sentence of former Local Rule 28(d) has also been deleted from Local Rule 32(b) because footnotes and narrow margins can no longer be used to circumvent the size limitations for briefs established by the new rules.

Former Local Rule 32(c) has been deleted because FRAP 32(a)(2)(F) requires counsel's phone number.

Rule 32.1. Citing judicial dispositions.

(a) **Citation permitted.** A court may not prohibit or restrict the citation of federal judicial opinions, orders, judgments or other written dispositions that have been:

(i) designated as "unpublished," "not for publication," "nonprecedential," "not precedent," or the like; and

(ii) issued on or after January 1, 2007.

(b) **Copies required.** If a party cites a federal judicial opinion, order, judgment, or other written disposition that is not available in a publicly accessible electronic database, the party must file and serve a copy of that opinion, order, judgment, or disposition with the brief or other paper in which it is cited. (Added amended June 1, 2006, effective December 1, 2006.)

Local Rule 32.1. Citation of unpublished dispositions.

Citation of this Court's unpublished dispositions issued prior to January 1, 2007, in briefs and oral arguments in this Court and in the district courts within this Circuit is disfavored, except for the purpose of establishing res judicata, estoppel, or the law of the case.

If a party believes, nevertheless, that an unpublished disposition of this Court issued prior to January 1, 2007, has precedential value in relation to a material issue in a case and that there is no published opinion that would serve as well, such disposition may be cited if the requirements of FRAP 32.1(b) are met. (Added June 1, 2006, effective December 1, 2006.)

Rule 33. Appeal conferences.

The court may direct the attorneys — and, when appropriate, the parties — to participate in one or more conferences to address any matter that may aid in disposing of the proceedings, including simplifying the issues and discussing settlement. A judge or other person designated by the court may preside over the conference, which may be conducted in person or by telephone. Before a settlement conference, the attorneys must consult with their clients and obtain as much authority as feasible to settle the case. The court may, as a result of the conference, enter an order controlling the course of proceedings or implementing any settlement agreement. (Amended by order adopted April 29, 1994, effective December 1, 1994; and by order adopted April 24, 1998, effective December 1, 1998.)

Local Rule 33. Circuit mediation conferences.

All civil and agency cases in which all parties are represented by counsel on appeal will be reviewed by a circuit mediator after the filing of the docketing statements required by Local Rule 3(b). The circuit mediator will determine whether a mediation conference may assist either the Court or the parties. Counsel for a party may also request a conference if counsel believes it will be of assistance to the Court or the parties. Counsel's participation is required at any scheduled conference. Mediation conferences will generally be conducted by telephone but may be conducted in person in the discretion of a circuit mediator. Mediation conferences may be adjourned from time to time by a circuit mediator. Purposes of the mediation conference include:

(a) Jurisdictional review;

(b) Simplification, clarification, and reduction of issues;

(c) Discussion of settlement; and

(d) Consideration of any other matter relating to the efficient management and disposition of the appeal.

Although the time allowed for filing of briefs is not automatically tolled by proceedings under this local rule, if the parties wish to pursue, or are engaged in, settlement discussions, counsel for any party may move to extend the briefing schedule. The mediator, through the Clerk of the Court, may enter orders which control the course of proceedings and, upon agreement of the parties, dispose of the case.

Statements and comments made during all mediation conferences, and papers or electronic information generated during the process, are not included in Court files except to the extent disclosed by orders entered under this local rule. Information disclosed in the mediation process shall be kept confidential and shall not be disclosed to the judges deciding the appeal or to any other person outside the mediation program participants. Confidentiality is required of all participants in the mediation proceedings. All statements, documents, and discussions in such proceedings shall be kept confidential. The mediator, attorneys, and other participants in the mediation shall not disclose such statements, documents, or discussions without prior approval of the Standing Panel on Attorney Discipline. Any alleged violations of this rule shall be referred to the Court's Standing Panel on Attorney Discipline for a determination pursuant to Local Rule 46(g) of whether imposition of discipline is warranted. All proceedings before the Standing Panel on Attorney Discipline involving confidential inofrmation under this procedure shall be confidential. (Amended by order effective March 12, 1998; and by order effective Dec. 11, 2001.)

COMMENT

Local Rule 33 has been amended to reflect the Court conference attorneys' preference for granting a definite extension rather than an indefinite suspension of a briefing schedule during settlement discussions.

Rule 34. Oral argument.

(a) **In general.** (1) Party's statement. Any party may file, or a court may require by local rule, a statement explaining why oral argument should, or need not, be permitted.

(2) Standards. Oral argument must be allowed in every case unless a panel of three judges who have examined the briefs and record unanimously agrees that oral argument is unnecessary for any of the following reasons:

(A) the appeal is frivolous;

(B) the dispositive issue or issues have been authoritatively decided; or

(C) the facts and legal arguments are adequately presented in the briefs and record, and the decisional process would not be significantly aided by oral argument.

(b) **Notice of argument; postponement.** The clerk must advise all parties whether oral argument will be scheduled, and, if so, the date, time, and place for it, and the time allowed for each side. A motion to postpone the argument or to allow longer argument must be filed reasonably in advance of the hearing date.

(c) **Order and content of argument.** The appellant opens and concludes the argument. Counsel must not read at length from briefs, records, or authorities.

(d) **Cross-appeals and separate appeals.** If there is a cross-appeal, Rule 28(h) determines which party is the appellant and which is the appellee for purposes of oral argument. Unless the court directs otherwise, a cross-appeal or separate appeal must be argued when the initial appeal is argued. Separate parties should avoid duplicative argument.

(e) **Nonappearance of a party.** If the appellee fails to appear for argument, the court must hear appellant's argument. If the appellant fails to appear for argument, the court may hear the appellee's argument. If neither party appears, the case will be decided on the briefs, unless the court orders otherwise.

(f) **Submission on briefs.** The parties may agree to submit a case for decision on the briefs, but the court may direct that the case be argued.

(g) **Use of physical exhibits at argument; removal.** Counsel intending to use physical exhibits other than documents at the argument must arrange to place them in the courtroom on the day of the argument before the court convenes. After the argument, counsel must remove the exhibits from the courtroom, unless the court directs otherwise. The clerk may destroy or dispose of the exhibits if counsel does not reclaim them within a reasonable time after the clerk gives notice to remove them. (Amended by order adopted April 30, 1979, effective August 1, 1979, by order effective July 1, 1986, by order adopted April 30, 1991, effective December 1, 1991, and by order adopted April 22, 1993, effective December 1, 1993; and by order adopted April 24, 1998, effective December 1, 1998.)

Local Rule 34(a). Oral argument; pre-argument review and summary disposition of appeals; statement regarding the need for oral argument.

In the interest of docket control and to expedite the final disposition of pending cases, the chief judge may designate a panel or panels to review any pending case at any time before argument for disposition under this rule.

In reviewing pending cases before argument, the panel will utilize the minimum standards set forth in FRAP 34(a)(2). If all of the judges of the panel to which a pending appeal has been referred conclude that oral argument is not to be allowed, they may make any appropriate disposition without oral argument including, but not limited to, affirmance or reversal.

Because any case may be decided without oral argument, all major arguments should be fully developed in the briefs. In furtherance of the disposition of pending cases under this rule, parties may include in their briefs at the conclusion of the argument a statement setting forth the reasons why, in their opinion, oral argument should be heard. (Amended by order effective December 1, 1998.)

Local Rule 34(b). Informal briefs.

Whenever an application for a certificate of appealability from the denial of a writ of habeas corpus or a motion under 28 U.S.C. § 2255 is filed, or whenever any pro se appeal is filed, the clerk shall notify the appellant that appellant shall file, within 21 days after service of such notice, an informal brief, listing the specific issues and supporting facts and arguments raised on appeal. Appellee is permitted, but not required, to file an informal response brief within 14 days after service of appellant's informal brief, and appellant is permitted, but not required, to file an informal reply brief within 10 days after service of appellee's informal response brief. Appellant's informal brief and any informal response and reply briefs filed by the parties shall be considered, together with the record and other relevant papers, by the panel to which the proceeding has been referred. The Court will limit its review to the issues raised in the informal brief.

The informal brief may be submitted on a form provided by the clerk and shall provide the specific information required by the form. The parties need not limit their briefs solely to the form. An additional supporting memorandum may be attached if a party deems it necessary in order to address adequately the issues raised, but the informal brief and any supporting memorandum shall not exceed the length limitations established by FRAP 32(a)(7). It is unnecessary to attach record excerpts since the record is before the Court. It is not necessary to cite cases in an informal brief. Unless additional copies are requested by the Clerk, only the original informal brief must be filed with the Court and copies served on the other parties to the case.

Once an informal briefing schedule has been established the parties may file a formal brief only with the permission of the Court. The Court initially reviews cases that are informally briefed under its procedures set forth in Local Rule 34(a) pertaining to pre-argument review.

If the panel reviewing an informal brief submitted by an indigent pro se litigant determines that further briefing and possible oral argument would be of assistance, counsel will be appointed and directed to file additional formal briefs. In any appeal that has been informally briefed, the Court may direct that additional briefs be filed prior to oral argument. (Amended by order effective December 1, 1998; by order effective April 1, 2008; and amended effective December 1, 2009.)

COMMENT

Local Rule 34(b) has been amended to delete the requirement of the Clerk sending the pro se party a copy of the local rule. Instead, the Clerk's office sends instructions on how to complete the informal briefing form.

Effect of amendments. — The 2008 amendment in the second paragraph in the third sentence substituted "informal brief and any supporting memorandum" for "the briefs with any attachments"; added the fourth sentence; and rewrote the last sentence regarding two copies to be filed and a copy to be mailed.

The 2009 amendment in the first paragraph substituted "21 days after service" for "twenty-one days after receipt" in the first sentence, added the second sentence, and substituted "response and reply briefs filed by the parties" for "brief filed by appellee" in the third sentence.

Local Rule 34(c). Court sessions and notification to counsel.

The Court sits in Richmond, Virginia, to hear cases during six to eight separate argument weeks scheduled between September and June. The Court also sits at law schools within the Circuit and at other special argument sessions. The Court's oral argument schedule is available on the Court's Internet site, www.ca4.uscourts.gov.

The Court initially hears and decides cases in panels consisting of three judges with the Chief Judge or most senior active judge presiding. Each panel regularly hears oral argument in four cases each day during court week; additional cases are added as required.

Attorneys appearing for oral argument must register with the Clerk's Office on the morning of argument to learn of courtroom assignment, order of appearance, and allocation of oral argument time. Counsel not already a member of the Fourth Circuit bar will be admitted to practice before the Court at that time upon compliance with the provisions of Local Rule 46(b).

The Court convenes at 9:30 a.m., with the exception of Friday, when it convenes at 8:30 a.m.

Preparation for the argument calendar begins in the Clerk's Office at least two months prior to argument. Upon receiving notice that a case has been tentatively assigned to an argument session, counsel must inform the clerk, within the time provided in the notice, of any conflict or other matter that would affect scheduling of the case for that session. After a case has been scheduled for argument, any motion that would affect the argument date must show good cause for the requested relief and that the relief could not have been requested within the period set by the Court for notice of conflicts. Continuance of an established oral argument date is not granted because of a prior professional commitment. Although a case will not be removed from the calendar because of a scheduling conflict by counsel after the notification of oral argument has been issued, the Court may direct another lawyer from the same firm to argue the appeal if counsel of record cannot be present. (Amended by order effective April 1, 2008.)

COMMENT

Local Rule 34(c) deletes reference to the January session of Court because Court is no longer held in January. The rule also adds that counsel will be admitted to the bar of the Court only when counsel complies with the provisions of Local Rule 46(b). Proposed Local Rule 34(c) also changes existing I.O.P. 34.1 to reflect that the registration and oral argument for cases on Fridays is 45 minutes earlier than on other days of the Court session. Proposed Local Rule 34(c) also reflects the preference of the Court, as a matter of practice, to receive notice of any scheduling conflict when counsel receives notice of the tentative calendaring of a case for oral argument.

Effect of amendments. — The 2008 amendment rewrote the first paragraph concerning the court schedule; deleted the last sentence of the third paragraph regarding the time of registration; and rewrote the last paragraph other than the first and last sentences.

Local Rule 34(d). Argument time.

Briefs for the cases assigned to a hearing panel are distributed by the clerk to the judges on a hearing panel at the time the hearing panel assignments are made. The members of the Court hearing oral argument will have read the briefs before the hearing and therefore will be familiar with the case. In oral argument, counsel should emphasize the dispositive issues.

Since the appellant is allowed to open and close the argument, counsel for appellant should indicate at registration before oral argument how much time counsel wants to reserve for rebuttal. It is recommended that no more than two attorneys argue per side. Each side is normally allowed 20 minutes, even in consolidated cases, but counsel may not need the full time allotted or the Court may shorten or extend the time allotted. In social security disability cases, black lung cases, and labor cases where the primary issue is whether the agency's decision is supported by substantial evidence and in criminal cases where the primary issue involves the application of the sentencing guidelines, each side is limited to 15 minutes. In black lung cases in which the Director, Office of Workers' Compensation Programs, has been granted leave to file a separate brief, the Director will share argument time with whichever side the Director's brief supports.

If counsel believes that more time is needed for oral argument, a written motion setting forth the reasons for additional time and whether the other parties consent must be submitted well in advance of the hearing date. The Court may sua sponte extend the allotted time during the argument or it may terminate the argument whenever in its judgment further argument is unnecessary. (Amended by order effective December 1, 1998; June 1, 1999.)

COMMENT

Proposed Local Rule 34(d) reflects the Court's current practice regarding the sharing of time for oral argument with the Director, Office of Workers' Compensation Programs, in black lung appeals.

Local Rule 34(d) was amended to provide that the court may reduce argument time from 30 minutes when extended argument is unnecessary.

Local Rule 34(e). Motion to submit on briefs.

As soon as possible upon completion of the briefing schedule or within 10 days of tentative notification of oral argument, whichever is earlier, any party may file a motion to submit the case on the briefs without the necessity of oral argument. Such motions are not granted as a matter of course. A motion to submit on briefs should not be used to alleviate a scheduling conflict after the notification of oral argument has been issued. (Amended by order effective December 1, 1998; by order effective December 1, 2002; and amended effective December 1, 2009.)

COMMENT

Local Rule 34(e) has been amended to conform to the court's practice of requiring that motions to submit on the briefs be filed within

ten days of notification to counsel that a case is tentatively calendared. This notification may occur before briefing is completed.

Effect of amendments. — The 2009 amendment substituted "10 days" for "10 calendar days" in the first sentence.

I.O.P. 34.1. Calendar assignments and panel composition.

The Clerk of Court maintains a list of mature cases available for oral argument and on a monthly basis merges those cases with a list of three-judge panels provided by a computer program designed to achieve total random selection.

The composition of each panel usually changes each day during court week except on those occasions where only one panel is sitting in a given geographical location. Every effort is made to assign cases for oral argument to judges who have had previous involvement with the case on appeal through random assignment to a preargument motion or prior appeal in the matter, but there is no guarantee that any of the judges who have previously been involved with an appeal will be assigned to a hearing panel. The varied assignment of judges to panels and the independent assignment of varied cases to panels is designed, insofar as practicable, to assure the opportunity for each judge to sit with all other judges an equal number of times, and to assure that both the appearance and the fact of presentation of particular types of cases to particular judges is avoided. (Redesignated by order effective December 1, 1995; amended by order effective February 1, 2001.)

I.O.P. 34.2. Disposition without oral argument.

A decision against oral argument must be unanimous, and if a case is decided without oral argument the decision on the merits must be unanimous also. Whenever at least one member of the review panel determines that oral argument would be of assistance, the panel notifies the clerk who places the case on the oral argument calendar.

I.O.P. 34.3. Audio files of oral argument.

Effective with its May 2011 argument session, the Court will make audio files of oral arguments available on the Court's Internet site, without charge, two days after argument. Counsel are reminded that the following information should not be included in argument to the Court:

(A) Personal data protected by Fed. R. App. P. 25(a)(5):

(1) social security and taxpayer identification numbers;

(2) dates of birth;

(3) names of minor children;

(4) financial account numbers; and

(5) home addresses in criminal cases.

(B) Criminal case information protected by the Judiciary's Privacy Policy for Electronic Case Files:

(1) unexecuted summonses or warrants;

(2) pretrial bail or presentence investigation reports;

(3) statements of reasons in the judgment of conviction;

(4) juvenile records;

(5) identifying information about jurors or potential jurors;

(6) financial affidavits filed under the Criminal Justice Act;

(7) ex parte requests to authorize services under the Criminal Justice Act; and

(8) sealed documents (e.g., motions for downward departure for substantial assistance, plea agreements indicating cooperation, or victim statements).

Any motion to seal argument must be filed on the public docket at least five days before oral argument, in accordance with Local Rule 25(c)(2). Audio files of sealed arguments will not be released absent an order of the Court unsealing the argument. (Added May 2, 2011, effective May 2, 2011.)

Rule 35. En banc determination.

(a) **When hearing or rehearing en banc may be ordered.** A majority of the circuit judges who are in regular active service may order that an appeal or other proceeding be heard or reheard by the court of appeals en banc. An en banc hearing or rehearing is not favored and ordinarily will not be ordered unless:

(1) en banc consideration is necessary to secure or maintain uniformity of the court's decisions; or

(2) the proceeding involves a question of exceptional importance.

(b) **Petition for hearing or rehearing en banc.** A party may petition for a hearing or rehearing en banc.

(1) The petition must begin with a statement that either:

(A) the panel decision conflicts with a decision of the United States Supreme Court or of the court to which the petition is addressed (with citation to the conflicting case or cases) and consideration by the full court is therefore necessary to secure and maintain uniformity of the court's decisions; or

(B) the proceeding involves one or more questions of exceptional importance, each of which must be concisely stated; for example, a petition may assert that a proceeding presents a question of exceptional importance if it involves an issue on which the panel decision conflicts with the authoritative decisions of other United States Courts of Appeals that have addressed the issue.

(2) Except by the court's permission, a petition for an en banc hearing or rehearing must not exceed 15 pages, excluding material not counted under Rule 32.

(3) For purposes of the page limit in Rule 35(b)(2), if a party files both a petition for panel rehearing and a petition for rehearing en banc, they are considered a single document even if they are filed separately, unless separate filing is required by local rule.

(c) **Time for petition for hearing or rehearing en banc.** A petition that an appeal be heard initially en banc must be filed by the date when the appellee's brief is due. A petition for a rehearing en banc must be filed within the time prescribed by Rule 40 for filing a petition for rehearing.

(d) **Number of copies.** The number of copies to be filed must be prescribed by local rule and may be altered by order in a particular case.

(e) **Response.** No response may be filed to a petition for an en banc consideration unless the court orders a response.

(f) **Call for a vote.** A vote need not be taken to determine whether the case will be heard or reheard en banc unless a judge calls for a vote. (Amended by order adopted April 30, 1979, effective August 1, 1979, and by order adopted April 29, 1994, effective December 1, 1994 and by order adopted April 24, 1998, effective December 1, 1998.)

Local Rule 35. En banc proceedings.

(a) **Petition for rehearing en banc.** A petition for rehearing en banc must be made at the same time, and in the same document, as a petition for rehearing. The request for en banc consideration shall be stated plainly in the title of the petition. Petitions for rehearing en banc will be distributed to all active and senior judges of the Court, and to any visiting judge who may have heard and decided the appeal.

(b) **Decision to hear or rehear a case en banc.** A majority of the circuit judges who are in regular active service may grant a hearing or rehearing en banc. For purposes of determining a majority under this rule, the term majority means of all judges of the Court in regular active service who are presently serving, without regard to whether a judge is disqualified. A poll on whether to rehear a case en banc may be requested, with or without a petition, by an active judge of the Court or by a senior or visiting judge who sat on on the panel that decided the case originally. Unless a judge requests that a poll be taken on the petition, none will be taken. If no poll is requested, the panel's order on a petition for rehearing will bear the notation that no member of the Court requested a poll. If a poll is requested and hearing or rehearing en banc is denied, the order will reflect the vote of each participating judge. A judge who joins the Court after a petition has been submitted to the Court, and before an order has been entered, will be eligible to vote on the decision to hear or rehear a case en banc.

(c) **Decision of cases heard or reheard en banc.** An en banc hearing will be before all eligible, active and participating judges of the Court. An en banc rehearing will be before all eligible and participating active judges, and any senior judge of the Court who sat on the panel that decided the case originally. An active judge who takes senior status after a case is heard or reheard by an en banc Court will be eligible to participate in the en banc decision. A judge who joins the Court after argument of a case to an en banc Court will not be eligible to participate in the decision of the case. A judge who joins the Court after submission of a case to an en banc Court without oral argument will participate in the decision of the case. Granting of rehearing en banc vacates the previous panel judgment and opinion; the rehearing is a review of the judgment or decision from which review is sought and not a review of the judgment of the panel. (The circuit takes the position that the change of wording in 28 U.S.C. § 46(c) referring to participation in en banc decisions does not alter the long-standing rule that the en banc court reviews the decision from which review is sought in this Court, not the decision of a panel.)

(d) **Additional copies of briefs and appendix for en banc hearing or rehearing.** The Court's order granting hearing or rehearing en banc may require the parties to file additional copies of the briefs and appendix. Each party will bear the initial cost of additional copies of its own briefs. The party that requested the hearing or rehearing en banc will bear the initial cost of filing additional copies of the appendix. In the event that cross petitions for hearing or rehearing en banc are granted, the parties will share equally the initial cost of preparing additional copies of the appendix. (Amended effective December 4, 1996; effective December 1, 1998; and by order adopted September 30, 2003, effective December 1, 2003.)

Effect of amendments. — The 2004 amendment, in (b), inserted, "A poll on whether to rehear a case en banc may be requested, with or without a petition, by an

active judge of the court or by a senior or
visiting judge who sat on on the panel that
decided the case originally."

Rule 36. Entry of judgment; notice.

(a) **Entry.** A judgment is entered when it is noted on the docket. The clerk must prepare, sign, and enter the judgment:

(1) after receiving the court's opinion — but if settlement of the judgment's form is required, after final settlement; or

(2) if a judgment is rendered without an opinion, as the court instructs.

(b) **Notice.** On the date when judgment is entered, the clerk must serve on all parties a copy of the opinion — or the judgment, if no opinion was written — and a notice of the date when the judgment was entered. (Amended by order adopted April 24, 1998, effective December 1, 1998; and by order adopted April 29, 2002, effective December 1, 2002.)

Local Rule 36(a). Publication of decisions.

Opinions delivered by the Court will be published only if the opinion satisfies one or more of the standards for publication:

i. It establishes, alters, modifies, clarifies, or explains a rule of law within this Circuit; or

ii. It involves a legal issue of continuing public interest; or

iii. It criticizes existing law; or

iv. It contains a historical review of a legal rule that is not duplicative; or

v. It resolves a conflict between panels of this Court, or creates a conflict with a decision in another circuit.

The Court will publish opinions only in cases that have been fully briefed and presented at oral argument. Opinions in such cases will be published if the author or a majority of the joining judges believes the opinion satisfies one or more of the standards for publication, and all members of the Court have acknowledged in writing their receipt of the proposed opinion. A judge may file a published opinion without obtaining all acknowledgements only if the opinion has been in circulation for ten days and an inquiry to the non-acknowledging judge's chambers has confirmed that the opinion was received. (Amended by order effective December 1, 2002; amended effective December 1, 2009.)

Effect of amendments. — The 2009 amendment substituted "ten days and an inquiry to the non-acknowledging judge's chambers has confirmed that the opinion was received" for "ten calendar days" in the last sentence of the last paragraph.

Local Rule 36(b). Unpublished dispositions; distribution of opinions.

Unpublished opinions give counsel, the parties, and the lower court or agency a statement of the reasons for the decision. They may not recite all of the facts or background of the case and may simply adopt the reasoning of the lower court. They are sent only to the trial court or agency in which the case originated, to counsel for all parties in the case, and to litigants in the case not represented by counsel. Any individual or institution may receive copies of all published opinions of the Court by paying an annual subscription fee for this service. In addition, copies of published opinions are sent to all circuit judges, district judges, bankruptcy judges, magistrate judges, clerks of district court, United States Attorneys, and Federal Public Defenders upon request. Published and unpublished opinions issued since January 1, 1996 are available free of charge at www.ca4.uscourts.gov.

Counsel may move for publication of an unpublished opinion, citing reasons. If such motion is granted, the unpublished opinion will be published without change in result. (Amended by order effective January 1, 1994; by order effective December 1, 1995; by order effective December 1, 2002; by order effective October 5, 2004; by order effective January 7, 2005; and amended effective December 1, 2009.)

COMMENT

Proposed Local Rule 36(b) changes EDOS to ABBS to reflect the new name of the Appellate Bulletin Board System. All opinions issued on or after January 1, 1995 will be maintained on the ABBS for a minimum of six months.

Effect of amendments. — The 2004 amendment, effective Oct. 5, 2004, with a notice period extending through November 30, 2004, and subject to amendment in light of comments received, in the fourth sentence deleted "and certain unpublished" following "published".

The 2005 amendment divided the former first paragraph into the current first and second paragraphs and substituted "published" for "such" in the first sentence of the second paragraph.

The 2009 amendment deleted the former sixth sentence of the first paragraph.

Local Rule 36(c). Citation of unpublished dispositions.
[Transferred]

Editor's note. — Former Local Rule 36(c) was amended and renumbered as Local Rule 32.1 June 1, 2006, effective Deceber 1, 2006.

I.O.P. 36.1. Opinion preparation assignments.

The custom of the Fourth Circuit is to reserve judgment at the conclusion of oral argument. A conference of the panel is held promptly after oral argument, usually immediately after the presentation of the case. Although a tentative decision may be reached at this conference, additional conferences are sometimes necessary. Opinion assignments are made by the Chief Judge on the basis of recommendations from the presiding judge of each panel on which the Chief Judge did not sit.

I.O.P. 36.2. Circulation of opinions in argued cases.

Although one judge writes the opinion, every panel member is equally involved in the process of decision. An appeal may be heard and decided by two of the three judges assigned to a panel, when one judge becomes unavailable. If a panel is reduced to two and the two cannot agree, however, the case will be reargued before a new three-judge panel which may or may not include prior panel members.

When a proposed opinion in an argued case is prepared and submitted to other panel members copies are provided to the non-sitting judges including the senior judges and their comments are solicited. The opinion is then finalized. The Clerk's Office never receives advance notice of when a decision will be rendered, so counsel should not call for such information. (Amended by order effective April 1, 2008.)

COMMENT

I.O.P. 36.2 has been amended to reflect that the Court no longer prints all opinions.

Effect of amendments. — The 2008 amendment deleted "and announcement of decision" in the title; and deleted the third paragraph regarding mailing copies of the opinion to counsel or calling counsel to provide information, but not reading the opinon over the telephone.

I.O.P. 36.3. Summary opinions.

If all judges on a panel of the Court agree following oral argument that an opinion in a case would have no precedential value, and that summary disposition is otherwise appropriate, the Court may decide the appeal by summary opinion. A summary opinion identifies the decision appealed from, sets forth the Court's decision and the reason or reasons therefor, and resolves any outstanding motions in the case. It does not discuss the facts or elaborate on the Court's reasoning.

Rule 37. Interest on judgments.

(a) **When the court affirms.** Unless the law provides otherwise, if a money judgment in a civil case is affirmed, whatever interest is allowed by law is payable from the date when the district court's judgment was entered.

(b) **When the court reverses.** If the court modifies or reverses a judgment with a direction that a money judgment be entered in the district court, the mandate must contain instructions about the allowance of interest. (Amended by order adopted April 24, 1998, effective December 1, 1998.)

Rule 38. Frivolous appeal — Damages and costs.

If a court of appeals determines that an appeal is frivolous, it may, after a separately filed motion or notice from the court and reasonable opportunity to respond, award just damages and single or double costs to the appellee. (Amended by order adopted April 29, 1994, effective December 1, 1994; and by order adopted April 24, 1998, effective December 1, 1998.)

Applied in Gaiters v. Lynn, 831 F.2d 51 (4th Cir. 1987); Bast v. Cohen, Dunn & Sinclair, 59 F.3d 492 (4th Cir. 1995).

Rule 39. Costs.

(a) **Against whom assessed.** The following rules apply unless the law provides or the court orders otherwise:

(1) if an appeal is dismissed, costs are taxed against the appellant, unless the parties agree otherwise;

(2) if a judgment is affirmed, costs are taxed against the appellant;

(3) if a judgment is reversed, costs are taxed against the appellee;

(4) if a judgment is affirmed in part, reversed in part, modified, or vacated, costs are taxed only as the court orders.

(b) **Costs for and against the United States.** Costs for or against the United States, its agency, or officer will be assessed under Rule 39 (a) only if authorized by law.

(c) **Costs of copies.** Each court of appeals must, by local rule, fix the maximum rate for taxing the cost of producing necessary copies of a brief or appendix, or copies of records authorized by Rule 30(f). The rate must not exceed that generally charged for such work in the area where the clerk's office is located and should encourage economical methods of copying.

(d) **Bill of costs; objections; insertion in mandate.** (1) A party who wants costs taxed must — within 14 days after entry of judgment — file with the circuit clerk, with proof of service, an itemized and verified bill of costs.

(2) Objections must be filed within 10 days after service of the bill of costs, unless the court extends the time.

(3) The clerk must prepare and certify an itemized statement of costs for insertion in the mandate, but issuance of the mandate must not be delayed for taxing costs. If the mandate issues before costs are finally determined, the district clerk must — upon the circuit clerk's request — add the statement of costs, or any amendment of it, to the mandate.

(e) **Costs on appeal taxable in the district court.** The following costs on appeal are taxable in the district court for the benefit of the party entitled to costs under this rule:

(1) the preparation and transmission of the record;

(2) the reporter's transcript, if needed to determine the appeal;

(3) premiums paid for a supersedeas bond or other bond to preserve rights pending appeal; and

(4) the fee for filing the notice of appeal. (Amended by order adopted April 30, 1979, effective August 1, 1979, and by order effective July 1, 1986; and by order adopted April 24, 1998, effective December 1, 1998.)

Discretion of court. — Under this Rule, an appellate court has wide discretion in the taxation of costs. Square Constr. Co. v. Washington Metro. Area Transit Auth., 800 F.2d 1256 (4th Cir. 1986).

Local Rule 39(a). Reproduction costs.

The cost of producing and binding necessary copies of briefs and appendices in the form required by Fed. R. App. P. 32 shall be taxable as costs at a rate equal to actual cost, but not higher than 15 cents per page for each copy required for filing and service by Local Rules 30(b)(4) and 31(d) or by order of the Court. (Amended effective December 1, 1998; amended effective September 1, 2011.)

COMMENT

Local Rule 39(a) has been amended to delete reference to printing costs for typeset briefs.

Effect of amendments. — The 2011 amendment substituted "Reproduction" for "Printing" in the section heading; and rewrote the text.

Local Rule 39(b). Bill of costs.

The verified bill of costs may be that of a party or counsel, and should be accompanied by the printer's itemized statement of charges. When costs are sought for or against the United States, counsel should cite the statutory authority relied upon. Taxation of costs will not be delayed by the filing of a petition for rehearing or other postjudgment motion. A late affidavit for costs must be accompanied by a motion for leave to file. The clerk rules on all bills of costs and objections in the first instance.

Local Rule 39(c). Recovery of costs in the district court.

The only costs generally taxable in the Court of Appeals are: (1) the docketing fee if the case is reversed; and (2) the cost of printing or reproducing briefs and appendices, including exhibits.

Although some costs are "taxable" in the Court of Appeals, all costs are recoverable in the district court after issuance of the mandate. If the matter of costs has not been settled before issuance of the mandate, the clerk will send a supplemental "Bill of Costs" to the district court for inclusion in the mandate at a later date.

Various costs incidental to an appeal must be settled at the district court level. Among such items are: (1) the cost of the reporter's transcript; (2) the fee for filing the notice of appeal; (3) the fee for preparing and transmitting the record; and (4) the premiums paid for any required appeal bond. Application for recovery of these expenses by the successful party on appeal must be made in the district court, and should be made only after issuance of the mandate by the Court of Appeals. These costs, if erroneously applied for in the Court of Appeals, will be disallowed without prejudice to the right to reapply for them in the district court.

COMMENT

Existing I.O.P. 39 has been reorganized into proposed Local Rules 39(b) and (c), with redundancies eliminated.

Rule 40. Petition for panel rehearing.

(a) **Time to file; contents; answer; action by the court if granted.**
(1) Time. Unless the time is shortened or extended by order or local rule, a petition for panel rehearing may be filed within 14 days after entry of judgment. But in a civil case, if the United States or its officer or agency is a party, the time within which any party may seek rehearing is 45 days after entry of judgment, unless an order shortens or extends the time.

(2) Contents. The petition must state with particularity each point of law or fact that the petitioner believes the court has overlooked or misapprehended and must argue in support of the petition. Oral argument is not permitted.

(3) Answer. Unless the court requests, no answer to a petition for panel rehearing is permitted. But ordinarily rehearing will not be granted in the absence of such a request.

(4) Action by the court. If a petition for panel rehearing is granted, the court may do any of the following:

(A) make a final disposition of the case without reargument;

(B) restore the case to the calendar for reargument or resubmission; or

(C) issue any other appropriate order.

(b) **Form of petition; length.** The petition must comply in form with Rule 32. Copies must be served and filed as Rule 31 prescribes. Unless the court permits or a local rule provides otherwise, a petition for panel rehearing must not exceed 15 pages. (Amended by order adopted April 30, 1979, effective August 1, 1979, and by order adopted April 29, 1994, effective December 1, 1994; and by order adopted April 24, 1998, effective December 1, 1998.)

Local Rule 40(a). Filing of petition.

Although petitions for rehearing are filed in a great many cases, few are granted. Filing a petition solely for purposes of delay or in order merely to reargue the case is an abuse of privilege. Whenever a request for rehearing en banc is contained in a petition, such fact must be stated plainly on the cover of and in the title of the document. Only the original petition for rehearing or rehearing en banc is required unless additional copies are requested by the Clerk. (Amended effective December 1, 1998; by order effective October 5, 2004; and by order effective April 1, 2008.)

Effect of amendments. — The 2004 amendment, effective Oct. 5, 2004, rewrote the third sentence in the third paragraph.

The 2008 amendment incorporated the second paragraph into the first paragraph and added the last sentence; and deleted the fomer last paragraph regarding numbers of copies required.

Local Rule 40(b). Statement of purpose.

A petition for rehearing must contain an introduction stating that, in counsel's judgment, one or more of the following situations exist:

i. A material factual or legal matter was overlooked in the decision.

ii. A change in the law occurred after the case was submitted and was overlooked by the panel.

iii. The opinion is in conflict with a decision of the United States Supreme Court, this Court, or another court of appeals and the conflict is not addressed in the opinion.

iv. The proceeding involves one or more questions of exceptional importance.

A petition should only be made to direct the Court's attention to one or more of the above situations. The points to be raised should be succinctly listed in counsel's statement of purpose. (Amended effective December 1, 1998.)

COMMENT

Local Rule 40(b) has been amended to add a fourth ground for filing a petition for rehearing. The local rule now incorporates the standard contained in FRAP 35(b)(1). Because the statement of purpose section of a petition for rehearing is not a requirement of FRAP, the provision in Local Rule 40(b) regarding rejection of a petition which fails to contain such a statement has been deleted.

Local Rule 40(c). Time limits for filing petitions.

The Court strictly enforces the time limits for filing petitions for rehearing and petitions for rehearing en banc. The Clerk's Office will deny as untimely any petition received in the Clerk's Office later than 45 days after entry of judgment in any civil case where the United States, or an agency or officer thereof is a party, or 14 days after the entry of judgment in any other case. The only grounds for an extension of time to file a petition, or to accept an untimely petition, are as follows:

i. the death or serious illness of counsel, or of a member of counsel's immediate family (or in the case of a party proceeding without counsel, the death or serious illness of the party or a member of the party's immediate family); or

ii. an extraordinary circumstance wholly beyond the control of counsel or of a party proceeding without counsel.

Petitions for rehearing and petitions for en banc rehearing from incarcerated persons proceeding without the assistance of counsel are deemed filed when they are delivered to prison or jail officials. All other such petitions are deemed filed only when received in the Clerk's Office. (Amended effective December 1, 1998.)

Local Rule 40(d). Papers filed after denial of a petition for rehearing.

Except for timely petitions for rehearing en banc, cost and attorney fee matters, and other matters ancillary to the filing of an application for writ of certiorari with the Supreme Court, the Office of the Clerk shall not receive motions or other papers requesting further relief in a case after the Court has denied a petition for rehearing or the time for filing a petition for rehearing has expired. (Amended effective December 1, 1998.)

I.O.P. 40.1. Submission of petitions for rehearing to the court.

The Clerk's Office will hold any petition for rehearing or petition for rehearing en banc, until the time for filing all such petitions, or any extension thereof granted in the particular case, has run. Thereafter, all petitions for rehearing in the same case will be distributed to the Court simultaneously. (Amended effective December 1, 1998.)

I.O.P. 40.2. Panel rehearing.

The panel of judges who heard and decided the appeal will rule on the petition for rehearing. Such panel may include a senior circuit judge or a visiting judge sitting in the Fourth Circuit by designation.

If a petition for rehearing is granted, the original judgment and opinion of the Court are vacated and the case will be reheard before the original panel. The Court may direct the filing of additional briefs, or the parties may seek leave of Court to file additional briefs.

COMMENT

Proposed I.O.P. 40.2 changes the reference to visiting judges in existing I.O.P. 40.5 to delete reference to district or federal appellate judges because visiting judges with this Court have included judges from the Court of International Trade pursuant to designation under 28 U.S.C. § 293. The I.O.P. also deletes the requirement of setting forth the vote of the panel on a petition for rehearing because the Court does not now disclose that information in its routine orders.

Rule 41. Mandate, contents, issuance and effective date; stay.

(a) **Contents.** Unless the court directs that a formal mandate issue, the mandate consists of a certified copy of the judgment, a copy of the court's opinion, if any, and any direction about costs.

(b) **When issued.** The court's mandate must issue 7 calendar days after the time to file a petition for rehearing expires, or 7 calendar days after entry of an order denying a timely petition for panel rehearing, petition for rehearing en banc, or motion for stay of mandate, whichever is later. The court may shorten or extend the time.

(c) **Effective date.** The mandate is effective when issued.

(d) **Staying the mandate.** (1) On petition for rehearing or motion. The timely filing of a petition for panel rehearing, petition for rehearing en banc, or motion for stay of mandate, stays the mandate until disposition of the petition or motion, unless the court orders otherwise.

(2) Pending petition for certiorari. (A) A party may move to stay the mandate pending the filing of a petition for a writ of certiorari in the Supreme Court. The motion must be served on all parties and must show that the certiorari petition would present a substantial question and that there is good cause for a stay.

(B) The stay must not exceed 90 days, unless the period is extended for good cause or unless the party who obtained the stay files a petition for the writ and so notifies the circuit clerk in writing within the period of the stay. In that case, the stay continues until the Supreme Court's final disposition.

(C) The court may require a bond or other security as a condition to granting or continuing a stay of the mandate.

(D) The court of appeals must issue the mandate immediately when a copy of a Supreme Court order denying the petition for writ of certiorari is filed. (Amended by order adopted April 29, 1994, effective December 1, 1994; by order adopted April 24, 1998, effective December 1, 1998; and by order adopted April 29, 2002, effective December 1, 2002.)

Local Rule 41. Motion for stay of the mandate.

A motion for stay of the issuance of the mandate shall not be granted simply upon request. Ordinarily the motion shall be denied unless there is a specific showing that it is not frivolous or filed merely for delay. The motion must present a substantial question or set forth good or probable cause for a stay. Stay requests are normally acted upon without a request for a response.

COMMENT

Proposed Local Rule 41 deletes the requirement in existing I.O.P. 41.2 that only one copy of a motion for stay of mandate need be filed. The preferred practice is that counsel file an original and three copies, like other pleading.

I.O.P. 41.1. Issuance of the mandate.

On the date of issuance of the mandate, the Clerk of the Court will issue written notice to the parties and the clerk of the lower court that the judgment of the Court of Appeals takes effect that day. The trial court record will be returned to the clerk of that court once the mandate has issued.

COMMENT

I.O.P. 41.1 has been changed to reflect the actual practice that records often go back to the lower court under separate cover within a few days of issuance of the mandate. This is especially true if the Clerk's office must get the records back from chambers or the Office of Staff Counsel.

I.O.P. 41.2. Petitions for writs of certiorari.

A petition for a writ of certiorari must be filed with the Supreme Court within 90 days of the entry of judgment in a criminal case or a civil case. The time for the petition does not run from the issuance of the mandate, but from the date of judgment which is also the opinion date. If a petition for rehearing or a petition for rehearing en banc is timely filed, the time runs from the date of denial of that petition. Counsel should consult the Rules of the Supreme Court for details on how to proceed with the petition.

The Rules of the Supreme Court do not require that the record accompany a petition for certiorari and the record will not be forwarded unless specifically requested by the petitioner or counsel. Requests to certify and transmit the record to the Supreme Court prior to action on the petition for a writ of certiorari are disfavored by the Supreme Court. The Clerk of the Supreme Court will request the record from the Court of Appeals when review of the record is desired by the Supreme Court prior to action on a petition for writ of certiorari or upon granting certiorari if the record has not been transmitted earlier. The same procedures are followed for Supreme Court review by certification pursuant to 28 U.S.C. § 1254(2).

If a case is remanded to the Court of Appeals from the Supreme Court, the case shall be reopened under the original docket number and the Court of Appeals may require additional briefs and oral argument, summarily dispose of the case or take any other action consistent with the Supreme Court's opinion. (Amended effective December 1, 1998.)

I.O.P. 41.2 is amended to clarify, consistent with amendments to FRAP 35, that a timely petition for rehearing en banc will now stay the time to petition for certiorari.

Rule 42. Voluntary dismissal.

(a) **Dismissal in the district court.** Before an appeal has been docketed by the circuit clerk, the district court may dismiss the appeal on the filing of a stipulation signed by all parties or on the appellant's motion with notice to all parties.

(b) **Dismissal in the court of appeals.** The circuit clerk may dismiss a docketed appeal if the parties file a signed dismissal agreement specifying how costs are to be paid and pay any fees that are due. But no mandate or other process may issue without a court order. An appeal may be dismissed on the appellant's motion on terms agreed to by the parties or fixed by the court. (Amended by order adopted April 24, 1998, effective December 1, 1998.)

Local Rule 42. Voluntary dismissals.

In civil cases, the stipulation of dismissal or motion for voluntary dismissal may be signed by counsel. In criminal cases, however, the agreement or motion must be signed or consented to by the individual party appellant personally or counsel must file a statement setting forth the basis for counsel's understanding that the appellant wishes to dismiss the appeal and the efforts made to obtain the appellant's written consent. Counsel must serve a copy of this statement on appellant.

Proposed Local Rule 42 adds language to existing I.O.P. 42.1 to reflect the Court's current practice regarding the additional steps necessary in a criminal case for counsel to obtain a voluntary dismissal.

Rule 43. Substitution of parties.

(a) **Death of a party.** (1) **After Notice of Appeal is Filed**. If a party dies after a notice of appeal has been filed or while a proceeding is pending in the court of appeals, the decedent's personal representative may be substituted as a party on motion filed with the circuit clerk by the representative or by any party. A party's motion must be served on the representative in accordance with Rule 25. If the decedent has no representative, any party may suggest the death on the record, and the court of appeals may then direct appropriate proceedings.

(2) **Before Notice of Appeal Is Filed — Potential Appellant**. If a party entitled to appeal dies before filing a notice of appeal, the decedent's personal representative — or, if there is no personal representative, the decedent's attorney of record — may file a notice of appeal within the time prescribed by these rules. After the notice of appeal is filed, substitution must be in accordance with Rule 43(a)(1).

(3) **Before Notice of Appeal Is Filed — Potential Appellee**. If a party against whom an appeal may be taken dies after entry of a judgment or order

in the district court, but before a notice of appeal is filed, an appellant may proceed as if the death had not occurred. After the notice of appeal is filed, substitution must be in accordance with Rule 43(a)(1).

(b) **Substitution for a reason other than death.** If a party needs to be substituted for any reason other than death, the procedure prescribed in Rule 43(a) applies.

(c) **Public officer: identification; substitution.** (1) **Identification of party**. A public officer who is a party to an appeal or other proceeding in an official capacity may be described as a party by the public officer's official title rather than by name. But the court may require the public officer's name to be added.

(2) **Automatic substitution of officeholder**. When a public officer who is a party to an appeal or other proceeding in an official capacity dies, resigns, or otherwise ceases to hold office, the action does not abate. The public officer's successor is automatically substituted as a party. Proceedings following the substitution are to be in the name of the substituted party, but any misnomer that does not affect the substantial rights of the parties may be disregarded. An order of substitution may be entered at any time, but failure to enter an order does not affect the substitution. (Amended by order effective July 1, 1986; and by order adopted April 24, 1998, effective December 1, 1998.)

Rule 44. Case involving a constitutional question when the United States or the relevant state is not a party.

(a) **Constitutional challenge to federal statute.** If a party questions the constitutionality of an Act of Congress in a proceeding in which the United States or its agency, officer, or employee is not a party in an official capacity, the questioning party must give written notice to the circuit clerk immediately upon the filing of the record or as soon as the question is raised in the court of appeals. The clerk must then certify that fact to the Attorney General.

(b) **Constitutional challenge to state statute.** If a party questions the constitutionality of a statute of a State in a proceeding in which that State or its agency, officer, or employee is not a party in an official capacity, the questioning party must give written notice to the circuit clerk immediately upon the filing of the record or as soon as the question is raised in the court of appeals. The clerk must then certify that fact to the attorney general of the State. (Amended by order adopted April 24, 1998, effective December 1, 1998; and by order adopted April 29, 2002, effective December 1, 2002.)

Rule 45. Clerk's duties.

(a) **General provisions.** (1) Qualifications. The circuit clerk must take the oath and post any bond required by law. Neither the clerk nor any deputy clerk may practice as an attorney or counselor in any court while in office.

(2) When court is open. The court of appeals is always open for filing any paper, issuing and returning process, making a motion, and entering an order. The clerk's office with the clerk or a deputy in attendance must be open during business hours on all days except Saturdays, Sundays, and legal holidays. A court may provide by local rule or by order that the clerk's office be open for

specified hours on Saturdays or on legal holidays other than New Year's Day, Martin Luther King, Jr.'s Birthday, Presidents' Day, Memorial Day, Independence Day, Labor Day, Columbus Day, Veterans' Day, Thanksgiving Day, and Christmas Day.

(b) **Records.** (1) The docket. The circuit clerk must maintain a docket and an index of all docketed cases in the manner prescribed by the Director of the Administrative Office of the United States Courts. The clerk must record all papers filed with the clerk and all process, orders, and judgments.

(2) Calendar. Under the court's direction, the clerk must prepare a calendar of cases awaiting argument. In placing cases on the calendar for argument, the clerk must give preference to appeals in criminal cases and to other proceedings and appeals entitled to preference by law.

(3) Other records. The clerk must keep other books and records required by the Director of the Administrative Office of the United States Courts, with the approval of the Judicial Conference of the United States, or by the court.

(c) **Notice of an order or judgment.** Upon the entry of an order or judgment, the circuit clerk must immediately serve a notice of entry on each party with a copy of any opinion, and must note the date of service on the docket. Service on a party represented by counsel must be made on counsel.

(d) **Custody of records and papers.** The circuit clerk has custody of the court's records and papers. Unless the court orders or instructs otherwise, the clerk must not permit an original record or paper to be taken from the clerk's office. Upon disposition of the case, original papers constituting the record on appeal or review must be returned to the court or agency from which they were received. The clerk must preserve a copy of any brief, appendix, or other paper that has been filed. (Amended by order adopted March 1, 1971, effective July 1, 1971; by order effective July 1, 1986; by order adopted April 24, 1998, effective December 1, 1998; and by order adopted April 29, 2002, effective December 1, 2002.)

Local Rule 45. Dismissals for failure to prosecute.

When an appellant in either a docketed or non-docketed appeal fails to comply with the Federal Rules of Appellate Procedure or the rules or directives of this Court, the clerk shall notify the appellant or, if appellant is represented by counsel, appellant's counsel that upon the expiration of 15 days from the date thereof the appeal will be dismissed for want of prosecution, unless prior to that date appellant remedies the default. Should the appellant fail to comply within said 15-day period, the clerk shall then enter an order dismissing said appeal for want of prosecution, and shall issue the mandate. In no case shall the appellant be entitled to reinstate the case and remedy the default after the same shall have been dismissed under this rule, unless by order of this Court for good cause shown. The dismissal of an appeal shall not limit the authority of this Court, in an appropriate case, to take disciplinary action against defaulting counsel. (Amended effective December 1, 1998; and by order effective April 1, 2008.)

Local Rule 45 eliminates the requirement that the clerk notify appellant personally of counsel's default before dismissing an appeal for failure to prosecute.

Effect of amendments. — The 2008 amendment deleted "a certified copy thereof to the clerk of the district court as and for" before "the mandate" in the third sentence.

I.O.P. 45.1. Clerk's Office.

The Clerk's Office is located on the fifth floor of the United States Courthouse Annex in Richmond, Virginia, and is open from 8:30 a.m. to 5:00 p.m. every weekday, except federal holidays. All correspondence concerning cases pending before the Court should be addressed to:

Clerk, United States Court of Appeals
for the Fourth Circuit
1100 East Main Street, Suite 501
Richmond, Virginia 23219
Telephone 804/771-2213

I.O.P. 45.2. Public information.

The Court's opinions, rules, procedures, forms, and argument calendar are available at **www.ca4.uscourts.gov**. Docket information is also available at **www.ca4.uscourts.gov** to users with a log-in name and password for the Judiciary's PACER system (Public Access to Court Electronic Records). Information concerning the status of appeals and the operation of rules and procedures may be obtained from the Clerk's Office by telephone inquiry. Matters of public record may be reviewed upon request at the Clerk's Office and case documents may be transmitted to the district court for review by counsel upon proper application to the Clerk's Office. (Amended by order effective December 1, 2002.)

Existing I.O.P. 45.3 was deleted as being redundant of Local Rule 45, after minor additions were made to the local rule.
Local Rule 45 eliminates the requirement that the clerk notify appellant personally of counsel's default before dismissing an appeal for failure to prosecute.

Rule 46. Attorneys.

(a) **Admission to the bar.** (1) Eligibility. An attorney is eligible for admission to the bar of a court of appeals if that attorney is of good moral and professional character and is admitted to practice before the Supreme Court of the United States, the highest court of a state, another United States court of appeals, or a United States district court (including the district courts for Guam, the Northern Mariana Islands, and the Virgin Islands).

(2) Application. An applicant must file an application for admission, on a form approved by the court that contains the applicant's personal statement

showing eligibility for membership. The applicant must subscribe to the following oath or affirmation:

"I, _____, do solemnly swear [or affirm] that I will conduct myself as an attorney and counselor of this court, uprightly and according to law; and that I will support the Constitution of the United States."

(3) Admission procedures. On written or oral motion of a member of the court's bar, the court will act on the application. An applicant may be admitted by oral motion in open court. But, unless the court orders otherwise, an applicant need not appear before the court to be admitted. Upon admission, an applicant must pay the clerk the fee prescribed by local rule or court order.

(b) **Suspension or disbarment.** (1) Standard. A member of the court's bar is subject to suspension or disbarment by the court if the member:

(A) has been suspended or disbarred from practice in any other court; or

(B) is guilty of conduct unbecoming a member of the court's bar.

(2) Procedure. The member must be given an opportunity to show good cause, within the time prescribed by the court, why the member should not be suspended or disbarred.

(3) Order. The court must enter an appropriate order after the member responds and a hearing is held, if requested, or after the time prescribed for a response expires, if no response is made.

(c) **Discipline.** A court of appeals may discipline an attorney who practices before it for conduct unbecoming a member of the bar or for failure to comply with any court rule. First, however, the court must afford the attorney reasonable notice, an opportunity to show cause to the contrary, and, if requested, a hearing. (Amended by order effective July 1, 1986; and by order adopted April 24, 1998, effective December 1, 1998.)

Local Rule 46(a). Legal assistance to indigents by law students.

An eligible law student with the written consent of an indigent and the attorney of record may appear in this Court on behalf of that indigent in any case. An eligible law student with the written consent of the United States Attorney or authorized representative may also appear in this Court on behalf of the United States in any case. An eligible law student with the written consent of the State Attorney General or authorized representative may also appear in this Court on behalf of that state in any case. In each case, the written consent shall be filed with the clerk.

An eligible law student may assist in the preparation of briefs and other documents to be filed in this Court, but such briefs or documents must be signed by the attorney of record. The student may also participate in oral argument with leave of the Court, but only in the presence of the attorney of record. The attorney of record shall assume personal professional responsibility for the law student's work and for supervising the quality of that work. The attorney should be familiar with the case and prepared to supplement or correct any written or oral statement made by the student.

In order to make an appearance pursuant to this rule, the law student must:

1. Be duly enrolled in a law school approved by the American Bar Association;

2. Have completed legal studies amounting to at least four (4) semesters, or the equivalent if the school is on some basis other than a semester basis;

3. Be certified by the dean of the student's law school as being of good character and competent legal ability which certification shall be filed with the clerk. This certification may be withdrawn by the dean at any time by mailing notice to the clerk or by termination by this Court without notice of hearing and without any showing of cause;

4. Be introduced to the Court by an attorney admitted to practice before this Court;

5. Neither ask for nor receive any compensation or remuneration of any kind from the person on whose behalf the student renders services, but this shall not prevent an attorney, legal aid bureau, law school, public defender agency, a State, or the United States from paying compensation to the eligible law student, nor shall it prevent any agency from making such charges for its services as it may otherwise properly require;

6. Certify in writing that he or she has read and is familiar with the Code of Professional Responsibility or Rules of Professional Conduct in force in the state in which the student's law school is located.

Local Rule 46(b). Admission to practice.

Only attorneys admitted to the bar of this Court may practice before the Court. An attorney may be named on a brief filed in this Court without being admitted to the bar of the Fourth Circuit, provided that at least one lawyer admitted to practice in this Court also appears on the brief. Any other document submitted by an attorney who is not a member of the bar of the Fourth Circuit will be accepted for filing conditioned on his or her qualifying for membership within a reasonable time.

Each applicant for admission to the bar of this Court shall file with the clerk an application on the form approved by the Court and furnished by the clerk. Thereafter, upon written or oral motion of a member of the bar of the Court, the Court will act upon the application. A qualified attorney may be admitted upon personal appearance in open court. It is not necessary that an applicant appear in open court for the purpose of being admitted unless the Court shall otherwise order.

The requisite $196 fee must accompany the application, but attorneys appointed by the Court to represent a party in forma pauperis, counsel for the United States and any agency thereof who has a case pending before this Court, and law clerks to the judges of the Court and to the district judges, magistrate judges, and bankruptcy judges within this Circuit shall be admitted to the bar of this Court without the payment of an admission fee. The clerk shall credit $176 of each $196 fee to the Judiciary's fee account and designate the remaining $20 for deposit to a fund maintained by the Court for the benefit of the bench and bar for the administration of justice.

A certificate indicating that an attorney has been admitted to practice before the Fourth Circuit will be sent to counsel by mail after admission. (Amended by order effective March 31, 2005; and by order effective November 1, 2011.)

Effect of amendments. — The 2005 amendment substituted "$170" for $40.00" in the first sentence of the third paragraph; added the last sentence of the third paragraph; and deleted the former first sentence of the last paragraph, concerning deposit of fees.

The 2011 amendment, in the third paragraph substituted "$196" for "$170" twice and "$176" for "$150."

Local Rule 46(c). Appearance of counsel; withdrawal; substitutions.

Each attorney of record must file a written appearance with the clerk within 14 days after the appeal is docketed or after being retained or appointed. At the time of docketing, the clerk will send to each counsel or party in the trial court a "designation of counsel" form. This form should be filled out and returned to the Clerk of the Fourth Circuit within 14 days. Thereafter, the Court will send correspondence, notices of oral argument, and copies of final decisions only to those attorneys who have filed their appearance forms. More than one attorney of the same firm may sign the same form. This form does not affect the credit line listed on printed opinions, as that information is furnished to publishing firms from those names listed on the briefs.

Once an appearance in an appeal has been filed, an attorney may not withdraw from representation without notice to the party he or she is representing and consent of the Court. A motion to withdraw should state fully the reason for the request. Substitution of counsel of record can be accomplished by submitting a counsel of record form or written appearance for new counsel along with existing counsel's motion to withdraw or strike appearance. (Amended by order effective December 1, 1995; and by order effective December 1, 2002.)

Local Rule 46(d). Appointment of counsel.

In any appeal in which appointment of counsel is mandated by section (a)(1) of the Criminal Justice Act, 18 U.S.C. § 3006A(a)(1), counsel is appointed upon the docketing of the appeal without prior notice to the attorney who represented the indigent in the case below. The duty of counsel appointed under the CJA extends through advising an unsuccessful appellant in writing of the right to seek review in the Supreme Court. If the appellant requests in writing that a petition for a writ of certiorari be filed and in counsel's considered judgment there are grounds for seeking Supreme Court review, counsel shall file such a petition. If appellant requests that a petition for a writ of certiorari be filed but counsel believes that such a petition would be frivolous, counsel may file a motion to withdraw with the Court of Appeals. The motion must reflect that a copy was served on the client and that the client was informed of the right to file a response to the motion within seven days. The Clerk will hold the motion after filing for fifteen days before submitting it to the Court to allow time for appellant's response, if any, to be received.

Assignment of counsel is discretionary in other indigent cases. Therefore, such cases receive a preliminary review before a decision is made regarding appointment of counsel. In assigning counsel, the Court may direct counsel to brief a particular issue, but counsel is free to address any additional issues which appear to be meritorious.

Payment of counsel appointed under the CJA is governed by 18 U.S.C. § 3006A(d) and this Circuit's Plan in Implementation of the Criminal Justice

Act. Unless compensation for legal services becomes available to assigned counsel by statute, the Court will pay counsel assigned for appellate representation not covered by the CJA a maximum fee of $750 plus expenses from the Attorney Admission Fund.

To receive payment from the Court, court-appointed or court-assigned counsel in all cases must submit to the Clerk's Office an itemized statement of expenses, with receipts, within sixty days of final disposition of the case. Depending upon the course of the case, this may be sixty days from (1) the date of judgment, (2) dismissal of the appeal, or (3) denial of a petition for rehearing. Before the expiration of the sixty-day time period the Court, for good cause shown, may grant counsel an extension of time to file the application for compensation and reimbursement. If court-appointed counsel files a petition for writ of certiorari with the Supreme Court, the 60-day period for applying for compensation and reimbursement runs from the date of filing the petition for writ of certiorari. (Amended and redesignated by order effective December 1, 1995; amended by order effective February 1, 2001.)

COMMENT

Proposed Local Rule 46(d) extends the time period for filing a CJA voucher until 60 days after filing of a petition for writ of certiorari. This is the preferred procedure over having court-appointed counsel file a supplemental voucher after filing of certiorari as set forth in existing I.O.P. 46.3. Proposed Local Rule 46(d) also adds the requirement that court-appointed counsel inform the client of the right to file a response to a motion to withdraw and reflects that the Clerk will hold the motion to withdraw for fifteen days before submitting it to the Court to allow time for the client's response.

Local Rule 46(e). Attorney's fees and expenses.

The Court may award attorney's fees and expenses whenever authorized by statute. Any application for an award must include a reference to the statutory basis for the request and a detailed itemization of the amounts requested. Court-appointed counsel may apply for an award of fees and expenses, but any award by the Court is in lieu of the regular appointment fees provided by the Court. In certain agency cases, counsel may submit the standard government form for fees and expenses provided by the agency for approval by the Court.

Local Rule 46(f). Proceeding pro se.

An individual may proceed without the aid of counsel, but should so inform the Court at the earliest possible time. In any pro se appeal, the clerk shall notify the parties that they shall file informal briefs as provided by Local Rule 34(b). The Court will limit its review to the issues raised in the informal briefs and will consider the need for the appointment of counsel when reviewing the appeal under Local Rule 334(a). Cases involving pro se litigants are ordinarily not scheduled for oral argument.

Local Rule 46(g). Rules of disciplinary enforcement.

(1) A member of the bar of this Court may be disciplined by this Court as a result of

(a) Conviction in any court of the United States, the District of Columbia, or any state, territory or commonwealth of the United States, of any felony or of any lesser crime involving false swearing, misrepresentation, fraud, willful failure to file income tax returns, deceit, bribery, extortion, misappropriation, or theft;

(b) Imposition of discipline by any other court of whose bar the attorney is a member, or an attorney's disbarment by consent or resignation from the bar of such court while an investigation into allegations of misconduct is pending;

(c) Conduct with respect to this Court which violates the rules of professional conduct or responsibility in effect in the state or other jurisdiction in which the attorney maintains his or her principal office, the Federal Rules of Appellate Procedure, the local rules of this Court, or orders or other instructions of this Court; or

(d) Any other conduct unbecoming a member of the bar of this Court.

(2) Discipline may consist of disbarment, suspension from practice before this Court, monetary sanction, removal from the roster of attorneys eligible for appointment as Court-appointed counsel, reprimand, or any other sanction that the Court may deem appropriate. Disbarment is the presumed discipline for conviction of a crime specified in paragraph (1)(a) above. The identical discipline imposed by another court is presumed appropriate for discipline taken as a result of that other court's action pursuant to paragraph (1)(b). A monetary sanction imposed on disciplinary grounds is the personal responsibility of the attorney disciplined, and may not be reimbursed by a client.

(3) The clerk reviews reports received from other courts concerning discipline imposed on members of the bar of this Court. He refers to the Court all disbarments, suspensions, resignations during the pendency of misconduct investigations, and other actions sufficient to cast doubt upon the member's continuing qualification to practice before this Court.

(4) The clerk issues a notice to show cause why a member of the bar shall not be disciplined by this Court upon receipt of official notification of an attorney's conviction of a crime specified in paragraph (1)(a) or of the imposition of discipline by another court referred to this Court pursuant to paragraph (3) above, or upon the Court's determination that cause may exist for discipline pursuant to paragraphs (1)(c) or (1)(d). Such notice is sent by certified mail, directs that a response be filed within 30 days of the date of the notice, and directs that the attorney complete and return to the clerk within that time a declaration of the names and addresses of other bars to which he or she is admitted, using the form supplied by the clerk, whether or not the attorney chooses otherwise to respond to the notice. The clerk also appends a copy of Local Rule 46(g).

(5) Upon receiving official notification that a member of the bar has been convicted of a crime specified in paragraph (1)(a), the clerk automatically will issue an order suspending the attorney's privilege to practice before this Court pending the Court's determination of appropriate discipline.

(6) An attorney to whom a notice to show cause has been sent may consent to disbarment, by filing with the clerk an affidavit stating that the attorney desires to consent to disbarment and that:

(a) The attorney's consent is freely and voluntarily rendered; the attorney is not being subjected to coercion or duress; the attorney is fully aware of the implications of so consenting;

(b) The attorney is aware that there is a presently pending proceeding involving allegations that there exist grounds for the attorney's discipline, the nature of which the attorney shall specifically set forth;

(c) The attorney acknowledges that the material facts so alleged are true; and

(d) The attorney so consents because the attorney knows that he or she cannot successfully defend himself or herself.

The order disbarring the attorney on consent is a matter of public record. However, the affidavit will not be publicly disclosed or made available for use in any other proceeding except upon order of this Court.

(7) If the attorney fails to respond to the notice within 30 days, or such other time as the court shall allow, the clerk enters an order imposing the presumptive discipline. If no presumptive discipline is specified for the conduct, the clerk notifies the Court of the attorney's non-response and the Court takes such action as it deems appropriate.

(8) All matters pertaining to discipline of attorneys are submitted to the Court's Standing Panel on Attorney Discipline, which consists of three active circuit judges, each of whom is appointed by the Chief Judge to serve on the Panel for a three-year term. The initial members of the Standing Panel are appointed for terms of one, two, and three years so that the Panel members' terms are staggered for continuity of decision making. If any member of the Standing Panel is unable to hear a particular matter, the clerk randomly designates another active circuit judge to the Panel for the purpose of disposing of that matter.

(9) The Standing Panel considers all materials submitted by an attorney to whom notice to show cause has issued. The Panel may request further information from a court that has previously imposed discipline on the attorney, or from its disciplinary agency. A copy of any such information is made available to the attorney or to his or her counsel. Should an attorney request a hearing on the matter it will be heard by the Standing Panel at a time and place of its choosing.

(10) The Court may at any time appoint counsel to investigate or prosecute a disciplinary matter, or to represent an indigent attorney instructed to show cause. The Court prefers to appoint as prosecuting counsel the disciplinary agency of the highest court of the state in which the attorney maintains his or her principal office. However, if the state disciplinary agency declines appointment, or the Court deems other counsel more appropriate, it may appoint any other member of the bar as prosecuting counsel. Counsel appointed either for prosecution or defense will be compensated for his or her services according to the Court's plan for appointment of counsel in criminal cases, from the attorney admission fund.

(11) The Court's order imposing discipline will set forth the nature of the discipline imposed; if disbarment or suspension from practice before the Court, the terms upon which reinstatement will occur or be considered by the Court; and any instructions to the clerk concerning the notification of the Court's action to be given to other courts or official bodies.

(12) The clerk is responsible for

(a) Automatically initiating show cause proceedings when official notice of an attorney's conviction of a crime specified in paragraph (1)(a) or discipline by another court pursuant to paragraph (3) is brought to his or her attention;

(b) Bringing to the attention of the Standing Panel instances of violations by members of the bar of this Court of the Federal Rules of Appellate Procedure, this Court's local rules or this Court's orders or other instructions that may warrant discipline;

(c) Obtaining declarations of the names and addresses of other bars of which an attorney possibly subject to discipline by this Court may be a member; and

(d) Unless directed otherwise by the Court, within 10 days of the imposition of discipline upon a member of the bar of this Court, notifying all other courts of those bars the attorney reports that he or she is a member, and the American Bar Association's National Disciplinary Data Bank, of the Court's action, enclosing a certified copy of the Court's order.

COMMENT

Proposed Local Rule 46(g) deletes the reference in existing I.O.P. 46.6 to violation of internal operating procedures as grounds for discipline because there are no more directives in the remaining internal operating procedures.

Rule 47. Rules of a court of appeals.

(a) **Local rules.** (1) Each court of appeals acting by a majority of its judges in regular active service may, after giving appropriate public notice and opportunity for comment, make and amend rules governing its practice. A generally applicable direction to parties or lawyers regarding practice before a court must be in a local rule rather than an internal operating procedure or standing order. A local rule must be consistent with — but not duplicative of — Acts of Congress and rules adopted under 28 U.S.C. § 2072 and must conform to any uniform numbering system prescribed by the Judicial Conference of the United States. Each circuit clerk must send the Administrative Office of the United States Courts a copy of each local rule and internal operating procedure when it is promulgated or amended.

(2) A local rule imposing a requirement of form must not be enforced in a manner that causes a party to lose rights because of a nonwillful failure to comply with the requirement.

(b) **Procedure when there is no controlling law.** A court of appeals may regulate practice in a particular case in any manner consistent with federal law, these rules, and local rules of the circuit. No sanction or other disadvantage may be imposed for noncompliance with any requirement not in federal law, federal rules, or the local circuit rules unless the alleged violator has been furnished in the particular case with actual notice of the requirement. (Amended by order adopted April 27, 1995, effective December 1, 1995; and by order adopted April 24, 1998, effective December 1, 1998.)

Local Rule 47(a). Procedures for adoption of local rules and internal operating procedures.

Following tentative approval of an amendment to its local rules or internal operating procedures, and consultation with its Advisory Committee on Rules and Procedures, the Court of Appeals will provide public notice of the proposed amendment and an opportunity for comment.

The Court will set a period for comment for each proposed amendment, based upon the urgency of the matter involved. If the Court determines that there is an immediate need for a rule, the Court may provide that an amendment take immediate effect, and promptly thereafter afford notice and opportunity for comment.

Notice of a proposed amendment will be provided by distribution of the proposed change to all district judges, bankruptcy judges, magistrate judges, district and bankruptcy clerks, United States Attorneys, and state bar associations within the Circuit. Notice will also be sent to all legal newspapers and bar journals within the Circuit. Such notice shall include the text of a proposed amendment, unless it is lengthy. If the amendment is lengthy, the notice will describe the purpose and effect of the proposed amendment, and advise interested parties to obtain copies of the text of the proposed amendment from the clerk. Any person or organization requesting routine notice of proposed amendments to the Court's rules and internal operating procedures may, by letter to the clerk, be placed on the mailing list for such proposed changes.

All comments will be addressed to the Clerk of the Court of Appeals. If comments are received, they will be circulated to all members of the Court prior to the effective date of the proposed amendment, unless the amendment was given immediate effect.

Local Rule 47(b). Advisory committee on rules and procedures.

The Court's Advisory Committee on Rules and Procedures shall consist of five attorneys, one from each of the states constituting the Fourth Circuit.

The members shall be appointed by the Chief Judge of the Circuit for three-year terms. The terms shall be staggered, so that no more than two members' terms expire in any year. No person may serve more than two full three-year terms.

The Chief Judge of the Circuit shall designate one of the members to serve as chair of the Committee. The clerk shall serve as the Court's principal liaison with the Committee.

The Committee shall study the Court's local rules and internal operating procedures, make recommendations concerning them, and advise the Court concerning all proposed changes to them.

I.O.P. 47.1. Judicial conference.

(a) There shall be held pursuant to 28 U.S.C. § 333 a conference of all the circuit and district judges, all bankruptcy judges and all full-time magistrate judges of the Circuit for the purpose of considering the business of the courts, advising means of improving the administration of justice within such Circuit, and discussion of ideas with respect to the administration of justice. It shall be the duty of every judge of the Circuit in active service and every full-time magistrate judge to attend such conference.

(b) The first day of the conference shall be devoted to a session for the judges alone, in which there shall be discussed matters affecting the state of the dockets and the administration of justice in their respective districts.

(c) Members of the bar to be designated, as hereafter set forth, shall be members of the conference. Such members, except members emeritus, shall participate in the conference's discussions and deliberations on the second and third days.

(d) Members of the conference from the bar shall be as provided in I.O.P. 47.2 as approved by the active circuit judges sitting from time to time in administrative session.

(e) The Circuit Executive of this Court shall be the secretary of the conference, and shall make and preserve an accurate record of its proceedings.

(f) Each member of the bar designated as a member of the conference shall pay an annual membership fee in an amount fixed by the Court of Appeals, to be applied to the payment of the expenses of the conference as approved by the Chief Judge of the Circuit. The payment of the annual membership fee shall be a condition to retention of conference membership. The Chief Judge is entitled to excuse payment of such fee in the proper circumstances.. (Amended effective Aug. 1, 2005; Dec. 1, 2008.)

Effect of amendments. — The 2005 amendment, effective August 1, 2005, substituted "pursuant to 28 U.S.C § 333" for "each year" and made minor stylistic changes in the first sentence of (a).

The 2009 amendment, effective December 1, 2008, rewrote (c); and in (f) substituted "designated as" for "chosen to be" in the first sentence; inserted "annual" preceding "membership" in the second sentence; and rewrote the last sentence.

I.O.P. 47.2. Membership in the judicial conference of the circuit.

Commencing with the 2009 conference, there shall be four types of members of the conference: ex officio members, invited members, permanent members, and members emeritus.

(A) Ex officio members.

(1) The Attorney General of the United States, or designee.

(2) The presidents of the state bar associations of the states of the Circuit. When two bar associations in the same state are both recognized under this rule, the president of each shall be entitled to attend, and the maximum number of members of the conference from the bar, from any state, under this provision, shall be limited to two. As long as there is only one state bar association in Maryland, the Bar Association of Baltimore City may be treated as a state bar association under this provision.

(3) One representative of the federal bar association elected to the Federal Bar Council from the Fourth Circuit, each conference year, on a rotational basis.

(4) All United States Attorneys in the Circuit.

(5) All Federal Public Defenders in the Circuit.

(6) All Community Defenders in the Circuit.

(7) All Chief Justices of the courts of last resort of the states comprising this Circuit.

(8) All Attorneys General of the states comprising this Circuit.

(9) The Chief Judge of the United States Court of Appeals for the Armed Forces.

(10) The Chief Judge of the United States Tax Court.

(11) One representative of each accredited law school within the Circuit.

(B) Members designated by judges.

(1) Invited members. Lawyers who are not permanent members of the conference as set forth under (B)(2) below are invited by the Chief Judge as guests of a scheduled conference upon designation by an active or senior circuit or district judge.

(a) Each active or senior circuit judge or district judge may designate two guests for invitation to the conference.

(b) Each new circuit or district judge attending his or her first two conferences as a judge may designate three guests for invitation to the conference.

(2) Permanent members. (a) By attending two biennial conferences (or, alternatively, one biennial and two annual conferences, or three annual conferences) as an invited member under (B)(1) above, a lawyer shall become a permanent member of the conference, entitled to attend future conferences. In order to retain such permanent member status, a permanent member must have, in a given year, paid the annual membership fee and, commencing after the 2009 conference, attended the most recent conference or at least one of the two conferences preceding it.

(b) A former or retired circuit or district judge of the Circuit shall be a permanent member of the conference, entitled for life to attend all conferences.

(3) Members emeritus. A permanent member for ten years or more shall become a member emeritus upon either:

(a) Failing to satisfy the requirements for retaining permanent member status under (B)(2) above; or

(b) Electing to assume member emeritus status and properly notifying the conference secretary of such decision.

In order to retain member emeritus status, a member emeritus must have, in a given year, paid the annual membership fee in the amount fixed for emeritus membership. A member emeritus will not be invited to attend future conferences, except as an invited member under (B)(1) above. A member emeritus may be reinstated as a permanent member by designation of the Chief Judge for good cause shown, or by again qualifying for permanent membership under (B)(2) above. (Amended effective August 1, 2005; by order effective April 16, 2007; by order effective December 1, 2008; and by order effective February 1, 2011.)

Effect of amendments. — The 2005 amendment, effective August 1, 2005, in the introductory paragraph substituted "2005" for "1997 annual"; added A.5 and redesignated the following sections accordingly; rewrote B.1; and in B.2. combined the two sentences, substituted "two" for "three," "a guest" for "guests" and "becomes a member of the conference," for "retains permanent membership in the conference. Permanent membership entitles the member".

The 2007 amendment substituted "2007 con-ference" for "2005 conference" in the introductory language; added (A)(3) and redesignated accordingly.

The 2008 amendment deleted "Bar" preceding "membership" in the rule heading; rewrote the introductory language; and rewrote (B)(1) heading and (B).

The 2011 amendment deleted "Commencing with the 2009 conference" in the introductory language of (B)(1) and rewrote (B)(1)(a) and (B)(1)(b).

Editor's note. — The publisher substituted

"biennial" for "biannual" twice in (B)(2)(a) following an editorial correction by the Court on March 13, 2009.

Rule 48. Masters.

(a) **Appointment; powers.** A court of appeals may appoint a special master to hold hearings, if necessary, and to recommend factual findings and disposition in matters ancillary to proceedings in the court. Unless the order referring a matter to a master specifies or limits the master's powers, those powers include, but are not limited to, the following:

(1) regulating all aspects of a hearing;

(2) taking all appropriate action for the effcient performance of the master's duties under the order;

(3) requiring the production of evidence on all matters embraced in the reference; and

(4) administering oaths and examining witnesses and parties.

(b) **Compensation.** If the master is not a judge or court employee, the court must determine the master's compensation and whether the cost is to be charged to any party. (Added by order adopted April 29, 1994, effective December 1, 1994; and by order adopted April 24, 1998, effective December 1, 1998.)

Editor's note. — The provisions of this rule are new. Former FRAP 48 is now codified as subdivision (c) of FRAP 1.

Form 1   4TH CIR. LOCAL & IOPS

NATIONAL FORMS.

Editor's note. — For a full list of Forms and Notices for the Fourth Circuit, see the Court's website at http:// www.ca4.uscourts.gov/forms.Nots.htm. Note that on the web site, many of the forms contain additional links to documentation that pertains to the particular form.

Form 1. Notice of appeal (District Court).

United States District Court for the _____

District of _____

File Number _____

	)	
v.	)	Notice of Appeal
	)	
	)	

Notice is hereby given that _____ (plaintiffs) (defendants) in the above named case,* hereby appeal to the United States Court of Appeals for the _____ Circuit (from the final judgment) (from the order (describing it)) entered in this action on the _____ day of _____, 20____.

(s) _____

Attorney for _____

Address: _____

(Amended by order adopted April 22, 1993, effective December 1, 1993; by order adopted March 27, 2003, effective December 1, 2003; and by order effective August 11, 2011.)

Form 2. Notice of appeal (Tax Court).

UNITED STATES TAX COURT
Washington, D.C.

_____, Petitioner	)	
	)	
v.	)	Docket No._____
	)	
Commissioner of Internal	)	
Revenue, Respondent	)	

Notice of Appeal

Notice is hereby given that _____ *, hereby appeal to the United States Court of Appeals for the _____ Circuit from (that part of) the decision of this court entered in the above captioned proceeding on the _____ day of _____, 20___, relating to _____

_____

* See Rule 3(c) for permissible ways of identifying appellants.

_____

_____ .

(s)_____
Counsel for _____
Address: _____

_____
_____

(Amended by order adopted April 22, 1993, effective December 1, 1993; by order adopted March 27, 2003, effective December 1, 2003; and by order effective June 30, 2011.)

Form 3. Petition for review of order of agency, board, commission or officer.

UNITED STATES COURT OF APPEALS
FOR THE _____ CIRCUIT

	)	
	)	
v.	)	Petition for Review
	)	
	)	

_____ hereby petition the court for review of the Order of the _____ Commission entered on _____, 20____.

_____
Attorney for Petitioners
Address: _____

_____

(Amended by order adopted April 22, 1993, effective December 1, 1993; by order adopted March 27, 2003, effective December 1, 2003; and by order effective June 30, 2011.)

Form 4. Application to appeal in forma pauperis.

Application to Appeal In Forma Pauperis

_____ v. _____ Appeal No. _____

District Court or Agency No. _____

A. Affidavit in Support of Motion

I swear or affirm under penalty of perjury that, because of my poverty, I cannot prepay the docket fees of my appeal or post a bond for them. I believe I am entitled to redress. I swear or affirm under penalty of perjury under United States laws that my answers on this form are true and correct. (28 U.S.C. § 1746; 18 U.S.C. § 1621.)

Form 4   4TH CIR. LOCAL & IOPS

Signed: _____

Instructions

Complete all questions in this application and then sign it. Do not leave any blanks: if the answer to a question is "0," "none," or "not applicable (N/A)," write in that response. If you need more space to answer a question or to explain your answer, attach a separate sheet of paper identified with your name, your case's docket number, and the question number.

Date: _____

B. My issues on appeal are (required):

1. *For both you and your spouse estimate the average amount of money received from each of the following sources during the past 12 months. Adjust any amount that was received weekly, biweekly, quarterly, semiannually, or annually to show the monthly rate. Use gross amounts, that is, amounts before any deductions for taxes or otherwise.*

Income source	Average monthly amount during the past 12 months		Amount expected next month	
	You	Spouse	You	Spouse
Employment	$_____	$_____	$_____	$_____
Self-employment	$_____	$_____	$_____	$_____
Income from real property (such as rental income)	$_____	$_____	$_____	$_____
Interest and dividends	$_____	$_____	$_____	$_____
Gifts	$_____	$_____	$_____	$_____
Alimony	$_____	$_____	$_____	$_____
Child support	$_____	$_____	$_____	$_____
Retirement (such as social security, pensions, annuities, insurance)	$_____	$_____	$_____	$_____
Disability (such as social security, insurance payments)	$_____	$_____	$_____	$_____
Unemployment payments	$_____	$_____	$_____	$_____
Public-assistance (such as welfare)	$_____	$_____	$_____	$_____
Other (specify):	$_____	$_____	$_____	$_____
Total monthly income:	$_____	$_____	$_____	$_____

1272

2. *List your employment history, most recent employer first. (Gross monthly pay is before taxes or other deductions.)*

Employer	Address	Dates of employment	Gross monthly pay
___	___	___	___
___	___	___	___
___	___	___	___

3. *List your spouse's employment history, most recent employer first. (Gross monthly pay is before taxes or other deductions.)*

Employer	Address	Dates of employment	Gross monthly pay
___	___	___	___
___	___	___	___
___	___	___	___

4. *How much cash do you and your spouse have?* $_____

Below, state any money you or your spouse have in bank accounts or in any other financial institution.

Financial institution	Type of account	Amount you have	Amount your spouse has
___	___	$ ___	$ ___
___	___	$ ___	$ ___
___	___	$ ___	$ ___

If you are a prisoner, you must attach a statement certified by the appropriate institutional officer showing all receipts, expenditures, and balances during the last six months in your institutional accounts. If you have multiple accounts, perhaps because you have been in multiple institutions, attach one certified statement of each account.

5. *List the assets, and their values, which you own or your spouse owns. Do not list clothing and ordinary household furnishings.*

Home (Value)	**Other real estate** (Value)	**Motor vehicle #1** (Value)
___	___	Make & year: ___
___	___	Model: ___
___	___	Registration #: ___

Motor vehicle #2 (Value)	**Other assets** (Value)	**Other assets** (Value)
Make & year: ___	___	___
Model: ___	___	___
Registration #: ___	___	___

6. *State every person, business, or organization owing you or your spouse money, and the amount owed.*

Person owing you or your spouse money	Amount owed to you	Amount owed to your spouse
_____	_____	_____
_____	_____	_____
_____	_____	_____

7. *State the persons who rely on you or your spouse for support.*

Name [or, if under 18, initials only]	Relationship	Age
_____	_____	_____
_____	_____	_____
_____	_____	_____

8. *Estimate the average monthly expenses of you and your family. Show separately the amounts paid by your spouse. Adjust any payments that are made weekly, biweekly, quarterly, semiannually, or annually to show the monthly rate.*

	You	Your Spouse
Rent or home-mortgage payment (include lot rented for mobile home)	$_____	$_____
Are real-estate taxes included? ☐ Yes ☐ No		
Is property insurance included? ☐ Yes ☐ No		
Utilities (electricity, heating fuel, water, sewer, and telephone)	$_____	$_____
Home maintenance (repairs and upkeep)	$_____	$_____
Food	$_____	$_____
Clothing	$_____	$_____
Laundry and dry-cleaning	$_____	$_____
Medical and dental expenses	$_____	$_____
Transportation (not including motor vehicle payments)	$_____	$_____
Recreation, entertainment, newspapers, magazines, etc.	$_____	$_____
Insurance (not deducted from wages or included in Mortgage payments)	$_____	$_____
Homeowner's or renter's	$_____	$_____
Life	$_____	$_____
Health	$_____	$_____
Motor Vehicle	$_____	$_____
Other: _____	$_____	$_____
Taxes (not deducted from wages or included in Mortgage payments) (specify): _____	$_____	$_____
Installment payments		
Motor Vehicle	$_____	$_____
Credit card (name): _____	$_____	$_____
Department Store (name): _____	$_____	$_____
Other: _____	$_____	$_____

Alimony, maintenance, and support
paid to others $_____ $_____
Regular expenses for operation of
business, profession, or farm
(attach detailed statement) $_____ $_____
Other (specify): _____ $_____ $_____
Total monthly expenses: $_____ $_____

9. *Do you expect any major changes to your monthly income or expenses or in
your assets or liabilities during the next 12 months?*
☐ Yes ☐ No If yes, describe on an attached sheet.

10. *Have you paid — or will you be paying — an attorney any money for services
in connection with this case, including the completion of this form?*
☐ Yes ☐ No

If yes, how much? $_____
If yes, state the attorney's name, address, and telephone number:

_____

_____

11. *Have you paid — or will you be paying — anyone other than an attorney
(such as a paralegal or a typist) any money for services in connection with this
case, including the completion of this form?*
☐ Yes ☐ No
If yes, how much? $_____
If yes, state the person's name, address, and telephone number:

_____

_____

12. *Provide any other information that will help explain why you cannot pay the
docket fees for your appeal.*

13. *Identify the city and state of your legal residence.*

City _____ State _____

Your daytime phone number: _____

Your age: _____ Your years of schooling: _____

Last four digits of your social security number: _____

(Amended effective May 18, 2004; and effective December, 2010.)

Form 5. Notice of appeal (Bankruptcy Court).

United States District Court for the _____ District of _____

In re _____,
       Debtor

)
)
v.   )   File No. _____
)
)
)

Notice of Appeal to United States Court of Appeals
for the _____ Circuit

_____, the plaintiff [or defendant or other party] appeals to the United States Court of Appeals for the _____ Circuit from the final judgment [or order or decree] for the district court of _____ [or bankruptcy appellate panel of the _____ circuit], entered in this case on _____ , 20__ [here describe the judgment, order, or decree] _____ .

The parties to the judgment [or order or decree] appealed from and the names and addresses of their respective attorneys are as follows:

Dated _____

Signed _____   _____
   Attorney for Appellant   Attorney for Appellant
   Address: _____   Address: _____
_____   _____

(Added by order adopted April 25, 1989, effective December 1, 1989; amended by order adopted March 27, 2003, effective December 1, 2003; and by order effective June 30, 2011.)

Form 6. Certificate of Compliance With Rule 32(a).

UNITED STATES COURT OF APPEALS

FOR THE FOURTH CIRCUIT

No. _____   Caption: _____

CERTIFICATE OF COMPLIANCE WITH RULE 28.1(e) OR 32(a)

Certificate of Compliance With Type-Volume Limitation,
Typeface Requirements, and Type Style Requirements

1. This brief complies with the type-volume limitation of Fed. R. App. P. 28.1(e) or 32(a)(7)(B) because:

[Appellant's Opening Brief, Appellee's Response Brief, and Appellant's Response/Reply Brief may not exceed 14,000 words or 1,300 lines; Appellee's

Opening / Response Brief may not exceed 16,500 words or 1,500 lines; any Reply or Amicus Brief brief may not exceed 7,000 words or 650 lines; line count may be used only with monospaced type]

☐ this brief contains _____ *[state the number of]* words, excluding the parts of the brief exempted by Fed. R. App. P. 32(a)(7)(B)(iii), *or*

☐ this brief uses a monospaced typeface and contains _____ *[state the number of]* lines of text, excluding the parts of the brief exempted by Fed. R. App. P. 32(a)(7)(B)(iii).

2. This brief complies with the typeface requirements of Fed. R. App. P. 32(a)(5) and the type style requirements of Fed. R. App. P. 32(a)(6) because:

[14-point font must be used with proportional typeface, such as Times New Roman or CG Times; 12-point font must be used with monospaced typeface, such as Courier or Courier New]

☐ this brief has been prepared in a proportionally spaced typeface using _____ *[state name and version of word processing program]* in _____ *[state font size and name of type style]*, *or*

☐ this brief has been prepared in a monospaced typeface using _____ *[state name and version of word processing program]* with _____ *[state number of characters per inch and name of type style]*.

(s) _____

Attorney for _____

Dated: _____

(Added by order adopted April 29, 2002, effective December 2002; ; amended effective March 30, 2011.)

FOURTH CIRCUIT FORMS.

Editor's note. — For a full list of Forms and Notices for the Fourth Circuit, see the Court's website at http://www.ca4.uscourts.gov/forms.Nots.htm.

Forms A through D appear in substantially the same form as in the past, and are retained in this publication.

Former Form E. Docketing Statement (Tax Court) no longer appears on the court's web site. Former Form F. Docketing Statement (Agency) and Form G. Docketing Statement (Civil or Criminal) have been amended to appear as Docketing Statement (Civil/Agency) and Docketing Statement (Criminal). Due to the changes and the expansion of forms available on the web site the publisher directs the user to the web site. Note that on the web site, many of the forms contain additional links to documentation that pertains to the particular form.

Form A. Disclosure of corporate affiliations and other entities with a direct financial interest in litigation.

Only one form needs to be completed for a party even if the party is represented by more than one attorney. Disclosures must be filed on behalf of *all* parties to a civil, agency, bankruptcy or mandamus case. Corporate defendants in a criminal or post-conviction case and corporate amici curiae are required to file disclosure statements. Counsel has a continuing duty to update this information.

No. _____Caption: _____

Pursuant to FRAP 26.1 and Local Rule 26.1, _____

(name of party/amicus)

who is _____,

(appellant/appellee/amicus)

makes the following disclosure:

1. Is party/amicus a publicly held corporation or other publicly held entity?
         ( ) YES   ( ) NO

2. Does party/amicus have any parent corporations?
         ( ) YES   ( ) NO

   If yes, identify all parent corporations, including grandparent and great-grandparent corporations:

3. Is 10% or more of the stock of a party/amicus owned by a publicly held corporation or other publicly held entity?
         ( ) YES   ( ) NO

   If yes, identify all such owners:

4. Is there any other publicly held corporation or other publicly held entity that has a direct financial interest in the outcome of the litigation (Local Rule 26.1(b))?
         ( ) YES   ( ) NO

   If yes, identify entity and nature of interest:

5. Is party a trade association? (amici curiae do not complete this question)

( ) YES   ( ) NO

If yes, identify any publicly held member whose stock or equity value could be affected substantially by the outcome of the proceeding or whose claims the trade association is pursuing in a representative capacity, or state that there is no such member:

6.   Does this case arise out of a bankruptcy proceeding?

( ) YES   ( ) NO

If yes, identify any trustee and the members of any creditors' committee:

_____   _____
         (signature)   (date)

CERTIFICATE OF SERVICE
****

I certify that on _____ the foregoing document was served on all parties or their counsel of record through the CM/ECF system if they are registered users or, if they are not, by serving a true and correct copy at the addresses listed below:
(Effective 2011.)

Form B. Appearance of counsel.
UNITED STATES COURT OF APPEALS FOR THE FOURTH CIRCUIT

APPEARANCE OF COUNSEL FORM
BAR ADMISSION & ECF REGISTRATION: If you have not been admitted to practice before the Fourth Circuit, you must complete and return an Application for Admission before filing this form. If you were admitted to practice under a different name than you are now using, you must include your former name when completing this form so that we can locate you on the attorney roll. Electronic filing by counsel is required in all Fourth Circuit cases. If you have not registered as a Fourth Circuit ECF Filer, please complete the required steps at www.ca4.uscourts.gov/cmecftop.htm.

_____

THE CLERK WILL ENTER MY APPEARANCE IN APPEAL NO. _____ as
☐Retained ☐Court-appointed(CJA) ☐Court-assigned(non-CJA)
☐Federal Defender ☐Pro Bono ☐Government

COUNSEL FOR: _____ as the
                             (party name)
☐appellant(s) ☐appellee(s) ☐petitioner(s) ☐respondent(s)

☐amicus curiae ☐intervenor(s)

_____
         (signature)

_____   _____
Name (printed or typed)   Voice Phone

Form B   4TH CIR. LOCAL & IOPS

_____   _____
Firm Name (if applicable)   Fax Number

_____   _____
Address   E-mail address (print or type)

_____

OR, I, _____**, AM NOT PARTICIPATING
IN THIS CASE.**
APPELLATE COUNSEL IS: _____.
                    (Name)   (Phone)

_____

CERTIFICATE OF SERVICE

I certify that on _____ the foregoing document was served on all parties
or their counsel of record through the CM/ECF system if they are registered
users or, if they are not, by serving a true and correct copy at the addresses
listed below:

_____   _____

Signature   Date

Form C. Certificate of death penalty case — Fourth Circuit Local Rule 22(b).

CERTIFICATE OF DEATH PENALTY CASE
Fourth Circuit Local Rule 22(b)

U.S. District Court for the

Case Caption:

Counsel for Petitioner/Defendant (name, address, phone)	Counsel for Respondent/Plaintiff: (name, address, phone)

Institution of Incarceration:

Explanation of Emergency Nature of Proceedings

Has petitioner/defendant previously filed cases in federal court?
[ ] No   [ ] Yes (give court, caption, number, filing date, disposition and disposition date)

Does petitioner/defendant have cases pending in other courts?
[ ] No   [ ] Yes (give court, caption, number, filing date and status)

I hereby certify under penalty of perjury that the petitioner/defendant is presently under a sentence of death and that the information provided on this form is currently accurate and correct.	
Date	Signature

Note: The Court of Appeals will periodically request case status reports. Counsel is under a continuing affirmative obligation to immediately notify the Fourth Circuit of any changes or additions to the information contained on this form. In cases with a pending execution date, counsel must provide the Court of Appeals with four copies of all documents filed in the U.S. District Court and any pertinent state court materials.

Form D. Application for admission to the bar.

UNITED STATES COURT OF APPEALS

FOR THE FOURTH CIRCUIT

APPLICATION FOR ADMISSION TO THE BAR

Instructions: Only attorneys admitted to the bar of the United States Court of Appeals for the Fourth Circuit may practice before the Court. In accordance with Fourth Circuit Rule 46(b), an attorney who is admitted to practice before the highest court of a state and who is of good moral and professional character may become a member of the bar by:

   1. providing the information requested below;

   2. having a member of the bar of the Court move admission by signing the Motion for Admission;

   3. swearing or affirming the Oath before the clerk, a deputy clerk, a notary public or the Court (admission by personal appearance before the Court is usually reserved for ceremonial occasions);

   4. paying the admission fee of $196.00 by credit card through CM/ECF or by check made payable to "Clerk, United States Court of Appeals." (The fee is waived for attorneys appointed to represent a party in forma pauperis, law clerks to federal judges within this Circuit, and counsel for the United States or any agency thereof who have a case pending before the Court. If a fee waiver is sought, add the Fourth Circuit docket number here: _____); and

   5. submitting the completed form through CM/ECF or mailing or delivering the completed form and check to the Clerk of the United States Court of Appeals, 1100 E. Main Street, Suite 501, Richmond, VA 23219-3517.

NAME (present practicing name):

Last _____

First _____   Middle _____

Generation (Jr., Sr., II, III, etc.) _____

Title (if applicable) _____

Prefix (Mr., Mrs., Miss, Ms., Professor, etc.) _____

STATE OF RESIDENCE (for use on your certificate): _____

FIRM: _____

BUSINESS ADDRESS: _____

_____

_____

City _____

State _____   Zip   Code _____ - _____   Phone (___) ___ - ___ Ext. _____

Fax ( ) - E-mail _____

YEAR OF BIRTH: _____

STATE COURT ADMISSIONS:

	Status (active, inactive)	Approx. Date Admitted (if available)
1.	_____	_____
2.	_____	_____
3.	_____	_____

FEDERAL COURT ADMISSIONS:

	Status (active, inactive)	Approx. Date Admitted (if available)
1.	_____	_____
2.	_____	_____
3.	_____	_____

DISCIPLINARY ACTIONS: Have you ever been disciplined, or are you the subject of any pending disciplinary proceeding, by the bar of any jurisdiction or by any court?

Yes [ ] No [ ] If yes, please explain in detail on a separate sheet of paper.

CRIMINAL CONVICTIONS: Have you ever been convicted of a criminal offense (other than a traffic offense)?

Yes [ ] No [ ] If yes, please explain in detail on a separate sheet of paper.

OATH

I, _____ , certify that, to the best of my knowledge and belief, the information on this application is true, correct, complete, and made in good faith. I do solemnly swear (or affirm) that I will conduct myself as an attorney and counselor of this court, uprightly and according to law; and that I will support the Constitution of the United States.

_____
(signature)

Subscribed and sworn to before me this _____ day of _____, 20_____

Notary commission expires:

_____   _____
(date)   (signature and title)

MOTION FOR ADMISSION

I, _____ , a member of the Bar of the United States Court of Appeals for the Fourth Circuit, hereby move the admission of the applicant to the Bar of the Court. I am satisfied that the applicant is of good moral and professional character and is admitted to practice before the highest court of a state.

_____   _____
(date)   (signature and title)

(Revised January 1, 2005; amended effective November 1, 2011.)

APPENDIX A. RESOLUTION RESPECTING BAR MEMBERSHIP IN THE JUDICIAL CONFERENCE OF THE CIRCUIT.

Transferred.

Editor's note. — By order dated April 30, 1992, former Appendix A was transferred to be I.O.P. 47.2, effective June 30, 1992.

APPENDIX B. GUIDELINES FOR PREPARATION OF APPELLATE TRANSCRIPTS IN THE FOURTH CIRCUIT.

Revision effective December 4, 1996; amended effective December 1, 2009.

I. INTRODUCTION

A. **Purpose.** These guidelines set forth in detail the following:

1. Duties of the district court clerk's office, appellant and appellee in ordering the transcript;

2. Responsibilities of the court reporter for preparing and timely filing the transcript;

3. Duties of the court of appeals for acknowledging transcript orders and monitoring the timeliness of the filing of transcripts;

4. Procedures for court reporters to follow in requesting extensions of time and waivers of fee sanctions;

5. Criteria to be used by the court of appeals in acting on requests for extensions and waivers;

6. Common problems that have been encountered by court reporters and the court of appeals in the ordering, preparation and filing of transcripts; and

7. Provisions for supplementation of these Guidelines by local procedures adopted by a district court.

B. **Relation to Federal Rules of Appellate Procedure.** Although Rule 11(b), Federal Rules of Appellate Procedure, requires transcripts to be filed within 30 days of the purchase order date, the court of appeals will use the time limits set forth in the district court reporter management plans governing the application of fee sanctions as the time periods within which transcripts will be due. All of the plans establish a 60-day period for preparation of transcripts without financial penalty. Exceptions are:

1. Special provisions adopted by the Fourth Circuit Judicial Council for appeals by incarcerated criminal defendants;

2. Special circumstances, such as

(a) bail appeals,

(b) death penalty cases,

(c) expedited sentencing appeals,

(d) recalcitrant witness appeals, or

(e) other expedited procedures.

The Table on the next page sets forth the time requirements in detail.

TABLE OF TRANSCRIPT DUE DATES AND APPLICABLE SANCTIONS

NATURE OF CASE	LENGTH OF TRANSCRIPT	TRANSCRIPT DUE	10% FEE SANCTION	20% FEE SANCTION
Direct criminal appeals, appellant incarcerated	1000 pages or less	within 30 days of transcript order or judgment and commitment order, whichever is later	if filed after 30th day	if filed after 60th day
	more than 1000 pages	as ordered by clerk following consultation with reporter and parties	if due date missed	if due date missed by more than 30 days
All other cases, in other than exceptional circumstances	any length	within 60 days of transcript order or judgment and commitment order, whichever is later	if filed after 60th day	if filed after 90th day
Exceptional circumstances (e.g., bail appeals, death penalty cases, expedited sentencing appeals, etc.)	any length	as ordered by clerk following consultation with reporter and parties	*	*

*Twenty percent fee sanction automatically imposed if due date missed. Letter to chief district judge, after consultation with chief circuit judge requiring immediate preparation of the transcript.

C. **Effective date.** These guidelines will take effect on June 1, 1986, and will apply to all Fourth Circuit cases subject to F.R.A.P. 11(b) in which the transcript is ordered after that date.

D. **Definitions.** For purposes of these Guidelines, references to appellant-appellee will refer to counsel for appellant-appellee unless appellant-appellee is proceeding pro se, in which case all duties and responsibilities are those of appellant-appellee individually.

II. ORDERING AND ACKNOWLEDGING TRANSCRIPTS

A. **Duties of district court clerk's office.** 1. When a notice of appeal is filed, the district court clerk's office will notify appellant of the availability of appellate forms from the court of appeals, www.ca4.uscourts.gov.

2. Upon entry of an order authorizing preparation of a transcript at government expense pursuant to the Criminal Justice Act or 28 U.S.C. § 753(f), the district court reporter coordinator or appeals deputy will notify the court of appeals of the date on which the order was entered.

3. When substitute reporters or contract reporters are used, the district court reporter coordinator or district court appeals deputy will furnish them

with copies of these guidelines and explain the procedures to be followed in preparing appellate transcripts.

4. When the transcript is filed, the district court clerk's office will transmit notice of the filing to the court of appeals through CM/ECF.

B. **Duties of appellant.** 1. Within 14 days after filing the notice of appeal, the appellant is required by F.R.A.P. 10(b)(1) to order from the court reporter such transcript of the proceedings as the appellant deems necessary. The notice of docketing issued by the court of appeals shall inform the appellant that the docketing statement and transcript order must be filed in the court of appeals within 14 days of the docketing notice.

2. By service of a copy of the Docketing Statement, appellant will notify appellee(s) that (a) a transcript is not needed for the appeal, (b) a transcript is already on file in the district court, or (c) less than the complete transcript will be ordered. The statement of issues in the Docketing Statement will satisfy the requirement of F.R.A.P. 10(b)(3).

3. Before a transcript can be ordered, the appellant must obtain from the court reporter an estimate of the length of the transcript and make appropriate financial arrangements with the reporter by immediate payment in full or by another payment arrangement acceptable to the reporter, such as filing a CJA 24 form with the district court for authorization of transcript in a criminal case pursuant to the Criminal Justice Act. [Local Rule 10(c)(1)]. Payment or other financial arrangements satisfactory to the reporter must accompany the court reporter's copy of the transcript order. [F.R.A.P. 10(b)(4)].

4. In criminal cases, counsel may seek authorization from the district court to order transcript after entry of verdict but prior to sentencing. The district court may authorize the early ordering of transcript if it determines that defense counsel has informed the defendant of the right to appeal and the defendant has instructed counsel to appeal regardless of the nature or length of the sentence imposed. The time requirements for the preparation of transcripts that are ordered before sentencing shall not begin to run until after entry of the judgment and commitment order.

5. To order a transcript, the appellant completes the transcript order form (and CJA 24 form as needed) and distributes the copies to the court reporter, the district court, the court of appeals (attached to docketing statement), and opposing counsel (attached to docketing statement).

A separate transcript order (and CJA 24 form) must be prepared for each court reporter from whom a transcript is requested.

6. Failure by the appellant to timely order a transcript, failure to make satisfactory financial arrangements with the court reporter, or failure to specify in adequate detail those proceedings to be transcribed will subject the appeal to dismissal by the clerk of the court of appeals for want of prosecution pursuant to Local Rule 45.

7. When supplemental transcripts are requested, appellant must complete another transcript order form, make satisfactory financial arrangements with the reporter, and distribute copies to the same persons to whom the original transcript order was sent.

8. If payment is waived by the reporter at the time of ordering the transcript, the appellant must make full payment upon receipt of the reporter's invoice. If payment is not made within a reasonable period of time, the appeal will be subject to dismissal by the clerk of the court of appeals pursuant to Local Rule 45.

9. Transcripts ordered under the Criminal Justice Act do not include opening and closing statements, voir dire, or jury instructions unless prior special authorization has been received by appellant. CJA 24 forms should be obtained from the district court or from www.ca4.uscourts.gov and submitted to the district court judge for approval. In multi-defendant cases involving CJA defendants, only original transcripts should be ordered from the court reporter(s). Requests for copies will be arranged by the district court or appointed counsel at commercially competitive rates. Contact the district court reporter coordinator or district court clerk's office for further instructions.

10. When an appellant has ordered a transcript, he or she is obligated to pay the reporter for it. If the appeal is dismissed voluntarily, the appellant is nonetheless responsible to the reporter for the cost of transcript prepared prior to the reporter's receipt of notification from the appellant of the appeal's dismissal.

11. Appellant is required to review the transcript upon filing in the district court and provide the court reporter with a statement of the personal data identifiers, including the page number, line number, and text to be redacted, in accordance with the Judicial Conference Policy on Privacy and Public Access to Electronic Case Files.

C. **Duties of appellee.** 1. If the appellee deems a transcript of other parts of the proceedings to be necessary, he or she is required by F.R.A.P. 10(b)(3), within 14 days after service of the Docketing Statement by the appellant, to file and serve on the appellant a designation of additional parts to be included. Unless within 14 days after service of such designation the appellant has ordered such parts, and has so notified the appellee, the appellee may within the following 14 days either order the parts or move the district court for an order requiring the appellant to do so.

2. If the appellee wishes to obtain a copy of the transcript which has been ordered by the appellant, he or she may do so by ordering the copy directly from the court reporter. Satisfactory financial arrangements must be completed with the reporter before obtaining the copy. It is not appellant's responsibility to order and pay for a copy of the transcript for appellee.

3. Appellee is required to review the transcript upon filing in the district court and provide the court reporter with a statement of the personal data identifiers, including the page number, line number, and text to be redacted, in accordance with the Judicial Conference Policy on Privacy and Public Access to Electronic Case Files.

D. **Duties of the court reporter.** 1. Upon receipt of the transcript order form and completion of satisfactory financial arrangements, the reporter must prepare the required transcript within the time set forth in the applicable district court reporter management plan.

2. The appellant attaches copies of the transcript order (and any CJA 24 form) to the docketing statement filed with the court of appeals. Upon receiving the transcript order, the court of appeals will complete and send to the reporter, and to the court reporter coordinator and the district court, a transcript order acknowledgment form to verify the transcript order. The acknowledgment will include a copy of the transcript order and any CJA 24 form and will show the date by which the transcript must be filed to avoid sanctions. The due date is computed from issuance of the transcript order acknowledgment in accordance with the time specified in the district court reporter management plans. Seven days are added to the applicable time period to permit confirmation of financial arrangements, including approval by the district court of the CJA 24 form. If the transcript order form is complete and accurate and financial arrangements are satisfactory, no response is required from the court reporter to the transcript order form or the transcript acknowledgment form.

3. If there is a problem, with financial arrangements (e.g., the CJA 24 form is not approved within 7 days of issuance of the transcript order acknowledgment), with identification of the transcript ordered, with proper designation of the court reporters involved in the case, or with any other aspect of the transcript order, the court reporter must complete and file a transcript order deficiency notice with the court of appeals within 14 days of issuance of the transcript order acknowledgment (time may be extended for vacation, serious illness or other unusual circumstances). The deficiency notice is served on the parties and the district court reporter coordinator through CM/ECF. The court reporter need not inform the court of appeals if he or she in fact received the transcript order early. The court reporter may use any additional time so created for preparation of the transcript without fear of incurring a sanction for late filing. The court of appeals' Acknowledgment constitutes an implied fee sanction waiver to the due date set forth on the form.

4. The deadline for completion of the transcript will be rescinded or extended upon filing of the transcript order deficiency notice, indicating a problem with the terms of the order, for whatever reasonable period of time is required for the reporter or district court reporter coordinator to resolve the problem with the appellant. The court of appeals transcript coordinator will be in touch with the reporter or district court reporter coordinator upon receipt of the transcript order deficiency notice to offer assistance, such as notification to the appellant that the appeal will be dismissed if the problem is not remedied promptly.

5. The court of appeals will send a revised transcript order acknowledgment or transcript extension order setting forth a new transcript filing date reflecting the delay caused by the problem with the original transcript order.

6. Unless the court of appeals is notified of a problem with the transcript order, or of some other reason why the information on the transcript order acknowledgment form prepared by the court of appeals is incorrect, the reporter will be held to the schedule set forth therein absent the granting of an extension of time. It is the court reporter's responsibility to notify the court of appeals of any problem.

7. If the transcript is estimated to be more than 1000 pages and is ordered in a criminal appeal in which the appellant is incarcerated, the reporter will receive an acknowledgment form with a due date which will be established by the court of appeals.

8. Transcript provided to counsel for use on appeal shall comply with appellate requirements for full-sized, rather than condensed, transcript and for identification of the testifying witness and type of testimony (e.g., direct, cross, deposition) at the top of each page of in-court and deposition testimony.

9. When the transcript has been completed and the court copy filed in the district court, notice of the filing must be sent to the court of appeals through CM/ECF. If the transcript was filed late, the court reporter must file a transcript certification form in the court of appeals showing that the proper fee reduction sanction was taken. A copy of the certification is served on the parties and the district court reporter coordinator through CM/ECF.

10. The court reporter must make any requested redactions to the transcript and file a redacted version of the transcript in the district court in accordance with the Judicial Conference Policy on Privacy and Public Access to Electronic Case Files. Notice of filing of the redacted version of the transcript must be sent to the court of appeals through CM/ECF.

11. Unless a written motion is filed by the appellant with the court of appeals, and an extension granted by the clerk of the court of appeals, requests by an appellant that a reporter suspend or delay preparation of a transcript that has been ordered will have no effect on the date the transcript is due, or on the appellant's obligation to pay for it when it is prepared. The only exception is when a motion for voluntary dismissal of the appeal has been granted; in that instance the appellant is responsible for paying only for that portion of the transcript completed prior to the reporter's receipt of notification from the appellant of the appeal's dismissal.

E. **Duties of Court of Appeals.** 1. F.R.A.P. 10(b)(1) requires the appellant to order the transcript within 14 days after filing the notice of appeal. If the completed form is not received by the court of appeals within 14 days of the court's notice of docketing of the appeal, the court of appeals will notify the appellant that no order has been received and that failure to comply with F.R.A.P. 10(b)(1) will subject the appeal to dismissal by the clerk for want of prosecution pursuant to Local Rule 45.

2. When the court of appeals receives the transcript order form, it will be reviewed for any obvious defects (e.g., multiple reporters on one form, or incompleteness as far as nature of proceedings requested or certification of satisfaction of financial requirements). If it appears to be in order, the court of appeals will prepare for the reporter a transcript order acknowledgment which will include the transcript order and any CJA 24 form and will show the due date, computed in accordance with the time limits set forth in the applicable district court reporter management plan. The court of appeals clerk's office will work together with reporters and parties to remedy any deficiencies in the transcript order that are brought to its attention by the reporter. (See Sections D. 3 - 8 for full description of procedures.)

III. REPORTS

Reports on outstanding transcripts will be generated monthly and will be distributed to the court reporters involved, as well as to the district court clerks or their court reporter coordinators. If the report shows a transcript outstanding when it has actually been filed, the reporter or district court reporter coordinator should call the court of appeals and report the date of filing. If everything in the report is correct and none of the transcripts are overdue, no response is required from the reporter.

IV. TIME LIMITS FOR FILING TRANSCRIPTS—
FEE REDUCTION SANCTIONS

A. **Requests for extensions of time.** As set forth in the district court reporter management plans, all requests for extensions of time for the filing of appellate transcripts (F.R.A.P. 11(b) transcripts) are submitted to the clerk of the court of appeals. They should be in writing, on the designated form. They are served on counsel through CM/ECF. A request for an extension of time will automatically constitute a corresponding request for a waiver of any applicable fee reduction sanction. Requests for extensions must be filed 10 days in advance of the deadline from which relief is sought, unless unforeseen circumstances make later requests necessary, in which case the reasons will be set out by the reporter in the request. When requesting an extension, the information furnished should be very specific. Failure to submit complete information will delay action on the request and lead to additional paperwork for the reporter. After reviewing the request for extension, the court of appeals will issue an order granting in part, or denying the request, which will set forth the resulting timeframes for purposes of fee sanction imposition. Counsel, the district court reporter coordinator, and the district court clerk will also receive copies of this order.

B. **Grounds for extensions of time.** 1. Excessive burden of transcript, considering length and complexity of the proceedings ordered within a short period of time. District court reporter coordinators are expected to make court reporter assignments within a district so as to anticipate and to avoid to the extent possible the imposition of excessive transcript loads on individual reporters. When these efforts are unsuccessful, reporters may apply for relief from applicable fee sanctions and have the court of appeals assign the relative priority to be given to competing appellate transcript orders. The fact that a reporter has accumulated orders for more than 3000 pages within three months will be presumed to establish the existence of an "excessive burden." The existence of outstanding overdue transcripts may or may not be grounds for extending the time for subsequently ordered transcripts. In computing the amount of transcript for purposes of demonstrating excessive burden, the reporter can include all transcripts ordered within ninety days of the request for extension. The reporter may include transcript obligations for the district court as well as those ordered for appellate purposes. However, the orders must be "firm orders". A "firm order" for an appellate transcript is one for which the court of appeals has received a transcript order from the appellant. For a district court transcript it is an order communicated by a judge or a party; it cannot be a reporter's speculation that an order will be forthcoming.

2. Vacation. A reporter can plan to take reasonable vacations, as authorized by the district court, and obtain extensions of deadlines that would fall within those periods or become impossible to meet in light of them.

3. Unavoidable, excessive time required for attendance in court. It is the responsibility of the district court reporter coordinator to adjust reporter assignments to ensure that the needs of the trial and appellate courts can be met. Occasions may arise, nonetheless, when a court reporter's courtroom obligations, including official travel required to reach the courtroom, prevent his or her meeting transcript obligations. Reasonable extensions of time will be given in such instances.

4. Incapacitation or serious illness. A reporter may certify to the clerk of the court of appeals that he or she has become temporarily incapacitated or seriously ill, and obtain reasonable relief from pending deadlines. This ground does not include common colds or other ailments that would not prevent attendance in court.

5. Unforeseen emergencies. Reporters may seek extensions for any other good cause which makes the completion of a transcript within the allotted time impossible.

V. SANCTIONS

A. **Fee reduction sanctions.** An official court reporter will be required to deduct from his or her charges for a completed transcript not timely filed with the district court the amount of any fee reduction sanction applicable by the terms of a district court reporter management plan.

B. **Removal from courtroom and request for substitute reporter.** The chief judge of the court of appeals, following consultation with the chief judge of the district court, may order a reporter to remain out of the courtroom, and pay the costs of a satisfactory substitute reporter, if a transcript is ninety days overdue.

VI. MONITORING OF TRANSCRIPT FILING

The clerk of the court of appeals will monitor the filing of all appellate transcripts and the fees charged by reporters when a transcript is filed untimely. The fee sanction mechanism exists by virtue of the district court reporter management plans which require reporters to take fee reductions if a transcript is not filed on time. Therefore, the court of appeals will not issue a sanction order. It is the reporter's duty to abide by the provisions of his or her district court reporter management plan and to take a fee reduction if one is applicable.

The court of appeals will take no action if the transcript is filed on time or, if not filed on time, the appropriate fee reduction has been taken as shown by the transcript certification form that the reporter submitted to the court of appeals when the transcript was filed. If a fee reduction was applicable and was not taken by the reporter, the court of appeals will send notice to the reporter setting forth the fee reduction that should have been taken. Copies of this notice will be sent to counsel, the district court reporter coordinator (if any) and the judge to whom the reporter reports or the chief district judge. If the certification is not submitted within a reasonable period after the filing of the transcript, the reporter will be requested to submit a copy of his or her invoice.

The court of appeals will also send a letter to the chief district judge when a transcript is sixty days overdue. The letter will identify the particular transcript involved and the date of the order. Copies of the letter will be sent to the judge (if any) to whom the reporter reports, the district court reporter coordinator, the district court clerk, and the reporter. The letter will alert the chief judge of the district court to the possibility that the reporter may be required to remain out of the courtroom, paying for a substitute reporter, until the transcript is completed, if the transcript becomes ninety days overdue.

VII. COMMON PROBLEMS

A. **Transcripts prepared at government expense.** 1. Criminal Justice Act [18 U.S.C. § 3006A(6)]. When the reporter receives the approved CJA form, preparation of the transcript should begin immediately. To allow time for the district court to act on the CJA 24 application, the court of appeals adds 7 days to the transcript deadline set upon receipt of its copy of the transcript order and CJA 24 forms. If the district court does not approve the CJA 24 form within 7 days, the court reporter may request rescission or extension of the deadline using the transcript order deficiency notice.

Pursuant to the Guidelines for the Administration of the Criminal Justice Act, in multi-defendant cases involving CJA defendants, no more than one original transcript should be purchased from the court reporter on behalf of CJA defendants. One of the appointed counsel or the district court should arrange for the duplication, at commercially competitive rates, of enough copies of the transcript(s) for each of the CJA defendants for whom a transcript has been approved.

2. In forma pauperis litigants [28 U.S.C. § 753(f)]. When an order is entered directing preparation of a transcript at government expense pursuant to 28 U.S.C. § 753(f), the transcript order date is the date the reporter receives the court's order authorizing preparation of the transcript.

B. **Supplemental transcripts.** Supplemental transcripts are usually ordered after the original transcript has been filed and a briefing schedule established by the court of appeals. Therefore, these transcripts should be expedited. Counsel is under an obligation to notify the court of appeals that a supplemental transcript has been ordered. The court of appeals will then send the transcript order acknowledgment form to the reporter with the request that the reporter prepare these transcripts as quickly as possible.

C. **Expedited proceedings.** When a transcript is requested for an expedited proceeding, the due date for filing the transcript is established by the court of appeals. If an expedited transcript is requested and prepared within 7 days after receipt or notification of the order, the court reporter may charge the higher rates for expedited transcripts.

Transcripts for appeals arising from a criminal sentence imposed under 18 U.S.C. § 3742 will only be expedited if a motion for expedited review of criminal sentence is granted by the court of appeals. Only those portions of the transcript pertinent to the appeal must be prepared on an expedited basis. The court reporter will be notified by the court of appeals when a motion to expedite has been granted.

In bail appeals, only the portion of the transcript dealing with the bail issue should be ordered on a rush basis. Even though there may be other portions of the transcript that the appellant has ordered, the portion dealing with the bail issue should be prepared first.

In expedited proceedings, a twenty percent fee sanction from the regular transcript rate will be imposed if the due date is missed. At the same time, a letter will be sent to the chief judge of the district court, advising of the delinquency and warning that the chief judge of the court of appeals may order the reporter to remain out of the courtroom, and pay the costs of a satisfactory substitute reporter, if the transcript is not filed immediately. IF THE COURT REPORTER ANTICIPATES A PROBLEM WITH PROMPT PREPARATION OF AN EXPEDITED TRANSCRIPT, THE DISTRICT COURT REPORTER COORDINATOR AND THE COURT OF APPEALS SHOULD BE NOTIFIED IMMEDIATELY.

D. **Payment for transcript.** The court of appeals approves of reporters' demanding a substantial deposit or full payment in advance for preparation of a transcript. In those instances where a reporter does not demand full payment in advance, and upon transcript completion has not been paid fully by the appellant, the following procedures should be followed:

1. Timely file the court copy of the transcript with the district court clerk's office.

2. Contact the court of appeals immediately and a letter will be sent to the appellant stating that if full payment is not made to the court reporter within fifteen days of the date of the letter, the appeal will be dismissed for failure to prosecute.

Fee reduction sanctions will be applicable if the court copy of the transcript is not timely filed. Problems with payment for the transcript after its completion will have no effect on the established due date.

E. **Substitute reporters.** When an official court reporter hires a substitute, the official reporter still retains responsibility for the timely filing of the transcript. All provisions applicable to an official court reporter will be applicable to the substitute. If there is a problem with the filing of a transcript, the official court reporter will be notified as well as the substitute reporter. All correspondence and orders by the court of appeals will be sent to both reporters. The substitute can request extensions of time and waivers of applicable fee sanctions from the court of appeals. However, all guidelines applicable to the official reporter will be applicable to the substitute reporter and the proper procedures for requesting extensions must be followed.

F. **Contract reporters.** Contractual reporting services in district courts are provided as supplements to the services of official staff. Contractual services are used after the district court reporter coordinator has determined that no official court reporter is available. Contract reporters must follow the procedures set out below.

1. All contractors are subject to the terms and conditions of their contacts with the district courts. Standard contract terms for delinquent transcript provide that the contract reporter may charge only 90% of the prescribed fee for transcript not delivered within 30 days of the date ordered (with payment arrangements made) and may charge only 80% of the prescribed fee for transcript not delivered within 60 days of the date ordered (with payment arrangements made).

2. Extensions of time for filing transcripts for F.R.A.P. 11(b) cases may be requested in writing following the procedures set forth in these guidelines. However, the court of appeals cannot waive the fee sanctions for contract reporters. A waiver of applicable fee reduction sanctions may be requested, in writing, from the contracting officer. A copy of the letter requesting a waiver of fee sanctions should be sent to the court of appeals.

G. **Filing of transcripts with the district court.** When the proceedings that are transcribed have been taken in another division of the district court, the reporter may file the court copy of the transcript in the district in which his or her office is located. That division will file stamp the copy and forward it to the appropriate division for inclusion in the record to be transmitted to the court of appeals.

VIII. ADDITIONAL LOCAL PROCEDURES

Following prior consultation with the clerk of the court of appeals, a district court may institute supplemental local procedures designed to adapt these Guidelines to the structure of court reporting services in place in that district.

FOURTH CIRCUIT TRANSCRIPT ORDER FORM

Case Style _____

Dist. Ct. No. _____ District _____

Date Notice of Appeal filed _____ Ct. of Appeals No. _____

Name of Court Reporter/Electronic Rec. (use separate form for each reporter)

_____

Address of Reporter _____

Appellant must order any necessary transcript, completing a separate transcript order form (and separate CJA 24 Form) for each reporter and submitting the order to the court reporter and the district court within 14 days of noting the appeal. The completed form must show that necessary financial arrangements have been made or that a CJA 24 Form has been submitted to the district judge for approval. Copies of the transcript order form must be attached to the docketing statement filed in the Court of Appeals and served on opposing counsel within 14 days of docketing of the appeal, or the appeal will be subject to dismissal pursuant to Local Rule 45. If appellee finds other parts of the proceedings necessary, appellee must designate the additional parts within 14 days after service of the transcript order. If appellant has not ordered the additional parts within 14 days, appellee may, within the following 14 days, order the additional parts or move in the district court for an order requiring appellant to do so. In sentencing appeals, a transcript of the sentencing hearing must be ordered. In *Anders* appeals, plea (or trial) and sentencing transcript must be ordered. If appellee wishes to obtain a copy of transcript ordered by appellant, appellee must order a copy from the court reporter. In multi-defendant cases involving CJA defendants, only one original trial transcript should be purchased from the court reporter on behalf of CJA defendants, and copies should thereafter be made at commercially competitive rates. Counsel must review transcript and notify the district court of any intention to direct redaction of personal data identifiers within 7 days of filing of the transcript, and thereafter submit a statement of redactions to the court reporter within 21 days of filing of the transcript, as required by the *Judicial Conference Policy on Privacy and Public Access to Electronic Case Files.* Counsel should verify that the witness name and type of examination appear in the top margin of each page of testimony, as required for inclusion in the appendix on appeal. Local Rule 30(b).

A. This constitutes an order of the transcript of the following proceedings. Check appropriate box(es), provide date of hearing, and indicate total number of estimated pages. Failure to specify in adequate detail the proceedings to be transcribed is grounds for dismissal. Specific authorization is required under the CJA for opening and closing statements, voir dire, or jury instructions.

PROCEEDING	HEARING DATE(S)
☐ Voir Dire	_____
☐ Opening Statement (Plaintiff)	_____
☐ Opening Statement (Defendant)	_____
☐ Closing Argument (Plaintiff)	_____
☐ Closing Argument (Defendant)	_____
☐ Opinion of Court	_____
☐ Jury Instructions	_____
☐ Sentencing	_____
☐ Bail Hearing	_____
☐ Pre-Trial Proceedings (specify)	_____
_____	_____
☐ Testimony (specify) _____	_____
_____	_____
☐ Other (specify) _____	_____
_____	_____

TOTAL ESTIMATED PAGES _____

B. I certify that I have contacted the court reporter (or coordinator if electronic recording from the District of Maryland) and satisfactory financial arrangements for payment of the transcript have been made.

☐ Private funds. (Deposit of $_____ enclosed with court reporter's copy. Check No. _____.)

☐ Criminal Justice Act. A CJA 24 Form has been submitted to the district court and a copy is attached.

☐ Government expense (civil case — IFP). Motion for transcript at government expense is pending with district judge.

☐ Advance payment waived by court reporter. Payment in full is due upon receipt of transcript.

☐ Federal Public Defender — no CJA 24 Form necessary.

☐ United States appeal —copy of litigation expense form attached, if applicable.

Signature _____ Typed Name _____
Address _____
Telephone No. _____ Date Sent to Reporter _____

Editor's note. — The Fourth Circuit Local Rules are amended effective December 1, 2009. These Rules reflect the proposed changes. Any changes resulting from the public comment period will appear in the next publication.

APPENDIX C. FOURTH CIRCUIT PLAN IN IMPLEMENTATION OF THE CRIMINAL JUSTICE ACT.

The Judicial Council of the Fourth Circuit adopts the following plan, in implementation of the Criminal Justice Act.

I. RIGHT TO COUNSEL

1. **Direct appeals.** In every direct appeal involving a person

(a) who is charged with a felony or misdemeanor (other than a petty offense), or with juvenile delinquency as defined in 18 U.S.C. § 5031, or with a violation of probation or supervised release; or who faces modification, reduction, or enlargement of a condition, or extension or revocation of a term of supervised release; or who is under arrest and representation is required by law; or who is subject to a mental condition hearing under Chapter 13 of Title 18; or who is held in custody as a material witness; or who appeals from parole proceedings conducted pursuant to 18 U.S.C. § 4106A; or,

(b) for whom the Sixth Amendment to the Constitution requires the appointment of counsel or for whom, in a case in which he faces the loss of liberty, any federal law requires the appointment of counsel,

whether the appeal be by a defendant from a judgment of conviction or other order, or by the United States from a judgment of acquittal or dismissal, a defendant shall be entitled to be represented by counsel as a matter of right.

If the appeal involves a petty offense for which confinement is authorized, the court may appoint counsel for a financially eligible person upon a determination that the interests of justice so require.

In these cases, unless an application for the appointment of counsel has already been received, or notice of appearance has been filed by retained counsel, the clerk of this court shall promptly notify the defendant of his right to counsel and shall inform him that counsel will be appointed if he is financially unable to obtain adequate representation. Where an attorney had previously been appointed to represent the defendant in district court, that attorney shall be reappointed, without prior notice, upon the docketing of the appeal in this court. If there is no such reappointment, either because defendant appeared pro se or was represented by retained counsel in the district court, the clerk shall appoint the attorney of record in the district court, where appropriate, or select an appointee from a panel of approved attorneys.

In pro se cases in which the appellant exercises his right to represent himself as suggested by *Faretta v. California*, 422 U.S. 806 [45 L Ed 2d 562] (1975); 28 U.S.C. § 1654, the court may find it appropriate to appoint standby counsel for the appellant to assist in the appeal to protect the integrity and ensure the continuity of the judicial proceedings. (*McKaskle v. Wiggins*, 465 U.S. 168 [79 L Ed 2d 122] (1984); *Faretta, supra*). Accordingly, if a pro se appellant is represented, at least in part, by standby counsel, compensation may be provided under the CJA.

2. **Collateral proceedings.** In an appeal in a post-conviction proceeding under 28 U.S.C. §§ 2254 or 2255, seeking to vacate or set aside a death sentence, a petitioner who is financially unable to obtain adequate representation shall be entitled to appointment of one or more attorneys. 18 U.S.C.A. § 3599(a)(2). In an appeal in a collateral proceeding brought by the petitioner from any other order denying the relief requested pursuant to 28 U.S.C. §§ 2241, 2254, or 2255, a petitioner shall not be entitled to be represented by counsel as a matter of right. In these cases, counsel will be appointed only after the court has decided to hear the case on the merits, as in the granting of leave to appeal or the issuance of a certificate of appealability. However, in an appeal brought by the United States or a state from an order granting the relief requested, a petitioner shall be entitled to representation as a matter of right.

In any non-capital case brought pursuant to 28 U.S.C. §§ 2241, 2254, or 2255, the court may, on motion of the petitioner or on its own motion, appoint counsel where the court determines that (a) petitioner is financially unable to obtain adequate representation and (b) the interests of justice require legal representation, as when petitioner needs the assistance of counsel to go forward with an apparently meritorious petition. The clerk shall thereupon appoint the attorney of record in the district court, where appropriate, or select an appointee from a panel of approved attorneys.

Where a petitioner is under sentence of death, the clerk shall appoint counsel upon receipt of the notice of appeal.

II. APPOINTMENT OF COUNSEL

1. **Court order.** Every appointment of counsel pursuant to the Criminal Justice Act and this Plan shall be made by an order of this court. A prerequisite to appointment shall be an affirmative finding by the court that a defendant is financially unable to employ counsel. However, where counsel was appointed in the lower court, this court will presume, until reason to the contrary appears, that the defendant remains financially unable to retain counsel, and no such finding shall be required.

The selection of counsel under the Criminal Justice Act shall be the exclusive responsibility of the court, and no person entitled to court-appointed counsel shall be permitted to select counsel to represent him.

2. **Retroactivity.** An appointment may be made retroactive to include any representation furnished to an indigent by an attorney prior to appointment pursuant to this Plan.

3. **Scope.** A person for whom counsel is appointed shall be represented at every stage of the proceedings, through appeal, including ancillary matters appropriate to the proceedings and including a petition for writ of certiorari to the Supreme Court if non-frivolous grounds exist for filing such a petition.

4. **Substitution of counsel.** The court may, in the interests of justice, substitute one appointed counsel for another at any stage of the proceedings. The total compensation to be paid both attorneys shall not exceed the statutory maximum for one appointment, unless the case involves extended or complex representation.

5. **One attorney for multiple defendants.** In appeals involving multiple defendants, separate counsel will normally be appointed for each defendant, unless there has been a waiver on the record by the defendants or good cause is shown. If one attorney is appointed to represent more than one defendant, a separate order of appointment shall be entered for each defendant. The attorney may be compensated for his services up to the maximum for each defendant represented; however, time spent in common on one or more defendants must be prorated.

6. **Multiple appointments for one defendant.** In capital cases, and in other cases of extreme difficulty where the interests of justice so require, the court may appoint an additional attorney to represent a defendant. Each attorney so appointed shall be eligible to receive the maximum compensation allowed under the Criminal Justice Act. Any defendant indicted for a capital offense is entitled to have two attorneys appointed. 18 U.S.C. § 3005.

7. **Defendant's objection to appointed attorney.** The court shall give consideration to a defendant's expression of dissatisfaction with his counsel only if specific grounds for dissatisfaction are stated. Appointed counsel shall be relieved only when the court, in its discretion, determines that the interests of justice so require.

8. **Withdrawal of counsel.** An attorney appointed to represent a defendant in the lower court is generally obliged to continue that representation upon appeal unless relieved by this court. *See infra* Part V.1. An attorney who does not desire to continue the representation must file a motion to withdraw with the clerk of this court promptly after filing the notice of appeal.

Counsel's request to be relieved from representation on appeal shall be given due consideration. While the court recognizes there may be benefits to maintaining continuity of counsel, it also recognizes that the skills necessary to proceed as appellate counsel may differ from those required for trial counsel. Substitution of counsel shall not reflect negatively in any way on the conduct of the lawyer involved.

In its discretion, this court may appoint the attorney who represented the eligible person in the district court, a Federal Public Defender's office from the circuit, or a lawyer from the court's Criminal Justice Act panel. *See infra* Part IV.4.

III. DEFENDANT'S FINANCIAL STATUS

1. **Filing application.** A defendant who, in the district court, was represented by employed counsel, or was unrepresented, or was represented by appointed counsel but has nonetheless been requested to file a new application in this court, may apply to this court for the appointment of counsel. Such application shall be accompanied by an affidavit disclosing the applicant's financial status and any resources available to him to compensate counsel.

2. **Re-examination by court.** The court, at any time, may re-examine a defendant's financial status as it bears upon the appointment of counsel and, thereupon, (a) appoint counsel to represent the defendant, if the defendant is not already represented or is unable to pay previously retained counsel, (b)

terminate the appointment of counsel, or (c) require a partial payment of counsel fees by the defendant. The defendant shall furnish such financial and related information as may be requested during the re-examination, unless he desires to proceed without counsel.

3. **Insufficiency of funds; partial payment.** If a defendant's net financial resources and anticipated income are in excess of the amount needed to provide him and his dependents with the necessities of life and to provide for his release on bond, but are insufficient to pay fully for retained counsel, this court will find the defendant eligible for the appointment of counsel but will direct him to pay the available excess funds to the clerk at the time of appointment. The court may increase or decrease the amount of such payments and impose appropriate conditions, where applicable. All such payments by the defendant shall be received pursuant to the prescriptions of subsection (f) of the Criminal Justice Act.

4. **Family resources.** Funds and property standing in the name of, or held by, members of a defendant's family will be considered available for the payment of the fees of retained counsel if there is a finding, upon a reasonable basis of fact, that the family has indicated a willingness and a financial ability to pay all or part of the costs of representation. The initial determination of a defendant's eligibility for the appointment of counsel should be made without regard to family resources unless the family plans and is financially able to retain counsel promptly.

5. **Attorney's information.** If at any time after appointment, counsel obtains information that a client is financially able to make payment, in whole or in part, for legal services in connection with his representation, and the source of the attorney's information is not protected as a privileged communication, counsel shall so advise this court.

IV. PANEL OF ATTORNEYS

1. **CJA Appellate Panel Committee.** A CJA appellate panel committee will be appointed by the court for the purpose of recommending minimum standards of eligibility for the CJA appellate panel, developing legal education and training opportunities for panel members, and otherwise improving CJA appellate representation.

2. **Panel composition.** The clerk, subject to this court's approval, shall prepare a list of attorneys from which appointments shall be made. Attorneys, to be eligible for appointment, must be admitted to practice before this court under Rule 46 of the Federal Rules of Appellate Procedure, and must meet the minimum standards of eligibility recommended by the CJA appellate panel committee and adopted by the court. In preparing a list, the clerk will review and consider the standards of eligibility adopted by the court and the court's experience with attorneys.

3. **Periodic revision.** The panel shall be revised periodically to ensure an adequate number of competent attorneys to provide effective representation to all persons entitled to appointed counsel.

4. **Appointments.** Appointments shall be made by the clerk on a rotational basis, subject to this court's discretion. Consideration will be given to the

nature of the case, the place of the trial, the residence of the indigent person if on bail, the place of confinement, and other relevant matters. In death penalty cases at least one attorney appointed must have been admitted to practice in the Fourth Circuit Court of Appeals for not less than five years, and must have had not less than three years experience in the handling of appeals in the Fourth Circuit in felony cases. For good cause however, the court may appoint another attorney whose background, knowledge, or experience would otherwise enable him or her to properly represent the petitioner, with due consideration to the seriousness of the possible penalty and to the unique and complex nature of the litigation. The Court will look to the factors articulated in the American Bar Association's guidelines for selection of appellate counsel in capital cases including the length of bar membership, general experience in criminal defense litigation, and specific experience in death penalty appeals and appeals of murder, aggravated murder or other serious felonies. The Court will also consider whether counsel has attended and successfully completed a recent training or educational program on criminal advocacy which focused on the appeal of cases in which a sentence of death was imposed. Finally, the Court will review the availability of ongoing consultation support to appointed counsel from experienced counsel.

When the court determines that the appointment of an attorney, who is not a member of the CJA panel, is appropriate in the interest of justice, judicial economy, or some other compelling circumstance warranting his or her appointment, the attorney may be admitted to the CJA panel pro hac vice and appointed to represent the appellant. These appointments should be made only in exceptional circumstances, such as the appointment in a death penalty case of an attorney furnished by a state or local public defender organization or legal aid agency where the attorney had represented the appellant during prior state court proceedings. Further, the attorney should possess such qualities as would qualify him or her for admission to the CJA panel in the ordinary course of panel selection.

5. **Removal from the panel.** An attorney may be removed from the panel by the clerk for twice refusing to accept an appointment or by the court for any good reason.

V. ATTORNEY'S DUTY TO CONTINUE REPRESENTATION

1. **Trial counsel.** Every attorney, including retained counsel, who represented a defendant in the district court shall continue to represent the client after termination of those proceedings, unless relieved of further responsibility by this court. Where counsel has not been relieved:

If there is a judgment of conviction or an order revoking probation, counsel shall inform the defendant of his right to appeal and of his right to have counsel appointed on appeal. If so requested by the defendant, counsel shall file a timely notice of appeal. Thereafter, unless the defendant otherwise so instructs, counsel shall take appropriate and timely steps to perfect and present the appeal, including, where appropriate, the ordering of such part of the transcript as may be necessary for consideration on appeal.

Similarly, if there is an appeal by the United States from an order or judgment adverse to it, counsel shall continue to represent the client.

In any case brought pursuant to 28 U.S.C. §§ 2241, 2254, or 2255 which results in an order by the district court denying the relief requested, counsel shall inform the petitioner of his right to appeal and of the court's authority to appoint appellate counsel in its discretion. If so requested by the petitioner, counsel shall file a timely notice of appeal and a motion for appointment of appellate counsel, and counsel's duty is thereby ended. On the other hand, if petitioner is granted the relief requested, counsel shall continue to represent the petitioner in the event the respondent appeals the judgment.

2. **Appellate counsel.** Every attorney, including retained counsel, who represents a defendant in this court shall continue to represent his client after termination of the appeal unless relieved of further responsibility by this court or the Supreme Court. Where counsel has not been relieved:

If the judgment of this court is adverse to the defendant, counsel shall inform the defendant, in writing, of his right to petition the Supreme Court for a writ of certiorari. If the defendant, in writing, so requests and in counsel's considered judgment there are grounds for seeking Supreme Court review, counsel shall prepare and file a timely petition for such a writ and transmit a copy to the defendant. Thereafter, unless otherwise instructed by the Supreme Court or its clerk, or unless any applicable rule, order or plan of the Supreme Court shall otherwise provide, counsel shall take whatever further steps are necessary to protect the rights of the defendant, until the petition is granted or denied.

If the appellant requests that a petition for writ of certiorari be filed but counsel believes that such a petition would be frivolous, counsel may file a motion to withdraw with this court wherein counsel requests to be relieved of the responsibility of filing a petition for writ of certiorari. The motion must reflect that a copy was served on the client.

If the United States seeks a writ of certiorari to review a judgement of this court, counsel shall take all necessary steps to oppose the United States' petition.

Similarly, in any proceeding brought pursuant to 28 U.S.C. §§ 2241, 2254, or 2255 which results in an order by this court, appointed counsel shall take those steps necessary, as set forth above, to protect the rights of the defendant in the Supreme Court.

VI. COMPENSATION AND REIMBURSEMENT OF EXPENSES

1. **Voucher.** Upon the completion of service in this court, appointed counsel shall submit a voucher for compensation and reimbursement on the Criminal Justice Act form currently approved by the Administrative Office of the United States Courts. Vouchers shall be submitted no later than 60 days after the final disposition of the case, unless good cause is shown. The clerk will determine the amount of compensation and reimbursement to be paid. The approved voucher will then be reviewed by the Circuit Executive, signed by the Chief Judge, and forwarded to the Administrative Office for payment or further handling.

2. **Hourly rates.** Counsel may be compensated at rates authorized by the Judicial Conference pursuant to 18 U.S.C. § 3006A(d)(1) for non-capital cases and pursuant to 18 U.S.C. § 3599(g)(1) for capital cases.

3. **Maximum compensation allowable.** Limitations on maximum compensation shall be as prescribed in 18 U.S.C. § 3006A(d)(2) for non-capital cases. In capital cases, maximum compensation limits do not apply, and compensation shall be in such amounts as the court determines to be reasonably necessary.

In all cases where there has been a substitution of counsel, or where multiple defendants have been represented by one attorney or multiple appointments have been made for one defendant, total compensation shall be determined pursuant to Section II, Paragraphs 4, 5, and 6.

Payment in excess of the prescribed limitations may be made to provide fair compensation in a case involving extended or complex representation, upon approval by the Chief Judge of this court or other active circuit judge designated by him. Counsel claiming in excess of the statutory maximum must submit with his voucher a detailed memorandum supporting and justifying counsel's claim that the representation given was in a complex or extended case, and that the excess payment is necessary to provide fair compensation. If the legal or factual issues in a case are unusual, thus requiring the expenditure of more time, skill and effort by the lawyer than would normally be required in an average case, the case is "complex". If more time is reasonably required for total processing than would normally be required in the average case, the case is "extended". Attorneys seeking compensation have the burden of providing sufficient details to support their claim that the case is more complex or time consuming than the average case. This burden also exists with regard to the reasonableness of hours claimed for representation.

4. **Reimbursable expenses.** Counsel shall be entitled to reimbursement for reasonably incurred out-of-pocket expenditures. Travel by privately owned automobile should be claimed at the mileage rate currently applicable to federal employee travel, plus parking fees and tolls. Transportation other than by privately owned automobile should be claimed on an actual expense basis. Necessary airline travel will be reimbursed only at coach class rates. Expenditures for meals and lodging, as well as for telephone toll calls, telegrams, and copying are reimbursable. The cost of photocopying or similar copying services is reimbursable, while the cost of printing is not. Where photocopying services are performed in counsel's office, the reimbursement shall be limited to out-of-pocket expenses, not to exceed 15 cents per copy. For photocopying and other services in preparation of briefs and appendices by commercial printers, reimbursement shall not exceed 35 cents per copy. All materials contained in appendices prepared by commercial printers in court-appointed cases will be reproduced on both sides of a sheet. No joint appendix in a court-appointed case shall exceed 250 sheets without advance permission from the Court. Compensation paid to law students for legal research is reimbursable, but expenses incurred by the law student in assisting counsel are not. When necessary for adequate representation in death penalty cases, reasonable employment and compensation of public and private organizations which

provide consulting services to counsel are reimbursable to assist in such areas as records completion, identification of potential issues, exhaustion of state remedies, and review of draft pleadings and briefs. Detailed receipts are required for all travel and lodging expenses, non-office copying services, and any other expense in excess of $50.00. Failure to provide detailed receipts may result in the expense being denied. Any expense in excess of $50.00 must be itemized in a manner which will permit a review of the amount expended.

5. **Representation to the Supreme Court.** Counsel's time and expenses involved in the preparation of a petition for a writ of certiorari to the Supreme Court, and in the protection of the defendant's rights up until the time that Court disposes of a petition, should be included in the voucher for services performed in this court.

6. **Number of copies.** Appointed counsel is required to file six copies of the brief and five copies of the appendix with the clerk of the court, with service of one copy on counsel for each party separately represented. Appointed counsel shall be entitled to reimbursement for the cost of photocopying required copies.

7. **Non-reimbursable expenses.** General office overhead, personal items and non-legal personal services for the person represented, filing fees, services of process, and printing are non-reimbursable. (A person represented under the Criminal Justice Act is not required to pay filing fees or costs, or give security therefore, nor must he file the 28 U.S.C. § 1915(a) affidavit, for an appeal.)

8. **Authorized transcripts.** Authorized transcripts should not be claimed in the voucher by an attorney. The Administrative Office will pay the appropriate court reporter directly.

9. **Interim payment of expenses.** This court, in rare cases, will entertain requests for interim reimbursement of extraordinary and substantial expenses.

10. **Direct payment from person represented.** No appointed counsel shall accept a payment or a promise of payment from a defendant for representation in this court without prior authorization from the court on an appropriate Criminal Justice Act form.

11. **Public defender.** Where a defendant is represented by a federal public defender, the defender shall be compensated solely by his federal salary and shall not submit a Criminal Justice Act form for compensation.

12. **Non-appointed co-counsel.** Non-appointed attorneys may not be compensated, but an appointed attorney may claim compensation for services furnished by a partner, associate, or co-counsel, within the maximum compensation allowed to the appointed attorney.

VII. RULES, REGULATIONS, FORMS

1. **Rules and regulations.** This Plan shall be subject to and held to have been amended pro tanto by any rule or regulation adopted by the Judicial Conference of the United States concerning the operation of plans under the Criminal Justice Act.

The Judicial Council or this court may adopt rules or regulations concerning the operation of this Plan, which, when promulgated, shall have the same force as provisions of this Plan.

2. **Forms.** Forms approved by the Administrative Office of the United States Courts for use in the administration of the Criminal Justice Act shall be used whenever appropriate. Where there are no approved forms, this court may approve and require the use of designated forms or other instruments.

VIII. ADMINISTRATION

Generally; clerk's office. Any act to be done by the court may be done by any judge of the court, by the clerk, or by a deputy clerk pursuant to delegated authority.

IX. DEFINITIONS

1. **Supreme Court.** Supreme Court of the United States.
2. **Administrative Office.** Administrative Office of the United States Courts.
3. **This Court; the Court.** The United States Court of Appeals for the Fourth Circuit.
4. **Criminal Justice Act.** Criminal Justice Act of 1964, 18 U.S.C. § 3006A, as amended.
5. **Defendant; defendants.** Where appropriate in this Plan, the word "defendant" or "defendants" shall be construed to include petitioner or petitioners in a collateral proceeding.
6. **Judicial Council.** Judicial Council of the Fourth Judicial Circuit of the United States.

X. AMENDMENTS

This Plan may be amended at any time by the Judicial Council effective when a copy of the amendatory resolution is filed with the Administrative Office or at such later date as may be specified in the resolution.

XI. EFFECTIVE DATE

This amended plan is effective October 1, 2008. (Amended May 1, 2002; amended effective July 14, 2005; amended effective January 1, 2006; amended by order August 14, 2008, effective October 1, 2008.)

Effect of amendments. — The 2002 amendment in 2. under VI., substituted "$90" for "$75" and "$90" for "$55" and "$90 — $125" for "$90 — $125" and substituted "May 1, 2002" for "April 1, 2001" and substituted "May 1, 2002" for "April 1, 2001" in XI.

The 2005 amendment, under VI., in 2. in the third sentence, substituted "up to $160 per hour for work performed on or after February 1, 2005" for "within the $75-$125 per hour range"; and in 3 substituted "December 8, 2004" for "November 13, 2000," and "$1,500" for "$1,200" in two places, and in the first sentence added "any appeal from a determination of the United States Parole Commission

under 18 U.S.C. § 4106A"; and deleted the former second paragraph as redundant following the amendment to the first paragraph; and in XI, substituted "July 14, 2005" for "May 1, 2002".

The 2006 amendment substituted "January 1, 2006" for "May 1, 2002" in the second paragraph; in 2. under VI., substituted "January 1, 2006" for "May 1, 2002", substitued "$92" for "$90" twice, substituted "$163" for "$160", and substituted "January 1, 2006" for "February 1, 2005."

The 2007 Order, effective September 17, 2007, in II.8, changed the heading, in the first sentence added "unless relieved by this court.

See *infra,* Part V.1.", deleted the third through fifth sentences, and added two new paragraphs; added IV.1 and redesignated accordingly, and rewrote the end of the second sentence and the third sentence related to minimum standards of eligibility; in VI.2, changed the date to "May 20, 2007" and raised the normal rate from $92 to $94 and the rate in death penalty cases from $163 to $166; and in XI. changed the effective date to September 17, 2007.

Thee 2008 order substituted "18 U.S.C.A. § 3599(a)(2)" for "21 U.S.C.A. § 848(q)" in I.2; rewrote VI.2; in VI.3., substituted the first paragraph for the former first and second paragraphs; and in XI, substituted "October 1, 2008'" for January 1, 2006".

Editor's note. — As to the Plan for the Composition and Administration of the CJA Appellate and Capital Appellate Panels (the Panel Composition Plan), see www.ca4.uscourts.gov.

APPENDIX D. DEATH PENALTY REPRESENTATION IN THE FOURTH CIRCUIT.

UNITED STATES COURT OF APPEALS

FOR THE FOURTH CIRCUIT

JUDICIAL COUNCIL

In the Matter of Death Penalty Representation   *

In the Fourth Circuit   *

No. 113

ORDER

The Report of the Death Penalty Committee, which is attached to and made a part of this Order, is hereby adopted by the Fourth Circuit Judicial Council. The official policy of the Fourth Circuit shall be:

(1) Federal Public Defenders may be appointed to represent individuals charged with federal capital crimes and collateral attacks on federal capital convictions and sentences.

(2) Federal Public Defenders shall not be appointed to represent criminal defendants petitioning pursuant to 28 U.S.C.A. Section 2254 for relief from a state death sentence.

(3) The limitations on time for decision set forth in 28 U.S.C.A. Section 2266 shall apply at the district and circuit court levels and the Circuit Executive is authorized to inquire into the reasons for any noncompliance with the limitations.

and it is so ORDERED.

FOR THE COUNCIL:

/s/ J. Harvie Wilkinson III

Chief Judge

Date: October 3, 1996
Amended: October 1, 2008

I. STATUTORY PROVISIONS PRESENTLY APPLICABLE
TO APPOINTMENT OF ATTORNEYS FOR
CAPITAL REPRESENTATION

A. APPOINTMENT OF COUNSEL FOR INDIGENT CAPITAL DEFEN-
DANTS IS STATUTORILY GUARANTEED FOR FEDERAL TRIALS,
DIRECT APPEAL FROM FEDERAL CONVICTIONS, § 2255 PRO-
CEEDINGS, AND § 2254 PROCEEDINGS.

Congress has enacted special provisions guaranteeing that "in every criminal action in which a defendant is charged with a crime which may be
punishable by death" and in "any post conviction proceeding under section
2254 or 2255 of Title 28, seeking to vacate or set aside a death sentence, any
defendant who is or becomes financially unable to obtain adequate representation … shall be entitled to the appointment of one or more attorneys." 18
U.S.C.A. § 3599(a)(1) & (2). Any defendant indicted for a federal capital crime
is entitled to have two attorneys appointed. 18 U.S.C.A. § 3005.

B. THE MINIMUM QUALIFICATIONS OF APPOINTED COUNSEL ARE
STATUTORILY DEFINED.

The lead attorney appointed to represent one indicted on an offense
punishable by death "must have been admitted to practice in the court in
which the prosecution is to be tried for not less than five years, and must have
had not less than three years experience in the actual trial of felony prosecutions in that court." 18 U.S.C.A. § 3599(b). And, at least one of the attorneys
appointed to represent a defendant indicted with a federal capital crime must
"be learned in the law applicable to capital cases." 18 U.S.C.A. § 3005.

A lead attorney appointed after conviction to represent a capital defendant
on direct appeal, or during § 2255 proceedings, "must have been admitted to
practice in the court of appeals for not less than five years, and must have had
not less than three years experience in the handling of appeals in that court in
felony cases." 18 U.S.C.A. § 3599(c).

A court may, for good cause shown, appoint another attorney who does not
meet the requirements set forth in 18 U.S.C.A. § 3599(b)-(c), but whose
experience otherwise enables him or her to adequately represent the defendant. 18 U.S.C.A. § 3599(d).

Attorneys that have been appointed typically continue the representation on
appeal. *See* 18 U.S.C.A. § 3599(e) (providing that once appointed attorneys
continue representation throughout subsequent proceedings); 18 U.S.C.A.
§ 3006A(c).

C. COMPENSATION FOR FEES IS PRESENTLY LIMITED ONLY TO A
"REASONABLE FEE" IN THE VIEW OF THE DISTRICT COURT.

Attorneys appointed pursuant to § 3599 may be compensated at the rate
authorized by the Judicial Conference pursuant to 3599(g)(1). Counsel is also
bound by the limitation of $7,500 for investigative, expert, and other reason-
ably necessary expenses unless a higher fee is approved by the court. 18
U.S.C.A. § 3599(g)(2).

II. RECOMMENDATIONS

A. SOLICIT QUALIFIED AND INTERESTED COUNSEL AND MAIN-
TAIN LISTS OF ATTORNEYS QUALIFYING FOR APPOINTMENT AS
LEAD COUNSEL AND SECOND-CHAIR COUNSEL.

<u>District Court</u>

** **It is recommended that a plan be adopted under which the
district court would contact the bar and solicit applications for a
panel of attorneys qualified to represent capital defendants.**

Some districts have experienced difficulty in locating qualified and interested counsel to undertake capital representation. But, it is believed that there
are many attorneys who would seek the opportunity for appointment if they
were made aware of that opportunity. Accordingly, it is recommended that on
a district-by-district basis, a program of solicitation of the bar should be
implemented in order to increase the number of attorneys seeking appointment.

** **It is recommended that the district courts maintain lists of those
attorneys qualified to represent capital defendants as lead counsel and as second-chair counsel and that these attorneys' expertise in trial, appellate, and habeas representation be identified.**

Because the statutory requirements for lead counsel are more stringent than
those for second-chair counsel, courts should maintain separate lists of those
attorneys who are qualified for each type of appointment. In addition to the
statutory qualifications, specialized skills and experience are necessary to
represent capital defendants in trial, appellate, and habeas proceedings.
Courts may find separate lists of attorneys with trial, appellate, and/or habeas
experience useful. Alternatively, courts may conclude that some other method
of identifying various types and levels of expertise is preferable.

In ascertaining which attorneys of those expressing an interest in capital
representation and seeking appointment are qualified to be placed on lists of
those available for appointment as lead and second-chair counsel, the court
may wish to consider appointment of an oversight committee composed of
district judges, magistrate judges, district court clerks, and the Federal Public
Defender, *see* 18 U.S.C.A. § 3005.

It is envisioned that over time attorneys chosen for appointment from the
second-chair counsel list will develop the qualifications to be placed on the lead
counsel list, and that appointment of second-chair attorneys is desirable in
order to develop a wider range of expertise available for lead counsel appointment. In addition, special consideration should be given to appointment of the
attorney who represented a § 2254 petitioner during state collateral proceedings, if interested in appointment and qualified for it. *See* 18 U.S.C.A.
§ 3599(d).

<u>Circuit Court</u>

** **It is recommended that the circuit court solicit the bar for
applications, maintain lists of those attorneys qualified to repre-**

sent capital defendants as lead counsel and as second-chair counsel, and identify attorneys' expertise in appellate and habeas representation.

Although attorneys that have been appointed at the district court level typically continue their representation on appeal, from time to time it is necessary to appoint attorneys pursuant to § 3599 during appellate proceedings. Consequently, it is recommended that a plan to solicit the bar for applications for appointment to capital representation be adopted and that lists of those attorneys qualified and interested in capital representation as lead and second-chair counsel be maintained.

B. USE FEDERAL PUBLIC DEFENDERS FOR REPRESENTATION OF FEDERAL CAPITAL CHARGES AND COLLATERAL ATTACKS ON FEDERAL CAPITAL CONVICTIONS AND SENTENCES; DO NOT UTILIZE FEDERAL PUBLIC DEFENDERS FOR PROSECUTION OF HABEAS PROCEEDINGS FILED BY STATE PRISONERS.

** **It is recommended that federal public defenders be utilized for representation of individuals charged with federal capital crimes and collateral attacks on federal capital convictions.**

Providing representation for defendants charged with federal crimes punishable by the death penalty is within the statutory responsibility of the Federal Public Defender (FPD) to provide representation for all indigents charged with federal crimes. It is contemplated that FPDs will be placed in the pool of attorneys available to represent capital defendants in federal capital trials, on direct appeal, and in § 2255 proceedings. For some period of time, until FPDs develop the qualifications and experience, their appointments may be limited to second-chair positions. *See* 18 U.S.C.A. § 3599(d). However, such appointments should be encouraged whenever possible in order to permit FPDs to attain expertise in this area.

** **It is recommended that FPDs not be appointed to represent criminal defendants petitioning pursuant to 28 U.S.C.A. § 2254 for relief from a state death sentence.**

The consensus of opinion among FPDs in the circuit is that FPD representation in § 2254 proceedings challenging a state sentence of death is undesirable for a number of reasons. First, the prospect of a federal agency opposing the validity of state convictions creates the appearance of an unacceptable conflict between separate and independent sovereigns. Second, although the FPD is authorized to represent defendants seeking a writ of habeas corpus, encouraging such representation is problematic because litigation of collateral state-court proceedings and issues may be necessary, raising the question of the appropriateness of FPDs appearing in state court and presenting issues outside their traditional area of expertise. Finally, appointing FPDs to represent § 2254 petitioners could be viewed as an attempt to circumvent the will of Congress, given its recent decision to withdraw funding from death penalty resource centers.

C. IMPOSE RESTRAINTS ON TIME FOR DECISION.

** **It is recommended that the limitations on time for decision set forth in 28 U.S.C.A. § 2266 be adopted at the district and circuit court levels and that the circuit executive be authorized to inquire into the reasons for any noncompliance with the limitations.**

Under 28 U.S.C.A. § 2266 (enacted by the Antiterrorism and Effective Death Penalty Act of 1996), proceedings brought pursuant to § 2254 that are governed by Chapter 154 of Title 28 and proceedings brought pursuant to § 2255 in which the defendant was sentenced to death must be decided by the district court and the circuit court within specified time limits. The district court is required to render a decision and enter a final judgment (including a resolution of any motion to alter or amend the judgment) within 450 days of the date on which the petition is filed or 60 days after the date on which the case is submitted for decision, whichever is earlier, subject to an extension of up to 30 days if the district court determines that the ends of justice would best be served by the delay. *See* 28 U.S.C.A. § 2266(a)-(b). The court of appeals is required to render a decision within 120 days of the date on which the reply brief is filed and to rule on any petition for rehearing or rehearing en banc within 30 days of the date the petition is filed or the date a response thereto is filed, whichever is later. *See* 28 U.S.C.A. § 2266(c). Furthermore, if the petition is granted, any hearing must be conducted and a final decision rendered within 120 days of the entry of the order granting rehearing. *Id.* And, following a remand by the court of appeals en banc or the Supreme Court for further proceedings, the period for decision runs from the date the remand is ordered. *Id.*

The time limitations imposed by § 2266 are applicable only in those § 2254 proceedings governed by Chapter 154, (*i.e.*, those challenging a state death sentence where the state has adopted specified procedures for appointment of counsel to represent the defendant in state post-conviction proceedings) and in § 2255 proceedings in which the defendant was sentenced to death. As such, the limitations presently will not apply to the majority of § 2254 petitions challenging a death sentence because of the relatively recent adoption of those mechanisms. *See Bennett v. Angelone*, No. 95-4004, 1996 WL 469705, at *4 (4th Cir. Aug. 20, 1996) (stating that question of whether Virginia's mechanism for appointment of counsel satisfied requirements for application of Chapter 154 was irrelevant because Chapter 154 would not apply when the mechanism was not in place during the petitioner's state collateral proceedings). Time constraints, however, are sorely needed at present. *See, e.g., Correll v. Thompson*, 63 F.3d 1279, 1285 n.4 (4th Cir. 1995), *cert. denied*, 116 S. Ct. 688 (1996) (noting that § 2254 petition was pending in district court for in excess of three years prior to final decision). Consequently, it is recommended that the time limitations for decision imposed by § 2266 be adopted and implemented by rule immediately. It is contemplated that the limitations would apply to cases pending when the rule became effective, but that the limitations would apply prospectively. (For example, an appeal in a § 2255 proceeding challenging a death sentence that had been argued to this court and was pending decision would have to be decided within 120 days of the date the rule becomes effective.)

Additionally, it is recommended that a mechanism be established to track cases to which the time limitations apply, and in the event that cases remain pending after the date on which they were due to be decided, the Circuit Executive be authorized to make appropriate inquiry on behalf of the Judicial Council to seek an explanation of the reasons why the judge or panel of judges faile to comply with the time limitation. (Amended by order August 14, 2008, effective October 1, 2008.)

Effect of amendments. — The 2008 amendment updated references throughout the order; and in second sentence of the first paragraph after the first recommendation in C, substituted "450 days" for "180 days" and added "or 60 days after the date on which the case is submitted for decision, whichever is earlier".

Index to Federal Rules of Appellate Procedure for United States Courts of Appeals; Local Rules and Internal Operating Procedures of the Fourth Circuit

INDEX

INDEX

INDEX

INDEX

1321

INDEX

INDEX

INDEX

INDEX

INDEX

RULES FOR JUDICIAL-CONDUCT AND JUDICIAL-DISABILITY PROCEEDINGS

As adopted March 11, 2008.

Preface

These Rules were promulgated by the Judicial Conference of the United States, after public comment, pursuant to 28 U.S.C. §§ 331 and 358, to establish standards and procedures for addressing complaints filed by complainants or identified by chief judges, under the Judicial and Disability Act, 28 U.S.C. §§ 351-364.

ARTICLE I. GENERAL PROVISIONS.

Rule 1. Scope.

These Rules govern proceedings under the Judicial Conduct and Disability Act, 28 U.S.C. §§ 351-364 (the Act), to determine whether a covered judge has engaged in conduct prejudicial to the effective and expeditious administration of the business of the courts or is unable to discharge the duties of office because of mental or physical disability.

In September 2006, the Judicial Conduct and Disability Act Study Committee, appointed in 2004 by Chief Justice Rehnquist and known as the "Breyer Committee," presented a report, known as the "Breyer Committee Report," 239 F.R.D. 116 (Sept. 2006), to Chief Justice Roberts that evaluated implementation of the Judicial Conduct and Disability Act of 1980, 28 U.S.C. §§ 351-364. The Breyer Committee had been formed in response to criticism from the public and the Congress regarding the effectiveness of the Act's implementation. The Executive Committee of the Judicial Conference directed the Judicial Conference Committee on Judicial Conduct and Disability to consider the recommendations made by the Breyer Committee and to report on their implementation to the Conference.

The Breyer Committee found that it could not evaluate implementation of the Act without establishing interpretive standards, Breyer Committee Report, 239 F.R.D. at 132, and that a major problem faced by chief judges in implementing the Act was the lack of authoritative interpretive standards. *Id.* at 212-15. The Breyer Committee then established standards to guide its evaluation, some of which were new formulations and some of which were taken from the "Illustrative Rules

Governing Complaints of Judicial Misconduct and Disability," discussed below. The principal standards used by the Breyer Committee are in Appendix E of its Report. *Id.* at 238.

Based on the findings of the Breyer Committee, the Judicial Conference Committee on Judicial Conduct and Disability concluded that there was a need for the Judicial Conference to exercise its power under Section 358 of the Act to fashion standards guiding the various officers and bodies who must exercise responsibility under the Act. To that end, the Judicial Conference Committee proposed rules that were based largely on Appendix E of the Breyer Committee Report and the Illustrative Rules.

The Illustrative Rules were originally prepared in 1986 by the Special Committee of the Conference of Chief Judges of the United States Courts of Appeals, and were subsequently revised and amended, most recently in 2000, by the predecessor to the Committee on Judicial Conduct and Disability. The Illustrative Rules were adopted, with minor variations, by circuit judicial councils, to govern complaints under the Judicial Conduct and Disability Act.

After being submitted for public comment pursuant to 28 U.S.C. § 358(c), the present Rules were promulgated by the Judicial Conference on March 11, 2008.

Rule 2. Effect and Construction.

(a) **Generally.** These Rules are mandatory; they supersede any conflicting judicial council rules. Judicial councils may promulgate additional rules to implement the Act as long as those rules do not conflict with these Rules.

(b) **Exception.** A Rule will not apply if, when performing duties authorized by the Act, a chief judge, a special committee, a judicial council, the Judicial Conference Committee on Judicial Conduct and Disability, or the Judicial Conference of the United States expressly finds that exceptional circumstances render application of that Rule in a particular proceeding manifestly unjust or contrary to the purposes of the Act or these Rules.

Unlike the Illustrative Rules, these Rules provide mandatory and nationally uniform provisions governing the substantive and procedural aspects of misconduct and disability proceedings under the Act. The mandatory nature of these Rules is authorized by 28 U.S.C. § 358(a) and (c). Judicial councils re-

tain the power to promulgate rules consistent with these Rules. For example, a local rule may authorize the electronic distribution of materials pursuant to Rule 8(b).

Rule 2(b) recognizes that unforeseen and exceptional circumstances may call for a different approach in particular cases.

Rule 3. Definitions.

(a) **Chief Judge.** "Chief judge" means the chief judge of a United States Court of Appeals, of the United States Court of International Trade, or of the United States Court of Federal Claims.

(b) **Circuit Clerk.** "Circuit clerk" means a clerk of a United States court of appeals, the clerk of the United States Court of International Trade, the clerk of the United States Court of Federal Claims, or the circuit executive of the United States Court of Appeals for the Federal Circuit.

(c) **Complaint.** A complaint is:

(1) a document that, in accordance with Rule 6, is filed by any person in his or her individual capacity or on behalf of a professional organization; or

(2) information from any source, other than a document described in (c)(1), that gives a chief judge probable cause to believe that a covered judge, as defined in Rule 4, has engaged in misconduct or may have a disability, whether or not the information is framed as or is intended to be an allegation of misconduct or disability.

(d) **Court of Appeals, District Court, and District Judge.** "Courts of appeals," "district court," and "district judge," where appropriate, include the United States Court of Federal Claims, the United States Court of International Trade, and the judges thereof.

(e) **Disability.** "Disability" is a temporary or permanent condition rendering a judge unable to discharge the duties of the particular judicial office. Examples of disability include substance abuse, the inability to stay awake during court proceedings, or a severe impairment of cognitive abilities.

(f) **Judicial Council and Circuit.** "Judicial council" and "circuit," where appropriate, include any courts designated in 28 U.S.C. § 363.

(g) **Magistrate Judge.** "Magistrate judge," where appropriate, includes a special master appointed by the Court of Federal Claims under 42 U.S.C. § 300aa-12(c).

(h) **Misconduct.** Cognizable misconduct:

(1) is conduct prejudicial to the effective and expeditious administration of the business of the courts. Misconduct includes, but is not limited to:

(A) using the judge's office to obtain special treatment for friends or relatives;

(B) accepting bribes, gifts, or other personal favors related to the judicial office;

(C) having improper discussions with parties or counsel for one side in a case;

(D) treating litigants or attorneys in a demonstrably egregious and hostile manner;

(E) engaging in partisan political activity or making inappropriately partisan statements;

(F) soliciting funds for organizations; or

(G) violating other specific, mandatory standards of judicial conduct, such as those pertaining to restrictions on outside income and requirements for financial disclosure.

(2) is conduct occurring outside the performance of official duties if the conduct might have a prejudicial effect on the administration of the business

of the courts, including a substantial and widespread lowering of public confidence in the courts among reasonable people.

(3) does not include:

(A) an allegation that is directly related to the merits of a decision or procedural ruling. An allegation that calls into question the correctness of a judge's ruling, including a failure to recuse, without more, is merits-related. If the decision or ruling is alleged to be the result of an improper motive, e.g., a bribe, ex parte contact, racial or ethnic bias, or improper conduct in rendering a decision or ruling, such as personally derogatory remarks irrelevant to the issues, the complaint is not cognizable to the extent that it attacks the merits.

(B) an allegation about delay in rendering a decision or ruling, unless the allegation concerns an improper motive in delaying a particular decision or habitual delay in a significant number of unrelated cases.

(i) **Subject Judge.** "Subject judge" means any judge described in Rule 4 who is the subject of a complaint.

COMMENT

Rule 3 is derived and adapted from the Breyer Committee Report and the Illustrative Rules.

Unless otherwise specified or the context otherwise indicates, the term "complaint" is used in these Rules to refer both to complaints identified by a chief judge under Rule 5 and to complaints filed by complainants under Rule 6.

Under the Act, a "complaint" may be filed by "any person" or "identified" by a chief judge. *See* 28 U.S.C. § 351(a) and (b). Under Rule 3(c)(1), complaints may be submitted by a person, in his or her individual capacity, or by a professional organization. Generally, the word "complaint" brings to mind the commencement of an adversary proceeding in which the contending parties are left to present the evidence and legal arguments, and judges play the role of an essentially passive arbiter. The Act, however, establishes an administrative, inquisitorial process. For example, even absent a complaint under Rule 6, chief judges are expected in some circumstances to trigger the process — "identify a complaint," *see* 28 U.S.C. § 351(b) and Rule 5 — and conduct an investigation without becoming a party. *See* 28 U.S.C. § 352(a); Breyer Committee Report, 239 F.R.D. at 214; Illustrative Rule 2(j). Even when a complaint is filed by someone other than the chief judge, the complainant lacks many rights that a litigant would have, and the chief judge, instead of being limited to the "four corners of the complaint," must, under Rule 11, proceed as though misconduct or disability has been alleged where the complainant reveals information of misconduct or disability but does not claim it as such. *See* Breyer Committee Report, 239 F.R.D. at 183-84.

An allegation of misconduct or disability filed under Rule 6 is a "complaint," and the Rule so provides in subsection (c)(1). However, both the nature of the process and the use of the term "identify" suggest that the word "complaint" covers more than a document formally triggering the process. The process relies on chief judges considering known information and triggering the process when appropriate. "Identifying" a "complaint," therefore, is best understood as the chief judge's concluding that information known to the judge constitutes probable cause to believe that misconduct occurred or a disability exists, whether or not the information is framed as, or intended to be an accusation. This definition is codified in (c)(2).

Rule 3(e) relates to disability and provides only the most general definition, recognizing that a fact-specific approach is the only one available.

The phrase "prejudicial to the effective and expeditious administration of the business of the courts" is not subject to precise definition, and subsection (h)(1) therefore provides some specific examples. Although the Code of Conduct for United States Judges may be informative, its main precepts are highly general; the Code is in many potential applications aspirational rather than a set of disciplinary rules. Ultimately, the responsibility for determining what constitutes misconduct under the statute is the province of the judicial council of the circuit subject to such review and limitations as are ordained by the statute and by these Rules.

Even where specific, mandatory rules exist — for example, governing the receipt of gifts by judges, outside earned income, and financial disclosure obligations — the distinction between the misconduct statute and the specific, mandatory rules must be borne in mind. For example, an inadvertent, minor violation of any one of these Rules, promptly remedied when called to the attention of the judge, might still be a violation but might not rise to the level of misconduct under the statute. By contrast, a pattern of such violations of the Code might well rise to the level of misconduct.

An allegation can meet the statutory standard even though the judge's alleged conduct did not occur in the course of the performance of official duties. The Code of Conduct for United States Judges expressly covers a wide range of extra-official activities, and some of these activities may constitute misconduct. For example, allegations that a judge solicited funds for a charity or participated in a partisan political event are cognizable under the Act.

On the other hand, judges are entitled to some leeway in extra-official activities. For example, misconduct may not include a judge being repeatedly and publicly discourteous to a spouse (not including physical abuse) even though this might cause some reasonable people to have diminished confidence in the courts. Rule 3(h)(2) states that conduct of this sort is covered, for example, when it might lead to a "substantial and widespread" lowering of such confidence.

Rule 3(h)(3)(A) tracks the Act, 28 U.S.C. § 352(b)(1)(A)(ii), in excluding from the definition of misconduct allegations "[d]irectly related to the merits of a decision or procedural ruling." This exclusion preserves the independence of judges in the exercise of judicial power by ensuring that the complaint procedure is not used to collaterally attack the substance of a judge's ruling. Any allegation that calls into question the correctness of an official action of a judge — without more — is merits-related. The phrase "decision or procedural ruling" is not limited to rulings issued in deciding Article III cases or controversies. Thus, a complaint challenging the correctness of a chief judge's determination to dismiss a prior misconduct complaint would be properly dismissed as merits-related — in other words, as challenging the substance of the judge's administrative determination to dismiss the complaint — even though it does not concern the judge's rulings in Article III litigation. Similarly, an allegation that a judge had incorrectly declined to approve a Criminal Justice Act voucher is merits-related under this standard.

Conversely, an allegation — however unsupported — that a judge conspired with a prosecutor to make a particular ruling is not merits-related, even though it "relates" to a ruling in a colloquial sense. Such an allegation attacks the propriety of conspiring with the prosecutor and goes beyond a challenge to the correctness

— "the merits" — of the ruling itself. An allegation that a judge ruled against the complainant because the complainant is a member of a particular racial or ethnic group, or because the judge dislikes the complainant personally, is also not merits-related. Such an allegation attacks the propriety of arriving at rulings with an illicit or improper motive. Similarly, an allegation that a judge used an inappropriate term to refer to a class of people is not merits-related even if the judge used it on the bench or in an opinion; the correctness of the judge's rulings is not at stake. An allegation that a judge treated litigants or attorneys in a demonstrably egregious and hostile manner while on the bench is also not merits-related.

The existence of an appellate remedy is usually irrelevant to whether an allegation is merits-related. The merits-related ground for dismissal exists to protect judges' independence in making rulings, not to protect or promote the appellate process. A complaint alleging an incorrect ruling is merits-related even though the complainant has no recourse from that ruling. By the same token, an allegation that is otherwise cognizable under the Act should not be dismissed merely because an appellate remedy appears to exist (for example, vacating a ruling that resulted from an improper *ex parte* communication). However, there may be occasions when appellate and misconduct proceedings overlap, and consideration and disposition of a complaint under these Rules may be properly deferred by a chief judge until the appellate proceedings are concluded in order to avoid, *inter alia*, inconsistent decisions.

Because of the special need to protect judges' independence in deciding what to say in an opinion or ruling, a somewhat different standard applies to determine the merits-relatedness of a non-frivolous allegation that a judge's language in a ruling reflected an improper motive. If the judge's language was relevant to the case at hand — for example a statement that a claim is legally or factually "frivolous" — then the judge's choice of language is presumptively merits-related and excluded, absent evidence apart from the ruling itself suggesting an improper motive. If, on the other hand, the challenged language does not seem relevant on its face, then an additional inquiry under Rule 11 is necessary.

With regard to Rule 3(h)(3)(B), a complaint of delay in a single case is excluded as merits-related. Such an allegation may be said to challenge the correctness of an official action of the judge — in other words, assigning a low priority to deciding the particular case. But, by the same token, an allegation of a habitual pattern of delay in a significant number of unrelated cases, or an allegation of deliberate delay in a single case arising out of an illicit motive, is not merits-related.

The remaining subsections of Rule 3 provide

technical definitions clarifying the application of the Rules to the various kinds of courts covered.

Rule 4. Covered Judges.

A complaint under these Rules may concern the actions or capacity only of judges of United States courts of appeals, judges of United States district courts, judges of United States bankruptcy courts, United States magistrate judges, and judges of the courts specified in 28 U.S.C. § 363.

COMMENT

This Rule tracks the Act. Rule 8(c) and (d) contain provisions as to the handling of complaints against persons not covered by the Act,

such as other court personnel, or against both covered judges and noncovered persons.

ARTICLE II. INITIATION OF A COMPLAINT.

Rule 5. Identification of a Complaint.

(a) **Identification.** When a chief judge has information constituting reasonable grounds for inquiry into whether a covered judge has engaged in misconduct or has a disability, the chief judge may conduct an inquiry, as he or she deems appropriate, into the accuracy of the information even if no related complaint has been filed. A chief judge who finds probable cause to believe that misconduct has occurred or that a disability exists may seek an informal resolution that he or she finds satisfactory. If no informal resolution is achieved or is feasible, the chief judge may identify a complaint and, by written order stating the reasons, begin the review provided in Rule 11. If the evidence of misconduct is clear and convincing and no informal resolution is achieved or is feasible, the chief judge must identify a complaint. A chief judge must not decline to identify a complaint merely because the person making the allegation has not filed a complaint under Rule 6. This Rule is subject to Rule 7.

(b) **Noncompliance with Rule 6(d).** Rule 6 complaints that do not comply with the requirements of Rule 6(d) must be considered under this Rule.

COMMENT

This Rule is adapted from the Breyer Committee Report, 239 F.R.D. at 245-46.

The Act authorizes the chief judge, by written order stating reasons, to identify a complaint and thereby dispense with the filing of a written complaint. *See* 28 U.S.C. § 351(b). Under Rule 5, when a chief judge becomes aware of information constituting reasonable grounds to inquire into possible misconduct or disability on the part of a covered judge, and no formal complaint has been filed, the chief judge has the power in his or her discretion to begin an appropriate inquiry. A chief judge's decision whether to informally seek a resolution and/or to identify a complaint is guided by the results of that inquiry. If the chief judge concludes that there is probable cause to be-

lieve that misconduct has occurred or a disability exists, the chief judge may seek an informal resolution, if feasible, and if failing in that, may identify a complaint. Discretion is accorded largely for the reasons police officers and prosecutors have discretion in making arrests or bringing charges. The matter may be trivial and isolated, based on marginal evidence, or otherwise highly unlikely to lead to a misconduct or disability finding. On the other hand, if the inquiry leads the chief judge to conclude that there is clear and convincing evidence of misconduct or a disability, and no satisfactory informal resolution has been achieved or is feasible, the chief judge is required to identify a complaint.

An informal resolution is one agreed to by

the subject judge and found satisfactory by the chief judge. Because an informal resolution under Rule 5 reached before a complaint is filed under Rule 6 will generally cause a subsequent Rule 6 complaint alleging the identical matter to be concluded, *see* Rule 11(d), the chief judge must be sure that the resolution is fully appropriate before endorsing it. In doing so, the chief judge must balance the seriousness of the matter against the particular judge's alacrity in addressing the issue. The availability of this procedure should encourage attempts at swift remedial action before a formal complaint is filed.

When a complaint is identified, a written order stating the reasons for the identification must be provided; this begins the process articulated in Rule 11. Rule 11 provides that once the chief judge has identified a complaint, the chief judge, subject to the disqualification provisions of Rule 25, will perform, with respect to that complaint, all functions assigned to the chief judge for the determination of complaints filed by a complainant.

In high-visibility situations, it may be desirable for the chief judge to identify a complaint without first seeking an informal resolution (and then, if the circumstances warrant, dismiss or conclude the identified complaint without appointment of a special committee) in order to assure the public that the allegations have not been ignored.

A chief judge's decision not to identify a complaint under Rule 5 is not appealable and is subject to Rule 3(h)(3)(A), which excludes merits-related complaints from the definition of misconduct.

A chief judge may not decline to identify a complaint solely on the basis that the unfiled allegations could be raised by one or more persons in a filed complaint, but none of these persons has opted to do so.

Subsection (a) concludes by stating that this Rule is "subject to Rule 7." This is intended to establish that only: (i) the chief judge of the home circuit of a potential subject judge, or (ii) the chief judge of a circuit in which misconduct is alleged to have occurred in the course of official business while the potential subject judge was sitting by designation, shall have the power or a duty under this Rule to identify a complaint.

Subsection (b) provides that complaints filed under Rule 6 that do not comply with the requirements of Rule 6(d), must be considered under this Rule. For instance, if a complaint has been filed but the form submitted is unsigned, or the truth of the statements therein are not verified in writing under penalty of perjury, then a chief judge must nevertheless consider the allegations as known information, and proceed to follow the process described in Rule 5(a).

Rule 6. Filing a Complaint.

(a) **Form.** A complainant may use the form reproduced in the appendix to these Rules or a form designated by the rules of the judicial council in the circuit in which the complaint is filed. A complaint form is also available on each court of appeals' website or may be obtained from the circuit clerk or any district court or bankruptcy court within the circuit. A form is not necessary to file a complaint, but the complaint must be written and must include the information described in (b).

(b) **Brief Statement of Facts.** A complaint must contain a concise statement that details the specific facts on which the claim of misconduct or disability is based. The statement of facts should include a description of:

(1) what happened;

(2) when and where the relevant events happened;

(3) any information that would help an investigator check the facts; and

(4) for an allegation of disability, any additional facts that form the basis of that allegation.

(c) **Legibility.** A complaint should be typewritten if possible. If not typewritten, it must be legible. An illegible complaint will be returned to the complainant with a request to resubmit it in legible form. If a resubmitted complaint is still illegible, it will not be accepted for filing.

(d) **Complainant's Address and Signature; Verification.** The complainant must provide a contact address and sign the complaint. The truth of the statements made in the complaint must be verified in writing under penalty of perjury. If any of these requirements are not met, the complaint will be accepted for filing, but it will be reviewed under only Rule 5(b).

(e) **Number of Copies; Envelope Marking.** The complainant shall provide the number of copies of the complaint required by local rule. Each copy should be in an envelope marked "Complaint of Misconduct" or "Complaint of Disability." The envelope must not show the name of any subject judge.

COMMENT

The Rule is adapted from the Illustrative Rules and is self-explanatory.

Rule 7. Where to Initiate Complaints.

(a) **Where to File.** Except as provided in (b),

(1) a complaint against a judge of a United States court of appeals, a United States district court, a United States bankruptcy court, or a United States magistrate judge must be filed with the circuit clerk in the jurisdiction in which the subject judge holds office.

(2) a complaint against a judge of the United States Court of International Trade or the United States Court of Federal Claims must be filed with the respective clerk of that court.

(3) a complaint against a judge of the United States Court of Appeals for the Federal Circuit must be filed with the circuit executive of that court.

(b) **Misconduct in Another Circuit; Transfer.** If a complaint alleges misconduct in the course of official business while the subject judge was sitting on a court by designation under 28 U.S.C. §§ 291-293 and 294(d), the complaint may be filed or identified with the circuit clerk of that circuit or of the subject judge's home circuit. The proceeding will continue in the circuit of the first-filed or first-identified complaint. The judicial council of the circuit where the complaint was first filed or first identified may transfer the complaint to the subject judge's home circuit or to the circuit where the alleged misconduct occurred, as the case may be.

COMMENT

Title 28 U.S.C. § 351 states that complaints are to be filed with "the clerk of the court of appeals for the circuit." However, in many circuits, this role is filled by circuit executives. Accordingly, the term "circuit clerk," as defined in Rule 3(b) and used throughout these Rules, applies to circuit executives.

Section 351 uses the term "the circuit" in a way that suggests that either the home circuit of the subject judge or the circuit in which misconduct is alleged to have occurred is the proper venue for complaints. With an exception for judges sitting by designation, the Rule requires the identifying or filing of a misconduct or disability complaint in the circuit in which the judge holds office, largely based on the administrative perspective of the Act. Given the Act's emphasis on the future conduct

of the business of the courts, the circuit in which the judge holds office is the appropriate forum because that circuit is likely best able to influence a judge's future behavior in constructive ways.

However, when judges sit by designation, the non-home circuit has a strong interest in redressing misconduct in the course of official business, and where allegations also involve a member of the bar — *ex parte* contact between an attorney and a judge, for example — it may often be desirable to have the judicial and bar misconduct proceedings take place in the same venue. Rule 7(b), therefore, allows transfer to, or filing or identification of a complaint in, the non-home circuit. The proceeding may be transferred by the judicial council of the filing or identified circuit to the other circuit.

1336

Rule 8. Action by Clerk.

(a) **Receipt of Complaint.** Upon receiving a complaint against a judge filed under Rule 5 or 6, the circuit clerk must open a file, assign a docket number according to a uniform numbering scheme promulgated by the Judicial Conference Committee on Judicial Conduct and Disability, and acknowledge the complaint's receipt.

(b) **Distribution of Copies.** The clerk must promptly send copies of a complaint filed under Rule 6 to the chief judge or the judge authorized to act as chief judge under Rule 25(f), and copies of complaints filed under Rule 5 or 6 to each subject judge. The clerk must retain the original complaint. Any further distribution should be as provided by local rule.

(c) **Complaints Against Noncovered Persons.** If the clerk receives a complaint about a person not holding an office described in Rule 4, the clerk must not accept the complaint for filing under these Rules.

(d) **Receipt of Complaint about a Judge and Another Noncovered Person.** If a complaint is received about a judge described in Rule 4 and a person not holding an office described in Rule 4, the clerk must accept the complaint for filing under these Rules only with regard to the judge and must inform the complainant of the limitation.

COMMENT

This Rule is adapted from the Illustrative Rules and is largely self-explanatory.

The uniform docketing scheme described in subsection (a) should take into account potential problems associated with a complaint that names multiple judges. One solution may be to provide separate docket numbers for each subject judge. Separate docket numbers would help avoid difficulties in tracking cases, particularly if a complaint is dismissed with respect to some, but not all, of the named judges.

Complaints against noncovered persons are not to be accepted for processing under these Rules but may, of course, be accepted under other circuit rules or procedures for grievances.

Rule 9. Time for Filing or Identifying a Complaint.

A complaint may be filed or identified at any time. If the passage of time has made an accurate and fair investigation of a complaint impractical, the complaint must be dismissed under Rule 11(c)(1)(E).

COMMENT

This Rule is adapted from the Act, 28 U.S.C. §§ 351, 352(b)(1)(A)(iii), and the Illustrative Rules.

Rule 10. Abuse of the Complaint Procedure.

(a) **Abusive Complaints.** A complainant who has filed repetitive, harassing, or frivolous complaints, or has otherwise abused the complaint procedure, may be restricted from filing further complaints. After giving the complainant an opportunity to show cause in writing why his or her right to file further complaints should not be limited, a judicial council may prohibit, restrict, or impose conditions on the complainant's use of the complaint procedure. Upon written request of the complainant, the judicial council may revise or withdraw any prohibition, restriction, or condition previously imposed.

(b) **Orchestrated Complaints.** When many essentially identical complaints from different complainants are received and appear to be part of an orchestrated campaign, the chief judge may recommend that the judicial council issue a written order instructing the circuit clerk to accept only a certain number of such complaints for filing and to refuse to accept further ones. The clerk must send a copy of any such order to anyone whose complaint was not accepted.

COMMENT

This Rule is adapted from the Illustrative Rules.

Rule 10(a) provides a mechanism for a judicial council to restrict the filing of further complaints by a single complainant who has abused the complaint procedure. In some instances, however, the complaint procedure may be abused in a manner for which the remedy provided in Rule 10(a) may not be appropriate. For example, some circuits have been inundated with submissions of dozens or hundreds of essentially identical complaints against the same judge or judges, all submitted by different complainants. In many of these instances, persons with grievances against a particular judge or judges used the Internet or other technology to orchestrate mass complaint-filing campaigns against them. If each complaint submitted as part of such a campaign were accepted for filing and processed according to these Rules, there would be a serious drain on court resources without any benefit to the adjudication of the underlying merits.

A judicial council may, therefore, respond to such mass filings under Rule 10(b) by declining to accept repetitive complaints for filing, regardless of the fact that the complaints are nominally submitted by different complainants. When the first complaint or complaints have been dismissed on the merits, and when further, essentially identical submissions follow, the judicial council may issue a second order noting that these are identical or repetitive complaints, directing the circuit clerk not to accept these complaints or any further such complaints for filing, and directing the clerk to send each putative complainant copies of both orders.

ARTICLE III. REVIEW OF A COMPLAINT BY THE CHIEF JUDGE.

Rule 11. Review by the Chief Judge.

(a) **Purpose of Chief Judge's Review.** When a complaint is identified by the chief judge or is filed, the chief judge must review it unless the chief judge is disqualified under Rule 25. If the complaint contains information constituting evidence of misconduct or disability, but the complainant does not claim it as such, the chief judge must treat the complaint as if it did allege misconduct or disability and give notice to the subject judge. After reviewing the complaint, the chief judge must determine whether it should be:

(1) dismissed;

(2) concluded on the ground that voluntary corrective action has been taken;

(3) concluded because intervening events have made action on the complaint no longer necessary; or

(4) referred to a special committee.

(b) **Inquiry by Chief Judge.** In determining what action to take under Rule 11(a), the chief judge may conduct a limited inquiry. The chief judge, or a designee, may communicate orally or in writing with the complainant, the subject judge, and any others who may have knowledge of the matter, and may review transcripts or other relevant documents. In conducting the inquiry, the chief judge must not determine any reasonably disputed issue.

(c) **Dismissal.** (1) Allowable grounds. A complaint must be dismissed in whole or in part to the extent that the chief judge concludes that the complaint:

(A) alleges conduct that, even if true, is not prejudicial to the effective and expeditious administration of the business of the courts and does not indicate a mental or physical disability resulting in inability to discharge the duties of judicial office;

(B) is directly related to the merits of a decision or procedural ruling;

(C) is frivolous;

(D) is based on allegations lacking sufficient evidence to raise an inference that misconduct has occurred or that a disability exists;

(E) is based on allegations which are incapable of being established through investigation;

(F) has been filed in the wrong circuit under Rule 7; or

(G) is otherwise not appropriate for consideration under the Act.

(2) Disallowed grounds. A complaint must not be dismissed solely because it repeats allegations of a previously dismissed complaint if it also contains material information not previously considered and does not constitute harassment of the subject judge.

(d) **Corrective Action.** The chief judge may conclude the complaint proceeding in whole or in part if:

(1) an informal resolution under Rule 5 satisfactory to the chief judge was reached before the complaint was filed under Rule 6, or

(2) the chief judge determines that the subject judge has taken appropriate voluntary corrective action that acknowledges and remedies the problems raised by the complaint.

(e) **Intervening Events.** The chief judge may conclude the complaint proceeding in whole or in part upon determining that intervening events render some or all of the allegations moot or make remedial action impossible.

(f) **Appointment of Special Committee.** If some or all of the complaint is not dismissed or concluded, the chief judge must promptly appoint a special committee to investigate the complaint or any relevant portion of it and to make recommendations to the judicial council. Before appointing a special committee, the chief judge must invite the subject judge to respond to the complaint either orally or in writing if the judge was not given an opportunity during the limited inquiry. In the chief judge's discretion, separate complaints may be joined and assigned to a single special committee. Similarly, a single complaint about more than one judge may be severed and more than one special committee appointed.

(g) **Notice of Chief Judge's Action; Petitions for Review.** (1) When special committee is appointed. If a special committee is appointed, the chief judge must notify the complainant and the subject judge that the matter has been referred to a special committee and identify the members of the committee. A copy of the order appointing the special committee must be sent to the Judicial Conference Committee on Judicial Conduct and Disability.

(2) When chief judge disposes of complaint without appointing special committee. If the chief judge disposes of the complaint under Rule 11(c), (d), or (e), the chief judge must prepare a supporting memorandum that sets forth the

reasons for the disposition. Except as authorized by 28 U.S.C. § 360, the memorandum must not include the name of the complainant or of the subject judge. The order and the supporting memorandum, which may be one document, must be provided to the complainant, the subject judge, and the Judicial Conference Committee on Judicial Conduct and Disability.

(3) Right of petition for review. If the chief judge disposes of a complaint under Rule 11(c), (d), or (e), the complainant and subject judge must be notified of the right to petition the judicial council for review of the disposition, as provided in Rule 18. If a petition for review is filed, the chief judge must promptly transmit all materials obtained in connection with the inquiry under Rule 11(b) to the circuit clerk for transmittal to the judicial council.

(h) **Public Availability of Chief Judge's Decision.** The chief judge's decision must be made public to the extent, at the time, and in the manner provided in Rule 24.

COMMENT

Subsection (a) lists the actions available to a chief judge in reviewing a complaint. This subsection provides that where a complaint has been filed under Rule 6, the ordinary doctrines of waiver do not apply. A chief judge must identify as a complaint any misconduct or disability issues raised by the factual allegations of the complaint even if the complainant makes no such claim with regard to those issues. For example, an allegation limited to misconduct in fact-finding that mentions periods during a trial when the judge was asleep must be treated as a complaint regarding disability. Some formal order giving notice of the expanded scope of the proceeding must be given to the subject judge.

Subsection (b) describes the nature of the chief judge's inquiry. It is based largely on the Breyer Committee Report, 239 F.R.D. at 243-45. The Act states that dismissal is appropriate "when a limited inquiry ... demonstrates that the allegations in the complaint lack any factual foundation or are conclusively refuted by objective evidence." 28 U.S.C. § 352(b)(1)(B). At the same time, however, Section 352(a) states that "[t]he chief judge shall not undertake to make findings of fact about any matter that is reasonably in dispute." These two statutory standards should be read together, so that a matter is not "reasonably" in dispute if a limited inquiry shows that the allegations do not constitute misconduct or disability, that they lack any reliable factual foundation, or that they are conclusively refuted by objective evidence.

In conducting a limited inquiry under subsection (b), the chief judge must avoid determinations of reasonably disputed issues, including reasonably disputed issues as to whether the facts alleged constitute misconduct or disability, which are ordinarily left to a special committee and the judicial council. An allegation of fact is ordinarily not "refuted" simply because the subject judge denies it. The limited inquiry must reveal something more in the way of refutation before it is appropriate to dismiss a complaint that is otherwise cognizable. If it is the complainant's word against the subject judge's — in other words, there is simply no other significant evidence of what happened or of the complainant's unreliability — then there must be a special-committee investigation. Such a credibility issue is a matter "reasonably in dispute" within the meaning of the Act.

However, dismissal following a limited inquiry may occur when the complaint refers to transcripts or to witnesses and the chief judge determines that the transcripts and witnesses all support the subject judge. Breyer Committee Report, 239 F.R.D. at 243. For example, consider a complaint alleging that the subject judge said X, and the complaint mentions, or it is independently clear, that five people may have heard what the judge said. *Id.* The chief judge is told by the subject judge and one witness that the judge did not say X, and the chief judge dismisses the complaint without questioning the other four possible witnesses. *Id.* In this example, the matter remains reasonably in dispute. If all five witnesses say the judge did not say X, dismissal is appropriate, but if potential witnesses who are reasonably accessible have not been questioned, then the matter remains reasonably in dispute. *Id.*

Similarly, under (c)(1)(A), if it is clear that the conduct or disability alleged, even if true, is not cognizable under these Rules, the complaint should be dismissed. If that issue is reasonably in dispute, however, dismissal under (c)(1)(A) is inappropriate.

Essentially, the standard articulated in subsection (b) is that used to decide motions for summary judgment pursuant to Fed. R. Civ. P. 56. Genuine issues of material fact are not resolved at the summary judgment stage. A material fact is one that "might affect the outcome of the suit under the governing law," and a dispute is "genuine" if "the evidence is such that a reasonable jury could return a verdict for the nonmoving party." *Anderson v. Liberty Lobby,* 477 U.S. 242, 248 (1986). Similarly, the chief judge may not resolve a genuine issue concerning a material fact or the existence of misconduct or a disability when conducting a limited inquiry pursuant to subsection (b).

Subsection (c) describes the grounds on which a complaint may be dismissed. These are adapted from the Act, 28 U.S.C. § 352(b), and the Breyer Committee Report, 239 F.R.D. at 239-45. Subsection (c)(1)(A) permits dismissal of an allegation that, even if true, does not constitute misconduct or disability under the statutory standard. The proper standards are set out in Rule 3 and discussed in the Commentary on that Rule. Subsection (c)(1)(B) permits dismissal of complaints related to the merits of a decision by a subject judge; this standard is also governed by Rule 3 and its accompanying Commentary.

Subsections (c)(1)(C)-(E) implement the statute by allowing dismissal of complaints that are "frivolous, lacking sufficient evidence to raise an inference that misconduct has occurred, or containing allegations which are incapable of being established through investigation." 28 U.S.C. § 352(b)(1)(A)(iii).

Dismissal of a complaint as "frivolous," under Rule 11(c)(1)(C), will generally occur without any inquiry beyond the face of the complaint. For instance, when the allegations are facially incredible or so lacking in indicia of reliability that no further inquiry is warranted, dismissal under this subsection is appropriate.

A complaint warranting dismissal under Rule 11(c)(1)(D) is illustrated by the following example. Consider a complainant who alleges an impropriety and asserts that he knows of it because it was observed and reported to him by a person who is identified. The judge denies that the event occurred. When contacted, the source also denies it. In such a case, the chief judge's proper course of action may turn on whether the source had any role in the allegedly improper conduct. If the complaint was based on a lawyer's statement that he or she had an improper *ex parte* contact with a judge, the lawyer's denial of the impropriety might not be taken as wholly persuasive, and it would be appropriate to conclude that a real factual issue is raised. On the other hand, if the complaint quoted a disinterested third party and that disinterested party denied that

the statement had been made, there would be no value in opening a formal investigation. In such a case, it would be appropriate to dismiss the complaint under Rule 11(c)(1)(D).

Rule 11(c)(1)(E) is intended, among other things, to cover situations when no evidence is offered or identified, or when the only identified source is unavailable. Breyer Committee Report, 239 F.R.D. at 243. For example, a complaint alleges that an unnamed attorney told the complainant that the judge did X. *Id.* The subject judge denies it. The chief judge requests that the complainant (who does not purport to have observed the judge do X) identify the unnamed witness, or that the unnamed witness come forward so that the chief judge can learn the unnamed witness's account. *Id.* The complainant responds that he has spoken with the unnamed witness, that the unnamed witness is an attorney who practices in federal court, and that the unnamed witness is unwilling to be identified or to come forward. *Id.* at 243-44. The allegation is then properly dismissed as containing allegations that are incapable of being established through investigation. *Id.*

If, however, the situation involves a reasonable dispute over credibility, the matter should proceed. For example, the complainant alleges an impropriety and alleges that he or she observed it and that there were no other witnesses; the subject judge denies that the event occurred. Unless the complainant's allegations are facially incredible or so lacking indicia of reliability warranting dismissal under Rule 11(c)(1)(C), a special committee must be appointed because there is a material factual question that is reasonably in dispute.

Dismissal is also appropriate when a complaint is filed so long after an alleged event that memory loss, death, or changes to unknown residences prevent a proper investigation.

Subsection (c)(2) indicates that the investigative nature of the process prevents the application of claim preclusion principles where new and material evidence becomes available. However, it also recognizes that at some point a renewed investigation may constitute harassment of the subject judge and should be foregone, depending of course on the seriousness of the issues and the weight of the new evidence.

Rule 11(d) implements the Act's provision for dismissal if voluntary appropriate corrective action has been taken. It is largely adapted from the Breyer Committee Report, 239 F.R.D. 244-45. The Act authorizes the chief judge to conclude the proceedings if "appropriate corrective action has been taken." 28 U.S.C. § 352(b)(2). Under the Rule, action taken after the complaint is filed is "appropriate" when it acknowledges and remedies the problem raised by the complaint. Breyer Committee Report, 239 F.R.D. at 244. Because the Act deals with the conduct of judges, the emphasis is on correction of the judicial conduct that was the subject of the complaint. *Id.* Terminating a complaint based on corrective action is premised on the implicit understanding that voluntary self-correction or redress of misconduct or a disability is preferable to sanctions. *Id.* The chief judge may facilitate this process by giving the subject judge an objective view of the appearance of the judicial conduct in question and by suggesting appropriate corrective measures. *Id.* Moreover, when corrective action is taken under Rule 5 satisfactory to the chief judge before a complaint is filed, that informal resolution will be sufficient to conclude a subsequent complaint based on the identical conduct.

"Corrective action" must be voluntary action taken by the subject judge. Breyer Committee Report, 239 F.R.D. at 244. A remedial action directed by the chief judge or by an appellate court without the participation of the subject judge in formulating the directive or without the subject judge's subsequent agreement to such action does not constitute the requisite voluntary corrective action. *Id.* Neither the chief judge nor an appellate court has authority under the Act to impose a formal remedy or sanction; only the judicial council can impose a formal remedy or sanction under 28 U.S.C. § 354(a)(2). *Id.* Compliance with a previous council order may serve as corrective action allowing conclusion of a later complaint about the same behavior. *Id.*

Where a judge's conduct has resulted in identifiable, particularized harm to the complainant or another individual, appropriate corrective action should include steps taken by that judge to acknowledge and redress the harm, if possible, such as by an apology, recusal from a case, or a pledge to refrain from similar conduct in the future. *Id.* While the Act is generally forward-looking, any corrective action should, to the extent possible, serve to correct a specific harm to an individual, if such harm can reasonably be remedied. *Id.* In some cases, corrective action may not be "appropriate" to justify conclusion of a complaint unless the complainant or other individual harmed is meaningfully apprised of the nature of the corrective action in the chief judge's order, in a direct communication from the subject judge, or otherwise. *Id.*

Voluntary corrective action should be proportionate to any plausible allegations of misconduct in the complaint. The form of corrective action should also be proportionate to any sanctions that a judicial council might impose under Rule 20(b), such as a private or public reprimand or a change in case assignments. Breyer Committee Report, 239 F.R.D at 244-45. In other words, minor corrective action will not suffice to dispose of a serious matter. *Id.*

Rule 11(e) implements Section 352(b)(2) of the Act, which permits the chief judge to "conclude the proceeding," if "action on the complaint is no longer necessary because of intervening events," such as a resignation from judicial office. Ordinarily, however, stepping down from an administrative post such as chief judge, judicial-council member, or court-committee chair does not constitute an event rendering unnecessary any further action on a complaint alleging judicial misconduct. Breyer Committee Report, 239 F.R.D. at 245. As long as the subject of the complaint performs judicial duties, a complaint alleging judicial misconduct must be addressed. *Id.*

If a complaint is not disposed of pursuant to Rule 11(c), (d), or (e), a special committee must be appointed. Rule 11(f) states that a subject judge must be invited to respond to the complaint before a special committee is appointed, if no earlier response was invited.

Subject judges, of course, receive copies of complaints at the same time that they are referred to the chief judge, and they are free to volunteer responses to them. Under Rule 11(b), the chief judge may request a response if it is thought necessary. However, many complaints are clear candidates for dismissal even if their allegations are accepted as true, and there is no need for the subject judge to devote time to a defense.

The Act requires that the order dismissing a complaint or concluding the proceeding contain a statement of reasons and that a copy of the order be sent to the complainant. 28 U.S.C. § 352(b). Rule 24, dealing with availability of information to the public, contemplates that the order will be made public, usually without disclosing the names of the complainant or the subject judge. If desired for administrative purposes, more identifying information can be included in a non-public version of the order.

When complaints are disposed of by chief judges, the statutory purposes are best served by providing the complainant with a full, particularized, but concise explanation, giving reasons for the conclusions reached. *See also* Commentary on Rule 24, dealing with public availability.

Rule 11(g) provides that the complainant and subject judge must be notified, in the case of a disposition by the chief judge, of the right to petition the judicial council for review. A copy of a chief judge's order and memorandum, which may be one document, disposing of a complaint must be sent by the circuit clerk to the Judicial Conference Committee on Judicial Conduct and Disability.

ARTICLE IV. INVESTIGATION AND REPORT BY SPECIAL COMMITTEE.

Rule 12. Composition of Special Committee.

(a) **Membership.** Except as provided in (e), a special committee appointed under Rule 11(f) must consist of the chief judge and equal numbers of circuit and district judges. If the complaint is about a district judge, bankruptcy judge, or magistrate judge, then, when possible, the district-judge members of the committee must be from districts other than the district of the subject judge. For the courts named in 28 U.S.C. § 363, the committee must be selected from the judges serving on the subject judge's court.

(b) **Presiding Officer.** When appointing the committee, the chief judge may serve as the presiding officer or else must designate a committee member as the presiding officer.

(c) **Bankruptcy Judge or Magistrate Judge as Adviser.** If the subject judge is a bankruptcy judge or magistrate judge, he or she may, within 14 days after being notified of the committee's appointment, ask the chief judge to designate as a committee adviser another bankruptcy judge or magistrate judge, as the case may be. The chief judge must grant such a request but may otherwise use discretion in naming the adviser. Unless the adviser is a Court of Federal Claims special master appointed under 42 U.S.C. § 300aa-12(c), the adviser must be from a district other than the district of the subject bankruptcy judge or subject magistrate judge. The adviser cannot vote but has the other privileges of a committee member.

(d) **Provision of Documents.** The chief judge must certify to each other member of the committee and to any adviser copies of the complaint and statement of facts in whole or relevant part, and any other relevant documents on file.

(e) **Continuing Qualification of Committee Members.** A member of a special committee who was qualified to serve when appointed may continue to serve on the committee even though the member relinquishes the position of chief judge, active circuit judge, or active district judge, as the case may be, but only if the member continues to hold office under Article III, Section 1, of the Constitution of the United States, or under 28 U.S.C. § 171.

(f) **Inability of Committee Member to Complete Service.** If a member of a special committee can no longer serve because of death, disability, disqualification, resignation, retirement from office, or other reason, the chief judge must decide whether to appoint a replacement member, either a circuit or district judge as needed under (a). No special committee appointed under these Rules may function with only a single member, and the votes of a two-member committee must be unanimous.

(g) **Voting.** All actions by a committee must be by vote of a majority of all members of the committee.

COMMENT

This Rule is adapted from the Act and the Illustrative Rules.

Rule 12 leaves the size of a special committee flexible, to be determined on a case-by-case basis. The question of committee size is one that should be weighed with care in view of the potential for consuming the members' time; a large committee should be appointed only if there is a special reason to do so.

Although the Act requires that the chief judge be a member of each special committee, 28 U.S.C. § 353(a)(1), it does not require that the chief judge preside. Accordingly, Rule 12(b) provides that if the chief judge does not preside, he or she must designate another committee member as the presiding officer.

Rule 12(c) provides that the chief judge must appoint a bankruptcy judge or magistrate judge as an adviser to a special committee at the request of a bankruptcy or magistrate subject judge.

Subsection (c) also provides that the adviser will have all the privileges of a committee member except a vote. The adviser, therefore, may participate in all deliberations of the committee, question witnesses at hearings, and write a separate statement to accompany the special committee's report to the judicial council.

Rule 12(e) provides that a member of a special committee who remains an Article III judge may continue to serve on the committee even though the member's status otherwise changes. Thus, a committee that originally consisted of the chief judge and an equal number of circuit and district judges, as re-

quired by the law, may continue to function even though changes of status alter that composition. This provision reflects the belief that stability of membership will contribute to the quality of the work of such committees.

Stability of membership is also the principal concern animating Rule 12(f), which deals with the case in which a special committee loses a member before its work is complete. The Rule permits the chief judge to determine whether a replacement member should be appointed. Generally, appointment of a replacement member is desirable in these situations unless the committee has conducted evidentiary hearings before the vacancy occurs. However, cases may arise in which a special committee is in the late stages of its work, and in which it would be difficult for a new member to play a meaningful role. The Rule also preserves the collegial character of the committee process by prohibiting a single surviving member from serving as a committee and by providing that a committee of two surviving members will, in essence, operate under a unanimity rule.

Rule 12(g) provides that actions of a special committee must be by vote of a majority of all the members. All the members of a committee should participate in committee decisions. In that circumstance, it seems reasonable to require that committee decisions be made by a majority of the membership, rather than a majority of some smaller quorum.

Rule 13. Conduct of an Investigation.

(a) **Extent and Methods of Special-Committee Investigation.** Each special committee must determine the appropriate extent and methods of the investigation in light of the allegations of the complaint. If, in the course of the investigation, the committee has cause to believe that the subject judge may have engaged in misconduct or has a disability that is beyond the scope of the complaint, the committee must refer the new matter to the chief judge for action under Rule 5 or Rule 11.

(b) **Criminal Conduct.** If the committee's investigation concerns conduct that may be a crime, the committee must consult with the appropriate prosecutorial authorities to the extent permitted by the Act to avoid compromising any criminal investigation. The committee has final authority over the timing and extent of its investigation and the formulation of its recommendations.

(c) **Staff.** The committee may arrange for staff assistance to conduct the investigation. It may use existing staff of the judicial branch or may hire special staff through the Director of the Administrative Office of the United States Courts.

(d) **Delegation of Subpoena Power; Contempt.** The chief judge may delegate the authority to exercise the committee's subpoena powers. The judicial council or special committee may institute a contempt proceeding under 28 U.S.C. § 332(d) against anyone who fails to comply with a subpoena.

This Rule is adapted from the Illustrative Rules.

Rule 13, as well as Rules 14, 15, and 16, are concerned with the way in which a special committee carries out its mission. They reflect the view that a special committee has two roles that are separated in ordinary litigation. First, the committee has an investigative role of the kind that is characteristically left to executive branch agencies or discovery by civil litigants. 28 U.S.C. § 353(c). Second, it has a formalized fact-finding and recommendation-of-disposition role that is characteristically left to juries, judges, or arbitrators. *Id.* Rule 13 generally governs the investigative stage. Even though the same body has responsibility for both roles under the Act, it is important to distinguish between them in order to ensure that appropriate rights are afforded at appropriate times to the subject judge.

One of the difficult questions that can arise is the relationship between proceedings under the Act and criminal investigations. Rule 13(b)

assigns responsibility for coordination to the special committee in cases in which criminal conduct is suspected, but gives the committee the authority to determine the appropriate pace of its activity in light of any criminal investigation.

Title 28 U.S.C. § 356(a) provides that a special committee will have full subpoena powers as provided in 28 U.S.C. § 332(d). Section 332(d)(1) provides that subpoenas will be issued on behalf of judicial councils by the circuit clerk "at the direction of the chief judge of the circuit or his designee." Rule 13(d) contemplates that, where the chief judge designates someone else as presiding officer of a special committee, the presiding officer also be delegated the authority to direct the circuit clerk to issue subpoenas related to committee proceedings. That is not intended to imply, however, that the decision to use the subpoena power is exercisable by the presiding officer alone. *See* Rule 12(g).

Rule 14. Conduct of Hearings by Special Committee.

(a) **Purpose of Hearings.** The committee may hold hearings to take testimony and receive other evidence, to hear argument, or both. If the committee is investigating allegations against more than one judge, it may hold joint or separate hearings.

(b) **Committee Evidence.** Subject to Rule 15, the committee must obtain material, nonredundant evidence in the form it considers appropriate. In the committee's discretion, evidence may be obtained by committee members, staff, or both. Witnesses offering testimonial evidence may include the complainant and the subject judge.

(c) **Counsel for Witnesses.** The subject judge has the right to counsel. The special committee has discretion to decide whether other witnesses may have counsel present when they testify.

(d) **Witness Fees.** Witness fees must be paid as provided in 28 U.S.C. § 1821.

(e) **Oath.** All testimony taken at a hearing must be given under oath or affirmation.

(f) **Rules of Evidence.** The Federal Rules of Evidence do not apply to special-committee hearings.

(g) **Record and Transcript.** A record and transcript must be made of all hearings.

This Rule is adapted from Section 353 of the Act and the Illustrative Rules.

Rule 14 is concerned with the conduct of fact-finding hearings. Special-committee hearings will normally be held only after the investigative work has been completed and the committee has concluded that there is sufficient evidence to warrant a formal fact-finding proceeding. Special-committee proceedings are primarily inquisitorial rather than adversarial. Accordingly, the Federal Rules of Evidence do not apply to such hearings. Inevitably, a hearing will have something of an adversary character. Nevertheless, that tendency should be moderated to the extent possible. Even though a proceeding will commonly have investigative and hearing stages, committee members should not regard themselves as prosecutors one day and judges the next. Their duty — and that of their staff — is at all times to be impartial seekers of the truth.

Rule 14(b) contemplates that material evidence will be obtained by the committee and presented in the form of affidavits, live testi-mony, etc. Staff or others who are organizing the hearings should regard it as their role to present evidence representing the entire picture. With respect to testimonial evidence, the subject judge should normally be called as a committee witness. Cases may arise in which the judge will not testify voluntarily. In such cases, subpoena powers are available, subject to the normal testimonial privileges. Although Rule 15(c) recognizes the subject judge's statutory right to call witnesses on his or her own behalf, exercise of this right should not usually be necessary.

Rule 15. Rights of Subject Judge.

(a) **Notice.** (1) Generally. The subject judge must receive written notice of:

(A) the appointment of a special committee under Rule 11(f);

(B) the expansion of the scope of an investigation under Rule 13(a);

(C) any hearing under Rule 14, including its purposes, the names of any witnesses the committee intends to call, and the text of any statements that have been taken from those witnesses.

(2) Suggestion of additional witnesses. The subject judge may suggest additional witnesses to the committee.

(b) **Report of the Special Committee.** The subject judge must be sent a copy of the special committee's report when it is filed with the judicial council.

(c) **Presentation of Evidence.** At any hearing held under Rule 14, the subject judge has the right to present evidence, to compel the attendance of witnesses, and to compel the production of documents. At the request of the subject judge, the chief judge or the judge's designee must direct the circuit clerk to issue a subpoena to a witness under 28 U.S.C. § 332(d)(1). The subject judge must be given the opportunity to cross-examine committee witnesses, in person or by counsel.

(d) **Presentation of Argument.** The subject judge may submit written argument to the special committee and must be given a reasonable opportunity to present oral argument at an appropriate stage of the investigation.

(e) **Attendance at Hearings.** The subject judge has the right to attend any hearing held under Rule 14 and to receive copies of the transcript, of any documents introduced, and of any written arguments submitted by the complainant to the committee.

(f) **Representation by Counsel.** The subject judge may choose to be represented by counsel in the exercise of any right enumerated in this Rule. As provided in Rule 20(e), the United States may bear the costs of the representation.

COMMENT

This Rule is adapted from the Act and the Illustrative Rules.

The Act states that these Rules must contain provisions requiring that "the judge whose conduct is the subject of a complaint ... be afforded an opportunity to appear (in person or by counsel) at proceedings conducted by the investigating panel, to present oral and documentary evidence, to compel the attendance of witnesses or the production of documents, to cross-examine witnesses, and to present argument orally or in writing." 28 U.S.C.

§ 358(b)(2). To implement this provision, Rule 15(e) gives the judge the right to attend any hearing held for the purpose of receiving evidence of record or hearing argument under Rule 14.

The Act does not require that the subject judge be permitted to attend all proceedings of the special committee. Accordingly, the Rules do not give a right to attend other proceedings — for example, meetings at which the committee is engaged in investigative activity, such as interviewing persons to learn whether they ought to be called as witnesses or examining for relevance purposes documents delivered pursuant to a subpoena duces tecum, or meetings in which the committee is deliberating on the evidence or its recommendations.

Rule 16. Rights of Complainant in Investigation.

(a) **Notice.** The complainant must receive written notice of the investigation as provided in Rule 11(g)(1). When the special committee's report to the judicial council is filed, the complainant must be notified of the filing. The judicial council may, in its discretion, provide a copy of the report of a special committee to the complainant.

(b) **Opportunity to Provide Evidence.** If the committee determines that the complainant may have evidence that does not already exist in writing, a representative of the committee must interview the complainant.

(c) **Presentation of Argument.** The complainant may submit written argument to the special committee. In its discretion, the special committee may permit the complainant to offer oral argument.

(d) **Representation by Counsel.** A complainant may submit written argument through counsel and, if permitted to offer oral argument, may do so through counsel.

(e) **Cooperation.** In exercising its discretion under this Rule, a special committee may take into account the degree of the complainant's cooperation in preserving the confidentiality of the proceedings, including the identity of the subject judge.

COMMENT

This Rule is adapted from the Act and the Illustrative Rules.

In accordance with the view of the process as fundamentally administrative and inquisitorial, these Rules do not give the complainant the rights of a party to litigation, and leave the complainant's role largely to the discretion of the special committee. However, Rule 16(b) provides that, where a special committee has been appointed and it determines that the complainant may have additional evidence, the complainant must be interviewed by a representative of the committee. Such an interview may be in person or by telephone, and the representative of the committee may be either a member or staff.

Rule 16 does not contemplate that the complainant will ordinarily be permitted to attend proceedings of the special committee except when testifying or presenting oral argument. A special committee may exercise its discretion to permit the complainant to be present at its proceedings, or to permit the complainant, individually or through counsel, to participate in the examination or cross-examination of witnesses.

The Act authorizes an exception to the normal confidentiality provisions where the judicial council in its discretion provides a copy of the report of the special committee to the complainant and to the subject judge. 28 U.S.C. § 360(a)(1). However, the Rules do not entitle the complainant to a copy of the special committee's report.

In exercising their discretion regarding the role of the complainant, the special committee and the judicial council should protect the confidentiality of the complaint process. As a consequence, subsection (e) provides that a special committee may consider the degree to which a complainant has cooperated in preserving the confidentiality of the proceedings in determining what role beyond the minimum required by these Rules should be given to that complainant.

Rule 17. Special-Committee Report.

The committee must file with the judicial council a comprehensive report of its investigation, including findings and recommendations for council action. The report must be accompanied by a statement of the vote by which it was adopted, any separate or dissenting statements of committee members, and the record of any hearings held under Rule 14. A copy of the report and accompanying statement must be sent to the Judicial Conference Committee on Judicial Conduct and Disability.

COMMENT

This Rule is adapted from the Illustrative Rules and is self-explanatory. The provision for sending a copy of the special-committee report and accompanying statement to the Judicial Conference Committee is new.

ARTICLE V. JUDICIAL-COUNCIL REVIEW.

Rule 18. Petitions for Review of Chief Judge Dispositions Under Rule 11(c), (d), or (e).

(a) **Petitions for Review.** After the chief judge issues an order under Rule 11(c), (d), or (e), a complainant or subject judge may petition the judicial council of the circuit to review the order. By rules promulgated under 28 U.S.C. § 358, the judicial council may refer a petition for review filed under this Rule to a panel of no fewer than five members of the council, at least two of whom must be district judges.

(b) **When to File; Form; Where to File.** A petition for review must be filed in the office of the circuit clerk within 35 days of the date on the clerk's letter informing the parties of the chief judge's order. The petition should be in letter form, addressed to the circuit clerk, and in an envelope marked "Misconduct Petition" or "Disability Petition." The name of the subject judge must not be shown on the envelope. The letter should be typewritten or otherwise legible. It should begin with "I hereby petition the judicial council for review of ..." and state the reasons why the petition should be granted. It must be signed.

(c) **Receipt and Distribution of Petition.** A circuit clerk who receives a petition for review filed within the time allowed and in proper form must:

(1) acknowledge its receipt and send a copy to the complainant or subject judge, as the case may be;

(2) promptly distribute to each member of the judicial council, or its relevant panel, except for any member disqualified under Rule 25, or make available in the manner provided by local rule, the following materials:

(A) copies of the complaint;

(B) all materials obtained by the chief judge in connection with the inquiry;

(C) the chief judge's order disposing of the complaint;

(D) any memorandum in support of the chief judge's order;

(E) the petition for review; and

(F) an appropriate ballot;

(3) send the petition for review to the Judicial Conference Committee on Judicial Conduct and Disability. Unless the Judicial Conference Committee

requests them, the clerk will not send copies of the materials obtained by the chief judge.

(d) **Untimely Petition.** The clerk must refuse to accept a petition that is received after the deadline in (b).

(e) **Timely Petition Not in Proper Form.** When the clerk receives a petition filed within the time allowed but in a form that is improper to a degree that would substantially impair its consideration by the judicial council — such as a document that is ambiguous about whether it is intended to be a petition for review — the clerk must acknowledge its receipt, call the filer's attention to the deficiencies, and give the filer the opportunity to correct the deficiencies within 21 days of the date of the clerk's letter about the deficiencies or within the original deadline for filing the petition, whichever is later. If the deficiencies are corrected within the time allowed, the clerk will proceed according to paragraphs (a) and (c) of this Rule. If the deficiencies are not corrected, the clerk must reject the petition.

COMMENT

Rule 18 is adapted largely from the Illustrative Rules.

Subsection (a) permits a subject judge, as well as the complainant, to petition for review of a chief judge's order dismissing a complaint under Rule 11(c), or concluding that appropriate corrective action or intervening events have remedied or mooted the problems raised by the complaint pursuant to Rule 11(d) or (e). Although the subject judge may ostensibly be vindicated by the dismissal or conclusion of a complaint, a chief judge's order may include language disagreeable to the subject judge. For example, an order may dismiss a complaint, but state that the subject judge did in fact engage in misconduct. Accordingly, a subject judge may wish to object to the content of the order and is given the opportunity to petition the judicial council of the circuit for review.

Subsection (b) contains a time limit of thirty-five days to file a petition for review. It is important to establish a time limit on petitions for review of chief judges' dispositions in order to provide finality to the process. If the complaint requires an investigation, the investigation should proceed; if it does not, the subject judge should know that the matter is closed.

The standards for timely filing under the Federal Rules of Appellate Procedure should be applied to petitions for review. *See* Fed. R. App. P. 25(a)(2)(A) and (C).

Rule 18(e) provides for an automatic extension of the time limit imposed under subsection (b) if a person files a petition that is rejected for failure to comply with formal requirements.

Rule 19. Judicial-Council Disposition of Petitions for Review.

(a) **Rights of Subject Judge.** At any time after a complainant files a petition for review, the subject judge may file a written response with the circuit clerk. The clerk must promptly distribute copies of the response to each member of the judicial council or of the relevant panel, unless that member is disqualified under Rule 25. Copies must also be distributed to the chief judge, to the complainant, and to the Judicial Conference Committee on Judicial Conduct and Disability. The subject judge must not otherwise communicate with individual council members about the matter. The subject judge must be given copies of any communications to the judicial council from the complainant.

(b) **Judicial-Council Action.** After considering a petition for review and the materials before it, a judicial council may:

(1) affirm the chief judge's disposition by denying the petition;

(2) return the matter to the chief judge with directions to conduct a further inquiry under Rule 11(b) or to identify a complaint under Rule 5;

(3) return the matter to the chief judge with directions to appoint a special committee under Rule 11(f); or

(4) in exceptional circumstances, take other appropriate action.

(c) **Notice of Council Decision.** Copies of the judicial council's order, together with any accompanying memorandum in support of the order or separate concurring or dissenting statements, must be given to the complainant, the subject judge, and the Judicial Conference Committee on Judicial Conduct and Disability.

(d) **Memorandum of Council Decision.** If the council's order affirms the chief judge's disposition, a supporting memorandum must be prepared only if the judicial council concludes that there is a need to supplement the chief judge's explanation. A memorandum supporting a council order must not include the name of the complainant or the subject judge.

(e) **Review of Judicial-Council Decision.** If the judicial council's decision is adverse to the petitioner, and if no member of the council dissented on the ground that a special committee should be appointed under Rule 11(f), the complainant must be notified that he or she has no right to seek review of the decision. If there was a dissent, the petitioner must be informed that he or she can file a petition for review under Rule 21(b) solely on the issue of whether a special committee should be appointed.

(f) **Public Availability of Judicial-Council Decision.** Materials related to the council's decision must be made public to the extent, at the time, and in the manner set forth in Rule 24.

COMMENT

This Rule is largely adapted from the Act and is self-explanatory.

The council should ordinarily review the decision of the chief judge on the merits, treating the petition for review for all practical purposes as an appeal. The judicial council may respond to a petition by affirming the chief judge's order, remanding the matter, or, in exceptional cases, taking other appropriate action.

Rule 20. Judicial-Council Consideration of Reports and Recommendations of Special Committees.

(a) **Rights of Subject Judge.** Within 21 days after the filing of the report of a special committee, the subject judge may send a written response to the members of the judicial council. The judge must also be given an opportunity to present argument through counsel, written or oral, as determined by the council. The judge must not otherwise communicate with council members about the matter.

(b) **Judicial-Council Action.** (1) Discretionary actions. Subject to the judge's rights set forth in subsection (a), the judicial council may:

(A) dismiss the complaint because:

(i) even if the claim is true, the claimed conduct is not conduct prejudicial to the effective and expeditious administration of the business of the courts and does not indicate a mental or physical disability resulting in inability to discharge the duties of office;

(ii) the complaint is directly related to the merits of a decision or procedural ruling;

(iii) the facts on which the complaint is based have not been established; or

(iv) the complaint is otherwise not appropriate for consideration under 28 U.S.C. §§ 351-364.

(B) conclude the proceeding because appropriate corrective action has been taken or intervening events have made the proceeding unnecessary.

(C) refer the complaint to the Judicial Conference of the United States with the council's recommendations for action.

(D) take remedial action to ensure the effective and expeditious administration of the business of the courts, including:

(i) censuring or reprimanding the subject judge, either by private communication or by public announcement;

(ii) ordering that no new cases be assigned to the subject judge for a limited, fixed period;

(iii) in the case of a magistrate judge, ordering the chief judge of the district court to take action specified by the council, including the initiation of removal proceedings under 28 U.S.C. § 631(i) or 42 U.S.C. § 300aa—12(c)(2);

(iv) in the case of a bankruptcy judge, removing the judge from office under 28 U.S.C. § 152(e);

(v) in the case of a circuit or district judge, requesting the judge to retire voluntarily with the provision (if necessary) that ordinary length-of-service requirements will be waived; and

(vi) in the case of a circuit or district judge who is eligible to retire but does not do so, certifying the disability of the judge under 28 U.S.C. § 372(b) so that an additional judge may be appointed.

(E) take any combination of actions described in (b)(1)(A)-(D) of this Rule that is within its power.

(2) Mandatory actions. A judicial council must refer a complaint to the Judicial Conference if the council determines that a circuit judge or district judge may have engaged in conduct that:

(A) might constitute ground for impeachment; or

(B) in the interest of justice, is not amenable to resolution by the judicial council.

(c) **Inadequate Basis for Decision.** If the judicial council finds that a special committee's report, recommendations, and record provide an inadequate basis for decision, it may return the matter to the committee for further investigation and a new report, or it may conduct further investigation. If the judicial council decides to conduct further investigation, the subject judge must be given adequate prior notice in writing of that decision and of the general scope and purpose of the additional investigation. The judicial council's conduct of the additional investigation must generally accord with the procedures and powers set forth in Rules 13 through 16 for the conduct of an investigation by a special committee.

(d) **Council Vote.** Council action must be taken by a majority of those members of the council who are not disqualified. A decision to remove a bankruptcy judge from office requires a majority vote of all the members of the council.

(e) **Recommendation for Fee Reimbursement.** If the complaint has been finally dismissed or concluded under (b)(1)(A) or (B) of this Rule, and if the subject judge so requests, the judicial council may recommend that the Director of the Administrative Office of the United States Courts use funds appropriated to the Judiciary to reimburse the judge for reasonable expenses incurred during the investigation, when those expenses would not have been incurred but for the requirements of the Act and these Rules. Reasonable expenses include attorneys' fees and expenses related to a successful defense or prosecution of a proceeding under Rule 21(a) or (b).

(f) **Council Action.** Council action must be by written order. Unless the council finds that extraordinary reasons would make it contrary to the interests of justice, the order must be accompanied by a memorandum setting forth the factual determinations on which it is based and the reasons for the council action. The order and the supporting memorandum must be provided to the complainant, the subject judge, and the Judicial Conference Committee on Judicial Conduct and Disability. The complainant and the subject judge must be notified of any right to review of the judicial council's decision as provided in Rule 21(b).

COMMENT

This Rule is largely adapted from the Illustrative Rules.

Rule 20(a) provides that within twenty-one days after the filing of the report of a special committee, the subject judge may address a written response to all of the members of the judicial council. The subject judge must also be given an opportunity to present oral argument to the council, personally or through counsel. The subject judge may not otherwise communicate with council members about the matter.

Rule 20(c) provides that if the judicial council decides to conduct an additional investigation, the subject judge must be given adequate prior notice in writing of that decision and of the general scope and purpose of the additional investigation. The conduct of the investigation will be generally in accordance with the procedures set forth in Rules 13 through 16 for the conduct of an investigation by a special committee. However, if hearings are held, the council may limit testimony or the presentation of evidence to avoid unnecessary repetition of testimony and evidence before the special committee.

Rule 20(d) provides that council action must be taken by a majority of those members of the council who are not disqualified, except that a decision to remove a bankruptcy judge from office requires a majority of all the members of the council as required by 28 U.S.C. § 152(e). However, it is inappropriate to apply a similar rule to the less severe actions that a judicial council may take under the Act. If some members of the council are disqualified in the matter, their disqualification should not be given the effect of a vote against council action.

With regard to Rule 20(e), the judicial council, on the request of the subject judge, may recommend to the Director of the Administrative Office of the United States Courts that the subject judge be reimbursed for reasonable expenses, including attorneys' fees, incurred. The judicial council has the authority to recommend such reimbursement where, after investigation by a special committee, the complaint has been finally dismissed or concluded under subsection (b)(1)(A) or (B) of this Rule. It is contemplated that such reimbursement may be provided for the successful prosecution or defense of a proceeding under Rule 21(a) or (b), in other words, one that results in a Rule 20(b)(1)(A) or (B) dismissal or conclusion.

Rule 20(f) requires that council action normally be supported with a memorandum of factual determinations and reasons and that notice of the action be given to the complainant and the subject judge. Rule 20(f) also requires that the notification to the complainant and the subject judge include notice of any right to petition for review of the council's decision under Rule 21(b).

ARTICLE VI. REVIEW BY JUDICIAL CONFERENCE COMMITTEE ON CONDUCT AND DISABILITY.

Rule 21. Committee on Judicial Conduct and Disability.

(a) **Review by Committee.** The Committee on Judicial Conduct and Disability, consisting of seven members, considers and disposes of all petitions for review under (b) of this Rule, in conformity with the Committee's jurisdictional statement. Its disposition of petitions for review is ordinarily final. The Judicial Conference of the United States may, in its sole discretion, review any such Committee decision, but a complainant or subject judge does not have a right to this review.

(b) **Reviewable Matters.** (1) Upon petition. A complainant or subject judge may petition the Committee for review of a judicial-council order entered in accordance with:

(A) Rule 20(b)(1)(A), (B), (D), or (E); or

(B) Rule 19(b)(1) or (4) if one or more members of the judicial council dissented from the order on the ground that a special committee should be appointed under Rule 11(f); in that event, the Committee's review will be limited to the issue of whether a special committee should be appointed.

(2) Upon Committee's initiative. At its initiative and in its sole discretion, the Committee may review any judicial-council order entered under Rule 19(b)(1) or (4), but only to determine whether a special committee should be appointed. Before undertaking the review, the Committee must invite that judicial council to explain why it believes the appointment of a special committee is unnecessary, unless the reasons are clearly stated in the judicial council's order denying the petition for review. If the Committee believes that it would benefit from a submission by the subject judge, it may issue an appropriate request. If the Committee determines that a special committee should be appointed, the Committee must issue a written decision giving its reasons.

(c) **Committee Vote.** Any member of the Committee from the same circuit as the subject judge is disqualified from considering or voting on a petition for review. Committee decisions under (b) of this Rule must be by majority vote of the qualified Committee members. If only six members are qualified to vote on a petition for review, the decision must be made by a majority of a panel of five members drawn from a randomly selected list that rotates after each decision by a panel drawn from the list. The members who will determine the petition must be selected based on committee membership as of the date on which the petition is received. Those members selected to hear the petition should serve in that capacity until final disposition of the petition, whether or not their term of committee membership has ended. If only four members are qualified to vote, the Chief Justice must appoint, if available, an ex-member of the Committee or, if not, another United States judge to consider the petition.

(d) **Additional Investigation.** Except in extraordinary circumstances, the Committee will not conduct an additional investigation. The Committee may return the matter to the judicial council with directions to undertake an additional investigation. If the Committee conducts an additional investigation, it will exercise the powers of the Judicial Conference under 28 U.S.C. § 331.

(e) **Oral Argument; Personal Appearance.** There is ordinarily no oral argument or personal appearance before the Committee. In its discretion, the Committee may permit written submissions from the complainant or subject judge.

(f) **Committee Decisions.** Committee decisions under this Rule must be transmitted promptly to the Judicial Conference of the United States. Other distribution will be by the Administrative Office at the direction of the Committee chair.

(g) **Finality.** All orders of the Judicial Conference or of the Committee (when the Conference does not exercise its power of review) are final.

COMMENT

This Rule is largely self-explanatory.

Rule 21(a) is intended to clarify that the delegation of power to the Judicial Conference Committee on Judicial Conduct and Disability to dispose of petitions does not preclude review of such dispositions by the Conference. However, there is no right to such review in any party.

Rules 21(b)(1)(B) and (b)(2) are intended to fill a jurisdictional gap as to review of dismissals or conclusions of complaints under Rule 19(b)(1) or (4). Where one or more members of a judicial council reviewing a petition have dissented on the ground that a special committee should have been appointed, the complainant or subject judge has the right to petition for review by the Committee but only as to that issue. Under Rule 21(b)(2), the Judicial Conference Committee on Judicial Conduct and Disability may review such a dismissal or conclusion in its sole discretion, whether or not

such a dissent occurred, and only as to the appointment of a special committee. No party has a right to such review, and such review will be rare.

Rule 21(c) provides for review only by Committee members from circuits other than that of the subject judge. To avoid tie votes, the Committee will decide petitions for review by rotating panels of five when only six members are qualified. If only four members are qualified, the Chief Justice must appoint an additional judge to consider that petition for review.

Under this Rule, all Committee decisions are final in that they are unreviewable unless the Judicial Conference, in its discretion, decides to review a decision. Committee decisions, however, do not necessarily constitute final action on a complaint for purposes of Rule 24.

Rule 22. Procedures for Review.

(a) **Filing a Petition for Review.** A petition for review of a judicial-council decision may be filed by sending a brief written statement to the Judicial Conference Committee on Judicial Conduct and Disability, addressed to:

> Judicial Conference Committee on Judicial Conduct and Disability
> Attn: Office of General Counsel
> Administrative Office of the United States Courts
> One Columbus Circle, NE
> Washington, D.C. 20544

The Administrative Office will send a copy of the petition to the complainant or subject judge, as the case may be.

(b) **Form and Contents of Petition for Review.** No particular form is required. The petition must contain a short statement of the basic facts underlying the complaint, the history of its consideration before the appropriate judicial council, a copy of the judicial council's decision, and the grounds on which the petitioner seeks review. The petition for review must specify the date and docket number of the judicial-council order for which review is sought. The petitioner may attach any documents or correspondence arising in the course of the proceeding before the judicial council or its special committee. A petition should not normally exceed 20 pages plus necessary attachments.

(c) **Time.** A petition must be submitted within 63 days of the date of the order for which review is sought.

(d) **Copies.** Seven copies of the petition for review must be submitted, at least one of which must be signed by the petitioner or his or her attorney. If the petitioner submits a signed declaration of inability to pay the expense of duplicating the petition, the Administrative Office must accept the original petition and must reproduce copies at its expense.

(e) **Action on Receipt of Petition for Review.** The Administrative Office must acknowledge receipt of a petition for review submitted under this Rule, notify the chair of the Judicial Conference Committee on Judicial Conduct and Disability, and distribute the petition to the members of the Committee for their deliberation.

COMMENT

Rule 22 is self-explanatory.

ARTICLE VII. MISCELLANEOUS RULES.

Rule 23. Confidentiality.

(a) **General Rule.** The consideration of a complaint by the chief judge, a special committee, the judicial council, or the Judicial Conference Committee on Judicial Conduct and Disability is confidential. Information about this consideration must not be disclosed by any judge or employee of the judicial branch or by any person who records or transcribes testimony except as allowed by these Rules. In extraordinary circumstances, a chief judge may disclose the existence of a proceeding under these Rules when necessary to maintain public confidence in the federal judiciary's ability to redress misconduct or disability.

(b) **Files.** All files related to complaints must be separately maintained with appropriate security precautions to ensure confidentiality.

(c) **Disclosure in Decisions.** Except as otherwise provided in Rule 24, written decisions of the chief judge, the judicial council, or the Judicial Conference Committee on Judicial Conduct and Disability, and dissenting opinions or separate statements of members of the council or Committee may contain information and exhibits that the authors consider appropriate for inclusion, and the information and exhibits may be made public.

(d) **Availability to Judicial Conference.** On request of the Judicial Conference or its Committee on Judicial Conduct and Disability, the circuit clerk must furnish any requested records related to a complaint. For auditing purposes, the circuit clerk must provide access to the Committee to records of proceedings under the Act at the site where the records are kept.

(e) **Availability to District Court.** If the judicial council directs the initiation of proceedings for removal of a magistrate judge under Rule

20(b)(1)(D)(iii), the circuit clerk must provide to the chief judge of the district court copies of the report of the special committee and any other documents and records that were before the judicial council at the time of its decision. On request of the chief judge of the district court, the judicial council may authorize release to that chief judge of any other records relating to the investigation.

(f) **Impeachment Proceedings.** If the Judicial Conference determines that consideration of impeachment may be warranted, it must transmit the record of all relevant proceedings to the Speaker of the House of Representatives.

(g) **Subject Judge's Consent.** If both the subject judge and the chief judge consent in writing, any materials from the files may be disclosed to any person. In any such disclosure, the chief judge may require that the identity of the complainant, or of witnesses in an investigation conducted by a chief judge, a special committee, or the judicial council, not be revealed.

(h) **Disclosure in Special Circumstances.** The Judicial Conference, its Committee on Judicial Conduct and Disability, or a judicial council may authorize disclosure of information about the consideration of a complaint, including the papers, documents, and transcripts relating to the investigation, to the extent that disclosure is justified by special circumstances and is not prohibited by the Act. Disclosure may be made to judicial researchers engaged in the study or evaluation of experience under the Act and related modes of judicial discipline, but only where the study or evaluation has been specifically approved by the Judicial Conference or by the Judicial Conference Committee on Judicial Conduct and Disability. Appropriate steps must be taken to protect the identities of the subject judge, the complainant, and witnesses from public disclosure. Other appropriate safeguards to protect against the dissemination of confidential information may be imposed.

(i) **Disclosure of Identity by Subject Judge.** Nothing in this Rule precludes the subject judge from acknowledging that he or she is the judge referred to in documents made public under Rule 24.

(j) **Assistance and Consultation.** Nothing in this Rule precludes the chief judge or judicial council acting on a complaint filed under the Act from seeking the help of qualified staff or from consulting other judges who may be helpful in the disposition of the complaint.

COMMENT

Rule 23 was adapted from the Illustrative Rules.

The Act applies a rule of confidentiality to "papers, documents, and records of proceedings related to investigations conducted under this chapter" and states that they may not be disclosed "by any person in any proceeding," with enumerated exceptions. 28 U.S.C. § 360(a). Three questions arise: Who is bound by the confidentiality rule, what proceedings are subject to the rule, and who is within the circle of people who may have access to information without breaching the rule?

With regard to the first question, Rule 23(a) provides that judges, employees of the judicial branch, and those persons involved in recording proceedings and preparing transcripts are obliged to respect the confidentiality requirement. This of course includes subject judges who do not consent to identification under Rule 23(i).

With regard to the second question, Rule 23(a) applies the rule of confidentiality broadly to consideration of a complaint at any stage.

With regard to the third question, there is no barrier of confidentiality among a chief judge, judicial council, the Judicial Conference, and the Judicial Conference Committee on Judicial Conduct and Disability. Each may have access to any of the confidential records for use in their consideration of a referred matter, a petition for review, or monitoring the administration of the Act. A district court may have similar access if the judicial council orders the district court to initiate proceedings to remove a magistrate judge from office, and Rule 23(e) so provides.

In extraordinary circumstances, a chief judge may disclose the existence of a proceeding under these Rules. The disclosure of such information in high-visibility or controversial cases is to reassure the public that the federal judiciary is capable of redressing judicial misconduct or disability. Moreover, the confidentiality requirement does not prevent the chief judge from "communicat[ing] orally or in writing with ... [persons] who may have knowledge of the matter," as part of a limited inquiry conducted by the chief judge under Rule 11(b).

Rule 23 recognizes that there must be some exceptions to the Act's confidentiality requirement. For example, the Act requires that certain orders and the reasons for them must be made public. 28 U.S.C. § 360(b). Rule 23(c) makes it explicit that memoranda supporting chief judge and council orders, as well as dissenting opinions and separate statements, may contain references to information that would otherwise be confidential and that such information may be made public. However, subsection (c) is subject to Rule 24(a) which provides the general rule regarding the public availability of decisions. For example, the name of a subject judge cannot be made public in a decision if disclosure of the name is prohibited by that Rule.

The Act makes clear that there is a barrier of confidentiality between the judicial branch and the legislative. It provides that material may be disclosed to Congress only if it is believed necessary to an impeachment investigation or trial of a judge. 28 U.S.C. § 360(a)(2). Accordingly, Section 355(b) of the Act requires the Judicial Conference to transmit the record of the proceeding to the House of Representatives if the Conference believes that impeachment of a subject judge may be appropriate. Rule 23(f) implements this requirement.

The Act provides that confidential materials may be disclosed if authorized in writing by the subject judge and by the chief judge. 28 U.S.C. § 360(a)(3). Rule 23(g) implements this requirement. Once the subject judge has consented to the disclosure of confidential materials related to a complaint, the chief judge ordinarily will refuse consent only to the extent necessary to protect the confidentiality interests of the complainant or of witnesses

who have testified in investigatory proceedings or who have provided information in response to a limited inquiry undertaken pursuant to Rule 11. It will generally be necessary, therefore, for the chief judge to require that the identities of the complainant or of such witnesses, as well as any identifying information, be shielded in any materials disclosed, except insofar as the chief judge has secured the consent of the complainant or of a particular witness to disclosure, or there is a demonstrated need for disclosure of the information that, in the judgment of the chief judge, outweighs the confidentiality interest of the complainant or of a particular witness (as may be the case where the complainant is delusional or where the complainant or a particular witness has already demonstrated a lack of concern about maintaining the confidentiality of the proceedings).

Rule 23(h) permits disclosure of additional information in circumstances not enumerated. For example, disclosure may be appropriate to permit a prosecution for perjury based on testimony given before a special committee. Another example might involve evidence of criminal conduct by a judge discovered by a special committee.

Subsection (h) also permits the authorization of disclosure of information about the consideration of a complaint, including the papers, documents, and transcripts relating to the investigation, to judicial researchers engaged in the study or evaluation of experience under the Act and related modes of judicial discipline. The Rule envisions disclosure of information from the official record of complaint proceedings to a limited category of persons for appropriately authorized research purposes only, and with appropriate safeguards to protect individual identities in any published research results that ensue. In authorizing disclosure, the judicial council may refuse to release particular materials when such release would be contrary to the interests of justice, or that constitute purely internal communications. The Rule does not envision disclosure of purely internal communications between judges and their colleagues and staff.

Under Rule 23(j), chief judges and judicial councils may seek staff assistance or consult with other judges who may be helpful in the process of complaint disposition; the confidentiality requirement does not preclude this. The chief judge, for example, may properly seek the advice and assistance of another judge who the chief judge deems to be in the best position to communicate with the subject judge in an attempt to bring about corrective action. As another example, a new chief judge may wish to confer with a predecessor to learn how similar complaints have been handled. In consulting with other judges, of course, the chief

judge should disclose information regarding
the complaint only to the extent the chief judge
deems necessary under the circumstances.

Rule 24. Public Availability of Decisions.

(a) **General Rule; Specific Cases.** When final action has been taken on a complaint and it is no longer subject to review, all orders entered by the chief judge and judicial council, including any supporting memoranda and any dissenting opinions or separate statements by members of the judicial council, must be made public, with the following exceptions:

(1) if the complaint is finally dismissed under Rule 11(c) without the appointment of a special committee, or if it is concluded under Rule 11(d) because of voluntary corrective action, the publicly available materials must not disclose the name of the subject judge without his or her consent.

(2) if the complaint is concluded because of intervening events, or dismissed at any time after a special committee is appointed, the judicial council must determine whether the name of the subject judge should be disclosed.

(3) if the complaint is finally disposed of by a privately communicated censure or reprimand, the publicly available materials must not disclose either the name of the subject judge or the text of the reprimand.

(4) if the complaint is finally disposed of under Rule 20(b)(1)(D) by any action other than private censure or reprimand, the text of the dispositive order must be included in the materials made public, and the name of the subject judge must be disclosed.

(5) the name of the complainant must not be disclosed in materials made public under this Rule unless the chief judge orders disclosure.

(b) **Manner of Making Public.** The orders described in (a) must be made public by placing them in a publicly accessible file in the office of the circuit clerk or by placing the orders on the court's public website. If the orders appear to have precedential value, the chief judge may cause them to be published. In addition, the Judicial Conference Committee on Judicial Conduct and Disability will make available on the Federal Judiciary's website, www.uscourts.gov, selected illustrative orders described in paragraph (a), appropriately redacted, to provide additional information to the public on how complaints are addressed under the Act.

(c) **Orders of Judicial Conference Committee.** Orders of this Committee constituting final action in a complaint proceeding arising from a particular circuit will be made available to the public in the office of the clerk of the relevant court of appeals. The Committee will also make such orders available on the Federal Judiciary's website, www.uscourts.gov. When authorized by the Committee, other orders related to complaint proceedings will similarly be made available.

(d) **Complaints Referred to the Judicial Conference of the United States.** If a complaint is referred to the Judicial Conference under Rule 20(b)(1)(C) or 20(b)(2), materials relating to the complaint will be made public only if ordered by the Judicial Conference.

COMMENT

Rule 24 is adapted from the Illustrative Rules and the recommendations of the Breyer Committee.

The Act requires the circuits to make available only written orders of a judicial council or the Judicial Conference imposing some form of sanction. 28 U.S.C. § 360(b). The Judicial Conference, however, has long recognized the desirability of public availability of a broader range of orders and other materials. In 1994, the Judicial Conference "urge[d] all circuits and courts covered by the Act to submit to the West Publishing Company, for publication in Federal Reporter 3d, and to Lexis all orders issued pursuant to [the Act] that are deemed by the issuing circuit or court to have significant precedential value to other circuits and courts covered by the Act." Report of the Proceedings of the Judicial Conference of the United States, Mar. 1994, at 28. Following this recommendation, the 2000 revision of the Illustrative Rules contained a public availability provision very similar to Rule 24. In 2002, the Judicial Conference again voted to encourage the circuits "to submit non-routine public orders disposing of complaints of judicial misconduct or disability for publication by on-line and print services." Report of the Proceedings of the Judicial Conference of the United States, Sept. 2002, at 58. The Breyer Committee Report further emphasized that "[p]osting such orders on the judicial branch's public website would not only benefit judges directly, it would also encourage scholarly commentary and analysis of the orders." Breyer Committee Report, 239 F.R.D. at 216. With these considerations in mind, Rule 24 provides for public availability of a wide range of materials.

Rule 24 provides for public availability of orders of the chief judge, the judicial council, and the Judicial Conference Committee on Judicial Conduct and Disability and the texts of any memoranda supporting their orders, together with any dissenting opinions or separate statements by members of the judicial council. However, these orders and memoranda are to be made public only when final action on the complaint has been taken and

any right of review has been exhausted. The provision that decisions will be made public only after final action has been taken is designed in part to avoid public disclosure of the existence of pending proceedings. Whether the name of the subject judge is disclosed will then depend on the nature of the final action. If the final action is an order predicated on a finding of misconduct or disability (other than a privately communicated censure or reprimand) the name of the judge must be made public. If the final action is dismissal of the complaint, the name of the subject judge must not be disclosed. Rule 24(a)(1) provides that where a proceeding is concluded under Rule 11(d) by the chief judge on the basis of voluntary corrective action, the name of the subject judge must not be disclosed. Shielding the name of the subject judge in this circumstance should encourage informal disposition.

If a complaint is dismissed as moot, or because intervening events have made action on the complaint unnecessary, after appointment of a special committee, Rule 24(a)(2) allows the judicial council to determine whether the subject judge will be identified. In such a case, no final decision has been rendered on the merits, but it may be in the public interest — particularly if a judicial officer resigns in the course of an investigation — to make the identity of the judge known.

Once a special committee has been appointed, and a proceeding is concluded by the full council on the basis of a remedial order of the council, Rule 24(a)(4) provides for disclosure of the name of the subject judge.

Finally, Rule 24(a)(5) provides that the identity of the complainant will be disclosed only if the chief judge so orders. Identifying the complainant when the subject judge is not identified would increase the likelihood that the identity of the subject judge would become publicly known, thus circumventing the policy of nondisclosure. It may not always be practicable to shield the complainant's identity while making public disclosure of the judicial council's order and supporting memoranda; in some circumstances, moreover, the complainant may consent to public identification.

Rule 25. Disqualification.

(a) **General Rule.** Any judge is disqualified from participating in any proceeding under these Rules if the judge, in his or her discretion, concludes that circumstances warrant disqualification. If the complaint is filed by a judge, that judge is disqualified from participating in any consideration of the complaint except to the extent that these Rules provide for a complainant's participation. A chief judge who has identified a complaint under Rule 5 is not automatically disqualified from considering the complaint.

(b) **Subject Judge.** A subject judge is disqualified from considering the complaint except to the extent that these Rules provide for participation by a subject judge.

(c) **Chief Judge Not Disqualified from Considering a Petition for Review of a Chief Judge's Order.** If a petition for review of a chief judge's order entered under Rule 11(c), (d), or (e) is filed with the judicial council in accordance with Rule 18, the chief judge is not disqualified from participating in the council's consideration of the petition.

(d) **Member of Special Committee Not Disqualified.** A member of the judicial council who serves on a special committee, including the chief judge, is not disqualified from participating in council consideration of the committee's report.

(e) **Subject Judge's Disqualification After Appointment of a Special Committee.** Upon appointment of a special committee, the subject judge is automatically disqualified from participating in any proceeding arising under the Act or these Rules as a member of any special committee, the judicial council of the circuit, the Judicial Conference of the United States, and the Judicial Conference Committee on Judicial Conduct and Disability. The disqualification continues until all proceedings on the complaint against the subject judge are finally terminated with no further right of review.

(f) **Substitute for Disqualified Chief Judge.** If the chief judge is disqualified from participating in consideration of the complaint, the duties and responsibilities of the chief judge under these Rules must be assigned to the most-senior active circuit judge not disqualified. If all circuit judges in regular active service are disqualified, the judicial council may determine whether to request a transfer under Rule 26, or, in the interest of sound judicial administration, to permit the chief judge to dispose of the complaint on the merits. Members of the judicial council who are named in the complaint may participate in this determination if necessary to obtain a quorum of the judicial council.

(g) **Judicial-Council Action When Multiple Judges Are Disqualified.** Notwithstanding any other provision in these Rules to the contrary,

(1) a member of the judicial council who is a subject judge may participate in its disposition if:

(A) participation by one or more subject judges is necessary to obtain a quorum of the judicial council;

(B) the judicial council finds that the lack of a quorum is due to the naming of one or more judges in the complaint for the purpose of disqualifying that judge or judges, or to the naming of one or more judges based on their participation in a decision excluded from the definition of misconduct under Rule 3(h)(3); and

(C) the judicial council votes that it is necessary, appropriate, and in the interest of sound judicial administration that one or more subject judges be eligible to act.

(2) otherwise disqualified members may participate in votes taken under (g)(1)(B) and (g)(1)(C).

(h) **Disqualification of Members of the Judicial Conference Committee.** No member of the Judicial Conference Committee on Judicial Conduct and Disability is disqualified from participating in any proceeding under the Act or these Rules because of consultations with a chief judge, a member of a special committee, or a member of a judicial council about the interpretation or application of the Act or these Rules, unless the member believes that the consultation would prevent fair-minded participation.

COMMENT

Rule 25 is adapted from the Illustrative Rules.

Subsection (a) provides the general rule for disqualification. Of course, a judge is not disqualified simply because the subject judge is on the same court. However, this subsection recognizes that there may be cases in which an appearance of bias or prejudice is created by circumstances other than an association with the subject judge as a colleague. For example, a judge may have a familial relationship with a complainant or subject judge. When such circumstances exist, a judge may, in his or her discretion, conclude that disqualification is warranted.

Subsection (e) makes it clear that the disqualification of the subject judge relates only to the subject judge's participation in any proceeding arising under the Act or these Rules as a member of a special committee, judicial council, Judicial Conference, or the Judicial Conference Committee. The Illustrative Rule, based on Section 359(a) of the Act, is ambiguous and could be read to disqualify a subject judge from service of any kind on each of the bodies mentioned. This is undoubtedly not the intent of the Act; such a disqualification would be anomalous in light of the Act's allowing a subject judge to continue to decide cases and to continue to exercise the powers of chief circuit or district judge. It would also create a substantial deterrence to the appointment of special committees, particularly where a special committee is needed solely because the chief judge may not decide matters of credibility in his or her review under Rule 11.

While a subject judge is barred by Rule 25(b) from participating in the disposition of the complaint in which he or she is named, Rule 25(e) recognizes that participation in proceedings arising under the Act or these Rules by a judge who is the subject of a special committee investigation may lead to an appearance of self-interest in creating substantive and procedural precedents governing such proceedings; Rule 25(e) bars such participation.

Under the Act, a complaint against the chief judge is to be handled by "that circuit judge in regular active service next senior in date of commission." 28 U.S.C. § 351(c). Rule 25(f) provides that seniority among judges other than the chief judge is to be determined by date of commission, with the result that complaints against the chief judge may be routed to a former chief judge or other judge who was appointed earlier than the chief judge. The Rules do not purport to prescribe who is to preside over meetings of the judicial council. Consequently, where the presiding member of the judicial council is disqualified from participating under these Rules, the order of precedence prescribed by Rule 25(f) for performing "the duties and responsibilities of the chief circuit judge under these Rules" does not apply to determine the acting presiding member of the judicial council. That is a matter left to the internal rules or operating practices of each judicial council. In most cases the most senior active circuit judge who is a member of the judicial council and who is not disqualified will preside.

Sometimes a single complaint is filed against a large group of judges. If the normal disqualification rules are observed in such a case, no court of appeals judge can serve as acting chief judge of the circuit, and the judicial council will be without appellate members. Where the complaint is against all circuit and district judges, under normal rules no member of the judicial council can perform the duties assigned to the council under the statute.

A similar problem is created by successive complaints arising out of the same underlying grievance. For example, a complainant files a complaint against a district judge based on alleged misconduct, and the complaint is dismissed by the chief judge under the statute. The complainant may then file a complaint against the chief judge for dismissing the first complaint, and when that complaint is dismissed by the next senior judge, still a third complaint may be filed. The threat is that the complainant will bump down the seniority ladder until, once again, there is no member of the court of appeals who can serve as acting chief judge for the purpose of the next complaint. Similarly, complaints involving the merits of litigation may involve a series of decisions in which many judges participated or in which a rehearing en banc was denied by the court of appeals, and the complaint may name a majority of the judicial council as subject judges.

In recognition that these multiple-judge complaints are virtually always meritless, the judicial council is given discretion to determine: (1) whether it is necessary, appropriate, and in the interest of sound judicial administration to permit the chief judge to dispose of a complaint where it would otherwise be impossible for any active circuit judge in the circuit to act, and (2) whether it is necessary, appropriate, and in the interest of sound judicial administration, after appropriate findings as to need and justification are made, to permit subject judges of the judicial council to participate in the disposition of a petition for review where it would otherwise be impossible to obtain a quorum.

Applying a rule of necessity in these situations is consistent with the appearance of justice. *See, e.g., In re Complaint of Doe*, 2 F.3d 308 (8th Cir. Jud. Council 1993) (invoking the rule of necessity); *In re Complaint of Judicial Misconduct*, No. 91-80464 (9th Cir. Jud. Council 1992) (same). There is no unfairness in permitting the chief judge to dispose of a patently insubstantial complaint that names all active circuit judges in the circuit.

Similarly, there is no unfairness in permitting subject judges, in these circumstances, to participate in the review of a chief judge's dismissal of an insubstantial complaint. The remaining option is to assign the matter to another body. Among other alternatives, the council may request a transfer of the petition under Rule 26. Given the administrative inconvenience and delay involved in these alternatives, it is desirable to request a transfer only if the judicial council determines that the petition is substantial enough to warrant such action.

In the unlikely event that a quorum of the judicial council cannot be obtained to consider the report of a special committee, it would normally be necessary to request a transfer under Rule 26.

Rule 25(h) recognizes that the jurisdictional statement of the Judicial Conference Committee contemplates consultation between members of the Committee and judicial participants in proceedings under the Act and these Rules. Such consultation should not automatically preclude participation by a member in that proceeding.

Rule 26. Transfer to Another Judicial Council.

In exceptional circumstances, a chief judge or a judicial council may ask the Chief Justice to transfer a proceeding based on a complaint identified under Rule 5 or filed under Rule 6 to the judicial council of another circuit. The request for a transfer may be made at any stage of the proceeding before a reference to the Judicial Conference under Rule 20(b)(1)(C) or 20(b)(2) or a petition for review is filed under Rule 22. Upon receiving such a request, the Chief Justice may refuse the request or select the transferee judicial council, which may then exercise the powers of a judicial council under these Rules.

COMMENT

Rule 26 is new; it implements the Breyer Committee's recommended use of transfers. Breyer Committee Report, 239 F.R.D. at 214-15.

Rule 26 authorizes the transfer of a complaint proceeding to another judicial council selected by the Chief Justice. Such transfers may be appropriate, for example, in the case of a serious complaint where there are multiple disqualifications among the original council, where the issues are highly visible and a local disposition may weaken public confidence in the process, where internal tensions arising in the council as a result of the complaint render disposition by a less involved council appropriate, or where a complaint calls into question policies or governance of the home court of appeals. The power to effect a transfer is lodged in the Chief Justice to avoid disputes in a council over where to transfer a sensitive matter and to ensure that the transferee council accepts the matter.

Upon receipt of a transferred proceeding, the transferee council shall determine the proper stage at which to begin consideration of the complaint — for example, reference to the transferee chief judge, appointment of a special committee, etc.

Rule 27. Withdrawal of Complaints and Petitions for Review.

(a) **Complaint Pending Before Chief Judge.** With the chief judge's consent, a complainant may withdraw a complaint that is before the chief judge for a decision under Rule 11. The withdrawal of a complaint will not prevent a chief judge from identifying or having to identify a complaint under Rule 5 based on the withdrawn complaint.

(b) **Complaint Pending before Special Committee or Judicial Council.** After a complaint has been referred to a special committee for investigation and before the committee files its report, the complainant may withdraw the complaint only with the consent of both the subject judge and either the special committee or the judicial council.

(c) **Petition for Review.** A petition for review addressed to a judicial council under Rule 18, or the Judicial Conference Committee on Judicial Conduct and Disability under Rule 22 may be withdrawn if no action on the petition has been taken.

COMMENT

Rule 27 is adapted from the Illustrative Rules and treats the complaint proceeding, once begun, as a matter of public business rather than as the property of the complainant. Accordingly, the chief judge or the judicial council remains responsible for addressing any complaint under the Act, even a complaint that has been formally withdrawn by the complainant.

Under subsection 27(a), a complaint pending before the chief judge may be withdrawn if the chief judge consents. Where the complaint clearly lacked merit, the chief judge may accordingly be saved the burden of preparing a formal order and supporting memorandum. However, the chief judge may, or be obligated under Rule 5, to identify a complaint based on allegations in a withdrawn complaint.

If the chief judge appoints a special committee, Rule 27(b) provides that the complaint may be withdrawn only with the consent of both the body before which it is pending (the special committee or the judicial council) and the subject judge. Once a complaint has reached the stage of appointment of a special committee, a resolution of the issues may be necessary to preserve public confidence. Moreover, the subject judge is given the right to insist that the matter be resolved on the merits, thereby eliminating any ambiguity that might remain if the proceeding were terminated by withdrawal of the complaint.

With regard to all petitions for review, Rule 27(c) grants the petitioner unrestricted authority to withdraw the petition. It is thought that the public's interest in the proceeding is adequately protected, because there will necessarily have been a decision by the chief judge and often by the judicial council as well in such a case.

Rule 28. Availability of Rules and Forms.

These Rules and copies of the complaint form as provided in Rule 6(a) must be available without charge in the office of the clerk of each court of appeals, district court, bankruptcy court, or other federal court whose judges are subject to the Act. Each court must also make these Rules and the complaint form available on the court's website, or provide an Internet link to the Rules and complaint form that are available on the appropriate court of appeals' website.

Rule 29. Effective Date.

These Rules will become effective 30 days after promulgation by the Judicial Conference of the United States.

Form JUDICIAL-CONDUCT PROCEEDINGS

APPENDIX

Judicial Council of the _____ Circuit

COMPLAINT OF JUDICIAL MISCONDUCT OR DISABILITY

To begin the complaint process, complete this form and prepare the brief statement of facts described in item 5 (below). The RULES FOR JUDICIAL-CONDUCT AND JUDICIAL-DISABILITY PROCEEDINGS, adopted by the Judicial Conference of the United States, contain information on what to include in a complaint (Rule 6), where to file a complaint (Rule 7), and other important matters. The rules are available in federal court clerks' offices, on individual federal courts' Web sites, and on www.uscourts.gov.

Your complaint (this form and the statement of facts) should be typewritten and must be legible. For the number of copies to file, consult the local rules or clerk's office of the court in which your complaint is required to be filed. Enclose each copy of the complaint in an envelope marked "COMPLAINT OF MIS-CONDUCT" or "COMPLAINT OF DISABILITY" and submit it to the appropriate clerk of court. **Do not put the name of any judge on the envelope.**

1. Name of Complainant: _____
   Contact Address: _____
   _____
   _____

   Daytime telephone: (____) _____

2. Name(s) of Judge(s): _____
   Court: _____

3. Does this complaint concern the behavior of the judge(s) in a particular lawsuit or lawsuits?
   [ ] Yes   [ ] No
   If "yes," give the following information about each lawsuit:
   Court: _____
   Case Number: _____
   Docket number of any appeal to the _____ Circuit: _____
   Are (were) you a party or lawyer in the lawsuit?
   [ ] Party   [ ] Lawyer   [ ] Neither
   If you are (were) a party and have (had) a lawyer, give the lawyer's name, address, and telephone number:
   _____
   _____
   _____

4. Have you filed any lawsuits against the judge?
   [ ] Yes   [ ] No
   If "yes," give the following information about each lawsuit:
   Court: _____
   Case number: _____

1364

Present status of lawsuit: _____

Name, address, and telephone number of your lawyer for the lawsuit against the judge:

_____

_____

_____

Court to which any appeal has been taken in the lawsuit against the judge:

_____

Docket number of the appeal: _____

Present status of the appeal: _____

5. **Brief Statement of Facts.** Attach a brief statement of the specific facts on which the claim of judicial misconduct or disability is based. Include what happened, when and where it happened, and any information that would help an investigator check the facts. If the complaint alleges judicial disability, also include any additional facts that form the basis of that allegation.

6. **Declaration and signature:**

I declare under penalty of perjury that the statements made in this complaint are true and correct to the best of my knowledge.

(Signature) _____ (Date) _____

Index to Rules for Judicial-Conduct and Judicial-Disability Proceedings

INDEX

INDEX

RULES OF THE UNITED STATES DISTRICT COURT FOR THE DISTRICT OF MARYLAND

As amended, July 2001; August 16, 2004; January 1, 2008; December 1, 2009; July 1, 2010; July 1, 2011.

I. Civil.

II. Criminal.

III. United States Magistrate Judges.

IV. Bankruptcy Proceedings.

V. Court Administration and Security.

VI. Miscellaneous.

VII. Attorney Admission, Assistance and Discipline.

VIII. Patents.

Editor's note. — These Rules supplement the Federal Rules of Civil Procedure, the Federal Rules of Criminal Procedure, the Supplemental Rules for Certain Admiralty and Maritime Claims, Rules of Procedure for the Trial of Misdemeanors before United States Magistrates and the Bankruptcy Rules.

RULES OF U.S. DISTRICT COURT (MD)

CROSS-REFERENCE TO UNIFORM NUMBERING SYSTEM

I. Scope of Rules

RULES OF U.S. DISTRICT COURT (MD)

RULES OF U.S. DISTRICT COURT (MD)

I. CIVIL.

Rule 101. Counsel.

1. **Who May Appear as Counsel; Who May Appear Without Counsel.**
a. Generally. Except as otherwise provided in this Rule and in L.R. 112.3 and 28 U.S.C. § 515, only members of the Bar of this Court may appear as counsel in civil cases. Individuals who are parties in civil cases may only represent themselves. Individuals representing themselves are responsible for performing all duties imposed upon counsel by these Rules and all other applicable federal rules of procedure. All parties other than individuals must be represented by counsel.

b. *Pro hac vice.*

i. Generally. The Court may permit any attorney (except any attorney who is a member of the Maryland Bar or maintains any law office in Maryland) who is a member in good standing of the Bar of any other United States Court or of the highest court of any state to appear and participate as counsel in a particular civil case. Such permission shall not constitute formal admission to the Bar of this Court. However, an attorney admitted *pro hac vice* is subject to the disciplinary jurisdiction of this Court. Any party represented by an attorney who has been admitted *pro hac vice* must also be represented by an attorney who has been formally admitted to the Bar of this Court who shall sign all documents and, unless excused by the presiding judge, be present at any court proceedings.

ii. Certification Requirement. The Motion for Admission *Pro Hac Vice* shall include a certification as to the number of times the attorney has been admitted *pro hac vice* during the twelve (12) months immediately preceding the filing of the motion and identify any other active cases in this Court in which the attorney is admitted *pro hac vice.*

iii. Limitation. Admission *pro hac vice* is not a substitute for admission to the Bar of this Court, but rather is intended to facilitate occasional appearances only. Unless otherwise ordered for good cause shown, no attorney may be admitted *pro hac vice* in more than three unrelated cases in any twelve (12)-month period, nor may any attorney be admitted *pro hac vice* in more than three (3) active unrelated cases at any one time.

iv Multi-District Litigation. Attorneys in multi-district litigation cases need not be members of this Court's Bar. Instead, an attorney may move for admission *pro hac vice* if the attorney is a member in good standing of the bar of any United States District Court. For purposes of this subsection only, attorneys requesting admission *pro hac vice* (1) are not required to have their admissions moved by an active member of this Court's bar, (2) do not need another member of this Court's bar to sign pleadings or enter appearances, and (3) are limited to practice in this Court in only the multi-district litigation proceeding.

c. Appearance for Obtaining Deposition Subpoenas. Unless otherwise ordered by the Court, it shall not be necessary for counsel to be admitted to the Bar of this Court in order to (1) obtain a subpoena for depositions to be taken in this District for cases pending in other Districts or (2) participate in proceedings to enforce or quash any such subpoena. However, an attorney exempted by this Rule from the requirement of being admitted to the bar of this Court is subject to the disciplinary jurisdiction of this Court.

d. Duty to Avoid Scheduling Conflicts. Before entering an appearance in a case, counsel must inquire whether any hearing date or a trial date has already been set in the case. If a date has been set and it conflicts with counsel's schedule in any respect, counsel shall not enter an appearance unless counsel first resolves the conflict by obtaining a continuance of one of the conflicting proceedings or, if counsel is a member of a firm, obtaining the client's consent to have another member of the firm appear on the client's behalf. After entering an appearance, counsel has a continuing duty to honor all scheduling commitments made to the Court.

2. **Withdrawal of Appearance.** a. Individuals. In the case of an individual, appearance of counsel may be withdrawn only with leave of Court and if (1) appearance of other counsel has been entered, or (2) withdrawing counsel files a certificate stating (a) the name and last known address of the client, and (b) that a written notice has been mailed to or otherwise served upon the client at least seven (7) days previously advising the client of counsel's proposed withdrawal and notifying the client either to have new counsel enter an appearance or to advise the Clerk that the client will be proceeding without counsel. If the withdrawal of counsel's appearance is permitted, the Clerk shall notify the party that the party will be deemed to be proceeding without counsel unless and until new counsel enters an appearance on behalf of the party.

b. Parties Other Than Individuals. In the case of any party other than an individual, including corporations, partnerships, unincorporated associations and government entities, appearance of counsel may be withdrawn only with leave of Court and if (1) appearance of other counsel has been entered, or (2) withdrawing counsel files a certificate stating (a) the name and last known address of the client, and (b) that the written notice has been mailed to or otherwise served upon the client at least seven (7) days previously advising the client of counsel's proposed withdrawal and notifying it that it must have new counsel enter an appearance or be subject to the dismissal of its claims and/or default judgment on claims against it. In the event that within thirty (30) days of the filing of the motion to withdraw, new counsel has not entered an appearance, the Court may take such action, if any, that it deems appropriate, including granting the motion to withdraw and dismissing any affirmative claim for relief asserted by the party and/or directing the party to show cause why a default should not be entered on claims asserted against it. (Amended Aug. 16, 2004, effective Aug. 16, 2004; by order effective January 1, 2008;

amended effective December 1, 2009; amended effective July 1, 2010; amended effective July 1, 2011.)

Effect of amendments. — The 2004 amendment, effective Aug. 16, 2004, in 1.b inserted "or maintains any law office in Maryland" and added "who shall sign all documents and, unless excused by the presiding judge, be present at any court proceedings"; and added 1.d.

The 2008 amendment in 1.a rewrote the second sentence and added the fourth sentence; added b.ii and b.iii; rewrote c; in d substituted "Duty to avoid scheduling" for "Checking for" in the heading.

The 2009 amendment substituted "seven (7) days" for "five days" in the first sentence of 2.a and 2.b; and made minor stylistic changes.

The 2010 amendment added 1.b.iv.

The 2011 amendment substituted "without counsel" for "pro se" throughout and made minor, stylistic changes.

Rule 102. General filing and service requirements.

1. **Signatures, identifying information and proof of service.** a. Signatures. i. Parties represented by counsel. When a party is represented by counsel, the Clerk shall accept for filing only documents signed by a member of the Bar of this Court whose appearance is entered on behalf of that party. Use of any of the methods for signing an electronic document established by the Court, including use of an attorney's login and password to electronically file a document, constitutes the attorney's signature on the document.

ii. Parties appearing without counsel. When a party is appearing without counsel, the Clerk will accept for filing only documents signed by that party. Attorneys who have prepared any documents which are submitted for filing by a self-represented litigant must be members of the Bar of this Court and must sign the document, state their name, address, telephone number and their bar number assigned by this Court.

b. Identifying information. i. Required on all Court documents. At the bottom of all Court documents, counsel and self-represented litigants shall state their name, address, telephone number, e-mail and fax number. Counsel shall also state their bar number assigned by this Court. This is not a substitute for compliance with L.R. 101.1.b.ii and L.R. 701.3.

ii. Duty of counsel to notify the Clerk of any change in address. Counsel must promptly notify the Clerk of any change of address, including e-mail address irrespective of any changes noted on a pleading or other document. This obligation is continuing and if counsel fails to comply, the Court may enter an order dismissing any affirmative claims for relief and may enter a default judgment.

iii. Duty of self-represented litigants to keep current address on file. Self-represented litigants must file with the Clerk in every case which they have pending a statement of their current address where case-related papers may be served. This obligation is continuing, and if any self-represented litigant fails to comply, the Court may enter an order dismissing any affirmative claims for relief filed by that party and may enter a default judgment on any claims asserted against that party.

c. Proof of service. Except as provided for in Rules 112.1 and 112.2, all Court documents other than the original complaint must bear a signed certificate signed by counsel stating that the service required by Fed. R. Civ. P. 5(a) has been made. If a document is filed electronically, the notice of electronic filing constitutes a certificate of service as to all parties to whom electronic notice is sent.

d. Electronic transmission. Electronic filing of documents is permitted in accordance with the policies and procedures established by the Court.

2. **Format of Court documents.** a. Caption. The case caption on all Court documents shall contain only a short title, consisting of the names of the first plaintiff and the first defendant only, and the civil action number. This Rule shall not apply to the original complaint (which shall contain the names and addresses of all parties and the county of residence of any Maryland party) or any pleading seeking to add a new party (which shall contain the short caption and the name and address of the parties sought to be added and the county of residence of any Maryland party sought to be added).

b. Margins, spacing and numbering and 2-hole punched. All documents filed with the Court shall not exceed 8 ½" x 11", with a top margin of at least 1 ½" and left-hand margin of 1" and a right-hand margin of ½". Lines of text shall be double spaced except for quotations and footnotes. Pages shall be numbered at the bottom of every page after the first page. Typed, printed or written material shall appear only on the front side of any page. All documents submitted in paper format shall be two-hole punched on the top of each page.

c. Legibility. No document shall be accepted for filing unless it is legible.

3. **Issuance of subpoenas in self-represented, in forma pauperis cases**. The Clerk shall not issue any subpoena under Fed. R. Civ. P. 45(a)(3) to any self-represented litigant proceeding *in forma pauperis* without first obtaining an order from the Court authorizing the issuance of the subpoena. Before entering any such order the Court may require the litigant to state the reasons why the subpoena should be issued, and the Court may refuse to authorize issuance of the subpoena if it concludes that the subpoena imposes undue burden or expense on the person subject to the subpoena or upon the U.S. Marshal or other court officer who would be required to serve it under 28 U.S.C. § 1915.

4. **Interdivisional filing.** Unless otherwise ordered by the Court, if a case designated to one division under the Court's standing order is assigned to a judge in the other division, any pleadings, motions, memoranda or other documents may be filed in the designated division and, if such filing is made within any applicable deadline, shall be deemed to be timely. (Amended Aug. 16, 2004, effective Aug. 16, 2004; by order effective January 1, 2008; amended effective December 1, 2009; amended effective July 1, 2011.)

Effect of amendments. — The 2004 amendment, effective Aug. 16, 2004, changed the subheading designations in 1.a.i, 1.a.ii, 2 and 2.c; in 1.a.i substituted "documents" for "papers" in the first sentence, and added the second sentence; in 1.b.i inserted "e-mail" and added the third sentence; divided 1.b.ii into 1.b.ii and 1.b.iii and rewrote accordingly; in 1.c substituted "documents" for "papers" in the first sentence and added the second sentence; and rewrote 1.d.

The 2008 amendment substituted "documents" for "papers" in 4.

The 2009 amendment made minor stylistic changes in 2.a.

The 2011 amendment substituted "without counsel" for "pro se" in the subheading and first sentence of 1.a.ii; substituted "self-represented" for "pro se" in the second sentence of 1.a.ii and in 1.b.i; rewrote 1.b.iii; and added the exception in 1.c.

Editor's note. — As to electronic filing of

documents with the United States District
Court for the District of Maryland (CM/ECF),
see www.mdd.uscourts.gov/CMECF.

Rule 103. Institution of suit and pleadings.

1. **Civil cover sheet/extra copies of complaint/designation of related cases.** a. Civil cover sheet and extra copies of complaint. i. Cases subject to electronic filing. The complaint, civil cover sheet and any other documents being filed should be submitted to the Clerk in accordance with the electronic filing procedures adopted by the Court.

ii. Cases exempt from electronic filing. When filing a complaint, counsel shall submit to the Clerk a complete civil cover sheet and two (2) copies of the complaint.

b. Related cases. i. Designation by plaintiff. If counsel for a plaintiff in a civil action believes that the action being filed and one or more other civil actions or proceedings previously decided or pending in this Court (1) arise from the same or identical transactions, happenings, or events; (2) involve the identical parties or property; (3) involve the same patent or trademark; or (4) for any other reason would entail substantial duplication of labor if heard by different judges, counsel shall indicate that fact by designating the case as a "related case" on the civil cover sheet. A copy of the cover sheet shall be served on all parties.

ii. Designation by defendant. If counsel for a defendant believes that a case is related to a prior case and that fact has not been noted on the civil cover sheet by plaintiff, counsel for the defendant shall bring that information to the attention of all parties and the Clerk, and the Clerk shall note it on the cover sheet and inform the judge to whom the new case has been assigned.

iii. Resolution of disputes. Any disputes regarding the designation of a case as being related to another case shall be presented by motion to the judge to whom the new or later case has been assigned.

2. **Process.** a. Number of copies. i. Cases subject to electronic filing. In cases subject to electronic filing, counsel shall submit to the Clerk the following number of copies when process is to be served; (a) one (1) copy of any summons for each party to be served, except that in cases where the United States, a federal agency or a federal employee in his official capacity is named as a defendant, five (5) copies of the summons should be submitted; (b) four (4) copies of a warrant for arrest or summons with process of maritime attachment and garnishment for tangible property or two (2) copies of such documents for intangible property; and (c) two (2) copies of all writs, including writs of possession, replevin, execution, garnishment and attachment before a judgment.

ii. Cases exempt from electronic filing. In cases exempt from electronic filing, counsel shall submit to the Clerk the following number of copies when process is to be served: (a) two (2) copies of any summons for each party to be served, except that in cases where the United States, a federal agency, or a federal employee in his official capacity is named as a defendant, six (6) copies of the summons should be submitted; (b) five (5) copies of a warrant for arrest or summons with process of maritime attachment and garnishment for tangible property or two copies of such documents for intangible property; and (c) three (3) copies of all writs, including writs of possession, replevin, execution, garnishment and attachment before a judgment.

b. When served by Marshal. Unless otherwise ordered by the Court, the United States Marshal shall not serve any process or subpoenas except the following: (a) all process for a party proceeding *in forma pauperis* without counsel, (b) warrants of arrests *in rem* or process of maritime attachment and garnishment, (c) writs of possession, replevin, execution, garnishment and attachment before a judgment, (d) process served under 28 U.S.C. § 2361, and (e) when requested by the plaintiff, process in suits where the plaintiff is authorized to proceed as a seaman under 28 U.S.C. § 1916. Unless otherwise ordered by the Court and except for a party who is proceeding *in forma pauperis* or as a seaman under 28 U.S.C. § 1916, the Marshal may require a party to pay or secure the fees and expenses before serving any process which this Rule requires that the Marshal serve.

c. Waiver procedure. Whenever the waiver procedure under Fed. R. Civ. P. 4(d) is invoked, counsel shall submit to the Clerk a notice identifying the defendant(s) to whom the notice and request to waive service of summons is being sent.

The notice shall be filed upon the filing of the complaint or such later date that counsel decides to invoke the waiver procedure.

3. **Disclosure of affiliations and financial interest.** When filing an initial pleading or promptly after learning of the information to be disclosed, counsel shall file a statement (separate from any pleading) containing the following information:

a. Corporate affiliation. The identity of any parent or other affiliate of a corporate party and the description of the relationship between the party and such affiliates.

b. Financial interests in the outcome of the litigation. The identity of any corporation, unincorporated association, partnership or other business entity, not a party to the case, which may have any financial interest whatsoever in the outcome of the litigation, and the nature of its financial interest. The term "financial interest in the outcome of the litigation" includes a potential obligation of an insurance company or other person to represent or to indemnify any party to the case. Any notice given to the Clerk under this Rule shall not be considered as an admission by the insurance company or other person that it does in fact have an obligation to defend the litigation or to indemnify a party or as a waiver of any rights that it might have in connection with the subject matter of the litigation.

4. **Security for costs.** Any party against whom affirmative relief (other than a compulsory counterclaim) is filed may file a motion requesting that the party seeking the affirmative relief give security for costs if that party is not a resident of this District. Upon the filing of the motion, the Court shall issue a show cause order to the party seeking affirmative relief. A party who does not show cause why such security should not be required shall deposit with the Clerk on the date that the show cause response is due or on such later date as may be set by the Court the sum of $150 or such higher amount as the Court

determines is appropriate. The Court may dismiss the claim of a party who fails to deposit the required security. This Rule shall not apply to any party proceeding *in forma pauperis* or as a seaman under 28 U.S.C. § 1916.

5. **Removal.** a. Certification of filing of State court documents. Any party effecting removal shall file with the notice true and legible copies of all process, pleadings, documents and orders which have been served upon that party. Within thirty (30) days thereafter the party shall file true and legible copies of all other documents then on file in the state court, together with a certification from counsel that all filings in the state court action have been filed in the United States District Court. In cases subject to electronic filing, the copies shall be filed in accordance with the electronic filing procedures adopted by the Court.

b. Filing memoranda regarding pending motions. If a motion is pending at the time of removal as to which a legal memorandum has not been submitted, the moving party shall file a supporting memorandum within fourteen (14) days of the date of removal. If at the time of removal a motion is pending as to which a legal memorandum has been submitted, the party opposing the motion shall file an opposition memorandum on the date that the opposition memorandum was due in the state court or within fourteen (14) days of the date of removal, whichever is earlier.

c. Disclosure of affiliations and financial interest. Within seven (7) days after the filing of a notice of removal, all parties shall make the disclosures required by L.R. 103.3.

d. Cases related to bankruptcy cases. Removals under 28 U.S.C. § 1452 or § 1441 in cases related to bankruptcy cases should be filed with the Bankruptcy Clerk.

6. **Amendments of pleadings.** a. Original of proposed amendment to accompany motion. Whenever a party files a motion requesting leave to file an amended pleading, the original of the proposed amended pleading shall accompany the motion. If the motion is granted, an additional copy of the amended pleading need not be filed. The amended pleading shall be deemed to have been served, for the purpose of determining the time for response under Fed. R. Civ. P. § 15(a), on the date that the Court grants leave for its filing.

b. Exhibits to amended pleadings. Unless otherwise ordered by the Court, only newly added exhibits are to be attached to an amended pleading. However, if the amended pleading adds a new party, counsel shall serve all exhibits referred to in the amended pleading upon the new party.

c. Identification of amendments. Unless otherwise ordered by the Court, the party filing an amended pleading shall file and serve (1) a clean copy of the amended pleading and (2) a copy of the amended pleading in which stricken material has been lined through or enclosed in brackets and new material has been underlined or set forth in bold-faced type.

d. Requested consent of other counsel. Before filing a motion requesting leave to file an amended pleading, counsel shall attempt to obtain the consent of other counsel. Counsel shall state in the motion whether the consent of other counsel has been obtained.

7. **Third-party complaints.** a. Filing. A third-party plaintiff shall file with the Clerk only the third-party complaint itself and not all the prior pleadings attached thereto.

b. Service. Unless otherwise ordered by the Court, a third party plaintiff shall serve upon a third party defendant copies of all documents (other than notices of previously held depositions) which the parties have previously served upon one another and shall make all previously conducted discovery materials available for review by the third party defendant.

8. **Dismissal for want of prosecution.** a. Failure to effect service. If a party demanding affirmative relief has not effected service of process within 120 days of filing the pleading seeking the affirmative relief, the Court may enter an order asking the party to show cause why the claim should not be dismissed. If the party fails to show good cause within fourteen (14) days of the entry of the order or such other time as may be set by the Court, the claim shall be dismissed without prejudice.

b. Dormancy of action for nine months. If no document has been filed in Court in any action for more than nine months, the Court may enter an order asking the parties to show cause why the case should not be dismissed. If good cause is not shown within fourteen (14) days of the entry of the show cause order or such other time as may be set by the Court, the case shall be dismissed without prejudice.

9. **Scheduling orders.** a. Categories of actions generally exempted from Fed. R. Civ. P. 16(b). All categories of actions in which ordinarily discovery is not conducted and additional parties are not added are exempted from Fed. R. Civ. P. 16(b). These categories of actions include petitions filed under 28 U.S.C. § 2254, motions filed under 28 U.S.C. § 2255, social security appeals, bankruptcy appeals, appeals on the record from administrative agencies, motions to enforce arbitration awards, forfeiture actions, actions seeking enforcement of judgments, and mortgage or deed of trust foreclosures. In all actions in which a scheduling order is not entered under Fed. R. Civ. P. 16(b), the presiding judge will enter such orders as are necessary to assure the prompt and expeditious resolution of the litigation.

b. Actions exempted from the consultation requirement of Fed. R. Civ. P. 16(b). All actions except ones which the presiding judge notifies the parties that he or she designates to be complex, e.g., antitrust, mass tort, patent infringement, RICO and securities fraud actions in which all parties are represented by counsel, are exempted from the requirement of Fed. R. Civ. P. 16(b) that the Court consult with counsel (or unrepresented parties) or await a report from the parties under Fed. R. Civ. P. 26(f) before entering a scheduling order. All scheduling orders, however, shall provide that any party who believes that any deadline set in the scheduling order is unreasonable may request in writing a modification of the order or that a conference be held for the purpose of seeking a modification of the order. (Amended Aug. 16, 2004, effective Aug. 16, 2004; amended effective December 1, 2009.)

Effect of amendments. — The 2004 amendment, effective Aug. 16, 2004, substituted "documents" or "document" for "papers" or "paper" throughout the Rule; and in 1.a. inserted i, redesignated the former text as ii and made minor changes; rewrote 2.a; and in

2.c. substituted "submit to the Clerk a notice" for "submit to the Clerk a written notice"; in the introductory language of 3 substituted "file a statement" for "submit to the Clerk two copies of a written statement" and made minor changes in the first sentence of 3.b; in 5, added the third sentence of 5.a., and added 5.c and 5.d; and in 6.c in the heading substituted "Identification" for "Highlighting" and substi-

tuted "pleading shall file and serve" for "pleading shall provide to all counsel and to the clerk".

The 2009 amendment made minor stylistic changes.

Editor's note. — As to electronic filing of documents with the United States District Court for the District of Maryland (CM/ECF), see www.mdd.uscourts.gov/CMECF.

Rule 104. Discovery.

1. **Limitation on number of requests for production and requests for admission.** Unless otherwise ordered by the Court, or agreed upon by the parties, no party shall serve upon any other party, at one time or cumulatively, more than thirty (30) requests for production, or more than thirty (30) requests for admission (other than requests propounded for the purpose of establishing the authenticity of documents or the fact that documents constitute business records), including all parts and sub-parts.

2. **Timely written discovery requests required.** Interrogatories, requests for production, motions for physical and mental examination, and written deposition questions must be made at a sufficiently early time to assure that they are answered before the expiration of the discovery deadline set by the Court. Unless otherwise ordered by the Court, no discovery deadline will be extended because written discovery requests remain unanswered at its expiration.

3. **Discovery to proceed despite existence of disputes.** Unless otherwise ordered by the Court, the existence of a discovery dispute as to one matter does not justify delay in taking any other discovery.

4. **Conference of counsel and commencement of discovery.** Unless otherwise ordered by the Court or agreed upon by the parties, the conference of counsel required by Fed. R. Civ. P. 26(f) need not take place and discovery shall not commence and disclosures need not be made until a scheduling order is entered.

5. **Discovery materials not to be filed with court.** Unless otherwise ordered by the Court, written discovery requests, responses thereto, notices of service of discovery requests or responses, depositions, and disclosures under Fed. R. Civ. P. 26(a) (1) and (2) shall not be filed with the Court. The party propounding written discovery or taking a deposition shall be responsible for retaining the original copies of the discovery materials (including the certificates of service) and shall make them available for inspection by any other party.

6. **Format of responses to interrogatories and requests for production.** Responses to interrogatories and requests for production shall set forth each interrogatory or request followed by the answer and/or a brief statement of the grounds for objection, including a citation of the main applicable authorities (if any).

7. **Conference of counsel required.** Counsel shall confer with one another concerning a discovery dispute and make sincere attempts to resolve the differences between them. The Court will not consider any discovery motion

unless the moving party has filed a certificate reciting (a) the date, time and place of the discovery conference, and the names of all persons participating therein, or (b) counsel's attempts to hold such a conference without success; and (c) an itemization of the issues requiring resolution by the Court.

8. **Procedure regarding motions to compel.** The following procedure shall be followed in litigating motions to compel answers to interrogatories and requests for production or entry upon land as to which a response has been served. This procedure shall not govern motions to compel (a) answers to interrogatories or to requests for production or entry upon land where no responses at all have been served, (b) answers to deposition questions or (c) responses to discovery requests directed to a non-party. Such latter motions shall be filed with the Court and treated as any non-discovery motion, except that, as to disputes concerning discovery directed to a non-party, unless otherwise directed by the Court, the Court will not consider the motion until a conference has been held under LR 104.8.b. and a certificate has been filed under LR 104.8.c.

a. Service of motions and memoranda. If a party who has propounded interrogatories or requests for production is dissatisfied with the response to them and has been unable to resolve informally (by oral or written communications) any disputes with the responding party, that party shall serve a motion to compel within thirty (30) days of the party's receipt of the response. The memorandum in support of the motion shall set forth, as to each response to which the motion is directed, the discovery request, the response thereto, and the asserted basis for the insufficiency of the response. The memorandum shall be succinct and need not include citation to legal authorities unless such citation is necessary in order to understand the issues presented. The opposing party shall serve a memorandum in opposition to the motion within fourteen (14) days thereafter. The moving party shall serve any reply memorandum within fourteen (14) days thereafter. The parties shall serve motions and memoranda under L.R. 104.8 in accordance with Fed. R. Civ. P. 5(a) and shall not serve them through the Court's electronic filing system nor file with the Court notices of service of the motion and memoranda. Extensions of time given by the parties to one another to serve any document hereunder need not be approved by the Court, provided, however, that no extension of time limits set in any scheduling order entered by the Court shall be made without the Court's prior approval.

b. Conference of counsel. Counsel are encouraged to confer with one another before or immediately after a motion to compel is served. If they are unable to resolve their disputes, counsel must hold the conference required by L.R. 104.7 after serving upon one another all of the documents relating to the motion to compel.

c. Filing of certificate of conference and motions and memoranda. i. Cases subject to electronic filing. If counsel fail to resolve their differences during their conference, the party seeking to compel discovery shall file the certificate required by L.R. 104.7, and shall append thereto a copy of the motion and memoranda previously served by the parties under L.R. 104.8.a.

ii. Cases exempt from electronic filing. If counsel fail to resolve their differences during their conference, the party seeking to compel discovery shall file (i) the certificate required by L.R. 104.7, and (ii) the original and two copies of its motion and memorandum concerning the motion to compel and three (3) copies of all other memoranda concerning the motion.

9. **Smoking during depositions prohibited.** Unless all persons present otherwise agree, smoking is prohibited in the room in which a deposition is being taken.

10. **Actions and witnesses exempted from provisions of Fed. R. Civ. P. 26(a)(2)(B).** Unless otherwise ordered by the Court a party must provide the disclosures required by Fed. R. Civ. P. 26(a)(2)(B) only as to experts retained or specially employed by a party to provide expert testimony. The disclosures need not be provided as to hybrid fact/expert witnesses such as treating physicians. The party must disclose the existence of any hybrid fact/expert witness pursuant to Fed. R. Civ. P. 26(a)(2)(A), and disclose the subject matter on which the witness is expected to present evidence under Fed. R. Evid. 702, 703, or 705, as well as a summary of the facts and opinions to which the hybrid fact/expert witness is expected to testify, pursuant to Fed. R. Civ. P. 26(a)(2)(C). In addition, an adverse party may obtain the opinions of such witnesses (to the extent appropriate) through interrogatories, document production requests, and depositions.

11. **Fees and costs.** a. Interpretation of Fed. R. Civ. P. 26(b)(4)(E). Unless otherwise ordered by the Court, any reasonable fee charged by an expert for the time spent in a discovery deposition and in traveling to and from the deposition shall be paid by the party taking the deposition. The fee charged by the expert for time spent preparing for the deposition shall be paid by the party designating the expert. The expert may not charge an opposing party for a discovery deposition a fee at any hourly rate higher than the rate that he or she charges for the preparation of his or her report.

b. Limitation on the amount of fees of treating physician. Unless otherwise ordered by the Court, a treating physician shall not charge a fee higher than the hourly fee that he or she customarily charges for in-office patient consultation or $325 per hour, whichever is lower, for any work that he or she performs in connection with any discovery matter or for the taking of a *de bene esse* deposition. Any party noticing a deposition of a treating physician shall (after conferring with opposing counsel) advise the physician of the number of hours that will be required for the deposition (both on direct and cross examination). The treating physician may not charge for any hours exceeding this estimate, provided that the deposition is completed within the estimate, and may terminate the deposition when the estimated time has elapsed.

c. Limitation on cost of photocopying. Unless otherwise ordered by the Court, the amount that a party or third-party witness may charge as a photocopying expense when producing documents in response to a discovery request or subpoena shall not exceed the rate established by the Court for taxation of costs.

12. **Familiarity with Discovery Guidelines.** Counsel should be familiar with the Discovery Guidelines that are an appendix to these Rules.

13. **Proposed confidentiality orders.** Any proposed confidentiality order shall include (a) a definition of confidentiality consistent with Fed. R. Civ. P.

26(c); (b) a method for challenging particular designations of confidentiality with the burden remaining on the party seeking confidentiality to justify it under Rule 26(c); (c) a provision that whenever materials subject to the confidentiality order (or any pleading, motion or memorandum referring to them) are proposed to be filed in the Court record under seal, the party making such filing must simultaneously submit a motion and accompanying order pursuant to L.R. 105.11; and (d) a provision permitting the Clerk to return to counsel or destroy any sealed material at the end of the litigation. (Amended Aug. 16, 2004, effective Aug. 16, 2004; by order effective January 1, 2008; amended effective December 1, 2009; amended effective December 1, 2010; amended effective July 1, 2011; amended effective September 21, 2011.)

Effect of amendments. — The 2004 amendment, effective Aug. 16, 2004, rewrote 4; in the first sentence of 5 inserted "notices of service of discovery requests or responses," and deleted the former second sentence; in the second sentence of 7 deleted "and any issues remaining to be resolved" following "discovery conference," added "and (c) an itemization of the issues requiring resolution by the Court" and made minor, related changes; in 8.a in the heading substituted "and Memoranda" for "Papers," divided the former sixth sentence into the present sixth and seventh sentences, rewrote the seventh sentence, and substituted "document" for "papers" in the eighth sentence; in 8.b in the second sentence, substituted "documents" for "papers"; in 8.c in the heading substituted "and Memoranda" for "Papers," inserted i, redesignated the existing text as ii and substituted "seeking to compel discovery" for "seeking the motion to compel"; and in 11.b in the first sentence substituted "$250" for "$200".

The 2008 amendment rewrote the sixth through eighth sentences in 8.a as one sentence; in 8.b substituted "served" for "filed"; rewrote the last sentence in 8.c.i; and in 13 deleted "(7)" after the first instance of "Fed. R. Civ. P. 26(c)".

The 2009 amendment in 4 added "Conference of Counsel and" in the heading and added "the conference of counsel required by Fed. R. Civ. P. 26(f) need not take place and"; in the fifth sentence of 8.a substituted "fourteen (14) days" for "eleven days"; in the first sentence of 11.b substituted "$325" for "$250"; and made minor stylistic changes.

The 2010 amendment by Standing Order 2010-05 added "disclose the subject matter ... In addition" in 10, applicable to cases filed or pending on or after December 1, 2010.

The amendment effective July 1, 2011, in the second sentence of 10 added "disclose the subject matter on which the witness ... pursuant to Fed. R. Civ. P. 26(a)(2)(C)"; and made a stylistic change at the beginning of the third sentence.

The amendment effective September 21, 2011, substituted "Fed. R. Civ. P. 26(b)(4)(E)" for "Fed. R. Civ. P. 26(b)(4)(C)" in the subheading of 11.

Editor's note. — As to electronic filing of documents with the United States District Court for the District of Maryland (CM/ECF), see www.mdd.uscourts.gov/CMECF.

Rule 105. Motions, briefs and memoranda.

1. Memoranda required; number of copies. Any motion and opposition to a motion shall be filed with the Clerk and be accompanied by a memorandum setting forth the reasoning and authorities in support of it.

a. Cases subject to electronic filing. The motion, memorandum and any exhibits or attachments should be filed electronically in accordance with the procedures adopted by the Court.

b. Cases exempt from electronic filing. The original and one (1) copy of all motions and memoranda shall be filed, except that two (2) copies of discovery motions and memoranda shall be filed. If, however, counsel considers it impractical to file a copy of voluminous exhibits appended to a motion or memorandum, counsel may contact the judge to whom the case is assigned to ask permission not to file such a copy.

2. **Filing schedule.** a. General. All motions must be filed within deadlines set by the Court. Unless otherwise ordered by the Court, all memoranda in opposition to a motion shall be filed within fourteen (14) days of the service of the motion and any reply memoranda within fourteen(14) days after service of the opposition memoranda. Unless otherwise ordered by the Court, surreply memoranda are not permitted to be filed.

b. Last-minute filing prohibited. In no event, unless otherwise ordered by the Court, is any memorandum to be filed after 4:00 p.m. on the afternoon before the last business day preceding the day on which the proceeding to which the memorandum relates is to be held. For example, a memorandum relating to a proceeding to be held on a Monday must be filed by 4:00 p.m. the previous Thursday.

c. Where more than one party plans to file summary judgment motions. In a two-party case, if both parties intend to file summary judgment motions, counsel are to agree among themselves which party is to file the initial motion. After that motion has been filed, the other party shall file a cross-motion accompanied by a single memorandum (both opposing the first party's motion and in support of its own cross-motion), the first party shall then file an opposition/reply, and the second party may then file a reply. If more than two (2) parties intend to file motions in a multi-party case, counsel shall submit a proposed briefing schedule when submitting their status report.

3. **Limitations on length.** Unless otherwise ordered by the Court, memoranda in support of a motion or in opposition thereto and trial briefs shall not exceed fifty (50) pages, and reply memoranda shall not exceed twenty-five (25) pages, exclusive of (a) affidavits and exhibits, (b) tables of contents and citations, and (c) addenda containing statutes, rules, regulations and similar material.

4. **When table of contents required.** A table of contents shall be included in any memorandum or brief exceeding twenty-five (25) pages in length.

5. **Appendices.** a. Appendix of cases not generally reported. Every memorandum or brief shall be accompanied by an appendix containing any opinions cited therein which are not reported in WESTLAW or in West's Federal or regional reports. A copy of the appendix shall be served upon other counsel.

b. Appendix of exhibits. If any motion, memorandum or brief is accompanied by more than five (5) exhibits, the exhibits shall be tabbed and indexed.

6. **Hearings.** Counsel may (but need not) file a request for hearing. Unless otherwise ordered by the Court, however, all motions shall be decided on the memoranda without a hearing.

7. **Trial briefs.** Unless otherwise ordered by the Court, counsel may (but need not) submit trial briefs.

8. **Motions for sanctions.** a. Not to be filed as a matter of course. The Court expects that motions for sanctions will not be filed as a matter of course. The Court will consider in appropriate cases imposing sanctions upon parties who file unjustified sanctions motions.

b. Responses required only upon Court order. Unless otherwise ordered by the Court, a party need not respond to any motion filed under Fed. R. Civ. P. 11 or 28 U.S.C. § 1927. The Court shall not grant any motion without requesting a response.

9. **Motions for extension of time.** Before filing a motion to postpone any proceeding or to extend the time for the filing of any document or the taking of any other required action counsel shall attempt to obtain the consent of other counsel and shall give notice of the motion to other counsel a reasonable time before presentation of the motion to the Court. Counsel shall state in the motion whether the consent of other counsel has been obtained. Where counsel deems it reasonably practicable, counsel also shall try to obtain the consent of an unrepresented party.

10. **Motions to reconsider.** Except as otherwise provided in Fed. R. Civ. P. 50, 52, 59, or 60, any motion to reconsider any order issued by the Court shall be filed with the Clerk not later than fourteen (14) days after entry of the order.

11. **Sealing.** Any motion seeking the sealing of pleadings, motions, exhibits or other documents to be filed in the Court record shall include (a) proposed reasons supported by specific factual representations to justify the sealing and (b) an explanation why alternatives to sealing would not provide sufficient protection. The Court will not rule upon the motion until at least fourteen (14) days after it is entered on the public docket to permit the filing of objections by interested parties. Materials that are the subject of the motion shall remain temporarily sealed pending a ruling by the Court. If the motion is denied, the party making the filing will be given an opportunity to withdraw the materials. Upon termination of the action, sealed materials will be disposed of in accordance with L.R. 113. (Amended Aug. 16, 2004, effective Aug. 16, 2004; by order effective January 1, 2008; amended effective December 1, 2009; and amended effective July 1, 2010.)

Effect of amendments. — The 2004 amendment, effective Aug. 16, 2004, in 1 redesignated the first sentence as introductory language, inserted 1.a, and designated the remaining previous second and third sentences as 1.b; in 2.a deleted the former third sentence; and in 2.b. substituted "4:00 p.m." for "5:00 p.m." in two places; in 9 and 11 in the first sentence substituted "documents" for "papers"; and in 11 added the fifth sentence.

The 2008 amendment made a minor, stylistic change in the heading for 2.c.

The 2009 amendment substituted the second instance of "fourteen (14) days" for "eleven days" in the second sentence of 2.a; in 10 substituted "fourteen (14) days" for "10 days"; and made minor stylistic changes.

The 2010 amendment substituted "Fed. R. Civ. P. 50, 52, 59, or 60" for "Fed. R. Civ. P. 60" in 10.

Editor's note. — As to electronic filing of documents with the United States District Court for the District of Maryland (CM/ECF), see www.mdd.uscourts.gov/CMECF.

Cited in Koffman v. Osteoimplant Technology, Inc., 182 Bankr. 115 (D. Md. 1995).

Rule 106. Pretrial procedure.

1. **When pretrial order required.** A pretrial order must be submitted in all cases except the following: (a) prisoner habeas corpus petitions; (b) prisoner civil rights cases; (c) collection cases brought by the United States; (d) land condemnation cases; (e) *in rem* forfeiture actions brought by the United States; (f) administrative appeals brought against the Secretary of the Department of Health and Human Services; (g) foreclosure actions; (h) petitions brought by the United States to enforce a summons of the Internal Revenue Service; (i) appeals from rulings of the Bankruptcy Court; and (j) suits to enforce or quash subpoenas.

2. **Contents of pretrial order.** A proposed pretrial order shall contain the following:

a. A brief statement of facts that each plaintiff proposes to prove in support of that plaintiff's claims, together with a listing of the separate legal theories relied upon in support of each claim.

b. A brief statement of facts that each defendant proposes to prove or rely upon as a defense thereto, together with a listing of the separate legal theories relied upon in support of each affirmative defense.

c. Similar statements as to any counterclaim, crossclaim, or third-party claim.

d. Any amendments required of the pleadings.

e. Any issue in the pleadings that is to be abandoned.

f. Stipulations of fact or, if the parties are unable to agree, requested stipulations of fact.

g. The details of the damages claimed or any other relief sought as of the date of the pretrial conference.

h. A listing of each document or other exhibit, including summaries of other evidence, other than those expected to be used solely for impeachment, separately identifying those which each party expects to offer and those which each party may offer if the need arises. The listing shall indicate which exhibits the parties agree may be offered in evidence without the usual authentication. This requirement may be met by attaching an exhibit list to the pretrial order.

i. A list for each party of the name, address and telephone number of each witness, other than those expected to be called solely for impeachment, separately identifying those whom the party expects to present and those whom the party may call if the need arises.

j. A list for each party of the name and specialties of experts the party proposes to call as witnesses including hybrid fact/expert witnesses such as treating physicians.

k. A list of the pages and/or lines of any portion of a deposition to be offered in a party's case in chief or any counter-designations under Fed. R. Civ. P. 32(a)(4).

l. Any other pretrial relief, including a reference to pending motions, which is requested.

m. Any other matters added by the Court.

3. **Responsibility for preparing pretrial order.** The plaintiff shall prepare the first draft of the pretrial order covering all matters which the plaintiff proposes to include in the pretrial order. Unless otherwise ordered by the Court or agreed upon by counsel, the plaintiff shall serve a copy of a draft upon opposing counsel fourteen (14) days before the proposed pretrial order is due to be filed. Unless otherwise ordered by the Court or agreed upon by counsel, opposing counsel shall serve any proposed revisions and additions upon plaintiff's counsel at least seven (7) days before the order is due to be filed. If counsel are unable to agree upon any particular provision of the proposed order, counsel for each party shall submit to the Judge by the filing date a draft proposal on the provision in dispute.

4. **Submission of pretrial order.** a. Time. Unless otherwise ordered by the Court, the pretrial order shall be submitted to the Judge seven (7) days before the pretrial conference is to be held.

b. Submission procedure. i. Cases subject to electronic filing. The proposed pretrial order should be filed in accordance with the Court's electronic filing procedures.

ii. Cases exempt from electronic filing. The original and one (1) copy of the pretrial order shall be submitted.

c. Fed. R. Civ. P. 26(a)(3) disclosures. Submission of a pretrial order containing the information required by L.R. 106.2 within the time limits prescribed by L.R. 106.3 and L.R. 106.4 shall be deemed to constitute compliance with Fed. R. Civ. P. 26(a)(3).

5. **Approval and entry of pretrial order.** After approving the pretrial order the Judge shall have the approval entered on the docket.

6. **Pretrial conference.** The pretrial conference shall be attended by at least one (1) of the attorneys for each of the parties who will actually participate in the trial. Attorneys attending the conference shall be familiar with all aspects of the case and shall confer with their clients before the conference to obtain authority from them to enter into stipulations. If the case involves numerous exhibits, counsel shall be prepared to discuss proposals for the orderly presentation of the exhibits at trial.

7. **Pretrial preparation of exhibits.** a. Pretrial numbering. Prior to trial counsel shall attach tags to all exhibits clearly identifying their proponent and number. Tags may be obtained from the Clerk. Counsel shall file with the Clerk and serve upon opposing counsel at least one (1) business day prior to the scheduled trial date an exhibit list. Counsel shall retain the exhibits until they are presented at trial. This Rule does not apply to exhibits to be used solely for impeachment.

b. Pretrial review of exhibits. Prior to trial counsel shall meet for the purpose of reviewing and making available for copying one another's proposed exhibits, except those to be used solely for impeachment. All exhibits which are proffered at trial shall be precisely the same in form and substance as the exhibits which were made available for review and copying prior to trial unless counsel otherwise indicates to opposing counsel.

8. **Jury instructions, voir dire questions, and special verdict forms.** a. Submission procedure. i. Cases subject to electronic filing. Unless otherwise ordered, proposed jury instructions, voir dire questions and special verdict forms should be filed electronically.

ii. Cases exempt from electronic filing. Unless otherwise ordered, the original and two (2) copies of proposed instructions, voir dire questions, and special verdict forms shall be filed with the Clerk.

b. Contents of proposed instructions. Proposed instructions shall be numbered and shall set forth in a separate paragraph or on a separate paper a citation to any authorities upon which they are based. Counsel may submit any proposed instructions which they deem appropriate but, unless otherwise ordered by the Court, counsel need not submit proposed instructions on general matters not particular to the case. Upon request the Court shall provide to counsel a copy of its customary general instructions prior to the instructions submission deadline. (Amended Aug. 16, 2004, effective Aug. 16, 2004; amended effective December 1, 2009.)

Effect of amendments. — The 2004 amendment, effective Aug. 16, 2004, in 2.j inserted "including hybrid fact/expert witnesses such as treating physicians"; in 4.b. in the heading substituted "Submission Procedure" for "Number of Copies," inserted 4.b.i and redesignated the former text as 4.b.ii; rewrote 5; in 7.a. in the third sentence deleted "two copies of" preceding "exhibit list"; rewrote 8.a. and in 8.b in the first sentence substituted "page" for "paper".

The 2009 amendment substituted "fourteen (14) days" for "fifteen days" in the second sentence of 3; in the third sentence of 3 and in 4.a substituted "seven (7) days" for "five days"; and made minor stylistic changes.

Editor's note. — As to electronic filing of documents with the United States District Court for the District of Maryland (CM/ECF), see www.mdd.uscourts.gov/CMECF.

Rule 107. Trial.

1. [Reserved for future use]

2. **Postponements — Client consent required.** No motion seeking the postponement of any trial shall be made by any counsel without the knowledge and consent of the client whom that counsel represents.

3. **Subpoenas — Timely service.** As provided in LR 103.2.b, unless ordered by the Court, the United States Marshal shall not serve trial subpoenas except for a party who is proceeding *in forma pauperis* without counsel.

4. **Imposition of jury costs for late settlement.** Except for good cause shown, whenever the settlement of an action tried by a jury causes a trial to be postponed, canceled or terminated before a verdict, all juror costs shall be imposed upon the parties unless counsel has notified the Court and the Clerk's Office of the settlement at least one (1) full business day prior to the day on which the trial is scheduled to begin. The costs shall be assessed equally against the parties and their counsel unless otherwise ordered by the Court.

5. **Exhibits.** a. Pretrial numbering and exchange of exhibits. Counsel are to number exhibits prior to trial in accordance with LR 106.7.a. At trial counsel need not hand to other counsel for review any exhibit which prior to trial was made available for review and copying in accordance with LR 106.7.b.

b. Admission into evidence. Unless otherwise ordered by the Court or unless counsel requests that a particular exhibit be marked for identification only, whenever an exhibit number is first mentioned by counsel during the examination of a witness at trial, the exhibit shall be deemed to be admitted into evidence unless opposing counsel then asserts an objection to it.

c. Circulation to jury. The Court may permit counsel to circulate exhibits among the jurors at trial. However, if such permission is granted, counsel shall be expected to continue with questioning of the witness while the exhibit is being circulated unless the Court otherwise orders. Counsel shall not abuse this procedure by seeking to circulate exhibits at the conclusion of the examination.

d. Disposition. [See. L.R. 113]

6. **Obligation to anticipate evidentiary objections.** Counsel are under an obligation to anticipate evidentiary objections and, whenever possible, bring them to the attention of the Court before they are formally asserted so that they can be resolved when the jurors are not present.

7. **Exclusion of witnesses.** Witnesses need not be excluded unless a party invokes the exclusion of witness rule. "Exclusion of witness rule" means that

only parties (or the designated representatives of parties), their counsel, and expert witnesses approved by the Court may be present in the courtroom during the course of trial and that no person may directly or indirectly advise a witness (other than a party or expert witness) of what the testimony of another witness has been. Subject to this constraint, counsel may prepare their witnesses for trial during the course of trial.

8. **Time limitations.** a. Presentations to jury. Unless otherwise ordered by the Court, no opening statement or closing argument (including rebuttal argument) shall exceed one hour.

b. Presentation of evidence. In cases which it deems exceptional, the Court may, after consultation with counsel and giving respect to their views, impose in advance reasonable time limitations on presentation of evidence.

9. **Courtroom etiquette.** a. Counsel to stand when addressing Court. Unless otherwise permitted by the Court, counsel shall stand whenever addressing the Court except in stating brief evidentiary objections.

b. Movement in the courtroom. i. Generally. Unless otherwise ordered by the Court, counsel may conduct their examination of witnesses from any reasonable location in the well of the Court.

ii. Approaching witnesses. Unless otherwise ordered by the Court, counsel may approach a witness to show an exhibit without prior approval of the Court but may not do so for any other reason.

c. Persons to be referred to by surname. Unless otherwise ordered by the Court, counsel shall refer by surname to all parties, witnesses or other persons whose names may be mentioned during the course of trial (except persons under the age of 18).

10. **One attorney per witness.** Only one (1) attorney for each party may conduct the examination of any witness. Only that attorney may object to questions asked by opposing counsel during the examination of that witness.

11. **Examination of witnesses.** a. Order of questioning and argument. Unless otherwise ordered by the Court, co-parties represented by different counsel will examine witnesses and present argument in the order in which they are named in the complaint, and third-party defendants will examine witnesses after defendants have done so.

b. Limitation on redundant cross-examination. In cases involving parties who share common interests, the judge may order that counsel for those parties designate one of themselves as "lead counsel" for each witness. The counsel so designated shall be the only counsel authorized to conduct cross-examination concerning matters which relate to the common interests shared by the parties.

12. [Reserved for Future Use]

13. **Witnesses excused at conclusion of testimony.** Unless counsel otherwise so indicate, a witness shall be excused at the conclusion of the witness's testimony.

14. **Speaking with witness on the stand.** Unless otherwise ordered by the Court, during all breaks and recesses counsel may speak with a witness while conducting a direct examination of the witness but (with the exceptions noted below) may not discuss testimony with the witness, including a party,

while the witness is on cross, re-direct or re-cross examination. Notwithstanding the foregoing, unless otherwise ordered by the Court, counsel representing a defendant in a criminal case may confer with the defendant during breaks and recesses, and a non-party witness may confer with the witness's own counsel at any time.

15. **Mistrial and imposition of costs for unfair conduct.** If any witness volunteers unfairly prejudicial testimony not fairly responsive to the question asked, or if counsel commits any prejudicial error during the course of trial (including failing to advise a witness of evidence which the Court has ruled is inadmissible with the result that the witness refers to such evidence), the Court may order a mistrial and impose upon the responsible person all jury costs thus far incurred.

16. **Interviews of jurors.** Unless permitted by the presiding judge, no attorney or party shall directly or through an agent interview or question any juror, alternate juror or prospective juror with respect to that juror's jury service. (Amended Aug. 16, 2004, effective Aug. 16, 2004; amended effective December 1, 2009.)

Effect of amendments. — The 2004 amendment, effective Aug. 16, 2004, deleted the text of 5.d and inserted a bracketed cross-reference indicator.

The 2009 amendment made minor stylistic changes.

Rule 108. Judgments.

1. **Judgment by confession.** a. Complaint, related documents, and attachments. A complaint requesting the entry of judgment by confession shall be filed by the plaintiff accompanied by the written instrument authorizing the confession of judgment and entitling the plaintiff to a claim for liquidated damages and supported by an affidavit made by the plaintiff or someone on that party's behalf stating the specific circumstances of the defendant's execution of said instrument and including, where known, the age and education of the defendant, and further including the amount due thereunder, and the post office address (including street address if needed to effect mail delivery) of the defendant.

b. Review by Court regarding entry of judgment. Upon review of the aforesaid documents, the Court may direct the entry of judgment upon a finding that the aforesaid documents prima facie establish (1) a voluntary, knowing, and intelligent waiver by the defendant of the right to notice and a prejudgment hearing on the merits of the claim of the plaintiff for liquidated damages and (2) a meritorious claim of the plaintiff for liquidated damages against the defendant.

c. Notice to defendants. Immediately upon the entry of a judgment pursuant to paragraph (b) above, the Clerk shall issue a notice for the defendant notifying said party of the entry of the judgment and requiring defendant to appear in the cause wherein it is entered within thirty (30) days or such other time as may be required by statute or rule after the service of the notice and show, if such be the case, that said party did not voluntarily, knowingly, and intelligently waive the right to notice and a prejudgment hearing on the merits of the claim or otherwise show cause why the judgment should be vacated, opened or modified.

d. *Application to vacate judgment.* Application to vacate, open or modify the judgment must be made by motion within thirty (30) days after service of the notice; or such other time as may be required by statute or rule. The motion shall be made on the ground that the defendant has a meritorious defense to the cause of action. It shall set forth fully the facts relied on for such defense. A copy of the motion shall be served on the plaintiff or his attorney. If no application is made within the time allowed, the judgment shall be final.

e. *Determination of motion.* The motion shall be considered and determined as promptly as possible by the Court. If the evidence presented establishes that there are substantial and sufficient grounds for an actual controversy as to the merits of the case, the Court shall order the judgment by confession vacated, opened or modified, with leave to the defendant to file a pleading, and the case shall stand for trial. If the evidence does not establish that there are substantial and sufficient grounds for actual controversy as to the merits of the case, the judgment shall stand to the same extent as a final judgment.

f. *Failure to effect service.* If the notice issued under section (c) is not served despite reasonable efforts to effect service, the Court, upon petition of the plaintiff setting forth an account of the efforts made to effect service, shall provide for notice to the defendant in the manner provided by statute or rule.

g. *Address of defendant unknown.* Where the affidavit indicates that the address of the defendant is unknown, a judgment shall not be entered except upon order of Court, and the Court shall provide notice to the defendant pursuant to statute or rule.

h. *Entry of judgment by confession.* Except as authorized by this Rule, judgment by confession shall be entered only upon order of Court, after such notice and upon such terms as the Court may direct.

i. *Sale on execution upon judgment by confession.* Unless otherwise ordered by the Court, a sale on execution upon a judgment by confession shall not be made until after judgment has become final under sections (c), (d), and (e) of this Rule. (Amended Aug. 16, 2004, effective Aug. 16, 2004; amended effective December 1, 2009.)

Effect of amendments. — The 2004 amendment, effective Aug. 16, 2004, substituted "documents" for "papers" in the heading of 1.a and in two places in 1.b.

The 2009 amendment made minor stylistic changes.

Rule 109. Post-trial proceedings.

1. **Bill of costs.** a. *Time for filing.* Unless provided by L.R. 109.2.c or otherwise ordered by the Court, a bill of costs shall be filed within fourteen (14) days of the entry of judgment, or of the entry of an order denying a motion, filed under Fed. R. Civ. P. 50(b), 52(b) or 59. A bill for costs incurred on appeal taxable in this Court should be filed within fourteen (14) days of the issuance of the mandate by the Court of Appeals or, in the event of review by the Supreme Court, within fourteen (14) days of the entry of judgment by the Supreme Court. Non-compliance with these time limits shall be deemed a waiver of costs.

b. Contents. In any case where any costs other than the fee for filing the action are being requested, the bill of costs shall be supported by affidavit and accompanied by a memorandum setting forth the grounds and authorities supporting the request. Any vouchers or bills supporting the cost being requested shall be attached as exhibits.

c. Objections. A party objecting to any requested costs shall submit a memorandum in opposition to the request within the time permitted by L.R. 105.2. If no such memorandum is filed within the required time, the Clerk may without notice or hearing tax all of the requested costs.

2. **Motions requesting attorneys' fees.** a. Time for filing. Unless otherwise provided by statute, LR 109.2.c. or otherwise ordered by the Court, any motion requesting the award of attorneys' fees must be filed within fourteen (14) days of the entry of judgment. The memorandum required by L.R. 109.2.b must be filed within thirty-five (35) days from the date the motion is filed; or (unless otherwise ordered by the Court) in the event an appeal is taken from the underlying judgment, within fourteen (14) days of the issuance of the mandate of the Court of Appeals. Any opposition to the motion shall be filed within fourteen (14) days of service of the memorandum. Non-compliance with these time limits shall be deemed to be a waiver of any claim for attorneys' fees.

b. Contents. Any motion requesting the award of attorneys' fees must be supported by a memorandum setting forth the nature of the case, the claims as to which the party prevailed, the claims as to which the party did not prevail, a detailed description of the work performed broken down by hours or fractions thereof expended on each task, the attorney's customary fee for such like work, the customary fee for like work prevailing in the attorney's community, a listing of any expenditures for which reimbursement is sought, any additional factors which are required by the case law, and any additional factors that the attorney wishes to bring to the Court's attention. If the Rules and Guidelines for Determining Attorneys' Fees in Certain Cases contained in Appendix B to these Rules are applicable, any motion for attorneys' fees also shall be prepared in accordance with such Rules and Guidelines.

c. Social security cases. The provisions of Rules 109.2.a and 109.2.b shall apply to motions requesting an award of attorneys' fees under 42 U.S.C. § 406(b) with the following exception and additions: (i) the motion must be filed within thirty (30) days of the entry of judgment; and (ii) the motion may not seek any award of fees for representation of the claimant in administrative proceedings. A motion for bill of costs in a social security benefits case must be filed within thirty (30) days of the entry of judgment. (Amended Aug. 16, 2004, effective Aug. 16, 2004; by order effective January 1, 2008; amended effective December 1, 2009; amended effective July 1, 2011.)

Effect of amendments. — The 2004 amendment, effective Aug. 16, 2004, deleted "an order remanding to state court any removed action" following "or 59" in the first sentence of 1.a. and following "109.2c" in the first sentence of 2.a.

The 2008 amendment in 2.b substituted "De-termining Attorneys' Fees in Certain Cases" for "Determining Lodestar Attorneys' Fees in Civil Rights and Discrimination Cases".

The 2009 amendment made minor stylistic changes.

The 2011 amendment rewrote the last sentence in 2.b.

Rule 110. Appeal.

1. **Bonds.** a. Amount. Unless otherwise ordered by the Court, the amount of any supersedeas bond filed to stay execution of a money judgment pending appeal shall be 120% of the amount of the judgment plus an additional $500 to cover costs on appeal.

b. Waiver for state and municipal agencies. Unless otherwise ordered by the Court, the state of Maryland, any of its political subdivisions, and any agents thereof shall not be required to post a supersedeas or appeal bond. (Amended effective December 1, 2009.)

Effect of amendments. — The 2009 amendment made minor stylistic changes in 1.b.

Rule 111. Settlement orders.

When the Court has been notified by counsel that a case has been settled, the Court may enter an order dismissing the case and providing for the payment of costs. Such an order of dismissal shall be without prejudice to the right of a party to move for good cause to reopen the case within a time set by the Court if the settlement is not consummated. Alternatively, the Court, upon being notified by counsel that a case has been settled, may require counsel to submit within sixty (60) days a proposed order providing for settlement, in default of which the Court may enter such judgment or other order as may be deemed appropriate.

An order entered pursuant to this Rule means that the entire case, including all claims, counter-claims, cross-claims, third-party claims and claims for attorneys' fees and costs has been settled, unless otherwise stated in the order.

Rule 112. Special proceedings.

1. **Habeas corpus petitions.** a. Applicability of general rules. Petitions for habeas corpus filed pursuant to 28 U.S.C. § 2254 and motions filed pursuant to 28 U.S.C. § 2255 shall be governed, respectively, by the Rules Governing § 2254 Cases in the United States District Courts and the Rules Governing § 2255 Proceedings in the United States District Courts.

b. Return of insufficient petitions. The Clerk of the Court may, upon Court order, return petitions that do not comply with Rules 2 and 3 of the above Rules but shall retain a copy of them as required by said Rules.

c. Form. Petitions shall be filed on forms as they are approved from time to time by order of the Court.

d. Filing fee for § 2254 actions. A filing fee of $5.00 shall be required for 28 U.S.C. § 2254 actions unless the Court authorizes the petitioner to proceed *in forma pauperis*. The Court generally will not authorize a petitioner who has $25.00 or more available after payment of the fee to proceed *in forma pauperis*.

e. No responses to § 2255 motions required without Court order. The Government need not respond to a motion filed under 28 U.S.C. § 2255 unless requested by the Court.

f. Filing. All communications shall be directed to and filed with the Clerk. At the time of filing a petition or motion under 28 U.S.C. § 2241, 28 U.S.C. § 2254, or 28 U.S.C. § 2255, self-represented prisoners must provide the Clerk's Office with one service copy of the petition or motion.

g. Service. All court documents — other than the original petition or motion — filed by self-represented prisoners under 28 U.S.C. § 2241, 28 U.S.C. § 2254, or 28 U.S.C. § 2255 are deemed "filed electronically" for L.R. 102.1.c purposes at the time the documents are electronically docketed by the Clerk's Office. For any response to a document filed electronically under this paragraph, any deadline for filing a response will be calculated from the date the document is electronically docketed by the Clerk's Office.

2. **Prisoner civil rights actions.** a. Forms. All self-represented civil rights actions brought by inmates of penal institutions shall be filed on forms approved from time to time by order of the Court. Petitions to proceed *in forma pauperis* shall likewise be filed on forms approved from time to time by the Court. The Court may authorize penal institutions to produce, stock or distribute such approved forms.

b. Filing and service. All communications shall be directed to and filed with the Clerk. At the time of filing the complaint, self-represented prisoners must provide the Clerk's Office with a service copy of the complaint as to each defendant.

c. Service. i. As to all defendants represented by counsel, all court documents — other than the original complaint — filed by self-represented prisoners in civil rights actions are deemed "filed electronically" for L.R. 102.1.c purposes at the time the documents are electronically docketed by the Clerk's Office. For any response to a document filed electronically under this paragraph, any deadline for filing a response will be calculated from the date the document is electronically docketed by the Clerk's Office.

ii. As to all defendants not represented by counsel, self-represented prisoners are responsible for serving a copy of all documents filed with the Court upon a defendant in accordance with Fed. R. Civ. P. 5. Self-represented prisoners are solely responsible both for determining which defendants are represented and for ensuring unrepresented defendants are served with a copy of any document filed with the Court.

3. **Multi-district litigation.** a. Numbering and docketing. A group of actions transferred to this district under 28 U.S.C. § 1407 shall be given the composite number previously assigned by the Multi-District Panel. Individual actions within the group shall be given specific civil action numbers.

b. Counsel need not be a member of the Bar of this Court. Counsel representing a party in a transferred action need not be a member of the Bar of this Court but shall follow Rule 101.b.iv for moving for admission *pro hac vice*. Parties in multi-district litigation cases need not have counsel who have been admitted to the Bar of this Court.

c. Notification of address. Upon receipt of an order of transfer, all counsel in the transferred action shall notify the Clerk of their names, addresses and telephone numbers.

4. **Condemnation cases — Request for immediate possession.** A plaintiff in a condemnation case seeking immediate possession of land shall submit a statement reciting (a) whether or not the land is improved and, if so,

a specific description of the improvements, (b) whether or not the land is occupied and, if so, the name and address of the occupant and (c) whether the owner and the occupant consent to plaintiff's taking immediate possession.

5. **Review of jeopardy assessments.** All actions arising under 26 U.S.C. § 7429 shall bear the designation "Review of Jeopardy Assessment" on the complaint next to the style of the case. A proposed show cause order shall be submitted with the complaint, and the Clerk shall immediately bring the action to the attention of the Court. Failure to comply with this Rule may result in dismissal of the action. (Amended Aug. 16, 2004, effective Aug. 16, 2004; amended effective December 1, 2009; amended effective July 1, 2010; amended effective July 1, 2011.)

Effect of amendments. — The 2004 amendment, effective Aug. 16, 2004, deleted the former second sentences of 3.a and 3.c; and rewrote 3.b.

The 2009 amendment made minor stylistic changes.

The 2010 amendment in 3.b substituted "Rule 101.b.iv for moving for admission pro hac vice" for "any modified procedures for pro

hac vice," substituted "Parties in multi-district litigation cases" for "admission established by the Court, and such a party" and made related and minor stylistic changes.

The 2011 amendment substituted "petitions" for "motions" in the heading of 1; added 1.f and 1.g; substituted "self-represented" for "pro se" in 2.a; rewrote 2.b; and added 2.c.

Rule 113. Disposition of exhibits and sealed materials.

1. **Trial and Hearing Exhibits.** a. Pending appeal. Unless otherwise ordered by the Court, at the conclusion of a trial or a hearing, the Clerk shall return all exhibits to counsel who submitted them. It is the responsibility of counsel to maintain the exhibits until the time for filing a notice of appeal has expired, or, in the event an appeal is taken, until the appeal is concluded. Upon request by counsel for another party or the Court, counsel having custody of the exhibits must make them available for inspection. Upon request, counsel must transmit the exhibits to the appellate court.

b. Upon final termination of action. Within thirty (30) days of the final termination of an action, counsel may request the return of any trial and hearing exhibits which are in the custody of the Clerk. If any counsel fails to request the return of exhibits, the Court may direct the return, destruction, or other disposition of the exhibits.

2. **Firearms, contraband and currency.** In any action to which the United States is a party, the United States shall maintain custody throughout the proceedings of any firearms, contraband, or currency which have been presented as exhibits and shall be responsible for their safekeeping.

3. **Sealed materials other than trial and hearing exhibits.** Within thirty (30) days of the final termination of an action, counsel may request the return of any sealed materials other than trial and hearing exhibits or request that the materials be unsealed. If counsel fails to request the return or unsealing of any sealed materials, the Court may direct the return, destruction or other disposition of the materials. (Amended Aug. 16, 2004, effective Aug. 16, 2004; and by order effective January 1, 2008; amended effective December 1, 2009.)

Effect of amendments. — The 2004 amendment, effective Aug. 16, 2004, rewrote this Rule.

The 2008 amendment added "and sealed materials" in the rule heading.

The 2009 amendment made minor stylistic changes.

II. CRIMINAL.

Rule 201. Counsel.

1. **Who may appear as counsel.** A defendant in a criminal case may be represented by [1] a member of the Bar of this Court or [2] an attorney who certifies that he or she is [a] a member in good standing of the Bar of the highest court of any state or the District of Columbia and [b] familiar with Federal Rules of Criminal Procedure, the Federal Rules of Evidence, the Federal Rules of Appellate Procedure and the Local Rules of this Court.

2. **Appointment of counsel.** Counsel for indigent defendants shall be appointed in accordance with the procedures established by the plan as adopted and amended by the Court from time to time pursuant to 18 U.S.C. § 3006A. The plan is available for public inspection through the Clerk's Office.

3. **Withdrawal of appearance.** Counsel for a defendant may withdraw their appearance only with leave of Court. (Amended Aug. 16, 2004, effective Aug. 16, 2004; by order effective January 1, 2008; and amended effective December 1, 2009.)

Effect of amendments. — The 2004 amendment, effective Aug. 16, 2004, in 2 in the second sentence substituted "through" for "in".

The 2008 amendment rewrote 1.

The 2009 amendment made minor stylistic changes in 1.

Rule 202. General filing and service requirements.

1. **Generally.** The provisions of L.R. 102 (other than the requirement of L.R. 102.1.a.i that where a party is represented by counsel, all papers filed with the Clerk must be signed by a member of the Bar of this Court) apply to criminal proceedings.

2. **Superseding Charging Documents.** The provisions of L.R. 103.6.c apply to any superseding charging documents. (Amended Aug. 16, 2004, effective Aug. 16, 2004)

Effect of amendments. — 2004 amendment, effective Aug. 16, 2004, added 2 and made minor changes.

Rule 203. Speedy trial plan.

The order establishing time limits and procedures to assure the prompt disposition of criminal cases and certain juvenile proceedings as adopted and amended from time to time by Court order is available for public inspection through the Clerk's Office. (Amended Aug. 16, 2004, effective Aug. 16, 2004.)

Effect of amendments. — The 2004 amendment, effective Aug. 16, 2004, substituted "through" for "in".

Rule 204. Release of information by attorneys.

1. **Generally.** An attorney shall not directly or indirectly release or authorize the public release of any information or opinion concerning any imminent or pending criminal litigation if there is a reasonable likelihood that the release of the information or opinion will interfere with a fair trial or otherwise prejudice the due administration of justice.

2. **Investigations.** Any attorney participating in any grand jury or other investigation shall not make any extra-judicial public statement which goes beyond the public record or which is not necessary to inform the public that the investigation is underway, to describe the general scope of the investigation, to obtain assistance in the apprehension of a suspect, to warn the public of any danger, or otherwise to aid in the progress of the investigation.

3. **Pretrial.** From the time of arrest, issuance of an arrest warrant or the filing of a complaint, information, or indictment in any criminal matter until the commencement of trial or disposition without trial, a lawyer associated with the prosecution or defense shall not release or authorize the release, for dissemination by any means of public communication, of any extra-judicial statement concerning:

a. The prior criminal record (including arrests, indictments, or other charges of crime), or the character or reputation of the accused, except that the lawyer may make a factual statement of the accused's name, age, residence, occupation, and family status, and if the accused has not been apprehended, a lawyer associated with the prosecution may release any information necessary to aid in the apprehension or to warn the public of any dangers that person may present;

b. The existence or contents of any confession, admission, or statement given by the accused, or the refusal or failure of the accused to make any statement;

c. The performance of any examinations or tests or the accused's refusal or failure to submit to an examination or test;

d. The identity, testimony, or credibility of prospective witnesses, except that the lawyer may announce the identity of the victim if the announcement is not otherwise prohibited by law;

e. The possibility of a plea of guilty to the offense charged or a lesser offense;

f. Any opinion as to the accused's guilt or innocence or as to the merits of the case or the evidence in the case.

The foregoing shall not be construed to preclude the lawyer, in the proper discharge of official or professional obligations, from announcing the fact and circumstances of arrest (including time and place of arrest, resistance, pursuit, and use of weapons), the identity of the investigating and arresting officer or agency, and the length of the investigation; from making an announcement, at the time of seizure of any physical evidence other than a confession, admission or statement, which is limited to a description of the evidence seized; from disclosing the nature, substance, or text of the charge, including a brief description of the offense charged; from quoting or referring without comment to public Court records in the case; from announcing the scheduling or result of any stage in the judicial process; from requesting assistance in obtaining evidence; or from announcing without further comment that the accused denies the charges which have been made.

4. **Trial.** During a jury trial, including the period of selection of the jury, no lawyer associated with the prosecution or defense shall give or authorize any extra-judicial statement or interview, relating to the trial or the parties or issues in the trial, for dissemination by any means of public communication, except that the lawyer may quote from or refer without comment to public Court records in the case.

5. **Scope of Rule.** Nothing in this Rule is intended to preclude the formulation or application of more restrictive rules relating to the release of information about juvenile or other offenders, to preclude the holding of hearings or the lawful issuance of reports by legislative, administrative, or investigative bodies, or to preclude any lawyer from replying to any public charges of misconduct that are made.

6. **Penalty.** Any violation of this Rule may be treated as a contempt of Court and may subject the violator to the disciplinary action of the Court.

Rule 205. Release of information by Court personnel.

No person associated with the Court, including any member of the Clerk's Office, of the U.S. Marshal's Office, the staff of any Judge or Magistrate Judge, and any court reporter shall directly or indirectly disclose to any person, without prior authorization by the Court, any information relating to a pending investigation or case which is not part of the public Court records. By way of illustration and not by way of limitation, no Court personnel shall divulge any information concerning arguments and hearings held in chambers or otherwise outside the presence of the public.

Rule 206. Bail.

1. **Grounds for insufficiency.** a. Property otherwise pledged. Unless otherwise ordered by the Court, property serving as security for bail pledged in any other Court shall not be accepted as security for bail ordered in this Court.

b. Person acting under power of attorney. Bail shall not be taken from a person under a power of attorney or other written instrument, save in cases of corporate surety, where the power of attorney or written instrument has first been filed with and approved by the Clerk.

2. **Traffic offenses.** If any person taken into custody for violation of any traffic law or regulation triable before a United States Magistrate Judge is a member of a travel club, automobile association or other organization providing its members with guaranteed appearance bond service and if the terms and conditions of such service are set forth on the defendant's membership card, the membership card may be accepted, in accordance with its terms and conditions and subject to its monetary limits, in lieu of cash or corporate undertaking. The card shall be retained by the judicial officer setting bail and shall be transmitted forthwith to the organization issuing it, according to its established procedures, in exchange for other security to be furnished to the Court.

3. **Forfeiture procedure.** a. General. When a bail is forfeited by order of the Court, the Clerk shall send to the defendant, defense counsel, and the

surety a copy of the forfeiture order by regular mail. Within fourteen (14) days of the date of the order, the surety shall either produce the defendant in Court or shall deposit in the registry of the Court the sum forfeited. A surety who fails to comply with this requirement within the fourteen (14)-day period shall be prohibited from writing any other bails in this Court until compliance has been accomplished. In the case of a corporate surety, this provision shall apply both to the bondsman and the corporate surety.

b. Judgment by default. Judgment by default upon any forfeiture shall be entered in accordance with the provisions of Fed. R. Crim. P. 46 (e) (3).

4. **Prepayment of fees.** The Marshal may require any party (other than one whom the Court has found to be indigent) to pay or secure fees and expenses before serving any writ. (Amended effective December 1, 2009.)

Effect of amendments. — The 2009 amendment in 3.a substituted "fourteen (14) days" for "ten days" in the second sentence and substituted "fourteen (14) day" for "ten-day" in the third sentence.

Rule 207. Motions.

The provisions of L.R. 105 (except L.R. 105.2.c and 105.11) apply to criminal proceedings. (Amended Aug. 16, 2004, effective Aug. 16, 2004.)

Effect of amendments. — The 2004 amendment, effective Aug. 16, 2004, substituted "105.2.c and 105.11" for "105.8".

Rule 208. Arrest to arraignment.

[Reserved for future use]

Rule 209. Discovery.

[Reserved for future use]

Rule 210. Pretrial procedure.

The provisions of L.R. 106.7 (to the extent that under otherwise applicable law exhibits must be disclosed prior to trial) and L.R. 106.8 apply to criminal proceedings.

Rule 211. Trial.

The provisions of L.R. 107.2, 107.5(a), and 107.5(b) (to the extent that under otherwise applicable law exhibits must be disclosed prior to trial), 107.5(c), 107.6, 107.7, 107.8, 107.9, 107.10, 107.11, 107.13, 107.14, and 107.16 apply to criminal proceedings. (Amended by order effective January 1, 2008.)

Effect of amendments. — The 2008 amendment deleted "107.12" after "107.11".

Rule 212. Post-trial motions.

[Reserved for future use]

Rule 213. Sentencing.

1. **Confidentiality of presentence, supervised release, and probation records.** a. Generally. Unless the Court orders that a presentence report, supervised release report, violation report, probation record, or portion thereof be placed in the public record, such report or record is a confidential internal Court document to which the public has no right of access. Except as otherwise authorized by Fed. R. Crim. P. 32(c), by this Rule or otherwise by law, the probation department shall not, unless otherwise ordered by the Court, disclose to any person any such report or record.

b. Procedure upon demand by judicial process. When the production of a presentence report, supervised release report, violation report, probation record, or portion thereof, or the testimony of a probation officer concerning information learned during the performance of official duty is commanded by subpoena or other judicial process, the probation officer shall seek instruction from the Court and request that the Court issue an appropriate order. Except in the most unusual circumstances, the Court shall order that the probation officer be excused from honoring the subpoena or other judicial process and that the requested disclosure not be made.

c. Limited disclosure by direction of the Chief Probation Officer. The Chief Probation Officer may authorize the disclosure of a presentence report, supervised release report, violation report, probation record, or portion thereof, to law enforcement agencies, rehabilitation agencies and bona fide research agencies for use in the normal course of their duties. If authorizing such a disclosure, the Chief U.S. Probation Officer shall promulgate written guidelines to assure the security and confidentiality of the disclosed information.

d. [Reserved for Future Use]

e. Non-disclosure of probation officer's recommendations. Unless otherwise ordered in a particular case by the Court, the probation officer's recommendation on the sentence is not to be disclosed to the defendant, the defendant's counsel, or the attorney for the government.

2. **Entry of scheduling order.** In any case governed by the Sentencing Guidelines promulgated by the United States Sentencing Commission, the Court shall enter an order relating to the sentencing process, in a form prescribed by the Court *en banc,* at the time of entry of a plea of *nolo contendere* or guilty or after a verdict of guilty after trial. The form of order is available for public inspection in the Clerk's Office.

3. **Misdemeanor cases.** Pursuant to § 6A1.2(d) of the Sentencing Guidelines and Policy Statements of the United States Sentencing Commission, in any case for which there has been no conviction above the level of a Class A misdemeanor, (which includes all misdemeanors and infractions), the judicial officer may permit the parties to make oral statements at or before sentencing of the sentencing factors to be relied upon at sentencing in lieu of a written statement.

Pursuant to § 6B1.4(c) of the Sentencing Guidelines and Policy Statements of the United States Sentencing Commission, a judicial officer taking a plea of guilty or *nolo contendere* pursuant to a plea agreement, for any offense or offenses not above the level of a Class A misdemeanor (which includes all misdemeanors and infractions), may permit the parties to make any required stipulation of facts relative to sentencing orally, on the record, at the time the plea agreement is offered, in lieu of a written stipulation. (Amended effective December 1, 2009.)

Effect of amendments. — The 2009 amendment made minor stylistic changes in 1.b.

Rule 214. Disposition of exhibits and sealed materials.

The provisions of L.R. 113 apply to criminal proceedings. (Amended Aug. 16, 2004, effective Aug. 16, 2004.)

Effect of amendments. — The 2004 amendment, effective Aug. 16, 2004, added "and sealed materials" to the heading.

III. UNITED STATES MAGISTRATE JUDGES.

Rule 301. Authority of United States Magistrate Judges.

1. **Geographical jurisdiction.** All Magistrate Judges have jurisdiction to try, hear and determine cases within their original and referred jurisdiction throughout the entire District of Maryland and in such cases arising in adjoining districts pursuant to separate authorizations.

2. **Recording.** All Court proceedings before Magistrate Judges shall be recorded either electronically or by a court reporter.

3. **Criminal cases.** All Magistrate Judges are specially designated to conduct criminal cases with the consent of the defendant, including trial, judgment, sentence, and revocation of probation or supervised release, in conformity with and subject to the limitations of 18 U.S.C. § 3401, Fed. R. Crim. P. 58, and any other applicable law of the United States. All full-time Magistrate Judges may conduct a jury trial in any misdemeanor case when the defendant so requests and is entitled to trial by jury under the Constitution and laws of the United States.

4. **Civil cases.** Pursuant to 28 U.S.C. § 636(c), with the consent of the parties, a District Judge may designate a full-time Magistrate Judge to conduct any or all proceedings, including trial, in a jury or non-jury civil matter, and to order the entry of final judgment in the case. Cases referred to a Magistrate Judge shall be randomly assigned.

Upon the filing of any civil case, the Clerk of Court shall notify the parties of their right to proceed by consent before a Magistrate Judge.

5. **Authority under 28 U.S.C. § 636(b).** a. Nondispositive matters. Pursuant to 28 U.S.C. § 636(b), a District Judge may designate a full-time Magistrate Judge to hear and determine (including the passage of final orders as to all or any part of) any pretrial matter pending before the Court except those listed in L.R. 301.5.b below. Nondispositive pretrial matters include, but are not limited to, discovery disputes and pretrial orders under Fed. R. Civ. P. 16.

Any objection to a Magistrate Judge's order must be served and filed within fourteen (14) days after service of the order. Unless otherwise ordered by the Magistrate Judge who issued the order or the District Judge who designated the Magistrate Judge to hear and determine the matter, the filing of objections to the Magistrate Judge's order shall not operate as a stay of any obligation or deadline imposed by the order. A District Judge may reconsider, modify, or set aside any portion of the Magistrate Judge's order found to be clearly erroneous or contrary to law.

b. Dispositive matters. Pursuant to 28 U.S.C. § 636(b), a District Judge may designate a full-time Magistrate Judge to conduct hearings, if necessary, including evidentiary hearings, and to submit to the District Judge proposed findings of fact and recommendations for action to be taken by the District Judge as to any of the following:

i. a motion for injunctive relief;

ii. a motion for judgment on the pleadings;

iii. a motion for summary judgment;

iv. a motion by a defendant to dismiss or quash an indictment or information;

v. a motion to suppress evidence in a criminal case;

vi. a motion to dismiss or permit maintenance of a class action;

vii. a motion to dismiss for failure to state a claim upon which relief can be granted;

viii. a motion to involuntarily dismiss an action;

ix. a motion to review an administrative determination as to Social Security or related benefits, pursuant to 42 U.S.C. § 405(g);

x. prisoner petitions challenging conditions of confinement; and

xi. applications for post-trial relief under 28 U.S.C. § 2254 and § 2255 made by individuals convicted of criminal offenses.

Any objections must be served and filed within fourteen (14) days after a copy of the proposed findings and recommendations is served on the party wishing to object, pursuant to Fed. R. Civ. P. 72(b). When the proceedings before the Magistrate Judge have been electronically recorded, transcription of the record shall not be necessary unless otherwise directed by the Court.

The District Judge shall make a *de novo* determination as to those portions of the proposed findings and recommendations to which specific objections are made. The District Judge may accept, reject, or modify the recommended decision, may receive further evidence, or may recommit the matter to the Magistrate Judge with instructions.

c. Designation as special master. A District Judge may designate a Magistrate Judge to serve as a special master pursuant to and in accordance with Fed. R. Civ. P. 53. With consent of the parties, such designation may be made without regard to the limitations of Fed. R. Civ. P. 53(b). Appeals from the decision of a Magistrate Judge designated as a special master pursuant to this Rule shall be taken in accordance with Fed. R. Civ. P. 53(e).

6. **Other duties.** All Magistrate Judges are specially designated to exercise all powers heretofore held by United States Commissioners, to exercise all other powers authorized by 28 U.S.C. § 636(a) and (g), or any other applicable

law, and to perform such additional duties as are not inconsistent with the Constitution and laws of the United States. These powers and duties include, but are not limited to, the following:

a. Consideration of criminal complaints and affidavits and issuance of arrest warrants or summonses pursuant to Fed. R. Crim. P. 3, 4, and 9.

b. Conduct of initial appearance proceedings for defendants pursuant to Fed. R. Crim. P. 5.

c. Conduct of preliminary examinations pursuant to Fed. R. Crim. P. 5.1 and 18 U.S.C. § 3060.

d. Receipt of grand jury returns pursuant to Fed. R. Crim. P. 6(f) and issuance of bench warrants on indictments pursuant to Fed. R. Crim. P. 9.

e. Acceptance of waivers of indictment pursuant to Fed. R. Crim. P. 7(b).

f. Conduct of preliminary hearings in probation or supervised release revocation proceedings pursuant to Fed. R. Crim. P. 32.1.

g. Conduct of initial proceedings pursuant to Fed. R. Crim. P. 5(c) for defendants charged in other districts.

h. Issuance of search and seizure warrants pursuant to Fed. R. Crim. P. 41.

i. Appointment of attorneys pursuant to 18 U.S.C. § 3006A and Fed. R. Crim. P. 44.

j. Issuance of orders concerning release or detention of defendants and material witnesses and forfeiture or exoneration of bond pursuant to 18 U.S.C. § 3141 *et seq.*, and Fed. R. Crim. P. 32.1, 40 and 46.

k. Direction of the payment of basic transportation and subsistence expenses for released persons financially unable to bear such costs, pursuant to 18 U.S.C. §§ 4282 and 4285.

l. Issuance of orders permitting dismissals, on the government's motion, of violation notices, complaints, informations, and indictments in criminal cases pursuant to Fed. R. Crim. P. 48(a).

m. Handling of arraignments in criminal cases pursuant to Fed. R. Crim. P. 10, including acceptance of not guilty pleas, scheduling of motions, scheduling of pretrial conferences and trials, and issuance of bench warrants for the arrest of a defendant who fails to appear for arraignment before the Magistrate Judge.

n. Conduct of initial proceedings upon the appearance of an individual accused of an act of juvenile delinquency pursuant to 18 U.S.C. § 5034.

o. Appointment of interpreters pursuant to 28 U.S.C. §§ 1827 and 1828 in cases initiated by the United States.

p. Under appropriate conditions and when an order is required, issuance of orders for lineups, photographs, fingerprinting, palmprinting, voice identification, mental or physical examination, the taking of blood, urine, fingernail, hair, or bodily secretion samples (with appropriate medical safeguards required by due process considerations), and handwriting exemplars.

q. Upon the request of the United States Attorney, (1) authorization of the installation of pen registers and trap and trace devices, and execution of orders directing the telephone company to assist the Government in such installation; (2) authorization of the installation of beeper devices ("transponders"), Global Positioning Satellite ("GPS") tracking devices, other tracking devices; and (3) authorization of the installation of devices ("clone beepers") which duplicate signals received on a contact beeper or similar device, and execution of orders directing the company or other person furnishing the contact beeper to assist the Government in such installation.

r. Issuance of orders (1) under the provisions of § 356 of the Tax Equity and Fiscal Responsibility Act of 1982 (P.L. 97-248) authorizing, pursuant to 26 U.S.C. § 6103 (as amended by P.L. 97-248), the disclosure of tax returns and return information for use in criminal proceedings, and (2) directing banks not to notify their customers of the issuance of subpoenas for financial records pursuant to 12 U.S.C. § 3409 or 12 U.S.C. § 3413(i).

s. Issuance of writs of habeas corpus *ad testificandum* and *ad prosequendum*.

t. Upon request of the United States Attorney, a Magistrate Judge shall have the authority to consider and approve an agreement between the Government and a defendant to defer prosecution in any petty offense or misdemeanor case for a period not to exceed one year from the date said agreement is approved by the Magistrate Judge.

u. Use of the services of the United States Probation Office for preparation of presentence investigations and other reports and recommendations.

v. Conduct of international extradition proceedings pursuant to 18 U.S.C. § 3184.

w. Appointment of counsel and performance of the verification functions set forth in 18 U.S.C. §§ 4107, 4108, and 4109 relating to proceedings for the transfer of offenders between the United States and foreign countries.

x. Issuance of warrants or orders permitting entry into and inspection of premises and/or seizure of property, as authorized by law, when properly requested by a government agency.

y. Issuance of show cause orders to enforce administrative summons or subpoenas.

z. Issuance of attachments, conduct of hearings, including evidentiary hearings, and submission to the District Judge of proposed findings of fact and recommendations with respect to the disposition of a petition to enforce compliance with a summons issued by the Internal Revenue Service.

aa. Consideration and granting or denial of motions of litigants to proceed *in forma pauperis*, with appeal to a District Judge.

ab. Appointment of counsel for indigent litigants pursuant to 28 U.S.C. § 1915(e)(1) and other statutes.

ac. Making special appointments to serve process pursuant to Fed. R. Civ. P. 4(c)(2).

ad. Organization of petit and grand juries.

ae. Conduct of voir dire and receipt of jury verdicts in civil and criminal cases being tried by a District Judge, on consent of the parties.

af. Supervision of proceedings on requests for letters rogatory in civil and criminal cases pursuant to 28 U.S.C. § 1782.

ag. Execution of exemplifications of Court records.

ah. Issuance of orders in mortgage foreclosure proceedings prior to ratification of sale.

ai. Ordering and conducting prejudgment remedy proceedings in accordance with 28 U.S.C. §§ 3101-3105.

aj. Ordering and conducting supplementary proceedings in accordance with Md. R. Proc. 2-633, upon the filing of an appropriate affidavit.

ak. Review and issuance of orders concerning confessed judgments pursuant to L.R. 108.1.b *supra.*

al. Review of default judgments and recommendations concerning damages.

am. Review of matters and issuance of orders under Local Admiralty Rule (LAR)(e)(4).

an. Issuance of orders for the deposit and withdrawal of registry funds in conjunction with matters over which Magistrate Judges exercise jurisdiction.

ao. Conduct of naturalization ceremonies.

ap. Admission of attorneys to the Bar of this Court.

aq. Any full-time Magistrate Judge is authorized to conduct proceedings for initial commitment of narcotics addicts under Title III of the Narcotics Addicts Rehabilitation Act.

The Magistrate Judge, after conducting such proceedings, shall recommend to the District Judge the commitment of the addict or shall state his reasons for recommending against commitment. In a case where the Magistrate Judge recommends against commitment, the addict shall have a right to a hearing *de novo* before a District Judge.

The Magistrate Judge's recommendation shall be transmitted forthwith to the Chambers Judge for appropriate action.

ar. All Magistrate Judges for the District of Maryland are specially designated to commit persons to St. Elizabeth's Hospital, Washington, D.C., in accordance with the provisions of the District of Columbia Code, § 21-902.

as. Issue orders for contempt of Court as authorized by the Federal Courts Improvement Act of 2000, 28 U.S.C. § 636(e).

7. **Part-time magistrate judges.** Nothing in these Local Rules shall be deemed an assignment to part-time Magistrate Judges of additional duties under 28 U.S.C. § 636(b) other than those permitted by Rule 7 of the Conflict of Interest Rules for Part-Time Magistrate Judges adopted by the Judicial Conference pursuant to 28 U.S.C. § 632(b). (Amended Aug. 16, 2004, effective Aug. 16, 2004; by order effective January 1, 2008; amended effective December 1, 2009; amended effective July 1, 2011.)

Effect of amendments. — The 2004 amendment, effective Aug. 16, 2004, in 6.g substituted "5(c)" for "40"; in 6.q inserted "Global Positioning Satellite ("GPS") tracking devices"; and in 6.ak substituted "108.1.b" for "108.b".

The 2008 amendment substituted "Section 5.b." for "§ 5.b." in the first paragraph of 5.a.

The 2009 amendment substituted "L.R. 301.5.b." for "Section 5.b." in the first sentence of the first paragraph of 5.a; in the first sentence of the second paragraph of 5.a and 5.b substituted "fourteen (14) days" for "ten days"; and made minor stylistic changes in 7.

The 2011 amendment substituted "after service of the order" for "of the entry of the order" in the second paragraph of 5.a.

Rule 302. Appeals from decisions by Magistrate Judges.

1. **Criminal cases.** Appeals in criminal cases shall be made to the District Court within fourteen (14) days from entry of the decision, order, judgment of conviction, or sentence in accordance with Fed. R. Crim. P. 58(g)(2) and other applicable statutes and rules.

Within thirty (30) days of the docketing of the appeal, the appellant shall file with the Clerk of Court and serve on the appellee a memorandum stating the exact points of law, facts, and authorities on which the appeal is based. The appellee shall file an answering memorandum within thirty (30) days thereafter. The Court may extend these times upon a showing of good cause. If an appellant fails to file a memorandum within the time provided, the Court may dismiss the appeal. All appeals shall be decided on the record and the parties' memoranda, unless the Court, in its discretion, orders oral argument.

2. **Civil cases.** Appeals in civil cases referred by consent shall be governed by Fed. R. Civ. P. 73. (Amended effective December 1, 2009.)

Effect of amendments. — The 2009 amendment in 1 substituted "fourteen (14) days" for "ten days" in the first paragraph and made minor stylistic changes.

Rule 303. Designation of Chief Magistrate Judge.

The Chief District Judge shall have the authority to designate one of the full-time Magistrate Judges as Chief United States Magistrate Judge for the District of Maryland. The Chief Magistrate Judge shall perform such duties in connection with the administration of the Magistrate Judges' system within this district as the Chief District Judge may, from time to time, assign. The Chief Magistrate Judge, or a person designated by the Chief Magistrate Judge, is authorized to reassign from one Magistrate Judge to another matters originally assigned by a District Judge to a Magistrate Judge pursuant to L.R. 301 and 28 U.S.C. § 636. (Amended effective December 1, 2009.)

Effect of amendments. — The 2009 amendment added the last sentence.

Rule 304. Forfeiture of collateral.

1. **General provisions.** a. The provisions of this Rule do not create or otherwise define an offense. This Rule applies to petty offenses which have otherwise been created and/or defined by federal statutes, regulations, or applicable state statutes lawfully assimilated by virtue of the Assimilative Crimes Act (18 U.S.C. § 13) which petty offenses are committed within the jurisdiction of the United States District Court for the District of Maryland.

b. When an asterisk (*) is inserted next to a listed violation, *no* forfeiture of collateral will be permitted. Forfeiture of collateral will not be permitted unless same is specifically authorized by the collateral schedule hereinafter provided, except as authorized by paragraph (d) below. For any offense not specifically listed, a mandatory appearance will be required except as may be authorized by paragraph (d) below.

c. In the event any non-mandatory offense is one of a number of multiple offenses, and any one of such multiple offenses is a mandatory appearance offense, the arresting officer or officer issuing a violation notice shall treat all offenses which otherwise would have been non-mandatory as a mandatory appearance offense. In the event any non-mandatory offense is deemed by the arresting officer or officer issuing a violation notice to be of an aggravated nature, the officer may treat the offense as a mandatory appearance offense. The arresting officer or officer issuing a violation notice may, within his discretion, always treat any offense as a mandatory appearance offense notwithstanding the fact that forfeiture of collateral may otherwise be permitted pursuant to this Rule.

d. Notwithstanding any other provision contained in this Rule, at the request or recommendation of, or with the consent of the prosecuting authority, the United States Magistrate Judge may set or authorize the setting of collateral for any petty offense. Notwithstanding any other provision contained in this Rule, at the request or recommendation of, or with the consent of the prosecuting authority, the United States Magistrate Judge may increase or decrease any collateral which may otherwise be authorized or set pursuant to this Rule. The United States Magistrate Judge may require a mandatory appearance for any petty offense so long as any collateral which may have been previously authorized and set pursuant to this Rule has not been received prior to the Magistrate Judge's issuance of a notice of mandatory appearance.

e. At no time may collateral be set in an amount greater than the maximum fine authorized for the offense charged, nor may collateral be less than any mandatory minimum fine which may be required as a penalty for the offense charged. Should any collateral erroneously be set higher than the authorized maximum fine then the collateral shall automatically be reduced to said authorized maximum fine. Should any collateral erroneously be set in an amount less than a required mandatory minimum fine, the amount of collateral shall automatically be increased to said mandatory minimum.

f. A collateral offense shall be processed by giving an alleged offender a violation notice or citation with mail-in envelope (comparable to DD Form 1805 in use on military installations or in such other form as may otherwise be approved by the Court), the notice or citation setting forth the offense, the date and location thereof, name of the issuing officer, the full name, address, date of birth, and any other identifying data, which may include social security number, concerning the offender and the amount of collateral which can be forfeited. It shall further contain instructions to pay the collateral to the Clerk of the Court, or if the offender wishes to contest the charge, to indicate the option to appear before a United States Magistrate Judge for trial or other appropriate proceedings, in either event by mailing the form to the Clerk of the Court within seven (7) days of receipt of the violation notice or citation. The violation notice or citation shall also set forth the date and time upon which the matter will be heard before a United States Magistrate Judge or otherwise indicate that the defendant will be notified when to appear in the future.

g. The Clerk shall establish a Central Violations Bureau for the processing of violation notices, citations and collateral. The address of the Central Violations Bureau shall be U.S. Courts - CVB, P.O. Box 70939, Charlotte, NC 28272-0939, or such other address as may be subsequently approved by the

Court. All violation notices and citations issued to alleged offenders shall show the appropriate address for the receipt of collateral or notice that a defendant desires a hearing before the United States Magistrate Judge.

h. For any petty offense in which collateral is not set, the defendant shall be issued a violation notice or citation containing the information required in paragraphs (f) and (g) above, except that in the space provided for the amount of collateral there shall be inserted the letters "M.A." which letters shall indicate mandatory appearance required, directing the defendant to appear before a United States Magistrate Judge at a specified date and time or otherwise indicating that the defendant will be notified when to appear in the future. However, if the arresting officer has reason to believe that the person charged with an offense may not appear as required, the officer may take the alleged offender before a United States Magistrate Judge or other judicial officer as set forth in 18 U.S.C. § 3041 without unnecessary delay for the purpose of setting appropriate conditions of release in accordance with the provisions of 18 U.S.C. § 3146.

i. Except in exceptional circumstances, a violation notice or citation shall charge only one offense. If an alleged offender is deemed to have committed more than one offense, each offense shall be charged on a separate violation notice or citation. Nothing contained in this Rule shall be deemed to prohibit the prosecution of a petty offense by means of a criminal complaint, criminal information, or indictment.

j. The payment of collateral for any offense in which collateral is set as authorized by this Rule, shall cause said collateral to be forfeited to the United States and payment and forfeiture of said collateral shall signify that the defendant does not contest the charge nor requires a hearing before a United States Magistrate Judge. If collateral is paid and forfeited, such action shall be tantamount to a finding of guilty, and the defendant shall be deemed convicted of any offense for which collateral is paid and forfeited. Upon conviction, the Clerk or United States Magistrate Judge shall certify the record of any conviction of a traffic violation, but not to include parking offenses, to the appropriate state Motor Vehicle Administration.

k. Whenever a check is returned to the Clerk as uncollectible for any reason within the control of the payor, the offense for which the collateral was posted shall be referred promptly to the appropriate United States Magistrate Judge for the scheduling of a mandatory appearance or such other action as may be deemed appropriate by the United States Magistrate Judge.

l. When any alleged offender fails to pay any collateral set pursuant to this Rule and fails to appear in response to a Notice to Appear or Summons, the United States Magistrate Judge may consider and treat the offense as a mandatory appearance offense, and thereafter refuse any tender of the payment of collateral and set the case for hearing, or in the Magistrate Judge's discretion, increase the amount of collateral. A United States Magistrate Judge may also issue a warrant for the arrest of the alleged offender as authorized by Fed. R. Crim. P. 58(d)(3) and/or set the case for hearing.

m. For offenses designated as "Hunting and Fishing," "Wildlife," or "Migratory Bird Treaty Act," in the case of an aggravated offense, multiple offenses, an offense involving a defendant who has previously been convicted of an offense in the above categories, or for any other reason deemed appropriate by the Office of the United States Attorney for the District of Maryland or any other attorney acting under the authority of the United States Attorney to represent the Government in proceedings before United States Magistrate Judges, the arresting officer or officer issuing a violation notice shall have the discretion to set collateral within the minimum and maximum limits hereinafter specified, subject to prior authorization from the Office of the United States Attorney for the District of Maryland or any other attorney acting under the authority of the United States Attorney for the District of Maryland. Otherwise, the collateral shall be the minimum amount provided for in the collateral schedule.

n. In the event the payment is received by the Clerk before the Violation Notice is forwarded to a Magistrate Judge for collection, the Clerk shall retain and process it. Should it be necessary for the Court or United States Magistrate Judge to issue an arrest warrant as a result of any alleged violator's failure to appear, the amount of collateral shall automatically triple from the amount originally set on the violation notice or citation. For good cause shown, the Court and/or United State [States] Magistrate Judge may reduce the collateral. Nothing contained herein shall prevent the United States Magistrate Judge from requiring a mandatory appearance.

o. In any mandatory appearance case or in the event that any authorized collateral is not forfeited, should any alleged violator fail to appear in response to a Notice to Appear or Summons, the United States Magistrate Judge, Clerk of the Court, Central Violations Bureau and/or the United States Marshal may, in coordination with the Maryland Department of Transportation Motor Vehicle Administration, utilize the Motor Vehicle Administration violation and flagging procedures so as to prohibit an alleged violator who fails to appear in connection with any parking or traffic offense from obtaining a current motor vehicle registration from the State of Maryland until such time as any outstanding offenses are disposed of according to law. The Clerk or United States Magistrate Judge shall not authorize the release of any flag upon the vehicle registration of an alleged violator until such time as all collateral is paid by cash, certified check or money order, and forfeited, except that in the event a trial is requested, no hearing or trial shall be held until such time as the total collateral is deposited with the Clerk or United States Magistrate Judge. Upon the deposit of said collateral, any flag upon the vehicle registration of the alleged violator shall be released. For good cause shown, in the interest of justice or in otherwise exceptional circumstances, the United States Magistrate Judge may reduce the amount of collateral to be paid and forfeited or deposited under this paragraph and authorize the release of any flag upon the vehicle registration of the alleged violator upon the payment or deposit of such reduced amount, unless it is determined by the United States Magistrate [Judge] that no payment or deposit shall be required.

p. The provisions of this Rule shall apply to petty offenses alleged to have been committed by a juvenile prior to the filing of the Attorney General's certification referred to in 18 U.S.C. § 5032 and 18 U.S.C. § 3401(g). After the filing of such certification, the provisions of this Rule shall apply only in the event that the juvenile, with the advice of counsel, files a written request to be prosecuted as an adult.

q. Nothing contained in this Rule shall prevent the issuance of a Warrant of Arrest in accordance with Fed. R. Crim. P. 58(d)(3) or any other lawful authority.

2. **Schedule of monetary collateral and mandatory appearance offenses.** The Court shall approve a schedule of monetary collateral and mandatory appearance offenses, which schedule shall be filed with the Clerk as a public document. The Court may amend the schedule from time to time. (Amended Aug. 16, 2004, effective Aug. 16, 2004; amended effective December 1, 2009.)

Effect of amendments. — The 2004 amendment, effective Aug. 16, 2004, in 1.f inserted a comma following "approved by the Court)".

The 2009 amendment substituted "U.S. Courts - CVB, P.O. Box 70939, Charlotte, NC 28272-0939" for "Central Violations Bureau, Clerk, United States District Court, United States Courthouse, Baltimore, Maryland 21201" in the second sentence of 1.g; and made minor stylistic changes.

IV. BANKRUPTCY PROCEEDINGS.

Rule 401. Rules in Bankruptcy Court proceedings.

Proceedings in the Bankruptcy Court shall be governed by Local Bankruptcy Rules as adopted from time to time by order of the Court.

Rule 402. Referral of bankruptcy cases and proceedings.

Pursuant to 28 U.S.C. § 157(a), all cases under Title 11 of the United States Code and proceedings arising under Title 11 or arising in or related to cases under Title 11 shall be deemed to be referred to the Bankruptcy Judges of this District.

Cited in In re Lewis, 170 Bankr. 861 (Bankr. D. Md. 1994); Koffman v. Osteoimplant Technology, Inc., 182 Bankr. 115 (D. Md. 1995).

Rule 403. Definition of transmittal.

As used in this chapter, transmittal of a document includes the forwarding of a paper document or copy; or providing access to an electronic document in accordance with the procedures adopted by the Court. (Added Aug. 16, 2004, effective Aug. 16, 2004.)

Rule 404. Appeals to the District Court.

1. **Manner of appeal.** a. Generally. Appeals to the District Court from the Bankruptcy Court shall be taken in the manner prescribed in Part VIII of the Bankruptcy Rules, Rules 8001 et seq.

b. Bankruptcy Court opinion and order. Appellant shall provide with the opening brief a copy of the Bankruptcy Court opinion and order from which the appeal is being taken.

2. **Dismissal for non-compliance with Bankruptcy Rule 8006.** Whenever the appellant fails to designate the contents of the record on appeal or to

file a statement of the issues to be presented on appeal within the time required by Bankruptcy Rule 8006, the Bankruptcy Clerk shall transmit forthwith to the Clerk of the District Court a partial record consisting of a copy of the order or judgment appealed from, the notice of appeal, a copy of the docket entries and such other documents as the Bankruptcy Clerk deems relevant to the appeal. (The District Court may thereafter order the Bankruptcy Clerk to transmit any other relevant documents to the Clerk of the District Court). When the partial record has been filed in the District Court the Court may, upon motion of the appellee (which is to be filed in the District Court) or upon its own initiative, dismiss the appeal for non-compliance with Bankruptcy Rule 8006 after giving the appellant an opportunity to explain the non-compliance and upon considering whether the non-compliance had prejudicial effect on the other parties.

3. **Dismissal for non-compliance with Bankruptcy Rule 8009.** Whenever the appellant fails to serve and file a brief within the time required by Bankruptcy Rule 8009, the District Court may, upon motion of the appellee (to be filed in the District Court) or upon its own initiative, dismiss the appeal after giving the appellant an opportunity to explain the non-compliance and upon considering whether the non-compliance had prejudicial effect on the other parties.

4. **Procedure regarding motion to stay pending appeal.** After seeking appropriate relief under Bankruptcy Rule 8005, an appellant seeking a stay pending appeal by the District Court of an order entered by the Bankruptcy Court shall file with the Clerk of the District Court a motion to stay and copies of all documents in the record of the Bankruptcy Court relevant to the appeal. Upon the filing of these documents, the Clerk of the District Court shall immediately open a civil file and the District Court shall give immediate consideration to the motion to stay. If the underlying appeal is ultimately perfected, it will be assigned the same civil action number as was assigned to the motion to stay.

5. **Bankruptcy Court certification regarding interlocutory appeal.** Whenever there has been filed in the District Court an application for leave to appeal an interlocutory order of the Bankruptcy Court, the Bankruptcy Court shall, upon request of the District Court, submit to the District Court a written certification stating whether, in its opinion, the interlocutory order involves a controlling question of law as to which there is substantial ground for difference of opinion and whether an immediate appeal of it may materially advance the ultimate termination of the case. The District Court shall thereafter determine whether to grant or deny the application for leave to appeal. (Amended Aug. 16, 2004, effective Aug. 16, 2004; amended effective December 1, 2009.)

Effect of amendments. — The 2004 amendment, effective Aug. 16, 2004, renumbered former Rule 403 to be this Rule; substituted "documents" for "papers" wherever the term occurs; in a.2 in the first sentence substituted "transmit" for "forward"; and in a.4 inserted "After seeking appropriate relief under Bankruptcy Rule 8005" at the beginning.

The 2009 amendment, effective December 1, 2009, made minor, stylistic changes.

Rule 405. Rules of procedure for withdrawal of reference.

1. **General rule.** When a case or proceeding has been referred by this Court to the Bankruptcy Court, all documents and pleadings in or related to such case or proceeding shall be filed with the Clerk in the Bankruptcy Court.

2. **Withdrawal of reference of bankruptcy case or proceeding.** a. Filing of motion for withdrawal of reference with bankruptcy clerk. A motion pursuant to 28 U.S.C. § 157(d) and Bankruptcy Rule 5011 to withdraw the reference of any bankruptcy case, contested matter or adversary proceeding referred to the Bankruptcy Court pursuant to 28 U.S.C. § 157(a) and L.R. 402 shall be filed with the Clerk in the Bankruptcy Court. If the motion requests withdrawal of only a portion of the case, a contested matter, or a portion of an adversary proceeding, the motion shall be accompanied by the filing of a designation of the documents and pleadings filed in the case or proceeding to which the motion relates.

b. Withdrawal of reference of bankruptcy cases. A motion to withdraw the reference of a case to the Bankruptcy Court must be timely filed, and in any event, before the case is closed.

c. Withdrawal of reference of adversary proceeding or contested matter. A motion to withdraw an adversary proceeding or a contested matter in a case which has been referred to the Bankruptcy Court must be filed by the earlier of fourteen (14) days before the date scheduled for the first hearing on the merits and;

i. in the case of an adversary proceeding, within twenty-one (21) days after the last pleading is permitted to be filed pursuant to Bankruptcy Rule 7012; or

ii. in the case of a contested matter, within twenty-one (21) days after the last responsive pleading or memorandum in opposition is permitted to be filed pursuant to Local Bankruptcy Rule 9013-1(b)(3).

3. Filing of pleadings after reference withdrawn. a. If the reference of an entire case has been withdrawn from the Bankruptcy Court to the District Court, all pleadings and documents in or related to such case shall be thereafter filed with the Clerk in the District Court.

b. Where the reference of only a portion of an entire case has been withdrawn, pleadings and documents with respect to the case (including any parts thereof that have been withdrawn or transferred) shall continue to be filed with the Clerk in the Bankruptcy Court. Any pleadings and documents which relate to any parts of the case which have been withdrawn or transferred to the District Court shall also be filed with the Clerk of the District Court.

c. Upon withdrawal or transfer of any complaint to the District Court, the plaintiff may forward to the defendant a notice and request to waive service of summons or the Clerk shall issue a District Court summons pursuant to Fed. R. Civ. P. 4(d) unless either of the aforementioned has already occurred pursuant to the Bankruptcy Rules.

d. This subsection (d) governs personal injury tort and wrongful death claims which must be tried in the District Court pursuant to 28 U.S.C. § 157(b)(5). Except for the procedures contained within this subsection, personal injury tort and wrongful death proceedings shall be filed with the

Clerk in the Bankruptcy Court. However, beneath the bankruptcy number, the pleading or other document shall designate the pleading or document as a "SECTION 157(b)(5) MATTER." When filing a complaint a completed District Court civil cover sheet (A.O. Form JS-44c) should be submitted beneath the Bankruptcy Court cover sheet required by Local Bankruptcy Rule 7003-1. No summons shall be issued until the proceeding is transferred to the District Court. Upon filing the complaint, the Clerk in the Bankruptcy Court shall immediately transfer the proceeding to the District Court and plaintiff may send to the defendant(s) a notice and request to waive service of summons pursuant to Fed. R. Civ. P. 4(d) or the Clerk of the District Court shall issue a summons.

4. **Motions concerning venue in bankruptcy cases and proceedings.** All motions concerning venue in cases arising under Title 11 or arising in or related to cases under Title 11 shall be determined by the Bankruptcy Court, except in those cases to be tried in the District Court pursuant to 28 U.S.C. § 157(b)(5). (Amended Aug. 16, 2004, effective Aug. 16, 2004; amended effective January 1, 2008; and amended effective December 1, 2009.)

Effect of amendments. — The 2004 amendment, effective Aug. 16, 2004, renumbered former Rule 404 to be this Rule; substituted "documents" for "papers" or "document" for "paper" wherever the terms occur; in 2.c.ii substituted "9013-1(b)(3)" for "9013-1(3)"; in 3.b. in the first sentence substituted "withdrawn or transferred" for "withdrawn, transferred or removed," inserted the present second sentence, and deleted the former third sentence; in 3.c. substituted "withdraw or transfer" for "withdrawal, transfer or removal" and deleted "or the Clerk shall issue a District Court summons" following "4(d)"; in 3.d in the first sentence substituted "(d)" for "(5)," in the fourth sentence substituted "7003-1" for "7005-1" and in the sixth sentence substituted "send" for "forward".

The 2008 amendment deleted the last sentence in 3.b regarding keeping a separate docket sheet of pleadings and documents transferred to the District Court.

The 2009 amendment, effective December 1, 2009, in 2.c substituted "fourteen (14)" for "eleven (11)"; and in 2.c.i and 2.c.ii substituted "twenty-one (21)" for "twenty (20)"; and made minor, stylistic changes.

Rule 406. Jury trial.

1. **Demand.** In any bankruptcy proceeding any party may demand a trial by jury of any issue triable of right by jury by (1) serving upon the other parties a demand therefor in writing at any time after the commencement of the action and not later than fourteen (14) days after the service of the last pleading directed to such issue, and (2) filing the demand as required by Bankruptcy Rule 9015. Such demand may be indorsed upon a pleading of the party. If the adversary proceeding is one that has been removed from another court, any demand previously made under the rules of that court shall constitute a demand for trial by jury under this Rule.

2. **Specification of issues.** In the demand a party may specify the issues which the party wishes so tried; otherwise the party shall be deemed to have demanded trial by jury for all the issues so triable. If the party has demanded trial by jury for only some of the issues, any other party within fourteen (14) days after service of the demand or such lesser time as the Court may order, may serve a demand for trial by jury of any other or all of the issues of fact in the action.

3. **Waiver.** The failure of a party to serve and file a demand as required by this Rule constitutes a waiver by the party of trial by jury. A demand for trial by jury made as herein provided may not be withdrawn without the consent of the parties.

4. **Consent to jury trial before United States Bankruptcy Judge.** Pursuant to 28 U.S.C. § 157(e), with the consent of the parties, a District Judge may designate a Bankruptcy Judge to conduct a jury trial. (Amended Aug. 16, 2004, effective Aug. 16, 2004; amended effective December 1, 2009.)

Effect of amendments. — The 2004 amendments, effective Aug. 16, 2004, renumbered former Rule 405 to be this Rule; in 1 substituted "9015" for "7005"; and added 4.

The 2009 amendment, effective December 1, 2009, substituted "fourteen (14) days" for "10 days" in 1 and 2; and made minor, stylistic changes.

Rule 407. Removal.

Removals under 28 U.S.C. § 1452 or § 1441 in cases related to bankruptcy cases should be filed with the Bankruptcy Clerk. (Added Aug. 16, 2004, effective Aug. 16, 2004.)

V. COURT ADMINISTRATION AND SECURITY.

Rule 501. Assignment of cases.

1. **In general.** This Rule governs the assignment of cases to Judges of the Court and among the two divisions of the Court. It is a rule of administrative convenience, and it is not intended to, nor does it, confer any rights upon any litigant. Notwithstanding the provisions of this Rule, the Court may assign a case to a Judge in a division other than the one specified in this Rule.

All cases will be assigned to one of the Judges of the Court. With the exception of cases referred to Magistrate Judges, all proceedings in a particular case will usually be held before the Judge to whom that case is assigned.

2. **Removals.** A case removed from a state tribunal shall be assigned to one of the Judges sitting in the division of the Court in which the state tribunal is located.

3. **Prisoner cases.** All District Judges shall be assigned a pro-rata share of all (i) habeas corpus cases, and (ii) civil rights cases filed by prisoners.

4. **Other civil cases.** Other civil cases shall be assigned in accordance with the provisions set forth in this paragraph, with priority accorded to the first provision that may be applicable. Any questions about a particular assignment shall be decided by the Court.

a. Cases involving government agencies. i. A case in which a Maryland local government or agency is a party shall be assigned to a Judge sitting in the division of the Court in which the principal office of the local government or agency is located.

ii A case in which the United States, the State of Maryland, or one of their agencies and a non-governmental entity or individual residing in Maryland are opposing parties shall be assigned to a Judge sitting in the division of the Court in which the non-governmental party resides.

b. Cases involving Maryland residents. i. A case in which all of the Maryland parties reside in the same division (a corporation's residence shall be its principal place of business in Maryland) shall be assigned to a Judge sitting in that division.

ii. A case in which the Maryland parties reside in different divisions of the Court shall be assigned to a Judge sitting in the division where a majority of the Maryland parties reside, but if there is not a majority resident in either division, then the case shall be assigned to a Judge sitting in the division of the Court in which the events described in the Complaint took place.

iii. A class action shall be assigned to a Judge sitting in the division of the Court where a majority of the named plaintiffs reside, but if there is not a majority resident in either division, then the case shall be assigned to a Judge sitting in the division of the Court in which the events described in the Complaint took place.

c. Cases in which no party resides in Maryland. A case in which no party is a resident of Maryland shall be assigned to a Judge sitting in the division in which the events described in the Complaint took place. (Amended Aug. 16, 2004, effective Aug. 16, 2004; by order effective January 1, 2008; and amended effective December 1, 2009.)

Effect of amendments. — The 2004 amendment, effective Aug. 16, 2004, designated the existing text as 1 and added 2-4.
The 2008 amendment added the first paragraph in 1; and rewrote 2 and 4.
The 2009 amendment made minor stylistic changes.

Rule 502. Jury selection plan.

The Jury Selection Plan as adopted and amended from time to time by Court order shall be available for public inspection in the Clerk's Office.

Rule 503. No attorneys or Court personnel as sureties.

No member of the Bar, of the Clerk's Office, of the U.S. Marshal's Office or of the staff of any Judge or Magistrate Judge shall act as surety on any bond or undertaking in any action or proceeding in the Court.

Rule 504. Hours of Clerk's Office.

1. **Hours of actual operation.** The Clerk's Office shall be open from 9:00 a.m. to 4:00 p.m. on all days except Saturdays, Sundays, the legal holidays specified in Fed. R. Civ. P. 77(c) and the day after Thanksgiving.

2. **After hours box.** For the convenience of litigants and counsel, an "after hours" or "night" box in which filings can be made outside of normal business hours is located on the first floor of each Courthouse. The hours during which each box is accessible are posted on the Court's website and at the entrance to each Courthouse.

3. **Emergency contact.** A representative of the Clerk's Office may be contacted in an emergency to arrange to accept filings. The appropriate telephone number(s) may be obtained by contacting the Clerk's Office during normal business hours or by consulting the website. The emergency contact number(s) are also posted at the entrance to each Courthouse. (Amended Aug. 16, 2004, effective Aug. 16, 2004.)

Effect of amendments. — The 2004 amendment, effective Aug. 16, 2004, in 1 substituted "4:00 p.m." for "5:00 p.m.".

Rule 505. Courthouse security.

1. **Inspection of entering persons.** All persons entering any federal court facility in this District and all items carried by them shall be subject to appropriate screening and checking by any United States Marshal or any security officer or any law enforcement officer on duty. Any person who refuses fully to cooperate in such screening or checking may be denied entrance to the Courthouse.

2. **Confiscation of weapons and contraband.** Any weapons (unless carried by law enforcement officers on their official duties) shall be impounded by the person conducting inspection. Property thus impounded may be retained for use as evidence and may be forfeited, destroyed or otherwise disposed of in accordance with law. Any person unlawfully carrying such property is subject to criminal prosecution. (Amended effective December 1, 2009.)

Effect of amendments. — The 2009 amendment made minor stylistic changes in 1.

Rule 506. Photographing and recording Court proceedings and courthouse spaces.

1. **Photographing, recording and transmitting Court proceedings.** Unless otherwise ordered by the Chief Judge, no Court proceeding may be photographed, video recorded, audio recorded, broadcast, televised or otherwise transmitted except as follows:

a. Persons presiding over naturalization proceedings may authorize the use of cameras or video recorders during the proceedings.

b. Judges presiding over ceremonial proceedings may authorize the use of cameras and video recorders during the proceedings.

c. Official court reporters and official electronic recorders employed by the Clerk's Office shall record Court proceedings, provided, however, that no court reporter or electronic recorder shall use or permit to be used any official recording of a Court proceeding in connection with any radio or television broadcast.

d. Any Judge may authorize a court reporter privately retained by one or more parties to record a Court proceeding if any official court reporter or official electronic recorder is unavailable or unable to perform the necessary recording.

2. **Photographing, video recording and televising courthouse spaces.** a. Courtrooms and other public spaces. Unless otherwise ordered by the Chief Judge, no courtroom or other public space in the courthouse may be photographed, video recorded or televised except as follows:

i. On the day of naturalization proceedings, persons being naturalized and their families and friends may use cameras in the public spaces on the first floor;

ii. On the day of receptions or other social events, persons attending the event may use cameras in the space where the event is being held; and

iii. Employees of the General Services Administration and GSA architects and contractors may use cameras in the courtrooms and other public spaces when Court is not in session.

b. Office spaces. Cameras may not be used in any office within the courthouse except with the approval of the person in charge of the office.

3. **Penalties.** Any camera, recording device or other equipment used in violation of this Rule may be impounded. Any violation of this Rule may be treated as a contempt of Court and any violator who is a member of the Bar may be subjected to the disciplinary action of the Court. (Amended effective December 1, 2009.)

Effect of amendments. — The 2009 amendment made minor stylistic changes in 1.d.

Rule 507. Copying and removal of Court papers.

1. **Copying.** Requests for copies of documents which are part of the public record may be processed by either the Clerk's Office or the copy service designated by the Court.

2. **Removal of original papers prohibited.** Unless otherwise ordered by the Court, no Court paper or any paper connected with the business of the Clerk shall be taken out of the Clerk's Office, provided, however, that authorized Court personnel may remove such papers for the purpose of carrying them to a courtroom or the chambers of a Judge or Magistrate Judge. (Amended Aug. 16, 2004, effective Aug. 16, 2004.)

Effect of amendments. — The 2004 amendment, effective Aug. 16, 2004, rewrote 1.

Rule 508. Investment of registry funds.

The Court shall by standing order set the amount of funds deposited in the Court Registry which shall be invested at interest. These funds shall be placed in an interest bearing account or such other investment as is ordered by the Court. Funds in any one case will be divided as necessary to assure full F.D.I.C. coverage of principal and interest. All funds invested at interest will be assessed a charge pursuant to the fee schedule set by the Judicial Conference of the United States.

In the event the Clerk is not present for service of the order required by Fed. R. Civ. P. 67, such service shall be made upon the Chief Deputy Clerk or the Finance Clerk, only.

Rule 509. Preservation of records in actions involving title to realty.

The official file in any case involving title to realty shall be deemed to be a permanent record of the Court and shall not be destroyed. (Amended Aug. 16, 2004, effective Aug. 16, 2004.)

Effect of amendments. — The 2004 amendment, effective Aug. 16, 2004, in the heading substituted "Preservation of records in actions involving title to realty" for "Records disposition", deleted 2 and made related changes.

Rule 510. Unclaimed funds in the registry.

Funds in the registry unclaimed for more than two (2) years shall be transferred, with the approval of the Court, to the Treasury. They may be withdrawn from the Treasury by the claimant pursuant to the procedure set forth in 28 U.S.C. § 2042. (Amended effective December 1, 2009.)

Effect of amendments. — The 2009 amendment made minor stylistic changes.

Rule 511. [Reserved for Future Use].

Rule 512. Lapse in appropriations.

This Rule shall become effective only when Congress fails to enact legislation to fund operations of the United States Courts. The Anti-Deficiency Act, 31 U.S.C. § 655 limits permissible government activities in the event of such a failure to those otherwise "authorized by law" or those needed to meet "cases of emergency involving the safety of human life or the protection of property."

This Court is directly involved in the judicial process, and under the Constitution and laws of the United States, it is always open to exercise the judicial power of the United States. Thus, the Court must continue, even in the absence of funding by Congress, to receive new cases, and hear and dispose of pending cases. Activities will, however, be limited as nearly as practical to those functions necessary and essential to continue the resolution of pending cases. The Court shall advise the United States Marshal and the General Services Administration of the level of building and security services necessary to maintain such Court operations.

The Court finds that District Judges' staff, Magistrate Judges' staff, the Clerk's Office, the CJA Supervising Attorney, the Staff Attorneys, the Probation Department, the Pretrial Services Office, the Federal Public Defender's Office, Criminal Justice Act Attorneys, official court reporters, and jurors are all essential to the continuation of Court operations. Work of all personnel shall be limited to those essential functions set forth above. In the event any personnel are not engaged in those services, they shall be furloughed for the period of lapsed appropriations.

The Court will recognize that the United States Attorney, as an officer of the Department of Justice, may have to restrict the role of the staff of the United States Attorney's Office to cases "essential to protect life and property." (Amended effective December 1, 2009.)

Effect of amendments. — The 2009 amendment made minor stylistic changes.

VI. MISCELLANEOUS.

Rule 601. Definitions.

1. **The "Court" and the "Judge".** Except in the Supplemental Admiralty and Maritime Rules (see LAR(a)(3)), the terms the "Court" and the "Judge" mean "United States Magistrate Judge" as to all proceedings pending before a United States Magistrate Judge.

2. **Statutory references.** All references in these Local Rules to specific statutes or rules of procedure shall be deemed to apply to any amended or renumbered versions of such statutes or rules as may be promulgated in the future.

Rule 602. Fines.

Any attorney who fails to appear at or who is late for a proceeding scheduled by the Court or who shall fail to submit a timely status report to the Court may be fined by the Court up to $250.00. The Clerk shall maintain a record of fines imposed under this Rule and shall refer to the Disciplinary and Admissions Committee of the Court for appropriate action the name of any attorney against whom more than two (2) fines have been imposed within five (5) years. Nothing contained in this Rule shall be construed as limiting the power of a Judge of this Court, in addition to imposing a fine hereunder, to assess costs against an attorney for a non-appearance or lateness, or to punish any such offending attorney in any other way for contempt of Court. (Amended effective December 1, 2009; amended effective July 1, 2011.)

Effect of amendments. — The 2009 amendment made minor stylistic changes. The 2011 amendment substituted "Disciplinary and Admissions Committee" for "Disciplinary Committee" in the second sentence.

Rule 603. Special orders in widely publicized and sensational cases.

In a widely publicized or sensational criminal or civil case, the Court, on motion of either party or on its own motion, in the exercise of its general powers, may issue a special order governing such matters as extrajudicial statements by parties and witnesses likely to interfere with the rights of the accused to a fair trial by an impartial jury, the seating and conduct in the courtroom of spectators and news media representatives, the management and sequestration of jurors and witnesses, and any other matters which the Court may deem appropriate for inclusion in such an order.

Rule 604. Suspension of Rules.

For good cause shown, the Court may in a particular case suspend the provisions of any of these Rules upon application of a party or upon its own motion and may order proceedings in accordance with its direction.

Cited in Koffman v. Osteoimplant Technology, Inc., 182 Bankr. 115 (D. Md. 1995).

Rule 605. Amendment of Rules.

1. **Regular procedure.** The Court shall consider proposed amendments to these Rules at least every three (3) years. Any person may submit proposed amendments to the Chief Judge. Any such proposals will be reviewed by the Rules Committee of the Court which will recommend to the Court as a whole any amendments which it believes should be adopted. At least ninety (90) days prior to the proposed effective date, the Court will cause to be published on the Court's web site notice of the substance of any amendment (subject to public notice and comment) which a majority of the members of the Court have agreed should be adopted. The Clerk shall maintain for public inspection copies of any proposed amendments. Any member of the public may submit comments on a proposed amendment to the Chief Judge within thirty (30) days of the first public notice of the proposed amendment or such later date as may be set by the Court. The Court will take final action upon the proposed amendments after giving consideration to any such comments which have been submitted. Unless otherwise ordered by the Court, the effective date of any amendment shall be July 1st of the year in which it is adopted.

2. **Emergency procedure.** The Court may adopt a rule necessary to meet any condition of emergency without complying with the procedure set forth in L.R. 605.1. If such an emergency rule is adopted, public notice of it shall be given promptly after its adoption and it shall be submitted for public consideration in accordance with L.R. 605.1 during the next regular amendment cycle. (Amended Aug. 16, 2004, effective Aug. 16, 2004; amended effective December 1, 2009.)

Effect of amendments. — The 2004 amendment, effective Aug. 16, 2004, in 1 in the first sentence deleted "annually" preceding "consider" and inserted "at least every three years"; at the end of the second sentence deleted "on or before November 30"; in the fourth sentence substituted "At least 90 days prior to the proposed effective date" for "On or before April 1st" and "on the Court's web site" for "in The Daily Record"; and in the fifth sentence deleted "at least five" preceding "copies".

The 2009 amendment made minor stylistic changes in 1.

Rule 606. Civility.

The Court expects all of its Judges and all counsel to conduct themselves in a professional and courteous manner in connection with all matters pending before the Court. (Amended effective December 1, 2009.)

Effect of amendments. — The 2009 amendment made minor stylistic changes.

Rule 607. Alternative dispute resolution.

1. **Authorization of ADR.** The Court authorizes the use of all alternative dispute resolution processes in civil actions, including adversary proceedings in bankruptcy. The Magistrate Judges of the Court shall constitute the panel of neutrals made available by the Court for use by the parties. The provisions of 28 U.S.C. § 455 shall govern the disqualification of a Magistrate Judge from serving as a neutral. The parties may agree to the use of a neutral other than a Magistrate Judge.

2. **Consideration of ADR.** Litigants in all civil cases shall consider using the ADR process provided by the Court at an appropriate stage in the litigation.

3. **Attendance at ADR proceedings.** Trial counsel for each party, as well as a party representative having full settlement authority, shall attend each settlement conference held by the Court. If insurance coverage may be applicable, a representative of the insurer, having full settlement authority, shall attend.

4. **Confidentiality.** The Court's ADR process is confidential. Unless otherwise agreed by the parties and the Court no disclosure shall be made to anyone, including the judicial officer to whom the case is assigned, of any dispute resolution communication that in any respect reveals the dispute resolution positions of the parties or advice or opinions of neutrals. No such communication shall be admissible in any subsequent proceeding except as permitted by the Federal Rules of Evidence.

5. **Arbitration.** Actions may be referred to arbitration only in accordance with the provisions of 28 U.S.C. § 654. Consent to arbitration must be freely and knowingly given. No party or attorney shall be prejudiced in any way for refusing to participate in arbitration. (Amended effective December 1, 2009.)

Effect of amendments. — The 2009 amendment made minor stylistic changes in the heading of 3.

VII. ATTORNEY ADMISSION, ASSISTANCE AND DISCIPLINE.

Rule 701. Admission.

1. **Qualifications.** a. General. Except as provided in subsections (c) and (d) of this Rule, an attorney is qualified for admission to the Bar of this District if the attorney is, and continuously remains, an active member in good standing of the highest court of any state (or the District of Columbia) in which the attorney maintains his or her principal law office, or of the Court of Appeals of Maryland; is of good private and professional character; is familiar with the Maryland Lawyers' Rules of Professional Conduct, the Federal Rules of Civil Procedure, the Federal Rules of Evidence, the Federal Rules of Appellate Procedure, and these Local Rules; is (to the extent relevant to his or her area(s) of practice) familiar with the Federal Rules of Criminal Procedure, the Federal Rules of Bankruptcy Procedure, and the Local Bankruptcy Rules; and is willing, available and competent to accept appointments by the Court to represent indigent parties in civil cases in this District unless the acceptance of such appointments is inconsistent with an attorney's professional employment obligations as, for example, a government attorney.

b. Federal government attorneys. An attorney who is a member of a Federal Public Defender's Office, the Office of the United States Attorney for this District, or other federal government lawyer, is qualified for admission to the Bar of this District for purposes relating to her or his employment if the attorney is an active member in good standing of the highest court of any state (or the District of Columbia), is of good private and professional character, is familiar with the Code of Professional Responsibility, the Federal Rules of Civil Procedure and Criminal Procedure, the Federal Rules of Evidence, the Federal Rules of Appellate Procedure and these Local Rules.

c. Reciprocity with other jurisdictions. No attorney, other than a member of the Maryland Bar, who maintains his or her principal law office outside the District of Maryland may be a member of the Bar of this District if the attorney is, or becomes, a member of the Bar of the United States District Court for the district in which the attorney maintains his or her principal law office if that district court has a local rule that denies membership in its bar to any attorney who is a member of the Maryland Bar maintaining his or her principal law office in Maryland.

d. Non-Maryland lawyers maintaining any law office in Maryland. An attorney who is not a member of the Maryland Bar is not qualified for admission to the Bar of this District if the attorney maintains any law office in Maryland.

e. Principal Office. The term "principal law office" as used in this Rule means "the chief or main office in which an attorney usually devotes a substantial period of his or her time to the practice of law during ordinary business hours in the traditional work week." In determining whether an office is the "principal law office," the Court shall consider the following non-exclusive factors:

i. The attorney's representations of his or her "principal law office" or "law office" for purposes of malpractice insurance coverage, tax obligations and client security trust fund obligations.

ii. The address utilized in pleadings, correspondence with clients, applications for malpractice insurance and bar admissions, advertising, letterhead and other business matters.

iii. The location of meetings with clients, conduct of depositions, research and employment of support staff and associates.

iv. Location of client files, accounting records, and other business records, library and communication facilities such as telephone and fax service.

v. Whether the attorney has other offices, their locations and their relative utilization.

vi. The laws under which the law practice is organized, such as the place of incorporation.

2. **Procedure.** a. Original applications. Each applicant for admission to the Bar shall file an application, accompanied by a motion filed by the applicant's sponsor. The application and motion shall be on forms prescribed by the Court and shall be made available by the Clerk to applicants upon request. The applicant's sponsor must be a member of the Bar of this Court and must have known the applicant for at least one year. The latter requirement may be waived if the sponsor sets forth sufficient grounds in the motion for admission to satisfy the Court that the sponsor has reason to know that the applicant is qualified for admission. Each applicant for admission shall also pay any original admission fee set by the Court.

b. Renewal applications. Each member of the Bar of this Court shall submit an application to renew her or his membership periodically as directed by the

Court. The application shall be on a form prescribed by the Court. Notice shall be sent by the Clerk to each member of the Bar of the Court at least thirty (30) days prior to the date on which the application is due. The applicant for renewal shall also pay any renewal fee set by the Court. A timely renewal application shall be granted if the applicant meets all of the qualifications for admission to the Bar of this Court and if she or he pays the renewal fee. Failure to submit a timely renewal application or to pay the renewal fee will cause the attorney's membership in the Bar of this Court to be changed to inactive status.

c. Request to resign or withdraw an application for admission. i. Request. A request to resign from, or to withdraw an initial or renewal application for admission to, the practice of law in this Court shall be submitted in writing under oath. The request shall state that the resignation or request to withdraw an original or renewal application is not being offered to avoid disciplinary action and that the attorney has no knowledge of any pending investigation, action, or proceedings in any jurisdiction involving allegations of professional misconduct by the attorney or the commission of a crime.

ii. When attorney may not resign or withdraw an application for admission. An attorney may not resign or withdraw an original or renewal application for admission while the attorney is the subject of a disciplinary investigation, action, or proceeding involving allegations of professional misconduct or the commission of a crime. A request to resign or to withdraw an original or renewal application does not prevent or stay any disciplinary action or proceeding against the attorney.

iii. Procedure. Upon receiving a copy of the request submitted in accordance with section (c)(i) of this Rule, the Disciplinary and Admissions Committee shall investigate the request and submit a recommendation to the full bench of the Court.

iv. Order of the Court. After considering the recommendation of the Disciplinary and Admissions Committee, the Court shall enter an order accepting or denying the resignation or request to withdraw an application. A resignation or withdrawal of an application is effective only upon entry of an order approving it.

v. Duty of Clerk. When the Court enters an order accepting an attorney's resignation or permitting the withdrawal of an application, the Clerk of the Court shall strike the name of the attorney from the register of attorneys in this Court.

vi. Effect of resignation or withdrawal of application for admission. An attorney may not practice law in this Court after entry of an order accepting the attorney's resignation or permitting the withdrawal of an application.

vii. Motion to vacate. After notice and opportunity to be heard, the Court may, at any time, vacate or modify the order in case of intrinsic or extrinsic fraud.

3. **Duty of counsel to notify the clerk of any change in address.** Counsel must promptly notify the Clerk of any change of address, including e-mail, address irrespective of any changes noted on a pleading or other document.

4. **Confidentiality of admission and renewal applications.** No information contained in any bar admission or renewal application shall be released by the Clerk of this Court without the order of the Chair of the Disciplinary and Admissions Committee of the Court or the presiding judge in a pending case, and only after consultation by the Committee Chair or the presiding judge with the full bench. (Amended Aug. 16, 2004, effective Aug. 16, 2004; by order effective January 1, 2008; amended effective December 1, 2009; amended effective July 1, 2011.)

Effect of amendments. — The 2004 amendment, effective Aug. 16, 2004, in 1.a inserted "and continuously remains" preceding "a member in good standing"; in 1.b inserted "for purposes relating to her or his employment" following "to the bar of this District"; added 1.d; in 2.b. in the first sentence substituted "periodically as directed by the Court." for "every three years from the date of her or his original admission" and rewrote the second sentence; and added 3.

The 2008 amendment added "and d" in the first sentence of 1.a; rewrote 1.c without substantive change; and added 1.e.

The 2009 amendment substituted "changed to inactive status" for "stricken" in the last sentence of 2.b; added 2.c and 4; and made minor stylistic changes.

The 2011 amendment substituted "an active member" for "a member" in 1.a. and 1.b; in 1.a. substituted "Maryland Lawyers' Rules of Professional Conduct" for "Code of Professional Responsibility", deleted "and Criminal" after "Civil", added "is (to the extent relevant to his or her area(s) of practice) familiar with the Federal Rules of Criminal Procedure, the Federal Rules of Bankruptcy Procedure, and the Local Bankruptcy Rules"; and made minor, stylistic changes.

Rule 702. Student practice.

1. **Eligibility.** Any eligible law student in a law school accredited by the American Bar Association may, under the conditions stated below, represent a party, and appear before any Bankruptcy Judge, Magistrate Judge, or District Court Judge in this District.

2. **Requirements.** For a student to be eligible to practice, the following requirements must be met:

a. The conduct of the case must be under the supervision of a member of the Bar of this District and that supervisor must be present with and prepared to assist the student at any Court appearances, assume full professional responsibility for the student's work, and read, approve and co-sign all documents filed with the Court.

b. The student must be in his or her final two (2) years of law school.

c. The student must be enrolled for credit in a law school clinical program.

d. The program must maintain professional liability insurance for its activities and those of its supervisors and participating students.

e. The student may not accept personal compensation from a client or other source, although the supervisor or the law school clinical program may accept compensation.

3. **Petition to practice.** Before a student shall be eligible under this Rule, the dean of the student's law school shall file with the Clerk of this Court a petition listing: the names of the enrolled students, the names of the supervisors and the address of an office to which the Court may send all notices in connection with this Rule. The petition shall include a certification that, in the opinion of the dean and the faculty, the students have adequate knowledge of the procedural rules and substantive law, and that the activities of the

students will be adequately supervised as required by this Rule. Upon written approval by the Chief Judge, or a designated Judge, of this District, to be filed with the Clerk of this Court, the listed students shall be authorized to practice pursuant to this Rule and subject to the further order of this Court. The written approval of the said Judge as to both students and supervisors shall remain in effect for twelve (12) months from the date of approval, unless withdrawn or unless, by further petition by the dean, the said Judge shall extend the privilege. (Amended Aug. 16, 2004, effective Aug. 16, 2004; amended effective December 1, 2009; amended effective July 1, 2010; amended effective July 1, 2011.)

Effect of amendments. — The 2004 amendment, effective Aug. 16, 2004, in 1 substituted "represent" for "interview, advise, negotiate with or on behalf of"; and in 2.a substituted "documents" for "papers".

The 2009 amendment made minor stylistic changes.

The 2010 amendment deleted "in this District" following "the address of an office" in the first sentence of 3.

The 2011 amendment added "Bankruptcy Judge" in 1; and deleted a colon after "listing" in the first sentence of 3.

Rule 703. Attorneys subject to discipline.

Any attorney practicing before this Court or who has practiced before this Court in any way shall be deemed thereby to have conferred disciplinary jurisdiction upon the Court for any alleged misconduct of that attorney. To the extent appropriate, all Rules set forth herein as applicable to attorneys admitted to practice before the Court shall also be deemed applicable to and enforceable against any attorney participating in any manner in any proceeding in this Court, whether or not admitted to practice before the Court.

Rule 704. Rules of Professional Conduct.

This Court shall apply the Rules of Professional Conduct as they have been adopted by the Maryland Court of Appeals.

Rule 705. Disciplinary proceedings.

1. **Allegations of Misconduct.** a. Referral for Investigation. When allegations of misconduct which, if substantiated, would warrant discipline of an attorney shall come to the attention of a Judge of this Court, the Judge shall refer the matter to the Court's Disciplinary and Admissions Committee. If the Disciplinary and Admissions Committee determines that further investigation is necessary, it may refer the matter to Maryland Bar Counsel to conduct an investigation. Alternatively, the Court, upon the recommendation of the Disciplinary and Admissions Committee, may appoint one or more members of the Bar of the Court as counsel to conduct the investigation. Notice of any such appointment shall be given to the respondent-attorney, and the respondent-attorney may move to disqualify counsel so appointed within fourteen (14) days after service of the notice.

b. Recommendation by Counsel. After the conclusion of the investigation, counsel shall submit to the Disciplinary and Admissions Committee a recommendation that a formal hearing be held or that the matter be disposed of by dismissal, admonition, deferral or otherwise. The Disciplinary and Admissions Committee shall take such action as it deems appropriate.

c. Initiation of Formal Proceedings. If formal disciplinary proceedings are to be initiated, the Court shall issue an order requiring the respondent-attorney to show cause within thirty (30) days after service of the order why the attorney should not be disciplined.

d. Disciplinary Hearing. If the respondent-attorney's answer to the show cause order raises any issue of fact or if the respondent-attorney wishes to be heard in mitigation, a disciplinary hearing shall be held before one (1) or more Judges of the Court. If the disciplinary proceeding is predicated upon the complaint of a Judge of this Court, the disciplinary hearing shall be conducted before a panel of three (3) other Judges of this Court appointed by the Chief Judge or, if there are less than three (3) Judges eligible to serve or the Chief Judge is the complainant, the panel shall be appointed by the Chief Judge of the Fourth Circuit Court of Appeals. For purposes of this subsection, "Judge" includes the District Judges, Magistrate Judges, and Bankruptcy Judges of this Court, and at least one (1) District Judge shall serve on each panel.

e Recommendation and Final Action. Following the disciplinary hearing, the panel shall prepare a report and recommendation for en banc consideration by the District Judges of the Court. The District Judges will review the report and recommendation and determine any final action in the matter. The Chief Judge will then issue any appropriate order on behalf of the District Judges.

f. Confidentiality. Proceedings under this section shall be confidential except that any opinion and order entered by the Court disbarring, suspending, or imposing other discipline upon an attorney shall be placed on the public record.

g. Disbarment by Consent While Under Disciplinary Investigation or Prosecution. i. Any respondent-attorney may consent to disbarment while a disciplinary investigation or proceeding is pending against that attorney, but only by delivering to the Court an affidavit stating that the attorney desires to consent to disbarment and that: (1) the attorney's consent is freely and voluntarily rendered; (2) the attorney is not being subjected to coercion or duress; (3) the attorney is fully aware of the implications of so consenting; (4) the attorney is aware that there is a presently pending investigation or proceeding involving allegations that there exist grounds for the attorney's discipline the nature of which the attorney shall specifically set forth; (5) the attorney acknowledges that the material facts so alleged are true, unless such acknowledgment would involve the admission of a crime; and (6) the attorney so consents because the attorney knows that if charges were predicated upon the matters under investigation, or if the proceeding were prosecuted, the attorney could not successfully defend himself.

ii. Upon receipt of the required affidavit, the Court shall enter an order disbarring the attorney.

iii. The order disbarring the attorney on consent shall be a matter of public record. However, the affidavit required under the provisions of this Rule shall not be publicly disclosed or made available for use in any other proceeding except upon order of the Court.

2. **Criminal Convictions.** a. Serious Crimes. i. Definition. For purposes of this Rule the term "serious crime" shall include any felony and any lesser

crime a necessary element of which, as determined by the statutory or common law definition of such crime in the jurisdiction where the judgment was entered, involved false swearing, misrepresentation, fraud, willful failure to file income tax returns, deceit, bribery, extortion, misappropriation, theft, or an attempt or a conspiracy or solicitation of another to commit any of the above.

ii. Suspension. Upon the filing with the Court of a certified copy of a judgment of conviction demonstrating that any attorney admitted to practice before the Court has been convicted in any Court of the United States, or the District of Columbia, or of any state, territory, commonwealth or possession of the United States of a serious crime, the Court shall enter an order immediately suspending that attorney, whether the conviction resulted from a plea of guilty or nolo contendere or from a verdict after trial or otherwise, and regardless of the pendency of any appeal. Such order shall direct the attorney to show cause within thirty (30) days why disbarment or some lesser punishment should not be imposed. A copy of such order shall immediately be served upon the attorney.

iii. Imposition of Discipline. After the show cause period has ended, the Court's Disciplinary and Admissions Committee will review the conviction, as well as any response. If the attorney's response includes a request for a hearing, the matter shall be assigned for a prompt disciplinary hearing as provided for in L.R. 705.1.d. Absent such a request, the Disciplinary and Admissions Committee may (a) refer the matter to counsel for investigation pursuant to L.R. 705.1.a; (b) conduct a disciplinary hearing pursuant to L.R. 705.1.d; or (c) recommend final action to the full bench, which may include any form of bar discipline up to and including disbarment.

iv. Lifting of Discipline. In the event that an attorney's underlying conviction is reversed or vacated and that attorney has had discipline imposed under the provisions of this Rule, the attorney will not be reinstated immediately but must apply for reinstatement under L.R. 705.4.

b. Other Crimes. The Disciplinary and Admissions Committee may, pursuant to L.R. 705.1, refer to counsel for investigation and initiation of disciplinary proceedings any attorney who has been convicted of any crime other than a serious crime.

3. **Discipline Imposed by Other Courts.** a. Attorney's Duty to Disclose. Any attorney admitted to practice before this Court shall, upon being subjected to public discipline or being enjoined from the practice of law by any other Court of the United States or the District of Columbia, or by a court of any state, territory commonwealth or possession of the United States, promptly inform the Clerk of this Court of such action.

b. Notification to Attorney. Upon the filing of a certified or exemplified copy of a judgment or order demonstrating that an attorney admitted to practice before this Court has been disciplined by another court, this Court shall forthwith issue a notice directed to the attorney containing:

i. a copy of the judgment or order from the other court;

ii. an order immediately suspending the attorney, in the event the discipline imposed by the other court consists of suspension or disbarment, or an order enjoining the attorney from the practice before this Court, in the event the attorney has been enjoined from the practice of law; and

iii. an order directing the attorney to show cause within thirty (30) days after service of the order why identical action by this Court would be unwarranted.

c. Stay. In the event the discipline imposed in the other jurisdiction has been stayed there, any reciprocal discipline imposed in this Court shall be deferred until such stay expires.

d. Imposition of Identical Discipline. This Court shall impose the identical discipline imposed by the other Court unless the respondent-attorney demonstrates, or this Court finds, that upon the face of the record upon which the discipline in another jurisdiction is predicated it clearly appears:

i. that the procedure was so lacking in notice or opportunity to be heard as to constitute a deprivation of due process; or

ii. that there was such an infirmity of proof establishing the misconduct as to give rise to the clear conviction that this Court could not, consistent with its duty, accept as final the conclusion of the other Court on that subject; or

iii. that the imposition of the same discipline by this Court would result in grave injustice; or

iv. that the misconduct established is deemed by this Court to warrant substantially different discipline or injunctive action.

Where this Court determines that any of said elements exist, it shall enter such other order as it deems appropriate.

4. **Reinstatement.** a. When Court Order Required. An attorney suspended for three (3) months or less shall be automatically reinstated at the end of the period of suspension upon the filing with the Court of an affidavit of compliance with the provisions of the order. An attorney suspended for more than three (3) months or disbarred may not resume practice until reinstated by order of this Court.

b. Time of Application Following Disbarment. A person who has been disbarred after hearing or by consent may not apply for reinstatement until the expiration of at least five (5) years from the effective date of the disbarment.

c. Hearing on Application. i. Petitions for reinstatement by a disbarred or suspended attorney, and three (3) copies of said petition, shall be filed with the Clerk of this Court. Upon receipt of the petition, the Chief Judge shall promptly refer the petition to the Court's Disciplinary and Admissions Committee to review the petition and to determine whether a hearing is necessary. If the Disciplinary and Admissions Committee finds good cause that reinstatement is appropriate without a hearing, then the Court, if in agreement, may grant the petition for reinstatement.

ii. Otherwise, the Chief Judge shall assign the matter for prompt hearing before one (1) or more Judges of this Court, provided, however, that if the disciplinary proceeding was predicated upon the complaint of a Judge of this Court, the hearing shall be conducted before a panel of three (3) other Judges of this Court appointed by the Chief Judge, or, if there are less than three (3) Judges eligible to serve or the Chief Judge was the complainant, by a panel appointed by the Chief Judge of the Court of Appeals of the Fourth Circuit. For purposes of this subsection, "Judge" includes the District Judges, Magistrate

Judges, and Bankruptcy Judges of this Court, and at least one (1) District Judge shall serve on each panel.

The Judge or Judges assigned to the matter shall, within thirty (30) days after referral, schedule a hearing at which the petitioner shall have the burden of demonstrating by clear and convincing evidence that he/she has the moral qualifications, competency and learning in the law required for admission to practice law before this Court and that his/her resumption of the practice of law will not be detrimental to the integrity and standing of the Bar or to the administration of justice, or subversive of the public interest.

d. Appointment of Counsel. The Court may, pursuant to L.R. 705.1.a, appoint counsel to investigate whether the petition for reinstatement should be granted and to participate in the reinstatement hearing.

e. Conditions of Reinstatement. If the petitioner is found unfit to resume the practice of law, the petition shall be dismissed. If the petitioner is found fit to resume the practice of law, the Court may enter an order of reinstatement, provided that the order may make reinstatement conditional upon the payment of all or part of the costs of the proceedings, and upon the making of partial or complete restitution to parties harmed by the petitioner whose conduct led to the suspension or disbarment. Provided further, that if the petitioner has been suspended or disbarred for five (5) years or more, reinstatement may be conditioned upon the furnishing of proof of competency and learning in the law, which proof may include certification by the bar examiners of a state or other jurisdiction of the attorney's successful completion of an examination for admission to practice subsequent to the date of suspension or disbarment.

f. Successive Petitions. No petition for reinstatement shall be filed within one (1) year following an adverse judgment upon a petition for reinstatement filed by or on behalf of the same person.

5. **Dissemination of Information.** a. To Other Courts. Whenever it appears that any person convicted of any crime or disbarred or suspended or censured or disbarred on consent by this Court is admitted to practice law in any other jurisdiction or before any other court, the Clerk of this Court shall, within fourteen (14) days of the conviction, disbarment, suspension, censure, or disbarment on consent, transmit to the disciplinary authority in such other jurisdiction, or for such other court, a certificate of the conviction or a certified or exemplified copy of the judgment or order of disbarment, suspension, censure or disbarment on consent, as well as the last known office and residence addresses of the defendant or respondent.

b. To the American Bar Association. The Clerk shall promptly notify the National Discipline Data Bank operated by the American Bar Association of any order imposing public discipline upon any attorney admitted to practice before this Court. (Amended by order effective January 1, 2008; amended effective December 1, 2009; amended effective July 1, 2010; amended effective July 1, 2011.)

Effect of amendments. — The 2008 amendment rewrote 3.b.ii; in 3.b.iii substituted "identical action" for "the imposition of identical discipline"; and at the end of 3.c.iv added "or injunctive action" at the end.

The 2009 amendment substituted "fourteen

(14) days" for "fifteen days" in the last sentence of 1.a; in 5.a substituted "fourteen (14) days" for "ten days"; and made minor stylistic changes.

The 2010 amendment in 1.d added "Disciplinary" or variant preceding "hearing" in the paragraph heading and twice in the text and added the last sentence; and added (e) and redesignated accordingly.

The 2011 amendment substituted "Disciplinary and Admissions Committee" for "Disciplinary Committee" throughout the Rule; rewrote the second sentence of 2.a.ii. and rewrote 2.a.iii and 2.a.iv; in 4.c added the i and ii designations; in 4.c.i. in the first sentence substituted "three (3) copies" for "seven (7) copies", rewrote the second sentence, and added the third sentence.

Rule 706. Fee agreements.

In any civil case, other than cases governed by the Prison Litigation Reform Act, where counsel is appointed by the Court to represent a party, counsel may request that the party to be represented enter into a contingent fee agreement. The agreement shall not require the payment of attorneys' fees in an amount greater than 25% of any recovery if the case is settled, nor greater than 33 ⅓% of any amount awarded after a trial. The agreement may not require the plaintiff to pay litigation expenses unless such payment is approved by the Court. In cases where there is a statutory provision for attorneys' fees, the contingent fee shall be reduced by any statutory fees. (Added Aug. 16, 2004, effective Aug. 16, 2004.)

VIII. PATENTS.

Rule 801. Scope.

Unless otherwise ordered by the Court, these rules apply to all civil actions filed in or transferred to this Court in which one or more parties (a) assert claims of patent infringement; (b) seek a declaratory judgment that a patent is not infringed, is invalid or is unenforceable; (c) seek an order pursuant to 35 U.S.C. § 256 directing the Director of Patents of the United States Patent Office to issue a certificate to correct an error regarding the identity of inventors; or (d) assert a claim pursuant to 35 U.S.C. § 292 for false marking. Section I of the Local Rules of this Court shall also apply to such actions, except to the extent that they are inconsistent with the Local Rules in this Section VIII. (Added effective July 1, 2011.)

Rule 802. Scheduling Conference.

Within seven (7) days after an Answer has been filed or, with respect to a case that has been transferred to this District, within seven (7) days after the case has been docketed, Plaintiffs counsel shall contact all counsel and Chambers to arrange a telephone conference between counsel for the parties and Chambers for the purpose of scheduling a Scheduling Conference. Counsel should be prepared to address the following issues during the Scheduling Conference:

a. Proposed modification of the obligations or deadlines set forth in Section VIII of the Local Rules;

b. The scope and timing of discovery, including expert witness disclosures, and expert witness depositions, and limits on the total number of hours of fact witness depositions;

c. The scope and timing of dispositive motions;

d. Limits on the number of patent claims that can be construed by each party;

e. The format of the Claim Construction Hearing, including whether the Court will hear live testimony, the order of presentation, and the estimated length of the hearing;

f. How the parties intend to educate the Court on the patent(s) at issue;

g. The need for any Confidentiality Order in accordance with L.R. 104.13;

h. Whether any party intends to seek discovery of electronically stored information and whether the parties have reached an agreement on such discovery. (The Court will expect that counsel will have reviewed the Suggested Protocol for Discovery of Electronically Stored Information, published on the Court's website.);

i. Whether the parties unanimously consent to proceed before a United States Magistrate Judge; and

j. Whether the parties jointly request an early settlement or ADR conference.

Unless justice requires otherwise, the Court will approve reasonable adjustments to the deadlines set forth in Section VIII of the Local Rules when (1) all parties agree to the adjustments; (2) a case involves particularly complex technologies or a large number of patents; (3) the parties include non-U.S. entities or individuals; or (4) a substantial portion of the testimonial or documentary evidence will require translation to English. (Added effective July 1, 2011.)

Rule 803. Discovery.

1. **Commencement.** Subject to L.R. 803.2, discovery shall be conducted in accordance with L.R. 104 and shall not commence until the issuance of a Scheduling Order.

2. **Objections.** Except as provided in this rule or as otherwise ordered, it shall not be a ground for objecting to an opposing party's discovery request (e.g., interrogatory, document request, request for admission, deposition question) that the discovery request or disclosure requirement is premature in light of, or otherwise conflicts with, Section VIII of the Local Rules. A party may object, however, to responding to the following categories of discovery requests on the ground that they are premature in light of the timetable provided in Section VIII of the Local Rules:

a. Requests seeking to elicit a party's claim construction position;

b. Requests seeking to elicit from the patent claimant a comparison of the asserted claims and the accused apparatus, product, device, process, method, act, or other instrumentality;

c. Requests seeking to elicit from an accused infringer a comparison of the asserted claims and the prior art; and

d. Requests seeking to elicit from an accused infringer the identification of any advice of counsel, and related documents.

Where a party properly objects to a discovery request as set forth above, that party shall provide the requested information on the date on which it is required to be provided to an opposing party under Section VIII of the Local Rules or as set by the Court, unless there are other legitimate grounds for objection. (Added effective July 1, 2011.)

Rule 804. Disclosures.

1. **Cases Involving Claims of Infringement.** Unless otherwise ordered by the Court, in all cases, other than those arising under the Hatch-Waxman Act (21 U.S.C. § 355), in which a party has asserted a claim of patent infringement, the parties shall make the following disclosures:

a. Initial Disclosure of Infringement Contentions. Thirty (30) days from the date of the Scheduling Order, any party claiming patent infringement shall serve on all parties an Initial Disclosure of Infringement Contentions, separately setting forth for each allegedly infringing party, the following information:

i. Each claim of each patent in suit that is allegedly infringed by each allegedly infringing party, including for each claim the applicable statutory subsections of 35 U.S.C. § 271 asserted;

ii. .Separately for each allegedly infringed claim, each accused apparatus, product, device, process, method, act, or other instrumentality ("Accused Instrumentality") of each allegedly infringing party of which the party is aware. This identification shall be as specific as possible. Each product, device, and apparatus shall be identified by name or model number, if known. Each method or process shall be identified by name, if known, or by any product, device, or apparatus which, when used, allegedly results in the practice of the claimed method or process;

iii. A chart identifying specifically where each limitation of each asserted claim is found within each Accused Instrumentality, including for each limitation that such party contends is governed by 35 U.S.C. § 112(6), the identity of the structure(s), act(s), or material(s) in the Accused Instrumentality that performs the claimed function;.

iv. For each claim which is alleged to have been indirectly infringed, an identification of any direct infringement and a description of the acts of the alleged indirect infringer that contribute to or are inducing that direct infringement. Insofar as alleged direct infringement is based on joint acts of multiple parties, the role of each such party in the direct infringement must be described;

v. Whether each limitation of each asserted claim is alleged to be literally present or present under the doctrine of equivalents in the Accused Instrumentality;

vi. For any patent that claims priority to an earlier application, the priority date to which each asserted claim allegedly is entitled;

vii. The date of conception and the date of reduction to practice of each asserted claim;

viii. If a party claiming patent infringement wishes to preserve the right to rely, for any purpose, on the assertion that its own apparatus, product, device, process, method, act, or other instrumentality practices the claimed invention, the party shall identify, separately for each asserted claim, each such apparatus, product, device, process, method, act, or other instrumentality that incorporates or reflects that particular claim; and

ix. If a party claiming patent infringement alleges willful infringement, the basis for such allegation.

b. Document Production Accompanying Initial Disclosure of Infringement Contentions. With the Initial Disclosure of Infringement Contentions, the party claiming patent infringement shall produce to each allegedly infringing party or make available for inspection and copying all documents relating to:

i. Any offers to sell or efforts to market each claimed invention prior to the date of the application for the patent; (A party's production of a document as required herein shall not constitute an admission that such document evidences or is prior art under 35 U.S.C. § 102);

ii. The standing of the party alleging infringement with respect to each patent upon which such allegations are based; and

iii. A copy of the file history for each patent in suit.

c. Initial Disclosure of Invalidity Contentions in Defense of Infringement Claims. Sixty (60) days from the date of the Scheduling Order, each party opposing a claim of patent infringement, shall serve on all parties its Invalidity Contentions, which shall contain the following information:

i. The identity of each item of prior art that allegedly anticipates each asserted claim or renders it obvious. Each prior art patent shall be identified by its number, country of origin, and date of issue. Each prior art publication shall be identified by its title, date of publication, and where feasible, author and publisher. Prior art under 35 U.S.C. § 102(b) shall be identified by specifying the item offered for sale or publicly used or known, the date the offer or use took place or the information became known, and the identity of the person or entity which made the use or which made and received the offer, or the person or entity which made the information known or to whom it was made known. Prior art under 35 U.S.C. § 102(f) shall be identified by providing the name of the person(s) from whom and the circumstances under which the invention or any part of it was derived. Prior art under 35 U.S.C. § 102(g) shall be identified by providing the identities of the person(s) or entities involved in and the circumstances surrounding the making of the invention before the patent applicant(s);

ii. Whether each item of prior art anticipates each asserted claim or renders it obvious. If obviousness is alleged, an explanation of why the prior art renders the asserted claim obvious, including an identification of any combinations of prior art showing obviousness;

iii. A chart identifying where specifically in each alleged item of prior art each limitation of each asserted claim is found, including for each limitation that such party contends is governed by 35 U.S.C. § 112(6), the identity of the structure(s), act(s), or material(s) in each item of prior art that performs the claimed function; and

iv. Any grounds of invalidity based on 35 U.S.C. § 101, indefiniteness under 35 U.S.C. § 112(2) or enablement or written description under 35 U.S.C. § 112(1) of any of the asserted claims.

d. Document Production Accompanying Initial Disclosure of Invalidity Contentions. With the Initial Disclosure of Invalidity Contentions, the party opposing a claim of patent infringement shall produce or make available for inspection and copying a copy of any prior art identified in the Initial Disclosure of Invalidity Contentions that does not appear in the file history of the patent(s) at issue. To the extent any such item is not in English, an English translation of the portion(s) relied upon shall be produced.

2. **Cases Seeking Declaratory Judgment of Invalidity.** Unless otherwise ordered by the Court, in all cases in which a party files a complaint or other pleading seeking a declaratory judgment that a patent is invalid, and there are no claims for patent infringement asserted by any party, the parties shall make the following disclosures:

a. Initial Disclosure of Invalidity Contentions. Thirty (30) days from the date of the Scheduling Order, the party seeking a declaratory judgment of invalidity shall serve upon each opposing party its Initial Disclosure of Invalidity Contentions that conform to L.R. 804.1.c.

b. Document Production Accompanying Initial Disclosure of Invalidity Contentions. With the Initial Disclosure of Invalidity Contentions, the party seeking a declaratory judgment that a patent is invalid shall produce or make available for inspection and copying the documents described in L.R. 804.1.d..

3. **Cases Arising Under the Hatch-Waxman Act [21 U.S.C. § 355].** Unless otherwise ordered by the Court, in all cases alleging patent infringement based upon a Paragraph IV certification under 21 U.S.C. § 355, the parties shall make the following disclosures:

a. Initial Disclosure of Invalidity Contentions. Thirty (30) days from the date of the Scheduling Order, the Defendant shall serve upon the Plaintiff its Initial Disclosure of Invalidity Contentions that conform to L.R. 804.1.c.

b. Initial Disclosure of Non-Infringement Contentions. With the Initial Disclosure of Invalidity Contentions, the Defendant shall serve upon the Plaintiff its Initial Disclosure of Non-Infringement Contentions for any patents referred to in Defendants Paragraph IV Certification which shall include a claim chart identifying each claim in the patent at issue in the case and each limitation of each claim and shall specifically identify for each claim which claim limitation(s) are literally absent from the Defendants allegedly infringing Abbreviated New Drug Application or New Drug Application.

c. Document Production Accompanying Initial Disclosures of Invalidity and Non-Infringement Contentions. Defendant shall produce or make available for inspection and copying and produce to the Plaintiff or make available for inspection and copying the documents described in L.R. 804.1.d, as well as a complete copy of the entire Abbreviated New Drug Application or New Drug Application that is the basis of the case in question and any document or thing that the Defendant intends to rely on in defense against any infringement contentions by Plaintiff.

d. Initial Disclosure of Infringement Contentions. Sixty (60) days from the date of the Scheduling Order, Plaintiff shall serve Defendant with an Initial Disclosure of Infringement Contentions, for all patents referred to in Defendants Paragraph IV Certification, which shall contain all disclosures required by L.R. 804.1.a.

e. Document Production Accompanying Initial Disclosure of Infringement Contentions. Plaintiffs Initial Disclosure of Infringement Contentions shall be accompanied by the production of documents required under L.R. 804.1.b.

4. **Cases Seeking Correction of Inventors (35 U.S.C. § 256).** Unless otherwise ordered by the Court, in all cases in which a party seeks an order directing the Director of Patents to correct the inventors on a certificate of patent pursuant to 35 U.S.C. § 256, the parties shall make the following disclosures:

a. Initial Disclosure of Contribution Contentions. Thirty (30) days from the date of the Scheduling Order, any party seeking an order directing the Director of Patents to correct a certificate of patent pursuant to 35 U.S.C.§ 256 by adding to or replacing the inventors identified on the certificate shall serve the opposing parties a claim chart identifying each claim in the patent(s) at issue in the case to which the party alleges a person or persons, not named as inventor or joint inventor on certificate(s) of patent, made a significant contribution in conception and/or reduction to practice, describing the contribution made by the alleged inventor or joint inventor(s), and identifying the date each such contribution was made.

b. Document Production Accompanying Initial Disclosure of Contribution Contentions. With the Initial Disclosure of Contribution Contentions, the party seeking correction of a certificate of patent shall produce or make available for inspection and copying and produce to opposing parties or make available for inspection and copying:

i. All documents upon which the party asserts its standing to bring the claim(s) pursuant to 35 U.S.C. § 256; and

ii. All documents reflecting the alleged inventor or joint inventor(s) contribution to the conception and/or reduction to practice of the inventions described in the claims identified in the Initial Disclosure of Contribution Contentions.

c. Documents Reflecting Conception and Reduction to Practice. Sixty (60) days from the date of the Scheduling Order, the opposing parties shall serve upon the disclosing party all documents reflecting or pertaining to the conception and reduction to practice of the inventions described in the claims identified in the Initial Disclosure of Contribution Contentions.

5. **Cases Alleging False Marking (35 U.S.C. § 292).** Unless otherwise ordered by the Court, in all cases in which a party alleges false marking pursuant to 35 U.S.C. § 292, the parties shall make the following disclosures.

a. Initial Disclosure of False Marking Contentions. Thirty (30) days from the date of the Scheduling Order, any party asserting a claim of false marking pursuant to 35 U.S.C.§ 292 shall serve the opposing parties a chart identifying each item or article that the party claims has been falsely marked, the patent numbers with which the item or article was allegedly marked, the alleged expiration date of each such patent, and, to the extent that the party contends that the item or article is not within the inventions claimed in each such patent, the basis for each such contention.

b. Response to Initial Disclosure of False Marking Contentions. Sixty (60) days from the date of the Scheduling Order, the opposing parties shall serve upon the disclosing party a chart listing each item or article identified in the Initial Disclosure of False Marking, identifying all patent numbers with which those items and articles were marked and the periods of time during which they were so marked, the number of units of each item and article that were sold during each such period, and the basis for the opposing party's contention that the items and articles were within the inventions claimed in each such patent.

6. **Amendment to Contentions.** A party may amend Contentions described in L.R. 804.1 through 804.5 upon written consent of all parties or, for good cause shown, upon leave of the Court.

7. **Advice of Counsel.** Unless otherwise ordered by the Court, not later than thirty (30) days after entry of the Court's claim construction order, each party relying upon advice of counsel as part of a patent-related claim or defense for any reason shall:

a. Produce or make available for inspection and copying any written advice and documents related thereto for which the attorney-client and work product protection have been waived;

b. Provide a written summary of any oral advice and produce or make available for inspection and copying that summary and documents related thereto for which the attorney-client and work product protection have been waived; and

c. Serve a privilege log identifying any documents other than those identified in L.R. 804.7.a above, except those authored by counsel acting solely as trial counsel, relating to the subject matter of the advice which the party is withholding on the grounds of attorney-client privilege or work product protection.

d. A party who does not comply with the requirements of this L.R. 804.7 shall not be permitted to rely on advice of counsel for any purpose absent a stipulation of all parties or by order of the Court. (Added effective July 1, 2011.)

Rule 805. Claim Construction.

1. **Cases Involving Claims of Infringement.** Unless otherwise ordered by the Court, in all cases, other than those arising under the Hatch-Waxman Act (21 U.S.C. § 355), in which a party has asserted a claim of patent infringement:

a. Sixty (60) days from the date of the Scheduling Order, the party asserting infringement shall serve on each alleged infringing party a Claim Chart containing the following information:

i. Each claim of any patent in suit which the party alleges was infringed;

ii. Separately for each allegedly infringed claim, the identity of each accused apparatus, product, device, process, method, act, or other instrumentality ("Accused Instrumentality") of each allegedly infringing party;

iii. Whether such infringement is claimed to be literal or under the doctrine of equivalents;

iv. Where each element of each infringed claim is found within each Accused Instrumentality; and

v. If the party alleging infringement wishes to preserve the right to rely on that party's own apparatus, product, device, process, method, act, or other instrumentality as evidence of commercial success, the party must identify, separately for each claim, each such apparatus, product, device, process, method, act, or other instrumentality that incorporates or reflects that particular claim.

b. Sixty (60) days from the date of the Scheduling Order, the party asserting infringement shall also serve on each alleged infringing party a Proposed Claim Construction Statement containing the following information for each claim in issue:

i. Identification of any special or uncommon meanings of words or phrases in the claim;

ii. All references from the specification that support, describe, or explain each element of the claim;

iii. All material in the prosecution history that describes or explains each element of the claim; and

iv. Any extrinsic evidence that supports the proposed construction of the claim, including, but not limited to, expert testimony, inventor testimony, dictionary definitions and citations to learned treatises, as permitted by law.

c. Ninety (90) days from the date of the Scheduling Order, the alleged infringing parties shall serve upon the party claiming infringement a Responsive Claim Chart containing the following:

i. The identity of each item of prior art that allegedly anticipates each asserted claim or renders it obvious. Each prior art patent shall be identified by its number, country of origin, and date of issue. Each prior art publication shall be identified by its title, date of publication, and where feasible, author and publisher. Prior art under 35 U.S.C. § 102(b) shall be identified by specifying the item offered for sale or publicly used or known, the date the offer or use took place or the information became known, and the identity of the person or entity which made the use or which made and received the offer, or the person or entity which made the information known or to whom it was made known. Prior art under 35 U.S.C. § 102(f) shall be identified by providing the name of the person(s) from whom and the circumstances under which the invention or any part of it was derived. Prior art under 35 U.S.C. § 102(g) shall be identified by providing the identities of the person(s) or entities involved in and the circumstances surrounding the making of the invention before the patent applicant(s);

ii. Whether the prior art anticipates the claim or renders it obvious. If a combination of prior art references makes a claim obvious, that combination must be identified;

iii. Where, specifically, within each item of prior art each element of the claim is found;

iv. All grounds of invalidity other than anticipation or obviousness of any of the claims listed in the Claim Chart. This identification must be as specific as possible. For example, each party asserting a best mode defense must set forth with particularity what constitutes the inventors best mode, specifically citing information or materials obtained in discovery to the extent feasible. Each party asserting an enablement defense must set forth with particularity what is lacking in the specification to enable one skilled in the art to make or use the invention; and

v. If the claimant has alleged willful infringement, the date and a document reference number for each opinion of counsel upon which the party relies to support a defense to the willfulness allegation, including, but not limited to, issues of validity, and infringement of any patent in suit.

d. Ninety (90) days from the date of the Scheduling Order, the alleged infringing parties shall serve upon the party claiming infringement a Responsive Claim Construction Statement containing the following:

1. Identification of any special or uncommon meanings of words or phrases in the claim in addition to those disclosed in the Proposed Claim Construction Statement;

ii. All references from the specification that support, describe, or explain each element of the claim in addition to or contrary to those described in the Proposed Claim Construction Statement;

iii. All material in the prosecution history that describes or explains each element of the claim in addition to or contrary to those described in the Proposed Claim Construction Statement; and

iv. Any extrinsic evidence that supports the proposed construction of the claim, including, but not limited to, expert testimony, inventor testimony, dictionary definitions and citations to learned treatises, as permitted by law.

e. Amendment of a Claims Chart or a Responsive Claims Chart may be made only on stipulation of all parties or by Order of the Court, which shall be entered only upon a showing of excusable subsequent discovery of new information or extraordinary good cause.

f. One hundred twenty (120) days from the date of the Scheduling Order, the parties, having met and conferred on claim construction, shall file a Joint Claim Construction Statement which shall contain the following information:

i. The construction of those claims and terms on which the parties agree;

ii. Each party's proposed construction of each disputed claim and term, supported by the same information that is required in the respective claim construction statements; and

iii. For any party who proposes to call one or more witnesses at any claim construction hearing, the identity of each such witness, the subject matter of his or her testimony, and an estimate of the time required for the testimony.

g. One hundred twenty (120) days from the date of the Scheduling Order, the parties shall file and serve opening briefs with supporting evidence and identification of any proposed Claim Construction Hearing witnesses.

h. One hundred fifty (150) days from the date of the Scheduling Order, the parties shall file and serve any responsive brief and supporting evidence directly rebutting their opponents supporting evidence and identifying any additional proposed Claim Construction Hearing witnesses.

2. **Cases Seeking Declaratory Judgment of Invalidity.** Unless otherwise ordered by the Court, in all cases in which a party files a complaint or other pleading seeking a declaratory judgment that a patent is invalid, and there are no claims for patent infringement asserted by any party:

a. Sixty (60) days from the date of the Scheduling Order, the party asserting invalidity shall serve on each alleged infringing party a Claim Chart containing the following information:

i. The identity of each item of prior art that allegedly anticipates each asserted claim or renders it obvious. Each prior art patent shall be identified by its number, country of origin, and date of issue. Each prior art publication shall be identified by its title, date of publication, and where feasible, author and publisher. Prior art under 35 U.S.C. § 102(b) shall be identified by specifying the item offered for sale or publicly used or known, the date the offer or use took place or the information became known, and the identity of the person or entity which made the use or which made and received the offer, or the person or entity which made the information known or to whom it was made known. Prior art under 35 U.S.C. § 102(f) shall be identified by providing the name of the person(s) from whom and the circumstances under which the invention or any part of it was derived. Prior art under 35 U.S.C. § 102(g) shall be identified by providing the identities of the person(s) or entities involved in and the circumstances surrounding the making of the invention before the patent applicant(s);

ii. Whether the prior art anticipates the claim or renders it obvious. If a combination of prior art references makes a claim obvious, that combination must be identified;

iii. Where, specifically, within each item of prior art each element of the claim is found; and

iv. All grounds of invalidity other than anticipation or obviousness of any of the claims listed in the Claim Chart. This identification must be as specific as possible. For example, each party asserting a best mode defense must set forth with particularity what constitutes the inventors best mode, specifically citing information or materials obtained in discovery to the extent feasible. Each party asserting an enablement defense must set forth with particularity what is lacking in the specification to enable one skilled in the art to make or use the invention.

b. Sixty (60) days from the date of the Scheduling Order, the party asserting invalidity shall also serve on each opposing party a Proposed Claim Construction Statement containing the following information for each claim in issue:

i. Identification of any special or uncommon meanings of words or phrases in the claim;

ii. All references from the specification that support, describe, or explain each element of the claim;

iii. All material in the prosecution history that describes or explains each element of the claim; and

iv. Any extrinsic evidence that supports the proposed construction of the claim, including, but not limited to, expert testimony, inventor testimony, dictionary definitions and citations to learned treatises, as permitted by law.

c. Ninety (90) days from the date of the Scheduling Order, the opposing parties shall serve upon the party claiming invalidity a Responsive Proposed Claim Construction Statement containing the following:

i. Identification of any special or uncommon meanings of words or phrases in the claim in addition to those disclosed in the Proposed Claim Construction Statement;

ii. All references from the specification that support, describe, or explain each element of the claim in addition to or contrary to those described in the Proposed Claim Construction Statement;

iii. All material in the prosecution history that describes or explains each element of the claim in addition to or contrary to those described in the Proposed Claim Construction Statement; and

iv. Any extrinsic evidence that supports the proposed construction of the claim, including, but not limited to, expert testimony, inventor testimony, dictionary definitions and citations to learned treatises, as permitted by law.

d. Amendment of a Claims Chart or a Responsive Claims Chart may be made only on stipulation of all parties or by Order of the Court, which shall be entered only upon a showing of excusable subsequent discovery of new information or extraordinary good cause.

e. One hundred twenty (120) days from the date of the Scheduling Order, the parties, having met and conferred on claim construction, shall file a Joint Claim Construction Statement which shall contain the following information:

i. The construction of those claims and terms on which the parties agree;

ii. Each party's proposed construction of each disputed claim and term, supported by the same information that is required in the respective claim construction statements; and

iii. For any party who proposes to call one or more witnesses at any claim construction hearing, the identity of each such witness, the subject matter of his or her testimony, and an estimate of the time required for the testimony.

f. One hundred twenty (120) days from the date of the Scheduling Order, the parties shall file and serve opening briefs with supporting evidence and identification of any proposed Claim Construction Hearing witnesses.

g. One hundred fifty (150) days from the date of the Scheduling Order, the parties shall file and serve any responsive brief and supporting evidence directly rebutting their opponents supporting evidence and identifying any additional proposed Claim Construction Hearing witnesses.

3. **Cases Arising Under the Hatch-Waxman Act (21 U.S.C. § 355).** Unless otherwise ordered by the Court, in all cases alleging patent infringement based upon a Paragraph IV certification under 21 U.S.C. § 355:

a. Sixty (60) days from the date of the Scheduling Order, the Defendant shall serve the Plaintiff with a Claim Chart containing the following:

i. The identity of each item of prior art that allegedly anticipates each asserted claim or renders it obvious. Each prior art patent shall be identified by its number, country of origin, and date of issue. Each prior art publication shall be identified by its title, date of publication, and where feasible, author and publisher. Prior art under 35 U.S.C. § 102(b) shall be identified by specifying the item offered for sale or publicly used or known, the date the offer or use took place or the information became known, and the identity of the person or entity which made the use or which made and received the offer, or the person or entity which made the information known or to whom it was made known. Prior art under 35 U.S.C. § 102(f) shall be identified by providing the name of the person(s) from whom and the circumstances under which the invention or any part of it was derived. Prior art under 35 U.S.C. § 102(g) shall be identified by providing the identities of the person(s) or entities involved in and the circumstances surrounding the making of the invention before the patent applicant(s);

ii. Whether the prior art anticipates the claim or renders it obvious. If a combination of prior art references makes a claim obvious, that combination must be identified;

iii. Where, specifically, within each item of prior art each element of the claim is found; and

iv. All grounds of invalidity other than anticipation or obviousness. This identification must be as specific as possible. For example, each party asserting a best mode defense must set forth with particularity what constitutes the inventors best mode, specifically citing information or materials obtained in discovery to the extent feasible. Each party asserting an enablement defense must set forth with particularity what is lacking in the specification to enable one skilled in the art to make or use the invention.

b. Sixty (60) days from the date of the Scheduling Order, the Defendant shall serve the Plaintiff with a Proposed Claim Construction Statement containing the following information for each claim in issue:

i. Identification of any special or uncommon meanings of words or phrases in the claim;

ii. All references from the specification that support, describe, or explain each element of the claim;

iii. All material in the prosecution history that describes or explains each element of the claim; and

iv. Any extrinsic evidence that supports the proposed construction of the claim, including, but not limited to, expert testimony, inventor testimony, dictionary definitions and citations to learned treatises, as permitted by law.

c. Ninety (90) days from the date of the Scheduling Order, the Plaintiff shall serve upon the Defendant a Responsive Proposed Claim Construction Statement containing the following:

i. Identification of any special or uncommon meanings of words or phrases in the claim in addition to those disclosed in the Proposed Claim Construction Statement;

ii. All references from the specification that support, describe, or explain each element of the claim in addition to or contrary to those described in the Proposed Claim Construction Statement;

iii. All material in the prosecution history that describes or explains each element of the claim in addition to or contrary to those described in the Proposed Claim Construction Statement; and

iv. Any extrinsic evidence that supports the proposed construction of the claim, including, but not limited to, expert testimony, inventor testimony, dictionary definitions and citations to learned treatises, as permitted by law.

d. Amendment of a Claims Chart or a Responsive Claims Chart may be made only on stipulation of all parties or by Order of the Court, which shall be entered only upon a showing of excusable subsequent discovery of new information or extraordinary good cause.

e. One hundred twenty (120) days from the date of the Scheduling Order, the parties, having met and conferred on claim construction, the parties shall file a Joint Claim Construction Statement which shall contain the following information:

i. The construction of those claims and terms on which the parties agree;

ii. Each party's proposed construction of each disputed claim and term, supported by the same information that is required in the respective claim construction statements; and

iii. For any party who proposes to call one or more witnesses at any claim construction hearing, the identity of each such witness, the subject matter of his or her testimony, and an estimate of the time required for the testimony.

f. One hundred twenty (120) days from the date of the Scheduling Order, the parties shall file and serve opening briefs with supporting evidence and identification of any proposed Claim Construction Hearing witnesses.

g. One hundred fifty (150) days from the date of the Scheduling Order, the parties shall file and serve any responsive brief and supporting evidence directly rebutting their opponents supporting evidence and indentifying any additional proposed Claim Construction Hearing witnesses

4. **Cases Seeking Correction of Inventors (35 U.S.C. § 256) and Cases Alleging False Marking (35 U.S.C. § 292).** Sixty (60) days from the date of the Scheduling Order, the parties, having met and conferred on claim construction, shall report to the Court as to whether there are any contested issues of claims construction and, if so, shall propose a schedule for serving Claim Construction Statements and Responsive Claim Construction Statements and filing a Joint Claim Construction Statement, opening claim construction briefs and responsive claim construction briefs. (Added effective July 1, 2011.)

Rule 806. Certification of Disclosures.

All statements, disclosures, and charts served in accordance with L.R. 804 and L.R. 805 shall be dated and signed by counsel of record. Counsel's signature shall constitute a certification that to the best of his or her knowledge, information and belief, formed after an inquiry that is reasonable under the circumstances, the information contained in the statement, disclosure or chart is complete and correct at the time it is made. (Added effective July 1, 2011.)

Rule 807. Motions for Stay Pending Reexamination.

No motion for stay pending reexamination of a patent by the Central Reexamination Unit ("CRU") of the USPTO shall be considered unless accompanied by a copy of (1) the Reexamination Order and (2) the First Office Action issued by the CRU. (Added effective July 1, 2011.)

IX. SUPPLEMENTAL ADMIRALTY AND MARITIME RULES.

Local Admiralty Rule (a). Scope, citation and definitions.

Local Admiralty Rule (a)(1). Scope.

These local admiralty rules apply only to civil actions that are governed by the Supplemental Rules for Certain Admiralty and Maritime Claims (Supplemental Rule or Rules). All other local rules are applicable in these cases, but to the extent that another local rule is inconsistent with the applicable local admiralty rules, the local admiralty rules shall govern.

Local Admiralty Rule (a)(2). Citation.

The local admiralty rules may be cited by the letters "LAR" and the lower case letters and numbers in parentheses that appear at the beginning of each section. The lower case letter is intended to associate the local admiralty rule with the Supplemental Rule that bears the same capital letter.

Local Admiralty Rule (a)(3). Definitions.

As used in the local admiralty rules, "Court" means the United States District Court for the District of Maryland; "judicial officer" means a United States District Judge or a United States Magistrate Judge; "Clerk of Court" means the Clerk of the United States District Court and includes deputy clerks of court; "Marshal" means the United States Marshal and includes deputy marshals; "keeper" means any person or entity appointed by the Marshal to take physical custody of and maintain the vessel or other property under arrest or attachment; and "substitute custodian" means the individual or entity who, upon motion and order of the Court, assumes the duties of the Marshal or keeper with respect to the vessel or other property arrested or attached. (Amended effective December 1, 2009.)

Effect of amendments. — The 2009 amendment made minor stylistic changes.

Local Admiralty Rule (b). Maritime attachment and garnishment.

Local Admiralty Rule (b)(1). "Found within the district".

A defendant is not found within the District unless the defendant, can be personally served therein by delivering process (i) in the case of an individual, to the individual personally, or by leaving a copy thereof at the individual's dwelling house or usual place of abode with some person of suitable age and discretion; (ii) in the case of a corporation, trust or association, to an officer, trustee, managing or general agent thereof; (iii) in the case of a partnership, to a general partner thereof; and (iv) in the case of a limited liability company, to a manager thereof. (Amended effective December 1, 2009.)

Effect of amendments. — The 2009 amendment deleted "at the time of the filing of the complaint" following "unless the defendant" in 1.

Local Admiralty Rule (b)(2). Affidavit that defendant is not found within the district.

The affidavit required by Supplemental Rule B(1) to accompany the complaint shall specify with particularity the efforts made by and on behalf of plaintiff to find and serve the defendant within the district.

Local Admiralty Rule (b)(3). Use of state procedure.

When the plaintiff invokes a state procedure in order to attach or garnish under Fed. R. Civ. P. 4(e), the process of attachment or garnishment shall so state.

Local Admiralty Rule (b)(4). Notice to defendant.

In default applications, the affidavit or other proof required by Supplemental Rule B(2)(c) from the plaintiff or the garnishee shall specify with particularity the efforts made to give notice of the action to the defendant.

Local Admiralty Rule (c). Actions in rem: Special provisions.

Local Admiralty Rule (c)(1). Intangible property.

The summons to show cause why property should not be deposited in the Court, issued pursuant to Supplemental Rule C(3)(c) shall direct the person having control of intangible property to show cause no later than fourteen (14) days after service why the intangible property should not be delivered to the Court to abide further order of the Court. A judicial officer for good cause shown may lengthen or shorten the time. Service of the warrant shall have the effect of arresting the intangible property and bringing it within the control of the Court. Service of the summons to show cause requires a garnishee wishing to retain possession of the property to establish grounds for doing so, including specification of the measures taken to segregate and safeguard the intangible property arrested. Upon order of the Court, the person who is served may deliver or pay over to the Clerk of Court the intangible property proceeded against to the extent sufficient to satisfy the plaintiff's claim. If such delivery or payment is made, the person served is excused from the duty to show cause. (Amended by order effective January 1, 2008; amended effective December 1, 2009.)

Effect of amendments. — The 2008 amendment added "(c)" after "C(3)" in the first sentence. The 2009 amendment substituted "fourteen (14) days" for "10 days" in the first sentence.

Local Admiralty Rule (c)(2). Publication of notice of action and arrest.

The notice required by Supplemental Rule C(4) shall be published at least once in a newspaper of general circulation in the division of the District where the property has been seized. The Clerk of Court shall maintain and make available a list of newspapers of general circulation for each division of the District. The plaintiff's attorney shall file with the Clerk of Court a copy of the notice as it was published. The notice shall contain:

  a. The court, title, and number of the action;

  b. The date of the arrest;

  c. The identity of the property arrested;

  d. The name, address, telephone number, and bar number of the attorney for plaintiff;

  e. A statement that a person asserting ownership interest in the property or a right of possession pursuant to Supplemental Rule C(6) must file a statement of such interest with the Clerk and serve it on the attorney for the plaintiff within fourteen (14) days after publication;

  f. A statement that an answer to the complaint must be filed and served within twenty-one (21) days after the filing of the statement of interest and that otherwise default may be entered and condemnation ordered;

  g. A statement that motions to intervene under Fed. R. Civ. P. 24 by persons asserting maritime liens or other interests shall be filed within a time fixed by the Court; and

  h. The name, address, and telephone number of the Marshal and the keeper or substitute custodian. (Amended effective December 1, 2009.)

Effect of amendments. — The 2009 amendment substituted "fourteen (14) days' for "10 days' in e; and in f substituted "twenty-one (21) days' for "20 days'.

Local Admiralty Rule (c)(3). Notice requirements.

  a. **Default judgments.** i. Notice given. A party seeking a default judgment in an action *in rem* must satisfy the judge that due notice of the action and arrest of the property has been given (1) by publication as required in LAR (c)(2); (2) by service of the complaint and warrant of arrest upon the Marshal and keeper, substitute custodian, master, or other person having custody of the property; and (3) by mailing such notice to every other person who has not appeared in the action and is known to the party seeking the default judgment to have an ownership interest in the property.

  ii. Notice attempted. (1) If the defendant property is a vessel documented under the laws of the United States, the plaintiff must attempt to notify all persons identified as having an interest in the vessel in the United States Coast Guard Certificate of Ownership or the General Index or Abstract of Title. (2) If the defendant property is a vessel numbered as provided in the Federal Boat Safety Act, the plaintiff must attempt to notify the owner as named in the records of the issuing authority.

  b. **Ship Mortgage Act.** For purposes of the Ship Mortgage Act, 46 U.S.C.A. § 31325, notice to the Master of a vessel, or the person having physical custody thereof, by service of the Warrant of Arrest and Complaint shall be deemed in compliance with the notice requirements of such Act, as to all persons, except as to those who have recorded a notice of claim of lien.

c. **Mailing.** The notification requirement is satisfied by mailing copies of the warrant of arrest and complaint to the person's address using any form of mail requiring a return receipt.

Local Admiralty Rule (c)(4). Entry of default and default judgment.

After the time for filing a claim or answer has expired, the plaintiff may move for entry of default under Fed. R. Civ. P. 55(a). Default will be entered upon showing by affidavit or certificate of counsel that:

Notice has been given as required by LAR (c)(3)(a)(i); and

a. Notice has been attempted as required by LAR (c)(3)(a)(ii), where appropriate; and

b. The time to answer by any person asserting a right of possession or any ownership interest in the property has expired; and

c. No answer has been filed and no one has appeared to defend on behalf of the property.

The plaintiff may move for judgment under Fed. R. Civ. P. 55(b) at any time after default has been entered. (Amended effective July 1, 2011.)

Effect of amendments. — The 2011 amendment deleted the a. designation and redesignated accordingly.

Local Admiralty Rule (d). Possessory, petitory, and partition actions.

Local Admiralty Rule (d). Return date.

In an action under Supplemental Rule D, a judicial officer may order that the statement of interest and answer be filed on a date earlier than twenty-one (21) days after arrest. The order may also set a date for expedited hearing of the action. (Amended effective December 1, 2009.)

Effect of amendments. — The 2009 amendment substituted "twenty-one (21) days" for "20 days" in the first sentence.

Local Admiralty Rule (e). Actions in rem and quasi in rem: General Provisions.

Local Admiralty Rule (e)(1). Itemized demand for judgment.

The demand for judgment in every complaint filed under Supplemental Rules B or C shall allege the dollar amount of the debt or damages for which the action was commenced. The demand for judgment shall also allege the nature of other items of damage.

Local Admiralty Rule (e)(2). Salvage action complaints.

In an action for a salvage award, the complaint shall allege the dollar value of the vessel, cargo, freight, and other property salved or any other basis for an award. The complaint shall also state the dollar amount of the award claimed.

Local Admiralty Rule (e)(3). Verification of pleadings.

Every complaint in Supplemental Rules B, C, and D actions shall be verified upon oath or solemn affirmation, or in the form provided by 28 U.S.C. § 1746, by a party or by an authorized officer of a corporate party. If no party or authorized corporate officer is readily available, verification of a complaint may be made by an agent, attorney in fact, or attorney of record, who shall state the sources of the knowledge, information and belief contained in the complaint; declare that the document verified is true to the best of that knowledge, information, and belief; state why verification is not made by the party or an authorized corporate officer; and state that the affiant or declarant is authorized so to verify. If the verification was not made by a party or authorized corporate officer, any interested party may move, with or without requesting a stay, for the personal oath of a party or an authorized corporate officer, which shall be procured by commission or as otherwise ordered.

Local Admiralty Rule (e)(4). Review by judicial officer.

Unless otherwise required by the judicial officer, the review of complaints and papers called for by Supplemental Rules B(1) and C(3) does not require the affiant or declarant, party or attorney to be present. Any complaint presented to a judicial officer for review shall be accompanied by a form of order to the Clerk which, upon signature by the judicial officer, shall direct the arrest, attachment, or garnishment sought by the applicant.

Local Admiralty Rule (e)(5). Exigent circumstances.

This certification of exigent circumstances by the plaintiff or his attorney under Supplemental Rules B and C shall consist of an affidavit or a declaration pursuant to 28 U.S.C. § 1746 describing in detail the facts establishing the exigent circumstances.

Local Admiralty Rule (e)(6). Instructions to the Marshal.

The party who requests a warrant of arrest or process of attachment or garnishment shall provide instructions to the Marshal.

Local Admiralty Rule (e)(7). Property in possession of United States officer.

When the property to be attached or arrested is in the custody of an employee or officer of the United States, the Marshal will deliver a copy of the complaint and warrant of arrest or summons and process of attachment or garnishment to that officer or employee if present, and otherwise to the custodian of the property. The Marshal will instruct the officer or employee or custodian to retain custody of the property until ordered to do otherwise by a judicial officer.

Local Admiralty Rule (e)(8). Adversary hearing.

An adversary hearing provided for in Supplemental Rule E(4)(f) following arrest or attachment or garnishment shall be conducted by the Court within three (3) days after a request for such hearing, unless otherwise ordered. (Amended effective December 1, 2009.)

Effect of amendments. — The 2009 amendment made minor, stylistic changes.

Local Admiralty Rule (e)(9). Security deposit for seizure of vessels.

The party(ies) who seek(s) arrest or attachment of a vessel or property aboard a vessel shall deposit with the Marshal $3,000 for vessels more than sixty-five (65) feet in length overall or $500 for vessels sixty-five (65) feet in length overall or less. These deposits shall be used to cover the expenses of the Marshal including, but not limited to, dockage, keepers, maintenance, and insurance. The party(ies) shall advance additional sums from time to time as requested by the Marshal to cover the estimated expenses until the property is released or disposed of as provided in Supplemental Rule E. (Amended effective December 1, 2009.)

Effect of amendments. — The 2009 amendment made minor, stylistic changes.

Local Admiralty Rule (e)(10). Intervenors' claims and sharing of Marshal's fees and expenses.

a. **Intervention before sale.** When a vessel or other property has been arrested, attached, or garnished, and is in the hands of the Marshal or custodian substituted therefore, anyone having a claim against the vessel or property is required to present the claim by filing an intervening complaint under Fed. R. Civ. P. 24, and not by filing an original complaint, unless otherwise ordered by a judicial officer. An order permitting intervention may be signed *ex parte* at the time of filing the motion, subject to the right of any party to object to such intervention within fourteen (14) days after receipt of a copy of the motion and proposed pleading. Such motions shall not be subject to the provisions of L.R. 105. Upon the signing of an order permitting intervention, the clerk shall forthwith deliver a conformed copy of the intervening complaint to the Marshal, who shall deliver the copy to the vessel or custodian of the property. Intervenors shall thereafter be subject to the rights and obligations of parties, and the vessel or property shall stand arrested, attached, or garnished by the intervenor. An intervenor shall not be required to advance a security deposit to the Marshal for seizure of a vessel as required by LAR (e)(9). Property arrested, attached, or garnished by an intervenor shall be released in accordance with Supplemental Rule E(5).

c. **Sharing Marshal's fees and expenses before sale.** Upon motion by any party, security deposits may be ordered to be paid or shared by any party who has arrested, attached, or garnished a vessel or property aboard a vessel in amount or proportions to be determined by a judicial officer.

c. **Intervention after sale.** After ratification of sale and payment of the purchase price, any person having a claim against the vessel or property that arose before ratification must present the same by intervening complaint, pursuant to LAR (e)(10)(a), against the proceeds of the sale and may not proceed against the vessel unless a judicial officer shall otherwise order for good cause shown. Where an intervening complaint prays service of process *in rem,* the filing of such intervening complaint with the clerk shall be deemed to be a claim against such proceeds without the issuance of an *in rem* process, unless a judicial officer shall otherwise order for good cause shown. The judicial officer shall allow a period of at least thirty (30) days after due ratification of the sale for the submission of such claims. (Amended effective December 1, 2009.)

Effect of amendments. — The 2009 amendment substituted "fourteen (14) days" for "15 days" in the second sentence of 10.a; twice in 11.c substituted "seven (7) days" for "120 hours"; in 12.b and in 12.e substituted "seven (7) days" or variant for "three days" in three places; in the first sentence of 12.f substituted "seven (7) days" for "five days"; and made minor stylistic changes.

Local Admiralty Rule (e)(11). Custody of property.

a. **Safekeeping of property.** When a vessel or other property is brought into the Marshal's custody by arrest or attachment, the Marshal shall arrange for adequate safekeeping, which may include the placing of keepers on or near the vessel. A substitute custodian in place of the Marshal may be appointed by order of the Court.

b. **Insurance.** The Marshal may order insurance to protect the Marshal, his deputies, keepers, and substitute custodians, from liabilities assumed in arresting and holding the vessel, cargo, or other property, and in performing whatever services may be undertaken to protect the vessel, cargo, or other property, and in maintaining the Court's custody. The premiums charged for the liability insurance shall be paid out of the security deposits advanced to the Marshal in accordance with LAR(e)(9).

c. **Employment of vessel's officers and crew by Marshal.** All officers and members of the crew employed on a vessel of 750 gross tons or more shall be deemed employees of the Marshal for the period of seven (7) days the attachment or arrest of the vessel unless the Marshal, pursuant to a Court order, has notified the officers and members of the crew that they are not so employed or unless the vessel is released from attachment or arrest. If the vessel is not released within seven (7) days, the Marshal shall, on request of the seizing party, immediately thereafter designate which, if any, officers and members of the crew he is continuing to employ to preserve the vessel and shall promptly notify the remaining officers and members of the crew that they are no longer in his employ and are no longer in the service of the vessel and are free to depart from the vessel. The notice required by the preceding sentence shall be by written notice posted in a prominent place in each of the mess rooms or dining salons used by the officers and unlicensed personnel aboard the vessel.

d. **Normal vessel operations and movement of the vessel.** Following arrest, attachment, or garnishment of a vessel or property aboard a vessel, normal vessel operations shall be permitted to commence or continue unless otherwise ordered by the Court. No movement of the vessel shall take place unless authorized by order of a judicial officer.

e. **Procedure for filing claims by suppliers for payment of charges.** A person who furnishes supplies or services to a vessel, cargo, or other property in custody of the Court who has not been paid and claims the right to payment as an expense of administration shall submit an invoice to the Clerk in the form of a verified claim within the time period set by the Court for intervention after sale pursuant to LAR (e)(10)(c). The supplier must serve copies of the claim on the Marshal, substitute custodian if one has been appointed, and all parties of record. The Court may consider the claims individually or schedule a single hearing for all claims. (Amended effective December 1, 2009.)

Effect of amendments. — The 2009 amendment substituted "seven (7) days" for "120 hours" twice in 11.c.

Local Admiralty Rule (e)(12). Sale of property.

a. **Notice.** Notice of sale of property in an action under Supplemental Rules B or C shall be published under such terms and conditions as set by the Court.

b. **Payment of bid.** These provisions apply unless otherwise ordered in the order of sale: The person whose bid is accepted shall immediately pay the Marshal the full purchase price if the bid is $1,000 or less. If the bid exceeds $1,000, the bidder shall immediately pay a deposit of at least $1,000 or 10% of the bid, whichever is greater, and shall pay the balance within seven (7) days after the day on which the bid was accepted. If an objection to the sale is filed within that seven (7)-day period, the bidder is excused from paying the balance of the purchase price until seven (7) days after the sale is confirmed. Payment shall be made in cash, by certified check, or by cashier's check drawn on banks insured by the Federal Deposit Insurance Corporation or the Federal Savings and Loan Insurance Corporation.

c. **Default.** If the successful bidder does not pay the balance of the purchase price within the time allowed, the bidder shall be in default. In such a case, the judicial officer may accept the second highest bid or arrange a new sale. The defaulting bidder's deposit shall be forfeited and applied to any additional costs incurred by the Marshal because of the default, the balance being retained in the registry of the Court awaiting its order.

d. **Report of sale by marshal.** At the conclusion of the sale, the Marshal shall forthwith file a written report with the Court of the fact of sale, the date, the price obtained, the name and address of the successful bidder, and any other pertinent information.

e. **Time and procedure for objection to sale.** An interested person may object to the sale by filing a written objection with the Clerk within seven (7) days following the sale, serving the objection on all parties of record, the successful bidder, and the Marshal, and depositing such sum with the Marshal as determined by him to be sufficient to pay the expense of keeping the property for at least seven (7) days. Payment to the Marshal shall be in cash, certified check, or cashier's check drawn on banks insured by the Federal Deposit Insurance Corporation or the Federal Savings and Loan Insurance Corporation.

f. **Confirmation of sale.** A sale shall be confirmed by order of the Court within seven (7) days, but no sooner than three (3) days, after the sale. If an objection to the sale has been filed pursuant to LAR (e)(12)(e), the Court shall hold a hearing on the confirmation of the sale. The Marshal shall transfer title to the purchaser upon the order of the Court.

g. **Disposition of deposits.** i. Objection sustained. If an objection is sustained, sums deposited by the successful bidder will be returned to the bidder forthwith. The sum deposited by the objector will be applied to pay the fees and expenses incurred by the Marshal in keeping the property until it is resold, and any balance remaining shall be returned to the objector. The objector will be reimbursed for the expense of keeping the property from the proceeds of a subsequent sale.

ii. Objection overruled. If the objection is overruled, the sum deposited by the objector will be applied to pay the expense of keeping the property from the day the objection was filed until the day the sale is confirmed, and any balance remaining will be returned to the objector forthwith. (Amended effective December 1, 2009.)

Effect of amendments. — The 2009 amendment substituted "seven (7) days" or variant for "three days" in 12.b in three places and in 12.e; in the first sentence of 12.f substituted "seven (7) days" for "five days"; and made minor stylistic changes.

Local Admiralty Rule (e)(13). Discharge of stipulations for value and other security.

When an order is entered in any cause marking the case "Dismissed" or "Agreed and Settled," or "Agreed, Settled and Satisfied," the entry shall operate as a cancellation of all stipulations for value or other security provided to release the property seized that were filed in the case, unless otherwise provided in the order or by the Court.

Local Admiralty Rule (f). Limitation of liability.

Local Admiralty Rule (f)(1). Security for costs.

The amount of security for costs under Supplemental Rule F(1) shall be $1,000, and it may be combined with the security for value and interest, unless otherwise ordered.

Local Admiralty Rule (f)(2). Order of proof at trial.

Where the vessel interests seeking statutory limitation of liability have raised the statutory defense by way of answer or complaint, the plaintiff in the former or the party asserting a claim against the vessel or owner in the latter shall proceed with its proof first, as is normal at civil trials.

ELECTRONIC FILING REQUIREMENTS AND PROCEDURES.

Editor's note. — As to electronic filing of documents with the United States District Court for the District of Maryland (CM/ECF), see www.mdd.uscourts.gov/CMECF. For specific filing requirements, see Administrative Order 11-03, amended October 5, 2011, effective November 1, 2011.

APPENDIX A
DISCOVERY GUIDELINES OF THE UNITED STATES DISTRICT COURT FOR THE DISTRICT OF MARYLAND.

Adopted September 11, 1995; amended effective December 1, 2009; amended effective July 1, 2011.

Guideline 1: Conduct of discovery.

a. The purpose of these Guidelines is to facilitate the just, speedy, and inexpensive conduct of discovery in civil cases before the Court, and these Guidelines will be construed and administered accordingly, with respect to all attorneys, parties, and nonparties involved in discovery of civil cases before the Court. Fed R. Civ. P. 26 requires that discovery be relevant to any party's claim or defense; proportional to what is at issue in a case; and not excessively burdensome or expensive as compared to the likely benefit of obtaining the discovery being sought.

The parties and counsel have an obligation to cooperate in planning and conducting discovery to tailor the discovery to ensure that it meets these objectives. Counsel have a duty to confer early and throughout the case as needed to ensure that discovery is planned and conducted consistent with these requirements and, where necessary, make adjustments and modifications in discovery as needed.

During the course of their consultation, counsel are encouraged to think creatively and to make proposals to one another about alternatives or modifications to the discovery otherwise permitted that would permit discovery to be completed in a more just, speedy, inexpensive way. By way of illustration only, such alternatives could include different or additional deadlines for the filing of motions or the completion of all or part of discovery; accelerated exchanges of disclosures, additional data or descriptions of the parties' claims and defenses; sampling techniques; and substantial limitations on, or even the elimination of, depositions, coupled with alternative methods of exchanging or obtaining factual information or the equivalent of deposition testimony.

b. The parties and their counsel are encouraged to submit to the Court for approval their agreements to expand or limit discovery. If, however, counsel are unable to reach agreement on a discovery plan that substantially modifies the normal course of discovery, and either side believes that the Court's assistance would be helpful in framing or implementing such a plan, then the Court will make itself available with reasonable promptness, in response to a brief, written request for a discovery management conference that identifies the issues for consideration.

c. Counsel are expected to have read the Federal Rules of Civil Procedure, Local Rules of the Court, these Guidelines, and, with respect to discovery of electronically stored information ("ESI"), the Suggested Protocol for Discovery of ESI, posted on the Court's website, www.mdd.uscourts.gov. Compliance with these Guidelines will be considered by the Court in resolving discovery disputes, including whether sanctions should be awarded pursuant to Fed. R. Civ. P. 37, or the Court's inherent powers.

d. Attorneys are expected to behave professionally and with courtesy towards all involved in the discovery process, including but not limited to opposing counsel, parties and non-parties. This includes cooperation and civil conduct in an adversary system. Cooperation and civility include, at a minimum, being open to, and reasonably available for, discussion of legitimate differences in order to achieve the just, speedy, and inexpensive resolution of the action and every proceeding. Cooperation and communication can reduce the costs of discovery, and they are an obligation of counsel.

e. All discovery requests, responses and objections are governed by the requirements of Fed. R. Civ. P. 26(g) and counsel and parties are expected to be familiar with the requirements of the Rule.

f. Whenever possible, attorneys are expected to communicate with each other in good faith throughout the discovery process to resolve disputes without the need for intervention by the Court, and should do so promptly after becoming aware of the grounds for the dispute. In the event that such good faith efforts are unsuccessful, an unresolved dispute should be brought to the Court's attention promptly after efforts to resolve it have been unsuccessful. A failure to do so may result in a determination by the Court that the dispute must be rejected as untimely. Counsel may bring the unresolved dispute to the Court's attention by filing a letter, in lieu of a written motion, that briefly describes the dispute, unless otherwise directed by the Court.

g. Upon being notified by the parties of the unresolved discovery dispute, the Court will promptly schedule a conference call with counsel, or initiate other expedited procedures, to consider and resolve the discovery dispute. If the Court determines that the issue is too complicated to resolve informally, it may set an expedited briefing schedule to ensure that the dispute can be resolved promptly.

h. To the extent that any part of these Guidelines conflicts with any Local Rules of the Court, or an order of the Court in a particular case, then the conflicting rule or order should be considered to be governing. (Amended effective July 1, 2011.)

Effect of amendments. — The 2011 amendment added the b. designation and re-designated accordingly.

Guideline 2: Stipulations setting discovery deadlines.

Subject to approval by the Court, attorneys are encouraged to enter into written discovery stipulations to supplement Court's scheduling order. During the scheduling process, the Court will consider requests to impose milestone dates for motions, such as spoliation motions, and motions *in limine* (including *Daubert* motions) that do not normally otherwise have automatically-imposed deadlines. The Court encourages parties to submit to the Court for approval joint suggestions made pursuant to the Suggested Protocol for Discovery of ESI.

Guideline 3: Expert witness fees.

a. Unless counsel agree that each party will pay its own experts, the party taking an expert witness's deposition ordinarily pays the expert's fee for the time spent in deposition and related travel. *See* L.R. 104.11.a. Accordingly, counsel for the party that designated the expert witness should try to assure that the fee charged by the expert to the party taking the deposition is fair and reasonable. In the event a dispute arises as to the reasonableness or other aspects of an expert's fee, counsel should promptly confer and attempt in good faith to resolve the dispute without the involvement of the Court. If counsel are unsuccessful, the expert's deposition should proceed on the date noted, unless the Court orders otherwise, and the dispute respecting payment should be brought to the Court's attention promptly. The factors that may be considered in determining whether a fee is reasonable include, but are not limited to: (1) the expert's area of expertise; (2) the expert's education and training; (3) the fee being charged to the party who designated the expert; and (4) the fees ordinarily charged by the expert for non-litigation services, such as office consultations with patients or clients.

b. Recognizing that a treating physician may be considered both a fact witness and an expert, the Court has chosen to impose a specific limitation on the fee a treating physician may charge to either party. It is implicit in L.R. 104.11.b, which requires counsel to estimate the hours of deposition time required, that the physician may charge a fee for the entire time he or she reserved in accordance with the estimate, even if counsel conclude the deposition early. Further, unless the physician received notice at least two business days in advance of a cancellation, the physician is entitled to be paid for any time reserved that cannot reasonably be filled. Every effort should be made to schedule depositions at a time convenient for the witness, and to use videotaped or other visually recorded *de bene esse* depositions rather than requiring the physician's presence at trial. Note that this Discovery Guideline does not limit the reasonable fee a treating physician may charge if required to testify in court.

c. The parties are encouraged not to designate multiple experts on the same or similar topics.

d. Guideline 4.d is applicable to expert witness depositions.

Guideline 4: Guidelines in scheduling depositions.

a. Attorneys are expected to make a good faith effort to coordinate deposition dates with opposing counsel, parties, and non-party deponents, before noting a deposition.

b. Before agreeing to a deposition date, an attorney is expected to attempt to clear the date with his/her client if the client is a deponent, or wishes to attend the deposition, and with any witnesses the attorney agrees to attempt to produce at the deposition without the need to have the witness served with a subpoena.

c. An agreed-upon deposition date is presumptively binding. An attorney seeking to change an agreed-upon date has a duty to coordinate a new date before changing the agreed date. Noncompliance with Guideline 4.d may rebut the presumption contained herein.

d. If an attorney making a good faith effort to coordinate deposition dates under Guideline 4.a anticipates requesting that the deponent produce ESI at the deposition, that anticipated request should be disclosed to the opposing counsel, parties, and non-party deponents at the time of the Guideline 4.a coordination effort, or as soon thereafter as it becomes anticipated. At a minimum, the discovering/requesting party should describe the scope and form of ESI that will be requested. Counsel are encouraged to review and, if applicable, comply with the Suggested Protocol For Discovery Of ESI.

e. Upon reasonable request, and where reasonably practicable, in order to expedite the deposition questioning, a deponent should produce documents including ESI, properly requested in a notice of deposition and accompanying subpoena, if any, a reasonable time prior to the deposition. Noncompliance with a reasonable and timely request for production of such documents prior to a deposition may be considered by the Court in a motion or request made pursuant to Fed. R. Civ. P. 30(d)(1) to determine whether additional time is needed to fairly examine the deponent or if the deponent, another person, or any other circumstance has impeded or delayed the examination.

Guideline 5: Designation by an organization of someone to testify on its behalf.

a. **Requested areas of testimony.** A notice or subpoena to an entity, association or other organization should accurately and concisely identify the designated area(s) of requested testimony, giving due regard to the nature, business, size and complexity of the entity being asked to testify. The notice or subpoena should ask the recipient to provide the name(s) of the designated person(s) and the areas that each person will testify to by a reasonable date before the deposition is scheduled to begin.

b. **Designating the best person to testify for the organization.** An entity, association or other organization responding to a deposition notice or subpoena should make a diligent inquiry to determine what individual(s) is (are) best suited to testify.

c. **More than one person may be necessary.** When it appears that more than one individual should be designated to testify without duplication on the designated area(s) of inquiry, each such individual should be identified, a reasonable period of time before the date of the deposition, as a designated witness along with a description of the area(s) to which he or she will testify.

Guideline 6: Deposition questioning, objections and procedure.

a. An attorney should not intentionally ask a witness a question that misstates or mischaracterizes the witness's previous answer.

b. During the taking of a deposition, it is presumptively improper for an attorney to make objections which are not consistent with Fed. R. Civ. P. 30(c)(2). Objections should be stated as simply, concisely and non-argumentatively as possible to avoid coaching or making suggestions to the deponent, and to minimize interruptions in the questioning of the deponent (for example: "objection, leading"; "objection, asked and answered"; "objection, compound question"; "objection, form"). If an attorney desires to make an objection for the record during the taking of a deposition that reasonably could have the effect of coaching or suggesting to the deponent how to answer, then the deponent, at the request of any of the attorneys present, or, at the request of a party if unrepresented by an attorney, should be excused from the deposition during the making of the objection.

c. An attorney should not repeatedly ask the same or substantially identical question of a deponent if the question already has been asked and fully and responsively answered by the deponent. Upon objection by counsel for the deponent, or by the deponent if unrepresented, it is presumptively improper for an attorney to continue to ask the same or substantially identical question of a witness unless the previous answer was evasive or incomplete.

d. It is presumptively improper to instruct a witness not to answer a question during the taking of a deposition unless under the circumstances permitted by Fed. R. Civ. P. 30(c)(2). However, it is also presumptively improper to ask questions clearly beyond the scope of discovery permitted by Fed. R. Civ. P. 26(b)(1), particularly of a personal nature, and continuing to do so after objection shall be evidence that the deposition is being conducted in bad faith or in such a manner as unreasonably to annoy, embarrass, or oppress the deponent or party, which is prohibited by Fed. R. Civ. P. 30(d)(3).

e. If requested to supply an explanation as to the basis for an objection, the objecting attorney should do so, consistent with Guideline 6(b) above.

f. While the interrogation of the deponent is in progress, neither an attorney nor the deponent should initiate a private conversation except for the purpose of determining whether a privilege should be asserted. To do so otherwise is presumptively improper.

g. During breaks in the taking of a deposition, no one should discuss with the deponent the substance of the prior testimony given by the deponent during the deposition. Counsel for the deponent may discuss with the deponent at such time whether a privilege should be asserted or otherwise engage in discussion not regarding the substance of the witness's prior testimony.

h. Unless otherwise ordered by the Court, the following persons may, without advance notice, attend a deposition: individual parties; a representative of non-individual parties; and expert witnesses of parties. Except for the persons identified above, counsel should notify other parties not later than seven (7) business days before the taking of a deposition if counsel desires to have a non-party present during a deposition. If the parties are unable to agree to the attendance of this person, then the person shall not be entitled to attend the deposition unless the party desiring to have the person attend obtains a Court order permitting him/her to do so. Unless ordered by the Court, however, a dispute regarding who may attend a deposition should not be grounds for delaying the deposition. All persons present during the taking of a deposition should be identified on the record before the deposition begins. Other than the deponent, counsel representing a party or unrepresented party, persons attending a deposition may not ask or answer questions during, or otherwise participate in the process of, the deposition.

i. Except for the person recording the deposition in accordance with Fed. R. Civ. P. 30(b), during the taking of a deposition no one may record the testimony without the consent of the deponent and all parties in attendance, unless otherwise ordered by the Court.

Intent of section (c). — Section (c) of this guideline was intended to strike a balance between an attorney's right to continue an inquiry where a deponent's response is evasive or incomplete with the defending attorney's legitimate desire to prevent the deposing attorney from employing the abusive tactic of repeatedly asking the same, or substantially the same, question, despite having received a complete and nonevasive answer. Boyd v. University of Md. Med. Sys., 173 F.R.D. 143 (D. Md. 1997).

Guideline 7: Assertions of privilege at depositions.

a. When a claim of privilege is asserted during a deposition, and information is not provided on the basis of such assertion:

b. In accordance with Fed. R. Civ. P. 26(b)(5), the person asserting the privilege should identify during the deposition the nature of the privilege (including work product) that is being claimed.

c. After a claim of privilege has been asserted, the person seeking disclosure should have reasonable latitude during the deposition to question the witness to establish other relevant information concerning the assertion of privilege, including: (i) the applicability of the particular privilege being asserted; (ii) any circumstances that, under Fed. R. Evid. 502, may demonstrate that a prior disclosure was or was not permitted without waiver of the privilege; (iii) any circumstances that may constitute an exception to the assertion of the privilege; and (iv) any circumstances which may result in the privilege having been waived.

d. In accordance with Fed. R. Civ. P. 26(b)(5), the party asserting the privilege, in providing the foregoing information, should not be required to reveal the information that is itself privileged or protected from disclosure. (Amended effective July 1, 2011.)

Effect of amendments. — The 2011 amendment added the a. designation and re-designated accordingly.

Guideline 8: Making a record of improper conduct during a deposition.

Upon request of any attorney, party unrepresented by an attorney, or the deponent if unrepresented by an attorney, the person recording the deposition in accordance with Fed. R. Civ. P. 30(b) should enter on the record a description by the requesting person of conduct of any attorney, party, or person attending the deposition which violates these guidelines, the Federal Rules of Civil Procedure, or the Local Rules of the Court.

Guideline 9: Delay in responding to discovery requests.

a. **Interrogatories, requests for production of documents, and requests for admission of facts and genuineness of documents.** The Federal Rules of Civil Procedure designate the time prescribed for responding to Interrogatories, Requests for Production of Documents, and Requests for Admission of Facts and Genuineness of Documents. Nothing contained in these guidelines modifies the time limits prescribed by the Federal Rules of

Civil Procedure. Attorneys should make good faith efforts to respond to discovery requests within the time prescribed by those rules.

Absent exigent circumstances, attorneys seeking additional time to respond to discovery requests should contact opposing counsel as soon as practical after receipt of the discovery request, but not later than three (3) days before the response is due. In multiple party cases, the attorney wanting additional time should contact the attorney for the party propounding the discovery.

A request for additional time which does not conflict with a scheduling deadline imposed by the Federal Rules of Civil Procedure, the Local Rules of the Court, or a Court order should not be unreasonably refused. If a request for additional time is granted, the requesting party should promptly prepare a writing which memorializes the agreement, which shall be served on all parties but need not be submitted to the Court for approval.

Unless otherwise provided by the Local Rules of the Court, no stipulation that modifies a Court-imposed deadline shall be deemed effective unless and until the Court approves the stipulation.

b. **Depositions.** Unless otherwise ordered by the Court or agreed upon by the parties, fourteen (14) days notice should be deemed to be "reasonable notice" within the meaning of Fed. R. Civ. P. 30(b)(1), for the noting of depositions.

Guideline 10: Interrogatories, requests for production of documents, answers to interrogatories, and written responses to document requests.

a. A party may object to an interrogatory, document request, or part thereof, while simultaneously providing partial or incomplete answers to the request. If a partial or incomplete answer is provided, the answering party shall state that the answer is partial or incomplete.

b. No part of an interrogatory or document request should be left unanswered merely because an objection is interposed to another part of the interrogatory or document request.

c. In cases where a party is represented by more than one attorney of record, no discovery motion, response or opposition should be filed unless a senior attorney of record has read the contents of the motion and any supporting memorandum and exhibits.

d. In accordance with Fed. R. Civ. P. 26(b)(5), where a claim of privilege is asserted objecting to any interrogatory, document request, or part thereof, and information is not provided on the basis of such assertion:

i. The party asserting the privilege shall, in the objection to the interrogatory, document request, or part thereof, identify with specificity the nature of the privilege (including work product) that is being claimed;

ii. The following information should be provided in the objection, if known or reasonably available, unless divulging such information would cause disclosure of the allegedly privileged information;

a. For oral communications:

(i) the name of the person making the communication and the names of persons present while the communication was made, and, where not apparent, the relationship of the persons present to the person making the communication;

(ii) the date and place of the communication; and

(iii) the general subject matter of the communication.

b. For documents:

(i) the type of document;

(ii) the general subject matter of the document;

(iii) the date of the document; and

(iv) such other information as is sufficient to identify the document, including, where appropriate, the author, addressee, custodian, and any other recipient of the document, and, where not apparent, the relationship of the author, addressee, custodian, and any other recipient to each other.

iii. The above information should be provided separately for each document for which privilege/protection is asserted, unless doing so would be excessively burdensome or expensive. In such instances, the party asserting privilege/protection should particularize why providing separate designations would be excessively burdensome or expensive, and then may identify by categories the voluminous documents or communications for which privilege/protection is asserted, providing the above information for each category. A party may only designate documents as privileged/protected by category if each document (1) is within the privilege/protection claimed, and (2) shares common characteristics such as sender, receiver, author, or specific subject matter. Where only part of a document or communication is privileged/protected, the unprivileged/unprotected portion should be disclosed if otherwise discoverable and within the scope of the discovery request.

iv. Reasonably promptly after receiving the information contained in Guideline 10.d.ii., the party seeking disclosure should notify the party from whom disclosure is sought of any deficiencies in the particularization of the basis for any privilege/protection asserted, including any "category designations" under Guideline 10.d.iii. Once done, the party from whom disclosure was sought shall, with reasonable promptness, provide sufficient factual information, including by affidavit, to establish the factual basis for each claim of privilege or protection that has been claimed. Failure to do so may result in a determination by the Court that the party asserting the privilege or work product protection has failed to particularize it as required by Fed. R. Civ. P. 26(b)(5), resulting in the waiver of any privilege/protection that has been claimed.

v. The parties are encouraged to confer and reach agreement regarding how to assert privilege/protection claims with respect to Email "chains" or "strings," and if unable to do so, to bring to the attention of the Court their disagreement for prompt resolution.

e. If a party asserts in response to an interrogatory, request for production of documents, or request for admission of facts, that electronically stored information is not reasonably accessible because of undue burden or cost, within the meaning of Fed. R. Civ. P. 26(b)(2)(B), or otherwise asserts that requested discovery is unduly burdensome or expensive, the party making that assertion is expected to disclose, promptly and with particularity, the facts on which it relies to support that contention.

f. In addition to paper copies, parties are encouraged to exchange discovery requests and responses in a commonly-accepted word processing format, if requested, in order to reduce the clerical effort required to prepare responses and motions.

APPENDIX B
RULES AND GUIDELINES FOR DETERMINING
ATTORNEYS' FEES IN CERTAIN CASES[1].

1. **Mandatory rules regarding billing format, time recordation, and submission of quarterly statements.** a. Time shall be recorded by specific task and lawyer or other professional performing the task as set forth more fully in L.R. 109.1.b.

b. Fee applications, accompanied by time records, shall be submitted in the following format organized by litigation phase[2]:

i. case development, background investigation and case administration (includes initial investigations, file setup, preparation of budgets, and routine communications with client, co-counsel, opposing counsel, and the Court);

ii. pleadings;

iii. interrogatories, document production, and other written discovery;

iv. depositions (includes time spent preparing for depositions);

v. motions practice;

vi. attending Court hearings;

vii. trial preparation and post-trial motions;

viii. attending trial;

ix. ADR; and

x. fee petition preparation.

c. Counsel for a party intending to seek fees if the party prevails shall submit to opposing counsel quarterly statements showing the amount of time spent on the case and the total value of that time. These statements need not be in the "litigation phase" format provided in Guideline 1.b or otherwise reflect how time has been spent. The first such statement is due at the end of the first quarter in which the action is filed. Failure to submit these statements may result in a denial or reduction of fees.[3]

d. Upon request by the Judge (or private mediator agreed upon by the parties) presiding over a settlement conference, counsel for all parties (with the exception of public lawyers who do not ordinarily keep time records) shall turn over to that officer (or mediator) statements of time and the value of that time in the "litigation phase" format provided in Guideline 1.b.

---

[1] These rules and guidelines apply to cases in which a prevailing party would be entitled, by applicable law or contract, to reasonable attorneys' fees based on a set of criteria including hours and rates. They do not apply to cases in which statutes or contracts authorize fees based on a fixed percentage or other formula, such as social security cases.

[2] In general, preparation time and travel time should be reported under the category to which they relate. For example, time spent preparing for and traveling to and from a Court hearing should be recorded under the category "Court hearings." Factual investigation should also be listed under the specific category to which it relates. For example, time spent with a witness to obtain an affidavit for a summary judgment motion or opposition should be included under the category "motions practice." Similarly, a telephone conversation or a meeting with a client held for the purpose of preparing interrogatory answers should be included under the category "Interrogatories, Document Production and Other Written Discovery." Of course, each of these tasks must be separately recorded in the back-up documentation in accordance with Guideline 1.a.

[3] Opposing counsel may not seek a denial or reduction of fees from the court if he/she did not first request that such statements be provided.

e. If during the course of a fee award dispute a Judge orders that the billing records of counsel for the party opposing fees must be turned over to the party requesting fees, those billing records shall be submitted in the "litigation phase" format.

2. **Guidelines regarding compensable and non-compensable time.**
a. Where plaintiffs with both common and conflicting interests are represented by different lawyers, there shall be a lead attorney for each task (e.g., preparing for and speaking at depositions on issues of common interest and preparing pleadings, motions, and memoranda), and other lawyers shall be compensated only to the extent that they provide input into the activity directly related to their own client's interests

b. Only one lawyer for each separately represented party shall be compensated for attending depositions[4].

c. Only one lawyer for each party shall be compensated for attending hearings[5].

d. Generally, only one lawyer is to be compensated for client, third party and intra-office conferences, although if only one lawyer is being compensated the time may be charged at the rate of the more senior lawyer. Compensation may be paid for the attendance of more than one lawyer where justified for specific purposes such as periodic conferences of defined duration held for the purpose of work organization, strategy, and delegation of tasks in cases where such conferences are reasonably necessary for the proper management of the litigation.

e. Travel. i. Whenever possible time spent in traveling should be devoted to doing substantive work for a client and should be billed (at the usual rate) to that client. If the travel time is devoted to work for a client other than the matter for which fees are sought, then the travel time should not be included in any fee request. If the travel time is devoted to substantive work for the client whose representation is the subject of the fee request, then the time should be billed for the substantive work, not travel time.

ii. Up to two (2) hours of travel time (each way and each day) to and from a court appearance, deposition, witness interview, or similar proceeding that cannot be devoted to substantive work may be charged at the lawyer's hourly rate.

iii. Time spent in long-distance travel above the two (2) hours limit each way, that cannot be devoted to substantive work, may be charged at one-half of the lawyer's usual rate.

---

[4] Departure from this guideline would be appropriate upon a showing of a valid reason for sending two attorneys to the deposition, e.g. that the less senior attorney's presence is necessary because he organized numerous documents important to the deposition but the deposition is of a critical witness whom the more senior attorney should properly depose. Departure from the guideline may be appropriate upon a showing that more than one retained attorney representing the defendant attended the deposition and charged the time for his/her attendance.

[5] The same considerations discussed in footnote 4 concerning attendance by more than one lawyer at a deposition also apply to attendance by more than one lawyer at a hearing. There is no guideline as to whether more than one lawyer for each party is to be compensated for attending trial. This must depend upon the complexity of the case and the role that each lawyer is playing. For example, if a junior lawyer is present at trial primarily for the purpose of organizing documents but takes a minor witness for educational purposes, consideration should be given to billing his/her time at a paralegal's rate.

3. **Guidelines regarding hourly rates**[6]. a. Lawyers admitted to the bar for less than five years (5): $ 150-190

b. Lawyers admitted to the bar for five (5) to eight (8) years: $165-250

c. Lawyers admitted to the bar for nine (9) to fourteen (14) years: $ 225-300

d. Lawyers admitted to the bar for fifteen (15) years or more: $ 275-400

e. Paralegals and law clerks: $ 95-115.

4. **Reimbursable expenses.** a. Generally, reasonable out-of-pocket expenses (including long-distance telephone calls, express and overnight delivery services, computerized on-line research and faxes) are compensable at actual cost.

b. Mileage is compensable at the rate of reimbursement for official government travel in effect at the time the expense was incurred.

c. Copy work is compensable at the rate established by the Court for taxation of costs. (Amended Aug. 16, 2004, effective Aug. 16, 2004; by order effective January 1, 2008; and by order effective December 1, 2009.)

Effect of amendments. — The 2004 amendment, effective Aug. 16, 2004, in 1.d and 1.e substituted "Judge" for "judicial officer".

The 2008 amendment rewrote the heading and its footnote; in 1.c added the last sentence with its footnote; in 2, deleted c and redesignated accordingly; and in 3, increased the hourly rates, rewrote c and added d and redesignated accordingly.

The December 1, 2009, amendment made minor, stylistic changes in 2.e., 3, and in the footnotes.

---

[6] These rates are intended solely to provide practical guidance to lawyers and judges when requesting, challenging and awarding fees. The factors established by case law obviously govern over them. One factor that might support an adjustment to the applicable range is an increase in the cost of legal services since the adoption of the guidelines. The guidelines, however, may serve to make the fee petition less onerous by narrowing the debate over the range of a reasonable hourly rate in many cases. These rates do not apply to cases governed by the Prison Litigation Reform Act, which sets an hourly rate by statute.

APPENDIX C
REGULATIONS GOVERNING THE REIMBURSEMENT OF EXPENSES IN PRO BONO CASES IN THE UNITED STATES DISTRICT COURT FOR THE DISTRICT OF MARYLAND.

I. **Eligibility for Reimbursement.** When an attorney has been appointed to represent an indigent party in a civil case before this Court, that attorney shall be allowed to petition the Court for reimbursement of certain expenses, incurred in the preparation and presentation of the case, subject to these regulations. The limit applicable to such expenses, unless otherwise requested by counsel and approved by the Court's Attorney Admissions Committee, is ten thousand dollars ($10,000.00).

II. **Restrictions on Eligibility.** A. Any costs that are either waived or recoverable under the provisions of Title 18, U.S. Code or Title 28, U.S. Code or which have been otherwise recovered shall not be reimbursed from the Admissions Fund.

B. In no case shall an appointed attorney for a party who has been awarded costs and/or fees pursuant to a judgment in a suit before this Court be eligible for reimbursement of those costs and/or fees from the Admissions Fund.

C. Only those costs associated with the preparation or presentation of a civil action in the United States District Court for the District of Maryland shall be approved for reimbursement. No costs associated with the preparation or presentation of an appeal to the U.S. Court of Appeals or the U.S. Supreme Court shall be reimbursed from the Admissions Fund.

III. **Procedures for Petitioning for Reimbursement.** A. Within thirty (30) days of the entry of a judgment, the appointed attorney shall file with the Judge a request for reimbursement of costs on a form approved by the Court and available from the Clerk. Where it is considered necessary and appropriate, the Judge may approve an interim reimbursement of extraordinary and substantial expenses.

B. In cases in which an appointed attorney has withdrawn or has been dismissed prior to the entry of a judgment, that attorney shall file a request for reimbursement within thirty (30) days of such withdrawal or dismissal. Any work product obtained with expenditures from the Admissions Fund shall subsequently be provided to the newly-appointed counsel or, where no new counsel is appointed, to the party for whom counsel was appointed.

C. In cases where interim reimbursements are approved and paid and appointed counsel subsequently recovers previously reimbursed expenses, counsel shall, within thirty (30) days from said recovery, return to the Admissions Fund an amount up to the amount previously reimbursed, depending on the amount of the recovery.

IV. **Reimbursable Expenses.** The following out-of-pocket expenses may be reimbursed upon approval by the Judge:

1. Depositions and Transcripts. The costs of depositions and transcripts may be reimbursed up to the rates, and subject to the limitations, established by the Court for the taxation of costs.

2. Investigative, Expert or Other Services. A. Counsel may request (in an *ex parte* application) investigative, expert or other services necessary for the adequate preparation of a matter. The Court, upon finding after appropriate *ex parte* inquiry that the services are necessary, may authorize them.

B. Without prior request, counsel may obtain, subject to later review, investigative, expert or other services necessary for the adequate preparation of the case. Counsel should note that approval of this type of expenditure is not automatic and should be prepared to defend his/her reasons for not requesting prior approval.

3. Travel Expenses. Travel may be reimbursed at actual cost if public transportation is used, or if a private vehicle is used, at the rate of reimbursement for official government travel in effect at the time the expense was incurred, plus parking, tolls, and similar expenses.

4. Service/Witness Fees. Service and witness fees that are not otherwise avoided, waived or recoverable may be reimbursed from the Admissions Fund.

5. Interpreter Services. Costs of interpreter services not otherwise avoided, waived or recoverable may be reimbursed from the Admissions Fund.

6. Photocopies, Photographs, Telephone Long Distance Calls, etc. Actual out-of-pocket expenses incurred for items such as photographs, long distance calls, express and overnight delivery services, and computerized on-line research necessary for the preparation of the case may be reimbursed from the Admissions Fund. Copy work may be reimbursed at the rate established by the Court for taxation of costs.

7. Other Expenses. Expenses other than those in sections one through six, above, may be approved by the Judge. For anticipated expenses over five hundred dollars ($500.00), counsel should seek *ex parte* approval from the presiding Judge prior to making the expenditure. When requesting reimbursement under this section, a detailed description of the expenses should be attached to the petition filed with the Judge.

V. **Restrictions on Reimbursement.** A. General office overhead is not reimbursable from the Admissions Fund.

B. The Judge may disallow reimbursement for any expense that is not documented.

C. The Judge may disallow reimbursement of expenses if he or she determines that appointed counsel did not pursue reasonable courses of recovery of expenses, including seeking statutorily permitted costs and fees, prior to application for reimbursement from the Admissions Fund.

D. Under no circumstances shall Admissions Fund funds be authorized to pay for costs or fees taxed against a party or appointed counsel, as a result of a Court ruling or as part of a judgment obtained by an adverse party in a civil action before this Court. (Amended Aug. 16, 2004, effective Aug. 16, 2004; by order effective December 1, 2009; and by order effective September 21, 2011.)

Effect of amendments. — The 2004 amendment, effective Aug. 16, 2004, substituted "Judge" for "presiding Judicial Officer" throughout the Appendix; in I substituted "Five Thousand ($5,000.00)" for "Twenty Five Hundred ($2500.00)"; in IV.3 deleted "for trips in excess of 50 miles each way" following "Travel"; in IV.4 substituted "Service/Witness" for "Service of Papers/Witness" in the heading and "Service and witness fees" for "Fees for service of papers and the appearance of witnesses"; in IV.6 in the heading substituted

"Long Distance" for "Toll"; in the first sentence substituted "long distance calls, express and overnight delivery services, and computerized on-line research" for "toll calls and telegrams"; in IV.7 rewrote the second sentence; and in V rewrote A.

The December 1, 2009, amendment made minor, stylistic changes.

The 2011 amendment substituted "ten thousand dollars ($10,000.00)" for "five thousand dollars ($5,000.00)" at the end of I.

APPENDIX D
STANDARD FORMS.

Guidelines for Uniform Instructions and Definitions for Use in Discovery Requests

These Guidelines set forth the full text of instructions and definitions for Interrogatories and Requests for Production of Documents. Parties may use any instructions, definitions, or rules of construction that are consistent with the Federal Rules of Civil Procedure. This Court has stated that the use of reasonable definitions may be helpful. *Diversified Products Corp. v. Sports Center Co.*, 42 F.R.D. 3, 4 (D. Md. 1967). This Court has also stated that unreasonable definitions may render interrogatories so burdensome that objections to the entire series should be sustained, with sanctions. *Id.*

The purpose of the Guidelines is to provide a presumptively proper "safe harbor." The Guidelines are appropriate for many cases and their use is encouraged. The Guidelines may not be appropriate in certain cases. Their use is purely and wholly optional. If they are used, the Court will likely consider them presumptively proper and a party objecting to them will have the burden of demonstrating that they are not proper. Compliance with the Guidelines will be considered by the Court in resolving discovery disputes, including whether sanctions should be awarded pursuant to Fed. R. Civ. P. 37.

The Guidelines are not intended to broaden or narrow the scope of discovery permitted by the Federal Rules of Civil Procedure.

The Instructions and Definitions of the Guidelines may be incorporated into a party's Interrogatories or Request for Production of Documents by the following statement: "The Uniform Instructions and Definitions For Use in Discovery Requests are incorporated herein." If this statement, or a substantially similar statement, is placed in the party's Interrogatories or Request for Production of Documents, the Court will deem the Instructions and Definitions of these Guidelines to be incorporated by reference therein. If a specific discovery request is incorporated into a party's Interrogatories or Request for Production of Documents, the request should state "(Standard Interrogatory No. _____)" or "(Standard Document Request No. _____)."

STANDARD INTERROGATORIES

IN THE UNITED STATES DISTRICT COURT
FOR THE DISTRICT OF MARYLAND

_____,   *
    Plaintiff   *
v.   *   Civil Action No.:
                                *
_____,   *   _____
    Defendant   *

****

INTERROGATORIES

Pursuant to Fed. R. Civ. P. 33, and L.R. 104, _____, by its undersigned attorneys, propounds these Interrogatories, to which _____ shall respond separately and fully, in writing and under oath, within the time prescribed by the Federal Rules of Civil Procedure, in accordance with the Instructions and Definitions set forth hereinafter.

INSTRUCTIONS

1. These instructions and definitions should be construed to require answers based upon the knowledge of, and information available to, the responding party as well as its agents, representatives, and, unless privileged, attorneys. It is intended that the following discovery requests will not solicit any material protected either by the attorney/client privilege or work product doctrine which was created by, or developed by, counsel for the responding party after the date on which this litigation was commenced. If any inquiry is susceptible of a construction which calls for the production of such material, that material need not be provided and no privilege log pursuant to Fed. R. Civ. P. 26(b)(5) or Discovery Guideline 9(a) will be required as to such material.

2. These Interrogatories are continuing in character, so as to require that supplemental answers be filed seasonably if further or different information is obtained with respect to any interrogatory.

3. Pursuant to Discovery Guideline 9(b), no part of an interrogatory should be left unanswered merely because an objection is interposed to another part of the interrogatory. Pursuant to Discovery Guideline 9(a), if a partial or incomplete answer is provided, the responding party shall state that the answer is partial or incomplete.

4. Pursuant to Discovery Guideline 9(c), in accordance with Fed. R. Civ. P. 26(b)(5), where a claim of privilege is asserted in objecting to any interrogatory or part thereof, and information is not provided on the basis of such assertion:

A. In asserting the privilege, the responding party shall, in the objection to the interrogatory, or part thereof, identify with specificity the nature of the privilege (including work product) that is being claimed;

B. The following information should be provided in the objection, if known or reasonably available, unless divulging such information would cause disclosure of the allegedly privileged information,

(1) For oral communications:

a. the name of the person making the communication and the names of persons present while the communication was made, and, where not apparent, the relationship of the persons present to the person making the communication;

b. the date and place of the communication; and

c. the general subject matter of the communication.

(2) For documents:

a. the type of document,

b. the general subject matter of the document,

c. the date of the document, and

d. such other information as is sufficient to identify the document, including, where appropriate, the author, addressee, custodian, and any other recipient of the document, and where not apparent, the relationship of the author, addressee, custodian, and any other recipient to each other.

5. If the responding party elects to specify and produce business records in answer to any interrogatory, the specification shall be in sufficient detail to permit the interrogating party to locate and identify, as readily as the responding party can, the business records from which the answer may be ascertained.

6. If, in answering these Interrogatories, the responding party encounters any ambiguities when construing a question, instruction, or definition, the responding party's answer shall set forth the matter deemed ambiguous and the construction used in answering.

DEFINITIONS

Notwithstanding any definition below, each word, term, or phrase used in these Interrogatories is intended to have the broadest meaning permitted under the Federal Rules of Civil Procedure.

1. *Concerning*: The term "concerning" means relating to, referring to, describing, evidencing, or constituting.

2. *Communication*: The term "communication" means the transmittal of information by any means.

3. *Document*: The terms "document" and "documents" are defined to be synonymous in meaning and equal in scope to the usage of the term "documents" in Fed. R. Civ. P. 34(a) and include(s) the term "writing". Unless the producing party demonstrates undue burden or other grounds sufficient to meet the requirements of Fed. R. Civ. P. 26(c), electronic mail is included within the definition of the term "document". The terms "writings", "recordings", and "photographs" are defined to be synonymous in meaning and equal in scope to the usage of those terms in Fed. R. Evid. 1001. A draft or non-identical copy is a separate document within the meaning of the term "document".

4. *Identify (with respect to persons)*: When referring to a person, to "identify" means to state the person's full name, present or last known address, and, when referring to a natural person, additionally, the present or last known

place of employment. If the business and home telephone numbers are known to the answering party, and if the person is not a party or present employee of a party, said telephone numbers shall be provided. Once a person has been identified in accordance with this subparagraph, only the name of the person need be listed in response to subsequent discovery requesting the identification of that person.

5. *Identify (with respect to documents)*: When referring to documents, to "identify" means to state the: (i) type of document; (ii) general subject matter; (iii) date of the document; and, (iv) author(s), addressee(s), and recipient(s) or, alternatively, to produce the document.

6. *Occurrence/Transaction*: The terms "occurrence" and "transaction" mean the events described in the Complaint and other pleadings, as the word "pleadings" is defined in Fed. R. Civ. P. 7(a).

7. *Parties*: The terms "plaintiff" and "defendant" (including, without limitation, third-party plaintiff, third-party defendant, counter claimant, cross-claimant, counter-defendant, and cross-defendant), as well as a party's full or abbreviated name or a pronoun referring to a party, mean that party and, where applicable, its officers, directors, and employees. This definition is not intended to impose a discovery obligation on any person who is not a party to the litigation or to limit the Court's jurisdiction to enter any appropriate order.

8. *Person*: The term "person" is defined as any natural person or any business, legal or governmental entity or association.

9. *You/Your*: The terms "you" or "your" include the person(s) to whom these requests are addressed, and all of that person's agents, representatives and attorneys.

10. The present tense includes the past and future tenses. The singular includes the plural, and the plural includes the singular. "All" means "any and all"; "any" means "any and all." "Including" means "including but not limited to." "And" and "or" encompass both "and" and "or." Words in the masculine, feminine or neuter form shall include each of the other genders.

STANDARD INTERROGATORIES TO A PLAINTIFF

STANDARD INTERROGATORY NO. 1: Identify all persons who are likely to have personal knowledge of any fact alleged in the complaint, and state the subject matter of the personal knowledge possessed by each such person.

STANDARD INTERROGATORY NO. 2: Identify all persons who have a subrogation interest in any claim set forth in the complaint, and state the basis and extent of such interest.

STANDARD INTERROGATORY NO. 3: Itemize and show how you calculate any damages claimed by you in this action, whether economic, non-economic, punitive or other.

STANDARD INTERROGATORIES TO A DEFENDANT

STANDARD INTERROGATORY NO. 4: If you contend that the Defendant is improperly identified, state Defendant's correct identification.

STANDARD INTERROGATORY NO. 5: Identify any persons or entities whom Defendant contends are persons needed for just adjudication within the meaning of Fed. R. Civ. P. 19, but who have not been named by Plaintiff.

STANDARD INTERROGATORY NO. 6: Identify all persons who are likely to have personal knowledge of any fact alleged in the complaint or in your answer to the complaint, and state the subject matter of the personal knowledge possessed by each such person.

STANDARD INTERROGATORY NO. 7: If you have knowledge of any person carrying on an insurance business that might be liable to satisfy part or all of a judgment that might be entered in this action or to indemnify or reimburse the payments made to satisfy the judgment, identify that person and state the applicable policy limits of any insurance agreement under which the person might be liable.

STANDARD INTERROGATORIES TO ANY PARTY

STANDARD INTERROGATORY NO. 8: For each witness identified by you in connection with the disclosures required by Fed. R. Civ. P. 26(a)(2)(A), provide a complete statement of the opinions to be expressed and basis and reasons therefore.

STANDARD INTERROGATORY NO. 9: For each witness you have retained or specially employed to provide expert testimony in this case, or employed by you whose duties regularly involve giving expert testimony and whom you expect to testify at trial, provide a complete statement of the opinions to be expressed and the basis and reasons therefore.

STANDARD INTERROGATORY NO. 10: State the facts concerning the matters alleged in [paragraph _____ of your Complaint] [paragraph _____ of your Answer to the Complaint] [your affirmative defense no. _____].

STANDARD INTERROGATORY NO. 11: If you contend that _____, state the facts concerning such contention.

STANDARD REQUESTS FOR PRODUCTION OF DOCUMENTS

IN THE UNITED STATES DISTRICT COURT
FOR THE DISTRICT OF MARYLAND

_____,	*	
Plaintiff	*	
v.	*	Civil Action No.:
_____,	*	_____
Defendant	*	

****

REQUEST FOR PRODUCTION OF DOCUMENTS

Pursuant to Fed. R. Civ. P. 34, and L.R. 104, _____, by its undersigned attorneys, requests that _____ respond to this Request within the time prescribed by the Federal Rules of Civil Procedure, and produce the following documents for inspection and copying on the _____ day of _____, _____, at ___ o'clock, a.m., and continuing from day to day thereafter, until completed, at the offices of _____,

(name and address)

or at such time and place as may be agreed upon by all counsel.

INSTRUCTIONS

1. If, in responding to this Request for Production, the responding party encounters any ambiguities when construing a request or definition, the response shall set forth the matter deemed ambiguous and the construction used in responding.

2. Whenever in this Request you are asked to identify or produce a document which is deemed by you to be properly withheld from production for inspection or copying:

A. If you are withholding the document under claim of privilege (including, but not limited to, the work product doctrine), please provide the information set forth in Fed. R. Civ. P. 26(b)(5) and Discovery Guideline 9(c)(ii)(b), including the type of document, the general subject matter of the document, the date of the document, and such other information as is sufficient to identify the document, including, where appropriate, the author, addressee, custodian, and any other recipient of the document, and where not apparent, the relationship of the author, addressee, custodian, and any other recipient to each other, in a manner that, without revealing the information claimed to be protected, will enable this party to assess the applicability of the privilege or protection claimed by you;

B. If you are withholding the document for any reason other than an objection that it is beyond the scope of discovery or that a request is unduly burdensome, identify as to each document and, in addition to the information requested in paragraph (2.A), above, please state the reason for withholding the document.

3. When a document contains both privileged and non-privileged material, the non-privileged material must be disclosed to the fullest extent possible without thereby disclosing the privileged material. If a privilege is asserted with regard to part of the material contained in a document, the party claiming the privilege must clearly indicate the portions as to which the privilege is claimed. When a document has been redacted or altered in any fashion, identify as to each document the reason for the redaction or alteration, the date of the redaction or alteration, and the person performing the redaction or alteration. Any redaction must be clearly visible on the redacted document.

4. It is intended that this Request will not solicit any material protected either by the attorney/client privilege or by the work product doctrine which was created by, or developed by, counsel for the responding party after the date on which this litigation was commenced. If any Request is susceptible of a construction which calls for the production of such material, that material need not be provided and no privilege log pursuant to Fed. R. Civ. P. 26(b)(5) or Discovery Guideline 9(a) will be required as to such material.

5. If production of any requested document(s) is objected to on the grounds that production is unduly burdensome, describe the burden or expense of the proposed discovery.

DEFINITIONS

Notwithstanding any definition set forth below, each word, term, or phrase used in this Request is intended to have the broadest meaning permitted under the Federal Rules of Civil Procedure. As used in this Request, the following terms are to be interpreted in accordance with these definitions:

1. *Communication*: The term "communication" means the transmittal of information by any means.

2. *Concerning*: The term "concerning" means relating to, referring to, describing, evidencing, or constituting.

3. *Document*: The terms "document" and "documents" are defined to be synonymous in meaning and equal in scope to the usage of the term "documents" in Fed. R. Civ. P. 34(a) and include(s) the term "writing." Unless the producing party demonstrates undue burden or other grounds sufficient to meet the requirements of Fed. R. Civ. P. 26(c), electronic mail is included within the definition of the term "document." The terms "writings," "recordings," and "photographs" are defined to be synonymous in meaning and equal in scope to the usage of those terms in Fed. R. Evid. 1001. A draft or non-identical copy is a separate document within the meaning of the term "document."

4. *Occurrence/Transaction*: The terms "occurrence" and "transaction" mean the events described in the Complaint and other pleadings, as the word "pleadings" is defined in Fed. R. Civ. P. 7(a).

5. *Parties*: The terms "plaintiff" and "defendant" (including, without limitation, third-party plaintiff, third-party defendant, counter claimant, cross-claimant, counter-defendant, and cross-defendant), as well as a party's full or abbreviated name or a pronoun referring to a party, mean that party and,

where applicable, its officers, directors, and employees. This definition is not intended to impose a discovery obligation on any person who is not a party to the litigation or to limit the Court's jurisdiction to enter any appropriate order.

6. *Person*: The term "person" is defined as any natural person or any business, legal or governmental entity, or association.

7. *You / Your*: The terms "you" or "your" include the person(s) to whom this Request is addressed, and all of that person's agents, representatives and attorneys.

8. The present tense includes the past and future tenses. The singular includes the plural, and the plural includes the singular. "All" means "any and all;" "any" means "any and all." "Including" means "including but not limited to." "And" and "or" encompass both "and" and "or." Words in the masculine, feminine or neuter form shall include each of the other genders.

9. If the requested documents are maintained in a file, the file folder is included in the request for production of those documents.

STANDARD DOCUMENT REQUESTS

1. All documents referred to in your Answers to Interrogatories.

2. All statements (as that term is used in Fed. R. Civ. P. 26(b)(3)(C)) which were previously made by this party and any of its present or former directors, officers, or employees, concerning the action or its subject matter.

3. All documents (including, but not limited to, correspondence, notes, memoranda, and journal entries) which relate to, describe, summarize, or memorialize any communication between you and [Name], or anyone known or believed by you to have been acting under the authority of [Name], concerning the occurrence.

4. All documents (including, but not limited to, fee agreements, reports, and correspondence) provided to, received from, or prepared by each witness identified by you in connection with the disclosures required by Fed. R. Civ. P. 26(a)(2)(A) or in connection with any witness identified in your Answer to Standard Interrogatory No. 8 or 9.

5. All contracts or agreements entered into between plaintiff and defendant concerning the occurrence or transaction.

6. All documents concerning your claim for damages or the methods used to calculate such alleged damages.

7. All documents concerning any release, settlement, or other agreement, formal or informal, pursuant to which the liability of any person or any entity for damage arising out of the occurrence which is the subject matter of this lawsuit has been limited, reduced, or released in any manner. This request includes all agreements by one party or person to indemnify another party or person for claims asserted in this litigation.

8. All insurance policies under which a person carrying on an insurance business might be liable to pay to you or on your behalf all or part of the damages sought in this action.

9. All documents received from or provided to any other party to this action since the filing of the Complaint, whether provided informally or in response to

a formal request. All documents referred to in the Complaint and other pleadings, as the word "pleadings" is defined in Fed. R. Civ. P. 7(a).

STIPULATED ORDER REGARDING
CONFIDENTIALITY OF DISCOVERY MATERIAL
AND INADVERTENT DISCLOSURE OF PRIVILEGED MATERIAL
(Local Rule 104.13)

Whereas, the parties have stipulated that certain discovery material be treated as confidential and that certain provisions of Fed. R. Evid. 502 be incorporated in an order;

Accordingly, it is this _____ day of _____, _____, by the United States District Court for the District of Maryland, ORDERED:

1. Designation of Discovery Materials as Confidential. All documents produced in the course of discovery, all Answers to Interrogatories, all Answers to Requests for Admission, all Responses to Requests for Production of Documents, and all deposition testimony and deposition exhibits shall be subject to this Order concerning confidential information, as set forth below:

(a) The designation of confidential information shall be made by placing or affixing on the document, in a manner which will not interfere with its legibility, the word "CONFIDENTIAL." One who provides material may designate it as "CONFIDENTIAL" only when such person in good faith believes it contains sensitive personal information, trade secrets or other confidential research, development, or commercial information which is in fact confidential. A party shall not routinely designate material as "CONFIDENTIAL," or make such a designation without reasonable inquiry to determine whether it qualifies for such designation. Except for documents produced for inspection at the party's facilities, the designation of confidential information shall be made prior to, or contemporaneously with, the production or disclosure of that information. In the event that documents are produced for inspection at the party's facilities, such documents may be produced for inspection before being marked confidential. Once specific documents have been designated for copying, any documents containing confidential information will then be marked confidential after copying but before delivery to the party who inspected and designated the documents. There will be no waiver of confidentiality by the inspection of confidential documents before they are copied and marked confidential pursuant to this procedure.

(b) Portions of depositions of a party's present and former officers, directors, employees, agents, experts, and representatives shall be deemed confidential only if they are designated as such when the deposition is taken or within seven business days after receipt of the transcript. Any testimony which describes a document which has been designated as "CONFIDENTIAL," as described above, shall also be deemed to be designated as "CONFIDENTIAL."

(c) Information or documents designated as confidential under this Order shall not be used or disclosed by the parties or counsel for the parties or any persons identified in subparagraph (d) below for any purposes whatsoever other than preparing for and conducting the litigation in which the information or documents were disclosed (including appeals). The parties shall not disclose information or documents designated as confidential to putative class members not named as plaintiffs in putative class litigation unless and until one or more classes has/have been certified.

(d) The parties and counsel for the parties shall not disclose or permit the disclosure of any documents or information designated as confidential under this Order to any other person or entity, except that disclosures may be made in the following circumstances:

(i) Disclosure may be made to counsel and employees of counsel for the parties who have direct functional responsibility for the preparation and trial of the lawsuit. Any such employee to whom counsel for the parties makes a disclosure shall be provided with a copy of, and become subject to, the provisions of this Order requiring that the documents and information be held in confidence.

(ii) Disclosure may be made only to employees of a party required in good faith to provide assistance in the conduct of the litigation in which the information was disclosed.

(iii) Disclosure may be made to court reporters engaged for depositions and those persons, if any, specifically engaged for the limited purpose of making photocopies of documents. Prior to disclosure to any such court reporter or person engaged in making photocopies of documents, such person must agree to be bound by the terms of this Order.

(iv) Disclosure may be made to consultants, investigators, or experts (hereinafter referred to collectively as "experts") employed by the parties or counsel for the parties to assist in the preparation and trial of the lawsuit. Prior to disclosure to any expert, the expert must be informed of and agree in writing to be subject to the provisions of this Order requiring that the documents and information be held in confidence.

(e) Except as provided in subparagraph (d) above, counsel for the parties shall keep all documents designated as confidential which are received under this Order secure within their exclusive possession and shall take reasonable efforts to place such documents in a secure area.

(f) All copies, duplicates, extracts, summaries, or descriptions (hereinafter referred to collectively as "copies") of documents or information designated as confidential under this Order or any portion thereof, shall be immediately affixed with the word "CONFIDENTIAL" if that word does not already appear.

2. Confidential Information Filed with Court. To the extent that any materials subject to this Confidentiality Order (or any pleading, motion or memorandum disclosing them) are proposed to be filed or are filed with the Court, those materials and papers, or any portion thereof which discloses confidential information, shall be filed under seal (by the filing party) with the Clerk of the Court in an envelope marked "SEALED PURSUANT TO ORDER OF COURT DATED _____," together with a simultaneous motion pursuant to L.R. 104.13(c) (hereinafter the "Interim Sealing Motion"). The Interim Sealing Motion shall be governed by L.R. 105.11. Even if the filing party believes that the materials subject to the Confidentiality Order are not properly classified as confidential, the filing party shall file the Interim Sealing

Motion; provided, however, that the filing of the Interim Sealing Motion shall be wholly without prejudice to the filing party's rights under paragraph (4) of this Confidentiality Order.

3. Party Seeking Greater Protection Must Obtain Further Order. No information may be withheld from discovery on the ground that the material to be disclosed requires protection greater than that afforded by paragraph (1) of this Order unless the party claiming a need for greater protection moves for an order providing such special protection pursuant to Fed. R. Civ. P. 26(c).

4. Challenging Designation of Confidentiality. A designation of confidentiality may be challenged upon motion. The burden of proving the confidentiality of designated information remains with the party asserting such confidentiality. The provisions of Fed. R. Civ. P. 37(a)(5) apply to such motions.

5. Return of Confidential Material at Conclusion of Litigation. At the conclusion of the litigation, all material treated as confidential under this Order and not received in evidence shall be returned to the originating party. If the parties so stipulate, the material may be destroyed instead of being returned. The Clerk of the Court may return to counsel for the parties, or destroy, any sealed material at the end of the litigation, including any appeals.

6. Non-waiver of privilege for inadvertently disclosed materials. Pursuant to Fed. R. Evid. 502(d), the inadvertent disclosure of any document that is subject to a legitimate claim that the document is subject to the attorney-client privilege or the work-product protection shall not waive the protection or the privilege for either that document or for the subject matter of that document.

7. Return of inadvertently disclosed materials. Except in the event that the requesting party disputes the claim, any documents the producing party deems to have been inadvertently disclosed and to be subject to the attorney-client privilege or the work-product protection shall be, upon written request, promptly returned to the producing party, or destroyed, at that party's option. If the claim is disputed, a single copy of the materials may be retained by the requesting party for the exclusive purpose of seeking judicial determination of the matter pursuant to Fed. R. Civ. P. 26(b)(5)(B) and Fed. R. Evid. 502.
[SIGNATURES OF COUNSEL]

UNITED STATES [DISTRICT] [MAGISTRATE] JUDGE

ORDER SEALING PORTIONS OF THE COURT RECORD
(Local Rule 105.11)

Whereas, the parties have filed a Joint Motion seeking a Protective Order Sealing Portions of the Court Record ("Joint Motion");

Whereas, in the Joint Motion, the parties have "proposed" reasons supported by specific factual representations to justify the [requested] "sealing," in accordance with L.R. 105.11;

Whereas, the parties have identified the following portion of the record as that portion which is subject to the Joint Motion [describe with particularity the portion to be sealed] (the "Sealed Record");

Whereas, the Court has considered the Joint Motion and any opposition thereto;

Whereas, the Court has not ruled on the Joint Motion for at least fourteen (14) days after it was entered on the public Court docket to permit the filing of objections by interested parties;

Whereas, the Court has considered any objections by interested parties, pursuant to L.R. 105.11;

Whereas, the parties have stated in the Joint Motion why alternatives to sealing would not provide sufficient protection;

Whereas, the Court finds and holds that alternatives to sealing would not provide sufficient protection;

Whereas, the Court finds and holds that sealing of a portion and/or portions of the record, specified herein, is appropriate;

Accordingly, it is this _____ day of _____, _____, by the United States District Court for the District of Maryland, ORDERED:

1. That the Joint Motion for Protective Order Sealing Portions of the Record be, and the same hereby is, GRANTED, as specifically set forth herein;

2. That the Sealed Record (as defined above) be, and hereby is, PLACED UNDER SEAL by the Clerk of the Court and that the Sealed Record shall be placed in an envelope or other container which is marked "SEALED, SUB-JECT TO ORDER OF COURT DATED _____."

3. A copy of this Order shall be mailed to all counsel of record and to any other person entitled to notice hereof, and shall be docketed in the Court file.

_____

UNITED STATES [DISTRICT] [MAGISTRATE] JUDGE

Index to Rules of the United States District Court for the District of Maryland

INDEX

INDEX

INDEX

INDEX

INDEX

INDEX

UNITED STATES BANKRUPTCY COURT FOR THE DISTRICT OF MARYLAND LOCAL BANKRUPTCY RULES

LOCAL BANKRUPTCY RULES

Effective November 1, 2007; amended effective September 1, 2011.

IN THE UNITED STATES BANKRUPTCY COURT FOR THE DISTRICT OF MARYLAND

LOCAL BANKRUPTCY RULES

BANKRUPTCY

PART I.

Rule 1002-1. Petition — General.

(a) The petition will be dismissed without a hearing if:

(1) the petition is not signed by the debtor(s);

(2) the party filing the petition neither pays the prescribed filing fee with the petition nor files with the petition an application to pay the required fee in installments, nor files an application requesting waiver of the filing fee if eligible to do so;

(3) the debtor does not file the master mailing matrix with the petition;

(4) a Chapter 11 debtor does not file the list of twenty (20) largest unsecured creditors with the petition;

(5) the petition is submitted by a debtor who is not an individual and is not represented by an attorney who is a member of the bar of the District Court;

(6) the petition is submitted by a person who, under either 11 U.S.C. § 109(g) or an order of court, may not be a debtor at the time of the submission of the petition.

(7) a voluntary petition is filed without the debtor's social security number being provided; or

(8) in cases for individuals, the Credit Counseling Statement or request for waiver pursuant to 11 U.S.C. § 109(h)(4) is not filed and debtor has not checked the block on Exhibit D to the petition stating that debtor received the approved budget and credit counseling during the 180-day period ending on the filing of the petition.

(b) **Other deficient petitions and papers — Notice of deficient filing.** The Clerk can issue a notice:

(1) specifying deficiencies — except those described in subsection (a) — in the petition, schedules, and associated papers; and

(2) stating that the petition, schedule or associated papers may be stricken or the case dismissed if the deficiencies are not corrected within fourteen (14)

days after the date of issuance of the deficiency notice. (Added Dec. 4, 2003, effective Jan. 1, 2004; amended September 27, 2006, effective September 27, 2006; amended April 27, 2007, effective May 1, 2007; amended effective December 1, 2009; amended Aug. 24, 2011, effective Sept. 1, 2011.)

Effect of amendments. — The Summary of Changes to Local Bankruptcy Rules, effective January 1, 2004, concerning (a) states, "This Rule has been changed so as to be compatible to the ECF process. Unlike a paper petition, the Clerk is unable to reject an electronic petition. An electronic petition will be dismissed without a hearing if it falls into any of the seven (7) categories described"; and concerning (b) states, "This Rule is changed to modify the time for remedying deficient papers to ten (10) calendar days."

The 2005 amendment by Administrative Order 05-04, October 17, 2005, effective from that date, in (a)(2) added "nor files an application requesting waiver of the filing fee"; and added (a)(8).

The 2006 amendment by Administrative Order 05-06, January 25, 2006, effective February 1, 2006, substituted "fifteen (15) business days" for "ten (10) business days."

The 2006 amendment by Administrative Order No. 05-04, effective September 27, 2006, reenacted (a)(2) without change and in (a)(8) added "and debtor has not checked the block on Exhibit D to the petition stating the the debtor received the approved budget and credit counseling during the 180-day period preceding the filing of the petition."

The 2007 amendment, in (a)(8), added "is not filed" after "§ 109(h)(4)", and substituted "received approved budget" for "received the approved budget"; and deleted "business" before "days" in (b)(2).

The 2009 amendment transferred "or" from the end of (a)(5) to the end of (a)(7) and made related changes; and substituted "fourteen (14) days" for "fifteen (15) days" in (b)(2).

The 2011 amendment substituted "ending on" for "preceding" in (a)(8).

Editor's note. — Administrative Order No. 05-04, effective September 27, 2006, provides that the amendments apply to cases filed after October 17, 2005.

Rule 1004-1. Voluntary petition — Partnership.

A person filing a bankruptcy case for a partnership must file a certificate that the filing is authorized under the entity's partnership or operating agreement and applicable law. (Added December 4, 2003, effective January 1, 2004; amended October 15, 2007, effective November 1, 2007.)

Effect of amendments. — The Summary of Changes to Local Bankruptcy Rules, effective January 1, 2004, states, "This Rule has been modified because of the revision of Federal Bankruptcy Rule 1004, effective December 1, 2002."

The 2007 Order, effective November 1, 2007, substituted "entity's partnership or operating agreement" for "partnership agreement".

Rule 1006-1. Filing fees — Installment payments.

(a) **Tender of payment.** The filing fee may be paid in cash or by cashier's check, certified check or negotiable money order made payable to "Clerk, United States Bankruptcy Court." Only counsel may pay filing fees by credit card. Payment by counsel's check will be accepted only if the check is drawn on the account of the attorney for the debtor or on the account of a law firm of which the attorney for the debtor is a member, partner, associate or of counsel. The Clerk shall maintain a list of attorneys and law firms whose checks have been dishonored and may refuse to accept the checks of such attorneys or firms.

(b) **Payment of fees in installments.** The Clerk may approve for the court an application by an individual to pay the filing and administrative fees in installments that proposes a payment plan with minimum payments in accordance with the following schedule:

	At Filing	Within 30 Days After Filing	Within 60 Days After Filing	Within 90 Days After Filing
Chapter 7	25%	25%	25%	25%
Chapter 11	50%	50%	—	—
Chapter 12	25%	25%	25%	25%
Chapter 13	25%	25%	25%	25%

(Amended effective Jan. 1, 2004.)

Rule 1007-1. Mailing list or matrix.

(a) **Matrix contents.** A debtor must file with the voluntary petition a master mailing matrix containing the names and addresses of the debtor and all creditors. In a case under Chapter 11, the debtor must include in the matrix the taxing authority for each county in which the debtor holds an interest in real estate.

(b) **Matrix form.** The master mailing matrix must be submitted in the form required by the Clerk.

(c) **Supplemental matrix.** The debtor must file a supplemental mailing matrix with any schedule or amended schedule that contains a change in address or an entity entitled to notice or adds the names of an entity not listed on the original matrix. If a scheduled creditor was omitted from, or incorrectly listed on, the mailing matrix, the debtor must file a supplemental mailing matrix that corrects the error promptly after it is discovered. The supplemental matrix must conform to the form required by the Clerk.

(d) **Verification.** The master mailing matrix and any supplemental mailing matrix must be dated and verified. The verification must state that to the best of the affiant's knowledge, information and belief, the matrices are accurate and complete. (Added Dec. 4, 2003, effective Jan. 1, 2004.)

Editor's note. — As to Administrative Order 08-03 which sets out an Interim Rule, 1007-I, to be in effect until the federal Bankruptcy Rule is enacted in 2010, see the Court's website, http://www.mdb.uscourts.gov, under the "Announcements" for December 17, 2008 in the archive.

Rule 1007-2. Verification of authority file — Corporations.

A certified copy of the resolution authorizing the filing of the bankruptcy petition must be filed with a corporate debtor's voluntary petition. The resolution must show approval by the corporate body empowered by applicable law to authorize filing a bankruptcy petition. (Added Dec. 4, 2003, effective Jan. 1, 2004.)

Rule 1007-3. Notice to creditors omitted from or incorrectly listed on master mailing matrix.

If a debtor files schedules or a supplemental mailing matrix after filing the petition, and if the debtor's schedules or a supplemental mailing matrix include one or more creditors that were not included, or were listed incorrectly, on the debtor's master mailing matrix filed with the petition, a debtor must comply with the following procedures:

(a) Notice to creditors. The debtor must send to each creditor that is added or whose address is corrected:

(1) a copy of the original Notice for Meeting of Creditors, and

(2) a copy of each order that establishes or extends a bar date for claims or for complaints to determine the dischargeability of certain debts or to object to the discharge of the debtor.

(b) Certificate of compliance. With the schedules and supplemental mailing matrix, the debtor must file a certificate of compliance with this Rule, together with a dated and clearly titled supplemental mailing matrix that lists only the names and correct mailing addresses of each newly scheduled creditor. (Added Dec. 4, 2003, effective Jan. 1, 2004.)

Rule 1007-4. Payment advices.

Copies of all payment advices or other evidence of payment received within 60 days before the date of the filing of the petition by the debtor from any employer of the debtor, (1) shall not be filed with the court unless otherwise ordered, and (2) shall be provided to the trustee, and any creditor who timely requests copies of the payment advices or other evidence of payment, at least seven (7) days before the date of the meeting of creditors conducted pursuant to 11 U.S.C. § 341. To be considered timely, a creditor's request must be received by the debtor at least fourteen (14) days before the first date set for the meeting of creditors.

If the debtor cannot provide copies of the required payment advices, debtor is required to file a Statement Under Perjury in the form set forth in Local Bankruptcy Form Q. Upon filing of a notice that the debtor has not provided a copy of all pay advices or other evidence of payment, or a Statement Under Perjury, as required herein above, an order of dismissal may be entered after fourteen (14) days notice to the debtor, counsel to the debtor, and the United States Trustee and an opportunity for hearing. (Added October 17, 2005, effective October 17, 2005; amended September 27, 2006, effective September 27, 2006; amended April 27, 2007, effective May 1, 2007; amended effective December 1, 2009.)

Effect of amendments. — The 2006 amendment by Administrative Order No. 05-04, effective September 27, 2006, added the second paragraph.

The 2007 amendment in the first sentence of the first paragraph, substituted "local office of the United States Trustee" for "trustee", substituted "date of the meeting of creditors" for "time of the meeting of creditors", added "by the debtor", and substituted "fifteen (15) days' notice to the debtor" for "(fifteen) 15 days' notice to the debtor".

The 2009 amendment in the first paragraph substituted "trustee" for "local Office of the United States Trustee" and added "(7)" after "seven"; and substituted "fourteen (14) days" for "15 days" once in each paragraph.

Editor's note. — Administrative Order No. 05-04, effective September 27, 2006, provides that the amendments apply to cases filed after October 17, 2005.

Rule 1007-5. Compliance with filing requirements.

The Clerk will docket a Certificate of Compliance for each case meeting all filing requirements under 11 U.S.C. § 521(a)(1), except payment advices under Section 521(a)(1)(B)(iv), or a Certificate of Non-compliance, as appropriate. (Added Oct. 17, 2005, effective Oct. 17, 2005; amended September 27, 2006, effective September 27, 2006; amended April 27, 2007, effective May 1, 2007.)

Effect of amendments. — The 2006 amendment by Administrative Order No. 05-04, effective September 27, 2006, added "except payment advices under Section 521(a)(1)(B)(iv)" and made related changes.

The 2007 amendment substituted "Non-compliance" for "non-compliance" near the end.

Editor's note. — Administrative Order No. 05-04, effective September 27, 2006, provides that the amendments apply to cases filed after October 17, 2005.

Rule 1009-1. Amendments to lists and schedules.

When filing amended schedules that add previously unscheduled creditors, a debtor must comply with the following procedures:

(a) Notice to United States Trustee. The debtor must send a copy of the amended schedule to the Office of the United States Trustee and to any trustee appointed in the case.

(b) Notice to creditors. The debtor must send to each creditor added or whose status is changed by the amended schedule.

(1) a copy of the amended schedule;

(2) a copy of the original Notice for Meeting of Creditors; and

(3) a copy of each order that establishes or extends a bar date for filing proofs of claims or complaints to determine the dischargeability of certain debts or to object to the discharge of the debtor.

(c) Certificate of compliance. With the amended schedule, the debtor must file a certificate of compliance with this Rule, together with a dated and clearly titled supplemental mailing matrix that lists only the names and correct mailing addresses of all newly scheduled creditors. (amended October 15, 2007, effective November 1, 2007.)

Effect of amendments. — The 2007 Order, effective November 1, 2007, in (b)(3) added "filing proofs of" and substituted "certain debts or to object to the discharge of the debtor" for "debts" at the end.

Rule 1015-1. Joint administration/consolidation.

The estates of spouses filing a joint petition will be deemed consolidated under § 302(b) of the Bankruptcy Code unless otherwise ordered on the motion of a party in interest made within thirty (30) days after conclusion of the meeting of creditors held under § 341 of the Bankruptcy Code.

Rule 1017-1. Dismissal of case.

Upon the filing of a notice that the debtor has not provided a copy of the Federal income tax return to the trustee pursuant to Sec. 521(e)(2)(A) of Title 11 U.S.C., an order of dismissal may be entered after fourteen (14) days notice to the debtor, counsel to the debtor, and the United States Trustee and an opportunity for hearing. (Amended Oct. 17, 2005, effective Oct. 17, 2005;

amended April 27, 2007, effective May 1, 2007; amended effective December 1, 2009.)

Effect of amendments. — The 2005 amendment, effective October 17, 2005, in the first sentence added "the Certification of Domestic Support Obligation and the Verification of Names of Dependents owed Domestic Support Obligation, if applicable,".

The 2007 amendment rewrote the Rule.

The 2009 amendment substituted "fourteen (14) days" for "fifteen (15) days".

PART II.

Rule 2002-1. Notice to creditors and other interested parties.

(a) **Noticing Period.** A debtor, creditor, official committee, and any other party in interest sending a notice of proposed action to other parties in interest must give recipients no less than twenty-one (21) days from the date of completion of service to file an objection to the action described in the notice, unless the Federal Bankruptcy Rules specifically require a different time or unless otherwise ordered by the court or these Rules.

(b) **Content.** In addition to the information required by specific notices, notices must contain sufficient information to enable a party in interest to make a reasonably well-informed decision whether to object to the action proposed in the notice. The notice must state: (1) the date by when objections must be filed; (2) the person upon whom objections must be served; (3) that the proposed action may be authorized without further order or notice if no timely objection is filed; (4) that the court, in its discretion, may conduct a hearing or determine the matter without a hearing regardless of whether an objection is filed; (5) that an objection must state the facts and legal grounds on which the objection is based; and (6) the name of the party giving notice or its attorney, together with the address, telephone number and email address of the party to be contacted if parties in interest have questions regarding the subject of the notice. A notice may not state that an objecting party must attend a court hearing in support of any objection made.

(c) **Certificate of service.** A party must file a certificate of service of a notice given under these Rules or the Federal Bankruptcy Rules within seven (7) days after completion of service.

(d) **Content of objections.** An objecting party must state the authority for the objection either in its filed objection or in an accompanying memorandum of fact and law. An objecting party must certify that copies of the objection and of any supporting memorandum have been sent to the opposing party or parties and their counsel.

(e) **Sales notices.** See Local Bankruptcy Rule 6004-1.

(f) **Technical requirements for notices.** A party sending a notice must show the date of completion of service conspicuously on the face of the notice.

(g) **Limitation of notice — Chapter 7.** A party required to give notice pursuant to Federal Bankruptcy Rule 2002(a) may limit notice as provided under Federal Bankruptcy Rule 2002(h) to (1) creditors that hold claims for which proofs of claim have been filed; and (2) such other creditors who may file timely claims.

(h) **Limitation of notice — Chapter 11.** In Chapter 11 cases, where official committees are appointed and the number of creditors exceeds thirty (30), notices of the actions described below can be limited to the debtor, the United States Trustee, the members of all official committees or committee counsel, if appointed, and to those creditors and equity security holders who file and serve on counsel for the debtor a written request for notices of:

(1) the proposed use, sale or lease of property of the estate other than in the ordinary course of business;

(2) the hearing on the approval of a compromise or settlement of a controversy — other than the approval of an agreement pursuant to Federal Bankruptcy Rule 4001(d);

(3) a hearing on an application for compensation or reimbursement of expenses; and

(4) such other notices as the Court orders.

(i) **Voluntary dismissal — Chapter 7 and 11.** Notices of a motion by debtor to dismiss a voluntary case under Chapter 7 or 11 must be sent to all parties in interest.

(j) **Continued meetings and hearings.** If a hearing or meeting of creditors is continued or rescheduled at the request of a party, or for reason of the failure of a party to appear or comply with applicable law or rules, that party must send notice of the continued or rescheduled hearing or meeting by the fastest means to avoid inconvenience to other parties entitled to notice. The party must file a certificate of service of that notice. (Amended April 27, 2007, effective May 1, 2007; amended October 15, 2007, effective November 1, 2007; amended effective December 1, 2009.)

Effect of amendments. — The April, 2007 amendment added "and email address" in (b)(6) and made related changes.

The 2007 Order, effective November 1, 2007, made minor changes in the heading of (e) and the introductory text of (h); in (g) substituted "A party required to give notice pursuant to" for "Notice to creditors in cases under Chapter 7 required by" and "limit notice' for "be limited'; and in (j) substituted "by the fastest means to avoid inconvenience to other parties entitled to notice" for "to all creditors and other entities entitled to notice and file a certificate of that notice" and added the second sentence related to filing the certificate of notice.

The 2009 amendment substituted "twenty-one (21) days" for "twenty (20) days" in (a); and in (c) substituted "seven (7) days" for "five (5) days".

Rule 2002-2. Notice to equity security holders.

Unless otherwise ordered by the Court, the debtor-in-possession (or trustee if applicable) is responsible for giving notices required by Federal Bankruptcy Rule 2002(d). (Added Dec. 17, 2009.)

Editor's note. — Administrative order 09-04, December 17, 2009, added this Rule.

Rule 2004-1. Examinations under Federal Bankruptcy Rule 2004.

(a) **Production request limits.** A party in interest may not request or compel an entity being examined under Federal Bankruptcy Rule 2004 to respond to more than thirty (30) requests for production.

(b) **Smoking during examinations prohibited.** No one can smoke in a room where an examination is being conducted, unless all persons agree.

(c) **Examination and production to proceed despite existence of disputes.** An examination or production dispute as to one matter does not justify delay in taking an examination or responding to other examination or production requests, unless otherwise ordered by the court.

(d) **Examination guidelines.** The court's Discovery Guidelines set forth in Appendix C govern scheduling and the conduct of examinations and requests for production, unless they are not applicable in context.

(e) **Conference of counsel required.** Counsel must confer concerning an examination or production dispute and make good faith attempts to resolve an examination or production disupte. The court will not consider a motion to compel or for sanctions unless the moving party has filed a certificate stating:

(1) the date, time, and place of a dispute resolution conference; the names of all persons participating; and any unresolved issues remaining; or

(2) the moving party's attempts to hold such a conference without success.

(f) **Copying expenses.** A party in interest requesting copies of documents that were produced for inspection under Federal Bankruptcy Rule 2004 must pay the actual, reasonable costs of copying. (Amended October 15, 2007, effective November 1, 2007; amended effective December 1, 2009.)

Effect of amendments. — The 2007 Order, effective November 1, 2007, in (d) added "scheduling and".

The 2009 amendment deleted "present" after "persons" in (b).

Rule 2015-1. Compensation by debtor in Chapter 11.

(a) The rate of compensation paid by debtor in possession to its officers, directors, members or partners shall not exceed the rate of compensation paid to those persons ninety (90) days prior to the filing of the petition, unless otherwise ordered by the court.

(b) The debtor shall file a statement containing the following information within twenty-one (21) days after filing a petition in a Chapter 11 case:

(1) a statement specifying the duties and positions of the following (to the extent compensated):

(A) the debtor, if an individual;

(B) the members of the partnership;

(C) the officers and directors of the corporation, and any other insiders (as defined by 11 U.S.C. §101); and

(D) the members of the limited liability company.

(2) the rate of compensation paid to each person identified in Local Bankruptcy Rules 2015-1(b)(1) ninety (90) days prior to and at the time of the filing of the petition; and,

(3) the rate of compensation of each as of the time the statement is filed. (Amended October 15, 2007, effective November 1, 2007; amended effective December 1, 2009.)

Effect of amendments. — The 2007 Order, effective November 1, 2007, in (b)(1) introduction added "(to the extent compensated)", in

(b)(1)(C) added "as defined by 11 U.S.C. § 101; and", added (b)(1)(D); and in (b)(2) added "person identified in Local Rules 2015-1(b)(1)".

The 2009 amendment added "members" in (a); substituted "twenty-one (21) days" for "twenty (20) days" in the introductory language of (b); and added "Bankruptcy" in (b)(2).

Rule 2016-1. Compensation of professionals.

(a) **Applications for compensation by professionals.** Unless the court orders otherwise, all professionals seeking compensation pursuant to §§ 327, 328, 330, and 331 of the Bankruptcy Code, including attorneys, accountants, examiners, investment bankers, financial advisors and real estate advisors, must prepare and submit their applications for compensation in accordance with the Guidelines attached as Appendix D to these Rules.

(b) **Disclosure of compensation.** An attorney representing a debtor in a case or in connection with a case must file a Federal Bankruptcy Rule 2016(b) disclosure statement with the petition. If an attorney commences representation of the debtor in a case or in connection with a case after the filing of the petition, such attorney must file the Federal Bankruptcy Rule 2016(b) disclosure statement at the time representation is commenced. (Amended April 27, 2007, effective May 1, 2007.)

Effect of amendments. — The 2007 amendment added "financial advisors" in (a) and made related changes; and rewrote (b).

Rule 2070-1. Administrative expenses.

Motions for the allowance or payment of administrative expenses must be served upon the debtor, trustee, members of any committee elected under § 705 or appointed under § 1102 of the Bankruptcy Code or its counsel, or in a Chapter 11 case, if no committee of unsecured creditors has been appointed, to those creditors on the list filed pursuant to Federal Bankruptcy Rule 1007(d), the United States Trustee, and to those parties in interest who have filed written requests for notice. (Amended April 27, 2007, effective May 1, 2007.)

Effect of amendments. — The 2007 amendment added "debtor," before "trustee", added "members of" before "any committee", and substituted "or its counsel" for "or its authorized agent".

Rule 2072-1. Notice to other courts with pending actions.

The debtor or other party filing a bankruptcy case must promptly send notice conforming to Local Bankruptcy Form A of the bankruptcy filing to the following persons:

(a) the clerk of any court where the debtor is a party to a pending civil action and all other parties of record; and

(b) any judge specially assigned to a pending civil action in which the debtor is a party.

Rule 2081-1. Chapter 11 — Scheduled claims.

The debtor in a Chapter 11 case must serve on each creditor whose claim is listed on a schedule as disputed, contingent, or unliquidated, notice of that listing within fourteen (14) days after filing the schedule or within fourteen (14) days after adding a disputed creditor to a previously filed schedule. The notice must state that such creditor has the right to file a proof of claim and the failure to do so timely may prevent the creditor from voting on a plan or participating in any distribution. The debtor must file a certificate of service of the notice within seven (7) days of service. (Amended effective December 1, 2009.)

Effect of amendments. — The 2009 amendment substituted "fourteen (14) days" for "fifteen (15) days" twice in the first sentence; and in the last sentence substituted "seven (7) days" for "five (5) days".

Rule 2081-2. Chapter 11 accelerated cases — Chapter 11(a).
[Abrogated effective May 1, 2007].

PART III.

Rule 3001-1. Supporting information for claims against individual debtors.

(a) **Open-end or revolving consumer credit agreements.** When a claim is based on an open-end or revolving consumer credit agreement, the last account statement sent to the debtor prior to the filing of the petition shall also be filed with the proof of claim. If the account statement has been lost or destroyed, a statement of the circumstances of the loss or destruction shall be filed with the proof of claim.

(b) **Additional requirements; sanctions for failure to comply.** In a case in which the debtor is an individual:

(1) If, in addition to its principal amount, a claim includes interest, fees, expenses, or other charges incurred before the petition was filed, an itemized statement of the interest, fees, expenses, or charges shall be filed with the proof of claim.

(2) If a security interest is claimed in property of the debtor, the proof of claim shall include a statement of the amount necessary to cure any default as of the date of the petition.

(3) If a security interest is claimed in property that is the debtor's principal residence and an escrow account has been established in connection with the claim, the proof of claim shall be accompanied by an escrow account statement prepared as of the date the petition was filed and in a form consistent with applicable nonbankruptcy law.

(4) If the holder of a claim fails to provide any information required by this Local Rule, the holder shall be precluded from presenting the omitted information, in any form, as evidence in any hearing or submission in any contested matter or adversary proceeding in the case, unless the court determines that the failure was substantially justified or is harmless. In addition to or in lieu of this sanction, the court may, after notice and hearing, award other appropriate relief, including reasonable expenses and attorney's fees caused by the failure. (Added effective December 1, 2009.)

Rule 3002-1. Notice relating to claims secured by security interest in the debtor's principal residence.

(a) **Notice of payment changes.** In a chapter 13 case, if a claim secured by a security interest in the debtor's principal residence is provided for under the debtor's plan pursuant to § 1322(b)(5) of the Code, the holder of the claim shall file and serve on the debtor, debtor's counsel, and the trustee notice of any change in the payment amount, including any change that results from an interest rate or escrow account adjustment at least 30 days before the first payment in the new amount is due.

(b) **Form and content.** A notice filed and served pursuant to subdivision (a) of this rule shall conform substantially to the form of notice under applicable nonbankruptcy law and the underlying agreement that would be given if the debtor were not a debtor in bankruptcy and be filed in the case as an attachment to a line. The creditor shall delete or redact any personal or confidential identifying information regarding any individual identified in the notice.

(c) **Notice of fees, expenses, and charges.** In a chapter 13 case, if a claim secured by a security interest in the debtor's principal residence is provided for under the debtor's plan pursuant to § 1322(b)(5) of the Code, the holder of the claim shall file and serve on the debtor, debtor's counsel, and the trustee a notice that itemizes all fees, expenses, or charges incurred in connection with the claim after the bankruptcy case was filed, and that the holder asserts are recoverable against the debtor or against the debtor's principal residence. The notice shall be filed as an attachment to a line in the bankruptcy case and served no later than 180 days after the date when the fees, expenses, or charges are incurred. On motion of the debtor or trustee filed no later than one year after service of the notice, the court shall, after notice and hearing, determine whether payment of the fees, expenses, or charges is required by the underlying agreement and applicable nonbankruptcy law to cure a default or maintain payments in accordance with § 1322(b)(5) of the Code.

(d) **Notice of final cure payment.** No later than 30 days after making final payment of any cure amount on a claim secured by a security interest in the debtor's principal residence, the trustee in a chapter 13 case shall file and serve upon the holder of the claim, the debtor, and debtor's counsel a notice stating that the amount required to cure the default has been paid in full. If the debtor contends that final cure payment has been made and the trustee does not timely file and serve the notice required by this subdivision, the debtor may file and serve upon the holder of the claim and the trustee a notice stating that the amount required to cure the default has been paid in full. The notice shall be served upon the holder of the claim in accordance with the Federal Bankruptcy Rules 9014 and 7004 and also must be served: (1) upon any attorney who has appeared for that claimant in the bankruptcy case and (2) upon the claimant at the address (and in care of the individual) shown on the proof of claim. If the claim has been assigned by an assignment filed with the court, the service under (2) above shall be made upon the assignee at the address designated upon the filed assignment. The notice must clearly state that if no response is filed as provided for under subparagraph (e) of this rule, the court may enter the order provided for in subparagraph (e) without further notice or hearing.

(e) **Response to notice of final cure payment.** No later than 30 days after service of the notice under subdivision (d) of this rule, the holder of a claim secured by a security interest in the debtor's principal residence may file and serve on the debtor, debtor's counsel, and the trustee a statement indicating (1) whether it agrees that the debtor has paid in full the amount required to cure the default, and (2) whether, consistent with § 1322(b)(5) of the Code, the debtor is otherwise current on all payments. If applicable, the statement shall itemize any required cure or postpetition amounts that the holder contends remain unpaid as of the date of the statement. The statement shall be filed as an attachment to a line in the main case. If the holder of a claim secured by a security interest in the debtor's principal residence fails to file and serve a timely response to the notice of final cure payment, the court shall promptly enter an order declaring that the debtor has cured the default and that no amounts are unpaid as of the date of the Notice of Final Cure Payment.

(f) **Motion and hearing.** On motion of the debtor or trustee filed no later than 30 days after service of the statement under subdivision (e) of this rule, the court shall, after notice and hearing, determine whether the debtor has cured the default and paid all required postpetition amounts in full.

(g) **Failure to notify.** If the holder of a claim secured by a security interest in the debtor's principal residence fails to provide any information required by subdivision (a), (c), or (e) of this rule, the holder shall be precluded from presenting the omitted information, in any form, as evidence in any hearing or submission in any contested matter or adversary proceeding in the case, unless the court determines that the failure was substantially justified or is harmless. In addition to or in lieu of this sanction, the court may, after notice and hearing, award other appropriate relief, including reasonable expenses and attorney's fees caused by the failure. (Added effective December 1, 2009.)

Rule 3003-1. Time for filing proofs of claim in Chapter 11 cases.

In a Chapter 11 case a proof of claim is timely filed if it is filed not later than ninety (90) days after the first date set for the meeting of creditors under 11 U.S.C. § 341(a), unless a different date is fixed by the court. (Added Dec. 4, 2003, effective Jan. 1, 2004.)

Effect of amendments. — The Summary of Changes to Local Bankruptcy Rules, effective January 1, 2004, states, "This new Rule provides a bar date for filing proofs of claim in Chapter 11."

Rule 3003-2. Wage claimants.

A wage claimant must provide claimant's full social security number directly to the trustee, in addition to filing a proof of claim for past wages with the court. (Added December 4, 2003, effective Jan. 1, 2004; amended effective December 1, 2009.)

Effect of amendments. — The 2009 amendment deleted "appointed in a business case" after "trustee."

Rule 3007-1. Claims — Objections.

In addition to the service required by Federal Bankruptcy Rules 9014 and 7004(b), a party objecting to a proof of claim must serve a copy of the objection and any supporting memorandum and affidavit on the claimant at the address (and in care of the individual) shown on the proof of claim and must certify that service to the court. The objection must conspicuously state that:

(a) within thirty (30) days after the date on the certificate of service of the objection, the claimant may file and serve a memorandum in opposition, together with any documents and other evidence the claimant wishes to attach in support of its claim, unless the claimant wishes to rely solely upon the proof of claim; and

(b) an interested party may request a hearing that will be held at the court's discretion. (Amended October 15, 2007, effective November 1, 2007; amended effective December 1, 2009.)

Effect of amendments. — The 2007 amendment, effective November 1, 2007, deleted (b) and redesignated accordingly. The 2009 amendment substituted "at the court's" for "in the Court's" in (b).

Rule 3007-2. Creditors holding secured claims.

In cases under Chapter 13, the holder or servicer of any secured claim must notify forthwith the debtor, the debtor's attorney, if any, and the Chapter 13 Trustee of changes in the amounts of future payments caused by changes in the interest rate, taxes, insurance or other sums required to be placed in escrow, and the effective date of the change. (Added October 15, 2007, effective November 1, 2007.)

Rule 3012-1. Avoidance of lien on principal residence under 11 U.S.C. § 506 — Chapter 13 only.

(a) **Form.** A motion to avoid a lien on a Chapter 13 debtor's principal residence under 11 U.S.C. § 506 may name only one creditor as a respondent. A separate motion is required for each creditor whose lien is sought to be avoided. The name, address and nature of ownership (e.g. tenancy in common, tenancy by the entirety) of any non-debtor owner of property must also be included.

(b) **Required material.** Debtor(s) must submit with the motion:

(1) Evidence of the value of the residence, and

(2) If no proof of claim has been filed by the holders of claims secured by senior interests in the principal residence, evidence of the amount of the claims so secured.

(c) **Service of motion and notice of hearing.** (1) The Clerk will maintain a list of dates available for hearings on motions to avoid lien for each judge of the court. The list will be posted on the court's website.

(2) Movant must select a hearing date from the list for the judge to whom the case is assigned that is more than forty-nine (49) days after the date of service.

(3) Movant must serve a copy of the motion to avoid lien on the respondent and any non-debtor owner in the manner required by Federal Bankruptcy Rules 9014 and 7004(b) and Local Bankruptcy Rule 3007-1(a) (that requires service upon the individual who signed a proof of claim filed by respondent), together with a hearing notice conforming to Local Bankruptcy Form G.

(d) **Filing of proof of service.** Movant must file with the motion a certificate of service of the motion to avoid lien and the notice of hearing. The certificate must comply with Local Bankruptcy Rule 9013-4.

(e) **Response to motion to avoid lien.** If no response to the motion to avoid lien is filed within thirty (30) days after the date of the service (plus any additional time required by Federal Bankruptcy Rules 9006(a) and (f)), the court may rule on the motion as unopposed. The Court Hearing Scheduler (CHS) Program on the court's website and CM/ECF filing screen for this type of motion will compute the date that an objection is due.

(f) **Proposed order.** Movant shall file with the motion a proposed order conforming to Local Bankruptcy Form H. If granted, avoidance of the lien shall occur at such time as debtor completes performance of debtor's confirmed Chapter 13 plan and receives a discharge under 11 U.S.C. § 1328(a). (Added December 4, 2003, effective January 1, 2004; amended October 15, 2007, effective November 1, 2007; November 10, 2008, effective December 1, 2008; amended effective December 1, 2009; amended November 12, 2010, effective November 12, 2010; amended Aug. 24, 2011, effective Sept. 1, 2011.)

Effect of amendments. — The Summary of Changes to Local Bankruptcy Rules, effective January 1, 2004, states, "This Rule has been modified so as to make it applicable only to liens on the Chapter 13 debtor's principal residence. The time for response has been extended from twenty-five(25) to thirty (30) days."

The 2007 Order, effective November 1, 2007, in (b)(1), second sentence, substituted "on the Court's website" for "published by such other means selected by the Clerk"; in (b)(3) added "(that requires service upon the individual who signed a proof of claim filed by respon-

dent)"; and made a minor grammatical change in (e).

The 2008 amendment substituted "avoid lien for each judge" for "on the calendar of each judge" in (b)(1); substituted "avoid lien" for "avoid the lien" in (c); and rewrote (d).

The 2009 amendment substituted "forty-nine (49)" for "fifty (50)" in (b)(2).

The 2010 amendment by Administrative Order 10-2 added the last sentence in (a) and "and any non-debtor owner" in (b)(3).

The 2011 amendment added (b) and redesignated accordingly.

Rule 3012-2. Valuation of collateral and avoidance of nonresidential liens — Chapter 13 only.

(a) **Form.** A motion under 11 U.S.C. § 506 in a Chapter 13 case to value collateral or to avoid a security interest in personal property or in real property that is not a debtor's principal residence may name only one creditor as a respondent. A separate motion is required for each creditor whose lien is sought to be avoided. The name, address and nature of ownership (e.g. tenancy in common, tenancy by the entirety) of any non-debtor owner of property must also be included.

(b) **Required material.** Debtor(s) must submit with the motion;

(1) Evidence of the value of the residence, and

(2) If no proof of claim has been filed by the holders of claims secured by senior interests in the principal residence, evidence of the amount of the claims so secured.

(c) **Service of motion and notice of hearing.** (1) The Clerk will maintain a list of dates available for hearings on motions under subsection (a) for each judge of the court. The list will be posted on the court's website.

(2) Movant must select a hearing date from the list for the judge to whom the case is assigned that is more than forty-nine (49) days after the date of service.

(3) Movant must serve a copy of the motion to avoid lien on the respondent and any non-debtor owner in the manner required by Federal Bankruptcy Rules 9014 and 7004(b) and Local Bankruptcy Rule 3007-1(a) (that requires service upon the individual who signed a proof of claim filed by respondent), together with a hearing notice conforming to Local Bankruptcy Form K.

(d) **Filing of proof of service.** Movant must file with the motion a certificate of service of the motion to avoid lien and the notice of hearing. The certificate must comply with Local Bankruptcy Rule 9013-4.

(e) **Responses to motion to avoid lien.** If no response to the motion to avoid lien is filed within thirty (30) days after the date of the service (plus any additional time required by Federal Bankruptcy Rules 9006(a) and (f)), the court may rule on the motion as unopposed. The Court Hearing Scheduler (CHS) Program on the court's website and CM/ECF filing screen for this type of motion will compute the date that an objection is due.

(f) **Proposed order.** Movant shall file with the motion a proposed order conforming to Local Bankruptcy Form L. If granted, avoidance of the security interest shall occur when debtor completes performance of debtor's confirmed Chapter 13 plan and receives a discharge under 11 U.S.C. § 1328(a). (Added December 4, 2003, effective January 1, 2004; amended October 15, 2007, effective November 1, 2007; November 10, 2008, effective December 1, 2008; effective December 1, 2009; amended November 12, 2010, effective November 12, 2010; amended Aug. 24, 2011, effective Sept. 1, 2011.)

Effect of amendments. — The 2007 Order, effective November 1, 2007, in (b)(1), second sentence, substituted "on the Court's website" for "published by such other means selected by the Clerk"; and in (b)(3) added "(that requires service upon the individual who signed a proof of claim filed by respondent)".

The 2008 Order, effective November 11, 2008, substituted "A motion" for "A motion" in the first sentence of (a); in (b)(1) substituted "for each judge" for "on the calendar of each judge" in the first sentence, and deleted "in the public area of each division and" following "be posted" in the second sentence; and rewrote (d).

The 2009 amendment substituted "forty-nine (49)" for "fifty (50)" in (b)(2).

The 2010 amendment by Administrative Order 10-2 added the last sentence in (a) and "and any non-debtor owner" in (b)(3).

The 2011 amendment added (b) and redesignated accordingly.

Editor's note. — The Summary of Changes to Local Bankruptcy Rules, effective January 1, 2004, states, "This is a new Rule applicable in Chapter 13 cases for the valuation of collateral and avoidance of non-residential liens. The procedure tracks the procedure used for residential liens."

Rule 3014-1. Bankruptcy Code § 1111(b) election in Chapter 11(a) reorganization cases.
[Abrogated effective May 1, 2007.]

Rule 3015-1. Chapter 13 plans — Form and service.

(a) A Chapter 13 plan must conform to Local Bankruptcy Form M, unless compelling circumstances require a deviation.

(1) All deviations in a plan from Local Bankruptcy Form M must be highlighted.

(2) The debtor must file all motions and objections that may impact the debtor's plan on or before the first date scheduled for the meeting of creditors under 11 U.S.C. § 341.

(b) If, after filing the petition, the debtor files an original plan, or an amended plan that does anything other than increase the amount payable under the plan, debtor must serve a copy of the plan upon each creditor and the Chapter 13 trustee, and file a certificate of service.

(c) All Chapter 13 Plans must be signed by the debtor and are subject to Local Rule 9011-2(b). (Added December 4, 2003, effective January 1, 2004; amended October 15, 2007, effective November 1, 2007.)

Effect of amendments. — The Summary of Changes to Local Bankruptcy Rules, effective January 1, 2004, states, "This Rule has been amended to have debtors file Chapter 13 plans that conform to Local Bankruptcy Form M, unless compelling circumstances require deviation."

The 2007 Order, effective November 1, 2007, in (a) introduction substituted "A Chapter 13 plan must conform" for "A debtor shall file a Chapter 13 plan that conforms" and deleted "and unusual" after "compelling".

Rule 3015-2. Chapter 13 — Confirmation.

(a) Debtors and their counsel must attend all scheduled confirmation hearings, unless excused by the Chapter 13 trustee or the court.

(b) Objections to the plan must be filed and copies served on the Chapter 13 Trustee, the debtor, and the debtor's attorney no later than seven (7) days before the date set for hearing on confirmation of the plan.

(c) Within seven (7) days prior to the date of the initial confirmation hearing, the debtor must file a Pre-Confirmation Certificate. If a confirmation hearing is continued, an updated Pre-Confirmation Certificate must be filed within seven (7) days prior to such hearing. (Added Dec. 4, 2003, effective Jan. 1, 2004; amended April 27, 2007, effective May 1, 2007; amended effective December 1, 2009.)

Effect of amendments. — The Summary of Changes to Local Bankruptcy Rules, effective January 1, 2004, concerning (b) states, "This Rule has been amended to set a date by which objections to Chapter 13 plans must be filed."

The 2007 amendment substituted "no later than 8 days… confirmation of the plan." for "by the later of 21 days after the filing of the plan or 45 days after the conclusion of the meeting of creditors."; and added (c).

The 2009 amendment substituted "seven (7) days" for "eight (8) days" each time it appears in (b) and (c).

Rule 3015-3. Pre-confirmation adequate protection and personal property lease payments.

(a) A Chapter 13 Plan must:

(1) provide for direct payments to the creditor of post-petition personal property lease payments and post-petition installment payments of secured claims; and

(2) identify the creditor(s) to whom payments are to be made showing:

(A) to whom the payment is to be made;

(B) the amount of the periodic payment; and

(C) the last four digits of the account number.

(b) No later than fourteen (14) days prior to the date of a confirmation hearing, debtor shall serve on the trustee and file with the court an affidavit stating all §1326(a)(1) pre-confirmation payments made by the debtor. The affidavit must state the details set forth in paragraph (a) above. A copy of the affidavit must be served on the creditors so paid in the manner provided for service of a summons and complaint by Federal Bankruptcy Rule 7004 and if a proof of claim has been filed, in care of the person signing the proof of claim at the address indicated on the proof of claim.

(c) Objections to the accuracy of the affidavit must be filed no later than fourteen (14) days after the filing and service of the affidavit.

(d) Unless otherwise ordered by the court or agreed to by the parties, pre-confirmation adequate protection payments for creditors holding claims secured by a motor vehicle shall be in a sum equal to the monthly contract payment. (Added October 15, 2007, effective November 1, 2007; amended effective December 1, 2009.)

Effect of amendments. — The 2009 amendment added a colon at the end of the introductory language in (a); deleted "calendar" before "days" and made stylistic changes in (b); and substituted "fourteen (14) days" for "ten (10) days" in (c).

Rule 3016-1. Chapter 11(a) accelerated case plan.

[Abrogated by order adopted October 17, 2005, effective October 17, 2005.]

Editor's note. — Rule 3016-1 was abrogated by order adopted October 17, 2005, effective October 17, 2005. This Rule has been deleted, effective May 1, 2007.

Rule 3016-2. Chapter 11(a) accelerated case disclosure statement.

[Abrogated by order adopted October 17, 2005, effective October 17, 2005.]

Editor's note. — Rule 3016-2 was abrogated by order adopted October 17, 2005, effective October 17, 2005. This Rule has been deleted, effective May 1, 2007.

Rule 3017-1. Conditional approval of disclosure statement, objections, and hearing in Chapter 11(a) accelerated case.

[Abrogated by order adopted October 17, 2005, effective October 17, 2005.]

Rule 3018-1. Tally of ballots — Chapter 11.

The tally of ballots must be filed with the Clerk no later than seven (7) days prior to the confirmation hearing. The tally must substantially conform to the form prescribed by the court and available from the Clerk. (Amended October 15, 2007, effective November 1, 2007, amended effective December 1, 2009.)

Effect of amendments. — The 2007 Order, effective November 1, 2007, deleted (b) and made related changes.

The 2009 amendment substituted "seven (7) days" for "the third business day" in the first sentence.

Rule 3019-1. Modifications of Confirmed Chapter 11 Plans of Individual Debtors.

If the debtor is an individual, a request to modify the plan under § 1127(e) of the Bankruptcy Code shall identify the proponent and shall be filed together with the proposed modification. The proponent of the modifications, or such other person as the court may direct, shall give the debtor, the trustee, and all creditors not less than twenty-one (21) days notice by mail of the time fixed to file objections and, if an objection is filed, the hearing to consider the proposed modification, unless the court orders otherwise with respect to creditors who are not affected by the proposed modification. A copy of the notice shall be transmitted to the United States trustee, together with a copy of the proposed modification. Any objection to the proposed modification shall be filed and served on the debtor, the proponent of the modification, the trustee, and any other entity designated by the court, and shall be transmitted to the United States trustee. An objection to a proposed modification is governed by Rule 9014. (Added December 4, 2003, effective January 1, 2004; amended September 27, 2006, effective September 27, 2006; amended April 27, 2007, effective May 1, 2007, amended effective December 1, 2009.)

Effect of amendments. — The 2006 amendment by Administrative Order No. 05-04, effective September 27, 2006, reenacted the rule without change.

The 2007 amendment rewrote the Rule.

The 2009 amendment added "Bankruptcy" before "Code" in the first sentence; and substituted "twenty-one (21) days" for "twenty (20) days" in the second sentence.

Editor's note. — Administrative Order No. 05-04, effective September 27, 2006, provides that the amendments apply to cases filed after October 17, 2005.

Rule 3022-1. Completion of the administration of confirmed Chapter 11 plans.

(a) **Fully administered plan.** A Chapter 11 plan will be deemed fully administered under Federal Bankruptcy Rule 3022:

(1) after the completion of the following:

(A) six (6) months have elapsed after the entry of a final order of confirmation that has become nonappealable;

(B) the deposits required by the plan have been distributed;

(C) the property proposed by the plan to be transferred has been transferred;

(D) the debtor or the successor of the debtor under the plan has assumed the business or the management of the property dealt with by the plan;

(E) payments under the plan have commenced; and

(F) all motions, contested matters, and adversary proceedings have been finally resolved; or

(2) for individual Chapter 11 debtors, upon the completion of all plan payments; or

(3) at another time specifically defined by the plan.

(b) **Certification.** A plan administrator of a confirmed plan that is fully administered must file forthwith a certification of full administration. The certification must include a final summary report of the disbursements, distributions, and transfers that have been made pursuant to the plan, together with a description of other acts taken to consummate the plan. The certification must also describe any matters involving consummation of the confirmed plan that have not been fully resolved.

(c) **Final decree.** The plan administrator must file with the court and serve on the United States Trustee, the Creditor's committee or its counsel or if there is no such Committee, upon the 20 largest Unsecured Creditors the court's form motion for a final decree (Local Bankruptcy Form N-1 for non-individuals and Local Bankruptcy Form N-2 which includes the motion for discharge for individuals) closing the case with the certification of full administration.

(d) **Progress reports.** The plan administrator shall file and serve on the United States Trustee reports of progress towards full administration of the plan until the plan administrator files a final certification and report. The first report must be filed six (6) months after the entry of the order of confirmation. Subsequent reports must be filed every six (6) months thereafter. (Added December 4, 2003, effective January 1, 2004; amended October 17, 2005, effective October 17, 2005; amended September 27, 2006, effective September 27, 2006; amended October 15, 2007, effective November 1, 2007; amended effective December 1, 2009; amended Aug. 24, 2011, effective Sept. 1, 2011.)

Effect of amendments. — The Summary of Changes to Local Bankruptcy Rules, effective January 1, 2004, concerning (c), states, "This Rule implements the Court's new Local Bankruptcy Form N, the Motion for a Final Decree in a case under Chapter 11."

The 2005 amendment, effective October 17, 2005, added (a)(2) and made related changes.

The 2006 amendment by Administrative Order No. 05-04, effective September 27, 2006, reenacted (a)(2) and (a)(3) without change.

The 2007 Order, effective November 1, 2007, made minor changes in (a)(2) and the third sentence in (b); and in (c) substituted "the Court's form motion for a final decree (Local Bankruptcy Form N-1 for nonindividuals and Local Bankruptcy Form N-2 for individuals)" for "an application".

The 2009 amendment added "or" at the end of (a)(2).

The 2011 amendment substituted "plan administrator" for "proponent" in the first sentence of (b) and (d); in the parenthetical in (c) added "the Creditor's committee ... Unsecured Creditors" and "which includes the motion for discharge".

Editor's note. — Administrative Order No. 05-04, effective September 27, 2006, provides that the amendments apply to cases filed after October 17, 2005.

The editorial staff of the publisher also changed "plan proponent" to "plan administrator" in (d) to conform the text to the directive in Administrative Order 11-01e included at the beginning of the rules order.

Rule 3070-1. Chapter 13 — Special procedures.

(a) A debtor in a case under Chapter 13 will be presumed to have provided adequate protection of collateral by continuing to make payments as and when due and maintaining required insurance for the collateral.

(b) Upon dismissal or conversion of a Chapter 13 case, any funds that the trustee holds in a case will be charged for the trustee's allowed expenses and any outstanding Clerk's fees. (Added Dec. 4, 2003, effective Jan. 1, 2004; amended October 15, 2007, effective November 1, 2007.)

Effect of amendments. — The Summary of Changes to Local Bankruptcy Rules, effective January 1, 2004, concerning (a), states, "Has been amended to provide that there is a presumption that debtors are providing adequate protection by continuing to make payments to secured creditors after filing."

The 2007 Order, effective November 1, 2007, deleted the subheadings in (a) and (b) and made a minor change in text in (a).

PART IV.

Rule 4001-1. Automatic stay — Relief from.

(a) **Form of motion.** (1) Generally a motion for relief from the automatic stay of 11 U.S.C. § 362(a) must be titled "Motion for Relief from Stay" or a similar phrase. The motion's caption must be in the format used in Official Bankruptcy Form 16D for an adversary proceeding. The motion may not be combined with a request for any other relief, except for adequate protection or for relief from the co-debtor stay of 11 U.S.C. § 1201(a) or § 1301(a).

(2) Prospective Relief. (A) Any motion for relief from stay that includes a request for the imposition of an equitable servitude, or any other prospective relief that would limit a stay arising under 11 U.S.C. § 362(a), must be titled in a manner that clearly and conspicuously so states.

(B) Any proposed order submitted by counsel, including any order consented to by adverse parties, must be titled in a manner that clearly and conspicuously so states.

(b) **Contents of motion for relief from stay.** The following material, when applicable, must be included in a motion for relief from stay:

(1) A detailed statement of the debt owed to the Movant;

(2) If periodic payments are in arrears, the amount of arrears accrued prepetition and postpetition;

(3) A description of the property encumbered;

(4) A description of the security interest involved, with attached documents that evidence the security interest and its perfection;

(5) A statement of the basis for the relief claimed, such as, a lack of adequate protection or the absence of equity and that the property is not necessary for an effective reorganization. The specific facts constituting cause shall be set forth if a motion is brought for cause;

(6) If Movant asserts a valuation of the subject property, the motion should state the amount of the valuation, the date, and the basis therefor (appraisal, blue book, etc.);

(7) The specific nature of the relief from stay that is requested.

(c) **Service of motion and notice of hearing.** (1) The Clerk will maintain a list of dates available for hearings on motions for relief from stay for each judge of the court. The list will be posted on the court's website.

(2) Movant must select a hearing date from the list for the judge to whom the case is assigned that is more than twenty-one (21) days after the date of service.

(3) Movant must serve the motion for relief from stay with a hearing notice conforming to Local Bankruptcy Form B.

(d) **Response to motion for relief from stay.** (1) Time. An opposition to a motion for relief from stay must be filed within fourteen (14) days after service of the motion (plus any additional time required by Federal Bankruptcy Rules 9006(a) and (f)). The Court Hearing Scheduler (CHS) Program on the court's website and CM/ECF filing screen for this type of motion will compute the date that an objection is due.

(2) Form. The caption of the response must be the same as the form for the caption of the motion as set out in paragraph (a) above.

(3) Pleading. A response must include detailed answers to each numbered paragraph of the motion, in conformity with the requirements of Federal Rules Civil Procedure 8(b) and (d). All defenses to the motion must be stated in the response.

(4) Response by Standing Chapter 12 and 13 Trustees. Standing Chapter 12 and Chapter 13 Trustees are served for informational purposes and are not required to respond to motions for relief from stay.

(e) **Unopposed motion.** If timely opposition is not filed, the court may grant or otherwise dispose of the motion prior to the scheduled hearing date.

(f) **Requirements under 11 U.S.C. § 362(e).** (1) Waiver. If Movant notices a hearing date more than thirty (30) days after the date of the filing of the motion, Movant is deemed to have consented to the inapplicability of 11 U.S.C. § 362(e) through the day of the hearing on the motion for relief from stay.

(2) Commencement of measuring period. A request for relief under 11 U.S.C. § 362(d) is complete to commence the thirty (30) day measuring period under § 362(e) only when filed and noticed in compliance with this Rule.

(g) **Deadline for pre-filing exhibits.** In cases under Chapter 11, exhibits must be pre-filed as required by Local Bankruptcy Rule 7016-1(c) no later than seven (7) days prior to the noticed hearing date. (Amended April 27, 2007, effective May 1, 2007; amended October 15, 2007, effective November 1, 2007; November 10, 2008, effective December 1, 2008; amended effective December 1, 2009.)

Effect of amendments. — The April, 2007 amendment added (a)(2) and made related changes; in (a)(1) added "Generally" and "§ 1201 (a) or"; in (c) substituted "on the court's website" for "published by such other means selected by the Clerk"; deleted (d) and redesignated accordingly; in (d)(1) substituted "service of the motion" for "the date of the notice of hearing"; and rewrote (e) without substantive change.

The 2007 Order, effective November 1, 2007, updated the designations in (a)(2).

The 2008 Order, effective December 1, 2008, substituted "Movant" for "movant" in (b)(1), (b)(6) and (f)(1); deleted "the amount of arrears accrued" following "prepetition and" in (b)(2); rewrote (c)(1) and (d)(1); substituted "Federal Rules of Civil Procedure 8(b)" for "Fed.R.Civ.P. 8(b)" in (d)(3); and substituted "If Movant" for "If a movant" in (f)(1).

The 2009 amendment in (g) substituted
"seven (7) days" for "the third business day"
and made a stylistic change.

Rule 4001-2. Automatic stay — Post-filing arrears.

Where an issue presented by a motion for relief from stay is the debtor's failure to make payments that became due after the filing of the bankruptcy case, the moving party shall file and serve a history of payments received post-petition upon the debtor at least seven (7) days before the date set for hearing. (Added Dec. 4, 2003, effective Jan. 1, 2004; amended October 15, 2007, effective November 1, 2007; amended effective December 1, 2009.)

Effect of amendments. — The Summary of Changes to Local Bankruptcy Rules, effective January 1, 2004, states, "This is a new Rule requiring that a party seeking relief from the stay file and serve a history of payments received post-petition upon the debtor where the motion is based in whole or part upon failure to receive post-petition payments."

The 2007 Order, effective November 1, 2007, made minor grammatical changes.

The 2009 amendment substituted "seven (7) days" for "eight (8) days".

Rule 4001-3. Action following foreclosure.

A party obtaining relief from the automatic stay and thereafter consummating a foreclosure sale that produces a surplus must:

(a) provide a copy of the Report of Sale and all Auditor's Reports to the bankruptcy trustee, and

(b) when filing the Report of Sale in a case under Chapter 7 or Chapter 13, notify the Auditor of the name and address of the bankruptcy trustee. (Added Dec. 4, 2003, effective Jan. 1, 2004; amended October 15, 2007, effective November 1, 2007.)

Effect of amendments. — The Summary of Changes to Local Bankruptcy Rules, effective January 1, 2004, states, "This is a new Rule requiring a party obtaining relief from the automatic stay and consummating a foreclosure to provide certain information to the trustee and to the state court Auditor."

The 2007 Order, effective November 1, 2007, in (b) made minor grammatical changes, added 'or Chapter 13', and deleted 'to whom the surplus must be paid' at the end.

Rule 4001-4. Obtaining credit/refinancing.

(a) Movant must provide the notice required by Federal Bankruptcy Rule 4001(c) for a motion to obtain credit.

(b) The notice must include a statement of the deadline for the filing of any opposition. The deadline date shall be no less than fourteen (14) days after service of the motion (plus any additional time required by Federal Bankruptcy Rules 9006(a) and (f)). The Court Hearing Scheduler (CHS) Program on the court's website and CM/ECF filing screen for this type of motion will compute the date that an objection is due.

(c) The notice must include a hearing date that the movant selects from a list of hearing dates that is maintained by the Clerk for the assigned judge on the court's website.

(d) The notice must also include a description of the essential terms of the proposed credit, including the amount, the interest rate, the lender's identity, the collateral pledged therefor, the repayment terms, the costs therefor, and the proposed use of the proceeds.

(e) The notice may include a statement that the court may grant relief without a hearing if no timely objection is filed.

(f) In any Chapter 13 case in which the deadline to file claims has expired, the title of the notice must include the following words:

AND SETTING DEADLINE TO AMEND FILED PROOFS OF CLAIMS

(g) In a Chapter 13 case in which the deadline to file proofs of claims has expired, the notice must include the following words:

In accordance with Local Bankruptcy Rule 4001-4(g), any amendment to a previously filed claim must be filed no later than twenty-one (21) days after the date of filing of this notice. Such amendments include amending a claim previously filed as a secured claim, to reflect an unsecured claim resulting from the effect of 11 U.S.C. § 506(a) and/or liquidation of the collateral.

(h) **Request to shorten time and/or expedited hearing.** (1) If Movant requests that the time to object should be shortened, or that a more expedited hearing is needed, Movant shall file contemporaneously a separate motion requesting that the court shorten the time within which responses may be filed and/or requesting that the court set an expedited hearing.

(2) If a motion is filed to shorten the time to object or to expedite the hearing thereon, Movant must include the following language in the notice:

MOVANT HAS ALSO FILED A MOTION TO SHORTEN THE TIME FOR RESPONSE AND/OR FOR AN EXPEDITED HEARING. IF THAT MOTION TO SHORTEN OR EXPEDITE IS GRANTED, THE TIME TO OBJECT AND/OR DATE FOR HEARING WILL BE CHANGED AS PROVIDED IN SUCH ORDER. (Added Dec. 4, 2003, effective Jan. 1, 2004; amended April 27, 2007, effective May 1, 2007; amended October 15, 2007, effective November 1, 2007; November 10, 2008, effective December 1, 2008; amended effective December 1, 2009.)

Effect of amendments. — The Summary of Changes to Local Bankruptcy Rules, effective January 1, 2004, states, "This governs applications to refinance loans and creates a process where parties may select a hearing."

The April, 2007 amendment substituted "fifteen (15) days'" for "twenty (20) days'" in (b); rewrote (c); substituted "if no timely objection is filed" for "if no objections are filed" in (e); and added (f) and (g).

The 2007 Order, effective November 1, 2007, added (h) to address requests to shorten time.

The 2008 Order, effective December 1, 2008, rewrote (b).

The 2009 amendment substituted "fourteen (14) days" for "fifteen (15) days" in the second sentence of (b); in (g) substituted "twenty-one (21) days" for "twenty (20) days"; and in (h) substituted "If Movant" for "If the Movant".

Rule 4001-5. Post petition payment notices and account access.

Creditors and lessors may continue to provide customary notices, including, but not limited to, monthly statements, payment coupons, escrow adjustment analyses to debtors regarding post-petition account activity. Further, to the extent available, creditors and lessors may allow debtors to access, obtain information, and make post-petition payments through electronic, telephonic and/or on-line means.

The creditor's or lessor's actions outlined in the immediately preceding paragraph shall not be considered a violation of the automatic stay. (Added

Oct. 17, 2005, effective Oct. 17, 2005; amended September 27, 2006, effective September 27, 2006; amended April 27, 2007, effective May 1, 2007; amended October 15, 2007, effective November 1, 2007.)

Effect of amendments. — The 2006 amendment by Administrative Order No. 05-04, effective September 27, 2006, reenacted the Rule without change.

The April, 2007 amendment rewrote the Rule.

The 2007 Order, effective November 1, 2007, added the second paragraph.

Editor's note. — Administrative Order No. 05-04, effective September 27, 2006, provides that the amendments apply to cases filed after October 17, 2005.

Rule 4002-1. Current address and telephone number of debtor.

(a) **Address of debtor.** Every debtor must maintain a statement of the debtor's current address with the Clerk. This obligation continues until the case is closed.

(b) **Debtor's telephone number.** A debtor proceeding in proper person must maintain a statement of the debtor's current telephone number with the Clerk. This obligation continues until the case is closed.

Rule 4003-1. Objection to claim of exemptions.

Required notice. An objection to the list of property claimed as exempt under § 522 of the Bankruptcy Code must contain conspicuous notice that: (1) any opposition to the objection must be filed and served within twenty-eight (28) days after the objection was served; and (2) the court may rule upon the objection and any response thereto without a hearing. (Added December 4, 2003, effective January 1, 2004; amended effective December 1, 2009.)

Effect of amendments. — The 2009 amendment substituted "twenty-eight (28)" for "thirty (30)."

Rule 4003-2. Lien avoidance under 11 U.S.C. § 522(f).

(a) **Form.** A motion to avoid a lien under 11 U.S.C. § 522(f) may name only one creditor as a respondent. A separate motion is required for each creditor whose lien is sought to be avoided. The name, address and nature of ownership (e.g. tenancy in common, tenancy by the entirety) of any non-debtor owner of property must also be included.

(b) **Service of motion and notice of hearing.** (1) The Clerk will maintain a list of dates available for hearings on motions to avoid lien for each judge of the court. The list will be posted in the public area of each division and on the court's website.

(2) Movant must select a hearing date from the list for the judge to whom the case is assigned that is more than forty-nine (49) days after the date of service.

(3) Movant must serve a copy of the motion to avoid lien on the respondent and any non-debtor owner in the manner required by Federal Bankruptcy Rules 9014 and 7004(b) and Local Bankruptcy Rule 3007-1(a) (that requires service upon the individual who signed the proof of claim filed by respondent) together with a hearing notice conforming to Local Bankruptcy Form C.

(c) **Filing of proof of service.** Movant must file with the motion a certificate of service of the motion to avoid lien and the notice of hearing. The certificate must comply with Local Bankruptcy Rule 9013-4.

(d) **Responses to motions to avoid liens.** The notice must include a statement of deadline for the filing of any opposition. The deadline date shall be no less than twenty-eight (28) days after service of the motion (plus any additional time required by Federal Bankruptcy Rules 9006(a) and (f)). The Court Hearing Scheduler (CHS) Program on the court's website and CM/ECF filing screen for this type of motion will compute the date that an objection is due. If no response to the motion to avoid lien is filed within twenty-eight (28) days after the date of the service (plus any additional time provided by Federal Bankruptcy Rules 9006(a) and (f)), the court may rule on the motion as unopposed. (Added December 4, 2003, effective January 1, 2004; amended October 15, 2007, effective November 1, 2007; November 10, 2008, effective December 1, 2008; amended effective December 1, 2009; amended November 12, 2010, effective November 12, 2010; amended Aug. 24, 2011, effective Sept. 1, 2011.)

Effect of amendments. — The Summary of Changes to Local Bankruptcy Rules, effective January 1, 2004, concerning (b)(3), states, "This Rule requires that motions for avoidance of liens under § 522(f) be served in the same fashion as objections to proofs of claim."

The 2007 Order, effective November 1, 2007, in (b)(1), second sentence, substituted "on the Court's website" for "published by such other means selected by the Clerk"; in (b)(3) added "(that requires service upon the individual who signed a proof of claim filed by respondent)"; and in (d)(2) substituted "rule on the motion without a hearing" for "dispose of an unopposed motion before the scheduled hearing date".

The 2008 Order, effective December 1, 2008, substituted "lien for each judge" for "liens on the calendar of each judge" in the first sentence in (b)(1); and rewrote (d).

The 2009 amendment substituted "forty-nine (49) days" for "fifty (50) days" in (b)(2); and "twenty-eight (28) days" for "twenty-five (25) days" twice in (d).

The 2010 amendment by Administrative Order 10-2 added the last sentence in (a) and "and any non-debtor owner" in (b)(3).

The 2011 amendment added the last sentence in (a) and "and any non-debtor owner" in (b)(3).

Rule 4007-1. Dischargeability complaints under 11 U.S.C. § 523(a)(15).

[Abrogated effective May 1, 2007.]

Rule 4008-1. Discharge in Chapter 13 cases.

The Debtor's Affidavit Requesting Discharge, Local Bankruptcy Form P, must be filed and served on the Chapter 13 Trustee and all creditors no later than ninety (90) days after the Chapter 13 Trustee files the notice of completion of plan payments. The failure to timely file this affidavit may result in the case being closed without a discharge. (Amended April 27, 2007, effective May 1, 2007; amended effective December 1, 2009.)

Effect of amendments. — The 2007 amendment rewrote the Rule.

The 2009 amendment substitutued "ninety (90) days" for "90 days"; and substituted "Trustee" for "trustee" twice.

PART V.

Rule 5001-1. Court administration — Lapse in appropriations.

This Rule will become effective only when Congress fails to enact legislation to fund operations of the United States Courts. The Anti-Deficiency Act, 31 U.S.C. § 1515, limits permissible government activities in the event of such a failure to those otherwise "authorized by law" or those needed to meet "cases of emergency involving the safety of human life or the protection of property."

This court is directly involved in the judicial process and under the Constitution and laws of the United States, it is always open to exercise the judicial power of the United States as a unit of the District Court. Thus, the court must continue, even in the absence of funding by Congress, to receive new cases, and to hear and dispose of pending cases. Activities will, however, be limited as nearly as practical to those functions necessary and essential to continue the resolution of pending cases. The court will advise the United States Marshal and the General Services Administration of the level of building and security services necessary to maintain such court operations.

The court finds that judges' staffs and the Clerk and the Clerk's staff are persons essential to the continuation of court operations. Work of all personnel shall be limited to those essential functions set forth above.

Rule 5001-2. Clerk — Office location/hours.

(a) **Office hours.** The office hours of the Clerk in the Greenbelt and Baltimore Divisions shall be from 8:00 a.m. to 4:00 p.m. on all days, except Saturdays, Sundays, and holidays observed by the United States District Court for the District of Maryland.

(b) **Night box.** A night box is located in the lobby of each of the United States Courthouses in Baltimore and in Greenbelt. Bankruptcy petitions, pleadings and other papers may be placed in the night box for filing after regular office hours, Monday through Friday (except holidays) and until the courthouse is closed to the public or midnight, whichever is earlier. The Garmatz Federal Courthouse in Baltimore is closed to the public at midnight while the Greenbelt Federal Courthouse is closed at 7:00 p.m. **The night box is intended as an after-hours convenience, and it is not intended as an alternative for filing papers during regular office hours.** All documents must be "date and time stamped" prior to being deposited in the secure night box.

(c) **After hours filing.** During periods outside the regular office hours of the Clerk's Office and when the night box is not available, arrangements may be made in advance for time sensitive filings by contacting a designated court representative. The contact information of the designated court representatives are posted on the court's web page, on each night box and on notice boards in the divisional offices.

(d) **Deadlines are not extended. The availability of the night box and after hours filing do NOT extend the "Last Day" as defined by Federal Bankruptcy Rule 9006(a)(4), which Last Day ends for filing, other than electronic filing, at 4:00 p.m. when the Clerk's Offices close.**

(e) **Division of business.** The division of business for the United States Bankruptcy Court for the District of Maryland is as follows:

(1) Cases originating in Allegany, Calvert, Charles, Frederick, Garrett, Montgomery, Prince George's, St. Mary's, and Washington Counties are assigned to the Greenbelt Divisional Office, 300 U.S. Courthouse, 6500 Cherrywood Lane, Greenbelt, Maryland, 20770, (301) 344-8018.

(2) Cases originating in Baltimore City, Anne Arundel, Baltimore, Caroline, Carroll, Cecil, Dorchester, Harford, Howard, Kent, Queen Anne's, Somerset, Talbot, Wicomico, and Worcester Counties are assigned to the Baltimore Divisional Office, 8530 U.S. Courthouse, 101 West Lombard Street, Baltimore, Maryland, 21201, (410) 962-2688.

(f) **Places for holding court.** (1) All court hearings in cases originating in Baltimore City, Anne Arundel, Baltimore, Carroll, Cecil, Harford, and Howard Counties will be scheduled in the Garmatz Federal Courthouse, 101 West Lombard Street, Baltimore, Maryland, 21201.

(2) All court hearings in cases originating in Allegany, Calvert, Charles, Frederick, Garrett, Montgomery, Prince George's, St. Mary's, and Washington Counties will be scheduled in the Federal Courthouse at 6500 Cherrywood Lane, Greenbelt, Maryland, 20770.

(3) All court hearings in cases under Chapters 7, 12 and 13 originating in Caroline, Dorchester, Kent, Queen Anne's, Somerset, Talbot, Wicomico, and Worcester Counties, including related adversary proceedings, and all Section 341 meetings of creditors therein, will be scheduled in the United States Courtroom, U.S. Post Office Building, Room 104, 129 East Main Street, Salisbury, Maryland 21801. A debtor in a case originating from Queen Anne's County may request by motion that all future court hearings, excluding Section 341 meetings of creditors, be conducted at the United States Courthouse in Baltimore. In Chapter 11 cases, the Section 341 meeting of creditors will be conducted by the U.S. Trustee in Baltimore; and court hearings will be scheduled in Salisbury, if possible, or in Baltimore at the request of a party, if necessary.

(4) In cases under Chapter 11 originating in Anne Arundel County, Baltimore City, Baltimore County, Caroline, Carroll, Cecil, Dorchester, Harford, Howard, Kent, Queen Anne's, Somerset, Talbot, Wicomico or Worcester County, the meeting of creditors held under Section 341 will be conducted by the United States Trustee in Baltimore. Court hearings may be scheduled in Salisbury or Baltimore at the direction of the court. The court will consider the convenience of the parties in selecting the venue. (Added December 4, 2003, effective January 1, 2004; amended April 27, 2007, effective May 1, 2007; amended October 15, 2007, effective November 1, 2007; amended November 10, 2008, effective December 1, 2008; amended effective December 1, 2009.)

Effect of amendments. — The Summary of Changes to Local Bankruptcy Rules, effective January 1, 2004, concerning (b), states, "The 'Night Box' procedure has been modified with respect to the file dating of non-emergency matters."

The April, 2007 amendment added (d).

The 2007 Order, effective November 1, 2007, in (c)(2) substituted "8308" for "8515" in the Court's address.

The 2008 Order, effective December 1, 2008, in (c)(2) substituted "8530" for "8308" in the Court's address; added "21801" at the end of the first sentence in (d)(3); and rewrote (d)(4).

The 2009 amendment rewrote the last sentence of (b) and deleted (b)(1) through (b)(3); added (c) and (d); and redesignated accordingly.

Rule 5005-1. Filing by electronic means.

The Court will accept for filing documents submitted, signed or verified by electronic means that comply with the Electronic Case Filing Procedures established by the Court as published on the Court's website. (Added October 15, 2007, effective November 1, 2007.)

Editor's note. — As to electronic filing of documents with United States Bankruptcy Court for the District of Maryland, see www.mdb.uscourts.gov.

Rule 5011-1. Abstention.

(a) **Adversary proceeding.** In an adversary proceeding, a motion for abstention pursuant to 28 U.S.C. § 1334(c), must be filed within the time prescribed for filing a response under Federal Bankruptcy Rule 7012(a).

(b) **Contested matter.** In a contested matter, a motion for abstention pursuant to 28 U.S.C. § 1334(c) must be filed within thirty (30) days from the date indicated on the certificate of service on the pleading initiating the contested matter.

Rule 5011-2. Withdrawal of reference.

A motion for withdrawal of reference is governed by Local Rule 405.2 of the United States District Court for the District of Maryland. See Appendix B. (Amended October 15, 2007, effective November 1, 2007.)

Effect of amendments. — The 2007 Order, effective November 1, 2007, substituted "405.2" for "404(A)(2)".

Rule 5071-1. Motions for postponement/continuances.

(a) **Court order required.** A court order is required for any postponement of a hearing, pretrial conference, or trial.

(b) **Notice to client and other parties.** A motion to postpone any matter before the court must certify that the client has prior notice of the filing of that motion. Notice of such motion, together with the reasons therefor, must be given by the fastest means to avoid inconvenience to other parties entitled to notice or their counsel before filing unless such notice is waived.

(c) **Conflicting engagement.** A motion for a postponement of a hearing or trial on the grounds of a prior conflicting engagement must be filed within fourteen (14) days after the date such conflict became apparent. Written evidence of the conflicting engagement must be attached to the motion.

(d) **Meeting of creditors.** A request for postponement of a meeting of creditors held under Bankruptcy Code § 341 shall be handled as follows:

(1) in Chapter 12 and 13 cases requests shall be made to the standing trustee assigned to the case;

(2) in Chapter 7 cases requests shall be made to the interim trustee; and

(3) in Chapter 11 cases requests shall be made to the Assistant United States Trustee assigned to the division of court where the case is pending.

(Amended April 27, 2007, effective May 1, 2007; amended October 15, 2007, effective November 1, 2007; amended effective December 1, 2009.)

Effect of amendments. — The April, 2007 amendment, effective May 1, 2007, rewrote (b).

The 2007 Order, effective November 1, 2007, in (b), second sentence, deleted "to all other parties" before "or their counsel"; and in (d)(1), added "12 and" after "Chapter".

The 2009 amendment substituted fourteen (14) days" for "ten (10) days" in the first sentence of (c); and "United States" for "U.S." in (d)(3).

Rule 5073-1. Photography, recording devices and broadcasting.

Unless otherwise ordered by the court, no court proceeding can be photographed, videotaped, televised, recorded, reproduced, or broadcast in any way except by an official court reporter.

PART VI.

Rule 6004-1. Sale of estate property.

(a) **Sale notices.** Notices of private sale of estate property must include the following:

(1) if an appraisal has been performed,

(A) the appraised value of the asset being sold;

(B) the date of the appraisal; and

(C) the name and address of the appraiser;

(2) if no appraisal has been performed, the scheduled value of the asset being sold;

(3) the purchaser's identity;

(4) a full description of any relationship between the purchaser and any party in interest;

(5) a statement of all consideration paid and to be paid by the purchaser and the payment terms;

(6) a statement of the deadline for the filing of any opposition. The deadline date shall be no less than twenty-one (21) days after service of the motion, plus any additional time required by Federal Bankruptcy Rules 9006(a) and (f). The Court Hearing Scheduler (CHS) Program on the court's website and CM/ECF filing screen for this type of motion will compute the date that an objection is due;

(7) a date selected from the court's website for a hearing if a timely objection is filed; and

(8) a statement that the property may be sold without further notice if a timely objection is not filed.

(b) **Request to shorten time and/or for expedited hearing.** (1) If Movant requests that the time to object should be shortened, or that a more expedited hearing is needed, Movant shall file contemporaneously a separate motion requesting that the court shorten the time within which responses may be filed and/or requesting that the court set an expedited hearing.

(2) If a motion is filed to shorten the time to object to the sale or to expedite the hearing thereon, Movant must include the following language in the Sale Notice described in subsection (a) of this rule:

MOVANT HAS ALSO FILED A MOTION TO SHORTEN THE TIME FOR RESPONSE AND/OR FOR AN EXPEDITED HEARING. IF THAT MOTION TO SHORTEN OR EXPEDITE IS GRANTED, THE TIME TO OBJECT AND/OR DATE FOR HEARING WILL BE CHANGED AS PROVIDED IN SUCH ORDER.

(c) **Disclosure of sale charges.** All charges and costs to be paid by the estate and all concessions to be made by the estate must be disclosed in the notice of sale.

(d) **Sale without objection.** If no timely written objection is filed, the sale shall be deemed authorized upon expiration of the notice period. This paragraph does not apply to sales free and clear of liens or of interests of persons other than the debtor.

(e) **Clerk's certificate.** Upon payment of the appropriate fee, the Clerk will furnish a certificate that no objection has been filed to a notice of sale.

(f) In any Chapter 13 case in which the deadline to file claims has expired, the title of the notice must include the following words:

AND SETTING DEADLINE TO AMEND FILED PROOFS OF CLAIMS

(g) In a Chapter 13 case in which the deadline to file proofs of claims has expired, the notice must include the following words:

In accordance with Local Bankruptcy Rule 6004-1(f), any amendment to a previously filed claim must be filed no later than twenty-one (21) days after the date of filing of this notice. Such amendments include amending a claim previously filed as a secured claim, to reflect an unsecured claim resulting from the effect of 11 U.S.C. § 506(a) and/or liquidation of the collateral. (Added December 4, 2003, effective January 1, 2004; amended April 27, 2007, effective May 1, 2007; amended October 15, 2007, effective November 1, 2007; November 10, 2008, effective December 1, 2008; amended effective December 1, 2009.)

Effect of amendments. — The Summary of Changes to Local Bankruptcy Rules, effective January 1, 2004, states, "This Rule governing the procedure for sale of estate property has been augmented so as to allow parties to select a date for a hearing if a timely objection is filed."

The April, 2007 amendment rewrote (b); and added (e) and (f).

The 2007 Order, effective November 1, 2007, added (b) to address requests to shorten time and redesignated the remaining subsections accordingly.

The 2008 Order, effective December 1, 2008 rewrote (a)(6).

The 2009 amendment substituted "twenty-one (21) days" for "twenty (20) days" in the second sentence of (a)(6) and in (g); in (b)(1) substitutued "If Movant" for "If the Movant".

Editor's note. — The heading for (b), as added by the September, 2007, order has been modified to conform to the text.

Rule 6006-1. Executory contracts — Unexpired leases.

(a) **Notice required.** Parties seeking the assumption, rejection, or assignment of an executory contract or unexpired lease must give notice of the proposed action to: (1) the other party to the executory contract or unexpired lease; (2) any official committee, or in the absence of a committee, to the holders of the ten (10) largest unsecured claims taken from debtor's list filed pursuant to Federal Bankruptcy Rule 1007(d) or Schedule F; (3) the trustee; (4) the United States Trustee; and (5) all parties requesting notice. The notice must state that the court may rule upon the request without a hearing if there is no timely request for a hearing.

(b) **Motion to reject a collective bargaining agreement.** A party moving to reject a collective bargaining agreement must file the following with the motion:

(1) an affidavit demonstrating compliance with Bankruptcy Code § 1113(b); and

(2) a certificate of service that the moving party has served the motion and affidavit on the authorized representative of the employees covered by the collective bargaining agreement.

Rule 6070-1. Tax refunds.

Notice to trustee and court. It is the duty of the debtor, within seven (7) days of receipt of a tax refund or notice of tax assessment or deficiency, to file with the court, and in Chapter 7 cases to send to the trustee, a copy of the refund check and transmittal letter and a copy of any tax assessment, deficiency notice, or other relevant documents. (Added Dec. 4, 2003, effective Jan. 1, 2004; amended effective December 1, 2009.)

Effect of amendments. — The Summary of Changes to Local Bankruptcy Rules, effective January 1, 2004, states, "This Rule has been amended to eliminate the authority of taxing authorities to deliver tax refunds directly to debtors."

The 2009 amendment substituted "seven (7) days" for "five (5) days".

PART VII.

Rule 7001-1. Trustees' filing fees.

Payment of the filing fee for an adversary proceeding filed by a trustee may be deferred pending acquisition of sufficient funds by the trustee to pay such fees in full or pro rata with other expenses of administration.

Rule 7003-1. Adversary cover sheet.

A party who is not represented by an authorized Filing User of the Electronic Case Filing system must file a completed adversary proceeding cover sheet when filing an adversary proceeding. (Added Dec. 4, 2003, effective Jan. 1, 2004.)

Effect of amendments. — The Summary of Changes to Local Bankruptcy Rules, effective January 1, 2004, states, "This Rule has been modified to require the filing of an adversary cover sheet only by a party not represented by an authorized user of the ECF system."

Rule 7003-2. Disclosure of corporate affiliates.

Each non-governmental corporate party to an adversary proceeding or contested matter shall file a statement identifying all its parent corporations and listing every publicly held company that owns 10% or more of the party's stock. A party shall file the statement with its initial pleading filed in the court and shall supplement the statement within a reasonable time of any change in the information. (Amended April 27, 2007, effective May 1, 2007.)

Effect of amendments. — The 2007 amendment substituted "an adversary pro-ceeding or contested matter" for "an adversary proceeding in this court" in the first sentence.

Rule 7005-1. Filing of discovery materials.

Unless otherwise ordered by the court, a party may not file with the court either written discovery requests, responses to discovery or depositions (other than as exhibits to motions). A party propounding written discovery or taking a deposition or providing a discovery response must file a notice stating: (a) the type of discovery or response served; (b) the date and type of service; and (c) the person(s) served. Parties must retain the original copies of the discovery materials and make them available for inspection by any other party.

Rule 7012-1. Core or non-core matters and consent.

(a) Prior to trial a party may move for a ruling that an adversary proceeding is core or non-core. The court will ordinarily allow adverse parties fourteen (14) days from service of the motion to file responses. Such a motion does not postpone any time periods unless ordered by the court.

(b) In addition to the provisions of Federal Rules of Bankruptcy Procedure 7008(a) and 7012(b), all parties in an adversary proceeding shall include in their initial pleading a statement as to whether the party consents to entry of final orders or judgments by the Bankruptcy Judge. (Added October 15, 2007, effective November 1, 2007; amended effective October 26, 2011.)

Effect of amendments. — The 2011 amendment rewrote (b).
Editor's note. — The 2007 Order, effective November 1, 2007, restored text previously deleted by the May 1, 2007, Order; amended effective October 26, 2011.

Rule 7015-1. Amended and supplemental pleadings.

Unless otherwise ordered by the court, the party filing an amended pleading shall file and serve (1) a clean copy of the amended pleading; and (2) a copy of the amended pleading in which stricken material has been lined through or enclosed in brackets and new material has been underlined or set forth in bold faced type. (Added November 12, 2010, effective November 12, 2010; and August 24, 2011, effective September 1, 2011.)

Rule 7016-1. Pretrial procedures.

(a) **General.** The court may, in any adversary proceeding or contested matter, direct the attorney for a party or a party appearing without counsel to appear before it for a preliminary scheduling or pretrial conference pursuant to Federal Bankruptcy Rule 7016.

(b) **Pretrial statement.** Where required by court order, each party will file a pretrial memorandum, with copies sent to all other attorneys of record or parties proceeding without counsel. Each party must state the following in its pretrial memorandum:

(1) a brief statement of facts that the party proposes to prove in support of a claim or defense, together with a statement of legal theories and citations of authorities;

(2) any required pleading amendments;

(3) any pleaded, but abandoned, issue;

(4) stipulations of fact;

(5) the details of the damage claimed or any other relief sought;

(6) a list of the documents and records to be offered in evidence by the party at the trial other than those expected to be used solely for impeachment, indicating which documents the party expects to introduce in evidence without the usual authentication;

(7) a list of the names and specialties of experts that the party proposes to call as witnesses; and

(8) a statement of any matter that must be resolved before trial.

(c) **Required pre-filing of exhibits.** (1) Adversary proceedings and Chapter 11 lift stays. In all adversary proceedings and in motions seeking relief from stay in Chapter 11 cases, each party must pre-file all exhibits which that party intends to introduce into evidence, except for exhibits to be offered solely for rebuttal. Each party must include in the pre-filed exhibits any report by an expert whom the party may call as a witness or, if no report has been prepared, an affidavit by such expert as to the expert's direct testimony. The exhibits must be filed and received by the opposing parties within the time limits set in the scheduling order. In adversary proceedings, if opposing parties do not file written objections to pre-filed exhibits by the time specified in the scheduling order, the exhibits will be admitted into evidence.

(2) Method of pre-filing of exhibits. All pre-filed exhibits must be filed within the time limits set in the scheduling order by submission of an original and two (2) copies. Each set of exhibits must be bound or affixed together and must have at the beginning an exhibit list identifying each exhibit by number. Each exhibit must be tabbed by exhibit number. An additional copy must be furnished to each other party in the matter.

(3) Size. To the extent possible, all exhibits must be reduced to 8-½ by 11 inches.

(4) Failure to pre-file exhibits. Exhibits that are not pre-filed as required by this Rule may be excluded from evidence.

(d) **Proof of amount of claim or debt.** (1) Required verified statement. In all adversary proceedings and all contested matters, a party seeking to prove the amount of a liquidated debt must offer as an exhibit an affidavit setting forth the amount of the alleged claim or debt, itemized by component, unless the information is contained in a previously filed pleading in the matter and verified pursuant to 28 U.S.C. § 1746. The declarant must be present in the courtroom for cross-examination, or an objection made pursuant to Federal Rule of Evidence 802 may be sustained.

(2) Pre-filing requirement. In adversary proceedings and Chapter 11 motions for relief from stay, the required affidavit or verified pleading must be pre-filed as an exhibit, in accordance with subsections (d)(1) of this Rule. (Amended October 15, 2007, effective November 1, 2007; amended effective December 1, 2009; amended Aug. 24, 2011, effective Sept. 1, 2011.)

Effect of amendments. — The 2007 Order, effective November 1, 2007, made a minor grammatical change in (a).

The 2009 order added a comma in (b)(3); transferred "and" from the end of (b)(6) to the end of (b)(7) and made related changes.

The 2011 amendment substituted "without counsel" for "pro se" in (a) and in the first sentence of the introductory language of (b).

Rule 7026-1. Discovery — General.

(a) **Discovery request limits.** A party may not serve on any other party in a contested matter or an adversary proceeding more than thirty (30) interrogatories and thirty (30) requests for production, including all parts and sub-parts.

(b) **Timely written discovery requests required.** All discovery requests must be made at a sufficiently early date to assure that the time for response expires before any discovery deadlines set by the court.

(c) **Discovery to proceed despite existence of disputes.** Unless otherwise ordered by the court, a discovery dispute as to one matter does not justify delay in taking or responding to any other discovery.

(d) **Discovery stayed pending resolution of Federal Bankruptcy Rule 7012(b) motion.** The filing of a motion pursuant to Federal Bankruptcy Rule 7012(b) stays discovery unless the movant presents matters outside the pleading.

(e) **Format of responses.** Responses to discovery must restate each request followed by the response or a brief statement of the grounds for objection.

(f) **Conference of counsel required.** Counsel must confer concerning a discovery dispute and make good faith attempts to resolve their differences. The court will not resolve a discovery dispute unless the moving party has filed a certificate stating:

(1) the date, time, and place of the discovery conference, the names of all persons participating and any unresolved issues remaining; or

(2) the moving party's attempts to hold such a conference without success.

(g) **Smoking during depositions prohibited.** Unless all persons present agree, no one can smoke in a room where a deposition is being taken.

(h) **Deposition of an expert.** The party taking the deposition of an expert shall pay a reasonable fee for the time spent by the expert in deposition and traveling to and from the deposition. The party designating the expert will pay any fee charged by the expert for time spent in preparing for the deposition.

(i) **Copying expenses.** A party in interest requesting copies of documents that were produced for inspection must pay the actual, reasonable costs of copying.

(j) **Discovery Guidelines.** Discovery Guidelines adopted by the court and set forth in Appendix C govern the conduct of discovery. (Added December 4, 2003, effective Jan. 1, 2004; amended April 27, 2007, effective May 1, 2007; amended effective December 1, 2009.)

Effect of amendments. — The Summary of Changes to Local Bankruptcy Rules, effective January 1, 2004, concerning (i), states, "This Rule deals with paying costs of copies of documents produced for inspection."

The 2007 amendment substituted "more than thirty (30) interrogatories and thirty (30) requests for production" for "more than thirty (30) interrogatories, more than thirty (30) requests for production, and thirty (30) requests for admissions" in (a).

The 2009 amendment deleted "entertain to" before "resolve" in the introductory language in (f).

Rule 7054-1. Allowance of costs.

No costs will be allowed in adversary proceedings in excess of filing fees unless the entitled party files a Bill of Costs within twenty-one (21) days after the entry of the judgment or order. (Amended effective December 1, 2009.)

Effect of amendments. — The 2009 amendment substituted "twenty-one (21) days" for "twenty (20) days".

Rule 7054-2. Attorneys' fees.

Unless a longer period is fixed by statute or by the court, motions by a prevailing party for an award of attorney's fees must be filed within twenty-one (21) days after the entry of judgment or order. (Amended effective December 1, 2009.)

Effect of amendments. — The 2009 amendment substituted "twenty-one (21) days" for "twenty (20) days".

Rule 7055-1. Default — Failure to prosecute.

(a) **Clerk's notice.** If, upon the expiration of six (6) months after the filing of the last pleading, it appears to the Clerk that no significant activity has since occurred in an adversary proceeding or contested matter in which there is no scheduled hearing, the Clerk will send written notice to all parties to the adversary proceeding or contested matter that the proceeding or matter will be denied or dismissed without prejudice unless, within thirty (30) days after the date of the notice, the plaintiff or movant presents good and sufficient cause in writing why the dismissal or denial should not be ordered.

(b) **Court action.** If there is no response to the Clerk's notice, an order of dismissal or denial may be entered.

Rule 7056-1. Where summary judgment is requested against party without counsel.

The notice of any motion seeking summary judgment in which the non-moving party is without counsel shall conform substantially to Official Form 20A and, in addition, shall set forth the requirement for a response in substantially the following form:

NOTICE

A motion for summary judgment is a request that one or more issues in a case be decided without holding a trial. Motions for summary judgment are governed by Rule 56, Federal Rules of Civil Procedure. Summary judgment may be granted if (a) the material facts are not genuinely disputed and (b) based on those facts, the party asking for summary judgment is entitled to judgment as a matter of law. If you wish to oppose the motion, you must file with the court and serve on the other party, a written response at least seven (7) days prior to the hearing. **If you fail to file a timely written response to the motion, the court may assume you do not oppose the motion and may grant the motion without holding a hearing.** This will result in the termination of the matter in favor of the moving party. If you disagree with any of the facts stated by the other party, you must include with your response sworn statements from yourself or other knowledgeable witnesses supporting your version of the facts. A sworn statement may take the form either of an affidavit or a declaration signed under penalty of perjury. Any documents you want the court to consider should be identified in, and attached to, the sworn statements. If you are unable to obtain sworn statements supporting your position, you must file a sworn statement stating why you are unable to obtain such statements at this time. (Added April 27, 2007, effective May 1, 2007; amended effective December 1, 2009; amended Aug. 24, 2011, effective Sept. 1, 2011.)

Effect of amendments. — The 2009 amendment substituted "seven (7) days" for "two (2) business days" in the fourth sentence of the Notice.

The 2011 amendment substituted "without counsel" for "pro se".

PART VIII.

Rule 8001-1. Appeals.
See Appendix B.

PART IX.

Rule 9001-1. Definitions and rules.
(a) **Definitions in Federal Bankruptcy Rules.** The definitions of words and phrases in Federal Bankruptcy Rule 9001 and the definitions adopted by reference therein apply in these Local Bankruptcy Rules.

(b) **Bankruptcy Code.** In these Local Bankruptcy Rules, reference to the Bankruptcy Code means Title 11 of the United States Code.

(c) **Federal Bankruptcy Rules.** Reference to Federal Bankruptcy Rule(s) means the Federal Rules of Bankruptcy Procedure.

(d) **District Court.** In these Local Bankruptcy Rules, reference to the District Court means the United States District Court for the District of Maryland.

(e) **File.** Where the word "file" appears in these Local Bankruptcy Rules, such filing is to be made electronically via ECF or with the appropriate divisional office of the Clerk of the United States Bankruptcy Court for the District of Maryland. (Amended December 4, 2003, effective January 1, 2004; amended effective December 1, 2009.)

Effect of amendments. — The 2009 amendment added "the" before "appropriate" in (e).

Rule 9004-1. Papers — Requirements of form; orders.
(a) **General.** All petitions, pleadings, schedules and other documents filed in paper form shall be 8½ by 11 inches in size, legibly typewritten, printed or reproduced. The papers shall be of standard weight and, except for proposed

orders, shall have an upper margin of not less than one half inch. No such document may be two-hole punched, stapled or similarly fastened so as to cause punctures in the paper. Original pleadings must be retained pursuant to Local Bankruptcy Rule 9011-3. Only copies should be submitted for filing with the Court.

(b) **Proposed orders.** The first page of all orders shall have an upper margin of not less than three (3) inches. The last line in the order must be, **"End of Order",** centered in the middle of the line. The signature line for the judge shall be omitted. (Added Dec. 4, 2003, effective Jan. 1, 2004.)

Effect of amendments. — The Summary of Changes to Local Bankruptcy Rules, effective January 1, 2004, states, "This Rule concerns the format of papers in order to facilitate the ECF system."

Rule 9009-1. Local Bankruptcy Forms.

The Local Bankruptcy Forms prescribed in these Rules are set out in Appendix A. They shall be observed and used with alterations as may be appropriate.

Rule 9010-1. Self-represented parties.

(a) **Who may appear self-represented.** Except for filing motions seeking to obtain funds deposited in the Registry of the Court, only individuals may represent themselves.

(b) **Responsibilities of parties appearing self-represented.** Individuals representing themselves are responsible for performing all duties imposed on counsel by the Bankruptcy Code, the Federal Bankruptcy Rules, these Rules, and applicable federal or state law. (Amended April 27, 2007, effective May 1, 2007; amended Aug. 24, 2011, effective Sept. 1, 2011.)

Effect of amendments. — The 2007 amendment added the exception in (a) and made a related change.

The 2011 amendment substituted "self-represented" for "pro se" in the subsection heading of (a) and (b).

Rule 9010-2. Current information.

(a) **Duty to keep current information on file.** Counsel and parties appearing without counsel must file and maintain a statement of current address and telephone number in every case in which such person appears. This obligation continues until the case is closed.

(b) **Excusable neglect.** Should any person fail to maintain a current address with the Clerk and as a result, either for lack of response or lack of an appearance, the court enters an order dismissing any affirmative claim for relief or enters a judgment by default or otherwise against such person or such person's client, the failure to maintain a current address shall not be considered excusable neglect. (Amended Aug. 24, 2011, effective Sept. 1, 2011.)

Effect of amendments. — The 2011 amendment substituted "without counsel" for "pro se" in the first sentence of (a).

Rule 9010-3. Attorneys — Who may appear as counsel.

(a) **Generally.** Except as otherwise provided in this Rule and 28 U.S.C. § 515, only members of the Bar of the District Court may appear as counsel.

(b) **Admission *pro hac vice*.** (1) The court can permit any attorney (except a member of the Maryland Bar) who is a member in good standing of the Bar of any other United States Court or of the highest court of any state to appear and participate as counsel in a particular bankruptcy case. Such permission will not constitute formal admission to the Bar of the District Court. An attorney admitted *pro hac vice* is subject to the disciplinary jurisdiction of the District Court and of this court.

(2) A party represented by an attorney who has been admitted *pro hac vice* must also be represented by an attorney who is a member of the Bar of the District Court.

(3) The application for admission *pro hac vice* shall comply with Local District Court Rule 101.1.b. The application shall conform to Local Bankruptcy Form F.

(c) **Certain actions not requiring admission to the Bar of the District Court.** An attorney not admitted to the Bar of the District Court may file (1) a proof of claim for a client; (2) a fee application as principal of a professional group; (3) a motion to retrieve funds from the Registry of the Court; or (4) a request for all notices.

(d) **Appearance for obtaining deposition subpoenas.** It is not necessary for counsel to be admitted to the Bar of the District Court in order to obtain a subpoena for depositions to be taken in this district for cases pending in other districts. However, an attorney seeking such a subpoena is subject to the disciplinary jurisdiction of the District Court and of this court. (Amended April 27, 2007, effective May 1, 2007; amended October 15, 2007, effective November 1, 2007.)

Effect of amendments. — The April, 2007 amendment added "and 28 U.S.C. § 515" in (a) and made a related change; and rewrote (b)(3) and (c).

The 2007 Order, effective November 1, 2007, added (c)(4).

Rule 9010-4. Withdrawal of appearance of an attorney.

(a) **When individuals are clients.** (1) An attorney may withdraw an appearance entered on behalf of an individual if another attorney has entered an appearance for and appears as attorney of record for that individual;

(2) Except as provided in subparagraph (1), the appearance of an attorney may be withdrawn only with leave of the court. A motion for leave to withdraw must be accompanied by a certificate stating:

(A) the name and last known address of the client; and

(B) that a written notice has been mailed to or otherwise served upon the client at least seven (7) days previously advising the client of counsel's proposed withdrawal and notifying the client either to have new counsel enter an appearance or to advise the Clerk that the client will be proceeding without counsel.

(b) **When clients are other than individuals.** If the client is other than an individual, including corporations, partnerships, unincorporated associations and government entities, appearances of counsel may be withdrawn only with leave of court and if:

(1) appearance of other counsel has been entered; or

(2) withdrawing counsel files a certificate stating:

(A) the name and last known address of the client; and

(B) that a written notice has been mailed to or otherwise served upon the client at least seven (7) days previously advising the client of counsel's proposed withdrawal and notifying the client that it must have new counsel enter an appearance or be subject to dismissal of its case, dismissal of its claims and/or judgment by default on claims against it. If new counsel has not entered an appearance within twenty-one (21) days after the filing of the motion to withdraw, the court may dismiss an affirmative claim for relief by, or enter a default against, the unrepresented party. (Added Dec. 4, 2003, effective Jan. 1, 2004; amended October 15, 2007, effective November 1, 2007; amended effective December 1, 2009.)

Effect of amendments. — The Summary of Changes to Local Bankruptcy Rules, effective January 1, 2004, states, "This Rule has been changed to eliminate the necessity of obtaining a court order where a successor attorney has entered an appearance."

The 2007 Order, effective November 1, 2007, in (b) introduction made a minor grammatical change; and in (b)(2)(B) in the second sentence deleted "and if the court grants the motion to withdraw" before "the court may dismiss".

The 2009 amendment substituted "seven (7) days" for "five (5) days" in (a)(2)(B) and in the first sentence of (b)(2)(B); and in the second sentence of (b)(2)(B) substituted "twenty-one (21) days" for "twenty (20) days".

Rule 9010-5. Attorneys for debtors — Duties.

(a) An attorney who files a petition in bankruptcy on behalf of a debtor, or who subsequently enters an appearance on behalf of a debtor other than as special counsel approved under Bankruptcy Code § 327(e), will be counsel of record in all matters arising during the administration of the case, such as adversary proceedings and motions for relief from stay, except as set forth below;

(b) In an individual case, representation will continue through discharge and continue as to any matter pending at the time of the discharge. However, an attorney representing an individual debtor may exclude adversary proceedings and United States Trustee audits provided that debtor's written acknowledgment of this limitation is filed with counsel's Federal Bankruptcy Rule 2016(b) statement. (Amended April 27, 2007, effective May 1, 2007.)

Effect of amendments. — The 2007 amendment in (b) deleted "commenced under or converted to Chapter 7" after "individual case", and added "and U.S. Trustee audits"; and deleted (c) through (f).

Rule 9010-6. Chapter 13 debtor's counsel.

Counsel for the debtor(s) in a Chapter 13 case shall abide by all requirements set forth in the Chapter 13 Debtor's Counsel Responsibilities and Fees in Appendix F. (Added April 27, 2007, effective May 1, 2007.)

Rule 9011-1. Signatures, federal bar number.

This Rule augments Federal Bankruptcy Rule 9011. An individual signing pleadings must include the signer's printed name, post office and business address, telephone number and, if available, facsimile and e-mail addresses. If the signer is an attorney admitted to practice before the United States District Court for the District of Maryland, the attorney shall include his or her federal bar number as listed on the Attorney Admission List. (Amended October 15, 2007, effective November 1, 2007.)

Effect of amendments. — The 2007 Order, effective November 1, 2007, in the first sentence added "and, if available, facsimile and email address" and made a related change.

Rule 9011-2. Signing of electronically transmitted pleadings; representations to the court.

(a) **Responsibility for use of login and password.** An attorney or other person who is assigned a court-issued login and password to file documents electronically is responsible for all documents filed using that login and password.

(b) **Signature and certification.** The transmission of a petition, pleading, motion or other paper by electronic means shall constitute both a signature by the attorney or other person responsible for transmitting it that is required by Federal Bankruptcy Rule 9011(a) and a certification within the meaning of Federal Bankruptcy Rule 9011(b). Such transmission shall also constitute a representation by the attorney or other person responsible for an electronic transmission to the court that he or she is in possession of the original petition, pleading, motion or other paper, with all original signatures thereon other than those papers signed solely by the filing user and co-counsel. (Added Dec. 4, 2003, effective Jan. 1, 2004.)

Effect of amendments. — The Summary of Changes to Local Bankruptcy Rules, effective January 1, 2004, states, "This Rule governs signing of electronically transmitted pleadings."

Rule 9011-3. Maintenance and production of original documents.

(a) **Maintenance.** The attorney or other person responsible for an electronic transmission to the court shall maintain the original petition, pleading, motion or other paper bearing original signatures other than that of the electronic filer, for three (3) years after the bankruptcy case is closed.

(b) **Production.** Upon reasonable request by the court or an interested party, the attorney or other person responsible for an electronic filing shall produce for inspection and copying the original petition, pleading, motion, or other paper filed by electronic means, with all original signatures thereon. (Added Dec. 4, 2003, effective Jan. 1, 2004; amended April 27, 2007, effective May 1, 2007.)

Effect of amendments. — The Summary of Changes to Local Bankruptcy Rules, effective January 1, 2004, states, "This Rule requires the person filing by electronic means to retain the paper containing the original signature for a period of three (3) years after the bankruptcy case is closed."

The 2007 amendment substituted "or other paper bearing original signatures other than that of the electronic filer, for three (3) years" for "or other paper filed by electronic means, including all original signatures, for a period ending three (3) years" in (a).

Editor's note. — As to electronic filing of

documents with United States Bankruptcy Court for the District of Maryland, see www.mdb.uscourts.gov.

Rule 9013-1. Motions practice.

(a) **Requirement of written motion.** All motions must be in writing and filed with the court, unless made during a hearing or trial.

(b) **Procedure for motions other than motions for relief from stay and motions to avoid lien.** (1) All motions must state with particularity the grounds therefor and the relief or order sought. Supplementing Local Bankruptcy Rule 9013-3 as to moving parties, responding parties must file with the court, at the time of filing a response, a proposed order stating the requested disposition.

(2) Parties may file with or append to their motion and memorandum, or to their responsive pleading and opposing memorandum, supporting affidavits or documents establishing the elements of entitlement to the relief sought or any defense.

(3) Any responsive pleading and memorandum in opposition to a motion must be filed within fourteen (14) days from the date of service of said motion.

(4) Except as otherwise provided in the Bankruptcy Code, the Federal Bankruptcy Rules, these Rules or by the court, a motion can be decided on the pleadings and memoranda filed.

Rule 9013-2. Briefs and memoranda of law.

A party must file with each motion a brief memorandum of fact and law entitling the movant to the relief claimed or a statement that no memorandum will be filed and that the movant will rely solely upon the motion.

Rule 9013-3. Orders — Proposed.

(a) All requests for relief, except motions for relief from the automatic stay, motions to dismiss or convert, and pleadings initiating adversary proceedings under Federal Bankruptcy Rule 7001, must be accompanied by a proposed order. The proposed order must contain a specific title describing the nature and effect of the order. The names and addresses of all counsel or other parties in interest who should receive copies of the order shall be set forth in the lower left-hand corner of the final page of the proposed order or carried over to another page. The chapter of the case shall be stated in the caption.

(b) Proposed orders for motions for relief from the automatic stay and responses thereto should be submitted to the court upon the earlier of:

(1) A consent being reached by all parties; or,

(2) After the conclusion of the hearing on the motion.

(c) When a proposed order is submitted to the court, copies shall be simultaneously transmitted to all other parties to the matter. (Amended April 27, 2007, effective May 1, 2007.)

Effect of amendments. — The Summary of Changes to Local Bankruptcy Rules, effective January 1, 2004, states, "This Rule has been modified so as to eliminate the requirement for filing the Order for Relief from Stay with the Motion for Relief from Stay."

The 2007 amendment rewrote (c).

Rule 9013-4. Certificate of service.

(a) Any required certificate of service for a pleading, notice, objection or other paper must be in compliance with Federal Rule of Civil Procedure 5 and applicable provisions of the Federal Bankruptcy Rules. Pursuant to Federal Bankruptcy Rules 5005(a)(2) and 7005, service pursuant to the ECF Guidelines also constitutes valid service.

(b) The certificate shall be placed at the end of the item served and endorsed by an attorney of record, the party's authorized agent, or by a party if not represented by an attorney.

(c) The certificate must state:

(1) the date and method of service;

(2) the names and addresses of the persons served; and

(3) if persons are served in a representative capacity, the parties whom they represent. (Amended Dec. 4, 2003, effective Jan. 1, 2004.)

Rule 9013-5. Responsibility for proper service.

(a) It is the obligation of an attorney or party that files a pleading to determine every party with a cognizable interest in the pleading that should receive a copy and the current address of each. A certificate of service signed by an attorney, by an attorney's authorized agent or by a party constitutes a representation to the court that all parties entitled to service have been included and have been served properly. Violation of this paragraph shall be subject to an appropriate sanction.

(b) It is the obligation of an attorney or party filing a motion to review any notice of a hearing on that motion prepared by the Clerk and to communicate forthwith to the Clerk any deficiency in the notice and any omission in the list of parties receiving notice. (Added Dec. 4, 2003, effective Jan. 1, 2004.)

Rule 9014-1. Discovery.

The initial disclosures required by Federal Bankruptcy Rule 7026(a) are not applicable to contested matters, unless the court directs otherwise.

Rule 9014-2. Default and dismissal for non-prosecution.

Local Bankruptcy Rule 7055-1 applies in contested matters.

Rule 9015-1. Time for filing consent to have jury trial conducted by bankruptcy judge.

A statement of consent to have a jury trial conducted by a bankruptcy judge under 28 U.S.C. § 157(e) must be filed before the conclusion of the initial pretrial conference.

Rule 9018-1. Privacy policy and transcript redaction procedures.
Transferred.

Cross references. — As to privacy policy and transcript redaction procedures, see Rule 9037-1 of the Local Bankruptcy Rules for the District of Maryland.

Editor's note. — The December 1, 2009, amendment redesignated this Rule as Rule 9037-1.

Rule 9019-1. Settlements and agreed orders.

(a) **Order.** Subject to the requirements of Federal Bankruptcy Rules 2002(a)(3), 4001(d), and 9019, when the court is advised by the moving party that an adversary proceeding or contested matter has been settled, the court can enter an order dismissing the adversary proceeding or contested matter and providing for the payment of costs. Such an order of dismissal will be without prejudice to the right of a party to move for good cause to reopen the proceeding or matter within a reasonable time after settlement should have occurred if the settlement is not consummated. Alternatively, the court, upon notification by counsel that a proceeding or matter has been settled, can require counsel to submit, within fourteen (14) days, a proposed order providing for the settlement, in default of which the court can enter judgment or other appropriate order.

(b) **Complete disposition.** An order entered pursuant to this Rule has the effect of noting the settlement of the entire adversary proceeding or contested matter, including all claims, counterclaims, third-party claims, and cross-claims, unless otherwise stated.

(c) In adversary proceedings, motions for approval of settlements must be filed in both the main case and the adversary case. (Amended April 27, 2007, effective May 1, 2007; amended effective December 1, 2009.)

Effect of amendments. — The 2007 amendment added (c).

The 2009 amendment substituted "fourteen (14) days" for "ten (10) days" in the last sentence of (a); and rewrote (c).

Rule 9019-2. Alternative dispute resolution.

A Bankruptcy Dispute Resolution Program ("BDRP") will be maintained and available to facilitate the resolution of disputes. The BDRP is to operate in such a way as to allow the participants to use a variety of alternative dispute resolution methods. These methods may include but are not limited to: mediation, negotiation, early neutral evaluation and settlement facilitation. The specific method or methods employed will be those that are appropriate, as determined by the Resolution Advocate and the parties.

(a) **Cases eligible for inclusion in the BDRP.** All controversies arising in an adversary proceeding, contested matter, or other dispute in a bankruptcy case, will be eligible for referral to the BDRP except:

(1) Employment and compensation of professionals;

(2) Compensation of trustees and examiners;

(3) Objections to discharge under 11 U.S.C. § 727, except where such objections are joined with disputes over dischargeability of debts under 11 U.S.C. § 523; and

(4) Matters involving contempt or other types of sanctions.

(b) **Panel of resolution advocates.** The court shall will maintain a panel of professionals (the "Panel") who have volunteered to serve as Resolution Advocates to assist in resolution of matters referred to the BDRP.

(1) An application to serve as a member of the Panel (see Local Bankruptcy Form J-1) must be submitted to the BDRP Administrator by the deadlines established by the court each year.

(2) In order to qualify for service as a Resolution Advocate, each applicant must certify that the applicant is willing; (A) to serve as a Resolution Advocate for a minimum of one year; and (B) to evaluate or mediate *pro bono* matters not more often than once in six (6) months, subject only to unavailability due to conflicts, personal or professional commitments, or other matters that would make service inappropriate;

(3) The Applicant may indicate the Applicant's availability to act as a Compensated Resolution Advocate in addition to the unpaid services described in paragraph (2) above. The Applicant should state the rates the Applicant would charge for such services;

(4) The court may limit panel membership to keep the Panel at an appropriate size and to ensure that the Panel is comprised of individuals with broad-based experience, superior skills and qualifications.

(c) **Administration of the BDRP.** A judge of this court will be appointed by the Chief Judge to serve as the BDRP Administrator. The BDRP Administrator will be aided by a staff member of the court, who will collect applications, maintain the roster of the Panel, track and compile results of the BDRP, and handle such other administrative duties as are necessary.

(d) **Assignment to dispute resolution.** (1) If requested in writing by the parties, a contested matter, adversary proceeding, or other dispute (hereinafter collectively referred to as "Matter" or "Matters") may be assigned to the BDRP by order of the court.

(2) While as a general rule participation in the BDRP is voluntary, any judge, acting *sua sponte* or on the request of a party, may designate specific Matters for inclusion in the program.

(3) If a Matter is assigned to the BDRP, the parties will be presented with the order assigning the Matter to the BDRP and a current roster of the Panel. The parties will be given the opportunity to confer and designate a mutually acceptable Resolution Advocate as well as an alternate Resolution Advocate.

(4) With the consent of the judge, the parties may select a Resolution Advocate who is not a member of the Panel, who shall be subject to the applicable provisions of this Rule.

(5) If the parties cannot agree, or if the judge deems selection by the court to be appropriate, the judge will select a Resolution Advocate.

(6) The order assigning a Matter to the BDRP will be Local Bankruptcy Form J-2(a). The Order Appointing Resolution Advocate will be Local Bankruptcy Form J-2(b). The original orders will be docketed and retained in the case or adversary proceeding file and copies mailed by the party so designated by the judge to the assigned Resolution Advocate, the alternate Resolution Advocate, the BDRP Administrator's staff assistant and to all parties with a cognizable interest in the dispute. Assignment to the BDRP does not alter or affect any time limits, deadlines, scheduling matters or orders in any adversary proceeding, contested matter or other proceeding, unless specifically ordered by the court.

(7) A Resolution Advocate must promptly determine all conflicts or potential conflicts in the same manner as under the applicable rules pertaining to the Resolution Advocate's profession. If the Resolution Advocate's firm has represented one or more of the parties, the Resolution Advocate must promptly disclose that circumstance to all parties in writing. A party who believes that the assigned Resolution Advocate has a conflict of interest may promptly bring that matter to the attention of the Resolution Advocate. If the Resolution Advocate does not withdraw from the assignment, the matter must be brought to the attention of the court by the Resolution Advocate or any party.

(e) **Dispute resolution procedures.** (1) Within seven (7) days of notification of appointment, the Resolution Advocate shall:

(A) give notice to the parties of the time and place for the BDRP Conference. The conference will commence not later than sixty (60) days following the date of appointment of the Resolution Advocate unless the Order of Appointment provides a different time period in which to commence the BDRP Conference, and which will be held in a suitable neutral setting, such as the office of the Resolution Advocate. The Resolution Advocate will circulate for signature the Confidentiality Agreement, Local Bankruptcy Form J-3 at this conference; or

(B) if the Resolution Advocate is not available to serve in the Matter, notify the parties, the alternate Resolution Advocate, and the BDRP Administrator's staff assistant of that unavailability. The alternate Resolution Advocate will thereafter serve as the Resolution Advocate. Upon written stipulation between the Resolution Advocate and the parties, the BDRP Conference may be continued for a period not to exceed thirty (30) days.

(2) Unless modified by the Resolution Advocate, no later than fourteen (14) days prior to the date of the BDRP Conference, each party must submit a written BDRP Statement directly to the Resolution Advocate. The plaintiff or movant will provide the Resolution Advocate with copies of the complaint or motion and the answer or opposition with respect to the contested matter along with the BDRP Statement. For good cause, the judge may order a different schedule. The Resolution Advocate must keep a BDRP Statement confidential and not disclose its contents to anyone without express written consent of the party submitting it.

(3) Such statements will not exceed ten (10) pages (not counting exhibits and attachments). While such statements may include any information that would be useful, they must:

(A) identify the person(s), in addition to counsel, who will attend the session as representative of the party with decision making authority;

(B) describe briefly the substance of the dispute;

(C) address whether there are legal or factual issues whose early resolution might appreciably reduce the scope of the dispute or contribute significantly to settlement;

(D) identify the discovery that could contribute most to equipping the parties for meaningful discussions;

(E) set forth the history of past settlement discussions, including disclosure of prior and any presently outstanding offers and demands;

(F) make an estimate of the cost and time to be expended for further discovery, pretrial motions, expert witnesses and trial; and

(G) indicate presently scheduled dates for further status conferences, pre-trial conferences, trial or otherwise.

(4) Parties may identify in the BDRP Statements persons connected to a party opponent (including a representative of a party opponent's insurance carrier) whose presence at the BDRP Conference would improve substantially the prospects for making the session productive; the fact that a person has been so identified, will not, by itself, result in an order compelling that person to attend the BDRP Conference. A separate motion and court order are required.

(5) Parties must attach to their written BDRP Statements copies of documents out of which the dispute has arisen, e.g., contracts and those documents whose availability would materially advance the purposes of the BDRP Conference.

(6) The BDRP Statements shall not be filed. The court shall not have access to them.

(7) Counsel for each party who is primarily responsible for the Matter (or the party who is proceeding without counsel) will personally attend the BDRP Conference and any adjourned sessions of that conference. Counsel for each party must come prepared to discuss resolution of the Matter in detail and in good faith.

(8) All individual parties, and representatives with authority to negotiate and to settle the Matter on behalf of parties other than individuals, shall attend the BDRP Conference in person, unless excused by the Resolution Advocate for cause. A party or lawyer who is excused from appearing in person at the BDRP Conference may be required to participate by telephone.

(9) The Resolution Advocate may direct parties to attend a second BDRP Conference, if in the judgment of the Resolution Advocate, a subsequent mediation session would promote resolution of the dispute.

(10) Willful failure to attend the BDRP Conference, or other violations of this Rule, shall be reported to the court by the Resolution Advocate and may result in the imposition of sanctions by the court.

(11)(A) All written and oral communications made in connection with or during any BDRP Conference, including the BRRP Statements, will be subject to all protections afforded by Federal Rules of Evidence 408. No such communication may be used in any present or future proceeding for any purpose. Nevertheless, if all of the parties to the BDRP and the Resolution Advocate agree in writing, such communications may be disclosed. Notwithstanding the foregoing, this paragraph 11(A) does not require the exclusion of any evidence:

(i) otherwise discoverable, merely because it is presented in the course of a BDRP Conference; or

(ii) offered for another purpose, such as providing bias or prejudice of a witness, negativing a contention of undue delay, or proving an effort to obstruct a criminal investigation or prosecution.

(B) Nothing in this section (e) will be construed to prevent parties, counsel or Resolution Advocates from responding in absolute confidentiality, to inquiries or surveys by persons authorized by this court to evaluate the BDRP. Nor will anything in this section be construed to prohibit parties from entering into written agreements resolving some or all of the Matter or entering or filing procedural or factual stipulations based on suggestions or agreements made in connection with a BDRP Conference.

(12) If the Resolution Advocate makes any oral or written suggestions as to the advisability of a change in any party's position with respect to settlement, the attorney for that party must promptly transmit that suggestion to the client.

(13) The Resolution Advocate has no obligation to make any written comments or recommendations, but may, as a matter of discretion, provide the attorneys for the parties with a written settlement recommendation memorandum. No copy of any such memorandum will be filed with the clerk or made available in whole or in part, directly or indirectly, to the court.

(14) The BDRP Conference will proceed informally. Rules of evidence do not apply. There will be no formal examination or cross-examination of witnesses. Where necessary, the Resolution Advocate may conduct continued BDRP Conferences after the initial session. As appropriate, the Resolution Advocate may:

(A) permit each party (through counsel or otherwise) to make an oral presentation of its position;

(B) help the parties identify areas of agreement and, where feasible, enter stipulations;

(C) assess the relative strengths and weaknesses of the parties' contentions and evidence, and explain as carefully as possible the reasoning of the Resolution Advocate that supports these assessments;

(D) assist the parties, through separate consultation or otherwise, in settling the dispute;

(E) estimate, where feasible, the likelihood of liability and the dollar range of damages;

(F) help the parties devise a plan for sharing the important information and/or conducting the key discovery that will equip them as expeditiously as possible to participate in meaningful settlement discussions or to posture the case for disposition by other means; and

(G) determine whether some form of follow-up to the conference would contribute to the case development process or to settlement.

(f) **Procedure upon completion of dispute resolution session.** Upon the conclusion of the BDRP Conference, the following procedure will be followed:

(1) If the parties have reached an agreement regarding the disposition of the Matter, the parties, with the advice of Resolution Advocate, will determine who will prepare the writing to dispose of the Matter, and they may continue the BDRP Conference to a date convenient to all parties and the Resolution Advocate as necessary. Where required by provisions of the Bankruptcy Code or other applicable law, they must promptly submit the fully executed stipulation to the court for approval. Where court approval is not required, the written agreement disposing of the matter will be enforceable pursuant to applicable law;

(2) The Resolution Advocate must file with the court and serve on the parties and the BDRP Administrator's staff assistant, within fourteen (14) days, Local Bankruptcy Form J-4, showing whether there has been compliance with the BDRP Conference requirements of this Rule, and whether or not a settlement has been reached. Regardless of the outcome of the BDRP Conference, the Resolution Advocate will *not* provide the court with any details of the substance of the conference; and

(3) In order to assist the BDRP Administrator in compiling useful data to evaluate the BDRP, and to aid the court in assessing the efforts of the members of the Panel, the Resolution Advocate will provide the BDRP Administrator's staff assistant with an estimate of the number of hours spent in the BDRP Conference and otherwise on the matter, which report must be on Local Bankruptcy Form J-5.

(g) **Compensated resolution advocacy.** In addition to serving as a Resolution Advocate on a *pro bono* basis, a panel member may act as a Compensated Resolution Advocate ("CRA") in other matters.

(1) The CRA will be appointed as set forth above in this Rule, but the appointing Order will set forth the terms of the CRA's engagement.

(2) If the CRA is to receive compensation from the bankruptcy estate,

(A) a notice shall be filed setting forth the identity of the Resolution Advocate (whether or not on the panel) and the terms and conditions of compensation (including hourly rate) with a right to object/comment on such terms and conditions, subject to such time limitations as the judge deems reasonable under the circumstances;

(B) if the proposed compensation to the Resolution Advocate is $3,000.00 or less, there is no need for further court order to authorize payment to the Resolution Advocate;

(C) if the proposed compensation to the Resolution Advocate is proposed to be more than $3,000.00, a notice for an award of final compensation shall be filed by or on behalf of the Resolution Advocate and served as an application under Bankruptcy Rule 2002(a)(6) with an opportunity for parties to object/comment within twenty-one (21) days after the filing of the notice; however, the inability of the BDRP to result in a settlement/stipulation shall not be a factor to be used in awarding less compensation than would be allowed based on an application of the terms and conditions of compensation upon retention of the Resolution Advocate; and

(D) the estate's share of such compensation shall be an administrative claim against the estate.

(3) Unless the appointing order provides for compensation solely by the bankruptcy estate, no CRA will be appointed without the consent of all parties to the controversy submitted to the BDRP. (Amended Dec. 4, 2003, effective Jan. 1, 2004; amended effective December 1, 2009; amended Aug. 24, 2011, effective Sept. 1, 2011.)

Effect of amendments. — The 2009 amendment substitutued "BDRP Conference" and "BDRP Statement" and variants throughout the Rule; in (d)(7), substituted "that matter" for "the matter"; deleted "calendar" before "days" in the introductory language of (e), (e)(A), and (f)(2); substituted "fourteen (14) days" for "eight (8) days" and deleted "of notification" before "prior" in the first sentence of (e)(2); transferred "and" from the end of (e)(3)(F) to the end of (e)(3)(G); substituted "who is" for "where" in the parenthetical in (e)(7); in the first sentence of (f)(2) substituted "fourteen (14) calendar days" for "ten (10) days"; and in (g)(2)(C) substituted "twenty-one (21) days" for "twenty (20) days"; and made minor stylistic changes.

The 2011 amendment substituted "without counsel" for "pro se" in the first sentence of (e)(7).

Rule 9029-1. Local Bankruptcy Rules — General.

Any judge of this court may suspend or modify a requirement or provision of any of these Rules in a particular case, adversary proceeding or contested matter on the court's own motion or on motion of a party. (Amended effective December 1, 2009.)

Effect of amendments. — The 2009 amendment substituted "may suspend" for "can suspend."

Rule 9033-1. Proposed findings of fact and conclusions of law in non-core proceeding.

When a party has objected to proposed findings or conclusions pursuant to Federal Bankruptcy Rule 9033(b), for the purpose of preparing the record and identifying the issues for the District Court, the parties will follow the procedures set forth in Federal Bankruptcy Rule 8006 by treating the objection(s) as an appeal. The bankruptcy judge may order the designated extract supplemented.

Rule 9036-1. Notice by electronic transmission.

In addition to service of notice by electronic transmission or by first-class mail, notice may be given by hand-delivery or facsimile transmission, except that the Clerk shall not accept for filing any facsimile transmission. All notices given by facsimile transmission shall be followed by hard copy notice with original signature mailed by the next business day. (Amended December 4, 2003, effective January 1, 2004; amended October 15, 2007, effective November 1, 2007.)

Effect of amendments. — The 2007 Order, effective November 1, 2007, deleted (b) to conform with Federal Rule 9036 as amended in 2005 with related changes, and substituted "service of notice by electronic transmission or by first-class mail" for "methods of notice available under the Federal Bankruptcy Rules".

Rule 9037-1. Privacy policy and transcript redaction procedures.

(a) **Privacy Policy.** The Judicial Conference of the United States has adopted a privacy policy to restrict the publication of certain personal data in documents filed with the court. The policy requires limiting social security and financial account numbers to the last four digits, using only initials for the names of minor children, and limiting dates of birth to the year. If such information is elicited during testimony in court proceedings, it will become available to the public when the official transcript in filed with the court unless, and until, it is redacted. The better practice is to avoid introducing this information into the record in the first place either through testimony or in exhibits. Counsel and self-represented litigants are advised to take this into account when questioning witnesses or making other statements in court or introducing exhibits into evidence. If a restricted item is mentioned or introduced in court, parties may ask to have it stricken from the record or partially redacted to conform to the privacy policy or the court may do so on its own motion.

(b) **Transcript redaction procedures.** Upon the receipt of a transcript, the Clerk will serve a Notice of Requirement to Review Transcript on all parties to the hearing. A filed transcript will be available at the Clerk's office for inspection only for a period of ninety (90) days after it is filed. During the ninety (90) day period, a copy of the transcript may be obtained from the transcriber at the rate established by the Judicial Conference, the transcript will be available within the court for internal use, and an attorney who obtains the transcript from the transcriber may obtain remote electronic access to the transcript via the court's CM/ECF system for purposes of creating hyperlinks to the transcript in court filings and for other purposes. Counsel, or self-represented litigants, will have seven (7) days from the date of filing of the transcript to file a Notice of Intent to Request Redaction with the court, stating an intention to review the transcript to determine whether to request redaction of sensitive private information before the transcript is made electronically available to the public. A copy of the notice must be served upon the transcriber. A party will have twenty-one (21) days from the date of the filing of the transcript to file a Request for Redaction of Transcript with the Court (which will be a private, restricted event) and send a copy to the transcriber, listing the entries by page and line where personal data appears that should be redacted. The deadline for filing the redacted version of the transcript is thirty-one (31) days from the filing date of the transcript. At the end of the ninety (90) day restriction period, the redacted version will be made available via remote electronic access and at the public terminals in the Clerk's office for viewing and printing. The unredacted version of the transcript will not be available via remote electronic access or at the Clerk's office upon the filing of the redacted transcript; it shall be maintained as a private, restricted event. An attorney who purchases the transcript during the ninety (90) day restricted period will be given remote electronic access to the transcript and any redacted version filed. (Added October 15, 2007, effective November 1, 2007; November 10, 2008, effective December 1, 2008; amended effective December 1, 2009; amended Aug. 24, 2011, effective Sept. 1, 2011.)

Effect of amendments. — The 2008 Order, dated November 10, 2008, effective December 1, 2008, corrected capitalization in the second and third sentences of (a); and in (b) substituted "seven (7) business days" for "5 business days" in the first sentence, and "twenty-one days" for "21 days" in the last sentence.

The 2009 amendment rewrote (b).

The 2011 amendment substituted "self-represented" for "pro se" in the fifth sentence of (a) and in the fourth sentence of (b).

Rule 9070-1. Exhibits.

(a) **Pending appeal.** From the conclusion of a hearing or trial to the expiration of the time within which to file a notice of appeal or, in the event that an appeal is taken, until the transmission of the record to the District Court, the Clerk will retain all documentary exhibits except ones of unusual bulk or weight. Documents of unusual bulk or weight and all non-documentary exhibits will remain in the custody of the attorney presenting them, who (1) will permit inspection of them by counsel for another party for the purpose of preparing the record on appeal; (2) will be responsible for their safekeeping; and (3) if requested, will send them to the appellate court.

(b) **Upon termination of action.** Upon the closing of a contested matter or adversary proceeding, the Clerk will send a notice to all counsel advising counsel to remove, within thirty (30) days, all trial and hearing exhibits and all sealed materials that counsel presented at any time during the pendency of the contested matter or adversary proceeding. If a party fails to retrieve exhibits within thirty (30) days, the exhibits will be discarded by the Clerk.

APPENDIX A. LOCAL BANKRUPTCY FORMS (LBF).

LBF-A: Notice of Filing of Case in Bankruptcy Court.

IN THE CIRCUIT COURT FOR
_____ COUNTY, MARYLAND

IN RE: :
                                          :
                                          :
         vs.   :   Civil No. _____
                                          :
                                          :

NOTICE OF FILING OF CASE IN BANKRUPTCY COURT

You are hereby notified of the filing of a case in the _____ Division of the United States Bankruptcy Court for the District of Maryland for the following debtor(s): _____ . The bankruptcy case no. is _____ . It is a case under Chapter _____ filed on _____ . The case is now pending.

Attorney for Debtor(s)	**OR**	Debtor(s), if without counsel
Name: _____		Name: _____
Address: _____		Address: _____
_____		_____
_____		_____
Tel. No. _____		Tel. No. _____

OR

Attorney for Petitioning Creditor(s) _____
Address: _____
Tel. No. _____
Petitioning Creditor(s) _____
_____
_____

*   *   *   *   *   *

I hereby certify that copies of the foregoing Notice of Filing of Bankruptcy Case were mailed this _____ day of _____, 20___, to the Judge of this court assigned this case and to the following counsel of record:

_____
Signature of Affiant

LBF-B: Notice of Motion for Relief from Stay and Hearing Thereon.

IN THE UNITED STATES BANKRUPTCY COURT
FOR THEDISTRICT OF MARYLAND AT _____ .

IN RE: :
                                          :   Case No. _____
                                          :   Chapter _____
                Debtor(s)   :
                                          :
                                          :
                Movant(s)   :
        vs.   :
                                          :
                                          :
                Respondent(s)   :

**NOTICE OF MOTION FOR RELIEF FROM STAY
AND HEARING THEREON**

_____ has filed papers with the court
seeking relief from the automatic stay of 11 U.S.C. § 362(a) to enable it to
proceed to _____ . Your rights may be
affected. You should read these papers carefully and discuss them with your
lawyer. (If you do not have a lawyer, you may wish to consult one.)

If you do not want the court to grant the motion for relief from stay, or if you
want the court to consider your views on the motion, then by
_____ * you or your lawyer must file a written response with
the Clerk of the Bankruptcy Court explaining your position and mail a copy to:

[Movant's attorney's name and address, or Movant's name
if without counsel]

[names and addresses of others to be served]

If you mail rather than deliver, your response to the Clerk of the Bankruptcy
Court for filing, you must mail it early enough so that the court will receive it
by the date stated above.

The hearing is scheduled for _____, at _____, ** in Courtroom
_____, United States Bankruptcy Court, _____ .

If you or your lawyer do not take these steps by the deadline, the court may
find that you do not oppose the relief sought in the motion and may grant or
otherwise dispose of the motion before the scheduled hearing date.

DATE: _____ ***   _____
                                Signature (Attorney or Movant if without
                                counsel)
                                Telephone No. _____

1553

[*]   Insert a date that is **14 days** after the date of this notice (service), plus any additional time provided by Federal Bankruptcy Rules 9006(a) and (f). The Court Hearing Scheduler (CHS) Program on the court's website and CM/ECF filing screen for this type of motion will compute the date that an objection is due. Use the date computed.

[**]   Insert a date and time from the list of dates available for the judge assigned to the case that is more than **21 days** after the date of this notice.

[***] Insert the date notice served.

CERTIFICATE OF SERVICE

I certify that on the _____ day of _____, 20____, copies of the notice and motion for relief from stay were served upon the party (parties) whose name(s) and address(es) are listed below:

(1)   (2)

(3)   (4)

(5)   (6)

_____
Signature

_____
Print Name

NOTE: Service must be made pursuant to Federal Bankruptcy Rule 7004

LBF-C: Notice of Debtor(s)' Motion to Avoid Lien Pursuant to 11 U.S.C. § 522(f) and Hearing Thereon.

_____

IN THE UNITED STATES BANKRUPTCY COURT
FOR THE DISTRICT OF MARYLAND AT _____

IN RE: :
                                  :   Case No. _____
                                  :   Chapter _____
            Debtor(s)   :
                                  :
                                  :
            Movant(s)   :

vs.   :
                                           :
                                           :
          Respondent   :
_____   :

NOTICE OF DEBTOR(S)' MOTION
TO AVOID LIEN PURSUANT TO 11 U.S.C. § 522(f)
AND HEARING THEREON

A motion was filed on behalf of the debtor(s) to avoid a lien held by
_____. Your rights may be affected. You
should read these papers carefully and discuss them with your lawyer. If you
do not have a lawyer, you may wish to consult one. A copy of the motion is
attached.

If you do not want the court to grant the motion avoiding the lien, or if you
want the court to consider your views on the motion, then by
_____ * you or your lawyer must file with the Clerk of the
Bankruptcy Court a response to the motion explaining your position and mail
a copy of the response to:

[Movant's attorney's name and address, or Movant's name and address if
without counsel]

If you mail, rather than deliver, your response to the Clerk of the Court for
filing, you must mail it early enough so that the court will receive it by the date
stated above.

If you file a timely response to the motion, the hearing on the motion will
take place on _____, at _____, ** in Courtroom _____, United States
Bankruptcy Court, _____.

If you or your lawyer do not file and serve a timely response to the motion,
the court may find that you do not oppose the relief sought in the motion and
may grant or otherwise dispose of the motion before the scheduled hearing
date.

DATE: _____ ***   _____
                                   Signature (Attorney or Movant if without
                                   counsel)
                                   Telephone No. _____

[*]   Insert a date that is at least **28 days** after the date this notice is mailed,
      plus any additional time provided by Federal Bankruptcy Rules 9006(a)
      and (f). The Court Hearing Scheduler (CHS) Program on the court's
      website and CM/ECF filing screen for this type of motion will compute
      the date that an objection is due. Use the date computed.
[**] Insert a date and time from the list of dates available for the judge
      assigned to the case that is at least **49 days** after the date of this notice.
[***] Insert the date notice was served.

CERTIFICATE OF SERVICE

I certify that on the _____ day of _____, 20_____, copies of the notice and motion to avoid lien were served upon the Respondent(s) whose name(s) and address(es) are set forth below.

(1)   (2)

(3)   (4)

(5)   (6)

_____
Signature

_____
Print Name

NOTE: Service must be made pursuant to Federal Bankruptcy Rule 7004 and Local Bankruptcy Rule 4003-2.

LBF-D: Financial Statement.

[Deleted.]

Editor's note. — The 2007 Order, effective November 1, 2007, deleted Form D.

LBF-E: Application for Supplemental Allowance of Attorney's Fees.

IN THE UNITED STATES BANKRUPTCY COURT
FOR THE DISTRICT OF MARYLAND

In re: *
                                *
                                *   Case No. _____
                                *   Chapter 13
                Debtor   *

APPLICATION FOR SUPPLEMENTAL ALLOWANCE OF ATTORNEY'S FEES

NOW COMES _____, Counsel to the Debtor(s), (hereinafter "Applicant") who makes this request for the allowance of attorney's fees for services rendered for the benefit of the Debtor and the bankruptcy estate, and in support thereof states as follows:

1. Applicant has served as counsel to the Debtor throughout the pendency of the Chapter 13 proceedings.

2. The fees sought in this application result from services rendered for or on behalf of the Debtor.

3. The fees sought to be paid to Applicant result from services rendered or required to be rendered for a matter which was not contemplated or included in the initial retainer agreement as evidenced by the Rule 2016(b) Disclosure Statement filed at the beginning of this case.

4. The services for which the additional fees are now sought by Applicant are described in the attached Supplemental 2016(b), which has been filed with the Court and is included herein by reference.

5. The services for which the additional fees are now sought by Applicant are reasonable and necessary services that benefit the Estate for the following reasons: _____.

6. In support of this Application, Applicant has attached relevant time records that identify the professionals who worked on this case, their hourly rates, the tasks performed, and the amount of time spent on each such task.

7. Prior to the filing of this Application, Applicant has been paid a total of $_____ in fees and $_____ in expenses in this case. Of those amounts, Applicant has received $_____ in fees and $_____ in expenses in distributions from the Trustee and $_____ in fees and $_____ in expenses in payments from the Debtor or on Debtor's behalf.

8. Applicant respectfully submits and hereby affirms to the Court that the fees and costs requested by this application were both reasonable and necessary.

9. Further, that the fees charged for the services described are reasonable based upon the customary fees charged and generally approved by this Court for services of this nature provided by comparably skilled professionals.

10. No agreement or understanding exists between Applicant and any other person for the division or sharing of compensation for services rendered or costs advanced in connection with Applicant's representation of the Debtor.

11. The Debtor(s) have requested that the services be provided by Counsel and that this Court allow the payment of the requested attorney's fees and, if necessary, approve the payment of the fees as an administrative expense through the Chapter 13 Plan.

12. Applicant avers the approval of the requested fees:
    ☐ will not affect distribution to creditors under the plan
    ☐ will affect distribution to creditors under the plan in the following manner:

_____

_____

WHEREFORE, Applicant prays that this Court approve the Attorney's fees and costs prayed for herein in the amount of $ _____, to be paid by the Debtor or to be paid by the Chapter 13 Trustee as an administrative expense through the Chapter 13 Plan.

Respectfully submitted,

/s/Attorney _____

                                    Attorney, Esquire
                                    Firm, LLC
                                    Address
                                    Address
                                    Address
                                    Telephone

                          Certificate of Service

    I hereby certify that the foregoing Application for Supplemental Allowance of Attorney's Fees has been mailed and/or electronically transmitted this _____ day of _____, 20___ to the (Debtor w/address), (Trustee w/address) and the following:

                                    /s/Attorney _____
                                    Attorney, Esquire

LBF-E-1: Notice of Application for Supplemental Allowance of Attorney's Fees.

              IN THE UNITED STATES BANKRUPTCY COURT
                 FOR THE DISTRICT OF MARYLAND

In re: *
                                          *
                                          *   Case No. _____
                                          *   Chapter 13
                    Debtor   *

NOTICE OF APPLICATION FOR SUPPLEMENTAL ALLOWANCE OF ATTORNEY'S FEES

    Pursuant to Local Bankruptcy Rule 2002-1 of the Maryland Bankruptcy Rules, Notice is hereby given that:

    1. An Application for Allowance of Attorney's Fees has been filed by the Debtor(s)' Counsel, (hereafter "Applicant").

    2. The Application seeks fees of $_____ for representation in legal matters made necessary by events which have occurred during the Chapter 13 proceedings.

    3. Pursuant to the Local Bankruptcy Rules the Applicant has filed a Supplemental 2016(b) Disclosure Statement along with the Application describing the services rendered on behalf of the Debtor.

    4. If the Court approves the Application, the Fees approved may be paid by the Chapter 13 Trustee as an administrative expense. Applicant avers the approval of the requested fees:

    ☐ will not affect distribution to creditors under the plan

    ☐ will affect distribution to creditors under the plan in the following manner:

_____

_____ .

5. Any objection to the Application must be filed within 21 days of the date of the Application with the Clerk, U.S. Bankruptcy Court for the District of Maryland, _____, with a copy sent to the undersigned Counsel, the Chapter 13 Trustee, and shall state the factual and legal grounds on which it is based.

6. The Application may be approved without further Order or Notice if no timely objection is filed, and the Court, in its discretion, may conduct a hearing or determine the matter without a hearing regardless of whether an objection is filed.

7. Parties in interest with questions may contact the undersigned.

Date of Notice _____, 20____

Respectfully submitted,

/s/Attorney _____
Attorney, Esquire
Firm, LLC
Address
Address
Address
Telephone

Certificate of Service

I hereby certify that the foregoing Notice of Application for Supplemental Allowance of Attorney's Fees has been mailed and/or electronically transmitted this _____ day of _____, 20____ to the (Debtor w/address), (Trustee w/address), all creditors on the mailing matrix and to the following:

/s/Attorney _____
Attorney, Esquire

LBF-E-2: Supplemental Disclosure of Compensation of Attorney for Debtor.

IN THE UNITED STATES BANKRUPTCY COURT
FOR THE DISTRICT OF MARYLAND

IN RE:

Debtor

*	
*	
*	Case No. _____
*	
*	Chapter _____

SUPPLEMENTAL DISCLOSURE OF COMPENSATION OF ATTORNEY FOR DEBTOR

1. Pursuant to 11 U.S.C. § 329(a) and Federal Bankruptcy Rule 2016(b), I certify that I am the attorney for the above-named debtor(s) and that

compensation paid, or agreed to be paid, to me after one year before the filing of the petition in bankruptcy for services rendered or to be rendered on behalf of the debtor(s) in contemplation of or in connection with the bankruptcy case in addition to any amounts already disclosed is as follows:

For legal services, I have agreed to accept ....$_____

Prior to the filing of this statement I have received ....$_____

Balance Due ....$_____

2. The source of the compensation paid to me was:

☐ Debtor   ☐ Other (specify):

3. The source of compensation to be paid to me is:

☐ Debtor   ☐ Other (specify):

4. ☐ I have not agreed to share the above-disclosed compensation with any other person unless they are members and associates of my law firm.

☐ I have agreed to share the above-disclosed compensation with another person or persons who are not members or associates of my law firm. A copy of the agreement, together with a list of the names of the people sharing in the compensation, is attached.

5. Since the filing of any prior 2016(b) statement in this case, counsel has agreed to perform the following additional services for the supplemental fees identified above:

_____

_____

6. By agreement with the debtor(s), the above-disclosed fee does not include the following services:

CERTIFICATION

I certify that the foregoing is a complete statement of any agreement or arrangement for payment to me for representation of the debtor(s) in this bankruptcy proceedings.

Date: _____   _____

                               Signature of Attorney

                               _____

                               Name of law firm

LBF-F: Motion for Admission Pro Hac Vice.

IN UNITED STATES BANKRUPTCY COURT
FOR THE DISTRICT OF MARYLAND
at _____

*

_____   *   Case No. _____

          Plaintiff(s),   *

v.   *

                              *

                              *   Adversary No. _____

                              *

_____   *

          Defendant(s).   *

MOTION FOR ADMISSION PRO HAC VICE

Pursuant to Local Bankruptcy Rule 9010-3(b) of this Court, and Local Rule 101.1(b) of the U.S. District Court for the District of Maryland, _____, Esquire, a member in good standing of the bar of this court, moves the admission of _____, Esquire, to appear _pro hac vice_ in the captioned proceeding as counsel for _____ _____.

Movant and the proposed admittee respectfully certify as follows:

1) The proposed admittee is not a member of the Bar of Maryland.

2) The proposed admittee is a member in good standing of the bar(s) of the following State and/or United States Courts:

State Court & Date of Admission   U.S. Court & Date of Admission

_____   _____

_____   _____

_____   _____

3) During the twelve (12) months immediately preceding the filing of this motion, the proposed admittee has been admitted _pro hac vice_ in this Court _____ times.

4) The proposed admittee has never been disbarred, suspended, or denied admission to practice law in any jurisdiction. (NOTE: If the proposed admittee has been disbarred, suspended, or denied admission to practice law in any jurisdiction, then he/she must submit a statement fully explaining all relevant facts.)

5) The proposed admittee is familiar with the Federal Bankruptcy Rules, the Local Bankruptcy Rules, the Federal Rules of Evidence, and the Maryland Lawyers' Rules of Professional Conduct, and understands that he/she shall be subject to the disciplinary jurisdiction of this court.

6) Co-counsel for the proposed admittee in this proceeding will be the undersigned or _____, Esquire, who has been formally admitted to the bar of the U.S. District Court for the District of Maryland.

7) It is understood that admission _pro hac vice_ does not constitute formal admission to the bar of the U.S. District Court for the District of Maryland.

8) The $50.00 fee for admission _pro hac vice_ is enclosed. (Payment may be made by check or money order payable to: Clerk of Court, United States District Court or by major credit card.)

9) We hereby certify under penalties of perjury that the foregoing statements are true and correct.

Respectfully submitted,

Movant —
Signature: _____
Printed Name: _____
Firm: _____
Address: _____
_____
_____

Proposed Admittee —
Signature: _____
Printed Name: _____
Firm: _____
Address: _____
_____
_____

Phone Number: _____
Email: _____
Maryland U.S. District Court Number:
_____

Phone Number: _____
Email: _____

LBF-G: Notice of Debtor(s)' Motion to Avoid Lien on Principal Residence Pursuant to 11 U.S.C. § 506 and Hearing Thereon.

IN THE UNITED STATES BANKRUPTCY COURT
FOR THE DISTRICT OF MARYLAND
at _____

IN RE: :
                                :   Case No. _____
                                :   Chapter 13
Debtor(s).   :
                                :
_____   :
                                :
Movant(s),   :
v.   :
                                :   Account No. _____
                                :   (Loan account number that
Respondent(s).   :   bears lien sought to be avoided)

NOTICE OF DEBTOR(S)' MOTION TO AVOID LIEN ON PRINCIPAL RESIDENCE PURSUANT TO 11 U.S.C. § 506 AND HEARING THEREON

A motion was filed on behalf of the debtor(s) to avoid a lien held by _____. Your rights may be affected. You should read these papers carefully and discuss them with your lawyer. If you do not have a lawyer, you may wish to consult one. A copy of the motion is attached.

If you do not want the court to grant the motion avoiding the lien, or if you want the court to consider your views on the motion, then by _____ * you or your lawyer must file with the Clerk of the Bankruptcy Court a response to the motion explaining your position and mail a copy of the response to:

[Movant's attorney's name and address, or Movant's name and address if without counsel]

If you mail rather than deliver your response to the Clerk of the Court for filing, you must mail it early enough so that the court will receive it by the date stated above.

If you file a timely response to the motion, the hearing on the motion will take place on _____, at _____, ** in Courtroom _____, United States Bankruptcy Court, _____.

If you or your lawyer do not file and serve a timely response to the motion, the court may find that you do not oppose the relief sought in the motion and may grant or otherwise dispose of the motion before the scheduled hearing date.

DATE: _____ ***   _____

Signature (Attorney or Movant if without counsel)

Telephone No. _____

[*]   Insert date that is at least **30 days** after the date this notice is mailed, plus any additional time provided by Federal Bankruptcy Rules 9006(a) and (f). The Court Hearing Scheduler (CHS) Program on the court's website and CM/ECF filing screen for this type of motion will compute the date that an objection is due. Use the date computed.

[**]   Insert a date and time from the list of dates available for the judge assigned to the case that is at least **49 days** after the date of this notice.

[***] Insert the date notice was served.

CERTIFICATE OF SERVICE

I certify that on the _____ day of _____, 20_____, copies of the notice and motion to avoid lien were served upon the Respondent(s) whose name(s) and address(es) are set forth below.

(1)   (2)

(3)   (4)

(5)   (6)

_____

Signature

_____

Print Name

NOTE: Service must be made pursuant to Federal Bankruptcy Rule 7004 and Local Bankruptcy Rule 3012-1.

LBF-H: Order Granting Motion to Avoid Lien on Debtor(s)' Principal Residence.

IN THE UNITED STATES BANKRUPTCY COURT
FOR THE DISTRICT OF MARYLAND
at _____

IN RE:	:	
	:	Case No. _____
	:	Chapter 13
Debtor(s)	:	
_____	:	
	:	
Movant(s)	:	
vs.	:	
	:	
	:	
Respondent(s)	:	

ORDER GRANTING MOTION TO AVOID LIEN ON DEBTOR(S)' PRINCIPAL RESIDENCE

Having considered debtor's Motion to Avoid Lien, and any response filed thereto, and it appearing that proper notice has been given, pursuant to 11 U.S.C. § 506 and for the reasons set forth in the case of *Johnson vs. Asset Management Group, LLC*, 226 B.R. 364 (D. Md. 1998), it is by the United States Bankruptcy Court for the District of Maryland,

ORDERED, that the claim of Respondent be and is hereby deemed wholly unsecured.

ORDERED, that at such time as a discharge Order is entered pursuant to 11 U.S.C. § 1328(a) in this case, the lien held in favor of Respondent on debtor's real property described as: _____,
shall be void, and it is further

ORDERED, that the claim of Respondent herein shall be allowed as a general unsecured claim under the debtor's plan.

cc: Trustee
   Debtor(s)
   Debtor(s)' Attorney
   Respondent
   U.S. Trustee

END OF ORDER

LBF-J-1: Application to Serve on BDRP Panel.

APPLICATION
UNITED STATES BANKRUPTCY COURT
DISTRICT OF MARYLAND
BANKRUPTCY DISPUTE RESOLUTION PROGRAM PANEL

Name: _____

Office Address: _____

    City   State   Zip

Office Phone: _____ Office Fax: _____

Education: _____

_____

_____

Professional licenses or memberships and accreditations:

_____

_____

Dispute Resolution Training: Yes _____   No _____
    (a) U.S. Bankruptcy Court Training _____
    (b) Other Training _____

Experience: _____

_____

_____

Counties in which you are willing to serve as a Resolution Advocate:

_____

If you are also applying to be a Compensated Resolution Advocate, rates charged:

_____

_____

Additional information: _____

_____

_____

    I hereby certify that the information set forth above is true and correct.[1] I agree to serve for a minimum of one year and to act as an unpaid Resolution Advocate, in matters not to exceed one matter per calendar quarter.

_____   _____

    Date   Signature

---

[1] It is the responsibility of the applicant to submit an amended application if any information contained on this application changes.

LBF-J-2a: Order Assigning Matter to the BDRP.

IN THE UNITED STATES BANKRUPTCY COURT
FOR THE DISTRICT OF MARYLAND
at _____

IN RE: :
                                      :   Case No. _____
                                      :   Chapter _____
            Debtor(s)   :
_____   :
                                      :
        Plaintiff(s)/Movant(s)   :
_____   :
        vs.   :   Adversary No. _____
                                      :   (if appropriate)
                                      :
                                      :
    Defendant(s)/Respondents   :

**ORDER ASSIGNING MATTER
TO THE BANKRUPTCY DISPUTE RESOLUTION PROGRAM**

In an effort to facilitate resolution of the dispute herein, and
_____ the parties having requested in writing
_____ the above-signed Judge having *sua sponte* determined
that the above-captioned contested matter/adversary proceeding/dispute be
assigned to the Bankruptcy Dispute Resolution Program, it is, by the United
States Bankruptcy Court for the District of Maryland

ORDERED, pursuant to Local Bankruptcy Rule 9019-2, that the matter that
is the subject of the instant dispute is assigned to the Bankruptcy Dispute
Resolution Program.
cc:

End of Order

LBF-J-2b: Order appointing resolution advocate.

IN THE UNITED STATES BANKRUPTCY COURT
FOR THE DISTRICT OF MARYLAND
at _____

IN RE: :
                                      :   Case No. _____
                                      :   Chapter _____
            Debtor(s)   :
_____   :
                                      :
        Plaintiff(s)/Movant(s)   :
_____   :

vs.   : Adversary No. _____
                                       :   (if appropriate)
                                       :
                                       :
Defendant(s)/Respondents   :

ORDER APPOINTING RESOLUTION ADVOCATE

This _____,
            (adversary proceeding)(name of dispute in main case)
having been assigned to the Bankruptcy Dispute Resolution Program of this
district, the following are hereby appointed as Resolution Advocate and
Alternate Resolution Advocate:

RESOLUTION ADVOCATE: ALTERNATE:

_____   _____
Name   Name

_____   _____
Address   Address

_____   _____
City, State, Zip   City, State, Zip

_____   _____
Telephone   Telephone

This matter concerns:
        ( ) Dischargeability   ( ) Objection to Claim   ( ) Lien Avoidance
        ( ) Other: _____
        _____
        _____

Special Instruction from the Court: _____
_____

**The attorneys for the parties are:

Attorney for _____ ;   Attorney for _____;

_____   _____
Name   Name

_____   _____
Address   Address

_____   _____
City, State, Zip   City, State, Zip

_____   _____
Telephone   Telephone

The Resolution Advocate is serving on a _____ basis. If the
Resolution Advocate is acting as a Compensated Resolution Advocate, following application and approval, compensation will be paid by the following
terms:

                _____ % From Plainiff
                _____ % From Defendant
                _____ % From the Bankruptcy Estate.

The Parties are to comply with the provisions of Local Bankruptcy Rule 9019-2. All individual parties, and representatives with authority to negotiate and to settle the Matter on behalf of parties other than individuals, must personally attend the BDRP conference unless excused by the Resolution Advocate for cause. Willful failure to attend the BDRP conference and other violations of this order may result in the imposition of sanctions by the court. The BDRP conference is to be completed by _____.

Counsel for _____ shall mail a copy of this order to the assigned Resolution Advocate, the Alternate Resolution Advocate, and all parties to the dispute and file a proof of such service within seven (7) days from the date of this Order.
cc:

End of Order
** **Use additional pages if there are more than two parties.**

LBF-J-3: Confidentiality Agreement.

United States Bankruptcy Court
District of Maryland
Bankruptcy Dispute Resolution Program

Confidentiality Agreement

This agreement is to be signed prior to the commencement of the Bankruptcy Dispute Resolution Program Conference (BDRP Conference) by all parties, their counsel and the Resolution Advocate.

All parties agree as follows:

1. All statements made during the BDRP Conference or otherwise in furtherance of the resolution process are protected by and subject to Federal Rule of Evidence 408 and are privileged and are not discoverable. The Resolution Advocate has, however, an affirmative duty to disclose any statements made which relate to the commission of a crime to the appropriate authorities.

2. Information provided and representations made for the first time during or in connection with the resolution process must be considered confidential unless otherwise agreed to in writing by all the parties with the exception of information or representations that relate to a crime.

3. The Resolution Advocate may not be compelled to testify in any civil proceeding as to any information provided or representations made during or in connection with the resolution process.

4. Nothing presented by another party in the course of a BDRP matter may be introduced into evidence or relied upon in any legal or quasi-legal proceeding, except for information, statements or documents relating to the commission of a crime or evidence otherwise admissible under Federal Rule of Evidence 408.

Nonliability of Resolution Advocate: Toward the desired goal of open and complete communication to enable parties to settle their disputes, all parties agree that the Resolution Advocate will not be held liable for any act or omission connected to the resolution process.

Breach of Confidentiality Agreement: In the event of a breach of this confidentiality agreement, the breaching party is liable for all costs, expenses, liabilities and fees including attorneys' fees which the non-breaching party and Resolution Advocate may incur as a result of the breach.

Date _____

Resolution Advocate   Parties

_____   _____

                                                        _____

IN THE UNITED STATES BANKRUPTCY COURT
FOR THE DISTRICT OF MARYLAND
at _____

IN RE: :
                                   :   Case No. _____
                                   :   Chapter _____
     Debtor(s)   :
_____   :
                                   :   Adversary No. _____
     Plaintiff(s)/Movant(s)   :   INITIAL MEDIATION
vs.   :   CONFIDENTIALITY
                                   :   AGREEMENT
                                   :   *CONFIDENTIAL -*
                                   :   *NOT TO BE FILED*
     Defendant(s)/Respondent(s)   :   *WITH THE COURT*
                                   :

This is an Agreement between the parties and the Mediator to enter into confidential discussions about the mediation of the following issues: _____

_____

_____

_____

[Attach additional page(s) if necessary.]

The undersigned understand and agree to the strict confidentiality of their mediation. Mediation discussions, any draft resolutions and any unsigned mediated agreements must not be disclosed to anyone not involved in the Mediation Program and will not be admissible in any court or administrative proceeding. Only an agreement signed by all parties may be so admissible.

The parties further agree not to call the Mediator to testify concerning the mediation nor to provide any materials from the Mediation Program in any court or administrative proceeding between the parties.

In addition, the Mediator will not be compelled to divulge any materials from the Mediation Program or to testify in regard to the mediation in any judicial or other proceeding.

Dated: _____   _____
                                (Name of Party)

                                _____
                                (Signature of Party)

Dated: _____   _____
                                (Name of Party's Counsel)

                                _____
                                (Signature of Party's Counsel)

Dated: _____   _____
                                (Name of Party)

                                _____
                                (Signature of Party)

Dated: _____   _____
                                (Name of Party's Counsel)

                                _____
                                (Signature of Party's Counsel)

Dated: _____   _____
                                (Name of Mediator)

                                _____
                                (Signature of Mediator)

[Attach additional page(s) if necessary.]

LBF-J-4: Certificate Re: BDRP Conference.

IN THE UNITED STATES BANKRUPTCY COURT
DISTRICT OF MARYLAND
at _____

IN RE: :
                                :   Case No. _____
                                :   Chapter _____
                    Debtor(s)   :
_____   :
                                :
                    Plaintiff(s) :
        vs.   :   Adversary No. _____
                                :
                                :

Defendant(s)   :

CERTIFICATE RE: BDRP CONFERENCE

1. I hereby certify that pursuant to an Order of Assignment by this Court to the Bankruptcy Dispute Resolution Program dated _____, a BDRP Conference was ____ was not ____ held.

(If Applicable)   Date: _____

Continued Date: _____

2. A settlement of this matter was ____ was not ____ reached.

Date: _____   _____

Resolution Advocate

_____

(Type or Print Name)

LBF-J-5: Resolution Advocate Report.

IN THE UNITED STATES BANKRUPTCY COURT
DISTRICT OF MARYLAND
at _____

IN RE: :
                                :   Case No. _____
            Debtor(s)   :   Chapter _____
_____   :
                                :
                                :
                                :
            Plaintiff(s)   :
   vs.   :   Adversary No. _____
                                :
            Defendant(s)   :
                                :

REPORT OF BDRP CONFERENCE

I, _____, Resolution Advocate for the Bankruptcy Dispute Resolution Program (BDRP), state:

1. A BDRP conference was held on _____ at _____ (attach attendance form(s)).

(If Applicable) Continued Date: _____ at _____.

2. The Rules governing the conference were _____ were not _____ complied with. If not, how? _____

_____.

3. A settlement of this matter was _____ was not _____ reached.

4. If a settlement/resolution was reached, _____ (plaintiff/defendant/other), prepared the written stipulation for settlement.

5. Prior to the preparation of a final written agreement, the parties chose to put the agreement on the court record. Yes _____ No _____

6. I spent _____ hours in preparing for and scheduling the conference(s).

7. I spent _____ hours attending the conference(s).

8. The dispute resolution procedure utilized was: (Check as many as applicable. If more than one is applicable, give the appropriate percentage of time spent on each).

      Early Neutral Evaluation _____

      Settlement Negotiation _____

      Mediation _____

9. Comments/Suggestions: _____

_____

_____

_____

Dated: _____   _____

                           (Resolution Advocate)

                          _____

                          (Type or Print Name)

BDRP SESSION ATTENDANCE FORM

Case Name: _____

Case No.: _____

Adversary Proceeding Name: _____

Adversary Proceeding No.: _____

Date of Session: _____

Resolution Advocate: _____

Instructions: Please have **all attorneys and client representatives** who attend the conference(s) provide the following information. The purpose of this information is to facilitate survey research of the value of the BDRP.

ATTORNEYS

Name: _____   Name: _____

Firm Name: _____   Firm Name: _____

_____   _____

Address: _____   Address: _____

_____   _____

Phone: ( ) _____   Phone: ( ) _____

Attorney for: _____   Attorney for: _____

Name: _____   Name: _____

Firm Name: _____   Firm Name: _____

_____   _____

Address: _____   Address: _____

_____   _____

Phone: ( ) _____   Phone: ( ) _____

Attorney for: _____   Attorney for: _____

CLIENT REPRESENTATIVES

Name: _____   Name: _____
Firm Name: _____   Firm Name: _____

_____   _____

Address: _____   Address: _____

_____   _____

Phone: (   ) _____   Phone: (   ) _____
Party Representing: _____   Party Representing: _____

Name: _____   Name: _____
Firm Name: _____   Firm Name: _____

_____   _____

Address: _____   Address: _____

_____   _____

Phone: (   ) _____   Phone: (   ) _____
Party Representing: _____   Party Representing: _____

Name: _____   Name: _____
Firm Name: _____   Firm Name: _____

_____   _____

Address: _____   Address: _____

_____   _____

Phone: (   ) _____   Phone: (   ) _____
Party Representing: _____   Party Representing: _____

LBF-K: Notice of Debtor(s)' Motion to Value Collateral and to Avoid Security Interest Pursuant to 11 U.S.C. § 506 and Hearing Thereon.

IN THE UNITED STATES BANKRUPTCY COURT
FOR THE DISTRICT OF MARYLAND
at _____

IN RE:	*	
	*	Case No. _____
Debtor(s).	*	Chapter 13
	*	
_____	*	
	*	
	*	
Movant(s),	*	
vs.	*	Account No. _____
	*	(Loan account number that
	*	bears lien sought to be
	*	avoided)
Respondent(s).	*	

NOTICE OF DEBTOR(S)' MOTION TO VALUE COLLATERAL AND TO AVOID SECURITY INTEREST PURSUANT TO 11 U.S.C. § 506 AND HEARING THEREON

A motion was filed on behalf of the debtor(s) to value collateral or to avoid a security interest held by _____. Your rights may be affected. You should read these papers carefully and discuss them with your lawyer. If you do not have a lawyer, you may wish to consult one. A copy of the motion is attached.

If you do not want the court to grant the motion avoiding the lien, or if you want the court to consider your views on the motion, then by _____* you or your lawyer must file with the Clerk of the Bankruptcy Court a response to the motion explaining your position and mail a copy of the response to:

> [Movant's attorney's name and address, or Movant's name and address if without counsel]

If you mail rather than deliver your response to the Clerk of the Court for filing, you must mail it early enough so that the court will receive it by the date stated above.

If you file a timely response to the motion, the hearing on the motion will take place on _____, at _____,** in Courtroom _____, United States Bankruptcy Court, _____.

If you or your lawyer do not file and serve a timely response to the motion, the court may find that you do not oppose the relief sought in the motion and may grant or otherwise dispose of the motion before the scheduled hearing date.

DATE: _____ *** _____

> Signature (Attorney or Movant if without counsel)
> Telephone No. _____

[*] Insert date that is at least **30 days** after the date this notice is mailed, plus any additional time provided by Federal Bankruptcy Rules 9006(a) and (f). The Court Hearing Scheduler (CHS) Program on the court's website and CM/ECF filing screen for this type of motion will compute the date that an objection is due. Use the date computed.

[**] Insert a date and time from the list of dates available for the judge assigned to the case that is at least **49 days** after the date of this notice.

[***] Insert the date notice was served.

CERTIFICATE OF SERVICE

I certify that on the _____ day of _____ , 20_____, copies of the notice and motion to value collateral or to avoid lien were served upon the Respondent(s) whose name(s) and address(es) are set forth below.

(1)   (2)

(3)   (4)

(5)   (6)

_____
Signature
_____
Print Name

NOTE: Service must be made pursuant to Federal Bankruptcy Rule 7004 and Local Bankruptcy Rule 3012-2.

LBF-L: Order Granting Motion to Value Collateral and to Avoid Security Interest.

· IN THE UNITED STATES BANKRUPTCY COURT
FOR THE DISTRICT OF MARYLAND
at _____

IN RE: *
                                *   Case No. _____
               Debtor(s).   *   Chapter 13
                                *
_____   *
                                *
                                *
               Movant(s),   *
        vs.   *
                                *
               Respondent(s).   *

**ORDER GRANTING MOTION TO VALUE COLLATERAL
AND TO AVOID SECURITY INTEREST**

Having considered debtor's motion, and any response filed thereto, and it appearing that proper notice has been given, pursuant to 11 U.S.C. § 506, it is by the United States Bankruptcy Court for the District of Maryland,

ORDERED, that the value of the collateral securing Respondent's claim is $_____ ; and it is further

ORDERED, that at such time as a discharge Order is entered in this case pursuant to 11 U.S.C. § 1328, the lien held in favor of Respondent on the property described below is void to the extent of Respondent's unsecured claim:

[List of collateral];

and it is further

ORDERED, that the claim of Respondent herein shall be treated under debtor's plan as an allowed secured claim in an amount not to exceed the value of Respondent's collateral and as an allowed, general unsecured claim for the balance.

cc: Trustee
    Debtor(s)
    Debtor(s)' Attorney
    Respondent
    U.S. Trustee

End of Order

LBF-M: Chapter 13 Plan.

IN THE UNITED STATES BANKRUPTCY COURT
FOR THE DISTRICT OF MARYLAND
at _____

IN RE: *

                      *   Case No. _____

                      *   Chapter 13

                      *

         Debtor   *

CHAPTER 13 PLAN

☐ Original Plan   ☐ Amended Plan   ☐ Modified Plan

The Debtor proposes the following Chapter 13 plan and makes the following declarations:

1. The future earnings of the Debtor are submitted to the supervision and control of the Trustee, and Debtor will pay as follows (select only one):

a. $ _____ per month for a term of _____ months. OR

b. $ _____ per month for _____ month(s),

    $ _____ per month for _____ month(s),

    $ _____ per month for _____ month(s), for a total term of _____ months. OR

c. $ _____ per month prior to confirmation of this plan, and

    $ _____ per month after confirmation of this plan, for a total term of _____ months (if this option is selected, complete 2.e.i).

2. From the payments received, the Trustee will make the disbursements in the order described below:

a. Allowed unsecured claims for domestic support obligations and trustee commissions.

b. Administrative claims under 11 U.S.C. § 507(a)(2), including attorney's fee balance of $ _____ (unless allowed for a different amount by an order of the Court).

c. Claims payable under 11 U.S.C. § 1326(b)(3). Specify the monthly payment: $ _____.

d. Other priority claims defined by 11 U.S.C. § 507(a)(3)-(10). The Debtor anticipates the following priority claims:

e. Concurrent with payments on non-administrative priority claims, the Trustee will pay secured creditors as follows:

i. Until the plan is confirmed, adequate protection payments and/or personal property lease payments on the following claims will be paid directly by the Debtor; and, after confirmation of the plan, the claims will be treated as specified in 2.e.ii and 2.e.iii, below (designate the amount of the monthly payment to be made by the Debtor prior to confirmation, and provide the redacted account number (last 4 digits only), if any, used by the claimant to identify the claim):

Claimant	Redacted Acct. No.	Monthly Payment

ii. Pre-petition arrears on the following claims will be paid through equal monthly amounts under the plan while the Debtor maintains post-petition payments directly (designate the amount of anticipated arrears, and the amount of the monthly payment for arrears to be made under the plan):

Claimant	Anticipated Arrears	Monthly Payment	No. of Mos.

iii. The following secured claims will be paid in full, as allowed, at the designated interest rates through equal monthly amounts under the plan:

Claimant	Amount	% Rate	Monthly Payment	Nos. of Mos.

iv. The following secured claims will be satisfied through surrender of the collateral securing the claims (describe the collateral); any allowed claims for deficiencies will be paid pro rata with general unsecured creditors; upon confirmation of the plan, the automatic stay is lifted, if not modified earlier, as to the collateral of the listed creditors:

v. The following secured claims are not affected by this plan and will be paid outside of the plan directly by the Debtor:

vi. If any secured claim not described in the previous paragraphs is filed and not disallowed, that claim shall be paid or otherwise dealt with outside the plan directly by the Debtor, and it will not be discharged upon completion of the plan.

vii. In the event that the trustee is holding funds in excess of those needed to make the payments specified in the Plan for any month, the trustee may pay secured claims listed in paragraphs 2.e.ii and 2.e.iii in amounts larger than those specified in such paragraphs.

f. After payment of priority and secured claims, the balance of funds will be paid *pro rata* on allowed general, unsecured claims. (If there is more than one class of unsecured claims, describe each class.)

3. The amount of each claim to be paid under the plan will be established by the creditor's proof of claim or superseding Court order. The Debtor anticipates filing the following motion(s) to value a claim or avoid a lien. (Indicate the asserted value of the secured claim for any motion to value collateral.):

4. Payments made by the Chapter 13 trustee on account of arrearages on pre-petition secured claims may be applied only to the portion of the claim pertaining to pre-petition arrears, so that upon completion of all payments due under the Plan, the loan will be deemed current through the date of the filing of this case. For the purposes of the imposition of default interest and post-petition charges, the loan shall be deemed current as of the filing of this case.

5. Secured Creditors holding claims subject to cramdown will retain their liens until the earlier of the payment of the underlying debt determined under nonbankruptcy law, or discharge under § 1328; and if the case is dismissed or converted without completion of the plan, the lien shall also be retained by such holders to the extent recognized under applicable nonbankruptcy law.

6. The following executory contracts and/or unexpired leases are assumed (or rejected, so indicate); any unexpired lease with respect to personal property that has not previously been assumed during the case, and is not assumed in the plan, is deemed rejected and the stay of §§ 362 and/or 1301 is automatically terminated:

7. Title to the Debtor's property shall revest in the Debtor when the Debtor is granted a discharge pursuant to 11 U.S.C. § 1328, or upon dismissal of the case, or upon closing of the case.

8. Non-standard Provisions:

Date   Debtor

Attorney for Debtor   Joint Debtor

LBF-N-1: Chapter 11 Final Report and Motion for Final Decree.

IN THE UNITED STATES BANKRUPTCY COURT
FOR THE DISTRICT OF MARYLAND

IN RE: *

                      *

                      *   Case No. _____

                      *   Chapter 11

         Debtor(s)   *

CHAPTER 11 FINAL REPORT AND MOTION FOR FINAL DECREE

The following is the report of payments made pursuant to the Plan, confirmed by this Court on _____ .

TOTAL DISTRIBUTION   _____

PERCENTAGE OF CLAIMS PAID OR PROPOSED TO BE PAID TO THE GENERAL CLASS OF UNSECURED CREDITORS WITHIN THE PLAN

_____ %

A. Gross Cash Receipts: _____

	Paid	Proposed	Total

B. Priority Payments of Expenses of Administration Other Than Operating Expenses:

1. Trustee's commission (if any)   _____ _____ _____
2. Fee and expenses, Trustee's Counsel   _____ _____ _____

C. Other Professional Fees and Expenses:

1. Fees and expenses, Accountants   _____ _____ _____
2. Fees and expenses, Auctioneers and Appraisers   _____ _____ _____
3. Fees and expenses, Attorneys for Debtor   _____ _____ _____
4. Other professional fees (specify)   _____ _____ _____
5. Taxes, fines, penalties, etc.   _____ _____ _____
6. Other expenses of administration (must be itemized: includes bond premiums, settlement costs, other expenses)   _____ _____ _____
7. Total   _____

D. Payments to creditors: (totals under each category sufficient)

1. Payments to secured creditors   _____ _____ _____
2. Payments to priority creditors   _____ _____ _____
3. Payments to unsecured creditors   _____ _____ _____
4. Payments to equity security holders   _____ _____ _____

E. Other payments: (including surplus payments to debtor)   _____ _____ _____

F. **TOTAL DISTRIBUTION**   _____

The Plan Proponent, (or Trustee if appointed) hereby avers that all provisions of the Plan have been substantially consummated. Wherefore, the Plan Proponent (or Trustee), having fully administered this estate, prays for entry of a Final Decree.

DATE: _____   _____
                                    Attorney for Plan Proponent
                                    (or Trustee)
cc: Creditor's Committee (or counsel), or
        20 largest Unsecured Creditors
    U.S. Trustee

LBF-N-2: Chapter 11 Final Report and Motion for Discharge and Final Decree [For Individual Debtor(s)].

IN THE UNITED STATES BANKRUPTCY COURT
FOR THE DISTRICT OF MARYLAND

IN RE: *
                                *
                                *   Case No. _____
                                *   Chapter 11
            Debtor(s)   *

CHAPTER 11 FINAL REPORT AND MOTION FOR DISCHARGE AND FINAL DECREE
[For Individual Debtor(s)]

The following is the report of payments made pursuant to the Plan, confirmed by this Court on _____ .

TOTAL DISTRIBUTION   _____

PERCENTAGE OF CLAIMS PAID OR PROPOSED TO BE PAID TO THE GENERAL CLASS OF UNSECURED CREDITORS WITHIN THE PLAN

_____ %

A. Gross Cash Receipts: _____

	Paid	Proposed	Total
B. Priority Payments of Expenses of Administration Other Than Operating Expenses:			
1. Trustee's commission (if any)	_____	_____	_____
2. Fee and expenses, Trustee's Counsel	_____	_____	_____
C. Other Professional Fees and Expenses:			
1. Fees and expenses, Accountants	_____	_____	_____
2. Fees and expenses, Auctioneers and Appraisers	_____	_____	_____
3. Fees and expenses, Attorneys for Debtor	_____	_____	_____
4. Other professional fees (specify)	_____	_____	_____
5. Taxes, fines, penalties, etc.	_____	_____	_____
6. Other expenses of administration (must be itemized: includes bond premiums,			

settlement costs, other expenses)   _____ _____ _____

7. Total   _____

D.   Payments to creditors: (totals
under each category sufficient)
1. Payment to secured creditors   _____ _____ _____
2. Payment to priority creditors   _____ _____ _____
3. Payments to unsecured creditors   _____ _____ _____
4. Payments to equity security holders _____ _____ _____

E.   Other payments: (including surplus
payments to debtor)   _____ _____ _____

F. **AMOUNT TO BE PAID UNDER PLAN**   _____

TOTAL DISTRIBUTION   _____

The Plan Administrator, (or Trustee if appointed) hereby avers that all provisions of the Plan have been substantially consummated, and plan payments have been completed. Furthermore, the Debtor(s) hereby certify, under penalty of perjury that the following statements are true and correct:

1. Debtor(s) have completed all payments under the Plan.
2. If 11 U.S.C. §1141(d)(3) applies, Debtor(s) have completed an instructional course concerning financial management as described in 11 U.S.C. § 111.
3. Debtor(s) did not have, either at the time of filing this bankruptcy or at the present time, equity in excess of $125,000 if the case was filed before April 1, 2007, or $136,875 if the case was filed between April 1, 2007 and April 1, 2010, and $146,450 for a case filed after April 1, 2010 , in the type of property described in 11 U.S.C. § 522(p)(1) [generally the debtor's homestead].
4. There is not currently pending any proceeding in which Debtor(s) may be found guilty of a felony of the kind described in 11 U.S.C. § 522(q)(1)(A) or liable for a debt of the kind described in 11 U.S.C. § 522(q)(1)(B).

Debtor: _____   DATE: _____
Debtor: _____   DATE: _____

Wherefore, the Plan Administrator (or Trustee), having fully administered this estate, prays for entry of an Order of Discharge and the entry of a Final Decree.

DATE: _____   _____

    Attorney for Plan Administrator
    (or Trustee)

cc: Creditor's Committee (or counsel), or
    20 largest Unsecured Creditors
    U.S. Trustee

LBF-O: Pre-Confirmation Certification.

IN THE UNITED STATES BANKRUPTCY COURT
FOR THE DISTRICT OF MARYLAND
at _____

IN RE: *
                                          *
                                          *   Case No. _____
                                          *   Chapter 13
                    Debtor(s)   *

PRE-CONFIRMATION CERTIFICATION

Debtor(s) hereby certify under penalty of perjury that the following state-ments are true and correct:

1. Debtor(s) has/have paid any fee, charge, amount required under Section 1930 of title 28, U.S.C., or by the plan (i.e. adequate protection payments) to be paid before confirmation.

2. Debtor(s) has/have paid all amounts that are required under a domestic support obligation and that first became payable after the date of the filing of the petition, if applicable.

3. Debtor(s) has/have filed all applicable Federal, State, and Local tax returns with the appropriate taxing authorities for all taxable periods ending during the 4-year period ending on the date of the filing of the petition.

Debtor(s) affirm that the plan is proposed in accordance with 11 U.S.C § 1325 and request said plan be confirmed.

_____	_____
Date	Debtor's Signature
_____	_____
Date	Joint Debtor's Signature

LBF-P: Debtor's Affidavit Requesting Discharge.

IN THE UNITED STATES BANKRUPTCY COURT
FOR THE DISTRICT OF MARYLAND
at _____

IN RE: *
                                          *
                                          *
                                          *   Case No. _____
                                          *
                                          *   Chapter 13
                    Debtor   *

DEBTOR'S AFFIDAVIT REQUESTING DISCHARGE

IN JOINT FILINGS, A SEPARATE AFFIDAVIT MUST BE COMPLETED BY EACH DEBTOR IN ORDER TO BE ELIGIBLE FOR A DISCHARGE

The Chapter 13 Trustee has filed a notice of completion in my case and I am hereby requesting that the Court issue a discharge. I testify under penalty of perjury to the following: (Complete all sections and provide *all* required information.)

1. The following creditors hold a claim that is not discharged under 11 U.S.C. § 523 (a)(2) or (a)(4) or a claim that was reaffirmed under 11 U.S.C. § 524(c): (*provide name, address, and telephone number of each such creditor*)

_____

_____

2. _____ I have not received a discharge in a Chapter 7, 11 or 12 bankruptcy case that was filed within 4 years prior to the filing of this Chapter 13 Bankruptcy.

3. _____ I have not received a discharge in another Chapter 13 bankruptcy case that was filed within 2 years prior to the filing of this Chapter 13 bankruptcy.

4. A. _____ I did not have either at the time of filing this bankruptcy or at the present time, equity in excess of $125,000 if the case was filed before April 1, 2007, or $136,875 if the case was filed between April 1, 2007 and April 1, 2010, and $146,450 for a case filed after April 1, 2010 , in the type of property described in 11 U.S.C. §522(p)(1) [generally the debtor's homestead].

B. _____ There is not currently pending any proceeding in which I may be found guilty of a felony of the kind described in 11 U.S.C. § 522(q)(1)(A) or liable for a debt of the kind described in 11 U.S.C. § 522(q)(1)(B).

5. COMPLETION OF INSTRUCTIONAL COURSE CONCERNING PERSONAL FINANCIAL MANAGEMENT PURSUANT TO 11 U.S.C. § 1328(g)(1)

[Complete one of the following statements]

I, _____ (printed name of debtor) _____, the debtor in the above-styled case hereby certify that on _____ (date) _____ I completed an instructional course in personal financial management provided by _____ (Name of Provider) _____, by an approved personal financial management instruction provider.

_____ Official Form 23 was filed previously with the court; OR

_____ A document attesting to my completion of the personal financial management instruction course is attached.

____ I, _____ (printed name of debtor) _____, the debtor in the above-styled case, hereby certify that no personal financial management course is required because: [check the appropriate box.]

☐   I am incapacitated or disabled, as defined in 11 U.S.C. § 109(h)(4);
☐   I am on active military duty in a military combat zone; or
☐   I reside in a district in which the United States Trustee has determined that the approved instructional courses are not adequate at this time to serve the additional individuals who would otherwise be required to complete such courses.

☐   CERTIFICATION REGARDING DOMESTIC SUPPORT OBLIGA-
TIONS PURSUANT TO 11 U.S.C § 1328(a)

[Complete one of the following statements]

____ I, _____ (printed name of debtor) _____ , the debtor in the above-styled case, hereby certify that I am not currently required, nor at any time during the period of this bankruptcy have I been required, by a judicial or adminis-trative order, or by statute, to pay a domestic support obligation.

____ I, _____ (printed name of debtor) _____ , the debtor in the above-styled case am required by judicial or administrative order, or by statute, to pay a domestic support obligation as defined in 11 U.S.C. § 101(14A). (This refers to a debt owed to or recoverable by a spouse, former spouse or child of the debtor or such child's parent, legal guardian or responsible relative or a governmental unit in the nature of alimony, maintenance or support.)

The name and address of each holder of a domestic support obligation follows:

_____

_____

_____

_____

_____

[check the appropriate box.]

____ I hereby certify that all amounts payable under such order or such statute that are due on or before the date of this affidavit (including amounts due before the petition was filed, but only to the extent provided for by the plan) have been paid; or

____ I have executed, and the court has approved, a written waiver of discharge pursuant to 11 U.S.C. § 1328(a).

My current address is:

_____

_____

_____

The name and address of my most recent/current employer is:

_____

_____

_____

I declare under penalty of perjury that all of the above statements are true and correct to the best of my knowledge, information, and belief, and that the Court may rely on the truth of each statement in determining whether to grant me a discharge in this case. I further understand that the court may revoke my discharge if such order of discharge was procured by fraud.

Signature of Debtor: _____   Date: _____

NOTICE OF OPPORTUNITY TO OBJECT

Any objections to the accuracy of this affidavit must be filed within fourteen (14) days of the date of service of this Affidavit. If no objection is filed, the Court will consider entering a discharge order in this case without further notice or hearing.

CERTIFICATE OF SERVICE

I hereby certify that this affidavit was served this _____ day of _____, 20_____, electronically to those recipients authorized to receive a Notice of Electronic Filing by the Court, and/or first class mail, postage prepaid to:

Chapter 13 Trustee
All creditors and parties in interest.

LBF-Q: Statement Under Penalty of Perjury Concerning Payment Advices Due Pursuant to U.S.C. § 521(a)(1)(B)(iv).

IN THE UNITED STATES BANKRUPTCY COURT
FOR THE DISTRICT OF MARYLAND

IN RE:

*
*
*   Case No. _____
*
Debtor(s)   *
*

STATEMENT UNDER PENALTY OF PERJURY CONCERNING PAYMENT ADVICES DUE PURSUANT TO 11 U.S.C. § 521(a)(1)(B)(iv)

I, _____ (Debtor's name[2]), state that I did not provide copies of all payment advices or other evidence of payment received within 60 days before the date of the filing of the petition, by me from any employer because:

_____ (1) I was not employed during the period immediately preceding the filing of the above-referenced case _____ (state the dates that you were not employed);

_____ (2) I was employed during the period immediately preceding the filing of the above-referenced case but did not receive any payment advices or other evidence of payment from my employer within 60 days before the filing of the petition;

_____ (3) I am self employed and do not receive any evidence of payment;

_____ (4) Other (please explain) _____.

I declare under penalty of perjury that I have read the foregoing statements and that they are true and accurate to the best of my knowledge, information and belief.

---

[2] A separate form must be filed for each Debtor

Dated this _____ day of _____, 20____.

_____ (Signature of Debtor)

Debtor

APPENDIX B. LOCAL DISTRICT COURT RULES FOR BANKRUPTCY PROCEEDINGS WITH CROSS-REFERENCE.

CROSS-REFERENCE
FEDERAL RULES OF BANKRUPTCY PROCEDURE
to
U.S. DISTRICT COURT OF MARYLAND LOCAL RULES

FRBP		LDCR
9029.1	Rules in Bankruptcy Court Proceedings	401
9029.2	Referral of Bankruptcy Cases and Proceedings	402
	Appeals to the District Court	404
8001.1	Manner of Appeal	404.1
8006.1	Dismissal for Non-Compliance with FRBP 8006	404.2
8009.1	Dismissal for Non-Compliance with FRBP 8009	404.3
8005.1	Procedure Re: Motion to Stay Pending Appeal	404.4
8003.1	Bankruptcy Court Certification Re:	404.5
	Interlocutory Appeal	
	Rules of Procedure Under 28 U.S.C. § 1334	405
9029.3	Filing of Pleadings and Papers/General Rule	405.1
5011.1	Withdrawal of Reference of Certain Bankruptcy	405.2a
	Proceedings/Filing of Motion for Withdrawal	
	of Reference with Bankruptcy Clerk	
5011.1(a)	Withdrawal of Reference of Bankruptcy Cases	405.2b
5011.1(b)	Withdrawal of Reference of Adversary	405.2c
	Proceeding or Contested Matter	
5011.1(c) /9027	Filing of Pleadings in Transferred Cases	405.3
1014 /9030	Motions Concerning Venue in Bankruptcy Cases and Proceedings	405.4
9015.1 /9029	Jury Trial/Demand	406.1
9015.2 /9029	Specification of Issues	406.2
9015.3 /9029	Waiver	406.3

Editor's note. — The Rules for bankruptcy proceedings used in the U.S. Bankruptcy Court for the District of Maryland are set out as Part IV, Rules 401 through 407, of the Rules of the U. S. District Court for the District of Maryland.

APPENDIX C. DISCOVERY GUIDELINES OF THE UNITED STATES DISTRICT COURT FOR THE DISTRICT OF MARYLAND.

Editor's note. — The discovery guidelines used in the U.S. Bankruptcy Court for the District of Maryland are set out as Appendix A of the Rules of the U. S. District Court for the District of Maryland.

APPENDIX D. COMPENSATION GUIDELINES FOR PROFESSIONALS IN THE UNITED STATES BANKRUPTCY COURT FOR THE DISTRICT OF MARYLAND.

The following guidelines apply to professional fee applications in all bankruptcy cases in the United States Bankruptcy Court for the District of Maryland. These guidelines shall apply to all professionals seeking compensation pursuant to 11 U.S.C. §§ 327, 328, 330 and 331, including attorneys, accountants, examiners, investment bankers and real estate advisors, unless the court, in the order employing such professional or other order, provides otherwise. These guidelines set forth information to be contained in both interim and final applications for the approval of fees and expenses.

Although conformity to these guidelines will ensure that certain necessary information is included to assist the court in its review of professional fee applications, it must be remembered that the following are guidelines only. Applications for compensation may vary from case to case, and each application must be reviewed on its own merits depending upon the facts and circumstances of the case. Familiarity with and adherence to the following guidelines will, it is hoped, promote the submission of more uniform professional fee applications containing adequate information, and facilitate a meaningful review process and more expeditious action by the court.

A. **Format of fee applications.** Bankruptcy Rule 2016(a) sets forth certain requirements with respect to professional fee applications. The application should set forth a detailed statement of (1) the services rendered, (2) the time expended, (3) the expenses incurred, (4) the amounts requested, (5) the rates charged for such services, (6) how the services rendered were necessary to the administration of, or beneficial at the time at which the services were rendered toward the completion of, the case, (7) information relevant to a determination that the services were performed within a reasonable amount of time commensurate with the complexity, importance and nature of the problem, issue or task addressed, and (8) an affirmation that the compensation requested is reasonable based upon the customary compensation and reimbursement of expenses charged by the applicant and comparably skilled professionals in nonbankruptcy matters. In addition, applications should include a statement as to what payments have been made or promised to the applicant, the source of the compensation paid or promised, whether there is any sharing arrangement and the particulars as to any such sharing arrangement. Applications should also set forth the date the order approving employment was entered and the dates of entry of any previous orders approving interim compensation to the applicant and the amounts of compensation previously approved. Finally, fee applications should include a "lodestar" analysis and discussion of the factors identified in *Johnson v. Georgia Highway Express, Inc.*, 488 F.2d 714 (5th Cir. 1974), and adopted by the Fourth Circuit in *Barber v. Kimbrell's, Inc.*, 577 F.2d 216 (4th Cir. 1978), *Anderson v. Booth,*

658 F.2d 246 (4th Cir. 1978) and *Harman v. Levin,* 772 F.2d 1150 (4th Cir. 1985).

B. **Description of services rendered and time expended.** Daily time sheets or a listing of daily time entries, in legible form, should be included in or attached to the application.[1] The time sheets or time entries should provide an itemized listing of all services performed by each professional and paraprofessional and the time spent on each matter indicated. The applicable billing rate for each professional and paraprofessional should be indicated.

Each professional and paraprofessional should record time in increments of tenths of an hour and keep contemporaneous time records. Time records should set forth in reasonable detail an appropriate narrative description of the services rendered. As a general rule, the description should include indications of the participants in and the length and nature of the activities undertaken. Examples of insufficient descriptions include "telephone call," "telephone call to X," "conference with client," "research," "review of documents," "review of pleadings," and "correspondence." Examples of satisfactory descriptions are set forth in footnote 3.

The broad "lumping" of services, or the grouping of different tasks within one block of time, should generally be avoided in favor of more specific descriptions.[2] In recording time for each day, each professional and paraprofessional may describe in one entry the nature of the services rendered on a given task during that day and the aggregate time expended that day on such task, provided, however, that if the professional or paraprofessional works more than one hour on a task on any given day, the time record for that day should include internally, within the description of services for that day, the amount of time spent on each particular activity. A hypothetical time record complying with the foregoing is included below.[3]

The description of services required to be set forth is not intended to require the disclosure of privileged or confidential information, provided, that if additional detail is required, the court may direct that such additional information be furnished subject to appropriate protective conditions. Information set forth in a fee application shall not operate as a waiver of any applicable privilege, including the attorney/client privilege or work product doctrine.

Charges for conferences between individuals in the same firm on the same case are not objectionable, if reasonable, necessary and limited. Similarly, more than one professional may charge for attending a meeting or hearing on behalf of the same client if such attendance is reasonable, necessary and

---

[1] Fee applications for matters handled on a contingent fee basis and applications required to be submitted pursuant to § 506(b) should also conform to the applicable format guidelines set forth herein.

[2] Notwithstanding the general prohibition of "lumping", time entries for periods of one hour or less on a given day may be grouped together provided that a reasonable description of the services rendered within such time entry is provided.

[3] A complying time entry would be:

"internal conference with X re cash collateral (.3); revise draft motion re cash collateral (.8); conf. call with Y and Z re cash collateral hearing (.5); review documents re cash collateral motion (1.1); legal research re cash collateral hearing (.5) ... Total Time 3.2"

limited. An explanation as to why more than one professional attended such meeting or hearing may in certain circumstances be required, particularly if such multiple professional attendance does not appear to be reasonable in a particular situation.[4]

Ordinarily, time entries should be organized by tasks and presented chronologically. An applicant should either organize the time sheets or present a time entry listing by discrete tasks where an application covers multiple tasks undertaken by the applicant during the time period covered by the application. Within each task identified, the time entries of all timekeepers working on such task should appear chronologically. In addition, the application should include a summary by timekeeper of the time spent on each task, the billing value for each timekeeper and a total billing amount for each task. Finally, the application should also include a brief narrative description as to why each task was undertaken, the current status thereof and the results or benefits achieved to date.

It is not the intent of these guidelines to set forth a definitive listing of what tasks should be separately identified in each case or each professional fee application. However, where a discrete activity can reasonably be expected to continue over a period of at least three months and can reasonably be expected to constitute 10-20% or more of the fees to be sought for an interim period, the professional should present a separate chronological listing of time entries for such matter to the extent reasonably practicable. Examples of categories which might comprise separate tasks in a particular case are set forth below.[5]

Subject to court approval, a trustee may employ himself or herself, or a firm with which the trustee is affiliated, as a professional. In such cases, applications for compensation should distinguish services rendered as trustee from those rendered by the professional seeking compensation.

Compensation sought for time spent traveling should indicate the mode and time of travel, the necessity for travel and whether any substantive work was

---

[4] In appropriate cases where there are multiple counsel from different firms representing the same party, such counsel may be required to submit their applications simultaneously.

[5] *Sample Task Listing for Attorneys*

Asset analysis and recovery.
Asset disposition/sales/leases/executory contracts.
Business operations.
Case administration.
Claims administration and objections.
Fee/employment applications and objections.
Financing/cash collateral.
Litigation [separately identify larger litigation matters as discrete tasks.]
Meetings of creditors.
Plan and disclosure statement.

Sample Task Listing for Accountants

Accounting/auditing.
Business analysis.
Corporate finance.
Data analysis.
Litigation consulting.
Tax issues.
Valuation/projections.

performed while traveling (*e.g.,* preparing for hearing). If excessive or unreasonable, compensation for travel time may be reduced. If time is spent during travel working on other matters, such travel time should not also be billed to the bankruptcy case.

Compensation for time spent preparing and defending fee applications is appropriate if reasonable. Compensation for the preparation of fee applications will be based on the level and skill reasonably required to prepare the application.

C. **Reimbursement for disbursements and expenses.** Disbursements and expenses for which reimbursement is sought should be summarized in the fee application by category and any unusual items explained. Excessive charges will not be reimbursed. The following are guidelines with respect to some (but not necessarily all) of the categories of reimburseable disbursements and expenses:

Photocopying. The applicable charge for photocopying should be the actual cost of such copying not to exceed 20¢ per page or, if an outside service is used, the actual cost of such copying.

Facsimile transmission. Charges for out-going facsimile transmissions to long-distance telephone numbers are reimburseable at the lower of (i) toll charges or (ii) if such amount is not readily determinable, $1.25 per page for domestic and $2.50 per page for international transmissions. Charges for incoming facsimile transmissions are not reimburseable.

Mileage. The applicable charge for automobile mileage should not exceed the government approved rate, plus actual parking charges incurred.

Travel. The actual expenses incurred for out-of-town travel are reimburseable. However, first-class airfare, luxury accommodations and deluxe meals are not reimburseable, nor are personal or incidental charges unless necessary as a result of unforeseen circumstances.

Computerized legal research. Reasonable expenses may be charged for computerized legal research, including Lexis and Westlaw, provided that there is a description of the legal research undertaken and the charges do not exceed the actual cost to the attorney.

Postage, telephone, courier and freight. The cost of postage, freight, overnight delivery, courier services and telephone toll charges may be reimburseable, if reasonably incurred. Only the long distance component of cellular telephone charges is reimbursible. Charges for services such as messengers and overnight mail should not be incurred indiscriminately. Charges for local telephone services are not reimburseable. If normal, routine first-class postage is not customarily charged to other clients, then such postage would not be reimburseable; however, special postage charges or bulk mailings would ordinarily be reimburseable.

Court costs. Court costs and disbursements are reimburseable.

Meals. Charges for meals are generally not reimburseable unless justified under appropriate circumstances or unless incurred as part of otherwise reimburseable out-of-town travel.

Overtime charges. Overtime for non-professional and paraprofessional staff is reimburseable only if specifically justified in the application as necessary under the circumstances. Overtime charges for professional staff is not reimburseable.

Word processing, proofreading, secretarial and other staff services. Daytime, ordinary business hour charges for word processing, proofreading, secretarial, library and other staff services (exclusive of paraprofessional services) are generally considered office overhead items and, therefore, not reimburseable unless specifically justified in exceptional circumstances.

With respect to all disbursements and expenses for which reimbursement is sought, it must be understood that they must be of a kind and at a rate customarily charged to and collected from other clients and subject to the test of reasonableness under the circumstances of each case.

Each professional fee application in which the applicant is seeking reimbursement for expenses should include a statement that, with respect to expenses for which reimbursement is sought, the applicant is familiar with and has submitted the application in conformity with the "Compensation Guidelines for Professionals in the United States Bankruptcy Court for the District of Maryland."

D. **Lodestar analysis, Johnson factors and billing judgment.** Each professional fee application should contain a "lodestar" analysis and discussion of the *Johnson v. Georgia Highway Express, Inc. (supra)* factors, as adopted by the Fourth Circuit in *Barber v. Kimbrell's, Inc. (supra)*, including a statement as to the professional's application of billing judgment to the compensation sought by such professional.

The "lodestar" analysis should include a summary listing the name of each professional and paraprofessional for whom compensation is sought, the number of hours worked by each identified individual, that individual's hourly rate (which should not exceed such individual's standard hourly rate in other bankruptcy and non-bankruptcy matters), the total compensation sought for each such individual and a total of all compensation sought for the period in question, before and after applying billing judgment to the compensation requested. A similar detailed summary of disbursements and expenses by category should also be presented.

The fee application should discuss the application of the twelve *Johnson v. Georgia Highway Express, Inc.* factors, to the extent that they apply in each particular case. Those factors may be summarized as follows:

1. the time and labor expended;
2. the novelty and difficulty of the questions raised;
3. the skill required to properly perform the professional services rendered;
4. the professional's opportunity costs in pursuing the matter;
5. the customary fee for like work;
6. the professional's expectations as to compensation at the outset of the matter;
7. the time limitations imposed by the client or circumstances;
8. the amount in controversy and the results obtained;
9. the experience, reputation and ability of the professional;
10. the desirability or undesirability of the case within the professional community in which the case arose;

11. the nature and length of the professional relationship between the professional and client; and

12. professional fee awards in similar cases.

Not all of the foregoing twelve factors will be applicable to every fee application. However, they should be considered in the professional's exercise of billing judgment and discussed in the fee application. If a particular factor is not considered to be applicable, the application should so state. In addition, if the professional believes that other factors are relevant to the compensation requested, the foregoing list is not intended to be exhaustive. Professionals are encouraged to state all facts and circumstances that such professional believes to be relevant to the compensation requested.

In the final analysis, in making its determination with respect to a fee application and the amount of compensation to be awarded, the court will consider the nature, the extent, and the value of the services rendered.

APPENDIX E. MARYLAND STATE BAR ASSOCIATION CODE OF CIVILITY.

In May 1997, the Maryland State Bar Association's Board of Governors approved the following aspirational Code of Civility for all lawyers and judges in Maryland. MSBA encourages all Maryland lawyers and judges to honor and voluntarily adhere to the standards set forth in these codes. Civility is the cornerstone of the legal profession.

LAWYERS' DUTIES

1. We will treat all participants in the legal process, in a civil, professional, and courteous manner and with respect at all times and in all communications, whether oral or written. These principles are intended to apply to all attorneys who practice law in the State of Maryland regardless of the nature of their practice. We will refrain from acting upon or manifesting racial, gender, or other bias or prejudice toward any participant in the legal process. We will treat all participants in the legal process with respect.

2. We will abstain from disparaging personal remarks or acrimony toward any participants in the legal process and treat everyone with fair consideration. We will advise our clients and witnesses to act civilly and respectfully to all participants in the legal process. We will, in all communications, speak and write civilly and respectfully to the Court, staff, and other court or agency personnel with an awareness that they, too, are an integral part of the judicial system.

3. We will not encourage any person under our control to engage in conduct that would be inappropriate under these standards if we were to engage in such conduct.

4. We will not bring the profession into disrepute by making unfounded accusations of impropriety or attacking counsel, and absent good cause, we will not attribute bad motives or improper conduct to other counsel.

5. We will strive for orderly, efficient, ethical and fair disposition of litigation, as well as disputed matters that are not yet the subject of litigation, and for the efficient, ethical, and fair negotiation and consummation of business transactions.

6. We will not engage in conduct that offends the dignity and decorum of judicial and administrative proceedings, bring disorder to the tribunal or undermines the image of the legal profession, nor will we allow clients or witnesses to engage in such conduct. We will educate clients and witnesses about proper courtroom decorum and to the best of our ability, prevent them from creating disorder or disruption in the courtroom.

7. We will not knowingly misrepresent, mischaracterize, or misquote fact or authorities cited.

8. We will be punctual and prepared for all scheduled appearances so that all matters may begin on time and proceed efficiently. Furthermore, we will also educate everyone involved concerning the need to be punctual and prepared, and if delayed, we will notify everyone involved, if at all possible.

9. We will attempt to verify the availability of necessary participants and witnesses so we can promptly reschedule appearances if necessary.

10. We will avoid ex parte communications with the court, including the judge's staff, on pending matters in person (whether in social, professional, or other contexts), by telephone, and in letters and other forms of written communication, unless authorized.

JUDGES' RESPONSIBILITIES

1. We will not use hostile, demeaning or humiliating words in opinions or in written or oral communications with lawyers, parties or witnesses.

2. We will be courteous, respectful and civil to lawyers, parties, witnesses, and court personnel. We will maintain control of all court proceedings, recognizing that judges have both the obligation and the authority to ensure that judicial proceedings are conducted with dignity, decorum and courtesy to all.

3. Within the practical limits of time, we will afford lawyers appropriate time to present proper arguments and to make a complete and accurate record.

4. We will make reasonable efforts to decide promptly all matters presented for decision.

5. We will be considerate of professional and personal time schedules of lawyers, parties, witnesses and court staff in scheduling hearings, meetings, and conferences, consistent with the efficient administration of justice.

6. We will be punctual in convening trials, hearings, meetings, and conferences; if they are not begun when scheduled; proper and prompt notification will be given.

7. We will inform counsel promptly of any rescheduling, postponement, or cancellation of hearings, meetings or conferences.

8. We will work cooperatively with all other judges and other jurisdictions with respect to availability of lawyers, witnesses, parties and court resources.

9. We will treat each other with courtesy and respect.

10. We will conscientiously assist and cooperate with other jurists to assure the efficient and expeditious processing of cases, while, when possible, accommodating the trial schedule of all lawyers, parties and witnesses.

APPENDIX F. CHAPTER 13 DEBTOR'S COUNSEL RESPONSIBILITIES AND FEES.

1. A copy of paragraphs 2. and 3. of this document, Chapter 13 Debtor's Counsel Responsibilities and Fees, must be delivered to the debtor(s) by counsel at the time counsel is employed, in addition to the retainer agreement by and between the debtor(s) and debtor's counsel.

2. With the exception of adversary proceedings, appeals, and U.S. Trustee audits, for which separate arrangements may be made, counsel must represent their client in all matters in the bankruptcy case as long as counsel is counsel of record. This includes defending motions, including motions for relief from stay, and bringing objections to claims and prosecuting motions on behalf of debtor. After the initial engagement, counsel may not demand payments from the debtor as a precondition to doing the work. Notwithstanding the foregoing, the Court may, upon prior application, allow counsel to enter a limited appearance, including, but not limited to, representation on a pro bono or reduced fee basis.

3. Counsel must remain as counsel of record until the entry of a court order allowing the withdrawal of appearance, or until the case is dismissed or closed. The failure to receive payment for services rendered or to be rendered may serve as the basis for counsel filing a motion to withdraw.

4. The following fee arrangements are presumed reasonable under Section 329 and allowable under Section 330 and require no application or approval, except as stated below. This presumption is rebuttable and the fee can be the subject of an order to justify the fee.

If no objection or order to justify fee is filed or entered, the presumptively reasonable fee is deemed allowed under 11 U.S.C. § 330 without the entry of an Order. However, if an objection or order to justify fee is filed or entered, the burden shall be upon debtor's counsel to prove that the fee should be allowed under 11 U.S.C. § 330 under the facts and circumstances of the case for which the fee is sought. The foregoing notwithstanding, any objection filed by a trustee or other party in interest shall describe the asserted factual basis for rebutting the presumption.

A. A flat fee, not to exceed $3,500.00 for representation of the debtor for all matters in the main case. However, Counsel may by application request approval of additional fees for work done upon matters that were both not reasonably expected and that are extraordinary, or for work done after 90 days following the entry of the order confirming plan until representation ends. Such application may be made on Local Form E with notice (Local Form E-1).

B. A flat fee, not to exceed $4,500.00 for representation for all matters in the main case. Except as stated in the following sentence, Counsel waives all opportunity to apply for additional work in the main case. Counsel may by application request approval of additional fees for work done upon matters that were not reasonably expected and that are extraordinary. Such application may be made on Local Form E with notice (Local Form E-1).

C. A flat fee, not to exceed $2,000.00 for representation of the debtor on all matters relating to plan confirmation. Counsel may apply for additional compensation for additional fees for prosecuting or defending motions not relating to the plan confirmation, including, without limitation, motions for relief from stay, or for claims objections. Such application may be made on Local Form E with notice (Local Form E-1). The requirement for representation in all matters in the bankruptcy case, stated in paragraph 2. above, applies without regard to the more limited coverage of the $2,000.00 fee arrangements set forth in this subparagraph.

D. In any fee arrangement described in subparagraphs A, B and C above, the plan may provide that the Trustee will disburse any unpaid fees to counsel and other claimants whose claims are described in 11 U.S.C. § 507(a)(2), before any disbursement by the Trustee to other creditors except claimants whose claims are described in 11 U.S.C. § 507(a)(1). Unless otherwise provided by the confirmed Plan, if, after payment to claimants whose claims are described in 11 U.S.C. § 507(a)(1), the remaining unpaid balance of the attorney's fee, the trustee's commission and other claims described in 11 U.S.C. § 507(a)(2) cannot be disbursed in full from the Plan payments due during the first twelve months of the Plan term, then the remaining unpaid balance of such fee shall be disbursed on a pro rata basis with any other priority and/or secured claims.[1]

5. All fees are subject to subsequent disgorgement upon an order of the court. No plan or confirmation order shall bar by res judicata or otherwise the subsequent review and potential disgorgement of the fee, upon objection or order to justify fee and notice thereof.

6. Full compliance with Federal Rule of Bankruptcy Procedure 2016(b) is required, including the filing of a Supplemental Disclosure on Local Form E-2 of additional funds received from any person, other than distributions from the Trustee under a confirmed plan. Counsel shall state in the Disclosure of Compensation filed pursuant to Federal Rule of Bankruptcy Procedure 2016(b) whether the fee arrangement is one of the flat fees described in subparagraphs A, B or C of paragraph 4 above, and, if so, which such fee arrangement applies.

7. Nothing in this Appendix F shall preclude, restrict, or prohibit counsel from entering into fee arrangements different from those arrangements described in Paragraph 4 above. Counsel must file an application for compensation in accordance with the Bankruptcy Code, Bankruptcy Rules, and the Rules of this Court for any fee arrangement that is different from the fee arrangements described in Paragraph 4 above.

---

[1] Nothing in subparagraph 4.D is intended to alter or amend any obligation counsel may have under nonbankruptcy law concerning escrowing, administering or accounting for any funds disbursed to counsel pursuant to these procedures.

Index to Rules of the United States Bankruptcy Court for the District of Maryland Local Bankruptcy Rules

INDEX

INDEX

INDEX

INDEX

MICHIE'S™ ANNOTATED CODE
OF THE PUBLIC GENERAL LAWS
OF MARYLAND

Maryland Rules
Volume 2

May 2012 Supplement
to the 2012 Edition

Prepared by the Editorial Staff of the Publishers

(Including amendments adopted through April 24, 2012, and annotations taken from Court of Appeals and Court of Special Appeals opinions issued through April 11, 2012)

LexisNexis®

701 East Water Street, Charlottesville, VA 22902

5259629

ISBN 978-1-4224-8851-5 (set)

(Pub. 43805)

Table of Contents

Volume 1

Volume 2

MARYLAND RULES

TITLE 9. FAMILY LAW ACTIONS

CHAPTER 100. ADOPTION; GUARDIANSHIP TERMINATING PARENTAL RIGHTS.

Rule 9-103. Petition.

Disability. — When a guardianship petition seeking termination of a mother's parental rights alleged the mother might have a disability, the granting of that petition pursuant to the mother's deemed consent, due to a failure to timely object to the petition, was reversed because (1) the mother had a right to appointed counsel, pursuant to § 5-307(a) of the Family Law Article and Md. R. 9-105(b), including the right to counsel's effective assistance, and (2) counsel did not provide effective assistance when counsel did not file a timely objection to the petition. In re Adoption/Guardianship of Chaden M., 422 Md. 498, 30 A.3d 935 (2011).

Rule 9-105. Show cause order; disability of a party; other notice.

Denial of effective assistance of counsel. — Granting of a guardianship petition seeking termination of a mother's parental rights alleging the mother might have a disability, pursuant to the mother's deemed consent, due to a failure to timely object to the petition, was reversed because (1) the mother had a right to appointed counsel, pursuant to § 5-307(a) of the Family Law Article and (b) of this Rule, including the right to counsel's effective assistance, and (2) counsel did not provide effective assistance when counsel did not file a timely objection to the petition. In re Adoption/Guardianship of Chaden M., 422 Md. 498, 30 A.3d 935 (2011).

Rule 9-107. Objection.

Denial of effective assistance of counsel. — Granting of a guardianship petition seeking termination of a mother's parental rights alleging the mother might have a disability, pursuant to the mother's deemed consent, due to a failure to timely object to the petition, was reversed because (1) the mother had a right to appointed counsel, pursuant to § 5-307(a) of the Family Law Article and Md. R. 9-105(b), including the right to counsel's effective assistance, and (2) counsel did not provide effective assistance when counsel did not file a timely objection to the petition. In re Adoption/Guardianship of Chaden M., 422 Md. 498, 30 A.3d 935 (2011).

TITLE 10. GUARDIANS AND OTHER FIDUCIARIES

Chapter 200. Guardian of Person.
Rule
10-202. Certificates.

CHAPTER 200. GUARDIAN OF PERSON.

Rule 10-202. Certificates.

(a) **Generally required.** Except as provided in section (d), if guardianship of the person of a disabled person is sought, the petitioner shall file with the petition signed and verified certificates of (1) two physicians licensed to practice medicine in the United States who have examined the disabled person, or (2) one licensed physician who has examined the disabled person and one licensed psychologist or certified clinical social worker who has seen and evaluated the disabled person. An examination or evaluation by at least one of the health care professionals under this subsection shall occur within 21 days before the filing of the petition.

(b) **Contents.** Each certificate shall state: (1) the name, address, and qualifications of the person who performed the examination or evaluation, (2) a brief history of the person's involvement with the disabled person, (3) the date of the last examination or evaluation of the disabled person, and (4) the person's opinion as to: (A) the cause, nature, extent, and probable duration of the disability, (B) whether institutional care is required, and (C) whether the disabled person has sufficient mental capacity to understand the nature of and consent to the appointment of a guardian.

(c) **Delayed filing of certificates.** (1) After refusal to permit examination. If the petition is not accompanied by the required certificate and the petition alleges that the disabled person is residing with or under the control of a person who has refused to permit examination by a physician or evaluation by a psychologist or certified clinical social worker, and that the disabled person may be at risk unless a guardian is appointed, the court shall defer issuance of a show cause order. The court shall instead issue an order requiring that the person who has refused to permit the disabled person to be examined or evaluated appear personally on a date specified in the order and show cause why the disabled person should not be examined or evaluated. The order shall be personally served on that person and on the disabled person.

(2) Appointment of health care professionals by court. If the court finds after a hearing that examinations are necessary, it shall appoint two physicians or one physician and one psychologist or certified clinical social worker to conduct the examinations or the examination and evaluation and file their reports with the court. If both health care professionals find the person to be disabled, the court shall issue a show cause order requiring the alleged disabled person to answer the petition for guardianship and shall require the petitioner to give notice pursuant to Rule 10-203. Otherwise, the petition shall be dismissed.

(d) **Beneficiary of the Department of Veterans Affairs.** If guardianship of the person of a disabled person who is a beneficiary of the United States

3

Department of Veterans Affairs is being sought, the petitioner shall file with the petition, in lieu of the two certificates required by section (a) of this Rule, a certificate of the Secretary of that Department or an authorized representative of the Secretary stating that the person has been rated as disabled by the Department in accordance with the laws and regulations governing the Department of Veterans Affairs. The certificate shall be prima facie evidence of the necessity for the appointment. (Amended Feb. 10, 1998, effective July 1, 1998; Oct. 5, 1999; Nov. 12, 2003, effective Jan. 1, 2004; Dec. 4, 2007, effective Jan. 1, 2008.)

Editor's note. — This Rule is set out to show the following change: in (a)(2) "licensed physician who" has been substituted for "licensed physician or who".

TITLE 11. JUVENILE CAUSES

Rule 11-113. Waiver of jurisdiction.

Cited in Gaines v. State, 201 Md. App. 1, 28
A.3d 706 (2011).

TITLE 12. PROPERTY ACTIONS

CHAPTER 100. GENERAL PROVISIONS.

Rule 12-102. Lis pendens.

Applicability.

Complaint seeking to establish a constructive trust on specified real property is an action whose nature is such that it directly involves the property and is a proceeding directly relating to the title to the property transferred or in which the ultimate interest and object is to subject the property in question to the disposal of a decree of the court; thus, such a complaint is within the ambit of Maryland's lis pendens doctrine. Stewart Title Guar. Co. v. Sanford Title Servs., LLC, — F. Supp. 2d — (D. Md. July 8, 2011).

In an action in which plaintiff, a title insurance company, alleged that certain real properties were illegitimately purchased with monies misappropriated from an escrow account and that plaintiff was required to make up a shortfall in the escrow account due to defendants' fraudulent conduct, plaintiff's complaint seeking to establish a constructive trust on the properties constituted a valid lis pendens on the properties because the complaint directly related to the title to the properties. Stewart Title Guar. Co. v. Sanford Title Servs., LLC, — F. Supp. 2d — (D. Md. July 8, 2011).

TITLE 14. SALES OF PROPERTY

CHAPTER 200. FORECLOSURE OF LIEN INSTRUMENTS.

Rule 14-201. Applicability; Other Remedies.

Cited in Maddox v. Cohn, 424 Md. 379, 36 A.3d 426 (2012); D'Aoust v. Diamond, 424 Md. 549, 36 A.3d 941 (2012).

Rule 14-204. Institution of action.

Cited in Maddox v. Cohn, 424 Md. 379, 36 A.3d 426 (2012); Svrcek v. Rosenberg, — Md. App. —, — A.3d — (Mar. 29, 2012).

Rule 14-205. Conditions precedent to the filing of an action.

Cited in Maddox v. Cohn, 424 Md. 379, 36 A.3d 426 (2012); Svrcek v. Rosenberg, — Md. App. —, — A.3d — (Mar. 29, 2012).

Rule 14-206. Petition for immediate foreclosure against residential property.

Court order directing sale held not to change nature of proceedings.
When trustees appointed to conduct a judicial sale of a condominium allegedly (1) sent the owner notice at an incorrect address, despite knowing the correct address, (2) affirmed in an affidavit that notice was properly sent, and (3) allegedly did not comply with promises to the owner to inform the court that the sale should not be ratified, the trustees were not entitled to qualified public official immunity because the trustees were not public officials, as the trustees did nothing "to make and enforce laws," nor were the trustees' acts performed in a "legislative or policymaking capacity." D'Aoust v. Diamond, 424 Md. 549, 36 A.3d 941 (2012).

When trustees appointed to conduct a judicial sale of a condominium allegedly (1) sent the owner notice at an incorrect address, despite knowing the correct address, (2) affirmed in an affidavit that notice was properly sent, and (3) allegedly did not comply with promises to the owner to inform the court that the sale should not be ratified, the trustees were not entitled to qualified judicial immunity because Maryland did not recognize such immunity. D'Aoust v. Diamond, 424 Md. 549, 36 A.3d 941 (2012).

Trustees' employer not immune for alleged Rule violations. — When trustees appointed to conduct a judicial sale of a condominium allegedly (1) sent the owner notice at an incorrect address, despite knowing the correct address, (2) affirmed in an affidavit that notice was properly sent, and (3) allegedly did not comply with promises to the owner to inform the court that the sale should not be ratified, the law firm that employed the trustees was not entitled to judicial immunity because the firm had no involvement in the process of conducting the judicial sale. D'Aoust v. Diamond, 424 Md. 549, 36 A.3d 941 (2012).

When trustees appointed to conduct a judicial sale of a condominium allegedly (1) sent the owner notice at an incorrect address, despite knowing the correct address, (2) affirmed in an affidavit that notice was properly sent, and (3) allegedly did not comply with promises to the owner to inform the court that the sale should not be ratified, the law firm that employed the trustees was not entitled to qualified public official immunity because the firm could not claim immunity based on any alleged immunity of the firm's employees, and the firm did not show an independent basis for such immunity. D'Aoust v. Diamond, 424 Md. 549, 36 A.3d 941 (2012).

Trustees not immune for alleged Rule violations. — When trustees appointed to conduct a judicial sale of a condominium allegedly (1) sent the owner notice at an incorrect address, despite knowing the correct address, (2) affirmed in an affidavit that notice was properly sent, and (3) allegedly did not comply with promises to the owner to inform the court that the sale should not be ratified, the trustees were not entitled to judicial immunity

because the trustees did not act as judicial officers at the time of the acts complained of, and the legislature had not granted such immunity. D'Aoust v. Diamond, 424 Md. 549, 36 A.3d 941 (2012).

Rule 14-207. Pleadings; service of certain affidavits, pleadings, and papers.

Requirements satisfied. — Substitute trustees were entitled to seek foreclosure because the trustees satisfied the requirements of § 7-105.1(d)(2) of the Real Property Article and (b) by filing (1) a copy of the deed of trust, supported by an affidavit that the deed of trust was a true and accurate copy, (2) a copy of the debt instrument, supported by an affidavit certifying ownership of the debt instrument, and (3) a copy of a deed of appointment of the substitute trustees, supported by an affidavit that the copy was a true and accurate copy of the deed of appointment. Svrcek v. Rosenberg,

— Md. App. —, — A.3d — (Mar. 29, 2012).

Substitute trustees' lawful possession of promissory note. — Substitute trustees lawfully possessed a promissory note under which the substitute trustees sought to foreclose, despite a lack of endorsements on the copy of the note filed, because a prior trustee established that the prior trustee was a person not in possession of an instrument who was entitled to enforce the instrument under § 3-309 of the Commercial Law Article, since the note was lost. Svrcek v. Rosenberg, — Md. App. —, — A.3d — (Mar. 29, 2012).

Rule 14-207.1. Court screening.

Cited in Maddox v. Cohn, 424 Md. 379, 36 A.3d 426 (2012).

Rule 14-209. Service in actions to foreclose on residential property; notice.

Cited in Svrcek v. Rosenberg, — Md. App. —, — A.3d — (Mar. 29, 2012).

Rule 14-211. Stay of the sale; dismissal of action.

University of Baltimore Law Forum. — For a note, "Recent Development: Bates v. Cohn," see 41 U. Balt. L. F. 177 (2011).

Abuse of discretion to stay proceedings. — It was an abuse of discretion for a trial court to stay foreclosure proceedings because, (1) under this section and controlling precedent, a stay was only proper if other pending litigation could affect a plaintiff's ability to foreclose, (2) (e) made it mandatory to deny a motion for a stay if no defense to the foreclosure were presented, and (3) the foreclosure proceeding was stayed pending resolution of subordination litigation, which dealt only with the validity of a subordination agreement, not the validity of the lien under which foreclosure was sought, such that the effect of the successful prosecution of the subordination litigation would only make the lien junior to that of a lienholder, rather than invalidating the lien under which foreclosure was sought. Bechamps v. 1190 Augustine Herman, LC, 202

Md. App. 455, 32 A.3d 542 (2011).

Untimely motion to dismiss. — Mortgagor's motion to dismiss foreclosure proceedings was untimely because (1) the motion was filed more than 15 days after service of an order to docket, and (2) the mortgagor did not show good cause for extending the filing time, as the mortgagor admitted the date on which the mortgagor was served with the order to docket, and the mortgagor's asserted ignorance of the requirement to respond within 15 days was not an excuse. Svrcek v. Rosenberg, — Md. App. —, — A.3d — (Mar. 29, 2012).

Res judicata. — Because the issue of the validity of the mortgagors' rescission claims had already been resolved in another action ending in a final judgment in a Maryland court in a foreclosure action, issue preclusion prevented a federal district court from considering the rescission claims once more. DeCosta v. U.S. Bancorp, — F. Supp. 2d — (D. Md. Sept. 27, 2010).

Quoted in Bates v. Cohn, 417 Md. 309, 9 A.3d 846 (2010).

Rule 14-212. Alternative dispute resolution.

Cited in Maddox v. Cohn, 424 Md. 379, 36 A.3d 426 (2012).

Rule 14-214. Sale.

Cited in Maddox v. Cohn, 424 Md. 379, 36 A.3d 426 (2012).

Rule 14-215. Post-sale procedures.

Cited in Maddox v. Cohn, 424 Md. 379, 36 A.3d 426 (2012).

Rule 14-216. Proceeds of sale.

Cited in Maddox v. Cohn, 424 Md. 379, 36 A.3d 426 (2012).

CHAPTER 300. JUDICIAL SALES.

Rule 14-302. Sales — Generally.

Cited in D'Aoust v. Diamond, 424 Md. 549, 36 A.3d 941 (2012).

Rule 14-303. Procedure prior to sale.

Cited in D'Aoust v. Diamond, 424 Md. 549, 36 A.3d 941 (2012).

Rule 14-305. Procedure following sale.

University of Baltimore Law Forum. — For a note, "Recent Development: Bates v. Cohn," see 41 U. Balt. L. F. 177 (2011).

Sale properly ratified. — Pursuant to § 7-105 of the Real Property Article and (d) of this Rule, a foreclosure sale was properly ratified and a property owner's exceptions thereto were properly overruled, as a concurrent interest holder had acquired the owner's promissory note, which was secured by a deed of trust on her one-half interest in the property, and when she defaulted on the note, her interest was freely devisable and properly foreclosed upon. Fagnani v. Fisher, 418 Md. 371, 15 A.3d 282 (2011).

When a mortgagor objected to the ratification of a foreclosure sale of the mortgagor's property on the grounds that an unauthorized fee was imposed on third-party purchasers, the sale was properly ratified because the mortgagor did not have standing to raise the issue, as (1) the mortgagor could only show injury if the mortgagor showed another bidder would pay more than the mortgagor owed but was deterred by an advertisement requiring the fee, which was not shown, and (2) the mortgagor did not show trustees committed fraud or acted deceptively by advertising the fee. Maddox v. Cohn, 199 Md. App. 63, 20 A.3d 153 (2011).

Defaulting purchaser only liable for shortage between original price and first resale price. — Trial court erred in ratifying an auditor's report, finding a purchaser who defaulted on a sale of foreclosed property was liable for the shortage between the original price and an eventual resale price to a third purchaser, as pursuant to (g), the purchaser was only liable for a shortage between the original price and the first resale; a shortage that resulted from the second purchaser's default at resale, prompting a third sale/second resale, was the second purchaser's responsibility. Simard v. Burson, 197 Md. App. 396, 14 A.3d 6 (2011).

Successful bidder was not liable for the risk and expense of a second resale, because, absent special circumstances, the defaulting purchaser at a foreclosure sale of property is liable, under (g), for only one resale due to his or her default; the default of the purchaser at the second resale was not a consequence arising naturally, i.e. according to the usual course of things. Burson v. Simard, 424 Md. 318, 35 A.3d 1154 (2012).

Motion for equitable abatement of interest.

Although a foreclosure sale purchaser was entitled to an equitable abatement of interest due to the filing of exceptions under (d)(1) by the former owners, a trial court abused its discretion in abating the interest from the date of the foreclosure sale to the date of settlement because only the time from the initial date set for final ratification to the actual date of final ratification constituted a delay caused by the former owners. Zorzit v. 915 W. 36th St., LLC, 197 Md. App. 91, 12 A.3d 698 (2011).

Defenses must be raised prior to foreclosure sale. — This rule and judicial opinions precluded the homeowner from challenging the lender's failure to satisfy loss mitigation requirements as an exception to the foreclosure sale; the homeowner had to assert known and ripe defenses to the conduct of the foreclosure sale prior to the sale. Bates v. Cohn, 417 Md. 309, 9 A.3d 846 (2010).

Sale procedurally proper. — Pursuant to this rule, a foreclosure sale was conducted properly procedurally, as the advertisement was sufficient because it adequately described the premises, and the price was not grossly inadequate in the circumstances. Fagnani v. Fisher, 418 Md. 371, 15 A.3d 282 (2011).

Cited in D'Aoust v. Diamond, 424 Md. 549, 36 A.3d 941 (2012); Svrcek v. Rosenberg, — Md. App. —, — A.3d — (Mar. 29, 2012).

TITLE 15. OTHER SPECIAL PROCEEDINGS

CHAPTER 1000. WRONGFUL DEATH.

Rule 15-1001. Wrongful death.

It was an abuse of discretion to dismiss a wrongful death complaint under (b), due to the failure of a decedent's widow and the widow's children to join, as a use plaintiff, a child the decedent had adopted during a prior marriage, whose whereabouts were unknown, within three years of the decedent's death, because (1) the wrongful death statute did not impose such a requirement, (2) under art. IV, § 1 of the Maryland Constitution, a procedural rule could not substantively alter a beneficiary's right, (3) while (b) was violated, the Rule did not provide a consequence for a violation, requiring that a consequence be determined in light of the totality of the circumstances and the purpose of the Rule, under Md. R. 1-201(a), and (4) the totality of the circumstances did not mandate dismissal. Univ. of Md. Med. Sys. Corp. v. Muti, — Md. —, 37 A.3d 956 (2012).

CHAPTER 1200. CORAM NOBIS.

Rule 15-1201. Applicability.

University of Baltimore Law Forum. — For a comment, "Innocence and Incarceration: A Comprehensive Review of Maryland's Post- conviction DNA Relief Statute and Suggestions for Improvement," see 42 U. Balt. L. F. 65 (2011).

TITLE 16. COURTS, JUDGES, AND ATTORNEYS

CHAPTER 300. CIRCUIT COURT CLERKS' OFFICES.

Rule 16-303. Payment of money into court.

Cited in Att'y Griev. Comm'n v. Tauber, 421 Md. 415, 26 A.3d 967 (2011).

CHAPTER 400. ATTORNEYS, OFFICERS OF COURT AND OTHER PERSONS.

Rule 16-404. Administration of court reporters.

Cited in McReady v. Univ. Sys. of Md., — Md. App. —, 37 A.3d 1018 (2012); McReady v. Univ. Sys. of Md., — Md. App. —, 37 A.3d 1018 (2012).

CHAPTER 600. ATTORNEY TRUST ACCOUNTS.

Rule 16-603. Duty to maintain account.

Disbarment was proper sanction. — Attorney was disbarred for violating this section and Md. Law. R. Prof. Conduct 1.1, 1.3, 1.15(a), (d), and (e), 1.16(d), 5.5(a) and (b), 8.4(b), (c), and (d), Md. R. 16-604 and 16-609, and § 10-306 of the Business Occupations and Professions Article, by commingling client funds with the attorney's own funds, failing to pay medical providers for clients, and practicing after the attorney lost the right for failure to pay Client Protection Fund assessment and failure to file a pro bono report. Att'y Griev. Comm'n v. Agiliga, 422 Md. 613, 31 A.3d 103 (2011).

Rule 16-604. Trust account — Required deposits.

Attorney disbarred.

Attorney violated this Rule and Md. Law. R. Prof. Conduct 1.2(a), 1.15(d), 8.4(c) and (d), Md. R. 16-609(c), and § 10-306 of the Business Occupations and Professions Article, and was disbarred, after misappropriating tens of thousands of dollars that should have been paid to a physical therapist and settling a client's claim without the client's knowledge or consent. Att'y Griev. Comm'n v. Stern, 419 Md. 525, 19 A.3d 904 (2011).

Attorney was disbarred for violating this section and Md. Law. R. Prof. Conduct 1.1, 1.3, 1.15(a), (d), and (e), 1.16(d), 5.5(a) and (b), 8.4(b), (c), and (d), Md. R. 16-603 and 16-609, and § 10-306 of the Business Occupations and Professions Article, by commingling client funds with the attorney's own funds, failing to pay medical providers for clients, and practicing after the attorney lost the right for failure to pay Client Protection Fund assessment and failure to file a pro bono report. Att'y Griev. Comm'n v. Agiliga, 422 Md. 613, 31 A.3d 103 (2011).

Attorney was disbarred for violating this section, and Md. Law. R. Prof. Conduct 1.4(a)(2) and (a)(3), 1.5(a), 1.15(c) and (d), 1.16(d), 8.1(b), 8.4(a) and (d), and 16-606.1(a)(3), by, inter alia, failing to deposit a client's checks into a trust account and make a recoding of such deposit. Att'y Griev. Comm'n of Md. v. Van Nelson, — Md. —, — A.3d — (Mar. 27, 2012).

Cited in Att'y Griev. Comm'n v. Tauber, 421 Md. 415, 26 A.3d 967 (2011).

Rule 16-606.1. Attorney trust account record-keeping.

Failure to create adequate records. — Attorney violated this Rule by failing to create a record for his trust account that chronologically showed all deposits and disbursements or describing the check number or other payment identification for disbursements. Att'y Griev. Comm'n v. Patterson, 421 Md. 708, 28 A.3d 1196 (2011).

Attorney was disbarred for violating (a)(3), and Md. Law. R. Prof. Conduct 1.4(a)(2) and (a)(3), 1.5(a), 1.15(c) and (d), 1.16(d), 8.1(b), 8.4(a) and (d), and 16-604, by, inter alia, failing to deposit a client's checks into a trust account and make a recoding of such deposit. Att'y Griev. Comm'n of Md. v. Van Nelson, — Md. —, — A.3d — (Mar. 27, 2012).

Rule 16-607. Commingling of funds.

Disbarment ordered.
Disbarment for violating this rule and Md. Law. R. Prof. Conduct 1.1, 1.3, 1.4(b), 1.15, 8.1(a) and (b), and 8.4(c) and (d), was appropriate based on a finding that the attorney's commitment to hiding to truth from Bar Counsel was systematic and unwavering and was not the product of mere mistake, and where there was no innocent explanation for the fabrication of documents or the alternation of bank records after Bar Counsel began its investigation. Att'y Griev. Comm'n v. Payer, — Md. —, 38 A.3d 378 (2012).

Rule 16-609. Prohibited transactions.

Intent not relevant to violation. — Attorney violated (c) when the attorney wrote checks for amounts that he knew exceeded the balance in his trust account, even though the second check was written after a bank teller told the attorney there was money in the account; there was no requirement that the attorney intentionally overdrew the account. Att'y Griev. Comm'n v. Patterson, 421 Md. 708, 28 A.3d 1196 (2011).

Attorney disbarred for violating rules.
Attorney was disbarred for admittedly violating Md. Law. R. Prof. Conduct 1.1, 1.15(a) and (c), and 8.4(a) — (d), as well as this Rule and § 10-306 of the Business Occupations and Professions Article, by misappropriating client funds to make it appear as though the attorney's collected fees were higher than those fees actually were, when the attorney was being considered for partner in the attorney's firm, and by failing to file complaints in clients' cases, misrepresenting that the complaints were filed, and fabricating documents to hide the misrepresentations, because (1) disbarment was the presumed sanction for the misappropriation, and (2) the attorney did not show "compelling extenuating circumstances" justifying a lesser sanction, as the attorney showed no serious and debilitating mental condition, since the attorney was not diagnosed with a mental illness, the attorney did not show such a condition was the "root cause" of the attorney's misconduct by making the attorney unable to do day-to-day activities in a normal manner, and the attorney did not show such a condition caused an utter inability to conform the attorney's conduct to the law and the Maryland Rules of Professional Conduct, so any psychological issues the attorney had at the time of the attorney's misconduct did not mitigate the attorney's sanction. Att'y Griev. Comm'n v. Palmer, 417 Md. 185, 9 A.3d 37 (2010).

Attorney violated (c) and Md. Law. R. Prof. Conduct 1.2(a), 1.15(d), 8.4(c) and (d), Md. R. 16-604, and § 10-306 of the Business Occupations and Professions Article, and was disbarred, after misappropriating tens of thousands of dollars that should have been paid to a physical therapist and settling a client's claim without the client's knowledge or consent. Att'y Griev. Comm'n v. Stern, 419 Md. 525, 19 A.3d 904 (2011).

Attorney was disbarred for violating this section and Md. Law. R. Prof. Conduct 1.1, 1.3, 1.15(a), (d), and (e), 1.16(d), 5.5(a) and (b), 8.4(b), (c), and (d), Md. R. 16-603 and 16-604, and § 10-306 of the Business Occupations and Professions Article, by commingling client funds with the attorney's own funds, failing to pay medical providers for clients, and practicing after the attorney lost the right for failure to pay Client Protection Fund assessment and failure to file a pro bono report. Att'y Griev. Comm'n v. Agiliga, 422 Md. 613, 31 A.3d 103 (2011).

Cited in Att'y Griev. Comm'n v. Khandpur, 421 Md. 1, 25 A.3d 165 (2011).

When an attorney deposited unearned funds received on a client's behalf in the attorney's operating account, rather than in a trust account, it was not error for a hearing judge not to find the attorney violated this Rule because (1) the attorney "drew against" the funds in the

13

attorney's operating account, and (2) nothing showed those funds included the funds paid for the client, so no reasonable trier of fact could find by clear and convincing evidence that the attorney made an unauthorized use of the funds. Att'y Griev. Comm'n v. Tauber, 421 Md. 415, 26 A.3d 967 (2011).

CHAPTER 700. DISCIPLINE AND INACTIVE STATUS OF ATTORNEYS.

Rule 16-701. Definitions.

Applied in Balt. County v. Barnhart, 201 Md. App. 682, 30 A.3d 291 (2011).

Rule 16-711. Attorney Grievance Commission.

Applied in Balt. County v. Barnhart, 201 Md. App. 682, 30 A.3d 291 (2011).

Rule 16-712. Bar Counsel.

Applied in Balt. County v. Barnhart, 201 Md. App. 682, 30 A.3d 291 (2011).

Rule 16-715. Costs.

Cited in Att'y Griev. Comm'n v. Usiak, 418 Md. 667, 18 A.3d 1 (2011); Att'y Griev. Comm'n v. Khandpur, 421 Md. 1, 25 A.3d 165 (2011); Att'y Griev. Comm'n v. Carithers, 421 Md. 28, 25 A.3d 181 (2011).

Rule 16-723. Confidentiality.

Applied in Att'y Griev. Comm'n v. Joseph, 422 Md. 670, 31 A.3d 137 (2011); Balt. County v. Barnhart, 201 Md. App. 682, 30 A.3d 291 (2011).
Stated in Kim v. Md. State Bd. of Physicians, 423 Md. 523, 32 A.3d 30 (2011).
Cited in Att'y Griev. Comm'n v. Usiak, 418 Md. 667, 18 A.3d 1 (2011); Att'y Griev. Comm'n v. Keiner, 421 Md. 492, 27 A.3d 153 (2011).

Rule 16-731. Complaint; investigation by Bar Counsel.

Applied in Balt. County v. Barnhart, 201 Md. App. 682, 30 A.3d 291 (2011).

Quoted in Att'y Griev. Comm'n v. Fox, 417 Md. 504, 11 A.3d 762 (2010).

Rule 16-732. Investigative subpoena.

Cited in Att'y Griev. Comm'n v. Keiner, 421 Md. 492, 27 A.3d 153 (2011).

Rule 16-734. Procedure upon completion of investigation.

Applied in Balt. County v. Barnhart, 201 Md. App. 682, 30 A.3d 291 (2011).

Rule 16-736. Conditional diversion agreement.

Admissibility of evidence. — When an attorney was alleged to have violated Md. Law. R. Prof. Conduct 1.4(a) and (b) and 8.4(a), (b), (c), and (d), as well as § 7-302 of the Criminal Law Article by altering the attorney's employer law firm's electronic files to facilitate taking certain of the firm's clients with the attorney when the attorney left the firm, it was not error to rule that the report of a peer review panel and communications between the attorney's counsel and Bar Counsel about the possibility of a conditional diversion agreement were inadmissible because (1) the report and communications were irrelevant to the attorney's charged conduct and mitigation of the attorney's sanction, (2) the report was merely a recommendation to the Attorney Grievance Commission, and not the Court of Appeals, and (3) there was no authority to support remanding the case to reconsider the availability of a conditional diversion agreement. Att'y Griev. Comm'n v. Keiner, 421 Md. 492, 27 A.3d 153 (2011).

Cited in Att'y Griev. Comm'n v. Khandpur, 421 Md. 1, 25 A.3d 165 (2011).

Rule 16-743. Peer review process.

Applied in Att'y Griev. Comm'n v. Joseph, 422 Md. 670, 31 A.3d 137 (2011).

Cited in Att'y Griev. Comm'n v. Keiner, 421 Md. 492, 27 A.3d 153 (2011).

Rule 16-751. Petition for disciplinary or remedial action.

Applied in Balt. County v. Barnhart, 201 Md. App. 682, 30 A.3d 291 (2011); Att'y Griev. Comm'n v. Maignan, 423 Md. 191, 31 A.3d 467 (2011); Att'y Griev. Comm'n v. Joseph, 422 Md. 670, 31 A.3d 137 (2011).

Quoted in Att'y Griev. Comm'n v. Lara, 418 Md. 355, 14 A.3d 650 (2011); Att'y Griev. Comm'n v. Coppola, 419 Md. 370, 19 A.3d 431 (2011); Att'y Griev. Comm'n v. Stern, 419 Md. 525, 19 A.3d 904 (2011); Att'y Griev. Comm'n v. Khandpur, 421 Md. 1, 25 A.3d 165 (2011); Att'y Griev. Comm'n v. Agiliga, 422 Md. 613, 31 A.3d 103 (2011).

Stated in Att'y Griev. Comm'n v. Zodrow, 419 Md. 286, 19 A.3d 381 (2011).

Cited in Att'y Griev. Comm'n v. Carithers, 421 Md. 28, 25 A.3d 181 (2011); Att'y Griev. Comm'n v. Keiner, 421 Md. 492, 27 A.3d 153 (2011); Att'y Griev. Comm'n v. Paul, 423 Md. 268, 31 A.3d 512 (2011); Att'y Griev. Comm'n of Md. v. Van Nelson, — Md. —, — A.3d — (Mar. 27, 2012).

Rule 16-752. Order designating judge.

Applied in Att'y Griev. Comm'n v. Joseph, 422 Md. 670, 31 A.3d 137 (2011).

Quoted in Att'y Griev. Comm'n v. Khandpur, 421 Md. 1, 25 A.3d 165 (2011); Att'y Griev. Comm'n v. Brady, 422 Md. 441, 30 A.3d 902 (2011).

Cited in Att'y Griev. Comm'n v. Palmer, 417 Md. 185, 9 A.3d 37 (2010); Att'y Griev. Comm'n v. Fox, 417 Md. 504, 11 A.3d 762 (2010); Att'y Griev. Comm'n v. Usiak, 418 Md. 667, 18 A.3d 1 (2011); Att'y Griev. Comm'n v. Zodrow, 419 Md. 286, 19 A.3d 381 (2011); Att'y Griev. Comm'n v. Carithers, 421 Md. 28, 25 A.3d 181 (2011); Att'y Griev. Comm'n v. Keiner, 421 Md. 492, 27 A.3d 153 (2011); Att'y Griev. Comm'n v. Patterson, 421 Md. 708, 28 A.3d 1196 (2011); Att'y Griev. Comm'n v. Agiliga, 422 Md. 613, 31 A.3d 103 (2011); Att'y Griev. Comm'n v. Paul, 423 Md. 268, 31 A.3d 512 (2011); Att'y Griev. Comm'n v. Smith, — Md. —, — A.3d — (Mar. 19, 2012).

Rule 16-753. Service of petition.

Quoted in Att'y Griev. Comm'n v. Brady, 422 Md. 441, 30 A.3d 902 (2011).

Rule 16-757. Judicial hearing.

Applied in Att'y Griev. Comm'n v. Fox, 417 Md. 504, 11 A.3d 762 (2010); Att'y Griev. Comm'n v. Sucklal, 418 Md. 1, 12 A.3d 650 (2011); Att'y Griev. Comm'n v. Joseph, 422 Md. 670, 31 A.3d 137 (2011); Balt. County v. Barnhart, 201 Md. App. 682, 30 A.3d 291 (2011); Att'y Griev. Comm'n v. Maignan, 423 Md. 191, 31 A.3d 467 (2011).

Quoted in Att'y Griev. Comm'n v. Lara, 418 Md. 355, 14 A.3d 650 (2011); Att'y Griev. Comm'n v. Coppola, 419 Md. 370, 19 A.3d 431 (2011); Att'y Griev. Comm'n v. Stern, 419 Md. 525, 19 A.3d 904 (2011); Att'y Griev. Comm'n v. Patterson, 421 Md. 708, 28 A.3d 1196 (2011); Att'y Griev. Comm'n v. Brady, 422 Md. 441, 30 A.3d 902 (2011); Att'y Griev. Comm'n of Md. v. Van Nelson, — Md. —, — A.3d — (Mar. 27, 2012).

Cited in Att'y Griev. Comm'n v. Palmer, 417 Md. 185, 9 A.3d 37 (2010); Att'y Griev. Comm'n v. Elliott, 417 Md. 659, 12 A.3d 105 (2011); Att'y Griev. Comm'n v. Zodrow, 419 Md. 286, 19 A.3d 381 (2011); Att'y Griev. Comm'n v. Carithers, 421 Md. 28, 25 A.3d 181 (2011); Att'y Griev. Comm'n v. Tauber, 421 Md. 415, 26 A.3d 967 (2011); Att'y Griev. Comm'n v. Keiner, 421 Md. 492, 27 A.3d 153 (2011); Att'y Griev. Comm'n v. Paul, 423 Md. 268, 31 A.3d 512 (2011); Att'y Griev. Comm'n v. Ambe, — Md. —, 38 A.3d 390 (2012).

Rule 16-758. Post-hearing proceedings.

Cited in Potomac Valley Orthopaedic Assocs. v. Md. State Bd. of Physicians, 417 Md. 622, 12 A.3d 84 (2011); Att'y Griev. Comm'n v. De La Paz, 418 Md. 534, 16 A.3d 181 (2011); Att'y Griev. Comm'n v. Paul, 423 Md. 268, 31 A.3d 512 (2011).

Rule 16-759. Disposition.

Findings of fact and conclusions of law accepted due to parties' failures to file exceptions. — In an attorney disciplinary matter, a hearing judge's findings of fact and conclusions of law were accepted, under (b)(2)(A) of this Rule, for purposes of determining an appropriate sanction because neither the Attorney Grievance Commission nor the attorney against whom charges were brought filed exceptions to those findings and conclusions. Att'y Griev. Comm'n v. De La Paz, 418 Md. 534, 16 A.3d 181 (2011).

Court accepted a judge's findings in an attorney disciplinary case because there were no exceptions filed; the lawyer was disbarred because he engaged in the unauthorized practice of law when, while under a prior suspension, he advised, counseled, and drafted documents and pleadings for the complainant and received at least $ 5,100 in legal fees from the complainant. Att'y Griev. Comm'n v. Maignan, 423 Md. 191, 31 A.3d 467 (2011).

Applied in .

Quoted in Att'y Griev. Comm'n v. Coppola, 419 Md. 370, 19 A.3d 431 (2011); Att'y Griev. Comm'n v. Stern, 419 Md. 525, 19 A.3d 904 (2011); Att'y Griev. Comm'n v. Brady, 422 Md. 441, 30 A.3d 902 (2011); Att'y Griev. Comm'n of Md. v. Van Nelson, — Md. —, — A.3d — (Mar. 27, 2012).

Cited in Att'y Griev. Comm'n v. Usiak, 418 Md. 667, 18 A.3d 1 (2011); Att'y Griev. Comm'n v. Carithers, 421 Md. 28, 25 A.3d 181 (2011); Att'y Griev. Comm'n v. Agiliga, 422 Md. 613, 31 A.3d 103 (2011); Att'y Griev. Comm'n v. Paul, 423 Md. 268, 31 A.3d 512 (2011); Att'y Griev. Comm'n v. Smith, — Md. —, — A.3d — (Mar. 19, 2012).

Rule 16-760. Order imposing discipline or inactive status.

Further representation after suspension.

Because (f) provided for the protection of the public by authorizing Bar Counsel to take further action against the attorney in the unlikely event that she ever again engaged in the unauthorized practice of law, and in light of her failing health and intent to return to Africa, disbarment was not necessary; rather, the indefinite suspension was continued. Att'y Griev. Comm'n v. Brisbon, 422 Md. 625, 31 A.3d 110 (2011).

Applied in Att'y Griev. Comm'n v. Sucklal, 418 Md. 1, 12 A.3d 650 (2011).

Stated in Att'y Griev. Comm'n v. Ambe, — Md. —, 38 A.3d 390 (2012).

Rule 16-761. Costs.

Applied in Att'y Griev. Comm'n v. Maignan, 423 Md. 191, 31 A.3d 467 (2011).

Cited in Att'y Griev. Comm'n v. Elliott, 417 Md. 659, 12 A.3d 105 (2011); Att'y Griev. Comm'n v. Tauber, 421 Md. 415, 26 A.3d 967

(2011); Att'y Griev. Comm'n v. Keiner, 421 Md. 492, 27 A.3d 153 (2011); Att'y Griev. Comm'n v. Paul, 423 Md. 268, 31 A.3d 512 (2011); Att'y Griev. Comm'n v. Payer, — Md. —, 38 A.3d 378 (2012).

Rule 16-773. Reciprocal discipline or inactive status.

Disbarment required.
In a reciprocal disciplinary action, the attorney, who had been suspended from the practice of law for one year and one day in Colorado, was disbarred for violating Md. Law. R. Prof. Conduct 3.3(a)(1), 3.4(c), and 8.4(a), (b), (c), and (d), based on the attorney's own admission that he failed to make pertinent disclosures

during a personal bankruptcy case and gave false testimony that case. Att'y Griev. Comm'n v. Zodrow, 419 Md. 286, 19 A.3d 381 (2011).

Cited in Att'y Griev. Comm'n v. Keiner, 421 Md. 492, 27 A.3d 153 (2011); Att'y Griev. Comm'n v. Paul, 423 Md. 268, 31 A.3d 512 (2011).

CHAPTER 800. MISCELLANEOUS.

Rule 16-801. Promulgation of rules.

University of Baltimore Law Forum. — For an article, "The Idealist Discourse of Legal Professionalism in Maryland: Delineating the

Omissions and Eloquent Silences as a Progressive Critique," see 41 U. Balt. L. F. 120 (2011).

Rule 16-811. Client Protection Fund of the Bar of Maryland.

Editor's note.
This rule is set out herein to correct an error appearing in the bound volume. "Rule 15 of the Rules Governing Admission to the Bar of

Maryland" has been substituted for "Rule 15 of Rules Governing Admission to Bar" in e.2.

Quoted in Att'y Griev. Comm'n v. Brady, 422 Md. 441, 30 A.3d 902 (2011).

Rule 16-812. Maryland Lawyers' Rules of Professional Conduct.

Cited in Att'y Griev. Comm'n v. Paul, 423 Md. 268, 31 A.3d 512 (2011).

Rule 16-813. Maryland Code of Judicial Conduct.

In banc hearing proper despite recusal of some judges and vacancy. — It was not error, under § 1-403(c) of the Courts Article, for the Maryland Court of Special Appeals to hear a case in banc when less than seven judges voted to do so because (1) three judges

recused themselves under Md. Code Jud. Conduct R. 2.11, (2) one seat was vacant, and (3) the statute's proper interpretation held a majority of those remaining could decide to hear the case in banc. Exxon Mobil Corp. v. Ford, — Md. App. —, — A.3d — (Mar. 6, 2012).

TITLE 17. ALTERNATIVE DISPUTE RESOLUTION

CHAPTER 100. PROCEEDINGS IN CIRCUIT COURT.

Rule 17-109. Mediation confidentiality.

Stated in Kim v. Md. State Bd. of Physicians, 423 Md. 523, 32 A.3d 30 (2011).

APPENDIX: THE MARYLAND LAWYERS' RULES OF PROFESSIONAL CONDUCT

Rule 1.0. Terminology.

Cited in Att'y Griev. Comm'n v. De La Paz, 418 Md. 534, 16 A.3d 181 (2011); Att'y Griev. Comm'n v. Keiner, 421 Md. 492, 27 A.3d 153 (2011).

CLIENT-LAWYER RELATIONSHIP.

Rule 1.1. Competence.

I. General Consideration.
II. Specific Acts.
III. Sanctions.

I. GENERAL CONSIDERATION.

Quoted in Att'y Griev. Comm'n of Md. v. Van Nelson, — Md. —, — A.3d — (Mar. 27, 2012).

II. SPECIFIC ACTS.

Incompetence found.
While the attorney's drafting of a complaint that did not specifically comply with all the technical requirements did not violate this section, the attorney did violate this section when the attorney failed to enter an appearance in an action until the trial date, did not learn of the looming trial date until the client informed the attorney of it several days before trial, and did not give the client accurate information about the status of the case. Att'y Griev. Comm'n v. Patterson, 421 Md. 708, 28 A.3d 1196 (2011).

Violation found.
Attorney violated this Rule in two cases because, (1) in a civil case in which the attorney was retained to defend a client, the attorney never entered the attorney's appearance or contact the plaintiff, and did not appear for a hearing, leaving the client to enter into a consent judgment without the aid of counsel, and, (2) in a personal injury case, after discovering that a defendant was deceased, the attorney did not open an estate or otherwise act to protect a client's claim, which was eventually dismissed for a failure to prosecute. Att'y Griev. Comm'n v. De La Paz, 418 Md. 534, 16 A.3d 181 (2011).

Where a suspended attorney agreed to represent two clients at their interview/meeting with The United States Citizenship and Immigration Services and engaged in an in-depth interview to obtain significant personal and other legal information with the obvious intention of developing information to prepare the appropriate forms, the attorney engaged in the practice of law in violation of Md. Law. R. Prof. Conduct 1.1, 1.4, 1.5, 5.5, and 8.4. Att'y Griev. Comm'n v. Brisbon, 422 Md. 625, 31 A.3d 110 (2011).

Attorney violated this section by failing to file a response to a motion to dismiss a client's complaint and failing to appear for a status conference. Att'y Griev. Comm'n v. Brady, 422 Md. 441, 30 A.3d 902 (2011).

III. SANCTIONS.

Disbarment was proper sanction.
Attorney violated this rule by completely neglecting a case after filing a complaint, such that the case was dismissed, and by effectively abandoning a second case for six years; the attorney was disbarred for violating this rule along with Md. Law. R. Prof. Conduct 1.2(a), 1.3, 1.4(a), 1.16(d), 8.1(b), and 8.4(a), (c), and (d). Att'y Griev. Comm'n v. Fox, 417 Md. 504, 11 A.3d 762 (2010).

Attorney was disbarred for admittedly violating Md. Law. R. Prof. Conduct 1.1, 1.15(a) and (c), and 8.4(a) — (d), as well as Rule 16-609 and § 10- 306 of the Business Occupations and Professions Article, by misappropriating client funds to make it appear as though the attorney's collected fees were higher than those fees actually were, when the attorney was being considered for partner in the attorney's firm, and by failing to file complaints in clients' cases, misrepresenting that the complaints were filed, and fabricating documents to hide the misrepresentations, because (1) disbarment was the presumed sanction for the misappropriation, and (2) the attorney did not show "compelling extenuating circumstances" justifying a lesser sanction, as the attorney showed no serious and debilitating mental condition, since the attorney was not diagnosed with a mental illness, the attorney did not show such a condition was the "root cause" of the attorney's misconduct by making the attorney unable to do day-to-day activities in a normal manner, and the attorney did not show such a condition caused an utter inability to conform the attorney's conduct to the law and the Maryland Rules of Professional Conduct, so any psychological issues the attorney had at the time of the attorney's misconduct did not mitigate the attorney's sanction. Att'y Griev. Comm'n v. Palmer, 417 Md. 185, 9 A.3d 37 (2010).

Attorney was disbarred for violating this section and Md. Law. R. Prof. Conduct 1.3, 1.15(a), (d), and (e), 1.16(d), 5.5(a) and (b), 8.4(b), (c), and (d), Md. R. 16-603, 16-604, and 16-609, and § 10-306 of the Business Occupations and Professions Article, by commingling client funds with the attorney's own funds,

failing to pay medical providers for clients, and practicing after the attorney lost the right for failure to pay Client Protection Fund assessment and failure to file a pro bono report. Att'y Griev. Comm'n v. Agiliga, 422 Md. 613, 31 A.3d 103 (2011).

Disbarment for violating this rule and Md. Law. R. Prof. Conduct 1.3, 1.4(b), 1.15, 8.1(a) and (b), and 8.4(c) and (d), and Md. R. 16-607 was appropriate based on a finding that the attorney's commitment to hiding to truth from Bar Counsel was systematic and unwavering and was not the product of mere mistake, and where there was no innocent explanation for the fabrication of documents or the alternation of bank records after Bar Counsel began its investigation. Att'y Griev. Comm'n v. Payer, — Md. —, 38 A.3d 378 (2012).

Rule 1.2. Scope of Representation and Allocation of Authority Between Client and Lawyer.

Failure to abide by represenation objectives.

Attorney violated this Rule because, (1) after a client signed a contract to be represented by the attorney's employer, the attorney did not respect that decision when the attorney asserted that the client hired the attorney personally, and (2) the attorney took action on the client's behalf that the client did not authorize when the attorney substituted the attorney's name as payee on the client's check made payable to the attorney's employer. Att'y Griev. Comm'n v. Elliott, 417 Md. 659, 12 A.3d 105 (2011).

Disbarment was proper sanction.

Attorney violated this rule by failing to abide by the decisions of his clients in one action and failing to pursue their matter after the complaint was filed, and by failing to consult with a client in a second action about the settlement agreement reached with an insurer; the attorney was disbarred for violating this rule along with Md. Law. R. Prof. Conduct 1.1, 1.3, 1.4(a), 1.16(d), 8.1(b), and 8.4(a), (c), and (d). Att'y Griev. Comm'n v. Fox,

417 Md. 504, 11 A.3d 762 (2010).

Attorney was disbarred for violating (d) and Md. Law. R. Prof. Conduct 8.4(a), (b), (c), and (d), when the attorney empowered a client's child to forge the client's signature on estate documents, notarized falsely executed and initialed estate documents, and directed the attorney's employees to falsely attest to the signature; the attorney suffered no cognitive deficits and new what he was doing was wrong. Att'y Griev. Comm'n v. Coppola, 419 Md. 370, 19 A.3d 431 (2011).

Attorney violated (a) and Md. Law. R. Prof. Conduct 1.15(d), 8.4(c) and (d), Md. R. 16-604 and 16-609(c), and § 10-306 of the Business Occupations and Professions Article, and was disbarred, after misappropriating tens of thousands of dollars that should have been paid to a physical therapist and settling a client's claim without the client's knowledge or consent. Att'y Griev. Comm'n v. Stern, 419 Md. 525, 19 A.3d 904 (2011).

Cited in State v. Northam, 421 Md. 195, 26 A.3d 344 (2011); In re Adoption/Guardianship of Chaden M., 422 Md. 498, 30 A.3d 935 (2011).

Rule 1.3. Diligence.

I. General Consideration.
II. Specific Acts.
III. Sanctions.

I. GENERAL CONSIDERATION.

Cited in Att'y Griev. Comm'n v. Paul, 423 Md. 268, 31 A.3d 512 (2011).

II. SPECIFIC ACTS.

Failure to handle clients' matters in a reasonably diligent manner.

Attorney violated this section when the attorney failed to enter an appearance in an action until the trial date, did not learn of the looming trial date until the client informed the attorney of it several days before trial, and did not give the client accurate information about the status of the case. Att'y Griev. Comm'n v. Patterson, 421 Md. 708, 28 A.3d 1196 (2011).

Failure to represent adequately.

Attorney violated this Rule in two cases because, (1) in a civil case in which the attorney was retained to defend a client, the attorney never entered the attorney's appearance or contact the plaintiff, and did not appear for a hearing, leaving the client to enter into a consent judgment without the aid of counsel, and, (2) in a personal injury case, after discovering that a defendant was deceased, the attorney did not open an estate or otherwise act to protect a client's claim, which was eventually dismissed for a failure to prosecute. Att'y Griev. Comm'n v. De La Paz, 418 Md. 534, 16 A.3d 181 (2011).

Failure to timely file asylum application. — Attorney violated this Rule by failing to file a client's asylum application on time; while the attorney argued that the late filing was due to the client's failure to timely provide essential information, the Court of Appeals concluded that a reasonably diligent attorney would have submitted as complete an application as possible before the deadline. Att'y Griev. Comm'n v. Khandpur, 421 Md. 1, 25 A.3d 165 (2011).

Violation found. — Attorney violated this section by failing to file a response to a motion to dismiss a client's complaint and failing to appear for a status conference. Att'y Griev. Comm'n v. Brady, 422 Md. 441, 30 A.3d 902 (2011).

Rule 1.4. Communication.

I. General Consideration.
II. Sanctions.

I. GENERAL CONSIDERATION.

Failure to communicate with client.

Attorney violated this Rule, in two cases, because (1) the attorney did not respond to clients' telephone messages or letters, (2) the

III. SANCTIONS.

Disbarment was proper sanction.

Attorney violated this rule by failing to diligently pursue an action for two clients after the complaint was filed and failing to monitor the action, and by allowing a second action to languish for over six years while an insurer sent over 50 checks to the attorneys' office; the attorney was disbarred for violating this rule along with Md. Law. R. Prof. Conduct 1.1, 1.2(a), 1.4(a), 1.16(d), 8.1(b), and 8.4(a), (c), and (d). Att'y Griev. Comm'n v. Fox, 417 Md. 504, 11 A.3d 762 (2010).

Attorney was disbarred for violating this section and Md. Law. R. Prof. Conduct 1.4(a) and (b), 1.15(a), (c), and (d), 1.16(d), 8.1(b), and 8.4(a) and (d), after the attorney received advance fee payments from two clients, deposited the money in a personal account, rather than a trust account, having not earned the fees, and abandoned the clients without performing work for the clients. Att'y Griev. Comm'n v. Lara, 418 Md. 355, 14 A.3d 650 (2011).

Attorney was disbarred for violating this section and Md. Law. R. Prof. Conduct 1.1, 1.15(a), (d), and (e), 1.16(d), 5.5(a) and (b), 8.4(b), (c), and (d), Md. R. 16-603, 16-604, and 16-609, and § 10-306 of the Business Occupations and Professions Article, by commingling client funds with the attorney's own funds, failing to pay medical providers for clients, and practicing after the attorney lost the right for failure to pay Client Protection Fund assessment and failure to file a pro bono report. Att'y Griev. Comm'n v. Agiliga, 422 Md. 613, 31 A.3d 103 (2011).

Disbarment for violating this rule and Md. Law. R. Prof. Conduct 1.1, 1.4(b), 1.7, 1.15, 8.1(a) and (b), and 8.4(c) and (d), and Md. R. 16-607 was appropriate based on a finding that the attorney's commitment to hiding to truth from Bar Counsel was systematic and unwavering and was not the product of mere mistake, and where there was no innocent explanation for the fabrication of documents or the alternation of bank records after Bar Counsel began its investigation. Att'y Griev. Comm'n v. Payer, — Md. —, 38 A.3d 378 (2012).

attorney did not tell a client that the client's case had been dismissed, and (3) the attorney did not tell clients the attorney had moved the attorney's practice or provide the clients with new contact information. Att'y Griev. Comm'n v. De La Paz, 418 Md. 534, 16 A.3d 181 (2011).

Attorney violated (b) when the attorney failed to give the client accurate information about the status of the case, in particular, when failing to tell the client that witnesses the client wished to have testify at trial wanted to be compensated as "experts." Att'y Griev. Comm'n v. Patterson, 421 Md. 708, 28 A.3d 1196 (2011).

Attorney violated this section by failing to keep the client informed of the status of the client's case, despite the client's repeated attempts to reach the attorney; among other things, the attorney never informed the client that a motion to dismiss her case had been filed or that a status conference had been scheduled. Att'y Griev. Comm'n v. Brady, 422 Md. 441, 30 A.3d 902 (2011).

Failure to disclose fee. — Respondent, who was not licensed to practice law in Maryland, violated Md. Law. R. Prof. Conduct 1.4(b) and 1.5(a) and (b) by suing a client for fees at an excessive hourly rate that she had not disclosed and he had not agreed to pay. Att'y Griev. Comm'n v. Sucklal, 418 Md. 1, 12 A.3d 650 (2011).

Failure to disclose suspension. — Where a suspended attorney agreed to represent two clients at their interview/meeting with The United States Citizenship and Immigration Services and engaged in an in-depth interview to obtain significant personal and other legal information with the obvious intention of developing information to prepare the appropriate forms, the attorney engaged in the practice of law in violation of this Rule as the attorney failed to disclose her suspension. Att'y Griev. Comm'n v. Brisbon, 422 Md. 625, 31 A.3d 110 (2011).

Attorney's unilateral decision to make firm's client attorney's personal client. — Attorney violated (a)(1) because (1) the attorney made a unilateral decision to make a client the attorney's personal client although the client had entered into a written agreement to retain the law firm which employed the attorney, and (2) the attorney decided to change the payee on the client's check from the firm to the attorney without discussing the change and obtaining the client's consent. Att'y Griev. Comm'n v. Elliott, 417 Md. 659, 12 A.3d 105 (2011).

When an attorney altered the attorney's law firm employer's electronic files to facilitate the attorney taking certain of the firm's clients with the attorney when the attorney left the firm, the attorney admittedly violated (a) and (b) because the attorney failed to communicate with the attorney's clients regarding a material change in the clients' representation. Att'y Griev. Comm'n v. Keiner, 421 Md. 492, 27 A.3d 153 (2011).

Quoted in Att'y Griev. Comm'n v. Khandpur, 421 Md. 1, 25 A.3d 165 (2011).

Cited in Att'y Griev. Comm'n v. Agiliga, 422 Md. 613, 31 A.3d 103 (2011); Att'y Griev. Comm'n v. Paul, 423 Md. 268, 31 A.3d 512 (2011).

II. SANCTIONS.

Disbarment was proper sanction.
Attorney violated this rule by failing to keep his clients informed about the status of their cases, including the dismissal of one case, which the attorney himself was not aware of, and by failing to respond promptly to requests for information about the subject actions; the attorney was disbarred for violating this rule along with Md. Law. R. Prof. Conduct 1.1, 1.2(a), 1.3, 1.16(d), 8.1(b), and 8.4(a), (c), and (d). Att'y Griev. Comm'n v. Fox, 417 Md. 504, 11 A.3d 762 (2010).

Attorney was disbarred for violating (a) and (b) and Md. Law. R. Prof. Conduct 1.3, 1.15(a), (c), and (d), 1.16(d), 8.1(b), and 8.4(a) and (d), after the attorney received advance fee payments from two clients, deposited the money in a personal account, rather than a trust account, having not earned the fees, and abandoned the clients without performing work for the clients. Att'y Griev. Comm'n v. Lara, 418 Md. 355, 14 A.3d 650 (2011).

When an attorney altered the attorney's law firm employer's electronic files to facilitate the attorney taking certain of the firm's clients with the attorney when the attorney left the firm, the proper sanction for the attorney's admitted violations of Md. Law. R. Prof. Conduct 8.4(a), (b), (c), and (d), and (a) and (b) of this Rule, as well as Md. Code Ann., Crim. Law § 7-302, was disbarment because (1) the attorney's conduct was dishonest, intentional, and solely motivated by a desire for personal gain, so disbarment was presumed, and (2) the attorney's mental disabilities of depression and alcohol dependency were not "compelling extenuating circumstances" warranting a lesser sanction as the disabilities did not result in an utter inability to conform the attorney's conduct to the law and the Rules of Professional Conduct. Att'y Griev. Comm'n v. Keiner, 421 Md. 492, 27 A.3d 153 (2011).

Disbarment for violating (b) and Md. Law. R. Prof. Conduct 1.1, 1.3, 1.7, 1.15, 8.1(a) and (b), and 8.4(c) and (d), and Md. R. 16-607 was appropriate based on a finding that the attorney's commitment to hiding to truth from Bar Counsel was systematic and unwavering and was not the product of mere mistake, and where there was no innocent explanation for the fabrication of documents or the alternation of bank records after Bar Counsel began its investigation. Att'y Griev. Comm'n v. Payer, — Md. —, 38 A.3d 378 (2012).

Attorney was disbarred for violating (a)(2) and (a)(3), and Md. Law. R. Prof. Conduct 1.5(a), 1.15(c) and (d), 1.16(d), 8.1(b), 8.4(a) and (d), and Md. R. 16-604 and 16-606.1(a)(3), by, inter alia, failing to communicate with a client regarding the disposition of a settlement check, despite numerous phone calls from the client requesting that information. Att'y Griev. Comm'n of Md. v. Van Nelson, — Md. —, — A.3d — (Mar. 27, 2012).

Rule 1.5. Fees.

I. GENERAL CONSIDERATION.

Percentage fees not allowed. — As a bank presented no evidence that it agreed to pay attorneys' fees other than on an hourly rate basis or concerning the fees it would incur in future collection efforts, the court did not err in awarding the bank only the reasonable fees it incurred as of the date of judgment instead of fees equal to 15 percent of principal amount owed, as the parties' loan agreement provided. Suntrust Bank v. Goldman, 201 Md. App. 390, 29 A.3d 724 (2011).

Applied in Friolo v. Frankel, 201 Md. App. 79, 28 A.3d 752 (2011).

Cited in Att'y Griev. Comm'n v. Agiliga, 422 Md. 613, 31 A.3d 103 (2011).

II. SPECIFIC ACTS.

"Excessive fee."
Attorney violated (a) when the attorney charged a client for the execution of a judgment, when there was no judgment. Att'y Griev. Comm'n v. Patterson, 421 Md. 708, 28 A.3d 1196 (2011).

Unreasonable fee.
Respondent, who was not licensed to practice law in Maryland, violated Md. Law. R. Prof. Conduct 1.4(b) and 1.5(a) and (b) by suing a client for fees at an $ 375 per hour, a rate that she had not disclosed and he had not agreed to pay. Att'y Griev. Comm'n v. Sucklal, 418 Md. 1, 12 A.3d 650 (2011).

Attorney violated this Rule because the attorney's fee, collected in advance, that was otherwise reasonable, became unreasonable when the attorney did no work to earn the fee. Att'y Griev. Comm'n v. De La Paz, 418 Md. 534, 16 A.3d 181 (2011).

Although the attorney's hourly rate of $ 220 was not unreasonable on its face, the attorney violated (a) by collecting $ 10,000 in fees without providing commensurate services, thus making the fees received wholly disproportionate and unreasonable in relation to the services provided. Att'y Griev. Comm'n v. Brady, 422 Md. 441, 30 A.3d 902 (2011).

Reasonable fee award.
When a tenant successfully sued a landlord, but the trial court's judgment was reversed and the case was remanded for a second trial, at which the tenant again prevailed, the tenant was entitled to an award of fees and costs incurred at the second trial because (1) the tenant did not engage in unreasonable conduct at the first trial which necessitated the second trial, and (2) the second trial was, instead, necessitated by the trial court's erroneous rulings at the first trial. Cong. Hotel Corp. v. Mervis Diamond Corp., 200 Md. App. 489, 28 A.3d 75 (2011).

Partial success.
It was not error for a trial court not to award a landlord the full amount of attorneys' fees the landlord requested in a lawsuit against a tenant because (1) most fees were incurred regarding an issue on which the tenant did not prevail, and (2) it was not error to find that the hourly rate charged by counsel was high for the county in which the litigation was brought. Carroll Indep. Fuel Co. v. Wash. Real Estate Inv. Trust, 202 Md. App. 206, 32 A.3d 128 (2011).

Calculation of fees in homeowners' association assessment dispute. — While lodestar method did not apply when calculating attorneys' fees in homeowners' associations' assessment dispute because no fee-shifting statute finding that such litigation promoted a public policy was involved, the trial court properly used the rubric of this rule to determining a reasonable fee. Monmouth Meadows Homeowners Ass'n v. Hamilton, 416 Md. 325, 7 A.3d 1 (Oct. 25, 2010).

Unauthorized practice of law. — Where a suspended attorney agreed to represent two clients at their interview/meeting with The United States Citizenship and Immigration Services and engaged in an in-depth interview to obtain significant personal and other legal information with the obvious intention of developing information to prepare the appropriate forms, the attorney engaged in the practice of law in violation of Md. Law. R. Prof. Conduct 1.1, 1.4, 1.5, 5.5, and 8.4. Att'y Griev. Comm'n v. Brisbon, 422 Md. 625, 31 A.3d 110 (2011).

III. EVIDENCE.

Post judgment attorney fees. — If a contract calls for the shifting of attorneys' fees incurred in post judgment collection efforts, and assuming that it does not avoid the doctrine of merger, a trial court should permit the requesting party to put on evidence of fees that will, with certainty, be incurred in addition to those actually incurred at that time. Suntrust Bank v. Goldman, 201 Md. App. 390, 29 A.3d 724 (2011).

IV. SANCTIONS.

Disbarment was proper sanction.

Lawyer was disbarred because he engaged in the unauthorized practice of law when, while under a prior suspension, he advised, counseled, and drafted documents and pleadings for the complainant and received at least

$ 5,100 in legal fees from the complainant; among other things, an attorney's suspension rendered a legal fee paid by a client unreasonable. This was the third time in seven years that the lawyer had violated the Rules of Professional Conduct. Att'y Griev. Comm'n v. Maignan, 423 Md. 191, 31 A.3d 467 (2011).

Attorney was disbarred for violating (a), and Md. Law. R. Prof. Conduct 1.4(a)(2) and (a)(3), 1.15(c) and (d), 1.16(d), 8.1(b), 8.4(a) and (d), and Md. R. 16-604 and 16-606.1(a)(3), by, inter alia, receiving a total of $ 19,285 in fees, despite earning only $ 9,825 under the fee agreement. Att'y Griev. Comm'n of Md. v. Van Nelson, — Md. —, — A.3d — (Mar. 27, 2012).

Rule 1.7. Conflict of Interest: General Rule.

Cited in Att'y Griev. Comm'n v. Payer, — Md. —, 38 A.3d 378 (2012).

Rule 1.9. Duties to Former Clients.

Editor's note. — This Rule is set out to reflect the following change: "about" was added at the beginning of (b)(2).

No conflict of interest found

Disqualification of an insured's attorney and her law firm was not warranted under Rules 1.9(a) and 1.10(a) where the insurer only showed that the attorney had previously represented other insureds; it failed to show that it also stood in an attorney-client relationship with the attorney. Pa. Nat'l Mut. Cas. Ins. Co. v. Perlberg, — F. Supp. 2d — (D. Md. May 20, 2011).

Disqualification of an insured's attorney was not warranted under (a) where the attorney's prior representation of other insureds was in matters that were not at all related to a coverage issue, which was the subject matter

of the present dispute that the insurer was involved in against other insureds. Pa. Nat'l Mut. Cas. Ins. Co. v. Perlberg, — F. Supp. 2d — (D. Md. May 20, 2011).

No violation. — As there were no facts indicating the former county attorney was involved in the manner in which the county calculated transferred retirement benefits during her tenure, and the trial court properly determined the county waived the ability to request the attorney's disqualification, the county failed to show a violation of Md. Law. R. Prof. Conduct 1.9 and 1.11 where the former attorney represented a county employee. Balt. County v. Barnhart, 201 Md. App. 682, 30 A.3d 291 (2011).

Cited in State v. Goldsberry, 419 Md. 100, 18 A.3d 836 (2011).

Rule 1.10. Imputation of Conflicts of Interest: General Rule.

No conflict of interest found. — Disqualification of an insured's attorney and her law firm was not warranted under Rules 1.9(a) and 1.10(a) where the insurer only showed that the attorney had previously represented other insureds; it failed to show that it also stood in an

attorney-client relationship with the attorney. Pa. Nat'l Mut. Cas. Ins. Co. v. Perlberg, — F. Supp. 2d — (D. Md. May 20, 2011).

Cited in Att'y Griev. Comm'n v. Carithers, 421 Md. 28, 25 A.3d 181 (2011).

Rule 1.11. Special Conflicts of Interest for Former and Current Government Officers and Employees.

Conflict of interest not shown.

As there were no facts indicating the former county attorney was involved in the manner in which the county calculated transferred retire-

ment benefits during her tenure, and the trial court properly determined the county waived the ability to request the attorney's disqualification, the county failed to show a violation of

Md. Law. R. Prof. Conduct 1.9 and 1.11 where the former attorney represented a county em-

ployee. Balt. County v. Barnhart, 201 Md. App. 682, 30 A.3d 291 (2011).

Rule 1.15. Safekeeping Property.

I. General Consideration.
  A. In General.
  C. Misappropriation or Mishandling of Funds.
II. Sanctions.

I. GENERAL CONSIDERATION.

A. In General.

Cited in Att'y Griev. Comm'n v. Tauber, 421 Md. 415, 26 A.3d 967 (2011).

C. Misappropriation or Mishandling of Funds.

Misappropriation of funds.
Attorney violated this Rule because (1) the attorney did not enter a client's name into the database of the firm by which the attorney was employed, (2) the attorney did not record the client's retainer payment, (3) the attorney did not forward that payment to the firm's main office, (4) the attorney substituted the attorney's name as payee on a check that the client issued to the firm, and deposited that check in the attorney's personal account, and (5) the attorney did not relinquish the funds deposited in the attorney's personal account to the firm until after the attorney was confronted by a supervisor. Att'y Griev. Comm'n v. Elliott, 417 Md. 659, 12 A.3d 105 (2011).

Attorney violated (a) of this Rule and 10-304(a) of the Business Occupations and Professions Article because, when the attorney maintained an unauthorized side practice while being employed "of counsel" for a law firm, the attorney (1) did not keep a trust account for clients represented in that practice, and (2) deposited unearned retainers from that practice in the attorney's personal account. Att'y Griev. Comm'n v. Carithers, 421 Md. 28, 25 A.3d 181 (2011).

Failure to deposit unearned funds into trust account. — Attorney violated (a) by failing to keep adequate records and failing to deposit a client's unearned deposit into his trust account; the trial judge did not believe that the attorney could have performed substantial work on the matter, entitling him to half of the total fee at the time the deposit was made. Att'y Griev. Comm'n v. Khandpur, 421 Md. 1, 25 A.3d 165 (2011).

Failure to provide accounting. — Attorney violate (d) when the attorney failed to provide a full accounting to a client who had demanded a refund of the fee paid. Att'y Griev. Comm'n v. Patterson, 421 Md. 708, 28 A.3d 1196 (2011).

II. SANCTIONS.

Disbarment was proper sanction.
Attorney was disbarred for admittedly violating Md. Law. R. Prof. Conduct 1.1, 1.15(a) and (c), and 8.4(a) — (d), as well as Rule 16-609 and § 10- 306 of the Business Occupations and Professions Article, by misappropriating client funds to make it appear as though the attorney's collected fees were higher than those fees actually were, when the attorney was being considered for partner in the attorney's firm, and by failing to file complaints in clients' cases, misrepresenting that the complaints were filed, and fabricating documents to hide the misrepresentations, because (1) disbarment was the presumed sanction for the misappropriation, and (2) the attorney did not show "compelling extenuating circumstances" justifying a lesser sanction, as the attorney showed no serious and debilitating mental condition, since the attorney was not diagnosed with a mental illness, the attorney did not show such a condition was the "root cause" of the attorney's misconduct by making the attorney unable to do day-to-day activities in a normal manner, and the attorney did not show such a condition caused an utter inability to conform the attorney's conduct to the law and the Maryland Rules of Professional Conduct, so any psychological issues the attorney had at the time of the attorney's misconduct did not mitigate the attorney's sanction. Att'y Griev. Comm'n v. Palmer, 417 Md. 185, 9 A.3d 37 (2010).

Attorney was disbarred for violating (a), (c) and (d), and Md. Law. R. Prof. Conduct 1.3, 1.4(a) and (b)1.16(d), 8.1(b), and 8.4(a) and (d), after the attorney received advance fee payments from two clients, deposited the money in a personal account, rather than a trust account, having not earned the fees, and abandoned the clients without performing work for the clients. Att'y Griev. Comm'n v. Lara, 418 Md. 355, 14 A.3d 650 (2011).

Attorney violated (d) and Md. Law. R. Prof. Conduct 1.2(a), 8.4(c) and (d), Md. R. 16-604 and 16-609(c), and § 10-306 of the Business Occupations and Professions Article, and was disbarred, after misappropriating tens of thousands of dollars that should have been paid to a physical therapist and settling a client's claim without the client's knowledge or consent. Att'y Griev. Comm'n v. Stern, 419 Md. 525, 19 A.3d 904 (2011).

Attorney was disbarred for violating (a), (d) and (e) of this section and Md. Law. R. Prof. Conduct 1.1, 1.3 1.16(d), 5.5(a) and (b), 8.4(b), (c), and (d), Md. R. 16-603, 16-604, and 16-609, and § 10-306 of the Business Occupations and Professions Article, by commingling client funds with the attorney's own funds, failing to pay medical providers for clients, and practicing after the attorney lost the right for failure to pay Client Protection Fund assessment and failure to file a pro bono report. Att'y Griev. Comm'n v. Agiliga, 422 Md. 613, 31 A.3d 103 (2011).

Disbarment for violating this rule and Md. Law. R. Prof. Conduct 1.1, 1.3, 1.4(b), 8.1(a)

and (b), and 8.4(c) and (d), and Md. R. 16-607 was appropriate based on a finding that the attorney's commitment to hiding to truth from Bar Counsel was systematic and unwavering and was not the product of mere mistake, and where there was no innocent explanation for the fabrication of documents or the alternation of bank records after Bar Counsel began its investigation. Att'y Griev. Comm'n v. Payer, — Md. —, 38 A.3d 378 (2012).

Attorney was disbarred for violating (c) and (d), and Md. Law. R. Prof. Conduct 1.4(a)(2) and (a)(3), 1.5(a), 1.16(d), 8.1(b), 8.4(a) and (d), and Md. R. 16-604 and 16-606.1(a)(3), by, inter alia, failing to remit to the client the portion of the settlement check to which the client was entitled. Att'y Griev. Comm'n of Md. v. Van Nelson, — Md. —, — A.3d — (Mar. 27, 2012).

Rule 1.16. Declining or Terminating Representation.

I. General Consideration.
II. Sanctions.

I. GENERAL CONSIDERATION.

Counsel properly allowed to withdraw. — Lender's counsel was properly allowed to withdraw because counsel complied with the requirements of Md. R. 2-132(b) by providing the lender with notice of counsel's intention to withdraw much more than five days prior to moving to withdraw, which notice advised the lender to have another attorney enter an appearance for the lender. Serio v. Baystate Props., LLC, — Md. App. —, — A.3d — (Mar. 8, 2012).

Abandonment of client.

Attorney violated this Rule in two cases because (1) the attorney moved the attorney's practice without notifying a client, and, upon termination of the client's case, did not return an unearned fee, and, (2) in a personal injury case in which it was learned that the defendant was deceased, the attorney did not open an estate or otherwise prevent the dismissal of a client's case for failure to prosecute. Att'y Griev. Comm'n v. De La Paz, 418 Md. 534, 16 A.3d 181 (2011).

Attorney violated this section when the attorney abandoned a client by failing to respond to a motion to dismiss the client's case, failing to appear at scheduled court dates, failing to inform the client the attorney intended to end the attorney's representation of the client, and failing to refund unearned fees. Att'y Griev. Comm'n v. Brady, 422 Md. 441, 30 A.3d 902 (2011).

Quoted in Att'y Griev. Comm'n v. Stern, 419 Md. 525, 19 A.3d 904 (2011).

Cited in Att'y Griev. Comm'n v. Patterson, 421 Md. 708, 28 A.3d 1196 (2011); Att'y Griev.

Comm'n v. Paul, 423 Md. 268, 31 A.3d 512 (2011); Att'y Griev. Comm'n v. Ambe, — Md. —, 38 A.3d 390 (2012).

II. SANCTIONS.

Disbarment was proper sanction.

Attorney violated this rule by effectively terminating his representation of clients in two action by abandoning the cases; the attorney was disbarred for violating this rule along with Md. Law. R. Prof. Conduct 1.1, 1.2(a), 1.3, 1.4(a), 8.1(b), and 8.4(a), (c), and (d). Att'y Griev. Comm'n v. Fox, 417 Md. 504, 11 A.3d 762 (2010).

Attorney was disbarred for violating (d) and Md. Law. R. Prof. Conduct 1.3, 1.4(a) and (b), 1.15(a), (c), and (d), 8.1(b), and 8.4(a) and (d), after the attorney received advance fee payments from two clients, deposited the money in a personal account, rather than a trust account, having not earned the fees, and abandoned the clients without performing work for the clients. Att'y Griev. Comm'n v. Lara, 418 Md. 355, 14 A.3d 650 (2011).

Attorney was disbarred for violating (d) and Md. Law. R. Prof. Conduct 1.1, 1.3, 1.15(a), (d), and (e), 5.5(a) and (b), 8.4(b), (c), and (d), Md. R. 16-603, 16-604, and 16-609, and § 10-306 of the Business Occupations and Professions Article, by commingling client funds with the attorney's own funds, failing to pay medical providers for clients, and practicing after the attorney lost the right for failure to pay Client Protection Fund assessment and failure to file a pro bono report. Att'y Griev. Comm'n v. Agiliga, 422 Md. 613, 31 A.3d 103 (2011).

ADVOCATE.

Rule 3.2. Expediting litigation.

Violation of Rule shown.
Attorney violated this section by failing to expedite a tort action, taking no effort to serve process upon either defendant and undertaking no discovery. Att'y Griev. Comm'n v. Patterson, 421 Md. 708, 28 A.3d 1196 (2011).

Rule 3.3. Candor Toward the Tribunal.

Misrepresentation in complaint.
Attorney who falsely represented that he was not a resident of California in the applications for admission pro hac vice, as he was a resident of California and had no property in Maryland and he had filed a pro se action noting that he was a California resident, violated Md. Law. R. Prof. Conduct 3.3(a) and 8.4(c). Att'y Griev. Comm'n v. Joseph, 422 Md. 670, 31 A.3d 137 (2011).

Disbarment appropriate.
In a reciprocal disciplinary action, the attorney, who had been suspended from the practice of law for one year and one day in Colorado, was disbarred for violating Md. Law. R. Prof. Conduct 3.3(a)(1), 3.4(c), and 8.4(a), (b), (c), and (d), based on the attorney's own admission that he failed to make pertinent disclosures during a personal bankruptcy case and gave false testimony that case. Att'y Griev. Comm'n v. Zodrow, 419 Md. 286, 19 A.3d 381 (2011).

Where an attorney's conduct of lying in order to obtain pro hac vice status in California lacked candor, was dishonest, misleading, prejudicial to the administration of justice, and beyond excuse, and there were no mitigating circumstances, the attorney was disbarred. Att'y Griev. Comm'n v. Joseph, 422 Md. 670, 31 A.3d 137 (2011).

Stated in Blake v. State, 418 Md. 445, 15 A.3d 787 (2011).

Cited in Att'y Griev. Comm'n v. Coppola, 419 Md. 370, 19 A.3d 431 (2011); State v. Northam, 421 Md. 195, 26 A.3d 344 (2011); Att'y Griev. Comm'n v. Paul, 423 Md. 268, 31 A.3d 512 (2011).

Rule 3.4. Fairness to Opposing Party and Counsel.

Rule violated.
In the course of the employee's deposition, the employee's counsel instructed the employee not to answer on grounds other than privilege or court-ordered limitation, in violation of Fed. R. Civ. P. 30(d)(3) and this Rule. Mezu v. Morgan State Univ., 269 F.R.D. 565 (D. Md. 2010).

Over the course of the employee's deposition, her counsel objected more than 50 times, and counsel interjected frequently to answer questions for the employee; the frequency of counsel's objections and interjections and the length of the ensuing discussions impeded the deposition and frustrated the examination of the employee in violation of this Rule. Mezu v. Morgan State Univ., 269 F.R.D. 565 (D. Md. 2010).

Disbarment appropriate. — In a reciprocal disciplinary action, the attorney, who had been suspended from the practice of law for one year and one day in Colorado, was disbarred for violating Md. Law. R. Prof. Conduct 3.3(a)(1), 3.4(c), and 8.4(a), (b), (c), and (d), based on the attorney's own admission that he failed to make pertinent disclosures during a personal bankruptcy case and gave false testimony that case. Att'y Griev. Comm'n v. Zodrow, 419 Md. 286, 19 A.3d 381 (2011).

Quoted in Att'y Griev. Comm'n v. Khandpur, 421 Md. 1, 25 A.3d 165 (2011).

Cited in Att'y Griev. Comm'n v. Paul, 423 Md. 268, 31 A.3d 512 (2011).

LAW FIRMS AND ASSOCIATIONS.

Rule 5.3. Responsibilities Regarding Nonlawyer Assistants.

Applied in Att'y Griev. Comm'n v. Ambe, — Md. —, 38 A.3d 390 (2012).

Cited in Att'y Griev. Comm'n v. Khandpur, 421 Md. 1, 25 A.3d 165 (2011).

Rule 5.5. Unauthorized Practice of Law; Multijurisdictional Practice of Law.

Engaging in practice of law.

Respondent violated Md. Law. R. Prof. Conduct 5.5, 7.1, and 7.5 by establishing a law firm in Maryland and holding herself out as an attorney without being licensed to practice there. Att'y Griev. Comm'n v. Sucklal, 418 Md. 1, 12 A.3d 650 (2011).

Where a suspended attorney agreed to represent two clients at their interview/meeting with The United States Citizenship and Immigration Services and engaged in an in-depth interview to obtain significant personal and other legal information with the obvious intention of developing information to prepare the appropriate forms, the attorney engaged in the practice of law in violation of Md. Law. R. Prof. Conduct 1.1, 1.4, 1.5, 5.5, and 8.4. Att'y Griev. Comm'n v. Brisbon, 422 Md. 625, 31 A.3d 110 (2011).

Unauthorized practice by attorney licensed in other jurisdictions.

Attorney, who was admitted to practice law in New York only, was reprimanded for violating this section and Md. Law. R. Prof. Conduct 7.1 and 8.4, after he assisted immigration clients in personal injury matters in Maryland, failed to change his letterhead and sign to indicate he was not licensed to practice in Maryland, and engaged in the unauthorized practice of law in Maryland. Att'y Griev. Comm'n v. Ambe, — Md. —, 38 A.3d 390 (2012).

Suspended license.

Lawyer was disbarred because he engaged in the unauthorized practice of law when, while under a prior suspension, he advised, counseled, and drafted documents and pleadings for the complainant and received at least $ 5,100 in legal fees from the complainant; among other things, the lawyer's exercise of legal knowledge, skills and education while suspended violated (a), and the lawyer's failure to inform the complainant of his suspension before May 2008 also demonstrated a violation of (a). This was the third time in seven years that the lawyer had violated the Rules of Professional Conduct. Att'y Griev. Comm'n v. Maignan, 423 Md. 191, 31 A.3d 467 (2011).

Disbarment.

Attorney was disbarred for violating (a) and (b) of this section and Md. Law. R. Prof. Conduct 1.1, 1.3, 1.15(a), (d), and (e), 1.16(d), 8.4(b), (c), and (d), Md. R. 16-603, 16-604, and 16-609, and § 10-306 of the Business Occupations and Professions Article, by commingling client funds with the attorney's own funds, failing to pay medical providers for clients, and practicing after the attorney lost the right for failure to pay Client Protection Fund assessment and failure to file a pro bono report. Att'y Griev. Comm'n v. Agiliga, 422 Md. 613, 31 A.3d 103 (2011).

Cited in Att'y Griev. Comm'n v. Smith, — Md. —, — A.3d — (Mar. 19, 2012).

PUBLIC SERVICE.

Rule 6.1. Pro Bono Publico Service.

Cited in Davis v. Petito, — Md. —, — A.3d — (Feb. 27, 2012).

INFORMATION ABOUT LEGAL SERVICES.

Rule 7.1. Communications Concerning a Lawyer's Services.

Letterhead information.

Attorney, who was admitted to practice law in New York only, was reprimanded for violating this section and Md. Law. R. Prof. Conduct 5.5 and 8.4, after he assisted immigration clients in personal injury matters in Maryland, failed to change his letterhead and sign to indicate he was not licensed to practice in Maryland, and engaged in the unauthorized practice of law in Maryland. Att'y Griev. Comm'n v. Ambe, — Md. —, 38 A.3d 390 (2012).

Unauthorized practice of law. — Respondent violated Md. Law. R. Prof. Conduct 5.5, 7.1, and 7.5 by establishing a law firm in Maryland and holding herself out as an attorney without being licensed to practice there. Potomac Valley Orthopaedic Assocs. v. Md. State Bd. of Physicians, 417 Md. 622, 12 A.3d 84 (2011).

Cited in Att'y Griev. Comm'n v. Carithers, 421 Md. 28, 25 A.3d 181 (2011).

Rule 7.5. Firm Names and Letterheads.

Unauthorized practice of law. — Respondent violated Md. Law. R. Prof. Conduct 5.5, 7.1, and 7.5 by establishing a law firm in Maryland and holding herself out as an attorney without being licensed to practice there.

Att'y Griev. Comm'n v. Sucklal, 418 Md. 1, 12 A.3d 650 (2011).

Cited in Att'y Griev. Comm'n v. Carithers, 421 Md. 28, 25 A.3d 181 (2011).

MAINTAINING THE INTEGRITY OF THE PROFESSION.

Rule 8.1. Bar Admission and Disciplinary Matters.

Failure to respond as grounds for sanction.

Hearing judge erred in failing to find a violation of this Rule, as the evidence showed the attorney did not produce financial records despite two clear and specific demands by Bar Counsel. Att'y Griev. Comm'n v. Khandpur, 421 Md. 1, 25 A.3d 165 (2011).

Cooperation with bar counsel

Attorney violated this Rule because the attorney did not respond to requests for information from the Attorney Grievance Commission about a client's disciplinary complaint. Att'y Griev. Comm'n v. De La Paz, 418 Md. 534, 16 A.3d 181 (2011).

Deliberate misrepresentations to disciplinary counsel.

Attorney violated (a) because (1) the attorney represented to Bar Counsel that a client had retained the attorney personally (as opposed to the firm by which the attorney was employed) when the attorney knew that the client had executed a written contract with the firm and the attorney had signed the same contract on behalf of the firm, and (2) the attorney misrepresented to Bar Counsel that the client had authorized the attorney to change the payee on a check the client issued to the firm. Att'y Griev. Comm'n v. Elliott, 417 Md. 659, 12 A.3d 105 (2011).

Violation and mitigating factor shown.

— Attorney violated/Aa(b) by failing to respond to Bar Counsel's demand for information, and the attorney established his multiple sclerosis as a mitigating factor for his violation of (b). Att'y Griev. Comm'n v. Patterson, 421 Md. 708, 28 A.3d 1196 (2011).

Disbarment required.

Attorney violated this rule by failing to timely respond to Bar Counsel's requests for information despite being granted two extensions and failing to produce a file duirng an interview, as requested ahead of time; the attorney was disbarred for violating this rule along with Md. Law. R. Prof. Conduct 1.1, 1.2(a), 1.3, 1.4(a), 1.16(d). and 8.4(a), (c), and (d). Att'y Griev. Comm'n v. Fox, 417 Md. 504, 11 A.3d 762 (2010).

Attorney was disbarred for violating (b) and Md. Law. R. Prof. Conduct 1.3, 1.4(a) and (b), 1.15(a), (c), and (d), 1.16(d), and 8.4(a) and (d), after the attorney received advance fee payments from two clients, deposited the money in a personal account, rather than a trust account, having not earned the fees, and abandoned the clients without performing work for the clients. Att'y Griev. Comm'n v. Lara, 418 Md. 355, 14 A.3d 650 (2011).

Disbarment for violating (a) and (b) and Md. Law. R. Prof. Conduct 1.1, 1.3, 1.4(b), 1.15, and 8.4(c) and (d), and Md. R. 16-607 was appropriate based on a finding that the attorney's commitment to hiding to truth from Bar Counsel was systematic and unwavering and was not the product of mere mistake, and where there was no innocent explanation for the fabrication of documents or the alternation of bank records after Bar Counsel began its investigation. Att'y Griev. Comm'n v. Payer, — Md. —, 38 A.3d 378 (2012).

Attorney was disbarred for violating (b), and Md. Law. R. Prof. Conduct 11.4(a)(2) and (a)(3), 1.5(a), 1.15(c) and (d), 1.16(d), 8.4(a) and (d), and Md. R. 16-604 and 16-606.1(a)(3), by, inter alia, repeatedly failing to respond to Bar Counsel's investigative requests, ignoring two letters and refusing to be interviewed by an investigator for the Attorney Grievance Commission. Att'y Griev. Comm'n of Md. v. Van Nelson, — Md. —, — A.3d — (Mar. 27, 2012).

Quoted in Att'y Griev. Comm'n v. Stern, 419 Md. 525, 19 A.3d 904 (2011); Att'y Griev. Comm'n v. Ambe, — Md. —, 38 A.3d 390 (2012).

Cited in Att'y Griev. Comm'n v. Brady, 422 Md. 441, 30 A.3d 902 (2011); Att'y Griev. Comm'n v. Joseph, 422 Md. 670, 31 A.3d 137 (2011); Att'y Griev. Comm'n v. Paul, 423 Md. 268, 31 A.3d 512 (2011).

Rule 8.2. Judicial and Legal Officials.

Cited in Att'y Griev. Comm'n v. Paul, 423 Md. 268, 31 A.3d 512 (2011).

Rule 8.4. Misconduct.

I. General Consideration.
II. What constitutes violation.
   A. In general.
   B. Criminal Acts.
   D. Handling clients' funds.
   E. Forgery, fraud, and false pretenses.
III. Evidence and sanctions.

I. GENERAL CONSIDERATION.

Actions reflecting adversely on fitness to practice law.

When an attorney altered the attorney's law firm employer's electronic files to facilitate the attorney taking certain of the firm's clients with the attorney when the attorney left the firm, the attorney admittedly violated (a), (b), (c), and (d) because (1) the attorney's acts of altering and deleting documents within the firm's client files constituted criminal acts in violation of § 7-302 of the Criminal Law Article and, therefore, violated these Rules, (2) the attorney's criminal conduct reflected adversely on the attorney's honesty, trustworthiness and fitness as a lawyer, (3) the attorney's conduct was deceitful and prejudicial to the administration of justice as the attorney carried out the deception after hours, when others would not observe the attorney's actions, as the attorney understood the attorney's actions to be inappropriate and unauthorized. Att'y Griev. Comm'n v. Keiner, 421 Md. 492, 27 A.3d 153 (2011).

Violation Found

Lawyer was disbarred because he engaged in the unauthorized practice of law when, while under a prior suspension, he advised, counseled, and drafted documents and pleadings for the complainant and received at least $ 5,100 in legal fees from the complainant; among other things, § 10-601 of the Business Occupations and Professions Article criminalized the unauthorized practice of law, so there was a violation of (a)-(d). This was the third time in seven years that the lawyer had violated the Rules of Professional Conduct. Att'y Griev. Comm'n v. Maignan, 423 Md. 191, 31 A.3d 467 (2011).

II. WHAT CONSTITUTES VIOLATION.

A. In general.

Violation of several Maryland Rules of Professional Conduct.

Attorney violated (a) because, when the attorney maintained an unauthorized side practice while being employed "of counsel" for a law firm, and deposited unearned retainers from clients in that side practice in the attorney's personal account, the attorney violated Md. R. Prof. Conduct 1.15(a) and (b) — (d) of this Rule. Att'y Griev. Comm'n v. Carithers, 421 Md. 28, 25 A.3d 181 (2011).

Failure to disclose nonattorney status.

Where a suspended attorney agreed to represent two clients at their interview/meeting with The United States Citizenship and Immigration Services and engaged in an in-depth interview to obtain significant personal and other legal information with the obvious intention of developing information to prepare the appropriate forms, the attorney engaged in the practice of law in violation of this Rule as she failed to disclose her non-attorney status. Att'y Griev. Comm'n v. Brisbon, 422 Md. 625, 31 A.3d 110 (2011).

Pro hac vice representation. — Attorney who falsely represented that he was not a resident of California in the applications for admission pro hac vice, as he was a resident of California and had no property in Maryland and he had filed a pro se action noting that he was a California resident, violated Md. Law. R. Prof. Conduct 3.3(a) and 8.4(c). Att'y Griev. Comm'n v. Joseph, 422 Md. 670, 31 A.3d 137 (2011).

Conduct prejducial to administration of justice.

When an attorney left a courtroom after a trial court disagreed with the attorney's position that the court had no authority to deny the State's uncontested motion to stet a criminal charge against the attorney's client, under Md. R. 4-248, despite the trial court's instruction that the case was not concluded, the attorney was properly found to have violated (d) because the attorney's conduct wasted judicial resources and was prejudicial to the administration of justice. Att'y Griev. Comm'n v. Usiak, 418 Md. 667, 18 A.3d 1 (2011).

When an attorney left a courtroom after a trial court disagreed with the attorney's position that the court had no authority to deny the State's uncontested motion to stet a criminal charge against the attorney's client, under Md. R. 4-248, despite the trial court's instruction that the case was not concluded, the attorney was properly found to have violated (d) because (1) the attorney's interpretation of Md. R. 4-248 was plainly wrong, and, (2) even if the attorney's interpretation were correct, the attorney's conduct was prejudicial to the administration of justice. Att'y Griev. Comm'n v. Usiak, 418 Md. 667, 18 A.3d 1 (2011).

Attorney violated (d) because, when the attorney maintained an unauthorized side practice while being employed "of counsel" for a law firm, the attorney (1) stole fees that were owed to the firm, when the attorney represented and received fees from clients who owed the firm fees. Att'y Griev. Comm'n v. Carithers, 421 Md. 28, 25 A.3d 181 (2011).

Attorney violated (d) by abandoning the client and making the client unable to reinstate the client's claims, thereby severely obstructing the administration of justice. Att'y Griev. Comm'n v. Brady, 422 Md. 441, 30 A.3d 902 (2011).

B. Criminal Acts.

Acts constituting felony theft.
Attorney violated (b) because, when the attorney maintained an unauthorized side practice while being employed "of counsel" for a law firm, the attorney engaged in criminal conduct, under § 7-104(a) of the Criminal Law Article, by stealing the firm's fees, when the attorney represented and received fees from clients who owed the firm fees. Att'y Griev. Comm'n v. Carithers, 421 Md. 28, 25 A.3d 181 (2011).

D. Handling clients' funds.

Mishandling attorney trust account.
Attorney violated (d) by falsely stating to the investigator that he had deposited prepaid funds into his trust account and by failing to produce complete records, in a timely manner, after a legitimate demand by Bar Counsel, to show the receipt and distribution of trust funds. Att'y Griev. Comm'n v. Khandpur, 421 Md. 1, 25 A.3d 165 (2011).

E. Forgery, fraud, and false pretenses.

Providing false information.
Attorney violated (a), (c), and (d) by submitting false documents in support of the attorney's application to practice law in the District of Columbia in order to conceal the attorney's non-compliance with that jurisdiction's requirements on the practice of law there by attorneys who were not admitted to the District of Columbia Bar because, (1) under (c) and (d), it was misconduct to engage in conduct involving dishonesty, fraud, deceit or misrepresentation or prejudicial to the administration of justice, (2) under (a), it was misconduct to violate the Maryland Lawyers' Rules of Professional Conduct, and (3) the attorney's fabrication to advance the attorney's misrepresentations about compliance with applicable rules involved deceit and was prejudicial to the administration of laws governing the practice of law. Att'y Griev. Comm'n v. Smith, — Md. —, — A.3d — (Mar. 19, 2012).

Stealing employer's fees. — Attorney violated (c) because, when the attorney maintained an unauthorized side practice while being employed "of counsel" for a law firm, the attorney (1) stole fees that were owed to the firm, when the attorney represented and received fees from clients who owed the firm fees, (2) used the firm's resources for the attorney's side practice, and (2) put unearned fees from the side practice in the attorney's personal account. Att'y Griev. Comm'n v. Carithers, 421 Md. 28, 25 A.3d 181 (2011).

III. EVIDENCE AND SANCTIONS.

Violation found.
Respondent violated (a) — (d) in her dealings with a client and a person from whom she borrowed money by, inter alia, falsely claiming to be licensed to practice law in Maryland. Att'y Griev. Comm'n v. Sucklal, 418 Md. 1, 12 A.3d 650 (2011).

Attorney violated this Rule in two cases because, (1) in a personal injury case in which it was learned that the defendant was deceased, the attorney's failure to petition to open an estate for the deceased defendant resulted in the dismissal of a client's complaint, and the attorney delayed the client's pursuit of the complaint by promising to petition to open the estate by a certain date, neglecting to do so, and then failing to inform the client of the complaint's dismissal, and, (2) in another case, despite soliciting a client, the attorney never entered the attorney's appearance on the client's behalf, and then failed to appear at a hearing for which the attorney was retained. Att'y Griev. Comm'n v. De La Paz, 418 Md. 534, 16 A.3d 181 (2011).

Attorney violated (a) — (d) because the attorney (1) intentionally took funds belonging to the firm by which the attorney was employed, consisting of a client's check issued to the firm, and placed the funds in the attorney's personal bank account, (2) commingled the funds with the attorney's own personal funds and later transferred a portion of the funds to another personal bank account without the knowledge or consent of the client or the law firm to whom the funds belonged, (3) failed to advise the law firm of payments made by the client, and (4) did not relinquish the funds to the firm until after the attorney was confronted by a supervisor. Att'y Griev. Comm'n v. Elliott, 417 Md. 659, 12 A.3d 105 (2011).

Violation not found.

When an attorney deposited unearned funds received on a client's behalf in the attorney's operating account, rather than in a trust account, it was not error for a hearing judge not to find the attorney violated (c) because the hearing judge (1) could accept the attorney's explanation that the attorney believed the attorney was allowed to deposit the funds in the operating account and that the attorney opened a trust account as soon as the attorney learned the attorney was required to have a trust account, (2) found no indication of the attorney's dishonest intent, and (3) based the finding on a credibility assessment of the attorney, so the finding was deferred to. Att'y Griev. Comm'n v. Tauber, 421 Md. 415, 26 A.3d 967 (2011).

Reciprocal discipline.

In a reciprocal disciplinary action, the attorney, who had been suspended from the practice of law for one year and one day in Colorado, was disbarred for violating Md. Law. R. Prof. Conduct 3.3(a)(1), 3.4(c), and 8.4(a), (b), (c), and (d), based on the attorney's own admission that he failed to make pertinent disclosures during a personal bankruptcy case and gave false testimony that case. Att'y Griev. Comm'n v. Zodrow, 419 Md. 286, 19 A.3d 381 (2011).

Reprimand was proper sanction.

When a lawyer violated (d) by filing a stipulation of dismissal falsely purporting to bear opposing counsel's signature, a reprimand was the proper sanction because (1) the lawyer and opposing counsel agreed to the dismissal's terms, so the lawyer's misconduct had no adverse impact on other parties' rights, (2) the lawyer honestly thought the lawyer's intentional alteration of the stipulation was authorized, so the lawyer's misconduct was not willful, and the lawyer's motive was not fraudulent, (3) the lawyer did not benefit from the lawyer's conduct, as the lawyer lost the lawyer's job, (4) the lawyer showed remorse, (5) the lawyer sought ethics counseling, reducing the likelihood that the conduct would be repeated, (6) the lawyer had no record of prior discipline, and (7) a suspension was not required, as, under the circumstances, a reprimand would protect the public and impress upon the lawyer the seriousness of the lawyer's misconduct. Att'y Griev. Comm'n v. Paul, 423 Md. 268, 31 A.3d 512 (2011).

Attorney, who was admitted to practice law in New York only, was reprimanded for violating this section and Md. Law. R. Prof. Conduct 5.5 and 7.1, after he assisted immigration clients in personal injury matters in Maryland, failed to change his letterhead and sign to indicate he was not licensed to practice in Maryland, and engaged in the unauthorized practice of law in Maryland. Att'y Griev. Comm'n v. Ambe, — Md. —, 38 A.3d 390 (2012).

Thirty-day suspension.

Attorney was suspended from the practice of law for 30 days for depositing unearned funds received on a client's behalf in an operating account, rather than a trust account, because (1) the attorney violated (d) by not having a trust account, (2) it was found the attorney mistakenly thought the attorney properly handled the funds and that the attorney's failure to put the funds in a trust account was not done with an intent to be dishonest, (3) there was a potential for injury, (4) an indefinite suspension was too harsh, as there was no misappropriation, and (5) a reprimand was inadequate. Att'y Griev. Comm'n v. Tauber, 421 Md. 415, 26 A.3d 967 (2011).

Evidence justified findings of misconduct, and disbarment was warranted.

Attorney was disbarred for violating (a) and (d), and Md. Law. R. Prof. Conduct 1.4(a)(2) and (a)(3), 1.5(a), 1.15(c) and (d), 1.16(d), and 8.1(b), and Md. R. 16-604 and 16-606.1(a)(3), by, inter alia, disregarding a client, refusing to pay the client the fees and expenses the client advanced, and refusing to cooperate in the investigation. Att'y Griev. Comm'n of Md. v. Van Nelson, — Md. —, — A.3d — (Mar. 27, 2012).

Disbarment required.

Attorney violated this rule by failign to diligently and competently oversee an action failing to communicate the clients in two actions, and failing to obtain a client's consent for settlement; the attorney was disbarred for violating this rule along with Md. Law. R. Prof. Conduct 1.1, 1.2(a), 1.3, 1.4(a), 1.16(d). and 8.1(b) Att'y Griev. Comm'n v. Fox, 417 Md. 504, 11 A.3d 762 (2010).

Attorney was disbarred for admittedly violating Md. Law. R. Prof. Conduct 1.1, 1.15(a) and (c), and 8.4(a) — (d), as well as Rule 16-609 and § 10- 306 of the Business Occupations and Professions Article, by misappropriating client funds to make it appear as though the attorney's collected fees were higher than those fees actually were, when the attorney was being considered for partner in the attorney's firm, and by failing to file complaints in clients' cases, misrepresenting that the complaints were filed, and fabricating documents to hide the misrepresentations, because (1) disbarment was the presumed sanction for the misappropriation, and (2) the attorney did not show "compelling extenuating circumstances" justifying a lesser sanction, as the attorney showed no serious and debilitating mental condition, since the attorney was not diagnosed with a mental illness, the attorney did not show such a condition was the "root cause" of the attorney's misconduct by making the attorney unable to do day-to-day activities in a normal manner, and the attorney did not show such a condition caused an utter inability to conform the attorney's conduct to the law and the Maryland Rules of Professional Conduct, so any psychological issues the attorney had at the time of the attorney's misconduct did not mitigate the attorney's sanction. Att'y Griev. Comm'n v. Palmer, 417 Md. 185, 9 A.3d 37 (2010).

Attorney was disbarred for violating (a) and (d) and Md. Law. R. Prof. Conduct 1.3, 1.4(a) and (b), 1.15(a), (c), and (d), 1.16(d), and 8.1(b), after the attorney received advance fee payments from two clients, deposited the money in a personal account, rather than a trust account, having not earned the fees, and abandoned the clients without performing work for the clients. Att'y Griev. Comm'n v. Lara, 418 Md. 355, 14 A.3d 650 (2011).

Attorney was disbarred for violating (a), (b), (c), and (d) and Md. Law. R. Prof. Conduct 1.2, when the attorney empowered a client's child to forge the client's signature on estate documents, notarized falsely executed and initialed estate documents, and directed the attorney's employees to falsely attest to the signature; the attorney suffered no cognitive deficits and new what he was doing was wrong. Att'y Griev. Comm'n v. Coppola, 419 Md. 370, 19 A.3d 431 (2011).

Attorney violated (c) and (d), and Md. Law. R. Prof. Conduct 1.2(a), 1.15(d), Md. R. 16-604 and 16-609(c), and § 10-306 of the Business Occupations and Professions Article, and was disbarred, after misappropriating tens of thousands of dollars that should have been paid to a physical therapist and settling a client's claim without the client's knowledge or consent. Att'y Griev. Comm'n v. Stern, 419 Md. 525, 19 A.3d 904 (2011).

When an attorney altered the attorney's law firm employer's electronic files to facilitate the attorney taking certain of the firm's clients with the attorney when the attorney left the firm, the proper sanction for the attorney's admitted violations of Md. Law. R. Prof. Conduct 1.4(a) and (b) and (a), (b), (c), and (d) of this Rule, as well as Md. Code Ann., Crim. Law § 7-302, was disbarment because (1) the attorney's conduct was dishonest, intentional, and solely motivated by a desire for personal gain, so disbarment was presumed, and (2) the attorney's mental disabilities of depression and alcohol dependency were not "compelling ex-

tenuating circumstances" warranting a lesser sanction as the disabilities did not result in an utter inability to conform the attorney's conduct to the law and the Rules of Professional Conduct. Att'y Griev. Comm'n v. Keiner, 421 Md. 492, 27 A.3d 153 (2011).

Attorney was disbarred for violating (b), (c), and (d) of this section and Md. Law. R. Prof. Conduct 1.1, 1.3, 1.15(a), (d), and (e), 1.16(d), 5.5(a) and (b), Md. R. 16-603, 16-604, and 16-609, and § 10-306 of the Business Occupations and Professions Article, by commingling client funds with the attorney's own funds, failing to pay medical providers for clients, and practicing after the attorney lost the right for failure to pay Client Protection Fund assessment and failure to file a pro bono report. Att'y Griev. Comm'n v. Agiliga, 422 Md. 613, 31 A.3d 103 (2011).

Where an attorney's conduct of lying in order to obtain pro hac vice status in California lacked candor, was dishonest, misleading, prejudicial to the administration of justice, and beyond excuse, and there were no mitigating circumstances, the attorney was disbarred. Att'y Griev. Comm'n v. Joseph, 422 Md. 670, 31 A.3d 137 (2011).

Disbarment for violating (c) and (d), and Md. Law. R. Prof. Conduct 1.1, 1.3, 1.4(b), 1.15, and 8.1(a) and (b), and Md. R. 16-607 was appropriate based on a finding that the attorney's commitment to hiding to truth from Bar Counsel was systematic and unwavering and was not the product of mere mistake, and where there was no innocent explanation for the fabrication of documents or the alternation of bank records after Bar Counsel began its investigation. Att'y Griev. Comm'n v. Payer, — Md. —, 38 A.3d 378 (2012).

When an attorney violated (a), (c), and (d) by submitting false documents in support of the attorney's application to practice law in the District of Columbia in order to conceal the attorney's non-compliance with that jurisdiction's requirements on the practice of law there by attorneys who were not admitted to the District of Columbia Bar, disbarment was the appropriate sanction because (1) disbarment was ordinarily imposed for submitting fabricated evidence to conceal a violation of disciplinary rules, and (2) no compelling extenuating circumstances justified a departure from that sanction, as the attorney's misconduct was a carefully contrived effort to mislead the D.C. Bar Admissions Committee to believe the attorney complied with applicable rules. Att'y Griev. Comm'n v. Smith, — Md. —, — A.3d — (Mar. 19, 2012).

FEDERAL RULES OF APPELLATE PROCEDURE FOR UNITED STATES COURTS OF APPEALS; LOCAL RULES AND INTERNAL OPERATING PROCEDURES OF THE FOURTH CIRCUIT

TITLE VI. HABEAS CORPUS; PROCEEDINGS IN FORMA PAUPERIS.

Local Rule 22(d). Motions for authorization.

Editor's note. — On February 6, 2012, the United States Court of Appeals for the 4th Circuit proposed amendments to Local Rules 22(d), 25(a), 25(b), 25(c), 30(b), 31(c) and 32(b), with the amended local rules superseding Administrative Order 08-01, effective April 16, 2012. However, on April 12, 2012, the 4th Circuit issued a notice stating that the court was "suspend[ing] the April 16, 2012, effective date of its proposed amendments to Local Rules 22(d), 25(a), 25(b), 25(c), 30(b), 31(c) & 32(b), and the superseding of Administrative Order 08-01, pending further review of public comments on the proposed amendments."

TITLE VII. GENERAL PROVISIONS.

Local Rule 25(a). Electronic case filing system.

Editor's note.
On February 6, 2012, the United States Court of Appeals for the 4th Circuit proposed amendments to Local Rules 22(d), 25(a), 25(b), 25(c), 30(b), 31(c) and 32(b), with the amended local rules superseding Administrative Order 08-01, effective April 16, 2012. However, on April 12, 2012, the 4th Circuit issued a notice stating that the court was "suspend[ing] the April 16, 2012, effective date of its proposed amendments to Local Rules 22(d), 25(a), 25(b), 25(c), 30(b), 31(c) & 32(b), and the superseding of Administrative Order 08- 01, pending further review of public comments on the proposed amendments."

Local Rule 25(b). Filing documents, use of facsimile equipment, service, certificate of service.

Editor's note. — On February 6, 2012, the United States Court of Appeals for the 4th Circuit proposed amendments to Local Rules 22(d), 25(a), 25(b), 25(c), 30(b), 31(c) and 32(b), with the amended local rules superseding Administrative Order 08-01, effective April 16, 2012. However, on April 12, 2012, the 4th Circuit issued a notice stating that the court was "suspend[ing] the April 16, 2012, effective date of its proposed amendments to Local Rules 22(d), 25(a), 25(b), 25(c), 30(b), 31(c) & 32(b), and the superseding of Administrative Order 08-01, pending further review of public comments on the proposed amendments."

Local Rule 25(c). Confidential and sealed materials.

Editor's note. — On February 6, 2012, the United States Court of Appeals for the 4th Circuit proposed amendments to Local Rules 22(d), 25(a), 25(b), 25(c), 30(b), 31(c) and 32(b), with the amended local rules superseding Administrative Order 08-01, effective April 16, 2012. However, on April 12, 2012, the 4th Circuit issued a notice stating that the court was "suspend[ing] the April 16, 2012, effective date of its proposed amendments to Local Rules 22(d), 25(a), 25(b), 25(c), 30(b), 31(c) & 32(b), and the superseding of Administrative Order 08-01, pending further review of public comments on the proposed amendments."

Local Rule 30(b). Appendix contents; number of copies.

Editor's note.

On February 6, 2012, the United States Court of Appeals for the 4th Circuit proposed amendments to Local Rules 22(d), 25(a), 25(b), 25(c), 30(b), 31(c) and 32(b), with the amended local rules superseding Administrative Order 08-01, effective April 16, 2012. However, on April 12, 2012, the 4th Circuit issued a notice stating that the court was "suspend[ing] the April 16, 2012, effective date of its proposed amendments to Local Rules 22(d), 25(a), 25(b), 25(c), 30(b), 31(c) & 32(b), and the superseding of Administrative Order 08- 01, pending further review of public comments on the proposed amendments."

Local Rule 31(c). Filing and service.

Editor's note. — On February 6, 2012, the United States Court of Appeals for the 4th Circuit proposed amendments to Local Rules 22(d), 25(a), 25(b), 25(c), 30(b), 31(c) and 32(b), with the amended local rules superseding Administrative Order 08-01, effective April 16, 2012. However, on April 12, 2012, the 4th Circuit issued a notice stating that the court was "suspend[ing] the April 16, 2012, effective date of its proposed amendments to Local Rules 22(d), 25(a), 25(b), 25(c), 30(b), 31(c) & 32(b), and the superseding of Administrative Order 08-01, pending further review of public comments on the proposed amendments."

Local Rule 32(b). Length of briefs.

Editor's note. — On February 6, 2012, the United States Court of Appeals for the 4th Circuit proposed amendments to Local Rules 22(d), 25(a), 25(b), 25(c), 30(b), 31(c) and 32(b), with the amended local rules superseding Administrative Order 08-01, effective April 16, 2012. However, on April 12, 2012, the 4th Circuit issued a notice stating that the court was "suspend[ing] the April 16, 2012, effective date of its proposed amendments to Local Rules 22(d), 25(a), 25(b), 25(c), 30(b), 31(c) & 32(b), and the superseding of Administrative Order 08-01, pending further review of public comments on the proposed amendments."

UNITED STATES BANKRUPTCY COURT FOR THE DISTRICT OF MARYLAND LOCAL BANKRUPTCY RULES

LOCAL BANKRUPTCY RULES

Effective November 1, 2007; amended effective September 1, 2011.

IN THE UNITED STATES BANKRUPTCY COURT FOR THE DISTRICT OF MARYLAND

LOCAL BANKRUPTCY RULES

PART III.

Rule 3001-1. Supporting information for claims against individual debtors.

(a) **Open-end or revolving consumer credit agreements.** When a claim is based on an open-end or revolving consumer credit agreement, the last account statement sent to the debtor prior to the filing of the petition shall also be filed with the proof of claim. If the account statement has been lost or destroyed, a statement of the circumstances of the loss or destruction shall be filed with the proof of claim.

(b) [Rescinded.] (Added effective December 1, 2009; amended Nov. 30, 2011, effective Dec. 1, 2011.)

Effect of amendments. — The 2011 amendment rescinded (b).

Rule 3002-1. Notice relating to claims secured by security interest in the debtor's principal residence.

Rescinded November 30, 2011, effective December 1, 2011.

Rule 3012-2. Valuation of collateral and avoidance of nonresidential liens — Chapter 13 only.

(a) **Form.** A motion under 11 U.S.C. § 506 in a Chapter 13 case to value collateral or to avoid a security interest in personal property or in real property that is not a debtor's principal residence may name only one creditor as a respondent. A separate motion is required for each creditor whose lien is sought to be avoided. The name, address and nature of ownership (e.g. tenancy in common, tenancy by the entirety) of any non-debtor owner of property must also be included.

(b) **Required material.** Debtor(s) must submit with the motion;

(1) Evidence of the value of the property, and

(2) If no proof of claim has been filed by the holders of claims secured by senior interests in the property, evidence of the amount of the claims so secured.

(c) **Service of motion and notice of hearing.** (1) The Clerk will maintain a list of dates available for hearings on motions under subsection (a) for each judge of the court. The list will be posted on the court's website.

(2) Movant must select a hearing date from the list for the judge to whom the case is assigned that is more than forty-nine (49) days after the date of service.

(3) Movant must serve a copy of the motion to avoid lien on the respondent and any non-debtor owner in the manner required by Federal Bankruptcy Rules 9014 and 7004(b) and Local Bankruptcy Rule 3007-1(a) (that requires service upon the individual who signed a proof of claim filed by respondent), together with a hearing notice conforming to Local Bankruptcy Form K.

(d) **Filing of proof of service.** Movant must file with the motion a certificate of service of the motion to avoid lien and the notice of hearing. The certificate must comply with Local Bankruptcy Rule 9013-4.

(e) **Responses to motion to avoid lien.** If no response to the motion to avoid lien is filed within thirty (30) days after the date of the service (plus any additional time required by Federal Bankruptcy Rules 9006(a) and (f)), the court may rule on the motion as unopposed. The Court Hearing Scheduler (CHS) Program on the court's website and CM/ECF filing screen for this type of motion will compute the date that an objection is due.

(f) **Proposed order.** Movant shall file with the motion a proposed order conforming to Local Bankruptcy Form L. If granted, avoidance of the security interest shall occur when debtor completes performance of debtor's confirmed Chapter 13 plan and receives a discharge under 11 U.S.C. § 1328(a). (Added December 4, 2003, effective January 1, 2004; amended October 15, 2007, effective November 1, 2007; November 10, 2008, effective December 1, 2008; effective December 1, 2009; amended November 12, 2010, effective November 12, 2010; amended Aug. 24, 2011, effective Sept. 1, 2011.)

Editor's note.
Pursuant to the court's announcement, "property" has been substituted for "residence" in (b)(1) and for "principal residence" in (b)(2).